MAIN CITIES OF EUROPE

2005

Selection of hotels and restaurants

Sélection d'hôtels et de restaurants

Auswahl an Hotels und Restaurants

Selezione di alberghi e ristoranti

Selección de hoteles y restaurantes

MICHELIN

MAIN CITIES OF EUROPE

3 *Introduction* English

13 *Introduction* Français

17 *Einführung* Deutsch

21 *Introduzione* Italiano

25 *Introducción* Espagnol

Dear Reader

The Michelin Guide offers a selection of the best hotels and restaurants in many categories of comfort and price. It is compiled by a team of professionally trained inspectors who travel the country visiting new establishments as well as those already listed in the guide. Their mission is to check the quality and consistency of the amenities and service provided by the hotels and restaurants throughout the year. The inspectors are full-time Michelin employees and their assessments, made anonymously, are therefore completely impartial and independent.

The amenities found in each establishment are indicated by symbols, an international language which enables you to see at a glance whether a hotel has a car park or swimming pool. To take full advantage of the wealth of information contained in the guide, consult the introduction. A short descriptive text complements the symbols.

Entry in the Michelin Guide is completely free of charge and every year the proprietors of those establishments listed complete a questionnaire giving the opening times and prices for the coming year. Nearly 100,000 pieces of information are updated for each annual edition.

Our readers also contribute through the 45,000 letters and e-mails received annually commenting on hotels and restaurants throughout Europe.

Thank you for your support and please continue to send us your comments. We hope you enjoy travelling with the Michelin Guide 2005.

Contents

37 **Austria** • *Österreich*
Vienna, *Mautern, Schützen am Gebirge*
Innsbruck
Salzburg, *Filzmoos, Werfen*

69 **Benelux** • *Belgium, Grand Duchy of Luxembourg, Netherlands*
Brussels, *Ellezelles*
Antwerp, *Kruiningen (Netherlands)*
Bruges, *Kruishoutem, De Panne, Waregem, Sluis (Netherlands), Zeebrugge*
Liège, *Namur, Tongeren, Maastricht (Netherlands)*
Luxembourg, *Echternach, Paliseul (Belgium)*
Amsterdam, *Giethoorn, Haarlem, Zwolle*
The Hague
Rotterdam, *Delft*

173 **Czech Republic** • *Česká Republika*
Prague

189 **Denmark** • *Danmark*
Copenhagen

203 **Finland** • *Suomi*
Helsinki

213 **France** • *Principality of Monaco*
Paris and Environs
(La Défense, Marne-la-Vallée/Disneyland Resort Paris, Orly and Roissy Airports, Rungis, Versailles)
Joigny, Rheims, Saulieu, Vézelay
Bordeaux, *Eugénie-les-Bains, Pauillac*
Cannes, *Grasse, Mougins, La Napoule*
Lille, *Béthune*
Lyons, *Annecy, Le Bourget-du-Lac, Chagny, Megève, Mionnay, Montrond-les-Bains, Roanne, St-Bonnet-le-Froid, Valence, Vienne, Vonnas*

Marseilles, *Aix-en-Provence, Les Baux-de-Provence, Lourmarin, Montpellier*
Monaco (Principality of)
Nice, *Beaulieu-sur-Mer, Èze, St-Martin-du-Var, La Turbie, Vence*
Strasbourg, *Baerenthal, Gundershoffen, Illhaeusern, Lembach, Marlenheim, Obernai*
Toulouse, *Laguiole, Puymirol*

345 **Germany** • *Deutschland*
Berlin
Cologne, *Bergisch-Gladbach, Bad Neuenahr-Ahrweiler, Wittlich, Perl*
Dresden
Düsseldorf, *Dortmund, Essen, Grevenbroich*
Frankfurt on Main, *Saarbrücken*
Hamburg, *Rendsburg, Sylt (Insel)*
Hanover, *Bad Nenndorf*
Leipzig
Munich, *Aschau im Chiemgau, Wernberg-Köblitz*
Stuttgart, *Baiersbronn, Sulzburg*

455 **Greece** • *Elláda*
Athens

467 **Hungary** • *Magyarország*
Budapest

479 **Ireland, Republic of** • *Eire*
Dublin

497 **Italy** • *Italia*
Rome, *Baschi*
Florence, *Colle di Val d'Elsa, San Casciano in Val di Pesa, San Vincenzo*
Milan, *Abbiategrasso, Bergamo, Canneto sull' Oglio, Concesio, Erbusco, Soriso*
Naples, *Island of Capri, Ravello, Sant'Agata sui Due Golfi*
Palermo, *Villafrati (Sicily)*
Taormina *(Sicily)*
Turin, *Torre Pellice*
Venice, *Isola Rizza, Rubano, Verona*

601 **Norway** • *Norge*
Oslo

611 **Poland** • *Polska*

Warsaw

623 **Portugal**

Lisbon

641 **Spain** • *España*

Madrid

Barcelona, *Girona, Roses, Sant Celoni, Sant Pol de Mar*

Bilbao, *Lasarte-Oria, Oiartzun, Donostia-San Sebastián*

Málaga, *Marbella*

Seville

València

723 **Sweden** • *Sverige*

Stockholm

Gothenburg

743 **Switzerland**

Suisse – Schweiz – Svizzera

Bern

Basle

Geneva, *Brent, Cossonay, Crissier, Cully, Vevey Vufflens-le-Château*

Zürich

779 **United Kingdom**

London, *Bray-on-Thames, Cambridge, Oxford*

Belfast

Birmingham, *Chagford, Cheltenham, Ludlow*

Edinburgh

Glasgow

Leeds, *Winteringham*

Liverpool

Manchester

In addition to those situated in the main cities, restaurants renowned for their excellent cuisine will be found in the towns printed in light type in the list above.

How the Guide Works

With the aim of giving the maximum amount of information in a limited number of pages Michelin has adopted a system of symbols complemented by short descriptive texts, which is renowned the world over. Without this system the present publication would run to several volumes. Judge for yourselves by comparing the descriptive text below with the equivalent extract from the Guide. In the following example prices are quoted in euro (€).

La Résidence (Paul) , ✆ 09 18 21 32 43, *laresidence@wanadoo.fr*
Fax 09 18 21 32 49, ← lake, ,
 ✂ – ⇝ . MC AE JCB BX a
March-November – **Meals** *(closed Sunday)* 53.50/99
 11.60 – **25 rm** 76/122.
◆ A 19c villa on a hillside surrounded by woodland. Ornate panelled dining room overlooking gardens. Bedrooms all have antiques and private patios.
Spec. Goujonnettes de sole. Poulet aux écrevisses. Profiteroles.
Wines. Vouvray, Bourgueil.

This demonstration clearly shows that each entry contains a great deal of information. The symbols are easily learnt and knowing them will enable you to understand the Guide. The text provides a further summary, enabling you to choose which establishments meet your needs.

A very comfortable hotel where you will enjoy a pleasant stay and be tempted to prolong your visit. The excellence of the cuisine, which is personally supervised by the proprietor Mr Paul, is worth a detour on your journey. The hotel is in a quiet secluded setting, away from built-up areas. To make a reservation phone 09 18 21 32 43 or e-mail laresidence@wanadoo.fr ; the Fax number is 09 18 21 32 49. The hotel affords a fine view of the lake ; in good weather it is possible to eat outdoors. The hotel has an indoor swimming pool and a private tennis court. Smoking is not allowed in certain areas of the hotel. Parking facilities, under cover, are available to hotel guests. The hotel accepts payment by MasterCard, American Express, and Japan Credit Bureau credit cards. Letters giving the location of the hotel on the town plan : BX a.
The hotel is open from March to November but the restaurant closes every Sunday. The set meal prices range from 53.50 € for the lowest to 99 € for the highest. The cost of continental breakfast served in the bedroom is 11.60 €. 25 bedroomed hotel. The high season charges vary from 76 € for a single to 122 € for the best double or twin bedded room. Included for the gourmet are some culinary specialities, recommended by the hotelier : Strips of deep-fried sole fillets, Chicken with crayfish, Choux pastry balls filled with ice cream and covered with chocolate sauce. In addition to the best quality wines you will find many of the local wines worth sampling : Vouvray, Bourgueil.

Hotels, Restaurants

Categories, standard of comfort

	XXXXX	*Luxury in the traditional style*
	XXXX	*Top class comfort*
	XXX	*Very comfortable*
	XX	*Comfortable*
	X	*Quite comfortable*
		Other recommended accommodation
		Traditional pubs serving food
		Tapas bars
	without rest	*The hotel has no restaurant*
	with rm	*The restaurant also offers accommodation*
		The **"Bib Hotel"** *: Good accommodation at moderate prices*

Atmosphere and setting

...	*Pleasant hotels*
XXXXX ... X,	*Pleasant restaurants*
	Very quiet or quiet secluded hotel
	Quiet hotel
sea,	*Exceptional view, Panoramic view*
	Interesting or extensive view

Cuisine

	Exceptional cuisine in the country, worth a special journey
	Excellent cooking : worth a detour
	A very good restaurant in its category
Meals	*The* **"Bib Gourmand"** *:* *Good food at moderate prices*
	A particularly interesting wine list

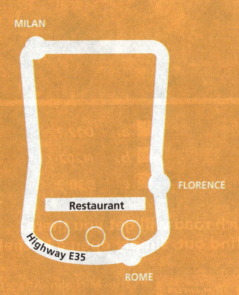

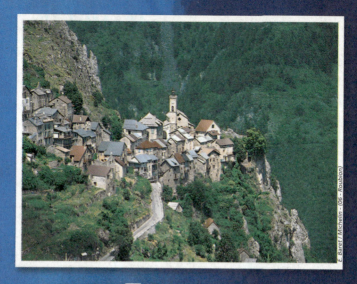

Cher lecteur

Le Guide Michelin vous propose, dans chaque catégorie de confort et de prix, une sélection des meilleurs hôtels et restaurants. Cette sélection est effectuée par une équipe d'inspecteurs, professionnels de formation hôtelière, qui sillonnent le pays toute l'année pour visiter de nouveaux établissements et ceux déjà cités afin d'en vérifier la qualité et la régularité des prestations. Salariés Michelin, les inspecteurs travaillent en tout anonymat et en toute indépendance.

Les équipements et services sont signalés par des symboles, langage international qui vous permet de voir en un coup d'œil si un hôtel dispose, par exemple, d'un parking ou d'une piscine. Pour bien profiter de cette très riche source d'information, plongez-vous dans l'introduction. Un texte décrivant l'atmosphère de l'hôtel ou du restaurant complète ces renseignements.

L'inscription dans le guide est totalement gratuite. Chaque année, les hôteliers et restaurateurs cités remplissent le questionnaire qui leur est envoyé, nous fournissant les dates d'ouverture et les prix pour l'année à venir.

Près de 100 000 informations sont mises à jour pour chaque édition (nouveaux établissements, changements de tarif, dates d'ouverture).

Une grande aide vient aussi des commentaires des lecteurs avec près de 45 000 lettres et Email par an, pour toute l'Europe.

Merci d'avance pour votre participation et bon voyage avec le Guide Michelin 2005.

Hôtels, Restaurants

Classe et confort

	XXXXX	*Grand luxe et tradition*
	XXXX	*Grand confort*
	XXX	*Très confortable*
	XX	*De bon confort*
	X	*Assez confortable*
		Autres formes d'hébergement conseillées
		Traditionnel "pub" anglais servant des repas
		Bars à tapas
	without rest	*L'hôtel n'a pas de restaurant*
	with rm	*Le restaurant possède des chambres*
		Le **"Bib Hôtel"** *: Bonnes nuits à petits prix*

L'agrément

...	*Hôtels agréables*
XXXXX ... X,	*Restaurants agréables*
	Hôtels très tranquille
	Hôtel tranquille
sea,	*Vue exceptionnelle*
	Vue intéressante

La table

✿✿✿	*Cuisine remarquable, cette table vaut le voyage*
✿✿	*Cuisine excellente, cette table mérite un détour*
✿	*Une très bonne cuisine dans sa catégorie*
Meals	*Le* **"Bib Gourmand"** *:* *Repas soignés à prix modérés*
	Carte des vins offrant un choix particulièrement attractif

L'installation

30 rm	*Nombre de chambres*
	Ascenseur – Télévision dans la chambre
	Non-fumeurs
	Air conditionné (dans tout ou partie de l'établissement)
	Prise Modem
	Tennis – Piscine : de plein air ou couverte
	Sauna – Salle de remise en forme – Wellness centre
	Jardin – Parc – Plage aménagée
	Repas servis au jardin ou en terrasse
	Ponton d'amarrage
P P	*Voiturier – Garage – Parc à voitures, parking clos*
	Etablissement en partie accessible aux personnes à mobilité réduite
	Équipements d'accueil pour les enfants
25-150	*Salles de conférences : capacité des salles*
4/40	*Salons particuliers : capacité minimale et maximale des salles*
	Accès interdit aux chiens

Les prix

Les prix sont indiqué dans la monnaie du pays. Établis pour l'année 2005, ils ne doivent être modifiés que si le coût de la vie subit des variations importantes.

Au restaurant

Meals 40/56	*Prix des repas à prix fixes*
Meals a la carte 48/64	*Prix des repas à la carte*
	Restaurants proposant des menus à prix attractifs servis avant ou après le théâtre
b.i.	*Boisson comprise*
	Vin de table en carafe
	Vin servi au verre

A l'hôtel

30 rm 120/239	*Prix minimum pour une chambre d'une personne et maximum pour la plus belle chambre occupée par deux personnes*
30 rm 60/120 140/239	*En Allemagne et en Autriche, les prix indiqués correspondent au prix minimum/maximum des chambres pour une personne et au prix minimum/maximum des chambres pour deux personnes, petit déjeuner compris.*
30 rm 135/270	*Prix des chambres petit-déjeuner compris*

Petit-déjeuner

16	*Prix du petit-déjeuner*

Cartes de paiement

AE GB JCB VISA	*Cartes de paiement acceptées*

Service et taxes

A l'exception de la Grèce, de la Hongrie, de la Pologne et de l'Espagne, les prix indiqués sont nets. Au Royaume Uni et en Irlande, s = service compris. En Italie, le service est parfois compté en supplément aux prix des repas. Ex. : (16 %).

Les Plans

Principaux signes conventionnels

Information touristique
Hôtel, restaurant – Lettre les repérant sur le plan
Monument intéressant et entrée principale } *Lettre les repérant sur le plan*
Église ou chapelle intéressante
Thiers (R.) *Rue commerçante – Parking – Parking Relais*
Tramway
Station de métro
Sens unique
Église ou chapelle
Bureau principal de poste restante et Téléphone
Édifices publics repérés par des lettres :
POL T M *Police (dans les grandes villes commissariat central) – Théâtre – Musée*
Gare routière – Aéroport – Hôpital – Marché couvert
Ruines – Monument, statue – Fontaine
Jardin, parc, bois – Cimetière, Cimetière israélite
Piscine de plein air, couverte – Hippodrome – Golf
Téléphérique – Funiculaire
Stade – Vue – Panorama

Les indications portées sur les plans sont dans la langue du pays, en conformité avec la dénomination locale.

Les curiosités

★★★ *Vaut le voyage*
★★ *Mérite un détour*
★ *Intéressante*

Lieber Leser

Der Michelin-Führer bietet Ihnen in jeder Komfort- und Preiskategorie eine Auswahl der besten Hotels und Restaurants. Diese Auswahl wird von einem Team von Inspektoren mit Ausbildung in der Hotellerie erstellt, die das Jahr hindurch das ganze Land bereisen. Ihre Aufgabe ist es, die Qualität und die Leistung der empfohlenen und der neu aufzunehmenden Hotels und Restaurants zu überprüfen. Als Angestellte bei Michelin arbeiten die Inspektoren anonym und völlig unabhängig.

Die Einrichtung und der gebotene Service der Betriebe wird durch Symbole gekennzeichnet- eine internationale Sprache, die auf einen Blick erkennen lässt, ob ein Hotel beispielsweise einen Parkplatz oder ein Schwimmbad besitzt. Um diese umfangreiche Information voll nutzen zu können, werfen Sie einen Blick in die Einleitung. Der Text, der die Atmosphäre eines Hotels oder Restaurants beschreibt, ergänzt die Symbole.

Die Empfehlung im Michelin-Führer ist absolut kostenlos. Alle empfohlenen Hotels und Restaurants füllen jedes Jahr einen Fragebogen aus, in dem uns die Schließungszeiten und die aktuellen Preise für das nächste Jahr genannt werden. Nahezu 100 000 Veränderungen für jede Ausgabe ergeben sich daraus (neue Betriebe, veränderte Preise und Schließungszeiten).

Eine sehr große Hilfe sind jedoch auch Sie, unsere Leser - mit beinahe 45 000 Briefen und E-Mails aus ganz Europa.

Wir bedanken uns im Voraus für Ihre Hilfe und wünschen Ihnen eine gute Reise mit dem Michelin-Führer 2005.

Hotels, Restaurants

Kategorien Komfort

	Großer Luxus und Tradition
	Großer Komfort
	Sehr komfortabel
	Mit gutem Komfort
	Mit Standard-Komfort
	Andere empfohlene Übernachtungsmöglichkeiten
	Traditionelle Pubs die Spsen anbieten
	Tapas bars
without rest	*Hotel ohne restaurant*
with rm	*Restaurant vermietet auch Zimmer*
	Der **"Bib Hôtel"** *Hier übernachten Sie gut und Preiswert*

Annehmlichkeiten

...	*Angenehme Hotels*
... ,	*Angenehme Restaurants*
	Sehr ruhiges oder abgelegenes und ruhiges Hotel
	Ruhiges Hotel
sea,	*Reizvolle Aussicht, Rundblick*
	Interessante oder weite Sicht

Küche

	Eine der besten Küchen des Landes : eine Reise wert
	Eine hervorragende Küche : verdient einen Umweg
	Eine sehr gute Küche : verdient Ihre besondere Beachtung
Meals	*Der* **"Bib Gourmand"** *:* *Sorgfältig zubereitete preiswerte Mahlzeiten*
	Weinkarte mit besonders attraktiven Angebot

Einrichtung

30 rm	*Anzahl der Zimmer*
	Fahrstuhl – Fernsehen im Zimmer
	Nichtraucher – Klimaanlage
	Modem-, Faxanschluss im Zimmer
	Tennis – Freibad – Hallenbad
	Sauna – Fitnessraum – Wellness centre
	Garten – Park – Strandbad
	Garten-, Terrassenrestaurant
	Bootssteg
	Wagenmeister – Garage – Parkplatz, gesicherter Parkplatz
	Für Körperbehinderte leicht zugängliche Zimmer
	Spezielle Einrichtungen/Angebote für Kinder
150	*Konferenzräume mit Höchstkapazität*
4/40	*Veranstaltungsräume (Mindest- und Höchstkapazität)*
	Hunde sind unerwünscht

Die Preise

Die Preise sind in der jeweiligen Landeswährung angegeben. Sie gelten für das Jahr 2005 und ändern sich nur bei starken Veränderungen der Lebenshaltungskosten.

Im Restaurant

Meals 40/56	*Feste Menupreise*
Meals a la carte 48/64	*Mahlzeiten "a la carte"*
	Restaurants mit preiswerten Menus vor oder nach dem Theaterbesuch
b.i.	*Getränke inbegriffen*
	Preiswerter Wein in Karaffen
	Wein glasweise ausgeschenkt

Im Hotel

30 rm 120/239	*Mindestpreis für ein Einzelzimmer und Höchstpreis für das schönste Doppelzimmer für zwei Personen.*
30 rm 60/120 140/239	*In Deutschland und Österreich beziehen sich die Zimmer-Preise auf Einzelzimmer und Doppelzimmer jeweils Mindest- und Höchstpreis inclusive Frühstück.*
30 rm 135/270	*Zimmerpreis inkl. Frühstück*

Frühstück

16	*Preis des Frühstücks*

Kreditkarten

JCB VISA	*Akzeptierte Kreditkarten*

Bedienungsgeld und Gebühren

Mit Ausnahme von Griechenland, Ungarn, Polen und Spanien sind die angegebenen Preise Inklusivpreise. In den Kapiteln über Großbritannien und Irland bedeutet s = Bedienungsgeld inbegriffen. In Italien wird für die Bedienung gelegentlich ein Zuschlag zum Preis der Mahlzeit erhoben, z.B. (16 %).

Stadtpläne

Erklärung der wichtigsten Zeichen

i	*Informationsstelle*
□ ⓐ ● ● a	*Hotel, Restaurant – Referenzbuchstabe auf dem Plan*
■ ■ ■ ■	*Sehenswertes Gebäude mit Haupteingang* } *Referenzbuchstabe auf dem Plan*
† † † ♁ ♁ B	*Sehenswerte Kirche oder Kapelle* } *Referenzbuchstabe auf dem Plan*
Thiers (R.) P P/R	*Einkaufsstraße – Parkplatz, Parkhaus – Park-and-Ride-Plätze*
—•—•—	*Straßenbahn*
⊖ ◓ ●	*U-Bahnstation*
→ ►	*Einbahnstraße*
† ♁	*Kirche oder Kapelle*
✉ ⊠ ☎	*Postlagernde Sendungen, Telegraph – Telefon*
■ ■	*Öffentliche Gebäude, durch Buchstaben gekennzeichnet :*
POL T M	*Polizei (in größeren Städten Polizeipräsidium) – Theater – Museum*
🚌 ✈	*Autobusbahnhof – Flughafen*
⊞ ✉	*Krankenhaus – Markthalle*
∴ ■ ◎	*Ruine – Denkmal, Statue – Brunnen*
▭ ▭ t t t ⊡	*Garten, Park, Wald – Friedhof, Jüd. Friedhof*
≈ ≈ ≈ ≈ 🏇	*Freibad – Hallenbad – Pferderennbahn*
⚑18	*Golfplatz und Lochzahl*
o-■-■-o o+++++o	*Seilschwebebahn – Standseilbahn*
◯ ⋞ ✳	*Sportplatz – Aussicht – Rundblick*

Die Angaben auf den Stadtplänen erfolgen, übereinstimmend mit der örtlichen Beschilderung, in der Landessprache.

Sehenswürdigkeiten

★★★	*Eine Reise wert*
★★	*Verdient einen Umweg*
★	*Sehenswert*

Caro lettore

La Guida Michelin le propone, per ogni categoria di confort e di prezzo, una selezione dei migliori alberghi e ristoranti effettuata da un'équipe di professionisti del settore. Gli ispettori, dipendenti Michelin, attraversano il paese tutto l'anno per visitare nuovi esercizi e verificare la qualità e la regolarità delle prestazioni di quelli già citati, lavorando nel più stretto anonimato e in tutta autonomia.

Le attrezzature ed i servizi sono indicati da simboli, un immediato linguaggio internazionale che ti permetterà di capire in un attimo se, per esempio, un albergo dispone di parcheggio o di piscina. Per trarre il meglio da questa ricca fonte d'informazioni, le consigliamo di consultare l'introduzione. Le indicazioni sono poi completate da un testo che descrive l'atmosfera dell'albergo o del ristorante.

L'iscrizione nella guida è completamente gratuita. Ogni anno gli albergatori e i ristoratori citati compilano un questionario inviato loro per fornirci i periodi di apertura e i prezzi per l'anno a venire. Circa 100 000 dati sono aggiornati ad ogni edizione (nuovi esercizi, variazioni di tariffe, periodi di apertura).

Di grande aiuto sono anche i commenti dei lettori che ci inviano circa 45 000 lettere ed e-mail all'anno da tutta l'Europa.

Grazie sin d'ora per la sua partecipazione e buon viaggio con la Guida Michelin 2005.

Alberghi, Ristoranti

Categorie

	XXXXX	*Gran lusso e tradizione*
	XXXX	*Gran confort*
	XXX	*Molto confortevole*
	XX	*Di buon confort*
	X	*Abbastanza confortevole*
		Forme alternative di ospitalità
		Pub con servizio cucina
		Tapas bars (in Spagna)
	without rest	*L'albergo non ha ristorante*
	with rm	*Il ristorante dispone di camere*
		Il **"Bib Hotel"** *: Buona sistemazione a prezzo contenuto*

Amenità e tranquillità

...	*Alberghi ameni*
XXXXX ... X,	*Ristoranti ameni*
	Albergo molto tranquillo, o isolato e tranquillo
	Albergo tranquillo
sea,	*Vista eccezionale – vista panoramica*
	Vista interessante o estesa

La Tavola

✿✿✿	*Una delle migliori tavole del Paese, vale il viaggio*
✿✿	*Tavola eccellente, merita una deviazione*
✿	*Un'ottima tavola nella sua categoria*
Meals	*Il* **"Bib Gourmand"** *:* *Pasti accurati a prezzi contenuti*
	Carta dei vini con proposte particolarmente interessanti

Installazioni

30 rm	*Numero di camere*
	Ascensore – Televisione in camera
	Riservato ai non fumatori – Aria condizionata
	Presa modem in camera
	Tennis – Piscina : all'aperto, coperta
	Sauna – Palestra – Wellness centre
	Giardino – Parco – Spiaggia attrezzata
	Pasti serviti in giardino o in terrazza – Pontile d'ormeggio
	Posteggiatore – Garage – Parcheggio : all'aperto, chiuso
	Camere accessibili a persone con difficoltà motoria
	Attrezzaturaper accoglienza e ricreazione dei bambini
150	*Sale per conferenze : capienza massima*
4/40	*Saloni particolari : capienza minima e massima*
	Accesso vietato ai cani

I Prezzi

I prezzi sono indicati nella moneta del paese. Stabiliti par l'anno 2005, essi non dovranno essere modificati tranne il caso in cui avvengano variazioni importanti nel costo della vita.

Pasti

Meals 40/56	*Menu a prezzo fisso (minimo, massimo)*
Meals à la carte 48/64	*Pasto alla carta*
	Ristoranti che offrono menù a prezzi ridotti prima e/o dopo gli spettacoli teatrali
b.i.	*Bevanda compresa*
	Vino sfuso – Vino servito a bicchiere

Camere

30 rm 120/239	*Prezzo per una camera singola e massimo per una camera per due persone in alta stagione.*
30 rm 60/120 140/239	*I prezzi riportati per la Germania e l'Austria si intendono rispettivamente riferiti al prezzo più basso e più alto sia per le camere singole che per le camere doppie, prima colazione inclusa.*
30 rm 135/270	*Prezzo della camera compresa la prima colazione*

Prima Colazione

16	*Prezzo della prima colazione*

Carte di credito

	Carte di credito accettate dall'esercizio

Servizio e tasse

A eccezione della Grecia, dell'Ungheria, della Polonia e della Spagna, i prezzi indicati sono netti.
Nel Regno Unito e in Irlanda, s = servizio compreso.
In Italia il servizio è talvolta calcolato come supplemento al prezzo del pasto. Es.: (15 %).

Le Piante

Simboli vari

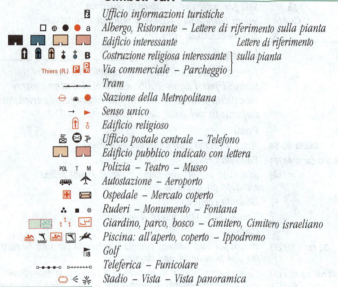

Ufficio informazioni turistiche
a *Albergo, Ristorante – Lettere di riferimento sulla pianta*
Edificio interessante — *Lettere di riferimento sulla pianta*
B *Costruzione religiosa interessante* — *Lettere di riferimento sulla pianta*
Thiers (R.) *Via commerciale – Parcheggio*
Tram
Stazione della Metropolitana
Senso unico
Edificio religioso
Ufficio postale centrale – Telefono
Edificio pubblico indicato con lettera
POL T M *Polizia – Teatro – Museo*
Autostazione – Aeroporto
Ospedale – Mercato coperto
Ruderi – Monumento – Fontana
Giardino, parco, bosco – Cimitero, Cimitero israeliano
Piscina: all'aperto, coperto – Ippodromo
18 *Golf*
Teleferica – Funicolare
Stadio – Vista – Vista panoramica

Le indicazioni riportate sulle piante sono nella lingua del paese.

Curiosità

★★★ *Vale il viaggio*
★★ *Merita una deviazione*
★ *Interessante*

Amigo lector

La Guía Michelin le propone, para cada categoría de confort y de precio, una selección de los mejores hoteles y restaurantes. Esta selección la lleva a cabo un equipo de inspectores, todos ellos profesionales de la hostelería, que recorren el país durante todo el año para visitar nuevos establecimientos y verificar que las prestaciones de los que ya están citados siguen manteniendo la calidad y la regularidad. Los inspectores de Michelin trabajan siempre en el anonimato para guardar su independencia.

Las infraestructuras y servicios aparecen señalados por símbolos, un lenguaje internacional que le permitirá ver rápidamente si un hotel tiene aparcamiento o piscina. Para sacarle el mejor partido a toda esta información no deje de leer la introducción. Un pequeño texto describe las principales características de cada establecimiento.

La inscripción en la guía es totalmente gratuita. Todos los años, los hosteleros y restauradores mencionados rellenan un cuestionario en el que nos señalan sus fechas de apertura y precios para el año siguiente. En cada edición se actualizan alrededor de 100.000 datos (nuevos establecimientos, cambios de tarifas, fechas de apertura).

También nos resultan de una inestimable ayuda los casi 45.000 mails y cartas que recibimos cada año con los comentarios y sugerencias de nuestros lectores de toda Europa.

Le agradecemos de antemano su colaboración y sólo nos queda desearle un buen viaje con la Guía Michelin 2005.

Hoteles, Restaurantes

Categorías

	XXXXX	*Gran lujo y tradición*
	XXXX	*Gran confort*
	XXX	*Muy confortable*
	XX	*Confortable*
	X	*Sencillo pero confortable*
		Otros tipos de alojamiento recomendados
		Pub tradicional inglés con servicio de comidas
		Bar de tapas
	without rest	*El hotel no dispone de restaurante*
	with rm	*El restaurante tiene habitaciones*
		El **"Bib Hotel"** *: Grato descanso a precio moderado*

Atractivo y tranquilidad

...	*Hoteles agradables*
XXXXX ... X,	*Restaurantes agradables*
	Hotel muy tranquilo, o aislado y tranquilo
	Hotel tranquilo
sea,	*Vista excepcional*
	Vista interesante o extensa

La Mesa

	Una de las mejores mesas del país, justifica el viaje
	Mesa excelente, vale la pena desviarse
	Muy buena mesa en su categoría
Meals	*El* **"Bib Gourmand"** *: Buenas comidas a precios moderados*
	Carta de vinos que ofrece una selección particularmente atractiva

La instalación

30 rm	*Número de habitaciones*
	Ascensor – Televisión en la habitación
	No fumadores – Aire acondicionado
	Toma de Modem
	Tennis – Piscina : al aire libre o cubierta
	Sauna – Fitness – Wellness centre
	Jardin – Parque – Playa equipada
	Comidas servidas en el jardín o en la terraza
	Embarcadero
	Aparcacoches – Garaje – Aparcamiento exterior – Aparcamiento cerrado
	Habitaciones adaptadas para minusválidos
	Instalaciones infantiles
150	*Salas de conferencias : capacidad de las salas*
4/40	*Salones particulares: capacidad mínima/máxima de las salas*
	Prohibidos los perros

Los precios

Los precios están expresados en la moneda del país. Las tarifas son válidas para 2005 salvo variaciones en el coste de bienes y servicios.

Comida

Meals 40/56	*Precios de las comidas a precio fijo*
Meals à la carte 48/64	*Precios de las comidas a la carta*
	Restaurantes con comidas a precios moderados servidas antes y después del espectáculo
b.i.	*Bebida incluida*
	Vino de mesa en jarra
	Vino servido por copas

Habitaciones

30 rm 120/239	*Precio mínimo de una habitacíon individual y precio máximo de la mejor habitacíon doble.*
30 rm 60/120 140/239	*Los precios indicados en Alemania y Austria corresponden al precio mínimo/máximo de una habitacíon individual y doble respectivamente, incluido desayuno.*
30 rm 135/270	*Precio de las habitaciones con desayuno incluido*

Desayuno

16	*Precio del desayuno*

Tarjetas de crédito

MC AE GB JCB VISA	*Tarjetas de crédito aceptadas*

Servicios e impuestos

A excepción de Grecia, Hungría, Polonia y España, los precios indicados son netos. En el Reino Unido e Irlanda, s = servicio incluido. En Italia, el servicio se añade a veces como suplemento a los precios de las comidas. Ej. : (16 %).

Los planos

Signos diversos

	Información turística
a	*Hotel, restaurante – Letra de referencia en el plano de la ciudad*
	Edificio interesante y entrada principal } *Letra de referencia en el plano de la ciudad*
B	*Edificio religioso interesante* } *Letra de referencia en el plano de la ciudad*
Thiers (R.)	*Calle comercial – Aparcamiento*
	Tranvía
	Estación de metro
	Sentido único
	Iglesia o capilla
	Oficina central de lista de correos – Teléfonos
	Edificio público localizado con letras :
POL T M	*Policía (en las grandes ciudades : Jefatura) – Teatro – Museo*
	Estación de autobuses – Aeropuerto
	Hospital – Mercado cubierto
	Ruinas – Monumento – Fuente
	Jardín, parque, bosque – Cementerio, Cementerio judío
	Piscina al aire libre o cubierta – Hipódromo
18	*Golf y número de hoyos*
	Teleférico, telecabina – Funicular
	Estadio – Vista – Panorama

Las indicaciones de los planos están señaladas en el idioma del país de acuerdo con la denominación local.

Las curiosidades

★★★	*De interés excepcional*
★★	*Muy interesante*
★	*Interesante*

NEW YORK

UTC - 5
(Universal time co-ordinated/ Greenwich Mean Time)

DIRECT DAILY FLIGHTS
Total time of journey from city centre to city centre (in hours)

Amsterdam	9 1/4
Athens	12
Barcelona	9 1/4
Berlin	12 3/4
Brussels	10 3/4
Budapest	11
Copenhagen	9 3/4
Dublin	8 3/4
Düsseldorf	9 1/4
Frankfurt	9 3/4
Geneva	9 1/2
Glasgow	10
Hamburg	11
Helsinki	12
Lisbon	8 3/4
London	9 1/2
Luxembourg	11 1/2
Madrid	9 1/4
Milan	9 3/4
Munich	11 3/4
Oslo	9 1/2
Paris	9 3/4
Rome	10 1/2
Stockholm	11 1/2
Vienna	10 1/2
Warsaw	12 1/2
Zürich	9 3/4

FIN
UTC + 2
Helsinki
N
Oslo
Stockholm
S
Gothenburg
DK
Copenhagen
Hamburg
Berlin
Warsaw
Hanover
PL
Leipzig
Düsseldorf
Dresden
Cologne
D
Prague
CZ
Frankfurt
Stuttgart
Vienna
trasbourg
Munich
Salzburg
Budapest
A
Zürich
asle
Innsbruck
H
CH
erne
Venice
Milan
Turin
Monaco
Florence
I
Rome
Naples
GR
Athens
Palermo
Taormina
A Austria
B Belgium
CH Switzerland
CZ Czech Republic
D Germany
DK Denmark
E Spain
F France
FIN Finland
GB United Kingdom
GR Greece
H Hungary
I Italy
IRL Ireland
L Luxembourg
N Norway
NL Netherlands
PL Poland
P Portugal
S Sweden

DISTANCES BY ROAD

(in kilometres)

	Amsterdam	Athens	Barcelona	Berlin	Bern	Bordeaux	Brussels	Budapest	Cologne	Copenhagen	Dublin	Edinburgh	Frankfurt	Geneva	Hamburg	Helsinki	Lisbon	London	Luxembourg	Lyons	Madrid	Manchester	Marseilles	Milan	Munich	Oslo	Paris	Prague	Rome	Stockholm	Strasbourg	Stuttgart	Venice	Vienna	Warsaw
Athens	2849																																		
Barcelona	1506	2081																																	
Berlin	663	2274	1855																																
Bern	804	1557	931	914																															
Bordeaux	1088	2223	564	1633	850																														
Brussels	205	2092	1310	767	643	892																													
Budapest	1408	1480	1898	856	1111	1926	1369																												
Cologne	261	2599	1350	573	586	1067	210	1159																											
Copenhagen	783	2666	2088	388	1225	1795	913	1247	740																										
Dublin	949	2815	1863	1511	1366	1151	781	2151	992	750																									
Edinburgh	742	2971	2019	978	1522	1365	937	2307	1148	491	404																								
Frankfurt	433	2414	1318	544	422	1149	394	974	184	806	1177	1333																							
Geneva	920	1527	752	1070	159	692	719	1267	708	1382	1328	1484	578																						
Hamburg	471	2563	1776	285	913	1483	601	1145	428	324	1346	705	494	1069																					
Helsinki	1737	3123	3142	1286	2201	2917	1868	1656	1860	958	1260	1002	1832	2357	1278																				
Lisbon	2251	3251	1246	2796	2013	1160	2056	3067	2232	2960	2316	2530	2314	1922	2648	4084																			
London	486	2352	1400	1048	903	982	318	1688	529	1195	456	642	713	865	883	1324	2145																		
Luxembourg	415	1879	1148	766	430	926	215	1191	204	942	995	1151	238	507	629	2053	2090	532																	
Lyons	928	1624	636	1223	310	536	728	1370	716	1454	1325	1481	686	152	1142	2510	1700	862	515																
Madrid	1778	2678	615	2323	1527	686	1583	2494	1758	2486	1842	2056	1840	1348	2174	3610	630	1667	1618	1232															
Manchester	212	2688	1736	874	1239	1024	654	2024	865	552	203	360	1049	1201	682	1087	2188	329	867	1197	1715														
Marseilles	1240	1607	506	1534	575	647	1039	1423	1027	1766	1637	1793	997	430	1454	2821	1675	1173	826	314	1102	1510													
Milan	1045	1204	974	1030	349	996	883	938	827	1424	1607	1763	663	321	1111	2317	2144	1144	670	441	1571	1480	500												
Munich	832	2061	1353	587	424	1257	721	689	583	943	1528	1685	398	581	788	1875	2421	1065	508	731	1949	1401	986	490											
Oslo	1277	3115	2582	837	1731	2289	1407	1697	1234	611	790	532	1312	1888	819	798	3452	829	1436	1949	2979	591	2260	1833	1392										
Paris	506	2053	997	1051	586	579	311	1496	487	1215	865	1021	578	534	902	2339	1742	402	355	458	1269	738	769	848	821	1708									
Prague	874	1938	1698	337	757	1603	891	520	681	728	1634	1790	496	913	608	1519	2766	1171	727	1064	2293	1085	1376	862	381	1178	1032								
Rome	1617	759	1329	1496	921	1470	1455	1193	1399	1852	2179	2335	1235	857	1653	2783	2498	1716	1242	945	1925	2052	854	568	905	2301	1385	1290							
Stockholm	1451	3175	2756	898	1893	2463	1581	1757	1408	672	973	716	1474	2049	991	316	3626	1012	1610	2123	3153	775	2434	1894	1453	529	1881	1238	2361						
Strasbourg	596	1689	1123	755	239	1061	434	1018	361	1021	1196	1352	218	396	709	2042	2224	733	221	489	1719	1069	801	481	360	1527	490	598	1052	1689					
Stuttgart	617	2296	1215	633	286	1079	512	880	367	971	1319	1475	203	443	659	1921	2243	856	299	616	1812	1192	859	494	222	1477	613	476	1056	1639	149				
Venice	1214	1082	1228	1045	602	1256	1135	687	965	1401	1859	2015	801	581	1203	2246	2398	1396	922	701	1825	1732	754	269	454	1851	1109	805	524	1911	729	605			
Vienna	1149	1666	1788	620	852	1685	1110	248	900	1012	1893	2049	715	1008	909	1673	2849	1429	932	1159	2384	1765	1314	828	430	1461	1237	284	1083	1521	758	620	577		
Warsaw	1220	2157	2335	594	1394	2189	1324	677	1130	911	2069	1570	1067	1550	877	979	3352	1606	1289	1702	2879	1431	2013	1509	996	1360	1607	616	1773	413	1235	1114	1267	693	
Zurich	793	1490	1051	846	123	955	631	995	575	1177	1355	1511	411	279	865	2134	2119	892	418	429	1648	1228	695	282	308	1683	591	680	854	1845	225	211	534	735	1327

Helsinki - Strasbourg

2042 km

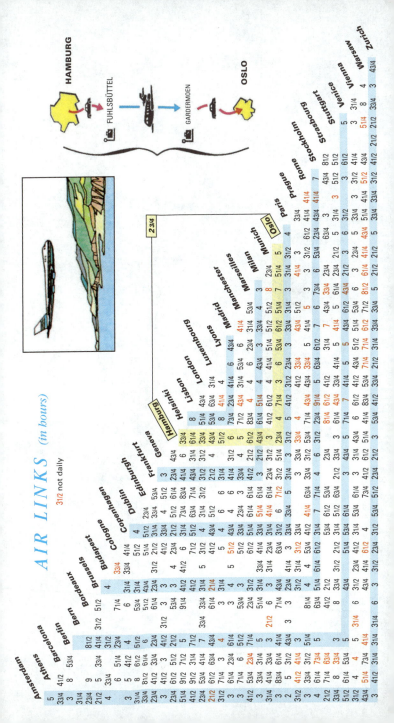

AIR LINKS *(in hours)*

31/2 not daily

	Amsterdam	Athens	Barcelona	Berlin	Bern	Bordeaux	Brussels	Budapest	Cologne	Copenhagen	Dublin	Edinburgh	Frankfurt	Geneva	Hamburg	Helsinki	Lisbon	London	Luxembourg	Lyons	Madrid	Manchester	Marseilles	Milan	Munich	Oslo	Paris	Prague	Rome	Stockholm	Strasbourg	Stuttgart	Venice	Vienna	Warsaw
Athens	5																																		
Barcelona	33/4	41/2																																	
Berlin	3	8	53/4																																
Bern	31/4																																		
Bordeaux	23/4	9		81/2																															
Brussels	21/2	5	33/4	41/4	31/2	51/2																													
Budapest	4	33/4		31/2			4																												
Cologne		6	51/4	23/4		71/4		**33/4**																											
Copenhagen	3	5	41/2	4		6	31/4	33/4	41/4																										
Dublin	31/4	8	61/2	51/2		53/4	31/4		51/2	4																									
Edinburgh	33/4	81/2	61/4	6		51/2	43/4		51/4	51/2	23/4																								
Frankfurt	23/4	41/2	33/4	23/4		61/4	23/4	31/2	21/2	31/4	33/4	53/4																							
Geneva	3	41/2	3	41/2	31/2	3	3		41/2	33/4	4	51/2	3																						
Hamburg	23/4	61/2	51/2	21/2		53/4	3	4	23/4	21/2	51/2	61/4	23/4	43/4																					
Helsinki	51/4	91/2	71/2	5		91/4	41/2	41/2	6	31/4	73/4	83/4	41/4	6	33/4																				
Lisbon	41/2	91/2	31/4	71/2			41/2		71/2	51/2	63/4	71/4	43/4	31/4	61/4	8																			
London	23/4	53/4	41/4	7	33/4	33/4	31/4	5	31/2	4	31/4	31/2	31/2	31/2	33/4	51/4	43/4																		
Luxembourg	**21/2**	61/2	63/4	43/4		61/4	**21/4**		41/2	43/4	51/2		21/2	4	43/4	53/4	63/4	31/4																	
Lyons	31/2	71/4	3	**4**		3	31/4		5	4	6	6	31/4		51/2	8	**41/4**	4																	
Madrid	3	61/4	23/4	61/4		3	4	5	**51/2**	43/4	4	6	41/4	31/2	6	73/4	23/4	41/4	6	43/4															
Manchester	3	71/4	6	51/2		53/4	3		51/2	33/4	23/4	3	33/4	4	5	71/2	**43/4**	31/4	53/4	6	**41/4**														
Marseilles	41/2	53/4	**23/4**	71/4		23/4	31/2		61/2	51/4	61/4	61/4	41/2	21/2	61/2	83/4	**4**	4	6	23/4	31/4	53/4													
Milan	3	33/4	31/4	5		51/4	31/4	33/4	41/4	33/4	**51/4**	61/4	3	21/2	43/4	61/4	**51/4**	4	43/4	3	33/4	4	3												
Munich	31/4	41/4	33/4	3	**21/2**	6	3	31/4	23/4	31/4	**41/4**	61/4	23/4	31/2	3	41/2	61/2	4	41/4	51/4	51/2	51/2	**8**	23/4											
Oslo	3	83/4	61/4	41/4		71/4	43/4		63/4	31/2	6	**71/2**	31/2	51/4	23/4	4	71/4	3	6	53/4	61/2	51/4	7	51/4	5										
Paris	2	5	31/2	43/4	3	3	23/4	41/4	3	33/4	33/4	5	31/4	3	31/2	5	41/2	31/2	23/4	3	33/4	31/4	3	31/4	31/2	4									
Prague	31/2	**41/2**	**41/4**	3			31/2	31/4	**31/2**	33/4			3	33/4	**33/4**	**4**		41/2	**33/4**		**43/4**	51/2		**41/4**	3		33/4								
Rome	3	33/4	31/2	51/4		81/4	4	4	53/4	41/2	**41/4**	63/4	33/4	31/2	53/4	71/4	**43/4**	43/4	**33/4**	5	41/4	**5**	3	3	31/2	61/2	41/4	**41/4**							
Stockholm	4	61/4	**73/4**	5		63/4	51/4	61/4	61/2	31/4	7	71/4	4	6	31/2	23/4	**91/4**	5	63/4	61/2	7	6	73/4	6	53/4	23/4	43/4	**41/4**	7						
Strasbourg	21/2	71/4	**63/4**			41/2	21/2			53/4	61/2	53/4		23/4		**81/4**	**61/2**	41/2		31/4	**7**	43/4	**33/4**	23/4		63/4	3		43/4	81/2					
Stuttgart	33/4	8	**33/4**	3		8	33/4	31/2	21/2	31/4	51/2	63/4	21/2	33/4	3	61/4	**43/4**	33/4	41/4	5	**41/4**	5	61/4	23/4	21/2	5	31/4	**3**	51/2	51/2					
Venice	51/2	61/4	53/4	5			43/4		51/4	53/4	61/4		3	43/4	5	71/4	**7**	41/4	5	**5**	43/4	61/2	**43/4**	21/2	3	6	31/2		3	61/2		5			
Vienna	31/2	4	**4**	5	**31/4**	6	31/2	23/4	41/2	31/4	53/4	61/4	3	31/4	43/4	6	61/2	41/2	43/4	51/2	51/4	53/4	6	3	23/4	5	33/4	3	31/2	41/4		3	31/4		
Warsaw	43/4	**51/4**	73/4	**41/4**			43/4	41/4	**61/2**	4		73/4	41/2	61/2	51/4	41/4	83/4	53/4	**71/4**	**71/4**	**61/2**	71/2	**81/2**	**61/4**	**41/4**	**43/4**	51/4	41/4	**51/2**	43/4		**51/4**	8	4	
Zurich	3	41/2	31/4	31/4	31/4	6	3	31/2	23/4	31/2	53/4	51/2	23/4	21/2	3	53/4	41/2	33/4	21/2	31/4	33/4	33/4	5	21/2	21/2	5	33/4	33/4	31/2	41/2	21/2	21/2	33/4	3	43/4

Hamburg – Oslo: 23/4

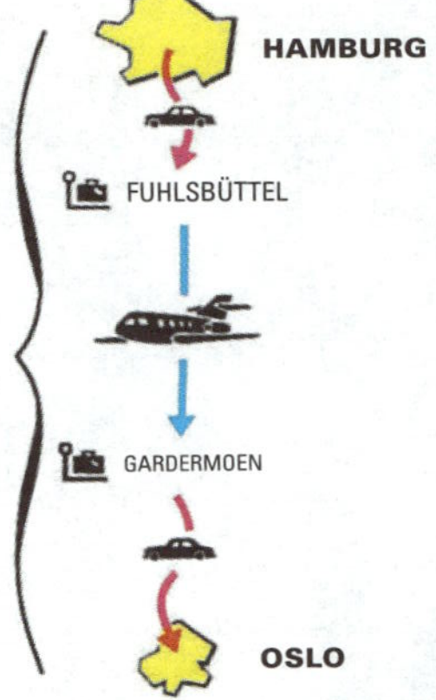

- a. ***Muséum National d'Histoire Naturelle (Paris)***
- b. ***Natural History Museum (London)***
- c. ***Museum für Naturkunde (Berlin)***

Can't decide ?

Then immerse yourself in the Michelin Green Guide !

- Everything to do and see
- The best driving tours
- Practical information
- Where to stay and eat

The Michelin Green Guide: the spirit of discovery.

MICHELIN
A better way forward

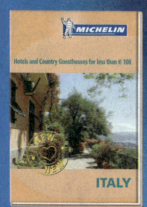

Austria

Österreich

VIENNA
INNSBRUCK – SALZBURG

PRACTICAL INFORMATION

LOCAL CURRENCY

1 euro (€) = 1,34 USD ($) (Dec. 2004)

TOURIST INFORMATION

In Vienna: *Österreich-Information, 1040 Wien, Margaretenstr. 1, ✆ (01) 587 20 00, oewwien@austria.info.at, Fax (01) 588 66 48*
Niederösterreich Touristik-Information, 1010 Wien, Fischhof 3/3, ✆ (01) 53 61 00, tourismus@noe.co.at, Fax (01) 536 10 60 62

Austrian National Holiday: *26 October*

AIRLINES

Austrian-Airlines: *1010 Wien, Kärntner Ring 18, ✆ (05) 17 89, Fax (05) 17 66 42 30*

Air France: *1010 Wien, Kärntner Str. 49, ✆ (01) 5 02 22 24 07, Fax (01) 5 02 22 24 07*

British Airways: *1010 Wien, Kärntner Ring 10, ✆ (01) 5 06 60, Fax (01) 5 04 20 84*

Japan Airlines: *1010 Wien, Kärntner Str. 11, ✆ (01) 512 75 22, Fax (01) 512 75 54*

Lufthansa City Center: *1010 Wien, Wienerbergstr. 5, ✆ (01) 607 10 70*

FOREIGN EXCHANGE

Hotels, restaurants and shops do not always accept foreign currencies and it is wise, therefore, to change money and cheques at the banks and exchange offices which are found in the larger stations, airports and at the border.

SHOPPING and BANK HOURS

Shops are open from 9am to 6pm, but often close for a lunch break. They are closed Sunday and Bank Holidays (except the shops in railway stations).
Branch offices of banks are open from Monday to Friday between 8am and 12.30pm (in Salzburg 12am) and from 1.30pm to 3pm (in Salzburg 2pm to 4.30pm), Thursday to 5.30pm (only in Vienna).
In the index of street names, those printed in red are where the principal shops are found.

BREAKDOWN SERVICE

ÖAMTC: *See addresses in the text of each city.*

ARBÖ: *in Vienna: Mariahilfer Str. 180, ✆ (01) 89 12 10, Fax (01) 89 12 12 36 in Salzburg: Münchner Bundesstr. 9, ✆ (0662) 43 36 01, in Innsbruck: Stadlweg 7, ✆ (0512) 3 45 12 30*
in Austria the ÖAMTC (emergency number ✆ 120) and the ARBÖ (emergency number ✆ 123) make a special point of assisting foreign motorists. They have motor patrols covering main roads.

TIPPING

Service is generally included in hotel and restaurant bills. But in Austria, it is usual to give more than the expected tip in hotels, restaurants and cafés. Taxi-drivers, porters, barbers and theatre attendants also expect tips.

SPEED LIMITS

The speed limit in built up areas (indicated by place name signs at the beginning and end of such areas) is 50 km/h - 31 mph; on motorways 130 km/h - 80 mph and on all other roads 100 km/h - 62 mph. Driving on Austrian motorways is subject to the purchase of a road tax obtainable from border posts and ÖAMTC.

SEAT BELTS

The wearing of seat belts in Austria is compulsory for drivers and all passengers.

VIENNA
(WIEN)

Austria **730** V 4 *– pop. 1 640 000 – alt. 156 m.*

Budapest 208 ④ – München 435 ⑦ – Praha 292 ① – Salzburg 292 ⑦ – Zagreb 362 ⑥.

Albertinaplatz, ✉ A-1010, ☎ (01) 2 45 55, Fax (01) 24 55 56 66, info@wien.info
ÖAMTC, ✉ A-1010, Schubertring 1, ☎ (01) 71 19 90.

18 GC Wien Freudenau 65a CY, *☎ (01) 7 28 95 64,*
18 Club Danube Golf Wien Weingartenallee 22 (Northeast: 10 km by Wagram Str. CX*), ☎ (01) 2 56 82 82*
9 C + C Golfclub At Wienerberg, Gutheil-Shroder-Gasse 9 BZ *☎ (01) 6 61 23*
✈ Wien-Schwechat by ③, ☎ (01) 7 00 70.
☎ (01) 58 00 29 89. – Exhibition Centre (Wiener Messe), Messestr. 1, ☎ (01) 727 20.

SIGHTS

THE HOFBURG★★★

Around the Hofburg: St Michael's Square★ – St Michael's Gate★ – Swiss Gate★ – Josef's square★ – Heroe's Square★
Souvenirs of the Habsburgs; Imperial Apartments★ – Sisi – Museum★ – Imperial porcelain and silver collection★ ; Milan centerpiece★★ – Imperial Treasury★★★; Rudolf Imperial Crown★★★; Insignia and regalia of the Holy Roman Germanic Empire★★; Imperial Crown★★★ – Holy Lance★★ – Spanish Riding School★★ – Austrian National Library★ – Albertina Collection of Graphic Art★★
Ephesos-Museum★★ (Frieze from the Parthian momument★★)
Museum of Ancient Musical Instruments★★ – Collection of Arms and Armour★★ – Ethnographic Museum★ – Papyrus Museum★ JR

SCHÖNBRUNN★★★

Palace of Schönbrunn; Tour of the Palace★★ – Great Gallery★★★ – Carriage Museum★ – Imperial Carriage★★ – Park★★ ⩽★ of the Gloriette★★ – Zoo★ – Palm House★ – Gloriette★★ AZ

BUILDINGS AND MONUMENTS

St. Stephen's Cathedral★★★ KR *– Stephansplatz★★*
Church of the Capucins: Imperial Crypt of the Habsburg pantheon★★ JR *Lower Belvedere★* FU *Museum of Austrian Medieval Art★ – Museum of Austrian Baroque Art★★*
Upper Belvedere★★ FV*: 19C and 20C Austrian and International Art★★ – State Opera★★* JS *– Church of Charles Borromero★★* CY *– Burgtheater★* HR *– St. Peter's Church★* JR *– Church of the Jesuits★* KR *– Church Maria am Gestade★* JP *– Abbey of the Scots★, Scotsaltar★★* JPR *– City Palace of Prince Eugene of Savoy★* KR

JUGENDSTIL AND SECESSION

Post Office Savings Bank★ LR *– Wagner-Pavillons★* JS *– Secession Pavilion★★* JS *– Buildings★ by Wagner on Linke Wienzeile – Wagner Villas★ (in Penzing)* FU *– Steinhof Church in Penzing★★* AY

STREETS, SQUARES AND PARKS

*The Tour of the Ring★★ – Graben★ (Plague Pillar★★)*JR *– Donner's Fountain★★* JR *– Volksgarten★* HR *– Spittelberg Quarter★* KS *– Prater★ (Giant Ferris Wheel★★)* GU *– Zoo of Lainz★ West by⑦*

MUSICAL VIENNA

Pasqualatihaus★ (Beethoven) HP *– Figaro-Haus★ (Mozart)* KR *Schubert-Memorial★* FT **M**[5] *– Haydn-Memorial★* EV **M**[10] *– Johann-StraußMemorial★* LP *– House of Music★★* KS

IMPORTANT MUSEUMS

Museum of Art History★★★ HS *– Quarter of Museums★★ (Leopold Museum★)* HS *– Art Gallery of the Academy of Fine Arts★★* JS *– Austrian Museum of Applied and Decorative Arts (MAK)★★* LR *– Historical Museum of the City of Vienna★* KS *Natural History Museum★* HR *– City of Vienna Jewish Museum★* JR *– Museum of Military History★* GV **M**[23] *– Treasure Chamber of the Grand Masters★* KR *– Clock and Watch Museum★* JR **M**[17] *– Technical Museum★* AZ **M**[2] *– Imperial Furniture Depot★* EU **M**[11] *– Cathedral Museum★* KR **M**[19] *– Liechtenstein Museum* FT **M**[27]

EXCURSIONS

UNO-City★ CY *– Danube Park★* CX *– Danube Tower ⩽★★* CX *– Kahlenberg★* BX *– Leopoldsberg★★ ⩽★★* BX *– Klosterneuburg Abbey★ (Altarpiece by Nicolas of Verdun★★); Museum of the Abbey★ – Essl Collection★ North: 13km – Heiligenkreuz★ South-West: 32 km by⑥ – Grinzing★* BX *– Wienerwald★ South-West by⑥ – Heiligenstadt★ (Karl-Marx-Hof★)*BX.

INDEX OF STREET NAMES IN WIEN

Adalbert-Stifter-Str. CX 3
Albertinapl. JS
Alser Str. EU
Alserbachstr. EFT 4
Altes Landgut CZ
Altmannsdorfer Str. AZ 6
Am Heumarkt KLS
Am Hof JR
Amundsenstr. AY
Annagasse JKS
Arsenalstr. FGV
Aspernbrücke LPR
Atzgerdorfer Pl. AZ
Auerspergstr. HR
Augartenbrücke JP
Babenbergerstr. HJS
Bäckerstr. KR 9
Ballhauspl. HJR
Bankgasse HJR
Bauernmarkt KR 10
Beatrixgasse LS
Beethovenpl. KS
Berggasse HP
Biberstr. LR
Billrothstr. ET 12
Blumauergasse LP
Börsegasse JP
Börselpl. JP
Bognergasse JR 13
Bräunerstr. JR 15
Breite Gasse HRS
Breitenfurter Str. AZ 16
Breitenleer Str. CX
Brigittenauer Lände FT
Brünner Str. CX
Burggasse HRS, EU
Burgring HR
Cobenzlgasse AX
Concordiapl. JP
Dampfschiffstr. LPR
Döblinger Hauptstr. BXY 21
Dominikanerbastei KR 22
Donaufelder Str. CX
Donaustadtstr. CXY 24
Dornbacher Str. AY
Dorotheergasse JR 25
Dr-Ignaz-Seipel-Pl. KR 27
Dr-Karl-Lueger-Ring HPR
Dr-Karl-Renner-Ring HR
Dresdner Str. CXY
Eichenstr. EV
Eipeldauerstr. CX
Engerthstr. GT
Erdberger Lände CYZ, GU 28
Erdbergstr. CY 30
Erzherzog-Karl-Str. CY 31
Europapl. EU
Exelbergstr. AXY
Falkestr. KLR 33
Favoritenstr. FV 34
Felderstr. HR
Fleischmarkt KR
Flötzersteig AY
Floridsdorfer Brücke CX 36
Flurschützstr. EV
Franz-Josefs-Kai KLPR
Freyung JR
Friedrich-Schmidt-Pl. HR
Friedrichstr. JS 38
Gablenzgasse AY
Garnisongasse HP
Georg-Coch-Pl. LR 40
Gersthofer Str. AY
Getreidemarkt HJS 42
Glockengasse LP
Graben JR
Gregor-Mendel-Str. ET 43
Grenzackerstr. CZ 45
Griechengasse KR 46
Grinzinger Allee BX 48
Grinzinger Str. BX 49
Grünbergstr. AZ, FGV
Gudrunstr. BCZ
Gumpendorfer Str. HS
Gutenberggasse HS 51
Hadikgasse AYZ
Hafenzufahrtstr. CY
Haidgasse KP
Handelskai CXY
Hasenauerstr. ET 54
Hauptallee CY
Hauptstr. AX
Heiligenkreuzer Hof KR 55
Heiligenstädter Lände FT 57
Heiligenstädter Str. FT 58
Heinestr. FGT
Heinrichsgasse JP
Hermesstr. AZ
Hernalser Hauptstr. AY
Herrengasse JR
Hetzendorfer Str. AZ
Hietzinger Kai AZ 60
Himmelpfortgasse KR 61
Hintere Zollamtsstr. LR
Hirschstettner Str. CX 63
Hoche Warte BX 64
Hörlgasse HJP
Hohenstr. AX
Hoher Markt KR
Hollandstr. KP
Hütteldorfer Str. ABY
Invalidenstr. LR
Jägerstr. FT
Johannesgasse KRS
Josefspl. JR
Josefstädter Str. EU
Judengasse KR 66
Judenpl. JR 67
Kärntner Ring JKS
Kärtner Str. JRS
Kahlenberger Str. BX
Karlspl. JS
Kohlmarkt JR 70
Krottenbachstr. ABX
Kulmgasse AY 23
Kundmanngasse GU 71
Laaer-Berg-Str. CZ
Lainzer Str. AZ
Landesgerichtsstr. HPR
Landstr. Gürtel FGV
Landstr. Hauptstr. LR, GUV 72
Lange Gasse EU 73
Lassallestr. CY, GT 74
Laxenburger Str. CZ, FV
Leopoldauer Str. CX
Leopoldsgasse KP
Lerchenfelder Str. EU
Lichtenfelsgasse HR
Lichtensteg KR 78
Liechtensteinstr. HP
Linke Bahngasse LS
Linke Wienzeile BYZ, EV
Linzer Str. AY
Löwelstr. HR 79
Löwengasse GU
Lothringerstr. KS
Lugeck KR
Marc-Aurel-Str. KPR 81
Margaretengürtel EFV
Margaretenstr. BCYZ 82
Maria-Theresien-Pl. HRS
Maria-Theresien-Str. HJP
Mariahilfer Str. HS, EU
Marienbrücke KP
Maurer Hauptpl. AZ
Maurer-Lange-Gasse AZ 83
Meidlinger Hauptstr. BZ 84
Michaelerpl. JR
Millöckergasse JS 29
Minoritenpl. JR
Mölkerbastei HP 85
Museumspl. HS
Museumstr. HR
Naglergasse JR
Neubaugasse EU 86
Neubaugürtel EU
Neuer Markt JR 87
Neustiftgasse HR 88
Neuwaldegger Str. AY 89
Nibelungengasse HJS
Nordbahnstr. CY
Nordbrücke CX
Nußdorfer Str. ET
Obere Augartenstr. FT
Obere Donaustr. KP
Operngasse JS
Opernring JS
Oppolzergasse HR 90
Parkring KLR
Philharmonikerstr. JS 91
Plankengasse JR 92
Postgasse KR
Prager Str. CX
Praterbrücke CY
Praterstr. LP, FGU
Prinz-Eugen-Str. CY, FUV 93
Raffineriestr. CY
Rathauspl. HR
Rautenweg CX
Raxstr. BZ 94
Rechte Bahngasse LS
Reichsbrücke CY
Reisnerstr. LS
Renngasse JPR 95
Rennweg CYZ
Rooseveltpl. HP
Roßauer Brücke JP
Rotensterngasse LP
Rotenturmstr. KR
Rudolf-Sallinger-Pl. LS
Rudolfspl. JKP
Salvatorgasse JPR 96
Salztorbrücke KP
Salztorgasse KP
Schauflergasse JR 97
Schlachthausgasse CY 98
Schlickpl. JP
Schönbrunner Str. ABZ, EV 99
Schönlaterngasse KR 100
Schottengasse HP 102
Schottenring JP
Schreyvogelgasse HR 103
Schubertring KS
Schüttelstr. CY, GU
Schulhof JR 105
Schwarzenbergpl. KS
Schwarzspanierstr. HP
Schwedenbrücke KPR
Schwertgasse JP 106
Seilerstätte KRS
Seitzergasse JR 107
Seyringer Str. CX
Siebenbrunnengasse EFV
Siebensterngasse HS
Siemensstr. CX
Sieveringer Str. AX
Simmeringer Hauptstr. CZ
Singerstr. KR
Sonnenfelsgasse KR 108
Sonnwendgasse FV
Speisinger Str. AZ 109
Spiegelgasse JR
Spitalgasse EU 111
Spittelauer Lände FT 112
Spittelberggasse HS 114
Stephanspl. KR 115
Stock-im-Eisen-Pl. JR 116
Stromstr. FT
Stubenbastei KR
Stubenring LR
Südosttangente CY
Taborstr. KLP
Tegetthoffstr. JR 117
Tiefer Graben JPR 120
Traisengasse FGT
Triester Str. BZ, FV
Tuchlauben JR 123
Türkenstr. HJP
Ungargasse LS
Universitätsstr. HP
Untere Donaustr. LP
Uraniastr. LR 124
Veitingergasse AZ 126
Vordere Zollamtsstr. LR
Währinger Gürtel ETU
Währinger Str. HP, ET
Wagramer Str. CXY
Wallnerstr. JR
Wattgasse AY
Webgasse EV 68
Weihburggasse KR
Weiskirchnerstr. LR 130
Weißgerberlände GU 129
Wiedner Gürtel FV 131
Wiedner Hauptstr. JS, FV 132
Wienerbergstr. BZ 134
Wipplingerstr. JPR
Wollzeile KR
Zieglergasse EU 135
Zirkusgasse LP

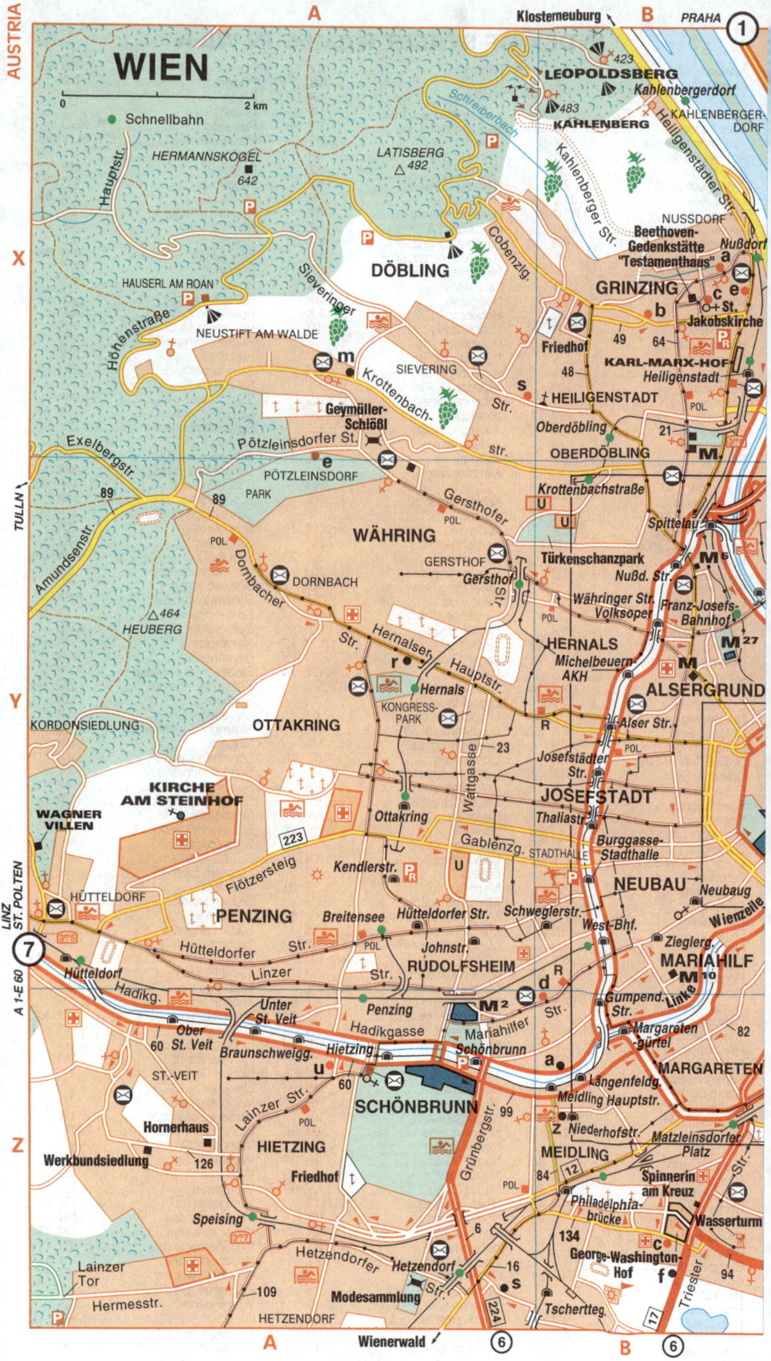
WIEN
AUSTRIA
Schnellbahn
0
2 km
Klosterneuburg
PRAHA
1
LEOPOLDSBERG
Kahlenbergerdorf
KAHLENBERG
KAHLENBERGER-DORF
Heiligenstädter Str.
Schreiberbach
Kahlenberger Str.
HERMANNSKOGEL
642
LATISBERG
492
Hauptstr.
NUSSDORF
Beethoven-Gedenkstätte "Testamenthaus"
Nußdorf
Cobenzlg.
DÖBLING
GRINZING
St. Jakobskirche
HAUSERL AM ROAN
Sieveringer
Höhenstraße
NEUSTIFT AM WALDE
Friedhof
KARL-MARX-HOF
Heiligenstadt
SIEVERING
Krottenbach-
Str.
HEILIGENSTADT
Geymüller-Schlößl
Exelbergstr.
Pötzleinsdorfer St.
Oberdöbling
OBERDÖBLING
PÖTZLEINSDORF
PARK
Krottenbachstraße
Gersthofer
TULLN
WÄHRING
Spittelau
Amundsenstr.
Dornbacher
DORNBACH
GERSTHOF
Gersthof
Türkenschanzpark
Nußd. Str.
Währinger Str. Volksoper
Franz-Josefs-Bahnhof
464
HEUBERG
Hernalser
Hauptstr.
HERNALS
Michelbeuern-AKH
Hernals
ALSERGRUND
KONGRESS-PARK
Alser Str.
KORDONSIEDLUNG
OTTAKRING
Wattgasse
Josefstädter Str.
KIRCHE AM STEINHOF
JOSEFSTADT
WAGNER VILLEN
Ottakring
Thaliastr.
223
Gablenzg.
STADTHALLE
Burggasse-Stadthalle
Flötzersteig
Kendlerstr.
NEUBAU
Neubaug
LINZ ST. PÖLTEN
HÜTTELDORF
PENZING
Breitensee
Hütteldorfer Str.
Schweglerstr.
West-Bhf.
Wienzeile
Hütteldorfer
Str.
Johnstr.
Zieglerg.
7
Hütteldorf
Linzer
Str.
RUDOLFSHEIM
MARIAHILF
Hadikg.
Unter St. Veit
Penzing
Gumpend. Str.
Linke
A 1-E 60
Ober St. Veit
Hadikgasse
Mariahilfer
Str.
Margareten-gürtel
Braunschweigg.
Hietzing
Schönbrunn
MARGARETEN
ST.-VEIT
Längenfeldg.
Lainzer Str.
SCHÖNBRUNN
Meidling Hauptstr.
Hornerhaus
HIETZING
Grünbergstr.
Niederhofstr.
Matzleinsdorfer Platz
Werkbundsiedlung
126
Friedhof
MEIDLING
Spinnerin am Kreuz
Philadelphia-brücke
Speising
Wasserturm
Lainzer Tor
Hetzendorfer
Str.
Hetzendorf
George-Washington-Hof
Hermesstr.
Modesammlung
Tscherttег.
Triester
HETZENDORF
Wienerwald
6
Z
X
Y
A
B

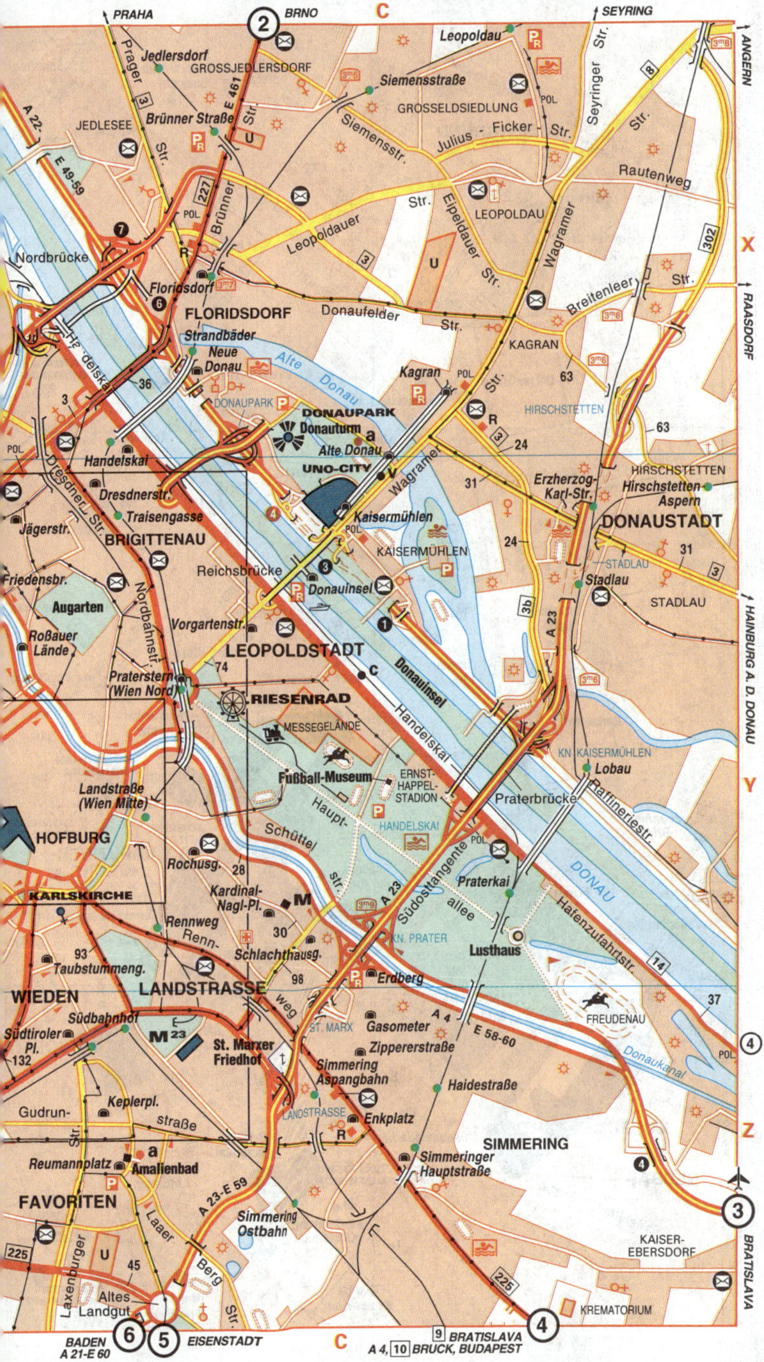

PRAHA
BRNO
C
SEYRING
ANGERN
Leopoldau
Jedlersdorf
GROSSJEDLERSDORF
Siemensstraße
GROSSELDSIEDLUNG
Seyringer Str.
JEDLESEE
Brünner Straße
E 461
Prager Str.
Siemensstr.
Julius - Ficker Str.
Rautenweg
A 22
E 49-59
Brünner Str.
Leopoldauer Str.
Eipeldauer Str.
LEOPOLDAU
Wagramer
302
X
Nordbrücke
Floridsdorf
FLORIDSDORF
Donaufelder Str.
Breitenleer Str.
RAASDORF
KAGRAN
Strandbäder
Neue Donau
Alte Donau
Kagran
DONAUPARK
Donauturm
Alte Donau
UNO-CITY
HIRSCHSTETTEN
Handelskai
Dresdnerstr.
Traisengasse
Jägerstr.
Dresdner Str.
BRIGITTENAU
Wagramer
Kaisermühlen
KAISERMÜHLEN
Erzherzog-Karl-Str.
Hirschstetten
HIRSCHSTETTEN
Aspern
DONAUSTADT
STADLAU
Stadlau
STADLAU
Friedensbr.
Reichsbrücke
Donauinsel
Augarten
Roßauer Lände
Nordbahnstr.
Vorgartenstr.
LEOPOLDSTADT
Donauinsel
A 23
HAINBURG A. D. DONAU
Praterstern (Wien Nord)
RIESENRAD
MESSEGELÄNDE
Handelskai
Fußball-Museum
ERNST-HAPPEL-STADION
KN KAISERMÜHLEN
Lobau
Landstraße (Wien Mitte)
HOFBURG
Schüttelstr.
Haupt-allee
HANDELSKAI
Praterbrücke
Raffineriestr.
Y
Rochusg.
Kardinal-Nagl-Pl.
KARLSKIRCHE
Südosttangente
Praterkai
DONAU
Rennweg
Renn-weg
Schlachthausg.
A 23
KN. PRATER
Lusthaus
Hafenzufahrtstr.
Taubstummeng.
WIEDEN
LANDSTRASSE
Erdberg
Südbahnhof
Südtiroler Pl.
ST. MARX
Gasometer
A 4
E 58-60
FREUDENAU
M 23
St. Marxer Friedhof
Zippererstraße
Simmering Aspangbahn
Haidestraße
Donaukanal
Gudrun-straße
Keplerpl.
LANDSTRASSE
Enkplatz
Z
Reumannplatz
Amalienbad
SIMMERING
Simmeringer Hauptstraße
FAVORITEN
A 23-E 59
Simmering Ostbahn
Laaer Berg Str.
KAISER-EBERSDORF
Laxenburger Str.
Altes Landgut
KREMATORIUM
BRATISLAVA
BADEN A 21-E 60
EISENSTADT
9 BRATISLAVA
A 4, 10 BRUCK, BUDAPEST

H
J
P
R
S
ALSERGRUND
Votivkirche
Roosevelt-platz
SIGMUND-FREUD-PARK
Universitätsstr.
Schottentor-Universität
Universität
Börse
Schottenring
Ringturm
Deutschmeister-Denkmal
Concordiapl.
MARIA AM GESTADE
Hohe Brücke
SCHOTTENSTIFT
Schotten-kirche
PASQUALATI-HAUS
Dreimäderl-haus
FREYUNG
Palais Kinsky
Römische Baureste
Altes Rathaus
Am Hof
RATHAUS
Neues Rathaus
Rathauspl.
Rathaus-park
Friedrich-Schmidt-Platz
BURG-THEATER
Minoriten-Kirche
Minoritenplatz
Bundeskanzleramt
Palais Mollard-Clary
PETERSKIRCHE
GRABEN
PESTSÄULE
Theseus-Tempel
Parlament
VOLKSGARTEN
Ballhaus-pl.
MICHAELER PL.
Michaeler Kirche
SISI MUSEUM
HOFBURG
HELDENPLATZ
KONGRESS-ZENTRUM
Äußeres Burgtor
Neue Burg
Stallburg
JOSEFS PL.
JÜDISCHES MUSEUM
DONNER BRUNNEN
KAPUZINER-KIRCHE
KAPUZINERGRUFT
ALBERTINA
Glashaus
Burggarten
Albertina-Platz
STAATSOPER
NATURHISTORISCHES MUSEUM
Maria-Theresien-Platz
KUNSTHISTORISCHES MUSEUM
Volkstheater
Palais Trautson
SPITTELBERG
MUSEUMSQUARTIER
NEUBAU
Mariahilfer Straße
AKADEMIE DER BILDENDEN KÜNSTE
Schiller-Denkmal
Café Museum
SECESSIONS-GEBÄUDE
Künstler-haus
Karlsplatz
Kunsthalle project space
WAGNER-PAVILLONS
WIEDEN
Theater an der Wien
Opern-Ring
Kärntner
Burgring
Dr. Karl-Lueger-Ring
Dr. K.-Renner-Ring
Lerchenfelder Str.
Museumstr.
Auerspergstr.
Babenbergerstr.
Nibelungeng.
Gumpendorfer Str.
Siebensterng.
Herrengasse
Wipplingerstr.
Naglergasse
Wallner-str.
Spiegelg.

K L

WIEN
0
200 m
Schnellbahn
LEOPOLDSTADT
Haidgasse
Glockeng.
Rotensterngasse
JOHANN-STRAUSS "GEDENKSTÄTTE"
Praterstr.
Zirkusg.
Nestroypl.
Hollandstr.
Obere
DONAUKANAL
Franz-Josefs-Kai
Rudolfs-pl.
Salztorbrücke
Donaustr.
Taborstraße
Praterstr.
Donaustr.
Untere
Salztorg.
Marienbr.
Ruprechtskirche
Schwedenbr.
Aspern brücke
Urania-Sternwarte
Dampfschiffstr.
Franz-Josefs-Kai
Schwedenpl.
HOHER MARKT
Römische Ruinen
Fleischmarkt
FLEISCHMARKT
Postg.
POST-SPARK.
Zollamtsstr.
Zollamts-str.
Lugeck
Rotenturmstr.
Alte Schmiede
JESUITEN-KIRCHE
Biberstr.
Regierungs-gebäude
Vordere
Hintere
STEPHANSDOM
Wollzeile
Postg.
Dominikaner-kirche
Alte Universität
Stubenring
MAK
Stephanspl.
FIGARO-HAUS
Deutschordens-haus
Singerstr.
Weihburg-
Stubenbastei
Stubentor
WIEN MITTE
Franziskaner-Kirche
Palais Colloredo
WIEN
Landstraße (Wien Mitte)
STADTPALAIS DES PRINZEN EUGEN
Johannes-Anna-Kirche
Annag.
Seilerstätte
gasse
Parkring
Stadtpark
Invalidenstr.
JOH.-STRAUSS-DENKMAL
KURSALON
Ungargasse
Linke
Rechte
Am Heumarkt
HAUS DER MUSIK
Schelling-gasse
RING
Schubertring
ÖAMTC
Johannesgasse
Café Schwarzenberg
Stadtpark
Rudolf-Sallinger-Pl.
Beatrixg.
Ring
Hotel Imperial
Beethovenplatz
Bahngasse
Reisnerstr.
Bahngasse
Ungargasse
KONZERT-HAUS
Heumarkt
Am
Musikvereins-gebäude
Lothringer
AM MODENA-PARK
HIST. MUSEUM
SCHWARZENBERG-PLATZ
P
R
S

K L

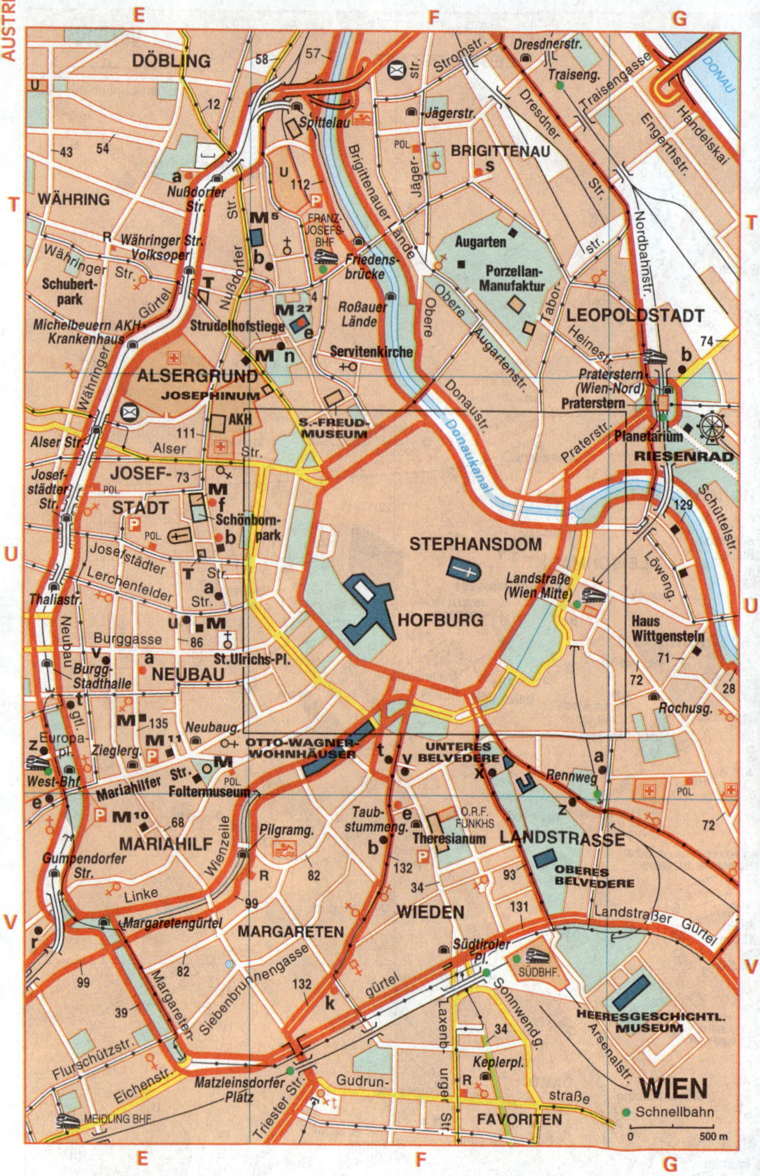

The rates shown may be revised
if the cost of living changes to any great extent.
Before making your reservation, confirm with the hotelier
the exact price that will be charged.

Town Centre, city districts (Stadtbezirke) 1 - 9 :

Imperial, Kärntner Ring 16, ✉ 1015, ☎ (01) 50 11 00, *Fax (01) 50110410, hotel.imperial@luxurycollection.com*, ⅃, – |‡|, ⇹ rm, ▤ TV ☏ – 🏛 120. AE ⓓ ⓜ VISA JCB. ✻ rest KS a
Imperial (booking essential) *(closed 4 weeks July - August) (dinner only)* **Meals** à la carte 43/76 ♀ – ***Café Imperial* : Meals** à la carte 30/45 – ⌂ 33 – **138 rm** 469/794 – 562/794 – 30 suites.
◆ The Württemberg Palace is a jewel in Vienna's architectural crown. Lavish, luxurious room décor plus fine antique furnishings breathing the spirit of the 19C. Exclusive ambience in the restaurant. Viennese coffee-house atmosphere in the Café Imperial.

Grand Hotel, Kärntner Ring 9, ✉ 1010, ☎ (01) 51 58 00, *Fax (01) 5151312, sales@grandhotelwien.com*, ⅃ – |‡|, ⇹ rm, ▤ TV ☏ ♿ 🚗 – 🏛 220. AE ⓓ ⓜ VISA JCB KS f
Le ciel *(closed Sunday)* **Meals** à la carte 40/63 ♀ – ***Unkai*** (Japanese) *(closed Monday lunch)* **Meals** 38/95, ♀ – ***Grand Café* : Meals** à la carte 24/45 ♀ – ⌂ 29 – **205 rm** 320/400 – 390/470 – 11 suites.
◆ The glories of the Belle Epoque have been brought to life again in this luxurious establishment whose superb décor and furnishings will appeal to all those with high standards of taste. The elegant Le Ciel above the rooftops. Sushi and Sashimi in the Unkai.

Palais Coburg, Coburgbastei 4, ✉ 1010, ☎ (01) 51 81 80, *Fax (01) 518181, hotel.residenz@palaiscoburg.com*, ⛱, 🏊, – |‡|, ⇹ rm, ▤ TV ☏ 🚗 – 🏛 150. AE ⓓ ⓜ VISA JCB. ✻ KR m
Meals see ***Restaurant Coburg*** below – ***Gartenpavillon*** *(lunch only)* **Meals** à la carte 16/25 ♀ – **35 suites** ⌂ 460/1920 – 460/1920.
◆ No expense has been spared in the restoration of this 1840 palace, with its refined, luxurious reception area, its individual, lavishly furnished suites with the latest technology.The garden pavilion, arranged as a winter garden, is attractively light.

Sacher, Philharmonikerstr. 4, ✉ 1010, ☎ (01) 51 45 60, *Fax (01) 51456810, wien@sacher.com* – |‡|, ⇹ rm, ▤ TV ☏ – 🏛 50. AE ⓓ ⓜ VISA JCB. ✻ rest JS x
Meals à la carte 33/62 ♀ – ⌂ 27 – **108 rm** 297/336 – 357/396 – 10 suites.
◆ This Vienna institution was opened in 1876. The establishment's atmosphere is enhanced by prize antiques and a famous painting collection. The classically elegant restaurant also serves typical Viennese fare such as Wiener Schnitzel and Sachertorte.

Bristol, Kärntner Ring 1, ✉ 1015, ☎ (01) 51 51 60, *Fax (01) 51516550, hotel.bristol@westin.com* – |‡|, ⇹ rm, ▤ TV ☏ – 🏛 80. AE ⓓ ⓜ VISA JCB. ✻ rest JS m
Meals see ***Korso*** below – ***Sirk*** *(closed July 3 weeks for lunch)* **Meals** à la carte 35/61 ♀ – ⌂ 30 – **140 rm** 405/688 – 10 suites.
◆ A very British hotel. Choice antiques and original works of art decorate the rooms, which also feature fine plasterwork, ceiling paintings and period furniture. Exclusive tower rooms. The Rotisserie Sirk with tasteful décor of the utmost discretion.

Le Méridien, Opernring 13, ✉ 1010, ☎ (01) 58 89 00, *Fax (01) 588909090, info.vienna@lemeridien.com*, ⅃, 🏊 – |‡| ⇹ ▤ TV ☏ ♿ 🚗 – 🏛 180. AE ⓓ ⓜ VISA JCB. ✻ rest JS c
***Shambala* : Meals** 25 (lunch)/65 and à la carte ♀ – ⌂ 23 – **294 rm** 305/435 – 355/435 – 17 Suiten.
◆ From the outside it looks like a traditional grand hotel, inside it is stylishly modern with appealing lines. Rooms are in attractive, bright colours, with the most up-to-date technology. Simple, elegant design and interesting lighting in the Shambala.

InterContinental, Johannesgasse 28, ✉ 1037, ☎ (01) 71 12 20, *Fax (01) 7134489, vienna@interconti.com*, ←, ⅃ – |‡|, ⇹ rm, ▤ TV ☏ ♿ 🚗 – 🏛 470. AE ⓓ ⓜ VISA JCB. ✻ rest KS p
Meals à la carte 26/48 ♀ – ⌂ 23 – **453 rm** 250/330 – 310/390 – 61 suites.
◆ Rooms with lovely warm colours and a touch of Mediterranean style. 10th-floor Club Lounge with exclusive ambience and spectacular city views. In the evening diners can enjoy Mediterranean cooking and a relaxed atmosphere.

Marriott, Parkring 12a, ✉ 1010, ☎ (01) 51 51 80, *Fax (01) 515186736, vienna.marriott.info@marriotthotels.com*, ⅃, 🏊 – |‡|, ⇹ rm, ▤ TV ☏ ♿ 🚗 – 🏛 300. AE ⓓ ⓜ VISA. ✻ rest KR d
Meals 26/45 and à la carte – ⌂ 23 – **313 rm** 270/320 – 5 suites.
◆ This hotel in the centre of Vienna is known for its comfort and highly professional management and service. Many rooms with a view of the City Park. Business floor. Classically welcoming atmosphere in the restaurant.

Hilton Vienna Plaza, Schottenring 11, ✉ 1010, ✆ (01) 31 39 00, *Fax (01) 3139022422, cb_vienna-plaza@hilton.com*, rm, - 60. AE VISA JCB JP a
La Scala *(closed lunch Saturday, Sunday and Bank Holidays)* **Meals** 33/62 and à la carte - 24 - **218 rm** 330 - 370 - 10 suites.
◆ In love with Art Deco and classical Modernism, this contemporary grand hotel has designer rooms that impress with their cool luxury. The Scala has attractive place settings in a contemporary milieu.

Radisson SAS Palais, Parkring 16, ✉ 1010, ✆ (01) 51 51 70, *Fax (01) 5122216, sales.vienna@radissonsas.com*, rm, - 190. AE VISA JCB. rest KR z
Le siècle *(closed 1 week Easter, July - August, Saturday lunch, Sunday, Monday dinner and Bank Holidays)* **Meals** à la carte 33/51 - ***Palais Café :*** **Meals** à la carte 18/32 - 22 - **247 rm** 280 - 45 suites.
◆ Stylish furnishings and discreetly patterned materials characterise the tasteful rooms in this pair of linked palaces opposite the City Park. The Le Siècle restaurant has an attractively traditional ambience. The Palais Café is a feature of the wintergarden.

Hilton Vienna, Am Stadtpark 3, ✉ 1030, ✆ (01) 7 17 00, *Fax (01) 7170011000, reservation.vienna@hilton.com*, rm, - 475. AE VISA. rest LR e
Meals à la carte 28/40 - 24 - **579 rm** 200/285 - 250/330 - 41 suites.
◆ You can revel in the city view from the upper-floor rooms of this conference hotel. Large, welcoming reception area and rooms with light wood furnishings. The restaurant has a contemporary and congenial design.

Renaissance Penta, Ungargasse 60, ✉ 1030, ✆ (01) 71 17 50, *Fax (01) 711758143, rhi.viese.sales@renaissancehotels.com*, rm, - 260. AE VISA JCB FU a
Meals à la carte 23/35 - 17 - **339 rm** 180/250.
◆ You don't have to be an experienced equestrian to stay in this neo-Classical listed building that was once the Imperial military riding school. Bright, functional natural wood furnishings. Diners made welcome in the elegant Borromäus restaurant.

Ambassador, Kärntner Str. 22, ✉ 1010, ✆ (01) 96 16 10, *Fax (01) 5132999, office@ambassador.at* - - 80. AE VISA JCB. rest JR s
Meals see ***Mörwald im Ambassador*** below - 20 - **86 rm** 225/412 - 285/516.
◆ Tradition and Viennese charm in a pleasing symbiosis with Hi-Tech. Individual rooms with welcoming colours, elegant décor and classical comfort in the most modern style.

Hotel im Palais Schwarzenberg, Schwarzenbergplatz 9, ✉ 1030, ✆ (01) 7 98 45 15, *Fax (01) 7984714, hotel@palais-schwarzenberg.com*, - 250. AE VISA JCB FU x
Meals 33 *(lunch)*/55 and à la carte - **44 rm** 255/350 - 330/450 - 4 suites.
◆ Enchanting aptly describes this former palace dating from 1732, with its wonderful private park, its classic, individually designed rooms with their period furniture and its unique Baroque function rooms. Elegant terrace restaurant overlooking the park.

Hotel de France, Schottenring 3, ✉ 1010, ✆ (01) 31 36 80, *Fax (01) 3195969, defrance@austria-hotels.at*, rm, - 80. AE VISA JCB HP b
Meals *(closed Saturday and Sunday)* à la carte 32/44 - **208 rm** 250/300 - 285/335.
◆ A particularly lovely, traditional city hotel. Guests are accommodated in well-presented rooms, mostly furnished with Viennese period pieces. Modern maisonettes on the top floor. Luxurious Belle Etage restaurant. A simpler style in the Bistro.

Das Triest, Wiedner Hauptstr. 12, ✉ 1040, ✆ (01) 58 91 80, *Fax (01) 5891818, rosi@dastriest.at*, rm, - 60. AE VISA JCB FU t
Meals *(closed end July - early August, 1 week early January, Saturday lunch and Sunday)* (Italian) 39/45 and à la carte - **72 rm** 195/295 - 249/310 - 3 suites.
◆ The Terence Conran designed rooms with blue chairs and desks with modem links are functional and comfortable without being fussy. Contemporary ambience in the restaurant with lots of mirrors and attractive lighting effects.

Arcotel Wimberger, Neubaugürtel 34, ✉ 1070, ✆ (01) 52 16 50, *Fax (01) 52165811, wimberger@arcotel.at*, rm, rm, - 650. AE VISA JCB EU t
Meals 22 *(buffet lunch)* and à la carte - 11 - **225 rm** 160 - 200 - 7 suites.
◆ Following fire damage to the old Hotel Wimberger, there are now modern rooms with natural wood furnishings devoted to the needs of business travellers. The Maskerade restaurant has been decorated with materials saved from the old ballroom.

NH Belvedere without rest, Rennweg 12a, ✉ 1030, ✆ (01) 2 06 11, *Fax (01) 2061115, nhbelvedere@nh-hotels.com*, AE VISA JCB FV z
13 - **114 rm** 115/175.
◆ Modern hotel occupying the neo-Classical building of the old State Printing Works. Attractive rooms, some with a view of the Botantical Gardens. Bistro with snacks.

PREMIER
À REIMS FRANCE

Sofitel, Am Heumarkt 35, 1030, (01) 71 61 60, *Fax (01) 71616844, h1276@accor.com* – rm, – 60. KS e
Meals *(closed lunch Saturday, Sunday and Bank Holidays)* à la carte 19/39 – 17 – **211 rm** 150/206 – 170/226.
◆ Art Nouveau features and Klimt reproductions give a welcoming feeling to these rooms with their timeless natural wood furnishings and modern technology. Central location. Restaurant with attractive place settings and Viennese specialities.

Hilton Vienna-Danube, Handelskai 269, 1020, (01) 7 27 77, *Fax (01) 72782200, info.vienna-danube@hilton.com*, – rm, – 200. rest CY c
Meals à la carte 26/37 – 19 – **367 rm** 240 – 270.
◆ This former warehouse on the Danube has rooms of sizeable dimensions, with excellent technical facilities. Conference area on the 8th floor with city view. Enjoy the outlook over the river while you dine in the restaurant.

Kaiserhof without rest, Frankenberggasse 10, 1040, (01) 5 05 17 01, *Fax (01) 505887588, info@hotel-kaiserhof.at*, – FU v
74 rm 125/170 – 155/230.
◆ The Richard family have been looking after travellers since 1577. Built in 1896, the Kaiserhof is the ideal place for their talents, full of fine design and Viennese charm.

Mercure Grandhotel Biedermeier without rest, Landstraßer Hauptstr. 28 (at Sünnhof), 1030, (01) 71 67 10, *Fax (01) 71671503, h5357-sl@accor.com* – – 60. LR d
15 – **203 rm** 142 – 160 – 14 suites.
◆ All the rooms in this establishment have been provided with cherrywood Biedermeier-style furnishings and are welcoming and extremely comfortable.

Kaiserin Elisabeth without rest, Weihburggasse 3, 1010, (01) 51 52 60, *Fax (01) 515267, info@kaiserinelisabeth.at* – – 20. KR a
63 rm 119/160 – 205.
◆ Mozart and Wagner were regular guests in this hotel near the Cathedral, which has provided accommodation since 1809. Elegant dark wood furnishings in turn-of-the-century style.

Altstadt Vienna without rest, Kirchengasse 41, 1070, (01) 5 26 33 99, *Fax (01) 5234901, hotel@altstadt.at* – . EU u
37 rm 109/129 – 159 – 7 suites.
◆ Each of the rooms in this patrician mansion has its own distinctive character. Tasteful décor, with high ceilings, parquet floors and contemporary Italian furnishings.

König von Ungarn, Schulerstr. 10, 1010, (01) 51 58 40, *Fax (01) 515848, hotel@kvu.at* – , rm, – 15. rest KR f
Meals *(dinner only)* à la carte 22/36 – **33 rm** 135/155 – 192.
◆ This stylish décor of this traditional 16C hotel behind the Cathedral features warm colours. The courtyard is well worth a look. Follow in Mozart's footsteps ; the great composer once lived here.

K+K Hotel Maria Theresia without rest, Kirchberggasse 6, 1070, (01) 5 21 23, *Fax (01) 5212370, kk.maria.theresia@kuk.at*, – , rm, – 40. HS a
123 rm 165 – 216.
◆ A hotel in the idyllic artistic district of Spittelberg, with prettily decorated rooms, some with glass-topped work-desks. The rooms with a city view are particularly lovely.

Rathaus without rest, Lange Gasse 13, 1080, (01) 4 00 11 22, *Fax (01) 400112288, office@hotel-rathaus-wien.at* – – 20. EU a
13 – **33 rm** 118/138 – 148/198.
◆ The old structure of this late 19C establishment has been successfully combined with tasteful, modern design. Each room is named after an Austrian winegrower.

Rathauspark without rest, Rathausstr. 17, 1010, (01) 40 41 20, *Fax (01) 40412761, rathauspark@austria-trend.at* – – 30. HP a
117 rm 136/169 – 195/244.
◆ A stucco-adorned reception area welcomes you to this smart establishment dating from 1880. The rooms, most of which have high ceilings, are furnished in a modern, elegant style. Take a ride in the original lift.

Falkensteiner Am Schottenfeld without rest, Schottenfeldgasse 74, 1070, (01) 5 26 51 81, *Fax (01) 5265181160, schottenfeld@falkensteiner.com*, – – 100. rest EU v
95 rm 129 – 164.
◆ Nestled in a terrace of houses everything in this hotel is modern, from the extensive reception area to the pleasant brightly furnished, functional rooms.

K+K Palais Hotel without rest, Rudolfsplatz 11, ✉ 1010, ℘ (01) 5 33 13 53, *Fax (01) 533135370, kk.palais.hotel@kuk.at* – AE VISA JCB JP h
66 rm 165/185 – 215.
◆ This historic Stadtpalais offers functional, yet welcoming, rooms and a breakfast room in warm colours. The Cathedral and Underground are close at hand.

Strudelhof without rest, Pasteurgasse 1, ✉ 1090, ℘ (01) 3 19 25 22, *Fax (01) 319252210020, seminarhotel@strudlhof.at*, – 150. AE VISA FT n
84 rm 128/164 – 174.
◆ This hotel offers its guests comfortable rooms with good technical facilities. The palace at the rear makes a stylish setting for business meetings.

Suite Hotel 900 m Zur Oper without rest, Wiedner Hauptstr. 44, ✉ 1040, ℘ (01) 5857211, *Fax (01) 585721128, hotel-oper900m@aon.at* – 30. AE VISA JCB FV b
29 rm 130/170 – 170 – 6 suites.
◆ All rooms in this traditional town house have solid cherrywood furnishings and good technical facilities. Café with art gallery.

Mercure Secession without rest, Getreidemarkt 5, ✉ 1060, ℘ (01) 58 83 80, *Fax (01) 58838212, h3532@accor.com* – rm, – 30. AE VISA JCB JS b
70 rm 140/161 – 174.
◆ Thanks to its central location, this establishment is an excellent base for your exploration of the city. Homely, comfortable rooms plus apartments.

Opernring without rest, Opernring 11, ✉ 1010, ℘ (01) 5 87 55 18, *Fax (01) 587551829, hotel@opernring.at* – AE VISA JCB JS a
35 rm 140/185 – 155/215.
◆ This establishment by the Opera has a lovely Art Nouveau facade. The spacious rooms combine liveability and comfort with the functionality of up-to-date accommodation.

Starlight Suiten Salzgries without rest, Salzgries 12, ✉ 1010, ℘ (01) 5 35 92 22, *Fax (01) 535922211, reservation@starlighthotel.com*, – AE VISA JCB JP e
13 – **50 suites** 139 – 169.
◆ If one room is not enough, stay in this modern hotel whose suites are both functional and with up-to-date technology. Quietly located in a side street in the city centre.

Tourotel without rest, Mariahilferstr. 156, ✉ 1150, ℘ (01) 89 23 33 50, *Fax (01) 8923335495, hotel.mariahilf@tourotel.at* – AE VISA EV e
65 rm 99/129 – 139/149.
◆ Not far from the West Station, this modern-looking city building has good, functional and practically furnished rooms.

Ibis Messe, Lassallestr. 7a, ✉ 1020, ℘ (01) 21 77 00, *Fax (01) 21770555, h2736@accor.com* – rm, – 100. AE VISA GT b
Meals à la carte 16/25 – 9 – **166 rm** 62 – 77.
◆ This establishment close to the Prater has contemporary, brightly furnished and functional rooms, well-equipped with technical facilities and generous work-desks.

Restaurant Coburg - Hotel Palais Coburg, Coburgbastei 4, ✉ 1010, ℘ (01) 51 81 88 00, *Fax (01) 51818818, restaurant@palais-coburg.com*, – AE VISA JCB. KR m
closed Monday, Sunday and Bank Holidays – **Meals** *(dinner only)* 62/92 and à la carte.
Spec. Variation vom Kalbskopf mit Rettich und Pfeffergelée. Gebratene Taube mit roten Rübenlinsen und Rahmgnocchi. Topfenschmarren mit Birnen.
◆ Beautifully restored vaults and lavish place settings contribute to the discreetly elegant ambience of the restaurant. The cuisine is classic with a creative touch.

Korso - Hotel Bristol, Kärntner Ring 1, ✉ 1010, ℘ (01) 51 51 65 46, *Fax (01) 51516575* – AE VISA JCB. JS m
closed 9 to 29 August and Saturday lunch – **Meals** 34 *(lunch)*/84 and à la carte.
Spec. Roh marinierter Kaisergranat mit Zitronenöl und Artischocken. Zander mit Polenta und Paprikasauce. Gebratene Bauernente mit glacierten Äpfeln und Rahmkraut.
◆ Reinhard Gerer's Viennese and French cuisine is served here in an atmosphere that is traditional and elegant.

Steirereck, Am Heumarkt 2 (in the citypark), ✉ 1030, ℘ (01) 7 13 31 68, *Fax (01) 71351682, wien@steirereck.at*, – AE VISA JCB LR c
closed Saturday and Sunday – **Meals** *(dinner only)* (booking essential) 77/85.
Spec. Gänseleberschnitte mit Rhabarber und Erdbeeren. Lamm mit karamelisierter Weizensauce und Schwammerlbaumkuchen. Schaftopfen und -joghurt mit Himbeeren.
◆ Following a move to new quarters in the middle of January Helmut Österreicher now serves his cuisine in the newly renovated rooms of this former dairy farm in the City Park. The location by the river is idyllic.

XXX ✿ **Mörwald im Ambassador**, Kärntner Str. 22 (first floor), ✉ 1010, ✆ (01) 96 16 11 61, *Fax (01) 96161160, ambassador@moerwald.at* – ▤. AE ⓓ MC VISA JCB. ⚹ JR s
closed Sunday and Bank Holidays – **Meals** (booking essential) 30 *(lunch)*/69 and à la carte ♀, ⚘.
Spec. Tauben-Gänseleber-Chartreuse. Szegediner Hummerkrautfleisch. Zander mit zweierlei Spinat.
◆ In a neo-Classical building, an elegant first floor restaurant reached through a smart bar, setting the tone for the enjoyment of local cuisine and some creative specialities. The large glass windows open for a hint of alfresco dining in the summer.

XXX **Drei Husaren**, Weihburggasse 4, ✉ 1010, ✆ (01) 51 21 09 20, *Fax (01) 512109218, office@drei.husaren.at* – AE ⓓ MC VISA JCB KR u
Meals à la carte 43/64.
◆ In a side street close to the Cathedral, this is an historic gourmet restaurant with cheerful yellow-painted walls. A refined version of classic Viennese cuisine is served.

XXX **Rubens Palais**, Fürstengasse 1 (Palais Liechtenstein), ✉ 1090, ✆ (01) 3 19 23 96 13, *Fax (01) 319239696, marionjambor@yahoo.de*, ⛱ – AE ⓓ MC VISA. ⚹ FT e
closed Sunday and Monday – **Meals** 62/95 and à la carte ♀, ⚘ – ***Ruben's Brasserie*** *(closed Tuesday)* **Meals** à la carte 20/41 ♀.
◆ This elegant restaurant with its very intimate atmosphere and professional service has flourished in an extension of the Liechtenstein Palace, built in 1711. Lovely forecourt. The contemporary Brasserie is a somewhat simpler alternative to Ruben's Palais.

XXX **Niky's Kuchlmasterei** with rm, Obere Weissgerberstr. 6, ✉ 1030, ✆ (01) 7 12 90 00, *Fax (01) 712900016, office@kuchlmasterei.at*, ⛱ – ⚹ rm. AE ⓓ MC VISA LR f
Meals *(closed Sunday and Bank Holidays, except December)* 30 *(lunch)*/51 and à la carte ♀, ⚘ – ☕ 13 – **7 suites** 220.
◆ The opulence and original features of the rooms in this unusual restaurant never fail to surprise. A lovely terrace and an enormous wine cellar. Individual, exclusive suites.

XXX **Julius Meinl am Graben**, Graben 19 (first floor), ✉ 1010, ✆ (01) 5 32 33 34 60 00, *Fax (01) 53233341290, julius.meinl@restaurant.com* – ▤. AE ⓓ MC VISA JCB JR e
closed Sunday and Bank Holidays – **Meals** (booking essential) 29 *(lunch)*/70 and à la carte ♀, ⚘.
◆ A glass lift transports diners up through the famous delicatessen to this secret restaurant with its elegant ambience and refined Austrian cuisine.

XXX **Grotta Azzurra**, Babenbergerstr. 5, ✉ 1010, ✆ (01) 5 86 10 44, *Fax (01) 586104415, office@grotta-azzurra.at* – AE ⓓ MC VISA JCB HS s
Meals (Italian) à la carte 27/42.
◆ Vienna's oldest Italian establishment is lent its special character by wonderfully crafted Venetian glass and mosaics. Seasonal menu featuring Italian regional cuisine.

XXX **Steirer Stub'n**, Wiedner Hauptstr. 111, ✉ 1050, ✆ (01) 5 44 43 49, *Fax (01) 5440888, steirerstuben@chello.at* – ▤. AE ⓓ MC VISA FV k
closed Sunday and Bank Holidays, July - August Saturday and Sunday – **Meals** (booking essential) à la carte 25/35 ♀.
◆ Typical Viennese dishes are proffered in an atmospheric setting, which the tastefully decorated, rustic dining rooms do much to enhance.

XX **Selina**, Laudongasse 13, ✉ 1080, ✆ (01) 4 05 64 04, *Fax (01) 4080459* – AE ⓓ MC VISA JCB EU f
closed Saturday lunch, dinner Sunday and Bank Holidays – **Meals** 82 and à la carte ♀.
◆ On the edge of the city centre, sophisticated cuisine served in an elegantly modern ambience accentuated by pictures and Classical features.

XX ✿ **Fabios**, Tuchlauben 6, ✉ 1010, ✆ (01) 5 32 22 22, *Fax (01) 5322225, fabios@fabios.at* – ▤. AE ⓓ MC VISA JR x
closed Sunday – **Meals** (Italian) (booking essential) à la carte 31/55 ♀.
Spec. Kurz gebratenes Thunfischfilet mit Sesamkrust und geschmortem Kohl. Ochsenbacken in Olivenöl geschmort mit karamellisierten Karotten. Warmer Schokoladenauflauf mit Blutorangensorbet.
◆ This fashionable Italian establishment offers not only fine cuisine but also sophisticated place settings and lovely, minimalist interior décor.

XX ✿ **Walter Bauer**, Sonnenfelsgasse 17, ✉ 1010, ✆ (01) 5 12 98 71, *Fax (01) 5129871, restaurant.walter.bauer@aon.at* – ▤. AE ⓓ MC VISA. ⚹ KR c
closed 1 week Easter, mid July - mid August, Saturday - Monday lunch and Bank Holidays – **Meals** (booking essential) 49/69 and à la carte ♀.
Spec. Hummerkrautfleisch. Oktopusrisotto mit konfierten Zitronen. Pyramide von der Valrhona Schokolade.
◆ This lovely vaulted restaurant is somewhat hidden away in a little alleyway not far from the Jesuits' Church - dating from the 14C, it was once a stables.

Vestibül, Dr. Karl-Lueger-Ring 2 (at Burgtheater), ✉ 1010, ☎ (01) 5 32 49 99, *Fax (01) 532499910, restaurant@vestibuel.at* – AE ⓓ ⓜ VISA HR d
closed Saturday lunch, Sunday and Bank Holidays – **Meals** à la carte 28/41 ♀.
◆ In a wing of the Burgtheater that was once the Emperor's private entrance, this stylish and elegant restaurant offers Viennese and Mediterranean cuisine.

Novelli, Bräunerstr. 11, ✉ 1010, ☎ (01) 5 13 42 00, *Fax (01) 5139974, novelli@haslauer.at*, – AE ⓓ ⓜ VISA JR b
closed Sunday – **Meals** (Italian) (booking essential) 25 *(lunch)*/49 and à la carte ♀.
◆ This is a place in which to enjoy a relaxed Italian atmosphere and appreciate classic food and drink from the shores of the Mediterranean.

Zum weißen Rauchfangkehrer, Weihburggasse 4, ✉ 1010, ☎ (01) 5 12 34 71, *Fax (01) 512347128, rauchfangkehrer@utanet.at* – ▤. ⓜ VISA KR e
closed July - August, 2 weeks January, Sunday and Monday – **Meals** *(dinner only)* (booking essential) à la carte 36/64 ♀.
◆ One of Vienna's loveliest old restaurants, divided into cheerful, attractively decorated rooms with corner seats. The choice on the menu is impressive.

Indochine 21, Stubenring 18, ✉ 1010, ☎ (01) 5 13 76 60, *Fax (01) 513766016, restaurant@indochine.at*, – ▤. AE ⓓ ⓜ VISA JCB LR b
Meals (Euro-Asian) 45/65 and à la carte ♀.
◆ In an excellent city location this chic establishment brings a touch of old Indochina to Vienna. Fusion cuisine - French with an Asian touch - served to a very high standard.

Zum Schwarzen Kameel, Bognergasse 5, ✉ 1010, ☎ (01) 5 33 81 25, *Fax (01) 533812510, info@kameel.at*, – ▤. AE ⓓ ⓜ VISA JCB JR m
closed Sunday and Bank Holidays – **Meals** (booking essential) à la carte 28/49 ♀.
◆ This fashionable and far from everyday restaurant is entered through a delicatessen. Lovely Art Nouveau style combines with Viennese charm to make it very special.

Buddha Club, Währinger Gürtel 172 (Metropolitan railway elbows), ✉ 1090, ☎ (01) 4 79 88 49, *Fax (01) 4799023, reservierung@buddha-club.at*. AE ⓓ ⓜ VISA JCB ET a
closed June - September, Sunday and Monday – **Meals** *(dinner only)* (booking essential) à la carte 31/39 ♀.
◆ The interior of this restaurant under the railway arches is a restful concoction of dark wood and stripped floors, Buddha statues and contemporary paintings.

Fadinger, Wipplingerstr. 29, ✉ 1010, ☎ (01) 5 33 43 41, *Fax (01) 5324451, restaurant@fadinger.at* – AE VISA JP f
closed Saturday, Sunday and Bank Holidays – **Meals** (booking essential) à la carte 24/48 ♀.
◆ Attractive city centre establishment close to the stock exchange. Bright watercolours, cheerful atmosphere and a mixture of local dishes and fine cuisine.

Livingstone, Zelinkagasse 4, ✉ 1010, ☎ (01) 5 33 33 93, *Fax (01) 53333935, office@livingstone.at*, – ⓓ ⓜ VISA JP m
Meals *(dinner only)* à la carte 25/40 ♀.
◆ This former textile warehouse in the Jewish quarter of Vienna now houses a colonial style restaurant. The Bar Planter's Club is very comfortable.

Harry's Time, An der Hülben 1, ✉ 1010, ☎ (01) 5 12 45 56, *Fax (01) 5124694, office@harrys-time.at*. AE ⓓ ⓜ VISA GR d
closed Saturday lunch, Sunday and Bank Holidays – **Meals** (booking essential) à la carte 23/39 ♀.
◆ Recommendations for this family-run bistro-style restaurant are the refined and pleasantly informal atmosphere, and the very friendly service.

Artner, Floragasse 6, ✉ 1040, ☎ (01) 5 03 50 33, *Fax (01) 5035034, restaurant@artner.co.at*, – AE ⓓ ⓜ VISA FV e
closed Christmas, lunch Saturday, Sunday and Bank Holidays – **Meals** 9 *(lunch)*/36 and à la carte ♀.
◆ Dark wooden floors and appealing lines describe the simple and modern furnishings in this restaurant. International and local cuisine, with a good value lunchtime set-menu.

Urania, Uraniastr. 1, ✉ 1010, ☎ (01) 7 13 30 66, *Fax (01) 7157297, office@barurania.com*, – AE ⓓ ⓜ VISA KR a
Meals (booking essential) 25/55 and à la carte ♀.
◆ Trendy restaurant in an observatory. A plain and simple interior in discreet colours behind a glazed-in façade. Lovely views of the Danube from the roof terrace in summer.

Tempel, Praterstr. 56, ✉ 1020, ☎ (01) 2 14 01 79, *Fax (01) 2140179, restaurant.tempel@utanet.at* – ⓜ VISA LP a
closed 22 December - 10 January, Sunday and Monday – **Meals** 27/36 and à la carte.
◆ This little bistro-style restaurant is tucked away in a courtyard. It serves local specialities as well as more refined dishes and is well worth looking for.

Schnattl, Lange Gasse 40, ✉ 1080, ☎ (01) 4 05 34 00, *Fax (01) 4053400*, – AE DC – *closed 2 weeks April, 2 weeks end August, Saturday, Sunday and Bank Holidays* – **Meals** 34/48 and à la carte. EU b
◆ This well-run little restaurant with its simple but not unattractive interior is located on the edge of the city centre. It's very pleasant sitting out in the courtyard.

Hedrich, Stubenring 2, ✉ 1010, ☎ (01) 5 12 95 88 LR a
closed August, Saturday, Sunday and Bank Holidays – **Meals** à la carte 10/22.
◆ Typical unfussy pub-type ambience and a menu full of carefully prepared local dishes. Personal service.

Gaumenspiel, Zieglergasse 54, ✉ 1070, ☎ (01) 5 26 11 08, *Fax (01) 526110830, essen@gaumenspiel.at* – MC VISA EU a
closed 3 weeks June, Saturday lunch and Sunday – **Meals** (booking essential) 28/49 and à la carte.
◆ A very simple-style Bistro with friendly, competent service. Wooden floors and warm red colours enhance the very pleasant atmosphere.

City districts (Stadtbezirke) 10 - 15 :

Holiday Inn Vienna South, Triester Str. 72, ✉ 1100, ☎ (01) 6 05 30, *Fax (01) 60530580, info@holiday-inn.co.at*, <, , – rm, – 210. AE DC MC VISA JCB BZ f
Meals à la carte 21/34 – 21 – **174 rm** 196 – 212 – 4 suites.
◆ This modern hotel with functional rooms is on the edge of town in a business park with a shopping centre. Rooms with fax and modem link. The high point of the Brasserie California restaurant is the vast hot and cold buffet.

Renaissance Wien, Linke Wienzeile/Ullmannstr. 71, ✉ 1150, ☎ (01) 89 10 20, *Fax (01) 89102300, rhi.viehw@renaissancehotels.com*, , – rm, – 200. AE DC MC VISA JCB BZ a
Meals à la carte 22/34 – 21 – **309 rm** 227 – 250.
◆ Guests are accommodated here in functional rooms with light wood furnishings. There's more space in the Executive Rooms. City panorama from the indoor pool on the 7th floor. The restaurant has an air of elegance.

Mercure Wien Westbahnhof, Felberstr. 4, ✉ 1150, ☎ (01) 98 11 10, *Fax (01) 98111930, h5358@accor.com*, – rm, – 30. AE DC MC VISA. rest EU z
Meals à la carte 17/34 – 14 – **253 rm** 145 – 165.
◆ Pink on the outside, this corner building has a meticulously refurbished interior, with comfortable rooms offering all the facilities to be expected in a contemporary hotel. The Café-Restaurant Klimt is particularly inviting.

Landhaus Tschipan without rest, Friedhofstr. 12, ✉ 1100, ☎ (01) 6 89 40 11, *Fax (01) 689401135, office@tschipan.at* – – 15. AE DC MC VISA.
closed 23 December - 3 January – **29 rm** 68/75 – 105/120.
◆ Attractive, well-run family establishment on the edge of town. Guests appreciate the well-kept, homely rooms with Italian period furnishings. by Laaer Berg Straße CZ

Gartenhotel Altmannsdorf, Hoffingergasse 26, ✉ 1120, ☎ (01) 8 01 23, *Fax (01) 8012351, office@gartenhotel.com*, , Park, – rm, – 60. AE DC MC VISA AZ s
Meals à la carte 27/42 – **95 rm** 130/170 – 160/180.
◆ Behind the yellow facade are modern, functional rooms mostly used by conference delegates. Those with a view of the park are particularly pleasant. A former greenhouse makes an attractive wintergarden-like setting for the hotel restaurant.

Reither without rest, Graumanngasse 16, ✉ 1150, ☎ (01) 8 93 68 41, *Fax (01) 8936835, hotel.reither@aon.at*, , – rm. AE DC MC VISA. EV r
closed 22 to 27 December – **50 rm** 95/110 – 135.
◆ The rooms in this family establishment are well maintained, furnished in a contemporary and practical style, some with balcony or terrace.

Brunners, Wienerbergstr. 7 (22th floor), ✉ 1100, ☎ (01) 6 07 65 00, *Fax (01) 6076510, office@brunners.at*, < Wien, – . AE DC MC VISA BZ c
closed Saturday lunch, Sunday and Bank Holidays – **Meals** (booking essential) 20 *(lunch)*/70 and à la carte.
◆ Head for the heights! This restaurant is on the very top floor of an office skyscraper. Dark wooden floors and a semi-circular glass frontage create a modern and elegant ambience. Very attractive place settings.

Hietzinger Bräu, Auhofstr. 1, ✉ 1130, ☎ (01) 87 77 08 70, *Fax (01) 877708722, hietzing@plachutta.at*, – . AE DC MC VISA AZ u
closed mid July - mid August – **Meals** (booking essential) à la carte 34/44.
◆ Behind the Art Nouveau façade is a temple devoted to the cult of beef. All kinds of famous Viennese beef specialities are served in this refined version of a typical pub.

Vikerl's Lokal, Würfelgasse 4, ✉ 1150, ☏ (01) 8 94 34 30, *Fax (01) 8924183* BYZ d
closed Sunday dinner and Monday, June - August Sunday and Monday – **Meals** *(weekdays dinner only)* (booking essential) à la carte 21/35 ♀.
◆ An enjoyable time is guaranteed at this family establishment, what with its rustic ambience and its hearty local dishes which vary according to the season. Friendly service.

Meixner's Gastwirtschaft, Buchengasse 64 / corner of Herndlgasse, ✉ 1100, ☏ (01) 6 04 27 10, *Fax (01) 6063400, k.meixner@aon.at*, – VISA CZ a
Meals à la carte 20/32 ♀.
◆ Traditional inn with cheerful décor, where the landlady is known for her authentic and very tasty way with the local cuisine. Attractive pub garden to the rear.

City districts (Stadtbezirke) 16 - 19 :

Landhaus Fuhrgassl-Huber without rest, Rathstr. 24, ✉ 1190, ☏ (01) 4 40 30 33, *Fax (01) 4402714, landhaus@fuhrgassl-huber.at*, – AE VISA AX m
closed 1 week early February – **38 rm** 77/85 – 115/125.
◆ A pleasant country-house atmosphere awaits guests to this family-run establishment with its comfortable and prettily decorated rooms. Excellent breakfast buffet.

Jäger without rest, Hernalser Hauptstr. 187, ✉ 1170, ☏ (01) 48 66 62 00, *Fax (01) 48666208, hoteljaeger@aon.at* – AE VISA AY r
17 rm 80/107 – 110/140.
◆ Well-run establishment with pretty front garden, family-owned for over 90 years. The rooms are furnished in various styles, some with air-conditioning.

Eckel, Sieveringer Str. 46, ✉ 1190, ☏ (01) 3 20 32 18, *Fax (01) 3206660, restaurant.eckel@aon.at*, – AE VISA AX s
closed 2 weeks August, 24 December - mid January, Sunday and Monday – **Meals** à la carte 22/46 ♀.
◆ This country house is partly traditional with dark wood panelling, partly bright and friendly. Regular visitors appreciate the lovely summer terrace as well as the local and classic cuisine.

Plachutta with rm, Heiligenstädter Str. 179, ✉ 1190, ☏ (01) 3 70 41 25, *Fax (01) 370412520, nussdorf@plachutta.at*, – AE VISA BX e
closed end July - early August – **Meals** à la carte 25/44 ♀ – 8 – **4 rm** 55 – 85.
◆ This friendly establishment has an amazing line in beef dishes such as hearty soups served from big copper cooking pots and filled with all kinds of delicious meaty morsels.

City district (Stadtbezirk) 22 :

Crowne Plaza, Wagramer Str. 21, ✉ 1220, ☏ (01) 26 02 00, *Fax (01) 2602020, crowneplazavienna@ichotelsgroup.com*, – rm, – 280. AE VISA JCB. rest CY v
Meals à la carte 24/35 – 19 – **252 rm** 230 – 260 – 3 suites.
◆ This establishment helps make life easy for the business traveller, what with a business centre, conference rooms with up-to-the-minute technology and functional rooms with work-desks and ISDN. In contemporary style, Stars Restaurant opens on to the foyer.

Mraz u. Sohn, Wallensteinstr. 59, ✉ 1200, ☏ (01) 3 30 45 94, *Fax (01) 3501536*, – P. VISA FT s
closed 7 to 29 August, 24 December - 6 January, Saturday, Sunday and Bank Holidays – **Meals** (booking essential) à la carte 33/49 ♀.
Spec. Karamellisierte rohe Gänseleber mit Cereals. Oxenfilet mit Feigensenf und Ofengemüse. Schoko - Tapas.
◆ A family-run restaurant with a modern design, a young motivated service team and exceptionally creative cuisine.

Sichuan, Arbeiterstrandbadstr. 122, ✉ 1220, ☏ (01) 2 63 37 13, *Fax (01) 2633714, info@sichuan.at*, – VISA CX a
Meals (Chinese) 9 *(lunch)*/25 and à la carte ♀.
◆ Built in Chinese style, this establishment is surrounded by an astonishingly beautiful traditional garden. The restaurant's name indicates the nature of the regional cuisine.

Heurigen and Buschenschänken (wine gardens) – (mostly self-service, hot and cold dishes from buffet, prices according to weight of chosen meals, therefore not shown below. Buschenschänken sell their own wines only) :

Schübel-Auer, Kahlenberger Str. 22 (Döbling), ✉ 1190, ☏ (01) 3 70 22 22, *Fax (01) 3702222, daniela.somloi@schuebel-auer.at*, – AE VISA BX a
closed 22 December - 8 February, Sunday and Monday – **Meals** *(dinner only)* (buffet only) ♀.
◆ This old building was once a wine-grower's house with a mill and a run of millstones. It was carefully restored in 1972 and lovingly fitted out. Internal courtyard.

Feuerwehr-Wagner, Grinzingerstr. 53 (Heiligenstadt), ✉ 1190, ✆ (01) 3 20 24 42, *Fax (01) 3209141, heuriger@feuerwehrwagner.at,* – AE MC VISA BX b
Meals *(dinner only)* (buffet only).
◆ This typical wine tavern with its cosy interior of dark wood and well-scrubbed tables is a great favourite with its regulars. The terraced garden is particularly attractive.

Mayer am Pfarrplatz, Pfarrplatz 2 (Heiligenstadt), ✉ 1190, ✆ (01) 3 70 12 87, *Fax (01) 3704714, mayer@pfarrplaz.at,* – MC VISA JCB BX c
closed 21 December - 15 January – **Meals** *(weekdays dinner only)* (buffet only).
◆ This is a wine tavern as it should be, with a rustic interior, a Viennese Schrammelmusik band and a pretty courtyard. Another point of interest - Beethoven lived here in 1817 !

at Vienna-Schwechat Airport *by ③ : 20 km :*

NH Vienna Airport, Hotelstr. 1 (at the airport), ✉ 1300 *Wien*, ✆ (01) 70 15 10, *Fax (01) 701519571, nhviennaairport@nh-hotels.com,* – rm, – 300. AE MC VISA JCB
Meals à la carte 29/38 – **499 rm** 200/296 – 245/312.
◆ This elegant establishment is a convenient resting place for birds of passage. An extensive reception area and rooms which are partly stylishly modern, partly traditional, all with excellent technical facilities. The restaurant is open plan with unfussy décor.

Mautern Niederösterreich 730 S 3 – *pop. 3 100 – alt. 201 m.*
Wien 78.

Landhaus Bacher with rm, Südtiroler platz 2, ✉ 3512 ✆ (02732) 8 29 37, *Fax (02732) 74337, info@landhaus-bacher.at,* – , – VISA
closed January – February – **Meals** *(closed Monday and Tuesday) 33 (lunch)/90 (dinner)* and à la carte, – **10 rm** 75/90 – 110/150.
Spec. Variation von der Gänseleber. Das Beste vom Milchlamm mit gefülltem Artischockenboden. Schokotorte mit Banyuls – Schaum und Himbeeren.
◆ This restaurant has been well known for its classic cuisine for years. Lisl Wagner-Bacher is busy at the stove, while her husband takes care of the well-stocked wine cellar.

Schützen am gebirge Burgenland 730 V 5 – *pop. 1 350 – alt. 124 m.*
Wien 60.

Taubenkobel (Eselböck) with rm, Hauptstr. 33, ✉ 7081 ✆ (02684) 22 97, *Fax (02684) 229718, taubenkobel@relaischateaux.at,* , – rest 15
closed 23 December – 22 February – **Meals** *(closed Monday and Tuesday)* (booking essential) 58/88, – **7 rm** 110/130 – 160/250.
Spec. Soproner Gänseleberterrine. Gefüllte Wachtel mit Zwetschgen und Trüffel. Schokoladenpraline mit Blattgold und Erdbeeren.
◆ Walter Eselbök's exceptional cuisine, prepared almost exclusively with local products, can be enjoyed in the lovingly decorated restaurant. A pretty garden.

INNSBRUCK Austria 730 G 7 – pop. 128 000 – alt. 575 m – wintersport : 575/2250 m 3 7 12.

See : *Old Town*★ CDZ - *Maria-Theresien-Strasse*★ CZ ≤★★ *on the Nordkette, Hungerburg*★ AY, *Belfry (Stadtturm)* CZ **B**, ★ *over the city – Little Golden Roof (Goldenes Dachl)*★ CZ – *Helblinghaus*★ CZ – *Dom (Inneres*★*, Grabmal von Erzherzog Maximilian*★*) - Hofburg*★ *(Riesensaal*★★*)* CZ – *Hofkirche* CZ *(Maximilian's Mausoleum*★★*, Silver Chapel* ★★*) – Tyrol Museum of Popular Art (Tiroler Volkskunstmuseum)*★★ CDZ – *"Ferdinandeum" Tyrol Museum (Tiroler Landesmuseum "Ferdinandeum")*★ DZ**M2** – *Wilten Basilica*★ AY – *Hungerburg*★ AY – *Hafelekar*★★ *with* AY – *Castle Ambras*★ BY.

Envir: *Hall in Tirol*★ *(East : 10 km) – Volders : Church Zum hl. Karl Borromäus*★ *(East : 15 km) – Wattens : Swarowski Crystal Worlds*★ *(East : 17 km) – Ellbögen road between Patsch and Matrei*★★ *(South : 10 km) – The Stubaital*★★ *(Southwest : 12 km).*

18 *Innsbruck-Igls, Rinn, Oberdorf 11 (Southeast : 10 km)* ✆ *(05223) 7 81 77 ;* 9 *Innsbruck-Igls, Lans, Sperberegg (Southeast : 15 km)* ✆ *(0512) 37 71 65.*

Innsbruck (West : 4,5 km), ✆ *(0512) 22 52 50.*

Amraser Straße.

Exhibition Centre, Falkstr. 2, ✆ *(0512) 5 38 30.*

Burggraben 3, ✉ *A-6020,* ✆ *(0512) 5 98 50, Fax (0512) 598507, info@innsbruck.tv b.co.at.*

Wien 445 – München 160 – Salzburg 153 – Bozen 117.

Plans on following pages

AUSTRIA

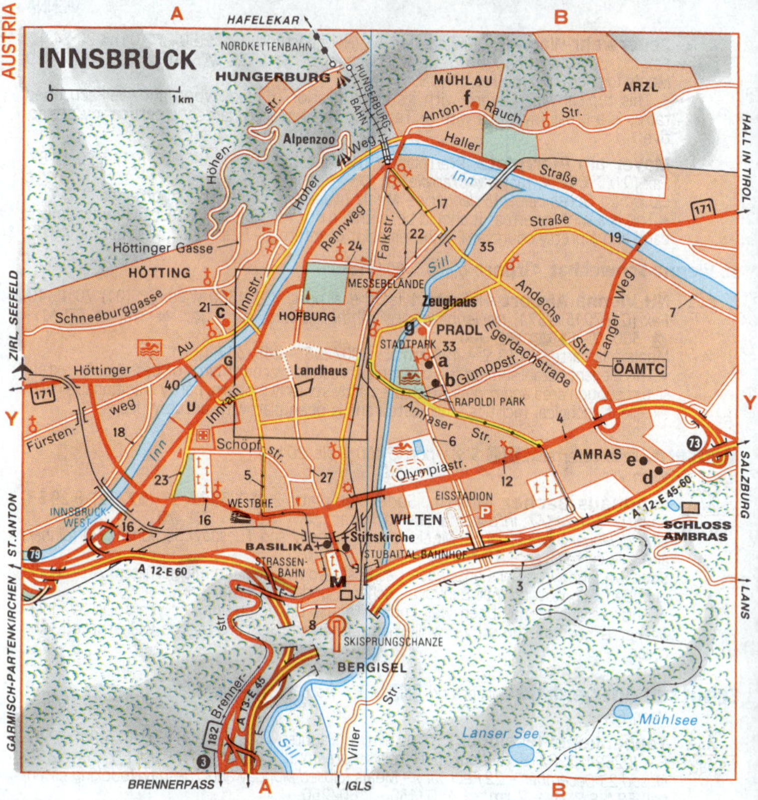

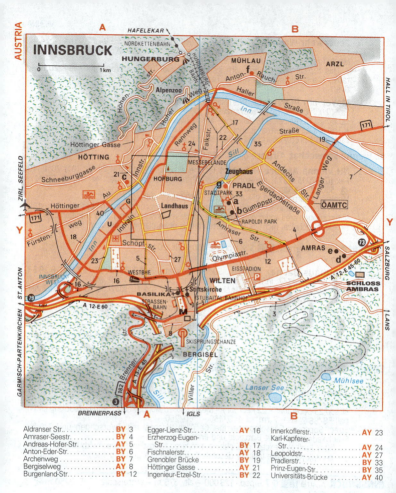

Aldranser Str. .... BY 3
Amraser-Seestr. .... BY 4
Andreas-Hofer-Str. .... AY 5
Anton-Eder-Str. .... BY 6
Archenweg .... BY 7
Bergiselweg .... AY 8
Burgenland-Str. .... BY 12
Egger-Lienz-Str. .... AY 16
Erzherzog-Eugen-Str. .... BY 17
Fischnalerstr. .... AY 18
Grenobler Brücke .... BY 19
Höttinger Gasse .... AY 21
Ingenieur-Etzel-Str. .... BY 22
Innerkoflerstr. .... AY 23
Karl-Kapferer-Str. .... AY 24
Leopoldstr. .... AY 27
Pradlerstr. .... BY 33
Prinz-Eugen-Str. .... BY 35
Universitäts-Brücke .... AY 40

Europa-Tyrol, Südtiroler Platz 2, ✉ 6020, ✆ (0512) 59 31, *Fax (0512) 587800, hotel@europatyrol.com*, – rm, – 200. AE VISA
DZ a

Meals see ***Europa-Stüberl*** below – **122 rm** 145/205 – 205/288 – 4 suites.

◆ This grand hotel of 1869 has been patronised by many famous personalities, among them Queen Elizabeth II. The splendid Baroque hall is especially worth seeing.

Hilton, Salurner Str. 15, ✉ 6010, ✆ (0512) 5 93 50, *Fax (0512) 5935220, info.innsbruck@hilton.com*, – rm, – 180. AE VISA JCB
CDZ b

Guggeryllis : **Meals** à la carte 26/39 – 20 – **176 rm** 150/185 – 180/215 – 4 suites.

◆ Right in the centre of town, this establishment has functional rooms offering superb views of the Alps. Guests can try their luck in the Casino. The elaborately decorated Guggeryllis gets its name from a 16C court jester.

The Penz without rest, Adolf-Pichler-Platz 3, ✉ 6020, ✆ (0512) 5 75 65 70, *Fax (0512) 5756579, office@thepenz.com* – – 120. AE VISA JCB.
CZ z

96 rm 130/160 – 150/210.

◆ With its glazed façade, this is a particularly stylish hotel, close to the Old Town and linked to a new shopping gallery. Modern design in the interior as well.

INNSBRUCK

Adolf-Pichler-Pl. . . . . CZ 2
Anichstr. . . . . CZ
Bozner Pl. . . . . DZ 10
Burggraben . . . . CZ 14
Dompl. . . . . CZ 15
Herzog-Friedrich-Str. . . . . CZ 20
Ingenieur-Etzel-Str. . . . . DZ 22
Kiesbachgasse . . . . CZ 25
Landhauspl. . . . . CZ 26
Leopoldstr. . . . . CZ 27
Maria-Theresein-Str. . . . . CZ
Marktgraben . . . . CZ
Meinhardstr. . . . . DZ 28
Meraner Str. . . . . CZ 30
Museumstr. . . . . CDZ
Pfarrgasse . . . . CZ 32
Stiftgasse . . . . CZ 37
Südbahnstr. . . . . DZ 38

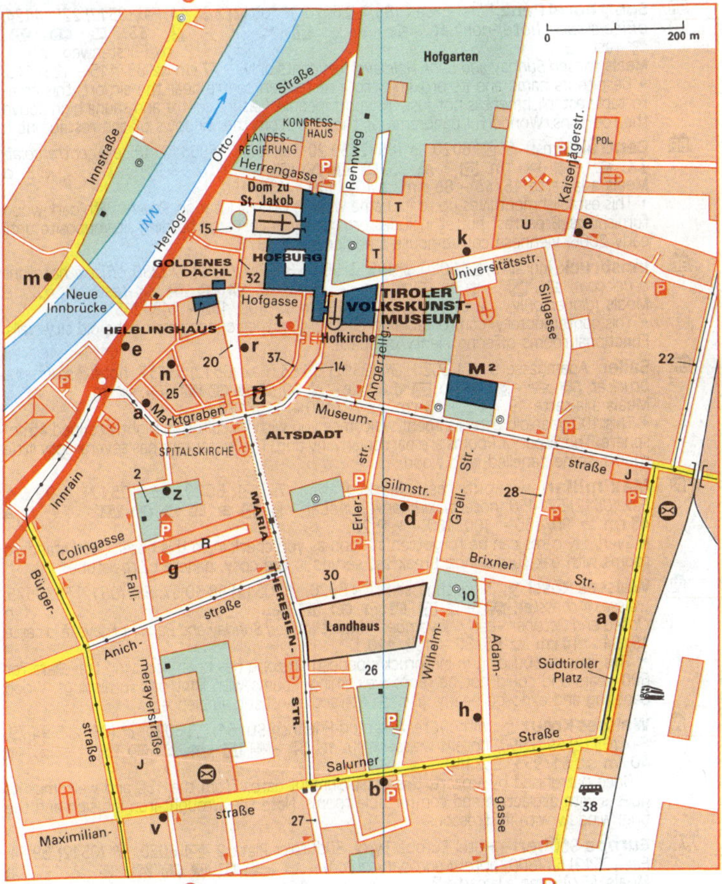

Romantik Hotel Schwarzer Adler, Kaiserjägerstr. 2, ✉ 6020, ✆ (0512) 58 71 09, *Fax (0512) 561697, info@deradler.com* – , rm, – 40. VISA JCB
Meals *(closed Sunday and Bank Holidays)* 50 and à la carte – **39 rm** 101/154 – 150/230 – 4 suites. DZ e

◆ Tradition and modernity go hand in hand here. The elegant, themed rooms are all different, some with designs by Versace and Swarovski, others in straightforward Tyrolean style. Guests dine in a cosy Tyrolean ambience beneath a splendid vault.

Neue Post, Maximilianstr. 15, ✉ 6020, ✆ (0512) 5 94 76, *Fax (0512) 581818, innsbruck@hotel-neue-post.at* – , rm, AE VISA. CZ v
Meals *(closed Saturday lunch, Sunday and Bank Holidays)* à la carte 25/43 – **50 rm** 98/125 – 118/200.

◆ Built in 1902 in traditional style and a favourite with sportspeople, this hotel has transformed itself from simple inn to classically tasteful city hotel. Guests can dine in the winter garden or in the Japanese restaurant.

Grauer Bär, Universitätsstr. 7, ✉ 6020, ✆ (0512) 5 92 40, *Fax (0512) 574535, grauer-baer@innsbruck-hotels.at*, – ... – 200. AE MC VISA JCB DZ k
Meals see ***Belle Époque** below* – **194 rm** 95/120 – 120/185 – 4 suites.
◆ Just 200m from the historic centre, this hotel consists of three town houses. Some of the rooms are very modern and all of them have excellent technical facilities and solid furnishings.

Sporthotel Penz, Fürstenweg 183, ✉ 6020, ✆ (0512) 2 25 14, *Fax (0512) 22514124, office@sporthotel-penz.at*, – ... – 35. AE MC VISA. rest by Fürstenweg AY
Meals *(closed Sunday and Bank Holidays)* (residents only) – **77 rm** 85/115 – 128/145.
◆ Despite its name and its proximity to a recreation centre near the airport, this comfortable establishment is not just for sportspeople. Leisure centre and sauna high above the rooftops. Wonderful panorama of the Alps from the windows of the restaurant.

Central, Gilmstr. 5, ✉ 6020, ✆ (0512) 59 20, *Fax (0512) 580310, office@central.co.at*, ... rm, – 25. AE MC VISA DZ d
Meals à la carte 15/33 – **85 rm** 105/140 – 130/150.
◆ This establishment lives up to its name with its central location. Rooms with dark wood furnishings. Breakfast buffet includes organic produce. Large building site opposite until early 2006. Viennese coffee-house tradition since 1875.

Innsbruck, Innrain 3, ✉ 6020, ✆ (0512) 59 86 80, *Fax (0512) 572280, office@hotelinnsbruck.com*, ... – 30. AE MC VISA. rest CZ e
Meals *(dinner only)* à la carte 19/36 – **113 rm** 109/168 – 148/243.
◆ This contemporary, comfortable hotel is built on the foundations of the old city walls. Functional rooms offering plenty of space.

Sailer, Adamgasse 8, ✉ 6020, ✆ (0512) 53 63, *Fax (0512) 53637, hotel@sailer-innsbruck.at*, ... rm, ... – 80. AE MC VISA JCB. rm DZ h
Meals à la carte 19/44 ♀ – **93 rm** 70/160 – 110/180.
◆ This 100-year-old establishment welcomes you with its cultured, slightly refined atmosphere. The Superior Rooms are particularly inviting. The restaurant has several cosy little rooms, some panelled with wood.

Maximilian without rest, Marktgraben 7, ✉ 6020, ✆ (0512) 5 99 67, *Fax (0512) 577450, hotel.maximilian@eunet.at* – ... AE MC VISA CZ a
43 rm 90/130 – 100/160 – ½ P 20.
◆ Everyday cares can be forgotten as soon as you check in to this hotel. Good standard rooms with oak furnishings. Breakfast served in the cosy, panelled Zirbelstube.

Weisses Rössl, Kiebachgasse 8, ✉ 6020, ✆ (0512) 58 30 57, *Fax (0512) 5830575, weisses@roessl.at*, – ... AE MC VISA JCB CZ n
closed end October - early November – **Meals** *(closed Sunday and Bank Holidays)* à la carte 19/34 – **14 rm** 65/80 – 102/120.
◆ This little old building in Innsbruck's pedestrian zone has been receiving travellers for 600 years and could not be more welcoming. Rooms with light oak furnishings. Wood panelling and exposed beams give an attractively rustic ambience.

Weisses Kreuz without rest, Herzog-Friedrich-Str. 31, ✉ 6020, ✆ (0512) 5 94 79, *Fax (0512) 5947990, hotel@weisseskreuz.at*, – ... AE MC VISA CZ r
40 rm 61/95 – 95/110.
◆ Once patronised by Mozart, this establishment dates from the 15C and welcomes its guests with attractive and comfortable rooms. Note the wrought-iron inn sign and the oriel window with its frescoes.

Europa-Stüberl - Hotel Europa-Tyrol, Südtiroler Platz 2, ✉ 6020, ✆ (0512) 59 31, *Fax (0512) 587800, hotel@europatyrol.com* – ... AE MC VISA. DZ a
Meals 35/45 and à la carte ♀.
◆ A comfortable Tyrolean style restaurant with friendly service. The various dining rooms, furnished in light wood, have a warm and congenial atmosphere.

Belle Époque - Hotel Grauer Bär, Universitätsstr. 7, ✉ 6020, ✆ (0512) 5 92 40, *Fax (0512) 574535, grauer-baer@innsbruck-hotels.at* – ... AE MC VISA JCB DZ k
closed Monday lunch, Sunday and Bank Holidays – **Meals** à la carte 22/51 ♀.
◆ A classic design of a restaurant with cross vaulted ceiling and red high-backed chairs, lovely table settings and chandeliers.

Wirtshaus Schöneck (Miller), Weiherburggasse 6, ✉ 6020, ✆ (0512) 27 27 28, *Fax (0512) 272729, info@wirtshaus-schoeneck.com*, ≤, – ... AE MC VISA JCB
closed end August - early September, end January - early February, Tuesday and Wednesday – **Meals** *(dinner only)* (booking essential) 48/68 and à la carte ♀. AY s
Spec. Gebratene Jakobsmuscheln mit Hummer und Tintenfischrisotto. Rehrücken mit Sellerie und Kartoffelpaunzen. Schokoladencanelloni mit Erdbeeren und Mangosorbet.
◆ This 19C inn has a lovely location overlooking the city. Classic cuisine is served in the 3 dining rooms, all cosily furnished in antique wood. Choose the one with the magnificent view.

Lichtblick, Maria-Theresienstr. 18 (Rathauspassage, 7th floor), ✉ 6020, ✆ (0512) 56 65 50, *office@restaurant-lichtblick.at*, ← Innsbruck, – AE Ⓓ MC VISA JCB CZ g
closed Sunday and Bank Holidays – **Meals** (booking essential) 30/40 and à la carte.
◆ The contemporary décor, the professional service and creative cuisine are this restaurant's recipe for success. Floor-to-ceiling windows give a wonderful view over the city.

Dengg, Riesengasse 13, ✉ 6020, ✆ (0512) 58 23 47, *Fax (0512) 936088, dengg@chello.at* – AE Ⓓ MC VISA CZ t
closed 2 weeks end May, Sunday and Bank Holidays – **Meals** à la carte 17/43.
◆ Restaurant occupying a venerable building in an Old Town alleyway. Three vaulted dining rooms with individual décor make an ideal setting for Cross-over-style food and drink.

at Innsbruck-Amras :

Kapeller, Philippine-Welser-Str. 96, ✉ 6020, ✆ (0512) 34 31 06, *Fax (0512) 34310668, office@kapeller.at*, – TV P – 20. AE Ⓓ MC VISA BY e
Meals *(closed 3 weeks July, Monday lunch, Sunday and Bank Holidays)* à la carte 20/40
36 rm 55/100 – 96/138.
◆ Particularly convenient location on the edge of town near the motorway. Comfortable furnishings with practical wooden furnishings. Traditional hospitality in the dining rooms of the restaurant.

Bierwirt, Bichlweg 2, ✉ 6020, ✆ (0512) 34 21 43, *Fax (0512) 3421435, bierwirt@aon.at*, , – , rm, TV P – 80. MC VISA BY d
Meals *(closed Saturday lunch and Sunday)* à la carte 14/28 – **63 rm** 59/75 – 92/115.
◆ This typical Alpine inn is one of the oldest and most historic of its kind in the area. Tlovingly furnished, rustic bedrooms. Several small dining rooms in the local style.

at Innsbruck-Mariahilf :

Mondschein without rest, Mariahilfstr. 6, ✉ 6020, ✆ (0512) 2 27 84, *Fax (0512) 2278490, office@mondschein.at* – TV – 30. AE Ⓓ MC VISA JCB CZ m
34 rm 87/90 – 119/145.
◆ Right by the inn and classified as a historical monument, the city's oldest row of buildings includes this hotel. Distinctive, Italian-style rooms with PC and modem links.

Trattoria da Peppino, Kirschentalgasse 6, ✉ 6020, ✆ (0512) 27 56 99, *Fax (0512) 275699* – AE Ⓓ MC VISA JCB AY c
closed 14 August - 5 September, Sunday and Monday – **Meals** *(dinner only)* (Italian) à la carte 27/34.
◆ This little restaurant in contemporary trattoria style has been established in a dwelling-house. Italian cuisine based on first-rate, fresh produce.

at Innsbruck-Pradl :

Parkhotel Leipzigerhof, Defreggerstr. 13, ✉ 6020, ✆ (0512) 34 35 25, *Fax (0512) 394357, info@leipzigerhof.at*, – , rm, TV P. AE Ⓓ MC VISA JCB BY b
Meals *(closed Sunday and Bank Holidays)* 15/47 and à la carte – **60 rm** 84/136 – 112/190.
◆ The Perger family's private hotel is located directly opposite the city park. Well-presented rooms with contemporary furnishings. Ask for one of the rooms with an oriel window. Nothing could be cosier than the Tyrolean-style restaurant.

Alpinpark, Pradlerstr. 28, ✉ 6020, ✆ (0512) 34 86 00, *Fax (0512) 364172, alpinpark@innsbruck-hotels.at*, – TV – 30. AE Ⓓ MC VISA JCB BY a
Meals à la carte 18/32 – **87 rm** 80/110 – 105/140.
◆ This yellow-coloured functional building on the edge of the city centre has solidly furnished rooms. In winter there is a shuttle service to the surrounding ski-slopes. Restaurant and rustic dining room.

Restaurant Altpradl - Hotel Altpradl, Pradlerstr. 8, ✉ 6020, ✆ (0512) 34 16 34, *Fax (0512) 341634*, – MC VISA JCB BY g
closed Monday – **Meals** *(weekdays dinner only)* 39/55 and à la carte.
◆ This sophisticated restaurant in the hotel of the same name is divided into a series of parlours, all decorated in rustic country style.

at Igls *South : 4 km, by Viller Straße AB :*

Schlosshotel, Viller Steig 2, ✉ 6080, ✆ (0512) 37 72 17, *Fax (0512) 377217198, hotel@schlosshotel-igls.com*, ← mountains, , , – TV P – 30. AE Ⓓ MC VISA. rest
closed mid March - mid April, mid October - mid December – **Meals** à la carte 29/50 – **18 rm** 210/300 – 360/400 – 6 suites.
◆ In its garden, this refined establishment in the style of a noblemanÆs residence offers sheer luxury, with extremely elegant rooms and suites and first-class service. Tradition and elegance combine harmoniously in the mahogany-panelled restaurant.

SALZBURG Austria 730 L 5 – pop. 146 000 – alt. 425 m.

See: *Old Town★★ YZ – ≤ ★★ over the town (from the Mönchsberg) Z and ≤★★ (from Hettwer Bastei) Y – Hohensalzburg ★★ X, Z : ≤★★ (from the Kuenburg Bastion), ✻★★ (from the Reck Tower), Museum (Burgmuseum)★ – St. Peter's Churchyard (Petersfriedhof)★★ Z – St. Peter's Church (Stiftskirche St. Peter)★★ Z – Residenz★★ Z – Natural History Museum (Haus der Natur)★★ Y* **M2** *– Franciscan's Church (Franziskanerkirche)★ Z* **A** *– Getreidegasse★ Y – Mirabell Garden (Mirabellgarten)★ V (Grand Staircase★★ of the castle) – Baroque Museum★ V* **M3** *– Cathedral (Dom)★ Z.*

Envir: *Road to the Gaisberg (Gaisbergstraße)★★ (≤★) by ① – Untersberg★ by ② : 12 km (with cable car) – Castle Hellbrunn (Schloss Hellbrunn) ★ (Volkskundemuseum ★) by Nonntaler Hauptstraße X.*

(9) *Salzburg-Wals, Schloss Klessheim, ✆ (0662) 85 08 51 ;*

(9) *Hof (by ① : 20 km), ✆ (06229) 23 90 ;*

(18) *St. Lorenz (by ① : 29 km), ✆ (06232) 3 83 50 ;*

(18) *Salzburg - Eugendorf (by ① : 11 km), ✆ (06225) 7 00 00.*

✈ *Innsbrucker Bundesstr. 95 (by ③), ✆ (0662) 8 58 00 - City Air Terminal (Autobus Station), Südtiroler Platz V.*

🚘 *Lastenstraße V.*

Exhibition Centre, Am Messezentrum 1, ✆ (0662) 2 40 40.

ℹ *Salzburg-Information, Mozartplatz 5, ✉ 5020, ✆ (0662) 88 98 73 30, Fax (0662) 8898732, tourist@salzburginfo.at.*

Wien 292 ① – Innsbruck 177 ③ – München 140 ④

Alter Markt	Y	2
Bürgerspitalgasse	Y	4
Dreifaltigkeitsgasse	Y	6
Getreidegasse	Y	
Hanusch-Pl.	Y	15
Herbert-von-Karajan-Pl.	Y	16
Judengasse	YZ	
Kaigasse	Z	
Kajetaner-Pl.	Z	21
Linzer Gasse	Y	
Makartpl.	Y	
Max-Reinhardt-Pl.	Z	33
Residenzpl.	Z	32
Sigmund-Haffner-Gasse	YZ	35
Theatergasse	Y	39
Universitätspl.	Y	40
Waagpl.	Z	43

SALZBURG

Auerspergstr. . . . . V 3	Gstättengasse . . . . X 12	Nußdorfer Str. . . . . X 31
Bürglsteinstr. . . . . X 5	Kaiserschützenstr. . . . . V 20	Rainerstr. V
Erzabt-Klotz-Str. . . . . X 9	Lindhofstr. . . . . V 22	Schießstattstr. . . . . V 33
	Mirabellpl. . . . . V 26	Schwatzstr. . . . . V 34
	Nonntaler Hauptstr. . . . . X 29	Späthgasse . . . . X 37

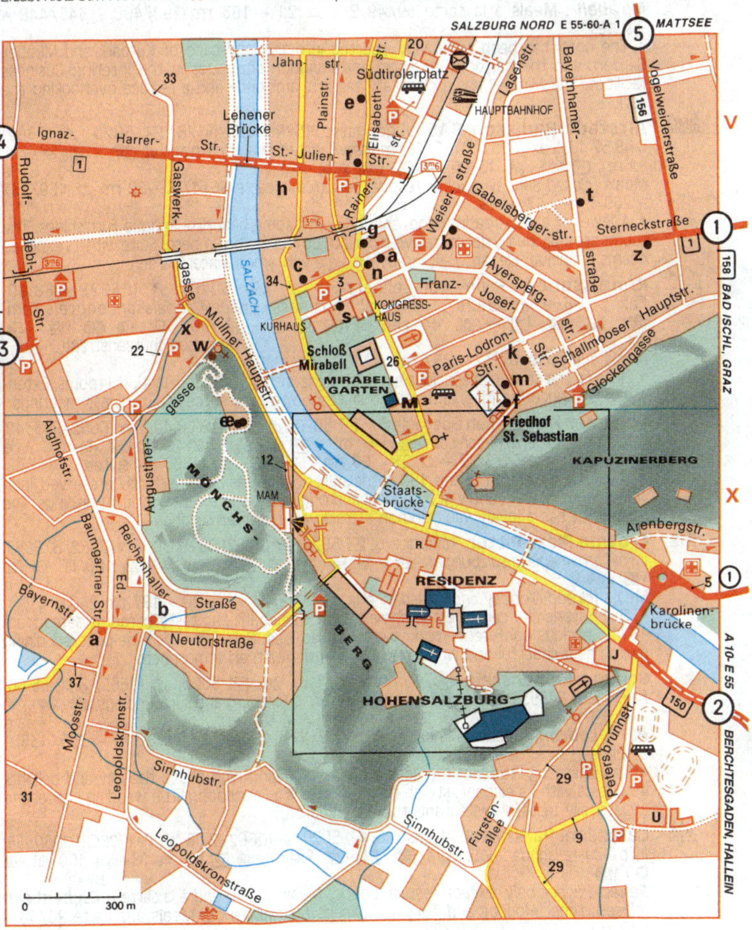

Sacher, Schwarzstr. 5, ✉ 5020, ✆ (0662) 8 89 77, *Fax (0662) 88977551, salzburg@sacher.com*, 🏋, ≘ – 🛗 ▤ 📺 📞 ♿ 🚗 – 🏛 80. AE ⓓ ⓜⓒ VISA JCB Y b
***Zirbelstube :* Meals** 45/68 and à la carte 🍷 – ***Salzachgrill :* Meals** 13 and à la carte, 🍷 – ☕ 26 – **118 rm** 170/556 – 329/556 – 3 suites.
◆ Built by Carl Freiherr von Schwarz, this historic grand hotel attracts guests from all over the world. Stylish elegance featuring every kind of luxury. Elegant, pine-panelled Alpine dining room. The Salzach Grill has a superb terrace overlooking the river.

Bristol, Makartplatz 4, ✉ 5020, ✆ (0662) 87 35 57, *Fax (0662) 8735576, hotel.bristol@salzburg.co.at* – 🛗, ⚹ rm, ▤ 📺 📞 – 🏛 60. AE ⓓ ⓜⓒ VISA JCB. ⚹ Y a
closed 1 February - 17 March – **Meals** *(closed Sunday, except festival period)* 28 *(lunch)*/58 *(dinner)* and à la carte – **60 rm** ☕ 142/357 – 204/420 – 9 suites.
◆ This stylish late-19C establishment stands in the heart of Mozart's home town. Individually decorated, tasteful rooms, some with luxurious bathrooms. Classic-style hotel restaurant.

Sheraton, Auerspergstr. 4, ✉ 5020, ☎ (0662) 88 99 90, *Fax (0662) 881776, sheraton.salzburg@sheraton.at*, , , entrance to the spa facilities, – , rm, – 50. AE VISA JCB V s
***Mirabell* : Meals** à la carte 39/49 – 21 – **163 rm** 292/408 – 345/448 – 9 suites.
◆ The hotel has been sensitively inserted into the landscape of Kurpark and Mirabell Garden, and the harmony of form and function continues in the interior. Business facilities. The Mirabell has a classically tasteful ambience and a terrace overlooking the park.

Altstadt Radisson SAS, Judengasse 15/Rudolfskai 28, ✉ 5020, ☎ (0662) 8 48 57 10, *Fax (0662) 8485716, radisson-altstadt@austria-trend.at*, – , rm, rm, – 40. AE VISA JCB. Y s
Meals *(closed Sunday, except festival period)* à la carte 36/47 – **62 rm** 169/337 – 269/513 – 13 suites.
◆ A jewel of a hotel dating from the 12C, with some beautiful antique furnishings. The rooms are individually decorated with period furniture - the Emperor Suite with its exposed beams is unique. Elegant restaurant with a lovely small winter garden.

Renaissance, Fanny-von-Lehnert-Str. 7, ✉ 5020, ☎ (0662) 4 68 80, *Fax (0662) 4688228, rhi.szgbr.business.center@renaissancehotels.com*, , , , – , rm, – 500. AE VISA JCB. by Kaiserschützenstraße V
Meals à la carte 16/32 – **257 rm** 169/308 – 193/332.
◆ Close to the station, a spacious establishment with stylish and functional rooms. Extensive conference facilities, and the latest technology for successful business meetings.

Goldener Hirsch, Getreidegasse 37, ✉ 5020, ☎ (0662) 8 08 40, *Fax (0662) 843349, welcome@goldenerhirsch.com* – , rm, – 50. AE VISA JCB Y e
Meals à la carte 34/61 – 25 – **69 rm** 258/450 – 274/600 – 4 suites.
◆ The romantic charm of this 15C patrician residence has been perfectly preserved. Individual rooms with country-style appeal and originality, some with period furnishings. The restaurant has a lovely vault and an attractively rustic atmosphere.

Crowne Plaza-Pitter, Rainerstr. 6, ✉ 5020, ☎ (0662) 88 97 80, *Fax (0662) 878893, info@crowneplaza-salzburg.at*, – , rm, – 180. AE VISA JCB V n
Meals *(closed Monday and Tuesday)* à la carte 28/43 – 20 – **187 rm** 240 – 410.
◆ This historic city centre establishment with its elegant and tasteful rooms dates from 1870. Spacious conference rooms with all facilities. Ballroom. The pine-panelled dining room has a cheerful and wonderfully authentic Austrian atmosphere.

Schloss Mönchstein, Mönchsberg Park 26, ✉ 5020, ☎ (0662) 8 48 55 50, *Fax (0662) 848559, salzburg@moenchstein.at*, ≤ Salzburg and surroundings, , , – – 25. AE VISA JCB. rest X e
***Paris Lodron* : Meals** à la carte 41/60 – **23 rm** 268/316 – 335/435 – 5 suites.
◆ This charming little castle enjoys a parkland setting high above the city and delights its guests with its elegant, stylish rooms. There is a fascinating little wedding chapel and a classically tasteful restaurant, the Paris Lodron.

Castellani Parkhotel, Alpenstr. 6, ✉ 5020, ☎ (0662) 2 06 00, *Fax (0662) 2060555, info@castellani-parkhotel.com*, , – , rm, – 100. AE VISA by ②
Salieri *(dinner only, except festival period)* **Meals** 50/70 and à la carte – ***Eschenbach*** *(closed dinner Monday and Tuesday, except festival period)* **Meals** à la carte 26/38 – **152 rm** 98/230 – 128/260.
◆ The modern hotel building is in fascinating contrast to the charming old patrician residence. Beyond the spacious foyer are tastefully decorated rooms. The Salieri in elegant contemporary style, the Eschenbach a mixture of modern and traditional

Zum Hirschen, St.-Julien-Str. 21, ✉ 5020, ☎ (0662) 88 90 30, *Fax (0662) 8890358, info@zumhirschen.at*, beer garden, – , rm, – 30. AE VISA JCB. V r
Meals *(closed Sunday)* à la carte 17/33 – **64 rm** 80/136 – 108/173.
◆ Close to the station. The hotel offers traditional Salzburg hospitality in a tasteful setting with Italian period furnishings. Extensive roof-terrace sauna. Restaurant with five attractively decorated dining rooms.

Dorint Novotel, Sterneckstr. 20, ✉ 5020, ☎ (0662) 8 82 03 10, *Fax (0662) 8820319, h5354@accor.com*, , – , rm, – 150. AE VISA JCB. rest V z
Meals à la carte 24/36 – **139 rm** 108/205 – 133/245 – 4 suites.
◆ This hotel can be recommended for its central location, only ten minutes on foot from the Old Town. Functional rooms. Conference facilities and ISDN technology. Restaurant Amadeo with garden terrace.

Imlauer, Rainerstr. 12, ✉ 5020, ☎ (0662) 8 89 92, *Fax (0662) 87769416, hotel@imlauer.com*, – |‡|, ⚟ rm, TV ☎ P – 100. AE ① MC VISA V g
***Stieglbräu* : Meals** à la carte 15/34 – **50 rm** ☐ 143/167 – 162/191.
◆ A contemporary reception area and stylish, modern rooms with light furnishings and excellent technical facilities welcome you in this centrally-located hotel. Traditional, elegant restaurant in the Hotel Stieglbräu.

NH Carlton without rest, Markus-Sittikus-Str. 3, ✉ 5020, ☎ (0662) 8 82 19 10, *Fax (0662) 88219188, nhcarlton@nh-hotels.com*, – |‡|, ⚟ rm, TV ☎ P. AE ① MC VISA V c
40 rm ☐ 110/140 – 146/200 – 13 suites.
◆ A delightful city centre residence with all the charm of a comfortable private villa. Spacious rooms with high ceilings and elegant knot-wood furnishings.

Altstadthotel Wolf-Dietrich, Wolf-Dietrich-Str. 7, ✉ 5020, ☎ (0662) 87 12 75, *Fax (0662) 8712759, office@salzburg-hotel.at*, , , – |‡| TV ☎ . AE ① MC VISA JCB V m
***Ährlich** (closed 1 February - 15 March, Sunday and Monday) (dinner only)* **Meals** à la carte 19/38 – **40 rm** ☐ 69/144 – 114/154 – 4 suites.
◆ Tasteful, elegant old residence in a traffic-calmed part of town. Comfortable rooms, some offering perfect peace and quiet. Four extravagant theme suites ! Restaurant run on organic principles using animal products only raised in humane conditions.

NH Salzburg, Franz-Josef-Str. 26, ✉ 5020, ☎ (0662) 88 20 41, *Fax (0662) 874240, nhsalzburg@nh-hotels.com*, – |‡|, ⚟ rm, TV ☎ P – 90. AE ① MC VISA V k
Meals *(dinner only)* à la carte 17/32 – **140 rm** ☐ 95/145 – 105/180.
◆ Not far from the Mirabell Garden, this establishment offers business travellers solidly furnished, functional rooms with work-desks plus modem link on request.

Markus Sittikus without rest, Markus-Sittikus-Str. 20, ✉ 5020, ☎ (0662) 8 71 12 10, *Fax (0662) 87112158, info@markus-sittikus.at* – |‡| TV ☎ – 15. AE ① MC VISA JCB V a
39 rm ☐ 65/94 – 105/126.
◆ City hotel with a yellow façade, named after Prince Bishop Markus Sittikus von Hohenems. Rooms are individually furnished, some with pretty colours and materials.

Lasserhof without rest, Lasserstr. 47, ✉ 5020, ☎ (0662) 87 33 88, *Fax (0662) 8733886, info@lasserhof.com* – |‡| ⚟ TV ☎. AE ① MC VISA JCB V b
28 rm ☐ 55/159 – 85/159.
◆ This impeccably run hotel accommodates its guests in stylish and comfortable rooms.

Haus Arenberg without rest, Blumensteinstr. 8, ✉ 5020, ☎ (0662) 64 00 97, *Fax (0662) 6400973, info@arenberg-salzburg.at*, <, – TV ☎ P. ① MC VISA
13 rm ☐ 69/145 – 119/145. by Arenbergstraße X
◆ This small hotel in a villa district at the edge of the city centre is run by the owners. With clean rooms in contemporary and functional design.

Altstadthotel Amadeus without rest, Linzer Gasse 43, ✉ 5020, ☎ (0662) 87 14 01, *Fax (0662) 8714017, salzburg@hotelamadeus.at* |‡| ⚟ TV ☎. AE ① MC VISA JCB V f
23 Zim ☐ 72/120 – 112/150.
◆ Situated in the middle of the Old Town this listed building, over 500 years old, has very tasteful rooms furnished in a variety of styles.

Hohenstauffen without rest, Elisabethstr. 19, ✉ 5020, ☎ (0662) 8 77 66 90, *Fax (0662) 87219351, hohenstauffen@aon.at* – |‡| ⚟ TV P. AE ① MC VISA JCB V e
31 rm ☐ 72/145 – 109/145.
◆ Close to the station, this hotel has been in the same family ownership since 1906. Rooms individually furnished, some with a four-poster.

Riedenburg, Neutorstr. 31, ✉ 5020, ☎ (0662) 83 08 15, *Fax (0662) 843923, reservierung@riedenburg.at*, – P. AE ① MC VISA X a
closed end February - early March, end October - early November, Sunday and Monday, except festival period – **Meals** (booking essential) 15 *(lunch)*/59 and à la carte ♀, .
Spec. Weißes Tomatenmousse und Essenz mit gebeizter Bio-Beiried. Milchkalbskotelett mit Gänseleber und Rucolarisotto. Verschiedenes von der Birne.
◆ Two attractive and elegant dining rooms designed with light wood and warm colours. Lovely place settings and immaculate service. Wine list has over 600 wines.

Alt Salzburg, Bürgerspitalgasse 2, ✉ 5020, ☎ (0662) 84 14 76, *Fax (0662) 8414764, altsalzburg@aon.at* – AE ① MC VISA JCB Y c
closed 1 week mid February, Sunday and Monday lunch, except festival period – **Meals** (booking essential for dinner) à la carte 25/40 ♀.
◆ Elegant country-style restaurant, fine for dining before or after the opera. Local cuisine with an international touch.

Gasthaus zu Schloss Hellbrunn, Fürstenweg 37, ✉ 5020, ✆ (0662) 82 56 08, *Fax (0662) 82560842, office@taste-gassner.com*, – P. AE ⊕ MC VISA by ②
closed February, Sunday and Monday – **Meals** *(dinner only)* 47/60 and à la carte ♀.
◆ In a setting of parkland and fountains this Renaissance summer residence houses a stylish Mediterranean restaurant. Ambitious creative cuisine in the evenings, simple traditional fare at lunchtime.

Bei Bruno im Ratsherrnkeller, Sigmund-Haffner-Gasse 4, ✉ 5020, ✆ (0662) 87 84 17, *Fax (0662) 8784174, bruno@restaurant-austria.net* – AE ⊕ MC VISA JCB Y g
closed 3 weeks February, 1 week end May, 1 week early June, Sunday and Bank Holidays, except festival period – **Meals** à la carte 28/56 ♀.
◆ Leather upholstery, attractively laid tables, and walls in a warm shade of orange give this vaulted restaurant an attractive, almost Mediterranean atmosphere.

Esszimmer, Müllner Hauptstr. 33, ✉ 5020, ✆ (0662) 87 08 99, *Fax (0662) 870833, office@esszimmer.com*, – ▤. AE MC VISA V x
closed Sunday and Monday – **Meals** (booking essential) 22 *(lunch)*/62 and à la carte ♀.
Spec. Krebserl-Chartreuse mit Avocados und Crème fraiche. Brust und Haxerl von der Taube mit Gnocchi und Eierschwammerln. Baumkuchen-Pfirsichtörtchen mit weissem Pralineneis.
◆ The restaurant design has an unusual quality, with appealing lines and strong colours. Diners can see into the kitchen, where traditional, creative cuisine with a local touch is prepared.

Culinarium, St.-Julien-Str. 2, ✉ 5020, ✆ (0662) 87 88 85, *Fax (0662) 879188, restaurantculinarium@gmx.at*. ⊕ MC VISA V h
geschl. 1 week mid June, 1 week mid September, Monday lunch, Sunday and Bank Holidays – **Meals** à la carte 28/39 ♀.
◆ Attractive, bright colours and beautiful basket chairs lend a touch of elegance to this restaurant. It has a kitchen that you can see into and attentive service.

K+K Restaurant am Waagplatz, Waagplatz 2 (1st floor), ✉ 5020, ✆ (0662) 84 21 56, *Fax (0662) 84215633, kk.restaurant@kuk.at*, – ▤. AE ⊕ MC VISA JCB Z h
closed 1 February - 6 March – **Meals** (booking essential) à la carte 22/37 ♀.
◆ Listed building with an interior subdivided into a number of cosy little dining rooms. Medieval dining and entertainment in the lovely vaulted cellars, by prior booking.

Magazin, Augustinergasse 13, ✉ 5020, ✆ (0662) 8 41 58 40, *Fax (0662) 8415844, office@magazin.co.at*, – ⊕ MC VISA V w
closed Monday, Sunday and Bank Holidays, except festival period – **Meals** (booking essential) 35/42 and à la carte ♀.
Spec. Wildentenbrust und Gänseleber mit Schalotten-Portweinmarmelade. Seeteufel mit Beluga-Linsen und Thymian-Specksauce. Schokoladenflan mit Himbeeren und Sabayone.
◆ The restaurant offers something a little bit different. Creative cuisine is served at one large table in a simply designed, vaulted room. With a bar area and a landscaped inner courtyard.

Perkeo, Priesterhausgasse 20, ✉ 5020, ✆ (0662) 87 14 72, *kibler@netway.at*, – MC VISA Y n
closed 1 week early September, 24 December - 6 January, Saturday and Sunday, except festival period – **Meals** *(dinner only)* 35/48 and à la carte ♀.
◆ A small, sophisticated evening restaurant with a friendly ambience. You can watch the dishes being creatively prepared in the kitchen. There is a Bistro-style eatery in the front area.

at Salzburg-Aigen *Southeast : 6 km, by Bürglsteinstraße X :*

Doktorwirt, Glaser Str. 9, ✉ 5026, ✆ (0662) 6 22 97 30, *Fax (0662) 62297325, schnoell@doktorwirt.co.at*, , (heated), , – TV P. – 35. AE ⊕ MC VISA JCB. rest
closed 2 weeks February and mid October - end November – **Meals** *(closed Monday, September - early May Sunday dinner and Monday)* 13 *(lunch)*/35 and à la carte ♀, – **41 rm** 68/100 – 105/195.
◆ This 12C building named after the doctor who bought it in 1670 is now a comfortable, country-style inn with a tasteful and welcoming ambience.The restaurant consists of two pine-panelled rooms from the eastern Tyrol.

Rosenvilla without rest, Höfelgasse 4, ✉ 5020, ✆ (0662) 62 17 65, *Fax (0662) 6252308, hotel@rosenvilla.com*, – TV P. AE ⊕ MC VISA
14 rm 65/145 – 146/226.
◆ A feng-shui garden has been laid out in front of this villa not far from the city centre. Each room has individual décor. The Exclusive Room is very spacious.

Gasthof Schloss Aigen, Schwarzenbergpromenade 37, 5026, (0662) 62 12 84, *Fax (0662) 6212844, schloss-aigen@elsnet.at, – closed 10 to 20 January, Wednesday and Thursday lunch, except festival period* – **Meals** à la carte 26/46.
◆ Once part of the castle estate, this rustic inn stands on the edge of the forest. Organic beef from the Pinzgau forms the basis of delicious dishes.

at Salzburg-Gnigl *East : 3,5 km, by ① :*

Pomodoro, Eichstr. 54, 5023, (0662) 64 04 38, – *closed August, Monday and Tuesday* – **Meals** (Italian) (booking essential) à la carte 25/35.
◆ This homely restaurant has been in the same ownership for over 20 years. Wooden panelling together with fish-nets spanning the ceiling contribute to the rustic atmosphere.

at Salzburg-Itzling *North : 1,5 km, by Kaiserschützenstraße V :*

Gasthof Auerhahn with rm, Bahnhofstr. 15, 5020, (0662) 45 10 52, *Fax (0662) 4510523, auerhahn@eunet.at,* – rest, *closed 1 week February, 2 weeks July* – **Meals** *(closed Sunday dinner and Monday, except festival period)* à la carte 19/36 – **11 rm** 43/48 – 72/82.
◆ This small hotel is in an older town house close to the Salzburg-Itzling railway station. Comfortable rustic restaurant with modern fireside room and well-kept, homely rooms.

at Salzburg-Leopoldskron *Southwest : 3 km, by Moosstraße X :*

Frauenschuh without rest, Gsengerweg 1a, 5020, (0662) 83 23 34, *Fax (0662) 83233440, pension@frauenschuh.at,* , – . – **17 Zim** 52/80 – 80/90.
◆ This contemporary, small hotel with rooms furnished in solid, country style antique wood is situated in a quiet side street. Enjoy breakfast on the terrace in the summer.

at Salzburg-Liefering *Northwest : 4 km, by ④ :*

Brandstätter, Münchner Bundesstr. 69, 5020, (0662) 43 45 35, *Fax (0662) 43453590, info@hotel-brandstaetter.com,* , , , – – 35.
closed 23 to 26 December – **Meals** *(closed 1 week early January, Sunday and Bank Holidays, except festival period)* (booking essential) 24/50 and à la carte – **36 rm** 72/95 – 91/130.
Spec. Flusskrebserl in Dillcreme auf Häuptelsalat. Kalbs-Rieslingbeuschel mit Knödel. Topfensoufflé mit Beerenmus und Sauerrahmeis.
◆ Personally run inn with lovingly decorated rooms and lots of local peasant furniture. Ask for one of the rooms with a balcony overlooking the garden. Cosy dining rooms where an array of local cuisine is served.

Salzburg-Maxglan *Southwest : 2 km, by Neutorstraße X :*

Zur Post without rest (with guest houses), Maxglaner Hauptstr. 45, 5020, (0662) 8 32 33 90, *Fax (0662) 8323395, info@hotelzurpost.info,* – .
24 rm 55/102 – 80/120.
◆ This lovely family business has rooms which are both homely and functional, offering excellent technical facilities and modern bathrooms. Bright, small breakfast room.

Astoria without rest, Maxglaner Hauptstr. 7, 5020, (0662) 83 42 77, *Fax (0662) 83427740, hotel.astoria@aon.at*
30 rm 60/85 – 88/104.
◆ Stylish, modern rooms, and a contemporary breakfast room with wooden floors are all part of the welcome in this well-run hotel.

at Salzburg-Morzg *South : 3 km, by Nonntaler Hauptstraße Z :*

Zum Buberl Gut, Gneiser Str. 31, 5020, (0662) 82 68 66, *Fax (0662) 826866,* – *closed 1 week May, 2 weeks September, 1 week January and Tuesday* – **Meals** (booking essential) à la carte 25/39.
◆ A 17C estate which was completely renovated in 1992. A combination of local and Italian cuisine is served in the country-style restaurant rooms.

at Salzburg-Nonntal :

Purzelbaum, Zugallistr. 7, 5020, (0662) 84 88 43, *Fax (0662) 84888433, info@purzelbaum.at,* – Z e
closed Sunday and Monday lunch, except festival period – **Meals** à la carte 34/48.
◆ This venerable old city building houses a contemporary style restaurant offering French cuisine and friendly service.

at Salzburg-Parsch *East : 5 km, by Bürgleinstraße* X :

Villa Pace without rest, Sonnleitenweg 9, ✉ 5020, ℘ (0662) 64 40 77, *Fax (0662) 64407770, info@villapace.at,* ← Salzburg and fortress, – rm, VISA
closed February – **12 rm** 73/99 – 127/173.
• An exquisitely elegant villa captivates with its individually-styled rooms, some of which are very spacious, and its high location overlooking Salzburg. Well-tended garden.

on the Heuberg *Northeast : 3 km, by* ① *- Hhe 565 m*

Schöne Aussicht, Heuberg 3, ✉ 5023 *Salzburg,* ℘ (0662) 64 06 08, *Fax (0662) 6406082, hotel@salzburgpanorama.at,* ←, – rm, – 20. AE VISA
closed mid January - mid February – **Meals** *(closed Wednesday)* à la carte 15/29 – **28 rm** 51/128 – 72/138.
• Around 300 years old, this farmstead stands on its own on the Heuberg hill and lives up to its name ("Beautiful View"). Ask for one of the rooms with a balcony. Country-style restaurant with a tiled stove, and a garden terrace for the view.

on the Gaisberg *East : 5 km, by* ① :

Vitalhotel Kobenzl, Am Gaisberg 11, *alt. 730 m,* ✉ 5020 *Salzburg,* ℘ (0662) 64 15 10, *Fax (0662) 642238, info@kobenzl.at,* – – 30. AE VISA. rest
closed 6 January - 6 March – **Meals** à la carte 42/53 – **41 rm** 156/356 – 182/414.
• High above the city in lovely leafy surroundings, this elegant mountain hotel features lots of gilt and old wood. The visitors' book has been signed by many of the great (e.g. Richard Nixon) and good. Guests dine in a stylish setting.

Romantik Hotel Gersberg Alm, Gersberg 37, *alt. 800 m,* ✉ 5023 *Salzburg-Gnigl,* ℘ (0662) 64 12 57, *Fax (0662) 644278, office@gersbergalm.at,* ←, – – 120. AE VISA JCB. rest
Meals (booking essential) à la carte 25/38 – **46 rm** 91/128 – 134/163 – 3 suites.
• This extended and secluded mountain inn with a wood-panelled façade dates back to 1860. Today's guests are accommodated in homely rooms, furnished in light wood. Restaurant with two cheerfully rustic dining rooms.

near Airport *Southwest : 5 km, by* ③ :

Airporthotel, Dr.-M.-Laireiter-Str. 9, ✉ 5020 *Salzburg-Loig,* ℘ (0662) 85 00 20, *Fax (0662) 85002044, airporthotel@aon.at,* – rm, – 20. AE VISA JCB. rest
Meals (residents only) – **39 rm** 95/125 – 135/155.
• This airport hotel consists of a pair of linked country houses offering functional rooms, some with a balcony.

Ikarus, Wilhelm-Spazier-Str. 7a (Hangar-7, 1st floor), ✉ 5020 *Salzburg,* ℘ (0662) 21 97 77, *Fax (0662) 21973786, ikarus@at.redbull.com,* ← – – 20. AE VISA JCB.
Meals (booking essential) 40 *(lunch)*/84 and à la carte.
Spec. Gebratener Loup de mer mit Seehecht-Brandade und Paprikacoulis. Sautiert Langostinos mit grünen Spargel und Mango. Geschmolzener Topfenködel mit gratiniertem Pistazienparfait.
• Built to shelter the Flying Bulls historic aircraft collection, Hangar 7 with its overarching, transparent canopy also sees guest chefs offering monthly themed menus.

at Anif *South : 7 km, by* ② :

Friesacher (with guest house Anifer Hof), Hellbrunner Str. 17, ✉ 5081, ℘ (06246) 89 77, *Fax (06246) 897749, first@hotelfriesacher.com,* – rm, – 40. AE VISA
Meals à la carte 16/35 – **90 rm** 75/100 – 125/210.
• This stylish, country-style house has been welcoming guests for 150 years. All rooms with balcony and ISDN. The restaurant is divided into a number of attractive little rooms.

Schlosswirt zu Anif (with guest house), Salzachtal Bundesstr. 7, ✉ 5081, ℘ (06246) 7 21 75, *Fax (06246) 721758, info@schlosswirt-anif.com,* – AE VISA JCB
closed 2 weeks February and 1 week end October – **Meals** *(closed Monday, except festival period)* à la carte 28/47 – **28 rm** 84 – 156.
• Like the neighbouring moated castle, this historic hotel dates back to 1350. It has been carefully restored and offers Biedermeier style rooms. The lord of the castle has had taverner's rights in the hotel restaurant since 1607.

at Bergheim *North : 7 km, by Elisabeth-Str.* V :

Gasthof Gmachl, Dorfstr. 35, ✉ 5101, ✆ (0662) 45 21 24, *Fax (0662) 45212468, info@gmachl.at,* , , , (heated), , – , 25. AE MC VISA
closed early to mid July – **Meals** 25/42 and à la carte – **68 rm** 78/112 – 136/180 – 7 suites.
◆ Historic, centrally located inn with cosy rooms and comfortable suites as well as an attractively laid out park with recreational facilities. Welcoming dining rooms in a variety of styles.

at Bergheim-Maria Plain *North : 7 km, by Elisabeth-Str.* V :

Zur Plainlinde (Brugger), Plainbergweg 30, ✉ 5101, ✆ (0662) 45 85 57, *Fax (0662) 458270, restaurant@plainlinde.at,* ←, – P. MC VISA
closed 1 week June, 1 week September, 3 weeks January, Monday and Tuesday (festival period only Monday) – **Meals** (booking essential) à la carte 27/53, .
Spec. Geräucherter Bachsaibling mit Sauerrahm und Zitronendressing. Heimischer Waller mit Püree und Ofentomaten am Zweig. Karamellisierte Topfen-Limonentarte.
◆ Very friendly and professional service, creative local cuisine prepared from excellent products and a pleasantly informal atmosphere.

at Hallwang-Söllheim *Northeast : 7 km, by ② and Linzer Bundesstraße :*

Pfefferschiff (Fleischhaker), Söllheim 3, ✉ 5300, ✆ (0662) 66 12 42, *Fax (0662) 661841, restaurant@pfefferschiff.at,* – P. AE VISA.
closed end June - mid July, Sunday and Monday, during festival period only Monday – **Meals** (booking essential) 30 *(lunch)*/61 *(dinner)* and à la carte .
Spec. Blunzenguglhupf mit schwarzen Trüffeln. Rehrücken mit Ingwerkirschen und Petersilienpüree. Topfenschmarren mit Äpfeln und Sauerrahmeis.
◆ Step aboard a 350-year-old rectory anchored in a leafy setting. Individual, stylish interior. Navigate your way through a menu featuring the best of local cuisine.

Filzmoos Salzburg 730 M 6 – pop. 1 350 – alt. 1 057 m.
Salzburg 75.

Hubertus (Maier) with rm, Am Dorfplatz 1, ✉ 5532, ✆ (06453) 82 04, *Fax (06453) 82046, info@hotelhubertus.at,* ←, , , (heatet), – , rm, P. AE MC VISA
closed 10 April - 10 May and November - 5 December – **Meals** *(closed Monday - Tuesday except Bank Holidays)(Wednesday - Friday dinner only)* 88 and à la carte – **14 rm** 90/170 – 150/220.
Spec. Saiblingfilet mit Krebserlravioli und Krebsnage. Taube in zwei Gängen serviert. Variation von Topfen.
◆ A charming alpine hotel : give yourself a treat in the elegant restaurant where chef Johanna Maier creates delicious regional dishes. Very beautiful country house style rooms.

Werfen Salzburg 730 L 6 – pop. 3 200 – alt. 600 m.
Salzburg 47.

Karl und Rudolf Obauer with rm, Markt 46, ✉ 5450, ✆ (06468) 5 21 20, *Fax (06468) 521212, ok@obauer.com,* – rm, rest, P – 25. AE
Meals *(closed Monday - Tuesday, except out of season and festival period)* (booking essential) 36 *(lunch)*/75 and à la carte , – **10 rm** 80/130 – 120/210.
Spec. Geräucherte Kalbsleber mit Forcher Speck und Safranapfel. Wachtel mit weißer Bohnencreme und Kresse. Himbeertörtchen mit Campari-Pfeffersorbet.
◆ Gourmets come here to enjoy the unique style of cuisine served in a modern and elegant restaurant by skilled, attentive staff. Lovely garden terrace. The breakfast served at the table is of exceptional quality.

Benelux

Belgium

BRUSSELS – ANTWERP – BRUGES – LIÈGE

Grand Duchy of Luxembourg

LUXEMBOURG

Netherlands

AMSTERDAM – The HAGUE – ROTTERDAM

PRACTICAL INFORMATION

LOCAL CURRENCY

1 euro (€ = 1,34 USD ($) (Déc. 2004)

TOURIST INFORMATION

Telephone numbers and addresses of Tourist Offices are given in the text of each city under 🅸 .

National Holiday: *Belgium: 21 July; Netherlands: 30 April; Luxembourg: 23 June.*

AIRPORTS

Brussels Airport at Zaventem, ☎ 0900 70000.
Schiphol Airport at Schiphol, ☎ (020) 794 08 00.
Luxembourg Airport, L-2987 Luxembourg, ☎ (00 352) 47 98 50 50.

FOREIGN EXCHANGE

In Belgium, *banks close at 4.30pm and weekends;*

in the Netherlands, *banks close at 5.00pm and weekends, Schiphol Airport exchange offices open daily from 6.30am to 11.30pm.*

TRANSPORT

Taxis: *may be hailed in the street, at taxi ranks or called by telephone.*
Bus, tramway: *practical for long and short distances and good for sightseeing.*

Brussels has a **Métro** *(subway) network. In each station complete information and plans will be found.*

POSTAL SERVICES – SHOPPING

Post offices open Monday to Friday from 9am to 5pm in Benelux.
Shops and boutiques are generally open from 9am to 7pm in Belgium and Luxembourg, and from 9am to 6pm in the Netherlands. The main shopping areas are:

in Brussels: *Rue Neuve, Porte de Namur, Avenue Louise, Avenue de la Toison d'Or, Boulevard de Waterloo, Rue de Namur - Also Brussels antique market on Saturday from 9am to 3pm, and Sunday from 9am to 1pm (around Place du Grand-Sablon) - Flower and Bird market (Grand-Place) on Sunday morning - Flea Market (Place du Jeu de Balles) – Shopping Centres: Basilix, Westland Shopping Center, Woluwé Shopping Center, City 2, Galerie Louise.*

in Luxembourg: *Grand'Rue and around Place d'Armes - Station Quarter.*

in Amsterdam: *Kalverstraat, Leidsestraat, Nieuwendijk, P.C. Hoofstraat, Beethovenstraat, Van Baerlestraat and Utrechtsestraat – Shopping Center, Magna Plaza – Second-hand goods and antiques (around Rijksmuseum and Spiegelgracht) – Flower Market – Amsterdam Flea Market (near Waterlooplein).*

BREAKDOWN SERVICE *24 hour assistance:*

Belgium: *TCB, Brussels ☎ 0 2 233 22 02 – VTB-VAB, Antwerp ☎ 0 3 253 63 63 – RACB, Brussels ☎ 0 2 287 09 11.*

Luxembourg: *ACL ☎ 45 00 451.*

Netherlands: *ANWB, The Hague ☎ (070) 314 71 47 – KNAC, The Hague ☎ (070) 383 16 12.*

TIPPING *In Benelux, prices include service and taxes.*

SPEED LIMITS – SEAT BELTS

In Belgium and Luxembourg, the maximum speed limits are 120 km/h-74 mph on motorways and dual carriageways, 90 km/h-56 mph on all other roads and 50 km/h-31 mph in built-up areas. In the Netherlands, 100/120 km/h-62/74 mph on motorways and "autowegen", 80 km/h-50 mph on other roads and 50 km/h-31 mph in built-up areas. In each country, the wearing of seat belts is compulsory for drivers and passengers.

BRUSSELS
(BRUXELLES/BRUSSEL)

1000 Région de Bruxelles-Capitale – Brussels Hoofdstedelijk Gewest 533 L 17 *and* 716 G 3 *– Pop. 997 126.*

Paris 308 – Amsterdam 204 – Düsseldorf 222 – Lille 116 – Luxembourg 219.

Plans of Brussels
- Suburbs .... pp. 2 and 3
- Brussels .... pp. 4 and 5
- Large scale plans .... p. 6

Places of interest .... p. 7

Alphabetical listing of hotels and restaurants .... pp. 8 to 10
- ★★★, ★★, ★ establishments .... p. 11
- List of establishments according to style of cuisine .... pp. 12 and 13

List of hotels and restaurants :
- Town centre .... pp. 14 to 22
- Suburbs .... pp. 22 to 30
- District .... pp. 30 to 35

TOURIST OFFICES

TIB Hôtel de Ville, Grand'Place, ✉ 1000, ✆ 0 2 513 89 40, tourism@brusselsinternational.be, Fax 0 2 514 45 38.
Office de Promotion du Tourisme (OPT), r. Marché-aux-Herbes 63, ✉ 1000, ✆ 0 2 504 02 00, info@opt.be, Fax 0 2 513 69 50.
Toerisme Vlaanderen, Grasmarkt 63, ✉ 1000, ✆ 0 2 504 03 90, info@toerismevlaanderen.be, Fax 0 2 504 02 70.

For more information on tourist attractions consult our Green Guide to Brussels and our Map N° 44.

BRUXELLES/ BRUSSEL

9ème de Ligne (Bd du) . . . . . EQ 271
Baudouin (Bd) . . . . EQ 16
Bienfaiteurs (Pl. des) . . . . . . GQ 21
Brabançonne (Av. de la) . . . . . GR 28
Édouard de Thibault (Av.) . . . . HS 72
Europe (Esplanade de l') . . . . . ES 89
Frans Courtens (Av.) . . . . HQ 102
Frère Orban (Square) . . . . FR 104
Froissart (R.) . . . . GS 106
Général Eisenhower (Av.) . . . GQ 108
Hal (Porte de) . . . . ES 114
Henri Jaspar (Av.) . . . . ES 117
Herbert Hoover (Av.) . . . . HR 118
Industrie (Quai de l') . . . . ER 126
Jan Stobbaerts (Av.) . . . . GQ 133
Jardin Botanique (Bd du) . . . . FQ 134
Jean Jacobs (Pl.) . . . . ES 135
Jean Volders (Av.) . . . . EST 138
Jeu de Balle (Pl. du) . . . . ES 139

Livourne (R. de) . . . . FT 158
Louise (Galerie) . . . . FS 162
Luxembourg (R. du) . . . . FS 165
Marie-Louise (Square) . . . . . . GR 171
Méridien (R. du) . . . . FQ 173
Midi (Bd du) . . . . ES
Mons (Chaussée de) . . . . ER 177
Nerviens (Av. des) . . . . GS 181
Ninove (Chaussée de) . . . . . . ER 183
Palmerston (Av.) . . . . GR 187
Porte de Hal
(Av. de la) . . . . ES 199
Prince Royal (R. du) . . . . FS 204
Reine (Av. de la) . . . . FQ 208
Rogier (Pl. Charles) . . . . FQ 213
Roi Vainqueur (Pl. du) . . . . HS 216
Saint-Antoine (Pl.) . . . . GT 220
Scailquin (R.) . . . . FR 228
Victoria Régina
(Av.) . . . . FQ 249
Waterloo (Chaussée de) . . . . . ET 256

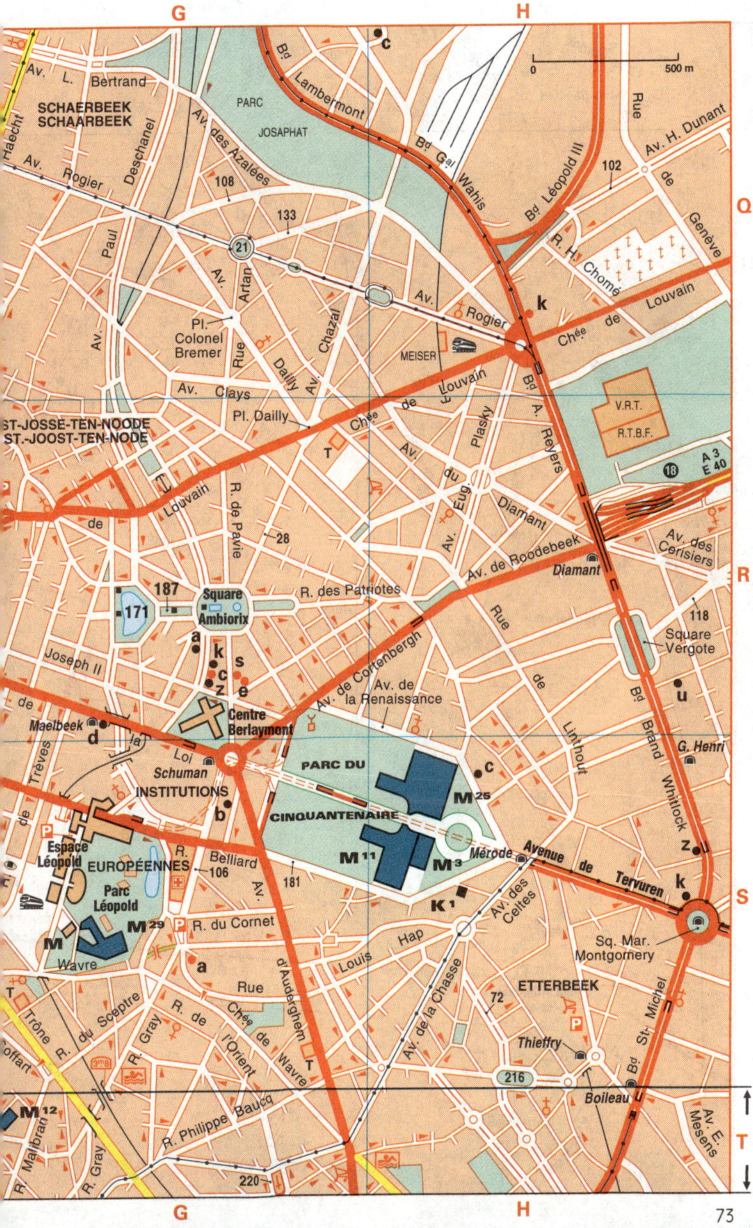

BRUXELLES/ BRUSSEL

2ème Régiment de Lanciers (Av. du) . . . . HU 265
7 Bonniers (Av. des) . . . . EV 270
Américaine (R.) . . . . FU 8
Auguste Rodin (Av.) . . . . GU 12
Besme (Av.) . . . . EV 18
Boondael (Drève de) . . . . . . GX 22
Cambre (Bd de la) . . . . GV 33
Coccinelles (Av. des) . . . . HX 40
Congo (Av. du) . . . . GV 48
Copernic (R.) . . . . FX 51
Dodonée (R.) . . . . FV 61
Dries . . . . HX 63
Émile de Beco (Av.) . . . . GU 79
Émile De Mot (Av.) . . . . GV 81
Éperons d'Or (Av. des) . . . . . GU 85

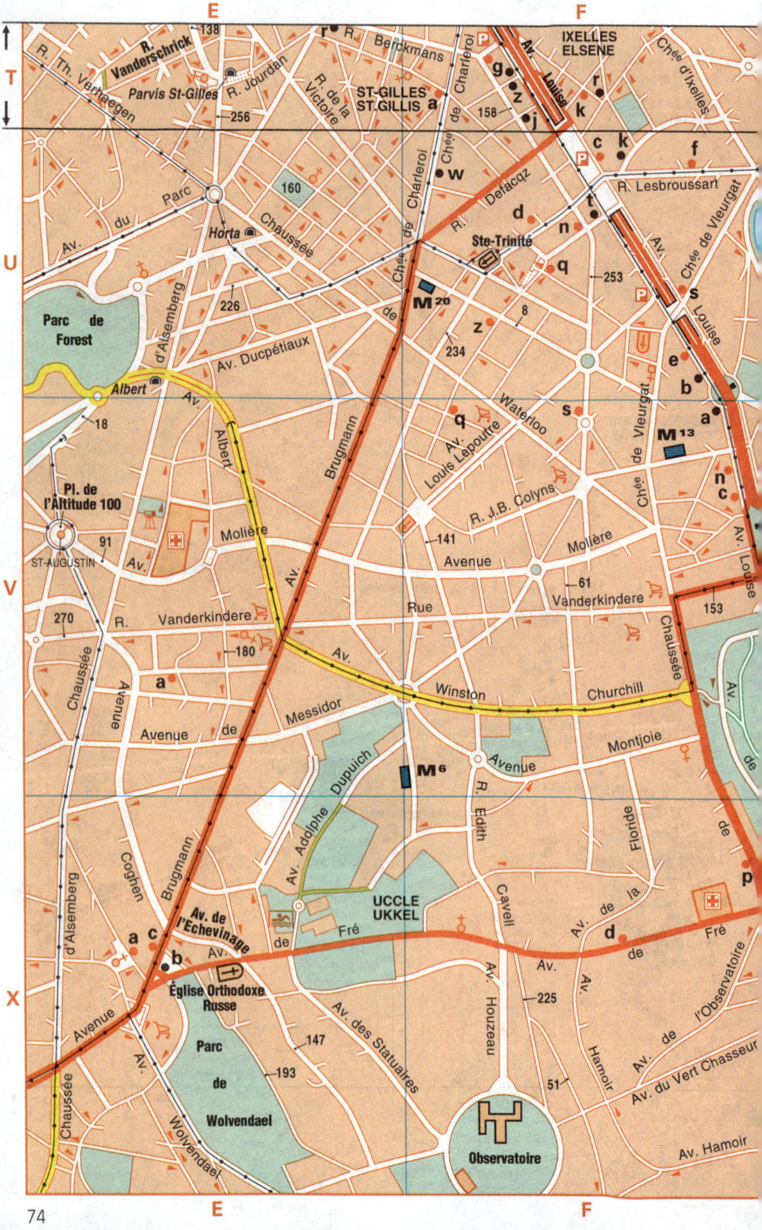

Everard (Av.) . . . . EV 91
Hippodrome (Av. de l') . . . . . . GU 120
Invalides (Bd des) . . . . HV 127
Jean Volders (Av.) . . . . ET 138
Joseph Stallaert (R.) . . . . FV 141
Juliette Wytsman (R.) . . . . . . GU 145
Kamerdelle (Av.) . . . . EX 147
Legrand (Av.) . . . . FV 153
Livourne (R. de) . . . . FT 158
Louis Morichar (Pl.) . . . . EU 160
Mutualité (R. de la) . . . . EV 180
Nouvelle (Av.) . . . . GU 184
Paul Stroobant (Av.) . . . . EX 193
Saint-Antoine (Pl.) . . . . GT 220
Saisons (Av. des) . . . . GV 223
Saturne (Av. de) . . . . FX 225
Savoie (R. de) . . . . EU 226
Tabellion (R. du) . . . . FU 234
Washington (R.) . . . . FU 253
Waterloo (Chaussée de) . . . . . ET 256

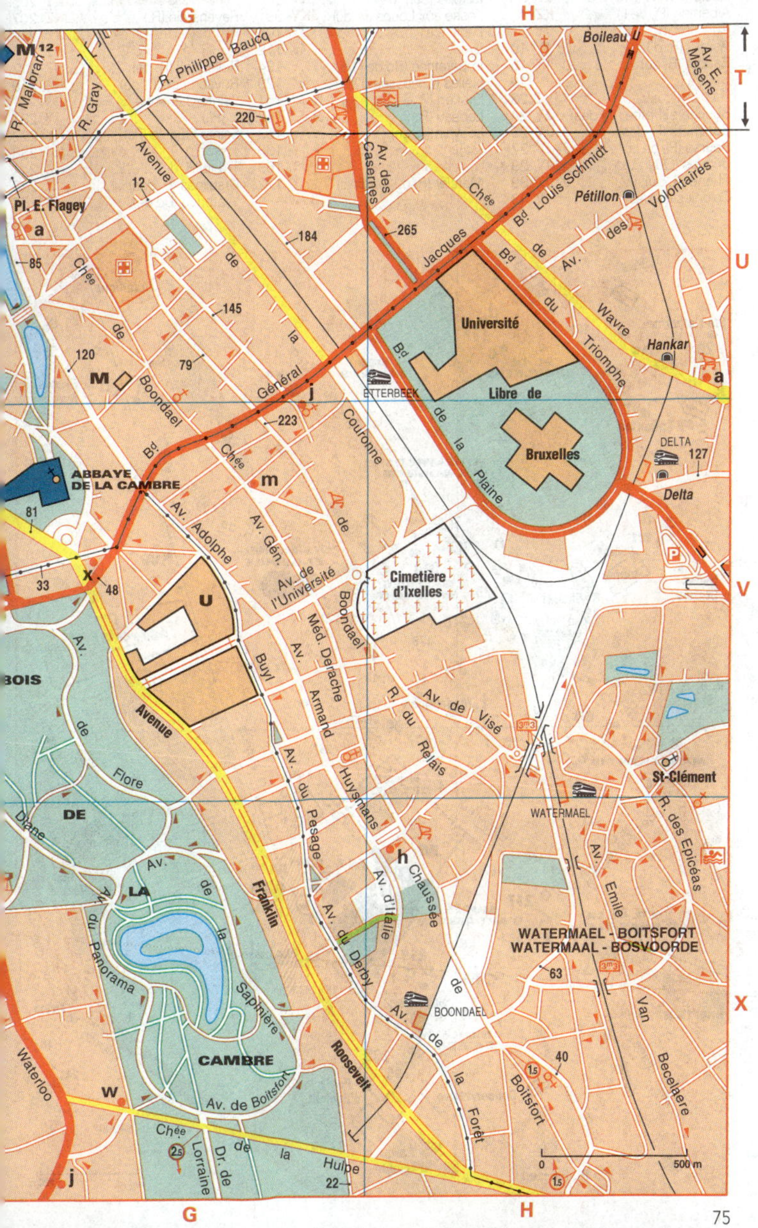

BRUXELLES/ BRUSSEL

6 Jeunes Hommes (R. des) KZ 268
Adolphe Max (Bd) JY 3
Albertine (Pl. de l') KZ 4
Anspach (Bd) JY
Assaut (R. d') KY 10
Baudet (R. du) KZ 15
Beurre (R. au) JY 19
Bortier (Galerie) JYZ 23
Bouchers (Petite rue des) JY 24
Bouchers (R. des) JY 25
Bourse (Pl. de la) JY 27
Briques (Quai aux) JY 29
Chêne (R. du) JZ 39
Colonies (R. des) KY 43
Comédiens (R. des) KY 45
Commerce (R. du) KZ 46
Croix de Fer (R. de la) KY 52
Duquesnoy (R.) JZ 66
Ernest Allard (R.) JZ 86
Étuve (R. de l') JZ 87
Europe (Carr. de l') KY 90
Fossé aux Loups (R. du) JKY 99
Fripiers (R. des) JY 105
Grand Sablon (Pl. du) KZ 112
Impératrice (Bd de l') KY 124
Ixelles (Chaussée d') KZ 129
Laeken (R. de) JY 151
Lebeau (R.) JZ 152
Louvain (R. de) KY 163
Marché aux Herbes (R. du) JY 168
Marché aux Poulets (R. du) JY 169
Mercier (R. du Cardinal) KY 172
Midi (R. du) JYZ
Montagne (R. de la) KY 178
Musée (Pl. du) KZ 179
Neuve (R.) JKZ
Nord (Passage du) JY 182
Petit Sablon (Pl. du) KZ 195
Presse (R. de la) KY 201
Princes (Galeries des) JKY 205
Ravenstein (R.) KZ 207
Reine (Galerie de la) JY 210
Roi (Galerie du) KY 214
Rollebeek (R. de) JZ 217
Ruysbroeck (R. de) KZ 219
Sainte-Catherine (Pl.) JY 221
Sainte-Gudule (Pl.) KY 222
Toison d'Or (Av. de la) KZ 238
Trône (R. du) KZ 241
Ursulines (R. des) JZ 243
Waterloo (Bd de) KZ 255

GOLF COURSES

18 9 Southeast : 14 km at Tervuren, Château de Ravenstein ☎ 0 2 767 58 01, Fax 0 2 767 28 41 – 18 Northeast : 14 km at Melsbroek, Steenwagenstraat 11 ☎ 0 2 751 82 25, Fax 0 2 751 84 25 – 18 at Anderlecht, Sports Area of la Pede, r. Scholle 1 ☎ 0 2 521 16 87, Fax 0 2 521 51 56 – 9 at Watermael-Boitsfort, chaussée de la Hulpe 53a ☎ 0 2 672 22 22, Fax 0 2 675 34 81 – 9 Southeast : 16 km at Overijse, Gemslaan 55 ☎ 0 2 687 50 30, Fax 0 2 687 37 68 – 9 West : 8 km at Itterbeek, J.M. Van Lierdelaan 24 ☎ 0 2 569 00 38, Fax 0 2 567 00 38 – 18 Northeast : 20 km at Kampenhout, Wildersedreef 56 ☎ 0 16 65 12 16, Fax 0 16 65 16 80 – 9 East : 18 km at Duisburg, Hertswegenstraat 59 ☎ 0 2 769 45 82, Fax 0 2 767 97 52.

PLACES OF INTEREST

BRUSSELS SEEN FROM ABOVE

Atomium★ – Basilica of the Sacred Heart★ – Arcades of the Royal Museum of the Army and Military History★ HS **M**[25].

FAMOUS VIEWS OF BRUSSELS

The Law Courts ES **J** – *Administrative sections of the City of Brussels* KY – *Place Royale★* KZ.

GREEN AREAS

Parks : Bruxelles, Wolvendael, Woluwé, Laeken, Cinquantenaire, Duden, Bois de la Cambre, Forêt de Soignes.

HISTORICAL MONUMENTS

Grand-Place★★★ JY – *Monnaie Theatre★* JY – *St Hubert Arcades★★* JKY – *Erasmus' House (Anderlecht)★★ – Castle and park (Gaasbeek)★★ (Southwest : 12 km) – Royal Greenhouses (Laeken)★★.*

CHURCHES

Sts-Michael's and Gudule's Cathedral★★ KY – *Church of N.-D. de la Chapelle★* JZ – *Church of N.-D. du Sablon★* KZ – *Abbey of la-Cambre (Ixelles)★★* FGV – *Church of Sts-Pierre and Guidon (Anderlecht)★.*

MUSEUMS

Museum of Ancient Art★★★ KZ – *Museum of the Cinquantenaire★★★* HS **M**[11] – *Museum of Modern Art★★* KZ **M**[2] – *Belgian Centre for Comic Strip Art★★* KY **M**[8] – *Autoworld★★* HS **M**[3] – *Natural Science Museum★★* GS **M**[29] – *Museum of Musical Instruments★★★* KZ **M**[21] – *Constantin Meunier Museum (Ixelles)★* FV **M**[13] – *Ixelles Community Museum (Ixelles)★★* GT **M**[12] – *Charlier Museum★* FR **M**[9] – *Bibliotheca Wittockiana (Woluwé-St-Pierre)★ – Royal Museum of Central Africa (Tervuren/district)★★ – Horta Museum (St-Gilles)★★* EFU **M**[20] – *Van Buuren Museum (Uccle)★* EFV **M**[6] – *Bellevue★* KZ **M**[28].

MODERN ARCHITECTURE

Atomium★ – Berlaymont Centre GR – *European Parliament* GS – *Arts Centre* KZ **Q**[1] – *Administrative sections of the City of Brussels* KY – *Garden-Cities Le Logis and Floréal (Watermael-Boitsfort) – Garden-Cities Kapelleveld (Woluwé-St-Lambert) – UCL Campus (Woluwé-St-Lambert) – Stoclet Palace (Tervuren/district)★ – Swift (La Hulpe/district) – Shop-front P. Hankar★* KY **W** – *Ixelles council building* FS **K**[2] – *Van Eetvelde Hotel★* GR 187 – *Old England★* KZ **N** – *Cauchie House (Etterbeek)★* HS **K**[1].

SCENIC AREAS

Grand-Place★★★ JY – *Grand and Petit Sablon★★* JZ – *St-Hubert Arcades★★* JKY – *Place du Musée* KZ – *Place Ste-Catherine* JY – *The Old Town (Halles St-Géry – vault of the Senne – Church of Riches Claires)* ER – *Rue des Bouchers★* JY – *Manneken Pis★★* JZ – *The Marolles District* JZ – *Galerie Bortier* JY.

Alphabetical listing of hotels and restaurants

A

31 Abbey
21 Agenda Louise
15 Agenda Midi
22 Alain Cornelis
15 Alban Chambon (L') (H. Métropole)
32 Aloyse Kloos
27 Amici miei
17 Amigo
29 Amis du Cep (Les)
31 Arconati (Host. d')
26 Argus
17 Aris
34 Arlecchino (L') (H. Aub. de Waterloo)
17 Armes de Bruxelles (Aux)
14 Astoria
18 Astrid Centre
21 Atelier de la Truffe Noire (L')
18 Atlas
24 Aub. de Boendael (L')
32 Aub. Napoléon
33 Aub. de Waterloo
30 auberg'in (l')

B

22 Balade Gourmande (La)
16 Balthazar
33 Barbizon
25 Beau-Site
14 Bedford
18 Belle Maraîchère (La)
23 Belson
25 Beverly Hills
32 Bijgaarden (De)
28 Blue Elephant
33 Boetfort
28 Bon-Bon
23 Brasserie de la Gare (La)
28 Brasseries Georges
20 Bristol Stephanie
22 Brouette (La)
24 Bruneau

C

24 Cambrils
17 Carrefour de l'Europe
26 Cascade
19 Castello Banfi
23 Caudalie (La)
17 Cerf (Le)
28 Chalet de la Forêt (Le)
15 Chambord
35 Château du Mylord
20 Châtelain (Le)
19 « Chez Marius » En Provence
24 Claude Dupont
19 Clef des Champs (La)
27 Comfort Art H. Siru
15 Comme Chez Soi
20 Conrad
27 County House
27 Crowne Plaza
30 Crowne Plaza Airport
16 Crowne Plaza Europa
28 Cuisine du 519 (La)

D

27 Dames Tartine (Les)
29 Da Mimmo
30 Deux Maisons (Les)
17 Dixseptième (Le)
21 Dome (Le)
16 Dorint

E

19 Écailler du Palais Royal (L')
22 Erasme
16 Eurovillage

F

23 Fierlant (De)
21 Floris Louise
25 Four Points Sheraton

18 François
26 French Kiss
28 Frères Romano (Les)

G

32 Gosset
26 Gd H. Mercure Royal Crown
34 Green Park
23 Grignotière (La)
34 Gril aux herbes (Le)
29 Grill (Le)

H

34 Hacienda (La)
19 Herbe Rouge (L')
14 Hesperia Grand'Place
19 Hilton
33 Hof ter Imde
31 Holiday Inn Airport
16 Holiday Inn Schuman
20 Hyatt Regency

I – J – K

20 Idiot du village (L')
16 In 't Spinnekopke
33 Istas
26 I Trulli
15 Jaloa
20 JB
19 Jolly du Grand Sablon
31 Kapblok (De)
31 Kasteel Gravenhof
18 Kelderke ('t)
23 Khaïma (La)
26 Khnopff
34 Kijk Uit
33 Koen Van Loven

L

29 Lambeau
27 Lambermont
20 Larmes du Tigre (Les)
25 Leopold
33 Lipsius
19 Lola
18 Loup-Galant (Le)
22 Lychee

M

19 Maison du Bœuf (H. Hilton)
17 Maison du Cygne (La)
24 Maison Félix
26 Manos Premier
15 Manufacture (La)
24 Marie
14 Marriott
17 Matignon
29 Maurice à Olivier (de)
30 Medicis
20 Melía Avenue Louise
28 Menus Plaisirs (Les)
23 Mercure
17 Méridien (Le)
14 Métropole
32 Michel
22 Ming Dynasty
30 Montgomery
29 Monty

N – O

23 New Asia
16 New Hotel Charlemagne
14 NH Atlanta
31 NH Brussels Airport
26 NH Brussels City Centre
15 NH Grand Place Arenberg
26 NH Stéphanie
31 Novotel Airport
17 Novotel off Grand'Place
18 Novotel Centre-Tour Noire
25 O' comme 3 Pommes
17 Ogenblik (de l')
33 Orangeraie Roland Debuyst (L')

P – Q

24 Pagode d'Or (La)
28 Pain et le Vin (Le)
16 Pappa e Citti
23 Park
35 Parkhof
28 Passage (Le)
25 Perles de Pluie (Les)
14 Plaza (Le)
21 Porte des Indes (La)
28 pré en bulle (le)
14 President Centre
21 President Nord

21 President World Trade Center
21 Prince de Liège (Le)
32 Pyramid
15 Queen Anne
25 Quincaillerie (La)

R

14 Radisson SAS
31 Rainbow Airport
31 Relais Delbeccha
34 Rembrandt (de)
25 Renaissance
29 Repos des Chasseurs (Au)
34 Rijckendael
34 Roseraie (La)
17 Roue d'Or (La)
34 Rouge Glamour
21 Rouge Tomate
16 Royal Windsor
27 Rue Royale
(Gd H. Mercure Royal Crown)

S

15 Sabina
22 Saint Guidon
15 Samourai
24 San Daniele
14 Scandic Grand'Place
15 Sea Grill (H. Radisson SAS)
27 Senza Nome
35 Sheraton Airport
27 Sheraton Towers
29 Sodehotel La Woluwe
25 Sofitel
30 Sofitel Airport
33 Soret
20 Stanhope
32 Ster (De)
23 Stirwen
35 Stockmansmolen
34 Stoveke ('t)
18 Strofilia

T

29 Table de Mamy
21 Tagawa
16 Take Sushi
32 Terborght
30 Tour d'Argent (La)
19 Trente rue de la Paille
30 Trois Couleurs (Des)
21 Truffe Noire (La)
27 Tulip Inn Boulevard
25 Tutto Pepe

U – V

22 Ustel
34 Val Joli
35 Via-Vai
29 Vieux Boitsfort (Au)
26 Vieux Pannenhuis (Rôtiss. Le)
26 Vigne... à l'Assiette (De la)
30 Vignoble de Margot (Le)
28 Villa d'Este
21 Villa Lorraine
18 Vincent
18 Viva M'Boma

W – Y

32 Waerboom
18 Welcome
24 Yen (Le)

Starred establishments

✿✿✿

15 XXX Comme Chez Soi

✿✿

32 XXXX Bijgaarden (De)
35 XXXX Château du Mylord
24 XXXX Bruneau
15 XXXX Sea Grill (H. Radisson SAS)
24 XXX Claude Dupont

✿

33 XXXX Barbizon
19 XXXX Maison du Bœuf (H. Hilton)
21 XXXX Villa Lorraine
29 XXX Vieux Boitsfort (Au)
19 XXX Écailler du Palais Royal (L')
32 XXX Michel
33 XXX Orangeraie Roland Debuyst (L')
22 XXX Saint Guidon
24 XXX San Daniele
21 XXX Truffe Noire (La)
30 XX Deux Maisons (les)
29 XX Maurice à Olivier (de)
32 XX Terborght
28 X Bon-Bon
24 X Marie
28 X Passage (Le)
27 X Senza Nome

Establishments according to style of cuisine

Buffets

20 Bistrol Stéphanie *Q. Louise*

19 Café d'Egmont (J. Hilton) *Q. Palais de Justice*

20 Café Wiltcher's (H. Conrad) *Q. Louise*

31 NH Brussels Airport *at Diegem*

27 Sheraton Towers *Q. Roger St-Josse-ten-Noode*

Grill

24 Aub. de Boendael (L') *Ixelles Q. Boondael*

32 Aub. Napoleon *at Meise*

30 auberg'in (l') *Woluwé-St-Pierre*

26 French Kiss *Jette*

29 Grill (Le) *Watermael-Boitsfort*

26 Vieux Pannenhuis (Rôtiss. Le) *Jette*

Pub rest – Brasseries

23 Brasserie de la Gare (La) *Berchem-Ste-Agathe*

28 Brasseries Georges *Uccle*

22 Erasme *Anderlecht*

33 Istas *Env. at Overijse*

31 Kasteel Gravenhof *Env. at Dworp*

19 Lola *Q. des Sablons*

15 NH Grand Place Arenberg

22 Prince de Liège (Le) *Anderlecht*

25 Quincaillerie (La) *Ixelles Q. Bascule*

17 Roue d'Or (La) *Q. Grand'Place*

32 Ster (De) *Env. at Itterbeek*

35 Stockmansmolen *Env. at Zaventem*

22 Ustel *Anderlecht*

26 Vigne... à l'Assiette (De la) *Ixelles Q. Louise*

Regional

16 In 't Spinnekopke

18 Kelderke ('t) *Q. Grand'Place*

Seafood – Oyster bar

18 Belle Maraîchère (La) *Q. Ste-Catherine*

28 Brasseries Georges *Uccle*

19 Écailler du Palais Royal (L') *Q. des Sablons*

18 François *Q. Ste-Catherine*

25 Quincaillerie (La) *Ixelles Q. Bascule*

15 Sea Grill (H. Radisson SAS)

34 Stoveke ('t) *Env. at Strombeek-Bever*

30 Vignoble de Margot (Le) *Woluwé-St-Pierre*

Chinese

22 Lychee *Q. Atomium*

22 Ming Dynasty *Q. Atomium*

23 New Asia *Auderghem*

Greek

18 Strofilia *Q. Ste-Catherine*

Indian

21 Porte des Indes (La) *Q. Louise*

Italian

27 Amici miei *Schaerbeek Q. Meiser*

17 Amigo *Q. Grand'Place*

34 Arlecchino (L') (H. Aub. de Waterloo) *Env. at Sint-Genesius-Rode*

21 Atelier de la Truffe Noir (L') *Q. Louise*

19 Castello Banfi *Q. des Sablons*

29 Da Mimmo *Woluwe-St-Lambert*

26 I Trulli *St-Gilles Q. Louise*

19 Jolly du Grand Sablon *Q. des Sablons*

29 Repos des Chasseurs (Au) *Watermael-Boitsfort*

24 San Daniele *Ganshoren*

27 Senza Nome *Schaerbeek*

25 Tutto Pepe *Ixelles Q. Louise*

35 Via-Vai *at Wemmel*

Japanese

19 Herbe Rouge (L') *Q. des Sablons*
15 Samourai
21 Tagawa *Q. Louise*
16 Take Sushi *Q. de l'Europe*

Moroccan

23 Khaïma (La) *Auderghem*

Spanish

34 Hacienda (La)

Thai

28 Blue Elephant *Uccle*
20 Larmes du Tigre (Les) *Q. Palais de Justice*
25 Perles de Pluie (Les) *Ixelles Q. Bascule*

Vietnamese

24 Pagode d'Or (La) *Ixelles Q. Boondael*
30 Tour d'Argent (La) *Woluwe-St-Pierre*
24 Yen (Le) *Ixelles*

BRUXELLES (BRUSSEL)

Radisson SAS, r. Fossé-aux-Loups 47, ✉ 1000, ☎ 0 2 219 28 28, *reservations.brussels@radissonsas.com, Fax 0 2 219 62 62,* – 25-450. AE VISA. KY f
Meals see ***Sea Grill*** below – ***Atrium*** Lunch 18 – a la carte 35/53 – 25 – **271 rm** 210/245, – 10 suites.
◆ A luxury hotel whose atrium bears remnants of the city's 12C fortifications. High-tech rooms varying in layout. "Comic strip" bar. Large restaurant crowned by a high dome. Themed food weeks. Resident pianist.

Astoria, r. Royale 103, ✉ 1000, ☎ 0 2 227 05 05, *H1154@accor.com, Fax 0 2 217 11 50,* – 25-210. AE VISA KY b
Meals ***Le Palais Royal*** *(closed 15 July-15 August and weekends)* 40/55 b.i. – 25 – **104 rm** 100/340, – 14 suites.
◆ Churchill and Dali have both stayed at this elegant Belle Époque palace. Sumptuous lounges and bedrooms adorned with period furniture. Top-class service. Opulent restaurant with mirrors, a marble fireplace, frescoes, and moulded and gilt fixtures and fittings.

Le Plaza, bd. A. Max 118, ✉ 1000, ☎ 0 2 278 01 00, *esterel@leplaza-brussels.be, Fax 0 2 278 01 01* – 25-800. AE VISA JCB FQ e
Meals *(closed Saturday lunch and Sunday).* Lunch 29 – a la carte 37/55 – 27 – **187 rm** 125/450, – 6 suites.
◆ Elegant rooms furnished with fine taste and a listed lounge-theatre are the main features of this 1930s hotel, whose plans were inspired by the George V in Paris. A wide cupola embellished with a celestial fresco adds a sense of space to the bar-restaurant.

Marriott, r. A. Orts 7 (opposite the Stock Exchange), ✉ 1000, ☎ 0 2 516 90 90 and 516 91 00 (rest), *mhrs.brudt.ays.mgr@marriotthotels.com, Fax 0 2 516 90 00,* – ch, – 25-450. AE VISA. rm JY z
Meals *(closed Sunday dinner).* Lunch 13 – a la carte 26/40 – 25 – **212 rm** 119/399, – 6 suites.
◆ Situated in front of the Stock Exchange and with an imposing turn-of-the-century façade, the interior of this hotel is modern and very comfortable. Rotisserie and modern brasserie where the usual international fare is freshly prepared.

Métropole, pl. de Brouckère 31, ✉ 1000, ☎ 0 2 217 23 00 , *info@metropolehotel.be, Fax 0 2 218 02 20* – 25-500. AE VISA JCB JY c
Meals see ***L'Alban Chambon*** below – **291 rm** 299/449, – 14 suites.
◆ This 19C palace on place de Brouckère was eulogised by Jacques Brel. Impressive foyer, sumptuous period lounges and delicate Art Nouveau frescoes discovered in 2004.

NH Atlanta, bd A. Max 7, ✉ 1000, ☎ 0 2 217 01 20 , *nhatlanta@nh-hotels.be, Fax 0 2 217 37 58,* – 25-160. AE VISA JY d
Meals *(closed lunch Saturday and Sunday)* – a la carte approx. 35 – 19 – **228 rm** 84/150, – 13 suites.
◆ Large-scale renovation work has given new life to this fine hotel built in the 1930s just a stone's throw from the nostalgic passage du Nord and place de Brouckère. The Atlanta's luxurious modern brasserie serves a range of French and Italian cuisine.

Bedford, r. Midi 135, ✉ 1000, ☎ 0 2 507 00 00, *info@hotelbedford.be, Fax 0 2 507 00 10,* – 25-550. AE VISA. ER k
Meals a la carte 37/55 – **318 rm** 230/320, – 8 suites.
◆ Just a short walk from the Manneken Pis and 500m/550yd from the Grand-Place, this chain hotel has a dozen apartments, as well as over 300 well-appointed standard rooms. The emphasis on the menu and wine-list is firmly French.

President Centre without rest, r. Royale 160, ✉ 1000, ☎ 0 2 219 00 65 , *gm@presidentcentre.be, Fax 0 2 218 09 10* – . AE VISA JCB.
73 rm 195/295. KY a
◆ Morpheus extends his welcoming arms in the comfortable, soundproofed rooms of the Hotel President Centre. Invaluable car attendants, attentive service and a cosy bar.

Hesperia Grand'Place without rest, r. Colonies 10, ✉ 1000, ☎ 0 2 504 99 10, *hotel@hesperia-grandplace.com, Fax 0 2 503 14 51* – – 25. AE VISA
47 rm 130/270. KY z
◆ An ideal location between the Gare Centrale and Saints-Michel-et-Gudule Cathedral. Modern, comfortable rooms, plus a bright breakfast room.

Scandic Grand'Place, r. Arenberg 18, ✉ 1000, ☎ 0 2 548 18 11 , *grand.place@scandic-hotels.com, Fax 0 2 548 18 20,* – ch, – 25-80. AE VISA JCB KY r
Meals *(closed lunch Saturday and Sunday)* – a la carte 22/34 – **100 rm** 99/269.
◆ 250m/275yd from the Grand-Place, and accessible via the Galeries St-Hubert, this late-19C mansion has 100 small but charming rooms promising a good night's sleep. A soberly-designed, yet welcoming modern brasserie.

NH Grand Place Arenberg, r. Assaut 15, ✉ 1000, ☎ 0 2 501 16 16, *nhgrandplace@nh-hotels.com, Fax 0 2 501 18 18* – AE ⓓ ⓜⓒ VISA. KY g
Meals (pub rest). *Lunch 10* – a la carte 22/37 – ☕ 17 – **155 rm** 69/220.
◆ This chain hotel is well-placed for exploring the heart of the city. Modern, functional bedrooms with standard furnishings.

Agenda Midi without rest, bd Jamar 11, ✉ 1060, ☎ 0 2 520 00 10, *midi@hotel-agenda.com, Fax 0 2 520 00 20* – AE ⓓ ⓜⓒ VISA ES z
35 rm ☕ 64/99.
◆ This renovated building on place Jamar is just a short distance from the Gare du Midi TGV railway station. Pleasant rooms and a brightly decorated breakfast room.

Chambord without rest, r. Namur 82, ✉ 1000, ☎ 0 2 548 99 10, *info@hotel-chambord.be, Fax 0 2 514 08 47* – AE ⓓ ⓜⓒ VISA JCB. KZ u
69 rm ☕ 60/160.
◆ A 1960s-style hotel alongside the porte de Namur. Spacious, adequately furnished rooms, with those to the rear generally quieter. Public car park a few yards away.

Queen Anne without rest, bd E. Jacqmain 110, ✉ 1000, ☎ 0 2 217 16 00, *Fax 0 2 217 18 38* – AE ⓓ ⓜⓒ VISA. EFQ a
60 rm ☕ 78/198.
◆ The Queen Anne is located on a major road linking the World Trade Center district and the old town. Plain, but carefully maintained bedrooms with double-glazing.

Sabina without rest, r. Nord 78, ✉ 1000, ☎ 0 2 218 26 37, *infos@hotelsabina.be, Fax 0 2 219 32 39* – AE ⓓ ⓜⓒ VISA KY c
24 rm ☕ 75/90.
◆ A modest hotel with quiet, plain rooms that are gradually being refurbished, situated between the colonne du Congrès and the place des Barricades. Pleasant breakfast room.

Sea Grill - Hotel Radisson SAS, r. Fossé-aux-Loups 47, ✉ 1000, ☎ 0 2 217 92 25, *seagrill@radissonsas.com, Fax 0 2 227 31 27,* Seafood – AE ⓓ ⓜⓒ VISA. KY f
closed 26 March-3 April, 1 to 28 August, 29 October-6 November, Saturday, Sunday and Bank Holidays – **Meals**. *Lunch 49* – 75/210 b.i., – a la carte 75/119
Spec. Saint-Jacques cuites à la vapeur d'algues, crème légère au cresson (15 September-April). Bar entier cuit en croûte de sel. Manchons de crabe de la mer de Barents tiédis au beurre de persil plat.
◆ A warm, Scandinavian-influenced ambience, ambitious fish-dominated menu, excellent wine cellar, plus a lounge offering a good choice of cigars. Friendly, impeccable service.

L'Alban Chambon - Hotel Métropole, pl. de Brouckère 31, ✉ 1000, ☎ 0 2 217 23 00, *info@metropolehotel.be, Fax 0 2 218 02 20* – AE ⓓ ⓜⓒ VISA JCB JY c
closed 18 July-16 August, Saturday, Sunday and Bank Holidays – **Meals**. *Lunch 35* – 55/90 b.i..
◆ The name of this restaurant pays homage to the Metropole's architect. Light, classic cuisine served in a former ballroom embellished with period furniture.

Comme Chez Soi (Wynants), pl. Rouppe 23, ✉ 1000, ☎ 0 2 512 29 21, *info@commechezsoi.be, Fax 0 2 511 80 52* – AE ⓓ ⓜⓒ VISA ES m
closed 3 July-1 August, Christmas-New Year, Sunday and Monday – **Meals** (booking essential) 64/159, – a la carte 64/236
Spec. Filet de sole farci au king crabe et son beurre, crustacés à l'estragon. Éventail de carré d'agneau de la Gaume aux herbes fraîches. Fine salade de fruits nobles, glace à la vanille et coulis tropical anisé.
◆ Despite the slightly cramped feel, the Belle Époque atmosphere, recreated in this Horta-inspired decor, is the perfect foil for the superb cuisine and magnificent wine list.

La Manufacture, r. Notre-Dame du Sommeil 12, ✉ 1000, ☎ 0 2 502 25 25, *info@manufacture.be, Fax 0 2 502 27 15,* , Open until 11 p.m. – AE ⓓ ⓜⓒ VISA ER e
closed Saturday lunch and Sunday – **Meals**. *Lunch 14* – a la carte 29/51.
◆ Metal, wood, leather and granite have all been used to decorate this trendy brasserie occupying the workshop of a renowned leather manufacturer. Contemporary cuisine.

Samourai, r. Fossé-aux-Loups 28, ✉ 1000, ☎ 0 2 217 56 39, *Fax 0 2 771 97 61,* Japanese cuisine – AE ⓓ ⓜⓒ VISA JCB. JY e
closed 15 July-16 August, Tuesday and Sunday lunch – **Meals**. *Lunch 22* – a la carte 42/84.
◆ A Japanese restaurant near the Théâtre de la Monnaie with a menu offering a comprehensive choice. Extensive selection of vintage Bordeaux wines.

Jaloa, pl. de la Vieille Halle aux Blés 31, ✉ 1000, ☎ 0 2 512 18 31, *contact@jaloa.com, Fax 0 2 512 18 31,* , Open until 11 p.m. – AE ⓜⓒ VISA JZ d
closed Saturday lunch and Sunday – **Meals**. *Lunch 14* – a la carte 40/59.
◆ A long, narrow dining room in an old house near the Brel Museum with minimalist modern decor and a view of the kitchen. Contemporary cuisine and background music.

In 't Spinnekopke, pl. du Jardin aux Fleurs 1, ✉ 1000, ☎ 0 2 511 86 95, *info@spinnekopke.be, Fax 0 2 513 24 97,* , Partly regional cuisine – . AE ① MC VISA ER d
closed Saturday lunch, Sunday and Bank Holidays – **Meals**. Lunch 14 b.i. – a la carte 24/48.
◆ This charming, typical tavern serves a wide choice of bistro-style cuisine, accompanied by some good wines and local beers. Service with a smile.

Quartier de l'Europe

Dorint, bd Charlemagne 11, ✉ 1000, ☎ 0 2 231 09 09, *H5344@accor.com, Fax 0 2 230 33 71,* – ch, – 25-150. AE ① MC VISA JCB. rest GR c
Meals ***L'Objectif*** *(closed lunch Saturday and Sunday)* Lunch 33 – a la carte 36/54 – 24 – **210 rm** 75/290, – 2 suites.
◆ This newly built chain hotel with a designer appearance comprises two inter-connected buildings with spacious, striking rooms. The modernity of the dining room is in keeping with the innovative and attractive cuisine. Exhibition of contemporary photography.

Crowne Plaza Europa, r. Loi 107, ✉ 1040, ☎ 0 2 230 13 33, *brussels@ichotelsgroup.com, Fax 0 2 230 03 26,* – – 25-350. AE ① MC VISA. GR d
Meals *(closed August and lunch Saturday and Sunday)* (open until 11 p.m.). Lunch 21 – a la carte 35/56 – 25 – **238 rm** 120/350, – 2 suites.
◆ The 1970s-built Europa, located a few steps from the main European institutions, has undergone large-scale renovation. Business centre and full conference facilities. Pleasant restaurant with buffet lunch options, eclectic à la carte menu and good wine-list.

Eurovillage, bd Charlemagne 80, ✉ 1000, ☎ 0 2 230 85 55, *sales@eurovillage.be, Fax 0 2 230 56 35,* , – – 25-130. AE ① MC VISA JCB. rest GR a
Meals *(closed August, 20 December-5 January, Saturday and Sunday lunch).* Lunch 25 – a la carte 23/42 – 17 – **100 rm** 100/200.
◆ A modern building alongside a verdant park with small but charming bedrooms, good seminar and business facilities, and spacious lounge areas. Plenty of menu choices, plus lunchtime buffets.

Holiday Inn Schuman, r. Breydel 20, ✉ 1040, ☎ 0 2 280 40 00, *hotel@holiday-inn-brussels-schuman.com, Fax 0 2 282 10 70,* – – 45. AE ① MC VISA JCB. rm GS b
Meals (dinner only) a la carte 26/36 – 20 – **56 rm** 45/250.
◆ A modern hotel at the heart of the city's administrative district named after this renowned pro-European politician. Guestrooms and suites offering high levels of comfort.

New Hotel Charlemagne, bd Charlemagne 25, ✉ 1000, ☎ 0 2 230 21 35, *brusselscharlemagne@new-hotel.be, Fax 0 2 230 25 10,* – – 30-50. AE ① MC VISA JCB. rest GR k
Meals (residents only) – 19 – **66 rm** 210/230.
◆ This practical small hotel between Square Ambiorix and the Centre Berlaymont is popular with EU staff. Reception, lounge-bar and breakfast room on the same floor.

Pappa e Citti, r. Franklin 18, ✉ 1000, ☎ 0 2 732 61 10, *pappaecitti@skynet.be, Fax 0 2 732 57 40,* , Italian cuisine – AE ① MC VISA. GR e
closed August, 18 December-6 January, Saturday, Sunday and Bank Holidays – **Meals**. Lunch 27 b.i. – a la carte 34/112.
◆ Popular with European civil servants who head for this small, friendly Italian restaurant to enjoy Sardinian specialities and wines. Two lunch sittings. Veranda.

Take Sushi, bd Charlemagne 21, ✉ 1000, ☎ 0 2 230 56 27, *Fax 0 2 231 10 44,* , Japanese cuisine with Sushi-bar – AE ① MC VISA. GR z
closed 25 to 31 December, Saturday and Sunday lunch – **Meals**. Lunch 14 – a la carte 22/70.
◆ A corner of Japan at the heart of the city's European institutions district. Japanese décor, background music and small garden. Popular sushi bar. Kimono-clad waitresses.

Balthazar, r. Archimède 63, ✉ 1000, ☎ 0 2 742 06 00, – AE MC VISA GR s
closed 23 December-2 January, Saturday lunch and Sunday – **Meals**. Lunch 10 – a la carte 30/48.
◆ A modern brasserie-style ambience where the focus is on Southern French and Italian dishes and wines from around the world. Multilingual service. Small garden.

Quartier Grand'Place (Ilot Sacré)

Royal Windsor, r. Duquesnoy 5, ✉ 1000, ☎ 0 2 505 55 55, *Fax 0 2 505 55 00,* – – 25-350. AE ① MC VISA. rest JYZ f
Meals. Lunch 17 – a la carte 33/46 – 25 – **248 rm** 325/420, – 17 suites.
◆ Luxury, comfort and refinement characterise this grand hotel in the historic centre. Quiet bedrooms with antique furniture, top-notch service and excellent facilities.

Le Méridien, Carrefour de l'Europe 3, ✉ 1000, ☎ 0 2 548 42 11, *info@meridien.be, Fax 0 2 548 40 80*, ←, Fō – 🛗 ✈ ▤ TV ♿ ch, 🚗 – 🏛 25-200. AE ① MC VISA JCB. ✗ KY h
Meals ***L'Épicerie*** *(closed 15 July-20 August and Sunday dinner)* Lunch 49 – a la carte 53/73 ♀ – ☕ 25 – **216 rm** 135/450, – 8 suites.
◆ The hotel's majestic neo-Classical façade stands opposite the Gare Centrale. Gleaming interior décor, with elegant bedrooms boasting the very latest in facilities. An interesting restaurant menu is complemented by buffet lunches and a popular Sunday brunch.

Amigo, r. Amigo 1, ✉ 1000, ☎ 0 2 547 47 47, *sales@hotelamigo.com, Fax 0 2 513 52 77*, Fō – 🛗 ✈ ▤ TV 🚗 – 🏛 25-200. AE ① MC VISA. ✗ JY x
Meals ***Bocconi*** (Italian cuisine) lunch 20-50 ♀ – ☕ 30 – **152 rm** 520/630, – 7 suites.
◆ This imposing building dating from 1958 shows Spanish Renaissance influence. Classic bedrooms with varied furnishings. Collection of works of art on display.

Le Dixseptième without rest, r. Madeleine 25, ✉ 1000, ☎ 0 2 502 17 17, *info@ledixseptieme.be, Fax 0 2 502 64 24* – 🛗 ✈ ▤ TV – 🏛 25. AE ① MC VISA. ✗ JY j
18 rm ☕ 130/240, – 6 suites.
◆ As its name indicates, this old town house dates from the 17C. Elegant lounges and large, homely bedrooms furnished with antiques from different periods.

Carrefour de l'Europe without rest, r. Marché-aux-Herbes 110, ✉ 1000, ☎ 0 2 504 94 00, *info@carrefoureurope.net, Fax 0 2 504 95 00* – 🛗 ✈ ▤ TV – 🏛 25-200. AE ① MC VISA JCB. ✗ JKY n
☕ 21 – **58 rm** 85/285, – 5 suites.
◆ This modern hotel just off the Grand-Place is in keeping with the harmony of the city's architecture. Bedrooms slightly on the drab side, but of a good standard nonetheless.

Novotel off Grand'Place, r. Marché-aux-Herbes 120, ✉ 1000, ☎ 0 2 514 33 33, *H1030@accor.com, Fax 0 2 511 77 23*, 🏖 – 🛗 ✈ ▤ TV – 🏛 25. AE ① MC VISA JCB. ✗ rest JKY n
Meals. Lunch 14 – a la carte 23/37 – ☕ 15 – **136 rm** 179/220.
◆ An ideal location just 200m/220yd from the Gare Centrale and Grand-Place. All the Novotel's bedrooms conform to the chain's latest quality standards.

Aris without rest, r. Marché-aux-Herbes 78, ✉ 1000, ☎ 0 2 514 43 00, *info@arishotel.be, Fax 0 2 514 01 19* – 🛗 ✈ ▤ TV ♿. ① MC VISA JY g
55 rm ☕ 75/220.
◆ This practical small hotel occupies a house close to the city's main square and the Galeries St-Hubert. 55 rooms offering modern comfort.

Matignon without rest, r. Bourse 10, ✉ 1000, ☎ 0 2 511 08 88, *Fax 0 2 513 69 27* – 🛗 TV. AE ① MC VISA JY q
37 rm ☕ 75/102.
◆ Half the cosy double-glazed rooms in this pleasant hotel offer attractive views over the Stock Exchange. Mainly popular with tourists.

La Maison du Cygne, r. Charles Buls 2, ✉ 1000, ☎ 0 2 511 82 44, *lecygne@skynet.be, Fax 0 2 514 31 48*, With L'Ommegang on the ground floor – ▤ 🅿. AE ① MC VISA JCB. ✗ JY w
closed 3 weeks August, late December, Saturday lunch and Sunday – **Meals**. Lunch 40 – 70/90 ♀ 🍇.
◆ This 17C house on the Grand-Place was originally the headquarters of the Butchers' Guild. Panelled interior and themed lounges. Traditional cuisine with modern flourishes.

Aux Armes de Bruxelles, r. Bouchers 13, ✉ 1000, ☎ 0 2 511 55 98, *arbrux@beon.be, Fax 0 2 514 33 81*, Open until 11 p.m. – ▤. AE ① MC VISA JY t
closed 19 June-19 July and Monday – **Meals**. Lunch 23 b.i. – 30/45.
◆ A veritable Brussels institution at the heart of the historic centre, where the focus is resolutely Belgian. Three rooms in traditional, modern and brasserie style.

Le Cerf, Grand'Place 20, ✉ 1000, ☎ 0 2 511 47 91, *Fax 0 2 546 09 59*, Open until 11.30 p.m. – ▤. AE ① MC VISA JY s
closed July, Saturday and Sunday – **Meals**. Lunch 22 b.i. – 46 b.i./54 b.i. ♀.
◆ This old aristocratic residence (1710) is a mix of wood, stained glass and warm fabrics, giving an overall intimate and hushed feel. Two tables overlooking the Grand-Place.

de l'Ogenblik, Galerie des Princes 1, ✉ 1000, ☎ 0 2 511 61 51, *ogenblik@tiscalinet.be, Fax 0 2 513 41 58*, 🏖, Open until midnight – AE ① MC VISA JY p
closed Sunday – **Meals** – a la carte 45/65 ♀.
◆ This old café-style restaurant is known for its fine, classic cuisine, chef's suggestions and daily specials. Popular with the local business community.

La Roue d'Or, r. Chapeliers 26, ✉ 1000, ☎ 0 2 514 25 54, *Fax 0 2 512 30 81*, Open until midnight – AE ① MC VISA JY y
Meals. Lunch 10 – a la carte 25/52 ♀.
◆ A typical old café with a convivial atmosphere where the culinary emphasis is on staple Belgian brasserie fare. Surrealist wall paintings in the genre of Magritte.

Vincent, r. Dominicains 8, ✉ 1000, ☎ 0 2 511 26 07, *info@restaurantvincent.com, Fax 0 2 502 36 93*, Open until 11.30 p.m. – AE VISA JY n
closed first 2 weeks August and 2 to 12 January – **Meals**. *Lunch 18* – a la carte 27/52.
◆ Savour the typical Brussels atmosphere of this nostalgic rotisserie adorned with painted ceramic-tile frescoes. Local dishes to the fore, with meat and mussel specialities.

't Kelderke, Grand'Place 15, ✉ 1000, ☎ 0 2 513 73 44, *Fax 0 2 546 09 59*, Regional cooking, open until 2 a.m. – AE VISA JY i
closed 1 to 14 July – **Meals** – a la carte 22/43.
◆ This quaint tavern-cum-restaurant occupies the vaulted cellar of a house on the Grand-Place. Copious cuisine with "local colour", plus an ambience to match.

Quartier Ste-Catherine (Marché-aux-Poissons)

Novotel Centre-Tour Noire, r. Vierge Noire 32, ✉ 1000, ☎ 0 2 505 50 50, *H2122@accor.com, Fax 0 2 505 50 00*, – – 25-350. AE VISA JCB JY r
Meals – a la carte 28/41 – 15 – **217 rm** 115/215.
◆ Discreet elegance and functional modernity best describe this hotel, which owes it name to one of the towers that made up the city's first defensive walls.

Welcome without rest, r. Peuplier 1, ✉ 1000, ☎ 0 2 219 95 46, *info@hotelwelcom e.com, Fax 0 2 217 18 87* – . VISA JY h
16 rm 85/160.
◆ A friendly hotel occupying an attractive corner house, inside which the new decor of each room calls to mind a different country. Silk Route-inspired decor in the suite.

Atlas without rest, r. Vieux Marché-aux-Grains 30, ✉ 1000, ☎ 0 2 502 60 06, *info@atlas.be, Fax 0 2 502 69 35* – – 30. AE VISA ER a
88 rm 75/199.
◆ This 18C hotel stands on a small square in a well-to-do neighbourhood full of fashion boutiques. Most of the rooms look onto an inner courtyard.

Astrid Centre without rest, pl. du Samedi 11, ✉ 1000, ☎ 0 2 219 31 19, *info@astridhotel.be, Fax 0 2 219 31 70* – – 25-80. VISA JY b
100 rm 75/150.
◆ A building of modern design between place Ste-Catherine and place de Brouckère. Facilities include standard, simply furnished rooms, a bar, lounge areas and conference rooms.

François, quai aux Briques 2, ✉ 1000, ☎ 0 2 511 60 89, , Oyster bar, seafood – . AE VISA JCB JY k
closed Sunday and Monday – **Meals**. *Lunch 25* – 32/37 ♀.
◆ Delicious fish and seafood, washed down with some great white wines, await customers at this in-vogue restaurant. The maritime interior is enlivened with nostalgic photos.

La Belle Maraîchère, pl. Ste-Catherine 11, ✉ 1000, ☎ 0 2 512 97 59, *Fax 0 2 513 76 91*, Seafood – . AE VISA JY k
closed 2 weeks carnival, mid July-early August, Wednesday and Thursday – **Meals** – 32/65 b.i. .
◆ Run by two brothers, the kitchen produces a consistently wide choice of dishes, with a preference for the sea. Enticing wine-list. Popular with business customers and locals.

Le Loup-Galant, quai aux Barques 4, ✉ 1000, ☎ 0 2 219 99 98, *Fax 0 2 219 99 98* – AE VISA JCB EQ a
closed 1 week Ascension, 1 to 15 August, 24 to 31 December, Sunday and Monday – **Meals**. *Lunch 20* – 25/50 b.i..
◆ Make sure you hear the legend surrounding this old house at one end of the Vismet. Wide choice of cuisine and wine. Chimney and exposed beams in the dining room.

Viva M'Boma, r. Flandre 17, ✉ 1000, ☎ 0 2 512 15 93, Regional cuisine – AE VISA. ER b
closed 15 July-15 August and Sunday – **Meals** (lunch only except Thursday and Friday). *Lunch 10* – a la carte approx. 27.
◆ This small restaurant in rue de Flandre near place Sainte-Catherine is well worth a visit for those wishing to sample typical Belgian/Brussels specialities.

Strofilia, r. Marché-aux-Porcs 11, ✉ 1000, ☎ 0 2 512 32 93, *strofilia@pi.be, Fax 0 2 512 09 94*, Greek cuisine, open until midnight – AE VISA. ER c
closed 25 July-15 August and Sunday – **Meals** (dinner only) a la carte 23/38.
◆ Named after a wine press, this upmarket "ouzerie" serves typical cuisine in its airy loft-style dining rooms showing touches of Byzantine decor. Good wine list.

Quartier des Sablons

Jolly du Grand Sablon, r. Bodenbroek 2, ✉ 1000, ✆ 0 2 518 11 00, *jollyhotelsablon@jollyhotels.be, Fax 0 2 512 67 66* – ≡ ch, – 25-150. AE ⓪ MC VISA. rest KZ p
Meals *(closed 1 to 25 August and 25 December-5 January)* (Italian cuisine) a la carte 45/55 ♀ – **192 rm** ☐ 299/320, – 1 suite.
• This Italian-owned hotel is located just a stone's throw from the city's prestigious royal museums. Well-appointed rooms, plus a conference centre with a range of tailor-made facilities. The restaurant offers Italian cuisine, buffets and daily specials.

L'Écailler du Palais Royal (Hahn), r. Bodenbroek 18, ✉ 1000, ✆ 0 2 512 87 51, *Fax 0 2 511 99 50*, Seafood – ≡. AE ⓪ MC VISA. KZ r
closed August, Christmas-New Year, Sunday and Bank Holidays – **Meals** a la carte 54/110
Spec. Ravioli de homard au curry léger. Bouillabaisse de poisons de la mer du Nord. Gratin de pamplemousses, sorbet à la kriek.
• The chef here successfully blends the flavours of the sea with beautiful presentation. Elegant grey décor and a choice of seating : benches, chairs or the bar-counter.

Trente rue de la Paille, r. Paille 30, ✉ 1000, ✆ 0 2 512 07 15, *info@resto-trenteruedelapaille.com, Fax 0 2 514 23 33* – ≡. AE ⓪ MC VISA JZ x
closed mid July-mid August, Christmas-New Year, Saturday and Sunday – **Meals.** *Lunch 31* – a la carte 57/74.
• An open fire, exposed beams, brickwork, drapery, floral bouquets and assorted crockery characterise this warm and welcoming restaurant in the antiques district.

Castello Banfi, r. Bodenbroek 12, ✉ 1000, ✆ 0 2 512 87 94, *Fax 0 2 512 87 94*, Partly Italian cuisine – ≡. AE ⓪ MC VISA KZ q
closed first week Easter, last 3 weeks August, Christmas-New Year, Sunday dinner and Monday – **Meals.** *Lunch 27* – a la carte 36/79.
• The menu at this gastronomic restaurant, hidden behind an 18C façade, encompasses specialities from both France and Italy. The name refers to a large Tuscan wine estate.

"Chez Marius" En Provence, pl. du Petit Sablon 1, ✉ 1000, ✆ 0 2 511 12 08, *chez.marius@skynet.be, Fax 0 2 512 27 89*, – AE ⓪ MC VISA. KZ s
closed 20 July-20 August, Saturday, Sunday and Bank Holidays – **Meals.** *Lunch 22* – 43/50 b.i..
• Memories of the south will come flooding back in this rustic-style restaurant, with its typically Provençal cuisine. In summer, why not enjoy a pastis on the terrace.

La Clef des Champs, r. Rollebeek 23, ✉ 1000, ✆ 0 2 512 11 93, *laclefdeschamps@resto.be, Fax 0 2 502 42 32*, – AE ⓪ MC VISA JZ k
closed Sunday dinner and Monday – **Meals.** *Lunch 15* – 30/49 b.i..
• A recommended address with a light, bright feel, where the welcome is always cheerful. Cuisine from around France.

Lola, pl. du Grand Sablon 33, ✉ 1000, ✆ 0 2 514 24 60, *restaurant.lola@skynet.be, Fax 0 2 514 26 53*, Brasserie, open until 11.30 p.m. – ≡. AE MC VISA. JZ z
Meals a la carte 29/55 ♀.
• This convivial brasserie with its contemporary décor devotes its energies to the latest culinary trends. Choose between sitting on benches, chairs or at the bar.

L'Herbe Rouge, r. Minimes 34, ✉ 1000, ✆ 0 2 512 48 34, *Fax 0 2 511 62 88*, Japanese cuisine, open until 11 p.m. – AE MC VISA JZ p
closed Monday – **Meals.** *Lunch 15* – a la carte approx. 42.
• A reasonably authentic and well-compiled Japanese menu is on offer in this simply furnished, contemporary-style restaurant ornamented with risqué Japanese prints.

Quartier Palais de Justice

Hilton, bd de Waterloo 38, ✉ 1000, ✆ 0 2 504 11 11 and 0 2 504 13 33 (rest), *bruhitwrm@hilton.com, Fax 0 2 504 21 11*, ≤ town, – ≡ – 45-650. AE ⓪ MC VISA JCB. FS s
Meals see ***Maison du Bœuf*** below – ***Café d'Egmont*** (partly buffets, open until midnight) *Lunch 35* – a la carte 36/58 ♀ – ☐ 32 – **419 rm** 155/480, – 13 suites.
• International business clientele will be well and truly pampered in this imposing Hilton built between the upper and lower towns. The hotel's Café d'Egmont offers buffets and themed food weeks beneath its Art Deco glass.

Maison du Bœuf - Hotel Hilton, 1st floor, bd de Waterloo 38, ✉ 1000, ✆ 0 2 504 13 34, *bruhitwrm@hilton.com, Fax 0 2 504 21 11*, ≤ – ≡ P. AE ⓪ MC VISA JCB. FS s
Meals. *Lunch 55* – 68, a la carte 63/180 ♀
Spec. Côte de bœuf rôtie en croûte de sel. Bar rôti au thym frais, crème d'échalotes. Tartare maison au caviar.
• The Hilton's gastronomic restaurant proposes a resolutely traditional à la carte menu in keeping with its opulent décor. Extensive wine-list. Views over the Parc d'Egmont.

JB, r. Grand Cerf 24, ✉ 1000, ☎ 0 2 512 04 84, *restaurantjb@vt4.net, Fax 0 2 511 79 30,* – AE VISA FS z
closed Saturday lunch, Sunday and Bank Holidays – **Meals** – 20/40 b.i..
◆ This friendly restaurant behind the affluent boulevard de Waterloo has nothing to do with the brand of whisky ! Good value à la carte and menus prepared with a modern touch.

L'Idiot du village, r. Notre Seigneur 19, ✉ 1000, ☎ 0 2 502 55 82, Open until 11 p.m. – AE VISA JZ a
closed 20 July-20 August, 23 December-3 January, Saturday and Sunday – **Meals**. Lunch 15 – a la carte 35/58.
◆ An intelligently-run bistro despite the name ! A warm ambience, cuisine with an original modern touch, astute wine-list and friendly, smiling service.

Les Larmes du Tigre, r. Wynants 21, ✉ 1000, ☎ 0 2 512 18 77, *Fax 0 2 502 10 03,* , Thai cuisine – AE VISA ES p
closed Tuesday and Saturday lunch – **Meals**. Lunch 11 – a la carte 25/36.
◆ Thai cuisine is the focus in this mansion close to the Palais de Justice. An extensive range of traditional dishes, plus a buffet option on Sundays. Typical Thai décor.

Quartier Léopold *(see also at Ixelles)*

Stanhope, r. Commerce 9, ✉ 1000, ☎ 0 2 506 91 11, *summithotels@stanhope.be, Fax 0 2 512 17 08,* – AE VISA KZ v
Meals ***Brighton*** *(closed Saturday and Sunday)* Lunch 39 – a la carte 53/91 – 25 – **80 rm** 275/375, – 15 suites.
◆ This town house offers a welcome change from the city's larger hotels with its superb bedrooms - some split-level - all with Internet access. Elegant restaurant where the emphasis is on contemporary cuisine. The enclosed terrace is an added bonus.

Quartier Louise *(see also at Ixelles and at St-Gilles)*

Conrad, av. Louise 71, ✉ 1050, ☎ 0 2 542 42 42, *brusselsinfo@conradhotels.com, Fax 0 2 542 42 00,* – – 25-450. AE VISA JCB FS f
Meals ***Loui*** *(closed August, Saturday lunch, Sunday and Monday)* Lunch 32 – a la carte 40/58 ♀ – ***Café Wiltcher's*** Lunch 22 – a la carte 34/72 – 30 – **254 rm** 595/670, – 15 suites.
◆ An upmarket hotel brilliantly arranged inside a 1900s mansion. Spacious bedrooms with classic furnishings, a full range of seminar and leisure facilities, plus a chic, glass-crowned café. The contemporary restaurant is popular with an upwardly mobile crowd.

Bristol Stephanie, av. Louise 91, ✉ 1050, ☎ 0 2 543 33 11, *hotel_bristol@bristol.be, Fax 0 2 538 03 07,* – – 25-400. AE VISA JCB. rest FT g
Meals *(closed 16 July-5 August, 16 December-8 January, Saturday and Sunday)* (partly buffets). Lunch 40 b.i. – a la carte 41/62 ♀ – 26 – **139 rm** 340/425, – 3 suites.
◆ This luxury property is spread across two interlinked buildings with large, elegant bedrooms. Typical Norwegian furniture adorns the hotel's suites. Contemporary dining in a Scandinavian-inspired ambience. Buffet options also available.

Le Châtelain , r. Châtelain 17, ✉ 1000, ☎ 0 2 646 00 55, *H9@le-chatelain.net, Fax 0 2 646 00 88,* – – 25-280. AE VISA JCB. rm FU t
Meals *(closed Saturday and Sunday lunch).* Lunch 17 – a la carte 34/47 – 25 – **105 rm** 310/430, – 2 suites.
◆ A new hotel with stylish, comfortable rooms featuring the very latest equipment and facilities. The restaurant offers a wide range of options with the emphasis on diversity.

Hyatt Regency, av. Louise 381, ✉ 1050, ☎ 0 2 649 98 00, *brussels@hyattintl.com, Fax 0 2 640 17 64* – – 25-50. AE VISA JCB.
Meals ***Barsey*** *(closed Saturday lunch and Sunday)* Lunch 19 – a la carte 38/55 – 22 – **96 rm** 97/327, – 3 suites. FV a
◆ A characterful hotel near the Bois de la Cambre skilfully refurbished in Second Empire style. Elegant public areas and tasteful, well-appointed rooms. Personalised service. Neo-Classical decor in the Jacques Garcia-designed restaurant-lounge. Trendy ambience.

Meliá Avenue Louise without rest, r. Blanche 4, ✉ 1000, ☎ 0 2 535 95 00, *karin.jongman@solmelia.com, Fax 0 2 535 96 00* – – 35. AE VISA. FT z
22 – **80 rm** 110/260.
◆ The Avenue Louise enjoys a good location a few yards from place Stéphanie. Cosy, individually styled rooms with tasteful furnishings. Impressive lounge adorned with a chimney.

Floris Louise without rest, r. Concorde 59, ✉ 1000, ☎ 0 2 515 00 60, *florislouise@busmail.net, Fax 0 2 503 35 19* – AE VISA. FS d
36 rm 90/214.
◆ This hotel occupies two houses slightly set back from avenue Louise. Modern, well-appointed accommodation and a pleasant breakfast room.

Agenda Louise without rest, r. Florence 6, ✉ 1000, ☎ 0 2 539 00 31, *louise@hotel-agenda.com, Fax 0 2 539 00 63* – AE VISA FT j
37 rm 114/126.
◆ Just 50m/55yd from the elegant avenue Louise, this completely renovated hotel offers guests a friendly welcome and well-appointed, reasonably-sized rooms.

La Porte des Indes, av. Louise 455, ✉ 1050, ☎ 0 2 647 86 51, *brussels@laportedesindes.com, Fax 0 2 640 30 59*, Indian cuisine – AE VISA. FV c
closed Sunday lunch – **Meals**. Lunch 20 – a la carte 22/59.
◆ If your taste-buds fancy a change, head for La Porte des Indes, with its exotic, deliciously flavoured cuisine. The restaurant interior is decorated with Indian antiques.

Tagawa, av. Louise 279, ✉ 1050, ☎ 0 2 640 50 95, *o.tagawa@tiscali.be, Fax 0 2 648 41 36*, Japanese cuisine – P. AE VISA JCB. FU e
closed Saturday lunch, Sunday and Bank Holidays – **Meals**. Lunch 11 – a la carte 22/80.
◆ This simply furnished Japanese restaurant is worth tracking down inside one of the city's shopping galleries. Western and Oriental (tatamis) comfort, plus a sushi bar.

L'Atelier de la Truffe Noire, av. Louise 300, ✉ 1050, ☎ 0 2 640 54 55, *luigi.ciciriello@truffenoire.com, Fax 0 2 648 11 44*, Partly Italian cuisine, open until 11 p.m. – AE VISA FU s
closed Sunday and Monday lunch – **Meals** – a la carte 40/57 ♀.
◆ A "hip" brasserie whose originality and success lie in its fast service and truffle-based gastronomic menu. A well-thought-out and varied à la carte showing Italian influence.

Rouge Tomate, av. Louise 190, ✉ 1050, ☎ 0 2 647 70 44, *rougetomate@skynet.be, Fax 0 2 646 63 10*, Open until 11.30 p.m. – AE VISA. FU c
Meals a la carte 28/46.
◆ Behind the façade of this 19C house is a bright, designer dining room serving contemporary cuisine popular with a well-heeled clientele. Terrace to the rear.

Quartier Bois de la Cambre

Villa Lorraine (Vandecasserie), av. du Vivier d'Oie 75, ✉ 1000, ☎ 0 2 374 31 63, *info@villalorraine.be, Fax 0 2 372 01 95*, – P. AE VISA JCB. GX w
closed last 3 weeks July and Sunday – **Meals**. Lunch 55 – 150 b.i., a la carte 57/170 ♀
Spec. Foie gras au sauternes et truffes. Émincé de bœuf à l'italienne. Fricassée de homard et huîtres au riesling (September-February).
◆ A father and son man the kitchens of this top restaurant on the edge of a wood. Classic cuisine, matching décor and a prestigious wine cellar. Pleasant shady terrace.

La Truffe Noire, bd de la Cambre 12, ✉ 1000, ☎ 0 2 640 44 22, *luigi.ciciriello@truffenoire.com, Fax 0 2 647 97 04* – AE VISA GV x
closed 1 week Easter, first 2 weeks August, Christmas-New Year, Saturday lunch and Sunday – **Meals**. Lunch 40 – 80/155 b.i., – a la carte 69/190 ♀
Spec. Carpaccio aux truffes fraîches à ma façon. Saint-Pierre aux poireaux et truffes. Truffe au chocolat noir en sucre filé et coulis de framboises.
◆ Truffle-lovers will feel well at home amid the foliage of the Cambre and the abbey of the same name. Elegant modern interior, refined cuisine and quality wines.

Quartier Botanique, Gare du Nord *(see also at St-Josse-ten-Noode)*

President World Trade Center, bd du Roi Albert II 44, ✉ 1000, ☎ 0 2 203 20 20, *sales.wtc@presidenthotels.be, Fax 0 2 203 24 40*, – 25-350. AE VISA JCB. rest FQ d
Meals. Lunch 18 – a la carte 34/58 – 20 – **286 rm** 250/260, – 16 suites.
◆ An imposing hotel offering high levels of comfort at one end of Brussels' "Manhattan", close to the Gare du Nord and the towers of the World Trade Center. The restaurant's classic menu includes several fixed options and good daily suggestions.

Le Dome (annex Le Dome II), bd du Jardin Botanique 12, ✉ 1000, ☎ 0 2 218 06 80, *dome@skypro.be, Fax 0 2 218 41 12*, – rm, – 25-80. AE VISA. FQ m
Meals. Lunch 16 – a la carte 30/42 – **125 rm** 105/250.
◆ The dome crowning the 1900s-style façade overlooks the lively place Rogier. Fresh Art Nouveau tones in the hotel's public areas. Pleasant, spacious bedrooms. A modern brasserie with mezzanine serving a range of elaborate and more simple dishes.

President Nord without rest, bd A. Max 107, ✉ 1000, ☎ 0 2 219 00 60, *gm@presidentnord.be, Fax 0 2 218 12 69* – AE VISA JCB. FQ k
63 rm 145/195.
◆ A corner hotel a short hop from the Cité Administrative and busy rue Neuve shopping street. Six floors of welcoming, well-appointed rooms, including fifteen junior suites.

Quartier Atomium (Centenaire - Trade Mart - Laeken)

XX **Ming Dynasty,** Parc des Expositions - av. de l'Esplanade BP 9, ✉ 1020, ☎ 0 2 475 23 45, *info@mingdynasty.be, Fax 0 2 475 23 50,* Chinese cuisine, open until 11 p.m. - ▤ P. AE ⓓ ⓜⓒ VISA
closed 15 July-15 August, Tuesday dinner and Saturday lunch – **Meals**. *Lunch 13* – a la carte 22/51.
◆ This Chinese restaurant opposite the parc des Expositions offers several fixed-menus, modern décor and appropriate background music. Respectable wine-list.

XX **Lychee,** r. De Wand 118, ✉ 1020, ☎ 0 2 268 19 14, *Fax 0 2 268 19 14,* Chinese cuisine, open until 11 p.m. – ▤. AE ⓓ ⓜⓒ VISA
closed 10 to 31 July – **Meals**. *Lunch 8* – 22/33.
◆ A wide choice of Chinese dishes and a very reasonably-priced lunch are available at this long-established restaurant. Dining room with veranda.

XX **La Balade Gourmande,** av. Houba de Strooper 230, ✉ 1020, ☎ 0 2 478 94 34, *Fax 0 2 479 89 52,* 🏡 – ♿. ⓓ ⓜⓒ VISA
closed 1 week carnival, 15 August-6 September, Wednesday dinner, Saturday lunch and Sunday – **Meals**. *Lunch 15* – 30.
◆ The à la carte and fixed-menu options at this local restaurant cover a cross-section of traditional dishes prepared with a modern eye. Decor dominated by red fabrics.

ANDERLECHT

Le Prince de Liège, chaussée de Ninove 664, ✉ 1070, ☎ 0 2 522 16 00, *princed eliege@coditel.be, Fax 0 2 520 81 85* – |‡|, ▤ rm, TV ⇨lunch only 🚗 – 🏛 25. AE ⓓ ⓜⓒ VISA
Meals *(closed 1 to 15 August, Saturday lunch and Sunday dinner)* (pub rest). *Lunch 16* – 25/45 – **32 rm** ☐ 65/102.
◆ The rooms at this family-run hotel located alongside a major road junction are functional, double-glazed and offer good value for money. Bar-restaurant serving classic à la carte choices, with menus and seasonal suggestions highlighted on slate boards.

Ustel, Square de l'Aviation 6, ✉ 1070, ☎ 0 2 520 60 53 and 0 2 522 30 25 (rest), *hot el.ustel@grouptorus.com, Fax 0 2 520 33 28,* 🏡 – |‡| ⇤ ▤ TV 🚗 – 🏛 25-100. AE ⓓ ⓜⓒ VISA. ✂ rest ES q
Meals *(closed mid July-mid August, Saturday and Sunday)* (brasserie, lunch only). *Lunch 14* – 25/34 b.i. – **114 rm** ☐ 95/168.
◆ This hotel along the city's inner ring road has 94 simply furnished rooms of varying size, including twenty or so "apartments" with their own kitchenette. The machinery of an old lock provides an original backdrop to the hotel brasserie.

Erasme, rte de Lennik 790, ✉ 1070, ☎ 0 2 523 62 82, *comfort@skynet.be, Fax 0 2 523 62 83,* 🏡, 🏋 – |‡| ⇤, ▤ rm, TV ♿ ch, P – 🏛 25-80. AE ⓓ ⓜⓒ VISA
Meals (pub rest) 16 – **73 rm** ☐ 62/119, – 1 suite.
◆ A chain hotel on the outskirts of the city, 1km/0.6mi beyond the ring road, with small but welcoming bedrooms with adequate soundproofing. Three seminar rooms. Varied international menu.

XXX ✿ **Saint Guidon** 2nd floor, in the R.S.C. Anderlecht football stadium, av. Théo Verbeeck 2, ✉ 1070, ☎ 0 2 520 55 36, *saint-guidon@skynet.be, Fax 0 2 523 38 27* – ▤ P – 🏛 25-500. ⓓ ⓜⓒ VISA. ✂
closed 24 December-1 January, 20 June-21 July, Saturday, Sunday, Bank Holidays and first league match days – **Meals** (lunch only) 55 b.i. a la carte 55/75
Spec. Ravioles de homard aux truffes. Sole meunière et petit stoemp aux poireaux et persil plat. Filet d'agneau poêlé à l'estragon (21 June-21 September).
◆ This typical restaurant is situated on the second floor of Anderlecht's football stadium. Refined cuisine which evolves with the seasons. Car park.

XX **Alain Cornelis,** av. Paul Janson 82, ✉ 1070, ☎ 0 2 523 20 83, *Fax 0 2 523 20 83,* 🏡 – AE ⓓ ⓜⓒ VISA. ✂
closed 1 week Easter, first 2 weeks August, 24 December-3 January, Wednesday dinner, Saturday lunch and Sunday – **Meals** 30/63 b.i. ♀.
◆ A classically bourgeois restaurant with a traditional wine-list. The terrace to the rear is embellished with a small garden. Fixed-menus, à la carte and dishes of the month.

XX **La Brouette,** bd Prince de Liège 61, ✉ 1070, ☎ 0 2 522 51 69, *info@labrouette.be, Fax 0 2 522 51 69* – AE ⓓ ⓜⓒ VISA
closed 28 March-3 April, 26 July-17 August, Saturday lunch, Sunday dinner and Monday – **Meals**. *Lunch 30* – 38/65 b.i. ♀ 🍇.
◆ La Brouette's steady flow of regulars appreciate the impeccable culinary skills of the kitchen as well as the harmony of the accompanying wine-list.

AUDERGHEM (OUDERGEM)

La Grignotière, chaussée de Wavre 2041, ✉ 1160, ☎ 0 2 672 81 85, *Fax 0 2 672 81 85* – AE ⓓ ⓜⓒ VISA
closed 1 to 20 August, Sunday and Monday – **Meals**. *Lunch 35* – 46.
• On the edge of the Forêt de Soignes, with décor that varies from the simple and modern to the more measured and traditional. Multi-choice menus. Separate small lounge.

La Caudalie, r. Jacques Bassem 111, ✉ 1160, ☎ 0 2 675 20 20, *Fax 0 2 675 20 80* – P. AE ⓓ ⓜⓒ VISA
closed Saturday lunch and Sunday – **Meals**. *Lunch 46* – a la carte 36/60 ♀.
• An inviting restaurant with a well-balanced wine list in perfect harmony with the cuisine. Spotless modern decor inside, plus an outdoor dining area to the rear.

New Asia, chaussée de Wavre 1240, ✉ 1160, ☎ 0 2 660 62 06, *Fax 0 2 675 67 28*, Chinese cuisine – ▤. AE ⓓ ⓜⓒ VISA. HU a
closed last 2 weeks July and Monday except Bank Holidays – **Meals**. *Lunch 9* – 14/25.
• A relaxed ambience pervades this local restaurant created over 20 years ago. Traditional Chinese décor provides the backdrop for a huge choice of dishes and menus.

La Khaïma, chaussée de Wavre 1390, ✉ 1160, ☎ 0 2 675 00 04, *Fax 0 2 675 12 25*, Moroccan cuisine – ▤. AE ⓜⓒ VISA.
closed August – **Meals** 27.
• Popular with aficionados of tagines and couscous, this small restaurant, with its typical pouffes, rugs and beaten copper, is housed beneath a Berber tent (khaïma).

BERCHEM-STE-AGATHE (SINT-AGATHA-BERCHEM)

La Brasserie de la Gare, chaussée de Gand 1430, ✉ 1082, ☎ 0 2 469 10 09, *Fax 0 2 469 10 09* – ▤ P. AE ⓓ ⓜⓒ VISA
closed Saturday lunch and Sunday – **Meals**. *Lunch 12* – 26 ♀.
• A lively and convivial brasserie opposite the Berchem-Ste-Agathe train station. Traditional cooking, an enticing wine list and amusing naïve paintings in the dining room.

ETTERBEEK

Stirwen, chaussée St-Pierre 15, ✉ 1040, ☎ 0 2 640 85 41, *alain.troubat@skynet.be*, *Fax 0 2 648 43 08* – AE ⓓ ⓜⓒ VISA JCB GS a
closed 2 weeks August, 2 weeks December, Saturday and Sunday – **Meals**. *Lunch 28* – a la carte 38/46.
• "White Star" (stirwen) in Breton, this welcoming brasserie with its hints of Belle Époque architecture serves traditional dishes from around France.

Quartier Cinquantenaire (Montgomery)

Park without rest, av. de l'Yser 21, ✉ 1040, ☎ 0 2 735 74 00, *info@parkhotelbrussels.be*, *Fax 0 2 735 19 67*, – ▤ – 25-65. AE ⓓ ⓜⓒ VISA JCB
51 rm ☕ 105/300. HS c
• An amalgam of two houses opposite the parc du Cinquantenaire, this hotel has 51 comfortable rooms, half of which are singles. The breakfast room looks onto a small garden.

EVERE

Belson without rest, chaussée de Louvain 805, ✉ 1140, ☎ 0 2 708 31 00, *resa@gresham-belsonhotel.com*, *Fax 0 2 708 31 66* – ▤ – 25. AE ⓓ ⓜⓒ VISA JCB.
☕ 22 – **132 rm** 95/310, – 3 suites.
• This chain hotel provides easy access to both the city centre and airport (Zaventem). Two categories of rooms plus a fitness area.

Mercure, av. Jules Bordet 74, ✉ 1140, ☎ 0 2 726 73 35, *H0958@accor-hotels.com*, *Fax 0 2 726 82 95* – ▤ rest, – 25-120. AE ⓓ ⓜⓒ VISA JCB
Meals *(closed 12 July-22 August)*. *Lunch 20 b.i.* – a la carte 25/42 ♀ – ☕ 17 – **112 rm** 175/250, – 7 suites.
• A typical Accor chain hotel offering standard Mercure comfort, just a few yards from NATO and five minutes from Zaventem airport. Seminar rooms. Plainly decorated restaurant enlivened by cartoon-strip illustrations.

FOREST (VORST)

De Fierlant without rest, r. De Fierlant 67, ✉ 1190, ☎ 0 2 538 60 70, *Fax 0 2 538 91 99* – AE ⓓ ⓜⓒ VISA.
40 rm ☕ 60/85.
• Conveniently located between the Gare du Midi and the Forest-National concert hall, this practical hotel occupies a small, modern building with standard, soundproofed rooms.

GANSHOREN

XXXX
✿✿
Bruneau, av. Broustin 75, ✉ 1083, ✆ 0 2 421 70 70, *Fax 0 2 425 97 26*, – ▤ dinner only P. AE ◑ MC VISA
closed 1 to 10 February, August, Bank Holiday Thursdays, Tuesday and Wednesday – **Meals**. *Lunch 45* – 95/150 b.i., – a la carte 75/202 ♀
Spec. Gaufrette de blinis au caviar osciètre farcie de crème aigre. Javanais de bar à la chair de langoustines et sabayon au jus de crustacés. Contrefilet de veau de lait farci soubise au lard fumé.
◆ This renowned restaurant has achieved a perfect creative balance while at the same time maintaining its commitment to local products. Prestigious wine-list. Summer terrace.

XXX
✿✿
Claude Dupont, av. Vital Riethuisen 46, ✉ 1083, ✆ 0 2 426 00 00, *claudedupont @resto.be, Fax 0 2 426 65 40* – AE ◑ MC VISA
closed July, Monday and Tuesday – **Meals**. *Lunch 45* – 65/130 b.i., – a la carte 57/91 ♀
Spec. Écrevisses sautées à la bordelaise. Timbale de homard en mousseline de jeunes poireaux. Canette de barbarie au cidre bouché et petites reinettes caramélisées.
◆ A master-class in culinary invention. The accolades and awards on display in the entrance hall are thoroughly deserved. Sumptuous cellar.

XXX
✿
San Daniele (Spinelli), av. Charles-Quint 6, ✉ 1083, ✆ 0 2 426 79 23, *Fax 0 2 426 92 14*, Partly Italian cuisine – ▤. AE ◑ MC VISA
closed 1 week Easter, 15 July-15 August, Sunday and Monday – **Meals** – 60, a la carte 43/57
Spec. Calamaretti, gamberetti et scampis en friture. Ris de veau en crépinette de chou-vert aux truffes. Soufflé d'ananas glacé à l'orange sanguine.
◆ The warm, friendly welcome, extensive Italian menu and alluring choice of wines from across the Dolomites continue to attract a loyal following.

XX
Cambrils 1st floor, av. Charles-Quint 365, ✉ 1083, ✆ 0 2 465 50 70, *restaurant.ca mbrils@skynet.be, Fax 0 2 465 76 63*, – ▤. AE MC VISA
closed 15 July-15 August, Sunday and dinner Monday and Thursday – **Meals**. *Lunch 23* – 30/52 b.i. ♀.
◆ The kitchens of this pleasant restaurant open out onto the dining room, which in turn looks onto avenue Charles-Quint. Traditional à la carte menu. Ground floor bar. Terrace.

IXELLES (ELSENE)

XX
Le Yen, r. Lesbroussart 49, ✉ 1050, ✆ 0 2 649 07 47, , Vietnamese cuisine – AE ◑ MC VISA. ✄ FU f
closed Saturday lunch and Sunday – **Meals**. *Lunch 9* – 23/30 b.i..
◆ Modern and simple Oriental décor provides the backdrop for this Vietnamese restaurant (yen translates as "the swallow") serving poetically named traditional dishes.

Quartier Boondael (University)

XX
L'Aub. de Boendael, square du Vieux Tilleul 12, ✉ 1050, ✆ 0 2 672 70 55, *auberge-de-boendael@resto.be, Fax 0 2 660 75 82*, , Grill rest – P. AE ◑ MC VISA HX h
closed Saturday, Sunday and Bank Holidays – **Meals**. *Lunch 48 b.i.* – a la carte 38/74.
◆ This rustic-style inn occupies a 17C house with a roaring fire in winter and a fine selection of grilled meats. Banquets at weekends.

X
La Pagode d'Or, chaussée de Boondael 332, ✉ 1050, ✆ 0 2 649 06 56, *Fax 0 2 649 09 00*, , Vietnamese cuisine, open until 11 p.m. – AE ◑ MC VISA JCB. ✄ GV m
closed Monday – **Meals**. *Lunch 9* – 23/35.
◆ A fine ambassador for Vietnamese cuisine with its clear and consistent menu, "rice table" options, and an intimate dining room with discreet exotic touches.

X
✿
Marie, r. Alphonse De Witte 40, ✉ 1050, ✆ 0 2 644 30 31, *Fax 0 2 644 27 37* – ▤. AE MC VISA. ✄ GU a
closed 17 July-16 August, 23 December-3 January, Saturday lunch, Sunday and Monday – **Meals**. *Lunch 16* – a la carte 46/60 ♀
Spec. Brandade de morue à l'huile d'olives, concassée de tomates et coulis de poivrons. Escalope de thon rouge grillée aux artichauts et parmesan (15 April-15 September). Selle d'agneau rôtie, jus à l'ail confit et tian d'aubergines.
◆ Traditional cuisine peppered with southern influences and an attractive selection of wines are the hallmarks of this pleasant, pocket-sized gourmet bistro.

Quartier Bascule, Châtelain, Ma Campagne

XX
Maison Félix 1st floor, r. Washington 149, ✉ 1050, ✆ 0 2 345 66 93, *Fax 0 2 344 92 85* – AE ◑ MC VISA. ✄ FV s
closed 1 to 22 August, 3 to 10 January, Sunday and Monday – **Meals**. *Lunch 24* – 38/48 ♀ .
◆ Customers will need to pass through Monsieur Félix's delicatessen in order to reach the dining room on the first floor. A high standard of cuisine plus a superb wine-list.

O' comme 3 Pommes, pl. du Châtelain 40, ✉ 1050, ✆ 0 2 644 03 23, *resto@oc3pommes.be, Fax 0 2 644 03 23*, – AE MC VISA FU q
closed Sunday – **Meals** (dinner only until 11 p.m.) 50.
• A fresh, modern restaurant with a slate menu teeming with stylish dishes enlivened with the occasional Asian touch.

La Quincaillerie, r. Page 45, ✉ 1050, ✆ 0 2 533 98 33, *info@quincaillerie.be, Fax 0 2 539 40 95*, Brasserie with oyster bar, open until midnight – P. AE MC VISA JCB FU z
closed lunch Saturday, Sunday and Bank Holidays – **Meals**. Lunch 13 – a la carte 30/52 ♀.
• A gleaming brasserie superbly laid out in this former Art Deco-style ironmonger's. Seafood bar and daily specials. Very professional service. Valet parking.

Les Perles de Pluie, r. Châtelain 25, ✉ 1050, ✆ 0 2 649 67 23, *info@lesperlesdepluie.be, Fax 0 2 644 07 60*, , Thai cuisine, open until 11 p.m. – MC VISA FU n
closed Monday and Saturday lunch – **Meals**. Lunch 15 – a la carte 26/41.
• This twin-roomed restaurant serves typical Thai cuisine. Typical interior décor embellished with traditional woodwork.

Tutto Pepe, r. Faider 123, ✉ 1050, ✆ 0 2 534 96 19, *tuttopepe@skynet.be, Fax 0 2 538 65 68*, Italian cuisine – . AE MC VISA. FU d
closed 20 July-20 August, 23 December-3 January, Saturday, Sunday and Bank Holidays – **Meals** a la carte 43/155.
• A tiny, authentic restaurant where the welcome is 100 % Italian and somewhat theatrical. The à la carte choices here are posted on menu boards.

Quartier Léopold *(see also at Bruxelles)*

Renaissance, r. Parnasse 19, ✉ 1050, ✆ 0 2 505 29 29, *rhi.brubr.renaissance@renaissancehotels.com, Fax 0 2 505 22 76*, , , , – ch, – 25-360. AE MC VISA. FS e
Meals *Symphony* *(closed lunch Saturday and Sunday)* Lunch 19 – a la carte 28/53 ♀ – 23 – **256 rm** 85/399, – 6 suites.
• The Renaissance enjoys a good location on the edge of the European institutions district. Modern, well-appointed rooms, excellent business, conference and leisure facilities, plus a full range of hotel services. Contemporary cuisine, including a lunch menu.

Leopold, r. Luxembourg 35, ✉ 1050, ✆ 0 2 511 18 28, *reservations@hotel-leopold.be, Fax 0 2 514 19 39*, – – 25-80. AE MC VISA FS y
Meals *Salon Les Anges* *(closed Saturday lunch and Sunday)* (lunch only July-August) Lunch 35 – a la carte 47/63 – 18 – **111 rm** 112/186.
• This continually expanding hotel boasts smart, comfortable bedrooms, smart public areas, a winter garden on a shady inner courtyard, and a peaceful atmosphere, mirrored in the hushed restaurant, with its classic menu and interesting wine-list.

Quartier Louise *(see also at Bruxelles and at St-Gilles)*

Sofitel without rest, av. de la Toison d'Or 40, ✉ 1050, ✆ 0 2 514 22 00, *H1071@accor.com, Fax 0 2 514 57 44*, – – 25-120. AE MC VISA FS r
25 – **166 rm** 135/330, – 4 suites.
• Discreet luxury and soft comfort characterise this renovated hotel popular with an international business clientele. Terrace and garden.

Four Points Sheraton, r. Paul Spaak 15, ✉ 1000, ✆ 0 2 645 61 11, *reservations.brussels@sheraton.com, Fax 0 2 646 63 44*, , – ch, – 25-40. AE MC VISA JCB. rest FU k
Meals (open until 11 p.m.). Lunch 15 – a la carte 25/37 ♀ – 19 – **128 rm** 83/265.
• A large chain hotel close to avenue Louise. Spacious, slightly outdated bedrooms, but with good facilities. Sauna, jacuzzi and garden in which guests can unwind. The dining room menu shows a clear liking for beef, as well as Swiss delicacies.

Argus without rest, r. Capitaine Crespel 6, ✉ 1050, ✆ 0 2 514 07 70, *reception@hotel-argus.be, Fax 0 2 514 12 22* – . AE MC VISA FS t
42 rm 100/120.
• The Argus has 41 standard, plainly furnished rooms with soundproofing. The breakfast room is decorated with Art Deco-style stained glass. Good value for money.

Beau-Site without rest, r. Longue Haie 76, ✉ 1000, ✆ 0 2 640 88 89, *beausite@coditel.net, Fax 0 2 640 16 11* – . AE MC VISA FT r
38 rm 99/169.
• 100m/110yd from the city's most elegant avenue. A small, attractive hotel where the welcome is friendly and the service attentive.

Beverly Hills without rest, r. Prince Royal 71, ✉ 1050, ✆ 0 2 513 22 22, *beverlyhills@infonie.be, Fax 0 2 513 87 77*, , – . AE MC VISA JCB FS b
35 rm 110/125.
• This hotel close to the avenue de la Toison d'Or offers rooms with comfortable facilities guaranteeing a good night's sleep. Fitness room and sauna.

De la Vigne... à l'Assiette, r. Longue Haie 51, ✉ 1000, ☎ 0 2 647 68 03, *Fax 0 2 647 68 03*, Bistro – AE MC VISA FT k
closed 21 July-20 August, Saturday lunch, Sunday and Monday – **Meals**. *Lunch 12* – 20/32.
◆ Wine-lovers will enjoy this restaurant, where the décor and ambience are plain and simple, the bistro-style menu well-balanced, and the advice from the wine-waiter invaluable.

JETTE

Rôtiss. Le Vieux Pannenhuis, r. Léopold Ier 317, ✉ 1090, ☎ 0 2 425 83 73, *levieuxpannenhuis@belgacom.net, Fax 0 2 420 21 20*, Partly grill rest – AE MC VISA
closed July, Saturday lunch and Sunday – **Meals**. *Lunch 21* – 30/64 b.i.
◆ This attractively preserved coaching inn exuding rustic charm offers a wide-ranging choice of classic dishes including meat grilled on an open fire in the dining room.

French Kiss, r. Léopold Ier 470, ✉ 1090, ☎ 0 2 425 22 93, *Fax 0 2 428 68 24*, Partly grill rest – AE MC VISA
closed 18 July-16 August, Christmas, New Year and Monday – **Meals**. *Lunch 17* – 27.
◆ A pleasant brick-built restaurant-grill peppered with the occasional modern flourish. Large, varied menu accompanied by a well-compiled wine-list. Very popular with locals.

ST-GILLES (SINT-GILLIS)

Cascade without rest, r. Berckmans 128, ✉ 1060, ☎ 0 2 538 88 30, *info@cascadehotel.be, Fax 0 2 538 92 79* – – 25. AE MC VISA. ES r
82 rm 215/470.
◆ Built around a large inner courtyard, this modern building has 82 neat and well-appointed bedrooms with carpets and double-glazing.

Knhopff, r. St-Bernard 1, ✉ 1060, ☎ 0 2 534 20 04, *info@khnopff.be, Fax 0 2 537 56 91*, Open until midnight – dinner only. AE MC VISA. rest FT a
closed 21 July-15 August, Saturday lunch and Sunday – **Meals**. *Lunch 13* – carte 30 à 51.
◆ The 19C Belgian symbolist artist Fernand Khnopff painted several canvases here, hence the restaurant's name. Charming hosts, contemporary cuisine and a trendy atmosphere.

Quartier Louise *(see also at Bruxelles and at Ixelles)*

Manos Premier (annex Manos Stéphanie 50 rm - 5 suites), chaussée de Charleroi 102, ✉ 1060, ☎ 0 2 537 96 82 and 0 2 533 18 30 (rest), *manos@manoshotel.com, Fax 0 2 539 36 55*, – rm, dinner only – 25-100. AE MC VISA. FU w
Meals ***Kolya*** *(closed 24 December-2 January, Saturday lunch and Sunday) Lunch 15* – 35/85 b.i. – **45 rm** 295/320, – 5 suites.
◆ A graceful late-19C town house adorned with sumptuous Louis XV and Louis XVI furniture. Veranda breakfast room, ornamental garden and fitness equipment. Chic restaurant with a hushed lounge, in addition to an attractive terrace with a cool patio.

NH Brussels City Centre, chaussée de Charleroi 17, ✉ 1060, ☎ 0 2 539 01 60, *nhbrussels.city.centre@nh-hotels.com, Fax 0 2 537 90 11* – – 25-75. AE MC VISA JCB. rm FS w
Meals. *Lunch 8* – a la carte 22/54 – 17 – **246 rm** 59/200.
◆ This squat building perched in the upper section of the city has several room categories, including a dozen "executive" bedrooms. Dynamic staff. The new brasserie offers varied lunch and dinner choices.

NH Stéphanie without rest, r. Jean Stas 32, ✉ 1060, ☎ 0 2 537 42 50, *nhstephanie@nh-hotels.be, Fax 0 2 539 33 79* – – 30. AE MC VISA FS a
17 – **68 rm** 69/220.
◆ Set back slightly from the bustling place Stéphanie, this hotel of the same name boasts a number of bright, modern rooms. Public car park nearby.

I Trulli, r. Jourdan 18, ✉ 1060, ☎ 0 2 537 79 30, *Fax 0 2 538 98 20*, Italian cuisine, open until 11 p.m. – AE MC VISA. FS c
closed 10 to 31 July and Sunday – **Meals**. *Lunch 16* – a la carte 40/68.
◆ This traditional Italian restaurant - named after the typical houses from Puglia depicted on the wall frescoes - specialises in dishes from the region. Buffet of antipasti.

ST-JOSSE-TEN-NOODE (SINT-JOOST-TEN-NODE)

Quartier Botanique *(see also at Bruxelles)*

Gd H. Mercure Royal Crown, r. Royale 250, ✉ 1210, ☎ 0 2 220 66 11, *H1728@accor.com, Fax 0 2 217 84 44*, – – 50-550. AE MC VISA FQ r
Meals see ***Rue Royale*** below – 20 – **309 rm** 120/235, – 4 suites.
◆ A comfortable chain hotel located close to the Botanique cultural centre, with its terraced gardens. Numerous conference rooms. Parking, bellboy and room service available.

XXX **Rue Royale** - Gd H. Mercure Royal Crown, r. Royale 250, ✉ 1210, ☎ 0 2 220 66 11, *H1728@accor.com, Fax 0 2 217 84 44, Open until 11 p.m.* - AE VISA FQ r
Meals - a la carte 28/44 ♀.
◆ This hotel restaurant is known for its "70s"-style atmosphere, contemporary cuisine, a well-put-together lunch menu, and enticing Mercure chain wine-list.

X **Les Dames Tartine,** chaussée de Haecht 58, ✉ 1210, ☎ 0 2 218 45 49, *Fax 0 2 218 45 49* - VISA FQ s
closed first 3 weeks August, Saturday lunch, Sunday and Monday - **Meals**. *Lunch 19* - 30/42 ♀.
◆ This small, intimate restaurant remains loyal to its past. Customers sit at sewing machine tables, surrounded by paintings of the owner's ancestors.

Quartier Rogier *(see also at Schaerbeek)*

Sheraton Towers, pl. Rogier 3, ✉ 1210, ☎ 0 2 224 31 11, *reservations.brussels@sheraton.com, Fax 0 2 224 34 56,* ch, - 25-600. AE VISA JCB. rest FQ n
Meals (partly buffets). *Lunch 31* - a la carte 40/51 ♀ - 25 - **489 rm** 105/320, - 44 suites.
◆ With its full range of facilities, the Sheraton is popular with business clientele. Spacious high-tech bedrooms, plus "smart rooms" combining a work environment with relaxation. Buffets, gastronomic theme weeks and attractive light cuisine in the restaurant.

Crowne Plaza, r. Gineste 3, ✉ 1210, ☎ 0 2 203 62 00, *info@cpbxl.be, Fax 0 2 203 55 55,* - 25-500. AE VISA FQ v
Meals *(closed lunch Saturday and Sunday). Lunch 15* - 35 - 25 - **355 rm** 320/370, - 1 suite.
◆ A Belle Époque-style palace embellished with period furniture in which several rooms have preserved the spirit of the 1900s. Seminar and business centre. Large Art Deco brasserie attracting a well-heeled clientele.

Comfort Art H. Siru without rest, pl. Rogier 1, ✉ 1210, ☎ 0 2 203 35 80, *art.hotel.siru@skynet.be, Fax 0 2 203 33 03* - 25-80. AE VISA FQ p
101 rm 70/250.
◆ The decor in each room of this Roaring Twenties building has been designed by a different contemporary Belgian artist. Popular in the past with the poets Verlaine and Rimbaud.

Tulip Inn Boulevard, av. du Boulevard 17, ✉ 1210, ☎ 0 2 205 15 11, *info.hotel@tulipinnbb.be, Fax 0 2 201 15 15,* ch, - 25-450. AE VISA JCB. FQ b
Meals (dinner residents only) - **450 rm** 85/212, - 4 suites.
◆ This brand-new hotel is the second largest in the city in terms of capacity. Attractive, well-appointed small rooms with wood or carpeted floors.

SCHAERBEEK (SCHAARBEEK)

X ✿ **Senza Nome** (Bruno), r. Royale Ste-Marie 22, ✉ 1030, ☎ 0 2 223 16 17, *senzanome@skynet.be, Fax 0 2 223 16 17,* Italian cuisine - VISA. FQ u
closed 21 July-25 August, Saturday lunch and Sunday - **Meals** a la carte approx. 47 ♀
Spec. Tagliata di tonno. Linguine Vongole. Branzino alla siciliana.
◆ Despite being established ten years ago, this small restaurant remains "nameless". A good range of Italian cuisine and wines, plus daily specials. Friendly, family atmosphere.

Quartier Meiser *(see also at St-Josse-ten-Noode)*

Lambermont without rest (annexes 61 rm -), bd Lambermont 322, ✉ 1030, ☎ 0 2 242 55 95, *info@lambermonthotels.com, Fax 0 2 215 36 13* - . AE VISA GHQ c
11 - **42 rm** 69/99.
◆ Despite being away from the centre, this comfortable hotel on a boulevard of the same name enjoys peace and quiet as well as easy access to the heart of the city.

X **Amici miei,** bd Général Wahis 248, ✉ 1030, ☎ 0 2 705 49 80, *Fax 0 2 705 29 65,* , Italian cuisine - AE VISA HQ k
closed Saturday lunch and Sunday - **Meals** - a la carte 32/49.
◆ Judging by the décor, "My Friends" is also a pal of showbiz and sports personalities! As the name would suggest, the focus here is on Italian cuisine.

UCCLE (UKKEL)

County House, square des Héros 2, ✉ 1180, ☎ 0 2 375 44 20, *countyhouse@skynet.be, Fax 0 2 375 31 22* - , rest, - 25-150. AE VISA. EX b
Meals. *Lunch 23* - a la carte 35/51 - **86 rm** 105/185, - 16 suites.
◆ This building on the northern edge of the Parc Wolvendael has 86 well-appointed rooms, all with a private terrace. Spacious restaurant, serving contemporary cuisine with special midweek menus.

XXXX **Le Chalet de la Forêt,** Drêve de Lorraine 43, ✉ 1180, ✆ 0 2 374 54 16, *chaletdelaforet@skynet.be, Fax 0 2 374 35 71,* – P – 30. AE ⓓ MC VISA
closed Saturday and Sunday – **Meals**. *Lunch 27* – a la carte 63/101 ♀.
• This former dairy on the edge of the Forêt de Soignes is now home to an attractive restaurant with modern decor, contemporary cuisine and a well-balanced wine list.

XXX **Les Frères Romano,** av. de Fré 182, ✉ 1180, ✆ 0 2 374 70 98, *Fax 0 2 374 04 18* – P. AE ⓓ MC VISA FX d
closed 2 weeks Easter, last 3 weeks August, Sunday and Bank Holidays – **Meals**. *Lunch 35* – a la carte 41/65.
• Three brothers are in charge of this elegant restaurant housed in a villa dating from the 1900s. The menu here is traditional, occasionally enlightened by a modern flourish.

XXX **Villa d'Este,** r. Etoile 142, ✉ 1180, ✆ 0 2 376 48 48, *Fax 0 2 376 48 48,* – P. AE ⓓ MC VISA
closed July, late December, Wednesday October-April, Sunday dinner and Monday – **Meals** – 30/50.
• This impressive villa surrounded by vineyards offers two excellent multi-choice menus ("tradition" and "prestige") as well as two wine-lists.

XX **Blue Elephant,** chaussée de Waterloo 1120, ✉ 1180, ✆ 0 2 374 49 62, *brussels@blueelephant.com, Fax 0 2 375 44 68,* Thai cuisine – P. AE ⓓ MC VISA. GX j
closed Saturday lunch – **Meals**. *Lunch 17* – 45/64 b.i..
• Country antiques, cane furniture, floral arrangements and local colour combine to create an exotic atmosphere in this Thai restaurant.

XX **Le Pain et le Vin,** chaussée d'Alsemberg 812a, ✉ 1180, ✆ 0 2 332 37 74, *info@painvin.be, Fax 0 2 332 17 40,* – AE MC VISA.
closed Easter, first week September, Christmas, New Year, Saturday lunch, Sunday and Monday – **Meals**. *Lunch 22* – a la carte 53/73 ♀.
• A modern, elegant restaurant concentrating on refined, seasonal dishes. Customers are spoilt for choice on the wine-list...with helpful advice from the sommelier.

XX **La Cuisine du 519,** av. Brugmann 519, ✉ 1180, ✆ 0 2 346 53 08, *lacuisinedu519@pro.tiscali.be, Fax 0 2 346 53 09,* – P. AE ⓓ MC VISA EX c
closed Saturday lunch, Sunday and Bank Holidays – **Meals**. *Lunch 15* – a la carte 33/54.
• A restaurant housed in an old mansion. If available, ask for a table in the dining room to the rear, embellished with an Ionic column, chimney and Indian door.

X **Bon-Bon** (Hardiquest), r. Carmélites 93, ✉ 1180, ✆ 0 2 346 66 15, *Fax 0 2 346 66 15* – AE ⓓ MC VISA. EV a
closed 21 July-15 August, 1 to 8 January, Saturday lunch, Sunday and Monday – **Meals**. *Lunch 30* – 55/75, – a la carte 62/88
Spec. Tartine de thon salé et fumé aux légumes croquants. Sole bretonne en habit de blettes. L'orange façon suzette.
• A backdrop of wall panelling, wood flooring, mirrors and grey velvet for modern cuisine prepared exclusively with ingredients of certified origin.

X **Brasseries Georges,** av. Winston Churchill 259, ✉ 1180, ✆ 0 2 347 21 00, *info@brasseriesgeorges.be, Fax 0 2 344 02 45,* , Oyster bar, open until midnight – P. AE ⓓ MC VISA FV n
Meals. *Lunch 15* – a la carte 25/44 ♀.
• One of the largest brasseries-seafood bars in the city. Parisian in style with an inexpensive lunchtime bar menu. Friendly service, plus useful valet parking.

Quartier St-Job

XX **Les Menus Plaisirs,** r. Basse 7, ✉ 1180, ✆ 0 2 374 69 36, *lesmenusplaisirs@belgacom.net, Fax 0 2 331 38 13,* – AE ⓓ MC VISA
closed 1 week Easter, last week August, late December, Saturday lunch, Sunday, Monday dinner and Bank Holidays – **Meals**. *Lunch 13* – 30/50.
• This small but stylish restaurant has developed a good local reputation for its personalised, modern cuisine. Pleasant garden for dining out in summer.

XX **le pré en bulle,** av. J. et P. Carsoel 5, ✉ 1180, ✆ 0 2 374 08 80, *Fax 0 2 372 93 67,* – P. AE MC VISA
closed Monday dinner and Tuesday – **Meals**. *Lunch 15* – 30/48 b.i. ♀.
• A small 17C farm with plain but attractive décor, a creative menu based on traditional dishes and several tempting menus. Pleasant terrace for the summer months.

X **Le Passage,** av. J. et P. Carsoel 13, ✉ 1180, ✆ 0 2 374 66 94, *restaurant@lepassage.be, Fax 0 2 374 69 26,* – P. AE ⓓ MC VISA
closed 3 weeks July, first week January, Saturday lunch, Sunday and Bank Holidays – **Meals**. *Lunch 20* – 40/50, – a la carte 41/71
Spec. Foie d'oie au torchon farci aux figues confites, chutney aux poires et safran. Escalopines de ris de veau croustillantes aux morilles. Blanc de turbotin cuit au lait épicé, mousseline de crevettes grises.
• A pocket-sized restaurant with a trendy dining room decorated in various shades of grey. Contemporary cuisine not lacking in refinement.

WATERMAEL-BOITSFORT (WATERMAAL-BOSVOORDE)

Au Repos des Chasseurs, av. Charle Albert 11, ✉ 1170, ☎ 0 2 660 46 72, *info@aureposdeschasseurs.be, Fax 0 2 674 26 76,* – TV – 25-80. AE MC VISA
Meals (partly Italian cuisine, open until 11 p.m.). *Lunch 21* – a la carte 24/63 – **11 rm** 65/139.
• Those in search of peace and quiet will undoubtedly find it at "Hunters' Rest", an old dairy on the edge of a wood. Comfortably renovated rooms. A choice of classic French and Italian dishes dominates the restaurant menu, with game in season. Large terrace.

Au Vieux Boitsfort (Gillet), pl. Bischoffsheim 9, ✉ 1170, ☎ 0 2 672 23 32, *Fax 0 2 660 22 94,* – AE MC VISA
closed 3 weeks August, Saturday lunch and Sunday – **Meals** (booking essential). *Lunch 40* – 65/85 b.i., – a la carte 56/75
Spec. Risotto de cèpes et foie d'oie poêlé. Vapeur de cabillaud à la mousseline de crevettes grises. Noix de ris de veau braisées aux agrumes.
• This lauded corner restaurant has exchanged its original décor for a resolutely modern interior. Refined, traditional cuisine and a well-stocked cellar.

Le Grill, r. Trois Tilleuls 1, ✉ 1170, ☎ 0 2 672 95 13, *Fax 0 2 660 22 94,* – AE MC VISA JCB
closed 2 weeks July, Saturday lunch and Sunday – **Meals** – 27.
• On the edge of the Forêt de Soignes, Le Grill offers a standard à la carte menu with an emphasis on grilled dishes. Contemporary-style dining room.

WOLUWE-ST-LAMBERT (SINT-LAMBRECHTS-WOLUWE)

Sodehotel La Woluwe , av. E. Mounier 5, ✉ 1200, ☎ 0 2 775 21 11, *sodehotel@sodehotel.be, Fax 0 2 770 47 80,* – TV ch, P – 25-200. AE MC VISA JCB. rest
Meals ***Leonard*** *Lunch 23* – a la carte 35/57 – 21 – **120 rm** 150/285, – 6 suites.
• Away from the centre, but with easy access, this chain hotel has 118 spacious rooms combining peace and quiet and modern comfort. Business and conference centre. Modern and refined restaurant with cuisine that matches the setting. Bright patio.

Monty without rest, bd Brand Whitlock 101, ✉ 1200, ☎ 0 2 734 56 36, *info@monty-hotel.be, Fax 0 2 734 50 05* – TV. AE MC VISA HS z
18 rm 90/140.
• This former private mansion has been skilfully renovated in modern style. The hotel's two main selling-points are its friendly staff and the designer fittings throughout.

Lambeau without rest, av. Lambeau 150, ✉ 1200, ☎ 0 2 732 51 70, *info@hotellambeau.com, Fax 0 2 732 54 90* – TV. AE MC VISA. HR u
24 rm 69/93.
• This small, family-run hotel is located in a residential district, just opposite a metro station. Compact, identically furnished modern rooms with plain furnishings.

Da Mimmo, av. du Roi Chevalier 24, ✉ 1200, ☎ 0 2 771 58 60, *mimmo1961@yahoo.it, Fax 0 2 771 58 60,* , Italian cuisine – AE MC VISA.
closed August, late December-early January, Saturday lunch and Sunday – **Meals**. *Lunch 45* – a la carte 44/71
• Da Mimmo prides itself on its true Italian cuisine with no concessions to Belgian tastes. Pleasant, modern-style dining room. Good choice of wines shipped direct from Italy.

de Maurice à Olivier (Detombe) in the back room of a bookshop, chaussée de Roodebeek 246, ✉ 1200, ☎ 0 2 771 33 98 – AE MC VISA
closed 15 to 31 July, Sunday and Monday dinner – **Meals**. *Lunch 22* – 50/60, – a la carte 45/64
Spec. Marbré de perdreau au foie gras, pistaches et tomates confites (September-October). Suprême de pigeonneau en croustille d'épices. Café glacé à la minute.
• A father and son are at the helm of this small brasserie with an unusual location behind the family bookshop. A bistro-style menu and a literary atmosphere.

La table de Mamy, av. des Cerisiers 212, ✉ 1200, ☎ 0 2 779 00 96, *Fax 0 2 779 00 96,* – AE MC VISA
closed 3 weeks August, Saturday lunch and Sunday – **Meals** – 27.
• Enjoy the traditional cuisine of yesteryear in this pleasant restaurant in which the nostalgic internal décor is a throwback to olden times.

Les Amis du Cep, r. Th. Decuyper 136, ✉ 1200, ☎ 0 2 762 62 95, *info@les-amis-du-cep.be, Fax 0 2 771 20 32,* – AE MC VISA
closed 5 to 20 September, 1 week Christmas, Sunday and Monday – **Meals**. *Lunch 16* – 30/58 b.i.
• This small villa which advertises itself as a gourmet bistro is known for its contemporary flair in the kitchen and a top-notch wine-list.

WOLUWE-ST-PIERRE (SINT-PIETERS-WOLUWE)

Montgomery, av. de Tervuren 134, ✉ 1150, ℘ 0 2 741 85 11, *hotel@montgomery.be, Fax 0 2 741 85 00,* – 35. AE VISA.
Meals *(closed Saturday lunch and Sunday). Lunch 18 b.c.* – 25 – 20 – **61 rm** 150/360, – 2 suites. HS k
◆ The tasteful, individually furnished rooms in this small luxury hotel are inspired by colonial, British and "Ralph Lauren" styles. Lounge-library, fitness room and sauna. The cuisine in the snug restaurant will find favour with aficionados of modern cuisine.

Des 3 Couleurs, av. de Tervuren 453, ✉ 1150, ℘ 0 2 770 33 21, *Fax 0 2 770 80 45,* – AE VISA
closed Easter holidays, 15 to 31 August, Saturday lunch, Sunday dinner and Monday – **Meals**. *Lunch 37* – 52/99 b.i..
◆ White beams and furniture, allied with Burgundy stone, add cachet to the interior décor of this elegant villa with an attractive terrace. Traditional à la carte choices.

Le Vignoble de Margot, av. de Tervuren 368, ✉ 1150, ℘ 0 2 779 23 23, *info@levignobledemargot.be, Fax 0 2 779 05 45,* , Partly oyster bar – AE VISA
closed 23 December-3 January, Saturday lunch, Sunday and Bank Holidays – **Meals** – a la carte 47/73.
◆ This former station-buffet encircled by its own "vineyard" enjoys views over a park and several ponds. Elaborate choice of classic dishes, plus a seafood bar. Banqueting room.

Les Deux Maisons (Demartin), Val des Seigneurs 81, ✉ 1150, ℘ 0 2 771 14 47, *lesdeuxmaisons@skynet.be, Fax 0 2 771 14 47,* – AE VISA
closed first week Easter, first 3 weeks August, Christmas-New Year, Sunday and Monday – **Meals** – 33/82 b.i., – a la carte 45/74
Spec. Langoustines rôties et légumes glacés en barigoule. Bar en croûte de sel au beurre blanc. Moelleux au chocolat.
◆ A plain dining room with a contemporary look is the backdrop for refined cuisine with a modern touch enhanced by a superb wine-list. "Dégustation" and "Tradition" menus.

Medicis, av. de l'Escrime 124, ✉ 1150, ℘ 0 2 779 07 00, *Fax 0 2 779 19 24,* – AE VISA.
closed Easter, Saturday lunch and Sunday – **Meals**. *Lunch 15* – 30/55.
◆ The Medicis occupies a noble-looking villa in which the modern menu is certain to sharpen your appetite. French-Italian wine list and a fine selection of desserts.

l'auberg'in, r. au Bois 198, ✉ 1150, ℘ 0 2 770 68 85, *Fax 0 2 770 68 85,* , Grill rest – P. AE VISA
closed Saturday lunch and Sunday – **Meals** – 31.
◆ This small, Brabant-style 19C farm has been converted into a convivial restaurant with neo-rustic décor and a roaring fire. Grilled specialities cooked in the dining room.

La Tour d'Argent, av. Salomé 1, ✉ 1150, ℘ 0 2 762 99 80, Vietnamese cuisne – VISA.
closed 4 to 7 April, 13 August-3 September, Wednesday and lunch Thursday and Saturday – **Meals**. *Lunch 11* – 19/24.
◆ A well-deserved name for this simple, family-run Vietnamese restaurant serving authentic dishes which will transport you to the Far East. Unfailingly friendly service.

BRUSSELS ENVIRONS

at Diegem *Brussels-Zaventem motorway A 201, Diegem exit* C *Machelen pop. 12 061* – ✉ *1831 Diegem :*

Crowne Plaza Airport, Da Vincilaan 4 ℘ 0 2 416 33 33, *cpbrusselsairport@ichotelsgroup.com, Fax 0 2 416 33 44,* ch, P – 25-400. AE VISA. rest
Meals (open until 11 p.m.). *Lunch 21* – a la carte 25/44 – 21 – **312 rm** 110/355, – 3 suites.
◆ Part of the Crowne Plaza chain, this hotel is located in a business park close to the airport. Comfortable and spacious rooms as well as good conference facilities. The restaurant offers a choice of contemporary cuisine including a buffet lunch option.

Sofitel Airport, Bessenveldstraat 15 ℘ 0 2 713 66 66, *H0548@accor.com, Fax 0 2 721 43 45,* P – 25-300. AE VISA. rest
Meals ***La Pléiade*** *(closed Friday dinner, Saturday and Sunday lunch) Lunch 22* – a la carte 28/61 – 21 – **125 rm** 99/360.
◆ A top-of-the-range chain hotel alongside a motorway 4km/2.5mi from Zaventem airport with quiet, newly renovated rooms and full conference and leisure facilities. The pleasant restaurant serves a range of appetising modern dishes.

Holiday Inn Airport, Holidaystraat 7 ✆ 0 2 720 58 65, *hibrusselsairport@ichotelsgroup.com, Fax 0 2 720 41 45,* – 25-400.
Meals (open until 11 p.m.). *Lunch 30* – a la carte 27/42 – 21 – **310 rm** 100/230.
• The Holiday Inn offers a range of facilities, such as conference and fitness rooms, sauna, hammam, solarium, pool and tennis court. Other advantages include proximity to the airport and quiet, restful rooms. Expansive restaurant menu with a few Tex-Mex dishes.

NH Brussels Airport, De Kleetlaan 14 ✆ 0 2 203 92 52, *nhbrusselsairport@nh-hotels.be, Fax 0 2 203 92 53,* ch, – 25-80.
Meals *(closed mid July-mid August, Friday, Saturday and Sunday)* (partly buffets). *Lunch 30* – a la carte 35/45 – 19 – **234 rm** 187/260.
• A modern construction close to the airport with up-to-date, comfortable rooms with good soundproofing, in keeping with the standards expected of the NH chain. Contemporary tastes are well-catered for in the hotel restaurant.

Novotel Airport, Da Vincilaan 25 ✆ 0 2 725 30 50, *H0467@accor.com, Fax 0 2 721 39 58,* rest, – 25-100.
Meals (open until midnight) a la carte 27/44 – 15 – **207 rm** 180/186.
• Ideal for those with an early flight to catch. No surprises in the identical bedrooms, which conform to the Novotel's usual criteria. Seminar rooms and outdoor pool.

Rainbow Airport, Berkenlaan 4 ✆ 0 2 721 77 77, *reservations@rainbowhotel.be, Fax 0 2 721 55 96,* rest, ch, – 25-100.
Meals *(closed Saturday and Sunday). Lunch 30* – a la carte 23/43 – 16 – **100 rm** 79/219.
• Despite being on the small side, the rooms here are attractive, well-maintained and spotlessly clean. Modern decor in the restaurant, where the emphasis is on conventional dishes. A haven of peace of quiet for stopover or transit passengers.

at Dilbeek *West : 7 km – pop. 38 782 – ✉ 1700 Dilbeek :*

Relais Delbeccha, Bodegemstraat 158 ✆ 0 2 569 44 30, *relais.delbeccha@skynet.be, Fax 0 2 569 75 30,* – 25-100.
Meals *(closed Sunday dinner). Lunch 30* – 35/52 b.i. – **12 rm** 81/120.
• A quiet hotel with just 12 rooms, where the welcome is warm and friendly. Pleasant interior, cosy lounge, comfortable rooms with classic furniture, meeting rooms and a garden. Reasonably stylish restaurant offering outdoor dining in the summer.

Host. d'Arconati with rm, d'Arconatistraat 77 ✆ 0 2 569 35 00, *arconati@hotmail.com, Fax 0 2 569 35 04,* – 40.
closed February – **Meals** *(closed Sunday dinner, Monday and Tuesday)* a la carte 43/53 – **4 rm** 78/87.
• A charming Art Deco villa with quaint rooms and a tree-shaded garden, ablaze with colour in summer, which provides the perfect setting in which to unwind.

De Kapblok, Ninoofsesteenweg 220 ✆ 0 2 569 31 23, *reservatie@dekapblok.be, Fax 0 2 569 67 23* –
closed Easter holidays, 22 July-15 August, Christmas holidays, Sunday and Monday – **Meals**. *Lunch 33* – 47/65.
• The "Butcher's Block" is a small, local restaurant serving good quality traditional cuisine, appetising menus and a highly respectable choice of wines.

at Dworp *(Tourneppe) South : 16 km Beersel pop. 23 152 – ✉ 1653 Dworp :*

Kasteel Gravenhof, Alsembergsesteenweg 676 ✆ 0 2 380 44 99, *info@gravenhof.be, Fax 0 2 380 40 60,* rm, – 25-120.
Meals (pub rest) a la carte 22/43 – 15 – **26 rm** 100/130.
• This impressive château is a 17C folly replete with old knick-knacks, period furniture, and spacious bedrooms overlooking a park with ornamental ponds. The charming tavern-restaurant is in the depths of the castle's old vaulted cellars.

at Grimbergen *North : 11 km – pop. 33 312 – ✉ 1850 Grimbergen :*

Abbey, Kerkeblokstraat 5 ✆ 0 2 270 08 88, *info@hotelabbey.be, Fax 0 2 270 81 88,* rest, – 30-200. rm
closed July – **Meals *'t Wit Paard*** *(closed Saturday and Sunday) Lunch 32* – a la carte 45/62 – **28 rm** 130/250.
• The Abbey's imposing architecture is reminiscent of a Flemish farm. Quiet, spacious guest rooms, plus meeting halls, bar, fitness area and sauna. Traditional restaurant fare, log fires in winter and outdoor dining on the terrace in summer.

at Groot-Bijgaarden *Northwest : 7 km* *Dilbeek pop. 38 782 – 1702 Groot-Bijgaarden :*

Waerboom, Jozef Mertensstraat 140 0 2 463 15 00, *info@waerboom.com, Fax 0 2 463 10 30,* – 25-270. AE VISA.
closed mid July-mid August – **Meals** (residents only) – **35 rm** 96/121.
• This Flemish farm has been tastefully converted into an attractive, family-run hotel. Conventional rooms, indoor pool, sauna and well-tended garden. Banquets and seminars.

Gosset, Gossetlaan 52 0 2 466 21 30, *info@gosset.be, Fax 0 2 466 18 50,* – 25-200. AE VISA. rm
closed last week December-first week January – **Meals**. *Lunch 10* – a la carte 26/39 – **48 rm** 100/125.
• This comfortable modern hotel with adequately soundproofed rooms occupies a small building on an industrial estate near the ring road. Large, contemporary dining room crowned with a fresco depicting a celestial scene. Shuttle bus to the city centre.

De Bijgaarden, I. Van Beverenstraat 20 0 2 466 44 85, *debijgaarden@skynet.be, Fax 0 2 463 08 11,* <, – AE VISA JCB
closed 27 March-3 April, 8 to 29 August, Saturday lunch and Sunday – **Meals**. *Lunch 50* – 65/125 b.i., – a la carte 75/156
Spec. Beignet de foie gras d'oie caramélisé au porto. Coffre de homard aux salsifis et truffe. Cochon de lait rôti à l'ancienne, sauce aux condiments.
• An enchanting residence in a bucolic setting, with an elegant interior, fine, traditional cuisine, magnificent wine cellar, and Groot-Bijgaarden Castle as a backdrop.

Michel (Van Landeghem), Gossetlaan 31 0 2 466 65 91, *restaurant.michel@belgacom.net, Fax 0 2 466 90 07,* – AE VISA
closed 29 March, 2 to 20 August, 23 December-3 January, Sunday and Monday – **Meals** – 48/87 b.i.
Spec. Œuf poché aux jets de houblon (mid February-March). Perdreau rôti à la feuille de vigne (15 September-15 November). Sole farcie au risotto et crevettes grises.
• The unassuming décor of this gastronomic restaurant is in sharp contrast to its refined cuisine, which follows classic lines. Good wine-list. Outdoor dining in summer.

at Hoeilaart *Southeast : 13 km – pop. 10 023 – 1560 Hoeilaart :*

Aloyse Kloos, Terhulpsesteenweg 2 (at Groenendaal) 0 2 657 37 37, *Fax 0 2 657 37 37,* – VISA
closed August, Saturday lunch, Sunday dinner and Monday – **Meals**. *Lunch 25* – 33/57 b.i. .
• Classic cuisine and superb wines are the hallmarks of this villa on the edge of the massif de Soignes. The renowned local hams are cured on the property.

at Huizingen *South : 12 km* *Beersel pop. 23 152 – 1654 Huizingen :*

Terborght (De Vlieger), Oud Dorp 16 0 2 380 10 10, *terborght@skynet.be, Fax 0 2 380 10 97* – – 50. AE VISA
closed 7 to 17 February, 25 July-11 August, Tuesday and Wednesday – **Meals**. *Lunch 28* – 39/75 b.i., – a la carte 46/83
Spec. Déclinaison de crevettes grises. Tout agneau. Nougat glacé, millefeuille de framboises.
• A 17C house with impressive crow-stepped gables and an interior which blends both rustic and contemporary decorative features. Refined modern cuisine.

at Itterbeek *West : 8 km* *Dilbeek pop. 38 782 – 1701 Itterbeek :*

De Ster, Herdebeekstraat 169 (locality Sint-Anna-Pede) 0 2 569 78 08, *rest.dester@skynet.be, Fax 0 2 569 37 97,* , Pub – VISA
closed 2 weeks August, Monday, Tuesday and lunch Saturday and Sunday – **Meals**. *Lunch 16* – 25/45.
• Recognisable by its attractive half-timbered façade, this old inn on a main road has several dining rooms laid out on various levels, in addition to a pleasant summer terrace.

at Machelen *Northeast : 12 km – pop. 12 061 – 1830 Machelen :*

Pyramid, Heirbaan 210 0 2 253 54 56, *rest.pyramid@skynet.be, Fax 0 2 253 47 65,* – AE VISA
closed 27 March-3 April, 18 July-7 August, Saturday lunch and Sunday – **Meals**. *Lunch 36* – 65/90 .
• A contemporary villa and renovated interior provide the setting for inventive cuisine. Summer terrace ornamented with a water feature and verdant pyramid.

at Meise *North : 14 km – pop. 18 449 – 1860 Meise :*

Aub. Napoléon, Bouchoutlaan 1 0 2 269 30 78, *Fax 0 2 269 79 98,* Grill rest – AE VISA
closed August and late December – **Meals**. *Lunch 36* – 56/74 b.i. .
• A small, welcoming inn on the approach to Meuse. Rustic-style interior decor based on the theme of Napoleon. Grilled specialities, plus an "imperial" wine cellar !

Hof ter Imde, Beekstraat 32 (Northwest : 3 km, locality Imde), 1861, 0 52 31 01 01, *info@hofterimde.be, Fax 0 52 31 05 50,*
closed carnival week, 20 July-4 August, 1 to 8 November, Saturday lunch, Sunday and Monday except Bank Holidays – **Meals**. Lunch 30 – 38/68 b.i..
• This rustically located former Brabant farmhouse is now a cosy restaurant with a contemporary-style dining room and outdoor section overlooking an orchard.

Koen Van Loven, Brusselsesteenweg 11 0 2 270 05 77, *koen.van.loven@proximedia.be, Fax 0 2 270 05 46,* 25-150.
closed building workers holidays, Monday and Tuesday – **Meals**. Lunch 30 – 41/73 b.i..
• This early-20C bourgeois residence is now home to a contemporary-style restaurant. Comprehensive cellar. Large room for banquets and seminars.

at Melsbroek *Northeast : 14 km C Steenokkerzeel pop. 10 567 – 1820 Melsbroek :*

Boetfort, Sellaerstraat 42 0 2 751 64 00, *boetfort@proximedia.be, Fax 0 2 751 62 00,* 25-50. DK p
closed carnival week, 21 July-15 August, Wednesday dinner, Saturday lunch and Sunday – **Meals**. Lunch 34 – 38/70 b.i..
• This 17C manor house with a park once hosted the Sun King himself. Much of the building's cachet lies in its strong historical links.

at Nossegem *East : 13 km C Zaventem pop. 27 967 – 1930 Nossegem :*

L'Orangeraie Roland Debuyst, Leuvensesteenweg 614 0 2 757 05 59, *orangeraie@biz.tiscali.be, Fax 0 2 759 50 08,* 35.
closed 1 week Easter, 1 to 15 August, Saturday lunch, Sunday and Monday – **Meals**. Lunch 35 – 41/99 b.i., – a la carte 66/100
Spec. Déclinaison de foie d'oie et Pata Negra. Tronçon de sole et foie d'oie aux girolles. Filet d'agneau des prés salés en tian de légumes à la sauge, croquette d'ail doux.
• A contemporary restaurant with soothing red and ecru decor and innovative cuisine based on premium ingredients. Summer dining under the pergola.

at Overijse *Southeast : 16 km – pop. 23 831 – 3090 Overijse :*

Soret, Kapucijnendreef 1 (at Jezus-Eik) 0 2 657 37 82, *hotel.soret.bvba@pandora.be, Fax 0 2 657 72 66,* 40.
Meals see ***Istas*** below – **39 rm** 65/105, – 1 suite.
• A brand-new hotel situated on the edge of the Forêt de Soignes. Smartly decorated rooms of varying shapes but generally with plenty of space. Peace and quiet guaranteed.

Barbizon (Deluc), Welriekendedreef 95 (at Jezus-Eik) 0 2 657 04 62, *barbizon@euronet.be, Fax 0 2 657 40 66,*
closed 12 July-3 August, 10 January-3 February, Tuesday and Wednesday – **Meals**. Lunch 36 – 50/110 b.i., – a la carte 69/123
Spec. Tournedos de langoustines juste raidi, compotée de tomates douces et roquette, crème au cresson. Filet de turbotin rôti, artichaut au Vin jaune et beurre de crevettes grises. Gibier (September-January).
• This Norman-style villa bordering the forest is in harmony with its bucolic setting. Exquisite, classic cuisine. Terrace and a delightful garden for warm summer days.

Lipsius, Brusselsesteenweg 671 (at Jezus-Eik) 0 2 657 34 32, *lipsius@skynet.be, Fax 0 2 657 31 47* –
closed 1 week after Easter, August, Christmas, New Year, Saturday lunch, Sunday dinner and Monday – **Meals**. Lunch 35 – 50/83 b.i..
• Ceruse beams, brick vaulting, chasuble chairs and co-ordinated tableware make up the decor at this respected restaurant named after a humanist born in Overijse.

Istas - Hotel Soret, Brusselsesteenweg 652 (at Jezus-Eik) 0 2 657 05 11, , Pub rest –
closed 1 week Easter, August, Wednesday and Thursday – **Meals** – a la carte 22/41.
• A century-old tavern-cum-restaurant a stone's throw from the Forêt de Soignes. Traditional cuisine and colourful local dishes served in a convivial atmosphere.

at Sint-Genesius-Rode *(Rhode-St-Genèse) South : 13 km – pop. 17 930 – 1640 Sint-Genesius-Rode :*

Aub. de Waterloo, chaussée de Waterloo 212 0 2 358 35 80, *aubergedewaterloo@skynet.be, Fax 0 2 358 38 06,* 25-70.
closed 1 to 15 August and late December – **Meals** see ***L'Arlecchino*** below – **84 rm** 70/191.
• This recently built hotel close to the site of Napoleon's downfall offers two categories of rooms, plus studios with Chinese or Syrian décor. Business clientele.

XX **L'Arlecchino** - Hotel Aub. de Waterloo, chaussée de Waterloo 212 ℘ 0 2 358 34 16, *Fax 0 2 358 28 96*, , Italian cuisine, partly trattoria - AE VISA
closed August and Monday - **Meals** - 33/48 b.i..
• The menu at this restaurant will delight lovers of all things Italian, as will the pizzas from the trattoria. Venetian decor in the hushed dining room. Good Italian wines.

at Sint-Pieters-Leeuw *Southwest : 13 km - pop. 30 384 - ✉ 1600 Sint-Pieters-Leeuw :*

Green Park, V. Nonnemanstraat 15 ℘ 0 2 331 19 70, *info@greenparkhotel.be, Fax 0 2 331 03 11*, , , - - 25-100. AE VISA. rest
closed July - **Meals** (residents only) - **18 rm** 74/110.
• Green Park was built a few years ago in this verdant, peaceful setting by a lake. Small fitness centre. Popular with business customers.

at Strombeek-Bever *North : 9 km Grimbergen pop. 33 312 - ✉ 1853 Strombeek-Bever :*

Rijckendael, J. Van Elewijckstraat 35 ℘ 0 2 267 41 24, *rijckendael@vhv-hotels.be, Fax 0 2 267 94 01*, , - , rm, - 25-40. AE VISA
Meals *(closed last 3 weeks July-first week August)*. Lunch 23 - 36/65 b.i. - **49 rm** 99/165.
• This hotel of modern design is located a short walk from the Atomium and Heysel stadium. Identical, well-appointed rooms. Private car park. Restaurant with a rustic feel laid out inside a small farm.

XX **'t Stoveke**, Jetsestraat 52 ℘ 0 2 267 67 25, , Seafood - AE VISA.
closed 3 weeks June, Sunday, Monday and Bank Holidays - **Meals**. Lunch 31 - a la carte 56/77.
• A family-run restaurant where the emphasis is on fish and seafood. Tiny dining room with views of the kitchen, plus a small terrace open to the elements.

XX **Val Joli**, Leestbeekstraat 16 ℘ 0 2 460 65 43, *info@valjoli.be, Fax 0 2 460 04 00*, - - 25-40. VISA
closed 2 weeks June, late October-early November, Monday and Tuesday - **Meals**. Lunch 15 - 32/64 b.i..
• A villa with a garden and terraces. From your table, you can watch the ducks frolicking on the lake. Varied cuisine.

at Vilvoorde *(Vilvorde) North : 17 km - pop. 36 170 - ✉ 1800 Vilvoorde :*

XXX **La Hacienda**, Koningslosteenweg 34 ℘ 0 2 649 26 85, *Fax 0 2 647 43 50*, , Spanish cuisine - - 25. AE VISA.
closed mid July-mid August - **Meals**. Lunch 24 - 39.
• This bright hacienda is tucked away in a cul-de-sac near the canal. Authentic Iberian cuisine with regional menus and grilled meats. Wide choice of Spanish wines.

XX **Kijk Uit**, Lange Molensstraat 60 ℘ 0 2 251 04 72, *kijkuit-vilvoorde@hotmail.com, Fax 0 2 751 09 01* - AE VISA.
closed 15 July-15 August, late December, Saturday, Sunday and Monday dinner - **Meals**. Lunch 30 - 49/69 b.i..
• The Kijk Uit is overlooked by a 15C watchtower. Decidedly trendy cuisine served in a renovated high-ceilinged dining room which has managed to preserve its original character.

XX **Rouge Glamour**, Fr. Rooseveltlaan 18 ℘ 0 2 253 68 39, *Fax 0 2 253 68 39* - VISA
closed Easter week, first 2 weeks August, All Saints'week, Monday, Tuesday dinner and lunch Saturday and Sunday - **Meals**. Lunch 20 - 30/69 b.i..
• Modern cuisine offered in a cabaret-style setting, with a plant-filled summer terrace at the back with dark wood furnishings.

at Wemmel *North : 12 km - pop. 14 405 - ✉ 1780 Wemmel :*

La Roseraie, Limburg Stirumlaan 213 ℘ 0 2 456 99 10 and 0 2 460 51 34 (rest), *hotel@laroseraie.be, Fax 0 2 460 83 20*, - AE VISA JCB
Meals *(closed Saturday lunch, Sunday dinner and Monday)*. Lunch 22 - a la carte 36/48 - **8 rm** 107/150.
• La Roseraie occupies a pretty villa with eight reasonably comfortable, individually furnished guest rooms with varying styles : African, Japanese, Roman etc. Friendly welcome. Traditionally furnished dining room serving cuisine with the occasional modern touch.

XXX **Le Gril Aux Herbes**, Brusselsesteenweg 21 ℘ 0 2 460 52 39, *Fax 0 2 461 19 12*, - AE VISA
closed 1 to 21 July, 24 December-2 January, Saturday lunch and Sunday - **Meals**. Lunch 30 - 45/85 b.i. .
• The cuisine at this small villa with a large garden is based on high-quality, carefully selected products. The wine-list does justice to the reputation of French vineyards.

XX **Parkhof,** Parklaan 7 ✆ 0 2 460 42 89, *info@parkhof.be, Fax 0 2 460 25 10,* – P. AE Ⓓ MC VISA
closed Easter, 2 weeks July, Monday and dinner Wednesday and Sunday – **Meals**. Lunch 16 – 35/83 b.i..
◆ Located in a public park close to the Beverbos nature reserve, the Oliartes has a pleasant terrace for dining outdoors in summer.

XX **Via-Vai,** Vijverslaan 1 ✆ 0 2 460 55 64, *Fax 0 2 460 13 92,* , Partly Italian cuisine, open until 11 p.m. – P. AE Ⓓ MC VISA.
Meals. Lunch 18 – a la carte 27/46.
◆ Il Brunello's extensive menu is mainly devoted to Italian cuisine. The contemporary interior is similarly influenced by Italy. Trattoria section, plus a summer restaurant.

at Zaventem *Brussels-Zaventem airport motorway A 201 – pop. 27 967 – ✉ 1930 Zaventem :*

Sheraton Airport, at airport ✆ 0 2 710 80 00, *info@sheraton.be, Fax 0 2 710 80 80,* – TV ch, P – 25-600. AE Ⓓ MC VISA JCB
Meals Concorde *(closed Saturday lunch)* Lunch 55 b.i. – a la carte 54/74 – 25 – **292 rm** 85/470, – 2 suites.
◆ The closest luxury hotel to the airport, the Sheraton is a popular choice with business customers from around the world. International à la carte menu and buffet lunches that are ideal for busy corporate travellers.

XX **Stockmansmolen** 1st floor, H. Henneaulaan 164 ✆ 0 2 725 34 34, *info@stockmansmolen.be, Fax 0 2 725 75 05,* Partly pub rest – P. AE Ⓓ MC VISA
closed last 2 weeks July-first week August, Christmas, New Year, Saturday and Sunday – **Meals**. Lunch 72 b.i. – 54/93 b.i..
◆ The brasserie and restaurant - the latter on the first floor - share the two parts of this 13C water mill, built using a combination of wood and stone.

ELLEZELLES (ELZELE) *7890 Hainaut* **533 H 18, 534 H 18** *and* **716 E 3** *– pop. 5 597.*
Bruxelles 55 km.

XXXX ✿✿ **Château du Mylord** (Thomaes brothers), r. St-Mortier 35 ✆ 0 68 54 26 02, *chateaudumylord@pi.be, Fax 0 68 54 29 33,* – P. AE Ⓓ MC VISA
closed 29 March-6 April, 16 to 31 August, 22 December-9 January, Monday lunch except Bank Holidays and dinner Sunday, Monday and Wednesday – **Meals**. Lunch 50 – 65/155 b.i., – a la carte 72/95 ♀
Spec. Morue confite à l'huile d'olives, purée aillée et calamars au jus de viande. Carpaccio de Saint-Jacques, foie d'oie et émulsion aux girolles (September-April). Selle d'agneau en persillade de fleurs de houblon (January-August).
◆ This splendid 19C manor house stands in the surroundings of a delightful park. Elegant décor, superb terrace, cuisine with modern nuances, and vintage wines. Exquisite !.

ANTWERP (ANTWERPEN) *2000* 533 L 15 *and* 716 G 2 *– pop. 454 172.*

See : *Around the Market Square and the Cathedral★★★ : Market Square★ (Grote Markt), Vlaaikensgang★* **FY**, *Cathedral★★★ and its tower★★★* **FY** *– Butchers' House★ (Vleeshuis) : Musical instruments★* **FY D** *– Rubens' House ★★ (Rubenshuis)* **GZ** *– Interior★ of St. James' Church (St-Jacobskerk)* **GY** *- Hendrik Conscience Place★ – St. Charles Borromeo's Church★ (St-Carolus Borromeuskerk)* **GY** *– St. Paul's Church (St-Pauluskerk) : interior★★* **FY** *– Zoo★★ (Dierentuin)* **DEU** *– Zurenborg Quarter★★* **EV** *– The port (Haven)* **FY**.
Museums : Maritime "Steen"★ (Nationaal Scheepvaartmuseum Steen) **FY** *– Ethnographic Museum★* **FY M**[1] *– Plantin-Moretus★★★* **FZ** *– Mayer Van den Bergh★★ : Mad Meg★★ (Dulle Griet)* **GZ** *– Rockox House★ (Rockoxhuis)* **GY M**[4] *– Royal Art Gallery★★★ (Koninklijk Museum voor Schone Kunsten)* **VCM**[5] *- Museum of Photography★* **CV M**[6] *– Open-air Museum of Sculpture Middelheim★ (Openluchtmuseum voor Beeldhouwkunst) – Provincial Museum Sterckshof-Zilvercentrum★.*

18 9 North : 15,5 km at Kapellen, G. Capiaulei 2 ✆ 0 3 666 84 56, - 18 South : 10 km at Aartselaar, Kasteel Cleydael, Cleydaellaan 36 ✆ 0 3 887 00 79 - 18 9 East : 10 km at Wommelgem, Uilenbaan 15 ✆ 0 3 355 14 00 - 18 9 East : 13 km at Broechem, Kasteel Bossenstein, Moor 16 0 3 485 64 46.

Grote Markt 13 ✆ 0 3 232 01 03, visit@antwerpen.be, Fax 0 3 231 19 37 – Tourist association of the province, Koningin Elisabethlei 16, ✉ 2018, ✆ 0 3 240 63 73, info@tpa.be, Fax 0 3 240 63 83.
Brussels 48 – Amsterdam 159 – Luxembourg 261 – Rotterdam 103.

Plans on following pages

ANTWERPEN

Amsterdamstr. ... DT 4
Ankerrui ... DT 6
Ballaerst. ... DV 12
Borsbeekbrug ... EX 16
Brialmontlei ... DV 21
Britselei ... DV 22
Broederminstr. ... CV 24
Brouwersvliet ... DT 25
Brusselstr. ... CV 27
Carnotstr. ... EU
Cassiersstr. ... DT 31
Charlottalei ... DV 33
Cockerillkaai ... CV 36
Cogels-Osylei ... EV 37
Cuperusstr. ... EV 38
Dambruggestr. ... ETU 39
de Gerlachekaai ... CV 67
de Keyserlei ... DU 103
Diksmuidelaan ... EX 43
Emiel Banningstr. ... CV 51
Emiel Vloorsstr. ... CX 52
Erwtenstr. ... ET 55
Falconpl. ... DT 58
Franklin Rooseveltpl. ... DU 60
Gemeentestr. ... DU 63
Gen. Armstrongweg ... CX 64
Gen. van Merlenstr. ... EV 65
Gerard Le Grellelaan ... DX 66
Gillisplaats ... CV 69
Gitschotellei ... EX 70
Graaf van Egmontstr. ... CV 72
Haantjeslei ... CDV 79
Halenstr. ... ET 81
Hessenpl. ... DT 84
Jan de Voslei ... CX 90
Jan van Gentstr. ... CV 91
Jezusstr. ... DU 96
Justitiestr. ... DV 97
Kasteelpleinstr. ... DV 102
Kloosterstr. ... CU 105
Kol. Silvertopstr. ... CX 106
Koningin Astridpl. ... DEU 109
Koningin Elisabethlei ... DX 110
Korte Winkelstr. ... DTU 114
Lambermontplaats ... CV 116
Lange Winkelstr. ... DT 118
Leopold de Waelpl. ... CV 120
Leopold de Waelstr. ... CV 121
Leysstr. ... DU 123
Londenstr. ... DT 124
Maria Henriettalei ... DV 125
Marnixplaats ... CV 129
Mercatorstr. ... DEV 130
Namenstr. ... CV 133
Offerandestr. ... EU 136
Ommeganckstr. ... EU 138
Orteliuskaai ... DT 141
Osystr. ... DU 142
Oude Leeuwenrui ... DT 148
Pelikaanstr. ... DU 151
Plantinkaai ... CU 153
Ploegstr. ... EU 154
Posthofbrug ... EX 157
Prins Albertlei ... DX 159
Provinciestr. ... EUV 162
Pyckestr. ... CX 163
Quellinstr. ... DU 165
Quinten Matsijslei ... DUV 166
Rolwagenstr. ... EV 171
Schijnpoortweg ... ET 174
Simonsstr. ... DEV 178
Sint-Bernardsesteenweg ... CX 180
Sint-Gummarusstr. ... DT 181
Sint-Janspl. ... DT 183
Sint-Jozefsstr. ... DV 186
Sint-Michielskaai ... CU 187
Turnhoutsebaan (BORGERHOUT) EU
van Aerdtstr. ... DT 3
van Breestr. ... DV 19
van den Nestlei ... EV 135
van Schoonhovestr. ... DEU 175
Viaduct Dam ... ET 202
Viséstr. ... ET 204
Volksstr. ... CV 207
Vondelstr. ... DT 208
Waterloostr. ... EV 210

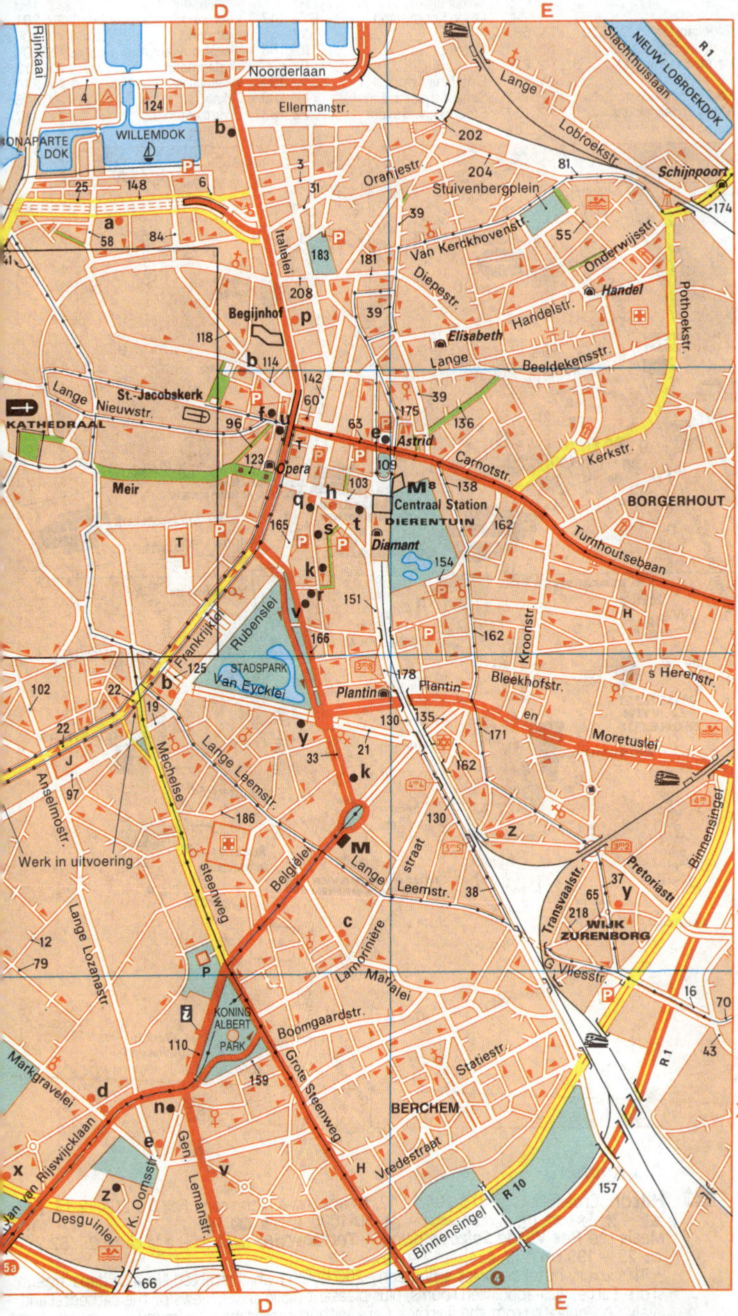
D
E
Rijnkaai
Noorderlaan
Ellermanstr.
BONAPARTE DOK
WILLEMDOK
NIEUW LOBROEKDOK
Slachthuislaan
R 1
Lange
Lobroekstr.
Oranjestr.
Stuivenbergplein
Schijnpoort
Italiëlei
Van Kerckhovenstr.
Onderwijsstr.
Diepestr.
Handel
Handelstr.
Pothoekstr.
Begijnhof
Elisabeth
Lange
Beeldekensstr.
St.-Jacobskerk
Lange Nieuwstr.
KATHEDRAAL
Meir
Opera
Astrid
Carnotstr.
Kerkstr.
Centraal Station
DIERENTUIN
Diamant
BORGERHOUT
Turnhoutsebaan
Frankrijklei
Rubenslei
STADSPARK
Van Eycklei
Plantin
Kroonstr.
Bleekhofstr.
s Herenstr.
en
Moretuslei
Mechelse steenweg
Lange Leemstr.
Anselmostr.
Werk in uitvoering
Belgiëlei
Lange Leemstr.
straat
Transvaalstr.
Pretoriastr.
WIJK ZURENBORG
Binnensingel
Lange Lozanastr.
Lamorinièrestr.
Marialei
G. Vliesstr.
KONING ALBERT PARK
Boomgaardstr.
Grote Steenweg
Statiestr.
Markgravelei
BERCHEM
Jan van Rijswijcklaan
Gen. Lemanstr.
K. Oomsstr.
Vredestraat
Desguinlei
Binnensingel
R 10
R 1
T
U
V
X
D
E

ANTWERPEN

Gildekamerstr. . . . . FY 68
Groenplaats . . . . FZ
Handschoenmarkt . . . . FY 82
Klapdorp . . . . GY
Korte Gasthuisstr. . . . . GZ 112
Maria Pijpelinckxstr. . . . . . . GZ 127
Meir . . . . GZ
Nationalestr. . . . . FZ
Oude Koornmarkt . . . . FYZ 147
Paardenmarkt . . . . GY
Repenstr. . . . . FY 168
Schoenmarkt . . . . FZ
Sint-Jansvliet . . . . FZ 184
Sint-Rochusstr. . . . . FZ 189
Steenhouwersvest . . . . FZ 193
Twaalf Maandenstr. . . . . GZ 199
Veemarkt . . . . FY 201
Vlasmarkt . . . . FYZ 205
Vleeshouwersstr. . . . . FY 206
Vrijdagmarkt . . . . FZ 213
Wisselstr. . . . . FY 214
Zirkstr. . . . . FY 216
Zwartzusterstr. . . . . FY 217

Old Antwerp

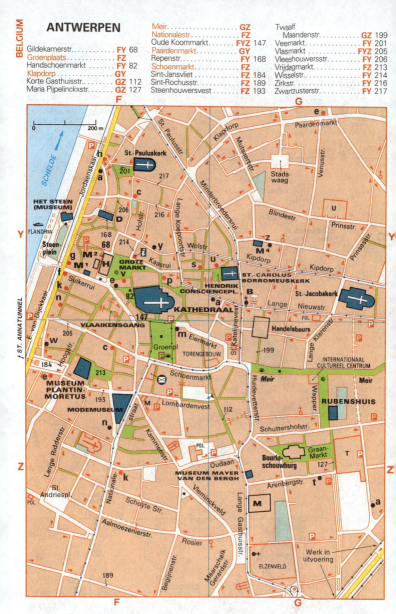

Hilton, Groenplaats ✆ 0 3 204 12 12, *fb-antwerp@hilton.com,* Fax *0 3 204 12 13,* – 30-1000. AE VISA FZ m

Meals see ***Het Vijfde Seizoen*** below – ***Terrace-Café*** *Lunch 25* – a la carte 29/52 – 25 – **199 rm** 179/434, – 12 suites.

◆ This luxury hotel occupies a fine early-20C building which started life as a department store. Large, well-appointed rooms, plus pleasant public areas. Views of the cathedral and lively Groenplaats from the Terrace Café with its comprehensive menu.

De Witte Lelie without rest, Keizerstraat 16 ☎ 0 3 226 19 66, *hotel@dewittelelie.be, Fax 0 3 234 00 19* – AE MC VISA JCB GY z
closed 18 December-6 January – **7 rm** 195/495, – 3 suites.
◆ Quiet and full of charm, this small "grand hotel" is spread across several 17C houses. Cosy, elegantly decorated rooms, in addition to an inviting patio.

't Sandt, Het Zand 17 ☎ 0 3 232 93 90, *info@hotel-sandt.be, Fax 0 3 232 56 13* – rm, – 25-100. AE MC VISA. FZ w
Meals *de kleine Zavel* *(closed Saturday lunch)* Lunch 20 – a la carte 29/50 – **27 rm** 135/240, – 2 suites.
◆ The fine Rococo façade of this impressive 19C residence contrasts vividly with the sober, contemporary décor of its interior. Delightful, Italianate winter garden, roomy, elegant guest accommodation, and good-quality bistro cuisine.

Theater, Arenbergstraat 30 ☎ 0 3 203 54 10, *info@theater-hotel.be, Fax 0 3 233 88 58,* – – 25-50. AE MC VISA. GZ t
Meals *(closed 18 July-16 August, Saturday lunch, Sunday and Bank Holidays).* Lunch 16 – a la carte 32/42 – **122 rm** 110/235, – 5 suites.
◆ A modern, comfortable hotel with an ideal location at the heart of the old city, just a short distance from the Bourla theatre and Rubens' house. Spacious bedrooms decorated in warm tones. Characterful restaurant featuring a small menu from around the world.

Rubens without rest, Oude Beurs 29 ☎ 0 3 222 48 48, *hotelrubens@microsun.es, Fax 0 3 225 19 40* – AE MC VISA JCB. FY y
35 rm 145/185, – 1 suite.
◆ A quiet and friendly renovated hotel near the Grand-Place and cathedral. Some rooms overlook the inner courtyard, which is flower-decked in summer.

Julien without rest, Korte Nieuwstraat 24 ☎ 0 3 229 06 00, *info@hotel-julien.com, Fax 0 3 233 35 70* – AE MC VISA. GY a
11 rm 160/250.
◆ An intimate hotel with a carriage entrance opening onto a tramlined street. Cosy interior decor blending classical, rustic and design features. Attractive modern bedrooms.

Villa Mozart, Handschoenmarkt 3 ☎ 0 3 231 30 31, *info@villamozart.be, Fax 0 3 231 56 85,* – AE MC VISA JCB FY e
Meals (pub rest). Lunch 15 – a la carte 23/43 – 13 – **25 rm** 99/148.
◆ Superbly located in the bustling heart of Antwerp between the Grand-Place and the cathedral (visible from some rooms), this small hotel is a pleasant and highly practical option. The brasserie is decorated in modern style.

Antigone without rest, Jordaenskaai 11 ☎ 0 3 231 66 77, *info@antigonehotel.be, Fax 0 3 231 37 74* – P. AE MC VISA JCB FY a
21 rm 75/95.
◆ A simple, but perfectly comfortable and adequate hotel housed in a bourgeois-style building near the Schelde River and Steen Museum. Individually decorated rooms.

't Fornuis (Segers), Reyndersstraat 24 ☎ 0 3 233 62 70, *Fax 0 3 233 99 03* – AE MC VISA. FZ c
closed August, 24 December-1 January, Saturday and Sunday – **Meals** (booking essential) a la carte 60/90
Spec. Salade de Saint-Jacques poêlées au foie d'oie. Sole farcie à la rhubarbe. Moelleux au chocolat et coulis d'oranges.
◆ This restaurant, occupying a fine 17C residence, offers an ambitious menu that is highly personalised and presented in theatrical fashion by the feisty chef ! Rustic decor.

Huis De Colvenier, St-Antoniusstraat 8 ☎ 0 3 226 65 73, *info@colvenier.be, Fax 0 3 227 13 14,* – P – 25 à 90. AE MC VISA FZ k
closed carnival week, August, Saturday lunch, Sunday and Monday – **Meals**. Lunch 50 – 60/100 b.i.
◆ This elegant 19C townhouse is embellished with attractive wall paintings, a charming winter garden and a cellar used for pre-dinner drinks. Attentive service.

Het Vijfde Seizoen - Hotel Hilton, Groenplaats 32 ☎ 0 3 204 12 12, *fb_antwerp@hilton.com, Fax 0 3 204 12 13* – . AE MC VISA FZ m
closed last week July-first 2 weeks August, Sunday and Monday – **Meals**. Lunch 38 – 45/95 b.i.
◆ This comfortable restaurant, popular with the business community, is part of a chain hotel. Refined decor and a resolutely traditional menu.

De Kerselaar (Michiels), Grote Pieter Potstraat 22 ☎ 0 3 233 59 69, *dekerselaar@pandora.be, Fax 0 3 233 11 49* – . AE MC VISA JCB FY n
closed last 2 weeks July, Sunday and lunch Monday and Saturday – **Meals**. Lunch 60 – 84 b.i., a la carte 55/83
Spec. Tartare de thon et crevettes à la tomate confite. Hamburger de saint-Pierre aux truffes et coulis de carottes. Pain d'épice façon pain perdu farci de figues et poires caramélisées.
◆ Food-lovers will feel pampered in this discreet house accessible via a small pedestrian street. Creative French cuisine, intimate atmosphere and stylish service.

XX **Neuze Neuze,** Wijngaardstraat 19 ☎ 0 3 232 27 97, *neuzeneuze@pandora.be, Fax 0 3 225 27 38* – AE ⓓ MC VISA JCB FY s
closed 2 weeks August, first week January, Sunday and lunch Wednesday and Saturday – **Meals**. *Lunch 25* – 50/75 b.i..
◆ An intimate setting where the clientele ranges from business people to romantic couples. Separate banqueting rooms. Copious cuisine and refined service.

XX **Orso D'oro - De Gulden Beer,** Grote Markt 14 ☎ 0 3 226 08 41, *Fax 0 3 232 52 09*, <, terrace, Italian cuisine – ▤. AE ⓓ MC VISA. ✻ FY v
Meals. *Lunch 25* – 37/85 b.i..
◆ This old house with its crow-step gables stands on the Grand-Place. Inviting Italian menu and pleasant views from the terrace and first floor.

XX **Het Nieuwe Palinghuis,** Sint-Jansvliet 14 ☎ 0 3 231 74 45, *hetnieuwepalinghuis@resto.be, Fax 0 3 231 50 53*, Seafood – ▤. AE ⓓ MC VISA. ✻ FZ e
closed June, 24 December-15 January, Monday and Tuesday – **Meals**. *Lunch 33* – 62/80 b.i..
◆ Fish and seafood take pride of place in this restaurant, whose walls are adorned with nostalgic images of old Antwerp. Good choice of affordable wines.

XX **'t Silveren Claverblat,** Grote Pieter Potstraat 16 ☎ 0 3 231 33 88, *Fax 0 3 231 31 46* – AE ⓓ MC VISA. ✻ FY k
closed 2 weeks August, Tuesday, Wednesday and lunch Monday and Saturday – **Meals**. *Lunch 35* – 60/70 b.i..
◆ A pleasant, small building in the old town. Its emblem, a silver four-leafed clover, is said to bring good luck. Classic à la carte choices based on quality ingredients.

XX **P'tit Vatelli,** Kammenstraat 75. ☎ 0 3 226 96 46, *Fax 0 3 226 96 46*, Open until 11 p.m. – ▤. AE ⓓ MC VISA JCB FZ r
closed last 2 weeks July, first week January, Sunday and Monday – **Meals**. *Lunch 22* – 30/70 b.i..
◆ A pleasantly arranged dining room and friendly ambience await guests behind the attractive façade dating from 1577. Classic dishes based on ingredients of the highest quality.

XX **La Rade** 1st floor, E. Van Dijckkaai 8 ☎ 0 3 233 37 37, *larade@skynet.be, Fax 0 3 233 49 63* – AE ⓓ MC VISA FY g
closed 7 to 13 February, 11 to 31 July, Saturday lunch, Sunday and Bank Holidays – **Meals**. *Lunch 38* – a la carte 39/55.
◆ An unusual restaurant housed in a bourgeois 19C residence. The main features of interest here are the masonic enthronement seat, mosaic dome and oriental room.

X **De Manie,** H. Conscienceplein 3 ☎ 0 3 232 64 38, *restaurant.demanie@pi.be, Fax 0 3 232 64 38*, terrace – AE ⓓ MC VISA GY u
closed carnival week, last 2 weeks August, Sunday lunch school holidays, Wednesday and Sunday dinner – **Meals**. *Lunch 25* – a la carte 46/62 ♀.
◆ On a pleasant square by the St-Charles-Borromée church, the De Manie's old façade is fronted by a summer terrace. Modern-rustic interior with mezzanine. Contemporary cuisine.

X **Dock's Café,** Jordaenskaai 7 ☎ 0 3 226 63 30, *info@docks.be, Fax 0 3 226 65 72*, terrace, Brasserie-Oyster bar, open until 11 p.m. – ▤. AE MC VISA. ✻ FY h
closed Saturday lunch – **Meals**. *Lunch 15* – 22/33 ♀.
◆ A sense of travel pervades this seafood bar-cum-brasserie with its futurist, ship-based décor. Dining room with mezzanine and neo-Baroque staircase. Reservation recommended.

X **De Reddende Engel,** Torfbrug 3 ☎ 0 3 233 66 30, *Fax 0 3 233 73 79*, terrace – AE ⓓ MC VISA JCB FY p
closed 17 and 18 April, 16 August-14 September, Tuesday, Wednesday and Saturday lunch – **Meals** – 24/39.
◆ A 17C house close to the cathedral is the setting for this friendly, rustic restaurant serving classic French cuisine with southern influence. Bouillabaisse a speciality.

X **Le Petit Zinc,** Veemarkt 9 ☎ 0 3 213 19 08, *Fax 0 3 213 19 08*, terrace, Bistro – AE MC VISA
closed 26 March-3 April, 15 to 31 August, Saturday, Sunday and Bank Holidays – **Meals**. *Lunch 20* – a la carte 45/66 ♀. FY b
◆ A convivial local bistro with closely packed small tables, slate menus featuring simple yet tasty dishes, and attentive service.

X **le Zoute Zoen,** Zirkstraat 17 ☎ 0 3 226 92 20, *Fax 0 3 231 01 30* – AE MC VISA. ✻
closed Monday and Saturday lunch – **Meals**. *Lunch 16* – 27/60 b.i.. FY c
◆ The menu in this cosy, intimate "gastro-bistro" offers unique value for money in Antwerp. A range of copious contemporary dishes served by efficient, friendly staff.

X **Hecker,** Kloosterstraat 13 ☎ 0 3 233 07 58, *info@hecker.be*, terrace – AE ⓓ MC VISA CU a
closed 15 to 30 August, Monday lunch and Wednesday – **Meals**. *Lunch 17* – a la carte 34/52.
◆ This modern bistro sharing its walls with an antiques shop offers a small menu which is both original and enticing. A good choice of wines from around the world.

Town Centre and Station

Astrid Park Plaza, Koningin Astridplein 7, 2018, 0 3 203 12 34, *Fax 0 3 203 12 51*, – 25-500. rest DEU e
Meals. *Lunch 20* – a la carte 21/42 – 20 – **225 rm** 150/450, – 3 suites.
• This four-star hotel, its original architectural design the work of Michael Graves, is on a busy square near the central railway station. Impeccable, spacious and well-appointed rooms and modern public areas. Bright restaurant serving contemporary recipes.

Radisson SAS Park Lane, Van Eycklei 34, 2018, 0 3 285 85 85, *Fax 0 3 285 85 00*, rest, – 25-600. rest DV y
Meals. *Lunch 30* – a la carte 36/62 – 23 – **160 rm** 137/195, – 14 suites.
• This luxury hotel is well-located on a main road away from the centre, opposite a public park. Full range of tailored facilities and services for its mainly business clientele. Small dining room serving classic international cuisine.

Hyllit without rest, De Keyserlei 28 (access by Appelmansstraat), 2018, 0 3 202 68 00, *info@hyllithotel.be, Fax 0 3 202 68 90*, – 25-150. DU q
17 – **122 rm** 100/196, – 4 suites.
• Intimate public areas, spacious bedrooms and junior suites, and a good view of Antwerp's rooftops from the bright breakfast room and two large terraces.

Alfa De Keyser without rest, De Keyserlei 66, 2018, 0 3 206 74 60, *info@dekeyserhotel.be, Fax 0 3 232 39 70*, – 25-120. DU t
20 – **120 rm** 145/170, – 3 suites.
• Easily accessible and advantageously located close to the railway station and a metro line. Cosy, modern bedrooms.

Plaza without rest, Charlottalei 49, 2018, 0 3 287 28 70, *book@plaza.be, Fax 0 3 287 28 71* – 25. DV k
80 rm 112/260.
• A warm, friendly atmosphere is the hallmark of this old-style hotel on the edge of the city centre. Large, elegant rooms, a grand English-style lobby and Victorian bar.

Carlton, Quinten Matsijslei 25, 2018, 0 3 231 15 15, *Fax 0 3 225 30 90* – 25-100. rest DU v
Meals *(closed 27 March-3 April, 26 December-8 January and Sunday)* (dinner only) 42/56 b.i. – **127 rm** 112/238, – 1 suite.
• A comfortable hotel near the diamond centre and a municipal park. Four guestroom categories with those on the higher floors offering pleasant views. Business centre. French cuisine tops the menu, in addition to a few Flemish-inspired dishes.

Astoria without rest, Korte Herentalsestraat 5, 2018, 0 3 227 31 30, *Fax 0 3 227 31 34*, DU r
closed 1 to 21 August and 24 December-8 January – **66 rm** 104/175.
• Although slightly away from the action, the Astoria has a reasonable location near the diamond district and Stadtspark. Granite lobby and façade, and well-appointed rooms.

Antverpia without rest, Sint-Jacobsmarkt 85 0 3 231 80 80, *antverpia@skynet.be, Fax 0 3 232 43 43* – DU f
closed 26 December-3 January – **18 rm** 99/125.
• A small, pleasant hotel with attractive, meticulously maintained rooms located between the railway station and the city's main shopping streets.

Alfa Empire without rest, Appelmansstraat 31, 2018, 0 3 203 54 00, *info@empirehotel.be, Fax 0 3 233 40 60* – DU s
70 rm 95/165.
• Nestled at the heart of the diamond district, the Alfa Empire offers 70 large rooms ensuring a good night's sleep. Interesting breakfast room decor.

Colombus without rest, Frankrijklei 4 0 3 233 03 90, *colombushotel@skynet.be, Fax 0 3 226 09 46*, – DU u
32 rm 68/118.
• Behind the hotel's classical façade are 32 rooms with good soundproofing and attractively decorated public areas. An excellent location just opposite the city's opera house.

Express by Holiday Inn without rest, Italiëlei 2a 0 3 221 49 49, *hotel@express-hiantwerpen.com, Fax 0 3 221 49 44* – 40. DT b
140 rm 74/115.
• This chain hotel was built in 2003 in the Dokken district, a former port area which has undergone considerable regeneration. Fresh, modern bedrooms with public areas to match.

Eden without rest, Lange Herentalsestraat 25, ✉ 2018, ℘ 0 3 233 06 08, *hotel.eden@skynet.be, Fax 0 3 233 12 28* – AE VISA JCB. DU k
66 rm 99/110.
◆ A basic, but well-maintained hotel with a prime location in the middle of the diamond district, close to the railway station. Identical, functional bedrooms.

De Barbarie, Van Breestraat 4, ✉ 2018, ℘ 0 3 232 81 98, *Fax 0 3 231 26 78,* – AE VISA JCB DV b
closed first week Easter holidays, 4 to 19 September, Saturday lunch, Sunday and Monday – **Meals**. Lunch 40 – a la carte 62/115.
◆ The creative menu here includes several duck specialities, accompanied by an attractive wine list. Fine collection of silver tableware. Outdoor restaurant.

La Luna, Italiëlei 177 ℘ 0 3 232 23 44, *info@laluna.be, Fax 0 3 232 24 41,* Multinational cuisines – dinner only. AE VISA DT p
closed 1 week Easter, last week July-first 2 weeks August, Christmas-New Year, Saturday lunch, Sunday and Monday – **Meals** – 33.
◆ The American brasserie-style atmosphere and cosmopolitan menu are popular with the city's upwardly mobile clientele. A refined, reasonably priced menu and excellent wine list.

HARMONY, Mechelsesteenweg 169, ✉ 2018, ℘ 0 3 239 70 05 – AE VISA DV n
closed 25 August-7 September, Wednesday and Saturday lunch – **Meals**. Lunch 23 – a la carte 44/58.
◆ The contemporary cuisine on offer here is in harmony with the decor of modern filtered lighting, fluted pilasters, lattice-work chairs and plain table setting.

Gran Duca 6th floor, De Keyserlei 28, ✉ 2018, ℘ 0 3 202 68 87, *granduca@pandora.be, Fax 0 3 225 51 99,* – AE VISA DU q
closed Saturday lunch and Sunday – **Meals**. Lunch 25 – a la carte 33/60.
◆ The extensive glass frontage of this Italian restaurant above the Hyllit Hotel opens onto three panoramic terraces. Bright, spacious dining room furnished with rattan chairs.

Dôme, Grote Hondstraat 2, ✉ 2018, ℘ 0 3 239 90 03, *info@domeweb.be, Fax 0 3 239 93 90* – AE VISA EV z
closed 24 December-5 January, Monday and lunch Tuesday and Saturday – **Meals**. Lunch 28 – a la carte 51/70.
◆ Fine inventive cuisine served under the impressive dome in this 19C Baroque house which was once a chic café. Faultless service and excellent sommelier. Ring bell for access.

't Peerd, Paardenmarkt 53 ℘ 0 3 231 98 25, *resto_t_peerd@yahoo.com, Fax 0 3 231 59 40,* – AE VISA GY e
closed 2 weeks Easter, Tuesday and Wednesday – **Meals**. Lunch 38 – a la carte 39/77.
◆ This characterful small restaurant is embellished in equestrian decor, providing a hint of the house specialities. Studied wine list, attentive service and local ambience.

O'Kontreir, Isabellalei 145, ✉ 2018, ℘ 0 3 281 39 76, *info@okontreir.com, Fax 0 3 237 92 06* – VISA. DV c
closed last week July-first week August, late December, Monday, Tuesday and lunch Saturday and Sunday – **Meals** 45/60 b.i..
◆ The O'Kontrier serves creative, contemporary and well-presented dishes in a distinctly modern setting in the city's Jewish quarter. Japanese tableware and background music.

Pazzo, Oude Leeuwenrui 12 ℘ 0 3 232 86 82, *pazzo@skynet.be, Fax 0 3 232 79 34,* Open until 11 p.m. – AE VISA DT a
closed 25 July-15 August, Christmas, New Year, Saturday, Sunday and Bank Holidays – **Meals**. Lunch 19 – a la carte 26/51.
◆ A lively restaurant occupying a former warehouse converted into a modern brasserie, where the emphasis is on contemporary dishes and wines chosen to complement the cuisine.

Yamayu Santatsu, Ossenmarkt 19 ℘ 0 3 234 09 49, *Fax 0 3 234 09 49,* Japanese cuisine with Sushi-bar – AE VISA JCB DTU b
closed first 2 weeks August, Sunday lunch and Monday – **Meals**. Lunch 12 – a la carte 34/72.
◆ This compact and constantly reliable Japanese restaurant and sushi bar is well known to aficionados of Asian cuisine. Quality products and an extensive menu choice.

North Quartier (Docks)

Novotel, Luithagen-haven 6 (Haven 200), ✉ 2030, ℘ 0 3 542 03 20, *H0465@accor.com, Fax 0 3 541 70 93,* – ch, – 25-180. AE VISA. rest
Meals a la carte 25/40 – 14 – **120 rm** 61/107.
◆ This mid-range chain hotel is situated to the northeast of the port area, close to a motorway junction and along a road that links it directly with the city centre.

Het Pomphuis, Siberiastraat, ✉ 2030, ☎ 0 3 770 86 25, *info@hetpomphuis.be, Fax 0 3 770 86 10*, <, Open until 11 p.m. – P – 25-200. AE MC VISA.
Meals. Lunch 25 – a la carte 24/65 ♀.
• This spacious, luxurious brasserie is housed in a huge early-20C redbrick former port building with three impressive bilge pumps on display inside.

South Quarter

Crowne Plaza, G. Legrellelaan 10, ✉ 2020, ☎ 0 3 259 75 00, *cpantwerp@ichotelsgroup.com, Fax 0 3 216 02 96*, – rest, P – 25-600. AE MC VISA JCB. rest
Meals ***Plaza One for two*** Lunch 28 – a la carte 34/47 – 21 – **256 rm** 114/245, – 6 suites.
• This international hotel close to a motorway exit offers pleasantly decorated, well-appointed rooms with a contemporary feel. Good conference facilities and 24-hour service. Lively lounge bar, plus a restaurant refurbished in 2004.

Corinthia, Desguinlei 94, ✉ 2018, ☎ 0 3 244 82 11, *Fax 0 3 216 47 12*, – rest, P – 25-590. AE MC VISA. rest DX z
Meals *(closed Sunday)* (open until midnight) a la carte 27/43 – 20 – **208 rm** 109/209, – 5 suites.
• This glass-fronted hotel is located close to the city's ring road with links to the Brussels motorway and historical centre. Sleek and spacious foyer, bright and spacious bedrooms, plus a contemporary-style dining room with appealing à la carte/menu options.

Firean, Karel Oomsstraat 6, ✉ 2018, ☎ 0 3 237 02 60, *info@hotelfirean.com, Fax 0 3 238 11 68* – . AE MC VISA JCB DX n
closed 23 July-16 August and 24 December-9 January – **Meals** see ***Minerva*** below – **15 rm** 131/163.
• A charming, quiet hotel with a patio occupying an Art Deco-style residence close to the Koning Albert Park. Rooms decorated with stylish antique furniture. Attentive service.

Industrie without rest, Emiel Banningstraat 52 ☎ 0 3 238 66 00, *hotelindustrie@telenet.be, Fax 0 3 238 86 88* – . AE MC VISA. CV a
12 **rm** 60/87.
• A well-maintained small hotel occupying two mansions close to two of the city's best museums. Compact but well-appointed rooms with a touch of individuality.

Minerva - Hotel Firean, Karel Oomsstraat 36, ✉ 2018, ☎ 0 3 216 00 55, *restaurantminerva@skynet.be, Fax 0 3 216 00 55* – . AE MC VISA JCB DX e
closed 25 July-16 August, 24 December-10 January, Sunday and Monday – **Meals** – a la carte 50/94.
• This modern, elegant restaurant has replaced the former garage that once stood here. Enticing traditional cuisine and seasonal suggestions. Easy parking in the evening.

Loncin, Markgravelei 127, ✉ 2018, ☎ 0 3 248 29 89, *info@loncinrestaurant.be, Fax 0 3 248 38 66*, – P. AE MC VISA DX d
closed Saturday lunch and Sunday – **Meals**. Lunch 35 – 50/95 b.i..
• A soberly elegant bourgeois restaurant serving a classic choice of quality dishes. Wine list featuring prestigious names, fine vintages and a good choice of half-bottles.

Liang's Garden, Markgravelei 141, ✉ 2018, ☎ 0 3 237 22 22, *Fax 0 3 248 38 34*, Chinese cuisine – . AE MC VISA DX d
closed mid July-mid August and Sunday – **Meals**. Lunch 24 – a la carte 26/37.
• This attractive mansion houses one of Antwerp's oldest Chinese restaurants. A bourgeois setting with a few Asian touches. Menu featuring Peking duck specialities.

Kommilfoo, Vlaamse Kaai 17 ☎ 0 3 237 30 00, *kommilfoo@resto.be, Fax 0 3 237 30 00* – . AE MC VISA. CV e
closed first 2 weeks July, Sunday and Monday – **Meals**. Lunch 30 – 40/65 b.i..
• Located opposite a large, free car park a stone's throw from three museums, this former warehouse is sober yet modern in design, with a menu that is equally contemporary.

Radis Noir, Desguinlei 186, ✉ 2018, ☎ 0 3 238 37 70, *Fax 0 3 238 39 07*. AE MC VISA. DX x
closed 1 week before carnival, first 2 weeks August, Saturday, Sunday and Bank Holidays – **Meals** carte 47/58.
• This bourgeois house on a busy street near the new Palais de Justice has been transformed into a restaurant with designer-influenced decor. Concise yet regularly updated menu.

Suburbs

at Berchem 🄲 *Antwerpen – ✉ 2600 Berchem :*

XXX **De Tafeljoncker,** Frederik de Merodestraat 13 ✆ 0 3 281 20 34, *restaurant.de-tafeljoncker@pandora.be, Fax 0 3 281 20 34,* – AE ⓓ ⓜ VISA DX f
closed 23 February-13 March, 31 August-11 September, Sunday dinner, Monday and Tuesday – **Meals**. *Lunch 50* – 63/90 b.i..
◆ This cosy restaurant occupying a bourgeois mansion offers guests two menus from which dishes can be ordered separately. Elegant table settings.

XX **Brasserie Marly,** Generaal Lemanstraat 64 ✆ 0 3 281 23 23, *info@marly.be, Fax 0 3 281 33 10* – P. AE ⓓ ⓜ VISA. DX c
closed 17 July-15 August, Saturday and Sunday – **Meals** 25 b.i./53 b.i. ♀.
◆ A welcoming brasserie located on the fringes of the city. Imaginative choices in which fish, oysters and Bresse poultry take centre-stage. Efficient valet parking.

XX **De Troubadour,** Driekoningenstraat 72 ✆ 0 3 239 39 16, *info@detroubadour.be, Fax 0 3 230 82 71* – P. AE ⓓ ⓜ VISA DX a
closed last 3 weeks August, Sunday and Monday – **Meals**. *Lunch 25* – 33 ♀.
◆ Intelligently composed menus are a strongpoint of this pleasantly modern restaurant where the charismatic owner ensures a warm and friendly atmosphere.

at Borgerhout *East : 3 km* 🄲 *Antwerpen – ✉ 2140 Borgerhout :*

Scandic, Luitenant Lippenslaan 66 ✆ 0 3 235 91 91, *info-antwerp@scandic-hotels.com, Fax 0 3 235 08 96,* – P. – 25-230. AE ⓓ ⓜ VISA JCB. rest
Meals *(closed lunch Saturday, Sunday and Bank Holidays). Lunch 20* – a la carte 27/40 ♀ – **200 rm** 92/257, – 4 suites.
◆ A renovated chain hotel with a good location along the ring road, close to Borgerhout railway station, the Sterchshof Museum (Zilvercentrum) and a golf course. Business centre. Modern brasserie with an equally contemporary menu and attractive teak terrace.

at Deurne *Northeast : 3 km* 🄲 *Antwerpen – ✉ 2100 Deurne :*

XX **De Violin,** Bosuil 1 ✆ 0 3 324 34 04, *deviolin@pandora.be, Fax 0 3 326 33 20,* – P. – 30. AE ⓓ ⓜ VISA.
closed Sunday and Monday dinner – **Meals**. *Lunch 41 b.i.* – a la carte 49/62.
◆ A charming restaurant occupying a small farm with painted shutters. Classic cuisine plus daily specials explained in person. Delightful Asia-inspired terrace in summer.

at Ekeren *North : 11 km* 🄲 *Antwerpen – ✉ 2180 Ekeren :*

X **De Mangerie,** Kapelsesteenweg 471 ✆ 0 3 605 26 26, *Fax 0 3 605 24 16,* – P. AE ⓓ ⓜ VISA
closed Saturday lunch – **Meals** – 29 ♀.
◆ An attractive, "Louisiana"-style façade, a maritime-inspired interior design and a choice of traditional and seasonal dishes. Mezzanine and terraces.

Environs

at Aartselaar *South : 10 km – pop. 14 253 – ✉ 2630 Aartselaar :*

Kasteel Solhof without rest, Baron Van Ertbornstraat 116 ✆ 0 3 877 30 00, *info@solhof.be, Fax 0 3 877 31 31,* – P. – 25-50. AE ⓜ VISA.
closed Christmas-New Year – 20 – **24 rm** 159/245.
◆ This impressive mansion surrounded by water and greenery south of Antwerp has a number of outbuildings and a terrace overlooking a public park. Quiet, well-appointed rooms.

at Boechout *Southeast : 9 km – pop. 11 947 – ✉ 2530 Boechout :*

XXX **De Schone van Boskoop** (Keersmaekers), Appelkantstraat 10 ✆ 0 3 454 19 31, *deschonevanboskoop@skynet.be, Fax 0 3 454 02 10,* – P. AE ⓓ ⓜ VISA JCB.
closed Easter week, last 3 weeks August, Christmas-New Year, Sunday and Monday – **Meals**. *Lunch 45* – 108 b.i., a la carte 80/145 ♀
Spec. Composition de thon et langoustine au foie d'oie et truffe. Cabillaud au chou et tempura de crabe. Quatre préparations à base de chocolat blanc et noir.
◆ A pleasant restaurant with an artistic and contemporary interior. Personalised menu with numerous daily specials. Lake and statue-adorned terrace.

X **l'Étoile,** Binnensteenweg 187 ✆ 0 3 454 53 23, *info@letoile.be, Fax 0 3 454 53 33,* Open until 11 p.m. – P. AE ⓓ ⓜ VISA.
Meals. *Lunch 18* – a la carte 31/49 ♀.
◆ This smart, trendy restaurant is further embellished by a large veranda, mezzanine and pleasant summer terrace. Relaxed yet dynamic service.

at Edegem *Southeast : 5 km – pop. 21 955 – ✉ 2650 Edegem :*

Ter Elst, Terelststraat 310 (by Prins Boudewijnlaan) ☎ 0 3 450 90 00, *info@terelst.be, Fax 0 3 450 90 90,* – 25-500.

Meals ***Couvert Classique*** *(closed 3 July-12 August and Sunday) Lunch 33* – 33/72 b.i. – **53 rm** 90/110.

◆ In a slightly isolated location to the south of Antwerp, the Ter Elst is a hotel of recent design linked to a sports centre. Modern auditorium and large, simply furnished rooms. Neo-rustic-style dining room serving traditional fare. Attractive wine list.

La Cabane (Vandersteen), Mechelsesteenweg 11 ☎ 0 3 454 58 98, *restaurantlacabane@skynet.be, Fax 0 3 455 34 26* –

closed 1 week Easter, mid July-mid August, first week January, Saturday lunch, Sunday and Monday – **Meals**. *Lunch 35* – 46/90 b.i., – a la carte 48/79 ♀

Spec. Risotto aux champignons des bois (21 September-21 December). Ris de veau braisé aux carottes et à la bière régionale. Riz condé de saison.

◆ Modern interior décor, refined cuisine flirting with modern trends, a lunch menu with good choice and a well-stocked cellar. An upmarket address, despite the name ! .

at Kapellen *North : 15,5 km – pop. 25 813 – ✉ 2950 Kapellen :*

De Bellefleur (Buytaert), Antwerpsesteenweg 253 ☎ 0 3 664 67 19, *Fax 0 3 665 02 01,* –

closed July, Saturday lunch and Sunday – **Meals**. *Lunch 55 b.i.* – 90/110 b.i., – a la carte 103/216 ♀

Spec. Navarin de sole aux chanterelles, cèpes et truffes. Selle de chevreuil rôtie, jus de gibier léger et jeunes légumes (August-March). Grouse d'Écosse et gratin de figues, son jus au pur malt (September-December).

◆ This high-quality restaurant serves traditional cuisine prepared with a modern flourish. In summer, dine on the pretty veranda, surrounded by a flower-filled garden.

at Schoten *Northeast : 10 km – pop. 33 125 – ✉ 2900 Schoten :*

Kleine Barreel, Bredabaan 1147 ☎ 0 3 645 85 84, *info@kleine-barreel.be, Fax 0 3 645 85 03* – 25-60.

Meals. *Lunch 33* – 40/64 b.i. ♀.

◆ Known to everyone in the city, the Kleine Barreel offers its customers a traditional menu which is updated monthly. Comfortable dining room with "club" chairs.

Uilenspiegel, Brechtsebaan 277 (3 km on N 115) ☎ 0 3 651 61 45, *Fax 0 3 652 08 08,* – 25.

closed 31 January-10 February, 11 to 28 July, Tuesday and Wednesday – **Meals**. *Lunch 20* – 30/45 ♀.

◆ Slate has now replaced the original thatch roof. Two dining rooms, one a veranda overlooking a pretty garden used in the summer for outdoor dining.

at Wijnegem *East : 10 km – pop. 8 819 – ✉ 2110 Wijnegem :*

Ter Vennen, Merksemsebaan 278 ☎ 0 3 326 20 60, *tervennen@skynet.be, Fax 0 3 326 38 47,* – 50.

Meals – 35/59 b.i..

◆ A classic address in a small farm nestled beneath tall trees. Well-balanced, multi-choice menu, wine cellar which can be visited upon request, plus an attractive teak terrace.

Kruiningen *Zeeland (Netherlands) Reimerswaal – pop. 20 839* 532 J 14 *and* 715 D 7.

Antwerpen 56 km.

Le Manoir, Zandweg 2 (West : 1 km), ✉ 4416 NA, ☎ (0 113) 38 17 53, *info@interscaldes.nl, Fax (0 113) 38 17 63,*

closed 1 week October and first 2 weeks January – **Meals** see ***Inter Scaldes*** below – 21 – **10 rm** 195/340, – 2 suites.

◆ This large, thatch-roofed villa stands on a polder dotted with lovingly-maintained orchards, hedges, rose gardens and fruit trees. Ten comfortable rooms.

Inter Scaldes (Brevet) - Hotel Le Manoir, Zandweg 2 (West : 1 km), ✉ 4416 NA, ☎ (0 113) 38 17 53, *info@interscaldes.nl, Fax (0 113) 38 17 63,*

closed 1 week October, first 2 weeks January, Monday, Tuesday and Saturday lunch – **Meals**. *Lunch 79* – 181 b.i., a la carte 97/157 ♀

Spec. Bar de ligne au laurier, sauce au verjus. Saint-Jacques lutées à la truffe. Soufflé au fromage blanc, citron et à la vanille.

◆ Following a serious fire, this chic restaurant renowned for its culinary flair has risen like a phoenix from the ashes. Delightful terrace-veranda and English garden.

BELGIUM

BRUGES (BRUGGE) *8000 West-Vlaanderen* 533 E 15 *and* 716 C 2 *– pop. 116 680.*

See : *Procession of the Holy Blood★★★ (De Heilig Bloedprocessie) – Historic centre and canals★★★ (Historisch centrum en grachten) – Market Square★★ (Markt)* AU*, Belfry and Halles★★★ (Belfort en Hallen) ≤★★ from the top* AU *– Market-town★★ (Burg)* AU *– Basilica of the Holy Blood★ (Basiliek van het Heilig Bloed) : low Chapel★ or St. Basiles Chapel (beneden- of Basiliuskapel)* AU **B** *– Chimney of the "Brugse Vrije"★ in the Palace of the "Brugse Vrije"* AU **S** *– Rosery quay (Rozenhoedkaai) ≤★★* AU **63** *– Dijver ≤★★* AU *– St. Boniface bridge (Bonifatiusbrug) : site★★* AU *– Beguinage★★ (Begijnhof)* AV *– Trips on the canals★★★ (Boottocht)* AU *– Church of Our Lady★ (O.-L.-Vrouwekerk) : tower★★, statue of the Madonna★★, tombstone★★ of Mary of Burgundy★★* AV **N.**

Museums : Groeninge★★★ (Stedelijk Museum voor Schone Kunsten) AU *– Memling★★★ (St. John's Hospital)* AV *– Gruuthuse★ : bust of Charles the Fifth★ (borstbeeld van Karel V)* AU **M¹** *– Arentshuis★* AU **M⁴** *– Folklore★ (Museum voor Volkskunde)* DY **M².**

Envir : *Southwest : 10,5 km at Zedelgem : baptismal font★ in the St. Lawrence's church – Northeast : 7 km : Damme★.*

Northeast : 7 km at Sijsele, Doornstraat 16 ☎ 0 50 35 89 25, Fax 0 50 35 89 25.

Burg 11 ☎ 0 50 44 86 86, toerisme@brugge.be, Fax 0 50 44 86 00 and at railway station, Stationsplein – Tourist association of the province, Koning Albert I-laan 120, ☎ 0 50 30 55 00, info@westtoer.be, Fax 0 50 30 55 90.

Brussels 96 – Ghent 45 – Lille 72 – Ostend 28.

Plans on following pages

Town Centre

Crowne Plaza, Burg 10 ☎ 0 50 44 68 44, *hotel@crowne-plaza-brugge.com, Fax 0 50 44 68 68*, ≤, ch, – 25-400. AE VISA JCB. AU a
Meals ***Het Kapittel*** *(closed Wednesday dinner, Saturday lunch and Sunday)* *Lunch 21* – 32/70 b.i. – ***De Linde*** *Lunch 9* – 22/32 b.i. – 21 – **93 rm** 232/276, – 3 suites.
◆ The Crowne Plaza offers a quiet base and high levels of comfort on Burg Square. The basement contains important vestiges and objects from medieval times. Gastronomic fare in the 't Kapittel restaurant. The De Linde doubles as a buffet-lunch venue and tea room.

de tuilerieën without rest, Dijver 7 ☎ 0 50 34 36 91, *info@hoteltuilerieen.com, Fax 0 50 34 04 00*, ≤, – 25-45. AE VISA JCB AU c
24 – **43 rm** 125/399, – 2 suites.
◆ The noble façade of this elegant hotel fronts one of the city's most picturesque canals. Cosy blend of modern-classic interior decor, spruce bedrooms and an attractive pool.

Relais Oud Huis Amsterdam without rest, Spiegelrei 3 ☎ 0 50 34 18 10, *info@oha.be, Fax 0 50 33 88 91*, ≤, – 25. AE VISA AT d
20 – **32 rm** 198/238, – 2 suites.
◆ This former 17C Dutch trading centre along the banks of a canal has been transformed into a charming hotel with rooms offering pleasant views. Locked garage 300m/330yd away.

de orangerie without rest, Kartuizerinnenstraat 10 ☎ 0 50 34 16 49, *info@hotelorangerie.com, Fax 0 50 33 30 16* – AE VISA JCB AU e
19 – **19 rm** 170/350, – 1 suite.
◆ A quiet hotel in an old house bordering a delightful canal overlooked by four of the hotel's rooms. Period furniture, plus a charming patio and terrace by the water's edge.

Die Swaene, Steenhouwersdijk 1 ☎ 0 50 34 27 98, *info@dieswaene.com, Fax 0 50 33 66 74*, ≤, – rm, – 30. AE VISA JCB AU p
Meals ***Storie*** *(closed 2 weeks July, 2 weeks January, Wednesday and Thursday lunch)* *Lunch 40* – 54/99 b.i. – 15 – **30 rm** 160/295, – 2 suites.
◆ A peaceful hotel full of character and period furniture with views of one of the city's canals. The guest bedrooms, romantic to a fault, are all individually furnished. Intimate gastronomic restaurant offering classic dishes with a modern twist.

Sofitel, Boeveriestraat 2 ☎ 0 50 44 97 11, *H1278@accor.com*, Fax 0 50 44 97 99, – 25-150. AE VISA CZ b
Meals ***Ter Boeverie*** *Lunch 31 b.i.* – 40 b.i./59 b.i. – 19 – **149 rm** 225.
◆ This attractive, centrally located hotel overlooks a large square. Spacious, pleasantly refurbished rooms furnished in a variety of styles. The restaurant's repertoire is extensive, covering standard fare, traditional dishes and a choice of vegetarian options.

Acacia without rest, Korte Zilverstraat 3a ☎ 0 50 34 44 11, *info@hotel-acacia.com, Fax 0 50 33 88 17*, – 25-40. AE VISA JCB.
closed 3 to 21 January – **46 rm** 120/190, – 2 suites. AU n
◆ Within a few yards of the Grand-Place, the Acacia is characterised by its impeccable appearance and the elegance of its furnishings. Spacious rooms, some split-level.

de' Medici, Potterierei 15, 0 50 33 98 33, *reservation@hoteldemedici.com, Fax 0 50 33 07 64*, ch, – 25-180. AE VISA JCB. CX g
Meals see ***Koto*** below – **81 rm** 174/209.
• A modern construction built away from the centre, facing a canal. A contemporary interior, with large, well-appointed rooms. Small Japanese garden.

Oud Huis de Peellaert without rest, Hoogstraat 20, 0 50 33 78 89, *info@depeellaert.be, Fax 0 50 33 08 16*, – 30. AE VISA JCB. ATU a
50 rm 115/275.
• This former town house close to the Grand'Place has been elegantly refurbished, with spacious traditional guestrooms offering the full range of modern comforts.

Relais Ravestein, Molenmeers 11, 0 50 47 69 47, *info@relaisravestein.be, Fax 0 50 47 69 48*, lunch only – 35. AE VISA. DY b
Meals. Lunch 27 – a la carte 39/170 – 20 – **15 rm** 175/275.
• This fine old residence was once the home of the descendants of Adolphe de Clèves, nephew of Philippe Le Bon. The restaurant's harmonious interior design enhances the house's former character. Modern restaurant with an attractive waterfront terrace.

Jan Brito without rest, Freren Fonteinstraat 1, 0 50 33 06 01, *info@janbrito.com, Fax 0 50 33 06 52*, – 25-40. AE VISA JCB AU j
23 rm 110/235, – 3 suites.
• Behind the hotel's typical façade are two floors - the larger, more luxurious rooms are on the first, the more modern, compact ones on the second. 16C-18C interior decor.

Pandhotel without rest, Pandreitje 16, 0 50 34 06 66, *info@pandhotel.com, Fax 0 50 34 05 56* – AE VISA JCB AU q
15 – **24 rm** 125/225.
• An elegant hotel, spread out over three houses with character in the city centre. The hotel's rooms and junior suites have all been furnished with a keen, aesthetic eye.

Heritage without rest, N. Desparsstraat 11, 0 50 44 44 44, *info@hotel-heritage.com, Fax 0 50 44 44 40*, – AE VISA JCB.
15 – **24 rm** 150/227. AT k
• This majestic 19C residence between the Grand-Place and the theatre is now a comfortable hotel with a hushed ambience. Attractive 14C cellar with fitness facilities.

Walburg without rest, Boomgaardstraat 13, 0 50 34 94 14, *info@hotelwalburg.be, Fax 0 50 33 68 84* – 30. AE VISA JCB. AT f
closed 3 January-3 February – **12 rm** 130/200, – 1 suite.
• Imposing neo-Classical architecture, with an old entrance leading to a monumental hall with two lofty galleries adorned with columns and balustrades. "King-size" rooms.

Novotel Centrum, Katelijnestraat 65b, 0 50 33 75 33, *H1033@accor.com, Fax 0 50 33 65 56*, – 50-400. AE VISA JCB. rest
Meals a la carte 25/38 – 14 – **126 rm** 100/140. AV h
• A modern chain hotel near the Beguine convent and Memling Museum. Recently refurbished standard rooms with good soundproofing. Pleasant lobby-bar. The restaurant offers a full menu for dinner, with a much-restricted choice at lunchtime.

Prinsenhof without rest, Ontvangersstraat 9, 0 50 34 26 90, *info@prinsenhof.com, Fax 0 50 34 23 21* – AE VISA JCB CY s
15 – **16 rm** 140/295.
• This small, refined and welcoming hotel occupies a renovated mansion away from the busy centre. Rooms of differing styles characterised by their cosy feel.

De Castillion (annex Het Gheestelic Hof - 14 rm), Heilige Geeststraat 1, 0 50 34 30 01, *info@castillion.be, Fax 0 50 33 94 75*, – rm, – 25-50. AE VISA JCB.
rest AU r
Meals *le Manoir Quatre Saisons* *(closed 24 July-12 August and Sunday dinner and lunch Monday and Tuesday except Bank Holidays)* Lunch 35 – 49/87 b.i. – **20 rm** 100/215.
• The former bishop's palace (1743) is now home to this quite charming hotel with crow-step gables, personalised rooms, an Art Deco lounge and an attractive inner courtyard. Modern dining room, furnished in Louis XVI style.

Montanus without rest, Nieuwe Gentweg 78, 0 50 33 11 76, *info@montanus.be, Fax 0 50 34 09 38*, – 40. AE VISA AV e
24 rm 120/180.
• A charming hotel occupying a mansion tucked away from the main sights of interest. Half of the stylish rooms overlook the garden and English-style pavilion.

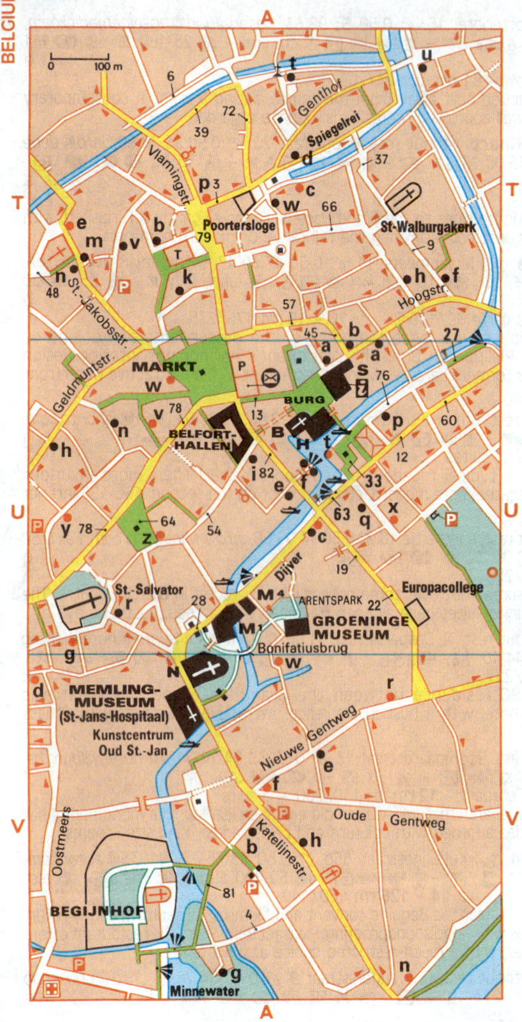

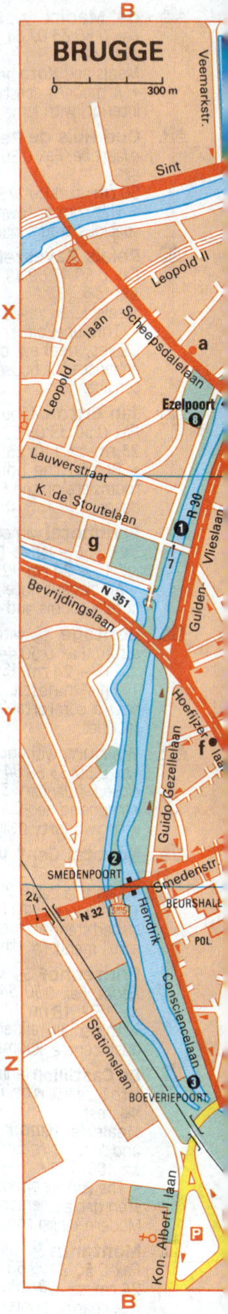

Academiestr.	AT 3	Moerstr.	CY, AT 48
Arsenaalstr.	AV 4	Noordzandstr.	CY 49
Augustijnenrei	AT 6	Noorweegsekaai	DX 51
Bloedput	BY 7	Oude Burg	AU 54
Boomgaardstr.	AT 9	Philipstockstr.	AT 57
Braambergstr.	AU 12	Predikherenstr.	AU 60
Breidelstr.	AU 13	Rolweg	DX 61
Eekhoutstr.	AU 19	Rozenhoedkaai	AU 63
Garenmarkt	AU 22	Simon Stevinpl.	AU 64
Geldmunstr.	AU	Sint-Jansstr.	AT 66
Gistelse Steenweg	BZ 24	Spanjaardstr.	AT 72
Gloribusstr.	CZ 25	Steenhouwersdijk	AU 76
Groene Rei	ATU 27	Steenstr.	AU 78
Gruuthusestr.	AU 28	Vlamingstr.	AT 79
Huidenvetterspl.	AU 33	Wijngaardstr.	AV 81
Koningstr.	AT 37	Wollestr.	AU 82
Kortewinkel	AT 39	Zuidzandstr.	CY 84
Maalse Steenweg	DY 43	Zwarte Leertouwersstr.	DY 85
Mallebergpl	ATU 45		

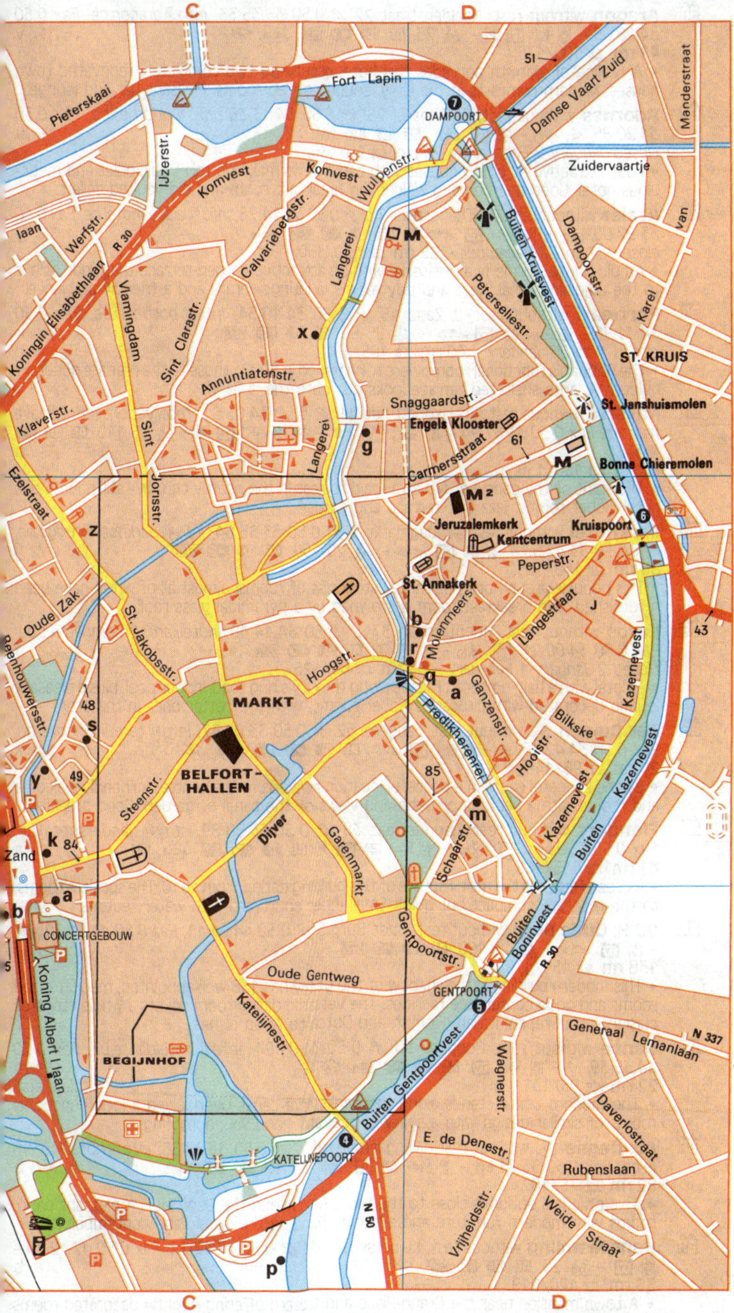
C
D
X
Y
Z
Pieterskaai
Fort Lapin
DAMPOORT
Damse Vaart Zuid
Manderstraat
Zuidervaartje
IJzerstr.
Komvest
Wulpenstr.
Langerei
Calvariebergstr.
Werfstr.
R 30
Koningin Elisabethlaan
Vlamingdam
Sint Clarastr.
Annuntiatenstr.
Buiten Kruisvest
Peterseliestr.
Dampoortstr.
Karel
van
ST. KRUIS
St. Janshuismolen
Snaggaardstr.
Engels Klooster
Carmersstraat
Bonne Chieremolen
Klaverstr.
Sint
Jorisstr.
Ezelstraat
Jeruzalemkerk
Kantcentrum
Kruispoort
Peperstr.
St. Annakerk
Oude Zak
St. Jakobsstr.
Molenmeers
Langestraat
Hoogstr.
MARKT
Ganzenstr.
Kazernevest
Bilkske
Predikherenrei
Hooistr.
BELFORT-HALLEN
Steenstr.
Dijver
Garenmarkt
Schaarstr.
Buiten Kazernevest
Zand
CONCERTGEBOUW
Gentpoortstr.
Buiten Boninvest
Koning Albert I laan
Oude Gentweg
GENTPOORT
Katelijnestr.
Generaal Lemanlaan
N 337
BEGIJNHOF
Buiten Gentpoortvest
Wagnerstr.
Daverlostraat
KATELIJNEPOORT
E. de Denestr.
Rubenslaan
Weide Straat
N 50
Vrijheidsstr.

Aragon without rest, Naaldenstraat 22 ✆ 0 50 33 35 33, *info@aragon.be, Fax 0 50 34 28 05* – AE VISA JCB. AT v
42 rm 100/175.
◆ A feeling of warmth pervades this hotel occupying two completely renovated town houses. Modern comforts in the cosy, soundproofed rooms. Pleasant bar and lounge.

Adornes without rest, St-Annarei 26 ✆ 0 50 34 13 36, *info@adornes.be, Fax 0 50 34 20 85*, – AE VISA AT u
closed January-8 February – **20 rm** 90/130.
◆ Four attractive adjoining houses with canal views make up this small, quiet and meticulous hotel. Good bedrooms, a welcoming breakfast room and old vaulted cellars.

Azalea without rest, Wulfhagestraat 43 ✆ 0 50 33 14 78, *info@azaleahotel.be, Fax 0 50 33 97 00*, – AE VISA JCB CY y
closed 22 to 27 December – **25 rm** 120/160.
◆ An old house, formerly a brasserie, with an attractive garden-terrace that adds colour to the adjoining canal. Neat and tidy rooms, a lounge-library and a friendly ambience.

Portinari without rest, 't Zand 15 ✆ 0 50 34 10 34, *info@portinari.be, Fax 0 50 34 41 80* – 25-80. AE VISA CY k
closed 1 to 26 January – **40 rm** 105/150.
◆ The Potinari's functional rooms were refurbished in 2002 ; those to the rear are generally quieter. A large sheltered terrace looks out onto the 't Zand.

Navarra without rest, St-Jakobsstraat 41 ✆ 0 50 34 05 61, *reservations@hotelnavarra.com, Fax 0 50 33 67 90*, – 25-110. AE VISA. AT n
87 rm 130/158.
◆ The spirit of the consul of Navarra - laid to rest in the nearby church - still haunts this hotel. Sober rooms, jazz bar, terrace and garden.

Parkhotel without rest, Vrijdagmarkt 5 ✆ 0 50 33 33 64, *info@parkhotelbrugge.be, Fax 0 50 33 47 63* – – 25-250. AE VISA CY j
86 rm 110/125.
◆ This popular group hotel has three categories of rooms, almost all of which have been refurbished. The breakfast room is crowned by a pyramidal glass roof.

Karos without rest, Hoefijzerlaan 37 ✆ 0 50 34 14 48, *hotelkaros@compaqnet.be, Fax 0 50 34 00 91*, – AE VISA BY f
closed 2 January-1 February – **58 rm** 65/125.
◆ A hotel with a half-timbered façade along the city's ring road. Indoor pool, plus a pleasant lounge decorated with birdcages. Sober rooms, with the better ones in the attic.

Ter Duinen without rest, Langerei 52 ✆ 0 50 33 04 37, *info@terduinenhotel.be, Fax 0 50 34 42 16*, – AE VISA JCB. CX x
20 rm 98/149.
◆ By the Langerei canal, in a peaceful location away from the centre. A friendly welcome and rooms with a veranda or patio and views of the canal or garden. Good breakfast.

Flanders without rest, Langestraat 38 ✆ 0 50 33 88 89, *stay@flandershotel.be, Fax 0 50 33 93 45*, – AE VISA JCB. DY a
41 rm 115/165.
◆ A green façade is the main feature of this building dating from 1910. The spotless rooms, to the rear, are compact but quiet. Small inner courtyard with water feature.

Gd H. Oude Burg without rest, Oude Burg 5 ✆ 0 50 44 51 11, *Fax 0 50 44 51 00*, – – 25-160. AE VISA AU i
138 rm 150/170.
◆ This modern building in the shadow of the belfry has 138 well-appointed, medium-sized rooms and good conference facilities. The versatile dining room covers a whole range of cuisine from French, Italian, Flemish and Dutch to Asian dishes.

Dante without rest, Coupure 30 ✆ 0 50 34 01 94, *info@hoteldante.be, Fax 0 50 34 35 39*, – AE VISA. DY m
22 rm 93/131.
◆ The modern Dante stands along the banks of a canal, overlooking a lock. Functional rooms of similar design with a spacious feel and good soundproofing.

Academie without rest, Wijngaardstraat 7 ✆ 0 50 33 22 66, *info@hotelacademie.be, Fax 0 50 33 21 66* – AE VISA AV b
82 rm 75/162.
◆ This practical option is close to the Lac d'Amour and the Begijnhof. A pleasant patio, rooms with modern furniture and a lounge blending the classic and contemporary.

Hans Memling without rest, Kuipersstraat 18 ✆ 0 50 47 12 12, *Fax 0 50 47 12 10* – – 25. AE VISA. AT b
36 rm 120/219.
◆ A town mansion near the Grand-Place and theatre offering brightly decorated rooms of uniform comfort and varying size. Bar-lounge and a wall-enclosed terrace.

Ter Brughe without rest, Oost-Gistelhof 2 ☎ 0 50 34 03 24, *info@hotelterbrughe.com, Fax 0 50 33 88 73* – ⇔ TV 🚗. AE ⓓ MC VISA AT a
46 rm ☕ 87/175.
• A late-Gothic-style residence just a few yards from the Speelmansrei Canal. Plain, but individually furnished rooms. Breakfast served in the original vaulted cellars.

Bryghia without rest, Oosterlingenplein 4 ☎ 0 50 33 80 59, *info@bryghiahotel.be, Fax 0 50 34 14 30* – |♦| TV. AE ⓓ MC VISA. ⚘ AT t
closed 18 December-16 February – **18 rm** ☕ 67/135.
• On a quiet square near a small bridge over the Speelmansrei Canal, this compact hotel has an attractive 15C façade and medium-sized rooms furnished in modern style.

Anselmus without rest, Ridderstraat 15 ☎ 0 50 34 13 74, *info@anselmus.be, Fax 0 50 34 19 16* – TV. AE MC VISA. ⚘ AT h
closed January – **16 rm** ☕ 77/102.
• Close to the Markt and the Burg, the hotel's main entrance opens onto a quite charming lounge. Classically furnished bedrooms.

Relais Bourgondisch Cruyce without rest, Wollestraat 41 ☎ 0 50 33 79 26, *info@relaisbourgondischcruyce.be, Fax 0 50 34 19 68*, < canals and old Flemish houses – |♦| ⇔ TV. AE MC VISA. ⚘ AU f
closed last 3 weeks January – ☕ 10 – **15 rm** 140/250.
• The timber-framed façade provides a unique view of canals lined by old Flemish houses. Refined decor in the guestrooms, plus a panoramic breakfast-cum-tearoom.

Egmond without rest, Minnewater 15 (by Katelijnestraat) ☎ 0 50 34 14 45, *info@egmond.be, Fax 0 50 34 29 40*, <, – TV P. ⚘ AV g
closed January – **8 rm** ☕ 92/125.
• This charming residence near the Lac d'Amour was formerly the office of a notary public. The hotel's guestrooms overlook a peaceful garden.

Biskajer without rest, Biskajersplein 4 ☎ 0 50 34 15 06, *info@hotelbiskajer.com, Fax 0 50 34 39 11* – |♦| TV. AE ⓓ MC VISA AT w
17 rm ☕ 80/130.
• This small, well-kept hotel is situated along the Spiegelrei Canal, in a relatively quiet district just 5 minutes from the centre. Basic but perfectly comfortable rooms.

't Putje (annex - 13 rm), 't Zand 31 ☎ 0 50 33 28 47, *hotelputje@pandora.be, Fax 0 50 34 14 23*, – |♦| ⇔ TV. AE ⓓ MC VISA CZ a
Meals (pub rest, open until 11 p.m.). *Lunch 9* – 31/43 b.i. – **27 rm** ☕ 67/105.
• At the entrance to the old city, near the 't Zand. The hotel's rooms are welcoming and modern but with varying levels of soundproofing. Limited services. Public parking. Refined, contemporary tavern, plus a more intimate restaurant. Front terrace in summer.

ter Reien without rest, Langestraat 1 ☎ 0 50 34 91 00, *info@hotelterreien.be, Fax 0 50 34 40 48* – |♦| TV. AE MC VISA. ⚘ DY r
closed January – **26 rm** ☕ 70/85.
• A waterfront hotel with smallish rooms, with the exception of the bridal suite. A dozen or so rooms enjoy views of the canal.

Bourgoensch Hof, Wollestraat 39 ☎ 0 50 33 16 45, *info@bourgoensch-hof.be, Fax 0 50 34 63 78*, < canals and old Flemish houses, , – |♦| TV ♿ ch, 🚗. MC VISA
closed 6 January-12 February – **Meals** *(closed Thursday)* – a la carte approx. 37 – **17 rm** ☕ 86/144. AU f
• This old Flemish house overlooks one of Bruges' most beautiful canals, which is visible from some of the hotel's rooms. Reasonable comfort. Bistro-style restaurant serving a range of local specialities, plus a popular terrace during the summer months.

Gd H. du Sablon, Noordzandstraat 21 ☎ 0 50 33 39 02, *info@sablon.be, Fax 0 50 33 39 08* – |♦| ⇔ TV – 25-100. AE MC VISA JCB AU h
Meals (residents only) – **36 rm** ☕ 89/120.
• An old building along a busy shopping street between the cathedral and the Grand-Place. Entrance hall, dating from 1900, crowned by an Art Deco dome. Well-maintained rooms.

De Barge, Bargeweg 15 ☎ 0 50 38 51 50, *info@debargehotel.com, Fax 0 50 38 21 25*, – TV P. AE ⓓ MC VISA. ⚘ rm CZ p
closed 23 December-3 January – **Meals** *(closed Sunday and Monday)*. *Lunch 20* – a la carte 35/70 ♀ – **23 rm** ☕ 95/165.
• This old barge moored on the canal linking Bruges with Ghent has been converted into a small floating hotel with guest "cabins" brightly decorated in nautical style. As you would expect, the cuisine at the captain's table is influenced by the sea.

Boterhuis, St-Jakobsstraat 38 ☎ 0 50 34 15 11, *boterhuis@pandora.be* – TV 🚗. AE ⓓ MC VISA AT m
Meals *(closed Sunday dinner October-March)* (open until 11 p.m.). *Lunch 14* – a la carte 25/41 – **13 rm** ☕ 65/110.
• This old hotel within a few hundred yards of the Markt is crowned by a small tower which houses the hotel's best two rooms, accessible via a spiral staircase.

Malleberg without rest, Hoogstraat 7 ✆ 0 50 34 41 11, *hotel@malleberg.be, Fax 0 50 34 67 69* – TV. AE MC VISA. ATU b
8 rm ☕ 70/94.
• The bedrooms of this small hotel just off the Place du Bourg are furnished in plain, modern style. The vaulted cellar now serves as the breakfast room.

De Karmeliet (Van Hecke), Langestraat 19 ✆ 0 50 33 82 59, *Fax 0 50 33 10 11*, – P. AE D MC VISA JCB. DY q
closed 26 June-13 July, 2 to 13 October, Tuesday lunch and Sunday dinner October-May, Sunday lunch June-September and Monday – **Meals**. Lunch 50 – 95/135 b.i., – a la carte 94/182 ♀
Spec. Tuile sucrée-salée aux grosses langoustines rôties. Dos de gros turbot piqué au jambon, sabayon de pommes de terre aux crevettes de Zeebrugge (21 June-21 September). Ravioli à la vanille et pommes caramélisées en chaud-froid.
• An exclusive, elegant restaurant occupying an aristocratic house with a refined, classically modern interior, veranda-lounge, contemporary art exhibits and enclosed terrace.

De Snippe with rm, Nieuwe Gentweg 53 ✆ 0 50 33 70 70, *info@desnippe.be, Fax 0 50 33 76 62*, – rm, TV P. AE D MC VISA AV r
Meals *(closed 9 January-4 February, Sunday and Monday lunch)*. Lunch 38 – a la carte 51/120 – **8 rm** *(closed 9 January-4 February and Sunday November-March)* ☕ 145/150.
• An attractive 18C house is the setting for this highly rated restaurant with charming wall décor, innovative cuisine, superb wine-list, themed bedrooms and a shady terrace.

Den Gouden Harynck (Serruys), Groeninge 25 ✆ 0 50 33 76 37, *goud.harynck@pandora.be, Fax 0 50 34 42 70* – P. AE D MC VISA AUV w
closed 1 week Easter, last 2 weeks July-first week August, last week December, Saturday lunch, Sunday and Monday – **Meals**. Lunch 50 – 62, a la carte 72/99
Spec. Langoustines braisées au Vin Jaune et primeurs. Foie d'oie poêlé au witlof et coulis de banyuls. Canard de challans à la fondue d'oignons, dattes et citron.
• The menu at this restaurant close to the city's main museums is both refined and inventive. Hushed atmosphere in the dining room. Pretty flower-decked courtyard in summer.

't Pandreitje, Pandreitje 6 ✆ 0 50 33 11 90, *info@pandreitje.be, Fax 0 50 34 00 70* – AE D MC VISA JCB AU x
closed 27 March-4 April, 10 to 24 July, 30 October-9 November, Wednesday and Sunday – **Meals**. Lunch 40 – 60/95 ♀.
• The emphasis at this small restaurant housed in stylish, comfortable surroundings near the tourist centre is on luxury products and creative cuisine. Comprehensive wine-list.

Duc de Bourgogne with rm, Huidenvettersplein 12 ✆ 0 50 33 20 38, *duc@ssi.be, Fax 0 50 34 40 37*, ≤ canals and typical houses – rest, TV. AE MC VISA AU t
closed 4 to 29 July and 3 to 28 January – **Meals** *(closed Monday and Tuesday lunch)*. Lunch 36 – 58 ♀ – **10 rm** ☕ 110/160.
• At the junction of the city's most picturesque canals, this rustic-style restaurant serving traditional cuisine is decorated with late Middle Ages-style wall paintings.

De Lotteburg, Goezeputstraat 43 ✆ 0 50 33 75 35, *lotteburg@pi.be, Fax 0 50 33 04 04*, Seafood – . AE D MC VISA JCB. AV d
closed 15 to 24 June, 31 August-9 September, 4 to 22 January, Monday, Tuesday and Saturday lunch – **Meals**. Lunch 30 – 48/87 b.i. ♀.
• A delightful shady terrace adorned with teak furniture is hidden behind the restaurant's white façade and blue shutters. The culinary focus here is resolutely seaward.

Patrick Devos, Zilverstraat 41 ✆ 0 50 33 55 66, *info@patrickdevos.be, Fax 0 50 33 58 67*, – P. AE D MC VISA JCB AU y
closed 21 July-11 August, 26 to 30 December, Saturday lunch and Sunday – **Meals**. Lunch 37 – 48/82 b.i. ♀.
• Features of note in this proud aristocratic mansion include a Louis XVI lounge, Art Nouveau decor in the dining room and a charming summer terrace-patio. Contemporary cuisine.

't Stil Ende, Scheepsdalelaan 12 ✆ 0 50 33 92 03, *stilende@skynet.be, Fax 0 50 33 26 22*, – . MC VISA BX a
closed carnival week, late July, All Saints, Saturday lunch, Sunday and Monday – **Meals** – 32/80 b.i.
• An address worth hunting down away from the main tourist haunts. Contemporary interior design, an extraordinary wine-cooling system, tasty menus and a summer terrace.

De Florentijnen, Academiestraat 1 ✆ 0 50 67 75 33, *info@deflorentijnen.be, Fax 0 50 67 75 33* – 25-60. AE MC VISA AT p
closed 20 July-5 August, 1 week November, 1 to 15 January, Sunday except Bank Holidays and Monday – **Meals**. Lunch 30 – 45/65 b.i. ♀.
• This spacious restaurant is housed in a former Florentine trading building, hence the name. The modern cuisine is matched by the contemporary-style interior design.

XX **Kardinaalshof,** St-Salvatorskerkhof 14 ✆ 0 50 34 16 91, *info@kardinaalshof.be, Fax 0 50 34 20 62* – AE ⓓ MC VISA AUV g
closed first 2 weeks July, Wednesday and Thursday lunch – **Meals**. *Lunch 35* – 48/84 b.i. ♀.
◆ Fish and seafood are the prominent features within the walls of this building with its distinctive Baroque-style façade close to the Markt. Cosy ambience.

XX **Den Dijver,** Dijver 5 ✆ 0 50 33 60 69, *info@dijver.be, Fax 0 50 34 10 64,* terrace, Beer cuisine – AE MC VISA AU c
closed July, Wednesday and Thursday lunch – **Meals**. *Lunch 30* – 39/89 b.i..
◆ A must for beer-lovers, where the cuisine is inspired by Belgium's favourite drink. A friendly ambience, in which each dish is best accompanied by a glass of the frothy stuff !

XX **Tanuki,** Oude Gentweg 1 ✆ 0 50 34 75 12, *info@tanuki.be, Fax 0 50 33 82 42,* Japanese cuisine with Teppan-Yaki and Sushi-bar – ▤. AE MC VISA JCB AV f
closed 1 week carnival, 2 weeks July, 1 week All Saints, Monday and Tuesday – **Meals**. *Lunch 17* – 50/65.
◆ One of the few Japanese restaurants in Bruges. Authentic cuisine, including an impressive Teppan-Yaki menu and a sushi bar. Typical Oriental décor.

XX **Aneth,** Maria van Bourgondiëlaan 1 (behind the Graaf Visart park) ✆ 0 50 31 11 89, *info@aneth.be, Fax 0 50 32 36 46,* Seafood – AE ⓓ MC VISA BY g
closed last 2 weeks August, first 2 weeks January, Saturday lunch, Sunday and Monday – **Meals**. *Lunch 45* – 55/100 b.i. ♀.
◆ The Aneth occupies an early-20C villa opposite a canal and public park, where fish and seafood take centre-stage. Elegant interior blending the classic and modern.

XX **Spinola,** Spinolarei 1 ✆ 0 50 34 17 85, *spinola@pandora.be, Fax 0 50 34 17 85,* terrace – ▤. ⓓ MC VISA AT c
closed last week January-first week February, last week June-first week July, Sunday and Monday lunch – **Meals** – 46.
◆ A pleasant, rustic-style restaurant near the Spiegelrei Canal and statue of Jan Van Eyck. The mouth-watering choice of dishes is complemented by a comprehensive wine-list.

XX **'t Zwaantje,** Gentpoortvest 70 ✆ 0 50 34 38 85, *hetzwaantje@skynet.be,* terrace – AE ⓓ MC VISA AV n
closed 8 to 22 July, Wednesday, Thursday and Saturday lunch – **Meals** – 38 ♀.
◆ Three small swans (zwaantjes) enliven the front of this charming restaurant with a veranda, rear terrace, romantic atmosphere and a menu inspired by current culinary trends.

X **Bhavani,** Simon Stevinplein 5 ✆ 0 50 33 90 25, *info@bhavani.be, Fax 0 50 34 89 52,* terrace, Indian cuisine – AE ⓓ MC VISA AU z
Meals. *Lunch 17* – a la carte 31/41.
◆ If you're tempted by some typical Indian cuisine while visiting the city, head for Place Simon Stevin, where the Bhavani offers a good choice, including vegetarian options.

X **Kurt's pan,** St-Jakobsstraat 58 ✆ 0 50 34 12 24, *kurt.vandaele@planetinternet.be, Fax 0 50 49 11 97* – ▤. AE MC VISA. ✻ AT e
closed last week June, 1 week November, 1 week January, Monday and Tuesday lunch – **Meals**. *Lunch 20* – 42 b.i./65 b.i..
◆ A simply furnished, family-run restaurant with a rustic feel in a small Flemish-style house near St-Jacob's Church. A varied choice of typical dishes.

X **Koto** - Hotel de' Medici, Potterierei 15 ✆ 0 50 44 31 31, *koto@hoteldemedici.com, Fax 0 50 33 05 71,* Japanese cuisine with Teppan-Yaki – P. AE ⓓ MC VISA JCB. ✻ CX g
closed 3 to 18 January, Monday and lunch Tuesday and Wednesday – **Meals**. *Lunch 24* – 42/77 b.i..
◆ The Hotel de' Medici's Japanese restaurant has developed a loyal following for its Teppan-Yaki, sushi and sashimi. Modern décor showing Oriental influence.

X **Cafedraal,** Zilverstraat 38 ✆ 0 50 34 08 45, *info@caferaal.be, Fax 0 50 33 52 41,* terrace, Open until 11 p.m. – AE MC VISA AU s
closed lunch Saturday and Sunday – **Meals**. *Lunch 13* – a la carte 42/90.
◆ The engaging menu at this lively brasserie occupying a charming historic building is certain to satisfy its hungry customers. "Cuban" bar and an attractive interior terrace.

X **Huyze Die Maene,** Markt 17 ✆ 0 50 33 39 59, *huyzediemaene@pandora.be, Fax 0 50 33 44 60,* terrace, Pub rest – ▤. AE ⓓ MC VISA AU w
closed February and lunch Saturday, Sunday and Bank Holidays – **Meals**. *Lunch 14* – 32.
◆ The success of this tavern-restaurant is due to its fabulous location on the Markt, its attractive façade, brasserie atmosphere and appealing menu with daily specials.

Suburbs

Northwest : *5 km – ✉ 8000* :

Scandic, Handboogstraat 1 (Sint-Pieters) ✆ 0 50 25 25 25, *res.brugge@scandic-hotels.com, Fax 0 50 25 25 27,* , – lunch only – 80. AE VISA. ER a
Meals *(closed Saturday lunch). Lunch 15* – carte 31 à 60 – **120 rm** 129/159.
• This chain hotel is housed in a modern building in the city's port district. Stylish contemporary rooms which are well equipped, bright and airy. Spacious contemporary dining room with tables spaced well apart.

De gouden Korenhalm, Oude Oostendsesteenweg 79a (Sint-Pieters) ✆ 0 50 31 33 93, *info@degoudenkorenhalm.be, Fax 0 50 31 18 96,* – AE VISA
closed late February-early March, late August-early September, Monday and Tuesday – **Meals**. *Lunch 31* – 45/74 b.i..
• This modern, Flemish-style building on the outskirts of the city has developed an enviable reputation for its varied menu of refined seasonal dishes. Quality French wine-list.

at Sint-Andries *Southwest : 4 km Bruges – ✉ 8200 Sint-Andries* :

Host. Pannenhuis , Zandstraat 2 ✆ 0 50 31 19 07, *hostellerie@pannenhuis.be, Fax 0 50 31 77 66,* , , – ch, – 25. AE VISA JCB
Meals *(closed 1 to 23 July, 15 January-2 February, Tuesday dinner and Wednesday). Lunch 34* – 46/71 b.i. – **19 rm** *(closed 15 January-2 February)* 95/125.
• A quaint hostelry dating from the 1930s that has recently been refurbished. Reasonably quiet, spacious bedrooms and a summer terrace overlooking the garden. The highly traditional menu includes several fish and lobster specialities.

Herborist (Hanbuckers) with rm, De Watermolen 15 (by ⑥ : 6 km, then on the right after E 40 - A 10) ✆ 0 50 38 76 00, *Fax 0 50 39 31 06,* , , – rest, AE VISA.
closed 21 March-1 April, 20 June-1 July, 19 September-4 October, 19 December-1 January, Monday and dinner Thursday and Sunday – **Meals** (set menu only). *Lunch 65 b.i.* – 85 – **4 rm** 100/150
Spec. Foie de canard chaud et confit d'agrumes aux sept poivres. Colvert aux pêches de vignes (September-mid November). Saint-Jacques au cappuccino de foie de canard (mid September-mid March).
• Nestled in a rural setting, this inn has been restored with great taste. Original and promising à la carte and menu options, enhanced by a prestigious cellar.

at Sint-Kruis *East : 6 km Bruges – ✉ 8310 Sint-Kruis* :

Wilgenhof without rest, Polderstraat 151 ✆ 0 50 36 27 44, *info@hotel-wilgenhof.be, Fax 0 50 36 28 21,* , , – AE VISA.
6 rm 80/150.
• This charming small farm stands along the Damse Vaart canal, amid a landscape of open countryside and polders. Faultless rooms and a roaring log fire in the lounge in winter.

Eethuis De Jonkman, Maalsesteenweg 438 (East : 2 km) ✆ 0 50 36 07 67, *resto@ronniejonkman.be, Fax 0 50 35 76 96,* – AE VISA JCB
closed 2 weeks May, 2 weeks October, Christmas-New Year, Sunday and Monday – **Meals** – 33/63 b.i..
• An attractive Flemish villa where the menu is contemporary, concise and based on the freshest products. Harmonious wine-list. Pleasant terraces with teak furniture.

at Sint-Michiels *South : 4 km Bruges – ✉ 8200 Sint-Michiels* :

Weinebrugge, Koning Albertlaan 242 ✆ 0 50 38 44 40, *weinebrugge@pi.be, Fax 0 50 39 35 63,* – AE VISA.
closed 1 to 15 July and Tuesday – **Meals**. *Lunch 29* – 45/75 bc.
• This comfortable restaurant, with a separate bar and lounge, occupies a Flemish villa on the edge of the Tillegem forest. Traditional cuisine with a modern flourish.

Casserole (Hotel school), Groene-Poortdreef 17 ✆ 0 50 40 30 30, *casserole@tergroenepoorte.be, Fax 0 50 40 30 35,* – – 35. AE VISA.
closed school holidays, Saturday and Sunday – **Meals** (lunch set menu only) 29/42 b.i..
• This restaurant is housed in a small farm in the middle of the country. Attractive country-style dining room, a menu that changes frequently and good, reasonably priced wines.

Hertog Jan, Torhoutse Steenweg 479 ✆ 0 50 67 34 46, *kalon@pandora.be, Fax 0 50 67 34 45,* – AE VISA
closed 3 to 11 avril, 11 July-8 August, 30 October-7 November, 25 December-2 January, Sunday and Monday – **Meals**. *Lunch 50 b.i.* – 50/100 b.i. .
• A popular haunt known for its "gastro-bistro" atmosphere, creative cuisine, international cellar and choice of wines by the glass. Kitchens in full view, plus dynamic service.

Environs

at Hertsberge *South by N 50 : 12,5 km* *Oostkamp pop. 21 371 – ✉ 8020 Hertsberge :*

Manderley, Kruisstraat 13 ☎ 0 50 27 80 51, *manderley@pandora.be, Fax 0 50 27 80 51,* – P. AE ① MC VISA
closed late September-early October, 3 weeks January, Tuesday dinner in winter, Sunday dinner and Monday – **Meals**. *Lunch 36* – 50/87 b.i. ♀.
• An old farm with a pleasant summer terrace overlooking a garden, a menu in tune with modern tastes and a large cellar. Roaring fires in winter.

at Varsenare *West : 6,5 km* *Jabbeke pop. 13 634 – ✉ 8490 Varsenare :*

Manoir Stuivenberg (Scherrens brothers) with rm, Gistelsteenweg 27 ☎ 0 50 38 15 02, *info@manoirstuivenberg.be, Fax 0 50 38 28 92,* – , rest, TV P – 25-300. AE ① MC VISA.
closed 18 July-4 August and 1 to 19 January – **Meals** *(closed Saturday lunch, Sunday dinner, Monday and Tuesday). Lunch 42* – 66/108 b.i., – a la carte 74/116 – **8 rm** *(closed Sunday evening and Monday)* 124/162, – 1 suite
Spec. Turbot braisé au citron et marmelade de tomates. Poitrine de pigeon en crapaudine. Gibier (in season).
• This chic manor house decorated with fine attention to detail is renowned for its modern take on traditional dishes and its attentive service.

at Waardamme *South by N 50 : 11 km* *Oostkamp pop. 21 371 – ✉ 8020 Waardamme :*

Ter Talinge, Rooiveldstraat 46 ☎ 0 50 27 90 61, *tertalinge@tiscali.be, Fax 0 50 28 00 52,* – P. AE MC VISA
closed last week February-first 3 weeks March, last week August-first week September, Wednesday, Thursday and dinner Monday and Tuesday – **Meals**. *Lunch 28* – 45/65 b.i..
• The teal (taling) has made its nest in this modern villa with a rustic-style interior and attractive terrace. Classic, traditional cuisine with a loyal band of regulars.

at Zedelgem *Southwest : 10,5 km – pop. 21 919 – ✉ 8210 Zedelgem :*

Zuidwege, Torhoutsesteenweg 128 ☎ 0 50 20 13 39, *angelo@zuidwege.be, Fax 0 50 20 17 39,* , – , rm, TV P – 25. AE ① MC VISA. rm
Meals *(closed first week July, Christmas holidays, Saturday and Sunday lunch)* (pub rest). *Lunch 10* – a la carte 22/44 – **20 rm** *(closed Christmas holidays)* 60/85.
• Located close to a main crossroads, the Zuidwege has 20 functional bedrooms with double-glazing. A well-maintained, modern hotel offering basic services. Buffet breakfast. Relaxed ambience in the restaurant.

Ter Leepe, Torhoutsesteenweg 168 ☎ 0 50 20 01 97, *Fax 0 50 20 88 54* – P – 220. AE MC VISA
closed 17 July-3 August, 15 to 25 January, Monday and dinner Wednesday and Sunday – **Meals**. *Lunch 38 b.i.* – 65 b.i..
• This villa is home to a restaurant with well-structured à la carte choices, a popular all-inclusive menu, and a selection of vintage wines. Banqueting room to the rear.

Kruishoutem *9770 Oost-Vlaanderen* 533 G 17 *and* 716 D 3 *– pop. 8 075.*
Bruges 44 km.

Hof van Cleve (Goossens), Riemegemstraat 1 (near N 459, motorway E 17 - A 14, exit ⑥) ☎ 0 9 383 58 48, *inof@hofvancleve.com, Fax 0 9 383 77 25,* ≤, – P. AE ① MC VISA.
closed 1 week Easter, 24 July-17 August, late December-early January, Sunday and Monday – **Meals**. *Lunch 65* – 110/175 b.i., – a la carte 100/210 ♀
Spec. Ravioli ouvert de joues de bœuf et champignons, sabayon à l'estragon. Pigeonneau au lard croustillant, parmentière aux truffes et banyuls. Poudre de chocolat et granite à l'orange et gingembre.
• One of the musts of Belgian gastronomy with its inventive cuisine served in an elegant small farm with views overlooking a verdant valley.

De Panne *(La Panne) 8660 West-Vlaanderen* 533 A 16 *and* 716 A 2 *– pop. 9 893.*
Bruges 55 km.

Host. Le Fox (Buyens) with rm, Walckierstraat 2 ☎ 0 58 41 28 55, *hotelfox@pandora.be, Fax 0 58 41 58 79* – TV . AE ① MC VISA
closed 7 to 23 April, 2 to 21 October, 28 November-2 December, 8 to 19 January, Monday except Bank Holidays and Tuesday October-June – **Meals**. *Lunch 40* – 70/105 b.i., – a la carte 65/85 ♀ – 11 – **13 rm** 50/95
Spec. Toast cannibale de langoustines écrasées au caviar. Savarin de bintjes et crevettes grises, œuf poché et crème de xères. Suprême de turbot en croûte, beurre nantais.
• One of the best restaurants on the coast, a few steps from the promenade. Refined and creative traditional cuisine, plus an enticing wine list. Guestrooms of similar quality.

Waregem *8790 West-Vlaanderen* **533** **F 17** *and* **716** **D 3** *– pop. 35 987. Bruges 47 km.*

XXXX ✿✿ **'t Oud Konijntje** (Mmes Desmedt), Bosstraat 53 (South : 2 km near E 17 - A 14) ✆ 0 56 60 19 37, *info@oudkonijntje.be, Fax 0 56 60 92 12,* – P. AE ① MC VISA
closed 1 week Easter, late July-early August, Christmas-New Year, Friday and dinner Thursday and Sunday – **Meals** – 85/110, – a la carte 69/115 ♀,
Spec. Potée de jeunes légumes à la crème de foie d'oie, croustillant de fleur de courgette. Tronçon de turbot aux noisettes grillées et truffe (December-February). Pigeonneau rôti au romarin et mousseline de pommes de terre surprise.
◆ Pleasant interior décor, an enchanting terrace with a fountain, and a flower-filled garden in summer provide a scenic backdrop to this high-class starred restaurant.

Zeebrugge *West-Vlaanderen* C *Brugge pop. 116 680* **533** **E 14** *and* **716** **C 1** – ✉ *8380 Zeebrugge (Brugge) – Bruges 15 km.*

XX ✿✿ **'t Molentje** (Horseele), Baron de Maerelaan 211 (South : 2 km on N 31) ✆ 0 50 54 61 64, *molentje@pi.be, Fax 0 50 54 79 94,* – P. AE MC VISA.
closed 7 to 12 March, 13 to 18 June, 5 to 24 September, 2 to 7 January, Wednesday and Sunday – **Meals** (booking essential). *Lunch 58* – 135 b.i., a la carte 89/137
Spec. L'abstrait d'anguille au vert et caviar oscièttre. Saint-Jacques à la plancha, beurre aux herbes. Saucisse de brochet et petits-gris, crème mousseuse de citron vert aux champignons des bois.
◆ An isolated but attractive small farm accessible via the expressway to Bruges. Tastefully furnished, with cuisine that is both creative and refined. A formidable wine cellar.

Sluis *Zeeland (Netherlands)* **532** **F 15** *and* **715** **B 8** *– pop. 24 791. Bruges 21 km.*

XXX ✿✿ **Oud Sluis** (Herman), Beestenmarkt 2, ✉ 4524 EA, ✆ (0 117) 46 12 69, *oudsluis@zeelandnet.nl, Fax (0 117) 46 30 05,* Seafood – AE ① MC VISA.
closed first week April, first 2 weeks June, 2 weeks October, last week December, Monday and Tuesday – **Meals**. *Lunch 45* – 90, a la carte 94/125 ♀,
Spec. 6 préparations d'huîtres de Zélande (September-April). Rouleaux de thon mariné et langoustines, crème de yaourt et caviar. Bar de ligne salé aux anchois, vinaigrette d'agrumes et mousseline au macvin (May-October).
◆ This typical auberge fronting a lively small square is known for its refined, original cuisine where the emphasis is firmly on seafood. Efficient service.

LIÈGE *4000* **533** **S 19,** **534** **S 19** *and* **716** **J 4** *– pop. 184 474.*

See : *Citadel* ≤★★ **DW** – *Cointe Park* ≤★ **CX** – *Old Town*★★ – *Palace of the Prince-Bishops*★ : *court of honour*★★ **EY** – *The Perron*★ *(market cross)* **EY A** – *Baptismal font*★★★ *of St. Bartholomew's church* **FY** – *Treasury*★★ *of St. Paul's Cathedral : reliquary of Charles the Bold*★★ **EZ** – *St. James church*★★ *: vaults of the nave*★★ **EZ** – *Altarpiece*★ *in the St. Denis church* **EY** – *Church of St. John : Wooden Calvary statues*★ **EY** – *Aquarium*★ **FZ D**.

Museums : Life in Wallonia★★ **EY** – *Religious and Roman Art Museum*★ **FY M⁵** – *Curtius and Glass Museum*★ *: evangelistary of Notger*★★★, *collection of glassware*★ **FY M¹** – *Arms*★ **FY M³** – *Ansembourg*★ **FY M²** – *Modern Art and Contemporary Art*★ **DX M⁷**.

Envir : *Northeast : 20 km : Blégny-Trembleur*★★ – *Southwest : 27 km : Baptismal font*★ *in the church*★ *of St. Severin – North : 17 km at Visé, Reliquary of St. Hadelin*★ *in the collegiate church.*

9 r. Bernalmont 2 ✆ 0 4 227 44 66, Fax 0 4 227 91 92 - 18 South : 8 km at Angleur, rte du Condroz 541 ✆ 0 4 366 20 21, Fax 0 4 337 20 26 - 18 Southeast : 18 km at Gomzé-Andoumont, Sur Counachamps, r. Gomzé 30 ✆ 0 4 360 92 07, Fax 0 4 360 92 06.

✆ 0 4 342 52 14, Fax 0 4 229 27 33.

En Féronstré 92 ✆ 0 4 221 92 21, office.tourisme@liege.be, Fax 0 4 221 92 22 and Gare des Guillemins ✆ 0 4 252 44 19 – Tourist association of the province, bd de la Sauvenière 77 ✆ 0 4 232 65 10, ftpl@prov-liege.be, Fax 0 4 232 65 11.

Brussels 97 – Amsterdam 242 – Antwerp 119 – Cologne 122 – Luxembourg 159 – Maastricht 32.

Plans on following pages

Bedford, quai St-Léonard 36 ✆ 0 4 228 81 11, *infolg@hotelbedford.be, Fax 0 4 227 45 75,* – rm, rm, rest, P – 25-240. AE ① MC VISA.
– **Meals**. *Lunch 25* – a la carte 25/39 – **147 rm** 210/235, - 2 suites. **DW g**
◆ Fronting a busy quay on the site of a former convent and mill. Pleasant soundproofed rooms and interior garden-terrace. The hotel dining room stands beneath an impressive 17C vaulted ceiling. Modern à la carte and menu choices, plus buffet of hors d'oeuvres.

XX **Héliport,** bd Frère Orban 37z (Meuse-side) ✆ 0 4 252 13 21, *info@restaurantheliport.be, Fax 0 4 252 57 50,* ←, 🍽 – ▤ P. AE MC VISA CX e
closed 1 week carnival, 2 weeks July, Sunday and Monday – **Meals.** *Lunch 28* – 40/50.
◆ A boat mast dominates the entrance to this nautically themed restaurant serving contemporary cuisine. Pleasant open-air restaurant overlooking the Meuse.

Old town

Mercure, bd de la Sauvenière 100 ✆ 0 4 221 77 11, *mercureliege.hotel@alliance-hospitality.com, Fax 0 4 221 77 01* – |♦| ⇆ ▤ TV 🚗 – 🏛 25-120. AE ⓓ MC VISA EY t
Meals *(closed Saturday lunch and Sunday)* (pub rest) a la carte 22/31 – **105 rm** ☕ 173/188.
◆ This chain hotel, with its quiet and comfortable rooms, enjoys a central location on one of the city's main boulevards, close to the lively "Le Carré". The cuisine at the Bar à Thym brasserie shows a predilection for spices.

XXX **Max,** pl. Verte 2 ✆ 0 4 222 08 59, *Fax 0 4 222 08 73,* 🍽, Seafood and oyster bar, open until 11 p.m. – 🏛 25. AE ⓓ MC VISA EY a
closed Saturday lunch – **Meals.** *Lunch 30* – a la carte 43/75.
◆ This elegant brasserie in the city centre has been decorated by Luc Genot. Its reputation is firmly rooted in its excellent fish and seafood. Oyster bar and heated terrace.

XXX **Au Vieux Liège,** quai Goffe 41 ✆ 0 4 223 77 48, *Fax 0 4 223 78 60* – ▤. AE ⓓ MC VISA FY a
closed mid July-mid August, Wednesday dinner, Sunday and Bank Holidays – **Meals.** *Lunch 29* – 40/59 b.i..
◆ This pretty 16C timber house is home to one of Liège's oldest restaurants. A rustic setting with classic choices enlivened by the occasional exotic touch. Collection of rums.

XX **Folies Gourmandes,** r. Clarisses 48 ✆ 0 4 223 16 44, 🍽 – AE ⓓ MC VISA EZ q
closed 1 week Easter, mid August-early September, Sunday dinner and Monday – **Meals** – 33/55 b.i.
◆ A small, family-run restaurant occupying an early-20C house with a garden terrace to the rear. Appetising fixed-menu choices and low-calorie options.

XX **Septime,** r. St-Paul 12 ✆ 0 4 221 03 06, *Fax 0 4 221 02 04,* Grill room – ▤. AE ⓓ MC VISA EZ c
Meals. *Lunch 20* – a la carte 28/45.
◆ Along a busy pedestrianised street, overlooked by the cathedral. Interior decor of "raw concrete and taupe-coloured velvet", a relaxed atmosphere and a meat-dominated menu.

XX **L'Écailler,** r. Dominicains 26 ✆ 0 4 222 17 49, *info@ecailler.be, Fax 0 4 387 63 74,* 🍽, Seafood – ▤. AE ⓓ MC VISA EY n
Meals. *Lunch 35* – a la carte 34/48.
◆ The brasserie's name (The Oyster Seller) is a clear indication of the culinary bias of this Parisian bistro-style brasserie with a nostalgic air on the edge of "Le Carré".

XX **aux goûts du jour,** En Bergerue 6 ✆ 0 4 250 08 80, *lautermansbruno@belgacom.net* – ▤. AE ⓓ MC VISA EYZ x
closed 15 July-August, late December, Monday and Tuesday – **Meals** – 29/64 ♀.
◆ This restaurant in the Carré district is known for its innovative and attractive dishes based on a delicate fusion of flavours. Modern design in keeping with the cuisine.

X 😋 **les petits plats canailles du beurre blanc,** r. Pont 5 ✆ 0 4 221 22 65, *beurre.blanc@belgacom.net, Fax 0 4 221 22 65* – AE ⓓ MC VISA FY c
closed Wednesday dinner and Sunday – **Meals.** *Lunch 23* – 30/43 b.i. ♀.
◆ A small restaurant ingeniously split into two contrasting yet equally intimate sections. The old half-timbered façade has been lovingly preserved in the room to the rear.

X 😋 **Il était une fois...,** r. Saint-Jean-en-Isle 3 ✆ 0 4 222 18 54, *philippesi@hotmail.com, Fax 0 4 222 18 54* – AE ⓓ MC VISA EZ f
closed first week Easter, first 2 weeks August, Monday and lunch Tuesday and Saturday – **Meals** – 31/61 b.i. ♀.
◆ Warm tones on the walls ranging from ochre red to turmeric yellow provide a pleasant backdrop to this restaurant serving refined contemporary cuisine.

X 😋 **Enoteca,** r. Casquette 5 ✆ 0 4 222 24 64, *info@enoteca.be,* Italian cuisine – ▤. MC VISA
closed Saturday lunch and Sunday – **Meals** (set menu only) 19/48 b.i. 🍇. EY g
◆ This pleasant Italian restaurant is known for its authentic cuisine and wine-list. Contemporary interior with a kitchen visible from the dining room. Good-value lunch menu.

X 😋 **Le Bistrot d'en face,** r. Goffe 8 ✆ 0 4 223 15 84, *Fax 0 4 223 15 86,* 🍽 – AE MC VISA FY h
closed Monday and Saturday lunch – **Meals** – a la carte 30/38.
◆ This delightful Lyon-style bistro with a fine wooden façade and warm, friendly atmosphere is located behind the former meat market.

LIÈGE
0
300m
C
D
W
X
Citadelle
PARC DE LA CITADELLE
PARC DE LA PAIX
Rue des Glacis
R. Pierreuse
Ste Walburge
Rue Montagne de Ste
Campine
R. Xhovémont
CENTRE SPORTIF
PARC DE XHOVÉMONT
Carrefour Fontainebleau
R. L. Fraigneux
MUSEE DE LA VIE WALLONNE
PALAIS DES PRINCES ÉVÊQUES
Sauvenière
R. Léopold
la Batte
Meuse
Quai des Tanneurs
Bd de la Constitution
Pl. du Congrès
OUTRE-MEUSE
R. J. d'Outremeuse
Q. van Beneden
Q. Roosevelt
R. de l'Université
St-Paul
Bd de la
Av. Destenay
ST-JACQUES
Bd Piercot
Laurent
St.
JONFOSSE
Gilles
R. Wazon
St
R.
Rue Louvrex
JARDIN BOTANIQUE
PARC D'AVROY
Orban
Bd Frère
Pont Albert Ier
Quai Marcellis
Palais des Congrès
Parc de la Boverie
Quai
LONGDOZ
R. d'Harscamp
Rue
R. Basse Wez
Grétry
GRIVEGNÉE
Bd R. Poincaré
Bd Frankignoul
R. Fabry
R. du Plan Incliné
R. de Joie
Av.
Av. Blonden
R. de Fragnée
R. de Sclessin
R. Varin
Quai de Rome
Q. Mativa
R. Mozart
R. de Fétinne
FÉTINNE
Pl. des Nations-Unies
des Vennes
Quai des Ardennes
Ourthe
Pont de Fragnée
GUILLEMINS
Bd de l'Observatoire
Kleyer
G. Parc de Cointe
COINTE
MONUMENT INTERALLIÉ
POL
A 602
163
69
87
94
141
18
22
43
16
9
10
156
34
35
21
108
54
84
73
115
162
40
66
148
15
49
57
G
g
M
M7
a
B
e
n

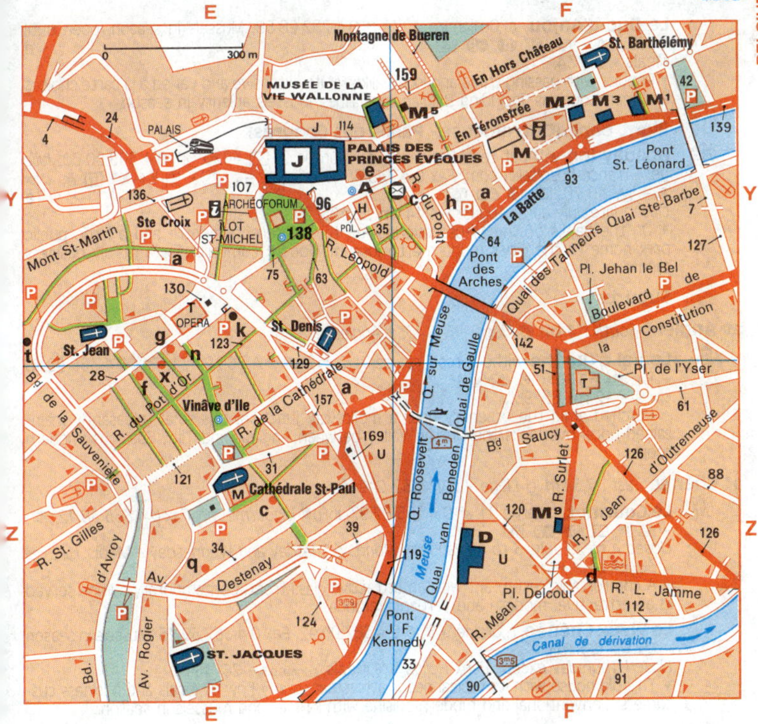

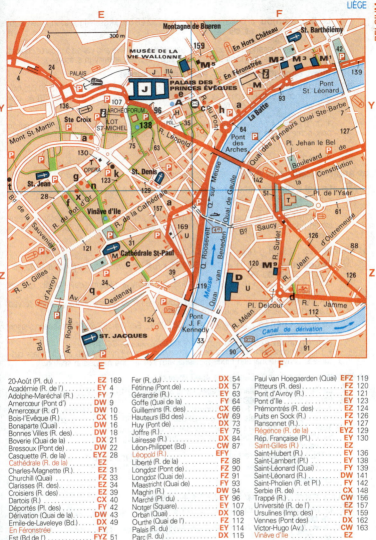

20-Août (Pl. du) EZ 169
Académie (R. de l') EY 4
Adolphe-Maréchal (R.) FY 7
Amercœur (Pont d') DW 9
Amercœur (R. d') DW 10
Bois-l'Evêque (R.) CX 15
Bonaparte (Quai) DW 16
Bonnes Villes (R. des) DW 18
Boverie (Quai de la) DX 21
Bressoux (Pont de) DW 22
Casquette (R. de la) EYZ 28
Cathédrale (R. de la) EZ
Charles-Magnette (R.) EZ 31
Churchill (Quai) FZ 33
Clarisses (R. des) EZ 34
Croisiers (R. des) EZ 39
Dartois (R.) CX 40
Déportés (Pl. des) FY 42
Dérivation (Quai de la) DW 43
Emile-de-Laveleye (Bd.) DX 49
En Féronstrée FY
Est (Bd de l') FYZ 51

Fer (R. du) DX 54
Fétinne (Pont de) DX 57
Gérardrie (R.) EY 63
Goffe (Quai de la) FY 64
Guillemins (R. des) CX 66
Hauteurs (Bd des) CW 69
Huy (Pont de) DX 73
Joffre (R.) EY 75
Lairesse (R.) DX 84
Léon-Philippet (Bd) CW 87
Léopold (R.) EFY
Liberté (R. de la) FZ 88
Longdoz (Pont de) FZ 90
Longdoz (Quai de) FZ 91
Maastricht (Quai de) FY 93
Maghin (R.) DW 94
Marché (Pl. du) EY 96
Notger (Square) EY 107
Orban (Quai) DX 108
Ourthe (Quai de l') FZ 112
Palais (R. du) EY 114
Parc (R. du) DX 115

Paul van Hoegaerden (Quai) EFZ 119
Pitteurs (R. des) FZ 120
Pont d'Avroy (R.) EZ 121
Pont d'Ile EY 123
Prémontrés (R. des) EZ 124
Puits en Sock (R.) FZ 126
Ransonnet (R.) FY 127
Régence (R. de la) EYZ 129
Rép. Française (Pl.) EY 130
Saint-Gilles (R.) EZ
Saint-Hubert (R.) EY 136
Saint-Lambert (Pl.) EY 138
Saint-Léonard (Quai) FY 139
Saint-Léonard (R.) DW 141
Saint-Pholien (R. et Pl.) FY 142
Serbie (R. de) CX 148
Trappé (R.) CW 156
Université (R. de l') EZ 157
Ursulines (Imp. des) FY 159
Vennes (Pont des) DX 162
Victor-Hugo (Av.) CW 163
Vinâve d'Ile EZ

As Ouhès, pl. du Marché 19 ✆ 0 4 223 32 25, *as.ouhes@skynet.be*, *Fax 0 4 237 03 77*, Brasserie, open until 11 p.m. – AE ⓓ ⓜⓒ VISA EY e
Meals – a la carte 22/38.
♦ "The Birds" is a Liège institution with a classic, brasserie-style menu including local dishes and daily specials. A central location near Le Perron, the symbol of the city.

Guillemins

Univers without rest, r. Guillemins 116 ✆ 0 4 254 55 55, *univers.hotel@skynet.be*, *Fax 0 4 254 55 00* – AE ⓓ ⓜⓒ VISA CX a
51 rm ☕ 65/78.
♦ This chain hotel near the Gare des Guillemins is a practical option for those with an early train to catch. Well-maintained rooms with good soundproofing.

Le Duc d'Anjou, r. Guillemins 127 ☎ 0 4 252 28 58, Mussels in season, open until 11.30 p.m. – AE VISA CX n
Meals – 22/34.
• Popular with passing trade and locals alike for its extensive and varied à la carte choices and menu options, including Belgian specialities. Mussels aplenty in season.

Right banc (Outremeuse - Palais des Congrès)

Holiday Inn without rest, Esplanade de l'Europe 2, ✉ 4020, ☎ 0 4 349 20 00, *hiliege@alliance-hospitality.com, Fax 0 4 343 48 10,* – 40-70. AE VISA DX a
closed late July-early August – **214 rm** 193/208, – 5 suites.
• On the banks of the Meuse overlooking the conference centre and a large public park home to the city's modern art museum. Modern comforts for a mainly business clientele.

Suburbs

at Angleur *South : 4 km* Ⓒ *Liège* – ✉ *4031 Angleur :*

Le Val d'Ourthe without rest, rte de Tiff 412 ☎ 0 4 365 91 71, *Fax 0 4 365 62 89* – VISA
9 – **12 rm** 82/95.
• Perched amid the greenery near a motorway junction, this small, pleasantly maintained hotel overlooks the Ourthe Valley between Angleur and Tilff. Spacious, modern rooms.

at Chênée *East : 7,5 km* Ⓒ *Liège* – ✉ *4032 Chênée :*

Le Gourmet, r. Large 91 ☎ 0 4 365 87 97, *info@legourmet.be, Fax 0 4 365 38 12,* – AE VISA
closed 4 to 29 July, 3 to 19 January, Monday, Tuesday and Wednesday – **Meals**. Lunch 25 – 30/64 b.i..
• A comfortable restaurant with an attractive glass front. Contemporary cuisine served in an attractive, modern and verdant veranda.

Le Vieux Chênée, r. Gravier 45 ☎ 0 4 367 00 92, *Fax 0 4 367 59 15,* Mussels in season – AE VISA
closed Thursday except Bank Holidays – **Meals**. Lunch 15 – 26/45 b.i..
• This old house with its typical decor attracts a steady flow of locals and business customers. Conventional and modern cuisine with lobster and mussels in season.

at Rocourt *North : 4 km* Ⓒ *Liège* – ✉ *4000 Rocourt :*

La Petite Table (Gillard), pl. Reine Astrid 3 ☎ 0 4 239 19 00, *lapetitetable@skynet.be, Fax 0 4 239 19 77* – VISA
closed 4 to 10 April, 1 to 19 August, 27 December-10 January, Monday, Tuesday and Saturday lunch – **Meals** (booking essential). Lunch 30 – 50/75 b.i., – a la carte 55/75
Spec. Émincé de Saint-Jacques sur un lit de couscous de chou-fleur. Ravioles de Saint-Jacques au salpicon homard. Croustillant d'agneau, gratin dauphinois aux poireaux.
• This small, discreet restaurant near a busy main road makes up in quality what it lacks in size ! Kitchen in view of diners, fine modern cuisine, with tables cheek by jowl.

Environs

at Ans *Northwest : 4 km – pop. 27 443 –* ✉ *4430 Ans :*

Le Marguerite, r. Walthère Jamar 171 ☎ 0 4 226 43 46, *Fax 0 4 226 38 35,* – AE VISA
closed late July-early August, Saturday lunch, Sunday and Monday dinner – **Meals**. Lunch 28 – 35/62 b.i. 𝕐.
• An esteemed restaurant which has been in business for 30 years. Seasonal contemporary cuisine with the accent on natural products. Elegant and refreshing interior decor.

La Fontaine de Jade, r. Yser 321 ☎ 0 4 246 49 72, *Fax 0 4 263 69 53,* Chinese cuisine, open until 11 p.m. – AE VISA
closed mid July-mid August and Tuesday – **Meals**. Lunch 13 – 22/51 b.i. 𝕐.
• Chinese restaurants are plentiful along this busy road. This one stands out for its affluent, exotic appearance, extensive menu and the quality of its cellar.

à Barchon *Northeast : 13,5 km* Ⓒ *Blégny pop. 12 662* – ✉ *4671 Barchon :*

La Pignata, rte de Légipont 20 (A 3-E 40, exit 36) ☎ 0 4 362 31 45, *info@lapignata.be, Fax 0 4 387 56 79,* , Partly Italian cuisine – 25. AE VISA
closed Monday, Wednesday dinner and Saturday lunch – **Meals**. Lunch 28 – 33/65 b.i..
• Mediterranean cuisine takes pride of place in this dashingly modern restaurant with the odd rustic touch. Pleasant terrace facing the garden and meadows. Italian wine list.

at Flémalle *Southwest : 16 km – pop. 25 362 – ✉ 4400 Flémalle :*

XXX **La Ciboulette,** chaussée de Chokier 96 ✆ 0 4 275 19 65, *la-ciboulette@teledisnet.be, Fax 0 4 275 05 81,* – ▤. AE MC VISA
closed last week July-first week August, 1 week January, Monday, Saturday lunch and dinner Sunday and Wednesday – **Meals**. *Lunch 30* – 49/103 b.i.
• An attractive group of Meuse-style houses is the setting for this refined restaurant offering a varied seasonal menu and wine list. Patio with garden-terrace views.

XX **Le Gourmet Gourmand,** Grand-Route 411 ✆ 0 4 233 07 56, *Fax 0 4 233 19 21,* – ▤. AE MC VISA
closed 21 July-10 August, Monday and Saturday lunch – **Meals** (lunch only except Friday and Saturday). *Lunch 30* – 40/60 b.i..
• A small, traditional establishment where the menu changes with the seasons and includes a range of local dishes. A wine cellar with the accent on Southwest France.

XX **Jacques Koulic,** chaussée de Chockier 82 ✆ 0 4 275 53 15, *jacques.koulic@cybernet.be,* – P. AE MC VISA
closed 1 to 15 September, Tuesday and Wednesday – **Meals**. *Lunch 34* – 65/95 b.i..
• An old house with a warm, rustic interior on the banks of the Meuse. Pleasantly modern cuisine, a diverse wine-list and wines by the glass. Terrace and enclosed garden.

at Herstal *Northeast : 6 km – pop. 36 466 – ✉ 4040 Herstal :*

XX **La Bergamote,** bd Ernest Solvay 72 (locality Coronmeuse) ✆ 0 4 342 29 47, *bergamote@sky.be, Fax 0 4 248 17 61,* – MC VISA
closed 28 January-7 February, 1 week Easter, last 2 weeks July, Sunday, Monday and Bank Holidays – **Meals**. *Lunch 29* – 41/75 b.i..
• This respected restaurant housed in a former post office has a "contemporary bistro" feel with menus in keeping with the overall ambience. Attractive terrace to the rear.

at Liers *North : 8 km C Herstal pop. 36 466 – ✉ 4042 Liers :*

X **La Bartavelle,** r. Provinciale 138 ✆ 0 4 278 51 55, *info@labartavelle.be, Fax 0 4 278 51 57,* – P – 25 à 60. AE MC VISA
closed carnival, 15 to 31 July, Saturday lunch and Sunday – **Meals** (lunch only except weekends) 30/50 b.i.
• A convivial restaurant with a Mediterranean feel. Provençal-inspired cuisine, wines from Southern France, contemporary art exhibits and a charming terrace facing the garden.

at Neuville-en-Condroz *South : 18 km C Neupré pop. 9 762 – ✉ 4121 Neuville-en-Condroz :*

XXXX ✿ **Le Chêne Madame** (Mrs Tilkin), av. de la Chevauchée 70 (Southeast : 2 km in Rognacs wood) ✆ 0 4 371 41 27, *Fax 0 4 371 29 43,* – P. AE MC VISA
closed August, Monday and dinner Thursday and Sunday – **Meals**. *Lunch 35* – 50/105 b.i., – a la carte 66/88
Spec. Homard canadien au lillet et poivre rose. Ravioles de céleri au foie gras et truffes. Suprême de pintade en crêpe croquante, sauce curry.
• This elegant country inn is one of the temples of Liège gastronomy. A classic choice of seasonal dishes using the very finest ingredients.

at Tilleur *Southwest : 8 km C St-Nicolas pop. 22 694 – ✉ 4420 Tilleur :*

X **Chez Massimo,** quai du Halage 78 ✆ 0 4 233 69 27, *Fax 0 4 234 00 31,* , Italian cuisine – 40. MC VISA
closed late December-early January, Saturday lunch, Sunday and Monday – **Meals** (set menu only) 28/40.
• This long-established Italian restaurant on the banks of the Meuse is renowned for its regional specialities and more run-of-the-mill national dishes.

Maastricht *Limburg (Netherlands)* 532 T 17 *and* 715 I 9 – *pop. 121 982.*
Liège 33 km.

Right banc (Wyck - Station - MECC) :

XXXX ✿✿ **Beluga** (Van Wolde), Plein 1992 nr 12 (Céramique Centre), ✉ 6221 JP, ✆ (0 43) 321 33 64, *info@rest-beluga.com, Fax (0 43) 326 03 56,* ← – ▤ P – 30. AE MC VISA JCB.
closed 5 to 14 February, 24 July-15 August, 27 December-2 January, Saturday lunch, Sunday and Monday – **Meals**. *Lunch 35* – 125 b.i. a la carte 88/118
Spec. Tajine de pigeon d'Anjou aux épices marocaines. Foie gras à la vapeur, gelée de pomme, crème de courge marinée et jambon ibérique. Croque-Monsieur au thon, caviar osciètre et vinaigrette à l'orange salée.
• In a revamped district next to a new bridge over the Maas. Elegant design features in the dining room provide the backdrop for personalised cuisine by a talented chef.

Namur *5000 Namur* 533 O 20, 534 O 20 *and* 716 H 4 *– pop. 105 842.*
Liège 61 km.

at Lives-sur-Meuse *East : 9 km* © *Namur –* ✉ *5101 Lives-sur-Meuse :*

XXXX ✿✿ **La Bergerie** (Lefevere) (hotel planned), r. Mosanville 100 ✆ 0 81 58 06 13, *marc@bergerielives.be, Fax 0 81 58 19 39* – ▤ P. AE ⓓ MC VISA
closed last 2 weeks February-early March, last 2 weeks August-early September, Sunday dinner, Monday and Tuesday – **Meals**. *Lunch 41* – 60/113 b.i., – a la carte 77/92 ♀,
Spec. Truites de notre vivier. Agneau rôti "Bergerie". Gâteau de crêpes soufflées.
◆ This elegant, Namur-style residence in a luxuriant, waterside setting is one of the country's best tables. Outstanding classic cuisine accompanied by an extensive wine-list.

Tongeren *3700 Limburg* 533 R 18 *and* 716 J 3 *– pop. 29 588.*
Liège 19 km.

at Vliermaal *North : 5 km* © *Kortessem pop. 8 063 –* ✉ *3724 Vliermaal :*

XXXXX ✿✿ **Clos St. Denis** (Denis), Grimmertingenstraat 24 ✆ 0 12 23 60 96, *info@closstdenis.be, Fax 0 12 26 32 07* – P. AE ⓓ MC VISA
closed 29 March-6 April, 18 July-3 August, 1 to 9 November, 29 December-10 January, Tuesday and Wednesday – **Meals**. *Lunch 50* – 99/182 b.i., – a la carte 92/155
Spec. Effiloché de crabe tourteau, marmelade de légumes marinés aux parfums du Sud et caviar d'aubergines. Pigeonneau royal poché, rôti et laqué. Délice au croustillant de pralin et chocolat pur Venezuela.
◆ Refined dining in a sumptuous 17C farm-château embellished with works of art. Charming terrace and adorable garden. A high-flying wine-list.

LUXEMBOURG – LËTZEBUERG

717 V 25 and 716 L 7 – pop. 77 325.

Amsterdam 391 – Bonn 190 – Brussels 219.

Plans of Luxembourg
Centre of Luxembourg .... pp. 2 and 3
List of hotels and restaurants .... pp. 4 to 9

TOURIST OFFICE

Luxembourg City Tourist Office, pl. d'Armes, ✉ 2011, ☎ 22 28 09, touristinfo@lcto.lu, Fax 46 70 70.
Air Terminus, gare centrale ✉ 1010, ☎ 42 82 82 20, info@ont.lu, Fax 42 82 82 30.
Airport at Findel ☎ 42 82 82 21, info@ont.lu, Fax 42 82 82 30.

GOLF COURSE

18 Hoehenhof (Senningerberg) near Airport, r. de Trèves 1, ✉ 2633, ☎ 34 00 90, Fax 34 83 91.

PLACES OF INTEREST

VIEWPOINTS

Place de la Constitution★★ F – *St-Esprit*★★ *Plateau* G – *Cliff Path*★★ G – *The Bock*★★ G – *Boulevard Victor Thorn*★ G 121 – *Three Acorns*★ DY.

MUSEUMS

National Museum of History and Art★ : *Gallo Roman section*★ *and Luxembourg Life section (decorative arts, folk art and traditions)*★★ G **M¹** – *Historical Museum of the City of Luxembourg*★ G **M³**.

OTHER THINGS TO SEE

Bock Casemates★★ G – *Grand Ducal Palace*★ G – *Cathedral of Our Lady*★ F – *Grand Duchess Charlotte Bridge*★ DY.

MODERN ARCHITECTURE

Plateau de Kirchberg : European Centre DEY.

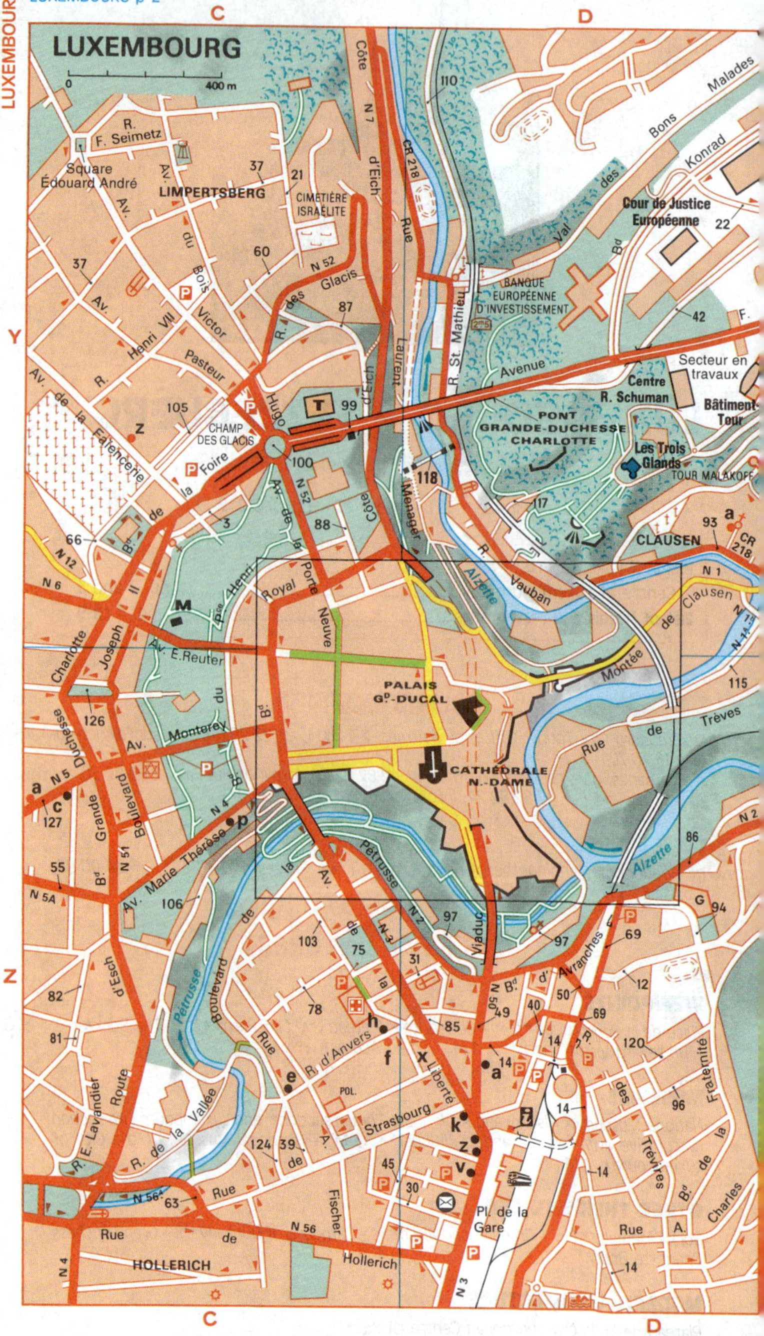
LUXEMBOURG
0
400 m
C
D
Y
Z
R. F. Seimetz
Square Édouard André
LIMPERTSBERG
CIMETIÈRE ISRAÉLITE
Côte d'Eich
Rue Laurent Ménager
R. St. Mathieu
N 7
CR 218
N 52
Glacis
Av. Victor Hugo
Av. Pasteur
Av. Henri VII
Av. du Bois
Av. de la Faïencerie
R. de la Foire
CHAMP DES GLACIS
Bd. Joseph II
Bd. Charlotte
Bd Grande Duchesse
Bd. Royal
Av. de la Porte Neuve
Av. E. Reuter
Av. Monterey
Bd. du Pce Henri
Av. Marie Thérèse
Bd. d'Esch
Route d'Esch
Boulevard
Pétrusse
Bd. de la Pétrusse
Av. de la Liberté
Viaduc
Bd. d'Avranches
R. d'Anvers
Rue de Strasbourg
Rue Fischer
Rue de Hollerich
HOLLERICH
R. E. Lavandier
R. de la Vallée
Pl. de la Gare
Bd. de la Pétrusse
Rue de Trèves
Bd. de la Fraternité
Rue A. Charles
Rue des Trévires
PALAIS Gd-DUCAL
CATHÉDRALE N.-DAME
Alzette
R. Vauban
CLAUSEN
Montée de Clausen
Avenue
PONT GRANDE-DUCHESSE CHARLOTTE
BANQUE EUROPÉENNE D'INVESTISSEMENT
Val des Bons Malades
Bd Konrad
Cour de Justice Européenne
Centre R. Schuman
Secteur en travaux
Bâtiment Tour
Les Trois Glands
TOUR MALAKOFF
N 1
N 2
N 3
N 4
N 5
N 5A
N 6
N 12
N 51
N 56
N 56A
N 50
POL.
M
T
a
c
e
f
h
k
p
v
x
z
G
3
12
14
21
22
30
31
37
39
40
42
45
49
50
55
60
63
66
69
75
78
81
82
85
86
87
88
93
94
96
97
99
100
103
105
106
110
115
117
118
120
124
126
127

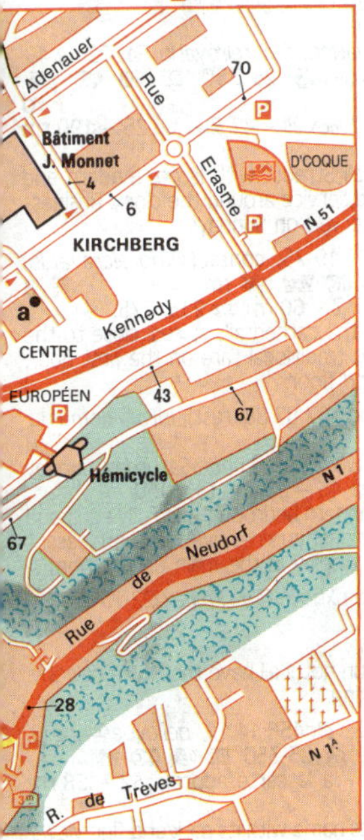

10-Septembre (Av. du) . . . CZ 127
Adames (R.) . . . . CY 3
Albert-Wehrer (R.) . . . . EY 4
Alcide-de-Gasperi (R.) . . . . EY 6
Aldringen (R.) . . . . F 7
Athénée (R. de l'Ancien) . . . F 9
Auguste-Lumière (R.) . . . . DZ 12
Bains (R. des) . . . . F 13
Bonnevoie (R. de) . . . . DZ 14
Boucherie (R. de la) . . . . . . G 15
Bruxelles (Pl. de) . . . . F 16
Capucins (R. des) . . . . F
Cerisiers (R. des) . . . . CY 21
Charles-Léon-Hammes (R.) . . . . DY 22
Chimay (R.) . . . . F 24
Clairefontaine (Pl.) . . . . FG 27
Clausen (R. de) . . . . EY 28
Commerce (R. du) . . . . . CDZ 30
Curé (R. du) . . . . F
Dicks (R.) . . . . CDZ 31
Eau (R. de l') . . . . G 33
Ermesinde (R.) . . . . CY 37
Etats-Unis (R. des) . . . . . . CZ 39
Fort Neipperg (R. du) . . . . DZ 40
Fort Niedergrünewald (R. du) . . . . DY 42
Fort Thüngen (R. du) . . . . EY 43
Fort Wedell (R. du) . . . . . CDZ 45
Fossé (R. du) . . . . F 46
Franklin-Roosevelt (Bd) . . . . F 48
Gare (Av. de la) . . . . DZ 49
Gaulle (Av. du Gén.-de) . . DZ 50
Grand-Rue . . . . F
Guillaume (Av.) . . . . CZ 55
Guillaume-Schneider (R.) . CY 60
J. P.-Probst (R.) . . . . CY 66
Jean-Baptiste-Merkels (R.) CZ 63
Jean-Ulveling (Bd) . . . . . . FG 64
Jules-Wilhem (R.) . . . . EY 67
Laboratoire (R. du) . . . . . . DZ 69
Léon-Hengen (R.) . . . . EY 70
Liberté (Av. de la) . . . . . . CDZ
Marché (Pl. du) . . . . G 72
Marché aux Herbes (R. du) . . . . FG 73
Martyrs (Pl. des) . . . . CZ 75
Michel-Rodange (R.) . . . . . CZ 78
Münster (R.) . . . . G 79
Nancy (Pl. de) . . . . CZ 81
Nassau (R. de) . . . . CZ 82
Notre-Dame (R.) . . . . F 84
Paris (Pl. de) . . . . DZ 85
Patton (Bd du Général) . . . DZ 86
Paul-Eyschen (R.) . . . . CY 87
Pescatore (Av.) . . . . CY 88
Pfaffenthal (Montée de) . . FG 90
Philippe-II (R.) . . . . F 91
Pierre-de-Mansfeld (Allée) DY 93
Pierre-et-Marie-Curie (R.) . DZ 94
Pierre-Hentges (R.) . . . . . . DZ 96
Porte Neuve (Av. de la) . . CY
Prague (R. de) . . . . DZ 97
Robert-Schuman (Bd) . . . CY 99
Robert-Schuman (Rond-Point) . . . . CY 100
Sainte-Zithe (R.) . . . . CZ 103
Scheffer (Allée) . . . . CY 105
Semois (R. de la) . . . . CZ 106
Sigefroi (R.) . . . . G 108
Sosthène Weis (R.) . . . . G 109
Stavelot (R. de) . . . . DY 110
Strasbourg (R. de) . . . . . . CDZ
Théâtre (Pl. du) . . . . F 114
Tour Jacob (Av. de la) . . DEY 115
Trois Glands (R. des) . . . . DY 117
Vauban (Pont) . . . . DY 118
Verger (R. du) . . . . DZ 120
Victor-Thorn (Bd) . . . . G 121
Willy-Georgen (R.) . . . . F 123
Wilson (R.) . . . . CZ 124
Winston-Churchill (Pl.) . . . CZ 126

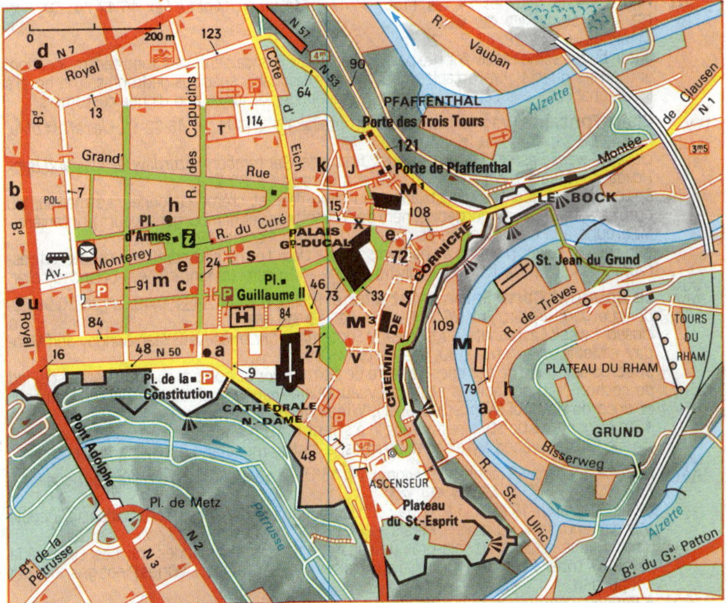

Luxembourg-Centre

Le Royal, bd Royal 12, ✉ 2449, ☎ 241 61 61, *reservations@hotelroyal.lu, Fax 22 59 48,* – AE VISA. rest F d
Meals see ***La Pomme Cannelle*** below – ***Le Jardin*** *Lunch 25* – 42 ♀ – ☐ 25 – **190 rm** 340/470, – 20 suites.
◆ A luxury hotel at the heart of Luxembourg's "Wall Street" with large, modern and superbly equipped bedrooms. Top-notch, personalised service around the clock. Business centre. Mediterranean-style brasserie. Buffet lunch served on Sundays.

Gd H. Cravat, bd Roosevelt 29, ✉ 2450, ☎ 22 19 75, *contact@hotelcravat.lu, Fax 22 67 11* – 25. AE VISA. rm F a
Meals *(closed August)* (pub rest). *Lunch 13* – 40/65 b.i. ♀ – **60 rm** ☐ 215/275.
◆ This small, classical palace stands in the shadow of the cathedral's spires, close to the city's pedestrianised area. Pleasant restaurant serving traditional fare on the first floor, in addition to a cosy tavern-restaurant on the ground floor.

Domus, av. Monterey 37, ✉ 2163, ☎ 467 87 81 and 467 87 88 (rest), *info@domus.lu, Fax 46 78 79,* – AE VISA. F u
Meals *le sot l'y laisse* *(closed 3 weeks August, last 2 weeks December, Saturday, Sunday and Bank Holidays) Lunch 12* – a la carte 22/50 ♀ – ☐ 15 – **38 rm** 135/150.
◆ A contemporary "apartment-hotel" with spacious, modern bedrooms and fully equipped kitchenettes. The brasserie-restaurant, serving traditional cuisine, overlooks a pleasant garden and terrace. Canvases by local artists are on display in the main dining room.

Rix without rest, bd Royal 20, ✉ 2449, ☎ 47 16 66, *rixhotel@vo.lu, Fax 22 75 35,* – VISA. F b
closed 17 December-2 January – **21 rm** ☐ 120/185.
◆ The stylish, identical rooms in this pleasant family-run hotel all have their own balcony. Impressive breakfast room and priceless private parking.

Parc-Belle-Vue , av. Marie-Thérèse 5, ✉ 2132, ☎ 456 14 11, *bellevue@hpb.lu, Fax 456 14 12 22,* – 25-350. AE VISA
Meals *(closed Saturday and Sunday lunch). Lunch 15* – a la carte approx. 32 – **58 rm** ☐ 115/130. CZ p
◆ This hotel slightly away from the centre lives up to its name with its park and fine views. The bedrooms are well furnished with good soundproofing, while the welcoming panoramic terrace provides the perfect setting for dining during the summer months.

Français, pl. d'Armes 14, ✉ 1136, ☎ 47 45 34, *hfinfo@pt.lu, Fax 46 42 74,* – 30. AE VISA F h
Meals. *Lunch 17* – 28/42 ♀ – **21 rm** ☐ 90/127.
◆ Run by the same family for the past 25 years, the Français enjoys a good central location, and offers guests comfortable, modern and reasonably spacious bedrooms. The hotel's traditional cuisine is certain to assuage the hunger of lunch and dinner customers.

Clairefontaine (Magnier), pl. de Clairefontaine 9, ✉ 1341, ☎ 46 22 11, *clairefo@pt.lu, Fax 47 08 21,* – AE VISA G v
closed 1 week Easter, 2 weeks August, first week September, Saturday, Sunday and Bank Holidays – **Meals**. *Lunch 60 b.i.* – 70/88, – a la carte 63/89 ♀
Spec. Gambas géantes croustillantes au chou-fleur et crème citronnée. Le meilleur du bœuf tradition luxembourgeoise, nem de champignons et hamburger saveurs printanières. Millefeuille à la crème anisée et céleri vert. **Wines** Riesling, Pinot blanc.
◆ In the old town, fronting a charming square close to the cathedral, this renowned restaurant is known for its ever-evolving cuisine and a complementary, well-balanced cellar.

Le Bouquet Garni Salon Saint Michel (Duhr), r. Eau 32, ✉ 1449, ☎ 26 20 06 20, *bouquetgarni@pt.lu, Fax 26 20 09 11* – AE VISA G e
closed 1 week Easter, late August-early September, Chritmas-New Year, Sunday and Monday – **Meals**. *Lunch 40 b.i.* – 80, a la carte 60/80 ♀
Spec. Salade tiède de pommes de terre de Noirmoutier et homard rôti (May-August). Pied de cochon farci de morilles et ris de veau. Dos de cabillaud piqué au thym cuit au four et coco de Paimpol (August-October). **Wines** Vin de la Barrique, Riesling.
◆ An elegant, rustic-style restaurant in a street running alongside the Palais Grand-Ducal. Classic fare enlivened by elegant touches, a tasting menu and appealing desserts.

Speltz, r. Chimay 8 (angle r. Louvigny), ✉ 1333, ☎ 47 49 50, *info@restaurant-speltz.lu, Fax 47 46 77,* – AE VISA F c
closed 20 March-18 April, 5 to 9 May, 31 July-15 August, 24 December-2 January, Sunday, Monday and Bank Holidays – **Meals** – 44/95 b.i. – a la carte 61/77 ♀
Spec. Boune schlupp au foie gras de canard, écrivisses et amandes fraîches. Lièvre à la royale (October-February). Tiramisu aux fraises (May-September). **Wines** Pinot gris, Riesling Koeppchen.
◆ Refined, contemporary cuisine served in two rooms with period furniture or, on sunny days, on the busy front terrace lining one of the city's pedestrian streets.

XXX **La Pomme Cannelle** - Hotel Le Royal, bd Royal 12, ✉ 2449, ☎ 241 61 67 36, *reservations@hotelroyal.lu, Fax 22 59 48* – ▤ ☞ 🅿. AE ⓓ VISA. ✻ F d
closed Saturday lunch, Sunday and Bank Holidays – **Meals**. *Lunch 45* – 65/120 b.i. ♀.
• Highly original cuisine in which high-quality ingredients and spices from the New World take pride of place. The chic, yet welcoming interior calls to mind exotic locations.

XXX **Jan Schneidewind,** r. Curé 20 (relocation planned to Kockelscheuer), ✉ 1368, ☎ 22 26 18, *info@schneidewind.lu, Fax 46 24 40,* ☂ – AE ⓓ MC VISA F s
closed Sunday and Monday – **Meals**. *Lunch 43* – 66/98 b.i. ♀.
• Customers can enjoy an appetising seasonal menu at this restaurant nestled between Place d'Armes and Place Guillaume II. The bare walls are enlivened with modern canvases.

XX **La Lorraine** 1st floor, pl. d'Armes 7, ✉ 1136, ☎ 47 14 36, *lorraine@pt.lu, Fax 47 09 64,* ☂, Partly oyster bar and seafood – ▤. AE ⓓ MC VISA. ✻ rest F e
closed Saturday lunch and Sunday – **Meals** a la carte 53/69 ♀.
• In a fine edifice on the place d'Armes, the Lorraine serves local cuisine, with oysters (in season) on the ground floor, and refined fare in an Art Deco room on the first.

X **Apoteca,** r. Boucherie 12, ✉ 1247, ☎ 26 47 82 45, *info@apoteca.lu, Fax 26 47 82 46,* ☂, Open until 11 p.m. – 🏛 25. AE ⓓ MC VISA G x
closed lunch Saturday and Sunday – **Meals**. *Lunch 25* – 48/74 b.i. ♀.
• This contemporary-style restaurant occupies a 19C house in the historical section of the upper town. Three small modern dining rooms embellished with rustic touches.

X **la fourchette à droite,** av. Monterey 5, ✉ 2163, ☎ 22 13 60, *Fax 22 24 95,* ☂ – AE ⓓ MC VISA F m
closed Saturday lunch – **Meals**. *Lunch 18* – 29/54 b.i. ♀.
• An attractive, popular restaurant located in the heart of the city. The menu in the wood-adorned "brasserie"-style dining room includes a good-value lunch option.

X **Wengé,** r. Louvigny 15, ✉ 1946, ☎ 26 20 10 58, *wenge@vo.lu, Fax 26 20 12 59,* ☂ – AE MC VISA F y
closed 12 to 19 April, 15 to 31 August, 1 to 11 January and Sunday – **Meals**. *Lunch 30* – 37/79 b.i. ♀.
• This fashionable restaurant is named after essence of wenge ; an exotic finewood. Intimate dining room where purple shades reign. Up-to-date dishes.

X **Thai Céladon,** r. Nord 1, ✉ 2229, ☎ 47 49 34, *Fax 37 91 75,* Thai cuisine – AE ⓓ MC VISA. ✻ FG k
closed Saturday lunch and Sunday – **Meals**. *Lunch 18* – 46.
• This central restaurant serves high-quality Thai cuisine and vegetarian dishes in an elegant and refined ambience. It takes its name from a glaze used by Oriental potters.

Luxembourg-Grund

XXXX ✿✿ **Mosconi,** r. Münster 13, ✉ 2160, ☎ 54 69 94, *Fax 54 00 43,* ☂, Italian cuisine – AE ⓓ MC VISA JCB G a
closed 1 week Easter, 7 to 29 August, Christmas-New Year, Saturday lunch, Sunday and Monday – **Meals**. *Lunch 34* – 45/85, – a la carte 66/83
Spec. Pâté de foie de poulet à la crème de truffes blanches. Risotto aux truffes blanches (October-December). Arista au Chianti (pork chop).
• A bourgeois house on the River Alzette serving fine Italian cuisine. A welcoming setting where the emphasis is on discreet luxury. Attractive terrace by the water's edge.

X **Kamakura,** r. Münster 4, ✉ 2160, ☎ 47 06 04, *kamakura@pt.lu, Fax 46 73 30,* Japanese cuisine – AE ⓓ MC VISA. ✻ G h
closed 1 week Easter, last 2 weeks August, Sunday and lunch Saturday and Bank Holidays – **Meals**. *Lunch 10* – 25/65.
• The Kamadura makes few concessions to the West with its minimalist ambience and design. Good sushi-bar and menus which remain loyal to Japanese customs. A firm favourite.

Luxembourg-Station

Gd H. Mercure Alfa, pl. de la Gare 16, ✉ 1616, ☎ 490 01 11, *H2058@accor.com, Fax 49 44 42* – |‡| ⇔ ▤ ▣ – 🏛 25-80. AE ⓓ MC VISA. ✻ rest DZ z
Meals (brasserie). *Lunch 21* – a la carte 30/53 – ☕ 18 – **140 rm** 175/220, – 1 suite.
• This completely refurbished chain hotel is a useful address for rail travellers. Pleasant rooms where a good night's sleep is guaranteed. The Parisian-style brasserie floats amid the vast Art Deco restaurant. International menu and fresh seafood.

President without rest, pl. de la Gare 32, ✉ 1024, ☎ 48 61 61, *president@pt.lu, Fax 48 61 80* – |‡| ⇔ ▤ ▣ 🅿 – 🏛 30. AE ⓓ MC VISA JCB. ✻ DZ v
42 rm ☕ 110/180.
• The rooms at this attractive, discreetly luxurious hotel in front of the station are comfortable and frequently refurbished. Personalised service and an intimate ambience.

City without rest, r. Strasbourg 1, ✉ 2561, ✆ 291 12 21, *mail@cityhotel.lu, Fax 29 11 33* – |‡| TV 🚗 – 🏛 25-80. AE ⓓ MC VISA DZ k
35 rm ☕ 87/160.
◆ This old building has a modern feel with spacious bedrooms equipped with every creature comfort and décor that bears the personal touch. Attentive service.

Christophe Colomb (annex Marco Polo - 18 rm) without rest, r. Anvers 10, ✉ 1130, ✆ 408 41 41, *mail@christophe-colomb.lu, Fax 40 84 08* – |‡| TV – 🏛 25. AE ⓓ MC VISA CZ h
24 rm ☕ 136/168.
◆ Just 500m/550yd from the station, this pleasant small hotel is ideal for those arriving in the city by train. Standard, reasonably spacious rooms with modern furnishings.

International, pl. de la Gare 20, ✉ 1616, ✆ 48 59 11, *info@hotelinter.lu, Fax 49 32 27* – |‡| ⅹ ▤ TV – 🏛 25-50. AE ⓓ MC VISA DZ z
Meals *(closed 20 December-6 January and Saturday lunch)* – 18/40 ♀ – **67 rm** ☕ 90/170, – 1 suite.
◆ Located opposite the railway station, the International offers the perfect location for guests travelling by train. Well-maintained rooms, in addition to an intimate restaurant adorned with wood panelling.

Le Châtelet (annex 🏠 - 9 rm) without rest, bd de la Pétrusse 2, ✉ 2320, ✆ 40 21 01, *contact@chatelet.lu, Fax 40 36 66* – |‡| TV. AE ⓓ MC VISA. ✗ rest CZ e
36 rm ☕ 88/120.
◆ Overlooking the Pétrusse Valley, this hotel is an amalgam of several houses, one of which is crowned by an imposing turret. Pine furniture throughout and good soundproofing.

Nobilis, av. de la Gare 47, ✉ 1611, ✆ 49 49 71, *info@hotel-nobilis.com, Fax 40 31 01* – |‡| ▤ TV – 🏛 50. AE ⓓ MC VISA DZ a
Meals. Lunch 17 – a la carte approx. 22 – ☕ 15 – **46 rm** 75/115.
◆ The Nobilis is part of a shopping centre complex located halfway between the railway station and the viaduct leading directly to the old town. Functional bedrooms.

XXX **Cordial** 1st floor, pl. de Paris 1, ✉ 2314, ✆ 48 85 38, *Fax 40 77 76* – AE MC VISA DZ x
closed 17 to 23 May, 19 July-12 August, 3 to 5 January, Saturday lunch, Sunday dinner and Monday – **Meals.** Lunch 33 – 42/90 b.i. ♀.
◆ A large, comfortable restaurant with a conventional layout and elegant ambience. Classic culinary options including a combination of menus and daily specials.

XX **Italia** with rm, r. Anvers 15, ✉ 1130, ✆ 486 62 61, *italia@euro.lu, Fax 48 08 07*, 🌳, Partly Italian cuisine – TV. AE ⓓ MC VISA CZ f
Meals – a la carte 30/49 – **20 rm** ☕ 70/90.
◆ The menu here is strong on Italian cuisine. The mainly Franco-Italian cellar includes some Moselle wines. Candlelit dinners with music on Fridays from September-June.

Suburbs

Airport *Northeast : 8 km* :

Ibis, rte de Trèves, ✉ 2632, ✆ 43 88 01, *H0974@accor.com, Fax 43 88 02*, ≤, 🌳 – |‡| ▤ TV ♿ ch, P – 🏛 25-80. AE ⓓ MC VISA
Meals. Lunch 11 b.i. – a la carte 22/36 – ☕ 10 – **120 rm** 65/95.
◆ A chain hotel with attractive lounge and dining areas plus a cheaper annexe for the budget-conscious. Despite limited space, the bedrooms offer the level of comfort you would expect from the Ibis name. A glass rotunda provides the backdrop for the restaurant.

Trust Inn without rest, r. Neudorf 679 (by rte de Trèves), ✉ 2220, ✆ 423 05 11, *trustinn@pt.lu, Fax 42 30 56* – ▤ TV. AE ⓓ MC VISA
7 rm ☕ 65/75.
◆ Despite a compact feel, the rooms are pleasant and well-equipped. As the hotel does not have a restaurant, breakfast - the only service available - is brought to your room.

XX **Le Grimpereau,** r. Cents 140, ✉ 1319, ✆ 43 67 87, *bridard@pt.lu, Fax 42 60 26*, 🌳 – P. AE ⓓ MC VISA
closed 1 week Easter, first 3 weeks August, Saturday lunch, Sunday dinner and Monday – **Meals** – 45 b.i./60.
◆ This neo-rustic restaurant in a foliage-adorned villa is named after the tree creepers that inhabit its walls. Popular with locals and airport staff. Excellent menu choice.

at Belair *West : 1,5 km* *Luxembourg :*

Albert Premier, without rest, r. Albert Ier 2a, 1117, 442 44 21, *info@albert1er.lu, Fax 44 74 41*, - - AE VISA CZ c
14 - **14 rm** 145/235.
• A "chic" hotel on the city's outskirts. Warm, English-style décor created with great attention to detail, charming, well-appointed rooms, and friendly, attentive service.

Parc Belair, av. du X Septembre 111, 2551, 442 32 31, *paribel@hpb.lu, Fax 44 44 84*, ≤, , , , - , rest, - 25-260. AE VISA JCB
Meals *Le Bistrot* *Lunch 10* - a la carte 22/44 - **53 rm** 220/280.
• This luxury hotel on the edge of a park is appreciated by guests for its cosy feel. Modern bedrooms and excellent facilities for seminars. The extensive menu at the small bistro across the street will more than satisfy the needs of the hungriest of customers.

Astoria, av. du X Septembre 44, 2550, 44 62 23, *Fax 45 82 96* - . AE VISA CZ a
closed Saturday and dinner Sunday and Monday - **Meals**. *Lunch 24* - a la carte 35/59.
• Housed in an attractive bourgeois residence at the entrance to the city, with a façade embellished with Art Deco features. Terrace-garden to the rear. Traditional menu.

Thailand, av. Gaston Diderich 72, 1420, 44 27 66, Thai cuisine -
closed 15 August-4 September, Monday and Saturday lunch - **Meals** a la carte 36/54.
• At the heart of Belair, this exotic restaurant is known for its myriad Thai recipes and typical, relatively tasteful décor, including parasols adorning the ceiling.

at Clausen *(Klausen)* *Luxembourg :*

les jardins du President with rm pl. Ste-Cunégonde 2, 1367, 260 90 71, *jardins@president.lu, Fax 26 09 07 73*, , - , rm, . AE VISA DY a
closed last week December-first week January - **Meals** *(closed Saturday lunch and Sunday)*. *Lunch 24* - a la carte 43/58 - **7 rm** 180/250.
• An elegant restaurant set amid an oasis of greenery producing dishes with a modern touch. The terrace overlooks a garden and waterfall. Individually designed bedrooms.

at Dommeldange *(Dummeldéng)* *North : 5,5 km* *Luxembourg :*

Hilton , r. Jean Engling 12, 1466, 4 37 81, *hilton.luxembourg@hilton.com, Fax 43 60 95*, ≤, , , - - 25-360. AE VISA JCB
Meals *Café Stiffchen* *Lunch 30* - a la carte 34/64 - 22 - **298 rm** 108/298, - 39 suites.
• This luxury hotel hugs the side of the valley on the edge of the forest. Bedrooms with every creature comfort, attentive service and a full range of conference facilities. Brasserie-style restaurant, plus buffet lunches Monday-Friday in the Café Stiffchen.

Host. du Grünewald, rte d'Echternach 10, 1453, 43 18 82, *hostgrun@pt.lu, Fax 42 06 46*, - , rest, - 25-40. AE VISA. rest
Meals *(closed 1 to 22 August, 1 to 18 January, Sunday and lunch Monday and Saturday)*. *Lunch 49* - 60/95 - **23 rm** 95/150, - 2 suites.
• A delightful, traditional-style hostelry with faded charm. Quaint bedrooms, all varying in shape and size. With its cosy feel, the overall atmosphere is quite romantic. A good classic menu and expansive wine list await guests in the restaurant.

Upland of Kirchberg *(Kiirchbierg)* :

Sofitel , r. Fort Niedergrünewald 6 (European Centre), 2015, 43 77 61, *H1314@accor.com, Fax 42 50 91* - ch, - 25-75. AE VISA EY a
Meals *Oro e Argento* *(closed Saturday)* a la carte 41/62 - 20 - **100 rm** 330, - 4 suites.
• This bold, oval-shaped hotel with a central atrium is located at the heart of the European institutions district. Comfortable, spacious rooms with service to match. The intimate Oro e Argento restaurant, with its hints of Venice, serves Italian cuisine.

Novotel , r. Fort Niedergrünewald 6 (European Centre), 2226, 429 84 81, *H1930@accor.com, Fax 43 86 58*, - ch, - 25-300. AE VISA EY a
Meals (open until midnight). *Lunch 23* - a la carte 22/38 - 15 - **259 rm** 190/195, - 1 suite.
• The Novotel is run by the same group as its neighbour, the Sofitel, and offers business customers a full range of seminar facilities as well as large, pleasant bedrooms.

at Limpertsberg *(Lampertsbierg)* C *Luxembourg* :

XX **Lagura,** av. de la Faïencerie 18, ✉ 1510, ✆ 26 27 67, *Fax 26 27 02 97*, – ▤. AE ⓓ ⓜ VISA CY z
closed Saturday lunch and Sunday – **Meals**. *Lunch 22* – a la carte 35/53 ♀.
◆ A trendy eatery with a minimalist ambience and eclectic globetrotting menu inspired by the Mediterranean and Asia. Pleasant terrace to the rear.

at Neudorf *(Neiduerf)* *Northeast : 4 km* C *Luxembourg* :

Ponte Vecchio without rest, r. Neudorf 271, ✉ 2221, ✆ 424 72 01, *vecchio@pt.lu, Fax 424 72 08 88* – |‡| ▤ TV P. AE ⓓ ⓜ VISA
46 rm ☕ 89/107.
◆ This old brewery has been redeveloped into impressive bedrooms (with and without kitchenettes) - including 9 split-level - and rooms adorned with charming Italianate frescoes.

at Rollingergrund *(Rolléngergronn)* *Northwest : 3 km* C *Luxembourg* :

Sieweburen, r. Septfontaines 36, ✉ 2534, ✆ 44 23 56, *Fax 44 23 53*, <, , – TV P. ⓜ VISA
Meals *(closed 24 December-8 January and Wednesday)* (pub rest). *Lunch 11* – a la carte 28/46 ♀ – **14 rm** ☕ 95/115.
◆ This half-timbered country house offers a choice of several sizes of bedroom, some of which are in the attic, all with adequate levels of comfort.

Environs

at Hesperange *(Hesper)* *Southeast : 5,5 km – pop. 11 177*

XXX ✿ **L'Agath** (Steichen), rte de Thionville 274 (Howald), ✉ 5884, ✆ 48 86 87, *restaurant@agath.lu, Fax 48 55 05*, – P. – 60. AE ⓓ ⓜ VISA
closed 1 to 16 August, 1 to 7 November, 1 to 10 January, Saturday lunch, Sunday and Monday – **Meals**. *Lunch 58* – a la carte 68/91 ♀
Spec. Ravioles de homard dans sa bisque mousseuse. Daurade royale dans son jus et légumes confits. Suprême de pigeon et millefeuille de chou vert. **Wines** Riesling, Chardonnay.
◆ The emphasis in this imposing villa set back from the road is on refined modern cuisine. A trompe-l'oeil decorates the cupola in the sumptuous dining room.

at Strassen *(Strossen)* *West : 4 km – pop. 6 021*

L'Olivier with apartments, rte d'Arlon 140a, ✉ 8008, ✆ 31 36 66, *olivier@mail.lu, Fax 31 36 27* – |‡| TV P. – 25-50. AE ⓓ ⓜ VISA
Meals see ***La Cime*** below – **38 rm** ☕ 77/184, – 4 suites.
◆ This building 400m/440yd from the motorway offers modern comforts, double-glazing and some split- level rooms with kitchenette. The view to the rear is pleasantly rural.

XX **La Cime** - Hotel L'Olivier, rte d'Arlon 140a, ✉ 8008, ✆ 31 88 13, *olivier@mail.lu, Fax 31 36 27*, – P. AE ⓓ ⓜ VISA
closed Saturday – **Meals**. *Lunch 35* – 22/30 ♀.
◆ A la carte options at this hotel restaurant include traditional dishes, plus several menus offering a choice of meat, fish and vegetarian dishes. Large, modern dining room.

XX **Le Nouveau Riquewihr,** rte d'Arlon 373, ✉ 8011, ✆ 31 99 80, *leriquewihr@email.lu, Fax 31 97 05*, – P. AE ⓓ ⓜ VISA
closed 24 December-2 January and Sunday – **Meals**. *Lunch 34* – a la carte 38/60 ♀.
◆ Comfortable Italian Renaissance-style dining room with a hushed, intimate ambience. Contemporary summer terrace in a verdant setting. Traditional seasonal menus.

at Walferdange *(Walfer)* *North : 5 km – pop. 6 628*

Moris, pl. des Martyrs, ✉ 7201, ✆ 330 10 51, *contact@morishotel.lu, Fax 33 30 70*, – |‡|, ▤ rest, TV P. – 50. AE ⓓ ⓜ VISA
closed 24 December-8 January – **Meals**. *Lunch 39* – a la carte 34/55 ♀ – **24 rm** ☕ 85/110.
◆ An octogonal hotel located at a crossroads near the village church. Functional, reasonably spacious rooms, albeit lacking soundproofing. Private car park. The welcoming, harmonious restaurant serves classic dishes and regional specialities.

XX **l'Etiquette,** rte de Diekirch 50, ✉ 7220, ✆ 33 51 68, *Fax 33 51 69*, – P. AE ⓓ ⓜ VISA
closed Tuesday and Sunday dinner – **Meals**. *Lunch 17* – 22/42 ♀.
◆ Originally a specialist wine store, which still exists to this day, l'Etiquette is now also known for its traditional cuisine and an exceptional cellar of regional wines.

Echternach *(Iechternach)* 717 X 24 *and* 716 M 6 – *pop. 4 480.*
Luxembourg 36 km.

at Geyershaff *(Geieschhaff) Southwest : 6,5 km by E 27* © *Bech pop. 935 :*

XXX ✿✿ **La Bergerie** (Phal), ✉ 6251, ✆ 79 04 64, *bergerie@relaischateaux.com, Fax 79 07 71,* ← – P. AE ⓓ MC VISA
closed 1 January-11 February, Sunday dinner and Monday – **Meals** (dinner only September-May except weekends) 110 b.i., a la carte 76/144 ♀
Spec. Foie gras aux cinq saveurs. Carré d'agneau de Sisteron grillé. Suprême de turbot, sauce au Champagne. **Wines** Pinot gris, Riesling.
◆ A charming restaurant known for its inventive cuisine nestled amid woods and fields. Excellent choice of local wines. Veranda-dining room overlooking a delightful park.

Paliseul *6850 Luxembourg belge (Belgium)* 534 P 23 *and* 716 I 6 – *pop. 4 999.*
Luxembourg 94 km.

XXX ✿✿ **Au Gastronome** (Libotte) with rm, r. Bouillon 2 (Paliseul-Gare) ✆ 0 61 53 30 64, *info@augastronome.be, Fax 0 61 53 38 91,* ⛱, – ▤ TV P. MC VISA
closed January-first week February, 27 June-8 July, Sunday dinner, Monday and Tuesday – **Meals**. Lunch 52 b.i. – 65/105, – a la carte 59/95 – **8 rm** ☐96/175
Spec. Cuisses de grenouilles au jus de persil, raviole frite de fromage de chèvre au radis. Canette en croûte d'amandes, navets à l'hydromel et dattes au citron. Pied de porc farci de ris de veau et de morilles grillé au romarin.
◆ This elegant Ardennes hostelry is renowned for its skilful reworking of traditional dishes. Hushed and elegant dining room, cosy bedrooms, plus a swimming pool in the garden.

AMSTERDAM

Noord-Holland 531 O 8 – ㉘ ㉙, 532 O 8 and 715 G 4 – ㉗ S – pop. 735 562.

Brussels 204 – Düsseldorf 227 – The Hague 60 – Luxembourg 419 – Rotterdam 76.

Places of interest .... p. 1 bis

Plans of Amsterdam

Centre of Amsterdam .... pp. 2 and 3

Street Index .... p. 4

Alphabetical listing of hotels and restaurants .... pp. 4 and 5

List of establishments according to style of cuisine .... p. 6

List of hotels and restaurants .... pp. 7 to 18

TOURIST OFFICE

VVV Amsterdam, Stationsplein 10, ✉ 1012 AB, ☎ (020) 201 88 00, info@atcb.nl, Fax (0 20) 625 28 69.

For more information on tourist attractions consult our Green Guide to Amsterdam and our Map Nº 36.

GOLF COURSES

18 West : 6 km at Halfweg, Machineweg 1b, ✉ 1165 NB, ☎ (0 23) 513 29 39, Fax (0 23) 513 29 35 – 9 South : 5 km at Duivendrecht, Zwarte Laantje 4, ✉ 1099 CE, ☎ (0 20) 694 36 50, Fax (0 20) 663 46 21 – 18 Buikslotermeerdijk 141, ✉ 1027 AC, ☎ (0 20) 632 56 50, Fax (0 20) 634 35 06 – 18 9 Southeast at Holendrecht, Abcouderstraatweg 46, ✉ 1105 AA, ☎ (0 294) 28 12 41, Fax (0 294) 28 63 47.

CASINO

Holland Casino KY, Max Euweplein 62, ✉ 1017 MB (near Leidseplein), ☎ (0 20) 521 11 11, Fax (0 20) 521 11 10.

PLACES OF INTEREST

VIEUWPOINTS

Keizersgracht★★ KVY *– from the sluice bridge on the Oudezijds Kolk and the Oudezijds Voorburgwal★* LX.

HISTORICAL MONUMENTS

Dam : Royal Palace★ KX *– Beguine Convent★★* KX *– Cromhout Houses★* KY **A**[4] *– Westerkerk★* KX *– Nieuwe Kerk★★* KX *– Oude Kerk★* LX.

HISTORICAL MUSEUMS

Amsterdam Historical Museum★★ KX *– Jewish Museum★* LY *– Allard Pierson Museum★ : archeological finds* LXY *– the House of Anne Frank★★* KX *– Netherlands Maritime History Museum★★* MX *– Tropical Museum★ – Van Loon Museum★* LY *– Willet-Holthuysen Museum★* LY.

FAMOUS COLLECTIONS

Rijksmuseum★★★ KZ *– Van Gogh Museum★★★ (Rijksmuseum)* JZ *– Museum of Modern Art★★★* JZ *– Amstelkring "Our Dear Lord in the Attic"★ (Museum Amstelkring Ons' Lieve Heer op Solder) : clandestine chapel* LX *– Rembrandt's House★ : works by the master* LX *– Cobra★ (Modern Art).*

MODERN ARCHITECTURE

Housing in the Jordaan district and around the Nieuwmarkt – Contemporary structures at Amsterdam Zuid-Oost (ING bank).

SCENIC AREAS AND PARKS

Old Amsterdam★★★ – Herengracht★★★ KVY *– Canals★★★ (Grachten) with hotel-boats (Amstel) – The Jordaan (Prinsengracht★★, Brouwersgracht★, Lijnbaansgracht, Looiersgracht, Egelantiersgracht★, Bloemgracht★)* KX *–* JKY *– Reguliersgracht★* LY *– Realeneiland – Dam★* KX *– Thin Bridge★ (Magere Brug)* LY *– The Walletjes★★ (red light district)* LX *– Sarphatipark – Oosterpark – Vondelpark* JZ *– Artis★* MY *(zoological park) – Singel★★* KY.

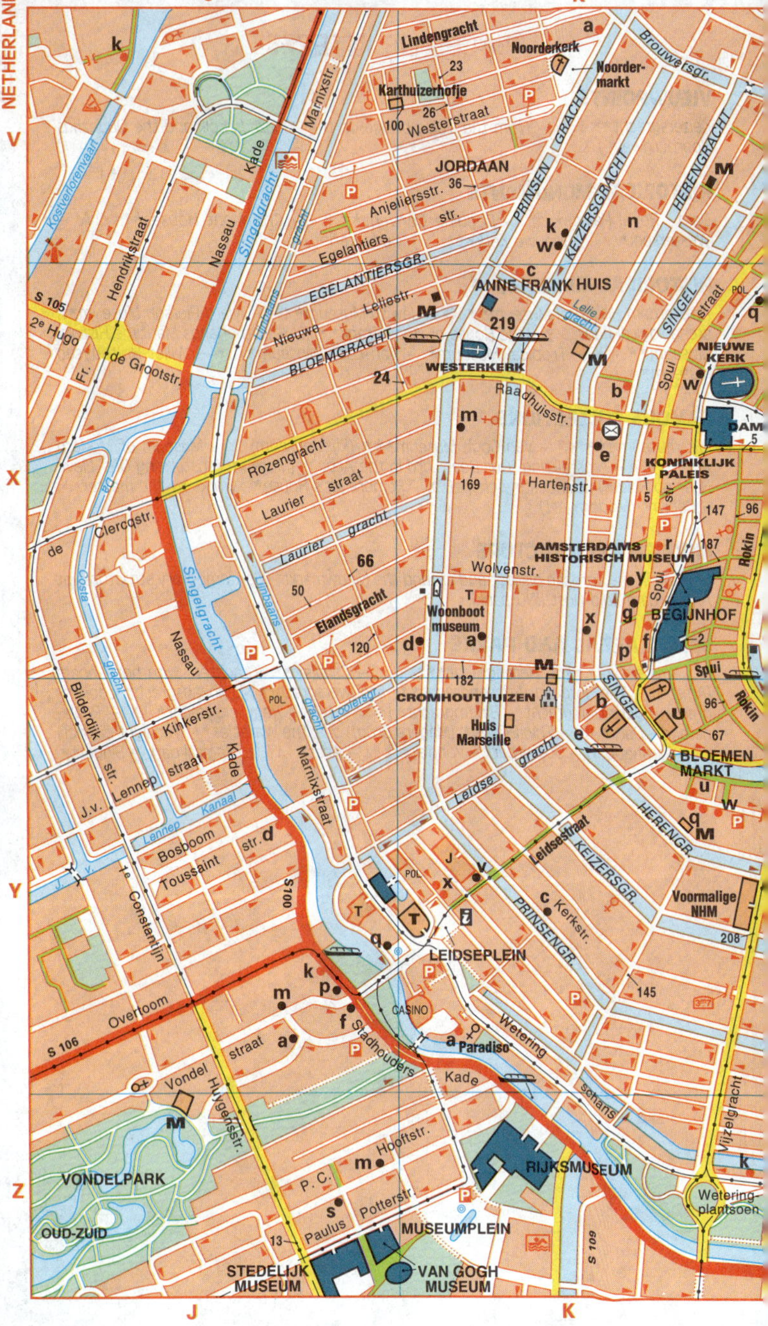
J
K
V
X
Y
Z
Lindengracht
Noorderkerk
Noorder-
markt
Brouwersgr.
Karthuizerhofje
23
26
100
Westerstraat
JORDAAN
Anjeliersstr.
36
str.
Egelantiers
gracht
EGELANTIERSGR.
Leliestr.
Nieuwe
BLOEMGRACHT
PRINSEN GRACHT
KEIZERSGRACHT
HERENGRACHT
ANNE FRANK HUIS
219
Lelie
gracht
WESTERKERK
24
Raadhuisstr.
SINGEL
straat
POL.
NIEUWE
KERK
DAM
5
KONINKLIJK
PALEIS
Spui
Kostverlorenvaart
Hendrikstraat
Nassau
Kade
Singelgracht
Marnixstr.
Lijnbaans
S 105
2e Hugo
de Grootstr.
Fr.
Rozengracht
Laurier
straat
gracht
169
Hartenstr.
5
str.
147
96
187
Rokin
AMSTERDAMS
HISTORISCH MUSEUM
66
50
Elandsgracht
Woonboot
museum
Wolvenstr.
BEGIJNHOF
2
120
182
CROMHOUTHUIZEN
Huis
Marseille
Spui
96
Rokin
67
BLOEMEN
MARKT
de
Clercqstr.
Costa
gracht
Singelgracht
Nassau
Bilderdijk
Kinkerstr.
Kade
Lijnbaans
gracht
Looiersgr.
Marnixstraat
straat
str.
J.v. Lennep
Kanaal
Lennep
Bosboom
Toussaint
str.
J. v.
1e Constantijn
S 100
Leidse
gracht
Leidsestraat
KEIZERSGR.
HERENGR.
PRINSENGR.
Kerkstr.
Voormalige
NHM
208
LEIDSEPLEIN
145
CASINO
Paradiso
Weteringschans
Vijzelgracht
Overtoom
S 106
straat
Vondel
Stadhouders
Kade
Huygensstr.
VONDELPARK
OUD-ZUID
Hooftstr.
P. C.
Paulus
Potterstr.
13
RIJKSMUSEUM
Wetering-
plantsoen
MUSEUMPLEIN
S 109
STEDELIJK
MUSEUM
VAN GOGH
MUSEUM

AMSTERDAM
0
200 m
L
M
V
X
Y
Z
de Ruijter Kade
HET IJ
IJ-tunnel
S 116
S 100
PASSAGIERS-TERMINAL
Centraal Station
Stationspl.
Open Haven Front
AIR TERMINAL
Werk in uitvoering
156
223
NIEUWE ZIJDE
Damrak
BEURS VAN BERLAGE
MUSEUM AMSTELKRING
Scheepvaart huis
Prins Hendrikkade
OOSTERDOK
NEMO
NEDERLANDS SCHEEPVAART MUSEUM
ARCAM
OUDE KERK
OUDE ZIJDE
Voorburg Wal
Achterburg Wal
Zeedijk
Geldersekade
Waals Eilandsgracht
Recht Boomssloot
Waag
Nieuw markt
POL
Montelbaanstoren
OUDE SCHANS
Uilenburgergracht
Prinsenhof
Oude Zijds
Kloveniers Burgwal
Zuiderkerk
REMBRANDT HUIS
Valkenburgerstr.
Entrepot dok
93
ALLARD PIERSON M.
Rokin
Muntplein
AMSTEL
Zwanenburg wal
Waterloopl.
Muziektheater
Waterlooplein
Mr. Visser Plein
Herengr.
Hortus Botanicus
Plantage
ARTIS
PLANTAGE
Middenlaan
166
Blauwbrug
Amstelstr.
REMBRANDTPL.
JOODS HISTORISCH MUSEUM
20
139
Nieuwe
AMSTELHOF
Keizers gracht
Plantage Muider gr.
MUSEUM WILLET-HOLTHUYSEN
Amstel
Utrechtsestr.
FOAM
MUSEUM VAN LOON
Kerkstr.
Amstel Kerk
REGULIERSGR.
De Duif
MAGERE BRUG
Weesperstr.
Prinsengracht
Roeters-str.
Achter
Amstelsluizen
Weesperplein
Sarphatistr.
Hogesluis Brug
Frederiksplein
Wetering-schans
Westeinde
Oosteinde
Mauritskade
Wibautstraat
Ruyschstr.
Singelgracht
Stadhouderskade
Amstel

INDEX OF STREET NAMES IN AMSTERDAM

1er Egelantiersdwarsstr. KV 36
2ème Boomdwarsstr. KV 26
2ème Lindendwarsstr. KV 23
Amstel LY
Amstelstr. LY
Amstelveld LY 9
Anjeliersstr. JKV
Beurspl. LX 19
Bilderdijkstr. JXY
Binnenkant MX 22
Blauwbrug LY
Bloemd-warsstr. (1e) JX 24
Bloemgracht JKX
Bosboom Toussaintstr. JY
Constantijn-Huygensstr. (1e) JY
Dam KX
Damrak LX
Damstr. LX 40
De Clercqstr. JX
De Ruijterkade LV
Egelantiersgracht JKX
Egelantiersstr. JVX
Elandsgracht JX 50
Elandsstr. JX
Entrepotdok MXY
Frederik-Hendrikstr. JVX
Frederikspl. LZ
Gedempte Begijnensloot KX 2
's-Gravelandseveer LY 58
Hartenstr. KX
Hazenstr. JX 66
Heiligeweg KY 67
Hekelveld LV 69
Herengracht KVY
Hogesluis-Brug LZ
Hugo-de-Grootstr. (2e) JX
Jacob-van-Lennepstr. JY
Jodenbreestr. LX 88
Jonas Daniël Meijerpl. MY 20
Kadijkspl. MX 93
Kalverstr. KXY 96
Karthuizersstr. JKV 100
Kattengat LV 105
Keizersgracht KVY
Kerkstr. KLY
Kinkerstr. JY
Langebrugsteeg LX 115
Laurierstr. JX
Leidsegracht KY
Leidsepl. KY
Leidsestr. KY
Leliegracht KX
Lijnbaansgracht JVX
Lindengracht JKV
Looiersdwarsstr. (1e) JX 120
Magerebrug LY
Marnixstr. JVY
Martelaarsgracht LV 126
Mauritskade MYZ
Mr. Visser Pl. MY
Muntpl. LY
Museumpl. KZ
Nassaukade JVY
Nieuwe Achtergracht MY
Nieuwe Amstelstr. LY 139
Nieuwe Doelenstr. LY 141
Nieuwe Herengracht LMY
Nieuwe Hoogstr. LX 142
Nieuwe Keizersgracht LMY
Nieuwe Leliestr. JKX
Nieuwe Prinsengracht LMY
Nieuwe Spiegelstr. KY 145
Nieuwendijk LVX
Nieuwezijds Voorburgwal KLX 147
Nieuwmarkt LX
Noordermarkt KV
Oosteinde LY
Oosterdokskade MX 156
Oude Doelenstr. LX 157
Oude Hoogstr. LX 159
Oude Schans LMX
Oude Turfmarkt LY 160
Oudebrugsteeg LX 162
Oudezijds Kolk LVX 223
Overtoom JY
Paleisstr. KX 5
Paulus-Potterstr. JKZ
Pieter-Corn-Hooftstr. JKZ
Plantage Kerklaan MY 166
Plantage Middenlaan MY
Prins-Hendrikkade MX
Prinsengracht KVY
Raadhuisstr. KX
Reestr. KX 169
Reguliersbreestr. LY 171
Reguliersdwarsstr. LY 172
Rembrandtpl. LY
Roetersstr. MY
Rokin LY
Rozengracht JX
Runstr. KX 182
Ruyschstr. MZ
Sarphatistr. LMZ
Singel KXY
Sint-Antoniesbreestr. LX 186
Sint-Luciënsteeg KX 187
Spui KXY
Spuistr. KX
Stadhouderskade JKY
Stationspl. LV
Stromarkt LV 195
Thorbeckepl. LY 198
Utrechtsestr. LY
Valkenburgerstr. MX
Van Baerlestr. JZ 13
Vijzelgracht KYZ
Vijzelstr. KY 208
Vondelstr. JY
Warmoesstr. LX 215
Waterloopl. LXY
Weesperstr. MY
Westeinde LZ
Westermarkt KX 219
Westerstr. KV
Weteringplantsoen KZ
Weteringschans KYZ
Wibautstr. MZ
Wolvenstr. KX
Zeedijk LX
Zuiderkerkhof LX 234
Zwanenburgwal LXY

Alphabetical listing of hotels and restaurants

A

9 Albus Gd H.
8 Ambassade
7 Amstel
9 Amsterdam

B

14 Bilderberg Garden
14 Blender
12 blue pepper
18 Bokkedoorms (De) (at Haarlem/Overveen)
12 Bordewijk
13 Brasserie van Baerle
11 Breitner

C

10 Café Roux (H. The Grand Sofitel Demeure)
9 Canal House
10 Christophe
14 Ciel bleu
10 City Center
16 Courtyard by Marriott-Amsterdam Airport
8 Crowne Plaza American
16 Crowne Plaza Amsterdam-Schiphol
7 Crowne Plaza City Centre

D

9 Dikker en Thijs Fenice
16 Dorint Novotel
17 Dorint Sofitel Airport
8 Dylan (The)
10 Dynasty

E - F - G

9 Eden
12 Entresol
9 Estheréa
7 Europe (de l')

10 Excelsior (H. Europe)
13 Filosoof (De)
13 Fita
13 Garage (Le)
16 Grand Hotel
7 Grand Sofitel Demeure (The)
12 Gresham Memphis (The)

H

12 Haesje Claes
16 Herbergh (De)
13 Hilton
17 Hilton Schiphol
15 Holiday Inn
14 Hollandais (Le)
11 Hosokawa

I – J

12 Indochine (L')
11 Indrapura
10 Inntel
12 Jan Luyken
17 Jagershuis ('t)
8 Jolly Carlton
16 Jonge Dikkert (De)

K – L

15 Kas (De)
17 Klein Paardenburg
10 Lancaster
18 Librije (De) (at Zwolle)
18 Lindenhof (De) (at Giethoorn)
15 Lloyd
17 Lute

M – N

11 Manchurian
14 Mangerie de Kersentuin (H. Bilderberg Garden)
16 Marktzicht
12 Marriott
15 Mercure Airport
14 Mercure a/d Amstel
9 Mercure Arthur Frommer
14 Meridien Apollo (Le)
12 NH Amsterdam Centre
7 NH Barbizon Palace
9 NH Caransa
9 NH City Centre
8 NH Doelen
7 NH Gd H. Krasnapolsky
9 NH Schiller
15 Novotel

O – P

13 Okura
17 Oude Toren (De)
15 Pakistan
11 Pêcheur (Le)
9 Port van Cleve (Die)
7 Pulitzer

R

13 Radèn Mas
7 Radisson SAS
17 Radisson SAS Airport
13 Ramada Museum Square
12 Relais (Le)
10 Rembrandt
7 Renaissance
16 Résidence Fontaine Royale (Grand Hotel)
10 Rive (La) (H. Amstel)
17 Ron Blaauw
15 Rosarium

S

16 Schiphol A4
11 Segugio
8 Seven One Seven
17 Sheraton Airport
11 Sichuan Food
8 Sofitel
13 Spring
8 Swissôtel

T

12 theeboom (d')
8 Toren
14 Tulip Inn Art
14 Tulip Inn City West
11 Tuynhuys (Het)

V – W – Y

15 VandeMarkt
11 Van Vlaanderen
10 Vermeer (H. Barbizon Palace)
8 Victoria
13 Villa Borgmann
14 visaandeschelde
13 Vondel
15 Voorbij het Einde
11 Vijff Vlieghen (d')
10 Wiechmann
14 Yamazato (H. Okura)

Establishments according to style of cuisine

Buffets

17 Greenhouse (H. Hilton Schiphol) *Env. at Schiphol*

Pub rest – Brasseries

7 Amstel Bar and Brasserie (The) (H. Amstel) *Centre*
13 Brasserie Camelia (H. Okura) *South and West Q.*
7 Brasserie De Palmboom (H. Radisson SAS) *Centre*
13 Brasserie van Baerle *Rijksmuseum*
11 Café Roux (H. The Grand Sofitel Demeure) *Centre*
8 Crowne Plaza American *Centre*
9 Eden *Centre*
13 Garage (Le) *Rijksmuseum*
9 NH City Centre *Centre*
9 NH Schiller *Centre*
15 Novotel *Buitenveldert*
9 Port van Cleve (Die) *Centre*
9 NH Schiller *Centre*

Seafood – Oyster bar

11 Pêcheur (Le) *Centre*
14 Sirène (La) (H. Le Meridien Apollo) *South and West Q.*
14 visaandeschelde *South and West Q.*

American

15 *H. Holiday Inn Buitenveldert*

Asian

17 East West (*H. Hilton Schiphol*) *Env. at Schiphol*
8 Dylan (The) *Centre*

Chinese

11 Sichuan Food *Centre*

Dutch regional

7 Dorrius (H. Crowne Plaza City Centre) *Centre*
19 Roode Leeuw (De) (H. Amsterdam) *Centre*

Indian

15 Pakistan *South and West Q.*

Indonesian

13 blue pepper *Centre*
11 Indrapura *Centre*
13 Radèn Mas *Rijksmuseum*

Italian

12 Bice (H. Golden Tulip Centre) *Rijksmuseum*
8 Caruso (H. Jolly Carlton) *Centre*
9 NH City Centre *Centre*
17 Radisson SAS Airport *Env. at Schiphol*
13 Roberto's (H. Hilton) *South and West Q.*
11 Segugio *Centre*
8 Swissôtel *Centre*

Japanese

11 Hosokawa *Centre*
13 Sazanka (H. Okura) *South and West Q.*
14 Yamazato (H. Okura) *South and West Q.*

Oriental

10 Dynasty *Centre*
11 Manchurian *Centre*

Vietnamese

12 Indochine (L') *Centre*

Centre

Amstel, Prof. Tulpplein 1, 1018 GX, (0 20) 622 60 60, *amstel@interconti.com, Fax (0 20) 622 58 08*, - 25-180. VISA JCB. MZ a
Meals see ***La Rive*** below – ***The Amstel Bar and Brasserie*** (open until 11.30 p.m.) a la carte 46/58 – 29 – **64 rm** 550/750, – 15 suites.
◆ This palace is a veritable haven of luxury and fine taste on the banks of the Amstel, its sumptuous rooms decorated with period furniture and magnificent detail. The cosy library-bar offers an appetising and cosmopolitan menu. Superb, attentive service.

The Grand Sofitel Demeure, O.Z. Voorburgwal 197, 1012 EX, (0 20) 555 31 11, *h2783@accor.com, Fax (0 20) 555 32 22*, - - 25-300. VISA. LX b
Meals see ***Café Roux*** below – 25 – **170 rm** 420/520, – 12 suites.
◆ Authentic Art Nouveau lounges, exquisite bedrooms and an inner garden await guests behind the magnificent façade of this building, which in the 16C hosted Maria de' Medici.

NH Gd H. Krasnapolsky, Dam 9, 1012 JS, (0 20) 554 91 11, *nhkrasnapolsky@nh-hotels.com, Fax (0 20) 622 86 07*, - - 25-750. VISA LX k
Meals ***Reflet*** *(closed 2 weeks Christmas-New Year)* (lunch by arrangement) 33 – **461 rm** 125/390, – 7 suites.
◆ This large hotel on the Dam offers a choice of "business" and "executive" rooms as well as apartments in modern or traditional style. The Reflet, created in 1883, has retained its original splendour and refined atmosphere. Delightful 19C winter garden.

de l'Europe, Nieuwe Doelenstraat 2, 1012 CP, (0 20) 531 17 77, *hotel@leurope.nl, Fax (0 20) 531 17 78*, - - 25-80. VISA JCB LY c
Meals see ***Excelsior*** and ***Le Relais*** below – 23 – **94 rm** 290/440, – 6 suites.
◆ A late-19C hotel-palace that combines both charm and tradition, with bedrooms decorated in fine taste. Collection of paintings by Dutch landscape artists. Attractive sea views.

NH Barbizon Palace, Prins Hendrikkade 59, 1012 AD, (0 20) 556 45 64, *nhbarbizonpalace@nh-hotels.com, Fax (0 20) 624 33 53*, - ch, - 25-300. VISA JCB. LV d
Meals see ***Vermeer*** below – ***Hudson's Terrace and Restaurant*** (open until 11 p.m.) Lunch 13 – a la carte approx. 47 – 20 – **267 rm** 185/290, – 3 suites.
◆ This comfortable hotel near the railway station has recently undergone substantial renovation in its guestrooms and public areas, with the superb colonnaded main hall. Modern cuisine and a vaguely nautical atmosphere in the Hudson's restaurant.

Radisson SAS, Rusland 17, 1012 CK, (0 20) 623 12 31, *reservations.amsterdam@radissonsas.com, Fax (0 20) 520 82 00*, - ch, - 25-180. VISA. rest LX h
Meals ***Brasserie De Palmboom*** Lunch 29 – a la carte approx. 41 – 22 – **242 rm** 260, – 1 suite.
◆ A modern chain hotel with an 18C presbytery in the atrium. Comfortable rooms, decorated in Scandinavian, Dutch, Oriental and Art Deco styles. Mediterranean restaurant with an emphasis on Italian cuisine, plus a modern brasserie with a relaxed atmosphere.

Renaissance, Kattengat 1, 1012 SZ, (0 20) 621 22 23, *renaissance.amsterdam@renaissancehotels.com, Fax (0 20) 627 52 45*, - ch, - 25-400. VISA. LV e
Meals *(closed Saturday and Sunday)*. Lunch 34 – a la carte 30/42 – 22 – **382 rm** 219/360, – 6 suites.
◆ A hotel offering superb conference facilities under the dome of a former Lutheran church. Modern comfort in the bedrooms, junior suites and suites. A wide range of guest services, plus a brasserie-restaurant serving a varied selection of international cuisine.

Crowne Plaza City Centre, N.Z. Voorburgwal 5, 1012 RC, (0 20) 620 05 00, *info@crownplaza.nl, Fax (0 20) 620 11 73*, - - 25-270. VISA. LV g
Meals ***Dorrius*** *(closed Sunday and Monday)* (partly Dutch regional cooking, dinner only) 38 – **268 rm** 125/395, – 2 suites.
◆ Near the station, the Crowne Plaza offers the comfort expected of this chain. View of Amsterdam's rooftops from the "lounge club" on the top floor. Attractive panelled restaurant and authentic 19C café. Traditional menu choices plus a range of local dishes.

Pulitzer, Prinsengracht 323, 1016 GZ, (0 20) 523 52 35, *sales.amsterdam@starwoodhotels.com, Fax (0 20) 627 67 53*, - - 25-150. VISA KX m
Meals ***Pulitzers*** a la carte 39/62 – 25 – **227 rm** 220/455, – 3 suites.
◆ A group of 25 17C-18C canal houses arranged around a central garden. Bedrooms offering welcome personal touches, and public areas embellished with works of art. A modern, original café-restaurant with humorous references to the painter Frans Hals.

Crowne Plaza American, Leidsekade 97, ✉ 1017 PN, ✆ (0 20) 556 30 00, *american@ichotelsgroup.com, Fax (0 20) 556 30 01,* , , , – , rm, ch, – 25-150. AE VISA JCB. JY q
Meals (Art deco style pub rest). *Lunch 28* – a la carte 28/41 ♀ – 18 – **172 rm** 130/365, – 2 suites.
◆ Hidden behind the imposing historic façade is this pleasant hotel with rooms that, although identically furnished, vary in size. The sophisticated entrance hall, with its touches of Art Deco, is the setting for the hotel's tavern-restaurant.

Victoria, Damrak 1, ✉ 1012 LG, ✆ (0 20) 623 42 55, *vicsales@parkplazahotels.nl, Fax (0 20) 625 29 97,* , , – ch, – 30-150. AE VISA JCB. LV j
Meals. *Lunch 23* – a la carte 35/70 ♀ – 20 – **295 rm** 99/315, – 10 suites.
◆ This classical palace, embellished by a new wing, is in an ideal location for those arriving in the city by train. Four room categories. The entrance hall is crowned by an attractive glass roof. Modern cuisine.

The Dylan, Keizersgracht 384, ✉ 1016 GB, ✆ (0 20) 530 20 10, *restaurant@blakes.nl, Fax (0 20) 530 20 30,* , , – , rm, – 30. AE VISA. KX a
Meals *(closed Saturday lunch and Sunday)* (partly Asian cuisine). *Lunch 28* – a la carte 55/81 – 21 – **38 rm** 255/995, – 3 suites.
◆ Luxury and peace and quiet best describe this residence with its surprising Oriental-inspired decor. Highly individual rooms, and a restaurant with a minimalist feel where the emphasis is on the flavours of the East.

Jolly Carlton, Vijzelstraat 4, ✉ 1017 HK, ✆ (0 20) 622 22 66 and 623 83 20 (rest), *banqueting.nl@jollyhotels.com, Fax (0 20) 626 61 83* – ch, – 25-150. AE VISA. LY n
Meals ***Caruso*** (Italian cuisine, dinner only until 11 p.m.) a la carte 52/65 ♀ – 17 – **218 rm** 125/470.
◆ This chain hotel, housed in a building from around 1900, is close to the flower market and Rembrandtplein. Standard rooms with soundproofing and Italian furnishings. Elegant restaurant serving Italian cuisine, including well-balanced lunches and fixed menus.

Swissôtel, Damrak 96, ✉ 1012 LP, ✆ (0 20) 522 30 00, *emailus.amsterdam@swissotel.com, Fax (0 20) 522 32 23,* – ch, – 25-45. AE VISA JCB. LX s
Meals (partly Italian cuisine) a la carte 22/41 ♀ – 20 – **101 rm** 299/360, – 5 suites.
◆ Various categories of guestrooms, including several junior suites, are on offer at this hotel near the Dam. Modern facilities, a business centre plus a trendy brasserie-restaurant with Mediterranean-inspired cuisine and a distinctly Italian slant.

Sofitel, N.Z. Voorburgwal 67, ✉ 1012 RE, ✆ (0 20) 627 59 00, *h1159@accor.com, Fax (0 20) 623 89 32,* – ch, – 25-55. AE VISA.
Meals a la carte 32/49 – 20 – **148 rm** 255/305. KX q
◆ This upmarket chain hotel, 500m/550yd from the main station, occupies an old mansion and an adjoining modern building. Recently refurbished façade and bedrooms. "Orient Express" atmosphere in the restaurant. Traditional menu.

Toren without rest, Keizersgracht 164, ✉ 1015 CZ, ✆ (0 20) 622 63 52, *info@hoteltoren.nl, Fax (0 20) 626 97 05,* – AE VISA KV w
12 – **39 rm** 135/240, – 1 suite.
◆ Anne Frank's House is just 200m/220yd from this family-run hotel with its tasteful, classic-style bedrooms. Elegant breakfast room next to the hotel's cosy bar.

NH Doelen without rest, Nieuwe Doelenstraat 24, ✉ 1012 CP, ✆ (0 20) 554 06 00, *nhdoelen@nh-hotels.com, Fax (0 20) 622 10 84,* , – – 25-100. AE VISA JCB. LY z
16 – **85 rm** 105/145.
◆ Built in 1856 on the banks of the Amstel, the Doelen is one of the oldest hotels in the city. English-style rooms with varying degrees of soundproofing.

Seven One Seven without rest, Prinsengracht 717, ✉ 1017 JW, ✆ (0 20) 427 07 17, *info@717hotel.nl, Fax (0 20) 423 07 17,* – . AE VISA.
8 rm 390/640. KY c
◆ If you're looking for a quiet, intimate hotel, this elegant 18C residence could be just for you, with its exquisite, individually furnished and spacious bedrooms.

Ambassade without rest, Herengracht 341, ✉ 1016 AZ, ✆ (0 20) 555 02 22, *info@ambassade-hotel.nl, Fax (0 20) 555 02 77,* , – . AE VISA KX x
16 – **51 rm** 165/195, – 8 suites.
◆ A group of typical 17C houses is the setting for this charming hotel bordered by two canals. Although varying in size, each bedroom is endowed with its own personal touch. Interesting library.

Estheréa without rest, Singel 305, ✉ 1012 WJ, ✆ (0 20) 624 51 46, *estherea@xs4all.nl*, *Fax (0 20) 623 90 01* – |‡| ⇋ TV. AE MC VISA JCB. ⚘ KX y
☐ 14 – **71 rm** 221/285.
• Set back from the hubbub of Amsterdam's central district, between the history museum and the Singel, this hotel is a complex of several adjoining houses with pleasant rooms.

Eden, Amstel 144, ✉ 1017 AE, ✆ (0 20) 530 78 78, *reso.eden@edenhotelgroup.com*, *Fax (0 20) 623 32 67* – |‡| ⇋, ▤ rm, TV ♿ ch,. AE ⊙ MC VISA JCB. ⚘ LY r
Meals (pub rest) 22/33 – ☐ 14 – **327 rm** 115/190.
• It's hard to believe that hidden behind the façade of these two narrow buildings along the banks of the Amstel is a hotel with over 300 rooms. Bar-restaurant with views of the river. Popular with both individual visitors and tour groups.

Amsterdam, Damrak 93, ✉ 1012 LP, ✆ (0 20) 555 06 66, *info@hotelamsterdam.nl*, *Fax (0 20) 620 47 16* – |‡| ⇋ ▤ TV. AE ⊙ MC VISA JCB. ⚘ LX s
Meals *De Roode Leeuw* (partly Dutch regional cooking) 27/30 – ☐ 11 – **79 rm** 95/310.
• This veteran Amsterdam hotel enjoys an unbeatable central location along the popular Damstraat. Rooms beyond reproach, with public parking nearby. The hotel brasserie serves a range of typically Dutch specialities.

NH Schiller, Rembrandtsplein 26, ✉ 1017 CV, ✆ (0 20) 554 07 00, *nhschiller@nh-hotels.com*, *Fax (0 20) 626 68 31*, ♣ – |‡| ⇋ TV. AE ⊙ MC VISA JCB. ⚘ LY x
Meals (brasserie). *Lunch 18* – 22/33 b.i. ♀ – ☐ 16 – **91 rm** 119/230, – 1 suite.
• A 1900s-style building fronting a lively square adorned with a statue of Rembrandt. Adequately equipped rooms with quality furnishings. Pleasant lobby. In the Art Deco brasserie, make sure you try the Frisse Frits, the bar's home-brewed beer.

Albus Gd H. without rest, Vijzelstraat 49, ✉ 1017 HE, ✆ (0 20) 530 62 00, *info@albusgrandhotel.com*, *Fax (0 20) 530 62 99* – |‡| ⇋ TV. AE ⊙ MC VISA JCB. ⚘ LY g
☐ 14 – **74 rm** 180/200.
• This hotel halfway between the flower market and Rembrandtplein provides good value for money and high levels of comfort. Ideal for guests in the city for business or leisure.

NH Caransa without rest, Rembrandtsplein 19, ✉ 1017 CT, ✆ (0 20) 554 08 00, *nhcaransa@nh-hotels.com*, *Fax (0 20) 626 68 31* – |‡| ⇋ TV – 🎤 25-100. AE ⊙ MC VISA JCB. ⚘ LY v
☐ 16 – **66 rm** 119/230.
• The Caransa's rooms are functional, well-maintained and reasonably sized. The warm furnishings add a cosy "British" feel. Four seminar rooms available for business meetings.

die Port van Cleve, N.Z. Voorburgwal 178, ✉ 1012 SJ, ✆ (0 20) 624 48 60, *salesmarketing@dieportvancleve.com*, *Fax (0 20) 622 02 40* – |‡| ⇋, ▤ rest, TV – 🎤 40. AE ⊙ MC VISA JCB. ⚘ KX w
Meals (brasserie). *Lunch 20* – a la carte 24/53 ♀ – ☐ 18 – **119 rm** 216/305, – 1 suite.
• The very first Dutch brewery group was established behind this imposing façade near the royal palace in the 19C. Noteworthy features today include the six junior suites and a charming Dutch-style bar. Grill-restaurant where steak holds pride of place.

Dikker and Thijs Fenice without rest, Prinsengracht 444, ✉ 1017 KE, ✆ (0 20) 620 12 12, *info@dtfh.nl*, *Fax (0 20) 625 89 86*, ⚓ – |‡| ⇋ TV. AE ⊙ MC VISA JCB
42 rm ☐ 125/345. KY v
• This classical building is located 100m/110yd from the Leidseplein, opposite a small bridge spanning the Princes' Canal, which is visible from a few of the rooms.

NH City Centre, Spuistraat 288, ✉ 1012 VX, ✆ (0 20) 420 45 45, *Fax (0 20) 420 43 00*, ≤, ⚓ – |‡| ⇋ TV ♿ ch, 🚗. AE ⊙ MC VISA JCB. ⚘ KX g
Meals (pub rest, partly Italian cuisine). *Lunch 20* – a la carte 22/35 ♀ – ☐ 16 – **209 rm** 120/190.
• Nestled between the Singel and the Begijnhof, this chain hotel offers rooms which have been newly refurbished in typical NH style. Spacious, comfortable lounge plus an informal restaurant serving Italian cuisine.

Mercure Arthur Frommer without rest, Noorderstraat 46, ✉ 1017 TV, ✆ (0 20) 622 03 28, *h1032@accor.com*, *Fax (0 20) 620 32 08* – |‡| ⇋ ▤ TV 🚗 P. AE ⊙ MC VISA. ⚘ LYZ j
☐ 14 – **90 rm** 105/170.
• A series of houses lining a quiet street close to both the Rijksmuseum and the Museum Van Loon. Fairly standard rooms, basic levels of service, but a useful car park.

Canal House without rest, Keizersgracht 148, ✉ 1015 CX, ✆ (0 20) 622 51 82, *info@canalhouse.nl*, *Fax (0 20) 624 13 17* – |‡|. ⊙ MC VISA JCB. ⚘ KV k
26 rm ☐ 140/190.
• This 17C canal-front residence has preserved all its old charm. Individually styled rooms, with good views at the front and less noise at the rear. Eclectic mix of furniture.

Inntel without rest, Nieuwezijdskolk 19, ✉ 1012 PV, ☎ (0 20) 530 18 18, *infoamsterdam@hotelinntel.com, Fax (0 20) 422 19 19* – AE Ⓓ MC VISA LVX a

☕ 18 – **236 rm** 99/290.

◆ A modern hotel at the heart of the busy Nieuwe Zijde shopping district near the station. Rooms with double-glazing and soundproofed doors.

Rembrandt without rest, Herengracht 255, ✉ 1016 BJ, ☎ (0 20) 622 17 27, *info@rembrandtresidence.nl, Fax (0 20) 625 06 30*, – . AE Ⓓ MC VISA JCB KX e

111 rm ☕ 100/175.

◆ An ideal location for those keen to explore the city centre and its canals. Accommodation of varying sizes, with more standardised guestrooms along the Singel.

City Center without rest, N.Z. Voorburgwal 50, ✉ 1012 SC, ☎ (0 20) 422 00 11, *info@ams.nl, Fax (0 20) 420 03 57* – . AE Ⓓ MC VISA. LV f

☕ 15 – **106 rm** 189.

◆ A modern building on the edge of the Nieuwe Zijde district, 400m/440yd from the main station. Basic, but well-maintained rooms. The underground car park is a major plus.

Wiechmann without rest, Prinsengracht 328, ✉ 1016 HX, ☎ (0 20) 626 33 21, *info@hotelwiechmann.nl, Fax (0 20) 626 89 62* – . MC VISA. KX d

37 rm ☕ 55/140.

◆ The Wiechmann occupies three small houses overlooking the Prinsengracht. The best, albeit slightly more rustic rooms are to be found on the corners of the building.

Lancaster without rest, Plantage Middenlaan 48, ✉ 1018 DH, ☎ (0 20) 535 68 88, *res.lancaster@edenhotelgroup.com, Fax (0 20) 535 68 89* – . AE Ⓓ MC VISA JCB. MY e

☕ 14 – **92 rm** 95/170.

◆ This completely renovated old residence stands opposite the zoo in a residential area away from the centre. Although differing in size, the rooms here are perfectly adequate.

XXXX ✿✿ **La Rive** - Hotel Amstel, Prof. Tulpplein 1, ✉ 1018 GX, ☎ (0 20) 520 32 64, *evert_groot@interconti.com, Fax (0 20) 520 32 66*, ≤, – . AE Ⓓ MC VISA JCB. MZ a

closed 25 July-15 August, 31 December-1 January, Saturday lunch, Sunday and Bank Holidays – **Meals**. Lunch 50 b.i. – 85/98, – a la carte 71/97 ♀

Spec. Terrine de jambon Jabugo, foie gras à la gelée de queue de bœuf. Pigeonneau grillé et poivron rouge, sauce au maïs. Feuilleté aux pommes, cannelle, glace vanille et caramel au beurre salé.

◆ Hushed tones, refined décor and incomparable comfort are the main features of the Amstel's gastronomic restaurant, from where guests can enjoy a superb view of the river.

XXXX **Excelsior** - Hotel de l'Europe, Nieuwe Doelenstraat 2, ✉ 1012 CP, ☎ (0 20) 531 17 05, *hotel@leurope.nl, Fax (0 20) 531 17 78*, ≤, , Open until 11 p.m., – . AE Ⓓ MC VISA JCB LY c

closed 1 to 15 January and lunch Saturday and Sunday – **Meals**. Lunch 45 – 65/95 b.i. ♀.

◆ This century-old palace provides a delightful backdrop to its pleasantly redecorated restaurant. Views of the Munttoren and the ever-busy Amstel River from the terrace.

XXXX ✿ **Vermeer** - Hotel NH Barbizon Palace, Prins Hendrikkade 59, ✉ 1012 AD, ☎ (0 20) 556 48 85, *vermeer@nh-hotels.nl, Fax (0 20) 624 33 53*, – . AE Ⓓ MC VISA. LV d

closed 27 July-26 August, 24 December-8 January, Saturday lunch and Sunday – **Meals**. Lunch 40 – 55/130 b.i. – a la carte 58/75 ♀

Spec. Ravioli de ris de veau aux écrevisses et mousse de citron. Risotto de bar à l'émulsion d'olives. Ananas rôti aux granny smith et glace au beurre noisette.

◆ Sadly, Vermeer never set up his easel at this restaurant which offers customers elegant, classically-based cuisine, enlivened by the occasional note of inventiveness.

XXX ✿ **Christophe** (Royer), Leliegracht 46, ✉ 1015 DH, ☎ (0 20) 625 08 07, *info@christophe.nl, Fax (0 20) 638 91 32* – . AE Ⓓ MC VISA KVX c

closed 1 to 8 January, Sunday and Monday – **Meals** (dinner only) 65/75, – a la carte 64/93 ♀

Spec. Lapin de quatre heures au foie gras et jus de cassis. Fricassée de homard aux haricots coco et piments d'Espelette. Noix de ris de veau au romarin et citron confit.

◆ Ambitious cuisine peppered with Mediterranean touches served in a luxurious setting. Central location on the Leliegracht, near Anne Frank's House and the Jordaan district.

XXX **Dynasty**, Reguliersdwarsstraat 30, ✉ 1017 BM, ☎ (0 20) 626 84 00, *Fax (0 20) 622 30 38*, , Oriental cuisine – . AE Ⓓ MC VISA. KY q

closed 27 December-27 January and Tuesday – **Meals** (dinner only) a la carte 32/50.

◆ Enjoy a wander through the flower market before sitting down to table at this Oriental restaurant with its refreshing, multi-coloured décor. Specialities from Southeast Asia.

XX **d'Vijff Vlieghen,** Spuistraat 294 (by Vlieghendesteeg1), ✉ 1012 VX, ☎ (0 20) 530 40 60, *restaurant@vijffvlieghen.nl, Fax (0 20) 623 64 04*, , – . AE ⓓ ⓜ VISA JCB. KX p
Meals (dinner only) 33/51 ♀.
◆ The "Five Flies" (Vijff Vlieghen) is a group of small 17C houses concealing a maze of charming, rustic-style rooms. Traditional à la carte choices and menus.

XX **Café Roux** - Hotel The Grand Sofitel Demeure, O.Z. Voorburgwal 197, ✉ 1012 EX, ☎ (0 20) 555 35 60, *h2783-fb@accor.com, Fax (0 20) 555 32 22*, – P. AE ⓓ ⓜ VISA. LX b
Meals. *Lunch 30* – 35/49 b.i. ♀.
◆ The Sofitel Demeure's Art Deco brasserie is known for its inventive modern cuisine. A mural by K. Appel, a member of the Cobra artistic group, is visible near the entrance.

XX **Het Tuynhuys,** Reguliersdwarsstraat 28, ✉ 1017 BM, ☎ (0 20) 627 66 03, *info@tuynhuys.nl, Fax (0 20) 423 59 99*, – . AE ⓓ ⓜ VISA JCB KY q
closed 31 December-1 January and lunch Saturday and Sunday – **Meals.** *Lunch 30* – 32/48.
◆ The menu is distinctly modern in this stylish split-level restaurant with an attractive garden terrace and contemporary dining room adorned with glazed ceramics.

XX **Indrapura,** Rembrandtplein 42, ✉ 1017 CV, ☎ (0 20) 623 73 29, *info@indrapura.nl, Fax (0 20) 624 90 78*, Indonesian cuisine – . AE ⓓ ⓜ VISA LY h
closed 31 December – **Meals** (dinner only) 25/39 ♀.
◆ A good choice of Indonesian dishes, including the inevitable"rijsttafel" (rice table). A broad mix of customers, including tourists, locals and groups.

XX ✿ **Sichuan Food,** Reguliersdwarsstraat 35, ✉ 1017 BK, ☎ (0 20) 626 93 27, *Fax (0 20) 627 72 81*, Chinese cuisine – . AE ⓓ ⓜ VISA. KY u
closed 31 December – **Meals** (dinner only, booking essential) 31/43, – a la carte 35/63
Spec. Dim Sum. Canard laqué à la pékinoise. Huîtres sautées maison.
◆ Hidden behind the ordinary façade is a temple of Asian gastronomy, where the flavours of Szechwan take pride of place. The décor is typical of any local Chinese restaurant.

XX **Hosokawa,** Max Euweplein 22, ✉ 1017 MB, ☎ (0 20) 638 80 86, *info@hosokawa.nl, Fax (0 20) 638 22 19*, Japanese cuisine with Teppan-Yaki – AE ⓓ ⓜ VISA JCB.
closed Sunday – **Meals** a la carte 34/66. KY a
◆ A sober, modern Japanese restaurant with eight teppanyaki (hotplates). Worth the trip just to admire the constant circulation of dishes in front of your eyes. Sushi bar.

XX ✿ **Van Vlaanderen** (Philippart), Weteringschans 175, ✉ 1017 XD, ☎ (0 20) 622 82 92, , – . AE ⓜ VISA KZ k
closed 24 July-15 August, 25 December-2 January, Sunday and Monday – **Meals** (dinner only, booking essential) 40/48, – a la carte 56/63 ♀
Spec. Méli-mélo de homard, Saint-Jacques et artichaut. Pigeon de Bresse farçi de foie de canard, sauce aux quatre épices. Millefeuille de poires, glace vanille aux cerneaux de noix et sauce caramel.
◆ Modern and refined French cuisine, coupled with the occasional Belgian-inspired recipe, awaits customers at this recommended address near the Museum Van Loon and Rijksmuseum.

XX **Breitner,** Amstel 212, ✉ 1017 AH, ☎ (0 20) 627 78 79, *Fax (0 20) 330 29 98* – AE ⓜ VISA JCB. LY p
closed 25 July-7 August, 25 December-3 January and Sunday – **Meals** (dinner only) a la carte 44/68 ♀.
◆ This restaurant takes its name from the Dutch impressionist artist. Modern cuisine, largely based on Mediterranean recipes. Wines from around the world. Views of the Amstel.

XX **Manchurian,** Leidseplein 10a, ✉ 1017 PT, ☎ (0 20) 623 13 30, *info@manchurian.nl, Fax (0 20) 626 21 05*, Oriental cuisine – . AE ⓓ ⓜ VISA JCB. KY x
closed 30 April and 31 December – **Meals** 30/70 b.i..
◆ This Asian restaurant on the busy Leidseplein specialises in Thai cuisine as well as Chinese dishes from Canton, Shanghai and Szechwan.

XX **Segugio,** Utrechtsestraat 96, ✉ 1017 VS, ☎ (0 20) 330 15 03, *Fax (0 20) 330 15 16*, Italian cuisine – . AE ⓓ ⓜ VISA. LY b
closed 23 December-2 January and Sunday – **Meals** (dinner only until 11 p.m.) a la carte 46/66 ♀.
◆ A good sense of smell is all you need to locate this "ristorante" which takes its name from a breed of hunting dog also used as a truffle hound. Good choice of Italian wines.

XX **Le Pêcheur,** Reguliersdwarsstraat 32, ✉ 1017 BM, ☎ (0 20) 624 31 21, *rien.vansanten@chello.nl, Fax (0 20) 624 31 21*, , Seafood – AE ⓜ VISA JCB. KY w
closed Saturday lunch and Sunday – **Meals.** *Lunch 31* – 40.
◆ As its name (The Fisherman) would suggest, fish and seafood take pride of place in this restaurant alongside the flower market. Terrace to the rear and parking nearby.

d'theeboom, Singel 210, ✉ 1016 AB, ✆ (0 20) 623 84 20, *info@theeboom.nl, Fax (0 20) 421 25 12,* – AE ① MC VISA JCB KX b
closed 24 December-5 January and Sunday – **Meals** (dinner only) 33/40.
◆ Firmly established along the Singel, 200m/220yd from the Dam, "The Tea-Room" is anything but ! It is in fact a restaurant with an interesting menu of inventive dishes.

Le Relais - Hotel de l'Europe, Nieuwe Doelenstraat 2, ✉ 1012 CP, ✆ (0 20) 531 17 77, *hotel@leurope.nl, Fax (0 20) 531 17 78,* Open until 11 p.m., – AE ① MC VISA JCB LY c
Meals. *Lunch 23* – 28 ♀.
◆ A small, elegant restaurant within a large hotel where you immediately feel in good hands. Traditional choices on a menu without any particular culinary theme.

Bordewijk, Noordermarkt 7, ✉ 1015 MV, ✆ (0 20) 624 38 99, *Fax (0 20) 420 66 03* – . AE ① MC VISA. KV a
closed mid July-mid August, 24 December-4 January and Monday – **Meals** (dinner only) a la carte 46/68.
◆ One of the trendiest addresses in the Jordaan district with a lively dining room furnished in a sober, yet modern style. Appetising menu and good wine list.

Haesje Claes, Spuistraat 275, ✉ 1012 VR, ✆ (0 20) 624 99 98, *info@haesjeclaes.nl, Fax (0 20) 627 48 17,* – . AE ① MC VISA JCB. KX f
closed 30 April and 25, 26 and 31 December – **Meals** 19/29 ♀.
◆ With its local atmosphere and loyal customers, this welcoming restaurant serves true Flemish fare : unfussy, generous and satisfying. 100m/110yd from the History Museum.

Entresol, Geldersekade 29, ✉ 1011 EJ, ✆ (0 20) 623 79 12, *entresol@chello.nl* – . MC VISA LX t
closed Monday and Tuesday – **Meals** (dinner only) a la carte 37/46.
◆ This charming, small family restaurant near Amsterdam's Chinatown occupies a house over 300 years old. Dutch-style décor in the dining rooms spread over two floors.

blue pepper, Nassaukade 366h, ✉ 1054 AB, ✆ (0 20) 489 70 39, *info@restaurantbluepepper.com,* Indonesian cuisine – AE ① MC VISA. JY d
closed Sunday – **Meals** (dinner only) a la carte 33/43 ♀.
◆ Filtered light, monochrome blues and delicate floral touches provide the basis of Blue Pepper's tranquil decor. Refined Javanese cuisine served on attractive tableware.

L'Indochine, Beulingstraat 9, ✉ 1017 BA, ✆ (0 20) 627 57 55, *kietle@wxs.nl,* Vietnamese cuisine – . AE ① MC VISA JCB. KY b
closed Monday – **Meals** (lunch by arrangement) a la carte 34/47.
◆ Embark upon a gastronomic journey between the gulfs of Siam and Tonkin in this small, simply furnished restaurant with a "colonial" name. Choice of French wines.

Rijksmuseum (Vondelpark)

Marriott, Stadhouderskade 12, ✉ 1054 ES, ✆ (0 20) 607 55 55, *amsterdam@mariotthotels.com, Fax (0 20) 607 55 11,* , , – ch, – 25-450. AE ① MC VISA JCB. JY f
Meals *(closed last 2 weeks July-first 2 weeks August, Sunday and Monday)* (dinner only) a la carte 34/44 ♀ – 24 – **387 rm** 199/249, – 5 suites.
◆ Impressive American-style hotel on one of the city's main roads. Huge rooms with a full range of creature comforts. Business centre and conference facilities.

NH Amsterdam Centre, Stadhouderskade 7, ✉ 1054 ES, ✆ (0 20) 685 13 51, *nhamsterdamcentre@nh-hotels.nl, Fax (0 20) 685 16 11* – ch, – 25-200. AE ① MC VISA JCB. JY p
Meals a la carte 22/41 – ***Bice*** *(closed 3 weeks August)* (Italian cuisine, dinner only) a la carte approx. 40 – 19 – **228 rm** 160/390, – 2 suites.
◆ This easily accessible, completely renovated chain hotel is located along the Singelgracht. Spacious, highly comfortable rooms with period furniture. Impressive restaurant serving Italian cuisine and a brasserie that stays open late.

The Gresham Memphis without rest, De Lairessestraat 87, ✉ 1071 NX, ✆ (0 20) 673 31 41, *info@gresham-memphishotel.nl, Fax (0 20) 673 73 12,* , – – 40. AE ① MC VISA JCB.
18 – **74 rm** 205/250.
◆ Pleasant rooms that are soundproofed and gradually being modernised. Attentive service. Tram number 16 runs from in front of the hotel to the centre of the city.

Jan Luyken without rest, Jan Luykenstraat 58, ✉ 1071 CS, ✆ (0 20) 573 07 30, *jan-luyken@bilderberg.nl, Fax (0 20) 676 38 41* – . AE ① MC VISA JCB
18 – **62 rm** 90/258. JZ m
◆ An elegant hotel made up of three buildings dating from 1900 with modern interior decor. Large, well-appointed rooms and a good location at the heart of the museum district.

Vondel (annex) without rest, Vondelstraat 28, ✉ 1054 GE, ℘ (0 20) 612 01 20, *info @hotelvondel.nl, Fax (0 20) 685 43 21,* – |‡| TV. AE ① MC VISA JCB JY m
17 – **70 rm** 139/239.
• The Vondel occupies five houses dating from the late 19C. The building housing the reception has the best rooms, decorated in "boutique" style. Elegant lounges.

Ramada Museum Square without rest, De Lairessestraat 7, ✉ 1071 NR, ℘ (0 20) 671 95 96, *info@ams.nl, Fax (0 20) 671 17 56* – |‡| TV. AE ① MC VISA JCB.
15 – **34 rm** 149/239.
• Despite its plain façade, this hotel is well-maintained and enjoys a superb location close to three of the city's most important museums. Spacious rooms with modern furniture.

Fita without rest, Jan Luykenstraat 37, ✉ 1071 CL, ℘ (0 20) 679 09 76, *info@fita.nl, Fax (0 20) 664 39 69* – |‡| TV. AE ① MC VISA. JZ s
closed 15 December-16 January – **16 rm** 90/140.
• A small hotel offering a perfect base for individual travellers with its three categories of functional bedrooms and great location close to Amsterdam's major museums.

De Filosoof without rest, Anna van den Vondelstraat 6, ✉ 1054 GZ, ℘ (0 20) 683 30 13, *reservations@hotelfilosoof.nl, Fax (0 20) 685 37 50* – |‡| TV – 25. AE MC VISA.
38 rm 99/150.
• An original hotel on a one-way street skirting the Vondelpark. The decor here is inspired by cultural and philosophical themes, which can be mused on further in the garden.

Villa Borgmann without rest, Koningslaan 48, ✉ 1075 AE, ℘ (0 20) 673 52 52, *info@hotel-borgmann.nl, Fax (0 20) 676 25 80* – |‡| TV. AE ① MC VISA.
10 – **15 rm** 75/135.
• This attractive, 1900s red-brick villa near the refreshing Vondelpark is family-run and offers a quiet alternative to the city centre. Large, modern rooms.

Radèn Mas, Stadhouderskade 6, ✉ 1054 ES, ℘ (0 20) 685 40 41, *Fax (0 20) 685 39 81,* Indonesian cuisine, open until 11 p.m. – ▤. AE ① MC VISA JCB. JY k
Meals a la carte 31/68.
• This Indonesian restaurant enjoys a flattering reputation for its embodiment of the culinary heritage of this former Dutch colony. Live pianist every evening except Tuesday.

Le Garage, Ruysdaelstraat 54, ✉ 1071 XE, ℘ (0 20) 679 71 76, *info@rest-legarage.nl, Fax (0 20) 662 22 49,* With streetfood in Le Garage en Pluche, open until 11 p.m. – ▤ dinner only. AE ① MC VISA JCB
closed 25 July-8 August – **Meals**. *Lunch 30* – 33/50 ♀.
• A theatrical atmosphere and cosmopolitan exuberance pervade this modern brasserie whose menu is both varied and imaginative. Lively tapas bar-restaurant next door.

Spring, Willemsparkweg 177, ✉ 1071 GZ, ℘ (0 20) 675 44 21, *info@restaurantspring.nl, Fax (0 20) 676 94 14,* – ▤. AE ① MC VISA JCB.
closed Saturday lunch and Sunday – **Meals**. *Lunch 30* – a la carte 45/57 ♀.
• This trendy eatery with a long and narrow designer dining room is cut in two by an unusual bench. Highly contemporary cuisine and a collection of canvases by Jasper Krabbé.

Brasserie van Baerle, Van Baerlestraat 158, ✉ 1071 BG, ℘ (0 20) 679 15 32, *Fax (0 20) 671 71 96,* , Open until 11 p.m. – AE ① MC VISA
closed 25 and 26 December, January and Saturday lunch – **Meals**. *Lunch 33* – a la carte 39/54 ♀.
• A typical restaurant popular with a loyal local clientele tempted by an attractive menu enhanced by a harmonious wine list. Sunday brunch.

South and West Quarters

Okura , Ferdinand Bolstraat 333, ✉ 1072 LH, ℘ (0 20) 678 71 11, *sales@okura.nl, Fax (0 20) 671 23 44,* , , , , – |‡| ▤ TV ♿ ch, P – 25-1200. AE ① MC VISA JCB.
Meals see ***Ciel Bleu*** and ***Yamazato*** below – ***Sazanka*** (Japanese cuisine with Teppan-Yaki, dinner only) 53/80 ♀ – ***Brasserie Le Camelia*** (open until 11 p.m.) a la carte approx. 46 ♀ – 26 – **357 rm** 170/380, – 12 suites.
• This luxury Japanese-style international hotel overlooks the Noorder Amstel canal. Superb health centre and extensive conference facilities. Japanese restaurant with dishes cooked on typical hobs. The Camelia brasserie serves a variety of French cuisine.

Hilton, Apollolaan 138, ✉ 1077 BG, ℘ (0 20) 710 60 00, *robertos.amsterdam@hilton.com, Fax (0 20) 710 60 80,* , , , , , , – |‡| ▤ TV ♿ ch, P – 25-550. AE ① MC VISA.
Meals *Roberto's* (Italian cuisine with buffet) a la carte 45/54 ♀ – 25 – **267 rm** 180/390, – 4 suites.
• Following a complete overhaul, the Hilton now offers smart new designer rooms, plus a canal-side garden and terraces. The pleasant Mediterranean-style Roberto's restaurant specialises in Italian cuisine with a choice of menus and antipasti buffets.

Bilderberg Garden, Dijsselhofplantsoen 7, ✉ 1077 BJ, ☎ (0 20) 570 56 00, *garden@bilderberg.nl, Fax (0 20) 570 56 54* – AE VISA JCB
Meals see ***Mangerie De Kersentuin*** below – 21 – **120 rm** 165/350, – 2 suites.
♦ This small-sized "grand hotel" combines discreet luxury and charm. Rooms with everything you could possibly need, decorated with taste and a fine sense of detail.

Le Meridien Apollo, Apollolaan 2, ✉ 1077 BA, ☎ (0 20) 673 59 22, *info.apollo@lemeridien.com, Fax (0 20) 570 57 44,* – 25-200. AE VISA JCB.
Meals ***La Sirène*** (seafood) *Lunch 33* – a la carte 43/83 – 21 – **217 rm** 305/390, – 2 suites.
♦ Located away from the frenetic pace of the centre at the junction of five canals, this upmarket chain hotel offers guests comfortable rooms and a full range of services. Spacious modern restaurant with a waterfront terrace and an emphasis on fish and seafood.

Tulip Inn City West, Reimerswaalstraat 5, ✉ 1069 AE, ☎ (0 20) 410 80 00, *info@tiamsterdamcw.nl, Fax (0 20) 410 80 30* – ch, – 25-70. AE VISA
Meals (dinner only) a la carte 22/35 – 14 – **162 rm** 135/150.
♦ This recently opened chain hotel is situated in a relatively quiet area of the city. Its main selling points are its spacious rooms and lounges, and the good parking facilities nearby. Although traditional, the restaurant menu shows contemporary influence.

Tulip Inn Art (annex Golden Tulip Art - 60 rm), Spaarndammerdijk 302 (Westerpark), ✉ 1013 ZX, ☎ (0 20) 410 96 70, *art@westlordhotels.nl, Fax (0 20) 681 08 02,* – – 25. AE VISA.
Meals (open until 11 p.m.) 25 b.i. – 15 – **130 rm** 170.
♦ A thoroughly modern hotel close to the ring-road with rooms designed with the modern business traveller in mind. Exhibition of paintings by contemporary artists. Trendy "brasserie"-style tavern-restaurant.

Ciel Bleu - Hotel Okura, 23rd floor, Ferdinand Bolstraat 333, ✉ 1072 LH, ☎ (0 20) 678 71 11, *restaurants@okura.nl, Fax (0 20) 678 77 88,* ville, – AE VISA JCB.
closed mid July-mid August and late December – **Meals** (dinner only) 55/93, – a la carte 77/102
Spec. Saint-Jacques rôties aux truffes. Agneau de trois façons. Parfait au whisky et beignets de cerises.
♦ This highly acclaimed restaurant, with its appetising and inventive menu, enjoys a superb view of the city's rooftops from the top of the Japanese-owned Okura Hotel.

Yamazato - Hotel Okura, Ferdinand Bolstraat 333, ✉ 1072 LH, ☎ (0 20) 678 83 51, *restaurants@okura.nl, Fax (0 20) 678 77 88,* Japanese cuisine, – AE VISA JCB.
Meals. *Lunch 49* – 50/90, – a la carte 39/69
Spec. Uminosachi Tempura (shrimps). Sukiyaki (beef). Usuzukuri (bass) (September-May).
♦ A minimalist ambience pervades this restaurant serving delicious traditional Japanese dishes under the watchful gaze of geisha girls. Lunch box menu also available.

visaandeschelde, Scheldeplein 4, ✉ 1078 GR, ☎ (0 20) 675 15 83, *info@visaandeschelde.nl, Fax (0 20) 471 46 53,* Seafood, open until 11 p.m. – dinner only AE VISA JCB.
closed 24 December-2 January and lunch Saturday and Sunday – **Meals**. *Lunch 29* – a la carte 40/72
♦ The model of the boat in the window clearly demonstrates this restaurant's culinary intentions. A bright, somewhat spartan dining room in maritime blue and white.

Mangerie De Kersentuin - Hotel Bilderberg Garden, Dijsselhofplantsoen 7, ✉ 1077 BJ, ☎ (0 20) 570 56 00, *garden@bilderberg.nl, Fax (0 20) 570 56 54,* – AE VISA JCB. rest
closed 31 December-1 January, Saturday lunch and Sunday – **Meals**. *Lunch 28* – 33 b.i./58
♦ A brasserie-style atmosphere pervades this "eatery", with its gleaming copper fittings and comfortable red benches. Inviting contemporary menu and welcoming summer terrace.

Blender, Van der Palmkade 16, ✉ 1051 RE, ☎ (0 20) 486 98 60, *info@blender.to, Fax (0 20) 486 98 51,* – AE VISA JV k
closed 1 January and Monday – **Meals** (dinner only until 11 p.m.) a la carte approx. 40
♦ Blender occupies the ground floor of a circular building where the atmosphere is distinctly young and trendy. A semi-circular counter and charming, attentive service.

Le Hollandais, Amsteldijk 41, ✉ 1074 HV, ☎ (0 20) 679 12 48, *lehollandais@planet.nl* – AE VISA JCB
closed Sunday – **Meals** (dinner only) a la carte 41/57
♦ An endearing local bistro-cum-restaurant attracting a professional/bohemian clientele. Modern cuisine in a plain, uncluttered setting.

Pakistan, Scheldestraat 100, ✉ 1078 GP, ✆ (0 20) 675 39 76, *Fax (0 20) 675 39 76*, Indian cuisine – AE ⓓ MC VISA
Meals (dinner only until 11 p.m.) 25/45.
◆ The popularity of this authentic Pakistani restaurant near the RAI remains high thanks to its range of copious menus. No pork on the menu, but plenty of beef.

East and Southeast Quarters

Mercure a/d Amstel, Joan Muyskenweg 10, ✉ 1096 CJ, ✆ (0 20) 665 81 81, *H1244@accor.com, Fax (0 20) 694 87 35*, ch, – 25-450. AE ⓓ MC VISA.
Meals. *Lunch 23* – a la carte 33/47 ♀ – 18 – **368 rm** 175/230.
◆ This hotel on the fringes of the city boasts excellent seminar facilities and rooms that match the standards expected of this worldwide chain. The restaurant offers a range of international dishes plus the standard Mercure wine-list.

Lloyd, Oostelijke Handelskade 34, ✉ 1019 BN, ✆ (0 20) 561 36 36, *post@lloydhotel.com, Fax (0 20) 561 36 00*, – ch, . AE ⓓ MC VISA.
Meals a la carte approx. 22 ♀ – 12 – **119 rm** 80/300.
◆ This imposing former shipbuilder's HQ dates from 1921. The artistic ambience is enhanced by the "cultural university", with its information and booking service. 14 of the hotel's rooms have shared bathrooms. Extensive international menu in the restaurant.

Voorbij het Einde, Sumatrakade 613, ✉ 1019 PS, ✆ (0 20) 419 11 43, *aperlot@wxs.nl, Fax (0 33) 479 31 92*, Open until 11 p.m. – AE MC VISA.
closed 27 December-12 January, Sunday, Monday and Tuesday – **Meals** (lunch by arrangement) a la carte 42/50 ♀.
◆ A pleasant surprise behind a row of austere buildings. Interesting mix of design furniture, bright partitions, an open kitchen and modern windows looking onto a small park.

De Kas, Kamerlingh Onneslaan 3, ✉ 1097 DE, ✆ (0 20) 462 45 62, *info@restaurantdekas.nl, Fax (0 20) 462 45 63*, ≤, – . AE ⓓ MC VISA.
closed 24 December-2 January, Saturday lunch and Sunday – **Meals** (set menu only). *Lunch 33* – 44.
◆ An unusual restaurant set out in an enormous greenhouse which produces a variety of market garden produce. The single menu, using the freshest of ingredients, changes daily.

VandeMarkt, Schollenbrugstraat 8, ✉ 1091 EZ, ✆ (0 20) 468 69 58, *bos.catering@wxs.nl, Fax (0 20) 463 04 54*, – AE ⓓ MC VISA.
closed 3 weeks building workers holidays, 25 December-3 January, Sunday and Monday – Meals (dinner only) 36/43 ♀.
◆ A resolutely contemporary brasserie well worth tracking down in a line of somewhat austere buildings. Canal-side summer terrace.

Buitenveldert (RAI)

Holiday Inn, De Boelelaan 2, ✉ 1083 HJ, ✆ (0 20) 646 23 00, *reservations.amsnt@ichotelsgroup.com, Fax (0 20) 517 27 64*, – ch, – 25-350. AE ⓓ MC VISA
Meals (American cuisine) a la carte 37/48 ♀ – 20 – **254 rm** 295, – 2 suites.
◆ Located close to the RAI exhibition centre, this chain hotel offers guests spacious and discreetly luxurious bedrooms and public areas. American-style dining, encompassing a highly varied menu and salad bar.

Novotel, Europaboulevard 10, ✉ 1083 AD, ✆ (0 20) 541 11 23, *wanda.boruus@accor.com, Fax (0 20) 646 28 23*, – ch, – 25-225. AE ⓓ MC VISA JCB
Meals (pub rest, open until midnight). *Lunch 20* – 22 ♀ – 17 – **611 rm** 120/219.
◆ This vast hotel is frequented by tour groups and business executives alike, with rooms of the standard you would expect from the Novotel name.

Rosarium, Amstelpark 1, ✉ 1083 HZ, ✆ (0 20) 644 40 85, *info@rosarium.net, Fax (0 20) 646 60 04*, ≤, – – 25-250. AE ⓓ MC VISA JCB.
closed Saturday and Sunday – **Meals.** *Lunch 30* – a la carte 38/51 ♀.
◆ This modern structure in the Amstelpark is home to a spacious modern restaurant, a wine-bar and eight meeting rooms. Polished designer decor.

by motorway The Hague (A 4 - E 19)

Mercure Airport, Oude Haagseweg 20 (exit ① Sloten), ✉ 1066 BW, ✆ (0 20) 617 90 05, *h1315@accor.com, Fax (0 20) 615 90 27* – ch, – 25-300. AE ⓓ MC VISA
Meals. *Lunch 20* – 25/30 ♀ – 18 – **152 rm** 139/159.
◆ A shuttle service covers the 3km/2mi between this hotel and Schiphol airport. Despite being on the motorway, the Mercure's large, comfortable rooms offer both peace and quiet.

Environs

at Amstelveen *South : 11 km – pop. 78 095*

Grand Hotel, Bovenkerkerweg 81 (South : 2,5 km direction Uithoorn), ✉ 1187 XC, ✆ (0 20) 645 55 58, *info@grandhotelamstelveen.nl, Fax (0 20) 641 21 21,* – AE VISA.
Meals see ***Résidence Fontaine Royale*** below, shuttle service – **97 rm** 153/173, – 2 suites.
• Situated alongside a main road five minutes from the airport, the Grand Hotel's rooms are spacious and modern with adequate soundproofing.

De Jonge Dikkert, Amsterdamseweg 104a, ✉ 1182 HG, ✆ (0 20) 643 33 33, *info@jongedikkert.nl, Fax (0 20) 645 91 62,* – AE VISA JCB
closed 24 and 31 December and 1 January – **Meals**. *Lunch 31* – 32/45 ♀.
• Innovative, stylish cuisine in a picturesque setting. Behind the neat façade, the rustic dining room has incorporated the base of a 17C windmill. Highly original ! .

Résidence Fontaine Royale - Grand Hotel, Dr Willem Dreesweg 1 (South : 2 km, direction Uithoorn), ✉ 1185 VA, ✆ (0 20) 640 15 01, *reservering@fontaineroyale.nl, Fax (0 20) 640 16 61,* – – 25-225. AE VISA.
closed Saturday lunch, Sunday and Monday dinner – **Meals**. *Lunch 24* – a la carte 39/48 ♀.
• The Grand Hotel's restaurant occupies a separate building 150m/165yd away, where the trend is distinctly modern. Facilities for banquets and seminars.

at Badhoevedorp *Southwest : 15 km* C *Haarlemmermeer pop. 122 902 :*

Dorint Novotel, Sloterweg 299, ✉ 1171 VB, ✆ (0 20) 658 81 11, *H5330@accor.com, Fax (0 20) 658 81 00,* – rm, ch, – 25-150. AE VISA. rest
Meals a la carte 30/49 ♀ – **211 rm** 95/215, – 9 suites.
• This modern chain hotel to the southwest of the city near the airport (shuttle service) provides modern comforts in its 211 large, soundproofed rooms.

De Herbergh with rm, Sloterweg 259, ✉ 1171 CP, ✆ (0 20) 659 26 00, *info@herbergh.nl, Fax (0 20) 659 83 90,* – rest, – 35. AE VISA. rm
Meals *(closed Saturday lunch)*. *Lunch 27* – a la carte 41/52 ♀ – 11 – **24 rm** 80/121.
• A hundred-year-old inn serving contemporary cuisine with good facilities for small business seminars. Functional bedrooms with a full array of creature comforts.

at Hoofddorp *by motorway A 4 - E 19 ④ -* C *Haarlemmermeer pop. 122 902 – see also at Schiphol.*

Binnenweg 20, ✉ 2132 CT, ✆ (0 23) 563 33 90, hoofddorp@vvvhollandsmidden.nl, Fax (0 23) 562 77 59

Crowne Plaza Amsterdam-Schiphol, Planeetbaan 2, ✉ 2132 HZ, ✆ (0 23) 565 00 00, *sales.amsap@ichotelsgroup.com, Fax (0 23) 565 05 21,* – – 25-350. AE VISA JCB
Meals. *Lunch 12* – a la carte 50 ♀ – 20 – **230 rm** 109/280, – 12 suites.
• A top-class hotel located between the centre of Hoofddorp and the motorway to Amsterdam-Schiphol airport. Rooms and suites with full amenities, plus a classic-contemporary restaurant serving innovative cuisine. Efficient service throughout.

Courtyard by Marriott - Amsterdam Airport, Kruisweg 1401, ✉ 2131 MD, ✆ (0 23) 556 90 00, *Fax (0 23) 556 90 09,* – ch, – 25-160. AE VISA.
Meals. *Lunch 15* – 22/40 b.i. ♀ – 16 – **148 rm** 145/225.
• This modern hotel on the edge of a large park between Haarlem and the airport is geared towards business clientele. Spacious, modern rooms, plus a sauna and fitness room.

Schiphol A 4, Rijksweg A 4 nr 3 (Sud : 4 km, Den Ruygen Hoek), ✉ 2132 MA, ✆ (0 252) 67 53 35, *info@schiphol.valk.nl, Fax (0 252) 62 92 45,* – ch, – 25-1500. AE VISA JCB
Meals. *Lunch 17* – a la carte 29/37 ♀ – 15 – **431 rm** 75/100, – 2 suites.
• A practical option for those with a plane to catch. Numerous room categories and a huge conference capacity. Part of the Van der Valk group, with its colourful Toucan logo.

Marktzicht, Marktplein 31, ✉ 2132 DA, ✆ (0 23) 561 24 11, *Fax (0 23) 563 72 91,* – AE VISA.
fermé dim. – **Meals**. *Lunch 30* – a la carte 38/57.
• This traditional "auberge" on the Markt dates from 1860 and was built during construction of the polder now home to Schiphol airport. Dutch dishes feature heavily on the menu.

at Ouderkerk aan de Amstel *South : 10 km* C *Amstelveen pop. 78 095* :

't Jagershuis, Amstelzijde 2, ✉ 1184 VA, ✆ (0 20) 496 20 20, *receptie@jagershuis.com*, *Fax (0 20) 496 45 41*, ←, ✈, – 30. AE ⓓ MC VISA JCB

closed 30 December-3 January – **Meals** *(closed Saturday lunch)*. Lunch 38 – a la carte 47/63 ♀ – **11 rm** ☕ 165/195.

◆ The summer terrace and cosy dining room of this auberge-cum-restaurant offer pleasant views of the Amstel. A substantial à la carte menu plus rooms with period furniture.

Ron Blaauw, Kerkstraat 56, ✉ 1191 JE, ✆ (0 20) 496 19 43, *info@ronblaauw.nl*, *Fax (0 20) 496 57 01*, – AE ⓓ MC VISA

closed 31 July-15 August, 31 December, 1 and 2 January, Saturday lunch, Sunday and Monday – **Meals**. Lunch 38 – 65/100 b.i. – a la carte 50/64 ♀

Spec. Rouget barbet grillé et tartare de langoustines (May-August). Foie d'oie aux épices et sauce madère (September-January). Tarte tatin.

◆ On the village square, in front of the church. With its subtle Japanese undertones, the ambitious, regularly updated menu blends in well with the modern setting.

Klein Paardenburg, Amstelzijde 59, ✉ 1184 TZ, ✆ (0 20) 496 13 35, *Fax (0 20) 472 32 57*, – P. AE ⓓ MC VISA

closed 31 December, Sunday lunch May-September and Saturday lunch – **Meals**. Lunch 38 – 48/55 b.i. ♀.

◆ This small temple of gastronomy is situated in a highly sought-after location along the Amstel. Striking dining room-cum-veranda dominated by a mix of brick, leather and wood.

Lute (with suites), De Oude Molen 5, ✉ 1184 VW, ✆ (0 20) 472 24 62, *info@luterestaurant.nl*, *Fax (0 20) 472 24 63*, – P. AE ⓓ MC VISA

closed 30 April, 26 December-1 January and lunch Saturday and Sunday – **Meals**. Lunch 30 – a la carte 49/64 ♀.

◆ A contemporary restaurant with an unusual location on the site of a former gunpowder factory. Loft-style, post-industrial architecture, glass aplenty and new suites.

at Schiphol *(international airport) Southwest : 15 km* C *Haarlemmermeer pop. 122 902 – see also at Hoofddorp – Casino, Schiphol airport - Terminal Centraal* ✆ *(0 23) 574 05 74, Fax (0 23) 574 05 77* :

Sheraton Airport, Schiphol bd 101, ✉ 1118 BG, ✆ (0 20) 316 43 00, *sales.amsterdam@starwoodhotels.com*, *Fax (0 20) 316 43 99*, – ch, – 25-500. AE ⓓ MC VISA

Meals ***Voyager*** Lunch 40 – a la carte 44/55 ♀ – ☕ 25 – **400 rm** 130/405, – 8 suites.

◆ The Schiphol Sheraton is designed predominantly for business clients, with six categories of rooms offering the latest in facilities. An attractive atrium, a comprehensive range of services, and a modern brasserie crowned by a blue cupola. Evening buffets.

Hilton Schiphol, Schiphol Bd 701, ✉ 1118 ZK, ✆ (0 20) 710 40 00, *hilton.schiphol@hilton.nl*, *Fax (0 20) 710 40 80*, – ch, P – 25-60. AE ⓓ MC VISA JCB.

Meals ***East West*** *(closed Saturday and Sunday)* (partly Asian cuisine, dinner only) a la carte 44/64 ♀ – ***Greenhouse*** (buffets, open until 11 p.m.) a la carte 37/68 ♀ – ☕ 25 – **278 rm** 169/349, – 2 suites.

◆ Facilities at the airport Hilton include rooms with high levels of comfort, top-notch service, a business centre and seminar rooms. The East West restaurant is known for its fusion of Western and Asian flavours, as well as its Japanese options.

Dorint Sofitel Airport, Stationsplein Zuid-West 951 (Schiphol-Oost), ✉ 1117 CE, ✆ (0 20) 540 07 77, *H5332.FB2@accor.com*, *Fax (0 20) 540 08 88*, – ch, – 25-640. AE ⓓ MC VISA JCB. rest

Meals ***Nadar*** *(closed lunch Saturday and Sunday)* Lunch 23 – a la carte 25/42 ♀ – ☕ 19 – **438 rm** 250, – 4 suites.

◆ This modern hotel and conference centre between the airport and Amsterdamse Bos is arranged around a large patio. Numerous "executive" rooms, plus a 24-hour English-style pub. The Nadar restaurant is named after a famous 19C French balloonist.

Radisson SAS Airport, Boeing Avenue 2 (South : 4 km by N 201 at Rijk), ✉ 1119 PB, ✆ (0 20) 655 31 31, *reservations.amsterdam.airport@radissonsas.com*, *Fax (0 20) 655 31 00*, – ch, P – 25-600. AE ⓓ MC VISA. rest

Meals a la carte 31/44 ♀ – ☕ 19 – **277 rm** 215/225, – 2 suites.

◆ With its proximity to the airport and motorway, large, friendly feel and well-equipped, discreetly luxurious rooms, the Radisson is the perfect base for a business trip. The menu in the Mediterranean restaurant shows a distinct fondness for all things Italian !

Giethoorn *Overijssel* 🄲 *Steenwijkerland pop. 42 358 :* 531 V 6 *and* 715 J 3.
Amsterdam 135 km.

XXX ✿✿ **De Lindenhof** (Kruithof), Beulakerweg 77 (Nord : 1,5 km), ✉ 8355 AC, ☎ (0 521) 36 14 44, *info@restaurantdelindenhof.nl, Fax (0 521) 36 05 95,* – P. AE ⓓ ⓜⓒ VISA JCB – *closed first 2 weeks March, last 2 weeks October and Thursday* – **Meals** (lunch by arrangement) 59/85, – a la carte 65/80 ♀,
Spec. Langoustines en aigre-doux de miel. Sandre au jus de truffes et mousseline de céleri-rave (except April-May). Cannellonis de queue de bœuf braisée aux morilles (21 September-21 March).
◆ This small thatched farmhouse surrounded by linden trees is now home to one of the leading restaurants in the Overijssel. Summer dining in the landscaped garden.

Haarlem *Noord-Holland* 531 M 8, 532 M 8 *and* 715 E 4 – *pop. 147 097.*
Amsterdam 20 km.

at Overveen *West : 4 km* 🄲 *Bloemendaal pop. 17 045 :*

XXXX ✿✿ **de Bokkedoorns,** Zeeweg 53 (West : 2 km), ✉ 2051 EB, ☎ (0 23) 526 36 00, *bokkedoorns@alliance.nl, Fax (0 23) 527 31 43,* ≤ lake, – P. AE ⓓ ⓜⓒ VISA JCB. – *closed 30 April, 5 and 24 December, 27 December-9 January, Monday and Saturday lunch* – **Meals**. *Lunch 45* – 58/114 b.i., – a la carte 67/95 ♀,
Spec. Salade de crabe de la mer du Nord et mousse au citron (May-October). Risotto aux truffes et huître de Zélande pochée (October-April). Déclinaison de ris de veau, sauce au vin rouge et crème de braisage.
◆ Modern architecture, interior design, wooded dunes and lake views from the terrace combine to create a magnificent setting for one of the best tables in North Holland.

Zwolle *Overijssel* 531 V 7 *and* 715 J 4 – *pop. 109 955.*
Amsterdam 111 km.

XXX ✿✿✿ **De Librije** (Boer), Broerenkerkplein 13, ✉ 8011 TW, ☎ (0 38) 421 20 83, *librije@alliance.nl, Fax (0 38) 423 23 29* – P. AE ⓜⓒ VISA.
closed 13 to 21 February, 31 July-22 August, 28 December-10 January, Sunday, Monday and lunch Tuesday and Saturday – **Meals**. *Lunch 55* – 76/165 b.i., – a la carte 98/117 ♀,
Spec. Quatre façons de manger le maquereau (September-January). Sole cuite au beurre fumé, jambon fermier et pommes de terre (August-March). Dos de cabillaud à la pomme de terre aux truffes (May-January).
◆ This celebrated restaurant in the wing of a 15C convent has been refurbished in modern style. Fine contemporary dining, where the emphasis is on flair and the personal touch.

The HAGUE (Den HAAG or 's GRAVENHAGE) *Zuid-Holland* 532 K 10 *and* 715 D 5 – *pop. 463 826.*

See : *Binnenhof★ : The Knight's Room★ (Ridderzaal)* JY – *Court pool (Hofvijver)* ≤★ HJY – *Lange Voorhout★* HJX – *Madurodam★★* – *Scheveningen★★*.
Museums : Mauritshuis★★★ JY – *Prince William V art gallery★ (Schilderijengalerij Prins Willem V)* HY M² – *Panorama Mesdag★* HX – *Mesdag★* – *Municipal★★ (Gemeentemuseum)* – *Bredius★* JY – *The seaside sculpture museum★★ (Museum Beelden aan Zee) at Scheveningen.*

Southeast : 5 km at Rijswijk, Delftweg 58, ✉ *2289 AL,* ☎ *(0 70) 319 24 24, Fax (0 70) 399 50 40* – *Northeast : 11 km at Wassenaar, Groot Haesebroekseweg 22,* ✉ *2243 EC,* ☎ *(0 70) 517 96 07, Fax (0 70) 514 01 71 and* *Dr Mansveltkade 15,* ✉ *2242 TZ,* ☎ *(0 70) 517 88 99, Fax (0 70) 551 93 02.*

✈ *Amsterdam-Schiphol Northeast : 37 km* ☎ *(0 20) 794 08 00 – Rotterdam Southeast : 17 km* ☎ *(0 10) 446 34 44, Fax (0 20) 446 34 99.*

Kon. Julianaplein 30, ✉ *2595 AA,* ☎ *0 900-340 35 05, info@vvvdenhaag.nl, Fax (0 70) 347 21 02.*

Amsterdam 55 – Brussels 182 – Rotterdam 27 – Delft 13.

Plan opposite

Centre

Crowne Plaza Promenade, van Stolkweg 1, ✉ 2585 JL, ☎ (0 70) 352 51 61, *info@crowneplazadenhaag.nl, Fax (0 70) 354 10 46,* ≤, – P. – 25-425. AE ⓓ ⓜⓒ VISA JCB. rest
Meals ***Brasserie Promenade*** *Lunch 30* – 35/40 ♀ – ***Trattoria dell'Arte*** (closed Sunday) (Italian cuisine, open until midnight and July-August dinner only) *Lunch 29* – a la carte approx. 48 – ☕ 23 – **93 rm** 165/310, – 1 suite.
◆ This large chain hotel alongside the inner ring road stands opposite a vast park. High levels of comfort, a collection of modern paintings and efficient service. A relaxed brasserie for those favouring a simple meal, plus a contemporary-style trattoria.

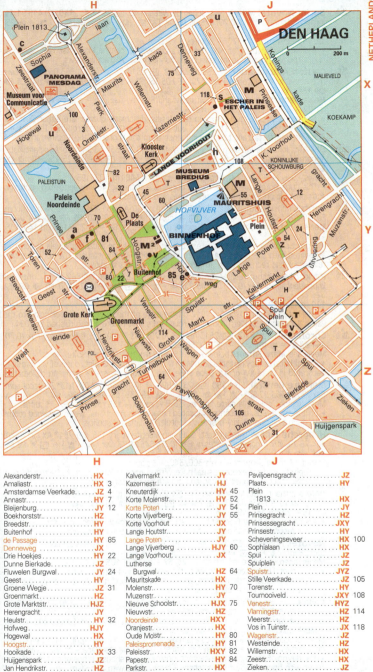

Alexanderstr. . . . . HX
Amaliastr. . . . . HX 3
Amsterdamse Veerkade . . . . . . JZ 4
Annastr. . . . . HY 7
Bleijenburg . . . . JY 12
Boekhorststr. . . . . HZ
Breedstr. . . . . HY
Buitenhof . . . . HY
de Passage . . . . HY 85
Denneweg . . . . JX
Drie Hoekjes . . . . HY 22
Dunne Bierkade . . . . JZ
Fluwelen Burgwal . . . . JY 24
Geest . . . . HY
Groene Wegje . . . . JZ 31
Groenmarkt . . . . HZ
Grote Marktstr. . . . . HJZ
Herengracht . . . . JY
Heulstr. . . . . HY 32
Hofweg . . . . HJY
Hogewal . . . . HX
Hoogstr. . . . . HY
Hooikade . . . . JX 33
Huijgenspark . . . . JZ
Jan Hendrikstr. . . . . HZ
Kalvermarkt . . . . JY
Kazernestr. . . . . HJ
Kneuterdijk . . . . HY 45
Korte Molenstr. . . . . HY 52
Korte Poten . . . . JY 54
Korte Vijverberg . . . . JY 55
Korte Voorhout . . . . JX
Lange Houtstr. . . . . JY
Lange Poten . . . . JY
Lange Vijverberg . . . . HJY 60
Lange Voorhout . . . . JX
Lutherse
Burgwal . . . . HZ 64
Mauritskade . . . . HX
Molenstr. . . . . HY 70
Muzenstr. . . . . JY
Nieuwe Schoolstr. . . . . HJX 75
Nieuwstr. . . . . HZ
Noordeinde . . . . HXY
Oranjestr. . . . . HX
Oude Molstr. . . . . HY 80
Paleispromenade . . . . HY 81
Paleisstr. . . . . HXY 82
Papestr. . . . . HY 84
Parkstr. . . . . HX
Paviljoensgracht . . . . JZ
Plaats . . . . HY
Plein
1813 . . . . HX
Plein . . . . JY
Prinsegracht . . . . HZ
Prinsessegracht . . . . JXY
Prinsestr. . . . . HY
Scheveningseveer . . . . HX 100
Sophialaan . . . . HX
Spui . . . . JZ
Spuiplein . . . . JZ
Spuistr. . . . . JYZ
Stille Veerkade . . . . JZ 105
Torenstr. . . . . HY
Tournooiveld . . . . JXY 108
Venestr. . . . . HYZ
Vlamingstr. . . . . HZ 114
Vleerstr. . . . . HZ
Vos in Tuinstr. . . . . JX 118
Wagenstr. . . . . JZ
Westeinde . . . . HZ
Willemstr. . . . . HX
Zeestr. . . . . HX
Zieken . . . . JZ

Dorint Novotel without rest, Johan de Wittlaan 42, 2517 JR, (0 70) 416 91 11, *info@dhd.dorint.nl, Fax (0 70) 416 91 00,* 25-2000.
19 – **214 rm** 310/370, – 2 suites.
• A strategic location "above" the city's conference centre. Modernist feel, spacious, bright rooms and a huge infrastructure for seminars. Attractive views.

Carlton Ambassador, Sophialaan 2, 2514 JP, (0 70) 363 03 63, *enouwens@ambassador.carlton.nl, Fax (0 70) 360 05 35,* 25-160. HX c
Meals ***Henricus*** *(closed lunch Saturday and Sunday)* Lunch 30 – a la carte 41/49 – 22 – **77 rm** 175/310, – 1 suite.
• The rooms in this small palace in the Mesdag diplomatic quarter are either Dutch or English in style. Plenty of character, but varying levels of soundproofing. The relaxed, floral-inspired restaurant takes its influence from the shores of the Mediterranean.

Bel Air, Johan de Wittlaan 30, 2517 JR, (0 70) 352 53 54, *info@goldentulipbelairhotel.nl, Fax (0 70) 352 53 53,* 25-250. rest
Meals. Lunch 23 – a la carte approx. 38 – 17 – **348 rm** 109/195.
• This huge hotel spread over nine floors has a total of 348 well-appointed rooms, in addition to impressively large public areas and lounges.

Sofitel, Koningin Julianaplein 35, 2595 AA, (0 70) 381 49 01, *h0755@accor.com, Fax (0 70) 382 59 27* – ch, 25-150.
Meals *(closed lunch Saturday and Sunday)*. Lunch 28 – 33/38 – 21 – **142 rm** 140/315, – 1 suite.
• A practical choice for rail travellers, the Sofitel offers the usual high levels of comfort associated with this chain in a modern building close to the station. The contemporary restaurant has recreated the atmosphere of an artist's studio.

Parkhotel without rest, Molenstraat 53, 2513 BJ, (0 70) 362 43 71, *info@parkhoteldenhaag.nl, Fax (0 70) 361 45 25,* 25-200. HY a
120 rm 125/275.
• This hotel was established in 1912 on the edge of the wooded park belonging to the Paleis Noordeinde. Modern rooms on four floors which were all refurbished in 2004.

Corona, Buitenhof 42, 2513 AH, (0 70) 363 79 30, *info@corona.nl, Fax (0 70) 361 57 85* – 25-100. HY v
Meals see ***Marc Smeets*** below – 16 – **35 rm** 109/179, – 1 suite.
• A small hotel occupying three houses on Buitenhof Square. Quaint rooms of varying sizes decorated in Louis XVI or Art Deco style. Popular with ministerial staff and diplomats.

Mercure Central, Spui 180, 2511 BW, (0 70) 363 67 00, *h1317@accor.com, Fax (0 70) 363 93 98* – 25-135. JZ v
Meals (dinner only) a la carte approx. 35 – 17 – **156 rm** 85/185, – 3 suites.
• Built in the 1980s, this centrally located hotel offers functional, well-maintained rooms with double-glazing. Mainly business clientele. "Minimalist" service.

Haagsche Suites without rest, Laan van Meerdervoort 155, 2517 AX, (0 70) 364 78 79, *info@haagschesuites.nl, Fax (0 70) 345 65 33,*
closed 17 to 31 January – **1 rm** 300/340, – 3 suites.
• A sophisticated and exclusive small hotel with an intimate interior created with a discreet aesthetic touch. Designer garden and private parking for guests.

Paleis without rest, Molenstraat 26, 2513 BL, (0 70) 362 46 21, *info@paleishotel.nl, Fax (0 70) 361 45 33* – HY f
15 – **20 rm** 135/195.
• A small luxury hotel fronted by an attractively bourgeois salmon pink façade. Bright, lavishly decorated guestrooms with impressive retro-style bathrooms.

Novotel, Hofweg 5, 2511 AA, (0 70) 364 88 46, *h1180@accor.com, Fax (0 70) 356 28 89* – 25-100. HJY e
Meals (open until 11 p.m.) a la carte 23/37 – 16 – **106 rm** 95/165.
• The Novotel is located just opposite the Binnenhof in a former cinema, and still retains a shopping arcade. Modern rooms, which received a facelift in 2004. The spacious restaurant is housed in the old projection room.

Calla's (van der Kleijn), Laan van Roos en Doorn 51a, 2514 BC, (0 70) 345 58 66, *Fax (0 70) 345 57 10* – JX u
closed 24 July-15 August, 25 December-5 January, Saturday lunch, Sunday and Monday – **Meals**. Lunch 38 – 56/91 b.i., – a la carte 73/97
Spec. Brochette de Saint-Jacques à la réglisse et witlof (October-April). Turbot en soufflé de pommes de terre aillées (May-December). Crêpes farcies glacées et glace vanille.
• The design of this modern restaurant, originally a warehouse, is one of cream and coral tones with open views of the kitchens. Classic cuisine with a modern bent.

XX **Saur,** Lange Voorhout 47, ✉ 2514 EC, ✆ (0 70) 346 25 65, *restaurant.saur@12move.nl, Fax (0 70) 362 13 13,* , Seafood – . AE ⓓ ⓜⓒ VISA JX h
closed 27 March, 16 May, 25 and 26 December, 1 January, Saturday lunch and Sunday – **Meals**. *Lunch* 30 – a la carte 50/73 ♀.
◆ A long-established culinary address in the city with a chic, contemporary brasserie-style atmosphere and oyster bar. Fish and seafood, particularly lobster, a speciality.

XX **Marc Smeets** - Hotel Corona, Buitenhof 42, ✉ 2513 AH, ✆ (0 70) 363 79 30, *rest.marcsmeets@planet.nl, Fax (0 70) 361 57 85,* – AE ⓓ ⓜⓒ VISA JCB. HY v
closed Sunday – **Meals**. *Lunch* 33 – a la carte 48/62 ♀.
◆ A chic restaurant on the ground floor of the Hotel Corona. Impressive Art Deco-inspired dining room with a muffled atmosphere. Contemporary menu.

XX **Julien,** Vos in Tuinstraat 2a, ✉ 2514 BX, ✆ (0 70) 365 86 02, *info@julien.nl, Fax (0 70) 365 31 47* – AE ⓓ ⓜⓒ VISA JCB JX s
closed Sunday – **Meals**. *Lunch* 30 – a la carte 46/75 ♀.
◆ The Julien's decor, including a sparkling 1900s-style mezzanine and bar, will thrill fans of Art Nouveau. A hushed ambience and traditional cuisine with seasonal influences.

XX **Rousseau,** Van Boetzelaerlaan 134, ✉ 2581 AX, ✆ (0 70) 355 47 43, – ⓜⓒ VISA
closed 6 to 14 February, 24 July-15 August, 24 December-2 January, Saturday lunch, Sunday and Monday – **Meals**. *Lunch* 25 – 30/89 b.i..
◆ The spirit of the 19C artist Jean Rousseau - the owner's namesake - lives on in this restaurant adorned with a pleasant Rousseau-style fresco. Imaginative seasonal menu.

XX **The Raffles,** Javastraat 63, ✉ 2585 AG, ✆ (0 70) 345 85 87, *Fax (0 70) 356 00 84,* Indonesian cuisine – . AE ⓓ ⓜⓒ VISA JCB.
closed late July-early August and Sunday – **Meals** (dinner only) a la carte 31/47 ♀.
◆ Delicious and authentic Indonesian cuisine is served in this typically decorated restaurant along the appropriately named Javastraat.

XX **Koesveld,** Maziestraat 10, ✉ 2514 GT, ✆ (0 70) 360 27 23, *Fax (0 70) 360 27 23,* – AE ⓓ ⓜⓒ VISA HX u
closed July-August, 15 December-3 January, Saturday lunch, Sunday and Monday – **Meals**. *Lunch* 20 – a la carte 33/43 ♀.
◆ This small restaurant between the Panorama Mesdag and Paleis Noordeinde is known for its modern, well-presented cuisine. Generous portions with a Mediterranean influence.

X **Shirasagi,** Spui 170 (relocation planned), ✉ 2511 BW, ✆ (0 70) 346 47 00, *shirasagi@planet.nl, Fax (0 70) 346 26 01,* Japanese cuisine with Teppan-Yaki – P. AE ⓓ ⓜⓒ VISA JCB. JZ v
closed 31 December-3 January and lunch Saturday, Sunday and Monday – **Meals**. *Lunch* 23 – 33/73.
◆ Part of the Mercure Central hotel, the Shirasagi's decor and cuisine is inspired by the land of the rising sun. Options here include fixed menus, à la carte, plus teppanyaki.

at Scheveningen C *'s-Gravenhage – Seaside resort★★ – Casino, Kurhausweg 1, ✉ 2587 RT, ✆ (0 70) 306 77 77, Fax (0 70) 306 78 88.*
Gevers Deynootweg 1134, ✉ 2586 BX, ✆ 0-900-340 35 05, vvvscheveningen@spdh.net, Fax (0 70) 352 04 26

Kurhaus, Gevers Deynootplein 30, ✉ 2586 CK, ✆ (0 70) 416 26 36, *info@kurhaus.nl, Fax (0 70) 416 26 46,* ←, , , – ch, P – 35-600. AE ⓓ ⓜⓒ VISA JCB. rest
Meals See ***Kandinsky*** below – ***Kurzaal*** (partly oyster bar) *Lunch* 25 – 28/41 b.i. ♀ – 22 – **245 rm** 215/291, – 10 suites.
◆ A sumptuous palace by the beach with a remarkable late-19C concert room now converted into a restaurant. Elegant rooms with modern comforts. Contemporary cuisine and oyster bar available under the Kurzaal's splendid cupola.

Europa, Zwolsestraat 2, ✉ 2587 VJ, ✆ (0 70) 416 95 95, *europa@bilderberg.nl, Fax (0 70) 416 95 55,* , , – , rest, – 25-460. AE ⓓ ⓜⓒ VISA JCB. rest
Meals ***Mangerie Oxo*** *(closed 25, 26 and 31 December)* (dinner only until 11 p.m.) 33 ♀ – 18 – **174 rm** 89/219.
◆ Standing at a crossroads near the dam, the recently renovated Europa has modern, well-appointed rooms with balconies (some with sea views) and soundproofing. The décor in the restaurant provides a trendy backdrop for a cuisine that is decidedly cutting-edge.

Carlton Beach, Gevers Deynootweg 201, ✉ 2586 HZ, ✆ (0 70) 354 14 14, *info@beach.carlton.nl, Fax (0 70) 352 00 20,* ←, , , , , – P – 25-250. AE ⓓ ⓜⓒ VISA JCB. rest
Meals (seafood) 30 – 21 – **183 rm** 190/245.
◆ A modern hotel at the end of the dam with well-soundproofed rooms and apartments overlooking the beach or car park. Full range of sports facilities, plus a restaurant crowned by an attractive glass roof. Choice of grilled dishes, including fish and seafood.

Badhotel, Gevers Deynootweg 15, ✉ 2586 BB, ☎ (0 70) 351 22 21, *info@badhotel scheveningen.nl, Fax (0 70) 355 58 70* – |♦| ⇆ ▤ TV P – 25-100. AE ① ⓪ VISA JCB
Meals (dinner only) 28/33 – ☕ 15 – **90 rm** 105/158.
◆ Halfway between the centre of Scheveningen and the port, this modern hotel overlooks the resort's main avenue. Slightly quieter rooms to the rear. Contemporary restaurant with an understandably maritime influence.

Seinpost, Zeekant 60, ✉ 2586 AD, ☎ (0 70) 355 52 50, *mail@seinpost.nl, Fax (0 70) 355 50 93*, ≤, Seafood – ▤. AE ① ⓪ VISA JCB
closed Saturday lunch, Sunday and Bank Holidays – **Meals**. Lunch 40 – 50/112 b.i. ♀.
◆ The god Neptune dominates this round building, where the menu is awash with fish and seafood. Comfortable dining room refurbished in contemporary style. Lovely sea views.

Kandinsky - Hotel Kurhaus, Gevers Deynootplein 30, ✉ 2586 CK, ☎ (0 70) 416 26 36, *info@kurhaus.nl, Fax (0 70) 416 26 46*, ≤, – ▤ P. AE ① ⓪ VISA JCB. ⚡
closed 31 December, Saturday lunch and Sunday – **Meals** (July-August dinner only). Lunch 30 – a la carte 50/79 ♀.
◆ An elegant modern restaurant which is part of the resort's flagship hotel. Comfortable dining room in beige shades with a classic menu with modern undertones.

Le Cirque (Kranenborg), Circusplein 50, ✉ 2586 CZ, ☎ (0 70) 416 76 76, *info@rest aurantlecirque.com, Fax (0 70) 416 75 37* – ▤ dinner only. AE ① ⓪ VISA. ⚡
✿ *closed 31 December, 1 January and Monday* – **Meals** (dinner only except Saturday and Sunday) 50/60 ♀
Spec. Ravioli de girolles à la crème d'ail. Saint-pierre laqué aux clémentines et limon. Crumble au beurre salé et poires confites.
◆ A new designer restaurant at the resort's Circustheater. Pre-show menus at 6pm, with more refined and creative cuisine from 8pm each evening.

Cap Ouest, Schokkerweg 37, ✉ 2583 BH, ☎ (0 70) 306 09 35, *info@capouest.nl, Fax (0 70) 350 84 54*, ≤, , Seafood – ▤. AE ① ⓪ VISA JCB
Meals. Lunch 20 – 40 ♀.
◆ Fish and seafood are the mainstays of this restaurant overlooking the port. The views from the modern dining room encompass the pleasure marina and fishing harbour.

Radèn Mas, Gevers Deynootplein 125, ✉ 2586 CR, ☎ (0 70) 354 54 32, *Fax (0 70) 350 60 42*, Partly Indonesian cuisine – ▤. AE ① ⓪ VISA. ⚡
Meals a la carte 31/65.
◆ The Far East takes pride of place on Scheveningen's main square, with Indonesian (including "rice tables") and Chinese dishes to the fore. "Javanese" ambience.

China Delight, Dr Lelykade 116, ✉ 2583 CN, ☎ (0 70) 355 54 50, *info@chinadelight.nl, Fax (0 70) 354 66 52*, Chinese cuisine – ① ⓪ VISA. ⚡
Meals (lunch by arrangement) a la carte 24/32.
◆ This spacious Chinese restaurant is housed in an old warehouse alongside one of the town's docks. A respectable menu geared towards the cuisine of Beijing and Szechwan.

à Kijkduin *West : 4 km* C *'s-Gravenhage :*

Atlantic, Deltaplein 200, ✉ 2554 EJ, ☎ (0 70) 448 24 82, *info@atlantichotel.nl, Fax (0 70) 368 67 21*, ≤, , , , – |♦| ⇆ TV P – 25-300. AE ① ⓪ VISA JCB. ⚡ rest
Meals. Lunch 28 – a la carte approx. 40 ♀ – **152 rm** ☕ 158/260.
◆ Most of the rooms and studios at this hotel by the dam have views of the beach or dunes. Facilities here include a swimming pool and relaxation area, and dining room with sea views. Friendly staff and service.

Environs

at Leidschendam *East : 6 km – pop. 73 747*

Green Park, Weigelia 22, ✉ 2262 AB, ☎ (0 70) 320 92 80, *info@greenpark.nl, Fax (0 70) 327 49 07*, ≤, , – |♦| TV – 25-250. AE ① ⓪ VISA
Meals see ***Chiparus*** below – ☕ 16 – **92 rm** 99/175, – 4 suites.
◆ This large chain hotel is built on piles on the edge of a lagoon. The bedrooms, laid out around a bright atrium, offer guests modern comfort. Pleasant service.

Villa Rozenrust, Veursestraatweg 104, ✉ 2265 CG, ☎ (0 70) 327 74 60, *villarozen rust@planet.nl, Fax (0 70) 327 50 62*, – P. AE ① ⓪ VISA
closed Tuesday, Wednesday and Saturday lunch – **Meals** (set menu only) 35/75 ♀.
◆ An attractive old villa with a romantic atmosphere is the backdrop for this restaurant offering just a single menu. Summer dining in the garden. Home-grown vegetables.

Chiparus - Hotel Green Park, Weigelia 22, ✉ 2262 AB, ☎ (0 70) 320 92 80, *info@gr eenpark.nl, Fax (0 70) 327 49 07*, ≤, – ▤. AE ① ⓪ VISA. ⚡
Meals. Lunch 30 – a la carte 33/52 ♀.
◆ The early-20C Romanian sculptor Chiparus lent his name to this restaurant facing the sea. A fashionable menu, strongly influenced by the Mediterranean. Lakeside terrace.

at Rijswijk South : 5 km – *pop.* 48 094

The Grand Winston Generaal Eisenhowerplein 1, ✉ 2288 AE, ☎ (0 70) 414 15 00, *info@grandwinston.nl, Fax (0 70) 414 15 10,* – – 25 à 200. AE ① MC VISA JCB
Meals see ***Imko Binnerts*** below – ***The Grand Canteen*** a la carte 30/50 ♀ – 18 – **245 rm** 109/215, – 7 suites.
• The reception of this new designer-style hotel by the Rijswijk station stands beneath the protective gaze of Sir Winston Churchill. The guestrooms here are split between two modern towers. Lounge bar and contemporary-style brasserie with a varied menu choice.

Imko Binnerts- Hotel The Grand Winston, 2nd floor Generaal Eisenhowerplein 1, ✉ 2288 AE, ☎ (0 70) 414 15 14, *info@grandwinston.nl, Fax (0 70) 414 15 10,* Seafood – . AE ① MC VISA JCB
closed 24 July-4 August, Saturday lunch and Sunday – **Meals**. Lunch 38 – 58/105 b.i., – a la carte 52/85 ♀
Spec. Rouget barbet au consommé de poivron rouge (April-September). Salade Niçoise maison. Turbot grillé et sa béarnaise.
• "Suspended" designer dining room with high-tech lighting via a glass wall which forms a virtual mosaic to filter external light. Fine cuisine mainly based on fish and seafood.

Savarin, Laan van Hoornwijck 29, ✉ 2289 DG, ☎ (0 70) 307 20 50, *info@savarin.nl, Fax (0 70) 307 20 55,* – – 25-120. AE ① MC VISA JCB
closed 27 December-1 January and lunch Saturday and Sunday – **Meals**. Lunch 30 – 35/45 ♀.
• This farm dating from 1916 is known for its inventive cuisine served in a dining room with rustic and designer decorative features. Summer restaurant and modern meeting rooms.

't Ganzenest, Delftweg 58 (near A 13 - E 19, exit ⑧ Rijswijk-Zuid), ✉ 2289 AL, ☎ (0 70) 414 06 42, *info@ganzenest.nl, Fax (0 70) 414 07 05,* ≤, – . AE ① MC VISA.
closed 2 weeks building workers holidays, late December-early January, Sunday, Monday and lunch Tuesday and Saturday – **Meals**. Lunch 28 – 38/102 b.i. ♀.
• The welcoming "Goose Nest" (Ganzenest) occupies a small farmhouse on the edge of a golf course. Dashing interior décor, an enticing contemporary menu and a delightful terrace.

Paul van Waarden, Tollensstraat 10, ✉ 2282 BM, ☎ (0 70) 414 08 12, *info@paulvanwaarden.nl, Fax (0 70) 414 03 91,* – AE MC VISA JCB
closed Sunday, Monday and lunch Saturday and Bank Holidays – **Meals**. Lunch 33 – 38/90 b.i., – a la carte 50/67 ♀
Spec. Quatre préparations de quatre foies différents. Cabillaud croquant au potage de pois cassés et anguille fumée (21 September-21 March). Tatin à la rhubarbe (March-August).
• Paul van Waarden serves his inventive dishes in one of several adjoining rooms in this modern, brasserie-style restaurant with its wall-enclosed terrace.

at Voorburg *East : 5 km – pop. 73 747*

Mövenpick, Stationsplein 8, ✉ 2275 AZ, ☎ (0 70) 337 37 37, *hotel-voorburg@moevenpick.com, Fax (0 70) 337 37 00,* , – ch, – 25-180. AE ① MC VISA JCB
Meals. Lunch 16 – a la carte 22/49 ♀ – 14 – **125 rm** 70/168.
• A chain hotel built along modern lines with well-dimensioned, pleasantly furnished functional rooms with good soundproofing. Service with a smile. Excellent choice at lunch and dinner, with buffets, grilled meats and fish, and various wok dishes.

Savelberg with rm, Oosteinde 14, ✉ 2271 EH, ☎ (0 70) 387 20 81, *info@restauranthotelsavelberg.nl, Fax (0 70) 387 77 15,* ≤, – – 35. AE ① MC VISA JCB
Meals *(closed Saturday lunch, Sunday and Monday)*. Lunch 43 – 60/120 b.i., – a la carte 66/97 ♀ – 16 – **14 rm** 138/195
Spec. Salade de homard maison. Turbot façon saisonnier. Pigeon de Bresse rôti au four, artichaut violette, tomates séchées et jus d'olives vertes.
• This magnificent 17C residence offers a treat for the senses with its traditional menu, vast wine list, terrace overlooking a park and individually furnished bedrooms.

Villa la Ruche, Prinses Mariannelaan 71, ✉ 2275 BB, ☎ (0 70) 386 01 10, *rest.villaruche@worldonline.nl, Fax (0 70) 386 50 64,* – . AE ① MC VISA
closed 25 December-10 January, Saturday lunch, Sunday and Monday – **Meals**. Lunch 29 – a la carte 43/72.
• A 19C villa is the setting for this restaurant with a classic layout and plane tree-shaded terrace. The emphasis here is on contemporary cuisine.

Brasserie Savelberg - De Koepel, Oosteinde 1, ✉ 2271 EA, ☎ (0 70) 369 35 72, *Fax (0 70) 360 32 14,* – AE ① MC VISA JCB
closed 30 December-2 January – **Meals** (dinner only until 11 p.m. except Sunday) 30/37.
• An opulent-looking brasserie in an impressive rotunda-shaped building crowned by an attractive cupola. Summer terrace, as well as a pleasant park for a post-prandial stroll.

Fouquet, Kerkstraat 52, ✉ 2271 CT, ☎ (0 70) 386 29 00, *voorburg@fouquet.nl, Fax (0 70) 386 55 92,* – ▤. MC VISA JCB
closed Monday – **Meals** (dinner only) 30/40.
◆ A welcoming, modern brasserie-style eatery occupying two 19C listed houses, with red seats, yellow walls, tables laid out side-by-side and a number of mirrors.

Papermoon, Herenstraat 175, ✉ 2271 CE, ☎ (0 70) 387 31 61, *info@papermoon.nl, Fax (0 70) 387 75 20,* – ▤. MC VISA
closed 31 December-1 January and Monday – **Meals** (dinner only) 28/52 b.i. ♀.
◆ This pleasant restaurant, with its hushed dining room ambience, offers a good choice of à la carte dishes and fixed menus.

at Wassenaar *Northeast : 11 km – pop. 25 662*

Aub. de Kieviet, Stoeplaan 27, ✉ 2243 CX, ☎ (0 70) 511 92 32, *receptie@de kieviet.nl, Fax (0 70) 511 09 69,* – ▤ TV ♿ ch, P – 25-90. AE MC VISA JCB
closed 31 December-1 January – **Meals** *(closed lunch Saturday and Sunday).* Lunch 25 – a la carte 43/63 ♀ – 15 – **23 rm** 110/190, – 1 suite.
◆ This auberge in a smart residential district is well worth tracking down for its modern comforts and redecorated rooms, some with a view of the flower-decked summer terrace. Classic cuisine served in a comfortable dining room. Leafy summer restaurant.

De Keuken van Waarde, Waalsdorperlaan 43, ✉ 2244 BN, ☎ (0 70) 328 11 67, *info@dekeukenvanwaarde.nl, Fax (0 70) 324 36 30,* – P. AE MC VISA JCB
closed late July-early August, late December-early January, Sunday and Monday – **Meals.** Lunch 35 – 38/77 b.i..
◆ Current culinary tastes are well catered for at this opulent villa with its bright, simply styled decor and teak-furnished front terrace. Friendly, professional service.

ROTTERDAM *Zuid-Holland* 532 L 11 *and* 715 E 6 – *pop. 599 651 – Casino* JY, *Plaza-Complex, Weena 624* ✉ *3012 CN,* ☎ *(0 10) 206 82 06, Fax (0 10) 206 85 00.*

See : *Lijnbaan★* JY – *St. Laurence Church (Grote- of St-Laurenskerk) : interior★* KY – *Euromast★ (Tower)* ★★, ≤★ JZ – *The harbour★★* KZ – *Willemsbrug★★* – *Erasmusbrug★★* KZ – *Delftse Poort (building)★* JY C – *World Trade Center★* KY Y – *The Netherlands architectural institute★* JZ W – *Boompjes★* KZ – *Willemswerf (building)★* KY.
Museums : History Museum Het Schielandshuis★ KY M[4] – *Boijmans-van Beuningen★★★* JZ – *History "De Dubbele Palmboom"★.*
Envir : *Southeast : 7 km, Kinderdijk Windmils★★.*

9 Kleiweg 480, ✉ *3045 PM,* ☎ *(0 10) 418 88 48, Fax (0 10) 418 46 98 - 9 Kralingseweg 200,* ✉ *3062 CG,* ☎ *(010) 452 22 83 18 East : 8 km at Capelle aan den IJssel, 's Gravenweg 311,* ✉ *2905 LB,* ☎ *(0 10) 442 21 09, Fax (0 10) 284 06 06 - 18 Southwest : 11 km at Rhoon, Veerweg 2a,* ✉ *3161 EX,* ☎ *(0 10) 501 80 58, Fax (0 10) 501 56 04.*
✈ ☎ *(0 10) 446 34 44, Fax (0 10) 446 34 99.*
Europoort to Hull : P and O North Sea Ferries Ltd ☎ *(0 181) 25 55 00 (information) and (0 181) 25 55 55 (reservations), Fax (0 181) 25 52 15.*
Coolsingel 67, ✉ *3012 AC,* ☎ *0 900-403 40 65, vvvrotterdam@anwb.nl, Fax (0 10) 413 01 24.*
Amsterdam 76 – The Hague 24 – Antwerp 103 – Brussels 148 – Utrecht 57.

Plan on next page

Centre

The Westin, Weena 686, ✉ 3012 CN, ☎ (0 10) 430 20 00, *rotterdam.westin@west in.com, Fax (0 10) 430 20 01,* ≤, – ▤ TV ♿ ch, – 25-100. AE MC VISA JCB. JY z
Meals *Lighthouse* (open until 11 p.m.) Lunch 19 – a la carte 37/53 ♀ – **227 rm** 300/330, – 4 suites.
◆ This new, futuristic skyscraper in front of the station offers a choice of spacious rooms with a full range of creature comforts. Conference rooms and business centre. Modern cuisine in a resolutely contemporary setting.

Hilton, Weena 10, ✉ 3012 CM, ☎ (0 10) 710 80 00, *sales-rotterdam@hilton.com, Fax (0 10) 710 80 80,* – ▤ TV ♿ – 25-325. AE MC VISA JCB JY s
Meals (open until 11 p.m.) a la carte 28/44 ♀ – 23 – **246 rm** 165/280, – 8 suites.
◆ A top chain hotel occupying a modern building near the World Trade Center with attractive, well-appointed rooms. The small restaurant in the lounge has an original, "artist's palette" wine list.

ROTTERDAM

Adrianastr. .... JY 4
Aert van Nesstr. .... JY 5
Beurspl. .... KY 9
Binnenwegpl. .... JY 10
Botersloot .... KY 13
Coolsingel .... JKY
Delftsepl. .... JY 21
Delftsestr. .... JY 22
Geldersekade .... KY 24
Grotekerkpl. .... KY 30
Haagseveer .... KY 33
Hartmanstr. .... JY 2
Hoogstr. .... GHU
Jonker Fransstr. .... KY 39
Karel Doormanstr. .... JY
Keizerstr. .... KY 40
Koningsdam .... KY 16
Korte Hoogstr. .... KY 46
Korte Lijnbaan .... JY 48
Kruiskade .... JY 51
Kruispl. .... JY 52
Leeuwenstr. .... KY 115
Lijnbaan .... JY
Nieuwstr. .... KY 70
Oude Binnenweg .... JY
Oude Hoofdpl. .... KY 20
Pompenburg .... JKY 78
Posthoornstr. .... KY 79
Regentessebrug .... KY 82
Rodezand .... KY 8
Scheepmakershaven .... KYZ 14
Scheepstimmermanslaan .... JZ 85
Schouwburgpl. .... JY 88
Spaansekade .... KY 89
Stadhuispl. .... JY 93
van Oldenbarneveltplaats .... JY 72
van Speykstr. .... JY 91
van Vollenhovenstr. .... JZ 107
Veerhaven .... JKZ 102
Veerkade .... JKZ 103
Westewagenstr. .... KY 116
Wijnbrug .... KY 112
Witte de Withstr. .... JZ 113

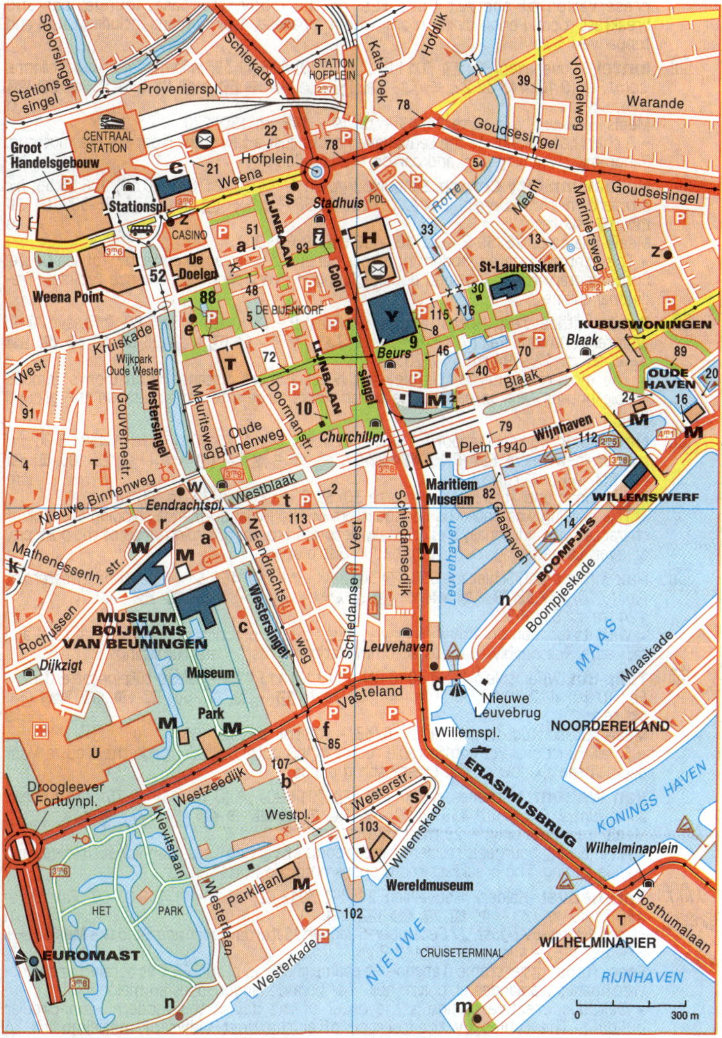

Parkhotel, Westersingel 70, ✉ 3015 LB, ☎ (0 10) 436 36 11, *parkhotel@bilderberg.nl, Fax (0 10) 436 42 12,* ≤, - 🛗 ⇔ ▤ TV P - 🏠 25-60. AE ⓓ ⓜⓒ VISA JCB. ✻ rest JZ a
Meals *(closed Saturday lunch). Lunch 34* – a la carte 29/44 ♀ – ☕ 21 – **187 rm** 65/289, – 2 suites.
◆ Six categories of chic rooms are on offer in this silver-grey tower dominating the museum quarter, just a stone's throw from the Lijnbaan shopping area. A fusion of blue, white and beige in the restaurant, with its "New Style", "Global" and "Classic" choices.

NH Atlanta Rotterdam without rest, Aert van Nesstraat 4, ✉ 3012 CA, ☎ (0 10) 206 78 00, *o.scheffers@nh-hotels.com, Fax (0 10) 411 74 23* – 🛗 ⇔ TV ♿ 🚗 – 🏠 25-325. AE ⓓ ⓜⓒ VISA JY r
☕ 16 – **213 rm** 85/205, – 2 suites.
◆ Large-scale renovation work in this 1930s hotel-palace has resulted in the preservation of the Art Deco feel of the lobby, staircase, lounge, bar and breakfast room. Period dining room, with a Japanese-inspired menu including sushi and teppanyaki.

Inntel, Leuvehaven 80, ✉ 3011 EA, ☎ (0 10) 413 41 39, *inforotterdam@hotelinntel.com, Fax (0 10) 413 32 22,* ≤, - 🛗 ⇔ ▤ TV – 🏠 25-250. AE ⓓ ⓜⓒ VISA JCB. ✻ KZ d
Meals. *Lunch 22* – a la carte 24/43 – ☕ 19 – **148 rm** 190/270.
◆ A chain hotel alongside the Leuvehaven docks, just a few steps from the Erasmusbrug. Panoramic swimming-pool and bar on the top floor.

Holiday Inn City Centre, Schouwburgplein 1, ✉ 3012 CK, ☎ (0 10) 206 25 55, *hiccrotterdam@bilderberg.nl, Fax (0 10) 206 25 50* – 🛗 ⇔ TV 🚗 – 🏠 25-300. AE ⓓ ⓜⓒ VISA. ✻ rest JY e
Meals a la carte 26/39 ♀ – ☕ 18 – **98 rm** 190/210.
◆ This centrally located modern hotel has benefited from a makeover by Adriaan Geuze. Contemporary furnishings and double-glazing in every room. Conference facilities. Traditional cuisine.

Savoy without rest, Hoogstraat 81, ✉ 3011 PJ, ☎ (0 10) 413 92 80, *info.savoy@edenhotelgroup.com, Fax (0 10) 404 57 12,* - 🛗 ⇔ ▤ TV – 🏠 25-60. AE ⓓ ⓜⓒ VISA JCB. ✻ ☕ 17 – **94 rm** 140/205. KY z
◆ The modern rooms in this pleasant hotel a short distance from Blom's famous "cubic houses" are spread across seven floors. Free internet access on the ground floor.

New York, Koninginnehoofd 1 (Wilhelminapier), ✉ 3072 AD, ☎ (0 10) 439 05 00, *info@hotelnewyork.nl, Fax (0 10) 484 27 01,* ≤, – 🛗 ⇔ TV 🚗 – 🏠 25-100. AE ⓓ ⓜⓒ VISA JCB. ✻ rm KZ m
Meals (open until midnight) a la carte 30/39 ♀ – ☕ 11 – **72 rm** 93/160.
◆ This building was once the headquarters of the Holland-America shipping line. Full of character with individually and originally decorated rooms affording views of the port, city or river. Large dining room furnished in bistro style.

Pax without rest, Schiekade 658, ✉ 3032 AK, ☎ (0 10) 466 33 44, *pax@bestwestern.nl, Fax (0 10) 467 52 78* – 🛗 ⇔ ▤ TV ♿ 🚗 – 🏠 25-80. AE ⓜⓒ VISA. ✻
124 rm ☕ 85/165.
◆ With its location on a major highway, the Pax is a practical option for both road and rail users. Reasonably spacious accommodation with standard furnishings.

Tulip Inn, Willemsplein 1, ✉ 3016 DN, ☎ (0 10) 413 47 90, *sales@tulipinnrotterdam.nl, Fax (0 10) 412 78 90,* ≤ – 🛗 ⇔, ▤ rest, TV – 🏠 25-60. AE ⓓ ⓜⓒ VISA JCB. ✻ rest KZ s
Meals *(closed August)* a la carte 26/36 – **108 rm** ☕ 110/185.
◆ Small, functional yet comfortable rooms in this hotel built alongside the Nieuwe Maas dock, in the shadow of the Erasmusbrug bridge.

Van Walsum, Mathenesserlaan 199, ✉ 3014 HC, ☎ (0 10) 436 32 75, *info@hotelvanwalsum.nl, Fax (0 10) 436 44 10* – 🛗 ⇔ TV P. AE ⓓ ⓜⓒ VISA JCB. ✻ rest
Meals (residents only) – **29 rm** ☕ 78/110.
◆ An imposing bourgeois residence with rooms of varying sizes, identical furnishings and double-glazing. The breakfast room opens onto the hotel terrace.

XXXX ✿✿✿ **Parkheuvel** (Helder), Heuvellaan 21, ✉ 3016 GL, ☎ (0 10) 436 07 66, *Fax (0 10) 436 71 40,* ≤, – P. AE ⓓ ⓜⓒ VISA JCB JZ n
closed 18 July-6 August, 27 December-5 January, Saturday lunch and Sunday – **Meals**. *Lunch 47* – 68/115, – a la carte 67/112 ♀
Spec. Turbot grillé, crème d'anchois et champignons au basilic. Filet et côtelettes de chevreuil panés d'amandes et poivre noir. Tempura de langoustines au melon.
◆ Delicious, creative cuisine is the order of the day in this modern, semi-circular building. The tables by the terrace offer the best views of maritime life. A real treat !.

XXX **Old Dutch,** Rochussenstraat 20, ✉ 3015 EK, ✆ (0 10) 436 03 44, *info@olddutch.net, Fax (0 10) 436 78 26,* – P. AE ⓓ MC VISA JZ r
closed Saturday dinner July-August, Saturday lunch, Sunday and Bank Holidays – **Meals**. *Lunch 33* – 48/83 b.i. ♀.
◆ A pleasant restaurant adorned with bourgeois furniture occupying an inn dating from 1932. Traditional cuisine with several menu options. Wines from around the world.

XX ✿ **La Vilette** (Mustert), Westblaak 160, ✉ 3012 KM, ✆ (0 10) 414 86 92, *Fax (0 10) 414 33 91* – ▤. AE ⓓ MC VISA JCB. JY t
closed 18 July-7 August, 24 December-1 January, Saturday lunch and Sunday – **Meals**. *Lunch 31* – 45, a la carte 43/57 ♀
Spec. Saint-Jacques et foie de canard aux pommes. Barbue et anguille, risotto et vinaigre à l'oseille. Éventail de chocolat et nougat.
◆ A refined brasserie ambience permeates this pleasant restaurant with an appetising modern menu and top-notch service. Public car park nearby.

XX **De Harmonie,** Westersingel 95, ✉ 3015 LC, ✆ (0 10) 436 36 10, *Fax (0 10) 436 36 08,* – 25-60. AE ⓓ MC VISA JCB JZ c
closed 26 December-2 January, Saturday lunch and Sunday – **Meals**. *Lunch 35* – a la carte 42/58 ♀.
◆ A pleasant restaurant by the Westersingel and Museumpark. Come the summer, the garden and terrace live up to the name. A refined setting for cuisine geared to modern tastes.

XX **ZeeZout,** Westerkade 11b, ✉ 3016 CL, ✆ (0 10) 436 50 49, *Fax (0 10) 225 18 47,* , Seafood – ▤. AE ⓓ MC VISA JZ e
closed 25 and 26 December, Saturday lunch, Sunday and Monday – **Meals**. *Lunch 28* – a la carte 41/64.
◆ The main attractions of this elegant brasserie are its fish and seafood recipes, hence its name (meaning "sea salt"), plus its terrace facing the Nieuwe Maas.

XX **Brancatelli,** Boompjes 264, ✉ 3011 XD, ✆ (0 10) 411 41 51, *pino@brancatelli.nl, Fax (0 10) 404 57 34,* Italian cuisine, open until 11 p.m. – ▤. AE ⓓ MC VISA KZ n
closed lunch Saturday and Sunday – **Meals**. *Lunch 32* – a la carte 30/48 ♀.
◆ This contemporary-style Italian restaurant on a lively quay offers an authentic choice of dishes accompanied by a good selection of wines received directly from Italy.

XX **Perla del Mare,** Van Vollenhovenstraat 15 (access by Westerlijk Handelsterrein), ✉ 3016 BE, ✆ (0 10) 241 04 00, *info@perladelmare.nl, Fax (0 10) 241 03 67,* Italian cuisine, seafood – ▤. AE ⓓ MC VISA JCB. JZ b
closed lunch Saturday and Sunday – **Meals**. *Lunch 38* – a la carte 45/79 ♀.
◆ As its name suggests, this nautically themed restaurant housed in an old warehouse specialises in Italian cuisine, with particular emphasis on fish and seafood.

X **Huson,** Scheepstimmermanslaan 14, ✉ 3011 BS, ✆ (0 10) 413 03 71, *lunch@huson.info, Fax (0 10) 412 49 38,* JZ f
closed last week July-first 2 weeks August, 1 to 10 January and Saturday – **Meals** (lunch only until 18 p.m.) a la carte approx. 35.
◆ This trendy restaurant furnished with plush leather benches offers a concise choice of simple dishes based on high-quality products. Non-stop service from 11am to 6pm.

X **Foody's,** Nieuwe Binnenweg 151, ✉ 3014 GK, ✆ (0 10) 436 51 63, *Fax (0 10) 436 54 42,* – ▤. AE ⓓ MC VISA. JZ k
closed Monday – **Meals** (dinner only until midnight) 35/46 ♀.
◆ A modern-style brasserie with kitchens in full view. The focus here is on "natural" modern cuisine using seasonal products. Good choice of wines by the glass.

X **de Engel,** Eendrachtsweg 19, ✉ 3012 LB, ✆ (0 10) 413 82 56, *restaurant@engel.com, Fax (0 10) 412 51 96* – ▤. AE ⓓ MC VISA JCB JZ z
closed Sunday – **Meals** (dinner only) a la carte 50/68 ♀.
◆ One of Rotterdam's current "in" places. A relaxed atmosphere, a dining room adorned with period furniture, and meticulous, seasonal cuisine with a modern touch.

X **Rosso,** Van Vollenhovenstraat 15 (access by Westerlijk Handelsterrein), ✉ 3016 BE, ✆ (0 10) 225 07 05, *Fax (0 10) 436 95 04* – ▤. AE MC VISA. JZ b
closed Sunday – **Meals** (dinner only until 11 p.m.) 33/40 ♀.
◆ A bar-restaurant in a trendily modernised former 19C warehouse. With its fashionable clientele and atmosphere, this is THE place to be seen.

Suburbs

Airport *North : 2,5 km :*

Airport, Vliegveldweg 59, ✉ 3043 NT, ✆ (0 10) 462 55 66, *info@airporthotel.nl, Fax (0 10) 462 22 66,* – 25-425. AE ⓓ ⓜⓒ VISA JCB.
Meals a la carte 27/39 ♀ – ▭ 16 – **96 rm** 165, – 2 suites.
◆ A modern airport hotel with functional, well-soundproofed bedrooms and a lounge and bar popular with a predominantly business clientele. Comfortable, contemporary dining room offering a range of traditional dishes. Shuttle service to the airport.

at Kralingen *East : 2 km* Ⓒ *Rotterdam :*

Novotel Brainpark, K.P. van der Mandelelaan 150 (near A 16), ✉ 3062 MB, ✆ (0 10) 253 25 32, *H1134@accor.com, Fax (0 10) 253 25 71* – ch, – 25-400. AE ⓓ ⓜⓒ VISA
Meals. *Lunch 18* – a la carte approx. 44 – ▭ 15 – **202 rm** 80/130.
◆ This contemporary tower-block stands in a business park on the outskirts of the city. Well-maintained rooms offering more space than is normally found across the chain. Restaurant options similar to other Novotels.

XXX **In den Rustwat,** Honingerdijk 96, ✉ 3062 NX, ✆ (0 10) 413 41 10, *rustwat@tiscali.nl, Fax (0 10) 404 85 40,* – . AE ⓓ ⓜⓒ VISA
closed building workers holidays, Christmas, 31 December-1 January, Sunday and Monday – **Meals.** *Lunch 30* – a la carte 44/53 ♀.
◆ This charming, recently extended thatch-roofed inn built in 1597 is located alongside an arboretum. Facilities include a terrace and flower-decked summer garden.

Europoort zone *West : 25 km :*

De Beer Europoort, Europaweg 210 (N 15), ✉ 3198 LD, ✆ (0 181) 26 23 77, *info@hoteldebeer.nl, Fax (0 181) 26 29 23,* dinner only – 25-180. AE ⓓ ⓜⓒ VISA
Meals. *Lunch 15* – 25/38 ♀ – **78 rm** ▭ 84/99.
◆ Set back from the lively Europoort, this medium-sized hotel has 78 functional rooms, half with canal views. Good sports and seminar facilities. The dining room and terrace face out towards the Hartelkanaal.

Environs

at Capelle aan den IJssel *East : 8 km – pop. 65 318*

NH Capelle, Barbizonlaan 2 (near A 20), ✉ 2908 MA, ✆ (0 10) 456 44 55, *info@nhcapelle.nh-hotels.nl, Fax (0 10) 456 78 58,* rm, – 25-250. AE ⓓ ⓜⓒ VISA JCB
Meals *(closed Sunday)* – a la carte 22/37 ♀ – ▭ 16 – **103 rm** 125/140 1 suite.
◆ A contemporary building near a ring road exit five minutes from the centre of Rotterdam. Central atrium, Scandinavian-style bedrooms and a nautically themed bar. "Southern" atmosphere in the restaurant, with summer dining on the terrace, overlooking a lake.

XX **Rivium Royale,** Rivium Boulevard 188, ✉ 2909 LK, ✆ (0 10) 202 56 33, *reserveren@riviumroyale.nl, Fax (0 10) 202 65 37,* – . ⓓ ⓜⓒ VISA
closed 22 July-15 August, 24 December-3 January, Saturday, Sunday and Bank Holidays – **Meals.** *Lunch 29* – a la carte 35/66 ♀.
◆ Beneath the building's contemporary dome is an impressive circular restaurant rising above an attractive mezzanine-lounge. Pleasant summer terrace overlooking the water.

at Rhoon *South : 10 km* Ⓒ *Albrandswaard pop. 18 737 :*

XXX **Biggo@het Kasteel van Rhoon,** Dorpsdijk 63, ✉ 3161 KD, ✆ (0 10) 501 88 96, *info@hetkasteelvanrhoon.nl, Fax (0 10) 506 72 59,* – – 25-100. AE ⓓ ⓜⓒ VISA JCB
closed Saturday lunch – **Meals.** *Lunch 33* – a la carte 51/62 ♀.
◆ This comfortable, modern restaurant occupies the outbuildings of a château. Fairly refined cuisine based along classical lines, plus a good wine list. Banqueting rooms.

at Schiedam *West : 6 km – pop. 75 802.*

Buitenhavenweg 9, 3113 BC, (0 10) 473 30 00, vvv.schiedam@kabelfoon.nl, Fax (0 10) 473 66 95

Novotel, Hargalaan 2 (near A 20), 3118 JA, (0 10) 471 33 22, *H0517@accor.com, Fax (0 10) 470 06 56,* , , – ch, – 25-200. AE VISA JCB
Meals – a la carte 22/38 – **134 rm** 81/159.
• A chain hotel in verdant surroundings at a crossroads close to the ring road. Functional rooms, summer terrace and garden with children's activities by the pool. Contemporary, brasserie-style restaurant.

Bistrot Hosman Frères, Korte Dam 10, 3111 BG, (0 10) 426 40 96, *Fax (0 10) 426 90 41* – . AE VISA JCB
closed 31 December-1 January, Monday and lunch Saturday and Sunday – **Meals** – 26/52 b.i.
• This charming inn, in a picturesque location near four old windmills in the old quarter, will delight customers with its "bistro-style" fare.

Delft *Zuid-Holland* 532 L 10 *and* 715 E 5 – *pop. 96 588.*
Rotterdam 16 km.

at Schipluiden *Southeast : 6 km* *Midden-Delfland pop.18 014 :*

De Zwethheul, Rotterdamseweg 480 (canalside), 2636 KB, (0 10) 470 41 66, *info@zwethheul.nl, Fax (0 10) 470 65 22,* , – AE VISA JCB
closed 25 December-9 January, Monday and lunch Saturday and Sunday – **Meals**. Lunch 45 – 63/130 b.i., – a la carte 54/127
Spec. Raviolis de poulet noir de Bresse aux langoustines sautées. Perdreau écossais en deux services (15 September-December). Composition de foie d'oie mariné aux bâtonnets de betteraves en aigre-doux.
• The culinary delights of this restored former auberge are enhanced by the riverfront views, particularly from the terrace, which comes into its own with the onset of spring.

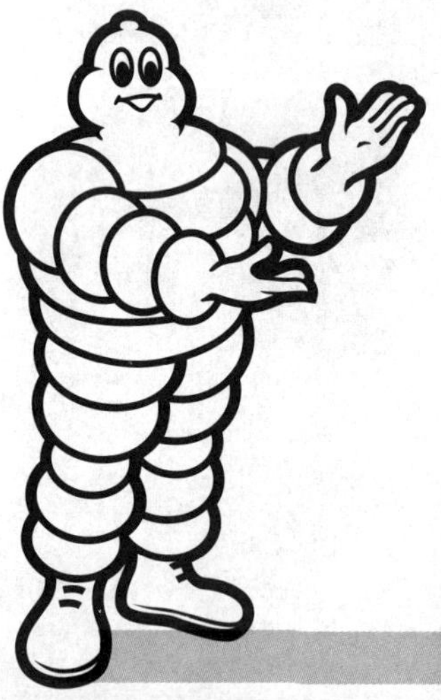

Czech Republic

Česká Republika

PRAGUE

PRACTICAL INFORMATION

LOCAL CURRENCY

Crown : *100 CZK = 3,25 euro (€) (Dec. 2004)*

National Holiday in the Czech Republic : *1 May, 8 May, 28 October, 17 November.*

PRICES

Prices may change if goods and service costs in the Czech Republic are revised and it is therefore always advisable to confirm rates with the hotelier when making a reservation.

FOREIGN EXCHANGE

It is strongly advised against changing money other than in banks, exchange offices or authorised offices such as large hotels, tourist offices, etc... Banks are usually open on weekdays from 9am to 5pm. Some exchange offices in the old city are open 24 hours a day.

HOTEL RESERVATIONS

In case of difficulties in finding a room through our hotel selection, it is always possible to apply to AVE Wilsonova 8, Prague 2, ☎ 224 223 521. CEDOK Na příkopě 18, Prague 1 ☎ 224 197 615.

POSTAL SERVICES

Post offices are open from 8am to 6pm on weekdays and 12 noon on Saturdays.

The **General Post Office** *is open 7am to 8pm : Jindřišska 14, Prague 1, ☎ 221 131 445. There is a 24 hr postal service at Hybernská 13 ☎ 224 225 845.*

SHOPPING IN PRAGUE

In the index of street names, those printed in red are where the principal shops are found. Typical goods to be bought include embroidery, puppets, Bohemian glass, porcelain, ceramics, wooden toys... Shops are generally open from 9am to 7pm.

TIPPING

Hotel, restaurant and café bills include service in the total charge but it is up to you to tip the staff.

CAR HIRE

The international car hire companies have branches in Prague. Your hotel porter should be able to give details and help you with your arrangements.

BREAKDOWN SERVICE

A 24 hour breakdown service is operated by Autoklub, Opletalova 29, Prague 1. ☎ 224 221 820.

SPEED LIMITS - SEAT BELTS - MOTORWAYS TAX

The maximum permitted speed on motorways is 130 km/h - 80 mph, 90 km/h 56 mph on other roads and 50 km/h - 31 mph in built up areas except where a lower speed limit is indicated.

The wearing of seat belts is compulsory for drivers and all passengers.

Driving on motorways is subject to the purchase of a single rate annual road tax obtainable from border posts and tourist offices.

In the Czech Republic, drivers must not drink alcoholic beverages at all.

PRAGUE
(PRAHA)

Česká Republika 731 F 3 – Pop. 1 203 230

Berlin 344 – Dresden 152 – Munich 384 – Nurnberg 287 – Wroclaw 272 – Vienna 291.

Prague Information Service : Na Příkope 20 (main office), Staroměstsk a radnice, and Main Railway Station ✆ 212 444 tourinfo@pis.cz

CEDOK : Na přikopě 18, Prague 1 ✆ 224 197 111, Fax 224 223 479.

Golf Club Praha, Motol-Praha 5, ✆ 257 216 584.

Ruzyně (Prague Airport) NW 20 km, by road nº 7 ✆ 220 113 314.

Bus to airport : Cedaz Bus at airlines Terminal Namesti Republicky ✆ 220 114 296.

CZECH AIRLINES (ČESKÉ AEROLINIE) V. Celnici 5, PRAGUE 1 ✆ 220 104 702.

See: Castle District★★★ (Hradčany) ABX : Prague Castle★★★ (Pražský Hrad) BX, St Vitus' Cathedral★★★ (Chram sv. Víta) BX, Old Royal Palace★★ (Královský palác) BX, St George's Convent★★ (National Gallery's Early Bohemian Art★★) (Bazilika sv. Jiří/Jiřský Klašter) BX, Hradčany Square★★ (Hradčanské náměstí) BX **37**, Schwarzenberg Palace★ (Schwarzenberský Palác) AX **R**[1], Loretto Shrine★★★ (Loreta) AX, Strahov Abbey★★ (Strahovský Klášter) AX – Lesser Town★★★ (Malá Strana) BX : Charles Bridge★★★ (Karluv Most) BCX, Lesser Town Square★ (Malostranské náměstí) BX, St Nicholas Church★★★ (Sv. Mikuláše) BX, Neruda Street★★ (Nerudova) BX, Wallenstein Palace★★ (Valdštejnský Palác) BX – Old Town★★★ (Staré Město) CX : Old Town Square★★★ (Staroměstské náměstí) CX, Astronomical Clock★★★ (Orloj) CX **R**[2], Old Town Hall★ – Extensive view★★ (Staroměstská radnice) CX **R**[2], St Nicholas'★★ (Sv. Mikuláše) CX, Týn Church★★ (Týnský chrám) CX, Jewish Quarter★★★ (Josefov) CX, Old-New Synagogue★★★ (Staranová Synagóga) CX, Old Jewish Cemetery★★★ (Starý židovský hřbitov) CX **R**[3], St Agnes Convent★★ (National Gallery's Collection of 19 C Czech Painting and Sculpture) (Anežský klášter) CX, Celetná Street★★ (Celetná) CX, Powder Tower★ (Prašná Brána) DX, House of the black Madonna★ (Dum u černe Matky boží) CX **E**, Municipal House★★★ (Obecní Dum) DX **N**[2] – New Town★ (Nové Město) CDY : Wenceslas Square★★★ (Václavské náměstí) CDXY.

Museums: National Gallery★★★ (Národní Galérie) AX, National Museum★ (Národní muzeum) DY, National Theatre★★ (Národní divadlo) CY **T**[2], Decorative Arts Museum★ (Umělecko prumyslové muzeum) CX **M**[6], City Museum★ (Prague model★★) (Muzeum hlavního města Prahy) DX **M**[3], Vila America★ (Dvořák Museum) DY.

Outskirts: Karlštejn Castle SW : 30 km ET – Konopiště Castle SW : 40 km FT.

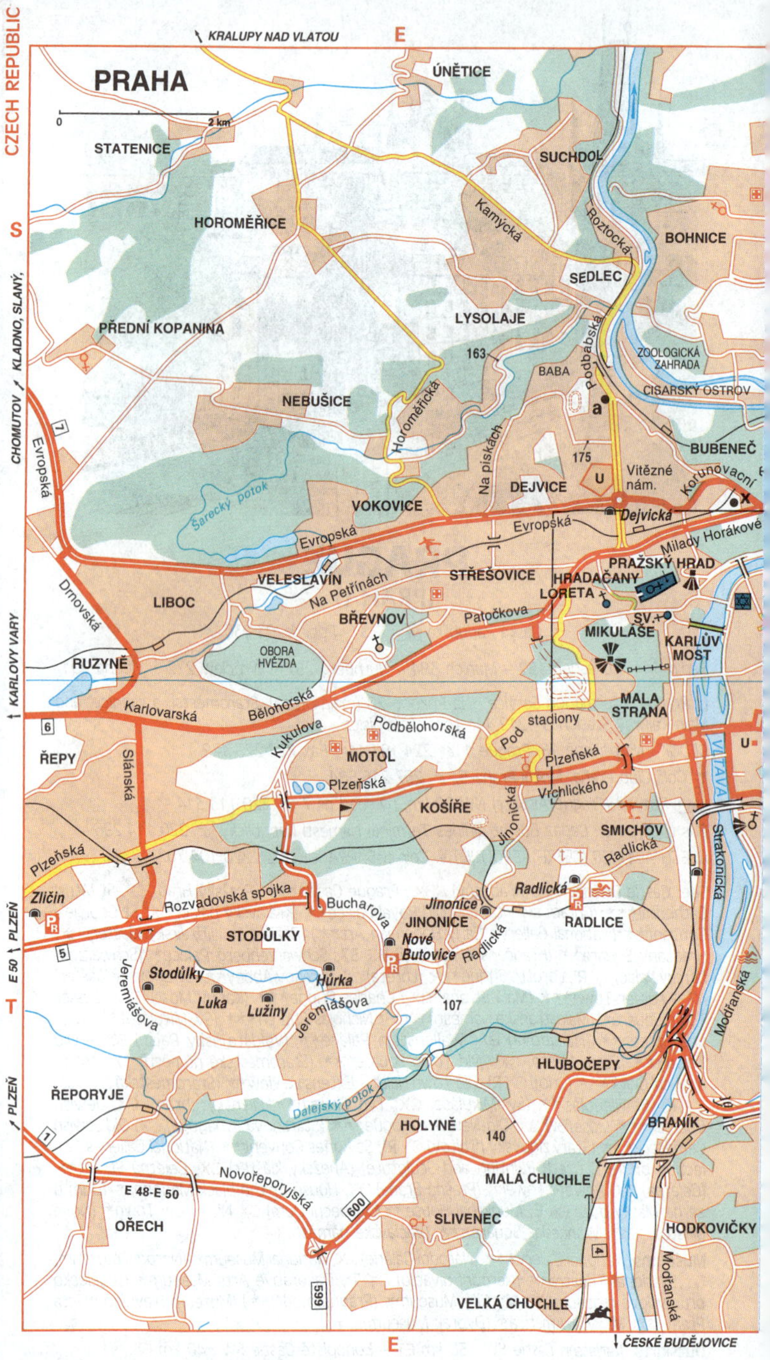

PRAHA
0
2 km
KRALUPY NAD VLATOU
E
ÚNĚTICE
STATENICE
SUCHDOL
HOROMĚŘICE
Kamýcká
Roztocká
BOHNICE
SEDLEC
PŘEDNÍ KOPANINA
LYSOLAJE
Podbabská
ZOOLOGICKÁ ZAHRADA
BABA
CISARSKÝ OSTROV
NEBUŠICE
Horoměřická
Na pískách
BUBENEČ
Evropská
Šárecký potok
VOKOVICE
DEJVICE
Vítězné nám.
Korunovační
Dejvická
Evropská
Milady Horákové
VELESLAVÍN
STŘEŠOVICE
PRAŽSKÝ HRAD
HRADČANY
LORETA
LIBOC
Na Petřinách
BŘEVNOV
Patočkova
Drnovská
SV. MIKULÁŠE
KARLŮV MOST
OBORA HVĚZDA
RUZYNĚ
MALA STRANA
Karlovarská
Bělohorská
Podbělohorská
Pod stadiony
Kukulova
MOTOL
ŘEPY
Slánská
Plzeňská
Plzeňská
VLTAVA
KOŠÍŘE
Vrchlického
Jinonická
SMICHOV
Radlická
Plzeňská
Strakonická
Radlická
Zličín
Rozvadovská spojka
Bucharova
Jinonice
JINONICE
RADLICE
STODŮLKY
Nové Butovice
Radlická
Jeremiášova
Stodůlky
Luka
Lužiny
Hůrka
Jeremiášova
107
Modřanská
HLUBOČEPY
ŘEPORYJE
Dalejský potok
HOLYNĚ
140
BRANÍK
MALÁ CHUCHLE
E 48-E 50
Novoreporyjská
600
OŘECH
SLIVENEC
HODKOVIČKY
Modřanská
599
VELKÁ CHUCHLE
E
ČESKÉ BUDĚJOVICE
CZECH REPUBLIC
S
CHOMUTOV
KLADNO, SLANÝ,
KARLOVY VARY
PLZEŇ
E 50
T
PLZEŇ
163
175
7
6
5
1
4

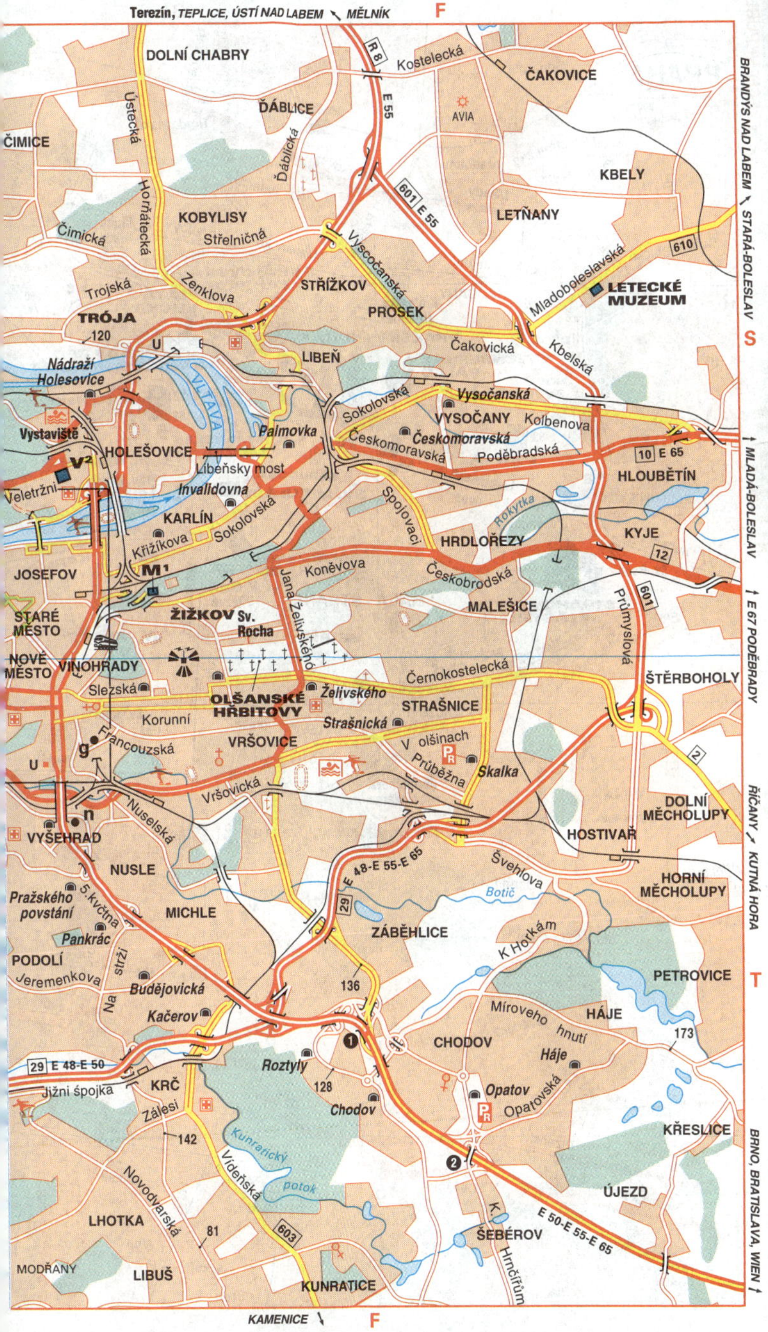
Terezín, TEPLICE, ÚSTÍ NAD LABEM ↖ MĚLNÍK
F
BRANDÝS NAD LABEM ↖ STARÁ-BOLESLAV
S
↑ MLADÁ-BOLESLAV
↑ E 67 PODĚBRADY
ŘÍČANY ↗ KUTNÁ HORA
T
BRNO, BRATISLAVA, WIEN ↑
KAMENICE ↘
F
DOLNÍ CHABRY
ĎÁBLICE
ČIMICE
Ústecká
Ďáblická
R 8
E 55
Kostelecká
ČAKOVICE
AVIA
KBELY
601 E 55
LETŇANY
KOBYLISY
Střelničná
Čimická
Hořňátecká
Trojská
Zenklova
STŘÍŽKOV
Vysočanská
PROSEK
Mladoboleslavská
610
LETECKÉ MUZEUM
TRÓJA
120
Čakovická
Kbelská
Nádraží Holešovice
LIBEŇ
VLTAVA
Sokolovská
Vysočanská
VYSOČANY
Kolbenova
Českomoravská
Českomoravská
Poděbradská
10 E 65
Vystaviště
Palmovka
HOLEŠOVICE
Libeňský most
V2
HLOUBĚTÍN
Veletržní
Invalidovna
Spojovací
Rokytka
KARLÍN
Sokolovská
Křižíkova
HRDLOŘEZY
KYJE
12
JOSEFOV
M1
Koněvova
Českobrodská
601
Průmyslová
MALEŠICE
STARÉ MĚSTO
ŽIŽKOV
Sv. Rocha
Jana Želivského
NOVÉ MĚSTO
VINOHRADY
Černokostelecká
ŠTĚRBOHOLY
Slezská
OLŠANSKÉ HŘBITOVY
Želivského
STRAŠNICE
Korunní
Strašnická
Francouzská
VRŠOVICE
V olšinach
Průběžná
Skalka
2
U
Vršovická
Nuselská
DOLNÍ MĚCHOLUPY
VYŠEHRAD
HOSTIVAŘ
NUSLE
E 48-E 55-E 65
Švehlova
HORNÍ MĚCHOLUPY
Pražského povstání
5. května
Botič
29
MICHLE
ZÁBĚHLICE
Pankrác
K Horkám
PODOLÍ
Jeremenkova
Na strži
136
PETROVICE
Budějovická
Mírového hnutí
HÁJE
Kačerov
CHODOV
173
29 E 48-E 50
Roztyly
Háje
Jižní spojka
KRČ
128
Opatov
Zálesí
Chodov
Opatovská
142
KŘESLICE
Kunratický potok
Novodvorská
Vídeňská
ÚJEZD
LHOTKA
81
K Hrnčířům
ŠEBEROV
E 50-E 55-E 65
603
MODŘANY
LIBUŠ
KUNRATICE

PRAHA
0
200 m
A
B
V
X
Y
Z
OŘECHOVKA
Generálá
Piky
Svatovítská
Dejvická
Bubenečská
Hradčanská
Badeniho
165
DEJVICE
Dělostřelecká
Pevnostní
Pod
hradbami
Milady
Horákové
Slunná
Na valech
Cukrovarnická
U Prašného
Mariánské
hradby
Chotkovy sady
43
Jelení
U Brusnice
KRÁLOVSKÁ ZAHRADA
141
HRADČANY
Královská Jízdárna
Míčovna
ZLATÁ ULIČKA
150
Patočkova
c
s
63
PRAŽSKÝ HRAD
JIŘSKÝ KLÁŠTER
mostu
ŠTERNBERSKÝ PALÁC
SV. VÍTA
ZAHRADY POD PRAŽSKÝM HRADEM
Keplerova
NOVÝ SVĚT
53
STARÝ KRÁLOVSKÝ PALÁC
f
168
Malostrans
Myslbekov
21
VALDŠTEJNSKÝ PALÁC
152
37
134
169
146
a
80
83
R1
MALOSTRANSKÉ NÁMĚSTÍ
154
LORETA
n
e
79
Vojanovy sady
a
Loretánská
NERUDOVA
z
Sv. Josefa
m
Parléřova
Úvoz
SV. MIKULÁŠE
e
t
97
10
b
b
147
n
18
P
Pohořelec
99
Dlabačov
x
122
w
VRTBOVSKÁ ZAHRADA
170
KARLŮV
Sv. Roch
87
Karmelitská
Kampě
STRAHOVSKÝ KLÁŠTER
MALÁ STRANA
P. Marie Vítězné
Na
KAMPA
Vaníčkova
PETŘÍN
v
Strahovská
Hladová zeď
Rozhledna
Čertovka
Sv. Vavřince
Újezd
RŮŽOVÝ SAD
Lanová
draha
Sv. Jana
STŘELECKÝ OSTROV
most
Vítězná
PETŘÍNSKÉ SADY
Štefánikova hvězdárna
STADION STRAHOV
Vaníčkova
Újezd
174
KINSKÉHO ZAHRADA
Petřínská
Janáčkovo
nám. Kinských
J
Atletická
Šermířská
Dětský ostrov
Sv. Michala
a
148
117
Na
Hřebenkách
Holečkova
Štefánikova
nábřeží
3
174
Jiráskův
Hřebenkách
Švédská
158
158
Na
SV. GABRIEL
Drtinova
93
b
Zapova
93
Mošnova
Kartouzská
SV. VÁCLAV
102
174
Plzeňská
Lidická
Holečkova
Plzeňská
Vrchlického
Duškova
Anděl
Na Bělidle
a
b
Mozartova
Radlická
Nádražní
Hořejší
Na
Věnečku
Zátlance
Kováků
Vltavská
Na Popelce
HUSOVY SADY
Ostrovského
Svornosti
nábřeží
U
Blaženky
Na
POL
A
B

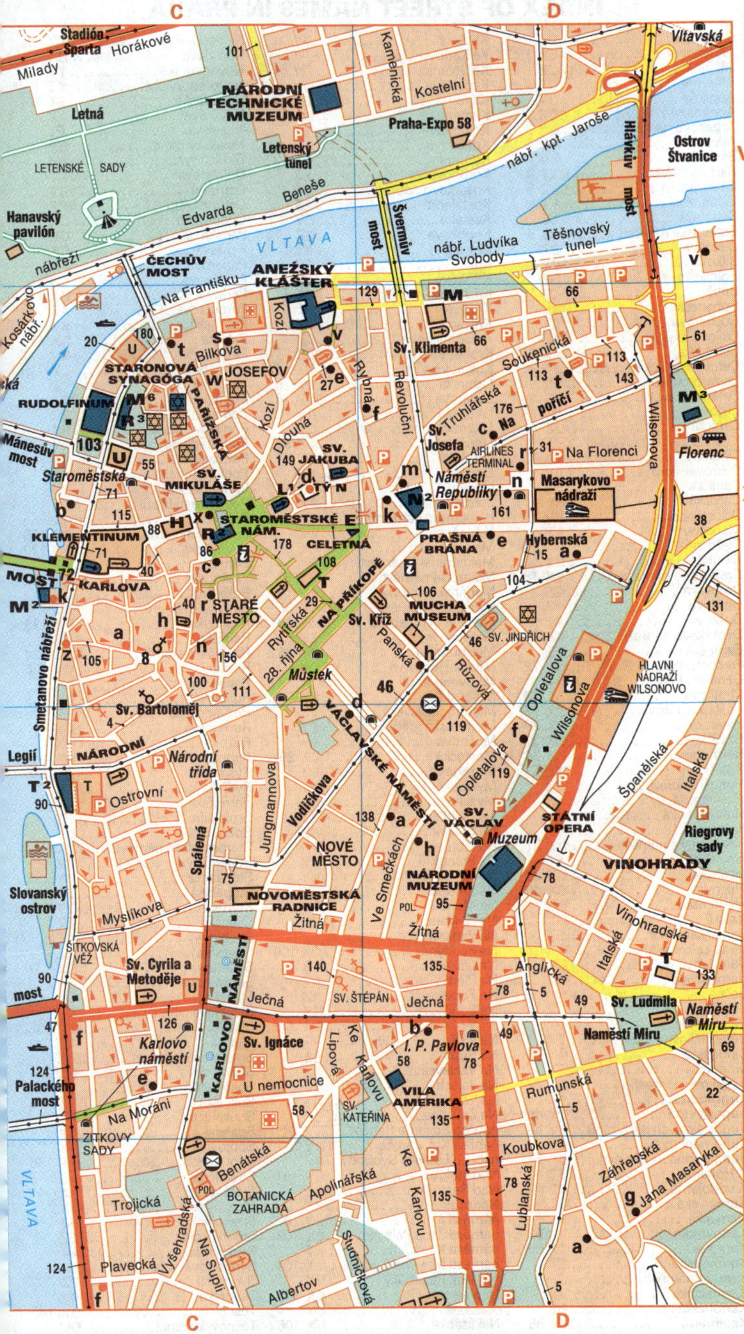
C
D
V
X
Y
Z
Stadión Sparta
Milady Horákové
Letná
LETENSKÉ SADY
Hanavský pavilón
NÁRODNÍ TECHNICKÉ MUZEUM
Letenský tunel
Kamenická
Kostelní
Praha-Expo 58
nábř. kpt. Jaroše
Vltavská
Ostrov Štvanice
Hlávkův most
Edvarda Beneše
VLTAVA
Švermův most
nábř. Ludvíka Svobody
Těšnovský tunel
Kosárkovo nábř.
nábřeží
ČECHŮV MOST
Na Františku
ANEŽSKÝ KLÁŠTER
STARONOVÁ SYNAGÓGA
JOSEFOV
Bílkova
PAŘÍŽSKÁ
RUDOLFINUM
Mánesův most
Staroměstská
Kozí
Dlouhá
Rybná
Revoluční
Sv. Klimenta
Soukenická
Na poříčí
Truhlářská
Sv. Josefa
AIRLINES TERMINAL
Na Florenci
Florenc
Wilsonova
Masarykovo nádraží
Náměstí Republiky
SV. MIKULÁŠE
SV. JAKUBA
TÝN
STAROMĚSTSKÉ NÁM.
CELETNÁ
KLEMENTINUM
KARLOVA
MOST
PRAŠNÁ BRÁNA
Hybernská
STARÉ MĚSTO
Rytířská
NA PŘÍKOPĚ
Sv. Kříž
MUCHA MUSEUM
Panská
SV. JINDŘICH
28. října
Můstek
HLAVNÍ NÁDRAŽÍ WILSONOVO
Smetanovo nábřeží
Sv. Bartoloměj
Opletalova
Růžová
VÁCLAVSKÉ NÁMĚSTÍ
Legií
NÁRODNÍ
Národní třída
Ostrovní
Jungmannova
Vodičkova
Spálená
NOVÉ MĚSTO
Ve Smečkách
SV. VÁCLAV
Muzeum
STÁTNÍ OPERA
Španělská
Italská
Riegrovy sady
VINOHRADY
Slovanský ostrov
NOVOMĚSTSKÁ RADNICE
NÁRODNÍ MUZEUM
Myslíkova
Žitná
Vinohradská
ŠITKOVSKÁ VĚŽ
Sv. Cyrila a Metoděje
NÁMĚSTÍ
Ječná
SV. ŠTĚPÁN
Anglická
Sv. Ludmila
Náměstí Míru
most
Karlovo náměstí
KARLOVO
Sv. Ignáce
Lípová
Ke Karlovu
I. P. Pavlova
VILA AMERIKA
Rumunská
Palackého most
U nemocnice
SV. KATEŘINA
Na Moráni
ZITKOVY SADY
Koubkova
Benátská
Záhřebská
Jana Masaryka
Apolinářská
Trojická
BOTANICKÁ ZAHRADA
Lublaňská
Vyšehradská
Na Slupi
Plavecká
Studničkova
Albertov

INDEX OF STREET NAMES IN PRAHA

5. května DZ
17. listopadu CX 180
28. října CX
Albertov CZ
Anglická DY
Apolinářská CDZ
Arbesovo náměstí BY 3
Atletická AY
Badeniho BV
Bartolomějská CXY 4
Bělehradská DYZ 5
Bělohorská ET
Benátská CZ
Betlémské náměstí CX 8
Bieblova BZ
Bilkova CX
Boleslavova DZ
Botič CZ
Bubenečská BV
Bucharova ET
Čakovická FS
Černínská AX 21
Černokostelecká FT
Českobrodská FS
Českomoravská FS
Čiklova DZ
Čimická FS
Celetná CDX
Cihelná BX 10
Cukrovarnická AV
Ďáblická FS
Dejvická BV
Dělostřelecká AV
Dlabačov AX
Dlážděná DX 16
Dlouhá CX
Dražického náměstí BX 18
Drnovská ES
Drtinova BY
Duškova AZ
Dvořákovo nábřeži CX 20
Evropská ES
Francouzská FT, DX 22
Generála Piky AV
Chotkova BV 43
Haštalské náměstí CX 27
Havířská CX 29
Havlíčkova DX 31
Heřmanova DV 34
Holečkova ABYZ
Hořejší nábřeží BZ
Horňátecká FS
Horoměřická ES
Horská CZ
Hradčanské náměstí AX 37
Hrnčířům FT
Husitská DX 38
Husova CX 40
Hybernská DX
Italská DY
Jana Masaryka DZ
Jana Želivského FST
Janáčkovo nábřeží BY
Jaromírova DZ
Ječná CDY
Jelení AV
Jeremenkova FT
Jeremiášova ET
Jindřišská DX 46
Jinonická ET
Jiráskovo náměstí CY 47
Jižni spojka FT
Jugoslávská DY 49
Jugoslávských partyzánů AV 50
Jungmannova CY
Jungmannovo náměstí CX 51
K Horkám FT
K vodojemu AZ
Kamenická DV
Kamýcká ES
Kanovnická AX 53
Kaprova CX 55
Karlovarská ET
Karlovo náměstí CY
Karmelitská BX
Kartouzská BY
Kateřinská CDY 58
Kbelská FS
Ke Karlovu DYZ
Ke Štvanici DX 61
Keplerova AX
Klárov BX 63
Klimentská DX 66
Kolbenova FS
Koněvova FS
Korunní FT, DY 69
Korunovační ES
Košarkovo nábřeží CX
Kostelecká FS
Kostelní DV
Koubkova DZ
Kováků BZ
Kozí CX
Křižíkova FS
Křižovnické náměstí CX 72
Křižová BZ
Křižovnická CX 71
Křesomyslova DZ
Krobova CDZ
Kukulova ET
Lazarská CY 75
Legerova DYZ 78
Letenská BX 79
Letenský tunel CV
Libušina CZ 80
Libušská FT 81
Lidická BZ
Lipová CY
Loretánska AX
Loretánské náměstí AX 83
Lublaňská DZ
Malé náměstí CX 86
Malostranské náměstí BX
Maltézské náměstí BX 87
Mariánské hradby BV
Mariánské náměstí CX 88
Masarykovo nábřeží CY 90
Matoušova BY 93
Mezibranská DY 95
Milady Horákové ABCV
Mirového hnuti FT
Míšeňská BX 97
Mladoboleslavská FS
Modřanská ET
Mošnova AY
Mostecká BX 99
Mozartova ABZ
Myslbekov AX
Myslíkova CY
Na Bělidle BZ
Na Březince ABZ
Na Florenci DX
Na Františku CY
Na Hřebenkách AY
Na Kampě BX
Na Moráni CY
Na Neklance BZ
Na Pankráci DZ
Na Perštýně CY 100
Na pískách ES
Na Pláni AZ
Na Popelce AZ
Na Poříčí DX
Na Příkopě CDX
Na strži FT
Na Supli CZ
Na Václavce AZ
Na valech BV
Na Věnečku AZ
Na Zatlance BZ
nábřeží Edvarda Beneše CV
nábřeží Kpt. Jaroše DV
nábřeží Ludvíka Svobody DV
Nad štolou CV 101
Nad Santoškou ABZ
Nádražní BZ
náměstí 4. října BY 102
náměstí Jana Palacha CX 103
náměstí Kinských BY
náměstí Maxima Gorkého DX 104
náměstí Republiky DX
Náprstkova CX 105
Národní CY
Nekázanka DX 106
Neklanova CZ
Nerudova BX
Novodvorská FT
Novořeporyjská ET
Novoveská ET 107
Nový Svět AX
Nuselská FT
Nuselský most DZ
Oldřichova DZ
Opletalova DXY
Ostrovni CY
Ostrovského ABZ
Ovocný trh CX 108
Panská DX
Pařížská CX
Parléřova AX
Patočkova AX, ES
Perlová CX 111
Peroutkova AZ
Petřínská BY
Petrská DX 113
Pevnostni AV
Platnéřská CX 115
Plavecká CZ
Plzeňská ABZ
Pod hradbami AV
Pod kesnerkou BZ
Pod Stadiony ET, AY 117
Podbabská ES
Podbělohorská ET
Poděbradská FS
Podolské nábřeží CZ
Pohořelec AX
Politických vězňů DY 119
Povltavská FS 120
Přímá AZ
Prokopská BX 122
Průběžna FT
Průmyslová FST
Řásnovka DX 129
Radlická ABZ
Rašínovo nábřeží CYZ 124
Resslova CY 126
Revoluční DX
Rostocká ES
Rozvadovská spojka ET
Rumunská DY
Růžova DX
Rybná DX
Ryšavého FT 128
Rytířská CX
Šermířská AY
Šmidkeho FT
Španělská DY
Staroměstské náměstí CX
Štefánikova BY
Štěpánská DY 138
Štěpařská ET 140
Štúrova FT 142
Švédská AY
Švehlova FT
Santoška BZ
Seifertova DX 131
Sekaninova DZ
Slánská ET
Slavojova CDZ
Slezská DY 133
Slunná AV
Smetanovo nábřeží CXY
Sněmovní BX 134
Sokolovská FS
Sokolská DYZ 135
Soukenická DX
Spálená CY
Spojovací FS
Spořilovská FT 136
Střelničná FS
Střešovická AX 141
Strahovská AX
Strakonická BZ
Studničkova CZ
Svatovitská AV
Svobodova CZ
Svornosti BZ
Táborská DZ
Těšnov DX 143
Těšnovský tunel DV

Tomášská .... BX 146
Trojícká .... CZ
Trojská .... FS
Truhlářská .... DX
Tržiště .... BX 147
Turistická .... AY 148
Tynská .... CX 149
U Blaženky .... AZ
U Bruských Kasáren .... BX 150
U Brusnice .... AVX
U Kasáren .... AX 152
U lužického semináře .... BX 154
U Malvazinky .... AZ
U Mrázovky .... AZ
U nemocnice .... CY
U Nikolajky .... AZ
U Prašného mostu .... BX
U Šalamounky .... AZ
U Santošky .... BZ
Uhelný trh .... CY 156
Újezd .... BXY
Ústecká .... FS
Úvoz .... AX
V botanice .... BY 158
V celnici .... DX 161
V Olšinach .... FT
V Sáreckém údolí .... ES 163
Václavkova .... AV 165
Václavské náměstí .... CDY
Valdštejnská .... BX 168
Valdštejnské náměstí .... BX 169
Vaníčkova .... AY
Ve Smečkách .... DY
Veletržní .... FS
Velkopřevorské náměstí .... BX 170
Videňská .... FT
Vinohradská .... DY
Vítězná .... BY
Vítězné náměstí .... ES
Vlašská .... BX
Vltavská .... BZ
Vnislavova .... CZ 171
Vodičkova .... CY
Vratislavova .... CZ
Vrchlického .... AZ
Vršovická .... FT
Vyšehradská .... CZ
Vysočanská .... FS
Výstavní .... FT 173
Wilsonova .... DXY
Xaveriova .... AZ
Železná .... CX 178
Žitná .... CY
Záhřebská .... DZ
Zálesi .... FT
Zapova .... AY
Zborovská .... BY 174
Zelená .... ES 175
Zenklova .... FS
Zlatnická .... DX 176

Four Seasons, Veleslavínova 1098/2a, 110 00, 221 427 000, *prg.reservations@fourseasons.com, Fax 221 426 000,* - - 120. CX b
Meals (see ***Allegro*** below) – 900 – **141 rm** 9300/18500, 20 suites.
• Four houses - modern, neo-Classical, Baroque and neo-Renaissance - make up this elegant riverside hotel. Luxuriously appointed modern rooms; state-of-the-art business facilities. Modern fine dining restaurant, softly lit and stylishly understated.

Inter-Continental, Nám. Curieových 43-45, 110 00, 296 631 111, *prague@interconti.com, Fax 224 811 216,* - rm, - 500. CX t
Meals (see ***Zlatá Praha*** below) – 665 – **283 rm** 11000/11460, 89 suites 13900/20000.
• Prague's first luxury hotel provides all of the facilities expected of an international hotel. Elegant bedrooms, most enjoy views of the river or the old part of the city.

Carlo IV, Senovážné Nám. 13, 110 00, 224 593 111, *reservation@carloiv.boscolo.com, Fax 224 593 000,* - rm, - 360. rest DX a
Box Block **: Meals** a la carte 945/2200 – 790 – **152 rm** 11600/13500.
• 19C converted bank with marbled lobby and ornate ceiling. Contemporary pool and health centre. All bedrooms have stylish furniture and modern facilities. A stylish restaurant serving modern dishes with a strong Mediterranean influence.

Radisson SAS Alcron, Štěpánská 40, 110 00, 222 820 000, *sales.prague@radissonsas.com, Fax 222 820 120,* - - 150. DY a
La Rotonde **: Meals** 1190 and a la carte 1130/1470 (see also ***Alcron*** below) – 660 – **192 rm** 7220, 19 suites.
• Built in 1930's and recently refurbished to a very high standard. Original Art Deco theme carried through to include the spacious and extremely comfortable bedrooms. Immaculately laid out restaurant with a stylish Art Deco theme and an outdoor summer terrace.

Aria, Trziste 9, 118 00, 225 334 111, *stay@aria.cz, Fax 225 334 131,* - rm, - 30. BX x
Coda **: Meals** a la carte 1165/1645 – **23 rm** 10400/12000, 29 suites 15200/30400.
• Stylish modern hotel in the castle district. Hi-tech bedrooms, each with its own musical theme from opera to jazz. Hotel has its own musical director. Choose from the stylish menu in intimate Coda or eat on the stunning roof top terrace.

Marriott, V Celnici 8, 110 00, 222 888 888, *prague.marriott@marriotthotels.com, Fax 222 888 823,* - rm, - 350. rest DX n
Meals a la carte approx 600 – 615 – **258 rm** 9055, 35 suites.
• International hotel, opened in 1999. First-class conference and leisure facilities. Committed service and modern, smart bedrooms with all the latest facilities. Brasserie offers a wide selection of cuisine from American, French to traditional Czech.

Hilton Prague, Pobřežní 1, ✉ 186 00, ☎ 222 841 111, *sales.prague@hilton.com, Fax 224 842 378,* <, 🏠, Fitness, sauna, swimming pool, squash – lift, ⊁ rm, ▤ TV ☎ ♿ 🚗 P – 🎤 1500. MC AE DC VISA JCB. ⊁ rest DV v
Czech House : **Meals** *(closed Sunday)* (dinner only) a la carte approx 1000 – ***Café Bistro :*** **Meals** a la carte approx 800 🍷 – ☕ 685 – **757 rm** 8235/10100, 31 suites.
◆ Adjacent to the International Business Centre, glass building with a spectacular atrium - the largest hotel in the country. Impressive leisure facilities. Modern, Mediterranean repertoire at Czech House. Informal Café Bistro.

Renaissance, V Celnici 7, ✉ 111 21, ☎ 221 822 100, *renaissance.prague@renaissancehotels.com, Fax 221 822 200,* Fitness, sauna, swimming pool – lift, ⊁ rm, ▤ TV ☎ ♿ 🚗 – 🎤 120. MC AE DC VISA JCB. ⊁ DX r
Seven : **Meals** a la carte approx 1000 🍷 – ***U Korbele*** *(☎ 221 822 433)* **: Meals** a la carte approx 600 🍷 – ☕ 615 – **314 rm** 8450.
◆ Luxury group hotel in the heart of the City. Geared to the modern corporate traveller ; well-equipped bedrooms, particularly those on the 'Renaissance Club' floor. Seven specialises in grills and seafood. Czech specialities in casual, relaxing U Korbele.

Palace, Panská 12, ✉ 111 21, ☎ 224 093 111, *info@palacehotel.cz, Fax 224 221 240,* sauna – lift, ⊁ rm, ▤ TV ☎ ♿ 🚗 – 🎤 150. MC AE DC VISA JCB. ⊁ rest DX h
Meals a la carte 1350/2580 🍷 – ***Gourmet Club Restaurant :*** **Meals** (dinner only) 1200/5600 and a la carte 1220/2230 🍷 – **114 rm** ☕ 10600/11300, 10 suites.
◆ Original façade dates back to 1906 and its Viennese Art Nouveau style. Elegant interior ; bedrooms combine period furniture with modern facilities and services. Brasserie and bar with all-day menu. Classic club ambience in the Gourmet Club Restaurant.

Savoy, Keplerova Ul. 6, ✉ 118 00, ☎ 224 302 430, *info@hotel-savoy.cz, Fax 224 302 128,* Fitness, sauna – lift, ⊁ rm, ▤ TV ☎ ♿ 🚗 – 🎤 60. MC AE DC VISA JCB. ⊁ rest AX a
Hradčany : **Meals** 660/1000 and a la carte 900/1950 🍷 – **59 rm** ☕ 9700, 2 suites.
◆ Elegant lobby and relaxing library bar suggesting a bygone era. Up-to-date bedrooms with all mod cons and large, marbled bathrooms. Elegant pillared room with tall windows open on fine days. Uniformed staff and immaculate settings ; international ingredients.

Le Palais, U Zvonařky 1, ✉ 120 00, ☎ 234 634 111, *info@palaishotel.cz, Fax 234 634 635,* 🏠, Fitness, sauna – lift, ⊁ rm, ▤ TV ☎ ♿ 🚗 – 🎤 90. MC AE DC VISA DZ a
Meals a la carte 970/1230 – **60 rm** ☕ 8340/11600, 12 suites.
◆ Elegant hotel in converted late 19C mansion in Belle Epoque style. Basement sauna, gym and treatment rooms. Luxurious bedrooms with modern comforts and equipment. Comfortable restaurant serving modern dishes and Czech specialities.

Corinthia Towers, Kongresová 1, ✉ 140 69, ☎ 261 191 111, *towers@corinthia.cz, Fax 261 225 011,* <, Fitness, sauna, swimming pool, squash – lift, ⊁ rm, ▤ TV ☎ ♿ 🚗 – 🎤 400. MC AE DC VISA FT n
Rickshaw : **Meals** - Asian - *(closed Sunday)* (dinner only) 790/1260 and a la carte 1600/2600 – ***Toscana :*** **Meals** - Italian - 470/1100 and a la carte 630/1000 🍷 – **532 rm** ☕ 8200, 12 suites.
◆ Modern corporate skyscraper, opposite the Congress Centre ; many rooms enjoy city views. Rickshaw serves a mix of Asian dishes. Toscana is a popular Italian restaurant.

Grand Hotel Bohemia, Králodvorská 4, ✉ 110 00, ☎ 234 608 111, *beranck@grandhotelbohemia.cz, Fax 222 329 545* – lift, ⊁ rm, ▤ TV ☎ ♿ – 🎤 140. MC AE DC VISA JCB DX k
Meals 770/925 and a la carte – **78 rm** ☕ 7100/14450.
◆ Classic 1920's hotel, in an ideal location for tourists, with a splendid neo-Baroque ballroom. Comfortable bedrooms are generously proportioned and service professional. Restaurant with large windows which add to the feeling of light and space.

Hoffmeister, Pod Bruskou 7, ✉ 118 00, ☎ 251 017 111, *hotel@hoffmeister.cz, Fax 251 017 120,* 🏠 – lift ▤ TV ☎ 🚗. MC AE DC VISA. ⊁ rest BX s
Meals 1000/1500 and a la carte 1090/1470 – **28 rm** ☕ 8550/9750, 10 suites.
◆ Charming residence at the foot of the Castle steps ; a 1920's feel and a huge collection of Adolf Hoffmeister art. Tasteful and comfortable. Elegant surroundings with original Adolf Hoffmeister cartoons. Attentive service ; French and Italian influenced cooking.

Andel's, Stroupeznického 21, ✉ 150 00, ☎ 296 889 688, *info@andelshotel.com, Fax 296 889 999,* Fitness, sauna – lift, ⊁ rm, ▤ TV ☎ ♿ 🚗 – 🎤 350. MC AE DC VISA JCB BZ a
Oscar's : **Meals** 149 (lunch) and a la carte – ***Nagoya*** *(☎ 251 511 724)* **: Meals** - Japanese - *(closed Sunday and Monday lunch)* a la carte approx 800 – **257 rm** ☕ 7400/8000, 33 suites.
◆ Modern hotel in large complex with cinema. Conference and fitness centres. Rooms are bright, modern and minimalist as are impressive new suites ; hi-tech facilities. Informal dining in Oscar brasserie ; simple menu. Nagoya offers traditional Japanese dishes.

Mövenpick, Mozartova 261/1, ✉ 150 00, ✆ 257 151 111, *hotel.prague@moevenpick.com, Fax 257 153 002,* ≤, ⛱, 🏋, ≘s, 🟩 – |♦|, ⇹ rm, ▤ TV ✆ ♿ 🚗 – 🏛 250. MC AE ◑ VISA JCB AZ b
***Il Giardino :* Meals** a la carte 530/1080 – ***Movenpick** (✆ 257 153 232) :* **Meals** - Mediterranean - (buffet lunch) 690/736 and a la carte 360/1090 – **436 rm** ☕ 6370/6990.
◆ Unique two-part hotel. From the ground floor, a funicular railway climbs uphill to larger, better equipped, balconied rooms with panoramic views - superior in both senses. Modern brasserie on the ground floor. Mediterranean influences in Il Giardino.

Crowne Plaza, Koulova 15, ✉ 160 45, ✆ 296 537 111, *hotel@crowneplaza.cz, Fax 296 537 535,* ⛱, 🏋, ≘s, 🟩 – |♦|, ⇹ rm, ▤ TV ✆ ♿ 🅿 – 🏛 250. MC AE ◑ VISA JCB. ✂ ES a
Meals 495 and a la carte approx 620 – **250 rm** ☕ 10925/11300, 4 suites.
◆ An imposing example of Socialist Realism architecture. Softened interior retains a grandeur, with tapestries, stained glass and mosaics. Refurbished, well-equipped bedrooms. Ornate decoration lends a period feel to the restaurant.

Mercure, Na Poříčí 7, ✉ 110 00, ✆ 221 800 800, *h3440@accor-hotels.com, Fax 221 800 801,* ⛱ – |♦|, ⇹ rm, ▤ TV ✆ ♿. MC AE ◑ VISA JCB DX c
***Felice :* Meals** *(closed lunch Saturday and Sunday)* 525/1000 and a la carte approx 820 – ☕ 445 – **173 rm** 6055/6425, 1 suite.
◆ Modern hotel behind ornate, period façade. Chapter Bar features works of famous Czech writers. Ask for a deluxe room ; more spacious. Booking advisable at this modern Parisian brasserie. Menus blend French and Czech classics.

Paříž, U obecního domu 1, ✉ 110 00, ✆ 222 195 195, *booking@hotel-pariz.cz, Fax 224 225 475,* ≘s – |♦|, ⇹ rm, ▤ TV ✆ 🚗 – 🏛 55. MC AE ◑ VISA JCB DX m
***Sarah Bernhardt :* Meals** 600 (lunch) and a la carte 830/1210 🍷 – ***Café de Paris :* Meals** a la carte 450/680 – ☕ 650 – **71 rm** 9950, 15 suites.
◆ A city landmark ; famed for its neo-Gothic, Art Nouveau architecture. Original staircase with preserved window panels. Neat and clean bedrooms. Fine example of Art Nouveau in Sarah Bernhardt restaurant. Simple French fare in Café de Paris.

Riverside without rest., Janáčkovo nábřeži 15, ✉ 150 00, ✆ 225 994 611, *info@riversideprague.com, Fax 225 994 615,* ≤ – |♦|, ⇹ rm, ▤ TV ✆ ♿. MC AE ◑ VISA JCB. ✂ BY b
42 rm ☕ 9000/9800, 3 suites.
◆ An early 20C façade facing the river conceals a modern sound-proofed hotel with bar and breakfast room. Stylish bedrooms with luxurious bathrooms ; many with views.

K + K Central, Hybernská 10, ✉ 110 00, ✆ 225 022 000, *hotel.central@kkhotels.cz, Fax 225 022 999,* 🏋, ≘s – |♦|, ⇹ rm, ▤ TV ✆ ♿ 🚗 – 🏛 60. MC AE ◑ VISA JCB DX e
Meals (meals in bar) a la carte 400/850 – **126 rm** ☕ 8450/9088, 1 suite.
◆ Beautifully restored property with extensions ; elegant Art Nouveau and ultra modern décor. Glass and steel breakfast gallery in old theatre. Larger rooms in original building.

K + K Fenix, Ve Smečkách 30, ✉ 110 00, ✆ 225 012 000, *hotel.fenix@kkhotels.cz, Fax 222 212 141,* 🏋, ≘s – |♦|, ⇹ rm, ▤ TV ✆ ♿ 🚗 – 🏛 40. MC AE ◑ VISA JCB. ✂ rest DY h
Meals (in bar) a la carte 500/830 🍷 – **127 rm** ☕ 7930/8545.
◆ Located in a quiet side street ; stylish and cosmopolitan interior behind a classic façade. Bedrooms vary in size and shape but all are smart, clean and comfortable. Open-plan café bar in the lobby ; tasty brasserie classics.

U Zlaté Studně 🐦, U Zlaté Studně 166/4, ✉ 118 00, ✆ 257 011 213, *hotel@zlatastudna.cz, Fax 257 533 320,* ≤ – |♦| ▤ TV ✆. MC AE ◑ VISA JCB BX f
Meals (see ***U Zlaté Studně*** below) – **17 rm** ☕ 6000/7100, 3 suites.
◆ 16C Renaissance building in quiet spot between the castle and Ladeburg Gardens. Inviting rooms with contemporary and reproduction furniture : richly furnished but uncluttered.

Residence Nosticova 🐦, Nosticova 1, Malá Strana, ✉ 118 00, ✆ 257 312 513, *info@nosticova.com, Fax 257 312 517* – |♦| TV ✆ 🅿. MC AE ◑ VISA JCB BX v
***Alchymist** (✆ 257 312 518) :* **Meals** 990 and a la carte 580/820 – ☕ 288 – **5 rm** 6464/7520, **5 suites** 8768/10240.
◆ Tastefully refurbished 17C townhouse in a quiet, cobbled side street. Stylish suites - all with their own kitchen - combine modern and antique furnishings and works of art.

Esplanade, Washingtonova 1600-19, ✉ 110 00, ✆ 224 501 111, *esplanade@esplanade.cz, Fax 224 229 306* – |♦|, ⇹ rm, ▤ rm, TV ✆ – 🏛 60. MC AE ◑ VISA JCB DY f
Meals 600/1210 (dinner) and a la carte 810/1000 🍷 – ☕ 470 – **74 rm** 3400/11000.
◆ Charming and atmospheric ; this Art Nouveau building is something of an architectural gem. Original features abound ; bedrooms enjoy style and a timeless elegance. Menu of traditional Czech and French specialities offered in friendly surroundings.

The Iron Gate, Michalská 19, ✉ 110 00, ☎ 225 777 777, *hotel@irongate.cz, Fax 225 777 778,* – |‡|, ▤ TV ☎ P. MC AE ◐ VISA JCB. ✂ rest CX r
***Zelezna Brata* : Meals** (live gypsy music) a la carte 630/1025 – ***Cafe Bogner* : Meals** a la carte approx 790 – **20 rm** ☐ 9600, **23 suites** ☐ 9600/32000.
◆ Distinctive part 14C Gothic house in cobbled street in Old Town; attractive central courtyard. Large rooms with antique furniture or painted beams; some duplex suites. Zelezna Brata in basement for Czech cuisine; gypsy music. Informal eating in Café Bogner.

Josef without rest., Rybná 20, ✉ 110 00, ☎ 221 700 111, *reservation@hoteljosef.com, Fax 221 700 999,* – |‡|, ✂ rm, ▤ TV ☎ ♿ – 🏛 70. MC AE ◐ VISA JCB. ✂ DX f
110 rm ☐ 6800/10800.
◆ Stylish designer hotel with light glass lobby, bar and breakfast room. Stylish bedrooms; deluxe rooms have ultra modern bathrooms.

U Prince, Staroměstské Nám. 29, ✉ 110 00, ☎ 224 213 807, *reserve@hoteluprince.cz, Fax 224 213 807,* < Prague, – |‡|, ✂ rm, ▤ TV. MC AE ◐ VISA JCB CX c
Meals a la carte 357/887 – **24 rm** ☐ 6590/16000.
◆ Restored 17C townhouse on main square with atmospheric rooms blending with mod cons and antique furnishings. Roof terrace with marvellous city views. Choose the half-panelled bar-restaurant for International cooking or the brick vaulted cellars for seafood.

Adria, Václavské Nám. 26, ✉ 110 00, ☎ 221 081 111, *mailbox@adria.cz, Fax 221 081 300* – |‡|, ✂ rm, ▤ TV ☎ ♿ – 🏛 70. MC AE ◐ VISA JCB. ✂
***Triton* : Meals** (dinner booking essential) 780 and a la carte 640/1550 – **80 rm** ☐ 3300/7300, 7 suites. CY d
◆ Ornate façade hides a labyrinth inside that connects five separate houses. Combines the nostalgic charm of Old Prague with modern, recently refurbished bedrooms. Eye-catching Art Nouveau grotto. Savour international dishes in unique, candlelit surroundings.

Maximilian without rest., Haštalská 14, ✉ 110 00, ☎ 225 303 120, *reservations@maximilianhotel.com, Fax 225 303 121* – |‡| ✂ ▤ TV ♿ – 🏛 50. MC AE ◐ VISA JCB CX e
71 rm ☐ 6300/7550.
◆ Tall, converted terraced house in a quiet square. Immaculately kept, with elegant and understated bedrooms and a smart breakfast room. Welcoming and friendly service.

Kinsky Garden, Holečkova 7, ✉ 150 00, ☎ 257 311 173, *info@hotelkinskygarden.cz, Fax 257 311 184* – |‡|, ✂ rm, ▤ TV ☎ ♿ – 🏛 25. MC AE ◐ VISA JCB. ✂ rest
Meals 420/490 and a la carte 460/850 ♀ – **60 rm** ☐ 5300/6500. BY a
◆ Overlooking the Park, with an attractive period façade. Smart little lobby and bar, with lots of marble. Comfortable and spacious bedrooms in warm, neutral colours. International and Italian-influenced cooking.

Zlatá Hvězda, Nerudova 48, Malá Strana, ✉ 118 00, ☎ 257 532 867, *hvezda@ok.cz, Fax 257 533 624,* – |‡| TV ☎. MC AE ◐ VISA AX e
Meals 220/320 (lunch) and a la carte 370/740 ♀ – **24 rm** ☐ 6300/7600, 2 suites.
◆ Imposing, part 18C burgher house in a delightful setting. Comfortable bedrooms and pleasant views of the town from the upper floors. Classic cooking from the traditional Czech repertory.

U Krále Karla, Uvoz 4, ✉ 118 00, ☎ 257 532 869, *ukrale@iol.cz, Fax 257 533 591* – |‡|, ✂ rm, TV. MC AE ◐ VISA AX n
Meals 600/900 and a la carte – **19 rm** ☐ 5300/8200.
◆ Rebuilt in 1639 into a Baroque house from an original Gothic building of a Benedictine Order. Features stained glass windows and antique oak furnishings. Panelled dining room and an ambience of Old Prague complemented by the traditional menu.

Blue Key without rest., Letenská 14, ✉ 118 00, ☎ 257 534 361, *bluekey@mbox.vol.cz, Fax 257 534 372,* – |‡| ✂ TV. MC AE ◐ VISA JCB BX a
22 rm ☐ 4200/5100, 6 suites.
◆ 18C house in heart of old town. The smart modern rooms, facing the central courtyard, are decorated in forest green or blue and white; some have kitchenettes.

Jalta, Václavské Nám. 45, ✉ 110 00, ☎ 222 822 111, *booking@jalta.cz, Fax 222 822 124* – |‡| ▤ TV ☎ – 🏛 100. MC AE ◐ VISA JCB DY e
Meals 620/1550 and a la carte – **89 rm** ☐ 7430/8050, 5 suites.
◆ Classic 1950's façade overlooking Wenceslas Square. Spacious feeling, extensive facilities and helpful staff. Good standard modern bedrooms. Elegant, sophisticated dining room with International and Czech dishes.

Novotel, Kateřinská 38, ✉ 120 00, ☎ 221 104 999, *h3194-re@accor-hotels.com, Fax 221 104 888,* – |‡|, ✂ rm, ▤ TV ☎ ♿ – 🏛 120. MC AE VISA JCB. ✂ rest DY b
Meals a la carte 600/935 ♀ – ☐ 390 – **146 rm** 5600/9200.
◆ 21C group hotel on the southern edge of the old town. Affordable accommodation, trim and practically designed, with spacious bedrooms. Modern restaurant with a neatly set terrace; well-known international dishes.

U Páva, U Lužického Semináře 30, ✉ 118 00, ☎ 257 533 360, *hotelupava@iol.cz, Fax 257 530 919,* – – rest BX m
Meals a la carte approx 700 – **15 rm** 5700/6200, 6 suites.
◆ Attractively located, converted 17C houses. Original stone columns in the hallways, nutwood furniture and ornately decorated rooms add to the character. Vaulted basement dining room has a warm and romantic feel. International menu with Czech specialities.

Questenberk without rest., Uvoz 15/155, ✉ 110 00, ☎ 220 407 600, *hotel@questenberk.cz, Fax 220 407 601,* – rm, AX b
30 rm 5900/12000.
◆ Converted 17C monastic hospital with ornate façade at the top of the Castle District. Arched corridors leading to sizable bedrooms with good facilities overlooking the city.

The Charles without rest., Josefská 1, ✉ 118 00, ☎ 257 532 913, *thecharles@bon.cz, Fax 257 532 910* – . BX e
31 rm 4200/6900.
◆ Elegant and ideally situated little hotel. Spacious bedrooms decorated with stripped floorboards, hand painted ceilings and Baroque style furnishings.

U Raka without rest., Cernínská 10, ✉ 118 00, ☎ 220 511 100, *uraka@login.cz, Fax 233 358 041,* – . AX c
6 rm 5600/7400.
◆ Two charming timbered cottages with flower-filled urns, troughs and millstones in a pretty rockery. Clean-lined, rustic rooms in warm brick and wood : cosy, inviting and romantic.

Art without rest., Nad Královskou oborou 53, ✉ 170 00, ☎ 233 101 331, *booking@arthotel.cz, Fax 233 101 311* – ES x
24 rm 5100/6900.
◆ Stylish, modern hotel in quiet district. Artists celebrated on each floor, including owner's father and grandfather. Roof-top view from front. Two attic suites with balconies.

Casa Marcello, Rásnovka 783, ✉ 110 00, ☎ 222 311 230, *booking@casa-marcello.cz, Fax 222 313 323,* , – rm, – 25. rest
Meals *(April-October)* a la carte 355/550 – **26 rm** 7800, 6 suites. CX v
◆ Beside the 1000 year old St Agnes Monastery ; bedrooms at this part 13C property were once the nuns' quarters. Several vaulted rooms with stately antique furniture. A traditional menu can be enjoyed on the secluded terrace or in the cosy panelled dining room.

Constans, Břetislavova 39, ✉ 118 00, ☎ 234 091 818, *hotel@hotelconstans.cz, Fax 234 091 860* – . BX b
Meals a la carte approx 350 – **32 rm** 4680/7170.
◆ Small hotel in narrow cobbled street in the Castle district. Good sized, light and airy bedrooms with locally made furniture. Simple café style restaurant-breakfast room-bar serving basic menu of international dishes.

Bellagio, U Milosrdnâch 2, ✉ 110 00, ☎ 221 778 999, *info@bellagiohotel.cz, Fax 221 778 900* – , rm, – 30. . CX s
Meals (dinner only) 695/795 and a la carte 645/1205 – **46 rm** 6552/8980.
◆ Converted pink apartment block near the river. Brick-vaulted bar/breakfast room. Stylish bedrooms in warm colours with modern furniture, attractive tiled bathrooms.

Biskupský Dům, Dražického Nám. 6, ✉ 118 00, ☎ 257 532 320, *biskup@ok.cz, Fax 257 531 840* – . BX t
Meals a la carte 395/800 – **45 rm** 6300/7600.
◆ In a small square near the Charles Bridge, a renovated townhouse hotel on the site of the 13C bishop's court. Simple rooms furnished in dark wood. Familiar Czech and international dishes.

Ametyst, Jana Masaryka 11, ✉ 120 00, ☎ 222 921 921, *mailbox@hotelametyst.cz, Fax 222 921 999,* – , rm, rest, DZ g
Meals (buffet lunch) 300/700 and a la carte 500/600 – **84 rm** 3600/5000.
◆ Bright, white six-storey building with a neat, precise feel. Smart bedrooms with all modern facilities. Choose Austrian fare in the wine bar or typical Czech and International dishes in the more formal 'Galleria'.

Cerná Liška, Mikulášská 2, Staroměstské Nám., ✉ 110 00, ☎ 224 232 250, *hotel@cernaliska.cz, Fax 224 232 249,* – . CX x
Meals a la carte approx 450 – **12 rm** 4000/6000.
◆ Delightful small hotel in the Old Town Square, a good base for exploring the city. All the bedrooms have character and charm. Simple ground floor café and 18C basement cellar restaurant with summer terrace ; vegetarian menu.

City H. Moran, Na Moráni 15, ✉ 120 00, ☎ 224 915 208, *bw-moran@login.cz, Fax 224 920 625* – , rm, . CY e
Meals a la carte approx 350 – **57 rm** 4080/4530.
◆ Modern interior behind a characterful, period façade. Small, discreet marbled lobby leads up to clean, well-kept, functional bedrooms. Useful city centre accommodation. Simple restaurant for modern, International and Czech cooking.

Bílá Labuť, Biskupská 9, ✉ 110 00, ✆ 222 324 540, *cchotels@login.cz, Fax 222 322 905,* – ⎮, rm, ♿. MC AE D VISA DX t
Meals a la carte approx 450 – **55 rm** 4700/6500.
◆ Converted from a large office block. Now offers simple, clean and well maintained accommodation in a central location. Popular with the business community. Modern bar and restaurant for Czech and International cooking.

Allegro (at Four Seasons H.), Veleslavínova 2a, ✉ 110 00, ✆ 221 426 880, – . MC AE D VISA JCB. CX b
Meals - Italian - 1200/1300 (lunch) and a la carte 1450/2185.
◆ Ground floor restaurant ; partial view of Charles Bridge ; beautiful summer terrace. Modern Italian menu based on classical dishes with seasonal specialities ; smooth service.

Zlatá Praha (at Inter-Continental H.), Nám. Curieových 43-45, ✉ 110 00, ✆ 296 630 914, *prague@interconti.com, Fax 296 631 207,* ≤ Prague, – . MC AE D VISA JCB. CX t
Meals a la carte 1165/1900.
◆ Stunning views of the city skyline provide a backdrop to this elegant, formal room. Extensive menu at well-spaced tables. Grills, fish specials on the terrace in summer.

Flambée, Husova 5, ✉ 110 00, ✆ 224 248 512, *flambee@flambee.cz, Fax 224 248 513* – . MC AE D VISA JCB CX h
Meals 1200 (lunch) and dinner a la carte 2200/2800 – ***Cafe Flambée :*** **Meals** a la carte 440/940.
◆ Elegant fine dining in established cellar restaurant : faultless, formal yet friendly service and well-judged classics - impressive selection of clarets. A little modern café-bistro open for coffees, desserts and brunch ; international dishes from main kitchen.

Alcron (at Radisson SAS Alcron H.), Štěpánská 40, ✉ 110 00, ✆ 222 820 038, *sales.prague@radissonsas.com, Fax 222 820 100* – . MC AE VISA JCB. DY a
closed Sunday – **Meals** - Seafood - (booking essential) (dinner only) a la carte 1630/2780.
◆ An Art Deco mural after de Lempicka dominates this intimate, semi-circular restaurant. Creative and classic seafood served by friendly, professional staff.

La Perle de Prague, Dancing House (7th floor), Rašínovo Nábřeží 80, ✉ 120 00, ✆ 221 984 160, *info@laperle.cz, Fax 221 984 179,* ≤, – ⎮ . MC AE D VISA JCB CY f
closed Sunday and lunch Monday – **Meals** - French - 590/2500 and a la carte 1050/1710.
◆ Eye-catching riverside building : free-form contours crowned by a mesh-metal onion dome. Superb terrace views and comfortable, strikingly modern decor. French-inspired menu.

Bellevue, Smetanovo Nábřeží 18, ✉ 110 00, ✆ 222 221 443, *bellevue@pfd.cz, Fax 222 220 453,* ≤, – MC AE VISA CX z
closed 24 December – **Meals** 1490/1890 and a la carte 1160/1970.
◆ On the first floor of an elegant building, affording views of the river and bridge. Pleasant terrace, comfortable surroundings, knowledgeable staff, contemporary cuisine.

Vinárna V Zátiší, Liliová 1, Betlémské Nám., ✉ 110 00, ✆ 222 221 155, *vzatisi@pfd.cz, Fax 222 220 629* – rest, . MC AE VISA. CX a
closed 24 December, lunch 31 December and lunch 1 January – **Meals** (dinner booking essential) 695/1575 and a la carte 1185/1485.
◆ Extensive menu includes traditional Czech flavours and more modern dishes. Friendly welcome. Divided into three rooms, each warmly decorated.

U Zlaté Studně (at U Zlaté Studně H.), U Zlaté Studně 4, ✉ 118 00, ✆ 257 011 213, *zlata.studne@email.cz, Fax 257 533 320,* ≤ Prague, – . MC AE D VISA JCB BX f
Meals a la carte 930/1670.
◆ Beautiful skyline views from a clean-lined top-floor restaurant and terrace, reached by its own lift. Affable staff ; full-flavoured modern dishes.

Le Terroir, Vejvodova 1, ✉ 110 00, ✆ 602 889 118, *rezervace@leterroir.cz,* – . MC AE D VISA JCB CX n
Meals - French - 950/1550 and a la carte 730/1120.
◆ Part 10C restored town house in Old Town with cobbled courtyard and steps descending past wine store to vaulted cellar. Evolving modern French style menu ; good value.

Kampa Park, Na Kampě 8b, ✉ 118 00, ✆ 257 532 685, *kontakt@kampapark.com, Fax 257 533 223,* ≤ Charles Bridge, – MC AE D VISA JCB BX w
closed 24-25 December – **Meals** (dinner booking essential) 395/475 (lunch) and a la carte 1235/1675.
◆ Popular restaurant stunningly located by Charles Bridge. Lively modern designer main room, outside terrace or covered waterside terrace. Modern menu with global influences.

Mlynec, Novotného Lávka 9, ✉ 110 00, ✆ 221 082 208, *mlynec@pfd.cz, Fax 221 082 391,* ≤ Charles Bridge, – MC AE D VISA JCB CX k
closed 24 December – **Meals** 1000/1600 (dinner) and a la carte 1035/1385.
◆ Spacious and contemporary : fine modern dishes combined with Czech classics - good Czech wines and terrace views of the Charles Bridge on fine summer evenings.

Pálffy Palác, Valdstejnska 14, ✉ 118 00, ✆ 257 530 522, *palffy@palffy.cz, Fax 257 530 522,* – MC AE VISA BX c
closed 24 December – **Meals** 300/1475 and a la carte 665/1475.
• First floor restaurant, a high ceilinged, ornate room in the 18C Prague Conservatory. A romantic setting in the evening ; delightful terrace in summer. Modern menu.

Rybí trh, Tânskâ dvůr 5, ✉ 110 00, ✆ 224 895 447, *info@rybitrh.cz, Fax 224 895 449,* – MC AE VISA. CX d
Meals - Seafood - a la carte 1370/3370.
• Modern restaurant which lives up to its name - Fish Market - with fresh seafood on crushed ice before open plan kitchen ; fish tanks, adjacent wine shop and tasting cellar.

U Patrona, Dražického Nám. 4, ✉ 118 00, ✆ 257 530 725, *upatrona@seznam.cz, Fax 257 530 723* – . MC AE VISA JCB BX n
Meals 350 (lunch) and a la carte 415/1240.
• Charming period house near Charles Bridge. Small ground floor restaurant or larger upstairs room with window into kitchen. French-influenced classics and Czech specialities.

Bistrot de Marlène, Plavecká 4, ✉ 120 00, ✆ 224 921 853, *info@bistrotdemarlene.cz, Fax 224 920 743* – MC AE VISA CZ f
closed 23 December-3 January, Sunday and Saturday lunch – **Meals** - French - (booking essential at dinner) a la carte 1020/1468 ♀.
• Still smoothly run by the eponymous owner, a likeable little neighbourhood restaurant. Sound, well-judged and unpretentious authentic French cuisine in the best bistro tradition.

Cafe La Veranda, Elišky Krásnohorské 2/10, ✉ 110 00, ✆ 224 814 733, *office@laveranda.cz, Fax 224 814 596* – . MC AE VISA JCB CX w
Meals a la carte 845/1395 ♀.
• Modern restaurant in the old Jewish district. Efficient service. Modern menu in keeping with the décor, fusing East and West to produce light dishes with interesting flavours.

Square, Malostranské Nám. 5/28, ✉ 118 00, ✆ 257 532 109, *squarerestaurant@squarerestaurant.cz, Fax 257 532 107,* – MC AE VISA JCB BX z
closed 24 December – **Meals** a la carte 555/785 ♀.
• Baroque building with contemporary décor and good view of square. Summer terrace and additional basement room. Modern menu with Mediterranean, mostly Italian, influence.

Denmark

Danmark

COPENHAGEN

PRACTICAL INFORMATION

LOCAL CURRENCY

Danish Kroner: *100 DKK = 13,46 euro (€) (Dec. 2004)*

TOURIST INFORMATION

The telephone number and address of the Tourist Information office is given in the text under **i**.

FOREIGN EXCHANGE

Banks are open between 9.30am and 4.00pm (6.00pm on Thursdays) on weekdays except Saturdays. The main banks in the centre of Copenhagen, the Central Station and the Airport have exchange facilities outside these hours.

AIRLINES

SAS/LUFTHANSA: *Air Terminal, ☎ 70 10 20 00*
AIR FRANCE: *Ved Versterpot 6, ☎ 33 12 76 76*
BRITISH AIRWAYS: *Rådhuspladsen 16, ☎ 33 14 60 00*

MEALS

At lunchtime, follow the custom of the country and try the typical buffets of Danish specialities (smørrebrød).

At dinner, the a la carte and set menus will offer you more conventional cooking.

SHOPPING IN COPENHAGEN

Strøget (Department stores, exclusive shops, boutiques).

Kompagnistræde (Antiques). Shops are generally open from 10am to 7pm (Saturday 9am to 4pm).

See also in the index of street names, those printed in red are where the principal shops are found.

THEATRE BOOKINGS

Your hotel porter will be able to make your arrangements or direct you to Theatre Booking Agents.

CAR HIRE

The international car hire companies have branches in Copenhagen. Your hotel porter should be able to give details and help you with your arrangements.

TIPPING

In Denmark, all hotels and restaurants include a service charge. As for the taxis, there is no extra charge to the amount shown on the meter.

SPEED LIMITS

The maximum permitted speed in cities is 50 km/h - 31 mph, outside cities 80 km/h - 50 mph and 130 km/h - 68 mph on motorways. Cars towing caravans 70 km/h – 44 mph and buses 80 km/h – 50 mph also on motorways.

Local signs may indicate lower or permit higher limits. On the whole, speed should always be adjusted to prevailing circumstances. In case of even minor speed limit offences, drivers will be liable to heavy fines to be paid on the spot. If payment cannot be made, the car may be impounded.

SEAT BELTS

The wearing of seat belts is compulsory for drivers and all passengers except children under the age of 3.

COPENHAGEN
(KØBENHAVN)

Danmark 711 Q 9 – pop. 501 664, Greater Copenhagen 1 810 000.

Berlin 385 – Hamburg 305 – Oslo 583 – Stockholm 630.

Copenhagen Tourist Information, Vesterbrogade 4 A, ✉ 1577 ☎ 70 22 24 42, Fax 70 22 24 52, touristinfo@woco.dk

Dansk Golf Union 56 ☎ 43 45 55 55.

Copenhagen/Kastrup SE : 10 km ☎ 32 31 32 31 – Air Terminal : main railway station ☎ 33 14 17 01.

Motorail for Southern Europe : ☎ 33 14 17 01.

Further information from the D S B, main railway station or tourist information centre (see above).

Øresund Bridge-high speed road and rail link between Denmark and Sweden.

See : Rosenborg Castle★★★ (Rosenborg Slot) CX – Amalienborg Palace★★ (Amalienborg) DY – Nyhavn★★★ (canal) DY – Tivoli★★ : May to mid September BZ – Christiansborg Palace★ (Christiansborg) CZ – Citadel★ (Kastellet) DX – Gråbrødretorv★ CY **28** – Little Mermaid★★ (Den Lille Havfrue) DX – Marble Bridge★ (Marmorbroen) CZ **50** – Marble Church★ (Marmorkirke) DY – Kongens Nytorv★ DX – Round Tower★ (Rundetårn) CY **E** – Stock Exchange★ (Børsen) CDZ – Strøget★ BCYZ – Town Hall (Rådhuset) BZ **H** : Jens Olsen's astronomical clock★ BZ **H** – Bibliothek★ CZ.

Museums : National Museum★★★ (Nationalmuseet) CZ – Ny Carlsberg Glyptotek★★★: art collection BZ – National Fine Arts Museum★★ (Statens Museum for Kunst) CX – Thorvaldsen Museum★★ (Thorvaldsens Museum) CZ **M**[1] – Den Hirschsprungske Samling★ CX – Davids Samling★ CY.

Outskirts : Ordrupgård★★: art collection (Ordrupgårdsamlingen) N : 10 km CX – Louisiana Museum of Modern Art★★★ (Museum for Moderne Kunst) N : 35 km CX – Arken Museum of Modern Art★★ SW : 17 km by 02 (BN) and 151 – Dragør★ SW : 13 km CZ – Rungstedlund★: Karen Blixen Museum N : 25 km CX – Open-Air Museum★ (Frilandsmuseet) NW : 12 km AX.

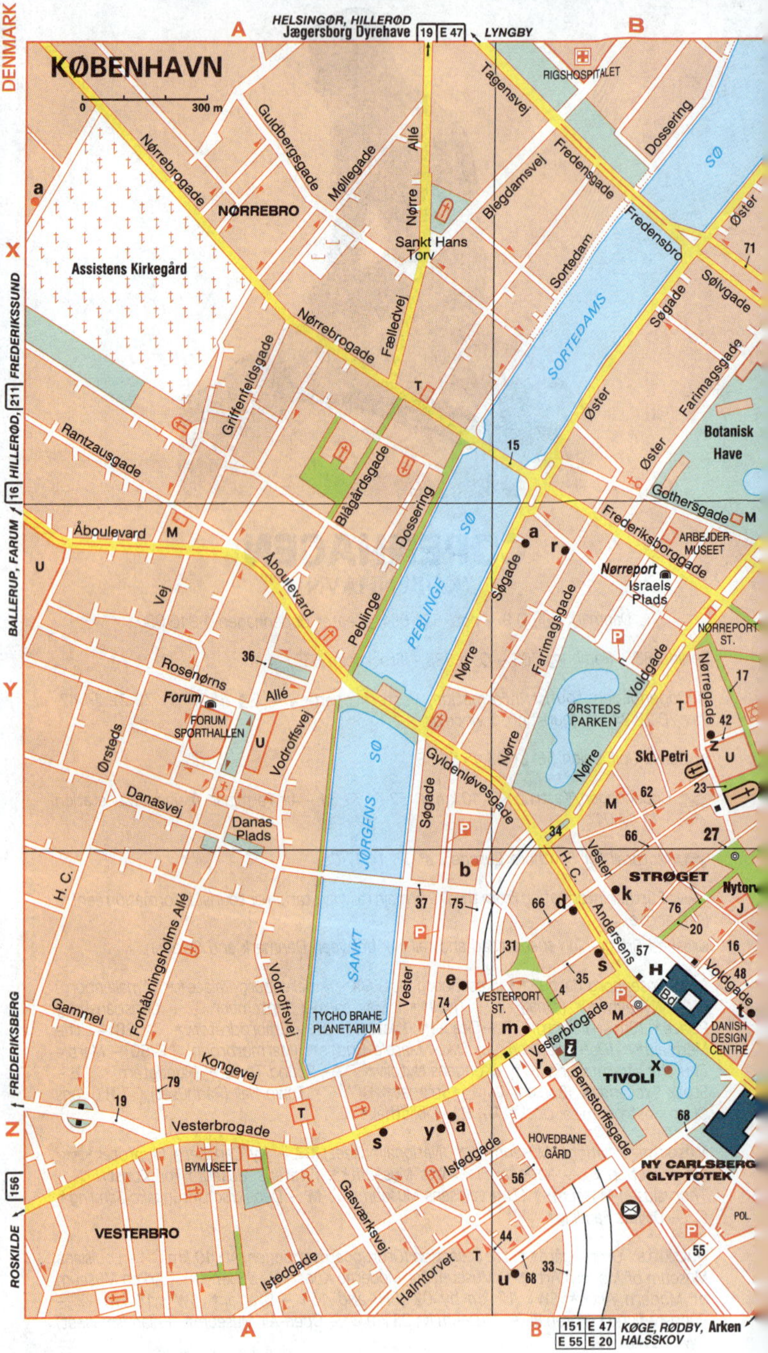
KØBENHAVN
0
300 m
A
B
X
Y
Z
HELSINGØR, HILLERØD
Jægersborg Dyrehave
19
E 47
LYNGBY
FREDERIKSSUND
211
HILLERØD,
16
BALLERUP, FARUM
FREDERIKSBERG
156
ROSKILDE
151
E 47
E 55
E 20
KØGE, RØDBY, Arken
HALSSKOV
RIGSHOSPITALET
Tagensvej
Dossering
SØ
Nørrebrogade
Guldbergsgade
Møllegade
Nørre
Allé
NØRREBRO
Blegdamsvej
Fredensgade
Fredensbro
Øster
Sankt Hans
Torv
Assistens Kirkegård
Sortedam
SORTEDAMS
Søgade
Sølvgade
Fælledvej
Griffenfeldsgade
Farimagsgade
Botanisk
Have
Rantzausgade
Blågårdsgade
Dossering
Gothersgade
Frederiksborggade
ARBEJDER-
MUSEET
Nørreport
Israels
Plads
Åboulevard
Vej
Peblinge
PEBLINGE
NØRREPORT
ST.
Rosenørns
Allé
Forum
FORUM
SPORTHALLEN
Vodroffsvej
ØRSTEDS
PARKEN
Nørregade
Voldgade
Ørsteds
Danasvej
Danas
Plads
JØRGENS
Gyldenløvesgade
Skt. Petri
H. C.
Vester
STRØGET
Nytorv
Andersens
Forhåbningsholms Allé
SANKT
Vestergade
VESTERPORT
ST.
Vesterbrogade
Gammel
Kongevej
TYCHO BRAHE
PLANETARIUM
DANISH
DESIGN
CENTRE
TIVOLI
Bernstorffsgade
Vesterbrogade
BYMUSEET
Istedgade
HOVEDBANE
GÅRD
NY CARLSBERG
GLYPTOTEK
Gasværksvej
Halmtorvet
VESTERBRO
POL.

C
152
HELSINGØR by Strandvejen
Ordrupgård
NORDHAVNEN
152
D
LANGELINIE
DENMARK
ŚWINOUJŚCIE
DEN LILLE HAVFRUE
Søgade
Farimagsgade
Stockholmsgade
13
Kristianiagade
Østbanegade
02
ØSTERPORT ST.
Folke Bernadottes Allé
Oslo Plads
ØSTER ANLÆG
KASTELLET
Øster
DEN HIRSCHSPRUNGSKE SAMLING
Øster Voldgade
Sølvgade
STATENS MUSEUM FOR KUNST
Skt. Albans
Churchill Parken
Grønningen
Esplanaden
GEOLOGISK MUSEUM
Sølvgade
Kronprinsessegade
Det Danske Kunstindustrimuseum
Øster Voldgade
ROSENBORG SLOT
Borgergade
Store Kongensgade
MEDICINSK HISTORISK MUSEUM
Amaliegade
Toldbodgade
MARMORKIRKEN
Dronningens Tværgade
Kongens Have
DAVIDS SAMLING
Bredgade
AMALIENBORG
X
Y
Z
Gothersgade
Kultorvet
Landemærket
Købmagergade
60
Amaliegade
OPERA
KONGENS NYTORV
NYHAVN
Toldbodgade
STRØGET
Østergade
Kongens Nytorv
FONDSBØRS
Kgl. Teater
Amagertorv
Holmens Kanal
NATIONAL BANKEN
INDERHAVNEN
Havnegade
BØRSEN
CHRISTIANSBORG
TØJHUSMUSEET
Brygge
KGL. BIBLIOTEK
NATIONALMUSEET
Vester Voldgade
H.C. Andersens Boulevard
Christians
INDERHAVNEN
Torvegade
Strandgade
Vandet
ORLOGSMUSEET
CHRISTIANSHAVN
CHRISTIANA
Vor Frelsers Kirke
Prinsessegade
B.W. MUSEUM
Overgaden neden
Overgaden oven
Vandet
Christianshavn
Langebrogade
SYDHAVNEN
Kalvebod Brygge
STADSGRAVEN
Vermlandsgade
KASTRUP DRAGØR
C
D

INDEX OF STREET NAMES IN COPENHAGEN

Aboulevard . . . . AY
Amager Boulevard . . . . CZ 2
Amagertorv (STRØGET) . . . CY
Amaliegade . . . . DXY
Amalienborg Plads . . . . DY 3
Axeltorv . . . . BZ 4
Bernstorffsgade . . . . BZ
Blegdamsvej . . . . BX
Blågårdsgåde . . . . AX
Borgergade . . . . DXY
Bredgade . . . . DY
Bremerholm . . . . CY 5
Børsgade . . . . DZ 7
Christan IX's Gade . . . . CY 8
Christians Brygge . . . . CZ
Christiansborg Slotsplads . . . CZ 9
Dag Hammarskjölds Allé . . . CX 13
Danas Plads . . . . AY
Danasvej . . . . AY
Dronning Louises Bro . . . . . BX 15
Dronningens Tværgade . . . CDY
Esplanaden . . . . DX
Farvergade . . . . BZ 16
Fiolstræde . . . . BY 17
Folke Bernadottes Allé . . . . DX
Forhåbningsholms Allé . . . . AZ
Fredensbro . . . . BX
Frederiksberg Allé . . . . AZ 19
Frederiksberggade (STRØGET) . . . . BZ 20
Frederiksborggade . . . . BY
Frederiksholms Kanal . . . . . CZ 21
Frue Plads . . . . BY 23
Fælledvej . . . . AX
Gammel Kongevej . . . . AZ
Gammel Mønt . . . . CY 24
Gammel Strand . . . . CZ 26
Gammeltorv . . . . BYZ 27
Gasværksvej . . . . AZ
Gothersgade . . . . BCY
Griffenfeldsgade . . . . AX
Grønningen . . . . DX
Gråbrødretorv . . . . CY 28
Guldbergsgade . . . . AX
Gyldenløvesgade . . . . AY
Halmtorvet . . . . AZ
Hambrosgade . . . . CZ 30
Hammerichsgade . . . . BZ 31
Havnegade . . . . DZ
H.C. Andersens Boulevard BCZ
H.C. Ørsteds Vej . . . . AY
Holmens Kanal . . . . CDZ
Højbro Plads . . . . CY 32
Ingerslevsgade . . . . BZ 33
Israels Plads . . . . BY
Istedgade . . . . AZ
Jarmers Plads . . . . BY 34
Jernbanegade . . . . BZ 35
Julius Thomsens Gade . . . . AY 36
Kalvebod Brygge . . . . CZ
Kampmannsgade . . . . AZ 37
Knippelsbro . . . . DZ 38
Kompagnistræde . . . . CZ 39
Kongens Nytorv . . . . DY
Kristen Bernikows Gade . . . CY 41
Kristianiagade . . . . DX
Kronprinsessegade . . . . . . CXY
Krystalgade . . . . BCY 42
Kultorvet . . . . CY
Kvægtorvsgade . . . . ABZ 44
Købmagergade . . . . CY
Landemaerket . . . . CY
Langebro . . . . CZ 45
Langebrogade . . . . CDZ
Læderstræde . . . . CYZ 46
Løngangstræde . . . . BZ 48
Løvstræde . . . . CY 49
Marmorbroen . . . . CZ 50
Møllegade . . . . AX
Niels Juels Gade . . . . DZ 51
Nybrogade . . . . CZ 52
Nygade STRØGET . . . . CYZ 53
Nyhavn . . . . DY
Nytorv . . . . BZ
Nørre Allé . . . . AX
Nørre Farimagsgade . . . . . . BY
Nørre Søgade . . . . ABY
Nørre Voldgade . . . . BY
Nørrebrogade . . . . AX
Nørregade . . . . BY
Oslo Plads . . . . DX
Overgaden neden Vandet . . DZ
Overgaden oven Vandet . . . DZ
Peblinge Dossering . . . . AY
Pistolstræde . . . . CY 54
Polititorvet . . . . BZ 55
Prinsessegade . . . . DZ
Rantzausgade . . . . AX
Reventlowsgade . . . . BZ 56
Rosenørns Allé . . . . AY
Rådhuspladsen . . . . BZ 57
Rådhusstræde . . . . CZ 59
Sankt Annæ Plads . . . . DY 60
Sankt Hans Torv . . . . AX
Sankt Peders Stræde . . . . . . BY 62
Skindergade . . . . CY 63
Sortedam Dossering . . . . . . BX
Stockholmsgade CX
Store Kannikestræde . . . . . . CY 64
Store Kongensgade . . . . . . DXY
Stormgade . . . . CZ
Strandgade . . . . DZ
Studiestræde . . . . BYZ 66
Sølvgade . . . . BCX
Sølvtorvet . . . . CX 67
Tagensvej . . . . BX
Tietgensgade . . . . BZ 68
Toldbodgade . . . . DXY
Torvegade . . . . DZ
Vandkunsten . . . . CZ 70
Ved Stranden . . . . CZ 72
Ved Vesterport . . . . AZ 74
Vermlandsgade . . . . DZ
Vester Farimagsgade . . . . . . AZ 75
Vester Søgade . . . . AYZ
Vester Voldgade . . . . BCZ
Vesterbrogade . . . . ABZ
Vestergade . . . . BZ 76
Vimmelskaftet (STRØGET) . CY 77
Vindebrogade . . . . CZ 78
Vodroffsvej . . . . AYZ
Værnedamsvej . . . . AZ 79
Webersgade . . . . BX 71
Østbanegade . . . . DX
Øster Farimagsgade . . . . . . BCX
Øster Søgade . . . . BCX
Øster Voldgade CX
Østergade (STRØGET) . . . . . CY

Angleterre, Kongens Nytorv 34, ✉ 1021 K, ☎ 33 12 00 95, *booking.hda@remmen.dk, Fax 33 12 11 18*, – rm, – 400. VISA. CDY t
Wiinblad *(☎ 33 37 06 45)* **: Meals** 355 (dinner) and a la carte 442/583 – 135 – **105 rm** 2170/3470, 18 suites.
• Elegant 18C grand hotel overlooking New Royal Square. Luxury in lobby sets tone throughout. Spacious rooms enjoy classic décor and antique furniture. Grand ballroom. Popular afternoon teas. Restaurant in marine blue décor ; Danish and French dishes.

Skt.Petri, Krystalgade 22, ✉ 1172 K, ☎ 33 45 91 00, *reservation@hotelsktpetri.com, Fax 33 45 91 10*, – rm, – 250. VISA JCB. rest BY z
***Brasserie Blu* : Meals** 325 (dinner) and a la carte 275/485 – 145 – **241 rm** 2095/2995, 27 suites.
• Former department store in central Copenhagen near old St Peter's Church. Large open plan atrium. Bright, stylish contemporary rooms with design features by Per Arnoldi. Informal restaurant ; international menu of classic brasserie dishes with Danish theme.

Radisson SAS Royal, Hammerichsgade 1, ✉ 1611 V, ☎ 33 42 60 00, *copenhagen@radissonsas.com, Fax 33 42 61 00*, Copenhagen, – rm, – 300. VISA JCB. rest BZ m
Alberto K* : Meals** *(closed Sunday)* (dinner only) (set menu only) 455 – ***Café Royal *(☎ 33 42 60 53)* **: Meals** (buffet lunch) 220 and a la carte 301/413 – 150 – **258 rm** 1995/2295, 2 suites.
• Large international hotel block dominating the skyline west of Tivoli and offering superb views. Scandinavian bedroom décor. Italian-influenced cuisine on 20th floor. Popular ground floor brasserie style café.

Copenhagen Marriott, Kalvebod Brygge 5, ✉ 1560, ☎ 88 33 99 00, *mhrs.cphdk.reservations@marriott.com, Fax 88 33 99 99,* ≤, , , – , rm, – 570. rest CZ b
***Terraneo* : Meals** - Mediterranean - (buffet lunch) 260/335 and a la carte 253/454 ♀ – 145 – **386 rm** 1795, 9 suites.
• Striking, glass-fronted hotel, its handsomely appointed rooms face the water or overlook the city and Tivoli. Top-floor executive rooms share a stylish private lounge. Lunchtime buffet and Mediterranean cuisine in the evening.

Radisson SAS Scandinavia, Amager Boulevard 70, ✉ 2300 S, ☎ 33 96 50 00, *copenhagen@radissonsas.com, Fax 33 96 55 00,* ≤ Copenhagen, , , , squash – , rm, – 1200. CZ s
Meals 180/280 and a la carte 250/440 ♀ – ***Blue Elephant*** (☎ *33 95 59 70*) **: Meals** - Thai - *(closed 23-26 December and Sunday)* (dinner only) 280/800 and a la carte 230/600 – ***Kyoto* : Meals** - Japanese - *(closed Christmas)* (dinner only) 290/500 and a la carte 220/430 (see also ***The Dining Room*** below) – 140 – **542 rm** 1495/1800.
• Tower-block hotel with spectacular views. Shops, casino and bar in busy lobby. Original bright bedrooms themed in six different styles. Traditional Danish to Italian dishes in dining room. Blue Elephant for authentic Thai cuisine. Kyoto for Japanese menu.

Sofitel Plaza Copenhagen, Bernstorffsgade 4, ✉ 1577 V, ☎ 33 14 92 62, *sofitel@accorhotel.dk, Fax 33 93 93 62* – , rm, – 30.
***Brasserie Flora Danica* : Meals** *(closed Sunday)* 245/845 and a la carte ♀ – 135 – **87 rm** 1859/2059, 6 suites. BZ r
• Venerable hotel commissioned in the early 20C by King Frederik VIII and overlooking Tivoli Gardens. Classic style room décor and atmospheric library bar. A modern, welcoming brasserie with a French-based menu.

Admiral, Toldbodgade 24-28, ✉ 1253, ☎ 33 74 14 14, *admiral@admiralhotel.dk, Fax 33 74 14 15,* ≤, – , rm, – 180. rest
Meals (see **Salt** below) – 108 – **366 rm** 1130/2170. DY s
• Converted 18C dockside warehouse. Maritime theme throughout. Bedrooms complement the rustic charm.

Imperial, Vester Farimagsgade 9, ✉ 1606 V, ☎ 33 12 80 00, *imperial@imperialhotel.dk, Fax 33 93 80 31* – , rm, rest, – 200. AZ e
***Imperial Garden* : Meals** *(closed last weekend June-first week August, 22 December-5 January and Sunday)* (dinner only) 410/415 and a la carte 390/625 – ***Imperial Brasserie* : Meals** *(closed 24 and 31 December)* (buffet lunch) 195/265 and a la carte 275/368 ♀ – 95 – **163 rm** 1495/2750, 1 suite.
• Large mid 20C hotel located on a wide city thoroughfare. Well serviced rooms range in size and are richly furnished in 1950s Danish designer style. Fine dining in attractive indoor "winter garden". Less formal dining in ground floor brasserie.

Kong Frederik, Vester Voldgade 25, ✉ 1552 V, ☎ 33 12 59 02, *kongfrederik@remmen.dk, Fax 33 93 59 01* – , rm, – 40. BZ k
***Frederiks* : Meals** *(closed Sunday and Bank Holidays)* 235/375 and a la carte 254/331 ♀ – 125 – **108 rm** 1040/1840, 2 suites.
• Classic elegant old building in good location. Traditional style décor with dark wood panelling. Comfortable rooms with old-fashioned furniture. Atrium style banquet hall. Wood-panelled, atmospheric brasserie offering traditional Danish cooking.

Kong Arthur, Nørre Søgade 11, ✉ 1370 K, ☎ 33 11 12 12, *hotel@kongarthur.dk, Fax 33 32 61 30,* , – , rm, – 50.
Sticks 'n' Sushi (☎ *33 11 14 07*) **: Meals** - Japanese - *(closed Sunday)* (dinner only) 150/450 and a la carte 240/485 – **107 rm** 930/2335. BY a
• Pleasant family run hotel on elegant late 19C residential avenue by Peblinge lake. Classic rooms equipped with modern facilities. Sticks 'n' Sushi for Japanese dishes.

First H. Vesterbro, Vesterbrogade 23-29, ✉ 1620 V, ☎ 33 78 80 00, *reception.copenhagen@firsthotels.dk, Fax 33 78 80 80* – , rm, . AZ s
***Restaurant* : Meals** *(closed Sunday)* (dinner only) a la carte approx 250 – 95 – **403 rm** 1799/1999.
• Large modern hotel with metal and glass façade on busy avenue. All bedrooms have good modern facilities in a contemporary style ; superior rooms are larger. Informal dining in front bar from International menu.

Phoenix, Bredgade 37, ✉ 1260 K, ☎ 33 95 95 00, *phoenixcopenhagen@arp-hansen.dk, Fax 33 33 98 33* – , rm, – 110. rest DY b
***Von Plessen* : Meals** (bar lunch)/dinner 300 and a la carte approx 295 – 130 – **210 rm** 1300/1725, 3 suites.
• Parts of this elegant hotel, located in the lively modern art and antiques district, date from the 17C. It features a grand marbled lobby and comfortable high ceilinged rooms.

The Square without rest., Rådhuspladsen 14, ✉ 1550 K, ☎ 33 38 12 00, *thesquare@arp-hansen.dk, Fax 33 38 12 01* – VISA JCB. BZ s
192 rm 1355/3195.
◆ Ideally located hotel in Town Hall Square. Breakfast room on 6th floor with view of city roofs. Good sized modern bedrooms with square theme in décor and fabrics.

71 Nyhavn, Nyhavn 71, ✉ 1051 K, ☎ 33 43 62 00, *71nyhavnhotel@arp-hansen.dk, Fax 33 43 62 01,* – rm, VISA JCB. rest DY z
Pakhus Kaelder **: Meals** *(closed Sunday)* (bar lunch)/dinner 325 and a la carte approx 394 – 130 – **142 rm** 1490/2350, 8 suites.
◆ Charming converted warehouse by the canal. Interior features low ceilings with wooden beams throughout. Compact comfortable bedrooms, many with views of passing ships.

Alexandra, H.C. Andersens Boulevard 8, ✉ 1553 V, ☎ 33 74 44 44, *jm@hotel-alexandra.dk, Fax 33 74 44 88,* – rm, VISA JCB. rest
closed 24-26 December – ***Mühlhausen*** **: Meals** *(closed Sunday lunch)* a la carte 277/325 – **61 rm** 1335/2035. BZ d
◆ Classic 19C hotel conveniently located for city centre. Some special design rooms feature Danish style furniture and fittings and an original painting in each. Banquettes and crisp linen in a stylish brasserie with a Mediterranean tone.

Strand without rest., Havnegade 37, ✉ 1058 K, ☎ 33 48 99 00, *copenhagenstrand@arp-hansen.dk, Fax 33 48 99 01* – VISA JCB DZ d
172 rm 1295/1595, 2 suites.
◆ Modern warehouse conversion on waterfront and a useful central location. Smart modern rooms with dark wood furniture and bright colours. Business centre.

DGI-byens, Tietgensgade 65, ✉ 1704 V, ☎ 33 29 80 00, *info@dgi-byen.dk, Fax 33 29 80 80,* – rm, – 80. VISA.
Vestauranten *(☎ 33 29 80 30)* **: Meals** (buffet lunch) 145/345 and a la carte 244/329 – **104 rm** 1295/1595. BZ u
◆ Turn of millennium hotel, part of huge, modern leisure complex with all the facilities. Minimalist bedrooms with simple, clean style and up-to-date facilities. Bright restaurant in original building offering a varied menu ; pleasant terrace.

City without rest., Peder Skrams Gade 24, ✉ 1054 K, ☎ 33 13 06 66, *hotelcity@hotelcity.dk, Fax 33 13 06 67* – VISA JCB DZ a
81 rm 995/1465.
◆ Well situated modern hotel between city centre and docks. Modern Danish style interior décor. Good technical facilities. Superior rooms are larger.

Comfort H. Mayfair without rest., Helgolandsgade 3, ✉ 1653 V, ☎ 70 12 17 00, *info.mayfair@comfort.choicehotels.dk, Fax 33 23 96 86* – VISA JCB. AZ a
closed 19 December-2 January – 95 – **103 rm** 1230/1730, 3 suites.
◆ Large well run hotel usefully located near station. Interior décor and furniture in classic English style. Neat rooms, well equipped with mod cons. Relaxing bar.

Clarion H. Neptun, Sankt Annae Plads 18-20, ✉ 1250 K, ☎ 33 96 20 00, *info.neptun@clarion.choicehotels.dk, Fax 33 96 20 66* – rm, – 40. VISA JCB DY a
closed 19-29 December – ***Gendarmen*** *(☎ 33 96 20 39)* **: Meals** *(closed Sunday)* (dinner only) 250/350 and a la carte 315/365 – 125 – **133 rm** 1425/2295.
◆ Converted from two characterful neighbouring houses in the popular Nyhavn district. Rooms are fitted with light wood furniture and offer good range of facilities. Rustic restaurant with wooden tables. Traditional Danish, seasonal menu.

Ibsens, Vendersgade 23, ✉ 1363 K, ☎ 33 13 19 13, *hotel@ibsenshotel.dk, Fax 33 13 19 16,* – rm, VISA JCB. BY r
La Rocca **: Meals** - Italian - *(closed 24-26 December and Bank Holidays)* 285 and a la carte 189/363 – ***Pintxos*** **: Meals** - Tapas - *(closed Sunday)* (dinner only) 285 and a la carte 189/363 – **118 rm** 755/1695.
◆ Large characterful converted apartment block next to sister hotel Kong Arthur. Variety of neat rooms with good facilities. Superior top floor bedrooms. Modern La Rocca for formal Italian dining. Pintxos offers authentic Spanish tapas dinner menu.

Danmark without rest., Vester Voldgade 89, ✉ 1552 V, ☎ 33 11 48 06, *hotel@hotel-danmark.dk, Fax 33 14 36 30* – VISA JCB. BZ t
88 rm 835/1455.
◆ Centrally located close to Tivoli Gardens, offers well kept functional rooms with traditional Scandinavian style décor. Newer rooms in older building are the best.

Top H. Hebron without rest., Helgolandsgade 4, ✉ 1653, ☎ 33 31 69 06, *tophotel@hebron.dk, Fax 33 31 90 67* – – 50. VISA JCB AZ y
closed 21 December-2 January – **93 rm** 750/1075, 6 suites.
◆ When it opened in 1900 it was one of the biggest hotels in the city and some of the original features remain. Bedrooms are surprisingly spacious for the price.

XXX **Prémisse,** Dronningens Tvaergade 2, ✉ 1302, ✆ 33 11 11 45, *mail@premisse.dk, Fax 33 11 11 68* – MC AE VISA JCB. ⚡ DY q
closed Easter, 15 July-15 August and Christmas – **Meals** (dinner only) a la carte 520/1055 ♀.
◆ 17C vaulted cellar restaurant with pillars ; modern décor. Wine cellar on view. Open plan kitchen serving uncompromisingly adventurous menu with original flavours.

XXX ✿ **Kong Hans Kaelder,** Vingårdsstraede 6, ✉ 1070 K, ✆ 33 11 68 68, *konghans@mail.tele.dk, Fax 33 32 67 68* – MC AE DC VISA JCB. ⚡ CY n
closed 1 week March, 3 weeks summer, last week December, Monday June-August, Sunday and Bank Holidays – **Meals** (booking essential) (dinner only) a la carte 660/700.
Spec. Cep bisque, wild mushroom tortellini. Roebuck in two preparations. Pumpkin and quince 'minestrone'.
◆ Discreetly located side street restaurant in vaulted Gothic cellar with wood flooring. Fine dining experience ; classically based cooking. Friendly and dedicated service.

XXX ✿ **Pierre André** (Houdet), Ny Østergade 21, ✉ 1101 K, ✆ 33 16 17 19, *Fax 33 16 17 72* – MC AE DC VISA. ⚡ CY s
closed Easter, 3 weeks summer, 24-27 December, 1 January, Sunday, Monday, Saturday lunch and Bank Holidays – **Meals** - French - (booking essential) 395/755 and a la carte 490/675 ♀.
Spec. Foie gras "Emilia Romagna". Huître en gelée, crème de raifort. Hot chocolate cake, Gianduja ice cream.
◆ Elegant, comfortable dining room with stylish décor in an attractive old building. Full-flavoured cuisine on a classical French base. Efficient and attentive service.

XXX **Restaurationen,** Møntergade 19, ✉ 1116 K, ✆ 33 14 94 95, *Fax 33 14 85 30* – MC AE DC VISA. ⚡ CY e
closed Easter, 3 July-29 August, 21 December-5 January, Sunday, Monday and Bank Holidays – **Meals** (booking essential) (dinner only except December) (set menu only) 640 ♀.
◆ A stylish and personally run restaurant. Accomplished modern Danish cooking using well sourced ingredients, accompanied by a comprehensive wine list.

XXX **Krogs,** Gammel Strand 38, ✉ 1202 K, ✆ 33 15 89 15, *krogs@krogs.dk, Fax 33 15 83 19* – ▤. MC AE DC VISA JCB. ⚡ CZ a
closed Sunday – **Meals** - Seafood - (booking essential) 350/950 and a la carte 660/1020 ♀.
◆ Characterful 18C house pleasantly located by canal. Classic room with high ceiling, well lit through large end window. Formal service ; seafood dishes attractively presented.

XX ✿ **Kommandanten,** Ny Adelgade 7, ✉ 1104 K, ✆ 33 12 09 90, *kommandanten@kommandanten.com, Fax 33 93 12 23* – ⚡. MC AE DC VISA JCB. ⚡ CY c
closed 4-25 July, 22 December-3 January, Sunday and Bank Holidays – **Meals** (booking essential) (dinner only) a la carte 600/790 ♀.
Spec. Roasted scallops, baby onions, smoked quail and caraway sauce. Chocolate desserts.
◆ Distinctive 18C townhouse : flowers, fine china, stylish contemporary décor and wrought-iron furniture. Exemplary service and original Danish and French cuisine.

XX ✿ **Formel B** (Jochumsen/Møller), Vesterbrogade 182, Frederiksberg, ✉ 1800 C, via Vesterbrogade ✆ 33 25 10 66, *info@formel-b.dk,* ☂ – MC AE DC VISA JCB. ⚡
closed 24-30 December and Sunday – **Meals** (set menu only) (lunch by arrangement)/dinner 600 ♀.
Spec. Turbot with black truffles. Quail with pointed cabbage and foie gras. Chocolate fondant, vanilla ice cream.
◆ Chic restaurant on the ground floor of an attractive period house. Sleek interior with sandstone and granite. Set menu : precise cooking with well chosen accompanying wines.

XX ✿ **Era Ora,** Overgaden neden Vandet 33B, ✉ 1414 K, ✆ 32 54 06 93, *era-ora@era-ora.dk, Fax 32 96 02 09* – MC AE DC VISA. ⚡ DZ c
closed 24-25 December, 1 January and Sunday – **Meals** - Italian - (booking essential) (set menu only) 280/880 ♀.
Spec. Antipasti selection. Home-made pasta.
◆ Stylish, discreetly located canalside restaurant offers an excellent overview of the best of Italian cuisine, by offering diners large array of small dishes. Good wine list.

XX ✿✿ **Ensemble** (Jensen/Maarbjerg), Tordenskjoldsgade 11, ✉ 1055 K, ✆ 33 11 33 52, *kontakt@restaurantensemble.dk* – MC AE DC VISA. ⚡ DY c
closed July, 9 days Christmas-New Year, Sunday and Monday – **Meals** (dinner only) (set menu only) 500 ♀.
Spec. Fjord shrimps with green asparagus. Fallow deer in three preparations. Braised shank of veal, wild mushrooms and watercress.
◆ Whites, greys and bright lighting add to the clean, fresh feel. Open-plan kitchen. Detailed and refined cooking from a set menu, with attentive and courteous service.

XXX ✿ **Noma** (Redzepi), Strandgade 93, ✉ 1401 K, ☎ 32 96 32 97, *noma@noma.dk*, *Fax 32 95 97 22* – MC AE DI VISA JCB. ✗ DY x
closed Easter, 3 weeks July, Christmas, Saturday lunch and Sunday – **Meals** 240/750 and a la carte 350/670.
Spec. Danish blue lobster, wild watercress. Wild rabbit with allspice. Marinated blueberries with blueberry sherbet.
• Converted 19C harbour warehouse with designer fittings. Talented chefs producing original and innovative dishes with ingredients from Iceland, Greenland and the Faroe Islands.

XXX **Kokkeriet,** Kronprinsessegade 64, ✉ 1306 K, ☎ 33 15 27 77, *info@kokkeriet.dk*, *Fax 33 15 27 75* – MC AE DI VISA JCB. ✗ CDX n
closed Easter, 25-31 July, 24-30 December, 1-2 January, Sunday and Monday – **Meals** (dinner only) (set menu only) 455/555 ♀.
• Smart, intimate restaurant with neighbourhood feel and stylish furnishings. Inventive modern menu offering 5-7 courses with wine to match. Enthusiastic service.

XXX **Il Grappolo Blu,** Vester Farimagsgade 35, ✉ 1606 V, ☎ 33 11 57 20, *ilgrappoloblu@ilgrappoloblu.com, Fax 33 12 57 20* – MC AE DI VISA JCB. ✗ AZ b
closed Easter, July, Christmas and Sunday – **Meals** - Italian - (dinner only) (set menu only) 280/595.
• Behind the unpromising façade lies this friendly restaurant, personally run by the owner. Ornate wood panelling and carving. Authentic Italian dishes that just keep on coming.

XXX **De Gaulle,** Kronborggade 3, ✉ 2200, ☎ 35 85 58 66, *restaurant@de-gaulle.dk*, *Fax 35 85 58 69* – MC AE DI VISA AX a
closed 1-29 July, 19 December-4 January, Sunday and Monday – **Meals** (dinner only) (set menu only) 360.
• In the Norrebro area, an intimate personally-run restaurant where young chef delivers some dishes to the table. Choice of 3-6 courses from set menu of modern French dishes.

XXX **The Dining Room** (at Radisson SAS Scandinavia H.), 25th Floor, Amager Boulevard 70, ✉ 2300 S, ☎ 33 96 58 58, *info@thediningroom.dk*, < Copenhagen – |‡| ✗ ▤ P. MC AE DI VISA CZ s
closed Sunday-Monday – **Meals** (dinner only) 300/800 and a la carte 345/560 ♀.
• Situated on the 25th floor of the hotel, but run independently, and providing diners with wonderful panoramic views of the city. Original and modern menu.

XXX **Extra,** Østerbrogade 64, ✉ 2100, via Oslo Plads ☎ 35 26 09 52, *extra@restaurant-extra.dk, Fax 35 26 09 54* – MC AE DI VISA. ✗
closed 3 weeks August, 1 week Christmas and Sunday – **Meals** (dinner only) (set menu only) 455/515.
• On main road not far from city centre. Basement restaurant below tapas bar. Artistic modern dishes with some unusual flavours and combinations prepared in open plan kitchen.

XXX **Frederiks Have,** Smallegade 41, ✉ 2000 Frederiksberg, West : 1 m. via Gammel Kongevej ☎ 38 88 33 35, *info@frederikshave.dk, Fax 38 88 33 37*, 🍽 – MC AE DI VISA JCB. ✗
closed 24-28 April, 23 December-8 January and Sunday – **Meals** 205/498 and a la carte 335/368.
• Established restaurant in leafy residential district. Homely ambience and delightful terrace. Monthly menus offer traditional and modern Danish cooking.

XXX **VB Square,** Oster Sogade 114, ✉ 2100, via Oster Sogade at junction with Oslo Plads ☎ 35 42 22 77, *Fax 35 42 22 70* – MC DI VISA. ✗
closed Christmas and New Year – **Meals** (lunch booking essential in summer) 295/445 and dinner a la carte 315/430 ♀.
• Relatively compact restaurant with a genuine neighbourhood feel. Contemporary colour scheme of browns and pastels. Knowledgeable service and modern Danish cooking.

XXX **Castel,** Gothersgade 35, ✉ 1123 K, ☎ 33 13 62 82, *admin@castel.dk, Fax 33 13 72 82* – ▤. MC DI VISA. ✗ CY a
closed 3 weeks July and Sunday – **Meals** (dinner only) 185/225 and a la carte 285/375.
• Magnificent glass ceiling, original woodwork and contemporary art in a 19C apothecary's shop. Balanced, flavourful dishes from an open-plan kichen in the converted laboratory.

XXX **Gammel Mont,** Gammel Mont 41, ✉ 1117 K, ☎ 33 15 10 60, *Fax 33 15 10 60* – MC AE DI VISA. ✗ CY b
closed July, Sunday and Bank Holidays – **Meals** 295/425 and a la carte 355/500 ♀.
• Half-timbered house from 1732 with striking red façade in smart commercial district. Traditional cuisine with seasonal variations and interesting range of herring dishes.

XXX ✿ **Rasmus Oubaek,** Store Kongensgade 52, ✉ 1264, ☎ 33 32 32 09, *rasmus-oubaek@mail.dk* – MC AE DI VISA. ✗ DY k
closed mid July-mid August, Christmas-New Year, Sunday and Monday – **Meals** (dinner only) (set menu only) 550 ♀.
Spec. Turbot and smoked queen scallop ravioli. Grilled rabbit with foie gras. Baked pineapple with dark rum and caramel.
• Unpretentious restaurant with simple but stylish décor offering accomplished classic dishes ; large and comprehensive list of quality wines ; pleasant and professional service.

Le Sommelier, Bredgade 63-65, ✉ 1260 K, ☎ 33 11 45 15, *mail@lesommelier.dk, Fax 33 11 59 79* – MC AE DC VISA JCB. ✈ DX c
closed 22 December-2 January and lunch Saturday and Sunday – **Meals** 265/350 and a la carte 325/455 ♀.
◆ Popular brasserie in the heart of the old town. The owners' passion for wine shows in posters, memorabilia and an excellent "by glass" list. Modern Danish cooking.

Salt (at Admiral H.), Toldbodgade 24-28, ✉ 1253, ☎ 33 74 14 44, *info@saltrestaurant.dk, Fax 33 74 14 16*, ≤, ☂ – P. MC AE DC VISA JCB DY s
Meals 325/345 and a la carte 352/395 ♀.
◆ Conran-designed restaurant in 18C warehouse ; outdoor summer tables. Only sea salt is used. Danish buffet and modern a la carte at midday ; more extensive modern dinner menu.

Godt (Rice), Gothersgade 38, ✉ 1123 K, ☎ 33 15 21 22, *restaurant.godt@get2net.dk* – MC DC VISA JCB. ✈ CY z
closed Easter, July, Christmas, New Year, Sunday, Monday and Bank Holidays – **Meals** (booking essential) (dinner only) (set menu only) 480/600.
Spec. Wild watercress soup with Danish lobster. Winter game with wild mushrooms. Pancake soufflé, caramelised pineapple and praline parfait.
◆ Small stylish modern two floor restaurant with grey décor, ceiling fans and old WWII shells as candle holders. Personally run. Excellently conceived daily menu of modern fare.

Kanalen, Christianshavn-Wilders Plads 2, ✉ 1403 K, ☎ 32 95 13 30, *info@restaurant-kanalen.dk, Fax 32 95 13 38*, ≤, ☂ – P. MC AE DC VISA JCB DZ b
closed 21-27 March, 24 December-2 January, Sunday and Bank Holidays – **Meals** (booking essential) (set menu only at dinner) 198/348 and lunch a la carte 331/358 ♀.
◆ Delightfully located former Harbour Police office on canalside. Simple elegant décor, informal yet personally run. Well balanced menu of modern Danish cooking.

Lumskebugten, Esplanaden 21, ✉ 1263 K, ☎ 33 15 60 29, *Fax 33 32 87 18*, ☂ – MC AE DC VISA JCB. ✈ DX b
closed 23 December-3 January, Sunday, Saturday lunch and Bank Holidays – **Meals** a la carte 328/875.
◆ Mid 19C café-pavilion near quayside and Little Mermaid. Interesting 19C maritime memorabilia and old paintings. Good traditional cuisine. Possibility of dining on boat.

M/S Amerika, Dampfaergevej 8 (Pakhus 12, Amerikakaj), ✉ 2100 K, via Folke Bernadettes Allée ☎ 35 26 90 30, *info@msamerika.dk, Fax 35 26 91 30*, ☂ – MC AE DC VISA JCB. ✈
closed 24 December-3 January, Sunday and Bank Holidays – **Meals** 228/345 and a la carte 360/455 ♀.
◆ Characterful 19C former warehouse in attractive quayside location, with popular terrace in the summer. Open plan kitchen provides fresh, appealing, modern Danish fare.

Guldanden, Sortedam Dossering 103, ✉ 2100 K, via Oslo Plads at junction of Sortedam Dossering and Osterbrogade ☎ 35 42 66 06, *mail@guldanden.dk, Fax 35 42 66 05*, ☂ – ▤. MC AE DC VISA JCB. ✈
closed 24-28 December and 1-3 January – **Meals** (set menu only at dinner) 245/350 and lunch a la carte approx 285 ♀.
◆ Glass-fronted restaurant with small summer terrace in residential district. Minimalist décor. Set menu with 3-7 course choice ; modern cooking with some unusual combinations.

TyvenKokkenHansKoneOgHendesElsker, Magstraede 16, ✉ 1204 K, ☎ 33 16 12 92, *post@tyven.dk* – MC AE DC VISA. ✈ CZ e
closed 20-28 March, 10 July-7 August and 23 December-2 January – **Meals** (dinner only) 495/595 and a la carte 495/655 ♀.
◆ 18C part timbered house in cobbled street. Named after the Peter Greenaway film. Set menu (5 courses) with small a la carte. French based dishes with Danish influence.

Viva, Langebrogade Kaj 570, ✉ 1411 K, ☎ 27 25 05 05, *viva@restaurantviva.dk*, ≤, ☂ – MC DC VISA. ✈ CZ c
closed 23 December-2 January – **Meals** 155/325 and a la carte 305/490 ♀.
◆ Converted German tug boat moored on the river ; stylish minimal interior and top deck terrace. Eclectic menu with strong Danish note at lunch.

Fiasco, Gammel Kongevej 176, Frederiksberg, ✉ 1850 C, via Gammel Kongevej ☎ 33 31 74 87, *Fax 33 31 74 87* – MC AE DC VISA
closed Christmas-New Year – **Meals** - Italian - 178/335 and lunch a la carte 255/335 ♀.
◆ Modern Italian restaurant to the west of the city centre. Bright room with fresh feel and large picture windows. Friendly young owners. Carefully prepared, authentic cuisine.

Grabrodre Torv 21, Grabrodre Torv 21, ✉ 1154 K, ☎ 33 11 47 07, *info@graabroedre21.dk, Fax 33 12 60 19,* – MC AE DC VISA JCB. CY r
closed 23 December-5 January and Sunday lunch – **Meals** 250/600 and a la carte 235/520 ♀.
◆ Pleasant little restaurant on corner of square. Light and airy décor with appealing terrace in the summer. Authentic rustic style traditional Danish specialities.

in Tivoli : *Vesterbrogade 3 ✉ 1620 V (Entrance fee payable)* :

The Paul (Cunningham), Vesterbrogade 3, ✉ 1630 K, ☎ 33 75 07 75, *info@thepaul.dk, Fax 33 75 07 76,* – MC AE DC VISA JCB. BZ x
12 April-18 September and dinner only Wednesday-Saturday 16 November-22 December – **Meals** *(closed Sunday)* (set menu only) 400/700 ♀.
Spec. Langoustine with macadamia, raspberry and tarragon. Grilled rabbit, cockles and tomato jam. Dark chocolate fondant, mango ice cream and Szechuan pepper.
◆ Elegant glass-domed 20C structure by the lake in Tivoli Gardens. Open-plan kitchen with chef's table. Set menu (3-7 courses) ; elaborate cooking using local produce.

SMØRREBRØD

The following list of simpler restaurants and cafés/bars specialize in Danish open sandwiches and are generally open from 10.00am to 4.00pm.

Amalie, Amaliegade 11, ✉ 1256, ☎ 33 12 88 10, – MC AE DC VISA JCB DY n
closed 2 weeks July, Christmas-New Year and Sunday – **Meals** (booking essential) (lunch only) a la carte 177/248.
◆ Located in a pretty 18C townhouse. Wood panelled walls and a clean, uncluttered style. Helpful service and ideal for those looking for an authentic, traditional Danish lunch.

Ida Davidsen, Store Kongensgade 70, ✉ 1264 K, ☎ 33 91 36 55, *ida.davidsen@cirque.dk, Fax 33 11 36 55* – MC AE DC VISA JCB. DY g
closed 4 July-1 August, 21 December-17 January, Saturday and Sunday – **Meals** (lunch only) a la carte 50/200.
◆ Family run for five generations, this open sandwich bar, on a busy city-centre street, is almost a household name in Denmark. Offers a full range of typical smørrebrød.

Sankt Annae, Sankt Annae Plads 12, ✉ 1250 K, ☎ 33 12 54 97, *Fax 33 15 16 61* – MC AE DC VISA. DY a
closed 24-26 December, 1 January, Sunday and Bank Holidays – **Meals** (lunch only) a la carte 45/148 ♀.
◆ Pretty terraced building in popular part of town. Simple décor with a rustic feel and counter next to kitchen. Typical menu of smørrebrød. Service prompt and efficient.

at Nordhavn *North : 3 km by Østbanegade* DX *and Road 2* – ✉ *Copenhagen*

Paustian, Kalkbraenderiløbskaj 2, ✉ 2100, ☎ 39 18 55 01, *mail@restaurantpaustian.dk* – P. MC DC VISA JCB
closed 4-24 July, 23 December-3 January and Sunday – **Meals** 300 (lunch) and a la carte 465/715.
◆ Stylish quayside restaurant located within Paustian, a furniture store not far from city centre by train. Choice of menus offering original creations. Impressive wine list.

at Hellerup *North : 7 ½ km by Østbanegade* DX *and Road 2* – ✉ *2900 Hellerup* :

Hellerup Parkhotel, Strandvejen 203, ✉ 2900, ☎ 39 62 40 44, *info@helleruparkhotel.dk, Fax 39 45 15 90,* – P – 150. MC AE DC VISA. rest
Via Appia* : Meals** - Italian - 179/359 and a la carte 249/359 (see also ***Saison below) – **71 rm** 1075/2700.
◆ Attractive classic hotel located in affluent suburb north of the city. Rooms vary in size and colour décor but offer same good standard of facilities and level of comfort. Popular local Italian restaurant on side of hotel with terrace.

Saison, Strandvejen 203, ✉ 2900, ☎ 39 62 48 42, *saison@saison.dk, Fax 39 62 20 30* – P. MC AE DC VISA.
closed Whitsun, Easter, 3 weeks July, 1 week Christmas, 1 January and Sunday – **Meals** 225/595 and a la carte 425/520 ♀.
◆ Run separately from the hotel in which it is located. Enjoys a bright and airy feel with high ceiling and large windows. Carefully prepared cooking using quality ingredients.

at Søllerød *North : 20 km by Tagensvej (take the train to Holte then taxi)* BX *and Road 19* – ✉ *2840 Holte* :

Søllerød Kro, Søllerødvej 35, ✉ 2840 K, ☎ 45 80 25 05, *mail@soelleroed-kro.dk, Fax 45 80 22 70,* – P. MC AE DC VISA JCB.
closed 3 weeks July, 24 December and 1 January – **Meals** 475/555 and a la carte 604/834.
◆ Characterful 17C thatched inn with attractive courtyard terrace and stylish Danish rustic-bourgeois décor. Classically based cooking with modern notes and excellent wine list.

at Kastrup Airport *Southeast : 10 km by Amager Boulevard* CZ – ✉ *2300 S :*

Hilton Copenhagen Airport, Ellehammersvej 20, Kastrup, ✉ 2770, ☎ 32 50 15 01, *res_copenhagen-airport@hilton.com, Fax 32 52 85 28,* <, Fø, ≘s, ☐ – |₿|, ⇔ rm, ▤ TV ✆ ♿ ⇔ – 🔬 450. MC AE ⓓ VISA. ⇔ rest

***Hamlet* : Meals** *(closed Sunday)* (dinner only) 495 and a la carte 325/528 ♀ – ***Horizon* : Meals** *(closed Saturday-Sunday)* (buffet meals) 189/219 ♀ – ☐ 140 – **382 rm** 2150.

◆ Glass walkway leads from arrivals to this smart business hotel. Bright bedrooms with light, contemporary Scandinavian furnishings and modern facilities. Hamlet is a formal open-plan restaurant with eclectic menu. Relaxed dining in Horizon beneath vast atrium.

Quality Airport H. Dan, Kastruplundgade 15, Kastrup, ✉ 2770, North : 2 ½ km by coastal rd ☎ 32 51 14 00, *Fax 32 51 37 01,* ⛱, Fø, ≘s – |₿|, ⇔ rm, ▤ rest, TV ✆ P – 🔬 60. MC AE ⓓ VISA JCB

Meals (dinner buffet only) – ☐ 95 – **228 rm** 1225/2125.

◆ Airport hotel not far from beach and countryside, popular with business travellers. All rooms with modern facilities ; some with views of canal. Traditional Danish cuisine in the restaurant.

Finland

Suomi

HELSINKI

PRACTICAL INFORMATION

LOCAL CURRENCY

1 euro (€) = 1,34 USD ($) (Dec. 2004)

TOURIST INFORMATION

The Tourist Office is situated near the Market Square, Pohjoisesplanadi 19 ☎ (09) 169 3757. Open from 2 May to 30 September, Monday to Friday 9am - 8pm, Saturday and Sunday 9am - 6pm, and from 1 October to 30 April, Monday to Friday 9am - 6pm Saturday and Sunday from 10am to 4pm. Hotel bookings are possible from a reservation board situated in the airport arrival lounge and in the main railway station; information is also available free.

National Holiday in Finland: *6 December.*

FOREIGN EXCHANGE

Banks are open between 9.15am and 4.15pm on weekdays only. Exchange offices at Helsinki-Vantaa airport and Helsinki harbour open daily between 6.30am and 11pm and at the railway station between 7am and 10pm.

MEALS

At lunchtime, follow the custom of the country and try the typical buffets of Scandinavian specialities.

At dinner, the a la carte and set menus will offer you more conventional cooking. Booking is essential.

Many city centre restaurants are closed for a few days over the Midsummer Day period.

SHOPPING IN HELSINKI

Furs, jewellery, china, glass and ceramics, Finnish handicraft and wood.

In the index of street names, those printed in red are where the principal shops are found. Your hotel porter will be able to help you with information.

THEATRE BOOKINGS

The following agents sell tickets for opera, theatre, concerts, cinema and sports events: Lippupalvelu ☎ 0600 108 00, Lippupiste ☎ 0600 900 900, Tiketti ☎ 0600 116 16.

CAR HIRE

The international car hire companies have branches in Helsinki and at Vantaa airport. Your hotel porter should be able to help you with your arrangements.

TIPPING

Service is normally included in hotel and restaurant bills. Doormen, baggage porters etc. are generally given a gratuity; taxi drivers are not usually tipped.

SPEED LIMITS

The maximum permitted speed on motorways is 120 km/h - 74 mph (in winter 100 km/h - 62 mph), 80 km/h - 50 mph on other roads and 50 km/h - 31 mph in built-up areas.

SEAT BELTS

The wearing of seat belts in Finland is compulsory for drivers and all passengers.

HELSINKI
(HELSINGFORS)

Finland **711** L 21 – *Pop. 546 317.*

Lahti 103 – Tampere 176 – Turku 165.

City Tourist Office Pohjoisesplanadi 19 ☎ (09) 169 37 57, Fax (09) 169 38 39, tourist.info@hel.fi.

Helsingin golfklubi ☎ (09) 550 235.

Helsinki-Vantaa N : 19 km ☎ 0200 14636 (information) – Finnair Head Office, Tietotie 11 A, ✉ 01053 ☎ 818 8383 – Air Terminal : Scandic H. Continental, Mannerheimintie 46 – Finnair City Terminal : Asema – Aukio 3, ☎ 0203 140 160 (reservations).

To Sweden, Estonia and boat excursions : contact the City Tourist Office (see above) – Car Ferry: Silja Line ☎ 0203 74 552 – Viking Line ☎ 123577 – Eckerö Line ☎ 228 8544 – Nordic Jetline ☎ 681 770 – Tallink ☎ 2282 1277.

See: *Senate Square*★★★ *(Senaatintori)* DY **53** – *Market Square*★★ *(Kauppatori* DY **26** – *Esplanadi*★★ CDY **8/43** – *Railway Station*★★ *(Rautatiesema)* CX – *Finlandia Hall*★★ *(Finlandia-talo)* BX – *National Opera House*★★ *(Kansallisoopera)* BX – *Church in the Rock*★★ *(Temppeliaukion kirkko)* BX – *Ateneum Art Museum*★★ *(Ateneum, Suomen Taiteen Museo)* CY **M**[1] – *National Museum*★★ *(Kansallismuseo)* BX **M**[2] – *Lutheran Cathedral*★★ *(Tuomiokirkko)* DY – *Parliament House*★ *(Eduskuntatalo)* BX – *Amos Anderson Collection*★ *(Amos Andersinin taidemuseo)* BY **M**[4] – *Uspensky Cathedral*★ *(Uspenskin katedraali)* DY – *Cygnaeus home and collection*★ *(Cynaeuksen galleria)* DZ **B** – *Mannerheim home and collection*★ *(Mannerheim-museo)* DZ **M**[5] – *Olympic Stadium*★ *(Olympiastadion)* ✳★★ BX **21** – *Museum of Applied Arts*★★ *(Taideteollisuusmuseo)* CZ **M**[6] – *Sibelius Monument*★ *(Sibelius-monumentti)* AX **S** – *Ice-breaker fleet*★ DX.

Outskirts: *Fortress of Suomenlinna*★★ *by boat* DZ – *Seurasaari Open-Air Museum*★★ BX – *Urho Kekkonen Museum*★ *(Urho Kekkosen museo)* BX.

TAMPERE 3 E 12
TURKU / ÅBO 1 E 18
A
B
X
Y
Z
SIBELIUKSEN-PUISTO
SIBELIUS-PARKEN
SUOMEN KANSALLISOOPPERA
FINLANDS NATIONALOPERA
Töölönlahti
Tölöviken
Taivallahti
Edesviken
Mechelininkatu/
Runebergsgatan
Runeberginkatu/
Mannerheimvägen
FINLANDIA-TALO
FINLANDIA-HUSET
Museokatu/
Museigatan
TEMPPELIAUKION KIRKKO
TEMPELPLATSENS KYRKA
EDUSKUNTATALO
RIKSDAGSHUSET
Hietaniemenkatu/
Sanduddsgatan
Arkadiankatu/
Arkadiagatan
Fredrikinkatu/
Runebergsgatan
Tennispalatsi
Lasipalatsi
Lapinlahti
Lappviken
Mechelingatan
TURKU / ÅBO 1 E 18
HANKO / HANGÖ 51
Kamppi Kampen
Kampintori/
Kamptorget
Annankatu/
Kalevagatan
Lönnrotsgatan
Fredriksgatan
Albertinkatu/
Albertsgatan
Kalevankatu/
Lönnrotinkatu/
Bulevardi/
Porkkalankatu/
Porkalagatan
Itämerenkatu/
Östersjögatan
Ruoholahti
Gräsviken
Ruoholahti
Gräsviken
Hietalahti
Sandviken
LÄNSISATAMA
VÄSTRA HAMMEN
Tehtaankatu/
EIRA
Merikatu/
HELSINKI
HELSINGFORS
0
300 m
LÄNSITERMINAALI
VÄSTRA TERMINALEN
TALLINNA
TALLINN

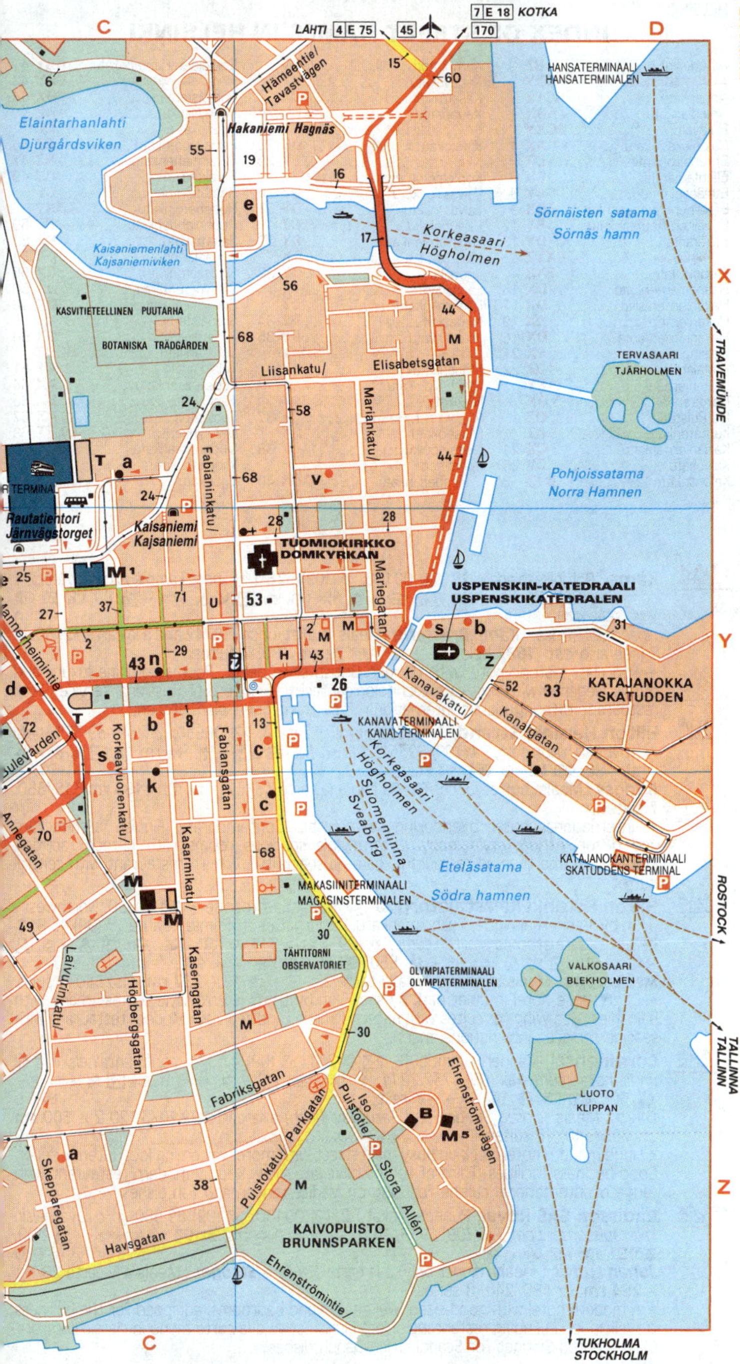
C
D
LAHTI 4 E 75
45
7 E 18 KOTKA
170
HANSATERMINAALI
HANSATERMINALEN
Elaintarhanlahti
Djurgårdsviken
Hämeentie/
Tavastvägen
Hakaniemi Hagnäs
Kaisaniemenlahti
Kajsaniemiviken
Korkeasaari
Högholmen
Sörnäisten satama
Sörnäs hamn
X
KASVITIETEELLINEN PUUTARHA
BOTANISKA TRÄDGÅRDEN
Liisankatu/
Elisabetsgatan
Mariankatu/
TERVASAARI
TJÄRHOLMEN
TRAVEMÜNDE
Fabianinkatu/
Pohjoissatama
Norra Hamnen
TERMINAL
Rautatientori
Järnvägstorget
Kaisaniemi
Kajsaniemi
TUOMIOKIRKKO
DOMKYRKAN
Mariegatan
USPENSKIN-KATEDRAALI
USPENSKIKATEDRALEN
Y
Mannerheimintie
KATAJANOKKA
SKATUDDEN
Kanavakatu
Kanalgatan
Bulevarden
KANAVATERMINAALI
KANALTERMINALEN
Korkeavuorenkatu/
Fabiansgatan
Korkeasaari
Högholmen
Suomenlinna
Sveaborg
Annegatan
Kasarmikatu/
Eteläsatama
Södra hamnen
KATAJANOKANTERMINAALI
SKATUDDENS TERMINAL
MAKASIINITERMINAALI
MAGASINSTERMINALEN
ROSTOCK
TÄHTITORNI
OBSERVATORIET
OLYMPIATERMINAALI
OLYMPIATERMINALEN
VALKOSAARI
BLEKHOLMEN
Laivurinkatu/
Högbergsgatan
Kaserngatan
Ehrenströmsvägen
TALLINNA
TALLINN
Fabriksgatan
Parkgatan
Iso Puistotie/
LUOTO
KLIPPAN
Stora Allén
Skepparegatan
Puistokatu/
Z
KAIVOPUISTO
BRUNNSPARKEN
Havsgatan
Ehrenströmintie/
C
D
TUKHOLMA
STOCKHOLM

INDEX OF STREET NAMES IN HELSINKI

Albertinkatu . . . . . BZ
Aleksanterinkatu . . . . . CDY 2
Annankatu . . . . . BCYZ
Arkadiankatu . . . . . ABX
Bulevardi . . . . . BCXY
Caloniuksenkatu . . . . . AX 4
Ehrenströmintie . . . . . DZ
Eläintarhantie . . . . . CX 6
Eteläesplanadi . . . . . CY 8
Eteläinen Hesperiankatu . . ABX 9
Eteläinen Rautatiekatu . . . . . BY 12
Eteläranta . . . . . DY 13
Fabianinkatu . . . . . CXYZ
Fredrikinkatu . . . . . BYZ
Haapaniemenkatu . . . . . DX 15
Hakaniemen silta . . . . . DX 17
Hakaniemen tori . . . . . DX 19
Hakaniemenranta . . . . . DX 16
Helsinginkatu . . . . . BX 21
Hietalahdenranta . . . . . BZ 22
Hietaniemenkatu . . . . . AXY
Hämeentie . . . . . DX
Iso Puistotie . . . . . DZ
Itämerenkatu . . . . . AZ
Kaisaniemenkatu . . . . . CX 24
Kaivokatu . . . . . CY 25
Kalevankatu . . . . . BYZ
Kampintori . . . . . BY
Kanavakatu . . . . . DXY
Kasarmikatu . . . . . CZ
Kauppatori . . . . . DY 26
Keskuskatu . . . . . CY 27
Kirkkokatu . . . . . DY 28
Kluuvikatu . . . . . CY 29
Korkeavuorenkatu . . . . . CYZ
Laivasillankatu . . . . . DZ 30
Laivastokatu . . . . . DY 31
Laivurinkatu . . . . . CZ
Lapinlahdenkatu . . . . . BY 32
Liisankatu . . . . . DX
Luotsikatu . . . . . DY 33
Länsiväylä . . . . . AYZ
Lönnrotinkatu . . . . . BZ
Mallaskatu . . . . . BZ 34
Malminkatu . . . . . BY 35
Mannerheimintie . . . . . BCXY
Mariankatu . . . . . DXY
Mechelininkatu . . . . . AXY
Merikatu . . . . . BCZ
Mikonkatu . . . . . CY 37
Museokatu . . . . . ABX
Neitsytpolku . . . . . CZ 38
Pohjoinen Hesperiankatu . . . . . ABX 40
Pohjoinen Rautatiekatu . . . ABY 41
Pohjoisesplanadi . . . . . CDY 43
Pohjoisranta . . . . . DX 44
Porkkalankatu . . . . . AZ
Puistokatu . . . . . DZ
Punavuorenkatu . . . . . BZ 46
Pursimiehenkatu . . . . . BZ 47
Ratakatu . . . . . CZ 49
Rautatientori . . . . . CY
Runeberginkatu . . . . . ABXY
Ruoholahdenkatu . . . . . BZ 50
Satamakatu . . . . . DY 52
Senaatintori . . . . . DY 53
Siltasaarenkatu . . . . . CX 55
Siltavuorenranta . . . . . DX 56
Snellmaninkatu . . . . . DX 58
Sörnäisten rantatie . . . . . DX 60
Tehtaankatu . . . . . BCDZ
Telakkakatu . . . . . BZ 61
Topeliuksenkatu . . . . . AX 64
Töölönkatu . . . . . BX 65
Töölöntori . . . . . AX 67
Unioninkatu . . . . . DXYZ 68
Uudenmaankatu . . . . . BCZ 70
Yliopistonkatu . . . . . CY 71
Yrjönkatu . . . . . BCY 72

Kämp, Pohjoisesplanadi 29, ✉ 00100, ℘ (09) 576 111, *hotelkamp@luxurycollection.com, Fax (09) 576 1122*, - rm, - 80. MC AE DC VISA JCB. CY n
closed Christmas – ***Kämp Brasserie* : Meals** (buffet lunch) 18/42 and a la carte 32/50.40 ♀ (see also ***est. 1887*** below) – 29 – **172 rm** 380, 7 suites.
• Top class historic hotel with de luxe British style décor. Rooms combine luxury and classic elegance with first rate technological facilities. Superb professional service. Sleek restaurant offering classic international fare from open plan kitchen.

Hilton Helsinki Strand, John Stenbergin Ranta 4, ✉ 00530, ℘ (09) 39 351, *helsinkistrand@hilton.com, Fax (09) 3935 3255*, rm, – 180. MC AE DC VISA. rest DX e
***Bridges* : Meals** (buffet lunch) 32/48 and a la carte 33/57 – 15 – **185 rm** 315/350, 7 suites.
• International hotel overlooking waterfront. Contemporary Finnish architecture and décor. Atrium style lobby. Comfortable spacious rooms with hi-tech facilities. Muted maritime themed restaurant, game a speciality, or main restaurant with central buffet.

Hilton Helsinki Kalastajatorppa, Kalastajatorpantie 1, ✉ 00330, Northwest : 5 km by Mannerheimintie, Tukholmankatu, Paciusgatan off Ramsaynranta ℘ (09) 45 811, *helsinkikalastajatorppa@hilton.com, Fax (09) 4581 2211*, rm, – 550. MC AE DC VISA JCB.
***Meritorppa* : Meals** (dinner only) a la carte 25/46 – 15 – **237 rm** 245/340, 1 suite.
• Conference hotel in quiet park by sea, 5km by tram. Nordic style rooms ; many with balconies ; Sea Wing for suites with hi-tech facilities and sea view. Modern restaurant with seaside terrace ; international menu.

Continental, Mannerheimintie 46, ✉ 00260, ℘ (09) 47 371, *continentalhelsinki@scandic-hotels.com, Fax (09) 4737 2211*, rm, – 600. MC AE DC VISA JCB. rest BX c
***Olivo* : Meals** *(closed Sunday and Saturday lunch)* a la carte 22.20/37.20 ♀ – **500 rm** 205/310, 12 suites.
• Huge modern hotel block on busy main street with more welcoming local interior décor. Good business facilities. Third of rooms have lake view. Roomy modern restaurant with range of international cuisine focusing on Mediterranean and fish dishes.

Radisson SAS Royal, Runeberginkatu 2, ✉ 00100, ℘ (09) 69 580, *info.royal.helsinki@radissonsas.com, Fax (09) 6958 7100*, rm, – 300. MC AE DC VISA JCB. BY b
***Johan Ludvig* : Meals** (dinner only) a la carte 38/41 – ***Ströget* : Meals** a la carte 28/31 – **254 rm** 180/240, 8 suites.
• A modern hotel with good-sized, well-maintained bedrooms, equipped for the business traveller. Johan Ludvig restaurant offers Finnish style a la carte menu in classic comfort. Glass-fronted Ströget for Scandinavian-Danish dishes.

Holiday Inn Helsinki City Centre, Elielinaukio 5, 00100, (09) 5425 5000, *helsinki.hihcc@restel.fi, Fax (09) 5425 5299,* rm, rest BX z
***Verde :* Meals** (dinner only) a la carte 32/45 – 17 – **174 rm** 233/258.
• Modern city centre hotel near railway station, post office and all main shopping areas. Modern well-equipped bedrooms ; good city view from 8th floor. Open style dining room serving popular menu using Finnish produce ; lighter dishes available at lunch time.

Radisson SAS Plaza, Mikonkatu 23, 00100, (09) 77 590, *info.plaza.helsinki@radissonsas.com, Fax (09) 7759 7100,* rm, – 100. CX a
Meals 16/50 and a la carte 30.40/46.70 – **301 rm** 190/250, 1 suite.
• Near the station, this sizeable modern business hotel maintains the reputation of this international group. Well-equipped rooms, in "Nordic", "Classic" or "Italian" style. Modern informal brasserie ; striking, painted windows.

Radisson SAS Seaside, Ruoholahdenranta 3, 00180, (09) 69 360, *info.seaside.helsinki@radissonsas.com, Fax (09) 693 2123,* rm, – 100. ABZ e
closed Easter and Christmas – ***Viola :* Meals** a la carte 23/36 – **358 rm** 220, 6 suites.
• Large contemporary hotel in quiet area ; view of harbour. Caters for business people and individuals ; also for groups. Modern rooms in three categories ; some with kitchenette. Modern restaurant offering mostly Mediterranean oriented dishes from open kitchen.

Holiday Inn Helsinki, Messuaukio 1 (near Pasila Railway Station), 00520, North : 4 km by Mannerheimintie, Nordenskiöldink, Savonkatu off Ratapihantie (09) 150 900, *holiday-inn@holidayinnhelsinki.fi, Fax (09) 150 901,* rm, – 120.
***Terra Nova :* Meals** (buffet lunch) 22.70/50 and a la carte – **239 rm** 215/239, 5 suites.
• Modern hotel in same building as congress centre ; popular for conferences. Take breakfast in the winter garden style atrium. Spacious well equipped rooms with modern décor. Cheerful modern brasserie-style restaurant, popular international cooking.

Simonkenttä, Simonkatu 9, 00100, (09) 68 380, *simonkentta@scandic-hotels.com, Fax (09) 683 8111,* – 80. BY c
***Simonkatu :* Meals** *(closed Sunday and Bank Holidays)* (buffet lunch) 20 and dinner a la carte 27/36 – **357 rm** 235/270, 3 suites.
• Ultra modern well located hotel with imposing glazed façade. Stylish designer décor with colourful fabrics and parquet flooring in all rooms. Some rooms with a view. Stylish restaurant offers range of popular traditional dishes.

Palace, Eteläranta 10, 00130, (09) 1345 6661, *reception@palacehotel.fi, Fax (09) 654 786,* – 350. DZ c
closed 23 December-15 January – **Meals** (see ***Palace Gourmet*** and ***Palacenranta*** below) – **37 rm** 235/350, 2 suites.
• 1950s hotel by harbour, occupying upper floors of building with street level reception. Spacious comfortable rooms with tasteful décor and modern facilites. Some views.

Marski, Mannerheimintie 10, 00100, (09) 68 061, *marski@scandic-hotels.com, Fax (09) 642 377,* rm, – 20. CY d
closed Christmas – **Meals** *(closed Sunday)* (buffet lunch) 19 and dinner a la carte 22/48 – **283 rm** 240/295, 6 suites.
• Large well run central hotel with imposing façade. Bright lobby with cosmopolitan coffee shop. Room styles are early and late 1990s and modern with good facilities. Welcoming bar and restaurant for traditional fare designed to appeal to all tastes.

Vaakuna, Asema-aukio 2, 00100, (09) 433 70, *sokos.hotels@sok.fi, Fax (09) 4337 7100,* rm, – 20. rest BY n
Meals a la carte 29/55 – **258 rm** 193/218, 12 suites.
• Modern accommodation, spacious, colourful and well-appointed, in this sizeable hotel, built for 1952 Olympics. Convenient for station. 10th-floor restaurant ; terrace for armchair dining - good view of station court and roofs ; lighter meals in coffee shop.

Torni, Yrjönkatu 26, 00100, (09) 43 360, *reception.torni@sok.fi, Fax (09) 4336 7100,* rm, – 35. rest BY r
closed Christmas – **Meals** *(closed Sunday, Saturday lunch and Bank Holidays)* 21.50/29 (lunch) and dinner a la carte 27/55 – **152 rm** 198/345.
• Traditional hotel in converted row of 1920s town houses in city centre. Rooms vary in size but all feature standard modern décor and facilities. Panoramic bar on 13th floor. Inviting restaurant overlooking street offering a traditional menu.

Pasila, Maistraatinportti 3 (near Pasila Railway Station), ✉ 00240, North : 4 km by Mannerheimintie, Nordenskiöldink off Vetuvitie ☎ (020) 123 4600, *pasila.helsinki@sokoshotels.fi, Fax (09) 143 771*, squash – rm, – 90. rest
closed Christmas and 31 December – ***Sevilla* : Meals** 12/20 and a la carte 15/28 ♀ – **172 rm** 141/194, 6 suites.
◆ Large, modern business hotel in tranquil district out of town, a short tram ride from city centre. Rooms feature contemporary local décor and furnishings. Informal Spanish-influenced restaurant ; popular menu with grills.

Grand Marina, Katajanokanlaitari 7, ✉ 00160, ☎ (09) 16 661, *grandmarina@scandic-hotels.com, Fax (09) 629 334*, – rm, – 500. rest DY f
***Makasiim* : Meals** *(closed Bank Holidays, lunch midsummer-1 August and Sunday lunch)* 26.50/30 (lunch) and dinner a la carte 16.40/38 ♀ – **446 rm** 197/232, 16 suites.
◆ Large harbourside hotel in converted warehouse opposite Marina Congress Centre. Practical rooms, functional fittings. Pub and coffee shop. Vast restaurant, modern Scandinavian décor. Extensive selection of international fare.

Rivoli Jardin without rest., Kasarmikatu 40, ✉ 00130, ☎ (09) 681 500, *rivoli.jardin@rivoli.fi, Fax (09) 656 988*, – CYZ k
55 rm 205/335.
◆ Well run traditional hotel in a quiet location close to city centre. Rooms are functional and comfortable, two on top floor have terrace. Winter garden style breakfast area.

Seurahuone, Kaivokatu 12, ✉ 00100, ☎ (09) 69 141, *seurahuone.cumulus@restel.fi, Fax (09) 691 4010*, – rm, – 60. rest CY e
closed 23-28 March and 21-28 December – **Meals** a la carte 25.10/38.80 ♀ – **118 rm** 198/232.
◆ Early 20C hotel, typical of its kind locally, opposite station. Décor and atmosphere reflect the charm of olden days. Rooms vary in size. Elegant restaurant retains a traditional charm. Offers menu featuring classic Finnish cuisine.

Olympia, Läntinen Brahenkatu 2, ✉ 00510, North : 2 km by Siltasaarenkatu ☎ (09) 69 151, *olympia.cumulus@restel.fi, Fax (09) 691 5219*, – rm, – 40. rest
Meals (dinner only) a la carte 19.50/40.80 – **101 rm** 125/150.
◆ Situated in a residential area near the amusement park 10min by tram from city centre. Modern bedrooms with standard décor and furnishings. Night club and Irish Pub. International menu in the restaurant.

G.W. Sundmans, Eteläranta 16 (1st floor), ✉ 00130, ☎ (09) 622 6410, *myyntipalvelu@royalravintolat.com, Fax (09) 661 331*, – – – 60. DY c
closed 22 December-8 January, Sunday, Saturday lunch and Bank Holidays – **Meals** 30/77 and a la carte 61/78.50 ♀ – ***Krog (ground floor)* : Meals** 17.50/46.50 and a la carte 36.20/46.80 ♀.
Spec. Fried langoustines with crayfish sauce. Lightly smoked Arctic char with morels. Mango soufflé, raspberry sorbet.
◆ 19C sea captain's Empire style mansion opposite harbour. Five classically decorated dining rooms with view. Elegant tables. Classically-based cuisine. Informal ground floor restaurant. Menu features local seafood and international dishes.

est. 1887, Pohjoisesplanadi 29, ✉ 00100, ☎ (09) 5761 1204, *mikko.jarvi@royalravintolat.com, Fax (09) 5761 1209*, – . CY n
closed Easter, midsummer, Christmas, Sunday, lunch Saturday and Bank Holidays – **Meals** 26/69.50 and a la carte 43/68 ♀.
◆ Elegant restaurant with Corinthian columns and 19C oil paintings. Immaculate tables. Interesting modern style dishes served by attentive and enthusiastic young team.

Nokka, Kanavaranta 7F, ✉ 00160, ☎ (09) 687 7330, *Fax (09) 6877 3330*, – . DY b
closed 25-28 March, 25-26 June, 5 November, 24 December-8 January, Sunday and Saturday lunch – **Meals** (booking essential) 27/69 and dinner a la carte 34.50/60.50 ♀.
◆ Converted warehouse divided into two striking rooms ; glazed wine cellar ; waterfront terrace. Watch the chefs prepare appealing, modern Finnish cuisine. Good service.

Palace Gourmet (at Palace H.), Eteläranta 10 (10th floor), ✉ 00130, ☎ (09) 1345 6715, *ilkka.rantanen@palaceravintolat.com, Fax (09) 657 474*, ← Helsinki and harbour, – . DZ c
closed Easter, July, Christmas, Saturday, Sunday and Bank Holidays – **Meals** 41/89 and dinner a la carte 65/72 ♀.
◆ 10th-floor restaurant with open view of harbour and sea ; splendid roof terrace. Local style décor and spacious layout. Serves traditional Finnish cuisine with hint of France.

XXX **Savoy,** Eteläesplanadi 14 (8th floor), ✉ 00130, ✆ (09) 684 4020, *terhi.oksanen@royalravintolat.com, Fax (09) 628 715,* ≤, – |≑| ▤. MC AE D VISA. ✈ CY b
closed Easter, midsummer, 2 weeks Christmas, Saturday and Sunday – **Meals** 56/98 and dinner a la carte 59/85 ♀.
◆ Panoramic restaurant in city centre with typical Finnish design dating from 1937. Classic traditional menu of local specialities. Ask for a table in the conservatory.

XX ✿ **George** (Aremo), Kalevankatu 17, ✉ 00100, ✆ (09) 647 662, *george@george.fi, Fax (09) 647 110* – ▤. MC AE D VISA JCB. ✈ BY e
closed 25-28 March, 24-26 June, 23-26 December, Sunday and Saturday lunch – **Meals** 26.50/49 and dinner a la carte 51/60 ♀.
Spec. Truffle sausage with fried apple. Pike and langoustine mousse in a cheese crust. Handmade chocolate truffles.
◆ 19C town house in residential district. Chilled chocolate truffle cabinet in bar. Elegant tableware. Classically-based cooking, using local produce with seasonal interest.

XX **Sipuli,** Kanavaranta 3 (2nd floor), ✉ 00160, ✆ (09) 6229 2811, *Fax (09) 6229 2840,* ≤ – 60. MC AE D VISA. ✈ DY s
closed Easter, 1 July-5 August, 23 December-10 January, Saturday and Sunday – **Meals** (dinner only) 40/60 and a la carte 42/66 ♀.
◆ Converted warehouse with view of Uspensky Orthodox cathedral through a picture window. Waterfront terrace bar. Serves selection of French inspired modern Finnish dishes.

XX **Bellevue,** Rahapajankatu 3, ✉ 00160, ✆ (09) 179 560, *info@restaurantbellevue.com, Fax (09) 636 985* – ▤. MC AE D VISA DY z
closed 1 week December and lunch July, 6 December, 1 January, Saturday and Sunday – **Meals** - Russian - 25/58 and dinner a la carte 34.60/62.60 ♀.
◆ Near Orthodox cathedral, restaurant in old town house with fairly sombre traditional Russian décor and cosy intimate atmosphere. Menu features Russian delicacies.

XX ✿✿ **Chez Dominique** (Valimaki), Ludviginkatu 3-5, ✉ 00130, ✆ (09) 612 7393, *info@chezdominique.fi, Fax (09) 6124 4220* – MC AE D VISA. ✈ CY s
closed July, 2 weeks Christmas, Sunday, Monday, Saturday lunch and Bank Holidays – **Meals** (booking essential) 39 (lunch) and a la carte 70/90 ♀.
Spec. Terrine of foie gras, cardamom sorbet. Anchovy butter fried monkfish, lobster tortellini. Pineapple ravioli, pastis and coconut jus.
◆ Small well run restaurant in old district. Plain minimalist décor and tiled floor. Refined modern cuisine with attention to detail ; special lunch menu.

XX **Palacenranta** (at Palace H.), Eteläranta 10 (1st floor), ✉ 00130, ✆ (09) 1345 6749, *palacenranta@palaceravintolat.com, Fax (09) 1345 6750,* ≤ Helsinki harbour – |≑| ▤. MC AE D VISA. ✈ DZ c
closed Sunday, Monday and Saturday lunch – **Meals** 27.50/85 and a la carte ♀.
◆ Stylish, modern restaurant with simple décor in neutral and dark tones and a wood panelled ceiling. Most tables have harbour views. Authentic Finnish cooking.

XX **Rivoli,** Albertinkatu 38, ✉ 00180, ✆ (09) 643 455, *kala.cheri@rivoli.inet.fi, Fax (09) 647 780* – ⊁ ▤. MC AE D VISA JCB. ✈ BZ a
closed 25-28 March, 24-26 June, 24-26 December, Saturday lunch, Sunday dinner and Bank Holidays – **Meals** 43 (dinner) and a la carte 23.70/50.60 ♀.
◆ Two different style dining rooms : smokers' is cosy with wood panelling ; non-smokers' is brasserie-style. Menu offers fusion of traditional, Finnish and French influences.

X ☺ **Lyon,** Mannerheimintie 56, ✉ 00260, ✆ (09) 408131, *ravintola.lyon@kolumbus.fi, Fax (09) 442074* – ▤. MC AE D VISA. ✈ BX x
restricted opening in summer and closed July, Sunday, Monday lunch, Saturday lunch and Bank Holidays – **Meals** (booking essential for dinner) 25/70 and a la carte 35/56.
◆ Traditional restaurant near the Opera serving French-style dishes made with fresh ingredients.

X **La Petite Maison,** Huvilakatu 28A, ✉ 00150, ✆ (09) 260 9680, *lapetite.maison@kolumbus.fi, Fax (09) 684 25 666* – MC AE D VISA. ✈ CZ a
closed Easter, Christmas and Sunday – **Meals** - French - (booking essential) (dinner only) 42/45 and a la carte 45.50/53.50 ♀.
◆ Cosy restaurant popular with local clientele in a quiet street known for its Art Deco architecture. Classic décor with strong French note. Good French-influenced classic fare.

X ☺ **Safka,** Vironkatu 8, ✉ 00170, ✆ (09) 135 7287, *safka@safka.fi* – ▤. MC AE D VISA. ✈ DX v
closed July, August, Christmas, Sunday, Saturday lunch and Monday dinner – **Meals** (booking essential) 30/45 (dinner) and a la carte 32/55.50 ♀.
◆ Modest local restaurant in converted shop near the cathedral in city centre. Cosy layout. Well run kitchen produces unfussy, fresh and seasonal, traditional Finnish food.

Serata, Bulevardi 32, 00120, (09) 680 1365, *serata@serata.net* – VISA. BZ b
closed 4 days Easter, 4 days midsummer, 17 December-1 January, Sunday, Monday dinner, Saturday in July, Saturday lunch and Bank Holidays – **Meals** - Italian - (booking essential) 20/50 and dinner a la carte 26/48.50.
• Converted shop in residential district. Open kitchen with some counter seating. Authentic Italian cooking with good value set menus including wine.

at Vantaa *North : 19 km by A 137* **DX** :

Vantaa, Hertaksentie 2 (near Tikkurila Railway Station), 01300, (09) 857 851, *reception.vantaa@sok.fi, Fax (09) 8578 5555*, , – , rm, – 280. VISA. rest
Sevilla : **Meals** a la carte approx 22.50 – **265 rm** 141/168.
• Beside the railway station and convenient for the airport ; a busy corporate hotel. Well equipped rooms in a modern Scandinavian style. Night club and pub. Modern restaurant, Spanish-influenced cooking and grills.

Holiday Inn Garden Court Helsinki Airport, Rälssitie 2, 01510, (09) 870 900, *airport.higc@restel.fi, Fax (09) 8709 0101*, , – , rm, – 25. VISA JCB. rest
Meals - Bistro - *(closed Saturday and Sunday lunch)* a la carte 29/44.05 – 15 – **280 rm** 185.
• Modern international hotel, suitable for business people. Standard bedrooms with modern décor and fittings in local style. Friendly, modern restaurant serves a simple range of traditional International dishes.

France

PARIS AND ENVIRONS – BORDEAUX
CANNES – LILLE – LYONS
MARSEILLES – PRINCIPALITY OF MONACO
NICE – STRASBOURG
TOULOUSE

PRACTICAL INFORMATION

LOCAL CURRENCY

Euro : 1 euro (€) = 1,30 USD ($) (Dec 2004)

TOURIST INFORMATION IN PARIS

Paris "Welcome" Office *(Office du Tourisme de Paris) : ✆ 08 92 68 30 00, 0,34 €/min. Gare de Lyon 20 bd Diderot, Gare du Nord 18 r. de Dunkerque, Opéra-grand magasin 11 bis rue Scribe, 9th, Montmartre place du Tertre, Tour Eiffel, Carrousel du Louvre.*

American Express *9 rue Auber, 9th, ✆ 01 47 77 72 00, Fax 01 42 68 17 17*

National Holiday in France : *14 July*

AIRLINES

AMERICAN AIRLINES : *109 rue du faubourg St-Honoré, 8th, ✆ 0810 87 28 72*

UNITED AIRLINES : *Roissy-Charles-de-Gaulle airport, T1 gate 36, ✆ 0810 72 72 72*

DELTA AIRLINES : *119 Champs-Élysées, 8th, ✆ 08 00 35 40 80*

BRITISH AIRWAYS : *Roissy-Charles-de-Gaulle airport, T2b, ✆ 0825 825 400*

AIR FRANCE : *119 avenue Champs-Élysées, 8th, ✆ 0820 820 820*

FOREIGN EXCHANGE OFFICES

Banks : *close at 4.30pm and at weekends*

Orly Sud Airport : *daily 6.30am to 11pm*

Roissy-Charles-de-Gaulle Airport : *daily 6am to 11.30pm*

TRANSPORT IN PARIS

Taxis : *may be hailed in the street when showing the illuminated sign-available day and night at taxi ranks or called by telephone*

Bus-Métro (subway) : *for full details see the Michelin Plan de Paris n° 11. The metro is quicker but the bus is good for sightseeing and practical for short distances.*

POSTAL SERVICES

Local post offices : *open Mondays to Fridays 8am to 7pm ; Saturdays 8am to noon*

General Post Office : *52 rue du Louvre, 1st : open 24 hours, ✆ 01 40 28 76 00*

SHOPPING IN PARIS

Department stores : *boulevard Haussmann, rue de Rivoli and rue de Sèvres*

Exclusive shops and boutiques : *faubourg St-Honoré, rue de la Paix and rue Royale, avenue Montaigne.*

Antiques and second-hand goods : *Swiss Village (avenue de la Motte Picquet), Louvre des Antiquaires (place du Palais Royal), Flea Market (Porte Clignancourt).*

TIPPING

Service is generally included in hotel and restaurants bills but you may choose to leave more than the expected tip to the staff. Taxi-drivers, porters, barbers and theatre or cinema attendants also expect a small gratuity.

BREAKDOWN SERVICE

Some garages in central and outer Paris operate a 24 hour breakdown service. If you breakdown the police are usually able to help by indicating the nearest one.

SPEED LIMITS

The maximum permitted speed in built up areas is 50 km/h - 31 mph ; on motorways the speed limit is 130 km/h - 80 mph and 110 km/h - 68 mph on dual carriageways. On all other roads 90 km/h - 56 mph.

SEAT BELTS

The wearing of seat belts is compulsory for drivers and all passengers.

PARIS AND ENVIRONS

Maps: 54, 55, 56, 57 G. Paris.

Map of arrondissements and districts	pp. 2 and 3
Maps	pp. 4 to 11
Sights	p. 12
Alphabetical list of hotels and restaurants	pp. 13 to 19
Hotels and restaurants of PARIS	pp. 20 to 65
Environs	pp. 66 to 70

Population : *Paris 2 147 857 ; Ile-de-France region : 10 952 011.*

Altitude : *Observatory : 60 m ; place Concorde : 34 m*

Air Terminals :

To ORLY

Orly Bus *(RATP) ✆ 08 36 68 77 14 from : place Denfert-Rochereau – 14th (exit RER)*

To ROISSY

Roissy Bus *(RATP) ✆ 08 36 68 77 14 from : Opéra, rue Scribe (angle rue Auber) 9th*
Orly *(Air France Bus) ✆ 01 41 56 89 00 from : Montparnasse, rue du Cdt-Mouchotte, Near SNCF station, 14th ; from : Invalides Aérogare, 2 rue Pelterie, 7th*
Roissy – CDG1 – CDG2 *(Air France Bus) from : Etoile, place Ch.-De-Gaulle, angle 1 avenue Carnot 17th, from : Porte Maillot, Palais des Congrès, near Méridien Hôtel, 17th*

Paris'Airports : *see Orly and Charles de Gaulle (Roissy)*

Railways, motorail : *information ✆ 01 53 90 20 20.*

ARRONDISSEMENTS

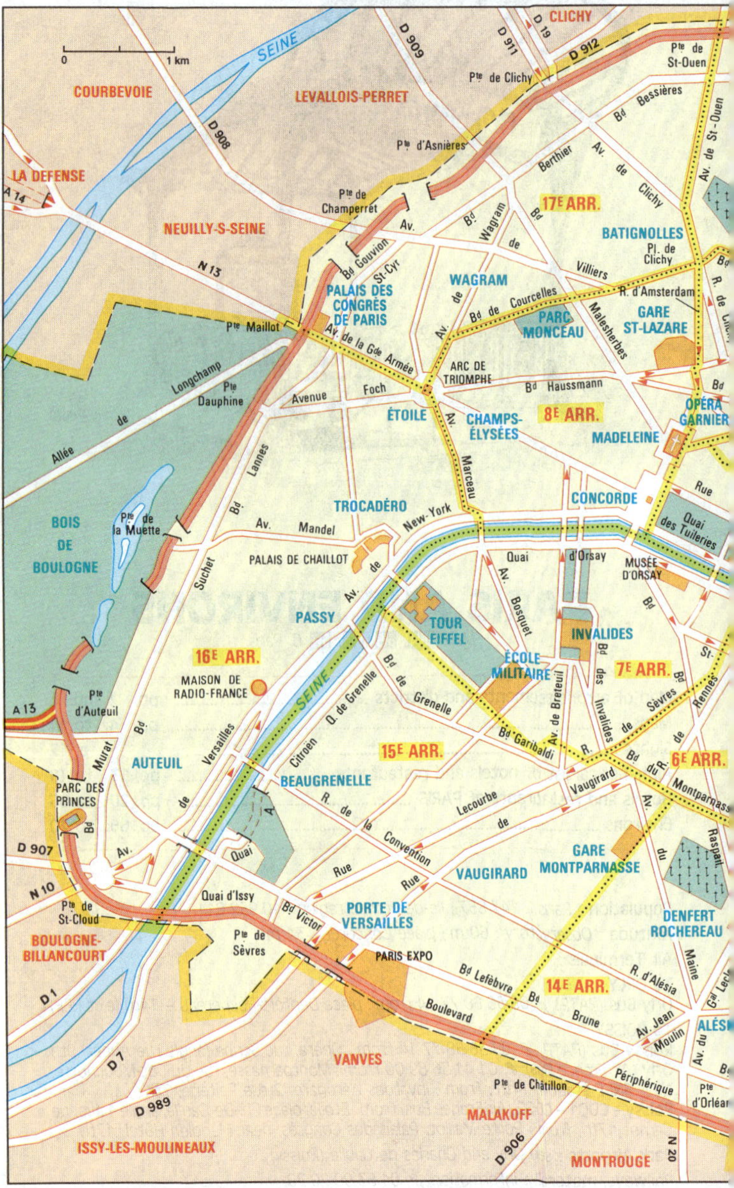

AND DISTRICTS

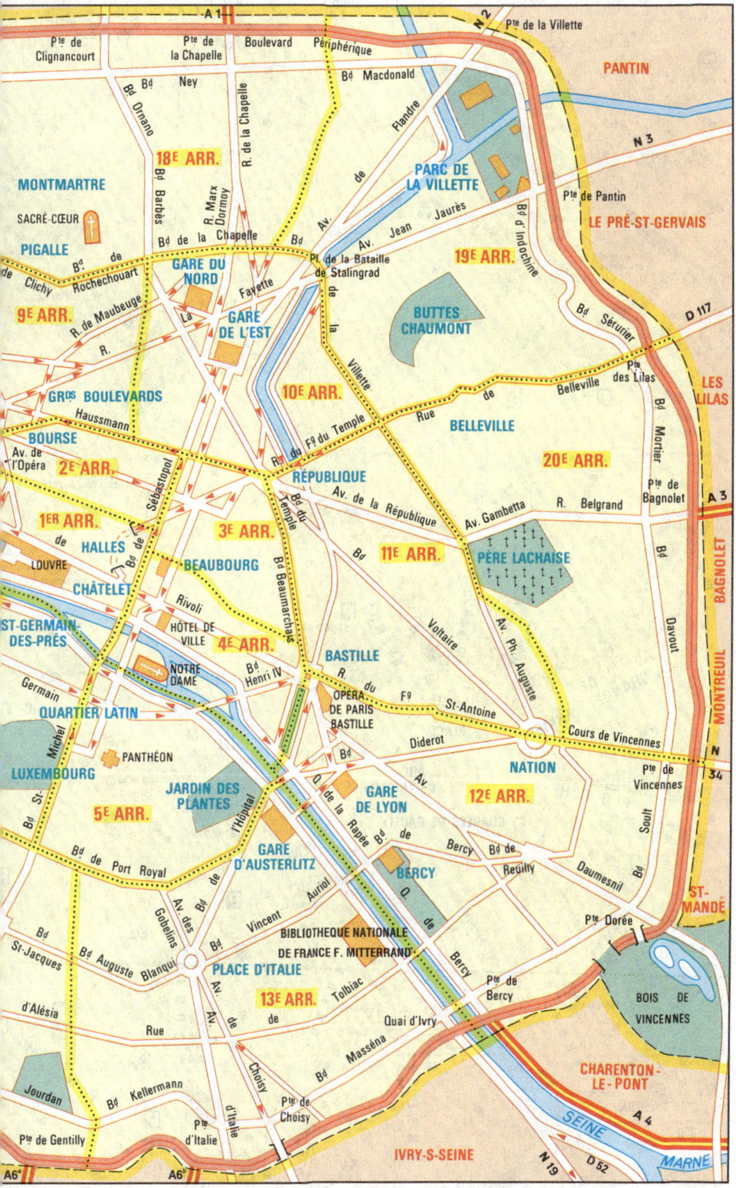

4
0
200 m
BERTHIER
BD
AV. GOURGAUD
R. de Courcelles
LYCÉE STE URSULE LOUISE DE BETTIGNIES
Sq. de l'Amerique Latine
Pl. de la Porte de Champerret
Pl. Stuart Merrill
Square J. Bellat
PORTE DE CHAMPERRET
AVENUE
Pl. du Mal Juin
PEREIRE-LEVALLOIS (R.E.R.)
PEREIRE
DE VILLIERS
Pl. du Brésil
WAGRAM
AV.
Pl. d'Israel
WAGRAM
R. G. Doré
Pl. J. Renard
Galvani
Laugier
Descombes
Tell
NIEL
D 7
D 8
PEREIRE
BOULEVARD
Square Bayen
R. Guillaume
Dumas
Faraday
R. de St Senoch
Demours
Pl. A. Maillart
MARCHÉ DES TERNES
Guersant
Bayen
AVENUE
R. G. Flaubert
Rennequin
Fourcroy
Poncelet
Banville
Prony
Courcelles
SVENSKA KYRKAN
LYCÉE TECHNOLOGIQUE
CLIN DU PARC MONCEAU
Pl. Tristan Bernard
AV.
DES TERNES
Pl. des Ternes
TERNES
E 8
BOULEVARD
COURCELLES
R. Saint Ferdinand
ST FERDINAND STE THÉRÈSE DE L'ENFANT JÉSUS
HÔPITAL MARMOTTAN
E 7
d'Armaillé
Acacias
ESPACE WAGRAM
MAC MAHON
AVENUE CARNOT
DE
Rue du Colonel Moll
LYCÉE ACTIVE BILINGUE ÉTOILE
CATHÉDRALE ST ALEXANDRE NEVSKY
SALLE PLEYEL
HOCHE
N.D. DE L'ANNONCIATION
Fg St Honoré
ST JOSEPH
ARGENTINE
AV. DE LA GRANDE ARMÉE
CH. DE GAULLE ÉTOILE (R.E.R.)
PLACE
ARC DE TRIOMPHE (R.E.R.)
CHARLES DE GAULLE
AVENUE
FRIEDLAND
Jardin de l'Hôtel Salomon de Rothschild
Pl. G. Guillaumin
Beaujon
CORPUS CHRISTI
CHAMBRE DE COMMERCE ET D'INDUSTRIE DE PARIS
Chateaubriand
FREDERIKSKIRKEN
F 8
Lord Byron
LIDO
Galerie Berri-Washington
AV. FOCH
F 7
AV. VICTOR HUGO
Lauriston
Rue du Dôme
CLIN V. HUGO
KLÉBER
CENTRE DE CONFÉRENCES INTERNATIONALES
La Pérouse
R. Newton
AIR FRANCE
GEORGE V
Galilée
Euler
DES
AVENUE
AV. D'IÉNA
ST GEORGE'S
Pl. de l'Uruguay
Kepler
Pl. H. Dunant
Pierre Charron
RESERVOIRS DE PASSY
Paul Valéry
Copernic
KLÉBER
Place des
Pl. de Beyrouth
SERBIE
Marbeuf
Galerie des Champs
Arcades du Lido

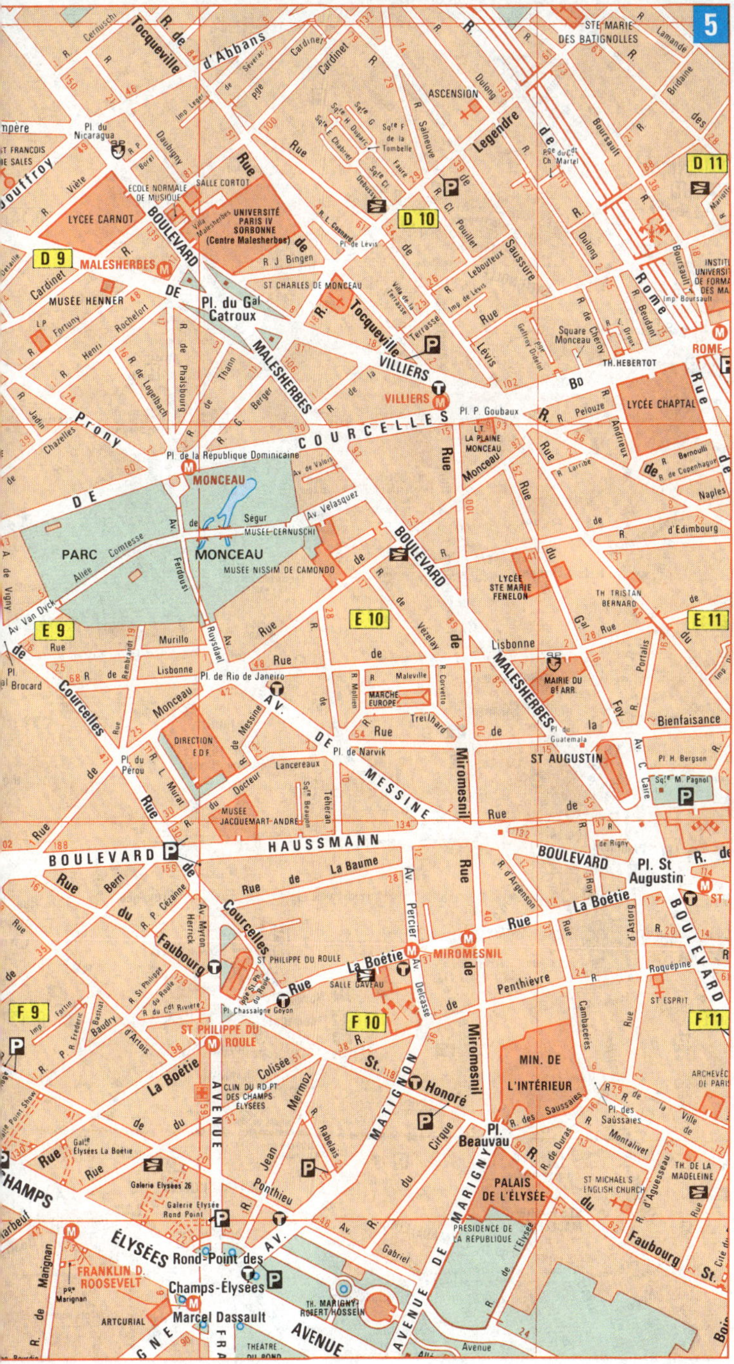
STE MARIE DES BATIGNOLLES
ASCENSION
Legendre
Tocqueville
d'Abbans
Cardinet
Dulong
Boursault
Rome
D 9
D 10
D 11
LYCEE CARNOT
ECOLE NORMALE DE MUSIQUE
SALLE CORTOT
UNIVERSITÉ PARIS IV SORBONNE (Centre Malesherbes)
MALESHERBES
MUSÉE HENNER
Pl. du Gal Catroux
ST CHARLES DE MONCEAU
BOULEVARD DE MALESHERBES
VILLIERS
TH. HEBERTOT
LYCÉE CHAPTAL
ROME
COURCELLES
Prony
Pl. de la République Dominicaine
MONCEAU
PARC MONCEAU
MUSEE CERNUSCHI
MUSEE NISSIM DE CAMONDO
LA PLAINE MONCEAU
LYCÉE STE MARIE FENELON
TH TRISTAN BERNARD
E 9
E 10
E 11
Lisbonne
Pl. de Rio de Janeiro
MARCHE EUROPE
MAIRIE DU 8e ARR
DIRECTION EDF
Pl. du Pérou
Pl. de Narvik
MESSINE
Miromesnil
ST AUGUSTIN
Bienfaisance
MUSEE JACQUEMART-ANDRE
HAUSSMANN
BOULEVARD
Pl. St Augustin
La Boétie
ST PHILIPPE DU ROULE
SALLE GAVEAU
MIROMESNIL
Penthièvre
F 9
F 10
F 11
MIN. DE L'INTÉRIEUR
CLIN DU RD PT DES CHAMPS ELYSÉES
St. Honoré
Pl. Beauvau
MATIGNON
PALAIS DE L'ÉLYSÉE
PRESIDENCE DE LA REPUBLIQUE
ST MICHAEL'S ENGLISH CHURCH
TH DE LA MADELEINE
ARCHEVÊCHÉ DE PARIS
Faubourg
CHAMPS ÉLYSÉES
Rond-Point des Champs-Élysées
FRANKLIN D. ROOSEVELT
Marcel Dassault
ARTCURIAL
TH. MARIGNY-ROBERT HOSSEIN
AVENUE
Gabriel

D 11
MAIRIE DU 17E ARR.
D 12
D 13
E 11
E 12
E 13
F 11
F 12
F 13
Rue Caulaincourt
THÉÂTRE DES 2 ÂNES
BAL DU MOULIN ROUGE
LYCÉE J. FERRY
Pl. Blanche
BLANCHE
COMÉDIE DE PARIS
PL. DE CLICHY
CLINIQUE VINTIMILLE
ESPACE EUROPEEN
INSTITUT UNIVERSITAIRE DE FORMATION DES MAITRES
DESCENTE DU ST-ESPRIT ET ÉGLISE RÉFORMÉE DES BATIGNOLLES
BATIGNOLLES
ROME
ST ANDRE DE L'EUROPE
Pl. de Dublin
R. de Parme
TH. DE L'ŒUVRE
LYCÉE ST LOUIS
FEDERATION PROTESTANTE DE FRANCE
DEUTSCHE EVANGELISCHE CHRISTUSKIRCHE
MUSÉE DE LA VIE ROMANTIQUE
TH. FONTAINE
CLIN. TURIN
LIÉGE
Constantinople
Pl. de l'Europe
EUROPE
CLIN. MILAN
PETIT THÉÂTRE DE PARIS
CASINO DE PARIS
TH. LA BRUYERE
MUSÉE GUSTAVE MOREAU
GARE ST LAZARE
Pl. de Budapest
Londres
STE TRINITE
TRINITÉ
Pl. d'Estienne d'Orves
LYCÉE RACINE
ST LAZARE
Pl. du Havre
Pl. G. Péri
R. de la Pépinière
LYCÉE CONDORCET
HAUSSMANN-ST LAZARE
TH. MOGADOR
Provence
ST AUGUSTIN
Sq. Louis XVI
CHAPELLE EXPIATOIRE
HAUSSMANN
TH. DES MATHURINS
TH. MICHEL
HAVRE CAUMARTIN
MAGASINS DU PRINTEMPS
GALERIES LAFAYETTE
CHAUSSÉE D'ANTIN
Mathurins
PARISTORIC
AUBER
OPÉRA GARNIER
TH. ATHÉNÉE L. JOUVET
COMÉDIE CAUMARTIN
MUSÉE DE LA PARFUMERIE
TH. ÉDOUARD VII SACHA GUITRY
OLYMPIA
ARCHEVÊCHE DE PARIS
Marché de la Madeleine
KIOSQUE-THÉÂTRE
MALESHERBES
TRONCHET
STE MARIE MADELEINE
MADELEINE
BD DE LA MADELEINE
BD DES CAPUCINES
OPÉRA
l'Opéra
QUATRE SEPTEMBRE
GALERIE DES TROIS QUARTIERS
CREDIT FONCIER DE FRANCE
MINISTERE DE LA JUSTICE
TH DAUNOU
TH. LA PÉPINIÈRE-OPÉRA
MICHELIN
TH. DES BOUFFES PARISIENS
ROYALE
St. Honoré
AVENUE

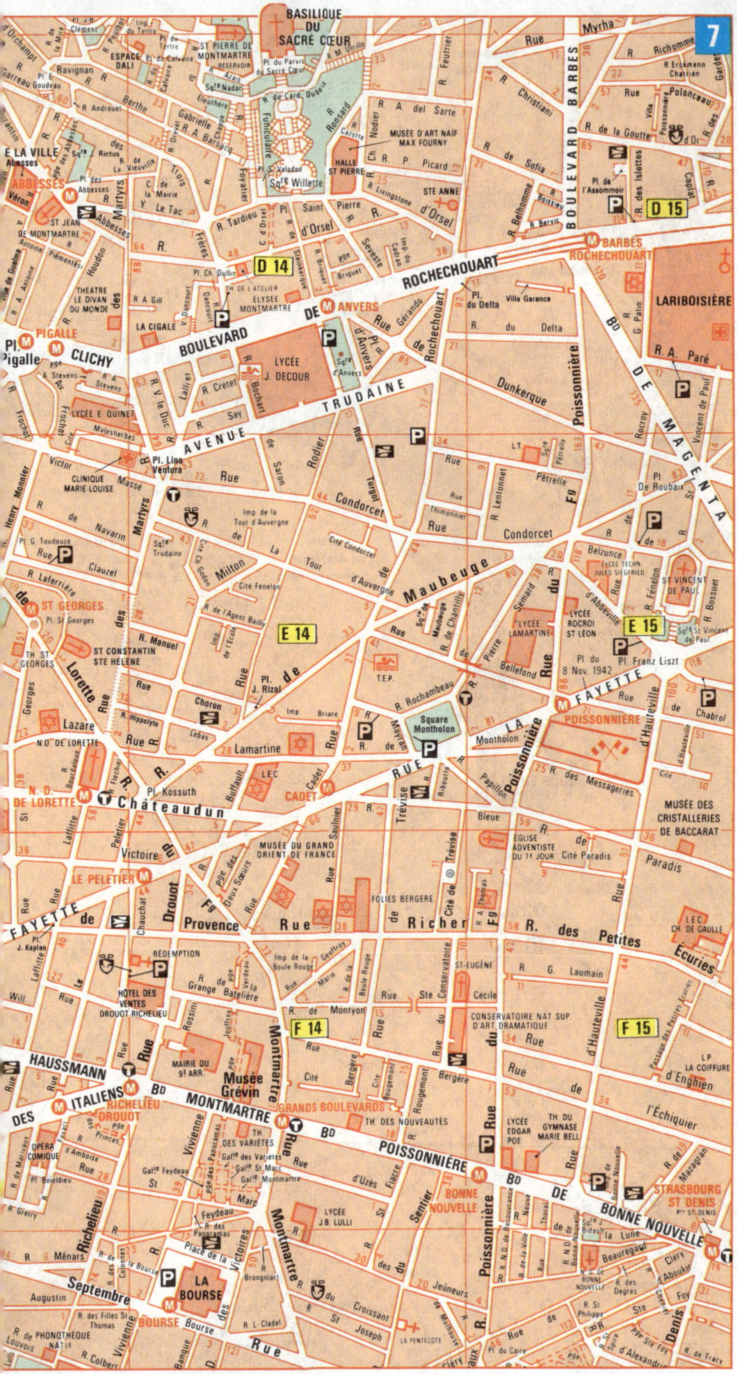
BASILIQUE DU SACRÉ CŒUR
ST PIERRE DE MONTMARTRE
ESPACE DALI
MUSÉE D'ART NAIF MAX FOURNY
HALLE ST PIERRE
Sq.re Willette
Funiculaire
ABBESSES
Pl. des Abbesses
ST JEAN DE MONTMARTRE
THEATRE LE DIVAN DU MONDE
LA CIGALE
PIGALLE
Pl. Pigalle
CLICHY
BOULEVARD DE ROCHECHOUART
ANVERS
D 14
D 15
BARBÈS ROCHECHOUART
BOULEVARD BARBÈS
LARIBOISIÈRE
Villa Garance
R. du Delta
LYCÉE J. DECOUR
AVENUE TRUDAINE
LYCEE E. QUINET
CLINIQUE MARIE-LOUISE
Pl. Lino Ventura
R. de Dunkerque
Rue Condorcet
Rue de Maubeuge
Rue de la Tour d'Auvergne
Rue Milton
Rue de Navarin
Rue Clauzel
ST GEORGES
Pl. St Georges
TH. ST GEORGES
ST CONSTANTIN STE HÉLÈNE
E 14
E 15
LYCÉE LAMARTINE
LYCÉE ROCROI ST LÉON
LYCÉE TECHN. JULES SIEGFRIED
ST VINCENT DE PAUL
Pl. Franz Liszt
Pl. du 8 Nov. 1942
BD DE MAGENTA
Rue La Fayette
POISSONNIÈRE
Square Montholon
Rue Rochambeau
Rue Lamartine
CADET
N.-D. DE LORETTE
Pl. Kossuth
Châteaudun
LE PELETIER
Rue de Provence
Rue Drouot
MUSÉE DU GRAND ORIENT DE FRANCE
FOLIES BERGÈRE
Rue Richer
Rue des Petites Écuries
R. de Paradis
MUSÉE DES CRISTALLERIES DE BACCARAT
ÉGLISE ADVENTISTE DU 7e JOUR
Cité Paradis
LEC CH. DE GAULLE
RÉDEMPTION
HÔTEL DES VENTES DROUOT RICHELIEU
ST-EUGÈNE
CONSERVATOIRE NAT. SUP. D'ART DRAMATIQUE
F 14
F 15
MAIRIE DU 9e ARR.
Musée Grévin
HAUSSMANN
RICHELIEU DROUOT
BD DES ITALIENS
BD MONTMARTRE
GRANDS BOULEVARDS
TH. DES NOUVEAUTÉS
TH. DES VARIÉTÉS
OPÉRA COMIQUE
BD POISSONNIÈRE
BONNE NOUVELLE
LYCÉE EDGAR POE
TH. DU GYMNASE MARIE BELL
BD DE BONNE NOUVELLE
STRASBOURG ST DENIS
Rue de l'Échiquier
Rue d'Enghien
LYCÉE J.B. LULLI
LA BOURSE
BOURSE
R. du Quatre Septembre
Rue Montmartre
PHONOTHÈQUE NAT.le
LA PENTECOTE
Rue du Croissant
Rue Réaumur

8
Place des États Unis
Pl. Amiral de Grasse
Pl. de Beyrouth
AMERICAN CATHEDRAL IN PARIS
G 7
G 8
BOISSIÈRE
LYCÉE ASSOMPTION
ST PIERRE DE CHAILLOT
Place Rochambeau
ST ETIENNE
Pl. P. Brisson
MUSÉE GUIMET
PALAIS GALLIERA
THÉATRE-STUDIO COMÉDIE DES CHAMPS ÉLYSÉES
CRAZY HORSE
ALMA MARCEAU
Place Marlène Dietrich
Pl. d'Iéna
IÉNA
Pl. de Tokyo
PRÉSIDENT
WILSON
Pl. de l'Alma
MUSÉE D'ART MODERNE
PALAIS DE TOKYO
SITE DE CRÉATION CONTEMPORAINE
UNION DE L'EUROPE OCCIDENTALE
CONSEIL ÉCONOMIQUE ET SOCIAL
NEW YORK
Pont de l'Alma
PALAIS DE CHAILLOT
JARDINS
Passerelle Debilly
Pt DE L'ALMA (R.E.R.)
Pl. de la Résistance
QUAI
BRANLY
H 7
H 8
MUSÉE DES ARTS PREMIERS (Secteur en travaux)
L'Université
Pl. de Varsovie
TROCADÉRO
Pont d'Iéna
LYCÉE ALMA
ST JEAN
RAPP
BOSQUET
TOUR EIFFEL
CHAMP DE MARS TOUR EIFFEL (R.E.R.)
STADE ÉMILE-ANTHOINE
DATAR
Pl. de Sydney
Pl. Jacques Rueff
J 7
J 8
Pl. du Général Gouraud
L.P G. EIFFEL
CHAMP DE MARS
Pl. de Kyoto
Pl. des Martyrs Juifs du Vélodrome d'Hiver
T.E.P.
BIR HAKEIM
DIRECTION JOURNAUX OFFICIELS
Pl. A. Sauvy
Fédération
ST LOUIS
ECOLE SUPRE DE GUERRE
BOULEVARD DE GRENELLE
Place Dupleix
ST LÉON
K 7
K 8
VILLAGE SUISSE
SUFFREN
ECOLE SUPRE D'INTENDANCE
Pl. Marcel Cerdan
DUPLEIX

G 10
G 11
G 9
H 9
H 10
H 11
J 9
J 10
J 11
K 9
K 10
K 11
ARTCURIAL
Marcel Dassault
AVENUE
CHAMPS ÉLYSÉES CLEMENCEAU
THEATRE DU ROND POINT
Sq^re de Berlin
Av. de Selves
Av. du Gal Eisenhower
Pl. Clemenceau
DES CHAMPS ÉLYSÉES
Allée
Avenue
Marcel
ESPACE PIERRE CARDIN
Gabriel
Proust
Carré Champs Elysées
Imp. Bourdin
CLIN. ELYSEE MONTAIGNE
MONTAIGNE
Rue
Imp. d'Antin
CHURCH OF SCOTLAND
Goujon
Rue Jean
Pl. François 1er
François 1er
Bayard
ÉGLISE ARMÉNIENNE
N.D. DE CONSOLATION
Albert 1er
Pl. du Canada
FRANKLIN D. ROOSEVELT
Sq^re J. Perrin
GRAND PALAIS
PALAIS DE LA DÉCOUVERTE
UNIVERSITÉ PARIS IV
Vallée Suisse
Av. W. Churchill
Av. Ch. Girault
Dutuit
PETIT PALAIS
Av. Edward Tuck
Cours la Reine
PL
DE
OBÉLI
CONCO
Port de la Conférence
Port des Champs Elysées
Port de la Concorde
Pont des Invalides
Pont Alexandre III
Pont de la Concorde
Gros Caillou
Port des Invalides
Quai d'Orsay
Quai
Esplanade Habib Bourguiba
THE AMERICAN CHURCH IN PARIS
D'ORSAY
Pl. de Finlande
R. Desgenettes
MAUBOURG
Fabert
R. Paul et Jean Lerolle
GALLIENI
AÉROGARE DES INVALIDES
(R.E.R.)
INVALIDES
R. Robert Esnault Pelterie
MIN. DES AFFAIRES ETRANGÈRES
MIN. DES AFFAIRES EUROPÉENNES
ASSEMBLÉE NATIONALE
PALAIS BOURBON
Bd
R. A. Briand
Rue
ASSEMBLÉE NATIONALE
Pl. du Prés! E. Herriot
R. du Colonel Combes
Moissan
R. Henri
Av. Sully Prudhomme
Schuman
CLIN. ALMA
Av. R.
Rue de l'Université
Jean Nicot
Pge Commun
Surcouf
ESPLANADE
DU MAL
Constantine
ST PIERRE DU GROS CAILLOU
Malar
Saint Dominique
R. de la Comète
TOUR MAUBOURG
DES INVALIDES
Rd-Pt du Bleuet de France
Pl. des Invalides
R. de Talleyrand
Pl. du Palais Bourbon
MAISON DE LA CHIMIE
Bourgogne
Saint
MINISTÈRE DE LA DÉFENSE
LYCÉE LA ROCHEFOUCAULT
Pge Jean Nicot
Rue Amélie
Cité du Gal Négrier
Grenelle
Pl. Salvador Allende
Square d'Ajaccio
INSTITUT GÉOGRAPHIQUE NATIONAL
R. de Champagny
R. de Martignac
Sq^re S. Rousseau
BASILIQUE STE CLOTILDE
Casimir Périer
Las Cases
Dom
ST JEAN
LA TOUR MAUBOURG
Sq^re Santiago du Chili
R. Valadon
R. E. Psichari
Jardin de l'Église évangélique luthérienne
PICQUET
MUSÉE DE L'ARMÉE
HÔTEL DES INVALIDES
ST LOUIS
MUSÉE DE L'ORDRE DE LA LIBÉRATION
INVALIDES
VARENNE
Rue de Varenne
MIN. DE L'EMPLOI ET DE LA SOLIDARITÉ
LYCÉE P. CLAUDEL
MIN. DE L'ÉDUCAT. NATIONA
MAIRIE DU 7e ARR.
Cité Martignac
MIN. DE L'AGRICULTURE ET DE LA PÊCHE
MIN. DES RELATIONS AVEC LE PARLEMENT
MIN. DE LA FONCTION PUBLIQUE
Champ de Mars
R. Bosquet
Cler
Duvivier
R. Chevert
R. Bougainville
Pge de la Vierge
MOTTE
ÉCOLE MILITAIRE
Rue
R. Amélie
L. Codet
R. J. Granier
Bd
MUSÉE RODIN
DES
Jardin de l'Intendant
ÉGLISE DU DÔME
Jardin de l'Abondance
HÔTEL MATIGNON
Vaneau
Cité Vaneau
C. Vaneau
de Jouy
R. de Chanaleilles
C. de Varenne
Pl. de l'École Militaire
Avenue de
Pl. D. Cochin
Pl. Vauban
Tourville
AVENUE LOWENDAL
R. Bixio
SÉGUR
Esplanade du Souvenir Français
AV. DE VILLARS
BOULEVARD
LYCÉE VICTOR DURUY
Barbet
CLIN. ST FRANÇOIS XAVIER
ST DOMINIQUE
PRÉFECTURE D'ILE DE FRANCE
Rue
ÉCOLE MILITAIRE
SECR^T D'ÉTAT À LA SANTÉ
DUQUESNE
DE BRETEUIL
d'Estrées
Rue
Pl. André Tardieu
ST FRANÇOIS XAVIER
R. Monsieur
Jardin Catherine Labouré
Imp. Oudinot
Pl. de Fontenoy
SECR^T D'ÉTAT AU LOGEMENT
MIN. DE L'AMÉNAGEMENT DU TERRITOIRE ET DE L'ENVIRONNEMENT
V. de Ségur
Pl. El Salvador
Pl. du Prés! P. de Gaulle
Mithouard
Sq^re de l'Abbé Esquerré
SECR^T D'ÉTAT À LA COOPÉRATION ET À LA FRANCOPHONIE
CLIN. DES RELIGIEUSES AUGUSTINES DE MEAUX
Oudinot
L.T. ALBERT DEMUN
MICHELIN
U.N.E.S.C.O.
AV.

G 11
G 12
G 13
H 11
H 12
H 13
J 11
J 12
J 13
K 11
K 12
MINISTERE DE LA JUSTICE
Place Vendôme
OPÉRA
MICHELIN
R. Danielle
Casanova
MUSÉE DES LUNETTES ET LORGNETTES
N D DE L'ASSOMPTION
Pl M Barrès
COUR DES COMPTES
MUSÉE BOUILHET CHRISTOFLE
HÔTEL CRILLON
HÔTEL DE LA MARINE
Galerie Royale
CONCORDE
PLACE DE LA CONCORDE
OBÉLISQUE
GALERIE NATIONALE DU JEU DE PAUME
RUE DE RIVOLI
R. de Castiglione
Saint
Thabor
R. du 29 Juillet
Passage des Jacobins
OFFICE DU TOURISME
PYRAMIDES
L'OPÉRA
ST ROCH
Honoré
Pl. des Pyramides
COMÉDIE FRANÇAISE RICHELIEU
Pl. A. Malraux
Pl. Colette
PALAIS ROYAL MUSÉE DU LOUVRE
Terrasse
JARDIN DES TUILERIES
TUILERIES
Feuillants
MUSÉE DE L'ORANGERIE
MUSÉE DE LA MODE ET DU TEXTILE
MUSÉE DES ARTS DÉCORATIFS
JARDIN DU CARROUSEL
ARC DE TRIOMPHE DU CARROUSEL
Pl. du Carrousel
PYRAMIDE
Napoléon
Cour
Terrasse des Tuileries
Av. du Gal Lemonnier
QUAI DES TUILERIES
Port des Tuileries
Passerelle Solférino
Quai Anatole France
Port du Bord de l'Eau
SEINE
Pont Royal
Pont du Carrousel
QUAI FRANÇOIS MITTERRAND
Port du Louvre
QUAI VOLTAIRE
QUAI MALAQUAIS
Port des Saints Pères
(R. E. R.) MUSÉE D'ORSAY
Pl. H. de Montherlant
PALAIS DE LA LÉGION D'HONNEUR
MUSÉE D'ORSAY
R. de la Légion d'Honneur
CAISSE DES DEPOTS ET CONSIGNATIONS
LA DOCUMENTATION FRANÇAISE
SECRT D'ÉTAT AUX P.M.E., AU COMMERCE ET A L'ARTISANAT
Rue de Bellechasse
R. de Poitiers
Rue de Lille
Rue de Verneuil
R. Allent
Rue du Bac
Rue de Beaune
INSTITUT DES LANGUES ET CIVILISATIONS ORIENTALES
Pl. J. Bainville
SOLFÉRINO
Dominique
Las Cases
Saint
R. de Villersexel
MIN. DE L'ÉQUIPEMENT, DES TRANSPORTS ET DU LOGEMENT
SECRT D'ÉTAT POUR L'EMPLOI
Imp. de Valmy
R. Montalembert
R. S. Bottin
DON CAMILO
E.N.A.
Rue de l'Université
ÉCOLE NATLE SUPRE DES BEAUX ARTS
Rue Bonaparte
R. des Beaux Arts
Rue des Saints Pères
MIN. DE L'ÉDUCATION NATIONALE
SECRT D'ÉTAT AUX ANCIENS COMBATTANTS
Pge de la Visitation
R. Simon
PENTEMONT
P.L. Courier
Imp. P.L. Courier
RUE DU BAC
ST THOMAS D'AQUIN
Pl. St Thomas d'Aquin
R. St Thomas d'Aquin
R. de Gribeauval
R. du Pré aux Clercs
ACADÉMIE NATLE DE MÉDECINE
UNIVERSITÉ PARIS V
R. Visconti
Jacob
Rue de Furstemberg
Grenelle
R. de Saint Simon
BOULEVARD
GERMAIN
R. de Luynes
Sqre de Luynes
Guillaume
R. Perronet
ST VLADIMIR LE GD
Sqre Taras Chevtchenko
MUSÉE MAILLOL
FONTAINE DES QUATRE SAISONS
LYCEE ST THOMAS D'AQUIN
FOND. NAT DES SCIENCES POLITIQUES
R. Guillaume Apollinaire
Pl. St Germain des Prés
Imp. des Deux Anges
St Benoît
MUSÉE EUGÈNE DELACROIX
R. de l'Abbaye
R. Cardinale
ST GERMAIN DES PRÉS
Pl. J.-P. Sartre S. de Beauvoir
Pl. du Québec
Varenne
C. de Varenne
LYCÉE D'HULST
Sqre de La Rochefoucauld
R. de Narbonne
R. de Commaille
R. de La Planche
R. de la Chaise
Square Récamier
Rue du Dragon
R. du Sabot
R. B. Palissy
R. Gozlin
Sqre F. Desruelles
Pl. J. Copeau
Pl. d'Acadie
MABILLON
R. de Montfaucon
R. Clément
SEMIN. DES MISSIONS ETRANGÈRES
Sqre des Missions Étrangères
R. Chomel
Babylone
R. Récamier
R. de Sèvres
Carref. de la Croix Rouge
Rennes
LE M VOX
Madame
Bonaparte
Four
R. des Canettes
R. Princesse
R. Mabillon
MARCHÉ ST GERMAIN
R. Guisarde
R. Lobineau
Saint
Square Boucicaut
Pl. Le Corbusier
SÈVRES BABYLONE
TH DU VIEUX COLOMBIER
R. du Vieux Colombier
ST SULPICE
Cherche Midi
N.D. DE LA MEDAILLE MIRACULEUSE
BON MARCHÉ
R. Velpeau
ST IGNACE
Pl. A. Deville
R. de Sèvres
R. M. Pape Carpantier
MAIRIE DU 6E ARR.
Pl. St Sulpice
ST SULPICE
Av. Révérend Père M. Riquet
R. Palatine
R. du Canivet
R. de Mézières
Rue de Rennes
UNIVERSITÉ PARIS V

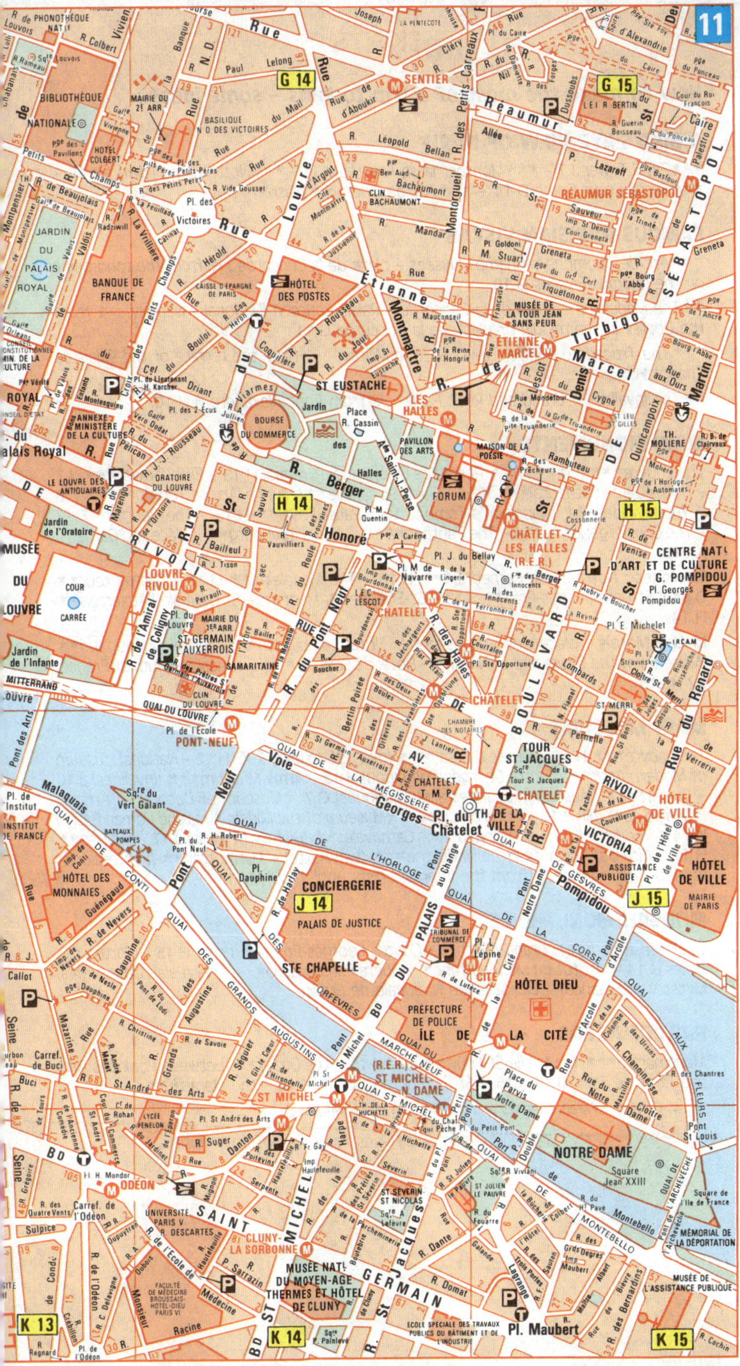
G 14
G 15
H 14
H 15
J 14
J 15
K 13
K 14
K 15
BIBLIOTHÈQUE NATIONALE
MAIRIE DU 2E ARR.
BASILIQUE N D DES VICTOIRES
SENTIER
Réaumur
RÉAUMUR SÉBASTOPOL
Pl. des Victoires
JARDIN DU PALAIS ROYAL
BANQUE DE FRANCE
HÔTEL DES POSTES
Étienne Marcel
ÉTIENNE MARCEL
Turbigo
MUSÉE DE LA TOUR JEAN SANS PEUR
ST EUSTACHE
BOURSE DU COMMERCE
LES HALLES
FORUM
PAVILLON DES ARTS
MAISON DE LA POÉSIE
ANNEXE MINISTÈRE DE LA CULTURE
LE LOUVRE DES ANTIQUAIRES
ORATOIRE DU LOUVRE
Jardin de l'Oratoire
MUSÉE DU LOUVRE
COUR CARRÉE
Jardin de l'Infante
LOUVRE RIVOLI
MAIRIE DU 1ER ARR.
ST GERMAIN L'AUXERROIS
SAMARITAINE
CHÂTELET LES HALLES
CENTRE NATL D'ART ET DE CULTURE G. POMPIDOU
IRCAM
TH. MOLIÈRE
BOULEVARD
SÉBASTOPOL
TOUR ST JACQUES
CHÂTELET
CHÂTELET T M P
Pl. du Châtelet
TH. DE LA VILLE
HÔTEL DE VILLE
MAIRIE DE PARIS
ASSISTANCE PUBLIQUE
RIVOLI
VICTORIA
POMPIDOU
PONT-NEUF
Sq. du Vert Galant
HÔTEL DES MONNAIES
INSTITUT DE FRANCE
CONCIERGERIE
PALAIS DE JUSTICE
STE CHAPELLE
TRIBUNAL DE COMMERCE
PRÉFECTURE DE POLICE
ÎLE DE LA CITÉ
HÔTEL DIEU
CITÉ
NOTRE DAME
Square Jean XXIII
Square de l'Ile de France
MÉMORIAL DE LA DÉPORTATION
ST MICHEL
ST MICHEL N. DAME
ODÉON
UNIVERSITÉ PARIS V R. DESCARTES
CLUNY-LA SORBONNE
MUSÉE NATL DU MOYEN-AGE THERMES ET HÔTEL DE CLUNY
SAINT GERMAIN
FACULTÉ DE MÉDECINE
ST SEVERIN ST NICOLAS
ST JULIEN LE PAUVRE
Pl. Maubert
MUSÉE DE L'ASSISTANCE PUBLIQUE
ECOLE SPECIALE DES TRAVAUX PUBLICS DU BATIMENT ET DE L'INDUSTRIE

SIGHTS

How to make the most of a trip to Paris – some ideas :

A BIRD'S-EYE VIEW OF PARIS

★★★ *Eiffel Tower* J 7 – ★★★ *Montparnasse Tower* LM 11 – ★★★ *Notre-Dame Towers* K 15 – ★★★ *Sacré Cœur Dome* D 14 – ★★★ *Arc de Triomphe platform* F 8.

FAMOUS PARISIAN VISTAS

★★★ *Arc de Triomphe – Champs-Élysées – place de la Concorde : ⩽ from the rond point on the Champs-Élysées* G 10.

★★ *The Madeleine – place de la Concorde – Palais Bourbon (National Assembly) : ⩽ from the Obelisk in the middle of place de la Concorde* G 11.

★★★ *The Trocadéro – Eiffel Tower – Ecole Militaire : ⩽ from the terrace of the Palais de Chaillot* H 7.

★★ *The Invalides – Grand and Petit Palais : ⩽ from Pont Alexandre III* H 10.

MAIN MONUMENTS

The Louvre★★★ *(Cour Carrée, Perrault's Colonnade, Pyramid)* H 13 – *Eiffel Tower*★★★ J 7 – *Notre-Dame Cathedral*★★★ K 15 – *Sainte-Chapelle*★★★ J 14 – *Arc de Triomphe*★★★ F 8 – *The Invalides*★★★ *(Napoleon's Tomb)* J 10 – *Palais-Royal*★★ H 13 – *The Opéra*★★ F 12 – *The Conciergerie*★★ J 14 – *The Panthéon*★★ L 14 – *Luxembourg*★★ *(Palace and Gardens)* KL 13.

Churches : *Notre-Dame Cathedral*★★★ K 15 – *The Madeleine*★★ G 11 – *Sacré Cœur*★★ D 14 – *St-Germain-des-Prés*★★ J 13 – *St-Etienne-du-Mont*★★ – *St-Germain-l'Auxerrois*★★ H 14.

In the Marais : *place des Vosges*★★★ – *Hôtel Lamoignon*★★ – *Hôtel Guénégaud*★★ *(Museum of the Chase and of Nature)* – *Hôtel de Soubise*★★ *(Historical Museum of France) by* HJ 15.

MAIN MUSEUMS

The Louvre★★★ H 13 – *Musée d'Orsay*★★★ *(mid-19C to early 20C)* H 12 – *National Museum of Modern Art*★★★ *(Centre Georges-Pompidou)* H 15 – *Army Museum*★★★ *(Invalides)* J 10 – *Guimet*★★★ *(musée national des arts asiatiques)* G 7 – *Museum of Decorative Arts*★★ *(107 rue de Rivoli)* H 13 – *Hôtel de Cluny*★★ *(Museum of the Middle Ages and Roman Baths)* K 14 – *Rodin*★★ *(Hôtel de Biron)* J 10 – *Carnavalet*★★ *(History of Paris)* J 17 – *Picasso*★★ H 17 – *Cité des Sciences et de l'Industrie*★★★ *(La Villette)* – *Marmottan*★★ *(Impressionist artists)* – *Orangerie*★★ *(from the Impressionists until 1930)* H 11.

MODERN MONUMENTS

La Défense★★ *(CNIT, Grande Arche)* – *Centre Georges-Pompidou*★★★ H 15 – *Forum des Halles* H 14 – *Institut du Monde Arabe*★ – *Opéra Paris-Bastille*★ – *Bercy (Palais Omnisports, Ministry of Finance)* – *Bibliothèque Nationale de France.*

PRETTY AREAS

Montmartre★★★ D 14 – *Ile St-Louis*★★ J 14 J 15 – *the Quays*★★ *(between Pont des Arts and Pont de Sully)* J 14 J 15 – *St Séverin district*★★ K 14 – *the Marais*★★★.

K 14, G 10 : *Reference letters and numbers on the town plans.*

Use MICHELIN Green Guide Paris for a well-informed visit.

ALPHABETICAL LIST (Hotels and restaurants)

A

40 A (Le)
28 Abbaye (L')
59 A et M Restaurant
36 Affriolé (L')
52 Aiglon (L')
26 Aiguière (L')
45 Al Ajami
41 Alain Ducasse au Plaza Athénée
47 Alba-Opéra
30 Albe (D')
46 Albert 1er
32 Alcazar
64 Allobroges (Les)
39 Amarante Champs Élysées
26 Ambassade d'Auvergne
41 Ambassadeurs (Les)
46 Ambassador
26 Ambroisie (L')
55 Ami Marcel (L')
60 Ampère
50 Anacréon
21 Angl'Opéra
44 Angle du Faubourg (L')
47 Anjou-Lafayette
41 Apicius
53 Apollinaire
53 Apollon Montparnasse
40 Arcade (L')
35 Arpège
27 Astier
38 Astor (L')
38 Astor Saint-Honoré
58 Astrance
61 Astrid
32 Atelier Maître Albert
51 Auberge Etchegorry
27 Auberge Pyrénées Cévennes
28 Aubusson (D')
25 Austin's
51 Avant Goût (L')
66 Avant Seine
68 Aviateurs

B

63 Ballon des Ternes
60 Balmoral
38 Balzac
60 Banville
22 Bar Vendôme
38 Baretto
27 Bascou (Au)
43 Bath's
62 Béatilles (Les)
36 Beato
25 Beaubourg
26 Beaumarchais
39 Bedford
28 Bel Ami St-Germain-des-Prés
28 Bélier (Le)
54 Benkay
26 Benoît
34 Bersoly's
62 Beudant
55 Beurre Noisette
51 Biche au Bois
55 Bistro d'Hubert
44 Bistrot du Sommelier
47 Blanche Fontaine
51 Bleu Marine
26 Bofinger
57 Bois (Du)
36 Bon Accueil (Au)
66 Botanic
32 Bouchons de François Clerc (Les)
44 Bouchons de François Clerc Étoile (Les)
25 Bourg Tibourg
33 Bourgogne et Montana

62 Braisière (La)
51 Brasserie
48 Brasserie Flo
45 Brasserie Haussmann
21 Brasserie Le Louvre
32 Brasserie Lipp
27 Brasserie Lutétia
25 Bretonnerie
37 Bristol, 112 rue du faubourg St-Honoré (Hotel)
41 Bristol, 112 rue du faubourg St-Honoré (Rest.)
28 Buci
32 Buisson Ardent

C

24 Cabaret
34 Cadran (Du)
48 Café de la Paix
24 Café Drouant
38 Café Faubourg
49 Café Ké
51 Café Lenôtre
45 Café Lenôtre-Pavillon Elysée
38 Café Terminus
68 Café Trianon
36 Caffé Minotti
40 Caffe Ristretto
63 Caïus
39 California
53 Carladez Cambronne
46 Carlton's Hôtel
25 Caron de Beaumarchais
54 Caroubier
43 Carpaccio
22 Carré des Feuillants
65 Cave Gourmande
63 Caves Petrissans
23 Céladon
55 Cerisaie
35 Chamarré
57 Chambellan Morgane
40 Chambiges Élysées
34 Champ-de-Mars
61 Champerret Élysées
38 Champs-Élysées Plaza
48 Chateaubriant (Au)
54 Chen-Soleil d'Est
36 Chez Eux (D')
43 Chiberta
53 Ciel de Paris
35 Cigale Récamier
41 "Cinq" (Le)
57 59 Poincaré
65 Clair de la Lune (Au)
36 Clos des Gourmets
42 Clovis
66 Communautés (Les)
60 Concorde La Fayette
38 Concorde St-Lazare
43 Copenhague
47 Corona
20 Costes
56 Costes K.
64 Cottage Marcadet
67 Country Inn and Suites
54 Coupole (La)
37 Cour Jardin (La)
67 Courtyard Marriott
37 Crillon
64 Crimée
58 Cristal Room Baccarat
26 Croix de Malte

D

53 Daguerre
64 Damrémont
39 Daniel
45 Daru
30 De Fleurie
39 De Sers
34 De Varenne
38 De Vigny
52 Delambre
32 Délices d'Aphrodite (Les)
62 Dessirier
66 2 Arcs (Les)
20 234 Rivoli
54 Dôme (Le)
26 Dôme du Marais (Le)
32 Dominique
23 Drouant
54 Duc (Le)
33 Duc de Saint-Simon

E

66 Échiquier (L')
21 Edouard VII
34 Eiffel Park Hôtel
42 Élysées (Les)
40 Élysées Céramic
56 Élysées Régencia
32 Emporio Armani Caffé
27 Enoteca (L')
63 Entredgeu (L')
32 Épi Dupin (L')
54 Épopée (L')
68 Escale (L')
22 Espadon (L')
28 Esprit St Germain
59 Essaouira
70 Étape Gourmande (L')
22 États-Unis Opéra
61 Étoile Park Hôtel
57 Étoile Residence Imperiale
67 Étoiles (Les)

F

59 Fakhr el Dine
70 Falher (Le)
38 Faubourg Sofitel Demeure Hôtels (Le)
44 Fermette Marbeuf 1900
61 Flaubert
43 Flora Danica
57 Floride Étoile
36 Florimond
23 Fontaine Gaillon
54 Fontanarosa
43 Fouquet's
37 Four Seasons George V
39 François 1er
47 Franklin

G

24 Gallopin
54 Gauloise
57 Gavarni
25 Général
24 Georges (Chez)
23 Gérard Besson
59 Géraud (Chez)
23 Goumard
68 Gourmet
62 Graindorge
26 Grand Hôtel Français
30 Grand Hôtel St-Michel
22 Grand Vefour
59 Grande Cascade
29 Grands Hommes
61 Guy Savoy

H - I

57 Hameau de Passy (Le)
31 Hélène Darroze
68 Hilton
37 Hilton Arc de Triomphe
66 Hilton La Défense
67 Hilton Orly
57 Hiramatsu
25 Holiday Inn11e
64 Holiday Inn19e
68 Holiday Inn
49 Holiday Inn Bastille
49 Holiday Inn Bibliothèque de France
64 Holiday Inn Garden Court Montmartre
52 Holiday Inn Paris Montparnasse
46 Holiday Inn Paris Opéra
22 Horset Opéra (L')
28 Hôtel (L')
63 Huîtrier (L')
48 I Golosi
23 Il Cortile
20 Inter-Continental
45 Intercontinental Le Grand Hôtel
53 Istria

J - K

31 Jacques Cagna
58 Jamin
50 Janissaire

42 Jardin
60 Jardin d'Ampère
20 Jardin d'Hiver (Le)
45 Jardin des Muses
34 Jardins d'Eiffel (Les)
55 Jardins Plein Ciel
50 Jean-Pierre Frelet
35 Jules Verne
51 Justine
33 K+K Hotel Cayré
44 Kinugawa

L

48 L'Hermitage
55 La Bonne Table (A)
60 La Fayette
46 Lafayette
37 Lancaster
31 Lapérouse
42 Lasserre
64 Laumière
42 Laurent
40 Lavoisier
35 Le Divellec
41 Ledoyen
29 Left Bank St-Germain
52 Lenox Montparnasse
33 Lenox Saint-Germain
63 Léon (Chez)
47 Libertel-Caumartin
53 Lilas Blanc
25 Little Palace
28 Littré
34 Londres Eiffel
21 Louvre
42 Lucas Carton
44 Luna
25 Lutèce
27 Lutétia
24 Lyonnais (Aux)

M

23 Macéo
28 Madison
61 Magellan
43 Maison Blanche
54 Maison Courtine
56 Majestic
29 Manoir St-Germain-des-Prés (Au)
21 Mansart
27 Mansouria
49 Manufacture
25 Marais Bastille
43 Marcande
42 Marée (La)
70 Marée de Versailles (La)
44 Marius et Janette
45 Market
38 Marriott
31 Marty
36 Maupertu
31 Mavrommatis
39 Meliá Royal Alma
21 Meliá Vendôme
67 Mercure
67 Mercure
70 Mercure
49 Mercure Gare de Lyon
64 Mercure Montmartre
47 Mercure Monty
53 Mercure Paris XV
52 Mercure Porte de Versailles
52 Mercure Raspail Montparnasse
46 Mercure Terminus Nord
52 Mercure Tour Eiffel
52 Mercure Tour Eiffel Suffren
61 Mercure Wagram Arc de Triomphe
60 Méridien Étoile
51 Méridien Montparnasse
20 Meurice
22 Meurice (Le)
62 Michel Rostang
67 Millenium
45 Millennium Opéra
29 Millésime Hôtel
40 Monna Lisa
39 Montaigne
33 Montalembert
53 Montparnasse 25
64 Moulin de la Galette
34 Muguet
24 Murano
47 Muses (Les)

N

39 Napoléon
36 New Jawad
22 Noailles
30 Notre Dame
52 Nouvel Orléans
68 Novotel
68 Novotel
49 Novotel Bercy
70 Novotel Château de Versailles
49 Novotel Gare de Lyon
66 Novotel La Défense
22 Novotel Les Halles
60 Novotel Porte d'Asnières
51 Novotel Tour Eiffel
52 Novotel Vaugirard

O

43 Obélisque (L')
30 Odéon Hôtel
48 Oenothèque (L')
36 Olivades (Les)
47 Opéra Cadet
60 Orenoc (L')
65 Oriental (L')
35 Ormes (Les)
33 Orsay (D')
59 Oscar
50 Oulette (L')

P

36 P'tit Troquet
57 Palais de Chaillot (Au)
23 Palais Royal
26 Pamphlet
62 Paolo Petrini
31 Paris
49 Paris Bastille
47 Paris-Est
30 Pas de Calais
58 Passiflore
57 Passy Eiffel
59 Paul Chêne
23 Pauline (Chez)
38 Pavillon
24 Pavillon de la Reine
46 Pavillon de Paris
22 Pavillon Louvre Rivoli
40 Pavillon Montaigne
54 Pavillon Montsouris
56 Pergolèse, 3 rue Pergolèse (Hotel)
58 Pergolèse, 40 rue Pergolèse (Rest.)
40 Pershing Hall
21 Petit Céladon
62 Petit Colombier
50 Petit Marguery
48 Petit Riche (Au)
48 Petite Sirène de Copenhague
54 Petites Sorcières (Les)
35 Pétrossian
62 Pétrus
24 Pied de Cochon (Au)
23 Pierre au Palais Royal
42 Pierre Gagnaire
30 Pierre Nicole
24 Pierrot
24 Pinxo
37 Plaza Athénée
21 Plaza Paris Vendôme
33 Pont Royal
58 Port Alma
70 Potager du Roy (Le)
65 Poulbot Gourmet
48 Pré Cadet
59 Pré Catelan
50 Pressoir (Au)
30 Prince de Conti

Q

60 Quality Pierre
40 Queen Mary
50 Quincy

R

40 Radisson SAS Champs Élysées
55 Raphael
55 Régalade

30 Régent
60 Regent's Garden
21 Regina
34 Relais Bosquet
28 Relais Christine
58 Relais d'Auteuil
53 Relais de Sèvres
64 Relais des Buttes
47 Relais du Pré
31 Relais Louis XIII
28 Relais Médicis
44 Relais Plaza
28 Relais St-Germain
30 Relais St-Jacques
29 Relais St-Sulpice
66 Renaissance
27 Repaire de Cartouche
56 Résidence Bassano (La)
70 Résidence du Berry (La)
29 Résidence Henri IV
46 Richmond Opéra
20 Ritz
29 Rives de Notre-Dame (Les)
64 Roma Sacré Coeur
32 Rotonde
37 Royal Monceau
21 Royal St-Honoré
29 Royal St-Michel

S

37 Safran
67 Saisons (Les)
55 Salle à Manger
31 Salon
38 San Régis
45 Scribe
48 16 Haussmann
30 Select
55 Severo
67 Sheraton
40 Signatures (Les)
59 6 New-York
68 Sofitel
38 Sofitel Arc de Triomphe
56 Sofitel Baltimore
21 Sofitel Castille
66 Sofitel Centre
40 Sofitel Champs-Élysées
68 Sofitel Château de Versailles
66 Sofitel Grande Arche
56 Sofitel Le Parc
49 Sofitel Paris Bercy
51 Sofitel Porte de Sèvres
62 Sormani
63 Soupière
60 Splendid Étoile
44 Spoon
56 Square
34 St-Germain
30 St-Germain-des-Prés
30 St-Jacques
56 St-James Paris
46 St-Pétersbourg
61 Star Hôtel Étoile
29 Ste-Beuve
44 Stella Maris
21 Stendhal
55 Stéphane Martin
44 Stresa
51 Sukhothaï

T

58 Table de Joël Robuchon (La)
58 Table du Baltimore (La)
43 Table du Lancaster (La)
41 Taillevent
59 Tang
48 Terminus Nord
63 Terrass'Hôtel
60 Terrasse
60 Terrasse (La)
37 Terrasse d'Été
22 Terrasse Fleurie
22 Thérèse
62 Timgad
31 Tour d'Argent
34 Tour Eiffel Invalides
29 Tour Notre-Dame
50 Touring Hôtel Magendie
33 Tourville
50 Train Bleu
50 Traversière
39 Trémoille
68 Trianon Palace

56 Trocadero Dokhan's
70 Trois Marches (Les)
47 Trois Poussins
55 Troquet
50 Trou Gascon (Au)
31 Truffière (La)

U - V

20 Vendôme
37 Vernet
33 Verneuil
70 Versailles (Le)
27 Victoria Palace
40 Vignon
61 Villa Alessandra
25 Villa Beaumarchais
29 Villa des Artistes
61 Villa des Ternes
61 Villa Eugénie
56 Villa Maillot (La)
46 Villa Opéra Drouot
29 Villa Panthéon
46 Villa Royale
52 Villa Royale Montsouris
45 Village d'Ung et Li Lam
26 Vin et Marée
35 Vin sur Vin
59 Vinci (Le)
35 Violon d'Ingres

W - X

43 W (Le)
34 Walt
38 Warwick
21 Washington Opéra
21 Westminster
57 Windsor Home

Y - Z

32 Yen
32 Yugaraj
32 Ze Kitchen Galerie
56 Zébra Square

HOTELS, RESTAURANTS

Listed by districts and arrondissements

(List of Hotels and Restaurants in alphabetical order, see pp 13 to 21)

G 12: These reference letters and numbers correspond to the squares on the Michelin maps : **plan Michelin Paris** no **54**. **Paris avec répertoire** no **55**. **Paris du Nord au Sud** no **56** et **Paris par Arrondissement** no **57**.

Consult any of the above publications when looking for a car park nearest to a listed establishment.

Opéra, Palais-Royal, Halles, Bourse.

1st and 2nd arrondissements.

1st: ✉ 75001

2nd: ✉ 75002

Ritz, 15 pl. Vendôme (1st) Ⓜ *Opéra* ✆ 01 43 16 30 30, *resa@ritzparis.com, Fax 01 43 16 36 68,* – 30 - 80. AE GB JCB. G 12
see ***L'Espadon*** below - ***Bar Vendôme*** : **Meals** a la carte 70/100 – 62 – **106 rm** 680/770, 56 suites.
◆ It was in 1898 that César Ritz inaugurated the "perfect hotel" of his dreams. Valentino, Proust, Hemingway and Coco Chanel have all stayed here. Matchless refinement. Superb swimming pool. The chic Bar Vendôme has a delightful terrace and serves afternoon tea.

Meurice, 228 r. Rivoli (1st) Ⓜ *Tuileries* ✆ 01 44 58 10 10, *reservations@meuricehotel.com, Fax 01 44 58 10 15,* – 40 - 70. AE GB JCB. rest G 12
see ***Le Meurice*** below - ***Le Jardin d'Hiver*** ✆ 01 44 58 10 44 **Meals** 50 – 45 – **121 rm** 600/800, 39 suites.
◆ One of the very first luxury hotels, founded in 1817 and turned into a palace in 1907. Sumptuous rooms and a superb top-floor suite with a staggering view over the city. Lovely Art Nouveau glass canopy and innumerable exotic plants in the Jardin d'Hiver.

Inter-Continental, 3 r. Castiglione (1st) Ⓜ *Tuileries* ✆ 01 44 77 11 11, *paris@interconti.com, Fax 01 44 77 14 60,* – 15 - 350. AE GB JCB G 12
234 Rivoli ✆ 01 44 77 10 40 **Meals** 35 – ***Terrasse Fleurie*** ✆ 01 44 77 10 40 *(May-September)* **Meals** a la carte 40/69 – 36,50 – **405 rm** 540/610, 33 suites.
◆ Splendid hotel of 1878 with rooms in all the styles of the 19C, some with a view of the Tuileries. Sumptuous Napoleon III-style lounges. Smart, convivial ambience at 234 Rivoli. Escape the clamour of the city in the Terrasse Fleurie facing the courtyard.

Costes, 239 r. St-Honoré (1st) Ⓜ *Concorde* ✆ 01 42 44 50 00, *hotel.costes@wanadoo.fr, Fax 01 42 44 50 01,* AE GB JCB G 12
Meals a la carte 50/85 – 30 – **76 rm** 350/600, 3 suites, 3 duplex.
◆ Revived Napoleon III-style in the gilt and purple bedrooms, delightful Italian courtyard and splendid leisure centre in this sumptuous palace, a favourite with the jet-set. The hotel restaurant is a stronghold of up-to-the-minute cuisine.

Vendôme without rest, 1 pl. Vendôme (1st) Ⓜ *Opéra* ✆ 01 55 04 55 00, *reservations@hoteldevendome.com, Fax 01 49 27 97 89* – AE GB JCB. G 12
30 – **19 rm** 480/610, 10 suites.
◆ The Place Vendôme is a fine setting for this 18C town mansion with its antique furnishings, marble, and up-to-the-minute facilities.

Plaza Paris Vendôme, 4 r. Mont-Thabor (1st) Ⓜ *Tuileries* ☎ 01 40 20 20 00, *reservations@plazaparisvendome.com, Fax 01 40 20 20 01,* – AE GB JCB G 12
see ***Pinxo*** below – ☕ 36 – **85 rm** 460/560, 12 suites.
◆ A 19C building transformed into a chic and refined modern hotel. Wood, beige and chocolate tones, and high-tech equipment in the bedrooms. Attractive Chinese bar.

Sofitel Castille, 33 r. Cambon (1st) Ⓜ *Madeleine* ☎ 01 44 58 44 58, *reservations@castille.com, Fax 01 44 58 44 00,* – 30. AE GB JCB G 12
see ***Il Cortile*** below – ☕ 28 – **86 rm** 475/600, 7 suites, 14 duplex.
◆ On the Opéra side, warm Italian Renaissance-style décor, smarter French ambience on the Rue de Rivoli side, enhanced by works by the famous 20C photographer Robert Doisneau.

Louvre, pl. A. Malraux (1st) Ⓜ *Palais Royal* ☎ 01 44 58 38 38, *hoteldulouvre@hoteldulouvre.com, Fax 01 44 58 38 01,* – 20 - 80. AE GB JCB. H 13
Brasserie Le Louvre ☎ 01 42 96 27 98 – **Meals** 33 🍷 – ☕ 21 – **170 rm** 450, 7 suites.
◆ Picasso stayed here, in what was one of the city's first grand hotels. Unique view from some rooms of the Avenue de l'Opéra and the Palais Garnier. In the Brasserie Le Louvre, both the cuisine and the turn-of-the-century décor pay homage to tradition.

Westminster, 13 r. Paix (2nd) Ⓜ *Opéra* ☎ 01 42 61 57 46, *resa.westminster@warwickhotels.com, Fax 01 42 60 30 66,* – 15 - 40. AE GB JCB G 12
see ***Céladon*** below - ***Petit Céladon*** (weekend only) *(closed August)* **Meals** 48 b.i. – ☕ 28 – **80 rm** 420/570, 21 suites.
◆ Once a convent, then a post hotel, this establishment took on the name of its celebrated ducal guest in 1846. Sumptuous bedrooms, luxurious apartments. At weekends, the Céladon becomes the Petit Céladon with a limited menu and informal service.

Royal St-Honoré without rest, 221 r. St-Honoré (1st) Ⓜ *Tuileries* ☎ 01 42 60 32 79, *rsh@hroy.com, Fax 01 42 60 47 44* – 15. AE GB JCB.
☕ 20 – **65 rm** 290/360, 5 suites. G 12
◆ This 19C edifice was built on the site of the old Hôtel de Noailles. Individual, very refined rooms. Louis XVI décor in the breakfast room.

Edouard VII, 39 av. Opéra (2nd) Ⓜ *Opéra* ☎ 01 42 61 56 90, *info@edouard7hotel.com, Fax 01 42 61 47 73* – rm, – 15 - 25. AE GB JCB G 13
Angl'Opéra ☎ 01 42 61 86 25 **Meals** 38/50 – ☕ 22 – **65 rm** 390/492, 4 suites.
◆ This was where the future Edward VII stayed when still Prince of Wales. Spacious, luxurious rooms. Dark panelling and stained-glass in the bar. Enjoy fusion-style cuisine in the modern, welcoming Angl Opéra restaurant.

Regina, 2 pl. Pyramides (1st) Ⓜ *Tuileries* ☎ 01 42 60 31 10, *reservation@regina-hotel.com, Fax 01 40 15 95 16,* – 20 - 60. AE GB JCB H 13
Meals *(closed August, Saturday, Sunday and Bank Holidays)* 40 🍷 – ☕ 28 – **116 rm** 335/455, 14 suites.
◆ Built in 1900, this hotel has kept its superb Art Nouveau foyer. Rooms filled with antique furnishings. Those on the patio side are quieter. Some with view of Eiffel Tower. Dining room with splendid fireplace, and a much appreciated courtyard in summer.

Meliá Vendôme without rest, 8 r. Cambon (1st) Ⓜ *Concorde* ☎ 01 44 77 54 00, *melia.vendome@solmelia.com, Fax 01 44 77 54 01* – 20. AE GB JCB. G 12
☕ 25 – **83 rm** 335/458.
◆ Opulent decor, stylish furniture and a hushed atmosphere dominate the recently refurbished rooms here. The elegant lounge is crowned by a Belle Époque glass roof.

Washington Opéra without rest, 50 r. Richelieu (1st) Ⓜ *Palais Royal* ☎ 01 42 96 68 06, *hotel@washingtonopera.com, Fax 01 40 15 01 12* – AE GB JCB. G 13
☕ 15 – **36 rm** 215/275.
◆ This old town mansion was once owned by Mme de Pompadour. Rooms with historic décor. Sixth-floor terrace with a lovely view over the garden of the Palais-Royal.

Stendhal without rest, 22 r. D. Casanova (2nd) Ⓜ *Opéra* ☎ 01 44 58 52 52, *h1610@accor-hotels.com, Fax 01 44 58 52 00* – AE GB JCB. G 12
☕ 17,50 – **20 rm** 281/305.
◆ Follow in the footsteps of the famous writer and stay in the "Rouge et Noir" suite of this characterful establishment. The refined rooms are all decorated in two colours.

Mansart without rest, 5 r. Capucines (1st) Ⓜ *Opéra* ☎ 01 42 61 50 28, *hotel.mansart@esprit-de-france.com, Fax 01 49 27 97 44* – AE GB JCB. G 12
☕ 10 – **57 rm** 127/300.
◆ This hotel has been renovated in a style that pays tribute to Louis XIV's architect, Mansart. Elegant rooms with Empire or Directoire furniture. Contemporary-style lounge.

L'Horset Opéra without rest, 18 r. d'Antin (2nd) Ⓜ *Opéra* ☎ 01 44 71 87 00, *loper a@paris-hotels-charm.com, Fax 01 42 66 55 54* – AE ⓓ GB JCB G 13
54 rm ☕ 230/260.
◆ Warm colours and light-wood furnishings characterise the spacious rooms of this traditional hotel close to the Opéra. Cosy atmosphere in the lounge.

Novotel Les Halles, 8 pl. M.-de-Navarre (1st) Ⓜ *Châtelet* ☎ 01 42 21 31 31, *h0785 @accor-hotels.com, Fax 01 40 26 05 79* – – 15 - 20. AE ⓓ GB JCB H 14
Meals a la carte approx. 30 🍷 – ☕ 15,50 – **271 rm** 228/282, 14 suites.
◆ Close to the Forum des Halles, this well-soundproofed hotel is up to the usual Novotel standards. Some rooms have been renovated and some have a view of the Church of St-Eustache. Palm-trees lend an exotic touch to the restaurant beneath its huge glass roof.

États-Unis Opéra without rest, 16 r. d'Antin (2nd) Ⓜ *Opéra* ☎ 01 42 65 05 05, *us-opera@wanadoo.fr, Fax 01 42 65 93 70* – – 25. AE ⓓ GB JCB. G 13
☕ 10 – **45 rm** 125/195.
◆ This hotel built in the 1930s offers a range of comfortable rooms renovated in modern style, some with period furniture.

Noailles without rest, 9 r. Michodière (2nd) Ⓜ *4 Septembre* ☎ 01 47 42 92 90, *golde ntulip.denoailles@wanadoo.fr, Fax 01 49 24 92 71,* – – 20. AE ⓓ GB JCB G 13
☕ 15 – **61 rm** 225/285.
◆ Resolutely contemporary elegance behind a sober old façade. Japanese-style décor in the spacious rooms, most of which overlook an attractive patio.

Thérèse without rest, 5-7 r. Thérèse (1st) Ⓜ *Pyramides* ☎ 01 42 96 10 01, *hotelthe rese@wanadoo.fr, Fax 01 42 96 15 22* – AE ⓓ GB JCB. G 13
☕ 12 – **43 rm** 134/210.
◆ Sober and refined decor in a modern style lightened with exotic touches, in this entirely renovated building. Charming rooms and breakfast room with vaulted ceiling.

Pavillon Louvre Rivoli without rest, 20 r. Molière (1st) Ⓜ *Pyramides* ☎ 01 42 60 31 20, *louvre@leshotelsdeparis.com, Fax 01 42 60 32 06* – . AE ⓓ GB JCB G 13
☕ 14 – **29 rm** 190/270.
◆ Well located between the Opéra and the Louvre, this comprehensively modernised hotel will please both art-lovers and shopaholics. Small but bright and colourful rooms.

Le Meurice - Hôtel Meurice, 228 r. Rivoli (1st) Ⓜ *Tuileries* ☎ 01 44 58 10 55, *restau ration@meuricehotel.com, Fax 01 44 58 10 15* – AE ⓓ GB JCB. G 12
✿✿
closed 1 to 29 August, Saturday lunch, Sunday and Monday – **Meals** 75 (lunch), 170/300 b.i. and a la carte 125/186 🍷
Spec. Petits ormeaux en fricassée, polenta coulante aux haricots blancs. Turbot rôti sur l'os à moelle. Millefeuille vanille, café, chocolat..
◆ 18C-style dining room directly inspired by the Grands Appartements of the Chateau of Versailles. Fine contemporary cuisine fit for a king !

L'Espadon - Hôtel Ritz, 15 pl. Vendôme (1st) Ⓜ *Opéra* ☎ 01 43 16 30 80, *food-bev@ ritzparis.com, Fax 01 43 16 33 75,* – AE ⓓ GB JCB. G 12
✿
closed 8 to 30 August – **Meals** 68 (lunch)/180 and a la carte 115/170 🍷
Spec. Tronçon de turbot aux cinq sauces. Lièvre à la royale (October-January). Soufflé au chocolat "tradition Ritz"..
◆ A foyer drenched in gilt and drapes, dazzling décor celebrating many famous guests, an attractive terrace and well-planted garden, altogether a very ritzy establishment.

Grand Vefour, 17 r. Beaujolais (1st) Ⓜ *Palais Royal* ☎ 01 42 96 56 27, *grand.vefour @wanadoo.fr, Fax 01 42 86 80 71* – AE ⓓ GB JCB. G 13
✿✿✿
closed 25 to 30 April, 1 to 29 August, 26 December-1 January, Friday dinner, Saturday and Sunday – **Meals** 75 (lunch)/255 and a la carte 172/204
Spec. Ravioles de foie gras à l'émulsion de crème truffée. Parmentier de queue de boeuf aux truffes. Palet noisette et chocolat au lait..
◆ In the Palais-Royal gardens, sumptuous late 18C interiors with splendid figures painted on glass pillars. Inspired, inventive cuisine worthy of a great historical monument.

Carré des Feuillants (Dutournier), 14 r. Castiglione (1st) Ⓜ *Tuileries* ☎ 01 42 86 82 82, *carre.des.feuillants@wanadoo.fr, Fax 01 42 86 07 71* – AE ⓓ GB JCB G 12
✿✿
closed August, Saturday and Sunday – **Meals** 65 (lunch)/150 and a la carte 110/155
Spec. Cèpes marinés, chapeau poêlé et pied en petit pâté chaud (Autumn). Noix de lotte en croûte de pomme de terre, caviar, fumet au raifort (Autumn-Winter). Chocolat noir fondant, chicorée mousseuse, moka en crème brûlée..
◆ This restaurant on the site of an old convent has a decidedly contemporary new look. Inventive cuisine with a Gascon touch. Impressive wine list.

Drouant, pl. Gaillon (2nd) Ⓜ *4 Septembre* ✆ 01 42 65 15 16, *drouantrv@elior.com, Fax 01 49 24 02 15* – AE GB JCB G 13
closed August, Saturday and Sunday – **Meals** see also ***Café Drouant*** 56 (lunch)/104 and a la carte 108/140
Spec. Ravioles d'oeuf de poule au coulis de truffe. Saint-Jacques à la coque au beurre demi-sel (October-May). Coeur de filet "Angus" poêlé, compote de queue de boeuf, pomme soufflées..
◆ Little Art Deco interiors around a majestic staircase designed by Jacques-Emile Ruhlmann. The Prix Goncourt jury has met in the Louis XVI room since 1914.

Goumard, 9 r. Duphot (1st) Ⓜ *Madeleine* ✆ 01 42 60 36 07, *goumard.philippe@wanadoo.fr, Fax 01 42 60 04 54* – AE GB JCB G 12
Meals 46 and a la carte 82/140
Spec. Langoustines du Guilvinec rôties (April-November). Tronçon de turbot de ligne, coques, jus iodé. Sorbet cacao amer, allumettes au chocolat..
◆ Intimate Art Deco interiors graced with seascape paintings. The original toilets designed by Louis Majorelle have survived and are well worth a look. Fine seafood.

Gérard Besson, 5 r. Coq Héron (1st) Ⓜ *Louvre Rivoli* ✆ 01 42 33 14 74, *gerard.besson4@libertysurf.fr, Fax 01 42 33 85 71* – AE GB JCB H 14
closed 1 to 8 May, 1 to 21 August, Monday lunch, Saturday lunch and Sunday – **Meals** 52 (lunch)/105 and a la carte 96/118
Spec. Fricassée de homard "Georges Garin". Carte de truffes (15 December-15 March). Gibier (season)..
◆ Just a step from Les Halles, an elegant and luxurious restaurant enhanced by beige tones, still-life paintings and Jouy fabrics. Classic cuisine with a contemporary touch.

Céladon - Hôtel Westminster, 15 r. Daunou (2nd) Ⓜ *Opéra* ✆ 01 47 03 40 42, *christophemoisand@leceladon.com, Fax 01 42 61 33 78* – AE GB JCB G 12
closed August, Saturday, Sunday and Bank Holidays – **Meals** 51 b.i. (lunch)/66 and a la carte 85/125
Spec. Pâté froid de lapin de garenne (15 September-15 January). Saint-Pierre rôti au beurre d'escargot. Soufflé williamine..
◆ Superb dining rooms with a décor featuring early 18C furniture, willow-green ("céladon") walls, and a collection of Chinese porcelain. Contemporary cuisine.

Il Cortile - Hôtel Sofitel Castille, 37 r. Cambon (1st) Ⓜ *Madeleine* ✆ 01 44 58 45 67, *ilcortile@castille.com, Fax 01 44 58 45 69,* – AE GB JCB G 12
closed 2 to 22 August, Saturday, Sunday and Bank Holidays – **Meals** 85 and a la carte 58/74
Spec. Risotto moelleux aux cèpes (September-December). Maltagliati à l'encre de seiche, coquillages. Souris d'agneau confit, rôti à la broche..
◆ A Villa d'Este of a dining room and a pretty tiled patio provide a fine setting for refined Italian cuisine. Enthusiastic service.

Fontaine Gaillon, pl. Gaillon (2nd) Ⓜ *4 Septembre* ✆ 01 47 42 63 22, *Fax 01 47 42 82 84,* – AE GB G 13
closed August, Saturday and Sunday – **Meals** 38 (lunch) and a la carte 50/61.
◆ Famous film stars Carole Bouquet and Gérard Depardieu are behind this elegant restaurant housed in a 17C private mansion, where the culinary emphasis is on fish and seafood.

Macéo, 15 r. Petits-Champs (1st) Ⓜ *Bourse* ✆ 01 42 97 53 85, *info@maceorestaurant.com, Fax 01 47 03 36 93* – GB. G 13
closed 8 to 21 August, Saturday lunch and Sunday – **Meals** 30/35 and a la carte 40/60.
◆ Striking fusion of Second Empire decor and contemporary furnishings. Inventive cuisine, vegetarian specialities and wines from around the world. Convivial lounge/bar.

Pierre au Palais Royal, 10 r. Richelieu (1st) Ⓜ *Palais Royal* ✆ 01 42 96 09 17, *pierreaupalaisroyal@wanadoo.fr, Fax 01 42 96 26 40* – . AE GB H 13
closed Saturday lunch and Sunday – **Meals** 28/35 and a la carte 40/50.
◆ Aubergine tones, artwork featuring the nearby Palais-Royal and attractively laid tables make up the simple, attractive decor of this restaurant serving seasonal cuisine.

Palais Royal, 110 Galerie de Valois - Jardin du Palais Royal (1st) Ⓜ *Bourse* ✆ 01 40 20 00 27, *palaisrest@aol.com, Fax 01 40 20 00 82,* – AE GB G 13
closed 20 December-15 January and Sunday – **Meals** a la carte 50/67.
◆ Beneath the windows of the flat where Colette once lived, a restaurant in Art Deco style with an idyllic terrace opening onto the gardens of the Palais-Royal.

Chez Pauline, 5 r. Villédo (1st) Ⓜ *Pyramides* ✆ 01 42 96 20 70, *chezpauline@wanadoo.fr, Fax 01 49 27 99 89* – . AE GB G 13
closed Saturday except dinner in July-August – **Meals** 35 (lunch)/42 and a la carte 46/85.
◆ In a quiet little street, this comfortable establishment has the character of an early 20C bistro. The first floor room is more intimate. Classic cuisine.

Café Drouant, pl. Galion (2nd) Ⓜ *4 Septembre* ✆ 01 42 65 15 16, *Fax 01 49 24 02 15,* – ▤ ☞. AE ⓓ GB JCB G 13
closed August, Saturday and Sunday – **Meals** a la carte 41/85 ♀.
◆ The little brother of the Restaurant Drouant offers seafood and "riff-raff" dishes beneath an unusual ceiling of silvered hair and plaster decorated with denizens of the deep.

Cabaret, 2 pl. Palais Royal (1st) Ⓜ *Palais Royal* ✆ 01 58 62 56 25, *Fax 01 58 62 56 40* – ▤ ☞ (dinner). AE GB. ✈ H 13
closed 1 to 22 August and Sunday – **Meals** (dinner only) a la carte 42/62 ♀.
◆ The basement has unusual décor featuring Indian drapes and African bar. At half-past midnight the restaurant becomes a club, much favoured by the "beautiful people".

Au Pied de Cochon (24 hr service), 6 r. Coquillière (1st) Ⓜ *Châtelet-Les Halles* ✆ 01 40 13 77 00, *de.pied-de-cochon@blanc.net, Fax 01 40 13 77 09,* – ▤. AE ⓓ GB – **Meals** a la carte 40/65 ♀. H 14
◆ The "Pig's Trotter" has been famous ever since its opening in 1946, not least for catering for night-owls. Unusual frescoes and chandeliers with fruit motifs.

Gallopin, 40 r. N.-D.-des Victoires (2nd) Ⓜ *Bourse* ✆ 01 42 36 45 38, *administration@brasseriegallopin.com, Fax 01 42 36 10 32* – ▤. AE ⓓ GB G 14
Meals 28/33,50 b.i. and a la carte 34/53 ♀.
◆ Together with its elaborate Victorian décor, Arletty and Raimu have contributed to the fame of this brasserie opposite the Palais Brongniart. Lovely glass canopy to the rear.

Chez Georges, 1 r. Mail (2nd) Ⓜ *Bourse* ✆ 01 42 60 07 11 – AE GB G 14
closed 29 July-19 August, Sunday and Bank Holidays – **Meals** a la carte 45/67.
◆ Full of the atmosphere of the Paris of 1900, this bistro is a local institution, with its traditional décor of zinc counter, benches, plasterwork and mirrors.

Pinxo - Hôtel Plaza Paris Vendôme, 9 r. Alger (1st) Ⓜ *Tuileries* ✆ 01 40 20 72 00, *Fax 01 40 20 72 02* – ▤ ☞. AE GB G 12
closed August – **Meals** a la carte 42/65.
◆ Stylish furniture, a black and white colour scheme and an open-view kitchen provide a simple yet chic backdrop for Alain Dutournier's excellent tapas creations.

Aux Lyonnais, 32 r. St-Marc (2nd) Ⓜ *Richelieu Drouot* ✆ 01 42 96 65 04, *auxlyonnais@online.fr, Fax 01 42 97 42 95* – AE GB F 14
closed 24 July-22 August, 24 December-3 January, Saturday lunch, Sunday and Monday – **Meals** (booking essential) 28 and a la carte 40/57.
◆ The bistro, founded in 1890, serves tasty Lyonnaise dishes which have a subtly modern touch, but still fit the delightfully retro style of the banquettes, mirrors and zinc bar.

Pierrot, 18 r. Étienne Marcel (2nd) Ⓜ *Etienne Marcel* ✆ 01 45 08 00 10 – ▤. AE GB H 15
closed 1 to 25 August, 25 December-4 January and Sunday – **Meals** a la carte 30/45 ♀.
◆ In the busy heart of the Sentier area, this cheerful bistro offers diners the authentic flavours of the Aveyron area. Small outdoor dining area in summer.

Bastille, République, Hôtel de Ville.

3rd, 4th and 11th arrondissements.
3rd: ✉ 75003
4th: ✉ 75004
11th: ✉ 75011

Pavillon de la Reine without rest, 28 pl. Vosges (3rd) Ⓜ *Bastille* ✆ 01 40 29 19 19, *contact@pavillon-de-la-reine.com, Fax 01 40 29 19 20* – ▤ TV – 25. AE ⓓ GB JCB J 17
25 – **31 rm** 385/495, 15 suites, 10 duplex.
◆ To the rear of one of the 36 brick mansions in the Place des Vosges, two buildings (one dating from the 17C) with refined rooms overlooking a courtyard or private garden.

Murano, 13 bd Temple (3rd) Ⓜ *Filles du Calvaire* ✆ 01 42 71 20 00, *paris@muranoresort.com, Fax 01 42 71 21 01,* – ▤ TV H 17
Meals a la carte 38/68 – 28 – **48 rm** 400/650, 4 suites.
◆ A new boutique hotel which sets itself apart with its immaculate designer decor and colour scheme, high-tech equipment, pop-art bar (150 brands of vodka) etc. Bright contemporary ambience in the restaurant, serving cuisine from around the globe. In-house DJ.

Holiday Inn, 10 pl. République (11th) Ⓜ *République* ☎ 01 43 14 43 50, *holiday.inn.paris.republique@ichotelsgroup.com, Fax 01 47 00 32 34,* – 25 - 150. AE GB JCB. rest G 17
Meals 17 (lunch)/35 – 22 – **318 rm** 215/245.
• In this fine 19C building a listed wrought-iron staircase leads to functional rooms, the best of which overlook the Napoleon III-style inner courtyard. The convivial atmosphere at the Belle Époque-style restaurant is enhanced by the pleasant veranda-terrace.

Villa Beaumarchais without rest, 5 r. Arquebusiers (3rd) Ⓜ *Chemin Vert* ☎ 01 40 29 14 00, *beaumarchais@leshotelsdeparis.com, Fax 01 40 29 14 01* – – 15. AE GB H 17
26 – **50 rm** 380/480.
• Well set-back from the bustle of the Boulevard Beaumarchais, this hotel has refined rooms with gilt furniture, all overlooking a pretty winter garden. Beneath its glass roof, the restaurant is drenched in greenery.

Bourg Tibourg without rest, 19 r. Bourg Tibourg (4th) Ⓜ *Hôtel de Ville* ☎ 01 42 78 47 39, *hotel@bourgtibourg.com, Fax 01 40 29 07 00* – . AE GB JCB. J 16
12 – **31 rm** 150/250.
• This charming hotel offers attractive refurbished rooms in a variety of styles - neo-Gothic, Baroque, or Oriental. A little gem in the heart of the Marais district.

Caron de Beaumarchais without rest, 12 r. Vieille-du-Temple (4th) Ⓜ *Hôtel de Ville* ☎ 01 42 72 34 12, *hotel@carondebeaumarchais.com, Fax 01 42 72 34 63* – . AE GB. J 16
9,80 – **19 rm** 152.
• The creator of Figaro lived in this historic street in the Marais quarter, and the décor of this charming establishment pays homage to him. Comfortable little rooms.

Little Palace, 4 r. Salomon de Caus (3rd) Ⓜ *Réaumur Sébastopol* ☎ 01 42 72 08 15, *info@littlepalacehotel.com, Fax 01 42 72 45 81* – . AE GB JCB
Meals *(closed August, 20 December-1 January, Friday dinner, Saturday and Sunday)* a la carte 25/35 – 12 – **49 rm** 140/156, 4 suites. G 15
• This early-20C building on a charming small square has enjoyed a recent facelift. Pleasant modern bedrooms - the best are on the 5th and 6th floors - with balconies and city views. Attractive wood panelling, light tones and refined furniture in the restaurant.

Général without rest, 5 r. Rampon (11th) Ⓜ *République* ☎ 01 47 00 41 57, *info@leg eneralhotel.com, Fax 01 47 00 21 56,* – . AE GB JCB G 17
12 – **47 rm** 150/220.
• Elegant decor and designer furniture add style to this exquisite hotel near place de la République. Wi-Fi technology, small business centre and pleasant fitness area.

Bretonnerie without rest, 22 r. Ste-Croix-de-la-Bretonnerie (4th) Ⓜ *Hôtel de Ville* ☎ 01 48 87 77 63, *hotel@bretonnerie.com, Fax 01 42 77 26 78* – . GB.
9,50 – **22 rm** 110/145, 4 suites, 3 duplex. J 16
• Some of the rooms in this elegant town mansion in the Marais district have canopied beds and exposed beams. Vaulted breakfast room.

Austin's without rest, 6 r. Montgolfier (3rd) Ⓜ *Arts et Métiers* ☎ 01 42 77 17 61, *austins.amhotel@wanadoo.fr, Fax 01 42 77 55 43* – . AE GB JCB. G 16
7 – **29 rm** 96/130.
• Situated in a quiet street opposite the Arts et Métiers museum. The rooms have been recently redecorated in a warm and bright style, some of them with original beams intact.

Marais Bastille without rest, 36 bd Richard Lenoir (11th) Ⓜ *Bréguet Sabin* ☎ 01 48 05 75 00, *maraisbastille@wanadoo.fr, Fax 01 43 57 42 85* – . AE GB JCB J18
10 – **36 rm** 130.
• The hotel faces onto the boulevard that has covered the Canal St-Martin since 1860. A renovated interior, with leather armchairs and oak furniture in the bedrooms.

Beaubourg without rest, 11 r. S. Le Franc (4th) Ⓜ *Rambuteau* ☎ 01 42 74 34 24, *htlbeaubourg@hotellerie.net, Fax 01 42 78 68 11* – . AE GB JCB.
7 – **28 rm** 110/140. H 15
• In a little street to the rear of the Pompidou Centre. Some of the welcoming and well-soundproofed rooms have exposed beams and stonework.

Lutèce without rest, 65 r. St-Louis-en-l'Ile (4th) Ⓜ *Pont Marie* ☎ 01 43 26 23 52, *hotel.lutece@free.fr, Fax 01 43 29 60 25* – . AE GB. K 16
11 – **23 rm** 164.
• The rustic charm of this hotel on the Ile-St-Louis is particularly appreciated by American visitors. Attractive, fairly quiet rooms. Fine antique wood panelling in the lounge.

Croix de Malte without rest, 5 r. Malte (11th) Ⓜ *Oberkampf* ✆ 01 48 05 09 36, *h2752-gm@accor-hotels.com, Fax 01 42 09 48 12* – TV. AE GB JCB H 17
10 – **29 rm** 115/125.
◆ The tropical atmosphere in the Maltese Cross is provided by colourful furniture, a stuffed parrot and a breakfast room designed to resemble a winter garden.

Grand Hôtel Français without rest, 223 bd Voltaire (11th) Ⓜ *Nation* ✆ 01 43 71 27 57, *grand-hotel-francais@wanadoo.fr, Fax 01 43 48 40 05* – TV. AE GB JCB K 20
10 – **36 rm** 95/135.
◆ This Haussmann-style corner building stands in a typically Parisian working class district. Recently renovated functional rooms, albeit lacking in finery. Good sound-proofing.

Beaumarchais without rest, 3 r. Oberkampf (11th) Ⓜ *Oberkampf* ✆ 01 53 36 86 86, *reservation@hotelbeaumarchais.com, Fax 01 43 38 32 86* – TV. AE GB JCB H 17
10 – **29 rm** 75/110.
◆ Despite their smallness, the brightly colourful rooms furnished with modern furniture have retained a certain charm. Leafy internal courtyard which is welcome in summer.

L'Ambroisie (Pacaud), 9 pl. des Vosges (4th) Ⓜ *St-Paul* ✆ 01 42 78 51 45 – AE GB. J 17
closed August, February Holidays, Sunday and Monday – **Meals** a la carte 178/228
Spec. Feuillantine de langoustines aux graines de sésame. Agneau de Lozère en nougatine d'amandes.Tarte fine sablée au chocolat, glace vanille.
◆ Beneath the arcades of the Place des Vosges, princely décor and a subtle cuisine not far from perfection - was not Ambrosia the food of the gods ?

Ambassade d'Auvergne, 22 r. Grenier St-Lazare (3rd) Ⓜ *Rambuteau* ✆ 01 42 72 31 22, *info@ambassade-auvergne.com, Fax 01 42 78 85 47* – . GB JCB
Meals 28 and a la carte 31/46 ♀. H 15
◆ As good as its name, this establishment is an excellent ambassador for its province, with authentically Auverngat décor, furnishings, food and wine.

Bofinger, 5 r. Bastille (4th) Ⓜ *Bastille* ✆ 01 42 72 87 82, *eberne@groupeflo.fr, Fax 01 42 72 97 68* – . AE GB JCB J 17
Meals 33,50 b.i. (lunch) and a la carte 35/65 ♀.
◆ Illustrious guests and remarkable décor lend a special atmosphere to this brasserie founded in 1864. Delicate cupola, and, on the upper floor, an interior decorated by Hansi.

L'Aiguière, 37bis r. Montreuil (11th) Ⓜ *Faidherbe Chaligny* ✆ 01 43 72 42 32, *patrick-masbatin1@libertysurf.com, Fax 01 43 72 96 36* – . AE GB JCB K 20
closed Saturday lunch, Sunday and Bank Holidays – **Meals** 24 b.i./60 b.i. and a la carte 55/82 ♀.
◆ Shades of yellow and elegant fabrics provide the attractive decor for this restaurant with a collection of pitchers, hence the name. Seasonal cuisine plus a fine wine list.

Benoît, 20 r. St-Martin (4th) Ⓜ *Châtelet* ✆ 01 42 72 25 76, *Fax 01 42 72 45 68* – . AE J 15
closed August – **Meals** 38 (lunch) and a la carte 55/91 ♀
Spec. Tête de veau ravigote. Cassoulet aux cocos de Paimpol. Gibier (season)..
◆ Forget the fast-food joints all around ! Here is a smart and busy bistro run by the same family since 1912, who know all about serving up carefully prepared traditional food.

Pamphlet, 38 r. Debelleyme (3rd) Ⓜ *Filles du Calvaire* ✆ 01 42 72 39 24, *Fax 01 42 72 12 53* – . GB H 17
closed 1 to 8 May, 8 to 27 August, 1 to 15 January, Saturday lunch, Monday lunch and Sunday – **Meals** 30/45 ♀.
◆ Attractive restaurant situated in the heart of the Marais. Rustic decor enlivened with bright paint and bullfighting posters. Traditional cuisine, with dishes from SW France.

Vin et Marée, 276 bd Voltaire (11th) Ⓜ *Nation* ✆ 01 43 72 31 23, *vin.maree@wanadoo.fr, Fax 01 40 24 00 23* – . AE GB K 21
Meals a la carte 35/55 ♀.
◆ Like its siblings elsewhere, pride of place on the menu is given to fish and seafood. The room to the rear, with its maritime décor, offers views of the kitchens.

Le Dôme du Marais, 53 bis r. Francs-Bourgeois (4th) Ⓜ *Rambuteau* ✆ 01 42 74 54 17, *Fax 01 42 77 78 17* – AE GB H16 J16
closed 1 to 25 August, Sunday and Monday – **Meals** 23 (lunch)/29 and a la carte 39/61 ♀.
◆ The tables here are set out beneath the lovely dome above the hall of the old Crédit Municipal building as well as in an interior like a winter garden. Contemporary cuisine.

Mansouria, 11 r. Faidherbe (11th) Ⓜ *Faidherbe Chaligny* ✆ 01 43 71 00 16, *Fax 01 40 24 21 97* – ⇽⇾ ▤. GB. ✈ K 19
closed 9 to 15 August, Monday lunch, Tuesday lunch and Sunday – **Meals** 29/44 b.i. and a la carte 31/60.
◆ Run by a former ethnologist who is now one of the city's leading names in Moroccan cuisine. The fragrant dishes are prepared by women and served amid typically Moorish décor.

Repaire de Cartouche, 99 r. Amelot (11th) Ⓜ *St-Sébastien Froissart* ✆ 01 47 00 25 86, *Fax 01 43 38 85 91* – GB H 17
closed 2 to 8 May, 1 to 21 August, 6 to 12 February, Sunday and Monday – **Meals** 24 (lunch) and a la carte 34/45.
◆ The late-17C-early-18C bandit Cartouche took refuge nearby while undertaking his criminal activities : the frescoes retrace some of his exploits. Enticing wine-list.

Auberge Pyrénées Cévennes, 106 r. Folie-Méricourt (11th) Ⓜ *République* ✆ 01 43 57 33 78 – ▤. AE GB G 17
closed 29 July-22 August, 1 to 7 January, Saturday lunch and Sunday – **Meals** 27 and a la carte 40/64 ♀.
◆ Rows of hanging hams and sausages, chequered tablecloths and tables huddled close together characterise this friendly restaurant serving hearty, local cuisine.

Au Bascou, 38 r. Réaumur (3rd) Ⓜ *Arts et Métiers* ✆ 01 42 72 69 25, *Fax 01 42 72 69 25* – AE GB G 16
closed 1 to 29 August, 24 December-2 January, Saturday and Sunday – **Meals** a la carte approx. 38 ♀.
◆ With its pleasingly textured walls, this is a place to come for the tasty cooking of the Basque country. Warm welcome plus freshly delivered produce from the region.

Astier, 44 r. J.-P. Timbaud (11th) Ⓜ *Parmentier* ✆ 01 43 57 16 35 – GB G 18
closed 24 April-3 May, 28 July-29 August, 23 Decembre-3 January, Saturday, Sunday and Bank Holidays – **Meals** (booking essential) 22 (lunch)/27.
◆ A pleasant ambience reigns in this typical bistro with its busy but friendly staff and high noise levels. A seasonal range of dishes, plus an expansive wine-list.

L'Enoteca, 25 r. Charles V (4th) Ⓜ *St-Paul* ✆ 01 42 78 91 44, *Fax 01 44 59 31 72* – GB
closed 13 to 18 August and lunch in August – **Meals** (booking essential) a la carte 29/47 ♀. J 16
◆ The highlight of this restaurant within 16C walls is its superb wine list of some 500 exclusively Italian wines. A lively atmosphere to go with the Italian cuisine.

Quartier Latin, Luxembourg, Jardin des Plantes.

5th and 6th arrondissements.
5th: ✉ 75005
6th: ✉ 75006

Lutétia, 45 bd Raspail (6th) Ⓜ *Sèvres Babylone* ✆ 01 49 54 46 46, *lutetia-paris@lutetia-paris.com, Fax 01 49 54 46 00* – |₿| ⇽⇾ ▤ TV ✆ – 🏛 300. AE ◐ GB JCB
see **Paris** below – ***Brasserie Lutétia*** ✆ 01 49 54 46 76 **Meals** 37 and a la carte approx. 56 ♀ – ☕ 22 – **206 rm** 480/550, 25 suites. K 12
◆ Built in 1907, this palatial Left Bank hotel has lost none of its glitter. Refined retro décor, Lalique chandeliers, fine sculpture. Refurbished rooms. Rendezvous of the Parisian elite. Splendid seafood menu in the Brasserie Lutétia.

Victoria Palace without rest, 6 r. Blaise-Desgoffe (6th) Ⓜ *St-Placide* ✆ 01 45 49 70 00, *info@victoriapalace.com, Fax 01 45 49 23 75* – |₿| ⇽⇾ ▤ TV ✆ ♿ 🚗 – 🏛 20. AE ◐ GB JCB L 11
☕ 18 – **62 rm** 305/365.
◆ Small luxury establishment of undeniable charm. Bedrooms with choice fabrics, period furniture and marble bathrooms, lounges with pictures, porcelain and lots of red velvet.

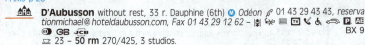

D'Aubusson without rest, 33 r. Dauphine (6th) Ⓜ *Odéon* ✆ 01 43 29 43 43, *reservationmichael@hoteldaubusson.com, Fax 01 43 29 12 62* – |♦| ✈ ▤ TV ✆ ♿ 🚗 P. AE ⓓ GB JCB BX 9
☕ 23 – **50 rm** 270/425, 3 studios.
◆ Refurbished 17C town mansion with individually decorated rooms, Versailles-style parquet floors, Aubusson tapestries, plus a bar that was once the city's first literary café.

Relais Christine without rest, 3 r. Christine (6th) Ⓜ *St-Michel* ✆ 01 40 51 60 80, *contact@relais-christine.com, Fax 01 40 51 60 81* – |♦| ✈ ▤ TV ✆ 🚗 – 🏛 20. AE ⓓ GB JCB J 14
☕ 25 – **35 rm** 345/440, 16 duplex.
◆ Lovely town mansion built on the site of a 13C convent - guests breakfast in the old vaulted kitchens. Attractive individually decorated and well-presented rooms.

Bel Ami St-Germain-des-Prés without rest, 7 r. St-Benoit (6th) Ⓜ *St-Germain des Prés* ✆ 01 42 61 53 53, *contact@hotel-bel-ami.com, Fax 01 49 27 09 33* – |♦| ▤ TV ✆ ♿. AE ⓓ GB JCB. ✂ J 13
☕ 20 – **115 rm** 290/410.
◆ Lovely 19C building next to the famous Flore and Deux Magots cafes. Resolutely contemporary décor with a touch of zen plus hi-tech facilities. A trendy establishment.

Buci without rest, 22 r. Buci (6th) Ⓜ *Mabillon* ✆ 01 55 42 74 74, *hotelbuci@wanadoo.fr, Fax 01 55 42 74 44* – |♦| ▤ TV ✆ ♿. AE ⓓ GB JCB. ✂ J 13
☕ 17 – **21 rm** 250/335, 3 suites.
◆ The hotel overlooks a picturesque street and its bustling market. Heavenly beds and English-style furniture in well-soundproofed, elegantly refurbished rooms. Piano bar.

L'Abbaye without rest, 10 r. Cassette (6th) Ⓜ *St-Sulpice* ✆ 01 45 44 38 11, *hotel.abbaye@wanadoo.fr, Fax 01 45 48 07 86* – |♦| ▤ TV ✆. AE GB. ✂ K 12
40 rm ☕ 216/320, 4 duplex.
◆ The charm of yesteryear, the comfort of today - what was once an 18C convent now has attractive rooms, some overlooking a patio. The duplex rooms have a terrace.

Littré without rest, 9 r. Littré (6th) Ⓜ *Montparnasse Bienvenüe* ✆ 01 53 63 07 07, *hotellittre@hotellitreparis.com, Fax 01 45 44 88 13* – |♦| ✈ ▤ TV ✆ – 🏛 20. AE ⓓ GB JCB. ✂ L 11
☕ 16 – **79 rm** 298/325, 11 suites.
◆ Halfway between Saint-Germain-des-Prés and Montparnasse, a classic building with reasonably spacious rooms, all attractively refurbished. Comfortable English bar.

L'Hôtel, 13 r. Beaux Arts (6th) Ⓜ *St-Germain des Prés* ✆ 01 44 41 99 00, *reservation@l-hotel.com, Fax 01 43 25 64 81,* Ꮀ – |♦| ▤ TV ✆. AE ⓓ GB JCB. ✂ J 13
(closed August, Sunday and Monday) 🍸 **- Le Bélier** ✆ 01 44 41 99 01 *(closed August, Sunday and Monday)* **Meals** a la carte 50/68 – ☕ 17 – **16 rm** 280/640, 4 suites.
◆ With its exuberant Baroque, Empire and Oriental decor by Garcia, the famous Hôtel is unique in its blend of joy and nostalgia. It was here that Oscar Wilde met his end. A decor of green and gold tones, old lanterns and stained glass adorn the the restaurant.

Esprit St Germain without rest, 22 av. St-Sulpice (6th) Ⓜ *Mabillon* ✆ 01 53 10 55 55, *contact@espritsaintgermain.com, Fax 01 53 10 55 56,* Ꮀ – |♦| ✈ ▤ TV ✆ ♿ K 13
☕ 16 – **30 rm** 350/550.
◆ Elegant, contemporary guestrooms offering a cheerful fusion of red, chocolate and beige, modern artwork and furniture, and bathrooms embellished with slate on the walls.

Relais St-Germain without rest, 9 carrefour de l'Odéon (6th) Ⓜ *Odéon* ✆ 01 43 29 12 05, *hotelrsg@wanadoo.fr, Fax 01 46 33 45 30* – |♦| kitchenette ▤ TV ✆. AE ⓓ GB JCB K 13
22 rm ☕ 210/360.
◆ Three 17C buildings now house a refined hotel where old beams, lustrous fabrics and period furniture add an attractive touch to the bedrooms.

Madison without rest, 143 bd St-Germain (6th) Ⓜ *St-Germain des Prés* ✆ 01 40 51 60 00, *resa@hotel-madison.com, Fax 01 40 51 60 01,* ≤ – |♦| ▤ TV ✆. AE ⓓ GB JCB J 13
54 rm ☕ 175/320.
◆ The writer Albert Camus was fond of this establishment, half of whose elegant rooms have a view of the church of St-Germain-des-Prés. Elegant Louis-Philippe lounge.

Relais Médicis without rest, 23 r. Racine (6th) Ⓜ *Odéon* ✆ 01 43 26 00 60, *reservation@relaismedicis.com, Fax 01 40 46 83 39* – |♦| ▤ TV ✆. AE ⓓ GB JCB. ✂ K 13
16 rm ☕ 188/258.
◆ This hotel close to the Théatre de l'Odéon has rooms with a cheerful Provençal touch. Those facing the patio are quieter. Furniture picked up from antique dealers.

Villa Panthéon without rest, 41 r. Écoles (5th) Ⓜ *Maubert Mutualité* ✆ 01 53 10 95 95, *pantheon@leshotelsdeparis.com, Fax 01 53 10 95 96* – AE GB JCB
25 – **59 rm** 310/710. K 14
• Parquet floors, brightly-coloured wall-hangings, exotic wood furniture and Liberty lamps lend foyer, rooms and bar of this hotel a distinctively British air.

Left Bank St-Germain without rest, 9 r. Ancienne Comédie (6th) Ⓜ *Odéon* ✆ 01 43 54 01 70, *lb@paris-hotels-charm.com, Fax 01 43 26 17 14* – . AE GB JCB K 13
31 rm 200/240.
• Damask, Jouy fabrics, Louis XIII-style furniture and old timbers give this 17C building a distinctive character. Some of the rooms offer a glimpse of Notre-Dame.

Millésime Hôtel without rest, 15 r. Jacob (6th) Ⓜ *St-Germain des Prés* ✆ 01 44 07 97 97, *reservation@millesimehotel.com, Fax 01 46 34 55 97* – . AE GB JCB J 13
16 – **22 rm** 185/220.
• Sunny tones and elegant furniture and fabrics contribute to the warm feel in the delightful bedrooms of this renovated hotel. Impressive 17C staircase.

Résidence Henri IV without rest, 50 r. Bernardins (5th) Ⓜ *Maubert Mutualité* ✆ 01 44 41 31 81, *reservation@residencehenri4.com, Fax 01 46 33 93 22* – kitchenette . AE GB JCB K 15
9 – **8 rm** 175/185, 5 suites.
• Building dating from 1879 with refurbished rooms that have kept the charm of yesteryear, with mouldings, friezes and marble chimneypieces. Overlooks a leafy square.

Les Rives de Notre-Dame without rest, 15 quai St-Michel (5th) Ⓜ *St-Michel* ✆ 01 43 54 81 16, *hotel@rivesdenotredame.com, Fax 01 43 26 27 09,* ← – . AE GB JCB J 14
13,70 – **10 rm** 213/550.
• Beautifully preserved 16C building with spacious Provençal-style rooms overlooking the Seine and Notre-Dame. Penthouse on the top floor.

Royal St-Michel without rest, 3 bd St-Michel (5th) Ⓜ *St-Michel* ✆ 01 44 07 06 06, *hotel.royal.st.michel@wanadoo.fr, Fax 01 44 07 36 25* – . AE GB JCB
15 – **39 rm** 220/250. K 14
• Right by the fountain on the famous Boulevard-St-Michel, the doors of this establishment open directly onto the bustle of the Latin Quarter. Modern, refurbished rooms.

Ste-Beuve without rest, 9 r. Ste-Beuve (6th) Ⓜ *Notre-Dame des Champs* ✆ 01 45 48 20 07, *saintebeuve@wanadoo.fr, Fax 01 45 48 67 52* – . AE GB JCB – 14 – **22 rm** 132/275. L 12
• With its intimate ambience, comfy sofas and open fires this establishment is more like a private residence than a hotel. Rooms a tasteful fusion of old and new.

Au Manoir St-Germain-des-Prés without rest, 153 bd St-Germain (6th) Ⓜ *St-Germain des Prés* ✆ 01 42 22 21 65, *msg@paris-hotels-charm.com, Fax 01 45 48 22 25* – . AE GB JCB J 12
32 rm 168/240.
• Period furniture, Jouy fabrics, frescoes and wood panelling add to the ambience of this hotel opposite two of the city's most famous cafes, Le Flore and Les Deux Magots.

Grands Hommes without rest, 17 pl. Panthéon (5th) Ⓜ *Luxembourg* ✆ 01 46 34 19 60, *reservation@hoteldesgrandshommes.com, Fax 01 43 26 67 32,* ← – – 20. AE GB JCB L 14
12 – **31 rm** 233/243.
• Facing the Panthéon, a pleasant hotel refurbished in late 18C style (mottled furniture). Most rooms look out over the last resting-place of France's great and good.

Tour Notre-Dame without rest, 20 r. Sommerard (5th) Ⓜ *Cluny la Sorbonne* ✆ 01 43 54 47 60, *tour-notre-dame@magic.fr, Fax 01 43 26 42 34* – . AE GB JCB – 12 – **48 rm** 155/229. K 14
• This hotel has a wonderful location almost next to the Museé de Cluny. Comfortable rooms featuring famous Jouy fabrics. Ask for one of the quieter ones at the back.

Villa des Artistes without rest, 9 r. Grande Chaumière (6th) Ⓜ *Vavin* ✆ 01 43 26 60 86, *hotel@villa-artistes.com, Fax 01 43 54 73 70* – . AE GB JCB. – 13 – **59 rm** 176. L 12
• The hotel's name pays homage to the artists who made Montparnasse what it is. Attractive rooms, many overlooking the courtyard. Glass-roofed breakfast room.

Relais St-Sulpice without rest, 3 r. Garancière (6th) Ⓜ *St-Sulpice* ✆ 01 46 33 99 00, *relaisstsulpice@wanadoo.fr, Fax 01 46 33 00 10* – – 20. AE GB JCB. – 12 – **26 rm** 170/205. K 13
• The decor of this establishment with its 19C façade strikes an exotic note with its seductive mixture of African and Asian motifs. The back rooms are particularly quiet.

Grand Hôtel St-Michel without rest, 19 r. Cujas (5th) *Luxembourg* 01 46 33 33 02, *grand.hotel.st.michel@wanadoo.fr, Fax 01 40 46 96 33* – AE GB JCB – 12 – **40 rm** 120/170, 5 suites. K 14
• A renovated Haussmann-style building with quiet rooms adorned with painted furniture. Architectural features include a Napoleon III-style lounge and vaulted breakfast room.

De Fleurie without rest, 32 r. Grégoire de Tours (6th) *Odéon* 01 53 73 70 00, *bonjour@hotel-de-fleurie.tm.fr, Fax 01 53 73 70 20* – AE GB. 10 – **29 rm** 145/265. K 13
• A striking 18C façade enhanced by statues in niches. Plush rooms with soft colours and attractive panelling. The quieter rooms are those overlooking the courtyard.

St-Germain-des-Prés without rest, 36 r. Bonaparte (6th) *St-Germain des Prés* 01 43 26 00 19, *hotel-saint-germain-des-pres@wanadoo.fr, Fax 01 40 46 83 63* – AE GB J 13
8 – **30 rm** 160/255.
• Floral fabrics and exposed beams lend a cheerful note to most of the rooms. The quieter ones face the courtyard. Breakfast room overlooking a remarkable floral display.

Notre Dame without rest, 1 quai St-Michel (5th) *St-Michel* 01 43 54 20 43, *hotel.lenotredame@libertysurf.fr, Fax 01 43 26 61 75,* – AE GB. 7 – **22 rm** 150/244, 4 duplex. K 14
• The comfortable little rooms of this hotel have all been refurbished and are air-conditioned and well-equipped. Most benefit from a view of Notre-Dame.

Relais St-Jacques without rest, 3 r. Abbé de l'Épée (5th) *Luxembourg* 01 53 73 26 00, *nevers.luxembourg@wanadoo.fr, Fax 01 43 26 17 81* – 10. AE GB JCB. – 17 – **23 rm** 195/250. L 14
• Rooms in Louis-Philippe or Directoire style, a breakfast room beneath a glass canopy, Louis XV lounge and 1920s bar - a random but very smart and successful fusion !

Prince de Conti without rest, 8 r. Guénégaud (6th) *Odéon* 01 44 07 30 40, *princedeconti@wanadoo.fr, Fax 01 44 07 36 34* – AE GB JCB. 13 – **26 rm** 165/195. J 13
• 18C building adjacent to the Hôtel de la Monnaie, ideal for anyone wanting to explore the famous art galleries of Montparnasse. Rooms and lounges with English-style décor.

Odéon Hôtel without rest, 3 r. Odéon (6th) *Odéon* 01 43 25 90 67, *odeon@odeonhotel.fr, Fax 01 43 25 55 98* – AE GB JCB. K 13
10 – **33 rm** 130/270.
• As well as the façade, the exposed beams and stone walls of the rooms are evidence of the great age of this 17C building. Brightly tiled bathrooms.

Régent without rest, 61 r. Dauphine (6th) *Odéon* 01 46 34 59 80, *hotel.leregent@wanadoo.fr, Fax 01 40 51 05 07* – AE GB JCB. J 13
12 – **25 rm** 140/210.
• Long, low façade dating from 1769. Luxurious, well-equipped rooms. Basement breakfast room with exposed beams and stonework.

Select without rest, 1 pl. Sorbonne (5th) *Cluny la Sorbonne* 01 46 34 14 80, *info@selecthotel.fr, Fax 01 46 34 51 79* – AE GB JCB K 14
6 – **67 rm** 175.
• Resolutely contemporary hotel in the heart of student Paris. Lounge embraces a leafy patio beneath a glass roof. Some of the rooms look out over the rooftops of the city.

D'Albe without rest, 1 r. Harpe (5th) *St-Michel* 01 46 34 09 70, *albehotel@wanadoo.fr, Fax 01 40 46 85 70* – AE GB JCB. K 14
12 – **45 rm** 120/175.
• Pleasant contemporary ambience in this hotel with somewhat small but bright and attractively decorated rooms. The Latin Quarter, the Ile de la Cité - Paris is at your feet !

Pas de Calais without rest, 59 r. Saints-Pères (6th) *St-Germain des Prés* 01 45 48 78 74, *infos@hotelpasdecalais.com, Fax 01 45 44 94 57* – AE GB JCB – 9 – **40 rm** 130/275. J 12
• This discreet hotel fronting a busy street has been well refurbished to include charming, individual bedrooms. Exposed beams on the top floor.

Pierre Nicole without rest, 39 r. Pierre Nicole (5th) *Port Royal* 01 43 54 76 86, *hotelpierre-nicole@voila.fr, Fax 01 43 54 22 45* – AE GB. M 13
6 – **33 rm** 70/90.
• The hotel is named after the famous Port-Royal theologian. Practical, moderately sized, yet well-maintained rooms at reasonable prices. Not far from the Jardin du Luxembourg.

St-Jacques without rest, 35 r. Écoles (5th) *Maubert Mutualité* 01 44 07 45 45, *hotelsaintjacques@wanadoo.fr, Fax 01 43 25 65 50* – AE GB JCB. 8 – **35 rm** 80/118. K 15
• The hotel's rooms are being progressively refurbished without losing any of their character (mouldings, fireplaces and period furnishings). Breakfast room with a fine fresco.

XXXXX ✿✿ **Tour d'Argent,** 15 quai Tournelle (5th) Ⓜ *Maubert Mutualité* ✆ 01 43 54 23 31, *resa@latourdargent.com, Fax 01 44 07 12 04,* < Notre-Dame – ▤ ⛟. AE ⓓ GB JCB K 16
closed Tuesday lunch and Monday – **Meals** 70 (lunch), 150/200 and a la carte 150/220
Spec. Quenelles de brochet "André Terrail". Canard "Tour d'Argent". Poire "Vie parisienne"..
◆ A favourite with celebrities since the 16C. Dining room with unique views of Notre-Dame, an exceptional wine list and famous Challans duck. A legendary establishment.

XXX ✿ **Jacques Cagna,** 14 r. Grands Augustins (6th) Ⓜ *St-Michel* ✆ 01 43 26 49 39, *jacquescagna@hotmail.com, Fax 01 43 54 54 48* – ▤ ⛟ (dinner). AE ⓓ GB JCB J 14
closed 30 July-24 August, Saturday lunch, Monday lunch and Sunday – **Meals** 39 (lunch)/85 and a la carte 89/118
Spec. Foie gras poêlé aux fruits de saison caramélisés. Coquilles Saint-Jacques (October-March).Noix de ris de veau en croûte de sel au romarin..
◆ In one of the city's oldest buildings, this comfortable dining room has massive beams, 16C panelling and Flemish pictures. Refined cuisine.

XXX ✿ **Paris** - Hôtel Lutétia, 45 bd Raspail (6th) Ⓜ *Sèvres Babylone* ✆ 01 49 54 46 90, *lutetia-paris@lutetia-paris.com, Fax 01 49 54 46 00* – ▤ ⛟. AE ⓓ GB JCB K 12
closed August, Saturday, Sunday and Bank Holidays – **Meals** 40 (lunch), 65/120 dinner and a la carte 84/117
Spec. Saint-Jacques au pistou (October-April). Turbot cuit sur le sel de Guérande. Pintade à l'embeurrée de choux (December-July).
◆ Faithfully reflecting the style of the hotel, the Art Deco restaurant was designed by Sonia Rykiel to resemble a lounge of the liner Normandie. Talented contemporary cuisine.

XXX ✿✿ **Relais Louis XIII** (Martinez), 8 r. Grands Augustins (6th) Ⓜ *Odéon* ✆ 01 43 26 75 96, *contact@relaislouis13.com, Fax 01 44 07 07 80* – ▤ ⛟ (dinner). AE GB JCB. ⚔
closed 1 to 30 August, Sunday and Monday – **Meals** 45 (lunch), 70/90 and a la carte 100/134 J 14
Spec. Ravioli de homard, foie gras et crème de cèpes. Caneton rôti aux épices douces et fortes. Millefeuille, crème légère à la vanille bourbon..
◆ In a 16C building, three intimate interiors in Louis XIII style, with balustrades, striped fabrics and exposed stonework. Subtle cuisine of today.

XXX ✿✿ **Hélène Darroze,** 4 r. d'Assas (6th) Ⓜ *Sèvres Babylone* ✆ 01 42 22 00 11, *helene.darroze@wanadoo.fr, Fax 01 42 22 25 40* – ▤ ⛟. AE GB K 12
closed Monday except dinner from mid-July-late August and Sunday – **Meals** *(only dinner from 17 July-31 August)* 65 (lunch), 168/220 b.i. and a la carte 100/167 – ***Salon*** *(closed 24 July-29 August, Tuesday lunch, Sunday and Monday)* **Meals** 30(lunch)79/99b.i. and a la carte 40/60
Spec. Soupe de palombe aux lentilles vertes duPuy (October-December). Oeuf coque, asperges, mousserons, foie gras, mouillettes à la truffe noire (Spring). Baba au Bas armagnac "Francis Darroze"..
◆ Near the Bon Marché department store, an establishment with bright, contemporary decor and delicious cuisine and wines from southwest France. Hélène Darroze holds court on the ground floor, dispensing tapas and snacks full of the flavour of the Landes.

XXX **Lapérouse,** 51 quai Grands Augustins (6th) Ⓜ *St-Michel* ✆ 01 43 26 68 04, *restaurantlaperouse@wanadoo.fr, Fax 01 43 26 99 39* – ▤ ⛟. AE ⓓ GB J 14
Meals 65 b.i. (lunch), 80 b.i./140 b.i. and a la carte 70/115 ♀.
◆ A smart city rendezvous since the late 19C and famous for its discreet and intimate interiors, this restaurant of 1766 has kept all its old spirit.

XX **Mavrommatis,** 42 r. Daubenton (5th) Ⓜ *Censier Daubenton* ✆ 01 43 31 17 17, *info@mavrommatis.fr, Fax 01 43 36 13 08* – ▤. AE GB JCB. ⚔ M 15
closed August, Sunday and Monday – **Meals** 32 and a la carte 36/48 ♀.
◆ This establishment provides Paris with the best of Greek cuisine. No folklore, but sobriety, elegance and comfort enhanced by subtle lighting. Attentive service. Terrace.

XX **La Truffière,** 4 r. Blainville (5th) Ⓜ *Place Monge* ✆ 01 46 33 29 82, *restaurant.latruffiere@wanadoo.fr, Fax 01 46 33 64 74* – ▤. AE ⓓ GB JCB L 15
closed 1 to 28 August, 19 to 25 December, Sunday and Monday – **Meals** 19 (lunch) and a la carte 59/98 ♀.
◆ This 17C house contains two rooms : one rustic in style with exposed beams, the other vaulted. Traditional cuisine rooted in SW France, plus an impressive wine list.

XX **Marty,** 20 av. Gobelins (5th) Ⓜ *Les Gobelins* ✆ 01 43 31 39 51, *restaurant.marty@wanadoo.fr, Fax 01 43 37 63 70* – ▤. AE ⓓ GB JCB M 15
Meals 36 and a la carte 40/57 ♀.
◆ This pleasant 1930s-style brasserie is adorned with mahogany panelling, chandeliers, stained glass, paintings and antique furniture. Traditional menu and seafood.

XX **Yugaraj,** 14 r. Dauphine (6th) *Odéon* 01 43 26 44 91, *contact@yugaraj.com, Fax 01 46 33 50 77* – AE D GB JCB J 14
closed August, 1-10 January, Thursday lunch and Monday – **Meals** 22,80 (lunch), 44,80/58.
• Wainscoting, decorative panels, silk fabrics and venerable objets d'art lend this stronghold of Indian cuisine something of the air of a museum. Well-informed menu.

XX **Alcazar,** 62 r. Mazarine (6th) *Odéon* 01 53 10 19 99, *contact@alcazar.fr, Fax 01 53 10 23 23* – AE D GB JCB J 13
Meals 17 b.i. (lunch)/38 b.i. and a la carte 41/66.
• What was once a showy cabaret theatre has been converted into a vast and trendy restaurant with designer décor. Tables with view of what's cooking, contemporary cuisine.

X **Yen,** 22 r. St-Benoît (6th) *St-Germain des Prés* 01 45 44 11 18, *restau-yen@wanadoo.fr, Fax 01 45 44 19 48* – AE D GB JCB J 13
closed 1 to 15 August, Sunday lunch, and Bank Holidays – **Meals** 55 and a la carte 25/60.
• Two dining rooms with minimalist Japanese décor, a little more cheerful on the first floor. The menu makes the most of soba, the chef's speciality (buckwheat noodles).

X **Brasserie Lipp,** 151 bd St-Germain (6th) *St-Germain des Prés* 01 45 48 53 91, *lipp@magic.fr, Fax 01 45 44 33 20* – AE D GB – **Meals** a la carte 37/63. J 13
• Founded in 1880, this brasserie is one of the great institutions of St-Germain. Dine in the downstairs room with its ceramics, painted ceilings and celebrities.

X **Atelier Maître Albert,** 1 r. Maître Albert (5th) *Maubert Mutualité* 01 56 81 30 01, *ateliermaitrealbert@guysavoy.com, Fax 01 53 10 83 23* – AE D GB JCB K 15
closed Christmas Holidays, Saturday lunch and Sunday lunch – **Meals** a la carte 40/56.
• A new team has breathed fresh life into this renowned restaurant, adding a design feel alongside the medieval chimney and exposed beams. Refined cuisine and grilled meats.

X **Rotonde,** 105 bd Montparnasse (6th) *Vavin* 01 43 26 68 84, *Fax 01 46 34 52 40* – AE GB JCB L 12
Meals 34 and a la carte 34/67.
• The history of this typical Parisian brasserie, popular with celebrities galore since it opened in 1903, is outlined on the back of the menu. Ideal for a post-theatre supper.

X **L'Épi Dupin,** 11 r. Dupin (6th) *Sèvres Babylone* 01 42 22 64 56, *lepidupin@wanadoo.fr, Fax 01 42 22 30 42*, – GB K 12
closed 31 July-26 August, Monday lunch, Saturday and Sunday – **Meals** (booking essential) 31.
• Beams and stonework for character, serried ranks of tables for conviviality, delicious dishes for your delight - this little restaurant has conquered the Bon Marché area.

X **Dominique,** 19 r. Bréa (6th) *Vavin* 01 43 27 08 80, *restaurant.dominique@mageos.com, Fax 01 43 27 03 76* – AE D GB JCB L 12
closed 25 July-24 August, Sunday and Monday – **Meals** (dinner only) 40 and a la carte 45/73.
• This stronghold of Russian cuisine is a vodka bar, grocery and restaurant all in one. Zakuski in the bistro, candlelit dining at the rear.

X **Les Délices d'Aphrodite,** 4 r. Candolle (5th) *Censier Daubenton* 01 43 31 40 39, *info@mavrommatis.fr, Fax 01 43 36 13 08* – AE GB JCB. M 15
closed Sunday – **Meals** a la carte 32/43.
• Tiny bistro with a holiday atmosphere - photos of Greek landscapes, bark-covered ceiling and cuisine redolent of the fruit of the olive tree.

X **Emporio Armani Caffé,** 149 bd St-Germain (6th) *St-Germain des Prés* 01 45 48 62 15, *Fax 01 45 48 53 17* – AE D GB JCB J 13
closed Sunday – **Meals** a la carte 47/81.
• On the first floor of the famous fashion shop a smart Italian café with attractively refurbished and comfortable decor and a very Left Bank clientele. Italian cuisine.

X **Ze Kitchen Galerie,** 4 r. Grands Augustins (6th) *St-Michel* 01 44 32 00 32, *zekitchen.galerie@wanadoo.fr, Fax 01 44 32 00 33* – AE D GB JCB J 14
closed Saturday lunch and Sunday – **Meals** 32 and a la carte 46/62.
• Zis is ZE place to come on the Left Bank quayside. Cool interior enlivened by works by contemporary artists, design furniture and modish dishes prepared as you watch.

X **Les Bouchons de François Clerc,** 12 r. Hôtel Colbert (5th) *Maubert Mutualité* 01 43 54 15 34, *Fax 01 46 34 68 07* – AE GB JCB K 15
closed Saturday lunch and Sunday – **Meals** 26/41 and a la carte approx. 46.
• What it lacks in space this 17C Parisian house makes up for in charm, with features including a roasting spit in the main dining room. Impressive, reasonably priced wine list.

X **Buisson Ardent,** 25 r. Jussieu (5th) *Jussieu* 01 43 54 93 02, *Fax 01 46 33 34 77*, – AE D GB L 15
closed August, Saturday lunch and Sunday – **Meals** 15/29 and a la carte approx. 35.
• A good-natured ambience pervades this compact local restaurant frequented at lunch-time by university students. Original frescoes dating from 1923. Traditional cuisine.

Faubourg-St-Germain, Invalides, École Militaire.

7th arrondissement.
7th: ✉ 75007

Pont Royal without rest, 7 r. Montalembert Ⓜ *Rue du Bac* ☎ 01 42 84 70 00, *hpr@hotel-pont-royal.com, Fax 01 42 84 71 00,* – 35. AE GB JCB J 12
26 – **64 rm** 380/430, 11 suites.
◆ Bold colours and mahogany panelling in the rooms - Left Bank Bohemianism combined with the comfort of a refined "literary hotel".

Duc de Saint-Simon without rest, 14 r. St-Simon Ⓜ *Rue du Bac* ☎ 01 44 39 20 20, *duc.de.saint.simon@wanadoo.fr, Fax 01 45 48 68 25* – AE GB. J 11
15 – **29 rm** 250/285, 5 suites.
◆ With bright colours, panelling, and antiques of various kinds, the atmosphere here is that of a fine residence of bygone days. Courteous reception plus tranquillity.

Montalembert, 3 r. Montalembert Ⓜ *Rue du Bac* ☎ 01 45 49 68 68, *welcome@montalembert.com, Fax 01 45 49 69 49,* – – 20. AE GB JCB J 12
Meals a la carte 40/66 – 28 – **48 rm** 340/430, 8 suites.
◆ Dark wood, leather, glass, steel, plus subtle shades of lilac, plum and tobacco, all the ingredients of contemporary style. Designer dining room, a terrace protected by a box hedge, and a two-stage cuisine to suit your appetite.

K+K Hotel Cayré without rest, 4 bd Raspail Ⓜ *Rue du Bac* ☎ 01 45 44 38 88, *reservations@kkhotels.fr, Fax 01 45 44 98 13* – AE GB JCB. J 12
22 – **124 rm** 350/410.
◆ An elegant lobby, fitness centre, free Internet access and modern, soundproofed rooms are some of the highlights of this hotel located on a busy thoroughfare.

Bourgogne et Montana without rest, 3 r. Bourgogne Ⓜ *Assemblée Nationale* ☎ 01 45 51 20 22, *bmontana@bourgogne-montana.com, Fax 01 45 56 11 98* – . AE GB JCB H 11
28 rm 150/240, 4 suites.
◆ Beauty and refinement in every room of this discreet 18C establishment. The top floor rooms have a superb view of the Palais-Bourbon.

Tourville without rest, 16 av. Tourville Ⓜ *Ecole Militaire* ☎ 01 47 05 62 62, *hotel@tourville.com, Fax 01 47 05 43 90* – . AE GB. J 9
12 – **30 rm** 165/310.
◆ Refined rooms with a happy combination of modern and period furniture, pictures, and décor featuring acid colours. Lounge decorated by David Hicks. Attentive service.

Verneuil without rest, 8 r. Verneuil Ⓜ *Musée d'Orsay* ☎ 01 42 60 82 14, *hotelverneuil@wanadoo.fr, Fax 01 42 61 40 38* – . AE GB. J 12
12 – **26 rm** 127/196.
◆ Old building in the "Left Bank Square" with décor like that of a private residence. Elegant rooms with engravings. A wall-plate at no 5bis indicates Serge Gainsbourg's home.

Lenox Saint-Germain without rest, 9 r. Université Ⓜ *St-Germain des Prés* ☎ 01 42 96 10 95, *hotel@lenoxsaintgermain.com, Fax 01 42 61 52 83* – . AE GB JCB. J 12
11 – **29 rm** 125/165, 5 suites.
◆ Discreetly luxurious rooms, which are not particularly spacious but are attractively decorated. "Egyptian" frescoes adorn the breakfast room. Art Deco-style bar.

D'Orsay without rest, 93 r. Lille Ⓜ *Solférino* ☎ 01 47 05 85 54, *hotel.orsay@esprit-de-france.com, Fax 01 45 55 51 16* – . AE GB JCB. H 11
10 – **41 rm** 125/175.
◆ The hotel occupies two lovely, recently refurbished buildings dating from the end of the 18C. Individually decorated rooms and attractive lounge with view of verdant patio.

Eiffel Park Hôtel without rest, 17bis r. Amélie Ⓜ *La Tour Maubourg* ✆ 01 45 55 10 01, *reservation@eiffelpark.com, Fax 01 47 05 28 68* – AE GB. J 9
15 – **36 rm** 155/185.
◆ Old-style painted furniture and Chinese and Indian antiques transport guests into an exotic atmosphere. Summer terrace and cosy lounge with an open fire. Attentive service.

Walt without rest, 37 av. de La Motte Picquet Ⓜ *Ecole Militaire* ✆ 01 45 51 55 83, *lewalt@inwoodhotel.com, Fax 01 47 05 77 59* – AE GB JCB J 9
12 – **25 rm** 270/320.
◆ Imposing Renaissance portraits above the headboards and contemporary furniture are just some of the original features in the rooms of this new hotel near the École Militaire.

Les Jardins d'Eiffel without rest, 8 r. Amélie Ⓜ *La Tour Maubourg* ✆ 01 47 05 46 21, *paris@hoteljardinseiffel.com, Fax 01 45 55 28 08* – AE GB JCB. H 9
15 – **80 rm** 117/161.
◆ Situated in a quiet street, this hotel comprises two buildings linked by a patio where breakfast is served in summer. Brightly decorated rooms, some of which have a balcony.

Relais Bosquet without rest, 19 r. Champ-de-Mars Ⓜ *Ecole Militaire* ✆ 01 47 05 25 45, *hotel@relaisbosquet.com, Fax 01 45 55 08 24* – AE GB JCB J 9
10,50 – **40 rm** 135/170.
◆ Discreet outside, this hotel has an attractively furnished interior in late 18C style. Refurbished rooms, all decorated with the same attention to detail. Attentive service.

Tour Eiffel Invalides without rest, 35 bd La Tour Maubourg Ⓜ *La Tour Maubourg* ✆ 01 45 56 10 78, *invalides@timhotel.fr, Fax 01 47 05 65 08* – AE GB JCB H 10
10 – **30 rm** 179/272.
◆ The rooms in this 19C establishment feature red and white brick, Louis XVI-style furniture, and reproductions of Impressionist paintings.

Muguet without rest, 11 r. Chevert Ⓜ *Ecole Militaire* ✆ 01 47 05 05 93, *muguet@wanadoo.fr, Fax 01 45 50 25 37* – AE GB. J 9
8,50 – **53 rm** 97/108.
◆ This small hotel on a quiet street has a modern lobby and rooms (three of which enjoy views of the Eiffel Tower and Les Invalides) adorned with Louis-Philippe-style furniture.

Londres Eiffel without rest, 1 r. Augereau Ⓜ *Ecole Militaire* ✆ 01 45 51 63 02, *info@londres-eiffel.com, Fax 01 47 05 28 96* – AE GB JCB. J 8
13 – **30 rm** 105/175.
◆ Close to the avenues of the Champ-de-Mars, this cosy hotel is decorated in bright colours. The second building beyond the little courtyard is quieter.

Du Cadran without rest, 10 r. Champ-de-Mars Ⓜ *Ecole Militaire* ✆ 01 40 62 67 00, *info@cadranhotel.com, Fax 01 40 62 67 13* – AE GB. J 9
10 – **42 rm** 165/178.
◆ Just a step from the busy market in the Rue Clerc. Modern rooms with a number of inspired Louis XVI touches. Leather-panelled lounge with 17C fireplace.

St-Germain without rest, 88 r. Bac Ⓜ *Rue du Bac* ✆ 01 49 54 70 00, *info@hotel-saint-germain.fr, Fax 01 45 48 26 89* – AE GB. J 11
12 – **29 rm** 190/210.
◆ This hotel owes its charm to its diversity, with Empire, Louis Philippe, and designer furniture, antiques, and contemporary paintings. Comfortable library, attractive patio.

De Varenne without rest, 44 r. Bourgogne Ⓜ *Varenne* ✆ 01 45 51 45 55, *info@hoteldevarenne.com, Fax 01 45 51 86 63* – AE GB. J 11
10 – **24 rm** 120/150.
◆ This relatively quiet hotel has been completely renovated and embellished with Empire and Louis XVI furniture. In summer, breakfast is served in a small leafy courtyard.

Champ-de-Mars without rest, 7 r. Champ-de-Mars Ⓜ *Ecole Militaire* ✆ 01 45 51 52 30, *stg@club-internet.fr, Fax 01 45 51 64 36* – GB. J 9
6,50 – **25 rm** 73/83.
◆ Between the Champ-de-Mars and the Invalides, a compact hotel with an English atmosphere. Green façade, cosy rooms and elegant, Liberty-style decor.

Bersoly's without rest, 28 r. Lille Ⓜ *Musée d'Orsay* ✆ 01 42 60 73 79, *hotelbersolys@wanadoo.fr, Fax 01 49 27 05 55* – AE GB J 13
closed August – 10 – **16 rm** 100/130.
◆ Impressionist nights in a 17C building - each room pays homage to a painter (Renoir, Gauguin...) with works that can be seen at the neighbouring Musée d'Orsay.

XXXX ✿✿✿ **Arpège** (Passard), 84 r. Varenne Ⓜ *Varenne* ✆ 01 45 51 47 33, *arpege.passard@wanadoo.fr, Fax 01 44 18 98 39* – ▤. AE ⓓ GB JCB J 10
closed Saturday and Sunday – **Meals** a la carte 150/240 ♀
Spec. "Collection légumière". Dragée de pigeonneau à l'hydromel. Ile flottante moka-mélisse..
◆ Precious woods and Lalique glass plus a masterchef's dazzling cuisine based on choice vegetables. Ask for a table in the elegant contemporary dining room.

XXXX ✿ **Le Divellec,** 107 r. Université Ⓜ *Invalides* ✆ 01 45 51 91 96, *ledivellec@noos.fr, Fax 01 45 51 31 75* – ▤ ⚿. AE ⓓ GB JCB. ✂ H 10
closed 23 July-22 August, Saturday and Sunday – **Meals** 65 (lunch) and a la carte 130/200
Spec. Homard bleu à la presse avec son corail. Gros turbot braisé aux truffes. Huîtres spéciales frémies à la laitue de mer..
◆ Smart nautical décor, with lots of blue and white, wave motifs on frosted glass, and a lobster tank. Fine seafood freshly shipped in from the shores of the Atlantic.

XXX ✿ **Jules Verne,** Eiffel Tower : 2nd platform, lift in south leg Ⓜ *Bir-Hakeim* ✆ 01 45 55 61 44, *Fax 01 47 05 29 41,* ≤ Paris – ▤ ⚿. AE ⓓ GB JCB. ✂ J 7
Meals 55 (lunch)/125 and a la carte 100/140
Spec. Deux tartares de cabillaud et de filet de boeuf. Fricassée de homard, ris de veau, jus de volaille. Fines feuilles au chocolat noir..
◆ The hi-tech décor of this establishment in the sky can hardly compete with the fantastic spectacle of Paris itself. To make the most of the experience, reserve a window seat.

XXX ✿ **Violon d'Ingres** (Constant), 135 r. St-Dominique Ⓜ *Ecole Militaire* ✆ 01 45 55 15 05, *violondingres@wanadoo.fr, Fax 01 45 55 48 42* – ▤. AE GB JCB J 8
closed Sunday and Monday – **Meals** 50 (lunch)/110 and a la carte 80/110
Spec. Foie gras de canard poêlé au pain d'épice. Suprême de bar croustillant aux amandes. Tatin de pied de porc caramélisée..
◆ Wainscoting helps create a warm ambience in this gourmet rendezvous famed for its virtuoso cuisine and its piano-playing chef.

XXX **Pétrossian,** 144 r. Université Ⓜ *Invalides* ✆ 01 44 11 32 32, *Fax 01 44 11 32 35* – ▤ ⚿. AE ⓓ GB JCB H 10
closed 8 to 30 August, Sunday and Monday – **Meals** 38 (lunch), 48/150 and a la carte 87/135 ♀.
◆ The Pétrossian family have been treating Parisians to Caspian caviar since 1920. Elegant restaurant over the shop serving inventive cuisine.

XX ✿ **Chamarré,** 13 bd La Tour-Maubourg Ⓜ *Invalides* ✆ 01 47 05 50 18, *chantallaval@wanadoo.fr, Fax 01 47 05 91 21* – ▤. AE GB JCB H 10
closed 8 to 22 August, 1 to 7 November, 16 to 22 February, Saturday lunch and Sunday – **Meals** 28 (lunch), 85/105 and a la carte 85/122
Spec. Poulpe d'Atlantique, vindaye confit, émincé de tentacules. Cochon de lait, peau croustillante, poitrine en rougail. Savarin punché au rhum, glace au riz au lait..
◆ Smart, modern decor with exotic wood panelling, friendly service, and a chef who is a master at melding the flavours of France and Mauritius (from where the owner hails).

XX ✿ **Les Ormes** (Molé), 22 r. Surcouf Ⓜ *La Tour Maubourg* ✆ 01 45 51 46 93, *Fax 01 45 50 30 11* – ▤. AE ⓓ GB H 9
Meals 35 (lunch)/44 and a la carte 47/60 ♀
Spec. Langoustines rôties aux épices douces. Poitrine de pigeon fermier farcie au foie gras. Soufflé au chocolat pur Caraïbes..
◆ Stéphane Molé has relocated Les Ormes from the 16th arrondissement to the former Bellecour, close to Les Invalides. An elegant setting in which to savour traditional cuisine.

XX **Cigale Récamier,** 4 r. Récamier Ⓜ *Sèvres Babylone* ✆ 01 45 48 87 87, *Fax 01 45 48 87 87,* ☂ – ▤. GB K 12
closed Sunday – **Meals** a la carte 40/55 ♀.
◆ The menu at this "literary" address popular with authors and publishers offers a wide choice of savoury and sweet soufflés. Quiet, pleasant terrace on a traffic-free street.

XX ✿ **Vin sur Vin,** 20 r. de Monttessuy Ⓜ *Ecole Militaire* ✆ 01 47 05 14 20 – ▤. GB H 8
closed 1 to 30 August, 22 Dec.-4 January, Monday except dinner from September to Easter, Saturday lunch and Sunday – **Meals** (booking essential) a la carte 55/82 🍇
Spec. Galette de pieds de cochon. Canard colvert (mid-September-late-January). Tourteau frais (May-September).
◆ Friendly service, elegant decor, delicious traditional cuisine and a full wine list (600 appellations) - top marks for this restaurant situated close to the Eiffel Tower !

New Jawad, 12 av. Rapp Ⓜ *Ecole Militaire* ☎ 01 47 05 91 37, *Fax 01 45 50 31 27* – ▤. AE ⓓ GB H 8
Meals 16/23 and a la carte 28/38 ♀.
◆ This restaurant near the Pont de l'Alma offers customers a luxurious ambience, attentive service and dishes from India and Pakistan.

Beato, 8 r. Malar Ⓜ *Invalides* ☎ 01 47 05 94 27, *beato.rest@wanadoo.fr, Fax 01 45 55 64 41* – ▤. AE GB H 9
closed 14 July-15 August, 24 December-1 January, Saturday lunch and Sunday – **Meals** 27 (lunch) and a la carte 36/63 ♀.
◆ Frescoes, columns that could have come from Pompeii, and neo-Classical chairs - a version of Italian décor for a chic restaurant. Dishes from Milan, Rome and elsewhere.

Caffé Minotti (Vernier), 33 r. Verneuil Ⓜ *Rue du Bac* ☎ 01 42 60 04 04, *caffeminotti@wanadoo.fr, Fax 01 42 60 04 05* – (dinner). AE GB J 12
closed August, Sunday and Monday – **Meals** a la carte 45/65 ♀
Spec. Les risotti. Gemelli aux cèpes. Tiramisu.
◆ Minimalist designer decor, including a stunning red Murano glass chandelier. Imaginative and delicate Italian cuisine with a balanced menu that is constantly evolving.

D'Chez Eux, 2 av. Lowendal Ⓜ *Ecole Militaire* ☎ 01 47 05 52 55, *Fax 01 45 55 60 74* – ▤. AE ⓓ GB J 9
closed 29 July-24 August and Sunday – **Meals** 40 (lunch) and a la carte 48/70 ♀.
◆ For over 40 years this restaurant has served copious portions inspired by the cuisine of Auvergne and southwest France. Provincial inn ambience and smock-coated staff.

Au Bon Accueil, 14 r. Monttessuy Ⓜ *Alma Marceau* ☎ 01 47 05 46 11 – ▤. GB H 8
closed Saturday and Sunday – **Meals** 27 (lunch)/31 and a la carte 46/67.
◆ In the shade of the Eiffel Tower, a modern interior or a small adjacent room with tasty food in contemporary style, well adapted to the season.

Les Olivades, 41 av. Ségur Ⓜ *Ségur* ☎ 01 47 83 70 09, *Fax 01 42 73 04 75* – ▤. AE GB JCB K 9
closed 4 to 27 August, Sunday, lunch Saturday and Monday – **Meals** 38/60 and a la carte 57/72.
◆ An establishment fragrant with the scent of olive oil, offering an appetising version of Mediterranean cuisine. Pleasing decor of pastel hues, modern art and rustic furniture.

Clos des Gourmets, 16 av. Rapp Ⓜ *Alma Marceau* ☎ 01 45 51 75 61, *Fax 01 47 05 74 20* – GB H 8
closed 10 to 25 August, Sunday and Monday – **Meals** 29 (lunch)/33.
◆ Recently redecorated in sunny colours, this modest place has its retinue of regulars who appreciate its appetising menu varied according to availability of fresh ingredients.

Maupertu, 94 bd La Tour Maubourg Ⓜ *Ecole Militaire* ☎ 01 45 51 37 96, *info@restaurant-maupertu-paris.com, Fax 01 53 59 94 83,* – GB J 10
closed 8 to 22 August and Sunday – **Meals** 28 ♀.
◆ The Invalides beckon whether you eat outside or in the veranda-like dining-room with its walls in sunny colours. Dishes inspired by the cuisine of Provence.

Florimond, 19 av. La Motte-Picquet Ⓜ *Ecole Militaire* ☎ 01 45 55 40 38, *Fax 01 45 55 40 38* – GB H 9
closed 1 to 8 May, 1 to 22 August, 24 December-3 January, Saturday and Sunday – **Meals** 19 (lunch)/33,50 and a la carte 41/61.
◆ Bearing the name of Monet's Giverny gardener, this tiny non-smoking establishment is decorated in bright colours and wood panelling. Dishes based on fresh market produce.

P'tit Troquet, 28 r. L'Exposition Ⓜ *Ecole Militaire* ☎ 01 47 05 80 39, *Fax 01 47 05 80 39* – GB. J 9
closed 1 to 23 August, 10 to 23 January, Sunday, lunch Saturday and Monday – **Meals** (booking essential) 27 (lunch)/29 ♀.
◆ Small it may be, but the "little innkeeper" has a lot going for it including a cheerful atmosphere, old posters, and a tasty cuisine based on produce fresh from the market.

L'Affriolé, 17 r. Malar Ⓜ *Invalides* ☎ 01 44 18 31 33, *Fax 01 44 18 91 12* – GB H 9
closed August, Christmas Holidays, Saturday and Sunday – **Meals** 29 (lunch)/32.
◆ Chef's suggestions on the daily specials' board, plus à la carte and fixed menu choices that change monthly according to seasonal availability.

Champs-Élysées, St-Lazare, Madeleine.

8th arrondissement.
8th: ✉ 75008

Plaza Athénée, 25 av. Montaigne Ⓜ *Alma Marceau* ☎ 01 53 67 66 65, *reservation @plaza-athenee-paris.com, Fax 01 53 67 66 66,* – 20 - 60. AE ⓓ GB JCB G 9
see ***Alain Ducasse au Plaza Athénée and Relais Plaza*** below **- *La Cour Jardin*** (terrace) ☎ 01 53 67 66 02 *(mid-May-mid-September)* **Meals** a la carte 75/95 – ☕ 46 – **143 rm** 555/750, 45 suites.
• Sumptuously refurbished rooms in classic or Art Deco style, "musical" teas in the Galerie des Gobelins, and a stunning designer bar - the epitome of the Parisian grand hotel. The Plaza's summer restaurant, the Cour Jardin, is a tranquil green oasis.

Four Seasons George V, 31 av. George V Ⓜ *George V* ☎ 01 49 52 70 00, *lecinq.p ar@fourseasons.com, Fax 01 49 52 70 10,* – 30 - 240. AE ⓓ GB JCB. rest F 8
see ***Le Cinq*** below **- *Terrasse d'Été*** ☎ 01 49 52 70 06 **Meals** a la carte 69/119 ♀ – ☕ 45 – **186 rm** 650/890, 59 suites.
• Now completely refurbished in 18C style, this hotel has luxurious and, by Parisian standards, huge rooms, wonderful art collections and a superb spa. The tables of the Terrasse d'Été are set out in the delightful inner courtyard.

Bristol, 112 r. Fg St-Honoré Ⓜ *Miromesnil* ☎ 01 53 43 43 00, *resa@lebristolparis.com, Fax 01 53 43 43 01,* rm, – 30 - 100. AE ⓓ GB JCB F 10
Meals see ***Bristol*** below – ☕ 47 – **126 rm** 620/780, 38 suites.
• Palatial 1925 grand hotel laid out around a magnificent garden. Luxurious rooms, mostly in Louis XV or XVI style and an exceptional boat-like pool on the top floor.

Crillon, 10 pl. Concorde Ⓜ *Concorde* ☎ 01 44 71 15 00, *crillon@crillon.com, Fax 01 44 71 15 02,* – 30 - 60. AE ⓓ GB JCB G 11
see ***Les Ambassadeurs*** and ***L'Obélisque*** below – ☕ 45 – **103 rm** 595/880, 44 suites.
• The lounges of this private hotel dating from the 18C have kept their splendid ornamentation. The panelled bedrooms are magnificent. Palatial living, French style.

Royal Monceau, 37 av. Hoche Ⓜ *Charles de Gaulle-Etoile* ☎ 01 42 99 88 00, *reserv ations@royalmonceau.com, Fax 01 42 99 89 90,* – 15 - 200. AE ⓓ GB JCB. E 8
see ***Jardin*** and ***Carpaccio*** below – ☕ 42 – **133 rm** 650/850, 47 suites.
• The recent refurbishment of this grand hotel (1928) is the work of Jacques Garcia. Superb foyer/lounge, elegant rooms and a well-equipped fitness centre with a swimming pool.

Hilton Arc de Triomphe, 51 r. Courcelles Ⓜ *Courcelles* ☎ 01 58 36 67 00, *info-a dt@hilton.com, Fax 01 58 36 67 84,* rm, – 15 - 800. AE ⓓ GB. rest E 9
Safran ☎ 01 58 36 67 96 **Meals** a la carte 42/77 – ☕ 30 – **438 rm** 730, 25 suites.
• Inspired by the liners of the 1930s, this new hotel has successfully conjured up the elegant luxury of bygone days with its elegant Art Deco bedrooms, patio-fountain etc. Modern cuisine influenced by the flavours and aromas of Asia in Le Safran. Fitness room.

Lancaster, 7 r. Berri Ⓜ *George V* ☎ 01 40 76 40 76, *reservations@hotel-lancaster.fr, Fax 01 40 76 40 00,* AE ⓓ GB. rest F 9
Meals see ***Table du Lancaster*** below – ☕ 32 – **49 rm** 350/590, 11 suites.
• B Pastoukhoff settled his bill here by painting pictures, thereby enriching the elegant décor of the venerable private hotel that was also a favourite of Marlene Dietrich.

Vernet, 25 r. Vernet Ⓜ *Charles de Gaulle-Etoile* ☎ 01 44 31 98 00, *reservations@ho telvernet.com, Fax 01 44 31 85 69* – AE ⓓ GB JCB. rest F 8
see ***Les Élysées*** below – ☕ 35 – **42 rm** 390/550, 9 suites.
• Lovely 1920s stone building with wrought-iron balconies. Empire or Louis XVI-style rooms. Trendy grill-bar.

Astor Saint-Honoré, 11 r. d'Astorg Ⓜ *St-Augustin* ☎ 01 53 05 05 05, *astor-resa@astor-st-honore.com, Fax 01 53 05 05 30,* – ♿ rm, . AE GB JCB. rest F 11
L'Astor ☎ 01 53 05 05 20 *(closed August, Saturday and Sunday)* **Meals** 45/65b.i. – 25 – **129 rm** 500/790, 5 suites.
◆ A successful fusion of Regency and Art Deco style in this cosy establishment much appreciated by a select circle of regular guests.

San Régis, 12 r. J. Goujon Ⓜ *Champs-Elysées Clemenceau* ☎ 01 44 95 16 16, *message@hotel-sanregis.fr, Fax 01 45 61 05 48* – . AE GB JCB. G 9
Meals *(closed August)* a la carte 46/71 – 22 – **33 rm** 315/565, 11 suites.
◆ Newly refurbished town mansion of 1857 with delightful rooms graced here and there with mottled furniture. Haute couture boutiques nearby. The San Régis restaurant - a real little gem - is in an intimate and luxurious lounge-cum-library.

Le Faubourg Sofitel Demeure Hôtels, 15 r. Boissy d'Anglas Ⓜ *Concorde* ☎ 01 44 94 14 14, *h1295@accor-hotels.com, Fax 01 44 94 14 28,* – ♿ . AE GB JCB. G 11
Café Faubourg ☎ 01 44 94 14 24 *(closed 1 to 22 August, Sunday lunch and Saturday)* **Meals** a la carte 60/80 – 28 – **174 rm** 530/600.
◆ The Faubourg-St-Honoré branch of Sofitel is housed in two 18C and 19C residences. Hi-tech rooms, 1930s-style bar and lounge beneath a glass roof. Up-to-the-minute decor, restful indoor garden and traditional cuisine at the Café Faubourg.

Sofitel Arc de Triomphe, 14 r. Beaujon Ⓜ *Charles de Gaulle-Etoile* ☎ 01 53 89 50 50, *h1296@accor-hotels.com, Fax 01 53 89 50 51* – ♿ – 40. AE GB JCB F 8
see ***Clovis*** below – 27 – **134 rm** 570/900.
◆ The building is from the Haussmann period, the decor inspired by the 18C, and the fixtures and fittings decidedly 21C. Elegant bedrooms, including the stunning "concept room".

De Vigny, 9 r. Balzac Ⓜ *Charles de Gaulle-Etoile* ☎ 01 42 99 80 80, *reservation@hoteldevigny.com, Fax 01 42 99 80 40* – rm, . AE GB JCB F 8
Baretto **: Meals** a la carte 52/83 – 25 – **26 rm** 395/495, 11 suites.
◆ A discreet, refined hotel with individual, cosy rooms close to the Champs-Élysées. The elegant, comfortable lounge is warmed by a blazing fire in winter. Le Baretto restaurant combines Art Deco style with traditional cuisine and a smart, hushed ambience.

Champs-Élysées Plaza without rest, 35 r. Berri Ⓜ *George V* ☎ 01 53 53 20 20, *info@champselyseesplaza.com, Fax 01 53 53 20 21* – ♿ AE GB JCB.
22 – **32 rm** 390/450. F 9
◆ The elegant and spacious bedrooms in this plush hotel close to the Champs-Elysées are all embellished with a chimney and Art Deco-style bathroom.

Concorde St-Lazare, 108 r. St-Lazare Ⓜ *St Lazare* ☎ 01 40 08 44 44, *stlazare@concordestlazare-paris.com, Fax 01 42 93 01 20* – – 250. AE GB JCB E 12
Café Terminus ☎ 01 40 08 43 30 **Meals** 33/47b.i. – 24 – **254 rm** 360/450, 12 suites.
◆ The monumental railway hotel of 1889 by the Gare St-Lazare has been completely refurbished. Its majestic foyer - a gem of 19C architecture and design - has been given a fresh new look. The Café Terminus has retro brasserie-style décor and bistro-type cuisine.

Marriott, 70 av. Champs-Élysées Ⓜ *Franklin D. Roosevelt* ☎ 01 53 93 55 00, *mhrs.pardt.ays@marriotthotels.com, Fax 01 53 93 55 01,* – ♿ – 15 - 165. AE GB JCB. F 9
Pavillon ☎ 01 53 93 55 00 *(closed Saturday)* **Meals** a la carte 40/54 – 29 – **174 rm** 775/1200, 18 suites.
◆ A combination of transatlantic efficiency and luxury in the rooms, some of which overlook the Champs Élysées. On the far side of the impressive atrium is the Pavillon, with a décor (lamps, frescoes) recalling a fondly imagined Paris of yesteryear.

Balzac, 6 r. Balzac Ⓜ *George V* ☎ 01 44 35 18 00, *reservation@hotelbalzac.com, Fax 01 44 35 18 05* – , rm, . AE GB JCB F 8
see ***Pierre Gagnaire*** below – 25 – **56 rm** 330/460, 14 suites.
◆ The hotel's name recalls the great 19C writer Honoré de Balzac who spent his last days at no 22 in this street. Elegant rooms, lounge with glass roof.

Warwick, 5 r. Berri Ⓜ *George V* ☎ 01 45 63 14 11, *resa.whparis@warwickhotels.com, Fax 01 43 59 00 98* – – 30 - 110. AE GB JCB. rest F 9
see ***Le W*** below – 28 – **144 rm** 450/580, 5 suites.
◆ The recent refurbishment of this hotel, which first opened in 1981, has seen the introduction of warm materials, contemporary furniture and fabrics hanging from the walls.

Napoléon, 40 av. Friedland *Charles de Gaulle-Etoile* 01 56 68 43 21, *napoleon@hotelnapoleonparis.com, Fax 01 56 68 44 40* – 15 - 80. AE GB JCB F 8
Meals *(closed August, dinner and weekends)* a la carte 40/57 – 26 – **75 rm** 350/600, 26 suites.
◆ Just a few steps from the Emperor's much-loved Étoile, this hotel evokes Napoleonic times with well-chosen pictures, figurines and autographs and with Directoire and Empire furniture. Luxurious, intimate bar/restaurant with limited menu and efficient service.

California, 16 r. Berri *George V* 01 43 59 93 00, *cal@hroy.com, Fax 01 45 61 03 62,* – – 20 - 100. AE GB JCB. rest F 9
Meals *(closed August, Saturday and Sunday)* (lunch only) 33/45 – 30 – **158 rm** 470/550, 16 duplex.
◆ Art-lovers appreciate this 1920s grand hotel, whose walls are hung with thousands of pictures. Another attraction is the display of 200 brands of whisky in the piano bar. Restaurant extending onto a delightful patio with greenery, mosaics, and fountain.

Trémoille, 14 r. Trémoille *Alma Marceau* 01 56 52 14 00, *reservation@hotel-tremoille.com, Fax 01 40 70 01 08,* – – 15. AE GB JCB. G 9
Meals *(closed Sunday and Monday)* 36 (lunch), 55/75 – 26 – **88 rm** 570, 5 suites.
◆ This hotel has recently been brought up-to-date and successfully manages to combine antiques with modern design. Well-equipped marble bathrooms ; elegant dining room with genteel atmosphere and seasonal menu.

Meliá Royal Alma without rest, 35 r. J. Goujon *Alma Marceau* 01 53 93 63 00, *melia.royal.alma@solmelia.com, Fax 01 53 93 63 01* – – 15. AE GB JCB
24 – **64 rm** 335/503. G 9
◆ Refined decor and Empire-style antique furniture in the recently renovated rooms. Panoramic views from the terrace on the top floor. Simple food and brunches on offer on the veranda with pretty little garden.

Bedford, 17 r. de l'Arcade *Madeleine* 01 44 94 77 77, *reservation@hotel-bedford.com, Fax 01 44 94 77 97* – – 15 - 50. AE GB JCB. rest F 11
Meals *(closed 1 to 28 August, Saturday and dinner)* (lunch only) 37 and a la carte 48/66 – 13,30 – **136 rm** 178/230, 10 suites.
◆ Built in 1860 in the elegant Madeleine district, the hotel has large, refurbished functional rooms. Ambience of 1900 with abundant decorative plasterwork and a lovely cupola in the restaurant, the Bedford's real jewel.

De Sers, 41 av. Pierre 1er de Serbie *George V* 01 53 23 75 75, *contact@hoteldesers.com, Fax 01 53 23 75 76,* , – – 35. G 8
Meals 30 (lunch) and a la carte 43/71 – 28 – **45 rm** 450/520, 7 suites.
◆ Wood panelling in the foyer and lounge, with old paintings on the walls. Several rooms have been renovated in classic style, with those facing the garden on the quieter side.

Montaigne without rest, 6 av. Montaigne *Alma Marceau* 01 47 20 30 50, *contact@hotel-montaigne.com, Fax 01 47 20 94 12* – . AE GB JCB G 9
19 – **29 rm** 300/450.
◆ Wrought-iron grilles, a fine flower-bedecked façade, and lovely décor make this a seductive place to stay. The avenue is a stronghold of the great couturiers.

Amarante Champs Élysées without rest, 19 r. Vernet *George V* 01 47 20 41 73, *amarante-champs-elysees@jjwhotels.com, Fax 01 47 23 32 15* – – 30. AE GB JCB F 8
25 – **42 rm** 330/450.
◆ A pretty canopy graces the smart façade of this corner building. Period furniture in the rooms. Luxurious lounge with piano bar and fine fireplace.

François 1er without rest, 7 r. Magellan *George V* 01 47 23 44 04, *hotel@hotel-francois1er.fr, Fax 01 47 23 93 43* – – 15. AE GB JCB F 8
21 – **40 rm** 320/460.
◆ Mexican marble, moulding, antique trinkets and furniture and numerous paintings contribute to the luxurious decor designed by Pierre-Yves Rochon. Substantial buffet breakfast.

Daniel without rest, 8 r. Frédéric Bastiat *St Philippe du Roule* 01 42 56 17 00, *hoteldanielparis@wanadoo.fr, Fax 01 42 56 17 01* – . AE GB JCB. F 9
28 – **22 rm** 230/390, 4 suites.
◆ Inspiration here comes from far and wide with furniture and objects from around the globe. With the addition of Jouy fabrics, the overall decor is both refined and welcoming.

Sofitel Champs-Élysées, 8 r. J. Goujon Ⓜ *Champs-Elysées Clemenceau* ✆ *01 40 74 64 64, h1184-re@accor-hotels.com, Fax 01 40 74 79 66,* - 15 - 150. AE GB JCB G 9
Les Signatures ✆ *01 40 74 64 94 (lunch only)(closed 30/07-28/08,24/12-01/01, Saturday, Sunday and Bank Holidays)* **Meals** 45 - 25 - **40 rm** 420/550.
• This private hotel dates from the time of Napoleon III. Refurbished contemporary rooms equipped with the very latest in facilities. Business centre. Cool decor and an attractive terrace in Les Signatures, which is particularly popular with journalists.

Radisson SAS Champs Élysées, 78 av. Marceau Ⓜ *Charles de Gaulle-Etoile* ✆ *01 53 23 43 43, reservations.paris@radissonsas.com, Fax 01 53 23 43 44,* - AE GB. F 8
Meals *(closed 1 to 22 August, Chrismas HolidayS, Saturday, Sunday and Bank Holidays)* 50 (dinner) and a la carte 60/80 - 22 - **46 rm** 315.
• A new hotel created in a building which once belonged to Louis Vuitton. Modern rooms, state-of-the-art equipment (plasma screen TVs) and efficient soundproofing. Dining by the bar or on the summer terrace. Concise à la carte menu showing Provençal influence.

Pershing Hall, 49 r. P. Charon Ⓜ *George V* ✆ *01 58 36 58 00, info@pershinghall.com, Fax 01 58 36 58 01* - - 60. AE GB JCB G 9
Meals *(closed Sunday dinner)* a la carte 42/85 - 34 - **20 rm** 390/1000, 6 suites.
• Once the residence of US General Pershing, a veterans' club and now a charming hotel redesigned by Andrée Putmann. Smart interior and delightful vertical garden. Beyond the curtain of glass pearls a restaurant with up-to-the-minute ambience and trendy menu.

Chambiges Élysées without rest, 8 r. Chambiges Ⓜ *Alma Marceau* ✆ *01 44 31 83 83, chamb@paris-hotels-charm.com, Fax 01 40 70 95 51* - AE GB JCB. - **26 rm** 250/330, 8 suites. G 9
• Wood panelling, wall hangings, luxurious soft-furnishings and romantic atmosphere in this entirely renovated hotel. Quiet, cosy rooms and pretty little interior garden.

Le A without rest, 4 r. Artois Ⓜ *St-Philippe du Roule* ✆ *01 42 56 99 99, hotel-le-a@wanadoo.fr, Fax 01 42 56 99 90* - - 21 - **26 rm** 320/439. F 9
• Artist Fabrice Hybert and design guru Frédéric Méchiche are behind this hotel in chic black and white. Soothing interior including a sitting room-library and lounge-bar.

L'Arcade without rest, 7 et 9 r. Arcade Ⓜ *Madeleine* ✆ *01 53 30 60 00, reservation@hotel-arcade.com, Fax 01 40 07 03 07* - - 25. AE GB JCB. 9,50 - **41 rm** 142/220, 4 duplex. F 11
• Marble and panelling in foyer and lounges, soft colours and choice furnishings in the bedrooms lend great charm to this discreet, elegant hotel near the Madeleine.

Monna Lisa, 97 r. La Boétie Ⓜ *St-Philippe du Roule* ✆ *01 56 43 38 38, contact@hotelmonnalisa.com, Fax 01 45 62 39 90* - AE GB JCB. F 9
Caffe Ristretto - Italian rest. *(closed August, Saturday and Sunday)* **Meals** 19(lunch)/46(lunch) and a la carte 46/58 - 17 - **22 rm** 245/265.
• This attractive hotel housed in a building dating from 1860 is a shop window for bold Italian design. Enjoy a gastronomic journey around the Italian peninsula in the delightfully contemporary surroundings of the Caffe Ristretto. Larger rooms facing the street.

Lavoisier without rest, 21 r. Lavoisier Ⓜ *St-Augustin* ✆ *01 53 30 06 06, info@hotellavoisier.com, Fax 01 53 30 23 00* - AE GB JCB. F 11
14 - **26 rm** 250/265, 4 suites.
• This hotel in the St-Augustin district has contemporary rooms, a small, cosy lounge-cum-library also serving as the bar, plus a vaulted breakfast room.

Queen Mary without rest, 9 r. Greffulhe Ⓜ *Madeleine* ✆ *01 42 66 40 50, hotelqueenmary@wanadoo.fr, Fax 01 42 66 94 92* - AE GB JCB F 12
17 - **36 rm** 145/199.
• A refined hotel with a very British ambience and a welcome sherry on arrival. Attractive patio, pretty breakfast room and cosy bedrooms.

Vignon without rest, 23 r. Vignon Ⓜ *Madeleine* ✆ *01 47 42 93 00, reservation@hotelvignon.com, Fax 01 47 42 04 60* - AE GB. F 12
20 - **28 rm** 275/340.
• Comfortable, contemporary rooms just a stone's throw from Place de la Madeleine; those on the top floor have been refurbished and are light and airy. Elegant breakfast room.

Élysées Céramic without rest, 34 av. Wagram Ⓜ *Ternes* ✆ *01 42 27 20 30, cerotel@aol.com, Fax 01 46 22 95 83* - AE GB JCB E 8
10 - **57 rm** 175/220.
• The stoneware Art Nouveau façade of 1904 is an architectural marvel, matched by the interior with furniture and décor inspired by the same style.

Pavillon Montaigne without rest, 34 r. J. Mermoz Ⓜ *Franklin D. Roosevelt* ✆ *01 53 89 95 00, hotelpavillonmontaigne@wanadoo.fr, Fax 01 42 89 33 00* - AE GB JCB. - 8 - **18 rm** 145/160. F 10
• Two buildings linked by a breakfast room with a glass roof. Rooms, some with exposed beams, have a mixture of antique and contemporary furnishings.

XXXXX ✿✿✿ **Le "Cinq"** - Hôtel Four Seasons George V, 31 av. George V Ⓜ *George V* ✆ 01 49 52 71 54, *lecinq.par@fourseasons.com, Fax 01 49 52 71 81,* – AE GB JCB. F 8
Meals 80 (lunch), 120/230 and a la carte 137/211
Spec. Gaspacho de laitue à la mozzarella et aux girolles. Turbot de ligne rôti au melon d'eau. Côte de veau de lait fermier aux câpres de Pantelleria.
• Majestic interior evoking the glories of the Grand Trianon and opening on to a delightful internal garden. Refined ambience and talented, classic cuisine.

XXXXX ✿✿ **Les Ambassadeurs** - Hôtel Crillon, 10 pl. Concorde Ⓜ *Concorde* ✆ 01 44 71 16 16, *restaurants@crillon.com, Fax 01 44 71 15 02* – AE GB JCB. G 11
closed 8 to 28 August, Monday lunch and Sunday – **Meals** 70 (lunch) and a la carte 152/210
Spec. Blanc à manger d'oeuf, truffe noire (January-March). Pigeonneau désossé, foie gras, jus à l'olive. Fraises des bois, lait concentré, jus de fraise façon chabrot.
• Once the ballroom of an 18C town mansion, the splendid interior is awash with gilded and marble decor reflected in huge mirrors. Refined cuisine.

XXXXX ✿✿✿ **Ledoyen,** carré Champs-Élysées (1st floor) Ⓜ *Champs-Elysées Clemenceau* ✆ 01 53 05 10 01, *ledoyen@ledoyen.com, Fax 01 47 42 55 01* – AE GB. G 10
closed 1 to 28 August, Monday lunch, Saturday, Sunday and Bank Holidays – **Meals** 73 (lunch), 168/244 b.i. and a la carte 144/200
Spec. Grosses langoustines bretonnes croustillantes, émulsion d'agrumes à l'huile d'olive. Blanc de turbot de ligne braisé, pommes rattes truffées. Noix de ris de veau en brochette de bois de citronnelle, jus d'herbes..
• Neo-Classical building erected in 1848 on the Champs-Élysées. Napoleon III decor, views of the gardens designed by Hittorff and fine cuisine featuring meat and fish dishes.

XXXXX ✿✿✿ **Alain Ducasse au Plaza Athénée** - Hôtel Plaza Athénée, 25 av. Montaigne Ⓜ *Alma Marceau* ✆ 01 53 67 65 00, *adpa@alain-ducasse.com, Fax 01 53 67 65 12* – AE GB JCB. G 9
closed 15 July-23 August, 23 to 31 December, Saturday, Sunday, lunch Monday, Tuesday and Wednesday – **Meals** 200/300 and a la carte 170/220
Spec. Langoustines rafraîchies, nage réduite, caviar osciètre. Volaille de Bresse, sauce albuféra aux tartufi di d'Alba (15 October-31 December). Coupe glacée de saison..
• The Plaza's sumptuous Regency decor has just been given a new fresh design look. Inventive dishes created by a team trained by Alain Ducasse. Comprehensive wine list.

XXXXX ✿✿ **Bristol** - Hôtel Bristol, 112 r. Fg St-Honoré Ⓜ *Miromesnil* ✆ 01 53 43 43 40, *resa@lebristolparis.com, Fax 01 53 43 43 01,* – AE GB JCB. F 10
Meals 75 (lunch)/160 and a la carte 100/208
Spec. Langoustines du Guilvinec rôties au thym-citron (except December-January). Poularde de bresse cuite en vessie au vin de Château-Chalon. Sabayon au chocolat noir, caramel mou aux épices, glace à l'infusion..
• With its oval shape and splendid panelling, the winter dining room resembles a little theatre. The summer dining room opens out on the hotel's magnificent garden.

XXXXX ✿✿✿ **Taillevent,** 15 r. Lamennais Ⓜ *Charles de Gaulle-Etoile* ✆ 01 44 95 15 01, *mail@taillevent.com, Fax 01 42 25 95 18* – AE GB JCB. F 9
closed 30 July-29 August, Saturday, Sunday and Bank Holidays – **Meals** (booking essential) 70 (lunch), 130/180 and a la carte 90/144
Spec. Barigoule d'artichauts poivrades aux langoustines. Tourte de ris de veau à la royale. Fruits de saison en cocotte lutée..
• Housed in a 19C town house which once belonged to the Duc de Morny, this restaurant has panelling, works of art, exquisite cuisine and a sumptuous cellar. A gastronomic must.

XXXXX ✿✿ **Apicius** (Vigato), 20 r. Artois Ⓜ *St Philippe du Roule* ✆ 01 43 80 19 66, *restaurant-apicius@wanadoo.fr, Fax 01 44 40 09 57,* – 10 - 15. AE GB JCB F 9
closed August, Saturday and Sunday – **Meals** 80 (lunch), 120/140 and a la carte 90/140
Spec. Foie gras de canard aux radis noirs confits. Milieu de très gros turbot rôti aux épices. Soufflé au chocolat noir..
• 19C Flemish paintings and 17C Indian sculptures ornament this elegant restaurant occupying a private town house. Contemporary à la carte menu, plus an outstanding wine list.

XXXXX ✿✿ **Lasserre,** 17 av. F.-D.-Roosevelt Ⓜ *Franklin D. Roosevelt* ✆ 01 43 59 53 43, *lasserre@lasserre.fr, Fax 01 45 63 72 23* – AE GB JCB. G 10
closed August, Sunday, lunch Saturday, Monday, Tuesday and Wednesday – **Meals** 75 (lunch)/185 and a la carte 120/190
Spec. Macaroni fourrés aux truffes et foie gras. Turbot aux cèpes et échalotes, palourdes gratinées (September-October). Pigeon André Malraux..
◆ One of the city's gastronomic institutions. The neo-Classical dining room is crowned by a stunning sunroof decorated with a troupe of dancers. Superb wine list.

XXXXX ✿✿ **Laurent,** 41 av. Gabriel Ⓜ *Champs Elysées Clemenceau* ✆ 01 42 25 00 39, *info@le-laurent.com, Fax 01 45 62 45 21,* – AE GB JCB. G 10
closed Saturday lunch, Sunday and Bank Holidays – **Meals** 70/150 and a la carte 131/196
Spec. Araignée de mer dans ses sucs en gelée, crème de fenouil. Grosses langoustines "tandoori" poêlées, copeaux d'avocat à l'huile d'amande. Flanchet de veau braisé, blettes à la moelle et au jus..
◆ Built by Jacques Hittorff, this antique-style pavilion with elegant leafy terraces and fine traditional cuisine is a little corner of paradise in the Champs-Élysées gardens.

XXXX ✿✿✿ **Lucas Carton** (Senderens), 9 pl. Madeleine Ⓜ *Madeleine* ✆ 01 42 65 22 90, *lucas.carton@lucascarton.com, Fax 01 42 65 06 23* – AE GB JCB. G 11
closed 1 to 24 August, 19 to 27 February, Sunday, lunch Monday and Saturday – **Meals** 76 (lunch), 144/380 b.i. and a la carte 138/229
Spec. Rouget barbet en croûte de sel. Râble de lièvre rôti, poivre de Séchouan et cacao. Macaron à la rose..
◆ Superb Art Nouveau panelling by Louis Majorelle in sycamore, maple and lemonwood enhanced by mirrors and exuberant floral ornamentation. Sublime synthesis of food and wine.

XXXX ✿ **Les Élysées** - Hôtel Vernet, 25 r. Vernet Ⓜ *Charles de Gaulle-Etoile* ✆ 01 44 31 98 98, *elysees@hotelvernet.com, Fax 01 44 31 85 69* – AE GB JCB. F 8
closed 23 July-22 August, 17 to 26 December, Monday lunch, Saturday and Sunday – **Meals** 55 (lunch), 72 b.i./130 (dinner) and a la carte 110/163
Spec. Foie gras de canard vapeur au gingembre. Buri cuit à la plaque façon "tataki". Pithiviers de perdrix, poule faisane et grouse au genièvre (October-December)..
◆ Inventive, masterly and subtly flavoured cuisine beneath a superb Belle Epoque glass roof designed by Gustave Eiffel which fills the interior with soft light.

XXXX ✿✿✿ **Pierre Gagnaire** - Hôtel Balzac, 6 r. Balzac Ⓜ *George V* ✆ 01 58 36 12 50, *p.gagnaire@wanadoo.fr, Fax 01 58 36 12 51* – AE GB F 8
closed 24/04-1/05, 23-30/10, 17-25/12, 4-12/02, Sunday lunch, Saturday and Bank Holidays – **Meals** 90 (lunch), 225/260 and a la carte 213/297
Spec. Langoustines de trois façons. Bar de ligne. Agneau de lozère..
◆ Smart, sober contemporary décor (pale panelling, modern works of art) can hardly compete with the spellbinding sounds of the resident jazzman.

XXXX ✿ **Jardin** - Hôtel Royal Monceau, 37 av. Hoche Ⓜ *Charles de Gaulle-Etoile* ✆ 01 42 99 98 70, *Fax 01 42 99 89 94,* – AE GB JCB. E 8
closed August, Monday lunch, Saturday and Sunday – **Meals** 49 (lunch)/99 and a la carte 88/130
Spec. Langoustines royales grillées. Lapin rôti aux écrevisses. Abricots du Rousillon rôtis aux amandes nouvelles..
◆ Resembling an elegant tent in Napoleonic style, this restaurant serves subtly-flavoured Mediterranean dishes. The terrace and garden have also been give a new look.

XXXX ✿ **La Marée,** 1 r. Daru Ⓜ *Ternes* ✆ 01 43 80 20 00, *lamaree@wanadoo.fr, Fax 01 48 88 04 04* – AE GB E 8
closed August, Sunday and Monday – **Meals** a la carte 75/125
Spec. Pressé de jarret de veau de lait aux langoustines. Menu tout "tout homard" en trois services. Bar en croûte de sel..
◆ A pretty half-timbered façade, stained-glass windows, Flemish paintings and warm panelling give this restaurant its refined character. Seafood specialities.

XXXX ✿ **Clovis** - Hôtel Sofitel Arc de Triomphe, 14 r. Beaujon Ⓜ *Charles de Gaulle-Etoile* ✆ 01 53 89 50 53, *h1296@accor-hotels.com, Fax 01 53 89 50 51* – AE GB JCB F 8
closed 24 July-24 August, 24 December-2 January, Saturday, Sunday and Bank Holidays – **Meals** 39 (lunch), 45/85 and a la carte 70/110
Spec. Tourteau et moules de bouchot en vapeur de chou. Blanc de Saint-Pierre en croûte truffée. Millefeuille au chocolat guanaja..
◆ With its classic décor brought up to date (shades of beige and brown), attentive, smiling service and refined cuisine, this establishment is a rendezvous for local gourmets.

La Table du Lancaster Hôtel Lancaster, 7 r. Berri Ⓜ *George V* ✆ 01 40 76 40 76, *reservations@hotel-lancaster.fr, Fax 01 40 76 40 00,* – AE GB. F 9
closed 23 July-22 August, lunch Saturday and Sunday – **Meals** a la carte 70/100
Spec. Toast de sardines aux truffes. Merlan aux noisettes. Tarte au sucre et beurre demi-sel..
◆ Astute, inventive cuisine supervised by Michel Troisgros in a pleasing contemporary setting adorned with Chinese prints and looking out onto the hotel garden.

Maison Blanche, 15 av. Montaigne (7th floor) Ⓜ *Alma Marceau* ✆ 01 47 23 55 99, *info@maison-blanche.fr, Fax 01 47 20 09 56,* ≤, – AE GB JCB G 9
closed lunch Saturday and Sunday – **Meals** 65 b.i. (lunch) and a la carte 86/121.
◆ On top of the Theatre des Champs-Élysées, a designer restaurant with an immense glass roof giving a view of the gilded dome of the Invalides. Languedoc influenced cuisine.

Fouquet's, 99 av. Champs Élysées Ⓜ *George V* ✆ 01 47 23 50 00, *fouquets@lucienbarriere.com, Fax 01 47 23 60 02,* – AE GB JCB F 8
Meals 42 (dinner)/78 and a la carte 80/120.
◆ A select clientele has been frequenting Le Fouquet's since 1899. Highlights include the dining room refurbished by J. Garcia, a popular outdoor terrace and brasserie cuisine.

Le W - Hôtel Warwick, 5 r. Berri Ⓜ *George V* ✆ 01 45 61 82 08, *lerestaurantw@warwickhotels.com, Fax 01 43 59 00 98* – AE GB JCB. F 9
closed August, 24 December-2 January, Saturday, Sunday and Bank Holidays – **Meals** 39 (lunch), 44/64 and a la carte 75/100
Spec. Huîtres juste raidies, émulsion iodée. Caneton rouennais aux deux cuissons. Allumettes croquantes aux figues caramélisées..
◆ "W" stands for the Warwick hotel, in the heart of which this restaurant with its contemporary décor serves a lovely sun-kissed cuisine.

Chiberta, 3 r. Arsène-Houssaye Ⓜ *Charles de Gaulle-Etoile* ✆ 01 53 53 42 00, *chiberta@guysavoy.com, Fax 01 45 62 85 08* – AE GB JCB F 8
closed August, Saturday lunch and Sunday – **Meals** 60/100 and a la carte 61/92
Spec. Crème de langoustines et carottes, citronnelle-gingembre. Saint-Pierre meunière à l'arête. Figue en trois préparations.
◆ The refurbished Chiberta owes its new look (dark tones and unusual "wall of bottles") to designer J-M Wilmotte and its innovative cuisine to G Savoy.

Carpaccio - Hôtel Royal Monceau, 37 av. Hoche Ⓜ *Charles de Gaulle-Etoile* ✆ 01 42 99 98 90, *reception@royalmonceau.com, Fax 01 42 99 89 94* – AE GB JCB E 8
closed 25 July-21 August – **Meals** 68/90 and a la carte 69/104
Spec. Larges pâtes fraiches aux cèpes et artichauts poivrade (September-October). Assortissement de poissons grillés, citron et safran. Langoustines aux tomates de Pachino..
◆ Beyond the foyer of the Royal Monceau hotel is this attractive restaurant full of Venetian atmosphere with Murano glass chandeliers and appetising Italian cuisine.

L'Obélisque - Hôtel Crillon, 6 r. Boissy d'Anglas Ⓜ *Concorde* ✆ 01 44 71 15 15, *restaurants@crillon.com, Fax 01 44 71 15 02* – . AE GB JCB G 11
closed 16 July-7 August, February Holidays and Bank Holidays – **Meals** 50.
◆ Interior featuring panelling, mirrors and decorative glass, plus diners packed tightly together. Never mind! The food is refined and tasty.

Marcande, 52 r. Miromesnil Ⓜ *Miromesnil* ✆ 01 42 65 19 14, *info@marcande.com, Fax 01 42 65 76 85,* – AE GB F 10
closed 8 to 21 August, 24 December-2 January, Friday dinner, Saturday except dinner from 04-09 and Sunday – **Meals** 39/90 b.i. and a la carte 48/79.
◆ Modest establishment favoured by a business clientele. Contemporary interior giving onto an attractive patio that is very popular in summer.

Copenhague, 142 av. Champs-Élysées (1st floor) Ⓜ *George V* ✆ 01 44 13 86 26, *floricadanica@wanadoo.fr, Fax 01 44 13 89 44,* – AE GB JCB F 8
closed 30 July-21 August, Saturday, Sunday and Bank Holidays – **Meals** 50 (lunch), 68/100 and a la carte 81/117 - ***Flora Danica :*** **Meals** 33 and a la carte 53/66 ♀
Spec. Carpaccio de Saint-Jacques aux grains de caviar (1 October-15 April). Saumon roulé au jambon de Skagen. Noisettes de renne rôties..
◆ This restaurant in the Maison du Danemark features Scandinavian cuisine, elegant Danish design, a view of the Champs-Élysées and a terrace overlooking a charming garden. In Flora Danica, both shop and menu make the most of salmon-based products.

Bath's, 9 r. La Trémoille Ⓜ *Alma Marceau* ✆ 01 40 70 01 09, *contact@baths.fr, Fax 01 40 70 01 22* – AE GB G 9
closed August, 24 to 27 December, Saturday, Sunday and Bank Holidays – **Meals** 30 (lunch)/70 and a la carte 82/106 ♀
Spec. Terrine de museau de porc cuit au foin, salade de lentilles. Saint-Pierre grillé, purée de pois au lard paysan. Fricassée de fraises gariguettes aux herbes (July-September..
◆ This restaurant, decorated with paintings and sculptures by the owner, has a hushed, elegant ambience. The menu focuses on specialities from the Auvergne. Good wine list.

XX **Spoon,** 14 r. Marignan Ⓜ *Franklin D. Roosevelt* ✆ 01 40 76 34 44, *spoonfood@aol.com, Fax 01 40 76 34 37* – ▤ ☞. AE ◑ GB JCB. ✗ G 9
closed 24 July-24 August, 24 December-5 January, Saturday and Sunday – **Meals** 45 (lunch) and a la carte 80/90 ♀.
◆ Minimalist, contemporary interior with designer furniture, exotic wood and a view of the kitchens. Flexible menu featuring dishes from around the globe.

XX ✿ **Luna,** 69 r. Rocher Ⓜ *Villiers* ✆ 01 42 93 77 61, *mchoisnluna@noos.fr, Fax 01 40 08 02 44* – ▤. AE GB E 11
closed 1 to 22 August and Sunday – **Meals** a la carte 63/90 ♀
Spec. Galette de langoustines aux jeunes poireaux. Cassolette de homard au lard fumé. Le "vrai baba" de Zanzibar..
◆ Sober Art Deco surroundings and cuisine based on daily deliveries of fine seafood from the shores of the Atlantic. Be sure to try the rum baba.

XX **Relais Plaza** - Hôtel Plaza Athénée, 25 av. Montaigne Ⓜ *Alma Marceau* ✆ 01 53 67 64 00, *reservation@plaza-athenee-paris.com, Fax 01 53 67 66 66* – ☞. AE ◑ GB JCB. ✗ G 9
closed August – **Meals** 43 and a la carte 75/116.
◆ Chic, intimate rendezvous for people from the neighbouring fashion houses. Subtle renovation has restored the Art Deco interior to its original glory. Refined classic cuisine.

XX **Fermette Marbeuf 1900,** 5 r. Marbeuf Ⓜ *Alma Marceau* ✆ 01 53 23 08 00, *fermettemarbeuf@blanc.net, Fax 01 53 23 08 09* – ▤. AE ◑ GB G 9
Meals 30 and a la carte 48/65 ♀.
◆ The extraordinary Art Nouveau decor of this glazed dining room dates from 1898 and was discovered only by chance in the course of restoration work. Traditional cuisine.

XX ✿ **Marius et Janette,** 4 av. George-V Ⓜ *Alma Marceau* ✆ 01 47 23 41 88, *Fax 01 47 23 07 19,* ☂ – ▤. AE ◑ GB G 8
Meals 60 b.i./100 (lunch) and a la carte 80/115 ♀
Spec. Merlan colbert (April-October). Loup grillé à l'écaille. Aïoli de morue..
◆ The restaurant's name evokes the Marseilles back country and the films of Robert Guédiguian. Nautical décor, attractive terrace, and a taste of the Mediterranean.

XX **Stella Maris,** 4 r. Arsène Houssaye Ⓜ *Charles de Gaulle-Etoile* ✆ 01 42 89 16 22, *stella.maris.paris@wanadoo.fr, Fax 01 42 89 16 01* – ▤. AE ◑ GB JCB. ✗ F 8
closed Saturday lunch, Sunday and lunch in August – **Meals** 79/115 and a la carte 83/107.
◆ This restaurant near the Arc de Triomphe offers classic, modern cuisine attractively presented by the talented Japanese chef. Warm welcome and cool, minimalist decor.

XX **Les Bouchons de François Clerc "Étoile",** 6 r. Arsène Houssaye Ⓜ *Charles de Gaulle-Etoile* ✆ 01 42 89 15 51, *siegebouchons@wanadoo.fr, Fax 01 42 89 28 67* – ▤. AE GB JCB. ✗ F 8
closed Saturday lunch and Sunday – **Meals** 43.
◆ The most recent of the François Clerc "Bouchon" restaurants, featuring fine seafood served in a setting evoking the oceans. Excellent choice of cost-price wines.

XX **Stresa,** 7 r. Chambiges Ⓜ *Alma Marceau* ✆ 01 47 23 51 62 – ▤. AE ◑ GB. ✗ G 9
closed 1 to 8 May, August, 20 December-3 January, saturday and Sunday – **Meals** (booking essential) a la carte 67/107.
◆ Set among the exclusive boutiques of the "Golden Triangle" this trattoria is favoured by artists and the jet-set and features works by the likes of Buffet and César.

XX **Bistrot du Sommelier,** 97 bd Haussmann Ⓜ *St-Augustin* ✆ 01 42 65 24 85, *bistrot-du-sommelier@noos.fr, Fax 01 53 75 23 23* – ▤. AE GB F 11
closed 1 to 23 August, 23 December-2 January, Saturday and Sunday – **Meals** 39 (lunch)/100 b.i. b.i. and a la carte 52/73 ♀.
◆ The bistro of Philippe Faure-Brac, recipient of the world's best sommelier award in 1992. A veritable temple of wine, with a quite outstanding cellar.

XX **Kinugawa,** 4 r. St-Philippe du Roule Ⓜ *St-Philippe du Roule* ✆ 01 45 63 08 07, *Fax 01 42 60 45 21* – ▤. AE ◑ GB JCB. ✗ F 9
closed 24 December-6 January, Saturday lunch and Sunday – **Meals** 54 (lunch), 72/108 and a la carte 65/90.
◆ Behind a modest façade close to the church of St-Philippe-du-Roule is a Japanese restaurant with a richly varied menu of specialities.

XX ✿ **L'Angle du Faubourg,** 195 r. Fg St-Honoré Ⓜ *Ternes* ✆ 01 40 74 20 20, *angledufaubourg@cavestaillevent.com, Fax 01 40 74 20 21* – ▤. AE ◑ GB JCB E 9
closed 30 July-29 August, Saturday, Sunday and Bank Holidays – **Meals** 35/70 and a la carte 51/69 ♀
Spec. Gelée de crustacés à l'anis étoilé. Épaule d'agneau braisée, légumes à la française. Croustillant au citron et basilic..
◆ On the corner of Rue Faubourg-St-Honoré and Rue Balzac this modern bistro with its cool interior offers classic cuisine brought up-to-date in a most acceptable manner.

Market, 15 av. Matignon Ⓜ *Franklin D. Roosevelt* ✆ 01 56 43 40 90, *prmarketsa@ao l.com, Fax 01 43 59 10 87* – AE GB F 10
Meals a la carte 47/74.
◆ A trendy restaurant with an upmarket address. Wood and stone predominate, with African masks adorning wall niches. The menu covers a range of French, Italian and Asian dishes.

Village d'Ung et Li Lam, 10 r. J. Mermoz Ⓜ *Franklin D. Roosevelt* ✆ 01 42 25 99 79, *Fax 01 42 25 12 06* – . AE GB JCB F 10
closed lunch Saturday and Sunday – **Meals** 19/35 and a la carte 35/44 ♀.
◆ Ung and Li welcome guests to this restaurant serving Thai and Chinese cuisine. Original Asian décor, with hanging aquariums and a molten glass floor with encrusted sand.

Al Ajami, 58 r. François 1er Ⓜ *George V* ✆ 01 42 25 38 44, *ajami@free.fr, Fax 01 42 25 38 39* – . AE GB JCB. G 9
Meals 21/38 and a la carte 30/50 ♀.
◆ The temple of Lebanese cuisine in the city, with recipes handed down from father to son since 1920. Oriental décor, friendly atmosphere and a faithful band of regulars.

Café Lenôtre-Pavillon Elysée, 10 Champs-Elysées Ⓜ *Champs-Elysées Clemenceau* ✆ 01 42 65 85 10, *Fax 01 42 65 76 23,* – . AE GB JCB. G 10
closed 5 to 25 August and Sunday dinner – **Meals** a la carte 43/68.
◆ Rejuvenated by a recent facelift, this elegant pavilion built for the 1900 World Exhibition is home to a cookery school and boutique, plus a resolutely modern restaurant.

Daru, 19 r. Daru Ⓜ *Courcelles* ✆ 01 42 27 23 60, *Fax 01 47 54 08 14* – . AE GB
closed August, Sunday and Bank Holidays – **Meals** 34 and a la carte 45/70. E 9
◆ Founded in 1918, Daru was the first Russian grocery store in Paris. Today, it continues to serve traditional zakouskis, blinis and caviar amid a décor of reds and black.

Opéra, Gare du Nord, Gare de l'Est, Grands Boulevards.

9th and 10th arrondissements.
9th: ✉ 75009
10th: ✉ 75010

Intercontinental Le Grand Hôtel, 2 r. Scribe (9th) Ⓜ *Opéra* ✆ 01 40 07 32 32, *legrand@interconti.com, Fax 01 42 66 12 51,* – – 20 - 120. AE GB JCB F 12
Meals see ***Café de la Paix*** below – 31 – **450 rm** 610/710, 28 suites.
◆ This famous palace dating from 1862 has just reopened after 18 months' renovation. The Second Empire feel has been maintained, and is now allied with more modern comforts.

Scribe, 1 r. Scribe (9th) Ⓜ *Opéra* ✆ 01 44 71 24 24, *h0663@accor.com, Fax 01 42 65 39 97* – – 50. AE GB JCB F 12
see ***Les Muses*** below - ***Jardin des Muses*** ✆ 01 44 71 24 19 **Meals** 32 – 28 – **206 rm** 470/680, 5 suites, 6 duplex.
◆ A discreetly luxurious hotel with English décor hidden behind the façade of a Haussmann-style building. It was here, in 1895, that the public were introduced to the film-making of the Lumière brothers. Brasserie menu at the Jardin des Muses in the basement.

Millennium Opéra, 12 bd Haussmann (9th) Ⓜ *Richelieu Drouot* ✆ 01 49 49 16 00, *opera@mill-cop.com, Fax 01 49 49 17 00,* – rm, – 80. AE GB JCB F 13
Brasserie Haussmann ✆ 01 49 49 16 64 **Meals** 26/36 ♀ – 25 – **150 rm** 400/500, 13 suites.
◆ This hotel dating from 1927 has lost little of its Roaring Twenties ambience, with tasteful bedrooms adorned with Art Deco furniture and modern comforts. A more trendy atmosphere reigns supreme in the Brasserie Haussmann, with its typical cuisine.

Ambassador, 16 bd Haussmann (9th) Ⓜ *Richelieu Drouot* ✆ 01 44 83 40 40, *ambas s@concorde-hotels.com, Fax 01 42 46 19 84* – – 110. AE GB JCB F 13
see ***16 Haussmann*** below – 22 – **282 rm** 360/495, 12 suites.
◆ Painted wood panels, crystal chandeliers, antique furniture and objets d'art adorn this elegant 1920s hotel with spacious and comfortable bedrooms.

Villa Opéra Drouot without rest, 2 r. Geoffroy Marie (9th) Ⓜ *Grands Boulevards* ✆ 01 48 00 08 08, *drouot@leshotelsdeparis.com, Fax 01 48 00 80 60* – . AE GB JCB F 14
20 – **29 rm** 229/299, 3 duplex.
◆ A subtle blend of Baroque décor and the latest in creature comforts await guests in rooms further embellished by drapes, velvet, silk and wood panelling.

Mercure Terminus Nord without rest, 12 bd Denain (10th) Ⓜ *Gare du Nord* ✆ 01 42 80 20 00, *h2761@accor-hotels.com, Fax 01 42 80 63 89* – – 70. AE GB JCB E 16
14 – **236 rm** 227/298.
◆ This hotel dating from 1865 has rediscovered its former glory following recent restoration. Art Nouveau glass, British decor and a cosy ambience add to the Victorian feel.

Holiday Inn Paris Opéra, 38 r. Échiquier (10th) Ⓜ *Bonne Nouvelle* ✆ 01 42 46 92 75, *information@hi-parisopera.com, Fax 01 42 47 03 97* – – 45. AE GB JCB F 15
Meals 37 b.i. – 19 – **92 rm** 305/365.
◆ A short walk from the city's major boulevards and their panoply of theatres and brasseries. Large rooms decorated in the spirit of the Belle Époque. The dining room is a jewel of the 1900s, with its mosaics, old glass, woodwork and fine Art Nouveau furniture.

Pavillon de Paris without rest, 7 r. Parme (9th) Ⓜ *Liège* ✆ 01 55 31 60 00, *mail@pavillondeparis.com, Fax 01 55 31 60 01* – . AE GB JCB D 12
16 – **30 rm** 240/296.
◆ Contemporary, minimalist décor and the latest in hotel technology (TV Internet access, fax and voice mail) are the key selling points of this sober, yet luxurious hotel.

Lafayette without rest, 49 r. Lafayette (9th) Ⓜ *Le Peletier* ✆ 01 42 85 05 44, *h2802-gm@accor-hotels.com, Fax 01 49 95 06 60* – kitchenette . AE GB JCB
14 – **96 rm** 174/209, 7 suites. F 14
◆ Elegant beige and wood furnishings in the lobby, plus bedrooms with a rustic, 18C feel and Liberty print fabrics. Winter garden atmosphere in the breakfast room.

St-Pétersbourg without rest, 33 r. Caumartin (9th) Ⓜ *Havre Caumartin* ✆ 01 42 66 60 38, *hotel.st-petersbourg@wanadoo.fr, Fax 01 42 66 53 54* – – 25. AE GB JCB F 12
100 rm 169/225.
◆ Most of the hotel's rooms, furnished in Louis XVI style, are spacious and overlook the courtyard. The opulent lounge, with its wood panelling, coffered ceilings and armchairs, is lit via a colourful glass ceiling. Hushed restaurant with an 1890s counter.

Richmond Opéra without rest, 11 r. Helder (9th) Ⓜ *Chaussée d'Antin* ✆ 01 47 70 53 20, *paris@richmond-hotel.com, Fax 01 48 00 02 10* – . AE GB JCB. F 13
10 – **59 rm** 147/167.
◆ Almost all the hotel's large and elegant bedrooms look onto the courtyard. The lounge is imposingly decorated in Empire style.

Carlton's Hôtel without rest, 55 bd Rochechouart (9th) Ⓜ *Anvers* ✆ 01 42 81 91 00, *carltons@club-internet.fr, Fax 01 42 81 97 04* – . AE GB JCB D 14
9 – **111 rm** 130/138.
◆ The Carlton's main features are its impressive location and rooftop terrace with views of the city. Comfortable rooms with good soundproofing in those facing the boulevard.

Villa Royale without rest, 2 r. Duperré (9th) Ⓜ *Pigalle* ✆ 01 55 31 78 78, *royale@leshotelsdeparis.com, Fax 01 55 31 78 70* – . AE GB JCB D 13
20 – **31 rm** 190/290.
◆ Antique and modern furniture and artefacts set against a backdrop of shimmering colourful decor. Recently redecorated and featuring the latest modern equipment.

Albert 1er without rest, 162 r. Lafayette (10th) Ⓜ *Gare du Nord* ✆ 01 40 36 82 40, *paris@albert1erhotel.com, Fax 01 40 35 72 52* – . AE GB JCB.
11 – **55 rm** 100/116. E 16
◆ A hotel with modern, well-appointed and constantly upgraded rooms with efficient double-glazing. Friendly atmosphere and service.

Opéra Cadet without rest, 24 r. Cadet (9th) Ⓜ *Cadet* ✆ 01 53 34 50 50, *infos@hotel-opera-cadet.fr, Fax 01 53 34 50 60* – 🛗 ▤ TV ✆ 🚗 – 🎤 50. AE ⓓ GB JCB
12 – **85 rm** 178/190, 3 suites. F 14
• Leave your car in the hotel garage, set up residence in this modern hotel, and take to the capital on foot. The rooms facing the garden are generally quieter.

Franklin without rest, 19 r. Buffault (9th) Ⓜ *Cadet* ✆ 01 42 80 27 27, *h2779@accor-hotels.com, Fax 01 48 78 13 04* – 🛗 ✈ TV ✆. AE ⓓ GB JCB. ✂ E 14
13 – **68 rm** 185/198.
• The elegant furnishings in the bedrooms are inspired by Napoleonic military campaigns. A good location in a quiet street plus an unusual naive trompe-l'oeil at reception.

Libertel-Caumartin without rest, 27 r. Caumartin (9th) Ⓜ *Havre Caumartin* ✆ 01 47 42 95 95, *h2811@accor-hotels.com, Fax 01 47 42 88 19* – 🛗 ✈ ▤ TV ✆. AE ⓓ GB JCB F 12
14 – **40 rm** 180/190.
• Attractively decorated rooms with contemporary light-wood furniture, plus a pleasant breakfast room ornamented with brightly coloured paintings.

Blanche Fontaine 🐌 without rest, 34 r. Fontaine (9th) Ⓜ *Blanche* ✆ 01 44 63 54 95, *tryp.blanchefontaine@solmelia.com, Fax 01 42 81 05 52* – 🛗 ✈ TV ✆ 🚗. AE ⓓ GB JCB
16 – **66 rm** 174, 4 suites. D 13
• Tucked away from the hustle and bustle of the city, the Blanche Fontaine offers guests spacious, reasonably renovated rooms, in addition to an attractive breakfast room.

Anjou-Lafayette without rest, 4 r. Riboutté (9th) Ⓜ *Cadet* ✆ 01 42 46 83 44, *hotel.anjou.lafayette@wanadoo.fr, Fax 01 48 00 08 97* – 🛗 TV ✆. AE ⓓ GB JCB E 14
11,50 – **39 rm** 125/150.
• A hotel with Second Empire-style ironwork close to the leafy Square Montholon. Comfortable, soundproofed rooms which have been completely renovated in modern style.

Paris-Est without rest, 4 r. 8 Mai 1945 (main courtyard Gare de l'Est)(10th) Ⓜ *Gare de l'Est* ✆ 01 44 89 27 00, *hotelparisest-bestwestern@autogrill.net, Fax 01 44 89 27 49* – 🛗 ▤ TV. AE ⓓ GB E 16
10 – **45 rm** 89/175.
• Although alongside a busy railway terminal, the hotel's renovated rooms face onto a quieter rear courtyard and have the benefit of efficient soundproofing.

Trois Poussins without rest, 15 r. Clauzel (9th) Ⓜ *St-Georges* ✆ 01 53 32 81 81, *h3p@les3poussins.com, Fax 01 53 32 81 82* – 🛗 kitchenette ✈ ▤ TV ✆ ♿. AE ⓓ GB JCB
10 – **40 rm** 135/185. E 13
• Charming bedrooms offering several levels of comfort, with views of Paris from the upper floors. Attractively vaulted breakfast room and a small terrace-courtyard.

Mercure Monty without rest, 5 r. Montyon (9th) Ⓜ *Grands Boulevards* ✆ 01 47 70 26 10, *hotel@mercuremonty.com, Fax 01 42 46 55 10* – 🛗 ✈ ▤ TV ✆ – 🎤 50. AE ⓓ GB JCB F 14
12,50 – **70 rm** 159/165.
• A fine 1930s façade, Art Deco ambience in the lobby and standard Mercure chain furnishings are the predominant features of this hotel close to the Folies Bergères.

Corona 🐌 without rest, 8 cité Bergère (9th) Ⓜ *Grands Boulevards* ✆ 01 47 70 52 96, *hotelcoronaopera@regetel.com, Fax 01 42 46 83 49* – 🛗 TV ✆ ♿. AE ⓓ GB JCB
12 – **56 rm** 140/180, 4 suites. F 14
• The façade of this building in a quiet and picturesque passageway built in 1825 is adorned with an elegant canopy. Burr elm furniture in the bedrooms, plus a homely lounge.

Alba-Opéra 🐌 without rest, 34 ter r. La Tour d'Auvergne (9th) Ⓜ *Pigalle* ✆ 01 48 78 80 22, *hotel-albaopera-residence@wanadoo.fr, Fax 01 42 85 23 13* – 🛗 kitchenette TV ✆. AE ⓓ GB JCB. ✂ E 14
10 – **25 rm** 109/148.
• It was in this hotel, at the end of a cul-de-sac, that the trumpet player Louis Armstrong lived during the 1930s. Several room categories offering varying degrees of comfort.

Relais du Pré without rest, 16 r. P. Sémard (9th) Ⓜ *Poissonnière* ✆ 01 42 85 19 59, *relaisdupre@wanadoo.fr, Fax 01 42 85 70 59* – 🛗 TV ✆. AE ⓓ GB E 15
10 – **34 rm** 82/102.
• Located close to its older siblings, this hotel offers the same refined levels of modern comfort in its guest rooms, in addition to a cosy and contemporary bar and lounge.

Les Muses - Hôtel Scribe, 1 r. Scribe (9th) Ⓜ *Opéra* ✆ 01 44 71 24 26, *h0663-re@accor-hotels.com, Fax 01 44 71 24 64* – ▤ ♿ 🍷. AE ⓓ GB JCB F 12
closed August, Saturday and Sunday – **Meals** 45 (lunch)/120 and a la carte 95/125 🍷
Spec. Crème brûlée au foie gras, melba, fleur de sel et pralin. Bar de ligne aux coquillages. Lièvre à la royale (season).
• This restaurant housed in the hotel basement is adorned with a fresco and several canvases depicting the Opéra district in the 19C. Enticing à la carte menu.

Café de la Paix -Intercontinental Le Grand Hôtel, 12 bd Capucines (9th) Ⓜ *Opéra*
☎ 01 40 07 36 36, *Fax 01 40 07 36 33* – ▤ ⊐. AE ◑ GB JCB. ✻ F 12
Meals 31 (lunch)/39 and a la carte 40/100.
◆ An opulent and famous brasserie adorned with fine frescoes, gilded panelling and furniture inspired by the style of the Second Empire. Recently renovated and open 7am-midnight.

Au Chateaubriant, 23 r. Chabrol (10th) Ⓜ *Gare de l'Est* ☎ 01 48 24 58 94, *Fax 01 42 47 09 75* – ▤. AE GB JCB E 15
closed 7 to 26 August, Sunday and Monday – **Meals** 29 and a la carte 38/68 ♀.
◆ A hushed ambience, attractively laid tables and a collection of modern paintings provide the setting for this restaurant where the cuisine is inspired by all things Italian.

16 Haussmann - Hôtel Ambassador, 16 bd Haussmann (9th) Ⓜ *Chaussée d'Antin* ☎ 01 44 83 40 40, *16haussmann@concorde-hotels.com, Fax 01 44 83 40 57* – ▤ ⊐ (lunch). AE ◑ GB F 13
closed 1 to 25 August, 1 to 11 November and Bank Holidays – **Meals** 38 and a la carte approx. 46.
◆ "Parisian" blues, golden yellows, sandy-coloured wood, red Starck-designed chairs and large bay windows looking onto the boulevard, the bustle of which adds to the ambience.

Au Petit Riche, 25 r. Le Peletier (9th) Ⓜ *Richelieu Drouot* ☎ 01 47 70 68 68, *aupetitriche@wanadoo.fr, Fax 01 48 24 10 79* – ▤. AE ◑ GB JCB F 13
closed Sunday – **Meals** 25,50/28,50 and a la carte 33/48 ♀.
◆ Graceful late-19C lounge/dining rooms embellished with mirrors. You might even end up sitting at the favourite table of Maurice Chevalier and other famous stars.

Brasserie Flo, 7 cour Petites-Écuries (10th) Ⓜ *Château d'Eau* ☎ 01 47 70 13 59, *Fax 01 42 47 00 80* – ▤ ⊐ (dinner). AE ◑ GB JCB F 15
Meals 23,50 b.i./33,50 b.i. and a la carte 45/72 ♀.
◆ At the heart of the picturesque cour des Petites-Écuries, the Flo's fine decor of plain wood, coloured glass and painted panels evokes Alsace at the beginning of the 20C.

Terminus Nord, 23 r. Dunkerque (10th) Ⓜ *Gare du Nord* ☎ 01 42 85 05 15, *Fax 01 40 16 13 98* – ▤. AE ◑ GB JCB E 16
Meals 32,90 b.i. and a la carte 35/60 ♀.
◆ The high ceiling, frescoes, posters and sculptures reflect in the mirrors of this brasserie which successfully blends Art Deco and Art Nouveau styles. Cosmopolitan clientele.

Petite Sirène de Copenhague, 47 r. N.-D. de Lorette (9th) Ⓜ *St-Georges* ☎ 01 45 26 66 66 – GB E 13
closed August, 23 December-2 January, Saturday lunch, Sunday, Monday and Bank Holidays – **Meals** (booking essential) 26/31 and a la carte 48/63.
◆ This restaurant with a simple dining room decor of whitewashed walls and filtered lighting serves a range of typical Danish dishes. Excellent service.

L'Oenothèque, 20 r. St-Lazare (9th) Ⓜ *Notre Dame de Lorette* ☎ 01 48 78 08 76, *loenotheque2@wanadoo.fr, Fax 01 40 16 10 27* – ▤. AE ◑ GB JCB E 13
closed 1 to 11 May, 9 to 31 August, Saturday and Sunday – **Meals** a la carte 35/66.
◆ A simple restaurant-cum-wine merchant offering a fine selection of vintages to accompany specials written up on the daily menu.

I Golosi, 6 r. Grange Batelière (9th) Ⓜ *Richelieu Drouot* ☎ 01 48 24 18 63, *i.golosi@wanadoo.fr, Fax 01 45 23 18 96* – ▤. GB F 14
closed 8 to 21 August, Saturday dinner and Sunday – **Meals** a la carte 29/43 ♀.
◆ The minimalist feel of this first-floor Italian restaurant is compensated for by the jovial service. A café, shop and tasting section are all found on the ground floor.

Pré Cadet, 10 r. Saulnier (9th) Ⓜ *Cadet* ☎ 01 48 24 99 64, *Fax 01 47 70 55 96* – ▤. AE ◑ GB JCB F 14
closed 1 to 8 May, 3 to 24 August, Christmas-New Year, Saturday lunch and Sunday – **Meals** (booking essential) 30/45 and a la carte 40/54.
◆ The success of this small eatery near the "Folies" is based on a pleasant ambience and service, and good-value dishes such as "tête de veau", the house speciality.

L'Hermitage, 5 bd Denain (10th) Ⓜ *Gare du Nord* ☎ 01 48 78 77 09, *restaurantlhermitage@wanadoo.fr, Fax 01 42 85 17 27* – ▤. AE ◑ GB E 15
closed 8 to 22 August, Monday lunch, Saturday lunch, Sunday and Bank Holidays – **Meals** 26 ♀.
◆ Named after the celebrated Rhône valley appellation in the owner's home region, L'Hermitage serves traditional seasonal cuisine amid a warm decor of red and orange tones.

Bastille, Gare de Lyon, Place d'Italie, Bois de Vincennes.

12th and 13th arrondissements.
12th: ✉ 75012
13th: ✉ 75013

Sofitel Paris Bercy, 1 r. Libourne (12th) Ⓜ *Cour St-Emilion* ✆ 01 44 67 34 00, *h2192@accor-hotels.com, Fax 01 44 67 34 01,* – – 250. AE GB JCB NP 20
Café Ké *(closed Saturday and Sunday* **Meals** 33 – 25 – **376 rm** 365/440, 10 suites, 10 duplex.
◆ An attractive glass façade, a modern interior in brown, beige and blue, plus the latest in facilities are the Sofitel's main features. Some rooms offer views of the city. The elegant Café Ké, with its refined cuisine, is a popular choice in the Bercy district.

Novotel Gare de Lyon, 2 r. Hector Malot (12th) Ⓜ *Gare de Lyon* ✆ 01 44 67 60 00, *h1735@accor-hotels.com, Fax 01 44 67 60 60,* – – 75. AE GB JCB L 18
Meals *(closed lunch Saturday and Sunday)* a la carte 23/36 – 13,50 – **253 rm** 185/206.
◆ This recently built hotel overlooks a quiet square. The functional bedrooms have a terrace on the 6th floor. 24-hour swimming pool with a well-equipped children's area. Contemporary, brasserie-style restaurant with benches, cubicles and bays. Traditional menu.

Holiday Inn Bastille without rest, 11 r. Lyon (12th) Ⓜ *Gare de Lyon* ✆ 01 53 02 20 00, *resa.hinn@guichard.fr, Fax 01 53 02 20 01* – – 75. AE GB JCB
14 – **125 rm** 152/198. L 18
◆ The façade of this hotel dates from 1913. Bedrooms decked out in wood panelling, attractive fabrics and a mix of period and modern furniture. Elegant Baroque-style lounge.

Novotel Bercy, 86 r. Bercy (12th) Ⓜ *Bercy* ✆ 01 43 42 30 00, *h0935@accor-hotels.com, Fax 01 43 45 30 60,* – rest, – 80. AE GB JCB
Meals 23 – 14 – **150 rm** 175/183. M 19
◆ The Novotel's rooms have just had a facelift in line with the chain's new standards. Good location close to the Bercy indoor stadium. Veranda dining-room plus a popular terrace in fine weather. Classic Novotel à la carte menu.

Mercure Gare de Lyon without rest, 2 pl. Louis Armand (12th) Ⓜ *Gare de Lyon* ✆ 01 43 44 84 84, *h2217@accor.com, Fax 01 43 47 41 94* – – 15 - 90. AE GB JCB L 18
14 – **315 rm** 180/190.
◆ A modern hotel overlooked by the tower of the Gare de Lyon, built in 1899. Refurbished bedrooms with ceruse wood furnishing and good soundproofing. Wine bar.

Holiday Inn Bibliothèque de France without rest, 21 r. Tolbiac (13th) Ⓜ *Bibliothèque F. Mitterrand* ✆ 01 45 84 61 61, *hibdf@wanadoo.fr, Fax 01 45 84 43 38* – – 25. AE GB JCB P 18
13 – **71 rm** 145/183.
◆ Fronting a busy street, 20m from the nearest metro station, this hotel has well-maintained, comfortable rooms with double-glazing. Restaurant open in the evening.

Paris Bastille without rest, 67 r. Lyon (12th) Ⓜ *Bastille* ✆ 01 40 01 07 17, *infosbastille@wanadoo.fr, Fax 01 40 01 07 27* – – 25. AE GB JCB K 18
12 – **37 rm** 149/192.
◆ Modern comfort, contemporary furniture and elegant fabrics characterise the rooms in this refurbished hotel opposite the Opéra ; those facing the courtyard are generally quieter.

Manufacture without rest, 8 r. Philippe de Champagne (13th) Ⓜ *Place d'Italie* ✆ 01 45 35 45 25, *lamanufacture.paris@wanadoo.fr, Fax 01 45 35 45 40* – . AE GB JCB N 16
10 – **57 rm** 139/239.
◆ Cordial service and elegant decor are the prime assets of this well-maintained hotel with rooms that verge on the small side. Provençal atmosphere in the breakfast room.

Touring Hôtel Magendie without rest, 6 r. Corvisart (13th) Ⓜ *Corvisart* ✆ 01 43 36 13 61, *magendie@vvf-vacances.fr, Fax 01 43 36 47 48* – 30. AE GB N 14
6,50 – **112 rm** 62/72.
◆ A hotel with small, soundproofed rooms furnished in laminated wood. Special efforts have been made here to accommodate guests with limited mobility.

Au Pressoir (Seguin), 257 av. Daumesnil (12th) Ⓜ *Michel Bizot* ✆ 01 43 44 38 21, *Fax 01 43 43 81 77* – GB JCB M 22
closed 1 to 29 August, Saturday and Sunday – **Meals** 76 and a la carte 75/106
Spec. Mitonnée de légumes verts au beurre salé. Lièvre à la royale (season). Coeur de filet de boeuf au coulis de truffe..
◆ A hushed ambience, attentive service and classic cuisine are the hallmarks of this restaurant full of provincial nostalgia, where the terrace fills up quickly at lunchtime.

Train Bleu, Gare de Lyon (12th) Ⓜ *Gare de Lyon* ✆ 01 43 43 09 06, *isabelle.car@compass-group.fr, Fax 01 43 43 97 96* – AE GB JCB L 18
Meals 43 b.i. and a la carte 48/69.
◆ This magnificent station buffet, opened in 1901, is adorned with gilding, stucco and frescoes recalling the famous PLM train line. Brasserie cuisine and classic French fare.

L'Oulette, 15 pl. Lachambeaudie (12th) Ⓜ *Cour St-Emilion* ✆ 01 40 02 02 12, *info@l-oulette.com, Fax 01 40 02 04 77,* – AE GB JCB N 20
closed Saturday and Sunday – **Meals** 32/80 b.i. and a la carte 45/64.
◆ This contemporary restaurant in the new Bercy district serves up inventive cuisine influenced by SW France. Shady terrace behind the thuya trees.

Au Trou Gascon, 40 r. Taine (12th) Ⓜ *Daumesnil* ✆ 01 43 44 34 26, *Fax 01 43 07 80 55* – AE GB JCB M 21
closed August, 25 December-2 January, Saturday and Sunday – **Meals** 40 (lunch)/100 and a la carte 60/80
Spec. Homard en rouleau végétal, jus coraillé (Summer-Autumn) Mignon et ris de veau, champignons sauvages en cannelloni (Autumn). Tarte fine de figues (Autumn)..
◆ The decor of this old 1900s-style bistro blends period mouldings, design furniture and grey tones. The culinary emphasis here is on SW France. Wines from the same region.

Petit Marguery, 9 bd Port-Royal (13th) Ⓜ *Gobelins* ✆ 01 43 31 58 59, *marguery@wanadoo.fr, Fax 01 43 36 73 34* – AE GB M 15
closed August, Sunday and Monday – **Meals** 25,20 (lunch)/33,60
◆ A convivial atmosphere pervades the pleasant retro-style dining rooms of this restaurant serving typical "bistro" dishes to a numerous band of regular customers.

Janissaire, 22 allée Vivaldi (12th) Ⓜ *Daumesnil* ✆ 01 43 40 37 37, *Fax 01 43 40 38 39,* – AE GB M 20
closed Saturday lunch and Sunday – **Meals** 13 (lunch), 23/50 and a la carte 24/44
◆ The sign depicting an elite soldier from the Ottoman infantry hints at the typical Turkish atmosphere and cuisine inside.

Traversière, 40 r. Traversière (12th) Ⓜ *Ledru Rollin* ✆ 01 43 44 02 10, *Fax 01 43 44 64 20* – AE GB JCB K 18
closed 1 to 20 August, Sunday dinner and Monday – **Meals** 23 (lunch), 29/39,50.
◆ A restaurant with the friendly atmosphere of a country inn (façade, exposed beams), but furnished in contemporary style. Traditional cuisine ; game in season.

Jean-Pierre Frelet, 25 r. Montgallet (12th) Ⓜ *Montgallet* ✆ 01 43 43 76 65, *marie_rene. relet@club-internet.fr* – GB L 20
closed August, February Holidays, Saturday lunch and Sunday – **Meals** 26 (dinner) and a la carte 36/53
◆ Plain décor, tables set close together to create a convivial ambience, and generous helpings of seasonal dishes best describe this popular local eatery.

Anacréon, 53 bd St-Marcel (13th) Ⓜ *Les Gobelins* ✆ 01 43 31 71 18, *Fax 01 43 31 94 94* – AE GB JCB M 16
closed 1 to 10 May, August, Wednesday lunch, Sunday and Monday – **Meals** 20 (lunch)/32.
◆ Named in honour of the Greek lyrical poet. Veranda-style dining room with paintings on the wall, friendly service and traditional cuisine with a touch of originality.

Quincy, 28 av. Ledru-Rollin (12th) Ⓜ *Gare de Lyon* ✆ 01 46 28 46 76, *Fax 01 46 28 46 76* – L 17
closed 10 August-10 September, Saturday, Sunday and Monday – **Meals** a la carte 44/72.
◆ A warm ambience reigns in this rustic bistro where the excellent cuisine, like the jovial owner "Bobosse", has plenty of character.

Biche au Bois, 45 av. Ledru-Rollin (12th) Ⓜ *Gare de Lyon* ☎ 01 43 43 34 38 – AE ⓓ GB K 18
closed 24 December-3 January, 23 July-22August, Monday lunch, Saturday and Sunday – **Meals** 22,90 and a la carte 24/38 ♀.
◆ Despite the noisy, smoky atmosphere and simple decoration, the service is attentive and the cuisine copious and traditional, including game in season.

L'Avant Goût, 26 r. Bobillot (13th) Ⓜ *Place d'Italie* ☎ 01 53 80 24 00, *Fax 01 53 80 00 77* – ▤. GB P 15
closed 1 to 9 May, 12 August-5 September, 1 to 10 January, Saturday, Sunday and Monday – **Meals** (booking essential) 28/40 and a la carte 29/40 ♀.
◆ The Foretaste is a modern bistro that always seems to be full. The reasons behind its success stem from its tasty seasonal cuisine, quality wine list and relaxed atmosphere.

Auberge Etchegorry, 41 r. Croulebarbe (13th) Ⓜ *Les Gobelins* ☎ 01 44 08 83 51, *Fax 01 44 08 83 69* – AE ⓓ GB JCB N 15
closed 8 to 23 August, Sunday and Monday – **Meals** 25/31,50 and a la carte 37/51 ♀.
◆ A brochure recounts the history of this Basque restaurant and its district. Sausages, hams, Espelette peppers and garlic hanging from the ceiling set the culinary tone.

Sukhothaï, 12 r. Père Guérin (13th) Ⓜ *Place d'Italie* ☎ 01 45 81 55 88 – GB P 15
closed 1 to 21 August, Monday lunch and Sunday – **Meals** 10,50 b.i. (lunch), 18 b.i./22 b.i. and a la carte 28/46.
◆ The former capital of a 13C-14C royal Thai kingdom has given its name to this restaurant serving both Thai and Chinese dishes under the watchful gaze of Buddha sculptures.

Vaugirard, Gare Montparnasse, Grenelle, Denfert-Rochereau.

14th and 15th arrondissements.
14th: ✉ 75014
15th: ✉ 75015

Méridien Montparnasse, 19 r. Cdt Mouchotte (14th) Ⓜ *Montparnasse Bienvenüe* ☎ 01 44 36 44 36, *meridien.montparnasse@lemeridien.com, Fax 01 44 36 49 00*, ≤, – |‡| ⇹ ▤ TV ☏ ♿ – 🏔 25 - 2 000. AE ⓓ GB JCB. ✻ rest M 11
see **Montparnasse 25** below - ***Justine*** ☎ 01 44 36 44 00 **Meals** 37(except Sunday lunch)/45(Sunday lunch only) and a la carte 40/50 ♀ – ☕ 24 – **916 rm** 410/460, 37 suites.
◆ Most of the spacious, modern rooms in this glass and concrete building have been revamped, with superb views of the capital from the upper floors. Winter garden décor in the Justine restaurant with its leafy terrace. Buffet-style menu options.

Sofitel Porte de Sèvres, 8 r. L. Armand (15th) Ⓜ *Balard* ☎ 01 40 60 30 30, *h0572@accor-hotels.com, Fax 01 45 57 04 22*, ≤, Fₛ, ▣ – |‡| ⇹ ▤ rest, TV ☏ ♿ 🚗 – 🏔 450. AE ⓓ GB JCB N 5
see ***Relais de Sèvres*** below - ***Brasserie*** ☎ 01 40 60 33 77 *(closed lunch Saturday and Sunday)* **Meals** a la carte 34/53 – ☕ 24 – **604 rm** 390/410, 14 suites.
◆ This hotel opposite the heliport offers soundproofed rooms, partly refurbished in elegant, contemporary style. Views of the west of Paris from the higher floors. The Brasserie, with its mosaics, cupola, benches etc, evokes the ambience of the Roaring Twenties.

Novotel Tour Eiffel, 61 quai Grenelle (15th) Ⓜ *Charles Michels* ☎ 01 40 58 20 00, *h3546@accor-hotels.com, Fax 01 40 58 24 44*, ≤, Fₛ, ▣ – |‡| ⇹ ▤ TV ☏ ♿ 🚗 – 🏔 500. AE ⓓ GB JCB K 6
Meals *Café Lenôtre* ☎ 01 40 58 20 75 **Meals** a la carte 45/65 ♀ – ☕ 20 – **752 rm** 350/410, 12 suites.
◆ An entirely renovated hotel with comfortable, modern rooms furnished with wood and bright colours, most with views of the Seine. The Café Lenôtre features pleasant, stylish decor, a contemporary à la carte menu and a delicatessen. High-tech conference centre.

Bleu Marine, 40 r. Cdt Mouchotte (14th) Ⓜ *Gaîté* ☎ 01 56 54 84 00, *montparnasse@bleumarine.fr, Fax 01 56 54 84 84*, , Fₛ – |‡| ⇹ ▤ rm, ♿ P – 🏔 80. AE ⓓ GB
Meals 25,50 ♀ – ☕ 13 – **354 rm** 250. M 11
◆ This brand-new hotel on place de Catalogne has gone the extra mile in creating its calm, refined guestrooms, inner garden, fitness centre and bar. Decked out in exotic woods and colourful fabrics, the restaurant offers buffet and à la carte options.

Mercure Tour Eiffel Suffren, 20 r. Jean Rey (15th) Ⓜ *Bir Hakeim* ✆ 01 45 78 50 00, *h2175@accor-hotels.com, Fax 01 45 78 91 42,* – 30 - 100. J 7
Meals 32 – 21 – **394 rm** 230/280.
◆ With decor that takes nature for its inspiration, this soundproofed hotel has recently undergone careful restoration. Some rooms have views over the Eiffel tower. The large dining room opens onto a pleasant terrace surrounded by trees and greenery.

Novotel Vaugirard, 253 r. Vaugirard (15th) Ⓜ *Vaugirard* ✆ 01 40 45 10 00, *h1978@accor-hotels.com, Fax 01 40 45 10 10,* – 25 - 300. M 9
Meals a la carte approx. 27 – 13 – **187 rm** 180/210.
◆ A vast chain hotel at the heart of the 15th arrondissement with large, modern rooms fitted with double-glazing. New contemporary decor, a leafy summer terrace, non-stop service and grilled daily specials in the Novotel Café.

L'Aiglon without rest, 232 bd Raspail (14th) Ⓜ *Raspail* ✆ 01 43 20 82 42, *hotelaiglon@wanadoo.fr, Fax 01 43 20 98 72* – M 12
8 – **38 rm** 129/150, 9 suites.
◆ Hidden behind L'Aiglon's discreet façade is a fine, Empire-style interior with pleasant rooms with efficient double-glazing. Some rooms are on the small side.

Mercure Tour Eiffel without rest, 64 bd Grenelle (15th) Ⓜ *Dupleix* ✆ 01 45 78 90 90, *hotel@mercuretoureiffel.com, Fax 01 45 78 95 55,* – 25 - 40. K 7
18 – **76 rm** 220/300.
◆ The rooms in the main building are furnished in line with the Mercure's normal standards ; those in the more recent wing offer superior comfort and numerous little extras.

Mercure Porte de Versailles without rest, 69 bd Victor (15th) Ⓜ *Porte de Versailles* ✆ 01 44 19 03 03, *h1131@accor-hotels.com, Fax 01 48 28 22 11* – 50 - 250. N 7
15 – **91 rm** 265/315.
◆ This 1970s hotel is handily placed opposite the Parc des Expositions. The refurbished rooms are the best choice, as the others are fairly plain and functional.

Villa Royale Montsouris without rest, 144 r. Tombe-Issoire (14th) Ⓜ *Porte d'Orléans* ✆ 01 56 53 89 89, *montsouris@leshotelsdeparis.com, Fax 01 56 53 89 80* – R 12
20 – **36 rm** 130/200.
◆ Beautiful hotel carefully decorated in Andalucian and Moorish styles. Small but cosy rooms, which are named after Moroccan cities.

Holiday Inn Paris Montparnasse without rest, 10 r. Gager Gabillot (15th) Ⓜ *Vaugirard* ✆ 01 44 19 29 29, *reservations@hiparis-montparnasse.com, Fax 01 44 19 29 39* – 30. M 9
13 – **60 rm** 145/205.
◆ A modern building in a quiet street, with a refurbished lobby and contemporary lounge crowned by a glass pyramid. The attractive, newly decorated rooms here are preferable.

Lenox Montparnasse without rest, 15 r. Delambre (14th) Ⓜ *Vavin* ✆ 01 43 35 34 50, *hotel@lenoxmontparnasse.com, Fax 01 43 20 46 64* – M 12
12 – **52 rm** 135/170.
◆ Popular with guests from the world of fashion. Stylish rooms with pleasant bathrooms, splendid suites on the 6th floor, and pleasant bar and lounges.

Nouvel Orléans without rest, 25 av. Gén. Leclerc (14th) Ⓜ *Mouton Duvernet* ✆ 01 43 27 80 20, *nouvelorleans@aol.com, Fax 01 43 35 36 57* – P 12
10 – **46 rm** 125/185.
◆ Named after the Porte d'Orléans, some 800m/880yd away, the hotel's 46 rooms are embellished with modern furniture and warm, colourful fabrics.

Delambre without rest, 35 r. Delambre (14th) Ⓜ *Edgar Quinet* ✆ 01 43 20 66 31, *delambre@club-internet.fr, Fax 01 45 38 91 76* – M 12
9 – **29 rm** 95.
◆ André Breton once stayed in this hotel on a quiet street near Montparnasse station. Contemporary decor, with plain, bright and for the most part spacious rooms.

Mercure Raspail Montparnasse without rest, 207 bd Raspail (14th) Ⓜ *Vavin* ✆ 01 43 20 62 94, *h0351@accor-hotels.com, Fax 01 43 27 39 69* – M 12
13 – **63 rm** 170/180.
◆ This Haussmann-style building enjoys an excellent location near the famous brasseries of the Montparnasse district. The hotel's rooms are modern with plain wood furnishings.

Apollinaire without rest, 39 r. Delambre (14th) Ⓜ *Edgar Quinet* ✆ 01 43 35 18 40, *infos@hotel.apollinaire.com, Fax 01 43 35 30 71* – AE GB M 12
7 – **36 rm** 107/130.
• The name pays homage to this poet who used to meet fellow writers and artists in Montparnasse. Colourful, functional and well-maintained bedrooms, plus a comfortable lounge.

Mercure Paris XV without rest, 6 r. St-Lambert (15th) Ⓜ *Boucicaut* ✆ 01 45 58 61 00, *h0903@accor-hotels.com, Fax 01 45 54 10 43* – – 30. AE GB M 7
11 – **56 rm** 141/147.
• 800m/880yd from the Porte de Versailles. The reception area and lounges are decorated in modern style, in keeping with the comfortable, well-maintained bedrooms.

Istria without rest, 29 r. Campagne Première (14th) Ⓜ *Raspail* ✆ 01 43 20 91 82, *hotelistria@wanadoo.fr, Fax 01 43 22 48 45* – AE GB. M 12
10 – **26 rm** 96/110.
• This hotel was immortalised by the French poet Aragon in "Il ne m'est Paris que d'Elsa". Small, basic rooms, a pleasant lounge, plus a breakfast room in the vaulted cellar.

Daguerre without rest, 94 r. Daguerre (14th) Ⓜ *Gaîté* ✆ 01 43 22 43 54, *hoteldaguerre@wanadoo.fr, Fax 01 43 20 66 84* – AE GB JCB. N 11
10 – **30 rm** 75/120.
• An early-20C building with somewhat small, but well-furnished rooms. Attractive breakfast room with exposed stonework in the old cellar.

Apollon Montparnasse without rest, 91 r. Ouest (14th) Ⓜ *Pernety* ✆ 01 43 95 62 00, *apollonm@wanadoo.fr, Fax 01 43 95 62 10* – AE GB JCB N 10-11
7 – **33 rm** 75/93.
• Courteous service, attractive rooms and proximity to Montparnasse and the Air France shuttle buses are the major plus-points of this hotel on a relatively quiet street.

Carladez Cambronne without rest, 3 pl. Gén. Beuret (15th) Ⓜ *Vaugirard* ✆ 01 47 34 07 12, *carladez@club-internet.fr, Fax 01 40 65 95 68* – AE GB JCB M 9
7,50 – **28 rm** 77,50/82.
• A new blue, salmon and green colour scheme has spruced up the small yet well-maintained rooms in this hotel renowned for the friendliness of its staff.

Lilas Blanc without rest, 5 r. Avre (15th) Ⓜ *La Motte Picquet Grenelle* ✆ 01 45 75 30 07, *hotellilasblanc@minitel.net, Fax 01 45 78 66 65* – GB K 8
closed August and 20 to 26 December – 7 – **32 rm** 63/75.
• A compact hotel in a street that is generally quiet at night. Small, colourful rooms with basic laminated furnishings ; those on the ground floor are generally darker.

XXXX ✿ **Montparnasse 25** - Hôtel Méridien Montparnasse, 19 r. Cdt Mouchotte (14th) Ⓜ *Montparnasse Bienvenüe* ✆ 01 44 36 44 25, *meridien.montparnasse@lemeridien.com, Fax 01 44 36 49 03* – P. AE GB JCB. M 11
closed 2 to 8 May, 11 July-28 August, 19 December-1 January, Saturday, Sunday andBank Holidays – **Meals** 49 (lunch)/105 and a la carte 83/118
Spec. Compression de bar et thon (Spring-Summer). Lièvre à la royale (season). Lasagne de foie gras aux cèpes.
• The contemporary black-lacquer décor may come as a shock, yet the overall effect is warm and cosy. Cuisine to suit modern tastes, plus a superb cheese trolley.

XXXX ✿ **Relais de Sèvres** - Hôtel Sofitel Porte de Sèvres, 8 r. L. Armand (15th) Ⓜ *Balard* ✆ 01 40 60 33 66, *h0572@accor-hotels.com, Fax 01 40 60 30 00* – P. AE GB JCB N 5
closed 13 July-29 August, 17 December-3 January, Friday dinner, Saturday, Sunday – **Meals** 57/72 b.i. and a la carte 74/107
Spec. Émietté de tourteau à la crème de fenouil. Filet d'esturgeon cuit au four au curry de Madras. Dégustation de quatre grands crus de chocolat.
• Elegant Sèvres blue decor acts as a backdrop to this impressive restaurant popular with gourmets and a business clientele. Contemporary cuisine and an impressive wine list.

XXX **Ciel de Paris,** Maine Montparnasse Tower, at 56th floor (15th) Ⓜ *Montparnasse Bienvenüe* ✆ 01 40 64 77 64, *ciel-de-paris.rv@elior.com, Fax 01 43 21 48 37,* < Paris – . AE GB JCB. M 11
Meals 32 (lunch)/54 and a la carte 75/150 .
• On clear days, the view from the pleasant modern dining room, looking out towards Les Invalides and the Eiffel Tower is hard to beat. A sky-high dining experience !

Le Duc, 243 bd Raspail (14th) Ⓜ *Raspail* ☎ 01 43 20 96 30, *Fax 01 43 20 46 73* – AE GB JCB M 12
closed 29 July-23 August, 24 December-2 January, Saturday lunch, Sunday and Monday – **Meals** 46 (lunch) and a la carte 62/100
Spec. Poissons crus. Saint-Jacques au naturel (October-April). Cabillaud en pavé et ses oeufs fumés (October-May).
◆ Le Duc serves simple but high-quality fish and seafood in a cosy yacht cabin-ambience based on mahogany panelling, maritime-inspired decoration and gleaming brass.

Benkay, 61 quai Grenelle (4th floor)(15th) Ⓜ *Bir-Hakeim* ☎ 01 40 58 21 26, *h3546@accor-hotels.com, Fax 01 40 58 21 30,* – P. AE GB JCB. K 6
Meals 26 (lunch), 60/225 and a la carte 51/107.
◆ Situated on the top floor, this restaurant has beautiful views over the Seine. Abstemious decor (marble and wood) ; sushis and teppanyakis on the menu.

Le Dôme, 108 bd Montparnasse (14th) Ⓜ *Vavin* ☎ 01 43 35 25 81, *Fax 01 42 79 01 19* – . AE GB JCB LM 12
closed Sunday and Monday in August – **Meals** a la carte 60/90.
◆ One of the haunts of bohemian writers and artists during the Roaring Twenties and now a chic restaurant which has preserved its Art Deco feel. Fish and seafood specialities.

Chen-Soleil d'Est, 15 r. Théâtre (15th) Ⓜ *Charles Michels* ☎ 01 45 79 34 34, *Fax 01 45 79 07 53* – . AE GB JCB K 6
closed August and Sunday – **Meals** 40 (lunch)/75 and a la carte 55/150
Spec. Ormeau one (Spring and autumn). Cuisses de grenouilles. Pigeonneau.
◆ Head away from the Seine to discover this authentic corner of Asia serving high-quality steamed and wok-based cuisine to a backdrop of furniture imported from China.

Maison Courtine (Charles), 157 av. Maine (14th) Ⓜ *Mouton Duvernet* ☎ 01 45 43 08 04, *Fax 01 45 45 91 35* – . AE GB. N 11
closed 1 to 28 August, 24 December-2 January, Sunday, lunch Saturday and Monday – **Meals** 36/40 ♀
Spec. Escalopes de foie gras de canard poêllées aux raisins. Homard rôti au piment d'espelette (May-June and September-November). Magret de canard au gros sel de Guérande.
◆ The menu here is a culinary Tour de France, served to a colourful, modern backdrop with Louis-Philippe-style furniture. Popular with a loyal group of aficionados.

Pavillon Montsouris, 20 r. Gazan (14th) Ⓜ *Cité Universitaire* ☎ 01 43 13 29 00, *Fax 01 43 13 29 02,* – . AE GB R 14
closed 15 February-2 March – **Meals** 49/69 ♀.
◆ This Belle Epoque building in the Parc Montsouris offers rural calm in the heart of Paris. Attractive glass, colonial-style decor and a terrace facing the park.

La Coupole, 102 bd Montparnasse (14th) Ⓜ *Vavin* ☎ 01 43 20 14 20, *lejeune@groupeflo.fr, Fax 01 43 35 46 14* – . AE GB L 12
Meals 33,50 b.i. and a la carte 38/65 ♀.
◆ The heart of old Montparnasse is still beating in this Art Deco brasserie with a lively ambience opened in 1927. 32 pillars decorated with works by artists from the period.

Gauloise, 59 av. La Motte-Picquet (15 th) Ⓜ *La Motte Picquet Grenelle* ☎ 01 47 34 11 64, *Fax 01 40 61 09 70,* – AE GB K 8
Meals 26,50 and a la carte 32/51 ♀.
◆ Judging by the signed photos on the walls, this century-old brasserie has played host to huge numbers of celebrities over the years. Pleasant pavement terrace.

Caroubier, 82 bd Lefèbvre (15th) Ⓜ *Porte de Vanves* ☎ 01 40 43 16 12, *Fax 01 40 43 16 12* – . AE GB N 11
closed 24 July-24 August and Monday – **Meals** 15 (lunch)/26,50 and a la carte 30/43 ♀.
◆ Contemporary decor enlivened by the occasional Oriental touch, a friendly, family atmosphere and generous Moroccan cuisine are the keys to the success of this restaurant.

Fontanarosa, 28 bd Garibaldi (15th) Ⓜ *Cambronne* ☎ 01 45 66 97 84, *Fax 01 47 83 96 30,* – . GB JCB L 9
Meals 20,30 (lunch) and a la carte 40/68 ♀.
◆ Escape the bustle of the city and relax on the attractive patio-terrace of this delightful trattoria serving Sardinian cuisine. Good choice of Italian wines.

L'Épopée, 89 av. É. Zola (15th) Ⓜ *Charles Michels* ☎ 01 45 77 71 37, *Fax 01 45 77 71 37* – AE GB JCB L 7
closed 28 July-28 August, 24 December-2 January, Saturday lunch and Sunday – **Meals** 32/40 ♀.
◆ A friendly and unpretentious small restaurant attracting a loyal following where the emphasis is on traditional cuisine. Impressive wine list.

Les Petites Sorcières, 12 r. Liancourt (14th) Ⓜ *Denfert Rochereau* ☎ 01 43 21 95 68, *Fax 01 43 21 95 68* – GB N 12
closed 18 July to 16 August, Sunday, lunch Monday and Saturday – **Meals** 30.
◆ Traditional cuisine is on offer in the "Little Witches". Located close to Denfert-Rochereau, with a decor in keeping with the name.

Stéphane Martin, 67 r. Entrepreneurs (15th) Ⓜ *Charles Michels* ✆ 01 45 79 03 31, *resto.stephanemartin@free.fr, Fax 01 45 79 44 69* – AE GB. L 7
closed 31 July-22 August, Sunday and Monday – **Meals** 27/32.
• A warm, friendly restaurant with a library-style decor (fresco depicting rows of books) serving seasonal, contemporary cuisine.

Bistro d'Hubert, 41 bd Pasteur (15th) Ⓜ *Pasteur* ✆ 01 47 34 15 50, *message@bistrodhubert.com, Fax 01 45 67 03 09* – AE GB JCB L 10
closed Sunday, lunch Saturday and Monday – **Meals** 35 and a la carte 39/65 ♀.
• Jars and bottles on the shelves, chequered tablecloths, and views of the kitchen add to the charm of this restaurant decorated in the style of a farm in Les Landes.

Beurre Noisette, 68 r. Vasco de Gama (15th) Ⓜ *Lourmel* ✆ 01 48 56 82 49, *Fax 01 48 56 82 49* – AE GB. N 6
closed 1 to 25 August, Sunday and Monday – **Meals** 20 (lunch)/29 ♀.
• Carefully prepared cuisine with a modern touch, plus seasonal suggestions on the specials board. Two plain yet contemporary dining rooms. Good choice of wine by the glass.

L'Ami Marcel, 33 r. G. Pitard (15th) Ⓜ *Plaisance* ✆ 01 48 56 62 06, *Fax 01 48 56 62 06* – AE GB JCB N 10
closed 10 to 30 August, Saturday lunch and Sunday – **Meals** 29 ♀.
• This friendly local bistro conjures up good and reasonably priced traditional cuisine. A zebrawood bar and paintings on the walls add a personal decorative touch.

Régalade, 49 av. J. Moulin (14th) Ⓜ *Porte d'Orléans* ✆ 01 45 45 68 58, *Fax 01 45 40 96 74* – GB R 11
closed August, Monday lunch, Saturday and Sunday – **Meals** (booking essential) 30.
• Smiling service and delicious country cooking are the main attributes of this small, simple but hugely popular bistro close to the Porte de Châtillon.

Troquet, 21 r. F. Bonvin (15th) Ⓜ *Cambronne* ✆ 01 45 66 89 00, *Fax 01 45 66 89 83* – GB. L 9
closed August, 24 December-2 January, Sunday and Monday – **Meals** 26 (lunch), 30/37 ♀.
• This typical Parisian "troquet" (bar) offers a single menu advertised on a slate board. A retro-style dining room provides the setting for fine seasonal cuisine.

Cerisaie, 70 bd E. Quinet (14th) Ⓜ *Edgar Quinet* ✆ 01 43 20 98 98, *Fax 01 43 20 98 98* – GB. M 11
closed 1 to 8 May, 25 July-25 August, 19 December-2 January, Saturday lunch, Sunday and Bank Holidays – **Meals** (booking essential) 28,80/31,80 and a la carte 30/40.
• A tiny restaurant in the heart of the "breton" district : the owner - and chef - chalks up a daily-changing menu of carefully prepared south-western dishes on the blackboard.

A La Bonne Table, 42 r. Friant (14th) Ⓜ *Porte d'Orléans* ✆ 01 45 39 74 91, *Fax 01 45 43 66 92* – AE GB JCB R 11
closed 17 to 31 July, 24 December-1 January, 27 February-6 March, Saturday lunch and Sunday – **Meals** 25 and a la carte 29/50.
• Despite his Japanese origins, the chef prepares traditional French cuisine enhanced by his Oriental culinary expertise. A comfortable elongated dining room with a retro feel.

Severo, 8 r. Plantes (14th) Ⓜ *Mouton Duvernet* ✆ 01 45 40 40 91 – GB N 11
closed 23 July-22 August, 19 December-3 January, Saturday dinner and Sunday – **Meals** a la carte 27/48 ♀.
• Meat delicacies from the Auvergne dominate the daily specials board in this friendly bistro with an eclectic wine list.

Passy, Auteuil, Bois de Boulogne, Chaillot, Porte Maillot.

16th arrondissement.
16th: ✉ 75016 or 75116

Raphael, 17 av. Kléber ✉ 75116 Ⓜ *Kléber* ✆ 01 53 64 32 00, *management@raphael-hotel.com, Fax 01 53 64 32 01,* – – TV – 50. AE GB JCB
Jardins Plein Ciel ✆ 01 53 64 32 30(7=t=h floor)-buffet *(May-October)* **Meals** 70(lunch)/90 ♀ – ***Salle à Manger*** ✆ 01 53 64 32 11 **Meals** 50 (lunch) and a la carte 64/82 ♀ – 35 – **44 rm** 325/550, 25 suites. F 7
• A superb wood-adorned gallery, elegant bedrooms, a panoramic rooftop terrace and an English bar are the treasures of the Raphaël, dating from 1925. Stunning view of Paris and buffet dining in the Jardins Plein Ciel and palatial decor in the Salle à Manger.

St-James Paris, 43 av. Bugeaud ✉ 75116 Ⓜ *Porte Dauphine* ☎ 01 44 05 81 81, *contact@saint-james-paris.com, Fax 01 44 05 81 82*, , - 25. AE GB JCB F 5
Meals *(closed weekends and Bank Holidays)* (residents only) 47 - 27 - **20 rm** 345/490, 28 suites590/750, 8 duplex.
◆ A fine mansion built by Madame Thiers in 1892 in the middle of a wooded garden. Majestic staircase, spacious bedrooms and a bar-library with the air of an English club.

Sofitel Le Parc, 55 av. R. Poincaré ✉ 75116 Ⓜ *Victor Hugo* ☎ 01 44 05 66 66, *h2797@accor-hotels.com, Fax 01 44 05 66 00*, , - - 40 - 250. AE GB JCB G 6
Meals see ***59 Poincaré*** below - 26 - **95 rm** 400/620, 21 suites, 3 duplex.
◆ The Parc's elegant "English"-style bedrooms are grouped around a garden-terrace and equipped with Wi-Fi technology. The decor in the bar is partly the work of Arman.

Sofitel Baltimore, 88bis av. Kléber ✉ 75116 Ⓜ *Boissière* ☎ 01 44 34 54 54, *welcome@hotelbaltimore.com, Fax 01 44 34 54 44*, - - 50. AE GB JCB G 7
see ***Table du Baltimore*** below - 27 - **102 rm** 350/775.
◆ Elegant furniture, "trendy" fabrics and old photos of the city of Baltimore contribute to the modern decor of the bedrooms, in contrast to the building's 19C architecture.

Costes K. without rest, 81 av. Kléber ✉ 75116 Ⓜ *Trocadéro* ☎ 01 44 05 75 75, *costes.k@wanadoo.fr, Fax 01 44 05 74 74*, - . AE GB JCB
20 - **83 rm** 300/550. G 7
◆ This discreet, ultra-modern hotel designed by Ricardo Bofill offers a serene haven for guests in its large, refined rooms arranged around a pretty Japanese-style patio.

Square, 3 r. Boulainvilliers ✉ 75016 Ⓜ *Mirabeau* ☎ 01 44 14 91 90, *hotel.square@wanadoo.fr, Fax 01 44 14 91 99* - - 20. AE GB JCB. K 5
Zébra Square ☎ 01 44 14 91 91 **Meals** a la carte 40/65 - 20 - **20 rm** 255/330.
◆ This flagship of contemporary architecture opposite the Maison de la Radio is a hymn to modern design with its curves, colours, high-tech equipment and abstract canvases. Striped designer decor and a contemporary menu in the hotel's fashionable restaurant.

Trocadero Dokhan's without rest, 117 r. Lauriston ✉ 75116 Ⓜ *Trocadéro* ☎ 01 53 65 66 99, *welcome@dokhans.com, Fax 01 53 65 66 88* - . AE GB JCB. G 6
27 - **41 rm** 480/540, 4 suites.
◆ It is impossible not to be won over by this charming early-20C private mansion built in Palladian style with a neo-Classical interior and 18C celadon panelling in the lounge.

La Villa Maillot without rest, 143 av. Malakoff ✉ 75116 Ⓜ *Porte Maillot* ☎ 01 53 64 52 52, *resa@lavillamaillot.fr, Fax 01 45 00 60 61* - - 25. AE GB JCB F 6
24 - **39 rm** 315/370, 3 suites.
◆ A stone's throw from Porte Maillot, this hotel offers comfortable rooms furnished in soft colours and with good soundproofing. Bright breakfast room overlooking greenery.

Majestic without rest, 29 r. Dumont d'Urville ✉ 75116 Ⓜ *Kléber* ☎ 01 45 00 83 70, *management@majestic-hotel.com, Fax 01 45 00 29 48* - . AE GB JCB
16 - **27 rm** 250/345, 3 suites. F 7
◆ A hotel with a discreet 1960s façade just a stone's throw from the Champs-Élysées. The guest rooms are spacious, quiet, traditionally furnished and impeccably maintained.

Pergolèse without rest, 3 r. Pergolèse ✉ 75116 Ⓜ *Argentine* ☎ 01 53 64 04 04, *hotel@pergolese.com, Fax 01 53 64 04 40* - . AE GB JCB E 6
18 - **40 rm** 220/380.
◆ An understated 16C façade with an unusual blue door that sets the tone for the designer interior featuring mahogany, glass bricks, chromes and bright colours.

Élysées Régencia without rest, 41 av. Marceau ✉ 75116 Ⓜ *George V* ☎ 01 47 20 42 65, *info@regencia.com, Fax 01 49 52 03 42* - - 20. AE GB JCB. G 8
18 - **43 rm** 215/275.
◆ Three styles of bedrooms are on offer behind the hotel's gracious façade : Louis XVI, Napoleon "return from Egypt", and contemporary. Elegant lounge, bar and library.

La Résidence Bassano without rest, 15 r. Bassano ✉ 75116 Ⓜ *George V* ☎ 01 47 23 78 23, *info@hotel-bassano.com, Fax 01 47 20 41 22* - . AE GB JCB - 18 - **28 rm** 195/245, 3 suites. G 8
◆ Although just a few hundred yards from the Champs-Élysées, the warm ambience, wrought-iron furniture and bright fabrics in this friendly hotel turn one's thoughts to Provence.

Étoile Residence Imperiale without rest, 155 av. de Malakoff ✉ 75116 Ⓜ *Porte Maillot* ☎ 01 45 00 23 45, *res.imperiale@wanadoo.fr, Fax 01 45 01 88 82* – AE GB JCB E 6
13 – **37 rm** 150/200.
• The refurbished, soundproofed rooms in this hotel are decorated in a range of styles (African, Asian etc) ; some have exposed beams, while others overlook the patio.

Passy Eiffel without rest, 10 r. Passy ✉ 75016 Ⓜ *Passy* ☎ 01 45 25 55 66, *contact@passyeiffel.com, Fax 01 42 88 89 88* – AE GB JCB J 6
10 – **49 rm** 130/160.
• A family-run hotel in a busy street. Functional, well-maintained rooms, either facing the road (some with views of the Eiffel Tower) or overlooking a flower-decked courtyard.

Chambellan Morgane without rest, 6 r. Keppler ✉ 75116 Ⓜ *George V* ☎ 01 47 20 35 72, *chambellan-morgane@wanadoo.fr, Fax 01 47 20 95 69* – 20. AE GB JCB GF 8
12 – **20 rm** 152/168.
• A small, tranquil hotel full of character with rooms that proudly display the colours of Provence. Pleasant Louis XVI lounge decorated with painted woodwork.

Floride Étoile without rest, 14 r. St-Didier ✉ 75116 Ⓜ *Boissière* ☎ 01 47 27 23 36, *floride.etoile@wanadoo.fr, Fax 01 47 27 82 87* – 30. AE GB JCB. G 7
12 – **63 rm** 145/205.
• Close to Trocadéro. Functional, newly renovated rooms ; those by the courtyard are smaller but quieter. Tastefully decorated, flower-decked lounge.

Du Bois without rest, 11 r. Dôme ✉ 75116 Ⓜ *Kléber* ☎ 01 45 00 31 96, *hoteldubois@wanadoo.fr, Fax 01 45 00 90 05* – AE GB JCB F 7
12 – **41 rm** 129/149.
• This cosy hotel stands in the 16C Montmartre street where Baudelaire breathed his last. Airy and stylish bedrooms, plus a Georgian-style lounge.

Windsor Home without rest, 3 r. Vital ✉ 75016 Ⓜ *La Muette* ☎ 01 45 04 49 49, *whpans@wanadoo.fr, Fax 01 45 04 59 50* – GB JCB H 6
11 – **8 rm** 110/160.
• A charming residence over a century old furnished like a private home with antique furniture, decorative mouldings, bright colours and modern touches. Small garden.

Gavarni without rest, 5 r. Gavarni ✉ 75116 Ⓜ *Passy* ☎ 01 45 24 52 82, *reservation@gavarni.com, Fax 01 40 50 16 95* – AE GB JCB. J 6
10 – **25 rm** 99/175.
• This red-brick hotel offers guests compact, but well-equipped and stylish rooms ; those on the upper two floors are more elegant.

Au Palais de Chaillot without rest, 35 av. R. Poincaré ✉ 75116 Ⓜ *Trocadéro* ☎ 01 53 70 09 09, *palaisdechaillot-hotel@magic.fr, Fax 01 53 70 09 08* – AE GB JCB. G 6
9 – **28 rm** 105/120.
• This hotel decorated in the colours of Provence enjoys a good location near Trocadéro. Small, bright and functional bedrooms, with wicker furniture in the breakfast room.

Le Hameau de Passy without rest, 48 r. Passy ✉ 75016 Ⓜ *La Muette* ☎ 01 42 88 47 55, *hameau.passy@wanadoo.fr, Fax 01 42 30 83 72* – AE GB JCB J 5-6
32 rm 109/124.
• Tucked away in the 16th district, this discreet "hamlet" (hameau) with its pretty courtyard guarantees guests a good night's sleep. Small, modern and well-maintained rooms.

Hiramatsu, 52 r. Longchamp ✉ 75016 Ⓜ *Trocadéro* ☎ 01 56 81 08 80, *paris@hiramatsu.co.jp, Fax 01 56 81 08 81* – AE GB JCB G 7
closed 1 to 21 August, 6 to 12 February, Saturday and Sunday – **Meals** 70 (lunch), 130/180 (booking essential) and a la carte 115/135
Spec. Foie gras de canard aux choux frisés, jus de truffe. Saint-Pierre cuit à la plancha, légumes de saison, sauce potagère. Variation autour du chocolat.
• New decor but the same high level of inventive cuisine from the Hiramatsu team following its move across the city. The epitome of fine gastronomy Japanese style.

59 Poincaré - Hôtel Sofitel Le Parc, 59 av. R. Poincaré ✉ 75116 Ⓜ *Victor Hugo* ☎ 01 47 27 59 59, *le59poincare@tiscali.fr, Fax 01 47 27 59 00,* – AE GB JCB G 6
closed 20 December to 31 December Saturday lunch, Sunday and Monday from OctoberAvril – **Meals** 49 (lunch)/115 and a la carte 60/105.
• On the ground floor of an enchanting town house dating from the Belle Époque, this restaurant has design flourishes by P Jouin and a menu featuring seasonal, classic cuisine.

XXX ✿✿ **Jamin** (Guichard), 32 r. Longchamp ✉ 75116 Ⓜ *Iéna* ✆ 01 45 53 00 07, *reservation @jamin.fr, Fax 01 45 53 00 15* – ▤. AE ⓓ GB. ✂ G 7
closed 30 April-8 May, 29 July-22 August, Saturday and Sunday – **Meals** 53 (lunch), 95/130 and a la carte 115/150
Spec. Ravioli de langoustines de petite pêche. Filet de grosse sole sauce normande. Pigeonneau grillé au foie gras.
◆ Behind this discreetly colourful façade, an elegant, simply decorated restaurant is the setting for an inventive menu that focuses on high-quality ingredients.

XXX ✿✿ **Relais d'Auteuil** (Pignol), 31 bd Murat ✉ 75016 Ⓜ *Michel Ange Molitor* ✆ 01 46 51 09 54, *pignol-p@wanadoo.fr, Fax 01 40 71 05 03* – ▤ ⇨. AE ⓓ GB JCB L 3
closed 31 July-24 August, Sunday, lunch Saturday and Monday – **Meals** 48 (lunch), 105/135 and a la carte 104/136
Spec. Petits chaussons de céleri-rave et truffes (November-February). Langoustines et topinambours infusés au bâton de citronnelle et marjolaine. Pigeon de Touraine désossé à la compotée de choux..
◆ Refined decor combining modern touches and period furniture. Sophisticated cuisine high on virtuosity and superb selection of wines.

XXX ✿ **La Table de Joël Robuchon,** 16 av. Bugeaud ✉ 75116 Ⓜ *Victor Hugo* ✆ 01 56 28 16 16, *latabledejoelrobuchon@wanadoo.fr, Fax 01 56 28 16 78* – ▤ ⇨. GB F 6
Meals a la carte 64/92 ♀
Spec. Oeuf mollet et friand au caviar. Merlan frit colbert. Soufflé aux brisures de nougat.
◆ Joël Robuchon works his culinary magic on classically inspired cuisine and tapas-style tasting dishes in this elegant setting.

XXX ✿ **La Table du Baltimore** - Hôtel Sofitel Baltimore, 1 r. Léo Delibes ✉ 75016 Ⓜ *Boissière* ✆ 01 44 34 54 34, *latable@hotelbaltimore.com, Fax 01 44 34 54 44* – ▤ ⇨. AE ⓓ GB JCB. ✂ G 7
closed 29 July-29 August, 23 December-1 January, Saturday, Sunday and Bank Holidays – **Meals** 45 b.i. (lunch)/95 and a la carte 52/75 ♀
Spec. Légumes d'automne (season). Foie gras de canard rôti en croûte d'oignons. Figue rôtie dans un jus d'épices (autumn).
◆ The decor here is a subtle mix of old wood panelling, contemporary furniture, warm colours and a collection of pictures on the walls. Fine cuisine to suit modern tastes.

XXX ✿ **Pergolèse** (Corre), 40 r. Pergolèse ✉ 75116 Ⓜ *Porte Maillot* ✆ 01 45 00 21 40, *lepergolese@wanadoo.fr, Fax 01 45 00 81 31* – ▤ ⇨. AE GB JCB F 6
closed 2 to 30 August, Saturday and Sunday – **Meals** 38/75 and a la carte 61/77
Spec. Ravioli de langoustines. Saint-Jacques rôties en robe des champs (October-April). Couscous de foie gras chaud (November-april).
◆ Yellow fabrics, light-coloured wood, mirrors and unusual sculptures combine to create this elegant setting a few yards from the select avenue Foch. Classic, refined cuisine.

XXX ✿ **Passiflore** (Durand), 33 r. Longchamp ✉ 75016 Ⓜ *Trocadéro* ✆ 01 47 04 96 81, *passiflore@club-internet.fr, Fax 01 47 04 32 27* – ▤ ⇨. AE GB JCB G 7
closed 1 to 23 August, Saturday lunch and Sunday – **Meals** 35 (lunch), 38/75 and a la carte 66/97
Spec. Ravioles de homard en mulligatowny. Risotto noir de Saint-Jacques au basilic thaï (October-April). Tournedos de pied de cochon.
◆ Ethnically-inspired plain yet elegant decor (shades of yellow and wood panelling) provides the setting for this restaurant serving classical cuisine with a personal touch.

XXX **Port Alma,** 10 av. New-York ✉ 75116 Ⓜ *Alma Marceau* ✆ 01 47 23 75 11, *Fax 01 47 20 42 92* – ▤. AE ⓓ GB JCB H 8
closed August, 24 December-2 January, Sunday and Monday – **Meals** a la carte 55/90 ♀.
◆ This veranda dining room with blue beams on the banks of the Seine is a safe bet for excellent fish and seafood. The freshest of products and smiling service.

XX **Cristal Room Baccarat,** 11 pl. des Etats-Unis ✉ 75116 Ⓜ *Boissière* ✆ 01 40 22 11 10, *cristalroom@baccarat.fr, Fax 01 40 22 11 99* – ▤ ⇨. AE ⓓ GB. ✂ G 7
closed Sunday – **Meals** (booking essential) a la carte 52/76.
◆ M.-L de Noailles held her salons in this residence now owned by Baccarat ; with decor in Philippe Starck style, modern menus and VIP prices, it's still the place to be seen.

XX ✿✿ **Astrance** (Barbot), 4 r. Beethoven ✉ 75016 Ⓜ *Passy* ✆ 01 40 50 84 40 – AE ⓓ GB. ✂ J 7
closed 1 to 7 May, 24 July-24 August, 6 to 14 November, February Holidays, Saturday, Sunday and Monday – **Meals** (booking essential) 70 (lunch)/150 and a la carte 92/130 ♀
Spec. Galette fine de champignons, foie gras mariné au verjus, citron rôti. Selle d'agneau grillée, aubergine au miso, fondue de parmesan. Les fruits rouges comme un vacherin.
◆ The inventive cuisine, "surprise" dinner menu, good wine list and modern decor at the Astrance (a flower, from the Latin aster, or star) have earned praise from across Paris.

Fakhr el Dine, 30 r. Longchamp ✉ 75016 Ⓜ *Trocadéro* ☎ 01 47 27 90 00, *resa@fakhreldine.com, Fax 01 53 70 01 81* – ▤ ☝. AE ⓓ GB. ✈ G 7
Meals 23/32 and a la carte 25/40.
◆ Mezzé, kafta and grilled meats all feature on the menu of this refined Lebanese restaurant worthy of Fakhr el Dine, one of the country's greatest princes.

Tang, 125 r. de la Tour ✉ 75116 Ⓜ *Rue de la Pompe* ☎ 01 45 04 35 35, *charlytang16@yahoo.fr, Fax 01 45 04 58 19* – ▤. AE GB H 5
closed 1 to 15 August, 24 December-3 January, 5 to 15 February, Sunday and Monday – **Meals** 39 (lunch), 65/98 and a la carte 60/102
Spec. Symphonie d'amuse-gueule. Saint-Jacques grillées, court-bouillon de pak-choi aux truffes (November-March). Pigeonneau laqué épicé aux cinq parfums.
◆ Behind the restaurant's wide bay windows is a high-ceilinged dining room with classical furnishings enlivened by the occasional oriental touch. Chinese and Thai specialities.

Paul Chêne, 123 r. Lauriston ✉ 75116 Ⓜ *Trocadéro* ☎ 01 47 27 63 17, *Fax 01 47 27 53 18* – ▤ ☝. AE ⓓ GB G 6
closed August, 23 December-1 January, Saturday lunch and Sunday – **Meals** 38/48 and a la carte 49/72.
◆ This restaurant has preserved its 1950s feel, with its old bar, comfortable benches, snug tables and lively atmosphere. Traditional dishes including the famous fried whiting.

Le Vinci, 23 r. P. Valéry ✉ 75116 Ⓜ *Victor Hugo* ☎ 01 45 01 68 18, *levinci@wanadoo.fr, Fax 01 45 01 60 37* – ▤ ☝. AE GB F 7
closed 1 to 22 August, Saturday and Sunday – **Meals** 31 and a la carte 50/68 ♀.
◆ Tasty Italian cuisine, a colourful interior and friendly service are the hallmarks of this small restaurant a short distance from the smart boutiques along avenue Victor-Hugo.

Essaouira, 135 r. Ranelagh ✉ 75016 Ⓜ *Ranelagh* ☎ 01 45 27 99 93, *Fax 01 45 27 56 36* – ✈ GB J 4
closed August, Monday lunch and Sunday – **Meals** a la carte 40/58 ♀.
◆ The Moroccan city has lent its name to this restaurant serving couscous, tajines and mechoui. Typical décor, including a mosaic fountain, rugs and other craft objects.

Chez Géraud, 31 r. Vital ✉ 75016 Ⓜ *La Muette* ☎ 01 45 20 33 00, *Fax 01 45 20 46 60* – GB H 5
closed 22 July-29 August, Saturday and Sunday – **Meals** 30 and a la carte 54/75.
◆ The façade and interior fresco, both created from Longwy faience, add a decorative edge to this chic bistro where pride of place is given to game (in season).

6 New-York, 6 av. New-York ✉ 75016 Ⓜ *Alma Marceau* ☎ 01 40 70 03 30, *Fax 01 40 70 04 77* – ▤ ☝. AE ⓓ GB JCB H 8
closed 2 to 23 August, Saturday lunch and Sunday – **Meals** 35 (lunch) and a la carte 47/60 ♀.
◆ A chic bistro with an eye-catching name, where the cuisine is in perfect harmony with the modern, refined setting.

A et M Restaurant, 136 bd Murat ✉ 75016 Ⓜ *Porte de St-Cloud* ☎ 01 45 27 39 60, *am-bistrot-16@wanadoo.fr, Fax 01 45 27 69 71*, 余 – ☝. AE GB JCB M 3
closed August, Saturday lunch and Sunday – **Meals** 30 and a la carte 32/44.
◆ A trendy modern bistro close to the river, with sober decor in tones of cream and Havana brown, designer lighting and refined contemporary cuisine.

Oscar, 6 r. Chaillot ✉ 75016 Ⓜ *Iéna* ☎ 01 47 20 26 92, *Fax 01 47 20 27 93* – ✈ AE ⓓ GB. ✈ G 8
closed 5 to 26 August, Saturday lunch, Sunday and Bank Holidays – **Meals** a la carte approx. 35 ♀.
◆ A bistro with a discreet façade, tables packed close together and a slate board featuring daily specials. Zero marketing, but a reputation that extends beyond the local area.

in the Bois de Boulogne :

Pré Catelan, rte Suresnes ✉ 75016 Ⓜ *Porte Dauphine* ☎ 01 44 14 41 14, *Fax 01 45 24 43 25*, 余, 🚗 – ▤ ☝ P. AE ⓓ GB JCB H 2
closed 23 October-2 November, 12 February-7 March, Sunday except lunch in season and Monday – **Meals** 60 (lunch), 120/160 and a la carte 126/176 ♀
Spec. L'os à moelle en deux façons. Le Homard rôti en feuilles d'algues, beurre aux zestes de citron vert. Le café expresso, en sabayon, ganache fouettée et crème glacée "brûlée".
◆ This elegant Napoleon III-style pavilion in the Bois de Boulogne has developed a worthy reputation for its inventive cuisine. Caran d'Ache décor, plus a delightful terrace.

Grande Cascade, allée de Longchamp (opposite the hippodrome) ✉ 75016 Ⓜ *Porte d'Auteuil* ☎ 01 45 27 33 51, *grandecascade@wanadoo.fr, Fax 01 42 88 99 06*, 余 – ☝ P. AE ⓓ GB JCB
closed 18 December-2 January and 20 February-5 March – **Meals** 70/165 and a la carte 135/175
Spec. Langoustines rôties au miel et vinaigre balsamique. Filets de sole au naturel, pommes de terre fondantes aux écrevisses. Pomme de ris de veau meunière, jus au madère.
◆ One of the capital's famed addresses, at the foot of the Bois de Boulogne's Grande Cascade. Refined cuisine, served in the splendid 1850 pavilion or on the exquisite terrace.

Clichy, Ternes, Wagram.

17th arrondissement.
17th: ✉ 75017

Méridien Étoile, 81 bd Gouvion St-Cyr Ⓜ *Neuilly-Porte Maillot* ✆ 01 40 68 34 34, *guest.etoile@lemeridien.com, Fax 01 40 68 31 31* – rest, – 50 - 1 200. AE GB JCB E 6
L'Orenoc ✆ 01 40 68 30 40 *(closed 25 July-25 August, Christmas Holidays, Sunday and Monday)* **Meals** 38 (lunch) and a la carte 53/77 ♀ – ***La Terrasse*** ✆ 01 40 68 30 85 *(closed Saturday)* **Meals** a la carte 42/65 ♀ – ☕ 24 – **1 008 rm** 450, 17 suites.
◆ This huge renovated hotel opposite the Palais des Congrès also comprises a jazz club, bar and shops. Black granite and beige in the bedrooms. Warm colonial-style decor and modern cuisine in L'Orenoc ; simple à la carte menu and buffet at the Terrasse.

Concorde La Fayette, 3 pl. Gén. Koenig Ⓜ *Porte Maillot* ✆ 01 40 68 50 68, *booking@concorde-hotels.com, Fax 01 40 68 50 43,* ← – – 40 - 2 000. AE GB JCB E 6
La Fayette ✆ 01 40 68 51 19 **Meals** 29/35 ♀ – ☕ 20 – **931 rm** 338/518, 19 suites.
◆ This 33-storey tower within the Palais des Congrès complex offers guests unbeatable views of the city from most bedrooms (all of which have been refurbished) and the panoramic bar. Buffet meals and stained glass in the La Fayette restaurant.

Splendid Étoile without rest, 1bis av. Carnot Ⓜ *Charles de Gaulle-Etoile* ✆ 01 45 72 72 00, *hotel@hsplendid.com, Fax 01 45 72 72 01* – – 18. AE GB F 7
☕ 22 – **53 rm** 260/290, 4 suites.
◆ A classical façade ornamented with elaborate balconies, behind which the 52 spacious rooms (some with views of the Arc de Triomphe) are furnished in Louis XV style.

Regent's Garden without rest, 6 r. P. Demours Ⓜ *Ternes* ✆ 01 45 74 07 30, *hotel.regents.garden@wanadoo.fr, Fax 01 40 55 01 42,* – . AE GB JCB. E 7
☕ 11 – **39 rm** 138/249.
◆ This elegant mansion, built by Napoleon III for his private physician, has 39 large, stylish rooms, some of which overlook a garden which is particularly pleasant in summer.

Balmoral without rest, 6 r. Gén. Lanrezac Ⓜ *Charles de Gaulle-Etoile* ✆ 01 43 80 30 50, *hotel@hotelbalmoral.fr, Fax 01 43 80 51 56* – . AE GB JCB E 7
☕ 10 – **57 rm** 115/170.
◆ Personalised service and a calm ambience typify this old hotel (1911) a short distance from Étoile. Bright tones in the bedrooms and fine decorative woodwork in the lounge.

Ampère, 102 av. Villiers Ⓜ *Pereire* ✆ 01 44 29 17 17, *resa@hotelampere.com, Fax 01 44 29 16 50,* – – 40 - 100. AE GB D 8
Jardin d'Ampère ✆ 01 44 29 16 54 *(closed 2 to 22 August and Sunday dinner)* **Meals** 33 and a la carte 45/70 ♀ – ☕ 15 – **100 rm** 240/285.
◆ A modern lobby, elegant piano-bar, high-tech web links and cosy rooms with a modern feel (some over the inner courtyard) are all features of this innovative hotel. Stylish decor and a pleasant terrace in the Jardin d'Ampère, with dinner concerts on fine days.

Novotel Porte d'Asnières, 34 av. Porte d'Asnières Ⓜ *Pereire* ✆ 01 44 40 52 52, *h4987@accorhotels.com, Fax 01 44 40 44 23* – – 250. AE GB JCB C 9
Meals a la carte approx. 35 ♀ – ☕ 14 – **140 rm** 155.
◆ Situated in a modern building near the périphérique, but very well insulated from the traffic noise and with pleasant views from the rooms. Restaurant with contemporary decor offering popular grill fare.

Banville without rest, 166 bd Berthier Ⓜ *Porte de Champerret* ✆ 01 42 67 70 16, *hotelbanville@wanadoo.fr, Fax 01 44 40 42 77* – . AE GB JCB D 8
☕ 15 – **38 rm** 150/215.
◆ This tastefully decorated building dating from 1926 has an inherent charm all of its own. Elegant lounges and stylish bedrooms with an individual touch.

Quality Pierre without rest, 25 r. Th.-de-Banville Ⓜ *Pereire* ✆ 01 47 63 76 69, *amarante-arcdetriomphe@jjwhotels.com, Fax 01 43 80 63 96* – – 30. AE GB JCB D 8
☕ 20 – **50 rm** 190/280.
◆ Popular with business clients. The hotel's bedrooms have been refurbished in Directoire-style, with some overlooking the patio.

Villa Alessandra without rest, 9 pl. Boulnois Ⓜ *Ternes* ✆ 01 56 33 24 24, *alessandra@leshoteldeparis.com, Fax 01 56 33 24 30* – AE GB JCB E 8
20 – **49 rm** 295/330.
◆ This hotel on a charming small square is a quiet and popular option. Rooms decorated in Mediterranean style with wrought-iron beds and colourful wood furniture.

Villa Eugénie without rest, 167 r. Rome Ⓜ *Rome* ✆ 01 44 29 06 06, *eugenie@leshotelsdeparis.com, Fax 01 44 29 06 07* – 20. AE GB JCB C 10
20 – **41 rm** 225/285.
◆ Empire furniture and toile de Jouy print wallpaper and fabrics combine to create a romantic atmosphere in the attractive bedrooms of this hotel. Cosy lounge.

Champerret Élysées without rest, 129 av. Villiers Ⓜ *Porte de Champerret* ✆ 01 47 64 44 00, *reservation@champerret-elysees.fr, Fax 01 47 63 10 58* – AE GB JCB. D 7
13 – **45 rm** 91/138.
◆ This "cyberhotel" with ADSL, Wi-Fi, two private telephone lines and fax facilities is bound to be popular with Internet-lovers. The quietest rooms overlook the courtyard.

Mercure Wagram Arc de Triomphe without rest, 3 r. Brey Ⓜ *Charles de Gaulle-Etoile* ✆ 01 56 68 00 01, *h2053@accor-hotels.com, Fax 01 56 68 00 02* – AE GB JCB. E 8
14,50 – **43 rm** 220/230.
◆ This hotel between Étoile and Les Ternes has a welcoming lobby and small but stylish rooms decorated in light-coloured wood and sparkling fabrics on a nautical theme.

Villa des Ternes without rest, 97 av. Ternes Ⓜ *Neuilly-Porte Maillot* ✆ 01 53 81 94 94, *hotel@hotelternes.com, Fax 01 53 81 94 95* – AE GB JCB E 6
13 – **39 rm** 170/260.
◆ A recently built hotel next to the Palais des Congrès, and as such popular with business travellers. Warm tones in the bedrooms, equipped with modern bathrooms.

Magellan without rest, 17 r. J.B.-Dumas Ⓜ *Porte de Champerret* ✆ 01 45 72 44 51, *paris@hotelmagellan.com, Fax 01 40 68 90 36,* – AE GB. D 7
12 – **72 rm** 102/146.
◆ Functional and spacious bedrooms are a feature of this fine 1900s hotel with a small pavilion at the end of the small garden. The hotel lounge is furnished in Art Deco style.

Étoile Park Hôtel without rest, 10 av. Mac Mahon Ⓜ *Charles de Gaulle-Etoile* ✆ 01 42 67 69 63, *ephot@easynet.fr, Fax 01 43 80 18 99* – AE GB JCB E 8
12 – **28 rm** 99/155.
◆ Superbly located just a few yards from the Arc de Triomphe. Behind the stone façade is an attractive interior renovated in contemporary style. Pleasant breakfast room.

Star Hôtel Étoile without rest, 18 r. Arc de Triomphe Ⓜ *Charles de Gaulle-Etoile* ✆ 01 43 80 27 69, *star.etoile.hotel@wanadoo.fr, Fax 01 40 54 94 84* – – 18. AE GB JCB E 7
12 – **62 rm** 120/160.
◆ Modern, medieval-inspired decor in the reception, lounge and breakfast room. Although the rooms are small, they are light, cheerful and relatively quiet.

Astrid without rest, 27 av. Carnot Ⓜ *Charles de Gaulle-Etoile* ✆ 01 44 09 26 00, *paris@hotel-astrid.com, Fax 01 44 09 26 01* – AE GB JCB E 7
10 – **41 rm** 116/142.
◆ Just 100m/110yd from the Arc de Triomphe, and run by the same family since 1936. Each room has a different style : Directoire, Tyrolian, Provençal etc.

Flaubert without rest, 19 r. Rennequin Ⓜ *Ternes* ✆ 01 46 22 44 35, *paris@hotelflaubert.com, Fax 01 43 80 32 34* – AE GB D 8
8 – **41 rm** 95/110.
◆ The major selling-point of this hotel with bright, modern decor is its peaceful and verdant patio, overlooked by a few rooms. Winter garden-style breakfast room.

Guy Savoy, 18 r. Troyon Ⓜ *Charles de Gaulle-Etoile* ✆ 01 43 80 40 61, *reserv@guysavoy.com, Fax 01 46 22 43 09* – AE GB JCB E 8
closed August, 24 December-2 January, Saturday lunch, Sunday and Monday – **Meals** 210/285 and a la carte 130/205
Spec. Soupe d'artichaut à la truffe noire, brioche feuilletée aux champignons et truffes. Côte de gros turbot à l'oeuf en salade et soupe. Ris de veau rissolés, "petits chaussons" de pommes de terre et truffes.
◆ A décor of glass, leather, wengé, African sculptures and works by leading names in modern art. Refined and inventive cuisine in this top, resolutely 21C restaurant.

Michel Rostang, 20 r. Rennequin Ⓜ *Ternes* ✆ 01 47 63 40 77, *rostang@relaischateaux.fr, Fax 01 47 63 82 75* – AE GB JCB D 8
closed 1 to 15 August, Sunday, lunch Monday and Saturday – **Meals** 75 (lunch), 175/230 and a la carte 128/198
Spec. "Menu truffe" (15 December-15 March). Langoustines rôties en brochettes de romarin (May-October). Pigeon rôti à l'amertume de cacao.
◆ An elegant and unusual setting in which decorative wood, Robj figurines, Lalique works and Art Deco stained-glass add to the luxurious decor. Excellent cuisine and wine list.

Sormani (Fayet), 4 r. Gén. Lanrezac Ⓜ *Charles de Gaulle-Etoile* ✆ 01 43 80 13 91, *Fax 01 40 55 07 37* – AE GB E 7
closed 29 July-21 August, Saturday, Sunday and Bank Holidays – **Meals** 44 (lunch) and a la carte 59/107
Spec. Tortelloni farci au parmesan et truffes blanches (October-December). Oeufs au plat, polenta et truffes noires. Ravioli aux langoustines et palourdes.
◆ A restaurant full of Latin charm and a "dolce vita" atmosphere near place de l'Étoile. Elegant Italian cuisine served to a backdrop of red decor and Murano glass.

Pétrus, 12 pl. Mar. Juin Ⓜ *Pereire* ✆ 01 43 80 15 95, *Fax 01 47 66 49 86* – AE GB JCB D 8
closed 10 to 25 August – **Meals** 42 and a la carte 50/78
◆ A profusion of excellent fresh fish and seafood is the order of the day in this pleasant, maritime-inspired restaurant.

Petit Colombier, 42 r. Acacias Ⓜ *Argentine* ✆ 01 43 80 28 54, *le.petit.colombier@wanadoo.fr, Fax 01 44 40 04 29* – AE GB E 7
closed 31 July-30 August, Saturday lunch and Sunday – **Meals** 35 and a la carte 67/83
◆ The patina of age, antique clocks and Louis XV chairs add provincial charm to this restaurant which recalls the visits of the world's heads of state.

Les Béatilles (Bochaton), 11 bis r. Villebois-Mareuil Ⓜ *Ternes* ✆ 01 45 74 43 80, *Fax 01 45 74 43 81* – GB E 7
closed August, Christmas Holidays, Saturday and Sunday – **Meals** 40 (lunch), 45/70 and a la carte 73/100
Spec. Nems d'escargots et champignons des bois. Pastilla de pigeon et foie gras aux épices. La "Saint-Cochon" (November-March)..
◆ Attentive service and imaginative and refined cuisine are the hallmarks of this restaurant with its simple and contemporary design.

Dessirier, 9 pl. Mar. Juin Ⓜ *Pereire* ✆ 01 42 27 82 14, *dessirier@michelrostang.com, Fax 01 47 66 82 07* – AE GB JCB D 8
closed 11 to 17 August, Saturday and Sunday in July-August – **Meals** 45 and a la carte 59/82
◆ A friendly brasserie-style restaurant where the armchairs, padded benches and fish- and seafood-inspired menu help to foster good humour and a convivial atmosphere.

Timgad, 21 r. Brunel Ⓜ *Argentine* ✆ 01 45 74 23 70, *Fax 01 40 68 76 46* – AE GB. E 7
Meals a la carte 40/61.
◆ The past splendour of the city of Timgad is revisited in this restaurant serving the perfumed cuisine of the Maghreb. Elegant, Moorish-inspired decor with Moroccan stucco.

Graindorge, 15 r. Arc de Triomphe Ⓜ *Charles de Gaulle-Etoile* ✆ 01 47 54 00 28, *le.graindorge@wanadoo.fr, Fax 01 47 54 00 28* – AE GB E 7
closed 1 to 21 August, Saturday lunch and Sunday – **Meals** 28 (lunch), 32/59 and a la carte 45/67
◆ Barley (orge) is the key ingredient in the beer which accompanies the copious Flemish dishes and seasonal fare served in this Art Deco-style restaurant. Wine also available !

La Braisière (Faussat), 54 r. Cardinet Ⓜ *Malesherbes* ✆ 01 47 63 40 37, *labraisiere@free.fr, Fax 01 47 63 04 76* – AE GB D 9
closed August, Saturday lunch and Sunday – **Meals** 30 (lunch) and a la carte 49/63
Spec. Gâteau de pommes de terre au foie gras. Épaule d'agneau de lait des Pyrénées (season). Mirliton aux figues.
◆ Comfortable restaurant in gentle pastels. The imaginative chef draws inspiration from the traditions of the south-west and takes his cue from the day's market specials.

Beudant, 97 r. des Dames Ⓜ *Rome* ✆ 01 43 87 11 20, *lebeudant@wanadoo.fr, Fax 01 43 87 27 35* – AE GB JCB. D 11
closed 23 July-22 August, Sunday and Monday – **Meals** 25 (lunch)/32 and a la carte 51/62.
◆ This Second Empire house just off the rue Beudant is home to two welcoming dining rooms furnished in light-coloured woodwork. Maritime slant to the menu.

Paolo Petrini, 6 r. Débarcadère Ⓜ *Porte Maillot* ✆ 01 45 74 25 95, *paolo.petrini@wanadoo.fr, Fax 01 45 74 12 95* – AE GB JCB. E 6
closed 1 to 21 August, Saturday lunch and Sunday – **Meals** 33/38 and a la carte 51/80
◆ Forget pizza and macaroni - this restaurant attracts discerning customers who come here to enjoy refined Italian cuisine. Contemporary decor enhanced by modern art.

XX **Ballon des Ternes,** 103 av. Ternes Ⓜ *Porte Maillot* ✆ 01 45 74 17 98, *leballondesternes@fr.oleane.com, Fax 01 45 72 18 84* – AE GB JCB E 6
closed 31 July-21 August – **Meals** a la carte 43/67 ♀.
◆ A pleasant brasserie with 1900s décor close to the Palais des Congrès. An emphasis on seafood and meat dishes, with attentive service.

XX **Chez Léon,** 32 r. Legendre Ⓜ *Villiers* ✆ 01 42 27 06 82, *chezleon32@wanadoo.fr, Fax 01 46 22 63 67* – AE GB D 10
closed August, Christmas Holidays, Saturday, Sunday and Bank Holidays – **Meals** 27 b.i. and a la carte 34/45 ♀.
◆ Popular with a faithful band of locals over a number of years, "the" bistro in the Batignolles district is known for its refined, traditional cuisine served on two floors.

X **Caïus,** 6 r. Armaillé Ⓜ *Charles de Gaulle-Etoile* ✆ 01 42 27 19 20, *Fax 01 40 55 00 93* – ▤. AE ⓓ GB JCB E 7
closed 6 to 19 August, Saturday lunch and Sunday – **Meals** 23 (lunch), 50/60 and a la carte 40/52 ♀.
◆ A chic bistro with a warm decor of wood, benches and photos on a coffee and spices theme. Appetising seasonally influenced cuisine with a personal touch.

X **Soupière,** 154 av. Wagram Ⓜ *Wagram* ✆ 01 42 27 00 73, *Fax 01 46 22 27 09* – ▤. AE GB D 9
closed 4 to 24 August, Saturday lunch and Sunday – **Meals** 28/55 and a la carte 43/59.
◆ An amiable local restaurant with attentive service and a classic à la carte, including "mushroom" menus in season. Trompe-l'oeil décor.

X **Caves Petrissans,** 30 bis av. Niel Ⓜ *Pereire* ✆ 01 42 27 52 03, *cavespetrissans@noos.fr, Fax 01 40 54 87 56,* 🌂 – ▤. AE GB D 8
closed 29 July-29 August, Saturday and Sunday – **Meals** (booking essential) 34 and a la carte 38/59.
◆ This hundred-year-old-plus establishment, which doubles as a wine shop and restaurant, was frequented in bygone days by famous literary figures. Well-presented bistro cuisine.

X **L'Huîtrier,** 16 r. Saussier-Leroy Ⓜ *Ternes* ✆ 01 40 54 83 44, *Fax 01 40 54 83 86* – ▤. AE GB JCB E 8
closed August, Sunday from May-July and Monday – **Meals** (lunch) a la carte 32/75 ♀.
◆ The seafood display at the entrance sets the tone for this contemporary-style restaurant, where diners can enjoy oysters and seafood at tightly spaced tables.

X **L'Entredgeu,** 83 r.Laugier Ⓜ *Porte de Champerret* ✆ 01 40 54 97 24, *Fax 01 40 54 96 62* D 7
closed Christmas Holidays, 2 to 22 August, Sunday and Monday – **Meals** 22 (lunch)/28.
◆ Friendly service, bistro-style furnishings, menus posted on slate boards and seasonal cuisine are the hallmarks of this restaurant with an unusual name well worth remembering.

Montmartre, La Villette, Belleville.

18th, 19th and 20th arrondissements.
18th: ✉ 75018
19th: ✉ 75019
20th: ✉ 75020

Terrass'Hôtel, 12 r. J. de Maistre (18th) Ⓜ *Place de Clichy* ✆ 01 46 06 72 85, *reservation@terrass-hotel.com, Fax 01 42 52 29 11,* 🌂 – 🛗 ⇆ ▤ 📺 📞 – 🏛 25 - 100. AE ⓓ GB JCB C 13
Terrasse ✆ 01 44 92 34 00 **Meals** 22,50/29 – ☕ 14 – **85 rm** 210/236, 15 suites.
◆ At the foot of the Sacré-Coeur. An unbeatable view of Paris from the upper-floor rooms facing the street. A warm, stylish interior with an attractive chimney in the lounge. Cosy Provençal dining room with a rooftop "Terrasse" offering views of the capital.

Holiday Inn, 216 av. J. Jaurès (19th) Ⓜ *Porte de Pantin* ✆ 01 44 84 18 18, *hilavillette@alliance-hospitality.com, Fax 01 44 84 18 20,* , – – 15 - 140. AE Ⓓ GB C 21
Meals *(closed Saturday and Sunday)* 18/52 ♀ – ☕ 15 – **182 rm** 275/345.
◆ A modern hotel opposite the Cité de la Musique and a few yards from the nearest métro stop. Spacious, soundproofed rooms with modern creature comforts. Sober brasserie-style dining room, plus a small terrace separated from the street by a curtain of greenery.

Mercure Montmartre without rest, 1 r. Caulaincourt (18th) Ⓜ *Place de Clichy* ✆ 01 44 69 70 70, *h0373@accor-hotels.com, Fax 01 44 69 70 71* – – 20 - 70. AE Ⓓ GB D 12
☕ 13,50 – **305 rm** 180/190.
◆ All the usual facilities one would expect of the Mercure in this hotel at the heart of Paris nightlife, a short walk from the Moulin-Rouge. Pleasant mahogany-coloured bar.

Holiday Inn Garden Court Montmartre without rest, 23 r. Damrémont (18th) Ⓜ *Lamarck Caulaincourt* ✆ 01 44 92 33 40, *hiparmm@aol.com, Fax 01 44 92 09 30* – – 20. AE Ⓓ GB JCB C 13
☕ 13 – **54 rm** 170.
◆ A fairly recent hotel on one of Montmartre's steep streets. Bright, functional rooms, plus a breakfast room decorated with an attractive trompe-l'oeil.

Roma Sacré Coeur without rest, 101 r. Caulaincourt (18th) Ⓜ *Lamarck Caulaincourt* ✆ 01 42 62 02 02, *hotel.roma@wanadoo.fr, Fax 01 42 54 34 92* – . AE Ⓓ GB JCB
☕ 7 – **57 rm** 77/97. C 14
◆ The Roma displays the full charm of Montmartre with a garden to the front, steps to the side and the Sacré-Coeur above. Colourful, recently refurbished rooms.

Laumière without rest, 4 r. Petit (19th) Ⓜ *Laumière* ✆ 01 42 06 10 77, *lelaumiere@wanadoo.fr, Fax 01 42 06 72 50* – . GB D 19
☕ 7,50 – **54 rm** 52/72.
◆ If you're looking for some urban greenery, this recently renovated hotel could fit the bill, with its attractive small garden and proximity to the Parc des Buttes-Chaumont.

Damrémont without rest, 110 r. Damrémont (18th) Ⓜ *Jules Joffrin* ✆ 01 42 64 25 75, *hotel.damremont@wanadoo.fr, Fax 01 46 06 74 64* – . Ⓓ GB B 13
☕ 7 – **35 rm** 75/85.
◆ This hotel near Montmartre offers modern, smallish but well-maintained rooms (those over the courtyard are quieter) with attractive mahogany-coloured furniture.

Crimée without rest, 188 r. Crimée (19th) Ⓜ *Crimée* ✆ 01 40 36 75 29, *hotelcrimee19@wanadoo.fr, Fax 01 40 36 29 57* – . AE Ⓓ GB JCB C 18
☕ 6 – **31 rm** 60/67.
◆ This hotel is situated 300m/330yd from the Canal de l'Ourcq. Good soundproofing in the functional rooms, some of which open on to a small garden.

Cottage Marcadet, 151 bis r. Marcadet (18th) Ⓜ *Lamarck Caulaincourt* ✆ 01 42 57 71 22, *Fax 01 42 57 71 22* – . GB. C 13
closed Easter Holidays, 7 to 14 August and Sunday – **Meals** 27/36,50 b.i. and a la carte 31/56.
◆ An intimate ambience awaits customers in this classical restaurant adorned with comfortable Louis XVI furniture. Refined, traditional cuisine.

Les Allobroges, 71 r. Grands-Champs (20th) Ⓜ *Maraîchers* ✆ 01 43 73 40 00, *Fax 01 40 09 23 22* – AE GB K 22
closed 1 to 9 May, August, 24 December-3 January, Sunday, Monday and Bank Holidays – **Meals** 19/32.
◆ Head off the beaten track to the Porte de Montreuil to discover this pleasant restaurant with its attractive but simple decor. Delicious contemporary cuisine.

Relais des Buttes, 86 r. Compans (19th) Ⓜ *Botzaris* ✆ 01 42 08 24 70, *Fax 01 42 03 20 44,* – GB E 20
closed August, 24 December-2 January, Saturday lunch and Sunday – **Meals** 31 and a la carte 42/60 ♀.
◆ A few yards from the Parc des Buttes-Chaumont. A warming fireplace in the modern dining room during the winter, plus a quiet courtyard terrace in summer. Traditional cuisine.

Moulin de la Galette, 83 r. Lepic (18th) Ⓜ *Abbesses* ✆ 01 46 06 84 77, *Fax 01 46 06 84 78,* – . AE Ⓓ GB JCB
closed Sunday dinner and Monday except lunch from April-October – **Meals** a la carte 38/55 ♀.
◆ This windmill dating from 1622 was to become a well-known dance hall painted by Renoir and Toulouse-Lautrec. Today, it is a pleasant restaurant with a charming terrace.

XX **Au Clair de la Lune,** 9 r. Poulbot (18th) Ⓜ *Abbesses* ☎ 01 42 58 97 03, *Fax 01 42 55 64 74* – AE GB JCB D 14
closed 20 August-19 September, Monday lunch and Sunday – **Meals** 29 and a la carte 35/65.
◆ Pierrot will extend a warm welcome to his auberge located just behind the Place du Tertre. A friendly atmosphere, with the backdrop of frescoes depicting old Montmartre.

X **Poulbot Gourmet,** 39 r. Lamarck (18th) Ⓜ *Lamarck Caulaincourt* ☎ 01 46 06 86 00 – GB C 14
closed 8 to 20 August and Sunday except – **Meals** 35 and a la carte 37/60.
◆ This bistro will take you back to the time when street urchins (poulbots) were a common sight in Montmartre. Classic cuisine that will satisfy the most discerning gourmet.

X **L'Oriental,** 76 r. Martyrs (18th) Ⓜ *Pigalle* ☎ 01 42 64 39 80 – AE GB. ✈ D 13-14
closed 22 July-28 August, Sunday and Monday – **Meals** 39 b.i. and a la carte 29/35.
◆ Smiling service and pleasing décor, including ornate mosaics and screens, typify this North African restaurant at the heart of cosmopolitan Pigalle.

X **Cave Gourmande,** 10 r. Gén. Brunet (19th) Ⓜ *Botzaris* ☎ 01 40 40 03 30, *la-cave-gourmande@wanadoo.fr, Fax 01 40 40 03 30* – ▤. GB E 20
closed August, February Holidays, Saturday and Sunday – **Meals** 32.
◆ Close to the Parc des Buttes-Chaumont, this friendly bistro is known for its varied range of daily specials. The decor here is a relaxed mix of wooden tables and bottle racks.

ENVIRONS

The outskirts of Paris up to 25Km

La Défense *92 Hauts-de-Seine* 311 J2 101 ⑭ – ✉ *92400 Courbevoie.* **See :** *Quarter★★ : perspective★ from the parvis.*
Paris 8,5.

Sofitel Grande Arche, 11 av. Arche, exit Défense 6 ✉ 92081 ☎ 01 47 17 50 00, *h3013@accor-hotels.com, Fax 01 47 17 55 66,* – 100. AE GB JCB. rest
Avant Seine ☎ 01 47 17 59 99 *(closed 1 to 21 August, 23 December-2 January, Friday dinner, Saturday, Sunday and Bank Holidays* – **Meals** a la carte approx. 48 – 23 – **368 rm** 395/445, 16 suites.
◆ Impressive ship prow architecture in glass and ochre-coloured stone. Spacious, elegant rooms, well-equipped lounges and auditorium (with interpreting booths). High-quality designer décor in the Avant Seine restaurant, where grilled meats are to the fore.

Renaissance, 60 Jardin de Valmy, by ring road, exit La Défense 7 ✉ 92918 *Puteaux* ☎ 01 41 97 50 50, *reservations@renaissancehotels.com, Fax 01 41 97 51 51,* – 160. AE GB JCB.
Meals *(closed Sunday lunch and Saturday)* 28/54 – 23 – **324 rm** 265/355, 3 suites.
◆ At the foot of the Carrara-marbled Grande Arche, this large modern hotel offers guests well-appointed rooms decorated with refinement. Old brasserie atmosphere in the wood-clad restaurant offering views over the Valmy gardens. Full fitness facilities.

Hilton La Défense, 2 pl. Défense ✉ 92053 ☎ 01 46 92 10 10, *parldhirm@hilton.com, Fax 01 46 92 10 50,* – 5 - 60. AE GB JCB. rest
Les Communautés ☎ 01 46 92 10 30 (lunch only) *(closed 5 to 25 August, Saturday, Sunday and Bank Holidays)* **Meals** 50/86 – ***L'Échiquier*** ☎ 01 46 92 10 35 **Meals** a la carte 35/54 – 26 – **148 rm** 280/540, 6 suites.
◆ This refurbished hotel stands within the confines of the CNIT conference centre. Warm, designer-style rooms, some with facilities for the business traveller. Modern cuisine and good views from Les Communautés restaurant ; traditional cuisine in L'Échiquier.

Sofitel Centre, 34 cours Michelet by ring road, exit La Défense 4 ✉ 92060 *Puteaux* ☎ 01 47 76 44 43, *h0912@accor.com, Fax 01 47 76 72 10,* – 100. AE GB. rest
Les 2 Arcs (lunch only) *(closed 29 July-22 August, 23 December-3 January, Friday dinner, Saturday, Sunday and Bank Holidays)* **Meals** 49/55 – ***Botanic*** ☎ 01 47 76 72 40 *(closed Friday dinner, Saturday and Sunday)* **Meals** a la carte approx. 42 – 24 – **151 rm** 345/480.
◆ A semi-circular building between the towers of La Défense. Large, well-equipped rooms, some of which have been refurbished. Hushed English-style bar, and contemporary decor and cuisine in Les 2 Arcs restaurant. Half-bar, half-brasserie ambience in Botanic.

Novotel La Défense, 2 bd Neuilly, exit Défense 1 ☎ 01 41 45 23 23, *h0747@accor.com, Fax 01 41 45 23 24* – 130. AE GB JCB
Meals *(closed lunch Saturday and Sunday)* a la carte 23/33 – 14 – **280 rm** 200/210.
◆ La Défense district, with its impressive architecture and sculpture, stands at the foot of this hotel with its comfortable and functional rooms, some offering views of Paris. Contemporary décor in the trendy dining room, which features a buffet section.

Marne-la-Vallée *77206 S.-et-M.* 312 E2 101 ⑲.
18 of Bussy-St-Georges (private) ☎ 01 64 66 00 00 ; 27 of Disneyland Paris at Magny-le-Hongre ☎ 01 60 45 68 90.
Paris 28.

at Disneyland Resort Paris *access by Highway A 4 and Disneyland exit.*
See : *Disneyland Resort Paris ★★★-Central reservation number for hotels : ☎ (00 33)01 60 30 60 30, Fax (00 33)01 64 74 57 50 – The rates for the hotels in Disneyland Resort Paris are based on a daily price that included entrance to the Parks – As these rates vary according to the season, we suggest that you call the central reservation number for current information*

Orly (Paris Airports) *94396 Val-de-Marne* 312 D3 101 ㉖ *– pop. 21 646 alt. 89.*
01 49 75 15 15.
Paris 15.

Hilton Orly, near airport station ✉ 94544 ✆ 01 45 12 45 12, *marylene.cedile@hilton.com, Fax 01 45 12 45 00,* – 280. AE GB JCB.
Meals 34 ♀ – 18 – **352 rm** 141/186.
◆ A 1960s hotel with subdued yet elegant rooms, and the latest high-tech equipment and facilities for business customers. Current décor, plus a choice of brasserie dishes, buffet options and a gastronomic à la carte menu in the restaurant.

Mercure, N 7, Z.I. Nord, Orlytech ✉ 94547 ✆ 01 49 75 15 50, *h1246@accor-hotels.com, Fax 01 49 75 15 51* – – 40. AE GB JCB
Meals 24 – 13 – **192 rm** 145/171.
◆ A convenient stopover hotel, particularly for business travellers, with its good facilities and well-maintained rooms. Contemporary bistro atmosphere, brasserie-style dishes and the standard "Mercure" chain wine-list in the restaurant.

See also *Rungis*

Roissy-en-France (Paris Airports) *95700 Val-d'Oise* 305 G6 101 ⑧ *– pop. 2 367 alt. 85.*
Roissy-Charles-de-Gaulle ✆ 01 48 62 22 80.
Paris 26.

at Roissy-Town :

Millennium, allée du Verger ✆ 01 34 29 33 33, *resa.cdg@mill-cop.com, Fax 01 34 29 03 05,* – – 150. AE GB JCB. rest
Meals 15 (lunch)/29 ♀ – 20 – **239 rm** 250/280.
◆ The excellent facilities here include a bar, Irish pub, fitness centre, impressive pool, meeting rooms, and a floor specifically for business clientele. The brasserie concentrates on buffets and international cuisine, with lighter snacks available in the bar.

Courtyard Marriott, allée du Verger ✆ 01 34 38 53 53, *Fax 01 34 38 53 54,* – – 500. AE GB JCB.
Meals 29 and a la carte approx. 40 ♀ – 17 – **296 rm** 169/300, 4 suites.
◆ The newest airport hotel offers modern facilities perfectly suited to business travellers in transit through Paris. The restaurant's classic cuisine is served to a backdrop of decor inspired by the City of Light's typical brasseries.

Country Inn and Suites, allée du Verger ✆ 01 30 18 21 00, *info-paris@countryinns.de, Fax 01 30 18 20 18,* – – 15 - 95. AE GB JCB
Meals *(closed lunch Saturday, Sunday and Bank Holidays)* a la carte 25/45 ♀ – 13 – **178 rm** 175/200.
◆ This recently built hexagonal and somewhat plain hotel offers guests spacious rooms of varying sizes with modern attractive decor. The restaurant menu features a mixture of French cuisine and dishes from the other side of the Atlantic. English-style bar.

Mercure, allée des Vergers ✆ 01 34 29 40 00, *h1245@accor-hotels.com, Fax 01 34 29 00 18,* – – 90. AE GB JCB
Meals 22,50 ♀ – 13 – **203 rm** 180/240.
◆ This chain hotel has had a recent facelift, with Provençal tones in the lobby, an old-style counter in the bar, and refurbished, soundproofed bedrooms offering plenty of space. The new-look dining room has been revamped with light-hearted bakery décor.

in Airport terminal nr 2 :

Sheraton , ✆ 01 49 19 70 70, *Fax 01 49 19 70 71,* – – 110. AE GB JCB
Les Étoiles *(closed Saturday, Sunday and Bank Holidays)* **Meals** 48,50(lunch)/55,50 – ***Les Saisons :*** **Meals** a la carte approx. 45 – 26 – **242 rm** 230/710, 12 suites.
◆ Step off the plane and into this futuristic hotel with its original architecture. Décor by Andrée Putman, views of the runway, peace and quiet, and elegant bedrooms. A modern setting and cuisine in Les Étoiles, with brasserie dishes in Les Saisons.

at Roissypole :

Hilton, 01 49 19 77 77, *cdghitwsal@hilton.com, Fax 01 49 19 77 78*, – 500. rest
Gourmet *(01 49 19 77 95) (closed July, August, Saturday and Sunday)* **Meals** 42/45 – ***Aviateurs*** (01 49 19 77 95) **Meals** 34 – 24 – **387 rm** 495, 4 suites.
◆ Bold architecture, space and light are the key features of this upmarket chain hotel with all the latest facilities, making it an ideal base for work and relaxation. Contemporary cuisine in Le Gourmet, plus a concise brasserie menu in the Aviateurs.

Sofitel, Zone centrale Ouest 01 49 19 29 29, *h0577@accor-hotels.com, Fax 01 49 19 29 00*, – – 60. rest
L'Escale : **Meals** a la carte 45/60 – 20 – **342 rm** 340/535, 8 suites.
◆ The major selling-points of this Sofitel between the two terminals are its personalised service, quiet ambience, seminar rooms, elegant bar and refined guest rooms. Nautical décor and cuisine in the pleasant and aptly named "Escale" (Port of Call) restaurant.

Novotel, 01 49 19 27 27, *h1014@accor-hotels.com, Fax 01 49 19 27 99* – – 60.
Meals 30/58 – 12 – **201 rm** 147/152.
◆ A mid-range chain hotel located opposite the airport's runways. The majority of its well-appointed rooms with double-glazing conform to the chain's new style. Restrained dining room designed with a brasserie feel, with modern furnishings and a simple layout.

Rungis

94150 Val-de-Marne 312 D3 101 ㉖ – *pop. 5 424 alt. 80.*
Paris 14.

at Pondorly : *Access : from Paris, Highway A 6 and take Orly Airport exit ; from outside of Paris, A 6 and Rungis exit :*

Holiday Inn, 4 av. Ch. Lindbergh 01 49 78 42 00, *hiorly.manager@alliance-hospitality.com, Fax 01 45 60 91 25* – – 15 - 150. rest
Meals 26 – 17 – **168 rm** 165/195.
◆ A comfortable hotel alongside the motorway, with large, modern rooms fitted with double-glazing. The dining room has been recently renovated in contemporary style with the occasional discreet touch of Art Deco. Traditional cuisine.

Novotel, Zone du Delta, 1 r. Pont des Halles 01 45 12 44 12, *h1628@accor-hotels.com, Fax 01 45 12 44 13*, – – 15 - 150.
Meals 24,50 – 12 – **181 rm** 144/156.
◆ The hotel's double-glazed bedrooms comply with the chain's normal standards. The bar is based on a comic strip theme ; the large restaurant on the city's wholesale markets.

Versailles

78000 Yvelines 311 I3 101 ㉓ – *pop. 85 726 alt. 130.*
See : *Palace*★★★ Y – *Gardens*★★★ *(fountain display*★★★ *(grandes eaux) and illuminated night performances*★★★ *(fêtes de nuit) in summer) – Ecuries Royales*★ Y – *The Trianons*★★ – *Lambinet Museum*★ Y **M.**
National at Guyancourt 01 30 43 36 00 by ⑤.
Tourist Office 2 bis av. Paris 01 39 24 88 88, Fax 01 39 24 88 89.
Paris 20 ①

Trianon Palace, 1 bd Reine 01 30 84 50 00, *reservation.0110h@westin.com, Fax 01 30 84 50 01*, – rm, – 15 - 200. rest
see ***Les Trois Marches*** below - ***Café Trianon :*** **Meals** a la carte 55/75 – 34 – **166 rm** 450/640, 26 suites.
◆ The classic architecture of this luxury hotel on the edge of the park is a fine example of early-20C elegance. Excellent fitness centre. The Café Trianon, with its attractive glass ceiling, continues to enjoy local popularity for its refined modern cuisine.

Sofitel Château de Versailles, 2 bis av. Paris 01 39 07 46 46, *h1300@accor-hotels.com, Fax 01 39 07 46 47*, – – 120. Y a
Meals *(closed 14 July-22 August, Friday and Saturday)* 35/48 – 22 – **146 rm** 390/410, 6 suites.
◆ Only the gate survives from the former artillery school here. Vast renovated rooms embellished with antique furniture and lithographs. The modern dining room, serving a range of French and international cuisine, is ornamented with Liberty print lambrequins.

VERSAILLES

Carnot (R.)	Y	
Chancellerie (R. de la)	Y	3
Clemenceau (R. Georges)	Y	7
Cotte (R. Robert de)	Y	10
États-Généraux (R. des)	Z	
Europe (Av. de l')	Y	14
Foch (R. du Mar.)	XY	
Gambetta (Pl.)	Y	17
Gaulle (Av. du Gén.-de-)	YZ	18
Hoche (R.)	Y	
Indép.-Américaine (R. de l')	Y	20
Leclerc (R. du Gén.)	Z	24
Mermoz (R. Jean)	Z	27
Nolhac (R. Pierre-de-)	Y	31
Orangerie (R. de l')	YZ	
Paroisse (R. de la)	Y	
Porte-de-Buc (R. de la)	Z	34
Rockfeller (Av.)	Y	37
Royale (R.)	Z	
Satory (R. de)	YZ	42
Vieux-Versailles (R. du)	YZ	47

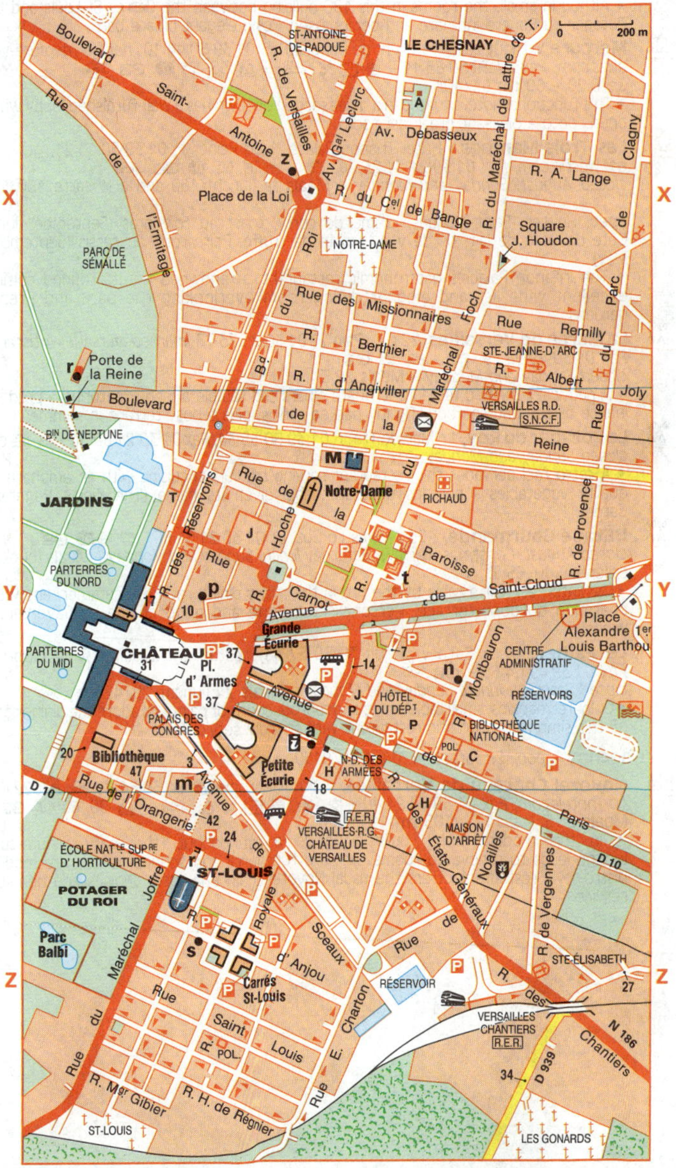

Le Versailles without rest, 7 r. Ste-Anne 01 39 50 64 65, *info@hotel-le-versailles.fr, Fax 01 39 02 37 85* – 25. AE GB JCB Y p
12 – **45 rm** 92/122.
• A combination of spacious rooms, Art Deco furniture, peace and quiet, a pretty terrace and attentive service explain the success of this pleasant and popular hotel.

La Résidence du Berry without rest, 14 r. Anjou 01 39 49 07 07, *resa@hotel-berry.com, Fax 01 39 50 59 40* – . AE GB JCB Z s
12 – **39 rm** 115/140.
• Although small, the rooms in this 18C building between the Carrés St-Louis and the Potager du Roi are intimate and personalised. Cosy, elegant billiard bar.

Mercure without rest, 19 r. Ph. de Dangeau 01 39 50 44 10, *hotel@mercure-versailles.com, Fax 01 39 50 65 11* – 35. AE GB JCB Y n
8,20 – **60 rm** 93/101.
• This functional hotel situated in a quiet section of town has a well-furnished lobby which opens onto a pleasant breakfast room.

Les Trois Marches - Hôtel Trianon Palace, 1 bd Reine 01 39 50 13 21, *gerard.vie@westin.com, Fax 01 30 21 01 25*, – . AE GB JCB X r
closed August, Sunday and Monday – **Meals** 58 (lunch)/160 and a la carte 160/205
Spec. Huîtres, Saint-Jacques, crème de curry, toast au foie gras (September-June). Côte de veau de lait, ris de veau, coulis de truffe. Poire rôtie au cassis (September-May).
• The Trianon Palace's gastronomic restaurant is renowned for its refined cuisine, excellent wine list and elegant dining room overlooking the park and French gardens.

La Marée de Versailles, 22 r. au Pain 01 30 21 73 73, *mareedeversailles@tiscali.fr, Fax 01 39 49 98 29*, – . AE GB Y t
closed Sunday and Monday – **Meals** 29.
• A nautically themed restaurant where diners can sample a menu featuring a predominance of fish and seafood. Tightly packed tables, plus a busy terrace in summer.

Le Potager du Roy, 1 r. Mar.-Joffre 01 39 50 35 34, *Fax 01 30 21 69 30* – . AE GB
closed Sunday and Monday – **Meals** 32/47. Z r
• A retro feel pervades this restaurant serving traditional cuisine with an emphasis on quality vegetables - perhaps understandable given its name (The King's Vegetable Garden) !

L'Étape Gourmande, 125 r. Yves Le Coz 01 30 21 01 63, – AE GB V n
closed August, Christmas Holidays, Saturday lunch, Sunday and Monday – **Meals** (booking essential) 40/65.
• In winter, ask for a table by the fire in the rustic dining room ; in summer, enjoy the charming outdoor terrace. Personalised cuisine and good choice of Savennières wines.

Le Falher, 22 r. Satory 01 39 50 57 43, *restaurant-le-falher@wanadoo.fr, Fax 01 39 49 04 66* – GB. Y m
closed Saturday lunch, Sunday and Monday – **Meals** 24 (lunch), 29/42.
• Coloured napkins, small table lamps and reproductions of paintings adorn the dining room of this simply styled rustic restaurant with friendly service.

at Le Chesnay – *pop. 28 530 alt. 120 –* *78150 :*

Novotel Château de Versailles, 4 bd St-Antoine 01 39 54 96 96, *h1022@accor-hotels.com, Fax 01 39 54 94 40* – 90. AE GB
Meals 21 – 12 – **105 rm** 115/141. X z
• In this modern hotel, built alongside a roundabout, the leafy atrium-cum-lounge leads to renovated rooms that are functional and soundproofed. The modern bistro-style restaurant offers the usual Novotel chain à la carte choices and non-stop service.

Joigny *89300 Yonne* **319** **D4** *– pop. 10 032 alt. 79.*
See *: Vierge au Sourire★ in St-Thibault's Church – Côte St-Jacques ≤★ 1,5 km by D 20.*
18 of Roncemay at Chassy ✆ 03 86 73 50 50.
Tourist Office 4 quai Ragobert ✆ 03 86 62 11 05, Fax 03 86 91 76 38.
Paris 147 – Auxerre 27 – Gien 75 – Montargis 59 – Sens 30 – Troyes 76.

La Côte St-Jacques (Lorain), 14 fg Paris ✆ 03 86 62 09 70, *lorain@relaischateaux.com, Fax 03 86 91 49 70,* ≤, – rest, – 12 - 25. AE GB JCB
closed 2 January-2 February – **Meals** *(closed lunch Monday and Tuesday from November-April except Bank Holidays)* (weekends booking essential) 75 b.i. (lunch), 147/175 and a la carte 116/154 – 28 – **32 rm** 140/400
Spec. Genèse d'un plat sur le thème de l'huître. Filet de turbot pané aux chanterelles, mousseline de châtaignes et sauce au verjus. Poularde de Bresse à la vapeur de champagne.. **Wines** Bourgogne blanc, Irancy.
◆ Luxury establishment on the River Yonne, with a pool, sauna, private boat (trips on the river) and shop. One of the great restaurants of France, with inventive cuisine served alongside traditional dishes, plus a constantly renewed procession of great wines.

Rheims (Reims) *51100 Marne* **306** **G7** *– pop. 187 206 alt. 85.*
See *: Cathedral★★★ – St-Remi Basilica★★ : interior★★★ – Palais du Tau★★ – Champagne cellars★★ – Place Royale★ – Porte Mars★ – Hôtel de la Salle★ – Foujita Chapel★ – Library★ of Ancien Collège des Jésuites – St-Remi Museum★★ – Hôtel le Vergeur Museum★ – Fine Arts Museum★.* **Envir.** *: Fort de la Pompelle : German helmets★ 9 km to the SE by N 44.*
18 Rheims-Champagne at Gueux ✆ 03 26 05 46 10 ; to the W by N 31-E 46 : 9,5 km.
Rheims-Champagne ✆ 03 26 07 15 15 : 6 km – ✆ 0892 35 35 33 – Tourist Office 2, r. Guillaume de Machault ✆ 03 26 77 45 00, Fax 03 26 77 45 19.
Paris 144 – Brussels 214 – Châlons-sur-Marne 48 – Lille 199 – Luxembourg 232.

Château les Crayères, 64 bd Vasnier ✆ 03 26 82 80 80, *crayeres@relaischateaux.com, Fax 03 26 82 65 52,* ≤, – AE GB JCB
closed mid-December-mid-January – **Meals** (booking essential) 65 (lunch), 200 b.i./230 b.i. and a la carte 116/145 – 26 – **17 rm** 275/475, 4 suites
Spec. Saint-Pierre cuit en croûte de coriandre. Piccata de veau de lait au sautoir. Ananas "Victoria" soufflé au rhum et raisins secs.. **Wines** Champagne.
◆ A fine noble residence in an English-style park close to the Gallo-Roman "crayères" (quarries) of the famous champagne houses. Luxurious bedrooms, sumptuous classical decor in the dining room, a terrace on the main courtyard, and traditional cuisine.

L'Assiette Champenoise (Lallement), à Tinqueux, 40 av. Paul Vaillant-Couturier ✉ 51430 ✆ 03 26 84 64 64, *assiette.champenoise@wanadoo.fr, Fax 03 26 04 15 69,* – rest, – 25. AE GB JCB. rest
Meals *(closed Tuesday and Wednesday lunch)* 55/85 and a la carte 72/99 – 14 – **55 rm** 128/178
Spec. Tourteau, pâte à kadaif frit, jus de crustacés. Pigeon fermier en tourte de ventrêche et épinards. Côte de veau de lait élevé sous la mère.. **Wines** Champagne, Bouzy..
◆ This aristocratic mansion in a flower-filled park has benefited from the recent addition of a new wing. Pleasantly renovated bedrooms, some with a lounge. Elegant dining room in pastel shades, charming terrace and delicious modern cuisine.

Saulieu *21210 Côte-d'Or* **320** **F6** *– pop. 2 837 alt. 535.* **See** *: St-Andoche Basilica★: capitals★★.*
Tourist Office 24 r. d'Argentine ✆ 03 80 64 00 21, Fax 03 80 64 21 96.
Paris 249 – Autun 41 – Avallon 38 – Beaune 64 – Clamecy 76 – Dijon 73.

Le Relais Bernard Loiseau, 2 r. Argentine ✆ 03 80 90 53 53, *loiseau@relaischateaux.com, Fax 03 80 64 08 92,* – rm, – 30. AE GB JCB
closed 11 January-10 February, Wednesday lunch and Tuesday from 9 November-23 March – **Meals** 92 b.i. (lunch), 120/172 and a la carte 120/200 – 28 – **23 rm** 195/330, 9 suites
Spec. Les "classiques" de Bernard Loiseau. Dos de féra à l'unilatérale sur fondue de cébettes (April-mid-October). Suprêmes de pigeon farcis et ses abats en croûte de pomme de terre, jus à la sauge (Summer-Autumn).. **Wines** Puligny-Montrachet, Chambolle-Musigny.
◆ This luxury 18C hostelry is the emblem of this small Burgundian town renowned for centuries for its hospitality. Fine innovative cuisine by a master chef and elegant rooms opening on to an English-style garden.

Vézelay 89450 Yonne 319 F7 - pop. 492 alt. 285.

Paris 221 - Auxerre 52 - Avallon 16 - Château-Chinon 58 - Clamecy 23.

at St-Père *South-East : 3 km by D 957 - pop. 385 alt. 148 - ✉ 89450.*

L'Espérance (Meneau) ⚘, ☎ 03 86 33 39 10, *marc.meneau@wanadoo.fr, Fax 03 86 33 26 15,* ←, ⛱, – rest, TV P – 15 - 50. AE GB JCB
closed late January-early March – **Meals** *(closed Wednesday lunch and Tuesday)* (booking essential) 89 b.i. (lunch), 129/175 and a la carte 155/190 ♀ – ☐ 30 – **20 rm** 120/260, 6 suites

Spec. Les quatre petits plats. Turbot en croûte de sel. Galets de pomme de terre, caviar.
Wines Bourgogne-Vézelay, Chablis.

• Traditional comfort in the main manor house, luxurious modernity in Le Pré des Marguerites, with more rusticity in Le Moulin. Conservatory-style restaurant with views of the delightful garden, and cuisine which blends the creative with the traditional.

BORDEAUX 33000 Gironde 335 H5 - pop. 215 363 alt. 4.

See : *18C Bordeaux : façades along the quayside★★* **EX**, *Esplanade des Quinconces* **DX**, *Grand Théâtre★★* **DX**, *Notre-Dame Church★* **DX**, *Allées de Tourny* **DX**, *– Cours Clemenceau* **DX**, *Place Gambetta* **DX**, *Cours de l'Intendance* **DX** *– Old Bordeaux★★ : Place de la Bourse★★* **EX**, *Place du Parlement★* **EX 109**, *St-Michel Basilica★* **EY**, *Great Bell★ (Grosse Cloche)* **EY D** *– Pey-Berland district : St-André Cathedral★* **DY** *(Pey-Berland Tower★ : ←★★ E) – Mériadeck district* **CY** *– Battle-Cruiser Colbert★★ – Museums : Fine Arts★ (Beaux-Arts)* **CDY M³**, *Decorative Arts★* **DY M²**, *Aquitaine★★* **DY M⁴** *– Entrepôt Lainé★★ : Museum of Contemporary Art★.*

18 Golf Bordelais ☎ 05 56 28 56 04 by av. d'Eysines : 4 km ; 36 of Bordeaux Lac ☎ 05 56 50 92 72, to the N by D 209 : 5 km ; 27 of Medoc at Louens ☎ 05 56 70 11 90 to the NW by D 6 : 6 km ; 27 Internat. of Bordeaux-Pessac ☎ 05 57 26 03 33 by N 250 ; 18 Bordeaux-Cameyrac ☎ 05 56 72 96 79 by N 89 : 18 km.

✈ *of Bordeaux-Mérignac : ☎ 05 56 34 50 50 to the W : 11 km.*

🚗 *☎ 0892 35 35 33.*

ℹ *Tourist Office 12 cours 30 Juillet ☎ 05 56 00 66 00, Fax 05 56 00 66 01 and St-Jean railway station ☎ 05 56 91 64 70.*

Paris 579 - Lyons 531 - Nantes 324 - Strasbourg 919 - Toulouse 245.

Burdigala, 115 r. G. Bonnac ☎ 05 56 90 16 16, *burdigala@burdigala.com, Fax 05 56 93 15 06* – TV – 25 - 100. AE GB JCB **CX** r
Jardin de Burdigala : **Meals** 33 – ☐ 18 – **68 rm** 175/270, 8 suites, 7 duplex.
• Period or contemporary furnishings, choice materials, the very latest facilities...the well soundproofed rooms of this luxury hotel breathe elegance and serenity. The circular Jardin de Burdigala restaurant offers refinement, a fountain, and sunken lighting.

Mercure Cité Mondiale ⚘, 18 parvis des Chartrons ☎ 05 56 01 79 79, *h2877@accor.hotels.com, Fax 05 56 01 79 00,* – TV – 25 - 800. AE GB JCB
closed 22 December-5 January – ***Le 20*** *(closed Friday dinner, Saturday and Sunday)* **Meals** a la carte approx. 25 ♀ – ☐ 12 – **96 rm** 106/126.
• Contemporary rooms, plus a panoramic terrace (where breakfast is served in summer) with a view over the whole of Bordeaux await guests inside the Cité Mondiale convention centre. Smart decor in the "20", with wine tasting and bistro-type fare.

Mercure Château Chartrons, 81 cours St-Louis ✉ 33300 ☎ 05 56 43 15 00, *h1810@accor-hotels.com, Fax 05 56 69 15 21,* – TV – 15 - 150. AE GB
Meals a la carte 20/25 ♀ – ☐ 12 – **150 rm** 102/130.
• Well-preserved, this lovely listed 18C structure was once a wine store. Spacious, comfortable rooms. The vines planted on the roof terrace are an amusing touch. Traditional menu served in a bistro-type ambience.

Mercure Mériadeck, 5 r.-Lateulade ☎ 05 56 56 43 43, *h1281@accor-hotels.com, Fax 05 56 96 50 59* – TV – 15 - 150. AE GB JCB **CY** v
Meals *(closed Saturday, Sunday and Bank Holidays)* 19 ♀ – ☐ 12 – **194 rm** 102/129.
• The décor of this establishment has a cinematic theme, with posters, photographs and other filmic items everywhere. Modern, welcoming rooms and excellent conference facilities. Le Festival pays homage to the silver screen, but local dishes are the stars.

Novotel Bordeaux-Centre, 45 cours Mar. Juin ☎ 05 56 51 46 46, *h1023@accor-hotels.com, Fax 05 56 98 25 56,* – TV – 80. AE GB JCB **CY** m
Meals 17 ♀ – ☐ 12 – **138 rm** 101/108.
• This Novotel has been carefully integrated into the Mériadeck district. The functional bedrooms are regularly refurbished and are well soundproofed. Soberly decorated dining room plus a terrace with a view of several typical old Bordeaux buildings.

Ste-Catherine without rest, 27 r. Parlement Ste-Catherine ✆ 05 56 81 95 12, *qualit y.bordeaux@wanadoo.fr, Fax 05 56 44 50 51* – 40. AE GB
11,50 – **82 rm** 75/177. DX m
• This charming 18C edifice is in the heart of the traffic-free city centre. Well-equipped rooms with colourful fabrics. A 17C well is a feature of the bar.

Majestic without rest, 2 r. Condé ✆ 05 56 52 60 44, *mail-majestic@hotel-majestic.com, Fax 05 56 79 26 70* – . AE GB JCB DX a
9 – **49 rm** 72/108.
• An elegant 18C hotel built in the typical style of the city. Plain but tastefully furnished rooms, comfortable lounge and attractive breakfast room.

Grand Hôtel Français without rest, 12 r. Temple ✆ 05 56 48 10 35, *infos@grand-hotel-français.com, Fax 05 56 81 76 18* – . AE GB JCB DX v
35 rm 90/154.
• This 18C residence has a façade enhanced by wrought-iron balconies. Public rooms and staircase in their original state, the comfortable bedrooms are more modern.

De la Presse without rest, 6 r. Porte Dijeaux ✆ 05 56 48 53 88, *info@hoteldelapresse.com, Fax 05 56 01 05 82* – . AE GB JCB. DX k
closed 25 December-2 January – 8 – **27 rm** 48/86.
• In the heart of the pedestrian area, this well-run and tastefully decorated hotel has a fine stone façade. Functional rooms. Controlled car access.

Continental without rest, 10 r. Montesquieu ✆ 05 56 52 66 00, *continental@hotel-le-continental.com, Fax 05 56 52 77 97* – . AE GB JCB DX b
closed 24 December-3 January – 7 – **50 rm** 56/95.
• Old town-mansion dating from the 18C located close to the Grands Hommes gallery. Pleasant rooms in bright colours. Comfortable, prettily furnished lounge.

La Maison du Lierre without rest, 57 r. Huguerie ✆ 05 56 51 92 71, *infos@maisondulierre.com, Fax 05 56 79 15 16* – . CX h
closed 7 to 23 January – 6,50 – **12 rm** 67/78.
• This pretty hotel takes its name from the ivy planted in the patio. Although small, the cosy rooms are furnished with antiques. Home-made breakfasts, A warm welcome assured.

Le Chapon Fin, 5 r. Montesquieu ✆ 05 56 79 10 10, *tmarx2@wanadoo.fr, Fax 05 56 79 09 10* – . AE GB JCB DX p
closed 28 February-7 March, 25 July-22 August, Sunday and Monday – **Meals** 27 (lunch), 48/76 and a la carte 75/96
Spec. Longuets toastés aux huitres et farce crépinette, jus à la coriandre. Bar aux noix de pécan. Canon d'agneau farci au beurre de sauge (April-November). **Wines** Côtes de Bourg, Pauillac.
• A real Bordeaux institution, famous and popular not only for its fine cuisine but also for the turn-of-the-century rocaille decor in the dining room.

Le Pavillon des Boulevards (Franc), 120 r. Croix de Seguey ✆ 05 56 81 51 02, *pavillon.des.boulevards@wanadoo.fr, Fax 05 56 51 14 58,* – . AE GB JCB
closed 8 to 29 August, 1 to 11 January, Sunday, lunch Monday and Saturday – **Meals** 60 and a la carte 74/93
Spec. Liégeois de caviar, homard à la crème de châtaignes. Turbot en cuisson douce, risotto d'encornets, jus au parmesan. Agneau de Pauillac, légumes "façon marocaine". **Wines** Côtes de Blaye, Graves.
• Kitchen utensils adorn the walls of this unusual contemporary restaurant, whose dining room opens on to a lovely summer terrace. Innovative cuisine.

Jean Ramet, 7 pl. J. Jaurès ✆ 05 56 44 12 51, *jean.ramet@free.fr, Fax 05 56 52 19 80* – . AE GB EX u
closed 1 to 9 May, 31 July-23 August, 1 to 10 January, Sunday and Monday – **Meals** 30 (lunch), 50/60 and a la carte 57/82
Spec. Asperges panées aux truffes (February-June). Rôti de camerons à la vanille, purée de petits pois. Sablé aux cerises (May-September). **Wines** Graves, Côtes de Castillon.
• The traditional cuisine of this establishment on the banks of the Garonne is popular with locals. The cheerful decor is in harmony with the fine furnishings and wall-hangings.

Le Vieux Bordeaux, 27 r. Buhan ✆ 05 56 52 94 36, *Fax 05 56 44 25 11,* – . AE GB EY a
closed 1 to 23 August, 6 to 21 February, Sunday, lunch Monday and Saturday – **Meals** 28/48 and a la carte 42/66.
• The country-style decor of this two-roomed restaurant is enhanced by contemporary touches. One room opens onto an attractive patio. Generous traditional cuisine.

L'Alhambra, 111bis r. Judaïque ✆ 05 56 96 06 91, *Fax 05 56 98 00 52* – . GB CX e
closed 20 July-20 August, Sunday, Bank Holidays, lunch Monday and Saturday – **Meals** 19 (lunch), 28/38 and a la carte 46/64
• Attractive restaurant in the style of a winter garden with decor based on shades of green and comfortable cane furnishings. Traditional cuisine.

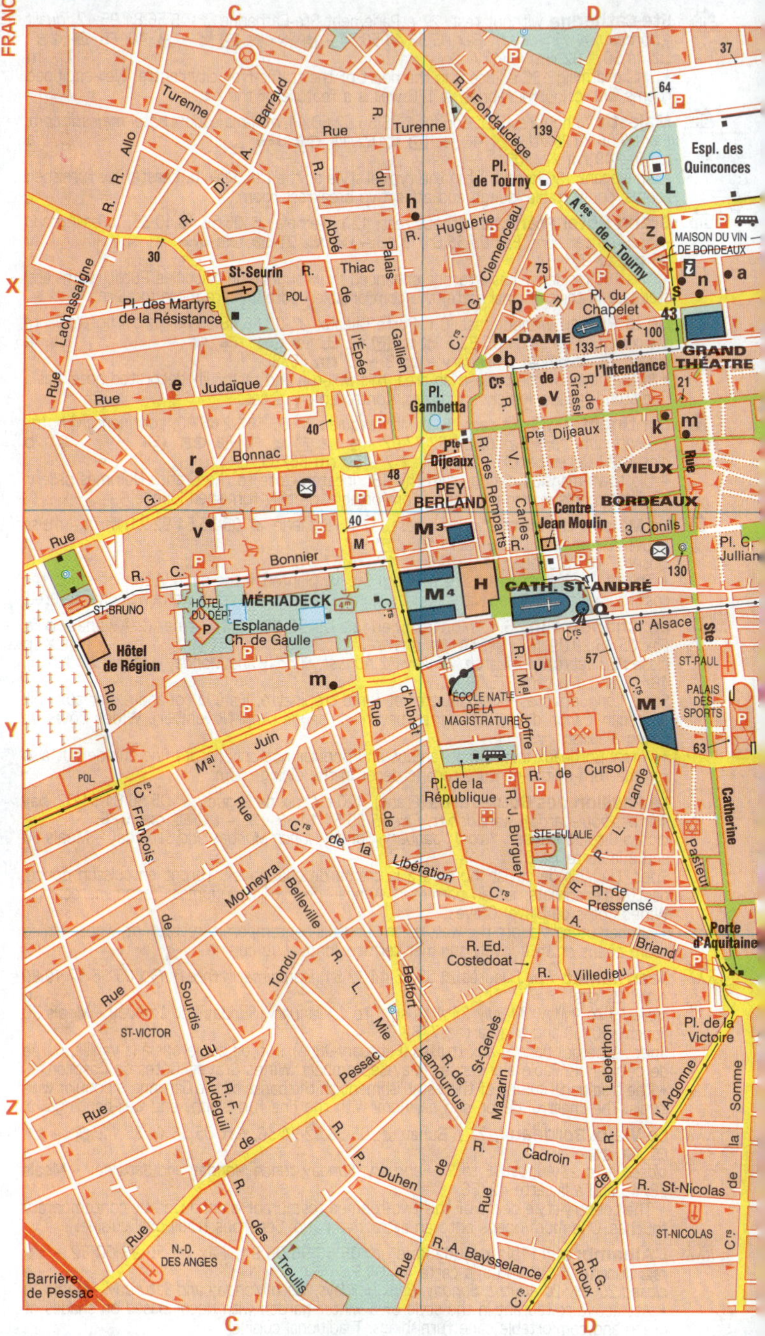
C
D
X
Y
Z
Turenne
Barraud
Rue
R.
du
Turenne
R. Fondaudège
139
37
64
Espl. des Quinconces
R. Allo
Dr.
A.
R.
Abbé
Palais
Pl. de Tourny
h
Huguerie
Clemenceau
A. des de Tourny
L
MAISON DU VIN DE BORDEAUX
z
30
Lachassaigne
St-Seurin
R.
Thiac
de
POL.
Pl. des Martyrs de la Résistance
l'Épée
Gallien
G.
C.rs
75
p
Pl. du Chapelet
n
a
s
43
100
N.-DAME
133
f
b
GRAND THÉATRE
l'Intendance
Rue
e
Judaïque
Pl. Gambetta
C.rs
de
v
R. de Grassi
21
R.
k
m
40
Pte Dijeaux
R. des Remparts
V.
Pte Dijeaux
Rue
VIEUX BORDEAUX
Bonnac
r
48
PEY BERLAND
Carles
Centre Jean Moulin
G.
Rue
v
40
M
M3
R.
3 Conils
Pl. C. Jullian
130
Bonnier
R.
C.
MÉRIADECK
M4
H
CATH. ST-ANDRÉ
ST-BRUNO
HÔTEL DU DÉPT
Esplanade Ch. de Gaulle
C.rs
C.rs
d' Alsace
Ste
Hôtel de Région
m
R.
Mal
u
57
ST-PAUL
PALAIS DES SPORTS
Rue
d'Albret
Rue
J
ÉCOLE NATLE DE LA MAGISTRATURE
Joffre
C.rs
M1
Juin
63
POL
Mal
C.rs
François
Rue
Pl. de la République
R. J. Burguet
R. de Cursol
Lande
Catherine
C.rs
de
de la
Libération
STE-EULALIE
P.
L.
Pasteur
Mouneyra
Belleville
R.
A.
Pl. de Pressensé
C.rs
de
R. Ed. Costedoat
Briand
Porte d'Aquitaine
Rue
Sourdis
Tondu
R.
L.
Mie
Belfort
R.
Villedieu
ST-VICTOR
du
Pessac
R. de Lamourous
St-Genès
Mazarin
Leberthon
Pl. de la Victoire
R. F. Audeguil
l'Argonne
Somme
Rue
de
R.
P.
Duhen
de
R.
Cadroin
R.
de
la
R.
Rue
de
R. St-Nicolas
de
Rue
N.-D. DES ANGES
des
Treuils
Rue
R. A. Bayssélance
R. G. Rioux
ST-NICOLAS
C.rs
C.rs
Barrière de Pessac

BORDEAUX
0
300 m
E
F
X
Y
Z
LA BASTIDE
Jardin Botanique
Rue Reignier
R. Nuyens
R. G. Carde
R. Serr
Quai des Queyries
STE-MARIE
Av. Thiers
R. P. Camelle
R. de la Bénauge
Pl. de Stalingrad
Pont de Pierre
Quai Deschamps
GARONNE
Q. Louis XVIII
Pl. J. Jaurès
PL. DE LA BOURSE
Musée national des Douanes
ST-PIERRE
Pte Cailhau
Bordeaux monumental
Pl. du Palais
Q. Richelieu
Lorraine
Pl. Lafargue
R. Neuve
Pte des Salinières
Quai des Salinières
Q. de la Grave
ST-ÉLOI
R. St-James
Victor Hugo
R. des Faures
St-François
ST-MICHEL
Pl. Duburg
Pl. Canteloup
R. Leyteire
R. du Mirail
Q. de la Monnaie
Q. Ste-Croix
Pont St-Jean
R. C. Sauvageau
THÉATRE PORT DE LA LUNE
CENTRE ANDRÉ MALRAUX
Ste-Croix
I.U.T. MONTAIGNE
Pl. Léon Duguit
R. du Hamel
Pl. des Capucins
R. des Douves
Pl. A. Meunier
R. Peyronnet
Q. de Paludate
R. de Tauzia
Crs de la Marne
Rue Kléber
Rue de Bègles
Rue de l'Yser
Rue Lafontaine
R. J. Steeg
Crs Barbey
Rue Malbec
R. Eug. le Roy
ST-JEAN
06
62
36
132
14
109
110
112
129
52
4
112
7
126
65
102
33
118
120
49
142

INDEX OF STREET NAMES IN BORDEAUX

3-Conils (R. des) . . . . DY
Abbé-de-l'Épée (R.) CX
Albret (Crs d') . . . . CY
Allo (R. R.) CX
Alsace-et-Lorraine (Crs d') DEY
Argentiers (R. des) . . . . EY 4
Argonne (Crs de l') . . . . DZ
Audeguil (R. F.) . . . . CZ
Ausone (R.) . . . . EY 7
Barbey (Crs) . . . . EFZ
Baysselance (R. A.) . . . . DZ
Bègles (R. de) . . . . EZ
Belfort (R. de) . . . . CYZ
Belleville (R.) . . . . CY
Bénauge (R. de la) . . . . FX
Bir-Hakeim (Pl. de) . . . . EY
Bonnac (R. G.) . . . . CXY
Bonnier (R. C.) . . . . CY
Bordelaise (Galerie) . . . . . . DX 21
Bourse (Pl. de la) . . . . EX
Briand (Crs A.) . . . . DYZ
Burguet (R. J.) . . . . DY
Cadroin (R.) . . . . DZ
Camelle (R. P.) . . . . FX
Canteloup (Pl.) . . . . EY
Capdeville (R.) . . . . CX 30
Capucins (Pl. des) . . . . EZ
Carde (R. G.) . . . . FX
Carles (R. V.) . . . . DXY
Carpenteyre (R.) . . . . EFY 33
Chapeau-Rouge (Crs) . . . . . EX 36
Chapelet (Pl. du) . . . . DX
Chartres (Allées de) . . . . . . DX 37
Château-d'Eau (R. du) . . . CXY 40
Clemenceau (Crs G.) . . . . . DX
Comédie (Pl. de la) . . . . DX 43
Costedoat (R. E.) . . . . DZ
Cursol (R. de) . . . . DY
Deschamps (Quai) . . . . FX
Dr-A.-Barraud (R.) CX
Dr-Nancel-Pénard (R.) . . . . . CX 48
Domercq (R. C.) . . . . FZ 49
Douane (Quai de la) . . . . . . EX 52
Douves (R. des) . . . . EZ
Duburg (Pl.) . . . . EY
Duffour-Dubergier (R.) . . . . DY 57
Duhen (R. P.) . . . . CDZ
Esprit-des-Lois (R. de l') . . . EX 62
Faures (R. des) . . . . EY
Ferme-de-Richemont (Pl. de la) . . . . DY 63
Foch (R. Mar.) . . . . DX 64
Fondaudège (R.) . . . . CDX
Fusterie (R. de la) . . . . EY 65
Gambetta (Pl.) . . . . DX
Gaulle (Espl. Ch.-de) . . . . . . CY
Grands-Hommes (Pl. des) . DX 75
Grassi (R. de) . . . . DX
Grave (Q. de la) . . . . EFY
Hamel (R. du) . . . . EZ
Huguerie (R.) . . . . DX
Intendance (Crs de l') . . . . . DX
Jean-Jaurès (Pl.) . . . . EX
Joffre (R. du Mar.) . . . . DY
Judaïque (R.) CX
Juin (Crs Mar.) . . . . CY
Jullian (Pl. C.) . . . . DY
Kléber (R.) . . . . EZ
Lachassaigne (R.) CX
Lafargue (Pl.) . . . . EY
Lafontaine (R.) . . . . EZ
Lamourous (R. de) . . . . . . CDZ
Lande (R. P.-L.) . . . . DY
Leberthon (R.) . . . . DZ
Leyteire (R.) . . . . EYZ
Libération (Crs de la) . . . . CDY
Louis-XVIII (Quai) . . . . EX
Malbec (R.) . . . . FZ
Marne (Crs de la) . . . . EZ
Martyrs-de-la-Résistance (Pl. des) CX
Mautrec (R.) . . . . DX 100
Mazarin (R.) . . . . DZ
Meunier (Pl. A.) . . . . FZ
Meynard (Pl.) . . . . EY 102
Mie (R. L.) . . . . CZ
Mirail (R. du) . . . . EY
Monnaie (Quai de la) . . . . . . FY
Mouneyra (R.) . . . . CYZ
Neuve (R.) . . . . EY
Nuyens (R.) . . . . FX
Orléans (Allées d') . . . . EX 106
Palais (Pl. du) . . . . EY
Palais Gallien (R. du) CX
Paludate (Quai de) . . . . FZ
Parlement (Pl. du) . . . . EX 109
Parlement St-Pierre (R. du) . . . . EX 110
Pas-St-Georges (R. du) . . . EXY 112
Pasteur (Crs) . . . . DY
Pessac (Barrière de) . . . . . . CZ
Pessac (R. de) . . . . CZ
Peyronnet (R.) . . . . FZ
Philippart (R. F.) . . . . EX 114
Pierre (Pont de) . . . . EFY
Porte de la Monnaie (R.) . . . . FY 118
Porte Dijeaux (R. de la) . . . . DX
Pressensé (Pl. de) . . . . DY
Queyries (Quai des) . . . . . EFX
Quinconces (Espl. des) . . . DX
Reignier (R.) . . . . FX
Remparts (R. des) . . . . DXY
Renaudel (Pl. P.) . . . . FZ 120
République (Pl. de la) . . . . . DY
Richelieu (Quai) . . . . EY
Rioux (R. G.) . . . . DZ
Rousselle (R. de la) . . . . EY 126
Roy (R. Eug. le) . . . . FZ
St-François (R.) . . . . EY
St-Genès (R. de) . . . . CDZ
St-James (R.) . . . . EY
St-Jean (Pont) . . . . FY
St-Nicolas (R.) . . . . DZ
St-Pierre (Pl.) . . . . EX 129
St-Projet (Pl.) . . . . DY 130
St-Rémi (R.) . . . . EX 132
Ste-Catherine (R.) . . . . DXY
Ste-Croix (Quai) . . . . FY
Salinières (Q. des) . . . . EY
Sarget (Passage) . . . . DX 133
Sauvageau (R. C.) . . . . EFY
Serr (R.) . . . . FX
Somme (Crs de la) . . . . DZ
Sourdis (R. F. de) . . . . CYZ
Stalingrad (Pl. de) . . . . FX
Steeg (R. J.) . . . . EZ
Tauzia (R. de) . . . . FZ
Thiac (R.) CX
Thiers (Av.) . . . . FX
Tondu (R. du) . . . . CZ
Tourny (Allées de) . . . . DX
Tourny (Pl. de) . . . . DX
Tourville (Av. de) . . . . BT 136
Treuils (R. des) . . . . CZ
Turenne (R.) . . . . CDX
Verdun (Crs de) . . . . DX 139
Victoire (Pl. de la) . . . . DZ
Victor-Hugo (Crs) . . . . EY
Vilaris (R.) . . . . EZ 142
Villedieu (R.) . . . . DZ
Yser (Crs de l') . . . . EZ

XX **La Tupina,** 6 r. Porte de la Monnaie ✆ 05 56 91 56 37, *latupina@latupina.com*, *Fax 05 56 31 92 11* – ⇨. AE ⓓ GB FY q
Meals 32 b.i. (lunch)/48 ♀.
◆ A relaxed atmosphere pervades this rustic restaurant specialising in dishes from SW France prepared over the stove or open fire as in bygone days. Comprehensive wine list.

XX **Gravelier,** 114 cours Verdun ✆ 05 56 48 17 15, *Fax 05 56 51 96 07* – ▤. AE ⓓ GB
closed 31 July-30 August, 12 to 19 February, Saturday and Sunday – **Meals** 20 (lunch), 24/40 ♀.
◆ Refined teak and zinc fittings, warm colours (aubergine, aniseed green, orange), successfully creating a congenial, minimalist ambience. Fine, inventive cuisine.

XX **Table Calvet,** 81 cours Médoc ✆ 05 56 39 62 80, *latablecalvet@calvet.com*, *Fax 05 56 39 62 80*, – ▤. AE GB.
closed 1 to 29 August, 1 to 9 January, Monday and Sunday - **Meals** 26/32 ♀.
◆ Created by the Maison Calvet wine company in an attractive former wine storehouse, this gourmet restaurant serves cuisine which is inspired by and evolves with the seasons.

X **L'Olivier du Clavel,** 44 r. C. Domercq (face gare St-Jean) ✆ 05 57 95 09 50, *fgclavel@wanadoo.fr*, *Fax 05 56 92 15 28* – ▤. AE ⓓ GB
closed August, 2 to 10 January, Saturday lunch, Sunday and Monday – **Meals** 27/45 ♀.
◆ The menu in this bistro is based on seasonal dishes prepared using different high-quality olive oils. Bright, spick-and-span decor and simply laid tables.

at Bordeaux-Lac *(Parc des Expositions) North of the town – ✉ 33300 Bordeaux :*

Sofitel Aquitania, av. J. G. Domergue ☎ 05 56 69 66 66, *h0669@accor-hotels.com, Fax 05 56 69 66 00,* – – 15 - 400. AE GB JCB
Flore : **Meals** 23/29 ♀ – 15 – **176 rm** 180, 7 suites.
◆ Hotel complex much favoured by business travellers thanks to its facilities for meetings and conferences. Spacious rooms, functional and well soundproofed. Neighbouring casino. There is a panoramic view of the lake from Le Flore and a terrace by the pool.

Novotel-Bordeaux Lac, av. J. G. Domergue ☎ 05 56 43 65 00, *h0403@accor-hotels.com, Fax 05 56 43 65 01,* – – 15 - 120. AE GB JCB – **Meals** a la carte 21/32 ♀ – 12 – **175 rm** 96/104.
◆ This 1970s hotel has the advantage of a location close to the exhibition grounds. Practical rooms, some with lake views. Garden with children's play facilities. Meals are served either in the Novotel Café or on the terrace by the swimming pool.

at Cenon *East, exit nr 25 – pop. 21 283 alt. 50 – ✉ 33150 :*

La Cape (Magie), allée Morlette ☎ 05 57 80 24 25, *Fax 05 56 32 37 46,* – AE GB
closed 1 to 23 August, Christmas Holidays, Saturday, Sunday and Bank Holidays – **Meals** 31 ♀
Spec. Cornet de Saint-Jacques au caviar d'Aquitaine et brochette rôtie. Filet de Saint-Pierre et grosse langoustine au citron confit. Millefeuille d'ananas rôti à la noix de coco. **Wines** Sainte-Foy-Bordeaux, Côtes de Blaye.
◆ This discreet building housing two modern, colourful dining rooms is further enhanced by a pleasant terrace-garden. Fine, inventive cuisine and wines direct from the estate.

at Bouliac *SE : 8 km – pop. 3 248 alt. 74 – ✉ 33270 :*

Hauterive et rest. St-James, pl. C. Hostein, near church ☎ 05 57 97 06 00, *reception@saint-james-bouliac.com, Fax 05 56 20 92 58,* < Bordeaux, – , rm, – 15. AE GB JCB. rest
Meals *(closed 2 April-9 May, 2 to 17 January, Sunday and Monday)* 55/120 and a la carte 87/113 ♀ - ***Le Bistroy*** ☎ 05 57 97 06 06 *(closed Sunday and lunch Wednesday and Saturday)* **Meals** 22 (lunch) and a la carte approx. 40 – 20 – **18 rm** 150/190
Spec. Tartare de melon et huîtres (May-July). Saint-Pierre au citron confit (September-November). Boîte chocolat noir et truffe noire (December-February). **Wines** Sainte-Foy-Bordeaux, Canon Fronsac.
◆ 17C wine-grower's house surrounded by buildings designed by J. Nouvel and inspired by tobacco-drying sheds. Zen-style designer rooms all with views of Bordeaux. Fine creative cuisine in the St-James ; local fare in the stripped-down bistro-style Bistroy.

at Martillac *S : 9 km by exit nr 18 and N 113 – pop. 2 020 alt. 40 – ✉ 33650 :*

Sources de Caudalie, chemin de Smith Haut-Lafitte ☎ 05 57 83 83 83, *sources@sources-caudalie.com, Fax 05 57 83 83 84,* – – 15 - 40. AE GB – ***La Grand'Vigne*** *(closed Monday and Tuesday)* **Meals** 57/87 b.i. – ***La Table du Lavoir :*** **Meals** 32/63 b.i. ♀ – 20 – **43 rm** 230/265, 6 suites.
◆ Luxurious rejuvenation among the vineyards : this establishment advocates a regime based on the "French Paradox", with delicious food washed down with red wine. Inventive dishes served in the 18C orangery. "La Table" is situated in a restored wine storehouse.

to the W :

at the airport of Mérignac *11 km by A 630 : from the North, exit nr 11=b, from the South, exit nr11 – ✉ 43700 Mérignac :*

Quality Suites Aéroport, 83 av. J. F. Kennedy ☎ 05 57 53 21 22, *choicequalitysuite@wanadoo.fr, Fax 05 57 53 21 23,* – kitchenette, rm, – 60. AE GB JCB AU b
L'Iguane ☎ 05 56 34 07 39 *(closed August, Saturday lunch and Sunday)* **Meals** 30/61 ♀ – ***L'Olive de Mer*** ☎ 05 56 12 99 99 **Meals** 22 ♀ – 11 – **154 rm** 172.
◆ Contemporary-themed cuisine and a comprehensive choice of the region's wines are on offer in this airport hotel's charming wood-clad restaurant. Trendy atmosphere in the Olive de Mer, with its sharp colours and designer furniture.

Mercure Aéroport, 1 av. Ch. Lindbergh ☎ 05 56 34 74 74, *H1508@accor-hotels.com, Fax 05 56 34 30 84,* – – 15 - 110. AE GB
Meals *(closed weekend and Bank Holidays)* 20 b.i. – 12 – **148 rm** 110/120.
◆ This hotel has been designed for those in need of a relaxing break between flights. Comfortable rooms, attractive lounge/bar and meeting rooms with decor on the theme of travel. Traditional cuisine served in an elegant dining room facing the terrace.

Novotel Aéroport, av. J. F. Kennedy ☎ 05 57 53 13 30, *h0402@accor-hotels.com, Fax 05 56 55 99 64,* – – 20 - 70. AE GB JCB
Meals a la carte approx. 30 ♀ – 12 – **137 rm** 102/110.
◆ Hotel separated from the airport by a pinewood. Rooms refurbished in Novotel's latest style. Good soundproofing. Outdoor children's play area. Restaurant with pleasant view of pool and garden and straightforward cuisine with emphasis on grills.

Eugénie-les-Bains *40320 Landes 335 I12 – pop. 507 alt. 65 – Spa (February.-November).*
les Greens d'Eugénie ☎ 05.
Tourist Office 147 r. René Vielle ☎ 05 58 51 13 16, Fax 05 58 51 12 02.
Bordeaux 151.

Les Prés d'Eugénie (Guérard), ☎ 05 58 05 06 07, *reservation@michelguerard.com, Fax 05 58 51 10 10,* – rm, – 40. AE GB.
closed 28 November-16 December and 2 January-25 March – (low-calorie menu for residents only) - ***rest. Michel Guérard*** (booking essential) *(closed lunch on week except 9/07-28/08 and Bank Holidays and Monday dinner)* **Meals** 90 /185 and a la carte 116/140 – 28 – **22 rm** 270/380, 6 suites
Spec. Caviar d'Aquitaine "Grand cru", tartare de pommes de terre à la crème de coquillages. Homard rôti, légèrement fumé au feu de bois. Galette feuilletée tiède aux grains de café. **Wines** Tursan blanc, Vin de pays des Terroirs Landais.
• This delightful 19C residence, incorporating a park and "farm" spa centre is a wonderful fusion of town and country. In his gastronomic restaurant Michel Guérard's elegant cuisine is inspired by Mother Nature.

Couvent des Herbes – AE GB. rest
closed 2 January-11 February – **Meals** see ***Les Prés d'Eugénie*** and ***Michel Guérard*** – 28 – **4 rm** 340/380, 4 suites470/500.
• Napoleon converted this pretty little 18C convent into a love-nest for his Eugénie. In a setting not unlike the Garden of Eden, its rooms will not fail to seduce you.

Maison Rose (see also ***rest. Michel Guérard***), ☎ 05 58 05 06 07, *reservation@michelguerard.com, Fax 05 58 51 10 10,* – kitchenette AE GB
closed 5 December-11 February – **Meals** (residents only) – 18 – **26 rm** 105/180, 5 studios.
• The "Pink House" blends restful pastel colours, white cane furniture, fresh-cut flowers, and a cosy lounge, creating an altogether welcoming guesthouse ambience.

Ferme aux Grives with rm, ☎ 05 58 05 05 06, *reservationmicheguerard.com, Fax 05 58 51 10 10,* – GB
closed 2 January-11 February – **Meals** *(closed Tuesday dinner and Wednesday except 9 July-28 August and Bank Holidays)* 40/42 – 25 – **1 rm** 340/380, 3 suites 470/500.
• Old village inn that has recaptured all the atmosphere of yesteryear. Kitchen garden, old beams and red floor tiles make a fine setting for revived local cuisine.

Pauillac *33250 Gironde 335 G3 – pop. 5 175 alt. 20.*
Bordeaux 53.

Château Cordeillan Bages , to the S : 1 km by D 2 ☎ 05 56 59 24 24, *cordeillan@relaischateaux.fr, Fax 05 56 59 01 89,* – AE GB JCB. rest
closed 10 December-14 February – **Meals** *(closed Monday, lunch Saturday and Tuesday)* 60 (lunch)/95 and a la carte 83/95 – 22 – **25 rm** 178/268, 4 suites
Spec. Pommes de terre cuites au foie gras, crème caramélisée au vinaigre de Xérès. Filet de boeuf blonde d'Aquitaine fumé aux sarments. Caramel de tomate, sorbet yaourt et coco râpé, jus de sangria réduit. **Wines** Saint-Estèphe, Moulis.
• This 17C charterhouse in the heart of the vineyards is also the headquarters of the École du Bordeaux wine school. Cosy, elegant rooms opening on to the courtyard. Non-smoking restaurant and terrace overlooking the château's vineyards. Stunning modern cuisine.

CANNES *06400 Alpes-Mar. 341 D6 – pop. 67 304 alt. 2 – Casinos Palm Beach X, Croisette BZ.*
See : *Site★★ – Seafront★★ : Boulevard★★ BCDZ and Pointe de la Croisette★ X – ★ from the Mont Chevalier Tower AZ* **V** *– The Castre Museum★★ (Musée de la Castre) AZ – Tour into the Hills★ (Chemin des Collines) NE : 4 km V – The Croix des Gardes X* **E** *★ W : 5 km then 15 mn.*
18 of Cannes-Mougins ☎ 04 93 75 79 13 by ④ : 9 km ; 27 of Mandelieu ☎ 04 92 97 32 00 by ② ; 18 Royal Mougins Golf Club at Mougins ☎ 04 92 92 49 69 by ④ : 10 km ; 18 Riviera Golf Club at Mandelieu ☎ 04 92 97 49 49 by ② : 8 km.
Tourist Office 1, bd de la Croisette ☎ 04 93 39 24 53, Fax 04 92 99 84 23.
Paris 903 ⑤ – Aix-en-Provence 146 ⑤ – Grenoble 312 ⑤ – Marseilles 159 ⑤ – Nice 32 ⑤ – Toulon 121 ⑤

Carlton Inter-Continental, 58 bd Croisette ☎ 04 93 06 40 06, *cannes@intercon ti.com, Fax 04 93 06 40 25,* – 25 - 250. AE GB JCB CZ e
Brasserie Carlton ☎ 04 93 06 40 21 **Meals** 36/44 – ***La Plage*** ☎ 04 93 06 44 94 *(April-15 October)* **Meals** a la carte 60/105 – 32 – **302 rm** 365/430, 36 suites.
• Hitchcock filmed some of "To Catch a Thief" in this famous hotel with its two cupolas. Luxurious Art Deco interior, a prestigious history, a world in itself. Belle Epoque decor and seasonal cuisine in the Brasserie Carlton with its view of the Croisette.

Majestic Barrière, 10 bd Croisette 04 92 98 77 00, *majestic@lucienbarriere.com, Fax 04 93 38 97 90,* ← – 40 - 400. BZ n
closed 15 November-30 December – see ***Villa des Lys*** below- ***Fouquet's*** 04 92 98 77 05 **Meals** 35/40b.i. – ***B. Sud*** 04 92 98 77 30 (lunch only) *(mid-May-end October)* **Meals** a la carte 40/75 – 29 – **285 rm** 475/870, 23 suites.
• The immaculate, majestic façade dates from the 1920s. Luxury and refinement on every floor. The best rooms have sea views. Bright and inviting dining room with a veranda overlooking the Croisette.

Martinez, 73 bd Croisette 04 92 98 73 00, *martinez@concorde-hotels.com, Fax 04 93 39 67 82,* ← – 40 - 600. DZ n
see ***La Palme d'Or*** below - ***Relais Martinez*** 04 92 98 74 12 **Meals** 31/60 b.i. – ***Plage*** 04 92 98 74 22 (lunch only) *(24 March-30 September)* **Meals** a la carte 33/80 – 35 – **385 rm** 500/850, 27 suites.
• This lovely Art Deco palace is where the stars of the film festival congregate. The luxury suites and attractive rooms with a view of the Croisette are extremely popular. The Relais Martinez has a smart, relaxed ambience, gourmet cuisine and a summer terrace.

Noga Hilton, 50 bd Croisette 04 92 99 70 00, *sales.cannes@hilton.com, Fax 04 92 99 70 11,* – 40 - 500. CZ b
La Scala 04 92 99 70 93 *(closed lunch 1 July-30 September)* **Meals** 38/49 – ***Plage*** 04 92 99 70 27 *(15 April-1 October)* **Meals** a la carte 42/60 – 25 – **187 rm** 699/969, 47 suites.
• This cube-like edifice is built on the site of the old Festival Palace. Very well-equipped rooms, remarkable atrium, 800-seat theatre, rooftop pool. Mediterranean dishes and wines from around the world in La Scala whose terrace enjoys a fine sea view.

Sofitel Méditerranée, 1 bd J. Hibert 04 92 99 73 00, *h0591-re@accor-hotels.com, Fax 04 92 99 73 29,* ← – 70. AZ n
Le Méditerranée (7th floor) 04 92 99 73 02 (dinner only in July-August) *(closed mid-November-mid-December, Sunday and Monday from September-June except Bank Holidays)* **Meals** 35/65 – ***Chez Panisse*** 04 92 99 73 10 **Meals** 25 – 25 – **149 rm** 222/337.
• 1930s hotel prettily decorated in Provençal style. Together with the rooftop pool, most of the rooms have a splendid view over Cannes and its bay. Superb panorama from the tables of Le Méditerranée. The cuisine of Provence is celebrated in the Panisse.

3.14 Hôtel, 5 r. F. Einesy 04 92 99 72 00, *Fax 04 92 99 72 12,* – 20. CZ u
Meals 43/104 – 23 – **81 rm** 570/600, 15 suites.
• Stunning multi-ethnic ambience in this recently revamped hotel, whose rooms are inspired by styles from all five continents. Attractive rooftop pool. The international theme continues in the restaurant where the Mediterranean cuisine is flavoured with spices.

Novotel Montfleury , 25 av. Beauséjour 04 93 68 86 86, *h0806@accor-hotels.com, Fax 04 93 68 87 87,* ← – 20 - 260. rest DY m
L'Olivier : **Meals** 35 – 20 – **181 rm** 180/210.
• This hotel is on the edge of the Californie area and its luxury villas. Modern rooms, refurbished in maritime or Provençal style. Lovely terrace and pool beneath the palm trees. Attractive, sunny decor, open kitchen and Mediterranean cuisine in L'Olivier.

Gray d'Albion, 38 r. Serbes 04 92 99 79 79, *graydalbion@lucienbarriere.com, Fax 04 93 99 26 10,* – 40 - 120. BZ d
Royal Gray 04 92 99 79 60 *(closed Sunday and Monday)* **Meals** 33(dinner)/42 – 20 – **192 rm** 285/400, 8 suites.
• This 1970s building houses an arcade of luxury shops as well as cosy rooms which are regularly refurbished. Discotheque, piano bar, private beach on the Croisette. Mediterranean cuisine awaits diners in the warm surroundings of the Royal Gray.

Croisette Beach without rest, 13 r. Canada 04 92 18 88 00, *croisettebea@aws.fr, Fax 04 93 68 35 38,* – DZ y
closed 22 November-27 December – 17 – **94 rm** 180/312.
• Spacious, well-soundproofed rooms with functional light-wood furnishings. Lounge and bar are regularly used for picture exhibitions.

Sun Riviera without rest, 138 r. d'Antibes 04 93 06 77 77, *info@sun-riviera.com, Fax 04 93 38 31 10,* – CZ h
closed 19 November-27 December – 15 – **42 rm** 154/247.
• In a street with lots of luxury shops, this hotel offers brightly decorated rooms furnished with period pieces. The best are those facing the garden (lovely palm tree).

CANNES

Albert-Édouard (Jetée) . . . . BZ
Alexandre-III (Bd) . . . . X 2
Alsace (Bd) . . . . BDY
Anc.-Combatants-d'Afrique-du-Nord (Av.) . . . . AYZ 4
André (R. du Cdt) . . . . CZ
Antibes (R. d') . . . . BCY
Bachaga-Saïd-Boualam (Av.) . . . AY 5
Beau-Soleil (Bd) . . . . X 10
Beauséjour (Av.) . . . . DYZ
Belges (R. des) . . . . BZ 12
Blanc (R. Louis) . . . . AYZ
Broussailles (Av. des) . . . . V 16
Buttura (R.) . . . . BZ 17
Canada (R. du) . . . . DZ
Carnot (Bd) X
Carnot (Square) . . . . V 20
Castre (Pl. de la) . . . . AZ 21
Chabaud (R.) . . . . CY 22
Clemenceau (R. G.) . . . . AZ
Coteaux (Av. des) V
Croisette (Bd de la) . . . . BDZ
Croix-des-Gardes (Bd) . . . . VX 29
Delaup (Bd) . . . . AY 30
Dr-Pierre Gazagnaire (R.) . . . . . AZ 32
Dr-R. Picaud (Av.) X
Dollfus (R. Jean) . . . . AZ 33
États-Unis (R. des) . . . . CZ 35
Favorite (Av. de la) . . . . X 38
Félix-Faure (R.) . . . . ABZ
Ferrage (Bd de la) . . . . ABY 40
Fiesole (Av.) . . . . X 43
Foch (R. du Mar.) . . . . BY 44
Gallieni (R. du Mar.) . . . . BY 48
Gaulle (Pl. Gén.-de) . . . . BZ 51
Gazagnaire (Bd Eugène) X
Grasse (Av. de) . . . . VX 53
Guynemer (Bd) . . . . AY
Hespérides (Av. des) . . . . X 55
Hibert (Bd Jean) . . . . AZ
Hibert (R.) . . . . AZ
Isola-Bella (Av. d') X
Jean-Jaurès (R.) . . . . BCY
Joffre (R. du Mar.) . . . . BY 60
Juin (Av. Mar.) . . . . DZ
Koening (Av. Gén.) . . . . DY
Lacour (Bd Alexandre) . . . . X 62
Latour-Maubourg (R.) . . . . DZ
Lattre-de-Tassigny (Av. de) . . . . AY 63
Laubeuf (Quai Max) . . . . AZ
Leader (Bd) . . . . VX 64
Lérins (Av. de) . . . . X 65
Lorraine (Bd de) . . . . CDY
Macé (R.) . . . . CZ 66
Madrid (Av. de) . . . . DZ
Meynadier (R.) . . . . ABY
Midi (Bd du) X
Mimont (R. de) . . . . BY
Mont-Chevalier (R. du) . . . . AZ 72
Montfleury (Bd) . . . . CDY 74
Monti (R. Marius) . . . . AY 75
Noailles (Av. J.-de) X
Observatoire (Bd de l') . . . . X 84
Oxford (Bd d') . . . . V 87
Pantiero (La) . . . . ABZ
Paradis-Terrestre (Corniches du) V 88
Pasteur (R.) . . . . DZ
Pastour (R. Louis) . . . . AY 90
Perier (Bd du) . . . . V 91
Perrissol (R. Louis) . . . . AZ 92
Petit-Juas (Av. du) VX
Pins (Bd des) . . . . X 95
Pompidou (Espl. G.) . . . . BZ
Prince-de-Galles (Av. du) . . . . . . X 97
République (Bd de la) X
Riou (Bd du) VX
Riouffe (R. Jean de) . . . . BY 98
Roi-Albert 1er (Av.) X
Rouguière (R.) . . . . BY 100
St-Antoine (R.) . . . . AZ 102
St-Nicolas (Av.) . . . . BY 105
St-Pierre (Quai) . . . . AZ
Sardou (R. Léandre) . . . . X 108
Serbes (R. des) . . . . BZ 110
Source (Bd de la) . . . . X 112
Stanislas (Pl.) . . . . AY
Strasbourg (Bd de) . . . . CDY
Teisseire (R.) . . . . CY 114
Tuby (Bd Victor) . . . . AYZ 115
Vallauris (Av. de) . . . . VX 116
Vallombrosa (Bd) . . . . AY 118
Vautrin (Bd Gén.) . . . . DZ
Vidal (R. du Cdt) . . . . CY 120
Wemyss (Av. Amiral Wester) . . . X 122

LE CANNET

Aubarède (Ch. de l') . . . . V 8
Bellevue (Pl.) . . . . V 13
Bréguières (Ch. de) . . . . V 14
Cannes (R. des) . . . . V 19
Carnot (Bd de) V
Cheval (Av. Maurice) . . . . V 23
Collines (Ch. des) V
Doumer (Bd Paul) V
Écoles (R. des) . . . . V 34
Four-à-Chaux (Bd du) . . . . V 45
Gambetta (Bd) . . . . V 50
Gaulle (Av. Gén.-de) V
Jeanpierre (Av. Maurice) . . . . . . V 58
Mermoz (Av. Jean) . . . . V 67
Monod (Bd Jacques) . . . . V 68
Mont-Joli (Av. du) . . . . V 73
N.-D.-des-Anges (Av.) . . . . V 79
Olivet (Ch. de l') . . . . V 85
Olivetum (Av. d') . . . . V 86
Paris (R. de) . . . . V 89
Pinède (Av. de la) . . . . V 94
Pompidou (Av. Georges) . . . . . . V 96
République (Bd de la) V
Roosevelt (Av. Franklin) . . . . . . V 99
St-Sauveur (R.) . . . . V 106
Victor-Hugo (R.) . . . . V 119
Victoria (Av.) V

VALLAURIS

Cannes (Av. de) . . . . V 18
Clemenceau (Av. G.) . . . . V 25
Golfe (Av. du) . . . . V 52
Isnard (Pl. Paul) . . . . V 56
Picasso (Av. Pablo) . . . . V 93
Rouvier (Bd Maurice) . . . . V 102
Tapis-Vert (Av. du) . . . . V 113

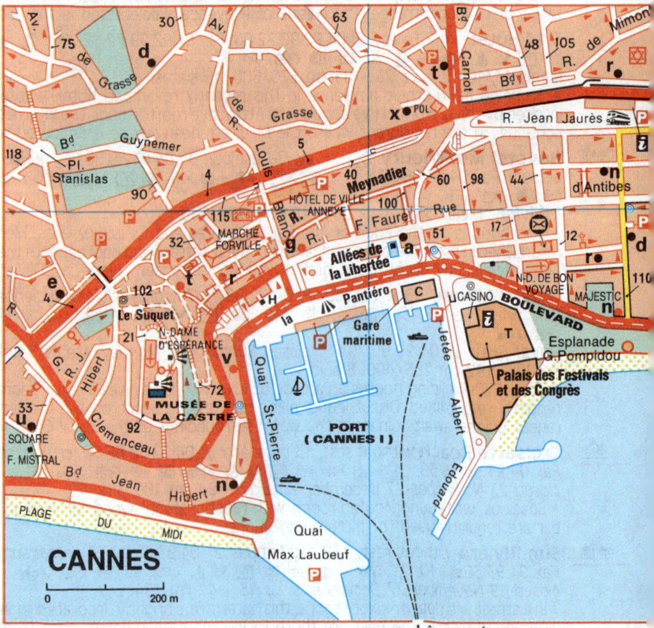

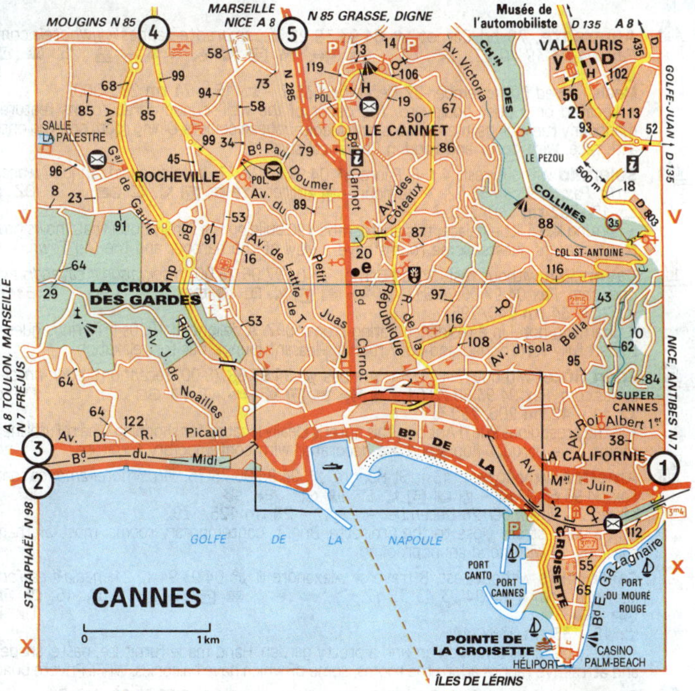
CANNES
MOUGINS N 85
MARSEILLE
NICE A 8
N 85 GRASSE, DIGNE
Musée de l'automobiliste
D 135
A 8
VALLAURIS
GOLFE-JUAN D 135
LE CANNET
ROCHEVILLE
SALLE LA PALESTRE
LA CROIX DES GARDES
Av. Victoria
CH.IN DES COLLINES
LE PEZOU
COL ST-ANTOINE
Bd Paul Doumer
Av. du Gal de Gaulle
Bd Carnot
Av. des Coteaux
Av. de Lattre de T.
Petit Juas
Bd Carnot
R. de la République
Av. d'Isola Bella
Bd du Riou
Av. J. de Noailles
Av. Dr R. Picaud
Bd du Midi
Bd DE LA CROISETTE
Av. Roi Albert 1er
LA CALIFORNIE
Av. Mal Juin
SUPER CANNES
NICE, ANTIBES N 7
A 8 TOULON, MARSEILLE N 7 FRÉJUS
ST-RAPHAËL N 98
GOLFE DE LA NAPOULE
PORT CANTO
PORT CANNES II
PORT DU MOURÉ ROUGE
Bd E. Gazagnaire
POINTE DE LA CROISETTE
HÉLIPORT
CASINO PALM-BEACH
ÎLES DE LÉRINS
500 m
0 1 km
V
X
C
D

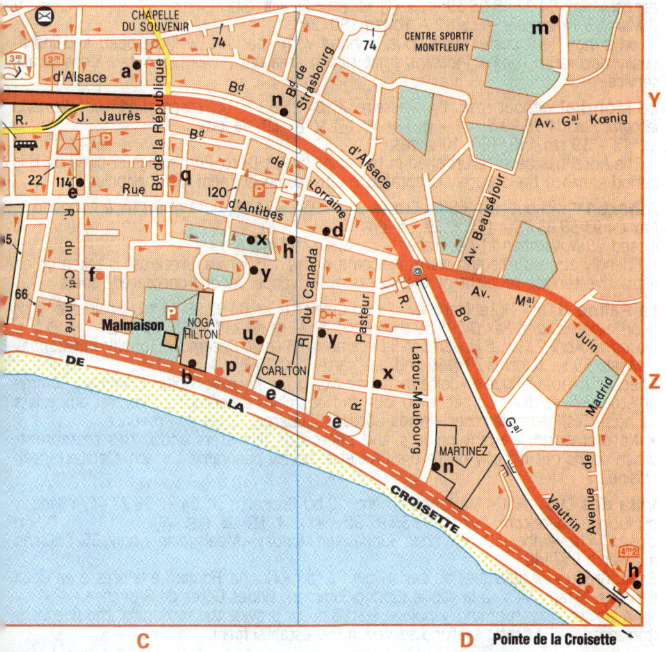
CHAPELLE DU SOUVENIR
CENTRE SPORTIF MONTFLEURY
d'Alsace
R. J. Jaurès
Bd d'Alsace
Bd de Strasbourg
Bd de la République
Bd de Lorraine
Rue d'Antibes
Av. Gal Kœnig
Av. Beauséjour
R. du Canada
R. Pasteur
R. Latour-Maubourg
R. du Cdt André
Malmaison
NOGA HILTON
CARLTON
MARTINEZ
Av. Mal Juin
Bd Gal Vautrin
Avenue de Madrid
DE LA CROISETTE
Pointe de la Croisette
Y
Z
C
D

Amarante, 78 bd Carnot ✆ 04 93 39 22 23, *amarante-cannes@jjwhotels.com, Fax 04 93 39 40 22,* , - ... - 25. AE GB JCB V e
Meals *(closed 30 November-27 December)* 35 – 15 – **71 rm** 280/300.
• Located on a busy boulevard. The décor of the well-soundproofed rooms features mahogany furnishings, mellow walls, and Mediterranean colours. Dining room opening onto a terrace, with décor and food in Provençal style.

Splendid without rest, 4 r. F. Faure ✆ 04 97 06 22 22, *hotel.splendid.cannes@wanadoo.fr, Fax 04 93 99 55 02,* harbour – kitchenette AE GB BZ a
17 – **62 rm** 110/220.
• Looking like a little palace, this aristocratic 19C building is a family hotel that knows how to pamper its guests. Some rooms have a view of the harbour and the Old Town.

Cavendish without rest, 11 bd Carnot ✆ 04 97 06 26 00, *reservation@cavendish-cannes.com, Fax 04 97 06 26 01* – AE GB BY t
20 – **34 rm** 240/295.
• Charming hotel in a residence dating from 1897. A delightful 1920s lift brings guests to carefully refurbished and cosy rooms. Pleasant lounge bar for relaxation.

Eden Hôtel without rest, 133 r. Antibes ✆ 04 93 68 78 00, *reception@eden-hotel-cannes.com, Fax 04 93 68 78 01* – AE GB DZ d
14 – **42 rm** 200/230.
• In the prestigious Rue d'Antibes, this hotel is ideally located for shopping. The refurbished rooms have parquet floors and are decorated with contemporary furniture.

America without rest, 13 r. St-Honoré ✆ 04 93 06 75 75, *info@hotel-america.com, Fax 04 93 68 04 58* – AE GB JCB. BZ r
closed 26 November-26 December – 12 – **28 rm** 125/179.
• In a quiet street close to the Croisette. Bright, contemporary rooms, most of them spacious, all with good soundproofing.

California's without rest, 8 traverse Alexandre III ✆ 04 93 94 12 21, *nadia@californias-hotel.com, Fax 04 93 43 55 17,* , – – 15. AE GB JCB DZ h
18 – **33 rm** 136/214.
• Lovely buildings arranged around a pretty garden. Hand-made furniture, pastel shades and attractive fabrics adorn the rooms, some of which have balconies. Wi-Fi. Private boat.

Fouquet's without rest, 2 rd-pt Duboys d'Angers ✆ 04 92 59 25 00, *info@le-fouquets.com, Fax 04 92 98 03 39* – AE GB CZ y
2 March-5 November – 12 – **10 rm** 180/230.
• On a not very busy roundabout, a hotel with spacious, well-equipped and individually decorated rooms. Pleasant small sitting area. Very well presented. Considerate service.

Le Mondial without rest, 1 r. Teisseire ✆ 04 93 68 70 00, *reservation@hotellemondial.com, Fax 04 93 99 39 11* – AE GB JCB CY e
12 – **39 rm** 110/180, 10 suites.
• The hotel has been refurbished in the spirit of Art Deco. Furnishings inspired by this period enhance the sprucely decorated rooms, some of them with balconies.

Albert 1er without rest, 68 av. Grasse ✆ 04 93 39 24 04, *hotel.albert1er@wanadoo.fr, Fax 04 93 38 83 75* – P. AE GB AY d
closed 28 November-11 December – 6,50 – **11 rm** 65/75.
• Friendly atmosphere and warm welcome in this 1930s villa. Breakfast is taken on an attractive terrace redolent of the scents of Provence. Soberly decorated rooms.

La Palme d'Or - Hôtel Martinez, 73 bd Croisette ✆ 04 92 98 74 14, *lapalmedor@concorde-hotels.com, Fax 04 93 39 03 38,* , – P. AE GB DZ n
closed 17 April-2 May, 6 November-5 December, 13 to 20 December, Sunday and Monday – **Meals** 55 b.i. (lunch), 70/160 and a la carte 95/180
Spec. Artichaut et figue en dolce forte, sabayon glacé aux olives noires (Summer). Comme un stockfish, sardines de pêche du jour en filets, chips de pérugine. Chocolat aux éclats de noisettes, gelée de roses. **Wines** Côtes du Luberon, Côtes de Provence.
• Natural wood, elegant colours and photos of film stars adorn this restaurant, which opens out directly on to the Croisette. Lovely panoramic terrace. Mediterranean cuisine.

Villa des Lys - Hôtel Majestic Barrière, 10 bd Croisette ✆ 04 92 98 77 41, *villadeslys@lucienbarriere.com, Fax 04 93 38 97 90* – AE GB JCB BZ n
closed 14 November-30 December, Sunday and Monday – **Meals** *(dinner only)* 65/150 and a la carte 95/140
Spec. Grosses langoustines au caviar, oeuf à l'armoricaine. Homard à la presse en deux services. "Traou Mad" à la vanille (Spring-Summer). **Wines** Côtes de Provence.
• An elegant glass roof and Napoleon III-style decor provide the setting for the fine Mediterranean and Atlantic seafood served in this establishment.

XXX **Le Mesclun,** 16 r. St-Antoine ✆ 04 93 99 45 19, *lemesclun@wanadoo.fr, Fax 04 93 47 68 29* – AE GB JCB AZ t
closed 20 November-20 December, 20 to 28 February and Wednesday – **Meals** (dinner only) 35 ♀.
◆ Luxurious ambience in this typical building of Old Cannes. Wainscoting, period furniture, pictures and discreet lighting form a lovely setting for intimate dinners.

XXX **Félix,** 63 bd Croisette ✆ 04 93 94 00 61, *cafe.felix.croisette@wanadoo.fr, Fax 04 93 94 06 90,* – AE GB DZ e
closed 20 November-20 December and lunch from 1 June-15 September – **Meals** 49 and a la carte 66/90.
◆ Charles Trenet was a regular, and this elegant brasserie-style restaurant in a superb location on the Croisette also featured in the film La Bonne Année. Prestigious terrace.

XX **Le Festival,** 52 bd Croisette ✆ 04 93 38 04 81, *contact@lefestival.fr, Fax 04 93 38 13 82,* – AE GB JCB CZ p
closed 21 November-27 December and February Holidays – **Meals** 35/40 ♀ - ***Grill :*** **Meals** a la carte 36/55.
◆ Cut-away ship drawings enliven the pale panelling of this huge brasserie. See and be seen on the terrace facing the Croisette ! Cool modern decor, convivial ambience and terrace in the Grill. Plain cuisine, grills, salads, daily menu etc.

XX **Mantel,** 22 r. St-Antoine ✆ 04 93 39 13 10, *noel.mantel@wanadoo.fr, Fax 04 93 39 13 10* – GB AZ c
closed 18 July-12 August, 10 to 20 November, Thursday lunch and Wednesday – **Meals** 23 (lunch), 32/54 ♀.
◆ One of a number of restaurants along a picturesque street in the old town (Le Suquet). Renowned for its reliable cuisine combining Provençal recipes and Italian influences.

XX **Gaston et Gastounette,** 7 quai St-Pierre ✆ 04 93 39 47 92, *Fax 04 93 99 45 34,* – AE GB AZ v
closed 1 to 20 December – **Meals** 20,50 (lunch)/36 ♀.
◆ The light-wood panelling of the two dining rooms is enhanced by colourful representations of Côte d'Azur landscapes. Attractive terrace facing the port.

X **Rendez-Vous,** 35 r. F. Faure ✆ 04 93 68 55 10, *Fax 04 93 38 96 21,* – AE GB
closed 8 to 17 January and 10 to 20 December – **Meals** 19,50/26,90 ♀. AZ g
◆ This smart establishment is a good place to meet after a highly perfumed morning spent in the neighbouring flower market. Traditional cuisine.

X **La Cave,** 9 bd République ✆ 04 93 99 79 87, *restaurantlacave@free.fr, Fax 04 93 46 15 12* – AE GB JCB CY c
closed 28 August-6 September and Sunday from October-May – **Meals** 28 ♀.
◆ Mirrors, posters, leatherette benches and open kitchens - you eat tightly packed together in this cheerful contemporary bistro. A slate shows the dishes of the day.

Grasse *06130 Alpes-Mar.* 341 C6 – *pop. 43 874 alt. 250.*

9 Victoria Golf Club ✆ 04 93 12 23 26 by D 4, D 3 and D 103 : 13 km ; 18 Gde Bastide at Châteauneuf-de-Grasse ✆ 04 93 77 70 08, E : 6 km by D7 ; 18 of St-Donat at Plan-de-Grasse ✆ 04 93 09 76 60 : 5 km ; 18 Opio-Valbonne ✆ 04 93 12 00 08 by D 4 : 11 km ; 9 St-Philippe Golf Academy at S. Antipolis ✆ 04 93 00 00 57, E : 12 km.
Tourist Office 22 Crs H. Cresp ✆ 04 93 36 66 66, Fax 04 93 36 86 36.
Cannes 17.

XXXX ✿✿ **Bastide St-Antoine** (Chibois) with rm, 48 av. H. Dunant (quartier St-Antoine) by road of Cannes : 1,5 km ✆ 04 93 70 94 94, *info@jacques-chibois.com, Fax 04 93 70 94 95,* ←, – 20 - 80. AE GB JCB. rm
Meals 53 (lunch), 130/170 and a la carte 91/128 ♀ – 23 – **11 rm** 235/330
Spec. Truffe en surprise d'habit blanc (season). Saint-Pierre en symphonie de pois gourmands et fenouil. Canette au jus de noix de tonka, cuite à l'étuvée. **Wines** Côtes de Provence, Bellet.
◆ This lovely 18C fortified house rises from a hill planted with ancient olive trees. Its tasty cuisine is a tribute to the capital of the perfume industry. Elegant rooms.

Mougins *06250 Alpes-Mar.* 341 C6 – *pop. 16 051 alt. 260.*

Cannes 8.

XXXX ✿✿ **Alain Llorca Le Moulin de Mougins** with rm, at Notre-Dame-de-Vie SE : 2,5 km by D 3 ✆ 04 93 75 78 24, *reservation@moulindemougins.com, Fax 04 93 90 18 55,* – P. AE GB
Meals *(closed Monday)* 48 (lunch), 98/150 and a la carte 110/165 ♀ – 25 – **3 rm** 140/190, 4 suites 300/330
Spec. Salade "façon riviera" aux rougets de roche. Morue de Bilbao en effeuillé, purée de pois chiches. Sabayon froid de turron, glace vanille. **Wines** Côtes de Provence, Bellet.
◆ Refined "Mediterranean cuisine" worth savouring in this 16C oil mill. The restaurant opens onto a delightfully scented garden with modern sculptures by renowned artists.

FRANCE

La Napoule *06210 Alpes-Mar.* 341 C6.

of Mandelieu ☎ 04 92 97 32 00 ; Riviera Golf Club at Mandelieu ☎ 04 92 97 49 49.

Tourist Office av. H.Clews ☎ 04 92 97 99 27, Fax 04 93 93 64 66.

Cannes 9,5.

L'Oasis (Raimbault), r. J. H. Carle ☎ 04 93 49 95 52, *oasis@relaischateaux.com, Fax 04 93 49 64 13,* – AE GB
closed 12 December-14 January, Sunday dinner and Monday from November-March and Monday lunch from April-October – **Meals** 45 (lunch), 68/148 and a la carte 100/125
Spec. Emietté d'esquinade à l'avocat en salade de langouste. Loup en croûte "Fernand Point". Carré d'agneau des Alpilles rôti et persillé, petits farcis niçois (Spring-Summer).
Wines Bellet, Coteaux d'Aix en Provence-les Baux.
◆ Lushly planted patio, elegant ambience, delicious Mediterranean cuisine with an oriental touch, a generous dessert trolley. No, it's not a mirage !

LILLE *59000 Nord* 302 G4 – *pop. 184 657 alt. 10.*

See : *Old Lille★★ : Old Stock Exchange★★ (Vieille Bourse)* EY, *Place du Général-de-Gaulle★* EY 66, *Hospice Comtesse★ (panelled timber vault★★)* EY, *– Rue de la Monnaie★* EY 120 *– Vauban's Citadel★* BV *– St-Sauveur district : Paris Gate★* EFZ, *<★ from the top of the belfry of the Hôtel de Ville* FZ *– Fine Arts Museum★★★ (Musée des Beaux-Arts)* EZ *– Général de Gaulle's Birthplace (Maison natale)* EY.

18 of Brigode at Villeneuve d'Ascq ☎ 03 20 91 17 86 : 9 km ; 36 of Bondues ☎ 03 20 23 20 62 : 9,5 km ; 9 of Flandres at Marcq-en-Baroeul ☎ 03 20 72 20 74 : 4,5 km ; 18 of Sart at Villeneuve d'Ascq ☎ 03 20 72 02 51 : 7 km ; 18 Lille Métropole at Ronchin ☎ 03 20 47 42 42.

of Lille-Lesquin : ☎ 03 20 49 68 68 : 8 km.

☎ 0892 35 35 33.

Tourist Office Pl. Rihour ☎ 03 59 57 94 00, Fax 03 59 57 94 14.

Paris 223 – Bruxelles 114 – Gent 75 – Luxembourg 310 – Strasbourg 530.

L'Hermitage Gantois, 224 r. Paris ☎ 03 20 85 30 30, *contact@hotelhermitagegantois.com, Fax 03 20 42 31 31* – – 20 - 60. AE GB JCB EZ b
Meals 39 – ***L'Estaminet*** *(closed Saturday lunch and Sunday)* **Meals** 19/26 – 18 – **67 rm** 245/285.
◆ This listed 14C hospice is now a fine hotel teeming with character with original decor enhanced by modern touches. Most rooms look on to pleasant patios. Traditional dining under the restaurant's red and gold vaults. Brasserie ambience in l'Estaminet.

Crowne Plaza, 335 bd Leeds ☎ 03 20 42 46 46, *contact@lille-crowneplaza.com, Fax 03 20 40 13 14,* <, – – 10 - 100. AE GB JCB
Meals 23 – 18 – **121 rm** 215/220. FY n
◆ This cube-like building opposite the TGV station is home to a brand-new hotel with spacious, modern rooms that are minimalist yet fully equipped. Starck-inspired decor, including an attractive library. Modern à la carte and buffet dining in the restaurant.

Carlton without rest, 3 r. Paris 59800 ☎ 03 20 13 33 13, *carlton@carltonlille.com, Fax 03 20 51 48 17,* – – 15 - 170. AE GB JCB EY u
17 – **60 rm** 165/252.
◆ An early-20C town mansion located opposite the Old Bourse. Luxury suites and Louis XV- and Louis XVI-style rooms with tasteful decor. English-style bar.

Alliance , 17 quai du Wault 59800 ☎ 03 20 30 62 62, *alliancelille@alliance-hospitality.com, Fax 03 20 42 94 25* – rm, – 35 - 100. AE GB JCB BV d
Meals *(closed Monday from 15 July-31 August)* 28/34 b.i. – 17 – **75 rm** 215, 8 suites.
◆ This 17C red-brick convent is halfway between Lille's historic centre and the Citadel. Rooms with contemporary décor around an indoor garden. A huge glass pyramid rises over the cloisters housing the restaurant. Piano bar.

Grand Hôtel Bellevue without rest, 5 r. J. Roisin ☎ 03 20 57 45 64, *grandhotelbellevue@wanadoo.fr, Fax 03 20 40 07 93* – – 50 - 100. AE GB JCB
12 – **60 rm** 115/150. EY a
◆ Beautiful stone building in the heart of the capital of French Flanders. Characterful rooms, attractively refurbished and with new furniture. Some overlook the Grand'Place.

Novotel Flandres, 49 r. Tournai 59800 ☎ 03 28 38 67 00, *h3165@accor-hotels.com, Fax 03 28 38 67 10,* – – 80. AE GB JCB FZ u
Meals a la carte 20/27 – 12 – **87 rm** 125/135, 6 suites.
◆ Next to Lille-Flandres railway station, this establishment conforms to the latest standards set by the Novotel chain. Huge foyer/lounge, modern, well-equipped rooms.

Mercure Opéra without rest, 2 bd Carnot ✉ 59800 ☎ 03 20 14 71 47, *h0802@accor-hotels.com, Fax 03 20 14 71 48* – 🛗 ⇔ ▤ TV ☎ – 🎤 25. AE ① GB JCB EY h
☕ 12 – **100 rm** 127/152.
• Exposed beams and old brickwork lend charm to the foyer and lounge of this venerable stone-built establishment. Contemporary-style rooms, refurbished with care.

De la Paix without rest, 46 bis r. Paris ✉ 59000 ☎ 03 20 54 63 93, *hotelpaixlille@aol.com, Fax 03 20 63 98 97* – 🛗 TV ☎. AE ① GB EY r
☕ 8,50 – **36 rm** 75/103.
• This hotel dates back to 1782. The owner is an enthusiastic art-lover who has filled the place with reproductions as well as painting the fresco adorning the breakfast room.

A L'Huîtrière, 3 r. Chats Bossus ✉ 59800 ☎ 03 20 55 43 41, *contact@huitriere.fr, Fax 03 20 55 23 10* – ▤. AE ① GB JCB EY g
closed 22 July-24 August, dinner Sunday and Bank Holidays – **Meals** 43 (lunch)/120 and a la carte 75/110 ♀
Spec. Huîtres (except July-August). Homard poêlé aux pommes de terre et à l'estragon. Tranche de gros turbot rôtie à la bière et aux endives.
• The ceramics where the fish are displayed are well worth a look and will certainly whet your appetite. Beyond, three luxury dining rooms are a high point of local gastronomy.

Le Sébastopol (Germond), 1 pl. Sébastopol ☎ 03 20 57 05 05, *n.germond@restaurant-sebastopol.fr, Fax 03 20 40 11 31* – ▤. AE GB JCB EZ a
closed 7 to 29 August, Sunday dinner, lunch Saturday and Monday – **Meals** 28 (lunch)/61 b.i. and a la carte 55/77 ♀
Spec. Crépinette de pieds de porc et foie gras aux cèpes (autumn). Filet de boeuf aux jets de houblon (spring). Vaporeux glacé à la chicorée.
• The elegant façade is enhanced by the landscaping and unusual awning. Refurbished dining room with warm, contemporary decor. Classic fine cuisine and good wine list.

L'Esplanade (Scherpereel), 84 façade Esplanade ✉ 59800 ☎ 03 20 06 58 58, *Fax 03 28 52 47 43* – ▤. AE ① GB BV x
closed Saturday lunch, Sunday and Bank Holidays – **Meals** 30 (lunch), 55/75 and a la carte 70/94 ♀
Spec. Saint-Jacques à la vinaigrette de coquillages (mid-October-late-February). Agneau en croûte de pommes de terre (March-August). Rouget à la plancha (April-September).
• Brick building next door to the "Queen of Citadelles". Comfortable, contemporary first floor dining room. Up-to-date cuisine accompanied by a splendid wine list.

Baan Thaï, 22 bd J.-B. Lebas ☎ 03 20 86 06 01, *Fax 03 20 86 72 94* – ▤. AE ① GB EZ s
closed Sunday except lunch from September-July and Saturday lunch – **Meals** 41/47 ♀.
• This restaurant installed in a fine town house invites diners to take a trip to the Kingdom of Siam. Elegant exotic decor and traditional Thai cuisine.

Clément Marot, 16 r. Pas ✉ 59800 ☎ 03 20 57 01 10, *clmarot@nordnet.fr, Fax 03 20 57 39 69* – ▤. AE ① GB JCB EY n
closed Sunday except lunch out of season – **Meals** 22 (lunch), 31/48.
• Little brick-built establishment run by descendants of the Cahors poet Clément Marot. Modern setting, pictures on the walls and convivial atmosphere.

Lanathaï, 189 r. Solférino ☎ 03 20 57 20 20, 🏞 – AE GB EZ s
closed Sunday – **Meals** 23/36.
• Elegant décor, with parquet floor, cane furniture, linen tablecloths, and an attractive teak terrace. Tasty, carefully prepared Thai cuisine.

Brasserie de la Paix, 25 pl. Rihour ☎ 03 20 54 70 41, *contact@brasserielapaix.com, Fax 03 20 40 15 52* – ▤. AE GB EY z
closed Sunday – **Meals** 17 (lunch)/25 ♀.
• With its ceramics, wainscoting, and serried ranks of tables and benches, this is an attractive brasserie only a few steps from the Tourist Office in the Palais Rihour.

L'Assiette du Marché, 61 r. Monnaie ☎ 03 20 06 83 61, *assiettedumarche@free.fr, Fax 03 20 14 03 75,* 🏞 – GB EY v
closed 1 to 21 August, Sunday and Bank Holidays – **Meals** 20 ♀.
• The new contemporary decor and glass roof over the inner courtyard bring to life this former 18C mint where the accent is on seasonally influenced cuisine.

La Coquille, 60 r. St-Étienne ✉ 59800 ☎ 03 20 54 29 82, *dadeleval@nordet.fr, Fax 03 20 54 29 82* – GB EY e
closed 1 to 15 August, Saturday lunch and Sunday – **Meals** (booking essential) 28 b.i. ♀.
• This 18C building has a striking brick façade. The interior is a harmonious combination of old beams, venerable walls and contemporary décor.

Alcide, 5 r. Débris St-Étienne ✉ 59800 ☎ 03 20 12 06 95, *bigarade@easynet.fr, Fax 03 20 55 93 83* – ▤. AE ① GB EY l
closed 18 July-15 August and Sunday dinner – **Meals** 20/27.
• Founded in 1830 in a lane by the famous Grand'Place, this brasserie has kept its original atmosphere - benches, serried ranks of tables, old panelling, and varied cuisine.

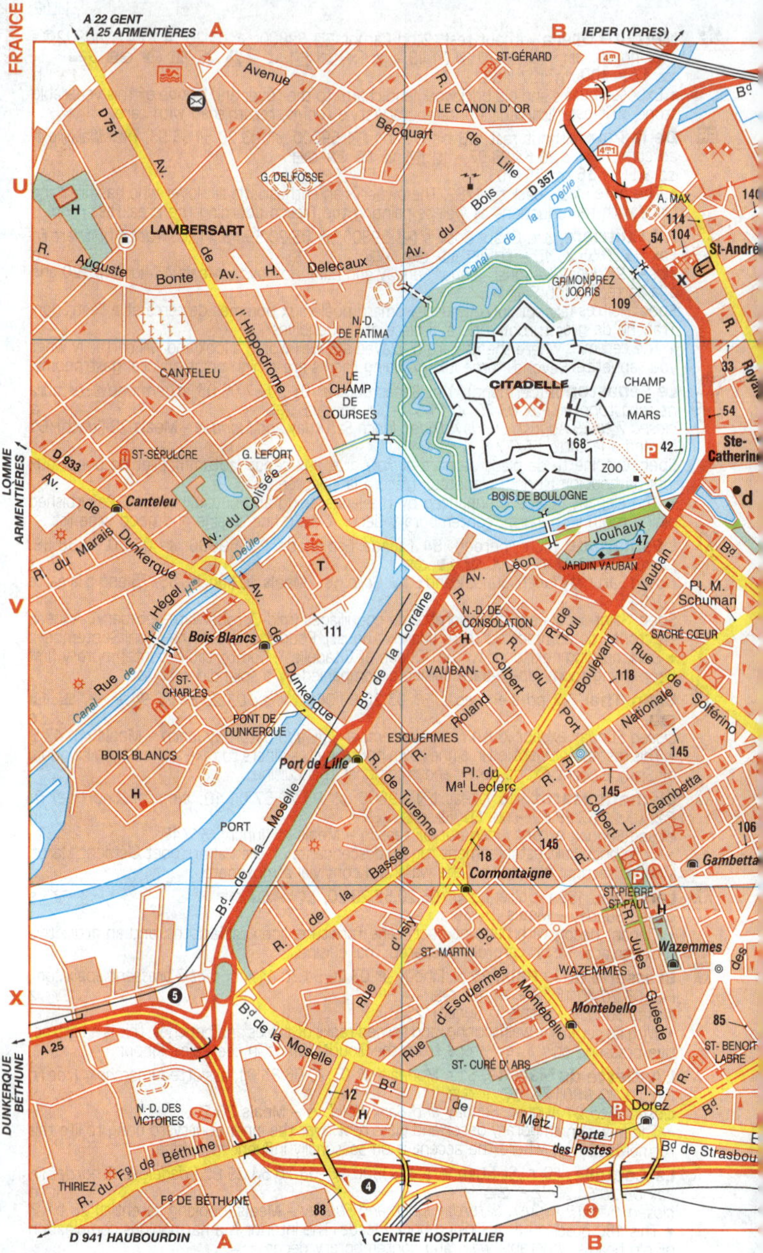

43e-Régt-d'Infanterie (Av. du) . . . . **BV** 168
Bapaume (R. de). . . . . **CX** 7
Beethoven (Av.) . . . . **AX** 12
Bernos (R.) . . . . **DV** 13
Bigo-Danel (Bd). . . . . **BV** 18
Carrel (R. Armand) . . . . **CX** 25
Colpin (R. du Lt) . . . . **BV** 33
Courmont (R.) . . . . **CX** 37
Cuvier (Av.) . . . . **BV** 42
Desmazières (R.) . . . . **BV** 47
Esplanade (Façade de l'). **BUV** 54
Fébvrier (Pl. J.) . . . . **CX** 56
Fontenoy (R. de) . . . . **CX** 60
Gaulle (R. du Gén.-de) . . . . **CU** 67

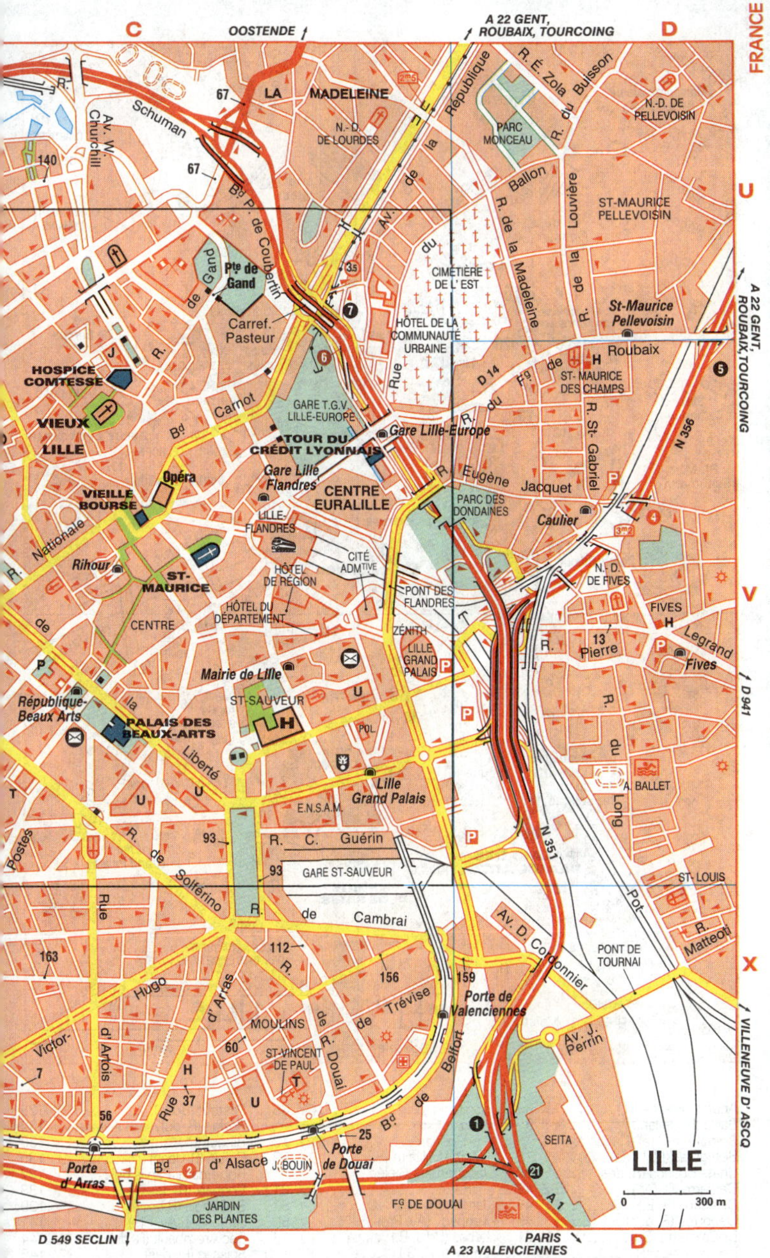

Justice (R. de la)	BX	85	Marronniers (Allée des)	BU	109	St-Sébastien (R.)	BCU	140
Lambret (Av. Oscar)	AX	88	Marx-Dormoy (Av.)	AV	111	Stations (R. des)	BV	145
Lebas (Bd J.-B.)	CV	93	Maubeuge (R. de)	CX	112	Valenciennes (R. de)	CX	156
Magasin (R. du)	BU	104	Max (Av. Adolphe)	BU	114	Verdun (Bd de)	DX	159
Manuel (R.)	BV	106	Meurein (R.)	BV	118	Wazemmes (R. de)	BCX	163

Anatole-France (R.) . . . . EY 3
Barre (R. de la) . . . . EY 9
Béthune (R. de) . . . . EYZ
Bettignies (Pl. L. de) . . . . . . EY 16
Chats-Bossus (R. des) . . . . EY 27
Debierre (R. Ch.) . . . . FZ 43
Delesalle (R. E.) . . . . EZ 45
Déportés (R. des) . . . . FY 46
Dr-Calmette (Bd) . . . . FY 51
Esquermoise (R.) . . . . EY
Faidherbe (R.) . . . . EY
Faubourg-de-Roubaix (R. du) . . . . FY 55
Fosses (R. des) . . . . EYZ 61
Gambetta (R. Léon) . . . . . DEZ
Gare (Pl. de la) . . . . FY 65
Gaulle (Pl. Gén.-de) . . . . EY 66
Grande-Chaussée (R. de la) . . . . EY 73
Hôpital-Militaire (R.) . . . . . . EY 78
Jacquemars-Giélée (R.) . . . . EZ 81
Jardins (R. des) . . . . EY 83
Kennedy (Av. Prés.) . . . . FZ 86
Lebas (Bd J. B.) . . . . FZ 93
Lefèvre (R. G.) . . . . FZ 100
Lepelletier (R.) . . . . EY 102
Maillotte (R.) . . . . EZ 105
Mendès-France (Pl.) . . . . . . EY 115
Monnaie (R. de la) . . . . EY 120
Nationale (R.) . . . . DEYZ
Neuve (R.) . . . . EY 123
Pasteur (Bd L.) . . . . FY 125
Réduit (R. du) . . . . FZ 132
Rihour (Pl.) . . . . EY 133
Roisin (R. Jean) . . . . EY 135
Rotterdam (Parvis de) . . . . . FY 137
Roubaix (R. de) . . . . EFY 138
St-Génois (R.) . . . . EY 139
St-Venant (Av. Ch.) . . . . FYZ 141
Sec-Arembault (R. du) . . . . EY 144
Suisses (Pl. des) . . . . FY 146
Tanneurs (R. des) . . . . EYZ 147
Tenremonde (R.) . . . . EY 148
Théâtre (Pl. du) . . . . EY 150
Trois-Mollettes (R. des) . . . . EY 154
Vieille-Comédie (R. de la) . . . . EY 162

at Marcq-en-Barœul – *pop. 37 177 alt. 15 – ✉ 59700 :*

Sofitel, av. Marne, by N 350 : 5 km ✆ 03 28 33 12 12, *h1099@accor-hotels.com, Fax 03 28 33 12 24* – 15 - 150.
L'Europe *(closed 22 July-28 August, Saturday lunch and Sunday dinner)* **Meals** 12,30/22,60 – 16 – **125 rm** 185/200.
• Close to a motorway junction, this 1970s establishment is surrounded by greenery. Attractive refurbished rooms, comfortable lounge and pleasant piano bar. Brasserie Europe with a slate displaying dishes of the day, plus a traditional menu and oyster bar.

at Lille-Lesquin airport *by A 1 : 8 km – ✉ 59810 Lesquin :*

Mercure Aéroport, ✆ 03 20 87 46 46, *h1098@accor-hotels.com, Fax 03 20 87 46 47,* – 900.
La Flamme : **Meals** 26/30 – 12 – **215 rm** 130.
• Imposing modern building opposite the airport. Spacious and very comfortable rooms, gradually being refurbished ; avoid those facing the motorway. Congenial atmosphere, traditional cuisine and excellent choice of meat dishes in the Flamme.

Novotel Aéroport, 55 route de Douai ✆ 03 20 62 53 53, *h0427@accor-hotels.com, Fax 03 20 97 36 12,* – 25 - 200.
Meals 24/29 – 11 – **92 rm** 93/98.
• This low structure was the first to be built (1967) by the company. Functional rooms refurbished in the style of more recent Novotels. Modern dining room with summer terrace overlooking the greenery. Usual Novotel menu.

Béthune *62400 P.-de-C. 301 I4 – pop. 27 808 alt. 34.*

Tourist Office Le Beffroi Gd Place ✆ 03 21 57 25 47, Fax 03 21 57 01 60.
Lille 39.

XXX ✿✿ **Meurin and Résidence Kitchener** with rm (due to move to Busnes in September), 15 pl. République ✆ 03 21 68 88 88, *marc.meurin@le-meurin.fr, Fax 03 21 68 88 89,* – kitchenette, rest,
closed July-August, Tuesday lunch, Sunday dinner and Monday – **Meals** 38 (lunch), 55/110 and a la carte 96/116 – 13 – **7 rm** 80/140
Spec. Galette de cèpes et champignons des bois (September-October). Rouget barbet sur toast d'aubergines à la mozzarella. Veau au jus réglissé.
• Lovely early 20C Flemish residence. Delightful dining rooms and terrace conservatory in Belle Epoque style. Inventive cuisine. Individually styled rooms.

LYONS (LYON) *69000 Rhône 327 I5 – pop. 445 452 alt. 175.*

See : *Site★★★ (panorama★★ from Fourvière) – Fourvière hill : Notre-Dame Basilica* EX, *Museum of Gallo-Roman Civilization★★ (Claudian tablet★★★)* EY **M³**, *Roman ruins* EY *– Old Lyons★★★ : Rue St-Jean★* FX, *St-Jean Cathedral★* FY, *Hôtel de Gadagne★ (Lyons Historical Museum★ and International Marionette Museum★)* EX **M¹** *– Guignol de Lyon* FX **N** *– Central Lyons (Peninsula) : to the North, Place Bellecour* FY, *Hospital Museum (pharmacy★)* FY **M⁸**, *Museum of Printing and Banking★★* FX **M⁶**, *– Place des Terreaux* FX, *Hôtel de Ville* FX, *Palais St-Pierre, Fine Arts Museum (Beaux-Arts)★★* FX **M⁴** *– to the South, St-Martin-d'Ainay Basilica (capitals★)* FY, *Weaving and Textile Museum★★★* FY **M²**, *Decorative Arts Museum★★* FY **M⁵** *– La Croix-Rousse : Silkweavers' House* FV **M¹¹**, *Trois Gaules Amphitheatre* FV **E** *– Tête d'Or Park★* GHV *– Guimet Museum of Natural History★★* GV **M⁷** *– Historical Information Centre on the Resistance and the Deportation★* FZ **M⁹**.

Envir. : *Rochetaillée : Henri Malartre Car Museum★★, 12 km to the North.*

18 Verger-Lyon at St-Symphorien-d'Ozon ✆ 04 78 02 84 20, S : 14 km ; 18 Lyon-Chassieu at Chassieu ✆ 04 78 90 84 77, E : 12 km by D 29 ; 18 Salvagny (private) at the Tour of Salvagny ✆ 04 78 48 88 48 ; junction Lyon-Ouest : 8 km ; 36 Golf Club of Lyon at Jons-Villette-d'Anthon ✆ 04 78 31 11 33.

of Lyon-Saint-Exupery ✆ 0826 800 826 to the E : 27 km.

✆ 0892 35 35 33.

Tourist Office pl. Bellecour ✆ 04 72 77 69 69, Fax 04 78 42 04 32.

Paris 462 – Geneva 151 – Grenoble 105 – Marseilles 313 – St-Étienne 60 – Turin 300.

Hotels

Town Centre (Bellecour-Terreaux) :

Sofitel, 20 quai Gailleton ✉ 69002 ✆ 04 72 41 20 20, *h0553@accor-hotels.com, Fax 04 72 40 05 50,* – 15 - 200. FY p
see ***Les Trois Dômes*** below ***Sofishop*** ✆ *04 72 41 20 80* **Meals** a la carte 31/40 – 24 – **137 rm** 285/405, 29 suites.
• The somewhat austere cubic exterior of this establishment contrasts with its luxurious interior. Ask for one of the refurbished rooms with their mahogany or light-wood furnishings. Typical brasserie ambience and cuisine in the Sofishop.

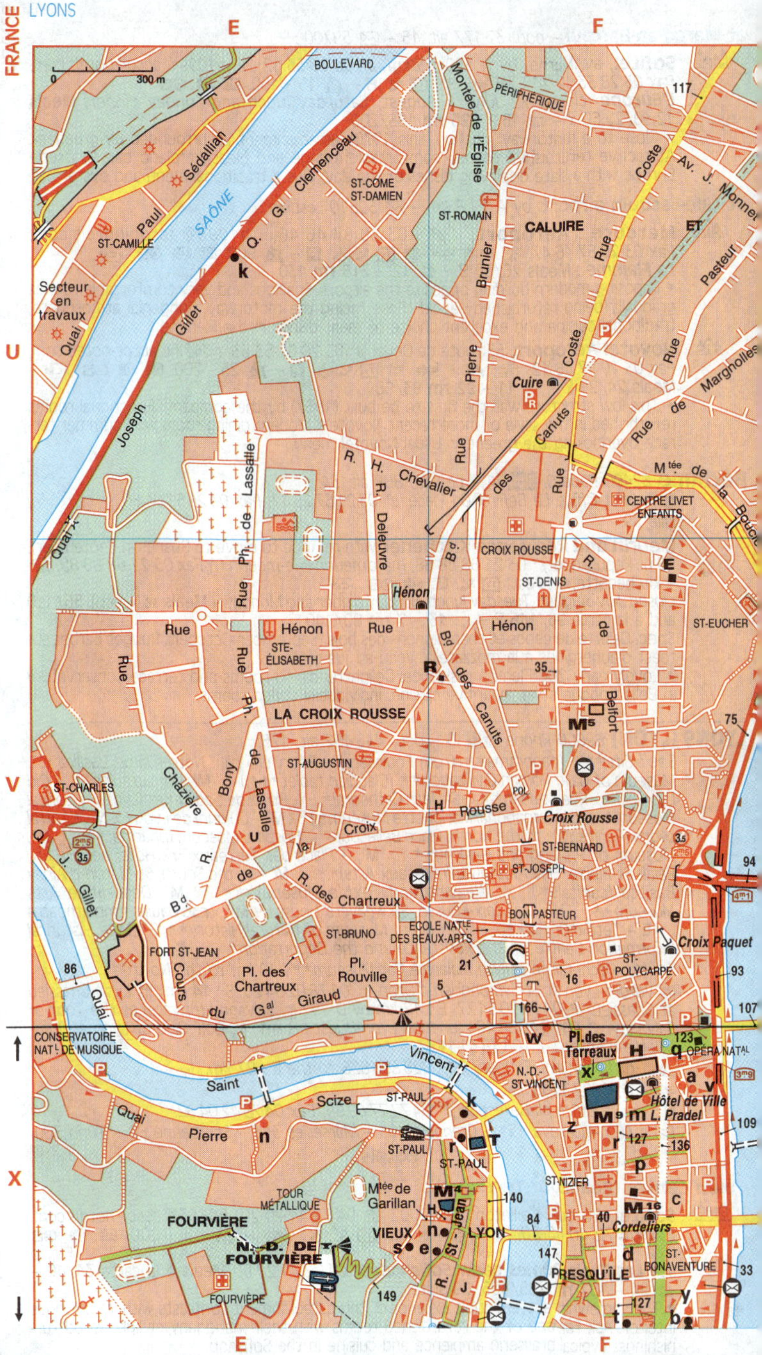
E
F
U
V
X
E
F
0
300 m
BOULEVARD
PÉRIPHÉRIQUE
Montée de l'Église
Sédallian
Paul
SAÔNE
Q. G. Clemenceau
ST-COME ST-DAMIEN
ST-ROMAIN
CALUIRE
ET
Coste
Av. J. Monnet
Rue Pasteur
ST-CAMILLE
Secteur en travaux
Quai
Gillet
Joseph
Brunier
Pierre
Rue
Cuire
Rue Coste
Rue de Margnolles
Canuts
Rue
Mtée de la Boucle
R. H. Chevalier
des
CENTRE LIVET ENFANTS
Quai
Rue Ph. de Lassalle
R. Deleuvre
Bd
CROIX ROUSSE
ST-DENIS
R.
de
Belfort
ST-EUCHER
Hénon
Rue
Hénon
Rue
Hénon
STE-ÉLISABETH
Bd des Canuts
35
Rue
Rue Ph.
LA CROIX ROUSSE
M5
75
ST-AUGUSTIN
Chazière
Bony
de Lassalle
ST-CHARLES
POL
Rousse
Croix Rousse
Croix
la
ST-BERNARD
R.
de
R. des Chartreux
ST-JOSEPH
94
Q. J. Gillet
Bd
BON PASTEUR
ECOLE NATLE DES BEAUX-ARTS
e
Croix Paquet
FORT ST-JEAN
ST-BRUNO
Cours
Pl. des Chartreux
Pl. Rouville
21
16
ST-POLYCARPE
93
86
Quai
du Gal Giraud
5
166
107
CONSERVATOIRE NATL DE MUSIQUE
Vincent
w
Pl. des Terreaux
H
123
q
OPÉRA NATAL
Saint
N.-D.-ST-VINCENT
x
a
v
Quai
Scize
ST-PAUL
k
Hôtel de Ville
L. Pradel
Pierre
n
ST-PAUL
r
T
M9
m
z
127
136
109
ST-PAUL
r
p
ST-NIZIER
X
TOUR MÉTALLIQUE
Mtée de Garillan
M4
140
M16
c
FOURVIÈRE
H
84
40
Cordeliers
VIEUX
n
LYON
St-Jean
N.-D. DE FOURVIÈRE
s
e
147
d
ST-BONAVENTURE
33
R.
J
PRESQU'ÎLE
149
FOURVIÈRE
127
y
t
b

G
H
Pasteur
FORT DE MONTESSUY
PARC J. CORBEL
Vignal
Chin de Boutary
163
Rte de Strasbourg
Pte DE ST-CLAIR
PÉAGE
STE-BERNADETTE
TUNNEL DE CALUIRE-ET-CUIRE A PÉAGE
Av.
St-Clair
de
CUIRE
Margnolles
rue
Rue de
Grande
Pont R. Poincaré
PARC DE LA FEYSSINE
Bd L. Bonnevay
U
ST-CLAIR
Bellevue
RHÔNE
CITÉ INTERNATIONALE
Gaulle
de
PALAIS DES CONGRÈS
MUSÉE D'ART CONTEMPORAIN
Briand
Aristide
Quai
Charles
UNIVERSITÉ CLAUDE BERNARD LYON I
VÉLODROME
GRANDE ROSERAIE
INTERPOL
Cours
Quai
PARC
Île du Souvenir
Stalingrad
Bd du 11 Novembre 1918
31
Pl. du Gal Leclerc
DE LA
JARDIN ZOOLOGIQUE
144
R. du Tonkin
Av. Galline
TÊTE D'OR
de la Bataille
Av. de Grande-Bretagne
Boulevard des
Rue
VILLEURBANNE
V
M20
STE-MADELEINE
Av.
SERRES
Cours
A. Philip
Duquesne
Av. Verguin
Rue
CHARPENNES
Bd
Rue
St-JOSEPH
57
R. G. Péri
RÉDEMPTION
Foch
de
R.
Sully
Belges
39
Cours É. Zola
Rue
Sully
Rue de
Vitton
Charpennes Charles Hernu
Rue
S
n
Cours
Z
Charmettes
Q. de Serbie
Pl. du Mal Foch
e
Roosevelt
la
Masséna
Bd des Brotteaux
Av.
V
F.
Cours Lyautey
x
H
ST-NICOLAS
CHARMETTES
Av.
Créqui
LES BROTTEAUX
Garibaldi
Tête
Bugeaud
Brotteaux
51
R. de la Viabert
Duguesclin
R.
ST-NOM-DE-JÉSUS
N.-D. DE BELLECOMBE
ST-POTHIN
POL.
Vauban
d'Or
48
Thiers
des
157
Rue
R.
X
Cours
Lafayette
Cours
Lafayette
Mal
Rue
Cours
b
Bonnel
TOUR CRÉDIT LYONNAIS
Rue
Rue de
s
Rue
LA PART DIEU
R. d'Aubigny
HÔTEL DU DÉPT
POL.
J
h
u
Part Dieu
a
G
H

E
F
X
Y
Z
CONSERVATOIRE NAT.L DE MUSIQUE
Quai
Saint
Pierre
Scize
Vincent
ST-PAUL
Pl. des Terreaux
N.-D.-ST-VINCENT
123
OPÉRA NAT.AL
Hôtel de Ville
L. Pradel
M9
127
136
109
ST-NIZIER
TOUR MÉTALLIQUE
M.tée de Garillan
M4
140
84
40
Cordeliers
M16
FOURVIÈRE
N.-D. DE FOURVIÈRE
VIEUX
LYON
R. St-Jean
147
PRESQU'ÎLE
ST-BONAVENTURE
33
149
127
ST-JEAN
Vieux Lyon
Cath. St-Jean
69
Aqueducs Romains
R. Radisson
M10
THÉÂTRES ROMAINS
MINIMES
ST-GEORGES
12
Tilsitt
Bellecour
Pl. Bellecour
136
HÔTEL DIEU
182
73
Pl. de Trion
R. de Trion
ST-JUST
10
POL
TUNNEL DE FOURVIÈRE
46
7
Fulchiron
Quai
ST-FRANÇOIS
176
M7
Ampère V. Hugo
M17
ST-IRÉNÉE
Chemin
St-Martin d'Ainay
Gailleton
Bernard
186
Choulan
de
82
Rue de Condé
STE-CROIX
du Docteur
171
Cl.
J. MOULIN LYON III
LUMIÈRE LYON II
Q.
85
Pl. Carnot
POL
Av. Debrousse
Q. des Étroits
Perrache
PERRACHE
ST-LUC
ST-JOSEPH
65
DEBROUSSE
Rambaud
Cours
POL.
Rousseau
SAÔNE
PRISONS
Suchet
Avenue
M1
STE-BLANDINE
Tramway 9-2005
Charlemagne
Perrache
R. G. Nadaud
Rue Lortet
Jean-Jacques
Quai
Quai
RHÔNE
Leclerc
Av.
Farge
Jean
Secteur
105
en
travaux
MARCHÉ DE GROS
Perrache
Cours
A7-E15
Yves
R.
Crépet
125
N.-D. DES ANGES
Pl. J. Jaurès
Av.
Rambaud
Quai
Av.
Leclerc
Boulevard
R. Clément Marot

G
H
X
Y
Z
LES BROTTEAUX
Cours Lyautey
Av. Créqui
R. Duguesclin
Garibaldi
Tête d'Or
Bugeaud
ST-NOM-DE-JÉSUS
Vauban
des Brotteaux
Brotteaux
R. de la Viabert
ST-NICOLAS
CHARMETTES
N.-D. DE BELLECOMBE
ST-POTHIN
POL.
157
Rue
Cours
Lafayette
Cours Lafayette
Thiers
Cours M.al
Rue de Bonnel
Cours
Rue de
TOUR CRÉDIT LYONNAIS
Part Dieu
LA PART DIEU
Rue
R. d'Aubigny
HÔTEL DU DEPT
IMMACULÉE CONCEPTION
Servient
CITÉ ADM.VE D'ÉTAT
R. de la Liberté
Pl. Guichard
PART DIEU
Av. G. Pompidou
178
101
ST-SACREMENT
Paul
Bert
Flandin
Av. Lacassagne
Pl. A. Jutard
Guillotière
Cours
Rue Duguesclin
Saxe
Créqui
ST-JACQUES
Garibaldi
Av. F. Faure
Faure
Saxe Gambetta
Grande
Marseille
ST-ANDRÉ
Jaurès
Av.
Félix
Garibaldi
Gambetta
PRISON MONTLUC
Béchevelin
N.-D. ST-LOUIS
Rue de
Jean
172
Pl. de Stalingrad
la
STE-MARIE DE LA GUILLOTIÈRE
Cours
J. MOULIN LYON III
Sans Souci
A. Thomas
LA GUILLOTIÈRE
L'ANNONCIATION
Guillotière
ST-MICHEL
R. M. Bloch
Chevreul
Pl. J. Macé
J. Macé
Av.
Garibaldi
Av. des Frères Lumière
Villon
131
Route
Tchécoslovaques
Berthelot
Rue
des
41
B.d
POL.
Rue
Rue
Avenue
M. Berliet
Jaurès
180
de
Gerland
CIMETIÈRE ISRAÉLITE
Villon
Berthelot
B.d des États-Unis
de
Vienne
Barret
Croix
Rue
Rue
ST-VINCENT DE PAUL
Musée urbain Tony-Garnier

INDEX OF STREET NAMES IN LYON

CALUIRE ET CUIRE

Boucle (Montée de la) FU
Boutary (Ch. de) HU
Briand (Cours A.) GUV
Brunier (R. P.) FU
Canuts (Bd des) FUV
Chevalier (R. H.) EFU
Clemenceau (Quai G.) EU
Coste (R.) FU
Église (Montée de l') FU
Margnolles (R. de) FGU
Monnet (Av. J.) FU
Pasteur (R.) FGU
Peissel (R. F.) FU 117
Saint Clair (Grande R. de) GHU
Soldats (Montée des) HU 163
Strasbourg (Rte de) CP
Vignal (Av. E.) GU

LA MULATIÈRE

J.-J. Rousseau (Quai) ZE

LYON

1re Div.-Fr.-Libre (Av. de la) EY 186
Annonciade (R. de l') FV 5
Antiquaille (R. de l') EY 7
Aubigny (R. d') HX
Barret (R. Croix) GZ
Basses Verchères (R. des) EY 10
Bataille de Stalingrad (Bd de la) HUV
Béchevelin (R.) GY
Belfort (R. de) FV
Belges (Bd des) GHV
Bellecour (Pl.) FY
Bellevue (Quai) GU
Berliet (R. M.) HZ
Bert (R. P.) GHY
Berthelot (Av.) GHZ
Bloch (R. M.) GZ
Bonaparte (Pt) FY 12
Bonnel (R. de) GX
Bony (R.) EV
Boucle (Montée de la) FU
Brotteaux (Bd des) HVX
Bugeaud (R.) HX
Burdeau (R.) FV 16
Canuts (Bd des) FUV
Carmélites (Mtée des) FV 21
Carnot (Pl.) FY
Charlemagne (Cours) EZ
Charmettes (R. des) HVX
Chartreux (Pl. des) EV
Chartreux (R. des) EV
Chazière (R.) EV
Chevalier (R. H.) EFU
Chevreul (R.) GYZ
Choulans (Ch. de) EY
Churchill (Pt W.) GV 31
Claude-Bernard (Q.) FY
Condé (R. de) FY
Courmont (Q. J.) FX 33
Crepet (R.) FZ
Créqui (R. de) GVY
Croix Rousse (Bd de la) EFV
Croix Rousse (Gde-R. de la) FV 35
Debrousse (Av.) EY
Deleuvre (R.) EUV
Dr-Gailleton (Q. du) FY
Duguesclin (R.) GVY
Duquesne (R.) GV
Épargne (R. de l') HZ 41
Étroits (Quai des) EY
Farge (Bd Y.) FZ
Farges (R. des) EY 46
Faure (Av. F.) GHY
Favre (Bd J.) HX 48
La-Fayette (Cours) GHX
La-Fayette (Pont) GX 88
Ferry (Pl. J.) HX 51
Flandin (R. M.) HXY
France (Bd A.) HV 57
Frères-Lumière (Av. des) HZ
Fulchiron (Q.) EY
Gallieni (Pt) FY 65
Gambetta (Cours) GHY
Garibaldi (R.) GVZ
Garillan (Montée du) EFX
Gaulle (Q. Ch.-de) GHU
Gerland (R. de) GZ
Gerlier (R. du Cardinal) EY 69
Gillet (Quai J.) EUV
Giraud (Cours du Gén.) EV
Grande-Bretagne (Av. de) GV
Grenette (R.) FX 71
Guillotière (Grande-R. de la) GYZ
Guillotière (Pt de la) FY 73
Hénon (R.) EFV
Herbouville (Cours d') FV 75
Jean-Jaurès (Av.) GY
Joffre (Quai du Mar.) EY 82
Juin (Pont Alphonse) FX 84
Jutard (Pl. A.) GY
Kitchener Marchand (Pt) EY 85
Koening (Pt Gén.) EV 86
Lassagne (Quai A.) FV 93
Lassalle (R. Ph. de) EUV
Lattre-de-Tassigny (Pt de) FV 94
Leclerc (Av.) EFZ
Leclerc (Pl. du Gén.) GV
Liberté (Cours de la) GXY
Lortet (R.) FZ
Lyautey (Pl. du Mar.) GVX
Marius-Vivier-Merle (Bd) HY 101
Marseille (R. de) GY
Montrochet (R. P.) EZ 105
Morand (Pont) FVX 107
Moulin (Quai J.) FX 109
Nadaud (R. G.) FZ
La Part Dieu HXY
Perrache (Quai) EZ
Pompidou (Av. G.) HY
Pradel (Pl. L.) FX 123
Pré Gaudry (R.) FZ 125
Prés.-Édouard-Herriot (R. du) FX 127
Radisson (R. Roger) EY
Rambaud (Quai) EYZ
Repos (R. du) GZ 131
République (R. de la) FXY 136
Rolland (Quai Romain) FX 140
Roosevelt (Cours F.) GVX
St-Antoine (Q.) FX 147
St-Barthélémy (Montée) EX 149
St-Jean (R.) FX
St-Vincent (Quai) EFX
Sarrail (Quai du Gén.) GX 157
Saxe (Av. du Mar. de) GXY
Scize (Quai P.) EX
Sédallian (Quai P.) EU
Serbie (Quai de) GV
Servient (R.) GY
Stalingrad (Pl. de) GHY
Suchet (Cours) EFZ
Sully (R.) GV
Tchécoslovaques (Bd des) HZ
Terme (R.) FV 166
Terreaux (Pl. des) FX
Tête d'Or (R. de la) GVX
Thiers (Av.) HVX
Tilsitt (Q.) FY
Trion (Pl. de) EY
Trion (R. de) EY
Université (Pont de l') FY 171
Université (R. de l') GY 172
Vauban (R.) GHX
Verguin (Av.) HV
Viabert (R. de la) HX
Victor-Hugo (R.) FY 176
Vienne (Rte de) GZ
Villette (R. de la) HY 178
Villon (R.) HZ
Vitton (Cours) HV
Vivier (R. du) GZ 180
Wilson (Pont) FY 182

VILLEURBANNE

11 Novembre 1918 (Bd du) HV
Bataille de Stalingrad (Bd de la) HUV
Bonnevay (Bd L.) HU
Charmettes (R. des) HVX
Dutriévoz (Av. A.) HV 39
Galline (Av.) HV
Péri (R. G.) HV
Philip (Cours A.) HV
Poincaré (Pt R.) HU
Rossellini (Av. R.) HV 144
Tonkin (R. du) HV
Zola (Cours Émile) HV

Sofitel Royal without rest, 20 pl. Bellecour ✉ 69002 ✆ 04 78 37 57 31, *h2952@accor-hotels.com, Fax 04 78 37 01 36* – AE GB JCB FY g
20 – **80 rm** 160/260.
• 19C building facing the most famous square in Lyon. Little "Clipper" rooms featuring brass and mahogany, larger rooms either functional or in Louis XV style.

Carlton without rest, 4 r. Jussieu ✉ 69002 ✆ 04 78 42 56 51, *h2950@accor-hotels.com, Fax 04 78 42 10 71* – AE GB JCB FX b
12,50 – **83 rm** 135/155.
• Purple and gold are a feature of this traditional hotel styled like a retro town mansion. The venerable lift cage has a certain charm too.

Mercure Plaza République without rest, 5 r. Stella ✉ 69002 ✆ 04 78 37 50 50, *h2951-gm@accor-hotels.com, Fax 04 78 42 33 34* – 20 - 35. AE GB JCB FY k
12 – **78 rm** 100/150.
• A grotesque face sits atop each window of this 19C building whose external appearance is in surprising contrast to the resolutely contemporary interior.

Globe et Cécil without rest, 21 r. Gasparin ✉ 69002 ☏ 04 78 42 58 95, *globe.et.cecil@wanadoo.fr, Fax 04 72 41 99 06* – |‡| ▤ TV ☏ – 🧑‍🏫 25. AE ⓓ GB JCB FY b
60 rm ☕ 118/145.
◆ The old 19C walls of this building conceal an establishment of great character. Individual rooms, furniture cadged from antique dealers and a panelled breakfast room.

Beaux-Arts without rest, 75 r. Prés. E. Herriot ✉ 69002 ☏ 04 78 38 09 50, *h2949@accor-hotels.com, Fax 04 78 42 19 19* – |‡| ⇹ ▤ TV ☏ – 🧑‍🏫 15. AE ⓓ GB JCB
☕ 12 – **75 rm** 135/143. FX t
◆ Fine building of 1900 with rooms mostly furnished in Art Deco style, though four of them have been decorated by contemporary artists.

Grand Hôtel des Terreaux without rest, 16 r. Lanterne ✉ 69001 ☏ 04 78 27 04 10, *ght@hotel-lyon.fr, Fax 04 78 27 97 75*, 🏊 – |‡| TV ☏. AE ⓓ GB FX u
☕ 9 – **53 rm** 72,50/115.
◆ A dignified façade gives little hint of the recently refurbished interior, with its colourful fabrics and furniture in various styles. Covered pool for relaxation.

La Résidence without rest, 18 r. V. Hugo ✉ 69002 ☏ 04 78 42 63 28, *hotel-la-residence@wanadoo.fr, Fax 04 78 42 85 76* – |‡| ▤ TV ☏. AE ⓓ GB JCB FY s
☕ 6,50 **67** rm 70.
◆ Establishment located in a traffic-free street close to Place Bellecour. Foyer and rooms in 1970s style, brighter, fresher decor in those recently refurbished.

Perrache :

Grand Hôtel Mercure Château Perrache, 12 cours Verdun ✉ 69002 ☏ 04 72 77 15 00, *h1292@accor-hotels.com, Fax 04 78 37 06 56* – |‡| ⇹ ▤ TV ☏ 🚗 P – 🧑‍🏫 20 - 200. AE ⓓ GB JCB EY a
Les Belles Saisons *(closed Saturday lunch)* **Meals** 30 🍷 – ☕ 14 – **111 rm** 97/187.
◆ The old PLM railway hotel has kept some of its Art Nouveau features, including the panelling in the foyer. Some rooms with original furnishings. The "Marjorelle" style really takes off in the superb Belles Saisons restaurant.

Charlemagne, 23 cours Charlemagne ✉ 69002 ☏ 04 72 77 70 00, *charlemagne@hotel-lyon.fr, Fax 04 78 42 94 84*, 🌳 – |‡| ▤ TV ☏ 🚗 P – 🧑‍🏫 15 - 120. AE ⓓ GB
Meals *(closed 1 to 22 August, 23 December-2 January, Friday dinner, Saturday and Sunday)* 19 – ☕ 9 – **116 rm** 90/110. EZ t
◆ Two buildings separated by a courtyard. The rooms in the second building are more spacious and attractive. Breakfast room in the style of a winter garden. Modern décor in the restaurant, plus a pleasant terrace and traditional, unpretentious cuisine.

Vieux-Lyon :

Villa Florentine 🐦, 25 montée St-Barthélémy ✉ 69005 ☏ 04 72 56 56 56, *florentine@relaischateaux.com, Fax 04 72 40 90 56*, ⩽ Lyon, 🏋, 🏊, 🌳 – |‡| ▤ TV ☏ ♿ 🚗 P – 🧑‍🏫 15. AE ⓓ GB JCB EFX s
see ***Les Terrasses de Lyon*** below – ☕ 30 – **20 rm** 190/350, 8 suites.
◆ This old hilltop convent with its Renaissance appearance is more than a match for the most sumptuous Tuscan villa.

Cour des Loges 🐦, 6 r. Boeuf ✉ 69005 ☏ 04 72 77 44 44, *contact@courdesloges.com, Fax 04 72 40 93 61*, 🌳, 🏋 – |‡| ▤ TV ☏ 🚗 – 🧑‍🏫 15 - 50. AE ⓓ GB JCB
Les Loges : **Meals** (lunch) 35 b.i. and a la carte dinner 🍷 – ☕ 22 – **52 rm** 230/590, 4 suites. FX n
◆ Contemporary artists and designers have created the striking decor of this group of 15C and 17C buildings laid out around a superb galleried courtyard. Inventive, personalised cuisine in the Aux Loges restaurant.

Tour Rose 🐦, 22 r. Boeuf ✉ 69005 ☏ 04 78 92 69 10, *contact@latour-rose.com, Fax 04 78 42 26 02* – |‡| ▤ TV ☏ 🚗 – 🧑‍🏫 25. AE ⓓ GB JCB EFX e
Meals *(closed lunch in August and Sunday)* 53/106 – ☕ 18 – **11 rm** 250/290, 8 suites.
◆ A group of houses typical of Old Lyon, with stair tower and terraced gardens. Wonderful rooms decorated by the city's foremost silk specialists. Lovely glass roof at the foot of the pink tower and a luxurious dining room offering creative and spicy cuisine.

Phénix Hôtel without rest, 7 quai Bondy ✉ 69005 ☏ 04 78 28 24 24, *reception@hotel-le-phenix.fr, Fax 04 78 28 62 86* – |‡| ▤ TV ☏ ♿ 🚗 – 🧑‍🏫 30. AE ⓓ GB JCB
☕ 11,50 – **36 rm** 120/162. FX k
◆ Venerable edifice on the banks of the Saône. Spacious rooms with contemporary décor, some with open fireplace. Attractive breakfast room beneath a glass roof.

Collège without rest, 5 pl. St Paul ✉ 69005 ☏ 04 72 10 05 05, *contact@college-hotel.com, Fax 04 78 27 98 84* – |‡| ⇹ ▤ TV ☏ ♿ 🚗 – 🧑‍🏫 20. AE GB JCB
☕ 11 – **39 rm** 105/135.
◆ The Collège Hôtel is a quite extraordinary concept, with its school desks, pommel horse and geographical maps recreating the feel of schooling in bygone days.

La Croix-Rousse (bank of the River Saône) :

Lyon Métropole, 85 quai J. Gillet ✉ 69004 ☎ 04 72 10 44 44, *metropole@lyonmetropole_concorde.com, Fax 04 72 10 44 42,* – P – 15 - 300. AE GB JCB EU k
Brasserie Lyon Plage ☎ 04 72 10 44 30 **Meals** 24 – 23 – **116 rm** 130/250.
• This 1980s establishment reflected in the water of the Olympic pool has excellent sports facilities, including a huge spa, gym, tennis courts and squash courts. Refurbished rooms. Lyon Plage Brasserie with maritime decor and a terrace overlooking the water.

Les Brotteaux :

Hilton, 70 quai Ch. de Gaulle ✉ 69006 ☎ 04 78 17 50 50, *rm-lyon@hilton.com, Fax 04 78 17 52 52,* – – 15 - 400. AE GB JCB GU a
Blue Elephant ☎ 04 78 17 50 00 *(closed 20 July-20 August, Saturday lunch and Sunday)* **Meals** 28(lunch), 42/57 – ***Brasserie*** ☎ 04 78 17 51 00 **Meals** 17/39 – 24 – **186 rm** 235/315, 5 suites.
• The Cité International includes this hotel as well as convention centre, casino, and modern art museum. Spacious rooms facing the Parc de la Tête d'Or or the Rhône. Thai specialities in the Blue Elephant, with more traditional cuisine in the Brasserie.

La Part-Dieu :

Radisson SAS, 129 r. Servient (32nd floor) ✉ 69003 ☎ 04 78 63 55 00, *info.lyon@radissonsas.com, Fax 04 78 63 55 20,* ← Lyons and Rhône Valley – – 15 - 110. AE GB JCB GX u
L'Arc-en-Ciel *(closed 15 July-25 August, Saturday lunch and Sunday)* **Meals** 38/55 b.i. – ***Bistrot de la Tour*** (ground floor) *(closed Friday dinner, Sunday lunch and Saturday)* **Meals** 18,50 – 18 – **245 rm** 220/270.
• Interior inspired by the traditional architecture of Lyon. Internal courtyard, galleries and ground-floor bistro. Panoramic views from the Arc-en-Ciel on the 32nd floor and the top of the tall 100m/330ft tower known as "The Pencil".

Novotel La Part-Dieu, 47 bd Vivier-Merle ✉ 69003 ☎ 04 72 13 51 51, *h0735@accor-hotels.com, Fax 04 72 13 51 99* – – 15 - 70. AE GB JCB HX a
Meals 19 – 12 – **124 rm** 134/147.
• Vast lounge/bar with internet facilities. Rooms are up to the Novotel group's current standards. Useful accommodation close to the station. The restaurant is popular with business people in between meetings or while awaiting a train.

Créqui Part-Dieu, 37 r. Bonnel ✉ 69003 ☎ 04 78 60 20 47, *inforesa@hotel-crequi.com, Fax 04 78 62 21 12* – – 30. AE GB GX s
Meals *(closed 1 to 21 August, Saturday and Sunday)* 17 – 11 – **46 rm** 125/140, 3 suites.
• This establishment is located opposite the law courts. Room decor inspired by the fabrics and colours of Provence, though a new wing is in a more contemporary style.

La Guillotière :

Libertel Wilson without rest, 6 r. Mazenod ✉ 69003 ☎ 04 78 60 94 94, *h2780@accor-hotels.com, Fax 04 78 62 72 01* – . AE GB JCB GY a
12 – **54 rm** 114/135.
• Contemporary furnishings in Art Deco style and the bright fabrics to be expected in the capital of silk give the rooms of this recent riverside hotel their special character.

Gerland :

Novotel Gerland, 70 av. Leclerc ✉ 69007 ☎ 04 72 71 11 11, *h0736@accor-hotels.com, Fax 04 72 71 11 00,* – – 90 - 150. AE GB
Meals 23/32 – 12 – **187 rm** 138/148.
• Modern building close to the Halle Tony-Garnier and the football stadium. Recently refurbished interior to current Novotel standards. The restaurant menu is in keeping with the chain's typical culinary format.

Montchat-Monplaisir :

Mercure Lumière, 69 cours A. Thomas ☎ 04 78 53 76 76, *h1535@accor-hotels.com, Fax 04 72 36 97 65* – – 25 - 50. AE GB JCB HZ e
Meals *(closed Sunday lunch, Saturday and Bank Holidays)* 25 – 12 – **78 rm** 118/127.
• This hotel built where the Lumière brothers' invented cinematography more than 100 years ago celebrates their achievement with a contemporary-style restaurant adorned with images from the silver screen.

at Bron – *pop. 37 369 alt. 204* – ✉ *69500* :

Novotel Bron, 260 av. J. Monnet ✆ 04 72 15 65 65, *h0436@accor-hotels.com, Fax 04 72 15 09 09*, – 15 - 500. AE GB
Meals a la carte 24/32 – 12 – **190 rm** 119/138.
◆ Between the A 43 motorway and the N 6 main road, a useful place to break your journey. Reasonably spacious rooms, good facilities for meetings, garden, pool. Restaurant up to the usual Novotel standard, conveniently located just outside Lyon.

Restaurants

XXXXX ✿✿✿ **Paul Bocuse,** bridge of Collonges N : 12 km by the banks of River Saône (D 433, D 51) ✉ 69660 *Collonges-au-Mont-d'Or* ✆ 04 72 42 90 90, *paul.bocuse@bocuse.fr, Fax 04 72 27 85 87* – AE GB JCB
Meals 110/190 and a la carte 92/122
Spec. Soupe aux truffes noires. Loup en croûte feuilletée. Volaille de Bresse en vessie..
Wines Pouilly-Fuissé, Moulin-à-Vent.
◆ Anyone who is anyone patronises the palatial inn of "Monsieur Paul", one of the greatest of epicureans. Historic dishes plus a wall-painting of "great chefs" in the courtyard.

XXXX ✿✿ **Léon de Lyon** (Lacombe), 1 r. Pleney ✉ 69001 ✆ 04 72 10 11 12, *leon@relaischateaux.com, Fax 04 72 10 11 13* – AE GB JCB FX r
closed 1 to 9 May, 31 July-22 August, Sunday and Monday – **Meals** 65 (lunch), 110/150 and a la carte 93/116
Spec. Cochon fermier du Cantal, foie gras et oignons confits. Quenelles de brochet, queues d'écrevisses, sauce nantua. Cinq petits desserts sur le thème de la praline de Saint-Genix..
Wines Saint-Véran, Chiroubles.
◆ The great traditions of the cuisine of Lyon live on in the dining rooms of this establishment with its wood panelling and its pictures celebrating kitchen culture. Terrific !

XXXX ✿ **Pierre Orsi,** 3 pl. Kléber ✉ 69006 ✆ 04 78 89 57 68, *orsi@relaischateaux.com, Fax 04 72 44 93 34*, – AE GB JCB GV e
closed Sunday and Monday except Bank Holidays – **Meals** 45 (lunch), 80/110 and a la carte 68/120
Spec. Ravioles de foie gras de canard au jus de porto et truffes. Homard en carapace. Pigeonneau en cocotte aux gousses d'ail confites.. **Wines** Meursault, Côte-Rôtie..
◆ This old building houses an elegant dining room and a terrace-cum-rose garden where fine Lyon cuisine is served. Splendid 200-year-old vaulted cellar.

XXX ✿ **Les Terrasses de Lyon** Hôtel Villa Florentine, 25 montée St-Barthélémy ✉ 69005 ✆ 04 72 56 56 56, *Fax 04 72 40 90 56*, ← Lyon, – (dinner) AE GB JCB EFX s
Meals 33 (lunch), 53 (dinner)/115 and a la carte 85/180
Spec. Foie gras frais de canard et ris de veau de Dordogne braisé, fine gelée au cidre. Homard rôti en cocotte, boulangère de pomme charlotte et tartare d'algues iodées. Onglet de boeuf de Salers, queue en parmentière et pommes soufflées. **Wines** Côtes du Vivarais, Saint-Joseph.
◆ A vaulted former convent refectory and glass-enclosed terrace provide the elegant backdrop for imaginative contemporary cuisine (reduced menu at lunchtime, except Sunday).

XXX ✿ **Christian Têtedoie,** 54 quai Pierre Scize ✉ 69005 ✆ 04 78 29 40 10, *restaurant@tetedoie.com, Fax 04 72 07 05 65* – AE GB EX n
closed 31 July-21 August, 26 February-5 March, Saturday lunch and Sunday – **Meals** 40/75 and a la carte 58/77
Spec. Parfait glacé de foie gras de canard. Saint Jacques rôties aux arômes de cacao et réglisse (October-March). Girolles confites aux coings, sorbet balsamique.. **Wines** Pouilly Fuissé, Crozes Hermitage..
◆ Behind the dignified façade an interior delicately decorated in a range of yellows. Some tables with a view of the River Saône. Contemporary cuisine. Cellar and wine sales.

XXX ✿ **Les Trois Dômes** Hôtel Sofitel, 20 quai Gailleton (at 8th floor) ✉ 69002 ✆ 04 72 41 20 97, *h0553@accor-hotels.com, Fax 04 72 40 05 50*, ← Lyon – AE GB JCB – *closed 24 July-22 August, Sunday and Monday* – **Meals** 51 (lunch), 71/114 b.i. and a la carte 75/110 FY p
Spec. Quenelle de brochet soufflée, écrevisses. Suprêmes de pigeon rôtis aux mangues. Trois grands crus de chocolat..
◆ Perched on the top floor of the Sofitel, the Trois Dômes offers its guests panoramic views and delicious, regionally influenced cuisine.

XXX ✿ **L'Auberge de Fond Rose** (Vignat), 23 quai G. Clemenceau ✉ 69300 *Caluire-et-Cuire* ✆ 04 78 29 34 61, *contact@aubergedefondrose.com, Fax 04 72 00 28 67*, – AE GB – *closed All Saints'Day Holidays, February Holidays, Sunday dinner and Monday* – **Meals** 59 and a la carte 76/91 EU v
Spec. Tataki de bonite aux pommes de terre et fenouil. Dos de sandre meunière. Selle d'agneau farcie.. **Wines** Condrieu, Saint-Joseph.
◆ 1920s residence nestling in a lovely well-shaded garden. Refurbished dining room with open fireplace and an attractive terrace. Fine classic cuisine.

XXX **Le St-Alban,** 2 quai J. Moulin ✉ 69001 ✆ 04 78 30 14 89, *Fax 04 72 00 88 82* – ▤. AE GB
closed 23 July-22 August, 1 to 6 January, Saturday lunch, Sunday and Bank Holidays – **Meals** 37/65 and a la carte 49/66 ♀. FX v
◆ Designs in silk showing the sights of Lyon enliven the smart interior of this vaulted dining room close to the Opera. Classic cuisine brought up to date.

XXX **La Mère Brazier,** 12 r. Royale ✉ 69001 ✆ 04 78 28 15 49, *info@lamerebrazier.com, Fax 04 78 28 63 63* – ▤. AE ⓓ GB FV e
closed 25 July-25 August, Monday out of season, Saturday except dinner in Winter and Sunday except lunch in Winter – **Meals** 46/55 and a la carte 50/75 ♀.
◆ This restaurant is a stronghold of Lyon culinary tradition, honouring the memory of the legendary Mère Brazier. A menu set in stone for all time.

XX ✿✿ **Auberge de l'Ile** (Ansanay-Alex), sur l'Ile Barbe ✉ 69009 ✆ 04 78 83 99 49, *info@aubergedelile.com, Fax 04 78 47 80 46* – ⟺ P. AE ⓓ GB JCB
closed 31 July-23 August, Sunday and Monday – **Meals** 75/120
Spec. Velouté de champignons comme un cappuccino, lardons de foie gras vapeur (Autumn). Mignon d'agneau de lait en croûte de sel (Spring). Crème glacée à la réglisse, cornet de pain d'épice.. **Wines** Condrieu, Côte-Rôtie..
◆ This 17C establishment tucked away on an island in the River Saône has a characterful interior (non-smoking) and offers a subtle version of contemporary cuisine.

XX ✿ **L'Alexandrin** (Alexanian), 83 r. Moncey ✉ 69003 ✆ 04 72 61 15 69, *Fax 04 78 62 75 57,* 🏠 – ▤. AE GB GX h
closed 1 to 9 May, 31 July-22 August, 24 December-3 January, Sunday, Monday and Bank Holidays – **Meals** 38 (lunch), 60/75 and a la carte 60/82
Spec. Fritots de carpe royale de la Dombes. Omble chevalier rôti aux épices indiennes (Spring-Summer). Aubergine confite à l'épaule d'agneau.. **Wines** Saint-Péray, Crozes-Hermitage..
◆ Contemporary decor, smiling service, good choice of Côtes-du-Rhône wines and innovative local cuisine, this establishment attracts the city's smart set.

XX ✿ **Nicolas Le Bec,** 14 r. Grolée ✉ 69002 ✆ 04 78 42 15 00, *restaurant@nicolaslebec.com, Fax 04 72 40 98 97* – ▤ ♿. AE ⓓ GB FX y
closed 1 to 20 August, 1 to 7 January, Sunday, Monday and Bank Holidays – **Meals** 45 (lunch), 85/105 and a la carte 70/110 ♀
Spec. Foie gras rôti aux fruits de saison. Bar à la vapeur d'eucalyptus et petits artichauts. Canetons de Challans cuits sur l'os, cébette au jus de gentiane (March-June).. **Wines** Condrieu.
◆ For lovers of all things Lyonnaise ! Smart, distinctly modern setting in beige and chocolate, subtly inventive cooking and a wine list which shows its true French colours.

XX **Le Passage,** 8 r. Plâtre ✉ 69001 ✆ 04 78 28 11 16, *restaurant@le-passage.com, Fax 04 72 00 84 34* – ▤. AE ⓓ GB JCB FX r
closed 8 to 23 August, Sunday, Monday and Bank Holidays – **Meals** 29/38 ♀.
◆ The bistro with cinema seating and a trompe l'oeil theatre curtain, the main dining room with club-type seats and luxurious decor - two seductive alternatives.

XX **Fleur de Sel,** 3 r. Remparts d'Ainay ✉ 69002 ✆ 04 78 37 40 37, *Fax 04 78 37 26 37* – GB FY q
closed August, Sunday and Monday – **Meals** 29, 33/48 ♀.
◆ Green and yellow net curtains filter the light entering this vast dining room. Well-spaced tables and modern seats. Individual cuisine inspired by Provençal cooking.

XX **Jardin des Saveurs,** 95 cours Docteur Long ✉ 69003 *Montchat-Monplaisir* ✆ 04 78 53 27 05, *Fax 04 72 34 67 48* – ▤. AE GB CQ a
closed 1 to 21 August and Sunday – **Meals** 29/55
◆ A former bar transformed into a hugely popular restaurant. Its success is based on its well-prepared dishes, an astute wine list, attentive service and sensible prices.

XX ✿ **Gourmet de Sèze** (Mariller), 129 r. Sèze ✉ 69006 ✆ 04 78 24 23 42, *legourmetdeseze@wanadoo.fr, Fax 04 78 24 66 81* – ▤. AE GB HV z
closed 1 to 9 May, 23 July-23 August, 20 to 26 February, Sunday, Monday and Bank Holidays – **Meals** (booking essential) 33/64 ♀
Spec. Croustillants de pieds de cochon. Coquilles Saint-Jacques d'Erquy (October-March). Grand dessert du gourmet.. **Wines** Pinot noir du Bugey, Saint-Joseph.
◆ Delightful little restaurant serving classic cuisine brought cleverly up to date. The gourmets of the Rue de Sèze are not alone in being seduced.

XX ✿ **Mathieu Viannay,** 47 av. Foch ✉ 69006 ✆ 04 78 89 55 19, *Fax 04 78 89 08 39* – ▤. AE GB GV s
closed 2 to 23 August, 24 December-2 January, Saturday and Sunday – **Meals** 28 (lunch)/55 ♀
Spec. Pâté de volaille de Bresse et foie gras. Ris de veau en croûte de truffes. Gros macaron au café..
◆ Resolutely contemporary restaurant with parquet floor, coloured seats, and unusual lighting by local designer Alain Vavro - all in harmony with the modern cuisine on offer.

XX **Maison Borie,** 3 pl. Antonin Perrin ✉ 69007 *Gerland* ✆ 04 72 76 20 20, *Fax 04 37 37 10 00,* – ▤ P. GB BQ d
closed 23 December-2 January and Sunday – **Meals** 28 (lunch), 48/75 ♀.
♦ Unusual contemporary decor, a trendy atmosphere and inventive cuisine are the main attractions inside this 19C house. More substantial dinner menu. Non-smoking dining rooms.

XX **La Tassée,** 20 r. Charité ✉ 69002 ✆ 04 72 77 79 00, *jpborgeot@latassee.fr, Fax 04 72 40 05 91* – ▤. AE GB FY u
closed Sunday – **Meals** 24 (lunch), 26/48 ♀.
♦ Painted in the 1950s, the medieval-style Bacchanalian fresco lends special character to the bistro close to the Place Bellecour. Classic cuisine and local Lyon specialities.

XX **Vivarais,** 1 pl. Gailleton ✉ 69002 ✆ 04 78 37 85 15, *Fax 04 78 37 59 49* – ▤. AE ⓓ GB JCB FY f
closed 24 July-22 August and Sunday – **Meals** 20 (lunch), 26/34 ♀.
♦ Wood panelling, old pictures... a fine setting in which to enjoy contemporary cuisine accompanied by a number of those tasty special delicacies from Lyon.

XX **La Voûte - Chez Léa,** 11 pl. A. Gourju ✉ 69002 ✆ 04 78 42 01 33, *Fax 04 78 37 36 41* – ▤. AE GB FY e
closed Sunday – **Meals** 27/38 ♀.
♦ The unchanging menu goes back to the time not so long ago when gastronomic life in Lyon was dominated by the famous "Mères". Retro decor downstairs, more refined upstairs.

X **Le Nord,** 18 r. Neuve ✉ 69002 ✆ 04 72 10 69 69, *Fax 04 72 10 69 68,* – ▤. AE ⓓ GB JCB FX p
closed 18 July-28 August – **Meals** 21/26 ♀.
♦ With its burgundy-coloured benches, mosaic floor, panelling and globe lighting, this establishment has all the atmosphere of a turn-of-the-century brasserie.

X **L'Est,** Gare des Brotteaux, 14 pl. J. Ferry ✉ 69006 ✆ 04 37 24 25 26, *Fax 04 37 24 25 25,* – ▤. AE ⓓ GB JCB HX v
Meals 21/26 ♀.
♦ Old station converted into a trendy brasserie, featuring electric trains and cuisine from around the world ; all aboard, globe-trotting gourmets !

X **L'Ouest,** 1 quai Commerce North along the banks of the Saône (D51) ✉ 69009 ✆ 04 37 64 64 64, *Fax 04 37 64 64 65,* – |‡| ▤. AE ⓓ GB JCB
Meals 21/26 ♀.
♦ Stunning modern brasserie combining wood, concrete and metal. Bar, giant screens, designer decor and a kitchen visible to all. A new addition to the Bocuse empire.

X **Le Sud,** 11 pl. Antonin Poncet ✉ 69002 ✆ 04 72 77 80 00, *Fax 04 72 77 80 01,* – ▤. AE ⓓ GB JCB FY d
Meals 21/26 ♀.
♦ One of Paul Bocuse's three establishments in Lyon, this brasserie brings the Mediterranean to town, with bright yellow décor and sun-kissed cuisine.

X **Francotte,** 8 pl. Célestins ✉ 69002 ✆ 04 78 37 38 64, *infos@francotte.fr, Fax 04 78 38 20 35* – ▤. AE GB FY r
closed Sunday, Monday and Bank Holidays – **Meals** 19/27 ♀.
♦ The ambience in this restaurant by the Célestins Theatre is part-traditional bouchon, part-bistro. Breakfast, afternoon tea and brasserie-style cuisine are served here.

X **La Machonnerie,** 36 r. Tramassac ✉ 69005 ✆ 04 78 42 24 62, *felix@lamachonnerie.com, Fax 04 72 40 23 32* – ▤. AE ⓓ GB EY n
closed Sunday and lunch except Saturday – **Meals** (booking essential) 18/40 b.i. ♀.
♦ Homely Lyon traditions are much in evidence in this restaurant, with its unpretentious service, convivial ambience and authentic cuisine.

X **La Terrasse St-Clair,** 2 Grande r. St-Clair ✉ 69300 *Caluire-et-Cuire* ✆ 04 72 27 37 37, *leon@relaischateaux.com, Fax 04 72 27 37 38,* – AE GB GU s
closed 1 to 17 January, 14 to 22 August, Monday dinner and Sunday – **Meals** 22,50 ♀.
♦ This restaurant has tried to replicate the atmosphere of one of those old-fashioned, informal French cafés with a dance floor. Pleasant terrace shaded by plane trees.

X **Le Théodore,** 34 cours Franklin Roosevelt ✉ 69006 ✆ 04 78 24 08 52, *Fax 04 72 74 41 21,* – ▤. AE ⓓ GB JCB GVX v
closed 7 to 21 August, Sunday and Bank Holidays – **Meals** 18,50 (lunch), 20,50/42,50.
♦ Behind the modest painted façade is an establishment with a seductive bistro-type atmosphere and Belle Epoque décor. Attractive summer terrace. Traditional cuisine.

X **Les Muses de l'Opéra,** pl. Comédie, 7th floor of the Opera ✉ 69001 ✆ 04 72 00 45 58, *Fax 04 78 29 34 01,* < Fourvière, – |‡| ▤. AE GB FX q
Meals 24/29.
♦ Designed by Jean Nouvel, a determinedly contemporary panoramic restaurant atop the Opera. View of the backs of the statues of the eight Muses on the cornice.

L'Étage, 4 pl. Terreaux (2nd floor) ✉ 69001 ✆ 04 78 28 19 59, *Fax 04 78 28 19 59* – ▤. GB FX x
closed 23 July-23 August, Sunday and Monday – **Meals** (booking essential) 18/51 ♀.
◆ This old silk workshop on the 2nd floor of a building without a lift is now a rather unusual, very contemporary place to dine, much in favour among local people.

Tablier de Sapeur, 16 r. Madeleine ✉ 69007 ✆ 04 78 72 22 40, *Fax 04 78 72 22 40* – ▤. AE ⓓ GB GY k
closed August, 25 December-2 January, Monday from October to June, Saturday from June to September and Sunday – **Meals** 20/40 ♀.
◆ Bright and welcoming family-run establishment offering refined traditional cuisine including local specialities like "tablier de sapeur" tripe plus a selection of open wines.

Daniel et Denise, 156 r. Créqui ✉ 69003 ✆ 04 78 60 66 53, *Fax 04 78 60 66 53* – ▤. AE GB GX s
closed August, Saturday, Sunday and Bank Holidays – **Meals** a la carte 27/46.
◆ In the setting of an old charcuterie, this rustic-style restaurant serves abundant, regional dishes. Old posters, photos and check tablecloths add to the ambience.

BOUCHONS : *Regional specialities and wine tasting in a Lyonnaise atmosphere*

Garet, 7 r. Garet ✉ 69001 ✆ 04 78 28 16 94, *legaret@wanadoo.fr, Fax 04 72 00 06 84* – ▤. AE GB – *closed 24 July-22 August, 24 December-2 January, Saturday and Sunday* – **Meals** (booking essential) 17 (lunch)/21 ♀. FX a
◆ Shirt-sleeves, dungarees, business suits, all mingle here to savour traditional local delicacies prepared without regard to faddy ideas of what constitutes a healthy diet.

Chez Hugon, 12 rue Pizay ✉ 69001 ✆ 04 78 28 10 94, *Fax 04 78 28 10 94* – AE GB
closed August, Saturday and Sunday – **Meals** (booking essential) 22/32 ♀. FX m
◆ In full view of her faithful customers, the lady chef watches her pots in a convivial atmosphere calculated to warm the cockles of any diner's heart.

Au Petit Bouchon "Chez Georges", 8 r. Garet ✉ 69001 ✆ 04 78 28 30 46 – GB
closed August, Saturday and Sunday – **Meals** 16/21 and dinner a la carte. FX a
◆ Eaten without ceremony, the specialities of this unpretentious establishment include tripe "tablier de sapeur", soufflé of quenelle, all washed down with jugs of Beaujolais.

Café des Fédérations, 8 r. Major Martin ✉ 69001 ✆ 04 78 28 26 00, *yr@lesfedeslyon.com, Fax 04 72 07 74 52* – ▤. GB JCB FX z
closed 23 July-21 August, Saturday and Sunday – **Meals** (booking essential) 20 (lunch)/23,50.
◆ Gingham tablecloths, diners cheek-by-jowl, giant sausages hanging from the ceiling, copious local cuisine - a real treat of a place !

Le Jura, 25 r. Tupin ✉ 69002 ✆ 04 78 42 20 57 – GB FX d
closed 21 July-21 August, Monday from September to April, Saturday from May to September and Sunday – **Meals** (booking essential) 19,30.
◆ Don't be put off by the sign, this is an authentic establishment that has kept its 1930s décor intact and provides diners with typical local treats.

Meunière, 11 r. Neuve ✉ 69001 ✆ 04 78 28 62 91, *Fax 04 78 28 62 91* – ▤. GB
closed 14 July-15 August, 25 December-2 January, Sunday, Monday and Bank Holidays – **Meals** (booking essential) 17,50 (lunch), 21/28 ♀. FX p
◆ The décor of this establishment in the Rue Neuve has remained unchanged since the 1920s. The appetising dishes often attract crowds of diners.

Environs

to the NE :

at Rillieux-la-Pape : *7 km by N 83 and N 84 – pop. 28 367 alt. 269 –* ✉ *69140 :*

Larivoire (Constantin), chemin des Iles ✆ 04 78 88 50 92, *bernard.constantin@larivoire.com, Fax 04 78 88 35 22,* – P. AE GB – *closed 16 to 28 August, 24 to 28 February, Tuesday, dinner Sunday and Monday* – **Meals** 32/80 and a la carte 65/90
Spec. Emietté d'araignée et tourteau en gelée de crustacés (Summer). Brochettes d'écrevisses en kadaif (May-September). Canette laquée "poire et miel".. **Wines** Saint-Véran, Chénas.
◆ Pretty pink building housing an attractive modernised restaurant, with antique furnishings. Pleasant shaded terrace. Local cuisine with a contemporary touch.

to the E :

at the Lyon St-Exupéry Airport : *27 km by A 43 –* ✉ *69125 Lyon St-Exupéry Airport :*

Sofitel Lyon Aéroport without rest, 3rd floor ✆ 04 72 23 38 00, *h0913@accor-hotels.com, Fax 04 72 23 98 00* – ▤. AE ⓓ GB JCB
☕ 19 – **120 rm** 204/244.
◆ This chain hotel in the main hall of the airport is the perfect choice for stopover passengers. Functional rooms, some with views of the runway, plus a "tropical" bar.

Le Bouchon, 1st floor in airport station ✆ 04 72 22 71 86, *Lyonaero@elior.com, Fax 04 72 22 71 72* – AE GB JCB – **Meals** 23 ♀.
◆ Styled on the city's typical restaurants (bouchons), the menu in this unpretentious brasserie revolves around local dishes. Fast service to suit its travelling clientele.

to the W :

at Tour-de-Salvagny *11 km by N 7 – pop. 3 402 alt. 356 – ✉ 69890 :*

La Rotonde, at Casino Le Lyon Vert ✆ 04 78 87 00 97, *restaurant-rotonde@g-partouche.fr, Fax 04 78 87 81 39* – AE GB JCB
closed 24 July-25 August, Sunday dinner, Tuesday lunch and Monday – **Meals** 38 (lunch), 78/118 and a la carte 90/106
Spec. Quatre foies pressés, salade de fonds d'artichauts crus et cuits. Tajine de homard entier aux petits farcis. Cannelloni de chocolat amer à la glace de crème brulée.. **Wines** Condrieu, Côte-Rôtie.
◆ Famous gourmet restaurant on the first floor of this celebrated casino established in 1882. The elegant Art Deco interior faces the abundant waters of a splendid fountain.

to the NW :

at Ecully : *7 km by A6 exit nÑ 36 – pop. 18 011 alt. 240 – ✉ 69130 :*

Saisons, Château du Vivier, 8 chem. Trouillat ✆ 04 72 18 02 20, *Fax 04 78 43 33 51* – AE GB AP c
closed 8 to 28 August, 19 December-2 January, Wednesday dinner, Saturday, Sunday and Bank Holidays – **Meals** 24 (lunch), 29/45.
◆ This 19C château, now an international hotel school founded in 1990 by Paul Bocuse, stands in its own park. The cuisine and service are provided by the school's students.

Porte de Lyon *- motorway junction A6-N6 : 10 km – ✉ 69570 Dardilly :*

Novotel Lyon Nord, ✆ 04 72 17 29 29, *h0437@accor-hotels.com, Fax 04 78 35 08 45,* – 25 - 75. AE GB JCB
Meals a la carte approx. 26 ♀ – 11,50 – **107 rm** 106/118.
◆ This 1970s Novotel is in the Dardilly business park. The rooms here have been refurbished and brought up to current Novotel standards. Traditional cuisine in the bistro-style dining room overlooking a landscaped garden.

Annecy *74000 H.-Savoie 328 J5 – pop. 50 348 alt. 448.*

See : *Old Annecy★★ : Descent from the Cross★ in church of St-Maurice, Palais de l'Isle★★, rue Ste-Claire★, bridge over the Thiou ≤★ – Château★ – Jardins de l'Europe★.*
Envir. : *Tour of the lake★★★ 39 km (or 1 hour 30 min by boat).*
18 of the lac d'Annecy at Talloires ✆ 04 50 60 12 89 : 10 km ; 27 of Giez lac d'Annecy ✆ 04 50 44 48 41 ; 9 of Belvédère at St-Martin-Bellevue ✆ 04 50 60 31 78.
of Annecy-Haute Savoie-Mont Blanc ✆ 04 50 27 30 06 by N 508 and D 14 : 4 km.
Tourist Office 1 r. J. Jaurès, Bonlieu ✆ 04 50 45 00 33, Fax 04 50 51 87 20.
Lyons 140.

at Veyrier-du-Lac *E : 5,5 km – pop. 2 063 alt. 504 – ✉ 74290*

La Maison de Marc Veyrat with rm, 13 Vieille rte des Pensières ✆ 04 50 60 24 00, *reservation@marcveyrat.fr, Fax 04 50 60 23 63,* ≤ lake, – AE GB
mid-May-mid-November and closed Tuesday except dinner in July-August, Monday and lunch except weekend – **Meals** 280/360 and a la carte 245/290 ♀ – 60 – **11 rm** 450/670
Spec. Pot de yaourt de foie gras, gelée végétale, myrthe odorante. Bonbons de caviar, chocolat blanc, écume de tussilage. Féra du lac fumée, écorce de sapin, boudin de riz craquant, pinceau de benoîte urbaine. **Wines** Roussette de Marestel, Mondeuse.
◆ This enchanting blue house offers stunning cuisine using Alpine herbs and flowers, superb Savoy-style decor and a splendid terrace overlooking the lake.

Le Bourget-du-Lac *73370 Savoie 333 I4 – pop. 3 945 alt. 240.*

Lyons 103.

Le Bateau Ivre - Hôtel Ombremont (Jacob), to the North, 2 km by N 504 ✆ 04 79 25 00 23, *ombremontbateauivre@wanadoo.fr, Fax 04 79 25 25 77,* ≤ lake and mountains, – AE GB JCB
mid-May-late October and closed Monday except dinner in July-August and lunch Tuesday and Thursday – **Meals** 55 (lunch), 80/150 and a la carte 99/137 ♀
Spec. Ecrevisses, chair d'araignée de mer, miel et vinaigre de Xérès. Lavaret doré, émulsion de fleurs de capucine, mousselinede carottes à l'orange. Ris de veau braisé en cocotte, fenouil, jus aux pamplemousses confits.. **Wines** Chignin, Mondeuse.
◆ Superb panorama of lake and Mont Revard from both the soberly elegant dining room and the attractive terrace. The cuisine of the "Drunken Boat" is far from abstemious.

Chagny *71150 S.-et-L.* 320 I8 *- pop. 5 591 alt. 215.*
Tourist Office 2 pl. des Halles 03 85 87 25 95, Fax 03 85 87 14 44.
Lyons 145.

Lameloise, 36 pl. d'Armes 03 85 87 65 65, *reception@lameloise.fr, Fax 03 85 87 03 57* – AE GB JCB
closed 21 December-26 January, Wednesday, lunch Thursday and Tuesday – **Meals** (booking essential) 90/125 and a la carte 85/128 – 20 – **16 rm** 130/285
Spec. Ravioli d'escargots de Bourgogne dans leur bouillon d'ail doux. Pigeonneau rôti à l'émietté de truffes. Griottines au chocolat noir sur une marmelade d'oranges amères.. **Wines** Rully blanc, Chassagne-Montrachet rouge.
◆ The modest exterior of this old Burgundian house belies its refined interior. Spacious rooms. Rustic elegance, warm welcome, and traditional dishes that have made the dining room (non-smoking) a byword for fine cuisine. Shop.

Megève *74120 H.-Savoie* 328 M5 *- pop. 4 509 alt. 1 113.*
Tourist Office r. Monseigneur Conseil 04 50 21 27 28, Fax 04 50 93 03 09.
Lyons 182.

La Ferme de mon Père (Veyrat) with rm, 367 rte du Crêt 04 50 21 01 01, *reservation@marcveyrat.fr, Fax 04 50 21 43 43* – AE GB
mid-December-mid-April and closed Monday except hotel and lunch except weekend – **Meals** 280/360 and a la carte 240/285 – 60 – **7 rm** 610/915
Spec. Crozets d'alpage sans féculent, bouillon de mer, crocus du Mont-Charvin. Saint-Jacques sautées, jus d'eucalyptus, nougatine de sésame, gâteau de coing. Poitrine de canette, jus de cacahuètes grillées, consommé d'abats de volaille au goût de terre. **Wines** Chignin-Bergeron, Apremont.
◆ A mountain farmstead featuring fine food flavoured with Alpine herbs and prepared by a chef ultra-conscious of the culinary heritage of Savoy. Superb rooms.

Mionnay *01390 Ain* 328 C5 *- pop. 2 109 alt. 276.*
Lyons 23.

Alain Chapel with rm, 04 78 91 82 02, *chapel@relaischateaux.com, Fax 04 78 91 82 37,* – AE GB JCB
closed 15 to 22 August, January, Friday lunch, Monday and Tuesday – **Meals** 60 (lunch), 103/140 and a la carte 110/155 – 17 – **12 rm** 110/130
Spec. Marinade froide de rougets et gelée de poissons de roche. Langoustines en gaufrettes de pommes de terre et charolais frais (Summer). Poulette de Bresse en vessie, sauce foie gras.. **Wines** Saint-Véran, Condrieu.
◆ Delicious traditional cuisine served in the charming, refined dining rooms of this elegant hostelry in the Dombes. Attractive rooms and carefully tended garden.

Roanne *42300 Loire* 327 D3 *- pop. 38 896 alt. 265.*
9 of Roannais at Villerest 04 77 69 70 60.
Roanne-Renaison 04 77 66 83 55 by D 9.
Tourist Office 1 Crs République 04 77 71 51 77, Fax 04 77 71 07 11.
Lyons 87.

Troisgros, pl. Gare 04 77 71 66 97, *info@troisgros.com, Fax 04 77 70 39 77,* – AE GB JCB
closed 2 to 17 August, 14 February-3 March, Monday lunch from November-February, Tuesday and Wednesday – **Meals** (booking essential) 140/175 and a la carte 150/173 – 24 – **12 rm** 165/300, 5 duplex
Spec. Panna fritta à la truffe. Aigre-doux de sardines marinées à la cannelle. Tarte au sucre et au beurre demi-sel, glace érable, pomme granny.. **Wines** Pouilly-Fuissé, Côte Rôtie.
◆ Charming bedrooms, a specialist gourmet library and collections of modern canvases are the hallmarks of this resolutely 21C station hotel. The holder of three stars since 1968, the Troisgros serves traditional cuisine with a modern twist. Excellent wine list.

St-Bonnet-le-Froid *43290 H.-Loire* 331 I3 *- pop. 194 alt. 1 126.*
Lyons 101.

Le Clos des Cimes (Marcon) , 04 71 59 93 72, *contact@regismarcon.fr, Fax 04 71 59 93 40,* <, – rest, AE GB
19 March-18 December and closed Monday dinner except from 13 June-3 November, Tuesday and Wednesday – ***Régis Marcon*** (due to move 350 m. in Spring) **Meals** 95/150 and a la carte 100/125 – ***Bistrot des Cimes*** (opening Spring) *(closed January, Sunday dinner, Monday and Tuesday)* **Meals** 18/30 – 18 – **10 rm** 160
Spec. Chaud-froid de champignons sauvages et homard en aigre-doux de fleurs. Rouget "retour de tuades" aux deux pommes. Menu "champignons" (Spring and Autumn).. **Wines** Saint-Joseph, Viognier de l'Ardèche.
◆ Charming bedrooms looking out onto countryside and a new restaurant with views of surrounding peaks. A perfect setting for enchanting cuisine inspired by the gastronomic treasures of the Auvergne, with mushrooms to the fore. Tasty local dishes in the Bistrot.

Valence *26000 Drôme 332 C4 – pop. 64 260 alt. 126.*

See : House of the Heads (Maison des Têtes)★ – Interior★ of the cathedral – Champ de Mars ≤★ – Red chalk sketches by Hubert Robert★★ in the museum.

of Chanalets at Bourg-les-Valence ☎ 04 75 83 16 23 ; New Golf of Bourget at Montmeyran ☎ 04 75 59 48 18, S : 16 ; of Valence-St-Didier(St-D. de Charpey) ☎ 04 75 59 67 01, E : 14km by D119.

of Valence-Chabeuil ☎ 04 75 85 26 26.

Tourist Office Parvis de la Gare ☎ 04 75 44 90 40, Fax 04 75 44 90 41.

Lyons 101.

Pic, 285 av. V. Hugo, Motorway exit signposted Valence-Sud ☎ 04 75 44 15 32, *pic@relaischateaux.com, Fax 04 75 40 96 03,* – 50. AE D GB JCB

closed to 3 to 26 January – **Meals** *(closed Tuesday from November-March, Sunday dinner and Monday)* (Sunday : booking essential) 50 (lunch), 115/145 and a la carte 120/200 – 23 – **12 rm** 175/280, 3 suites

Spec. Transparence de Saint-Jacques en gelée de céleri, crème glacée à la truffe noire (Winter). Loup de Méditerranée et caviar osciètre à la façon de mon père. Pintade fermière de la Drôme, foie gras et ravioles de légumes (Summer).. **Wines** Saint-Péray, Crozes-Hermitage.

• A delightful, relaxed and friendly "auberge" with a Provençal air. The elegant dining rooms and charming garden-terrace provide the perfect backdrop for delicate cuisine with a Mediterranean flavour.

Vienne *38200 Isère 333 C4 – pop. 29 975 alt. 160.*

See : Site★ – St-Maurice cathedral★★ – Temple of Augustus and Livia★★ – Roman Theatre★ – Church★ and cloisters★ of St-André-le-Bas – Mont Pipet Esplanade ≤★ – Old church of St-Pierre★ : lapidary museum★ – Gallo-roman city★ of St-Romain-en-Gal – Sculpture group★ in the church of Ste-Colombe.

Tourist Office 3 Crs Brillier ☎ 04 74 53 80 30, Fax 04 74 53 80 31.

Lyons 31.

La Pyramide (Henriroux), 14 bd F. Point ☎ 04 74 53 01 96, *pyramide.f.point@wanadoo.fr, Fax 04 74 85 69 73,* – 25. AE D GB JCB

closed February – **Meals** *(closed Sunday dinner and Monday except Bank Holidays)* 52 (lunch), 90/130 and a la carte 120/160 – 19 – **21 rm** 170/220, 4 suites

Spec. Découverte de homard aux cinq saveurs. Sartagnade de rouget à l'huile d'ail et chorizo. Piano au chocolat en "ut" praliné.. **Wines** Condrieu, Vin de Vienne.

• This famous restaurant, founded by the late and great Fernand Point, one of the world's most renowned chefs, occupies an attractive house built in local style with stylish rooms and a pleasant garden. The inventive cuisine here is worthy of the master himself.

Vonnas *01540 Ain 328 C3 – pop. 2 422 alt. 200.*

Lyons 63.

Georges Blanc, place du marché ☎ 04 74 50 90 90, *blanc@relaischateaux.com, Fax 04 74 50 08 80,* – 40. AE D GB JCB

closed January – **Meals** *(closed Wednesday lunch, Monday and Tuesday except Bank Holidays)* (booking essential) 98/220 and a la carte 110/160 – 24 – **35 rm** 170/420, 3 suites

Spec. Saint-Jacques rôties aux cèpes, aux épices et savagnin (October-March). Poulet de Bresse aux gousses d'ail, sauce foie gras. Panouille bressane glacée à la confiture de lait.. **Wines** Mâcon-Azé, Moulin à vent.

• Nestling in a flowery garden on the banks of the Veyle, this regional-style residence offers spacious, personalised bedrooms. The superlative cuisine and magnificent wine cellar combine to create one of the jewels of French gastronomy. Non-smoking restaurant.

MARSEILLES (MARSEILLE) *13000 B.-du-R. 340 H6 – pop. 798 430.*

See : Site★★★ – N.-D.-de-la-Garde Basilica ✳★★★ – Old Port★★ : Fish market (quai des Belges ET 5*) – Palais Longchamp★* GS *: Fine Arts Museum★, Natural History Museum★ – St-Victor Basilica★ : crypt★★* DU *– Old Major Cathedral★* DS **N** *– Pharo Park ≤★* DU *– Hôtel du département et Dôme-Nouvel Alcazar★ – Vieille Charité★★ (Mediterranean archeology)* DS **R** *– Museums : Grobet-Labadié★★* GS **M**⁷*, Cantini★* FU **M**⁵*, Vieux Marseille★* DT **M**²*, History of Marseilles★* ET **M**¹ *–* Envir. *: Corniche road★★ of Callelongue S : 13 km along the sea front –* Exc. *: – Château d'If★★ (✳★★★) 1 h 30.*

of Aix-Marseilles at les Milles ☎ 04 42 24 20 41 to the N : 22 km ; of Allauch (private) ☎ 04 91 07 28 22 ; junction Marseilles-East : 15 km, by D 2 and D 4=A ; of Marseilles-la Salette ☎ 04 91 27 12 16 by A 50.

Marseilles-Provence : ☎ 04 42 14 14 14 to the N : 28 km.

☎ 0892 35 35 33.

Tourist Office 2 rue Beauvau ☎ 04 91 13 89 00, Fax 04 91 13 89 00 20 and St-Charles railway station ☎ 04 91 50 59 18.

Paris 772 – Lyons 312 – Nice 188 – Turin 407 – Toulon 64 – Toulouse 401.

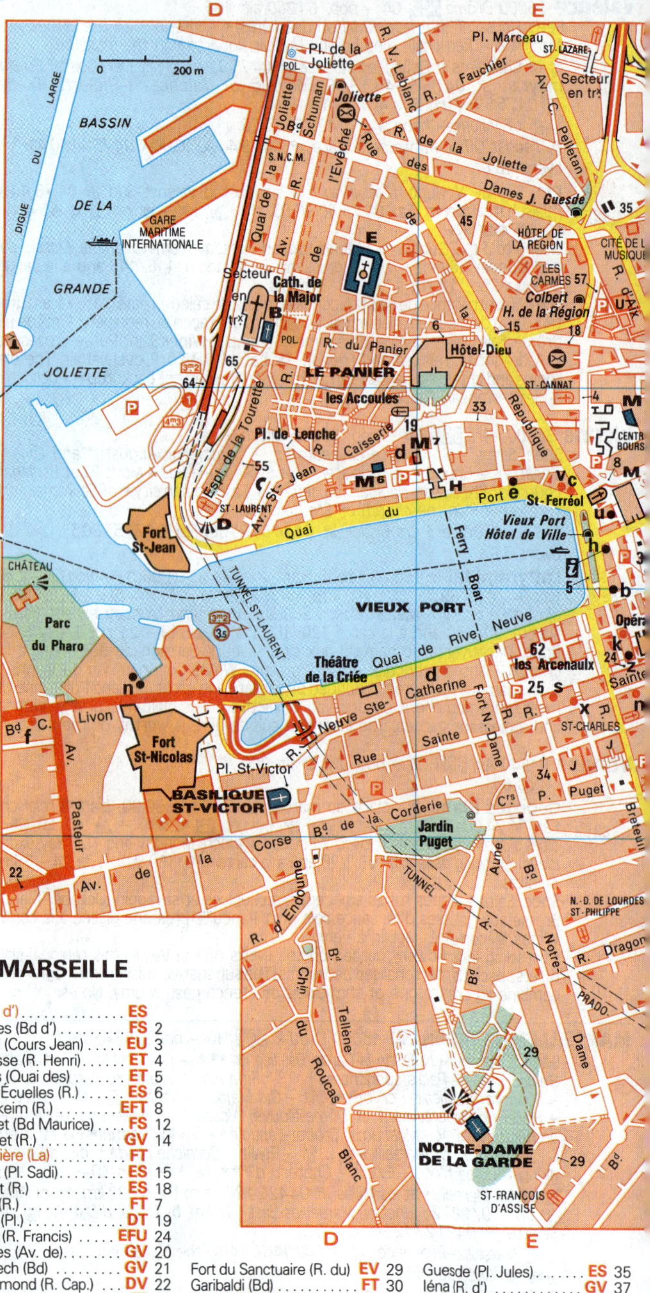

MARSEILLE

Aix (R. d') . . . . ES
Athènes (Bd d') . . . . FS 2
Ballard (Cours Jean) . . . . . EU 3
Barbusse (R. Henri) . . . . . . ET 4
Belges (Quai des) . . . . ET 5
Belles Écuelles (R.) . . . . . . ES 6
Bir-Hakeim (R.) . . . . EFT 8
Bourdet (Bd Maurice) . . . . FS 12
Busquet (R.) . . . . GV 14
Canebière (La) . . . . FT
Carnot (Pl. Sadi) . . . . ES 15
Colbert (R.) . . . . ES 18
Curiol (R.) . . . . FT 7
Daviel (Pl.) . . . . DT 19
Davso (R. Francis) . . . . . EFU 24
Delphes (Av. de) . . . . GV 20
Delpuech (Bd) . . . . GV 21
Dessemond (R. Cap.) . . . . DV 22
Dugommier (Bd) . . . . FT 23
Estienne-d'Orves (Crs d') . EU 25
Fabres (R. des) . . . . FT 27
Fort du Sanctuaire (R. du) EV 29
Garibaldi (Bd) . . . . FT 30
Gaulle (Pl. Gén.-de) . . . . . . ET 31
Grand'Rue . . . . ET 33
Grignan (R.) . . . . EU 34
Guesde (Pl. Jules) . . . . ES 35
Iéna (R. d') . . . . GV 37
Liberté (Bd de la) . . . . FS 42
Moisson (R. F.) . . . . ES 45
Montricher (Bd) . . . . GS 46

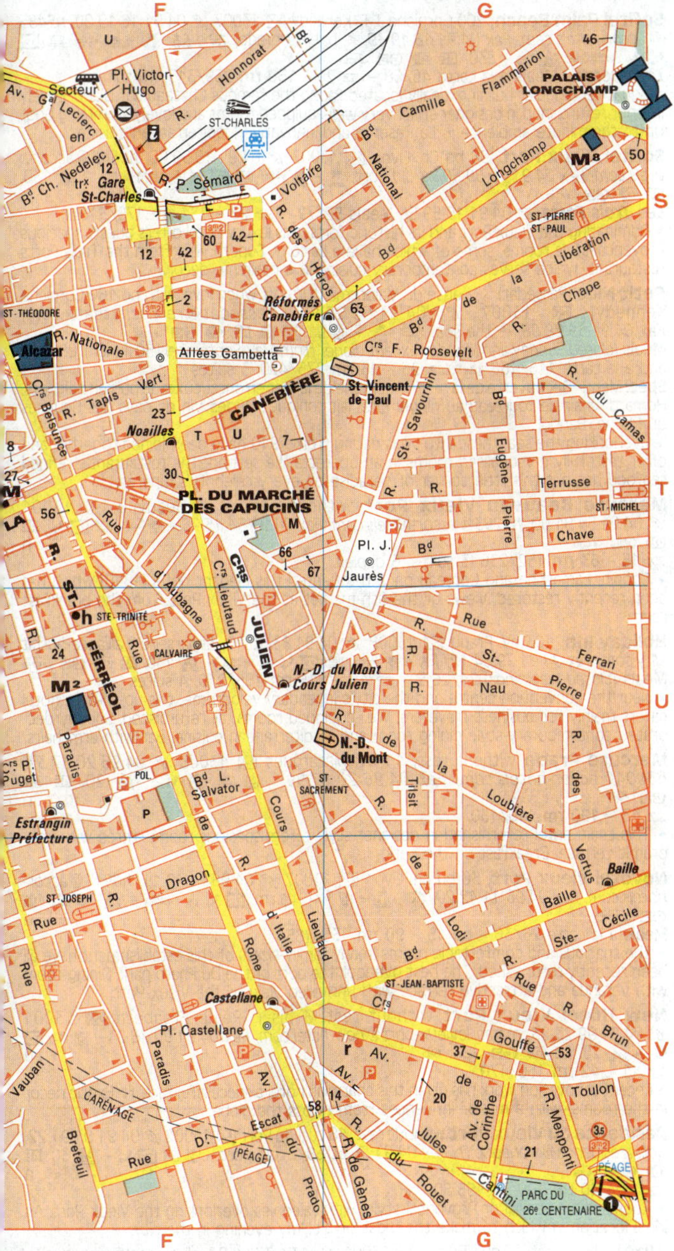

Paradis (R.) . . . . FUV
Philipon (Bd) . . . . GS 50
Raynouard (Traverse) . . . . GV 53
St-Ferréol (R.) . . . . FTU
St-Laurent (R.) . . . . DT 55
St-Louis (Cours) . . . . FT 56
Ste-Barbe (R.) . . . . ES 57
Ste-Philomène (R.) . . . . . . FV 58
Sembat (R. Marcel) . . . . . . FS 60
Sibié (R.) . . . . FT 67
Thiars (Pl.) . . . . EU 62
Thierry (Crs J.) . . . . GS 63
Tourette (Quai) . . . . DS 64
Trois Mages (R. des) . . . . . FT 66
Vaudoyer (Av.) . . . . DS 65

Sofitel Palm Beach, 200 Corniche J.-F. Kennedy 13007 04 91 16 19 00, *h3485@accor-hotels.com, Fax 04 91 16 19 39,* baie du prado, - - 15 - 330.
***La Réserve* : Meals** a la carte 46/68 - 21 - **150 rm** 239/315, 10 suites.
• Squat rectangular building ideally located facing the famous Chateau d'If Island. Lovely interior refurbished in designer style. Very well-equipped rooms and lovely swimming pool. Up-to-the-minute ambience in La Réserve and innovative Mediterranean cuisine.

Sofitel Vieux Port, 36 bd Ch. Livon 13007 04 91 15 59 00, *h0542@accor-hotels.com, Fax 04 91 15 59 50,* old Port, - - 130. DU n
Les Trois Forts 04 91 15 59 56 **Meals** 52/72 - 22 - **131 rm** 179/310.
• Dominating the Vieux Port and its historic forts, this luxury hotel offers guests spacious Provençal-style rooms, some of which have a balcony. Superb view from the Trois Forts restaurant, which serves contemporary cuisine in a maritime decor.

Petit Nice (Passédat), anse de Maldormé (turn off when level with no 160 Corniche Kennedy) 13007 04 91 59 25 92, *passedat@relaischateaux.com, Fax 04 91 59 28 08,* the sea, -
Meals *(closed Sunday and Monday except dinner from May-September)* 50 (lunch), 85/170 and a la carte 116/166 - 25 - **13 rm** 275/470, 3 suites
Spec. Menu "Découverte de la mer". Anémone de la mer en onctueux iodé puis en beignets. Homard, chair de tourteau au gingembre, lait tonique.. **Wines** Vin de pays des Bouches du Rhône, Bandol.
• Overlooking the sea, these two villas dating from 1910 have been joined together and offer tastefully personalised rooms in an operetta-like setting. The restaurant's refined seafood has put this little corner of paradise on every celebrity's itinerary.

Mercure Beauvau Vieux Port without rest, 4 r. Beauvau 13001 04 91 54 91 00, *h1293@accor-hotels.com, Fax 04 91 54 15 76* - ET h
15 - **63 rm** 152/236, 3 suites, 6 duplex.
• Chopin, Lamartine and Cocteau once frequented this elegant hotel (1816) which has been recently restored. Views of the fish market at the Vieux Port from the breakfast room.

Holiday Inn, 103 av. Prado 13008 04 91 83 10 10, *himarseille@alliance-hospitality.com, Fax 04 91 79 84 12,* - - 130.
Meals *(closed weekends)* 24/26 - 15 - **115 rm** 165/210, 4 suites.
• Near the convention centre and the city's legendary velodrome, this up-to-date hotel caters mainly for business travellers. Well-equipped rooms, all refurbished. Soberly decorated contemporary-style dining room and Mediterranean cuisine. Bar with armchairs.

Mercure Prado without rest, 11 av. Mazargues 13008 04 96 20 37 37, *h3004@accor-hotels.com, Fax 04 96 20 37 99* - - 20. BZ n
13 - **100 rm** 110/130.
• This chain hotel refurbished in designer style offers spacious rooms, three with panoramic terrace. Breakfast on the patio.

Novotel Vieux Port, 36 bd ch. Livon 13007 04 96 11 42 11, *h0911@accor-hotels.com, Fax 04 96 11 42 20,* - rm, - 50. DU n
Meals a la carte 26/36 - 15 - **90 rm** 135/165.
• The spacious and comfortable rooms (many family-sized) of this establishment have all been recently refurbished. The best overlook the port or the Du Pharo park. Dining-room with veranda and attractive terrace with unrivalled view of the Vieux Port.

New Hôtel Vieux Port without rest, 3 bis r. Reine Élisabeth 13001 04 91 99 23 23, *marseillevieux-port@new-hotel.com, Fax 04 91 90 76 24* - - 25. ET u
11 - **42 rm** 150/170.
• Recent renovation work has given this charming hotel a successful facelift. Exotic decor in the rooms, with a mix of influences from across the globe.

Résidence du Vieux Port without rest, 18 quai du Port 13002 04 91 91 91 22, *hotel.residence@wanadoo.fr, Fax 04 91 56 60 88,* old port - - 30. ET a
11 - **40 rm** 100,50/155,50.
• Rooms in traditional or Provençal style, with balconies overlooking the Vieux Port. An ideal location in which to make the most of a balmy evening in the city.

Alizé without rest, 35 quai Belges 13001 04 91 33 66 97, *alize-hotel@wanadoo.fr, Fax 04 91 54 80 06,* - ETU b
7 - **39 rm** 60/85.
• This functional establishment is situated opposite the city's famous fish market. The best rooms, with a view of the port, are at the front.

Une Table au Sud (Lévy), 2 quai Port (1st floor) ✉ 13002 ☎ 04 91 90 63 53, *une tableausud@wanadoo.fr, Fax 04 91 90 63 86,* ← – 🛗 ▤. AE GB ET c
closed 30 July-23 August, Sunday and Monday – **Meals** 30 (lunch), 39/78
Spec. Crumble de mulet au combava et gingembre. Rouget poêlés à la marjolaine, aubergines à l'huile d'argan. L'huile d'olive dans tous ses états.
• This restaurant with its bright decor offers diners good Mediterranean cuisine and fine views of the city's forts and "Bonne Mère" statue.

Miramar, 12 quai Port ✉ 13002 ☎ 04 91 91 10 40, *contact@bouillabaisse.com, Fax 04 91 56 64 31,* – ▤. AE ⓓ GB ET v
closed Sunday and Monday – **Meals** a la carte 60/80 ♀.
• Bouillabaisse and other fish specialities are served in this restaurant opposite the Vieux Port. The varnished wood decor and red chairs create a very 1960s ambience.

Ferme, 23 r. Sainte ✉ 13001 ☎ 04 91 33 21 12, *Fax 04 91 33 81 21* – ▤. AE ⓓ GB JCB EU m
closed August, Saturday lunch and Sunday – **Meals** 28 (lunch)/38 and a la carte 43/67.
• Trompe l'oeil effects and subtle lighting enhance the intimate layout of this plush restaurant close to the Cantini Museum. Traditional cuisine with a Provençal flavour.

L'Épuisette, Vallon des Auffes ✉ 13007 ☎ 04 91 52 17 82, *contact@l-epuisette.com, Fax 04 91 59 18 80,* ← Frioul Islands and Château d'If – ▤. AE GB
closed 7 August-7 September, Sunday and Monday – **Meals** 43/90 and a la carte 76/106 ♀
Spec. Risotto carnaroli aux truffes (October-March). Ravioles de homard (15 June-30 September). Filet de Saint-Pierre grillé (15 June-30 September).. **Wines** Coteaux d'Aix-en-Provence, Cassis.
• Anchored on the rocks of the enchanting Auffes valley, this glass vessel promises diners an exceptional culinary voyage. Bright decor in blue, white, and wood.

Péron, 56 corniche Kennedy ✉ 13007 ☎ 04 91 52 15 22, *info@restaurant-peron.com, Fax 04 91 52 17 29,* ← Frioul islands and Château d'If, – ✈ AE ⓓ GB JCB AY a
Meals 47/59 ♀.
• This restaurant offers superb sea views plus elegant, contemporary interiors made even more appealing by pictures painted by local artists. Modern, regional cuisine.

Les Arcenaulx, 25 cours d'Estienne d'Orves ✉ 13001 ☎ 04 91 59 80 30, *restaurant@les-arcenaulx.com, Fax 04 91 54 76 33,* – ▤. AE ⓓ GB JCB EU s
closed Monday in July-August and Sunday – **Meals** 28,50/49,50 ♀.
• In the 17C storehouses where galleys once tied up, there is a bookshop, a publisher's, and a restaurant offering a cuisine kissed by the southern sun.

Les Mets de Provence "Chez Maurice Brun", 18 quai de Rive Neuve (2nd floor) ✉ 13007 ☎ 04 91 33 35 38, *Fax 04 91 33 05 69* – ▤. GB EU d
closed 10 to 25 August, Sunday, lunch Monday and Saturday – **Meals** 37 b.i. (lunch)/53.
• Famous establishment set in an old convent in the Vieux Port. Lovely rustic Provençal ambience. Unique menu varied daily and explained verbally.

René Alloin, 9 pl. Amiral Muselier (by prom. G. Pompidou) ✉ 13008 ☎ 04 91 77 88 25, *alloinfilipe@aol.com, Fax 04 91 71 82 46,* – ▤. GB
closed Saturday lunch, Sunday dinner and Tuesday – **Meals** 21 (lunch), 38/49.
• Facing the Prado beach and with contemporary Provençal decor, this stronghold of fine cuisine has managed to hold its own among the massed bars and pizzerias.

Cyprien, 56 av. Toulon ✉ 13006 ☎ 04 91 25 50 00, *Fax 04 91 25 50 00* – ▤. GB GV r
closed 14/07-26/08, 23/12-5/01, Monday except dinner from June-September, Saturday lunch, Sunday and Bank Holidays – **Meals** 24/65.
• Fine food in a classic setting close to the place Castellane. Paintings and floral decoration adorn on the walls.

Michel-Brasserie des Catalans (Visciano), 6 r. Catalans ✉ 13007 ☎ 04 91 52 30 63, *Fax 04 91 59 23 05* – ▤. AE GB
Meals a la carte 44/74
Spec. Bouillabaisse. Supions sautés ail et persil. Bourride provençale. **Wines** Cassis, Bandol.
• This renovated restaurant facing the plage des Catalans is popular with locals for its bouillabaisse. The fish is also excellent, with the daily catch on display in a boat.

Café des Épices, 4 r. Lacydon ✉ 13002 ☎ 04 91 91 22 69, *cafedesepices@yahoo.fr* – ✈ AE GB. ✂ DT d
closed August, 24 December-2 January, Saturday lunch, Sunday and Monday – **Meals** (booking essential) 18 (lunch)/30.
• Despite seating just fifteen non-smoking diners, this intimate restaurant is popular for its refined, inventive cuisine and contemporary decor.

Chez Vincent, 25 r. Glandeves ✉ 13001 ☎ 04 91 33 96 78 EU k
closed August and Monday – **Meals** a la carte approx. 32.
• A modest façade, simple decor, and the same lady owner since the 1940s. This Marseille institution offers generous portions of local cuisine and pizzas cooked in a wood oven.

Aix-en-Provence
13100 B.-du-R. 340 H4 – pop. 134 222 alt. 206.

18 of Ste-Victoire at Fuveau ✆ 04 42 29 83 43 by N96 and D6 : 14 km ; 9 Set ✆ 04 42 29 63 69, O : 6 km by D17.

Tourist Office 2 pl. Général.-de-Gaulle ✆ 04 42 16 11 61, Fax 04 42 16 11 62.
Marseilles 31.

XXX ✿✿ **Clos de la Violette** (Banzo), 10 av. Violette ✆ 04 42 23 30 71, *restaurant@closdelaviolette.fr, Fax 04 42 21 93 03,* – (dinner).
closed 4 to 18 August, February Holidays, Monday except dinner from 1 June-30 September and Sunday – **Meals** (booking essential) 54 (lunch)/120 and a la carte 98/118
Spec. Charlotte croustillante de truffes (December-March). Petits farcis de légumes provençaux (June-October). Menu "Ballade Gourmande".. **Wines** Coteaux d'Aix-en-Provence.
◆ Away from the town's bustle, a lovely villa with garden invites diners to try the thousand and one delights of a characterful version of local cuisine. Elegant setting.

Les Baux-de-Provence
13520 B.-du-R. 340 D3 – pop. 434 alt. 185.

See : *Site★★★ – Château ※★★ – Charloun Rieu monument ≤★ – Place St-Vincent★ – Rue du Trencat★ – Paravelle Tower ≤★ – Yves-Brayer museum★ (in Hôtel de Porcelet) – Shepherds' Festival★★ (Christmas midnight mass) – Cathédrale d'Images★ N : 1 km on the D 27 – ※★★★ of the village N : 2,5 km on the D 27.*

9 of les Baux-de-Provence ✆ 04 90 54 40 20, S : 2 km.

Tourist Office Maison du Roy ✆ 04 90 54 34 39, Fax 04 90 54 51 15.
Marseilles 83.

in the Vallon :

XXXXX ✿✿ **Oustaù de Baumanière** (Charial) with rm, ✆ 04 90 54 33 07, *baumaniere@relaischateaux.fr, Fax 04 90 54 40 46,* ≤, – JCB
closed 9/01-3/03, Wednesday lunch in October and in April, Thursday lunch and Wednesday from November-March – **Meals** 90/149 and a la carte 109/134 – 20 – **12 rm** 270/499, 4 suites
Spec. Loup cuit doucement aux fleurs et feuilles aromatiques. Pigeonneau au jus de vin des Baux. Plié au chocolat.. **Wines** Coteaux d'Aix-en-Provence-les Baux.
◆ Venerable, vaulted 16C residence, a superb terrace with the Alpilles as a backdrop, this is a magical location. Fine cuisine redolent of the sun plus a sumptuous wine list.

Manoir ≤, – JCB
Meals see ***Oustaù de Baumanière*** – 19,50 – **7 rm** 263/284, 7 suites 425/457.
◆ The rooms of this elegant fortified house combine comfort, refinement and old-fashioned Provençal charm. Wooded park (with an ancient plane tree) and formal garden.

Lourmarin
84160 Vaucluse 332 F11 – pop. 1 119 alt. 224.

Tourist Office 9 av. Ph.-de-Girard ✆ 04 90 68 10 77, Fax 04 90 68 11 01.
Marseilles 63.

✿✿ **Moulin de Lourmarin** (Loubet), r. Temple ✆ 04 90 68 06 69, *info@moulindelourmarin.com, Fax 04 90 68 31 76,* – JCB
closed 9 January-9 Febrary – **Meals** *(closed Tuesday, lunch Wednesday and Thursday)* 52/148 and a la carte 100/130 – 15 – **16 rm** 300/430, 3 suites
Spec. Complicité de foie gras. Loup de ligne à l'unilatéral, infusion de sauge et orange. Carré d'agneau au serpolet, jus au thym citronné.. **Wines** Côtes du Luberon.
◆ Near the chateau, this charming 18C oil-mill has delightful rooms. Vaulted restaurant in the old press-house, a lovely terrace, and an inventive cuisine paying subtle homage to the flavours and colours of the Luberon.

Montpellier
34000 Hérault 339 I7 – pop. 225 392 alt. 27.

18 of Coulondres at St-Gely-du-Fesc ✆ 04 67 84 13 75, N : 12 km ; 18 of Fontcaude at Juvignac ✆ 04 67 45 90 10, O : 9 km ; 18 of Montpellier-Massane at Baillargues ✆ 04 67 87 87 89, E : 13 km.

of Montpellier-Méditerranée ✆ 04 67 20 85 00 to the SE : 7 km.

Tourist Office 30, allée Jean de Lattre de Tassigny ✆ 04 67 60 60 60, Fax 04 67 60 60 61.
Marseilles 171.

XXXX ✿✿ **Jardin des Sens** (Jacques et Laurent Pourcel) with rm, 11 av. St-Lazare ✆ 04 99 58 38 38, *contact@jardindessens.com, Fax 04 99 58 38 39,* – – 25.
closed 2 to 9 January – **Meals** *(closed 2 to 16 January, Monday except dinner in 07/08, Tuesday lunch except 07/08, Wednesday lunch and Sunday)* (booking essential) 50 (lunch), 125/190 and a la carte 114/194 – 22 – **12 rm** 180/260, 3 suites
Spec. Pressé de homard et légumes au jambon de canard. Filet de loup cuit au four et doré aux citrons, vinaigrette tiède au citron confit. Filets de pigeon rôtis, jus au cacao.. **Wines** Coteaux du Languedoc, Corbières.
◆ The tiered non-smoking dining room in designer style opens on to a spiral garden. Aesthetically pleasing decor and tempting cuisine.

FRANCE

MONACO (Principality of) (Principauté de) 341 F5 115 272 – pop. 29 972 alt. 65 – Casino.

Monaco *Capital of the Principality* 341 F5 – ✉ 98000.

See : Tropical Garden★★ (Jardin exotique) : ≤★ – Observatory Caves★ (Grotte de l'Observatoire) – St-Martin Gardens★ – Early paintings of the Nice School★★ in Cathedral – Recumbent Christ★ in the Misericord Chapel – Place du Palais★ – Prince's Palace★ – Museums : oceanographic★★ (aquarium★★, ≤★★ from the terrace), Prehistoric Anthropology★, Napoleon and Monaco History★, Royal collection of vintage cars★.

Urban racing circuit.

Paris 956 – Nice 21 – San Remo 44.

at Fontvieille

Columbus Hôtel, 23 av. Papalins ☎ (00-377) 92 05 90 00, *info@columbushotels.com, Fax (00-377) 92 05 91 67,* ≤, – – 25 - 80. AE GB JCB
Meals a la carte 60/75 – 30 – **153 rm** 295/335, 28 suites.
• A chic and contemporary boutique hotel with bedrooms (the majority with a balcony) featuring stylish furnishings, relaxing colour schemes and views of either the port or a landscaped park. Modern, Italian brasserie-style restaurant and a pleasant terrace.

Monte-Carlo *Fashionable resort of the Principality* 341 F5 – *Casinos Grand Casino, Monte-Carlo Sporting Club, Sun Casino.*

See : Terrace★★ of the Grand Casino – Museum of Dolls and Automata★.
Monte-Carlo ☎ (00-377) 93 41 09 11 to the N by D 53 : 11 km.
Tourist Office 2 bd des Moulins ☎ (00-377) 92 16 61 16, Fax (00-377) 92 16 61 16.

Paris, pl. Casino ☎ (00-377) 92 16 30 00, *hp@sbm.mc, Fax (00-377) 92 16 38 50,* ≤, – – 70. AE GB JCB. rest see ***Le Louis XV-Alain Ducasse*** and ***Grill*** below - ***Salle Empire*** ☎ (00-377) 92 16 29 52 (dinner only) *(open July-August)* **Meals** a la carte 83/141 – ***Côté Jardin*** ☎ (00-377) 92 16 68 44 (lunch only) **Meals** 50 – 35 – **147 rm** 470/690, 44 suites.
• An idyllic location, sumptuous furnishings, rich history and celebrity guests have cemented the legendary reputation of Monaco's most prestigious hotel, built in 1864. Majestically opulent Empire Room. Views of the Rock from the terrace of the Côté Jardin.

Hermitage, square Beaumarchais ☎ (00-377) 92 16 40 00, *hh@sbm.mc, Fax (00-377) 92 16 38 52,* ≤, – – 80. AE GB JCB. rest see ***Vistamar*** below ***Limun Bar*** *(lunch only)* **Meals** a la carte 45/60 – 34 – **251 rm** 490/750, 29 suites.
• Italian frescoes and loggias adorn the hotel's splendid façade facing the port. Inside, admire Eiffel's cast-iron and glass cupola. Luxurious bedrooms. Refined, lemon-inspired decor and regional cuisine in the Limùn bar, which also acts as a tea-room.

Métropole, 4 av. Madone ☎ (00-377) 93 15 15 15, *metropole@metropole.com, Fax (00-377) 93 25 24 44,* – – 60. AE GB JCB
Meals (restaurant not listed) – 35 – **131 rm** 500/990, 15 suites.
• Built in 1886 and remodelled towards the end of the 20C, this palatial hotel has recently received a new facelift, this time the work of designer Jacques Garcia

Méridien Beach Plaza, av. Princesse Grace, à la Plage du Larvotto ☎ (00-377) 93 30 98 80, *reservations.montecarlo@lemeridien.com, Fax (00-377) 93 50 23 14,* ≤, – rm, – 20 - 300. AE GB JCB
Meals a la carte 50/80 – 31 – **338 rm** 380.
• The street-side façade gives little hint of the superb spa facilities that face out to sea. Modern, tastefully decorated bedrooms, plus a luxurious conference centre. Buffet-style dining, with recipes unsurprisingly inspired by the Mediteranean.

Port Palace, 7 av. J. F. Kennedy ☎ (00-377) 97 97 90 00, *reservation@portpalace.com, Fax (00-377) 97 97 90 01,* ≤ Port et Rocher, – P. AE GB JCB DY t
Meals *Grand Large* *(closed lunch Saturday and Sunday in July-August)* **Meals** 80 – 29, 50 suites700/2100.
• The contemporary architecture of the latest addition to Monaco's hotel list stands alongside the harbour, its superbly equipped rooms providing impressive views of the Rock. Modern decor and traditional cuisine in the top-floor panoramic restaurant.

Monte-Carlo Grand Hôtel, 12 av. Spélugues ☎ (00-377) 93 50 65 00, *mail@montecarlograndhotel.com, Fax (00-377) 93 30 01 57,* ≤, – – 1 500. AE GB JCB
L'Argentin* : Meals** a la carte 70/90 – ***Pistou *(14 March-1 December and closed Tuesday dinner)* **Meals** a la carte 45/75 – 23 – **599 rm** 320/500, 20 suites.
• A vast hotel complex which includes a casino, cabaret, boutiques and conference centre. Mediterranean decor in the bedrooms, contrasting with the South American influence in L'Argentin. French and Italian cuisine in Le Pistou, with its sea-facing terrace.

Balmoral, 12 av. Costa ✆ (00-377) 93 50 62 37, *resa@hotel-balmoral.mc, Fax (00-377) 93 15 08 69,* ← – rm, – 20. AE GB JCB.
Meals *(closed November, Sunday dinner and Monday)* 27 – 16 – **53 rm** 210/300, 12 suites.
◆ Owned by the same family since 1896, the Balmoral is traditional in feel with comfortable bedrooms, half with views of the port, and a lounge furnished in Empire style.

Alexandra without rest, 35 bd Princesse Charlotte ✆ (00-377) 93 50 63 13, *hotelalexandra@monaco377.com, Fax (00-377) 92 16 06 48* – . AE GB JCB.
14 – **56 rm** 125/170.
◆ The richly ornamented façade bears witness to the ostentation of the Belle Époque. Breakfast is only served in guest bedrooms, which have a pleasantly old-fashioned feel.

Le Louis XV-Alain Ducasse - Hôtel de Paris, pl. Casino ✆ (00-377) 92 16 29 76, *lelouisxv@alain-ducasse.com, Fax (00-377) 92 16 69 21,* – AE GB JCB.
closed 29 November-29 December, 14 February-2 March, Wednesday except dinner from 22 June-24 August and Tuesday – **Meals** *(closed lunch from 1 March-15 May except Saturday, Sunday, Wednesday except dinner from 23/06-25/08 and Tuesday)* 90 b.i. (lunch), 150/190 and a la carte 180/220
Spec. Légumes des jardins de Provence à la truffe noire écrasée. Loup de Méditerranée en filet à la plancha, jus à l'artichaut. "Louis XV" au croustillant de pralin.. **Wines** Bellet blanc, Bandol rouge.
◆ Sumptuous classical decor, sublime Mediterranean flavours, a truly outstanding wine cellar, plus a terrace overlooking the famous casino. A veritable feast for the senses!

Grill de l'Hôtel de Paris, pl. Casino ✆ (00-377) 92 16 29 66, *hp@sbm.mc, Fax (00-377) 92 16 38 40,* ← the Principality, – AE GB JCB
closed 5 to 22 January and lunch from 7 July-28 August – **Meals** 70 (lunch) and a la carte 77/185
Spec. Langoustines royales rôties. Carré d'agneau. Poussin de nid rôti au thym frais.. **Wines** Côtes de Provence.
◆ On the 8th floor of this spectacular hotel, with the Mediterranean as a backdrop. The perfect vantage-point from which to view the Principality. Open-air terrace in season.

Vistamar - Hôtel Hermitage, pl. Beaumarchais ✆ (00-377) 92 16 27 72, *hh@sbm.mc, Fax (00-377) 92 16 38 43,* ← Harbour and Principality, – AE GB JCB
closed lunch in July-August – **Meals** 62 and a la carte 90/170
Spec. Quenelle de purée de potiron au gingembre, langoustines rôties à la noisette. Noix de Saint-Jacques au gril, sauté de salsifis à la truffe noire. Macaron de rose fourré de compote de rhubarbe et fruits rouges (Summer).. **Wines** Bandol.
◆ Exquisite fish dishes and stunning sea views from the delightful panoramic terrace and bay-windowed dining room are the keys to the Vistamar's continued success.

Bar et Boeuf, av. Princesse Grace, au Sporting-Monte-Carlo ✆ (00-377) 92 16 60 60, *b.b@sbm.mc, Fax (00-377) 92 16 60 61,* ←, – AE GB JCB
18 May-17 September and closed Monday from 18 May-20 June and from 29 August-17 September – **Meals** (dinner only) a la carte 83/110
Spec. "Tomate et tomates". Coeur de filet de bar aux condiments à la sicilienne. Cheese-cake, compotée de fruits rouges, sorbet fromage blanc.. **Wines** Côtes de Provence.
◆ A Philippe Starck-designed restaurant whose menu favours sea bass (bar), beef (boeuf) and wines from around the world. A popular late-night haunt for serious gourmets.

Saint Benoit, 10ter av. Costa ✆ (00-377) 93 25 02 34, *lesaintbenoit@montecarlo.mc, Fax (00-377) 93 30 52 64,* ← Harbour and Monaco, – . AE GB JCB
closed 20 December-4 January, Sunday dinner and Monday – **Meals** 28/38 and a la carte 42/64
◆ Not the easiest place to find, but well worth the effort for the view from the terrace. Modern, spacious dining room.

L'Hirondelle, 2 av. Monte-Carlo (aux Thermes Marins) ✆ (00-377) 92 16 49 30, *Fax (00-377) 92 16 49 02,* ← Harbour and rock, – . AE GB JCB.
closed 12 to 19 December – **Meals** (lunch only) 50 (low-calorie menu) and a la carte 64/83.
◆ Part of the prestigious Thermes Marins, the bright dining room and terrace enjoy a fine view of the port and rock. A range of classic dishes and health-conscious cuisine.

Café de Paris, pl. Casino ✆ (00-377) 92 16 25 54, *cp@sbm.mc, Fax (00-377) 92 16 38 58,* – . AE GB JCB
Meals a la carte 44/87
◆ In 1897, Édouard Michelin made a notable entrance here...at the wheel of his motor car! A Belle Époque-style brasserie with a lively outdoor terrace in summer.

Zébra Square, 10 av. Princesse Grace (Grimaldi Forum : 2nd floor by lift) ✆ (00-377) 99 99 25 50, *Fax (00-377) 99 99 25 60,* ←, – . AE GB JCB
closed 6 February-2 March – **Meals** a la carte 50/72
◆ The same designer decor, trendy atmosphere and contemporary cuisine as its Paris sibling, with the bonus of a charming terrace with views of the Mediterranean.

Maison du Caviar, 1 av. St-Charles ✆ (00-377) 93 30 80 06, *Fax (00-377) 93 30 23 90,* – AE GB
closed August, Saturday lunch and Sunday – **Meals** 24 (lunch)/28 ♀.
◆ A long-time favourite with locals, this family restaurant has been serving traditional dishes amid a decor of wrought iron, bottle racks and rustic furniture since 1954.

Polpetta, 2 r. Paradis ✆ (00-377) 93 50 67 84, *Fax (00-377) 93 50 67 84* – . AE GB
closed 10 to 30 June, Saturday lunch and Tuesday – **Meals** 23.
◆ A small Italian restaurant with three distinct atmospheres : the street terrace, the rustic main dining room, and a more refined and intimate section to the rear.

at Monte-Carlo Beach *North-East* BU *: 2,5 km – ✉ 06190 Roquebrune-Cap-Martin :*

Monte-Carlo Beach Hôtel, av. Princesse Grace ✆ 04 93 28 66 66, *bh@sbm.mc, Fax 04 93 78 14 18,* ≤ sea and Monaco, , , , – – 30. AE GB JCB. rest
4 March-12 November – ***Salle à Manger et sa Terrasse*** ✆ 04 93 28 66 72 **Meals** a la carte 60/100 – ***Le Deck*** ✆ 04 93 28 66 43 (lunch only) *(10 April-11 October)* **Meals** a la carte 65/85 ♀ – ***La Vigie*** ✆ 04 93 28 66 44 *(24 June-30 August)* **Meals** 41(lunch)/52 – ***Le Sea Lounge*** ✆ 04 93 28 66 42 *(25 May-15 September)* **Meals** a la carte 45/65 – 32 – **44 rm** 610/765, 3 suites.
◆ Created in 1929, this attractive, typically "monégasque" spa complex has welcomed stars such Nijinski, Cocteau etc. Italian-style bedrooms looking out on to the Rock and the open sea. Small but cosy fresco-adorned Salle à Manger. Open-air La Vigie restaurant.

NICE *06000 Alpes-Mar.* **341** E5 – *pop. 342 738 alt. 6 – Casino Ruhl* FZ.

See : *Site★★ – Promenade des Anglais★★* EFZ *– Old Nice★ : Château ≤★★* JZ*, Interior★ of church of St-Martin-St-Augustin* HY **D** *– Balustraded staircase★ of the Palais Lascaris* HZ **K***, Interior★ of Ste-Réparate Cathedral –* HZ **L***, St-Jacques Church★* HZ **N***, Decoration★ of St-Giaume's Chapel* HZ **R** *– Mosaic★ by Chagall in Law Faculty* DZ **U** *– Palais des Arts★* HJY *– Miséricorde Chapel★* HZ **S** *– Cimiez : Monastery★ (Masterpieces★★ of the early Nice School in the church)* HV **Q***, Roman Ruins★* HV *– Museums : Marc Chagall★★* GX*, Matisse★★* HV **M2***, Fine Arts Museum★★* DZ **M***, Masséna★* FZ **M1** *– Modern and Contemporary Art★★* HY *– Parc Phoenix★ – Carnival★★★ (before Shrove Tuesday).*

Envir. : *St-Michel Plateau ≤★★ 9,5 km.*

of Nice-Côte d'Azur ✆ 0820 423 333 : 7 km.

✆ 0892 35 35 33.

Tourist Office 5 prom. des Anglais ✆ 08 92 70 74 07, SNCF Station ✆ 08 92 70 74 07 and Airport, Terminal 1 ✆ 08 92 70 74 07.

Paris 932 – Cannes 32 – Genova 194 – Lyons 472 – Marseilles 188 – Turin 220.

Négresco, 37 promenade des Anglais ✆ 04 93 16 64 00, *direction@hotel-negresco.com, Fax 04 93 88 35 68,* ≤, , – – 30 - 200. AE GB JCB
see ***Chantecler*** below - ***La Rotonde :*** **Meals** 30 ♀ – 28 – **121 rm** 315/525, 12 suites.
◆ Built in 1913 by Henri Negresco, the son of a Romanian innkeeper, this majestic, almost mythical museum of a hotel is full of artworks and extravagant in every detail. The Rotonde is a striking brasserie with merry-go-round decor. FZ k

Palais Maeterlinck, 30 bd Maeterlinck, 6 km by Inferior Corniche ✉ 06300 ✆ 04 92 00 72 00, *info@palais-maeterlinck.com, Fax 04 92 04 18 10,* ≤ the coast, , , , , – kitchenette – 25 - 80. AE GB JCB.
Mélisande ✆ 04 92 00 72 01 *(closed Sunday dinner and Monday from October-May)* **Meals** 43/75 ♀ – 28 – **16 rm** 420/720, 13 suites, 11 duplex.
◆ Once the home of a Flemish poet, this establishment is in a mixture of Baroque and Florentine neo-Classical styles. Garden and pool project over the sea. The Mélisande has a gallery of 19C Orientalist pictures and a terrace overlooking the city shoreline.

Palais de la Méditerranée, 13 prom. Anglais ✆ 04 92 14 77 00, *reservation@lepalaisdelamediterranée.com, Fax 04 92 14 77 14,* ≤, , – rm, – 20 - 500. AE GB. rest FZ g
Meals ***Le Padouk*** *(dinner only from 15 July-15 August)* **Meals** 46(lunch)/70 ♀ – ***Pingala Bar*** *(lunch only)* **Meals** a la carte approx. 50 ♀ – 30 – **182 rm** 375/780, 6 suites.
◆ This legendary building with its listed Art Deco façade is now home to a brand-new hotel with modern, spacious rooms. Contemporary cuisine and warm decor in the Padouk restaurant, while the more modern Pingala Bar concentrates on cuisine from around the world.

Méridien, 1 promenade des Anglais ✆ 04 97 03 44 44, *reservations.nice@lemeridien.com, Fax 04 97 03 44 45,* ≤, , – – 300. AE GB JCB FZ d
Le Colonial Café ✆ 04 97 03 40 36 **Meals** a la carte 45/65 ♀ – ***La Terrasse du Colonial*** *30 March-1 November* **Meals** a la carte 45/65 ♀ – 23 – **301 rm** 210/240, 17 suites.
◆ The highlight of this contemporary palace is its rooftop pool facing the Baie des Anges. Lovely rooms in Mediterranean colours, beauty salon, hi-tech business facilities. Ethnic décor and world cuisine in the Colonial Café. Sea views from the Terrasse.

NICE

Alberti (R.) . . . . GHY 2
Alsace-Lorraine (Jardin d') EZ 3
Armée-du-Rhin (Pl. de l') . . JX 5
Auriol (Pont V.). . . . . JV 7
Bellanda (Av.) . . . . HV 10
Berlioz (R.) . . . . FY 12
Bonaparte (R.) . . . . JY 13
Carnot (Bd) . . . . JZ 15
Desambrois (Av.). . . . . GHX 18
Diables-Bleus (Av. des). . . JX 19
Europe (Parvis de l') . . . . . JX 21
Félix-Faure (Av.) . . . . GZ 22
France (R. de) . . . . DFZ
Gallieni (Av.) . . . . HJX 24
Gambetta (Bd) . . . . EXZ
Gautier (Pl. P.) . . . . HZ 25
Gioffredo (R.) . . . . HY
Hôtel-des-Postes (R. de l') HY 30
Ile-de-Beauté (Pl.) . . . . . . JZ 31
Jean-Jaurès (Bd) . . . . HYZ 32
Liberté (R. de la) . . . . GZ 35
Lunel (Quai) . . . . JZ 37
Masséna (Pl. et Espace) . GZ
Masséna (R.) . . . . FGZ 43
Médecin (Av. J.) . . . . FGY 44
Meyerbeer (R.) . . . . FZ 45
Monastère (Av. Pl.) . . . . . . HV 46
Moulin (Pl. J.) . . . . HY 47
Paradis (R.) . . . . GZ 55
Passy (R. F.). . . . . EY 57
Pastorelli (R.) . . . . GY 58
Phocéens (Av. des). . . . . . GZ 59
Ray (Av. du) . . . . FV 63

République (Av. de la) .. **JXY** 64
Rivoli (R. de) .... **FZ** 65
St-François-de-Paule (R.) **GHZ** 72
St-Jean-Baptiste (Av.) .... **HY** 73
Saleya (Cours) .... **HZ** 82
Sauvan (R. H.) .... **EZ** 84
Verdun (Av. de) .... **FGZ** 89
Walesa (Bd Lech) ...... **JYZ** 91
Wilson (Pl.) .... **HY** 92

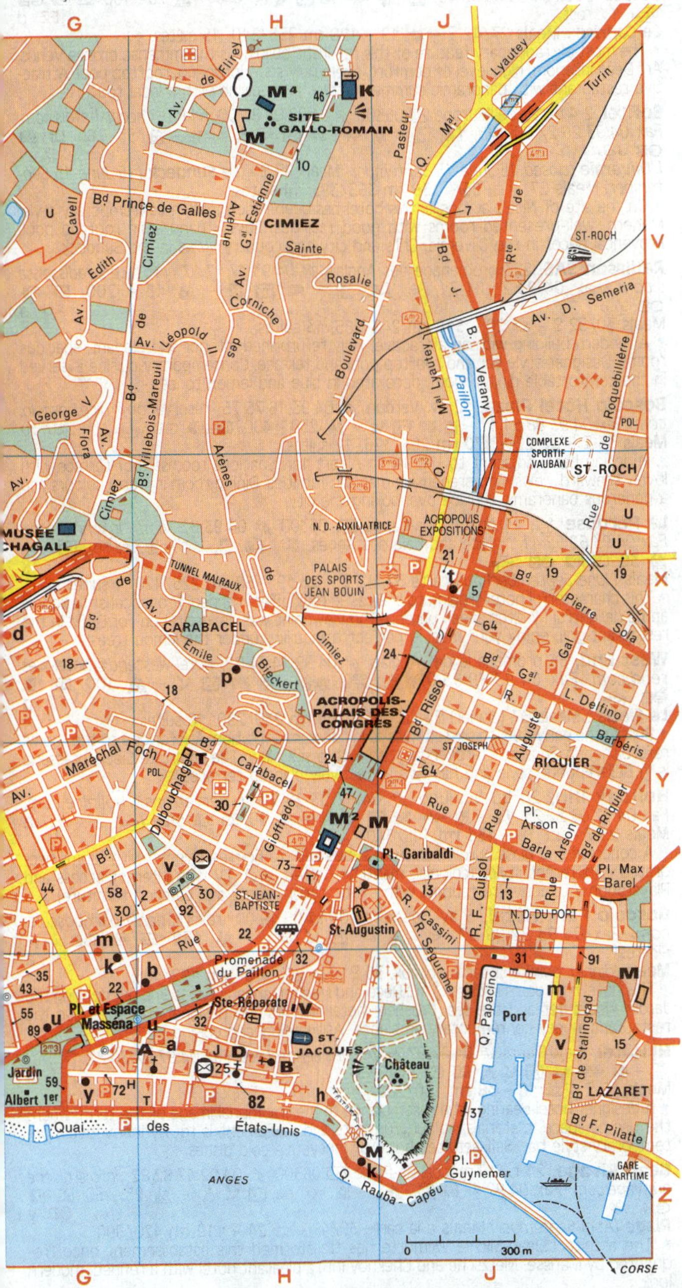

Élysée Palace, 59, promenade des Anglais ✆ 04 93 97 90 90, *reservation@elyseepalace.com, Fax 04 93 44 50 40,* - rest - 70 - 100. EZ d
***Le Caprice* : Meals** 27/42 - 19 - **128 rm** 255/310, 15 suites.
◆ The most extraordinary feature of this futuristic building is the immense bronze Venus. Art Deco interiors, high level of comfort, exemplary soundproofing, rooftop pool. Attractive restaurant with panoramic summer terrace and cuisine with a local touch.

Sofitel, 2-4 parvis de l'Europe ✉ 06300 ✆ 04 92 00 80 00, *h1119@accor-hotels.com, Fax 04 93 26 27 00,* - 35 - 80. JX t
L'Oliveraie *(closed 15 June-15 September)* **Meals** 27 - ***Le Sundeck*** *(15 June-15 September)* **Meals** 27 - 23 - **138 rm** 365/385, 14 suites.
◆ On the site of Nice's acropolis, this hotel has been redesigned in contemporary style. Modern, well-presented rooms with good facilities. Lovely panoramic rooftop pool. Provençal décor in the Oliveraie. Grills and city and country views in the Sundeck.

Radisson SAS, 223 promenade des Anglais ✆ 04 93 37 17 17, *info.nice@radissonsas.com, Fax 04 93 71 21 71,* - 15 - 200. AU n
Meals 30/52 - 20 - **318 rm** 240/285, 13 suites.
◆ A modern building with an attractive, fully refurbished interior and elegant, spacious rooms. Designer-style bar and rooftop pool and terrace. Contemporary cuisine is served in the comfortable dining room, decorated in blue and lemon tones.

Boscolo Hôtel Plaza, 12 av. Verdun ✆ 04 93 16 75 75, *reservation@nice.boscolo.com, Fax 04 93 88 61 11* - 250 - 400. GZ u
Meals 35 - 22 - **170 rm** 263/326, 12 suites.
◆ Imposing hotel adjacent to the Jardin Albert 1er. Spacious rooms. Roof-terrace with lovely seaward views. Comprehensive meeting facilities. Dining room in warm colours and a generous panoramic terrace overlooking the city.

La Pérouse , 11 quai Rauba-Capéu ✉ 06300 ✆ 04 93 62 34 63, *lp@hroy.com, Fax 04 93 62 59 41,* Nice and Baie des Anges, rm, - 30. HZ k
Meals *(June-September)* a la carte 32/42 - 19 - **58 rm** 225/420, 4 suites.
◆ This characterful hotel clinging to the castle rock offers refined, Provençal-style rooms and a delightful Mediterranean garden. The viewpoint was an inspiration for Dufy. In the restaurant-grill, enjoy your meal in perfect tranquillity under the lemon trees.

West End, 31 promenade des Anglais ✆ 04 92 14 44 00, *hotel-westend@hotel-westend.com, Fax 04 93 88 85 07,* - 100. FZ p
***Le Siècle* : Meals** 37 (dinner) - 18 - **109 rm** 230/290, 16 suites.
◆ Built in the early 19C, this listed hotel is in constant evolution. Ask for one of the rooms refurbished in English or Provençal style with a sea view. The smart Le Siècle brasserie is in Belle Epoque style and has two attractively planted terraces.

Holiday Inn, 20 bd V. Hugo ✆ 04 97 03 22 22, *reservations@holinice.com, Fax 04 97 03 22 23,* - 90. FY a
Meals 25 - 18 - **131 rm** 145/340.
◆ A concrete and glass building close to shops and traffic-free streets, with rooms decorated in different styles (colonial, maritime, taffeta etc). TV with internet access and Playstation. Attractive restaurant with exotic decor (plants and bamboo furniture).

Boscolo Park Hôtel, 6 av. Suède ✆ 04 97 03 19 00, *reservation@park.boscolo.com, Fax 04 93 82 29 27,* - 150. rest FZ a
Meals *(dinner only)* a la carte approx. 30 - 20 - **104 rm** 192/405.
◆ This hotel has rooms in classic, Art Deco and Mediterranean style, some overlooking the Jardin Albert 1er and the sea. Brushed metal, mirrors and designer furniture give the restaurant a very contemporary ambience. Asian-influenced cuisine.

Hi Hôtel, 3 av. Fleurs ✆ 04 97 07 26 26, *hi@hi-hotel.net, Fax 04 97 07 26 27,* EZ a
Meals 19 - 18 - **38 rm** 160/280.
◆ A designer hotel bearing little resemblance to the traditional image of the term, where the use of space, materials, colour, furniture and equipment is totally innovative. Contemporary-style bar. Self-service choice of innovative cold dishes.

Beau Rivage, 24 r. St-François-de-Paule ✉ 06300 ✆ 04 92 47 82 82, *info@nicebeaurivage.com, Fax 04 92 47 82 83,* - 25 - 30. GZ y
Plage *(April-September)* **Meals** a la carte 39/45 - 24 - **119 rm** 420/990.
◆ The architect Jean-Michel Wilmotte has transformed this establishment once frequented by Matisse, Nietzsche and Chekhov into a pleasant hotel with a refined, modern look.

Mercure Centre Notre Dame without rest, 28 av. Notre-Dame ✆ 04 93 13 36 36, *h1291@accor-hotels.com, Fax 04 93 62 61 69,* – ✉ 90. AE ⓓ GB JCB FXY q
☕ 15 – **201 rm** 145/175.
◆ In addition to pretty, contemporary-style rooms, this completely refurbished Mercure hotel has a 2nd floor hanging garden, beauty salon and rooftop terrace and pool.

Grimaldi without rest, 15 r. Grimaldi ✆ 04 93 16 00 24, *zedde@le-grimaldi.com, Fax 04 93 87 00 24* – AE ⓓ GB FY s
☕ 20 – **46 rm** 125/185.
◆ Provençal furnishings, wrought iron and lovely Souleûado fabrics give these rooms with little terraces on the top floor a personal touch. Very cosy foyer/bar/lounge.

Windsor, 11 r. Dalpozzo ✆ 04 93 88 59 35, *contact@hotelwindsornice.com, Fax 04 93 88 94 57,* – AE GB. rest FZ f
Meals *(closed lunch and Sunday)* a la carte approx. 34 – ☕ 10 – **57 rm** 105/155.
◆ Twenty fascinating "artists' rooms" including one bearing the signature of the local painter Ben. Exotic garden, plus leisure facilities which include massage and a steam room. Meals at the bar in winter and among the palms and bougainvillaea in summer.

Petit Palais without rest, 17 av. E. Bieckert ✆ 04 93 62 19 11, *petitpalais@provence-riviera.com, Fax 04 93 62 53 60,* ≤ Nice and sea – AE ⓓ GB JCB HX p
☕ 10 – **25 rm** 96/144.
◆ This villa of 1900 high up on the Cimiez hill was once lived in by Sacha Guitry. Most of the rooms look down over the rooftops of Nice's old town towards the Baie des Anges.

Durante without rest, 16 av. Durante ✆ 04 93 88 84 40, *info@hotel-durante.com, Fax 04 93 87 77 76,* – kitchenette AE GB FY b
☕ 9 **24 rm** 69/100.
◆ Newly renovated hotel with pretty bedrooms: the side road is so quiet that you can sleep with the windows open and let the scent of the orange trees waft in from the garden.

Chantecler - Hôtel Négresco, 37 promenade des Anglais ✆ 04 93 16 64 00, *direction@hotel-negresco.com, Fax 04 93 88 35 68* – AE ⓓ GB JCB FZ k
closed 3 January-8 February – **Meals** 45 (lunch), 75/90 and a la carte 98/161 ♀
Spec. Subrics de chair de tourteau, bouquet de brocolis sur émulsion d'orange. Homard cuit en carcasse dans un bouillon de citronnelle. Filet de boeuf poêlé aux câpres de l'île de Pantelleria.. **Wines** Vins de pays des Alpes Maritimes.
◆ Sumptuous panelling, Aubusson tapestries, Old Master paintings and damask curtains enhance the appeal of this early 18C interior. Delicious, highly individual cuisine.

L'Ane Rouge (Devillers), 7 quai Deux-Emmanuel ✉ 06300 ✆ 04 93 89 49 63, *anerouge@free.fr, Fax 04 93 89 49 63* – AE ⓓ GB JZ m
closed 6 to 14 July, February, Thursday lunch and Wednesday – **Meals** 26 (lunch), 55/75 and a la carte 58/88
Spec. Soupe glacée de tomate, fleur de courgette garnie aux calamars (April-October). Les poissons du jour. Tarte au chocolat, glace vanille.. **Wines** Vin de pays des Alpes-Maritimes, Bellet.
◆ Recently refurbished dining room with views of the castle rock and the activity in the yacht harbour - an attractive setting in which to savour tasty meat and fish dishes.

Don Camillo, 5 r. Ponchettes ✉ 06300 ✆ 04 93 85 67 95, *vianostephane@wanadoo.fr, Fax 04 93 13 97 43* – AE ⓓ GB HZ h
closed 19 to 27 December, Sunday and Monday lunch – **Meals** 32/56 and a la carte 40/60 ♀.
◆ Harmonious décor, subtle colours and a welcoming atmosphere are the attractions of this restaurant in a quiet street. Local cuisine plus Italian specialities.

Les Viviers, 22 r. A. Karr ✆ 04 93 16 00 48, *viviers.bretons@wanadoo.fr, Fax 04 93 16 04 06* – AE GB. FY k
closed August and Sunday – **Meals** 35/70 and a la carte 55/80 ♀.
◆ One dining room with elegant light-wood panelling, another with nautical decor - both serving identical food featuring fish, shellfish and daily specials.

L'Univers-Christian Plumail, 54 bd J. Jaurès ✉ 06300 ✆ 04 93 62 32 22, *plumailunivers@aol.com, Fax 04 93 62 55 69* – AE ⓓ GB HZ u
closed Sunday, lunch Saturday and Monday – **Meals** (booking essential) 42 and a la carte 56/71 ♀
Spec. Gamberonis poêlés à la coriandre fraîche. Chapon de mer poché au jus de bouille. Soufflé aux citrons du pays.. **Wines** Vin de pays des Alpes-Maritimes, Bellet.
◆ The decor of this establishment is enhanced by pictures and modern sculpture. Individual local cuisine, which is very popular with locals.

Auberge de Théo, 52 av. Cap de Croix ✆ 04 93 81 26 19, *aubergedetheo@wanadoo.fr, Fax 04 93 81 51 73* – GB BS u
closed 20 August-10 September, 24 December-3 January, Sunday dinner from September-April and Monday – **Meals** 19,50 (lunch)/30,50 ♀.
◆ On the city heights, this trattoria resembles nothing so much as Rome's famous Trastevere establishments. Rustic interior with beams and a real Neapolitan crib. Italian food.

XX **Brasserie Flo,** 4 r. S. Guitry ✆ 04 93 13 38 38, *c.sordillon@groupeflo.fr, Fax 04 93 13 38 39* – ▤. AE ⓓ GB JCB GYZ m
Meals 29,90 b.i. ♀.
◆ In the style of a Paris brasserie, this establishment occupies an old theatre and presents a lively spectacle at all times, teeming with diners and hosts of serving staff.

XX **Les Épicuriens,** 6 pl. Wilson ✆ 04 93 80 85 00, *Fax 04 93 85 65 00,* ☂ – ▤. AE GB *closed 6 August-2 September, Saturday lunch and Sunday* – **Meals** a la carte 34/48 ♀.
◆ Refined bistro-style decor, prettily planted terrace, up-to-the-minute cuisine with specials chalked up daily, much favoured by the business community. HY v

XX **Les Pêcheurs,** 18 quai des Docks ✆ 04 93 89 59 61, *jbarbate@wanadoo.fr, Fax 04 93 55 47 50,* ☂ – ▤. AE ⓓ GB JZ v
closed November-mid December, Tuesday dinner from December-April, Thursday lunch from May-October and Wednesday – **Meals** 28 ♀.
◆ In the yacht harbour, this establishment seems to sum up the Cote d'Azur, with nautical décor, boats bobbing outside, and delicious seafood gracing your plate.

X **Mireille,** 19 bd Raimbaldi ✆ 04 93 85 27 23 – ▤. AE GB GX d
closed 20 June-5 July, 15 to 23 August, Monday and Tuesday – **Meals** 27.
◆ Bang in the middle of Italian "Nizza", a restaurant with Hispanic décor and a real Provençal name. The only dish is paella, presented in a gleaming copper dish.

X **La Merenda,** 4 r. Terrasse ✉ 06300 – ▤ – *closed 1 to 15 June, 1 to 15 August, Saturday and Sunday* – **Meals** (booking essential) a la carte 32/40 ♀. HZ a
◆ Uncomfortable stools, no credit cards accepted, payment in cash only... but it's worth it for the pleasure of savouring the real taste of Nice !

at the airport : *7 km – ✉ 06200 Nice :*

Novotel Arenas, 455 promenade des Anglais ✆ 04 93 21 22 50, *h0478@accor-hotels.com, Fax 04 93 21 63 50* – |‡|, ⇔ ▤ TV ✆ ♿ 🚗 – 🏛 25 - 150. AE ⓓ GB
Meals a la carte 24/34 – ☕ 12 – **131 rm** 120/130.
◆ With plenty of space, functional furnishings, good soundproofing and numerous meeting rooms, this well-presented Novotel is much appreciated by business travellers. More intimate atmosphere than usual in the restaurant. Provençal cuisine.

Beaulieu-sur-Mer *06310 Alpes-Mar.* 341 F5 – *pop. 3 675 – Nice 8.*

✿✿ **Réserve de Beaulieu** 🔇, bd Mar. Leclerc ✆ 04 93 01 00 01, *reservation@reservebeaulieu.com, Fax 04 93 01 28 99,* < sea, ☂, 🏊, 🏋, 🏖 – |‡|, ▤ rm, TV ✆ 🚗. AE ⓓ GB
closed 30 November-22 December – **Meals** (dinner only from 1 June-30 September) 60/150 and a la carte 136/220 – ☕ 28 – **33 rm** 475/1000, 6 suites
Spec. Terrine de carottes nouvelles à l'écorce d'orange (April-June). Paupiettes de loup de ligne à l'olive (June-September). Carré d'agneau rôti et pithiviers de légumes méditerranéens.. **Wines** Côtes de Provence.
◆ Refined luxury by the seaside in a Florentine Renaissance-style palace dating from 1880. Beauty salon, indoor garden, private landing stage. Enjoy inventive Provençal cuisine in the elegant dining room or on the terrace with its magical view of the bay.

Èze *06360 Alpes-Mar.* 341 F5 – *pop. 2 509 alt. 390.*

ℹ *Tourisme Office pl. du Général de Gaulle* ✆ *04 93 41 26 00, Fax 04 93 41 04 80.*
Nice 12.

✿✿ **Château de la Chèvre d'Or** 🔇, r. Barri (pedestrian access) ✆ 04 92 10 66 66, *reservation@chevredor.com, Fax 04 93 41 06 72,* < coast and peninsula, ☂, 🏋, 🏖, 🌳 – ▤ TV ✆ P – 🏛 20. AE ⓓ GB JCB
4 March-early November – **Meals** *(closed Wednesday in March and November)* (booking essential) 60 (lunch)/150 and a la carte 155/205 ♀ – ☕ 40 – **32 rm** 301/680, 8 suites
Spec. Oursin, araignée de mer et Saint-Jacques en oursinade glacée et tartare (Winter). Epaule d'agneau confite aux épices, caillé de brebis parfumé au citron de Menton (Spring). Rouget de roche poêlé au jus d'olives niçoises (Summer).. **Wines** Côtes de Provence..
◆ With its hanging gardens high up on a rocky perch overlooking the Mediterranean, this enchanting establishment promises its guests an unforgettable experience. As well as delighting the eye, it's a treat for the taste-buds - a gastronomic paradise.

St-Martin-du-Var *06670 Alpes-Mar.* 341 E5 – *pop. 2 197 alt. 110 – Nice 26.*

XXXX ✿✿ **Jean-François Issautier,** on Nice road (N 202) 3 km ✆ 04 93 08 10 65, *jf.issautier@wanadoo.fr, Fax 04 93 29 19 73* – ▤ P. AE ⓓ GB
closed 3 to 12 October, early January-early February, Sunday dinner, Monday and Tuesday – **Meals** 49 b.i./100 and a la carte 85/115 ♀
Spec. Pied de cochon croustillant. Pêche du jour et légumes en "bagna cauda". Cul d'agneau rôti rosé au jus de menthe.. **Wines** Bellet, Côtes de Provence.
◆ This discreet restaurant, well-known to gourmets, is screened from the road by a conifer hedge. A fine classical repertoire favouring regional cuisine. Sophisticated setting.

La Turbie *06320 Alpes-Mar.* 341 F5 – *pop. 3 021 alt. 495.*
Nice 16.

Hostellerie Jérôme (Cirino) with rm, 20 r. Comte de Cessole ✆ 04 92 41 51 51, *hostellerie.jerome@wanadoo.fr, Fax 04 92 41 51 50,* ←, – rm, GB
closed 1 to 19 December, Monday, Tuesday except July-August and Bank Holidays – **Meals** 40 (lunch), 50/95 and a la carte 84/124 ♀ – ☕ 16 – **5 rm** 90/150
Spec. Tarte potagère aux gamberoni à l'huile d'olive. Foie gras de canard rôti aux agrumes de Menton (Winter). Loup de mer à la compotée de fleurs et feuilles de courgettes.. **Wines** Côtes de Provence, Bellet.
◆ Handsome 13C building in a village better known for the Trophée des Alpes monument. Trim dining room with Italian decor and Mediterranean cuisine.

Vence *06140 Alpes-Mar.* 341 D5 – *pop. 16 982 alt. 325.*
Tourist Office, 8 pl. Grand-Jardin ✆ 04 93 58 06 38, Fax 04 93 58 91 81 and 2, rue Grande ✆ 04 93 32 86 95, Fax 04 93 32 60 27.
Nice 23.

Jacques Maximin, 689 chemin de La Gaude, by road of Cagnes : 3 km ✆ 04 93 58 90 75, *info@jacques-maximin.com, Fax 04 93 58 22 86,* , – AE GB
closed mid Nov.-mid Dec., lunch in 07/08 except Sunday, Monday and Tuesday out of season except Bank Holidays – **Meals** (booking essential) 50 b.i. and a la carte 90/130
Spec. Loup sauvage rôti à la niçoise. Caviar de seiche du pays et d'aubergines anisé. Canard rôti à l'ail doux, en poivrade devin.. **Wines** Bellet, Coteaux Varois.
◆ Surrounded by luxurious vegetation, this 19C house adorned with works of art created by renowned artists is the setting for cuisine that is as delicious as it is creative.

STRASBOURG *67000 B.-Rhin* 315 K5 – *pop. 264 115 alt. 143.*
See : *Cathedral★★★ : Astronomical clock★ – La Petite France★★ : rue du Bains-aux-Plantes★★* HJZ *– Barrage Vauban ✲★★ – Ponts couverts★ – Place de la Cathédrale★* KZ **26** *: Maison Kammerzell★* KZ **e** *– Mausoleum★★ in St-Thomas Church* JZ *– Place Kléber★ – Hôtel de Ville★* KY **H** *– Orangery★ – Palais de l'Europe★ – Museum of Oeuvre N.-Dame★★* KZ **M¹** *– Boat trips on the Ill river and the canals★* KZ *– Museums★★ (decorative Arts, Fine Arts, Archeology) in the Palais Rohan★* KZ *– Alsatian Museum★★* KZ **M²**.
27 at Illkirch-Graffenstaden (private) ✆ 03 88 66 17 22 ; 18 of the Wantzenau at Wantzenau (private) ✆ 03 88 96 37 73 ; N by D 468 : 12 km ; 18 of Kempferhof at Plobsheim ✆ 03 88 98 72 72, S by D 468 : 15 km. – ✈ of Strasbourg-International : ✆ 03 88 64 67 67 by D 392 : 12 km FR *–* ✆ **0892 35 35 33.**
Tourist Office 17 pl. de la Cathédrale ✆ 03 88 52 28 28, Fax 03 88 52 28 29, pl.gare ✆ 03 88 32 51 49, Pont de l'Europe ✆ 03 88 61 39 23.
Paris 490 – Basle 145 – Bonn 360 – Bordeaux 915 – Frankfurt 218 – Karlsruhe 81 – Lille 545 – Luxembourg 223 – Lyons 485 – Stuttgart 157.

Régent Petite France, 5 r. Moulins ✆ 03 88 76 43 43, *rpf@regent-hotels.com, Fax 03 88 76 43 76,* ←, , – – 30 - 80. AE GB JCB
Meals *(closed Sunday from October-April and Monday from May-September)* 30 ♀ – ☕ 19 – **61 rm** 230/305, 7 suites, 4 duplex. JZ z
◆ Metal, glass, designer furniture and high-tech gadgetry dominate this modern hotel in an old refrigeration plant on the banks of the Ill. A trendy interior and a pleasant view of the river and old town are the main attractions of the restaurant.

Hilton, av. Herrenschmidt ✆ 03 88 37 10 10, *contact@hilton-strasbourg.com, Fax 03 88 36 83 27,* – – 25 - 350. AE GB JCB
La Table du Chef ✆ 03 88 37 41 42 (lunch only) *(closed 14 July-31 August, Saturday and Sunday)* **Meals** 38 ♀ – ***Le Jardin du Tivoli*** ✆ 03 88 35 72 61 **Meals** 25/28 ♀ – ☕ 21 – **237 rm** 225/311, 6 suites.
◆ A slender glass and steel building with rooms renovated with care. Multimedia centre, bars and a foyer with shops. British feel in La Table du Chef - a traditional restaurant at lunchtime and wine bar in the evening. Pleasant terrace at the Jardin du Tivoli.

Sofitel, pl. St-Pierre-le-Jeune ✆ 03 88 15 49 00, *h0568@accor-hotels.com, Fax 03 88 15 49 99,* – – 100. AE GB JCB JY s
L'Alsace Gourmande ✆ 03 88 15 49 10 **Meals** 30/35 b.i. ♀ – ☕ 29 – **155 rm** 255/375.
◆ The first Sofitel built in France (1964) is today a hotel combining modern comforts and excellent facilities. Smart bedrooms, plus a lobby that opens onto a patio. Soberly styled wood in the restaurant, where the focus is on locally influenced modern cuisine.

Holiday Inn, 20 pl. Bordeaux ✆ 03 88 37 80 00, *histrasbourg@alliance-hospitality.com, Fax 03 88 37 07 04,* , – – 300. AE GB JCB. rest
Meals *(closed lunch Saturday and Sunday)* 25 ♀ – ☕ 16 – **170 rm** 220/280.
◆ An ideal business and seminar hotel with well-appointed rooms near the European courts and conference centre. Traditional cuisine with Provençal touches served amid "Louisiana"-style décor.

STRASBOURG

22-Novembre (R. du). HJYZ
Abreuvoir (R. de l') . . . . . LZ 3
Arc-en-Ciel (R. de l') . . . KLY 7
Austerlitz (R. d') . . . . KZ 10
Auvergne (Pont d') . . . . . LY 12
Bateliers (R. des) . . . . . . LZ 14
Bonnes-Gens (R. des) . . JY 19
Bouclier (R. du) . . . . JZ 20
Castelnau (R. Gén.-de) . . KY 25
Cathédrale (Pl. de la) . . . . KZ 26
Chaudron (R. du) . . . . . . KY 28
Cheveux (R. des) . . . . JZ 29
Corbeau (Pl. du) . . . . KZ 31
Cordiers (R. des) . . . . KZ 32
Courtine (R. de la) . . . . . . LY 34
Dentelles (R. des) . . . . . . JZ 36
Division-Leclerc (R.) . . . JKZ
Écarlate (R. de l') . . . . . . JZ 43
Escarpée (R.) . . . . JZ 45
Étudiants (R. et Pl. des) . KY 46
Faisan (Pont du) . . . . JZ 47
Fonderie (Pont de la) . . . KY 52
Fossé-des-Tanneurs (R. du) . . . . JZ 57
Fossés-des-Treize (R. du) . . . . KY 58
Francs-Bourgeois (R. des) . . . . JZ 60
Frey (Quai Charles) . . . . . JZ 63
Grande-Boucherie (Pl. de la) . . . . KZ 76
Grandes-Arcades (R. des) . . . . JKY
Gutenberg (R.) . . . . JKZ 78
Hallebardes (R. des) . . . . KZ 80
Haute-Montée (R.) . . . . . JY 82
Homme de Fer (Pl. de l') JY 90
Hôpital-Militaire (R. de l'). LZ 91
Humann (R.) . . . . HZ 94
Ill (Quai de l') . . . . HZ 95
Kellermann (Quai) . . . . . . JY 100
Kléber (Pl.) . . . . JY
Krutenau (R. de la) . . . . . LZ 106
Kuss (Pont) . . . . HY 108
Lamey (R. Auguste) . . . . LY 109
Lezay-Marnésia (Quai) . . LY 114
Luther (R. Martin) . . . . . . JZ 117
Maire Kuss (R. du) . . . . . HY 120

Marché-aux-Cochons-de-Lait (Pl. du) . . . . KZ 124
Marché-aux-Poissons (Pl. du) . . . . KZ 125
Marché-Gayot (Pl. du) . KYZ 126
Marché-Neuf (Pl. du) . . KYZ 127
Maroquin (R. du) . . . . KZ 129
Mercière (R.) . . . . KZ 135
Mésange (R. de la) . . . . JKY 136
Monnaie (R. de la) . . . . . . JZ 141
Munch (R. Ernest) . . . . . . LZ 142
Noyer (R. du) . . . . JY 147
Nuée-Bleue (R. de la) . . . KY
Obernai (R. d') . . . . HZ 150
Outre (R. de l') . . . . KY 153
Paix (Av. de la) . . . . KLY 154
Parchemin (R. du) . . . . . . KY 156
Pierre (R. du Fg-de) . . . . . JY 160
Pontonniers (R. des) . . . . LY 167
Récollets (R. des) . . . . . KLY 172
St-Étienne (Quai) . . . . LY 183
St-Michel (R.) . . . . HZ 187
St-Nicolas (Pont) . . . . KZ 189
St-Pierre-le-Jeune (Pl.) . . . . JKY 190
Ste-Madeleine (Pont et R.) . . . . KLZ 192
Salzmann (R.) . . . . JZ 193
Sanglier (R. du) . . . . KY 194
Saverne (Pont de) . . . . . HY 195
Schoelcher (Av. Victor) . . LY 199
Sébastopol (R. de) . . . . . . JY 202
Serruriers (R. des) . . . . JKZ 205
Temple-Neuf (Pl. du) . . . KY 213
Temple-Neuf (R. du) . . . . KY 214
Théâtre (Pont du) . . . . . . KY 216
Thomann (R. des) . . . . . . JY 217
Tonneliers (R. des) . . . . . KZ 220
Turckheim (Quai) . . . . . . HZ 225
Vieil-Hôpital (R. du) . . . . . KZ 228
Vieux-Marché-aux-Poissons (R. du) . . . . KZ 229
Vieux-Marché-aux-Vins (R. et Pl. du) . . . . JY 230
Vieux-Seigle (R. du) . . . . . JZ 231
Wasselonne (R.) . . . . HZ 238
Wodli (R. Georges) . . . . . HY 242

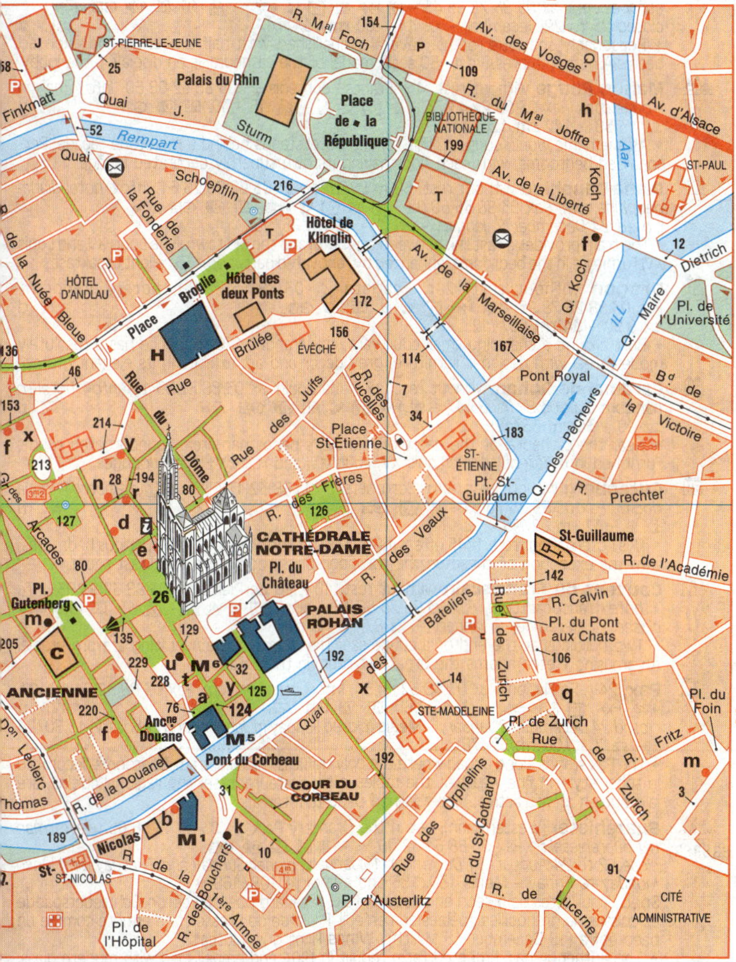

Régent Contades without rest, 8 av. Liberté ✆ 03 88 15 05 05, *rc@regent-hotels.com, Fax 03 88 15 05 15* – 17,50 – **47 rm** 170/270. LY f

◆ A 19C private mansion with an elegant decor of decorative panelling in the lounge and ubiquitous canvases. Spacious bedrooms, plus a Belle Epoque-style breakfast room.

Beaucour without rest, 5 r. Bouchers ✆ 03 88 76 72 00, *beaucour@hotel-beaucour.com, Fax 03 88 76 72 60* – – 25. 11 – **49 rm** 91/128. KZ k

◆ These two 18C Alsatian houses are laid out around a flowery patio. Elegant furnishings with bedrooms that blend the rustic with the contemporary.

Novotel Centre Halles, 4 quai Kléber ✆ 03 88 21 50 50, *h0439@accor-hotels.com, Fax 03 88 21 50 51* – – 15 - 80. JY k

Meals a la carte 29/36 – 12,80 – **98 rm** 135/145.

◆ Located within the Les Halles shopping centre, this chain hotel offers functional rooms, some with views of the old town. Cinema-inspired bar decor, plus an inviting restaurant with original decor which has moved away from the standard Novotel look.

De l'Europe without rest, 38 r. Fossé des Tanneurs ✆ 03 88 32 17 88, *info@hotel-europe.com, Fax 03 88 75 65 45* – – 30. *closed 23 to 29 December* – 11 – **60 rm** 73/174. JZ v

◆ Reasonably spacious rooms, several embellished with half-timbering and exposed beams.A hugely impressive 1 : 50 scale model of the cathedral is on display in the lobby.

Maison Rouge without rest, 4 r. Francs-Bourgeois ✆ 03 88 32 08 60, *info@maison-rouge.com, Fax 03 88 22 43 73* – – 15 - 30. JZ g

13,50 – **142 rm** 126/143.

◆ As the name would suggest, this refined hotel stands behind a red-stone façade. Personalised bedrooms, with each floor having its own superbly decorated lounge.

Diana-Dauphine without rest, 30 r. 1e Armée ✆ 03 88 36 26 61, *info@hotel-diana-dauphine.com, Fax 03 88 35 50 07* – . *closed 24 December-2 January* – 9 – **45 rm** 85/95.

◆ The tram provides a fast link between this hotel and the old town. Fine Louis XV and Louis XVI furniture in the bedrooms, enhanced by renovated bathrooms. Excellent breakfast.

Dragon without rest, 2 r. Ecarlate ✆ 03 88 35 79 80, *hotel@dragon.fr, Fax 03 88 25 78 95* – . JZ d

9,90 – **34 rm** 69/112.

◆ Built around a charming small courtyard, this tranquil 17C residence has a resolutely modern feel with designer furniture, grey decor and art exhibits in its elegant rooms.

Cardinal de Rohan without rest, 17 r. Maroquin ✆ 03 88 32 85 11, *info@hotel-rohan.com, Fax 03 88 75 65 37* – . KZ u

10 – **36 rm** 65/129.

◆ Near the cathedral at the heart of the city's pedestrian area. Soundproofed rooms furnished in different styles (Louis XV, Louis XVI and rustic). Elegant lounges.

Gutenberg without rest, 31 r. Serruriers ✆ 03 88 32 17 15, *hotel.gutenberg@wanadoo.fr, Fax 03 88 75 76 67* – . KZ m

8 – **42 rm** 62/95.

◆ This hotel dating from 1745 offers its guests comfortable, relatively spacious bedrooms, with the exception of those on the top floor. Glass roof in the breakfast room.

Couvent du Franciscain without rest, 18 r. Fg de Pierre ✆ 03 88 32 93 93, *info@hotel-franciscain.com, Fax 03 88 75 68 46* – – 15. *closed 24 December-8 January* – 8,50 – **43 rm** 64/66. JY e

◆ Two buildings at the end of a cul-de-sac. The rooms in the new wing are preferable. An amusing fresco adorns the breakfast room in the cellar.

Pax, 24 r. Fg National ✆ 03 88 32 14 54, *info@paxhotel.com, Fax 03 88 32 01 16,* – – 15 - 60. HYZ u

closed 24 December-2 January – **Meals** *(closed Sunday in January and February)* 13,50/24 – 7 – **106 rm** 57/78.

◆ The Pax stands along a road where the only traffic is the local tram. Bedrooms decorated in sober style. In fine weather, the tables in the restaurant, serving regional cuisine, are laid out on an attractive, vine-adorned patio-cum-terrace.

Buerehiesel (Westermann), set in the Orangery Park ✆ 03 88 45 56 65, *westermann@buerehiesel.fr, Fax 03 88 61 32 00,* – .

closed 2 to 24 August, 31 December-19 January, dinner Sunday and Tuesday, and lunch Monday to Friday – **Meals** 130/156 and a la carte 108/160

Spec. Aiguillettes de pigeon en salade et foie de canard poêlé au citron. Schniederspaetle et cuisses de grenouilles poêlées au cerfeuil. Poularde de Bresse cuite entière comme un baeckeoffa (15 December-15 March).. **Wines** Pinot gris, Muscat.

◆ This authentic half-timbered farm rebuilt in 1904 and embellished with modern glass, is hidden amid the greenery of the Parc de l'Orangerie. A paradise of Alsatian gastronomy !

XXXX ✿✿ **Au Crocodile** (Jung), 10 r. Outre ✆ 03 88 32 13 02, *info@au-crocodile.com, Fax 03 88 75 72 01* – ▤. AE ⓓ GB JCB. ⚘ KY x
closed 10 July-1 August, 24 December-10 January, Sunday and Monday – **Meals** 56 (lunch), 83/126 b.i. and a la carte 94/122 ♀
Spec. Foie de canard en croûte de sel, pommes boulangères truffées. Sandre et laitance de carpe au mille-choux à la coriandre. Tartelette "Crocodile" aux pommes et framboises.
Wines Riesling, Pinot gris.
◆ With its splendid wood décor, canvases and the famous crocodile brought back from the Egyptian campaign by an Alsatian captain, the setting is as refined as the cuisine.

XXX **Vieille Enseigne,** 9 r. Tonneliers ✆ 03 88 32 58 50, *info@la-vieille-enseigne.com, Fax 03 88 75 63 80* – ▤. AE ⓓ GB JCB KZ f
closed Saturday lunch and Sunday – **Meals** 33 (lunch), 61/78 and a la carte 63/99.
◆ Refined, in-vogue cuisine, an extensive wine cellar, and a hushed, elegant setting characterise this restaurant housed within the walls of a fine 17C Alsatian mansion.

XXX **Estaminet Schloegel,** 19 r. Krütenau ✆ 03 88 36 21 98, *Fax 03 88 36 21 98* – ▤. GB – *closed August, Sunday, lunch Saturday and Monday* – **Meals** 37/46 ♀. LZ q
◆ Set back from the historic centre, this former tavern is colourfully decorated with tasteful contemporary furnishings. A spiral wooden staircase adds further embellishment.

XXX **Maison Kammerzell and Hôtel Baumann** with rm, 16 pl. Cathédrale ✆ 03 88 32 42 14, *info@maison-kammerzell.com, Fax 03 88 23 03 92* – |♦| ▤ TV ✆ – 🏛 80 - 100. AE ⓓ GB JCB KZ e
hotel : closed February – **Meals** 29,50/45 and a la carte 33/51 ♀ – ☕ 10 – **9 rm** 69/110.
◆ Wall paintings, stained glass, wood sculptures and Gothic vaults provide a museum feel to this 16C Strasbourg institution serving typical Alsatian dishes.

XXX **Maison des Tanneurs dite "Gerwerstub",** 42 r. Bain aux Plantes ✆ 03 88 32 79 70, *maison.des.tanneurs@wanadoo.fr, Fax 03 88 22 17 26* – AE ⓓ GB JZ t
closed 30 December-25 January, Sunday and Monday – **Meals** a la carte 40/64.
◆ Ideally situated on the banks of the Ill, this typical Alsatian house in the Petite France district is one of the best addresses in town for an authentic sauerkraut.

XX **L'Atable 77,** 77 Grand'Rue ✆ 03 88 32 23 37, *Fax 03 88 32 50 24* – ▤. AE ⓓ GB JZ h
closed 1 to 9 May, 24 July-15 August, 12 to 20 February, Sunday and Monday – **Meals** 28/70 ♀.
◆ A refined contemporary look, attractive designer layout, exhibition of paintings and appetising cuisine with a modern theme characterise this appealing restaurant.

XX **Julien,** 22 quai Bateliers ✆ 03 88 36 01 54, *restaurant.julien@wanadoo.fr, Fax 03 88 35 40 14* – ▤. AE ⓓ GB KZ x
closed 27 March-4 April, 24 July-15 August, 1 to 10 January, Sunday and Monday – **Meals** 35/62 ♀.
◆ A fine 18C Alsatian house in which the decor of benches and glossy walls takes its inspiration from the bistros of the Belle Époque period. A classic culinary repertoire.

XX **S'Staefele,** 2 pl. St-Thomas ✆ 03 88 32 39 03, *Fax 03 88 21 90 80*, 🏠 – AE GB JZ k
closed 15 to 29 August, 31 December-3 January, Sunday and Monday – **Meals** 24/34 ♀.
◆ Meats, contemporary dishes and Mediterranean cuisine form the backbone of the menu in this rustic, bistro-style dining room. The terrace overlooks a pretty, small square.

XX ✿ **Serge and Co** (Burckel), 14 r. Pompiers ✉ 67300 *Schiltigheim* ✆ 03 88 18 96 19, *serge.burckel@wanadoo.fr, Fax 03 88 83 41 99* – ▤. GB BS g
closed 1 to 15 August, Saturday lunch, Sunday and Monday – **Meals** 24,50 (lunch), 42/95 ♀
Spec. Gelée de grenouilles à la purée de pois chiche. Noix de ris de veau rôtie, carrottes braisées. "cigare au chocolat".
◆ Serge Burckel has returned to his home turf after a long sojourn in Asia and the US to set up this pleasant modern restaurant serving inventive dishes inspired by his travels.

XX **Pont des Vosges,** 15 quai Koch ✆ 03 88 36 47 75, *pontdesvosges@noos.fr, Fax 03 88 25 16 85*, 🏠 – AE GB LY h
closed Sunday – **Meals** 30/40 ♀.
◆ This restaurant on the ground floor of an old building, is arranged in a semi-circle. A mix of retro and modern decor in which to enjoy a brasserie-style menu.

XX **Brasserie Kirn,** 6/8 r. de l'Outre ✆ 03 88 52 03 03, *Fax 03 88 52 01 00* – ▤. AE ⓓ GB KY f
closed Sunday – **Meals** 21 (lunch)/28 ♀.
◆ This former butcher's is now home to a large dining room decorated in early-20C style with a fine central dome and embellished with artistic stained glass. Brasserie cuisine.

X **S'Burjerstuewel (Chez Yvonne),** 10 r. Sanglier ✆ 03 88 32 84 15, *info@chez-yvonne.com, Fax 03 88 23 00 18* – AE ⓓ GB KYZ r
Meals (booking essential) a la carte 28/40.
◆ A chic wine-bar atmosphere pervades this Strasbourg institution where dining is somewhat cheek by jowl. Regional cuisine supplemented by contemporary daily specials.

WINSTUBS : *Regional specialities and wine tasting in a typical Alsatian atmosphere :*

Ami Schutz, 1 r. Ponts Couverts ✆ 03 88 32 76 98, *info@ami-schutz.com, Fax 03 88 32 38 40,* – AE GB HZ r
closed Christmas Holidays – **Meals** 22,80/45 b.i. ♀.
◆ This beer tavern between the branches of the River Ill has a pleasant shaded terrace. The charming dining rooms have a warm atmosphere and superb antique wood panelling.

S'Muensterstuewel, 8 pl. Marché aux Cochons de Lait ✆ 03 88 32 17 63, *muensterstuewel@wanadoo.fr, Fax 03 88 21 96 02,* – AE GB KZ y
closed 24/04 to 2/05, 17/07 to 1/08, 28/08 to 5/09, 30/10 to 7/11, 1 to 5/01, 6 to 14/02, Sunday and Monday – **Meals** 25 (lunch), 30/45.
◆ A former butcher's decorated in pure "winstub" style with pleasant rustic furniture. In summer, sit out on the terrace in front of a small square popular with tourists.

Le Clou, 3 r. Chaudron ✆ 03 88 32 11 67, *Fax 03 88 21 06 43* – AE GB KY n
closed Wednesday lunch, Sunday and Bank Holidays – **Meals** a la carte 30/50 ♀.
◆ This typical Alsatian wine-bar near the cathedral is known for its traditional décor and convivial atmosphere. Popular with celebrities, as shown by the photos on the walls.

Au Pont du Corbeau, 21 quai St-Nicolas ✆ 03 88 35 60 68, *corbeau@reperes.com, Fax 03 88 25 72 45* – GB KZ b
closed August, February Holidays, Sunday lunch and Saturday except December – **Meals** a la carte 25/36 ♀.
◆ On the banks of the river, next to the Musée Alsacien (popular art), this originally decorated restaurant is inspired by the Renaissance style of the area. Local specialities.

Fink'Stuebel, 26 r. Finkwiller ✆ 03 88 25 07 57, *finkstuebel@noos.fr, Fax 03 88 36 48 82* – GB JZ x
closed 5 to 28 August, Sunday and Monday – **Meals** a la carte 32/50 ♀.
◆ Half-timbers, painted wood, local furniture and flowered tablecloths provide the décor in this typical "winstub". Regional cuisine, with pride of place given to foie gras.

Zum Strissel, 5 pl. Gde Boucherie ✆ 03 88 32 14 73, *Fax 03 88 32 70 24* – AE GB KZ a
closed 7 July-3 August, 3 to 13 February, Sunday and Monday – **Meals** 10,40/22,50 ♀.
◆ This authentic "winstub" run by the same family since 1920 enjoys an attractive setting enhanced by works of wrought-iron and stained-glass showing Alsace's wine industry.

Hailich Graab "Au St-Sépulcre", 15 r. Orfèvres ✆ 03 88 32 39 97, *Fax 03 88 32 39 97* – GB KZ d
closed 14 to 31 July, Sunday and Monday – **Meals** a la carte 25/40.
◆ An archetypal wine bar and restaurant that faithfully respects the traditions of Alsace in both its décor and cuisine. A friendly atmosphere guaranteed.

Environs

at La Wantzenau *NE by D 468 : 12 km – pop. 5 462 alt. 130 – ✉ 67610 :*

Relais de la Poste (Daull) with rm, 21 r. Gén. de Gaulle ✆ 03 88 59 24 80, *info@relais-poste.com, Fax 03 88 59 24 89,* – rest, – 15. AE GB JCB
closed 25 July-7 August and 2 to 22 January – **Meals** *(closed Saturday lunch, Sunday dinner and Monday)* 42 b.i./110 and a la carte 61/110 – 11 – **18 rm** 69/122
Spec. Foie gras frais à la gelée de muscat. Paupiette de sandre soufflée au coulis de homard. Caille désossée farcie, sauce morilles. **Wines** Pinot gris, Rouge d'Ottrott.
◆ A typical Alsatian hostelry with elegant woodwork, frescoes and coffered ceilings. Personalised rooms, plus a veranda that looks out on to the countryside. Good wine list.

Baerenthal *57 Moselle* 307 Q5 *– pop. 702 alt. 220 – ✉ 57230 Bitche.*
Strasbourg 64.

at Untermuhlthal *SE : 4 km by D 87 – ✉ 57230 Baerenthal :*

L'Arnsbourg (Klein), ✆ 03 87 06 50 85, *l.arnsbourg@wanadoo.fr, Fax 03 87 06 57 67,* – AE GB JCB
closed 5 to 13 April, 6 to 22 September, 31 December-25 January, Tuesday and Wednesday – **Meals** (weekends booking essential) 52 (lunch), 105/130 and a la carte 95/120 ♀
Spec. Emulsion de pommes de terre et truffe (November-February). Saint-Pierre infusé au laurier en croûte de sel. Poitrine de pigeon relevé au wasabi. **Wines** Gewürztraminer, Muscat.
◆ Right by the ruins of Arnsbourg castle, a lovely isolated house among the Vosges forests. Elegant dining room (non-smoking) above the Zinsel. Inventive, delicious cuisine.

Gundershoffen *67110 B.-Rhin* 315 J3 – *pop. 3 490 alt. 180.*
Strasbourg 45.

Au Cygne (Paul), 35 Gd Rue ☎ 03 88 72 96 43, *sarl.lecygne@wanadoo.fr, Fax 03 88 72 86 47* – GB
closed 1 to 22 August, 17 February-7 March, Monday and Dinner, Thursday and Sunday – **Meals** 39/79 and a la carte 65/82
Spec. Jambonnettes de Grenouilles, schniederspaedle aux oignons confits. Langoustines sur compotée de légumes à l'orientale. Côtes et filet d'agneau en croûte d'herbes et d'épices. **Wines** Tokay-Pinot gris, Pinot noir.
• This fine half-timbered house is home to an elegant dining room embellished with woodwork, painted ceilings and floral compositions. Refined and inventive cuisine.

Illhaeusern *68970 H.-Rhin* 315 I7 – *pop. 646 alt. 173.*
Strasbourg 60.

Clairière without rest, rte Guémar ☎ 03 89 71 80 80, *hotel.la.clairiere@wanadoo.fr, Fax 03 89 71 86 22,* – GB
closed 3 January-6 March – 13 – **25 rm** 77/202.
• On the edge of the Forêt de l'Ill, this huge building inspired by the architecture of Alsace has quiet and spacious rooms, all with distinctive décor and some with balconies.

Auberge de l'Ill (Haeberlin), 2 rue de Collonges ☎ 03 89 71 89 00, *auberge-de-l-ill@auberge-de-l-ill.com, Fax 03 89 71 82 83,* flowered gardens, – AE GB
closed 3 to 11 January, 31 January-3 March, Monday and Tuesday – **Meals** (booking essential) 90 (lunch)/138 and a la carte 108/146
Spec. Saumon soufflé. Homard "prince Wladimir". Noisettes de chevreuil, compote de fruits secs, champignons sauvages et knepffla au fromage blanc. **Wines** Muscat, Pinot blanc.
• The lovely landscaped banks of the River Ill provide a fine backdrop to the elegant dining room of this establishment. Traditional cuisine featuring sublime Alsatian dishes.

Hôtel des Berges ☎ 03 89 71 87 87, *hotel-des-berges@wanadoo.fr, Fax 03 89 71 87 88,* – rm, – 15 - 25. AE GB
closed 2 to 12 January, 30 January-4 March and Tuesday – **Meals** see ***Auberge de l'Ill*** – 40 – **7 rm** 270/287, 6 suites.
• Attractively rebuilt tobacco-drying shed at the end of the garden belonging to the Auberge de l'Ill. Refined rooms, outdoor jacuzzi, and breakfast served on a boat !

Lembach *67510 B.-Rhin* 315 K2 – *pop. 1 689 alt. 190.*
Tourist Office 23 rte Bitche ☎ 03 88 94 43 16, Fax 03 88 94 20 04.
Strasbourg 55.

Auberge du Cheval Blanc (Mischler) with rm, 4 rte Wissembourg ☎ 03 88 94 41 86, *info@au-cheval-blanc.fr, Fax 03 88 94 20 74,* – 25. AE GB
closed 22 August-8 September and 23 January-9 February) – **Meals** *(closed Friday lunch, Monday and Tuesday)* 34/87 and a la carte 62/80 ***D'Rössel Stub*** *(closed Wednesday and Thursday)* **Meals** 24,50 and a la carte approx. 32 – 9,20 – **3 rm** 107/138, 3 suites 199
Spec. Farandole de quatre foies d'oie chauds. Trilogie de grenouilles. Médaillons de chevreuil à la moutarde de fruits rouges (May-February).. **Wines** Riesling, Pinot blanc.
• A lovely paved courtyard leads to the huge dining room of this 18C inn. Coffered ceiling, open fireplace, antique furniture and innovative Alsatian cuisine. The charming D'Rössel Stub bistro occupies a tastefully restored old farmhouse. Personalised bedrooms.

Marlenheim *67520 B.-Rhin* 315 I5 – *pop. 3 365 alt. 195.*
Strasbourg 20.

Cerf (Husser), 30 rue du Général de Gaulle ☎ 03 88 87 73 73, *info@lecerf.com, Fax 03 88 87 68 08,* – 20. AE GB
Meals *(closed Tuesday and Wenesday)* 39 (lunch), 85/125 and a la carte 75/105 – 15 – **13 rm** 90/200
Spec. Ravioli de foie gras de canard fumé en pot-au-feu. Brochette d'anguille et escargots grillés à la plancha. Saotoubo aux chocolats "grands crus". **Wines** Riesling, Crémant d'Alsace.
• Old post hotel transformed into an elegant establishment consisting of several buildings around a prettily planted courtyard. Well-presented rooms. Restaurant with panelling and pictures from the regional school of painting. Fine Alsatian cuisine of today.

Obernai *67210 B.-Rhin* 315 I6 – *pop. 10 471 alt. 185.*
Strasbourg 31.

La Fourchette des Ducs (Stamm), 6 r. Gare ☎ 03 88 48 33 38, *Fax 03 88 95 44 39* – AE GB
closed 1 to 8 May, 24/07-19/08, 27/12-6/01, 30/01-7/02, Sunday dinner, Monday and lunch except Sunday – **Meals** (booking essential) 75/95 and a la carte 73/100
Spec. Duo de langoustines en tartare et gelée. Saint-Pierre et brochette d'escargots au sésame. Pigeonneau d'Alsace à la réduction de pinot noir. **Wines** Riesling, Tokay-Pinot gris.
• Two opulent dining rooms, one with English-style panelling and decor by Lalique, Bugatti and Spindler, the second more contemporary. Original and inventive Alsace cuisine.

TOULOUSE *31000 H.-Gar.* 343 G3 – *pop. 390 350 alt. 146.*

at Vieille-Toulouse ✆ 05 61 73 45 48, S by D 4 : 8 km ; of Toulouse-la-Ramée(Tournefeuille) ✆ 05 61 07 09 09, W by D632 : 8km ; of St-Gabriel at Montrabé ✆ 05 61 84 16 65, E by D 112 : 9 km.

of Toulouse-Blagnac ✆ 0825 38 00 00.

✆ 0892 35 35 33.

Tourist Office Donjon du Capitole ✆ 05 61 11 02 22, Fax 05 61 22 03 63.

Paris 699 – Bordeaux 248 – Lyons 536 – Marseilles 407 – Nantes 569.

Sofitel Centre, 84 allées J. Jaurès ✆ 05 61 10 23 10, *h1091@accor-hotels.com, Fax 05 61 10 23 20* – 150. FX v
Meals ***SW Café* : Meals** a la carte 30/46 – 20 – **105 rm** 240, 14 suites.
• This hotel occupies eight floors of an imposing glass and red-brick building. Discreetly luxurious bedrooms with good soundproofing. Business centre and good seminar area. A contemporary feel in the SW Café with cuisine based on spices and regional products.

Crowne Plaza, 7 pl. Capitole ✆ 05 61 61 19 19, *hicptoulouse@alliance-hospitality.com, Fax 05 61 23 79 96,* – 60. EY t
Meals 23/54 – 22 – **162 rm** 305/410, 10 suites.
• This luxury hotel enjoys an excellent location on the famous Place du Capitole. Attractive, renovated rooms, some of which overlook the city hall. Intimate atmosphere in the restaurant, which opens on to a pleasant Florentine-style patio.

Grand Hôtel de l'Opéra without rest, 1 pl. Capitole ✆ 05 61 21 82 66, *contact@grand-hotel-opera.com, Fax 05 61 23 41 04,* – 15 - 40. EY a
22 – **57 rm** 147/272, 3 suites.
• Serenity and charm emanate from this hotel housed in a 17C convent. Attractive rooms adorned with wood panelling and red and yellow velvet. Pleasant lounge-bar.

Holiday Inn Centre, 13 pl. Wilson ✆ 05 61 10 70 70, *hi@capoul.com, Fax 05 61 21 96 70,* – 50. FY n
Brasserie le Capoul ✆ 05 61 21 08 27 **Meals** 23,50 – 14 – **130 rm** 160.
• The main features of this long-established hotel on a lively square are its glass-crowned lobby and contemporary-style bedrooms with highly original bathrooms. At Le Capoul, the culinary focus is on seafood, specialities from the southwest, and daily specials.

Brienne without rest, 20 bd Mar. Leclerc ✆ 05 61 23 60 60, *hoteldebrienne@wanadoo.fr, Fax 05 61 23 18 94* – 25. DV n
9 – **71 rm** 75/87.
• The façade of this hotel, named after the nearby canal, is a blend of brick and glass. Clean, colourful, refurbished bedrooms, plus a verdant lobby opening on to a patio.

Mercure Atria, 8 espl. Compans Caffarelli ✆ 05 61 11 09 09, *h1585@accor-hotels.com, Fax 05 61 23 14 12,* – 200. DV k
Meals 24/37 – 11,50 – **136 rm** 115/120.
• With its direct link to the city's conference centre, this hotel with its modern, spacious and quiet bedrooms is a popular choice with business travellers. The restaurant affords pleasant views of the adjacent public park.

Novotel Centre, 5 pl. A. Jourdain ✆ 05 61 21 74 74, *h0906@accor-hotels.com, Fax 05 61 22 81 22,* – 100. DV u
Meals a la carte approx. 30 – 11 – **135 rm** 130/136.
• Designed in the style of the region, this hotel stands alongside a Japanese garden. Spacious bedrooms (currently being renovated), some with a terrace. A festival of colour in the dining room, with its leafy outlook and mix of traditional and local cuisine.

Courtois without rest, 22 descente de la Halle aux Poissons ✆ 05 34 31 94 80, *contact@hotelcourtois.com, Fax 05 34 31 94 81* – EY d
18 – **14 rm** 125/175.
• This old building in the city's historic quarter has a contemporary interior of stained oak flooring, designer furniture, silk fabrics and discreet Japanese touches.

Beaux Arts without rest, 1 pl. Pont-Neuf ✆ 05 34 45 42 42, *contact@hoteldesbeauxarts.com, Fax 05 34 45 42 43,* – EY v
16 – **19 rm** 92/192.
• This tastefully transformed 18C house has 19 cosily elegant bedrooms, some with views of the Garonne. A charming insight into the colour and style of Occitania.

Grand Hôtel Jean Jaurès "Les Capitouls" without rest, 29 allées J. Jaurès ✆ 05 34 41 31 21, *info@hotel-capitouls.com, Fax 05 61 63 15 17* – – 20. FX g
13 – **51 rm** 110/150.
• An old mansion by a busy and central metro station. Impressive red-brick vaulting in the lobby, and bedrooms offering TV Internet access.

Mermoz without rest, 50 r. Matabiau ✆ 05 61 63 04 04, *reservation@hotel-mermoz, Fax 05 61 63 15 64* – kitchenette – 30. AE GB JCB
10 – **52 rm** 101. DV f
• The hotel's décor recalls the heroic pilots of the Aéropostale airmail service. Bedrooms lacking in refinement. A backdrop of flowered glass or a shaded terrace at breakfast.

Président without rest, 43 r. Raymond IV ✆ 05 61 63 46 46, *contact@hotel-president.com, Fax 05 61 62 83 60* – . AE GB JCB FX k
closed 1 to 8 May, 1 to 14 August and 26 December-1 January – 9,50 – **31 rm** 55/75.
• The rooms in this hotel, some of which are air-conditioned, are all attractively arranged around verdant patios on the ground floor. Contemporary decor.

Albert 1er without rest, 8 r. Rivals ✆ 05 61 21 17 91, *toulouse@hotel-albert1.com, Fax 05 61 21 09 64* – – 15. AE GB EX r
9,50 – **50 rm** 59/98.
• A good choice for those planning on exploring the "ville rose" on foot. Ask for one of the attractive, recently refurbished rooms - those to the rear are quieter.

Toulousy-Les Jardins de l'Opéra, 1 pl. Capitole ✆ 05 61 23 07 76, *info@toulousy.com, Fax 05 61 23 63 00* – . AE GB EY g
closed August, Sunday and Monday – **Meals** 42 (lunch), 68/98 and a la carte 90/125
Spec. Queues de langoustines poêlées à la réglisse. Pomme de ris de veau à la truffe. Vrai millefeuille servi tiède.
• Elegant, glass-canopied dining rooms decorated in Florentine style and separated by a pool dedicated to Neptune. A skilful interpretation of inventive cuisine.

Michel Sarran, 21 bd A. Duportal ✆ 05 61 12 32 32, *restaurant@michel-sarran.com, Fax 05 61 12 32 33,* – . AE GB DV m
closed 30 July-31 August, 18 to 25 December, Wednesday lunch, Saturday and Sunday – **Meals** (booking essential) 45 (lunch), 75/140 and a la carte 75/125
Spec. Soupe tiède de foie gras à l'huître. Liégeois de bar. Filet de porc noir de Bigorre en cocotte au thym.. **Wines** Gaillac, Côtes de Duras.
• This charming 19C residence offers an elegant setting in which to enjoy the very best flavours of the south. Car parking valet at lunchtime.

Le Pastel (Garrigues), 237 road of St-Simon, to the SW : 6 km ✉ 31100 ✆ 05 62 87 84 30, *lepastel@wanadoo.fr, Fax 05 61 44 29 22,* , – . AE GB.
closed Sunday and Monday – **Meals** (booking essential) 29 (lunch), 38/98 and a la carte 70/90
Spec. Saint-Jacques rôties "Jubilatoire" (October-April). Brick d'agneau de lait au citron confit (December-June). Crème rafraîchie de girolles aux copeaux de foie gras (May-September).
• This fine 19C building, with its pleasant garden-terrace, is the backdrop for generous personalised cuisine and a comprehensive wine list from southwest France.

7 Place St-Sernin, 7 pl. St-Sernin ✆ 05 62 30 05 30, *Fax 05 62 30 04 06* – . AE GB
closed Saturday lunch and Sunday – **Meals** 23/60 b.i. EX v
• In a house built in typical Toulouse style, this flamboyantly decorated and elegantly furnished restaurant is adorned with modern canvases. Cuisine with a modern flourish.

Brasserie Flo " Les Beaux Arts", 1 quai Daurade ✆ 05 61 21 12 12, *Fax 05 61 21 14 80,* – AE GB JCB EY v
Meals 30 b.i.
• This brasserie on the banks of the Garonne, frequented in past years by Ingres, Matisse and Bourdelle, is a popular evening venue. Pleasant retro decor and a varied menu.

Le 19, 19 descente de la Halle aux Poissons ✆ 05 34 31 94 84, *contact@restaurantle19.com, Fax 05 34 31 94 85* – AE GB. EY h
closed 1 to 8 May, 5 to 22 August, 24 December-9 January, Sunday, lunch Saturday and Monday – **Meals** 19 (lunch), 27/33
• Welcoming dining rooms, including one beneath a superb 16C ribbed vault. The open wine cellar and smoking room adopt a resolutely modern style. Cuisine from near and far.

Émile, 13 pl. St-Georges ✆ 05 61 21 05 56, *restaurant-emile@wanadoo.fr, Fax 05 61 21 42 26,* – . AE GB FY r
closed 24 December-10 January, Monday (except dinner in summer) and Sunday – **Meals** 18 (lunch), 35/45 .
• This popular restaurant created in the 1940s offers customers a range of local and fish dishes, plus an impressive wine list. The outdoor terrace is always full in summer.

Brasserie de l'Opéra, 1 pl. Capitole ✆ 05 61 21 37 03, *Fax 05 62 27 16 49,* – .
AE GB EY a
closed Sunday – **Meals** 26 .
• A chic, 1930s-style brasserie frequented by the city's smart set and stars who have marked their presence with a signed photo. The veranda converts into a pleasant terrace.

TOULOUSE

3-Piliers (R. des) . . . . EX 164
3-Journées (R. des) . . . FY 162
Alsace-Lorraine (R. d') EXY
Arnaud-Bernard (R.) . . . EX 4
Astorg (R. d') . . . . FY 5
Baronie (R.) . . . . EY 9
Billières (Av. E.) . . . . . . DV 13
Bonrepos (Bd) . . . . DV 16
Boulbonne (R.) . . . . FY 18
Bouquières (R.) . . . . FZ 19
Bourse (Pl. de la) . . . . . EY 20
Cantegril (R.) . . . . FY 23
Capitole (Pl. du) . . . . . . EY
Cartailhac (R. E.) . . . . . . EX 26
Chaîne (R. de la) . . . . . . EX 31
Cugnaux (R. de) . . . . . . DV 35
Cujas (R.) . . . . EY 36
Daurade (Quai de la) . . . EY 38
Demoiselles (Allée des) DV 40
Esquirol (Pl.) . . . . EY 54
La-Fayette (R.) . . . . EY
Fonderie (R. de la) . . . . EZ 60
Frères-Lion (R. des) . . . FY 62
Griffoul-Dorval (Bd) . . . DV 72
Henry-de-Gorsse (R.) . . EZ 76
Jules-Chalande (R.) . . . . EY 79
Lapeyrouse (R.) . . . . FY 85
Leclerc (Bd Mar.) . . . . . DV 87
Magre (R. Genty) . . . . . EY 91
Malcousinat (R.) . . . . . . EY 92
Marchands (R. des) . . . EY 95
Mercié (R. A.) . . . . EY 103
Metz (R. de) . . . . EFY
Peyras (R.) . . . . EY 113
Pleau (R. de la) . . . . FZ 114
Poids-de-l'Huile (R.) . . . EY 115
Polinaires (R. des) . . . . . EZ 116
Pomme (R. de la) . . . . . EFY 117
Pompidou (Allée) . . . . . DV 118
Rémusat (R. de) . . . . . . EX
République (R. de la) . . DV 124
Riguepels (R.) . . . . FY 127
Romiguières (R.) . . . . . . EY 129
Roosevelt (Allées) . . . FXY 130
St-Antoine-du-T. (R.) . . . . FY
St-Etienne (Port) . . . . . DV 133
St-Michel (Gde-R.) . . . . DV 134
St-Rome (R.) . . . . EY
Ste-Ursule (R.) . . . . EY 137
Sébastopol (R. de) . . . . DV 139
Semard (Bd P.) . . . . DV 142
Suau (R. J.) . . . . EY 146
Temponières (R.) . . . . . EY 147
Trinité (R. de la) . . . . . . EY 149
Vélane (R.) . . . . FZ 158
Wilson (Pl. Prés.) . . . . . FY

D

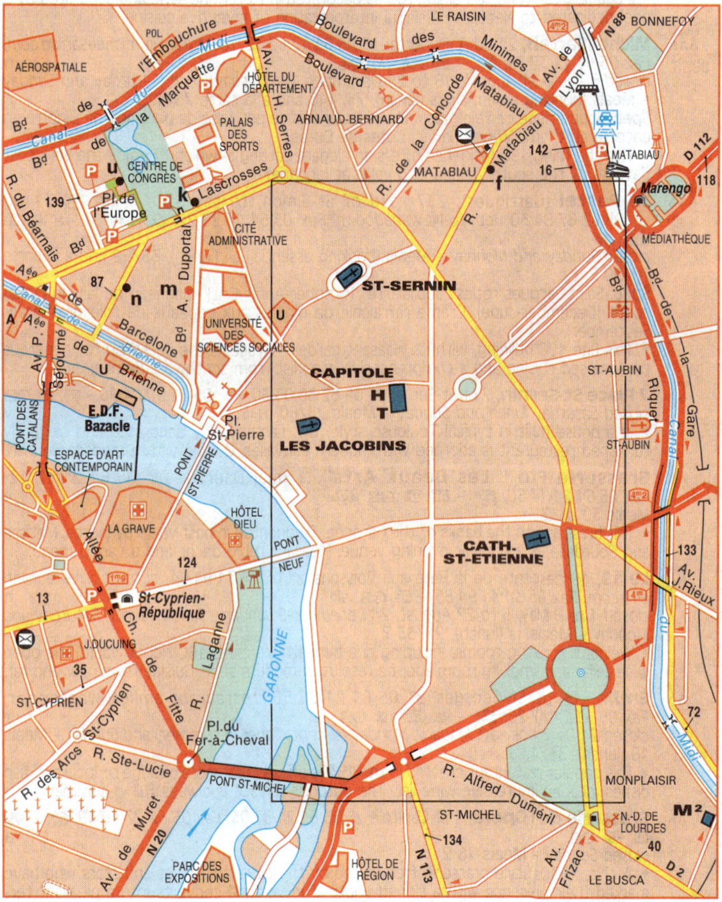

E
F
X
Y
Z
Pl. Arnaud Bernard
Bd d'Arcole
R. de la Concorde
R. C. Pauilhac
Matabiau
Raymond IV
Bayard
MATABIAU
Merly
R. Gatien-Arnoult
Pl. Jeanne d'Arc
Rue de
Bd de Strasbourg
R. B. de Born
Pl. de Belfort
R. de Belfort
BASILIQUE ST-SERNIN
MUSÉE ST-RAYMOND
Pl. St-Sernin
R. du Périgord
R. Dentert-Rochereau
Jaurès
R. Lautmann
R. des Lois
R. du Taur
R. de Rémusat
Lorraine
Pl. V. Hugo
R. d'Austerlitz
Jean Jaurès
Allées J. Jaurès
Pl. A. France
R. Déville
N.-Dame-du-Taur
R. La Fayette
Place Wilson
R. Gabriel Péri
R. Pargaminières
CAPITOLE
Capitole
Pl. du Capitole
Donjon
LES JACOBINS
R. Lakanal
R. Gambetta
R. St Rome
R. de la Colombette
R. M. Fonvielle
Rue Lazare
R. d'Aubuisson
Place Occitane
ST-GEORGES
Hôtel de Bernuy
R. d'Alsace
R. St-Antoine du T.
Pl. St.Georges
POL.
R. Peyrolières
R. du May
Pl. de la Daurade
MUSÉE DES AUGUSTINS
R. de Metz
Carnot
HÔTEL D'ASSÉZAT
R. de la Bourse
R. des Changes
Esquirol
Arts
Pont Neuf
R. de Metz
R. des Filatiers
Pl. Rouaix
R. Croix-Baragnon
R. Tolosane
R. Fermat
CATH. ST-ÉTIENNE
Allées François Verdier
R. des Potiers
R. des Couteliers
N.-D. la Dalbade
Languedoc
R. Mage
R. Perchepinte
R. St-Jacques
R. Ninau
Quai de la Garonnette
GARONNE
Pl. des Carmes
MUSÉE PAUL DUPUY
R. Espinasse
Pl. Montoulieu
R. de Tounis
R. de la Dalbade
R. Pharaon
R. du Languedoc
R. Ozenne
Grande-R. Nazareth
Jardin Royal
Grand Rond
Pl. du Salin
Allées Jules Guesde
Av. M. Hauriou
Pl. du Parlement
ST-EXUPÉRY
MUSÉUM D'HISTOIRE NATURELLE
Allées Frédéric Mistral
Allées P. Feuga
Pont St-Michel
R. Alfred Duméril
Jardin des Plantes
Mt de la Résistance
Pl. A. Lafourcade
0
200 m

Cosi Fan Tutte (Donnay), 8 r. Mage ✆ 05 61 53 07 24, *Fax 05 61 52 27 92* – GB FZ v
closed 1 to 9 May, 1 to 22 August, 23 to 30 December, Sunday and Monday – **Meals** (dinner only)(booking essential) 44/75 and a la carte 55/74
Spec. Saint-Jacques poêlées, crème de laitue et truffes (15 December-15 March). Selle d'agneau aux cornes d'abondance. Cannoli à la ricotta et fruits confits.
◆ A small restaurant with red drapes, "leopard-skin" carpet and original paintings. Delicious seasonal cuisine prepared according to Italian traditions. Italian wines.

Au Gré du Vin, 10 r. Pléau ✆ 05 61 25 03 51, *Fax 05 61 25 03 51* – GB. FZ t
closed August, Christmas-New Year, Saturday, Sunday and Bank Holidays – **Meals** (booking essential) 16 (lunch), 27/40 ♀.
◆ This unassuming restaurant opposite the Musée Paul Dupuy has a rustic feel, red-brick walls, friendly ambience, simple and tasty cuisine and a choice of wines by the glass.

at Rouffiac-Tolosan *by ② : 12 km – pop. 1 404 alt. 210 – ✉ 31180 :*

Ô Saveurs (Biasibetti), 8 pl. Ormeaux (au village) ✆ 05 34 27 10 11, *o.saveurs@free.fr, Fax 05 62 79 33 84,* – . AE ⓓ GB
closed 1 to 9 March, Easter Holidays, 11 to 31 August, Saturday lunch, Sunday dinner, and Monday – **Meals** 30/70 and a la carte 56/75 ♀
Spec. Fricassée de langoustines, foie gras et pleurotes au coulis de corail. Têtes de cèpes farcies au foie gras, petit ragoût de queues de cèpes (September-November). Assiette de grands crus de chocolat.. **Wines** Fronton, Gaillac.
◆ Set in a picturesque village, this delightful little house specialises in flavourful cooking with an up-to-date touch, served in welcoming dining rooms or on the terrace.

at Colomiers *: 10 km by exit nr 4 and Cornebarieu – pop. 28 538 alt. 182 – ✉ 31770 :*

L'Amphitryon (Delpech), chemin de Gramont ✆ 05 61 15 55 55, *amphitryon@wanadoo.fr, Fax 05 61 15 42 30,* <, – P. AE ⓓ GB
Meals 30 (lunch), 45/90 and a la carte 68/110 ♀
Spec. Sardine fraîche taillée au couteau, crème de morue et caviar de hareng. Anguille marinée et cuite dans un cassoulet de haricots de maûs du Béarn. Soufflé au chocolat blanc, marmelade de citron jaune.. **Wines** Gaillac, Côtes du Frontonnais.
◆ This large modern building houses a welcoming dining room with natural light streaming in through the glass roof. Views of the countryside from the terrace. Inventive cuisine.

at Blagnac *North-West : 7 km – pop. 20 586 alt. 135 – ✉ 31700 :*

Sofitel, 2 av. Didier Daurat, by road of airport, exit nr 3 ✆ 05 34 56 11 11, *h0565@accor-hotels.com, Fax 05 61 30 02 43,* , , , – TV P – 90. AE ⓓ GB JCB AS e
Caouec *(closed weekends)* **Meals** 30 ♀ – 19 – **100 rm** 230/250.
◆ A luxury chain hotel with a shuttle service to the airport. Elegant renovated bedrooms with yellow the dominant colour scheme. Pool and tennis court for those with time between flights. The sophisticated Le Caouec specialises in the cuisine of the southwest.

Holiday Inn Airport, pl. Révolution ✆ 05 34 36 00 20, *tlsap@ichotelsgroup.com, Fax 05 34 36 00 30,* , , – TV P – 15 - 150. AE ⓓ GB JCB AS h
Meals *(closed Friday dinner, Saturday and Sunday)* 21/37 ♀ – 18 – **150 rm** 210/245.
◆ The main features of the hotel's rooms are the warm, relaxing tones and contemporary furnishings. Pleasant brasserie-style restaurant decorated with frescoes paying homage to the olive tree. Fully equipped seminar area, plus an airport shuttle service.

Du cercle d'Oc, 6 pl. M. Dassault ✆ 05 62 74 71 71, *cercledoc@wanadoo.fr, Fax 05 62 74 71 72,* , – P. AE ⓓ GB AS t
closed 1 to 21 August, 26 December to 1 January, Saturday and Sunday – **Meals** 30 b.i./43 ♀.
◆ This pretty 18C farm is a haven of greenery at the heart of a busy shopping area. The atmosphere of an English club in the lounge and elegant dining room. Charming terrace.

Le Pré Carré, Toulouse-Blagnac airport (2nd floor) ✆ 05 61 16 70 40, *Fax 05 61 16 70 50,* < – AE ⓓ GB JCB. AS n
closed 14 July-15 August, Sunday dinner and Saturday – **Meals** 27 b.i./46.
◆ On the second floor of the airport, overlooking the runway. Designer décor with the emphasis on wood and reddish tones. Traditional à la carte menu.

Bistrot Gourmand, 1 bd Firmin Pons ✆ 05 61 71 96 95, *bistrot-gourmand@bistrot-gourmand.com, Fax 05 61 15 68 21,* – AE ⓓ GB AS v
closed 7 to 28 August, 25 December-2 January, Saturday lunch, Sunday, Monday and Bank Holidays – **Meals** 11,50/33.
◆ In the older part of Blagnac, with two rooms laid out on two floors. Pleasant terrace upstairs. The menu varies according to the season. Reasonable prices.

Laguiole *12210 Aveyron 338 J2 – pop. 1 248 alt. 1 004.*
Tourist Office pl. du Foirail ✆ 05 65 44 35 94, Fax 05 65 44 35 76.
Toulouse 208.

to the East *6 km by road of Aubrac (D 15)*

Michel Bras, ✆ 05 65 51 18 20, *michel.bras@wanadoo.fr, Fax 05 65 48 47 02,* Landscapes of Aubrac – , rest, AE GB JCB.
April-October and closed Monday except July-August – **Meals** *(closed lunch Tuesday and Wednesday except July-August and Monday)* (booking essential) 96/153 and a la carte 113/157 – 24 – **15 rm** 205/345
Spec. "Gargouillou" de jeunes légumes. Pièce de boeuf Aubrac rôtie à la braise. Biscuit tiède de chocolat coulant.. **Wines** Gaillac, Marcillac.
◆ This establishment looks like a spacecraft lost among the harsh landscapes of the Aubrac. Diners contemplate the scene while savouring an inspired version of local cuisine. Pure lines, bare rock, serene white surfaces, vast windows, plus designer cocktails.

Puymirol *47270 L.-et-G. 336 G4 – pop. 864 alt. 153.*
Toulouse 104.

Les Loges de l'Aubergade (Trama), 52 r. Royale ✆ 05 53 95 31 46, *trama@aubergade.com, Fax 05 53 95 33 80,* , – – 25. AE GB JCB.
closed February Holidays, Monday, Sunday dinner out of season and Tuesday except dinner in season – **Meals** 66 (lunch), 76/140 and a la carte 103/204 – 25 – **11 rm** 180/290
Spec. Papillote de pomme de terre en habit vert à la truffe. Hamburger de foie gras chaud aux cèpes, jus de canard corsé. Assiette des cinq sens.. **Wines** Côtes de Duras blanc, Buzet.
◆ Contemporary design inside two charming houses : one from the 17C, the other the 13C former seat of the counts of Toulouse. A breathtaking Garcia-designed baroque room, terrace-cloister, delicious, imaginative cuisine and fine cigars. A feast for the senses !

Germany

Deutschland

BERLIN – COLOGNE – DRESDEN

DÜSSELDORF – FRANKFURT ON MAIN

HAMBURG – HANOVER – LEIPZIG

MUNICH – STUTTGART

PRACTICAL INFORMATION

LOCAL CURRENCY

1 euro (€) = 1,34 USD ($) (Dec. 2004)

TOURIST INFORMATION

Deutsche Zentrale für Tourismus (DZT):
Beethovenstr. 69, 60325 Frankfurt, ✆ (069) 97 46 41 18, Fax (069) 97 46 42 34
National Holiday in Germany: *3 October.*

AIRLINES

DEUTSCHE LUFTHANSA AG: *✆ (01803) 803803*
AIR CANADA: *✆ (069) 27 11 51 11*
AIR FRANCE: *✆ (0180) 5 83 08 30*
AMERICAN AIRLINES: *✆ (01803) 242 324*
BRITISH AIRWAYS: *✆ (01805) 26 65 22*
JAPAN AIRLINES: *✆ (0180) 22 28 700*
AUSTRIAN AIRLINES: *✆ (0180) 300 05 20*

FOREIGN EXCHANGE

In banks, savings banks and at exchange offices.
Hours of opening from Monday to Friday 8.30am to 12.30pm and 2.30pm to 4pm except Thursday 2.30pm to 6pm.

SHOPPING

In the index of street names, those printed in red are where the principal shops are found.

BREAKDOWN SERVICE

ADAC: *for the addresses see text of the towns mentioned*

AvD: *Lyoner Str. 16, 60528 Frankfurt-Niederrad, ✆ (069) 6 60 60, Fax (069) 660 67 89*
In Germany the ADAC (emergency number (01802) 22 22 22), and the AvD (emergency number (0800) 9 90 99 09), make a special point of assisting foreign motorists. They have motor patrols covering main roads.

TIPPING

In Germany, prices include service and taxes. You may choose to leave a tip if you wish but there is no obligation to do so.

SPEED LIMITS

The speed limit, generally, in built up areas is 50 km/h - 31 mph and on all other roads it is 100 km/h - 62mph. On motorways and dual carriageways, the recommended speed limit is 130 km/h - 80 mph.

SEAT BELTS

The wearing of seat belts is compulsory for drivers and all passengers.

BERLIN

L Berlin 542, I 24 – pop. 3 400 000 – alt. 40 m.

Frankfurt/Oder 105 – Hamburg 289 – Hannover 288 – Leipzig 183 – Rostock 222.

Berlin Tourismus Marketing, Am Karlsbad 11, ✉ 10785, (030) 25 00 25, information@btm.de

Tourist Info Center (at Brandenburger Tor), side-wing, Pariser Platz, ✉ 10787 Berlin

Tourist Info Café, Am Alexander Platz (at TV tower), Panoramastr. 1a, ✉ 10178 Berlin

Tourist Info Center (at Europa Center), Budapester Str. 45, ✉ 10787 Berlin-Charlottenburg

ADAC, Berlin-Wilmersdorf, Bundesallee 29.

18 9 Berlin-Wannsee, Golfweg 22, (030) 8 06 70 60 – 18 Berlin-Gatow, Kladower Damm 182, (030) 3 65 00 06 – 18 9 Gross Kienitz (South : 25 km), (033708) 5 37 70 – 18 9 Börnicke, Am Kallin 1 (Northwest : 32 km), (033230) 89 40 – 9 Mahlow, Kiefernweg (South : 20 km), (033379) 37 05 95 – 18 18 Wildenbruch, Großer Seddiner See (Southwest : 37 km), (033205) 73 20 – 18 Stolpe, Am Golfplatz 1 (Northwest : 20 km), (03303) 54 92 14 – 9 Großbeeren, Am Golfplatz 1 (South 22 km), (033701) 3 28 90.

Berlin-Tegel EX, (0180) 5 00 01 86

Berlin-Schönefeld (South : 25 km), (0180) 5 00 01 86

Berlin-Tempelhof GZ, (0180) 5 00 01 86

Deutsche Lufthansa City Center, Kurfürstendamm 21, (030) 88 75 38 00.

Berlin-Wannsee, Reichsbahnstraße.

Exhibition Centre (Messegelände am Funkturm) BU, (030) 3 03 80, Fax (030) 30 38 23 25.

3
BERLIN
0
1km
S. Bahn
Bauarbeiten
E
F
X
Y
Z
BERLIN-TEGEL
A 105
A 111
E 26
Kurt-Schumacher-Damm
Hohenzollernkanal
Saatwinkler
VOLKSPARK
JUNGFERNHEIDE
Damm
Maria Regina Martyrum
Gedenkstätte Plötzensee
SIEMENSSTADT
Siemensdamm
AB DR. CHARLOTTENBURG
628
A 100
Westhafenkanal
WESTHAFEN
Quitzowstr.
Str.
Berlin - Spandauer
VOLKSPARK
REHBERGE
Transvaalstraße
Müller-
Holländer-
str.
SCHILLER
PARK
Barfus-
Seestraße
WEDDING
Müller-
straße
See-
651
SPREE
Olbersstr.
Sickingenstr.
Beussel-str.
698
704
Perleberger
TIERGARTEN
Turm-
str.
FRITZ-SCHLOSS-PARK
621
Belvedere
SCHLOSS-GARTEN
Tegeler Weg
Huttenstr.
Kaiserin-Augusta-Allee
Alt-Moabit
Alt-
Moabit
SCHLOSS CHARLOTTENBURG
699
Spandauer
Damm
Otto-
Levetzowstr.
SPREE
616
Landwehrkanal
609
Suhr-
Allee
Schloß Bellevue
Paul-
str.
West-end
637
M16
M2
M13
Schloßstr.
699
HANSA-VIERTEL
17.
des
DEUTSCHE OPER BERLIN
Straße
Juni
713
Kaiser-
damm
Bismarck-
str.
Ernst-Reuter-Pl.
Hardenberg-
Neuer See
TIERGARTEN
654
FUNKTURM
Lietzen
Kantstraße
see
625
Leibniz-
str.
Kantstraße
ZOOLOGISCHER GARTEN
str.
636
679
Messe-gelände
660
666
642
Lützowufer
AB. DR. FUNKTURM
KURFÜRSTENDAMM
Tauentzienstr.
A 115
Lietzenburger
Straße
Bülow-
640
str.
Str.
Hohenstaufenstr.
Straße
607
damm
Bundesallee
Potsdamer
allee
640
zollern-
Hubertus-see
Paulsborner
WILMERSDORF
Hohen-
Uhland-
Luther-
Grunewaldstr.
Koenigs-
Hubertus-allee
Berliner
639
SCHÖNEBERG
straße
Hohenzollerndamm
692
allee
Forckenbeck-
606
VOLKSPARK
Martin-
612
a
711
str.
Wex-str.
SCHMARGENDORF
Hagenstr.
A 100
Sachsen-
Clay-allee
Rheinbaben-allee
Wiesbadener Str.
Laubacher Str.
Bundes-
687
Haupt-
AB. KR. SCHÖNEBERG
708
FRIEDENAU

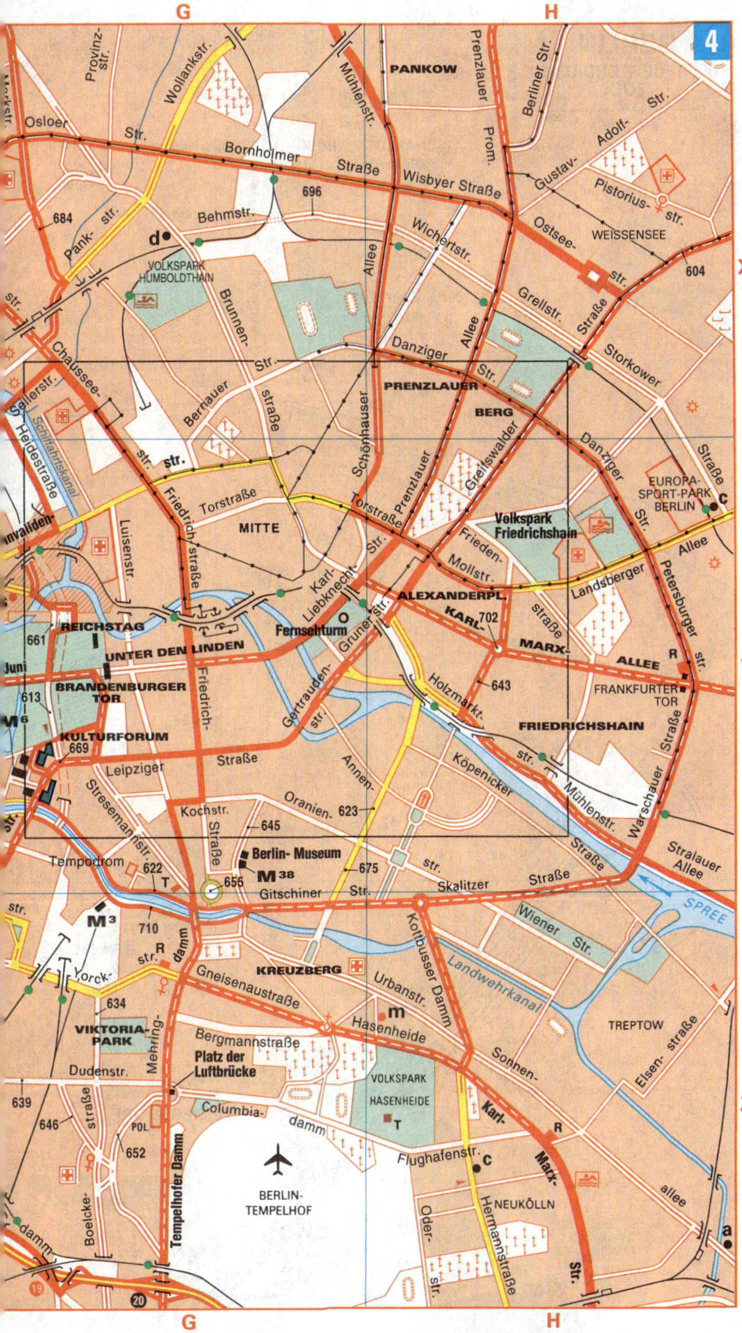
G
H
4
X
Y
Z
PANKOW
Mühlenstr.
Prenzlauer Prom.
Berliner Str.
Provinz-str.
Wollankstr.
Osloer
Str.
Bornholmer
Straße
Wisbyer Straße
Gustav-Adolf-Str.
Pistorius-str.
696
684
Behmstr.
Pank-str.
Wichertstr.
Ostsee-str.
WEISSENSEE
604
d
VOLKSPARK HUMBOLDTHAIN
Brunnen-straße
Allee
Grellstr.
Straße
Danziger
Storkower
Chaussee-str.
Sellerstr.
Heidestraße
Schiffahrtskanal
Str.
Bernauer
PRENZLAUER BERG
Schönhauser
Greifswalder
Danziger Str.
Straße
EUROPA-SPORT-PARK BERLIN
c
Torstraße
MITTE
Luisenstr.
Friedrichstraße
Prenzlauer
Torstraße
Volkspark Friedrichshain
Frieden-str.
Mollstr.
Landsberger Allee
Petersburger Str.
Invaliden-
Karl-Liebknecht-Str.
ALEXANDERPL.
702
Straße
KARL-MARX-ALLEE
REICHSTAG
Fernsehturm
Gruner Str.
661
UNTER DEN LINDEN
Juni
613
BRANDENBURGER TOR
Friedrich-straße
Gertrauden-str.
Holzmarkt-str.
643
FRANKFURTER TOR
R
FRIEDRICHSHAIN
M6
KULTURFORUM
669
Leipziger
Straße
Stresemannstr.
Annen-str.
Köpenicker str.
Mühlenstr.
Warschauer Straße
Oranien-
623
Kochstr.
645
Straße
Berlin-Museum
M38
Tempodrom
622
T
655
675
Gitschiner
Str.
Skalitzer
str.
Straße
Stralauer Allee
SPREE
M3
710
str.
R
damm
Wiener Str.
Landwehrkanal
Yorck-
KREUZBERG
Gneisenaustraße
Urbanstr.
Kottbusser Damm
634
m
Hasenheide
VIKTORIA-PARK
Mehring-
Bergmannstraße
Sonnen-
TREPTOW
Elsen-straße
Dudenstr.
Platz der Luftbrücke
VOLKSPARK HASENHEIDE
639
Columbia-damm
646
straße
T
Karl-Marx-Str.
R
POL.
652
Flughafenstr.
c
Tempelhofer Damm
BERLIN-TEMPELHOF
NEUKÖLLN
allee
damm
Boelcke-
Oder-str.
Hermannstraße
a
19
20

5
BERLIN
KURFÜRSTENDAMM
ZOO
0
400 m
S.Bahn
J
K
X
Y
Z
CHARLOTTENBURG
Bismarckstr.
Deutsche Oper
DEUTSCHE OPER BERLIN
Sophie-Ch.-Pl.
Sophie-Charlotte-Pl.
Kaiserdamm
Bismarckstraße
SCHILLER-THEATER
Zillestraße
Kaiser-Friedrich-Straße
R.-Wagner-Str.
Schloßstr.
Schillerstr.
Wilmersdorfer Str.
Krumme Straße
Leibnizstr.
Otto-Suhr-Allee
Fraunhoferstr.
609
Wundt-str.
LIETZENSEE PARK
Lietzensee
Neue Kantstraße
Kantstraße
Pestalozzistr.
Suarezstr.
Windscheidstraße
Amtsgerichtsplatz
Leonhardtstr.
Rönnestraße
625
705
CHARLOTTENBURG
Wilmersdorfer Str
SAVIGNYPLATZ
Mommsenstr.
Schlüterstr.
Bleibtreustr.
Holtzendorffplatz
Gervinusstr.
Droysenstr.
Dahlmannstr.
Lewishamstr.
Adenauerpl.
Heilbronner Str.
Damaschkestr.
Georg-Wilhelm-Straße
KURFÜRSTENDAMM
Xantener Str.
Lietzenburger Straße
Pariser Str.
Brandenburgische Straße
Düsseldorfer Straße
600
667
HALENSEE
Westfälische
Joachim-Friedrich-Straße
Nestorstraße
Hochmeisterplatz
Paulsborner Straße
Eisenzahnstraße
Konstanzer Str.
PREUSSEN PARK
Württembergische
Sächsische
Emser Str.
Emser Platz
BAB Stadtring
Grieser Pl.
Seesener Straße
Fehrbelliner Platz
Fehrbelliner Pl.
Hohenzollerndamm
HOHENZOLLERNDAMM
Konstanzer Str.
Sigmaringer Str.
Cunostr.
Rudolstädter
BAB Abzweig
Berliner Straße
WILMERSDORF
Blissestr.
Viktoria-
Auguste-
A 100
EISSTADION
STADION
AB. KR. WILMERSDORF
VOLKSPARK
Barstraße
Mecklenburgische Straße
Heidelbgr. Pl.
HEIDELBERGER PL.
Steglitz
Cunostraße
Forckenbeckstraße
POL

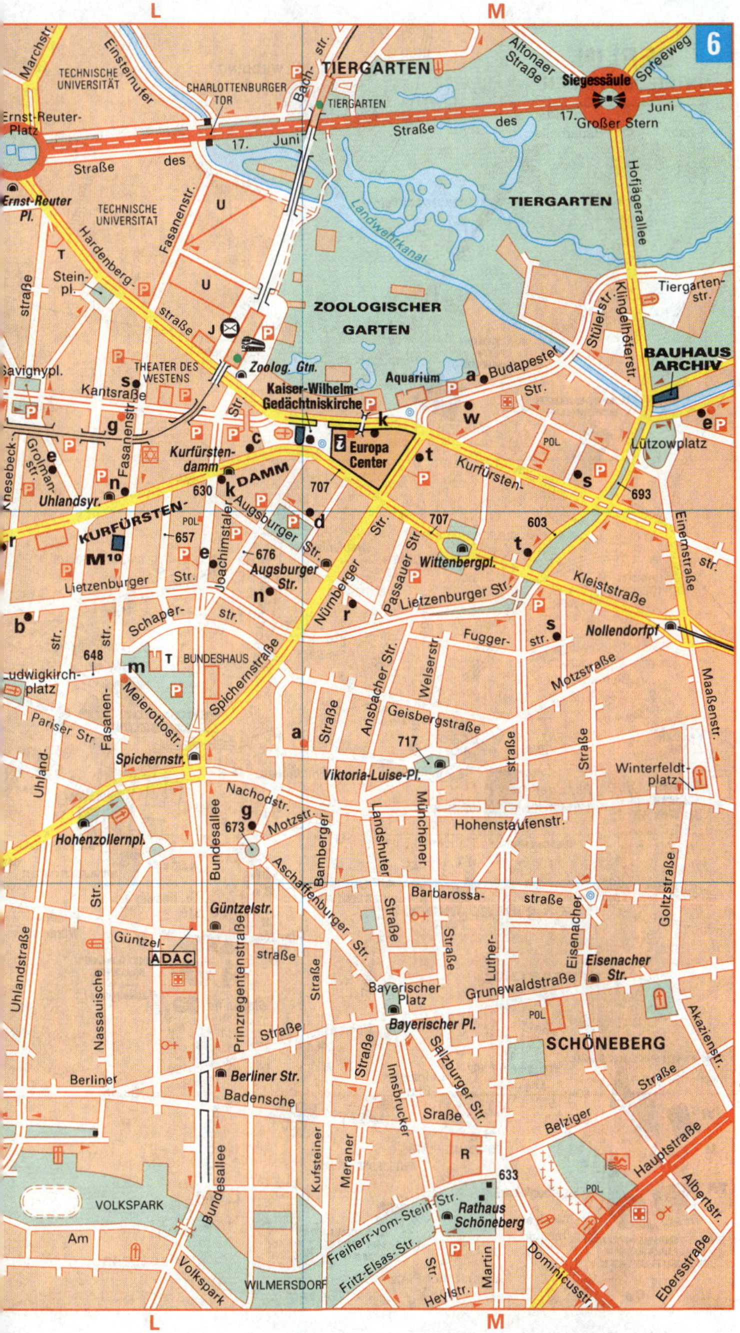
L
M
6
X
Y
Z
TIERGARTEN
Siegessäule
Großer Stern
17. Juni
Straße des 17. Juni
Spreeweg
Altonaer Straße
TECHNISCHE UNIVERSITÄT
Einsteinufer
CHARLOTTENBURGER TOR
Bachstr.
Marchstr.
Ernst-Reuter-Platz
Ernst-Reuter Pl.
Hofjägerallee
Landwehrkanal
Fasanenstr.
Hardenbergstraße
Steinpl.
ZOOLOGISCHER GARTEN
Tiergartenstr.
Stülerstr.
Klingelhöferstr.
BAUHAUS ARCHIV
Savignypl.
THEATER DES WESTENS
Zoolog. Gtn.
Kantstraße
Aquarium
Budapester Str.
Kaiser-Wilhelm-Gedächtniskirche
Europa Center
Lützowplatz
Kurfürstendamm
KURFÜRSTENDAMM
Kurfürstenstr.
Knesebeckstr.
Grolmanstr.
Uhlandstr.
Joachimstaler Str.
Augsburger Str.
Nürnberger Str.
Passauer Str.
Wittenbergpl.
Kleiststraße
Einemstraße
Lietzenburger Str.
Schaperstr.
Nollendorfpl.
Fuggerstr.
Motzstraße
BUNDESHAUS
Ludwigkirchplatz
Meierottostr.
Spichernstraße
Pariser Str.
Welserstr.
Geisbergstraße
Ansbacher Str.
Maaßenstr.
Viktoria-Luise-Pl.
Spichernstr.
Winterfeldtplatz
Nachodstr.
Motzstr.
Hohenstaufenstr.
Hohenzollernpl.
Bundesallee
Landshuter Str.
Münchener Str.
Bamberger Str.
Aschaffenburger Str.
Barbarossastraße
Goltzstraße
Güntzelstr.
Güntzelstraße
ADAC
Prinzregentenstraße
Eisenacher Str.
Lutherstr.
Grunewaldstraße
Bayerischer Platz
Bayerischer Pl.
SCHÖNEBERG
Akazienstr.
Salzburger Str.
Innsbrucker Str.
Nassauische Str.
Uhlandstraße
Berliner Str.
Badensche Straße
Belziger Straße
Hauptstraße
Albertstr.
Kufsteiner Str.
Meraner Str.
Rathaus Schöneberg
Freiherr-vom-Stein-Str.
Fritz-Elsas-Str.
Heylstr.
Martin-Luther-Str.
Dominicusstr.
Eberstraße
VOLKSPARK
Am Volkspark
WILMERSDORF
POL
630
657
676
707
693
603
648
717
673
633
M10

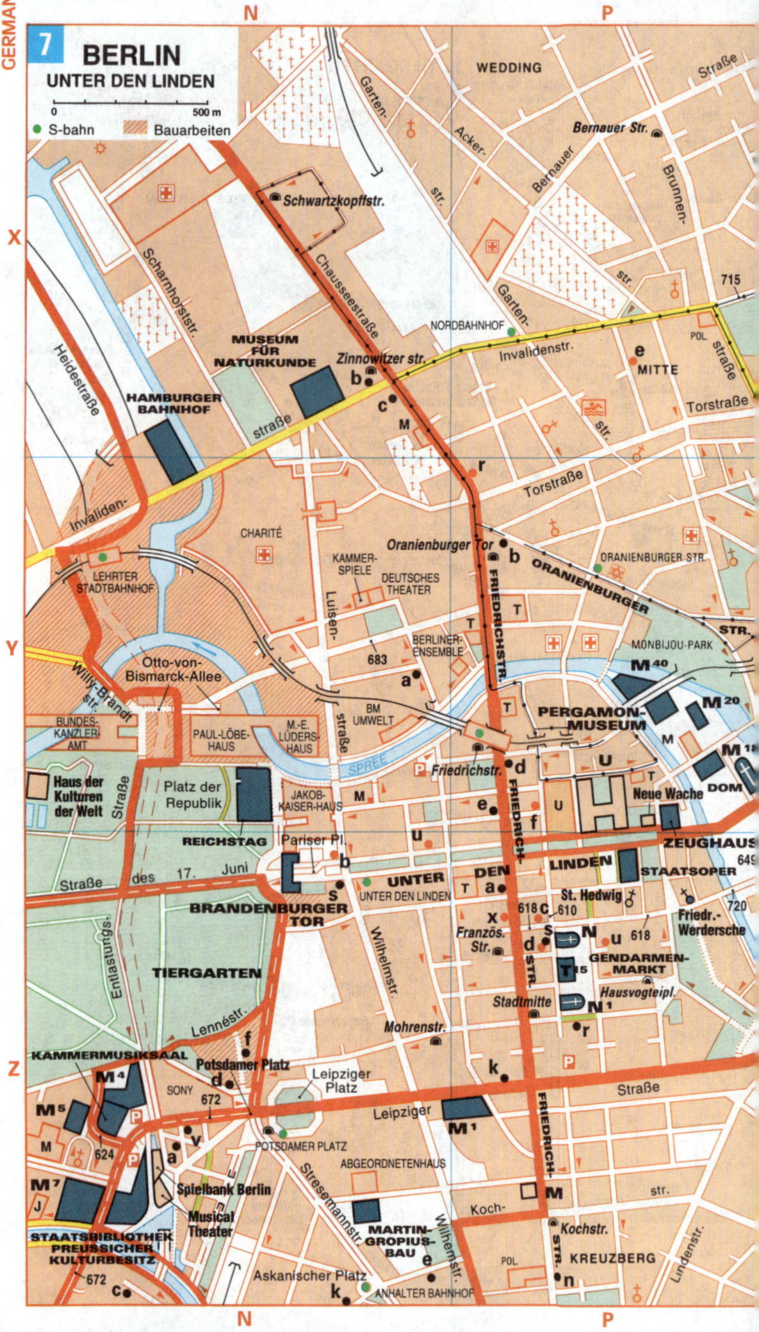
7
BERLIN
UNTER DEN LINDEN
0
500 m
S-bahn
Bauarbeiten
N
P
X
Y
Z
WEDDING
Garten-
Acker-
str.
Bernauer
Bernauer Str.
Brunnen-
Straße
str.
Schwartzkopffstr.
Chausseestraße
Scharnhorststr.
Heidestraße
MUSEUM
FÜR
NATURKUNDE
Zinnowitzer str.
NORDBAHNHOF
Invalidenstr.
715
POL
e
MITTE
Torstraße
HAMBURGER
BAHNHOF
straße
Invaliden-
Torstraße
CHARITÉ
Oranienburger Tor
ORANIENBURGER STR.
ORANIENBURGER
STR.
KAMMER-
SPIELE
DEUTSCHES
THEATER
FRIEDRICHSTR.
LEHRTER
STADTBAHNHOF
Luisen-
BERLINER-
ENSEMBLE
683
MONBIJOU-PARK
Otto-von-
Bismarck-Allee
Willy-Brandt
str.
BUNDES-
KANZLER-
AMT
PAUL-LÖBE-
HAUS
M.-E.
LÜDERS-
HAUS
straße
BM
UMWELT
SPREE
PERGAMON-
MUSEUM
Friedrichstr.
Haus der
Kulturen
der Welt
Straße
Platz der
Republik
JAKOB-
KAISER-HAUS
FRIEDRICH-
Neue Wache
DOM
ZEUGHAUS
REICHSTAG
Pariser Pl.
LINDEN
STAATSOPER
649
Straße
des
17.
Juni
UNTER
UNTER DEN LINDEN
DEN
St. Hedwig
720
BRANDENBURGER
TOR
618
610
Friedr.-
Werdersche
Französ.
Str.
618
Entlastungs-
Wilhelmstr.
STR.
GENDARMEN-
MARKT
15
TIERGARTEN
Hausvogteipl.
Stadtmitte
Lennéstr.
Mohrenstr.
KAMMERMUSIKSAAL
Potsdamer Platz
Leipziger
Platz
Straße
SONY
672
Leipziger
M 4
M 5
M 1
M 20
M 40
FRIEDRICH-
624
POTSDAMER PLATZ
ABGEORDNETENHAUS
M 7
Spielbank Berlin
Stresemannstr.
str.
Musical
Theater
Koch-
Kochstr.
STAATSBIBLIOTHEK
PREUSSISCHER
KULTURBESITZ
MARTIN-
GROPIUS-
BAU
Wilhelmstr.
STR.
KREUZBERG
Lindenstr.
POL
672
Askanischer Platz
ANHALTER BAHNHOF
N
P

R
S
8
X
Y
Z
Danziger
ERNST-
THALMANN-
PARK
Greifswalder Str.
Straße
Danziger Str.
PRENZLAUER BERG
Knaack-
Schwedter
allee
Kastanien-
Allee
Str.
Schönhauser
Str.
Allee
str.
a
627
Straße
Fehrbelliner
Choriner
POL
Senefelderpl.
T
Prenzlauer
POL
Greifswalder
Rosenthaler Pl.
Straße
Torstraße
Friedrichshain
Am
Torstraße
MARCHENBRUNNEN
Volkspark
Friedrichshain
690
R.-Luxemburg-
Pl.
T
Frieden-
Weinmeisterstr.
Moll-
Straße
689
718
Str.
Braun-
Str.
str.
664
658
P
POL
Otto-
Landsberger Allee
S-BAHN
ALEXANDER-
PLATZ
e
Pl. der Vereinten
Nationen
HACKESCHER
MARKT
Liebknecht-
Karl-
Schillingstr.
Str.
str.
a
Marienkirche
Fernsehturm
b
KONGRESS-
HALLE
Marx-
Karl-
Spandauer
L
R
Gruner
J
P
Alexanderstr.
POL
Strausberger
Platz
678
Str.
Allee
Klosterstr.
str.
NIKOLAI-
VIERTEL
663
Jannowitzbrücke
P
Lichtenberger
Breite
STADTBIBLIOTHEK
Stralauer
Str.
Str.
FRIEDRICHS - HAIN
MÄRKISCHES
MUSEUM
JANNOWITZBRÜCKE
P
Gertraudenstr.
b
615
Andreas-
u
c
Märk. Mus.
e
M
a
r
Brückenstr.
Holzmarkt-
P
Z
Spittelmarkt
Str.
Michaelkirchstr.
H.-Heine-Straße
Köpenicker
SPREE
OSTBAHNHOF
Annen-
Heine-
str.
str.
Str.
WALDECK-
PARK
Heinrich-
Engeldamm
Oranienstr.
Moritzplatz
R
S

INDEX OF STREET NAMES IN BERLIN

Ackerstr. 7 .. PX
Adenauerpl. 5 .. JY
Akazienstr. 6 .. MZ
Albertstr. 6 .. MZ
Albrecht-Achilles-Str. 5 .. JY 600
Alexanderpl. 8 .. RY
Alexanderstr. 8 .. SY
Alt-Moabit 3 .. FY
Altonaer Str. 6 .. MX
Am Friedrichshain 8 .. SX
Am Volkspark 6 .. LZ
Amtsgerichtspl. 5 .. JX
An der Urania 6 .. MY 603
Andreasstr. 8 .. SZ
Annenstr. 8 .. RZ
Ansbacher Str. 6 .. MY
Aschaffenburger Str. 6 .. MZ
Askanischer Pl. 7 .. NZ
Augsburger Str. 6 .. LY
Auguste-Viktoria-Str. 5 .. JZ
Bachstr. 6 .. MX
Badensche Str. 6 .. LZ
Bamberger Str. 6 .. MY
Barbarossastr. 6 .. MZ
Barfusstr. 3 .. FX
Barstr. 5 .. KZ
Bayerischer Pl. 6 .. MZ
Behmstr. 4 .. GX
Belziger Str. 6 .. MZ
Bergmannstr. 4 .. GZ
Berliner Allee 4 .. HX 604
Berliner Str. (PANKOW) 4 .. HX
Berliner Str. 6 .. LZ
Bernauer Str. (WEDDING) 7 .. PX
Beusselstr. 3 .. FY
Bismarckstr. 5 .. JX
Bleibtreustr. 5 .. KX
Blissestr. 3 .. FZ 606
Boelckestr. 4 .. GZ
Bornholmer Str. 4 .. GX
Brandenburgische Str. 3 .. EZ 607
Breite Str. 8 .. RZ
Brückenstr. 8 .. RZ
Brunnenstr. 7 .. PX
Budapester Str. 6 .. MX
Bülowstr. 3 .. FZ
Bundesallee 6 .. LY
Cauerstr. 5 .. KX 609
Charlottenstr. 7 .. PZ 610
Chausseestr. 7 .. NX
Choriner Str. 8 .. RX
Clayallee 3 .. EZ
Columbiadamm 4 .. GZ
Cunostr. 5 .. JZ
Dahlmannstr. 5 .. JY
Damaschkestr. 5 .. JY
Danziger Str. 8 .. RSX
Dominicusstr. 3 .. FZ 612
Droysenstr. 5 .. JY
Dudenstr. 4 .. GZ
Düsseldorfer Str. 5 .. KY
Einemstr. 6 .. MY
Einsteinufer 6 .. LX
Eisenacher Str. 6 .. MZ
Eisenzahnstr. 5 .. JY
Elsenstr. 4 .. HZ
Emser Pl. 5 .. KZ
Emser Str. 5 .. KY
Engeldamm 8 .. SZ
Entlastungsstr. 4 .. GY 613
Ernst-Reuter-Pl. 6 .. LX
Fasanenstr. 6 .. LX
Fehrbelliner Pl. 5 .. KZ
Fehrbelliner Str. 8 .. RX
Fischerinsel 8 .. RZ 615
Forckenbeckstr. 5 .. JZ
Franklinstr. 3 .. FY 616
Französische Str. 7 .. PZ 618
Fraunhoferstr. 5 .. KX
Freiherr-vom-Stein-Str. 6 .. MZ
Friedenstr. 8 .. SY
Friedrichstr. 7 .. PY
Fritz-Elsas-Str. 6 .. MZ
Fürstenbrunner Weg 3 .. EY 621
Fuggerstr. 6 .. MY
Gartenstr. 7 .. NX
Geisbergstr. 6 .. MY
Gendarmenmarkt 7 .. PZ
Georg-Wihelm-Str. 5 .. JY
Gertraudenstr. 8 .. RZ
Gervinusstr. 5 .. JX
Gitschiner Str. 4 .. GZ
Gneisenaustr. 4 .. GZ
Goltzstr. 6 .. MZ
Greifswalder Str. 8 .. SX
Grellstr. 4 .. HX
Grieser Pl. 5 .. JZ
Grolmanstr. 6 .. LX
Großer Stern 6 .. MX
Grunerstr. 8 .. RY
Grunewaldstr. 6 .. MZ
Güntzelstr. 6 .. LZ
Gustav-Adolf-Str. 4 .. HX
Hagenstr. 3 .. EZ
Hallesches Ufer 4 .. GY 622
Hardenbergstr. 6 .. LX
Hasenheide 4 .. HZ
Hauptstr. (SCHÖNEBERG) 6 .. MZ
Heidestr. 7 .. NX
Heilbronner Str. 5 .. JY
Heinrich-Heine-Str. 4 .. HY 623
Herbert-von-Karajan-Str. 7 .. NZ 624
Hermannstr. 4 .. HZ
Heylstr. 6 .. MZ
Hochmeisterpl. 5 .. JY
Hofjagerallee 6 .. MX
Hohenstaufenstr. 6 .. MY
Hohenzollerndamm 5 .. KZ
Holländerstr. 3 .. FX
Holtzendorffpl. 5 .. JY
Holtzendorffstr. 3 .. EY 625
Holzmarktstr. 8 .. SZ
Hubertusallee 3 .. EZ
Huttenstr. 3 .. FY
Immanuelkirchstr. 8 .. SX 627
Innsbrucker Str. 6 .. MZ
Invalidenstr. 7 .. NY
Jacob-Kaiser-Pl. 3 .. EX 628
Joachim-Friedrich-Str. 5 .. JY
Joachimstaler Pl. 6 .. LX 630
Joachimstaler Str. 6 .. LY
John-F.-Kennedy-Pl. 6 .. MZ 633
Kaiser-Friedrich-Str. 5 .. JX
Kaiserdamm 5 .. JX
Kaiserin-Augusta-Allee 3 .. EY
Kantstr. 5 .. JX
Karl-Liebknecht-Str. 8 .. RY
Karl-Marx-Allee 8 .. RY
Karl-Marx-Str. 4 .. HZ
Kastanienallee 8 .. RX
Katzbachstr. 4 .. GZ 634
Kleiststr. 6 .. MY
Klingelhöferstr. 3 .. FX 636
Knaackstr. 8 .. RX
Knesebeckstr. 6 .. LX
Kochstr. 7 .. PZ
Königin-Elisabeth-Str. 3 .. EY 637
Koenigsallee 3 .. EZ
Köpenicker Str. (MITTE) 8 .. SZ
Kolonnenstr. 3 .. FZ 639
Konstanzer Str. 3 .. EZ 640
Kottbusser Damm 5 .. HZ
Krumme Str. 5 .. JX
Kufsteiner Str. 6 .. MZ
Kurfürstendamm 5 .. JY
Kurfürstenstr. 3 .. FY 642
Kurt-Schumacher-Damm 3 .. FX
Landsberger Allee 8 .. SY
Landshuter Str. 6 .. MY
Laubacher Str. 3 .. FZ
Leibnizstr. 5 .. KX
Leipziger Pl. und Str. 7 .. NZ
Leitzenburger Str. 6 .. LY
Lennestr. 7 .. NZ
Leonhardtstr. 5 .. JX
Levetzowstr. 3 .. FY
Lewishamstr. 5 .. JY
Lichtenberger Str. 4 .. HY 643
Lindenstr. (KREUZBERG) 4 .. GY 645
Loewenhardtdamm 4 .. GZ 646
Ludwigkirchpl. 6 .. LY
Ludwigkirchstr. 6 .. LY 648
Lützowpl. 6 .. MX
Lützowufer 3 .. FX
Luisenstr. 7 .. NY
Lustgarten 7 .. PZ 649
Luxemburger Str. 3 .. FX 651
Maaßenstr. 6 .. MY
Manfred-von-Richthofen-Str. 4 .. GZ 652
Marchstr. 6 .. LX
Markstr. 4 .. GX
Martin-Luther-Str. 6 .. MZ
Masurenallee 3 .. EY 654
Mecklenburgische Str. 5 .. KZ
Mehringdamm 4 .. GZ
Mehringpl. 4 .. GY 655
Meierottostr. 6 .. LY
Meinekestr. 6 .. LY 657
Memhardstr. 8 .. RY 658
Meraner Str. 6 .. MZ
Messedamm 3 .. EY 660
Michaelkirchstr. 8 .. RZ
Mollstr. 8 .. RY
Moltkestr. 4 .. GY 661
Mommsenstr. 5 .. JX
Motzstr. 6 .. LY
Mühlendamm 8 .. RZ 663
Mühlenstr. (FRIEDRICHSHAIN) 4 .. HY
Mühlenstr. (PANKOW) 4 .. GX
Müllerstr. 3 .. FX
Münchener Str. 6 .. MY
Münzstr. 8 .. RY 664
Nachodstr. 6 .. LY
Nassauische Str. 6 .. LZ
Nestorstr. 5 .. JY
Neue Kantstr. 3 .. EY 666
Nürnberger Str. 6 .. MY
Oderstr. 4 .. HZ
Olbersstr. 3 .. EY
Oranienburger Str. (MITTE) 7 .. PY
Oranienstr. 8 .. RZ
Osloer Str. 4 .. GX
Ostseestr. 4 .. HX
Otto-Braun-Str. 8 .. RY
Otto-Suhr-Allee 5 .. KX
Paderborner Str. 5 .. JY 667
Pankstr. 4 .. GX
Pariser Pl. 7 .. NZ
Pariser Str. 5 .. KY
Passauer Str. 6 .. MY
Paulsborner Str. 5 .. JZ
Paulstr. 3 .. FY
Perleberger Str. 3 .. FY
Pestalozzistr. 5 .. JX
Petersburger Str. 4 .. HY
Platz der Republik 7 .. NY
Platz der Vereinten Nationen 8 .. SY
Potsdamer Pl. 4 .. GY 669

Potsdamer Str. (SCHÖNEBERG) . . . . 7 . . NZ 672
Prager Pl. . . . . 6 . . LY 673
Prenzlauer Allee . . . . . 8 . . RX
Prenzlauer Promenade 4 . . HX
Prinzenstr. . . . . 4 . . GY 675
Prinzregentenstr. . . . . 6 . . LZ
Provinzstr. . . . . 4 . . GX
Quitzowstr. . . . . 3 . . FX
Rankestr. . . . . 6 . . LY 676
Rathausstr. . . . . 8 . . RY 678
Rauchstr. . . . . 6 . . MX
Reichpietschufer . . . . . 3 . . FY 679
Reinhardtstr. . . . . 7 . . NY 683
Reinickendorfer Str. . . . 4 . . GX 684
Rheinbabenallee . . . . . 3 . . EZ
Rheinstr. . . . . 3 . . FZ 687
Richard-Wagner-Str. . . . 5 . . JX
Rönnestr. . . . . 5 . . JX
Rosa-Luxemburg-Str. . . 8 . . RY 689
Rosenthaler Str. . . . . . 8 . . RY 690
Rudolstädter Str. . . . . . 3 . . EZ 692
Saatwinkler Damm . . . . 3 . . EX
Sachsendamm . . . . 3 . . FZ
Sächsische Str. . . . . . . 5 . . KY
Salzburger Str. . . . . . . 6 . . MZ
Savignypl. . . . . 6 . . LX
Schaperstr. . . . . 6 . . LY
Scharnhorststr. . . . . . . 7 . . NX
Schillerstr. . . . . 5 . . JX
Schillstr. . . . . 6 . . MX 693
Schivelbeiner Str. . . . . 4 . . GX 696
Schloßstr. (CHARLOTTENBURG) 5 JX
Schlüterstr. . . . . 5 . . KX
Schönhauser Allee . . . . 8 . . RX
Schwedter Str. . . . . . . 8 . . RX
Seesener Str. . . . . 5 . . JY
Seestr. . . . . 3 . . FX
Sellerstr. . . . . 4 . . GX
Sickingenstr. . . . . 3 . . FY
Siemensdamm . . . . 3 . . EX
Siemensstr. . . . . 3 . . FY 698
Sigmaringer Str. . . . . . 5 . . KZ
Skalitzer Str. . . . . 4 . . HY
Sonnenallee . . . . 4 . . HZ
Sophie-Charlotten-Pl. . . 5 . . JX
Sophie-Charlotten-Str. . . 3 . . EY 699
Spandauer Damm . . . . . 3 . . EY
Spandauer Str. . . . . . . 8 . . RY
Spichernstr. . . . . 6 . . LY
Spreeweg . . . . 6 . . MX
Steinpl. . . . . 6 . . LX
Storkower Str. . . . . . . 4 . . HX
Stralauer Allee . . . . . . 4 . . HY
Stralauer Str. . . . . 8 . . RZ
Straße des 17. Juni . . . 6 . . MX
Strausberger Pl. . . . . . 4 . . HY 702
Stresemannstr. . . . . . . 7 . . NZ
Stromstr. . . . . 3 . . FY 704
Stülerstr. . . . . 6 . . MX
Stuttgarter Pl. . . . . . . 5 . . JX 705
Suarezstr. . . . . 5 . . JX
Südwestkorso . . . . 3 . . EZ 708
Tauentzienstr. . . . . . . 6 . . MX 707
Tegeler Weg . . . . 3 . . EY
Tempelhofer Damm . . . . 4 . . GZ
Tempelhofer Ufer . . . . . 4 . . GZ 710
Teplitzer Str. . . . . 3 . . EZ 711
Theodor-Heuss-Pl. . . . . 3 . . EY 713
Tiergartenstr. . . . . 6 . . MX
Torstr. . . . . 7 . . PX
Transvallstr. . . . . 3 . . FX
Turmstr. . . . . 3 . . FY
Uhlandstr. . . . . 6 . . LZ
Unter den Linden . . . . . 7 . . NZ
Urbanstr. . . . . 4 . . GZ
Veteranenstr. . . . . 7 . . PX 715
Viktoria-Luise-Pl. . . . . . 6 . . MY 717
Warschauer Str. . . . . . . 4 . . HY
Weinmeisterstr. . . . . . . 8 . . RY 718
Welserstr. . . . . 6 . . MY
Werderstr. . . . . 7 . . PZ 720
Westfälische Str. . . . . . 5 . . JY
Wexstr. . . . . 3 . . FZ
Wichertstr. . . . . 4 . . HX
Wiener Str. . . . . 4 . . HZ
Wiesbadener Str. . . . . . 3 . . EZ
Wilhelmstr. (MITTE) . . . 7 . . NZ
Wilmersdorfer Str. . . . . 5 . . JX
Windscheidstr. . . . . . . 5 . . JX
Winterfeldtpl. . . . . 6 . . MY
Wisbyer Str. . . . . 4 . . HX
Wittenbergpl. . . . . 6 . . MY
Wollankstr. . . . . 4 . . GX
Württembergische Str. . . 5 . . KY
Wundtstr. . . . . 5 . . JX
Xantener Str. . . . . 5 . . JY
Yorckstr. . . . . 4 . . GZ
Zillestr. . . . . 5 . . JX

SIGHTS

MUSEUMS, GALLERIES, COLLECTIONS

Museum Island (Museumsinsel)★★★ PY: *National Gallery (Alte Nationalgalerie)★★★* **M[20]** *(Paintings of Caspar David Friedrich★★★, paintings of Adolph Menzel★★★), Pergamon-Museum (Pergamonmuseum)★★★, Collection of Antiquities (Antikensammlung)★★★ : Altar of Pergamon (Pergamonaltar)★★★; Middle East Museum (Vorderasiatisches Museum)★★; Gate of Ishtar (Ischtartor)★★★; Museum of Islamic Art (Museum für Islamische Kunst)★★, Old Museum (Altes Museum)★★* **M[18]** *; Collection of Antiquities (Antikensammlung)★★★: Hildesheim silverware treasure (Hildesheimer Silberfund)★★★ – Forum of Culture (Kulturforum)★★★* NZ: *Philharmonie and Chamber Music Hall (Kammermusiksaal)★★★, Musical Instruments Museum (Musikinstrumenten-Museum)★* **M[4]**, *Museum of Decorative Arts (Kunstgewerbemuseum)★★,* **M[5]** *Guelph Treasure (Welfenschatz)★★★, Lüneburg Treasure (Lüneburger Ratssilber)★★★, Gallery of Paintings (Gemäldegalerie)★★★* **M[6]** *(Altars of Rogier van der Weyden)★★★, Collection of drawings (Kupferstichkabinett – Sammlung der Zeichnungen und Druckgraphik)★, New National Gallery (Neue Nationalgalerie)★★* **M[7]**, *Prussian State Library (Staatsbibliothek Preußischer Kulturbesitz)★ – Dahlem Museums (Museen Dahlem – Kunst und Kulturen der Welt)* BV: *Museum of Ethnography (Ethnologisches Museum)★★★, Division American archaeology (Abteilung Amerikanische Archäologie)★★★: Stone sculptures of Bilbao (Steinplastiken von Bilbao)★★★, Gold Room (Goldkammer)★★★, Museum of Indian Art (Museum für indische Kunst)★★, Collection of East Asian art (Museum für Ostasiatische Kunst★, European Culture Museum (Museum Europäischer Kulturen)★ – Charlottenburg Castle (Schloss Charlottenburg)★★★* EY: *Old Castle (Altes Schloss)★★, New Wing (Neuer Flügel)★★, Gersaint's Shop Sign (Ladenschild des Kunsthändlers Gersaint)★★★, Embarcation for Cythera (Einschiffung nach Kythera)★★★, Museum of Pre-and Proto-History (Museum für Vor- und Frühgeschichte)★, Garden (Schlossgarten)★★ New Pavilion (Neuer Pavillon★, Belvedere★, Mausoleum★) – Egyptian Museum and Collection of Papyrus (Ägyptisches Museum und Papyrussammlung)★★★* EY **M[2]**, *Nefertiti (Nofretete)★★★, Amarna founds (Amarna-Funde)★★★ – Collection Berggruen – Picasso and his time (Sammlung Berggruen – Picasso und seine Zeit)★★* EY **M[16]** *– Hamburg Station Museum (Hamburger Bahnhof – Museum für Gegenwart)★★* NX *– German Museum of Technique (Deutsches Technikmuseum Berlin)★★* GZ **M[3]** *– Jewish Museum (Jüdisches Museum)★★* GZ **M[38]** *– Nature Museum (Museum für Naturkunde)★★* NX *– March Museum (Märkisches Museum/Stadtmuseum Berlin)★★* RZ *– Bröhan-Museum★* EY **M[13]** *– Communications Museum (Museum für Kommunikation Berlin)★★* PZ **M[1]** *– Friedrichswerder Church (Friedrichswerdersche Kirche)★* PZ *– Museum of the artistic movement "Brücke" (Brücke-Museum)★ by Clay Allee* EZ **M[36]** *– Bauhaus Museum (Bauhaus-Archiv – Museum für Gestaltung)★* MX *– Museum of Cinema (Filmmuseum) (at Sony Center)★* NZ *– Botanical Museum (Botanisches Museum)★ by Rheinbabenallee* EZ

PARKS, GARDENS, LAKES

Zoological Garden (Zoologischer Garten)★★★ MX *– Tiergarten★★* MX *– Victory Column (Siegessäule)★ Panorama (Aussicht)★★ – Grunewald★★ by Clay-Allee* EZ: *Hunting Lodge (Jagdschloss Grunewald)★* **M[28]** *– Peacook Island (Pfaueninsel)★★ by Clay-Allee* EZ *– Park★★, Summer residence (Lustschloss)★ – Wannsee★★ by Clay-Allee* EZ *– Großer Müggelsee★★ by Stralauer Allee* HYZ *– Botanical Gardens (Botanischer Garten)★★ by Rheinbabenallee* EZ *– Viktoria-Park★* GZ

HISTORIC BUILDINGS, STREETS, SQUARES

Potsdam Square (Potsdamer Platz)★★ NZ *– Quartier DaimlerChrysler★ (Sony Center)★★ (roof)★★★ – Martin-Gropius-Bau★★* NZ *– Band des Bundes★★* NY *– Chancellor's office (Bundeskanzleramt)★★ – Parliament (Reichstag)★★* NY *(Panoramic platform (Panorama-Plattform))★★ – Brandenburg Gate (Brandenburger Tor)★★* NZ *– Gendarmenmarkt★★,* PZ *– Schauspielhaus★★, French Cathedral (Französischer Dom)★ (Panorama Ausblick)★★, German Cathedral (Deutscher Dom)★ – Unter den Linden★★* NPZ *– Administration building of DZ-Bank (Hauptverwaltung der DZ-Bank)★★, Prussian National Library (Staatsbibliothek-Preußischer Kulturbesitz)★, Monument of Frederick II (Reiterdenkmal Friedrichs II)★, Forum Fridericianum★★ (State Opera Unter den Linden Staatsoper Unter den Linden)★, Old Library (Alte Bibliothek)★, St-Hedwigs Cathedral (Sankt-Hedwigs-Kathedrale)★, New guardroom (Neue Wache)★, Arsenal (Zeughaus)★★, Crown Prince's Palace (Kronprinzenpalais)★ – Castle bridge (Schlossbrücke)★* PYZ *– Cathedral (Berliner Dom)★* PY *– Alexander Square (Alexanderplatz)★* RY *– Television Tower (Fernsehturm)★ (view Aussicht)★★★, Red Town Hall (Rotes Rathaus)★ – Nicolai District (Nikolaiviertel)★* RYZ *– Nicolai Church (Nikolaikirche)★, Knoblauchhaus Museum (Knoblauchhaus)★, Ephraim Palace (Ephraim-Palais)★ – Kurfürstendamm★★* LXY *– Kaiser-Wilhelm Memorial Church (Kaiser-Wilhelm-Gedächtniskirche)★★ – KaDeWe Shopping Centre★* MY *– Radio Tower (Funkturm)★ (Panorama (Aussicht))★★★* EY *– Olympic Stadium (Olympiastadion)★ by Spandauer Damm* EY *– Citadel (Zitadelle Spandau)★ by Siemensdamm* EX *– St.-Nichola's Church Spandau (St-Nikolai-Kirche Spandau)★ by Siemensdamm* EX

Town Centre : Charlottenburg, Mitte, Schöneberg, Tiergarten, Wilmersdorf

Adlon, Unter den Linden 77, ✉ 10117, ☎ (030) 2 26 10, *Fax (030) 22612222, adlon @kempinski.com*, – rm, – 300. AE VISA JCB. rest NZ s
Meals see ***Lorenz Adlon*** below – ***Quarré :*** **Meals** à la carte 37/57 ♀ – ***Adlon Stube*** *(closed 19 July - 18 August and Sunday dinner)* **Meals** à la carte 28/40 ♀ – ☐ 29 – **357 rm** 320/440 – 370/490 – 30 suites.
◆ A legend lives again ! The mother of all grand hotels has been rebuilt in its original palatial style. The Quarré is classically elegant. The Adlon Stube is In the style of an English gentleman's club.

The Ritz-Carlton, Potsdamer Platz 3, ✉ 10785, ☎ (030) 33 77 77, *Fax (030) 337775555, berlin@ritzcarlton.com*, – rm, – 450. AE VISA JCB. rest NZ d
Vitrum *(closed 2 weeks January, July, Sunday and Monday) (dinner only)* **Meals** 78/98 and à la carte ♀ – ***Brasserie Desbrosses :*** **Meals** à la carte 24/46 – ☐ 28 – **302 rm** 250/280 – 280/310 – 40 suites.
◆ Utterly exquisite, from the lavishly designed reception area with its freestanding flight of steps and gold-leaf décor, right up to the spacious rooms with high quality furnishings. The Vitrum is a picture of Venetian elegance. Original French Brasserie.

Grand Hyatt, Marlene-Dietrich-Platz 2, ✉ 10785, ☎ (030) 25 53 12 34, *Fax (030) 25531235, berlin@hyatt.de*, – rm, – 320. AE VISA JCB. NZ a
Vox : **Meals** à la carte 41/59 ♀ – ☐ 24 – **342 rm** 210/230 – 240/260 – 12 suites.
◆ Bold architectural forms on the rebuilt Potsdamer Platz. The contemporary architectural theme is carried through into the rooms with their authentic designer décor. The Vox has a subtly Asian atmosphere.

Grand Hotel Esplanade, Lützowufer 15, ✉ 10785, ☎ (030) 25 47 80, *Fax (030) 254788222, info@esplanade.de*, – rm, – 260. AE VISA JCB. rest MX e
Meals see ***Vivo*** below – ***Eckkneipe :*** **Meals** à la carte 18/44 – ☐ 20 – **386 rm** 230/280 – 255/310 – 23 suites.
◆ This grand hotel could almost be an exhibit in a modern design exhibition ! Paintings by the "Wild Berliners" adorn the walls. Conference ship with landing stage. Solid Berlin specialities served at the wooden tables of the "Eckkneipe" corner pub.

Palace, Budapester Str. 45, ✉ 10787, ☎ (030) 2 50 20, *Fax (030) 25021119, hotel @palace.de*, – rm, – 350. AE VISA JCB MX k
Meals see ***First Floor*** below – ☐ 20 – **282 rm** 205 – 360 – 19 suites.
◆ Luxury with a personal touch on the famous Kurfürstendamm. Every room has an individual character ; some overlook the Memorial Church, others the Zoo.

Swissôtel, Augsburger Str. 44, ✉ 10789, ☎ (030) 22 01 00, *Fax (030) 220102222, emailus.berlin@swissotel.com*, – rm, – 220. AE VISA JCB. rest LX k
44 : **Meals** à la carte 37/68 ♀ – ☐ 21 – **316 rm** 210/275 – 230/295.
◆ Berlin likes to think of itself as cosmopolitan and open to the world, and so does this newly built hotel in Postmodern style in the heart of the city. Cool elegance in the Restaurant 44.

Kempinski Hotel Bristol, Kurfürstendamm 27, ✉ 10719, ☎ (030) 88 43 40, *Fax (030) 8836075, reservations.bristol@kempinski.com*, – rm, – 280. AE VISA JCB. LX n
Kempinski Grill *(closed 5 weeks July - August, Saturday lunch, Sunday and Monday)* **Meals** à la carte 48/67 ♀ – ***Kempinski-Eck :*** **Meals** à la carte 26/31 – ☐ 23 – **301 rm** 290 – 330 – 21 suites.
◆ A red carpet leads directly from the Kurfürstendamm into this elegant and luxurious 1950s establishment, a favourite with such guests as John F Kennedy and Sophia Loren. Legendary Kempinski Grill with exquisite décor. Brasserie-style Kempinski-Eck.

The Westin Grand, Friedrichstr. 158, ✉ 10117, ☎ (030) 2 02 70, *Fax (030) 20273149, info@westin-grand.com*, – rm, – 160. AE VISA JCB PZ a
Friedrichs : **Meals** à la carte 28/47 – ***Stammhaus :*** **Meals** à la carte 23/35 – ☐ 23 – **358 rm** 222/375 – 247/400 – 18 suites.
◆ In the very heart of old Berlin, the hotel's foyer has an imposing 30m-high glass roof. This is an establishment of great elegance and nostalgic charm. Traditional ambience in Friedrich's, Berlin specialities in the Stammhaus.

InterContinental, Budapester Str. 2, ✉ 10787, ☎ (030) 2 60 20, *Fax (030) 26022600, berlin@ichotelsgroup.com*, – rm, 860. AE VISA JCB. rest MX a
Meals see ***Hugos*** below – ***L.A. Cafe*** : Meals à la carte 23/34 – 20 – **584 rm** 199/269 – 254/319 – 42 suites.
◆ From foyer to conference suite, this is a most impressive establishment. Tasteful, elegant rooms, those in the east wing in an attractively contemporary style. Splendidly equipped Vitality Club. American-style LA Café with lovely glass dome.

Hilton, Mohrenstr. 30, ✉ 10117, ☎ (030) 2 02 30, *Fax (030) 20234269, info.berlin@hilton.com*, – rm, 300. AE VISA JCB PZ r
Fellini (Italian) *(closed end July - mid August) (dinner only)* **Meals** à la carte 29/40 – ***Mark Brandenburg*** : **Meals** à la carte 28/41 – ***Trader Vic's*** (Polynesian) *(dinner only)* **Meals** à la carte 31/50 – 22 – **575 rm** 150/265 – 150/285 – 14 suites.
◆ A splendid foyer welcomes guests to this prestigious establishment. All rooms facing the street overlook the Gendarmenmarkt. Lavish fitness facilities. Italian cuisine in Fellini, Mark Brandenburg with traditional décor.

Marriott, Inge-Beisheim-Platz 1, ✉ 10785, ☎ (030) 22 00 00, *Fax (030) 220001000, berlin@marriotthotels.de*, – rm, 420. AE VISA JCB NZ f
Meals à la carte 22/45 – 22 – **379 rm** 159 – 219 – 9 suites.
◆ Most of the rooms, comfortably furnished in American cherrywood, are arranged around the extensive atrium, which is your point of welcome to this modern business hotel. Bistro-style restaurant with a show kitchen and large glass façade.

Radisson SAS-Hotel, Karl-Liebknecht-Str. 3, ✉ 10178, ☎ (030) 23 82 80, *Fax (030) 2382810, info.berlin@radissonsas.com*, – rm, 220. AE VISA JCB. rest RY b
Meals à la carte 23/40 – 21 – **427 rm** 160/180 – 22 suites.
◆ What an entrance ! A 25m high cylindrical aquarium soars up from the modernistic purity of the atrium lobby. The rooms too are furnished in bold, simple lines. A light and modern hotel restaurant with an open kitchen. Southeast Asian fare in the Noodle bar.

Dorint Sofitel Schweizerhof, Budapester Str. 25, ✉ 10787, ☎ (030) 2 69 60, *Fax (030) 26961000, info.bersch@dorint.com*, – rm, 460. AE VISA JCB MX w
Meals 28/39 à la carte 30/36 – 20 – **384 rm** 195/235 – 220/260 – 10 suites.
◆ The ultra-modern foyer is glimpsed through the hotel's glass façade. Full range of business facilities. Wellness Centre with 25m pool. Warm colours and bold paintings in the Bistro-Restaurant.

Steigenberger, Los-Angeles-Platz 1, ✉ 10789, ☎ (030) 2 12 70, *Fax (030) 2127117, berlin@steigenberger.de*, – rm, 300. AE VISA JCB. rest MY d
Louis *(closed July - August, Sunday and Monday) (dinner only)* **Meals** à la carte 40/53 – ***Berliner Stube*** : **Meals** à la carte 19/30 – 21 – **396 rm** 169 – 339 – 11 suites.
◆ A spacious foyer gives a foretaste of the standard of comfort of this old city establishment. Executive Floor with Club Lounge on the 6th floor. Varied bars. Restaurant Louis with refined atmosphere and creative cuisine. Cheerful "Berliner Stube" pub.

Brandenburger Hof, Eislebener Str. 14, ✉ 10789, ☎ (030) 21 40 50, *Fax (030) 21405100, info@brandenburger-hof.com*, – rm, 30. AE VISA JCB LY n
Meals see ***Die Quadriga*** below – ***Der Wintergarten*** : **Meals** à la carte 32/49 – **82 rm** 170/250 – 245/285 – 4 suites.
◆ The contrast between the Classical façade and the Bauhaus-style interior of this sophisticated establishment is handled with great verve. The light and airy Wintergarten restaurant is laid out around a Japanese courtyard.

Louisa's Place without rest, Kurfürstendamm 160, ✉ 10709, ☎ (030) 63 10 30, *Fax (030) 63103100, info@louisas-place.de*, . AE VISA JCB JY a
18 – **47 suites** 120 – 225.
◆ Tasteful, spacious suites with kitchenettes and the very friendly service are the distinguishing features of this exclusively furnished hotel. The Breakfast Room and library are very stylish.

Ramada Plaza, Pragerstr. 12, ✉ 10779, ☎ (030) 2 36 25 00, *Fax (030) 236250550, berlin.plaza@ramada-treff.de*, direct entrance to the Elexia-Wellness centre – rm, 70. AE VISA JCB. rest LY g
Meals à la carte 20/38 – 15 – **184 rm** 139 – 179 – 81 suites.
◆ The rooms and suites of this modern business hotel have elegant American cherrywood furnishings and the latest technical facilities. Executive Floor on the 6th floor. Classic-style restaurant.

Maritim proArte, Friedrichstr. 151, ✉ 10117, ✆ (030) 2 03 35, *Fax (030) 20334209, info.bpa@maritim.de*, – rm, – 600. AE VISA JCB PY e
Atelier *(dinner only)* **Meals** 60/90 and à la carte 36/49 – ***Bistro media*** *(lunch only)* **Meals** à la carte 19/30 – ***Galerie*** *(closed Saturday and Sunday)* **Meals** 26 (buffet lunch only) – 19 – **403 rm** 149/265 – 168/278 – 12 suites.
◆ A stone's throw from the prestigious thoroughfare of Unter den Linden, this avant-garde hotel offers rooms with the full range of technical facilities. Paintings by the "Young Wilds" throughout the hotel. The Atelier is designer in style through and through.

Jolly Hotel Vivaldi, Friedrichstr. 96, ✉ 10117, ✆ (030) 2 06 26 60, *Fax (030) 206266999, vivaldi.jhb@jollyhotels.de*, – rm, – 60. AE VISA PY d
Meals (Italian) 32/45 and à la carte 30/41 – 16 – **254 rm** 145/245 – 170/270.
◆ A spacious foyer welcomes guests to this modern, impeccably run hotel. Choice wood furnishings and attractive colours in the comfortable rooms. Bright open-plan restaurant.

Madison, Potsdamer Str. 3, ✉ 10785, ✆ (030) 5 90 05 00 00, *Fax (030) 590050500, welcome@madison-berlin.de*, – rm, – 20. AE VISA. NZ v
Meals see ***Facil*** below – 22 – **166 rm** 140/250 – 175/275 – 17 suites.
◆ In the media district close to Sony, cinema and shopping mall. Apartment hotel with rooms with cooking facilities and shopping service.

Dorint Sofitel am Gendarmenmarkt, Charlottenstr. 50, ✉ 10117, ✆ (030) 20 37 50, *Fax (030) 20375100, info.bergen@dorint.com*, – rm, – 80. AE VISA PZ s
Aigner **: Meals** 35/45 and à la carte 30/43 – 23 – **92 rm** 215/300 – 245/300.
◆ Directly opposite the French Cathedral on the Gendarmenmarkt. Dating from GDR times but completely refurbished in straightforward contemporary style. The Aigner Restaurant has original features from a Viennese coffee-house.

Crowne Plaza, Nürnberger Str. 65, ✉ 10787, ✆ (030) 21 00 70, *Fax (030) 2132009, info@cp-berlin.com*, – rm, – 350. AE VISA JCB. rest MX t
Meals *(closed Saturday lunch and Sunday dinner)* à la carte 25/37 – 18 – **423 rm** 160/250 – 180/270 – 10 suites.
◆ Well-located for a stroll along the Kurfuerstedamm or a visit to the KaDeWe department store. Distinctive but practical furnishings. Conference facilities including congress centre. Restaurant with wide range of international cuisine.

Sorat Hotel Spree-Bogen, Alt-Moabit 99, ✉ 10559, ✆ (030) 39 92 00, *Fax (030) 39920999, spree-bogen@sorat-hotels.com*, – rm, – 200. AE VISA JCB. rest FY b
Meals *(lunch only)* à la carte 23/34 – **221 rm** 128/237 – 166/272.
◆ Perfect peace on the banks of the River Spree. Within the walls of an old dairy building is a series of surprisingly modern interiors. Private landing-stage. The restaurant combines old brick walls with the latest in design.

Savoy, Fasanenstr. 9, ✉ 10623, ✆ (030) 31 10 30, *Fax (030) 31103333, info@hotel-savoy.com*, – rm, – 40. AE VISA LX s
Meals *(closed Sunday)* à la carte 24/34 – **125 rm** 142/222 – 152/232 – 18 suites.
◆ Charming city hotel with 70 years of experience. Mentioned in his writings by Thomas Mann and still favoured by the celebrities of today. Cigar Lounge. Classic interiors including restaurant with easy chairs.

Mondial, Kurfürstendamm 47, ✉ 10707, ✆ (030) 88 41 10, *Fax (030) 88411150, hotel-mondial@t-online.de*, – rm, – 50. AE VISA JCB
Meals à la carte 20/34 – **75 rm** 110/195 – 140/245. KY e
◆ Right on the Ku'Damm and ideally placed for forays into its bustling shopping activity. Subsequent recovery aided by relaxation in your comfortable soundproofed rooms. Restaurant with timeless décor and buffet with vast choice.

Alexander Plaza, Rosenstr. 1, ✉ 10178, ✆ (030) 24 00 10, *Fax (030) 24001777, info@hotel-alexander-plaza.de*, – rm, – 70. AE VISA RY a
Meals *(closed Sunday) (dinner only)* à la carte 20/30 – 15 – **92 rm** 140/170 – 150/180.
◆ Very handy for the fashionable Hackesche Hoefe area, the hotel was built in 1897 for a dealer in furs. The mosaic floor in the hall is an unmissable feature. The restaurant is strikingly furnished with black leather sofas and red chairs.

NH Berlin-Mitte, Leipziger Str. 106, ✉ 10117, ✆ (030) 20 37 60, *Fax (030) 20376600, nhberlinmitte@nh-hotels.com*, – rm, – 150. AE VISA. rest PZ k
Meals à la carte 23/48 – 16 – **392 rm** 136 – 164.
◆ Hotel with spacious foyer, modern, functional and comfortable rooms and an excellent central location. Leisure facilities on the 8th floor. Bistro-style restaurant opening on to the foyer.

Angleterre, Friedrichstr. 31, ✉ 10569, ✆ (030) 20 21 37 00, *Fax (030) 20213777, info@gold-inn.de*, rm, – 250. PZ b
***Speakers' Corner* : Meals** à la carte 15/27 – ☕ 13 – **156 rm** 115/185 – 125/195 – 4 suites.
◆ Enjoy the plush comfort of one of the rooms or suites to be found in the part of the hotel which was a Palace building in 1891. The old staircase is especially lovely. Speaker's Corner derives its name from the one in London's Hyde Park.

Grosser Kurfürst, Neue Roßstr. 11, ✉ 10179, ✆ (030) 24 60 00, *Fax (030) 24600300, grosserkurfuerst@deraghotels.de*, rm, – 20. RZ e
Meals *(closed Saturday and Sunday) (dinner only)* à la carte 24/39 – **144 rm** ☕ 140/195 – 175/240 – 7 suites.
◆ Smart, well equipped modern rooms, some facing the Spree River, lead off from an impressive lobby beneath a landmark glass tower. Elegant Mediterranean restaurant with a menu to match.

Henriette, Neue Roßstr.13, ✉ 10179, ✆ (030) 24 60 09 00, *Fax (030) 24600940, henriette@deraghotels.de*, – rm, – 40. RZ e
Meals (Indian) à la carte 14/20 – **53 rm** ☕ 135/213 – 165/225.
◆ Bedrooms and apartments are grouped around a four-storey light-well. Their décor makes use of fine materials to create a tasteful and comfortable atmosphere.

Alsterhof, Augsburger Str. 5, ✉ 10789, ✆ (030) 21 24 20, *Fax (030) 2183949, info@alsterhof.com*, beer garden, rm, – 120. MY r
Meals *(closed Sunday dinner)* à la carte 24/50 – ***Zum Lit-Fass*** *(dinner only)* **Meals** à la carte 16/30 – ☕ 16 – **200 rm** 100.
◆ This corner building with a glazed roof-pavilion offers exceptionally comfortable rooms and a small but attractive 6th floor leisure area. Internet terminals. Basement hotel restaurant. The more informal Zum Lit-Fass with a leafy beer garden.

Seehof, Lietzensee-Ufer 11, ✉ 14057, ✆ (030) 32 00 20, *Fax (030) 32002251, info@hotel-seehof-berlin.de*, – rm, – 30. JX r
Meals à la carte 25/39 – **75 rm** ☕ 135/190 – 165/220.
◆ Well-run hotel on the leafy banks of the Lietzensee. Elegant, tasteful rooms, some with mahogany furniture, others with period pieces. Restaurant with classical ambience and lovely lakeside terrace.

President, An der Urania 16, ✉ 10787, ✆ (030) 21 90 30, *Fax (030) 2186120, president@cca-hotels.de*, rm, – 70. MY t
Meals à la carte 26/32 – ☕ 14 – **177 rm** 123 – 141.
◆ As well as functional Economy and Business rooms with pc connection the hotel has Club Rooms with extra-large desks and comfortable leather chairs. Redesigned restaurant with wicker furniture.

Art'otel Berlin Mitte, Wallstr. 70, ✉ 10179, ✆ (030) 24 06 20, *Fax (030) 24062222, aobminfo@artotels.de* – rm, rm, – 35. RZ c
Meals à la carte 25/35 – ☕ 15 – **109 rm** 130/190 – 190/210.
◆ A wonderful synthesis of old patrician residence and ultramodern purpose-built hotel. Full-blooded designer interiors.

Hollywood Media Hotel without rest, Kurfürstendamm 202, ✉ 10719, ✆ (030) 88 91 00, *Fax (030) 88910280, info@filmhotel.de* – – 90. LY r
185 rm ☕ 115/182 – 137/204 – 12 suites.
◆ Hollywood comes to Berlin in Artur Brauner's hotel, making every guest a star. Rooms evoke the world of film. Own cinema.

Domicil, Kantstr. 111a, ✉ 10627, ✆ (030) 32 90 30, *Fax (030) 32903299, info@hotel-domicil-berlin.de*, – rm, – 50. JX v
Meals à la carte 18/28 – **70 rm** ☕ 108/143 – 153/184 – 6 suites.
◆ A curving glass façade distinguishes this corner building. Elegant pine furnishings give the rooms a sunny, Italian atmosphere. Bright tiling and mosaic in the bathrooms. Rooftop restaurant with garden.

Hecker's Hotel, Grolmanstr. 35, ✉ 10623, ✆ (030) 8 89 00, *Fax (030) 8890260, info@heckers-hotel.de* – rm, – 25. LX e
Cassambalis *(closed Sunday lunch)* **Meals** à la carte 32/42 – ☕ 16 – **69 rm** 125/160 – 150/180.
◆ This establishment combines individuality and personal service. Some rooms are comfortably functional, others in contemporary designer style or with tasteful themed decor. Mediterranean cuisine served with flair in Cassamblis.

Bleibtreu, Bleibtreustr. 31, ✉ 10707, ☎ (030) 88 47 40, *Fax (030) 88474444, info@bleibtreu.com*, – , rm, . KY s
Meals à la carte 28/37 – 15 – **60 rm** 142/152 – 152/167.
• Restored city residence dating from the Kaiser's times. Contemporary furnishings throughout, specially designed for the hotel by German and Italian firms. Stylish bistro-type restaurant opening on to the foyer.

Ku'Damm 101 without rest, Kurfürstendamm 101, ✉ 10711, ☎ (030) 5 20 05 50, *Fax (030) 520055555, info@kudamm101.com*, – , rm, – 60. . JY k
13 – **170 rm** 101/161 – 118/178.
• Uncompromising designer style throughout. Rooms in contemporary colours, with big windows and excellent technical facilities. 7th floor breakfast room with city views.

Luisenhof without rest, Köpenicker Str. 92, ✉ 10179, ☎ (030) 2 41 59 06, *Fax (030) 2792983, info@luisenhof.de* – – 30. RZ a
27 rm 120/180 – 150/250.
• Fine old 1822 town house with a fascinating history, including period as a depot for horse tramway. Elegantly furnished with period items.

Arcotel Velvet, Oranienburger Str. 52, ✉ 10117, ☎ (030) 2 78 75 30 (hotel) 24 78 10 78 (rest.), *Fax (030) 278753800, velvet@arcotel.at*, – , rm, – 20. PY n
***Lutter & Wegener* : Meals** à la carte 20/34 – 15 – **85 rm** 130/250 – 150/250.
• This hotel with its modern glass façade is right next to the Tacheles cultural centre. All rooms have warm red colours, portraits of famous personages and floor-to-ceiling windows. The Bistro-style Lutter & Wegener has a delicatessen counter and wine racks.

Dorint Novotel Berlin Mitte, Fischerinsel 12, ✉ 10179, ☎ (030) 20 67 40, *Fax (030) 20674111, h3278@accor.com*, , – , rm, – 220. . rest RZ b
Meals à la carte 19/35 – 15 – **238 rm** 139/189 – 154/214.
• This up-to-date establishment is located in a major building complex. Modern, functional rooms and a business centre on the top floor.

Mercure an der Charité, Invalidenstr. 38, ✉ 10115, ☎ (030) 30 82 60, *Fax (030) 30826100, h5341@accor.com* – , rm, – 85. NX b
Meals à la carte 21/29 – 13 – **246 rm** 77/106 – 86/116.
• This modern hotel close to the natural history museum devotes itself wholeheartedly to business travellers. Rooms and corridors graced by enlargements of postcards.

Art'otel Berlin City Center West, Lietzenburger Str. 85, ✉ 10719, ☎ (030) 8 87 77 70, *Fax (030) 887777777, aobwinfo@artotels.de* – , rm, – 25. LY b
Meals à la carte 21/26 – 13 – **91 rm** 120/167 – 130/177.
• New, contemporary hotel. The Andy Warhols are set off by the colourful interiors, with bedrooms in lime green and violet and public spaces in shades of red. In very much the same spirit, the restaurant with its vast glazed façade.

Hamburg, Landgrafenstr. 4, ✉ 10787, ☎ (030) 26 47 70, *Fax (030) 2629394, hoham@t-online.de*, – , rm, – 50. . rest MX s
Meals à la carte 23/33 – **191 rm** 99/166 – 132/200.
• Just a short walk from the Tiergarten. Spacious foyer with open fireplace. Sailors will enjoy the atmosphere in the Hanse Bar. Restaurant with winter garden.

Kanthotel without rest, Kantstr. 111, ✉ 10627, ☎ (030) 32 30 20, *Fax (030) 3240952, info@kanthotel.com* – – 15. JX e
70 rm 140/185 – 170/185.
• This well-run hotel with its comfortable, functional rooms is located between the International Congress Centre and the Memorial Church.

Sorat Art'otel without rest, Joachimstaler Str. 29, ✉ 10719, ☎ (030) 88 44 70, *Fax (030) 88447700, art-otel@sorat-hotels.com* – – 25. LY e
133 rm 124/148 – 146/168.
• Good location in central western Berlin. The whole building has been designed in avant-guard style by Wolf Vostell. Contemporary pictures adorn the walls.

Adrema without rest, Gotzkowskystr. 20, ✉ 10555, ☎ (030) 20 21 34 00, *Fax (030) 20213444, info.beradr@gold-inn.de* – . FY x
12 – **53 rm** 79/119 – 89/129.
• Crisp lines and functional fittings characterise the designer rooms of this establishment. Breakfast served at loft level with views of the River Spree.

Kronprinz without rest, Kronprinzendamm 1, 10711, (030) 89 60 30, *Fax (030) 8931215, reception@kronprinz-hotel.de* – 25. JY d
76 rm 115/130 - 145.
◆ Well known for its tasteful interior and situated on the western edge of town close to the International Congress Centre. Beer garden beneath ancient chestnut trees.

Schlosspark-Hotel, Heubnerweg 2a, 14059, (030) 3 26 90 30, *Fax (030) 326903600, schlossparkhotel@t-online.de*, – rm, – 30. EY a
Meals à la carte 14/24 – **40 rm** 92/150 – 112/170.
◆ Excellent starting point for visiting the nearby museums as well as the castle and its inviting park. It's a good idea to reserve a room facing the park. Restaurant-Café with rustic interior and conservatory.

Ramada, Chausseestr. 118, 10115, (030) 2 78 75 50, *Fax (030) 278755550, berlin.mitte@ramada-treff.de*, – rm, – 20. NX c
Meals à la carte 18/33 – 15 – **145 rm** 97.
◆ Mainly catering for business travellers, this hotel has contemporary, functional rooms. Glass handbasins are an original touch.

Albrechtshof, Albrechtstr. 8, 10117, (030) 30 88 60, *Fax (030) 30886100, albrechtshof@albrechtshof-hotels.de*, – rm, – 45. NY a
Meals à la carte 29/35 – **100 rm** 118/169 – 148/199.
◆ This comfortable establishment is one of the Christian Hotels chain. It has a chapel which can be used for weddings and christenings as well as for prayer and contemplation.

Boulevard without rest, Kurfürstendamm 12, 10719, (030) 88 42 50, *Fax (030) 88425450, info@hotel-boulevard.com* – – 15. LX c
57 rm 95/112 - 96/128.
◆ The hotel takes its name from the cosmopolitan thoroughfare on which it is located. Roof terrace with café and fine views of city life.

Scandotel Castor without rest, Fuggerstr. 8, 10777, (030) 21 30 30, *Fax (030) 21303160, scandotel@t-online.de* – MY s
78 rm 70/107 - 80/135.
◆ Ku'Damm and KaDeWe, cinemas and cafes, are all close to this contemporary establishment with its functional and well-equipped rooms

Kurfürstendamm am Adenauerplatz without rest, Kurfürstendamm 68, 10707, (030) 88 46 30, *Fax (030) 8825528, info@hotel-kurfuerstendamm.de* – – 30. JY n
34 rm 94 - 140.
◆ Rooms identically furnished in cherrywood. The building also houses a catering college.

Fjord Hotel without rest, Bissingzeile 13, 10785, (030) 25 47 20, *Fax (030) 25472111, fjordhotelberlin@t-online.de* – NZ c
57 rm 95/110 - 115/125.
◆ Family-run hotel just a stone's throw from Potsdamer-Platz. Contemporary décor. Breakfast served on the roof terrace when it's fine.

Lorenz Adlon - Hotel Adlon, Unter den Linden 77, 10117, (030) 22 61 19 60, *Fax (030) 22612222, adlon@kempinski.com* – NZ s
closed 17 July - 17 August, Sunday and Monday – **Meals** *(dinner only)* 95/150 and à la carte.
Spec. Parfait von der Gänsestopfleber mit Sauternesgelée und Kirschconfit. Suprême vom Atlantik Steinbutt mit jungem Gemüse und Château-Chalon-Sauce. Gebratenes Kalbsfilet mit Trüffeln und glasiertem Chicorée.
◆ Circular first-floor restaurant with view of the Brandenburg Gate. Stylishly elegant interior, impeccable service, lavish classic cuisine.

First Floor - Hotel Palace, Budapester Str. 45, 10787, (030) 25 02 10 20, *Fax (030) 25021129, hotel@palace.de* – MX k
closed 12 July - 7 August and Saturday lunch – **Meals** 40 *(lunch)*/105 and à la carte 54/67.
Spec. Gratinierte Jakobsmuscheln mit gebratener Lauchterrine. Kabeljau auf Kartoffel-Limonen-Püree mit Kapern und Strauchtomaten. Kalbskotelett mit Kalbsbries und Gänseleber gefüllt.
◆ First class cuisine from the brilliant Matthias Buchholz, with silver service and a French menu varying with the seasons.

XXXX ✿ **Hugos** - Hotel InterContinental, Budapester Str. 2, ✉ 10787, ✆ (030) 26 02 12 63, *Fax (030) 26021239, mail@hugos-restaurant.de*, ≤ Berlin – ▤. AE ⓓ ⓜ VISA JCB. ✈ MX a
closed 2 weeks January, 4 weeks July - August and Sunday – **Meals** *(dinner only)* 75/127 and à la carte 63/76 ♀, ✿.
Spec. Glasierte Gänsestopfleber mit Pattaya Mango. Rücken vom Müritzlamm mit Bohnen-Olivengemüse. Dessertvariation "Hugos".
◆ A wonderful combination of elegant modern design, fine settings, and the creative cuisine of Thomas Kammeier. Superb, roof-top dining!

XXXX ✿ **Margaux**, Unter den Linden 78 (entrance Wilhelmstraße), ✉ 10117, ✆ (030) 22 65 26 11, *Fax (030) 22652612, hoffmann@margaux-berlin.de*, ☂ – ▤. AE ⓓ ⓜ VISA. ✈ NZ b
closed Sunday and Monday lunch – **Meals** 35 *(lunch)*/95 and à la carte 60/88 ♀, ✿.
Spec. Dicke Bohnen im Gelée von Bresse Geflügel mit Salat von der Taube. Glattbutt mit Badoitgelée und geeistem Olivenöl. Lammschulter mit Paprika und Minze im Pergament serviert.
◆ Dishes range from classic to avantgarde, served in a sumptuous setting of gilt, velvet, rosewood, honey-coloured onyx and black marble.

XXX ✿ **FACIL** - Hotel Madison, Potsdamer Str. 3 (5th floor), ✉ 10785, ✆ (030) 5 90 05 12 34, *Fax (030) 590050500, welcome@facil.de*, ☂ – ▤. AE ⓓ ⓜ VISA. ✈ NZ v
closed 1 to 23 January, 23 July - 7 August, Saturday and Sunday – **Meals** 36 *(lunch)*/100 and à la carte 65/77 ♀.
Spec. Geräucherter Schwertfisch und Lachs mit Kartoffelstampf. Rehrücken mit gefülltem Kartoffelbaumkuchen und Himbeerjus. Passionsfruchtsoufflé mit Kokos und Guave-Sauerrahm-Sorbet.
◆ A glass life transports diners to this fully glazed restaurant on the 5th floor, characterised by its cool elegance and its leafy surroundings.

XXX ✿ **Die Quadriga** - Hotel Brandenburger Hof, Eislebener Str. 14, ✉ 10789, ✆ (030) 21 40 56 50, *Fax (030) 21405100, info@brandenburger-hof.com* – AE ⓓ ⓜ VISA JCB. ✈ LY n
closed 1 to 16 January, 11 July - 14 August, Saturday and Sunday – **Meals** *(dinner only)* 95 and à la carte 53/71 ♀, ✿.
Spec. Carpaccio von der Kalbshaxe mit gebratenem Hummer. Rehrücken mit Kirschkraut und Grießplätzchen. Geeister Krokantspitz mit eingelegten Kumquats.
◆ To the accompaniment of piano music, diners sit on Frank Lloyd Wright chairs and eat delightful delicacies off Berlin porcelain.

XXX **Vivo** - Grand Hotel Esplanade, Lützowufer 15, ✉ 10785, ✆ (030) 2 54 78 86 30, *Fax (030) 254788617, info@esplanade.de*, ☂ – ▤. AE ⓓ ⓜ VISA JCB. ✈ MX e
Meals *(dinner only)* 50/120 ♀.
◆ Following extensive renovation Restaurant Vivo opened in autumn 2004. Natural stonework, dark wood and warm colours create a Mediterranean atmosphere.

XXX **Wolter's am Kurfürstendamm**, Kurfürstendamm 160, ✉ 10799, ✆ (030) 89 04 91 87, *Fax (030) 89049189, info@restaurant-wolters.de*, ☂ – AE ⓓ ⓜ VISA JY a
closed Saturday lunch and Sunday – **Meals** 49 and à la carte 29/53.
◆ A classic and elegant restaurant with light parquet floors and attractive table settings. The establishment also has a delicatessen.

XX ✿ **VAU**, Jägerstr. 54, ✉ 10117, ✆ (030) 2 02 97 30, *Fax (030) 20297311, restaurant@vau-berlin.de*, ☂ – AE ⓓ ⓜ VISA. ✈ PZ u
closed Sunday – **Meals** 36 *(lunch)*/115 and à la carte 66/80 ♀.
Spec. Marinierte Flusskrebse auf gegrilltem Spargel mit Spargelemulsion (season). Gebratener St. Pierre mit Blumenkohl und Ochsenmark. Geschmortes und Gebratenes vom Lamm mit Brennesselspinat und Dörrtomate.
◆ The architecture and design of this bistro-style establishment are as much a feast as its appetising cuisine.

XX **Ana e Bruno**, Sophie-Charlotten-Str. 101, ✉ 14059, ✆ (030) 3 25 71 10, *Fax (030) 3226895, info@a.et.b.de* – ▤. AE. ✈ EY s
closed Sunday and Monday, except exhibitions – **Meals** *(dinner only)* (Italian) à la carte 51/62, ✿.
◆ Proprietor and chef Bruno Pellegrini explains to his guests how his menu has been composed and recommends appropriate wines. Elegant contemporary ambience.

XX **Alt Luxemburg**, Windscheidstr. 31, ✉ 10627, ✆ (030) 3 23 87 30, *Fax (030) 3274003, info@altluxemburg.de* – ▤. AE ⓓ ⓜ VISA JX s
closed Sunday – **Meals** *(dinner only)* (booking essential) 65/72 and à la carte 47/59.
◆ Pleasant late 19C ambience enhanced by fabrics by Josef Hoffmann, the great Viennese Art Nouveau designer. Classical cuisine served in an establishment of great individuality.

Bocca di Bacco, Friedrichstr. 167, ✉ 10117, ✆ (030) 20 67 28 28, *Fax (030) 20672929, info@boccadibacco.de* – AE MC VISA. PZ x
closed Sunday lunch – **Meals** (Italian) 20 *(lunch)* and à la carte 30/42.
◆ "The Mouth of Bacchus" is a stylish modern restaurant offering friendly service and fine Italian food. Opulent paintings and smart bar.

Guy, Jägerstr. 59 (courtyard), ✉ 10117, ✆ (030) 20 94 26 00, *Fax (030) 20942610, info@guy-restaurant.de,* – AE MC VISA. PZ d
closed Saturday lunch and Sunday – **Meals** 20 *(lunch)* and à la carte 39/48 ♀.
◆ Charm abounds on all four levels of this stylish establishment, with its restaurant, imposing courtyard, wine cellar, bar and banqueting hall.

Paris-Moskau, Alt-Moabit 141, ✉ 10557, ✆ (030) 3 94 20 81, *Fax (030) 3942602, restaurant@paris-moskau.de,* GY s
closed lunch Saturday and Sunday – **Meals** (booking essential) 52/82 and à la carte 34/50 ♀.
◆ This old timber-framed building is close to where the Wall once ran. Timeless, tasteful ambience, and dishes imaginatively varied by season.

Maothai, Meierottostr. 1, ✉ 10719, ✆ (030) 8 83 28 23, *Fax (030) 88675658,* – AE MC VISA. LY m
Meals *(Monday - Friday dinner only)* (Thai) à la carte 19/44.
◆ This neo-Classical building with its elegant façade is just round the corner from the Fasanenplatz. Comprehensive menu and Thai music.

Rutz, Chausseestr. 8, ✉ 10115, ✆ (030) 24 62 87 60, *Fax (030) 24628761, info@rutz-weinbar.de,* – AE D MC VISA PY r
closed early to mid January and Sunday – **Meals** *(dinner only)* 43/56 and à la carte 40/45 ♀.
◆ Laid out on two floors, the Rutz has achieved a coolly contemporary look. A highlight is the wine list with 1001 items.

Ottenthal, Kantstr. 153, ✉ 10623, ✆ (030) 3 13 31 62, *Fax (030) 3133732, restaurant@ottenthal.com* – AE MC VISA LX g
Meals *(dinner only)* (Austrian)(booking essential) 23 and à la carte 24/37.
◆ Welcoming restaurant named after a small wine-growing area in Lower Austria. The old steeple clock, which is an ornamental feature of the simply-styled room, also comes from this area.

Die Eselin von A., Kulmbacher Str. 15, ✉ 10777, ✆ (030) 2 14 12 84, *Fax (030) 21476948, info@die-eselin-von-a.de,* MY a
closed early to mid January and end July - early August – **Meals** *(dinner only)* 36/42 and à la carte 31/38 ♀.
◆ Bistro-style restaurant much appreciated by its many regulars for friendly service, relaxed atmosphere and contemporary international cuisine made from fresh ingredients.

Borchardt, Französische Str. 47, ✉ 10117, ✆ (030) 20 38 71 10, *Fax (030) 20387150,* – AE MC VISA PZ c
Meals à la carte 30/46.
◆ This is the place to see and be seen, in a fashionable setting enhanced by stucco ceilings and gilded capitals. Attractive courtyard.

Maxwell, Bergstr. 22 (entrance in courtyard), ✉ 10115, ✆ (030) 2 80 71 21, *Fax (030) 28599848, maxwell.berlin@t-online.de,* – AE D MC VISA JCB PX e
closed lunch Saturday and Sunday – **Meals** (booking essential) à la carte 28/37.
◆ This establishment occupies the courtyard of an old brewery. The building with its lovely neo-Gothic façade is worth a visit in itself. Attractive courtyard terrace.

Weinstein, Mittelstr. 1, ✉ 10117, ✆ (030) 20 64 96 69, *Fax (030) 20649699, weinstein-mitte@gmx.de,* – AE D MC VISA PY f
closed 2 weeks July, Saturday lunch and Sunday – **Meals** 29/41 and à la carte.
◆ The interior evokes the atmosphere of an exclusive Parisian bistro with an appealing touch of Art Deco. Ambitious cuisine with a Mediterranean flavour.

Lindenlife, Unter den Linden 44, ✉ 10117, ✆ (030) 2 06 29 03 33, *Fax (030) 206290335, info@lindenlife.de,* – AE MC VISA NZ u
Meals à la carte 26/33 – ***Weinlife* : Meals** à la carte 19/29.
◆ Contemporary and simple in style this restaurant is arranged over two floors in the parliament building - which also has a TV studio. You'll enjoy the bistro character of "Weinlife" - the snacks are served on boards.

Lutter und Wegner, Charlottenstr. 56, ✉ 10117, ✆ (030) 2 02 95 40, *Fax (030) 20295425, reservierung@lutter-wegner-gendarmenmarkt.de,* – AE MC VISA PZ e
Meals à la carte 28/41.
◆ The theme here is "wine, women and song", exemplified by the big columns painted by contemporary artists. Cheerful wine cellar.

at Berlin-Friedrichshain :

Inn Side Residence-Hotel, Lange Str. 31, ✉ 10243, ✆ (030) 29 30 30, *Fax (030) 29303199, berlin@innside.de*, – rm, – 35. AE Ⓓ ⓂⒸ VISA JCB. rest SZ r
Meals à la carte 22/30 – 14 – **133 rm** 135/160 – 155/180.
◆ An amazing interaction of shapes and colours characterises the spacious interiors of this establishment, laid out over six floors laden with a variety of art objects. Basement restaurant with winter garden overlooking the courtyard.

NH Berlin-Alexanderplatz, Landsberger Allee 26, ✉ 10249, ✆ (030) 4 22 61 30, *Fax (030) 422613300, nhberlinalexanderplatz@nh-hotels.com*, – rm, – 160. AE Ⓓ ⓂⒸ VISA JCB SY e
Meals à la carte 18/32 – 14 – **225 rm** 100 – 115.
◆ Grandly-conceived reception area. Rooms identically furnished in pale natural woods and well fitted-out for the business traveller. Sophisticated bistro-style restaurant.

at Berlin-Grunewald :

Schlosshotel im Grunewald, Brahmsstr. 10, ✉ 14193, ✆ (030) 89 58 40, *Fax (030) 89584800, info@schlosshotelberlin.com*, – rm, – 40. AE Ⓓ ⓂⒸ VISA JCB. rest EZ a
Vivaldi : **Meals** à la carte 68/84 ♀ – 23 – **54 rm** 250/310 – 280/340 – 12 suites.
◆ No, it's not a dream. Karl Lagerfeld was responsible for these amazing interiors. You can only stand and marvel. Alternatively, dine superlatively-well among the chandeliers, stucco and gorgeous gilt of the Vivaldi restaurant.

at Berlin-Kreuzberg :

Mövenpick, Schönebergerstr. 3, ✉ 10963, ✆ (030) 23 00 60, *Fax (030) 23006199, hotel.berlin@moevenpick.com*, – rm, – 175. AE Ⓓ ⓂⒸ VISA NZ k
Meals à la carte 23/34 – 17 – **243 rm** 170/245 – 180/265.
◆ This listed former Siemens building has a most unusual interior, a successful combination of contemporary design and historic features. The restaurant is in a courtyard with an opening glass roof.

relexa Hotel Stuttgarter Hof, Anhalter Str. 8, ✉ 10963, ✆ (030) 26 48 30, *Fax (030) 26483900, berlin@relexa-hotel.de*, – rm, – 160. AE Ⓓ ⓂⒸ VISA JCB NZ e
Meals à la carte 24/33 – **206 rm** 130/180 – 160/195 – 10 suites.
◆ A large reception area welcomes you to this new hotel extension, complemented by modern rooms with light beechwood furnishings and warm colours. The restaurant has a friendly atmosphere.

Le Cochon Bourgeois, Fichtestr. 24, ✉ 10967, ✆ (030) 6 93 01 01, *Fax (030) 6943480*, HZ m
closed 1 week early January, Sunday and Monday – **Meals** *(dinner only)* 36/45 and à la carte 29/38 ♀.
◆ With a character all its own, this unique establishment successfully combines boldly rustic décor with fine French cuisine.

at Berlin-Lichtenberg *East : 5 km, by Karl-Marx-Allee* HY :

Abacus Tierpark Hotel, Franz-Mett-Str. 3, ✉ 10319, ✆ (030) 5 16 20, *Fax (030) 5162400, info@abacus-hotel.de*, – rm, – 250. AE Ⓓ ⓂⒸ VISA
Meals à la carte 22/42 – **278 rm** 99/145 – 125/200.
◆ Right by Europe's largest open-air animal park, this is an ideal place for animal-lovers to stay. Functional rooms ; informal bistro-cafeteria style restaurant.

at Berlin-Lichterfelde *Southwest : 7 km, by Boelcke Straße* GZ :

Villa Toscana without rest, Bahnhofstr. 19, ✉ 12207, ✆ (030) 7 68 92 70, *Fax (030) 7734488, hotel@villa-toscana.de*, – . AE Ⓓ ⓂⒸ VISA JCB.
16 rm 80/110 – 100/120.
◆ Turn-of-the-century villa with a distinctively Italian atmosphere, laqueur furniture and a Tuscan-style garden. Garden pool where koi carp perform their leisurely manoeuvres.

at Berlin-Mariendorf *South : 7 km, by Tempelhofer Damm* GZ :

Landhaus Alpinia, Säntisstr. 32, ✉ 12107, ✆ (030) 76 17 70 (hotel) 7 41 99 98 (rest.), *Fax (030) 7419835, info@alpina-berlin.de*, – rm, – 20. AE ⓂⒸ VISA
Villa Rossini (Italian) *(dinner only)* **Meals** à la carte 21/32 – **58 rm** 93/135 – 115/160.
◆ For anyone wanting to get away from the hectic atmosphere of the city centre and yet remain within easy reach, this establishment with its traditional, country-style interiors is ideal. Pale pine and rustic fittings in the restaurant.

at Berlin-Neukölln :

Estrel, Sonnenallee 225, ✉ 12057, ☎ (030) 6 83 10, *Fax (030) 68312345, hotel@estrel.com*, beer garden, Fitness, Sauna – Lift, ⇹ rm, Air-cond. TV ☏ ♿ ⛹ Garage – ⛌ 2700. AE D MC VISA JCB. ✂ rest HZ a
Sans Souci *(dinner only)* **Meals** à la carte 26/33 – ***Portofino*** (Italian) **Meals** à la carte 22/45 – ***Sun Thai*** (Thai) *(dinner only)* **Meals** à la carte 21/32 – ☕ 15 – **1125 rm** 125 – 130 – 70 suites.
◆ Germany's biggest hotel is a world in itself, with a glazed-over piazza, its own convention and festival centre, rail station and landing stage. International cuisine in the Sans Souci, pizza and pasta in the Portofino.

Mercure, Hermannstr. 214, ✉ 12049, ☎ (030) 62 78 00, *Fax (030) 62780111, h1894@accor.com*, Fitness, Sauna – Lift, ⇹ rm, Air-cond. TV ☏ Garage – ⛌ 250. AE D MC VISA JCB. ✂ rest HZ c
Meals à la carte 23/32 – ☕ 15 – **216 rm** 106/122 – 116/132.
◆ Particularly convenient for travellers using Tempelhof airport, this establishment incorporates a cinema, hairdresser and beauty salon, shopping mall and offices.

at Berlin Prenzlauer Berg :

Park Plaza, Storkower Str. 162, ✉ 10407, ☎ (030) 42 18 10, *Fax (030) 42181111, ppbinfo@parkplazahotels.de* – Lift, ⇹ rm, Air-cond. TV ☏ ♿ – ⛌ 50. AE D MC VISA HY c
Meals *(closed Sunday) (dinner only)* à la carte 22/31 – **155 rm** ☕ 100/120 – 120/140.
◆ This hotel and office complex is located directly opposite the Europa Sport Park, ideal for those following the 6-day race in the Velodrom.

Zander, Kollwitzstr. 50, ✉ 10405, ☎ (030) 44 05 76 79, *Fax (030) 44057632, rolalbrecht@aol.com*, Terrace – AE MC VISA RX a
closed Sunday and Monday – **Meals** *(dinner only)* 27/40 and à la carte 28/39 ♀.
◆ Straightforward restaurant laid out on two levels with bistro-type seating, freshly prepared international dishes and a menu changed weekly.

at Berlin-Reinickendorf :

Mercure Airport Hotel, Gotthardstr. 96, ✉ 13403, ☎ (030) 49 88 40, *Fax (030) 49884555, h5348@accor.com* – Lift, ⇹ rm, TV ♿ Garage P – ⛌ 70. AE D MC VISA JCB. ✂ FX c
Meals à la carte 20/35 – ☕ 12 – **303 rm** 80/129 – 90/141.
◆ The Tegel airport bus stops here and there are good public transport connections to the rest of the city. Italian-style interiors.

at Berlin-Siemensstadt *Northwest : 12 km, by Siemensdamm EX :*

Holiday Inn Berlin-Esplanade, Rohrdamm 80, ✉ 13629, ☎ (030) 38 38 90, *Fax (030) 38389900, info@hiberlin-esplanade.de*, Terrace, Sauna, Pool – Lift, ⇹ rm, Air-cond. TV ☏ ♿ Garage – ⛌ 170. AE D MC VISA JCB. ✂ rest
Meals à la carte 24/36 – ☕ 16 – **336 rm** 133/214 – 158/255 – 4 suites.
◆ To enter the splendidly spacious foyer of this modern hotel is a wonderful relief after being cooped up in a plane or train. Bauhaus-style interiors throughout. Bright, contemporary restaurant.

Novotel, Ohmstr. 4, ✉ 13629, ☎ (030) 3 80 30, *Fax (030) 3819403, h0483@accor.com*, Pool – Lift, ⇹ rm, TV ☏ ♿ – ⛌ 200. AE D MC VISA. ✂ rest
Meals à la carte 18/31 – ☕ 14 – **119 rm** 99/105 – 99/120.
◆ This functional business hotel is right next to the Siemens complex. Rooms with generously dimensioned desks, inviting garden with pool.

at Berlin-Steglitz *Southwest : 5 km, by Hauptstraße FZ :*

Steglitz International, Albrechtstr. 2 (corner of Schloßstraße), ✉ 12165, ☎ (030) 79 00 50, *Fax (030) 79005550, info@steglitz.bestwestern.de* – Lift, ⇹ rm, Air-cond. rest, TV ♿ – ⛌ 270. AE D MC VISA. ✂ rest
Meals à la carte 22/30 – **200 rm** ☕ 98/110 – 120/134 – 3 suites.
◆ Privileged location with city bustle to one side, the tamed Nature of the Botanical Gardens to the other. Meeting and events rooms.

Edogawa, Lepsiusstr. 36, ✉ 12063, ☎ (030) 79 70 62 40, *Fax (030) 79706240, sino.com@t-online.de*, Terrace – AE D MC VISA JCB
Meals *(Monday - Friday dinner only)* (Japanese) à la carte 15/31.
◆ Japanese minimalism creates this establishment's special allure, just the right setting in which to appreciate specialities from the land of the rising sun.

at Berlin-Tegel :

Sorat Hotel Humboldt-Mühle, An der Mühle 5, ✉ 13507, ☎ (030) 43 90 40, *Fax (030) 43904444, humboldt-muehle@sorat-hotels.com*, – ♿ rm, – 🏛 50. AE ① ⓪ VISA JCB
Meals à la carte 25/42 – **120 rm** ☐ 109/149 – 134/174.
◆ Its wheel may no longer turn, but Humbolt's Mill dates back to the 13C. Some rooms with views of millstream or Tegel harbour. Hotel has a private yacht. Restaurant reached via a slender bridge over a canal. Northwest : 13 km, by Müllerstraße FX

Novotel Berlin Airport, Kurt-Schumacher-Damm 202 (by airport approach), ✉ 13405, ☎ (030) 4 10 60, *Fax (030) 4106700, h0791@accor.com*, – rm, – 🏛 150. AE ① ⓪ VISA EX r
Meals à la carte 21/32 – ☐ 14 – **184 rm** 111 – 127.
◆ This Novotel is good at taking those tired of flying under its wing ; there's a reviving pool and a relaxing sauna.

In this guide a symbol or a character, printed in ***red*** *or* ***black*** *does not have the same meaning.*
Pay particular attention to the explanatory pages.

COLOGNE (KÖLN) *Nordrhein-Westfalen* 543 N 4 – *pop. 1 020 100 – alt. 65 m.*

See : *Cathedral (Dom)★★★ (Magi's Shrine★★★, Gothic stained glass windows★ Cross of Gero (Gerokreuz)★, South chapel (Marienkapelle) : Patron Saints altar★★★, stalls★, treasury★* GY – *Roman-Germanic Museum (Römisch-Germanisches Museum)★★ (Dionysos Mosaic★, Roman glassware collection★★)* GY **M1** – *Wallraf-Richartz-Museum-Fondation Corboud★★* GZ **M12** *Museum Ludwig★★* FV **M2** – *Diocesan Museum (Diözesean Museum)★* GY **M3** – *Schnütgen-Museum★★* GZ **M4** – *Museum of East-Asian Art (Museum für Ostasiatische Kunst)★★ by HahnenstraßeAnd Richard Wagner Straße* EV – *Museum for Applied Art (Museum für Angewandte Kunst)★* GYZ **M6** – *St. Maria Lyskirchen (frescoes★★)* FX – *St. Severin (interior★)* FX – *St. Pantaleon (rood screen★)* EX – *St. Kunibert (stained glass windows★)* FU – *St. Mary the Queen (St. Maria Königin) : wall of glass★ by Bonnerstraße* FX – *St. Aposteln (apse★)* EV *K – St. Ursula (treasury★)* FU – *St. Mary of the Capitol (St. Maria im Kapitol)★ (Romanesque wooden church door★, trefoil chancel★)* GZ – *Imhoff-Stollwerck-Museum★* FX – *Old Town Hall (Altes Rathaus)★* GZ – *St. Gereon★ (Dekagon★)* EV.

⛳9 ⛳9 *Köln-Marienburg, Schillingsrotter Weg (South : 3 km), ☎ (0221) 38 40 53 ;* ⛳18 *Köln-Rogendorf, Parallelweg 1 (by Erftstraße and A 57 : 16 km), ☎ (0221) 78 40 18 ;* ⛳18 *Bergisch-Gladbach-Refrath, Golfplatz 2 (East : 17 km), ☎ (02204) 9 27 60 ;* ⛳18 *Pulheim Gut Lärchenhof, Hahnenstraße (Northwest : 19 km), ☎ (02238) 92 39 00.*
✈ *Köln-Bonn at Wahn (Southeast : 17 km) ☎ (02203) 4 00.*
*Exhibition Centre (Messegelände) by Deutzer Brücke (*FV*), ☎ (0221) 82 10, Fax (0221) 8212574.*
ℹ *Köln Tourismus, Unter Fettenhennen 19, ✉ 50667, ☎ (0221) 22 13 04 00, Fax (0221) 22120410, koelntourismus@stadt-koeln.de.*
ADAC, *Luxemburger Str. 169.*
Berlin 566 – Düsseldorf 39 – Aachen 69 – Bonn 32 – Essen 68.

Plans on following pages

Excelsior Hotel Ernst, Domplatz, ✉ 50667, ☎ (0221) 27 01, *Fax (0221) 135150, info@excelsiorhotelernst.de*, – ♿ rm, – 🏛 80. AE ① ⓪ VISA JCB. ✗ rm GY a
Meals see ***Hanse-Stube*** and ***Taku*** below – **152 rm** ☐ 210/285 – 280/380 – 9 suites.
◆ The best address in Cologne, directly opposite the Cathedral and steeped in tradition. Stylish rooms. Lovely marble foyer. Piano bar.

InterContinental, Pipinstr. 1, ✉ 50667, ☎ (0221) 2 80 60, *Fax (0221) 28061111, cologne@ichotelsgroup.com* – ♿ rm, – 🏛 200. AE ① ⓪ VISA JCB. ✗ rest GZ d
Meals à la carte 35/51 ♀ – ☐ 20 – **262 rm** 230/255 – 9 suites.
◆ Modern design and harmonious colour schemes throughout, from the spacious foyer to the comfortable suites and rooms. Exclusive leisure area (fee). 1st floor Maulbeer restaurant with panoramic windows.

Im Wasserturm, Kaygasse 2, ✉ 50676, ☎ (0221) 2 00 80, *Fax (0221) 2008888, info@hotel-im-wasserturm.de*, – ♿ rm, rest, – 🏛 120. AE ① ⓪ VISA JCB. ✗ rest FX c
Meals see ***La Vision*** below – ***dʌblju "W"*** **: Meals** à la carte 24/36 – ☐ 18 – **88 rm** 180/265 – 240/335 – 7 suites.
◆ Once Europe's tallest water-tower, this imposing brick edifice is now an elegant modern hotel. The 11m-high foyer is particularly striking. Designer style. Refined "W" bistro.

KÖLN
0
200 m
E
F
U
V
X
MEDIA-PARK
HANSAHOCHHAUS
Hansaring
Maybach-str.
Hansaring
Erftstr.
ALTE STADTMAUER
Kyotostr.
Christophstr.
Christophstr./ Mediapark
Gereonstr.
St. Gereon
Appellhofpl.
Friesenpl.
RÖMER TURM
Albertusstr.
Breite Str.
Ehrenstr.
Hohenzollern-ring
Mittelstr.
Rudolfpl.
HAHNENTOR
Neumarkt
Neumarkt
Cäcilien-
Hahnen-straße
Mauritius-
Hohenstaufen-ring
Jahnstraße
steinweg
Poststr.
Poststr.
Neue
Weyerstr.
Rothgerberbach
St.Pantaleon
Barbarossaplatz
Luxemburger Str.
Trierer Str.
Salierring
Waisenhaus-gasse
Eifelstraße
Eifelstraße
Sachsenring
ALTE STADTMAUER
Volksgartenstraße
VOLKSGARTEN
Vorgebirgstraße
Sachsenring
Ulrepforte
Ulrichgasse
St.Severin
Severinstor
Chlodwigplatz
Ubierring
Bonner Str.
Severinswall
BAYENTURM
Bayenstraße
RHEINAUHAFEN
Annostr.
Severinstr.
Sionstal
Im
markt
Severinsbr.
Severinstr.
Severinstr.
Perlengraben
POL
Süd-Fahrt
Nord-straße
Pipinstr.
Deutzer Br.
Mühlenbach
Hohe Pforte
St.Georg
Follerstr.
Holz-
St. Maria in Lyskirchen
MALAKOFFTURM
KÖLN-DÜSSELDORFER
HISTOR. RATHAUS
Groß St. Martin
Hohe Str.
Tunis-str.
DOM
Hohenzollernbr.
RHEIN
Goldgasse
Machabäerstr.
St.Kunibert
Konrad-Adenauer-Ufer
WECKSCHNAPP
BASTEI
Theodor-Heuss-Ring
Theodor-Heuss-Ring
Ebertpl.
Ebertpl.
Krefelder Str.
Hansaring
Weidengasse
EIGELSTEINTOR
Eigelstein
Eintrachtstr.
Turiner Str.
Dom-straße
St.Ursula

KÖLN

Am Bayenturm .... FX 3
Am Leystapel .... GZ 4
Am Malzbüchel .... GZ 5
An den Dominikanern .. GY 8
An der Malzmühle ..... FX 9
An St.-Katharinen ...... FX 14
Apostelnstr. .... EV 15
Auf dem Berlich .... EV 16
Augustinerstr. .... GZ 19
Bechergasse .... GZ 22
Bischofsgarten-Str. .... GY 26
Blaubach .... FX 28
Breite Str. .... GZ
Brückenstr. .... GZ 32
Dompropst-Ketzer-Str. .. GY 38
Drususgasse .... GY 39
Ehrenstr. .... EV
Eigelstein .... FU
Gertrudenstr. .... EV 47
Gladbacher Str. .... EU 48
Glockengasse .... GZ 50
Große Budengasse .... GZ 52
Große Neugasse ...... GY 54
Gürzenichstr. .... GZ 55
Habsburgerring .... EV 57
Hahnenstr. .... EV
Heinrich-Böll-Pl. .... GY 58
Hohe Str. .... GYZ
Hohenstaufenring ...... EX
Hohenzollernring .... EV
Kaiser-Wilhelm-Ring .... EV 62
Kardinal-Frings-Str. .... EV 65
Karolingerring .... FX 66
Kattenbug .... EV 67
Kleine Budengasse .... GZ 68
Kleine Witschgasse .... FX 69
Komödienstr. .... GY 71
Kurt-Hackenberg-Pl. .... GY 72
Mathiasstr. .... FX 74
Mechtildisstr. .... FX 76
Minoritenstr. .... GZ 79
Mittelstr. .... EV
Neumarkt .... EV
Neusser Str. .... FU 86
Offenbachpl. .... GZ 90
Pfälzer Str. .... EX 96
Quatermarkt .... GZ 99
Richmodstr. .... EV 100

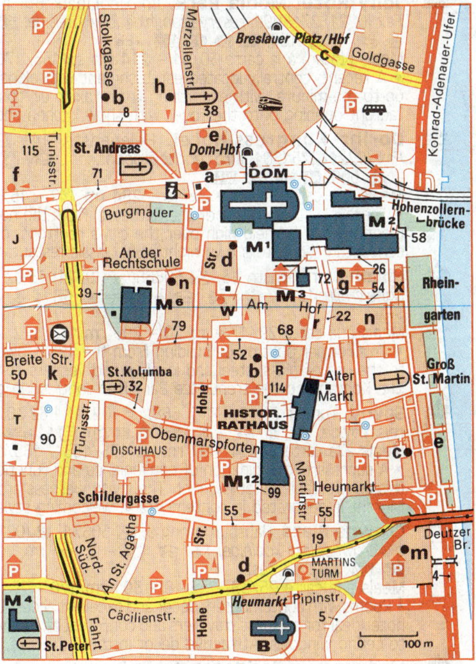

Riehler Str. .... FU 102
Roonstr. .... EX 104
Sankt-Apern-Str. .... EV 108
Schildergasse .... GZ
Severinstr. .... FX
Tel-Aviv-Str. .... FX 111
Unter Goldschmied .... GZ 114
Unter Sachsenhausen .... GY 115
Ursulastr. .... FU 116
Victoriastr. .... FU 117
Zeppelinstr. .... EV 118
Zeughausstr. .... EV 122

Dom Hotel, Domkloster 2a, ✉ 50667, ☎ (0221) 2 02 40, *Fax (0221) 2024444, sales@dom-hotel.com*, – rm, – 60. AE MC VISA JCB. rest GY d
Meals à la carte 38/52 – 20 – **124 rm** 340 – 395 – 6 suites.
◆ Tradition with perhaps a touch of nostalgia envelops residents in this stylish grand hotel dating from the Belle Epoque and located right by the Cathedral. Palm trees and cane furniture add to the Mediterranean atmosphere in the restaurant. Terrace with views.

Renaissance, Magnusstr. 20, ✉ 50672, ☎ (0221) 2 03 40, *Fax (0221) 2034777, sales.cologne@renaissancehotels.com*, , , – , rm, – 205. AE MC VISA JCB. rest EV b
***Raffael* : Meals** à la carte 23/37 – ***Valentino* : Meals** à la carte 22/28 – 19 – **236 rm** 175 – 205.
◆ A warmly coloured and intimate foyer greets guests on arrival. The beautiful rooms offer comfort, convenience and elegance. Refined atmosphere and lovely place settings characterise the Raffael. The Valentino has a bistro-like atmosphere.

Maritim, Heumarkt 20, ✉ 50667, ☎ (0221) 2 02 70, *Fax (0221) 2027826, info.kol@maritim.de*, , , , – , rm, – 1630. AE MC VISA JCB. rest GZ m
Bellevue* : Meals** à la carte 42/55 – ***La Galerie *(closed 4 July - 31 August, Sunday and Monday) (dinner only)* **Meals** à la carte 26/38 – **454 rm** 145/315 – 163/340 – 12 suites.
◆ With its glass roof and granite floor the foyer is an architectural masterpiece. Enjoy a stroll through the hotel's more than ample public spaces. The Bellevue offers a view over the Rhine and Cologne's Old Town. La Galerie is in the foyer.

Jolly Hotel Media Park, Im Mediapark 8b, ✉ 50670, ✆ (0221) 2 71 50, *Fax (0221) 2715999, reservation.jhk@jollyhotels.de*, rm, – 180. EU a
Meals (Italian) à la carte 30/41 – **214 rm** 135/170 – 160/195.
◆ A recent, centrally-located establishment with elegant rooms. Technical facilities are up-to-the-minute, with everything from fax to air conditioning and trouser-press. Restaurant opening onto the foyer with show kitchen and Italian atmosphere.

Dorint Kongress-Hotel, Helenenstr. 14, ✉ 50667, ✆ (0221) 27 50, *Fax (0221) 2751301, info.cgnchc@dorint.com*, rm, – 500. EV p
Meals à la carte 31/40 – 16 – **284 rm** 142 – 157 – 12 suites.
◆ There is a striking view of the Cathedral from the hotel's 12th floor. Conferences and meetings can be held high over the city's rooftops, or you can dance to your heart's content in the hotel's own night-club. Classic restaurant.

Hilton, Marzellenstr. 13, ✉ 50668, ✆ (0221) 13 07 10, *Fax (0221) 1307120, info.cologne@hilton.com*, – 300. GY h
Meals à la carte 29/47 – 20 – **296 rm** 152/172 – 154/174.
◆ This former post office building from the 1950s owes its special character as a hotel to the use of glass, steel and lovely wood veneers combined with subtle earth-colours. The Konrad and the trendy Ice Bar offer contrasting gastronomic experiences.

Savoy, Turiner Str. 9, ✉ 50668, ✆ (0221) 1 62 30, *Fax (0221) 1623200, office@hotelsavoy.de*, rm, rm, – 70.
Meals à la carte 24/34 – **97 rm** 135/155 – 165/187 – 3 suites. FU s
◆ A successful combination of convenience and functionality characterise the rooms of this comfortable establishment. The lavish wellness area is a bonus. Diva's Bar and Restaurant is decorated in contemporary, welcoming style.

Crowne Plaza, Habsburgerring 9, ✉ 50674, ✆ (0221) 22 80, *Fax (0221) 251206, info@crowneplaza-koeln.de*, rm, – 240. rest by Hahnenstraße EV
Meals à la carte 25/38 – 18 – **301 rm** 170 – 205.
◆ Rooms with contemporary décor and excellent access by public transport make this large hotel ideal for business travellers and conferences. Refined 1st-floor restaurant with floor-to-ceiling windows. Attractive décor in the Entrecote.

Lindner Dom Residence, An den Dominikanern 4a (entrance Stolkgasse), ✉ 50668, ✆ (0221) 1 64 40, *Fax (0221) 1644440, info.domresidence@lindner.de*, rm, – 120. GY b
closed 22 December - 2 January – ***La Gazetta*** *(closed Sunday dinner)* **Meals** à la carte 20/37 – 16 – **125 rm** 140 – 160.
◆ Modern atrium building with balconies and plenty of glass. The 7th floor rooms have a terrace. Furnishings in functional style make this eminently suitable for business travellers. The glazed façade of La Gazetta allows a fine view of the courtyard.

Dorint Sofitel Mondial Am Dom, Kurt-Hackenberg-Platz 1, ✉ 50667, ✆ (0221) 2 06 30, *Fax (0221) 2063527, h1306@accor.com*, rm, – 120. GY g
Meals à la carte 31/43 – 18 – **207 rm** 250 – 275.
◆ Close to the Cathedral in an excellent central location, this hotel has modern, functional rooms with good technical facilities. Especially spacious suites and deluxe rooms. Contemporary style restaurant with tapas bar.

Holiday Inn (with guest house), Belfortstr. 9, ✉ 50668, ✆ (0221) 7 72 10, *Fax (0221) 7721259, hibelfortstrasse@eventhotels.com*, rm, – 70. FU b
Meals à la carte 23/36 – **78 rm** 147 – 173.
◆ The great attraction of this establishment is its proximity to city centre and trade fair grounds. All rooms have attractive modern furnishings. Classic décor and place settings await diners in the Restaurant Quirinal.

Mercure Severinshof, Severinstr. 199, ✉ 50676, ✆ (0221) 2 01 30, *Fax (0221) 2013666, h1206@accor.com*, rm, – 220. FX a
Meals à la carte 18/29 – **253 rm** 132 – 166 – 8 suites.
◆ Well-run business and conference hotel in central location. Standard, functional rooms, plus superior "Club Rooms" on the 4th and 5th floors. Spacious bar area.

Lyskirchen without rest, Filzengraben 26, ✉ 50676, ✆ (0221) 2 09 70, *Fax (0221) 2097718, lyskirchen@eventhotels.com*, rest. FX u
closed 23 December - 2 January – **103 rm** 118 – 150.
◆ Carefully refurbished establishment in the middle of the historic riverside district. Functional rooms with contemporary furnishings - mostly lightwood.

Ascot without rest, Hohenzollernring 95, 50672, (0221) 9 52 96 50, *Fax (0221) 952965100, info@ascot.bestwestern.de*, – rm, VISA EV a
closed 22 December - 1 January – **46 rm** 105/115 – 132.
◆ This city centre hotel has retained its traditional façade, while its interior is in English country-house style. Cinemas, theatres and shops are right at hand.

Classic Hotel Harmonie without rest, Ursulaplatz 13, 50668, (0221) 1 65 70, *Fax (0221) 1657200, harmonie@classic-hotels.com* – VISA JCB FU g
72 rm 75/95 – 105.
◆ This beautifully restored former monastery now offers guests a relaxing setting with an Italian flair. Contemporary furniture and warm Mediterranean colours set the tone.

Viktoria without rest, Worringer Str. 23, 50668, (0221) 9 73 17 20, *Fax (0221) 727067, hotel@hotelviktoria.com* – VISA.
closed 23 December - 1 January – **47 rm** 90/100 – 113.
◆ This hotel with individual rooms boasts a magnificent Art Nouveau façade and was originally a museum of musical history. Elegant atrium-style breakfast room. by Konrad-Adenauer-Ufer FU

NH Köln, Holzmarkt 47, 50676, (0221) 2 72 28 80, *Fax (0221) 272288100, nhkoeln@nh-hotels.com*, – rm, – 130. VISA JCB. rest FX d
Meals à la carte 21/33 – 16 – **205 rm** 130.
◆ This modern hotel by the Severin bridge over the Rhine was opened in 2002. The rooms offer cool lines, functional furnishings and marble-topped desks. The contemporary-style restaurant has a conservatory overlooking the courtyard.

Dorint Novotel City, Bayenstr. 51, 50678, (0221) 80 14 70, *Fax (0221) 80147148, h3127@accor.com*, – rm, – 130. VISA FX n
Meals à la carte 22/31 – 15 – **222 rm** 130 – 145.
◆ Newly-built and up to the usual Novotel standard, with functional and contemporary rooms with natural lightwood furnishings.

Four Points Hotel Central, Breslauer Platz 2, 50668, (0221) 1 65 10, *Fax (0221) 1651333, fourpoints.koeln@arabellasheraton.de* – rm, VISA GY c
Meals à la carte 21/28 – **116 rm** 150/160 – 170 – 5 suites.
◆ Only a few minutes' walk from the Cathedral and the lively city centre.The hotel's discreet elegance and high level of comfort are appreciated by business travellers.

Senats Hotel, Unter Goldschmied 9, 50667, (0221) 2 06 20, *Fax (0221) 2062200, info@senats-hotel.de* – rm, – 230. VISA JCB GZ b
closed 23 December - 2 January – ***Falstaff*** *(closed Saturday lunch, Sunday and Bank Holidays)* **Meals** à la carte 22/42 – **59 rm** 79/92 – 115.
◆ From the modern-style foyer a splendidly spacious - listed - staircase leads up to contemporary-style rooms. Aperitif and beer bar. Bright and welcoming restaurant with a touch of country style.

Cristall without rest, Ursulaplatz 9, 50668, (0221) 1 63 00, *Fax (0221) 1630333, info@hotelcristall.de* – VISA JCB. FU r
closed 23 to 29 December – **84 rm** 102 – 133.
◆ This establishment has an extraordinarily varied décor. Fans of designer furniture will enjoy a stay here, especially if they try sitting in one of highly unusual sofas !

Coellner Hof, Hansaring 100, 50670, (0221) 1 66 60, *Fax (0221) 1666166, info@coellnerhof.de*, – rm, rest, – 30. VISA FU k
Meals *(closed Saturday and Sunday) (dinner only)* à la carte 17/38 – **70 rm** 70/95 – 90/105.
◆ What do you prefer? Country-style or contemporary? The individually furnished rooms give you the choice. Well-run establishment with a personal touch. Restaurant with tasteful wood décor.

Euro Garden Cologne without rest, Domstr. 10, 50668, (0221) 1 64 90, *Fax (0221) 1649333, sekretariat@eurotels.de*, – – 30. VISA FU a
85 rm 115/125 – 145.
◆ Well-run establishment not far from the city centre. Solidly furnished, functional rooms and ample buffet in the stylish breakfast room.

Königshof without rest, Richartzstr. 14, 50667, (0221) 2 57 87 71, *Fax (0221) 2578762, hotel@hotelkoenigshof.com* – VISA JCB GY n
82 rm 80/85 – 100.
◆ This exceptionally well-run establishment is just a few steps from the Cathedral and the main shopping streets. Impeccable rooms with good facilities.

Esplanade without rest, Hohenstaufenring 56, ✉ 50674, ☎ (0221) 9 21 55 70, *Fax (0221) 216822, info@hotelesplanade.de* – AE VISA JCB EX a
closed 22 December - 3 January – **32 rm** 90/105 – 116.
◆ Lavish décor in a cool, contemporary style. Some rooms have a balcony with a view of Cathedral or boulevard. Interesting glazed façade and splendid entrance area.

Antik Hotel Bristol without rest, Kaiser-Wilhelm-Ring 48, ✉ 50672, ☎ (0221) 13 98 50, *Fax (0221) 131495, hotel@antik-hotel-bristol.de* – AE VISA EU m
closed Christmas and Easter – **44 rm** 83/99 – 118.
◆ Ever dreamt of a night in a four-poster? This attractive, well-run hotel is full of antique furniture in a variety of styles including Empire style.

Santo without rest, Dagobertstr. 22, ✉ 50668, ☎ (0221) 9 13 97 70, *Fax (0221) 913977777, info@hotelsanto.de* – AE VISA JCB
69 rm 128/138 – 149. FU c
◆ This unusual establishment blends lovely wood veneers, natural floor materials and a specially designed lighting system into an avant-garde living concept of great comfort.

Hopper St. Antonius, Dagobertstr. 32, ✉ 50668, ☎ (0221) 1 66 00(hotel), 1 66 05 00 (rest.), *Fax (0221) 1660166, st.antonius@hopper.de*, – rm, – 15. AE VISA FU n
L. Fritz im Hopper *(closed lunch Saturday and Sunday)* **Meals** à la carte 27/36 – **54 rm** 100/130 – 140 – 5 suites.
◆ Urban heritage and contemporary design are perfectly blended here. The listed building has rooms with beautifully-styled modern teak furnishings. Dining is in an attractive, bistro-like setting.

Hopper, Brüsseler Str. 26, ✉ 50674, ☎ (0221) 92 44 00, *Fax (0221) 924406, hotel@hopper.de*, – rm, AE VISA
closed 24 to 28 March, 13 to 16 May and 17 December - 2 January – **Meals** *(closed Saturday lunch and Sunday)* à la carte 25/33 – **49 rm** 90/100 – 120.
◆ Outside, monastic charm ; inside, refined aesthetics and contemporary elegance. Unconventional accommodation with marble bathrooms and parquet floors. Sauna in vaulted cellars. A striking feature in the bistro-style restaurant is the impressive altar-painting. by Hahnenstraße EV

CityClass Hotel Caprice without rest, Auf dem Rothenberg 7, ✉ 50667, ☎ (0221) 92 05 40, *Fax (0221) 92054100, caprice@cityclass.de*, – – 20. AE VISA – **53 rm** 105 – 135. GZ c
◆ Centrally located in Cologne's Altstadt, this hotel is an ideal starting point for exploring the city. Contemporary rooms, good standard overall.

Ibis Barbarossaplatz without rest, Neue Weyerstr. 4, ✉ 50676, ☎ (0221) 2 09 60, *Fax (0221) 2096199, h1449@accor.com* – AE VISA EX d
9 – **208 rm** 59.
◆ Standard tour-group establishment with convenient, contemporary accommodation. Welcoming foyer and inviting bistro bar.

Hanse Stube - Excelsior Hotel Ernst, Dompropst-Ketzer-Str. 2, ✉ 50667, ☎ (0221) 2 70 34 02, *Fax (0221) 135150, ehe@excelsiorhotelernst.de*, – AE VISA JCB. GY e
Meals 29 *(lunch)* and à la carte 44/70 ♀.
◆ Stylish atmosphere in this elegant restaurant, where creative French cuisine is served to diners by the well-trained staff.

La Vision - Hotel Im Wasserturm, Kaygasse 2, ✉ 50676, ☎ (0221) 2 00 80, *Fax (0221) 2008888, info@hotel-im-wasserturm.de*, – AE VISA JCB. FX c
closed 2 weeks early January, 7 July - 19 August, Sunday and Monday – **Meals** 53/83 and à la carte 54/73 ♀.
Spec. Röllchen vom hausgebeiztem Lachs mit Störmousse. Crépinette von der Taube auf glasiertem Spargel und Sauche Rouennaise. Soufflé vom Topfen auf Erdbeer-Orangencoulis mit Tahiti-Vanille.
◆ Designer style restaurant on the 11th floor of a water-tower. Fantastic city views from the roof garden.

Börsen-Restaurant Maître (Schäfer), Unter Sachsenhausen 10, ✉ 50667, ☎ (0221) 13 30 21, *Fax (0221) 133040* – AE VISA. EV r
closed 21 March - 3 April, 4 weeks July - August, Saturday lunch, Sunday and Bank Holidays – **Meals** 48/90 and à la carte 53/70 ♀ – ***Börsen-Stube*** *(closed Saturday dinner – Sunday and Bank Holidays)* **Meals** à la carte 28/38 ♀.
Spec. Gänseleberterrine mit karamellisierten Apfelspalten und Auslesegelee. Tournedos vom Simmenthaler Rind mit Ochsenmark und Fleur de Sel. Warmes Schokoladensoufflé mit Beeren in Orangen-Vanille-Glaçage.
◆ The IHK (Chamber of Commerce) has a stylish and elegant restaurant offering refined, classic cuisine. The cellar Börsen-Stube with terrace is a more straightforward alternative.

XXX **Ambiance**, Komödienstr. 50, ✉ 50667, ℘ (0221) 9 22 76 52, *restaurant@ambiance-kokje.de* – AE ⓓ MC VISA GY f
closed 29 July - 19 August, Saturday, Sunday and Bank Holidays – **Meals** 37 *(lunch)*/69 and à la carte 47/55.
◆ This fine old city building houses a classically elegant restaurant with lovely place settings, attentive service, and creative cooking.

XXX **Grande Milano**, Hohenstaufenring 29, ✉ 50674, ℘ (0221) 24 21 21, *Fax (0221) 244846, info@grandemilano.com*, 余 – ▤. AE ⓓ MC VISA JCB EX v
closed July - August, Saturday lunch and Sunday – **Meals** (Italian) à la carte 32/63 ♀ – ***Pinot di Pinot :*** **Meals** 13 (lunch) and à la carte 19/28.
◆ Diners sit at beautifully presented tables in this elegant Italian restaurant. The cuisine is refined, specialising in dishes with truffles. A lighter, bistro-like ambience in the Pinot di Pinot.

XX **Domerie**, Buttermarkt 42, ✉ 50667, ℘ (0221) 2 57 40 44, *Fax (0221) 2574269, stefanruessel@t-online.de*, 余 – MC VISA. ⛌ GZ e
closed carnival and Monday, except exhibitions – **Meals** à la carte 25/37.
◆ To dine in this 15C building among antique furnishings and beneath the beautiful ceiling is quite an experience. Summer terrace with Rhine views.

XX **Fischers**, Hohenstaufenring 53, ✉ 50674, ℘ (0221) 3 10 84 70, *Fax (0221) 31084789, info@fischers-wein.com*, 余 – 🚶 40. ⓓ MC VISA EX n
closed end December - early January, Saturday lunch, Sunday and Bank Holidays – **Meals** à la carte 36/43 ♀, 🍇.
◆ A contemporary restaurant with an open kitchen and attentive service. Especially noted for its extensive range of wines. A charming terrace to the rear.

XX ✿ **Capricorn i Aries Restaurant**, Alteburger Str. 34, ✉ 50678, ℘ (0221) 32 31 82, *Fax (0221) 323182* FX m
closed carnival, Easter, 2 weeks July, Monday and Tuesday – **Meals** *(dinner only)* (booking essential) 75/85 and à la carte 59/74 ♀.
Spec. Dorade royale mit Tian à la catalane und Sternanisbutter. Geschmorte Kalbshaxe mit Trüffeln. Taube mit Belugalinsen.
◆ An air of refinement and elegance characterises this tiny little establishment where white is the dominant colour. Dishes from a creative kitchen presented on lovely crockery.

XX **Alfredo**, Tunisstr. 3, ✉ 50667, ℘ (0221) 2 57 73 80, *Fax (0221) 2577380, info@ristorante-alfredo.com* – AE GZ k
closed 3 weeks July - August, Saturday lunch, Sunday and Bank Holidays – **Meals** (booking essential) à la carte 36/46 ♀.
◆ This elegant little Italian restaurant is something of a Cologne institution, where a second generation of owners treats guests to a refined, constantly changing menu.

XX **Bizim**, Weidengasse 47, ✉ 50668, ℘ (0221) 13 15 81, *Fax (0221) 131581* – MC VISA. ⛌ FU d
closed 2 weeks February, 3 weeks July - August, Saturday lunch, Sunday and Monday – **Meals** (Turkish) (booking essential for dinner) 29 *(lunch)*/50 and à la carte 41/50.
◆ In the heart of the multicultural city centre, this Turkish restaurant serves typical dishes in a contemporary ambience.

XX **Em Krützche**, Am Frankenturm 1, ✉ 50667, ℘ (0221) 2 58 08 39, *Fax (0221) 253417, info@em-kruetzche.de*, 余 – AE ⓓ MC VISA. ⛌ GY x
closed Holy Week and Monday – **Meals** (booking essential for dinner) à la carte 29/42.
◆ Diners have been served in the nooks and crannies of this old city centre establishment for more than 400 years. Traditionally run family business.

XX **Taku** - Excelsior Hotel Ernst, Domplatz, ✉ 50667, ℘ (0221) 2 70 39 10, *Fax (0221) 135150* – ▤. AE ⓓ MC VISA. ⛌ rest GY a
closed 4 weeks July - August, Sunday and Monday – **Meals** (Asian) 29 *(lunch)* and à la carte 38/67 ♀.
◆ Asian delights served in a cool and elegant modern setting. A glass walkway and an aquarium set into the floor are among the unusual features of this establishment.

XX **L'escalier**, Brüsseler Str. 11, ✉ 50674, ℘ (0221) 2 05 39 98, *Fax (02232) 5691280, info@lescalier.restaurant.de*, 余 – ▤ by Hahnenstr. EV
closed Sunday, lunch Saturday and Monday – **Meals** 34/52 and à la carte ♀.
◆ This restaurant is characterised by its cool, contemporary ambience and its no-frills classic cuisine based on fine ingredients.

Bosporus, Weidengasse 36, ✉ 50668, ✆ (0221) 12 52 65, *Fax (0221) 9123829, restaurant.bosporus@t-online.de,* – AE MC VISA FU v
Meals (Turkish) à la carte 27/38.
◆ Something of the atmosphere of A Thousand And One Nights pervades this classic interior, together with a hint of Turkish delights. The Bosporus links Cologne with the Orient.

Le Moissonnier, Krefelder Str. 25, ✉ 50670, ✆ (0221) 72 94 79, *Fax (0221) 7325461* – MC VISA FU e
closed 1 week Easter, 3 weeks July - August, 24 December - early January, Sunday and Monday – **Meals** (booking essential) à la carte 40/57 ♀.
Spec. Foie gras de canard. Fricassée de pigeonneau au Maury. Crème maison.
◆ This highly original Art Nouveau bistro will transport you instantly to the heart of France with its creative offerings of refined French cuisine.

Capricorn i Aries Brasserie, Alteburgerstr. 31, ✉ 50678, ✆ (0221) 3 97 57 10, *Fax (0221) 323182* FX b
closed Saturday lunch and Sunday – **Meals** à la carte 26/35 ♀.
◆ Informal version of the establishment of the same name opposite. Elegant contemporary bistro atmosphere and polished service.

Daitokai, Kattenbug 2, ✉ 50667, ✆ (0221) 12 00 48, *Fax (0221) 137503, kol@daitokai.de* – AE DC MC VISA JCB. EV e
closed Monday and Tuesday lunch – **Meals** (Japanese) à la carte 36/46.
◆ The Daitokai, where chefs deploy their skills at the Teppan-Yaki and diners eat with chopsticks, brings an authentically Japanese atmosphere to the heart of the city.

Cologne brewery inns :

Höhn's Dom Brauerei Ausschank, Goltsteinstr. 83 (Bayenthal), ✉ 50968, ✆ (0221) 3 48 12 93, *Fax (0221) 3978572, m.k.hoehn@t-online.de,*
Meals 24/32 and à la carte 22/35 ♀. by Borner Straße FX
◆ Well-scrubbed wooden tables and solid local cuisine continue long-established Cologne traditions, together, of course, with the obligatory glass of Kölsch. Pretty terrace overlooking the inner courtyard.

Peters Brauhaus, Mühlengasse 1, ✉ 50667, ✆ (0221) 2 57 39 50, *Fax (0221) 2573962, info@peters-brauhaus.de,* – GZ n
Meals à la carte 17/29.
◆ Rustic beer-hall in traditional style. Take a good look around, since each nook and cranny of the place has its own character. Tasty food to go with your glass of "Kölsch".

Brauhaus Sion, Unter Taschenmacher 5, ✉ 50667, ✆ (0221) 2 57 85 40, *Fax (0221) 2582081, info@brauhaus-sion.de,* – AE DC MC VISA GZ r
Meals à la carte 17/30.
◆ Spacious interiors, with barrel-staves and hop-sacks on the walls. A "Kölsch" or three taste all the better after a session on the skittle-alley.

Früh am Dom, Am Hof 12, ✉ 50667, ✆ (0221) 2 61 32 11, *Fax (0221) 2613299, gastronomie@frueh.de,* beer garden GY w
Meals à la carte 17/32.
◆ Traditional beer-hall from 1904, with larger-than-life waiters darting about as in the days of yore. The cellars where the beer was brewed have recently been opened up.

at Cologne-Deutz *East : 1 km, by Deutzer Brücke FV :*

Hyatt Regency, Kennedy-Ufer 2a, ✉ 50679, ✆ (0221) 8 28 12 34, *Fax (0221) 8281370, cologne@hyatt.de,* ≤, beer garden, – rm, – 260. AE DC MC VISA JCB.
Graugans (Euro-Asian) *(closed mid July - mid August, Saturday lunch and Sunday)* **Meals** 35 (lunch) and à la carte 48/67 ♀ – ***Glashaus*** (Italian) **Meals** 28 (lunch) and à la carte 38/53 ♀ – 19 – **305 rm** 135/175 – 160/200 – 17 suites.
◆ This late 1980s hotel stands directly on the Rhine. Beyond the impressively spacious foyer are comfortably furnished rooms. The Graugans restaurant is casually elegant, while the Glashaus has been designed like a gallery.

Radisson SAS, Messe Kreisel 3, ✉ 50679, ✆ (0221) 27 72 00, *Fax (0221) 2777010, info.cologne@radissonsas.com,* – rm, – 250. AE DC MC VISA JCB
Meals à la carte 31/40 – 17 – **393 rm** 130/155.
◆ Convenient for the trade fairs, an extremely imposing and sophisticated establishment, built on a V-shaped plan. Fascinating 15m high glass structure and luxuriously appointed modern rooms, buffet restaurant, Paparazzi with open pizza oven.

Dorint Sofitel an der Messe, Deutz-Mülheimer-Str. 22, ✉ 50679, ☎ (0221) 80 19 00, *Fax (0221) 80190800, h5367@accor.com*, , , , – , rm, – 360. AE VISA JCB. rest
L'Adresse *(closed mid July - mid August, Sunday and Monday) (dinner only)* **Meals** à la carte 34/53 – ***Bell Arte*** (lunch only) **Meals** à la carte 21/40 – 17 – **313 rm** 199/333 – 31 suites.
◆ Contemporary elegance and excellent technical facilities in the rooms of this new hotel directly opposite the entrance to the trade fair grounds. Lavish fitness area. Cool elegance in L'Adresse. Bright and welcoming Bell Arte.

fair & more without rest, Adam-Stegerwald-Str. 9, ✉ 51063, ☎ (0221) 6 71 16 90, *Fax (0221) 67116910, info@fairandmore.com* – AE VISA JCB. rest
closed 18 December - 3 January – **58 rm** 70/85 – 87/97.
◆ What was once a youth hostel and then an office building is now a modern, well-run business hotel with functional rooms, ideal for trade fair delegates.

at Cologne-Ehrenfeld *West : 3 km, by Rudolfplatz EV and Aachener Straße :*

Holiday Inn City West, Innere Kanalstr. 15, ✉ 50823, ☎ (0221) 5 70 10, *Fax (0221) 5701999, city-west@eventhotels.com*, , – , rm, – 180. AE VISA JCB
closed 23 to 29 December – **Meals** à la carte 23/35 – **205 rm** 158/183 – 178/203.
◆ In an accessible location, modern glass building with functionally furnished and sensibly decorated rooms ideal for business travellers. Spacious restaurant with tall windows.

Imperial, Barthelstr. 93, ✉ 50823, ☎ (0221) 51 70 57, *Fax (0221) 520993, hotel@hotel-imperial.de*, – , rm, – 25. AE VISA JCB. rest
Meals à la carte 20/31 – **35 rm** 102/152 – 152/230.
◆ Hotel in a residential area on the outer ring road with good access. Soberly decorated rooms, mostly with mahogany furnishings. Tasteful restaurant.

at Cologne-Holweide *Northeast : 10 km, by Konrad-Adenauer-Ufer FU and Mülheimer Brücke :*

Isenburg, Johann-Bensberg-Str. 49, ✉ 51067, ☎ (0221) 69 59 09, *Fax (0221) 698703, info@isenburg.info*, – VISA JCB
closed carnival, mid July - mid August, Christmas, Saturday lunch, Sunday and Monday – **Meals** (booking essential) à la carte 30/47.
◆ The ivy-covered walls of this old moated castle are well worth a visit. The festive, medieval restaurant offers refined cuisine. Attractive outside terrace in summer.

at Cologne-Junkersdorf *West : 9 km, by Rudolfplatz EV and Aachener Straße :*

Brenner'scher Hof , Wilhelm-von-Capitaine-Str. 15, ✉ 50858, ☎ (0221) 9 48 60 00, *Fax (0221) 94860010, hotel@brennerscher-hof.de* – – 25. AE VISA
Pino's Osteria (Italian) **Meals** à la carte 17/41 – ***Anno Pomm*** (only potato dishes) **Meals** à la carte 18/25 – **42 rm** 135 – 160 – 7 suites.
◆ An individual, attractive place, with estate buildings dating from 1754. Mediterranean flair, with Italian period furniture, terracotta floors and rooms with fireplaces. Pino's Osteria overlooks the lovely courtyard. Anno Pomm in rustic Mediterranean style.

Mercure Junkersdorf, Aachener Str. 1059, ✉ 50858, ☎ (0221) 4 89 80, *Fax (0221) 48981000, h5365@accor.com* – , rm, – 80. AE VISA
Meals *(closed Sunday dinner)* à la carte 22/31 – 14 – **145 rm** 104 – 114.
◆ Modern hotel in accessible location. Functional rooms. Soundproofed windows guarantee a good night's rest.

at Cologne-Lindenthal *West : 4,5 km, by Rudolfplatz EV and B 264 :*

Holiday Inn Am Stadtwald, Dürener Str. 287, ✉ 50935, ☎ (0221) 4 67 60, *Fax (0221) 433765, info.hi-cologne-amstadtwald@queensgruppe.de*, beer garden – , rm, – 250. AE VISA. rest
Meals à la carte 25/46 – 15 – **150 rm** 110/118 – 130/146.
◆ This establishment is right on the lake in Cologne's city forest. Comfort is the hallmark of the interior. Business travellers will appreciate the functional room facilities.

Osteria Toscana, Dürener Str. 218, ✉ 50931, ☎ (0221) 40 80 22, *Fax (0221) 4009897* – . AE VISA
closed 10 to 31 August and Monday, except exhibitions – **Meals** à la carte 24/30.
◆ The restaurant's name hints at the kind of food to be expected. Inside, the atmosphere is bright and elegant, light and welcoming.

at Cologne-Marienburg *South : 4 km, by Bonner Straße FX :*

Marienburger Bonotel, Bonner Str. 478, ✉ 50968, ☎ (0221) 3 70 20, *Fax (0221) 3702132, info@bonotel.de*, – rm, – 40. AE VISA JCB
Meals *(dinner only)* à la carte 22/44 – **93 rm** 100 – 125.
◆ Conference and business establishment run to a high standard. Rooms furnished throughout with natural lightwood. Accessible location. Meals served in the Piano Lounge.

at Cologne-Marsdorf *West : 8 km, by Rudolfplatz EV and B 264 :*

Novotel Köln-West, Horbeller Str. 1, ✉ 50858, ☎ (02234) 51 40, *Fax (02234) 514106, h0705@accor.com*, , beer garden, , , , – rm, – 120. AE VISA JCB, rest
Meals à la carte 21/32 – 14 – **193 rm** 97 – 112.
◆ The hotel is just by the Frechen exit off the motorway. Rooms are convenient and functional. Garden swimming-pool with sun terrace.

at Cologne - Porz-Grengel *Southeast : 16 km, by Severin Brücke, follow signs to airport :*

Holiday Inn Airport, Waldstr. 255 (at Cologne/Bonn Airport), ✉ 51147, ☎ (02203) 56 10, *Fax (02203) 5619, reservation.hi-cologne-bonn-airport@queensgruppe.de*, beer garden – , rm, – 80. AE VISA JCB
Meals à la carte 25/47 – 15 – **177 rm** 139 – 174.
◆ Only 500m away from the airport and a good place for the airborne to land and refuel, not least because of the very liveable rooms and the atmospheric Münchhausen Bar.

at Cologne - Porz-Langel *South : 17 km, by Severinsbrücke FX and Siegburger Straße :*

Zur Tant (Hütter), Rheinbergstr. 49, ✉ 51143, ☎ (02203) 8 18 83, *Fax (02203) 87327*, , – AE VISA
closed Thursday, except Bank Holidays – **Meals** 55/70 and à la carte 43/56 ♀ – ***Hütter's Piccolo*** *(closed Thursday, except Bank Holidays)* **Meals** à la carte 26/34 ♀.
Spec. Chartreuse von Garnelen mit Tomatenrisotto. Seeteufel mit Bananen-Trüffelsauce und Vanillezwiebeln. Taubenkotelette mit Gänseleber und Selleriepüree.
◆ This restaurant is housed in a pretty half-timbered building. The generous window-space gives a fine view of the Rhine. Hütter's Piccolo is a contemporary-style bistro - a few steps above the Zur Tant.

at Cologne-Rodenkirchen *South : 8 km, by Bayernstraße FX and Agrippina Ufer :*

Atrium-Rheinhotel without rest (with guest house), Karlstr. 2, ✉ 50996, ☎ (0221) 93 57 20, *Fax (0221) 93572222, info@atrium-rheinhotel.de*, – – 15. AE VISA
closed 23 December - 3 January – **68 rm** 110 – 160.
◆ The hotel stands in a quiet little lane close to the riverside in the old fishing village of Rodenkirchen. Choose between comfortable or more simply furnished rooms.

Bergisch Gladbach *Nordrhein-Westfalen* 543 N 5 – *pop. 104 000 – alt. 86 m.*

Köln 17.

Restaurant Dieter Müller - Schlosshotel Lerbach, Lerbacher Weg, ✉ 51465, ☎ (02202) 20 40, *Fax (02202) 204940, info@schlosshotel-lerbach.com* – AE VISA,
closed 31 July - 22 August, 1 to 17 January, Sunday and Monday – **Meals** (booking essential) 60 *(lunch)*/130 and à la carte 80/113 ♀.
Spec. Confiertes Steinbuttfilet mit Olivenöl und eingemachter Zitrone. Variation vom Salzgraslamm mit Chorizofumet und frittierten Pimentos. Auflauf von Schokolade und schwarzen Oliven mit marinierten Feigen.
◆ Discreet elegance, attentive service and lavish table settings create an atmosphere of great refinement, which is matched by the excellent French cuisine.

at Bergisch Gladbach-Bensberg :

Vendôme - Grandhotel Schloss Bensberg, Kadettenstraße, ✉ 51429, ☎ (02204) 42 19 41, *Fax (02204) 42985, vendome@schlossbensberg.com* - AE VISA.
closed 2 weeks carnival, 3 weeks August - September, Monday and Tuesday – **Meals** 80 *(lunch)*/130 and à la carte 75/105 ♀.
Spec. Frühgemüse im Schweinebratensaft geschmort mit glaciertem Schweinekinn. Steinbutt an der Gräte mit Gemüse á la Escabèche und Kalbskutteln. Rehrücken mit Olivenkrokant und grünen Wacholdertomaten.
◆ Housed in a nobleman's residence, this gourmet restaurant provides attentive service and fine place settings. Well-chosen, classic dishes.

Neuenahr-Ahrweiler, Bad *Rheinland-Pfalz* 543 O 5 – *pop. 28 000 – alt. 92 m.*
Köln 63.

at Bad Neuenahr-Ahrweiler-Heppingen *East : 5 km :*

XXX ✿✿ **Steinheuers Restaurant Zur Alten Post** with rm, Landskroner Str. 110 (entrance Konsumgasse), ✉ 53474, ☎ (02641) 9 48 60, *Fax (02641) 948610, steinheuers.restaurant@t-online.de,* – rest, rm
Meals *(closed 3 weeks July - August, Tuesday and Wednesday)* 80/115 and à la carte
– *Landgasthof Poststuben* *(closed 1 week January, Tuesday and Wednesday)* **Meals** 36/49 and à la carte 28/42 – **11 rm** 80/130 – 125/140.
Spec. Variation von der Gänsestopfleber. Steinbutt in Traubenkernöl gegart mit Kräuterwurzelpüree. Eifeler Reh.
◆ Taste and elegance are reflected in the clean lines of the furnishings, seasonal and French influences characterise the cuisine. Attractive rooms, some ultra-modern, for an overnight stay. Refined local cuisine in the Poststuben in the style of a country inn.

Wittlich *Rheinland-Pfalz* 543 Q 4 – *pop. 18 000 – alt. 155 m.*
Köln 160.

at Dreis *Southwest : 8 km :*

XXXX ✿✿✿ **Waldhotel Sonnora** (Thieltges) with rm, Auf dem Eichelfeld, ✉ 54518, ☎ (06578) 9 82 20, *Fax (06578) 1402, info@hotel-sonnora.de,* –
closed 4 to 20 July and 27 December - 26 January – **Meals** *(closed Monday and Tuesday) (booking essential)* 98/118 and à la carte 64/86 – **20 rm** 80/100 – 110/170.
Spec. Felsenrotbarbe und Meeresfrüchte auf mariniertem Fenchel. Steinbutt und Kaisergranat im knusprigen Pastilla-Teig. Brust von der Challans-Blutente mit Gewürzhaut und glacierten Nektarinen.
◆ An aura of classic elegance pervades the restaurant, where a master-chef displays his outstanding talents. There are also well-looked after rooms and a lovely garden.

Perl *Saarland* 543 R 3 – *pop. 12 000 – alt. 254 m.*
Köln 230.

at Perl-Nennig *North : 10 km by B 419 :*

XXXX ✿✿ **Schloss Berg** with rm, Schlosshof 7, ✉ 66706, ☎ (06866) 7 91 18, *Fax (06866) 79458, info@schlossberg-nennig.de,* – rm,
closed 2 weeks July, 1 week October and 2 weeks January – **Meals** *(closed Monday and Tuesday)* 99/123 and à la carte 79/95 – **17 rm** 135 – 165 – 3 suites.
Spec. Landaiser Gänseleber "kalt-warm". Gedämpfte Langustinen-Chartreuse und pochierte Austern im Citronellsud. Rinderschulter 60 Std. sanft gegart mit Filet.
◆ Haute cuisine celebrated in an aristocratic setting. Treat yourself to one of the novel creations of chef Christian Bau, then spend the night in one of the stylish rooms.

DRESDEN L *Sachsen* 544 M 25 – *pop. 480 200 – alt. 105 m.*

See : *Zwinger*** : Picture Gallery Old Masters*** (Gemäldegalerie Alte Meister), Wallpavilion**, Nymphs' Bath**, Porcelain Collection**, Mathematical-Physical Salon**, Armoury*** AY – *Semper Opera*** AY – *Former court church** (Hofkirche)* BY – *Schloss : royal houses* (Fürstenzug-Mosaik), Long Passage* (Langer Gang)* BY – *Albertinum : Picture Gallery New Masters*** (Gemäldegalerie Neue Meister), Green Vault*** (Grünes Gewölbe)* BY – *Prager Straße** ABZ – *Museum of History of Dresden* (Museum für Geschichte der Stadt Dresden)* BY **L** – *Church of the Cross* (Kreuzkirche)* BY – *Japanese Palace* (Japanisches Palais) : garden ≤** ABX – *Museum of Saxonian Folk Art* (Museum für Sächsische Volkskunst)* BX **M 2** – *Great Garden* (Großer Garten)* CDZ – *Russian-Orthodox Church* (Russisch-orthodoxe Kirche) by Leningrader Str.* BZ – *Brühl's Terrace ≤* (Brühlsche Terrasse)* BY – *Equestrian statue of Augustus the Strong * (Reiterstandbild Augusts des Starken)* BX **E** – *Pfunds dairy (Pfunds Molkerei) (interior*) Bautzener Straße 97*CX.

Envir. : *Schloss Moritzburg* (Northwest : 14 km by Hansastraße* BX*)* – *Schloss Pillnitz* (Southeast : 15 km by Bautzner Straße* CX *)* – *Saxon Swiss*** (Sächsische Schweiz) : Bastei*** ≤**, Bad Schandau*, Festung Königstein**, Großsedlitz : Baroque Garden*.*

18 *Possendorf, Ferdinand-von-Schill-Str. 4 (South : 13 km),* ☎ *(035206) 24 30 ;* 18 *Ullersdorf, Am Golfplatz 1 (East : 8 km),* ☎ *(03528) 4 80 60.*

✈ *Dresden-Klotzsche (North : 13 km),* ☎ *(0351) 8 81 33 60.*

ℹ *Tourist-Information, Prager Str. 2a,* ✉ *01069,* ☎ *(0351) 49 19 20, Fax (0351) 49192116, info@dresden-tourist.de.*

ℹ *Tourist-Information, Schinkelwache, Theaterplatz,* ✉ *01067,* ☎ *(0351) 49 19 20.*

ADAC, *Striesener Str. 37.*

Berlin 192 – Chemnitz 70 – Görlitz 98 – Leipzig 111 – Praha 152.

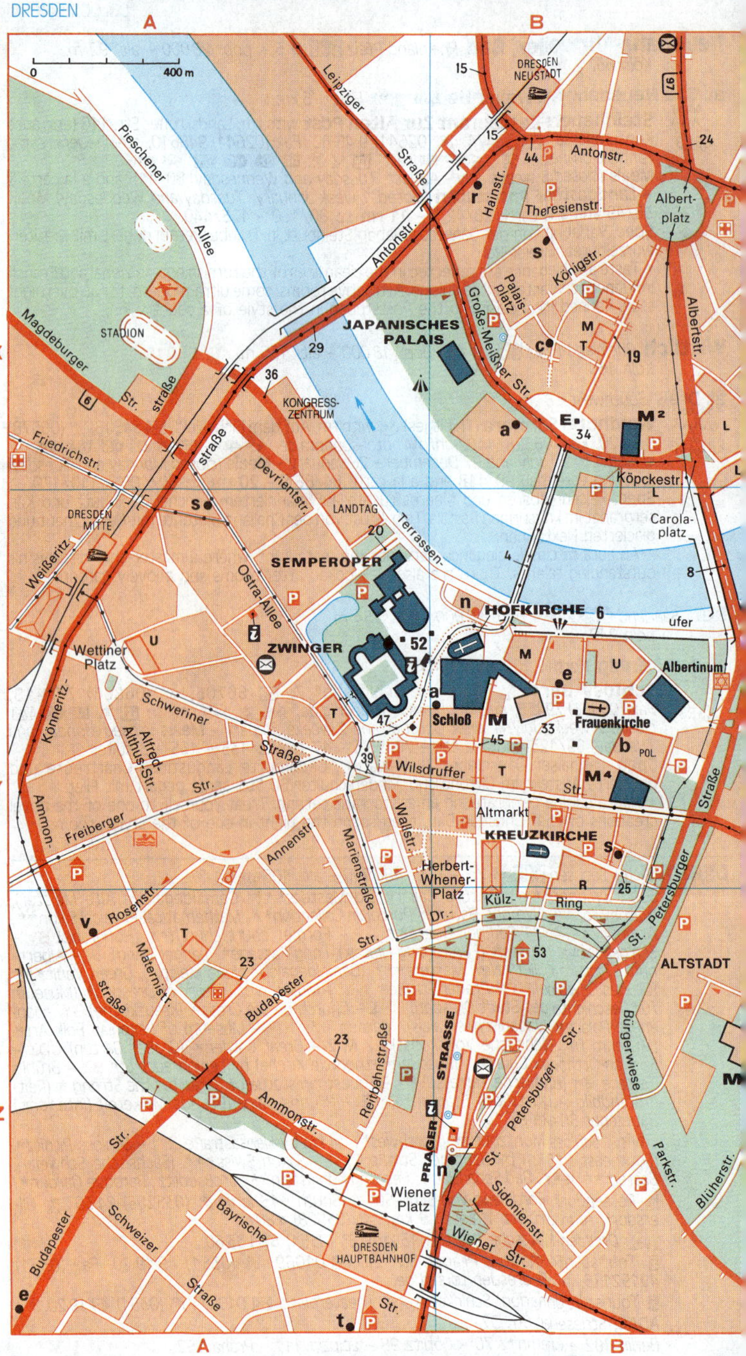
A
B
X
Y
Z
0
400 m
DRESDEN NEUSTADT
15
97
24
44
Antonstr.
Albert-platz
Theresienstr.
Hainstr.
Leipziger Straße
Pieschener Allee
Antonstr.
Palais platz
Königstr.
Albertstr.
Große Meißner Str.
JAPANISCHES PALAIS
STADION
Magdeburger Str.
straße
29
36
19
KONGRESS-ZENTRUM
34
Friedrichstr.
straße
Devrientstr.
Köpckestr.
LANDTAG
Terrassen-
Carola-platz
DRESDEN MITTE
Weißeritz
Ostra-Allee
20
SEMPEROPER
4
8
HOFKIRCHE
6
ufer
ZWINGER
52
Albertinum
Wettiner Platz
Schweriner
Alfred-Althus-Str.
Straße
47
Schloß
33
Frauenkirche
45
POL.
39
Wilsdruffer
Str.
Könneritz-
Ammon-
Freiberger
Str.
Annenstr.
Marienstraße
Wallstr.
Altmarkt
KREUZKIRCHE
Herbert-Whener-Platz
Külz-
Ring
25
Dr.-
Straße
Petersburger
St.
Rosenstr.
Maternistr.
23
Budapester
Str.
53
ALTSTADT
straße
23
Reitbahnstraße
PRAGER STRASSE
Bürgerwiese
Ammonstr.
St. Petersburger Str.
Str.
Parkstr.
Bühlerstr.
Wiener Platz
Sidonienstr.
DRESDEN HAUPTBAHNHOF
Wiener Str.
Budapester
Schweizer Straße
Bayrische Str.
A
B

DRESDEN

Albertbrücke	CX	2
Augustusbrücke	BY	4
Brühlsche Terrasse	BY	6
Carolabrücke	BY	8
Dr.-Külz-Ring	BYZ	
Hansastr.	BX	15
Hauptstr.	BX	19
Holländische Str.	AY	20
Josephinenstr.	AZ	23
Königsbrücker Str.	BX	24
Königstr.	BX	
Kreuzstr.	BYZ	25
Marienbrücke	AX	29
Neumarkt	BY	33
Neustädter Markt	BX	34
Ostra-Ufer	AX	36
Postpl.	AY	39
Prager Str.	ABZ	
Reichpietschufer	CX	40
Rothenburger Str.	CX	42
Sachsenallee	CY	43
Schlesischer Pl.	BX	44
Schloßstr.	BY	45
Sophienstr.	AY	47
Theaterpl.	BY	52
Waisenhausstr	BZ	53
Wilsdruffer Str.	ABY	

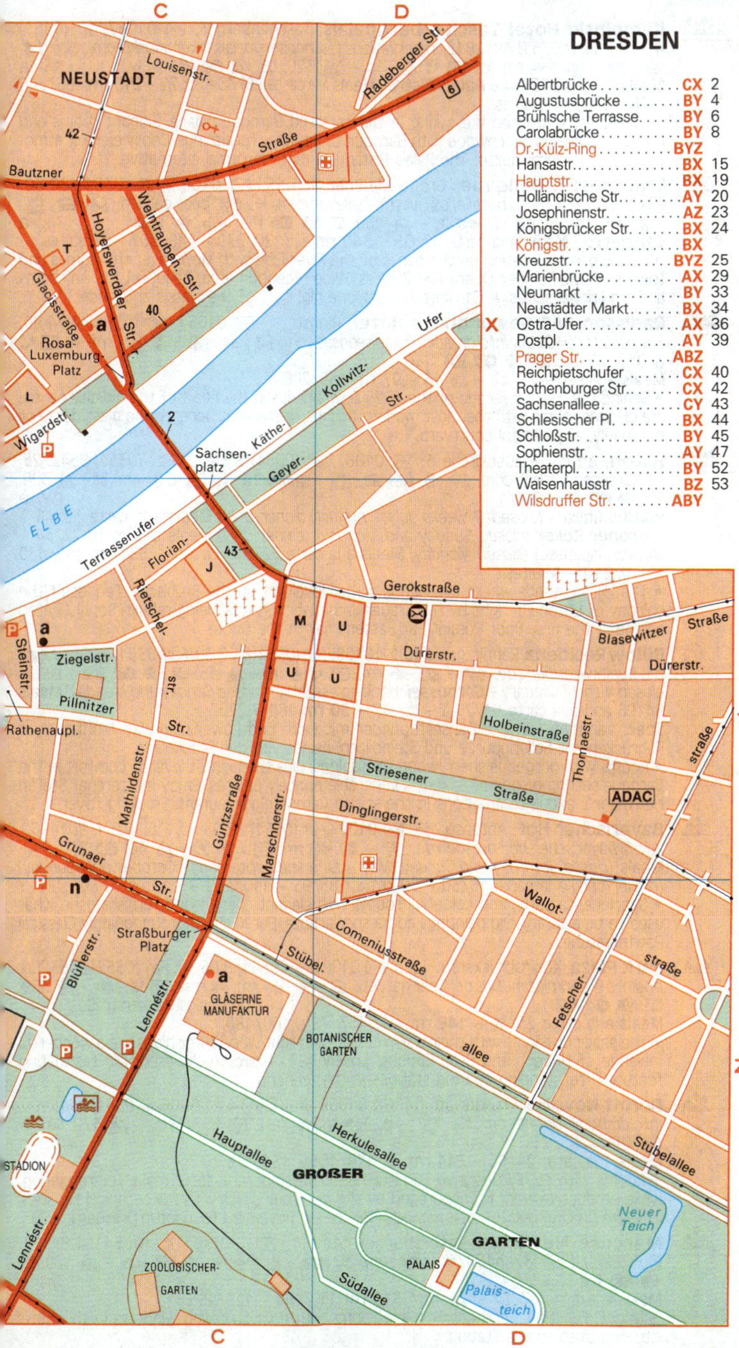

Kempinski Hotel Taschenbergpalais, Taschenberg 3, ✉ 01067, ✆ (0351) 4 91 20, *Fax (0351) 4912812, reservations.taschenbergpalais@kempinski.com*, – 🅿, 📺 – 320. AE ⊙ MC VISA JCB BY a
Meals à la carte 39/54 – ***Palais Bistro* : Meals** à la carte 26/33 – ☐ 22 – **215 rm** 255/340 – 285/370 – 12 suites.
• The guest is treated like a king in this restored Baroque palace. Elegant rooms and luxurious suites in beechwood with Baroque or designer furnishings. Coolly elegant atmosphere in the Intermezzo. The Palais Bistro is a more informal alternative.

The Westin Bellevue, Große Meißner Str. 15, ✉ 01097, ✆ (0351) 80 50, *Fax (0351) 8051609, hotelinfo@westin-bellevue.com*, ≤, beer garden, – rm, 📺 – 430. AE ⊙ MC VISA JCB. rest BX a
***Canaletto* : Meals** à la carte 42/55 – **340 rm** ☐ 120/279 – 140/307 – 19 suites.
• Lovely garden location on the banks of the River Elbe with views over the domes and towers of the Semper Opera and Schloss. Wide reception area, beautiful, stylish rooms and traditional suites. A Canaletto is just one highlight of the classic ambience.

Radisson SAS Gewandhaus Hotel, Ringstr. 1, ✉ 01067, ✆ (0351) 4 94 90, *Fax (0351) 4949490, info.dresden@radissonsas.com*, – rm, 📺 – 60. AE ⊙ MC VISA JCB BY s
Meals à la carte 27/42 – ☐ 16 – **97 rm** 135/200.
• Behind the historic façade of the 1525 Gewandhaus in the heart of the old city centre are elegant rooms with the most modern fittings. Restaurant beneath the glass dome of the lovely, airy central courtyard.

Hilton, An der Frauenkirche 5, ✉ 01067, ✆ (0351) 8 64 20, *Fax (0351) 8642725, info.dresden@hilton.com*, – rm, 📺 – 320. AE ⊙ MC VISA JCB BY e
Rossini (Italian) *(closed 2 weeks July - August)(dinner only)* **Meals** à la carte 32/46 – ***Wettiner Keller*** *(closed Sunday and Monday) (dinner only)* **Meals** à la carte 22/34 – ***Ogura*** (Japanese) *(closed Monday)* **Meals** à la carte 22/38 – ☐ 19 – **333 rm** 115/130 – 170/210 – 4 suites.
• The Hilton stands where Dresden is at her loveliest, on the Brühlsche Terrasse ("the balcony of Europe"), right by the Frauenkirche which is now being rebuilt. Sophisticated cuisine in the first floor Rossini. Far Eastern flair in the Ogura.

Bülow Residenz, Rähnitzgasse 19, ✉ 01097, ✆ (0351) 8 00 30, *Fax (0351) 8003100, info@buelow-residenz.de*, – rm, 📺 – 15. AE ⊙ MC VISA BX c
closed 4 to 17 January – ***Caroussel*** (booking essential) *(closed Sunday and Monday)* **Meals** 64/96 and à la carte 61/71 ♀ – ☐ 17 – **30 rm** 180 – 220.
Spec. Variation von der Gänsestopfleber mit Feld- und Löwenzahnsalat. Moritzburger Rehrücken mit Selleriepüree und Steinpilzen. Feines von der Schokolade.
• Rooms with gorgeous cherrywood furnishings, plus the highest level of comfort in the Baroque setting of one of Saxony's venerable princely palaces. Enjoy masterchef Stefan Herrmann's exquisite creations in the stylish Caroussel restaurant. Smoking foyer.

Bayerischer Hof, Antonstr. 33, ✉ 01097, ✆ (0351) 82 93 70, *Fax (0351) 8014860, info@bayerischer-hof-dresden.de*, – rm, 📺 – 40. MC VISA JCB
Meals *(closed Saturday and Sunday, May - June and September - October only Sunday) (dinner only)* à la carte 15/30 – **50 rm** ☐ 85/95 – 110/130 – 5 suites. BX r
• Spacious, tasteful, and colourful rooms with elegant cherrywood furnishings in what used to be a library. Old paintings add a special note. Eat in the thoroughgoingly Classical Patrizierstube.

Park Plaza, Königsbrückerstr. 121a, ✉ 01099, ✆ (0351) 8 06 30, *Fax (0351) 8063200, ppdinfo@parkplazahotels.de*, beer garden, – rm, rest, 📺 – 350. AE ⊙ MC VISA by Königsbrückerstraße BX
Meals à la carte 23/36 – **148 rm** ☐ 145/175 – 160/180.
• The spacious rooms with their warm colours and light wood furnishings are a wonderful melange of Hi-Tech and Belle Epoque. Lovely 1891 ballroom. An especially fascinating feature : freestanding cooking stations in the Szenario.

Dorint Novotel, Grunaer Str. 14, ✉ 01069, ✆ (0351) 4 91 50, *Fax (0351) 4915100, info.drshdd@dorint.com*, – rm, rest, 📺 – 170. AE ⊙ MC VISA JCB CYZ n
Meals à la carte 24/36 – **244 rm** ☐ 114/151 – 134/176.
• Rooms with solidly designed furniture and contemporary décor make for relaxation, while productive work is encouraged by the generous desks with full technical facilities. The "Die Brücke" restaurant is named after the art movement founded in Dresden in 1905.

Mercure Newa, St. Petersburger Str. 34, ✉ 01069, ✆ (0351) 4 81 40, *Fax (0351) 4955137, h1577@accor.com*, – rm, 📺 – 180. AE ⊙ MC VISA JCB BZ n
Meals à la carte 17/37 – ☐ 14 – **319 rm** 110/140 – 125/155.
• Bright, functional and comfortable rooms with floor-to-ceiling windows in this hotel situated close to the station.

Holiday Inn, Stauffenbergallee 25a, ✉ 01099, ✆ (0351) 8 15 10, *Fax (0351) 8151333, info@holiday-inn-dresden.de*, – rm, – 160. by Königsbrücker Straße BX
Meals à la carte 20/30 – **120 rm** 105/160 – 110/175.
• Conveniently situated a little outside the centre, with contemporary and functional rooms. The Club floor is particularly comfortable

Elbflorenz without rest, Rosenstr. 36, ✉ 01067, ✆ (0351) 8 64 00, *Fax (0351) 8640100, info@hotel-elbflorenz.de*, – – 150. AZ v
227 rm 105/155 – 125/175.
• "Florence on the Elbe" invites its guests to spend the night in Tuscan-style rooms with metal bedsteads and imitation stone walls. Delightfully leafy courtyard.

Comfort Hotel without rest, Buchenstr. 10, ✉ 01097, ✆ (0351) 8 15 15 00, *Fax (0351) 8151555, info@comfort-hotel-dresden.de*, – – 15. by Königsbrücker Straße BX
86 rm 65/120 – 80/135.
• Beechwood, modern design and good technical facilities make for a pleasant and comfortable stay. Well-located in Dresden-Neustadt with good public transport connections.

Art'otel, Ostra-Allee 33, ✉ 01067, ✆ (0351) 4 92 20, *Fax (0351) 4922777, aodrinfo@artotels.de*, – rm, – 300. AY s
Meals *(closed Sunday lunch)* à la carte 26/31 – **174 rm** 85/120 – 98/160.
• Modern art enthusiasts will not be disappointed by the exuberant design of this establishment with its attached art gallery. Unusual rooms with fascinating features like a "magic window" to the bathroom. Restaurant combines art and contemporary fittings.

Am Terrassenufer, Terrassenufer 12, ✉ 01069, ✆ (0351) 4 40 95 00, *Fax (0351) 4409600, hat@hotel-terrassenufer.de*, – rm, – 25. CY a
Meals à la carte 16/26 – **196 rm** 77/145 – 97/190 – 6 suites.
• Spacious rooms with light furniture, generous working facilities and, thanks to location on the famous Brühlsche Terrasse, wonderful views of the Elbe, city centre, and Saxon Switzerland. Dine in the glazed Pavillon-Restaurant with its contemporary fittings.

Leonardo, Bamberger Str. 14, ✉ 01187, ✆ (0351) 4 66 00, *Fax (0351) 4660100, info@leonardo.bestwestern.de*, – rm, – 35. rest by Budapester Str. AZ
Meals à la carte 18/30 – **92 rm** 84/124 – 114/154.
• Modern hotel with contemporary décor featuring attractive Mediterranean colours. Comfortable rooms with all technical facilities.Welcoming restaurant on two levels.

Martha Hospiz, Nieritzstr. 11, ✉ 01097, ✆ (0351) 8 17 60, *Fax (0351) 8176222, marthahospiz.dresden@t-online.de* – – 20. rm BX s
closed 22 to 27 December – **Kartoffelkeller** *(dinner only)* **Meals** à la carte 12/24 – **50 rm** 74/90 – 105/115.
• Traditional establishment run by the Protestant Church. Stylish rooms with classic, honey-coloured furniture, partly in Biedermeier style. Seven rooms with disabled facilities. Cosy restaurant, formerly a coal and potato cellar.

Achat without rest, Budapester Str. 34, ✉ 01069, ✆ (0351) 47 38 00, *Fax (0351) 47380999, dresden@achat-hotel.de* – – 20. AZ e
12 – **157 rm** 58/88.
• By the main railway station in the city centre, functional rooms with natural wood furnishings. Apartments with kitchenettes for longer term guests.

Privat, Forststr. 22, ✉ 01099, ✆ (0351) 81 17 70, *Fax (0351) 8013953, hotel-privat@t-online.de*, – – 25.
Meals à la carte 11/20 – **30 rm** 61/63 – 82/89. by Bautzener Str. DX
• Personally run, private hotel offering its guests functional rooms with all the amenities of contemporary accommodation. Bright restaurant with conservatory and attractive small terrace.

Kipping, Winckelmannstr. 6, ✉ 01069, ✆ (0351) 47 85 00, *Fax (0351) 4785099, reception@hotel-kipping.de*, – AZ t
Meals *(closed Sunday dinner)* à la carte 15/24 – **20 rm** 75/95 – 90/115.
• This well-run, restored town house in a side street to the rear of the main station offers individually decorated, comfortable rooms.

Lesage, Lennéstr. 1, ✉ 01069, ✆ (0351) 4 20 42 50, Fax (0351) 4204994, – CZ a
Meals 27 and à la carte 25/36.
• This restaurant has a unique location in the glass-walled Volkswagen works. Crisp design and elegant bistro style characterise the ambience.

Italienisches Dörfchen, Theaterplatz 3, ✉ 01067, ✆ (0351) 49 81 60, *Fax (0351) 4981688, gastro.theaterplatz@t-online.de,* , beer garden – AE VISA JCB BY n
Bellotto (Italian) **Meals** à la carte 23/40 – ***Wein- und Kurfürstenzimmer*** : Meals à la carte 19/35.
◆ The modern Bellotto restaurant is part of Dresden's "Italian Village", once home to the workmen who helped build the city. Elegant wine-cellar with fine plasterwork and warm red décor. Spectacular ceiling in the Kurfürstenzimmer.

Coselpalais, An der Frauenkirche 12, ✉ 01067, ✆ (0351) 4 96 24 44, *Fax (0351) 4989805, info@rank-buettig.de,* – . AE VISA BY b
Meals à la carte 19/35.
◆ This restored palace dating from 1763 is a dream both inside and out. The interior has a coffee-house character which harmonises well with the building as a whole.

Ars Vivendi, Bürgerstr. 14, ✉ 01127, ✆ (0351) 8 21 19 00, *Fax (0351) 8211901, frank.ollhoff@t-online.de* – AE VISA JCB by Leipziger Straße AX
closed Sunday and Monday – **Meals** *(dinner only)* 33/62 and à la carte.
◆ This attractive restaurant with its three little rooms resembles a wine cellar, with vaulting, welcoming lighting and cheerful atmosphere. Professional service.

Am Glacis, Glacisstr. 8, ✉ 01099, ✆ (0351) 8 03 60 33, *Fax (0351) 8036034, restaurant@am-glacis.de,* – AE VISA JCB CX a
closed 1 to 15 January, Saturday lunch and Sunday – **Meals** à la carte 26/42.
◆ This elegant contemporary restaurant is in the same building as the Mercure-Hotel Albertbrücke, and is guaranteed to take you on a fascinating gastronomic tour of France.

Alte Meister, Theaterplatz 1a, ✉ 01067, ✆ (0351) 4 81 04 26, *Fax (0351) 4810479, info@altemeister.net,* – AE VISA. AY e
Meals à la carte 23/31.
◆ Bright, high-ceilinged interiors and a vaulted ceiling with frescoes set the tone here. Splendid terrace with views of Opera and Theaterplatz.

Villandry, Jordanstr. 8, ✉ 01099, ✆ (0351) 8 99 67 24, *Fax (0351) 8996746, mail@villandry-restaurant.de,* – AE VISA by Königsbrücker Str. BX
closed 2 weeks February, 2 weeks August and Sunday – **Meals** *(dinner only)* (booking essential) à la carte 23/28.
◆ Mediterranean bistro-style ambience in this restaurant offering tasty international dishes as well as a relaxed atmosphere and live music.

at Dresden-Blasewitz *East : 5 km, by Blasewitzer Straße* DY :

Am Blauen Wunder, Loschwitzer Str. 48, ✉ 01309, ✆ (0351) 3 36 60, *Fax (0351) 3366299, reservierung@habw.de,* – – 20. VISA
closed 3 to 16 January – ***La Strada*** (Italian) *(closed Saturday and Sunday) (dinner only)* **Meals** à la carte 26/38 – **39 rm** 85/110 – 105/140.
◆ You certainly won't feel blue here! Very tasteful rooms, decorated in warm, Mediterranean colours, with excellent technical facilities. La Strada is furnished in bistro style.

at Dresden-Cotta *West : 5 km, by Magdeburger Straße (B 6)* AX :

Mercure Elbpromenade, Hamburger Str. 64 (B 6), ✉ 01157, ✆ (0351) 4 25 20, *Fax (0351) 4252420, h0479@t-online.de,* , – , rm, – 60. AE VISA JCB. rest
Meals *(closed Sunday lunch)* à la carte 16/44 – **103 rm** 81/116 – 101/116.
◆ Your residence in Dresden, the "Pearl of the North", is right on the Elbe. Spacious rooms with modern, bright furnishings in natural wood plus blue writing desks with excellent technical facilities.

Residenz Alt Dresden, Mobschatzer Str. 29, ✉ 01157, ✆ (0351) 4 28 10, *Fax (0351) 4281988, residenzaltdresden@ringhotels.de,* , , – – 100. AE VISA JCB
Meals à la carte 26/35 – **124 rm** 83/114 – 98/140.
◆ Functional rooms with modern furnishings in a mixture of yellow and orange. Longer-term guests accommodated in the annexe. Breakfast in the winter garden. Straightforward, bistro-style restaurant.

at Dresden-Kemnitz *Northwest : 6 km, by Magdeburger Straße* AX *and Bremer Straße* :

Romantik Hotel Pattis, Merbitzer Str. 53, ✉ 01157, ✆ (0351) 4 25 50, *Fax (0351) 4255255, info@pattis.de,* , , , – , rm, rest, – 80. AE VISA
Gourmet-Restaurant *(closed 2 weeks February, 2 weeks August, Sunday and Monday) (dinner only)* **Meals** 63/83 and à la carte – ***Vitalis*** : **Meals** à la carte 28/36 – **47 rm** 110/150 – 150/190 – 3 suites.
◆ A touch of luxury: extremely tastefully decorated rooms with Art Nouveau furnishings, plus a remarkable wellness area, and a small park. Gourmet restaurant with elegant interior. Vitalis restaurant has a pavilion-like character.

at Dresden-Klotzsche *Northeast : 9 km, by Königsbrücker Straße* BX :

Airport Hotel, Karl-Marx-Str. 25, ✉ 01109, ℘ (0351) 8 83 30, *Fax (0351) 8833333, bestwestern@airporthoteldresden.com*, – rm, rest, – 50.
Meals à la carte 21/30 – **100 rm** 97/128 – 114/128 – 7 suites.
♦ Happy landings in modern rooms arranged around an atrium and with solidly designed contemporary wooden furniture plus work desks with excellent facilities. Friendly restaurant with attractive room dividers.

at Dresden-Laubegast *East : 9 km, by Striesener Straße* DY :

Ramada-Treff Resident Hotel, Brünner Str. 11, ✉ 01279, ℘ (0351) 2 56 20, *Fax (0351) 2562800, resident.dresden@ramada-treff.de* – rm, – 45. rest
Meals *(weekdays dinner only)* à la carte 19/29 – **122 rm** 70/90 – 86/102.
♦ Relax in cosy, pastel-coloured rooms, functionally designed and ideal for the business traveller.

at Dresden-Leubnitz-Neuostra *Southeast : 5,5 km, by Parkstraße* BCZ *and Teplitzer Straße :*

Treff Hotel Dresden, Wilhelm-Franke-Str. 90, ✉ 01219, ℘ (0351) 4 78 20, *Fax (0351) 4782550, dresden@treff-hotels.de*, – rm, – 350.
Meals à la carte 24/33 – 13 – **262 rm** 68/88.
♦ Built in a semi-circle and close to the city centre, the Treff Hotel Dresden has comfortable rooms with tasteful furnishings in pale cherrywood. Large restaurant with sober contemporary décor.

at Dresden-Lockwitz *Southeast : 11 km, by Sankt Petersburger Straße* BZ *and B 172 :*

Landhaus Lockwitzgrund, Lockwitzgrund 100, ✉ 01257, ℘ (0351) 2 71 00 10, *Fax (0351) 27100130, tkaiser@landhaus-lockwitzgrund.de*, , beer garden – – 35.
closed 3 weeks January – **Meals** *(closed Monday)* à la carte 17/34 – **12 rm** 50 – 65.
♦ This country-house hotel in the romantic Lockwitz valley makes a wonderful setting for relaxation. Comfortable rooms with many original details. Restaurant in the well-preserved vaulted stables.

at Dresden-Loschwitz *Northeast : 6 km, by Bautzner Straße* CDX :

Schloß Eckberg (with separate hotel wing), Bautzner Str. 134, ✉ 01099, ℘ (0351) 8 09 90, *Fax (0351) 8099199, email@hotel-schloss-eckberg.de*, ⩤ Dresden and Elbe, – rm, – 70. rest
Meals 23 *(lunch)* and à la carte 35/44 – **84 rm** 85/180 – 118/235.
♦ Consisting of a neo-Gothic castle and a modern gentleman's residence, this is a fascinating place to stay, set in an extensive park and with rooms furnished with fine antiques. The stylish, traditional restaurant fits in well with the historical surroundings.

at Dresden-Niedersedlitz *Southeast : 10 km by Parkstraße* BZ *and B 172, off Lockwitztalstraße :*

Ambiente, Meusegaster Str. 23, ✉ 01259, ℘ (0351) 20 78 80, *Fax (0351) 2078836, info@hotel-ambiente.de* – . rest
Meals *(closed Sunday) (dinner only)* (residents only) – **20 rm** 71/91 – 86/118.
♦ This personally run hotel has interiors of great sophistication and elegance. Rooms with cherrywood furniture, famously comfortable Treca beds, and tasteful fabrics.

at Dresden-Strehlen *South : 4 km, by Parkstraße* CZ *and B 172, off Caspar-David-Friedrich-Straße :*

Four Points Hotel Königshof, Kreischaer Str. 2 (Wasaplatz), ✉ 01219, ℘ (0351) 8 73 10, *Fax (0351) 8731499, fourpoints.koenigshof@arabellasheraton.com*, – rm, – 180.
Meals à la carte 18/28 – 12 – **93 rm** 103 – 123 – 9 suites.
♦ In a listed building, this welcoming establishment has rooms with lovely beechwood furnishings and up-to-the-minute working facilities. Ask for a room with a four-poster. Cosy restaurant with bistro atmosphere.

at Dresden-Weixdorf *Northeast : 10 km, by Königsbrücker Straße* BX :

Quintessenz, Hohenbusch Markt 1, ✉ 01108, ℘ (0351) 88 24 40, *Fax (0351) 8824444, hotel.quintessenz@t-online.de*, – rm, – 60. rest
Meals *(closed Sunday) (dinner only)* à la carte 13/23 – **75 rm** 69/84 – 87/99.
♦ On the edge of town on the way to the A3 autobahn, this good hotel in a modern shopping centre offers comfortable rooms. Pictures of Italian landscapes grace the walls of the little Toskana restaurant.

DÜSSELDORF

L Nordrhein-Westfalen 543 M 4 – pop. 570 000 – alt. 40 m.

See : Königsallee★ EZ – Hofgarten★ DEY and Castle Jägerhof (Goethe-Museum★ EY **M1**) – Hetjensmuseum★ DZ **M4** – Museum of Art (museum kunst palast)★ (Glass Collection★★) DY **M2** – Collection of Art (Kunstsammlung NRW)★ DY **M3** – Löbbecke-Museum and Aquazoo★ by Kaiserswerther Straße AU – Hetjens-Museum★ DZ **M4.**

Envir. : Schloss Benrath (Parc★) South : 10 km by Siegburger Straße CX.

Düsseldorf-Grafenberg, Rennbahnstr. 26, ℘ (0211) 9 64 49 50 ; Gut Rommeljans, Rommeljansweg 12 (Northeast : 12 km), ℘ (02102) 8 10 92 ; Düsseldorf-Hubbelrath, Bergische Landstr. 700 (East : 12 km), ℘ (02104) 7 21 78 ; Düsseldorf-Hafen, Auf der Lausward 51, ℘ (0211) 41 05 29.

Düsseldorf-Lohausen (North : 8 km), ℘ (0211) 42 10.

Hauptbahnhof.

Exhibition Centre (Messegelände), ℘ (0211) 45 60 01, Fax (0211) 4560668.

Tourist-Information, Immermannstr. 65b, ✉ 40210, ℘ (0211) 17 20 22 2, Fax (0211) 1720234, tourist@duesseldorf.de.

ADAC, Himmelgeister Str. 63.

Berlin 552 – Amsterdam 225 – Essen 31 – Köln 40 – Rotterdam 237.

Plans on following pages

Steigenberger Parkhotel, Corneliusplatz 1, ✉ 40213, ℘ (0211) 1 38 10, Fax (0211) 1381592, duesseldorf@steigenberger.de, – |‡|, ⇔ rm, ▤ TV – 100. AE ⓓ ⓜⓒ VISA JCB. rest EY p
Menuett : **Meals** à la carte 39/64 ♀ – **133 rm** ☐ 195/320 – 270/390 – 6 suites.
◆ The first building on the square stands in a little city centre park. Beyond the classically beautiful façade is an elegant marble foyer and luxuriously appointed rooms. Dine in the stylish and comfortable setting of the Menuett.

Nikko, Immermannstr. 41, ✉ 40210, ℘ (0211) 83 40, Fax (0211) 161216, frontoffice@nikko-hotel.de, , – |‡|, ⇔ rm, ▤ TV – 220. AE ⓓ ⓜⓒ VISA JCB. rest
Benkay (Japanese) **Meals** 22(lunch)/80 – ☐ 17 – **301 rm** 172 – 272.
◆ The sushi-bar and a branch of the Mitsukoshi department store lend an exotically Oriental touch. Bird's-eye view over the city from swimming pool and sauna. Experience the expertise of Japanese chefs in the Benkay restaurant. BV g

Holiday Inn, Ludwig-Erhard-Allee 3, ✉ 40227, ℘ (0211) 7 77 10, Fax (0211) 7771777, info.hl.duesseldorf@queensgruppe.de, – |‡|, ⇔ rm, ▤ TV – 45. AE ⓓ ⓜⓒ VISA JCB BV s
closed 24 December - 3 January – **Meals** à la carte 23/33 – ☐ 18 – **134 rm** 145/160 – 175/190 – 5 suites.
◆ Priding itself on its timeless elegance, this modern business hotel is well-located close to the central railway station. The lovely whirlpool bath is one of the highlights of the leisure area. You are invited to dine in the classical setting of Ludwig's.

Holiday Inn City Centre-Königsallee, Graf-Adolf-Platz 8, ✉ 40213, ℘ (0211) 3 84 80, Fax (0211) 3848390, info.hl-duesseldorf-citycentre@queensgruppe.de, , – |‡|, ⇔ rm, ▤ rm, TV – 140. AE ⓓ ⓜⓒ VISA JCB EZ t
Meals à la carte 28/39 – ☐ 20 – **253 rm** 205 – 245.
◆ Smart, functional establishment on the Königsallee in the city centre, with exemplary conference and meeting facilities. Finnish sauna ideal for relaxing after a busy day.

Majestic without rest, Cantadorstr. 4, ✉ 40211, ℘ (0211) 36 70 30, Fax (0211) 3670399, info@majestic.bestwestern.de, – |‡| ⇔ TV – 30. AE ⓓ ⓜⓒ VISA JCB. BV a
closed 23 December - 1 January – ☐ 14 – **52 rm** 110/130 – 130/140.
◆ City centre establishment with a secluded and comfortable atmosphere. Two allergen-free rooms. Düsseldorf's frenetic night-life just a short step away.

Savoy without rest, Oststr. 128, ✉ 40210, ℘ (0211) 38 83 80, Fax (0211) 38838555, info@savoy.bestwestern.de, , – |‡| ⇔ ▤ TV – 50. AE ⓓ ⓜⓒ VISA EZ w
114 rm ☐ 97 – 143.
◆ Behind its historic façade this city hotel offers functional and contemporary rooms, equipped with the latest technology - just the ticket for business travellers.

Günnewig Hotel Esplanade without rest, Fürstenplatz 17, ✉ 40215, ℘ (0211) 38 68 50, Fax (0211) 38685555, hotel.esplanade@guennewig.de, , – |‡| ⇔ TV – 60. AE ⓓ ⓜⓒ VISA JCB BX s
80 rm ☐ 85/150 – 110/160.
◆ Business hotel in a tranquil but very central location on the Fürstenplatz, its spacious foyer much appreciated by its regular clientele.

DÜSSELDORF

Am Wehrhahn . . . . EY 3
Berliner Allee . . . . EZ
Blumenstr. . . . . EZ 7
Bolkerstr. . . . . DY 8
Citadellstr. . . . . DZ 13
Corneliusstr. . . . . EZ 15
Elberfelder Str. . . . . EY 21
Ernst-Reuter-Pl. . . . . EZ 23
Fischerstr. . . . . EY 27
Flinger Str. . . . . DY 28
Friedrich-Ebert-Str. . . . . EZ 29
Grabbepl. . . . . DY 32
Graf-Adolf-Str. . . . . EZ
Heinr.-Heine-Allee . . . . EY 42
Hofgartenrampe . . . . DY 45
Jan-Wellem-Pl. . . . . EY 51
Königsallee . . . . EZ
Marktpl. . . . . DY 68
Martin-Luther-Pl. . . . . EZ 69
Max.-Weyhe-Allee . . . . EY 70
Mühlenstr. . . . . DY 73
Ratinger Str. . . . . DY 88
Schadowpl. . . . . EY 90
Schadowstr. . . . . EY 91
Schneider-Wibbel-Gasse . . DY 95
Schulstr. . . . . DZ 96
Schwanenmarkt . . . . DZ 97
Tonhallenstr. . . . . EY 101
Vagedesstr. . . . . EY 104
Venloer Str. . . . . EY 105

A
B
U
V
X
GOLZHEIM
Reeser Pl.
Kaiserswerther Str.
Th.-Heuss-Brücke
THEODOR-HEUSS-BRÜCKE
Uerdinger Str.
ADAC
Cecilien-
Kaiserswerther
Golzheimer Platz
KÖLN-DÜSSELDORFER
RHEIN-
PARK
Kennedydamm
Johannstr.
Roßstr.
Heinrich-Ehrhardt Str.
Ulmen-
str.
Rather
Straße
Grashofstr.
Münsterstr.
DERENDORF
Brehmstr.
Gruner-
str
Collenbachstr.
Klever Straße
Münsterstr.
Moltkestr.
S.-BAHN
D.-ZOO
Rethelstr.
Kaiser-
Friedrich-
Ring
Joseph-Beuys-Ufer
allee
Klever Str.
Nordstr.
Prinz-Georg-Str.
Duisburger Str.
Kaiserstr.
Bagelstr.
Schinkelstr.
Rethelstr.
Schumannstr.
Grafenberger
RHEIN
OBERKASSEL
Luegallee
Luegplatz
OBERKASSELER BRÜCKE
HOF-GARTEN
Jägerhofstr.
HOF-GARTEN
Adlerstr.
D.-WEHRHAHN
Ackerstr.
Kaiser-Wilhelm-Ring
Schlossturm
ALTSTADT
Kölner
Rheinufertunnel
Königsallee
Berliner
Allee
Worringer
str.
RHEINKNIEBRÜCKE
LANDTAG RHEINTURM
Stromstr.
HAFEN
Handelszentrum
Hauptbahnhof
Stahlwerkstr.
Karl-
Str.
Graf-
Adolf-
Hüttenstr.
Eisenstr.
POL
Reichsstr.
Fürstenwall
Kronprinzenstr.
Elisabethstr.
Fürstenwall
Corneliusstr.
Ellerstr.
Oberbilker Markt
Lessingplatz
Kruppstraße
D.-FRIEDRICHSTADT
Bilker
Allee
D.-VÖLKLINGER STR.
Bachstr.
S.-BAHN
D.-BILK
D.-VOLKSGARTEN
Oberbilker
Allee
S.-BAHN
VOLKSGARTEN
Hennekamp
Mecum-
Aachener
Straße
Merowingerstr.
Auf'm
straße
Völklinger
Volmerswerther
Südring
Südring
ADAC
Stoffeler Kapellenweg
A
B

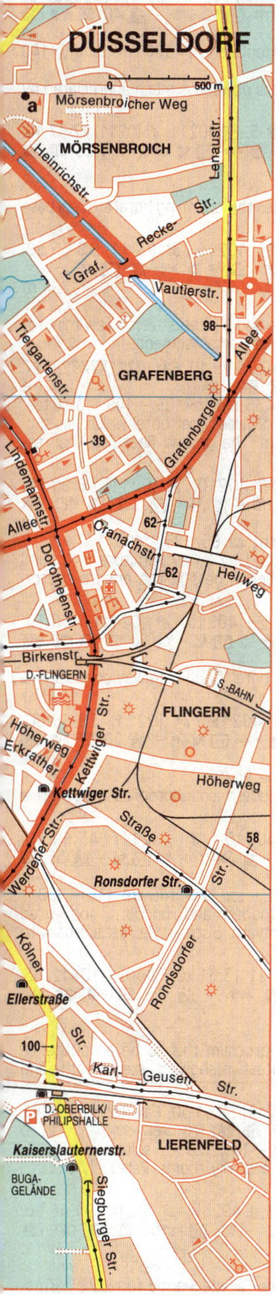

INDEX OF STREET NAMES IN DÜSSELDORF

Aachener Str. AX
Achenbachstr. BV 2
Ackerstr. BV
Adlerstr. BV
Am Wehrhahn EY 3
Auf'm Hennekamp BX
Bachstr. AX
Bagelstr. BV
Bastionstr. DZ
Benrather Str. DZ
Benzenbergstr. AX 5
Berger Allee DZ
Berliner Allee EZ
Bilker Allee AX
Bilker Str. DZ
Birkenstr. CV
Bismarckstr. EZ
Blumenstr. EZ 7
Bolkerstr. DY 8
Brehmpl. BU 9
Brehmstr. BU
Breite Str. EZ
Brunnenstr. BX 12
Burgpl. DY
Cecilienallee AU
Citadellstr. DZ 13
Collenbachstr. BU
Corneliusstr. EZ 15
Cranachstr. CV
Danziger Str. AU 16
Dorotheenstr. CV
Duisburger Str. EY
Eisenstr. BV
Elberfelder Str. EY 21
Elisabethstr. DZ
Ellerstr. BX
Erasmusstr. BX 22
Erkrather Str. CV
Ernst-Reuter-Pl. EZ 23
Eulerstr. BU 24
Fischerstr. EY 27
Flinger Str. DY 28
Friedrich-Ebert-Str. EZ 29
Friedrichstr. EZ
Fritz-Roeber-Str. DY
Fürstenpl. BX 30
Fürstenwall AX
Gartenstr. EY
Gladbacher Str. AX 31
Grabbepl. DY 32
Graf-Adolf-Pl. EZ
Graf-Adolf-Str. EZ
Graf-Recke-Str. CU
Grafenberger Allee BV
Grashofstr. BU
Grunerstr. BU
Hans-Sachs-Str. CV 39
Harkortstr. BV 40
Haroldstr. DZ
Heinr.-Ehrhardt-Str. BU
Heinr.-Heine-Allee EY 42
Heinrichstr. CU
Hellweg CV
Heresbachstr. BX 43
Herzogstr. BX 44
Höherweg CV
Hofgartenrampe DY 45
Homberger Str. AU 46
Hubertusstr. DZ
Hüttenstr. BX
Immermannstr. EY
Inselstr. DY
Jacobistr. EY
Jägerhofstr. EY
Jan-Wellem-Pl. EY 51
Johannstr. AU
Joseph-Beuys-Ufer DY
Jülicher Str. BU 52
Jürgenspl. AX 54
K.-Adenauer-Pl. BV 59
Kaiser-Friedrich-Ring AU
Kaiser-Wilhelm-Ring AV
Kaiserstr. EY
Kaiserwerther Str. AU
Karl-Geusen-Str. CX
Karlpl. DZ
Karlstr. BV
Kasernenstr. DZ
Kavalleriestr. DZ
Kennedydamm AU
Kettwiger Str. CV
Klever Str. AU
Klosterstr. BV 56
Kölner Str. BV
Königsallee EZ
Königsberger CV 58
Kopernikusstr. AX 60
Kronprinzenstr. AX
Kruppstr. BX
Lenaustr. CU
Lessingpl. BX
Lichtstr. CV 62
Lindemannstr. CV
Lorettostr. AX 64
Luegallee AV
Luisenstr. EZ
Marktpl. DY 68
Martin-Luther-Pl. EZ 69
Max.-Weyhe-Allee EY 70
Mecumstr. BX
Merowingerstr. AX
Mintropstr. BV 71
Mörsenbroicher Weg CU
Moltkestr. BU
Mühlenstr. DY 73
Münsterstr. BU
Nördl.Zubringer BU 77
Nordstr. EY
Oberbilker Allee BX
Oberbilker Markt BX 80
Oberkasseler Br. DY
Oststr. EZ
Pempelforter Str. BV 84
Plockstr. AX 86
Poststr. DZ
Prinz-Georg-Str. EY
Rather Str. BU
Ratinger Str. DY 88
Reichsstr. AX
Rethelstr. BV
Ronsdorfer Str. CX
Roßstr. BU
Schadowpl. EY 90
Schadowstr. EY 91
Scheurenstr. BV 92
Schillerpl. BV 93
Schinkelstr. BV
Schirmestr. BV 94
Schneider-Wibbel-Gasse DY 95
Schulstr. DZ 96
Schumannstr. BV
Schwanenmarkt DZ 97
Siegburger Str. CX
Simrockstr. CU 98
Sonnenstr. BX 99
Steinstr. EZ
Sternstr. EY
Stoffeler Kapellenweg BX
Stoffeler Str. CX 100
Stresemannstr. EZ
Stromstr. AV
Südring AX
Th.-Heuss-Br. AU
Tiergartenstr. CU
Tonhallenstr. EY 101
Uerdinger Str. AU
Ulmenstr. BU
Vagedesstr. EY 104
Vautierstr. CU
Venloer Str. EY 105
Victoriapl. DY
Völklinger Str. AX
Volmerswerther Str. AX
Werdener Str. CV
Witzelstr. BX 114
Worringer Pl. BV 115
Worringer Str. BV

Madison I, Graf-Adolf-Str. 94, ✉ 40210, ✆ (0211) 1 68 50, *Fax (0211) 1685328, reservierung@madison-hotels.de*, – rm, – 40. AE VISA BV n
Meals *(closed Saturday and Sunday) (dinner only)* (residents only) – **100 rm** 110/140 – 130/170.
◆ The birthplace of the great actor Gustav Gründgens is nowadays much appreciated by travellers for its comfortable, country-style rooms.

Günnewig Hotel Uebachs without rest, Leopoldstr. 5, ✉ 40211, ✆ (0211) 17 37 10, *Fax (0211) 17371555, hotel.uebachs@guennewig.de* – – 25. AE VISA JCB BV r
82 rm 85/99 – 110.
◆ A quiet side-street location in central Düsseldorf makes this charming hotel an ideal base for exploring this fascinating city.

Stadt München without rest, Pionierstr. 6, ✉ 40215, ✆ (0211) 38 65 50, *Fax (0211) 38655900, info@hotel-stadt-muenchen.de*, – – 30. VISA EZ m
90 rm 65/100 – 100/130.
◆ Contemporary, functional rooms, impeccable service and a location just a few minutes walk from the Altstadt are the great advantages of this establishment.

Burns Art Hotel, Bahnstr. 76, ✉ 40210, ✆ (0211) 7 79 29 10, *Fax (0211) 77929177, info@hotel-burns.de* – , rm, . AE VISA. EZ e
Sila Thai (Thai) **Meals** 40/43 and à la carte 23/37 – **35 rm** 125 – 145 – 3 suites.
◆ Behind the spruced-up 1898 façade pulses the life of a designer hotel which has successfully combined Italian charm and Asian minimalism. The ground floor Sila Thai restaurant adds to the fascinating mixture.

Madison II without rest, Graf-Adolf-Str. 47, ✉ 40210, ✆ (0211) 38 80 30, *Fax (0211) 3880388, c.bohacek@madison-hotels.de* – . AE VISA JCB EZ a
closed end December - early January and July – **24 rm** 85/125 – 105/150.
◆ A comfortable, country-house atmosphere is created by lovely furniture in natural wood. Residents of both Madison hotels can test their fitness in the private sports-club.

Carat Hotel without rest, Benrather Str. 7a, ✉ 40213, ✆ (0211) 1 30 50, *Fax (0211) 322214, info-d@carat-hotel.de*, – – 20. AE VISA
73 rm 125/135 – 150/155.
◆ Reliable, well looked-after accommodation in a city hotel. Good tramway connections. Secretarial and translations services available. DZ r

Antares without rest, Corneliusstr. 82, ✉ 40215, ✆ (0211) 38 65 60, *Fax (0211) 382050, info@antares-duesseldorf.de* – – 20. AE VISA JCB BX s
closed 20 December - 3 January – **48 rm** 71/78 – 91/98.
◆ This solidly built city centre establishment offers modern, soundproofed rooms for a relaxed stay. Office facilities for business travellers.

InterCityHotel, Graf-Adolf-Str. 81, ✉ 40210, ✆ (0211) 43 69 40, *Fax (0211) 43694499, duesseldorf@intercityhotel.de* – , rm, – 55. AE VISA JCB. rest BV k
Meals *(closed Saturday and Sunday)* à la carte 17/21 – 12 – **146 rm** 115 – 130.
◆ Two interconnecting town houses accommodate modern and functional good-sized rooms, with a bright breakfast room facing the courtyard. Bistro-style restaurant with glass façade overlooking the street.

Asahi without rest, Kurfürstenstr. 30, ✉ 40211, ✆ (0211) 3 61 20, *Fax (0211) 3612345, info@hotel-asahi.com*, – – 15. AE VISA JCB BV t
53 rm 125 – 145.
◆ Newspapers, breakfasts, special kinds of tea all proclaim this to be an authentically Japanese establishment. New sauna with the latest in showers, steam baths and solarium.

Astoria without rest, Jahnstr. 72, ✉ 40215, ✆ (0211) 38 51 30, *Fax (0211) 372089, info@hotel-astoria-dus.de* – . AE VISA JCB. BX b
closed 18 December - 3 January – **26 rm** 84/90 – 105/120 – 3 suites.
◆ Behind the venerable façade are welcoming, light and airy rooms. Relatively tranquil location. Impeccably run. Private parking.

Windsor without rest, Grafenberger Allee 36, ✉ 40237, ✆ (0211) 91 46 80, *Fax (0211) 9146840, dkiermeier@t-online.de*, – . AE VISA JCB BV c
18 rm 90 – 100.
◆ Fine Old-Town residence with a traditional sandstone façade. Period furniture harmonises with lovingly restored arched doorways and plaster ceilings.

Orangerie without rest, Bäckergasse 1, 40213, (0211) 86 68 00, *Fax (0211) 8668099, hotelorangerie@t-online.de* – – 30. DZ n
27 rm 100/150 – 126/180.
◆ In the very centre of the Old Town stands this neo-Classical edifice, framed by historic buildings like the Speesche Palais, the old Orangery, and the Maxkirche.

An der Kö without rest, Talstr. 9, 40217, (0211) 37 10 48, *Fax (0211) 370835, hotelanderkoe@t-online.de* – . EZ n
45 rm 87 – 123.
◆ Contemporary décor combined with professional office facilities, including dictation, typing, fax and translation. Private parking in the city centre an additional advantage.

Residenz without rest, Worringer Str. 88, 40211, (0211) 5 50 48 80, *Fax (0211) 55048877, info@residenzhotelduesseldorf.de* – . BV z
34 rm 75 – 95.
◆ In the heart of Düsseldorf with direct bus and metro connections to airport and trade fair grounds. Functional rooms with cherrywood furniture. One non-smoking floor.

Victorian, Königstr. 3a (1st floor), 40212, (0211) 8 65 50 22, *Fax (0211) 8655013, info@restaurant-victorian.de* – . EZ c
closed Sunday and Bank Holidays – **Meals** (booking essential) 35 *(lunch)* and à la carte 53/73, – ***Bistro im Victorian*** *(closed Sunday dinner and Bank Holidays)* **Meals** à la carte 25/38.
Spec. Dreierlei von der Gänsestopfleber mit Essig von der Trockenbeerenauslese. Steinbutt auf Mandelpolenta mit geschmorten Bohnen und Haselnusscrêpe. Baeckeofe von der Lammschulter mit La Ratte-Kartoffeln und Wildkräutern.
◆ Enjoy classic cooking in the elegant, English-style restaurant. Agreeable atmosphere created by chandeliers, mirrors, leather seats and benches. The bistro one floor lower down is no less stylish.

Weinhaus Tante Anna, Andreasstr. 2, 40213, (0211) 13 11 63, *Fax (0211) 132974, info@tanteanna.de* – DY c
closed Sunday and Bank Holidays, except exhibitions – **Meals** *(dinner only)* (booking essential) à la carte 31/47, .
◆ The 1593 chapel of a Jesuit monastery is now a cosy and characterful restaurant, with fine old paintings and antique furnishings.

La Terrazza, Königsallee 30 (3th floor), 40212, (0211) 32 75 40, *Fax (0211) 320975* – . EZ v
closed Sunday and Bank Holidays, except exhibitions – **Meals** (booking essential) 70 and à la carte 47/64, .
◆ With its glass walls, this is an excellent place to stop during your stroll round town. Mediterranean atmosphere and food with an Italian touch.

La Lampada, Hüttenstr. 9, 40215, (0211) 37 47 92, *Fax (0211) 377799, info@lalampada.de*, – EZ a
closed Saturday lunch and Sunday, except exhibitions – **Meals** à la carte 22/35.
◆ Diners are cordially invited to take their places at attractively-laid tables in this restaurant's refined setting. Fresh produce is the basis of the Italian cuisine.

Nippon Kan, Immermannstr. 35, 40210, (0211) 17 34 70, *Fax (0211) 3613625, nippon-kan@dnk.jis.de* – . BV g
closed Sunday – **Meals** (Japanese) (booking essential) 36/92 and à la carte 22/49.
◆ This is the place for enjoying Japanese delicacies in a totally authentic setting - ikebana-decorated tatami rooms, rice matting, cushions and low-slung tables.

Brewery-inns :

Zum Schiffchen, Hafenstr. 5, 40213, (0211) 13 24 21, *Fax (0211) 134596, info.schiffchen@stockheim.de*, – DZ f
closed 23 December - 1 January, Sunday and Bank Holidays, except exhibitions – **Meals** à la carte 23/39.
◆ 350-plus years old, this venerable beer-hall serves traditional Rhineland dishes at well-scrubbed tables as well as in the famous and attractive beer garden.

at Düsseldorf-Angermund *North : 15 km, by Danziger Straße* AU :

Haus Litzbrück, Bahnhofstr. 33, 40489, (0203) 99 79 60, *Fax (0203) 9979653, info@hotel-litzbrueck.de*, , , , – – 30. rest
Meals *(closed Monday, except Bank Holidays)* à la carte 23/40 – **22 rm** 78/89 – 98.
◆ Litzbrück stands in its own park in the idyllic landscape of the Lower Rhine. Guests are accommodated in an aristocratic edifice dating from the 1930s. Classic restaurant in a refined setting, charming side rooms. Garden terrace.

at Düsseldorf-Derendorf :

Villa Viktoria without rest, Blumenthalstr. 12, ✉ 40476, ℘ (0211) 46 90 00, *Fax (0211) 46900601, info@villaviktoria.com*, – 15. BU c
closed 23 December - 5 January – 18 – **40 suites** 155 – 235.
◆ This architectural gem from 1914 offers tastefully decorated suites to discerning guests. Garden terrace with a garland of columns.

Lindner Hotel Rhein Residence, Kaiserswerther Str. 20, ✉ 40477, ℘ (0211) 4 99 90, *Fax (0211) 4999100, info.rheinresidence@lindner.de*, rm, – 15. ABU f
closed 23 December - 1 January – **Meals** à la carte 23/33 – 15 – **126 rm** 140 – 165.
◆ Close to the Rhine promenade and the Königsallee this city hotel provides Economy, Business and First Class rooms with bright designs and good technical facilities. Contemporary restaurant with international cuisine.

NH Düsseldorf-Messe, Münsterstr. 230, ✉ 40470, ℘ (0211) 2 39 48 60, *Fax (0211) 239486100, nhduesseldorfmesse@nh-hotels.com*, rm, – 250. BU a
Meals à la carte 25/34 – 16 – **330 rm** 117.
◆ This hotel has contemporary written all over it, from the large reception area with practical design features to the functional furnishings of the rooms.

Gildors Hotel without rest (with guest house), Collenbachstr. 51, ✉ 40476, ℘ (0211) 5 15 85 00, *Fax (0211) 51585050, mail@gildors-hotel.de* –
closed 24 December - 1 January **50 rm** 92 – 155.
◆ Close to the centre, this establishment has a spacious breakfast room with views into the courtyard. Trade fair grounds, main station and airport only minutes away. BU n

Cascade without rest, Kaiserswerther Str. 59, ✉ 40477, ℘ (0211) 49 22 00, *Fax (0211) 4922022, info@hotel-cascade.de* –
closed Christmas - early January – **29 rm** 78/82 – 92/102. AU c
◆ Functional rooms with good facilities. Central location on the edge of the Old Town ideal for business people and tourists alike.

at Düsseldorf-Düsseltal :

Tafelspitz 1876, Grunerstr. 42a, ✉ 40239, ℘ (0211) 1 71 73 61, *Fax (0211) 1717361*, – BU b
closed Sunday and Monday – **Meals** *(dinner only)* 35/60 and à la carte.
◆ The striped wallpaper, the black, leather chairs and the clean lines proclaim the discreet elegance of this restaurant housed in an office and residential building.

at Düsseldorf-Golzheim :

Hilton, Georg-Glock-Str. 20, ✉ 40474, ℘ (0211) 4 37 70, *Fax (0211) 43772519, info.duesseldorf@hilton.com*, rm, – 890. rest AU r
Meals à la carte 35/49 – 20 – **375 rm** 140/195 – 160/215.
◆ Completely rebuilt in 2003, this exclusive establishment presents its glittering new face to the world. Warm colour schemes add a touch of luxury to the bedrooms. Elegant restaurant.

Radisson SAS Hotel, Karl-Arnold-Platz 5, ✉ 40474, ℘ (0211) 4 55 30, *Fax (0211) 4553110, info.duesseldorf@radissonsas.com*, – rm, – 450. rest AU q
Meals à la carte 32/48 – 18 – **309 rm** 159 – 7 suites.
◆ The hotel boasts a 10th floor conference centre with a fabulous view over the city. Guests can relax in the Pool-Club with whirlpool bath, fitness centre and massage. Light and airy atmosphere in Le Jardin restaurant.

Rosati, Felix-Klein-Str. 1, ✉ 40474, ℘ (0211) 4 36 05 03, *Fax (0211) 452963, remo@rosati.de*, – AU s
closed Saturday lunch and Sunday, except exhibitions – **Meals** (booking essential) 55 and à la carte 35/47 – ***Rosatidue*** : **Meals** à la carte 25/36.
◆ Renzo and Remo Rosati have been treating their guests to classic Italian dishes for decades. Informal but elegant bistro-style atmosphere, comfortable furnishings, and an open kitchen add to the Rosati experience.

at Düsseldorf-Kaiserswerth *North : 10 km, by Kaiserswerther Straße* AU :

Barbarossa without rest, Niederrheinstr. 365, ✉ 40489, ℘ (0211) 4 08 09 20, *Fax (0211) 40809270, info@hotel-barbarossa.com*, – – 50.
13 – **50 rm** 89/92 – 99.
◆ All the rooms in this refurbished hotel have been delightfully decorated and furnished in Italian country-house style. Some boast splendid brass bedsteads.

Im Schiffchen (Bourgueil), Kaiserswerther Markt 9 (1st floor), ✉ 40489, ✆ (0211) 40 10 50, *Fax (0211) 403667, restaurant.imschiffchen@t-online.de* – AE ⓓ MC VISA. *closed Holy Week, 3 weeks July - August, Sunday and Monday* – **Meals** *(dinner only)* (booking essential) à la carte 76/100 ♀.
Spec. Salat vom Hummer mit Staudensellerie und Meerrettichschaum. Gegrillte Gauthier-Taube mit Schnepfenjus. Bitter Moon.
♦ The classically elegant "Schiffchen" is on the first floor of an historic high-gabled house. Some of the country's finest French cuisine.

Bistro Jean-Claude im Schiffchen, Kaiserswerther Markt 9 (ground floor), ✉ 40489, ✆ (0211) 40 10 50, Fax (0211) 403667, *restaurant.imschiffchen@t-online.de* –
closed Holy Week, 3 weeks July - August, Sunday and Monday – **Meals** *(dinner only)* (booking essential) à la carte 40/47.
♦ White predominates in this informal version of the highly rated Schiffchen restaurant, where Maître Bourgueil offers international, French-influenced dishes.

at Düsseldorf-Lörick *West : 6 km, by Luegallee AV and Arnulfstraße :*

Fischerhaus, Bonifatiusstr. 35, ✉ 40547, ✆ (0211) 59 79 79, *Fax (0211) 5979759, mail@fischerhaus-hotel.de* – rm, TV P. ⓓ MC VISA
closed 23 December - 2 January – **Meals** see ***Hummerstübchen*** below – 8 – **41 rm** 80 – 105.
♦ This brick-built hotel enjoys a central but tranquil location in a leafy setting. Footpaths and yacht harbour right by the door.

Hummerstübchen (Nöthel) - Hotel Fischerhaus, Bonifatiusstr. 35, ✉ 40547, ✆ (0211) 59 44 02, *Fax (0211) 5979759, mail@hummerstuebchen.de* – P. ⓓ MC VISA
closed 27 December - 6 January, Sunday and Bank Holidays, except exhibitions – **Meals** *(dinner only)* (booking essential) 95/109 and à la carte 70/89 ♀.
Spec. Hummer-Menu. Hummersuppe mit Champagner. Loup de mer auf der Haut gebraten mit Zimt-Vanille-Fumet.
♦ The "Lobster Parlour" is as good as its name, though Peter Nöthel and his team offer a whole variety of tempting and expertly prepared dishes in this elegant setting.

at Düsseldorf-Lohausen *North : 8 km, by Danziger Straße AU :*

ArabellaSheraton Airport Hotel, at the airport, ✉ 40474, ✆ (0211) 4 17 30, *Fax (0211) 4173707, airporthotel.duesseldorf@arabellasheraton.com* – rm, TV – 120. AE ⓓ MC VISA JCB. rest
Meals à la carte 36/48 – 19 – **200 rm** 185/240 – 210/265.
♦ Whether you want to get a taste of the big wide world or are just passing through, this airport hotel is conveniently connected with both the arrival and departure halls. Semi-circular restaurant on two floors with splendid panoramic windows.

at Düsseldorf-Mörsenbroich :

Renaissance, Nördlicher Zubringer 6, ✉ 40470, ✆ (0211) 6 21 60, *Fax (0211) 6216666, rhi.dusrn.dos@renaissancehotels.com*, – rm, TV – 260. AE ⓓ MC VISA JCB BU e
Meals à la carte 23/42 – 17 – **244 rm** 129 – 3 suites.
♦ Secluded, private atmosphere in the sixth-floor Club. Active relaxation in the penthouse swimming-pool with a view over Düsseldorf's rooftops. Also sauna, solarium and steam-bath. The restaurant opens out into the bright and airy reception hall.

at Düsseldorf-Oberbilk :

NH Düsseldorf, Kölner Str. 186, ✉ 40227, ✆ (0211) 7 81 10, *Fax (0211) 7811800, nhduesseldorf@nh-hotels.com*, – rm, TV – 90. AE ⓓ MC VISA JCB BV b
Meals à la carte 25/38 – 16 – **338 rm** 77 – 77/97.
♦ With its central and very accessible location, this imposing glass-fronted atrium hotel is ideal for business travellers. All rooms with PC facilities. The foyer restaurant is the place for a buffet lunch.

at Düsseldorf-Oberkassel *West : 5 km, by Luegallee AV :*

Lindner Congress Hotel, Lütticher Str. 130, ✉ 40547, ✆ (0211) 5 99 70, *Fax (0211) 59971111, info.congresshotel@lindner.de*, – rm, TV P – 240. AE ⓓ MC VISA. rest
closed 22 December - 2 January – **Meals** à la carte 23/37 – 15 – **254 rm** 130/150 – 140/170.
♦ Up-to-the-minute business establishment. Functional rooms with fax, modem and internet connection, some with PC. Conference facilities with the latest technology. Contemporary décor gives the Belle Etoile restaurant a bistro-like character.

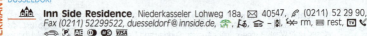

Inn Side Residence, Niederkasseler Lohweg 18a, ✉ 40547, ☎ (0211) 52 29 90, *Fax (0211) 52299522, duesseldorf@innside.de*, – rm, rest, AE VISA
Meals *(closed Saturday lunch and Sunday)* à la carte 27/46 – **126 rm** 146 – 180 – 6 suites.
• This conveniently situated hotel offers a fascinating experience in modern living with innovative design and elegant lines characterising everything, from the capacious reception area to your own room. Contemporary restaurant in the style of a dining room.

Mercure Seestern, Fritz-Vomfelde-Str.38, ✉ 40547, ☎ (0211) 53 07 60, *Fax (0211) 53076444, h2199@accor.com*, – rm, – 80. AE VISA JCB
Meals (Italian) à la carte 23/36 – **160 rm** 139 – 169.
• The spacious reception area sets the tone for the contemporary style which pervades this hotel, located in the commercial district. First-floor restaurant with cool, modern décor.

Courtyard by Marriott, Am Seestern 16, ✉ 40547, ☎ (0211) 59 59 59, *Fax (0211) 593569, courtyard.duesseldorf@courtyard.com*, – rm, – 120. AE VISA JCB
Meals à la carte 22/31 – 14 – **221 rm** 99 – 144.
• Spacious rooms offer every comfort as well as all the facilities a business traveller could wish for. Eight non-smoking floors. Classically stylish restaurant.

Novotel-City-West, Niederkasseler Lohweg 179, ✉ 40547, ☎ (0211) 52 06 00, *Fax (0211) 52060888, h3279@accor.com*, – rm, – 275. AE VISA. rest
Meals à la carte 23/34 – **232 rm** 140/150 – 170/180.
• Opened in 2001, this functional, modern establishment is perfectly attuned to the needs of business travellers and conference participants.

Hanseat without rest, Belsenstr. 6, ✉ 40545, ☎ (0211) 5 50 27 20, *Fax (0211) 55027277, info@hotel-hanseat.de* – AE VISA
37 rm 90/95 – 115/130.
• A touch of elegance behind a lovely Art Nouveau façade, with antique furniture and individual details enhancing comfortable rooms and public spaces. Attractive garden terrace.

De' Medici, Amboßstr. 3, ✉ 40547, ☎ (0211) 59 41 51, *Fax (0211) 592612, demedici@aol.com* – AE VISA
closed Saturday lunch, Sunday and Bank Holidays, except exhibitions – **Meals** (Italian) (booking essential) 42/45 and à la carte 27/45.
• Well-run by the Pocaterra family for many years. Personal recommendations complement the classically Italian written menu.

at Düsseldorf-Pempelfort :

Rossini, Kaiserstr. 5, ✉ 40479, ☎ (0211) 49 49 94, *Fax (0211) 4910819, info@restaurant-rossini.de*, – AE VISA JCB. EY r
closed 3 weeks July - August, Sunday and Bank Holidays, except exhibitions – **Meals** (Italian) 64/82 and à la carte 48/65 ♀.
• Much-favoured meeting place, with gourmet Italian cuisine and superb wine cellar. Elegant atmosphere with terracotta tiling in modern business premises.

at Düsseldorf-Unterbilk :

Courtyard by Marriott, Speditionstr. 11, ✉ 40221, ☎ (0211) 4 93 90, *Fax (0211) 49392000, cy.dushf.sales.mgr@courtyard.com*, – rm, – 90. AE VISA by Gladbacher Straße AX
Meals à la carte 27/39 – 15 – **139 rm** 125 – 140 – 6 suites.
• Opened in 2001, this establishment has a homely atmosphere thanks to the contemporary furnishings and warm earth-colours of the décor in rooms and suites.

Sorat, Volmerswerther Str. 35, ✉ 40221, ☎ (0211) 3 02 20, *Fax (0211) 3022555, duesseldorf@sorat-hotels.com*, – rm, – 130. AE VISA JCB AX c
Meals *(closed Sunday, except exhibitions)* à la carte 24/31 – **160 rm** 118/128 – 148/168.
• Comfortable rooms with warm colours and up-to-the-minute design features may tempt you to linger longer in what used to be the port area and is now the media and administrative district. Bistro-style modern restaurant.

Berens am Kai, Kaistr. 16, ✉ 40221, ☎ (0211) 3 00 67 50, *Fax (0211) 30067515, info@berensamkai.de*, – AE VISA AX d
closed 1 to 7 January, Saturday lunch, Sunday and Bank Holidays – **Meals** à la carte 57/73.
• Thanks to an imposing glass façade and a harbourside location, diners choosing this up-to-the-minute establishment will enjoy a lovely view of the Rhine.

XX **Schorn** with rm, Martinstr. 46a, ✉ 40223, ☎ (0211) 3 98 19 72, *Fax (0211) 8766155* – TV. MC. rm AX s
closed 2 weeks July - August – **Meals** *(closed Sunday and Monday) (dinner only)* (booking essential) à la carte 34/67 ♀, – **4 rm** ☐ 105 – 150.
◆ Fine French-inspired cuisine is served in what was once a patisserie near St Martin's Church. Prettily decorated rooms available for overnight guests.

XX **Rheinturm Top 180**, Stromstr. 20, ✉ 40221, ☎ (0211) 8 48 58, *Fax (0211) 325619, rheinturm@guennewig.de,* ※ Düsseldorf and Rhein (|, charge) – – 40. AE MC VISA JCB. AV a
Meals à la carte 34/53.
◆ It takes less than 60 seconds to whizz up to the 172-metre-high restaurant, which slowly rotates around its axis, giving you a superb all-round panorama.

at Düsseldorf-Unterrath *North : 7 km, by Ulmenstraße* BU *:*

Lindner Hotel Airport, Unterrather Str. 108, ✉ 40468, ☎ (0211) 9 51 60, *Fax (0211) 9516516, info.airport@lindner.de,* – |, rm, TV P – 130. AE MC VISA JCB
Meals à la carte 25/38 – ☐ 16 – **201 rm** 89/124 – 99/134.
◆ Weary travellers can wing their way here and refuel in the fitness centre, which also offers hydrojet massage and a relaxation programme specially designed for frequent flyers. The restaurant opening onto the hall is contemporary in style.

Avidon without rest, Unterrather Str. 42, ✉ 40468, ☎ (0211) 95 19 50, *Fax (0211) 95195333, hotel@avidon.de* – | TV P – 15. AE MC VISA JCB
34 rm ☐ 139 – 159.
◆ Rooms with high-quality contemporary décor and ample work-desks, well-located in relation to airport, trade fair grounds and city centre. 24-hour bar.

at Meerbusch-Büderich *Northwest : 7 km, by Luegallee* AV *and Neusser Straße :*

XX **Landhaus Mönchenwerth**, Niederlöricker Str. 56 (at the boat landing stage), ✉ 40667, ☎ (02132) 75 76 50, *Fax (02132) 757638, contact@moenchenwerth.de,* ≤, , beer garden – P – 20. AE MC VISA
closed Monday – **Meals** *(weekdays dinner only)* à la carte 44/54.
◆ This modernised country house stands right on the Rhine. Contemporary, welcoming restaurant with subtle decor. Classic dishes are the order of the day.

X **Lindenhof**, Dorfstr. 48, ✉ 40667, ☎ (02132) 26 64, *Fax (02132) 10196, service@lindenhof-restaurant.de,* – AE MC VISA
closed Monday – **Meals** (booking essential for dinner) à la carte 23/37.
◆ Brick-built establishment with country-style interior and changing picture collection. Local dishes, served in summer in a little beer garden.

at Meerbusch - Langst-Kirst *Northwest : 14 km, by Luegallee* AV *and Neusser Straße :*

Rheinhotel Vier Jahreszeiten , Zur Rheinfähre 14, ✉ 40668, ☎ (02150) 91 40, *Fax (02150) 914900, info@rheinhotel-meerbusch.de,* , beer garden, – |, rm, TV P – 120. AE MC VISA JCB
closed 20 December - 2 January – ***Bellevue*** *(closed October - April Monday - Tuesday) (October - April dinner only)* **Meals** à la carte 36/44 – ***Orangerie*** **Meals** 25 (only buffet lunch) – ***Langster Fährhaus*** *(closed Monday - Tuesday)* **Meals** à la carte 19/26 – **75 rm** ☐ 113/129 – 133/143.
◆ This country hotel stands right by the landing-stage on the Rhine opposite airport and trade fair grounds. Rooms have all amenities. The bright and elegant Bellevue restaurant is in the villa, while the Langster Fährhaus has a more earthy character.

Dortmund *Nordrhein-Westfalen* 543 L 6 – *pop. 598 000 – alt. 87 m.*
Düsseldorf 78.

at Dortmund-Syburg *Southwest : 13 km :*

XXXX ✿✿ **La Table**, Hohensyburgstr. 200 (at the casino), ✉ 44265, ☎ (0231) 7 74 07 37, *Fax (0231) 774077, latable@westspiel.de,* – P. AE MC VISA JCB.
closed 3 weeks July - August, 1 to 10 January, Monday - Tuesday and Bank Holidays – **Meals** *(dinner only)* (booking essential) 68/108 and à la carte 59/89 ♀, .
Spec. Variation von der Gänsestopfleber mit glasierten Äpfeln. Rochenflügel und mild geräucherte Makrele mit Ratatouille en gelée. Teegeräuchertes Filet vom Wagyu Rind mit Pecannüssen und Chinakohl.
◆ A careful combination of tradition and modernity gives this establishment its special quality. Exquisite French cuisine and attentive service.

Essen Nordrhein-Westfalen 543 L 5 – pop. 587 000 – alt. 120 m.
Düsseldorf 37.

at Essen-Kettwig South : 11 km :

Résidence (Bühler) with rm, Auf der Forst 1, ✉ 45219, ✆ (02054) 9 55 90, Fax (02054) 82501, info@hotel-residence.de, – P. AE VISA
closed 3 weeks July - August and 1 to 6 January – **Meals** (closed Sunday and Monday) (dinner only) (booking essential) 109 and à la carte 64/86 – 14 – **18 rm** 99 – 125.
Spec. Mit Gänseleber und Trüffel gefüllter Schmorapfel. Warm geräucherter Hummer mit Batatepüree und Brunnenkressesalat. Steinbutt mit Tomaten und Oliven überbacken auf Tintenfisch-Bolognese.
◆ A winning formula ! Classic elegance in this Art Nouveau villa, exemplary service, lavishly decorated tables and creative French cuisine.

Grevenbroich Nordrhein-Westfalen 543 M 3 – pop. 62 000 – alt. 60 m.
Düsseldorf 28.

Zur Traube (Kaufmann) with rm, Bahnstr. 47, ✉ 41515, ✆ (02181) 6 87 67, Fax (02181) 61122, zurtraube-grevenbroich@t-online.de – P. AE VISA. rm
closed 22 March - 12 April, 15 July - 9 August, 24 December - 6 January – **Meals** (closed Sunday and Monday) (booking essential) 48 (lunch)/108 and à la carte 61/97 – **6 rm** 118/145 – 150/190.
Spec. Terrine von der Bresse Taube mit Artischockensalat. Variation vom Bretonischem Hummer in rosa Champagner. Gratiniertes Limonenparfait mit Himbeeren.
◆ You will appreciate the classically elegant ambience of this temple to fine dining. Expertly made from the finest ingredients, your meal is served with impeccable style.

FRANKFURT ON MAIN (FRANKFURT AM MAIN) Hessen 543 P 10 – pop. 650 000 – alt. 95 m.

See : Zoo★★ FX – Goethe's House (Goethehaus)★ GZ – Cathedral (Dom)★ : Gothic Tower★★, Choir-stalls★, Museum★ HZ – Tropical Garden (Palmengarten)★ CV – Senckenberg-Museum★ (Department of Palaeontology★★) CV **M9** – Städel Museum (Städelsches Kunstinstitut und Städtische Galerie) ★★ GZ – Museum of Applied Arts (Museum für Angewandte Kunst)★ HZ – German Cinema Museum (Deutsches Filmmuseum)★ GZ **M7** – Museum of Modern Art (Museum für moderne Kunst)★ HY **M10**.

18 Frankfurt-Niederrad, Golfstr. 41 (by Kennedy-Allee CDX), ✆ (069) 6 66 23 17 ; 9 Frankfurt-Niederrad, Schwarzwaldstr. 127 (by Kennedy-Allee CDX), ✆ (069)96 74 13 53 ; 18 Hanau-Wilhelmsbad, Wilhelmsbader Allee 32 (East : 12 km by Hanauer Landstraße FX), ✆ (06181) 8 20 71 ; 18 Dreieich, Hofgut Neuhof (South : 13 km by A 661), ✆ (06102) 32 70 10.

Rhein-Main (Southwest : 12 km), ✆ (069) 69 00.
at Neu-Isenburg, Kurt-Schumacher-Str., (South : 7 km).
Exhibition Centre (Messegelände) (CX), ✆ (069) 7 57 50, Fax (069) 75756433.
Tourist Information, Main Station (Hauptbahnhof), ✉ (069) 21 23 88 00, Fax (069) 21237880.
Tourist Information, im Römer, ✉ 60311, ✆ (069) 21 23 88 00, Fax (069) 21237880, info@tcf.frankfurt.de.
ADAC, Schillerstr. 12.
Berlin 537 – Wiesbaden 41 – Bonn 178 – Nürnberg 226 – Stuttgart 204.

Plans on following pages

Steigenberger Frankfurter Hof, Am Kaiserplatz, ✉ 60311, ✆ (069) 2 15 02, Fax (069) 215900, frankfurter-hof@steigenberger.de, , – , rm, – 300. AE VISA JCB. rest GZ e
Meals see also ***Français*** below – ***Oscar's*** (closed Sunday lunch) **Meals** à la carte 27/35 – ***Iroha*** (closed Sunday and Bank Holidays, except exhibitions) **Meals** 35/87 and à la carte – 24 – **332 rm** 395/495 – 445/495 – 10 suites.
◆ A lavish refurbishment has restored the old Steigenberger headquarters, the grand hotel of 1876, to its original glory, visible throughout. Eat in Oscar's in bistro-style, or orientally in the Iroha.

Hessischer Hof, Friedrich-Ebert-Anlage 40, ✉ 60325, ✆ (069) 7 54 00, Fax (069) 75402924, info@hessischer-hof.com – , rm, P – 120. AE VISA JCB. rest CX p
Meals à la carte 46/55 – 19 – **117 rm** 213 – 520 – 3 suites.
◆ Exclusive antiques from the Prince of Hessen make a stay here a real experience. Contemporary rooms of great comfort and elegance will satisfy the most demanding guest. Sèvres porcelain and trompe l'oeil paintings lend the restaurant a special character.

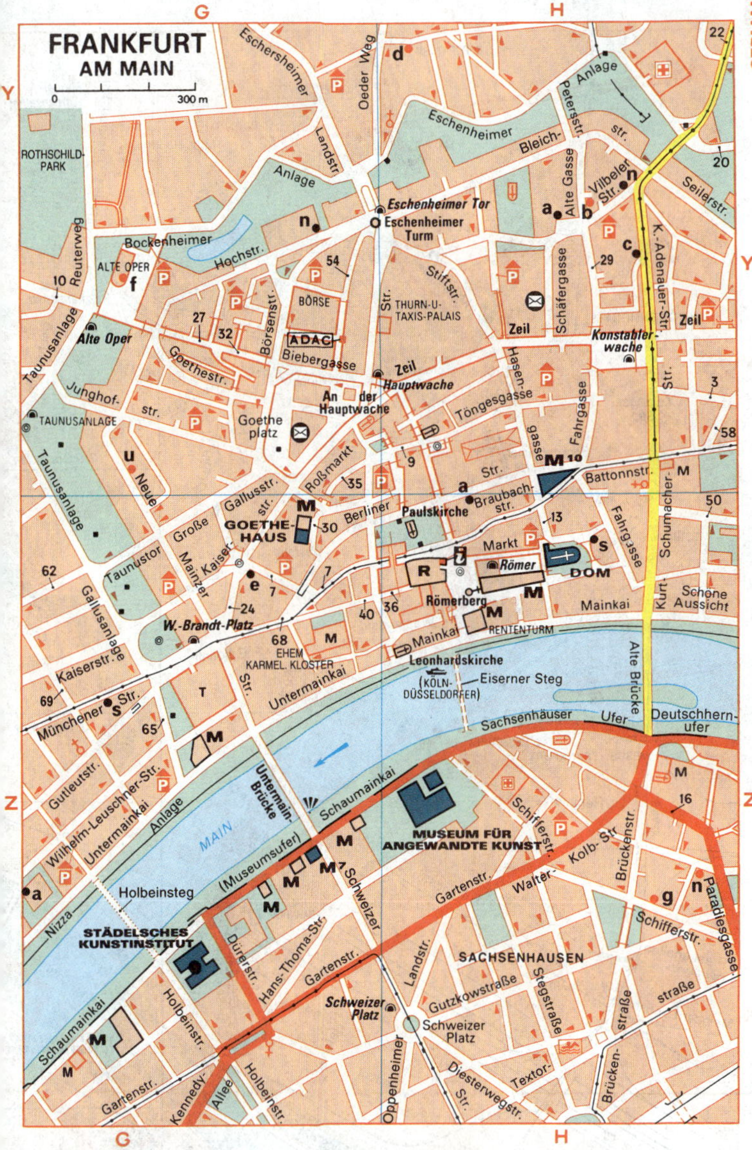

Allerheiligenstr. . . . . HY 3
An der Hauptwache . . . GHY
Bethmannstr. . . . . GZ 7
Bleidenstr. . . . . HY 9
Bockenheimer
Landstr. . . . . GY 10
Domstr. . . . . HZ 13
Elisabethenstr. . . . . HZ 16
Friedberger Anlage . . . . . HY 20
Friedberger Landstr. . . . . HY 22
Friedensstr. . . . . GZ 24
Goethestr. . . . . GY
Gr. Bockenheimer Str. . . . GY 27
Große Friedbergerstr. . . . HY 29
Großer Hirschgraben . . . . GZ 30
Kaiserstr. . . . . GZ
Kalbächer Gasse . . . . GY 32
Kleiner Hirschgraben . . . . GY 35
Limpurgergasse . . . . HZ 36
Münchener Str. . . . . GZ
Münzgasse . . . . GZ 40
Rechneigrabenstr. . . . . . . HZ 50
Roßmarkt . . . . GY
Schillerstr. . . . . GY 54
Stolzestr. . . . . HY 58
Taunusstr. . . . . GZ 62
Untermainanlage . . . . GZ 65
Weißfrauenstr. . . . . GZ 68
Weserstr. . . . . GZ 69
Zeil . . . . HY

C
D
V
X
A 66
EUROPATURM
Miquel- / Adickesallee
Miquelallee
Eschersheimer
Landstr.
Eysseneckstr.
Frauenlobstr.
Franz-Rücker-Allee
Sophienstr.
BOCKENHEIM
Miquelallee
BOTANISCHER GARTEN
GRÜNEBURG-PARK
Holzhausenstr.
12
Str.
Eschersheimer
Fürstenberger
PALMEN-GARTEN
Grüneburgweg
Grüneburgweg
Grüneburgweg
Leipziger Str.
Sophienstr.
Gräfstr.
Bockenheimer Warte
Siesmayerstr.
Liebigstr.
Schloß-
Adalbertstr.
Bockenheimer
Landstr.
WESTBAHNHOF
straße
Gräfstr.
Beethoven-
Westend
ROTHSCHILD PARK
M9
Senckenberganlage
Westendstr.
ALTE OPER
Hochstr.
Hamburger Allee
Th.-Heuss-Allee
Friedrich-Ebert-Anlage
straße
Westendstr.
Guiollettstr.
Neue
Mainzer
Taunusanlage
Goetheplatz
CONGRESS CENTER
MESSETURM
MESSE
MESSE FRANKFURT
Mainzer
Landstr.
Hemmerichsweg
S-BAHN
POL.
Platz der Republik
14
33
Taunusstr.
Str.
Landstr.
Hafenstr.
HAUPT-BAHNHOF
Frankenallee
Frankenallee
Mainzer
GALLUSWARTE
Mainzer Landstr.
Baseler Str.
Untermainkai
Schaumainkai (Museumsufer)
STÄDELSCHES KUNSTINSTITUT
Hafenstr.
Gutleutstr.
Friedensbr.
WESTHAFEN
MAIN
Stresemann-
Allee
allee
Gartenstr.
Gutleutstr.
Kennedy
43-44
STRESEMANNALLEE
FRANKFURT f. AM MAIN
0
500 m

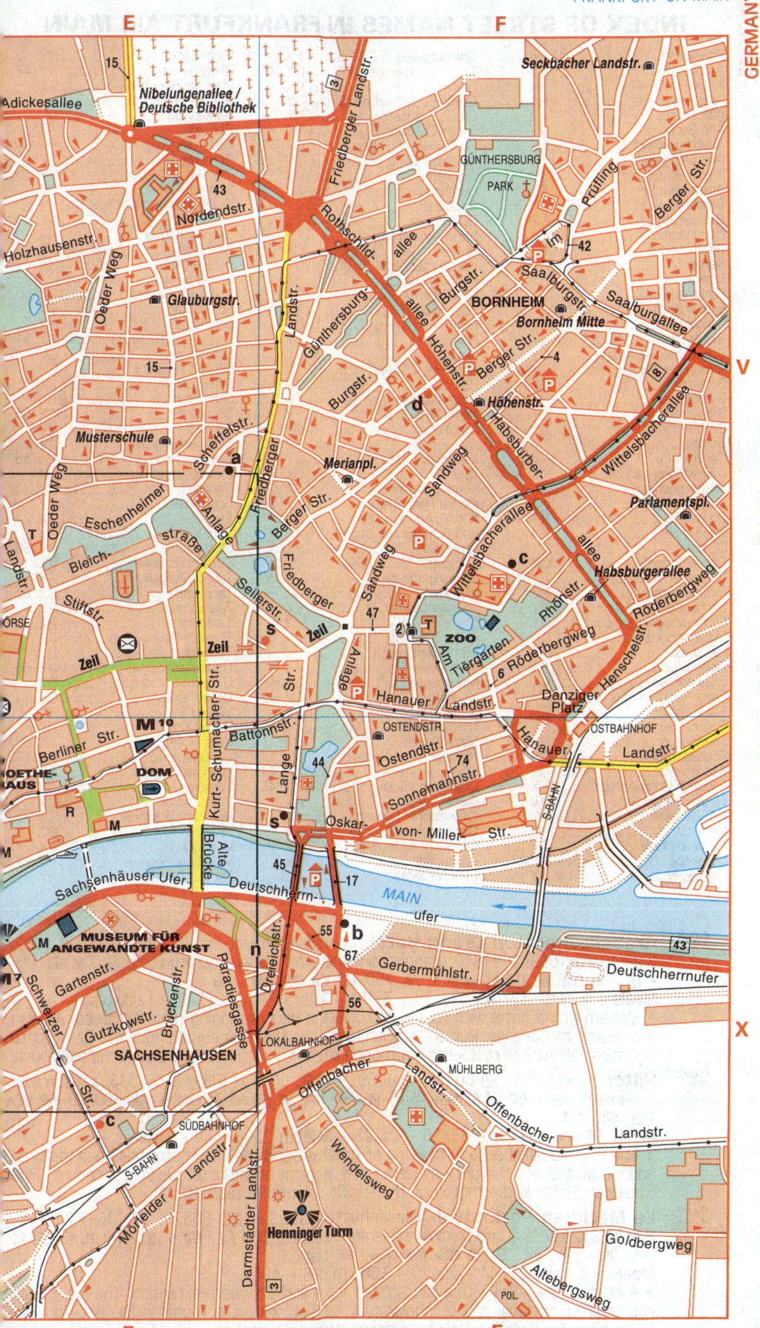
E
F
V
X
Adickesallee
Nibelungenallee /
Deutsche Bibliothek
Seckbacher Landstr.
Friedberger Landstr.
GÜNTHERSBURG
PARK
Prüfling
Berger Str.
Nordendstr.
Holzhausenstr.
Rothschild-
allee
Im
Saalburgstr.
Saalburgallee
Oeder Weg
Glauburgstr.
Günthersburg-
allee
Burgstr.
BORNHEIM
Bornheim Mitte
Höhenstr.
Landstr.
Musterschule
Scheffelstr.
Friedberger
Merianpl.
Habsburger-
allee
Wittelsbacherallee
Sandweg
Parlamentspl.
Eschenheimer
Anlage
Berger Str.
Bleich-
straße
Stiftstr.
Seilerstr.
Friedberger
Anlage
Zeil
Habsburgerallee
Röderbergweg
Rhönstr.
ZOO
Am Tiergarten
Henschelstr.
Danziger
Platz
Hanauer
Landstr.
OSTENDSTR.
OSTBAHNHOF
Berliner Str.
Battonnstr.
Ostendstr.
Sonnemannstr.
DOM
Kurt- Schumacher- Str.
Lange
Oskar-
von- Miller
Str.
S-BAHN
Alte
Brücke
Sachsenhäuser Ufer
Deutschherrn-
ufer
MAIN
MUSEUM FÜR
ANGEWANDTE KUNST
Gartenstr.
Schweizer
Str.
Paradiesgasse
Dreieichstr.
Brückenstr.
Gutzkowstr.
Gerbermühlstr.
Deutschherrnufer
SACHSENHAUSEN
LOKALBAHNHOF
Offenbacher
MÜHLBERG
Landstr.
SÜDBAHNHOF
S-BAHN
Mörfelder
Landstr.
Wendelsweg
Darmstädter Landstr.
Henninger Turm
Goldbergweg
Altebergsweg
POL

INDEX OF STREET NAMES IN FRANKFURT AM MAIN

Adalbertstr. CV
Adickesallee . . . . . EV
Alfred-Brehm-Pl. . . . . FV 2
Allerheiligenstr. . . . . HY 3
Alte Brücke . . . . . HZ
Alte Gasse . . . . . HY
Altebergsweg . . . . . FX
Am Tiergarten . . . . . FV
An der Hauptwache . . . . . GHY
Arnsburger Str. . . . . FV 4
Bärenstr. . . . . FV 6
Baseler Str. CX
Battonnstr. . . . . HY
Beethovenstr. CV
Berger Str. . . . . FV
Berliner Str. . . . . GHZ
Bethmannstr. . . . . GZ 7
Biebergasse . . . . . GY
Bleichstr. . . . . HY
Bleidenstr. . . . . HY 9
Bockenheimer Anlage . . . . . GY
Bockenheimer Landstr. . . . . GY 10
Börsenstr. . . . . GY
Braubachstr. . . . . HZ
Bremer Str. . . . . DV 12
Brückenstr. . . . . HZ
Burgstr. . . . . FV
Danziger Pl. . . . . FV
Darmstädter Landstr. . . . . EFX
Deutschherrnufer . . . . . HZ
Diesterwegstr. . . . . HZ
Domstr. . . . . HZ 13
Dreieichstr. . . . . FX
Dürerstr. . . . . GZ
Düsseldorfer Str. . . . . CX 14
Eckenheimer Landstr. . . . . EV 15
Elisabethenstr. . . . . HZ 16
Eschenheimer Anlage . . . . . HY
Eschersheimer Landstr. . . . . GY
Eyssenecksstr. . . . . DV
Fahrgasse . . . . . HYZ
Flößerbrücke . . . . . FX 17
Frankenallee CX
Franz-Rücker-Allee CV
Frauenlobstr. CV
Friedberger Anlage . . . . . HY 20
Friedberger Landstr. . . . . HY 22
Friedensbrücke CX
Friedensstr. . . . . GZ 24
Friedrich-Ebert-Anlage CVX
Fürstenberger Str. . . . . CDV
Gallusanlage . . . . . GZ
Gartenstr. . . . . GHZ
Gerbermühlstr. . . . . FX
Goethepl. . . . . GY
Goethestr. . . . . GY
Goldbergweg . . . . . FX
Gr. Bockenheimer Str. . . . . GY 27
Gräfstr. CV
Große Eschenheimer Str. . . . . GY
Große Friedbergerstr. . . . . HY 29
Große Gallusstr. . . . . GYZ
Großer Hirschgraben . . . . . GZ 30
Grüneburgweg . . . . . CDV
Guiollettstr. CV
Gunthersburgallee . . . . . FV
Gutleutstr. . . . . GZ
Gutzkowstr. . . . . HZ
Habsburgerallee . . . . . FV
Hafenstr. CX
Hamburger Allee CV
Hanauer Landstr. . . . . FX
Hans-Thoma-Str. . . . . GZ
Hasengasse . . . . . HY
Hemmerichsweg CX
Henschelstr. . . . . FV
Hochstr. . . . . GY
Höhenstr. . . . . FV
Holbeinstr. . . . . GZ
Holzhausenstr. . . . . EV
Im Prüfling . . . . . FV
Junghofstr. . . . . GY
Kaiserstr. . . . . GZ
Kalbächer Gasse . . . . . GY 32
Karlstr. . . . . CX 33
Kennedy-Allee . . . . . GZ
Kleiner Hirschgraben . . . . . GY 35
Konrad-Adenauer-Str. . . . . HY
Kurt-Schumacher-Str. . . . . HYZ
Lange Str. . . . . FX
Leibigstr. CV
Limpurgergasse . . . . . HZ 36
Mainkai . . . . . HZ
Mainzer Landstr. CVX
Markt . . . . . HZ
Miquelallee CV
Mörfelder Landstr. . . . . EX
Münchener Str. . . . . GZ
Münzgasse . . . . . GZ 40
Neebstr. . . . . FV 42
Neue Mainzer Str. . . . . GYZ
Nibelungenallee . . . . . EFV 43
Nizza Anlage . . . . . GZ
Nordendstr. . . . . EV
Obermainanlage . . . . . FX 44
Obermainbrücke . . . . . FX 45
Oeder Weg . . . . . GY
Offenbacher Landstr. . . . . FX
Oppenheimer Landstr. . . . . HZ
Oskar-von-Miller-Str. . . . . FX
Ostendstr. . . . . FX
Paradiesgasse . . . . . HZ
Petersstr. . . . . HY
Pfingstweidstr. . . . . FV 47
Platz der Republik CX
Rechneigrabenstr. . . . . HZ 50
Reuterweg . . . . . GY
Rhönstr. . . . . FV
Röderbergweg . . . . . FV
Römerberg . . . . . HZ
Roßmarkt . . . . . GY
Rothschildallee . . . . . FV
Saalburgallee . . . . . FV
Saalburgstr. . . . . FV
Sachsenhäuser Ufer . . . . . HZ
Sandweg . . . . . FV
Schäfergasse . . . . . HY
Schaumainkai (Museumsufer) . . . . . GHZ
Scheffelstr. . . . . EV
Schifferstr. . . . . HZ
Schillerstr. . . . . GY 54
Schloßstr. CV
Schöne Aussicht . . . . . HZ
Schweizer Pl. . . . . HZ
Schweizer Str. . . . . GHZ
Seehofstr. . . . . FX 55
Seilerstr. . . . . HY
Senckenberganlage CV
Siemensstr. . . . . FX 56
Siesmayerstr. CV
Sonnemannstr. . . . . FX
Sophienstr. CV
Stegstr. . . . . HZ
Stiftstr. . . . . HY
Stolzestr. . . . . HY 58
Stresemannallee . . . . . DX
Taunusanlage . . . . . GY
Taunusstr. . . . . GZ 62
Taunustor . . . . . GZ
Textorstr. . . . . HZ
Theodor-Heuss-Allee CV
Töngesgasse . . . . . HY
Untermainanlage . . . . . GZ 65
Untermainbrücke . . . . . GZ
Untermainkai . . . . . GZ
Vilbeler Str. . . . . HY
Walter-Kolb-Str. . . . . HZ
Wasserweg . . . . . FX 67
Weißfrauenstr. . . . . GZ 68
Wendelsweg . . . . . FX
Weserstr. . . . . GZ 69
Westendstr. CV
Wilhelm-Leuschner-Str. . . . . GZ
Windeckstr. . . . . FX 74
Wittelsbacherallee . . . . . FV
Zeil . . . . . HY

ArabellaSheraton Grand Hotel, Konrad-Adenauer-Str. 7, ✉ 60313, ☎ (069) 2 98 10, *Fax (069) 2981810, grandhotel.frankfurt@arabellasheraton.com*, – rm, – 280. HY c
Meals à la carte 32/42 – 24 – **378 rm** 250/515 – 270/540 – 12 suites.
◆ Modern grand hotel with rooms and suites in decors ranging from Art Deco, Arabian and Asiatic to Bavarian. Roman "spa landscape" in the "Balneum Romanum". Giving onto the main hall, Atrium restaurant with open kitchen and food with a Mediterranean touch.

Hilton, Hochstr. 4, ✉ 60313, ☎ (069) 1 33 80 00, *Fax (069) 13381338, sales_frankfurt@hilton.com*, – rm, – 300. VISA. rest GY n
Meals 33 and à la carte 33/55 – 26 – **342 rm** 229 – 449 – 3 suites.
◆ The fine old bathhouse in the ring of green around the city centre has been restored and integrated into this ultra-modern hotel, where it houses a unique fitness centre. "Fine American Style" is the motto of the Pacific Colours Restaurant.

Le Méridien Parkhotel, Wiesenhüttenplatz 28, ✉ 60329, ☎ (069) 2 69 70, *Fax (069) 2697884, info.frankfurt@lemeridien.com*, – rm, – 180. VISA JCB. rest CX k
Meals à la carte 27/44 – 20 – **300 rm** 165 – 185.
◆ A historic city hotel with a sandstone façade and a modern extension. The Art + Tech rooms are functional and technologically perfect, while the rooms in the Art Nouveau Palais have fine interiors. Informal bistro-style restaurant.

Marriott, Hamburger Allee 2, ✉ 60486, ☎ (069) 7 95 50, *Fax (069) 79552432, info.frankfurt@marriotthotels.com,* < Frankfurt, Fб, ≘s – |‡|, ⇹ rm, ▤ TV ☎ ⇔ – 🎙 600. AE ⓓ MC VISA JCB. ⚘ rest CV a
Meals à la carte 28/39 – ☕ 20 – **588 rm** 155 – 10 suites.
◆ This skyscraper rises high into the clouds opposite the trade fair grounds. It features Frankfurt's biggest ballroom and bedrooms with broadband facilities. Enjoy specialities from the American South West in the Arizona restaurant.

Maritim, Theodor-Heuss-Allee 3, ✉ 60486, ☎ (069) 7 57 80, *Fax (069) 75781000, info.fra@maritim.de,* Fб, ≘s, 🏊 – |‡|, ⇹ rm, ▤ TV ☎ ♿ ⇔ – 🎙 210. AE ⓓ MC VISA JCB. ⚘ rest CVX c
Classico *(closed lunch Saturday and Sunday)* **Meals** à la carte 36/50 – ***SushiSho*** (Japanese) *(closed Saturday and Sunday)* **Meals** à la carte 25/39 – ☕ 21 – **543 rm** 250 – 490 – 8 suites.
◆ Standing among the skyscrapers of the city centre, this hotel offers fantastic views from its upper floors. Tall folk benefit from the extra long beds provided. International cuisine in the elegant Classico, seductive Oriental specialities in the SushiSho.

InterContinental, Wilhelm-Leuschner-Str. 43, ✉ 60329, ☎ (069) 2 60 50, *Fax (069) 252467, frankfurt@interconti.com,* 🏖, Fб, ≘s, 🏊 – |‡|, ⇹ rm, ▤ TV ☎ ♿ – 🎙 400. AE ⓓ MC VISA JCB. ⚘ GZ a
Signatures: **Meals** à la carte 35/49 🍷 – ☕ 21 – **770 rm** 395/445 – 415/465 – 35 suites.
◆ Period furnishings, attractive colours and lovely materials give this hotel on the River Main its individual character. Wonderful city views from the 21st floor conference rooms. Signatures restaurant with warm and elegant decor. Smart conservatory.

Steigenberger Metropolitan, Poststr. 6, ✉ 60329, ☎ (069) 5 06 07 00, *Fax (069) 506070555, metropolitan@steigenberger.de,* Fб, ≘s – |‡|, ⇹ rm, ▤ TV ☎ ♿ ⇔ – 🎙 220. AE ⓓ MC VISA JCB. ⚘ rest CX m
Meals 24 *(lunch)* and à la carte 19/28 – ***Fine Dining:*** **Meals** à la carte 35/53 – **131 rm** ☕ 239/264 – 283 – 3 suites.
◆ Practicality, modernity and elegance are the successful ingredients of this comfortable hotel, concealed behind the smart façade of a 19C city palace. Hotel restaurant in contemporary style. The Fine Dining is classic and discreetly elegant.

Alexander am Zoo without rest, Waldschmidtstr. 59, ✉ 60316, ☎ (069) 94 96 00, *Fax (069) 94960720, info@alexanderamzoo.de,* ≘s – |‡| ⇹ TV ☎ ⇔ – 🎙 30. AE ⓓ MC VISA JCB FV c
66 rm ☕ 125 – 150 – 9 suites.
◆ Modern corner building with contemporary décor, not far from Frankfurt Zoo. During breaks from business meetings enjoy fine views of the city skyline from the hotel terraces.

An der Messe without rest, Westendstr. 104, ✉ 60325, ☎ (069) 74 79 79, *Fax (069) 748349, hotel.an.der.messe@web.de,* 🌳 – |‡| ▤ TV ☎ ⇔. AE ⓓ MC VISA JCB CV e
45 rm ☕ 123 – 149.
◆ Lacquered and gilded bedside tables, inlaid period furniture or gleaming modern veneers give each of the rooms in this establishment a highly individual character.

Palmenhof, Bockenheimer Landstr. 89, ✉ 60325, ☎ (069) 7 53 00 60, *Fax (069) 75300666, info@palmenhof.com* – |‡| TV ☎ P. AE ⓓ MC VISA JCB CV m
closed 23 December - 2 January – **Meals** see ***L'Artichoc*** below – ☕ 15 – **46 rm** 100/130 – 140/160.
◆ With a fascinating mixture of antique and modern furniture, each room here is unique. The rooms at the front have a fine view of old chestnut trees.

NH Frankfurt-City, Vilbelerstr. 2, ✉ 60313, ☎ (069) 9 28 85 90, *Fax (069) 928859100, nhfrankfurtcity@nh-hotels.com,* ≘s – |‡|, ⇹ rm, ▤ TV ☎ ♿ – 🎙 120. AE ⓓ MC VISA JCB HY n
Meals à la carte 23/35 – ☕ 17 – **256 rm** 115 – 145 – 8 suites.
◆ This well-run hotel is located in the city centre with the pedestrian zone just around the corner. Good technical facilities in the contemporary, comfortable rooms. First-floor restaurant with extensive buffet.

Villa Orange without rest, Hebelstr. 1, ✉ 60318, ☎ (069) 40 58 40, *Fax (069) 40584100, contact@villa-orange.de* – |‡| ⇹ TV ☎ – 🎙 30. AE ⓓ MC VISA
38 rm ☕ 120/140 – 140/150.
◆ An establishment of real charm: behind the orange-coloured façade is a tasteful interior combining comfortable contemporary elegance with tradition. EV a

Steigenberger Frankfurt-City, Lange Str. 5, ✉ 60311, ☎ (069) 21 93 00, *Fax (069) 21930599,* Fб – |‡|, ⇹ rm, ▤ TV ☎ ♿ ⇔ P – 🎙 120. AE ⓓ MC VISA JCB. ⚘ rest FX s
Meals à la carte 19/36 – **149 rm** ☕ 156 – 202.
◆ Opened in 2001, this hotel is particularly appreciated by business travellers. Tastefully decorated rooms with up-to-date technology, some with skyline views. Restaurant with open kitchen.

Imperial, Sophienstr. 40, ✉ 60487, ☎ (069) 7 93 00 30, *Fax (069) 79300388, info@imperial.bestwestern.de,* – |♦|, rm, AE VISA JCB CV t
closed Christmas - early January – **Meals** *(dinner only)* à la carte 18/29 – **68 rm** 125 – 155.
◆ Spacious air-conditioned rooms close to the Palmengarten park and only minutes on foot from the financial district, trade fair grounds, university and Metro. Shopping centre nearby. Cosy hotel restaurant with beer bar.

Mercure, Voltastr. 29, ✉ 60486, ☎ (069) 7 92 60, *Fax (069) 79261606, h1204@accor.com,* , – |♦|, rm, – 80. AE VISA JCB by Th.-Heuss-Allee CV
Meals à la carte 20/41 – **336 rm** 139/169 – 168/198 – 8 suites.
◆ Modern establishment facing the trade fair grounds. Spacious Club rooms on top floor. Long-term guests accommodated in the apartment block opposite.

Liebig-Hotel without rest, Liebigstr. 45, ✉ 60323, ☎ (069) 72 75 51, *Fax (069) 727555, hotelliebig@t-online.de* – . AE VISA. CV z
closed 24 December - 1 January – 12 – **20 rm** 103/152 – 128/179.
◆ Ask for a room on the second or third floor ; they have period English and Italian furniture as well as stylish traditional bathroom fittings.

Novotel Frankfurt City West, Lise-Meitner-Str. 2, ✉ 60486, ☎ (069) 79 30 30, *Fax (069) 79303930, h1049@accor.com,* , – |♦|, rm, – 150. AE VISA JCB CV r
Meals à la carte 20/28 – 15 – **235 rm** 135/155 – 165/170.
◆ The functional rooms behind the modern façade of this corner hotel impress with their spacious and well-lit work facilities.

Bristol without rest, Ludwigstr. 15, ✉ 60327, ☎ (069) 24 23 90, *Fax (069) 251539, bristol-hotel@t-online.de* – |♦| – 20. AE VISA JCB CX a
145 rm 60/65 – 70/85.
◆ Right by the main station and close to the city centre, this is an up-to-date establishment with modern rooms and all facilities for the business traveller.

InterCityHotel, Poststr. 8, ✉ 60329, ☎ (069) 27 39 10, *Fax (069) 27391999, frankfurt@intercityhotel.de* – |♦|, rm, – 80. AE VISA JCB CX e
Meals à la carte 22/30 – 13 – **384 rm** 110/197 – 134/244.
◆ With functionally designed interiors and bright, timeless furnishings, this hotel is located on the north side of Frankfurt's main station.

Plaza without rest, Esslinger Str. 8, ✉ 60329, ☎ (069) 2 71 37 80, *Fax (069) 237650, info@plaza-frankfurt.bestwestern.de* – |♦| . AE VISA JCB CX v
11 – **45 rm** 87/97 – 113/123.
◆ What was once a social-security centre now has a friendly and welcoming atmosphere with modern interiors in pale wood, well-crafted detailing and warmly coloured fabrics.

Express by Holiday Inn without rest, Gutleutstr. 296, ✉ 60327, ☎ (069) 50 69 60, *Fax (069) 50696100, express.frankfurtmesse@ichotelsgroup.com* – |♦| – 35. AE VISA CX f
175 rm 99.
◆ A boon for the business traveller. Furnished in a contemporary and functional style, this hotel is conveniently situated close to the trade fair grounds and station.

Atlantic without rest, Düsseldorfer Str. 20, ✉ 60329, ☎ (069) 27 21 20, *Fax (069) 27212100, info@atlantic.pacat.com* – |♦| . AE VISA JCB CX b
closed 23 December - 3 January – **60 rm** 90 – 120.
◆ Trendily designed reception area in sea-green. The theme is continued in the contemporary décor of the rooms with their brightly coloured bed-linen and pale green furniture.

Memphis without rest, Münchener Str. 15, ✉ 60329, ☎ (069) 2 42 60 90, *Fax (069) 24260999, memphis-hotel@t-online.de* – |♦| . AE VISA GZ s
42 rm 110 – 130.
◆ In the middle of Frankfurt's trendy arts district, this designer hotel is a charming melange of forms and colours. The courtyard-facing rooms are very quiet.

Miramar without rest, Berliner Str. 31, ✉ 60311, ☎ (069) 9 20 39 70, *Fax (069) 92039769, info@miramar-frankfurt.de* – |♦| . AE VISA JCB HZ a
closed 22 to 31 December – **39 rm** 90/110 – 120/140.
◆ Between the Römer and the Zeil shopping streets, this hotel has well-kept, welcoming rooms with lovely dark furniture. Good technical features including internet connection.

Domicil without rest, Karlstr. 14, ✉ 60329, ☎ (069) 27 11 10, *Fax (069) 253266, info@domicil-frankfurt.bestwestern.de* – |♦| . AE VISA JCB CX d
11 – **67 rm** 87/97 – 110/120.
◆ Perfectly located for access to the airport by rail and underground and on foot to the trade fair grounds and main station.

Manhattan without rest, Düsseldorfer Str. 10, ✉ 60329, ☎ (069) 2 69 59 70, *Fax (069) 269597777, manhattan-hotel@t-online.de* – AE MC VISA CX r

60 rm 80/110 – 90/130.

• Modern style throughout, from bright foyer with its parquet floor to smartly decorated rooms. Trade fair grounds, banks, cultural institutions all easily reached on foot.

Scala without rest, Schäfergasse 31, ✉ 60313, ☎ (069) 1 38 11 10, *Fax (069) 284234, info@scala.bestwestern.de* – AE MC VISA JCB HY a

11 – **40 rm** 89/94 – 110/120.

• This is the place if you are looking for somewhere central to spend the night. Recently refurbished, the hotel has a contemporary look plus up-to-date technical facilities.

Am Dom without rest, Kannengießergasse 3, ✉ 60311, ☎ (069) 1 38 10 30, *Fax (069) 283237, info@hotelamdom.de* – AE MC VISA HZ s

31 rm 85/95 – 110.

• Theatre people will find this city centre side street establishment very convenient. Ask for one of the rooms with a view of the Cathedral, the hotel's next-door neighbour.

Français - Hotel Steigenberger Frankfurter Hof, Am Kaiserplatz, ✉ 60311, ☎ (069) 21 51 18, *Fax (069) 215119, frankfurterhof@steigenberger.de* – AE MC VISA JCB. GZ e

closed 1 to 9 January, Easter, 10 July - 22 August, Sunday and Monday – **Meals** *(dinner only)* (booking essential) 72/105 and à la carte 49/62 ♀.

• The restaurant belonging to the imposing Frankfurter Hof grand hotel is a classically elegant institution, chandeliers and fine paintings giving it an aristocratic air.

Villa Merton, Am Leonhardsbrunnen 12, ✉ 60487, ☎ (069) 70 30 33, *Fax (069) 7073820, jb@kofler-company.de*, – AE MC VISA JCB. CV n

closed 23 December - 13 January, Saturday, Sunday and Bank Holidays – **Meals** (booking essential) 28 *(lunch)*/75 and à la carte 54/65 ♀.

Spec. Strammer Max von der Gänseleber. Schaum von jungen Erbsenschoten mit dreierlei Tatar und Kaviar. Kalbsbäckchen 24 Std. geschmort mit Spargelspitzen.

• Built in 1925 as an exclusive club for residents of the diplomatic quarter, this establishment is now a classically elegant restaurant for all to enjoy.

Tiger-Restaurant, Heiligkreuzgasse 20, ✉ 60313, ☎ (069) 92 00 22 25, *Fax (069) 92002217, info@tigerpalast.com* – AE MC VISA. FV s

closed 24 July - 23 August, Sunday and Monday – **Meals** *(dinner only)* (booking essential) 62/90 and à la carte 57/84 ♀ – ***Palast-Bistrot*** *(closed Monday) (dinner only)* **Meals** 38/46 and à la carte 34/46 ♀.

Spec. Tatar von Taschenkrebs aromatisiert mit Bittermandel in Limonengelée. Halber gebratener Langustenschwanz auf Basmatireis mit Madras-Currysauce. Roulade von der Tauben- und Wachtelbrust im Croissantteig gebacken.

• This cellar restaurant is a popular after-show rendezvous for fans of the in-house theatre as well as for others who appreciate its artistic décor, creative cooking, and the cheerful atmosphere generated beneath the historic brick vaults of the Palast Bistro.

Opéra, Opernplatz 1, ✉ 60313, ☎ (069) 1 34 02 15, *Fax (069) 1340239, info@opera-restauration.de*, – AE MC VISA GY f

Meals à la carte 29/45 ♀.

• The old opera-house foyer with its parquet floor, plaster ceilings, wall decorations, and Art Nouveau chandeliers has been lavishly restored. Terrace with city views.

Aubergine, Alte Gasse 14, ✉ 60313, ☎ (069) 9 20 07 80, *Fax (069) 9200786* – AE MC VISA HY b

closed 3 weeks July - August, Saturday lunch and Sunday – **Meals** (booking essential) 27 *(lunch)*/65 *(dinner)* and à la carte 44/54 ♀.

• This historic town mansion with its stained glass windows and modern art invites its guests to enjoy dishes with an Italian touch served on Versace tableware.

La Trattoria, Fürstenberger Str. 179, ✉ 60322, ☎ (069) 55 21 30, *Fax (069) 552130, info@latrattoria-ffm.de*, – AE MC VISA DV s

closed 23 July - 7 August, 24 December - 3 January, Saturday and Sunday, except exhibitions – **Meals** (Italian) (booking essential) 62/67 à la carte 51/59.

• Attractively-laid tables and competent service await diners in this Mediterranean-style restaurant in a corner building from the turn of the century.

L'Artichoc - Hotel Palmenhof, Bockenheimer Landstr. 91, ✉ 60325, ☎ (069) 90 74 87 71, *Fax (069) 90748772, info@lartichoc.de* – AE MC VISA CV b

closed 23 December - 10 January, Saturday-Sunday and Bank Holidays – **Meals** 28 and à la carte 33/53 ♀.

• In the red-walled cellars of the Palmenhof Hotel, this restaurant serving fusion cuisine devotes itself to "Love of Kitchen and Cookery".

Main Tower Restaurant, Neue Mainzer Str. 52 (53th floor), ✉ 60311, ☎ (069) 36 50 47 77, *Fax (069) 36504871, maintower.restaurant@compass-group.de,* ⇐ Frankfurt – |♦|. AE MC VISA. GY u
closed Monday – **Meals** *(dinner only)* (booking essential) 55/98 and à la carte.
• High above the city roofs, diners eat in a cool contemporary setting, with floor-to-ceiling windows making the best of the views.

Gargantua, Liebigstr. 47, ✉ 60323, ☎ (069) 72 07 18, *Fax (069) 71034695, info@gargantua.de,* – AE D MC VISA JCB CV s
closed Christmas - early January, Saturday lunch, Sunday and Bank Holidays – **Meals** (booking essential) 28 *(lunch)*/65 and à la carte 39/62.
• The small villa in the banking district houses an attractive restaurant with pretty table settings, wooden flooring and contemporary pictures. Cook-book collection on display.

Ernos Bistro, Liebigstr. 15, ✉ 60323, ☎ (069) 72 19 97, *Fax (069) 173838,* – AE MC VISA CV k
closed 23 July - 17 August, 22 December - 10 January, Saturday - Sunday and Bank Holidays – **Meals** (booking essential) 31 *(lunch)*/80 and à la carte 57/75 ♀.
Spec. Hausgemachte Gänsestopfleber "à la cuillère". Ragout vom Hummer mit Charlotte-Kartoffeln und Morcheln (season). Lammnüsschen und -kotelett mit Couscous.
• Bistro-style establishment with something of the countryside about it on the edge of Frankfurt's west end. Diners are treated to solid, tasty French cuisine.

Cyrano, Leibnizstr. 13, ✉ 60385, ☎ (069) 43 05 59 64, *Fax (069) 43055965, info@cyrano-restaurant.de,* – MC VISA. FV d
closed 24 December - 8 January – **Meals** *(dinner only)* à la carte 36/45 ♀.
• Stone flooring, benches and chairs in dark wood and attractively laid tables create a pleasingly contemporary ambience, complemented by friendly and professional service.

Estragon, Jahnstr. 49, ✉ 60318, ☎ (069) 5 97 80 38, *Fax (069) 5978038* – AE MC VISA
closed 3 weeks June and Sunday – **Meals** *(dinner only)* 34/45 and à la carte 26/41 ♀.
• This is an attractive and welcoming little bistro-style place, with warm colours and refined décor. Classic international dishes, some with a Mediterranean touch. HY d

Frankfurter Äppelwoilokale *(mainly light meals only)* :

Zum Rad, Leonhardsgasse 2 (Seckbach), ✉ 60389, ☎ (069) 47 91 28, *Fax (069) 47885057, info@zum-rad.de,* by Im Prüfling and Seckbacher Landstraße FV
closed Tuesday, August - April Monday and Tuesday – **Meals** *(weekdays open from 5.00 pm, Sunday and Bank Holidays from 3.00 pm)* à la carte 13/25.
• In the village of Seckbach, this 200-year old establishment boasts its own cider press, and guests can learn something of the secrets of Frankfurt's favourite tipple.

Klaane Sachsehäuser, Neuer Wall 11 (Sachsenhausen), ✉ 60594, ☎ (069) 61 59 83, *Fax (069) 622141, klaanesachse@web.de,* FX n
closed Sunday – **Meals** *(open from 4 pm)* à la carte 12/19.
• This earthy tavern has been making its own cider since 1876 and there's hearty Frankfurt food as well. You won't sit on your own here for very long !

Zum gemalten Haus, Schweizer Str. 67 (Sachsenhausen), ✉ 60594, ☎ (069) 61 45 59, *Fax (069) 6031457,* – MC VISA EX c
closed 19 July - 9. August and Monday – **Meals** à la carte 12/20.
• In a setting of painted walls and ancient implements the drinkers down their mugs of cider which, miraculously, seem never to empty !

Fichtekränzi, Wallstr. 5 (Sachsenhausen), ✉ 60594, ☎ (069) 61 27 78, *Fax (069) 612778,* HZ n
Meals *(open from 5 pm)* à la carte 14/25.
• With its wooden benches and rustic décor this tavern has a particularly cheerful atmosphere. There are international dishes as well as cider and Frankfurt specialities.

at Frankfurt-Bergen-Enkheim *East : 8 km, by Wittelsbacherallee* FV :

Amadeus, Röntgenstr. 5, ✉ 60388, ☎ (06109) 37 00, *Fax (06109) 370720, reservation@hotel-amadeus-frankfurt.de,* – |♦|, ⇆ rm, ▤ TV ☎ ♿ 🚗 P – 🏛 100. AE MC VISA
Meals à la carte 19/33 – ☐ 15 – **160 rm** 119/137 – 157.
• Modern, star-shaped conference hotel in the eastern part of the city with rooms in a contemporary version of Art Deco. Kitchenette apartments for longer stays.

at Frankfurt-Griesheim *West : 8 km, by Th.-Heuss-Allee* CV :

Courtyard by Marriott, Oeserstr. 180, ✉ 65933, ☎ (069) 3 90 50, *Fax (069) 3808218, cy.fracv.sales@courtyard.com,* ≘s, 🏊 – |♦|, ⇆ rm, ▤ rest, TV ☎ P – 🏛 230. AE D MC VISA JCB
Meals à la carte 25/32 – ☐ 15 – **236 rm** 105 – 125.
• Well-located in the green belt between airport and city centre. The 12th floor has a fitness centre and terrace with superb views of the Frankfurt skyline.

at Frankfurt-Höchst *West : 10 km, by Mainzer Landstraße* CX :

Lindner Congress Hotel, Bolongarostr. 100, ✉ 65929, ☎ (069) 3 30 02 00, *Fax (069) 33002999, info.frankfurt@lindner.de*, rm, – 160. AE VISA JCB. rest
Meals à la carte 25/42 – 18 – **285 rm** 305/315 – 335/345.
◆ This hotel prides itself on its technical amenities and all its rooms are well-equipped with internet access and the very latest in on-line facilities.

at Frankfurt-Niederrad *Southwest : 6 km, by Kennedy-Allee* CDX :

ArabellaSheraton Congress Hotel, Lyoner Str. 44, ✉ 60528, ☎ (069) 6 63 30, *Fax (069) 6633667, congress@arabellasheraton.com*, rm, – 290. AE VISA JCB
Meals à la carte 21/39 – **396 rm** 205/345 – 240/370 – 4 suites.
◆ Optimal business location in the Niederrad office district, plus a combination of professional conference facilities and comfortable accommodation. Frankfurt's vast city-forest right at the door. Two restaurants serving à la carte international dishes.

Holiday Inn, Isenburger Schneise 40, ✉ 60528, ☎ (069) 6 78 40, *Fax (069) 6784190, info.hi-frankfurt-airportnorth@queensgruppe.de*, beer garden, rm, – 250. AE VISA JCB
Meals à la carte 29/44 – **295 rm** 155/290 – 192/312.
◆ In a green setting in the middle of Germany's most extensive city-forest, this conference hotel has an enviable location midway between the airport and the centre of Frankfurt. Rooms with cherrywood furnishings, contemporary restaurant, and English-style bar.

Weidemann, Kelsterbacher Str. 66, ✉ 60528, ☎ (069) 67 59 96, *Fax (069) 673928, weidemann@t-online.de*, – AE VISA by Gartenstraße CX
closed Saturday lunch, Sunday and Bank Holidays – **Meals** (booking essential) 28 *(lunch)* and à la carte 40/53 ♀.
◆ Angelo Vega has realised his dream of his own restaurant and offers diners international fare prepared according to traditional recipes in a stylish and welcoming ambience.

at Frankfurt-Rödelheim : *Northwest : 10 km, by Leipziger Straße* CV *and Rödelheimer Landstraße :*

Osteria Enoteca, Arnoldshainer Str. 2/corner of Lorscher Straße, ✉ 60489, ☎ (069) 7 89 22 16, *Fax (069) 7892216*, – AE VISA.
closed 22 December - 7 January, Saturday lunch, Sunday and Bank Holidays – **Meals** 50/65 and à la carte 47/69 ♀.
Spec. Crudités vom Thunfisch mit Früchten und Oliven. Parmesan-Ravioli mit Erbsencreme und Minze. Gefüllter Kaninchenrücken mit Velouté von Bohnen.
◆ Ring the bell to gain entry to this stylish establishment, sit yourself down, and let yourself be treated to expertly prepared Italian delicacies.

at Frankfurt-Sachsenhausen :

Holiday Inn, Mailänder Str. 1, ✉ 60598, ☎ (069) 6 80 20, *Fax (069) 6802333, info.hi-frankfurt-citysouth@queensgruppe.de*, rm, – 200. AE VISA JCB. rest by Darmstädter Landstraße (B 3) FX
Meals à la carte 27/45 – 19 – **436 rm** 165 – 195.
◆ Bright rooms with cherrywood décor await guests opposite the Henninger office tower. There is a superb panorama of the city from the 25th floor. The elegant Le Chef restaurant offers fine international cuisine.

Maingaustuben, Schifferstr. 38, ✉ 60594, ☎ (069) 61 07 52, *Fax (069) 61995372, maingau@t-online.de* – AE VISA JCB HZ g
closed 2 weeks early August, Saturday lunch, Sunday dinner and Monday – **Meals** 12 *(lunch)*/72 and à la carte 27/43 ♀.
◆ Enjoy tasty international delicacies in an elegant, contemporary setting, then stroll along the nearby Museum Embankment or visit Frankfurt's famous "cider district".

at Eschborn *Northwest : 12 km, by A66* CV :

Mercure, Frankfurter Str. 71 (at industrial area south), ✉ 65760, ☎ (06196) 7 79 00, *Fax (06196) 7790500, h3128@accor.com* – rm, – 65. AE VISA. rest
Meals à la carte 19/38 – 14 – **125 rm** 110 – 125.
◆ This modern, functional building with its domed atrium is located in a business area and provides impeccable service. The attractive bistro-style restaurant has a light and airy atmosphere.

Novotel, Helfmann-Park 10, ✉ 65760, ☎ (06196) 90 10, *Fax (06196) 901900, h0491@accor.com*, (heated), – rm, – 200. AE MC VISA JCB
Meals à la carte 20/35 – 14 – **224 rm** 115 – 130.
◆ Spacious and functional rooms help guarantee a good night's rest. Families with children will appreciate the hotel's own pool, sunbathing lawn and play area.

Mercure Helfmann Park, Helfmann Park 1, ✉ 65760, ☎ (06196) 9 69 70, *Fax (06196) 9697100, h5379@accor.com*, – rm, – 100. AE MC VISA JCB
Meals à la carte 22/38 – **179 rm** 129/159 – 158/188.
◆ New, functional building and rooms with contemporary décor, particularly suitable for business travellers. Bistro-style Olive Tree restaurant with lavish buffet.

at Neu-Isenburg - Gravenbruch *Southeast : 11 km, by Darmstädter Landstraße* FX *and B 459 :*

Kempinski Hotel Gravenbruch, Graf zu Ysenburg und Büdingen-Platz 1, ✉ 63263, ☎ (069) 38 98 80, *Fax (069) 38988900, fb.gravenbruch@kempinski.com*, (heated), – rm, – 180. AE MC VISA JCB. rest
Meals 39/45 and à la carte – ***L'olivo*** (Italian) *(closed Saturday and Sunday) (dinner only)* **Meals** à la carte 24/33 – 23 – **283 rm** 245/445 – 300/470 – 15 suites.
◆ The winter garden overlooking the hotel's private lake is an experience in itself. This former country estate is still set in idyllic parkland and has spacious rooms and luxurious suites.

near Rhein-Main airport *Southwest : 12 km, by Kennedy-Allee* CX *:*

Sheraton, Hugo-Eckener-Ring 15 (terminal 1), ✉ 60549 *Frankfurt*, ☎ (069) 6 97 70, *Fax (069) 69772209, reservationsfrankfurt@sheraton.com*, – rm, – 700. AE MC VISA JCB. rest
Flavors : **Meals** à la carte 34/52 – ***Taverne*** *(closed Saturday and Sunday)* **Meals** à la carte 32/43 – **1006 rm** 310/575 – 345/610 – 28 suites.
◆ From table to plane or from jet to bed, this functional, soundproofed hotel is only separated by a glass bridge from the airport terminal. Varied international cuisine in Flavors. Grill and show-kitchens in the Taverne.

Steigenberger Airport, Unterschweinstiege 16, ✉ 60549 *Frankfurt*, ☎ (069) 6 97 50, *Fax (069) 69752419, info@airporthotel.steigenberger.de*, – rm, – 270. AE MC VISA JCB
Waldrestaurant Unterschweinstiege : **Meals** à la carte 24/59 – ***Faces*** *(closed Sunday and Monday)(dinner only)* **Meals** à la carte 37/49 – 19 – **573 rm** 225/325 – 245/345 – 20 suites.
◆ A spacious, elegant reception area in light marble leads through to comfortable rooms with excellent technical facilities, some with designer baths. Comfortable country-style atmosphere in the Schweinstiege restaurant. Faces is a classic-style bistro.

InterCityHotel Frankfurt Airport, Cargo City Süd, ✉ 60549 *Frankfurt*, ☎ (069) 69 70 99, *Fax (069) 69709444, frankfurt-airport@intercityhotel.de*, – rm, – 100. AE MC VISA JCB
Meals à la carte 24/32 – 16 – **361 rm** 125 – 145.
◆ Cool, no frills design in soundproofed, spacious rooms whose functional décor does not prevent them from being comfortable and welcoming. The restaurant welcomes diners into its colourful, contemporary ambience.

Saarbrücken *Saarland* 543 S 5 – *pop. 190 000 – alt. 191 m.*

Frankfurt 189.

XXX ✿✿ **GästeHaus**, Mainzer Str. 95, ✉ 66121, ☎ (0681) 9 58 26 82, *Fax (0681) 9582684, kontakt@gaestehaus-erfort.de*, – – 25. MC VISA JCB
closed 2 weeks September, 3 weeks January, Saturday lunch, Sunday and Monday – **Meals** (booking essential) 66/82 and à la carte 55/76.
Spec. Gänsestopfleber im Salzteig gegart mit glasierten Äpfeln (2 Pers.). Gebackenes Ei mit Imperial Kaviar und Kartoffel-Mousseline. Milchlammkeule mit Aromaten gebraten in zwei Gängen serviert (2 Pers.).
◆ Set in a beautiful location in a small park this 19C villa has a modern and elegant atmosphere. Excellent classic cuisine. The open-air terrace is especially lovely.

The rates shown may be revised if the cost of living changes to any great extent. Before making your reservation, confirm with the hotelier the exact price that will be charged.

HAMBURG L *Stadtstaat Hamburg* 541 F 14 – *pop.* 1 800 000 – *alt.* 10 *m.*

See : *Jungfernstieg*★ GY – *Außenalster*★★★ GHXY – *Hagenbeck Zoo (Tierpark Hagenbeck)*★★ *by Schröderstiftstr.* EX – *Television Tower (Fernsehturm)*★ (✻★★) EX – *Fine Arts Museum (Kunsthalle)*★★ HY **M1** – *St. Michael's church (St. Michaelis)*★ *(tower* ✻★*)* EFZ – *Stintfang* (≤★) EZ – *Port (Hafen)*★★ EZ – *Decorative Arts and Crafts Museum (Museum für Kunst und Gewerbe)*★ HY **M2** – *Historical Museum (Museum für Hamburgische Geschichte)*★ EYZ **M3** – *Communications Museum*★ FY **M4** – *Planten und Blo-en Park*★ EFX – *Museum of Ethnography (Hamburgisches Museum für Völkerkunde)*★ *by Rothenbaumchaussee* FX.

Envir. : *Altona : Northern Germany Museum (Norddeutsches Landesmuseum)*★★ *by Reeperbahn* EZ – *Altona Balcony (Altonaer Balkon)* ≤★ *by Reeperbahn* EZ – *Elbchaussee*★ *by Reeperbahn* EZ.

18 Hamburg-Blankenese, Falkenstein, In de Bargen 59 (West : 17 km), ✆ *(040) 81 21 77 ; 18 Hamburg-Lehmsahl, Treudelberg, Lemsahler Landstr. 45 (North : 16 km),* ✆ *(040) 60 82 25 00 ; 27 Hamburg-Wendlohe, Oldesloer Str. 251 (North : 14 km),* ✆ *(040) 5 52 89 66 ; 18 Wentorf-Reinbek, Golfstr. 2 (Southeast : 20 km),* ✆ *(040) 72 97 80 68.*

Hamburg-Fuhlsbüttel (North : 15 km), ✆ *(040) 5 07 50.*

Hamburg-Altona, Präsident-Krahn-Straße.

Exhibition Centre (Messegelände), St. Petersburger Str. 1 (EFX), ✆ *(040) 3 56 90, Fax (040)35692180.*

Tourist-Information im Hauptbahnhof, ✉ *20099,* ✆ *(040) 30 05 13 00.*

Tourist-Information am Hafen, Landungsbrücke 4-5, ✉ *20459,* ✆ *(040) 30 05 12 03, Fax (040) 313578, info@hamburg-tourismus.de.*

ADAC, *Amsinckstr. 39.*

Berlin 284 – Bremen 120 – Hannover 151.

Plans on following pages

Town centre : Eimsbüttel, Harvestehude, Rotherbaum, Uhlenhorst

Raffles Hotel Vier Jahreszeiten, Neuer Jungfernstieg 9, ✉ 20354, ✆ (040) 3 49 40, *Fax (040) 34942600, emailus.hvj@raffles.com,* ≤ Binnenalster, Fб, ≘s – |₫|, ⇔ rm, ▤ TV ✆ ♿ ⇔ – 🏛 110. AE ⓓ ⓜⓒ VISA JCB. ✗ GY v
Meals see ***Haerlin*** below – ***Doc Cheng's*** (Euro-Asian) *(closed Monday, lunch Saturday and Sunday)* **Meals** 39 and à la carte 33/45 – ***Jahreszeiten Grill :*** **Meals** à la carte 32/61 – ☕ 24 – **156 rm** 215/290 – 265/340 – 11 suites.
◆ On the banks of the Innenalster, this is one of the last truly grand Grand Hotels, where luxurious late 19C ambience blends with modern comfort. Doc Cheng's offers a wonderful combination of Eastern and Western cuisine, while the Grill is classically elegant.

Kempinski Hotel Atlantic, An der Alster 72, ✉ 20099, ✆ (040) 2 88 80, *Fax (040) 247129, hotel.atlantic@kempinski.com,* ≤ Außenalster, 🍽, ≘s, 🏊 – |₫|, ⇔ rm, TV ✆ ⇔ – 🏛 220. AE ⓓ ⓜⓒ VISA JCB. ✗ rest HY a
Meals *(closed Sunday lunch)* 29 (lunch)/82 and à la carte 46/63 – ☕ 22 – **252 rm** 230/430 – 270/470 – 11 suites.
◆ The "White Giant" has been a rendezvous of city society since 1909. Rooms with stucco ceilings and period furnishings, some with a view of the Alster. Restaurant with tasteful, elegant ambience. Attractive courtyard terrace.

Park Hyatt, Bugenhagenstr. 8, ✉ 20095, ✆ (040) 33 32 12 34, *Fax (040) 33321235, hamburg@hyatt.de,* 🍽, ⓦ, Fб, ≘s, 🏊 – |₫|, ⇔ rm, ▤ TV ✆ ♿ ⇔ – 🏛 120. AE ⓓ ⓜⓒ VISA JCB. ✗ HYZ t
Apples *(closed lunch Saturday and Sunday)* **Meals** 28 (lunch) and à la carte 47/66 – ☕ 22 – **252 rm** 195 – 220 – 5 suites.
◆ The Hyatt occupies a classic Hamburg brick building. Inside is a coolly elegant world of precious fabrics, Canadian cherrywood, and bathrooms designed by Philippe Starck. Stylish modernity gives Apples its inimitable charms.

Le Royal Méridien, An der Alster 52, ✉ 20099, ✆ (040) 2 10 00, *Fax (040) 21001111, info.lrmhamburg@lemeridien.com,* Fб, ≘s, 🏊 – |₫|, ⇔ rm, ▤ TV ✆ ♿ ⇔ – 🏛 200. AE ⓓ ⓜⓒ VISA JCB. ✗ rest HY d
Meals 22/51 and à la carte 37/49 ♀ – ☕ 19 – **284 rm** 195 – 345 – 7 suites.
◆ Exclusive atmosphere throughout, from the spacious foyer to the tastefully decorated rooms combining hi-tech facilities and contemporary art. The 8th-floor Le Ciel restaurant offers fantastic views over the Aussenalster lake.

Dorint Sofitel, Alter Wall 40, ✉ 20457, ✆ (040) 36 95 00, *Fax (040) 36951000, inf o.hamalt@dorint.com,* 🍽, ⓦ, Fб, ≘s, 🏊 – |₫|, ⇔ rm, ▤ TV ✆ ♿ ⇔ – 🏛 250. AE ⓓ ⓜⓒ VISA. ✗ rest FZ g
Meals à la carte 27/45 – ☕ 20 – **241 rm** 190/240 – 190/270 – 10 Suites.
◆ Designer hotel in an old postal bank on a waterway. Interior a fascinating mixture of marble, exposed concrete, fine veneers and modern technology. Restaurant an example of "opulent Purism".

E
F
X
Y
Z
STERNSCHANZENPARK
Schröderstiftstr.
Rentzelstr.
Bundesstr.
Grindelallee
Johns-
allee
72
An der Verbindungsbahn
Sternschanze
Sternschanze
Moorweidenstr.
Edmund-Siemers-Allee
Tiergartenstr.
FERNSEHTURM
PARK
"PLANTEN UN BLOMEN"
Lagerstr.
CONGRESS CENTRUM HAMBURG
Th-Heuss-Platz
St. Petersburger Str.
Karolinenstr.
MESSEGELÄNDE
Marseiller Str.
S. BAHN DAMMTOR
ALTER BOTANISCHER GARTEN
23
Bei den Kirchhöfen
Jungiusstr.
Stephanspl.
Messehallen
Marktstraße
46
KLEINE WALLANLAGEN
Gorch-Fock-Wall
Colonnaden
STAATSOPER
Dammtorwall
Dammtor-str.
Feldstr.
Feldstraße
Sievekingplatz
MUSIKHALLE
Gänsemarkt
Valentinskamp
Gänse-markt
Kaiser-Wilhelm-Str.
ABC Str.
29
WILHELM-KOCH-STADION
Post-
HEILIGENGEISTFELD
GROSSE WALLANLAGEN
Pilatuspool
Poolstr.
Bleichen
Glacischaussee
Holstenwall
HUMMEL DENKMAL
Hohe
33
Hütten
Thielbek
Wexstraße
77
Budapester Straße
Bleichenfleet
Wall
St. Pauli
Neuer Steinweg
Alter Steinweg
Neuer
Alsterfleet
62
70
Ludwig-Erhard-Str.
S. BAHN STADTHAUSBR.
Alter Wall
31
BISMARCK-DENKMAL
ST. MICHAELIS
Rödingsmarkt
35
43
54
Ost-West-Str.
Seewartenstr.
16
NEUSTADT
Schaarmarkt
Stintfang
Herrengrabenfleet
Deichstr.
Landungsbr.
Ditmar-Koel-Str.
Nikolaifleet
ALT-
10
Kajen
21
9
Johannisbollwerk
Vorsetzen
Hohe Brücke
Hafenrundfahrt
ELBE
BINNENHAFEN
NIEDERHAFEN
Baumwall
HAFEN

HAMBURG
0
200 m
G
H
X
Y
Z
AUSSENALSTER
BINNENALSTER
ROTHERBAUM
MOORWEIDE
ST. GEORG
HAMMERBROOK
OBERHAFEN
Fontenay
Mittelweg
Heimhuder Str.
Alsterufer
Warburgstraße
Alsterglacis
Esplanade
Kennedybrücke
Lombardsbrücke
Neuer Jungfernstieg
ALSTERRUNDFAHRT ANLEGESTELLE
ALSTERPAVILLON
JUNGFERNSTIEG
Jungfernstieg
Ballindamm
Ferdinandstr.
Glockengießerwall
Hermannstr.
Bergstr.
Mönckeberg-str.
Mönckebergstr.
Spitalerstr.
Steintorwall
Hauptbf. Nord
Hauptbf. Süd
Holzdamm
An der Alster
Koppel
Lange Reihe
Kirchenallee
Hansa-platz
Steindamm
Kreuz-weg
Kurt-Schumacher-Allee
Altmann-brücke
Steinstr.
Rathaus-markt
BÖRSE
St. Petrikirche
St. Jacobikirche
Speersort
Burchard-platz
Domstr.
Neß
Klosterwall
Meßberg
Deichtorplatz
Amsinckstr.
Högerdamm
Ost-West-Str.
Dovenfleet
Speicherstadt
St. Katharinenkirche
Bei den Mühren
Zollkanal
fleet
M¹
M²

INDEX OF STREET NAMES IN HAMBURG

ABC Str. FY
Adenauerallee HY 2
Alsterarkaden GY 3
Alsterglacis GX
Alsterufer GX
Alter Steinweg FZ
Alter Wall FZ
Altmannbrücke HYZ
Amsinckstr. HZ
An der Alster HX
An der Verbindungsbahn EFX
Ballindamm GY
Bei dem Neuen Krahn FZ 9
Bei den Kirchhöfen FX
Bei den Mühren GZ
Bei den St.-Pauli-Landungsbrücken EZ 10
Bergstr. GY
Böhmkenstr. EZ 16
Börsenbrücke GZ 18
Budapester Str. EY
Bundesstr. FX
Burchardpl. GZ
Colonnaden FY
Cremon FZ 21
Dammtordamm FX 23
Dammtorstr. FY
Dammtorwall FY
Deichstr. FZ
Deichtorpl. HZ
Ditmar-Koel-Str. EZ
Domstr. GZ
Dovenfleet GZ
Edmund-Siemers-Allee FX
Esplanade GY
Feldstr. EY
Ferdinandstr. GY
Fontenay GX
Gänsemarkt FY
Gerhofstr. FY 29
Glacischaussee EY
Glockengießerwall GHY
Gorch-Fock-Wall FY
Graskeller FZ 31
Grindelallee FX
Große Bleichen FY 33
Große Burstah FZ 35
Große Johannisstr. GZ 34
Große Reichenstr. GZ 37
Hachmannpl. HY 39
Hansapl. HY
Heimhuder Str. GX
Helgoländer Allee EZ 43
Hermannstr. GY
Högerdamm HZ
Hohe Bleichen FY
Hohe Brücke FZ
Holstenglacis EY 46
Holstenwall EY
Holzdamm HY
Hütten EY
Johannisbollwerk EZ
Johnsallee FX
Jungfernstieg GY
Kaiser-Wilhelm-Str. FY
Kajen FZ
Karolinenstr. EX
Kennedybrücke GY
Kirchenallee HY
Kleine Reichenstr. GZ 50
Klingberg GZ 51
Klosterwall HZ
Koppel HX
Krayenkamp FZ 54
Kreuzweg HY
Kurt-Schumacher-Allee HY
Lagerstr. EX
Lange Reihe HY
Lombardsbrücke GY
Ludwig-Erhard-Str. EFZ
Marktstr. EY
Marseiller Str. FX
Millerntordamm EZ 62
Mittelweg GX
Mönckebergstr. GHY
Moorweidenstr. FX
Neß GZ
Neuer Jungfernstieg GY
Neuer Steinweg EFZ
Neuer Wall FYZ
Ost-West-Str. FGZ
Pilatuspool EFY
Poolstr. FY
Poststr. FY
Pumpen HZ 68
Rathausmarkt GYZ
Rathausstr. GZ 69
Reeperbahn EZ 70
Reesendamm GY 71
Rentzelstr. EX
Rothenbaumchaussee FX 72
Schaarmarkt EFZ
Schleusenbrücke GY 75
Schmiedestr. GZ 76
Schröderstiftstr. EX
Seewartenstr. EZ
Sievekingpl. EFY
Speersort GZ
Spitalerstr. GHY
St-Petersburger Str. EFX
Stadthausbrücke FY 77
Steindamm HY
Steinstr. GHZ
Steintordamm HY 79
Steintorpl. HY 80
Steintorwall HYZ
Sternschanze EX
Theodor-Heuss-Pl. FX
Thielbek FY
Tiergartenstr. FX
Valentinskamp FY
Vorsetzen EFZ
Warburgstr. GX
Wexstr. FYZ
Zippelhaus GZ 88

Steigenberger, Heiligengeistbrücke 4, ✉ 20459, ☎ (040) 36 80 60, *Fax (040) 36806777, hamburg@steigenberger.de*, – , rm, – 180. rest FZ s
Calla *(closed 1 week early January, 30 June - 10 August, Sunday - Monday and Bank Holidays) (dinner only)* **Meals** à la carte 29/48 – ***Bistro am Fleet*** **: Meals** à la carte 21/33 – 19 – **234 rm** 180/225 – 206/251 – 4 suites.
• Dream location on the Alster Canal. Elegant establishment with a splendid red-brick façade. Conference rooms overlooking Hamburg's rooftops. Calla with a mix of European and Oriental flavours plus views of passing pleasure steamers. Bistro for those in a rush.

InterContinental, Fontenay 10, ✉ 20354, ☎ (040) 4 14 20, *Fax (040) 41422299, hamburg@interconti.com*, ≤ Hamburg and Alster, , , , , – , rm, – 300. GX r
Windows *(closed 4 to 31 July, 1 to 14 January and Sunday) (dinner only)* **Meals** 99 and à la carte 52/70 – ***Signatures*** **: Meals** à la carte 24/40 – 20 – **281 rm** 180 – 235 – 12 suites.
• Beautifully located on the Alster, this hotel combines refined ambience with international flair and contemporary-style functional rooms. Wonderful panorama from the elegant Windows restaurant on the 9th floor. Bright and airy Signatures wintergarden.

Renaissance Hamburg Hotel, Große Bleichen, ✉ 20354, ☎ (040) 34 91 80, *Fax (040) 34918919, rhi.hamrn.info@renaissancehotels.com*, , , – , rm, – 80. rest FY e
Meals à la carte 25/36 – 18 – **205 rm** 195 – 240.
• Tradition plus up-to-the-minute elegance. The old brick edifice with its wrought-iron balconies has spacious rooms with contemporary décor in warm shades of red, yellow, and orange. Restaurant with show-kitchen and bar area.

Elysée, Rothenbaumchaussee 10, ✉ 20148, ☎ (040) 41 41 20, *Fax (040) 41412733, info@elysee-hamburg.de*, , , , – , rm, – 325. FX m
Piazza Romana (Italian) **Meals** à la carte 33/38 – ***Brasserie*** **: Meals** 22 and à la carte 20/31 – 14 – **305 rm** 136 – 156 – 4 suites.
• Sophisticated establishment with classic elegance and comfortable rooms. Library in the style of an English gentleman's club with international newspapers. The Italian restaurant serves fine cuisine in a Mediterranean atmosphere. Brasserie with Parisian flair.

SIDE, Drehbahn 49, ✉ 20354, ℘ (040) 30 99 90, *Fax (040) 30999399, info@side-hamburg.de*, Fb, ≘s, ⊠ – |‡|, ⇹ rm, ▤ ⊡ ✆ ♿ ⇔ – ♚ 160. AE ⓓ ⓜ VISA JCB FY h
Meals à la carte 32/48 – ⊒ 20 – **178 rm** 180 – 205 – 10 suites.
♦ This is a newly built hotel with a far from everyday décor by Matteo Thun. Rooms and suites are spacious and have the latest technical facilities. Cool lines and minimalist décor set the tone in the Fusion restaurant.

Marriott, ABC-Str. 52, ✉ 20354, ℘ (040) 3 50 50, *Fax (040) 35051777, hamburg.marriott@marriotthotels.com*, ⛱, Fb, ≘s, ⊠ – |‡|, ⇹ rm, ▤ ⊡ ✆ ♿ ⇔ – ♚ 160. AE ⓓ ⓜ VISA JCB FY b
Meals à la carte 26/40 – ⊒ 19 – **277 rm** 179 – 5 suites.
♦ Right on Hamburg's Gänsemarkt (Goose Market), comfortable rooms brightly refurbished with colourful fabrics and Italian period furniture. Let yourself be tempted in the extraordinarily long American Place restaurant.

Europäischer Hof, Kirchenallee 45, ✉ 20099, ℘ (040) 24 82 48, *Fax (040) 24824799, info@europaeischer-hof.de*, ⓦ, Fb, ≘s, ⊠ Squash – |‡|, ⇹ rm, ▤ rest, ⊡ ✆ ⇔ – ♚ 200. AE ⓓ ⓜ VISA. ⚘ HY e
Meals *(closed Sunday - Monday) (Tuesday - Thursday dinner only)* à la carte 28/41 – ***Paulaner's* : Meals** à la carte 16/25 – **320 rm** ⊒ 105/171 – 135/183.
♦ Luxurious rooms with warm colours and lovely veneers. The leisure area features a splendid six-storey high waterslide. Paulaners has a touch of country style.

Crowne Plaza, Graumannsweg 10, ✉ 22087, ℘ (040) 22 80 60, *Fax (040) 2208704, reservations.cphamburg@ichotelsgroup.com*, Fb, ≘s, ⊠ – |‡|, ⇹ rm, ▤ ⊡ ✆ ♿ ⇔ – ♚ 140. AE ⓓ ⓜ VISA JCB by Lange Reihe HX
Meals 27 and à la carte 26/35 – ⊒ 16 – **285 rm** 176.
♦ Daylight streams through the cupola into the atrium which is surrounded by elegant, English-style rooms in warm colours. Diners in the Blue Marlin restaurant enjoy a welcoming ambience.

Garden Hotel ⛭ without rest (with guest houses), Magdalenenstr. 60, ✉ 20148, ℘ (040) 41 40 40, *Fax (040) 4140420, garden@garden-hotel.de*, ⛱ – |‡| ⇹ ⊡ ✆ ⇔ – ♚ 15. AE ⓜ VISA by Mittelweg GX
⊒ 12 – **58 rm** 125/155 – 145/175.
♦ The location is about as chic as they come here. Guests reside in three attractive houses, fascinating in themselves and with imaginatively decorated, elegantly modern rooms.

Radisson SAS Hotel, Marseiller Str. 2, ✉ 20355, ℘ (040) 3 50 20, *Fax (040) 35023440, reservations.hamburg@radissonsas.com*, ≤ Hamburg, Fb, ≘s, ⊠ – |‡|, ⇹ rm, ▤ ⊡ ✆ ♿ ⇔ – ♚ 350. AE ⓓ ⓜ VISA JCB FX a
Meals à la carte 20/31 – ***Trader Vic's*** *(dinner only)* **Meals** à la carte 30/49 – ⊒ 15 – **560 rm** 125 – 20 suites.
♦ Skyscraper in the "Planten und Blomen" park, linked to the Congress Centre. Spacious interior and functional rooms. Popular top-floor Tower-Bar. Restaurant with attractive place settings and cream-coloured leather seats. South seas atmosphere in Trader Vic's.

Abtei ⛭, Abteistr. 14, ✉ 20149, ℘ (040) 44 29 05, *Fax (040) 449820, abtei@relaischateaux.com*, ⛱, ⛱ – ▤ rest, ⊡ ✆. AE ⓜ VISA. ⚘ rest
closed 24 to 27 December – **Meals** *(closed Sunday and Monday) (dinner only)* (booking essential) 80/92 and à la carte 56/74 – **11 rm** ⊒ 135/180 – 180/240. by Rothenbaumchaussee FX
♦ Well-chosen antiques complement the interior of this lovely, deliciously secluded villa, calculated to charm all comers, not only those in search of a nostalgic experience. Intimate restaurant with a refined, English-style atmosphere.

relexa Hotel Bellevue, An der Alster 14, ✉ 20099, ℘ (040) 28 44 40, *Fax (040) 28444222, hamburg@relexa-hotel.de* – |‡|, ⇹ rm, ⊡ ⇔ P – ♚ 45. AE ⓓ ⓜ VISA HX d
Meals à la carte 25/33 – **92 rm** ⊒ 100/120 – 145/185.
♦ Traditional white hotel building. Mostly facing the Alster, rooms in the original section are especially attractive. Small but solid single rooms in the St Georg. Lunch with a view over the Alster, dine in the tasteful basement restaurant.

Hafen Hamburg (with Classic Residenz), Seewartenstr. 9, ✉ 20459, ℘ (040) 31 11 30, *Fax (040) 31113755, info@hotel-hamburg.de*, ≤, ⛱ – |‡|, ⇹ rm, ⊡ ⇔ P – ♚ 200. AE ⓓ ⓜ VISA JCB EZ y
Meals à la carte 26/36 – ⊒ 13 – **355 rm** 90 – 200.
♦ Overlooking the harbour from a lordly height, this is an impressive establishment. As well as functional rooms in 2 categories, there is also the modern, comfortable Classic Residenz. The spacious restaurant has a fine view over the port.

Mercure an der Messe, Schröderstiftstr. 3, ✉ 20146, ✆ (040) 45 06 90, *Fax (040) 450691000, info.hammes@dorint.com* – rm, – 70. AE VISA JCB EX a
Meals *(closed Sunday dinner)* à la carte 22/31 – 14 – **180 rm** 95/155 – 105/165.
◆ This business hotel right by the trade fair grounds is just a few steps from the television tower. Modern design, functional fittings.

Vorbach without rest, Johnsallee 63, ✉ 20146, ✆ (040) 44 18 20, *Fax (040) 44182888, info@hotel-vorbach.de* – – 20. AE VISA JCB FX b
116 rm 85/135 – 105/150.
◆ Three turn-of-the century town houses have evolved into this present-day hotel. Rooms are à la mode and well maintained.

InterCityHotel Hauptbahnhof, Glockengießerwall 14, ✉ 20095, ✆ (040) 24 87 00, *Fax (040) 24870111, reservierung@hamburg.intercityhotel.de* – rm, – 60. AE VISA. rest HY m
Meals 13 *(buffet lunch)* and à la carte 21/28 – 13 – **155 rm** 115/130 – 130/145.
◆ Ideally located diagonally opposite the main station, with rooms furnished in a functional and contemporary style. Bistro-style restaurant with lunchtime buffet.

Berlin, Borgfelder Str. 1, ✉ 20537, ✆ (040) 25 16 40, *Fax (040) 25164413, rezeption@hotel-berlin-hamburg.de*, – – 25. AE VISA. rest
Meals à la carte 16/30 – **93 rm** 95/107 – 111/134. by Adenauerallee HY
◆ Even at first glance this star-shaped hotel makes a striking impression, and its original style is continued in the contemporary and colourful décor of the beautifully designed rooms. Restaurant and terrace are in equally good taste.

Senator without rest, Lange Reihe 18, ✉ 20099, ✆ (040) 24 12 03, *Fax (040) 2803717, info@hotel-senator-hamburg.de* – . AE VISA JCB HY u
56 rm 99/149 – 119/175.
◆ Pale wood and lovely pastel-coloured fabrics give the interior décor of this establishment its harmonious character. Waterbeds in some rooms guarantee a good night's rest.

Baseler Hof, Esplanade 11, ✉ 20354, ✆ (040) 35 90 60, *Fax (040) 35906918, info@baselerhof.de* – rm, – 55. AE VISA JCB. GY x
Kleinhuis **: Meals** à la carte 24/34 – **167 rm** 79/119 – 115/135.
◆ This hotel midway between Aussenalster and Botanical Gardens forms part of the Christian Hotels chain. Well-kept rooms with varied furnishings - from mahogany to cane. The Kleinhuis is an attractive, bistro-style restaurant.

Arcadia, Spaldingstr. 70 (by Nordkanalstraße), ✉ 20097, ✆ (040) 23 65 04 00, *Fax (040) 23650629, arcadiahotel@compuserve.com*, – rm, – 40. AE VISA by Kurt-Schumacher-Straße HY and Nagelsweg
Meals *(closed Sunday)* à la carte 19/34 – **98 rm** 76/100 – 86/130.
◆ This former office building was converted into a hotel in 2000. Centrally located, it offers functional, well-equipped bedrooms. The Aquarius restaurant has a cool, contemporary look.

Novotel City Süd, Amsinckstr. 53, ✉ 20097, ✆ (040) 23 63 80, *Fax (040) 234230, h1163@accor.com*, – rm, – 60. AE VISA JCB by Amsinckstraße HZ
Meals à la carte 25/33 – 15 – **185 rm** 90/95 – 100/109.
◆ Bright, welcoming rooms offer plenty of space to relax and work in, and are especially suitable for business travellers. Restaurant with large show kitchen.

Wedina without rest (with guest houses), Gurlittstr. 23, ✉ 20099, ✆ (040) 2 80 89 00, *Fax (040) 2803894, info@wedina.com*, – . AE VISA HY b
59 rm 85/130 – 105/150.
◆ Hotel consisting of several buildings, all in bright Bauhaus colours. Attractive interiors too, with much use of natural materials.

Ambassador, Heidenkampsweg 34, ✉ 20097, ✆ (040) 2 38 82 30, *Fax (040) 230009, mail@ambassador-hamburg.de*, , – rm, – 110. AE VISA by Amsinckstraße HZ and Süderstraße
Meals à la carte 18/26 – **122 rm** 89/135 – 129/155.
◆ This city-centre hotel was completely renovated in 2000 and as well as a lovely reception area offers comfortable rooms in contemporary décor. Bistro-style restaurant.

Nippon, Hofweg 75, ✉ 22085, ✆ (040) 2 27 11 40, *Fax (040) 22711490, reservations@nippon-hotel-hh.de* – rm, – 20. AE VISA JCB. by An der Alster HX and Mundsburger Damm, off Papenhuder Str.
closed 23 December - 2 January – **Meals** *(closed Monday) (dinner only)* (Japanese) à la carte 24/40 – 10 – **42 rm** 95/118 – 113/146.
◆ Attractive, sober décor in this typically Japanese establishment, with lots of lightwood furnishings, pure colours, tatami floors, shoji partitions in front of the windows, and futons. The Way-Yo with its sushi-bar is a must for lovers of Japanese food.

Alster-Hof without rest, Esplanade 12, ✉ 20354, ☎ (040) 35 00 70, *Fax (040) 35007514, info@alster-hof.de* – ▮ TV ☎. AE ⓓ MC VISA JCB GY x
closed 23 December - 2 January – **117 rm** ☕ 70/96 – 99/131.
◆ This city centre hotel close to the Alster offers its guests solidly furnished, functional rooms. Some have traditional furnishings, others have been renovated.

Haerlin - Hotel Vier Jahreszeiten, Neuer Jungfernstieg 9, ✉ 20354, ☎ (040) 34 94 33 10, *Fax (040) 34942608, emailus.hvj@raffles.com*, ≤ Binnenalster – ▤. AE ⓓ MC VISA JCB. ✗ GY v
closed 4 weeks July - August, 1 weeks early January, Sunday and Monday – **Meals** *(dinner only)* 60/88 à la carte 56/73 ♀.
Spec. Gegrillter Petersfisch mit marinierter Rote Beete und Imperial Kaviar. Bretonischer Hummer mit geeistem Singapore Sling und Mango-Chilisalat. Lammrücken in Estragonkruste mit kandiertem Knoblauch.
◆ Elegant, stylish setting, with attentive, highly professional service and outstanding classic cuisine. Fine view over the Binnenalster.

Insel am Alsterufer, Alsterufer 35 (1st floor), ✉ 20354, ☎ (040) 4 50 18 50, *Fax (040) 45018511, info@insel-am-alsterufer.de*, 🏠 – 👥 40. AE ⓓ MC VISA GX c
Meals 19 *(lunch)* and à la carte 33/53 ♀.
◆ The dignified façade of the lovely white villa is floodlit to great effect in the evening. Elegant, coolly modern interior, plus French cusine.

Sgroi, Lange Reihe 40, ✉ 20099, ☎ (040) 28 00 39 30, *Fax (040) 28003931*, 🏠 – MC VISA JCB HY f
closed Saturday lunch, Sunday and Monday – **Meals** 55/65 and à la carte 44/51.
Spec. Warmer Salat von Jakobsmuscheln und Steinpilzen. Ausgelöste Taube mit Sellerie und rotem Zwiebelconfit. Milchlamm aus dem Ofen mit Sizilianischer Peperonata.
◆ Delightfully located on a little square, this restaurant has an attractive contemporary feel to it. Mediterranean fare with Italian origins.

Tirol, Milchstr. 19, ✉ 20148, ☎ (040) 44 60 82, *Fax (040) 44809327*, 🏠 – AE MC VISA
closed Sunday – **Meals** à la carte 29/44. by Mittelweg GX
◆ The Alpine atmosphere of this establishment and the Austrian delicacies provided will quickly dispel any depression brought about by North German drizzle !

Anna, Bleichenbrücke 2, ✉ 20354, ☎ (040) 36 70 14, *Fax (040) 37500736*, 🏠 – AE MC VISA. ✗ FY v
closed Sunday and Bank Holidays – **Meals** à la carte 31/41.
◆ Tuscan flair rules here, with parquet floor, wicker seats and red-green fabrics, but the cuisine is more eclectic, ranging from borscht to sour-cream pancakes.

San Michele, Englische Planke 8, ✉ 20459, ☎ (040) 37 11 27, *Fax (040) 378121, info@san-michele.de* – AE ⓓ MC VISA JCB EZ n
closed mid July - early August – **Meals** (Italian) 21 *(lunch)* and à la carte 35/50.
◆ Italianissimo ! This most Italian of Italian restaurants directly opposite St Michael's Church serves classic Neapolitan cuisine in a bright and cheerful Mediterranean setting.

Brook, Bei den Mühren 91, ✉ 20457, ☎ (040) 37 50 31 28, *Fax (040) 37503127* – AE
closed Sunday – **Meals** 29/33 and à la carte 31/43.
◆ Modern establishment with intentionally austere décor offering friendly service and a fine view of the spectacular warehouses of the floodlit Speicherstadt. GZ f

La Mirabelle, Bundesstr. 15, ✉ 20146, ☎ (040) 4 10 75 85, *Fax (040) 4107585*. AE MC VISA FX n
closed 2 weeks July - August and Sunday – **Meals** *(dinner only)* à la carte 34/42.
◆ A likeable little place with a laid-back atmosphere and a touch of Gallic flair. The owner talks his guests through the daily specials with real enthusiasm !

Fischküche, Kajen 12, ✉ 20459, ☎ (040) 36 56 31, *Fax (040) 36091153*, 🏠 – AE ⓓ MC VISA FZ c
closed Saturday lunch, Sunday and Bank Holidays – **Meals** (booking essential) à la carte 32/52.
◆ With a contrasting combination of bright yellow walls and blue and white tiling, this unusual bistro by the harbourside has an open kitchen specialising in fish dishes.

Fischmarkt, Ditmar-Koel-Str. 1, ✉ 20459, ☎ (040) 36 38 09, *Fax (040) 362191*, 🏠 – AE MC VISA EZ r
closed Saturday lunch – **Meals** (booking essential) 26/44 and à la carte 25/47.
◆ Just 300m from the harbour waters this restaurant is decorated in a subtle, light Mediterranean style, with a bistro atmosphere and open kitchen. Mainly fish dishes.

Le Plat du Jour, Dornbusch 4, ✉ 20095, ☎ (040) 32 14 14, *Fax (040) 4105857, jacqueslemercier@aol.com* – AE ⓓ MC VISA GZ v
closed 23 December - 7 January, Sunday, July - August Saturday and Sunday – **Meals** (booking essential) 26 *(dinner)* and à la carte 24/36.
◆ Welcoming French bistro with wooden seats and black and white photos. By Hamburg standards, the French dishes represent excellent value.

Casse-Croûte, Büschstr. 2, ✉ 20354, ☎ (040) 34 33 73, *Fax (040) 3589650, info@cassecroute.de* – AE MC VISA FY s
closed lunch Sunday and Bank Holidays – **Meals** 24 and à la carte 24/35.
• Attractive, bistro-style restaurant with open kitchen, contemporary ambience, and relaxed atmosphere.

Cox, Lange Reihe 68, ✉ 20099, ☎ (040) 24 94 22, *Fax (040) 28050902, info@restaurant-cox.de* HY v
closed lunch Saturday and Sunday – **Meals** (booking essential for dinner) à la carte 26/34.
• Diners sit on striking red leather seats and are served creative international dishes in a welcoming atmosphere in this establishment close to Hamburg's principal theatre.

Matsumi, Colonnaden 96 (1st floor), ✉ 20354, ☎ (040) 34 31 25, *Fax (040) 344219* – AE D MC VISA JCB FY r
closed 1 to 5 January, Sunday and Bank Holidays lunch – **Meals** (Japanese) à la carte 20/36.
• Diners can experience a wide range of authentic Japanese dishes here, magically created by Hideaki Morita to tempt connoisseurs and beginners alike.

Jena Paradies, Klosterwall 23, ✉ 20095, ☎ (040) 32 70 08, *Fax (040) 327598, jena-paradies@t-online.de* HZ a
closed Bank Holidays – **Meals** à la carte 18/31 ♀.
• The lofty hall of the Academy of Arts is now a restaurant with Bauhaus-style décor serving international cuisine. Lunchtime menu featuring solid and inexpensive German dishes.

at Hamburg-Alsterdorf *North : 8 km, by Grindelallee* FX *and Breitenfelder Straße :*

Alsterkrug Hotel, Alsterkrugchaussee 277, ✉ 22297, ☎ (040) 51 30 30, *Fax (040) 51303403, rez@alsterkrug.bestwestern.de*, – 🏋 – |‡|, ⇸ rm, TV 📞 🚗 P – 🏠 50. AE D MC VISA JCB
Meals à la carte 26/36 – ☕ 14 – **105 rm** 105 – 205.
• Let yourself be charmed by the Mediterranean flair of this establishment. Rooms in warm colours, with wickerwork chairs and abundant plants. Desks with fax and modem points. Warm colours too in the comfortable and welcoming restaurant.

at Hamburg-Altona *West : 5 km, by Reeperbahn* EZ *:*

Rema Hotel Domicil without rest, Stresemannstr. 62, ✉ 22769, ☎ (040) 4 31 60 26, *Fax (040) 4397579, domicil@remahotel.de* – |‡| ⇸ TV 📞 🚗. AE D MC VISA JCB by Budapester Straße EY
☕ 13 – **75 rm** 55 – 70.
• This hotel's rooms are decorated in lively colours, notably black and lilac ! Original details emphasise the individuality of the spacious rooms.

InterCityHotel, Paul-Nevermann-Platz 17, ✉ 22765, ☎ (040) 38 03 40, *Fax (040) 38034999, hamburg-altona@intercityhotel.de* – |‡|, ⇸ rm, TV 📞 ♿ – 🏠 60. AE D MC VISA
Meals *(closed Sunday dinner)* à la carte 20/27 – ☕ 13 – **133 rm** 107.
• Right by the Altona main railway station, this establishment boasts contemporary rooms with light wood furnishings. The room price includes use of the city public transport system. Bistro-style restaurant.

Landhaus Scherrer, Elbchaussee 130, ✉ 22763, ☎ (040) 8 80 13 25, *Fax (040) 8806260, info@landhausscherrer.de* – ▤ P. AE D MC VISA
closed Easter, Whit Sunday, Whit Monday and Sunday – **Meals** à la carte 42/70 ♀, –
***Bistro* : Meals** 28 and à la carte 30/40 ♀.
Spec. Bonito-Variation mit Teriyakimarinade. Gebratener Hummer mit Bohnen und Hummerjus. Schellfisch mit Hamburger Senfbutter.
• Erotic paintings on walls contrast with the otherwise country-house style of this establishment. Both the orgiastic paintings of Bachmann and the French cuisine lead guests into temptation. Senses and taste-buds are further led astray in the elegant Bistro.

Fischereihafen-Restaurant, Große Elbstr. 143, ✉ 22767, ☎ (040) 38 18 16, *Fax (040) 3893021, info@fischereihafen-restaurant-hamburg.de*, <, – P. AE D MC VISA
Meals (seafood only) (booking essential) 18 *(lunch)* and à la carte 28/55.
• A favourite of celebrities, who appreciate its classical ambience and its offerings of sophisticated local specialities mostly featuring fish and various crustaceans.

Au Quai, Grosse Elbstr. 145 b-d, ✉ 22767, ☎ (040) 38 03 77 30, *Fax (040) 38037732, info@au-quai.com*, – AE D MC VISA
closed lunch Saturday and Sunday – **Meals** à la carte 33/46.
• This trendy establishment with its waterside terrace is right on the harbour. Striking contemporary décor with designer items and holographic objects.

IndoChine, Neumühlen 11, ✉ 22763, ☎ (040) 39 80 78 80, *Fax (040) 39807882, info@indochine.de*, ≤, – P. AE MC VISA JCB
Meals (Asian) à la carte 29/45.
• This contemporary, elegant restaurant is to be found on the 3rd and 4th floors of an office building. Traditional Asian cuisine enhanced by the fine views. Riverside terrace.

Tafelhaus, Neumühlen 17, ✉ 22763, ☎ (040) 89 27 60, *Fax (040) 8993324, anfrage@tafelhaus.de*, ≤, – AE D MC VISA
closed lunch Saturday and Sunday – **Meals** 35 *(lunch)* and à la carte 43/60 ♀.
Spec. Kabeljau mit Orangenaroma. Gegrilltes Kalbskotelett mit Steinpilzsauce. Mascarpone-Sherrymousse mit Himbeeren.
• Smart, trendy restaurant in a glazed office building close to the container terminal. Contemporary interior, imaginative cooking. Riverside terrace.

Stocker, Max-Brauer-Allee 80, ✉ 22765, ☎ (040) 38 61 50 56, *Fax (040) 38615058, manfred.stocker@t-online.de*, – D MC VISA
closed 1 to 10 January, Monday, lunch Saturday and Sunday – **Meals** 18 *(lunch)*/59 and à la carte 28/43.
• Playful frescoes form an attractive pictorial background to Manfred Stocker's innovative interpretation of classic Austrian dishes, cleverly enhanced with contemporary touches.

La Vela, Große Elbstr. 27, ✉ 22767, ☎ (040) 38 69 93 93, *Fax (040) 38086788, la-vela@t-online.de*, ≤, – AE MC VISA – **Meals** à la carte 31/37.
• Right next to the Fischmarkt, this recently opened bistro-style restaurant is known for its friendly service. Terrace overlooking the River Elbe.

Henssler & Henssler, Große Elbstr. 160, ✉ 22767, ☎ (040) 38 69 90 00, *Fax (040) 38699055*, – AE
closed 2 weeks July, Christmas - early January, Sunday and Bank Holidays – **Meals** (Japanese) à la carte 23/38.
• Smart restaurant in what used to be a covered fish market. Japanese inspired black and white interior. Sushi bar and Japanese cuisine with a Californian touch.

Rive Bistro, Van-der-Smissen-Str. 1 (Cruise-Centre), ✉ 22767, ☎ (040) 3 80 59 19, *Fax (040) 3894775, info@rive.de*, ≤, – AE
Meals (booking essential) 19 *(lunch)*/48 and à la carte 23/47.
• This is the place to enjoy local seafood dishes, close to the fish market and with a harbour view. Unusual décor featuring metallic leaves. Fresh oysters at the bar.

at Hamburg-Bahrenfeld *West : 7 km, by Budapester Straße EY and Stresemannstraße :*

Gastwerk, Beim Alten Gaswerk 3/corner of Daimlerstraße, ✉ 22761, ☎ (040) 89 06 20, *Fax (040) 8906220, info@gastwerk-hotel.de*, – |‡|, ⇔ rm, TV P – 100. AE D MC VISA
Meals *(closed Saturday lunch and Sunday)* (Italian) à la carte 34/40 – 15 – **135 rm** 125 – 165 – 3 suites.
• The splendid old gasworks has become a loft-style designer hotel inviting you to stay in one of its spacious rooms. Natural materials and a host of lovely details. Relaxed atmosphere in the bistro-type restaurant with its red upholstered benches.

NH Hamburg-Altona, Stresemannstr. 363, ✉ 22761, ☎ (040) 4 21 06 00, *Fax (040) 421060100, nhhamburgaltona@nh-hotels.com*, – |‡| ⇔ TV – 150. AE D MC VISA
Meals à la carte 22/31 – 14 – **237 rm** 110 – 142.
• Brick building opened in 2001, featuring standard rooms with contemporary decor and good technical facilities. Modern restaurant with bountiful buffet.

25hours Hotel without rest, Paul-Dessau-Str. 2, ✉ 22761, ☎ (040) 85 50 70, *Fax (040) 85507100, info@25hours-hotel.de* – |‡|, ⇔ rm, TV P – 20. AE D MC VISA – 9 – **65 rm** 99 – 108.
• A simple, modern design combined with the retro-look is the trademark of this hotel close to the gas works - a former warehouse now extended. The bar serves snacks.

Das kleine Rote (Hinz), Holstenkamp 71, ✉ 22525, ☎ (040) 89 72 68 13, *Fax (040) 89726814*, – P
closed 1 to 17 January, Saturday lunch, Sunday and Monday – **Meals** (booking essential) 29 *(lunch)*/65 *(dinner)* and à la carte 43/48 ♀.
Spec. Terrine von der Entenstopfleber. Filet vom St. Pierre mit Lauch und Langustinen. Topfensoufflé mit Rhabarber.
• A dear little red building with a pretty garden is the home of this modern, lightly elegant restaurant with a Mediterranean air.

Atlas, Schützenstr. 9a (Entrance Phoenixhof), ✉ 22761, ☎ (040) 8 51 78 10, *Fax (040) 8517811, atlas@atlas.at*, – P. MC VISA
Meals 16 *(lunch)*/26 *(dinner)* and à la carte 28/36 ♀.
• This old fish smokehouse is now a well-run restaurant in contemporary bistro style. Small, ivy-clad outdoor eating area to the rear.

at Hamburg-Barmbek *Northeast : 6 km, by An der Alster* HX *and Mundsburger Damm :*

Mercure Hotel Meridian without rest, Holsteinischer Kamp 59, ✉ 22081, ☎ (040) 2 91 80 40, *Fax (040) 2983336, h4993@accor.com*, – – 25. AE VISA
13 – **67 rm** 85/135 – 95/145.
◆ Original colourful details and dark wood furniture give the décor here a special something. The spacious rooms have excellent working facilities.

at Hamburg-Billbrook *East : 8 km, by Amsinckstraße* HZ *and Billstraße :*

Böttcherhof, Wöhlerstr. 2, ✉ 22113, ☎ (040) 73 18 70, *Fax (040) 73187899, info@boettcherhof.com*, – rm, – 150. AE VISA.
rest
Meals à la carte 25/38 – 13 – **155 rm** 103/131 – 124/152.
◆ This modern, well-run establishment offers bright and tasteful rooms with colourful décor and solid cherrywood furnishings. Welcoming restaurant.

at Hamburg-Blankenese *West : 16 km, by Reeperbahn* EZ *and Elbchaussee :*

Süllberg - Seven Seas (Hauser) with rm, Süllbergsterrasse 12, ✉ 22587, ☎ (040) 8 66 25 20, *Fax (040) 866625213, info@suellberg-hamburg.de*, – – 100. AE VISA JCB
Meals *(closed 3 weeks January, Monday and Tuesday) (weekdays dinner only)* 56/108 and à la carte – ***Bistro*** : **Meals** à la carte 26/37 – 8 – **11 rm** 130/180 – 180/190.
Spec. Mit Rooibusch und Pfeffer hausgeräucherter Atlantik-Lachs. Velouté von französischen Berglinsen mit Kaninchen. Imperial Taube mit Steinpilzen soufflert.
◆ The luxurious Seven Seas fine dining restaurant is the centrepiece of the superbly renovated Süllberg complex, wonderfully located above the Elbe. The ballroom, available for parties, reflects the glories of former times. Modern und friendly Bistro.

at Hamburg-Eppendorf *North : 5 km, by Grindelallee* FX *and Breitenfelder Straße :*

Piment (Nouri), Lehmweg 29, ✉ 20251, ☎ (040) 42 93 77 88, *Fax (040) 42937789*, – VISA
closed 14 to 26 March and Sunday – **Meals** *(dinner only)* 40/65 and à la carte 53/64.
Spec. Gänseleberei mit Topinambur-Carpaccio. Geschmorte Kalbsbäckchen, gebratenes Kalbsfilet und gebackene Kalbshaxe. Topfenknödel mit Sauerrahmeis und glaciertem Williamsbirnen-Tatar.
◆ This lovely Art Nouveau establishment has been immaculately restored by the couple who run it, and who serve classic dishes with a North African touch.

Poletto, Eppendorfer Landstr. 145, ✉ 20251, ☎ (040) 4 80 21 59, *Fax (040) 41406993*,
closed 1 week July, Saturday lunch, Sunday - Monday and Bank Holidays – **Meals** 45/63 and à la carte 44/69.
Spec. Tramezzini mit gebratener Gänseleber und Gewürzapfel-Ragout. Steinbutt in Olivenöl gegart mit Fenchelpüree und geschmolzenen Tomaten. Das Beste von der Heidschnucke mit violetten Artischocken.
◆ Lovely place settings and Hussen chairs set the tone in this establishment with its stylish white walls. Cornelia Poletto cooks Mediterranean dishes with an Italian touch.

at Hamburg-Flottbek *West : 9 km, by Budapester Straße* EY *and Stresemannstraße :*

Landhaus Flottbek, Baron-Voght-Str. 179, ✉ 22607, ☎ (040) 8 22 74 10, *Fax (040) 82274151, info@landhaus-flottbek.de*, – – 30. AE VISA
Meals à la carte 27/38 – ***Club-House*** *(closed Monday - Thursday)* **Meals** à la carte 22/32 – **25 rm** 99/120 – 135/155.
◆ No ordinary hotel this, but a group of 18C farmhouses with a pretty garden and individual rooms lovingly decorated in country-house style. A characterful restaurant has been established in the old stables, and the Club-House Bistro is equally attractive.

at Hamburg-Fuhlsbüttel *North : 8 km, by Grindelallee* FX *and Breitenfelder Straße :*

Airport Hotel, Flughafenstr. 47 (at the airport), ✉ 22415, ☎ (040) 53 10 20, *Fax (040) 53102222, service@airporthh.com*, – rm, rest, – 140. AE VISA
Meals à la carte 27/39 – 15 – **159 rm** 140/160 – 165/185 – 11 suites.
◆ Only 500m from the runway, this charming country-style hotel offers harmonious, colourfully decorated and functional rooms. Wonderful trompe l'oeil murals in the swimming-pool. Tired flyers will enjoy recuperating in the hotel restaurant.

at Hamburg-Harburg *South : 15 km, by Amsinckstraße HZ and Wilhelmsburger Reichsstraße :*

Lindtner, Heimfelder Str. 123, ✉ 21075, ☎ (040) 79 00 90, *Fax (040) 79009482, info@lindtner.com*, – rm, rest, – 450. AE MC VISA

Meals à la carte 34/49 – 13 – **115 rm** 120/145 – 145/155 – 7 suites.

• A spacious foyer greets guests to this cooly elegant modern hotel with its light interiors. Contemporay art collection. Restaurant partly with ceiling-high windows and show kitchen, partly with country-style ambience.

at Hamburg-Langenhorn *North : 8 km, by Grindelallee FX and Breitenfelder Straße :*

Mercure-Airport-Nord, Langenhorner Chaussee 183, ✉ 22415, ☎ (040) 53 20 90, *Fax (040) 53209600, h5393@accor.com*, – rm, – 80. AE MC VISA JCB

Meals 24/26 *(buffet)* – **146 rm** 126/176 – 162/212.

• Not far from the airport, this architecturally impressive edifice has glazed corridors and leafy courtyards. Guests are accommodated in functional, contemporary rooms.

at Hamburg-Lemsahl-Mellingstedt *Northeast : 16 km, by An der Alster HX and B 4 :*

Marriott Hotel Treudelberg, Lemsahler Landstr. 45, ✉ 22397, ☎ (040) 60 82 20, *Fax (040) 60822444, info@treudelberg.com*, 18 – rm, – 160. AE MC VISA. rest

Meals à la carte 28/40 – 15 – **135 rm** 130/158.

• Fine views of the Alster valley are conducive to restful absorption in the historic atmosphere of Treudelberg. Elegant hotel with excellent recreational facilities. Relaxed atmosphere in the restaurant with its view of the hotel's golf course.

Stock's Fischrestaurant, An der Alsterschleife 3, ✉ 22399, ☎ (040) 6 02 00 43, *Fax (040) 6020028, info@stocks.de*, – AE MC VISA

closed Monday and Saturday lunch – **Meals** (booking essential) 20 *(lunch)*/43 and à la carte 31/43.

• This thatched timber-framed building dating from the 18C has been restored to its original glory after a fire and provided with a conservatory.

at Hamburg-Niendorf : *North : 12 km, by Grindelallee FX and Garstedter Weg :*

Lutz und König, König-Heinrich-Weg 200, ✉ 22455, ☎ (040) 55 59 95 53, *Fax (040) 55599554*, – AE MC VISA JCB

closed end July - early August, Monday and Saturday lunch – **Meals** (booking essential) 15 *(lunch)*/45 and à la carte 28/45.

• "Lutz" is your host, and you, the guest, are "König" (king), in this tastefully decorated country house, where he serves refined regional cuisine with a Mediterranean touch.

at Hamburg-Nienstedten *West : 13 km, by Reeperbahn EZ and Elbchaussee :*

Louis C. Jacob, Elbchaussee 401, ✉ 22609, ☎ (040) 82 25 50, *Fax (040) 82255444, jacob@hotel-jacob.de*, Harbour and Elbe, – rm, – 120. AE MC VISA JCB. rest

Meals (booking essential) 61 *(lunch)*/98 and à la carte 55/85 – 20 – **85 rm** 185/395 – 235/395 – 8 suites.

Spec. Sautierte Jakobsmuscheln mit Gurkencarpaccio und Sauce Verveine. Ochsenschwanzragout mit Baroloessigjus und Polentaschaum. Vierländer Ente in zwei Gängen serviert.

• Luxury establishment with restrained décor. Rooms are elegantly furnished with period pieces and all have individual colour schemes. Superb location overlooking the Elbe.Light, subtle tones and lovely table settings in the restaurant. Terrace with lime trees.

at Hamburg-Rothenburgsort *Southwest : 3 km, by Amsinckstraße HZ :*

Holiday Inn, Billwerder Neuer Deich 14, ✉ 20539, ☎ (040) 7 88 40, *Fax (040) 78841000, info@hi-hamburg.de*, – – 90. AE MC VISA

Meals à la carte 28/37 – 15 – **385 rm** 115/145 – 135/145 – 12 suites.

• Right on the Elbe, the Holiday Inn is a good place to lay up at night. Ideal for business travellers looking for comfortable and well-equipped rooms with all facilities. Restaurant with terrace giving river views.

at Hamburg-St. Pauli :

NH Hamburg - City without rest, Feldstr. 53, ✉ 20357, ☎ (040) 43 23 20, *Fax (040) 43232300, nhhamburg@nh.hotels.com*, – AE MC VISA JCB EY a

14 – **119 rm** 88/170 – 88/188.

• All of the rooms in this hotel are arranged as apartments, with up-to-date facilities - kitchenette, dining and living areas. PC, fax and modem on request.

at Hamburg-Schnelsen :

Ökotel, Holsteiner Chaussee 347, ✉ 22457, ☎ (040) 5 59 73 00, *Fax (040) 55973099, info@oekotel.de* – 15. R m
Meals *(closed Saturday and Sunday) (dinner only)* (residents only) – **23 rm** 57/95 – 77/115 – 3 suites.
◆ A comfortable alternative for environmentally conscious travellers, this hotel is designed and run on ecological principles. Attractive rooms, some with balcony.

at Hamburg-Stellingen *Northwest : 7 km, by Schröderstiftstraße FX :*

Holiday Inn, Kieler Str. 333, ✉ 22525, ☎ (040) 54 74 00, *Fax (040) 54740100, hihamburg-fo@ichotelsgroup.com,* – rm, – 25.
Meals à la carte 19/35 – **105 rm** 85 – 99.
◆ Plenty of space in these contemporary rooms, which include lightwood furniture and colourful modern pictures. Bus stop in front of the hotel. The restaurant also has a contemporary feel.

at Hamburg-Stillhorn *South : 11 km, by Amsinckstraße HZ and A 1 :*

Le Méridien, Stillhorner Weg 40, ✉ 21109, ☎ (040) 75 01 50, *Fax (040) 75015501, info.hhstillhorn@lemeridien.com,* – rm, rest, – 120.
Meals à la carte 29/38 – 12 – **146 rm** 145.
◆ Designed especially for the business traveller, this hotel presents a spacious reception area and functional rooms, in a convenient location just off the motorway. Classic-style restaurant.

at Hamburg-Winterhude *North : 5 km, by Mittelweg GX :*

Allegria, Hudtwalckerstr. 13, ✉ 22299, ☎ (040) 46 07 28 28, *Fax (040) 46072607, info@allegria-restaurant.de,*
closed Monday – **Meals** *(weekdays dinner only)* 46/65 and à la carte 27/44 ♀.
◆ Right by the Fährhaus Theatre in the suburb of Winterhude, this modern, brightly-lit and colourful establishment offers refined international cuisine with an Austrian touch.

Rendsburg *Schleswig-Holstein* 541 D 12 – *pop. 28 000 – alt. 7 m.*
Hamburg 102.

at Bistensee *Northeast : 12 km :*

Seehotel Töpferhaus (with guest house), Am See, ✉ 24791 *Alt-Duvenstedt,* ☎ (04338) 9 97 10, *Fax (04338) 997171, info@toepferhaus.com,* ← Bistensee, – rm, – 65.
Meals *(closed Sunday and Monday)* 55/78 and à la carte 50/75 ♀ – ***Pesel* : Meals** 25 and à la carte 28/34 ♀ – **46 rm** 90/125 – 135/170½ P 25.
Spec. Filet vom Steinbutt mit mariniertem Spargel. Backen vom Simmentaler Rind in Burgunder geschmort. Lakritz-Bavaroise mit Birnensorbet und Tonkabohnen-Sabayon.
◆ This hotel is typical of the region. In a lovely lakeside setting, it has pretty rooms, charm and style. The country-style restaurant is comfortable, serving classic French food. Beautiful terrace.

Sylt (Insel) *Schleswig-Holstein* 541 B 8.
Hamburg 204.

at Rantum – *pop. 470*

Dorint Sofitel Söl'ring Hof, Am Sandwall 1, ✉ 25980, ☎ (04651) 83 62 00, *Fax (04651) 8362020, info.gwtrat@dorint.com,* – rm,
Meals *(closed end January - early February and Sunday)(dinner only)* (booking essential) 75/98 and à la carte ♀, – **15 rm** 265/395 – 295/495.
Spec. Vorspeisen-Variation. Steinbutt an der Gräte gegart mit geschmortem Fenchel und Kalbskopfjus. Warme Schokoladentarte mit Früchten der Saison.
◆ Set in the picturesque Rantumer dunes, this establishment combines classic elegance and modern design. There is a nice little fitness centre. Sumptuous fare is served from the kitchen ; classic dishes are given a creative touch

Write to us...
If you have any comments on the contents of this Guide.
Your praise as well as your criticisms will receive careful consideration and, with your assistance, we will be able to add to our stock of information and, where necessary, amend our judgments.
Thank you in advance!

HANOVER (HANNOVER) L *Niedersachsen* 541 I 13 – *pop.* 515 200 – *alt.* 55 m.

See : *Herrenhausen Gardens (Herrenhäuser Gärten)★★ : Großer Garten★★, Berggarten★* CV – *Kestner-Museum★* DY **M1** – *Market Church (Marktkirche) : Altarpiece★★* DY – *Museum of Lower Saxony (Niedersächsisches Landesmuseum) : Prehistorical department★* EZ **M2** – *Sprengel-Museum★* EZ – *Historical Museum (Historisches Museum Hannover)★* DY.

Garbsen, Am Blauen See 120 (West : 14 km), *(05137) 73068 ; Isernhagen, Gut Lohne 22, (North : 14 km),* *(05139) 89 31 85 ; Langenhagen, Hainhaus 22 (North : 19 km),* *(0511) 73 68 32 ; Laatzen-Gleidingen, Am Golfplatz 1 (Southeast : 9 km),* *(05102) 30 55.*

Hanover-Langenhagen (North : 11 km), *(0511) 977 12 23.*

Exhibition Centre (Messegelände) (by Bischofsholer Damm FY *and Messe Schnellweg),* *(0511) 8 90, Fax (0511) 8931216.*

Tourismus-Service, Ernst-August-Platz 2, *30159,* *(0511) 12 34 51 11, Fax (0511) 12345112, info@hannover-tourism.de.*

ADAC, *Nordmannpassage 4.*

Berlin 289 – Bremen 123 – Hamburg 151.

Plans on following pages

Kastens Hotel Luisenhof, Luisenstr. 1, 30159, (0511) 3 04 40, *Fax (0511) 3044807, info@kastens-luisenhof.de* – rm, – 90. AE VISA JCB. rest EX b
Meals *(closed Sunday July - August)* à la carte 31/56 – **149 rm** 149/335 – 178/390 – 5 suites.
◆ Individual and elegant furnishings in Hanover's most venerable hotel, in family ownership since 1856. Tower Suite with city views. Modern conference and meeting facilities. A variety of eating places cater for every requirement.

Maritim Grand Hotel, Friedrichswall 11, 30159, (0511) 3 67 70, *Fax (0511) 325195, info.hgr@maritim.de,* – rm, – 250. AE VISA JCB. rest DY a
L'Adresse - Brasserie : **Meals** à la carte 30/51 – ***Wilhelm-Busch-Stube*** *(closed Saturday and Sunday) (dinner only)* **Meals** à la carte 19/32 – 15 – **285 rm** 126 – 148 – 14 suites.
◆ Central location, plus tasteful and elegant rooms, splendid public spaces for events of all kinds, and a tasteful lobby with open fire. L'Adresse restaurant is stylish, a lighter touch prevails in the Brasserie. Rustic setting in the Wilhelm-Busch-Stube.

Maritim Stadthotel, Hildesheimer Str. 34, 30169, (0511) 9 89 40, *Fax (0511) 9894900, info.hnn@maritim.de,* , , – rm, – 250. AE VISA JCB. rest EZ b
Meals à la carte 22/34 – 16 – **291 rm** 127 – 151.
◆ Living up to its name, the hotel greets you in classically maritime style at reception and bar. Rooms are functional and ideal for the business traveller. Traditional ambience in the restaurant.

Courtyard by Marriott, Arthur-Menge-Ufer 3, 30169, (0511) 36 60 00, *Fax (0511) 36600555, cy.hajcy.sales.mgr@courtyard.com,* , , – rm, – 190. AE VISA JCB DZ b
Julian's *(dinner only)* **Meals** à la carte 17/29 – ***Grand Café :*** **Meals** à la carte 17/20 – 14 – **149 rm** 113 – 5 suites.
◆ In this one-time casino, guests have the choice between comfortable functional rooms facing the Maschsee lake or the city centre. Fascinating pictures adorn the walls of Julian's restaurant.

Crowne Plaza Schweizerhof, Hinüberstr. 6, 30175, (0511) 3 49 50, *Fax (0511) 3495102, mail@crowneplaza-hannover.de* – rm, – 220. AE VISA EX d
Meals à la carte 27/41 – 16 – **201 rm** 110 – 155 – 4 suites.
◆ The contemporary atrium structure encompasses a welcoming and expansive reception area. Rooms are stylishly furnished with excellent technical facilities, and some have a glazed oriel window. An attractively light restaurant with an open kitchen.

Congress Hotel am Stadtpark, Clausewitzstr. 6, 30175, (0511) 2 80 50, *Fax (0511) 814652, info@congress-hotel-hannover.de,* , , – rm, – 1300. AE VISA. rest by Hans-Böckler Allee FY
Parkrestaurant : **Meals** à la carte 19/34 – **258 rm** 105/160 – 181 – 3 suites.
◆ A star-shaped hotel with functional rooms on 18 floors close to the congress centre. Take a dip in the highest pool in town, on the 17th floor ! Then rendezvous in the hotel's large Park restaurant nearby.

Central-Hotel Kaiserhof, Ernst-August-Platz 4, 30159, (0511) 3 68 30, *Fax (0511) 3683114, info@centralhotel.de,* – – 50. AE VISA JCB. rest – **Meals** à la carte 17/30 – **78 rm** 106/145 – 145/155. EX a
◆ Classic, recently renovated hotel building diagonally opposite the station. Comfortable rooms, tastefully decorated in country-house style, with attractive bathrooms. Restaurant with open kitchen and Viennese café.

C
D
V
X
Y
Z
HERRENHÄUSER GÄRTEN
Schneiderberg
PRINZENGARTEN
WELFENGARTEN
UNIVERSITÄT HANNOVER
Universität
Astern-
Im Moore
Am Kleinen Felde
Engelbosteler Damm
Weidendamm
Christuskirche
Oberstr.
Gustav-Adolf-Str.
Arndtstr.
Nordfelder Reihe
Vahrenwalder Str.
Hagenstr.
Hamburger Allee
Weltenstr.
Herschelstr.
Nikolaistr.
Celler Str.
Nienburger Str.
Herrenhäuser Allee
Jägerstr.
GEORGENGARTEN
Wilhelm-Busch-Str.
Schloßwender Str.
Am Klagesmarkt
Körnerstr.
Bremer Damm
Königsworther Platz
Brüderstr.
Otto-Brenner-Str.
Goseriede
Lange Laube
Steintor
Kurt-Schumacher-Str.
ADAC
Schillerstr.
Georgstr.
Kröpcke
Brühlstr.
Königsworther Str.
LEINE
Goethestr.
Clevetor
Glocksee
Braunstr.
Goethepl.
Clemensstr.
Leibnizufer
Schmiedestr.
Osterstr.
Marktkirche
Markthalle
Karmarschstr.
Marktstr.
Spinnereistr.
Limmerstr.
Küchengarten
Blumenauer Str.
Humboldtstr.
Calenberger Str.
Stephanusstr.
Minister-Stüve-Str.
Adolfstr.
Gustav-Bratke-Allee
Lavesallee
Waterloo
WATERLOOPLATZ
Falkenstr.
Lindener Marktplatz
Schwarzer Bär
Deisterstr.
Von-Alten-Allee
Posthornstr.
Waterloostr.
Culemannstr.
MASCHPARK
IHME
Auestr.
Rickinger Str.
Ritter-Brüning-Str.
Krankenhaus Siloah
Allerweg
Deisterplatz
SCHÜTZENPLATZ
Bruchmeisterallee
Arthur-Menge-Ufer
AWD-ARENA
Beuermannstr.
MASCH-

Aegidientorpl. . . . . EY 2
Am Küchengarten . . . . CY 3
Am Marstall . . . . DX 4
Am Steintor . . . . DX 5
Bahnhofstr. . . . . EX 7
Bischofsholer Damm . . FY 8
Braunschweiger Pl. . . . FY 9
Emmichpl. . . . . FX 12
Ernst-August-Pl. . . . . . . EX 13
Friederikenpl. . . . . DY 15
Friedrichswall . . . . . . DEY 16
Georgstr. . . . . DEX
Göttinger Str. . . . . CZ 17
Große Packhofstr. . . . . DX 18
Hans-Böckler-Allee . . . . FY 19
Hartmannstr. . . . . FZ 20
Joachimstr. . . . . EX 21
Karmarschstr. . . . . DY
Königsworther Pl. . . . CX 23
Lindener Marktpl. . . . . CY 24
Opernpl. . . . . EY 25
Scharnhorststr. . . . . . . FX 28
Thielenpl. . . . . EX 29
Volgersweg . . . . EX 30

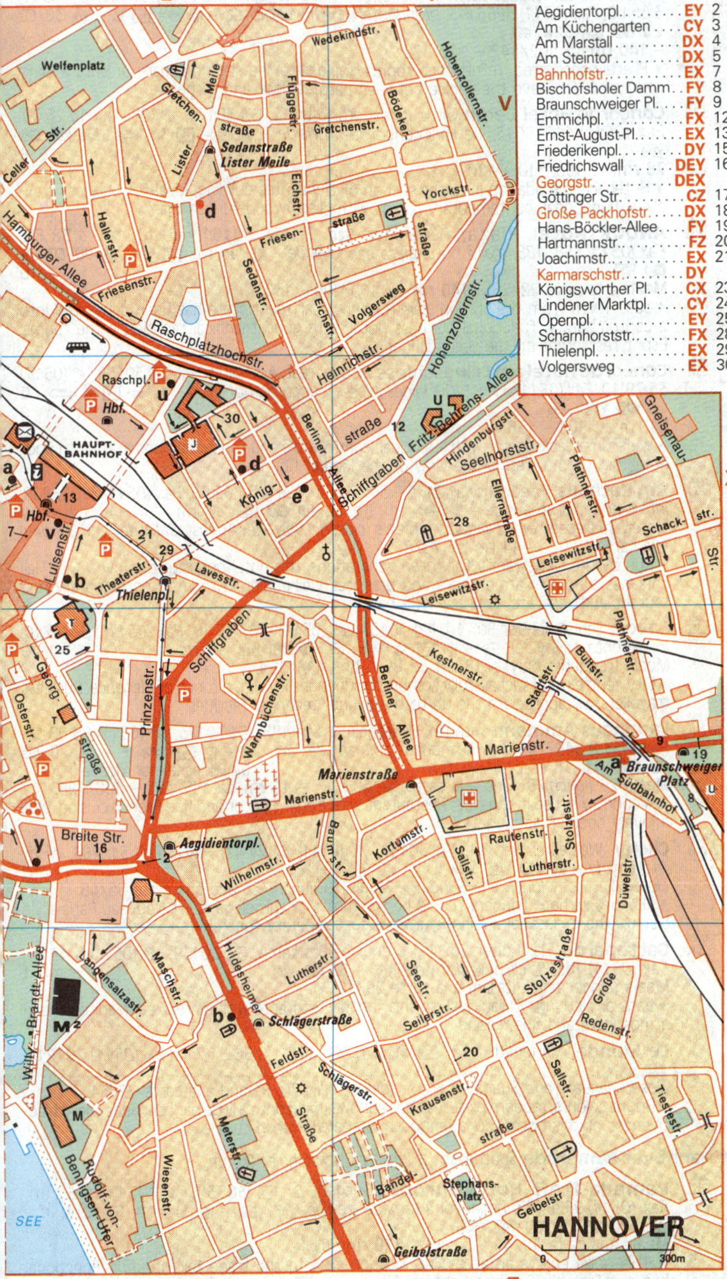

Grand Hotel Mussmann without rest, Ernst-August-Platz 7, ✉ 30159, ✆ (0511) 3 65 60, *Fax (0511) 3656145, grandhotel@hannover.de*, – |♦|, ✈ rm, TV ✆ – 🏛 30. AE ⓓ MC VISA JCB. ✂ EX v
– **140 rm** ☐ 102/142 – 142/172.
◆ Prettily-decorated, refurbished rooms giving onto the station square or onto a leafy courtyard. You have the choice between parquet floor and carpets.

Concorde Hotel Berlin without rest, Königstr. 12, ✉ 30175, ✆ (0511) 4 10 28 00, *Fax (0511) 41028013, berlin@concorde-hotels.de* – |♦| ✈ TV ✆ 🚗. AE ⓓ MC VISA EX e
78 rm ☐ 100/110 – 120.
◆ Hotel accommodation in upper section of city centre building, ideal for business travellers. Functional, contemporary rooms with cherrywood furnishings.

ANDOR Hotel Plaza, Fernroder Str. 9, ✉ 30161, ✆ (0511) 3 38 80, *Fax (0511) 3388188, mail@hotel-plaza-hannover.de* – |♦|, ✈ rm, TV ✆ – 🏛 90. AE ⓓ MC VISA EX u
Meals à la carte 22/28 – **140 rm** ☐ 100/120 – 130.
◆ Just 100m from the station, this former department store has been converted into a contemporary, functional business hotel, with good technical facilities in the rooms. Esprit restaurant on the second floor.

Concorde Hotel am Leineschloss without rest, Am Markte 12, ✉ 30159, ✆ (0511) 35 79 10, *Fax (0511) 35791100, leineschloss@concorde-hotels.de* – |♦| ✈ TV ✆ 🚗. AE ⓓ MC VISA JCB DY e
81 rm ☐ 101 – 136.
◆ Well-run establishment with individual, comfortable and functional rooms. The 4th floor breakfast room offers a fine view of the Market Church.

Am Rathaus, Friedrichswall 21, ✉ 30159, ✆ (0511) 32 62 68, *Fax (0511) 32626968, info@hotelamrathaus.de* – |♦|, ✈ rm, TV. AE ⓓ MC VISA. ✂ rm EY y
closed 23 December - 2 January – **Meals** *(closed 1 July - 28 August, Saturday and Sunday)* à la carte 17/42 – **44 rm** ☐ 75/83 – 100/120.
◆ Run by the same family for three generations, this hotel opposite the lovely City Hall park has a homely atmosphere and practical, well-equipped rooms. Contemporary restaurant and separate, country-style bar.

Savoy, Schloßwender Str. 10, ✉ 30159, ✆ (0511) 1 67 48 70, *Fax (0511) 16748710, info@hotel-savoy.de*, – |♦| TV ✆ 🚗. AE ⓓ MC VISA. ✂ rm CV e
Meals (residents only) – **18 rm** ☐ 89/129 – 114/154.
◆ City centre hotel successfully combining functionality with a touch of elegance. Business travellers will appreciate the up-to-the-minute technical facilities.

Landhaus Ammann with rm, Hildesheimer Str. 185, ✉ 30173, ✆ (0511) 83 08 18, *Fax (0511) 8437749, mail@landhaus-ammann.de*, 🌳, – |♦| TV 🚗 P – 🏛 70. AE ⓓ MC VISA. ✂ rest by Hildesheimer Straße EFZ
Meals 29 *(lunch)*/96 and à la carte 42/69 ♀, – **15 rm** ☐ 135/170 – 168/198.
◆ A country house in the city ! Restaurant with elegant décor and fine French cuisine, plus a lovely open-air section.

Clichy, Weißekreuzstr. 31, ✉ 30161, ✆ (0511) 31 24 47, *Fax (0511) 318283, clichy @clichy.de* – AE MC VISA JCB EV d
closed Saturday lunch and Sunday – **Meals** 39 *(lunch)*/56 and à la carte 35/48.
◆ "Luxury without frippery" could be the motto of this elegant Art Nouveau Paris-style bistro, where classical cuisine is given a contemporary touch.

Gattopardo, Hainhölzer Str. 1 / corner of Postkamp, ✉ 30159, ✆ (0511) 1 43 75, *Fax (0511) 14375, clichy@clichy.de*, 🌳 – AE MC VISA DV f
Meals *(dinner only)* (Italian) à la carte 29/39.
◆ Fans of all things Italian flock to this friendly ristorante with its relaxed, Mediterranean atmosphere and fine cuisine.

Le Monde, Marienstr. 117, ✉ 30171, ✆ (0511) 8 56 51 71, *Fax (0511) 781211*, 🌳 FY a
closed January and Sunday – **Meals** *(dinner only)* 20/31 and à la carte 22/34.
◆ Bright colours, modern pictures and windows giving onto a little park enhance the attractiveness of this bistro. Conscientiously prepared French cuisine.

at Hannover-Bemerode *Southeast : 8 km, by Bischofsholer Damm* FY :

Ramada-Treff Hotel Europa, Bergstr. 2, ✉ 30539, ✆ (0511) 9 52 80, *Fax (0511) 9528488, hannover@ramada-treff.de*, 🌳, – |♦|, ✈ rm, TV ✆ ♿ P – 🏛 180. AE ⓓ MC VISA JCB
Meals à la carte 19/41 – ☐ 13 – **179 rm** 105.
◆ This hotel enjoys an accessible location close to the trade fair grounds. Functional but comfortably furnished rooms. Fitness area. Entertainment programme for hotel guests.

at Hanover-Buchholz *Northeast : 7 km, by Bödekerstraße* FV *and Podbielskistraße :*

Mercure Atrium, Karl-Wiechert-Allee 68, ✉ 30625, ✆ (0511) 5 40 70, *Fax (0511) 5407826, h1701@accor.com*, – |‡|, ⇔ rm, – 🚗 ℗ – 🚶 120. AE ⓓ MC VISA JCB

Meals à la carte 28/37 – ☕ 15 – **220 rm** 99 – 109 – 6 suites.

◆ Glazed lifts transport guests to their contemporary-style rooms. Carefully planned conference area including secretarial and translation services and room with revolving stage.

Gallo Nero, Groß Buchholzer Kirchweg 72b, ✉ 30655, ✆ (0511) 5 46 34 34, *Fax (0511) 548283, mail@gisyvino.de*, – ℗. AE MC VISA *closed 2 weeks July, Saturday lunch and Sunday* – **Meals** (Italian) (booking essential for dinner) à la carte 34/47.

◆ 18C farmhouse with exposed beams and vinotheque. The mark of a fine wine, the black cockerel ("gallo nero") here stands for excellent cuisine. Permanent picture collection.

at Hanover-Döhren :

Wichmann, Hildesheimer Str. 230, ✉ 30519, ✆ (0511) 83 16 71, *Fax (0511) 8379811, gastw.wichmann@htp-tel.de*, – ℗. AE MC VISA by Hildesheimer Straße EFZ

Meals à la carte 38/68.

◆ This timber-framed house has a lovely courtyard garden. Diners choose among nine rooms - from country-style to elegant - in which to enjoy classic cuisine.

Die Insel, Rudolf-von-Bennigsen-Ufer 81, ✉ 30519, ✆ (0511) 83 12 14, *Fax (0511) 831322, n.schu@dieinsel.com*, <, – ℗. AE MC VISA

Meals (booking essential) 26 *(lunch)*/59 *(dinner)* and à la carte 31/52 ♀.

◆ This former swimming-pool building enjoys a fine view over the Maschsee lake. The long bar and generous windows give it a contemporary feel. Refined regional cuisine. by Rudolf-von Benningsen-Ufer EZ

at Hanover-Flughafen (Airport) *North : 11 km, by Vahrenwalder Straße* DV *:*

Maritim Airport Hotel, Flughafenstr. 5, ✉ 30669, ✆ (0511) 9 73 70, *Fax (0511) 9737590, info.hfl@maritim.de*, – |‡|, ⇔ rm, – 🚶 900. AE ⓓ MC VISA JCB. ⚡ rest

Meals (buffet only) 24 – ***Bistro Bottaccio*** *(closed Sunday and Monday)* **Meals** à la carte 28/45 – ☕ 16 – **528 rm** 135 – 150 – 30 suites.

◆ Built like a plane, this hotel looks ready to take off! Elegant décor and high level of comfort. Club Lounge with view of runways. Tastefully decorated restaurant.

Holiday Inn Airport, Petzelstr. 60, ✉ 30662, ✆ (0511) 7 70 70, *Fax (0511) 737781, reservation.hi-hannover-airport@queensgruppe.de*, – |‡|, ⇔ rm, ℗ – 🚶 150. AE ⓓ MC VISA JCB

Meals 20 *(buffet lunch)* and à la carte 28/45 – **211 rm** ☕ 99 – 129.

◆ Right by the airport (shuttle-bus), this establishment offers tastefully refurbished rooms and modern facilities for meetings and conferences.

at Hanover-Kirchrode *Southeast : 8 km, by Hans-Böckler Allee* FY *:*

Queens, Tiergartenstr. 117, ✉ 30559, ✆ (0511) 5 10 30, *Fax (0511) 5103510, info.qhannover@queensgruppe.de*, – |‡|, ⇔ rm, 🚗 ℗ – 🚶 140. AE ⓓ MC VISA JCB

Meals à la carte 22/40 – ☕ 14 – **178 rm** 110/136 – 153/179 – 3 suites.

◆ 1960s building surrounded by the Tiergarten park. Bright, welcoming rooms with good facilities - some with balcony. Restaurant with pleasant views of the leafy surroundings.

at Hanover-Lahe *Northeast : 10 km, by Bödekerstraße* FV *and Podbielskistraße :*

Holiday Inn, Oldenburger Allee 1, ✉ 30659, ✆ (0511) 6 15 50, *Fax (0511) 6155555, hannover@eventhotels.com*, – |‡|, ⇔ rm, rm, 🚗 ℗ – 🚶 280. AE ⓓ MC VISA. ⚡ rest

Meals à la carte 18/29 – ☕ 13 – **150 rm** 102.

◆ Accessible location in the northeastern part of town. Contemporary, functional rooms. Executive rooms cater for the needs of business travellers.

at Hanover-List *Northeast : 5 km, by Bödekerstraße* FV *:*

ArabellaSheraton Pelikan, Pelikanplatz 31, ✉ 30177, ✆ (0511) 9 09 30, *Fax (0511) 9093555, pelikanhotel@arabellasheraton.com*, – |‡|, ⇔ rm, 🚗 ℗ – 🚶 140. AE ⓓ MC VISA JCB

5th Avenue **: Meals** à la carte 26/34 – ☕ 16 – **147 rm** 151 – 7 suites.

◆ Carefully converted factory building. Where once famous "Pelikan" pens were produced, guests now stay in an ambience enlivened with an array of amusing details. Cool design contributes to the restaurant's contemporary look.

Dorint Novotel, Podbielskistr. 21, ✉ 30163, ☎ (0511) 3 90 40, *Fax (0511) 3904100, info.hajhan@dorint.com*, , – |‡|, ⇹ rm, ▤ rm, TV ☎ ♿ – 🎤 200. AE ⓓ ⓜ VISA JCB
Meals à la carte 22/37 ♀ – ☕ 16 – **206 rm** 120 – 130 – 4 suites.
◆ A famous biscuit factory once stood here. Nowadays there is an impressive combination of historical steam engines, avant-garde architecture and modern, comfortable rooms. Bright, elegant restaurant serving international dishes.

at Hanover-Messe (near Exhibition Centre) *Southeast : 9 km, by Hildesheimer Straße EFZ :*

Radisson SAS, Expo Plaza 5 (at Exhibition Centre), ✉ 30539, ☎ (0511) 38 38 30, *Fax (0511) 383838000, info.hannover@radissonsas.com*, – |‡|, ⇹ rm, ▤ TV ☎ ♿ – 🎤 220. AE ⓓ ⓜ VISA JCB
Meals à la carte 22/32 – ☕ 15 – **250 rm** 89/109 – 89/119.
◆ This establishment offers guests a choice of contemporary themed rooms - Hi-Tech, Italian, Maritime, or Scandinavian. In the lobby, the restaurant is divided into a buffet and an à la carte area.

Parkhotel Kronsberg (with guest house), Gut Kronsberg 1 (at Exhibition Centre), ✉ 30539, ☎ (0511) 8 74 00, *Fax (0511) 867112, parkhotel@kronsberg.bestwestern.de*, , , , – |‡|, ⇹ rm, ▤ rest, TV ☎ P – 🎤 150. AE ⓓ ⓜ VISA JCB
Meals *(closed 27 December - 2 January)* à la carte 28/37 – **200 rm** ☕ 85/160 – 130/186.
◆ A lovely Mediterranean-style foyer with a glass dome welcomes guests to this comfortable establishment. Guests can check into a room chosen according to their star sign. A choice of restaurants and a garden terrace cater for every culinary aspiration.

at Hanover-Vahrenwald *North : 4 km, by Vahrenwalder Straße DV :*

Fora, Großer Kolonnenweg 19, ✉ 30163, ☎ (0511) 6 70 60, *Fax (0511) 6706111, reservation.hannover@fora.de*, , – |‡|, ⇹ rm, ▤ rest, TV ☎ ♿ – 🎤 100. AE ⓓ ⓜ VISA JCB
Meals à la carte 21/31 – **142 rm** ☕ 98/118 – 118/138.
◆ Functional accommodation for the business traveller, with generous work areas and your own fax to make things easy. Conference rooms are also provided, with modern facilities.

at Laatzen *South : 9 km, by Hildesheimer Straße EFZ :*

Copthorne, Würzburger Str. 21, ✉ 30880, ☎ (0511) 9 83 60, *Fax (0511) 9836666, sales.hannover@mill-cop.com*, , , , – |‡|, ⇹ rm, ▤ rm, TV ☎ ♿ P – 🎤 300. AE ⓓ ⓜ VISA JCB
Meals à la carte 22/36 – **222 rm** ☕ 150 – 190.
◆ A hotel only five minutes on foot from the trade fair grounds. Many prominent guests have already enjoyed the tasteful comforts of this modern establishment. The glass pyramid helps create the attractively bright ambience in Bentley's.

at Langenhagen *North : 10 km, by Vahrenwalder Straße DV :*

Airport Congress Hotel without rest, Walsroder Str. 105, ✉ 30853, ☎ (0511) 7 71 96 10, *Fax (0511) 77196196, info@achh.de* – |‡| ⇹ TV ☎ – 🎤 200. AE ⓜ VISA JCB
74 rm ☕ 80/90 – 95.
◆ The world in a room! You have the freedom to decide whether to spend the night in English, Mexican, Moorish or Mediterranean style.

Ambiente, Walsroder Str. 70, ✉ 30853, ☎ (0511) 7 70 60, *Fax (0511) 7706111, hotel@ambiente.com* – |‡|, ⇹ rm, TV ☎ P – 🎤 20. AE ⓓ ⓜ VISA
closed 23 December - 2 January – **Meals** *(closed Saturday and Sunday lunch)* à la carte 18/32 – **67 rm** ☕ 92/104 – 117/119.
◆ Modern, comfortable establishment with excellent technical facilities including internet connection and PC on demand. Tasteful ambience in the Kamin-Bar restaurant.

at Ronnenberg-Benthe *Southwest : 10 km, by Deisterplatz CZ Bornumer Straße and B 65 :*

Benther Berg , Vogelsangstr. 18, ✉ 30952, ☎ (05108) 6 40 60, *Fax (05108) 640650, info@hotel-benther-berg.de*, , , – |‡|, ▤ rest, TV P – 🎤 60. AE ⓓ ⓜ VISA
Meals 26 *(lunch)*/42 and à la carte 31/45 – **70 rm** ☕ 76/97 – 92/128.
◆ This idyllic establishment consists of three parts: you can choose from the homely Altes Haus (an 1894 manor house), the functional Neues Haus and the comfortable Landhaus. Elegant gastronomy with an international repertoire.

at Isernhagen *North : 14 km, by Podbielskistraße B and Sutelstraße :*

Engel without rest, Burgwedeler Str. 151 (HB), ✉ 30916, ☎ (0511) 97 25 60, *Fax (0511) 9725646, info@hotel-engel-isernhagen.de* – ⇹ TV P – 🎤 20. AE ⓓ ⓜ VISA
28 rm ☕ 46/102 – 72/112.
◆ This highly recommended country-house style establishment offers tasteful, comfortable bedrooms and an attractive room for your varied breakfast buffet.

at Garbsen-Frielingen *Northeast : 19 km, by Bremer Damm CV and Westschnellweg :*

Bullerdieck (with guest house), Bgm.-Wehrmann-Str. 21, ✉ 30826, ☎ (05131) 45 80, *Fax (05131) 458222, info@bullerdieck.de*, beer garden, – rm, – 35. AE MC VISA – **Meals** à la carte 18/36 – **56 rm** 65/75 – 90/100.
◆ This spacious establishment has been owned by the same family since 1869. Comfortable and individually decorated rooms. Beauty parlour with wide range of services. Relaxed atmosphere in the rustic restaurant.

Nenndorf, Bad *Niedersachsen* 541 I 12 – *pop. 10 700 – alt. 70 m.*

Hannover 33.

at Bad Nenndorf-Riepen *Northwest : 4,5 km, by B 65 :*

La Forge (Gehrke) - Schmiedegasthaus Gehrke, Riepener Str. 21, ✉ 31542, ☎ (05725) 9 44 10, *Fax (05725) 944141, info@schmiedegasthaus.de* – AE VISA.
closed 3 weeks July - August, 2 weeks January, Monday and Tuesday – **Meals** *(dinner only)* (booking essential) 39/89.
Spec. Speckwickel vom Kabeljau mit Schweinskopf-Bohnenragout und Majoransauce. Piccata vom Kaninchenrücken mit pochierter Gänsestopfleber. Schokoladendessert mit Ananasterrine und Kokossuppe.
◆ Bright, elegant and friendly restaurant with lovely table settings, courteous service and creative cuisine.

LEIPZIG *Sachsen* 544 L 21 – *pop. 500 000 – alt. 118 m.*

See : *Old Town Hall★ (Altes Rathaus) BY – Old Stock Exchange★ (Alte Börse) BY – Museum of Fine Arts★★ (Museum der Bildenden Künste) BZ – St. Thomas' Church (Thomaskirche)★ BZ – Grassi Museum (Museum of Fine Art★, Museum of Ethnography★, Musical Instrument Museum★) CZ.*

Leipzig-Seehausen, Bergweg 10 (North : 8 km by Eutritzscher Straße), ☎ (034242) 5 21 74 42 ; Markkleeberg, Mühlweg (South : 9 km by Harkortstraße and B 2), ☎ (0341) 3 58 26 86 ; Machern, Plagwitzer Weg 6d (East : 15 km by Dresdner Str. and B2) ☎ (034292) 6 80 32.

Leipzig-Halle (Northwest : 15 km by Gerberstraße and Eutritzscher Straße BY), ☎ (0341) 22 40.

Exhibition Grounds (Neue Messe), Messe Allee 1 (by Eutritzscher Straße BY), ✉ 04356, ☎ (0341) 67 80, Fax (0341) 6788762 – Tourist Service, Richard-Wagner Str. 1, ✉ 04109, ☎ (0341) 7 10 42 60, Fax (0341) 7104271, info@lts-leipzig.de.

ADAC, *Augustusplatz 5/6.*

Berlin 180 – Dresden 109 – Erfurt 126.

Plans on following pages

Fürstenhof, Tröndlinring 8, ✉ 04105, ☎ (0341) 14 00, *Fax (0341) 1403700, fuerstenhof.leipzig@arabellasheraton.com*, – rm, – 60. AE MC VISA JCB BY c
Meals *(closed Sunday) (dinner only)* 70 and à la carte 49/64 – 19 – **92 rm** 195/235 – 220/260 – 4 suites.
◆ Beyond the façade of this neo-Classical town mansion of 1770 is an interior of luxurious elegance and exquisite service. Luxury pool. Aristocratic décor and fine furniture in the restaurant.

Marriott, Am Hallischen Tor 1, ✉ 04109, ☎ (0341) 9 65 30, *Fax (0341) 9653999, leipzig.marriott@marriotthotels.com*, – rm, – 200. AE MC VISA JCB BY n
Meals à la carte 24/41 – **231 rm** 99/121 – 115/137 – 11 suites.
◆ In the heart of the city, guests are accommodated in rooms lacking nothing in terms of comfort, convenience and technology ; all have internet access, modem point and answerphone. Allie's American Grill provides good food for every taste.

The Westin, Gerberstr. 15, ✉ 04105, ☎ (0341) 98 80, *Fax (0341) 9881229, info@westin-leipzig.com*, beer garden, – rm, – 360. AE MC VISA JCB. rest BY a
Meals *(closed August and Sunday)* à la carte 34/52 – ***Yamato*** (Japanese) **Meals** 20/70 and à la carte – 15 – **447 rm** 168/198 – 183/213 – 21 suites.
◆ Overnight guests can arrive here by helicopter if they wish. Luxurious rooms. The Club rooms are particularly suitable for business travellers. Coolly elegant restaurant. Japanese delicacies in the Yamato.

Renaissance, Großer Brockhaus 3, ✉ 04103, ☎ (0341) 1 29 20, *Fax (0341) 1292800, renaissance.leipzig@renaissancehotels.com*, – rm, – 350. AE MC VISA JCB DY a
Meals 18 *(lunch)* and à la carte 27/37 – **356 rm** 100 – 116.
◆ A superb, light and airy foyer greets guests to this impeccably run hotel. Bright, welcoming and comfortable rooms. International cuisine with an Oriental touch in the elegant Ambiente.

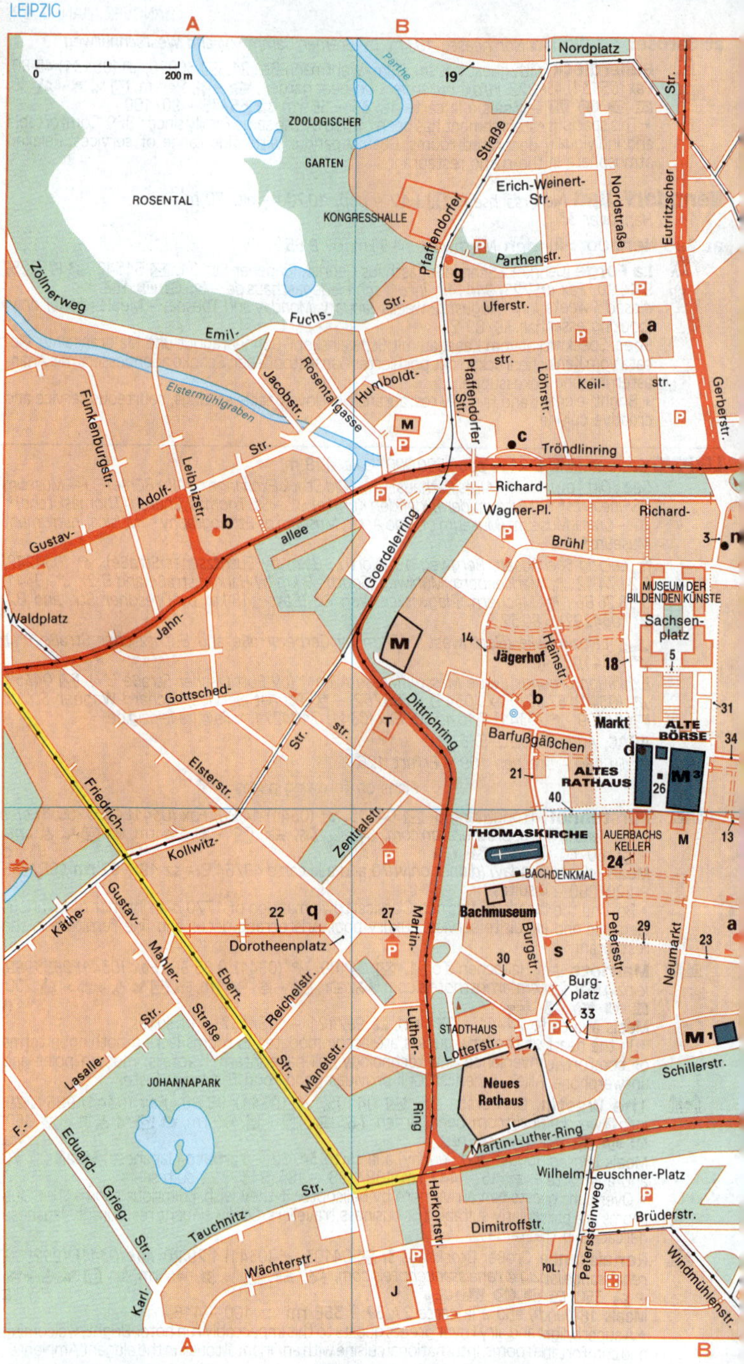
A
B
0
200 m
Nordplatz
Parthe
ZOOLOGISCHER
GARTEN
ROSENTAL
KONGRESSHALLE
Straße
Pfaffendorfer
Erich-Weinert-Str.
Nordstraße
Eutritzscher
Str.
Parthenstr.
Zöllnerweg
Emil-
Fuchs-
Str.
Uferstr.
str.
Keil-
str.
Löhrstr.
Gerberstr.
Jacobstr.
Rosentalgasse
Humboldt-
Pfaffendorfer Str.
Elstermühlgraben
Funkenburgstr.
Leibnizstr.
Str.
Tröndlinring
Richard-Wagner-Pl.
Richard-
Brühl
Adolf-
Gustav-
allee
Goerdelerring
MUSEUM DER BILDENDEN KÜNSTE
Sachsenplatz
Waldplatz
Jahn-
Jägerhof
Hainstr.
Gottsched-
str.
Dittrichring
Markt
ALTE BÖRSE
Barfußgäßchen
ALTES RATHAUS
Elsterstr.
Friedrich-
Str.
Zentralstr.
THOMASKIRCHE
AUERBACHS KELLER
Kollwitz-
BACHDENKMAL
Bachmuseum
Käthe-
Gustav-
Mahler-
Straße
Dorotheenplatz
Martin-Luther-Ring
Burgstr.
Petersstr.
Neumarkt
Ebert-
Str.
Reichelstr.
Burgplatz
STADTHAUS
Lotterstr.
Schillerstr.
Lasalle-
Manetstr.
JOHANNAPARK
Neues Rathaus
Martin-Luther-Ring
F.-
Eduard-
Grieg-
Str.
Wilhelm-Leuschner-Platz
Tauchnitz-
Str.
Harkortstr.
Dimitroffstr.
Brüderstr.
Petersteinweg
Windmühlenstr.
Wächterstr.
POL.
Karl-
Y
Z

LEIPZIG

Street	Grid	No.
Am Hallischen Tor	BY	3
Böttchergaßchen	BY	5
Dörrienstr.	DY	8
Grimmaische Str.	BCYZ	13
Grimmaischer Steinweg	CZ	12
Große Fleischergasse	BY	14
Katharinenstr.	BY	18
Kickerlingsberg	BY	19
Klostergasse	BY	21
Kolonnadenstr.	AZ	22
Kupfergasse	BZ	23
Mädlerpassage	BZ	24
Mecklenburger Str.	DY	25
Naschmarkt	BY	26
Otto-Schill-Str.	BZ	27
Preußergäßchen	BZ	29
Ratsfreischulstr.	BZ	30
Reichsstr.	BY	31
Reudnitzer Str.	DY	32
Schloßgasse	BZ	33
Schützenstr.	DY	37
Schuhmachergäßchen	BCY	34
Specks Hof	BCY	38
Steibs Hof	CY	39
Thomasgasse	BYZ	40
Wintergartenstr.	CY	42

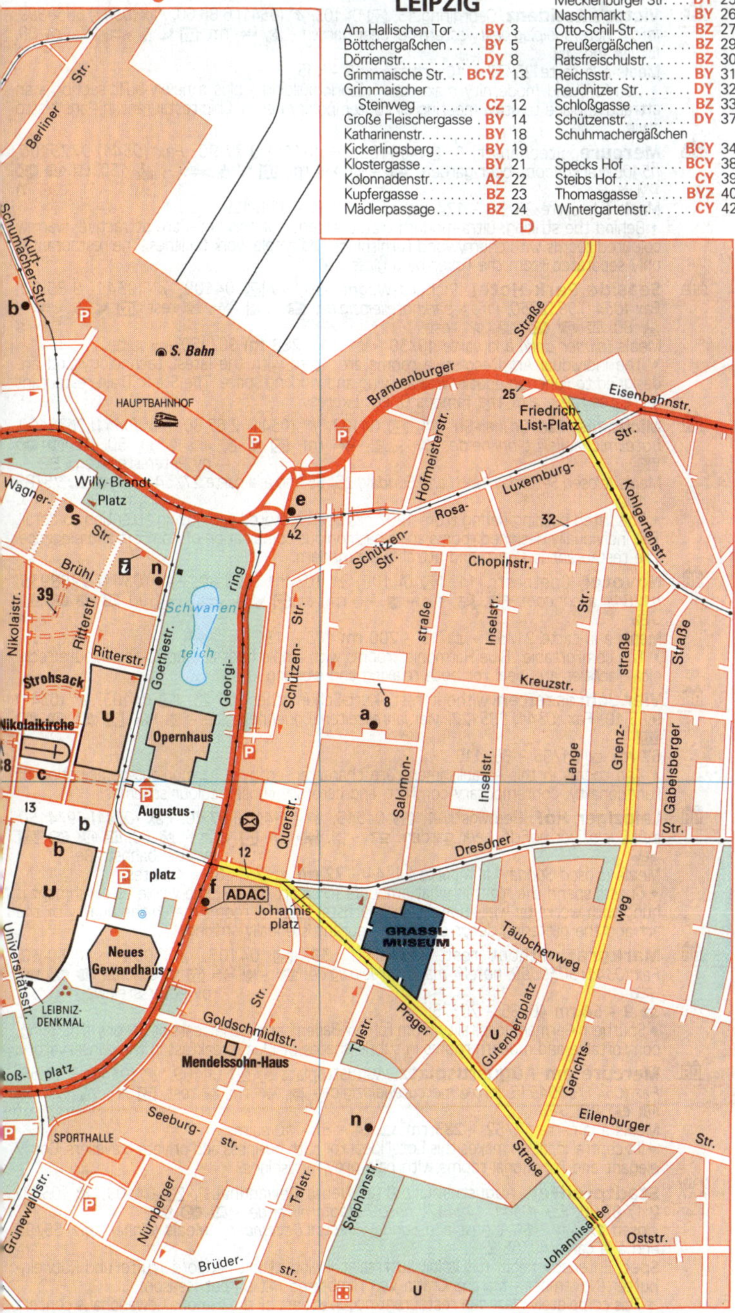

Victor's Residenz, Georgiring 13, ✉ 04103, ☎ (0341) 6 86 60, *Fax (0341) 6866899, info@victors-leipzig.bestwestern.de*, beer garden – |♦|, ⇔ rm, TV ☎ ♿ 🚗 P – 🎓 80. AE ◑ MC VISA CY e
Meals à la carte 23/37 – **101 rm** ☐ 115 – 135.
◆ Comfort and modernity make this historic building - plus a newly-built section - an attractive place to stay, meeting all contemporary needs. Chic restaurant in Paris bistro style.

Mercure, Stephanstr. 6, ✉ 04103, ☎ (0341) 9 77 90, *Fax (0341) 9779100, h5406@accor.com*, beer garden, ≘s – |♦|, ⇔ rm, TV ☎ ♿ 🚗 – 🎓 150. AE ◑ MC VISA JCB DZ n
Meals à la carte 26/36 – **174 rm** ☐ 104/111 – 121/129.
◆ Behind the striking, ultra-modern glazed exterior of this hotel are attractive, warmly coloured rooms with cherrywood furnishings and ample work facilities. The restaurant is only separated from the foyer by a glass wall.

Seaside Park Hotel, Richard-Wagner-Str. 7, ✉ 04109, ☎ (0341) 9 85 20, *Fax (0341) 9852750, info@parkhotelleipzig.de*, ≘s – |♦| ⇔, ▤ rest, TV ☎ ♿ 🚗 – 🎓 80. AE ◑ MC VISA. ⚘ rest CY s
Meals *(dinner only)* à la carte 18/36 – ☐ 14 – **288 rm** 90/150 – 5 suites.
◆ The individual Art Deco-style rooms are fitted with the latest technology and are designed to function equally well as living and working space. The Steak Train restaurant recreates the era of the famous Orient Express.

Michaelis, Paul-Gruner-Str. 44, ✉ 04107, ☎ (0341) 2 67 80, *Fax (0341) 2678100, hotel.michaelis@t-online.de*, 🏠 – |♦|, ⇔ rm, TV ☎ ♿ 🚗 – 🎓 50. AE ◑ MC VISA by Peterssteinweg BZ
Meals *(closed Saturday lunch and Sunday)* 25/35 and à la carte 27/34 – **59 rm** ☐ 75/85 – 100.
◆ This listed building dating from 1907 has been restored with loving attention to detail. The individually designed rooms are a harmonious combination of comfort and elegance. The restaurant is stylish and attractively modern.

Novotel, Goethestr. 11, ✉ 04109, ☎ (0341) 9 95 80, *Fax (0341) 9958935, h1784@accor.com*, 🏠, 🏋, ≘s – |♦|, ⇔ rm, ▤ TV ☎ ♿ 🚗 – 🎓 90. AE ◑ MC VISA JCB CY n
Meals à la carte 21/31 – ☐ 13 – **200 rm** 103 – 131.
◆ The comfortable "Blue Harmonie" rooms with ample beds and up-to-the-minute technical facilities are ideal for both relaxing and working.

Vier Jahreszeiten without rest, Kurt-Schumacher-Str. 23, ✉ 04105, ☎ (0341) 9 85 10, *Fax (0341) 985122, vier.jahreszeiten@guennewig.de* – |♦| ⇔ TV. AE ◑ MC VISA CY b
67 rm ☐ 61/95 – 85/115.
◆ The rooms in this establishment are characterised by a harmonious combination of functionality, contemporary comfort, and carefully chosen colour schemes.

Leipziger Hof, Hedwigstr. 1, ✉ 04315, ☎ (0341) 6 97 40, *Fax (0341) 6974150, info@leipziger-hof.de*, beer garden, ≘s – |♦|, ⇔ rm, TV ☎ P – 🎓 60. AE ◑ MC VISA JCB by Eisenbahnstraße DY
Meals *(closed Sunday)* à la carte 21/44 – **72 rm** ☐ 73 – 85 – 4 suites.
◆ Guests spend the night in what amounts to an art gallery ; the whole establishment is hung with works by well-known Leipzig artists. Tasteful rooms match the quality of the art and the glittering décor of the restaurant is equally striking.

Markgraf without rest, Körnerstr. 36, ✉ 04107, ☎ (0341) 30 30 30, *Fax (0341) 3030399, hotel@markgraf-leipzig.de*, ≘s – |♦| ⇔ TV ☎ 🚗. AE ◑ MC VISA JCB by Peterssteinweg BZ
☐ 9 – **54 rm** 40/65 – 70/75.
◆ Southern German hospitality from far-off Baden here in the heart of Saxony. Charming, comfortable and modern rooms in subtle shades of blue. Breakfast in the conservatory.

Mercure am Augustusplatz, Augustusplatz 5, ✉ 04109, ☎ (0341) 2 14 60, *Fax (0341) 9604916, info@mercure-leipzig.de* – |♦|, ⇔ rm, ▤ rest, TV P – 🎓 120. AE ◑ MC VISA JCB CZ f
Meals à la carte 17/32 – **283 rm** ☐ 74 – 87 – 10 suites.
◆ Its central location makes this hotel ideal for both business and private travellers. Coolly elegant and functional rooms with pale grey furnishings.

Stadtpfeiffer, Augustusplatz 8 (at Neues Gewandhaus), ✉ 04109, ☎ (0341) 2 17 89 20, *Fax (0341) 1494470, info@stadtpfeiffer.de* – AE MC VISA CZ
closed 17 July - 14 August and Sunday, except December – **Meals** *(dinner only)* 55/95 and à la carte 49/65 ♀.
Spec. Entenstopfleber mit Wildkräutersalat. Steinbutt mit Périgord Trüffel und Rotweinbutter (November - March). Gratin von Himbeeren mit Sorbet (season).
◆ This completely glazed-in restaurant occupies part of the famous Gewandhaus concert hall. Bright and friendly contemporary interior with designer seating.

Kaiser Maximilian, Neumarkt 9, ✉ 04109, ☎ (0341) 9 98 69 00, *Fax (0341) 9986901, webmaster@kaiser-maximilian.de*, – AE MC VISA BZ a
closed 1 week early January – **Meals** 50 and à la carte 33/39.
◆ With its contemporary décor the pillar room in the historic Städtisches Kaufhaus is bright and welcoming. Refined cuisine with an Italian touch.

allee, Jahnallee 28, ✉ 04109, ☎ (0341) 9 80 09 47, *Fax (0341) 9839180*, AY b
closed early - mid January, 3 weeks August and Monday – **Meals** *(dinner only)* (booking essential) 49 and à la carte 28/53 ♀.
◆ A contemporary restaurant with high quality furnishings in appealing lines and warm hues, enhanced by indirect lighting. Attractive place settings and impeccable service.

Auerbachs Keller, Grimmaische Str. 2 (Mädler-Passage), ✉ 04109, ☎ (0341) 21 61 00, *Fax (0341) 2161011, info@auerbachs-keller-leipzig.de* – AE ① MC VISA BYZ
Historische Weinstuben *(closed Sunday and Bank Holidays) (dinner only)* **Meals** 34/62 and à la carte 31/41 – ***Großer Keller :*** **Meals** à la carte 16/38.
◆ Diners have been coming to Auerbach's Cellar since 1525, among them Goethe, who set a famous scene in his Faust here. Faust rode into the wine cellar on a barrel. Art Nouveau atmosphere in the Grosser Keller. Traditional dishes served with special flair.

La Cachette, Pfaffendorfer Str. 26, ✉ 04105, ☎ (0341) 5 62 98 67, *Fax (0341) 5629869, leipzig@restaurant-la-cachette.de*, – AE ① MC VISA JCB. BY g
closed Sunday and Monday – **Meals** à la carte 22/38 ♀.
◆ Wood fittings, warm colours and works by Alfons Mucha give this hospitable jewel its cosy ambience. Professional presentation of Mediterranean cuisine.

Panorama Restaurant, Augustusplatz 9 (29 th floor of MDR-Building), ✉ 04109, ☎ (0341) 7 10 05 90, *Fax (0341) 7100589, info@panorama-leipzig.de*, ≤ Leipzig – AE MC VISA CZ b
Meals à la carte 17/32.
◆ On the 29th floor of the MDR radio building, this elegant modern restaurant maintains an appropriately high standard. Floor-to-ceiling windows with fine views over the city.

Medici, Nikolaikirchhof 5, ✉ 04109, ☎ (0341) 2 11 38 78, *Fax (0341) 9839399, medici-leipzig@t-online.de* – AE ① MC VISA JCB CY c
closed Sunday and Bank Holidays – **Meals** 42/52 and à la carte 35/48.
◆ Refined and creative Mediterranean cuisine served in a contemporary bistro-like atmosphere, next to the Nikolai Church. A striking steel structure supports a dining gallery.

Coffe Baum, Kleine Fleischergasse 4, ✉ 04109, ☎ (0341) 9 61 00 61, *Fax (0341) 9610030, coffebaum@t-online.de*, – AE MC VISA BY b
Lusatia (1st floor) *(closed August and Sunday)* **Meals** à la carte 31/37 – ***Lehmannsche Stube und Schuhmannzimmer :*** **Meals** à la carte 18/31.
◆ This temple to coffee has been kept much as it was in the 15C, when it was one of the first places to be licensed to sell coffee and chocolate. Solid traditional cooking, plus a coffee museum. Historic atmosphere in the blue-panelled Lusatia.

Apels Garten, Kolonnadenstr. 2, ✉ 04109, ☎ (0341) 9 60 77 77, *Fax (0341) 9607779, info@apels-garten.de*, – 30. AE MC VISA AZ q
closed dinner Sunday and Bank Holidays – **Meals** à la carte 14/25.
◆ Rich in traditional atmosphere, this restaurant serves Saxon dishes made according to historical recipes. Décor featuring dolls. The covered terrace is an attractive feature.

Lotter & Widemann, Markt 1, ✉ 04109, ☎ (0341) 1 49 79 01, *Fax (0341) 2251266, info@lotter-widemann.de* – AE MC VISA BY d
Meals à la carte 20/29.
◆ This vaulted establishment is named after the builders of Leipzig's lovely old city hall in which it is located. Sit here and soak up the brasserie atmosphere.

Thüringer Hof, Burgstr. 19, ✉ 04109, ☎ (0341) 9 94 49 99, *Fax (0341) 9944933, reservierung@thueringer-hof.de*, – AE MC VISA BZ s
Meals à la carte 17/26.
◆ Dating from 1454, this is one of the oldest beer-halls in the city, offering tasty morsels such as famous Thuringian sausages. Modern section in the courtyard.

at Leipzig-Breitenfeld *Northwest : 8 km, by Euritzscher Straße* BX *:*

Breitenfelder Hof, Lindenallee 8, ✉ 04158, ☎ (0341) 4 65 10, *Fax (0341) 4651133, info@breitenfelderhof.de*, , – rm, – 80. AE ① MC VISA
closed 24 December - 2 January – ***Gustav's :*** **Meals** à la carte 19/31 – 13 – **75 rm** 69/112.
◆ Stylish country hotel and separate villa in extensive parkland. Comprehensive leisure provision with hot-air balloon ascents, archery, badminton and competitive angling. The refurbished villa houses Gustav's restaurant.

at Leipzig-Connewitz *South : 2,5 km, by Harkort-Straße* BZ *and Richard-Lehmann-Straße :*

Leonardo Hotel und Residenz, Windscheidstr. 21, ✉ 04277, ☎ (0341) 3 03 30 (Hotel) 3 03 35 14 (Rest.), *Fax (0341) 3033555, info@hotel-leonardo.de*, – |♦|, ⇎ rm, ▤ rest, 📺 📞 ♿ – 🏋 30. AE ⓓ MC VISA JCB
Mona Lisa (Italian) *(closed Saturday lunch and Sunday)* **Meals** à la carte 18/38 – **53 rm** ☕ 85/95 – 100 – 3 suites.
♦ With Italian period furniture, king-size beds, generous desks with granite surfaces, and granite bath-tubs, this is a truly luxurious establishment. The Mona Lisa captivates with its sophisticated Italian atmosphere.

at Leipzig-Gohlis *North : 2,5 km, by Pfaffendorfer Straße* BY *:*

De Saxe, Gohliser Str. 25, ✉ 04155, ☎ (0341) 5 93 80, *Fax (0341) 5938299, hoteldesaxe@aol.com* – |♦| 📺 📞 P. AE ⓓ MC VISA JCB
Meals à la carte 12/28 – **33 rm** ☕ 57 – 68.
♦ Behind the sandstone facade of this city establishment are well-kept rooms, mostly furnished in honey-coloured cherrywood.

at Leipzig-Grosszschocher *Southwest : 7 km, by Käthe-Kollwitz-Straße* AZ *and Erich-Zeigner-Allee :*

Windorf, Ernst-Meier-Str. 1, ✉ 04249, ☎ (0341) 4 27 70, *Fax (0341) 4277222, info@windorf.bestwestern.de*, – |♦|, ⇎ rm, 📺 📞 P – 🏋 55. AE ⓓ MC VISA JCB
Meals à la carte 16/25 – **90 rm** ☕ 65 – 75.
♦ The bright and spacious rooms with natural wood furnishings throughout extend a friendly welcome. Ample work desks with all technical facilities. The restaurant and winter garden stand ready with a selection of local and international dishes.

at Leipzig-Leutzsch *West : 5,5 km, by Friedrich-Ebert-Straße* AY *:*

Lindner Hotel, Hans-Driesch-Str. 27, ✉ 04179, ☎ (0341) 4 47 80, *Fax (0341) 4478478, info.leipzig@lindner.de*, – |♦|, ⇎ rm, 📺 📞 – 🏋 85. AE ⓓ MC VISA
Meals à la carte 29/36 – ☕ 14 – **200 rm** 83/133 – 103/153 – 7 suites.
♦ Modern establishment, recommended for conferences and meetings, and featuring beautiful knotwood furnishings of superior quality. Excellent technical facilities. Striking use of glass in the foyer. Bright and cheerful bistro-style restaurant.

at Leipzig-Lindenau *West : 5 km, by Jahn-Allee* AY *:*

Lindenau, Georg-Schwarz-Str. 33, ✉ 04177, ☎ (0341) 4 48 03 10, *Fax (0341) 4480300, info@hotel-lindenau.de*, – |♦|, ⇎ rm, 📺 📞 P – 🏋 20. MC VISA
closed 24 December - 2 January – **Meals** *(closed Saturday and Sunday) (dinner only)* à la carte 15/23 – **51 rm** ☕ 54 – 74.
♦ With its lovely facade, this family-run hotel is in a vibrant city-centre location. Welcoming, functionally equipped rooms. Restaurant in subtle pastel tones.

at Leipzig-Paunsdorf *East : 5 km, by Dresdner Straße* DZ *and Wurzner Straße :*

Ramada Treff Hotel, Schongauer Str. 39, ✉ 04329, ☎ (0341) 25 40, *Fax (0341) 2541550, leipzig@ramada-treff.de*, – |♦|, ⇎ rm, ▤ 📺 📞 ♿ P – 🏋 630. AE ⓓ MC VISA JCB
Meals à la carte 19/33 – ☕ 13 – **291 rm** 79.
♦ Light but solid contemporary furniture and little built-in sitting areas with red and blue striped fabrics. Tasteful rooms enhanced by up-to-the-minute technical facilities.

at Leipzig-Portitz *Northeast : 10 km, by Berliner Straße* CY *:*

Accento, Tauchaer Str. 260, ✉ 04349, ☎ (0341) 9 26 20, *Fax (0341) 9262100, welcome@accento-hotel.de*, – |♦|, ⇎ rm, ▤ rest, 📺 📞 P – 🏋 80. AE ⓓ MC VISA JCB
closed 22 to 31 December – **Meals** à la carte 17/28 – ☕ 13 – **113 rm** 59 – 125.
♦ The living is stylish here, with many contemporary designer features including colourfully upholstered furniture. All rooms with modem and fax points. The bright and airy restaurant too is strikingly designed with strongly geometrical lines.

at Leipzig-Seehausen *North : 8 km, by Eutritzscher Straße* BY *and Theresienstraße :*

Im Sachsenpark, Walter-Köhn-Str. 3, ✉ 04356, ☎ (0341) 5 25 20, *Fax (0341) 5252528, info@sachsenparkhotel.de*, – |♦|, ⇎ rm, ▤ 📺 📞 ♿ P – 🏋 60. AE ⓓ MC VISA.
Meals à la carte 16/32 – **112 rm** ☕ 76 – 82.
♦ Tempting location for trade fair visitors, only 100m from the Sachsenpark and 500m from the golf course. Reduced green fee for guests. Rooms with lightwood furnishings. Bright and airy restaurant with contemporary décor.

at Leipzig-Stötteritz *Southeast : 5 km, by Prager Straße DZ and Stötteritzer Straße :*

Balance Hotel Alte Messe, Breslauer Str. 33, ✉ 04299, ☎ (0341) 8 67 90, *Fax (0341) 8679444, info@balancehotel-leipzig.de*, , – , rm, rest, – 30. AE MC VISA
Meals à la carte 17/31 – 12 – **126 rm** 69 – 9 suites.
◆ Close to the centre, in a quiet 19C residential area close to the Battle of the Nations Memorial. Comfortable, spacious rooms and suites with lightwood furnishings.

at Leipzig-Wahren *Northwest : 5 km, by Eutritzscher Straße BY and B 6 :*

Amadeo without rest, Georg-Schumann-Str. 268 (B 6), ✉ 04159, ☎ (0341) 91 02 00, *Fax (0341) 9102091, info@amadeo-leipzig.de* – – 15. AE MC VISA.
closed 20 December - 5 January **34 rm** 49/55 – 69/75.
◆ Contemporary furnishings in varieties of cane and wood characterise the comfortable rooms of this establishment. Buffet breakfast in attractive setting.

at Leipzig-Wiederitzsch *North : 7 km, by Eutritzscher Straße BY and Delitzscher Straße :*

NH Leipzig Messe, Fuggerstr. 2, ✉ 04448, ☎ (0341) 5 25 10, *Fax (0341) 5251300, nhleipzigmesse@nh-hotels.com*, , – , rm, – 220. AE MC VISA
Meals à la carte 26/38 – **308 rm** 92 – 104.
◆ This hotel is particularly devoted to the needs of business travellers. The functional rooms feature warm tones of orange and lightwood furnishings.

Hiemann, Delitzscher Landstr. 75, ✉ 04158, ☎ (0341) 5 25 30, *Fax (0341) 5253154, info@hotel-hiemann.de*, , – , rm, – 25. AE MC VISA
Meals à la carte 17/28 – **37 rm** 54/69 – 67/82.
◆ Family run hotel offering attractive maisonettes with good work facilities, plus modern rooms, some with cane furniture and sculptures, some with lightwood furnishings.Contemporary restaurant with plenty of greenery and a light, airy ambience.

at Wachau *Southeast : 8 km, by Prager Straße DZ and Chemnitzer Straße :*

Atlanta Hotel, Südring 21, ✉ 04416, ☎ (034297) 8 40, *Fax (034297) 84999, info@atlanta-hotel.de*, – , rm, – 250. AE MC VISA
Meals à la carte 19/28 – 10 – **196 rm** 57 – 72 – 6 suites.
◆ This establishment benefits from the nearby parklands such as the Agra Park. Rooms and suites in contemporary style with baths of Carrara marble. The restaurant too is stylishly contemporary.

MUNICH (MÜNCHEN) L *Bayern* 546 V 18 – *pop.* 1 300 000 – *alt.* 520 m.

See : *Old Town★★ KYZ, Marienplatz★ KZ – Church of Our Lady (Frauenkirche)★, (Memorial of Bavarian Emperor Ludwig★, tower ★) KZ – Schack-Galerie★ P35LY – German Museum (Deutsches Museum)★★★ LZ – Palace (Residenz)★★ (Treasury★★, Residenz Museum★★, Palace Theatre★) KY – Church of Asam Brothers (Asamkirche)★ KZ – Nymphenburg★★ (Castle★, Gallery of Beauties★, Parc★, Amalienburg★★, Botanical Garden (Botanischer Garten)★★) by Arnulfstr. EV – New Art Gallery (Neue Pinakothek)★★ KY - Old Art Gallery (Alte Pinakothek)★★★ KY - Gallery of Modern Art (Pinakothek der Moderne)★★ KY – City Historical Museum (Münchener Stadtmuseum)★ (Moorish Dancers★★) KZ* **M7** *– Villa Lenbach Collections (Städt. Galerie im Lenbachhaus)★ JY* **M4** *– Antique Collections (Staatliche Antikensammlungen)★ JY* **M3** *– Glyptothek★ JY* **M2** *– St Michael's Church (Michaelskirche)★ KYZ – Theatine Church (Theatinerkirche)★ KY – German Hunting and Fishing Museum (Deutsches Jagd- und Fischereimuseum)★ KZ* **M1** *– Olympic Park (Olympia-Park) (Olympic Tower ★★★) by Schleißheimer Straße FU – English Garden (Englischer Garten)★ (≤ from Monopteros Temple★) LY - Bavarian National Museum (Bayerisches Nationalmuseum)★★ LY* **M5** *– Hellabrunn Zoo (Tierpark Hellabrunn)★ by Lindwurmstraße (B 11) EX.*

9 München-Riem, Graf-Lehndorff Str. 36, (East : 10 km), ☎ (089) 94 50 08 00 ; 9 München-Thalkirchen, Zentralländstr. 40, (South : 6 km), ☎ (089) 7 23 13 04 ; 27 Straßlach, Tölzerstr. 95 (South : 17 km), ☎ (08170) 9 29 18 11 ; 18 Eschenried, Kurfürstenweg 10 (Northwest : 16 km), ☎ (08131) 5 67 40.

Flughafen Franz-Josef Strauß (Northeast : 29 km by Ungererstraße HU), ☎ (089) 9 75 00, City Air Terminal, Arnulfstraße (Main Station).

Ostbahnhof, Friedenstraße (HX).

Exhibition Centre (Messegelände) (by ③), ✉ 81823, ☎ (089) 9 49 01, Fax (089) 94920729.

Tourist Information am Bahnhofsplatz, ✉ 80335, ☎ (089) 2 33 03 00, Fax (089) 23330233, tourismus@muenchen.de.

ADAC, *Sendlinger-Tor-Platz 9.*

Berlin 586 – Innsbruck 162 – Nürnberg 165 – Salzburg 140 – Stuttgart 222.

INDEX OF STREET NAMES IN MÜNCHEN

Ackermannstr. . . . . FU
Adalbertstr. . . . . GU
Albrechtstr. . . . . EU
Alter Messepl. . . . . EX 3
Am Gasteig . . . . LZ 4
Amalienstr. . . . . KY
Amirapl. . . . . KY 6
An der Hauptfeuerwache . . JZ 7
Arcisstr. . . . . JY
Arnulfstr. . . . . EV
Asamstr. . . . . GX
Auenstr. . . . . GX
Auerfeldstr. . . . . GX
Augustenstr. . . . . JY
Aventinstr. . . . . KZ
Baaderstr. . . . . KLZ
Bahnhofpl. . . . . JY
Baldepl. . . . . GX 14
Barer Str. . . . . JKY
Baumgartnerstr. . . . . EX 17
Bavariaring . . . . EFX
Bayerstr. . . . . JY
Beethovenpl. . . . . JZ
Beethovenstr. . . . . JZ 20
Belgradstr. . . . . GU
Biedersteiner Str. . . . . HU 25
Blumenstr. . . . . KZ
Blutenburgstr. . . . . EV
Bonner Pl. . . . . GU
Bonner Str. . . . . GU 26
Brienner Str. . . . . JKY
Burgstr. . . . . KZ 30
Clemensstr. . . . . GU
Corneliusbrücke . . . . KZ
Corneliusstr. . . . . KZ
Dachauer Str. . . . . JY
Damenstiftstr. . . . . JZ 32
Denninger Str. . . . . HV 34
Dienerstr. . . . . KZ 36
Dietlindenstr. . . . . GHU
Dom-Pedro-Str. . . . . EU
Eduard-Schmid-Str. . . . . KLZ
Ehrengutstr. . . . . FX
Einsteinstr. . . . . HX
Eisenmannstr. . . . . KZ 39
Elisabethstr. . . . . FGU
Elisenstr. . . . . JY
Elsässer Str. . . . . HX 42
Emil-Riedel-Str. . . . . HV 45
Erhardtstr. . . . . KLZ
Feilitzschstr. . . . . GU
Flurstr. . . . . HX 49
Franz-Joseph-Str. . . . . GU
Franz-Joseph-Strauß-Ring . . LY 50
Franziskanerstr. . . . . GX
Frauenstr. . . . . KZ
Fraunhoferstr. . . . . KZ
Friedenstr. . . . . HX
Friedrichstr. . . . . GU 52
Gabelsberger . . . . JKY
Gärtnerpl. . . . . KZ
Galileipl. . . . . HV 53
Ganghoferstr. . . . . EX
Gebsattelstr. . . . . GX 55
Georgenstr. . . . . FGU 59
Giselastr. . . . . GU 60
Görresstr. . . . . FU
Goethestr. . . . . JZ
Gohrenstr. . . . . GU 61
Grasserstr. . . . . EV 63
Grillparzestr. . . . . HX
Hackerbrücke . . . . EV 65
Häberlstr. . . . . JZ
Hans-Sachs-Str. . . . . KZ
Haydnstr. . . . . JZ
Heimeranstr. . . . . EX

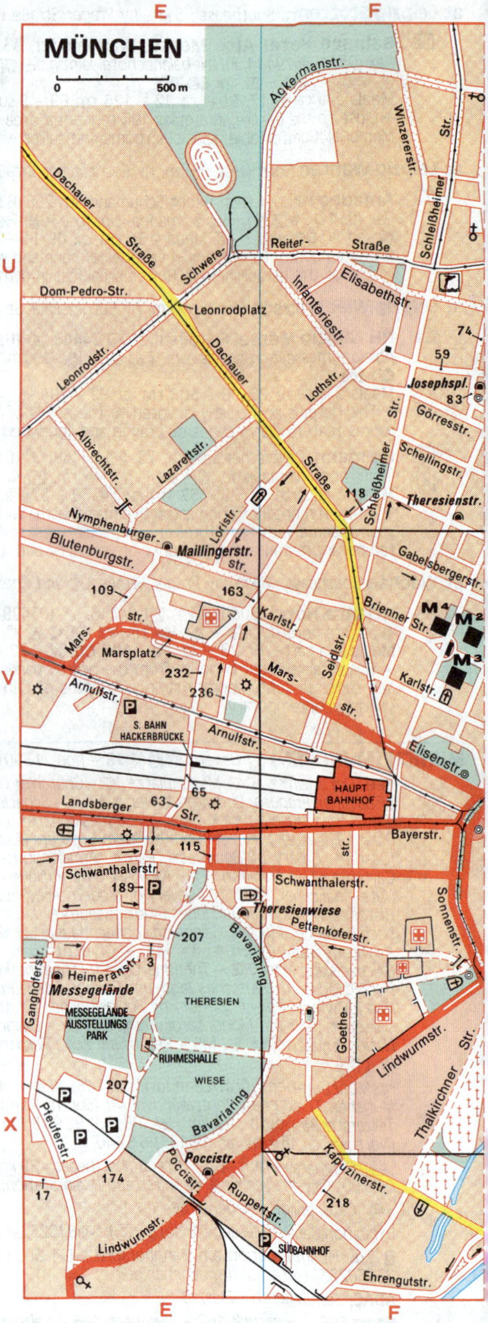

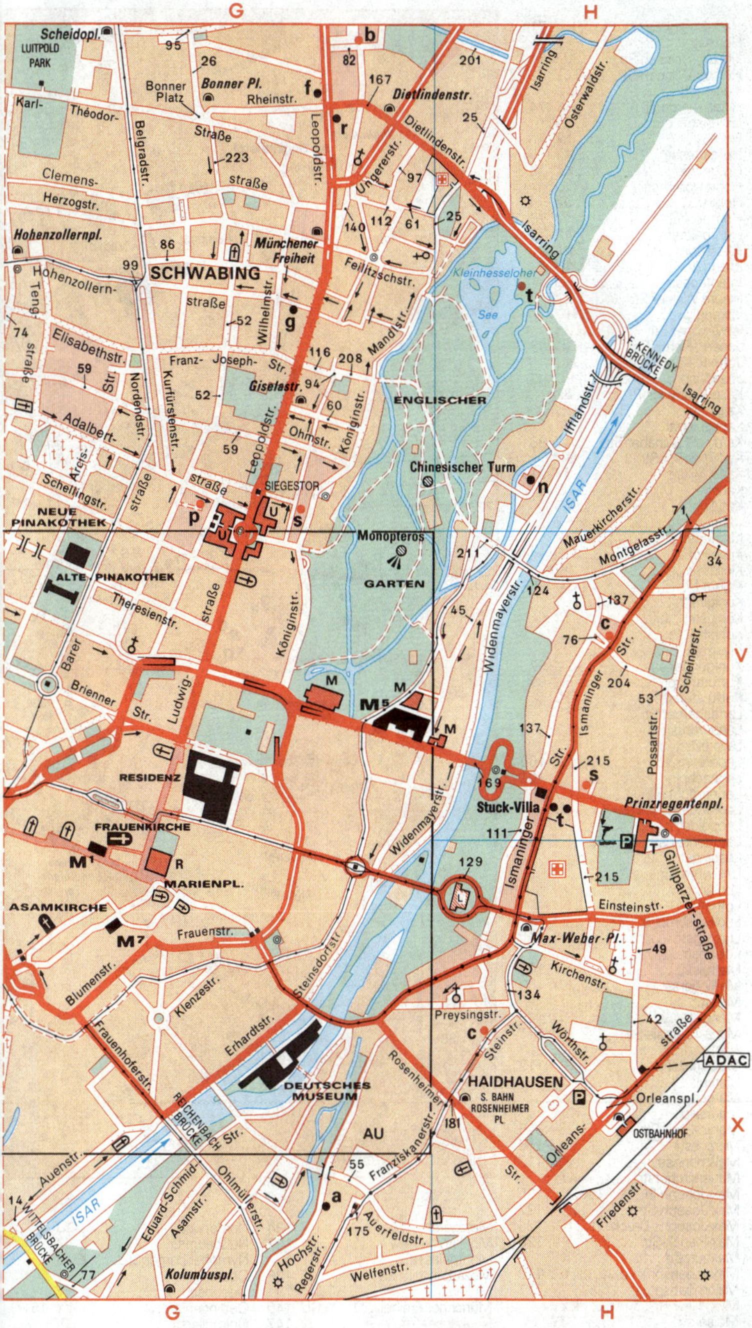
G
H
U
V
X
SCHWABING
ENGLISCHER
GARTEN
Chinesischer Turm
Monopteros
NEUE PINAKOTHEK
ALTE PINAKOTHEK
RESIDENZ
FRAUENKIRCHE
MARIENPL.
ASAMKIRCHE
DEUTSCHES MUSEUM
HAIDHAUSEN
AU
Stuck-Villa
Prinzregentenpl.
Max-Weber-Pl.
Orleanspl.
OSTBAHNHOF
ADAC
S. BAHN ROSENHEIMER PL
SIEGESTOR
LUITPOLD PARK
Scheidopl.
Bonner Pl.
Dietlindenstr.
Hohenzollernpl.
Münchener Freiheit
Giselastr.
Kleinhesseloher See
J.F. KENNEDY BRÜCKE
Isarring
ISAR
REICHENBACH BRÜCKE
WITTELSBACHER BRÜCKE
Kolumbuspl.
Leopoldstr.
Ludwigstr.
Brienner Str.
Widenmayerstr.
Ismaninger Str.
Grillparzerstraße
Einsteinstr.
Rosenheimer Str.
Frauenhoferstr.
Blumenstr.
Steinsdorfstr.
Erhardtstr.

Herkomerpl. .... HU 71
Herrnstr. .... LZ
Herzog-Heinrich-Str. .... JZ
Herzog-Wilhelm-Str. .... JZ
Herzogstr. .... GU
Hiltenspergerstr. .... FGU 74
Hirtenstr. .... JY
Hochstr. .... LZ
Hofgartenstr. .... KY
Hofgraben .... KZ 75
Hohenzollernstr. .... GU
Holzstr. .... JZ
Hompeschstr. .... HV 76
Humboldtstr. .... GX 77
Ickstattstr. .... KZ
Ifflandstr. .... HU
Infanteriestr. .... FU
Innere Wiener Str. .... LZ 79
Isarring .... HU
Ismaninger Str. .... HVX
Johann-Fichte-Str. .... GU 82
John-F.-Kennedy-Br. .... HU
Josephspl. .... FU 83
Kaiser-Ludwigs-Pl. .... JZ
Kaiserstr. .... GU 86
Kapuzinerstr. .... JZ
Kardinal-Faulhaber-Str. .... KY 88
Karl-Theodor-Str. .... GU
Karlspl.Stachus .... JY 91
Karlstr. .... JY
Karolinenpl. .... KY
Kaufingerstr. .... KZ
Kirchenstr. .... HX
Kißkaltpl. .... GU 94
Klenzestr. .... KZ
Kölner Pl. .... GU 95
Königinstr. .... LY
Königspl. .... JY
Kohlstr. .... KLZ
Kreuzstr. .... JZ
Kunigundenstr. .... GU 97
Kurfürstenpl. .... GU 99
Kurfürstenstr. .... GU
Landsberger Str. .... EV
Landwehrstr. .... JZ
Lazarettstr. .... EU
Ledererstr. .... KZ 100
Lenbachpl. .... KY 101
Leonrodpl. .... EU
Leonrodstr. .... EU
Leopoldstr. .... GU
Lerchenfeldstr. .... LY 102
Lessingstr. .... JZ
Lindwurmstr. .... JZ
Loristr. .... EUV
Lothstr. .... FU
Ludwigsbrücke .... LZ
Ludwigstr. .... KY
Luisenstr. .... JY
Maffeistr. .... KY 106
Maillingerstr. .... EV 109
Maistr. .... JZ
Mandlstr. .... GU
Maria-Theresia-Str. .... HV 111
Marienpl. .... KZ
Marschallstr. .... GU 112
Marspl. .... EV
Marsstr. .... JY
Marstallpl. .... KLY
Martin-Greif-Str. .... EX 115
Martiusstr. .... GU 116
Maßmannstr. .... FU 118
Mauerkircherstr. .... HUV
Max-Joseph-Pl. .... KY 125
Max-Joseph-Str. .... KY 127
Max-Josephs-Brücke .... HV 124
Max-Planck-Str. .... HX 129
Maxburgstr. .... KY
Maximiliansbrücke .... LZ 119
Maximilianspl. .... KY 121
Maximilianstr. .... KYZ
Meiserstr. .... JY

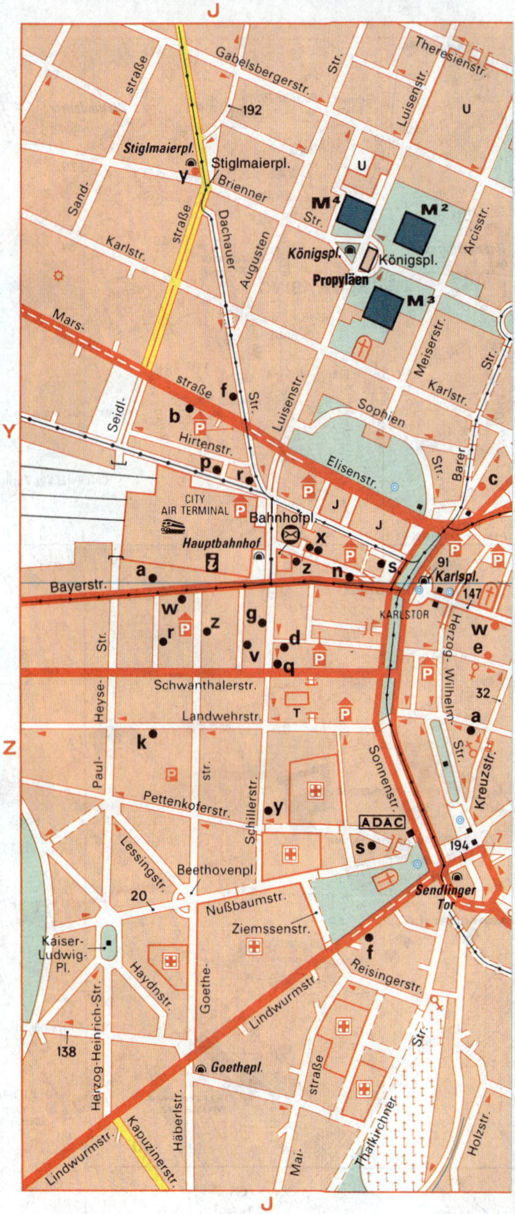

Metzgerstr. .... HX 134
Möhlstr. .... HV 137
Montgelasstr. .... HUV
Mozartstr. .... JZ 138
Müllerstr. .... KZ
Münchner Freiheit .... GU 140
Neuhauser Str. .... JZ 147
Nordendstr. .... GU
Nußbaumstr. .... JZ
Nymphenburger Str. .... EUV
Oberanger .... KZ
Odeonspl. .... KY
Oettingenstr. .... LY 151
Ohlmüllerstr. .... GX

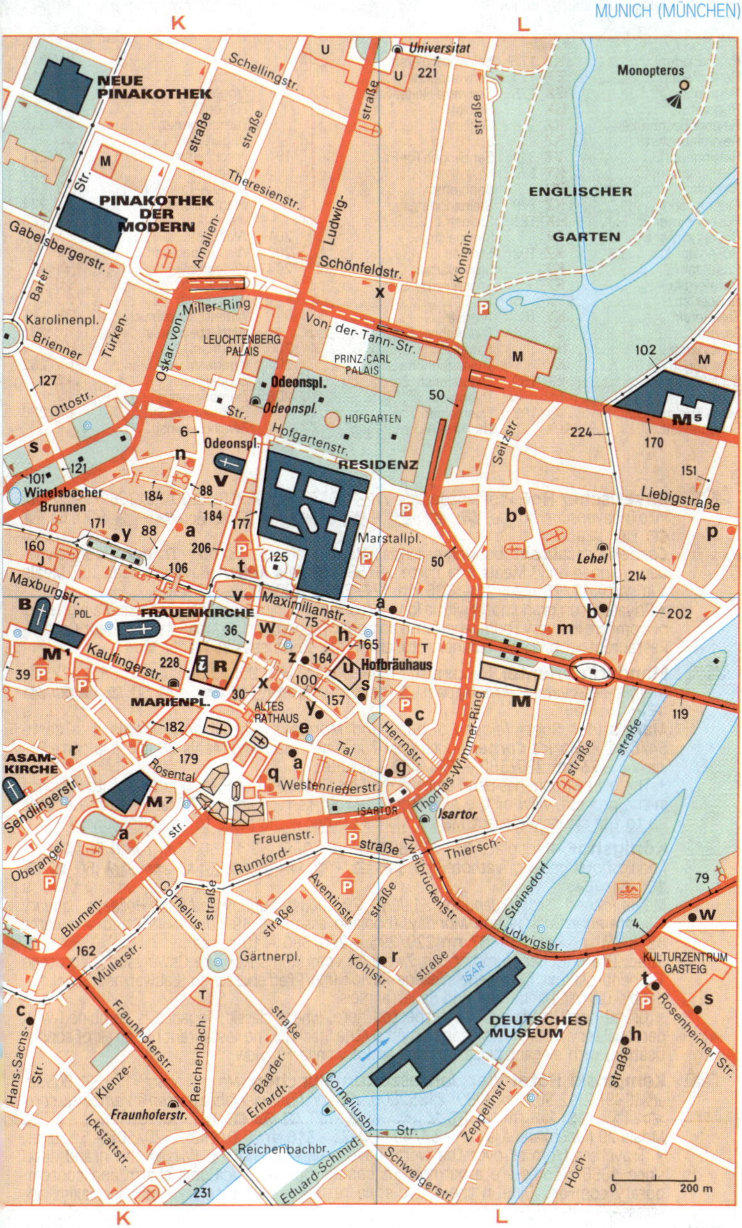

Ohmstr. .... GU
Orlandostr. .... KZ 157
Orleanspl. .... HX
Orleansstr. .... HX
Oskar-von-Miller-Ring .... KY
Osterwaldstr. .... HU
Ottostr. .... KY
Pacellistr. .... KY 160
Papa-Schmid-Str. .... KZ 162
Pappenheimstr. .... EV 163
Paul-Heyse-Str. .... JZ
Pettenkoferstr. .... JZ
Pfeuferstr. .... EX
Pfisterstr. .... KZ 164
Platzl .... KZ 165
Poccistr. .... EX
Possartstr. .... HV
Potsdamer Str. .... GU 167
Preysingstr. .... HX
Prinzregentenbrücke .... HV 169
Prinzregentenstr. .... LY 170

Promenadepl.	KY	171
Radlkoferstr.	EX	174
Regerpl.	GX	175
Regerstr.	GX	
Reichenbachbrüke	KZ	
Reichenbachstr.	KZ	
Reisingerstr.	JZ	
Residenzstr.	KY	177
Rheinstr.	GU	
Rindermarkt	KZ	179
Rosenheimer Pl.	HX	181
Rosenheimer Str.	LZ	
Rosenstr.	KZ	182
Rosental	KZ	
Rumfordstr.	KZ	
Ruppertstr.	EFX	
Salvatorstr.	KY	184
Sandstr.	JY	
Scheinerstr.	HV	
Schellingstr.	KY	
Schießstättstr.	EX	189
Schillerstr.	JZ	
Schleißheimer Str.	JY	192
Schönfeldstr.	KLY	
Schwanthalerstr.	JZ	
Schweigerstr.	LZ	
Schwere-Reiter-Str.	EFU	
Seidlstr.	JY	
Seitzstr.	LY	
Sendlinger Str.	KZ	
Sendlinger-Tor-Pl.	JZ	194
Sonnenstr.	JZ	
Sophienstr.	JY	
Steinsdorfstr.	LZ	
Steinstr.	HX	
Stengelstr.	HU	201
Sternstr.	LZ	202
Sternwartstr.	HV	204
Stiglmaierpl.	JY	
Tal	KZ	
Tengstr.	GU	
Thalkirchner Str.	JZ	
Theatinerstr.	KY	206
Theresienhöhe	EX	207
Theresienstr.	JK	
Thiemestr.	GU	208
Thierschstr.	LZ	
Thomas-Wimmer-Ring	LZ	
Tivolistr.	HV	211
Triftstr.	LY	214
Trogerstr.	HVX	215
Türkenstr.	KY	
Tumblingerstr.	FX	218
Ungererstr.	GU	
Veterinärstr.	LY	221
Viktoriastr.	GU	223
Von-der-Tann-Str.	KLY	
Wagmüllerstr.	LY	224
Weinstr.	KZ	228
Welfenstr.	GX	
Westenriederstr.	KZ	
Widenmayerstr.	GHV	
Wilhelmstr.	GU	
Winzererstr.	FU	
Wittelsbacherbrücke	GX	
Wittelsbacherstr.	KZ	231
Wörthstr.	HX	
Wredestr.	EV	232
Zeppelinstr.	LZ	
Ziemssenstr.	JZ	
Zirkus-Krone-Str.	EV	236
Zweibrückenstr.	LZ	

Bayerischer Hof, Promenadeplatz 2, ✉ 80333, ☎ (089) 2 12 00, *Fax (089) 2120906*, *info@bayerischerhof.de*, – rm, – 850. AE MC VISA JCB KY y
Garden-Restaurant (booking essential) **Meals** à la carte 35/60 – ***Trader Vic's*** (Polynesian) *(dinner only)* **Meals** à la carte 28/58 – ***Palais Keller*** (Bavarian beer inn) **Meals** à la carte 17/28 – 21 – **386 rm** 177/249 – 286/425 – 17 suites.
• Privately run grand hotel with a long history, combining personal charm and a high level of comfort in every room whether traditional, modern, or country-style. Elegant Garden-Restaurant with classic cuisine. A touch of the south seas in Trader Vic's.

Mandarin Oriental, Neuturmstr. 1, ✉ 80331, ☎ (089) 29 09 80, *Fax (089) 222539*, *momuc-reservations@mohg.com*, (heated) – – 50. AE MC VISA JCB KZ s
Mark's (1st floor) *(closed Sunday and Monday) (dinner only)* **Meals** à la carte 54/80 – ***Mark's Corner*** *(lunch only Tuesday - Saturday)* **Meals** 28 and à la carte – 24 – **73 rm** 280/380 – 330/430 – 6 suites.
• The old ballroom has been transformed into a luxury hotel, losing none of its brilliance in the process. View of the Alps from the roof-terrace and pool. Marble staircase leads up to the stylishly elegant Mark's. Mark's Corner is the place to meet for lunch.

Königshof, Karlsplatz 25, ✉ 80335, ☎ (089) 55 13 60, *Fax (089) 55136113*, *koenigshof@geisel-privathotels.de*, – rm, – 60. AE MC VISA JCB JY s
Meals *(closed 1 to 10 January, 31 July - 29 August, Sunday and Bank Holidays, January - September Sunday and Monday)* (booking essential) 39 *(lunch)*/118 and à la carte 52/84 – 20 – **87 rm** 220/295 – 270/380 – 10 suites.
Spec. Bretonischer Hummer mit Zweierlei vom Blumenkohl im Gewürzsud. Gebratene Taubenbrust mit Gänseleber-Sellerie-Ravioli und Pfefferkirschen. Lauwarmes Schokoladenbiskuit mit Himbeeren und Sauerrahmeis.
• Grand hotel traditions are respected here, where classic elegance is combined with personal service. Enviable location right by the Stachus. The restaurant has an air of sophistication, with elegant place settings and a wonderful view.

Kempinski Hotel Vier Jahreszeiten München, Maximilianstr. 17, ✉ 80539, ☎ (089) 2 12 50, *Fax (089) 21252000*, *reservations.vierjahreszeiten@kempinski.com*, – rm, – 230. AE MC VISA. rest LZ a
Meals 29 *(lunch)* and à la carte 33/49 – 25 – **316 rm** 300/460 – 370/505 – 51 suites.
• Travellers from all over the world have been enjoying the flair of this grand hotel since 1858. Rooms are a harmonious combination of traditional charm and contemporary comfort. Dine in the bistro-style restaurant with its view of the Maximilianstrasse.

Dorint Sofitel Bayerpost, Bayerstr. 12, ✉ 80335, ☎ (089) 59 94 80, *Fax (089) 599481000*, *info.mucbay@dorint.com*, – rm, – 450. AE MC VISA JCB. rest JY a
Meals à la carte 29/47 – 20 – **396 rm** 205/235 – 230/260 – 26 suites.
• The sandstone facade conceals a contemporary hotel. Dark colours and subdued lighting emphasise the avant garde design of this new establishment close to the main station.

Le Méridien, Bayerstr. 41, ✉ 80335, ☎ (089) 2 42 20, *Fax (089) 24221111, info.muenchen@lemeridien.com*, , , , , – , rm, – 160. AE VISA JCB JZ w
Meals à la carte 32/46 ₸ – ☕ 20 – **381 rm** 335/435 – 9 suites.
◆ Cool elegance accompanies you all the way from the lobby to the rooms of this modern hotel with appealing lines and lovely materials throughout. Ample windows in the restaurant give a wonderful view of the attractive, leafy courtyard,

Park Hilton, Am Tucherpark 7, ✉ 80538, ☎ (089) 3 84 50, *Fax (089) 38452588, info.munich@hilton.com*, beer garden, , – , rm, – 690. AE VISA JCB HU n
Meals à la carte 30/44 – ***Tse Yang*** (Chinese) *(closed Monday)* **Meals** à la carte 24/43 – ☕ 22 – **479 rm** 165/255 – 190/280 – 3 suites.
◆ This establishment is appreciated both for its tranquil location by the Englischer Garten, Munich's "green lung", and for its contemporary rooms, well equipped with technical facilities - including Business and Executive rooms. Bistro-style restaurant.

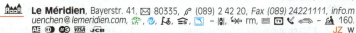

Excelsior, Schützenstr. 11, ✉ 80335, ☎ (089) 55 13 70, *Fax (089) 55137121, excelsior@geisel-privathotels.de*, – , rm, – 25. AE VISA JCB JY z
Geisel's Vinothek *(closed Sunday lunch)* **Meals** à la carte 30/34 ₸ – ☕ 16 – **114 rm** 150/230 – 190/230.
◆ Perhaps it is the rustically elegant ambience of foyer and rooms that give the impression of being in the heart of the countryside rather than in the middle of a bustling, cosmopolitan city. Country-style vinotheque with painted vaults.

Maritim, Goethestr. 7, ✉ 80336, ☎ (089) 55 23 50, *Fax (089) 55235901, info.mun@maritim.de*, , , – , rm, – 250. AE VISA JCB JZ z
Meals à la carte 24/36 – ☕ 18 – **339 rm** 154/170 – 176/209 – 5 suites.
◆ Close to the Deutsches Theater, the Stachus and the Oktoberfest grounds, this establishment provides every comfort in elegant and tastefully decorated rooms. Rotisserie and bistro offer international dishes.

ArabellaSheraton Westpark, Garmischer Str. 2, ✉ 80339, ☎ (089) 5 19 60, *Fax (089) 51963000, westpark@arabellasheraton.com*, , , – , rm, – 70. AE VISA JCB by Leopoldstraße GU
closed 23 December - 9 January – **Meals** à la carte 23/35 – ☕ 17 – **258 rm** 185 - 210 – 6 suites.
◆ Among the features of this contemporary hotel are functional rooms with the latest communication facilities and a bright and cheerful leisure area. Elegant ambience in the restaurant.

Eden-Hotel-Wolff, Arnulfstr. 4, ✉ 80335, ☎ (089) 55 11 50, *Fax (089) 55115555, sales@ehw.de*, – , rm, rm, – 140. AE VISA JCB JY p
Meals à la carte 21/37 – **216 rm** ☕ 133/148 – 172/188.
◆ Reside in elegant surroundings, rich in tradition, right in the middle of Bavaria's capital city. Seven allergen-free rooms with parquet floors. Authentic Bavarian atmosphere in the Zirbelstube, with a choice of international cuisine or tasty local fare.

King's Hotel without rest, Dachauer Str. 13, ✉ 80335, ☎ (089) 55 18 70, *Fax (089) 55187300, 1stclass@kingshotels.de* – – 35. AE VISA JCB JY f
closed 23 to 27 December – ☕ 15 – **86 rm** 125/140.
◆ Wood, wherever you look ! Its elegant Alpine style makes this a particularly welcoming hotel. And there's a four-poster in every room !

Exquisit without rest, Pettenkoferstr. 3, ✉ 80336, ☎ (089) 5 51 99 00, *Fax (089) 55199499, info@hotel-exquisit.com*, – – 25. AE VISA JZ s
50 rm ☕ 125/155 – 165 – 5 suites.
◆ In the very centre of town, this functional establishment has rooms with dark mahogany furniture. Marienplatz, Stachus and Oktoberfest grounds all within walking distance.

Anna, Schützenstr. 1, ✉ 80335, ☎ (089) 59 99 40, *Fax (089) 59994333, anna@geisel-privathotels.de* – , rm, . AE VISA JCB JYZ n
Meals à la carte 24/32 ₸ – **56 rm** ☕ 150 – 170.
◆ Right by the Stachus in Munich's Altstadt, this well-appointed hotel features contemporary design, attractive colour schemes and state-of-the-art technical facilities. Modern, bistro-type restaurant with sushi bar.

Platzl, Sparkassenstr. 10, ✉ 80331, ☎ (089) 23 70 30, *Fax (089) 23703800, info@platzl.de*, beer garden, Lб, ≘ – |‡|, ⋟ rm, TV ✆ ♿ 🚗 – 🎤 70. AE ⓓ MC VISA KZ z
Pfistermühle *(closed Sunday)* **Meals** à la carte 26/43 – ***Ayingers*** **: Meals** à la carte 18/33 – **167 rm** ☕ 96/145 – 157/230.
• Comfortable rooms in traditional Bavarian style in the historic heart of the city. The rooms facing the courtyard enjoy peace and quiet. Spa area in the style of the Moorish Kiosk of Ludwig II. All the atmosphere of old Munich in the vaulted Pfistermühle.

Drei Löwen without rest, Schillerstr. 8, ✉ 80336, ☎ (089) 55 10 40, *Fax (089) 55104905, info@hotel3loewen.de* – |‡| ⋟ TV ✆ – 🎤 15. AE ⓓ MC VISA JCB JZ m
☕ 14 – **96 rm** 105 – 130 – 3 suites.
• In the city centre close to the main station, this hotel has comfortable modern rooms tastefully furnished in wood.

Stadthotel Asam without rest, Josephspitalstr. 3, ✉ 80331, ☎ (089) 2 30 97 00, *Fax (089) 23097097, info@hotel-asam.de* – |‡| ⋟ TV ♿ 🚗. AE ⓓ MC VISA JZ a
closed 24 December - 6 January – ☕ 13 – **25 rm** 129/145 – 158/174 – 8 Suites.
• A small city centre hotel with more than a touch of luxury, offering rooms with many a stylish and tasteful detail.

Cortiina without rest, Ledererstr. 8, ✉ 80331, ☎ (089) 2 42 24 90, *Fax (089) 242249100, info@cortiina.com* – |‡| ⋟ ▤ TV ✆ 🚗. AE ⓓ MC VISA KZ y
35 rm ☕ 126/146 – 186.
• Cool furnishings and parquet floors in contemporary style rooms with state-of-the-art technical facilities. The attractive bar also serves light meals.

Torbräu, Tal 41, ✉ 80331, ☎ (089) 24 23 40(hotel) 22 80 75 23(rest.), *Fax (089) 24234235, info@torbraeu.de*, beer garden – |‡|, ⋟ rm, ▤ rm, TV ✆ 🚗 P – 🎤 30. AE MC VISA LZ g
La Famiglia (Italian) **Meals** à la carte 34/44 – **92 rm** ☕ 135/155 – 170/240 – 3 suites.
• This historic 15C building is reputedly the city's oldest hotel. Well-kept rooms with ample space, all with air-conditioning. Tuscan flair and Italian cuisine in the La Famiglia restaurant with its terracotta tiled floor.

Mercure City, Senefelder Str. 9, ✉ 80336, ☎ (089) 55 13 20, *Fax (089) 596444, h0878@accor.com*, beer garden – |‡|, ⋟ rm, ▤ TV ✆ 🚗 – 🎤 50. AE ⓓ MC VISA JCB. ⋟ rest
Meals à la carte 21/34 – **167 rm** ☕ 134/153 – 169/188. JZ v
• Spacious, contemporary and functional rooms in this city centre establishment close to the main station.

Admiral without rest, Kohlstr. 9, ✉ 80469, ☎ (089) 21 63 50, *Fax (089) 293674, info@hotel-admiral.de* – |‡| ⋟ TV ✆ 🚗. AE ⓓ MC VISA JCB LZ r
33 rm ☕ 115/165 – 145/195.
• Just a short walk from the city centre, this hotel has functional rooms, some offering peace and quiet. Breakfast served in the little garden when fine.

King's Hotel Center without rest, Marsstr. 15, ✉ 80335, ☎ (089) 51 55 30, *Fax (089) 51553300, center@kingshotels.de* – |‡| ⋟ TV ✆ ♿. AE ⓓ MC VISA JY b
☕ 12 – **90 rm** 98/120.
• A panelled foyer welcomes guests to this establishment close to the city centre. Comfortable rooms with elaborate four-posters.

NH Deutscher Kaiser without rest, Arnulfstr. 2, ✉ 80335, ☎ (089) 5 45 30, *Fax (089) 54532255, nhdeutscherkaiser@nh-hotels.com* – |‡| ⋟ TV ✆ – 🎤 80. AE ⓓ MC VISA JY r
☕ 15 – **174 rm** 124/139.
• Well-adapted to the requirements of business travellers, this hotel stands on the north side of the main station. Bright rooms with ample desks and comfortable chairs.

Drei Löwen Residenz without rest, Aldolf-Kolping-Str. 11, ✉ 80336, ☎ (089) 55 10 40, *Fax (089) 55104905, info@hotel3loewen.de* – |‡| ⋟ TV ✆. AE ⓓ MC VISA JCB JZ d
☕ 12 – **63 rm** 90 – 115.
• A few steps away is a sister establishment of the same name. Welcoming, comfortable rooms ; those to the rear are very quiet.

Atrium without rest, Landwehrstr. 59, ✉ 80336, ☎ (089) 51 41 90, *Fax (089) 535066, info@atrium-hotel.de*, ≘ – |‡| ⋟ TV ✆ 🚗 – 🎤 20. AE ⓓ MC VISA JCB JZ k
162 rm ☕ 142 – 172.
• Mirrors and marble distinguish the foyer of this elegant establishment. Rooms with natural wood furnishings and excellent technical facilities. Leafy little courtyard.

Splendid-Dollmann without rest, Thierschstr. 49, ✉ 80538, ☎ (089) 23 80 80, *Fax (089) 23808365, splendid-muc@t-online.de* – |‡| TV ✆. AE ⓓ MC VISA JCB LZ b
☕ 11 – **37 rm** 120/150 – 150/160.
• The book-lined reception area in this 19C town residence could be a library. Individual rooms, partly furnished with antiques and a pretty breakfast room with vaulted ceiling.

Domus without rest, St.-Anna-Str. 31, ✉ 80538, ☎ (089) 22 17 04, *Fax (089) 2285359, reservation@domus-hotel.de* – AE MC VISA LY b
closed 23 to 27 December – **45 rm** 105/118 – 128/135.
◆ Between the Maximilianstrasse and the Prinzregentenstrasse, this tastefully decorated hotel couldn't be better placed for shops, art, and culture.

Carat-Hotel without rest, Lindwurmstr. 13, ✉ 80337, ☎ (089) 23 03 80, *Fax (089) 23038199, info-m@carat-hotel.de* – 15. AE MC VISA JZ f
70 rm 107/117 – 137/152.
◆ Contemporary, functional rooms, primarily intended for business travellers. Most with modem connection, some with air-conditioning.

Kraft without rest, Schillerstr. 49, ✉ 80336, ☎ (089) 5 50 59 40, *Fax (089) 55059479, info@hotel-kraft.com* – AE MC VISA JCB JZ y
33 rm 80 – 95.
◆ Very liveable establishment, partly furnished with antique items. In the university clinic district, easy access to station, Oktoberfest, public transport and city centre.

Concorde without rest, Herrnstr. 38, ✉ 80539, ☎ (089) 22 45 15, *Fax (089) 2283282, info@concorde-muenchen.de* – AE MC VISA LZ c
closed Christmas - early January – **71 rm** 98 – 128.
◆ This attentively run hotel in the Altstadt has well-kept practical rooms furnished in a variety of styles. Some face the quiet courtyard.

Apollo without rest, Mittererstr. 7, ✉ 80336, ☎ (089) 53 95 31, *Fax (089) 534033, info@apollohotel.de* – P. AE MC VISA JCB JZ r
74 rm 89 – 99.
◆ This city centre hotel offers mahogany furnished rooms - spacious and comfortable. Ask for one facing the quiet courtyard.

Präsident without rest, Schwanthalerstr. 20, ✉ 80336, ☎ (089) 5 49 00 60, *Fax (089) 54900628, hotel.praesident@t-online.de* – 15. AE MC VISA JCB JZ q
42 rm 79/84 – 95.
◆ Ideal for theatre-goers, this completely rebuilt establishment is diagonally opposite Munich's Deutsches Theater. Contemporary rooms with bright, natural wood furniture.

Schlicker without rest, Tal 8, ✉ 80331, ☎ (089) 2 42 88 70, *Fax (089) 296059, schlicker-munich@t-online.de* – P. AE MC VISA KZ a
closed 22 December - 7 January – **69 rm** 85/105 – 115/170.
◆ Within sight of City Hall with its world-famous glockenspiel, this venerable 16C building is now a modern hotel. Elegant or spacious rooms.

Olympic without rest, Hans-Sachs-Str. 4, ✉ 80469, ☎ (089) 23 18 90, *Fax (089) 23189199* – AE MC VISA KZ c
38 rm 90/125 – 140.
◆ Partly furnished in Biedermeier style, most of the rooms here overlook leafy and tranquil inner courtyards. Close to Marienplatz, Deutsches Museum and Metro station.

Meier without rest, Schützenstr. 12, ✉ 80335, ☎ (089) 5 49 03 40, *Fax (089) 549034340, info@hotel-meier.de* – AE MC VISA JCB JY x
closed 23 to 29 December – **50 rm** 75/88 – 95/116.
◆ Completely refurbished in the late 1990s, this upper-floor establishment now offers its guests standard, functional rooms.

Schuhbeck's in den Südtiroler Stuben, Platzl 6, ✉ 80331, ☎ (089) 2 16 69 00, *Fax (089) 21669025, info@schuhbeck.de* – AE MC VISA KZ u
closed Monday lunch, Sunday and Bank Holidays – **Meals** 53 *(lunch)*/99 *(dinner)* and à la carte.
Spec. Gegrillter Zander auf Sellerie-Friséesalat. Gefüllte Kaninchenkeule mit Brennessel-Spinat und Pfifferlingen. Topfenpalatschinken mit Aprikosenröster.
◆ Elegance and country style happily combined. Wall panelling, plaster ceilings, and fine table settings make for a pleasant dining experience. Cooking school.

Boettner's, Pfisterstr. 9, ✉ 80331, ☎ (089) 22 12 10, *Fax (089) 29162024*, – . AE MC VISA KZ h
closed 15 April - 15 September Saturday - Sunday and Bank Holidays – **Meals** (booking essential) 32 *(lunch)*/74 and à la carte 42/74 – ***Boettner's Atrium*** : **Meals** à la carte 19/28.
◆ Boettner's is a Munich institution. You dine in one of several rooms with elegant, traditional décor, some of them with venerable wooden panelling. Classic cuisine.

Halali, Schönfeldstr. 22, ✉ 80539, ☎ (089) 28 59 09, *Fax (089) 282786, halali-muenchen@t-online.de* – AE MC VISA LY x
closed 3 weeks August, Saturday lunch, Sunday and Bank Holidays – **Meals** (booking essential) 22 *(lunch)* and à la carte 30/45.
◆ This historic, flower-bedecked 19C inn has a tasteful, rustic interior featuring plenty of wood panelling.

XX **Ederer**, Kardinal-Faulhaber-Str. 10, ✉ 80333, ✆ (089) 24 23 13 10, *Fax (089) 24231312, restaurant-ederer@t-online.de,* – ▤. AE MC VISA KY a
closed 2 weeks Whitsun, 1 week Christmas, Sunday and Bank Holidays – **Meals** (booking essential) 25 *(lunch)*/85 and à la carte 39/64.
◆ Surrounded by exclusive shops and boutiques, this high-ceilinged establishment offers diners a smart, contemporary setting.

XX **Hunsinger's Pacific**, Maximiliansplatz 5 (entrance Max-Joseph-Straße), ✉ 80333, ✆ (089) 55 02 97 41, *Fax (089) 55029742* – ▤. AE D MC VISA JCB KY s
closed Saturday lunch and Sunday – **Meals** à la carte 28/43.
◆ What used to be the "Aubergine" has now been transported to the Pacific Rim, with trompe l'oeil paintings lit by chandeliers. International cuisine with an Asian touch.

XX **Austernkeller**, Stollbergstr. 11, ✉ 80539, ✆ (089) 29 87 87, *Fax (089) 223166* – AE D MC VISA JCB LZ e
Meals *(dinner only)* (booking essential) à la carte 30/46.
◆ This is the place to come for shellfish and other freshly caught denizens of the deep. With a décor of porcelain plates, these vaulted cellars are a listed historic monument.

XX **Dallmayr**, Dienerstr. 14 (1st floor), ✉ 80331, ✆ (089) 2 13 51 00, *Fax (089) 2135443, gastro@dallmayr.de* – ▤. AE D MC VISA JCB KZ w
closed Monday - Wednesday from 7 pm, Thursday and Friday from 8 pm, Saturday from 4 pm, Sunday and Bank Holidays – **Meals** 33/48 and à la carte 38/52.
◆ This is the restaurant of the famous delicatessen patronised by kings and emperors. The freshness and naturalness of its products have become a byword.

XX **Nymphenburger Hof**, Nymphenburger Str. 24, ✉ 80335, ✆ (089) 1 23 38 30, *Fax (089) 1233852,* – AE MC VISA. EV a
closed 23 December - 15 January, Saturday lunch, Sunday and Bank Holidays – **Meals** (booking essential) 18 *(lunch)*/55 and à la carte 30/47 ♀.
◆ Bright and welcoming restaurant with a terrace. Pastel-coloured décor, plenty of flowers, and a refined cuisine with many local or Austrian-influenced specialities.

XX **Blauer Bock**, Sebastiansplatz 9, ✉ 80331, ✆ (089) 45 22 23 33, *Fax (089) 45222330, mail@restaurant-blauerbocl.de* – AE MC VISA KZ a
closed Saturday and Sunday lunch – **Meals** 19 *(lunch)* and à la carte 30/44.
◆ Just a few steps from the food market will take you to this modern restaurant. Its interior is a mix of simplicity and warm colours. Cuisine is international with French origins.

XX **Lenbach**, Ottostr. 6, ✉ 80333, ✆ (089) 5 49 13 00, *Fax (089) 54913075, info@lenbach.de,* – AE D MC VISA JY c
closed Sunday and Bank Holidays – **Meals** 15 *(lunch)*/48 and à la carte 32/54.
◆ Part of the Lenbach Palace redesigned by Sir Terence Conran to house vast and fashionable dining-spaces including a sushi-bar and a contemporary restaurant.

XX **Galleria**, Sparkassenstr. 11 / corner of Ledererstraße, ✉ 80331, ✆ (089) 29 79 95, *Fax (089) 2913653, info@ristorante-galleria.de* – ▤. AE D MC VISA KZ x
closed Sunday, except exhibitions and December – **Meals** (Italian) (booking essential) 27 *(lunch)* and à la carte 31/46 ♀.
◆ Intimate setting and wonderfully colourful décor. Changing selection of pictures. Cuisine based on classic Italian recipes.

XX **Weinhaus Neuner**, Herzogspitalstr. 8, ✉ 80331, ✆ (089) 2 60 39 54, *Fax (089) 266933, weinhaus-neuner@t-online.de* – AE MC VISA JZ e
closed Sunday and Bank Holidays – **Meals** à la carte 27/33.
◆ This vaulted establishment of 1852 is claimed to be Munich's oldest wine restaurant. Splendid wall-paintings. Traditional and local dishes.

XX **Les Cuisiniers**, Reitmorstr. 21, ✉ 80538, ✆ (089) 23 70 98 90, – D MC VISA LZ p
closed Saturday lunch and Sunday – **Meals** 17 *(lunch)* and à la carte 23/33 ♀.
◆ A bright and welcoming bistro-style restaurant with modern paintings on the walls. Simple Mediterranean cuisine.

X **Vinorant Alter Hof**, Alter Hof 3, ✉ 80331, ✆ (089) 24 24 37 33, *Fax (089) 24243734, mail@alter-hof-muenchen.de,* – MC VISA KZ w
closed dinner Sunday and Bank Holidays – **Meals** à la carte 19/34 ♀.
◆ This former residence of the Wittelsbach family, one of Munich's most venerable buildings, has two function rooms, each decorated in a contemporary and simple style, with a beautiful vaulted ceiling. Vinotek and large bar area in the cellar.

X **Dukatz**, Salvatorplatz 1, ✉ 80333, ✆ (089) 2 91 96 00, *Fax (089) 29196028, info@dukatz.de* KY n
closed Sunday dinner – **Meals** (booking essential) à la carte 25/35 ♀.
◆ In the "Literature House", a former indoor market dating from 1870, a range of international dishes is served in lovely vaulted rooms on two levels.

Zum Alten Markt, Dreifaltigkeitsplatz 3, 80331, (089) 29 99 95, *Fax (089) 2285076, lehner.gastro@zumaltenmarkt.de,* KZ q
closed Sunday and Bank Holidays – **Meals** (booking essential for dinner) à la carte 22/36.
◆ With its homely Tyrolean atmosphere, this pub-type establishment on the Viktualienmarkt boasts lavish wood panelling, some of it authentic and more than 400 years old.

Brewery-inns :

Spatenhaus an der Oper, Residenzstr. 12, 80333, (089) 2 90 70 60, *Fax (089) 2913054, spatenhaus@kuffler.de,* – AE MC VISA KY t
Meals à la carte 27/40.
◆ This century-old town mansion has a number of cheerful first floor rooms with varying décor and a ground floor with an Alpine feel about it.

Weisses Brauhaus, Tal 7, 80331, (089) 2 90 13 80, *Fax (089) 29013815, info@weisses-brauhaus.de,* – 30. MC VISA KZ e
Meals à la carte 16/30.
◆ Built around 1900, this establishment in the historic centre of town has a lovely façade. Inside, authentic local specialities served in a congenial atmosphere.

Augustiner Gaststätten, Neuhauser Str. 27, 80331, (089) 23 18 32 57, *Fax (089) 2605379, augustinerstammhaus@yahoo.de,* – AE MC VISA JZ w
Meals à la carte 16/32.
◆ Beer was brewed here in the Augustiner headquarters right up to 1885. Arcade Garden and Shell Hall are among the great achievements of Munich Art Nouveau. Fine beer garden.

Altes Hackerhaus, Sendlinger Str. 14, 80331, (089) 2 60 50 26, *Fax (089) 2605027, hackerhaus@aol.com,* – AE MC VISA JCB KZ r
Meals à la carte 12/35.
◆ This establishment has many faces, including the lively beer garden, the romantic covered courtyard, the cheerful councillors' parlour, and the vaults of the Schäfflergewölbe.

Zum Franziskaner, Residenzstr. 9/Perusastr. 5, 80333, (089) 2 31 81 20, *Fax (089) 23181244, zum.franziskaner@t-online.de,* – . AE MC VISA KYZ v
Meals à la carte 18/32.
◆ Traditional hospitality in spacious surroundings close to the main post office. Bavarian delicacies ranging from famous "white sausage" to the produce of rivers and lakes.

Bratwurstherzl, Dreifaltigkeitsplatz 1 (at Viktualienmarkt), 80331, (089) 29 51 13, *Fax (089) 29163751, bratwurst@t-online.de,* beer garden – MC VISA KZ q
closed Sunday and Bank Holidays – **Meals** à la carte 13/20.
◆ The big draw here are the sausages you grill yourself. "Beginners" get six, "Advanced students" eight, and "Regulars" are served straightaway with a round dozen.

at Munich-Allach *Northwest : 12 km, by Arnulfstraße EV and Menzinger Straße :*

Lutter without rest, Eversbuschstr. 109, 80999, (089) 8 12 70 04, *Fax (089) 8129584, hotel-lutter@t-online.de* – . MC VISA.
closed 16 December - 9 January – **27 rm** 67/82 – 77/105.
◆ Impeccably run establishment with functional rooms in the northwestern part of the city. Good value for the price.

at Munich-Bogenhausen :

ArabellaSheraton Grand Hotel, Arabellastr. 6, 81925, (089) 9 26 40, *Fax (089) 92648009, grandhotel.muenchen@arabellasheraton.com,* <, beer garden, , , , – , rm, – 650. AE MC VISA.
rest by Ismaninger Straße HVU
Meals *(closed Sunday) (lunch only)* 26 *(buffet)* and à la carte 26/34 – ***Die Ente vom Lehel*** *(closed August, Sunday and Monday) (dinner only)* **Meals** à la carte 49/62 – ***Paulaner's*** *(closed lunch Saturday, Sunday and Bank Holidays)* **Meals** à la carte 20/37 – 21 – **643 rm** 200/285 – 225/310 – 14 suites.
◆ Refurbished grand hotel with imposing foyer and beautifully decorated rooms. Opposite is the Arabellapark with its boutiques, bistros, cinemas and night-club. Opening onto the foyer, the Ente vom Lehel restaurant has a lively atmosphere.

Palace, Trogerstr. 21, 81675, (089) 41 97 10, *Fax (089) 41971819, palace@kuffler.de,* , , – , rm, – 25. AE MC VISA JCB HV t
Meals à la carte 32/43 – 15 – **74 rm** 155/225 – 200/280 – 3 suites.
◆ Elegant hotel with an exceptionally high standard of décor. All rooms with Louis XVI furniture, some with parquet floors. Roof-terrace and garden are well worth a visit when the sun shines. Elegant and stylish Palace Restaurant.

Prinzregent am Friedensengel without rest, Ismaninger Str. 42, ✉ 81675, ✆ (089) 41 60 50, *Fax (089) 41605466, friedensengel@prinzregent.de,* – AE VISA HV t
65 rm 129/185 – 149/215.
◆ This hotel is only five minutes from Munich's famous Englischer Garten. Attractive and comfortable, Alpine-style rooms. Lovely panelled breakfast room with conservatory.

Rothof without rest, Denninger Str. 114, ✉ 81925, ✆ (089) 9 10 09 50, *Fax (089) 915066, rothof@t-online.de,* – AE VISA
closed 23 December - 9 January – **37 rm** 121/131 – 152/172.
◆ Well-run hotel offering bright, spacious and welcoming rooms with large windows and modern working facilities - some pleasantly situated to the rear of the building. by Ismaninger Straße HUV

Bogenhauser Hof, Ismaninger Str. 85, ✉ 81675, ✆ (089) 98 55 86, *Fax (089) 9810221, bogenhauser-hof@t-online.de,* – AE VISA HV c
closed 25 March - 4 April, 23 December - 7 January, Sunday and Bank Holidays – **Meals** (booking essential) 63 and à la carte 41/58.
◆ This hunting lodge dating from 1825 serves a refined version of classic Munich cuisine, which can also be savoured in the idyllic surroundings of the summer garden.

Acquarello, Mühlbaurstr. 36, ✉ 81677, ✆ (089) 4 70 48 48, *Fax (089) 476464, info@acquarello.com,* – AE. by Prinzregentenstraße HV
closed 1 to 3 January, Saturday lunch, Sunday and Bank Holidays – **Meals** (Italian) 27 *(lunch)*/79 and à la carte 39/65.
Spec. Vitello Tonnato. Rinderschmorbraten mit Barolosauce und Selleriepüree. Schokoladenravioli mit Minzeis und Orangensauce.
◆ The chef has succeeded in creating wonderfully contrasting variations on the theme of Italian cuisine. Walls painted in subtle colours enhance the Mediterranean ambience.

Käfer Schänke, Prinzregentenstr. 73, ✉ 81675, ✆ (089) 4 16 82 47, *Fax (089) 4168623, kaeferschaenke@feinkost-kaefer.de,* – 15. AE VISA JCB HV s
closed July - August, Sunday and Bank Holidays – **Meals** (booking essential) à la carte 33/54.
◆ Cheerful restaurant plus a whole series of differently decorated little parlours, ranging from the cutlery parlour to a tiny tobacco parlour.

at Munich-Denning *East : 8 km, by Denninger Straße* HV :

Casale, Ostpreußenstr. 42, ✉ 81927, ✆ (089) 93 62 68, *Fax (089) 9306722,* – P. AE VISA
Meals (Italian) 23 *(lunch)*/49 and à la carte 28/44.
◆ Classic Italian cuisine awaits you in this bright and welcoming restaurant with its conservatory. Colourful pictures enhance the Mediterranean atmosphere.

at Munich-Haidhausen :

Hilton City, Rosenheimer Str. 15, ✉ 81667, ✆ (089) 4 80 40, *Fax (089) 48044804, info.munich@hilton.com,* – rm, – 180. AE VISA JCB LZ s
Meals à la carte 25/37 – 22 – **480 rm** 139/239 – 175/254 – 4 suites.
◆ Close to the Philharmonic Hall and the Gasteig culture centre, this establishment has functional rooms intended above all for business travellers. Restaurant in Alpine style with a choice of local or international cuisine.

Preysing without rest, Preysingstr. 1, ✉ 81667, ✆ (089) 45 84 50, *Fax (089) 45845444, info@hotel-preysing.de,* – – 15. AE VISA JCB LZ w
closed 24 December - 6 January – **76 rm** 130 – 180 – 5 suites.
◆ Rooms with natural wood furnishings and exquisite attention to detail. The cares of the day can soon be dispersed in pool, jacuzzi or sauna.

Dorint Novotel München City, Hochstr. 11, ✉ 81669, ✆ (089) 66 10 70, *Fax (089) 66107999, h3280@accor.com,* – rm, – 120. AE VISA LZ h
Meals à la carte 22/37 – **307 rm** 129 – 159.
◆ Ask for one of the rooms which have a splendid view of the city centre in this business hotel. Rooms are pleasantly furnished with refreshing colours and elegant lines. Bright, contemporary restaurant.

Holiday Inn Munich - City Centre, Hochstr. 3, ✉ 81669, ✆ (089) 4 80 30, *Fax (089) 4488277, muchb@ichotelsgroup.com,* – rm, – 350. AE VISA. rest LZ t
Meals à la carte 22/32 – 18 – **580 rm** 169 – 189.
◆ Modern conference hotel with spacious rooms, solid furnishings and a vast 2100sq metre conference area. Bistro-style restaurant and rustic beer lounge.

Vinaiolo, Steinstr. 42, ✉ 81667, ℘ (089) 48 95 03 56, *Fax (089) 48068011* – MC VISA HX c
closed Monday lunch – **Meals** (Italian) (booking essential for dinner) à la carte 36/42 ♀.
◆ The menu here is composed using fresh produce from the market, while the wines are displayed on the restored shelving of the old pharmacy that used to occupy the building.

at Munich-Neu Perlach *Southeast : 10 km, by Rosenheimer Straße* HX *and Otto-Brunner-Straße :*

Mercure Orbis, Karl-Marx-Ring 87, ✉ 81735, ℘ (089) 6 32 70, *Fax (089) 6327407, h1374@accor.com*, – rm, – 120. AE MC VISA JCB
Meals à la carte 19/29 – **185 rm** 127 – 151 – 4 suites.
◆ Smart upkeep is the keynote here, from the elegant lobby to the well-furnished bedrooms, usefully equipped with technological mod cons.

Villa Waldperlach without rest, Putzbrunner Str. 250 (Waldperlach), ✉ 81739, ℘ (089) 6 60 03 00, *Fax (089) 66003066, hotel@villa-waldperlach.de* –
AE MC VISA JCB
21 rm 80 – 95.
◆ All the rooms have contemporary oakwood furnishings, plus ample work-desks and excellent technical facilities. Exposed beams in some of the cosy top-floor rooms.

at Munich-Oberföhring *Northwest : 4 km, by Ismaninger Straße* HUV *:*

Freisinger Hof with rm, Oberföhringer Str. 189, ✉ 81925, ℘ (089) 95 23 02, *Fax (089) 9578516, freisinger.hof@t-online.de*, beer garden – AE MC VISA
Meals à la carte 24/44 – **13 rm** 98/115 – 130.
◆ Despite modernisation, this 1875 inn has kept its charm and character. Local specialities served in a rustic setting. Cosy country-style rooms.

at Munich-Riem :

Prinzregent an der Messe, Riemer Str. 350, ✉ 81829, ℘ (089) 94 53 90, *Fax (089) 94539566, messe@prinzregent.de*, , beer garden, – rm, – 40. AE MC VISA by Einsteinstr. HX
Meals à la carte 28/36 – **92 rm** 129 – 149 – 4 suites.
◆ This 18C building blends in well with its modern extension. The rooms are comfortable and well furnished ; nice, relaxing lounge. The cosy restaurant is in the historical part of the house.

Dorint Novotel München Messe, Willy-Brandt-Platz 1, ✉ 81829, ℘ (089) 99 40 00, *Fax (089) 99400100, info.mucmes@dorint.com*, – rm, – 230. AE MC VISA JCB by Einsteinstr. HX
Meals à la carte 24/33 – 15 – **278 rm** 125.
◆ Built on a former airport base, right by the trade fair grounds, this hotel is furnished in a modern style right through from the spacious reception area to all the rooms. Welcoming, light restaurant with glass façade.

at Munich-Schwabing :

Marriott, Berliner Str. 93, ✉ 80805, ℘ (089) 36 00 20, *Fax (089) 36002200, muenchen.marriott@marriotthotels.com*, – rm, – 300. AE MC VISA JCB. rest by Ungererstraße (B 11) HU
Meals à la carte 26/38 – 19 – **348 rm** 159 – 4 suites.
◆ This grand-hotel style establishment boasts a conference floor with up-to-the-minute technical facilities. Attractively decorated rooms with floral fabrics. American-style restaurant with open kitchen and large and splendid buffet.

Holiday Inn City Nord, Leopoldstr. 194, ✉ 80804, ℘ (089) 38 17 90, *Fax (089) 38179888, reservation.hi-munich-citynorth@queengruppe.de*, – – 320. AE MC VISA by Leopoldstraße GU
Meals à la carte 24/36 – 18 – **365 rm** 88/97 – 99/108.
◆ In Munich's arts and entertainment district, this modern business hotel has an array of amenities including Roman spa, sauna, solarium, massage, pool-side bar and sun terrace.

Renaissance Hotel, Theodor-Dombart-Str. 4 (corner of Berliner Straße), ✉ 80805, ℘ (089) 36 09 90, *Fax (089) 360996900, rhi.mucbr.reservations@renaissancehotels.com*, – rm, – 30. AE MC VISA JCB. rest by Ungererstraße (B 11) HU
Meals à la carte 21/32 – 16 – **261 rm** 145 – 87 suites.
◆ Close to the Englischer Garten and the Olympic Stadium. Attractive rooms and elegant suites offer a high level of comfort. For relaxing there is the "recreational oasis". Mediterranean-style Bistro 46-47.

🏨 **Four Points Hotel Olympiapark München**, Helene-Mayer-Ring 12, ✉ 80809, ℘ (089) 35 75 10, Fax (089) 35751800, fourpoints.olympiapark@arabellasheraton.com, 🌳 – 📶, 🙌 rm, 📺 ☎ 🅿 – 🔬 30. 🆎 ⓪ 🐮 VISA JCB
closed 24 December - 9 January – **Meals** (closed Sunday and Bank Holidays) à la carte 18/31 – ☑ 14 – **105 rm** 140 – 165. by Schleißheimer Straße **FU**
♦ Bang in the middle of the Olympia Park ! Elegant and functional rooms just a few steps away from the very best in sporting events and cultural highlights.

🏨 **Cosmopolitan** without rest, Hohenzollernstr. 5, ✉ 80801, ℘ (089) 38 38 10, Fax (089) 38381111, cosmo@cosmopolitan-hotel.de – 📶 🙌 📺 ☎ ⇔. 🆎 ⓪ 🐮 VISA JCB
71 rm ☑ 100 – 110. **GU** g
♦ In the heart of Schwabing, this hotel consists of two linked buildings offering modern rooms with designer furnishings and excellent technical facilities.

🏨 **Mercure** without rest, Leopoldstr. 120, ✉ 80802, ℘ (089) 3 89 99 30, Fax (089) 349344, h1104@accor.com – 📶 🙌 📺 ⇔. 🆎 ⓪ 🐮 VISA JCB **GU** r
☑ 12 – **65 rm** 82/117 – 106/126.
♦ Not far from the Englischer Garten and close to Old Schwabing with its cabarets and pubs, functional rooms up to the usual standard of Mercure establishments.

🏨 **Leopold** without rest, Leopoldstr. 119, ✉ 80804, ℘ (089) 36 04 30, Fax (089) 36043150, hotel-leopold@t-online.de, 🕿 – 📶 🙌 📺 ☎ ⇔ 🅿 – 🔬 20. 🆎 ⓪ 🐮 VISA JCB **GU** f
closed 23 to 30 December – **65 rm** ☑ 95/120 – 100/135.
♦ Charming hotel that has been in the same family for generations, located in the heart of the artistic district of Schwabing. Ask for a room with a view of the idyllic garden.

🍴🍴🍴🍴 / ❀❀ **Tantris**, Johann-Fichte-Str. 7, ✉ 80805, ℘ (089) 3 61 95 90, Fax (089) 36195922, info@tantris.de, 🌳 – 📶 🅿. 🆎 ⓪ 🐮 VISA. 🙌 **GU** b
closed 1 to 10 January, Sunday - Monday and Bank Holidays – **Meals** (booking essential) 60 (lunch)/128 (dinner) and à la carte 64/91 ☑, 🍷.
Spec. Bretonischer Hummer mit geschmortem Fenchel und Erbsenravioli. Kalbskopf im Ciabatta gebraten mit Steinpilzen und Feldsalat. Seewolf in Olivenöl pochiert mit Kartoffelschaum und Paprikamarinade.
♦ Number One on every Munich gourmet's list, and guarded by fabulous beasts, this black and orange temple to fine dining serves the magical dishes of an innovative chef.

🍴🍴 **Seehaus**, Kleinhesselohe 3, ✉ 80802, ℘ (089) 3 81 61 30, Fax (089) 341803, seehaus@kuffler.de, ⇐, 🌳, beer garden – 🅿. 🆎 🐮 VISA **HU** t
Meals à la carte 22/40.
♦ In an idyllic setting on the Kleinhesseloher lake, this establishment dishes up both German and international cuisine. The delightful lakeside terrace is a great asset.

🍴 **Bistro Terrine**, Amalienstr. 89 (Amalien-Passage), ✉ 80799, ℘ (089) 28 17 80, Fax (089) 2809316, terrine.bistro@t-online.de, 🌳 – 🆎 🐮 VISA **GU** p
closed 1 to 6 January, Bank Holidays, Sunday, lunch Monday and Saturday – **Meals** (booking essential for dinner) 23 (lunch) and à la carte 37/49.
♦ This restaurant is full of French bistro-style flair, right down to the Art Nouveau lamps. Classic French cuisine prepared from the freshest of ingredients.

at Munich-Sendling Southwest : 6 km, by Lindwurmstraße (B 11) **EX** :

🏨 **Holiday Inn München-Süd**, Kistlerhofstr. 142, ✉ 81379, ℘ (089) 78 00 20, Fax (089) 78002672, reservation@holiday-inn-muenchen-sued.de, 🌳, 🎿, 🕿, 🏊, 🌿 – 📶, 🙌 rm, 📶 ☎ ⇔ – 🔬 90. 🆎 ⓪ 🐮 VISA JCB
Meals à la carte 24/41 – ☑ 17 – **320 rm** 149 – 199.
♦ Modern business hotel with functional conference facilities. Business centre with internet provision, photocopier, PC and printer. Air-conditioned rooms with balconies.

🏨 **K+K Hotel am Harras** without rest, Albert-Rosshaupter-Str. 4, ✉ 81369, ℘ (089) 74 64 00, Fax (089) 7212820, info@kkhotels.de – 📶 🙌 📺 ☎ ⇔. 🆎 ⓪ 🐮 VISA JCB
106 rm ☑ 148/180 – 175/210.
♦ This establishment's many advantages include not only contemporary comforts and an attractive atmosphere but also a convenient location with good road and rail access.

at Munich-Untermenzing Northwest : 12 km, by Dachauer Straße **EU** and Baldur Straße :

🏨 **Romantik Hotel Insel Mühle**, Von-Kahr-Str. 87, ✉ 80999, ℘ (089) 8 10 10, Fax (089) 8120571, insel-muehle@t-online.de, 🌳, beer garden, 🌿 – 📺 ☎ ⇔ 🅿 – 🔬 30. 🆎 🐮 VISA
Meals 18 (lunch) and à la carte 32/39 – **38 rm** ☑ 95/120 – 141/174.
♦ This restored 16C watermill houses comfortable, country-house style rooms featuring warm colours and natural wood furnishings. Pleasant restaurant with lovely terrace overlooking the River Würm.

at Unterhaching *South : 10 km, by Kapuzinerstraße GX and Tegernseer Landstraße :*

Holiday Inn, Inselkammer Str. 7, 82008, (089) 66 69 10, *Fax (089) 66691600, info@holiday-inn-muenchen.de*, beer garden, – rm, rest, – 220.
Meals à la carte 29/39 – 16 – **270 rm** 130/156 – 156/182 – 3 suites.
• Located in an industrial area, this large modern hotel offers contemporary, functional rooms and comfortable suites and maisonettes.

Schrenkhof without rest, Leonhardsweg 6, 82008, (089) 6 10 09 10, *Fax (089) 61009150, hotel-schrenkhof@t-online.de*, – – 30.
closed Easter and 22 December - 9 January – **25 rm** 100 – 130.
• This Alpine-style establishment offers tasteful, highly individual rooms, some with fine wood panelling, some with lovely four-posters.

NH Unterhaching without rest, Leipziger Str.1, 82008, (089) 66 55 20, *Fax (089) 66552200, nhmuenchenunterhaching@nh-hotels.com*, –
14 – **80 rm** 120 – 129.
• This foyer of this hotel is a bright and airy atrium. Functionally designed rooms, with living and sleeping areas separated by a sliding door.

at Aschheim *Northeast : 13 km, by Prinzregentenstraße HV and Riem :*

Schreiberhof, Erdinger Str. 2, 85609, (089) 90 00 60, *Fax (089) 90006459, info@schreiberhof.de*, , – rm, – 90.
***Alte Gaststube* : Meals** à la carte 31/41 – **87 rm** 116 – 156.
• The spacious, elegant and functional rooms are provided with splendid, natural stone bathrooms. The light and airy winter garden is ideal for that special meeting or conference. The cosy Alte Gaststube serves local and international cuisine.

at Aschheim-Dornach *Northeast : 12 km, by Prinzregentenstraße HV and Riem :*

Inn Side Residence-Hotel, Humboldtstr. 12 (Industrialpark-West), 85609, (089) 94 00 50, *Fax (089) 94005299, muenchen@innside.de*, , – rm, rest, – 80.
closed 24 December - 1 January – **Meals** *(closed lunch Saturday and Sunday)* à la carte 20/32 – **134 rm** 149/199 – 183/233.
• Interesting rooms with some extraordinary design features, among others free-standing glazed showers. Allow yourself to be inspired by the highly original artworks on display. The Bistrorant Pappagallo has fusion cuisine with emphasis on Oriental dishes.

at airport Franz-Josef-Strauß *Northeast : 37 km, by A 9 and A 92 :*

Kempinski Airport München, Terminalstraße Mitte 20, 85356 *Munich*, (089) 9 78 20, *Fax (089) 97822610, info@kempinski-airport.de*, , , – rm, – 280.
Meals à la carte 22/33 – 24 – **389 rm** 181 – 195 – 46 suites.
• This outstanding example of the hotel architecture of today boasts a huge glazed atrium with 17m-high palm trees reaching upwards. The rooms are of an equivalent standard. Discreet elegance and contemporary style characterise the restaurant.

Aschau im Chiemgau *Bayern 546 W 20 – pop. 5 200 – alt. 615 m.*
München 82.

Restaurant Heinz Winkler - Residenz Heinz Winkler, Kirchplatz 1, 83229, (08052) 1 79 91 52, *Fax (08052) 179966, info@residenz-heinz-winkler.de*, –
Meals 110/135 and à la carte 59/95.
Spec. Langustinen mit Ruccola-Mandelsalat und Kaviar. Taubenbrust in der Brotkruste mit Pastinaken-Mousseline. Lavendeleis mit Birnen und Himbeeren.
• The creative and highly individual use of seasonal specialities makes a visit to this superlative and very welcoming restaurant an experience to remember.

Wernberg-Köblitz *Bayern 546 R 20 – pop. 5 000 – alt. 377 m.*
München 193.

Kastell - Hotel Burg Wernberg, Schloßberg 10, 92533, (09604) 93 90, *Fax (09604) 939139, hotel@burg-wernberg.de* –
closed 2 to 28 January, Monday and Tuesday – **Meals** *(dinner only)* (booking essential) 92/112 and à la carte.
Spec. Salat vom Kaninchen mit marinierter Gänseleber und Périgord Trüffel. St. Petersfisch mit Parmaschinken und Weißkrautrisotto. Kaffeedessert "Kastell".
• It's a real treat to sample French seasonal cuisine in this elegant establishment with its whitewashed vaults and polished service.

STUTTGART

Baden-Württemberg 545 T 11 – pop. 593 500 – alt. 245 m.

See : Linden Museum ★★ KY M1 – Park Wilhelma★ HT and Killesberg-Park★ GT – Television Tower (Fernsehturm) ✻★ HX – Stuttgart Gallery (Otto-Dix-Collection★) LY M4 – Old Castle (Altes Schloss) (Renaissance courtyard★) – Württemberg Regional Museum★ LY M3 – State Gallery★★ (Old Masters Collection★★) LY M2 – Collegiate church (Stiftskirche) (Commemorative monuments of dukes★) KY A – State Museum of Natural History (Staatl. Museum für Naturkunde) (Löwentor Museum★) HT M5 – Mercedes-Benz Museum★ JV M6 – Porsche Museum★ by Heilbronner Straße GT – Castle Solitude★ by Rotenwaldstraße FX.

Envir. : Bad Cannstatt Spa Park (Kurpark)★ East : 4 km JT.

Kornwestheim, Aldinger Str. 975 (North : 11 km), (07141) 87 13 19 ; Schwieberdingen, Nippenburg 21 (Northwest : 15 km), (07150) 3 95 30 ; Mönsheim, Schlossfeld (Northwest : 30 km by A 8), (07044) 9 11 04 10.

Stuttgart-Echterdingen, by Obere Weinsteige (B 27) GX, (0711) 94 80, City-Air-Terminal, Stuttgart, Lautenschlagerstr. 14 (LY).

Exhibition Centre (Messegelände Killesberg) (GT), (0711) 2 58 90, Fax (0711) 2589440.

Tourist-Info, Königstr. 1a, ✉ 70173, (0711) 2 22 82 40, Fax (0711) 2228216, info@stuttgart-tourist.de.

ADAC, Am Neckartor 2.

Berlin 630 – Frankfurt am Main 204 – Karlsruhe 88 – München 222 – Strasbourg 156.

Plans on following pages

Steigenberger Graf Zeppelin, Arnulf-Klett-Platz 7, ✉ 70173, (0711) 2 04 80, Fax (0711) 2048542, stuttgart@steigenberger.de, – rm, – 300. AE VISA JCB LY v

Meals see also ***Olivo*** below – ***Zeppelin Stüble*** *(closed Sunday dinner)* **Meals** à la carte 22/33 – ***Zeppelino's*** : **Meals** à la carte 25/38 – 20 – **192 rm** 195/225 – 220/240.

• A mixture of modernity and tradition is concealed behind this building's sober façade. Exclusive rooms in three varieties - classic, elegant or avantgarde. Eat informally in the cheerful Zeppelin-Stube.

Am Schlossgarten, Schillerstr. 23, ✉ 70173, (0711) 2 02 60, Fax (0711) 2026888, info@hotelschlossgarten.com, – rm, – 100. AE VISA. rest LY u

Meals see ***Zirbelstube*** below – ***Schlossgarten-Restaurant*** *(closed Friday and Saturday)* **Meals** à la carte 38/47 – ***Vinothek*** *(closed Sunday and Monday)* **Meals** 24 and à la carte 29/37 – 18 – **116 rm** 155/284 – 258/284 – 4 suites.

• Splendid location between shopping centre, state theatre and the lovely leafy Schlossgarten. Elegant, luxurious rooms with delightfully colourful fabrics. Restaurant with an elegant country-style ambience, plus a magnificent terrace overlooking the park.

Maritim, Seidenstr. 34, ✉ 70174, (0711) 94 20, Fax (0711) 9421000, info.stu@maritim.de, – rm, – 400. AE VISA JCB FV r

Meals *(end July - August dinner only)* à la carte 22/37 – 16 – **555 rm** 159/194 – 183/218 – 12 suites.

• With space for 800, the late 19C Riding Hall attached to this establishment is ideal for conferences and banquets. The Piano Bar has become a favourite Stuttgart rendezvous. Something for every taste in the Rotisserie and the Bistro Reuchlin.

Mercure City-Center, Heilbronner Str. 88, ✉ 70191, (0711) 25 55 80, Fax (0711) 25558100, h5424-re@accor.de – rm, – 120. AE VISA GU c

Meals à la carte 20/35 – 14 – **174 rm** 125/135 – 135/145.

• Bright and welcoming contemporary accommodation, particularly appreciated by business travellers - all rooms have ample work desks and PC and fax points. The Mediterranean-style restaurant brings a touch of the South to the establishment.

Royal, Sophienstr. 35, ✉ 70178, (0711) 6 25 05 00, Fax (0711) 628809, royalhotel@t-online.de – rm, – 50. AE VISA JCB KZ b

Meals *(closed 1 to 22 August, Sunday and Bank Holidays)* à la carte 21/45 – **100 rm** 96/135 – 125/145 – 3 suites.

• Well-run establishment with welcoming atmosphere. Tranquil, tasteful rooms, with integrated furnishings in either maple knotwood or cherrywood.

Wörtz zur Weinsteige, Hohenheimer Str. 28, ✉ 70184, (0711) 2 36 70 00, Fax (0711) 2367007, info@hotel-woertz.de, – rm, AE VISA JCB LZ p

Meals *(closed 3 weeks January, 3 weeks August, Sunday-Monday and Bank Holidays, except Christmas)* à la carte 27/43 – **33 rm** 85/120 – 100/140.

• The pride of this attentively run hotel is the Schloesschen, its elegant rooms featuring Italian furnishings. Comfortable, rustic rooms in the main building. Wood carving and wrought-iron lend the restaurant its distinctive character.

STUTTGART

Arnulf-Klett-Pl. . . . . LY 6
Augustenstr. . . . . KZ 7
Blumenstr. . . . . LZ 10
Bolzstr. . . . . LY 15
Calwer Str. . . . . KYZ 18
Charlottenpl. . . . . LZ 20
Dorotheenstr. . . . . LZ 24
Eberhardstr. . . . . KLZ 25
Friedrichspl. . . . . KY 27
Hauptstätter Str. . . . . KZ 30
Hegelpl. . . . . KY 32
Heilbronner Str. . . . . LY 34
Holzstr. . . . . LZ 40
Karlspl. . . . . LY 43
Karlstr. . . . . LZ 44
Katharinenpl. . . . . LZ 45
Kirchstr. . . . . LZ 46
Königstr. . . . . KLYZ
Konrad-Adenauer-Str. . . . . LY 47
Kronenstr. . . . . KLY 48
Kronprinzstr. . . . . KYZ 49
Leonhardspl. . . . . LZ 50
Marktpl. . . . . KLZ 52
Marktstr. . . . . LZ 53
Österreichischer Pl. . . . . KZ 57
Pfarrstr. . . . . LZ 61
Rotebühlpl. . . . . KZ 66
Rotebühlstr. . . . . KZ 70
Schloßpl. . . . . LY 72
Schulstr. . . . . KZ 75
Silberburgstr. . . . . KZ 76
Sophienstr. . . . . KZ 78
Theodor-Heuss-Str. . . . . KYZ 80
Torstr. . . . . KZ 82
Wilhelmspl. . . . . LZ 86
Wilhelmstr. . . . . LZ 88
Willi-Bleicher-Str. . . . . KY 91

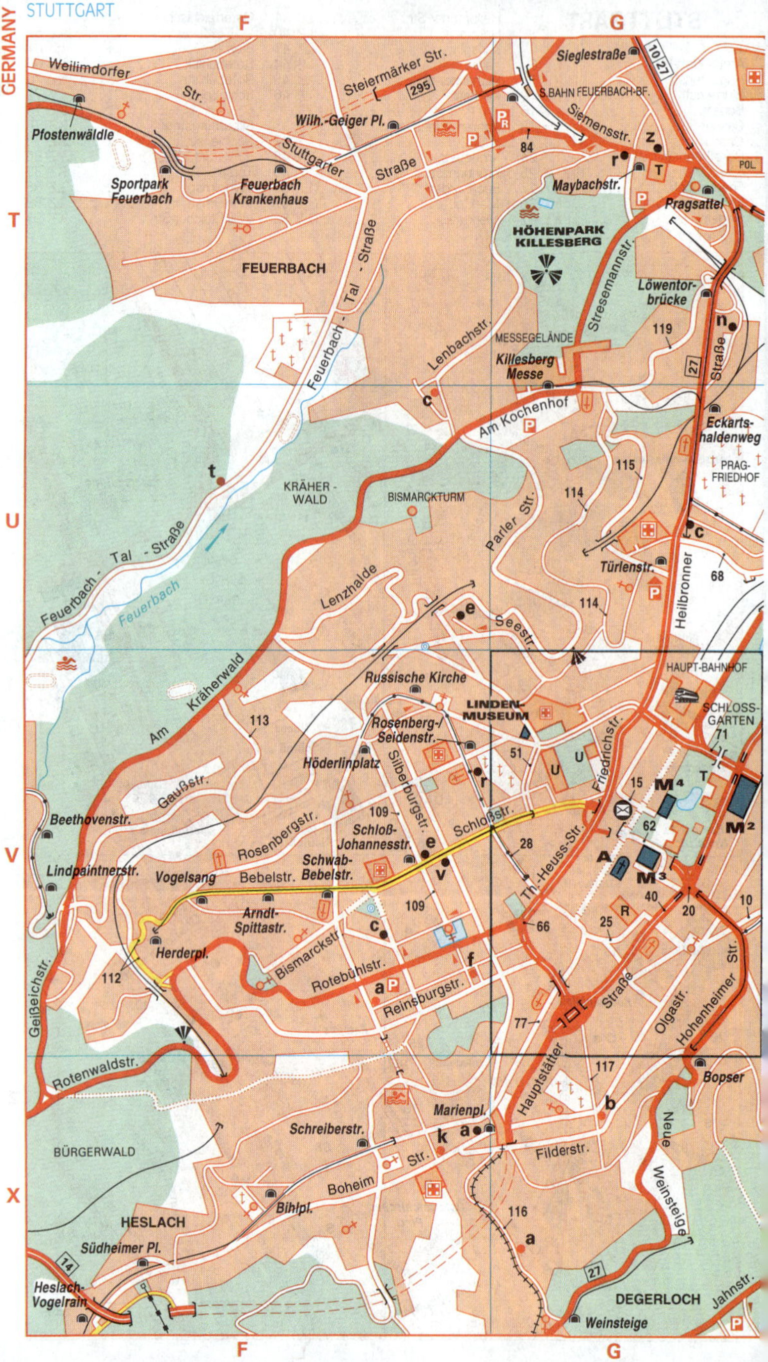
F
G
T
U
V
X
Weilimdorfer Str.
Steiermärker Str.
295
Sieglestraße
10 27
S.BAHN FEUERBACH-BF.
Siemensstr.
Wilh.-Geiger Pl.
Stuttgarter Straße
84
Pfostenwäldle
Sportpark Feuerbach
Feuerbach Krankenhaus
Maybachstr.
POL
Pragsattel
HÖHENPARK KILLESBERG
FEUERBACH
Feuerbach - Tal - Straße
Stresemannstr.
Löwentor-brücke
119
Lenbachstr.
MESSEGELÄNDE
Killesberg Messe
27
Straße
Am Kochenhof
Eckarts-haldenweg
PRAG-FRIEDHOF
115
114
KRÄHER - WALD
BISMARCKTURM
Parler Str.
Feuerbach - Tal - Straße
Feuerbach
Türlenstr.
Heilbronner
68
Lenzhalde
Seestr.
HAUPT-BAHNHOF
SCHLOSS-GARTEN
71
Russische Kirche
LINDEN-MUSEUM
Am Kräherwald
113
Rosenberg-/ Seidenstr.
51
Friedrichstr.
Höderlinplatz
Gaußstr.
Silberburgstr.
15
M4
M2
Beethovenstr.
109
Schloßstr.
62
Rosenbergstr.
Schloß-Johannesstr.
28
Th.-Heuss-Str.
A
M3
Lindpaintnerstr.
Vogelsang
Bebelstr.
Schwab-Bebelstr.
40
20
10
Arndt-Spittastr.
109
R
25
66
Herderpl.
Bismarckstr.
Rotebühlstr.
Straße
Olgastr.
Hohenheimer Str.
112
Reinsburgstr.
77
Geißeichstr.
Rotenwaldstr.
Hauptstätter
117
Bopser
Marienpl.
Schreiberstr.
Filderstr.
Neue Weinsteige
BÜRGERWALD
Boheim Str.
116
HESLACH
Bihlpl.
Südheimer Pl.
14
27
Heslach-Vogelrain
DEGERLOCH
Jahnstr.
Weinsteige

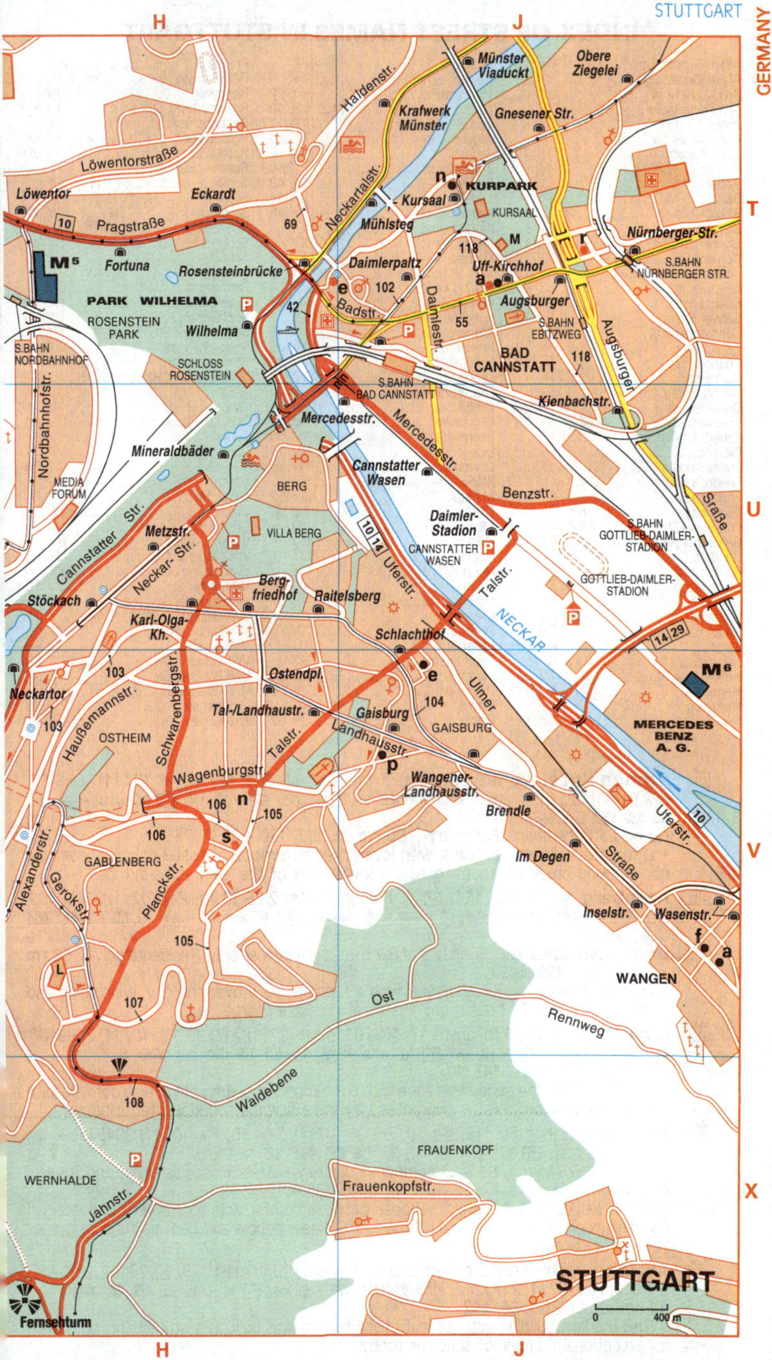
H
J
T
U
V
X
Münster Viaduckt
Obere Ziegelei
Haldenstr.
Krafwerk Münster
Gnesener Str.
Löwentorstraße
Neckartalstr.
KURPARK
Löwentor
Eckardt
Kursaal
KURSAAL
Mühlsteg
10
Pragstraße
69
M
Nürnberger-Str.
118
Uff-Kirchhof
S.BAHN NÜRNBERGER STR.
M5
Fortuna
Rosensteinbrücke
Daimlerpaltz
102
Augsburger
PARK WILHELMA
ROSENSTEIN PARK
42
Badstr.
Daimlestr.
55
S.BAHN EBITZWEG
Wilhelma
S.BAHN NORDBAHNHOF
SCHLOSS ROSENSTEIN
S.BAHN BAD CANNSTATT
BAD CANNSTATT
118
Augsburger
Kienbachstr.
Nordbahnhofstr.
Mercedesstr.
Mercedesstr.
Mineraldbäder
MEDIA FORUM
BERG
Cannstatter Wasen
Benzstr.
Straße
Cannstatter Str.
Metzstr.
VILLA BERG
10 14
Daimler-Stadion
S.BAHN GOTTLIEB-DAIMLER-STADION
Neckar-Str.
CANNSTATTER WASEN
Talstr.
GOTTLIEB-DAIMLER-STADION
Stöckach
Berg-friedhof
Raitelsberg
Uferstr.
NECKAR
Karl-Olga-Kh.
Schlachthof
14 29
M6
103
Ostendpl.
Neckartor
Haußemannstr.
Schwarenbergstr.
Tal-/Landhausstr.
Gaisburg
104
Ulmer
MERCEDES BENZ A. G.
103
OSTHEIM
GAISBURG
Landhausstr.
Talstr.
Wagenburgstr.
Wangener-Landhausstr.
106
105
Brendle
Uferstr.
10
106
Alexanderstr.
GABLENBERG
Gerokstr.
Planckstr.
Im Degen
Straße
Inselstr.
Wasenstr.
105
WANGEN
107
Ost
Rennweg
Waldebene
108
FRAUENKOPF
WERNHALDE
Frauenkopfstr.
Jahnstr.
STUTTGART
0
400 m
Fernsehturm

INDEX OF STREET NAMES IN STUTTGART

Albert-Schalfe-Str. . . . . HV 107
Alexanderstr. . . . . LZ, HV
Am Kochenhof . . . . FGU
Am Kräherwald . . . . FUV
Arnulf-Klett-Pl. . . . . LY 6
Augsburger Str. . . . . JTU
Augustenstr. . . . . KZ 7
Badstr. . . . . HJT
Bebelstr. . . . . FV
Benzstr. . . . . JU
Birkenwaldstr. . . . . GU 114
Bismarckstr. . . . . FV
Blumenstr. . . . . LZ, GV 10
Boheim Str. . . . . FX
Bolzstr. . . . . LY, GV 15
Brückenstr. . . . . HT 69
Büchsenstr. . . . . KY
Calwer Str. . . . . KYZ 18
Cannstatter Str. . . . . LY, HU
Charlottenpl. . . . . LZ, GV 20
Charlottenstr. . . . . LZ
Daimlestr. . . . . JTU
Danneckerstr. . . . . LZ
Dorotheenstr. . . . . LZ 24
Eberhardstr. . . . . KLZ, GV 25
Feuerbach-Tal-Str. . . . . FTU
Filderstr. . . . . FG
Frauenkopstr. . . . . HXJV
Friedrich-Ebert-Str. . . . . GTU 119
Friedrichspl. . . . . KY 27
Friedrichstr. . . . . KY, GV
Fritz-Elsas-Str. . . . . KYZ, GV 28
Gablenberger Haupstr. . . . . HV 105
Gaußstr. . . . . FV
Geißeichstr. . . . . FVX
Gerberstr. . . . . KZ
Gerokstr. . . . . HV
Haldenstr. . . . . HJT
Hauptstätter Str. . . . . KZ, GV 30
Hegelpl. . . . . KY 32
Hegelstr. . . . . KY
Heilbronner Str. . . . . LY, GTV 34
Herdersstr. . . . . FV 112
Herdweg . . . . . KY
Heusteigstr. . . . . KLZ
Hirschstr. . . . . KZ
Hohenheimer Str. . . . . LZ, GV
Holzgartenstr. . . . . KY
Holzstr. . . . . LZ, GV 40
Immen hofer Str. . . . . GVX 117
Jägerstraße . . . . . KY
Jahnstr. . . . . GHX
Johannesstr. . . . . FV 109
Karlspl. . . . . LY 43
Karlstr. . . . . LZ 44
Katharinenpl. . . . . LZ 45
Katharinenstr. . . . . LZ
Keplerstraße . . . . . KY
Kirchstr. . . . . LZ 46
Königstr. . . . . KLYZ
Köning-Karl-Str. . . . . JT 102
Konrad-Adenauer-Str. . . . . LY 47
Kriegsbergstr. . . . . KY
Kronenstr. . . . . KLY 48
Kronprinzstr. . . . . KYZ 49
Landhausstr. . . . . HUV, HJV 103
Lange Str. . . . . KYZ
Lautenschlagerstr. . . . . LY
Lenbachstr. . . . . GTU
Lenzhalde . . . . . FU
Leonhardspl. . . . . LZ 50
Libanonstr. . . . . HV 106
Löwentorstr. . . . . HT
Marienstr. . . . . KZ
Marktpl. . . . . KLZ 52
Marktstr. . . . . LZ 53
Mercedesstr. . . . . JU
Neckar-Str. . . . . HU
Neckartalstr. . . . . HJT
Neue Weinsteige . . . . . GX
Nordbahnhofstr. . . . . HU
Österreichischer Pl. . . . . KZ 57
Olgastr. . . . . LYZ, GVX
Panoramastr. . . . . KY
Parler Str. . . . . FGU
Paulinenstr. . . . . KZ
Pfarrstr. . . . . LZ 61
Pischekstr. . . . . HVX 108
Planckstr. . . . . HV
Planie . . . . . GV 62
Pragstr. . . . . GHT
Reinsburgstr. . . . . KZ, FGV
Rennweg . . . . . JV
Robert-Mayer-Str. . . . . GU 115
Rosenbergstr. . . . . FV
Rotebühlpl. . . . . KZ, GV 66
Rotebühlstr. . . . . KZ 70
Rotenwaldstr. . . . . FVX
Schillerpl. . . . . KLY
Schillerstr. . . . . LY
Schloßpl. . . . . LY 72
Schloßstr. . . . . KY, FGV
Schönestr. . . . . HT 42
Schulstr. . . . . KZ 75
Seestr. . . . . KY, FGV
Siemensstr. . . . . GT
Silberburgstr. . . . . KZ 76
Sophienstr. . . . . KZ 78
Steiermärker Str. . . . . FT
Stresemannstr. . . . . GT
Stuttgarter Str. (FEUERBACH) . . . . . FT
Talstr. . . . . HJV
Taubenheim-Str. . . . . JTU 118
Theodor-Heuss-Str. . . . . KYZ, GV 80
Torstr. . . . . KZ 82
Tübinger Str. . . . . KZ, GVX 77
Tunnelstr. . . . . GT 84
Uferstr. . . . . HJV
Ulmer Str. . . . . JUV
Ulrichstr. . . . . KLY
Urbanstr. . . . . LY
Wagenburgstr. . . . . HV
Waiblinger Str. . . . . JT 55
Waldebene Ost . . . . . HXV
Wangener Str. . . . . JV 104
Weilimdorfer Str. . . . . FT
Weinsteige . . . . . GX 116
Weißenburgstr. . . . . KZ
Wilhelmspl. . . . . LZ 86
Wilhelmstr. . . . . LZ 88
Willi-Bleicher-Str. . . . . KY 91
Willy-Brandt-Str. . . . . LY
Wolframstr. . . . . GU 68
Zeppelinstr. . . . . FV 113

Kronen-Hotel without rest, Kronenstr. 48, ✉ 70174, ✆ (0711) 2 25 10, *Fax (0711) 2251404, info@kronenhotel-stuttgart.de,* – 20. AE VISA JCB KY m
closed 23 December - 6 January – **80 rm** 102/120 – 133/175.
• Distinctively designed rooms, with lovely tiled bathrooms in pastel colours. From the non-smoking breakfast room there is a lovely view of the leafy surroundings.

Azenberg, Seestr. 114, ✉ 70174, ✆ (0711) 2 25 50 40, *Fax (0711) 22550499, info@hotelazenberg.de,* – rm, – 20. AE VISA JCB. rest FU e
Meals *(closed Saturday - Sunday and Bank Holidays) (dinner only)* (residents only) – **58 rm** 95/125 – 129/149.
• On the slope of the Killesberg hill with a fantastic view over the city. Welcoming and up-to-date rooms. 24-hour room service at no extra charge.

Unger without rest, Kronenstr. 17, ✉ 70173, ✆ (0711) 2 09 90, *Fax (0711) 2099100, info@hotel-unger.de* – – 15. AE VISA JCB LY a
95 rm 102/128 – 143/179.
• Directly behind the pedestrian zone with contemporary comfort in every room. Despite the central location, quiet is guaranteed by the efficiently soundproofed windows.

Wartburg, Lange Str. 49, ✉ 70174, ✆ (0711) 2 04 50, *Fax (0711) 2045450* – rm, rest, – 40. AE VISA. rest KY g
closed 25 to 28 March and 24 December - 7 January – **Meals** *(closed Saturday and Sunday) (lunch only)* à la carte 17/27 – **76 rm** 82/95 – 127/139.
• Small, well-run establishment. Choose between comfortable rooms with dark-stained furnishings or others in natural light wood. Business people and bankers tend to gather here at lunchtime.

Abalon without rest, Zimmermannstr. 7 (approach by Olgastr. 79), ✉ 70182, ✆ (0711) 2 17 10, *Fax (0711) 2171217, info@abalon.de* – . AE VISA LZ x
42 rm 71/86 – 96/112.
• This modern building with its leafy roof terrace was built as a student hostel, hence its exceptional number of spacious rooms.

Central Classic without rest, Hasenbergstr. 49a, ✉ 70176, ☏ (0711) 6 15 50 50, *Fax (0711) 61550530, central-classic@gmx.de* – AE VISA. FV c
closed 23 December - 8 January – **34 rm** 70/85 – 90/95.
• This little hotel by the Feuersee lake is much appreciated by business people because of its individual work desks with fax and PC points as well as ISDN phone.

City-Hotel without rest, Uhlandstr. 18, ✉ 70182, ☏ (0711) 21 08 10, *Fax (0711) 2369772, info@cityhotel-suttgart.de* – P. AE VISA. LZ a
31 rm 79/85 – 95/115.
• Looking like a private house from the outside, this hotel has clean, well-presented rooms. The breakfast room with its conservatory is a particularly attractive feature.

Rieker without rest, Friedrichstr. 3, ✉ 70174, ☏ (0711) 22 13 11, *Fax (0711) 293894, info@hotel-rieker.de* – . AE VISA JCB LY d
66 rm 97 – 122.
• Located opposite the main station, this hotel has comfortably furnished rooms and offers its guests a cleaning and ironing service.

Ibis am Löwentor without rest, Presselstr. 15, ✉ 70191, ☏ (0711) 25 55 10, *Fax (0711) 25551150, h2202@accor.com* – . AE VISA
9 – **132 rm** 66. GT n
• Ideal location between city centre and motorway, this is a newly-built hotel with bright, well-presented rooms. 24-hour reception.

Ibis am Marienplatz without rest, Marienplatz 8, ✉ 70178, ☏ (0711) 12 06 40, *Fax (0711) 12064160, h3284@accor.com* – . AE VISA
9 – **104 rm** 66. FX a
• This city centre establishment is a practical choice especially for business travellers, since the rooms have work desks and all necessary points.

Bellevue, Schurwaldstr. 45, ✉ 70186, ☏ (0711) 48 07 60, *Fax (0711) 4807631, info@bellevue-stuttgart.de* – P. AE VISA JV p
Meals *(closed mid August - early September, Tuesday and Wednesday)* à la carte 17/32 – **12 rm** 52/59 – 77.
• This family establishment dates back to 1913. Well-run and carefully maintained, it is located in a quiet residential area. A morning paper is provided for every guest. Cheerful and welcoming hotel restaurant.

Zirbelstube - Hotel Am Schlossgarten, Schillerstr. 23, ✉ 70173, ☏ (0711) 2 02 68 28, *Fax (0711) 2026888, info@hotelschlossgarten.com*, ≤, – . AE VISA. LY u
closed 1 to 11 January, 15 August - 5 September, Sunday and Monday – **Meals** 82/109 and à la carte 58/92 ♀, .
Spec. Variation von der Pelati-Tomate mit Gambas. Jakobsmuscheln asiatisch auf Curry-Glasnudeln. Taubenkotelett gefüllt mit Trüffel und Gänsestopfleber.
• This is one of the top places to eat in Stuttgart. Gourmets appreciate the classic menu with a Mediterranean touch and the carefully chosen wines. Terrace with lovely view.

Olivo - Hotel Steigenberger Graf Zeppelin, Arnulf-Klett-Platz 7 (1st floor), ✉ 70173, ☏ (0711) 2 04 82 77, *Fax (0711) 2048542, stuttgart@steigenberger.de* – . AE VISA JCB. LY v
closed August - 6 September, 1 to 10 January, Sunday - Monday and Bank Holidays – **Meals** (Italian) 68/122 and à la carte 39/47 ♀.
Spec. Sizilianischer Gemüsesalat mit gebratener Entenbrust. Filet vom Wolfsbarsch mit Fenchel und Rosmarinkartoffeln. Gefüllter Pfirsich mit Zabaione und weißem Kaffee-Eis.
• Décor featuring soft colours gives this restaurant an elegantly Mediterranean character. Sophisticated presentation of Thomas Heilemann's fine Italian cuisine.

Kern's Pastetchen, Hohenheimer Str. 64, ✉ 70184, ☏ (0711) 48 48 55, *Fax (0711) 487565, kerns.pastetchen@t-online.de* LZ v
closed Sunday and Monday – **Meals** *(dinner only)* 48/58 and à la carte 36/49.
• Elegant ambience with a touch of country style about it. International dishes influenced by the traditional cuisine of France and Austria.

Délice (Gutscher), Hauptstätter Str. 61, ✉ 70178, ☏ (0711) 6 40 32 22 KZ a
closed 24 December - 6 January, Saturday, Sunday and Bank Holidays – **Meals** *(dinner only)* (booking essential) 70 and à la carte 40/55 ♀, .
Spec. Marinierte Gänsestopfleberterrine mit Bratapfel. Bretonischer St. Pierre mit getrüffeltem Kohlrabi. Gefülltes Schokoladensoufflé mit Marillensauce.
• This vaulted establishment with its open kitchen makes an elegant impression. The menu is introduced by the chef in person. Walls graced by contemporary art.

La Fenice, Rotebühlplatz 29, ✉ 70178, ☏ (0711) 6 15 11 44, *Fax (0711) 6151146, g.vincenzo@t-online.de*, – AE VISA. KZ e
closed Monday, lunch Saturday and Sunday – **Meals** (Italian) 43 and à la carte 31/43.
• The Gorgoglione sisters have realised the dream of their own restaurant in this old post office building where Rosa serves excellent Italian dishes.

XX **Di Gennaro**, Kronprinzstr. 11, ✉ 70173, ☎ (0711) 2 22 96 03, *Fax (0711) 2229604O, kp@digennaro.de* – AE ⓓ ⓜ VISA. ✻ KZ n
closed Sunday and Bank Holidays – **Meals** (Italian) à la carte 33/41.
◆ This modern city building with its glass façade is home to both an Italian restaurant and a delicatessen. Contemporary bistro-style interior.

XX **Da Franco**, Calwer Str. 23 (1st floor), ✉ 70173, ☎ (0711) 29 15 81, *Fax (0711) 294549, info@dafrancostuttgart.de* – ▤. AE ⓜ VISA KYZ s
closed Monday – **Meals** (Italian) à la carte 29/50.
◆ An immaculately-run first floor establishment with a view down Stuttgart's main promenade. Contemporary décor and lots of white on the walls.

XX **La nuova Trattoria da Franco**, Calwer Str. 32, ✉ 70173, ☎ (0711) 29 47 44, *Fax (0711) 294549, info@dafrancostuttgart.de*, 🏕 – ▤. AE ⓜ VISA KYZ c
Meals (Italian) à la carte 25/37.
◆ See and be seen is the motto here. On two floors, with more refined Italian dishes available as well as the usual pasta and pizza.

XX **La Scala**, Friedrichstr. 41 (1st floor, 🛗), ✉ 70174, ☎ (0711) 29 06 07, *Fax (0711) 2991640* – ▤. AE ⓓ ⓜ VISA KY e
closed 2 weeks August, Sunday and Bank Holidays lunch – **Meals** (Italian) 24/36 and à la carte 23/36.
◆ Classic first floor Italian establishment with typical cuisine plus a special something because of the panelled walls and direct view of the famous Friedrichsbau.

X **Der Zauberlehrling** with rm, Rosenstr. 38, ✉ 70182, ☎ (0711) 2 37 77 70, *Fax (0711) 2377775, kontakt@zauberlehrling.de* – ⇆ rm, TV ☎ 🚗. ✻ LZ c
Meals *(closed Bank Holidays, lunch Saturday and Sunday)* à la carte 27/47 ♀ – **9 rm** ☕ 100/135 – 135/160.
◆ Refined country-style ambience. Diners sit at wooden tables and choose from a small but carefully composed menu of international dishes. Modern, designer rooms.

X **Vetter**, Bopserstr. 18, ✉ 70180, ☎ (0711) 24 19 16, *Fax (0711) 60189640*, 🏕
closed 3 weeks September - October, Sunday and Bank Holidays – **Meals** *(dinner only)* (booking essential) à la carte 23/36. LZ s
◆ This cheerful and well-run establishment in a city centre side street has contemporary décor and offers a choice of local and international specialities.

X **Augusten Stüble**, Augustenstr. 104, ✉ 70197, ☎ (0711) 62 12 48, 🏕 FV a
closed Sunday and Bank Holidays – **Meals** *(dinner only)* (booking essential) à la carte 20/25 ♀.
◆ Located just outside the city centre this bistro-style restaurant, bedecked in a profusion of dark wood, offers a wide range of wines and local cuisine up until midnight.

Swabian wine taverns (Weinstuben) *(mainly light meals only)* :

X **Weinstube Schellenturm**, Weberstr. 72, ✉ 70182, ☎ (0711) 2 36 48 88, *Fax (0711) 2262699, juergenwurst@t-online.de*, 🏕 LZ u
closed 24 December - 3 January, Sunday and Bank Holidays – **Meals** *(dinner only)* à la carte 19/33 ♀.
◆ This 16C fortified tower is the place to come and enjoy a typically Swabian atmosphere, with good wine and local specialities like Spätzle and Maultaschen.

X **Weinstube Klösterle**, Marktstr. 71 (Bad Cannstatt), ✉ 70372, ☎ (0711) 56 89 62, *Fax (0711) 558606*, 🏕 – ⓜ HJT e
Meals *(open from 5 pm)* à la carte 17/29.
◆ The historic monastery building of 1463 is one of the oldest inhabited structures in Stuttgart, its rustic character enhanced by its décor.

X **Stuttgarter Stäffele**, Buschlestr. 2a, ✉ 70178, ☎ (0711) 61 72 76, *Fax (0711) 613535, staeffele@aol.com*, 🏕 – AE ⓜ VISA FV f
closed lunch Saturday and Sunday – **Meals** (booking essential) à la carte 17/43.
◆ With wood panelling and red-and-white striped curtains, this is an archetypal wine tavern. The menu features Swabian dishes and Württemberg wines.

X **Weinstube Klink**, Epplestr. 1 (Degerloch), ✉ 70597, ☎ (0711) 7 65 32 05, *Fax (0711) 760307*, 🏕 by Obere Weinsteige GX
closed end August - early September, Saturday, Sunday and Bank Holidays – **Meals** *(open from 5 pm)* (booking essential) à la carte 24/40.
◆ You have to look carefully for the entrance to this establishment which is tucked away in a courtyard. An original feature is the daily menu, displayed on a blackboard.

X **Weinstube Träuble**, Gablenberger Hauptstr. 66 (entrance Bussenstraße), ✉ 70186, ☎ (0711) 46 54 28, *Fax (0711) 4207961*, 🏕 – ✻ HV s
closed 1 week September, 1 week January, Sunday and Bank Holidays – **Meals** *(open from 5 pm)* (only cold and warm light meals).
◆ This little place is 200 years old and looks a bit like a doll's house. It's great fun taking a glass or three next to the tiled stove in the cosy wood-panelled parlour.

Weinstube Kochenbas, Immenhofer Str. 33, ✉ 70180, ✆ (0711) 60 27 04, *Fax (0711) 602704, kochenbas@t-online.de,* GX b
closed end August - mid September and Monday – **Meals** (booking essential) à la carte 16/21.
• Stuttgart's second oldest wine tavern is an appealing place, its rustic décor giving it a typical Swabian atmosphere. The kitchen conjures up tasty local specialities.

Weinhaus Stetter, Rosenstr. 32, ✉ 70182, ✆ (0711) 24 01 63, *Fax (0711) 240193, post@weinhaus-stetter.de,* LZ e
closed mid August - early September, 24 December - 6 January, Sunday and Bank Holidays – **Meals** *(open Monday to Friday from 3 pm, Saturday 11 am to 3 pm)* (only cold and warm light meals).
• You'd have to go a long way to find a longer list of wines - the choice here is enormous, and includes excellent wines from abroad as well. You can buy as well as taste.

at Stuttgart-Büsnau *West : 9 km, by Rotenwaldstraße* FX *:*

relexa Waldhotel Schatten, Magstadter Straße 2 (Solitudering), ✉ 70569, ✆ (0711) 6 86 70, *Fax (0711) 6867999, stuttgart@relexa-hotel.de,* – rm, – 80. AE VISA JCB
La Fenêtre *(closed August - 5 September, Monday, Sunday and Bank Holidays) (dinner only)* **Meals** 36/40 and à la carte – ***Kaminrestaurant :*** **Meals** à la carte 21/30 – **136 rm** 105 – 139.
• This 200-year-old establishment stands outside the gates of the town, and is a successful synthesis of old and new. Some of the rooms are graced with antique furniture. The La Fenêtre restaurant has an elegant touch, the Kaminrestaurant is more down to earth.

at Stuttgart-Bad Cannstatt :

Mercure, Teinacher Str. 20, ✉ 70372, ✆ (0711) 9 54 00, *Fax (0711) 9540630, h1704@accor.com,* – rm, – 100. AE VISA JT n
Meals à la carte 24/39 – 13 – **156 rm** 97/123 – 117/149.
• This hotel offers comfortable, contemporary rooms. If you need extra space, ask for one of the very generously designed suites or apartments.

Krehl's Linde with rm, Obere Waiblinger Str. 113, ✉ 70374, ✆ (0711) 5 20 49 00, *Fax (0711) 52049013, info@krehl-gastronomie.de,* – – 50. AE VISA JT r
closed 3 weeks August - September – **Meals** *(closed Sunday and Monday)* 23/75 and à la carte 27/45 – **15 rm** 50/75 – 75/95.
• This traditional place has been in the same family since 1875. Stylish setting and a choice of local specialities or refined French delicacies. Solidly furnished rooms.

at Stuttgart-Degerloch :

Wielandshöhe (Klink), Alte Weinsteige 71, ✉ 70597, ✆ (0711) 6 40 88 48, *Fax (0711) 6409408,* – AE VISA GX a
closed Monday, January - November Sunday and Monday – **Meals** (booking essential) 64/98 *(dinner)* and à la carte 47/74.
Spec. Bretonischer Hummer mit Kartoffelsalat. Loup de mer in der Salzkruste. Lammrücken mit Kräutern der Alb.
• A famous chef is in charge here, a master of the classical repertoire with Mediterranean and local influences. Elegant ambience and wonderful view.

Das Fässle, Löwenstr. 51, ✉ 70597, ✆ (0711) 76 01 00, *Fax (0711) 764432, info@faessle.de,* – – 20. AE VISA by Jahnstraße GX
closed Sunday and Monday lunch – **Meals** (booking essential) 30 and à la carte 23/41.
• This country-style restaurant provides versions of international and local cuisine. Cheerful atmosphere with lattice windows and lots of panelling.

at Stuttgart-Fasanenhof *South : 10 km, by Obere Weinsteige* GX *and B 27 :*

Fora Hotel, Vor dem Lauch 20, ✉ 70567, ✆ (0711) 7 25 50, *Fax (0711) 7255666, reservation.fasanenhof@fora.de,* – rm, – 55. AE VISA
Meals à la carte 18/41 – **101 rm** 120 – 136.
• Modern establishment right in the middle of Stuttgart's Businesspark catering almost exclusively for business travellers. Fax in room on request.

at Stuttgart-Feuerbach :

Messehotel Europe, Siemensstr. 33, ✉ 70469, ✆ (0711) 81 00 40 (hotel) 8 10 04 24 55 (rest.), *Fax (0711) 810042555, info.str@europe-hotels-int.de* – rm, AE VISA GT r
Landhausstuben *(dinner only)* **Meals** à la carte 22/32 – **114 rm** 102 – 130.
• The pride of this modern trade-fair hotel is the lobby with its glass-sided lifts and landscaped water feature. Comfortable, contemporary rooms. Country-style restaurant with welcoming atmosphere.

Kongresshotel Europe, Siemensstr. 26, ✉ 70469, ☎ (0711) 81 00 40, *Fax (0711) 810041444, info.str@europe-hotels-int.de*, , – , rm, – 120. AE MC VISA GT z
Meals *(closed lunch Saturday and Sunday)* à la carte 21/39 – **144 rm** 78/110 – 120/138 – 3 suites.
◆ Almost all the rooms have Spanish-style décor in warm colours. The rooms on the business floor have fax and modem points.

Landgasthof im schönsten Wiesengrund with rm, Feuerbacher-Tal-Str. 200, ✉ 70469, ☎ (0711) 1 35 37 20, *Fax (0711) 13537210, info@landgasthof-wiesengrund.de*, , beer garden – rm, – 20. MC VISA FU t
Meals à la carte 24/45 – **12 rm** 65 – 85.
◆ Traditional décor and a menu based on local dishes supplemented by seasonal specialities. Bright, modern guest rooms.

at Stuttgart-Flughafen (Airport) *South : 15 km, by Obere Weinsteige GX and B 27 :*

Mövenpick-Hotel, Flughafenrandstr. 7, ✉ 70629, ☎ (0711) 7 90 70, *Fax (0711) 793585, hotel.stuttgart.airport@moevenpick.com*, , – , rm, – 40. AE MC VISA JCB. rest
Meals à la carte 22/38 – 16 – **229 rm** 149 – 174.
◆ Conveniently located only 200m from the airport terminal. Comfortable rooms with optimal soundproofing. Close to the S-Bahn rapid transit station.

top air, at the airport (terminal 1, level 4), ✉ 70629, ☎ (0711) 9 48 21 37, *Fax (0711) 7979210, top-air.stuttgart@woellhaf-airport.de* – . AE MC VISA
closed August - early September, end December - mid January, Saturday, Sunday and Bank Holidays – **Meals** 42 *(lunch)*/90 and à la carte.
Spec. Gänsestopfleber "kalt und warm" mit glasiertem Löwenzahn. Kokon vom Atlantik Steinbutt mit Langustinen-Basilikumbrandade. Bresse Taube im Blätterteig mit Portweinsauce.
◆ You can watch the planes taxiing past while being treated to the delightful French specialities of this uniquely located restaurant. Exquisite contemporary ambience.

at Stuttgart-Hoheheim *South : 10 km, by Mittlere Filderstraße HX :*

Speisemeisterei (Öxle), Am Schloss Hohenheim, ✉ 70599, ☎ (0711) 4 56 00 37, *Fax (0711) 4560038* –
closed 27 July - 12 August, 1 to 12 January, Monday and Tuesday – **Meals** *(weekdays dinner only)* (booking essential) 64/128 , .
Spec. St. Petersfisch mit weißem Zwiebelconfit und Koriandersauce. Entenbrust mit Gewürzhaut und Flan von eigener Leber. Gratiniertes Rehnüsschen mit Kirsch-Nussauflauf.
◆ Even the most jaded palate will be revived in the magnificent surroundings of Schloss Hohenheim, where the cuisine is as refined and aristocratic as the ambience.

at Stuttgart-Möhringen *Southwest : 8 km, by Obere Weinsteige GX and B 27 :*

Millennium Hotel and Resort (with **Sl**), Plieninger Str. 100, ✉ 70567, ☎ (0711) 72 10, *Fax (0711) 7212950, sales.stuttgart@mill-cop.com*, , beer garden, direct entrance to the recreation centre Schwaben Quelle – , rm, – 500. AE MC VISA
Meals (19 different restaurants, bars and cafes) à la carte 21/48 – 16 – **454 rm** 165/185 – 185/205.
◆ This modern high building stands opposite the Musical-Theaters. Elegant, tasteful rooms, and, a lavishly equipped leisure area. You can choose among 19 different themed restaurants and bars.

Gloria, Sigmaringer Str. 59, ✉ 70567, ☎ (0711) 7 18 50, *Fax (0711) 7185121, info@hotelgloria.de*, beer garden, – , rm, – 50. AE MC VISA
Möhringer Hexle *(closed Thursday and Sunday dinner)* **Meals** à la carte 17/36 – **90 rm** 67/85 – 90/113.
◆ A lovely bright foyer welcomes guests to this family-run hotel, which offers a choice of rooms, contemporary-functional or traditional-comfortable. An attractive aspect of the traditional Möhringer Hexle restaurant is its winter garden.

Fora Hotel without rest, Filderbahnstr. 43, ✉ 70567, ☎ (0711) 71 60 80, *Fax (0711) 7160850, reservation.moehringen@fora.de* – . AE MC VISA JCB
41 rm 86/91 – 107.
◆ This hotel is set back from the main road. Guests stay in well-presented furnished rooms, their welcoming appearance enhanced by the use of bright colours.

Zur Linde, Sigmaringer Str. 49, ✉ 70567, ☎ (0711) 7 19 95 90, *Fax (0711) 7199592, info@gasthauszurlin.de*, – AE MC VISA
closed Saturday lunch – **Meals** à la carte 20/38 .
◆ If you enjoy hearty food with a home-cooked flavour, the cheerful "Lime Tree" is the place for you. Tempting Swabian morsels lovingly prepared from traditional recipes.

at Stuttgart-Obertürkheim *East : 6 km, by Augsburger Straße* JU :

Brita Hotel, Augsburger Str. 671, 70329, (0711) 32 02 30, *Fax (0711) 32023400, info@brita-hotel.de* – rm, – 80. AE VISA
Meals *(closed August and Friday - Sunday)* à la carte 23/28 – **70 rm** 72/95 – 125.
• Friendly establishment with contemporary comforts. All rooms with soundproofed windows. Oversize beds on request. Good traditional cooking in the country-style Poststüble or the Kutscherstube.

at Stuttgart-Stammheim *North : 10 km, by Heilbronner Straße* GT :

Novotel-Nord, Korntaler Str. 207, 70439, (0711) 98 06 20, *Fax (0711) 98062137, h0501@accor.com*, , , (heated) – rm, – 130. AE VISA JCB. rest
Meals à la carte 19/28 – 13 – **109 rm** 94 – 123.
• This hotel is well-located in relation to the motorway. Rooms to the usual Novotel standard, with bright and functional furniture.

at Stuttgart-Vaihingen *Southwest : 9,5 km, by Böblinger Straße* FX :

Mercure Fontana, Vollmoellerstr. 5, 70563, (0711) 73 00, *Fax (0711) 7302525, h5425@accor.com*, , , , , – rm, – 250. AE VISA JCB. rest
Meals à la carte 22/42 – 16 – **252 rm** 167 – 182.
• Stylish rooms on 18 floors, tastefully and comprehensively furnished with work desks, little living areas, and exquisitely comfortable beds. Choose between the elegant and country-style sections of the restaurant.

at Stuttgart-Weilimdorf *Northwest : 12 km, by Steiermärker Straße* FT *and B 295* :

Holiday Inn, Mittlerer Pfad 25, 70499, (0711) 98 88 80, *Fax (0711) 988889, strgc.reservations@ichotelsgroup.com*, beer garden, , – rm, – 160. AE VISA. rest
Meals à la carte 22/36 – 16 – **321 rm** 160 – 7 suites.
• Standard rooms with comfortable, contemporary furnishings, all with tea- and coffee-making facilities. It's best to reserve a room in the main building.

at Stuttgart-Zuffenhausen *North : 8 km, by Heilbronner Straße* GT *and B 10* :

Achat without rest, Wollinstr. 6, 70439, (0711) 82 00 80, *Fax (0711) 82008999, stuttgart@achat-hotel.de* – . AE VISA JCB
12 – **104 rm** 48/98.
• This modern hotel was built in 1997. Attractive rooms with bright and welcoming décor, many with kitchenette.

at Fellbach *Northeast : 8 km, by Nürnberger Straße (B 14)* JT :

Classic Congress Hotel, Tainer Str. 7, 70734, (0711) 5 85 90, *Fax (0711) 5859304, info@cch-bw.de*, , – rm, – 55. AE VISA
closed 24 December - 8 January – **Meals** see ***Eduard M.*** below – **149 rm** 145/149 – 168.
• The hotel is linked to the Schwabenlandhalle by an underground passageway. Recently refurbished rooms with bright and cheerful furniture.

Zum Hirschen with rm, Hirschstr. 1, 70734, (0711) 9 57 93 70, *Fax (0711) 95793710, info@zumhirschen-fellbach.de*, – . VISA.
Meals *(closed early - mid August, Sunday and Monday)(dinner only)* (booking essential) 65/86 and à la carte 52/64 – ***Finca*** *(closed Sunday and Monday)* **Meals** à la carte 30/37 – **9 rm** 65/85 – 95/118.
Spec. Langostinos und Kalbskopf mit Tonkabohne. Bresse-Taube mit Petersilientapenade und Portweinjus. Schmandtörtchen mit Rhabarber und Erdbeersorbet.
• This extremely well run, elegant, modern galleried restaurant in the centre of the Old Town occupies a 16C timber-framed building. Classic wine list. Finca restaurant has vaulted ceiling and bare wooden tables. Mediterranean and local cuisine.

Eduard M. - Classic Congress Hotel, Tainer Str. 7 (Schwabenlandhalle), 70734, (0711) 5 85 94 11, *Fax (0711) 5859427, restaurant@eduardm.de*, – . AE VISA
closed 24 December - 8 January – **Meals** 25 and à la carte 24/48.
• The redesigned restaurant of the Classic Congress Hotel makes a attractive impression with its bright and welcoming décor and split levels.

Aldinger's Weinstube Germania, Schmerstr. 6, 70734, (0711) 58 20 37, *Fax (0711) 582077, aldingers@t-online.de*, –
closed 2 weeks carnival, 3 weeks August - September, Sunday and Monday – **Meals** (booking essential) 29/45 and à la carte 25/38.
• This wine tavern with a modern touch is run personally by the chef, an expert with local and seasonal dishes. Dining on the terrace when weather permits.

at Korntal-Münchingen *Northwest : 9 km, by Heilbronner Straße* GT *and B 10 :*

Mercure, Siemensstr. 50, ✉ 70825, ☎ (07150) 1 30, *Fax (07150) 13266, h0685@accor.com*, beer garden, ≘s, – ✉, ⇔ rm, TV ☎ ♿ P – 🏠 180. AE ① MC VISA
Meals à la carte 22/35 – **200 rm** ☐ 108/149 – 132/162.
◆ Conference delegates appreciate this hotel's proximity to the motorway. Functional rooms all with work desks and some with living areas.

at Leinfelden-Echterdingen *South : 13 km, by Obere Weinsteige* GX *and B 27 :*

Am Park, Lessingstr. 4 (Leinfelden), ✉ 70771, ☎ (0711) 90 31 00, *Fax (0711) 9031099, info@hotelampark-leinfelden.de*, beer garden – ✉, ⇔ rm, TV ☎ P – 🏠 15. AE MC VISA
closed 24 December - 10 January – **Meals** *(closed Saturday - Sunday and Bank Holidays)* à la carte 23/38 – **42 rm** ☐ 80 – 96.
◆ This welcoming establishment stands in a tranquil cul-de-sac surrounded by magnificent trees. Bright and attractively furnished rooms. Choose from the restaurant's range of well-prepared southern German specialities.

Filderland without rest, Tübinger Str. 16 (Echterdingen), ✉ 70771, ☎ (0711) 9 49 46, *Fax (0711) 9494888, hotel-filderland@t-online.de* – ✉ ⇔ TV ☎ 🚗 – 🏠 15. AE ① MC VISA. ✱
closed 24 December - 6 January – **48 rm** ☐ 63/69 – 83/89.
◆ Behind the attractive façade is a well-run hotel not far from the airport. Comfortable, contemporary interior.

Baiersbronn *Baden-Württemberg* 545 U 9 – *pop. 16 500 – alt. 550 m.*
Stuttgart 100.

Schwarzwaldstube - Hotel Traube Tonbach, Tonbachstr. 237, ✉ 72270, ☎ (07442) 49 26 65, *Fax (07442) 492692, tischreservierung@traube-tonbach.de*, ← – ▤ P. AE ① MC VISA. ✱
closed 1 to 26 August, 10 January - 4 February, Monday and Tuesday – **Meals** (booking essential) 105/130 and à la carte 75/98 ♀, ✿.
Spec. Gebratene Gänseleberscheiben mit Ananas-Mangochutney und Balsamicoglace. Lammrücken mit Ingwer und rotem Paprikaöl gratiniert. Kartoffel-Parmesanschaum mit einer Rosette von Sommertrüffeln.
◆ Harald Wohlfahrt's creative cuisine, prepared in a refined and harmonious manner, can be enjoyed in a rustically elegant setting. Very attentive service.

Restaurant Bareiss - Hotel Bareiss, Gärtenbühlweg 14, ✉ 72270, ☎ (07442) 4 70, *Fax (07442) 47320, info@bareiss.com*, ←, – ▤ P. AE ① MC VISA. ✱
closed 31 July - 26 August, 9 January - 4 February, Monday and Tuesday – **Meals** (booking essential) 98/118 and à la carte 65/93 ♀, ✿.
Spec. Rosette von gratinierten Jakobsmuscheln mit Imperial Kaviar. Atlantik Lotte mit Pastis flambiert auf Gewürzfenchel. Lammrücken von der Älbler Wacholderheide mit Gremolata.
◆ Maître Claus-Peter Lumpp's classic cuisine, a stylish ambience and attentive service are the recipe for success. Wine tastings in the cellar.

Sulzburg *Baden-Württemberg* 545 W 7 – *pop. 2 600 – alt. 474 m.*
Stuttgart 229.

Hirschen (Steiner) with rm, Hauptstr. 69, ✉ 79295, ☎ (07634) 82 08, *Fax (07634) 6717, hirschen-sulzburg@t-online.de*
closed 25 July - 11 August and 7 to 27 January – **Meals** *(closed Monday - Tuesday)* (booking essential) 36 *(lunch)*/98 and à la carte 55/82, ✿ – **9 rm** ☐ 72/108 – 92/128.
Spec. Variation von der Gänseleber mit Gelée. Schweinefuß mit Langustine gefüllt und Krustentiersauce. Crépinette vom Rehrücken mit Pfeffersauce und Apfelstrudel.
◆ This 18C inn fits in unobtrusively into the street scene. Inside, there are fine antiques and period furniture, as well as a kitchen producing superlative fare.

Greece

Elláda

ATHENS

PRACTICAL INFORMATION

LOCAL CURRENCY

1 euro (€) = 1,34 USD ($) (Dec 2004)

TOURIST INFORMATION

National Tourist Organisation (EOT): *26a, Amalia St, info_desk@gnto.gr, ✆ (210) 331 03 92. Hotel reservation: Hellenic Chamber of Hotels, 24 Stadiou, ✆ (210) 323 71 93, grhotels@otenet.gr. Fax (210) 322 54 49, also EOT at Athens International Airport ✆ (210) 353 04 45 - Tourist Police: 4 Stadiou ✆ 171.*

National Holidays in Greece: *6 January, 25 March, 15 August and 28 October.*

FOREIGN EXCHANGE

Banks are usually open on weekdays from 8am to 2pm. A branch of the National Bank of Greece is open daily from 8am to 2pm (from 9am to 1pm at weekends) at 2 Karageorgi Servias (Sindagma).

AIRLINES

OLYMPIC AIRWAYS: *96 Singrou 117 41 Athens, ✆ (210) 801 11 44/444, 3 Kotopouli (Omonia), 15 Filellinon (Sindagma) ✆ (210) 966 66 66.*
AIR FRANCE: *18 Vouliagmenis, Glyfada 166 75 Athens, ✆ (210) 960 11 00.*
BRITISH AIRWAYS: *1 Themistokleous Street 166 74 Glyfada ✆ (210) 890 6666.*
JAPAN AIRLINES: *22 Voulis 105 63 Athens, ✆ (210) 324 82 11.*
LUFTHANSA: *10 Ziridi St Maroussi ✆ (210) 617 52 00.*
SWISS INTERNATIONAL AIRLINES: *Athens International Airport, ✆ (210) 353 74 00.*

TRANSPORT IN ATHENS

Taxis: *may be hailed in the street even when already engaged; it is always advisable to pay by the meter (double fare after midnight).*
Bus: *good for sightseeing and practical for short distances.*
Metro: *Three lines cross the city from North east (Kifissia) to South west (Pireas) : from Northwest (Sepolia) to South (Dafni) and from Syntagma (Parliament Square) to Ethniki Amyna.*

POSTAL SERVICES

General Post Office: *100 Apellou (Kotzia Square) with poste restante, and also at Sindagma (Mitropoleos St).*
Telephone (OTE): *15 Stadiou and 85 Patission (all services).*

SHOPPING IN ATHENS

In summer, shops are usually open from 8am to 1.30pm, and 5.30 to 8.30pm. They close on Sunday, and at 2.30pm on Monday, Wednesday and Saturday. In winter they open from 9am to 5pm on Monday and Wednesday, from 10am to 7pm on Tuesday, Thursday and Friday, from 8.30am to 3.30pm on Saturday. Department Stores in Patission and Eolou are open fron 8.30 am to 8 pm on weekdays and 3 pm on Saturdays. The main shopping streets are to be found in Sindagma, Kolonaki, Monastiraki and Omonia areas. Flea Market (generally open on Sunday) and Greek Handicraft in Plaka and Monastiraki.

TIPPING

Service is generally included in the bills but it is usual to tip employees.

SPEED LIMITS

The speed limit in built up areas is 50 km/h (31 mph); on motorways the maximum permitted speed is 100 km/h (62 mph) and 80 km/h (50 mph) on other roads.

SEAT BELTS

The wearing of seat belts is compulsory for drivers and front seat passengers.

BREAKDOWN SERVICE

The ELPA (Automobile and Touring Club of Greece, ✆ (210) 60 68 800) operate a 24 hour breakdown service: 10400 for emergency road service.

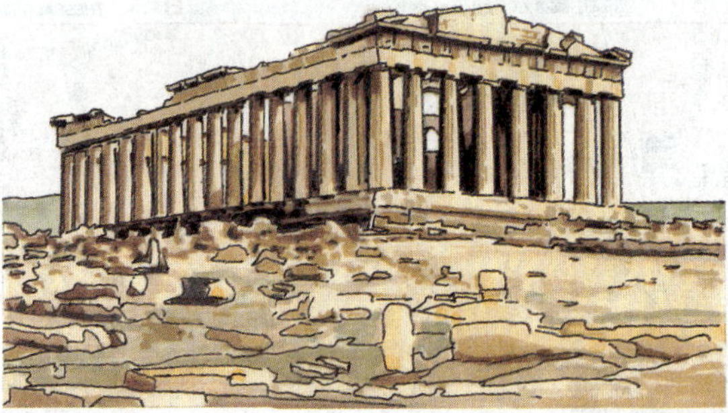

ATHENS
(ATHÍNA)

Atikí 737 ㉚ *– Pop. 3 192 606 (Athens and Piraeus area).*

Igoumenítsa 581 – Pátra 215 – Thessaloníki 479.

Tourist Information (EOT), 26a, Amalia St ☎ (210) 331 03 92 info_desk@gnto.gr
ELPA (Automobile and Touring Club of Greece), 395 Messogion ☎ (210) 606 88 00.

18 Glyfada 11610 ☎ (210) 894 68 20, Fax (210) 894 37 21.

E : 35 km, Athens International Airport ☎ (210) 353 00 00.

1 Karolou ☎ (210) 529 77 77.

SIGHTS

Views of Athens: Lycabettos (Likavitós) ☼ ★★★ DX *– Philopappos Hill (Lófos Filopápou) ≤ ★★★* AY.

ANCIENT ATHENS

Acropolis★★★ (Akrópoli) ABY *– Theseion★★ (Thissío)* AY *and Agora★ (Arhéa Agorá)* AY *– Theatre of Dionysos★★ (Théatro Dionissou)* BY *and Odeon of Herod Atticus★ (Odío Iródou Atikoú)* AY *– Olympieion★★ (Naós Olimbíou Diós)* BY *and Hadrian's Arch★ (Píli Adrianoú)* BY *– Tower of the Winds★* BY **A** *in the Roman Forum (Romaïkí Agorá).*

OLD ATHENS AND THE TURKISH PERIOD

Pláka★★ : Old Metropolitan★★ BY **P**[1] *– Monastiráki★ (Old Bazaar) : Kapnikaréa (Church)* BY **K**, *Odós Pandróssou★* BY **29**, *Monastiráki Square★* BY.

MODERN ATHENS

Sindagma Square★ CY *: Greek guard on sentry duty – Academy, University and Library Buildings★ (Akadimía* CX, *Panepistímio* CX, *Ethnikí Vivliothíki* BX*) – National Garden★ (Ethnikós Kípos)* CY.

MUSEUMS

National Archaelogical Museum★★★ (Ethnikó Arheologikó Moussío) BX *– Acropolis Museum★★★* BY **M**[5] *– Museum of Cycladic and Ancient Greek Art★★* DY **M**[10] *– Byzantine Museum★★ (Vizandinó Moussío)* DY *– Benaki Museum★★ (Moussío Benáki, private collection of antiquities and traditional art)* CDY *– Museum of Traditional Greek Art★* BY **M**[7] *– National Historical Museum★* BY **M**[2] *– Jewish Museum of Greece★* BY **M**[3] *– National Gallery and Soutzos Museum★ (painting and sculpture)* DY **M**[1].

EXCURSIONS

Cape Sounion★★★ (Soúnio) SE : 71 km BY *– Kessariani Monastery★★, E : 9 km* DY *– Daphne Monastery★★ (Dafní) NW : 10 km* AX *– Aigina Island★ (Égina) : Temple of Aphaia★★, 3 hours return.*

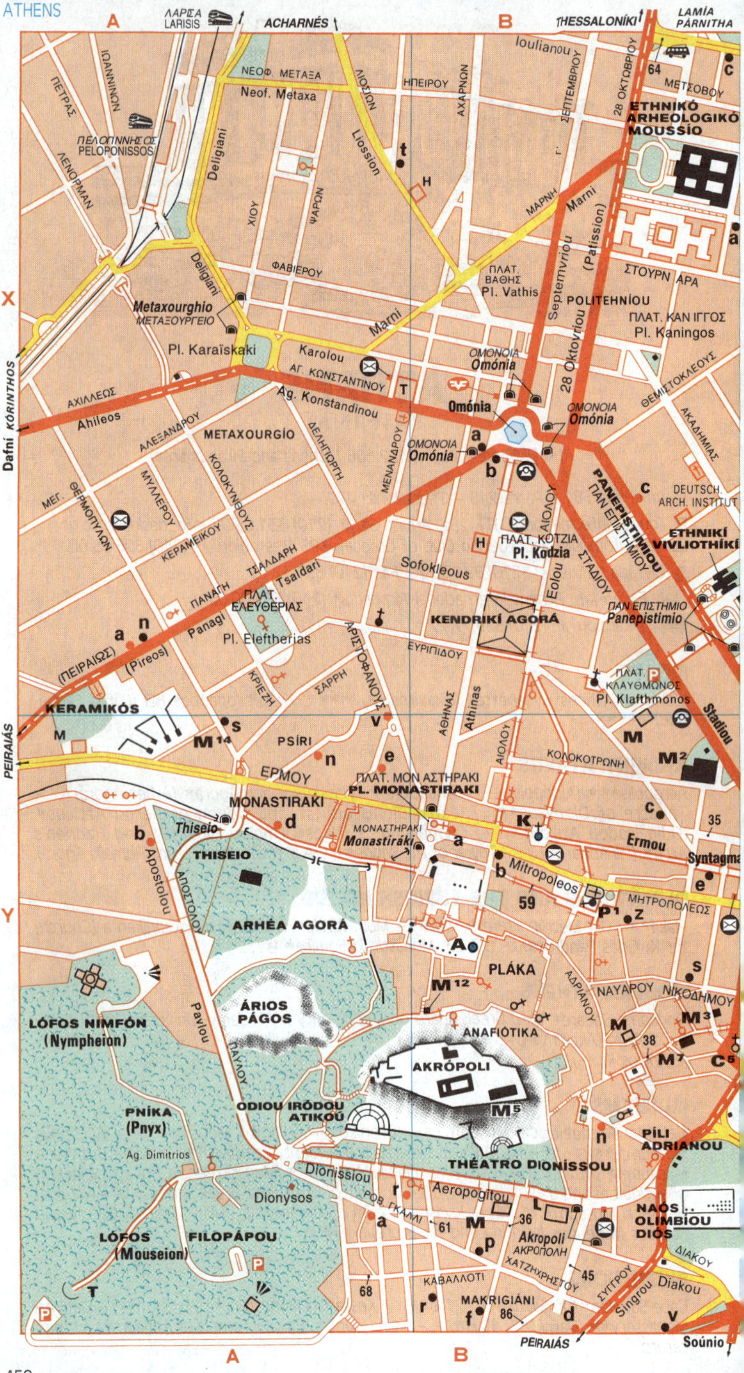
A
B
X
Y
ΛΑΡΣΑ
LARISIS
ACHARNÉS
THESSALONÍKI
LAMÍA
PÁRNITHA
ΙΩΑΝΝΙΝΩΝ
ΠΕΤΡΑΣ
ΠΕΛΟΠΟΝΝΗΣΟΣ
PELOPONISSOS
ΛΕΝΟΡΜΑΝ
ΝΕΟΦ. ΜΕΤΑΞΑ
Neof. Metaxa
Deligiani
ΛΙΟΣΙΩΝ
Liossion
ΗΠΕΙΡΟΥ
ΑΧΑΡΝΩΝ
Ioulianou
ΣΕΠΤΕΜΒΡΙΟΥ
28 ΟΚΤΩΒΡΙΟΥ
64
ΜΕΤΣΟΒΟΥ
ETHNIKÓ
ARHEOLOGIKÓ
MOUSSÍO
ΧΙΟΥ
ΨΑΡΩΝ
ΜΑΡΝΗ
Marni
(Patission)
Septemvriou
ΦΑΒΙΕΡΟΥ
ΠΛΑΤ. ΒΑΘΗΣ
Pl. Vathis
ΣΤΟΥΡΝ ΑΡΑ
POLITEHNÍOU
ΠΛΑΤ. ΚΑΝ ΙΓΓΟΣ
Pl. Kaningos
Metaxourghio
ΜΕΤΑΞΟΥΡΓΕΙΟ
Pl. Karaïskaki
Karolou
ΑΓ. ΚΩΝΣΤΑΝΤΙΝΟΥ
Ag. Konstandinou
ΟΜΟΝΟΙΑ
Omónia
28 Oktovriou
ΘΕΜΙΣΤΟΚΛΕΟΥΣ
ΑΚΑΔΗΜΙΑΣ
Dafní
KÓRINTHOS
ΑΧΙΛΛΕΩΣ
Ahileos
ΑΛΕΞΑΝΔΡΟΥ
METAXOURGÍO
ΚΟΛΟΚΥΝΘΟΥΣ
ΔΕΛΗΓΙΩΡΓΗ
ΜΕΝΑΝΔΡΟΥ
PANEPISTIMIOU
ΠΑΝ ΕΠΙΣΤΗΜΙΟΥ
DEUTSCH.
ARCH. INSTITUT
ΜΕΓ.
ΘΕΡΜΟΠΥΛΩΝ
ΜΥΛΛΕΡΟΥ
ΚΕΡΑΜΕΙΚΟΥ
ΑΙΟΛΟΥ
ΠΛΑΤ. ΚΟΤΖΙΑ
Pl. Kodzia
ETHNIKÍ
VIVLIOTHÍKÍ
ΤΣΑΛΔΑΡΗ
Tsaldari
Sofokleous
ΣΤΑΔΙΟΥ
Eolou
ΠΑΝΑΓΗ
Panagi
ΠΛΑΤ. ΕΛΕΥΘΕΡΙΑΣ
Pl. Eleftherias
KENDRIKÍ AGORÁ
ΠΑΝ ΕΠΙΣΤΗΜΙΟ
Panepistimio
ΑΡΙΣΤΟΦΑΝΟΥΣ
ΕΥΡΙΠΙΔΟΥ
(ΠΕΙΡΑΙΩΣ)
(Pireos)
ΚΡΙΕΖΗ
ΣΑΡΡΗ
ΑΘΗΝΑΣ
Athinas
ΠΛΑΤ. ΚΛΑΥΘΜΩΝΟΣ
Pl. Klafthmonos
Stadiou
KERAMIKÓS
PEIRAIÁS
PSIRI
ΚΟΛΟΚΟΤΡΩΝΗ
ΕΡΜΟΥ
ΠΛΑΤ. ΜΟΝ ΑΣΤΗΡΑΚΙ
PL. MONASTIRAKI
MONASTIRAKÍ
Thiseio
ΜΟΝΑΣΤΗΡΑΚΙ
Monastiráki
Ermou
35
Syntagma
Apostolou
THISEIO
Mitropoleos
59
ΜΗΤΡΟΠΟΛΕΩΣ
ΑΠΟΣΤΟΛΟΥ
ARHÉA AGORÁ
PLÁKA
ΑΔΡΙΑΝΟΥ
ΝΑΥΑΡΟΥ
ΝΙΚΟΔΗΜΟΥ
ÁRIOS
PÁGOS
ANAFIÓTIKA
LÓFOS NIMFÓN
(Nympheion)
Pavlou
ΠΑΥΛΟΥ
38
AKRÓPOLI
ODIOU IRÓDOU
ATIKOÚ
PNÍKA
(Pnyx)
Ag. Dimitrios
PÍLI
ADRIANOU
THÉATRO DIONÍSSOU
Dionissiou
Aeropogitou
Dionysos
ΡΟΒ. ΓΚΑΛΛΙ
61
36
NAÓS
OLIMBÍOU
DIÓS
LÓFOS
(Mouseion)
FILOPÁPOU
Akropoli
ΑΚΡΟΠΟΛΗ
ΧΑΤΖΗΧΡΗΣΤΟΥ
45
ΣΥΓΓΡΟΥ
Singrou
ΔΙΑΚΟΥ
Diakou
68
ΚΑΒΑΛΛΟΤΙ
MAKRIGIÁNI
86
PEIRAIÁS
Soúnio

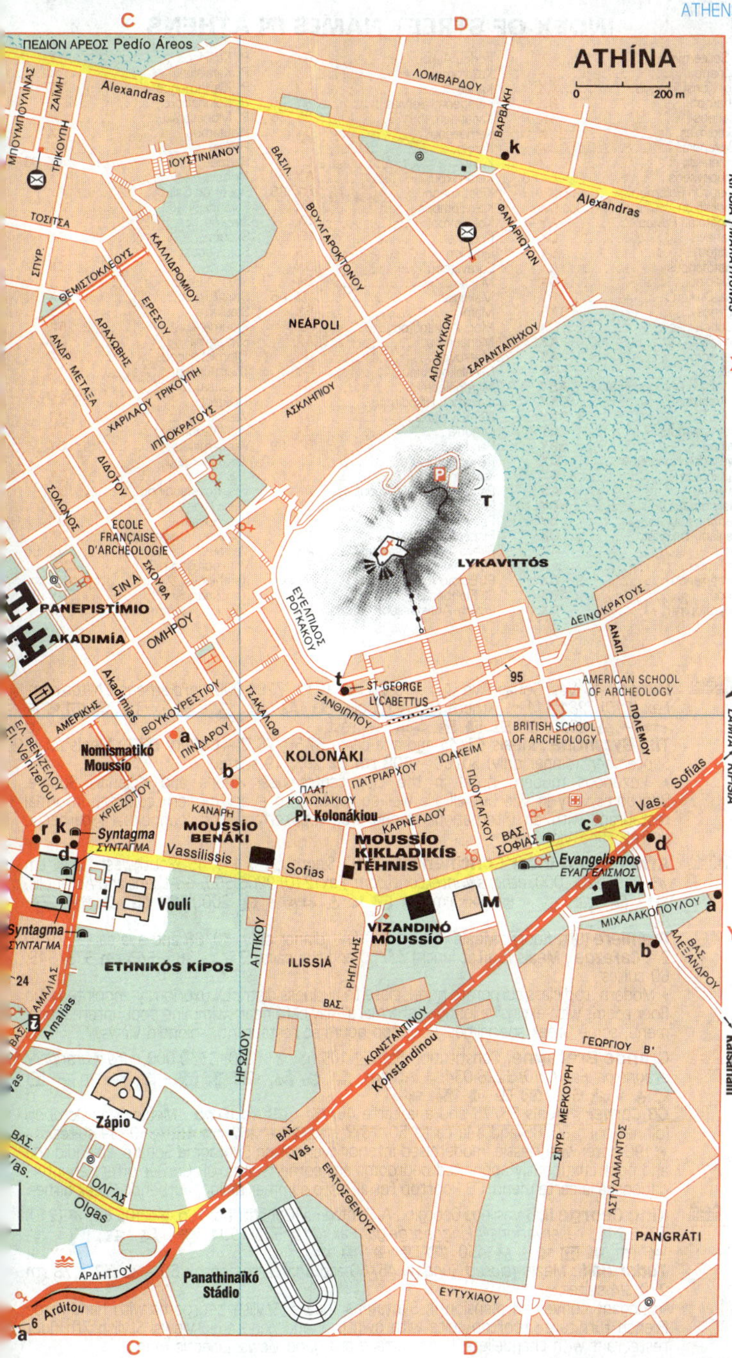
ATHÍNA
0
200 m
C
D
X
Y
ΠΕΔΙΟΝ ΑΡΕΟΣ Pedío Áreos
Alexandras
ΛΟΜΒΑΡΔΟΥ
ΒΑΡΒΑΚΗ
ΙΟΥΣΤΙΝΙΑΝΟΥ
ΒΑΣΙΛ.
ΜΠΟΥΜΠΟΥΛΙΝΑΣ
ΖΑΙΜΗ
ΤΡΙΚΟΥΠΗ
ΤΟΣΙΤΣΑ
ΣΠΥΡ.
ΘΕΜΙΣΤΟΚΛΕΟΥΣ
ΚΑΛΛΙΔΡΟΜΙΟΥ
ΒΟΥΛΓΑΡΟΚΤΟΝΟΥ
ΦΑΝΑΡΙΩΤΩΝ
ΕΡΕΣΟΥ
ΑΡΑΧΩΒΗΣ
ΑΝΔΡ ΜΕΤΑΞΑ
NEÁPOLI
ΑΠΟΚΑΥΚΩΝ
ΣΑΡΑΝΤΑΠΗΧΟΥ
ΧΑΡΙΛΑΟΥ ΤΡΙΚΟΥΠΗ
ΑΣΚΛΗΠΙΟΥ
ΙΠΠΟΚΡΑΤΟΥΣ
ΔΙΔΟΤΟΥ
ΣΟΛΩΝΟΣ
ECOLE FRANÇAISE D'ARCHEOLOGIE
ΣΚΟΥΦΑ
ΣΙΝ Α
PANEPISTÍMIO
AKADIMÍA
ΟΜΗΡΟΥ
ΕΥΕΛΠΙΔΟΣ ΡΟΓΚΑΚΟΥ
LYKAVITTÓS
T
ΔΕΙΝΟΚΡΑΤΟΥΣ
ΑΝΑΠ.
95
AMERICAN SCHOOL OF ARCHEOLOGY
ΠΟΛΕΜΟΥ
BRITISH SCHOOL OF ARCHEOLOGY
t
ST-GEORGE LYCABETTUS
ΞΑΝΘΙΠΠΟΥ
ΤΣΑΚΑΛΩΦ
ΒΟΥΚΟΥΡΕΣΤΙΟΥ
Akadimias
ΑΜΕΡΙΚΗΣ
ΠΙΝΔΑΡΟΥ
a
b
KOLONÁKI
ΠΑΤΡΙΑΡΧΟΥ
ΙΩΑΚΕΙΜ
ΠΛΟΥΤΑΡΧΟΥ
ΠΛΑΤ. ΚΟΛΩΝΑΚΙΟΥ
Pl. Kolonákiou
ΚΑΡΝΕΑΔΟΥ
ΕΛ. ΒΕΝΙΖΕΛΟΥ
El. Venizelou
Nomismatikó Moussío
ΚΡΙΕΖΩΤΟΥ
ΚΑΝΑΡΗ
MOUSSÍO BENÁKI
MOUSSÍO KIKLADIKÍS TÉHNIS
ΒΑΣ. ΣΟΦΙΑΣ
Vas. Sofias
c
d
r
k
Syntagma
ΣΥΝΤΑΓΜΑ
Vassilissis
Sofias
Evangelismos
ΕΥΑΓΓΕΛΙΣΜΟΣ
M¹
M
Voulí
ΜΙΧΑΛΑΚΟΠΟΥΛΟΥ
VIZANDINÓ MOUSSÍO
ΒΑΣ. ΑΛΕΞΑΝΔΡΟΥ
ETHNIKÓS KÍPOS
ΑΤΤΙΚΟΥ
ILISSIÁ
ΡΗΓΙΛΛΗΣ
ΒΑΣ.
ΚΩΝΣΤΑΝΤΙΝΟΥ
Konstandinou
ΓΕΩΡΓΙΟΥ Β'
24
ΑΜΑΛΙΑΣ
Amalias
ΗΡΩΔΟΥ
ΣΠΥΡ. ΜΕΡΚΟΥΡΗ
ΑΣΤΥΔΑΜΑΝΤΟΣ
Zápio
ΟΛΓΑΣ
Olgas
ΕΡΑΤΟΣΘΕΝΟΥΣ
PANGRÁTI
ΑΡΔΗΤΤΟΥ
Arditou
6
Panathinaïkó Stádio
ΕΥΤΥΧΙΔΟΥ
KIFISIÁ MARATHÓNAS
LAMÍA KIFISIÁ
Kaisarianí

INDEX OF STREET NAMES IN ATHENS

3-Septemvriou . . . BX
Adrianou . . . BY
Ag. Konstandinou . . . AX
Aharnon . . . BX
Ahilleos . . . AX
Akadimias . . . BCX
Alexandras . . . CDX
Amerikis . . . CXY
Anapavseos . . . CY 6
Anapiron Polemou . . . DXY
Apokafkon . . . DX
Apostolou Pavlou . . . AY
Arahovis . . . CX
Arditou . . . CY
Aristofanous . . . AX
Asklipiou . . . DX
Ath. Diakou . . . BY
Athinas . . . BXY
Bouboulinas . . . CX
Deligiani . . . AX
Deligiorgi . . . AX
Didotou . . . CX
Dionissiou Areopagitou . . . ABY
El. Venizelou . . . CXY
Eolou . . . BXY
Eratosthenous . . . DY
Ermou . . . ABY
Evelpidos Rongakou . . . DX
Fanarioton . . . DX
Favierou . . . AX
Filelinon . . . BCY 24
Hadzihristou . . . BY
Harilaou Trikoupi . . . CX
Hiou . . . AX
Ioulianou . . . AX
Ioustinianou . . . CX
Ipirou . . . ABX
Ipokratous . . . CX
Irodou Atikou . . . DY
Kalidromiou . . . CX
Kanari . . . CY
Karageorgi Servias . . . BY 35
Kariatidon . . . BY 36
Karneadou . . . DY
Karolou . . . AX
Kavaloti . . . BY
Keramikou . . . AX
Kidathineon . . . BY 38
Kolokinthous . . . AX
Kolokotroni . . . BY
Kriezotou . . . CY
Liossion . . . AX
Lomvardou . . . DX
Makri . . . BY
Makrigiani . . . BY 45
Marni . . . ABX
Meg. Alexandrou . . . AX
Menandrou . . . AX
Metsovou . . . BX
Mihalakopoulou . . . DY
Mitropoleos . . . BY
Navarhou Nikodimou . . . BY
Neof. Metaxa . . . AX
Omonia . . . BX
Pandrossou . . . BY 59
Panepistimiou . . . BX
Parthenonos . . . BY 61
Patission (28 Oktovriou) . . . BX
Patr. Ioakim . . . DY
Pedío Áreos . . . CX
Pindarou . . . CY
Pireos (Panagi Tsaldari) . . . AX
Pl. Anexartissias (Vathis) . . . BX
Pl. Egiptou . . . BX 64
Pl. Eleftherias . . . AX
Pl. Eth. Antistasseos (Kodzia) . BX
Pl. Kaningos . . . BX
Pl. Karaïskaki . . . AX
Pl. Klafthmonos . . . BX
Pl. Kolonakiou . . . DY
Pl. Monastiráki . . . ABY
Ploutarhou . . . DX
Psaron . . . AX
Radzieri . . . AY 68
Rigilis . . . DY
Rovertou Gali . . . AY
Sarandapihou . . . DX
Singrou . . . BY
Skoufa . . . CX
Sofokleous . . . ABX
Solonos . . . CX
Spir. Merkouri . . . DY
Spir. Trikoupi . . . CX
Stadiou . . . BXY
Stournara . . . BX
Syntagma . . . CY
Themistokleous . . . BCX
Thermopilon . . . AX
Tossitsa . . . CX
Tsakalof . . . DXY
Varvaki . . . DX
Vas. Alexandrou . . . DY
Vas. Amalias . . . CY
Vas. Georgiou B' . . . DY
Vas. Konstandinou . . . DY
Vas. Olgas . . . CY
Vas. Sofias . . . CDY
Vassiliou Voulgaroktonou . . . DX
Veïkou . . . BY 86
Voukourestiou . . . CXY
Xanthipou . . . DXY
Xenokratous . . . DY 95
Zaïmi . . . CX

Hilton, 46 Vas. Sofias Ave, ✉ 115 28, ℘ (210) 7281 000, *info.athens@hilton.com, Fax (210) 7281 111,* < Athens and Acropolis, , , , – , rm, – 2000. VISA JCB. rest DY d
***The Byzantine* : Meals** 32/35 and a la carte 37.50/76 ♀ – ***Galaxy BBQ* : Meals** *(May-September)* (dinner only) 50/60 – **508 rm** ☕ 295, 19 suites.
• Luxurious modern hotel in the city centre near shops and Kolonaki Square. Bedrooms vary in size but all are well-equipped with every modern comfort. Informal restaurant with an international menu. Rooftop terrace and lounge/bar ; barbecue buffet ; fine views.

Athenaeum Inter-Continental, 89-93 Singrou, ✉ 117 45, Southwest : 2 ¾ km ℘ (210) 9206 000, *athens@interconti.com, Fax (210) 9206 500,* < Athens and Acropolis, , , , – , rm, – 2000. VISA JCB.
***Première* (9th floor) : Meals** *(closed Sunday)* (dinner only) 50/68 and a la carte 50/70 ♀ – ***Cafezoe* : Meals** (buffet lunch) 33/50 and a la carte ♀ – ☕ 28 – **543 rm** 375/545, 60 suites.
• Modern, top class corporate hotel, close to business district. Luxuriously-appointed club floor rooms with exclusive lounge. Informal all-day café near swimming pool ; international menu, some Greek specialities. Roof-top gourmet restaurant ; splendid views.

Grande Bretagne, Constitution Sq, ✉ 105 63, ℘ (210) 3330 000, *info@grandebretagne.gr, Fax (210) 3228 034,* < Athens, , , , , , – , rm, – 380. VISA. CY d
***GB Corner* : Meals** 55/75 and a la carte 46/73 – ***GB Rooftop* : Meals** *(May-October)* (dinner only) 60/85 and a la carte 50/73 ♀ – ☕ 28 – **262 rm** 460/550, 59 suites.
• 19C hotel with classic, modernised interior overlooking Syntagma Square. Splendid spa and pool. Luxuriously-appointed bedrooms and corner suites. GB Corner offers an international à la carte menu. GB Rooftop for alfresco summer dining, authentic Greek dishes.

King George II, 3 Vasileos Georgiou A, Syntagma (Constitution) Sq, ✉ 105 64, ℘ (210) 3222 210, *reservations@kinggeorge.gr, Fax (210) 3250 504,* , , , – , rm, – 450. VISA. CY k
***Tudor Hall* : Meals** *(closed Sunday)* 45/60 and a la carte approx 60 – ☕ 32 – **78 rm** 270, 24 suites.
• Elegant converted mansion in Syntagma Square. Stylish bedrooms with hand-made French furniture ; rooftop suite with own pool and panoramic views. Stylish 7th floor restaurant with chandeliers, large terrace and good views. Eclectic menu.

Ledra Marriott, 115 Singrou, 117 45, Southwest : 3 km (210) 9300 000, *athensledramarriott@marriotthotels.com, Fax (210) 9559 153,* Athens, - rm, - 620.
***Kona Kai* : Meals** - Polynesian and Japanese - *(closed Sunday)* (dinner only) 40/50 and a la carte 38.50/78.50 – ***Zephyros* : Meals** - Mediterranean and Greek - (buffet lunch) 19.80/42 and a la carte 24/40 – 20 – **296 rm** 410/490, 18 suites.
◆ Commercial hotel with panoramic views from rooftop terrace. Executive rooms have exclusive lounge and high-tech extras. Authentic Japanese dishes in Kona Kai basement restaurant. Zephyros on 1st floor for traditional and international buffet.

Metropolitan, 385 Singrou, 175 64, Southwest : 7 km (210) 9471 000, *metropolitan@chandris.gr, Fax (210) 9471 010,* - rm, - 450.
***Trocadero* : Meals** (buffet lunch Monday-Friday) 21/31 and a la carte – 18 – **350 rm** 290, 24 suites.
◆ Striking, modern corporate hotel with easy access into and out of the city. Spacious, comfortable rooms with state-of-the-art facilities. Popular for business conventions. International or Italian fare can be taken overlooking the garden or beside the pool.

Divani Caravel, 2 Vas. Alexandrou, 161 21, (210) 7207 000, *divanis@divanicaravel.gr, Fax (210) 7236 683,* Athens, - rm, - 1000. DY b
***Brown's* : Meals** (dinner only) a la carte 54.50/80 – ***Café Constantinople* : Meals** (buffet lunch) 28/30 and a la carte 37/64 – 27 – **427 rm** 550/600, 44 suites.
◆ Modern hotel with spacious, marbled lobby. Conference facilities. Attractive roof garden with far-reaching views. Well-equipped rooms. Brown's for stylish dining and elegant cigar lounge. Café Constantinople open all-day for local and international dishes.

NJV Athens Plaza, 2 Vas. Georgiou A, Sindagma Sq., 105 64, (210) 3352 400, *sales_njv@grecotel.gr, Fax (210) 3235 856* - rm, - 250. CY r
***The Parliament* : Meals** 30 and a la carte – 25 – **159 rm** 320/550, 23 suites.
◆ Modern hotel handy for the shopping and business districts. Local stone adorns the contemporary lobby and bar. Boldly decorated, hi-tech bedrooms and luxurious suites. Modern menu of international dishes on 1st floor, overlooking Syntagma Square.

Park H. Athens, 10 Alexandras Ave, 106 82, (210) 8894 515, *sales@athensparkhotel.gr, Fax (210) 8238 420,* Athens, - - 750. BX c
***Alexandra's* : Meals** a la carte approx 40 – ***Park Café* : Meals** a la carte approx 30 – ***St'Astra* : Meals** *(closed Sunday)* (dinner only) 50/90 and a la carte – **138 rm** 190/220, 12 suites.
◆ Modern, family owned hotel between the archeological museum and Pedio Areos Park. Smartly fitted rooms, suites with spa baths. Dine in Alexandra's with piano accompaniment. All-day Park Café for a light meal. Enjoy the view from St'Astra by the rooftop pool.

Divani Palace Acropolis, 19-25 Parthenonos, 117 42, (210) 9280 100, *divanis@divaniacropolis.gr, Fax (210) 9214 993,* - - 180. BY r
***Aspassia* : Meals** 35/60 and a la carte 35/60 – ***Roof Garden* : Meals** *(closed mid October-mid May and Tuesday)* (live music) (buffet dinner only) 50 – 27 – **242 rm** 260, 8 suites.
◆ Near the Parthenon yet fairly quiet with parts of Themistocles' wall in the basement. Particularly comfortable suites. Aspassia for formal meals. Roof Garden for barbecue buffet with live music.

Stratos Vassilikos, Mihalakopoulou 114, 115 27, (210) 7706 611, *info@airotel.gr, Fax (210) 7708 137,* - - 150.
Meals 20/60 and a la carte 30/120 – **82 rm** 172, 6 suites.
◆ Elegant, modern hotel with coin-bar in reception. Spacious well-furnished bedrooms. Riva restaurant in the atrium for lunch or formal dinner.

St George Lycabettus, 2 Kleomenous, 106 75, (210) 7290 712, *Fax (210) 7290 439,* Athens, - - 210. DX t
***Le Grand Balcon* : Meals** *(closed Sunday)* (dinner only) a la carte approx 50 – ***Frame* : Meals** a la carte approx 30 – 26.50 – **152 rm** 313/469, 6 suites.
◆ Elevated position on Lycabettus Hill. Greek artwork and artifacts throughout. Roof-top pool. South rooms with balconies and view of the Acropolis and Athens skyline. Le Grand Balcon roof-top restaurant for international menu. All-day Frame for Greek dishes.

Electra Palace, 18 Nikodimou St, 105 57, (210) 3370 000, *aelectrapalace@ath.forthnet.gr, Fax (210) 3241 875* - - 60 BY s
95 rm, 7 suites.
◆ Modern interior behind a classical façade in Plaka. Ultra modern bedrooms and suites with classical décor ; some with view of the Acropolis. First-floor restaurant serving American buffet breakfast and a la carte lunch and dinner.

Zafolia, 87-89 Alexandras, ✉ 114 74, ✆ (210) 6449 002, *info@zafoliahotel.gr, Fax (210) 6442 042,* ← Athens, – – 180. DX k

Meals 22/40 – **185 rm** 149/162, 7 suites.

• Privately owned, commercial hotel on east side of city. Well-equipped bedrooms with modern amenities; suites with private balcony. Rooftop bar and pool. Ellinikon is a modern first floor restaurant; Greek and international menu and a busy lunchtime buffet.

Holiday Inn, 50 Mihalakopoulou, ✉ 115 28, ✆ (210) 7278 000, *info@hiathens.com, Fax (210) 7278 600,* – rm, – 650. DY a

Meals 22/25 and a la carte 35/45 – 22 – **192 rm** 469/512.

• Modern corporate hotel with state-of-the-art conference facilities. Executive bedrooms with ample work space and 3 suites. Plaza Restaurant offers international menu; light meals in summer in poolside roof garden commanding far-reaching city views.

Holiday Suites without rest., 4 Arnis St, ✉ 115 28, by Mihalakopoulou ✆ (210) 7278 000, *info@hiathens.com, Fax (210) 7278 600* –

Meals (see ***Holiday Inn*** above) – 18 – **34 rm** 560.

• Converted apartments in quiet residential area. Spacious rooms each with kitchenette and work area, superbly equipped with CD/DVD/fax. Breakfast here or at Holiday Inn.

Andromeda, 22 Timoleontos Vassou St, ✉ 115 21, via Vas. Sofias off Soutsou D. ✆ (210) 6415 000, *reservations@andromedaathens.gr, Fax (210) 6466 361* – rm, – 100.

Andromeda : **Meals** a la carte 29.64/47.53 – **21 rm** 145, 10 suites 175/400.

• Striking glass fronted 'boutique' hotel in a tranquil residential road. Blends contemporary style and traditional services. Individually designed rooms and annexe apartments. Modern restaurant with ornate décor and menu ranging from Asian to Italian.

Alexandros, 8 Timoleontos Vas., ✉ 115 21, via Vas. Sofias off Soutsou D. ✆ (210) 6430 464, *airotel@otenet.gr, Fax (210) 6441 084,* – – 340.

Don Giovanni : **Meals** 14/25 and a la carte 27/40 – **90 rm** 132, 3 suites.

• A relaxed, contemporary hotel behind a church in quiet residential area. Boldly decorated, comfortably appointed rooms. Don Giovanni is an elegant little restaurant with marble décor offering international and Mediterranean cuisine with some Greek specialities.

The Athenian Callirhoe, 52 Kallirois Ave and Petmeza, ✉ 117 43, ✆ (210) 9215 353, *hotel@tac.gr, Fax (210) 9215 342,* ← Athens, – – 110. BY v

Meals (see ***Etrusco*** below) – 15 – **84 rm** 450/500.

• A bright, contemporary boutique hotel with subtle Art Deco styling. City views from the rooftop terrace and balconies of the smartly fitted executive rooms.

Eridanus without rest., 78 Pireaus Ave, Keramikos, ✉ 104 35, ✆ (210) 5205 360, *eridanus@eridanus.gr, Fax (210) 5200 550,* – – 60. AX n

Meals (see ***Varoulko*** below) – 18 – **38** 190/350.

• Contemporary design hotel connected to the Varoulko. Luxurious bedrooms with high-tech equipment and hydro massage showers; some with views of the Acropolis.

Novotel, 4-6 Michail Voda, ✉ 104 39, ✆ (210) 8200 700, *h0866@accor-hotels.com, Fax (210) 8200 777,* ✱ Athens, – – 850. rest AX t

Meals a la carte 17.50/35 – 16 – **189 rm** 136/170, 6 suites.

• Busy conference and family friendly hotel convenient for Larissa station and the National Museum. Bedrooms are clean and functional. Open-plan restaurant or lighter meals served on rooftop setting in summer.

Omonia Grand, 2 Pireos, Omonia Sq, ✉ 105 52, ✆ (210) 5235 230, *salesacr@grecotel.gr, Fax (210) 5282 159* – BX a

Meals a la carte 25.70/39.50 – 20 – **115 rm** 300/350.

• Beyond the bronze sculptured door and impressive marbled lobby is a bright and up-to-date hotel. Many of the interior-designed bedrooms overlook the bustling square. Appealing, modern first floor restaurant with international menu.

Athens Acropol, 1 Pireos, Omonia Sq, ✉ 105 52, ✆ (210) 5282 100, *salesacr@grecotel.gr, Fax (210) 5282 159,* – – 350. BX b

Meals a la carte 19.50/28.50 – 20 – **164 rm** 300/350, 3 suites.

• Sister hotel to Omonia, blending modern and classic styling. Soundproofed bedrooms and suites offer sanctuary from the hustle and bustle of the city centre below. Spacious Acropol restaurant with extensive international menu or lighter snacks in bar.

Herodion, 4 Rovertou Galli, ✉ 117 42, ☎ (210) 9236 832, *herodion@herodion.gr, Fax (210) 9211 650,* ← Acropolis – lift ▤ TV – 50. MC VISA JCB. BY p
Meals 22/25 and a la carte - **90 rm** 200/320.
◆ Privately owned and popular tourist hotel a short walk from the Acropolis. Roof garden with panoramic views. Modern, well-equipped, rear rooms offer more seclusion. Pleasant conservatory-style restaurant with international menu or coffee shop for light snacks.

Electra, 5 Ermou, ✉ 105 63, ☎ (210) 3378 000, *electrahotels@ath.forthnet.gr, Fax (210) 3220 310* – lift ▤ TV – 70 BY e
109 rm.
◆ Popular tourist hotel within the lively pedestrianised shopping area. Soundproofed bedrooms are thoughtfully equipped and well maintained, some have spa baths. Mezzanine restaurant for Mediterranean cuisine, which has a loyal local following for lunch.

Plaka without rest., 7 Kapnikareas and Mitropoleos St, ✉ 105 56, ☎ (210) 3222 096, *plaka@tourhotel.gr, Fax (210) 3222 412,* ← Athens – lift ▤ TV. MC AE VISA. BY b
67 rm 115/145.
◆ Privately owned hotel among shops and tavernas, with a rooftop bar overlooking the old town. Spotless, sensibly priced modern rooms ; ask for one with a view of the Acropolis.

Hermes without rest., 19 Apollonos St, ✉ 105 57, ☎ (210) 3235 514, *hermes@tourhotel.gr, Fax (210) 3222 412* – lift ▤ TV. MC AE VISA. BY z
45 rm 115/145.
◆ Small modern hotel in Plaka near the shops and the Acropolis. Spacious lobby and breakfast room. Bedrooms have balcony or terrace and all mod cons.

Jason Inn, 12 Assomaton St Thission, ✉ 105 53, ☎ (210) 3251 106, *douros@otenet.gr, Fax (210) 3243 132* – lift ▤ TV. MC VISA. AY s
Meals 16 – **57 rm** 90/110.
◆ A busy, simple tourist hotel close to the Agora and a short distance from the flea market. Compact, yet well-equipped rooms ; outer rooms with balconies, quieter rooms at rear. Roof-top garden café-restaurant with a splendid view of the Acropolis.

Achilleas without rest., 21 Lekka St, ✉ 105 62, ☎ (210) 3233 197, *achilleas@tourhotel.gr, Fax (210) 3222 412* – lift ▤ TV. MC AE VISA. BY c
34 rm 115/145.
◆ Privately owned hotel close to Syntagma Square, a popular tourist choice. Compact but usefully equipped bedrooms - quieter at the rear ; also spacious family rooms ; good value.

Philippos without rest., 3 Mitseon, ✉ 117 42, ☎ (210) 9223 611, *philippos@herodion.gr, Fax (210) 9223 615* – lift ▤ TV – 80. MC VISA JCB. BY f
50 rm 150/210.
◆ Superior budget accommodation handy for the Acropolis, Pláka and the ancient theatre. Bedrooms in pastel colours with family rooms available. Ideal visiting base.

Museum without rest., 16 Bouboulinas St, ✉ 106 82, ☎ (210) 3805 611, *reservations30@yahoo.com, Fax (210) 3800 507* – lift ▤ TV. MC AE VISA. CX a
93 rm 70/110.
◆ Overlooking the National Archaeological Museum and offering comfortable accommodation. Bedrooms are a uniform size but all benefit from balconies and good facilities.

XXX ✿ **Spondi,** 5 Pyronos, off Varnava Sq, Pangrati, ✉ 116 36, via Eratosthenous behind the old Olympic Stadium ☎ (210) 7564 021, *info@spondi.gr, Fax (210) 7567 021,* – ▤ P. MC AE VISA JCB
closed 1 week Easter and 10-16 August – **Meals** - French Mediterranean - (dinner only) 85/110 and a la carte 59/82 ♀.
Spec. Medallion of pork with truffles and straw baked potatoes. 'Forgotten' vegetables with tonka bean infusion. Fin kaki au parfum de basilico.
◆ Attractive converted villa creating an intimate atmosphere in its elegant rooms and external courtyard and terraces. Outstanding modern French/Mediterranean cooking.

XXX ✿ **Varoulko** (Lefteris), 80 Piraios St, Keramikos, ✉ 104 35, ☎ (210) 5228 400, *Fax (210) 5228 800,* – lift ▤. MC AE VISA JCB. AX a
closed Sunday – **Meals** - Seafood - (booking essential) (dinner only) 40/50 and a la carte 37/48 ♀.
Spec. Fillet of catfish with Corinthian raisin sauce. John Dory, courgette chips and lime. Grouper with white truffles and almonds.
◆ Modern, stylish restaurant in converted house with roof terrace and view of the Acropolis. Surprise tasting menu of finest local seafood. Accomplished cooking.

XXX **Etrusco,** 32 Kallirois Ave, ✉ 117 43, ☎ (210) 9223 923, *hotel@tac.gr, Fax (210) 9215 342,* – lift ▤. MC AE VISA JCB BY v
closed Sunday – **Meals** (dinner only) 50/80 and a la carte approx 60 ♀.
◆ Stylish contemporary restaurant with roof terrace for dining in summer, situated in the Callirhoe Hotel. Innovative modern Greek cooking and international fusion cuisine.

Boschetto, Evangelismou, off Vas. Sofias, ✉ 116 76, ☎ (210) 7210 893, *Fax (210) 7223 598,* – ▤. MC AE ◑ VISA. DY c
closed 25 April-1 May, 8-28 August, 25 December, 1 January and Sunday – **Meals** - Italian influences - (dinner only) a la carte approx 50.
◆ Attractive summer house secluded within the neatly trimmed hedge of this small city park. Polished service of an elaborate international menu with strong Italian influences.

Edodi, 80 Veikou, ✉ 117 41, via Makrigiani ☎ (210) 9213 013, *Fax (210) 9213 013* – MC AE ◑ VISA.
closed 28 April-2 May, July-August and Sunday – **Meals** (booking essential) (dinner only) a la carte 47/59.
◆ Restored 19C town house. Diners are presented with the day's specials instead of a menu from which to make their choice. Owners provide attentive and personal service.

Hytra, Navarhou Apostoli 7, Psirri, ☎ (210) 3316 767, *Fax (210) 3316 767* – ▤. MC AE ◑ VISA JCB. AY n
closed 10 May-15 October and Sunday – **Meals** (dinner only) 48 and a la carte 34.50/59.
◆ Vibrant modern restaurant in trendy Psirri decorated with large pots (Hytra in Greek). Modern Greek menu using lots of herbs ; à la carte or 7 course surprise menu or meze.

Kiku, 12 Dimokritou St, ✉ 103 45, ☎ (210) 3647 033, *Fax (210) 3626 239* – ▤. MC AE ◑ VISA. CY a
closed 4 days Easter, August, 25 December, 1 January and Sunday – **Meals** - Japanese - (dinner only) 48/58 and a la carte 41.50/61.50 ♀.
◆ Stylish and authentic Japanese restaurant. Minimalist interior in shades of black and white with screens and soft lighting. Extensive selection of sushi and sashimi.

Taverna Strofi, 25 Rovertou Galli, ✉ 117 42, ☎ (210) 9214 130, ← Acropolis, – MC VISA. AY a
closed Sunday – **Meals** (dinner only) a la carte 20/25.
◆ Personally run by the same owners since the 1970's, this taverna offers rustic and home-cooked Greek cooking. In summer, 2nd floor terrace has splendid Acropolis views.

Prytanio, 7 Millioni St, Kolonaki, ✉ 106 73, ☎ (210) 3643 353, *kolonaki@prytaneion.gr, Fax (210) 8082 577,* – ▤. MC AE ◑ VISA JCB. CY b
Meals a la carte 26/44.50.
◆ Watch the fashionable shoppers go by from a table on the terrace or choose the more intimate interior or the garden. Pleasant service and modern Mediterranean-influenced menu.

Oraia Penteli, Iroon Sq (Psiri), ✉ 105 54, ☎ (210) 3218 627, *Fax (210) 3218 627,* – MC VISA AXY v
Meals a la carte 16/26.70.
◆ Historic building in the centre of Psirri converted into café-restaurant preparing traditional Greek recipes ; live Greek music mid-week evenings and weekend afternoons.

Taverna Sigalas, 2 Monastiraki Sq, ✉ 105 55, ☎ (210) 3213 036, *Fax (210) 3252 448,* – MC AE ◑ VISA BY a
Meals a la carte 10.50/14.60.
◆ Energetic service of robust local dishes and live music attract locals and tourists alike. Atmospheric taverna with walls hung with photographs of celebrities and statesmen.

To Kouti, 23 Andrianou St, Thissio, ✉ 105 55, ☎ (210) 3213 229, *Fax (210) 3314 116* – ▤. MC AE VISA AY d
closed Easter Sunday, 25 December and 1 January – **Meals** a la carte 26.50/35.50.
◆ Enjoys a popular local following, attracted by its slightly quirky décor and friendly, busy atmosphere. Menus written in children's books and offer simple, fresh dishes.

Environs

at Kifissia *Northeast : 15 km by Vas. Sofias* DY :

Pentelikon , 66 Diligianni St, Kefalari, ✉ 145 62, off Harilaou Trikoupi, follow signs to Politia ☎ (210) 6230 650, *pentelik@otenet.gr, Fax (210) 8019 223,* , , – , rm, ▤ TV – 250. MC AE ◑ VISA.
La Terrasse : **Meals** a la carte 35.70/54.60 ♀ (see also ***Vardis*** below) – 24 – **86 rm** 295/445, 7 suites.
◆ Imposing late 19C mansion in affluent residential suburb. Opulence and antiques throughout. Most charming and tranquil rooms overlook the gardens. Traditional service. Conservatory restaurant with a Mediterranean theme offering full range of dishes.

Theoxenia Palace, 2 Filadelfeos St, ✉ 145 62, ☎ (210) 6233 622, *reservations@theoxeniapalace.com, Fax (210) 6231 675,* , , – , rm, ▤ TV – 350. MC AE ◑ VISA.
Meals a la carte 36/47 – **69 rm** 280/420, 2 suites.
◆ Renovated 1920's hotel with imposing façade. Spacious well-equipped rooms. Good leisure and large conference/banqueting facilities. Brasserie for meals.

Theoxenia House without rest., 42 Harilaou Trikoupi St and 9 Pentelis St, ✉ 145 62, ☎ (210) 6233 622, *reservations@theoxeniapalace.com, Fax (210) 6231 675* – MC AE DC VISA.
11 rm 300/320, 1 suite.
• Stylish house in pleasant suburb converted to provide very large, well-equipped rooms, each with lounge area and kitchenette, and full use of the facilities at the Palace.

The Kefalari Suites without rest., 1 Pentelis and Kolokotroni St, Kefalari, ✉ 145 62, ☎ (210) 6233 333, *info@kefalarisuites.gr, Fax (210) 6233 330* – MC AE DC VISA.
11 suites 232/543.
• Early 20C villa set in a smart, quiet suburb ; stylish, airy, thoughtfully appointed rooms, each on a subtle, imaginative theme, most with lounge and veranda. Rooftop spa bath.

Vardis (at Pentelikon H.), 66 Diligianni, Kefalari, ✉ 145 62, off Harilaou Trikoupi, follow signs to Politia ☎ (210) 6230 660, *vardis@hotelpentelikon.gr, Fax (210) 8019 223*, – MC AE DC VISA.
closed Sunday – **Meals** - French - (dinner only) 62.50/100.50 and a la carte 65/92.
Spec. Millefeuille of scallops and mustard leaves. Steamed sole fillet with lime and baby fennel. Coconut milk cappuccino, chestnut mousseline.
• Elegant, ornately decorated restaurant with extensive terrace. Fine table settings. Formal and polished service of elaborate classic French/Mediterranean influenced cuisine.

at Athens International Airport *East : 35 km by Vas Sofias DY :*

Sofitel, ✉ 190 19, ☎ (210) 3544 000, *h3167-fb@accor.com, Fax (210) 3544 444*, – rm, – 600. MC AE DC VISA
***Karavi :* Meals** - French - (dinner only) a la carte 64/98 – ***Mesoghaia :* Meals** - Greek and Mediterranean - 32 and a la carte 36/56 – 22 – **332 rm** 245/270, 13 suites.
• First hotel at the new airport. Modern and very well equipped from clubby library bar to exclusive leisure club. Spacious rooms and impressive bathrooms. Fine dining on the 9th floor in Karavi. Informal brightly decorated Mesoghaia ground floor restaurant.

Holiday Inn Attica, Attica Ave, Paiania (between exits 17 and 18 of Airport Highway), ✉ 190 02, ☎ (210) 6689 000, *atticainfo@hiathens.com, Fax (210) 6689 500*, – rm, – 200. MC AE DC VISA JCB.
Meals 22/25 and a la carte 35/45 – 22 – **191 rm** 469/512, 3 suites.
• Corporate chain hotel near the international airport. Spacious, contemporary public areas and good leisure facilities. Large, comfortable and hi-tech bedrooms.

at Lagonissi *Southeast : 40 km by Singrou BY :*

Grand Resort Lagonissi, Sounio Ave, ✉ 190 10, ☎ (22) 9107 6000, *grandresort@grandresort.gr, Fax (22) 9102 4534*, Saronic Gulf, heated, – 180. MC AE DC VISA. rest
Meals - Mediterranean - a la carte 33/38 – ***Kohylia :* Meals** - Polynesian and Japanese - a la carte 67/95 – ***Captain's House :* Meals** - Italian - (dinner only) a la carte 37/57 – ***Ouzeri :* Meals** - Greek - a la carte 34.50/50 – **182 rm** 435/480, 99 suites.
• Luxurious, stunning resort on a private peninsula. 16 beaches ; suites with private pools. Service to satisfy the most demanding. Mediterraneo for seafood. Polynesian and Japanese cuisine in Kohylia. Captain's House for Italian dishes. Greek cooking in Ouzeri.

at Vouliagmeni *South : 18 km by Singrou BY :*

Divani Apollon Palace, 10 Ag. Nicolaou and Iliou St (Kavouri), off Athinas, ✉ 166 71, ☎ (210) 8911 100, *divanis@divaniapollon.gr, Fax (210) 9658 010*, Saronic Gulf, – 1200. MC AE DC VISA.
***Mythos :* Meals** (dinner only) 80/120 and a la carte 50/121 – ***Anemos :* Meals** 30/50 and a la carte 55/61 – **279 rm** 360/710, 7 suites.
• Modern hotel in fashionable resort. Poolside lounge. Spa and thalassotherapy centre. Executive bedrooms with balconies overlooking the Saronic Gulf. Small private beach. Dine in Mythos on the beach with local dishes. Anemos is modern with global fare.

The Margi, 11 Litous St, off Athinas by Apollonos, ✉ 166 71, ☎ (210) 8929 000, *themargi@themargi.gr, Fax (210) 8960 229*, – 500. MC AE DC VISA JCB.
Meals a la carte approx 30 – **90 rm** 220/600.
• A stylish hotel that combines contemporary elegance with a colonial feel. Breakfast is taken on the poolside terrace. Bedrooms have antique pieces and smart marble bathrooms. Informal restaurant with its eclectic menu is popular with the 'in crowd'.

at Kalamaki *Southwest : 14 km by Singrou BY :*

Akrotiri, Vas. Georgiou B5, Agios Kosmas, Elliniko, ✉ 167 77, ☎ (210) 9859 147, *akrotiri@enternet.gr, Fax (210) 9859 149*, – MC AE DC VISA JCB.
Meals (dinner only) a la carte 49/64.
• A seaside restaurant combining simplicity and luxury. Candlelit dinners on the pool terrace ; DJ music. Menu of good quality international cuisine with French influence.

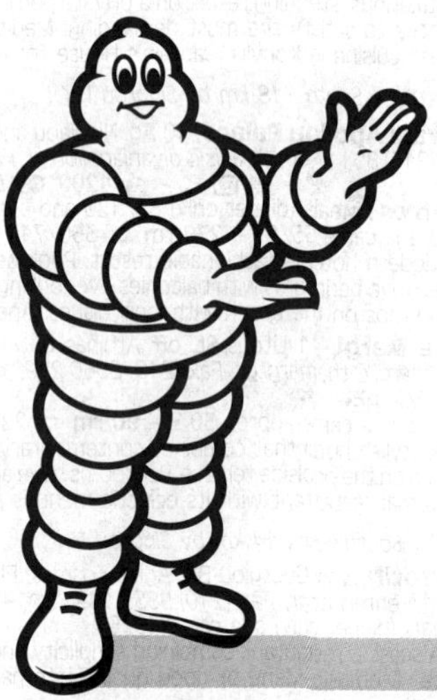

Hungary

Magyarország

BUDAPEST

PRACTICAL INFORMATION

LOCAL CURRENCY

Forint: *100 HUF = 0,40 euro (€) (Dec. 2004)*

National Holidays in Hungary: *15 March, 20 August, and 23 October.*

PRICES

Prices may change if goods and service costs in Hungary are revised and it is therefore always advisable to confirm rates with the hotelier when making a reservation.

FOREIGN EXCHANGE

It is strongly advised against changing money other than in banks, exchange offices or authorised offices such as large hotels, tourist offices, etc... Banks are usually open on weekdays from 8.30am to 4pm.

HOTEL RESERVATIONS

In case of difficulties in finding a room through our hotel selection, it is always possible to apply to the Tourist Information Offices (Liszt Ferenc square 11, ☎ 361 322 40 98, liszt@budapestinfo.hu).

POSTAL SERVICES

Main post offices are open from 8am to 7pm on weekdays, and 8am to 1pm on Saturdays. Post offices with longer opening hours:
Teréz körút 51. (Mon-Sat: 7am-9pm; Sun: 8am-8pm)
Baross tér – Eastern Railway Station (Mon-Sat: 7am-9pm).

SHOPPING IN BUDAPEST

In the index of street names, those printed in red are where the principal shops are found. Typical goods to be bought include embroidery, lace, china, leather goods, paprika, salami, Tokay (Tokaij), palinka, foie-gras... Shops are generally open from 10am to 6pm on weekdays (7pm on Thursday) and 9am to 1pm on Saturday.

TIPPING

Hotel, restaurant and café bills often do not include service in the total charge. In these cases it is usual to leave the staff a gratuity which will vary depending upon the service given.

CAR HIRE

The international car hire companies have branches in Budapest. Your hotel porter should be able to give details and help you with your arrangements.

BREAKDOWN SERVICE

A breakdown service is operated by MAGYAR AUTÓKLUB ☎ 188.

SPEED LIMIT

On motorways, the maximum permitted speed is 130 km/h – 80 mph, 100 km/h – 62 mph on main roads, 90 km/h – 55 mph on others roads and 50 km/h – 31 mph in built up areas.

SEAT BELTS

In Hungary, the wearing of seat belts is compulsory for drivers and front seat passengers. On motorways : all passengers.

TRANSPORT

The three metro lines (yellow, red and blue) and the trams and buses make up an extensive public transport network. Tickets must be purchased in advance. Daily, weekly and monthly passes are available.
Airport buses : apply to your hotel porter.

TAXIS

Only use authorised taxis displaying clear signage and yellow number plates.

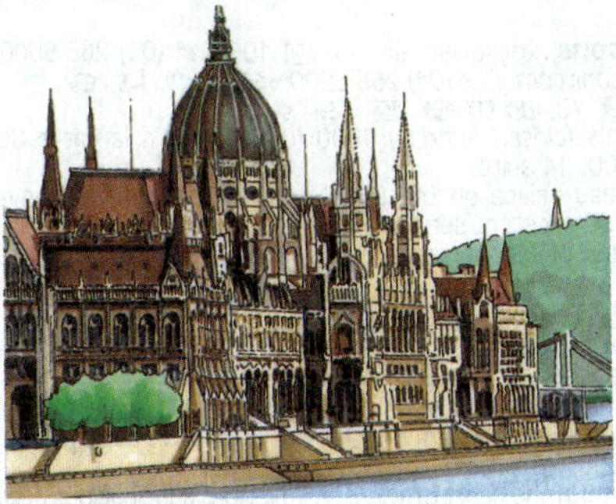

BUDAPEST

Hungary 732 D 8 – Pop. 1 909 000.

Munich 678 – Prague 533 – Venice 740 – Vienna 243 – Zagreb 350

Tourist Office of Budapest, Király Útca 93, ✉ 1077 ☎ (01) 352 98 04, Fax (01) 352 14 33 – IBUSZ Head Office, Liszt Ferenc square 11, ☎ (01) 322 40 98 liszt@budapestinfo.hu

✈ Ferihegy SE : 16 km by Üllo"i DZ, ☎ (01) 296 96 96 (information), Bus to airport : from International Bus station, Erzsébet tér, Station 6 Budapest 5th and Airport Minibus Service LRI – MALEV, Roosevelt tér 2, Budapest 5th ☎ (01) 296 85 55

Views of Budapest

Citadel (Citadella)★★★ GX – St. Gellert Monument (Szt. Gellért szobor)★★ GX – Liberation Monument (Szabadság szobor)★★ GX – Fishermen's Bastion (Halászbástya) ≤★★ FU.

BUDA

Gellert Thermal Baths (Gellért Gyógyfürd"o)★★★ GX – Matthias Church★★ (Mátyástemplom) FU – Attractive Streets★★ (Tancsics Mihaly utca – Fortuna utca – Uri utca) EFU – Royal Palace★★★ (Budavári palota) FV – Hungarian National Gallery★★ – Király Baths (Király Gyógyfürd"o)★★ CY.

PEST

Parliament Building★★★ (Országház) GU – Museum of Fine Arts★★★ (Szépm"uvészeti Múzeum) DY **M**[13] *– Hungarian National Museum★★ (Magyar Nemzeti Múzeum) HVX – Museum of Applied Arts★★ (Iparm"uvészeti Múzeum) CZ* **M**[5] *– Széchenyi Thermal Baths★★★ (Széchenyi Gyógyfürd"o) DY* **Q** *– Hungarian State Opera House★★ (Magyar Állami Operaház) HU – Chain Bridge (Széchenyi Lánchíd)★★ FGV – Liberty Bridge (Szabadság híd)★★ GHX – Ethnographical Museum (Néprajzi Múzeum)★★ GU – Former Post Office Savings Bank (Posta Takarékpénztár)★★ GU – Central Market Hall (Vásárcsarnok)★★ HX – Dohány utca Synagogue (Dohány utcai zsinagóga)★★ HV – Café New York★★ CZ* **A**.

ADDITIONAL SIGHTS

Margaret Island★★ (Margit-sziget) CY – Aquincum Museum★ (Aquincumi Muzéum) N : 12 km by Szentendrei út CY – St. Ann's Church★ (Szent Anna templom) FU.

Envir.: *Szentendre★★ N : 20 km – Visegrád N : 42 km : Citadel, view★★★*

Four Seasons, Roosevelt tér 5-6, 1051, (01) 268 6000, *budapest.reservations@fourseasons.com, Fax (01) 268 5000*, – rm, – 70. rest GV x
***Páva* : Meals** *(closed Sunday)* 9800 (dinner) and a la carte 8600/11500 – **165 rm** 66000/71000, 14 suites.
• Art nouveau palace on the Danube in business district converted into an elegant, modern hotel ; excellent service and spa treatments. Riverside dining room and terrace ; seasonal menu of Mediterranean and traditional Hungarian dishes with a contemporary twist.

Kempinski H. Corvinus, Erzsébet tér 7-8, 1051, (01) 429 3777, *hotel.corvinus@kempinski.com, Fax (01) 429 4777*, – rm, – 450. rest GV a
***Ristorante Giardino* : Meals** - Italian - (dinner only) a la carte 9900/12400 – ***Bistro Jardin* : Meals** (buffet lunch) 5500 and a la carte 7300/11500 – 6650 – **337 rm** 64000/111000, 28 suites.
• Modern hotel in the heart of the city. Luxurious and spacious accommodation, providing top class comfort and facilities, with service to match. Mediterranean style Ristorante Giardino. Bistro Jardin buffet restaurant.

Corinthia Grand H. Royal, Erzsébet krt 43-49, 1073, (01) 479 4000, *royal@corinthia.hu, Fax (01) 479 4333* – rm, . rest HU c
***Brasserie Royale* : Meals** 4500/15000 and a la carte 6500/9200 – ***Rickshaw* : Meals** - Japanese - *(closed Monday)* (dinner only) 6000/9000 and a la carte 5000/8500 – 4900 – **383 rm** 58600/68500, 31 suites.
• Early 20C grand hotel with impressive reception. Well-appointed bedrooms - spacious or compact - with modern décor in warm colours. Brasserie Royale for formal dining. Rickshaw for Japanese dishes and sushi bar.

Hilton , Hess András tér 1-3, 1014, (01) 889 6600, *hiltonhu@hungary.net, Fax (01) 889 6644*, Danube and Pest, – rm, – 650. rest FU a
***Dominican* : Meals** (dinner only) (pianist) a la carte 3985/17930 – ***Corvina* : Meals** (buffet lunch) 5975/10215 and a la carte 3610/10215 – ***Sushi Bar* : Meals** - Japanese - (dinner only) a la carte 3735/9715 – 5480 – **299 rm** 47315, 23 suites.
• Large hotel in historic castle district with stunning views. Remains of 13C Dominican church and cellars. Spacious, well equipped rooms. Dominican, elegant dining room with superb views. Informal Corvina dining room. Sushi Bar with minimalist oriental décor.

Le Meridien, Erzsébet tér 9-10, 1051, (01) 429 5500, *info@le-meridien.hu, Fax (01) 429 5555*, – rm, – 200. GV c
***Le Bourbon* : Meals** 6100 (lunch) and a la carte 5650/10000 – 6100 – **192 rm** 78000, 26 suites.
• Top class hotel, ideally located for both business and leisure. Classically furnished, very comfortable bedrooms and particularly smart bathrooms. Atrium styled restaurant with Art Deco glass dome and wood panelling.

Sofitel Atrium, Roosevelt tér 2, 1051, (01) 266 1234, *h3229-re@accor.com, Fax (01) 266 8271*, – rm, – 400. rest GV e
***Atrium Terrace* : Meals** (buffet lunch) 4500 and a la carte 5500/9000 – ***Focaccia* : Meals** - Mediterranean - 4500/9800 and a la carte 5500/9000 – 5000 – **328 rm** 44000/50100, 23 suites.
• Modern hotel near Chain Bridge. Impressive atrium with over 3000 plants and bi-plane suspended from roof. Comfortable, well equipped rooms. Stepped terrace leads up to elegant Atrium Terrace restaurant. Focaccia restaurant with Mediterranean menu and style.

Inter-Continental, Apáczai Csere János útca 12-14, 1368, (01) 327 6333, *budapest@interconti.com, Fax (01) 327 6357*, Danube and Buda, – rm, – 900 GV n
383 rm, 15 suites.
• Large hotel tower on river bank with good views from most rooms which have modern décor and all mod cons. Popular with business travellers. Viennese style coffee house. The Corso is restaurant, grill, café and bar all in one, with pleasant modern décor.

Marriott, Apáczai Csere János útca 4, 1052, (01) 266 7000, *marriott.budapest@axelero.hu, Fax (01) 266 5000*, Danube and Buda, , squash – rm, – 800. GV r
***Duna Grill* : Meals** (buffet lunch) 4400 and a la carte 5200/8500 – 4900 – **351 rm** 55200, 11 suites.
• Huge American-style hotel on river bank where every room has a balcony. Late 20C style décor in lobby, bar and comfortable rooms. Informal Duna Grill, open all day, international menu.

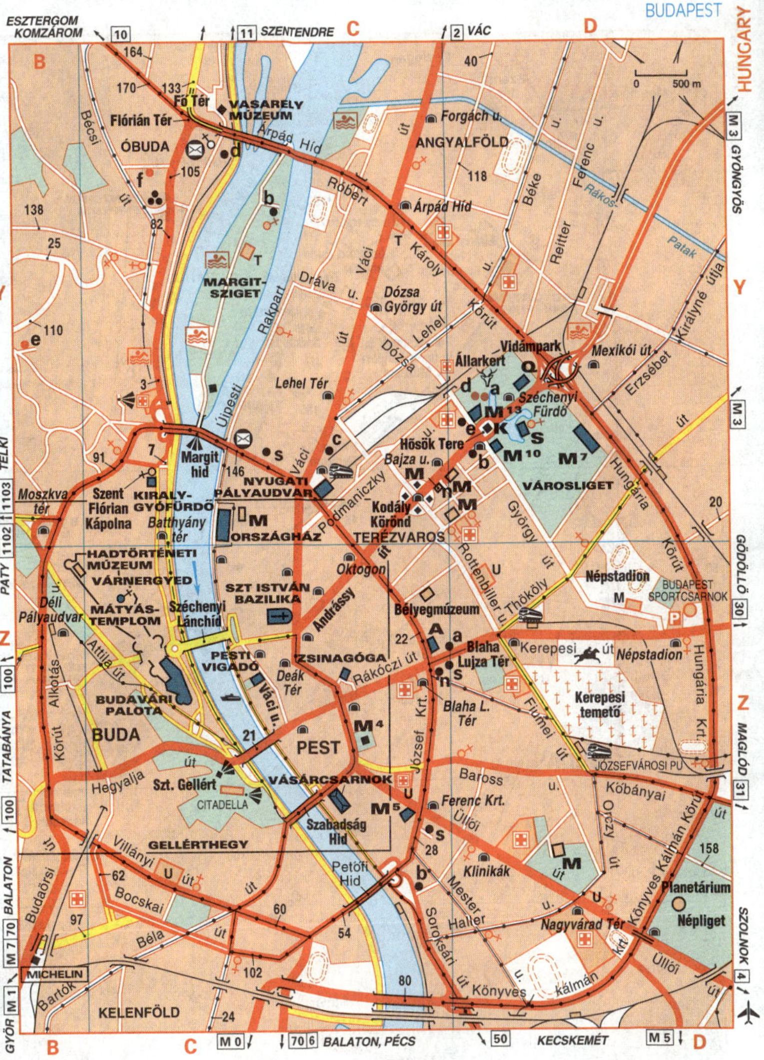

Corinthia Aquincum, Árpád Fejedelem útca 94, ✉ 1036, ✆ (01) 436 4706, *reservation@aqu.hu*, *Fax (01) 436 4119*, ≤, Ⓦ, 🏋, ≋s, 🏊 – 🛗, ⊁ rm, ▤ TV ✆ ♿ 🚗 🅿 – 🏛 260. MC AE ◑ VISA JCB. ⊁ rest HU c

Apicius **: Meals** a la carte 3200/7150 – **302 rm** ▭ 54000/56500, 8 suites.

◆ Modern hotel on west bank north of centre with own comprehensive thermal spa and therapy centre. Open plan lobby. Rooms are comfortable and offer good facilities. Apicius restaurant with smart modern décor in warm tones and a pleasant atmosphere.

Danubius Thermal 🌿, Margitsziget, ✉ 1138, ✆ (01) 889 4700, *resind@margitsziget.danubiusgroup.com*, *Fax (01) 889 4988*, ≤, 🌳, Ⓦ, 🏋, ≋s, 🏊 heated, 🏊, 🌳 – 🛗, ⊁ rm, ▤ TV ✆ ♿ 🚗 🅿 – 🏛 300. MC AE ◑ VISA JCB. ⊁ rest CY b

Platan **: Meals** (buffet lunch) 3700/5500 and a la carte 3500/8500 – **259 rm** ▭ 40000/44500, 8 suites.

◆ Concrete hotel set in island gardens in the Danube. Conference facilities. Huge thermal spa : heat, massage and water treatments. Modern bedrooms with a view. Buffet meals available at any time in Platan.

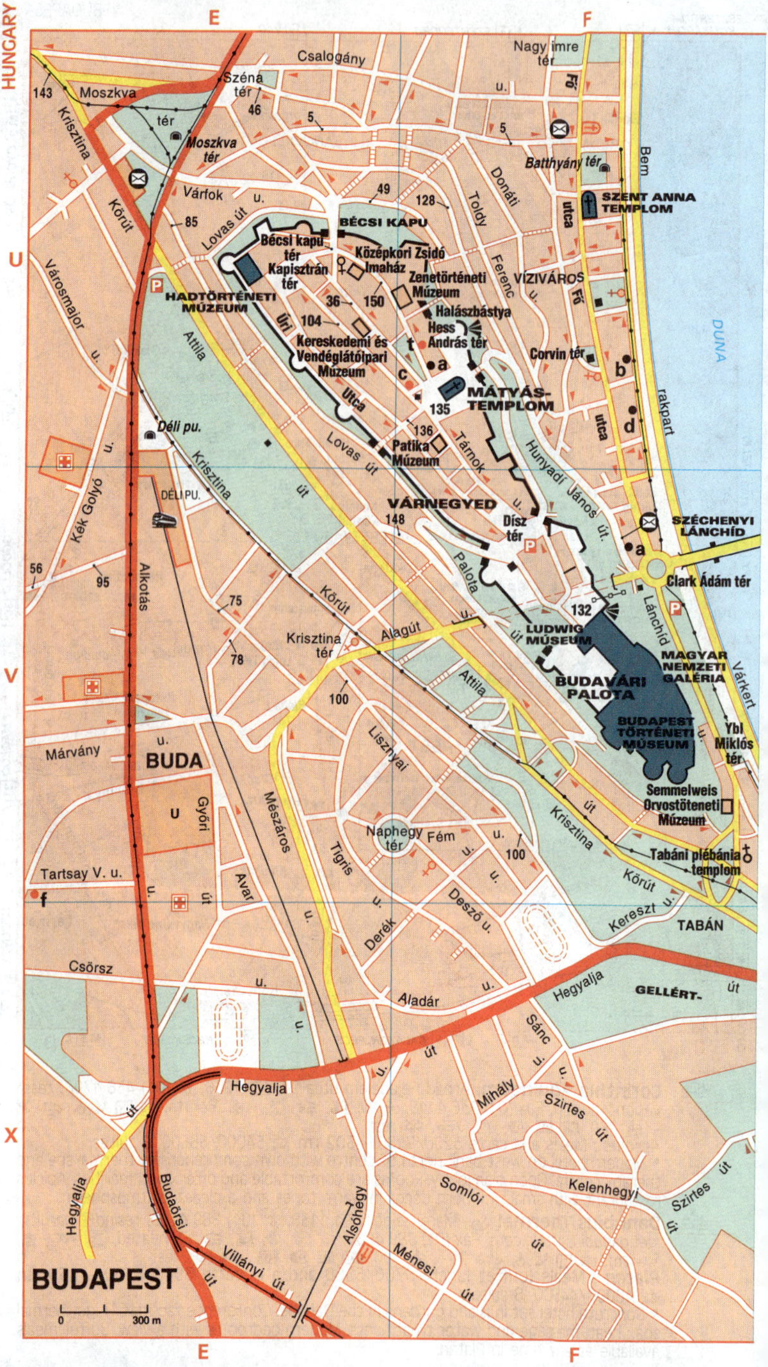
E
F
U
V
X
BUDAPEST
0
300 m
BUDA
VÁRNEGYED
VÍZIVÁROS
TABÁN
GELLÉRT-
DUNA
Csalogány
Széna tér
Moszkva
Moszkva tér
Krisztina
Körút
Várfok u.
Lovas út
Nagy Imre tér
Fő utca
Batthyány tér
Bem rakpart
SZENT ANNA TEMPLOM
BÉCSI KAPU
Bécsi kapu tér
Kapisztrán tér
Középkori Zsidó Imaház
Zenetörténeti Múzeum
HADTÖRTÉNETI MÚZEUM
Úri utca
Kereskedemi és Vendéglátóipari Múzeum
Halászbástya
Hess András tér
Corvin tér
MÁTYÁS-TEMPLOM
Patika Múzeum
Tárnok u.
Toldy Ferenc u.
Donáti
Hunyadi János út
Dísz tér
Palota út
SZÉCHENYI LÁNCHÍD
Clark Ádám tér
Lánchíd u.
LUDWIG MÚSEUM
MAGYAR NEMZETI GALÉRIA
BUDAVÁRI PALOTA
BUDAPEST TÖRTÉNETI MÚSEUM
Várkert
Ybl Miklós tér
Semmelweis Orvostöteneti Múzeum
Tabáni plébánia templom
Városmajor u.
Attila út
Déli pu.
DÉLI PU.
Kék Golyó u.
Alkotás u.
Krisztina tér
Alagút
Márvány u.
Győri u.
Tartsay V. u.
Avar u.
Mészáros u.
Lisznyai
Naphegy tér
Fém u.
Tigris u.
Derék
Dezső u.
Kereszt u.
Csörsz u.
Aladár
Hegyalja út
Sánc u.
Mihály
Szirtes út
Somlói út
Kelenhegyi út
Alsóhegy
Ménesi út
Budaörsi út
Villányi út
143
46
5
49
128
85
36
150
104
135
136
148
132
75
78
56
95
100
a
b
c
d
f
t

G
H
U
V
X
ORSZÁGHÁZ
NÉPRAJZI MÚZEUM
Kossuth Lajos tér
Alkotmány u.
Honvéd
FÖLDMŰVELÉSÜGYI MINISZTERIUM
Báthory
58
Vadász u.
Hold u.
Kossuth tér
Vértanúk tere
Szabadság tér
POSTA TAKARÉKPÉNZTAR
Zoltán
Akadémia
Nádor
Széchenyi
Széchenyi u.
Arany
Bank
Hercegprímás
János
Október 6 u.
Sas
Szent István tér
SZENT ISTVÁN BAZILIKA
Zrínyi u.
Roosevelt tér
József Attila
József Nádor tér
Erzsébet tér
Dorottya
Vörösmarty tér
Deák tér
Deák Ferenc tér
POL
Bécsi
PESTI VIGADÓ
Vörösmarty tér
Vigadó tér
Váci
Belgrád
Duna
korzó
rakpart
Petőfi tér
Párizsi udvar
Ferences templom
Ferenciek tere
Belvárosi plébániatemplom
Erzsébet híd
EGYETEMI TEMPLOM
Veres Pálné u.
Molnár
Váci u.
Szt. Gellért
RUDAS GYÓGYFÜRDŐ
HEGY
Citadella
Citadella Sétány
Szabadság szobor
Jubileumi park
Sziklakápolna
GELLÉRTFÜRDŐ
Kelenhegyi út
Szent Gellért tér
SZABADSÁG HÍD
DUNA
Szt. Gellért rakpart
Belgrád rakpart
Vámház
VÁSÁRCSARNOK
Csarnok tér
Mátyás
Kinizsi
Lónyai
Erkel
Ráday
Üllői út
Kálvin tér
Baross u.
Múzeum
Múzeum Körút
MAGYAR NEMZETI MÚZEUM
Petőfi Irodalmi Múzeum
Bródy Sándor u.
Astoria
Kossuth L. u.
Rákóczi
Puskin
Szentkirályi u.
PESTI MEGYEI TANÁCS
Károly Körút
ZSINAGÓGA
Dohány
Wesselényi
Dob
Nagy Diófa u.
Klauzál tér
Klauzál u.
Kazinczy u.
Kis Diófa u.
Király u.
Csányi u.
PEST
Paulay
Bajcsy-Zs. út
Postamúzeum
Andrássy
Székely M. u.
Zsilinszky út
Bajcsy-
Révay u.
Lázár
Opera
MAGYAR ALLAMI OPERAHÁZ
Arany János u.
Zichy
Hajós
Nagymező
Podmaniczky
Lovag
Dessewffy u.
Jókai
Jenő
Mozsár u.
Oktogon
Jókai tér
Liszt Ferenc tér
Liszt Ferenc Zeneművészeti Föiskola
Szondi u.
Csengery
Teréz
Aradi
LISZT FERENC EMLÉKMÚZEUM
Vörösmarty u.
Hunyadi tér
Ede
Kertész u.
120
16
4
142
38
8
2
108
160
116
106
44
70
32
112
88
90
64
52
140
66
159

INDEX OF STREET NAMES IN BUDAPEST

Akadémia u. GU
Aladár u. FX
Alagút u. EFV
Alkotás u. EV
Alkotmány u. GU
Alsóhegy u. EFX
Andrássy út. CZ, HU
Apáczai Csere János u. GV 2
Aradi u. HU
Arany János u. GU
Árpád Fejedelem útja. CY 3
Árpád híd CY
Árpád út DY
Attila u. DY
Attila út. EFV
Avar u. EVX
Bajcsy-Zsilinszky út GU
Bank u. GU
Bárczy István u. GV 4
Baross u. DZ, HX
Bartók Béla u. BCZ
Báthory u. GU
Batthyány tér FU
Batthyány u. EFU 5
Bécsi Kapu tér EU
Bécsi u. GV
Bécsi út BCY
Béke u. DY
Belgrád rakpart GVH
Bem József tér CY 7
Bem rakpart FUV
Blaha Lujza tér CDZ
Bocskai út CZ
Bródy Sándor u. HV
Budaörsi út BZ, EX
Csalogány u. EFU
Csányi u. HU
Csarnok tér HX
Csengery u. HU
Csörsz u. EX
Citadella Sétány GX
Clark Ádám tér FV
Corvin tér FU
Deák Ferenc tér GHV
Deák Ferenc u. GV 16
Derék u. FVX
Dessewffy u. HU
Dezső u. FVX
Dísz tér FV
Dob u. HUV
Dohány u. HV
Donáti u. FU
Dorottya u. GV
Dózsa György út DYZ
Dráva u. CY
Duna Korzó GV
Egressy út DY 20
Erkel u. HX
Erzébet híd GX, CZ 21
Erzébet Királyné utja DY
Erzébet krt CZ 22
Erzébet tér GV
Fehérvári út CZ 24
Felső Zöldmáli út BCY 25
Fém u. FV
Ferenc krt CZ 28
Ferenciek tere GHV 32
Fő tér CY
Fő u. FUV
Fortuna u. EU 36
Győri út EVX
Gerlóczy HV 38
Göncöl u. DY 40
Hajós u. HU
Haller u. DZ
Haris Köz GV 44
Hattyú u. EU 46
Hegyalja út CZ, FX
Hess András tér FU
Hold u. GU
Honvéd u. GU
Hunyadi János út FUV
Hunyadi tér HU
Hunfalvy u. EFU 49
Hungária körút DYZ
Irányi u. GX 52
Irinyi József u. CZ 54
Istenhegyi út BYZ, EV 56
Jókai tér HU
József krt DZ
József Nádor tér GV
József Attila u. GV
Kálmán Imre u. GU 58
Kálvin tér HX
Kapisztrán tér EU
Karinthy Frigyes út CZ 60
Karolina út BCZ 62
Károly körút DY, HV
Károlyi Mihály u. HVX 64
Kazinczy u. HV
Kecskeméti u. HX 66
Kék Golyó u. EUV
Kelenhegyi út FGX
Kerepesi út DZ
Kereszt u. FVX
Kertész u. HU
Kétújfalu u. BZ
Kigyó utca GV 70
Kinizsi u. HX
Király u. HUV
Kis Diófa u. HUV
Klauzál tér HV
Klauzál u. HV
Kőbányai út DZ
Könyves Kálmán krt DZ
Kosciuszko Tádé u. EV 75
Kossuth Lajos tér GU
Kossuth Lajos u. HV
Krisztina Körút CDV
Krisztina tér EV
Kuny Domokos u. EV 78
Lágymányosi híd CZ 80
Lajos u. CY 82
Lánchíd u. FV
Lázár u. HU
Lehel u. CDY
Lisznyai u. EFV
Liszt Ferenc tér HU
Logodi u. EU 85
Lónyai u. HX
Lovag u. HU
Lovas út EFU
Magyar u. HV 88
Március 15 tér GV 90
Margit híd CY
Margit krt CY 91
Márvány u. EV
Mátyás u. HX
Ménesi út FX
Mészáros u. EVX
Mester u. CDZ
Mihály u. FX
Molnár u. GX
Moszkva tér EU
Mozsár u. HU
Múzeum krt HVX
Múzeum u. HX
Nádor u. GU
Nagy Diófa u. HV
Nagy imre tér FU
Nagyenyed u. EV 95
Nagymező u. HU
Nagyszőlős u. BCZ 97
Naphegy tér EFV
Naphegy u. EFV 100
Október 6 u. GU
Október 23 u. CZ 103
Orczy út DZ
Ordas köz DZ
Országház u. EFU 104
Pacsirtamező u. CY 105
Palota út FV
Párizsi u. GV 106
Paulay Ede u. HU
Petőfi híd GZ
Petőfi Sándor u. GY 108
Petőfi tér GV
Podmaniczky u. CY, HU
Pusztaszeri út BCY 110
Puskin u. HVX
Ráday u. HX
Rákóczi út CZ, HU
Reáltanoda u. HV 112
Régi posta u. GV 116
Reitter Ferenc u. DY
Révay u. HU
Röppentyű DY 118
Roosevelt tér GV
Rottenbiller u. CDZ
Rumbach Sebestyén u. HV 120
Szabadság tér GU
Szabadság híd GHX
Szabó Ilonka u. EFU 128
Széchenyi Lánchíd FVG
Széchenyi rakpart GU
Széchenyi u. GU
Széher út ABY
Székely M. u. HU
Széna tér EU
Szent György tér FV 132
Szent Gellért tér GX
Szent István tér GU
Szentendrei út CY 133
Szentháromság tér FU 135
Szentháromság út FU 136
Szentkirályi u. HV
Szépvölgyi út BCY 138
Szerb u. HX 140
Szervita tér GV 142
Szilágyi Erzsébet fasor EU 143
Szirtes út FX
Szondi u. HU
Szt. Gellert rakpart GX
Szt. István krt CY 146
Sánc u. FX
Sas u. GUV
Somlói út FX
Soroksári út CDZ
Tábor u. EFV 148
Táncsics Mihály u. EFU 150
Tárnok u. FUV
Tartsay V. u EV
Teréz krt HU
Thököly út DYZ
Tigris u. EFV
Toldy Ferenc u. FU
Üllői út CDZ, HX
Újpesti rakpart CY
Úri u. EU
Váci u. GHVX
Váci út CDY
Vadász u. GU
Vajda Péter u. DZ 158
Vákert rakpart GV
Vámház krt HX
Várfok u. EU
Városház u. GHV 160
Városmajor u. BZ, EU
Veres Pálné u. HX
Vértanúk tere GV 159
Vigadó tér GV
Vihar u. CY 164
Villányi út CZ, EX
Vörösmarty tér GV
Vörösmarty u. HU
Vörösvári út CY 170
Wesselényi u. HV
Ybl. Miklós tér FV
Zichy Jenő u. HU
Zoltán u. GU
Zrínyi u. GU

Hilton WestEnd, Váci útca 1-3, ✉ 1069, ✆ (01) 288 5500, *info.budapest-westend@hilton.com, Fax (01) 288 5588,* – rm, – 350. rest CY c
Arrabona : **Meals** (buffet lunch) 6250/9000 and a la carte 5100/7200 – 5500 – **230 rm** 52500.
◆ 21C hotel incorporated in large adjoining indoor shopping centre. Comprehensive business facilities, roof garden ; spacious bedrooms. A bright and contemporary dining room on the first floor of the hotel, with a Mediterranean theme.

Art'otel, Bem Rakpart 16-19, ✉ 1011, ✆ (01) 487 9487, *budapest@artotel.hu, Fax (01) 487 9488,* – rm, – 160. rest FU b
Chelsea : **Meals** a la carte 3600/6650 – **156 rm** 48500/53500, 9 suites.
◆ Half new building, half converted baroque houses. Stylish and original interior in cool shades and clean lines. Features over 600 pieces of original art by Donald Sultan. Bright dining room with vaulted ceiling topped with glass and modern artwork.

Danubius Grand H. , Margitsziget, ✉ 1138, ✆ (01) 889 4700, *sales.budapest-spa@danubiusgroup.com, Fax (01) 889 4988,* – rm, – 120. rest CY b
Széchenyi : **Meals** a la carte approx 7500 – **154 rm** 41250/46650, 10 suites.
◆ Grand 19C building pleasantly located on Margaret Island with direct access to thermal spa and therapy centre. All rooms have views and reflect the style of the house. Grand and formal restaurant with pleasant décor and very appealing terrace in summer.

Radisson SAS Béke, Teréz körút 43, ✉ 1067, ✆ (01) 889 3900, *sales.budapest@radissonsas.com, Fax (01) 889 3915,* – rm, – 330. rest HU a
Szondi Lugas : **Meals** (buffet lunch) 4900/7500 and dinner a la carte – 4150 – **239 rm** 34200, 8 suites.
◆ Classic façade with mosaic fronts large international hotel in busy shopping street. Rear bedrooms quieter.Tea salon is one of the best in the city. Spacious restaurant with classic modern décor and eye-catching murals.

N.H.Budapest, Vigszinház u. 3, ✉ 1137, ✆ (01) 814 0000, *nhbudapest@nh-hotels.com, Fax (01) 814 0100,* – rm, – 100. CY s
Meals 2455/3200 and a la carte 4420/6880 – 3930 – **160 rm** 44720.
◆ Modern hotel in city suburbs. Conference facilities ; gym and sauna. Bright, modern, well-furnished rooms in bold colours with extra touches ; some with balconies. Simple restaurant ; dishes show Mediterranean influences.

K + K Opera , Révay útca 24, ✉ 1065, ✆ (01) 269 0222, *kk.hotel.opera@kkhotels.hu, Fax (01) 269 0230,* – rm, – 80 HU f
203 rm, 2 suites.
◆ Well run hotel in quiet street in business district near opera. Stylish modern interior design. Good size rooms smartly furnished and well equipped. Informal dining in bar with bright modern décor and pale wood furniture ; bistro style menu.

Andrássy, Andrássy útca 111, ✉ 1063, ✆ (01) 462 2118, *welcome@andrassyhotel.com, Fax (01) 322 9445,* – rm, . DY b
Zebrano : **Meals** a la carte 1880/3380 – **62 rm** 68000/79000, 8 suites.
◆ A classical Bauhaus building converted into a hotel in 2001. Stylish lobby with marbled columns and large murals. Bright and contemporary bedrooms, most with balconies. Small, friendly and informal restaurant which doubles as a bar and café.

Mercure Korona, Kecskeméti útca 14, ✉ 1053, ✆ (01) 486 8800, *h1765@accor.com, Fax (01) 318 3867,* – – 100. . rest HX s
Meals (dinner only) 4430 and a la carte approx 5415 – 4200 – **413 rm** 34450, 11 suites.
◆ Well equipped quite modern business hotel close to Hungarian National Museum. Contemporary rooms with all mod cons. Cavernous lobby. Coffee bar on bridge spanning street. Large, fairly sombre restaurant above hotel lobby with tiled floor, columns and plants.

Novotel, Rákóczi út 43-45, ✉ 1088, ✆ (01) 477 5400, *h3560@accor.com, Fax (01) 477 5454,* – rm, – 350. CDZ s
Palace : **Meals** (buffet lunch) 4650/5900 and a la carte 4050/6400 – 3700 – **227 rm** 34200.
◆ Early 20C Art Deco hotel with extensions, in the business district. Conference facilities ; basement leisure club. Spacious, well-fitted and modern bedrooms. The ornate, classic Palace restaurant serves an international menu.

Mercure Nemzeti, József Körút 4, ✉ 1088, ☎ (01) 477 2000, *h1686@accor.com, Fax (01) 477 2001* – |♦|, ⇔ rm, ▤ rm, TV ☎ – 🏗 60. MC AE D VISA JCB. ✻ rest CZ n
Meals a la carte 2900/6200 ♀ – ☕ 3200 – **75 rm** 24200, 1 suite.
♦ Commercial hotel near city centre in elegant 19C building featuring impressive Art Nouveau décor. Bedrooms are modern and well equipped, offering most mod cons. Restaurant boasts elegant Art Nouveau décor and a particularly splendid coloured glass ceiling.

Taverna, Váci útca 20, ✉ 1052, ☎ (01) 485 3100, *hotel@hoteltaverna.hu, Fax (01) 485 3111*, ≘s – |♦|, ⇔ rm, ▤ TV 🚗 – 🏗 100. MC AE D VISA JCB. ✻ rest GV h
***Cambrinus* : Meals** (dinner only) (gypsy music) a la carte approx 6000 ♀ – ***Holsten Brasserie* : Meals** a la carte approx 2500 ♀ – **223 rm** ☕ 33000/42000, 4 suites.
♦ Business and tourist hotel located on main pedestrianised shopping street. Extensive facilities offering something for everyone. Rooms are comfortable. Cambrinus restaurant with hunting scenes on walls. Convivial atmosphere at the Holsten Brasserie.

Mercure Metropol, Rákóczi útca 58, ✉ 1074, ☎ (01) 462 8100, *h2997@accor-hotels.com, Fax (01) 462 8181* – |♦|, ⇔ rm, ▤ TV ☎ ♿ – 🏗 50. MC AE D VISA JCB. ✻ CDZ a
Meals a la carte approx 3000 ♀ – ☕ 3185 – **130 rm** 25725.
♦ Opened in 2000, a newly constructed hotel lying in the heart of the business district. Bright bedrooms with fitted work desks and all the appropriate facilities. Small, simple restaurant behind the reception area with its own adjoining bar.

Uhu Villa 🐦, Keselyü I/a, ✉ 1025, Northwest : 8 km by Szilágyi Erzsébet fasor ☎ (01) 275 1002, *uhuvilla@uhuvilla.hu, Fax (01) 398 0571*, ←, 🌳, ≘s, 🏊, 🌿 – ▤ TV P – 🏗 25. MC AE VISA JCB. ✻
Meals *(closed Sunday)* (buffet lunch) 7500 and a la carte 6200/8500 – **11 rm** ☕ 22000/39100, 1 suite.
♦ Early 20C villa set in gardens in quiet location in the Buda Hills. Basement leisure centre with sauna and pool. Smart, contemporary bedrooms, with individual décor. Formal restaurant with terrace and view serving Italian influenced dishes.

Sissi without rest., Angyal útca 33, ✉ 1094, by Tuzoltó útca ☎ (01) 215 0082, *hsissi@axelero.hu, Fax (01) 216 6063*, 🌿 – |♦| ⇔ TV ♿ 🚗 – 🏗 25. MC AE D VISA CZ s
44 rm ☕ 27200/44535.
♦ Bedrooms are decorated in warm yellows and blues; some have wooden floors and a Scandinavian feel. Breakfast served in a conservatory overlooking a small garden at the rear.

Victoria without rest., Bem Rakpart 11, ✉ 1011, ☎ (01) 457 8080, *victoria@victoria.hu, Fax (01) 457 8088*, ← Danube and Pest, ≘s – |♦| ▤ TV ☎ P. MC AE D VISA JCB FU d
27 rm ☕ 25000/26200.
♦ Family-run hotel, popular with tourists, in a row of town houses just below the castle. Rooms are spacious, equipped with good range of facilities and all offer fine views.

Carlton without rest., Apor Péter útca 3, ✉ 1011, ☎ (01) 224 0999, *carltonhotel@axelero.hu, Fax (01) 224 0990* – |♦| ⇔ ▤ TV ☎ 🚗 – 🏗 25. MC AE D VISA FV a
95 rm ☕ 24500/32000.
♦ Usefully located hotel on Buda side of river, offering straightforward accommodation for the cost-conscious traveller. Rooms are functional and comfortable. Small bar.

Liget, Dózsa György útca 106, ✉ 1068, ☎ (01) 269 5300, *hotel@liget.hu, Fax (01) 269 5329*, 🌳, ≘s – |♦|, ⇔ rm, ▤ TV 🚗 P – 🏗 200. MC AE D VISA JCB. ✻ rest DY e
Meals 2960/3455 (lunch) and a la carte – **139 rm** ☕ 25900/56750.
♦ Inexpensive modern hotel with salmon pink exterior and green roof near Heroes' Square. Bedrooms identical throughout, with modern functional décor and fittings. Small bar. Original paintings, all for sale to diners, brighten the simple, friendly restaurant.

Ibis Centrum without rest., Raday útca 6, ✉ 1092, ☎ (01) 456 4100, *h2078@accor-hotels.com, Fax (01) 456 4116* – ⇔ ▤ TV ☎ ♿. MC AE D VISA JCB HX n
☕ 2000 **126 rm** 18500.
♦ Modern hotel well located for city and national museum. Good functional accommodation with all necessary facilities. Lounge, small bar, bright breakfast room, roof garden.

Mercure Relais Duna without rest., Soroksári út 12, ✉ 1095, ☎ (01) 455 8300, *h2025@accor.com, Fax (01) 455 8385* – |♦| ⇔ ▤ TV ☎ – 🏗 40. MC AE D VISA JCB. ✻ CZ b
☕ 3000 – **130 rm** 20800/22000.
♦ Modern hotel catering well for business people and tourists, close to river and city. Fair sized bedrooms offer simple but modern comforts and reasonable level of mod cons.

XXXX **Gundel,** Állatkerti utca 2, ✉ 1146, ☎ (01) 468 4040, *info@gundel.hu, Fax (01) 363 1917,* – P – 200. MC AE VISA. DY d
closed 24 December – **Meals** (booking essential) 2990/3900 (lunch) and a la carte 7750/15270 ♀ – ***1894* : Meals** *(closed Sunday-Monday)* (dinner only) a la carte 2960/7210♀.
◆ Hungary's best known restaurant, an elegant classic. Spacious main room with walnut panelling and ornate ceiling. Traditional cuisine. Summer terrace. Live music at dinner.

XXX **Vadrózsa,** Pentelei Molnár útca 15, ✉ 1025, via Römer Flóris útca ☎ (01) 326 5817, *vadrozsa@hungary.net, Fax (01) 326 5809,* – . MC AE VISA JCB BY e
closed 24-26 December – **Meals** 4800/12400 and a la carte 4460/10200 ♀.
◆ Pleasant villa just out of town. Elegant dining room with wood panelling. Display of raw ingredients presented with the menu. Attractive summer terrace. Detailed service.

XXX **Alabárdos,** Országház útca 2, ✉ 1014, ☎ (01) 356 0851, *alabardos@axelero.hu, Fax (01) 214 3814,* – . MC AE VISA JCB. FU c
closed Sunday – **Meals** (booking essential) (buffet lunch) 3500/8000 and a la carte 7300/14100 ♀.
◆ Well run restaurant in vaulted Gothic interior of characterful 17C building with covered courtyard in castle square. Extensive menu of good traditional Hungarian classics.

XXX **Fortuna,** Hess András tér 4, ✉ 1014, ☎ (01) 355 7177, *fortuna@hu.inter.net, Fax (01) 375 6857,* – – . MC AE VISA JCB. FU t
Meals (buffet lunch) 4500/10000 and dinner a la carte 5700/8900 ♀.
◆ Attractive period building with Gothic style interior and 13C Champagne cellar. Good range of traditional dishes with some modern influence ; medieval banquets a speciality.

XXX **Légrádi Antique,** Bárczy István útca 3-5 (first floor), ✉ 1052, ☎ (01) 266 4993 – MC AE VISA GV b
closed 24 December, Saturday lunch and Sunday – **Meals** (booking essential) a la carte 8450/12500.
◆ Restaurant above small antiques shop has elegant décor, vaulted ceiling, marble balustrades and intimate ambience. Classic menu of robust traditional fare. Gypsy music.

XX **Fausto's,** Dohány útca 5, ✉ 1072, ☎ (01) 269 6806, *faustos@axelero.hu, Fax (01) 269 6806* – . MC AE VISA. HV k
closed Easter, 3 weeks August, 24-26 December, first week January, Sunday and Bank Holidays – **Meals** - Italian - 3350/15000 and a la carte 4800/17200.
◆ Popular, personally run restaurant in tree-lined avenue next to impressive synagogue with smart décor and slick service. Attractive menu of Italian classics.

XX **Premier,** Andrássy út 101, ✉ 1062, ☎ (01) 342 1768, *premier-restaurant@axelero.hu, Fax (01) 322 1639,* – . MC AE VISA JCB CDY n
closed 24 December and Sunday October-April – **Meals** a la carte 3900/7900 ♀.
◆ Early 20C Art nouveau villa with three basement rooms and a pleasant outdoor terrace. Attentive service. Menu of traditional and international dishes with weekly specials.

XX **Képiró,** Képiró u. 3, ✉ 1053, ☎ (01) 266 0430, *info@kepirorestaurant.com, Fax (01) 266 0425* – . MC AE VISA HX r
closed Sunday and Saturday lunch – **Meals** a la carte 2900/6900 ♀.
◆ Glass-fronted restaurant, in narrow street near city centre, divided by central bar. Approachable and friendly service. Modern style cooking with seasonal menus.

XX **Robinson,** Városligeti tó, ✉ 1146, ☎ (01) 422 0222, *robinson@axelero.hu, Fax (01) 422 0072,* – MC AE VISA JCB DY a
Meals a la carte 3940/9350 ♀.
◆ Pavilion on tiny island in park ; fountains in lake. Spacious room with large picture windows ; large terrace. Extensive menu of traditional fare. Guitar music at dinner.

XX **Bagolyvár,** Allatkerti ut 2, ✉ 1146, ☎ (01) 468 3110, *bagolyvar@gundel.hu, Fax (01) 363 1917,* – MC AE VISA DY d
closed 25 December – **Meals** (music at dinner) a la carte 3020/6190 ♀.
◆ Unusual Austro-Hungarian castle style building next to its sister - Gundel. All female team serve home-style traditional fare prepared by all female kitchen.

XX **Kárpátia,** Ferenciek tere 7-8, ✉ 1053, ☎ (01) 317 3596, *restaurant@karpatia.hu, Fax (01) 318 0591* – . MC AE VISA JCB HV a
closed 24 December – **Meals** a la carte 5400/10600.
◆ One of the city's oldest restaurants with characterful vaulted Gothic style interior, beautifully painted walls and works of art. Extensive menu of good traditional cuisine.

Lou Lou, Vigyázó Ferenc útca 4, 1051, (01) 312 4505, *lou-lou.restaurant@axelero.hu, Fax (01) 472 0595* – GU a
closed 25 December, Sunday and Saturday lunch – **Meals** a la carte 4200/8400.
◆ Divided into two rooms ; one with walls covered with pictures, the other brighter and in terracotta colours. Well-judged service ; modern cooking with strong presentation.

Múzeum, Múzeum körút 12, 1088, (01) 338 4221, *Fax (01) 338 4221* – HV e
Meals a la carte 3200/9700.
◆ Founded in 1885, next to National Museum. High ceilings, tiled walls and large windows. Formally attired staff serve large portions of traditional Hungarian cooking.

Cyrano, Kristóf tér 7-8, 1052, (01) 266 3096, *cyrano@citynet.hu, Fax (01) 266 6818,* – GV t
closed 24-25 and 31 December – **Meals** a la carte 4170/8170.
◆ Popular informal restaurant just off main shopping street with unusual dramatic modern designer style décor. Serves selection of good modern European and Hungarian food.

Belcanto, Dalszínház útca 8, 1061, (01) 269 2786, *restaurant@belcanto.hu, Fax (01) 311 9547* – HU f
closed 25 December – **Meals** (booking essential) 3700/9800 and a la carte 4400/8800.
◆ Next to the opera and famous for classical and operatic evening recitals, including impromptu performances by waiters ! Atmosphere is lively and enjoyable. Hungarian food.

Baraka, Magyar útca 12-14, 1053, (01) 483 1355, *desboek@yahoo.com, Fax (01) 266 8808* – HV q
closed 24-25 December, 1 January and Sunday – **Meals** (booking essential) (dinner only) a la carte 5350/8400.
◆ Small restaurant with simple décor and corner bar ; quieter tables on mezzanine floor. Modern, international dishes showing French and Asian influences ; blackboard specials.

Kisbuda Gyöngye, Kenyeres útca 34, 1034, (01) 368 9246, *gyongye@remiz.hu, Fax (01) 368 9227,* – CY f
closed 24-26 December, 1 January and Sunday – **Meals** (booking essential) (music at dinner) a la carte 5800/9000.
◆ A genuine neighbourhood restaurant in a residential street. Wood panelling and murals. Attentive and very helpful service. Good value, carefully prepared and authentic food.

Krizia, Mozsár útca 12, 1066, (01) 331 8711, *Fax (01) 331 8711* –
closed 15-18 June, 24-26 December and Sunday – **Meals** - Italian - (buffet lunch) 2600/10000 and a la carte 3400/8500. HU b
◆ A pleasant intimate atmosphere, with candlelight and friendly service. Carefully prepared Italian cooking with the menu supplemented by regularly changing specials.

La Fontaine, Mérleg útca 10, 1051, (01) 317 3715, *restaurant@lafontaine.hu, Fax (01) 318 8562* – GV s
closed Sunday and Saturday lunch – **Meals** - French - a la carte 5400/8700.
◆ Authentic Gallic charm : even the tables are imported from France. High ceiling and tiled flooring adds to the airy feel. Traditional French menu with blackboard specials.

Náncsi Néni, Ördögárok útca 80, Hüvösvölgy, 1029, Northwest : 10 km by Szilágyi Erzsébetfasor (01) 397 2742, *info@nancsineni.hu, Fax (01) 397 2742,* –
closed 24 December – **Meals** (gypsy music at dinner) a la carte 2460/5650.
◆ Interior similar to a Swiss chalet, with gingham tablecloths, convivial atmosphere and large terrace. Well-priced home-style Hungarian cooking. Worth the drive from the city.

Arcade Bistro, Kiss Janos Alt u. 38, 1126, (01) 225 1969, *arcadebistrol@freestart.hu, Fax (01) 225 1968,* – EV f
closed 24-26 December and Sunday – **Meals** (booking essential) a la carte 3560/7220.
◆ Small local restaurant with central column water feature and colourful modern art décor. Seasonal menu of modern cuisine : daily specials and Mediterranean influences.

Remiz, Budakeszi útca 5, 1021, Northwest : 5 km by Szilágyi Erzsébet favor (01) 275 1396, *remiz@remiz.hu, Fax (01) 200 3843,* –
closed 24 December – **Meals** a la carte 4700/6700.
◆ On the outskirts of town and popular with the locals. Dine in the conservatory or on the large summer terrace. Efficient service from large brigade. Classic Hungarian dishes.

Republic of Ireland

Eire

DUBLIN

PRACTICAL INFORMATION

LOCAL CURRENCY

1 euro (€) = 1,34 USD ($) (Dec 2004)

TOURIST INFORMATION

The telephone number and address of the Tourist Information office is given in the text under **i**.

National Holiday in the Republic of Ireland: *17 March.*

FOREIGN EXCHANGE

Banks are open between 10am and 4pm on weekdays only.

Banks in Dublin stay open to 5pm on Thursdays and banks at Dublin and Shannon airports are open on Saturdays and Sundays.

SHOPPING IN DUBLIN

In the index of street names, those printed in red are where the principal shops are found.

CAR HIRE

The international car hire companies have branches in each major city. Your hotel porter should be able to give details and help you with your arrangements.

TIPPING

Many hotels and restaurants include a service charge but where this is not the case an amount equivalent to between 10 and 15 per cent of the bill is customary. Additionally doormen, baggage porters and cloakroom attendants are generally given a gratuity.

Taxi drivers are tipped between 10 and 15 per cent of the amount shown on the meter in addition to the fare.

SPEED LIMITS

The maximum permitted speed in the Republic is 60 mph (97 km/h) except where a lower speed limit is indicated.

SEAT BELTS

The wearing of seat belts is compulsory if fitted for drivers and front seat passengers. Additionally, children under 12 are not allowed in front seats unless in a suitable safety restraint.

ANIMALS

It is forbidden to bring domestic animals (dogs, cats...) into the Republic of Ireland.

SMOKING

In the Republic of Ireland the law prohibits smoking in all pubs, restaurants and hotel public areas.

DUBLIN

(Baile Átha Cliath) *Dublin* 712 N 7 – *pop. 1 004 614.*

Belfast 103 – Cork 154 – Londonderry 146.

Bord Failte Offices, Baggot Street Bridge ✆ (01) 602 4000 ; information@dublintourism.ie – Suffolk St – Arrivals Hall, Dublin Airport – The Square Shopping Centre, Tallaght.

Elm Park, Nutley House, Donnybrook ✆ (01) 269 3438 – Milltown, Lower Churchtown Rd, ✆ (01) 497 6090, EV *– Royal Dublin, North Bull Island, Dollymount, ✆ (01) 833 6346, NE : by R 105 – Forrest Little, Cloghran ✆ (01) 840 1763 – Lucan, Celbridge Rd, Lucan ✆ (01) 628 2106 – Edmondstown, Rathfarnham ✆ (01) 493 2461 – Coldwinters, Newtown House, St Margaret's ✆ (01) 864 0324.*

Dublin Airport ✆ (01) 814 1111, N : 5 1/2 m. by N 1 – Terminal : Busaras (Central Bus Station) Store St

to Holyhead (Irish Ferries) 2 daily (3 h 15 mn) – to Holyhead (Stena Line) 1-2 daily (3 h 45 mn) – to the Isle of Man (Douglas) (Isle of Man Steam Packet Co Ltd.) (2 h 45 mn/4 h 45) – to Liverpool (SeaCat February-November) (4 h) – to Liverpool (P & O Irish Sea) (8 h).

SIGHTS

See: *City★★★ – Trinity College★★* JY *– Old Library★★★ (Treasury★★★, Long Room★★) – Dublin Castle★★ (Chester Beatty Library★★★)* HY *– Christ Church Cathedral★★* HY *– St Patrick's Cathedral★★* HZ *– Marsh's Library★★* HZ *– National Museum★★ (The Treasury★★)* KZ *– National Gallery★★* KZ *– Newman House★★* JZ *– Bank of Ireland★★* JY *– Custom House★★* KX *– Tailors' Hall★* HY *– City Hall★* HY *– Temple Bar★* HJY *– Liffey Bridge★* JY *– Merrion Square★* KZ *– Number Twenty-Nine★* KZ **D** *– Grafton Street★* JYZ *– Powerscourt Centre★* JY *– Rotunda Hospital Chapel★* JX *– O'Connell Street★ (GPO Building★)* JX *– Hugh Lane Municipal Gallery of Modern Art★* JX **M**[4] *– Pro-Cathedral★* JX.

Envir.: *The Ben of Howth★ (≤★), NE: 6 m. by R 105* KX.

Exc.: *Powerscourt★★ (Waterfall★★* **AC***), S: 14 m. by N 11 and R 117* EV *– Russborough House★★★, SW: 22 m. by N 81* DV.

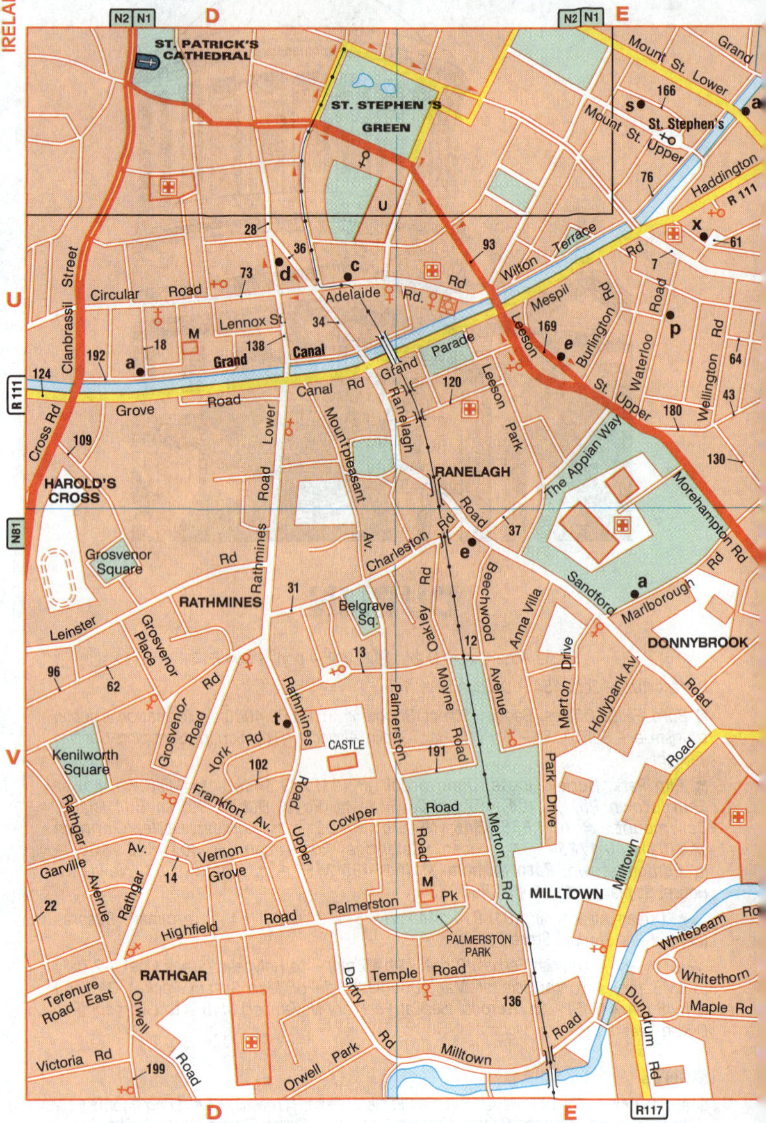

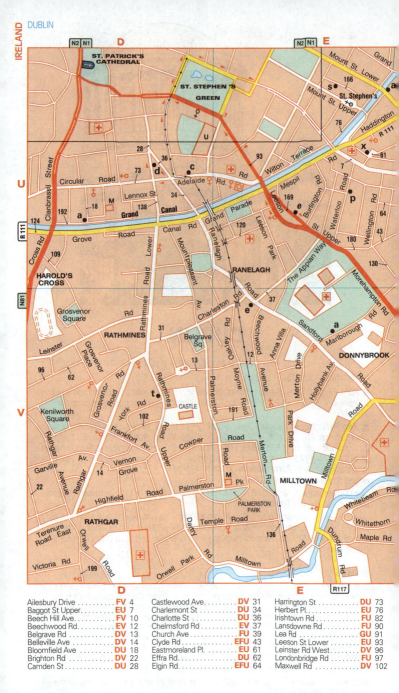

Ailesbury Drive .... FV 4
Baggot St Upper.......... EU 7
Beech Hill Ave.......... FV 10
Beechwood Rd.......... EV 12
Belgrave Rd .... DV 13
Belleville Ave .... DV 14
Bloomfield Ave .... DU 18
Brighton Rd .... DV 22
Camden St.......... DU 28
Castlewood Ave.......... DV 31
Charlemont St .... DU 34
Charlotte St .... DU 36
Chelmsford Rd .... EV 37
Church Ave.......... FU 39
Clyde Rd.......... EFU 43
Eastmoreland Pl. .... EU 61
Effra Rd.......... DU 62
Elgin Rd.......... EFU 64
Harrington St .... DU 73
Herbert Pl.......... EU 76
Irishtown Rd .... FU 82
Lansdowne Rd .... FU 90
Lea Rd .... GU 91
Leeson St Lower .... EU 93
Leinster Rd West.......... DV 96
Londonbridge Rd .... FU 97
Maxwell Rd .... DV 102

F G

Merlyn Park	GV	105	Richmond Ave South	EV	136	Stephen's Lane	EU	166
Mount Drummond Ave.	DU	109	Richmond St South	DU	138	Sussex Rd.	EU	169
Newbridge Ave.	FU	115	St Alban's Park	GV	142	Trimbleston Ave.	GV	175
Newgrove Ave.	GU	117	St John's Rd East	GV	145	Victoria Ave	FV	177
Northbrook Rd	EU	120	Seafort Ave	GU	153	Wellington Pl.	EU	180
Nutgrove Park	FV	121	Sean Moore Rd	GU	154	Windsor Rd	EV	191
Parnell Rd	DU	124	Serpentine Av.	FU	156	Windsor Terrace	DU	192
Pembroke Park	EU	130	Simmonscourt Rd	FU	160	Wynnsward Drive	FV	198
Raglan Rd	FU	133	South Lotts Rd	FU	163	Zion Rd	DV	199

DUBLIN

Anne St South . . . . JYZ 6
Brunswick St North . . . . HX 24
Buckingham St. . . . . KX 25
Bull Alley . . . . HZ 27
Chancery St . . . . HY 33
Clanbrassil St . . . . HZ 40
College Green . . . . JY 45
College St . . . . JY 46
Cornmarket. . . . . HY 49
D'Olier St. . . . . JY 51
Dawson St . . . . JYZ
Dorset St . . . . HX 55
Duke St . . . . JY 58
Earlsford Terrace. . . . . JZ 60
Essex Quay . . . . HY 65
Essex St . . . . HY 66
Fishamble St. . . . . HY 67
Fleet St . . . . JY 68
George's Quay . . . . KY 69
Golden Lane . . . . HZ 70
Grafton St . . . . JYZ
Henrietta St . . . . HX 75
Henry St . . . . JX
High St . . . . HY 78
Ilac Centre . . . . HJX
Irish Life Mall Centre . . . . . . JKX
Jervis Centre . . . . HJX
Kevin St Upper . . . . HZ 85
Kildare St. . . . . JKZ 87
King St South . . . . JZ 88
Marlborough St. . . . . JX 100
Merchants Quay . . . . HY 103
Merrion St . . . . KZ 104
Montague St . . . . JZ 106
Mount St Upper . . . . KZ 112
Nicholas St . . . . HY 118
North Great George's St . . . . JX 119
O'Connell St . . . . JX
Parnell Square East . . . . JX 126
Parnell Square North . . . . . . JX 127
Parnell Square West . . . . . . HJX 129
St Mary's Abbey St . . . . HY 148
St Patrick Close . . . . HZ 150
Stephen St . . . . HJY 165
Stephens Green . . . . JZ
Tara St. . . . . KY 171
Wellington Quay . . . . HJY 181
Werburgh St. . . . . HY 183
Westland Row . . . . KY 186
Westmoreland St . . . . JY 187
Wexford St . . . . HZ 189
Whitefriar St . . . . HZ 190
Winetavern St . . . . HY 193
Wood Quay . . . . HY 196

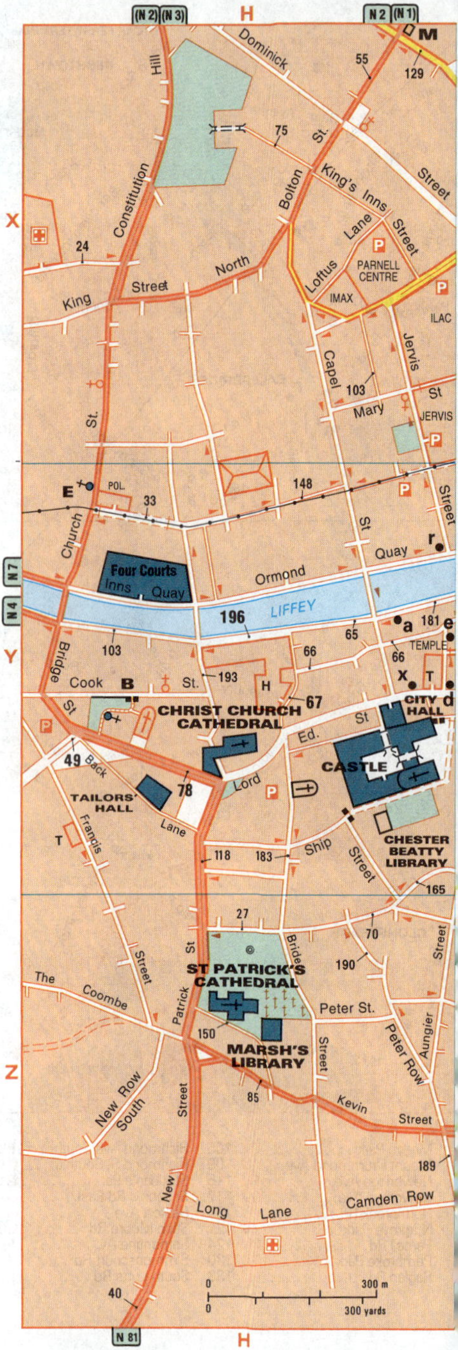

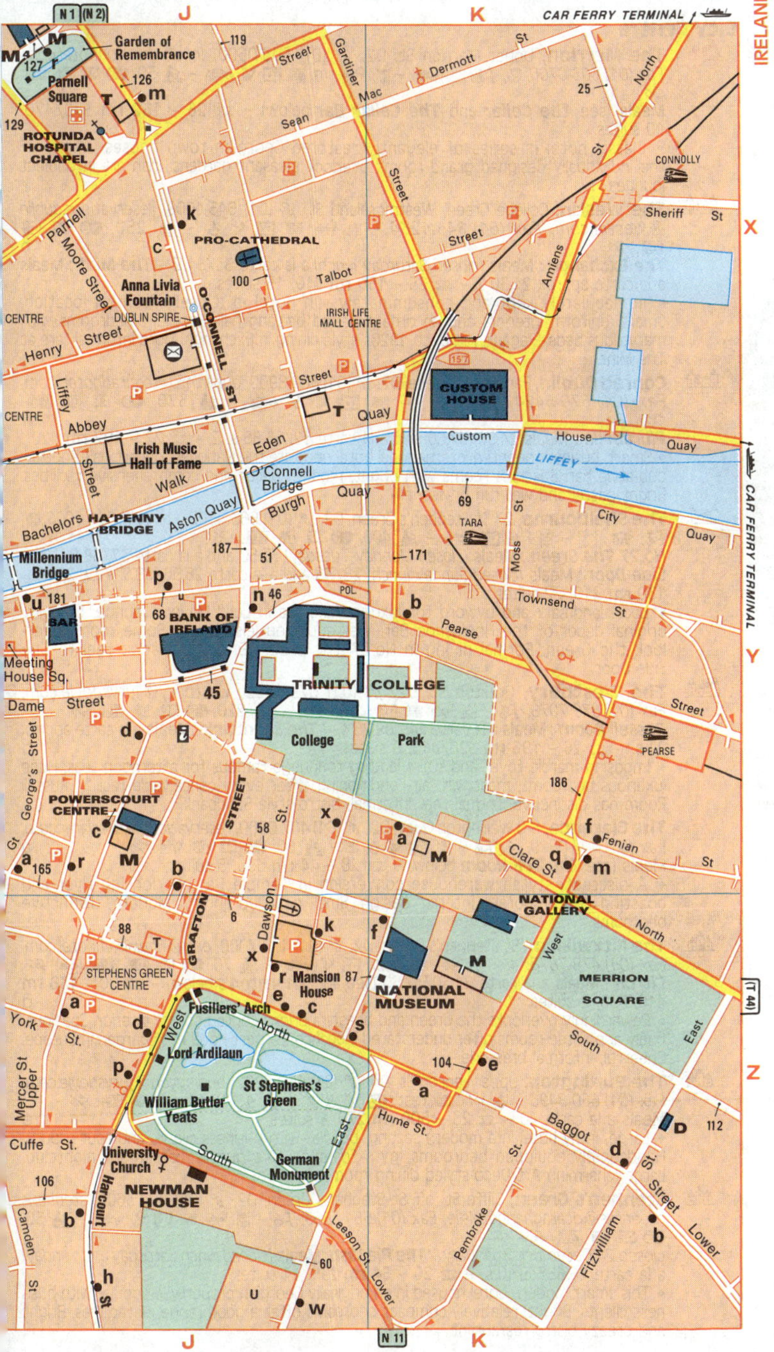

N 1
N 2
J
K
CAR FERRY TERMINAL
IRELAND
Garden of Remembrance
Parnell Square
ROTUNDA HOSPITAL CHAPEL
PRO-CATHEDRAL
Anna Livia Fountain
DUBLIN SPIRE
O'CONNELL ST
Moore Street
Parnell
Henry Street
CENTRE
IRISH LIFE MALL CENTRE
Talbot Street
Sean Mac Dermott St
Gardiner Street
North St
Amiens
CONNOLLY
Sheriff St
CUSTOM HOUSE
Custom House Quay
LIFFEY
Abbey Street
Eden Quay
Irish Music Hall of Fame
O'Connell Bridge
Burgh Quay
Bachelors Walk
Aston Quay
HA'PENNY BRIDGE
Millennium Bridge
TARA
City Quay
Moss St
Townsend St
Pearse Street
PEARSE
BANK OF IRELAND
Meeting House Sq.
Dame Street
TRINITY COLLEGE
College Park
POWERSCOURT CENTRE
George's Street
GRAFTON STREET
Dawson St.
Clare St
Fenian St
NATIONAL GALLERY
Mansion House
NATIONAL MUSEUM
MERRION SQUARE
North
West
South
East
STEPHENS GREEN CENTRE
York St.
Fusiliers' Arch
Lord Ardilaun
St Stephens's Green
William Butler Yeats
German Monument
University Church
NEWMAN HOUSE
Mercer St Upper
Cuffe St.
Harcourt St
Camden St
Hume St.
Baggot Street Lower
Leeson St. Lower
Pembroke St.
Fitzwilliam St.
N 11
T 44
X
Y
Z

City Centre

The Merrion, Upper Merrion St, D2, (01) 603 0600, *info@merrionhotel.com, Fax (01) 603 0700,* – rm, – 50. KZ e
Meals (see ***The Cellar*** and ***The Cellar Bar*** below) – 26 – **132 rm** 370/470, 10 suites.
• Classic hotel in series of elegantly restored Georgian town houses ; many of the individually designed grand rooms overlook pleasant gardens. Irish art in opulent lounges.

The Westin, College Green, Westmoreland St, (01) 645 1000, *reservations.dublin@westin.com, Fax (01) 645 1234* – – 250. JY n
***The Exchange* : Meals** *(closed Saturday lunch)* a la carte 33/51 – ***The Mint* : Meals** a la carte approx 21.50 – 25 – **150 rm** 410, 13 suites.
• Immaculately kept and consummately run hotel in a useful central location. Smart, uniform interiors and an ornate period banking hall. Excellent bedrooms with marvellous beds. Elegant, Art Deco 1920s-style dining in Exchange. More informal fare at The Mint.

Conrad Dublin, Earlsfort Terrace, D2, (01) 602 8900, *dublininfo@conradhotels.com, Fax (01) 676 5424,* – – 370. JZ w
***Plurabelle* : Meals** 24.50/37.50 and a la carte 32/55.65 **s.** – 22 – **192 rm** 420.
• Smart, business oriented international hotel opposite the National Concert Hall. Popular, pub-style bar. Spacious rooms with bright, modern décor and comprehensive facilities. Bright pastel and well-run brasserie.

The Shelbourne, 27 St Stephen's Green, D2, (01) 663 4500, *Fax (01) 661 6006,* – – 400. JZ s
***No.27 The Green* : Meals** *(closed Monday-Tuesday)* 33.50 and a la carte 37/68 – ***The Side Door* : Meals** *(closed Sunday lunch)* 28/35 and a la carte 26.50/38 – 22.50 – **130 rm** 210, 22 suites.
• Local landmark and byword for luxury. Take tea in Lord Mayor's lounge, or enjoy original décor of the Horseshoe Bar. Well-equipped leisure spa. Some rooms overlook the Green. Formal dining in No.27 The Green. Bright brasserie feel to The Side Door.

The Westbury, Grafton St, D2, (01) 679 1122, *westbury@jurysdoyle.com, Fax (01) 679 7078,* – – 220.
***Russell Room* : Meals** a la carte approx 25 **s.** – ***The Sandbank* : Meals** a la carte approx 21 **s.** – 26 – **196 rm** 320/410, 8 suites. JY b
• Imposing marble foyer and stairs leading to lounge famous for afternoon teas. Huge luxurious bedrooms, most with air-conditioning, offer every conceivable facility. Russell Room has distinctive, formal feel. Informal, bistro-style Sandbank.

The Clarence, 6-8 Wellington Quay, D2, (01) 407 0800, *reservations@theclarence.ie, Fax (01) 407 0820,* – – 60. HY a
Meals (see ***The Tea Room*** below) – 28 – **44 rm** 330, 5 suites.
• A discreet, stylish warehouse conversion in Temple Bar overlooking river and boasting contemporary interior design. Small panelled library. Modern, distinctive bedrooms.

The Fitzwilliam, St Stephen's Green, D2, (01) 478 7000, *enq@fitzwilliamhotel.com, Fax (01) 478 7878,* – , rest, – 70.
Citron* : Meals** a la carte 21.50/32.50 (see also ***Thornton's below) – 20 – **138 rm** 310/350, 2 suites. JZ d
• Rewardingly overlooks the Green and boasts a bright contemporary interior. Spacious, finely appointed rooms offer understated elegance. Largest hotel roof garden in Europe. Cheerful, informal brasserie.

The Burlington, Upper Leeson St, D4, (01) 660 5222, *burlington@jurysdoyle.com, Fax (01) 660 8496* – , rest, – 1500.
Meals a la carte 40 – 23 – **500 rm** 270, 6 suites. EU e
• Large, lively hotel in a modern setting, popular with business clients and tour groups. Handsomely equipped bedrooms, gym for executive guests ; basement nightclub. Large, charming Art Deco-styled dining room.

Stephen's Green, Cliffe St, off St Stephen's Green, D2, (01) 607 3600, *stephensgreenres@ocallaghanhotels.ie, Fax (01) 661 5663,* – – 50. JZ f
closed 24 December-2 January – ***The Pie Dish* : Meals** *(closed lunch Saturday and Sunday)* a la carte 26.65/39.10 **s.** – 20 – **64 rm** 295, 11 suites.
• This smart modern hotel housed in an originally Georgian property is popular with business clients. Bright, relatively compact bedrooms offer a good range of facilities. Bright and breezy bistro restaurant.

Brooks, Drury St, D2, (01) 670 4000, *sales@brookshotel.ie, Fax (01) 670 4455*, – – 30. . JY r
***Francesca's* : Meals** (dinner only) 15.75/19.75 and a la carte 17.95/37.50 – 18 – **98 rm** 205/285.
◆ Commercial hotel in modern English town house style. Smart lounges and spacious rooms with tasteful feel and good facilities. Extras in top range rooms, at a supplement. Ground floor Francesca's restaurant with open kitchen for chef-watching.

The Alexander, Fienian St, Merrion Sq, D2, (01) 607 3700, *alexanderres@ocallaghanhotels.ie, Fax (01) 661 5663*, – – 400. . KY f
closed 24 December-2 January – ***Caravaggio's* : Meals** (bar lunch Saturday and Sunday) a la carte 24.90/38.85 **s.** – 20 – **98 rm** 295, 4 suites.
◆ This bright corporate hotel, well placed for museums and Trinity College, has a stylish contemporary interior. Spacious comfortable rooms and suites with good facilities. Stylish contemporary restaurant with wide-ranging menus.

The Davenport, Lower Merrion St, off Merrion Sq, D2, (01) 607 3500, *davenportres@ocallaghanhotels.ie, Fax (01) 661 5663*, – – 275. . KY m
***Lanyon* : Meals** *(closed lunch Saturday and Sunday)* a la carte 27.90/36.60 – 20 – **113 rm** 295, 2 suites.
◆ Sumptuous Victorian gospel hall façade heralds elegant hotel popular with business clientèle. Tastefully furnished, well-fitted rooms. Presidents bar honours past leaders. Dining room with formal, Georgian interior.

The Gresham, 23 Upper O'Connell St, D1, (01) 874 6881, *info@thegresham.com, Fax (01) 878 7175*, – , rest, – 400. .
***23* : Meals** (dinner only) a la carte 33/52 – ***The Aberdeen* : Meals** a la carte 33/52 – 19.05 – **283 rm** 320, 6 suites. JX k
◆ Long established restored 19C property in a famous street offers elegance tinged with luxury. Some penthouse suites. Well-equipped business centre, lounge and Toddy's bar. The Aberdeen boasts formal ambience. 23 is named after available wines by glass.

Clarion H. Dublin IFSC, Excise Walk International Financial Services Centre, D1, (01) 433 8800, *info@clarionhotelifsc.com, Fax (01) 433 8811*, , , , – – 120. . by Custom House Quay KX
closed 24-26 December – ***Sinergie* : Meals** *(closed Saturday lunch)* 28 and a la carte 35/40 **s.** – ***Kudos* : Meals** - Asian - a la carte 19/24 **s.** – 20 – **154 rm** 280, 8 suites.
◆ In the heart of a modern financial district, a swish hotel for the business person : smart gym and light, spacious, contemporary rooms, some with balconies. Busy bar leads to clean-lined Sinergie with glass walls onto the kitchen. Kudos serves Asian menus.

Morrison, Lower Ormond Quay, D1, (01) 887 2400, *info@morrisonhotel.ie, Fax (01) 878 3185* – , rm, . HY r
Meals (see ***Halo*** below) – 21.50 – **90 rm** 270/305, 4 suites.
◆ Modern riverside hotel with ultra-contemporary interior by acclaimed fashion designer John Rocha. Hi-tech amenities in rooms. "Lobo" late-night club and sushi bar.

brownes townhouse, 22 St Stephen's Green, D2, (01) 638 3939, *info@brownesdublin.com, Fax (01) 638 3900* – . JZ c
Meals (see ***brownes brasserie*** below) – 17.50 – **11 rm** 175/250.
◆ Restored Georgian town house with original fittings in situ. Combines traditional charm with modern comfort. Bedrooms are well-appointed and stylish, some with view.

La Stampa H., 35 Dawson St, D2, (01) 677 4444, *hotel@lastampa.ie, Fax (01) 677 4411* – rest, . JZ x
closed 25-26 December – ***Tiger Becs* : Meals** - Thai - (dinner only) a la carte 27/39 (see also ***La Stampa*** below) – **23 rm** 200.
◆ A privately owned and discreetly stylish boutique hotel, close to St Stephen's Green. Individually appointed bedrooms with designer touches. Quieter rooms at rear. Atmospheric Tiger Becs with Thai dishes.

The Morgan without rest, 10 Fleet St, D2, (01) 679 3939, *reservations@themorgan.com, Fax (01) 679 3946* – , rest, . JY p
closed 24-26 December – 17.70 – **65 rm** 215, 1 suites.
◆ Discreet designer contemporary hotel in vibrant area emphasises style. Simple elegant foyer contrasts with large, busy bar. Sleek minimalist décor in well-equipped bedrooms.

Mont Clare, Lower Merrion St, off Merrion Sq, D2, (01) 607 3800, *info@ocallaghanhotels.ie* – , rest, – 120. . KY q
closed 24-30 December – ***Goldsmiths* : Meals** *(closed lunch Saturday and Sunday)* a la carte 22.50/33.45 – 20 – **74 rm** 205.
◆ Classic property with elegant panelled reception and tasteful comfortable rooms at heart of Georgian Dublin. Corporate suites available. Traditional pub style Gallery bar. Formal restaurant with tried-and-tested menus.

Chief O'Neills, Smithfield Village, Smithfield, D7, ✆ (01) 817 3838, *reservations@chiefoneills.com, Fax (01) 817 3839* – ▮ ⇔ TV ✆ ♿ P – 🏛 240. MC AE VISA. ✻
closed 23-26 December – ***Kelly & Ping* : Meals** - Asian - *(closed Sunday)* a la carte 25/35.50 – **73 rm** ☐ 180/250. by King St HX
◆ Based in cultural hub. Interactive music centre celebrates traditional Irish music. Sleek modern rooms with hi-fi. Viewing tower with wonderful vistas of the surrounding city. Asian restaurant in sleek modish setting adjacent to Jameson distillery.

Cassidys, Cavendish Row, Upper O'Connell St, D1, ✆ (01) 878 0555, *stay@cassidyshotel.com, Fax (01) 878 0687* – ▮ ⇔, ▤ rest, TV ✆ P – 🏛 80. MC AE ⓓ VISA. ✻
closed 24-26 December – ***Number Six* : Meals** (dinner only) 20.50/25 and a la carte 26/44.50 **s.** – **87 rm** ☐ 120/220, 1 suite. JX m
◆ Classic Georgian redbrick town house makes an elegant backdrop for modern comfort. Cheerful room décor. Limited on-street guest parking. Popular Groomes bar open to public. Bright, stylish dining room sports a homely ambience.

The Mercer, Mercer Street Lower, D2, ✆ (01) 478 2179, *stay@mercerhotel.ie, Fax (01) 478 0328* – ▮ ⇔ ▤ TV ♿ 🚗 – 🏛 100. MC AE ⓓ VISA. ✻ JZ a
***Cusack's* : Meals** *(closed Sunday)* a la carte 22/30 **s.** – **41 rm** 170/210.
◆ This modern boutique hotel, hidden away next to the Royal College of Surgeons, is pleasant and stylish. It offers comprehensive amenities including air conditioning. Smart yet relaxing restaurant.

Trinity Capital, Pearse St, D2, ✆ (01) 648 1000, *info@trinitycapital-hotel.com, Fax (01) 648 1010* – ▮ ⇔, ▤ rest, TV ✆ ♿ – 🏛 40. MC AE ⓓ VISA. ✻ KY b
closed 24-27 December – ***Siena* : Meals** (bar lunch)/dinner 24.95 and a la carte 20.85/32 – ☐ 15 – **82 rm** 165/192.
◆ Spacious lobby with striking modern furnishings leads off to stylish, soft-toned bedrooms, generously supplied with mod cons. A few minutes walk from Trinity College. Relaxed and fashionably styled dining room filled with natural light.

Buswells, Molesworth St, D2, ✆ (01) 614 6500, *buswells@quinn-hotels.com, Fax (01) 676 2090,* Fø – ▮ ⇔, ▤ rest, TV ✆ P – 🏛 85. MC AE ⓓ VISA. ✻
closed 24-26 December – ***Trumans* : Meals** (carvery lunch)/dinner a la carte 32/45 **s.** – **66 rm** ☐ 155/225, 2 suites. KZ f
◆ Elegant little hotel in quiet central location offering modern amenities while retaining its Georgian charm. Relax in cushioned lounge or cosy, pleasingly furnished rooms. Smart Trumans for formal dining.

Camden Court, Camden St, D2, ✆ (01) 475 9666, *sales@camdencourthotel.com, Fax (01) 475 9677,* Fø, ≘s, ⊡ – ▮ ⇔, ▤ rest, TV ✆ ♿ 🚗 – 🏛 125. MC AE VISA JCB. ✻ DU d
***The Court* : Meals** *(closed Sunday lunch)* (carving lunch)/dinner 23.95/32 and a la carte 27.65/36.50 – **246 rm** ☐ 210/280.
◆ A vaulted passageway leads to this smart, popular hotel in a thriving locality. Colourful soft furnishings in cosy, well-equipped rooms. Cheerful bar on an Irish myth theme. Open, informal restaurant with polished wood and popular menus.

Longfield's, 10 Lower Fitzwilliam St, D2, ✆ (01) 676 1367, *info@longfields.ie, Fax (01) 676 1542* – ▮ TV ✆. MC AE ⓓ VISA. ✻ KZ d
Meals (see ***Number Ten*** below) – **26 rm** ☐ 90/235.
◆ Classic Georgian town house on reputedly Europe's longest Georgian road. Spacious lounge ; stylish, individually furnished rooms of good size, all redolent of times gone by.

Harrington Hall without rest., 70 Harcourt St, D2, ✆ (01) 475 3497, *harringtonhall@eircom.net, Fax (01) 475 4544* – ▮ ⇔ TV ✆ P. MC AE ⓓ VISA JCB JZ h
28 rm ☐ 133/173.
◆ Two usefully located mid-terrace Georgian town houses. Friendly and well-run. Bright, spacious bedrooms with soundproofing, ceiling fans, access to fax and internet.

Trinity Lodge without rest., 12 South Frederick St, D2, ✆ (01) 617 0900, *trinitylodge@eircom.net, Fax (01) 617 0999* – ▤ TV. MC AE ⓓ VISA. ✻ JY x
closed 22-27 December – **12 rm** ☐ 95/180.
◆ Elegant Georgian town houses with local landmarks nearby. Spacious, well-furnished bedrooms with good level of comfort. Modern suites and de luxe rooms. Good value.

Eliza Lodge without rest., 23-24 Wellington Quay, D2, ✆ (01) 671 8044, *info@dublinlodge.com, Fax (01) 671 8362,* ← – ▮ ⇔ ▤ TV ✆. MC AE VISA. ✻ JY u
closed 22 December-3 January – **18 rm** ☐ 76/152.
◆ Ideally placed for Temple Bar nightlife. Lounge with video facilities and internet access ; comfortable, practical rooms : the balconied penthouse floor has fine river views. Glass-fronted restaurant facing the Liffey and Millennium Bridge.

Kilronan House without rest., 70 Adelaide Rd, D2, ✆ (01) 475 5266, *info@dublinn.com, Fax (01) 478 2841* – ⇔ TV. MC AE VISA. ✻ DU c
12 rm ☐ 76/170.
◆ Iln the heart of Georgian Dublin, a good value, well-kept town house run by knowledgeable, friendly couple. Individually styled rooms ; sustaining breakfasts.

XXXX **Patrick Guilbaud,** 21 Upper Merrion St, D2, (01) 676 4192, *restaurantpatrickguilbaud@eircom.net, Fax (01) 661 0052* – ⇔ ▤. MC AE ◑ VISA KZ e
✿✿ *closed 1 week Christmas, 17 March, Good Friday, Sunday and Monday* – **Meals** 45 (lunch) and a la carte 80/116 **s.** ♀.
Spec. Pig's trotter carpaccio, Meaux mustard ice cream. Sea bass with artichoke, coriander salad, carrots and cockles. Assiette of chocolate.
◆ Top class restaurant run by consummate professional offering accomplished Irish influenced dishes in elegant Georgian town house. Contemporary Irish art collection.

XXXX **Thornton's** (at The Fitzwilliam H.), 128 St Stephen's Green, D2, (01) 478 7008, *thorntonsrestaurant@eircom.net, Fax (01) 478 7009* – ⇔ ▤ 🚗. MC AE ◑ VISA
✿✿ *closed 1 week Christmas, Sunday and Monday* – **Meals** 30/40 (lunch) and a la carte 91/101 ♀. JZ d
Spec. Sautéed prawns with prawn bisque, truffle sabayon. Suckling pig with trotter, poitin sauce. Fruit parfait pyramid with glazed berries, orange sauce.
◆ Stylish modern restaurant on second floor offers exciting culinary ideas drawing on Irish, French and Italian cuisine, and interesting views too. Good value lunch menus.

XXX **Shanahan's on the Green,** 119 St Stephen's Green, D2, (01) 407 0939, *info@shanahans.ie, Fax (01) 407 0940* – ⇔ ▤. MC AE ◑ VISA JZ p
closed 22 December-12 January – **Meals** (booking essential) (dinner only and Friday lunch) a la carte 69/92 ♀.
◆ Sumptuous Georgian town house : upper floor window tables survey the Green. Supreme comfort enhances your enjoyment of strong seafood dishes and choice cuts of Irish beef.

XXX **L'Ecrivain** (Clarke), 109A Lower Baggot St, D2, (01) 661 1919, *enquiries@lecrivain.com, Fax (01) 661 0617,* 🌳 – ⇔ ▤. MC AE VISA KZ b
✿ *closed 23 December-4 January, Easter, Saturday lunch, Sunday and Bank Holidays* – **Meals** (booking essential) 40/65 and dinner a la carte approx 84.50 ♀.
Spec. Boudin of black pudding with Cashel Blue cheese and cider sorbet. Peppered loin of tuna, red pepper escabèche, avocado and lime purée. Roast rump of lamb, tomato and mint chutney, white onion mousseline.
◆ Soft piano notes add to the welcoming ambience. Robust, well prepared, modern Irish food with emphasis on fish and game. Private dining room has agreeable wine selection.

XXX **Chapter One,** The Dublin Writers Museum, 18-19 Parnell Sq, D1, (01) 873 2266, *info@chapteronerestaurant.com, Fax (01) 873 2330* – ⇔ ▤. MC AE ◑ VISA JX r
closed first 2 weeks August, 24 December-8 January, Sunday and Monday – **Meals** 28.50 (lunch) and dinner a la carte 48/60 🎭 ♀.
◆ In basement of historic building, once home to whiskey baron. Comfortable restaurant with Irish art on walls. Interesting menus focus on good hearty food : sample the oysters.

XX **The Tea Room** (at The Clarence H.), 6-8 Wellington Quay, D2, (01) 407 0813, *tearoom@theclarence.ie, Fax (01) 407 0826* – ⇔. MC AE ◑ VISA HY a
closed 25-26 December and Saturday lunch – **Meals** (booking essential) 32.00/75.00 and dinner a la carte 43/65.50 ♀.
◆ Spacious elegant ground floor room with soaring coved ceiling and stylish contemporary décor offers interesting modern Irish dishes with hint of continental influence.

XX **Halo** (at Morrison H.), Ormond Quay, D1, (01) 887 2421, *Fax (01) 887 2499* – ⇔ ▤. MC AE ◑ VISA HY r
closed lunch Monday-Friday except December – **Meals** 32.00 and a la carte 40/57.95 ♀.
◆ Ultramodern, minimal, split level restaurant designed by John Rocha, offering talented Asian and French influenced cuisine featuring interesting and original dishes.

XX **brownes brasserie** (at brownes townhouse H.), 22 St Stephen's Green, D2, (01) 638 3939, *info@brownesdublin.ie, Fax (01) 638 3900* – ⇔ ▤. MC AE ◑ VISA JZ c
closed Saturday lunch and Bank Holidays – **Meals** (booking essential) a la carte 37.50/69 **s.** ♀.
◆ Smart, characterful, with a Belle Epoque feel. On the ground floor of the eponymous Georgian town house with interesting and appealing classic dishes. A good value location.

XX **The Cellar** (at The Merrion H.), Upper Merrion St, D2, (01) 603 0630, *Fax (01) 603 0700* – ⇔ ▤ 🚗. MC AE ◑ VISA JCB KZ e
closed Saturday lunch – **Meals** 24.95 (lunch) and dinner a la carte 29/60.50 ♀.
◆ Smart open-plan basement restaurant with informal ambience offering well prepared formal style fare crossing Irish with Mediterranean influences. Good value lunch menu.

XX **One Pico,** 5-6 Molesworth Pl, D2, (01) 676 0300, *eamonnoreilly@ireland.com, Fax (01) 676 0411* – ⇔ ▤. MC AE ◑ VISA JZ k
closed 1-14 August, 23 December-7 January and Sunday – **Meals** 25/45 and dinner a la carte 45.35/55.30 ♀.
◆ Wide-ranging cuisine, classic and traditional by turns, always with an elaborate, eclectic edge. Décor and service share a pleasant formality, crisp, modern and stylish.

XX **Les Frères Jacques,** 74 Dame St, D2, ☎ (01) 679 4555, *info@lesfreresjacques.com, Fax (01) 679 4725* – ⋟⋞. MC AE VISA HY x
closed 25 December-2 January, Saturday lunch, Sunday and Bank Holidays – **Meals** - French - 22/35 and a la carte 38.50/66.95 ♀.
◆ Smart popular family-run bistro offering well prepared simple classic French cuisine with fresh fish and seafood a speciality, served by efficient team of French staff.

XX **Number Ten** (at Longfield's H.), 10 Lower Fitzwilliam St, D2, ☎ (01) 676 1367, *Fax (01) 676 1542* – ⋟⋞. MC AE ◑ VISA KZ d
closed Saturday lunch, Sunday and Monday – **Meals** 24.50 (lunch) and dinner a la carte 25.50/42 ♀.
◆ This bijou basement establishment with an atmosphere of understated elegance offers well cooked interesting menus combining traditional European cuisine with local flair.

XX **La Stampa** (at La Stampa H.), 35 Dawson St, D2, ☎ (01) 677 8611, *lastampa@eircom.net, Fax (01) 677 336* – ⋟⋞. MC AE VISA JZ x
closed 24-26 December and Good Friday – **Meals** (booking essential) (dinner only) 32 and a la carte 🎭 ♀.
◆ 19C former ballroom retains its vast mirrors and superbly intricate mosaic ceiling. Flavourful modern Irish dishes. Fine collection of Graham Knuttel originals adorns the bar.

XX **Peploe's,** 16 St Stephen's Green, D2, ☎ (01) 676 3144, *reservations@peploes.com, Fax (01) 676 3154* – ⋟⋞ ▤. MC AE VISA JZ e
closed 25-28 December and 1-2 January – **Meals** a la carte 25.25/41.50.
◆ Fashionable restaurant - a former bank vault - by the Green. Irish wall mural, Italian leather chairs, suede banquettes. Original dishes with pronounced Mediterranean accents.

XX **Saagar,** 16 Harcourt St, D2, ☎ (01) 475 5060, *info@saagarindianrestaurants.com, Fax (01) 475 5741* – ⋟⋞. MC AE ◑ VISA JCB JZ b
closed 25 December, Saturday and Sunday lunch – **Meals** - Indian - a la carte 15.85/23.40.
◆ Well-run restaurant serving subtly toned, freshly prepared Indian fare in basement of Georgian terraced house. Main road setting. Ring bell at foot of stairs to enter.

XX **Locks,** 1 Windsor Terrace, Portobello, D8, ☎ (01) 4543391, *Fax (01) 4538352* – ⋟⋞. MC AE ◑ VISA DU a
closed 25 December-8 January, Saturday lunch, Sunday and Bank Holidays – **Meals** 28.95/48.95 and a la carte 61.45/88.95.
◆ Street corner mainstay for 20 years; watch the swans swimming by on adjacent canal. Offers wide range, from simple one course dishes to more elaborate classic French fare.

XX **Jacobs Ladder,** 4-5 Nassau St, D2, ☎ (01) 670 3865, *dining@jacobsladder.ie, Fax (01) 670 3868* – ⋟⋞. MC AE ◑ VISA KY a
closed 2 weeks Christmas-New Year, 1 week August, 17 March, Sunday, Monday and Bank Holidays – **Meals** (booking essential) 37.00 (dinner) and a la carte 36.50/58.85 **s.** ♀.
◆ Up a narrow staircase, this popular small first floor restaurant with unfussy modern décor and a good view offers good value modern Irish fare and very personable service.

XX **Siam Thai,** 14-15 Andrew St, D2, ☎ (01) 677 3363, *siam@eircom.net, Fax (01) 670 7644* – ⋟⋞. MC AE VISA JCB JY d
closed 25-26 December and Sunday – **Meals** 33 (dinner) and a la carte 26.50/37.
◆ Centrally located restaurant with a warm, homely feel, embodied by woven Thai prints. Basement room for parties. Daily specials; Thai menus with choice and originality.

XX **Jaipur,** 41 South Great George's St, D2, ☎ (01) 677 0999, *dublin@jaipur.ie, Fax (01) 677 0979* – ⋟⋞. MC AE VISA JY a
closed 25-26 December – **Meals** - Indian - (dinner only and lunch Thursday-Saturday) 20 and a la carte 20/40.
◆ Vivid modernity in the city centre; run by knowledgable team. Immaculately laid, linen-clad tables. Interesting, freshly prepared Indian dishes using unique variations.

XX **Bang Café,** 11 Merrion Row, D2, ☎ (01) 676 0898, *Fax (01) 676 0899* – ⋟⋞ ▤. MC AE ◑ VISA KZ a
closed 24 December-5 January, Sunday and Bank Holidays – **Meals** (booking essential) a la carte 21.25/42.10.
◆ Stylish, mirror-lined lounge bar, closely set linen-topped tables and an open kitchen lend a lively, contemporary air. Flavourful menu balances the classical and the creative.

X **Bleu,** Joshua House, Dawson St, D2, ☎ (01) 676 7015, *Fax (01) 676 7027* – ⋟⋞ ▤. MC AE ◑ VISA JZ r
closed 25-26 December – **Meals** 19.95/30 and a la carte 26.85/42.85 **s.** ♀.
◆ Distinctive modern interior serves as chic background to this friendly all-day diner. Appealing bistro fare, well executed and very tasty. Good selection of wines by glass.

Dobbin's, 15 Stephen's Lane, off Lower Mount St, D2, (01) 676 4679, *dobbinswinebistro@eircom.net, Fax (01) 661 3331,* – . EU s
closed 1 week Christmas-New Year, Sunday, Monday dinner, Saturday lunch and Bank Holidays – **Meals** - Bistro - (booking essential) 18.50/24.50 (lunch) and dinner a la carte 52.50/67.
• In the unlikely setting of a former Nissen hut in a residential part of town, this popular restaurant, something of a local landmark, offers good food to suit all tastes.

Pearl Brasserie, 20 Merrion St Upper, D2, (01) 661 3572, *info@pearl-brasserie.com, Fax (01) 661 3629* – . KZ n
closed first week January, lunch Saturday-Monday and Bank Holidays – **Meals** - French - 25 (lunch) and dinner a la carte 32/51.50.
• A metal staircase leads down to this intimate, vaulted cellar brasserie and oyster bar. Franco-Irish dishes served at granite-topped tables. Amiable and helpful service.

The Bistro, 4-5 Castlemarket, D2, (01) 671 5430, *Fax (01) 6703379,* – . JY c
closed 25-26 December, 1 January and Good Friday – **Meals** a la carte 23.50/50.00.
• Friendly and buzzing in the heart of the city. Exposed floor boards, coir carpeting and vividly coloured walls. Additional terrace area. Interesting, modern dishes.

Eden, Meeting House Sq, Temple Bar, D2, (01) 670 5372, *Fax (01) 670 3330,* – . HY e
closed 25-30 December and Bank Holidays – **Meals** 19/24 (lunch) and dinner a la carte 29.50/44.50.
• Modern minimalist restaurant with open plan kitchen serves good robust food. Terrace overlooks theatre square, at the heart of a busy arty district. Children welcome.

Mermaid Café, 69-70 Dame St, D2, (01) 670 8236, *info@mermaid.ie, Fax (01) 670 8205* – . HY d
closed 25-26 and 31 December, 1 January and Good Friday – **Meals** (booking essential) 23.95 (lunch) and a la carte 34.85/49.85.
• This small informal restaurant with unfussy décor and wood floors offers an interesting and well cooked selection of robust modern dishes. Good service.

Cafe Mao, 2-3 Chatham Row, D2, (01) 670 4899, *info@cafemao.com* – . JZ r
closed Good Friday and 25-26 December – **Meals** - South East Asian - (bookings not accepted) a la carte 25.85/31.20.
• Well run trendy modern restaurant serving authentic southeast Asian fusion cuisine in an informal setting buzzing with action and atmosphere. Tasty food at tasty prices.

La Maison des Gourmets, 15 Castlemarket, D2, (01) 672 7258, *lamaison@indigo.ie, Fax (01) 864 5672* – . JY c
closed 1 week Christmas, Sunday and Bank Holidays – **Meals** (lunch only) a la carte 19/26.50 **s.**
• Simple, snug restaurant on the first floor above an excellent bakery offering high quality breads and pastries. Extremely good value meals using fine local ingredients.

The Cellar Bar (at The Merrion H.), Upper Merrion St, D2, (01) 603 0631, *info@merrionhotel.com, Fax (01) 603 0700* – . KZ e
Meals (live music Sunday brunch) (lunch only) (carving lunch) a la carte 23.25/28.75.
• Characterful stone and brick bar-restaurant in the original vaulted cellars with large wood bar. Popular with Dublin's social set. Offers wholesome Irish pub lunch fare.

Ballsbridge

Dublin 4.

Four Seasons, Simmonscourt Rd, D4, (01) 665 4000, *sales.dublin@fourseasons.com, Fax (01) 665 4099,* , , , , – – 800. FU e
***Seasons* : Meals** 28/65 (dinner) and a la carte 56/73 **s.** – ***The Cafe* : Meals** a la carte 36/54 **s.** – 28 – **192 rm** 355/435, 67 suites 670/2200.
• Every inch the epitome of international style - supremely comfortable rooms with every facility ; richly furnished lounge ; a warm mix of antiques, oils and soft piano études. Dining in Seasons guarantees luxury ingredients. Informal comforts in The Café.

The Berkeley Court, Lansdowne Rd, D4, (01) 6653200, *berkeleycourt@jurysdoyle.com, Fax (01) 6617238* – – 450.
***Berkeley Room* : Meals** *(closed Saturday lunch and Sunday dinner)* 33 (lunch) and a la carte 37.95/50.60 **s.** – ***Palm Court Café* : Meals** a la carte approx 27.50 **s.** – 24 – **182 rm** 275/380, 5 suites. FU c
• Luxurious international hotel in former botanical gardens ; two minutes from the home of Irish rugby. Large amount of repeat business. Solidly formal feel throughout. Berkeley Room for elegant fine dining. Breakfast buffets a feature of Palm Court Café.

The Towers, Lansdowne Rd, D4, (01) 667 0033, *towers@jurysdoyle.com, Fax (01) 660 5324*, heated – . **Meals** 50 – 20 – **100 rm** 260/350, 4 suites. FU p
◆ Comfortable, unstintingly equipped bedrooms, in keeping with the discreet service and the air of pleasing exclusivity. Private cocktail lounge, and use of Jurys facilities. Classic formal dining room with rich elegant décor.

Jurys Ballsbridge, Pembroke Rd, D4, (01) 660 5000, *ballsbridge@jurysdoyle.com, Fax (01) 660 5540*, heated – , rest, – 800. FU p
Meals 50 – 20 – **300** 295, 3 suites.
◆ Well located hotel popular with business people. Bustling glass roofed lobby. Large well appointed rooms. Long-running Irish cabaret. Relaxed Raglans proud of its real Irish dishes.

Herbert Park, D4, (01) 667 2200, *reservations@herbertparkhotel.ie, Fax (01) 667 2595*, – – 100. FU m
***The Pavilion* : Meals** *(closed dinner Sunday and Monday)* 23.50 (lunch) and dinner a la carte 37/53 **s.** – 19 – **150 rm** 230/275, 3 suites.
◆ Stylish contemporary hotel. Spacious, open, modern lobby and lounges. Excellent, well-designed rooms with tasteful décor. Some offer views of park. Good business facilities. French-windowed restaurant with al fresco potential ; oyster/lobster specialities.

The Wingate Hibernian, Eastmoreland Pl, D4, (01) 668 7666, *info@hibernianhotel.com, Fax (01) 660 2655* – – 30. EU x
closed 24-28 December – ***Patrick Kavanagh Room* : Meals** *(closed Sunday)* 17/35 and a la carte approx 27 – **41 rm** 120/270.
◆ Stately Victorian red brick house in suburbs which prides itself on its hospitality. Traditional, comfortable rooms with warmly elegant fittings. Small sun lounge. Well-presented modern European and Irish cuisine in restaurant.

The Schoolhouse, 2-8 Northumberland Rd, D4, (01) 667 5014, *reservations@schoolhousehotel.com, Fax (01) 667 5015*, – .
closed 24-26 December – ***The Canteen* : Meals** (bar lunch Saturday and Sunday) a la carte 22/42 – **31 rm** 165/300. EU a
◆ Spacious converted 19C schoolhouse, close to canal, boasts modernity and charm. Rooms contain locally crafted furniture. Inkwell bar has impressive split-level seating area. Old classroom now a large restaurant with beamed ceilings.

Ariel House without rest., 50-54 Lansdowne Rd, D4, (01) 668 5512, *reservations@ariel-house.net, Fax (01) 668 5845* – . FU n
closed 23-27 December – **37 rm** 99/150.
◆ Restored, listed Victorian mansion in smart suburb houses personally run, traditional small hotel. Rooms feature period décor and original antiques ; some four poster beds.

Bewley's, Merrion Rd, D4, (01) 668 1111, *bb@bewleyshotels.com, Fax (01) 668 1999*, – , rest, – 30. FU a
closed 24-26 December – ***O'Connells*** *((01) 647 3400)* **: Meals** (carvery lunch)/dinner 25/32.50 and a la carte 24.85/35.40 – 9.90 – **220 rm** 99.
◆ Huge hotel offers stylish modern accommodation behind sumptuous Victorian façade of former Masonic school. Location, facilities and value for money make this a good choice. Informal modern O'Connells restaurant, cleverly constructed with terrace in stairwell.

Butlers Town House, 44 Lansdowne Rd, D4, (01) 667 4022, *info@butlers-hotel.com, Fax (01) 667 3960* – . FU v
closed 23 December-10 January – **Meals** (room service only) – **20 rm** 145/195.
◆ Restored red brick town house in heart of embassy quarter. Individually styled rooms designed to recreate Victorian atmosphere while offering modern facilities and comfort.

Aberdeen Lodge, 53-55 Park Ave, D4, (01) 283 8155, *aberdeen@iol.ie, Fax (01) 283 7877*, – . GV e
Meals (light meals) (residents only) a la carte 23/33.50 – **17 rm** 99/140.
◆ Neat red brick house in smart residential suburb. Comfortable rooms with Edwardian style décor in neutral tones, wood furniture and modern facilities. Some garden views. Comfortable, traditionally decorated dining room.

Pembroke Townhouse without rest., 90 Pembroke Rd, D4, (01) 660 0277, *info@pembroketownhouse.ie, Fax (01) 660 0291* – .
closed 20 December-2 January – **48 rm** 165/210. FU d
◆ Period-inspired décor adds to the appeal of a sensitively modernised, personally run Georgian terrace town house in the smart suburbs. Neat, up-to-date accommodation.

Waterloo House without rest., 8-10 Waterloo Rd, D4, (01) 660 1888, *waterloohouse@eircom.ie, Fax (01) 667 1955*, – . EU p
closed 23-28 December – **17 rm** 59/165.
◆ Pair of imposing Georgian town houses. Elegant breakfast room with conservatory. Large comfortable rooms with coordinated heavy drapes and fabrics in warm modern colours.

Merrion Hall, 54-56 Merrion Rd, D4, ✆ (01) 668 1426, *merrionhall@iol.ie*, *Fax (01) 668 4280*, – ⫶ ⇹ ▤ TV ☏ P – 40. MC AE DC VISA. FU b
Meals (light meals) (residents only) a la carte 23/33.50 **s.** – **30 rm** 99/140, 4 suites.
• Red brick house on main road in suburbs. Welcoming lounge with open fires and homely ornaments. Well-equipped, pastel hued bedrooms with modern facilities.

Glenogra House without rest., 64 Merrion Rd, D4, ✆ (01) 668 3661, *glenogra@indigo.ie, Fax (01) 668 3698* – TV P. MC AE VISA. FU w
closed 1 week Christmas – **12 rm** 75/115.
• Neat and tidy bay windowed house in smart suburb. Personally run guesthouse with bedrooms attractively decorated in keeping with a period property. Modern facilities.

Anglesea Town House without rest., 63 Anglesea Rd, D4, ✆ (01) 668 3877, *helen@63anglesea.com, Fax (01) 668 3461* – TV. MC AE VISA. FV x
7 rm 80/140.
• Red brick Edwardian residence in smart suburb with many pieces of fine period furniture. Individually styled rooms with good facilities. Parking can be a challenge.

66 Townhouse without rest., 66 Northumberland Rd, D4, ✆ (01) 660 0333, *Fax (01) 660 1051* – TV P. MC VISA. FU z
closed 23 December-6 January – **8 rm** 70/120.
• Attractive Victorian red brick house with extension in smart suburb. Comfortable homely atmosphere. Good size rooms with tasteful décor and modern facilities.

Siam Thai, Sweepstake Centre, D4, ✆ (01) 660 1722, *siam@eircom.net* – ▤. MC AE VISA FU h
closed 25-26 December, lunch Saturday and Sunday and Good Friday – **Meals** - Thai - 17.95/45 and a la carte 29.95/39.
• Unerringly busy restaurant that combines comfort with liveliness. Smart waiters serve authentic Thai cuisine, prepared with skill and understanding. Good value lunches.

Roly's Bistro, 7 Ballsbridge Terrace, D4, ✆ (01) 668 2611, *ireland@rolysbistro.ie*, *Fax (01) 660 8535* – ▤. MC AE DC VISA FU r
closed Christmas – **Meals** (booking essential) 18.95 (lunch) and a la carte 33.95/46.95 .
• A Dublin institution : this roadside bistro is very busy and well run, with a buzzy, fun atmosphere. Its two floors offer modern Irish dishes and a very good value lunch.

Bella Cuba, 11 Ballsbridge Terrace, D4, ✆ (01) 660 5539, *info@bella-cuba.com*, *Fax (01) 660 5539* – . MC AE VISA FU r
closed 25 December – **Meals** - Cuban - (booking essential) (dinner only and lunch Thursday-Friday) 20/25 (lunch) and a la carte 26.65/37.75 **s.** .
• Family-owned restaurant with an intimate feel. Cuban memoirs on walls, fine choice of cigars. Authentic Cuban dishes, employing many of the island's culinary influences.

Donnybrook
Dublin 4.

Marble Hall without rest., 81 Marlborough Rd, D4, ✆ (01) 497 7350, *marblehall@eircom.net* – TV P. EV a
closed 21 December-5 January – **3 rm** 65/100.
• Georgian townhouse with effusive welcome guaranteed. Individually styled throughout, with plenty of antiques and quality soft furnishings. Stylish, warmly decorated bedrooms.

Ernie's, Mulberry Gdns, off Morehampton Rd, D4, ✆ (01) 269 3300, *Fax (01) 269 3260* – ▤. MC AE DC VISA FV k
closed 1 week Christmas-New Year, Saturday lunch, Sunday and Monday – **Meals** 15.50/38 and dinner a la carte 22/57.50 .
• Discreet professionally run restaurant in tranquil location offering classic Irish fare. Bright room with garden aspect, modern feel and contemporary Irish art collection.

Ranelagh *Dublin.*

Mint, 47 Ranelagh, D6, ✆ (01) 497 8655, *Fax (01) 497 9035* – ▤. MC AE VISA EV e
closed Monday and Bank Holidays – **Meals** 25.00 (lunch) and dinner a la carte 37.50/49.50.
• Modern, minimalist restaurant south of city centre. Mix of banquettes and slim, beige leather chairs. Modern fine dining, with French influences to the fore.

Rathgar
Dublin 6.

St Aiden's without rest., 32 Brighton Rd, D6, ✆ (01) 490 2011, *staidens@eircom.net*, *Fax (01) 492 0234* – TV P. MC VISA. DV n
closed 22-31 December – **8 rm** 65/110.
• Friendly, family run guesthouse in early Victorian mid-terrace. Comfortable lounge with tea, coffee and books. Ample rooms with simple décor and furniture. Good facilities.

Rathmines
Dublin 6.

Uppercross House, 26-30 Upper Rathmines Rd, D6, (01) 4975486, *enquiries@uppercrosshousehotel.com, Fax (01) 4975361* – closed 24-28 December – ***The Restaurant :*** **Meals** (dinner only and lunch Saturday-Sunday) a la carte 25/33 – **50 rm** 85/130. DV d
Privately run suburban hotel in three adjacent town houses with modern extension wing. Good size rooms and standard facilities. Live music midweek in traditional Irish bar. Restaurant offers a mellow and friendly setting with welcoming wood décor.

Zen, 89 Upper Rathmines Rd, D6, (01) 4979428, *Fax (01) 4979428* – DV t
closed 25-27 December – **Meals** - Chinese (Szechuan) - (dinner only and lunch Thursday, Friday and Sunday) 15 (lunch) and a la carte 24/30 **s.**
Renowned Chinese restaurant in the unusual setting of an old church hall. Imaginative, authentic oriental cuisine with particular emphasis on spicy Szechuan dishes.

Terenure *Dublin.*
Dublin 6.

Vermilion, 1st Floor above Terenure Inn, 94-96 Terenure Road North, D6, South : 6 m. by N 81 (01) 499 1400, *mail@vermilion.ie, Fax (01) 499 1300* –
closed 25-26 December and Good Friday – **Meals** - Indian - (dinner only and Sunday lunch) a la carte 27.40/44.85.
Smart restaurant above a busy pub in a residential part of town. Vividly coloured dining room and efficient service. Well-balanced, modern Indian food with a Keralan base.

at Dublin Airport *North : 6 ½ m. by N 1 DU and M 1 – Dublin*

Crowne Plaza, Northwood Park, Santry Demesne, Santry, D9, South : 2 m. on R 132 (01) 862 8888, *info@crowneplazadublin.ie, Fax (01) 862 8800,* – 240.
Touzai : **Meals** - Asian influences - *(closed Saturday lunch)* (buffet lunch)/dinner 16.95/40 **s.** – ***Cinnabar :*** **Meals** a la carte 26.45/38.90 – 21 – **202 rm** 295/315, 2 suites.
Next to Fingal Park, two miles from the airport. Hotel has predominant Oriental style, extensive meeting facilities, and modern, well-equipped rooms, some of Club standard. Touzai for Asian specialities. Stylish Cinnabar has extensive, eclectic menu range.

Great Southern, (01) 844 6000, *res@dubairport-gsh.com, Fax (01) 844 6001* – 450.
closed 24-26 December – ***Potters :*** **Meals** 15/25 and dinner a la carte 26.50/37.45 **s.** – ***O'Deas Bar :*** **Meals** (carvery lunch)/dinner a la carte 19.65/29 **s.** – 15 – **227 rm** 262.50, 2 suites.
Modern hotel catering for international and business travellers. Range of guest rooms, all spacious and smartly furnished with wood furniture and colourful fabrics. Potters has a spacious, formal feel. O'Deas Bar for intimate carvery menus.

Holiday Inn Dublin Airport, (01) 808 0500, *reservations-dublinairport@ichotelsgroup.com, Fax (01) 844 6002* – rest, – 130.
Bistro : **Meals** a la carte 18/29 **s.** – ***Sampan's :*** **Meals** - Asian - *(closed Bank Holidays)* (dinner only) a la carte 18/29 **s.** – 19 – **247 rm** 214.
Modern commercial hotel offers standard or Millennium rooms, all with colourful feel and good facilities. Free use of leisure centre. Live music at weekends in Bodhran bar. Informal Bistro restaurant with monthly themed menus. Oriental specials at Sampan's.

at Clontarf *Northeast : 3 ½ m. by R 105 KX – Dublin*

Clontarf Castle, Castle Ave, D3, (01) 833 2321, *info@clontarfcastle.ie, Fax (01) 833 2279,* – 500.
closed 25 December – ***Templars Bistro :*** **Meals** (carvery lunch Monday-Saturday)/dinner a la carte 28.35/35.50 – 20 – **108 rm** 250/285, 3 suites.
Set in an historic castle, partly dating back to 1172. Striking medieval style entrance lobby. Modern rooms and characterful luxury suites, all with cutting edge facilities. Restaurant with grand medieval style décor reminiscent of a knights' banqueting hall.

at Stillorgan *Southeast : 5 m. on N 11 GV – Dublin*

Radisson SAS St Helen's, Stillorgan Rd, D4, (01) 218 6000, *info.dublin@radissonsas.com, Fax (01) 218 6010,* – 350.
Talavera : **Meals** - Italian - (dinner only) 38.50 and a la carte 29.70/51 – 24 – **130 rm** 350/750, 21 suites.
Imposing part 18C mansion with substantial extensions and well laid out gardens. Well run with good level of services. Smart modern rooms with warm feel and all facilities. Delicious antipasti table at basement Talavera.

Stillorgan Park, Stillorgan Rd, (01) 288 1621, *sales@stillorganpark.com, Fax (01) 283 1610* – 600.
closed 24-25 December – ***Purple Sage :*** **Meals** (carvery lunch)/dinner 36.50 and a la carte approx 27.95 **s.** – **125 rm** 170/195.
• Modern commercial hotel in southside city suburb. Spacious rooms with modern facilities. Interesting horse theme décor in large stone floored bar with buffet. Purple Sage restaurant with mosaics, frescos and hidden alcoves.

at Monkstown *Southeast : 6 ½ m. by R 118* GV – *Dublin*

Siam Thai, 8a The Crescent, (01) 284 3309, *corcorantm@eircom.net, Fax (01) 4935841* –
Meals - Thai - (dinner only) 20/30 and a la carte approx 30.
• Popular Thai restaurant on main street opposite a church. Cosy interior with dark glossy décor and friendly ambience. Full range of authentic and popular Thai cuisine.

at Foxrock *Southeast : 7 ½ m. by N 11* GV – *Dublin*

Bistro One, 3 Brighton Rd, D18, (01) 289 7711, *bistroone@eircom.ie, Fax (01) 289 9858* –
closed 25 December-2 January, Sunday and Monday – **Meals** (booking essential) (dinner only) a la carte 32/43.
• Pleasantly set in residential area. Homely, with beams and walls of wine racks. Simple menu offers well-prepared classic Irish fare and Italian or Asian influenced dishes.

Bewleys, Central Park, D18, (01) 293 5000, *leop@bewleyshotels.com, Fax (01) 293 5099* – rest, – 30.
closed 24-26 December – ***Brasserie :*** **Meals** *(closed Saturday lunch)* (carvery lunch)/dinner 25 and a la carte 27.50/33 – 11 – **306 rm** 79.
• Handily placed next to racecourse, this modern hotel boasts smart bar with leather armchairs, decked terrace, and comfy, uniform bedrooms with good facilities. Informal brasserie with neutral, stylish tones.

at Clondalkin *Southwest : 8 m. by N 7* HY *on R 113* – *Dublin*

Red Cow Moran, Naas Rd, D22, Southeast : 2 m. on N 7 at junction with M 50 (01) 459 3650, *info@morangroup.ie, Fax (01) 459 1588* – – 700.
closed 24-26 December – ***The Winter Garden :*** **Meals** 20/25 (lunch) and dinner a la carte 36/46 **s.** – **120 rm** 185/250, 3 suites.
• Splendid sweeping lobby staircase gives a foretaste of this smart commercial hotel's mix of traditional elegance and modern design. Landmark Red Cow inn and Diva nightclub. Large characterful Winter Garden restaurant with bare brick walls and warm wood floor.

Bewley's H. Newlands Cross, Newlands Cross, Naas Rd (N 7), D22, (01) 464 0140, *res@bewleyshotels.com, Fax (01) 464 0900* – rest,
closed 24-26 December – **Meals** (carving lunch)/dinner 25 and a la carte 25/35 – 6.95 – **258 rm** 79.
• Well run, busy, commercial hotel popular with business people. Spacious rooms with modern facilities can also accommodate families. Represents good value for money. Large, busy café-restaurant with traditional dark wood fittings and colourful décor.

Italy

Italia

ROME – FLORENCE – MILAN – NAPLES
PALERMO – TAORMINA – TURIN – VENICE

PRACTICAL INFORMATION

LOCAL CURRENCY

1 euro (€) = 1,34 USD ($) (Dec 2004)

TOURIST INFORMATION

Welcome Office *(Azienda Promozione Turistica):*
– Via Parigi 5 - 00185 ROMA (closed Saturday afternoon and Sunday), ✆ 06 36 00 43 99, Fax 06 481 93 16
– Via Marconi 1 - 20123 MILANO, ✆ 02 72 52 43 01, Fax 02 72 52 43 50
See also telephone number and address of other Tourist Information offices in the text of the towns under **ℹ**.
American Express:
– Largo Caduti di El Alamein 9 - 00173 ROMA, ✆ 06 722801, Fax 06 72 22 30
– Via Larga 4 - 20122 MILANO, ✆ 02 72 10 41, Fax 02 89 00 990
National Holiday in Italy: *25 April.*

AIRLINES

ALITALIA: *Via Bissolati 13 - 00187 ROMA, ✆ 06 656 28 331, Fax 06 656 28 441*
Via Albricci 5 - 20122 MILANO, ✆ 02 24992700, Fax 02 805 67 57

AIR FRANCE: *Via Sardegna 40 - 00187 ROMA, ✆ 848884466, Fax 06 483803*
Piazza Cavour 2 - 20121 MILANO, ✆ 02 760731, Fax 02 760 73 355

DELTA AIRLINES: *via Malpensa 2000 - 20100 MILANO, ✆ 02 58 58 11 23, Fax 02 58 58 10 68*

FOREIGN EXCHANGE

Money can be changed at the Banca d'Italia, other banks and authorised exchange offices (Banks close at 1.30pm and at weekends).

POSTAL SERVICES

Local post offices: *open Monday to Friday 8.30am to 2.00pm (Saturday to noon)*

General Post Office *(open 24 hours only for telegrams):*
– Viale Europa 190 00144 ROMA – Piazza Cordusio 20123 MILANO

SHOPPING

In the index of street names, those printed in red are where the principal shops are found. In Rome, the main shopping streets are: Via del Babuino, Via Condotti, Via Frattina, Via Vittorio Veneto; in Milan: Via Dante, Via Manzoni, Via Monte Napoleone, Corso Vittorio Emanuele, Via della Spiga, Via Torino.

BREAKDOWN SERVICE

Certain garages in the centre and outskirts of towns operate a 24 hour breakdown service. If you break down the police are usually able to help by indicating the nearest one.

TIPPING

As well as the service charge, it is the custom to tip employees. The amount can vary depending upon the region and the service given.

SPEED LIMITS

On motorways, the maximum permitted speed is 130 km/h - 80 mph. On other roads, the speed limit is 90 km/h - 55 mph.

ROME
(ROMA)

00100 563 Q 19 38 – Pop. 2 540 829 – alt. 20.

Distances from Rome are indicated in the text of the other towns listed in this Guide.

via Parigi 5 ✉ 00185 ☎ 06 36 00 43 99, Fax 06 481 93 16 ;

A.C.I. *via Cristoforo Colombo 261 ✉ 00147 ☎ 06 514 971 and via Marsala 8 ✉ 00185 ☎ 06 49981, Fax 06 499 822 34.*

18 and 9 Parco de' Medici (closed Tuesday) ✉ 00148 Roma SW : 4,5 km ☎ 06 655 34 77 – Fax 06 655 33 44.

18 Parco di Roma via Due Ponti 110 ✉ 00191 Roma N : 4,5 km. ☎ 06 33 65 33 96, Fax 06 33 66 09 31.

18 and 9 Marco Simone at Guidonia Montecelio ✉ 00012 Roma W : 7 km ☎ 0774 366 469, Fax 0774 366 476.

18 and 9 Arco di Costantino (closed Monday) ✉ 00188 Roma N : 15 km ☎ 06 33 62 44 40, Fax 06 33 61 29 19.

18 and 9 (closed Monday) at Olgiata ✉ 00123 Roma NW : 19 km ☎ 06 308 89 141, Fax 06 308 89 968.

18 Fioranello (closed Wednesday) at Santa Maria delle Mole ✉ 00040 Roma SE : 19 km ☎ 06 713 80 80, Fax 06 713 82 12.

Ciampino SW : 15 km ☎ 794941.

Leonardo da Vinci di Fiumicino SE : 26 km ☎ 06 65631.

SIGHTS

How to make the most of a trip to Rome – some ideas :

Borghese Gallery★★★ – Villa Giulia★★★ DS *– Catacombs★★★ – Santa Sabina★★* MZ *– Villa Borghese★★* NOU *– Baths of Caracalla★★★* ET *– St Lawrence Without the Walls★★* FST **E** *– St Paul Without the Walls★★ – Old Appian Way★★ – National Gallery of Modern Art★* DS **M**[7] *– Mausoleum of Caius Cestius★* DT *– St Paul's Gate★* DT **B** *– San'Agnese and Santa Costanza★* FS **C** *– Santa Croce in Gerusalemme★* FT **D** *– San Saba★* ET *– E.U.R.★ – Museum of Roman Civilisation★★.*

ANCIENT ROME

Colosseum★★★ OYZ *– Roman Forum★★★* NOY *– Basilica of Maxentius★★★* OY **B** *– Imperial Fora★★★* NY *– Trajan's Column★★★* NY **C** *– Palatine Hill★★★* NOYZ *– Pantheon★★★* MVX *– Largo Argentina Sacred Precinct★★* MY *– Altar of Augustus★★* LU *– Domus Aurea★★* PY *– Temple of Apollo Sosianus★★* MY **X** *– Theatre of Marcellus★★* MY *– Tempio della Fortuna Virile★* MZ **Y** *– Tempio di Vesta★* MZ **Z** *– Isola Tiberina★* MY.

CHRISTIAN ROME

Gesù Church★★★ MY *– St Mary Major★★★* PX *– St John Lateran★★★* FT *– Santa Maria d'Aracoeli★★* NY **A** *– San Luigi dei Francesi★★* LV *– Sant'Andrea al Quirinale★★* OV **F** *–*

*St Charles at the Four Fountains*** OV **K** – *St Clement's Basilica*** PZ – *Sant'Ignazio*** MV **L** – *Santa Maria degli Angeli*** PV **N** – *Santa Maria della Vittoria*** PV – *Santa Susanna*** OV – *Santa Maria in Cosmedin*** MNZ – *Basilica of St Mary in Trastevere*** KZ **S** – *Santa Maria sopra Minerva*** MX **V** – *Santa Maria del Popolo*** MU **D** – *New Church** KX – *Sant'Agostino** LV **G** – *St Peter in Chains** OY – *Santa Cecilia** MZ – *San Pietro in Montorio** JZ ≤ *** – *Sant'Andrea della Valle*** LY **Q** – *Santa Maria della Pace** KV **R**.

PALACES AND MUSEUMS

*Capitoline Museums**** *; New Palace**** NY **H** – *Castel Sant'Angelo**** JKV – *National Roman Museum**** *: Aula Ottagona**** PV **M^9**, *Palazzo Massimo alle Terme* PV *and Altemps Palace**** KLV – *Chancery Palace*** KX **A** – *Farnese Palace*** KY – *Quirinal Palace*** NOV – *Barberini Palace*** OV – *Villa Farnesina*** KY – *Palazzo Venezia** MY **M^3** – *Palazzo Braschi** KX **M^4** – *Palazzo Doria Pamphili** MX **M^5** – *Palazzo Spada** KY – *Museo Napoleanico** KV.

THE VATICAN

*St Peter's Square**** HV – *St Peter's Basilica**** *(Dome* ≤ ****)* GV – *Vatican Museums**** *(Sistine Chapel*****)* GHUV – *Vatican Gardens**** GV.

PRETTY AREAS

Pincian Hill ≤ *** MU – *Capitol Square**** MNY – *Spanish Square**** MNU – *Piazza Navona**** LVX – *Fountain of the Rivers**** LV **E** – *Trevi Fountain**** NV – *Victor Emmanuel II Monument (Vittoriano)* ≤ ** MNY – *Quirinale Square*** NV – *Piazza del Popolo*** MU – *Gianicolo** JY – *Via dei Coronari** KV – *Ponte Sant'Angelo** JKV – *Piazza Bocca della Verità** MNZ – *Piazza Campo dei Fiori** KY **28** – *Piazza Colonna** MV **46** – *Porta Maggiore** FT – *Piazza Venezia** MNY.

INDEX OF STREET NAMES IN ROMA

4 Novembre (V.) 11 NX 201
20 Settembre (V.) 8 PU
24 Maggio (V.) 7 NX
30 Aprile (Viale) 10 JZ 202
Acaia (V.) 4 FT
Adriana (Pza) 6 JKV
Albania (Pza) 11 NZ
Albenga (V.) 4 FT 4
Alberteschi (Lungotevere) 11 MZ 6
Aldrovandi (V. U.) 4 ES
Altoviti (Lungotevere degli) 6 JV 7
Amba Aradam (V. d.) 12 PZ
Angelico (Viale) 5 HU
Anguillara (Lungotevere d.) 11 LY 9
Aosta (V.) 4 FT 10
Arenula (V.) 11 LY
Armi (Lungotev. d.) 3 DS
Augusta (Lungotevere in) 6 LU
Aurelia Antica (V.) 9 GZ
Aventino (Lungotev.) 11 MZ
Aventino (Viale) 11 NZ
Babuino (V. del) 7 MU
Baccelli (Viale Guido) 4 ET 12
Banchi Nuovi (V. d.) 6 KV 13
Banchi Vecchi (V. d.) 6 KX 15
Banco S. Spirito (V. d.) 6 JV 16
Barberini (V.) 8 OV
Bari (V.) 4 FS
Barletta (V.) 5 HU
Barrili (V.) 3 CT
Bassi (V. U.) 10 JZ
Battisti (V. C.) 11 NX 19
Beccaria (V. C.) 7 LU
Belle Arti (Viale d.) 3 DS
Belli (Pza G. G.) 10 LYZ 21
Bissolati (V. L.) 8 OU
Bocca della Verità (Pza della) 11 NZ
Boncompagni (V.) 8 OPU
Bonghi (V. R.) 12 PY
Botteghe Oscure (V. d.) 11 MY 22
Brasile (Piazzale) 7 OU
Brescia (Lungotev. A. da) 6 KU
Britannia (V.) 4 FT 24
Brofferio (V. A.) 6 JU
Buozzi (Viale B.) 4 ES
Busiri-Vici (V. A.) 9 HZ 25
Cadlolo (V. A.) 3 CS
Calabria (V.) 7 PU 27
Campania (V.) 8 OPU
Campidoglio (Pza d.) 11 MY
Campo dei Fiori (Pza) 10 KY 28
Candia (V.) 5 GU
Canonica (Viale P.) 7 NU
Cappellari (V. d.) 6 KX 30
Caravita (V.) 7 MV 31
Carini (V. G.) 6 JZ
Carso (Viale) 3 CS
Casilina (V.) 4 FT 33
Castello (Lungotev.) 6 KV 34
Castrense (Viale) 4 FT 36
Castro Pretorio (Viale) 4 FS 37
Catania (V.) 4 FS
Cavalieri di Vittorio Veneto (Viale d.) 3 CS 39
Cavalli Marini (Vle d.) 4 ES 40
Cavour (Ponte) 6 KV
Cavour (Pza) 6 KV
Cavour (V.) 12 OY
Cenci (Lungotev. d.) 11 MY
Cerchi (V. d.) 11 NZ
Cesi (V. F.) 6 KU
Cestio (Ponte) 11 MZ
Chiana (V.) 4 FS
Cicerone (V.) 6 KU
Cinque Lune (Pza) 6 LV 43
Cinquecento (Pza d.) 8 PV
Cipro (V.) 5 GU
Circo Massimo (V. d.) 11 NZ
Claudia (V.) 12 PZ
Clementino (V. d.) 7 MV 45
Clodia (Circonvallazione) 3 CS
Collina (V.) 8 PU
Colonna (Pza) 7 MV 46
Colonna (V. M. A.) 6 JKU
Colonna (V. V.) 6 KV 48
Conciliazione (V. d.) 6 JV
Condotti (V. dei) 7 MV
Consolazione (V. d.) 11 NY 49
Conte Verde (V.) 4 FT 51
Coronari (V. dei) 6 KV
Corridoni (V. F.) 3 CS 52
Corridori (V. d.) 5 HV 54
Corso (V. dell) 7 MU
Crescenzio (V.) 6 JU
Damiata (V.) 6 JU
Dandolo (V.) 10 KZ
D'Annunzio (Vle G.) 7 MU 55
De Rossi (V. G. B.) 4 FS
Della Rovere (Pza) 6 JV 57
Depretis (V. A.) 8 PV
Dezza (V. G.) 9 HZ
Dogana Vecchia (V. della) 7 LV 58
Domus Aurea (V.) 12 PY
Doria (V. Andrea) 5 GU
Druso (V.) 4 ET
Due Macelli (V.) 7 NV
Duilio (V.) 6 JU 60
Einaudi (Viale L.) 8 PV 61
Eleniana (V.) 4 FT 63
Emo (V. A.) 5 GU
Eroi (Piazzale d.) 5 GU
Esquilino (Pza d.) 8 PV
Etruria (V.) 4 FT
Fabricio (Ponte) 11 MY 64
Farnesina (Lungotevere d.) 10 KY
Fedro (V.) 3 CS
Felice (V. C.) 4 FT
Ferrari (V. G.) 6 JU
Ferratella in Laterano (V. d.) 4 ET 67
Filiberto (V. E.) 4 FT 69
Fiorentini (Lungotevere d.) 6 JV 70
Fiume (Pza) 7 PU
Flaminia (V.) 7 LU 73
Flaminio (Lungotev.) 3 DS
Florida (V.) 11 MY
Fontanella Borghese (V.) 7 MV 76

Fonteiana (V.) 9 GZ
Fori Imperiali (V. d.) 12 OY
Fornaci (V. d.) 9 HYZ
Foro Olitorio (V. d.) 11 MY 78
Franklin (V. B.) 3 DT
Frattina (V.) 7 MV
Gallia (V.) 12 PZ
Galvani (V.) 3 DT
Garibaldi (Ponte) 10 LY 81
Garibaldi (V.) 10 JY
Gelsomini (Viale) 3 DT 82
Germanico (V.) 6 JU
Gianicolense (Lungotevere) 6 JX
Gianicolo (Passeggiata di) 9 HY
Gianicolo (V. d.) 5 HX 85
Giolitti (V.) 4 FT
Giotto (Viale) 4 ET
Giovannelli (V. R.) 4 ES 87
Giubbonari (V. dei) 10 LY
Giulia (V.) 10 KY
Giuliana (V. dei) 5 GU
Giulio Cesare (Viale) 6 JU
Glorioso (Viale) 10 KZ
Gomenizza (V.) 3 CS
Gorizia (Viale) 4 FS
Governo Vecchio (V. d.) 6 KV 88
Gracchi (V. d.) 6 JU
Greca (V. d.) 11 MZ 90
Gregorio VII (Viale) 9 GY
Induno (V. G.) 10 KZ
Ippocrate (Viale) 4 FS
Ipponio (V.) 12 PZ
Italia (Cso d') 7 PU
Jugario (Vico) 11 MY 91
La Malfa (Piazzale U.) 11 NZ
La Spezia (V.) 4 FT
Labicana (V.) 12 PZ
Lanciani (V. R.) 4 FS
Lanza (V. G.) 12 PY
Lepanto (V.) 6 JU
Libertà (Pza d.) 6 KU
Liegi (Viale) 4 ES
Lucania (V.) 7 PU 94
Lucce (V. d.) 11 LZ
Ludovisi (V.) 8 OU
Lungara (V. d.) 10 JY
Lungaretta (V. d.) 10 KZ 96
Magna Grecia (V.) 4 FT
Magnolie (Viale d.) 7 NU
Mameli (V. G.) 10 KZ
Manara (V. L.) 10 KZ
Manzoni (Viale) 4 FT
Maresciallo Pilsudski (Viale) 3 DS 102
Margutta (V.) 7 MU
Marmorata (V. della) 3 DT
Marsala (V.) 4 FT
Marzio (Lungotev.) 6 LV
Mascherone (V. d.) 10 KY 103
Massina (V. A.) 10 JZ 105
Mazzini (Ponte) 10 JY
Mazzini (Viale G.) 3 DS
Mecenate (V.) 12 PY
Medaglie d'Oro (V.) 5 GU
Medici (V. G.) 10 JZ
Mellini (Lungotev.) 6 LU
Merulana (V.) 12 PY
Michelangelo (Lungotevere) 6 KU
Milano (V.) 8 OX
Milizie (Viale d.) 6 JU
Monserrato (V.) 10 KY 106
Montebello (V.) 8 PU
Monza (V.) 4 FT 108
Morgagni (V.) 4 FS 109
Morosini (V. E.) 10 KZ
Mte Brianzo (V.) 7 LV 107
Mura Aurelie (Viale d.) 9 HY
Muro Torto (Viale del) 7 MU
Museo Borghese (Viale d.) 8 OU
Navi (Lungotev. d.) 3 DS
Navicella (V. d.) 12 PZ
Navona (Pza) 6 LX
Nazionale (V.) 8 OV
Nenni (Ponte P.) 6 KU 111
Nizza (V.) 8 PU
Nomentana (V.) 4 FS
Oberdan (Lungotev.) 3 DS
Oslavia (V.) 3 CS
Ottaviano (V.) 5 HU
Paglia (V. d.) 10 KZ 114
Palatino (Ponte) 11 MZ
Panama (V.) 4 ES
Panisperna (V.) 12 PX
Parioli (Viale d.) 4 ES
Petroselli (V. L.) 11 MZ
Piave (V.) 8 PU
Piemonte (V.) 8 OU
Pierleoni (L. dei) 11 MZ 117
Pinciana (V.) 8 OU
Pio (Borgo) 6 JV
Piramide Cestia (Viale) 3 DT 118
Pisani (V. V.) 5 GU
Platone (Viale) 5 GU 120
Plebiscito (V. d.) 11 MY 121
Po (V.) 8 OU
Poerio (V. A.) 3 CT
Policlinico (V. d.) 4 FS 123
Pompeo Magno (V.) 6 KU
Popolo (Pza d.) 7 MU
Porta Angelica (V. del) 5 HV 126
Porta Capena (Pza di) 12 OZ
Porta Lavernale (V.) 11 MZ 127
Porta Maggiore (Pza di) 4 FT
Porta Metronia (Pza di) 12 PZ
Porta Pinciana (V.) 7 NU
Porta Portese (Pza) 11 LZ
Porta Portese (V.) 10 LZ 129
Portico d'Ottavia (V.) 11 MY 130
Portuense (V.) 10 KZ
Prati (Lungotevere) 6 LV
Pretoriano (Viale) 4 FT 133
Principe A. Savoia Aosta (Ponte) 6 JV 135
Principe Amedeo (Galleria) 5 HV
Principe Amedeo (V.) 8 PVX
Province (V. d.) 5 FS
Pta Cavalleggeri (V. di) 5 GV
Publicii (Clivo d.) 11 NZ 136
Quattro Fontane (V. d.) 8 OV
Quirinale (Pza d.) 7 NV
Quirinale (V. d.) 8 OV 138
Ravenna (V.) 4 FS
Regina Elena (V.) 4 FS
Regina Margherita (Ponte) 6 KU 139
Regina Margherita (Viale) 4 FS
Regolo (V. A.) 6 JU 141
Repubblica (Pza d.) 8 PV
Rienzo (V. Cola di) 6 JU
Rinascimento (Cso d.) 6 LX 142
Ripa (Lungotev.) 11 MZ
Ripa Grande (Porto di) 11 LMZ
Ripetta (V. di) 7 MU
Risorgimento (Ponte d.) 3 DS 144
Risorgimento (Pza) 5 HU
Rossetti (V. G.) 10 JZ
Rotonda (V.) 7 MX 147
Rovigo (V.) 4 FS 148
S. Alessio (V.) 11 NZ
S. Angelo (Borgo) 6 JV 151
S. Angelo (Ponte) 6 KV
S. Chiara (V.) 7 MX 153
S. Cosimato (Pza) 10 KZ
S. Francesco d'Assisi (Pza) 10 LZ
S. Francisco a Ripa (V. di) 10 KZ
S. Giovanni in Laterano (V. d.) 12 PZ
S. Gregorio (V. d.) 12 OZ
S. Ignazio (Pza) 7 MV 156
S. Marco (V.) 11 MY 157
S. Maria del Pianto (V.) 11 MY 159
S. Maria Maggiore (V.) 12 PX 160
S. Pancrazio (V.) 9 HZ
S. Pietro (Pza) 5 HV
S. Prisca (V. di) 11 NZ 162
S. Sabina (V. di) 11 MZ
S. Sonnino (Pza) 10 LZ
S. Spirito (Borgo) 6 JV
S. Stefano Rotondo (V. di) 12 PZ
S. Teodoro (V.) 11 NY
S. Uffizio (V. d.) 5 HV 165
Saffi (Viale A.) 10 KZ 150
Sallustiana (V.) 8 PU
Sangallo (Lungotevere d.) 6 JX
Sanzio (L. R.) 10 LY
Sassia (Lungotevere in) 6 JV
Savoia (V. F. di) 7 LU 166
Savoia (V. L. di) 7 LU
Scala (V. d.) 10 KY
Scalo S. Lorenzo (V.) 4 FT
Scipioni (V. d.) 6 JU
Scrofa (V. della) 7 LV
Seminario (V. d.) 7 MV 168
Sistina (V.) 7 NV
Sisto (Ponte) 10 KY
Spagna (Pza di) 7 NU
Sprovieri (V. F. S.) 9 HZ 171
Statuto (V. d.) 12 PY
Stelletta (V. d.) 7 MV 174
Sublicio (Ponte) 11 LZ
Tassoni (Largo) 6 JV
Teatro di Marcello (V. del) 11 MY 175
Tebaldi (Lungotev. d.) 10 KY
Terme Deciane (V.) 11 NZ 177
Terme di Caracalla (Viale delle) 12 OZ
Testaccio (Lungotev.) 11 LZ 178
Teulada (V.) 3 CS
Tevere (V.) 8 PU
Tiziano (Viale) 3 DS
Tomacelli (V.) 7 MV
Tor di Nona (Lungotevere) 6 KV
Torlonia (V.) 4 FS
Torre Argentina (V.) 11 MY 180
Traforo (V. del) 7 NV 181
Trastevere (Vle di) 10 KZ
Tre Madonne (V.) 4 ES 183
Trieste (Cso) 4 FS
Trinità dei Monti (Viale) 7 NU
Trionfale (Circ.) 5 GU
Tritone (V. del) 7 NV
Tuscolana (V.) 4 FT 184
Uffici del Vicario (V.) 7 MV 186
Umberto I (Ponte) 6 KV
Università (Viale d.) 4 FS
Vallati (L. d.) 10 LY
Valle Giulia (Viale) 4 ES 187
Valle Murcia (V.) 11 NZ 189
Vascello (V. d.) 9 HZ
Vaticano (Lungotevere) 6 JV 190
Vaticano (Viale) 5 GV
Venezia (Pza) 11 NY
Venezian (V. G.) 10 KZ 192
Vercelli (V.) 4 FT
Villa Massimo (Vle di) 4 FS 193
Villa Pamphili (Vle) 9 HZ
Viminale (V. d.) 8 PV
Virgilio (V.) 6 JU
Vitellia (V.) 9 GZ
Vittoria (Lungotevere d.) 3 CS
Vittorio Emanuele II (Cso) 6 KX
Vittorio Emanuele II (Ponte) 6 JV 195
Vittorio Emanuele Orlando (V.) 8 PV 196
Vittorio Veneto (V.) 8 OU
Volturno (V.) 8 PV 198
XXI Aprile (Viale) 4 FS
Zanardelli (V.) 6 KV 199

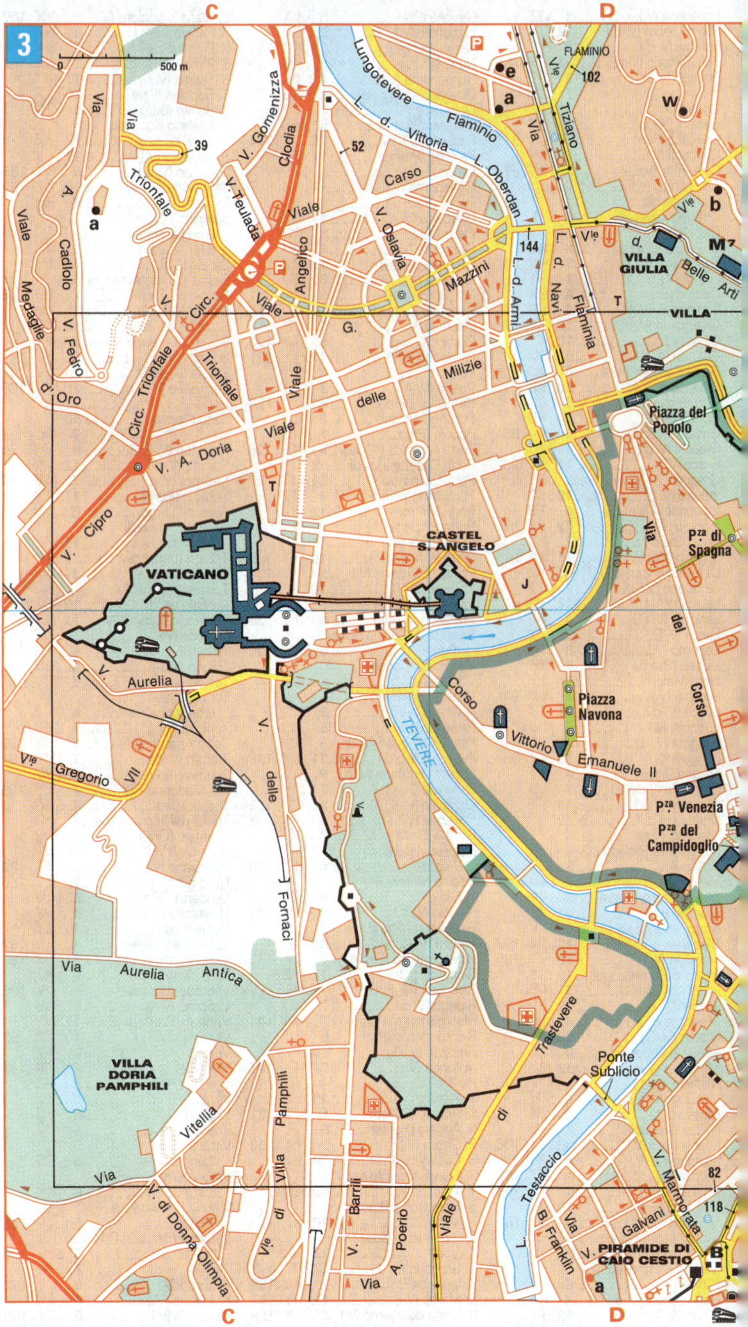
3
C
D
S
T
500 m
FLAMINIO
102
39
52
144
82
118
Via Trionfale
V. Gomenizza
Clodia
Lungotevere Flaminio
L. d. Vittoria
L. Oberdan
Via Tiziano
V. Teulada
Viale Angelico
Carso
V. Oslavia
Mazzini
L. d. Armi
L. d. Navi
Flaminia
VILLA GIULIA
Belle Arti
Viale Cadlolo
Viale Medaglie d'Oro
V. Fedro
Circ. Trionfale
Viale G.
Milizie
Viale delle
V. A. Doria
V. Cipro
Piazza del Popolo
Pza di Spagna
CASTEL S. ANGELO
VATICANO
Via del Corso
Aurelia
Vle Gregorio VII
V. delle Fornaci
Corso Vittorio Emanuele II
TEVERE
Piazza Navona
Pza Venezia
Pza del Campidoglio
Via Aurelia Antica
VILLA DORIA PAMPHILI
Vitellia
Via Pamphili
Via di Villa
Vle di
V. Barrili
Via A. Poerio
V. di Donna Olimpia
Viale di Trastevere
Ponte Sublicio
L. Testaccio
B. Franklin
Via Galvani
V. Marmorata
PIRAMIDE DI CAIO CESTIO

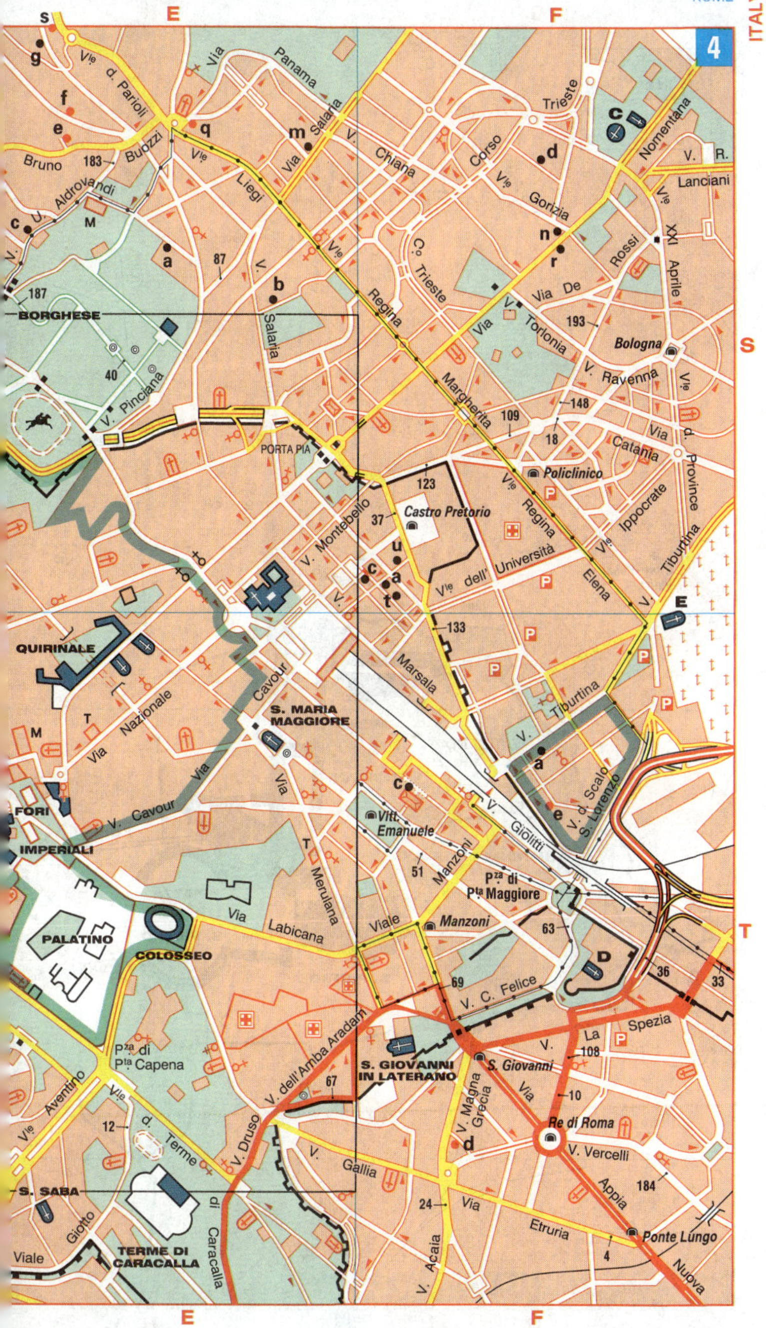
E
F
S
T
BORGHESE
PORTA PIA
Castro Pretorio
Policlinico
Bologna
QUIRINALE
S. MARIA MAGGIORE
FORI IMPERIALI
PALATINO
COLOSSEO
S. GIOVANNI IN LATERANO
S. Giovanni
Vitt. Emanuele
Manzoni
P.za di P.ta Maggiore
Re di Roma
Ponte Lungo
P.za di P.ta Capena
S. SABA
TERME DI CARACALLA
V.le d. Parioli
Buozzi
Bruno
Aldrovandi
V.le Liegi
Via Panama
Via Salaria
V. Chiana
Corso Trieste
V.le Gorizia
Nomentana
V. R. Lanciani
V.le XXI Aprile
Via De Rossi
V. Torlonia
C.o Trieste
Via Regina Margherita
V. Ravenna
Via Catania
V.le d. Province
V.le Ippocrate
Tiburtina
V.le Regina Elena
V.le dell' Università
V. Pinciana
V. Montebello
Marsala
V. Tiburtina
V. d. Scalo S. Lorenzo
V. Giolitti
Via Cavour
V. Cavour
Via Nazionale
Via Merulana
Via Labicana
Viale Manzoni
V. C. Felice
V. La Spezia
Via Appia Nuova
V. Vercelli
V. Magna Grecia
V. dell' Amba Aradam
V. Druso
V. Gallia
Via Etruria
V. Acaia
V.le Aventino
V.le d. Terme di Caracalla
Viale Giotto

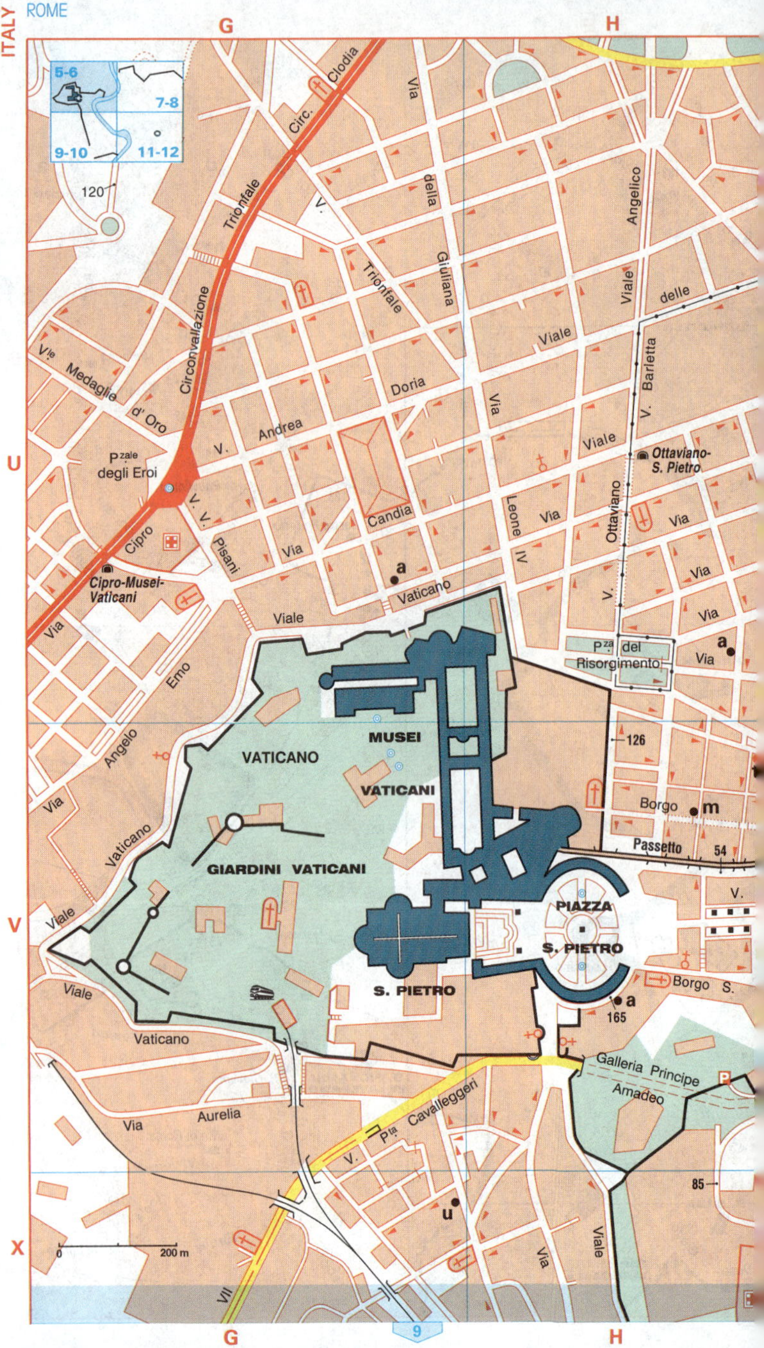
G
H
U
V
X
5-6
7-8
9-10
11-12
120
Circ.
Clodia
Trionfale
Circonvallazione
Via
della
Giuliana
Trionfale
Angelico
Viale
delle
Viale
V.
Barletta
Vle Medaglie d' Oro
Pzale degli Eroi
V. Andrea
Doria
Via
Viale
Ottaviano-S. Pietro
Candia
Leone IV
Via
V. V. Pisani
Cipro
Cipro-Musei-Vaticani
Via
a
Vaticano
V. Ottaviano
Via
Via
Via
Viale
Pza del Risorgimento
Via
a
Emo
Angelo
Via
MUSEI
VATICANI
VATICANO
126
Borgo
m
Vaticano
Passetto
54
GIARDINI VATICANI
Viale
V.
PIAZZA
S. PIETRO
S. PIETRO
Borgo S.
Viale
a
165
Vaticano
Galleria Principe Amadeo
P
Via
Aurelia
Pta Cavalleggeri
V.
85
u
0
200 m
Viale
Via
VII
9

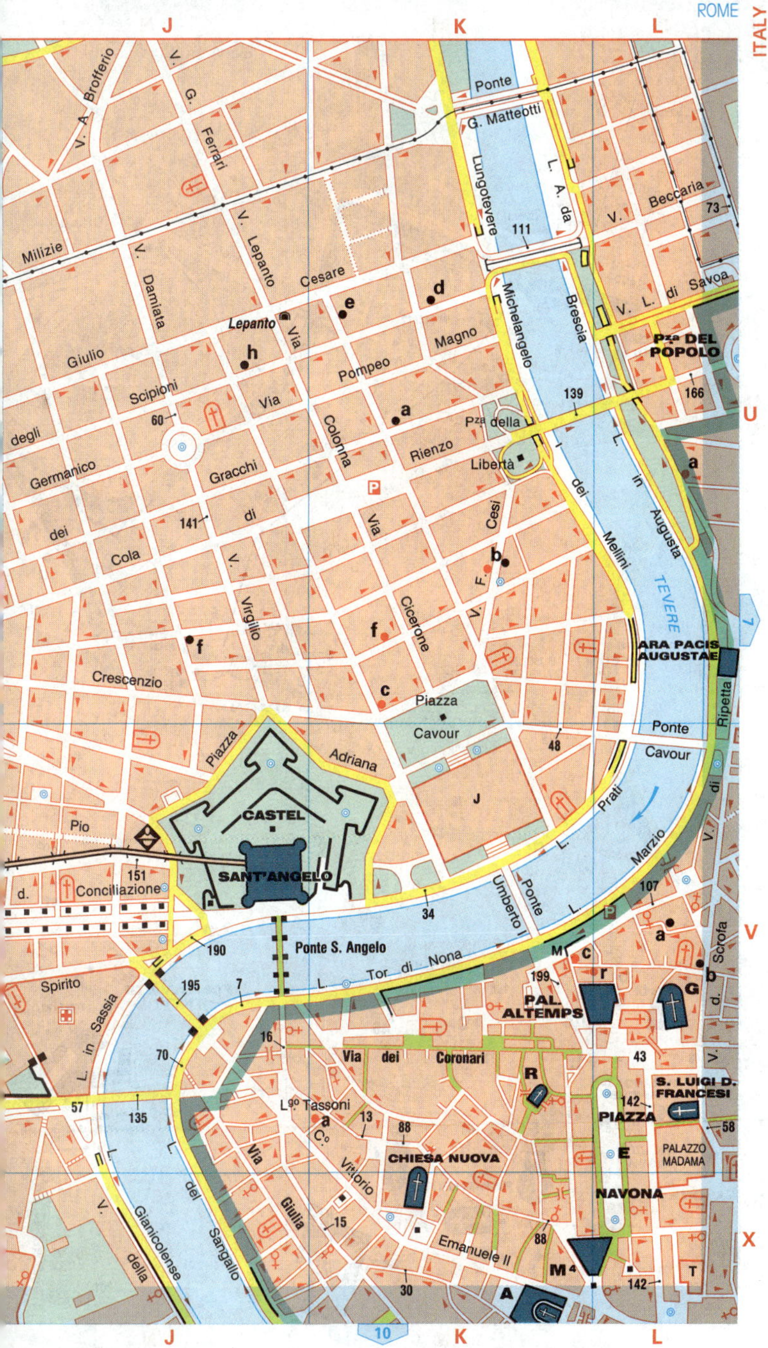
J
K
L
U
V
X
7
10
V. A. Brofferio
V. G. Ferrari
Ponte
G. Matteotti
Lungotevere
L. A. da
Brescia
Michelangelo
V. Beccaria
73
111
Milizie
V. Damiata
V. Lepanto
Cesare
Lepanto
Via
e
d
h
Giulio
Scipioni
Pompeo
Magno
V. L. di Savoia
Pza DEL POPOLO
166
139
60
degli
Germanico
Via
Colonna
a
Pza della
Libertà
Rienzo
Gracchi
141
dei
Cola
di
V.
Virgilio
Via
Cesi
V. F.
b
L. dei Mellini
L. in Augusta
TEVERE
Cicerone
f
c
ARA PACIS AUGUSTAE
Crescenzio
Piazza
Cavour
Ripetta
Ponte
Cavour
48
Piazza
Adriana
J
CASTEL
SANT'ANGELO
Prati
Marzio
V. di
Pio
151
d.
Conciliazione
34
Umberto I
Ponte
L.
107
a
Scrofa
190
Ponte S. Angelo
L. Tor di Nona
M
c
r
b
G
d.
Spirito
195
7
199
PAL. ALTEMPS
Sassia
in
L.
16
Via dei Coronari
43
70
R
S. LUIGI D. FRANCESI
57
135
Lgo Tassoni
a
Co
13
88
142
PIAZZA
58
E
PALAZZO MADAMA
Via
Vittorio
CHIESA NUOVA
L. del Sangallo
Giulia
NAVONA
V. della Gianicolense
15
Emanuele II
88
M4
142
T
30
A

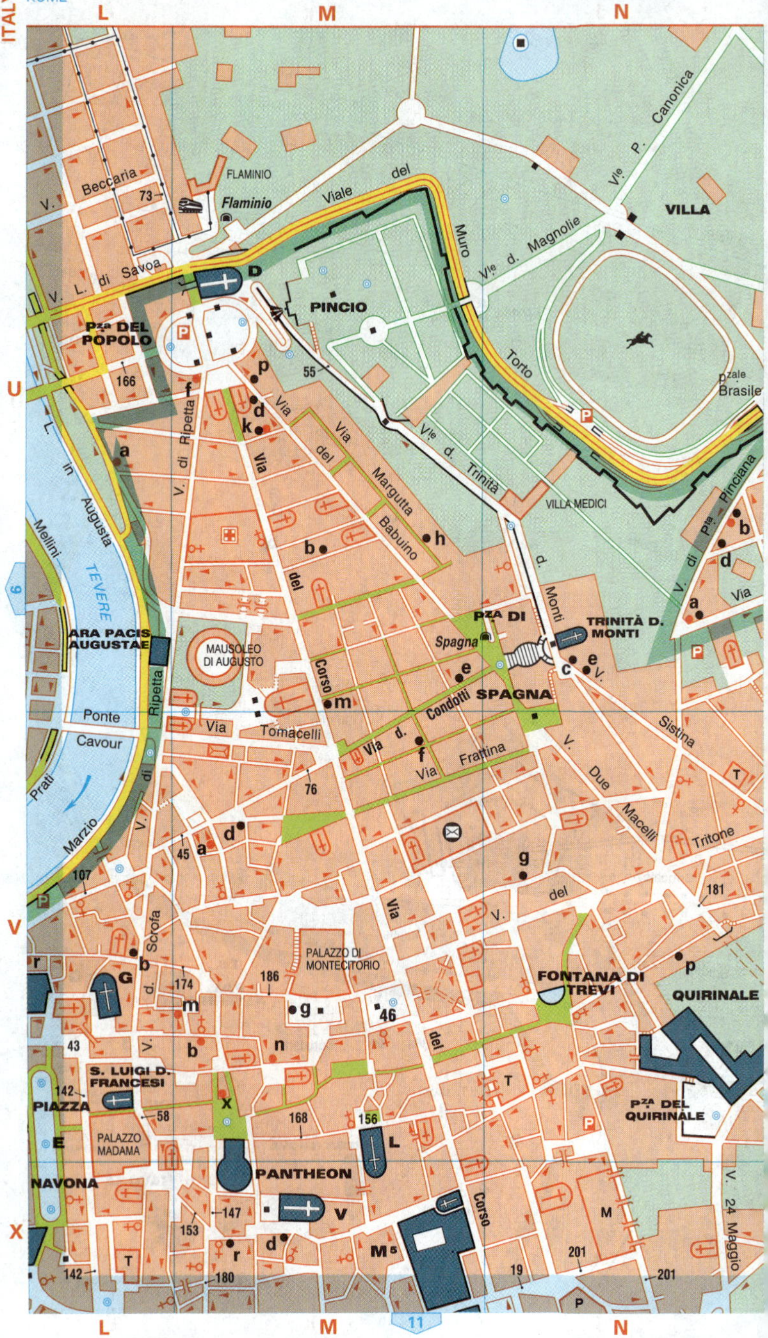

L
M
N
U
V
X
9
11
FLAMINIO
Flaminio
V. Beccaria
73
V. L. di Savoia
D
Viale del Muro Torto
PINCIO
V^le d. Magnolie
V^le P. Canonica
VILLA
P^zale Brasile
P^za DEL POPOLO
166
55
V. di Ripetta
f
p
d
k
a
Via del Babuino
Via Margutta
V^le d. Trinità d. Monti
VILLA MEDICI
L. in Augusta
Mellini
TEVERE
h
b
Via del Corso
P^za DI Spagna
TRINITÀ D. MONTI
SPAGNA
V. di P^ta Pinciana
Via
b
d
a
ARA PACIS AUGUSTAE
MAUSOLEO DI AUGUSTO
e
c
e
V. Sistina
m
Via Condotti
Ponte Cavour
Via Tomacelli
Via d. Frattina
f
Prati
Marzio
76
V. Due Macelli
Tritone
T
d
45
a
g
107
V. del
181
V
PALAZZO DI MONTECITORIO
b
V. d. Scrofa
p
r
G
174
186
FONTANA DI TREVI
QUIRINALE
m
g
46
43
b
n
S. LUIGI D. FRANCESI
142
PIAZZA
58
x
168
156
L
T
P^za DEL QUIRINALE
E
PALAZZO MADAMA
PANTHEON
NAVONA
147
v
V. 24 Maggio
M
153
r
d
M^5
Corso
201
T
142
180
19
201
P
L
M
N

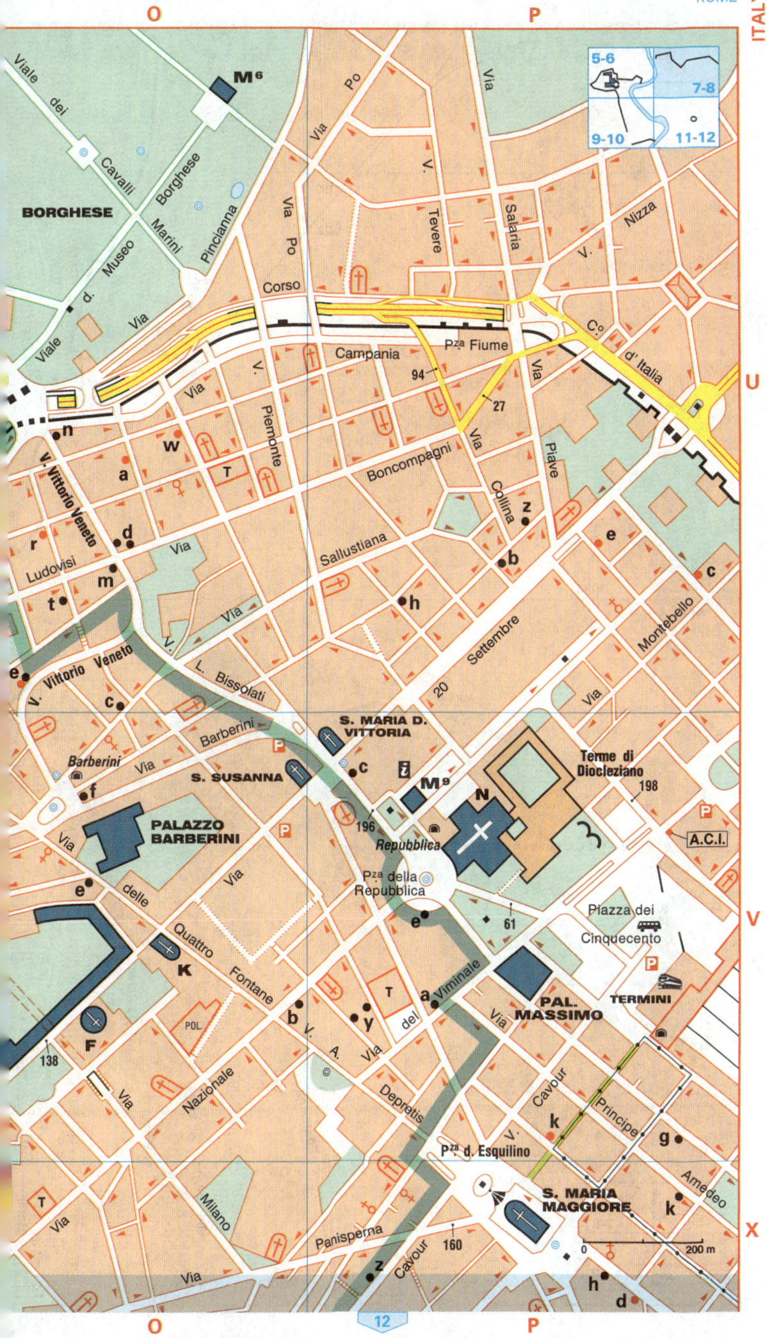
O
P
BORGHESE
Viale dei Cavalli Marini
Borghese
Pinciana
Viale d. Museo
Via
Via Po
Via Po
V. Tevere
Via Salaria
V. Nizza
Corso
Pza Fiume
Campania
Via
V. Piemonte
Via
Boncompagni
Via Collina
Piave
Co d'Italia
V. Vittorio Veneto
Ludovisi
Via
Sallustiana
Via
V. Vittorio Veneto
L. Bissolati
20 Settembre
Via Montebello
S. MARIA D. VITTORIA
Barberini
Via
Barberini
S. SUSANNA
Terme di Diocleziano
198
A.C.I.
PALAZZO BARBERINI
Repubblica
Pza della Repubblica
196
61
Piazza dei Cinquecento
Via
delle Quattro Fontane
Via
V. A. Depretis
Viminale
del
Via
PAL. MASSIMO
TERMINI
Via Cavour
Principe Amedeo
Nazionale
Via
138
POL.
Pza d. Esquilino
S. MARIA MAGGIORE
Milano
Via
Panisperna
Cavour
160
Via
0
200 m
12
5-6
7-8
9-10
11-12
U
V
X
94
27

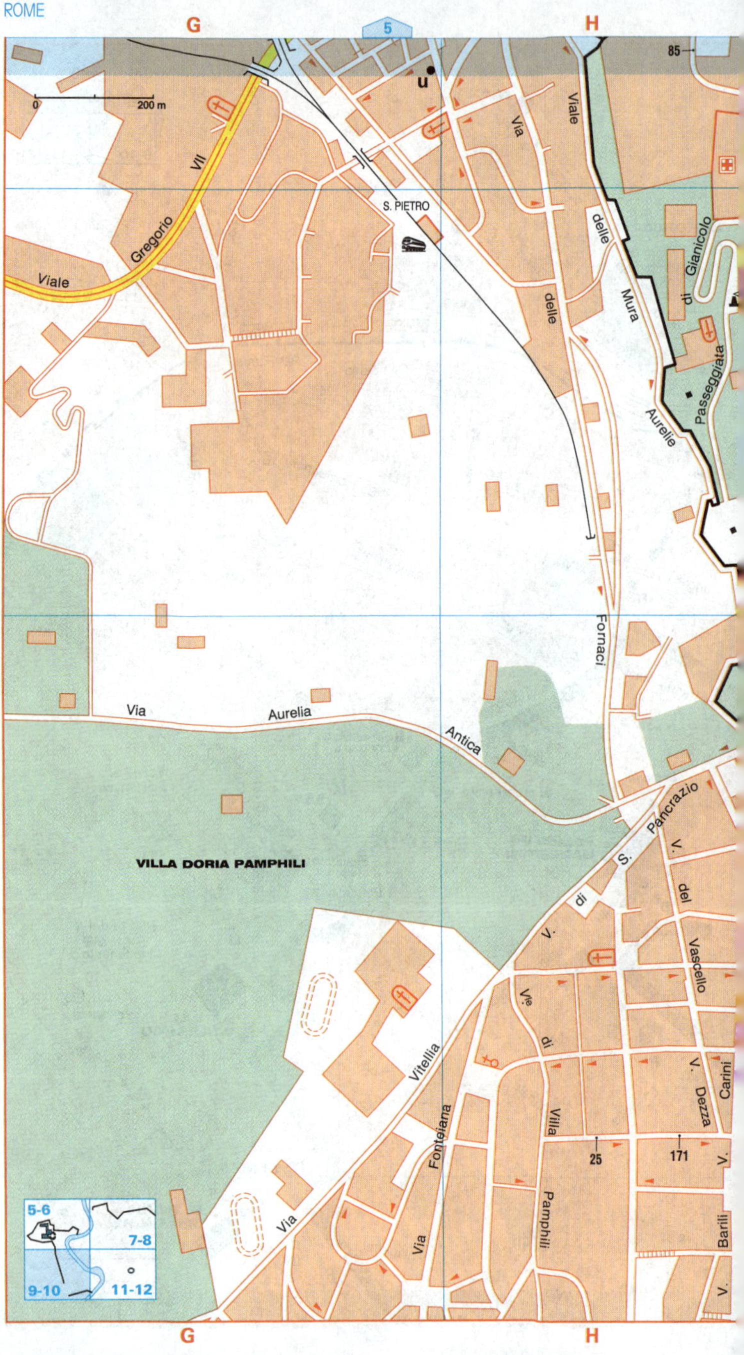
G
5
H
X
Y
Z
0
200 m
85
u
Viale Gregorio VII
S. PIETRO
Via
Viale delle Mura Aurelie
Via delle Fornaci
di Gianicolo
Passeggiata
Via Aurelia Antica
VILLA DORIA PAMPHILI
V. di S. Pancrazio
V. del Vascello
V.le di Villa Pamphili
Via Vitellia
Via Fonteiana
V. Dezza
Carini
V. Barili
V.
25
171
5-6
7-8
9-10
11-12
G
H

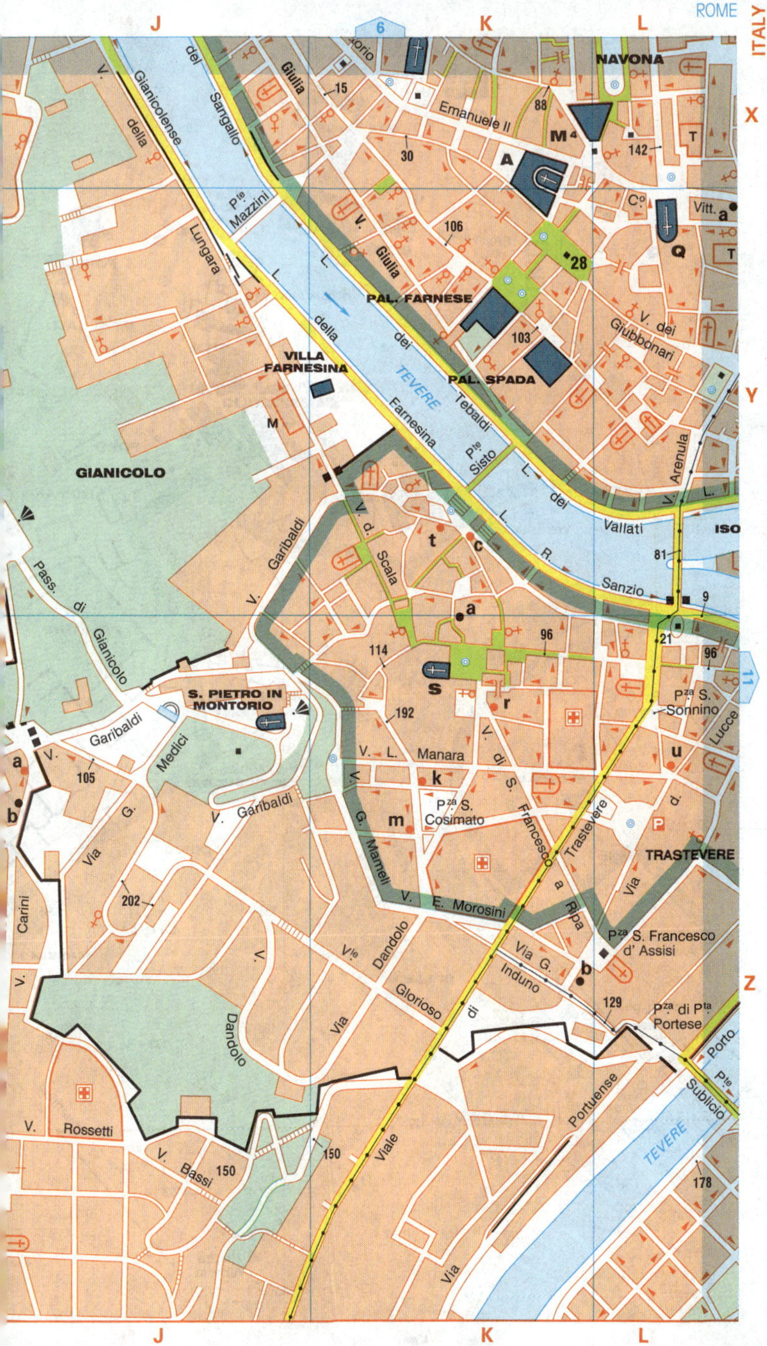
J
K
L
6
X
Y
Z
11
NAVONA
Giulia
15
Emanuele II
88
M4
30
A
142
C°
Vitt.
a
Q
T
V. Giulia
106
28
PAL. FARNESE
V. dei Giubbonari
103
PAL. SPADA
V. della Gianicolense
del Sangallo
Pte Mazzini
Lungara
L. della Farnesina
dei Tebaldi
TEVERE
VILLA FARNESINA
M
GIANICOLO
Pte Sisto
L. dei Vallati
Arenula
ISO
L. R. Sanzio
81
9
21
96
V. d. Scala
t
c
a
V. Garibaldi
Pass. di Gianicolo
114
S
r
S. PIETRO IN MONTORIO
Garibaldi
Medici
105
192
V. L. Manara
k
V. di S. Francesco a Ripa
Pza S. Sonnino
Lucce
u
Pza S. Cosimato
m
V. G. Mameli
V. Garibaldi
Via G.
202
Carini
V. E. Morosini
Trastevere
Via
d.
P
TRASTEVERE
Pza S. Francesco d' Assisi
b
Vle Dandolo
Via G. Induno
Glorioso
Via
Dandolo
di
129
Pza di Pta Portese
Porto
Pte Sublicio
V.
Rossetti
V. Bassi
150
Viale
Portuense
TEVERE
178
Via

L
M
N
7
X
Y
Z
10
PANTHEON
NAVONA
Corso
V. 24 Maggio
PIAZZA VENEZIA
Vitt.
Emanuele II
GESÙ
VITTORIANO
FORI
IMPERIALI
Via
V. dei Giubbonari
P.za DEL CAMPIDOGLIO
FORO
Via
ROMANO
Sacra
Arenula
L. dei Cenci
TEATRO DI MARCELLO
Vallati
ISOLA TIBERINA
Sanzio
P.te Cestio
V. Petroselli
V. di S. Teodoro
PALATINO
P.te Palatino
P.za S. Sonnino
Lucce
P.za Bocca d. Verità
S. MARIA IN COSMEDIN
S. CECILIA
Ripa
Lungotevere
Aventino
TRASTEVERE
Via
CIRCO
Via dei Cerchi
V. del
P.zale U. La Malfa
MASSIMO
P.za S. Francesco d' Assisi
Sabina
Circo
Massimo
S. SABINA
P.za di P.ta Portese
Porto di Ripa Grande
Lungotevere
V. di S.
P.te Sublicio
TEVERE
AVENTINO
V. S. Alessio
V.le Aventino
V. Marmorata
Piazza Albania
147
153
142
180
121
157
22
75
159
175
130
49
91
64
81
9
78
117
21
96
6
90
136
189
177
129
162
127
178
19
201

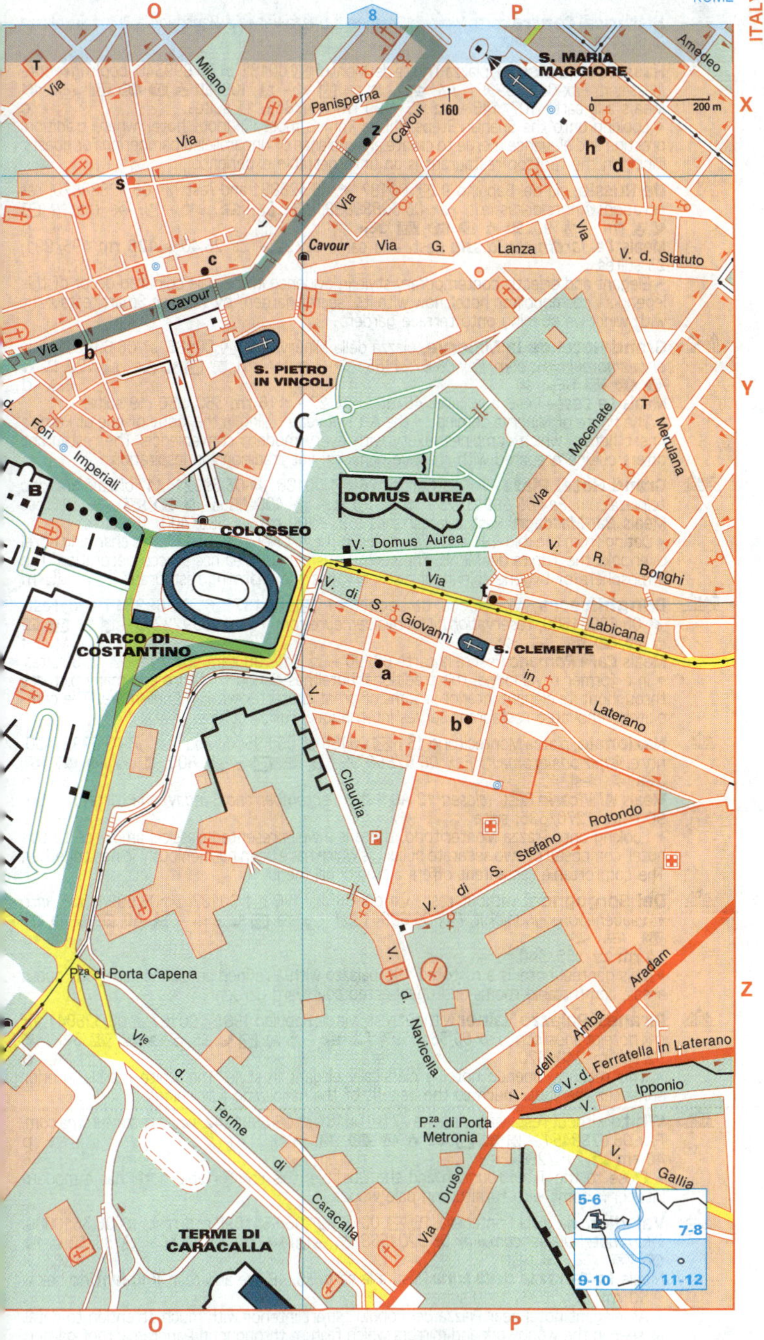
O
8
P
X
Y
Z
S. MARIA MAGGIORE
Amedeo
Milano
Via
Panisperna
Cavour
160
200 m
Via
Via
Cavour
Via G. Lanza
V. d. Statuto
Via
Cavour
Via
S. PIETRO IN VINCOLI
Fori Imperiali
Mecenate
Merulana
DOMUS AUREA
COLOSSEO
V. Domus Aurea
Via
V. R. Bonghi
V. di S. Giovanni in Laterano
Labicana
S. CLEMENTE
ARCO DI COSTANTINO
Claudia
V. di S. Stefano Rotondo
V. d. Navicella
Aradam
V. dell' Amba
V. d. Ferratella in Laterano
V. Ipponio
Pza di Porta Capena
Vle d. Terme di Caracalla
Pza di Porta Metronia
Via Druso
V. Gallia
TERME DI CARACALLA
5-6
7-8
9-10
11-12

Historical Centre corso Vittorio Emanuele, piazza Venezia, Pantheon e Quirinale, piazza di Spagna, piazza Navona :

Hassler Villa Medici, piazza Trinità dei Monti 6 00187 06 699340, *booking@hotelhassler.it, Fax 06 6789991,* – 100. **NU c**
Meals a la carte 107/146 – 45 – **99 rm** 484/869, 13 suites.
◆ Looking onto the Spanish Steps, this is Rome's most luxurious hotel, where tradition, prestige and elegance merge to create an ambience of unparalleled pampering for guests. Dining in the rooftop restaurant is an unforgettable experience.

De Russie, via del Babuino 9 00187 06 328881 and rest. 06 32888870, *reservations@hotelderussie.it, Fax 06 32888888,* – rm, rm – 90. **MU p**
Meals *Le Jardin du Russie* Rest. a la carte 62/92 – 26,40 – **125 rm** 495/891, 23 suites.
◆ Elegant and eclectic contemporary style in evidence in the pale coloured décor of this legendary cosmopolitan hotel, now with its "secret garden" by Valadier. Smart restaurant with windows opening onto terrace garden.

Grand Hotel de la Minerve, piazza della Minerva 69 00186 06 695201, *minerva@hotel-invest.com, Fax 06 6794165,* – rm, – 120. **MX d**
Meals *La Cesta* Rest. a la carte 46/86 – 27 – **116 rm** 360/550, 19 suites.
◆ The figure of Minerva dominates the Art Nouveau ceiling in the lobby of one of Rome's finest hotels, which combines luxury with every modern convenience. The restaurant offers cuisine prepared with creative panache, yet traditional in inspiration.

Grand Hotel Plaza, via del Corso 126 00186 06 69921111, *plaza@grandhotelplaza.com, Fax 06 69941575* – – 400. rest
Meals *Bar-Mascagni* Rest. a la carte 42/58 – **200 rm** 350/400, 15 suites.
◆ Dating from the mid-19C and remodelled in the Art Nouveau period, this charming hotel overlooks the Trinità dei Monti. The sumptuous lounge area has stucco decoration. The atmosphere of bygone splendour also pervades the charming restaurant. **MU m**

D'Inghilterra, via Bocca di Leone 14 00187 06 699811 and rest. 06 69981500, *reservation.hir@royaldemeure.com, Fax 06 69922243* – **MV f**
Meals *Cafè Romano* Rest. a la carte 67/90 – 31 – **98 cam** 304,70/562,10, 8 suites.
◆ In a former royal lodge, this traditional hotel has period furniture and many pictures throughout its elegant interior ; rooms of great character with an English feel. The completely renovated restaurant serves international fusion cuisine.

Nazionale, piazza Montecitorio 131 00186 06 695001 and rest. 06 69925530, *hotel@nazionaleroma.it, Fax 06 6786677* – – 800. rest **MV g**
Meals *Al Vicario* Rest. *(closed 12 August-3 September and Sunday)* a la carte 37/55 – **90 rm** 270/325, suite.
◆ Looking onto Piazza Montecitorio, there is a well-presented classical ambience to this hotel, composed of two separate buildings which have been harmoniously joined together. The comfortable restaurant offers a traditional menu.

Dei Borgognoni without rest., via del Bufalo 126 00187 06 69941505, *info@vaabeneborgognoniok.it, Fax 06 69941501* – – 60. **NV g**
54 rm 255/340.
◆ This genteel hotel is a restored 19C palazzo with a refined ambience ; spacious public areas, comfortable rooms and unexpected courtyard garden.

Piranesi-Palazzo Nainer without rest., via del Babuino 196 00187 06 328041, *info@hotelpiranesi.com, Fax 06 3610597,* – **MU d**
32 rm 240/320.
◆ This recently opened hotel is classically elegant in style. The white marble interior enhances the light, much to the benefit of the handsome furnishings.

White without rest., via In Arcione 77 00187 06 6991242, *white@travelroma.com, Fax 06 6788451* – **NV p**
40 rm 215/280.
◆ Close to the Trevi fountain and the Quirinale, this comfortable hotel has a modern interior ; rooms with furniture in pale woods.

Valadier, via della Fontanella 15 00187 06 3611998 and rest. 06 3610880, *info@hotelvaladier.com, Fax 06 3201558,* – rm, – 35. rest **MU k**
Meals *La Terrazza della Luna* Rest. a la carte 38/48 see also rest. ***Il Valentino*** below – **50 rm** 270/370, 10 suites.
◆ An elegant hotel near Piazza del Popolo ; smart interior with much attention to detail as seen in the woodwork and mirrors which feature throughout. Panoramic roof-garden.

The Inn at the Spanish Steps without rest., via dei Condotti 85 ✉ 00187 ℘ 06 69925657, *spanishstep@tin.it, Fax 06 6786470* – AE MO VISA JCB. MU e
18 rm 550/850.
◆ In the same building as the famous Caffè Greco, this hotel fulfils the requirements of even the most romantic of visitors to the Eternal City.

Santa Chiara without rest., via Santa Chiara 21 ✉ 00186 ℘ 06 6872979, *stchiara@tin.it, Fax 06 6873144* – 40. AE MO VISA JCB. MX r
96 rm 143/215, 3 suites.
◆ Since 1830, an uninterrupted tradition of family hospitality has reigned in this now totally restored hotel near the Pantheon ; pleasing, classically elegant, ambience.

Della Torre Argentina without rest., corso Vittorio Emanuele 102 ✉ 00186 ℘ 06 6833886, *info@dellatorreargentina.com, Fax 06 68801641* – AE MO VISA JCB. LY a
60 rm 157/225.
◆ Located between the old centre and the ancient sites, a refurbished hotel offering good facilities ; functional yet much attention to detail.

Forte without rest., via Margutta 61 ✉ 00187 ℘ 06 3207625, *info@hotelforte.com, Fax 06 32002707* – AE MO VISA JCB. MU h
15 rm 180/230.
◆ Occupying the first floor of a fine 18C palazzo at the top of the arty Via Margutta, this hotel has limited public areas, but charming and spacious rooms.

Portoghesi without rest., via dei Portoghesi 1 ✉ 00186 ℘ 06 6864231, *info@hotelportoghesiroma.com, Fax 06 6876976* – MO VISA. LV b
29 rm 150/190.
◆ Next to Sant'Antonio dei Portoghesi, a classically stylish hotel which, following its total refit combines modern comfort with a genteel ambience.

Mozart without rest., via dei Greci 23/b ✉ 00187 ℘ 06 36001915, *info@hotelmozart.com, Fax 06 36001735* – AE MO VISA. MU b
56 rm 170/235.
◆ Occupying a centrally-located 19C palazzo, this refurbished hotel has elegant period furnishings throughout ; attractive sun terrace.

Fontanella Borghese without rest., largo Fontanella Borghese 84 ✉ 00186 ℘ 06 68809504, *fontanellaborghese@interfree.it, Fax 06 6861295* – AE MO VISA JCB. MV d
24 rm 140/220.
◆ Peaceful yet centrally situated on the second and third floors of a historic building overlooking the Palazzo Borghese, this genteel and refined hotel is stylishly fitted out.

Hostaria dell'Orso di Gualtiero Marchesi, via dei Soldati 25/c ✉ 00186 ℘ 06 68301192, *info@hdo.it, Fax 06 68217063*, Elegant rest. – AE MO VISA. KV c
closed August and Sunday – **Meals** (dinner only) (booking essential) a la carte 52/80.
Spec. Riso, piselli e capesante. Ravioli di formaggio di pecora al ragù fine di agnello. Pollo alla romana.
◆ Revisit the bygone splendours of Roman high society in this elegant 15C building decorated in period style : restaurant, piano-bar and disco.

El Toulà, via della Lupa 29/b ✉ 00186 ℘ 06 6873498, *toula2@libero.it, Fax 06 6871115*, Elegant rest. – AE MO VISA JCB. MV a
closed August, 24 to 26 December, Sunday, Monday and Saturday lunch – **Meals** (booking essential) a la carte 47/78 (15 %).
◆ In Rome's government district, a wonderful, long-established restaurant ; delightfully elegant with modern dishes on offer alongside more traditional Venetian fare.

Antico Bottaro, via Passeggiata di Ripetta 15 ✉ 00186 ℘ 06 3236763, *anticobottaro@anticobottaro.it, Fax 06 3236763* – AE MO VISA JCB. LU a
closed 4 to 25 August and Monday – **Meals** a la carte 63/94.
◆ This 17C palazzo has terracotta floors and pink stucco walls. In business for around 130 years, the restaurant is under dynamic new management.

Il Convivio-Troiani, vicolo dei Soldati 31 ✉ 00186 ℘ 06 6869432, *info@ilconviviotroiani.com, Fax 06 6869432* – AE MO VISA JCB. KLV r
closed 9 to 15 August and Sunday – **Meals** *(dinner only)* (booking essential) a la carte 75/100.
Spec. Fiori di zucchina farciti con mozzarella ed alici, sorbetto agrodolce al peperone rosso (spring-summer). Vermicelli di Gragnano all'amatriciana sfumati al balsamico. Piccione arrostito, salsa allo sherry (autumn-spring).
◆ A modern creative slant to the meat and fish dishes served in the three elegant rooms of this restaurant, tucked away in an alley in the old centre.

XXX **L'Altro Mastai,** via Giraud 53 ang. via dei Bianchi Nuovi ✉ 00186 ✆ 06 68301296, *restaurant@laltromastai.it, Fax 06 6861303* – ▤. AE ⑤ ⓓ ⓜ VISA. ✻ KV a
closed 7 to 31 August – **Meals** (booking essential) a la carte 62/84.
◆ Opened in late 2003, this restaurant looks set to make its mark on the Roman culinary scene in spectacular style. Refined ambience, extensive wine list and top quality service.

XXX **Enoteca Capranica,** piazza Capranica 99/100 ✉ 00186 ✆ 06 69940992, *Fax 06 69940989* – ▤. AE ⑤ ⓓ ⓜ VISA JCB. ✻ MV n
closed Saturday lunch and Sunday ; in August open dinner only – **Meals** (booking essential for dinner) a la carte 50/74.
◆ Close to Montecitorio, this former wine bar has been transformed into an elegantly exclusive restaurant ; traditional Mediterranean dishes and an excellent wine list.

XXX **Il Valentino** - Hotel Valadier, via della Fontanella 14 ✉ 00187 ✆ 06 3610880, *Fax 06 3201558* – ▤. AE ⑤ ⓓ ⓜ VISA JCB. ✻ MU k
Meals a la carte 36/48.
◆ Pale woods and warm colours distinguish this refined restaurant. Its well-planned, creative menu is well suited to the elegant ambience ; good service.

XX ✿ **La Rosetta,** via della Rosetta 9/8 ✉ 00187 ✆ 06 6861002, *larosetta@tin.it, Fax 06 68215116* – ▤. AE ⑤ ⓓ VISA JCB. ✻ MV x
closed 10 to 30 August and lunch Saturday-Sunday – **Meals** (booking essential) seafood a la carte 43/120.
Spec. Antipasti di mare crudi, cotti e caldi. Linguine con gamberi rossi, basilico e mollica tostata piccante. Follia al cioccolato.
◆ The day's catch is displayed alluringly at the entrance of this restaurant ; luckily its popularity has not affected the quality of the cuisine or its pleasant ambience.

XX **Dal Bolognese,** piazza del Popolo 1/2 ✉ 00187 ✆ 06 3611426, *dalbolognese@virgilio.it, Fax 06 3222799,* 🏠 – ▤. AE ⑤ ⓜ VISA. ✻ MU f
closed 5 to 25 August, Christmas, New Year and Monday – **Meals** a la carte 47/61.
◆ Taste the finest Emilian cuisine at this establishment, one of the most renowned restaurants in the city. Summer dining out in the piazza.

XX ✿ **Quinzi Gabrieli,** via delle Coppelle 6 ✉ 00186 ✆ 06 6879389, *quinziegabrieli@tin.it, Fax 06 6874940,* 🏠 – ▤. AE ⓓ VISA. ✻ MV b
closed 3 weeks in August, Christmas and Sunday – **Meals** (dinner only) (booking essential) seafood a la carte 80/105 (10 %).
Spec. Capesante al profumo di menta. Paccheri di Gragnano all'amatriciana di triglia con scaglie al pecorino di fossa. Insalata di aragostina sarda all'arancia.
◆ All the fragrances and flavours of the sea in the middle of the city ; this quality restaurant is always busy and in vogue.

XX **Da Pancrazio,** piazza del Biscione 92 ✉ 00186 ✆ 06 6861246, *dapancrazio@tin.it, Fax 06 97840235* – ⊁. AE ⑤ ⓓ ⓜ VISA JCB LY e
closed 5 to 25 August, Christmas and Wednesday – **Meals** a la carte 35/48.
◆ Two thousand years of history permeate this charming establishment built in part on the ruins of the ancient Teatro di Pompeo ; a taverna-museum serving country cuisine.

XX **Myosotis,** vicolo della Vaccarella 3/5 ✉ 00186 ✆ 06 6865554, *marsili@libero.it, Fax 06 6865554* – ▤. AE ⑤ ⓓ ⓜ VISA JCB. ✻ MV m
closed 10 to 24 August, 2 to 9 January, Sunday and Monday lunch – **Meals** a la carte 31/53.
◆ In a green and peaceful setting, this well restored late 19C villa offers a genteel family ambience and high standards of comfort.

XX **Vecchia Roma,** via della Tribuna di Campitelli 18 ✉ 00186 ✆ 06 6864604, *Fax 06 6864604,* 🏠 – ▤. AE ⓓ VISA. ✻ MY c
closed 10 to 25 August and Wednesday – **Meals** Roman and seafood rest. a la carte 45/64.
◆ In the Campidoglio district, this traditional restaurant is made up of small, stylish, yet cosy rooms ; cuisine is seafood and Roman specialities.

Termini Railway Station via Vittorio Veneto, via Nazionale, Viminale, Santa Maria Maggiore, Porta Pia :

🏨 **St. Regis Grand,** via Vittorio Emanuele Orlando 3 ✉ 00185 ✆ 06 47091 and rest. ✆ 06 47092736, *stregisgrandrome@stregis.com, Fax 06 4747307,* 🏋, ⇔ – 🛗 ▤ 📺 ✆ ♿ – 🏛 300. AE ⑤ ⓓ ⓜ VISA JCB. ✻ PV c
Meals *Vivendo* Rest. *(closed August and Sunday)* a la carte 54/76 – ☕ 43 – **138 rm** 750/970, 23 suites.
◆ Frescoes, textiles and Empire furniture in the luxurious rooms and opulent public areas of this hotel, which retains the splendour of its earliest days (opened in 1894). Grand atmosphere of bygone days in the restaurant.

The Westin Excelsior, via Vittorio Veneto 125 ✉ 00187 ℘ 06 47081, *excelsiorrome@westin.com, Fax 06 4826205*, – rm, – 600. OU d
Meals *Doney* Rest. a la carte 50/70 – 43 – **284 rm** 760/815, 32 suites.
• This large, prestigious hotel is run along traditional lines for a smart, discerning clientele. The sumptuous interior is well appointed with antique items ; Italy's largest suite is in this hotel. The elegantly modern restaurant also serves light meals and post theatre.

Eden, via Ludovisi 49 ✉ 00187 ℘ 06 478121, *reservations@hotel-eden.it, Fax 06 4821584*, – – 80. NU a
Meals (see rest. **La Terrazza** below) – 49,50 – **121 rm** 528/858, 13 suites.
• Stylish simplicity in this hotel where the elegant ambience does not dispel the warmth of the welcome. Service and accommodation to satisfy even the most demanding guest.

Sofitel, via Lombardia 47 ✉ 00187 ℘ 06 478021, *prenotazioni.sofitelroma@accor-hotels.it, Fax 06 4821019* – rm, – 45. NU d
Meals a la carte 40/51 – **113 rm** 334/496.
• A historic building on the Via Veneto with a Neo-classical interior including an abundance of statues and busts. Fine view from the terrace. Elegant restaurant with vaulted ceilings in the old stable block.

Majestic, via Vittorio Veneto 50 ✉ 00187 ℘ 06 421441, *info@hotelmajestic.com, Fax 06 4880984*, – rm – 150. OU e
Meals *La Veranda* Rest. *(closed August, Sunday and Monday)* a la carte 47/80 see also rest.-bistrot ***La Ninfa*** below – 40 – **90 rm** 490/610, 8 suites.
• Cosmopolitan luxury combines with Italian hospitality in the elegant atmosphere of this smart hotel, one of the capital's finest. Linen and silverware in the refined yet welcoming La Veranda restaurant.

Splendide Royal, porta Pinciana 14 ✉ 00187 ℘ 06 421689, *reservations@splendideroyal.com, Fax 06 42168800*, – – 90. NU b
Meals (see rest. **Mirabelle** below) – **59 rm** 400/600, 9 suites.
• Gilding, damask and fine antique furniture grace the interior of this exclusive modern hotel, located in a former palazzo.

Regina Hotel Baglioni, via Vittorio Veneto 72 ✉ 00187 ℘ 06 421111, *regina.roma@baglionihotels.com, Fax 06 42012130* – rm, – 80. OU m
Meals a la carte 66/84 – 27,50 – **137 rm** 495/605, 6 suites.
• This hotel, occupying a restored building, has a stylish Art Deco ambience and top quality service ; the splendid rooms are elegant in their simplicity. A refined yet warm atmosphere in the restaurant, serving international cuisine.

Exedra, piazza della Repubblica 47 ✉ 00185 ℘ 06 48938020, *reservation@exedra.boscolo.com, Fax 06 48938000*, – rm, – 120. rest PV e
Meals *Tazio* Rest. a la carte 60/158 – 26 – **235 rm** 583, 3 suites.
• Situated in one of Rome best-known piazzas, this superior hotel is spacious with comfortable and well-equipped rooms. Its Tazio restaurant can accommodate business functions ; alternatively there is La Frusta, open evenings only.

Marriott Grand Hotel Flora, via Vittorio Veneto 191 ✉ 00187 ℘ 06 489929, *Fax 06 4820359*, – rm, rm – 150. OU b
Meals buffet lunch only and a la carte 41/82 – 25 – **155 rm** 478, 6 suites.
• Following a complete refit, this hotel at the end of Via Veneto is a harmonious and functional combination of simple elegance and modern refinement. Parquet floors and other decorative features in wood lend an ambience of warmth to the restaurant.

Aleph, via San Basilio 15 ✉ 00187 ℘ 06 422901, *reservation@aleph.boscolo.com, Fax 06 42290000*, – rm, rm – 60. rest OU c
Meals *Maremoto* Rest. a la carte 106/186 – 22 – **92 rm** 389, 4 suites.
• A prestigious establishment in the design hotel mould ; unusual lobby with distinctive colour scheme. Innovatively styled rooms and good health spa. Modern cuisine and minimalist décor in the restaurant.

Bernini Bristol, piazza Barberini 23 ✉ 00187 ℘ 06 488931 and rest. ℘ 06 488933288, *reservationsbb@sinahotels.it, Fax 06 4824266*, – rm, – 100. OV f
Meals *L'Olimpo* Rest. a la carte 78/101 – 28,60 – **110 rm** 342,10/528, 10 suites.
• A perfect balance between bygone glories and modern comforts in one of Rome's most elegant hotels. Rooftop restaurant offers outside dining and fine views over the Eternal City.

De la Ville Inter-Continental, via Sistina 69 ✉ 00187 ☎ 06 67331, *rome@intercontl.com, Fax 06 6784213,* – ◎ – ▦ ▣ – 84. AE ⊕ ◎ MC VISA. NU e
Meals a la carte 75/122 – ☐ 29 – **169 rm** 660/750, 23 suites.
• This establishment has all the ingredients for an unforgettable stay ; a recent successful revamp throughout has not eroded its historic charm. Elegant restaurant with efficient service serving Roman specialities as well as national and international dishes.

Empire Palace Hotel, via Aureliana 39 ✉ 00187 ☎ 06 421281, *gold@empirepalacehotel.com, Fax 06 42128400,* – ◎, rm, ▦ ▣ – 50. AE ⊕ ◎ MC VISA JCB. PU h
Meals ***Aureliano*** Rest. *(closed Sunday)* a la carte 41/66 – **113 rm** ☐ 275/396, 5 suites.
• A sophisticated hybrid of 19C building and contemporary design, with modern art displayed in the public areas ; simple elegance in the rooms. Red and blue chandeliers and cherrywood decorate the dining room.

Rose Garden Palace, via Boncompagni 19 ✉ 00187 ☎ 06 421741, *info@rosegardenpalace.com, Fax 06 4815608,* modern and minimalist design – ◎ ▦ ▣ – 50. AE ⊕ ◎ MC VISA JCB OU d
Meals (residents only) a la carte 30/44 – **65 rm** ☐ 247,50/437,80.
• Minimalist design has inspired the interiors of this new hotel, occupying an early 19C palazzo ; unusual.

Ambra Palace, via Principe Amedeo 257 ✉ 00185 ☎ 06 492330, *booking@ambrapalacehotel.com, Fax 06 49233100* – ◎ ▦ ▣ rm – 40. AE ⊕ ◎ MC VISA JCB. rest FT c
Meals (dinner only) (residents only) a la carte 40/68 – **78 rm** ☐ 206/289.
• Occupying a mid-19C palazzo, this well-appointed hotel is especially popular with business people.

Canada without rest., via Vicenza 58 ✉ 00185 ☎ 06 4457770, *info@hotelcanadaroma.com, Fax 06 4450749* – ◎ ▦ ▣. AE ⊕ ◎ MC VISA JCB. FS u
70 rm ☐ 134/158.
• In a period building near the station, this hotel has a simple elegance. Tastefully furnished, stylish rooms ; ask for one with a canopy bed.

Mecenate Palace Hotel without rest., via Carlo Alberto 3 ✉ 00185 ☎ 06 44702024, *info@mecenatepalace.com, Fax 06 4461354* – ◎ ▦ ▣ rm – 45. AE ⊕ ◎ MC VISA JCB. PX h
62 rm ☐ 250/280, 3 suites.
• The elegant 19C-style interior makes for a welcoming ambience in this recently built hotel, with high standards of comfort and service.

Barberini without rest., via Rasella 3 ✉ 00187 ☎ 06 4814993, *info@hotelbarberini.com, Fax 06 4815211* – ◎ ▦ ▣ – 50. AE ⊕ ◎ MC VISA JCB. OV e
☐ 20 – **31 rm** 229/304, 4 suites.
• Near the Barberini palace, this recently opened hotel is a restored historic building ; fine marble, opulent fabrics and decorative features in wood throughout.

Britannia without rest., via Napoli 64 ✉ 00184 ☎ 06 4883153, *info@hotelbritannia.it, Fax 06 48986316* – ◎ ▦ ▣. AE ⊕ ◎ MC VISA JCB PV y
33 rm ☐ 210/290.
• Competent family management at this small hotel where much attention to detail is evident. Unusual rooms in eclectic style ; very comfortable.

Artemide, via Nazionale 22 ✉ 00184 ☎ 06 489911, *hotelartemide@hotelartemide.it, Fax 06 48991700* – ◎, rm, ▦ ▣ rm – 120. AE ⊕ ◎ MC VISA JCB. OV b
Meals 30/55 – **85 rm** ☐ 250/345.
• Occupying an attractively restored Art Nouveau building, this classically stylish hotel offers all modern comforts ; good conference facilities.

Ariston without rest., via Turati 16 ✉ 00185 ☎ 06 4465399, *hotelariston@hotelariston.it, Fax 06 4465396,* – ◎ ▦ ▣ rm – 100. AE ⊕ ◎ MC VISA JCB. PV g
97 rm ☐ 180/240.
• Conveniently located near the station, a traditional family-run hotel ; well-appointed and offering high standards of service.

Marcella Royal Hotel without rest., via Flavia 106 ✉ 00187 ☎ 06 42014591, *info@marcellaroyalhotel.com, Fax 06 4815832,* – ◎ ▦ ▣. AE ⊕ ◎ MC VISA. PU z
85 rm ☐ 200/300.
• Close to the station and city centre, this hotel is comfortable and well-presented throughout ; breakfast served on the panoramic roof-garden terrace.

Venezia without rest., via Varese 18 ✉ 00185 ☎ 06 4457101, *info@hotelvenezia.com, Fax 06 4957687* – ◎ ▣. AE ⊕ ◎ MC VISA JCB. FS t
60 rm ☐ 118/160.
• A warm and professional approach from the family management of this hotel, which has spacious public areas with fine furniture and fabrics.

Astoria Garden, via Bachelet 8/10 ✉ 00185 ☎ 06 4469908, *astoria.garden@flashnet.it, Fax 06 4453329,* – . FS c
Meals (dinner only) (residents only) – **34 rm** 100/150.
◆ This recently refurbished hotel near the station has a welcoming ambience and a large, peaceful courtyard garden ; ask for a room with Jacuzzi bath.

The Bailey's Hotel without rest., via Flavia 39 ✉ 00187 ☎ 06 42020486, *info@hotelbailey.com, Fax 06 42020170* – . PU b
29 rm 180/284.
◆ Rooms with fine furniture and marble baths ; a refined and tasteful look, and every modern convenience. Well-restored to high standards.

Royal Court without rest., via Marghera 51 ✉ 00185 ☎ 06 44340364, *theroyal@tin.it, Fax 06 4469121* – . FS a
24 rm 160/200.
◆ Well-presented and stylish, this refurbished hotel has a friendly ambience and every modern comfort. Situated in a residential area close to the station.

Columbia without rest., via del Viminale 15 ✉ 00184 ☎ 06 4883509, *info@hotelcolumbia.com, Fax 06 4740209* – . PV a
45 rm 145/160.
◆ Warm and welcoming accommodation at this completely refurbished and comfortable hotel near Stazione Termini ; breakfast served on the roof terrace.

La Terrazza - Hotel Eden, via Ludovisi 49 ✉ 00187 ☎ 06 47812752, *reservations@hotel-eden.it, Fax 06 47812718* – . NU a
Meals (booking essential) a la carte 79/150.
◆ The focal point of this elegant, modern restaurant with roof garden is the charming panoramic view of Rome, an ideal backdrop against which to enjoy memorable cuisine.

Mirabelle - Hotel Splendide Royal, porta Pinciana 14 ✉ 00187 ☎ 06 42168838, – . NU b
Meals (booking essential) a la carte 65/93.
◆ A luxurious and historic feel to this charming restaurant overlooking Rome ; dining outside in summer. Modern cuisine with Mediterranean roots.

Agata e Romeo, via Carlo Alberto 45 ✉ 00185 ☎ 06 4466115, *ristorante@agataeromeo.it, Fax 06 4465842* – . PX d
closed 6 to 27 August, 1 to 16 January, Saturday and Sunday – **Meals** (booking essential) a la carte 65/89.
Spec. Sformato di formaggio di fossa con salsa di pere e miele (autumn-winter). Variazione di pomodoro (summer). Raviolini di caprino e asparagi selvatici (spring).
◆ This small restaurant, well-presented and elegant, draws together traditional cuisine and creativity. One of the finest wine-lists in Rome.

La Ninfa - Hotel Majestic, via Vittorio Veneto 50 ✉ 00187 ☎ 06 421441 – . OU e
Meals (booking essential) a la carte 44/68.
◆ Under the same roof as the Hotel Majestic, this first class restaurant serves interesting cuisine ; carefully prepared dishes, an elegant ambience and leisurely opening hours.

Al Grappolo d'Oro, via Palestro 4/10 ✉ 00185 ☎ 06 4941441, *info@algrappolodoro.it, Fax 06 4452350,* – . PU c
closed August, Saturday lunch and Sunday – **Meals** a la carte 32/47.
◆ Close to the Baths of Diocletian, this classic restaurant has been improved by recent refurbishment ; an extensive traditional menu.

Papà Baccus, via Toscana 32/36 ✉ 00187 ☎ 06 42742808, *papabaccus@papabaccus.com, Fax 06 42010005,* – . OU w
closed 15 days in August, Saturday lunch and Sunday – **Meals** (booking essential) Tuscan rest. a la carte 48/62.
◆ Near Via Veneto, this popular traditional restaurant serves seafood and Tuscan specialities (Chianina beef and Sienese pork).

Monte Caruso Cicilardone, via Farini 12 ✉ 00185 ☎ 06 483549 – . PV k
closed August, Sunday and Monday lunch – **Meals** Lucan rest. a la carte 29/47.
◆ The emphasis is on the flavours of the south in this warm and welcoming family-run restaurant ; menu based on Basilicatan dishes prepared authentically and simply.

Hostaria da Vincenzo, via Castelfidardo 6 ✉ 00185 ☎ 06 484596, *Fax 06 4870092* – PU e
closed August and Sunday – **Meals** a la carte 23/39.
◆ A classic restaurant, in terms of atmosphere and cuisine, with an emphasis on seafood. Pleasant friendly ambience ; many regulars and popular with business people.

Peppone, via Emilia 60 ✉ 00187 ☎ 06 483976, *Fax 06 483976*, Traditional rest. – ▤. AE ⊕ ◑ MC VISA JCB. ✻ OU r
closed Christmas, Easter, 15 to 30 August, Saturday and Sunday in July-August, only Sunday during other months – **Meals** a la carte 30/48 (15 %).
◆ Run by the same family since 1890, this is the quintessential place to savour traditional cuisine in an atmosphere of classic style.

Giovanni, via Marche 64 ✉ 00187 ☎ 06 4821834, *Fax 06 4817366* – ▤ ♿. AE ⊕ ◑ MC VISA OU a
closed August, Friday dinner and Saturday – **Meals** a la carte 38/55.
◆ The tone of this establishment is unmistakably that of the Marche region, as indeed are its specialities. A friendly ambience with many regulars; Roman cuisine also served.

Uno e Bino, via degli Equi 58 ✉ 00185 ☎ 06 4460702 – ▤. ⊕ ◑ MC VISA
closed Monday – **Meals** (dinner only) a la carte 33/49. FT e
◆ This welcoming restaurant best feature is the excellent value for money which it represents; its bistro feel makes for a friendly and informal atmosphere.

Ancient Rome Colosseo, Fori Imperiali, Aventino, Terme di Caracalla, Porta San Paolo, Monte Testaccio :

Capo d'Africa without rest., via Capo d'Africa 54 ✉ 00184 ☎ 06 772801, *info@hotelcapodafrica.com, Fax 06 77280801,* ⚒ – |‡| ▤ TV ☏ ♿ rm – 🏛 70. AE ⊕ ◑ MC VISA JCB. ✻ PZ b
65 rm ⊐ 300/320, suite.
◆ With a choice of larger or smaller rooms, this hotel is distinguished throughout by its fine furnishings and modern décor; close to the Colosseum.

Villa San Pio ⛱, via di Santa Melania 19 ✉ 00153 ☎ 06 5743547, *info@aventinohotels.com, Fax 06 5741112,* 🌳, 🌲 – |‡| ▤ TV P – 🏛 25. AE ⊕ ◑ MC VISA JCB. ✻
Meals *(closed Saturday)* (residents only) – **79 rm** ⊐ 180/220. MZ b
◆ Sharing a pleasant garden with two other establishments under the same management; this hotel has the feel of a genteel private home. A fine large lobby and modern rooms.

Borromeo without rest., via Cavour 117 ✉ 00184 ☎ 06 485856, *borromeo@ludovicigroup.com, Fax 06 4882541* – |‡| ▤ TV. AE ⊕ ◑ MC VISA JCB PX z
30 rm ⊐ 230/260, 2 suites.
◆ Near Santa Maria Maggiore, this comfortable hotel has well-appointed rooms with traditional furnishings, and a pleasant roof terrace.

Celio without rest., via dei Santi Quattro 35/c ✉ 00184 ☎ 06 70495333, *info@hotelcelio.com, Fax 06 7096377* – ⇹ ▤ TV. AE ⊕ ◑ MC VISA JCB PZ a
19 rm, ⊐ 250/300, suite.
◆ Combining refinement, comfort and atmosphere this welcoming hotel has elegant rooms of character; well located for the Colosseum.

Cilicia without rest., via Cilicia 5/7 ✉ 00179 ☎ 06 7005554, *info@hotelcilicia.it, Fax 06 77250016,* 🌲 – |‡| ▤ TV ♿ P – 🏛 100. AE ⊕ ◑ MC VISA. ✻
62 rm ⊐ 138/189. by viale delle Terme di Caracalla OPZ
◆ Opened in 2000 after careful refurbishment, this comfortable establishment has handy parking; the interior has fine wood-panelling and rooms with every modern convenience.

Duca d'Alba without rest., via Leonina 12/14 ✉ 00184 ☎ 06 484471, *info@hotelducadalba.com, Fax 06 4884840* – |‡| ▤ TV ☏. AE ⊕ ◑ MC VISA JCB OY c
27 rm ⊐ 150/195.
◆ In the picturesque quarter formerly known as the Suburra, this completely refurbished hotel has well-appointed rooms with classically elegant furnishings.

Mercure Hotel Roma Delta Colosseo without rest., via Labicana 144 ✉ 00184 ☎ 06 770021, *mercurehotelsroma@accor-hotels.it, Fax 06 7005781,* ⛱ – |‡| ⇹ ▤ TV – 🏛 60. AE ⊕ ◑ MC VISA. ✻ PYZ t
160 rm ⊐ 171/274.
◆ A curious contrast between the sites of ancient Rome and this contemporary-style hotel. The most striking feature is its swimming pool with terrace overlooking the Colosseum.

Domus Aventina ⛱ without rest., via Santa Prisca 11/b ✉ 00153 ☎ 06 5746135, *info@domus-aventina.com, Fax 06 57300044* – ▤ TV. AE ⊕ ◑ MC VISA JCB. ✻ NZ k
26 rm ⊐ 125/205.
◆ Close to the Circus Maximus in the Aventino district, this hotel has large, modern rooms. Cramped but comfortable public areas.

Solis Invictus without rest., via Cavour 311 ✉ 00184 ☎ 06 69920587, *info@hotelsolis.it, Fax 06 69923395* – |‡| ▤ TV. AE ⊕ ◑ MC VISA. ✻ OY b
16 rm ⊐ 110/185.
◆ This genteel, small hotel near the Colosseum now has a ground floor lobby; well-proportioned rooms with good furnishings and every modern convenience.

Checchino dal 1887, via Monte Testaccio 30 ✉ 00153 ☎ 06 5743816, *checchin o-roma@tin.it, Fax 06 5743816,* Historic building – AE VISA JCB. DT a
closed August, 24 December-2 January, Sunday and Monday – **Meals** (booking essential) Roman rest. a la carte 34/57.
◆ Located in the distinctive Testaccio quarter, this is a historic backdrop against which to savour the largely meat- and offal-based specialities of Roman cuisine.

Maharajah, via dei Serpenti 124 ✉ 00184 ☎ 06 4747144, *maharajah@maharajah.it, Fax 06 47885393* – AE VISA JCB. OY s
Meals Indian rest. a la carte 33/40.
◆ Subdued lighting, rugs, and Indian prints and fabrics create the appropriate atmosphere in this restaurant ; authentic Indian dishes, rather than pale European imitations.

Papok, salita del Grillo 6/b ✉ 00184 ☎ 06 69922183, *papok@tiscali.it, Fax 06 69922183* – AE VISA JCB NY c
closed 3 to 31 August and Monday – **Meals** a la carte 36/50.
◆ Near the Fori, this well-managed restaurant has a classic rustic ambience ; principally traditional seafood, but meat dishes also available.

St. Peter's Basilica (Vatican City) Gianicolo, Monte Mario, Stadio Olimpico :

Cavalieri Hilton, via Cadlolo 101 ✉ 00136 ☎ 06 35091, *roberta.rossi@hilton.com, Fax 06 35092241,* ≤ city, Private art collection, – rm, TV – 2000. AE VISA JCB. rest CS a
Meals *Il Giardino dell'Uliveto* Rest. a la carte 76/106 see also rest. ***La Pergola*** below – 35 – **354 rm** 865/920, 17 suites.
◆ Fine views over the city, sun-terraces and pool with gardens ; these are some of the features of this great hotel which excels in every respect. An informal poolside restaurant offers dining with cabaret.

Jolly Hotel Villa Carpegna, via Pio IV 6 ✉ 00165 ☎ 06 393731, *roma-villacarpe gna@jollyhotels.it, Fax 06 636856,* – rm, TV P – 330. AE VISA JCB. rest by via Cipro CS
Meals a la carte 40/54 – **201 rm** 256, 2 suites.
◆ The latest hotel in this chain's Roman contingent is a modern development with pool, convenient parking and good conference facilities. In summer the traditional restaurant serves meals by the pool.

Visconti Palace without rest., via Federico Cesi 37 ✉ 00193 ☎ 06 3684, *info@vis contipalace.com, Fax 06 3200551* – rm, TV rm – 150. AE VISA JCB. KU b
234 rm 280/320, 13 suites.
◆ A large 1970s building, this fully modernised, elegantly functional hotel appeals to business people and tourists alike ; large rooms with every modern convenience.

Jolly Leonardo da Vinci, via dei Gracchi 324 ✉ 00192 ☎ 06 328481, *roma-leon ardodavinci@jollyhotels.it, Fax 06 3610138* – rm, TV – 180. AE VISA KU a
Meals (residents only) a la carte 34/46 – **239 rm** 220/275, 5 suites.
◆ A very comfortable hotel which is equally popular with business people and tourists. Lobby and much of the accommodation refurbished.

Giulio Cesare without rest., via degli Scipioni 287 ✉ 00192 ☎ 06 3210751, *giulioce @uni.net, Fax 06 3211736,* – TV – 40. AE VISA. KU d
78 rm 280/300.
◆ An elegantly simple fa e masks a welcoming interior at this former patrician villa with courtyard garden ; smart Louis XVI-style furniture.

Farnese without rest., via Alessandro Farnese 30 ✉ 00192 ☎ 06 3212553, *hotel.fa rnese@mclink.it, Fax 06 3215129* – TV P. AE VISA. KU e
23 rm 190/250.
◆ In a restored patrician palace, this hotel is situated in the quiet Prati quarter, yet only 50m from the metro ; elegant and well-presented interior.

Starhotel Michelangelo, via Stazione di San Pietro 14 ✉ 00165 ☎ 06 398739, *michelangelo.rm@starhotels.it, Fax 06 632359* – rm, TV rm – 150. AE VISA JCB. rest GX u
Meals a la carte 50/80 – **171 rm** 260, 8 suites.
◆ Close to St Peter's, this comfortable hotel conforms to the standards expected of its rating ; period furniture, both in the public areas and rooms. The restaurant also possesses an ambience of simple elegance.

Residenza Paolo VI without rest., via Paolo VI 29 ✉ 00193 ☎ 06 68134108, *info @residenzapaoloVI.com, Fax 06 6867428,* ≤ – TV. AE VISA. HV a
29 rm 195/249.
◆ One of the Eternal City finest and rarest views, looking out over St Peter may be enjoyed from the terrace of this restaurant, located in a charming and graceful former monastery.

Dei Consoli without rest., via Varrone 2/d ✉ 00193 ☎ 06 68892972, *info@hoteldeiconsoli.com, Fax 06 68212274* – HU a
28 rm ☕ 220/320.
◆ Opened in 2000, this totally refurbished former palace is a now a cosy hotel with much attention to detail in evidence, and a smart clientele ; elegant empire-style rooms.

Sant'Anna without rest., borgo Pio 133 ✉ 00193 ☎ 06 68801602, *santanna@travel.it, Fax 06 68308717* – HV m
20 rm ☕ 150/210.
◆ Unusual trompe l'œil décor and a charming inner courtyard at this small and welcoming hotel, occupying a 16C palace close to St Peter's.

Gerber without rest., via degli Scipioni 241 ✉ 00192 ☎ 06 3216485, *info@hotelgerber.it, Fax 06 3217048* – JU h
27 rm ☕ 105/140.
◆ This family-run traditional hotel is close to the metro ; pale wood in the pleasant public areas and the simple but appealing rooms.

Arcangelo without rest., via Boezio 15 ✉ 00192 ☎ 06 6874143, *hotel.arcangelo@travel.it, Fax 06 6893050*, ← St Peter's Basilica – JU f
33 rm ☕ 140/211.
◆ Tasteful decoration and attention to detail in the wood-panelled public areas of this 19C former palace ; sun terrace with view of St Peter's.

Alimandi without rest., via Tunisi 8 ✉ 00192 ☎ 06 39723948, *alimandi@tin.it, Fax 06 39723943*, – GU a
closed 8 January-10 February – **35 rm** ☕ 90/155.

La Pergola - Hotel Cavalieri Hilton, via Cadlolo 101 ✉ 00136 ☎ 06 35092152, *lapergola.rome@hilton.com, Fax 06 35092165*, ← city, –
closed 7 to 22 August, 1 to 24 January, Sunday and Monday – **Meals** (dinner only) (booking essential) a la carte 98/151. CS a
Spec. Carpaccio tiepido di spigola su verdure mediterranee. Fiore di zucca in pastella su fondo di scampi con tartufo nero. Variazione di cioccolato.
◆ Luxurious yet refined elegance, impeccable service, and a delightful view of the Eternal City ; dinner at this rooftop restaurant is unforgettable.

L'Arcangelo, via Giuseppe Gioacchino Belli 59/61 ✉ 00193 ☎ 06 3210992, *Fax 06 3210992* – KU f
closed August, Saturday lunch, Sunday and Bank Holidays – **Meals** (booking essential) a la carte 39/58 (10 %).
◆ Rustic yet well presented, this cosy restaurant is competently run ; traditional meat and fish dishes with a modern twist.

Il Simposio-di Costantini, piazza Cavour 16 ✉ 00193 ☎ 06 32111131, *Fax 06 3211502*, Wine bar and rest. – KU c
closed August, Saturday lunch and Sunday – **Meals** a la carte 42/68.
◆ This restaurant-wine bar offers the choice between a drink at the bar or dining in the elegant restaurant ; hot and cold dishes, and a good cheese selection.

Antico Arco, piazzale Aurelio 7 ✉ 00152 ☎ 06 5815274, *anticoarco@tiscali.it, Fax 06 5815274* – JZ a
closed 8 to 22 August and Sunday – **Meals** (booking essential) a la carte 36/52.
◆ Refurbished along minimalist lines, this is a popular spot which is always very busy. Just inside is the bar, while the restaurant is split over two levels ; good service.

Taverna Angelica, piazza Amerigo Capponi 6 ✉ 00193 ☎ 06 6874514, Post theatre restaurant, open until late – JV t
closed 10 to 20 August and lunch except Sunday – **Meals** (booking essential) a la carte 31/43.
◆ Ideal for a romantic candlelit meal, perhaps after the theatre ; a friendly and intimate ambience with some imaginative interpretations of classic Italian dishes.

L'Antico Porto, via Federico Cesi 36 ✉ 00193 ☎ 06 3233661, *luca@mclink.net, Fax 06 3203483* – KU b
closed August, Saturday lunch and Sunday – **Meals** a la carte 36/68.
◆ The reliably professional management here has focused on fish dishes with great success. Classical style and cosiness combined.

Parioli via Flaminia, Villa Borghese, Villa Glori, via Nomentana, via Salaria :

Grand Hotel Parco dei Principi, via Gerolamo Frescobaldi 5 ✉ 00198 ☎ 06 854421, *principi@parcodeiprincipi.com, Fax 06 8845104*, ←, heated, – – 900. ES a
Meals *Pauline Borghese* Rest. *(closed Sunday lunch)* a la carte 56/78 – **183 rm** ☕ 500/600, 32 suites.
◆ Overlooking the parkland of the Villa Borghese, this hotel is an oasis of verdant calm in the heart of Rome ; elegant warm interiors, with much attention to detail in evidence and excellent service. Exclusive restaurant offering well-presented eclectic cuisine.

Aldrovandi Palace, via Ulisse Aldrovandi 15 ✉ 00197 ☎ 06 3223993 and rest. ☎ 06 3216126, *hotel@aldrovandi.com, Fax 06 3221435,* – rm P – 300. AE VISA JCB. ES c
Meals ***Baby*** Rest. *(closed Monday)* a la carte 58/80 – ☕ 29,70 – **121 rm** 412/561, 13 suites.
◆ Occupying an elegant late-19C palazzo with views of the Villa Borghese, this hotel has a small shaded park with pool, opulent interiors and genteel rooms.

Lord Byron , via De Notaris 5 ✉ 00197 ☎ 06 3220404, *info@lordbyronhotel.com, Fax 06 3220405* – . AE VISA JCB. DS b
Meals ***Sapori del Lord Byron*** Rest. *(closed Sunday)* a la carte 49/67 – **32 rm** ☕ 363/495, 3 suites.
◆ Feeling more like an exclusive private residence than a hotel, this refined establishment has rooms combining luxury with modern comforts and faultless service. The smart dining room is equally suitable for intimate meals or meetings.

The Duke Hotel, via Archimede 69 ✉ 00197 ☎ 06 367221, *theduke@thedukehotel.com, Fax 06 36004104* – rm – 80. AE VISA JCB. DS w
Meals (residents only) a la carte 46/62 – **78 rm** ☕ 366/430, 7 suites.
◆ The discreet, understated ambience of an English club is created in the stylish interiors of this well-appointed new hotel ; afternoon tea served in front of the fire.

Mercure Roma Corso Trieste without rest., via Gradisca 29 ✉ 00198 ☎ 06 852021, *mercure.romatrieste@accor-hotels.it, Fax 06 8412444,* – rm – 30. AE VISA. FS d
97 rm ☕ 180/200.
◆ Comfortable, spacious and modern rooms in this hotel, unusually situated in a residential quarter. Gym and sun deck on top floor.

Albani without rest., via Adda 45 ✉ 00198 ☎ 06 84991, *hotelalbani@flashnet.it, Fax 06 8499399* – – 90. AE VISA JCB. ES b
157 rm ☕ 186/250.
◆ Overlooking the parkland of the Villa Albani near the Via Veneto, this modern-style hotel has comfortable public areas, especially the fine and airy lobby.

Degli Aranci, via Oriani 11 ✉ 00197 ☎ 06 8070202, *hotel.degliaranci@flashnet.it, Fax 06 8070704,* – cam. – 40. AE VISA JCB. ES g
Meals a la carte 37/65 – **54 rm** ☕ 140/180, 2 suites.
◆ Not far from Viale Parioli, this genteel hotel is situated in a quiet, leafy area ; pleasant, stylish public areas and very comfortable rooms. The restaurant looks out over the grounds.

Fenix, viale Gorizia 5 ✉ 00198 ☎ 06 8540741, *info@fenixhotel.it, Fax 06 8543632,* , – , rm, – 32. AE VISA JCB. FS n
Meals *(closed August, Saturday dinner and Sunday)* (residents only) a la carte 24/40 – **73 rm** ☕ 130/200, 8 suites.
◆ Close to the parkland of Villa Torlonia, this establishment has smart well-presented public areas, and comfortable rooms which are tastefully furnished ; pleasant courtyard garden. Understated décor in the restaurant.

Villa Glori without rest., via Celentano 11 ✉ 00196 ☎ 06 3227658, *info@hotelvillaglori.it, Fax 06 3219495* – . AE VISA JCB. DS e
57 rm ☕ 105/160.
◆ Well located close to the Tiber, this friendly and informal hotel benefits from a simple yet genteel interior, and well-appointed rooms.

Villa Grazioli without rest., via Salaria 241 ✉ 00199 ☎ 06 8416587, *info@villagrazioli.it, Fax 06 8413385* – . AE VISA ES m
30 rm ☕ 160/200.
◆ Situated between the parks of Villa Ada and Villa Borghese, this new hotel has attractive public areas with unusual coffered ceilings, and comfortable rooms.

Villa del Parco withou rest., via Nomentana 110 ✉ 00161 ☎ 06 44237773, *info@hotelvilladelparco.it, Fax 06 44237572,* – . AE VISA JCB. FS r
29 rm ☕ 120/160.
◆ Occupying a charming late-19C villa with its own gardens, this welcoming family-run hotel offers excellent levels of service.

Astrid without rest., largo Antonio Sarti 4 ✉ 00196 ☎ 06 3236371, *info@hotelastrid.com, Fax 06 3220806* – . AE VISA JCB. DS a
48 rm ☕ 150/200.
◆ Managed competently and cordially, this hotel offers refurbished accommodation with every modern comfort, and serves a memorable breakfast on its panoramic terrace.

Gallura, via Giovanni Antonelli 2 ✉ 00197 ☎ 06 8072971, *Fax 06 8078110,* – . AE VISA JCB. ES f
closed 10 to 25 August, 1 to 10 January and Monday – **Meals** a la carte 68/92.
◆ Delightful summer dining outside at this well-located establishment, somewhat elevated from street level. Predominantly seafood cuisine.

Al Ceppo, via Panama 2 ✉ 00198 ☎ 06 8551379, *info@ristorantealceppo.it, Fax 06 85301370* – ▤. AE ⓢ ⓓ VISA JCB. ✻ ES q
closed 8 to 24 August and Monday – **Meals** (booking essential) a la carte 34/58.
◆ A rustic yet stylish feel to this restaurant serving Mediterranean cuisine, some of which is modern in style ; friendly atmosphere with many regulars.

La Scala, viale dei Parioli 79/d ✉ 00197 ☎ 06 8083978, *Fax 06 8084463*, – ▤. AE ⓢ ⓓ MC VISA JCB. ✻ ES s
closed 6 to 21 August and Wednesday – **Meals** Rest. and evening pizzeria a la carte 27/40.
◆ Run by the same family for over 30 years, this classic restaurant offers traditional Italian fare ; pizzas also available in the evenings.

Coriolano, via Ancona 14 ✉ 00198 ☎ 06 44249863, *Fax 06 44249724*, Elegant trattoria – ▤. AE ⓢ ⓓ MC VISA PU d
closed 8 August-1 September – **Meals** (booking essential) a la carte 38/59.
◆ Named after its proprietor, who has recently celebrated 50 years in charge of this elegant trattoria, which has a friendly and courteous ambience.

Ambasciata d'Abruzzo, via Pietro Tacchini 26 ✉ 00197 ☎ 06 8078256, *info@ambasciata-di-abruzzo.it, Fax 06 8074964*, – ▤. AE ⓢ ⓓ MC VISA JCB ES e
closed 23 August-7 September and 9 to 23 January – **Meals** a la carte 35/59.
◆ Specialising in the cuisine of the Abruzzo, but also serving Lazio dishes and seafood, this rustic and welcoming restaurant offers summer dining outside.

Trastevere area (typical district) :

Santa Maria without rest., vicolo del Piede 2 ✉ 00153 ☎ 06 5894626, *hotelsantamaria@libero.it, Fax 06 5894815*, – ▤ TV ♿. AE ⓢ ⓓ MC VISA JCB. ✻ KYZ a
20 rm 165/210.
◆ Laid out around a courtyard garden, this peaceful new hotel occupies the site of a 15C cloister. Nearby is Santa Maria in Trastevere.

San Francesco without rest., via Jacopo de' Settesoli 7 ✉ 00153 ☎ 06 58300051, *hotelsanfrancesco@tin.it, Fax 06 58333413* – ▤ TV. AE ⓢ ⓓ MC VISA JCB. ✻ KZ b
24 rm 175/205.
◆ Formerly a hostel attached to the neighbouring church, the building has now been rebuilt as a hotel. Pleasant breakfast room, modern well-appointed accommodation.

Alberto Ciarla, piazza San Cosimato 40 ✉ 00153 ☎ 06 5818668, *alberto@albertociarla.com, Fax 06 5884377*, – ▤. AE ⓢ ⓓ MC VISA JCB. ✻ KZ k
closed 1 week in August, 1 week in January and Sunday – **Meals** (dinner only) (booking essential) seafood a la carte 52/64.
◆ Roman cuisine is offered alongside traditional seafood specialities in this elegant restaurant in the heart of the Trastevere district. Excellent wine-list.

Corsetti-il Galeone, piazza San Cosimato 27 ✉ 00153 ☎ 06 5816311, *Fax 06 5896255*, – ▤. AE ⓢ ⓓ MC VISA JCB KZ m
closed Wednesday lunch – **Meals** Roman and seafood rest. 27/32 and a la carte 28/53.
◆ Set in an old galleon, this restaurant has a unique atmosphere. Run by the same family since 1922 ; Roman cuisine and seafood specialities.

Enoteca Ferrara, via del Moro 1/a ✉ 00153 ☎ 06 58333920, *info@enotecaferrara.it, Fax 06 5803769* – ⓢ ⓓ MC VISA JCB. ✻ KY c
Meals (dinner only except July-August) a la carte 48/61.
◆ Originally a wine bar, this establishment has evolved to offer cuisine which interprets traditional dishes with contemporary flair. Huge choice of Italian wines.

Sora Lella, via di Ponte Quattro Capi 16 (Isola Tiberina) ✉ 00186 ☎ 06 6861601, *Fax 06 6861601* – ▤. AE ⓢ ⓓ MC VISA JCB. ✻ MY g
closed August, 24 to 26 December, 1 to 8 January and Sunday – **Meals** Traditional Roman rest. a la carte 46/68.
◆ The son and grandchildren of the famous original proprietor maintain the traditions of a warm welcome and classic Roman cuisine at this restaurant.

Paris, piazza San Callisto 7/a ✉ 00153 ☎ 06 5815378, *Fax 06 5815378*, – ▤. AE ⓢ ⓓ MC VISA JCB. ✻ KZ r
closed August, Sunday dinner and Monday – **Meals** Roman rest. a la carte 32/62.
◆ In the heart of the Trastevere district, this cosy and genteel establishment offers polished interpretations of classic Roman cuisine. Very good wine-list.

Pastarellaro, via di San Crisogono 33 ✉ 00153 ☎ 06 5810871, *Fax 06 5810871*, Rest. wine bar with live piano music at dinner – ▤. AE ⓢ ⓓ MC VISA. ✻ LZ u
Meals (dinner only except Sunday) Roman and seafood rest. a la carte 36/51 (12 %).
◆ This restaurant-wine bar has live music in the evening ; the menu offers flavoursome traditional Roman cuisine and fish dishes.

Asinocotto, via dei Vascellari 48 ✉ 00153 ☎ 06 5898985, *gb@giulianobrenna.com, Fax 06 5898985* – ▤. AE ⊙ ⓓ MC VISA MZ a
closed 15 to 31 January and Monday – **Meals** (dinner only except Sunday) a la carte 45/63.
◆ Welcoming and well-run in its simplicity, this establishment offers creatively prepared traditional cuisine incorporating only the highest quality ingredients.

Checco er Carettiere, via Benedetta 10 ✉ 00153 ☎ 06 5817018, *osteria@tin.it, Fax 06 5884282,* – ▤. AE ⊙ ⓓ MC VISA KY t
closed Sunday dinner also Monday lunch July-August – **Meals** Roman and seafood rest. a la carte 36/55.
◆ Situated in the picturesque Trastevere district, this classic trattoria serves seafood and Roman dishes ; pleasantly rustic ambience.

North-Western area via Flaminia, via Cassia, Balduina, Prima Valle, via Aurelia :

Colony without rest., via Monterosi 18 ✉ 00191 ☎ 06 36301843, *info@colonyhotel.it, Fax 06 36309495,* – ▤ TV P – 90. AE ⊙ ⓓ MC VISA
72 rm 125/150. by viale Maresciallo DS
◆ Not too far out of the centre, this hotel is popular with business people and tourists alike. Comfortable colonial-style rooms and good meeting rooms.

Zone Hotel without rest., via A. Fusco 118 ✉ 00136 ☎ 06 35404111, *info@zonehotel.com, Fax 06 35420322, Shuttle service to the centre* – ▤ TV P – 30. AE ⊙ ⓓ MC VISA JCB by via Trionfale CS
54 rm 140/200.
◆ Not far from the Vatican, this hotel is quietly located in a residential area. Classic comfort in a modern setting ; shuttle service to centre.

Sisto V without rest., via Lardaria 10 ✉ 00168 ☎ 06 35072185, *hotel.sistov@tiscali.net.it, Fax 06 35072186* – ▤ TV. AE ⊙ ⓓ MC VISA. by via Trionfale CS
42 rm 110/140.
◆ Close to the Policlinico Gemelli, this hotel was opened in 2000 ; garage parking and comfortable modern rooms ; standards in keeping with its category.

L'Ortica, via Flaminia Vecchia 573 ✉ 00191 ☎ 06 3338709, *Fax 06 3338709,* – ▤. AE ⊙ ⓓ MC VISA JCB. by viale Maresciallo Pilsudski DS
closed 1 week in August and Sunday ; from October-April open Sunday lunch – **Meals** (dinner only) Neapolitan rest. a la carte 41/53.
◆ A good place to try Neapolitan dishes and other Campanian cuisine ; warm friendly ambience, decorated with unusual modern collectibles.

North-Eastern area via Salaria, via Nomentana, via Tiburtina :

la Giocca, via Salaria 1223 ✉ 00138 ☎ 06 8804411 and rest. ☎ 06 8804503, *hotel@lagiocca.it, Fax 06 8804495,* – ▤ TV P – 180. AE ⊙ ⓓ MC VISA. by via Salaria ES
Meals ***Pappa Reale*** Rest. Roman and seafood rest. a la carte 25/42 – **88 rm** 136,34/167,85, 3 suites.
◆ Modern efficiency and comfort in this recently refurbished hotel ; well-suited to business travellers. Classic style in the refitted rooms. Sizeable restaurant with pizzeria.

Carlo Magno without rest., via Sacco Pastore 13 ✉ 00141 ☎ 06 8603982, *desk@carlomagnohotel.com, Fax 06 8604355* – ▤ TV – 40. AE ⊙ ⓓ MC VISA JCB by via Salaria ES
60 rm 100/120.
◆ Well situated on Via Nomentana, this hotel has a smart and comfortable interior after a complete refit ; large top-floor terrace.

La Pergola without rest., via dei Prati Fiscali 55 ✉ 00141 ☎ 06 8107250, *info@hotellapergola.com, Fax 06 8124353,* – ▤ TV. AE ⊙ ⓓ MC VISA
96 rm 130/160. by via Salaria ES
◆ Family management makes for a homely atmosphere in this comfortable hotel near Via Salaria ; the well-presented pastel coloured rooms have modern furnishings.

Gabriele, via Ottoboni 74 ✉ 00159 ☎ 06 4393498, *ristorantegabriele@virgilio.it, Fax 06 43535366* – ▤. AE ⊙ ⓓ MC VISA. by via Tiburtina FS
closed August, Saturday, Sunday and Bank Holidays – **Meals** (booking essential) a la carte 40/55.
◆ A classic restaurant with modern style ; under the same management for 40 years. Traditional Roman and other Italian dishes, both meat and seafood ; good wine-list.

Mamma Angelina, viale Arrigo Boito 65 ✉ 00199 ☎ 06 8608928, *mammangelina@libero.it* – ▤. AE ⊙ ⓓ MC VISA. by via Salaria ES
closed August and Wednesday – **Meals** a la carte 21/40.
◆ Although the emphasis here is on fish, meat dishes are also available. Good value for money, classically stylish yet informal ambience.

South-Eastern area via Appia Antica, via Appia Nuova, via Tuscolana, via Casilina :

Appia Park Hotel without rest., via Appia Nuova 934 ✉ 00178 ✆ 06 716741, *info@appiaparkhotel.it, Fax 06 7182457*, – 150. by via Appia Nuova FT
110 rm 138/168.
◆ Set in its own gardens not far from the archaeological site of Appia Antica, ideal for those wanting a hotel out of the city centre. Classically stylish, comfortable rooms.

Rinaldo all'Acquedotto, via Appia Nuova 1267 ✉ 00178 ✆ 06 7183910, *info@rinaldoallacquedotto.it, Fax 06 7182968*, – 80. by via Appia Nuova FT
closed 10 to 20 August and Tuesday – **Meals** a la carte 35/55.
◆ A bright modern restaurant serving traditional cuisine and seafood ; the unusual veranda room has sliding doors and two trees growing through the roof.

Giuda Ballerino !, via Marco Valerio Corvo 135 ✉ 00174 ✆ 06 71584807, *info@giudaballerino.it* – by via Appia Nuova FT
closed August, Wednesday and Thursday lunch – **Meals** (booking essential) a la carte 35/49.
◆ Diners should not be discouraged by the exterior appearance and outlying location of this well presented little establishment, its walls decorated with comic strip illustrations. Innovative dishes.

Alfredo a via Gabi, via Gabi 36/38 ✉ 00183 ✆ 06 77206792, *Fax 06 77206792*, – FT d
closed August and Tuesday – **Meals** a la carte 26/30.
◆ This old-style trattoria, in the same hands since 1952, offers robust traditional Lazio and other Italian cuisine ; seafood and meat dishes.

South-Western area via Aurelia Antica, E.U.R., Città Giardino, via della Magliana, Portuense :

Sheraton Roma Hotel, viale del Pattinaggio 100 ✉ 00144 ✆ 06 54531, *res497.sheraton.roma@sheraton.com, Fax 06 5940689*, – rm, – 2000. by viale Aventino ES
Meals a la carte 58/93 – **631 rm** 329/403, 13 suites.
◆ This imposing modern development has well-appointed and varied accommodation ; adaptable meeting rooms well-suited to conferences. The elegant restaurant serves Italian and international cuisine.

Crowne Plaza Rome St. Peter's, via Aurelia Antica 415 ✉ 00165 ✆ 06 66420 and rest. ✆ 06 6642169, *cpstpeter@hotel-invest.com, Fax 06 6637190*, – rm, – 260. by viale Gregorio VII CT
Meals ***Le Jardin d'Hiver*** Rest. international specialities a la carte 45/61 – 18 – **321 rm** 277/327.
◆ A large hotel with ample parking and peaceful gardens with pool, offering high standards of comfort both in its public areas and in its spacious rooms. The Jardin d'Hiver restaurant offers a varied menu.

Melià Roma Aurelia Antica, via degli Aldobrandeschi 223 ✉ 00163 ✆ 06 665441, *melia.roma@solmelia.com, Fax 06 66544467*, – – 750. by viale Gregorio VII GY
Meals a la carte 35/56 – **270 rm** 285/305, suite.
◆ Despite having been constructed in record time, this hotel is extremely comfortable and well appointed ; very good conference facilities. The restaurant is of a high standard.

Atahotel Villa Pamphili, via della Nocetta 105 ✉ 00164 ✆ 06 6602, *prenotazioni@hotelvillapamphili.com, Fax 06 66157747*, – rm, – 500. by viale Gregorio VII CT
Meals a la carte 42/58 – **248 rm** 203/287, 10 suites.
◆ Peacefully-located adjacent to the parkland of Villa Doria Pamphili, this modern building has pleasant grounds ; shuttle service available to Piazza Risorgimento. The modern restaurant has two welcoming rooms.

Grand Hotel del Gianicolo without rest., viale Mura Gianicolensi 107 ✉ 00152 ✆ 06 58333405, *info@grandhotelgianicolo.it, Fax 06 58179434*, – – 120. JZ b
48 rm 320/360.
◆ Occupying an elegant small palazzo with well-kept garden and pool, this smart hotel offers comfortable, spacious accommodation and elegant public areas.

Shangri Là-Corsetti, viale Algeria 141 ✉ 00144 ℘ 06 5916441, *info@shangrilacorsetti.it, Fax 06 5413813,* ⛱, 🌳 – ⇔ rm, ▤ TV P – 🏛 80. AE $ ⊙ MC VISA JCB by viale Aventino ET
Meals (see rest. ***Shangri Là-Corsetti*** below) – **52 rm** ☕ 170/216.
◆ White domed ceilings, marble and sofas in the lobby of this 1960s hotel located in the EUR district, mainly used by business travellers ; attractive wooded gardens.

Dei Congressi, viale Shakespeare 29 ✉ 00144 ℘ 06 5926021, *info@hoteldeicongressiroma.com, Fax 06 5911903,* 🌳 – |\$|, ⇔ rm, ▤ TV – 🏛 250. AE $ ⊙ MC VISA. ⚘ by viale Aventino ET
closed 30 July-30 August – **Meals *La Glorietta*** Rest. *(closed 28 July-25 August and Saturday)* a la carte 35/49 – **105 rm** ☕ 145/200.
◆ Close to the EUR palazzo dei Congressi, this functional hotel offers comfortable accommodation and numerous meeting rooms. The restaurant serves classic dishes and offers outdoor dining in summer.

Shangri-Là Corsetti, viale Algeria 141 ✉ 00144 ℘ 06 5918861, *Fax 06 5914581,* 🌳 – ▤ P. AE $ ⊙ MC VISA JCB by viale Aventino ET
closed 13 to 29 August – **Meals** Roman and seafood specialities a la carte 38/59.
◆ Laid out over three well-presented and comfortable rooms, with summer dining outside ; menu includes traditional fare, seafood and international cuisine.

Outskirts of Rome

at Spinaceto *Suouth : 13 km :*

Four Points Hotel Sheraton Roma West, via Eroi di Cefalonia 301 ℘ 06 50834111, *info@fourpointsheratonroma.com, Fax 06 50834701,* Ⅎ\$, ≘s, ⛱ – |\$|, ⇔ rm, ▤ TV ✆ ♿ 🚗 – 🏛 450. AE $ ⊙ MC VISA. ⚘ rest
Meals a la carte 36/72 – **240** ☕ 220/286, 6 suites.
◆ On a single storey layout, this hotel is attractively modern in feel, and is ideal for conferences and business travellers. Its classic restaurant is light and spacious.

Baschi *05023 Terni* **563 N 18** – *pop. 2 692 alt. 165.*
Roma 118 – Orvieto 10 – Terni 70 – Viterbo 46.

Vissani, North : 12 km ✉ 05020 Civitella del Lago ℘ 0744 950206, *Fax 0744 950186* – ⇔ ▤ P AE $ ⊙ MC VISA JCB. ⚘
closed August, Sunday dinner, Wednesday and Thursday lunch – **Meals** (booking essential) a la carte 85/150 (15 %) 🍇.
Spec. Ravioli di grano saraceno farciti di anguilla e uva bianca, mantecato di piselli con farina d'arancia. Maialino da latte croccante con fagioli cannellini, salsa di astice. Crema fritta alla veneziana con salsa al rabarbaro e cubo di cioccolato al caffè.
◆ Antiques and modern decorative items combine to provide an elegant and individualistic style throughout, with creative cuisine notable for its quality of ingredients.

Ladispoli *00055 Roma* **563 Q 18** – *pop. 32 114.*
ℹ *piazza della Vittoria 11 ℘ 06 9913049, unpli@tiscalinet.it, Fax 06 913049.*
Roma 39 – Civitavecchia 34 – Ostia Antica 43 – Tarquinia 53 – Viterbo 79.

La Posta Vecchia 🐎, località Palo Laziale South : 2 km ℘ 06 9949501, *info@lapostavecchia.com, Fax 06 9949507,* ≤, ⛱, 🏖 – |\$| ▤ TV P – 🏛 50. AE $ ⊙ MC VISA. ⚘
19 March-14 November – **Meals** (booking essential) a la carte 76/117 – ☕ 25 – **16 rm** 580, 3 suites.
◆ The luxurious interior of this 17C building has a harmonious warmth ; set among parkland in a seafront location, it feels more like a patrician residence than a hotel. Of particular opulence is the dining room with views over the sea.

Write to us...
If you have any comments on the contents of this Guide.
Your praise as well as your criticisms will receive careful consideration and, with your assistance, we will be able to add to our stock of information and, where necessary, amend our judgments.
Thank you in advance!

FLORENCE (FIRENZE) 50100 P 563 L 15 *G. Tuscan – pop. 352 940 alt. 49.*

See : *Cathedral*** (Duomo)* **Y** *: east end***, dome*** (※**) – Campanile**** **Y B** *: ※** – Baptistry**** **Y A** *: doors***, mosaics*** – Cathedral Museum*** **Y M5** *– Piazza della Signoria*** **Z** *– Loggia della Signoria*** **Z K** *: Perseus*** by B. Cellini – Palazzo Vecchio**** **Z H** *– Uffizi Gallery**** **EU M3** *– Bargello Palace and Museum**** **EU M10** *– San Lorenzo**** **DU V** *: Church**, Laurentian Library**, Medici Tombs*** in Medicee Chapels** – Medici-Riccardi Palace*** **EU S2** *: Chapel***, Luca Giordano Gallery** – Church of Santa Maria Novella*** **DU W** *: frescoes by Ghirlandaio*** – Ponte Vecchio*** **Z** *– Pitti Palace*** **DV** *: Palatine Gallery***, Silver Museum**, Works by Macchiaioli** in Modern Art Gallery* – Boboli Garden** **DV** *: ※* from the Citadel Belvedere – Porcelain Museum** **DV** *– Monastery and Museum of St. Mark*** **ET** *: works*** by Beato Angelico – Academy Gallery*** **ET** *: Michelangelo gallery*** – Piazza della Santissima Annunziata** **ET 168** *: frescoes* in the church, portico** decorated with terracotta Medallions** in the Foundling Hospital* – Church of Santa Croce*** **EU** *: Pazzi Chapel** – Excursion to the hills** : ※*** from Michelangelo Square* **EFV***, Church of San Miniato al Monte*** **EFV***– Strozzi Palace*** **DU S4** *– Rucellai Palace*** **DU S3** *– Masaccio's frescoes*** in the Chapel Brancacci a Santa Maria del Carmine* **DUV** *– Last Supper of Fuligno** **DT***, Last Supper of San Salvi** **BS G** *– Orsanmichele** **EU R** *: tabernacle** by Orcagna – La Badia* **EU E** *: campanile*, delicate relief sculpture in marble**, tombs*, Madonna appearing to St. Bernard* by Filippino Lippi – Sassetti Chapel** and the Chapel of the Annunciation* in the Holy Trinity Church* **DU X** *– Church of the Holy Spirit** **DUV** *– Last Supper* of Sant'Apollonia* **ET** *– All Saints' Church* **DU** *: Last Supper* by Ghirlandaio – Davanzanti Palace** **Z M4** *– New Market Loggia** **Z L** *– Museums : Archaeological** (Chimera from Arezzo**, Françoise Vase**)* **ET***, Science** **EU M6** *– Marino Marini Museum** **Z M** *– Bardini Museum** **EV** *– La Specola Museum** **DV**.

See also : *Casa Buonarroti** **EU M1** *– Semi-precious Stone Workshop** **ET M9** *– Crucifixion* by Perugino* **EU C** *– Museo Horne** **EUV M11.**

Envir. : *Medicee Villas** : villa della Petraia*, villa di Castello*, villa di Poggio a Caiano** by via P. Toselli* **CT** *: 17 km, villa LaFerdinanda* di Artimino by via Pisana* **CU** *: 20 km – Galluzzo Carthusian Monastery** by via Senese* **CV**.

9 Parco di Firenze ☎ 3480058590, Fax 055 785627, North : 4 km;

18 Dell'Ugolino (closed Monday March-September), to Grassina ✉ 50015 ☎ 055 2301009, Fax 055 2301141, South : 12 km **BS**.

✈ *Amerigo Vespucci North-West : 4 km by via P. Toselli* **CT** *☎ 055 30615, Fax 055 318716.*

via Cavour 1 r ✉ 50129 ☎ 055 290832, infoturismo@provincia.fi.it, Fax 055 2760383 – piazza della Stazione 4 ✉ 50123 ☎ 055 212245, turismo3@comune.fi.it, Fax 055 2381226.

A.C.I. *viale Amendola 36 ✉ 50121 ☎ 055 24861, Fax 055 486234.*
Roma 277 – Bologna 105 – Milano 298.

Plans on following pages

The Westin Excelsior, piazza Ognissanti 3 ✉ 50123 ☎ 055 27151 and rest. ☎ 055 27152785, *excelsiorflorence@westin.com, Fax 055 210278* – 🛗, ⇔ rm, ▤ TV ☎ ♿ rm – 🏛 180. AE ⑤ ⑩ MO VISA JCB. ⛔ **DU b**
Meals *Il Cestello* Rest. a la carte 54/70 – ☕ 39 – **151 rm** 527/710, 11 suites.
• Sumptuous interiors within this former aristocratic residence on the banks of the Arno, where tradition and the most modern comforts blend to create a rarefied ambience. A regal atmosphere to the dining room ; coffered ceilings and Carrara marble.

Grand Hotel, piazza Ognissanti 1 ✉ 50123 ☎ 055 27761 and rest. ☎ 055 217400, *grandflorence@luxurycollection.com, Fax 055 217400,* 🌳, 🏋 – 🛗, ⇔ rm, ▤ TV ☎. AE ⑤ ⑩ MO VISA JCB **DU a**
Meals *Incanto Cafè Restaurant* Rest. a la carte 62/79 – ☕ 39 – **100 rm** 546/737, 7 suites.
• The atmosphere of Renaissance Florence combines with 21C comfort in the elegant surroundings of this prestigious titan of the hotel world. The sophisticated restaurant, which has been recently revamped, incorporates a terrace onto the piazza and on-show kitchen.

Savoy, piazza della Repubblica 7 ✉ 50123 ☎ 055 27351, *reservations@hotelsavoy.it, Fax 055 2735888,* 🌳 – 🛗, ⇔ rest, ▤ TV ☎ ♿ – 🏛 70. AE ⑤ ⑩ MO VISA JCB. ⛔ **Z q**
Meals *L'Incontro* Rest. a la carte 39/70 – ☕ 25 – **98 rm** 341/847, 9 suites.
• After total refurbishment, this great hotel (founded 1893) has been revitalised, offering a mix of elegance, comfort and high-tech gadgetry. Run by a young chef with an excellent track record, the brasserie style restaurant opens onto the piazza in summer.

J.K. Place without rest., piazza Santa Maria Novella 7 ✉ 50123 ☎ 055 2645181, *jkplace@jkplace.com, Fax 055 2658387,* ≤ – 🛗 ▤ TV ☎. AE ⑤ ⑩ MO VISA JCB **Y e**
20 rm ☕ 315/350, 2 suites.
• Of recent construction, this is a refined hotel with an atmosphere of modern elegance. Great care has been taken in choosing the high quality contemporary style furnishings.

Regency, piazza Massimo D'Azeglio 3 ✉ 50121 ☎ 055 245247, *info@regency-hotel.com, Fax 055 2346735,* – |‡|, ▤ TV ☏. AE ⓢ ◐ ◎ VISA JCB. ✂ rest FU a
Meals *Relais le Jardin* Rest. (booking essential) a la carte 40/66 – **34 rm** ☐ 363/605, suite.
◆ An atmosphere of charm and comfort offering respite from the tourist trail. Guests can relax in the pampered environment of the elegant lounge or the hidden calm of the garden, which may be seen from the more informal of the two dining rooms.

Albani, via Fiume 12 ✉ 50123 ☎ 055 26030, *hotel.albani@firenzealbergo.it, Fax 055 211045,* – |‡|, ✂ rm, ▤ TV ☏ – 350. AE ⓢ ◐ ◎ VISA JCB. ✂ rest
Meals (residents only) a la carte 41/50 – **98 rm** ☐ 345/360, 4 suites. DT a
◆ Close to the station, in a prestigious early 20C building, a refined Neo-classical style permeates throughout this charming hotel.

Helvetia e Bristol, via dei Pescioni 2 ✉ 50123 ☎ 055 26651, *information.hbf@royaldemeure.com, Fax 055 288353* – |‡| ▤ TV. AE ⓢ ◐ ◎ VISA JCB. ✂ Z b
Meals a la carte 46/69 – ☐ 30,80 – **45 rm** 314,60/580,80, 13 suites.
◆ The elegant allure of days gone by in an imposing 19C building, furnished with authentic antiques and 17C Florentine pictures. Very near Palazzo Strozzi.

Plaza Hotel Lucchesi, lungarno della Zecca Vecchia 38 ✉ 50122 ☎ 055 26236, *phl@plazalucchesi.it, Fax 055 2480921,* ← – |‡| ▤ TV – 160. AE ⓢ ◐ ◎ VISA JCB. ✂ rest EV b
Meals (residents only) a la carte 39/56 – **97 rm** ☐ 237/387.
◆ This elegant riverside hotel has been restored in keeping with the building which it occupies. Many rooms look onto the river and Santa Croce.

Grand Hotel Minerva, piazza Santa Maria Novella 16 ✉ 50123 ☎ 055 27230, *info@grandhotelminerva.com, Fax 055 268281,* – |‡|, ✂ rm, ▤ TV ☏ – 80. AE ⓢ ◐ ◎ VISA JCB. ✂ rest Y n
Meals *I Chiostri* Rest. a la carte 32/61 – **97 rm** ☐ 270/350, 5 suites.
◆ Next to the church of Santa Maria Novella, a very comfortable modern hotel, with well-proportioned public areas. Lovely view from the terrace with pool. A huge window looks onto the internal garden from the larger of the dining rooms, decorated in modern style

Continentale without rest., vicolo dell'Oro 6 r ✉ 50123 ☎ 055 27262, *continentale@lungarnohotels.com, Fax 055 283139,* – |‡|, ✂ rm, ▤ TV ☏ ♿. AE ⓢ ◐ ◎ VISA JCB. ✂ Z y
43 rm ☐ 381/405, suite.
◆ Situated at the base of a medieval tower, this sophisticated hotel has splendid views of the Ponte Vecchio, from both its flower-bedecked terrace and some of its fine rooms.

Lungarno, borgo Sant'Jacopo 14 ✉ 50125 ☎ 055 27261 and rest. ☎ 055 281661, *lungarno@lungarnohotels.com, Fax 055 268437,* ← – |‡|, ✂ rm, ▤ TV ☏ – 25. AE ⓢ ◐ ◎ VISA JCB. ✂ Z s
Meals *Borgo San Jacopo* Rest. *(closed August)* a la carte 35/61 – **60 rm** ☐ 380/415, 13 suites.
◆ Rooms with priceless views in a hotel on the very banks of the Arno, where the management's attention to detail is evident throughout. Fine collection of modern pictures. Bright restaurant with river terrace.

Brunelleschi, piazza Santa Elisabetta 3 ✉ 50122 ☎ 055 27370, *info@hotelbrunelleschi.it, Fax 055 219653,* ← – |‡|, ✂ rm, ▤ TV ☏ – 100. AE ⓢ ◐ ◎ VISA JCB. ✂ rest
Meals *(closed Sunday)* (residents only) – **87 rm** ☐ 245/360, 9 suites. Z c
◆ It seems possible to touch Brunelleschi's dome from some of the rooms in this elegant, unusual hotel. The tower dating to Byzantine times houses its own small museum.

Lorenzo il Magnifico without rest., via Lorenzo il Magnifico 25 ✉ 50129 ☎ 055 4630878, *info@lorenzoilmagnifico.net, Fax 055 4630878,* – |‡| ▤ TV ☏ ♿ P – 35. AE ⓢ ◐ ◎ VISA JCB. ✂ ET f
28 rm ☐ 230/280, suite.
◆ Once a convent, this elegant villa set among gardens has been competently restored ; high standards of comfort and hospitality.

Sofitel Firenze, via de' Cerretani 10 ✉ 50123 ☎ 055 2381301, *sofitel.firenze@accor-hotels.it, Fax 055 2381312* – |‡|, ✂ rm, ▤ TV ☏ ♿ rm. AE ⓢ ◐ ◎ VISA JCB. ✂
Meals *Il Patio* Rest. a la carte 34/47 – **83 rm** ☐ 380/420, suite. Y r
◆ A 17C patrician palace, now restored to offer all mod cons including very effective soundproofing, a real benefit given the central location ; the elegant restaurant is set in a glass-roofed terrace.

Gallery Hotel Art, vicolo dell'Oro 5 ✉ 50123 ☎ 055 27263 and rest. ☎ 055 27266987, *gallery@lungarnohotels.com, Fax 055 268557* – |‡|, ✂ rm, ▤ TV ☏ ♿. AE ⓢ ◐ ◎ VISA JCB. ✂ Z u
Meals *The Fusion Bar-Shozan Gallery* Rest. *(closed Monday)* a la carte 35/50 – **69 rm** ☐ 347/380, 5 suites.
◆ Contemporary design by a leading architect and cosmopolitan artwork displayed along art gallery lines are the ingredients making this truly modern hotel so unusual. A sophisticated, trendy restaurant with fusion cuisine.

FIRENZE
LIVORNO, GENOVA
PISA LIVORNO
SIENA
FORTEZZA DA BASSO
PORTA AL PRATO
ARNO
Ognissanti
PONTE VECCHIO
Corridoio Vasariano
S. SPIRITO
S. MARIA DEL CARMINE
Piazza del Carmine
Piazza S. Spirito
Piazza dei Pitti
PALAZZO PITTI
MUSEO LA SPECOLA
GIARDINO DI BOBOLI
VIOTTOLONE
PIAZZALE D. ISOLOTTO
Forte del Belvedere
MUSEO DELLE PORCELLANE
PORTA ROMANA
Viale N. Machiavelli
PASSEGGIATA AI COLLI
Cenacolo di Fuligno
PAL. D. CONGRESSI
PAL. D. AFFARI
Pza d. Indipendenza
Pza Vittorio Veneto
Pza Gaddi
Pza T. Tasso
Lungarno Amerigo Vespucci
Ponte Vespucci
Pte alla Carraia
L. Corsini
L. Guicciardini
Borgo S. Frediano
V. S. Spirito
V. Maggio
S. Felicita
300 m

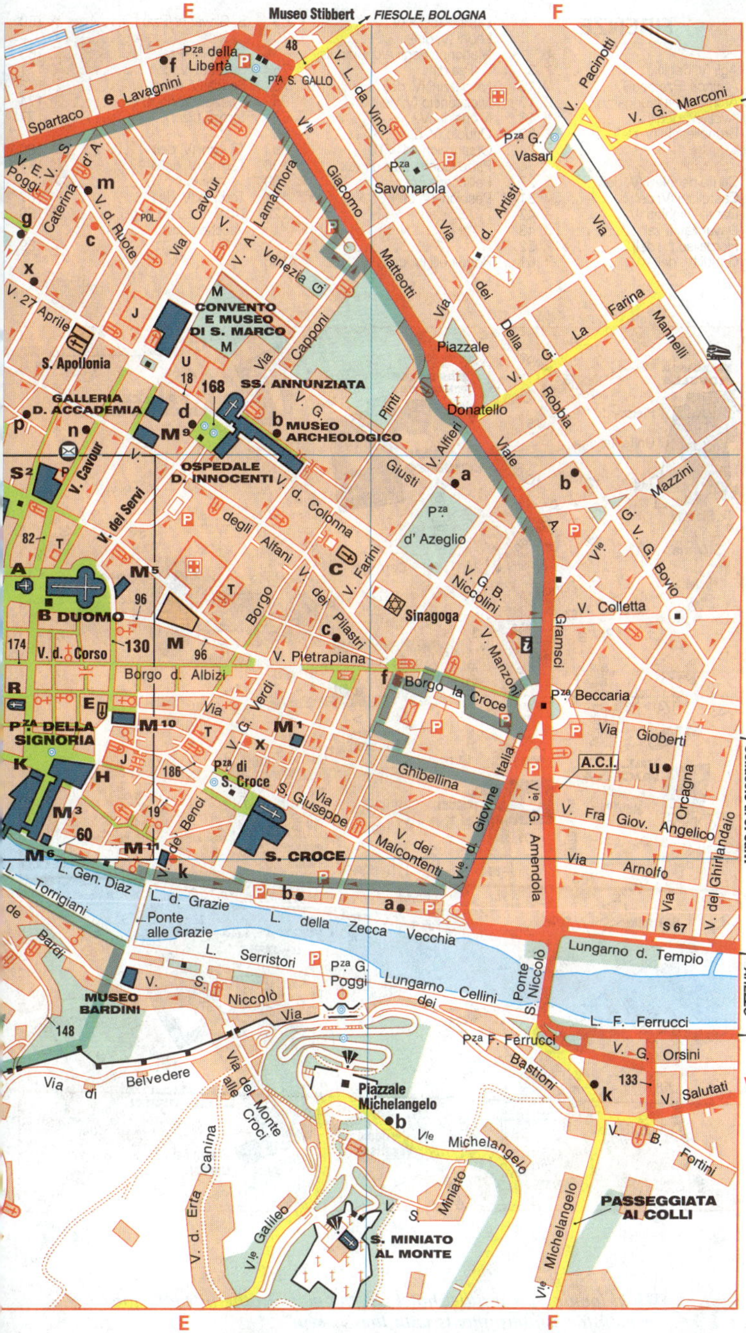
Museo Stibbert
FIESOLE, BOLOGNA
Pza della Libertà
Pta S. Gallo
Lavagnini
Spartaco
V. L. da Vinci
Vle Giacomo Matteotti
Pza Savonarola
Pza G. Vasari
V. Pacinotti
V. G. Marconi
FIESOLE
Via Cavour
V. A. Lamarmora
V. Venezia
V. G. Capponi
V. d. Ruote
Caterina d'A.
V. 27 Aprile
CONVENTO E MUSEO DI S. MARCO
S. Apollonia
GALLERIA D. ACCADEMIA
SS. ANNUNZIATA
MUSEO ARCHEOLOGICO
OSPEDALE D. INNOCENTI
Piazzale Donatello
Via Pinti
V. Alfieri
V. Giusti
Pza d' Azeglio
V. della Robbia
Via La Farina
V. Mannelli
Viale Mazzini
V. G. B. Niccolini
Sinagoga
V. Colletta
V. Manzoni
Gramsci
Pza Beccaria
Via Gioberti
A.C.I.
Orcagna
V. Fra Giov. Angelico
Via Arnolfo
V. del Ghirlandaio
Cenacolo di S. Salvi
V. Cavour
V. dei Servi
V. d. Colonna
V. degli Alfani
V. Farini
Borgo Pinti
V. dei Pilastri
DUOMO
V. d. Corso
Borgo d. Albizi
V. Pietrapiana
Borgo la Croce
Ghibellina
Via G. Verdi
Pza di S. Croce
Via S. Giuseppe
V. dei Malcontenti
Vle d. Giovine Italia
Vle G. Amendola
Pza DELLA SIGNORIA
S. CROCE
V. de Benci
L. Gen. Diaz
L. Torrigiani
L. d. Grazie
Ponte alle Grazie
L. della Zecca Vecchia
Lungarno d. Tempio
AREZZO
L. Serristori
Pza G. Poggi
Lungarno Cellini
Ponte S. Niccolò
V. de Bardi
V. S. Niccolò
MUSEO BARDINI
L. F. Ferrucci
V. G. Orsini
V. Salutati
Pza F. Ferrucci
Bastioni
Via di Belvedere
Via del Monte alle Croci
Piazzale Michelangelo
Vle Michelangelo
V. B. Fortini
V. S. Miniato
V. d. Erta Canina
Vle Galileo
S. MINIATO AL MONTE
Vle Michelangelo
PASSEGGIATA AI COLLI
E
F
T
U
V

FIRENZE

Agli (V. degli) . . . . Y 3
Antinori (Pza degli) . . . . Y 10
Archibusieri (Lungarno) . . . . . Z 12
Avelli (V. degli) . . . . Y 16
Brunelleschi (V. de') . . . . . . YZ 22
Calimala (V.) . . . . Z 24
Calzaiuoli (V. dei) . . . . YZ
Canto de' Nelli (V. del) . . . . . . Y 27
Castellani (V. de') . . . . Z 31
Dante Alighieri (V.) . . . . Z 42
Davanzati (Pza) . . . . Z 43
Fiordaliso (V. del) . . . . Z 52
Gondi (V. dei) . . . . Z 61
Lambertesca (V.) . . . . Z 69
Leoni (V. dei) . . . . Z 70
Madonna degli Aldobrandini (Pza di) . . . . Y 75
Magazzini (V. dei) . . . . Z 76
Melarancio (V. del) . . . . Y 85
Monalda (V.) . . . . Z 88
Oriuolo (V. d.) . . . . Y 96
Orsanmichele (V.) . . . . Z 99
Parte Guelfa (Pza di) . . . . Z 106
Pellicceria (V.) . . . . Z 109
Pescioni (V. de') . . . . YZ 111
Por S. Maria (V.) . . . . Z 126
Porta Rossa (V.) . . . . Z
Roma (V.) . . . . YZ
Rondinelli (V. de') . . . . Y 138
S. Giovanni (Pza) . . . . Y 150
S. Jacopo (Borgo) . . . . Z
S. Trinità (Pza) . . . . Z 163
Sassetti (V. de') . . . . Z 171
Spada (V. della) . . . . Z 173
Speziali (V. degli) . . . . Z 174
Strozzi (Pza) . . . . Z 177
Strozzi (V. degli) . . . . Z
Tavolini (V. dei) . . . . Z 180
Terme (V. delle) . . . . Z 181
Tornabuoni (V.) . . . . Z
Trebbio (V. del) . . . . Y 187
Uffizi (Piazzale degli) . . . . Z 188
Vaccchereccia (V.) . . . . Z 189
Vecchio (Ponte) . . . . Z

Traffic restricted in the town centre.

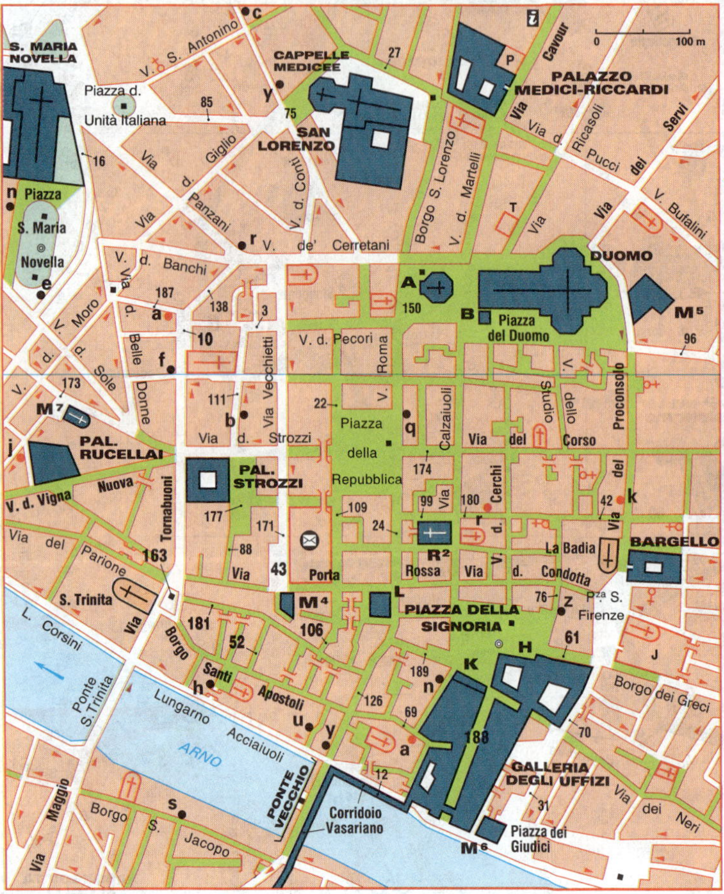

When looking for a quiet hotel use the maps in the introduction or look for establishments with the [symbol] *sign*

INDEX OF STREET NAMES IN FIRENZE

27 Aprile (V.) ET
Acciaiuoli (Lungarno) Z
Agli (V. degli) Y 3
Alamanni (V. L.) DT
Albizi (Borgo degli) EU
Aleardi (Viale A.) CU
Alfani (V. degli) ETU
Alfieri (V. V.) FTU
Amendola (Viale G.) FUV
Antinori (Pza degli) Y 10
Archibusieri (Lungarno) Z 12
Ariosto (Viale F.) CU 15
Arnolfo (V.) FV
Artisti (V. degli) FT
Avelli (V. degli) Y 16
Azeglio (Pza d') FU
Banchi (V. del) Y
Bardi (V. de) DEV
Bastioni (V. dei) EFV
Battisti (V. C.) ET 18
Beccaria (Pza) FU
Belfiore (Viale) CT
Belle Donne (V. delle) Y
Bellosguardo (V. di) CV
Belvedere (V. di) EV
Benci (V. de') EUV
Bentaccordi (V.) EU 19
Bovio (V. G.) FU
Brunelleschi (V. de') YZ 22
Bufalini (V.) Y
Calimala (V.) Z, DU 24
Calzaiuoli (V. dei) YZ
Canto de' Nelli (V. del) Y 27
Capponi (V. G.) ET
Carmine (Pza del) DU
Carraia (Ponte alla) DU
Casone (V. del) CV
Castellani (V. de') Z 31
Cavallotti (V. F.) CU
Cavour (V.) Y, ET
Cellini (Lungarno) FV
Cerchi (V. de') Z
Cerretani (V. de') Y, DU 34
Colletta (V. P.) FU
Colonna (V. della) EU
Condotta (V. della) Z
Conti (V. de') Y, DU 39
Corsini (Lungarno) Z, DU
Corso (V. del) Z, EU
Croce (Borgo la) FU
Dante Alighieri (V.) Z 42
Davanzati (Pza) Z 43
Della Robbia (V. dei) FT
Diacceto (V. J. da) DT
Diaz (Lungarno Generale) EV
Don G. Minzoni (Viale) ET 48
Donatello (Piazzale) FT
Duomo (Pza del) Y
Faenza (V.) DTU
Farina (V. G. La) FT
Farini (V.) EFU
Ferrucci (Lungarno F.) FV
Ferrucci (Pza F.) FV
Fiordaliso (V. del) Z 52
Fonderia (V. della) CU
Fortini (V. B.) FV
Foscolo (V. U.) CV
Fossi (V. de') DU
Fra G. Angelico (V.) FU
Fratelli Rosselli (Viale) CDT
Gaddi (Pza) CU
Galileo (Viale) EV
Galliano (V. G.) CT
Ghibellina (V.) EFU
Ghirlandaio (V. del) FUV
Giglio (Via del) Y
Gioberti (Via V.) FU
Giovine Italia (Viale della) FUV
Giudici (Pza dei) Z, EU 60
Giusti (V. G.) EFTU
Gondi (V. dei) Z 61
Gramsci (Viale) FTU
Grazie (Lungarno delle) EV
Grazie (Ponte alle) EV
Greci (Borgo dei) Z
Guelfa (V.) DET
Guicciardini (Lungarno) DU
Guicciardini (V. de') DV 66
Indipendenza (Pza della) DT
Italia (Cso) CU
Lamarmora (V. A.) ET
Lambertesca (V.) Z 69
Lavagnini (Viale S.) DET
Leoni (V. dei) Z 70
Libertà (Pza della) ET
Machiavelli (Viale N.) CDV
Madonna degli Aldobrandini (Pza di) Y 75
Magazzini (V. dei) Z 76
Maggio (V.) Z, DV
Malcontenti (V. dei) UV
Mannelli (V.) FT
Manzoni (V. A.) FU
Marcello (V. B.) CT
Marconi (V. G.) FT
Martelli (V. de') Y, EU 82
Matteotti (Viale G.) EFT
Mazzetta (V.) DV 84
Mazzini (Viale G.) FU
Melarancio (V. del) Y 85
Michelangelo (Piazzale) EFV
Michelangelo (Viale) FV
Monaco (V. G.) CDT
Monalda (V.) Z 88
Monte alle Croci (V. del) EV
Montebello (V.) CTU
Moro (V. del) Y
Nazionale (V.) DT
Neri (V. dei) Z
Niccolini (V. G. B.) FU
Ognissanti (Borgo) DU 93
Orcagna (V.) FUV
Oriuolo (V. d.) Y, EU 96
Orsanmichele (V.) Z 99
Orsini (V. G.) FV
Orto (V. d.) CU
Pacinotti (V. A.) FT
Palazzoulo (V.) DU
Panzani (V.) Y, DU 102
Parione (V. del) Z
Parte Guelfa (Pza di) Z 106
Pecori (V. de') Y
Pellicceria (V.) Z 109
Pescioni (V. de') YZ 111
Petrarca (Viale F.) CV
Pietrapiana (V.) EU
Pilastri (V. dei) EU
Pinti (Borgo) EFTU
Pisana (V.) CU
Pitti (Pza dei) DV
Poggi (Pza G.) EV
Poggi (V. E.) ET
Ponte alle Mosse (V. del) CT
Ponte Sospeso (V. del) CU 124
Por S. Maria (V.) Z 126
Porta Rossa (V.) Z
Porte Nuove (V. delle) CT
Prato (il) CT
Proconsolo (V. del) ZY
Pucci (V. de') Y
Redi (Viale F.) CT
Repubblica (Pza della) Z, DU 132
Ricasoli (V.) Y
Ricorborli (V. di) FV 133
Ridolfi (V. C.) DT 135
Roma (V.) YZ, DU 136
Romana (V.) CDV
Rondinelli (V. de') Y, DU 138
Ruote (V. delle) ET
S. Agostino (V.) DV 145
S. Antonino (V.) Y
S. Caterina d'Alessandria (V.) ET
S. Croce (Pza di) EU
S. Firenze (Pza) Z
S. Frediano (Borgo) CDU
S. Giorgio (Costa di) EV 148
S. Giovanni (Pza) Y 150
S. Giuseppe (V. di) EU
S. Jacopo (Borgo) Z, DU 153
S. Lorenzo (Borgo) Y
S. Maria Novella (Pza) Y
S. Miniato (V.) FV
S. Monaca (V.) DU 156
S. Niccolò (Ponte) FV
S. Niccolò (V.) EV
S. Rosa (Lungarno di) CU
S. Spirito (Pza) DV
S. Spirito (V.) DU
S. Trinita (Ponte) Z
S. Trinita (Pza) Z 163
Salutati (V.) FV
Saluti (V. C.) FV
Santi Apostoli (Borgo) Z, DU 166
Santissima Annunziata (Pza della) ET 168
Sanzio (Viale R.) CU
Sassetti (V. de') Z 171
Savonarola (Pza) FT
Scala (V. della) DTU
Serragli (V. de') DUV
Serristori (Lungarno) EV
Servi (V. dei) Y, EU
Signoria (Pza della) Z, EU
Soderini (Lungarno) CDU
Sole (V. del) YZ
Spada (V. della) Z 173
Speziali (V. degli) Z, EU 174
Strozzi (Pza) Z 177
Strozzi (V. degli) Z, DU 178
Strozzi (Viale F.) DT
Studio (V. dello) YZ
Tasso (Pza T.) CUV
Tavolini (V. dei) Z 180
Tempio (Lungarno del) FV
Terme (V. delle) Z, DU 181
Tornabuoni (V.) Z, DU 184
Torrigiani (Lungarno) EV
Torta (V.) EU 186
Toselli (V. P.) CT
Trebbio (V. del) Y 187
Uffizi (Piazzale degli) Z 188
Unità Italiana (Pza d.) Y
Vaccheréccia (V.) Z 189
Valfonda (V.) DT
Vasari (Pza G.) FT
Vecchietti (V. de') YZ
Vecchio (Ponte) Z, DU
Veneto (Pza Vittorio) CT
Venezia (V.) ET
Verdi (V. G.) EU
Vespucci (Lungarno A.) CDU
Vespucci (Ponte) CU
Vigna Nuova (V. della) Z, DU 193
Villani (V.) CV
Vinci (V. L. da) EFT
Vittoria (Ponte della) CU
Zecca Vecchia (Lungarno della) EFV

Anglo American, via Garibaldi 9 ✉ 50123 ☎ 055 282114, *reservation.ghr@framon-hotels.it, Fax 055 268513* – 100. – CU a
Meals a la carte 40/57 – **111 rm** 209/253, 4 suites.
◆ Central but surprisingly tranquil, close to the Lungarno. A cosy, welcoming atmosphere, with an unusual glass gallery lounge area. Evocations of days gone by in the dining room, serving Tuscan and Mediterranean dishes.

Starhotel Michelangelo, viale Fratelli Rosselli 2 ✉ 50123 ☎ 055 2784, *michelangelo.fi@starhotels.it, Fax 055 2382232* – rm, – 250. CT f
Meals 25 – **117 rm** 270, 2 suites.
◆ After a total refit this is effectively a brand new hotel, with accommodation boasting every comfort (even TV in the bathrooms) ; well-equipped conference rooms. An atmosphere of refinement in the cellars.

De la Ville without rest., piazza Antinori 1 ✉ 50123 ☎ 055 2381805, *info@hoteldelaville.it, Fax 055 2381809* – – 50. Y f
71 rm 240/415, 4 suites.
◆ Situated in the most exclusive shopping district, this hotel of distinction has been refitted. Offers spacious and stylish accommodation with modern bathrooms.

Adler Cavalieri without rest., via della Scala 40 ✉ 50123 ☎ 055 277810, *info@hoteladlercavalieri.com, Fax 055 27781509,* – DU x
60 rm 205/290.
◆ Close to the station, this hotel of studied elegance is excellently soundproofed and has fine wood panelling throughout. Efficient young management.

Palazzo Magnani Feroni without rest., borgo San Frediano 5 ✉ 50124 ☎ 055 2399544, *info@florencepalace.it, Fax 055 2608908,* – DU f
12 suites **320/590.**
◆ Occupying a 16C patrician palazzo with a small courtyard, this hotel offers fine all round views of the city from its terraces.

Londra, via Jacopo da Diacceto 18 ✉ 50123 ☎ 055 27390, *info@hotellondra.com, Fax 055 210682,* – rm, – 200. rest DT h
Meals a la carte 37/54 – **166 rm** 250/335.
◆ Located near the station, this comfortable and functional modern hotel has spacious public areas, a business centre and conference rooms. A contemporary-style dining room, with an adjoining terrace offering a more romantic setting.

J and J without rest., via di Mezzo 20 ✉ 50121 ☎ 055 26312, *jandj@dada.it, Fax 055 240282* – EU c
15 rm 315/430, 5 suites.
◆ An eclectic feel pervades throughout this atmospheric and original hotel, which was once a 16C convent.

UNA Hotel Vittoria, via Pisana 59 ✉ 50143 ☎ 055 22771, *una.vittoria@unahotels.it, Fax 055 22772* – rm, – 100. CU b
Meals a la carte 35/46 – **84 rm** 417/490.
◆ An unusual techno-hotel combining comfort with innovation. The imaginative design brief has created a charming and unique ambience. Original dining room with refectory table.

Grand Hotel Adriatico, via Maso Finiguerra 9 50123 ☎ 055 27931 and rest. ☎ 055 294447, *info@hoteladriatico.it, Fax 055 289661,* – rm, rm – 180. DU d
Meals 20/35 – **116 rm** 260/290, 3 suites.
◆ This recently refitted hotel benefits from a very central location, private parking, and a spacious, comfortable interior ; rooms in both modern and antique style. An attractive classical-style feel to two dining rooms serving Tuscan and national cuisine.

Berchielli without rest., lungarno Acciaiuoli 14 ✉ 50123 ☎ 055 264061, *info@berchielli.it, Fax 055 218636,* – – 80. Z h
76 rm 310/345, 4 suites.
◆ To not only be in the heart of Florence, but also on the Arno with a view of the Ponte Vecchio ; such is the enviable location of this comfortable hotel of distinction.

Il Guelfo Bianco without rest., via Cavour 29 ✉ 50129 ☎ 055 288330, *info@ilguelfobianco.it, Fax 055 295203* – ET n
30 rm 135/210.
◆ This small but distinguished hotel is close to the Duomo, housed in a restored 16C palazzo ; fine rooms, some with coffered ceilings.

Cellai without rest., via 27 Aprile 14 ✉ 50129 ☎ 055 489291, *info@hotelcellai.it, Fax 055 470387* – ET x
55 rm 150/225.
◆ A welcoming feel to this particularly well presented hotel, which hosts regular art exhibitions and has some fine furniture.

Porta Faenza without rest., via Faenza 77 ✉ 50123 ☎ 055 217975, *info@hotelporta faenza.it, Fax 055 210101* – DT d
25 rm 206.
• This welcoming hotel occupies an 18C building near Palazzo dei Congressi ; well-equipped comfortable rooms with fine furnishings.

Loggiato dei Serviti without rest., piazza SS. Annunziata 3 ✉ 50122 ☎ 055 289592, *info@loggiatodeiservitihotel.it, Fax 055 289595* – ET d
38 rm 140/205, 4 suites.
• Occupying the 16C twin of Brunelleschi's foundling hospital, this hotel has preserved its historic charm throughout.

Botticelli without rest., via Taddea 8 ✉ 50123 ☎ 055 290905, *info@hotelbotticelli.it, Fax 055 294322* – ET p
34 rm 140/225.
• Near San Lorenzo market, in a 16C palazzo, a charming hotel with frescoed vaulting in its public areas and a small covered terrace ; rooms with modern furnishings

Inpiazzadellasignoria without rest., via de' Magazzini 2 ✉ 50122 ☎ 055 2399546, *info@inpiazzadellasignoria.it, Fax 055 2676616* – Z z
10 rm 210/260.
• As the name suggests, this establishment overlooks Piazza della Signoria, the very heart of Florence ; the welcoming interior has an elegant air.

Palazzo Benci without rest., piazza Madonna degli Aldobrandini 3 ✉ 50123 ☎ 055 213848, *info@palazzobenci.com, Fax 055 288308*, – 30. Y y
35 rm 140/195.
• Next to San Lorenzo ; traces of the original 16C structure can still be seen in the public areas of this hotel which has a charming inner courtyard and comfortable rooms.

Relais Uffizi without rest., chiasso de' Baroncelli-chiasso del Buco 16 ✉ 50122 ☎ 055 2676239, *info@relaisuffizi.it, Fax 055 2657909* – Z n
8 rm 160/200.
• This medieval palazzo has eight tasteful rooms, and a breakfast room unique in Florence for its marvellous view of Piazza della Signoria.

Caravaggio without rest., piazza Indipendenza 5 ☎ 055 496310, *info@hotelcaravaggio.it, Fax 055 4628827* – DT e
37 rm 140/160.
• Having evolved from three former pensioni, this comfortable modern hotel is close to the centre. A family atmosphere of refinement.

Malaspina without rest., piazza dell'Indipendenza 24 ✉ 50129 ☎ 055 489869, *info@malaspinahotel.it, Fax 055 474809* – ET g
31 rm 130/199.
• An attractive hotel founded ten years ago after the reconstruction of an old palazzo ; welcoming public areas and stylish rooms.

Royal without rest., via delle Ruote 52 ✉ 50129 ☎ 055 483287, *info@hotelroyalfirenze.it, Fax 055 490976*, – ET m
39 rm 120/200.
• This former aristocratic residence with its fine garden and handy parking is pleasantly tranquil despite its central location ; comfortable rooms.

De Rose Palace without rest., via Solferino 5 ✉ 50123 ☎ 055 2396818, *firenze@hotelderose.it, Fax 055 268249* – CU c
18 rm 135/220.
• In a restored 19C palace, an elegant hotel with period furnishings and some fine Venetian lamps ; relaxing family atmosphere.

Select without rest., via Giuseppe Galliano 24 ✉ 50144 ☎ 055 330342, *info@selecthotel.it, Fax 055 351506* – 25. CT t
closed 20 to 27 December – 39 rm 190/210.
• Located away from the city centre and equally popular with tourists and business clients, this hotel has limited yet well presented public areas and rooms with wood furnishings. Courtyard pay parking.

Grifone without rest., via Pilati 22 ✉ 50136 ☎ 055 623300, *info@hotelgrifonefirenze.com, Fax 055 677628* –
61 rm 117/179, 10 suites. by lungarno del Tempio FV
• Located away from the city centre, this hotel caters for a predominantly business clientele ; plenty of free parking, wood furnishings in the rooms and apartments with kitchen facilities.

Della Robbia without rest., via della Robbia 7/9 ✉ 50132 ☎ 055 2638570, *info@hoteldellarobbia.it, Fax 055 2466371* – |♦| ▤ TV ☎ P. AE ⚬ ⓓ MC VISA JCB. ✗ FU b
closed August – **19 rm** ☕ 129/245.
◆ An Art Nouveau feel to both the fa e and the genteel interior of this new establishment occupying an early 20C small villa, run by its owners.

Morandi alla Crocetta without rest., via Laura 50 ✉ 50121 ☎ 055 2344747, *welcome@hotelmorandi.it, Fax 055 2480954* – ▤ TV. AE ⚬ ⓓ MC VISA JCB ET b
☕ 12 – **10 rm** 120/180.
◆ The cosy atmosphere of a grand private house pervades this stylishly furnished hotel with many period details ; in the centre near the Museo Archeologico.

River without rest., lungarno della Zecca Vecchia 18 ✉ 50122 ☎ 055 2343529, *info@hotelriver.com, Fax 055 2343531,* ← – |♦| ▤ TV ☎. AE ⚬ ⓓ MC VISA. ✗ FV a
closed 12 to 27 December – **38 rm** ☕ 190.
◆ Well located in a 19C palazzo on the Arno. The top floor rooms overlooking the river benefit from a delightful terrace. Attractively restored.

Enoteca Pinchiorri, via Ghibellina 87 ✉ 50122 ☎ 055 242777, *ristorante@enotecapinchiorri.com, Fax 055 244983,* ☂ – ✗ ▤. AE ⚬ MC VISA JCB EU x
closed August, Christmas, 31 December, Sunday, Monday and lunch Tuesday-Wednesday – **Meals** (booking essential) a la carte 165/235 ♠.
Spec. Capesante alla griglia, le loro barbine "cotte come la trippa" e raviolo farcito di zucchine all'origano. Spaghetti alla chitarra con crema di peperoni dolci e sgombro marinato. Maialino da latte con scalogni in agrodolce, insalata di patate e soprassata.
◆ Impeccable food, service and atmosphere ; summer dining outside. Sublime cuisine and a famously peerless wine list.

Cibrèo, via A. Del Verrocchio 8/r ✉ 50122 ☎ 055 2341100, *cibreo.fi@tin.it, Fax 055 244966* – ▤. AE ⚬ ⓓ MC VISA JCB FU f
closed 26 July-6 September, 31 December-6 January, Sunday and Monday – **Meals** (booking essential) a la carte 64/74 see also rest. ***Trattoria Cibrèo-Cibreino.***
◆ Perennially fashionable restaurant popular for its informal elegance ; young, relaxed staff and a dedicated, imaginative culinary style.

Don Chisciotte, via Ridolfi 4 r ✉ 50129 ☎ 055 475430, *Fax 055 485305* – ✗ ▤. AE ⚬ ⓓ MC VISA JCB. ✗ DT x
closed August, Sunday and Monday lunch – **Meals** (booking essential) a la carte 45/69.
◆ Close to the Fortezza da basso, an elegant atmosphere pervades in what is one of the city's finest restaurants ; creative modern twists to classic dishes.

Taverna del Bronzino, via delle Ruote 25/27 r ✉ 50129 ☎ 055 495220, *tavernadelbronzino@rabottiumberto.191.it, Fax 055 4620076* – ▤. AE ⚬ ⓓ MC VISA ET c
closed Easter, August, Christmas and Sunday – **Meals** (booking essential) a la carte 60/73 ♠.
◆ In a 15C palazzo, courteous hospitality and the historic setting set the tone for fine traditional cuisine.

Buca Lapi, via del Trebbio 1 r ✉ 50123 ☎ 055 213768, *Fax 055 284862* – ▤. AE ⚬ ⓓ MC VISA JCB Y a
closed August and Sunday – **Meals** (dinner only) (booking essential) a la carte 50/64 (10 %).
◆ In the ancient cellars of the palazzo Antinori, with well-presented typical Tuscan dishes. Very atmospheric.

Angels, via del Proconsolo 29/31 ✉ 50123 ☎ 055 2398762, *info@ristoranteangels.it, Fax 055 2398123, Rest. and american-bar* – ▤. AE ⚬ ⓓ MC VISA JCB. ✗ Z k
Meals (dinner only) a la carte 43/58 ♠.
◆ Run by a dedicated young couple, this modern establishment is set against an historic backdrop. Buffet lunches, with a more sophisticated evening menu.

Beccofino, piazza Scarlatti 1 r ✉ 50125 ☎ 055 290076, *info@beccofino.com, Fax 055 2728312* – ▤. ⚬ MC VISA. ✗ DU g
closed Monday – **Meals** (dinner only except Sunday) a la carte 40/49.
◆ A popular spot, modern in style with relaxed yet efficient service. The cuisine is contemporary and includes vegetarian dishes.

Il Cavaliere, viale Lavagnini 20/A ✉ 50129 ☎ 055 471914, *Fax 055 471914,* ☂ – ▤. AE ⚬ ⓓ MC VISA ET e
closed Wednesday – **Meals** (booking essential) a la carte 26/36.
◆ Small restaurant with stylish touches ; courtyard garden ideal for summer dining. Good value for money.

Paoli, via dei Tavolini 12 r ✉ 50122 ☎ 055 216215, *Fax 055 216215* – ▤. AE ⚬ ⓓ MC VISA JCB. ✗ Z r
closed August and Tuesday – **Meals** (booking essential) a la carte 29/59.
◆ Situated between the Duomo and Piazza della Signoria, this rustic establishment is notable for its 14C style architectural décor ; Tuscan and national dishes.

Il Guscio, via dell'Orto 49 ✉ 50124 ☎ 055 224421, *fgozzini@tiscali.it055 23220* – ⋇. AE ⓢ ⓓ MC VISA CU d
closed August, Saturday and Sunday in July, Sunday and Monday in other months – **Meals** (dinner only) a la carte 25/39.
◆ Run by the same family for many years, this establishment specialises in authentic country fare which is of good quality and tasty.

Trattoria Cibrèo-Cibreino, via dei Macci 122/r ✉ 50122 ☎ 055 2341100, *cibre o.fi@tin.it* – ▤. AE ⓢ ⓓ MC VISA JCB FU f
closed 26 July-6 September, 31 December-6 January, Sunday and Monday – **Meals** (few tables available ; no booking) a la carte 23/28 see also rest. ***Cibrèo*** below.
◆ An offshoot of Cibreo ; an informal atmosphere where, having successfully negotiated the queue, diners are served imaginative dishes at intimate tables.

Del Fagioli, corso Tintori 47 r ✉ 50122 ☎ 055 244285, *Fax 055 244285*, Typical Tuscan trattoria – ▤. EV k
closed August, Saturday and Sunday – **Meals** a la carte 22/29.
◆ A genuine welcome at this classic, family-run Tuscan trattoria offering traditional Florentine dishes.

Antico Fattore, via Lambertesca 1/3 r ✉ 50122 ☎ 055 288975, *Fax 055 283341* – ⋇ ▤. AE ⓢ ⓓ MC VISA Z a
closed 15 July-15 August and Sunday – **Meals** a la carte 26/42 (12 %).
◆ This trattoria close to the Uffizi has two well-presented traditional dining rooms ; Tuscan dishes predominate.

Il Santo Bevitore, via Santo Spirito 64/66 r ✉ 50125 ☎ 055 211264, *ilsantobevi tore@firenze.net, Fax 055 222493* – ⋇. ⓢ MC VISA DU h
closed Sunday – **Meals** a la carte 20/36.
◆ Located in the Sanfrediano district, just across the Arno from the centre ; traditional Tuscan cuisine with creative touches.

Il Latini, via dei Palchetti 6 r ✉ 50123 ☎ 055 210916, *torlatin@tin.it, Fax 055 289794*, Typical trattoria – ♿. AE ⓢ ⓓ MC VISA JCB. Z j
closed 24 December-5 January and Monday – **Meals** a la carte 35/40.
◆ The quintessential Florentine trattoria, not only because of its cuisine, but also on account of its cheerful, friendly service and informal atmosphere.

on the hills *South : 3 km :*

Villa la Vedetta, viale Michelangiolo 78 ✉ 50125 ☎ 055 681631, *info@villalavede ttahotel.com, Fax 055 6582544*, ≤ town and countryside, ⛱, – |‡| ▤ TV ♿ P. AE ⓢ ⓓ MC VISA JCB. rest FV b
Meals *Onice Lounge Bar* Rest. *(closed Monday) (dinner only)* a la carte 60/100 – **10 rm** ☕ 418/869, 8 suites 1859.
Spec. Variazione di baccalà e stoccafisso. Bocconcini di animelle in agrodolce su carpaccio di girello, mousse fredda di fegato grasso e vinaigrette al farro. Filetti di triglia con crocchetta d'ostrica, crema di burrata e crescione.
◆ Each room is individually styled at this luxurious establishment. Outside, the classic Italianate gardens include verdant stepped terracing and a pool. Elaborate, sophisticated cuisine prepared with lavish care.

Grand Hotel Villa Cora ⛰, viale Machiavelli 18 ✉ 50125 ☎ 055 2298451, *reser vations@villacora.it, Fax 055 229086*, ⛱, Shuttle service to city centre, – |‡| ▤ TV P – 150. AE ⓢ ⓓ MC VISA JCB. rest DV b
Meals *Taverna Machiavelli* Rest. a la carte 71/99 – **38 rm** ☕ 430/450, 10 suites.
◆ This 19C Neo-renaissance hotel is a succession of frescoed rooms with marble, stucco work and statues. Situated in its own parkland with swimming pool. The restaurant has a sophisticated menu ; outside dining on the veranda in summer.

Villa Belvedere ⛰ without rest., via Benedetto Castelli 3 ✉ 50124 ☎ 055 222501, *reception@villa-belvedere.com, Fax 055 223163*, ≤ town and hills, – |‡| ▤ TV P. AE ⓢ ⓓ MC VISA JCB. by via Senese CV
March-20 November – **23 rm** ☕ 130/207, 3 suites.
◆ This 1930s villa with extensive gardens, swimming pool and fine views, offers tranquillity in a stylish and friendly atmosphere.

Classic without rest., viale Machiavelli 25 ✉ 50125 ☎ 055 229351, *info@classichotel.it, Fax 055 229353*, – |‡| ▤ TV P. AE ⓢ ⓓ MC VISA DV c
☕ 8 – **19 rm** 110/150.
◆ Along the passeggiata ai colli ; a 19C villa with gardens, transformed ten years ago into a welcoming hotel ; charming, well-appointed rooms.

at Arcetri *South : 5 km*

Villa Montartino , via Silvani 151 ✆ 055 223520, *info@montartino.com, Fax 055 223495,* < the hills, countryside and the Certosa, , heated, – ▤ TV P – 35. AE Ⓓ MC VISA JCB.
closed 2 to 31 December – **Meals** (residents only) (booking essential) 25/100 – **7 rm** 235/286.
• This elegant historic villa in the hills is furnished with some fine antiques creating the atmosphere of a grand private house. Sensitively restored to its former glory.
by viale Michelangelo FV

at Galluzzo *South : 6,5 km*

Marignolle Relais Charme without rest., via di San Quirichino 16, località Marignolle ✉ 50124 ✆ 055 2286910, *info@marignolle.com, Fax 055 2047396,* < the hills and countryside, , – ▤ TV P. AE Ⓓ MC VISA JCB.
7 rm 195/255.
• A sophisticated blend of colourful fabrics distinguish the individually styled, attractive rooms of this rustic establishment set in the hills ; fine views from the poolside.
by viale Petrarca CV

Colle di Val d'Elsa *53034 Siena* 563 L 15 *G. Toscana – pop. 19 786 alt. 223.*
via Campana 43 ✆ 0577 922791, Fax 0577 922621.
Roma 255 – Arezzo 88 – Firenze 50 – Pisa 87 – Siena 24.

Arnolfo with rm, via XX Settembre 50/52 ✆ 0577 920549, *arnolfo@arnolfo.com, Fax 0577 920549,* – ▤ TV. AE Ⓓ MC VISA.
closed 26 July-10 August and 17 January-2 March – **Meals** *(closed Tuesday, Wednesday, Christmas dinner and New Year lunch)* (booking essential) a la carte 75/100 – **4 rm** 160.
Spec. Caciucco rivisitato con gallinella di mare, scampi e mazzancolle (summer). Cappelletti di anatra muta con brodo ristretto al Chianti e torcione al fegato d'oca (winter). Carrè e coscio di maialino di cinta senese con variazione di mele verdi (autumn-winter).
• An impressive and self-confident style of cuisine mixing traditional with contemporary ; set in a 16C building with two elegant dining rooms and a terrace for summer evenings.

Fiesole *50014 Firenze* 563 K 15 *G. Toscana – pop. 14 122 alt. 295.*
via Portigiani 3 ✆ 055 598720, info.turismo@comune.fiesole.it, Fax 055 598822.
Roma 285 – Arezzo 89 – Firenze 8 – Livorno 124 – Milano 307 – Pistoia 45 – Siena 76.

Villa San Michele , via Doccia 4 ✆ 055 5678200, *reservation@villasanmichele.net, Fax 055 5678250,* < Florence and hills, *Shuttle service to Florence*, , heated, ▤ TV P. AE Ⓓ MC VISA JCB.
24 March-27 November – **Meals** a la carte 80/115 – **42 rm** 679,80/1052,70, 4 suites.
• An elegant 15C building set among gardens and parkland, this charming former monastery has a fine fa e and stunning views. Cookery courses available. Splendid dining room ; in summers meals are served on the magnificent terrace overlooking Florence.

Villa Fiesole, via Beato Angelico 35 ✆ 055 597252, *info@villafiesole.it, Fax 055 599133,* < Florence and hills, , heated, – ▤ TV P. AE Ⓓ MC VISA
Meals (residents only) a la carte 42/56 – **32 rm** 320/350.
• Comprising a restored conservatory and a typical 19C Tuscan villa with frescoed ceilings, this genteel hotel also offers cookery courses.

San Casciano in Val di Pesa *50026 Firenze* 563 L 15 *G. Toscana – pop. 16 284 alt. 306.*
Roma 283 – Firenze 17 – Livorno 84 – Siena 53.

a Cerbaia *North-West : 6 km –* ✉ *50020 :*

La Tenda Rossa, piazza del Monumento 9/14 ✆ 055 826132, *latendarossa@tin.it, Fax 055 825210* – ▤. AE Ⓓ MC VISA JCB.
closed 10 to 31 August, Christmas, 1 to 15 January, Sunday and Monday lunch – **Meals** (booking essential) a la carte 71/101
Spec. Mazzancolle in mantello di formaggio e calamaretti farciti (spring-summer). Tortelli di zucca al sentore di affumicato con ricotta di capra stagionata e tartufo bianco (autumn-winter). Trancio di spigola gratinato al pane aromatizzato allo zafferano, budino al pomodoro.
• Several very organised members of the same family run this well known establishment ; an elegant ambience in which to enjoy gastronomic cuisine.

San Vincenzo 57027 Livorno 563 M 13 G. Toscana – pop. 6 562.

via Beatrice Alliata 2 ℘ 0565 701533, apt7sanvincenzo@costadeglietruschi.it, Fax 0565 706914.

Roma 260 – Firenze 146 – Grosseto 73 – Livorno 60 – Piombino 21 – Siena 109.

XXX ✿✿ **Gambero Rosso,** piazza della Vittoria 13 ℘ 0565 701021, *Fax 0565 704542*, ← – ▤. AE ⓓ ⓞ MC VISA JCB
closed 27 October-10 January, Monday and Tuesday – **Meals** (booking essential) a la carte 80/115.
Spec. Passatina di ceci con gamberi. Zuppa di burrata con ravioli di cefalo.Spigola con pancetta di cinta senese.
• Occupying a historic building, this elegant restaurant on the quayside of San Vincenzo has a refined menu which successfully balances creativity with practicality.

When looking for a quiet hotel use the maps in the introduction or look for establishments with the sign

---

MILAN (MILANO) 20100 P 561 F 9 G. Italy – pop. 1 247 052 alt. 122.

See : *Cathedral*★★★ *(Duomo)* MZ – *Cathedral Museum*★★ MZ **M1** – *Via and Piazza Mercanti*★ MZ **155** – *La Scala Opera House*★★ MZ – *Manzoni House*★ MZ **M7** – *Brera Art Gallery*★★★ KV – *Castle of the Sforza*★★★ JV – *Ambrosian Pinacoteca*★★ MZ : *Raphael's cartoons*★★★ *and Basket of fruit*★★★ *by Caravaggio – Poldi-Pezzoli Museum*★★ KV **M2** : *portrait of a woman*★★★ *(in profile) by Pollaiolo – Palazzo Bagatti Valsecchi*★★ KV **L** – *Natural History Museum*★ LV **M6** – *Leonardo da Vinci Museum of Science and Technology*★ HX **M4** – *Church of St. Mary of Grace*★ HX : *Leonardo da Vinci's Last Supper*★★★ – *Basilica of St. Ambrose*★★ HJX : *altar front*★★ – *Church of St. Eustorgius*★ JY : *Portinari Chapel*★★ – *General Hospital*★ KXY **U** – *Church of St. Satiro*★ : *dome*★ MZ – *Church of St. Maurice*★★ JX – *Church of St. Lawrence Major*★ JY.

Envir. : *Chiaravalle Abbey*★ *South-East : 7 km by corso Lodi* FGS – *Motor-Racing circuit at Monza Park North : 20 km ℘ 039 24821.*

27 (closed Monday) at Monza Park ✉ 20052 Monza ℘ 039 303081, Fax 039 304427, North : 20 km;

18 Molinetto (closed Monday) at Cernusco sul Naviglio ✉ 20063 ℘ 02 92105128, Fax 02 92106635, North-East : 14 km;

18 Barlassina (closed Monday) via Privata Golf 42 ✉ 20030 Birago di Camnago, ℘ 0362 560621, Fax 0362 560934, North : 26 km;

18 (closed Monday) at Zoate di Tribiano ✉ 20067 ℘ 02 90632183, Fax 02 90631861, South-East : 20 km;

18 Le Rovedine (closed Monday) at Noverasco di Opera ✉ 20090 ℘ 02 57606420, Fax 02 57606405, by via Ripamonti FS.

Forlanini of Linate East : 8 km ℘ 02 74852200.

Malpensa North-West : 45 km ℘ 02 74852200.

via Marconi 1 ✉ 20123 ℘ 02 72524301, aptinfo@libero.it, Fax 02 72524350 – Central Station ✉ 20124 ℘ 02 72524360.

A.C.I. *corso Venezia 43 ✉ 20121 ℘ 02 77451, Fax 02 781844.*

Roma 572 – Genève 323 – Genova 142 – Torino 140.

Plans on following pages

Historical centre – Duomo, Scala, Sforza Castle, corso Magenta, via Torino, corso Vittorio Emanuele, via Manzoni

Four Seasons, via Gesù 6/8 ✉ 20121 ℘ 02 77088, *milano@fourseasons.com, Fax 02 77085000*, – cam. – 280. AE ⓓ ⓞ MC VISA. KV a
Meals *La Veranda* Rest. a la carte 49/90 see also rest. ***Il Teatro*** below – 31 – **78 rm** 638/748, 25 suites 5148.
• Within Milan's golden triangle, this former 15C convent retains some of its original features, and is the most exclusive and elegant hotel in the city. Its refined restaurant overlooks a courtyard garden.

Grand Hotel et de Milan, via Manzoni 29 ✉ 20121 ℘ 02 723141, *infos@grandhoteletdemilan.it, Fax 02 86460861*, – – 50. AE ⓓ ⓞ VISA JCB KV g
Meals *Caruso* Rest. *(closed dinner)* a la carte 51/70 see also rest ***Don Carlos*** below – 35 – **95 rm** 528/616, 8 suites.
• The spirit of Verdi, who lived here, still lingers within this prestigious hotel's sumptuous late-19C interiors. Well-presented rooms with fine antique furniture. Well-lit restaurant dedicated to the maestro.

MILANO

Alcuino (V.) .... DQ 5
Anguissola (V. S.) ..... DR 6
Belisario (Viale) .... DR 21
Berengario (Viale) ..... DR 26
Bodio (Viale L.) .... EQ 32
Bodoni (V.)........... DQ 33
Boezio (Viale S.) ...... DR 35
Brianza (Viale) .... GQ 41
Buonarroti (V. M.) ..... DR 42
Calvi (V. P.)........... GR 47
Cassiodoro (Viale) ..... DR 54
Concordia (Cso) ..... FGR 71
Costa (V. A.) .... GQ 75
Duilio (Viale).......... DR 81
Eginardo (Viale) .... DR 84
Elia (Viale E.)........ DQR 86
Ezio (Viale) .... DR 87
Gallarate (V.) .... DQ 96
Gavirate (V.) .... DR 99
Gran Sasso (V.)........ GQ 106
Imbriani (V. degli)...... EQ 113
Indipendenza (Cso).... GR 114
Lauria (V. R. di) .... DQ 123
Leoncavallo (V.) ...... GQ 126
Lomellina (V.) .... GR 131
Maffei (V. A.) .... FR 135
Mar Jonio (Viale)........... DR 141
Melzo (V.) .... FGR 152
Migliara (Viale)........... DR 159
Misurata (Viale).......... DS 164
Monte Ceneri (Viale) ...... DQ 170
Murillo (Viale) .... DR 182

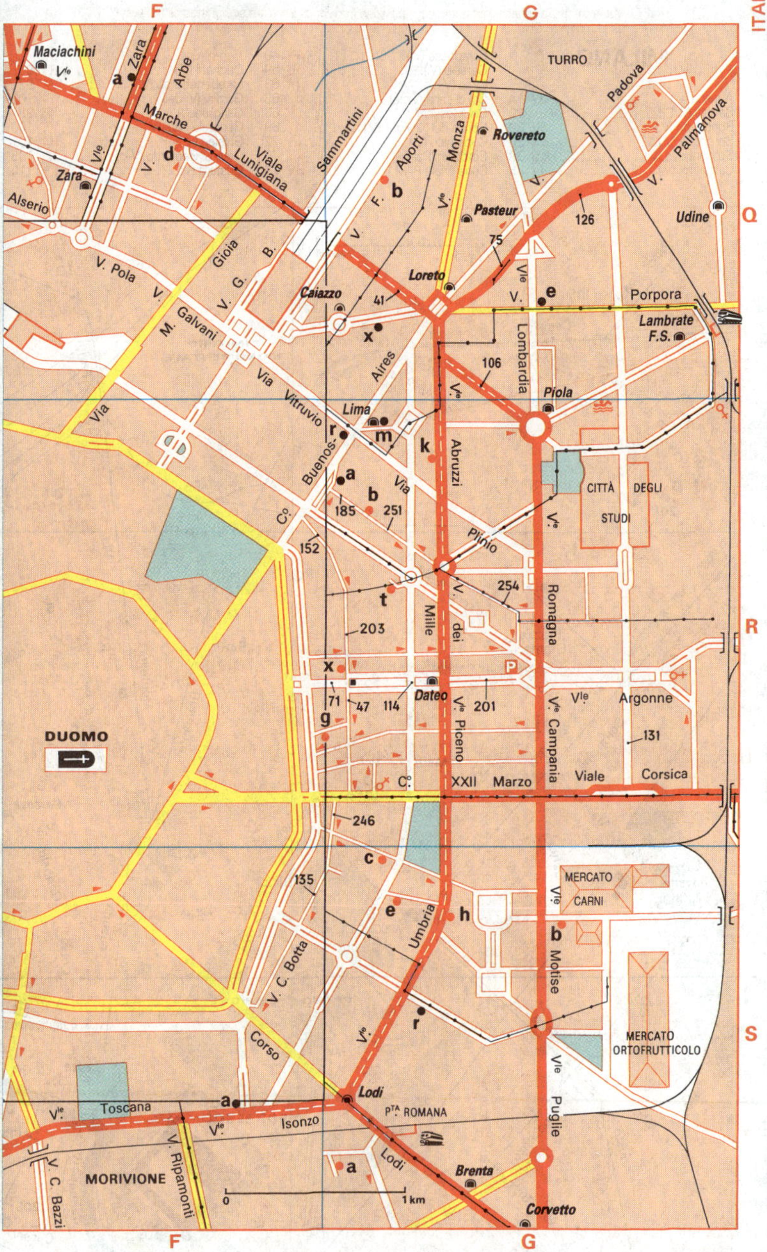

Omboni (V.) . . . . GR 185
Plebisciti (Cso) . . . . GR 201
Poerio (V.) . . . . GR 203
Ranzoni (Viale D.) . . . . DR 210
Rubens (V.) . . . . DR 222
Scarampo (V. L.) . . . . DQ 245
Sciesa (V. A.) . . . . FGR 246
Stoppani (V. A.) . . . . GR 251
Tiepolo (V.) . . . . GR 254
Trivulzio (V. A. T.) . . . . DR 261
Vigliani (V. P. O.) . . . . DQR 273
Washington (V. G.) . . . . . . DRS 279

Within the green shaded area, the city is divided into zones wich are signposted all the way round. Once entered, it is not possible to drive from one zone into another

MILANO

Aurispa (V.) . . . . JY 14
Battisti (V. C.) . . . . KLX 20
Bocchetto (V.) . . . . JX 30
Borgogna (V.) . . . . KX 36
Borgonuovo (V.) . . . . KV 38
Calatafimi (V.) . . . . JY 45
Caradosso (V.) . . . . HX 49
Ceresio (V.) . . . . JU 59
Circo (V.) . . . . JX 63
Col di Lana (Viale) . . . . JY 65
Col Moschin (V.) . . . . JY 66
Conca del Naviglio (V.) . . . . JY 69
Copernico (V.) . . . . LT 72
Cordusio (Pza) . . . . KX 73
Curie (Viale P. M.) . . . . HV 77
Dante (V.) . . . . JX
Dugnani (V.) . . . . HY 80
Fatebenefratelli (V.) . . . . KV 92
Gardini (V. dei) . . . . KV 102
Garigliano (V.) . . . . KT 98
Generale Fara (V.) . . . . KT 100
Ghisleri (V. A.) . . . . HY 101
Gran S. Bernardo (V.) . . . . HT 105
Gustalla (V.) . . . . KX 110

Induno (V. Flli) . . . . HT 116
Lambertenghi (V. P.) . . . . KT 122
Lepetit (V.) . . . . LTU 128
Maffei (V. A.) . . . . LY 135
Manzoni (V. A.) . . . . KV
Melzo (V.) . . . . LU 152
Mercato (V.) . . . . JV 158
Modestino (V.) . . . . HY 165
Moliere (Viale E.) . . . . HV 167
Monte Napoleone (V.) . . . . KV
Muratori (V. L.) . . . . LY 180
Oggiono (V. M. d') . . . . HJY 183
Orseolo (V.) . . . . HY 189
Paleocapa (V.) . . . . JV 191
Pastrengo (V.) . . . . KT 195
Perasto (V.) . . . . KT 198
Poliziano (V.) . . . . HTU 204
Ponte Vetero (V.) . . . . JV 205
Quadrio (V. M.) . . . . JT 207
Restelli (Viale F.) . . . . KT 214
Ruffini (V. Flli) . . . . HX 225
S. Babila (Pza) . . . . KX 228
S. Calimero (V.) . . . . KY 230
Savoia (Viale F. di) . . . . KU 243
Spiga (V. della) . . . . KV
Tivoli (V.) . . . . HV 255
Torchio (V.) . . . . JX 257
Torino (V.) . . . . MZ
Torriani (V. N.) . . . . LU 258
Trau (V.) . . . . KT 260
Valtellina (V.) . . . . JT 266
Vercelli (Cso) . . . . HX 267
Verdi (V.) . . . . KV 269
Vittorio Emanuele II (Cso) . . . . . NZ
Vittorio Veneto (Viale) . . . . KLU 278
Zezon (V.) . . . . LU 281

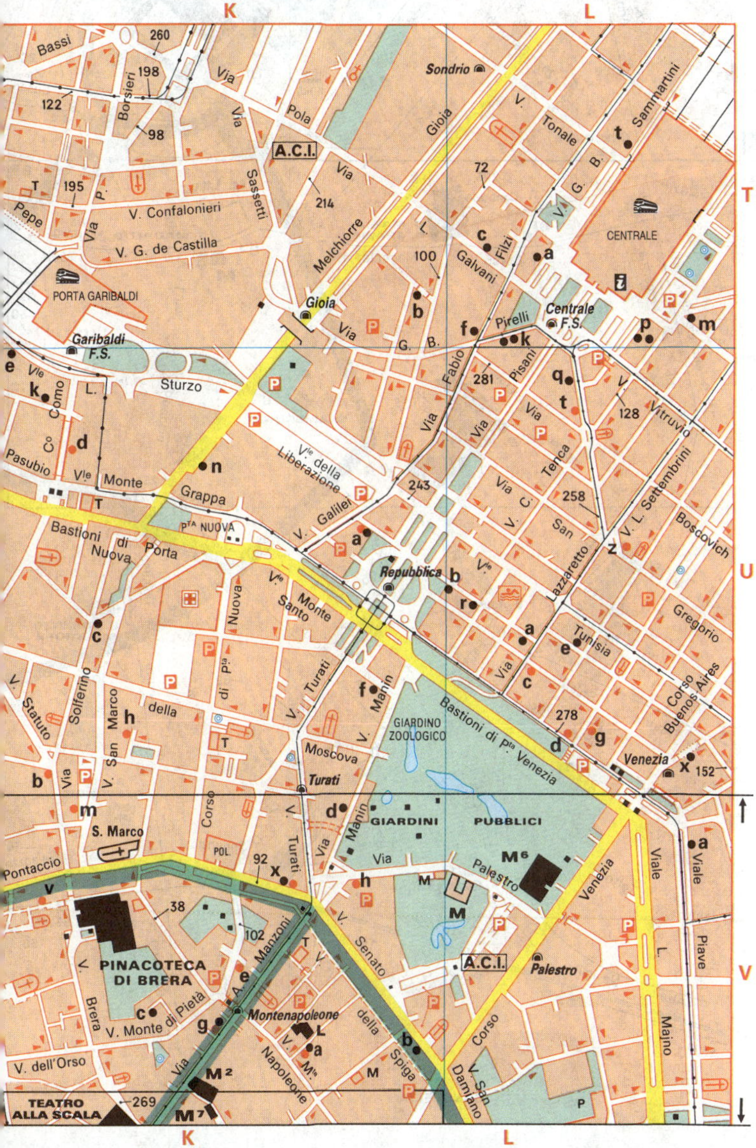

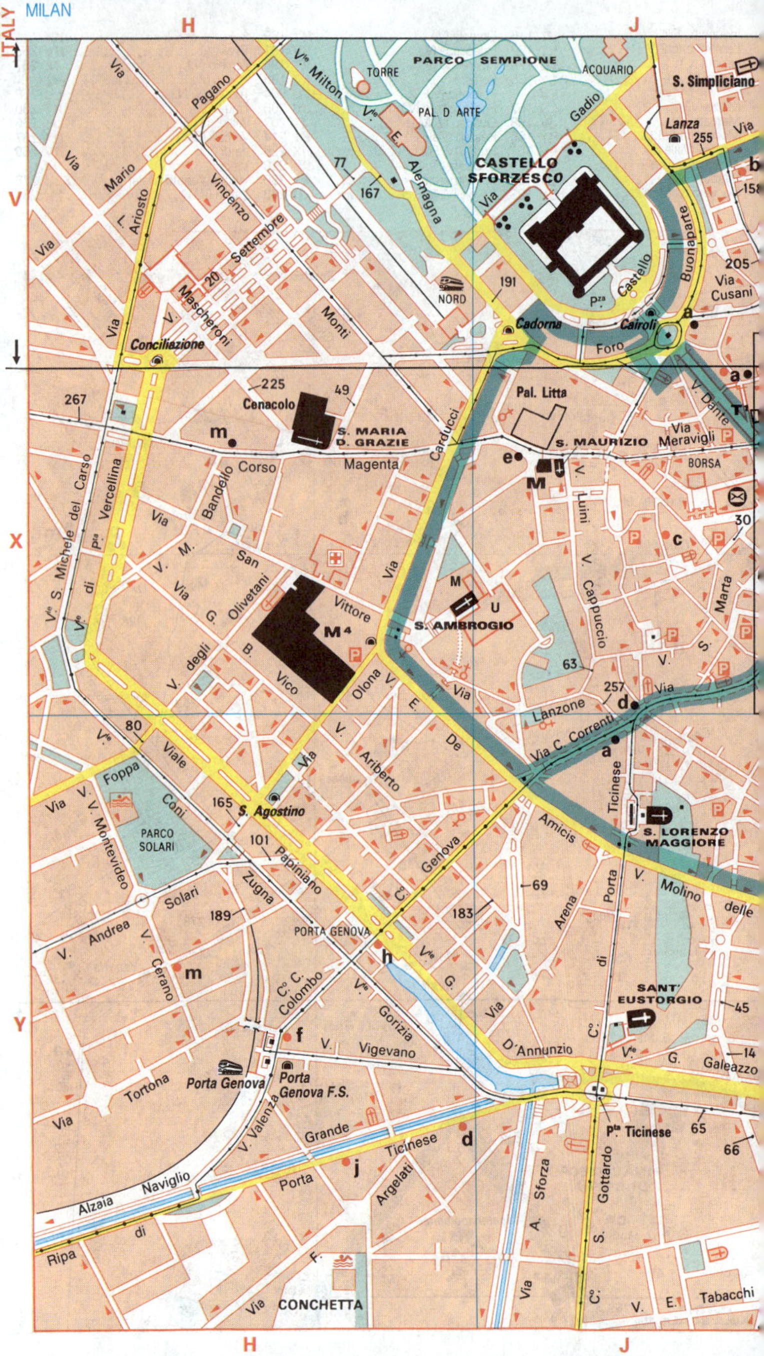
H
J
V
X
Y
PARCO SEMPIONE
TORRE
ACQUARIO
S. Simpliciano
PAL. D. ARTE
Vle Milton
Vle E. Alemagna
Gadio
Lanza
255
Via
CASTELLO SFORZESCO
Via Pagano
Via Mario
Via L. Ariosto
Via Vincenzo
77
167
158
Via
20 Settembre
Buonaparte
205
Via Cusani
V. Mascheroni
Monti
NORD
191
Pza Castello
Via
Conciliazione
Cadorna
Cairoli
Foro
225
49
Pal. Litta
267
Cenacolo
S. MARIA D. GRAZIE
Carducci
V. Dante
Via Meravigli
m
Corso Magenta
S. MAURIZIO
e
BORSA
Bandello
M
V. Luini
Vle S. Michele del Carso
Pza Vercellina
Via San
V. M.
30
c
Via
V. Cappuccio
Marta
Vle di
Via G. Olivetani
Vittore
M
U
S. AMBROGIO
M4
S.
V. degli
B.
Vico
Olona
V.
Via
63
V.
257
Via
d
Lanzone
E.
De
80
Vle
Viale
Coni
V.
Ariberto
Via C. Correnti
a
Foppa
Via
Ticinese
Via V.
V. Montevideo
PARCO SOLARI
165
S. Agostino
Amicis
S. LORENZO MAGGIORE
101
Papiniano
Zugna
Genova
C.
69
Solari
Via
Arena
Porta
V.
Molino
delle
V. Andrea
189
PORTA GENOVA
183
V. Cerano
m
h
Vle
G.
di
Cso C. Colombo
Vle Gorizia
Via
SANT' EUSTORGIO
45
f
V. Vigevano
D'Annunzio
Cso
Vle
G.
Galeazzo
14
Tortona
Porta Genova
Porta Genova F.S.
Pta Ticinese
65
66
Via
V. Valenza
Grande
Ticinese
d
j
Porta
Argelati
A. Sforza
Gotthardo
S.
Alzaia
Naviglio
di
Ripa
F.
Via
CONCHETTA
Via
Cso
V.
E.
Tabacchi
H
J

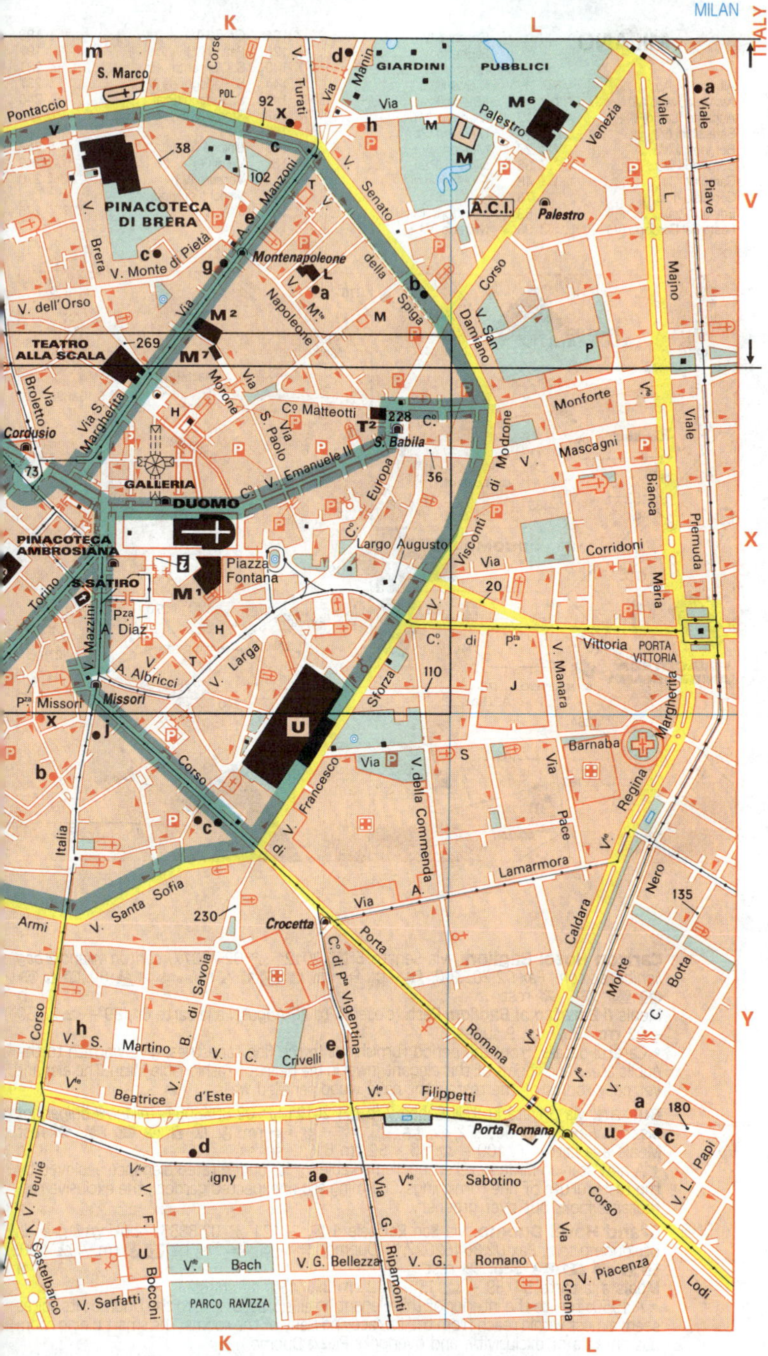
K
L
V
X
Y
S. Marco
Pontaccio
GIARDINI PUBBLICI
Via Manin
V. Turati
Via Palestro
Venezia
Viale Piave
Viale Majno
PINACOTECA DI BRERA
V. Brera
V. Monte di Pietà
A. Manzoni
Montenapoleone
V. Senato
della Spiga
A.C.I.
Palestro
Corso Venezia
V. San Damiano
V. dell'Orso
Via Napoleone
V. M.te
TEATRO ALLA SCALA
Via Broletto
Via S. Margherita
Cordusio
Via Morone
Co Matteotti
S. Babila
Monforte
Mascagni
Viale Bianca Maria
Viale Premuda
Via S. Paolo
Co. V. Emanuele II
Co. Europa
Largo Augusto
Visconti di Modrone
Corridoni
GALLERIA
DUOMO
PINACOTECA AMBROSIANA
Piazza Fontana
S. SATIRO
Torino
Mazzini
Pza A. Diaz
V. Larga
A. Albricci
Missori
Pza Missori
Co. di Pta Vittoria
PORTA VITTORIA
V. Manara
Margherita
Sforza
Corso
Via Francesco
V. della Commenda
Barnaba
Via Pace
Regina
Italia
V. Santa Sofia
Armi
Crocetta
Porta Romana
Lamarmora
Via A.
Caldara
Nero
Monte
Botta
C.
C. di Pta Vigentina
Romana
Corso
h
V. S. Martino
B. di Savoia
V. C. Crivelli
Vle Beatrice d'Este
Vle Filippetti
Porta Romana
V. L. Papi
Sabotino
V. Teulié
V. Castelbarco
V. Sarfatti
Bocconi
Vle Bach
PARCO RAVIZZA
V. G. Bellezza
Via G. Ripamonti
Romano
V. Piacenza
Crema
Lodi
Corso
Vle
igny
M
M1
M2
M6
M7
T2
U
H
J
P
S
28
36
38
73
92
102
110
135
180
20
228
230
269

MILANO

Albricci (V. A.) . . . . MZ 3
Arcivescovado (V.) . . . . . . MNZ 10
Augusto (Largo) . . . . NZ 12
Baracchini (V.) . . . . MZ 17
Bergamini (V.) . . . . NZ 27
Borgogna (V.) . . . . NZ 36
Cantù (V. C.) . . . . MZ 48
Cordusio (Pza) . . . . MZ 73
Edison (Pza) . . . . MZ 83
Festa del Perdono (V.) . . . . . . NZ 93
Gonzaga (V.) . . . . MZ 104
Laghetto (V.) . . . . NZ 120
Manzoni (V. A.) . . . . MZ 140
Marconi (V.) . . . . MZ 144
Marino (Pza) . . . . MZ 147
Mengoni (V.) . . . . MZ 153
Mercanti (Pza) . . . . MZ 155
Mercanti (V.) . . . . MZ 156
Missori (Pza) . . . . MZ 162
Monte Napoleone (V.) . . . . NZ 171
Montforte (Cso) . . . . NZ 168
Morone (V.) . . . . MNZ 176
Orefici (V.) . . . . MZ 188
Pattari (V.) . . . . NZ 197
S. Clemente . . . . NZ 231
S. Radegonda (V.) . . . . MZ 237
S. Stefano (Pza) . . . . NZ 240
Sforza (V. F.) . . . . NZ 248
Torino (V.) . . . . MZ
Unione (V.) . . . . MZ 264
Verdi (V.) . . . . MZ 269
Verziere (V.) . . . . NZ 270
Visconti di Modrone (V.) . . . . NZ 275
Vittorio Emanuele II (Cso) . . . NZ

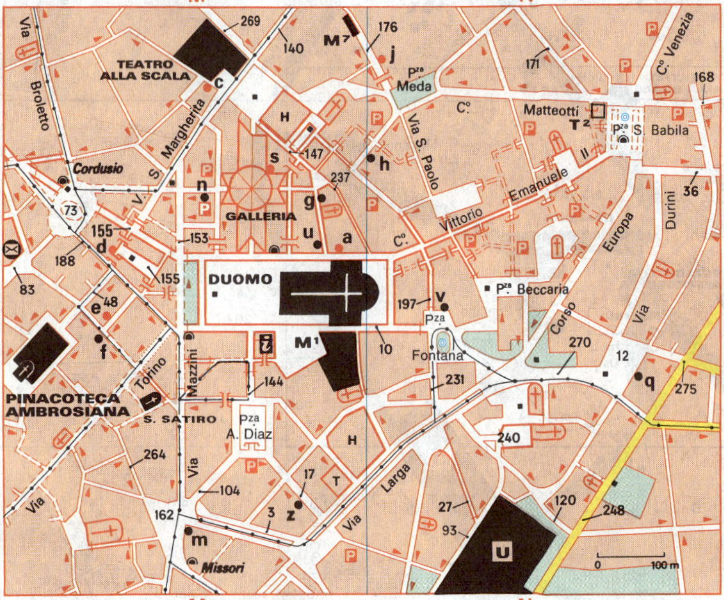

Carlton Hotel Baglioni, via Senato 5 ✉ 20121 ☎ 02 77077, *carlton.milano@baglionihotels.com, Fax 02 783300*, – rm, rm. – 80. AE VISA JCB. rest KV b
Meals *Il Baretto al Baglioni* Rest. *(closed 5 to 26 August)* a la carte 64/89 – 25,30 – **92 rm** 385/605, 9 suites.
◆ Careful details, from the period furnishings to the fine tapestries, give warmth to the public areas and rooms of this elegant jewel in the heart of fashionable Milan. The elegant yet cosy rooms of the restaurant have wood panelled walls.

Bulgari, via privata Fratelli Gabba 7/b ✉ 20121 ☎ 02 8058051, *milano@bulgarihotels.com, Fax 02 805805222*, – rm, . AE VISA. rest KV c
Meals a la carte 56/100 – 30 – **52 rm** 616, 7 suites.
◆ A new star on Milan hotel scene, remarkable for its understated elegance achieved by the tasteful use of fine furnishings. Charming and unexpected garden ; the exclusive restaurants looks out over greenery.

Grand Hotel Duomo, via San Raffaele 1 ✉ 20121 ☎ 02 8833, *bookings@grandhotelduomo.com, Fax 02 86462027*, ≤ Duomo, – rm, rm. – 100. AE VISA JCB. rest MZ u
Meals a la carte 54/69 – 15 – **162 rm** 290/430, 17 suites.
◆ A 1950s feel to the interior of this elegant hotel, situated next to the Duomo ; its spires seem almost within reach from the terrace and many of the rooms. The smart dining room has an aura of exclusivity, and overlooks Piazza Duomo.

Starhotel Rosa, via Pattari 5 ✉ 20122 ✆ 02 8831, *rosa.mi@starhotels.it, Fax 02 8057964,* – 🛗, ⇔ rm, ▤ 📺 ✆ – 🏛 130. AE ⑤ ⓪ ⓂⒸ VISA JCB. ✻ NZ v
Meals a la carte 46/56 – **246 rm** ☕ 385, 2 suites.
◆ Situated close to the Duomo, this recently refurbished establishment has large and elegant public areas with much marble and stucco work, and comfortable rooms. Well-equipped conference centre. The restaurant offers a traditional dining experience.

Jolly Hotel President, largo Augusto 10 ✉ 20122 ✆ 02 77461, *milano-president @jollyhotels.com, Fax 02 783449* – 🛗, ⇔ rm, ▤ 📺 ✆ – 🏛 100. AE ⑤ ⓪ ⓂⒸ VISA JCB. ✻ rest NZ q
Meals *Il Verziere* Rest. a la carte 37/55 – **234 rm** ☕ 275/333, 7 suite.
◆ In a central location, this large international hotel has conference rooms, and spacious public areas. Every convenience to be expected in a hotel of this category is apparent. Elegantly genteel restaurant.

Brunelleschi, via Baracchini 12 ✉ 20123 ✆ 02 88431, *Fax 02 804924* – 🛗 ▤ 📺 ♿ rm. AE ⑤ ⓪ ⓂⒸ VISA JCB. ✻ MZ z
closed 31 July-29 August – **Meals** a la carte 35/59 – **123 rm** ☕ 270/290, 7 suites.
◆ Black and white marble gives an air of rigorous austerity to the well-lit lobby of this Neo-classically-inspired modern hotel ; a softer look in evidence in the comfortably elegant rooms. Columns, glass and mirrors in the smart restaurant downstairs.

UNA Hotel Cusani, via Cusani 13 ✉ 20121 ✆ 02 85601, *una.cusani@unahotels.it, Fax 02 8693601* – 🛗 ▤ 📺 ✆ 🚗. AE ⑤ ⓪ ⓂⒸ VISA JCB. ✻ JV a
Meals a la carte 45/70 – **87 rm** ☕ 387/454, 5 suites.
◆ Occupying a fine position opposite the Castello Sforzesco, this comfortable hotel has large rooms with mahogany furnishings and decorated with pastels. The small restaurant is light and stylish.

Park Hotel Hyatt, via Tommaso Grossi 1 ✉ 20121 ✆ 02 88211234, *milano@hyattintl.com, Fax 02 88211235,* – 🛗 ⇔ ▤ 📺 ✆ ♿ – 🏛 60. AE ⑤ ⓪ ⓂⒸ VISA JCB. ✻ rest MZ n
Meals *The Park* Rest. *(closed August)* a la carte 65/87 – ☕ 32 – **91 rm** 649/704, 26 suites.
◆ Occupying a palace built in 1870 and next to the Galleria Vittorio Emanuele, this is the flagship of the Hyatt group in Italy. Inside, the feel is contemporary with ample use of travertine. The elegant modern look is also in evidence in the restaurant.

De la Ville, via Hoepli 6 ✉ 20121 ✆ 02 8791311 and rest. ✆ 02 8051231, *reservationsdlv@sinahotels.it, Fax 02 866609,* , ⛆, 🏊 – 🛗, ⇔ rm, ▤ 📺 ✆ ♿ rm. – 🏛 60. AE ⑤ ⓪ ⓂⒸ VISA JCB. ✻ NZ h
Meals *L'Opera* Rest. *(closed Sunday)* a la carte 40/52 – **108 rm** ☕ 335,50/360,80, suite.
◆ A warm English drawing room feel with panelling, velvet and wood floors in evidence. This very central hotel has well-appointed rooms and a smart restaurant.

The Gray, via San Raffaele 6 ✉ 20121 ✆ 02 7208951, *info.thegray@sinahotels.it, Fax 02 866526,* ⛆ – 🛗 ▤ 📺 ✆. AE ⑤ ⓪ ⓂⒸ VISA JCB. ✻ MZ g
Meals a la carte 48/72 – ☕ 27,50 – **21 rm** 330/660.
◆ An exercise in class and style, with a wealth of attention to detail and each room individually designed ; some look onto the Galleria. Painstaking care has also been taken with the small restaurant.

Spadari al Duomo, via Spadari 11 ✉ 20123 ✆ 02 72002371, *reservation@spadarihotel.com, Fax 02 861184* – 🛗, ⇔ rm, ▤ 📺 ✆. AE ⑤ ⓪ ⓂⒸ VISA JCB. ✻ MZ f
closed Christmas – **Meals** snacks only – **40 rm** ☕ 258/288, suite.
◆ Italy's first art hotel is ten years old ; small, elegant and exclusive, it houses a fine collection of contemporary art and design.

Cavour, via Fatebenefratelli 21 ✉ 20121 ✆ 02 620001, *booking@hotelcavour.it, Fax 02 6592263* – 🛗, ⇔ rm, ▤ 📺 ✆ – 🏛 80. AE ⑤ ⓪ ⓂⒸ VISA JCB. ✻ KV x
closed August and 24 December-6 January – **Meals** (see rest. ***Conte Camillo*** below) – **113 rm** ☕ 215/247, 5 suites.
◆ A large colonnaded lobby introduces visitors to this establishment, run for decades by the same family of leading Milanese hoteliers. Excellent recently refitted rooms.

Dei Cavalieri, piazza Missori 1 ✉ 20123 ✆ 02 88571, *hc@hoteldeicavalieri.com, Fax 02 8857241* – 🛗, ⇔ rm, ▤ 📺 ✆ – 🏛 250. AE ⑤ ⓪ ⓂⒸ VISA JCB. ✻ MZ m
Meals a la carte 48/61 – **177 rm** ☕ 289/379, 2 suites.
◆ This hotel celebrated its fiftieth birthday in 1999. Slightly cramped public areas, but a recent refit has created a pleasant space in which to entertain, and there is a fine terrace. The well-proportioned restaurant is traditionally stylish.

Regina without rest., via Cesare Correnti 13 ✉ 20123 ✆ 02 58106913, *info@hotelregina.it, Fax 02 58107033* – 🛗 ▤ 📺 ♿ – 🏛 40. AE ⑤ ⓪ ⓂⒸ VISA JCB. ✻ JY a
closed August and 23 December-7 January – **43 rm** ☕ 185/250.
◆ The courtyard of an 18C building covered by a glass pyramid is the lobby of this modern-style hotel ; parquet floors in the well-presented rooms.

Carrobbio without rest., via Medici 3 ✉ 20123 ☎ 02 89010740, *info@hotelcarrobbio.it, Fax 02 8053334* – |$| ▤ TV ♿ – 🏛 30. AE ⓈOD MC VISA JCB JX d
closed August and 22 December-6 January – **56 rm** ☐ 180/256.
◆ Central, but in a secluded location, this good quality, if functional, hotel has recently been renovated. Well-appointed rooms with good furnishings.

Ascot without rest., via Lentasio 3/5 ✉ 20122 ☎ 02 58303300, *info@hotelascotmilano.it, Fax 02 58303203* – |$| ▤ TV ☏ – 🏛 75. AE ⓈOD MC VISA. ✱ KY c
closed 23 December-6 January – **64 rm** ☐ 235/465.
◆ Under competent new management, this central hotel has comfortable public areas and small but well-appointed rooms which are nicely furnished.

King without rest., corso Magenta 19 ✉ 20123 ☎ 02 874432, *info@hotelkingmilano.com, Fax 02 89010798* – ▤ TV ☏. AE ⓈOD MC VISA JCB JX e
48 rm ☐ 148/215.
◆ From the upper floors of this totally refurbished and opulently furnished hotel there are views of the Duomo and the Castello. The rooms are not large but are comfortable.

Lloyd without rest., corso di Porta Romana 48 ✉ 20122 ☎ 02 58303332, *info@lloydhotelmilano.it, Fax 02 58303365* – |$| ▤ TV – 🏛 100. AE ⓈOD MC VISA JCB. ✱ KY c
closed 17 December-9 January – **56 rm** ☐ 235/350, suite.
◆ Opposite San Nazaro Maggiore, this recently refitted hotel is comfortably functional ; small meeting rooms.

Zurigo without rest., corso Italia 11/a ✉ 20122 ☎ 02 72022260, *zurigo@brerahotels.it, Fax 02 72000013* – |$| ▤ TV ☏. AE ⓈOD MC VISA JCB. ✱ KY j
40 rm ☐ 150/220.
◆ Near Piazza Missori, a historic building completely refurbished inside, with well-appointed quiet rooms ; courtesy bikes available.

XXXX **Savini,** galleria Vittorio Emanuele II ✉ 20121 ☎ 02 72003433, *savini@thi.it, Fax 02 72022888,* Elegant traditional decor – ▤. AE ⓈOD MC VISA JCB MZ s
closed 6 to 27 August, 1 to 6 January and Sunday – **Meals** (booking essential) a la carte 56/82 (12 %).
◆ A traditional historic setting in the prestigious Galleria. Redolent of the luxury of times gone by, with red velvet, crystal lamps and mirrors.

XXXX ✿✿ **Cracco-Peck,** via Victor Hugo 4 ✉ 20123 ☎ 02 876774, *cracco-peck@peck.it, Fax 02 861040* – ▤. AE ⓈOD MC VISA JCB. ✱ MZ e
closed 3 weeks in August, 22 December-10 January, Sunday and Saturday lunch, also Saturday dinner from 15 June to August – **Meals** (booking essential) a la carte 74/110 🍇.
Spec. Tuorlo d'uovo marinato con fonduta leggera di parmigiano. Risotto allo zafferano con midollo alla piastra. Vitello impanato alla milanese con pomodoro al forno e sedano candito.
◆ A legendary name in Milanese cuisine and a famous chef ; a winning combination for a new restaurant. Classic elegance, perfect service and excellent food.

XXXX **Il Teatro** - Hotel Four Seasons, via Gesù 8 ✉ 20121 ☎ 02 77088, *milano@fourseasons.com, Fax 02 77085000* – ▤. AE ⓈOD MC VISA. ✱ KV a
closed August, 1 to 7 January and Sunday – **Meals** (dinner only) (booking essential) a la carte 84/138.
◆ A very elegant and exclusive ambience in this restaurant among the stunning surroundings of the Four Seasons hotel. Creatively prepared cuisine.

XXX **Don Carlos** - Grand Hotel et de Milan, via Manzoni 29 ✉ 20121 ☎ 02 72314640, *banqueting@grandhoteletdemilan.it, Fax 02 86460861,* Late night dinners – ▤. AE ⓈOD MC VISA JCB KV g
closed August – **Meals** (dinner only) (booking essential) a la carte 64/100.
◆ An atmosphere of snug luxury with panelling, red lamps, and drawings and photos of the Verdi era ; varied, creative cuisine including seasonal dishes and Milanese favourites.

XXX **Conte Camillo** - Hotel Cavour, via Fatebenefratelli 21 (galleria di Piazza Cavour) ✉ 20121 ☎ 02 6570516, *booking@hotelcavour.it, Fax 02 6592263* – ▤. AE ⓈOD MC VISA JCB. ✱ KV x
closed August, 24 December-6 January and Sunday lunch – **Meals** a la carte 37/49.
◆ Attentive service and elegant surroundings, together with an intimate welcoming atmosphere ; traditional cuisine with a modern twist, with themed menus available.

XXX **Marino alla Scala,** piazza della Scala 5 (Trussardi palace) ✉ 20121 ☎ 02 80688201, *ristorante@marinoallascala.it, Fax 02 80688287* – |$| ▤. AE ⓈOD MC VISA MZ c
closed 7 to 31 August, Saturday lunch and Sunday – **Meals** (booking essential) a la carte 41/71.
◆ Tradition and innovation meet in the cuisine of this design-conscious establishment ; a stylish restaurant close by Milan's famous opera house.

XXX **Antico Ristorante Boeucc,** piazza Belgioioso 2 ✉ 20121 ☎ 02 76020224, *Fax 02 796173* – ▤. AE. ✻ NZ j
closed 13 to 17 April, August, 24 December-2 January, Saturday and Sunday lunch – **Meals** (booking essential) a la carte 51/66.
• In the stable block of the 18C Palazzo Belgioioso, an elegant and historic establishment; the choice of Milan's elite for 300 years; traditional cuisine.

XX **Armani/Nobu,** via Pisoni 1 ✉ 20121 ☎ 02 62312645, *Fax 02 62312674* – ⇔ ▤. AE $ ⓓ ⓜⓒ VISA JCB. ✻ KV e
closed August, 25 December-7 January, Sunday and Monday lunch – **Meals** (booking essential) Japanese rest. with South American influences a la carte 48/76 (10 %).
• An exotic marriage of fashion with gastronomy; Japanese fusion cuisine with South American influences, served in stylishly simple surroundings inspired by Japanese design.

XX **Nabucco,** via Fiori Chiari 10 ✉ 20121 ☎ 02 860663, *info@nabucco.it, Fax 02 8361014* – ⇔ ▤. AE $ ⓓ ⓜⓒ VISA JCB KV v
Meals (booking essential) a la carte 41/56 (10 %).
• In one of the Brera district's characteristic alleyways, this restaurant offers some interesting and unusual dishes; candlelit dining in the evenings.

XX **L'Assassino,** via Amedei 8, angolo via Cornaggia ✉ 20123 ☎ 02 8056144, *lamberto@ristorantelassassino.it, Fax 02 86467374* – ▤. AE $ ⓜⓒ VISA. ✻ KY x
closed 23 December-2 January and Monday – **Meals** (booking essential) a la carte 32/55 (10 %).
• Situated in the palazzo Recalcati, this classic venue is always very popular. Traditional cuisine; the fresh, home made pasta is especially good.

XX **Alla Collina Pistoiese,** via Amedei 1 ✉ 20123 ☎ 02 877248, *Fax 02 877248* – ▤. AE $ ⓓ ⓜⓒ VISA. ✻ KY x
closed Easter, 10 to 20 August, 24 December-2 January, Friday and Saturday lunch – **Meals** a la carte 36/57.
• The spirit of old Milan in a historic setting, run by the same family since 1938; the menu shows all aspects of Italy's cuisine but specialises in Tuscan and Milanese dishes.

XX **Al Mercante,** piazza Mercanti 17 ✉ 20123 ☎ 02 8052198, *Fax 02 86465250*, 🍽 – ▤. AE $ ⓓ ⓜⓒ VISA. ✻ MZ d
closed 1 to 27 August, 1 to 7 January and Sunday – **Meals** a la carte 35/43.
• A lively establishment charmingly situated in a medieval square offering summer dining outside; country cuisine and a fine buffet of antipasti.

X **La Felicità,** via Rovello 3 ✉ 20121 ☎ 02 865235, *fangleivalerio@hotmail.com, Fax 02 865235* – ▤. AE $ ⓓ ⓜⓒ VISA JCB. ✻ JX a
Meals Chinese rest. 15/20 and a la carte 19/26.
• Cantonese cuisine and a wide variety of other South East Asian dishes in this smart oriental restaurant; the mezzanine floor offers the cosiest and most romantic ambience.

X **La Tavernetta-da Elio,** via Fatebenefratelli 30 ✉ 20121 ☎ 02 653441, *ristorante@tavernetta.it, Fax 02 6597610* – ▤. AE $ ⓓ ⓜⓒ VISA JCB KV c
closed August, 24 December-2 January, Saturday lunch, Sunday and Bank Holidays – **Meals** Tuscan rest. a la carte 32/42.
• Under the same management for over forty years, this simple, friendly and lively restaurant has a strong local following; classic dishes and Tuscan specialities.

X **Hostaria Borromei,** via Borromei 4 ✉ 20123 ☎ 02 86453760, *Fax 02 86452178*, 🍽 – AE $ ⓓ ⓜⓒ VISA. ✻ JX c
closed 8 August-1 September, 24 December-7 January, Saturday lunch and Sunday – **Meals** (booking essential) Mantuan specialities a la carte 35/46.
• Delightful summer dining in the courtyard of a historic building in the centre; seasonal Lombard cuisine with an emphasis on the Mantova region.

Directional centre – via della Moscova, via Solferino, via Melchiorre Gioia, viale Zara, via Carlo Farini

🏨 **Grand Hotel Verdi,** via Melchiorre Gioia 6 ✉ 20124 ☎ 02 62371, *reservation.ver@framon.hotels.it, Fax 02 6237050* – |♿| ▤ TV ☏ 🚗 – 🔑 25. AE $ ⓓ ⓜⓒ VISA JCB. ✻ KU n
Meals a la carte 37/58 – **96 rm** ☕ 332, 3 suites.
• A recently built and well-appointed hotel. Deep red predominates in the modern interior which also evokes the decoration inside La Scala. Good quality cuisine in the elegant restaurant which has a smart red and white colour scheme.

🏨 **Atahotel Executive,** viale Luigi Sturzo 45 ✉ 20154 ☎ 02 62942807, *prenotazioni@hotel-executive.com, Fax 02 62942713* – |♿|, ⇔ rm, ▤ TV ☏ – 🔑 800. AE $ ⓓ ⓜⓒ VISA JCB. ✻ KU e
Meals a la carte 40/55 – **414 rm** ☕ 305/335, 6 suites.
• Opposite the stazione Garibaldi, a large 1970s hotel with excellent conference facilities (18 meeting rooms); pleasant well-lit rooms, many of which have been refitted. Elegant modern restaurant.

UNA Hotel Tocq, via A. de Tocqueville 7/D ✉ 20154 ☎ 02 62071, *una.tocq@unahotels.it, Fax 02 6570780* – |‡|, ▤ TV ☎ – 🏛 110. AE ⊙ ⓞ MC VISA JCB. ✻ KU k
Meals a la carte 34/44 – **122 rm** ☕ 329/387, suite.
◆ Sophisticated design and modern technology are the central themes of this minimalist-style hotel with a strong contemporary feel. The main area of the restaurant is brightly decorated with a parquet floor in natural Danish oak.

Four Points Sheraton Milan Center, via Cardano 1 ✉ 20124 ☎ 02 667461, *booking@fourpointsmilano.it, Fax 02 6703024,* 🏋 – |‡|, ⇹ rm, ▤ TV ☎ ♿ – 🏛 180. AE ⊙ ⓞ MC VISA JCB. ✻ rest KT b
Meals a la carte 45/56 – ☕ 18 – **250 rm** 270/320, 10 suites.
◆ Inside this modern building is an elegantly decorated interior with restful public areas ; good comfortable rooms, all recently refurbished. Large windows give plenty of light in the tastefully decorated dining room.

Sunflower without rest., piazzale Lugano 10 ✉ 20158 ☎ 02 39314071, *sunflower.hotel@tiscalinet.it, Fax 02 39320377* – |‡| ▤ TV ♿ 🚗 – 🏛 100. AE ⊙ ⓞ MC VISA JCB. ✻ EQ c
closed 31 July-22 August and 24 December-6 January – ☕ 12 – **55 rm** 124/176.
◆ Recently opened, this large hotel offers comfortable, functional accommodation ; rooms have wooden furnishings and ceramic floors.

Holiday Inn Milan Garibaldi Station, via Farini angolo via Ugo Bassi ✉ 20154 ☎ 02 6076801 and rest. ☎ 02 66823667, *reservations@hmilangaribaldi.com, Fax 02 6880764,* 🏋 – |‡| ⇹ ▤ TV ☎ ♿ rm. 🚗 – 🏛 50. AE ⊙ ⓞ MC VISA JCB. ✻ JT a
Meals ***L'Altra Fermata*** Rest. a la carte 31/41 – **131 rm** ☕ 230/290.
◆ Extensive restoration has created a light and welcoming hotel where minimalist design prevails. Attractive breakfast room with glass roof, and small restaurant serving fusion cuisine.

Santini, via San Marco 3 20121 ☎ 02 6555587, *info@ristorantesantini.it, Fax 02 6592589* – ▤ 🚗. AE ⊙ ⓞ MC VISA JCB KV m
closed 9 to 25 August, Saturday lunch and Sunday – **Meals** 35 b.i (lunch only) 75 and a la carte 59/90 🍇.
◆ An elegant establishment with modern overtones, but also offering two lounge areas more classically traditional in feel ; imaginatively fused flavours distinguish the cuisine.

Casa Fontana-23 Risotti, piazza Carbonari 5 ✉ 20125 ☎ 02 6704710, *trattoria@23risotti.it, Fax 02 66800465* – ▤. AE ⊙ ⓞ MC VISA. ✻ FQ d
closed Easter, August, Christmas, 1 to 6 January, Monday, Saturday lunch and Saturday dinner-Sunday in July – **Meals** (booking essential) risotto specialities a la carte 38/46.
◆ Worth seeking out is this small friendly restaurant slightly away from the centre ; the ritual 25-minute wait is necessary for preparation of one of their trademark risottos.

Alla Cucina delle Langhe, corso Como 6 ✉ 20154 ☎ 02 6554279, *Fax 02 29006859* – ⇹ ▤. AE ⊙ ⓞ MC VISA JCB. ✻ KU d
closed August, Sunday also Saturday in July – **Meals** Lombardy and Piedmontese specialities a la carte 37/51.
◆ Classic trattoria in terms of both ambience and menu ; excellent traditional cuisine with speciality Lombard and Piedmontese dishes.

Rigolo, largo Treves ang. via Solferino 11 ✉ 20121 ☎ 02 804589, *ristorante.rigolo@tiscalinet.it, Fax 02 86463220* – ⇹ ▤. AE ⊙ ⓞ MC VISA. ✻ KU b
closed August and Monday – **Meals** a la carte 30/45.
◆ Run by the same family for over 40 years, this recently refurbished restaurant in a fashionable district has many regulars, and serves meat and fish dishes.

Antica Trattoria della Pesa, viale Pasubio 10 ✉ 20154 ☎ 02 6555741, *Fax 02 29015157* – ▤. AE ⊙ ⓞ MC VISA JCB. ✻ JU s
closed Sunday – **Meals** Lombardy rest. a la carte 46/64.
◆ A pleasantly dated ambience in this old Milanese trattoria so typical of bygone Italy, serving dishes native to the city and Lombardy.

Serendib, via Pontida 2 ✉ 20121 ☎ 02 6592139, *Fax 02 6592139* – ▤. ⊙ MC VISA
closed 10 to 20 August – **Meals** (dinner only) (booking essential) Indian and Sinhalese rest. 11/18 and a la carte 23/26. JU b
◆ Singhalese and Indian cuisine authentically prepared and décor to match in this pleasant restaurant, which bears the ancient name of Sri Lanka.

Fuji, viale Montello 9 ✉ 20154 ☎ 02 29008349 – ▤. ⊙ ⓞ MC VISA JCB. ✻
closed Easter, 1 to 23 August, 24 December-2 January and Sunday – **Meals** (dinner only) (booking essential) Japanese rest. a la carte 38/56. JU a
◆ A successful joint venture between an Italian and a Japanese ; now approaching its tenth anniversary this no-frills Oriental restaurant also has a sushi bar.

Central Station – corso Buenos Aires, via Vittor Pisani, piazza della Repubblica

Principe di Savoia, piazza della Repubblica 17 ✉ 20124 ☎ 02 62301, *principe@hotelprincipedisavoia.com, Fax 02 6595838,* – 700. KU a
Meals (see rest. ***Galleria*** below) – 45 – **341 rm** 801/976, 63 suites.
◆ Opulence on a grand scale throughout this showcase hotel, with its fine furnishings and unparalleled attention to tasteful detail ; regal suites with own pool.

The Westin Palace, piazza della Repubblica 20 ✉ 20124 ☎ 02 63361, *palacemilan@westin.com, Fax 02 654485,* – rm, cam. – 250. LU b
Meals ***Casanova Grill*** Rest. *(dinner only in August)* (booking essential) a la carte 58/78 – 33 – **235 rm** 415/580, 7 suites.
◆ Modern skyscraper with sumptuous interior of brocades, gilding, panelling and fine details ; all the grandeur of a hotel of the highest quality. Well-spaced tables, comfortable seating and soft tones make for a pampered ambience in the restaurant.

Excelsior Gallia, piazza Duca d'Aosta 9 ✉ 20124 ☎ 02 67851, *sales@excelsiorgallia.it, Fax 02 66713239,* – rm, – 700. LT a
Meals 39 – 33 – **224 rm** 445/545, 13 suites.
◆ Next to the railway station, this giant of the Milanese hotel scene has been a byword for discreet hospitality, uncompromising luxury, and a prestigious clientele since opening in 1932. The sophisticated restaurant is located on the top floor.

Hilton Milan, via Galvani 12 ✉ 20124 ☎ 02 69831, *sales.milan@hilton.com, Fax 02 66710810,* – rm, – 180. LT c
Meals a la carte 48/61 – 27 – **317 rm** 465/485, 2 suites.
◆ Following a recent refit, this modern hotel is well appointed and extremely comfortable, both in its public areas and in its rooms ; a new conference centre has also been added. The restaurant is contemporary in style.

Starhotel Ritz, via Spallanzani 40 ✉ 20129 ☎ 02 2055, *ritz.mi@starhotels.it, Fax 02 29518679* – rm, – 180. GR a
Meals ***La Loggia*** Rest. a la carte 55/65 – **195 rm** 279/360, 6 suites.
◆ Central but quiet, this modern hotel has been refurbished and offers high levels of comfort and attention to detail throughout.

UNA Hotel Century, via Fabio Filzi 25/b ✉ 20124 ☎ 02 675041, *una.century@unahotels.it, Fax 02 66980602* – rm, – 80. LT f
Meals (residents only) a la carte 36/50 – 144 suites 394/464.
◆ This 17-storey modern hotel is very well appointed ; the rooms, all en-suite, can be divided to provide separate day areas. A relaxing atmosphere in the elegant dining room.

Michelangelo, via Scarlatti 33 ang. piazza Luigi di Savoia ✉ 20124 ☎ 02 67551, *michelangelo@milanhotel.it, Fax 02 6694232* – rm, – 500. LT s
Meals a la carte 47/71 – **306 rm** 232/272, 4 suites.
◆ An unprepossessing fa e to a hotel with spacious rooms of a sober elegance offering every modern convenience ; excellent well-equipped conference centre. A sophisticated ambience to the dining room.

Jolly Hotel Touring, via Tarchetti 2 ✉ 20121 ☎ 02 6335, *milano-touring@jollyhotels.it, Fax 02 6592209* – rm, – 120. KU f
Meals ***Amadeus*** Rest. a la carte 39/50 – **283 rm** 310, 6 suites.
◆ Between Piazza della Republica and the Via Palestro gardens, this quality hotel is well suited to conferences ; fine rooms, most of which have been recently refurbished. A stylish yet cosy atmosphere to the restaurant, with round tables and fitted carpets.

Sheraton Diana Majestic, viale Piave 42 ✉ 20129 ☎ 02 20581 and rest. ☎ 02 20582034, *sheraton.diana.majestic@starwood.com, Fax 02 20582058,* – rm, – 180. LV a
closed August – **Meals** ***Il Milanese Curioso*** Rest. a la carte 47/71 – 37 – **107 rm** 373/473, 3 suites.
◆ An early 20C feel and all modern comforts combine in this historic hotel, which has recently been well restored ; fine shaded garden. An elegant restaurant offering outdoor dining in the summer.

Jolly Hotel Machiavelli, via Lazzaretto 5 ✉ 20124 ☎ 02 631141 and rest ☎ 02 63114921, *machiavelli@jollyhotels.it, Fax 02 6599800* – rm, rest. – 70. rest LU a
Meals ***Caffè Niccolò*** Rest. a la carte 33/51 – 18 – **103 rm** 319.
◆ An airy and harmonious design taking in all the public areas of this modern hotel lends it a contemporary and comfortable style. The rooms are attractively furnished. Smart bistro-style restaurant which also has a wine bar.

Doria Grand Hotel, viale Andrea Doria 22 ✉ 20124 ☎ 02 67411411, *info@doriagrandhotel.it, Fax 02 6696669* – |♦|, ⚡ rm, ▤ TV ☎ ♿ rm. – 🏟 120. AE ⓢ ⓞ ⓜ VISA
Meals *(closed 18 July-21 August and 24 December-6 January)* a la carte 45/64 – **122 rm** ☕ 305/400, 2 suites. GQ x
◆ A caring management at this comfortable new hotel ; public areas decorated in an early-20C style, while a warmer, softer look is used in the rooms. Pale wood panelling and mirrors in the stylish restaurant.

Manin, via Manin 7 ✉ 20121 ☎ 02 6596511, *info@hotelmanin.it, Fax 02 6552160,* 🌳 – |♦|, ⚡ rm, ▤ TV ☎ – 🏟 100. AE ⓢ ⓞ ⓜ VISA JCB. ✗ rest KV d
closed 5 to 28 August – **Meals *Il Bettolino*** Rest. *(closed Saturday)* a la carte 53/67 – **118 rm** ☕ 210/290.
◆ A garden complete with plane trees is an unexpected pleasure at this hotel, soon to celebrate its centenary and recently refurbished ; stylish, well-appointed rooms. A smart yet cosy atmosphere in the excellent restaurant.

Bristol without rest., via Scarlatti 32 ✉ 20124 ☎ 02 6694141, *hotel.bristol@hotelbristolmil.it, Fax 02 6702942* – |♦| ▤ TV ☎ – 🏟 60. AE ⓢ ⓞ ⓜ VISA. ✗ LT m
closed August and 24 December-2 January – **68 rm** ☕ 150/200.
◆ Welcoming public areas tastefully furnished with antiques and rooms of classic style offering every modern convenience in this hotel near the station.

Sanpi without rest., via Lazzaro Palazzi 18 ✉ 20124 ☎ 02 29513341, *info@hotelsanpimilano.it, Fax 02 29402451,* 🏋, 🌳 – |♦|, ⚡ rm, ▤ TV ♿ rm. – 🏟 30. AE ⓢ ⓞ ⓜ VISA JCB. ✗ LU e
closed 9 to 25 August and 24 December-2 January – **79 rm** ☕ 235/295.
◆ Fine attention to detail in the public areas and a charming garden. A pleasant modern hotel with soft pastel rooms.

Auriga without rest., via Pirelli 7 ✉ 20124 ☎ 02 66985851, *auriga@auriga-milano.com, Fax 02 66980698* – |♦|, ⚡ rm, ▤ TV ☎ – 🏟 25. AE ⓢ ⓞ ⓜ VISA JCB. ✗ LTU k
closed 5 to 28 August and 23 December-1 January – **52 rm** ☕ 200/260.
◆ An interesting mixture of colours and styles in this hotel, from its striking fa e through to its extravagant interiors and more classically styled rooms.

Augustus without rest., via Napo Torriani 29 ✉ 20124 ☎ 02 66988271, *info@augustushotel.it, Fax 02 6703096* – |♦| ▤ TV. AE ⓢ ⓞ ⓜ VISA JCB LU q
closed 5 to 16 August and 23 to 27 December – **56 rm** ☕ 165/215.
◆ Among many other hotels near the station, this establishment has comfortable public areas and peaceful, welcoming rooms, decorated in soft tones.

Galles, via Ozanam 1 ang. corso Buenos Aires ✉ 20124 ☎ 02 204841, *reception@galles.it, Fax 02 2048422,* 🏋, ≘s – |♦|, ⚡ rm, ▤ TV ☎ – 🏟 120. AE ⓢ ⓞ ⓜ VISA JCB. ✗ GR m
Meals a la carte 32/44 – ☕ 13 – **187 rm** 276/386, 4 suites.
◆ In a historic palazzo in a city business district, this hotel is modern in concept following a recent refit ; well-maintained interior and versatile meeting rooms. Airy dining room overlooking Milan's rooftops and surrounded by its own roof garden.

Grand Hotel Puccini without rest., corso Buenos Aires 33, galleria Puccini ✉ 20124 ☎ 02 29521344, *reservation@grandhotelpuccini.it, Fax 02 2047825* – |♦|, ⚡ rm, ▤ TV ☎ ♿ rm. AE ⓢ ⓞ ⓜ VISA JCB GR r
65 rm ☕ 135/186.
◆ An elegant and atmospheric hotel which has recently been refurbished ; each floor has its own colour scheme and is named after a Puccini opera.

Fenice without rest., corso Buenos Aires 2 ✉ 20124 ☎ 02 29525541, *fenice@hotelfenice.it, Fax 02 29523942* – |♦| ▤ TV. AE ⓢ ⓞ ⓜ VISA JCB. ✗ LU x
46 rm ☕ 120/176.
◆ In a cosmopolitan area, this recently opened hotel is elegant and welcoming ; functional, well-appointed rooms.

Albert without rest., via Tonale 2 ang. via Sammartini ✉ 20125 ☎ 02 66985446, *albertotel@libero.it, Fax 02 66985624* – |♦| ▤ TV ♿ – 🏟 35. AE ⓢ ⓞ ⓜ VISA JCB. ✗ LT t
closed two weeks in August and two weeks at Christmas – **62 rm** ☕ 130/180.
◆ Next to the station, this relaunched historic hotel is a comfortable establishment with genteel, well-presented rooms.

Mini Hotel Aosta without rest., piazza Duca d'Aosta 16 ✉ 20124 ☎ 02 6691951, *aosta@minihotel.it, Fax 02 6696215* – |♦| ▤ TV. AE ⓢ ⓞ ⓜ VISA JCB. ✗ LT p
63 rm ☕ 120/180.
◆ This hotel facing the main station may be slightly dated inside but it is still comfortable ; many rooms recently redecorated and breakfast room with a fine view.

New York without rest., via Pirelli 5 ✉ 20124 ☎ 02 66985551, *info@hotelnewyorkspa.com, Fax 02 6697267* – |♦| ▤ TV. AE ⓢ ⓞ ⓜ VISA. ✗ LTU k
closed 1 to 28 August and 24 December-5 January – **69 rm** ☕ 124/195.
◆ Situated among many other hotels, this establishment is comfortable throughout ; a modern look to the rooms. Those which face inwards are quieter.

Sempione, via Finocchiaro Aprile 11 20124 02 6570323 and rest. 02 6552715, *hsempione@hotelsempione.it, Fax 02 6575379* – rest LU r
closed August – **Meals** ***Piazza Repubblica*** Rest. a la carte 31/45 – **43 rm** 130/190.
• Set in a historic building, this family-run hotel has been established for over thirty years ; simple but comfortable, its unfussy rooms have modern furniture. The restaurant has a formal ambience.

Florida without rest., via Lepetit 33 20124 02 6705921, *info@hotelfloridamilan.com, Fax 02 6692867* – LT p
56 rm 120/180, suite.
• In a quiet street near the main station, this comfortable hotel appeals to business travellers. Modern furnishings throughout.

Galleria - Hotel Principe di Savoia, piazza della Repubblica 17 20124 02 62301 – KU a
closed Saturday and Sunday lunch – **Meals** a la carte 72/98.
• Under the same roof as one of Milan finest hotels, this restaurant has an air of regal luxury, with fine furniture and antiques.

La Terrazza di Via Palestro, via Palestro 2 20121 02 76002186, *terrazza palestro@esperiaristorazione.it, Fax 02 76003328,* – – 200. KV h
closed 8 to 28 August, 23 December-8 January, Saturday and Sunday – **Meals** (booking essential) a la carte 50/65.
• Refined modern elegance with dining on the terrace in summer ; Among its innovative dishes, do not miss the Mediterranean sushi, an Italian spin on the Japanese classic.

Piccolo Sogno, via Stoppani 5 angolo via Zambelletti 20129 02 204603 – . GR b
closed 20 days in August, 1 to 10 January, Saturday lunch and Sunday – **Meals** (booking essential) a la carte 45/68.
• A recent change of management and name at this well-presented restaurant ; a warm welcome and traditional cuisine.

Mediterranea, piazza Cincinnato 4 20124 02 29522076, *ristmediterranea@fastwebnet.it, Fax 02 201156* – . LU z
closed 5 to 25 August, 27 December-7 January, Sunday and Monday lunch – **Meals** seafood a la carte 43/60 .
• A maritime feel here thanks to the blue glass throughout and the shellfish tanks ; simple flavoursome seafood.

Joia, via Panfilo Castaldi 18 20124 02 29522124, *joia@joia.it, Fax 02 2049244* – . LU c
closed 4 to 25 August, Saturday lunch and Sunday – **Meals** (booking essential) Vegetarian and seafood rest. a la carte 50/82 .
Spec. Variazione di tonno con gusti diversi (summer-winter). Ravioli di verdura con calamari, cozze e peperone dolce (summer winter). Tortino croccante di patate e peperoni, spuma soffice di zucchine e taleggio.
• Dark wood floors and skylights in the non-smoking main area ; creative seafood and conceptual vegetarian cuisine which looks and tastes great.

Torriani 25, via Napo Torriani 25 20124 02 67078183, *acena@torriani25.it, Fax 02 67479548* – . LU t
closed 12 to 20 August, 24 to 31 December, Saturday lunch and Sunday – **Meals** (booking essential) seafood a la carte 34/57.
• A spacious modern restaurant with an open kitchen and a buffet just inside, to whet the appetite of arriving diners in search of the elaborate cuisine on offer.

I Malavoglia, via Lecco 4 20124 02 29531387 – .
closed Easter, 1 May, August, 24 December-4 January and Sunday – **Meals** (dinner only) (booking essential) Sicilian and seafood rest. a la carte 38/54. LU g
• Run by the same husband and wife team since 1973, this pleasant, smart and tastefully presented restaurant specialises in Sicilian dishes and seafood with a modern twist.

Da Ilia, via Lecco 1 20124 02 29521895, *ristdailia@tin.it, Fax 02 29409165,* – LU d
closed Easter, August, 26 December-5 January, Friday and Saturday lunch – **Meals** a la carte 34/52.
• An informal atmosphere to this family-run restaurant, serving classic dishes with a strong Milanese influence.

Da Giannino-L'Angolo d'Abruzzo, via Pilo 20 20129 02 29406526, *Fax 02 29406526* – . GR t
closed Monday – **Meals** (booking essential for dinner) Abruzzi specialities a la carte 20/28.
• This family-run restaurant, in the same hands for over 45 years, has a welcoming, light and airy ambience ; authentic Abruzzo cuisine at modest prices.

La Cantina di Manuela, via Poerio 3 ✉ 20129 ☎ 02 76318892, *cantina4@virgilio.it, Fax 02 76312971*, , Rest. wine-bar – AE ✪ MC VISA. ✻ GR x
closed Sunday – **Meals** a la carte 26/33 .
◆ Quality ingredients and interesting choices in a relaxed ambience ; all dishes on the traditional menu are very gratifying, from meats through to cheeses

Romana-Vittoria – corso Porta Romana, corso Lodi, corso XXII Marzo, corso Porta Vittoria

Grand Visconti Palace, viale Isonzo 14 ✉ 20135 ☎ 02 540341, *info@grandviscontipalace.com, Fax 02 54069523*, , , , – rm, – 250. AE MC VISA. ✻ FS a
Meals ***Al Quinto Piano*** Rest. a la carte 53/81 – **166 rm** 400/470, 6 suites.
◆ This classically elegant hotel occupies a large building, formerly an industrial mill. Good health spa and conference facilities. The fifth floor restaurant is a jewel in dove-grey hues.

UNA Hotel Mediterraneo, via Muratori 14 ✉ 20135 ☎ 02 550071, *una.mediterraneo@unahotel.it, Fax 02 550072217* – , rm, – 75. AE ✪ MC VISA JCB. ✻ LY c
Meals a la carte 40/50 – **93 rm** 251/296.
◆ In the Porta Romana district near the metro a completely refurbished hotel with a comfortable modern feel throughout ; quiet and relaxing rooms.

Da Giacomo, via B. Cellini angolo via Sottocorno 6 ✉ 20129 ☎ 02 76023313, *Fax 02 76024305* – . AE ✪ MC VISA. ✻ FGR g
closed August, 23 December-7 January, Monday and Tuesday lunch – **Meals** seafood a la carte 47/69.
◆ Well-presented family-run trattoria with closely spaced tables ; fish dominates the varied menu but meat dishes are also available.

Isola dei Sapori, via Anfossi 10 ✉ 20135 ☎ 02 54100708, *Fax 02 54100708* – . AE MC VISA JCB. ✻ GS c
closed August, 23 December-3 January, Sunday and Monday lunch – **Meals** (booking essential for dinner) a la carte 33/46.
◆ A welcome newcomer to the Milan scene, opened two years ago by three young Sardinians, specialising in seafood ; modern decoration.

Masuelli San Marco, viale Umbria 80 ✉ 20135 ☎ 02 55184138, *masuelli.trattoria@tin.it, Fax 02 54124512* – . AE ✪ MC VISA JCB GS h
closed 3 weeks in August, 25 December-6 January, Sunday and Monday lunch – **Meals** (booking essential for dinner) Lombardy-Piedmontese rest. a la carte 30/41.
◆ A genteel rustic atmosphere in this traditional trattoria, in the same hands since 1921 ; cuisine in the Lombard-Piedmontese tradition.

Trattoria la Piola, via Perugino 18 ✉ 20135 ☎ 02 55195945, *info@lapiola.it, Fax 02 2481090* – . AE ✪ MC VISA. ✻ GS e
closed Easter, August, 24 December-2 January and Sunday – **Meals** (dinner only) seafood a la carte 34/46.
◆ The strongpoint of this simple establishment is the freshness of its ingredients ; among its appealing seafood cuisine are raw fish dishes.

Dongiò, via Corio 3 ✉ 20135 ☎ 02 5511372, *Fax 02 5401869* – . AE ✪ MC VISA LY u
closed August, Saturday lunch and Sunday – **Meals** (booking essential) a la carte 25/37.
◆ One of the last authentic trattorias, unfussy and family-run ; the specialities are fresh pasta, meat dishes and Calabrian cuisine.

Giulio Pane e Ojo, via Muratori 10 ✉ 20135 ☎ 02 5456189, *info@giuliopaneojo.com, Fax 02 36504603*, – . AE ✪ MC VISA JCB LY a
closed 24 Decemer-1 January and Sunday – **Meals** (booking essential) Roman rest. a la carte 27/32.
◆ A small, informal establishment run by young management offering typical Roman cuisine at competitive prices. Deservedly popular, booking is essential in the evenings.

Navigli – via Solari, Ripa di Porta Ticinese, viale Bligny, piazza XXIV Maggio

D'Este without rest., viale Bligny 23 ✉ 20136 ☎ 02 58321001, *reception@hoteldestemilano.it, Fax 02 58321136* – – 80. AE ✪ MC VISA. ✻ KY d
79 rm 150/220.
◆ A well-lit, 1980s-style lobby and spacious public areas in this hotel ; rooms decorated in a variety of styles, but all are equally comfortable and quiet.

Crivi's without rest., corso Porta Vigentina 46 ✉ 20122 ☎ 02 582891, *crivis@tin.it, Fax 02 58318182* – – 120. AE ✪ MC VISA JCB KY e
closed August and Christmas – **86 rm** 170/240, 3 suites.
◆ Centrally located and near the metro station, an agreeable hotel with pleasant public areas ; modern furnishings in the rooms, which are reasonably spacious and comfortable.

Liberty without rest., viale Bligny 56 ✉ 20136 ☎ 02 58318562, *reserve@hotelliberty-milano.com, Fax 02 58319061* – |♦| ▤ TV. AE ● ● ● VISA JCB. ✂ KY a
closed 1 to 24 August – **52 rm** ☕ 132/252.
♦ The public areas of this elegant hotel, near the Bocconi university, are Art Nouveau in style with antique furniture; many rooms with jacuzzi baths.

Des Etrangers without rest., via Sirte 9 ✉ 20146 ☎ 02 48955325, *info@hoteldesetrangers.it, Fax 02 48955325* – ✂ ▤ TV ☎ 🚗 – 🏛 50. AE ● ● ● VISA DS y
96 rm ☕ 95/150.
♦ Access down a flight of steps to this totally renovated establishment on a quiet street; practicality and comfort in evidence throughout. Convenient underground garage.

XXX ✿✿ **Sadler,** via Ettore Troilo 14 angolo via Conchetta ✉ 20136 ☎ 02 58104451, *sadler@sadler.it, Fax 02 58112343,* 🌳 – ▤. AE ● ● ● VISA JCB ES a
closed 8 August-2 September, 1 to 12 January and Sunday – **Meals** (dinner only) (booking essential) a la carte 67/102 🍇.
Spec. Tortelli di zucca con scaloppa di foie gras, mandorle e timo (spring-autumn). Filetto di San Pietro in casseruola ai sapori mediterranei (summer).Lombatina di maialino di cinta senese ai fiori di finocchio, salsa chiantigiana (winter).
♦ Stylish both in design and cuisine, this elegant modern restaurant is a famous name among its Milanese peers; a creative menu.

XX **Al Porto,** piazzale Generale Cantore ✉ 20123 ☎ 02 89407425, *alportodimilano@acena.it, Fax 02 8321481* – ▤. AE ● ● ● VISA JCB HY h
closed August, 24 December-3 January, Sunday and Monday lunch – **Meals** (booking essential) seafood a la carte 42/61.
♦ In the old 19C customs house of Porta Genova. This rustic, exclusively seafood, restaurant is a city favourite.

XX **Osteria di Porta Cicca,** ripa di Porta Ticinese 51 ✉ 20143 ☎ 02 8372763, *osteriadiportacicca@hotmail.com, Fax 02 8372763* – ▤. AE ● ● ● VISA JCB. ✂ HY j
closed Saturday lunch and Sunday – **Meals** (booking essential) a la carte 29/42.
♦ Opened in 1995, this smart and welcoming restaurant run by young management offers a modern spin to traditional cuisine.

XX **Tano Passami l'Olio,** via Vigevano 32/a ✉ 20144 ☎ 02 8394139, *info@tanopassamilolio.it, Fax 02 83240104* – ▤. AE ● ● ● VISA. ✂ HY f
closed August, 24 December-6 January and Sunday – **Meals** (dinner only) (booking essential) a la carte 59/81.
♦ Soft lighting and a romantic atmosphere in this cosy restaurant, with a menu of light meat and fish dishes using extra virgin olive oil.

XX **Il Torchietto,** via Ascanio Sforza 47 ✉ 20136 ☎ 02 8372910, *info@il.torchietto.com, Fax 02 8372000* – ▤. AE ● ● ● VISA. ✂ ES b
closed August, 26 December-3 January, Saturady lunch and Monday – **Meals** Mantuan rest. a la carte 36/45.
♦ Elegant and spacious trattoria on the Naviglio Pavese which has been recently refurbished; menu offers seasonal dishes and regional (especially Mantuan) specialities.

XX **Il Navigante,** via Magolfa 14 ✉ 20143 ☎ 02 89406320, *info@navigante.it, Fax 02 89420897* – ▤ P. AE ● ● ● VISA JCB JY c
closed August, Sunday lunch and Monday – **Meals** a la carte 36/72.
♦ Close to the Naviglio, this restaurant has live music every night. Run by a former ship cook, there is an unusual underfloor aquarium and plenty of seafood.

XX **Le Buone Cose,** via San Martino 8 ✉ 20122 ☎ 02 58310589, *lebuonecose@hotmail.com, Fax 02 58310589* – ▤. ● ● VISA. ✂ KY h
closed August, Saturday lunch and Sunday – **Meals** (booking essential) seafood a la carte 30/59.
♦ Small, elegant and welcoming, this informal establishment has many regulars; traditional but flavoursome seafood.

X **Trattoria Trinacria,** via Savona 57 ✉ 20144 ☎ 02 4238250, *trattoria.trinacria@libero.it* – ▤. AE ● ● ● VISA. ✂ DS w
closed Sunday – **Meals** (dinner only) (booking essential) Sicilian rest. a la carte 28/40.
♦ This recently opened Sicilian restaurant is pleasingly simple and modern; the menu is in dialect with Italian subtitles.

X **Trattoria Aurora,** via Savona 23 ✉ 20144 ☎ 02 8323144, *trattoriaaurora@libero.it, Fax 02 89404978,* 🌳 – AE ● ● VISA HY m
closed Monday – **Meals** Piedmontese rest. 15 (lunch only) 35 b.i. (dinner only).
♦ An atmospheric restaurant which in summer opens onto a fine garden to provide outdoor dining; many regulars, drawn by the classic Piedmontese cuisine.

Ponte Rosso, Ripa di Porta Ticinese 23 ✉ 20143 ✆ 02 8373132, *stefigian@tiscali.it, Trattoria-bistrot* – AE Ⓢ MC VISA. HY d
closed August, Sunday and Monday lunch – **Meals** a la carte 32/46.
◆ The exuberant proprietor has created a classic trattoria-bistro atmosphere, complete with a display of modern collectibles ; specialises in Triestino and Milanese dishes.

Fiera-Sempione – corso Sempione, piazzale Carlo Magno, via Monte Rosa, via Washington

Hermitage, via Messina 10 ✉ 20154 ✆ 02 318170, *hermitage.res@monrifhotels.it, Fax 02 33107399* – rm, TV rm. – 180. AE Ⓢ MC VISA JCB. HU q
closed August – **Meals** (see rest. ***Il Sambuco*** below) – **119 rm** 260/315, 8 suites.
◆ Refinement and comfort are the key words at this hotel which combines a classically stylish interior with every modern convenience ; popular with models and VIPs.

Melià Milano, via Masaccio 19 ✉ 20149 ✆ 02 44406, *melia.milano@solmelia.com, Fax 02 44406600,* – rm, TV rm. – 500. AE Ⓢ MC VISA. DR p
Meals *Alacena* Rest. *(closed August)* Spanish rest. a la carte 57/84 – 29 – **288 rm** 375/425, 4 suites.
◆ A prestigious modern hotel ; marble, crystal chandeliers and antique tapestries in the lobby, and imposing but very comfortable rooms ; excellent-quality Spanish cuisine in the smart "Alacena" restaurant.

Milan Marriott Hotel, via Washington 66 ✉ 20146 ✆ 02 48521 and rest ✆ 02 48522834, *marriott.booking@virgilio.it, Fax 02 4818925,* – rm, TV – 1300. AE Ⓢ MC VISA JCB. DR d
Meals *La Brasserie de Milan* Rest. a la carte 36/79 – 20 – **322 rm** 440, suite.
◆ An unusual contrast between the modern fa e and the classically elegant interiors in this hotel, which hosts many corporate events. Well-presented functional rooms. Traditional-style dining room with open kitchen.

Atahotel Fieramilano, viale Boezio 20 ✉ 20145 ✆ 02 336221, *prenotazioni@grandhotelfieramilano.com, Fax 02 314119* – TV rm. – 220. AE Ⓢ MC VISA JCB. DR e
closed August – **Meals *Ambrosiano*** Rest. (dinner only) a la carte 36/49 – **236 rm** 255/315, 2 suites.
◆ Opposite the Fiera, this recently refitted hotel has every modern convenience and a high level of comfort ; in summer breakfast is served in the gazebo outside. Quiet, elegant dining room.

Enterprise Hotel, corso Sempione 91 ✉ 20154 ✆ 02 318181 and rest ✆ 02 31818855, *info@enterprisehotel.com, Fax 02 31818811* – rm, TV cam. – 350. AE Ⓢ MC VISA JCB DQ c
Meals *Sophia's* Rest. *(closed August)* a la carte 48/60 – **120 rm** 265/332, 2 suites.
◆ A marble and granite exterior, coupled with made-to-measure furnishings give a strong geometrical theme to this elegant hotel where the emphasis is on design and detail. An unusual yet pleasant ambience for lunch or dinner.

UNA Hotel Scandinavia, via Fauchè 15 ✉ 20154 ✆ 02 336391, *una.scandinavia@unahotels.it, Fax 02 33104510,* – rm, TV – 170. AE Ⓢ MC VISA JCB. HT c
Meals *Una Restaurant* Rest. a la carte 32/42 – **153 rm** 310/364, suite.
◆ An elegant hotel near the Fiera which offers stylish accommodation and well equipped conference facilities. The smart dining room features marble and mahogany, and overlooks the courtyard garden.

Capitol Millennium, via Cimarosa 6 ✉ 20144 ✆ 02 438591, *info@capitolmillenium.com, Fax 02 4694724,* – TV – 70. AE Ⓢ MC VISA JCB. rest DR a
Meals (residents only) a la carte 40/53 – 18,50 – **61 rm** 250/375, 5 suites.
◆ Rising from the ashes of its predecessor, this small elegant hotel is a modern jewel. Excellent attention to detail throughout.

Regency without rest., via Arimondi 12 ✉ 20155 ✆ 02 39216021, *regency@regency-milano.com, Fax 02 39217734* – TV – 50. AE Ⓢ MC VISA JCB. DQ b
closed 5 to 25 August and 24 December-7 January – **71 rm** 190/240.
◆ This late-19C aristocratic residence with its genteel courtyard is charming and very tastefully decorated throughout ; it has a particularly pleasant lounge with roaring fire.

Poliziano Fiera without rest., via Poliziano 11 ✉ 20154 ✆ 02 3191911, *info@hotelpolizianofiera.it, Fax 02 3191931* – rm, TV – 90. AE Ⓢ MC VISA. HT a
closed 25 July-25 August and 18 December-7 January – **98 rm** 293/337, 2 suites.
◆ This small, modern hotel has been totally refurbished ; polite and attentive management ; well-proportioned, pleasantly decorated rooms.

Domenichino without rest., via Domenichino 41 ✉ 20149 ☎ 02 48009692, *hd@hoteldomenichino.it, Fax 02 48003953* – 60. DR f
closed 5 to 21 August and 23 December-1 January – **77 rm** 140/200, 2 suites.
• On a tree-lined road close to the Fiera, this elegant hotel has high standards of service ; confined public areas but comfortable rooms with modern furnishings.

Mozart without rest., piazza Gerusalemme 6 ✉ 20154 ☎ 02 33104215, *info@hotelmozartmilano.it, Fax 02 33103231* – 35. HT b
closed 31 July-22 August and 24 December-2 January – **119 rm** 199,50/252, 3 suites.
• Classical elegance and attentive service at this recently refurbished hotel near the Fiera ; modern furniture in the well-appointed rooms.

Metrò without rest., corso Vercelli 61 ✉ 20144 ☎ 02 4987897, *hotelmetro@tin.it, Fax 02 48010295* – DR x
40 rm 150/210.
• This family-run establishment is well placed for shopping ; pleasant public areas and elegant well-appointed rooms.

Astoria without rest., viale Murillo 9 ✉ 20149 ☎ 02 40090095, *info@astoriahotelmilano.com, Fax 02 40074642* – 40. DR m
closed 28 July-28 August – **69 rm** 130/210.
• Situated on a busy road, this recently refitted hotel is popular with tourists and business people alike ; modern rooms with excellent soundproofing.

Mini Hotel Tiziano without rest., via Tiziano 6 ✉ 20145 ☎ 02 4699035, *tiziano@minihotel.it, Fax 02 4812153* – DR k
54 rm 140/200.
• Near the Fiera but in a quiet location, this hotel has the advantage of its own gardens to the rear ; comfortable rooms.

Berlino without rest., via Plana 33 ✉ 20155 ☎ 02 324141, *hotelberlino@traveleurope.it, Fax 02 39210611* – DQ b
48 rm 90/120.
• Popular with business travellers, this comfortable hotel near the Fiera has traditionally-stylish public areas, with its (largely refurbished) rooms along more modern lines.

Lancaster without rest., via Abbondio Sangiorgio 16 ✉ 20145 ☎ 02 344705, *h.lancaster@tin.it, Fax 02 344649* – HU c
closed July, August, Christmas and New Year – **30 rm** 116/184.
• This 19C building is in a quiet residential district ; a pleasant hotel with welcoming, if cramped, public areas and well-maintained, smart rooms.

Certosa without rest., viale Certosa 26 ✉ 20155 ☎ 02 3271311, *info@hotel-certosa.it, Fax 02 3270456* – DQ d
27 rm 130/200.
• Opened in 2003, this hotel has limited public areas including lobby and breakfast room, in contrast to the spaciousness of its well-equipped accommodation. Courteous and efficient service

Antica Locanda Leonardo without rest., corso Magenta 78 ✉ 20123 ☎ 02 48014197, *info@anticalocandaleonardo.com, Fax 02 48019012,* – HX m
closed 5 to 25 August and 31 December-6 January – **20 rm** 95/195.
• A combination of genteel surroundings and warm welcome at this hotel, which looks onto a small courtyard ; close by is Leonardo's Last Supper.

Il Sambuco - Hotel Hermitage, via Messina 10 ✉ 20154 ☎ 02 33610333, *info@ilsambuco.it, Fax 02 33611850* – HU q
closed Easter, 1 to 20 August, 25 December-3 January, Saturday lunch and Sunday – **Meals** seafood a la carte 47/92.
• Like the hotel in which it is located, this restaurant is elegant and has high service standards ; renowned for its seafood cuisine, limited to stew on Mondays.

Montecristo, corso Sempione angolo via Prina ✉ 20154 ☎ 02 3495049, *Fax 02 312760* – HU j
closed August, 25 December-2 January, Tuesday and Saturady lunch – **Meals** seafood a la carte 41/57.
• A choice of dining on the ground floor with fish tanks, or in the more intimate basement taverna, at this restaurant serving traditional flavoursome seafood.

Arrow's, via Mantegna 17/19 ✉ 20154 ☎ 02 341533, *Fax 02 33106496,* – HU f
closed August, Sunday and Monday lunch – **Meals** (booking essential) seafood a la carte 36/66.
• Packed at lunchtime, largely with business diners, but more intimate during the evenings, this restaurant near Corso Sempione specialises in traditional seafood.

El Crespin, via Castelvetro 18 ✉ 20154 ☎ 02 33103004, *Fax 02 33103004* – ▤. AE ⓢ ⓓ ⓜ VISA. ✗ HT p
closed August, 26 December-7 January, Saturday lunch and Sunday – **Meals** (booking essential) a la carte 40/51.
♦ Old photos decorate the entrance area of this tastefully presented restaurant, where the menu is dictated by the changing seasons.

Da Stefano il Marchigiano, via Arimondi 1 angolo via Plana ✉ 20155 ☎ 02 33001863 – ▤. AE ⓢ ⓓ ⓜ VISA JCB. ✗ DQ d
closed August, Friday dinner and Saturday – **Meals** a la carte 30/44.
♦ For over twenty years this restaurant has been a favourite for lovers of good traditional cuisine ; meat and seafood dishes using quality ingredients.

Osteria del Borgo Antico, via Piero della Francesca 40 ✉ 20154 ☎ 02 3313641, *osteria@borgoantico.net* – ▤. AE ⓢ ⓓ ⓜ VISA. ✗ HT v
closed August, Saturday lunch and Sunday – **Meals** seafood a la carte 42/63.
♦ Opened a couple of years ago, this small well-run restaurant is nicely decorated and has a friendly atmosphere ; especially good seafood.

Le Pietre Cavate, via Castelvetro 14 angolo via Pier della Francesca ✉ 20154 ☎ 02 344704, *Fax 02 344704* – ✗ ▤. AE ⓢ ⓓ ⓜ VISA. ✗ HT p
closed August, 26 December-2 January, Tuesday and Wednesday lunch – **Meals** a la carte 34/48.
♦ This pleasant classic restaurant has been in the same hand for twenty years ; its extensive menu is Tuscan in style and includes meat, mushrooms and truffles, although fish dishes predominate.

Montina, via Procaccini 54 ✉ 20154 ☎ 02 3490498, ☂ – ▤. AE ⓢ ⓓ ⓜ VISA
closed 8 August-1 September, 30 December-9 January, Sunday and Monday lunch – **Meals** a la carte 19/36. HU d
♦ Pleasant bistro atmosphere with closely spaced tables and soft lighting in this restaurant run by twin brothers ; seasonal cuisine which is mainly Milanese.

Pace, via Washington 74 ✉ 20146 ☎ 02 43983058, *Fax 02 468567* – ▤. AE ⓢ ⓓ ⓜ VISA. ✗ DR z
closed Easter, 1 to 24 August, 24 December-5 January, Saturday lunch and Wednesday – **Meals** a la carte 25/35.
♦ This family-run trattoria, simple yet well presented, has been offering diners a warm welcome for over 30 years ; traditional meat and fish dishes.

Outskirts of Milan

North-Western area – viale Fulvio Testi, Niguarda, viale Fermi, viale Certosa, San Siro, via Novara

Grand Hotel Brun, via Caldera 21 ✉ 20153 ☎ 02 452711, *brun.res@monrifhotels.it*, *Fax 02 48204746* – |‡|, ✗ rm, ▤ TV ☎ – 🏛 500. AE ⓢ ⓓ ⓜ VISA. ✗
closed 23 December-4 January – **Meals** ***Don Giovanni*** Rest. *(closed Saturday and Sunday)* (dinner only) a la carte 50/75 and ***La Terrazza Rest.*** a la carte 30/40 – **309 rm** ☐ 260/330, 6 suites. by via S. Stratico DR
♦ In a peaceful location away from the centre, this hotel with its spacious public areas, functional rooms and well-proportioned meeting rooms, is ideal for business people. The pastel coloured dining room is decorated with trompe l'oeil scenes.

Rubens, via Rubens 21 ✉ 20148 ☎ 02 40302, *rubens@antareshotels.com*, *Fax 02 48193114*, 🏋 – |‡|, ✗ rm, ▤ TV ☎ P – 🏛 35. AE ⓢ ⓓ ⓜ VISA JCB. ✗ rest
Meals (residents only) – **87 rm** ☐ 195/270. DR g
♦ Contemporary artwork on the walls in the public areas and rooms of this elegant, functional hotel ; much attention to detail in evidence throughout.

Accademia, viale Certosa 68 ✉ 20155 ☎ 02 39211122, *accademia@antareshotels.com*, *Fax 02 33103878* – |‡| ✗ ▤ TV ☎ – 🏛 70. AE ⓢ ⓓ ⓜ VISA JCB. ✗ DQ g
Meals (residents only) 20/50 – **67 rm** ☐ 225/295.
♦ Endowed with great character, this hotel mixes modernity with classic style throughout its comfortable public areas and rooms, decorated with modern trompe l'oeil scenes.

Blaise e Francis, via Butti 9 ✉ 20158 ☎ 02 66802366, *info@blaiseefrancis.it*, *Fax 02 66802909* – |‡|, ✗ rm, ▤ TV ☎ ♿ – 🏛 200. AE ⓢ ⓓ ⓜ VISA. ✗ EQ a
Meals (dinner only) (residents only) a la carte 35/48 – **110 rm** ☐ 260/295.
♦ Located away from the centre, the top floors of this relatively new 14-storey hotel have fine views over the city ; comfortable rooms.

Novotel Milano Nord-Cà Granda, viale Suzzani 13 ✉ 20162 ☎ 02 641151, *novotelmilanonord@accor-hotels.it*, *Fax 02 66101961*, 🏋, ⛱ – |‡|, ✗ rm, ▤ TV ☎ ♿ P – 🏛 500. AE ⓢ ⓓ ⓜ VISA JCB. ✗ rest by viale Zara FQ
Meals a la carte 30/40 – **172 rm** ☐ 200/247.
♦ Out of town but well located, this recently built hotel has good standards of comfort and service. Rooms in keeping with the group's standards ; functional and no frills. A modern and spacious dining room with an eclectic menu.

Mirage, viale Certosa 104/106 ✉ 20156 ℘ 02 39210471, *mirage@gruppomirage.it, Fax 02 39210589* – rm – 100. AE VISA DQ z
closed 30 July-22 August – **Meals** *(closed Friday and Saturday)* (residents only) 30 – **86 rm** 180/240.
◆ Out of town but not far from the Fiera, ideal for the business traveller ; currently being extended, this hotel has modern public areas and comfortable rooms.

Valganna without rest., via Varè 32 ✉ 20158 ℘ 02 39310089, *info@hotelvalganna.it, Fax 02 39312566* – . AE VISA JCB by via degli Imbriani EQ
35 rm 113/165.
◆ Near the new Bovisa campus and one stop from the airport on the Malpensa Express, this comfortable family-run hotel offers good value for money.

Innocenti Evasioni, via privata della Bindellina ✉ 20155 ℘ 02 33001882, *ristorante@innocentievasioni.com, Fax 02 33001882,* , – . AE VISA JCB. DQ a
closed August, 3 to 9 January, Sunday and Monday – **Meals** (dinner only) (booking essential) a la carte 37/46.
◆ An unpromising exterior hides a pleasant modern restaurant, with soft lighting and windows onto a small garden ; whimsical creative cuisine.

La Pobbia 1850, via Gallarate 92 ✉ 20151 ℘ 02 38006641, *lapobbia@tiscali.it, Fax 02 38000724,* , Ancient Milanese rest. – – 30. AE VISA DQ w
closed August and Sunday – **Meals** a la carte 35/50.
◆ Well-established urbane restaurant (opened in 1920), with an elegant rustic ambience and al fresco dining in summer. Lombard and international cuisine.

Al Molo 13, via Rubens 13 ✉ 20148 ℘ 02 4042743, *Fax 02 40072616* – . AE VISA JCB DR b
closed 2 August-2 Septemer, 31 December-9 January, Sunday and Monday lunch – **Meals** seafood a la carte 35/59.
◆ This welcoming modern establishment best advert is the display of fresh fish which diners pass on the way in ; seafood and Sardinian specialities.

North-Eastern area – viale Monza, via Padova, via Porpora, viale Romagna, viale Argonne, viale Forlanini

Concorde, viale Monza 132 ✉ 20125 ℘ 02 26112020, *concorde@antareshotels.com, Fax 02 26147879* – – 160. AE VISA JCB.
Meals (residents only) a la carte 42/62 – **120 rm** 208/298.
◆ This comfortable out-of-town hotel is ideal for business people and corporate events ; recently refurbished rooms and versatile meeting rooms. by viale Monza GQ

Starhotel Tourist, viale Fulvio Testi 300 ✉ 20126 ℘ 02 6437777, *tourist.mi@starhotels.it, Fax 02 6472516,* – , rm, – 150. AE VISA JCB. by viale Zara FQ
Meals a la carte 40/50 – **140 rm** 230.
◆ Away from the centre, but well placed for motorway access, this hotel conforms to its group's standards ; a spacious refitted ground floor with well-appointed meeting rooms. Smart restaurant with bar.

Lombardia, viale Lombardia 74 ✉ 20131 ℘ 02 2824938, *hotelomb@tin.it, Fax 02 2893430* – , rm, – 100. AE VISA JCB. rest GQ e
closed 6 to 23 August – **Meals** *(closed Saturday and Sunday)* (dinner only) (residents only) 22/32 – **80 rm** 140/190.
◆ This well-presented hotel in the Piazzale Loreto district has a light spacious lobby and quiet, inner-facing rooms with modern furnishings.

Agape without rest., via Flumendosa 35 ✉ 20132 ℘ 02 27200702, *info@agapehotel.com, Fax 02 27203435* – – 30. AE VISA JCB
43 rm 135/180. by via Palmanova GQ
◆ Conveniently situated in a residential area with good road links, this hotel is run in a competent and businesslike fashion, with great weekend deals.

Tre Pini, via Tullo Morgagni 19 ✉ 20125 ℘ 02 66805413, *Fax 02 66801346,* – . AE VISA by via Arbe FQ
closed 9 to 22 August and Saturday – **Meals** (booking essential) char-grilled specialities a la carte 38/49.
◆ Completely refurbished, this spacious restaurant has doors opening out onto a terrace for summer dining ; roast meats a speciality, prepared in an open kitchen.

Centro Ittico, via Ferrante Aporti 35 ✉ 20125 ℘ 02 26823449, *Fax 02 26143774* – . VISA JCB GQ b
closed August, 25 December-7 January, Sunday and Monday lunch – **Meals** (booking essential for dinner) seafood a la carte 29/51.
◆ Beneath the platforms of the main station, this former fish market is unfussy in presentation and serves fresh seafood cuisine at its best.

South-Eastern area – viale Molise, corso Lodi, via Ripamonti, corso San Gottardo

Atahotel Quark, via Lampedusa 11/a ✉ 20141 ☎ 02 84431, *commerciale@quarkhotel.com, Fax 02 8464190,* – rm, – 1000. rest
by via C. Bazzi FS
closed 13 to 17 August and 1 to 8 January – **Meals** a la carte 49/78 – **190 rm** 212/260, 92 suites 352.
◆ A large recently built hotel, originally conceived as flats and thus offering spacious rooms and many suites ; it has one of the city's largest conference centres. Large windows and pastel décor in the restaurant.

Starhotel Business Palace, via Gaggia 3 ✉ 20139 ☎ 02 53545, *business.mi@starhotels.it, Fax 02 57307550,* – – 300.
by corso Lodi FGS
Meals (residents only) a la carte 35/50 – **215 rm** 230/245, 33 suites.
◆ Well placed for road and metro links, a fine example of a formal industrial building converted for hotel use. Spacious public areas and good conference facilities.

Mec without rest., via Tito Livio 4 ✉ 20137 ☎ 02 5456715, *hotelmec@tiscali.it, Fax 02 5456718,* – . GS r
40 rm 150/200.
◆ Away from the centre but close to the metro, this small and friendly hotel is run by a dynamic young management ; recently restored, it has a modern and functional interior.

La Plancia, via Cassinis 13 ✉ 20139 ☎ 02 5390558, *info@laplancia.it, Fax 02 5390558* – .
by corso Lodi FGS
closed August, 1 to 6 January and Sunday – **Meals** seafood and pizzeria a la carte 27/40.
◆ This bright modern pizzeria-style restaurant, with fish tank displays, offers the choice of pizzas or seafood ; also open for lunch.

Trattoria del Nuovo Macello, via Cesare Lombroso 20 ✉ 20137 ☎ 02 59902122, *info@trattoriadelnuovomacello.it, Fax 02 59902122* – . GS b
closed 14 August-6 September, 24 December-3 January, Saturday and Sunday – **Meals** (booking essential) 18/24 and a la carte 32/45.
◆ This local trattoria has been in business since 1940 ; it was fully refurbished in 1998 and offers a friendly ambience with creative cuisine rooted in rural tradition.

Taverna Calabiana, via Calabiana 3 ✉ 20139 ☎ 02 55213075, *taverna.calabiana@fastwebnet.it* – . . GS a
closed Easter, August, 24 December-5 January, Sunday and Monday – **Meals** Rest. and pizzeria a la carte 24/32.
◆ A welcoming rustic atmosphere with heavy wooden tables ; seasonal cuisine from various regions and authentic pizzas.

South-Western area – viale Famagosta, viale Liguria, via Lorenteggio, viale Forze Armate, via Novara

Holiday Inn Milan, via Lorenteggio 278 ✉ 20147 ☎ 02 413111, *sales@holidayinn-milano.it, Fax 02 413113,* – rm – 85.
by via Foppa DES
Meals ***Il Molinetto*** Rest. a la carte 43/60 – 20 – **119 rm** 255/285.
◆ A recent glass and concrete structure along American lines, offering a comfortable ambience in keeping with the group's standards ; well-appointed rooms. Italian and international cuisine in the welcoming dining room.

Il Luogo di Aimo e Nadia, via Montecuccoli 6 ✉ 20147 ☎ 02 416886, *info@aimoenadia.com, Fax 02 48302005* – .
by via Foppa DES
closed August, 1 to 8 January, Saturday lunch and Sunday – **Meals** (booking essential) 33 (lunch except Bank Holidays) 77 and a la carte 77/127.
Spec. Insalata tiepida di scampi, rigaglie di galletto, lingua di vitello e fagioli di Sorana (spring-autumn). Piccione alla birra, uva e nocciole con fagottino di melanzane e purea di ceci. Semifreddo alle arance, limoni canditi in guscio di cioccolato con sorbetto di pistacchi.
◆ A leading light of the city's culinary scene, this restaurant, with an impressive display of modern works of art, has cuisine memorable for its creativity.

L'Ape Piera, via Lodovico il Moro 11 ✉ 20143 ☎ 02 89126060, *info@ape-piera.com* – . DS a
closed 3 August-3 September, Saturday lunch and Sunday – **Meals** (booking essential) a la carte 30/42.
◆ In a historic setting redolent of old Milan, this is the ideal spot for diners in search of discreet elegance. Creatively inspired cuisine.

on national road 35-Milanofiori *by via Ascanio ES : 10 km :*

Royal Garden Hotel, via Di Vittorio ✉ 20090 Assago ☎ 02 457811, *garden.res@monrifhotels.it, Fax 02 45702901*, – ⊞ ▤ 📺 🅿 – 180. AE ⊕ ⊙ ⊕ VISA JCB.
closed 29 July-22 August and 23 December-6 January – **Meals** a la carte 58/80 – **151 rm** 230/290, 3 suites.
◆ The unusual style of this hotel is evident on entering the 25m-high lobby with its fountain and escalators ; innovation and comfort in tandem. The restaurant also has a quirky modernist ambience.

Abbiategrasso

20081 Milano 561 F 8 – *pop. 28 057 alt. 120.*
Roma 590 – Alessandria 80 – Milano 24 – Novara 29 – Pavia 33.

at Cassinetta di Lugagnano *North : 3 km – ✉ 20081 :*

Antica Osteria del Ponte, piazza G. Negri 9 ☎ 02 9420034, *info@anticaosteriadelponte.it, Fax 02 9420610*, – ▤. AE ⊕ ⊙ ⊕ VISA.
closed August, 25 December-12 January, Sunday and Monday – **Meals** (booking essential) a la carte 88/138.
Spec. Gamberi di San Remo marinati con cipollotto fresco e caviale oscietra. Risotto con zucchine in fiore e zafferano di Navelli (May-October). Guanciale di vitello all'amarone, cardamono e zenzero (October-March).
◆ This 16C bridge over the Naviglio now houses a gourmet's paradise ; wonderful creative cuisine and a stylish welcome in historic surroundings with exposed beams.

Bergamo

24100 P 561 E 11 *G. Italy – pop. 113 415 alt. 249.*
parco dei Colli ☎ 035 250033, Fax 035 4326540;
Bergamo L'Albenza (closed Monday) at Almenno San Bartolomeo ✉ 24030 ☎ 035 640028, Fax 035 643066.
La Rossera (closed Tuesday) at Chiuduno ✉ 24060 ☎ 035 838600, Fax 035 4427047.
Orio al Serio ☎ 035 326111.
viale Vittorio Emanuele II 20 ✉ 24121 ☎ 035 210204, aptbg@apt.bergamo.it, Fax 035 230184.
A.C.I. *via Angelo Maj 16 ✉ 24121 ☎ 035 285985, Fax 035 247635.*
Roma 601 – Brescia 52 – Milano 47.

Da Vittorio, viale Papa Giovanni XXIII 21 ✉ 24121 ☎ 035 213266, *info@davittorio.com, Fax 035 210805* – ▤. AE ⊕ ⊙ ⊕ VISA
closed August and Wednesday – **Meals** (booking essential) 45 (lunch only except Sunday)/110 and a la carte 76/141.
Spec. Patate gratinate con uovo, caviale e crema acida. Maialino croccante con salsa Madera. Cremoso al frutto della passione con spuma di cioccolato bianco.
◆ Named after its enthusiastic proprietor who passionately escorts his clients on a creative journey through the highlights of Italian cuisine.

Canneto sull'Oglio

46013 Mantova 561 G 13 – *pop. 4 511 alt. 35.*
Roma 493 – Brescia 51 – Cremona 32 – Mantova 38 – Milano 123 – Parma 44.

at Runate *North-West : 3 km : ✉ 46013 Canneto sull'Oglio :*

Dal Pescatore, ☎ 0376 723001, *santini@dalpescatore.com, Fax 0376 70304*, Elegant installation, – ▤ 🅿. AE ⊕ ⊙ ⊕ VISA JCB.
closed 15 August-9 September, 1 to 21 January, Monday, Tuesday and Wednesday lunch – **Meals** (booking essential) a la carte 100/150.
Spec. Zuppa di lumache, erbette, farfalle di pasta e tartufo nero (March-September). Cappello di prete di manzo al barbera e polenta gialla. Soufflè alla vaniglia con coulis al frutto della passione.
◆ A Lombard farm with authentic homely cuisine ; an elegant mix of warm welcome and sophistication makes for an unforgettable experience ; garden dining in summer.

Concesio

25062 Brescia 561 F 12 – *pop. 12 933 alt. 218.*
Roma 544 – Bergamo 50 – Brescia 10 – Milano 91.

Miramonti l'Altro, via Crosette 34, località Costorio ☎ 030 2751063, *info@miramontilaltro.it, Fax 030 2753189* – ▤ 🅿. ⊕ ⊙ ⊕ VISA.
closed 5 to 20 August and Monday – **Meals** (booking essential) a la carte 52/80.
Spec. Sfogliatina di lumache, finferli e pomodori alla curcuma (October-July). Risotto ai funghi e formaggi dolci di montagna (June-November). Crescendo di agnello con finale di suo carrè.
◆ Against a modern, Neo-classical-style backdrop, tradition and innovation combine to provide a memorable gastronomic experience.

Erbusco *25030 Brescia* 561 F 11 *– pop. 6 926 alt. 251.*
Roma 578 – Bergamo 35 – Brescia 22 – Milano 69.

XXXX ✿✿ **Gualtiero Marchesi,** via Vittorio Emanuele 11 (North : 1,5 km) ✆ 030 7760562, *ristorante@marchesi.it, Fax 030 7760379,* ≤ lake and mountains, Elegant installation – ▤ P. AE ⓢ ⓞ ⓜ VISA JCB. ✂
closed 3 January-10 February, Sunday dinner and Monday – **Meals** (booking essential) a la carte 77/127 ✿.
Spec. Insalata di spaghetti al caviale, erba cipollina. Raviolo aperto. Filetto di vitello alla Rossini secondo Gualtiero Marchesi.
◆ A temple to Italian gastronomy, this place is a joy to behold in all its refined simplicity. Mouthwatering menu.

Soriso *28018 Novara* 561 E 7 *– pop. 735 alt. 452.*
Roma 654 – Arona 20 – Milano 78 – Novara 40 – Stresa 35 – Torino 114 – Varese 46.

XXXX ✿✿✿ **Al Sorriso** with rm, via Roma 18 ✆ 0322 983228, *sorriso@alsorriso.com, Fax 0322 983328* – ✂ ▤ TV. AE ⓢ ⓞ ⓜ VISA JCB. ✂ rest
closed 3 to 28 August and 7 to 28 January – **Meals** *(closed Monday and Tuesday)* (booking essential) a la carte 98/138 ✿ – **8 rm** ☐ 120/190.
Spec. Zucchina con fonduta di porri di Cervere e riccioli di sogliola con caviale asetra (November-April). Gnocchetti di ricotta e spinaci con quadrucci di fegato d'oca, salsa di gorgonzola dolce e tartufo d'Alba (September-January). Coscietta di gallina faraona farcita e laccata al miele di rododendro con frittelle di mele e topinambur.
◆ Culinary artistry in this temple to gastronomy ; peerless imaginative cuisine in a beautifully presented ambience of refined elegance. An unforgettable experience.

NAPLES (NAPOLI) *80100* P 564 E 24 *G. Italy – pop. 1 008 419.*

See : *National Archaeological Museum★★★ KY – New Castle★★ KZ – Port of Santa Lucia★★ BU : ≤★★ of Vesuvius and bay – ≤★★★ at night from via Partenope of the Vomero and Posillipo FX – San Carlo Theatre★ KZ T – Piazza del Plebiscito★ JKZ – Royal Palace★ KZ – Carthusian Monastery of St. Martin★★ JZ.*
Spaccanapoli and Decumano Maggiore★★ KLY – Tomb★★ of King Robert the Wise and Cloisters★★ in Church of Santa Chiara★ KY – Cathedral★ (Duomo) LY – Sculptures★ in Chapel Sansevero KY – Arch★, Tomb★ of Catherine of Austria, apse★ in Church of St. Lawrence Major LY – Capodimonte Palace and National Gallery★★.
Mergellina★ : ≤★★ of the bay – Villa Floridiana★ EVX : ≤★ – Catacombs of St. Gennaro★★ – Church of Santa Maria Donnaregina★ LY – Church of St. Giovanni a Carbonara★ LY – Capuan Gate★ LMY – Cuomo Palace★ LY – Sculptures★ in the Church of St. Anne of the Lombards KYZ – Posillipo★ – Marechiaro★ – ≤★★ of the bay from Virgiliano Park (or Rimembranza Park).

Exc. : *Bay of Naples★★★ – Campi Flegrei★★ – Sorrento Penisula★★ Island of Capri★★★ Island of Ischia★★★.*

⛳9 (closed Tuesday) at Arco Felice ✉ 80078 ✆ 081 412881, Fax 081 2520438, West : 19 km.

✈ Ugo Niutta of Capodichino North-East : 6 km ✆ 081 7805697.

⛴ to Capri (1 h 15 mn), Ischia (1 h 25 mn) e Procida (1 h), daily – Caremar-Travel and Holidays, molo Beverello ✉ 80133 ✆ 081 5513882, Fax 081 5522011; to Cagliari 19 June-14 July Thursday and Saturday, 15 July-11 September Thursday and Tuesday (15 h 45 mn) and Palermo daily (11 h) – Tirrenia Navigazione, Stazione Marittima, molo Angioino ✉ 80133 ✆ 081 2514740, Fax 081 2514767 ; to Ischia daily (1 h 20 mn) – Linee Lauro, molo Beverello ✉ 80133 ✆ 081 5522838, Fax 081 5513236; to Aeolian Island Wednesday and Friday, 15 June-15 September Monday, Tuesday, Thursday, Friday, Saturday and Sunday (14 h) – Siremar-Genovese Agency, via De Petris 78 ✉ 80133 ✆ 081 5512112, Fax 081 5512114.

⛴ to Capri (45 mn), Ischia (45 mn) and Procida (35 mn), daily – Caremar-Travel and Holidays, molo Beverello ✉ 80133 ✆ 081 5513882, Fax 081 5522011; to Ischia (30 mn) and Capri (40 mn), daily – Alilauro, via Caracciolo 11 ✉ 80122 ✆ 081 7611004, Fax 081 7614250 and Linee Lauro, molo Beverello ✉ 80133 ✆ 081 5522838, Fax 081 5513236; to Capri daily (40 mn) – Navigazione Libera del Golfo, molo Beverello ✉ 80133 ✆ 081 5520763, Fax 081 5525589; to Capri (45 mn), to Aeolian Island June-September (4 h) and Procida-Ischia daily (35 mn) – Aliscafi SNAV, via Caracciolo 10 ✉ 80122 ✆ 081 7612348, Fax 081 7612141.

ℹ via San Carlo 9 ✉ 80132 ✆ 081 402394, info@inaples.it – Central Station ✉ 80142 ✆ 081 268779, ept@netgroup.it – piazza del Gesù Nuovo 7 ✉ 80135 ✆ 081 5523328 - Stazione Mergellina ✉ 80122 ✆ 081 7612102.

A.C.I. *piazzale Tecchio 49/d ✉ 80125 ✆ 081 7253811, Fax 081 5933644.*
Roma 219 – Bari 261

Grand Hotel Vesuvio, via Partenope 45 ✉ 80121 ℘ 081 7640044, *info@vesuvio.it, Fax 081 7644483,* < gulf and Castel dell'Ovo, – rm, rm – 400. FX n
Meals *Caruso Roof Garden* Rest. *(closed 1 to 20 August and Monday)* a la carte 42/78 – **142 rm** 330/410, 17 suites.
• The timeless charm of bygone splendour in this elegant setting, which has been a byword for Neapolitan hospitality since 1882; views over the sea and Castel dell'Ovo.

Excelsior, via Partenope 48 ✉ 80121 ℘ 081 7640111 and rest. ℘ 081 7649804, *info@excelsior.it, Fax 081 7649743,* – rm, rest
Meals *La Terrazza* Rest. *(closed 15 days in August and Sunday)* a la carte 49/67 – **124 rm** 280/340, 9 suites. GX w
• Echoes of elegant days gone by throughout in this jewel among Naples hotels, which has preserved an ambience of long-forgotten opulence. Luxurious rooms and a breath-taking view of the sea and Castel dell'Ovo from the rooftop restaurant.

Grand Hotel Santa Lucia, via Partenope 46 ✉ 80121 ℘ 081 7640666, *reservations-santalucia@thi.it, Fax 081 7648580,* < gulf and Castel dell'Ovo – rm, rm – 100. GX c
Meals a la carte 54/73 – **88 rm** 255/285, 8 suites.
• Splendid views over the sea and Castel dell'Ovo and a refined and stylish ambience to this late 19C hotel; attentive service and excellent rooms.

Grand Hotel Parker's, corso Vittorio Emanuele 135 ✉ 80121 ℘ 081 7612474, *info@grandhotelparkers.it, Fax 081 663527,* < city and gulf – rm, – 250. EX r
Meals *George's* Rest. a la carte 46/69 – **74 rm** 290/360, 9 suites.
• A harmonious marriage of modern comfort and classical elegance in this traditional hotel; each floor is furnished in a different style and all suites are duplex. Amazing views over the sea from the fine restaurant.

Mediterraneo, via Nuova Ponte di Tappia 25 ✉ 80133 ℘ 081 7970001, *info@mediterraneonapoli.com, Fax 081 2520079,* – rm, – 110. rest KZ a
Meals *La Terrazza* Rest. *(closed August and Sunday)* a la carte 45/55 – 20 – **223 rm** 210/270, 7 suites.
• Public areas dotted over several floors represent one of the dynamic new management innovations. All rooms are recently refurbished and the service is cordial and efficient. Top floor restaurant offering panoramic views.

San Francesco al Monte, corso Vittorio Emanuele 328 ✉ 80135 ℘ 081 4239111, *info@hotelsanfrancesco.it, Fax 081 2512485,* < city and gulf, – – 200. JZ c
Meals a la carte 30/50 – **35 rm** 255/285.
• This hotel makes splendid use of the building ecclesiastical origins; its charming rooms, formerly monastic cells, all have fine views. Overlooking the Golfo di Napoli, the restaurant gives diners the impression of being suspended in mid air.

Majestic, largo Vasto a Chiaia 68 ✉ 80121 ℘ 081 416500, *info@majestic.it, Fax 081 410145* – rm, – 120. rest FX b
Meals *(closed Sunday)* a la carte 46/58 – **106 rm** 190/240, 6 suites.
• Very centrally-located close to Via dei Mille, this genteel hotel has completely refitted rooms which are functional yet welcoming. The restaurant has a pleasant atmosphere and good service.

New Europe, via Galileo Ferraris 40 ✉ 80142 ℘ 081 3602111, *info@neweuropehotel.it, Fax 081 200758* – rm, rm – 800. rest HV b
Meals 30 – **156 rm** 175/215.
• Close to the station, this up to the minute hotel is popular with business travellers and offers every modern convenience to its guests. The dining room is modern but not without a certain elegance.

Miramare without rest., via Nazario Sauro 24 ✉ 80132 ℘ 081 7647589, *info@hotelmiramare.com, Fax 081 7640775,* < gulf and Vesuvius – GX e
18 rm 199/314.
• Formerly an aristocratic residence, this early 20C building with roof garden and fine views towards the sea and Vesuvius, is an elegant hotel of considerable character.

Villa Capodimonte, via Moiariello 66 ✉ 80131 ℘ 081 459000, *villacap@tin.it, Fax 081 299344,* <, – – 130. rest
Meals a la carte 28/43 – **58 rm** 175/220. by corso Amedeo di Savoia GU
• Taking its name from the hill on which it sits, this hotel in its own grounds with fine sea views has everything one might expect in a historic villa; elegant, large, well-appointed rooms. Restaurant offers the chance to dine outside in summer.

Traffic restricted in the town centre.

NAPOLI

Arcoleo (V. G.) . . . . FX 5
Arena della Sanità (V.) . . . . GU 6
Artisti (Pza degli) . . . . EV 9
Bernini (V. G. L.) . . . . EV 12
Bonito (V. G.) . . . . FV 13
Carducci (V. G.) . . . . FX 20
Chiatamone (V.) . . . . FX 25
Cirillo (V. D.) . . . . GU 27
Colonna (V. Vittoria) . . . . FX 29
Crocelle ai Vergini (V.) . . . . GU 35
D'Auria (V. G.) . . . . FV 40
Ferraris (V. Galileo) . . . . HV 54
Gaetani (V.) . . . . FX 61
Gen. Pignatelli (V.) . . . . HU 63
Giordano (V. L.) . . . . EV 64
Martini (V. Simone) . . . . EV 75
Mazzocchi (V. Alessio) . . . . HU 76
Menzinger (V. G.) . . . . EV 77
Morelli (V. D.) . . . . FX 84

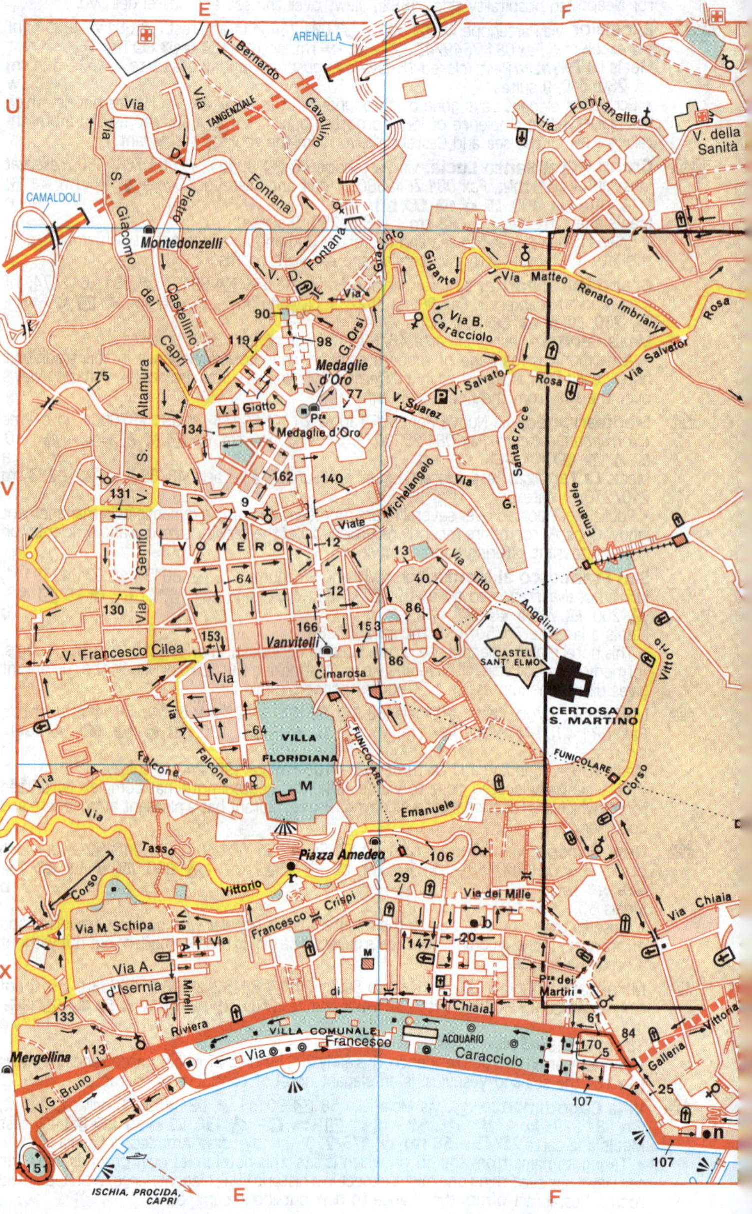

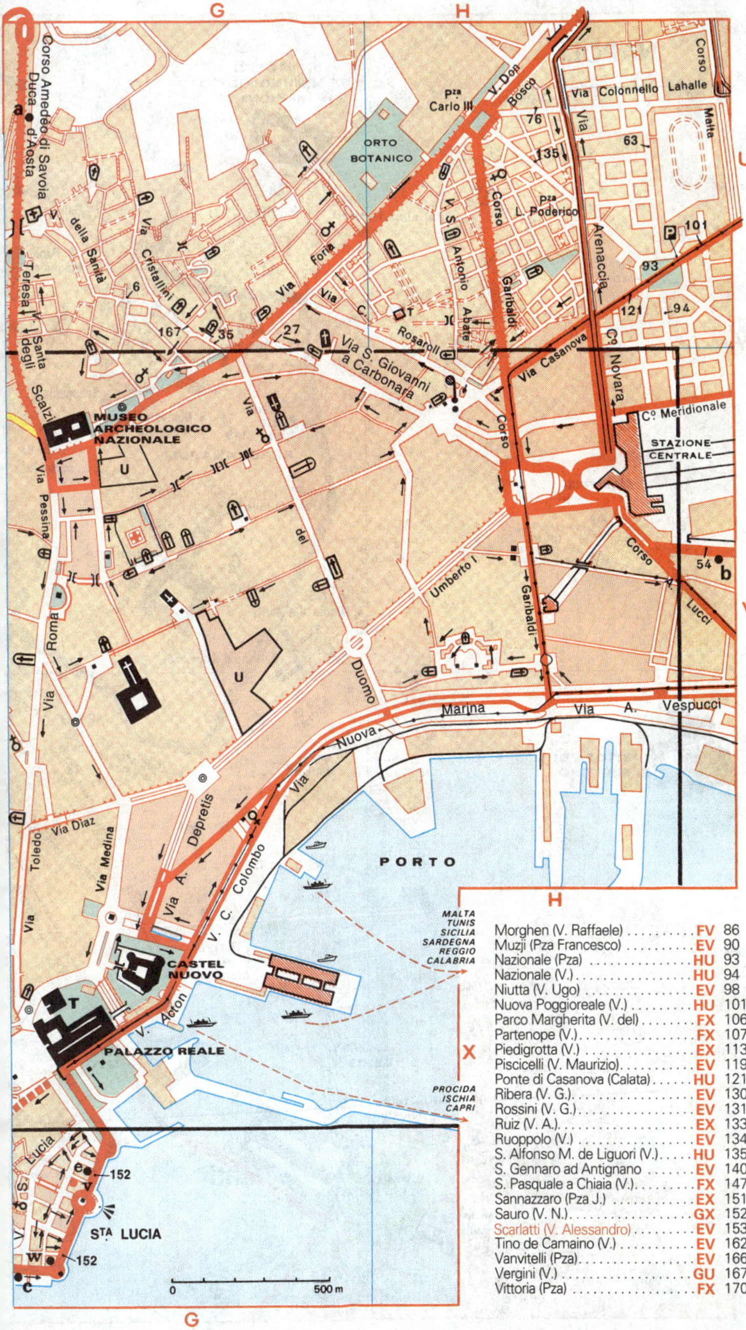

Morghen (V. Raffaele) .... FV 86
Muzji (Pza Francesco) .... EV 90
Nazionale (Pza) .... HU 93
Nazionale (V.) .... HU 94
Niutta (V. Ugo) .... EV 98
Nuova Poggioreale (V.) .... HU 101
Parco Margherita (V. del) .... FX 106
Partenope (V.) .... FX 107
Piedigrotta (V.) .... EX 113
Piscicelli (V. Maurizio) .... EV 119
Ponte di Casanova (Calata) .... HU 121
Ribera (V. G.) .... EV 130
Rossini (V. G.) .... EV 131
Ruiz (V. A.) .... EX 133
Ruoppolo (V.) .... EV 134
S. Alfonso M. de Liguori (V.) .... HU 135
S. Gennaro ad Antignano .... EV 140
S. Pasquale a Chiaia (V.) .... FX 147
Sannazzaro (Pza J.) .... EX 151
Sauro (V. N.) .... GX 152
Scarlatti (V. Alessandro) .... EV 153
Tino de Camaino (V.) .... EV 162
Vanvitelli (Pza) .... EV 166
Vergini (V.) .... GU 167
Vittoria (Pza) .... FX 170

NAPOLI
0
300 m
J
K
Y
Z
MUSEO ARCHEOLOGICO NAZIONALE
Cavour-Museo
Piazza Cavour
V. S. Teresa degli Scalzi
Rosa
Salvator
67
Via
V. S. Monica
V. Salvatore Tommasi
Pessina
88
145
U
Via Pisanelli
Via Anticaglia
V. S. Rosa
Pza Mazzini
Emanuele
Francesco
Saverio
Correra
Salita
Pontecorvo
Enrico
33
Sapienza
Via del Sole
S. Paolo Maggiore
S. Maria Maggiore
Tribunali
Via
Ventaglieri
Vittorio
G. Brombeis
b
Pza V. Bellini
148
Pza Miraglia
Sansevero
PTA ALBA
123
Dante
Piazza Dante
149
S. Domenico Maggiore
139
V. S.
Pzetta del Nilo
SPACCANAPOLI
Tarsia
Montesanto
83
Toledo
Pza del Gesù Nuovo
B. Croce
Corso
Scale Montesanto
STAZIONE CUMANA E FERROVIA CIRCUMFLEGREA
Via Porta Medina
Via Forno Vecchio
S. CHIARA
Via S. Chiara
Mezzocannone
MONTESANTO
15
72
136
165
V. P. Scura
V. d. Pignasecca
S. Nicola alla Carità
82
85
S. Anna d. Lombardi
V. Monteoliveto
154
Via Francesco Girardi
Piazza d. Carità
Via C. Battisti
Pza G. Bovio
34
CERTOSA DI S. MARTINO
c
31
Pza G. Matteotti
Via Cardinale G. Sanfelice
73
e
Depretis
Diaz
POL.
Via M. Cervantes
Medina
Via Alcide Gasperi
Speranzella
a
V. S. Giacomo
Cristoforo
FUNICOLARE
d
V. P.-E. Imbriani
H
Piazza Municipio
Corso
Via S. Mattia
CENTRALE
138
171
V. G. Verdi
T
W
Galleria Umberto I
S. Carlo
CASTEL NUOVO
Acton
Ferdinando
T1
Pza Trento e Trieste
MOLO BEVERELLO
PORTO
Via Chiaia
V. G. Nicotera
57
PZA DEL PLEBISCITO
PALAZZO REALE
S. Francesco di Paola
V. Monte di Dio
Pza dei Martiri
M
GALLERIA DELLA VITTORIA
V. Cesario Console
V. F. Acton
MOLO

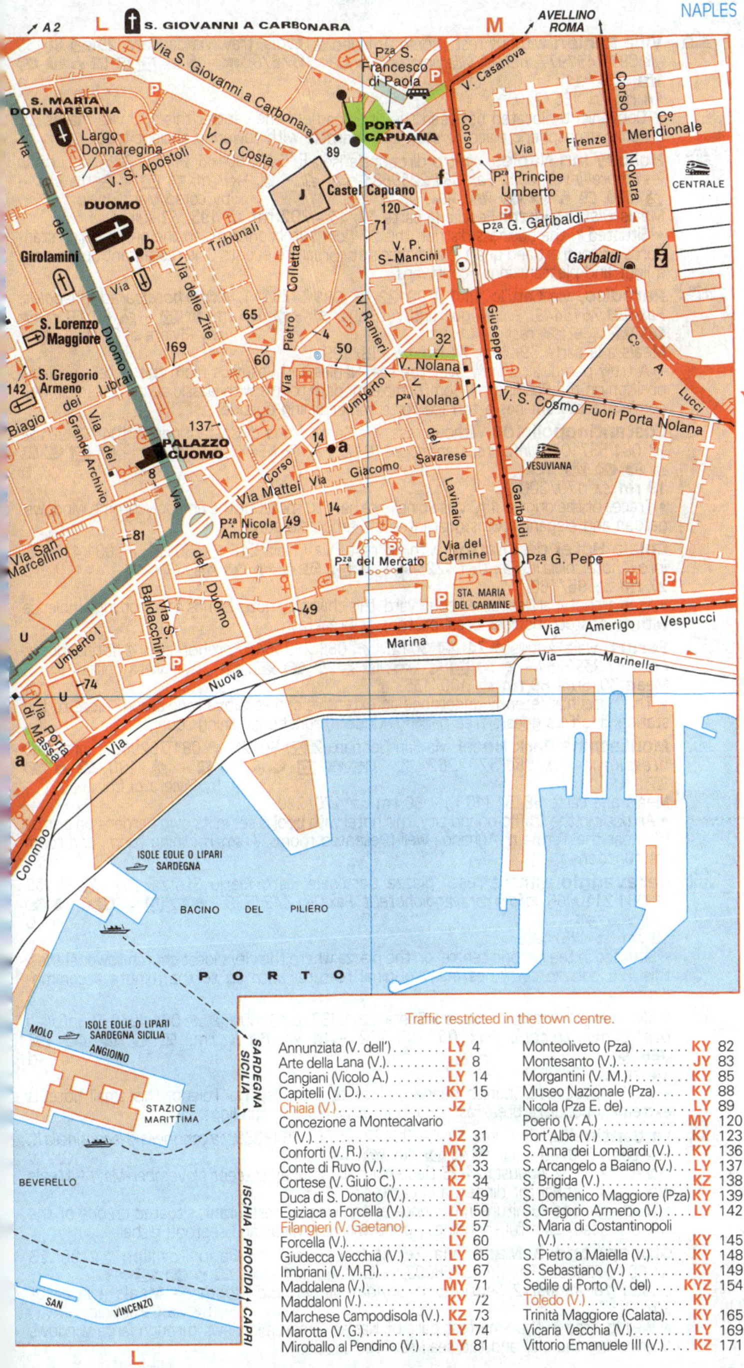

Traffic restricted in the town centre.

Street	Grid	No.
Annunziata (V. dell')	LY	4
Arte della Lana (V.)	LY	8
Cangiani (Vicolo A.)	LY	14
Capitelli (V. D.)	KY	15
Chiaia (V.)	JZ	
Concezione a Montecalvario (V.)	JZ	31
Conforti (V. R.)	MY	32
Conte di Ruvo (V.)	KY	33
Cortese (V. Giuio C.)	KZ	34
Duca di S. Donato (V.)	LY	49
Egiziaca a Forcella (V.)	LY	50
Filangieri (V. Gaetano)	JZ	57
Forcella (V.)	LY	60
Giudecca Vecchia (V.)	LY	65
Imbriani (V. M.R.)	JY	67
Maddalena (V.)	MY	71
Maddaloni (V.)	KY	72
Marchese Campodisola (V.)	KZ	73
Marotta (V. G.)	LY	74
Miroballo al Pendino (V.)	LY	81
Monteoliveto (Pza)	KY	82
Montesanto (V.)	JY	83
Morgantini (V. M.)	KY	85
Museo Nazionale (Pza)	KY	88
Nicola (Pza E. de)	LY	89
Poerio (V. A.)	MY	120
Port'Alba (V.)	KY	123
S. Anna dei Lombardi (V.)	KY	136
S. Arcangelo a Baiano (V.)	LY	137
S. Brigida (V.)	KZ	138
S. Domenico Maggiore (Pza)	KY	139
S. Gregorio Armeno (V.)	LY	142
S. Maria di Costantinopoli (V.)	KY	145
S. Pietro a Maiella (V.)	KY	148
S. Sebastiano (V.)	KY	149
Sedile di Porto (V. del)	KYZ	154
Toledo (V.)	KY	
Trinità Maggiore (Calata)	KY	165
Vicaria Vecchia (V.)	LY	169
Vittorio Emanuele III (V.)	KZ	171

Villa Ranieri without rest., corso Amedeo di Savoia, trav. via Cagnazzi 29 ✉ 80135 ✆ 081 7437977, *hotel@villaranieri.it, Fax 081 7437978,* – ▤ TV P. AE VISA JCB. GU a
14 rm ☕ 165/210.
• Conveniently located between the ring road and the centre, this 17C villa makes for a richly atmospheric place to stay. Lush gardens with towering ancient trees.

Holiday Inn Naples, centro direzionale Isola E/6 ✉ 80143 ✆ 081 2250111, *hinaples@hotel-invest.com, Fax 081 2250683,* – rm, ▤ TV rm – 320. AE VISA JCB. by corso Meridionale MY
Meals *Bistrot Victor* Rest. a la carte 31/43 – **292 rm** ☕ 195, 32 suites.
• Situated in the business district, this 22-floor hotel conforms to the group's high standards of comfort and quality, and excels at corporate events. The restaurant opens onto a light and pleasant inner courtyard.

Paradiso, via Catullo 11 ✉ 80122 ✆ 081 2475111, *info@hotelparadisonapoli.it, Fax 081 7613449,* < city, gulf and Vesuvius, – rm, ▤ TV – 80. AE VISA JCB. rest by Riviera di Chiaia EFX
Meals a la carte 39/49 – **74 rm** ☕ 118/199.
• A truly paradisaical view over the sea, Naples and Vesuvius from this hotel's enviable position on the Posillipo hill. Comfortable modern rooms with classic style. The small, welcoming restaurant has a terrace for summer dining outside.

Costantinopoli 104 without rest., via Santa Maria di Costantinopoli 104 ✉ 80138 ✆ 081 5571035, *info@costantinopoli104.it, Fax 081 5571051,* – ▤ TV. AE VISA JCB KY b
19 rm ☕ 170/200.
• Traces of the original 19C Villa Spinelli are hard to spot, but the fine polychrome windows, garden and elegant rooms guarantee a memorable stay.

Chiaja Hotel de Charme without rest., via Chiaia 216 ✉ 80121 ✆ 081 415555, *info@hotelchiaia.it, Fax 081 422344* – ▤ TV. AE VISA JCB. JZ a
27 rm ☕ 95/160.
• In an archetypal Neapolitan courtyard, this charming hotel blends a welcoming ambience with an aristocratic feel. Local pastries at breakfast.

Serius, viale Augusto 74 ✉ 80125 ✆ 081 2394844, *prenotazioni@hotelserius.it, Fax 081 2399251* – ▤ TV. AE VISA. by Riviera Chiaia EFX
Meals 30/50 – **69 rm** ☕ 100/135.
• This hotel has recently undergone an extensive and sensitive renovation ; close to the station, it offers guests free parking. Modern, functional dining room.

Montespina Park Hotel, via San Gennaro 2 ✉ 80125 ✆ 081 7629687, *info@montespina.it, Fax 081 5702962,* – ▤ TV rm P – 100. AE VISA. by Riviera di Chiaia EFX
Meals a la carte 38/51 (10 %) – **60 rm** ☕ 170/220.
• An oasis in the traffic-bound city, this hotel with pool is set in its own gardens on a small hill, near the Terme di Agnano ; well-presented rooms. A smart dining room, and room for functions.

Caravaggio without rest., piazza Cardinale Sisto Riario Sforza 157 ✉ 80139 ✆ 081 2110066, *info@caravaggiohotel.it, Fax 081 4421578* – ▤ TV. AE VISA JCB. LY b
18 rm ☕ 125/190.
• Situated in the historic centre, on the piazza where the city oldest church tower stands, this 17C palazzo combines many original features with up to the minute accommodation.

Il Convento without rest., via Speranzella 137/a ✉ 80132 ✆ 081 403977, *info@hotelilconvento.com, Fax 081 400332* – ▤ TV rm. AE VISA JCB. JZ d
14 rm ☕ 104/160.
• In the evocative Spanish quarter, close to the busy Via Toledo, this small hotel is extremely popular ; breakfast served in delightful surroundings.

La Cantinella, via Cuma 42 ✉ 80132 ✆ 081 7648838, *la.cantinella@lacantinella.it, Fax 081 7648769* – ▤. AE VISA JCB. GX v
closed 12 to 27 August, 24-25 December and Sunday (except November-May) – **Meals** (booking essential for dinner) a la carte 43/74.
• Much bamboo furniture in evidence at this elegant restaurant, situated on one of the world's most beautiful shorelines ; good wine-list, meat and seafood dishes.

Giuseppone a Mare, via Ferdinando Russo 13-Capo Posillipo ✉ 80123 ✆ 081 5756002, *Fax 081 5756002,* < city and gulf – ▤. AE VISA.
closed 16 August-2 September, Sunday dinner and Monday – **Meals** a la carte 30/50. by via Caracciolo FX
• Well located in the smartest part of Naples. Panoramic views through large windows overlooking the city and the sea ; seafood cuisine.

XX **Ciro a Santa Brigida,** via Santa Brigida 73 ✉ 80132 ✆ 081 5524072, Fax 081 5528992 – ▤. AE ⓢ ⓓ ⓜ VISA JCB JZ w
closed 7 to 25 August and Sunday (except December) – **Meals** Rest. and pizzeria a la carte 29/39.
◆ In the heart of old Naples, this animated pizzeria-restaurant is a city institution, modern in style but rooted in tradition ; meat and seafood dishes.

XX **Rosolino-Il Posto Accanto,** via Nazario Sauro 2/7 ✉ 80132 ✆ 081 7649873, *info@rosolino.it, Fax 081 7649870* – ▤ – 100. AE ⓢ ⓓ ⓜ VISA JCB. GX a
closed Sunday dinner – **Meals** Rest. and pizzeria a la carte 29/48.
◆ This versatile pizzeria-restaurant has rooms large and small, offering a variety of ambiences in which to eat ; a good choice of seafood and Neapolitan dishes.

XX **Transatlantico,** via Lucullíana-borgo Marinari ✉ 80132 ✆ 081 7648842, *transa.tlantico@libero.it, Fax 081 7649201,* – AE ⓢ ⓓ ⓜ VISA JCB.
closed 21 January-4 February and Tuesday – **Meals** a la carte 24/43.
◆ Overlooked by Castel dell'Ovo, this charming establishment is classically elegant ; outside dining in summer on the quayside of Santa Lucia. Traditional cuisine. by via Nazario Sauro GX

XX **Mimì alla Ferrovia,** via Alfonso d'Aragona 21 ✉ 80139 ✆ 081 5538525, *info@mimiallaferrovia.it, Fax 081 289004* – ▤. AE ⓢ ⓓ ⓜ VISA MY f
closed 13 to 22 August and Sunday – **Meals** a la carte 25/32 (15 %).
◆ Close to the station, this lively and elegant restaurant is popular with showbusiness people and has been restored recently. Traditional fish and local dishes.

XX **Le Due Palme,** via Agnano Astroni 30 ✉ 80125 ✆ 081 5706040, *info@leduepalme.it, Fax 081 7626128,* , – ▤ P. AE ⓢ ⓓ ⓜ VISA JCB. by Riviera Chiaia EFX
closed Monday – **Meals** (dinner only except Sunday in August) a la carte 26/40.
◆ Next to the Terme di Agnano, this light and spacious family-run restaurant has parking and serves meals outside in summer ; seafood and seasonal dishes.

X **L'Europeo di Mattozzi,** via Campodisola 4/6/8 ✉ 80133 ✆ 081 5521323, Fax 081 5521323 – ▤. AE ⓢ ⓓ ⓜ VISA JCB KZ e
closed 15 to 31 August, Sunday, also Saturday in July and the evening September-June (except the eve of Bank Holidays) Monday-Wednesday – **Meals** Rest. and pizzeria a la carte 30/42 (12 %).
◆ Regulars and first-timers alike receive the same red carpet treatment from the owner of this busy, simple pizzeria, run by the same family for decades ; local cuisine.

Island of Capri *80073 Napoli* 564 F 24 *G. Italy – pop. 13 189 alt.*

The limitation of motor-vehicles' access is regulated by legislative rules.

Grand Hotel Quisisana, via Camerelle 2 ✆ 081 8370788, *info@quisi.com, Fax 081 8376080,* ← sea and Certosa, , , , , , , , – ▤ TV – 550. AE ⓢ ⓓ ⓜ VISA.
March-October – **Meals *La Colombaia*** Rest. and pizzeria *(25 March-2 November ; closed dinner except 15 April to September)* a la carte 45/62 see also rest. ***Quisi*** below – **136 rm** 590, 13 suites.
◆ A historic and luxurious window on the world, this hotel is a byword for the highest standards of comfort ; garden with pool. An elegant atmosphere in the candle-lit La Colombaia restaurant ; Mediterranean cuisine.

Casa Morgano without rest., via Tragara 6 ✆ 081 8370158, *info@casamorgano.com, Fax 081 8370681,* ← sea and Certosa, heated – ▤ TV. AE ⓢ ⓓ ⓜ VISA JCB
April-October – **28 rm** 490.
◆ Situated on one of Capri best streets, between villas in lush grounds, this hotel's rooms are decorated with painted tiles and the terrace offers fine views.

Scalinatella without rest., via Tragara 8 ✆ 081 8370633, *info@scalinatella.com, Fax 081 8378291,* ← sea and Certosa, heated – ▤ TV. AE ⓢ ⓜ VISA.
15 March-5 November – **30 rm** 430/600.
◆ The flagship of a family-run group, this hotel with its exclusive reputation nestles in the hillside ; luxurious rooms.

Punta Tragara , via Tragara 57 ✆ 081 8370844, *info@hoteltragara.it, Fax 081 8377790,* ← Faraglioni and coast, , , heated – ▤ TV. AE ⓢ ⓓ ⓜ VISA JCB.
25 March-16 October – **Meals** 46/60 – **43 rm** 420/460, 16 suites.
◆ This Le Corbusier-designed hotel is the quintessence of Capri refinement. Lunch can be outside on the poolside terrace, followed by dinner in the well-presented dining room.

Luna , viale Matteotti 3 ✆ 081 8370433, *luna@capri.it, Fax 081 8377459,* ← sea, Faraglaioni e Certosa, , , – ▤ TV. AE ⓢ ⓓ ⓜ VISA JCB.
Easter-October – **Meals** (residents only) – **50 rm** 160/380, 4 suites.
◆ Perched high on the cliffs, the hotel has a large garden and terrace from which to admire the sea, the Faraglioni and the Certosa ; ask for a room with a view.

Villa Brunella, via Tragara 24 081 8370122, *villabrunella@capri.it, Fax 081 8370430,* sea and coast, heated – VISA JCB.
Easter-6 November – **Meals** (booking essential) a la carte 36/61 (12 %) – **20 rm** 250/290.
• A succession of planted terraces descend towards the sea ; a heated pool, enchanting panoramic views and classically elegant rooms.

La Certosella, via Tragara 13/15 081 8370713, *certosella@infinito.it, Fax 081 8376113,* heated, – VISA JCB.
Meals *(June-September)* a la carte 39/64 – **18 rm** 230/255.
• A small and charming garden invites lingering at this hotel, set among wisteria, lemon and orange trees. The spacious accommodation is housed in a Neo-classical building.

Canasta without rest., via Campo di Teste 6 081 8370561, *canasta@capri.it, Fax 081 8376675,* – VISA JCB.
April-October – **17 rm** 110/220.
• A charming family-run establishment near the Certosa di San Giacomo ; an elegant reception area and bright, simple rooms with good quality tasteful furnishings.

Syrene, via Camerelle 51 081 8370102, *syrene@capri.it, Fax 081 8370957,* – rm, VISA JCB.
April-October – **Meals** *(closed Tuesday except June to September)* a la carte 35/43 – **32 rm** 252/346.
• Located on one of Capri's main shopping streets, this comfortable hotel has generously proportioned public areas ; the rooms vary from classical to modern in style. The fine garden has a pool and lemon trees. Imposing columns in the dining room.

Quisi - Gd H. Quisisana, via Camerelle 2 081 8370788, *info@quisi.com, Fax 081 8376080,* – VISA.
March-October ; closed lunch and Sunday June-September – **Meals** a la carte 67/93.
• Comfortable seats, candles, all-encompassing attention to detail and an elegant ambience in this evenings only restaurant. High quality international cuisine.

La Cantinella, Parco Augusto, viale Matteotti 8 081 8370616, *la.cantinella@lacantinella.it, Fax 081 8370300,* Faraglioni, – VISA JCB.
April-October ; closed Tuesday except June-September – **Meals** a la carte 43/74.
• Steps between the Monastery and Augustus? Gardens lead up to a terrace from where the Faraglioni landscape appears, best admired from a table at the front.

Aurora, via Fuorlovado 18 081 8370181, *aurora@capri.it, Fax 081 8376533,* – VISA.
closed January-March – **Meals** Rest. and pizzeria a la carte 37/65 (15 %).
• A table outside is much in demand here, a long-established family-run restaurant of considerable charm. Seafood, meat dishes and pizzas.

La Capannina, via Le Botteghe 12 bis/14 081 8370732, *capannina@capri.it, Fax 081 8376990* – VISA.
10 March-10 November ; closed Wednesday except May-September – **Meals** (booking essential for dinner) a la carte 45/61 (15 %).
• This establishment, founded in the 1930s, remains perennially fashionable ; a wide variety of local dishes, somewhat refined to appeal to the international clientele.

at Anacapri *alt. 275 – 80071 :*

Capri Palace Hotel, via Capodimonte 2 081 9780111, *info@capri-palace.com, Fax 081 8373191,* Rooms with small private swimming pools, heated, – – 200. VISA JCB.
March-November – **Meals** (see rest. ***L'Olivo*** below) – **77 rm** 685/1070, 10 suites.
• Stone floors, vaulting and fabrics blend to create a refined interior of soft, creamy tones overlooking planted terraces and swimming pool.

Caesar Augustus, via Orlandi 4 081 8373395, *info@caesar-augustus.com, Fax 081 8371444,* – – 70. VISA JCB.
April-October – **Meals** a la carte 50/66 – **52 rm** 405/450, 5 suites.
• This hotel terrace, perched above the waves, offers breathtaking views and evokes a desire to take to the skies ; the refitted rooms are pleasant and comfortable.

Il Girasole without rest., via Linciano 47 081 8372351, *ilgirasole@capri.it, Fax 081 8373880,* Shuttle service previous booking, – – 80. VISA JCB.
March-October – **23 rm** 90/160.
• Overlooking the sea, with terraced gardens and pool, this small establishment set amid the verdant tranquillity of Anacapri will appeal to those in quest of peaceful isolation.

XXXX ✿ **L'Olivo** - Capri Palace Hotel, via Capodimonte 2 ✆ 081 9780111, *info@capri-palace.com, Fax 081 8373191,* – AE ⓘ MC VISA JCB
19 March-October – **Meals** a la carte 76/121.
Spec. Scaloppa di foie gras con mango allo zenzero e salsa di cassis. Ravioli capresi con pomodorini e basilico. Agnello da latte al forno con patate e carciofi.
◆ Traditional local style enhanced by a profusion of fabrics. An ambience of soft lighting in which island specialities are served alongside mainland dishes.

XX **La Rondinella,** via Orlandi 245 ✆ 081 8371223, *Fax 081 8373222,* – AE ⓘ MC VISA JCB
closed January and February – **Meals** Rest. and evening pizzeria a la carte 29/42 (10 %).
◆ Attentive service at this restaurant offering a rustic ambience in winter, and an attractive planted summer terrace ; seafood, Caprese dishes and also pizzas in the evening.

at Marina Grande – ✉ *80073 :*

XX **Da Paolino,** via Palazzo a Mare 11 ✆ 081 8376102, *dapaolino@iol.it, Fax 081 8375611,* – AE ⓘ MC VISA JCB
21 April-October ; closed lunch June to September – **Meals** a la carte 39/51.
◆ A bright, rustic feel to this pleasantly spacious establishment ; in summer diners eat among lush lemon trees. Country cuisine.

Ravello *84010 Salerno* 564 F 25 *G. Italy – pop. 2 524 alt. 350.*

piazza Duomo 10, ✆ 089 857096, aziendaturismo@ravcello.it, Fax 089 857977.
Roma 276 – Amalfi 6 – Napoli 59 – Salerno 29 – Sorrento 40.

XXXX ✿✿ **Rossellinis** - Hotel Palazzo Sasso, via San Giovanni del Toro 28 ✆ 089 818181, *info@palazzosasso.com, Fax 089 858900,* . AE ⓘ MC VISA JCB.
March-October – **Meals** (dinner only) a la carte 67/96.
Spec. Trio di scampi cotti e crudi su carpaccio di spigola (summer). Ziti (pasta) ripieni di caprino con coniglio alla cacciatora (spring-summer). Rossellinis gran dessert al cioccolato.
◆ Top marks for views, cuisine and ambience in the charming surroundings of Palazzo Sasso ; sophisticated interpretations of classic local fare share the menu with international dishes.

Sant'Agata sui due Golfi *80064 Napoli* 564 F 25 *G. Italy – alt. 391.*

Roma 266 – Castellammare di Stabia 28 – Napoli 55 – Salerno 56 – Sorrento 9.

XXX ✿✿ **Don Alfonso 1890** with rm, corso Sant'Agata 11 ✆ 081 8780026, *donalfonso@syrene.it, Fax 081 5330226,* – rest, rest, TV P. AE ⓘ MC VISA JCB.
closed 7 January-15 March, November and 24-25 December – **Meals** *(closed Monday and Tuesday lunch June-September, Monday and Tuesday in other months)* (booking essential) a la carte 79/106 – 5 suites 200.
Spec. Totanetti ripieni di formaggi locali con passata di peperoni alla griglia e semi di finocchietto selvatico (spring-autumn). Vesuvio di rigatoni di Maria Orsini Natale. Sfogliatella napoletana con salsa alle amarene.
◆ This hospitable establishment serves imaginatively prepared cuisine making the most of local ingredients. Interesting and robust dishes.

PALERMO (Sicily) *90100* P 565 M 22 *G. Italy – pop. 682 901.*

See : *Palace of the Normans★★ : the palatine Chapel★★★, mosaics★★★, Ancient Royal Apartments★★* AZ *– Oratory of St Dominic's Rosary★★★* BY **N** *– Oratory of St Cita★★★* BY **N** *– Church of St. John of the Hermits★★ : cloister★* AZ *– Piazza Pretoria★★* BY *– Piazza Bellini★* BY *: Martorana Church★★, Church of St. Cataldo★★ – Abatellis Palace★ : Regional Gallery of Sicily★★* CY **G** *– Magnolia fig trees★★ in Garibaldi Gardens* CY *– International Museum of Marionetes★★* CY **M** *– Archaeological Museum★ : metopes from the temples at Selinus★★, the Ram★★* BY **M** *– Villa Malfitano★★ – Botanical garden★ : magnolia fig trees★★* CDZ *– Capuchin Catacombs★★ – Villa Bonanno★* AZ *– Cathedral★* AYZ *– Quattro Canti★* BY *– Gancia, interior★* CY *– Magione : facade★* CZ *– St Francis of Assisi★* CY *– Mirto Palace★* CY *– Chiaramonte Palace★* CY *– St Mary of the chain★* CY **S** *– Gallery of Modern Art E. Restivo★* AX *– Villino Florio★ – St John of the Lepers★ – Zisa★ – Cuba★.*
Envir. : *Monreale★★★ by Corso Calatafimi : 8 km* AZ *– Addura's Caves★ North-East.*
✈ *Falcone-Borsellino East : 30 km ✆ 091 7020127, Fax 091 7020394.*
⛴ *to Genova daily except Sunday (20 h) and to Livorno Tuesday, Thursday and Saturday (17 h) – Grimaldi-Grandi Navi Veloci, calata Marinai d'Italia ✉ 90133 ✆ 091 587404, Fax 091 6110088; to Napoli daily (11 h), to Genova Monday, Wednesday and Friday and Sunday 18 June-31 December (24 h) and Cagliari Saturday (13 h 30 mn) – Tirrenia Navigazione, calata Marinai d'Italia ✉ 90133 ✆ 1478 99000, Fax 091 6021221.*
⛴ *to Aeolian Island June-September daily (1 h 50 mn) – SNAV Barbaro Agency, piazza Principe di Belmonte 51/55 ✉ 90139 ✆ 091 586533, Fax 091 584830.*
piazza Castelnuovo 34 ✉ 90141 ✆ 091 583847, info@palermotourism.com, Fax 091 586338 – Falcone-Borsellino Airport at Cinisi ✆ 091 591698 – piazza Giulio Cesare (Central Station) ✉ 90127 ✆ 091 6165914 – salita Belmonte 1 (Villa Igea) ✆ 091 6398011, info@aziendaturismopalermomonreale.it, Fax 091 6375400.
A.C.I. *via delle Alpi 6 ✉ 90144 ✆ 091 305227, Fax 091 300472. – Messina 235.*

A
B
X
Y
Z
Catania
Via Siracusa
S 113
V. della Libertà
V. G. Mazzini
Pza Nasce
Scinà
V. Puglisi
La Lumia
V. Messina
XX Settembre
E. Parisi
V. Marconi
Via XII Gennaio
V. Nicolò Garzilli
Villafranca
Via Dante
Piazza L. Sturzo
Via Emerico Amari
Principe di Belmonte
Via Stabile
AIR TERMINAL
GALLERIA D'ARTE MODERNA
Via Principe di Scordia
Via Onorato
Via Crispi
V. Mariano Stabile
V. R. Pilo
Via Ruggero Settimo
Pza S. Oliva
Pza Cavour
S. Giorgio dei Genovesi
S. Cita
Via Roma
Via Goethe
V. N. Turrisi
Via Volturno
Teatro Massimo
Pza Verdi
Via Meli
S. Domenico
V. Bandiera
Corso Alberto
S. Agostino
Via S. Agostino
V. Napoli
Via dei Candelai
Maqueda
Pza PRETORIA
QUATTRO CANTI
S. Giuseppe ai Teatini
Pza BELLINI
MARTORANA
S. CATALDO
Via Papireto
CATTEDRALE
Emanuele
Vittorio
SS. Salvatore
Pal. Marchesi
Chiesa d. Gesù
Pal. Comitini
Divisi
Amedeo
Porta Nuova
VILLA BONANNO
POL.
PALAZZO DEI NORMANNI
Porta di Castro
Pza Ballarò
CAPPELLA PALATINA
Piazza Indipendenza
Chiesa d. Carmine
Mercato di Ballarò
Mongitore
S. GIOVANNI DEGLI EREMITI
Lav. in Corso
Cº Re Ruggero
Parco D'Orléans
Via Tukory
S. ANTONINO
Via Oreto
V. Maggiore Perni
V. G. Arcoleo
V. d. Scienze

C
D
PALERMO
0
300 m
STAZIONE MARITTIMA
PORTO
MOLO SUD
GOLFO
DI
PALERMO
X
Y
Z
F. Patti
TORRE MASTRA
LA CALA
Via Castello
Cala
S 3
M 3
Porta Felice
Foro Umberto I°
Passeggiata delle Cattive
Palazzo Branciforti-Butera
Pza Marina
Giardino Garibaldi
PALAZZO CHIARAMONTE
Butera
Emanuele
PAL. MIRTO
S. FRANCESCO D'ASSISI
Alloro
La Gancia
G
Porta dei Greci
Pza d. Kalsa
Via
Pza Magione
S. Maria d. Spasimo
Pza d. Spasimo
La Magione
Lincoln
VILLA GIULIA
ORTO BOTANICO
GIARDINO TROPICALE
Pza Tumminello
Via Ponte di Mare
Corso Roma
Via Lincoln
V. dei
Via U
AIR TERMINAL
Pza Giulio Cesare
CENTRALE
Via G. F. Ingrassia
Archirafi
Cipolla
Mille
Segno
Via Tiro a
Oreto
S 113
V. S. Boccone
57
28
109
85
147
127
96
6
7
117
141
136
34
58

INDEX OF STREET NAMES IN PALERMO

Albergheria (V.) .... BZ 3
Alloro (V.) .... CY
Amari (V. E.) .... BX
Amedeo (Cso A.) .... AYZ
Aragona (Pza) .... CY 6
Aragona (V.) .... CY 7
Archimede (V.) .... AX 9
Archirafi (V.) .... CZ
Arcoleo (V. G.) .... BZ
Ballarò (Pza) .... BZ
Bandiera (V.) .... BY
Beati Paoli (Piazza) .... AY 124
Beati Paoli (V.) .... AY 10
Bellini (Pza) .... BY
Benedettini (V. d.) .... AZ 12
Boccone (V. S.) .... CZ
Bologni (Pza) .... BYZ 13
Butera (V.) .... CY
Cala (V.) .... CY
Calatafimi (Cso) .... AZ 16
Candelai (V. d.) .... BY
Cappuccinelle (V. d.) .... AY 20
Cappuccini (V.) .... AZ 19
Caracciolo (Pza) .... BY 22
Carini (V. I.) .... AX 24
Carmine (Pza d.) .... BZ 25
Cassa di Risparmio (Pza) .... BY 27
Cassari (V.) .... BCY 28
Castello (Pza) .... BCY
Castelnuovo (Pza) .... AX 30
Catania (V.) .... AX
Cattedrale (Pza d.) .... AZ 31
Cavalieri di Malta (Largo) .... BY 33
Cavour (V.) .... BXY
Cervello (V.) .... CY 34
Cipolla (V.) .... CZ
Collegio di Maria (V.) .... BX 36
Colonna Rotta (V.) .... AZ 37
Crispi (V.) .... BX
Croce dei Vespri (Pza d.) .... BY 39
Dante (V.) .... AX
Divisi (V.) .... BZ
Don Sturzo (Pza) .... ABX
Donizetti (V. G.) .... ABY 43
Errante (V. V.) .... BZ 49
Filiciuzza (V.) .... ABZ 52
Finocchiaro Aprile (Cso C.) .... AY 54
Fonderia (Pza) .... CY 57
Garibaldi (V.) .... CZ 58
Garzilli (V. N.) .... AX
Gasometro (Pza) .... DZ
Generale Cadorna (V.) .... AZ 59
Giudici (Discesa d.) .... BY 63
Giullio Cesare (Pza) .... CZ
Goethe (V.) .... AY
Indipendenza (Pza) .... AZ
Ingrassia (V. G. F.) .... CZ
Juvara Cluviero (V.) .... AY 67
Kalsa (Pza d.) .... CY
La Lumia (V. I.) .... AX
Latini (V. B.) .... AX 69
Libertà (V. d.) .... AX
Lincoln (V.) .... CZDY
Maggiore Perni (V.) .... BZ
Magione (Pza d.) .... CYZ
Maqueda (V.) .... BYZ
Marconi (V.) .... AX
Marina (Pza) .... CY
Marino (V. S.) .... BZ 73
Mazzini (V. G.) .... AX
Meccio (V. S.) .... AX 75
Meli (V.) .... BY
Messina (V.) .... AX
Mille (Cso d.) .... CZ
Mongitore (V. A.) .... ABZ
Monteleone (V.) .... BY 82
Mosca (V. G.) .... AZ 84
Mura del Cattive (Salita) .... CY 85
Napoli (V.) .... BY
Nasce (Pza) .... AX
Onorato (V.) .... BX
Oreto (V.) .... BZ
Orleans (Pza) .... AZ 90
Orlogio (V.) .... BY 91
Papireto (V.) .... AYZ
Parisi (V. E.) .... AX
Paternostro (V. A.) .... BCY 96
Paternostro (V. P.) .... AX 97
Patti (V. F.) .... BCX
Peranni (Pza D.) .... AY 99
Pignatelli d'Aragona (V.) .... AY 102
Pilo (V. R.) .... BXY
Pisani (Cso P.) .... AZ 103
Ponte di Mare (V.) .... DZ
Ponticello (V.) .... BZ 105
Porta di Castro (V.) .... ABZ
Porta Montalto (Pza) .... AZ 106
Porta S. Agata (V.) .... BZ 108
Porto Salvo (V.) .... CY 109
Pretoria (Pza) .... BY
Principe di Belmonte (V.) .... BX
Principe di Scordia (V.) .... BX
Principe Granatelli (V.) .... ABX 111
Puglisi (V.) .... AX
Quattro Canti (Pza Vigliena) .... BY
Rao (V. C.) .... CZ
Rivoluzione (Pza) .... CZ 117
Roma (V.) .... BXCZ
Ruggero Settimo (Pza) .... AX 118
Ruggero Settimo (V.) .... AXY
S. Agata (V.) .... AY 120
S. Agostino (V.) .... AYZ
S. Anna (Pza) .... BY 121
S. Antonino (Pza) .... BZ 123
S. Domenico (Pza) .... BY 126
S. Francesco da Paola (Pza) .... AY 127
S. Francesco d'Assisi (Pza) .... CY 129
S. Giorgio dei Genovesi (Pza) .... BY 130
S. Giovanni Decollato (Piazzetta) .... AZ 132
S. Isidoro alla Guilla (Pza) .... AY 133
S. Oliva (Pza) .... AX
S. Orsola (Vicolo) .... BZ 134
S. Sebastiano (V.) .... BY 135
S. Teresa (V.) .... CY 136
Sammartino (V.) .... AX 138
Scienze (V. d.) .... AZ
Scina (V.) .... BX
Scuole (V. d.) .... AZ 139
Siracusa (V.) .... AX
Spasimo (Pza d.) .... CYZ
Spasimo (V. d.) .... CY 141
Spirito Santo (V. d.) .... ABY 142
Squarcialupo (V.) .... BY 144
Stabile (V. M.) .... AYBX
Stazzone (Pza) .... AZ 145
Tiro a Segno (V.) .... DZ
Torremuzza (V.) .... CY 147
Tukory (Cso) .... ABZ
Tumminello (Pza) .... DZ
Turrisi (V. N.) .... AY
Turrisi Colonna (V.) .... AX 148
Umberto I (Foro) .... CYDZ
Valverde (V.) .... BY 149
Verdi (Pza) .... ABY
Villafranca (V.) .... AX
Virgilio (Pza) .... AX 150
Vittoria (Pza d.) .... AZ 151
Vittorio Emanuele (V.) .... AZCY
Volturno (V.) .... AY
XII Gennaio (V.) .... AX
XIII Vittime (Pza) .... BX 153
XX Settembre (V.) .... AX

Villa Igiea Grand Hotel, salita Belmonte 43 ✉ 90142 ☎ 091 6312111, *villa-igiea @amthotels.it, Fax 091 547654,* heated, – rm, rm – 400. VISA JCB. by via Crispi BX
Meals a la carte 61/79 – **113 rm** 177/436, 5 suites.
◆ Bygone splendour abounds in this Art Nouveau villa with planted terraces running down towards the sea ; this hotel is a refined environment offering all the comforts of modern hospitality. The restaurant is equally elegant and impressive.

Centrale Palace Hotel, corso Vittorio Emanuele 327 ✉ 90134 ☎ 091 336666, *info@centralepalacehotel.it, Fax 091 334881,* – rm – 120. VISA JCB. BY b
Meals *(closed Sunday)* (dinner only) a la carte 32/66 – **94 rm** 178/256, 9 suites.
◆ The sumptuous surroundings of an 18C aristocratic residence mask the presence of every modern convenience in this sensitively restored hotel. Delightful dining on the terrace in summer, with splendid views.

Astoria Palace Hotel, via Montepellegrino 62 ✉ 90142 ☎ 091 6281111, *astoria@ghshotels.it, Fax 091 6371227* – rm, – 750. VISA.
Meals a la carte 27/43 – **301 rm** 144/177, 14 suites. by via Crispi BX
◆ Friendly, cheerful staff and high standards of comfort at this modern hotel, with large and pleasant public areas ; state-of-the-art conference facilities. An air of elegant modernity in the restaurant.

Grand Hotel Federico II, via Principe di Granatelli 60 ✉ 90139 ☎ 091 7495052, *grandhotelfedericoII@classicahotels.com, Fax 091 6092500,* – 50. AX f
Meals a la carte 40/53 – **64 rm** 185/276.
◆ A hotel of subdued elegance, with fine furnishings, wood panelling and Empire style pieces. Spacious rooms and top floor restaurant with pleasant terrace.

Principe di Villafranca, via G. Turrisi Colonna 4 ✉ 90141 ☎ 091 6118523, *info@principedivillafranca.it, Fax 091 588705,* – rm, – 140. AX d
Meals *(closed August, Sunday and Monday lunch)* a la carte 36/48 – **34 rm** 130/185.
◆ Rising from the ashes of a previous hotel on this site, this new establishment was opened in 1998. Classically stylish throughout with period furnishings in abundance. The restaurant shares the same elegant atmosphere.

Vecchio Borgo without rest., via Quintino Sella 1/7 ✉ 90139 ☎ 091 6111446, *hotelvecchioborgo@classicahotels.com, Fax 091 6093318* – rm, rm. BX b
34 rm 134/176.
◆ An intimately proportioned establishment offering good service ; elegant lobby, breakfast room and accommodation with much attention to detail in evidence.

Cristal Palace, via Roma 477 ✉ 90139 ☎ 091 6112580, *cristal@shr.it, Fax 091 6112589,* – – 30. BX c
Meals a la carte 20/30 – **87 rm** 100/150.
◆ Recently refitted along contemporary lines, this modern hotel offers sober, well laid out accommodation and has a small health spa. Recommended for business travellers.

San Paolo Palace, via Messina Marine 91 ✉ 90123 ☎ 091 6211112, *hotel@sanpaolopalace.it, Fax 091 6215300,* <, – – 1600. by via Ponte di Mare DZ
Meals a la carte 20/31 – **274 rm** 113/139, 10 suites.
◆ A panoramic lift gives access to a wonderful roof-garden with pool at this modern hotel, located a little way from the city centre with fine views over the sea. Roof-garden dining in summer.

Massimo Plaza Hotel without rest., via Maqueda 437 ✉ 90133 ☎ 091 325657, *booking@massimoplazahotel.com, Fax 091 325711* – . BY e
15 rm 140/190.
◆ Occupying a palazzo in the centre opposite the Teatro Massimo, this smart modern hotel is well-presented and elegant throughout.

Tonic without rest., via Mariano Stabile 126 ✉ 90139 ☎ 091 581754, *hoteltonic@hoteltonic.com, Fax 091 585560* – rm. BX g
44 rm 80/100.
◆ Situated in the historic centre, this hotel has wood furnishings and very spacious rooms. Efficient and courteous management ; recently refurbished.

Residenza d'Aragona without rest., via Ottavio d'Aragona 25 ✉ 90139 ☎ 091 6622222, *residenzadaragona@libero.it, Fax 091 6622273* – . BX a
20 rm 125/175.
◆ This fully restored 19C building in the centre is now a small, warm and friendly hotel with attractively furnished, comfortable and spacious rooms.

Villa d'Amato, via Messina Marine 180 ✉ 90123 ☎ 091 6212767, *villadamato@jumpy.it, Fax 091 6212767,* – – 150. by via Ponte di Mare DZ
Meals *(closed Sunday lunch)* a la carte 26/32 – **37 rm** 90/120.
◆ Well located on the city outskirts between the sea and the Messina road, this comfortable hotel has a large garden ; bright rooms with modern furnishings. Relaxing restaurant.

Posta without rest., via Antonio Gagini 77 ✉ 90133 ☎ 091 587338, *info@hotelpostapalermo.it, Fax 091 587347* – . BY c
30 rm 85/100.
◆ Close to the busy Via Roma, this well-restored hotel has been in the same hands since 1921 ; popular with actors performing at the theatre nearby.

La Scuderia, viale del Fante 9 ✉ 90146 ☎ 091 520323, *la.scuderia@tiscalinet.it, Fax 091 520467,* – . by via C.A. Dalla Chiesa AX
closed 13 to 30 August and Sunday – **Meals** a la carte 35/52.
◆ Located in the Parco della Favorita, the spacious and stylish interior of this historic restaurant is adorned with columns and large windows ; traditional cuisine.

XX **Lo Scudiero,** via Turati 7 ✉ 90139 ✆ 091 581628, *Fax 091 581628* – ▤. AE ⓢ ⓓ MC VISA JCB. ✻ AX c
closed 7 to 23 August and Sunday – **Meals** a la carte 25/49.
◆ An elegant and welcoming environment with beamed ceilings opposite the Teatro Politeama ; excellently run with good courteous service and traditional cuisine.

XX **Regine,** via Trapani 4/a ✉ 90141 ✆ 091 586566, *regine@ristoranteregine.it, Fax 091 586566* – ▤. AE ⓢ ⓓ MC VISA JCB. ✻ AX e
closed August and Sunday – **Meals** a la carte 33/40.
◆ An eye catching seafood and starters buffet in this elegantly modern restaurant ; the ideal environment in which to savour Sicilian and other Italian dishes.

XX **Bellotero,** via Giorgio Castriota 3 ✉ 90139 ✆ 091 582158, *Fax 091 582158* – ▤. AE ⓢ MC VISA JCB. ✻ by via della Libertà AX
closed Monday – **Meals** (booking essential) a la carte 29/41.
◆ Located in the cellars of a palazzo, this restaurant is traditional in both style and cuisine, focusing on classic Sicilian dishes. Contemporary artworks displayed on the walls.

XX **Cucina Papoff,** via Isidoro La Lumia 32 ✉ 90139 ✆ 091 586460, *cucinapapoff@virgilio.it, Fax 091 586460* – ▤. AE ⓢ ⓓ MC VISA. ✻ AX b
closed August, Saturday lunch and Sunday – **Meals** a la carte 29/52.
◆ Early 20C high coffered ceilings in carved wood make for a rustic yet elegant dining room ; strictly Sicilian, traditional cuisine.

XX **Santandrea,** piazza Sant'Andrea 4 ✉ 90133 ✆ 091 334999, 🏛 – ▤. AE ⓢ MC VISA JCB BY d
closed January and Sunday – **Meals** (dinner only) (booking essential) local dishes a la carte 28/37.
◆ Exposed beams and woodwork abound in this oasis of hospitality in the midst of Vucciria market's picturesque chaos ; hearty regional cuisine in keeping with the location.

at Borgo Molara *West : 8 km* – ✉ *90126 Palermo :*

Baglio Conca d'Oro, via Aquino 19 c/d ✆ 091 6406286, *hotelbaglio@libero.it, Fax 091 6408742,* 🏛 – ▤ ✻ ▤ TV ♿ rm P – 🏔 400. AE ⓢ ⓓ MC VISA. ✻
Meals *(closed Sunday)* (booking essential) a la carte 34/52 – **27 rm** ☕ 138/164.
◆ This sensitively restored 18C paper-mill retains many original features and is now a charming hotel offering style, elegance and comfort. The smart restaurant is in keeping with the refined interiors of the rest of the establishment.

at Sferracavallo *North-West : 12 km* – ✉ *90148 Palermo :*

X **Il Delfino,** via Torretta 80 ✆ 091 530282, *trattorialdelfino@virgilio.it, Fax 091 6914256* – ▤. AE ⓢ ⓓ MC VISA JCB. ✻
closed Monday – **Meals** seafood 21.
◆ Always busy, this simple restaurant spares customers the trouble of choosing for themselves ; a fine set-menu of exclusively fish dishes.

Villafrati *90030 Palermo* 565 N 22 – *pop. 3 334 alt. 450.*
Palermo 36 – Agrigento 87 – Caltanissetta 100.

XXX ✿✿ **Mulinazzo,** strada statale 121, località Bolognetta North : 9 Km ✆ 091 8724870, *mulinazzo@libero.it, Fax 091 8737533* – ✻ ▤ P. AE ⓢ ⓓ MC VISA
closed 3 weeks July, 15 days January, Monday and dinners Sunday, Easter, Christmas and New Year – **Meals** a la carte 41/67.
Spec. Salsicciotti di tonno alla menta. Minestra di aragosta con spaghetti spezzati. Filetto di maialino in crosta di pistacchi di Bronte, salsa al cacao.
◆ This country villa has a pleasantly elegant ambience ; the menu is rooted in country cuisine, creatively interpreted by the chef with excellent results.

TAORMINA (Sicily) *98039 Messina* 565 N 27 *G. Italy – pop. 10 782 alt. 250.*

See : *Site★★★ – Greek Theatre★★★ : ≤★★★* BZ *– Public garden★★* BZ *– ✻★★ from the Square 9 Aprile* AZ *– Corso Umberto★* ABZ *– Castle : ≤★★* AZ.

Exc. : *Etna★★★ South-West : for Linguaglossa Mola Castle★ North-West : 5 km Alcantara Gorge★.*

Picciolo (closed Tuesday) via Picciolo 1 ✉ 95030 Castiglione di Sicilia ✆ 0942 986252, Fax 0942 986252, West : 25 km.

piazza Santa Caterina (Corvaja palace) ✆ 0942 23243, info@gate2taormina.com, Fax 0942 24941.

Catania 52 ② – Enna 135 ② – Messina 52 ① – Palermo 255 ② – Siracusa 111 ② – Trapani 359 ②

Grand Hotel Timeo, via Teatro Greco 59 ☎ 0942 23801, *reservation.tim@framon-hotels.it, Fax 0942 628501*, ← sea, coast and Etna, – 200. AE VISA JCB. BZ x
Meals *Il Dito e La Luna* Rest. a la carte 62/106 – **73 rm** 340/490, 11 suites.
◆ Fine gardens and planted terraces surround this hotel, synonymous with Sicily's famed hospitality ; a magical splendour pervades the superbly comfortable interiors. The restaurant looks onto the Greek theatre, affording diners one of the world's finest views.

San Domenico Palace, piazza San Domenico 5 ☎ 0942 613111, *san-domenico@thi.it, Fax 0942 625506*, heated, – rm – 400. AE VISA JCB. AZ m
Meals a la carte 59/81 – **105 rm** 250/540, 7 suites.
◆ It is difficult to describe this marvellous hotel, a former convent dating from the 15C set in beautiful gardens with exceptional views of Mount Etna and the sea. The restaurant is outstanding and has a charming terrace.

Villa Diodoro, via Bagnoli Croci 75 ☎ 0942 23312, *diodoro@gaishotels.com, Fax 0942 23391*, ← sea, coast and Etna, – rm – 400. AE VISA. BZ q
Meals a la carte 35/48 – **102 rm** 196/274, 3 suites.
◆ A large pool dominates the marvellous terrace, which appears to stretch far out towards Mount Etna. This well-restored hotel has many fine features, and a charming restaurant.

Grand Hotel Miramare, via Guardiola Vecchia 27 ☎ 0942 23401, *ghmiramare@tiscali.it, Fax 0942 626223*, ← sea and coast, – AE VISA. CZ c
March-October – **Meals** a la carte 36/56 – 19 – **66 rm** 170/220, 2 suites.
◆ This imposing structure, pleasantly located in parkland, has particularly appealing public areas adorned with Empire-style furniture. Large restaurant and well-kept grounds.

Villa Fabbiano, via Pirandello 81 ☎ 0942 626058, *info@villafabbiano.com, Fax 0942 23732*, ← sea and coast, – VISA. CZ a
March-October – **Meals** (lunch only) (residents only) 25/40 – **26 rm** 150/285, 4 suites.
◆ An early 20C aristocratic residence stylishly decorated and passionately run ; all rooms offer fine views, as does the attractively planted terrace.

Villa Ducale without rest., via Leonardo da Vinci 60 ☎ 0942 28153, *info@villaducale.com, Fax 0942 28710*, ← sea, coast and Etna – AE VISA JCB
closed 5 to 20 December and 10 January-18 February – **18 rm** 200/250. AZ p
◆ In a delightful situation, this charming hotel, formerly a family villa, has atmosphere and great character ; well run by an enterprising young couple.

Villa Sirina without rest., contrada Sirina ☎ 0942 51776, *info@villasirina.com, Fax 0942 51671*, – AE VISA.
21 March-9 November – **16 rm** 100/160. 2 km by via Crocifisso AZ
◆ In the lower part of the town, near the entrance to the public gardens, this restored villa offers comfortable accommodation. Furnished in keeping with the local style.

Villa Belvedere, via Bagnoli Croci 79 ☎ 0942 23791, *info@villabelvedere.it, Fax 0942 625830*, ← gardens, sea and Etna, – VISA. rest
10 March-26 November – **Meals** *(10 April-October ; closed dinner)* (residents only) – **49 rm** 129,50/205, suite. BZ b
◆ Well-designed public areas and simple yet presentable rooms ; breathtaking views, grounds planted with palms, and a pool are further features of this hotel.

Villa Schuler without rest., piazzetta Bastione ☎ 0942 23481, *schuler@tao.it, Fax 0942 23522*, ←, – AE VISA JCB. BZ d
5 March-13 November – **29 rm** 136.
◆ Opened in 1905 and run by the same family to this day ; close to the historic centre, with Mediterranean style gardens and sea views. The ideal place to relax.

Andromaco without rest., via Fontana Vecchia ☎ 0942 23834, *info@andromaco.it, Fax 0942 24985*, ←, – VISA by via Cappuccini BZ
24 rm 90/130.
◆ This informal hotel is situated in a quiet residential area with fine views. The well-appointed interiors make good use of space ; efficient and friendly management.

La Giara, vico La Floresta 1 ☎ 0942 23360, *info@lagiarataormina.com, Fax 0942 23233*, ←, Rest. and piano bar – AE VISA. BZ f
closed January and Sunday (in August dinner only) – **Meals** (booking essential) a la carte 43/68.
◆ Undoubtedly the town's most fashionable restaurant with soft lights, good service, and views over rooftops and terraces. Popular piano-bar in the evenings ; stylish clientele.

Casa Grugno, via Santa Maria de' Greci ☎ 0942 21208, *info@casagrugno.it*, – AE VISA JCB. AZ a
closed 20 November-25 December, 5 January-28 February and Wednesday (except April-September) – **Meals** a la carte 49/67.
◆ This recently opened restaurant prides itself on its creative seafood cuisine, offering interesting flavour combinations. A refined atmosphere ; located in the town centre.

XX **Al Duomo,** vico Ebrei 11 ✆ 0942 625656, *info@ristorantealduomo.it,* – ▤. AE ⑤ ⓓ ⓜ VISA. AZ q
closed December, January and Monday – **Meals** (booking essential) Sicilian rest. a la carte 34/45.
◆ After approaching along an alley and entering this restaurant, customers find themselves in smart surroundings overlooking the Piazza del Duomo. Summer dining on the terrace.

XX **La Griglia,** corso Umberto 54 ✆ 0942 23980, *intelisano@tao.it, Fax 0942 23980* – ▤. AE ⑤ ⓓ ⓜ VISA. BZ c
closed 20 November-20 December and Tuesday – **Meals** a la carte 21/36.
◆ Situated on the town's main street, this classic restaurant is generously strewn with plants. Traditional cuisine along seasonal lines.

XX **Vicolo Stretto by Charly,** via Vicolo Stretto 6 ✆ 0942 24995, *vicolostretto@virgilio.it,* – ▤. AE ⑤ ⓓ ⓜ VISA JCB. BZ m
March-November – **Meals** a la carte 43/54.
◆ Fish couscous is the signature dish here, where the cuisine of the western part of the island predominates. Attractive restaurant run by friendly and enthusiastic youngsters.

X **Il Baccanale,** piazzetta Filea 1 ✆ 0942 625390, *Fax 0942 623266,* – ▤. ⑤ ⓜ VISA BZ e
closed Thursday except April-November – **Meals** a la carte 22/34.
◆ The option to dine outside in the square or indoors at closely-spaced tables in this simple establishment, which has an atmosphere of genuine rusticity. Popular with tourists.

at Capotaormina *South : 4 km* – ✉ *98030 Mazzarò :*

Atahotel Capotaormina, via Nazionale 105 ✆ 0942 572111, *prenotazioni@capotaorminahotel.com, Fax 0942 625467,* sea water – |‡|, rm, ▤ TV ✆ P – 450. AE ⑤ ⓓ ⓜ VISA JCB.
April-October – **Meals** a la carte 46/76 – **196 rm** 293/430, 4 suites.
◆ A splendid clifftop location makes for some of the finest views in the area. Among the many natural beauties is the beach with an unusual cave. The restaurant serves meals on the delightful terrace overlooking the sea.

Traffic restricted in the town centre.

TAORMINA

Carmine (Pza d.)	AZ	3
Don Bosco (V.)	BZ	6
Duomo (Pza d.)	AZ	7
Fazzelo (V.)	AZ	9
Giardinazzo (V.)	BZ	10
Ginnasio (V. d.)	BZ	12
Giovanni (V. d.)	BZ	13
Guardiola Vecchia (V.)	BCZ	15
Jallia Bassia (V.)	BZ	16
S. Antonio (Pza)	AZ	18
S. Caterina (Largo)	BZ	19
S. Domenico (Piazzale)	AZ	21
Umberto I (Cso)	ABZ	
Von Gloeden (V. W.)	AZ	22

at Mazzarò *East : 5,5 km* CZ – ✉ *98030 :*

Grand Hotel Mazzarò Sea Palace, via Nazionale 147 ✆ 0942 612111, *info@mazzaroseapalace.it, Fax 0942 626237,* ≤ small bay, – rm, – 100. AE VISA JCB. CZ b
March-November – **Meals** a la carte 37/92 – **88 rm** 239/420, 9 suites.
◆ Elegant interiors, luxurious furnishings, numerous terraces, and a pool with fine views are some of the ingredients which make such a harmonious whole at this fine hotel. Smart restaurant with terrace for candlelit dining.

Atlantis Bay , via Nazionale 161 ✆ 0942 618011, *info@atlantisbay.it, Fax 0942 23194,* – – 200. AE VISA JCB.
March-November – **Meals** 49 – **78 rm** 350/420, 7 suites.
◆ This recently opened hotel is elegant and sophisticated, with sumptuous interiors and spacious rooms, all with sea views, offering every comfort. Splendid pool with terrace and private beach. Attention to detail evident in the excellent restaurant.

Da Giovanni, via Nazionale ✆ 0942 23531, ≤ sea and Isolabella – AE VISA JCB.
closed 7 January-10 February and Monday – **Meals** a la carte 32/47.
◆ Classic seaside restaurant with dishes based on fresh locally caught fish prepared along traditional lines. Panoramic situation offering fine views of Isola Bella.

Il Delfino-da Angelo, via Nazionale ✆ 0942 23004, *Fax 0942 23004,* ≤ small bay, – AE VISA JCB
15 March-October – **Meals** a la carte 22/40.
◆ Located between an attractive garden and the famous local beach, this establishment is the ideal place to savour the flavours of the sea, and enjoy a dip.

at Lido di Spisone *North-East : 1,5 km – ✉ 98030 Mazzarò :*

Caparena, via Nazionale 189 ☎ 0942 652033, *caparena@gaishotels.com, Fax 0942 36913,* ←, – rm – 200. AE VISA.
20 March-October – **Meals** a la carte 35/48 – **88 rm** 177/280.
◆ The seaside at its best ; elegance, comfort, palm trees, clear water, fine furnishings and a pleasant atmosphere. The ideal solution for tourists and conference delegates alike. The restaurant offers outside dining in the large, well-planted gardens.

at Castelmola *North-West : 5 km* AZ *– alt. 550 – ✉ 98030 :*

Villa Sonia , via Porta Mola 9 ☎ 0942 28082, *intelisano@tao.it, Fax 0942 28083,* ← Etna, – cam. – 110. AE VISA JCB.
closed November-20 December and 6 January-February – **Meals** ***Parco Reale*** Rest. a la carte 52/62 – 15 – **37 rm** 120/170, 3 suites.
◆ Occupying a restored historic villa on the way into a pretty little town, this hotel's interior is adorned with antiques and Sicilian craftware. The soberly smart restaurant is also furnished with period items.

TURIN (TORINO) *10100* P 561 G 5 *G. Italy – pop. 861 644 alt. 239.*

See : *Piazza San Carlo★★* CXY *– Egyptian Museum★★★, Sabauda Gallery★★ in Academy of Science* CX **M1** *– Cathedral★* VX *: relic of the Holy Shroud★★★ – Mole Antonelliana★ : Museum of Cinema★★★* DX *– Madama Palace★★ : museum of Ancient Art★★* CX **A** *– Royal Palace★ : Royal Armoury★* CDVX *– Risorgimento Museum★★ in Carignano Palace★★* CX **M2** *– Carlo Biscaretti di Ruffia Motor Museum★★ – GAM-Modern Art Gallery★★ – Model medieval village★ in the Valentino Park★★* CDZ.

Envir. : *Royal Residences★★ – Basilica of Superga★ : ←★★★ – Sacra di San Michele ★★★ – Tour to the pass, Colle della Maddalena★ : ←★★ of the city from the route Superga-Pino Torinese, ←★ of the city from the route Colle della Maddalena-Cavoretto.*

27, I Roveri (March-November ; closed Monday) at La Mandria ✉ 10070 Fiano Torinese ☎ 011 9235719, Fax 011 9235669, North : 18 km;

18, 18 Torino (closed Monday, January and February), at Fiano Torinese ✉ 10070 ☎ 011 9235440, Fax 011 9235886, North : 20 km;

18 Le Fronde (closed Tuesday, January and February) at Avigliana ✉ 10051 ☎ 011 9328053, Fax 011 9320928, West : 24 km;

9 Stupinigi (closed Monday), corso Unione Sovietica 506/a ✉ 10135 Torino ☎ 011 3472640, Fax 011 3978038.

Turin Airport of Caselle North : 15 km ☎ 011 5676361.

piazza Solferino (Atrium) ✉ 10122 ☎ 011 535181, info@turismotorino.org, Fax 011 530070 – Porta Nuova Railway Station ✉ 10125 ☎ 011 531327, Fax 011 5617095 – Turin Airport of Caselle ✉ 10123 ☎ 011 5678124.

A.C.I. *via Giovanni Giolitti 15 ✉ 10123 ☎ 011 57791, Fax 011 5779268.*

Roma 669 – Briançon 108 – Chambéry 209 – Genève 252 – Genova 170 – Grenoble 224 – Milano 140 – Nice 220.

Plans on following pages

Le Meridien Lingotto, via Nizza 262 ✉ 10126 ☎ 011 6642000, *reservations@lemeridien-lingotto.it, Fax 011 6642001,* – rm, rm – 40. AE VISA. by via Nizza CZ
Meals ***Torpedo*** Rest. a la carte 41/56 – **240 rm** 350, suite.
◆ This hotel, carved out of the Lingotto industrial complex, has its own tropical garden ; luxurious rooms with design features. Comfortable seating in the bright and elegant restaurant serving first class cuisine.

Grand Hotel Sitea, via Carlo Alberto 35 ✉ 10123 ☎ 011 5170171, *sitea@thi.it, Fax 011 548090* – – 100. AE VISA JCB. rest CY t
Meals a la carte 42/53 – **114 rm** 209/280, 2 suites.
◆ Hospitality, atmosphere, antique furniture ; a harmonious refinement is evident throughout at this traditional grand hotel (opened 1925) which has been recently renovated. Pleasant views from the subtly elegant restaurant.

Turin Palace Hotel, via Sacchi 8 ✉ 10128 ☎ 011 5625511, *palace@thi.it, Fax 011 5612187* – – 200. AE VISA. rest CY u
Meals *(closed August, Saturday and Sunday lunch)* a la carte 28/49 – **120 rm** 230/295, 2 suites.
◆ Style and tradition abound in this classic grand hotel which has been part of the city's life for more than a century ; a warm atmosphere and simple period elegance throughout. A refined ambience in the genteel and welcoming restaurant ; excellent service.

Le Meridien Art+Tech, via Nizza 230 ✉ 10126 ☎ 011 6642000, *reservations@lemeridien-lingotto.it, Fax 011 6642004* – rm – 150. AE MC VISA. by via Nizza CZ
Meals a la carte 41/56 – **141** 410, suite.
• A glass lift rises from the small lobby up to the balcony level, leading to the rooms. The effect created by this original design is impressive. Embellished by cherrywood, the restaurant is elegant yet informal.

Starhotel Majestic, corso Vittorio Emanuele II 54 ✉ 10123 ☎ 011 539153, *majestic.to@starhotels.it, Fax 011 534963* – rm, rm – 500. AE MC VISA JCB. CY e
Meals ***le Regine*** Rest. a la carte 43/65 – **160 rm** 200/235, 2 suites.
• Spacious and comfortable throughout, this centrally-located elegant hotel has been recently refitted. A large dome of coloured glass dominates the attractive dining room; international cuisine.

Jolly Hotel Ambasciatori, corso Vittorio Emanuele II 104 ✉ 10121 ☎ 011 5752, *torino-ambasciatori@jollyhotels.it, Fax 011 544978* – rm, – 350. AE MC VISA. rest BX a
Meals ***Il Diplomatico*** Rest. a la carte 39/65 – **195 rm** 220/255, 4 suites.
• Occupying an angular modern building, this hotel is continuously updated to meet the requirements of its corporate-function clientele; comfortable rooms, in keeping with the group's standards. Bright restaurant with a stylish atmosphere.

Atahotel Concord, via Lagrange 47 ✉ 10123 ☎ 011 5176756, *prenotazioni@hotelconcord.com, Fax 011 5176305* – – 200. AE MC VISA JCB. rest
Meals a la carte 32/46 – **135 rm** 260/310, 4 suites. CY s
• Centrally located near Porta Nuova, this comfortable establishment with its spacious interior is well suited to corporate events. Classic restaurant with an elegant ambience, plus an American-style bar.

Boston, via Massena 70 ✉ 10128 ☎ 011 500359, *direzione@hotelbostontorino.it, Fax 011 599358* – rm, – 50. AE MC VISA BZ c
Meals (see rest. ***Casa Vicina below)*** – **82 rm** 150/220, 5 suites.
• Restoration has combined high standards of comfort with tasteful decoration in this hotel; art works displayed in the lobby and oriental-style furnishings in the new rooms.

Victoria without rest., via Nino Costa 4 ✉ 10123 ☎ 011 5611909, *reservation@hotelvictoria-torino.com, Fax 011 5611806* – . AE MC VISA. CY v
106 rm 138/183.
• Antique furniture, a harmonious colour scheme and canopy beds; much attention to detail in evidence at this elegant hotel which oozes atmosphere and charm.

Pacific Hotel Fortino, strada del Fortino 36 ✉ 10152 ☎ 011 5217757, *hotelfortino@pacifichotels.it, Fax 011 5217749* – rm, – 450. AE MC VISA JCB CV d
Meals *(closed Sunday)* (dinner only) a la carte 31/50 – 13 – **92 rm** 176/232, 8 suites.
• Modern hotel designed to meet the needs of the business traveller. Several suites available fitted with the latest in Information Technology gadgetry. The spacious restaurant forms part of the hotel dedicated conference facilities.

Novotel Torino , corso Giulio Cesare 338/34 ✉ 10154 ☎ 011 2601211, *novotel.torino@accor-hotels.it, Fax 011 200574,* rm, rm – 200. AE MC VISA by corso Giulio Cesare DV
Meals a la carte 28/59 – **162 rm** 160/190.
• Not far from the motorway junction on the outskirts, this well laid out modern hotel has bright, spacious rooms, all of which incorporate sofa beds and large desks. The breakfast room and dining room occupy a single space.

Diplomatic, via Cernaia 42 ✉ 10122 ☎ 011 5612444, *info@hotel-diplomatic.it, Fax 011 540472* – rm, – 180. AE MC VISA. rest BX g
Meals *(closed Saturday and Sunday)* (dinner only) (residents only) – **126 rm** 200/260.
• Near Porta Susa station, concealed behind the 19C porticoes so characteristic of Turin, is the modern entrance lobby of this new hotel; small but very comfortable rooms.

City without rest., via Juvarra 25 ✉ 10122 ☎ 011 540546, *city.to@bestwestern.it, Fax 011 548188* – rm – 60. AE MC VISA JCB. BV e
15 – **57 rm** 180/400.
• Unusual contemporary style gives character to this conveniently located hotel near Porta Susa station; quiet, well-appointed rooms.

Holiday Inn Turin City Centre, via Assietta 3 ✉ 10128 ☎ 011 5167111, *hi.torit@libero.it, Fax 011 5167699* – rm, rm – 40. AE MC VISA. rest CY a
Meals (dinner only) 22 – **57 rm** 160/218.
• Occupying a restored 19C palazzo, this well-situated hotel offers every modern comfort including jacuzzis, power showers and saunas in its rooms. The restaurant is also designed along contemporary lines.

TORINO

4 Marzo (V.)	CX	93
20 Settembre (V.)	CXY	96
Alfieri (V.)	CY	6
Cadorna (Lungo Po L.)	DY	10
Carignano (Pza)	CX	12
Carlo Emanuele II (Pza)	CY	13
Carlo Felice (Pza)	CY	16
Casale (Cso)	DY	18
Castello (Pza)	CX	19
Cesare Augusto (Pza)	CV	23
Consolata (V. della)	CV	27
Diaz (Lungo Po A.)	DY	32
Gran Madre di Dio (Pza)	DY	38
Milano (V.)	CV	46
Napoli (Lungo Dora)	CV	50
Palazzo di Città (Pza del)	CX	51
Repubblica (Pza della)	CV	62
Roma (V.)	CXY	
S. Carlo (Pza)	CXY	
S. F. d'Assisi (V.)	CX	66
Solferino (Pza)	CX	75
Vitt. Emanuele I (Ponte)	DY	55
Vitt. Emanuele II (Lungo)	BCY	90

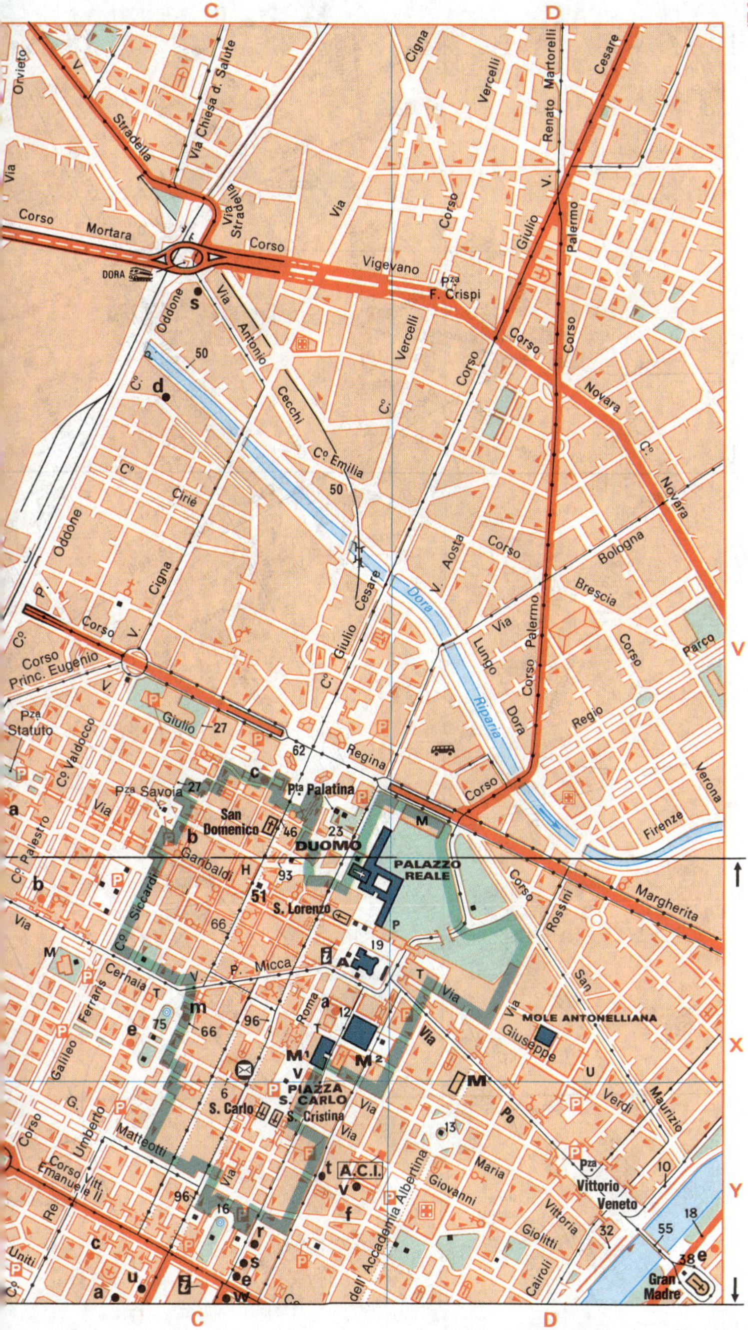
C
D
V
X
Y
Orvieto
Via Chiesa d. Salute
Cigna
Vercelli
Renato Martorelli
Cesare
Stradella
Via
Corso
Mortara
Via Stradella
Corso
Via
Corso
V.
Giulio
Palermo
DORA
Vigevano
Pza F. Crispi
Oddone
s
Via
Antonio
50
C.
d
Vercelli
Corso
Corso
Corso
Novara
Cecchi
C°
C° Emilia
Novara
C°
Ciriè
50
Oddone
V. Aosta
Corso
Bologna
Cigna
Dora
Cesare
Brescia
P.
Corso
Giulio
Via
Corso
Parco
C°
V.
Lungo
Palermo
V
Corso Princ. Eugenio
C°
Corso
Riparia
V.
Regio
Pza Statuto
Giulio
27
Dora
62
Regina
Verona
C° Valdocco
c
Pta Palatina
Corso
Pza Savoia
27
Firenze
Via
San Domenico
46
23
M
a
b
DUOMO
C° Palestro
Garibaldi
H
93
PALAZZO REALE
b
51
Corso
Margherita
Siccardi
S. Lorenzo
Rossini
Via
66
P
19
M
C°
Micca
San
Cernaia
T
P.
A
T
Via
Ferraris
m
a
Via
96
Roma
12
MOLE ANTONELLIANA
e
75
66
Via
Giuseppe
Galileo
M1
M2
T
V
M
U
PIAZZA S. CARLO
Verdi
G.
6
Via
Po
Maurizio
Corso
Umberto
S. Carlo
S. Cristina
Via
13
Matteotti
Maria
Pza Vittorio Veneto
10
Corso Vitt. Emanuele II
t
A.C.I.
v
Giovanni
Via
f
Vittoria
Re
96
16
dell' Accademia Albertina
18
Giolitti
32
55
c
r
Uniti
s
38 e
C°
u
Cairoli
a
e
w
Gran Madre
C
D

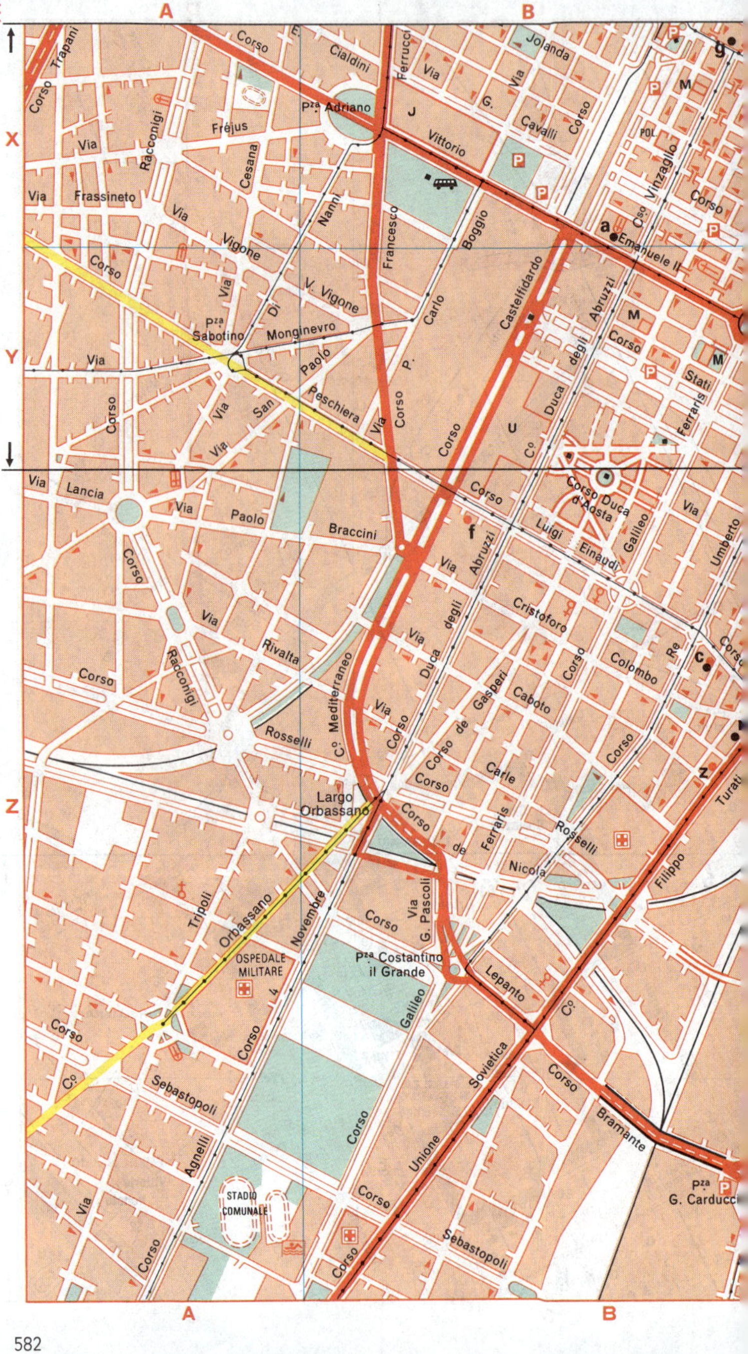

A
B
X
Y
Z
Corso Trapani
Corso Cialdini
Pza Adriano
Via Ferrucci
Via G. Jolanda
Via Cavalli
Corso Vittorio Emanuele II
Via Racconigi
Fréjus
Via Cesana
Via Frassineto
Via Vigone
Via Nanni
Via Francesco
Boggio
Corso Vinzaglio
POL
Pza Sabotino
Corso Di V. Vigone
Monginevro
Via San Paolo
Peschiera
Corso P. Carlo
Castelfidardo
Cso Duca degli Abruzzi
Corso Stati
Ferraris
Corso
Via Lancia
Via Paolo
Braccini
Corso Duca d'Aosta
Corso Luigi Einaudi
Via Galileo
Via Umberto
Via Duca degli Abruzzi
Cristoforo Colombo
Via Rivalta
Corso Racconigi
Corso Rosselli
Co. Mediterraneo
Via Corso
Corso de Gasperi
Caboto
Corso Re
Carle
Largo Orbassano
Corso de Ferraris
Nicola
Rosselli
Corso Filippo Turati
Tripoli
Orbassano
Novembre
4
OSPEDALE MILITARE
Corso
Via G. Pascoli
Pza Costantino il Grande
Lepanto
Galileo
Co. Sebastopoli
Corso Agnelli
Corso Unione Sovietica
Corso Bramante
Pza G. Carducci
STADIO COMUNALE
Corso Sebastopoli
Via
Corso
J
M
P
U
a
c
f
g
z

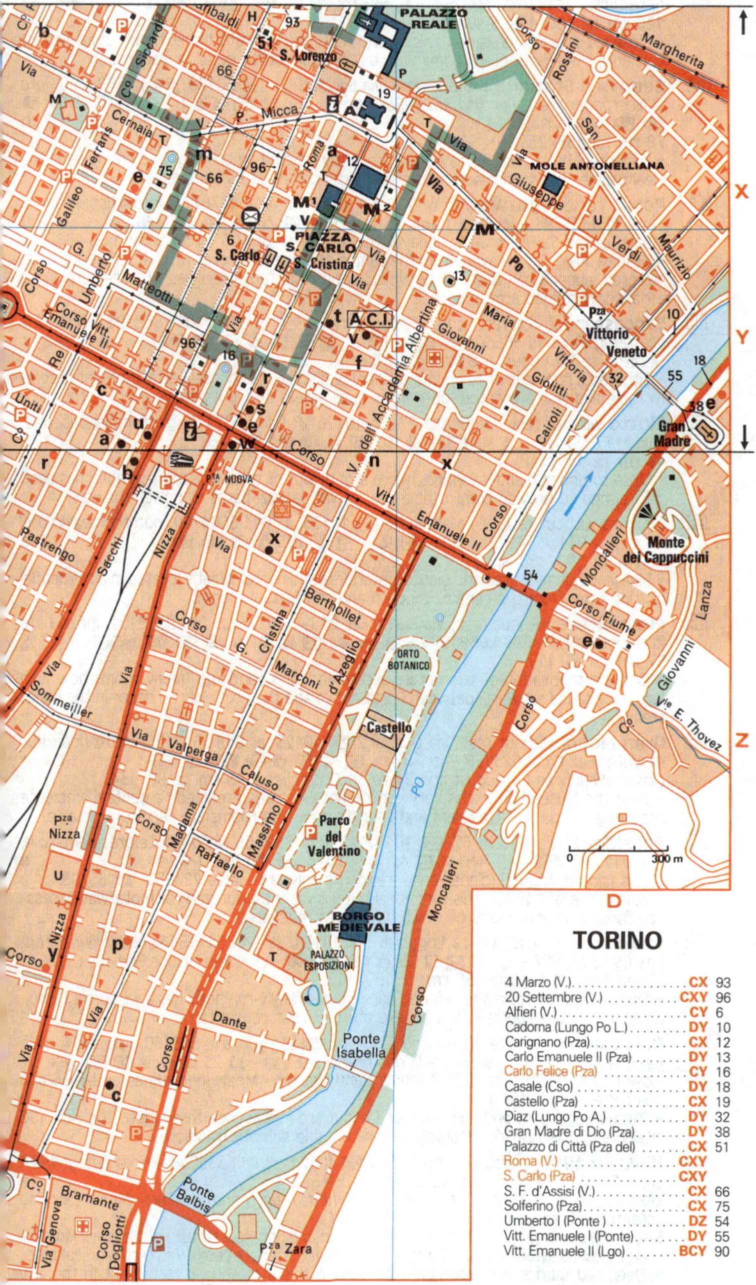

TORINO

4 Marzo (V.)	CX	93
20 Settembre (V.)	CXY	96
Alfieri (V.)	CY	6
Cadorna (Lungo Po L.)	DY	10
Carignano (Pza)	CX	12
Carlo Emanuele II (Pza)	DY	13
Carlo Felice (Pza)	CY	16
Casale (Cso)	DY	18
Castello (Pza)	CX	19
Diaz (Lungo Po A.)	DY	32
Gran Madre di Dio (Pza)	DY	38
Palazzo di Città (Pza del)	CX	51
Roma (V.)	CXY	
S. Carlo (Pza)	CXY	
S. F. d'Assisi (V.)	CX	66
Solferino (Pza)	CX	75
Umberto I (Ponte)	DZ	54
Vitt. Emanuele I (Ponte)	DY	55
Vitt. Emanuele II (Lgo)	BCY	90

Genio without rest., corso Vittorio Emanuele II 47 ✉ 10125 ℘ 011 6505771, *info@hotelgenio.it, Fax 011 6508264* – rm, – 80. CYZ w
120 rm 100/138, 3 suites.
◆ Close to Porta Nuova station, this recently enlarged and refurbished hotel has an elegant ambience ; well-presented rooms with much attention to detail in evidence.

Genova e Stazione without rest., via Sacchi 14/b ✉ 10128 ℘ 011 5629400, *info@albergogenova.it, Fax 011 5629896* – rm, rm – 70. CZ b
78 rm 135/233.
◆ A genteel hotel near Porta Nuova ; recently refitted to provide its clientele with the ideal balance between modern comfort and a classic, stylish interior.

Royal, corso Regina Margherita 249 ✉ 10144 ℘ 011 4376777, *info@hotelroyal.to, Fax 011 4376393* – – 600. BV u
Meals *(closed Saturday and Sunday lunch)* a la carte 36/46 – **75 rm** 115/160.
◆ Despite being slightly away from the centre, this pleasant hotel, which has recently been restored, appeals to guests of all types ; good conference facilities. The restaurant has a classically refined atmosphere.

Lancaster without rest., corso Filippo Turati 8 ✉ 10128 ℘ 011 5681982, *hotel@lancaster.it, Fax 011 5683019* – – 60. BZ r
closed 5 to 20 August – **83 rm** 106/140.
◆ Situated a little out of town in a residential district, this genteel establishment is comfortable and well presented, both in its public areas and in its above-average rooms.

Giotto without rest., via Giotto 27 ✉ 10126 ℘ 011 6637172, *giottohotel@libero.it, Fax 011 6637173* – – 30. CZ c
48 rm 115/148.
◆ Close to Lingotto and Valentino, hence slightly out of town, this modern hotel has been refurbished to provide comfortable rooms with jacuzzi baths or power showers.

Crimea without rest., via Mentana 3 ✉ 10133 ℘ 011 6604700, *hotel.crimea@hotelres.it, Fax 011 6604912* – – 35. DZ e
48 rm 100/180, suite.
◆ Pleasantly understated and elegant interiors in this hotel, quietly located in a residential district away from the centre ; modern and comfortable rooms.

Piemontese without rest., via Berthollet 21 ✉ 10125 ℘ 011 6698101, *info@hotelpiemontese.it, Fax 011 6690571* – CZ x
37 rm 96/119.
◆ Ongoing renovation of this hotel's accommodation continues (many rooms now with jacuzzi or sauna-shower) ; between Porta nuova and the Po. Colourful décor in the public areas.

Gran Mogol without rest., via Guarini 2 ✉ 10123 ℘ 011 5612120, *info@hotelgranmogol.it, Fax 011 5623160* – CY r
closed 29 July to 24 August and 24 to 31 December – **45 rm** 98/134.
◆ Near the Museo Egizio, this very central hotel has been refitted ; a genteel ambience appealing to business travellers and tourists alike. The rooms are very comfortable.

President, via Cecchi 67 ✉ 10152 ℘ 011 859555, *info@hotelpresident-to.it, Fax 011 2480465* – CV s
Meals *(closed August)* (dinner only) (residents only) a la carte 22/35 – 65/98.
◆ Built in the late 1970s, this functional hotel is fairly well located for motorway access ; comfortable rooms, many of which have been renovated.

Cairo without rest., via La Loggia 6 ✉ 10134 ℘ 011 3171555, *hcairo@ipsnet.it, Fax 011 3172027* – by corso Unione Sovietica BZ
closed 1 to 28 August – **56 rm** 100/140.
◆ Situated out of town and offering parking, this family-run hotel has a welcoming ambience ; the newer rooms in the annexe are the most comfortable.

Del Cambio, piazza Carignano 2 ✉ 10123 ℘ 011 543760, *cambio@thi.it, Fax 011 535282,* , Historic traditional restaurant – – 25.
closed 12 to 18 August, 1 to 7 January and Sunday – **Meals** (booking essential) 66 and a la carte 45/70 (15 %). CX a
◆ Turin's regal past and the spirit of Cavour are in evidence throughout the rich 19C interiors of this historic establishment with a fine culinary tradition.

Vintage 1997, piazza Solferino 16/h ✉ 10121 ℘ 011 535948, *info@vintage1997.com, Fax 011 535948* – . CX e
closed 6 to 31 August, 1 to 7 January, Saturday lunch and Sunday – **Meals** (booking essential) a la carte 40/58.
Spec. Insalata di gallina con robiola di Murazzano, melograno e tartufo di stagione. Rigatoni con scampetti e punte d'asparagi (spring-summer). Scampi e coniglio su crema di scalogno..
◆ Deep red fabrics and wood-panelled walls in this atmospheric restaurant in the city centre ; caring personal service and creative cuisine.

XXX **La Cloche,** strada al Traforo del Pino 106 ✉ 10132 ☎ 011 8992851, *la cloche@tiscalinet.it, Fax 011 8981522,* – – 100. AE VISA JCB by corso Moncalieri CDZ
closed 1 week in August, Sunday dinner and Monday – **Meals** a la carte 36/78.
◆ A rural setting in the foothills for this warm and elegant restaurant ; good banqueting room. Piedmontese cuisine following seasonal lines.

XXX **La Pista,** via Nizza 294 ✉ 10126 ☎ 011 6313523, *ristorante@lapista.to.it, Fax 011 6313708* – AE VISA JCB by via Nizza CZ
closed three weeks in August and one week in January – **Meals** (booking essential) 50/60 and a la carte 54/74.

XXX **Neuv Caval 'd Brôns,** piazza San Carlo 151 ✉ 10123 ☎ 011 5627483, *info@neuvcaval.com, Fax 011 543610* – AE VISA JCB. CX v
closed 10 to 24 August, Saturday lunch and Sunday – **Meals** (booking essential) a la carte 36/66.
◆ Beneath the arches of one of Piazza San Carlo 19C palazzi, this elegant and exclusive city restaurant has regained its historic exalted status.

XXX **La Barrique,** corso Dante 53 ✉ 10126 ☎ 011 657900, *Fax 011 657995* – . AE VISA CZ y
closed Sunday in June-September, also Monday in other months – **Meals** (booking essential) 19,50 (dinner only except Bank Holidays)/40,50 and a la carte 42/66.
Spec. Vitella piemontese in diverse maniere. Suprema di anatra confit con il suo fegato grasso, misticanza all'agro di lamponi. Variazione al cioccolato..
◆ A small and friendly oasis of peace and elegance in a somewhat busy district ; good service and imaginative cuisine using quality ingredients.

XXX **Marco Polo,** via Marco Polo 38 ✉ 10129 ☎ 011 599900, *ristorantemarcopolo@libero.it, Fax 011 50842266* – . AE VISA JCB BZ f
Meals (dinner only) (booking essential) seafood and japanese rest a la carte 40/65.
◆ A number of different rooms over two floors make up this restaurant, offering original cuisine : Japanese dishes, roast meats, and seafood.

XX **Moreno La Prima dal 1979,** corso Unione Sovietica 244 ✉ 10134 ☎ 011 3179191, *laprimamoreno@libero.it, Fax 011 3143423* – . AE VISA. GU c
closed 20 days in August and Monday lunch – **Meals** (booking essential) a la carte 50/70.
◆ From the ring road an unexpected lane leads to this well-presented and elegant establishment. The tables overlooking the gardens are especially pleasant ; traditional cuisine.

XX **Al Garamond,** via Pomba 14 ✉ 10123 ☎ 011 8122781 – . AE VISA JCB CY f
closed Saturday lunch and Sunday – **Meals** (booking essential) 40/60 and a la carte 47/62.
◆ Named after an officer of Napoleon's army, this establishment, run by a youthful but professional staff, serves imaginative modern dishes.

XX **Locanda Mongreno,** strada Mongreno 50 ✉ 10132 ☎ 011 8980417, *pikuz@libero.it, Fax 011 8227345,* – AE VISA by corso Moncalieri DZ
closed 25 August-10 September, 26 December-10 January and Monday – **Meals** (dinner only) (booking essential) 45/68 and a la carte 32/45.
Spec. Rombo arrostito con fave e cipollotto, salsa al limoncello, polvere di tè e fiocchi di pesce affumicato. Scamone di sanato dorato con cocktail di patate affumicate e zabaione freddo alla senape. I cinque gusti (dolce).
◆ A passionate young management has transformed this former rustic establishment into a stylish restaurant serving innovative, characterful cuisine.

XX **Al Gatto Nero,** corso Filippo Turati 14 ✉ 10128 ☎ 011 590414, *info@gattonero.it, Fax 011 502245* – . AE VISA. BZ z
closed August and Sunday – **Meals** a la carte 45/58.
◆ Cats of all kinds gaze from the periphery of this perennially popular restaurant with many celebrity regulars ; traditional Tuscan cuisine.

XX **'L Birichin,** via Vincenzo Monti 16/A ✉ 10126 ☎ 011 657457, *batavia@birichin.it, Fax 011 657457* . AE VISA JCB. CZ p
closed 6 to 26 August and Sunday – **Meals** (booking essential) a la carte 37/53.
◆ Close to the Lingotto exhibition centre, this welcoming little restaurant has two warmly decorated dining rooms. Informal with a gastronomic and often creative menu.

XX **Savoia,** via Corte d'Appello 13 ✉ 10122 ☎ 011 4362288, *r.savoia97@libero.it, Fax 011 4362288* – . AE VISA. CV b
closed Saturday lunch and Sunday – **Meals** (booking essential) a la carte 31/51.
◆ Fanciful and surprising modern dishes at this long established restaurant. Elegantly furnished, good service and atmosphere.

XX **Ij Brandè,** via Massena 5 ✉ 10128 ✆ 011 537279, *ijbrande@yahoo.it, Fax 011 5180668* – ▤. AE ⑤ ⓓ ⓜⓒ VISA JCB CY c
closed Sunday and Monday lunch – **Meals** (booking essential for dinner) a la carte 27/47.
◆ A warm, friendly restaurant with real fire in the Porta Nuova district ; traditional dishes interpreted with imagination and style.

XX **Galante,** corso Palestro 15 ✉ 10122 ✆ 011 537757, *galante@ristoratori.it, Fax 011 532163* – ▤. AE ⑤ ⓓ ⓜⓒ VISA JCB CX b
closed August, Saturday lunch and Sunday – **Meals** (booking essential) a la carte 30/50.
◆ Pale colours and upholstered seating in this small Neo-classical jewel ; many roast specialities, both meat and fish, on the menu.

XX **Porta Rossa,** via Passalacqua 3/b ✉ 10122 ✆ 011 530816, *Fax 011 530816* – ▤. AE ⑤ ⓓ ⓜⓒ VISA. ✂ CV a
closed August, 26 December-6 January, Saturday lunch and Sunday – **Meals** (booking essential) seafood a la carte 32/65.
◆ Near Piazza Statuto, this animated modern restaurant has closely-spaced tables and a wide selection of wonderfully-fresh fish dishes.

XX **Al Bue Rosso,** corso Casale 10 ✉ 10131 ✆ 011 8191393, *Fax 011 8191393* – ▤. AE ⑤ ⓜⓒ VISA. ✂ DY e
closed August, Saturday lunch and Monday – **Meals** a la carte 36/46 (10 %).
◆ In the same competent hands for over 30 years, this classically elegant restaurant near the Gran Madre church is on the banks of the Po ; rustic cuisine.

XX **Casa Vicina,** via Massena 66 ✉ 10128 ✆ 011 590949, *casavicina@libero.it* – AE ⑤ ⓓ ⓜⓒ VISA BZ c
closed 5 July-1 August, Sunday dinner and Monday – **Meals** (dinner only) a la carte 50/70.
◆ Formerly at the Canavese, the solid family management team have here preserved the name, style and traditional Piedmontese cuisine.

XX **Locanda Botticelli,** strada Arrivore 9 ✉ 10154 ✆ 011 2422012, *locandabotticelli@libero.it, Fax 011 2464662* – P. AE ⑤ ⓓ ⓜⓒ VISA JCB by corso Giulio Cesare DV
closed August and Sunday – **Meals** (booking essential) a la carte 30/40.
◆ Once through the gates, the uninspiring suburban setting is forgotten as diners are presented with a friendly ambience serving a wide range of meat and fish dishes.

XX **Perbacco,** via Mazzini 31 ✉ 10123 ✆ 011 882110 – ▤. AE ⑤ ⓓ ⓜⓒ VISA DZ x
closed August and Sunday – **Meals** (dinner only) 28.
◆ Centrally located, pleasant restaurant (evenings only) with an elegant modern atmosphere ; à la carte menu of seasonal Piedmontese cuisine.

XX **L'Agrifoglio,** via Accademia Albertina 38/D ✉ 10123 ✆ 011 837064 – AE ⑤ ⓓ ⓜⓒ VISA. ✂ CZ n
closed Sunday and Monday (except July) – **Meals** (dinner only) (booking essential) a la carte 30/44.
◆ This cosily small modern trattoria enjoys a well-deserved reputation ; checked tablecloths and cuisine which blends imagination and tradition.

XX **Solferino,** piazza Solferino 3 ✉ 10121 ✆ 011 535851, *Fax 011 535195* – AE ⑤ ⓓ ⓜⓒ VISA. ✂ CX m
closed 27-28 March, 25 December-2 January, Friday dinner and Saturday – **Meals** a la carte 27/36.
◆ Situated in an attractive Turin piazza, this classic restaurant has been in the same capable hands for nearly 30 years ; its traditional cuisine is of such renown that it is very busy even at lunchtime.

XX **Il 58,** via Valeggio 9 ✉ 10128 ✆ 011 505566, *ristoranteil58@libero.it, Fax 011 505566* – ▤. ⑤ ⓜⓒ VISA JCB CZ a
closed September and Monday – **Meals** seafood 31 and a la carte 32/45.
◆ Genteel restaurant with two elegant and welcoming rooms ; relaxed service and excellent ingredients evident in the cuisine (predominantly seafood). Youthful management.

XX **Tre Galline,** via Bellezia 37 ✉ 10122 ✆ 011 4366553, *info@3galline.it, Fax 011 4360013* – ✂. AE ⑤ ⓓ ⓜⓒ VISA CV c
closed 10 to 20 August, 1 to 8 January, Sunday and Monday lunch – **Meals** a la carte 36/52.
◆ Well presented rustic ambience with wood beamed ceilings in this historic city restaurant ; classic and flavoursome Piedmontese cooking.

X **Taverna delle Rose,** via Massena 24 ✉ 10128 ✆ 011 538345, *Fax 011 538345* – ▤. AE ⑤ ⓓ ⓜⓒ VISA JCB CZ r
closed August, Saturday lunch and Sunday – **Meals** a la carte 30/42.
◆ An enchanting ambience in this restaurant offering a wide range of traditional dishes ; for evening dining choose the romantic room with exposed brickwork and soft lights.

Torre Pellice *10066 Torino* 561 H 3 – *pop. 4 565 alt. 516.*

via Repubblica 3 ☎ 0121 91875, torrepellice@montagnedoc.it, Fax 0121 933353.

Roma 708 – Cuneo 64 – Milano 201 – Sestriere 71 – Torino 58.

XXX ✿✿ **Flipot** with rm, corso Gramsci 17 ☎ 0121 953465, *flipot@flipot.com, Fax 0121 91236* – TV. AE VISA.
closed 10 to 30 June and 24 December-10 January – **Meals** *(closed Monday and Tuesday, only Tuesday July-August)* a la carte 64/88 – **8 rm** 80/100.
Spec. Trota cotta nella corteccia di abete. Agnoli di mostardella (sanguinaccio) su porri in crema e croccanti. Carrè di agnello da latte cotto nel fieno maggengo e prustinenga (frattaglie) valdese.
• Deep in the Valli Valdesi, this establishment seems lost in bygone times ; a welcoming family environment with creative dishes drawing on timeless flavours.

VENICE (VENEZIA) *30100* P 562 F 19 *G. Venice – pop. 269 566.*

See : *St. Marks Square★★★ KZ : Basilica★★★ LZ – Doges Palace★★★ LZ – Campanile★★ : ★★ KLZ* **Q** *– Correr Museum★★ KZ* **M** *– Bridge of Sighs★★ LZ.*
Santa Maria della Salute★★ DV – St. Giorgio Maggiore★ : ★★★ from campanile FV – St. Zanipolo★★ LX – Santa Maria Gloriosa dei Frari★★★ BTU – St. Zaccaria★★ LZ – Interior decoration★★ by Veronese in the Church of St. Sebastiano BV – Ceiling★ of the Church of St. Pantaleone BU – Santa Maria dei Miracoli★ KLX – St. Francesco della Vigna★ FT – Ghetto★★ BT.
Scuola di St. Rocco★★★ BU – Scuola di St. Giorgio degli Schiavoni★★★ FU – Scuola dei Carmini★ BV – Scuola di St. Marco★ LX – Palazzo Labia★★ BT – Murano★★ : Glass Museum★, Church of Santi Maria e Donato★★ – Burano★★ – Torcello★★ : mosaics★★ in the basilica of Santa Maria Assunta.
Grand Canal★★★ : Rialto Bridge★★ KY – Ca' d'Oro★★★ JX – Academy of Fine Arts★★★ BV – Ca' Rezzonico★★ BV – Ca' Dario★ DV – Grassi Palace★ BV – Vendramin-Calergi Palace★ CT – Peggy Guggenheim Collection★★ in Palace Venier dei Leoni DV – Ca' Pesaro★ JX.

18 *(closed Monday) at Lido Alberoni ✉ 30011 ☎ 041 731333, Fax 041 731339, 15 mn by boat and 9 km;*

18 *et* 9 *Cà della Nave (closed Tuesday) at Martellago ✉ 30030 ☎ 041 5401555, Fax 041 5401926, North-West : 12 km;*

27 *Villa Condulmer (closed Monday), at Mogliano Veneto ✉ 30020 ☎ 041 457062, Fax 041 457062, North : 17 km.*

Marco Polo of Tessera, North-East : 13 km ☎ 041 2606111.

to Lido San Nicolò from piazzale Roma (Tronchetto) daily (30 mn); to isola di Pellestrina-Santa Maria del Mare from Lido Alberoni daily (10 mn).

to Punta Sabbioni from Riva degli Schiavoni daily (40 mn) ; to islands of Burano (30 mn), Torcello (40 mn), Murano (1 h 10 mn) from Punta Sabbioni daily; to islands of Murano (10 mn), Burano (45 mn), Torcello (50 mn) from Fondamenta Nuove daily; to Treporti di Cavallino from Fondamenta Nuove daily (1 h); to Venezia-Fondamenta Nuove from Treporti di Cavallino daily (1 h) to islands of Murano (50 mn), Burano (15 mn), Torcello (5 mn) daily – Information : Actv, Cannaregio 3935 ✉ 30131 ☎ 041 2722111, Fax 041 5207135.

calle Ascensione-San Marco 71/f ✉ 30124 ☎ 041 5297811, info@turismovenezia.it, Fax 041 5230399 – Santa Lucia Railway station ✉ 30121 ☎ 041 5298727, Fax 041 5281246 – Marco Polo Airport ☎ 041 5298711.

Roma 528 ① – Bologna 152 ① – Milano 267 ① – Trieste 158 ①

Plans on following pages

Cipriani, isola della Giudecca 10, 5 minutes by private shuttle from San Marco's pier ✉ 30133 ☎ 041 5207744, *info@hotelcipriani.it, Fax 041 5203930*, heated, – – TV – 200. AE VISA JCB. FV h
18 March-23 October – **Meals** a la carte 90/130 see also rest. ***Cip's Club*** – **70 rm** 1250, 7 suites.
• Situated serenely in its own private gardens with heated pool, this exclusive and luxurious grand hotel never fails to satisfy even the most exacting guests. Two dining options ; either the elegant restaurant inside, or the romantic terrace.

Palazzo Vendramin e Palazzetto, isola della Giudecca 10 ✉ 30133 ☎ 041 5207744, *info@hotelcipriani.it,* Giudecca canal and San Marco – TV. AE VISA JCB. FV c
closed until 17 February – **Meals** (see hotel ***Cipriani*** and ***Cip's Club*** below) – **10 rm** 1250, 5 suites 3945.
• Of recent origin, these two prestigious annexes of the Cipriani offer the atmosphere of a luxurious private residence, with high staffing levels to ensure maximum pampering.

2 Aprile (V.) .... ET 85
Accademia (Pte dell') .... BV 3
Bandiera e Moro (Campo) .. FV 6
Capello (Ramo) .... FT 10
Gallina (Calle Larga G.) ..... FT 18
Leoncini (Pzetta dei) .... EV 21
Libertà (Pte della) .... AT 24
Nuova (Str.) .... DET 28
Orologio (Merceria dell') ..... EV 31
Pescaria (Campo della) ..... DT 34
S. Bartolomeo (Campo) .... ET 39
S. Giovanni Crisostomo (Salizzada) .... ET 43
S. Lorenzo (Calle Larga) .... FT 46
S. Marco (Calle Larga) ..... EV 49

S. Marco (Pzetta) .... EV 52	S. Simeon Profeta (Campo) .... BT 66	Santi Apostoli (Rio Terà dei) .... ET 75
S. Maurizio (Campo) ...... DV 55	S. Zulian (Merceria) .... EU 67	Seriman (Salizzada) .... ET 78
S. Moisé (Salizzada) .... EV 58	Sáuro (Campo N.) .... BT 76	Traghetto (Campo del) ..... DV 79
S. Salvador (Merceria) ..... EU 61	Sant' Angelo (Campo) ..... DV 70	Verona (Calle della) .... DV 82
S. Samuele (Campo) ...... BV 64		

San Clemente Palace, isola di San Clemente 1, 10 minutes by private shuttle from San Marco's pier 30124 041 2445001, *sanclemente@thi.it, Fax 041 2445800*, , Golf 3 coursis, , , heated, , – , rm, rm – 450.
Meals ***Ca' dei Frati*** Rest. *(closed Sunday and Monday)* (dinner only) a la carte 91/121 and ***Le Maschere*** Rest. a la carte 86/111 – **205 rm** 478,50/599, 32 suites.
• Luxury and the highest standards of comfort pervade throughout this charming establishment, located on an island 15 minutes by boat from Piazza San Marco. Splendid view from the Cà dei Frati restaurant.

Gritti Palace, campo Santa Maria del Giglio 2467, San Marco 30124 041 794611, *grittipalace@luxurycollection.com, Fax 041 5200942*, Grand Canal, , – , rm, . JZ a
Meals ***Club del Doge*** Rest. a la carte 110/160 – 50 – **86 rm** 819, 6 suites.
• The exclusive charm of bygone days in this delightful jewel of the Venetian hotel scene ; effusive yet discreet in its hospitality and luxury. Fine fabrics, marble and wooden ceilings in the very elegant restaurant.

Danieli, riva degli Schiavoni 4196, Castello 30122 041 5226480, *danieli@luxurycollection.com, Fax 041 5200208*, San Marco Canal, , – – 150. LZ a
Meals a la carte 80/103 – 50 – **233 rm** 426/880, 12 suites.
• The sumptuous lobby in the Venetian-style covered courtyard, once a market for oriental spices and textiles, prepares the visitor for this unique and charming hotel. Fine views from the rooftop restaurant with terrace for summer dining.

Bauer Il Palazzo e Bauer Hotel, campo San Moisè 1459, San Marco 30124 041 5207022, *booking@bauervenezia.it, Fax 041 5207557*, , , , – , rm, – 150. KZ h
Meals ***De Pisis*** Rest. a la carte 88/123 – 41,80 – **190 rm** 630/790, 58 suites.
• The prestigious original hotel, occupying an opulent historic building, has now been enhanced by the addition of an 18C palazzo providing even more luxurious accommodation. The restaurant offers dining on the terrace, with views over the Grand Canal.

Luna Hotel Baglioni, calle larga dell'Ascensione 1243, San Marco 30124 041 5289840, *luna.venezia@baglionihotels.com, Fax 041 5287160*, – – 150. rest KZ p
Meals ***Canova*** Rest. a la carte 54/85 – **108 rm** 419,10/700,70, 20 suites.
• Once probably a lodging for pilgrims and templars, this unostentatious hotel has a dignified and refined ambience ; early-18C frescoed ceiling by School of Tiepolo. The elegant restaurant offers well presented eclectic cuisine.

Monaco e Grand Canal, calle Vallaresso 1332, San Marco 30124 041 5200211, *malibox@hotelmonaco.it, Fax 041 5200501*, Grand Canal and Santa Maria della Salute Church – cam.. . KZ e
Meals ***Grand Canal*** Rest. a la carte 62/78 – **98 rm** 290/510, 8 suites.
• Occupying a panoramic position, this comfortable hotel has a refined ambience ; well-presented rooms and a new wing which is more modern in style. Simple elegance in the restaurant which has a summer terrace on the Grand Canal.

Grand Hotel dei Dogi , Fondamenta Madonna dell'Orto 3500, Cannaregio 30121 041 2208111, *reservation@deidogi.boscolo.com, Fax 041 722278*, , – – 50. rest by Madonna dell'Orto DT
Meals ***Il Giardino di Luca*** Rest. a la carte 90/140 – **68 rm** 650, 2 suites.
• Off the tourist trail, this 17C palazzo set in its own grounds overlooking the lagoon is now a fine hotel with elegant airy interiors. A simple yet stylish look in the restaurant, with exposed beams and stone floors.

Metropole, riva degli Schiavoni 4149, Castello 30122 041 5205044, *venice@hotelmetropole.com, Fax 041 5223679*, San Marco Canal, , , – – 100. rest FV t
Meals ***Met*** Rest. a la carte 70/85 – **66 rm** 390/485, 4 suites.
• A prestigious location for this smart hotel on the lagoon, which has an unusual collection of antique objects (crucifixes, clocks, armour). Restaurant with pleasant atmosphere and eclectic menu.

Londra Palace, riva degli Schiavoni 4171 30122 041 5200533, *info@hotelondra.it, Fax 041 5225032*, San Marco Canal, – . LZ t
Meals ***Do Leoni*** Rest *(closed January)* (booking essential) a la carte 45/63 – **53 rm** 575/585.
• An abundance of charm and fine detail in this recently refurbished Neo-classical-style hotel, which prides itself on having 100 windows overlooking the lagoon. Restaurant with panoramic summer dining terrace on the lagoon.

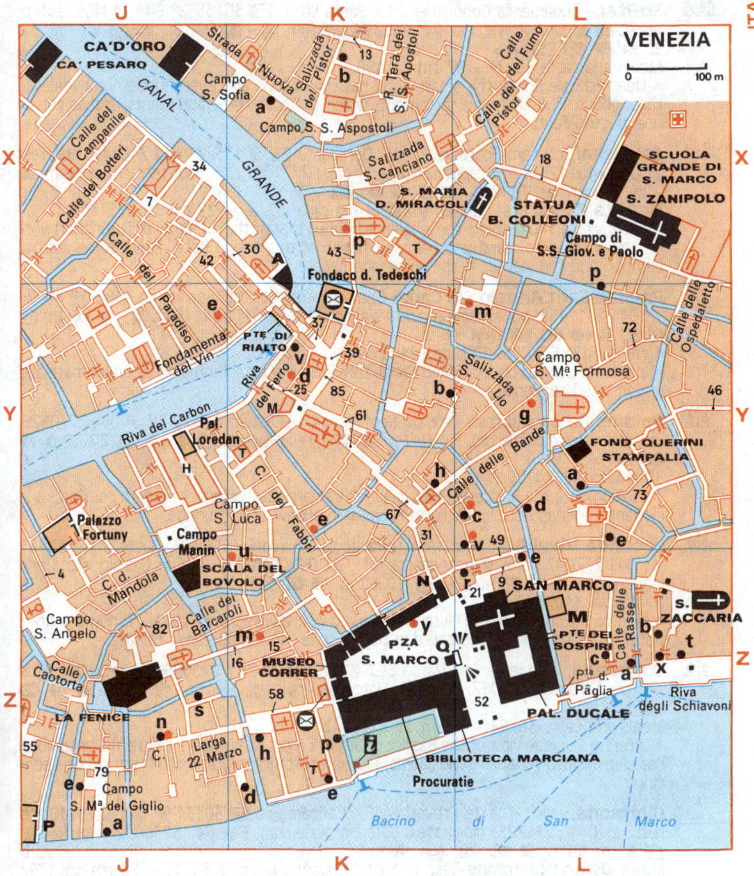

2 Aprile (V.) . . . . **KY** 85
22 Marzo (Calle Larga) . . . . . **JZ**
Avvocati (Calle degli) . . . . **JZ** 4
Beccarie (Campo delle) . . . . **JX** 7
Canonica (Calle di) . . . . **LZ** 9
Franceschi (Rio Terà dei) . . . **KX** 13
Frezzeria (Piscina di) . . . . **KZ** 16
Frezzeria . . . . **KZ** 15
Gallina (Calle Larga G.) . . . . . **LX** 18
Leoncini (Piazzetta dei) . . . . . **LZ** 21
Mazzini (Calle Larga) . . . . **KY** 25
Orefici (Ruga degli) . . . . **KX** 30
Orologio (Merceria dell') . . . . **KY** 31
Pescaria (Campo della) . . . . . **JX** 34
Pio X (Salizzada) . . . . **KY** 37
Rialto (Ponte di) . . . . **KY**
S. Bartolomeo (Campo) . . . . **KY** 39
S. Giovanni Crisostomo (Salizzada) . . . . **KX** 43
S. Lorenzo (Calle Larga) . . . . **LY** 46
S. Marco (Calle Larga) . . . . **LYZ** 49
S. Marco (Piazzetta) . . . . **LZ** 52
S. Marco (Pza) . . . . **KZ**
S. Maurizio (Campo) . . . . **JZ** 55
S. Moisé (Salizzada) . . . . **KZ** 58
S. Salvador (Merceria) . . . . . **KY** 61
S. Zulian (Merceria) . . . . **KY** 67
San Giovanni (Ruga Vecchia) . . . . **JX** 42
Santa Maria Formosa (Calle Lunga) . . . . **LY** 72
Santa Maria Formosa (Ruga Giuffa) . . . . **LY** 73
Traghetto (Campo del) . . . . . **JZ** 79
Verona (Calle della) . . . . **JZ** 82

The Westin Europa e Regina, corte Barozzi 2159, San Marco ✉ 30124
☎ 041 2400001, *RES075.europaregina@westin.com*, *Fax 041 5231533*,
< Grand Canal, 🍽, ⚓ – 🛗 ✈ ▤ TV – 👥 120. AE 💳 ① MC VISA JCB.
rest **KZ d**

Meals *La Cusina* Rest. a la carte 90/130 – ☕ 50 – **175 rm** 423/850, 9 suites.

◆ Marble, damask, glass and stucco work adorn the opulent, spacious interiors of this hotel on the Grand Canal, which, following refitting, offers high standards of comfort throughout. Open kitchen off the richly decorated restaurant ; canalside summer terrace.

Sofitel, Fondamenta Condulmer 245, Santa Croce ✉ 30135 ✆ 041 710400, *sofitel.venezia@accor-hotels.it, Fax 041 710394,* , , – , rm, – 50. AE VISA JCB BT k
Meals a la carte 50/77 – **97 rm** 490.
◆ Near Piazzale Roma, this smart hotel has classic style and every modern convenience throughout. The charming restaurant, which has cork trees and plants, makes for an unexpected feature.

Ca' Pisani, rio terà Foscarini 979/a, Dorsoduro ✉ 30123 ✆ 041 2401411 and rest ✆ 041 2401425, *info@capisanihotel.it, Fax 041 2771061,* , roof-terrace solarium, – , rm, AE VISA JCB. BV g
Meals *La Rivista* Rest. *(closed Monday)* a la carte 39/51 – **29 rm** 275/306.
◆ Occupying a 14C building, the ambience inside is that of the 1930s, with futurist artwork on the walls ; a bold and unusual combination at this design hotel. Polychrome marble, bamboo and red leather in the "wine and cheese bar".

Palazzo Sant'Angelo Sul Canal Grande without rest., San Marco 3488 ✉ 30124 ✆ 041 2411452, *palazzosantangelo@sinahotels.it, Fax 041 2411557,* – . AE VISA JCB. CUV d
4 rm 423,50/506, 10 suites 814.
◆ In a small palazzo on the Grand Canal, this charming establishment has an intimate and understated ambience.

Colombina without rest., calle del Remedio 4416, Castello ✉ 30122 ✆ 041 2770525, *info@hotelcolombina.com, Fax 041 2776044,* – – 20. AE VISA JCB LY d
32 rm 360/420.
◆ Looking onto the Bridge of Sighs canal, this smart hotel offers all modern comforts and elegant Venetian décor ; ask for a room with a view of the bridge.

Locanda Vivaldi without rest., riva degli Schiavoni 4150/52, Castello ✉ 30122 ✆ 041 2770477, *info@locandavivaldi.it, Fax 041 2770489,* < San Giorgio Island and lagoon, – – 50. AE VISA FV u
27 rm 310/440.
◆ Next to the church of the Pieta, this building where Vivaldi once studied is now a genteel hotel with large rooms decorated in period style ; small panoramic terrace.

Concordia, calle larga San Marco 367 ✉ 30124 ✆ 041 5206866, *venezia@hotelconcordia.it, Fax 041 5206775,* < San Marco Square – , rm, . AE VISA. rest LZ r
Meals a la carte 38/64 – **57 rm** 326/345.
◆ Offering a unique view of the Basilica of St Mark from its windows, this refurbished hotel has elegant 18C Venetian-style rooms. The new restaurant looks onto Piazzetta dei Leoncini.

Giorgione, calle Larga dei Proverbi 4587, Cannaregio ✉ 30131 ✆ 041 5225810 and rest. ✆ 041 5221725, *giorgione@hotelgiorgione.com, Fax 041 5239092* – rm. AE VISA JCB. KX b
Meals *Osteria Giorgione* Rest. *(closed Monday)* a la carte 35/49 – **76 rm** 179/265.
◆ Near the Ca' d'Oro, this smart hotel has a pleasant courtyard garden ; elegant antique furniture in both the public areas and the rooms.

Bellini without rest., lista di Spagna 116, Cannaregio ✉ 30121 ✆ 041 5242488, *reservation@bellini.boscolo.com, Fax 041 715193* – . AE VISA JCB. BT f
15 – **97 rm** 420/450.
◆ This refined hotel near the station has high standards of service ; rooms ranging from simple to sumptuous, some with views of the Grand Canal.

Saturnia e International, calle larga 22 Marzo 2398, San Marco ✉ 30124 ✆ 041 5208377, *info@hotelsaturnia.it, Fax 041 5207131,* – , rm, rm – 60. AE VISA JCB JZ n
Meals (see rest. ***La Caravella*** below) – **93 rm** 285/450.
◆ This delightful hotel, occupying a 14C patrician palace, has been run by the same family since 1908 ; period furnishings in the rooms and a sun deck with fine views.

Sant'Elena without rest., calle Buccari 10, Sant'Elena ✉ 30132 ✆ 041 2717811, *mailbox@hotelsantelena.com, Fax 041 2771569,* – rm AE VISA JCB by Riva dei 7 Martiri GV
76 rm 150/180.
◆ Situated in one of Venice greenest spots, this minimalist style hotel, a restored 1930s ecclesiastical building, offers high standards of comfort.

Bisanzio without rest., calle della Pietà 3651, Castello ✉ 30122 ☎ 041 5203100, *email@bisanzio.com, Fax 041 5204114,* – VISA JCB FV d
44 rm 260/280.
• In a quiet alley, this recently restored hotel is a successful fusion of ancient and modern ; smart interiors and welcoming rooms.

Savoia e Jolanda, riva degli Schiavoni 4187, Castello ✉ 30122 ☎ 041 5206644, *info@hotelsavoiajolanda.com, Fax 041 5207494,* ← San Marco Canal, – VISA. LZ x
Meals a la carte 33/64 (12 %) – **51 rm** 270/289, suite.
• Fine views over the Canale di San Marco and the island of San Giorgio from this attractively renovated hotel, occupying an 18C building ; richly elegant rooms. The fine restaurant also has a pleasant terrace.

Ai Mori d'Oriente without rest., fondamenta della Sensa 3319, Cannaregio ✉ 30121 ☎ 041 711001, *info@hotelaimoridoriente.it, Fax 041 714209,* – VISA by Madonna dell'Orto DT
55 rm 250/300, suite.
• Close to the church of Madonna dell to and its works by Tintoretto, this new hotel is furnished in Moorish style and occupies a historic palazzo.

Kette without rest., piscina San Moisè 2053, San Marco ✉ 30124 ☎ 041 5207766, *info@hotelkette.com, Fax 041 5228964,* – VISA. JZ s
63 rm 380/400, 2 suites.
• Close to La Fenice, this completely restored hotel overlooks a canal ; furnished to a high standard throughout.

Rialto, riva del Ferro 5149, San Marco ✉ 30124 ☎ 041 5209166, *info@rialtohotel.com, Fax 041 5238958,* ← Rialto bridge, – VISA JCB. KY v
Meals *(April-October)* a la carte 35/53 (12 %) – **79 rm** 206/232.
• A memorable view of the Rialto bridge from the windows of this elegant hotel with high service standards ; rooms in classic Venetian style. Modern restaurant and terrace looking onto the Grand Canal.

Gabrielli Sandwirth, riva degli Schiavoni 4110, Castello ✉ 30122 ☎ 041 5231580, *hotelgabrielli@libero.it, Fax 041 5209455,* – VISA JCB. rest FV b
closed 27 November-16 February – **Meals** 35/54 – **100 rm** 250/440.
• This genteel hotel in a historic palazzo on the lagoon has a terrace overlooking the Canale di San Marco, and a small courtyard garden, where meals are served during the summer.

Amadeus, lista di Spagna 227, Cannaregio ✉ 30121 ☎ 041 2206000, *amadeus@gardenahotels.it, Fax 041 2206020,* – , rest, – 120. VISA JCB. BT b
Meals ***Mirai*** Rest. *(closed Monday)* (dinner only) Japanese rest. a la carte 35/50 – **63 rm** 255/335.
• Located close to Santa Lucia station, this smart hotel has a garden and function room ; 18C Venetian-style furnishings in the rooms. Highly regarded and popular Japanese restaurant.

Montecarlo, calle dei Specchieri 463, San Marco ✉ 30124 ☎ 041 5207144, *mail@venicehotelmontecarlo.com, Fax 041 5207789* – VISA JCB LY c
Meals (see rest. ***Antico Pignolo*** below) – **48 rm** 190/235.
• Near Piazza San Marco, this hotel offers excellent service ; after a refit the rooms are of a good standard and tastefully decorated in traditional Venetian style.

Cà dei Conti without rest., fondamenta Remedio 4429, Castello ✉ 30122 ☎ 041 2770500, *info@cadeiconti.com, Fax 041 2770727,* – VISA LY a
15 rm 310/413.
• Near San Marco, this charming canalside hotel offers very comfortable accommodation furnished in 18C Venetian style.

Al Ponte dei Sospiri without rest., calle larga San Marco 381 ✉ 30124 ☎ 041 2411160, *info@alpontedeisospiri.com, Fax 041 2410268* – VISA JCB LZ e
8 rm 380/439.
• This newly opened hotel is in a 17C palazzo in a delightful position ; rooms with space to relax in, and rich fabrics and antique furniture.

Abbazia without rest., calle Priuli dei Cavalletti 68, Cannaregio ✉ 30121 ☎ 041 717333, *info@abbaziahotel.com, Fax 041 717949,* – ⇌ ▤ TV. AE ⓢ ⓞ ⓜ VISA JCB
BT a
50 rm ☕ 225/250.
◆ Occupying a restored Carmelite Friary, this charming hotel has a simple style, as evident in its bar, formerly a refectory with choir stalls and pulpit.

Ala without rest., campo Santa Maria del Giglio 2494, San Marco ✉ 30124 ☎ 041 5208333, *info@hotelala.it, Fax 041 5206390,* – ⇕ ⇌ ▤ TV ☏. AE ⓢ ⓞ ⓜ VISA JCB.
JZ e
85 rm ☕ 170/320.
◆ Situated in a little square not far from San Marco, this recently refurbished hotel has comfortable rooms and a small collection of arms and armour.

San Zulian without rest., campo de la Guerra 527, San Marco ✉ 30124 ☎ 041 5225872, *info@hotelsanzulian.it, Fax 041 5232265* – ⇕ ▤ TV ♿. AE ⓢ ⓞ ⓜ VISA JCB.
KY h
22 rm ☕ 230.
◆ A warm, welcoming hotel in the heart of the city which has recently been well refurbished ; good service and spacious well-equipped rooms with typical Venetian furnishings.

Antico Panada without rest., calle dei Specchieri 646, San Marco ✉ 30124 ☎ 041 5209088, *info@hotelpanada.com, Fax 041 5209619* – ⇕ ▤ TV. AE ⓢ ⓞ ⓜ VISA JCB
LY v
48 rm ☕ 185/260.
◆ A very central, charming hotel with attractive public areas such as its characteristic bar with wood panelling and antique mirrors ; welcoming period-style rooms.

Santa Chiara without rest., fondamenta Santa Chiara 548, Santa Croce ✉ 30125 ☎ 041 5206955, *conalve@doge.it, Fax 041 5228799* – ⇕ ▤ TV ♿ P. AE ⓢ ⓞ ⓜ VISA.
AT c
40 rm ☕ 137/220.
◆ Unique in Venice, this hotel is accessible by car and overlooks the Grand Canal. Welcoming rooms with classical furnishings ; newer, more spacious accommodation in the annexe.

Gardena without rest., fondamenta dei Tolentini 239, Santa Croce ✉ 30135 ☎ 041 2205000, *info@gardenahotels.it, Fax 041 2205020,* – ⇕ ▤ TV. AE ⓢ ⓞ ⓜ VISA JCB.
BT s
19 rm ☕ 175/265.
◆ Bright contemporary wall paintings decorate the public areas and rooms of this recently refurbished establishment, occupying a historic canalside building.

Pensione Accademia-Villa Maravage without rest., fondamenta Bollani 1058, Dorsoduro ✉ 30123 ☎ 041 5237846, *info@pensioneaccademia.it, Fax 041 5239152,* – ▤ TV. AE ⓢ ⓞ ⓜ VISA JCB.
BV b
27 rm ☕ 125/235.
◆ Situated in a pretty garden among the alleys and canals of old Venice, this 17C villa has a charm all of its own ; spacious well-presented interior decorated in period style.

American without rest., fondamenta Bragadin 628, Dorsoduro ✉ 30123 ☎ 041 5204733, *reception@hotelamerican.com, Fax 041 5204048,* – ⇌ ▤ TV ☏. AE ⓢ ⓜ VISA.
CV b
30 rm ☕ 250/270.
◆ A quiet canalside setting, smart public areas with wood panels and classical furnishings, and rooms in traditional Venetian style ; many with balconies overlooking the water.

Belle Arti without rest., rio terà Foscarini 912/A, Dorsoduro ✉ 30123 ☎ 041 5226230, *info@hotelbellearti.com, Fax 041 5280043,* – ⇕ ▤ TV ♿. AE ⓢ ⓜ VISA
BV g
65 rm ☕ 150/215.
◆ Near the Accademia, this comfortable modern hotel has a pleasant garden and a spacious interior ; the rooms offer every modern comfort.

Tre Archi without rest., fondamenta di Cannareggio 923, Cannaregio ✉ 30121 ☎ 041 5244356, *info@hoteltrearchi.com, Fax 041 5244356,* – ⇌ ▤ TV ♿. AE ⓢ ⓜ VISA
BT
24 rm ☕ 220/250.
◆ In Cannaregio where tourists are fewer and the ambience is authentically Venetian, this recently opened hotel has a courtyard garden, period furnishings and comfortable rooms.

La Calcina, fondamenta zattere ai Gesuati 780, Dorsoduro ✉ 30123 ☎ 041 5206466, *la.calcina@libero.it, Fax 041 5227045,* ← canal and Giudecca island, – ▤ TV. AE VISA JCB. BV f
Meals *(closed Monday)* a la carte 42/52 – **27 rm** 106/186.
◆ The relaxed atmosphere of old Venice pervades this charming hotel offering subtly understated hospitality ; bar with fine terrace on the Giudecca and a small, pleasant restaurant with canal views.

Santo Stefano without rest., campo Santo Stefano 2957, San Marco ✉ 30124 ☎ 041 5200166, *info@hotelsantostefanovenezia.com, Fax 041 5224460* – ▤ TV. AE VISA CV c
11 rm 220/280.
◆ Occupying a 15C tower in Campo Santo Stefano, this atmospheric hotel has very smart rooms with painted furniture and Murano glass lamps.

Canaletto without rest., calle de la Malvasia 5487, Castello ✉ 30122 ☎ 041 5220518, *info@hotelcanaletto.com, Fax 041 5229023* – ▤ TV. AE VISA KY b
38 rm 250.
◆ A comfortable hotel named after the famous artist who once lived here ; located between the Rialto and Piazza San Marco, the refurbished accommodation has period furnishings.

Locanda la Corte without rest., calle Bressana 6317, Castello ✉ 30122 ☎ 041 2411300, *info@locandalacorte.it, Fax 041 2415982* – ▤ TV. AE VISA. LY p
18 rm 140/230.
◆ Takes its name from its picturesque courtyard, where breakfast is served in summer ; rooms decorated in classic Venetian style.

Campiello without rest., calle del Vin 4647, Castello ✉ 30122 ☎ 041 5239682, *Fax campiello@hcampiello.it041 5205798* – ▤ TV. AE VISA. LZ b
15 rm 130/190.
◆ Close to Piazza San Marco and San Zaccaria, this small genteel hotel is run by a polite and efficient management ; limited public areas and well-presented rooms.

XXXX **Caffè Quadri,** piazza San Marco 120 ✉ 30124 ☎ 041 5222105, *quadri@quadrivenice.com, Fax 041 5208041,* ← – ▤. AE VISA. KZ y
closed Monday November-March – **Meals** (booking essential) a la carte 79/110.
◆ Situated in the smartest part of the city, this historic establishment boasts a wealth of stucco work, Murano glass and fine fabrics ; fine Venetian and other Italian cuisine.

XXX ✿ **Osteria da Fiore,** calle del Scaleter 2202/A, San Polo ✉ 30125 ☎ 041 721308, *reservation@dafiore.com, Fax 041 721343* – ▤. AE VISA JCB CT a
closed August, 25 December-15 January, Sunday and Monday – **Meals** (booking essential) seafood a la carte 79/108.
Spec. Grancevola con salsa al corallo. Ravioli di pesce. Filetto di branzino all'aceto balsamico tradizionale.
◆ Perennially fashionable and popular with locals and tourists alike, this welcoming modern restaurant serves original interpretations of traditional seafood dishes.

XXX **La Caravella** - Hotel Saturnia e International, calle Larga 22 Marzo 2397, San Marco ✉ 30124 ☎ 041 5208901, *caravella@hotelsaturnia.it, Fax 041 5205858,* , Typical rest. – ▤. AE VISA JCB. JZ n
Meals (booking essential) a la carte 63/89.
◆ The interior of this establishment is reminiscent of a galleon's lower decks with wood panelling everywhere ; meals also served on the outside terrace. Traditional dishes.

XXX **La Colomba,** piscina di Frezzeria 1665, San Marco ✉ 30124 ☎ 041 5221175, *colomba@sanmarcohotels.com, Fax 041 5221468,* – ▤ – 60. AE VISA JCB. KZ m
closed Wednesday and Thursday lunch except May-Ocotber – **Meals** a la carte 62/91 (15 %).
◆ Creative interpretations of traditional fare in this contemporary atmosphere ; walls hung with biennale artwork.

XX **Antico Pignolo,** calle dei Specchieri 451, San Marco ✉ 30124 ☎ 041 5228123, *info@anticopignolo.com, Fax 041 5209007,* , – ▤. AE VISA JCB. LY v
Meals a la carte 72/109 (12 %).
◆ A classically elegant restaurant at its best in the evenings ; traditional Venetian cuisine along seasonal lines. Good wine-list.

Fiaschetteria Toscana, San Giovanni Grisostomo 5719, Cannaregio ✉ 30121 ✆ 041 5285281, *Fax 041 5285521*, – . KX p
closed 24 July-13 August, Monday lunch and Tuesday – **Meals** a la carte 43/62.
◆ Good service and a lively ambience in this restaurant, which has nothing to do with Tuscany, serving robust meat and fish dishes. Outside dining in summer.

Do Forni, calle dei Specchieri 457/468, San Marco ✉ 30124 ✆ 041 5237729, *info@doforni.it, Fax 041 5288132* – . LY c
Meals (booking essential) a la carte 55/80 (12 %).
◆ This long established restaurant is popular with tourists and office workers alike ; a choice of rooms and ambiences, from intimate to spacious. Traditional local cuisine.

Cip's Club - Hotel Cipriani, fondamenta de le Zitelle 10, Giudecca ✉ 30133 ✆ 041 5207744, *info@hotelcipriani.it, Fax 041 2408519*, – . FV c
closed until 17 February – **Meals** a la carte 85/106.
◆ This restaurant has an informal yet elegant atmosphere and in summer offers dining outside on the Giudecca. Traditional meat and fish dishes, with Venetian specialities.

Hostaria da Franz, fondamenta San Giuseppe 754, Castello ✉ 30122 ✆ 041 5220861, *Fax 041 2419278*, – .
closed 11 November-24 December and 11 January-11 February – **Meals** seafood a la carte 56/78. by riva dei 7 Martiri GV
◆ Situated away from the tourist trail in the Castello district, this recently reopened family-run restaurant has a rustic ambience ; seafood cuisine.

Al Covo, campiello della Pescaria 3968, Castello ✉ 30122 ✆ 041 5223812, *Fax 041 5223812*, – . FV s
closed 15 December-15 January, Wednesday and Thursday – **Meals** 63/79.
◆ Close to Riva degli Schiavoni, this elegantly rustic establishment is very much in vogue and popular with tourists ; three variations to the a la carte menu.

Al Graspo de Ua, calle dei Bombaseri 5094/A, San Marco ✉ 30124 ✆ 041 5200150, *graspo.deua@flashnet.it, Fax 041 5209389* – . KY d
closed Monday – **Meals** (booking essential) a la carte 58/75 (12 %).
◆ A historic Venetian restaurant being restored to its former glory by an enthusiastic and competent new management ; meat and fish dishes.

Le Bistrot de Venise, calle dei Fabbri 4685, San Marco ✉ 30124 ✆ 041 5236651, *info@bistrotdevenise.com, Fax 041 5202244*, – . KY e
Meals a la carte 32/60 (15 %).
◆ A cosy ambience and closely spaced tables in this restaurant of character ; traditional cuisine and a tempting wine list (some available by the glass).

Ai Mercanti, corte Coppo 4346/A, San Marco ✉ 30124 ✆ 041 5238269, *info-aimercanti@libero.it, Fax 041 5238269*, – . KZ u
closed Sunday and Monday lunch – **Meals** a la carte 50/73.
◆ Centrally-located in a small and peaceful courtyard a little away from the main tourist trail, this smart, unostentatious restaurant mainly serves seafood.

Ai Gondolieri, fondamenta de l'Ospedaleto 366, Dorsoduro ✉ 30123 ✆ 041 5286396, *aigond@gpnet.it, Fax 041 5210075* – . DV d
closed Tuesday – **Meals** (dinner only July-August) (booking essential for dinner) beef dishes only a la carte 53/77.
◆ Next to the Guggenheim, this rustic establishment with wood-panelled walls concentrates on serving classic meat dishes from the Veneto region.

L'Osteria di Santa Marina, campo Santa Marina 5911, Castello ✉ 30122 ✆ 041 5285239, *ostsmarina@libero.it, Fax 041 5285239*, – . LY m
closed 1 to 17 August, 7 to 25 January, Sunday and Monday lunch – **Meals** seafood a la carte 45/62.
◆ A dedicated young management run this restaurant which, despite its no frills appearance, serves good, imaginative seafood alongside more traditional fare.

Vini da Gigio, fondamenta San Felice 3628/a, Cannaregio ✉ 30131 ✆ 041 5285140, *info@vinidagigio.com, Fax 041 5228597*, Inn serving food – . DT e
closed 15 to 31 August, 15 to 31 January and Monday – **Meals** (booking essential) a la carte 40/56.
◆ Located in the Cannaregio district, this simple restaurant has an informal rustic atmosphere with open kitchen serving meat and seafood ; good wine-list.

Trattoria alla Madonna, calle della Madonna 594, San Polo ✉ 30125 ☎ 041 5223824, *Fax 041 5210167*, Venetian trattoria – AE MC VISA JCB. JY e
closed 4 to 17 August, 24 December-January and Wednesday – **Meals** a la carte 29/40 (12 %).
◆ Near the Rialto, this traditional Venetian trattoria is always busy ; a simple yet animated environment in which to savour typical local dishes.

Anice Stellato, fondamenta della Sensa 3272, Cannaregio ✉ 30121 ☎ 041 720744 – MC VISA by fondamenta della Misericordia CDT
closed 9 to 15 March, 17 August-6 October, Monday and Tuesday – **Meals** (booking essential) a la carte 27/46.
◆ Off the beaten track, this restaurant is popular with Venetians, offering authentic seafood cuisine. Informal ambience and service ; friendly and efficient family management.

Alle Testiere, calle del Mondo Novo 5801, Castello ✉ 30122 ☎ 041 5227220, *Fax 041 5227220*, Inn serving food – MC VISA. LY g
closed 25 July-25 August, 24 December-12 January, Sunday and Monday – **Meals** (booking essential) seafood a la carte 48/66.
◆ This refined "bacaro" (wine bar) has simple wooden tables and a pleasant, informal atmosphere ; seafood only, prepared with care and imagination.

Osteria al Bacco, fondamenta Capuzine 3054, Cannaregio ✉ 30121 ☎ 041 721415, *Fax 041 717493*, *Inn serving food* – AE MC VISA JCB
closed 10 to 25 August, 10 to 25 January and Monday – **Meals** (booking essential) a la carte 28/42. by via Fondamenta della Misericordia CDT
◆ Away from the tourist trail in the unspoilt Cannaregio district, this restaurant retains its original early 20C fittings ; Venetian seafood dishes.

in Lido : *15 mn by boat from San Marco* KZ – ✉ *30126 Venezia Lido.*
Car access throughout the year from Tronchetto.
(June-September) Gran Viale S. M. Elisabetta 6 ☎ 041 5298711 :

The Westin Excelsior, lungomare Marconi 41 ☎ 041 5260201, *Fax 041 5267276*, rm, rm – 600. AE MC VISA JCB
15 March-20 November – **Meals** a la carte 85/119 – **196 rm** 610/816, 19 suites.
◆ In a beachfront location, this crenellated, vaguely Moorish style edifice has opulent charm and has been fashionable since opening in 1908. The elegant restaurant is in keeping with the splendour of the entire hotel.

Villa Mabapa, riviera San Nicolò 16 ☎ 041 5260590, *info@villamabapa.com*, *Fax 041 5269441*, – 60. AE MC VISA JCB
Meals *(closed lunch except June-October)* a la carte 41/61 – **70 rm** 180/299, suite.
◆ This genteel and spacious hotel occupies a 1930s villa and is directly managed by the proprietors ; tastefully furnished rooms. Classically elegant restaurant ; summer dining outside.

Quattro Fontane, via 4 Fontane 16 ☎ 041 5260227, *info@quattrofontane.com*, *Fax 041 5260726*, – – 40. AE MC VISA. rest
April-14 November – **Meals** a la carte 71/93 – **59 rm** 400/420.
◆ The evidence of over 60 years of collecting and travelling by its owners is on show throughout this hotel. A large and pleasant garden where guests may dine in summer.

Hungaria Palace Hotel, Gran Viale S.M. Elisabetta 28 ☎ 041 2420060, *info@hungaria.it*, *Fax 041 5264111*, – rm, – 60. AE MC VISA JCB
Meals (dinner only) a la carte 53/75 (15 %) – **79 rm** 220/378, 3 suites.
◆ One of the great names of the Lido, this establishment has, after a period of closure and extensive refurbishment, returned to centre stage of the Venetian hotel scene ; lots of charm and atmosphere. Elegant restaurant with classic dishes and plenty of seafood.

Le Boulevard without rest., Gran Viale S. M. Elisabetta 41 ☎ 041 5261990, *boulevard@leboulevard.com*, *Fax 041 5261917*, – AE MC VISA JCB
45 rm 230/360.
◆ Occupying a period building, this centrally located hotel has undergone recent refitting ; elegant public areas and functional rooms.

Villa Tiziana without rest., via Andrea Gritti 3 ☎ 041 5261152, *info@hoteltiziana.com*, *Fax 041 5262145* – AE MC VISA.
16 rm 215/265.
◆ This peaceful hotel in a refitted modern building has superior standards of comfort throughout (full courtesy pack, including bathrobes).

Trattoria Favorita, via Francesco Duodo 33 ✆ 041 5261626, *Fax 041 5261626,* – AE VISA JCB
closed 15 January-15 February, Monday and Tuesday lunch – **Meals** seafood a la carte 41/55.
◆ This family-run rustic trattoria has two welcoming rooms and space outside for summer dining ; seafood cuisine and Venetian specialities.

Al Vecio Cantier, via della Droma 76, località Alberoni South : 10 km ✉ 30011 Alberoni ✆ 041 5268130, *bahia2@libero.it, Fax 041 5268130,* – VISA JCB.
closed 15 November-15 December, 15 January-15 February, Monday and Tuesday, June-September open Tuesday dinner – **Meals** (booking essential) seafood a la carte 36/58.
◆ A friendly welcome and informal ambience at this trattoria with nautical-themed décor ; extremely fresh good quality ingredients evident in its seafood dishes.

in Murano *10 mn by boat from Fondamenta Nuove* EFT *and 1 h 10 mn by boat from Punta Sabbioni* – ✉ *30141* :

Ai Frati, Fondamenta Venier 4 ✆ 041 736694, *Fax 041 739346,* – VISA
closed 7 days in August, 15 days in February and Thursday – **Meals** a la carte 31/46 (12 %).
◆ In business as a bar since the mid-19C and serving food for half a century, this seafood trattoria is an important feature of Murano life ; summer dining on the canal terrace.

in Burano *50 mn by boat from Fondamenta Nuove* EFT *and 32 mn by boat from Punta Sabbioni* – ✉ *30012* :

Da Romano, via Galuppi 221 ✆ 041 730030, *info@daromano.it, Fax 041 735217,* – AE VISA JCB.
closed 15 December-5 February, Sunday dinner and Tuesday – **Meals** a la carte 38/62.
◆ Famed for its lace, the island of Burano has enjoyed this restaurant's cuisine for over 100 years. Contemporary art on the walls and flavoursome seafood.

Al Gatto Nero-da Ruggero, Fondamenta della Giudecca 88 ✆ 041 730120, *info@gattonero.it, Fax 041 735570,* , Typical trattoria – AE VISA
closed 15 to 30 November, 15 to 31 January and Monday – **Meals** a la carte 35/66.
◆ An informal and relaxed atmosphere in this classic trattoria with pleasant terrace ; Venetian dishes and seafood using only the finest ingredients.

in Torcello *45 mn by boat from Fondamenta Nuove* EFT *and 37 mn by boat from Punta Sabbioni* – ✉ *30012 Burano* :

Locanda Cipriani, piazza Santa Fosca 29 ✆ 041 730150, *info@locandacipriani.com, Fax 041 735433,* , – AE VISA
closed January-15 February and Tuesday – **Meals** 41/75 and a la carte 65/86.
◆ This trattoria has a charming, old-fashioned ambience and a refined, traditional menu ; dining in the garden in summer is a delightful experience.

Isola Rizza *37050 Verona* 562 G 15 – *pop. 2 924 alt. 23.*

Roma 487 – Ferrara 91 – Mantova 55 – Padova 84 – Verona 27.

Perbellini, via Muselle 130, exit highway 434 to Legnano ✆ 045 7135352, *ristorante@perbellini.com, Fax 045 7135899* – P. AE VISA
closed 7 August-1 September, 10 days in January, Sunday dinner, Monday and Tuesday lunch ; July-August also Sunday lunch – **Meals** (booking essential) 55 (lunch only except Bank Holidays) 110 and a la carte 86/119.
Spec. Wafer al sesamo con tartare di branzino, caprino all'erba cipollina, senzazioni di liquirizia. Risotto mantecato alla parmigiana, pere alla senape e sedano croccante. Guancia di vitello brasato su purè di patate con scaloppa di fegato grasso.
◆ Creative seafood drawing on the quality local produce ; a gourmet's delight in surprisingly elegant and exclusive surroundings, given the unlikely industrial location.

Rubano *35030* 562 F 17 – *pop. 13 859 alt. 18.*

Roma 490 – Padova 8 – Venezia 49 – Verona 72 – Vicenza 27.

Le Calandre, strada statale 11, località Sarmeola ✆ 049 630303, *alajmo@calandre.com, Fax 049 633000* – P. AE VISA.
closed 6 to 31 August, 25 December-20 January, Sunday and Monday – **Meals** (booking essential) a la carte 73/125.
Spec. Cappuccino di seppie al nero. Risotto allo zafferano con polvere di liquirizia. Degustazione di dolci.
◆ A classically modern, bright environment, this restaurant is renowned for its attention to detail in the preparation of imaginative and interesting cuisine.

Verona *37100* P 562 F 14 G. Italy - *pop. 256 110 alt. 59.*

Verona (closed Tuesday) at Sommacampagna ✉ 37066 ☎ 045 510060, Fax 045 510242, West : 13 km.

of Villafranca South-East : 14 km ☎ 045 8095666, Fax 045 8095706.

via degli Alpini 9 ☎ 045 8068680, iatbra@tiscali.it, Fax 045 8003638 – Porta Nuova Railway station ☎ 045 8000861, iatfs@tiscali.it – Villafranca Airport ☎ 045 8619163, iataeroporto@tiscali.it, Fax 045 8619163.

A.C.I. *via della Valverde 34 ✉ 37122 ☎ 045 595003, Fax 045 8619163.*

Roma 503 – Milano 157 – Venezia 114.

XXX ✿✿ **Il Desco,** via Dietro San Sebastiano 7 ✉ 37121 ☎ 045 595358, *Fax 045 590236* – VISA JCB.
closed Easter, 15 to 30 June, 25 December-10 January, Sunday and Monday ; open Monday dinner in July-August and December – **Meals** (booking essential) a la carte 76/112.

Spec. Millefoglie di coda di rospo e fegato grasso d'oca con salsa di alchechengi. Maltagliati con burrata melanzane, pomodoro e basilico. Filetto di San Pietro con porcini, carciofi fritti e salsa al limone e timo.

◆ One of the brightest stars in Italy's gastronomic firmament, this restaurant succeeds in combining an elegant, period atmosphere with creative and imaginative cuisine.

Norway

Norge

OSLO

PRACTICAL INFORMATION

LOCAL CURRENCY

Norwegian Kroner: *100 NOK = 12,28 euro (€) (Dec. 2004)*

TOURIST INFORMATION

The telephone number and address of the Tourist Information office is given in the text under **i**.

National Holiday in Norway: *17 May.*

FOREIGN EXCHANGE

In the Oslo area banks are usually open between 8.15am and 3.30pm but in summertime, 15/5 - 31/8, they close at 3pm. Saturdays and Sundays closed.
Most large hotels, main airports and Tourist information office have exchange facilities. At Oslo Airport the bank is open from 6.30am to 8pm (weekdays), 6.30am to 6pm (Saturday), 7am to 8pm (Sunday), all year round.

SHOPPING IN OSLO

Knitware, silverware, pewter and glassware.

Your hotel porter should be able to help you with information.

CAR HIRE

The international car hire companies have branches in each major city. Your hotel porter should be able to give details and help you with your arrangements. Cars can also be hired from the Tourist Information Office.

TIPPING IN NORWAY

A service charge is included in hotel and restaurant bills and it is up to the customer to give something in addition if he wants to.

The cloakroom is sometimes included in the bill, sometimes an extra charge is made.

Taxi drivers don't expect to be tipped. It is up to you if you want to give a gratuity.

SPEED LIMITS

The maximum permitted speed within built-up areas is 50 km/h - 31mph. Outside these areas it is 80 km/h - 50mph. Where there are other speed limits (lower or higher) they are signposted.

SEAT BELTS

The wearing of seat belts in Norway is compulsory for drivers and all passengers.

SMOKING

In Norway the law prohibits smoking in all restaurants and hotel public areas.

OSLO

Norge 711 M 7 – pop. 507 467.

Hamburg 888 – København 583 – Stockholm 522.

ℹ The Tourist Information Centre in Oslo, Fridtjof Nansens plass 5, ✉ 0160 ✆ 24 14 77 00, Fax 22 42 92 22 – KNA (Kongelig Norsk Automobilklub) Royal Norwegian Automobile Club, Cort Adelers gt 16 ✆ 21 60 49 00 – NAF (Norges Automobil Forbund), Storg. 2 ✆ 22 34 14 00.

18 Oslo Golfklubb ✆ 22 51 05 60.

✈ Oslo-Gardermoen NE: 45 km ✆ 64 81 20 00 – SAS Booking Office: ✆ 815 20 400 – Air Terminal: Galleri Oslo, Schweigaards gate 6.

⛴ Copenhagen, Frederikshavn, Kiel, Hirtshals : contact tourist information centre (see above).

See: Bygdøy ABZ Viking Ship Museum★★★ (Vikingskipshuset) ; Folk Museum★★★ (Norsk Folkemuseum) ; Fram Museum★★ (Frammuseet) ; Kon-Tiki Museum★★ (Kon-Tiki Museet) ; Maritime Museum★★ (Norsk Sjøfartsmuseum) – Munch Museum★★ (Munch-Museet) DY – National Gallery★★★ (Nasjonalgalleriet) CY **M**[1] – Vigelandsparken★ (Vigeland sculptures and museum) AX – Akershus Castle★ (Akershus Festning : Resistance Museum★) CZ **M**[2] – Oslo Cathedral (Domkirken: views★★ from steeple) CY – Ibsen-museet★ BY **M**[4].

Outskirts: Holmenkollen★ (NW: 10 km): view from ski-jump tower and ski museum BX – Sonia Henie-Onstad Art Centre★★ (Sonia Henie-Onstad Kunstsenter) (W: 12 km) AY.

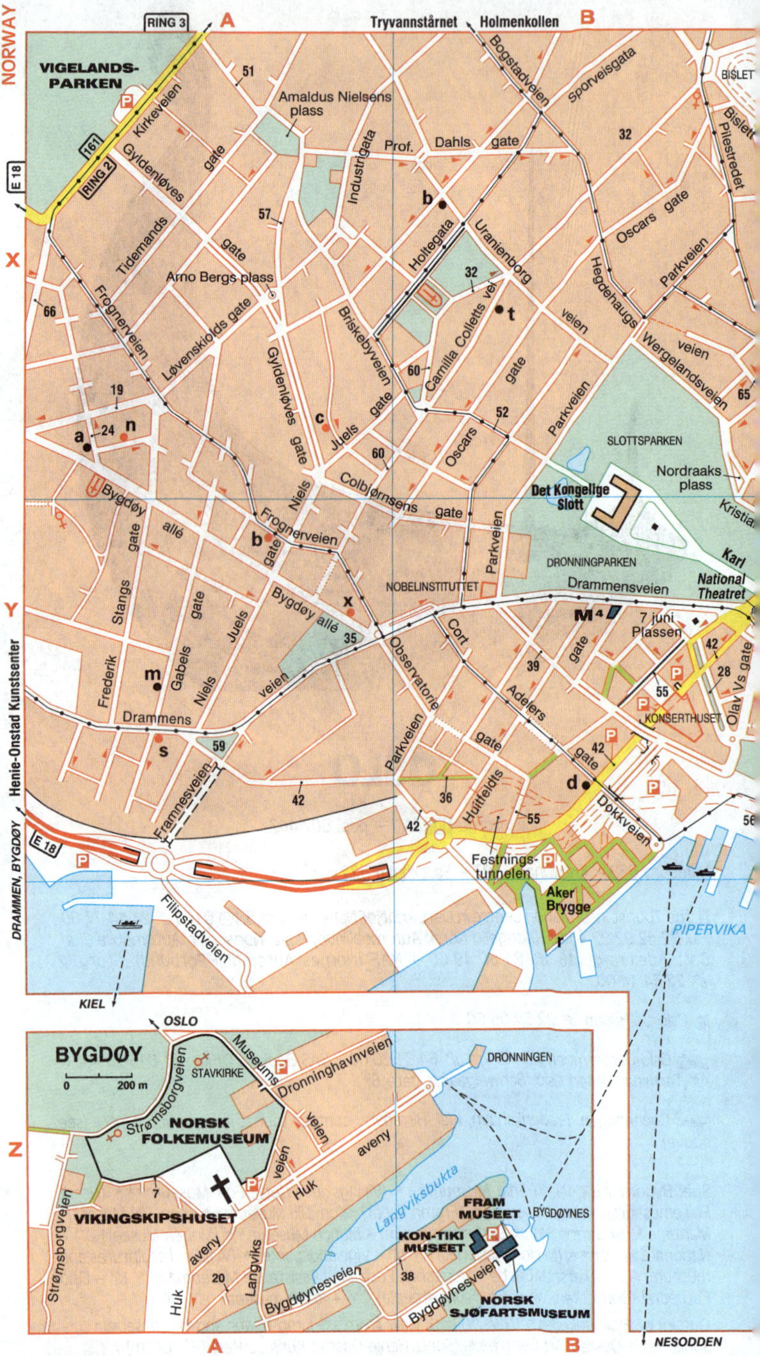

RING 3
A
Tryvannstårnet
Holmenkollen
B
VIGELANDS-PARKEN
Kirkeveien
Gyldenløves gate
Amaldus Nielsens plass
Prof. Dahls gate
Industrigata
Bogstadveien
Sporveisgata
BISLET
Bislett
Pilestredet
Oscars gate
Parkveien
Hegdehaugsveien
Wergelandsveien
Uranienborg
Holtegata
Camilla Colletts vei
Tidemands
Arno Bergs plass
Frognerveien
Løvenskiolds gate
Briskebyveien
Gyldenløves gate
Juels gate
Oscars gate
Parkveien
SLOTTSPARKEN
Nordraaks plass
Det Kongelige Slott
Kristian
Karl
National Theatret
DRONNINGPARKEN
Drammensveien
NOBELINSTITUTTET
Colbjørnsens gate
Niels
Frognerveien
Bygdøy allé
Stangs gate
Frederik
Gabels gate
Niels Juels
Drammens veien
Observatorie
Cort Adelers gate
7 juni Plassen
KONSERTHUSET
Olav Vs gate
Parkveien
Huitfeldts
Dokkveien
Festnings-tunnelen
Aker Brygge
PIPERVIKA
Framnesveien
Filipstadveien
Henie-Onstad Kunstsenter
DRAMMEN, BYGDØY
E 18
RING 2
KIEL
NESODDEN
OSLO
BYGDØY
0
200 m
STAVKIRKE
Museumsveien
Dronninghavnveien
DRONNINGEN
Strømsborgveien
NORSK FOLKEMUSEUM
VIKINGSKIPSHUSET
Huk aveny
Langviksbukta
FRAM MUSEET
BYGDØYNES
KON-TIKI MUSEET
Langviks
Bygdøynesveien
NORSK SJØFARTSMUSEUM
X
Y
Z

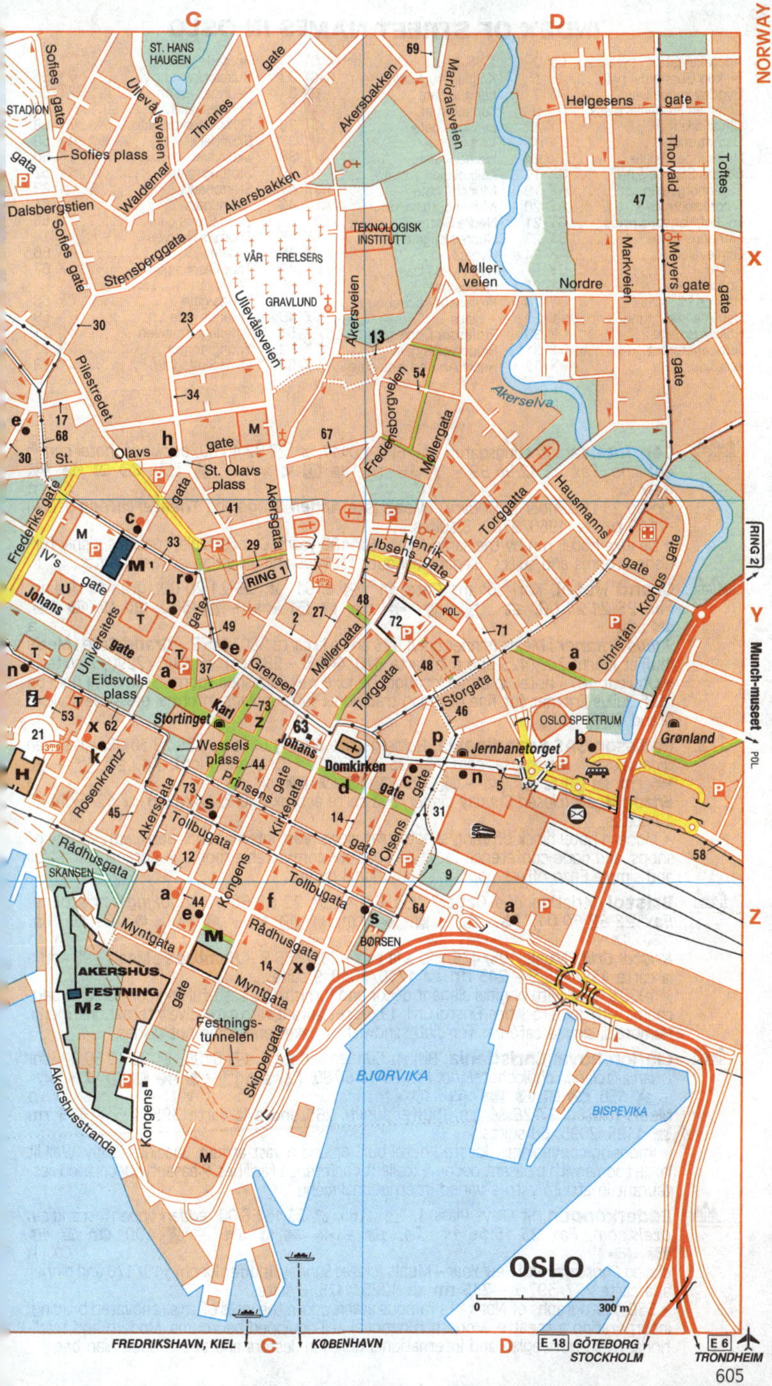
C
D
X
Y
Z
OSLO
0
300 m
ST. HANS HAUGEN
STADION
Sofies gate
Sofies plass
Ullevålsveien
Thranes gate
Akersbakken
Maridalsveien
Helgesens gate
Thorvald Meyers gate
Toftes gate
Waldemar
Dalsbergstien
Stensberggata
VÅR FRELSERS GRAVLUND
TEKNOLOGISK INSTITUTT
Møllerveien
Nordre gate
Markveien
Akersveien
Pilestredet
Fredensborgveien
Møllergata
Akerselva
St. Olavs gate
St. Olavs plass
Akersgata
Fredriks gate
Torggata
Hausmanns gate
Henrik Ibsens gate
RING 1
RING 2
Universitets gate
Johans gate
Grensen
Christian Krohgs gate
POL
Munch-museet
Eidsvolls plass
Stortinget
Karl Johans gate
Wessels plass
Storgata
OSLO SPEKTRUM
Grønland
Jernbanetorget
Domkirken
Rosenkrantz
Prinsens gate
Kirkegata
Tollbugata
Olsens gate
Rådhusgata
SKANSEN
Kongens gate
Myntgata
BØRSEN
AKERSHUS FESTNING
Festningstunnelen
Skippergata
BJØRVIKA
BISPEVIKA
Akershusstranda
FREDRIKSHAVN, KIEL
KØBENHAVN
E 18 GÖTEBORG STOCKHOLM
E 6 TRONDHEIM

INDEX OF STREET NAMES IN OSLO

Apotekergata . . . . CY 2
Biskop Gunnerus' gate . . . DY 5
Bygdøy kappellvei. . . . . AZ 7
Christian Frederiks plass . . DY 9
Christiana torv. . . . . CY 12
Damstredet . . . . CDX 13
Dronningens gate . . . . . . CYZ 14
Edvard Storms gate . . . . . . CX 17
Elisenbergveien . . . . AX 19
Fredriksborgveien. . . . . AZ 20
Fridtjof Nansens plass . . . . CY 21
Frimanns gate. . . . . CX 23
Gimleveien . . . . AX 24
Grensen . . . . CY
Grubbegata . . . . CY 27
Haakon VII's gate . . . . BY 28
Hammersborgtunnelen . . . CY 29
Holbergs Gate . . . . CX 30
Jernbanetorget. . . . . DY 31
Josefines gate . . . . ABX 32
Karl Johans gate . . . . . . BCDY
Kristian Augusts gate . . . BCY 33
Langés gate . . . . CX 34
Lapsetorvet. . . . . AY 35
Lassons gate . . . . BY 36
Lille Grensen. . . . . CY 37
Løchenveien. . . . . ABZ 38
Løkkeveien . . . . BY 39
Munchs gate . . . . CXY 41
Munkedamsveien . . . . . . ABY 42
Nedre Slottsgate . . . . CYZ 44
Nedre Vollgate . . . . CY 45
Nygata. . . . . DY 46
Olaf Ryes plass . . . . DX 47
Pløens gate. . . . . DY 48
Professor Aschehougs plass . . . . CY 49
Professor Dahls gate . . . . . AX 51
Riddervolds gate . . . . BX 52
Roald Amundsens gate . . . CY 53
Rosteds gate . . . . DX 54
Ruseløkkveien . . . . ABY 55
Rådhusplassen . . . . BCY 56
Schives gate. . . . . AX 57
Schweigaards gate . . . . . . DY 58
Skillebekk . . . . AY 59
Skovveien . . . . ABX 60
Stortingsgata. . . . . CY 62
Stortorvet . . . . CY 63
Strandgata. . . . . DZ 64
Sven Bruns gate. . . . . BX 65
Thomas Heftyes gate . . . . AX 66
Thor Olsens gate . . . . CX 67
Torggata. . . . . CDY
Tullins gate . . . . CY 68
Uelands gate . . . . DX 69
Vaterlandtunnelen . . . . DY 71
Youngstorget . . . . DY 72
Øvre Slottsgate. . . . . CY 73

Continental, Stortingsgaten 24-26, ✉ 0117, ☎ 22 82 40 00, *booking@hotel-continental.no, Fax 22 42 96 89* – |♦|, ⇔ rm, – 350. JCB. CY n
closed 23 December-2 January – **Meals** (see ***Annen Etage*** and ***Theatercaféen*** below) – **146 rm** 1960/2780, 8 suites.
◆ De luxe hotel, run by the same family for 100 years. Comfortable, spacious, richly furnished rooms and suites. Elegant banquet facilities and selection of restaurants.

Grand Hotel, Karl Johans Gate 31, ✉ 0101, ☎ 23 21 20 00, *grand@rica.no, Fax 23 21 21 00*, – |♦|, ⇔ rm, – 300. rest CY a
Julius Fritzner **: Meals** (dinner only) 525 and a la carte 580/615 ♀ – ***Grand Café*** **: Meals** (buffet lunch) 265/425 and a la carte 370/445 ♀ – **282 rm** 1845/2290, 7 suites.
◆ Opulent 1874 hotel, in prime location. De luxe well furnished rooms. Swimming pool on roof. Julius Fritzner for fine dining in traditional surroundings. Informal brasserie-style in Grand Café.

Radisson SAS Scandinavia, Holbergsgate 30, ✉ 0166, ☎ 23 29 30 00, *sales.scandinavia.oslo@radissonsas.com, Fax 23 29 30 01*, ≤ Oslo and Fjord, – |♦|, ⇔ rm, – 720. rest CX e
Enzo **: Meals** *(closed Sunday dinner)* a la carte approx 350 ♀ – **476 rm** 1245/1445, 12 suites.
◆ Modern hotel block offering spectacular views. Vast international lobby with variety of shops, and good conference facilities. Spacious comfortable rooms. Panoramic bar. Small and simple Enzo offers popular international dishes.

Bristol, Kristian IV's Gate 7, ✉ 0164, ☎ 22 82 60 00, *booking@bristol.no, Fax 22 82 60 01*, – |♦|, ⇔ rm, – 500. JCB. CY b
Bristol Grill **: Meals** 195/475 and a la carte 265/365 ♀ – ***Hambro's*** **: Meals** 295 and a la carte 435/585 ♀ – **243 rm** 1730/2030, 9 suites.
◆ 1920's hotel with original elegant décor and furnishings. Tasteful and comfortable bedrooms with good facilities. Bristol Grill, 1920s restaurant with extensive international menu. Hambro's, simple café-bar for club sandwiches, cakes and some hot dishes.

Clarion Royal Christiania, Biskop Gunnerus' Gate 3, ✉ 0106, ☎ 23 10 80 00, *christiania@clarion.choicehotels.no, Fax 23 10 80 80*, – |♦| ⇔ – 450. JCB. DY p
Meals *(closed 27-28 March)* (buffet lunch) 265 and a la carte 395/495 – **435 rm** 1195/2095, 68 suites.
◆ Imposing conveniently located hotel built around a vast atrium. Spacious lobby. Well lit large rooms with pleasant décor. Excellent conference facilities. Pleasantly decorated restaurant in atrium with a varied international menu.

Edderkoppen, St Olavs Plass 1, ✉ 0165, ☎ 23 15 56 00, *edderkoppen@scandic-hotels.com, Fax 23 15 56 11*, – ⇔ – 100. JCB CX h
closed Christmas and New Year – **Meals** *(closed Sunday)* (buffet lunch) 110/170 and dinner a la carte 277/397 ♀ – **235 rm** 1225/1425, 6 suites.
◆ 550 photographs of Norway's famous actors adorn the walls of this renovated building, incorporating a theatre. Modern functional well-equipped bedrooms. Modern and traditional fresh Norwegian and international dishes in Jesters and in the open plan bar.

Radisson SAS Plaza, Sonja Henies Plass 3, ✉ 0134, ✆ 22 05 80 00, *Fax 22 05 80 10,* < Oslo and Fjord, ⌂, ▣ – |‡|, ⇹ ▤ TV ✆ ♿ 🚗 – 🏛 950. MC AE ⓓ VISA JCB. ✗ rest DY b
Meals 190/550 and a la carte 300/535 ♀ – **654 rm** ☐ 1635/1995, 19 suites.
◆ Business-oriented hotel block, the tallest in Norway, with footbridge link to congress centre. Well furnished modern rooms. Superb views from top of tower. Panoramic bar. First floor restaurant and bar offering a modern menu of Mediterranean dishes.

Opera, Christian Frederiks plass 5, ✉ 0103, ✆ 24 10 30 00, *opera@rainbow-hotels.no, Fax 24 10 30 10,* <, 🏋, ⌂ – |‡|, ⇹ rm, ▤ TV ✆ ♿ – 🏛 240. MC AE ⓓ VISA. ✗ DZ a
closed 23 December-2 January – **Meals** (buffet lunch) 285/440 and dinner a la carte ♀ – **432 rm** ☐ 990/1825, 2 suites.
◆ A recent arrival in town, located next to the railway station and overlooking the harbour. Large modern building with functional yet contemporary furnishings and décor. Restaurant with huge windows affording panoramic views. Elaborate traditional cooking.

Rica Oslo, Europarådets Plass 1, ✉ 0154, ✆ 23 10 42 00, *rica.oslo.hotel@rica.no, Fax 23 10 42 10,* 🏋, ⌂ – |‡|, ⇹ rm, ▤ TV ✆ ♿ – 🏛 100. MC AE ⓓ VISA JCB. ✗ rest
Bjørvigen **: Meals** *(closed Sunday and Bank Holidays)* (buffet lunch) 185/350 and a la carte 313/438 – **173 rm** ☐ 1335/1535, 2 suites. DY c
◆ Modern hotel in three connected buildings close to station. Sound-proofed bedrooms have charming décor and paintings by local artists on walls. Cosy English style bar. Wood furnished restaurant offering a concise selection of traditional Norwegian dishes.

Rica Victoria, Rosenkrantzgate 13, ✉ 0121, ✆ 24 14 70 00, *booking.victoria@rica.no, Fax 24 14 70 01* – |‡|, ⇹ rm, ▤ TV ♿ 🚗 – 🏛 50. MC AE ⓓ VISA. ✗ rest
closed Christmas – **Meals** *(closed Saturday-Sunday)* (lunch only) (buffet only) 155 ♀ – **195 rm** ☐ 1295/1495, 4 suites. CY k
◆ Large modern hotel popular with business people, built around glazed-in atrium. Spacious comfortable rooms with sound-proofing, good quality fittings and modern facilities. Offers a simple menu of traditional cuisine on the enclosed patio.

Noble House without rest., Kongens Gate 5, ✉ 0153, ✆ 23 10 72 00, *noble.house @firsthotels.no, Fax 23 10 72 10,* 🏋, ⌂ – |‡| ⇹ TV ✆ 🚗. MC AE ⓓ VISA. ✗
53 rm ☐ 1399/1599, 16 suites. CZ e
◆ Charming hotel in good location. Spacious rooms with parquet floors, top quality furniture and modern facilities. All rooms equipped with kitchenette. Pleasant roof terrace.

Bastion without rest., Skippergaten 7, ✉ 0152, ✆ 22 47 77 00, *booking@hotelbast ion.no, Fax 22 47 77 99,* 🏋, ⌂ – |‡|, ⚓ ⇹ ▤ TV ✆ P – 🏛 50. MC AE ⓓ VISA CZ x
closed Christmas-New Year – **93 rm** ☐ 1295, 6 suites.
◆ Comfortable modern hotel handily placed for motorway. Welcoming rooms with good comforts and facilities. Furniture and paintings in part reminiscent of English style.

Rica H. Bygdoy Allé without rest., Bygdoy Allé 53, ✉ 0207, ✆ 23 08 58 00, *rica. hotel.bygdoey.alle@rica.no, Fax 23 08 58 08* – |‡| ⇹ TV ✆ – 🏛 40. MC AE ⓓ VISA
57 rm ☐ 1130/1695. AX a
◆ Neo-Gothic hotel (1890's) with elegant façade and period character in residential area. Period paintings in lounge and lobby. Beautifully decorated rooms with personal touch.

Stefan, Rosenkrantzgate 1, ✉ 0159, ✆ 23 31 55 00, *stefan@rainbow-hotels.no, Fax 23 31 55 55* – |‡| ⇹ ▤ TV ♿. MC AE ⓓ VISA. ✗ CY r
Meals a la carte approx 350 – **150 rm** ☐ 1100/1400.
◆ Modern hotel on convenient corner site. Rooms are well equipped with functional furniture and good facilties. Good variety of room types. Families and groups catered for. Eighth floor restaurant with small terrace. Popular buffets.

Gabelshus 🍃 without rest., Gabelsgate 16, ✉ 0272, ✆ 23 27 65 00, *booking.gabe lshus@comfort.choicehotels.no, Fax 23 27 65 60,* ⌂ – |‡| ⇹ TV ✆ P – 🏛 50. MC AE ⓓ VISA. ✗ AY m
closed Christmas – **112 rm** ☐ 1395/1595, 2 suites.
◆ Attractive early 20C vine-clad hotel with extension in quiet district. Modern public rooms. Large well-fitted bedrooms ; some on front with balconies, quieter at the rear.

Millennium, Tollbugaten 25, ✉ 0157, ✆ 21 02 28 00, *millennium@firsthotels.no, Fax 21 02 28 30* – |‡|, ⇹ rm, TV ♿. MC AE ⓓ VISA. ✗ CY s
Meals *(closed Sunday)* (dinner only) (coffee shop) a la carte 350/550 – **102 rm** ☐ 1349/1549, 10 suites.
◆ Functional modern hotel near harbour and restaurants. Internet access. Spacious well equipped rooms ; top floor with balconies ; quietest on inside although overlooked. Grill type kitchen open to room offers simple range of international bar snacks.

Børsparken without rest., Tollbugaten 4, ✉ 0152, ✆ 22 47 17 17, *booking.boersparken @comfort.choicehotels.no, Fax 22 47 17 18* – |‡| ⇹ TV ♿ – 🏛 75. MC AE ⓓ VISA. ✗
198 rm ☐ 1230/1430. CDZ s
◆ Modern functional chain hotel on corner site in city centre. Pleasant lobby opening onto tree-lined square. Compact practical rooms, well equipped for business clientele.

Byporten without rest., Jernbanetorget 6, 0154, 23 15 55 00, *byporten@scandic-hotels.com, Fax 23 15 55 11* – DY n
236 rm 1375/1575, 4 suites.
• Modern hotel in vast office/commercial centre block by station. Functional soundproofed rooms with environmentally friendly decor. Breakfast in nearby public restaurant.

Savoy, Universitetsgata 11, 0164, 23 35 42 00, *savoy@quality.choicehotels.no, Fax 23 35 42 01* – CY c
closed Christmas – **Meals** (see **restauranteik** below) – **93 rm** 1395/1795.
• Classic early 20C hotel in the city centre behind the museum. Stylish public areas. Spacious well-kept bedrooms with good facilities.

Norlandia Saga without rest., Eilert Sundtsgt. 39, 0259, 22 43 04 85, *service@saga.norlandia.no, Fax 22 44 08 63* – 25. BX b
closed 18-29 March and 16 December-2 January – **37 rm** 975/1175.
• Family-run hotel in quiet area. Cosy winter lounge with fire. Well lit rooms with classic furnishings and facilities ; rear rooms are quietest. Complimentary mid-week supper.

Spectrum without rest., Brugata 7, 0133, 23 36 27 02, *spectrum@rainbow-hotels.no, Fax 23 36 27 50* – DY a
closed 16 December-2 January – **151 rm** 995/1245.
• Conveniently located hotel in pedestrian street not far from station. Two styles of room : "old" are fairly functional ; "new" have more interesting décor and furniture.

Vika Atrium, Munkedamsveien 45, 0121, 22 83 33 00, *vika.atrium@rainbow-hotels.no, Fax 22 83 09 57,* – rm, – 240. rest BY d
Meals *(closed weekends and Bank Holidays)* (buffet lunch) 150/300 and a la carte 180/430 – **91 rm** 1295/1795.
• Located in large office block built around an atrium. Comfortable lobby lounge. Well serviced rooms with functional modern fittings. Good conference facilities.

Norrøna without rest., Grensen 19, 0159, 23 31 80 00, *norrona@rainbow-hotels.no, Fax 23 31 80 01* – – 120. CY e
closed 20-28 March – **93 rm** 1060/1310.
• Located right in the city centre, ideal for shopping and exploring on foot. Comfortable functional hotel with pleasant Scandinavian décor. Conference facilities. Busy coffee-shop popular with locals, offering selection of traditional local fare and soups.

Annen Etage (at Continental H.), Stortingsgaten 24-26, 0117, 22 82 40 70, *annen.etage@hotel-continental.no, Fax 22 42 70 09* – CY n
closed Easter, July, 23 December-2 January and Sunday – **Meals** (dinner only) 575/895 and a la carte 620/825.
Spec. Scallops with sunchoke, apple and truffle aigre-doux. Fillet of veal, glazed shin and red wine gravy. Apple soufflé, pain d'épice ice cream.
• Elegant formal dining room decorated in early 1920s style in a comfortable setting. Gourmet menu offers interesting range of attractively presented contemporary cuisine.

Bagatelle (Hellstrøm), Bygdøy Allé 3, 0257, 22 12 14 40, *bagatelle@bagatelle.no, Fax 22 43 64 20* – AY x
closed 1 week Easter, 10 July-8 August, 1 week Christmas and Sunday – **Meals** (booking essential) (dinner only) 680 and a la carte 720/840.
Spec. Grand menu dégustation. Coquilles St. Jacques 'sucre-salé'. Homard 'noir' aux endives.
• Highly reputed classic restaurant with colourful contemporary décor and numerous paintings on walls. Excellent traditional cuisine. Wine cellar may be viewed by diners.

Statholdergaarden (Stiansen), Rådhusgate 11, (entrance by Kirkegate) 1st floor, 0151, 22 41 88 00, *post@statholdergaarden.no, Fax 22 41 22 24* – CZ f
closed 20-28 March, 17 July-8 August, 23 December-3 January and Sunday – **Meals** (booking essential) (dinner only) 695/950 and a la carte 670/745 (see also ***Statholderens Krostue*** below).
Spec. Lobster and monkfish carpaccio. Venison glazed with black pepper, cranberry sauce. Praline tart, with cream cheese and lime ice cream.
• Fine 17C house offers elegant 1st floor dining room with original décor beneath beautiful period stucco ceilings, whose motifs reappear on the china. High quality cuisine.

Le Canard, President Harbitz Gate 4, 0259, 22 54 34 00, *lecanard@lecanard.no, Fax 22 54 34 10,* – AX c
closed Easter, Christmas, Monday 1 July-1 September and Sunday – **Meals** (dinner only) 565 and a la carte 645/890.
Spec. Grilled scallops with foie gras and orange syrup. Roast duck in two servings. Game and fowl in season.
• Tastefully decorated 1900 villa in residential district. Elegant dining room has beautiful antiques, a wall fresco and Baroque décor. Cuisine for the discerning gourmet.

XXX **Spisestedet Feinschmecker,** Balchensgate 5, ✉ 0265, ☎ 22 12 93 80, *kontakt@feinschmecker.no, Fax 22 12 93 88* – ⊭ ▤. MC AE ⓓ VISA. ✻ AX n
closed Easter, 3 weeks in summer and Sunday – **Meals** (booking essential) (dinner only) 595/845 and a la carte 640/720 ♀.
Spec. Baked turbot. Roast scallops and crawfish. Rack of lamb.
◆ Busy restaurant in residential building with inviting façade and tasteful colourful décor. Spacious dining room has warm, cosy atmosphere. Expertly cooked contemporary fare.

XXX **Oro,** Tordenskioldsgate 6A, ✉ 0160, ☎ 23 01 02 40, *post@restaurantoro.no, Fax 23 01 02 48* – ⊭ ▤. MC AE ⓓ VISA JCB. ✻ CY x
closed 23 December-3 January and Sunday – **Meals** (booking essential) 150/275 (lunch) and dinner a la carte 500/700 ♀ – ***Del i Oro*** **: Meals** - Tapas - 20/300 and a la carte 100/150 ♀.
◆ Elegant, modern designer décor in muted tones with an informal atmosphere. Open-plan kitchen offers inventive cuisine with a Mediterranean influence. Booking a must. Del i Oro, the adjoining tapas bar with a large counter displaying cold and some warm dishes.

XX **Det Gamle Raadhus,** Nedre Slottsgate 1, ✉ 0157, ☎ 22 42 01 07, *gamle.raadhus@gamle-raadhus.no, Fax 22 42 04 90*, 🏡 – MC AE ⓓ VISA JCB. ✻ CZ a
closed 1 week Easter, 3 weeks July, 1 week Christmas and Sunday – **Meals** (dinner only) 415/575 and a la carte 378/581 ♀.
◆ Well run restaurant operating for over a century located in Oslo's original City Hall, dating from 1641. Elegant rustic interior décor and English style atmosphere in bar.

XX **restauranteik,** Universitetsgata 11, ✉ 0164, ☎ 22 36 07 10, *eikefjord@restauranteik.no, Fax 22 36 07 11* – ⊭ ▤. MC AE ⓓ VISA. ✻ CY c
closed Easter, 4 weeks summer, Christmas, Sunday and Monday – **Meals** (dinner only) (set menu only) 335/445.
◆ Restaurant in striking minimalist style ; open plan kitchen with chef's table. Good value set menu of 3 or 5 courses of interesting dishes.

XX **Baltazar,** Dronningensgt 2-7, ✉ 0154, ☎ 23 35 70 60, *baltazar@baltazar.no, Fax 23 35 70 61*, 🏡 – ⊭ ▤. MC AE ⓓ VISA. ✻ CY d
closed 20-29 March, 17 May, 24 July-15 August, 21 December-3 January and Sunday – **Meals** - Italian - (dinner only) 475 and dinner a la carte 475/695 ♀ – ***Enoteca*** **: Meals** a la carte 316/381.
◆ In courtyard off Karl Johans gate beside cathedral. Serious Italian wine list ; small a la carte or concise chef's menu : home-made pasta, fine Italian produce and local fish. The rustic décor of the wine bar is just right for an informal lunch.

XX **Theatercaféen** (at Continental H.), Stortingsgaten 24-26, ✉ 0117, ☎ 22 82 40 50, *theatercafeen@hotel-continental.no, Fax 22 41 20 94* – ⊭. MC AE ⓓ VISA JCB. ✻ CY n
closed lunch July and Sunday – **Meals** (light lunch) 275/740 and a la carte 423/675 ♀.
◆ An institution in the city and the place to see and be seen. Elaborate lunchtime sandwiches make way for afternoon/evening brasserie specials.

XX **Mares,** Frognesveien 12B, ✉ 0263, ☎ 22 54 89 80, *mares@mares.no, Fax 22 54 89 85* – MC AE ⓓ VISA JCB. ✻ AY b
closed 1 week Easter and 23 December-4 January – **Meals** - Seafood - (booking essential) (dinner only) 435/675 and a la carte 345/585 ♀.
◆ Fish restaurant in traditional house in residential area. Well lit pleasant interior with modern designer décor, black and white photos on walls and local atmosphere.

X **Brasserie Hansken,** Akersgata 2, ✉ 0158, ☎ 22 42 60 88, *Fax 22 42 24 03* – ▤. MC AE ⓓ VISA JCB. ✻ CY v
closed 1 week Easter, 1 week Christmas and Sunday – **Meals** (booking essential) 275/595 and a la carte 444/613 ♀.
◆ Busy restaurant in lively district with strictly contemporary bistro-style décor and dark wood fittings. Good quality brasserie fare. Terrace bar on the square in summer.

X **A Touch of France,** Øvre Slottsgate 16, ✉ 0157, ☎ 23 10 01 65, *dartagnan@dartagnan.no, Fax 23 10 01 61*, 🏡 – ▤. MC AE ⓓ VISA JCB. ✻ CY z
closed Easter and 22 December-2 January – **Meals** (dinner only except Saturday and in summer) 320/500 and a la carte 345/490 ♀.
◆ French brasserie style dining room at D'Artagnan ; entrance from pedestrian street. Wall benches, bistro chairs and open kitchen at end of room. Interesting French dishes.

X **Statholderens Krostue,** Radhusgate 11, ✉ 0151, ☎ 22 41 88 00, *post@statholdergaarden.no, Fax 22 41 22 24* – ⊭. MC AE ⓓ VISA. ✻ CZ f
closed 20-28 March, 10 July-8 August, 23 December-3 January, Sunday and Monday – **Meals** 295/495 and a la carte 440/500.
◆ Three vaulted basement rooms with bistro-style décor and warm candle-lit ambience. Changing themed menus for dinner and a la carte for light lunch ; friendly service.

Lofoten Fiskerestaurant, Stranden 75, ✉ 0250, ✆ 22 83 08 08, *lofoten@fiskerestaurant.no, Fax 22 83 68 66,* ← – MC AE D VISA JCB. BZ r
Meals - Seafood - 200/460 and a la carte 342/550 ♀.
• A firm favourite with locals ; attractive, modern fjord-side restaurant at Aker Brygge. Chef patron offers a tempting array of seafood and shellfish.

Hos Thea, Gabelsgate 11, ✉ 0272, ✆ 22 44 68 74, *Fax 22 44 68 74* – MC AE D VISA JCB. AY s
closed 4 days Easter and 24-25 December – **Meals** (dinner only) 350/400 and a la carte 339/490 ♀.
• Discreet black façade in residential area conceals this typical little restaurant fitted out with simple Scandinavian style décor. Family atmosphere. Appealing menu.

at Lillestrøm *Northeast : 18 km by E 6 DZ :*

Arena, Nesgata 1, ✉ 2004, ✆ 66 93 60 00, *arena@rainbow-hotels.no, Fax 66 93 63 00,* – 1000. MC AE D VISA JCB. rest
closed 19 December-2 January – ***Madame Thrane* : Meals** (dinner only) a la carte 285/495 – ***Amfi* : Meals** (buffet lunch) 285/395 – **262 rm** 990/1745, 16 suites.
• Large modern hotel in trade fair centre with direct train access to airport and city centre. Spacious, contemporary rooms with every possible facility ; a few singles. Madame Thrane for interesting contemporary dishes. Buffet style service at the informal Amfi.

at Holmenkollen *Northwest : 10 km by Bogstadveien BX Sørkedalsveien and Holmenkollveien :*

Holmenkollen Park, Kongeveien 26, ✉ 0787, ✆ 22 92 20 00, *holmenkollen.park.hotel.rica@rica.no, Fax 22 14 61 92,* ← Oslo and Fjord, – 500. MC AE D VISA. rest
closed 22 December-4 January – ***De Fem Stuer* : Meals** (buffet lunch) 275/555 and dinner a la carte 480/685 ♀ – ***Galleriet* : Meals** *(closed Sunday dinner)* (buffet lunch) 275/295 and a la carte 305/375 ♀ – **209 rm** 1295/1395, 11 suites.
• Smart hotel near Olympic ski jump ; superb views. Part built (1894) in old Norwegian "dragon style" decorated wood. Chalet style rooms, some with balconies or views or saunas. International cuisine in De Fem Stuer. Informal Galleriet for a more popular menu.

at Oslo Airport *Northeast : 45 km by E 6 DZ at Gardermoen :*

Radisson SAS Airport, ✉ 2061, ✆ 63 93 30 00, *sales.airport.oslo@radissonsas.com, Fax 63 93 30 30,* – rm, – 220. MC AE D VISA JCB. rest
Meals a la carte 450/495 ♀ – **346 rm** 1750/1950, 4 suites.
• Ultra-contemporary business hotel on a semi-circular plan overlooking runway, but well sound-proofed. Rooms are a good size, well equipped and have varied décor. Modern restaurant offering a variety of international dishes to appeal to all comers.

Clarion Oslo Airport, West : 6 km, ✉ 2060, ✆ 63 94 94 94, *oslo.airport@clarionchoicehotels.no, Fax 63 94 94 95,* – rm, – 450. MC AE D VISA JCB. rest
Meals (buffet lunch) 250/295 and a la carte – **357 rm** 1395/1495, 1 suite.
• Modern Norwegian design hotel in wood and red tiles on star plan. Compact functional rooms with good modern facilities. Well equipped for conferences. Families at weekend. Vast restaurant offers a standard range of international dishes to cater for all tastes.

Trugstad Gård, Trugstadveien 10, ✉ 2034 Holter, Southwest : 10 km by Road 120 ✆ 63 99 58 90, *restaurant@trugstad.no, Fax 63 99 50 87* – MC AE D VISA JCB.
closed July and Christmas – **Meals** (booking essential) 280/535 and a la carte 495/650 ♀.
• Attractive and lovingly restored farmhouse yet only a short distance from the airport. Attentive and friendly service of modern set menu using the finest local ingredients.

Poland

Polska

Warsaw

PRACTICAL INFORMATION

LOCAL CURRENCY

Zloty : *100 PLN = 23,98 euro (€) (Dec. 2004)*

National Holidays in Poland: *1 and 3 May, 15 August, 1 and 11 November.*

PRICES

Prices may change if goods and service costs in Poland are revised and it is therefore always advisable to confirm rates with the hotelier when making a reservation.

FOREIGN EXCHANGE

It is strongly advised against changing money other than in banks, exchange offices or authorised offices such as large hotels and Kantor. Banks are usually open on weekdays from 8am to 6pm.

HOTEL RESERVATIONS

In case of difficulties in finding a room through our hotel selection, it is always possible to apply to the Tourist Office, (022) 94 31, Fax (022) 524 11 43, open 8am to 8pm.

POSTAL SERVICES

Post offices are open from 8am to 8pm on weekdays.

The **General Post Office** *is open 7 days a week and 24 hours a day : Poczta Glówna, Świetokrzyska 31/33.*

SHOPPING IN WARSAW

In the index of street names, those printed in red are where the principal shops are found. They are generally open from 10am to 7pm on weekdays and 9am to 3pm on Saturday.

THEATRE BOOKING

Your hotel porter will be able to make your arrangements or direct you to a theatre booking office: Kasy ZASP, Al Jerozolimskie 25 ☎ (022) 621 93 83, open on weekdays from 11am to 6.30pm.

TIPPING

Hotel, restaurant and café bills often do not include service in the total charge. In these cases it is usual to leave the staff a gratuity which will vary depending upon the service given.

CAR HIRE

The international car hire companies have branches in Warsaw. Your hotel porter should be able to give details and help you with your arrangements.

BREAKDOWN SERVICE

A 24 hour breakdown service is operated calling ☎ (022) 9637.

SPEED LIMIT

On motorways, the maximum permitted speed is 110 km/h – 68 mph, 90 km/h – 56 mph on other roads and 60 km/h – 37 mph in built up areas. In Warsaw the maximum speed limit is 31 mph, 50 km/h.

SEAT BELTS

In Poland, the wearing of seat belts is compulsory for drivers and all passengers.

WARSAW
(WARSAWA)

Polska 720 E 13 – Pop. 1 900 000.

Berlin 591 – Budapest 670 – Gdansk 345 – Kiev 795 – Moscow 1253 – Zagreb 993.

Warsaw Tourist Information Centres, Krakowskie Przedmieście 89, Al. Jerozolimskie 54 (in railway station) Warsaw Airport (Arrivals Hall) (022) 94 31 Fax (022) 524 11 43 info@warsawtour.pl.

First Warsaw Golf Club and Country Club, Rajszew 70, 05-110 Jabłonna (022) 782 45 55. Fax (022) 782 41 63

Warsaw Frederic Chopin Airport SW 10 km, by Żwirki i Wigury (022) 650 41 00.

Bus to airport: from major hotels in the town centre (ask the reception).

Polish Airlines (LOT) Al Jerozolimiskie 65/79, Warsaw (022) 577 99 52.

SIGHTS

OLD TOWN★★★ (STARE MIASTO) BX

Castle Square★ (Plac Zamkowy) BX 33 – Royal Palace★★ (Zamek Królewski) BX – Beer Street (Ulica Piwna) BX – Ulica Świetojańska BX 57 – St John's Cathedral★ (Katedra Św. Jana) BX – Old Town Marketplace★★★ (Rynek Starego Miasta) BX 54 – Warsaw History Museum★ (Muzeum Historyczne Warsawy) BX M[1] – Barbakan BX A.

NEW TOWN★ (NOWE MIASTO) ABX

New Town Marketplace (Rynek Nowego Miasta) ABX 36 – Memorial to the Warsaw Uprising (Pomnik Powstania Warzszawskiego) AX D.

ROYAL WAY★ (TRAKT KRÓLEWSKI)

St Anne's Church (Kościół Św. Anny) BX - Krakow's District Street (Krakowskie Przedmieście) BXY – New World Street (Nowy Świat) BYZ – Holy Cross Church (Św. Krzyoza) BY – National Museum★★ (Muzeum Narodowe) CZ.

LAZIENKI PARK★★★ (PARK ŁAZIENKOWSKI) FUV

Chopin Memorial (Pomnik Chopina) – Palace-on-the-Water★★ (Pałac na Wodzie) – Belvedere Palace (Belweder).

WILANÓW★★★ GV

ADDITIONAL SIGHTS

John Paul II Collection★★ (Muzeum Kolekcji im. Jana Pawła II) AY – Palace of Culture and Science (Pałac Kultury i Nauki): view★★ from panoramic gallery AZ.

D
PŁOCK
5
OLSZTYN, GDAŃSK
6
OSTROŁĘKA
E
E 77
7
WÓLKA WĘGLOWA
MŁOCINY
61
Modlińska
PIEKIEŁKO
Wybrzeże
Marymoncka
WAWRZYSZEW
Arkuszowa
RADIOWO
T
PARK
LEŚNY
BEMOWO
BIELANY
Wólczyńska
CHOMICZÓWKA
3
63
Jagiellońska
Gdyńskie
MARYMONT
7
PIASKI
ŻOLIBORZ
8
Śląskich
BOERNEROWO
CYTADELA
a
NOWE MIASTO
OGRÓD ZOOLOGICZNY
POWĄZKI
BEMOWO
STARE MIASTO
MURANÓW
Ratusz
Zamek Królewski
KOŁO
Okopowa
TRAKT
MŁYNÓW
Solidarności
R
M
T
U
T
Warszawska
Górczewska
Świętokrzyska
b
Powstańców
Al.
MIRÓW
Centrum
Towarowa
KRÓLEWSKI
M
Wolska
U
JELONKI
46
WOLA
ŚRÓDMIEŚCIE
E 30
2
ODOLANY
66
a
n
34
f
e
Połczyńska
Politechnika
POZNAŃ
4
ŁÓDŹ
Wawelska
Al.
Armii
4
OCHOTA
a
h
Pole Mokotowskie
STARE
Jerozolimskie
Grójecka
Wigury
Puławska
Racławicka
40
RAKÓW
Łopuszańska
URSUS
8
WYGLĘDOW
Wierzbno
V
Al.
WŁOCHY
p
634
34
a
F.
Hynka
MICHELIN
7
Wilanowska
719
OPACZ-KOLONIA
Krakowska
c
30
Al.
Żwirki
49
PRUSZKÓW
MICHAŁOWICE-OSIEDLE
E 77
7
8
e
SŁUŻEWIEC
Służew
RASZYN
Al.
WARSAW FREDERIC CHOPIN AIRPORT
WARSZAWA
Ursynów
0
2 km
79
3
8
E 67 WROCŁAW
KRAKÓW
D
E
GÓRA KALWARIA

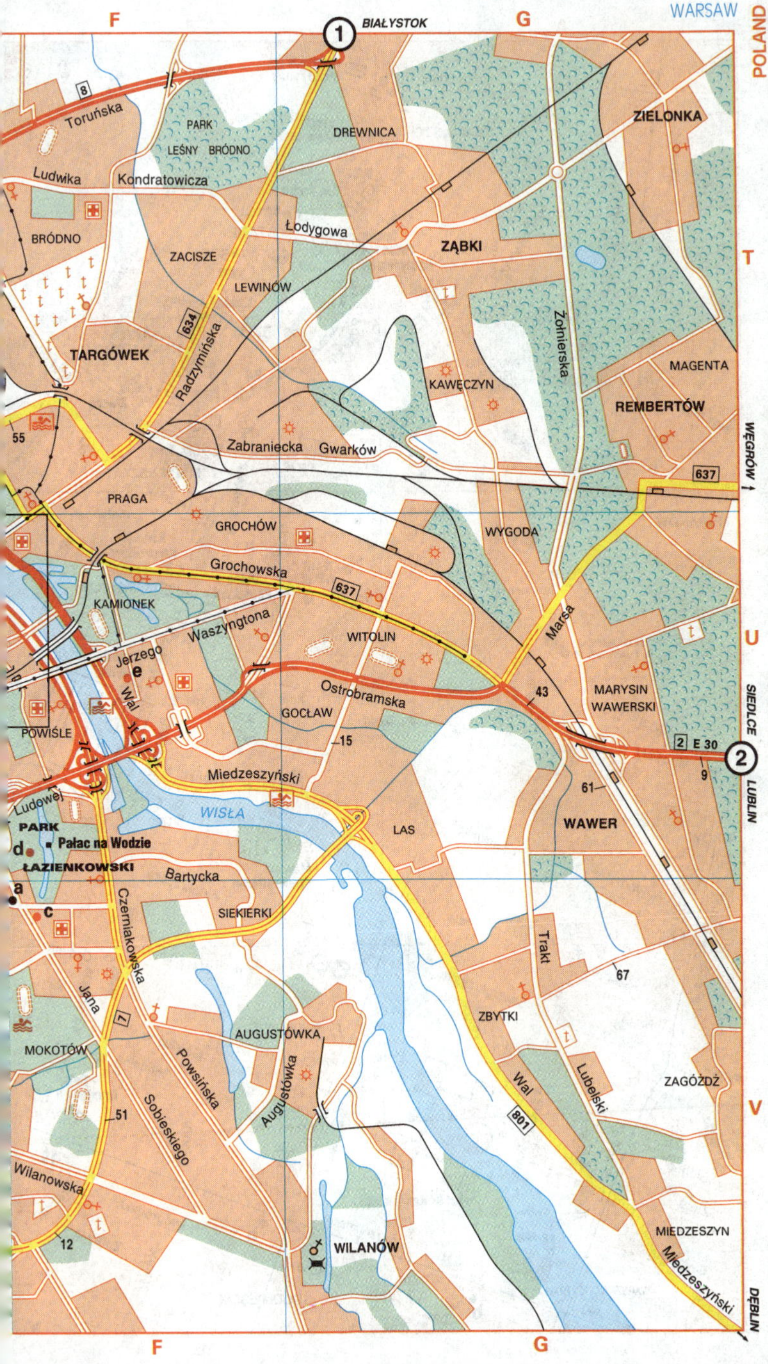
F
G
T
U
V
BIAŁYSTOK
1
2
8
Toruńska
PARK
LEŚNY BRÓDNO
DREWNICA
ZIELONKA
Ludwika
Kondratowicza
Łodygowa
BRÓDNO
ZACISZE
ZĄBKI
LEWINÓW
634
Radzymińska
TARGÓWEK
Żołnierska
MAGENTA
KAWĘCZYN
REMBERTÓW
55
Zabraniecka
Gwarków
637
WĘGRÓW
PRAGA
GROCHÓW
WYGODA
Grochowska
KAMIONEK
Waszyngtona
WITOLIN
Marsa
Jerzego
e
Wał
Ostrobramska
43
MARYSIN
WAWERSKI
SIEDLCE
POWIŚLE
GOCŁAW
15
2
E 30
9
Miedzeszyński
61
LUBLIN
Ludowej
WISŁA
LAS
WAWER
PARK
d
Pałac na Wodzie
ŁAZIENKOWSKI
a
Bartycka
c
Czerniakowska
SIEKIERKI
Trakt
67
Jana
7
ZBYTKI
AUGUSTÓWKA
MOKOTÓW
Powsińska
Augustówka
Lubelski
ZAGÓŹDŹ
Wał
801
51
Sobieskiego
Wilanowska
12
WILANÓW
MIEDZESZYN
Miedzeszyński
DĘBLIN

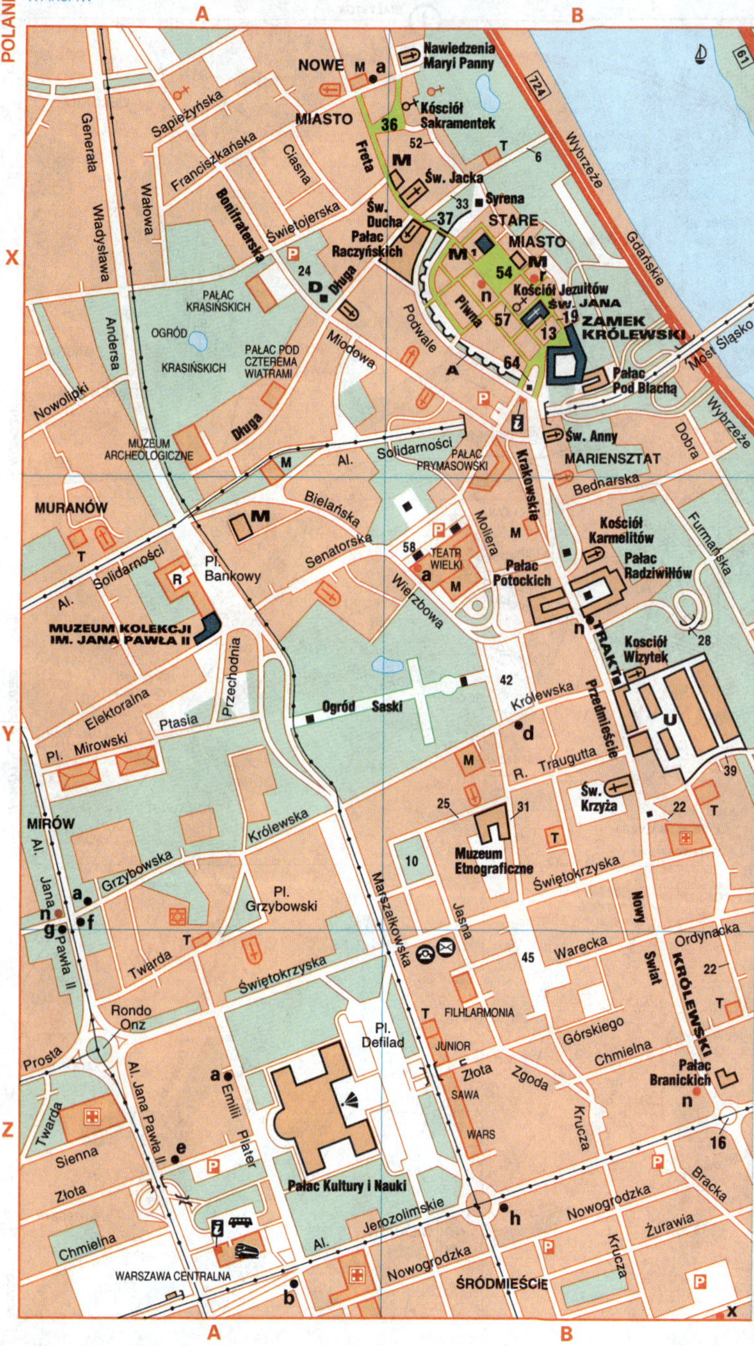
A
B
X
Y
Z
NOWE
MIASTO
Nawiedzenia Maryi Panny
Kościół Sakramentek
Sapieżyńska
Franciszkańska
Generała Władysława Andersa
Wałowa
Ciasna
Freta
Św. Jacka
Bonifraterska
Świętojerska
Św. Ducha
Pałac Raczyńskich
Syrena
STARE MIASTO
Wybrzeże Gdańskie
Kościół Jezuitów
Św. Jana
Piwna
ZAMEK KRÓLEWSKI
Most Śląsko
Pałac Pod Blachą
Podwale
Miodowa
Długa
PAŁAC KRASIŃSKICH
OGRÓD KRASIŃSKICH
PAŁAC POD CZTEREMA WIATRAMI
Nowolipki
MUZEUM ARCHEOLOGICZNE
Al. Solidarności
PAŁAC PRYMASOWSKI
Krakowskie
Św. Anny
MARIENSZTAT
Dobra
Wybrzeże
Bednarska
MURANÓW
Bielańska
Senatorska
Moliera
Kościół Karmelitów
Pałac Radziwiłłów
Furmańska
Pl. Bankowy
TEATR WIELKI
Pałac Potockich
MUZEUM KOLEKCJI IM. JANA PAWŁA II
Wierzbowa
TRAKT
Kościół Wizytek
Przechodnia
Elektoralna
Ptasia
Ogród Saski
Królewska
Przedmieście
Pl. Mirowski
R. Traugutta
Św. Krzyża
MIRÓW
Grzybowska
Muzeum Etnograficzne
Świętokrzyska
Al. Jana Pawła II
Pl. Grzybowski
Marszałkowska
Jasna
Nowy Świat
Ordynacka
Twarda
Warecka
KRÓLEWSKI
FILHARMONIA
Rondo Onz
Pl. Defilad
JUNIOR
Górskiego
Chmielna
Prosta
Złota
Zgoda
SAWA
Pałac Branickich
Emilii Plater
Krucza
WARS
Sienna
Pałac Kultury i Nauki
Bracka
Nowogrodzka
Al. Jerozolimskie
Żurawia
WARSZAWA CENTRALNA
ŚRÓDMIEŚCIE
724
61
36
37
52
33
6
24
54
57
13
19
64
58
42
28
39
25
31
22
10
45
16

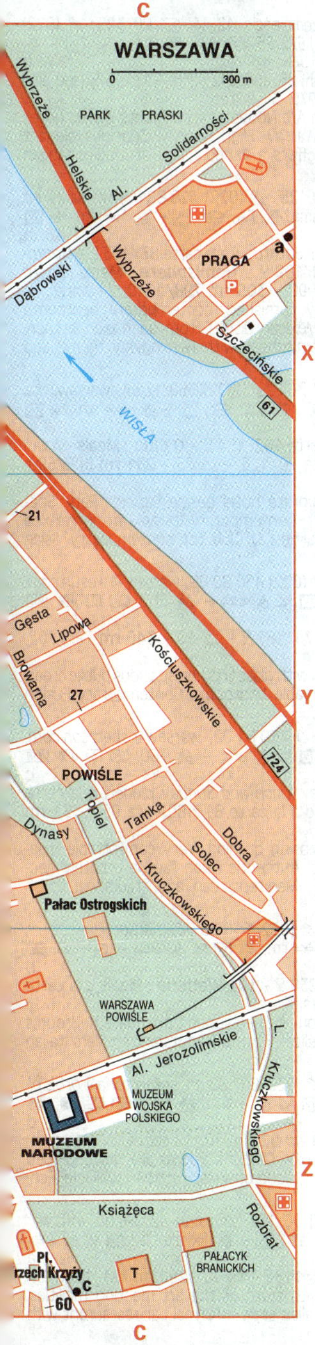

INDEX OF STREET NAMES IN WARSZAWA

Andersa (ul. Gen. Wł.) . AX
Arkuszova (ul.) . . . . DT
Armii Krajowej (al.) . . . DET 3
Armii Ludowej (al.) . . . EFU
Augustówka (ul.). . . . . FGV
Bankowy (pl.) . . . . AY
Bartycka (ul.) . . . . FU
Bednarska (ul.) . . . . . . BXY
Bielańscka (ul.) . . . . AY
Bitwy Warszawskiej (ul.) . . . . DU 4
Boleść (ul.) . . . . BX 6
Bonifraterska (ul.) . . . . . AX
Bracka (ul.) . . . . BZ
Broniewskiego (ul.). . . DET 7
Browarna (ul.) . . . . CY
Chmielna (ul.) . . . . ABZ
Ciasna (ul.) . . . . AX
Czecha (ul. Br.). . . . . GU 9
Czerniakowska (ul.) . . . . FV
Dąbrowskiego (pl.J. H.) BY 10
Defilad (pl.). . . . . ABZ
Długa (ul.) . . . . ABX
Dobra (ul.). . . . . BX
Dolina Służewiecka (ul.). . . . . EFV 12
Dynasy (ul.). . . . . CY
Dziekania (ul.). . . . . BX 13
Elektoralna (ul.) . . . . AY
Emilii Plater (ul.) . . . . AZ
Fieldorfa (ul. Gen. Emila) . . . . GU 15
Franciszkańska (ul.). . . . AX
Freta (ul.). . . . . AX
Furmańska (ul.) . . . . BY
Gaulla (Rondo Gen. Ch. De) . BZ 16
Gęsta (ul.) . . . . CY
Górczewska (ul.) . . . . . . DU
Górskiego (ul.) . . . . BZ
Grójecka (ul.) . . . . DEV
Grochowska (ul.) . . . . FGU
Grzybowska (ul.) . . . . . . AY
Grzybowski (pl.) . . . . AY
Hynka Franciszka (ul.) . . DV 18
Jagiellońska (ul.) . . . . . . ET
Jana Pawła II (al.) . . . . AYZ
Jasna (ul.) . . . . BYZ
Jerozolimskie (al.) . . ABCZ
Kanonia (ul.) . . . . BX 19
Karowa (ul.) . . . . CY 21
Kondratowicza (ul. L.) . . FT
Kopernika (ul. M.) . . . . BYZ 22
Krakowska (al.) . . . . DV
Krakowskie Przedmiescie (ul.) . . . . BXY
Krasińskich (pl.) . . . . AX 24
Kredytowa (ul.) . . . . BY 25
Królewska (ul.) . . . . ABY
Krucza (ul.) . . . . BZ
Kruczkowskiego (ul. L.) . . . . CYZ
Książęca (ul.) . . . . CZ
Łodygowa (ul.) . . . . . . FGT
Łopuszańska (ul.). . . . . . DV
Leszczyńska (ul.) . . . . . . CY 27
Lipowa (ul.). . . . . CY
Markiewicza (wiadukt) . BY 28
Marsa (ul.) . . . . GU
Marszałkowska (ul.) . ABYZ
Marynarska (ul.). . . . . . . EV 30
Mazowiecka (ul.) . . . . . . BY 31
Miodowa (ul.) . . . . . . ABX
Mirowski (pl.) . . . . AY
Modlińska (ul.) . . . . ET
Moliera (ul.) . . . . BY
Mostowa (ul.). . . . . BX 33
Niepodległości (al.) . . EUV 34
Nowego Miasta (rynek) . . . . ABX 36
Nowogrodzka (ul.) . . . . . BZ
Nowolipki (ul.) . . . . AX
Nowomiejska (ul.) . . . . . BX 37
Nowy Świat (ul.) . . . . . BYZ
Oboźna (ul.) . . . . BCY 39
Odyńca Antoniego (ul.) EV 40
ONZ (rondo) . . . . AZ
Ordynacka (ul.) . . . . BY
Ostrobramska (ul.) . . . . GU
Piłsudskiego (pl. J.) . . . . BY 42
Piwna (ul.) . . . . BX
Plowiecka (ul.) . . . . GU 43
Podwale (ul.) . . . . BX
Połczyńska (ul.) . . . . DU
Powsińska (ul.) . . . . FV
Powstańców Slaskich (ul) . . . . DTU
Powstańców Warszawy (pl.). . . . . BYZ 45
Prosta (ul.) . . . . AZ
Prymasa Tysiąclecia (al.) . . . . DU 46
Przechodnia (ul.) . . . . . . AY
Ptasia (ul.) . . . . AY
Puławska (ul.) . . . . EUV 48
Radzymińska (ul.). . . . . . FT
Rozbrat (ul.) . . . . CZ
Rzymowskiego (ul. W.). EV 49
Śląsko-Dąbrowski (most) . . . . BCX
Świętojańska (ul.) . . . . . BX 57
Świętojerska (ul.) . . . . . . AX
Świętokrzyska (ul.) . . ABYZ
Sapieżyńska (ul.) . . . . . . AX
Senatorska (ul.) . . . . . . ABY
Sienna (ul.) . . . . AZ
Sikorskiego (al. Gen. W.) . . . . FV 51
Sobieskiego Jana (ul.) . FV
Solec (ul.) . . . . CY
Solidarności (al.) . . . ACXY
Stara (ul.) . . . . BX 52
Starego Miasta (rynek). BX 54
Starzyńskiego (ul. Stefana) . . . . EFT 55
Tamka (ul.) . . . . CY
Teatralny (pl.) . . . . BY 58
Topiel (ul.). . . . . CY
Toruńska (ul.) . . . . EFT
Trakt Lubelski (ul.) . . . GUV
Traugutta (ul. R.) . . . . . . BY
Twarda (ul.) . . . . AYZ
Ujazdovskie (al.) . . . . CZ 60
Wał Miedzeszyński (ul.). . . . . FGUV
Wałowa (ul.). . . . . AX
Warecka (ul.) . . . . BYZ
Warszawska (ul.) . . . . . . DU
Waszyngtona Uerzego (ul.). . . . . FU
Wawelska (ul.) . . . . EU
Widoczna (ul.) . . . . GU 61
Wierzbowa (ul.) . . . . BY
Wilanowska (al.) . . . . . EFV
Wólczyńska (ul.). . . . . DT
Wolska (ul.) . . . . DU
Wybrzeże Gdańskie (ul.). . . . . BX, DET
Wybrzeże Helskie (ul.) . CX
Wybrzeże Kosciuszkowskie (ul.) . . . . BCXY
Wybrzeże Szczecińskie (ul.). CX
Wysockiego (ul. P.). . . . . ET 63
Zamkowy (pl.) . . . . BX 64
Zawiszy (pl.) . . . . EU 66
Zgoda (ul.) . . . . BZ
Złota (ul.) . . . . ABZ
Zołnierska (ul.) . . . . GT
Zurawia (ul.) . . . . BZ
Zwirki i Wigury (ul.) . . EUV
Zwoleńska (ul.) . . . . GV 67

Le Royal Meridien Bristol, Krakowskie Przedmieście 42-44, ✉ 00 325, ℘ (022) 551 10 00, *bristol@lemeridien.com.pl, Fax (022) 625 25 77,* – rm, – 180. BY n
Marconi **: Meals** - Mediterranean - (buffet lunch) 95 and a la carte 94/186 (see also ***Malinowa*** below) – 101 – **174 rm** 1655/1975, 31 suites.
◆ Imposing late 19C façade, partly decorated in Art Nouveau style fronts classic hotel, a byword for luxury and meeting place for Warsaw High Society. Spacious elegant rooms. Fairly informal restaurant with terrace offers a varied menu of Mediterranean fare.

Intercontinental, Ul. Emilii Plater 49, ✉ 00 125, ℘ (022) 328 88 88, *warsaw@interconti.com, Fax (022) 328 88 89,* City panorama, – rm, – 500. AZ a
Frida **: Meals** - Mexican - *(closed Sunday and lunch Saturday)* a la carte 83/103 – ***Downtown*** **: Meals** (lunch only) 59 and a la carte 74/108 – ***Hemisphere*** **: Meals** *(closed Monday)* (dinner only) a la carte 66/135 – 90 – **305 rm** 798/1040, 21 suites.
◆ Architecturally striking high-rise hotel. Richly furnished, contemporary bedrooms. Stunning 44th floor wellness centre. Frida for Mexican dishes from open plan kitchen. Cosmopolitan New York style in Downtown. Hemisphere with Hemingway theme and live music.

Hyatt Regency, Belwederska Ave 23, ✉ 00 761, ℘ (022) 558 12 34, *warsaw.reservations@hyattintl.com, Fax (022) 558 12 35,* – rm, – 350. FV a
Venti Tre **: Meals** - Italian - 85 (lunch) and a la carte 102/154 – ***Q Club*** **: Meals** - Asian - *(closed Saturday-Sunday)* (dinner only) a la carte 70/126 – 75 – **231 rm** 648/690, 19 suites.
◆ Striking glass fronted and ultra modern corporate hotel beside Lazienki Park. Spacious bedrooms with every facility and comfort. Contemporary Italian fare in relaxed Venti Tre. Open kitchen with wood fired specialities. Q Club for contemporary Asian menu.

The Westin, Al. Jana Pawła II 21, ✉ 00 854, ℘ (022) 450 80 00, *warsaw@westin.com, Fax (022) 450 81 11,* – rm, – 560. rest AYZ g
Fusion **: Meals** (buffet lunch) 65 and a la carte 74/161 – 90 – **346 rm** 792/902, 15 suites.
◆ Impressive modern façade, splendid glass atrium with glass lifts and spacious public areas. 'Heavenly beds' and modern facilities in comfortable bedrooms. Contemporary Fusion offers culinary delights as East meets West.

Sheraton, Ul. B. Prusa 2, ✉ 00 493, ℘ (022) 450 61 00, *warsaw@sheraton.com, Fax (022) 450 62 00,* – rm, – 700. CZ c
The Oriental **: Meals** - Asian - *(closed Saturday lunch and Sunday dinner)* a la carte 124/272 – ***Lalka*** **: Meals** (buffet lunch) 90 and a la carte 81/180 – 95 – **331 rm** 645/860, 19 suites.
◆ Up-to-date business hotel in well located imposing building. Very comfortable, spacious modern rooms with latest hi-tech facilities. Authentic Asian fare in ornately decorated Oriental. All-day bistro ; Old City mural ; Mediterranean and traditional Polish dishes.

Marriott, Al. Jerozolimskie 65-79, ✉ 00 697, ℘ (022) 630 63 06, *marriott@it.com.pl, Fax (022) 830 03 11,* City, – rm, – 700. AZ b
Parmizzano's **: Meals** - Italian - a la carte 133/230 – ***Lila Weneda*** **: Meals** a la carte 54/108 – 86 – **491 rm** 645/817, 31 suites.
◆ Modern high-rise business hotel opposite station. Well equipped up-to-date bedrooms with city views ; good facilities for business travellers. Formal Parmizzano's offers Italian fare. Classic Polish cooking in Lila Weneda.

Sofitel Victoria, Ul. Krølewska 11, ✉ 00 065, ℘ (022) 657 80 11, *sof.victoria@orbis.pl, Fax (022) 657 80 57,* – rm, – 650. rest BY d
Canaletto **: Meals** a la carte 99/200 – **329 rm** 924/1010, 12 suites.
◆ Large hotel overlooking Pilsudski Square and Saxon Gardens. Rooms are well equipped and comfortable with muted classic modern décor. Good business facilities available. Formal restaurant with Italian influence.

Radisson SAS Centrum, Grzybowska 24, ✉ 00 132, ℘ (022) 321 88 88, *info.warsaw@radissonsas.com, Fax (022) 321 88 89,* – rm, – 400. rest AY a
Latino Brasserie at Ferdy's **: Meals** a la carte 78/118 – 90 – **292 rm** 721, 19 suites.
◆ Popular corporate hotel in business district with state of the art meeting facilities. Modern bedrooms in maritime, Scandinavian or Italian style. Informal bar-restaurant with Latin American influences.

Le Régina, Ul. Kościelna 12, ✉ 00 218, ☎ (022) 531 60 00, *info@leregina.com, Fax (022) 531 60 01,* – |‡|, rm, – 100. VISA. AX a
La Rotisserie : **Meals** a la carte 128/252 – ☕ 90 – **59 rm** 1064/1645, 2 suites.
◆ Boutique hotel close to the OldTown ; neo-18C exterior but stylish, contemporary interior. Pleasant courtyard. Individually decorated, spacious high-tech bedrooms. Small, intimate restaurant offering original modern cuisine.

Jan III Sobieski, Plac Artura Zawiszy 1, ✉ 02 025, ☎ (022) 579 10 00, *hotel@sobieski.com.pl, Fax (022) 659 88 28,* – |‡|, rm, – 400. VISA JCB. rest EU a
Meals a la carte 84/186 ♀ – **392 rm** ☕ 761/1105, 35 suites.
◆ Up-to-date business hotel on busy thoroughfare. Pleasant first-floor terrace garden. Comfortable well equipped bedrooms. Good conference facilities. Restaurant offers classic menu of traditional local fare with international overtones.

Holiday Inn, Ul. Złota 48-54, ✉ 00 120, ☎ (022) 697 39 99, *holiday@orbis.pl, Fax (022) 697 38 99,* – |‡|, rm, – 220. VISA. rest AZ e
Symfonia : **Meals** a la carte 92/145 ♀ – ***Brasserie :*** **Meals** (buffet only) 89 ♀ – ☕ 69 – **326 rm** 709/795, 10 suites.
◆ Business hotel in the shadow of the Palace of Culture ; ideal for shopping. Comfortable bedrooms with good level of facilities. International cuisine in Symfonia accompanied by piano music. Brasserie for buffet lunch.

Mercure Fryderyk Chopin, Al. Jana Pawła II 22, ✉ 00 133, ☎ (022) 620 02 01, *mercure@perytnet.pl, Fax (022) 620 87 79,* – |‡|, rm, – 300. VISA JCB. rest AY f
Stanislas Brasserie : **Meals** a la carte 65/134 – ☕ 68 – **242 rm** 675/743, 7 suites.
◆ Up-to-date hotel located in business district, catering for business clientele. Practically appointed rooms. Comfortable brasserie-style restaurant for international dishes.

Novotel Centrum, Ul. Nowogrodzka 24-26, ✉ 00 511, ☎ (022) 621 02 71, *nov.warszawa@orbis.pl, Fax (022) 625 04 76* – |‡|, rm, – 450. VISA JCB BZ h
Meals (buffet lunch) 59 and a la carte 50/90 ♀ – ☕ 30 – **724 rm** 568/632, 10 suites.
◆ 1970s style high-rise hotel in central but noisy location on central shopping street. Contemporary style, well serviced bedrooms ; all with city views. Traditional style restaurant for international cuisine.

Rialto, Ul. Wilcza 73, ✉ 00 670, ☎ (022) 584 87 00, *info@hotelrialto.com.pl, Fax (022) 584 87 01,* – |‡| – 25. VISA JCB.
Meals (see ***Kurt Scheller's*** below) – ☕ 72 – **33 rm** 1089/1161, 11 suites. EU f
◆ Boutique hotel with superb Art Deco features in converted 1906 building in discreet location. Individually decorated bedrooms with the latest in comfort and facilities.

Hetman, Klopotowskiego 36, ✉ 03 717, ☎ (022) 511 98 00, *hetman@hotelhetman.pl, Fax (022) 618 51 39* – |‡|, rm, – 110. VISA. rest CX a
Meals (dinner only) a la carte 47/92 ♀ – **68 rm** ☕ 350/410.
◆ Modern hotel in a converted 19C apartment block, short walk over the river from the Old Town and city centre. Jacuzzi suite open to residents. Large up-to-date bedrooms. International cuisine in Hetman.

Ibis Stare Miasto, Ul. Muranowska 2, ✉ 00 209, ☎ (022) 310 10 00, *h3714@accor-hotels.com, Fax (022) 310 10 10* – |‡|, rm, – 40. VISA
l'Estaminet : **Meals** a la carte 67/109 – ☕ 28 – **333 rm** 259/310. ET a
◆ Modern hotel close to the Old Town with 24-hour bar and business centre. Spacious, comfortable bedrooms with en suite shower ; larger rooms on 6th floor with balconies. Bistro-style restaurant providing simple traditional European dishes.

Ibis Centrum, Al. Solidarności 165, ✉ 00 876, ☎ (022) 520 30 00, *h2894@accor.com, Fax (022) 520 30 30* – |‡|, rm, – 60. VISA EU b
l'Estaminet : **Meals** a la carte 57/90 – ☕ 26 – **189 rm** 249.
◆ Located at intersection of two main roads by Warsaw Trade Tower. Good size rooms are light and airy, well sound-proofed, with modern functional fittings. Bistro-style restaurant providing simple traditional European dishes.

Malinowa (at Le Royal Meridien Bristol H.), Krakowskie Przedmieście 42-44, ✉ 00 325, ☎ (022) 55 11 832, *Fax (022) 55 11 827* – . VISA JCB. BY n
Meals (dinner only) a la carte 185/376.
◆ Formal dining room with Art Nouveau décor and chandeliers adding opulence. Elaborate gourmet menu offers international cuisine with a strong French influence.

Belvedere, Ul. Agrykoli 1 (entry from Parkowa St), ✉ 00 460, ☎ (022) 841 22 50, *restauracja@belvedere.com.pl, Fax (022) 841 71 35,* ≤, – P. VISA JCB
Meals (booking essential) a la carte 82/174 ♀. FU d
◆ Elegant restaurant occupying late 19C orangery in Lazienkowski park. Dining room filled with statuesque plants. French-influenced International and Polish cuisine.

Restauracja Polska "Tradycja", Belwederska Ave 18A, 00 762, (022) 840 09 01, *restpolska@poczla.com.pl, Fax (022) 840 09 50,* – . JCB. FU c
Meals (booking essential) a la carte 57/113.
• Several homely dining rooms offer traditional Polish atmosphere ; live piano, candles and lace tablecloths. Professional service. Well prepared traditional Polish cooking.

Dom Polski, Ul. Francuska 11, 03 906, (022) 616 24 32, *restauracjadompolski@wp.pl, Fax (022) 616 24 88,* – . JCB. FU e
Meals a la carte 65/127.
• Elegant house in city suburb with pleasant terrace-garden. Comfortable dining rooms on two floors with welcoming ambience. Interesting well presented traditional cuisine.

Restauracja Polska, Ul. Nowy Swiat 21 (in the basement of the Polish Sculptors Union's Gallery), 00 029, (022) 826 38 77, *restpolska@poczla.com.pl, Fax (022) 828 31 32* – . JCB. BZ n
Meals a la carte 57/113.
• Atmospheric basement dining room with local style décor, colourful table linen and subdued lighting augmented by candles. Menu offers variety of traditional cuisine.

U Fukiera, Rynek Starego Miasta 27, 00 272, (022) 831 10 13, *ufukiera@ufukiera.pl, Fax (022) 831 58 08,* – . JCB. BX n
Meals a la carte 74/164.
• On historic central city square, well known restaurant with character ; 17C vaulted cellar and pleasant rear courtyard. Traditional Polish cuisine.

La Bohème, Plac Teatralny 1, 00 077, (022) 692 06 81, *mail.restauracja.laboheme@laboheme.com.pl, Fax (022) 692 06 84,* – . JCB BY a
Meals 60 (lunch) and a la carte 70/165.
• Elegant bar-restaurant with intimate vaulted cellar and attractive terrace located at Grand Theatre ; classic cuisine with international influences ; pre and post theatre menu.

Restauracja Polska, Chocimska 7, (022) 848 12 25, *Fax (022) 848 15 90,* – . JCB. EV a
Meals a la carte 57/113.
• Typical of the Restauracja Polska style ; traditional homely ambience ; professional service ; classic Polish cuisine.

Kurt Scheller's (at Rialto H.), Ul. Wilcza 73, 00 670, (022) 584 87 00, *restaurant@hotelrialto.com.pl, Fax (022) 584 87 01* – . JCB. EU f
Meals a la carte 80/135.
• Superb Art Deco style with reproduction 1930s furniture and posters. Modern slant on traditional Polish cooking by Kurt Scheller.

Casa Valdemar, Ul. Piekna 7-9, 00 539, (022) 628 81 40, *restauracja@casavaldemar.pl, Fax (022) 622 88 96,* – . EU e
Meals - Spanish influences - a la carte 47/127.
• Elegant Spanish style installation inside and out with pleasant wooden terrace to front. Authentic Spanish cooking ; try the meat and fish from the clay oven.

Flik, Ul. Puławska 43, 02 508, (022) 849 44 34, *restauracja@flik.com.pl, Fax (022) 849 44 06,* – . JCB EV h
Meals (buffet lunch) 48.50 and a la carte 67/113.
• Welcoming neighbourhood restaurant with Polish art collection, overlooking park. Good reputation and friendly service. Good quality well prepared traditional fare.

Swietoszek, Ul. Jezuicka 6-8, 00 281, (022) 831 56 34, *info@swietoszek.com.pl, Fax (022) 635 59 47* – BX r
Meals a la carte 68/99.
• Characterful restaurant in charming vaulted cellar in historic district. Rustic furniture, spot lights and candles add to ambience. Serves tasty traditional specialities.

Restaurant 99, Al. Jana Pawła II 23, 00 854, (022) 620 1999, *nn@restaurant99.com, Fax (022) 620 1998,* – . JCB AY n
Meals 59 (lunch) and a la carte 87/183.
• Lively noisy restaurant with informal atmosphere. Eclectic menu with dishes from wood burning oven and rotisserie. Stylish bar and lounge popular in the evening.

Absynt, Ul. Wspólna 35, 00 519, (022) 621 18 81, *absynt@siesta.com.pl, Fax (022) 622 11 01* – . BZ x
Meals - French - a la carte 79/133.
• Informal restaurant with a strong 'French' accent ; more intimate basement. Friendly service. Good value classic French dishes.

Inaba, Ul. Nowogrodzka 84-86, 02 018, (in the basement) (022) 622 59 55, *inaba@inaba.com.pl, Fax (022) 622 59 56* – . JCB. EU n
closed Easter and Christmas – **Meals** - Japanese - 60/190 and a la carte 42/87.
• Choose from the lively sushi-bar or the relaxed restaurant in this discreetly located basement restaurant. Authentic Japanese cuisine prepared with skill and precision.

at Warsaw Frederick Chopin Airport *Southwest : 10 km by Zwirki i Wigury :*

Courtyard by Marriott, Ul. Zwirki i Wigury 1, 00 906, (022) 650 01 00, *wcy@courtyard.com, Fax (022) 650 01 01,* – , rm, – 420. DEV e

Brasserie : **Meals** a la carte 50/122 – 77 – **219 rm** 580/600, 7 suites.

• Modern hotel opposite the airport entrance. Bar and cyber café with internet access ; conference facilities. Well-equipped modern bedrooms with effective sound proofing. Mezzanine brasserie offering an eclectic range of international dishes.

Airport H. Okęcie, Ul. 17 Stycznia 24, 02 146, (022) 456 80 00, *reservation@airporthotel.pl, Fax (022) 456 80 29,* , , – , rm, – 200. rest EV c

Mirage : **Meals** a la carte 51/101 – **173 rm** 513/625, 7 suites.

• Bright and modern corporate hotel 800 metres from the airport. Spacious meeting and bedrooms have both the international traveller and conference delegate in mind. Lively and popular 'Mirage' with open plan kitchen and buffet.

Lord, Al. Krakowska 218, 02 219, (022) 574 20 20, *okecie@hotellord.com.pl, Fax (022) 574 20 01,* , , – – 220. rest

Meals a la carte 60/80 – **87 rm** 310/350, 5 suites. DV a

• Bright and modern corporate hotel convenient for Warsaw Frederick Chopin Airport. Well kept and functional bedrooms. 6th floor café bar with terrace and city views. Elegant dining room offers classic Polish cooking.

Novotel Warszawa Airport, Ul. 1 Sierpnia 1, 02-134, (022) 575 60 00, *nov.airport@orbis.pl, Fax (022) 575 69 99,* , , , – , rm, – 300. rest EV p

Meals a la carte 53/117 – 45 – **269 rm** 477, 1 suite.

• Modern functional hotel not far from airport, which caters well for families and business people. Rooms are of adequate size, practical and well maintained. Private garden. Bright and modern restaurant specialises in international cuisine to suit all tastes.

Portugal

LISBON

PRACTICAL INFORMATION

LOCAL CURRENCY

1 euro (€) = 1,34 USD ($) (Dec 2004)

National Holiday in Portugal: *10 June.*

FOREIGN EXCHANGE

Hotels, restaurants and shops do not always accept foreign currencies and the tourist is therefore advised to change cheques and currency at banks, saving banks and exchange offices. The general opening times are as follows: banks 8.30am to 3pm (closed on Saturdays, Sundays, and Bank Holidays), money changers 9.30am to 6pm (usually closed on Sundays and Bank Holidays).

TRANSPORT

Taxis may be hailed when showing the green light or "Livre" sign on the windscreen. Metro (subway) network. In each station complete information and plans will be found.

SHOPPING IN LISBON

Shops and boutiques are generally open from 9am to 7pm. In Lisbon, the main shopping streets are: Rua Augusta, Rua do Carmo, Rua Garett (Chiado), Rua do Ouro, Rua da Prata, Av. de Roma, Av. da Liberdade, Shopping Center Amoreiras, Shopping Center Colombo.

TIPPING

Hotels, restaurants and café bills always include service in the total charge. Nevertheless it is usual to leave the staff a small gratuity which may vary depending upon the district and the service given. Doormen, porters and taxi-drivers are used to being tipped.

SPEED LIMITS

The maximum permitted speed on motorways is 120 km/h - 74 mph, on other roads 90 km/h - 56 mph and in built up areas 50 km/h - 37 mph.

SEAT BELTS

The wearing of seat belts is compulsory for drivers and all passengers.

THE FADO

The Lisbon Fado (songs) can be heard in restaurants in old parts of the town such as the Alfama, the Bairro Alto and the Mouraria. A selection of fado cabarets will be found at the end of the Lisbon restaurant list.

LISBON
(LISBOA)

(LISBOA) P 733 P 2 – *Pop. 662 782 – alt. 111.*

Paris 1785 – Madrid 624 – Bilbao 902 – Porto 310 – Sevilla 402.

Palácio Foz, Praça dos Restaudores ✉ 1250-187 ☎ 21 346 33 14, Fax 21 346 87 72 – Santa Apolónia Station (International Arrivals), ✉ 1100-105, ☎ 21 882 16 04, and airport ✉ 1700-111, ☎ 21 845 06 60, Fax 21 845 06 58 – A.C.P. Rua Rosa Araújo 49, ✉ 1250-195, ☎ 21 318 01 10, Fax 21 318 02 27.

18, 9 *Estoril* **W** *: 25 km ☎ 21 468 01 76, Fax 21 468 27 96 –* 18 *Lisbon Sports Club* **NW** *20 km ☎ 21 431 00 77 –* 18 *Club de Campo da Aroeira* **S** *: 15 km ☎ 21 297 91 10 Aroeira, Charneca da Caparica.*

Lisbon Airport **N** *: 8 km from city centre ☎ 21 841 35 00 – T.A.P., Pr. Marquês de Pombal 15-1º, ✉ 1979-134, ☎ 21 317 91 00 – Portugalia, Rua C – Edifício 70, Lisbon airport ✉ 1749-078, ☎ 21 842 55 00 and airport ☎ 21 841 50 00.*
Santa Apolónia ☎ 21 881 61 21 MX.

SIGHTS

VIEWS OVER LISBON

⩽★★ from the Suspension Bridge (Ponte 25 de Abril★) **S**: *by Av. da Ponte* EU – *☀★★ from Christ in Majesty (Cristo Rei)* **S**: *by Av. da Ponte* EU – *St. Georges Castle★★ (Castelo de São Jorge: ⩽★★★)* LX – *Santa Luzia Belvedere★ (Miradouro de Santa Luzia): ⩽★★* LY **L[1]** – *Santa Justa Lift★ (Elevador de Santa Justa): ⩽★* KY – *São Pedro de Alcântara Belvedere★ (Miradouro de São Pedro de Alcâtara): ⩽★★* JX **L[2]** – *Alto de Santa Catarina Belvedere★* JZ **A[1]** – *Senhora do Monte Belvedere (Miradouro da Senhora do Monte): ☀★★★* LV – *Largo das Portas do Sol★: ⩽★★* LY – *Church & Convent of Our Lady of Grace Belvedere (Igreja e Convento de Nossa Senhora da Graça, Miradouro★)* LX

MUSEUMS

Museum of Ancient Art★★★ (Museum Nacional de Arte Antiga; polyptych da Adoração de São Vicente★★★, Tentação de Santo Antão★★★, Japanese folding screens★★, Twelve' Apostles★, Anunciação★, Chapel★) EU **M[16]** – *Gulbenkian Foundation (Calouste Gulbenkian Museum★★★* FR, *Modern Art Centre★* FR **M[2]**) – *Maritime Museum★★ (Museu de Marinha: model boats★★★)* **W**: *by Av. 24 de Julho* EU – *Azulejo Museum★★ (Madre de Deus Convent: Church★★, chapter house★)* **NE**: *by Av. Infante D. Henrique* MX – *Water Museum EPAL★ (Museu da Água da EPAL)* HT **M[5]** – *Costume Museum★ (Museu Nacional do Traje)* **N**: *by Av. da República* GR – *Theatre Museum★ (Museu Nacional do Teatro)* **N**: *by Av. da República* GR – *Military Museum (Museu Militar; cellings★)* MY **M[15]** – *Museum of Decorative Arts★★ (Museu de Artes Decorativas: Fundação Ricardo do Espírito Santo Silva)* LY **M[13]** – *Archaeological Museum (Igreja do Carmo★)* KY **M[4]** – *São Roque Arte Sacra Museum★ (vestments★)* JKX **M[11]** – *Chiado Museum★ (Museu Nacional do Chiado)* KZ **M[18]** – *Music Museum★ (Museu da Música)* **N**: *by Av. da República* GR – *Rafael Bordalo Pinheiro Museum (ceramics★)* **N**: *by Av. da Republica* GR.

CHURCHES AND MONASTERIES

Cathedral★★ (Sé: gothic tombs★, grille★, tresor★) LY – *Hieronymite Monastery★★★ (Monasteiro dos Jerónimos): Santa Maria Church★★★ (vaulting★★, cloister★★★; Archaeological Museum: treasury★)* **W**: *by Av. 24 de Julho* EU – *São Roque Church★ (São João Baptista Chapel★★, interior★)* JX – *São Vicente de Fora Church (azulejos★)* MX – *Estrela Basilica★ (garden★)* EU **A[2]** – *Old Conception Church (Igreja da Conceição Velha: south front★)* LZ **D[1]** – *Santa Engrácia Church★* MX.

HISTORIC QUARTERS

Belém★★ (Culture Centre★) **W**: *by Av. 24 de Julho* EU – *The Baixa★★* JKXYZ – *Alfama★★* LY – *Chiado and Bairro Alto★* JKY.

PLACES OF INTEREST

Praça do Comércio★★ (or Terreiro do Paço) KZ – *Belém Tower★★★ (Torre de Belém)* **W**: *by Av. 24 de Julho* EU – *Marquis Fronteira Palace★★ (Palácio dos Marqueses de Fronteira: azulejos★★)* ER – *Rossio★ (station: neo-manuelina façade★)* KX – *Do Carmo st. and Garrett st. (Rua do Carmo and Rua Garrett)* KY – *Liberdade Ave★ (Avenida da Liberdade)* JV – *Edward VII Park★ (Parque Eduardo VII: ⩽★, greenhouse★)* FS – *Zoological Garden★★ (Jardin Zoológico)* ER – *Águas Livres Aqueduct★ (Aqueduto das Águas Livres)* ES – *Botanic Garden★ (Jardim Botánico)* JV – *Monsanto Park★ Belvedere (Parque Florestal de Monsanto: Miradouro: ☀★)* ER – *Campo de Santa Clara★* MX – *Santo Estêvão stairway and terrace★ (⩽★)* MY – *Ajuda Palace★ (Palacio da Ajuda)* **W**: *by Av. 24 de Julho* EU – *Arpad Szenes-Vieira da Silva Foundation★* EFS – *Boat trip on the river Tagus★ (⩽★★)* – *Vasco da Gama bridge★★* **NE**: *by Av. Infante D. Henrique* MX – *Lisbon oceanarium★★* **NE**: *by Av. Infante D. Henrique* MX – *East Station★ (Estação de Oriente)* **NE**: *by Av. Infante D. Henrique* MX.

INDEX OF STREET NAMES IN LISBOA

24 de Julho (Av.) . . . . FU
Afonso Costa (Av.) . . . . HR
Alecrim (R. do) . . . . JZ
Alegria (R. da) . . . . JX
Alexandre Herculano (R.) . . FT 7
Alfândega (R. da) . . . . LZ 10
Almeida e Sousa (R.) . . . . . ET
Almirante Reis (Av.) . . . . . . HR
Amoreiras (R. das) . . . . FT 13
Angelina Vidal (R.) LV
António Augusto de Aguiar (Av.) . . . . FR 15
António José de Almeida (Av.) . . . . GR 18
António Maria Cardoso (R.) JZ 21
António Pereira Carrilho (R.) HR 22
Arco do Carvalhão (R. do) . . ET
Arco do Cego (R. do) . . . . . GR 25
Arsenal (R. do) . . . . KZ
Artilharia Um (R. da) . . . . . FS 27
Atalaia (R. da) . . . . JY 28
Augusta (R.) . . . . KY
Augusto Rosa (R.) . . . . LY 31
Barão (R. do) . . . . LY 33
Barão de Sabrosa (R.) . . . . HR
Barata Salgueiro (R.) . . . . . FT 34
Barbadinhos (Calç. dos) . . . MV
Bartolomeu de Gusmão (R.) LY 36
Beneficência (R. da) . . . . . FR 40
Berna (Av. de) . . . . FR 42
Boavista (R. da) . . . . JZ
Bombarda (R.) LV
Borges Carneiro (R.) . . . . . FU
Braancamp (R.) . . . . FS 48
Cais de Santarém (R.) . . . . LZ 49
Calouste Gulbenkian (Av.) . ER
Calvário (L. do) . . . . EU 54
Campo das Cebolas . . . . . . LZ
Campo de Ourique (R. de) . ET 57
Campo de Santa Clara . . . MX
Campo dos Mártires da Pátria . . . . KV
Carmo (R. do) . . . . KY 63
Casal Ribeiro (Av.) . . . . GR 66
Cascais (R.) . . . . EU 67
Castilho (R.) . . . . FS
Cavaleiros (R. dos) LX
Chafariz de Dentro (L. do) . MY 71
Chão da Feira (R. do) . . . . . LY 70
Chiado (L. do) . . . . KY 72
Combro (Calç. do) . . . . JY
Comércio (Pr. do) . . . . KZ
Conceição da Glória (R.) . . . JX 75
Conde de Almoster (R.) . . . ER
Conde de Redondo (R.) . . . GS 78
Conde de Valbom (Av.) . . . . FR 76
Conselheiro F. de Sousa (Av.) . . . . ES 79
Correeiros (R. dos) . . . . KY 82
Corvos (R. dos) . . . . MX 85
Costa do Castelo LX
Cruzes da Sé (R.) . . . . LZ 90
Damasceno Monteiro (R.) . LV
Diário de Notícias (R. do) . . JY 91
Dom Afonso Henriques (Alam.) . . . . HR 93
Dom Carlos I (Av.) . . . . FU 94
Dom João da Câmara (Pr.) . KX 97
Dom Luís I (Pr.) . . . . JZ
Dom Pedro IV (Pr.) . . . . KX
Dom Pedro V (R.) . . . . JX
Domingos Sequeira (R.) . . . ET 106
Dona Estefânia (R. de) . . . . GS
Dona Filipa de Vilhena (Av.) GR 109
Duque de Ávila (Av.) . . . . . . GR
Duque de Loulé (Av.) . . . . . GS 111
Duque de Saldanha (Pr.) . . GR 112
Duque de Terceira (Pr.) . . . . JZ
Engenheiro Arantes e Oliveira (Av.) . . . . HR 114
Escola do Exército (R.) . . . . HS 117
Escola Politécnica (R. da) . . FT 120
Escolas Gerais (R. das) . . . . LY 118
Espanha (Pr. de) . . . . FR 124
Estrela (Calç. da) . . . . FU
Fanqueiros (R. dos) . . . . KY 127
Febo Moniz (R.) . . . . HS 129
Ferreira Borges (R.) . . . . ET 132
Figueira (Pr. da) . . . . KX
Fontes Pereira de Melo (Av.) . . . . GS 139
Forno do Tijolo (R.) . . . . HS 147
Francisco Gentil Martins (R.) . . . . ER
Francisco Sá Carneiro (Pr.) . HR
Funil (Trav. do) . . . . LY 148
Furnas (R. das) . . . . ER
Garcia de Horta (R.) . . . . . . FU 150
Garrett (R.) . . . . KY
General Domingos de Oliveira (Pr.) . . . . EU
General Roçadas (Av.) . . . . HS
Glória (Calç. da) . . . . JX 151
Glória (R. da) . . . . JX
Gomes Freire (R.) . . . . GS
Graça (Calç. da) . . . . LX 152
Graça (L. da) LX
Graça (R. da) LV
Guilherme Braga (R.) . . . . . . LY 154
Imprensa Nacional (R.) . . . . FT 157
Infante D. Henrique (Av.) . . MY
Infante Santo (Av.) . . . . EU
Instituto Bacteriológico (R. do) . . . . KV 160
Ivens (R.) . . . . KY
Jacinta Marto (R.) . . . . GS 162
Janelas Verdes (R. das) . . . EU 163
Jardim do Tabaco (R. do) . MY 165
João XXI (Av.) . . . . HR
Joaquim António de Aguiar (R.) . . . . FS 171
José Fontana (Pr.) . . . . GS
José Malhôa (Av.) . . . . ER
Lagares (R. dos) LX
Lapa (R. da) . . . . EU
Laranjeiras (Estr. das) . . . . . ER 172
Leite de Vasconcelos (R.) . . MX
Liberdade (Av. da) . . . . JV
Limoeiro (R. do) . . . . LY 175
Lóios (L. dos) . . . . LY
Luís de Camões (Pr.) . . . . . . JY
Madalena (R. da) . . . . KY
Manuel da Maia (Av.) . . . . . . HR 178
Maria Andrade (R.) . . . . HS 180
Maria da Fonte (R.) LV
Maria Pia (R.) . . . . ET
Marquês de Pombal (Pr.) . . FS
Martim Moniz (L.) . . . . KX 184
Mayer (Parque) . . . . JV
Miguel Bombarda (Av.) . . . . GR 186
Mirante (R. do) . . . . MX
Misericórdia (R. da) . . . . JY 190
Monte (Trav. do) LV
Morais Soares (R.) . . . . HR
Mouzinho de Albuquerque (Av.) . . . . HS
Norberto de Araújo (R.) . . . . LY 193
Nova do Almada (R.) . . . . . . KY
Olaias (Rot. das) . . . . HR
Ouro (R. do) . . . . KY
Paço da Rainha (L.) . . . . HS 195
Palma (R. da) . . . . KV
Paraíso (R. do) . . . . MX
Passos Manuel (R.) . . . . HS 198
Pedro Álvares Cabral (Av.) . FT 199
Penha de França (R. da) . . . HS
Poço dos Mouros (Calç. do) . . . . HR 204
Poço dos Negros (R. do) . . FU 205
Poiais de S. Bento (R.) . . . . FU 207
Ponte (Av. da) . . . . ET
Portas de Santo Antão (R.) KX
Portas do Sol (L. das) . . . . . LY 210
Possidónio da Silva (R.) . . . EU
Prata (R. da) . . . . KY
Presidente Arriaga (R.) . . . . EU 211
Príncipe Real (Pr. do) . . . . . JX 213
Prior (R. do) . . . . EU
Quelhas (R. do) . . . . FU
Ramalho Ortigão (R.) . . . . . FR
Rato (L. do) . . . . FT
Regueira (R. da) . . . . LY 214
Remédios (R. dos) . . . . MY
Restauradores (Pr. dos) . . . KX
Ribeira das Naus (Av. da) . . KZ
Ribeiro Sanches (R.) . . . . . . EU
Rodrigo da Fonseca (R.) . . . FS 219
Rodrigues de Freitas (L.) . . LX 220
Rosa (R. da) . . . . JY
Rovisco Pais (Av.) . . . . GR 222
S. Bernardo (R. de) . . . . FT 238
S. Caetano (R. de) . . . . EU
S. Domingos (L. de) . . . . KX 240
S. Filipe Neri (R. de) . . . . . . FT 241
S. Francisco (Calç. de) . . . . KZ 243
S. João da Mata (R.) . . . . . . FU 244
S. João da Praça (R. de) . . . LY 246
S. José (R. de) . . . . JV
S. Lázaro (R. de) . . . . KX
S. Marçal (R. de) . . . . FT 247
S. Miguel (R. de) . . . . LY 249
S. Paulo (R. de) . . . . JZ
S. Pedro (R. de) . . . . LY 250
S. Pedro de Alcântara (R. de) . . . . JX 252
S. Tiago (R. de) . . . . LY 253
S. Tomé (R. de) . . . . LX 255
S. Vicente (Calç. de) . . . . . . LX 256
S. Vicente (R. de) LX
Saco (R. do) . . . . KV
Sacramento (Calç. do) . . . . KY 225
Salitre (R. do) . . . . JV
Salvador (R. do) . . . . LY 226
Sampaio Bruno (R.) . . . . ET
Santa Catarina (R. de) . . . . . JY 228
Santa Justa (R. de) . . . . KY 229
Santa Luzia (Trav. de) . . . . . LY 231
Santana (Calç. de) . . . . KX
Santo André (Calç. de) LX
Santo António (R. de) . . . . . EU 232
Santo António da Sé (L.) . . . LY 233
Santo António dos Capuchos (R.) . . . . KV 234
Santo Estêvão (Escadinhas de) . . . . MY 236
Sapadores (R. dos) . . . . MV
Sapateiros (R. dos) . . . . KY 258
Saudade (R. da) . . . . LY
Século (R. do) . . . . JX
Senhora da Glória (R.) . . . . MV
Serpa Pinto (R.) . . . . KZ 262
Sodré (Cais do) . . . . JZ
Sol (R. do) . . . . FT 264
Telhal (R. do) . . . . KV
Terreiro do Trigo (R. do) . . . . LY 267
Vale de Sto António (R. do) MV
Verónica (R. da) . . . . MX
Vigário (R. do) . . . . MY 270
Vítor Cordon (R.) . . . . KZ
Voz do Operário (R.) LX

E
F
R
S
T
U
JARDIM ZOOLÓGICO
R. Conde de Almoster
R. das Furnas
R. Fr. Gentil Martins
SETE RIOS
PALÁCIO DE FRONTEIRA
Av. Columbano Bordalo Pinheiro
Av. José Malhôa
Pr. de Espanha
MUSEU GULBENKIAN
PARQUE FLORESTAL DE MONSANTO
Rua de Gulbenkian
Calouste
R. Ram. Ortigão
S. Sebastião
Campolide
R. Marquês da Fronteira
AQUEDUTO DAS ÁGUAS LIVRES
Av.
CAMPOLIDE
Rua
Parque
PARQUE EDUARDO VII
Pr. Marquês de Pombal
R. Castilho
Carvalhão
Pacheco
Duarte
Av. Engenheiro
Amoreiras
E.P.A.L.
R. Dom João V
Rato
L. do Rato
RATO
R. do Arco do Pia
CAMPO DE OURIQUE
R. Sampaio Bruno
R. Almeida e Sousa
Ceuta
Av. de Maria
Ponte
de Carvalho
R. Saraiva
JARDIM DA ESTRELA
R. de São Bento
Calç. da Estrela
R. Possidónio da Silva
Santo
LAPA
R. Borges Carneiro
R. do Q. Quelhas
R. da Lapa
R. de S. Caetano
MADRAGOA
Av. da Rua de Ceuta
Av.
Pr. Gen D. de Oliveira
Av. Infante
R. Ribeiro Sanches
R. do Prior
Av. 24 de Julho
ALCÂNTARA
Av.
211 de
M 16
M
M²
A²
172
64
40
42
15
124
76
171
48
79
27
219
241
13
7
34
57
132
264
120
199
238
157
247
106
232
207
205
94
244
150
163
54
67

G
H
LISBOA
0
500 m
Areeiro
Pr. F. Sá Carneiro
Av.
João
XXI
Afonso
Costa
Pr. de
Londres
Reis
C. Pequeno
CAIXA GERAL
DE DEPÓSITOS
25
R.
Barão
114
Olaias
Rotunda
das Olaias
Alameda
Almirante
93
de
Sabrosa
Arroios
Rua
Morais
ALTO DO PINA
República
de
Outubro
5
Duque
de
Ávila
Saldanha
R. de Dona
Estefânia
112
M
s
Picoas
Pr. J
Fontana
Pascoal
de
Melo
204
198
Avenida
Anjos
R. da Penha
de França
Roçadas
General
Av.
Soares
Av.
Mouzinho
de
Albuquerque
Afonso
B. LOPES
SAPADORES
Gomes
Freire
R.
162
129
117
147
180
R. A. Vidal
195
Intendente
R. dos
Sapadores
Calç. dos Barbadinhos
M5
Salitre
JARDIM
BOTÂNICO
AV.
DA
LIBERDADE
R. da Palma
R. da Graça
GRAÇA
R. D.
Pedro V
Pr. dos
Restauradores
CASTELO DE
SÃO JORGE
CAMPO
DE STA CLARA
SÃO ROQUE
ROSSIO
BAIRRO
ALTO
M15
CHIADO
R.
GARRETT
BAIXA
R.
do
Ouro
R.
da
Prata
ALFAMA
D.
Henrique
Infante
Calç. do
Combro
SÉ
R. de
S.Paulo
POL
H
Avenida
Julho
Av. da Ribeira
das Naus
PR. DO
COMÉRCIO
Estação Fluvial
TEJO
CACILHAS
BARREIRO, MONTIJO, SEIXAL
R
S
T
U
186
109
222
66
139
111
78
7
178
18
22

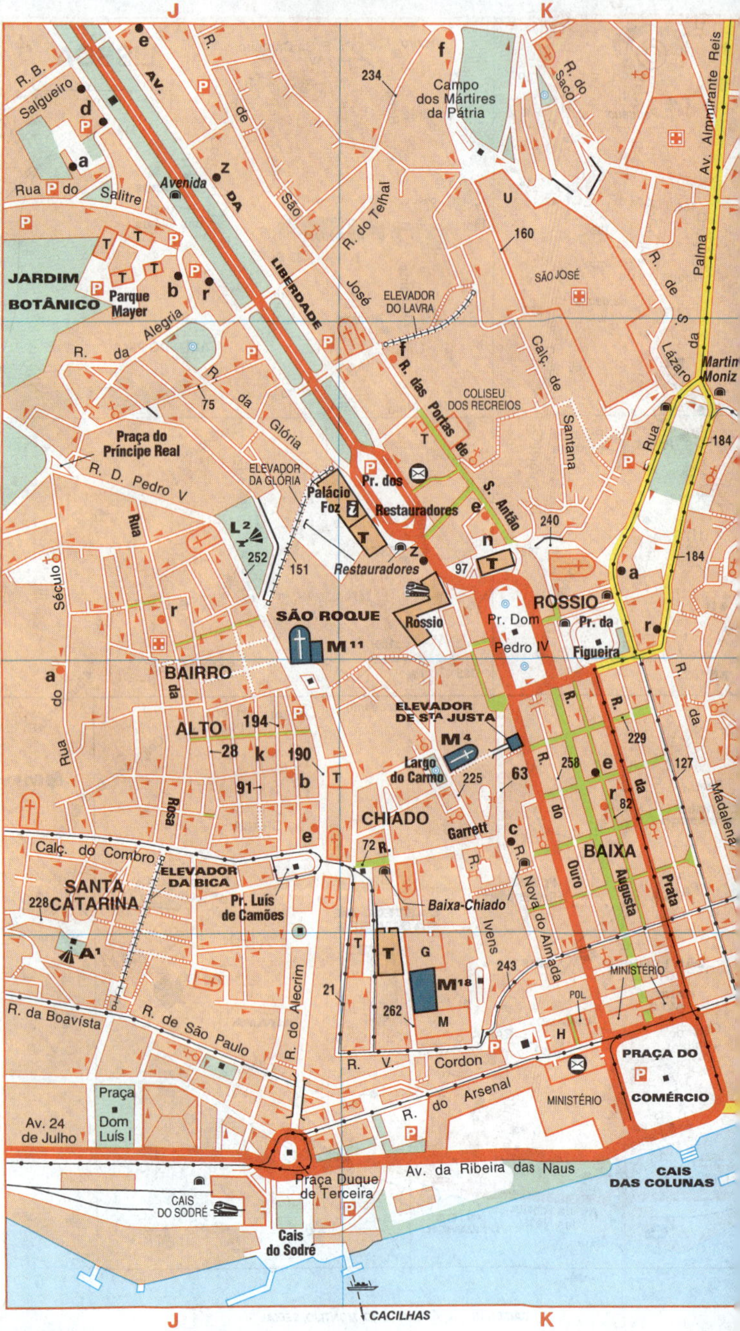

J
K
V
X
Y
Z
R. B.
Salgueiro
Rua do Salitre
Av. da Liberdade
Avenida
R. de São José
R. do Telhal
Campo dos Mártires da Pátria
234
R. do Saco
Av. Almirante Reis
Palma
R. de S. Lázaro
Martin Moniz
U
160
SÃO JOSÉ
JARDIM BOTÂNICO
Parque Mayer
ELEVADOR DO LAVRA
R. da Alegria
R. da Glória
R. das Portas de S. Antão
Calç. de Santana
COLISEU DOS RECREIOS
Rua
184
75
Praça do Príncipe Real
R. D. Pedro V
ELEVADOR DA GLÓRIA
Palácio Foz
Pr. dos Restauradores
Restauradores
240
Rua
Século
252
151
97
ROSSIO
Pr. Dom Pedro IV
Pr. da Figueira
Rossio
SÃO ROQUE
M 11
BAIRRO ALTO
Rua da
194
28
190
91
Rosa
ELEVADOR DE STA JUSTA
M 4
Largo do Carmo
225
63
R. da Madalena
229
127
258
82
R. do Ouro
R. Augusta
R. da Prata
BAIXA
CHIADO
Garrett
72
R.
R. Nova do Almada
Ivens
Calç. do Combro
ELEVADOR DA BICA
SANTA CATARINA
228
Pr. Luís de Camões
Baixa-Chiado
A 1
M 18
243
MINISTÉRIO
POL.
R. da Boavista
R. de São Paulo
R. do Alecrim
21
262
R. V. Cordon
R. do Arsenal
PRAÇA DO COMÉRCIO
MINISTÉRIO
Praça Dom Luís I
Av. 24 de Julho
Praça Duque de Terceira
Av. da Ribeira das Naus
CAIS DAS COLUNAS
CAIS DO SODRÉ
Cais do Sodré
CACILHAS

SAPADORES
GRAÇA
MOURARIA
ALFAMA
MIRADOURO DA SENHORA DO MONTE
Largo da Graça
Convento N.S. da Graça
São Vicente de Fora
CAMPO DE STA CLARA
SANTA ENGRÁCIA
SANTA APOLÓNIA
CASTELO DE SÃO JORGE
Museu Militar
Sto Estêvão
S. Miguel
L. dos Lóios
SÉ
Casa do Fado e da Guitarra Portuguesa
Campo das Cebolas
MINISTÉRIO
Estação Fluvial
CAIS DA ALFÂNDEGA
ALFÂNDEGA
Doca do Terreiro do Trigo
Doca da Marinha
TEJO
LISBOA
300 m
CACILHAS
BARREIRO, MONTIJO, SEIXAL

Centre : Av. da Liberdade, Praça dos Restauradores, Praça Dom Pedro IV (Rossio), Praça do Comércio, Rua Dom Pedro V, Rua de Santa Catarina, Campo de Santa Clara, Rua dos Sapadores

Tivoli Lisboa, Av. da Liberdade 185, ✉ 1269-050, ✆ 21 319 89 00, *htlisboa@mail.telepac.pt, Fax 21 319 89 50,* ← city from the terrace, , heated – 40/200. AE MC VISA. JV d
***Terraço :* Meals** a la carte 48/54 – **300 rm** 400/420, 29 suites.
• Elegant, comfortable and with fine views from the top floor. Pleasant, tastefully decorated and well-equipped bedrooms. The Terraço restaurant is both smart and traditional.

Sofitel Lisboa, Av. da Liberdade 127, ✉ 1269-038, ✆ 21 322 83 00, *h1319@accor-hotels.com, Fax 21 322 83 60* – , rm, – 25/300. AE MC VISA JV r
Meals 30 – 18 – **165 rm** 235/265, 5 suites.
• A friendly welcome, comfortable and with a contemporary classic feel. Enjoy a pleasant stay in agreeable surroundings.

Lisboa Plaza, Travessa do Salitre 7, ✉ 1269-066, ✆ 21 321 82 18, *plaza.hotels@heritage.pt, Fax 21 347 16 30* – – 25/140. AE MC VISA JCB. JV b
Meals 24 – 14 – **94 rm** 210/230, 12 suites.
• Near the famous Avenida da Liberdade. Very traditional with distinguished and tasteful atmosphere and classic décor. A large buffet is available in the dining room.

Mundial, Rua D. Duarte 4, ✉ 1100-198, ✆ 21 884 20 00, *info@hotel-mundial.pt, Fax 21 884 21 10,* ← – – 25/120. AE MC VISA JCB. KX a
***Varanda de Lisboa :* Meals** a la carte 30/43 – **373 rm** 140/150.
• Refurbished with all mod cons. Pleasant, well-appointed bedrooms in the heart of the Baixa Pombalina area. There are splendid views from the Varanda restaurant on the 8th floor.

Tivoli Jardim, Rua Julio Cesar Machado 7, ✉ 1250-135, ✆ 21 359 10 00, *htjardim@mail.telepac.pt, Fax 21 359 12 45,* – P – 25/40. AE MC VISA. JV a
Meals 15 – **119 rm** 310/320.
• Modern efficiency for the business traveller. A large foyer, conference rooms and pleasantly decorated bedrooms. The brightly-lit dining room offers traditional dishes.

Lisboa Regency Chiado without rest, Rua Nova do Almada 114, ✉ 1200-290, ✆ 21 325 61 00, *regencychiado@madeiraregency.pt, Fax 21 325 61 61* – . AE MC VISA. KY c
40 rm 190/200.
• Pleasantly situated in a building in the old part of the city. Friendly, professional service, with bedrooms decorated in oriental style.

Lisboa coffee shop only, Rua Barata Salgueiro 5, ✉ 1166-069, ✆ 21 350 00 00, *reservas-hotlis@netcabo.pt, Fax 21 355 41 39* – . AE MC VISA JCB. JV e
55 rm 125/150, 6 suites.
• An ideal hotel for the business traveller in an important business district. Comfort, tradition and efficiency in a small, former palace. Well-equipped bedrooms.

Avenida Palace without rest, Rua 1° de Dezembro 123, ✉ 1200-359, ✆ 21 321 81 00, *reservas@hotel-avenida-palace.pt, Fax 21 342 28 84* – – 25/100. AE MC VISA JCB. KX z
64 rm 180/205, 18 suites.
• An attractive and well-run hotel in the cultural and commercial quarter. Service, quality and a classic old-world ambience.

NH Liberdade, Av. da Liberdade 180-B, ✉ 1250-146, ✆ 21 351 40 60, *nhliberdade@nh-hotels.es, Fax 21 314 36 74,* – – 25/35. AE MC VISA JCB. JV z
Meals 25 – **83 rm** 280.
• Situated in Lisbon's most important business district. A comfortable and functional hotel with all the quality and characteristic style of this hotel chain.

Veneza without rest, Av. da Liberdade 189, ✉ 1250-141, ✆ 21 352 26 18, *comercial@3khoteis.com, Fax 21 352 66 78* – P. AE MC VISA JCB. JV d
37 rm 105/135.
• In a small former palace with a lovely façade. A perfect balance of old grandeur and modern day functionality.

Solar do Castelo without rest, Rua das Cozinhas 2, ✉ 1100-181, ✆ 21 887 09 09, *solar.castelo@heritage.pt, Fax 21 887 09 07* – . AE MC VISA JCB. LY c
14 – **14 rm** 260/290.
• A small 18C palace in an area with lots of historic monuments. A comfortable and completely renovated interior. Modern bedrooms with attractive design details.

Solar dos Mouros without rest, Rua do Milagre de Santo António 6, ✉ 1100-351, ☎ 218 85 49 40, *reservation@solardosmouros.pt, Fax 218 85 49 45*, ≤ – ▤ TV. AE ⓓ MC VISA. ✻ LY x
8 rm ☐ 186/240.
• A typical house which has been modernised and furnished with personal touches, including four paintings by the owner himself. Colourful bedrooms, some with excellent views.

Albergaria Senhora do Monte without rest, Calçada do Monte 39, ✉ 1170-250, ☎ 21 886 60 02, *senhoradomonte@hotmail.com, Fax 21 887 77 83*, ≤ São Jorge castle, town and river Tagus – |♦| ▤ TV. AE ⓓ MC VISA. ✻ LV c
28 rm ☐ 105/129.
• Quiet accommodation in the residential district of Graça. A small, attractive and well-run hotel. Pleasant bedrooms with classic décor, some with balcony.

Lisboa Tejo without rest, Rua dos Condes de Monsanto 2, ✉ 1100-159, ☎ 21 886 61 82, *hotellisboatejo.reservas@evidenciagrupo.com, Fax 21 886 51 63* – |♦| ▤ TV. AE ⓓ MC VISA JCB. ✻ KX r
58 rm ☐ 100/135.
• Moderate prices and pleasant, well-appointed bedrooms in the Baixa Pombalina district. A modern, refurbished and central hotel with a traditional atmosphere and elegant décor.

Insulana without rest, Rua da Assunção 52, ✉ 1100-044, ☎ 21 342 76 25, *insulana@netc.pt, Fax 21 342 89 24* – |♦| ▤ TV. AE ⓓ MC VISA. ✻ KY e
32 rm ☐ 50/60.
• In the heart of the Baixa Pombalina district with reasonable prices. A pleasant, comfortable and well-situated hotel with adequate facilities.

XXXX **Clara,** Campo dos Mártires da Pátria 49, ✉ 1150-225, ☎ 21 885 30 53, *clararestaurant@mail.telepac.pt, Fax 21 885 20 82*, 佘 – ▤. AE ⓓ MC VISA JCB. ✻ KV f
closed 1 to 15 August, Saturday lunch and Sunday – **Meals** a la carte approx. 45.
• In the city centre and with a beautiful terrace-garden and attractive décor. An elegant, friendly and very comfortable restaurant in a pleasant setting.

XXX **Tavares,** Rua da Misericórdia 37, ✉ 1200-000, ☎ 213 42 11 12, *reservas@tavaresrico.pt, Fax 213 47 81 25* – ▤. AE ⓓ MC VISA. ✻ JY e
closed Saturday lunch and Sunday – **Meals** a la carte 46/65.
• Founded in 1784, Lisbon's oldest restaurant has retained all its aristocratic elegance and ambience. A sumptuous decor of gilded work, mirrors and chandeliers.

XXX **Gambrinus,** Rua das Portas de Santo Antão 25, ✉ 1150-264, ☎ 21 342 14 66, *Fax 21 346 50 32* – ▤. AE MC VISA. ✻ KX n
Meals a la carte 72/86.
• In the historic centre of the city near the Rossio district. A restaurant with a well-established reputation backed up by fine cuisine and an excellent wine list.

XXX **Consenso,** Rua da Académia das Ciências 1-A, ✉ 1200-003, ☎ 21 343 13 13, *reservas@restauranteconsenso.com, Fax 21 343 13 12* – ▤. AE ⓓ MC VISA JCB JY a
closed Sunday – **Meals** - dinner only - a la carte 23/36.
• Good modern Portuguese cuisine. A pleasant dining room with modern décor and a relaxed atmosphere.

XXX **Escorial,** Rua das Portas de Santo Antão 47, ✉ 1150-160, ☎ 21 346 44 29, *Fax 21 346 37 58*, 佘 – ▤. AE ⓓ MC VISA JCB. ✻ KX e
Meals a la carte 25/34.
• Near the Rossio district. A well-established and well-run restaurant with pleasant décor and furnishings. Attentive and friendly service.

XXX **Casa do Leão,** Castelo de São Jorge, ✉ 1100-129, ☎ 21 887 59 62, *guest@pousadas.pt, Fax 21 887 63 29*, ≤, 佘 – ▤. AE ⓓ MC VISA. ✻ LXY s
Meals a la carte approx. 40.
• Situated in the walls of the castle of Sao Jorge. An elegant restaurant in traditional Portuguese-style with an exclusive ambience.

XX **Via Graça,** Rua Damasceno Monteiro 9-B, ✉ 1170-108, ☎ 21 887 08 30, *restauranteviagraca@hotmail.com, Fax 21 887 03 05*, ≤ São Jorge castle, town and river Tagus – ▤. AE ⓓ MC VISA JCB. ✻ LV d
closed Saturday lunch and Sunday – **Meals** - dinner only 16 to 30 August - a la carte 31/41.
• On the outskirts of Alfama with a magnificent panorama. Excellent cuisine in a busy, friendly and comfortable restaurant.

XX **O Faz Figura,** Rua do Paraíso 15-B, ✉ 1100-396, ☎ 21 886 89 81, *faz.figura@mail.telepac.pt, Fax 21 882 21 03*, ≤, 佘 – ▤. AE ⓓ MC VISA JCB. ✻ MX n
closed Saturday lunch and Sunday – **Meals** a la carte 30/38.
• Beside the church of Santa Engrácia on the outskirts of Alfama. A well-run establishment in a traditional and elegant setting.

Solar dos Presuntos, Rua das Portas de Santo Antão 150, ✉ 1150-269, 21 342 42 53, *restaurante@solardospresuntos.com, Fax 21 346 84 68* – AE MC VISA. KX b
closed August, Sunday and Bank Holidays – **Meals** a la carte 34/39.
• A locally-run, comfortable restaurant with a wide selection of well-prepared traditional dishes and some specialities from Minho.

O Múni, Rua dos Correeiros 115, ✉ 1100-163, 21 342 89 82 – AE MC VISA. KY r
closed September, Saturday, Sunday and Bank Holidays – **Meals** a la carte 26/33.
• A small and friendly restaurant in the centre of Baixa Pombalina. A relaxed and pleasant atmosphere with pleasant décor and furnishings.

Mercado de Santa Clara, Campo de Santa Clara (at market), ✉ 1170, 21 887 39 86, *Fax 21 887 39 86* – AE MC VISA. MX c
closed Sunday dinner and Monday – **Meals** a la carte 29/36.
• Near the Campo de Santa Clara. A comfortable restaurant with a relaxed atmosphere, an old-fashioned feel and subtle charm.

East : Praça Marquês de Pombal, Av. da Liberdade, Av. Almirante Reis, Av. João XXI, Av. da República, Av. Estados Unidos de América, Av. de Berlim

Tivoli Tejo, Av. D. João II (Parque das Nações), ✉ 1990-083, 21 891 51 00, *htte jo@tivoli.pt, Fax 21 891 53 45,* – – 25/250. AE MC VISA JCB. North-East : by Av. Infante D. Henrique MX
A VIII Colina* Meals** a la carte 31/38 - ***O Ardina *(lunch only)* **Meals** a la carte 26/30 – **262 rm** 175/190, 17 suites.
• Facing the Tajo estuary. Modern bedrooms and small bathrooms. Smallish, but pleasantly decorated public rooms. Fine views from the A VIII Colina restaurant.

Altis Park H., Av. Engenheiro Arantes e Oliveira 9, ✉ 1900-221, 21 843 42 00, *reservations@altisparkhotel.com, Fax 21 846 08 38* – – 25/600. AE MC VISA. rest HR z
Meals 17,50 – **285 rm** 135/150, 15 suites – PA 45.
• In a main business district. Modern, very well-run hotel with excellent facilities. Ideal for conferences and business meetings. Fine cuisine in the Navegadores restaurant.

Suites do Marquês, Av. Duque de Loulé 45, ✉ 1050-086, 21 351 04 80, *lisboa .com@barcelo.com.pt, Fax 21 353 18 65,* – – 25/50. AE MC VISA. GS z
Meals *(closed Sunday)* a la carte 22/30 – **80 rm** 196/216, 4 suites.
• Central location near the famous Praça Marquês de Pombal square. All the comfort and characteristic style of the Meliá chain in large, quiet and functional bedrooms.

Holiday Inn Lisbon, Av. António José de Almeida 28-A, ✉ 1000-044, 21 004 40 00, *hil@grupo-continental.com, Fax 21 793 66 72,* – – 25/300. AE MC VISA JCB. GR c
Meals 24 – **161 rm** 180/220, 8 suites.
• Centrally located : ideal for the business or leisure traveller. Few public rooms but comfortable bedrooms. A pleasant dining room with wickerwork furniture and a buffet.

AC Palacio Sottomayor, Av. Fontes Pereira de Melo 16, ✉ 1050-121, 210 05 09 30, *acpsottomayor@ac-hotels.com, Fax 210 05 09 31,* – – 25/60. AE MC VISA. GS x
Meals a la carte approx. 27 – **81 rm** 126,50/137,50, 2 suites.
• Located in the rear part of the palace, this hotel has a modern façade and a reception area that is typical of the AC chain. Pleasant lounge and meeting areas, plus modern, well-appointed bedrooms. An attractive, albeit soberly decorated restaurant.

Roma, Av. de Roma 33, ✉ 1749-074, 21 796 77 61, *info@hotelroma.pt, Fax 21 793 29 81,* – – 25/230. AE MC VISA JCB.
Meals 15 – **263 rm** 85/95 – PA 30. North : by Av. Almirante Reis HR
• On a major avenue. A modern hotel with large, comfortable rooms that promise a restful stay. Sixty executive bedrooms.

Dom Carlos Park coffee shop only, Av. Duque de Loulé 121, ✉ 1050-089, 21 351 25 90, *comercial@domcarloshoteis.com, Fax 21 352 07 28* – – 25/40. AE MC VISA JCB. GS n
76 rm 117/152.
• Traditional and elegant hotel in a very good location with restful ambience. Pleasant rooms with bathrooms decorated in marble and a small sitting area.

A.S. Lisboa without rest, Av. Almirante Reis 188, ✉ 1000-055, 21 842 93 60, *inf o@hotel-aslisboa.com, Fax 21 842 93 74* – – 25/80. AE MC VISA JCB.
75 rm 74,07/85,04. HR e
• In an interesting and lively area of the city. Comfort, a pleasant atmosphere and attentive, friendly service in a modern, functional style hotel.

Dom João without rest, Rua José Estêvão 43, ✉ 1150-200, ☎ 21 314 41 71, *Fax 21 352 45 69* – |‡| ▤ TV. AE ◐ MC VISA. ✻ HS e
18 rm ☕ 50/60.
◆ A small hotel with a friendly and pleasant traditional atmosphere. The majority of rooms have bathrooms fitted with showers.

D'Avis, Rua do Grilo 98, ✉ 1900-707, ☎ 21 868 13 54, *Fax 21 868 13 54* – ▤. AE ◐ MC VISA. ✻ East : by Av. Infante D. Henrique MX
closed Sunday – **Meals** - Alentejo rest - a la carte 18/23.
◆ A small but well-run traditional restaurant. Interesting cooking at good prices, served in pleasant surroundings with décor in the style of the beautiful Alentejo region.

West : Av. da Liberdade, Av. 24 de Julho, Av. da India, Largo de Alcântara, Av. da India, Av. Infante Santo, Praça Marquês de Pombal, Av. António Augusto de Aguiar, Av. de Berna, Praça de Espahna

Four Seasons H. Ritz Lisbon, Rua Rodrigo da Fonseca 88, ✉ 1099-039, ☎ 21 381 14 00, *ritzfourseasons@mail.telepac.pt, Fax 21 383 17 83,* <, ☂, ℒ₅ – |‡| ▤ TV ♿ 🚗 P – 🏛 25/500. AE ◐ MC VISA JCB. ✻ rest FS b
Meals 50 - ***Varanda* : Meals** a la carte 49/62 – ☕ 24 – **262 rm** 425/450, 20 suites.
◆ Luxury is the keynote in these exquisite bedrooms, more than matched by the superb public rooms. The exclusive restaurant in classic style serves sophisticated, immaculately presented cuisine.

Sheraton Lisboa H. & Towers, Rua Latino Coelho 1, ✉ 1069-025, ☎ 21 312 00 00, *sheraton.lisboa@sheraton.com, Fax 21 354 71 64,* <, ℒ₅, ⛱ heated – |‡| ▤ TV ♿ 🚗 – 🏛 25/550. AE ◐ MC VISA. ✻ rest GR s
Panorama *(dinner only)* **Meals** a la carte 47/62 - ***Caravela*** *(lunch only)* **Meals** a la carte 32/47 – ☕ 17 – **376 rm** 290/305, 8 suites.
◆ Business travellers should ask for the wonderful, fully equipped executive bedrooms. Conferences, receptions and dinners catered for. The Panorama restaurant is a very pleasant setting in which to sample finely prepared dishes.

Lapa Palace 🐦, Rua do Pau de Bandeira 4, ✉ 1249-021, ☎ 21 394 94 94, *info@lapa-palace.com, Fax 21 395 06 65,* <, ☂, ℒ₅, ⛱, ⛱, 🌳 – |‡| ▤ TV ♿ 🚗 P – 🏛 25/250. AE ◐ MC VISA JCB. ✻ rest EU a
***Hotel Cipriani* : Meals** a la carte 47/58 – **92 rm** ☕ 500, 9 suites.
◆ Classic splendour on a hill with the river Tajo in the distance. A restored 19C palace, with secluded corners and evocative gardens with a waterfall among the trees. The restaurant offers very carefully prepared Italian cuisine in a refined ambience.

Pestana Palace 🐦, Rua Jau 54, ✉ 1300-314, ☎ 21 361 56 00, *carlton.palace@pestana.com, Fax 21 361 56 01,* ℒ₅, ⛱, ⛱, 🌳 – |‡| ▤ TV ♿ 🚗 – 🏛 25/520. AE ◐ MC VISA JCB. ✻ West : by Av. 24 de Julho EU
***Valle Flor* : Meals** a la carte 44/69 – **173 rm** ☕ 410/430, 17 suites.
◆ A beautiful 19C palace, restored and decorated in period style with grand public rooms and bedrooms with careful detail. A restaurant which is magnificent as much for its cuisine as for the luxury of its dining rooms.

Le Meridien Park Atlantic Lisboa, Rua Castilho 149, ✉ 1099-034, ☎ 21 381 87 00, *reservas.lisboa@lemeridien.pt, Fax 21 389 05 05,* < – |‡|, ⊁ rm, ▤ TV ♿ 🚗 – 🏛 25/550. AE ◐ MC VISA JCB. ✻ rest FS a
***L'Appart* : Meals** a la carte 42/50 – ☕ 20 – **313 rm** 460, 17 suites.
◆ A full range of facilities and professional service in the comfort of modern bedrooms and suites. Bathrooms fitted with marble and high quality furnishings. A pleasantly decorated restaurant offering à la carte, buffet or dish of the day.

Altis, Rua Castilho 11, ✉ 1269-072, ☎ 21 310 60 00, *reservations@hotel-altis.pt, Fax 21 310 62 62,* ℒ₅, ⛱ – |‡| ▤ TV ♿ 🚗 – 🏛 25/700. AE ◐ MC VISA. ✻ FT z
Girassol* : Meals** a la carte 38/47 - ***Grill Dom Fernando *(closed Sunday)* **Meals** a la carte 49/61 – **290 rm** ☕ 250/300, 53 suites.
◆ A long-established hotel situated near to the Praça Marquês de Pombal square. Very classic rooms in pleasant modern style. In the Girassol restaurant guests help themselves to a large buffet.

Holiday Inn Lisbon Continental, Rua Laura Alves 9, ✉ 1069-169, ☎ 21 004 60 00, *hic@grupo-continental.com, Fax 21 797 36 69* – |‡| ▤ TV ♿ 🚗 – 🏛 25/180. AE ◐ MC VISA JCB. ✻ FR q
Meals 22,50 – ☕ 10,50 – **210 rm** 180/205, 10 suites.
◆ A hotel with a modern exterior that is very popular for business meetings. Pleasant, well-appointed bedrooms and adequate public areas. The dining room is not up to the standards of the rest of the hotel.

Real Parque, Av. Luís Bivar 67, ✉ 1069-146, ☎ 21 319 90 00, *info@hoteisreal.com, Fax 21 357 07 50* – |♦| ▤ TV ♿ 🚗 – 🔈 25/100. AE ① MC VISA JCB. ✱ FR a
***Cozinha do Real* : Meals** a la carte 28/37 – **147 rm** ☕ 155/175, 6 suites.
◆ Ideal for meetings, business and leisure travel. Elegant furnishings, quality and good taste everywhere. A modern exterior, classic contemporary décor and a charming lounge area. Good food served in a pleasant dining room.

Real Palacio, Rua Tomás Ribeiro, ✉ 1050-228, ☎ 213 19 95 00, *info@hoteisreal.com, Fax 213 19 95 01*, 🏋 – |♦|, ⇄ rm, ▤ TV ♿ 🚗 – 🔈 25/230. AE ① MC VISA JCB. ✱
Meals 35,50 – **143 rm** ☕ 215/240, 4 suites. FR s
◆ The Real Palacio is a mix of the modern and traditional with its stylish marble and elegant woodwork. Panelled meeting rooms and fully-equipped bedrooms. Options in the restaurant include the à la carte menu and an extensive buffet.

Villa Rica, Av. 5 de Outubro 295, ✉ 1600-035, ☎ 21 004 30 00, *Fax 21 004 34 99*, 🏋, 🏊 – |♦| ▤ TV ♿ 🚗 – 🔈 25/500. AE ① MC VISA. ✱
***Ouro Preto* : Meals** a la carte 45/61 – **166 rm** ☕ 126/141, 5 suites.
◆ An original hotel both architecturally and for the modern design of its furnishings and décor. Well-lit public areas. The Ouro Preto restaurant offers a choice of high quality dishes. North : by Av. da República GR

Sana Metropolitan Park H., Rua Soeiro Pereira Gomes-parcela 2, ✉ 1600-198, ☎ 21 798 25 00, *comer@metropolitan-lisboa-hotel.pt, Fax 21 795 08 64* – |♦| ▤ TV ♿ 🚗 – 🔈 25/250. AE ① MC VISA JCB. ✱ North : by Av. da República GR
Meals 16 – **315 rm** ☕ 165/195.
◆ Modern efficiency for the business traveller. A large foyer, well-equipped conference rooms and pleasantly decorated modern bedrooms.

Fénix, Praça Marquês de Pombal 8, ✉ 1269-133, ☎ 21 386 21 21, *fenixlisbia@fenixlisboa.com, Fax 21 386 01 31* – |♦| ▤ TV ♿ – 🔈 25/100. AE ① MC VISA JCB. ✱ FS g
***Bodegón* : Meals** a la carte 20/28 – **119 rm** ☕ 140/160, 4 suites.
◆ A classic hotel right on the Praça Marquês de Pombal square. The pleasant public rooms are matched by the well-appointed comfort of the hotel in general. A restaurant with elegant details and décor of soft colours.

Marquês de Pombal coffee shop only, Av. da Liberdade 243, ✉ 1250-143, ☎ 21 319 79 00, *info@hotel-marquesdepombal.pt, Fax 21 319 79 90* – |♦| ▤ TV ♿ 🚗 – 🔈 25/120. AE ① MC VISA JCB. ✱ FS e
123 rm ☕ 166/178.
◆ A recently built hotel. Conferences and business meetings in an atmosphere of modern efficiency. Elegantly furnished with up-to-date technology and conference hall.

Sana Reno H. without rest, Av. Duque d'Ávila 195-197, ✉ 1050-082, ☎ 21 313 50 00, *sanareno@sanahotels.com, Fax 21 313 50 01*, 🏊 – |♦| ▤ TV ♿ 🚗 – 🔈 25/115. AE ① MC VISA. ✱ FR m
89 rm ☕ 120/130, 3 suites.
◆ Professional service on the edge of the Eduardo VII park. Refurbished and extended in 1998, with an elegant foyer and comfortably functional bedrooms.

Barcelona without rest, Rua Laura Alves 10, ✉ 1050-138, ☎ 21 795 42 73, *reservas@3khoteis.com, Fax 21 795 42 81* – |♦| ▤ TV ♿ 🚗 – 🔈 25/230. AE ① MC VISA JCB. ✱ FR z
120 rm ☕ 125/150, 5 suites.
◆ An up-to-date hotel in the financial district of the city. Modern surroundings with avant-garde touches. Cheerful colourful décor and good level of comfort.

Mercure Lisboa Malhoa, Av. José Malhoa-lote 1684, ✉ 1099-051, ☎ 21 720 80 00, *h3346@accor-hotels.com, Fax 21 720 80 89*, 🏊 – |♦|, ⇄ rm, ▤ TV ♿ 🚗 – 🔈 25/200. AE ① MC VISA. ✱ ER b
Meals 14 – ☕ 7,50 – **103 rm** 92/98, 1 suite.
◆ Bedrooms with avant-garde design combining pleasant surroundings and optimum comfort. Panoramic views from the attractive swimming-pool. Dining room with an informal feel and a choice of à la carte or buffet.

Quality H., Campo Grande 7, ✉ 1700-087, ☎ 21 791 76 00, *quality.lisboa@netcabo.pt, Fax 21 795 75 00*, 🏋 – |♦| ▤ TV ♿ 🚗 – 🔈 25/70. AE ① MC VISA. ✱
Meals 19,20 – **80 rm** ☕ 250/280, 2 suites. North : by Av. da República GR
◆ A functional-style hotel with well-equipped bedrooms. A modern and practical atmosphere ; popular for large business meetings.

Amazónia Jamor, Av. Tomás Ribeiro 129 Queijas, ✉ 2795-891 Linda-A-Pastora, ☎ 21 417 56 38, *reservas@amazoniahoteis.com, Fax 21 417 56 30*, ≤, 🏋, 🏊, 🏊, 🎾 – |♦| ▤ TV ♿ 🚗 P – 🔈 25/200. AE ① MC VISA JCB. ✱ West : 10 km by Av. Engenheiro Duarte Pacheco ES
Meals a la carte 25/33 – **93 rm** ☕ 120/140, 4 suites.
◆ Spacious rooms in a modern style, the best with Jacuzzi. Good facilities. Conferences, meetings, dinners and receptions catered for.

Flórida without rest, Rua Duque de Palmela 34, ✉ 1250-098, ☎ 21 357 61 45, *sales@hotel-florida.pt, Fax 21 314 13 47* – |♦| ▤ TV – 🏔 25/100. AE ⊕ MC VISA JCB. ✈
72 rm ☕ 120/135. FS x
◆ A traditional hotel recently refurbished. The bedroom furniture is a bit outdated, although, in compensation, the bathrooms have marble fittings. A bright breakfast room.

Vila Galé Ópera, Travessa do Conde da Ponte, ✉ 1300-141, ☎ 21 360 54 00, *reserv.opera@vilagale.pt, Fax 21 360 54 50,* Ⅎ₆, 🏊 – |♦|, ⇔ rm, ▤ TV ♿ 🚗 – 🏔 25/230. AE ⊕ MC VISA JCB. ✈ West : by Av. 24 de Julho JZ
Meals 25 – **243 rm** ☕ 96/120, 16 suites.
◆ A predominantly business clientele due to its location next to a conference centre. Spacious foyer, modern, functional bedrooms and a fully equipped fitness area. Contemporary in style, the decor in the hotel restaurant is inspired by the world of music.

Amazónia Lisboa without rest, Travessa Fábrica dos Pentes 12, ✉ 1250-106, ☎ 21 387 70 06, *reservas@amazoniahoteis.com, Fax 21 387 90 90,* 🏊 heated – |♦| ▤ TV ♿ 🚗 – 🏔 25/200. AE ⊕ MC VISA JCB. ✈ FS d
192 rm ☕ 105/180.
◆ Near the Praça Marquês de Pombal square. Modern suites and functional-style bedrooms, the best with balconies. Professionally managed.

Clarión Suites coffee shop only, Rua Rodrigo da Fonseca 44, ✉ 1250-193, ☎ 21 004 66 00, *clarion.suites@grupo-continental.com, Fax 21 386 30 00,* 🏊 – |♦| ▤ TV 🚗. AE ⊕ MC VISA JCB. ✈ FS m
☕ 9 – **57 suites** 88/94.
◆ Limited space in the hotel's lounge and reception areas, although the suites on offer here are comfortable and functional, with contemporary decor and furnishings.

York House, Rua das Janelas Verdes 32, ✉ 1200-691, ☎ 21 396 24 35, *reservations@yorkhouselisboa.com, Fax 21 397 27 93,* 🌳 – ▤ TV – 🏔 25/90. AE ⊕ MC VISA JCB. ✈ FU e
Meals a la carte 33/40 – ☕ 14 – **32 rm** 160/175.
◆ In a 16C convent. The rooms have period furniture and individual décor with a Portuguese feel. Charm, modern comfort and distinguished elegance. There is a quiet and pleasant dining terrace shaded by trees.

Novotel Lisboa, Av. José Malhoa 1642, ✉ 1099-051, ☎ 21 724 48 00, *Ho784@accor-hotels.com, Fax 21 724 48 01,* <, 🌳, 🏊 – |♦|, ⇔ rm, ▤ TV ♿ 🚗 – 🏔 25/300. AE ⊕ MC VISA JCB ER e
Meals 17 – ☕ 7 – **246 rm** 78/86.
◆ Functional décor. Adequate facilities, modern service and well-appointed rooms. Conferences, dinners and receptions catered for. A large buffet is available in the dining room.

Sana Classic Executive H. without rest, Av. Conde Valbom 56, ✉ 1050-069, ☎ 21 795 11 57, *sana-classic.executive@sanahotels.com, Fax 21 795 11 66* – |♦| ▤ TV ♿ 🚗 – 🏔 25/55. AE ⊕ MC VISA. ✈ FR g
72 rm ☕ 67/77.
◆ Good location and ideal for the business traveller. Practical and functional. A modern foyer-reception, comfortable, well-equipped rooms and bathrooms with marble fittings.

Miraparque, Av. Sidónio Pais 12, ✉ 1050-214, ☎ 21 352 42 86, *hotel@miraparque.com, Fax 21 357 89 20* – |♦| ▤ TV. AE ⊕ MC VISA. ✈ FS k
Meals 16,50 – **96 rm** ☕ 90/100 – PA 30.
◆ In spite of this hotel's outdated style, its atmosphere has a pleasant, friendly and timeless feel. The façade has been redecorated and the rooms are of a reasonable standard.

Eduardo VII, Av. Fontes Pereira de Melo 5, ✉ 1069-114, ☎ 21 356 88 22, *sales@hoteleduardovii.pt, Fax 21 356 88 33,* < – |♦| ▤ TV – 🏔 25/100. AE ⊕ MC VISA JCB. ✈
Varanda **: Meals** a la carte 22/38 – ☕ 6 – **137 rm** 74/97, 1 suite. FS p
◆ Beside the Eduardo VII park. This hotel surprises with its classic, pleasant style. Smallish rooms which, nevertheless, offer high standards of comfort and careful décor. There are spectacular panoramic views over the city from the Varanda restaurant.

Marquês de Sá, Av. Miguel Bombarda 130, ✉ 1050-167, ☎ 21 791 10 14, *reservas.oms@dinippohotels.com, Fax 21 793 69 86* – |♦| ▤ TV 🚗 – 🏔 25/150. AE ⊕ MC VISA JCB. ✈ FR c
Meals 15,50 – **164 rm** ☕ 135/165.
◆ Beside the Gulbenkian Foundation. Business and pleasure in a pleasant atmosphere of quality. Friendly service and well-appointed rooms. Well-lit dining room with décor in blue tones and a large foyer.

As Janelas Verdes without rest, Rua das Janelas Verdes 47, ✉ 1200-690, ☎ 21 396 81 43, *janelas.verdes@heritage.pt, Fax 21 396 81 44* – |♦| ▤ TV. AE ⊕ MC VISA JCB. ✈ FU e
☕ 14 – **29 rm** 260/290.
◆ A late-18C mansion house with a beautiful patio and a charming function room. Traditional, romantic atmosphere.

Nacional without rest, Rua Castilho 34, ✉ 1250-070, ☎ 21 355 44 33, *hotelnacional@mail.telepac.pt*, *Fax 21 356 11 22* – AE VISA. FST s
59 rm 83/96, 2 suites.
◆ Up-to-date in style with professional management and friendly service. Bedrooms a little on the small side but modern and well equipped.

Sana Rex H. without rest, Rua Castilho 169, ✉ 1070-050, ☎ 21 388 21 61, *sanarex@sanahotels.com*, *Fax 21 388 75 81* – 25/50. AE VISA. FS a
68 rm 120/130.
◆ Refurbished in 1996. A modern and friendly hotel right in the city centre. A pleasant atmosphere, a charming reception area and well-appointed rooms. Dining room with a rustic feel and décor in wood where you can combine à la carte and buffet.

Da Torre, Rua dos Jerónimos 8, ✉ 1400-211, ☎ 21 361 69 40, *hoteldatorre.belem@mail.telepac.pt*, *Fax 21 361 69 46* – 25/50. AE VISA JCB. West : by Av. 24 de Julho EU
Meals see rest. ***São Jerónimo*** below – **59 rm** 80/95.
◆ In Belém near the los Jerónimos monastery. Attractive lounge area in classic Portuguese-style and small but very adequate rooms with beautiful wood and tile décor.

Berna without rest, Av. António Serpa 13, ✉ 1069-199, ☎ 21 781 43 00, *hotelberna@viphotels.com*, *Fax 21 793 62 78* – 25/180. AE VISA JCB.
7,50 – **240 rm** 64,50/70. GR a
◆ A hotel for either business or pleasure in the city centre. Small but well-equipped rooms, bathrooms a little reduced in size and adequate public areas.

Real Residência, Rua Ramalho Ortigão 41, ✉ 1070-228, ☎ 21 382 29 00, *info@hoteisreal.com*, *Fax 21 382 29 30* – 25/70. AE VISA JCB.
Meals 27,50 – **24 suites** 155/187,50. FR e
◆ Quality, comfort and elegance. Large, well-equipped apartments : bathrooms fitted with marble, traditional décor of good quality furnishings and fittings. The smallish dining room is pleasant and combines modern elements with attractive rustic details.

Ibis Lisboa Liberdade without rest, Rua Barata Salgueiro 53, ✉ 1250-043, ☎ 21 330 06 30, *h3137@accor-hotels.com*, *Fax 21 330 06 31* – rm, AE VISA FT a
5 – **70 rm** 64.
◆ All the true style of this hotel chain in the heart of the city. A small lounge and a functional dining room for breakfast and bedrooms equipped with the basics.

Nazareth without rest, Av. António Augusto de Aguiar 25-4°, ✉ 1050-012, ☎ 21 354 20 16, *reservas@residencianazareth.com*, *Fax 21 356 08 36* – AE VISA JCB. FRS y
3 – **32 rm** 48/60.
◆ This hotel has a welcoming feel with pleasant, well-appointed bedrooms and fully-equipped bathrooms. A friendly atmosphere in the centre of Lisbon.

Casa da Comida, Travessa das Amoreiras 1, ✉ 1250-025, ☎ 21 388 53 76, *reservas@casadacomida.pt*, *Fax 21 387 51 32* – AE VISA JCB. FT e
closed Saturday lunch, Sunday and Monday lunch – **Meals** a la carte 45/67.
◆ Don't miss out on this gem of a restaurant ! Refined and imaginative cuisine with professional service and a beautiful plant-filled patio. Elegant and welcoming.

Pabe, Rua Duque de Palmela 27-A, ✉ 1250-097, ☎ 21 353 74 84, *Fax 21 353 64 37* – AE VISA JCB. FS x
Meals a la carte 44/50.
◆ An attractive English pub in a welcoming rustic style which has three comfortable and pleasant public areas. The best is the bar area. Great ambience !

Conventual, Praça das Flores 45, ✉ 1200-192, ☎ 21 390 91 96, *Fax 21 390 91 96* – AE VISA FT m
closed August, Saturday lunch, Sunday and Monday lunch – **Meals** a la carte 30/47.
◆ Don't leave Lisbon without trying this elegant and well-established restaurant. Pleasant furnishings and décor, an exclusive atmosphere and a good menu.

São Jerónimo - *Hotel Da Torre*, Rua dos Jerónimos 12, ✉ 1400-211, ☎ 21 364 87 97, *Fax 21 363 26 92* – AE VISA JCB. West : by Av. 24 de Julho EU
closed Saturday lunch and Sunday – **Meals** a la carte 24/35.
◆ This restaurant belongs to the Hotel Da Torre. A spacious bar and waiting area and welcoming décor with modern decoration. Carefully prepared dishes and professional service.

XL, Calçada da Estrela 57, ✉ 1200-661, ☎ 21 395 61 18, *Fax 21 395 85 12* – AE VISA. FU n
closed 1 to 21 August and Sunday – **Meals** - dinner only, booking essential - a la carte approx. 32.
◆ A comprehensive list of Spanish wines and delicious young lamb are the highlights of this restaurant with an ingenious, maze-like layout and charming colonial atmosphere.

XX **Saraiva's,** Rua Engenheiro Canto Resende 3, ✉ 1050-104, ☎ 21 354 06 09, *Fax 21 353 19 87* – ▤. AE ⓓ ⓜ VISA JCB. ✻ FR v
closed Saturday and Bank Holidays – **Meals** a la carte 22/29.
• Carpeted floors and elegant modern-style furnishings. Very professional service, a well-heeled clientele and a lively ambience.

XX **Estufa Real,** Jardim Botânico da Ajuda - Calçada do Galvão, ✉ 1400, ☎ 21 361 94 00, *estufa.real@clix.pt, Fax 21 361 90 18* – ▤ P. AE ⓓ ⓜ VISA. ✻
closed Saturday lunch – **Meals** - lunch only - a la carte 22/39.
• A relaxing location in the Jardim Botânico da Ajuda. A lovely glassed-in conservatory with attractive modern design details. West : by Av. 24 de Julho EU

XX **Adega Tia Matilde,** Rua da Beneficência 77, ✉ 1600-017, ☎ 21 797 21 72, *Fax 21 797 21 72* – ▤ ⇔. AE ⓓ ⓜ VISA. ✻ FR h
closed Saturday dinner and Sunday – **Meals** a la carte 23/28.
• A popular establishment, friendly and professional. Portuguese specialities. Classic-modern style with plants and fresh flowers on the tables.

XX **Varanda da União,** Rua Castilho 14 C-7º, ✉ 1250-069, ☎ 21 314 10 45, *Fax 21 314 10 46,* ≤ – |‡| ▤. AE ⓓ ⓜ VISA JCB. ✻ FT b
closed Sunday – **Meals** a la carte approx. 35.
• A fine panorama of Lisbon rooftops from the 7th floor of a residential building. A large number of waiting staff and success based on the quality of the cuisine.

XX **O Polícia,** Rua Marquês Sá da Bandeira 112, ✉ 1050-150, ☎ 21 796 35 05, *Fax 21 796 97 91* – ▤. AE ⓓ ⓜ VISA. ✻ FR c
closed Saturday dinner, Sunday and Bank Holidays – **Meals** a la carte 26/35.
• Renowned for fish. Well-decorated establishment, with large dining room, friendly service and a busy atmosphere. Reservation recommended.

X **Sua Excelência,** Rua do Conde 34, ✉ 1200-367, ☎ 21 390 36 14, *sua xcelencia@mail.telepac.pt, Fax 21 396 75 85,* 🏠 – ▤. AE ⓜ VISA JCB EU t
closed September and Wednesday – **Meals** a la carte 26/48.
• Simple and pleasant. Comfortable and friendly, offering cooking with an individual touch. Patio with a canopy.

X **Caseiro,** Rua de Belém 35, ✉ 1300-354, ☎ 21 363 88 03, *Fax 21 364 23 39* – ▤. AE ⓓ ⓜ VISA. ✻ West : by Av. 24 de Julho EU
closed August and Sunday – **Meals** a la carte 24/34.
• Traditional establishment serving delicious, simply prepared dishes which have made this restaurant well known in the locality.

The fado restaurants :

XX **Clube de Fado,** São João da Praça 94, ✉ 1100-521, ☎ 21 885 27 04, *info@clube-de-fado.com, Fax 21 888 26 94* – ▤. AE ⓓ ⓜ VISA JCB. ✻ LYZ h
Meals - dinner only - a la carte 32/43.
• A restaurant with a well-cared for appearance, a pleasant ambience and a bar with a friendly atmosphere. Simple décor.

XX **Sr. Vinho,** Rua do Meio-à-Lapa 18, ✉ 1200-723, ☎ 21 397 26 81, *restsrvinho@telepac.pt, Fax 21 395 20 72* – ▤. AE ⓓ ⓜ VISA JCB. ✻ FU r
closed Sunday – **Meals** - dinner only - a la carte approx. 50.
• Traditional cuisine of the region to the classic Lisbon sound of fado in a pleasant and welcoming setting. The dining room is a little crowded but the menu is good.

XX **A Severa,** Rua das Gáveas 51, ✉ 1200-206, ☎ 21 342 83 14, *Fax 21 346 40 06* – ▤. AE ⓓ ⓜ VISA JCB. ✻ JY b
closed Thursday – **Meals** a la carte 35/50.
• A traditional fado restaurant run by a large family who base their success on good cuisine. Comfortable and with classic Portuguese décor.

X **Adega Machado,** Rua do Norte 91, ✉ 1200-284, ☎ 21 322 46 40, *Fax 21 346 75 07* – ▤. AE ⓓ ⓜ VISA JCB. ✻ JY k
closed Monday – **Meals** - dinner only - a la carte 36/44.
• Pleasant décor in a typical restaurant of the region where the singing of fado tends to predominate over the cuisine. Rather small tables.

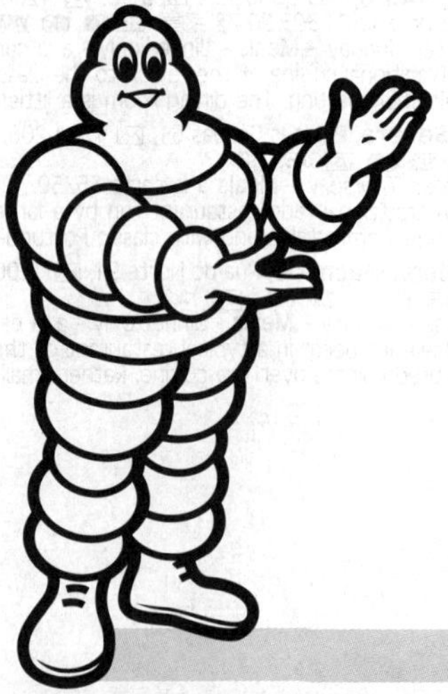

Spain

España

MADRID – BARCELONA – BILBAO
MÁLAGA – SEVILLE – VALÈNCIA

PRACTICAL INFORMATION

LOCAL CURRENCY

1 euro (€) = 1,34 USD ($) (Dec 2004)

National Holiday in Spain: *12 October*

TOURIST INFORMATION

The telephone number and address of the Tourist Information offices is given in the text of the towns under ℹ.

FOREIGN EXCHANGE

Banks are usually open from 8.30am to 2pm (closed on Saturdays and Sundays in summer).
Exchange offices in Sevilla and Valencia airports open from 9am to 2pm, in Barcelona airport from 9am to 2pm and 7 to 11pm. In Madrid and Málaga airports, offices operate a 24-hour service.

TRANSPORT

Taxis may be hailed when showing the green light or "Libre" sign on the windscreen. Madrid, Barcelona, Bilbao and Valencia have a Metro (subway) network. In each station complete information and plans will be found.

SHOPPING

In the index of street names, those printed in red are where the principal shops are found.
The big stores are easy to find in town centres; they are open from 10am to 9.30pm. Exclusive shops and boutiques are open from 10am to 2pm and 5 to 8pm. In Madrid they will be found in Serrano, Princesa and the Centre; in Barcelona, Passeig de Gràcia, Diagonal and the Rambla de Catalunya.
Second-hand goods and antiques: El Rastro (Flea Market), Las Cortes, Serrano in Madrid; in Barcelona, Les Encantes (Flea Market), Gothic Quarter.

TIPPING

Hotel, restaurant and café bills always include service in the total charge. Nevertheless it is usual to leave the staff a small gratuity which may vary depending upon the district and the service given. Doormen, porters and taxi-drivers are used to being tipped.

SPEED LIMITS

The maximum permitted speed on motorways is 120 km/h - 74 mph, and 90 km/h - 56 mph on other roads.

SEAT BELTS

The wearing of seat belts is compulsory for drivers and all passengers.

"TAPAS"

Bars serving "tapas" (typical Spanish food to be eaten with a glass of wine or an aperitif) will usually be found in central, busy or old quarters of the following selected cities.

MADRID

Madrid 28000 P 576 K 19, 575 K 19 and 121 H 7 – Pop. 2 957 058 – alt. 646.

Paris (by Irún) 1276 – Barcelona 617 – Bilbao 395 – A Coruña/La Coruña 684 – Lisboa 625 – Málaga 494 – Porto 609 – Sevilla 531 – València 352 – Zaragoza 322.

Duque de Medinaceli 2, ✉ 28014, ☎ 902 100 007, turismo@madrid.org, Fax 91 429 37 05, Pl. Mayor 3, ✉ 28012, ☎ 91 588 16 36, inforturismo@munimadrid.es, Fax 91 366 54 77, Puerta de Toledo Market, ✉ 28005, ☎ 902 100 007, turismo@madrid.org, Fax 91 364 24 32, Atocha Station, ✉ 28007, ☎ 902 100 007, turismo@madrid.org, Fax 91 530 79 55 Chamartín Station, ✉ 28036, ☎ 902 100 007 turismo @madrid.org, Fax 91 323 79 51 and Madrid-Barajas airport ✉ 28042, ☎ 902 100 007, turismo @madrid.org, Fax 91 305 41 95 – R.A.C.E. Isaac Newton – Parque Technológico de Madrid (PTM), ✉ 28760 Tres Cantos (Madrid), ☎ 91 594 74 00, Fax 91 594 72 49.

18 18 9 Club de Campo-Villa de Madrid, North-west by Av. de la Victoria ☎ 91 550 20 10 DU
18 18 La Moraleja, North : 11 km by Pas. de la Castellana ☎ 91 650 07 00 GR – 9 Club Barberán, South-west : 10 km by Av. de Portugal ☎ 91 509 11 40 DX
18 9 Las Lomas – El Bosque, South-west : 18 km by Av. de Portugal and detour to Boadilla del Monte ☎ 91 616 75 00 DX
18 Real Automóvil Club de España, North : 28 km by Pas. de la Castellana ☎ 91 657 00 11 GR
18 Nuevo Club de Madrid, Las Matas, West : 26 km by Av. de la Victoria ☎ 91 630 08 20 DU
9 Somosaguas, West : 10 km by Puente del Rey ☎ 91 352 16 47 DX
9 18 Club Olivar de la Hinojosa, North-east by Av. de América and detour to M 40 ☎ 91 721 18 89
18 La Dehesa, Villanueva de la Cañada, West : 28 km by Av. de la Victoria and detour to El Escorial ☎ 91 815 70 22 DU
18 18 Real Sociedad Hipica Española Club de Campo, North : 28 km by Pas. de la Castellana ☎ 91 657 10 18 GR.

✈ Madrid-Barajas E : 12 km ☎ 902 353 570 – Iberia : Velázquez 130, ✉ 28006, ☎ 91 587 87 87 HUV, Santa Cruz de Marcenado 2, ✉ 28015, ☎ 902 400 500 EV and at airport, ✉ 28042, ☎ 91 587 87 87.
Chamartín 🚗 ☎ 902 24 02 02 HR.

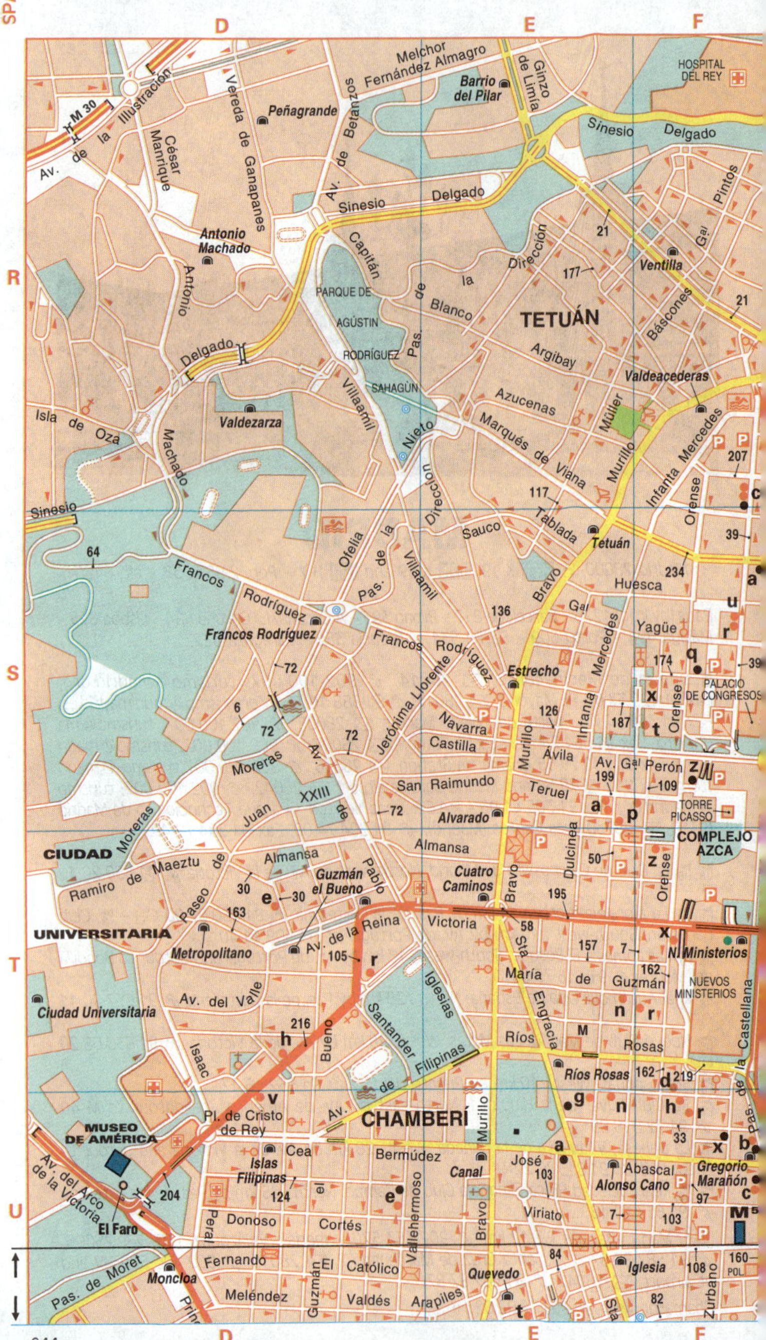
D
E
F
R
S
T
U
D
E
F
M 30
Av. de la Ilustración
César Manrique
Vereda de Ganapanes
Peñagrande
Melchor Fernández Almagro
Av. de Betanzos
Barrio del Pilar
Ginzo de Limia
HOSPITAL DEL REY
Sinesio Delgado
Antonio Machado
Antonio Machado
Capitán Blanco
PARQUE DE AGÚSTIN RODRÍGUEZ SAHAGÚN
Pas. de la Dirección
TETUÁN
Ventilla
Gal Pintos
Báscones
Argibay
Valdeacederas
Azucenas
Marqués de Viana
Müller
Murillo
Infanta Mercedes
Isla de Oza
Valdezarza
Villaamil
Nieto
Dirección
Orense
117
Tablada
Tetuán
Sauco
Ofelia
Pas. de la Villaamil
Bravo
64
Francos Rodríguez
Francos Rodríguez
136
Huesca
Yagüe
Gal
234
207
39
21
177
174
39
PALACIO DE CONGRESOS
Estrecho
Jerónima Llorente
Navarra
Castilla
126
Murillo
Ávila
Infanta Mercedes
187
Orense
Av. Gal Perón
199
109
72
6
72
72
Moreras
Av. XXIII
Juan
San Raimundo
Teruel
Alvarado
TORRE PICASSO
COMPLEJO AZCA
CIUDAD UNIVERSITARIA
Moreras
Ramiro de Maeztu
Paseo de Juan XXIII
Almansa
Almansa
Guzmán el Bueno
Pablo Iglesias
Cuatro Caminos
Bravo
Dulcinea
50
195
Orense
30
30
163
Metropolitano
Av. de la Reina Victoria
58
157
7
105
Nuevos Ministerios
162
NUEVOS MINISTERIOS
Ciudad Universitaria
Av. del Valle
Santander
Iglesias
Sta María de Guzmán
Engracia
Ríos Rosas
216
Bueno
Isaac Peral
Av. de Filipinas
Ríos Rosas
162
219
Pas. de la Castellana
MUSEO DE AMÉRICA
Pl. de Cristo de Rey
CHAMBERÍ
Murillo
33
Cea Bermúdez
Islas Filipinas
Canal
José Abascal
103
Alonso Cano
Gregorio Marañón
97
Av. del Arco de la Victoria
204
124
el
Vallehermoso
Bravo
Viriato
103
7
El Faro
Donoso Cortés
M5
Pas. de Moret
Moncloa
Fernando El Católico
Meléndez Valdés
Guzmán
Arapiles
Quevedo
84
Iglesia
108
160
POL
82
Zurbano
Sta
Princesa

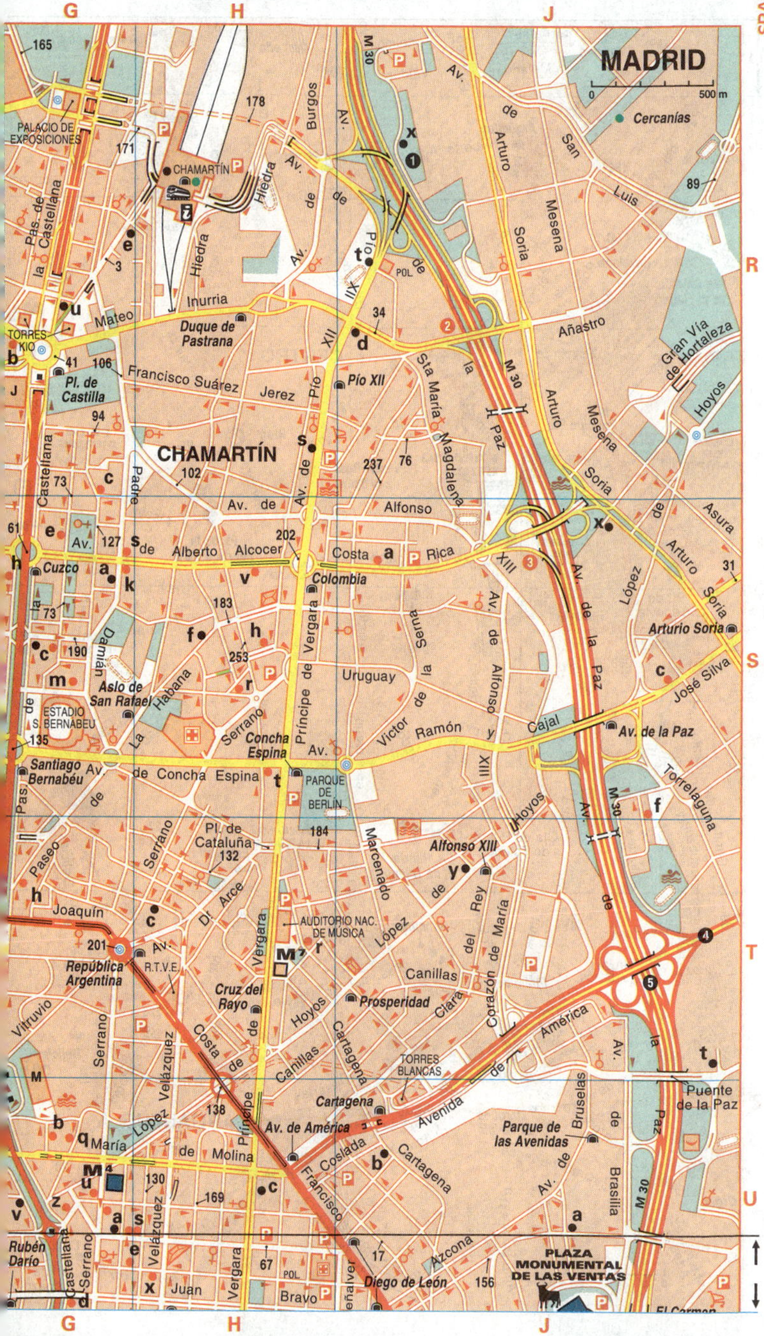
MADRID
0
500 m
Cercanías
G
H
J
R
S
T
U
PALACIO DE EXPOSICIONES
CHAMARTÍN
TORRES KIO
Pl. de Castilla
Duque de Pastrana
Pío XII
Av. de Burgos
Av. de Pío XII
Hiedra
Inurria
Mateo
Francisco Suárez
Jerez
Pas. de la Castellana
Padre Damián
Av. de Alberto Alcocer
Av. de Alfonso XIII
Costa Rica
Colombia
Cuzco
Santa María Magdalena
Av. de la Paz
M 30
Añastro
Arturo Soria
Mesena
San Luis
Av. de San Luis
Gran Vía de Hortaleza
Hoyos
López de Hoyos
Asura
Arturio Soria
José Silva
Av. de la Paz
Torrelaguna
Uruguay
Víctor de la Serna
Ramón y Cajal
Aslo de San Rafael
ESTADIO S. BERNABEU
La Habana
Serrano
Concha Espina
Av. de Concha Espina
Santiago Bernabéu
Paseo de la Castellana
PARQUE DE BERLÍN
Príncipe de Vergara
Marcenado
Alfonso XIII
Pl. de Cataluña
Dr. Arce
Joaquín Costa
República Argentina
R.T.V.E.
AUDITORIO NAC. DE MÚSICA
Cruz del Rayo
Prosperidad
Canillas
Clara del Rey
Corazón de María
Cartagena
TORRES BLANCAS
Avenida de América
Av. de América
Vitruvio
Velázquez
María de Molina
Parque de las Avenidas
Av. de Bruselas
Av. de Brasilia
Puente de la Paz
Francisco Silvela
Coslada
Azcona
Rubén Darío
Diego de León
Juan Bravo
Eñalver
PLAZA MONUMENTAL DE LAS VENTAS
El Carmen
POL

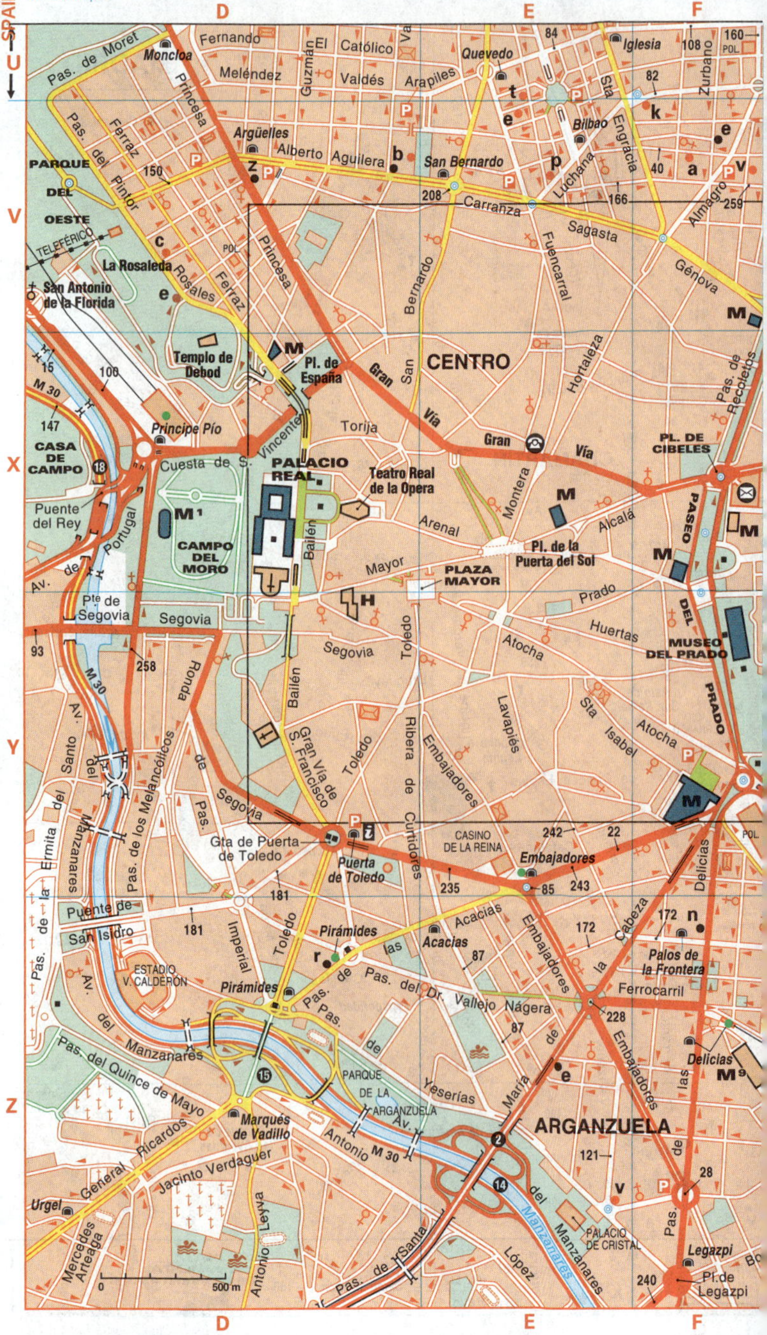
D
E
F
U
V
X
Y
Z
Pas. de Moret
Moncloa
Fernando
Meléndez
El Católico
Valdés
Guzmán
Arapiles
Quevedo
Iglesia
Zurbano
Princesa
Ferraz
Pas. del Pintor
Argüelles
Alberto Aguilera
San Bernardo
Bilbao
Luchana
Sta Engracia
Almagro
PARQUE DEL OESTE
TELEFÉRICO
La Rosaleda
Rosales
San Antonio de la Florida
Carranza
Sagasta
Génova
Fuencarral
Bernardo
Hortaleza
Templo de Debod
Pl. de España
CENTRO
Gran Vía
San
Pas. de Recoletos
Príncipe Pío
CASA DE CAMPO
Cuesta de S. Vincente
Torija
PALACIO REAL
Teatro Real de la Ópera
Montera
PL. DE CIBELES
Puente del Rey
CAMPO DEL MORO
Portugal
Bailén
Arenal
Pl. de la Puerta del Sol
Alcalá
PASEO DEL PRADO
Mayor
PLAZA MAYOR
Prado
Av. de Portugal
Pte de Segovia
Segovia
Huertas
Atocha
MUSEO DEL PRADO
Toledo
Ronda de Segovia
Lavapiés
Sta Isabel
Gran Vía de S. Francisco
Ribera de Curtidores
Embajadores
Av. del Manzanares
Pas. de los Melancólicos
Pas. de la Ermita del Santo
Gta de Puerta de Toledo
Puerta de Toledo
CASINO DE LA REINA
Embajadores
Delicias
Puente de San Isidro
Imperial
Pirámides
Acacias
Palos de la Frontera
Pas. de la Cabeza
ESTADIO V. CALDERÓN
Pas. de las Acacias
Pas. del Dr. Vallejo Nágera
Ferrocarril
Pas. del Quince de Mayo
PARQUE DE LA ARGANZUELA
Yeserías
María de Molina
Pas. de las Delicias
ARGANZUELA
Marqués de Vadillo
Av. Antonio
M 30
General Ricardos
Jacinto Verdaguer
Urgel
Mercedes Arteaga
Antonio Leyva
Pas. de Santa María de la Cabeza
del Manzanares
López
PALACIO DE CRISTAL
Legazpi
Pl. de Legazpi
0
500 m

SPAIN
G
H
J
U
V
X
Y
Z
PLAZA MONUMENTAL DE LAS VENTAS
Diego de León
Azcona
Rubén Darío
Castellana
Serrano
Velázquez
Vergara
Juan Bravo
N. de Balboa
SALAMANCA
Lista
Peñalver
Conde
Ortega y Gasset
José
Ayala
Hermosilla
Goya
Jorge Juan
Príncipe de Vergara
Av. de los Toreros
Silvela
Ventas
El Carmen
Alcalá
Pl. de Manuel Becerra
Manuel Becerra
Parque de la Quinta Fuente del Berro
Av. de la Paz
PALACIO DE LOS DEPORTES
O'Donnell
TORRE ESPAÑA
R.T.V.E.
Baranda
Esquerdo
PUERTA DE ALCALÁ
Retiro
P. de Vergara
Narváez
Ibiza
Alcalde
Sáinz de Baranda
Sainz
Juan Esplandiú
PARQUE DE ROMA
Estanque
Alfonso XII
Menéndez Pelayo
EL PARTERRE
PARQUE DEL BUEN RETIRO
Palacio de Cristal
LA CHOPERA
OBSERVATORIO ASTRONÓMICO
RETIRO
Av. de Nazaret
Doctor
Astros
Estrella
Pl. Corregidor Alonso de Aguilar
Pl. de Mariano de Cavia
Conde de Casal
Pl. Conde de Casal
Avenida Cavanilles
Av. del Mediterráneo
A 3
M 30
Atocha Renfe
ATOCHA
PANTEÓN
Av. de Menéndez Pelayo
Valderribas
Comercio
Av. de la Ciudad de Barcelona
Doctor Esquerdo
Pacífico
Toledana
Sierra
Camino de Valderribas
Méndez Álvaro
Bustamante
Bosch
Pedro
P.te de Vallecas
Av. de la Albufera
Nueva Numancia
Arroyo del Olivar
Portazgo
Monte Igueldo
Monte Perdido
Av. de la Paz
PARQUE DE LAS DELICIAS
PLANETARIO
CINE IMAX
M 12
POL.

K
L
V
X
Y
Z
Princesa
Palacio de Liria
V. Rodríguez
Conde Duque
Montserrat
Amaniel
San Bernardo
Divino
Pastor
Glorieta de Bilbao
Bilbao
Sagasta
Fuencarral
Apodaca
Barceló
Pl. Dos de Mayo
CENTRO CULTURAL CLARA DEL REY
Palma
MALASAÑA
Espíritu
Tribunal
San Mateo
Santo
San Pablo
Noviciado
TORRE DE MADRID
EDIFICIO ESPAÑA
Ferraz
MUSEO CERRALBO
Plaza de España
Reyes
Pez
Madera
Baja de San
Colón
Luna
Pizarro
Corredera
Barco
Puebla
Hortaleza
Pelayo
Gran Vía
Leganitos
Cuesta de San Vicente
PALACIO DEL SENADO
Santo Domingo
Jardines de Sabatini
Torija
Bailén
Bola
Callao
Infantas
LA ENCARNACIÓN
PALACIO REAL
Teatro Real de la Opera
LAS DESCALZAS REALES
Carmen
Montera
Jardines
Pl. de Oriente
Pl. de Isabel II
Ópera
Arenal
Alcalá
Sevilla
Pl. de la Armería
Pl. de Canalejas
Catedral N. S. de la Almuneda
Mayor
Sol
Pl. de la Puerta del Sol
PL. DE LA VILLA
PLAZA MAYOR
Pl. de la Provincia
Carretas
Cruz
Arco de Cuchilleros
SAN MIGUEL
Sacramento
Segovia
Pl. J. Benavente
Atocha
Huertas
San Pedro
Jardines de las Vistillas
Pl. de la Paja
Capilla del Obispo
S. Isidro
Colegiata
Antón Martín
Magdalena
Toledo
Pl. de Tirso de Molina
La Latina
Don Pedro
San Francisco el Grande
Pl. de Cascorro
Pl. de la Cebada
Jesús y María
Mesón de Paredes
Lavapiés
Olivar
Ave María
Calatrava
el Rastro
Ribera de Curtidores
Embajadores
Gran Vía de San Francisco
Zurita
Argumosa
Valencia
200 m
Cercanías

MADRID

Alcalá . . . . MX
Alvarez Gato . . . . LY 9
Arenal . . . . KY
Arrieta . . . . KX 18
Augusto Figueroa . . . . . . MV 24
Ayala . . . . NV 25
Bárbara de Braganza . . . . NV 27
Bordadores . . . . KY 32
Callao (Pl. del) . . . . LX 36
Carmen LX
Cava Alta . . . . KZ 42
Cava Baja . . . . KZ 43
Cava de San Miguel . . . . . KY 45
Ciudad de Barcelona
(Av. de la) . . . . NZ 46
Colón (Pl. de) . . . . NV 49
Concepción Jerónima . . . . LY 52
Conde de Romanones . . . LY 53
Cordón (Pl. del) . . . . KY 54
Cortes (Pl. de las) . . . . . . MY 57
Cuchilleros . . . . KY 60
Duque de Alba . . . . LZ 78
Duque de Medinaceli . . . MY 79
Echegaray . . . . LY 81
Espoz y Mina . . . . LY 88
Estudios . . . . KZ 91
Felipe IV . . . . NY
Fernando el Santo . . . . . . NV 99
Fuencarral LV
General Vara del Rey
(Pl. del) . . . . KZ 112
Goya . . . . NV 114
Gran Vía LX
Herradores (Pl. de los) . . . KY 116
Hortaleza LX
Independencia (Pl. de la) . NX 118
Infanta Isabel (Pas. de la) . NZ 119
Jesús del Valle . . . . LV 123
Libreros . . . . KX 133
Madrazo . . . . MY 141
Marqués de Cubas . . . . . MY 145
Mayor (Pl.) . . . . KY
Mayor . . . . KY
Mejía Lequerica . . . . LMV 159
Montera LX
Núñez de Arce . . . . LY 168
Preciados . . . . LX 186
Príncipe . . . . LY 188
Puerta Cerrada (Pl. de) . . . KY 191
Puerta de Moros (Pl. de) . KZ 192
Puerta del Sol (Pl. de la) . . LY
Recoletos . . . . NX 196
San Bernardino . . . . KV 211
San Francisco (Carrera de) KZ 214
San Jerónimo
(Carrera de) . . . . LMY 218
San Justo . . . . KY 220
San Lorenzo . . . . LV 222
San Millán . . . . KZ 225
Santa Engracia . . . . MV 226
Santo Domingo
(Cuesta de) . . . . KX 230
Santo Domingo (Pl. de) . . KX 231
Sevilla . . . . LY 232
Tudescos . . . . LX 238
Valverde . . . . LV 246
Ventura de la Vega . . . . . . LY 249
Ventura Rodríguez . . . . . . KV 250
Vergara . . . . KY 252
Villa de París (Pl. de la) . . . NV 255
Virgen de los Peligros . . . . LX 256

INDEX OF STREET NAMES IN MADRID

Acacias (Pas. de las) EZ
Agustín de Foxá GR 3
Alberto Aguilera DV
Alberto Alcocer (Av. de) HS
Albufera (Av. de la) JZ
Alcalá MX
Alcalde Sáinz de Baranda JX
Alcántara JV 4
Alfonso XI NX
Alfonso XII NX
Alfonso XIII (Av. de) JS
Almagro FV
Almansa DT
Almirante Francisco Moreno DS 6
Almirante MV
Alonso Cano ET 7
Alonso Martínez (Pl. de) MV
Alvarez Gato LY 9
Amaniel KV
América (Av. de) JT
Añastro JR
Ancora GZ 10
Aniceto Marinas DX 15
Antonio Leyva DZ
Antonio López DZ
Antonio Machado DR
Antonio Maura NY
Apodaca LV
Arapiles EU
Arco de la Victoria (Av. del) DU
Ardemans JU 17
Arenal KY
Argensola MV
Argumosa LZ
Arrieta KX 18
Arroyo de la Media Legua JY 19
Arroyo del Olivar JZ
Arturo Soria JRS
Astros JY
Asturias (Av. de) ER 21
Asura JS
Atocha (R. de) EY 22
Atocha LY
Augusto Figueroa MV 24
Ave María LZ
Ávila ES
Ayala NV 25
Azcona JU
Azucenas ER
Bailén KY
Bárbara de Braganza NV 27
Barceló LV
Barco LV
Barquillo MX
Báscones FR
Beata María Ana de Jesús (Pl. de la) FZ 28
Beatriz de Bobadilla DT 30
Belisana JS 31
Betanzos (Av. de) DR
Bilbao (Glta de) LV
Bola KX
Bolívar GZ
Bordadores KY 32
Brasilia (Av. de) JU
Bravo Murillo EU
Bretón de los Herreros FU 33
Bruselas (Av. de) JU
Burgos (Av. de) HR
Bustamante GZ
Caídos de la División Azul JR 34
Calatrava KZ
Callao (Pl. del) LX 36
Camino de los Vinateros JY 37
Canalejas (Pl. de) LY
Canillas JT
Cánovas del Castillo (Pl. de) MY
Capitán Blanco Argibay ER
Capitán Haya FS 39
Caracas FV 40
Carmen LX
Carranza EV
Carretas LY
Cartagena JU
Cascorro (Pl. de) LZ
Castellana (Pas. de la) NV
Castilla (Pl. de) GR 41
Castilla ES
Cataluña (Pl. de) HT
Cava Alta KZ 42
Cava Baja KZ 43
Cava de San Miguel KY 45
Cavanilles JY
Cea Bermúdez DU
Cebada (Pl. de la) KZ
César Manrique DR
Cibeles (Pl. de) MX
Ciudad de Barcelona (Av. de la) NZ 46
Clara del Rey JT
Claudio Coello GV 48
Claudio Moyano NZ
Colegiata LZ
Colón (Pl. de) NV 49
Colón LV
Comandante Zorita ET 50
Comercio HZ
Concepción Jerónima LY 52
Concha Espina (Av. de) HS
Conde de Casal (Pl. del) JY
Conde de Peñalver JU
Conde de Romanones LY 53
Conde Duque KV
Corazón de María JT
Cordón (Pl. del) KY 54
Corredera Baja de San Pablo LV
Corregidor Alonso de Aguilar (Pl. del) JY
Corregidor Diego Cabeza de Vaca JY 55
Cortes (Pl. de las) MY 57
Coslada JU
Costa Rica JS
Cristo Rey (Pl. de) DU
Cruz LY
Cuatro Caminos (Glta de) ET 58
Cuchilleros KY 60
Cuzco (Pl. de) GS 61
Daroca (Av. de) JV 63
Dehesa de la Villa (Carret. de la) DS 64
Delicias (Pas. de las) FYZ
Diego de León HU 67
Dirección (Pas. de la) ER
Divino Pastor LV
Doce de Octubre JX 69
Doctor Arce (Av. del) HT
Doctor Castelo JX 70
Doctor Esquerdo JY
Doctor Federico Rubio y Gali (Av. del) DS 72
Doctor Fléming GS 73
Doctor Vallejo Nágera (Pas. del) EZ
Don Pedro KZ
Don Ramón de la Cruz HV 75
Donoso Cortés DU
Dos de Mayo (Pl. del) LV
Drácena JR 76
Dulcinea ET
Duque de Alba LZ 78
Duque de Medinaceli MY 79
Echegaray LY 81
Eduardo Dato (Pas. de) FU 82
Eloy Gonzalo EU 84
Embajadores (Glta de) EY 85
Embajadores LZ
Emperador Carlos V (Pl. del) NZ
Ermita del Santo (Pas. de la) DY
Espalter NZ
España (Pl. de) KV
Esperanza (Pas. de la) EZ 87
Espíritu Santo LV
Espoz y Mina LY 88
Estación de Hortaleza (Carret. a la) JR 89
Estrella Polar JY 90
Estudios KZ 91
Extremadura (Pas. de) DY 93
Felipe IV NY
Félix Boix GR 94
Fernán González JX 96
Fernández de la Hoz FU 97
Fernando El Católico DU
Fernando el Santo NV 99
Fernando VI MV
Ferraz DV
Ferrocarril FZ
Filipinas (Av. de) ET
Florida (Pas. de la) DX 100
Francisco Silvela HU
Francisco Suárez HR
Francos Rodríguez DS
Fray Bernardino Sahagún HR 102
Fúcar MZ
Fuencarral LV
Ganapanes (Vereda de) DR
García de Paredes EU 103
General Ibáñez de Ibero DT 105
General López Pozas GR 106
General Martínez Campos (Pas. del) FU 108
General Moscardó FS 109
General Perón (Av. del) FS
General Pintos FR
General Ricardos DZ
General Vara del Rey (Pl. del) KZ 112
General Yagüe FS
Génova NV
Ginzo de Limia ER
Goya NV 114
Gran Vía LX
Gravina MV
Guzmán El Bueno DU
La Habana (Pas. de) HS
Hermosilla HV
Herradores (Pl. de los) KY 116
Hiedra HR
Hierbabuena ER 117
Hortaleza (Gran Vía de) JR
Hortaleza LX
Huertas LY
Huesca ES
Ibiza JX
Ilustración (Av. de la) DR
Imperial (Pas.) DZ
Independencia (Pl. de la) NX 118
Infanta Isabel (Pas. de la) NZ 119
Infanta Mercedes ES
Infantas LX
Isaac Peral DT
Isabel II (Pl. de) KX
Isla de Oza DR
Jacinto Benavente (Pl. de) LY
Jacinto Verdaguer DZ
Jaime El Conquistador EZ 121
Jardines LX
Jerez HR
Jerónima Llorente DS

Jesús del Valle LV 123
Jesús y María LZ
Jesús MY
Joaquín Costa GT
Joaquín María López DU 124
Jorge Juan HX
José Abascal EU
José Ortega y Gasset HV
José Silva JS
Juan Bravo HU
Juan de Olías ES 126
Juan Esplandiú JX
Juan Ramón Jiménez GS 127
Juan XXIII (Pas. de) DS
Julio Camba JV 129
Lagasca HV 130
Lavapiés LZ
Lealtad (Pl. de la) NY
Leganitos KX
Legazpi (Pl. de) FZ
Leizarán HT 132
Libreros KX 133
Lima (Pl. de) GS 135
Lope de Haro ES 136
López de Hoyos (Glta de) HU 138
López de Hoyos JT
Luchana EV
Luis Mitjans JZ 139
Luna KV
Madera LV
Madrazo MY 141
Magdalena LZ
Manuel Becerra (Pl. de) JV
Manzanares (Av. del) DEYZ
Marcenado JT
María de Guzmán ET
María de Molina HU
Mariano de Cavia (Pl. de) HY
Marqués de Cubas MY 145
Marqués de Monistrol (Pas. del) DX 147
Marqués de Salamanca (Pl. del) HV 148
Marqués de Urquijo DV 150
Marqués de Viana ER
Marqués de Zafra (Pas. del) JV 151
Marqués del Riscal GV 153
Martínez de la Riva JZ 155
Martínez Izquierdo JU 156
Mateo Inurria HR
Maudes ET 157
Mayor (Pl.) KY
Mayor KY
Mediterráneo (Av. del) JY
Mejía Lequerica LV 159
Melancólicos (Pas. de los) DY
Melchor Fernández Almagro DR
Meléndez Valdés DU
Méndez Álvaro HZ
Menéndez Pelayo (Av. de) HX
Mercedes Arteaga DZ
Mesena JR
Mesón de Paredes LZ
Miguel Angel FU 160
Modesto Lafuente FT 162
Moncloa (Av. de la) DT 163
Monforte de Lemos (Av. de) GR 165
Montalbán NX
Monte Igueldo (Av. del) JZ
Monte Perdido JZ
Montera LX
Montserrat KV
Moratín MZ
Moreras DS
Moret (Pas. de) DU
Moreto NY
Müller ER
Murillo (Pl. de) NZ
Narváez HX
Navarra ES
Nazaret (Av. de) JY
Nicasio Gallego EV 166
Núñez de Arce LY 168
Núñez de Balboa HV 169
O'Donnell JX
Ofelia Nieto DS
Olivar LZ
Orense FS
Oriente (Pl. de) KX
Pablo Iglesias (Av. de) DT
Padre Damián GS
Padre Francisco Palau y Quer GR 171
Paja (Pl. de la) KZ
Palma LV
Palos de la Frontera FZ 172
La Paz (Av. de) JV
La Paz (Puente de) JU
Pedro Bosch HZ
Pedro Teixeira FS 174
Pelayo MV
Pez Volador JY 175
Pez LV
Pinos Alta ER 177
Pintor Rosales (Pas. del) DV
Pío Baroja JY 180
Pío XII (Av. de) HR
Pío XII (Túnel de) HR 178
Pizarro LV
Pontones (Pas. de los) DZ 181
Portugal (Av. de) DX
Potosí HS 183
Pradillo HT 184
Prado (Pas. del) NZ
Prado MY
Preciados LX 186
Presidente Carmona (Av. del) ES 187
Prim NV
Princesa KV
Príncipe de Vergara HS
Príncipe LY
Profesor Waksman GS 190
Provincia (Pl. de la) LY
Puebla LV
Puerta Cerrada (Pl. de) KY 191
Puerta de Moros (Pl. de) KZ 192
Puerta de Toledo (Glta de) DY
Puerta del Sol (Pl. de la) LY
Puerto de Canfranc JZ 193
Quince de Mayo (Pas. del) DZ
Raimundo Fernández Villaverde ET 195
Ramiro de Maeztu DT
Ramón y Cajal (Av. de) JS
Recoletos (Pas. de) NV
Recoletos NX 196
Reina Cristina (Pas. de la) HY 198
Reina Mercedes ES 199
Reina Victoria (Av. de la) DET
República Argentina (Pl. de la) GT 201
República Dominicana (Pl. de la) HS 202
Rey (Puente del) DX
Reyes Católicos (Av. de los) DU 204
Reyes KV
Ribera de Curtidores KZ
Río KV
Ríos Rosas ET
Rosario Pino FR 207
Ruiz Jiménez (Glta de) EV 208
Sacramento KY
Sagasta LV
Salvador Dalí (Pl. de) JX 210
San Bernardino KV 211
San Bernardo KV
San Francisco (Carrera de) KZ 214
San Francisco (Gran Vía de) KZ
San Francisco de Sales (Pas. de) DT 216
San Isidro (Pte de) DZ
San Jerónimo (Carrera de) LY 218
San Juan de la Cruz (Pl. de) FT 219
San Justo KY 220
San Lorenzo LV 222
San Luis (Av. de) JR
San Marcos MX
San Mateo LV
San Millán KZ 225
San Raimundo ES
San Vicente (Cuesta de) DX
Santa Bárbara (Pl. de) MV
Santa Engracia MV 226
Santa Isabel MZ
Santa María de la Cabeza (Glta de) EZ 228
Santa María de la Cabeza (Pas. de) DFZ
Santa María Magdalena JR
Santander DT
Santo Domingo (Cuesta de) KX 230
Santo Domingo (Pl. de) KX 231
Sauco ES
Segovia (Puente de) DY
Segovia (Ronda de) DY
Segovia DY
Serrano NV
Sevilla LY 232
Sierra Toledana JZ
Sinesio Delgado DR
Sor Angela de la Cruz FS 234
Tablada ES
Teruel ES
Tirso de Molina (Pl. de) LZ
Toledo (Ronda de) EY 235
Toledo KZ
Toreros (Av. de los) JV
Torija KX
Torpedero Tucumán JR 237
Torrelaguna JS
Tudescos LX 238
Uruguay JS
Vado de Santa Catalina FZ 240
Valderribas (Camino de) JZ
Valderribas JZ
Valencia (Ronda de) EY 243
Valencia EY 242
Valle (Av. del) DT
Vallehermoso DU
Valverde LV 246
Velázquez HU
Ventura de la Vega LY 249
Ventura Rodríguez KV 250
Vergara KY 252
Victor Andrés Belaunde HS 253
Victor de la Serna JS
Villa (Pl. de la) KY
Villa de París (Pl. de la) NV 255
Villaamil DR
Villanueva NV
Virgen de los Peligros LX 256
Virgen del Puerto (Pas. de la) DY 258
Viriato EU
Vitruvio GT
Yeserías (Pas. de) EZ
Zurbano FU
Zurbarán FV 259
Zurita LZ

SIGHTS

VIEW OVER MADRID

Moncloa Beacon (Faro de Madrid): ☼ ★★ DU.

MUSEUMS

Prado-Museum ★★★ NY – *Thyssen Bornemisza Museum* ★★★ MY M6 – *Royal Palace* ★★ *(Palacio Real)* KXY *(Palace* ★*: Throne Room* ★, *Royal Armoury* ★★, *Royal Carriage Museum* ★ DX M1*)* – *National Archaeological Museum* ★★ *(Dama de Elche* ★★★*)* NV – *Lázaro Galdiano Museum* ★★ *(collection of enamels and ivories* ★★★*)* GU M4 – *Casón del Buen Retiro* ★ *(annexe to the Prado)* NY – *Reina Sofia Art Museum* ★ *(Picasso's Guernica* ★★★*)* MZ – *Army Museum* ★ *(Museo del Ejército)* NY – *Museum of the Americas* ★ *(Museo de América; Treasure of Los Quimbayas* ★, *Cortesano Manuscript* ★★★*)*, DU – *San Fernando Royal Fine Arts Academy* ★ *(Real Academia de Bellas Artes de San Fernando)* LX M2 – *Cerralbo Museum* ★ KV – *Sorolla Museum* ★ FU M5 – *City Museum (Museo de la Ciudad : models* ★*)* HT M7 – *Naval Museum (ship models* ★, *map of Juan de la Cosa* ★★*)* NXY M3 – *National Museum of Decorative Arts*★ NX M8 – *Municipal Museum (facade* ★★, *model of Madrid* ★*)* LV M10 – *National Museum of Science and Technology (ballestilla* ★★*)* FZ M9.

CHURCHES AND MONASTERIES

Descalzas Reales Monastery ★★ KLX – *San Francisco el Grande Church (stall* ★ *in chancel and sacristy)* KZ – *Royal Convent of the Incarnation* ★ *(Real Monasterio de la Encarnación)* KX – *San Antonio de la Florida Chapel* ★ *(frescoes* ★★*)* DV – *Saint Michael Church* ★ KY

THE OLD TOWN

Eastern Quarter ★★ *(Barrio de Oriente)* KVXY – *Bourbon Madrid* ★★ MNXYZ – *Old Madrid* ★ KYZ

PLACES OF INTEREST

Plaza Mayor ★★ KY – *Buen Retiro Park* ★★ HY – *Zoo-Aquarium* ★★ *West : by Casa de Campo Park* ★ DX – *Plaza de la Villa* ★ KY – *Vistillas Gardens (Q* ★*)* KYZ – *Campo del Moro Winter Garden* ★ DX – *University City* ★ *(Ciudad Universitaria)* DT – *Casa de Campo (Park)* ★ DX – *Plaza de Cibeles* ★ MNX – *Paseo del Prado* ★ MNXYZ – *Alcalá Arch* ★ *(Puerta de Alcalá)* NX – *Bullring* ★ *(Plaza Monumental de las Ventas)* JUV – *West Park* ★ *(Parque del Oeste)* DV

THEMATIC PARK

Warner Bros Park★ *South-East: 30 km: by Av. Del Manzanares* EZ

Centre : Paseo del Prado, Puerta del Sol, Gran Vía, Alcalá, Paseo de Recoletos, Plaza Mayor

The Westin Palace, pl. de las Cortes 7, ✉ 28014, ☎ 91 360 80 00, *reservation.palacemadrid@westin.com, Fax 91 360 81 00,* – rm, – 25/500. rest MY e
Meals a la carte 42/66 – 25 – **417 rm** 369, 48 suites.
• An elegant historic building in front of the Congreso de Diputados with a lovely patio in the middle and a Modernist-style glass dome. A harmonious blend of tradition and luxury.

Villa Real, pl. de las Cortes 10, ✉ 28014, ☎ 91 420 37 67, *villareal@derbyhotels.es, Fax 91 420 25 47,* – – 35/220. rest MY c
***Europa* : Meals** a la carte 33/44 – 19 – **96 rm** 316/354, 19 suites.
• This hotel has a valuable collection of Greek and Roman art on display in its public areas. The comfortable bedrooms have attractive decorative details and mahogany furnishings. A pleasant restaurant with contemporary lithographs.

Crowne Plaza Madrid City Centre, pl. de España, ✉ 28013, ☎ 91 454 85 00, *reservas@crowneplazamadrid.com, Fax 91 548 23 89,* – – 25/220. KV s
Meals a la carte 28/39 – 17 – **295 rm** 270/294, 11 suites.
• A traditional-style hotel in a cultural quarter of the city. Comfortable and well-appointed bedrooms and several lounges. A very good restaurant with beautiful views.

Tryp Ambassador, Cuesta de Santo Domingo 5, ✉ 28013, ☎ 91 541 67 00, *ambasador@trypnet.com, Fax 91 559 10 40* – – 25/300. KX k
Meals a la carte approx. 36 – 17 – **159 rm** 144/178, 24 suites.
• A rather grand hotel in keeping with the tone of this area of the city. A beautiful covered interior patio and comfortable rooms with elegant and high-quality furnishings. With its glass roof, the restaurant has the feel of a winter garden.

NH Nacional, paseo del Prado 48, ✉ 28014, ☎ 91 429 66 29, *nhnacional@nh-hotels.com, Fax 91 369 15 64* – – 25/150. NZ r
Meals *(closed 15 July to 5 September, Saturday and Sunday)* a la carte 28/41 – 17 – **213 rm** 176/211, 1 suite.
• A hotel with an attractive façade and a privileged location. A large foyer-reception and welcoming rooms with light toned décor and modern comfort.

Quo Puerta del Sol without rest, Sevilla 4, ✉ 28014, ☎ 91 532 90 49, *puertadelsol@hotelesquo.com, Fax 91 531 28 34* – . LY e
13 – **61 rm** 156/195, 1 suite.
• What the hotel lacks in lounge and public areas is compensated by the magnificent bedrooms with their avant-garde design and high technical specification.

Liabeny, Salud 3, ✉ 28013, ☎ 91 531 90 00, *info@hotelliabeny.com, Fax 91 532 74 21* – – 25/125. LX c
Meals 21 – 14 – **222 rm** 109/147.
• A hotel in a busy commercial area. The old-fashioned English-style bar lends a touch of class to the public areas. Comfortable rooms with classic functional décor and furnishings. The restaurant has an intimate ambience.

Senator España, Gran Vía 70, ✉ 28013, ☎ 91 522 82 65, *senator.espana@playasenator.com, Fax 91 522 82 64,* – rm, – 25/200. KV a
Meals 16 – 12 – **171 rm** 130/150.
• Excellent leisure facilities, which include a beauty salon and hydromassage pool. The hotel's guestrooms are well-appointed, and offer full soundproofing.

Santo Domingo, pl. de Santo Domingo 13, ✉ 28013, ☎ 91 547 98 00, *reserva@hotelsantodomingo.com, Fax 91 547 59 95* – – 25/200. KX a
Meals 31,50 – 11,50 – **120 rm** 162/215.
• Numerous works of art decorate the walls of this hotel. Comfortable rooms with modern bathrooms, some with hydro-massage baths.

Palacio San Martín, pl. San Martín 5, ✉ 28013, ☎ 91 701 50 00, *sanmartin@intur.com, Fax 91 701 50 10,* – – 25. KX t
Meals 35 – 15 – **93 rm** 133/163, 1 suite.
• A historic building which in the 1950s was the United States Embassy. A patio with a glass roof serves as a lounge area. Traditional-style bedrooms, plus a panoramic restaurant on the top floor.

H10 Villa de la Reina, Gran Vía 22, ✉ 28013, ☎ 91 523 91 01, *h10.villa.delareina@h10.es, Fax 91 521 75 22* – – 25/40. LX t
Meals 24 – 15 – **73 rm** 180/195, 1 suite.
• An attractive building dating from the early 20C with an elegant foyer-reception decked in marble and fine wood. All the charm of former times and comfortable rooms.

Preciados, Preciados 37, ✉ 28013, ☎ 91 454 44 00, *preciadoshotel@preciadoshotel.com, Fax 91 454 44 01* – – 25/100. KX u
Meals 18 – 12 – **68 rm** 117,20/186, 5 suites.
• The severe 19C Classicism of this hotel's architecture is in complete contrast to its modern and well-appointed facilities. A small but pleasant lounge.

Arosa coffee shop only, Salud 21, ✉ 28013, ☎ 91 532 16 00, *arosa@hotelarosa.com, Fax 91 531 31 27* – ⧉ ▤ TV – 25/45. AE ⓓ ⓜⓞ VISA JCB LX q
☕ 13 – **134 rm** 134/205.
◆ A wide range of cultural and leisure activities on your doorstep. The rooms have been modernised to improve comfort and décor.

Mayorazgo, Flor Baja 3, ✉ 28013, ☎ 91 547 26 00, *comercial@hotelmayorazgo.com, Fax 91 541 24 85* – ⧉ ▤ TV – 25/250. AE ⓓ ⓜⓞ VISA JCB. KV c
Meals 26 – ☕ 13 – **200 rm** 140/175.
◆ Close to the Plaza de España with a classic foyer, elegant rooms and pleasant décor. Facilities include a shop, boutique and a hairdressing salon. An intimate and elegant dining room with both a buffet and à la carte dishes.

A. Gaudí, Gran Vía 9, ✉ 28013, ☎ 91 531 22 22, *gaudi@hoteles-catalonia.es, Fax 91 531 54 69,* – ⧉ ▤ TV ♿ – 25/120. AE ⓓ ⓜⓞ VISA. LX s
Meals 15 – ☕ 13 – **185 rm** 136/177.
◆ Right in the centre of Madrid with an attractive early 20C façade behind which is a lively and modern interior. Well-lit, comfortable and modern rooms.

Senator Gran Vía, Gran Vía 21, ✉ 28013, ☎ 91 531 41 51, *senator.granvia@playasenator.com, Fax 91 524 07 99,* – ⧉ ▤ TV ♿ – 25. AE ⓓ ⓜⓞ VISA JCB.
Meals 16 – ☕ 13 – **136 rm** 120/140. LX b
◆ Behind the Senator's distinctive classical façade is an interior with the latest in modern comforts, including avant-garde bedrooms. Dining options include a simply styled restaurant offering à la carte and buffet dining, and a spacious cafeteria.

Lope de Vega without rest, Lope de Vega 49, ✉ 28014, ☎ 91 360 00 11, *lopedevega@hotellopedevega.com, Fax 91 429 23 91* – ⧉ ▤ TV – 25/50. AE ⓓ ⓜⓞ VISA JCB. MY d
☕ 11,77 – **59 rm** 140/180.
◆ A modern hotel with a marble foyer-reception and an adjoining convention centre. Contemporary-style bedrooms with written references to the playwright and 17C Madrid.

Suecia, Marqués de Casa Riera 4, ✉ 28014, ☎ 91 531 69 00, *bookings@hotelsuecia.com, Fax 91 521 71 41* – ⧉ ▤ TV – 25/150. AE ⓓ ⓜⓞ VISA. MX r
Meals 24 – ☕ 14 – **119 rm** 146/184, 9 suites.
◆ Opened in 1956, the Suecia has welcomed many famous guests, including Ernest Hemingway. The hotel's rooms are a successful mix of antique furniture and modern touches. The welcoming restaurant is part of the spacious, multi-purpose entrance hall-cum-reception.

Catalonia Moratín, Atocha 23, ✉ 28012, ☎ 91 369 71 71, *moratin@hoteles-catalonia.es, Fax 91 360 12 31* – ⧉ ▤ TV ♿ – 25/30. AE ⓓ ⓜⓞ VISA JCB. LY b
Meals 15 – ☕ 13 – **59 rm** 136/177, 4 suites.
◆ This 18C building combines original features, such as the staircase, with others of a more modern, practical design, including the stylish bedrooms. Attractive inner patio, as well as a pleasant restaurant in the basement serving refined cuisine.

Tryp Atocha without rest, Atocha 83, ✉ 28012, ☎ 91 330 05 00, *tryp.atocha@solmelia.com, Fax 91 420 15 60* – ⧉ ▤ TV – 25/210. AE ⓓ ⓜⓞ VISA. MZ a
☕ 14,50 – **150 rm** 132/150.
◆ This small palace dating from 1913 offers guests modern, functional facilities. The spacious lounge areas include the glass-adorned "salón de actos" and a superb staircase.

Atlántico without rest, Gran Vía 38, ✉ 28013, ☎ 91 522 64 80, *informacion@hotelatlantico.es, Fax 91 531 02 10* – ⧉ ▤ TV. AE ⓓ ⓜⓞ VISA JCB. LX e
116 rm ☕ 112/150.
◆ The comfort in this centrally located mansion has increased following a recent expansion. Harmonious decor in the bedrooms with matching wallpaper and curtains.

Casón del Tormes without rest, Río 7, ✉ 28013, ☎ 91 541 97 46, *hotormes@infonegocio.com, Fax 91 541 18 52* – ⧉ ▤ TV. AE ⓓ ⓜⓞ VISA. KV v
☕ 7 – **63 rm** 81/100.
◆ Large, bright and well-renovated public areas. Although lacking the best decor, the hotel's bedrooms have modern bathrooms and facilities expected of this category.

El Prado without rest, Prado 11, ✉ 28014, ☎ 91 369 02 34, *hotelprado@pradohotel.com, Fax 91 429 28 29* – ⧉ ▤ TV – 25/35. AE ⓓ ⓜⓞ VISA JCB. LY a
☕ 10 – **49 rm** 135/161.
◆ Modern and central and in an area which is lively at night. Rooms functional but equipped in keeping with their category. Coffee shop with a separate entrance.

Tryp Gran Vía without rest, Gran Vía 25, ✉ 28013, ☎ 91 522 11 21, *tryp.gran.via@solmelia.com, Fax 91 521 24 24* – ⧉ ▤ TV ♿ – 25/50. AE ⓓ ⓜⓞ VISA JCB. LX z
☕ 12 – **175 rm** 130/155.
◆ A landmark hotel frequented by Ernest Hemingway. Facilities here include a small foyer, a good breakfast room and pleasant bedrooms with marble bathrooms.

Carlos V without rest, Maestro Vitoria 5, ✉ 28013, ☎ 91 531 41 00, *recepcion@hotelcarlosv.com, Fax 91 531 37 61* – |♦| ▤ TV. AE ⓓ ⓜ VISA JCB. ✂ LX f
67 rm ☕ 94/124.
• The classic decor in the hotel lounge creates an atmosphere that is both warm and welcoming. The bedrooms here are pleasant, albeit on the functional side.

Los Condes without rest, Los Libreros 7, ✉ 28004, ☎ 91 521 54 55, *info@hotel-loscondes.com, Fax 91 521 78 82* – |♦| ▤ TV. AE ⓓ ⓜ VISA JCB. ✂ KLV g
☕ 9 – **68 rm** 86,92/135,50.
• Los Condes has a small reception area, pleasant lounge and a functional cafeteria for breakfast, along with bedrooms furnished and decorated in simple style.

Alexandra without rest, San Bernardo 29, ✉ 28015, ☎ 91 542 04 00, *alexhot@teleline.es, Fax 91 559 28 25* – |♦| ▤ TV – 25/90. AE ⓓ ⓜ VISA JCB. ✂ KV z
☕ 8 – **68 rm** 75/95.
• This hotel is discreetly run by friendly staff. The bedrooms have somewhat functional decor with standard furnishings and modern bathrooms.

La Terraza del Casino, Alcalá 15-3º, ✉ 28014, ☎ 91 521 87 00, *laterraza@casinodemadrid.es, Fax 91 523 44 36,* – |♦| ▤. AE ⓓ ⓜ VISA JCB. ✂ LX v
closed Holy Week, August, Saturday lunch, Sunday and Bank Holidays – **Meals** 100 and a la carte 63/71.
Spec. Yemas de espárragos blancos con trufa de verano y su sopa (primavera-verano). San Pedro con puré de limón y huevas de bacalao. Espalditas de cordero con chalotas a la naranja.
• In the 19C Madrid Casino building. The lounges have a classy feel and the very attractive terrace is a delightful setting in which to eat.

Paradis Madrid, Marqués de Cubas 14, ✉ 28014, ☎ 91 429 73 03, *paradis_madrid@paradis.es, Fax 91 429 32 95* – ▤. AE ⓓ ⓜ VISA JCB. ✂ MY v
closed Holy Week, Saturday lunch, Sunday and Bank Holidays – **Meals** a la carte 36/49.
• Located next to the Palacio de Congresos, this modern restaurant with one large dining room and two private dining rooms beyond is accessed via a delicatessen shop.

Café de Oriente, pl. de Oriente 2, ✉ 28013, ☎ 91 541 39 74, *cafeoriente@grupolezama.com, Fax 91 547 77 07* – ▤. AE ⓓ ⓜ VISA JCB. ✂ KXY w
Meals a la carte 44/51.
• In front of the Palacio Real and with a luxury café and an attractive wine cellar-style dining room. International menu with a modern twist.

La Manduca de Azagra, Sagasta 14, ✉ 28004, ☎ 91 591 01 12, *Fax 91 591 01 13* – ▤ LV b
closed August, 3 to 9 January and Sunday – **Meals** a la carte approx. 38.
• A privileged central location for this spacious restaurant with a minimalist feel in both its design and lighting. The cuisine here is based on quality products.

Moaña, Hileras 4, ✉ 28013, ☎ 91 548 29 14, *Fax 91 541 65 98* – |♦| ▤ 🚗. AE ⓓ ⓜ VISA JCB. ✂ KY r
Meals - Galician rest - a la carte 42/58.
• A comfortable, elegant restaurant in a central and historic area. A busy, popular bar, various private rooms and a large fish-tank containing a tempting selection of seafood.

Bajamar, Gran Vía 78, ✉ 28013, ☎ 91 548 48 18, *bajamar@iservicesmail.com, Fax 91 559 13 26* – ▤. AE ⓓ ⓜ VISA JCB. ✂ KV r
Meals - Seafood - a la carte 46/60.
• Beside the Plaza de España and with fish and seafood on display in the window. Very popular with foreign tourists. Very good fish and seafood dishes.

Errota-Zar, Jovellanos 3-1º, ✉ 28014, ☎ 91 531 25 64, *errota@errota-zar.com, Fax 91 531 25 64* – ▤. AE ⓓ ⓜ VISA. ✂ MY s
closed Holy Week, 3 weeks in August and Sunday – **Meals** - Basque rest - a la carte 34/40.
• In front of the Zarzuela theatre. The sober but elegant dining room serves Basque cuisine accompanied by an extensive wine and cigar list. One private room is also available.

El Asador de Aranda, Preciados 44, ✉ 28013, ☎ 91 547 21 56, *Fax 91 556 62 02* – ▤. AE ⓓ ⓜ VISA. ✂ KX z
closed 15 July-8 August and Monday dinner – **Meals** - Roast lamb - a la carte approx. 28.
• An attractive Castilian restaurant with beautiful wood ceilings. Traditional dishes and roast meats cooked in a wood fired oven a speciality.

Casa Matías, San Leonardo 12, ✉ 28015, ☎ 91 541 76 83, *Fax 91 541 93 70* – ▤. AE ⓓ ⓜ VISA. ✂ KV b
closed Sunday dinner – **Meals** - Braised meat specialities - a la carte 36/43.
• This Basque-style cider-house, adorned with large casks of its trademark brew for customers to taste, has two spacious rustic-modern rooms, one with an open grill.

XX **Julián de Tolosa,** Cava Baja 18, ✉ 28005, ℘ 91 365 82 10, *Fax 91 366 33 08* – ▤. AE ① MC VISA JCB. ✂ KZ c
closed Sunday dinner – **Meals** - Braised meat specialities - a la carte approx. 36.
• A pleasant restaurant in neo-rustic style offering the best T-bone steaks in the city. The limited menu is more than compensated for by the quality of the food.

XX **La Ópera de Madrid,** Amnistía 5, ✉ 28013, ℘ 91 559 50 92, *Fax 91 559 50 92* – ▤. AE ① MC VISA JCB. ✂ KY g
closed August, Sunday and Monday dinner – **Meals** a la carte 25/32.
• A good place to start an evening out or to discuss a play seen in the nearby theatre while enjoying something delicious. Elegant décor and a well-balanced menu.

XX **Pinocchio Bel Canto,** Sánchez Bustillo 5, ✉ 28012, ℘ 91 468 73 73, *restaurante@pinocchio.es, Fax 91 662 18 65,* Lively evening meals – ▤. AE ① MC VISA. ✂ NZ t
closed August, Saturday lunch and Sunday – **Meals** a la carte approx. 30.
• A very good location in front of the Centro de Arte Reina Sofia. Classic-modern décor and Italian influenced cuisine to the sound of bel canto.

XX **El Mentidero de la Villa,** Santo Tomé 6, ✉ 28004, ℘ 91 308 12 85, *info@mentiderodelavilla.com, Fax 91 651 34 88* – ▤. AE ① MC VISA. ✂ MV b
closed August, Saturday lunch, Sunday and Bank Holidays – **Meals** a la carte 32/39.
• A friendly, intimate restaurant with original and tasteful decor. Very carefully prepared and bold international cuisine.

XX **El Landó,** pl. Gabriel Miró 8, ✉ 28005, ℘ 91 366 76 81, *ellandomadrid@hotmail.com, Fax 91 366 25 56* – ▤. AE ① MC VISA. ✂ KZ a
closed Holy Week, August and Sunday – **Meals** a la carte 38/47.
• Near to the Basílica de San Francisco el Grande, this restaurant has a bar, dining room in the basement, and private room, all classically furnished with a profusion of wood.

XX **El Rincón de Esteban,** Santa Catalina 3, ✉ 28014, ℘ 91 429 92 89, *Fax 91 365 87 70* – ▤. AE ① MC VISA. ✂ MY a
closed August and Sunday – **Meals** a la carte 47/56.
• Frequented by politicians because of its proximity to the Palacio de Congresos. Intimate and elegant and offering traditional-style dishes.

XX **La Cava del Faraón,** Segovia 8, ✉ 28005, ℘ 91 542 52 54, *Fax 91 457 45 30* – ▤. AE ① MC VISA JCB. ✂ KY s
closed Monday – **Meals** - Egyptian rest, dinner only - a la carte 25/30.
• A typical Egyptian setting, with a tea-room, domed ceilings and a dining room where you can sample the cuisine of the country and enjoy a belly-dancing performance.

X **La Barraca,** Reina 29, ✉ 28004, ℘ 91 532 71 54, *Fax 91 523 82 73* – ▤. AE ① MC VISA JCB. ✂ LX a
Meals - Rice dishes - a la carte 26/35.
• Popular with tourists because of its renown and its location. Traditional Valencian décor with lots of ceramic tiles. Rice dishes a speciality.

X **La Vaca Verónica,** Moratín 38, ✉ 28014, ℘ 91 429 78 27 – ▤. AE ① MC VISA MZ e
closed Saturday lunch – **Meals** a la carte 20/28.
• This delightfully intimate and friendly restaurant is decorated in original style with colourful paintings, mirrored ceilings and candles on every table.

X **La Bola,** Bola 5, ✉ 28013, ℘ 91 547 69 30, *Fax 91 541 71 64* – ▤. ✂ KX r
closed Sunday dinner – **Meals** - Madrid style stew - a la carte approx. 25.
• A long-established Madrid tavern with the flavour of old Madrid. Traditional stewed dishes a speciality. Try the meat and chickpea stew.

X **La Esquina del Real,** Amnistía 2, ✉ 28013, ℘ 91 559 43 09 – ▤. AE MC VISA. ✂ KY e
closed 15 August-15 September, Saturday lunch and Sunday – **Meals** a la carte 38/45.
• An intimate and pleasant rustic-style restaurant with stone and brick walls. Friendly service and French dishes.

X **Taberna Carmencita,** Libertad 16, ✉ 28004, ℘ 91 531 66 12, *patxolezama@grupolezama.es, Fax 91 522 48 38* – ▤. AE ① MC VISA JCB. ✂ MX u
closed August-9 September, Saturday lunch and Sunday – **Meals** a la carte 19/28.
• A small restaurant founded in 1850 with dining areas on two levels. A traditional menu and some Basque specialities. Good ambience.

🍷 **La Botillería,** pl. de Oriente 4, ✉ 28013, ℘ 91 548 46 20, *cafeoriente@grupolezama.com, Fax 91 547 77 07,* 🏞 – ▤. AE ① MC VISA. ✂ KX w
Tapa 4,50 – **Ración** approx. 6,50.
• In an area that is very lively at night. Traditional Viennese café-style décor and a wide variety of canapes accompanied by good wines served by the glass.

🍷 **Prada a Tope,** Príncipe 11, ✉ 28012, ℘ 91 429 59 21 – ▤. MC VISA. ✂ LY u
closed August and Monday – **Tapa** 6 – **Ración** - Dishes from El Bierzo - approx. 8.
• A traditional establishment with a bar and rustic-style tables. Wood décor, photos on the walls and the opportunity to buy various products.

Taberna de San Bernardo, San Bernardo 85, ✉ 28015, ☎ 91 445 41 70 – ▤. MC VISA. ✻ – **Ración** approx. 5,80. LV m
◆ An informal, rustic tavern with three separate sections. Popular house specialities include two vegetarian dishes - papas con huevo and fritura de verduras.

Bocaito, Libertad 6, ✉ 28004, ☎ 91 532 12 19, *bocaito@bocaito.com, Fax 91 522 56 29* – ▤. ◑ MC VISA. ✻ MX b
closed August, Saturday lunch and Sunday – **Tapa** 2,50 – **Ración** approx. 9.
◆ A taurine atmosphere and décor. Ideal for sampling tapas either at the splendid bar or at a table. Deep fried and egg-based tapas are specialities.

Typical atmosphere :

Posada de la Villa, Cava Baja 9, ✉ 28005, ☎ 91 366 18 60, *povisa@posadadelavilla.com, Fax 91 366 18 80* – ▤. AE ◑ MC VISA JCB. ✻ KZ v
closed August and Sunday dinner except May – **Meals** a la carte 24/38.
◆ An old inn with a friendly ambience and Castilian décor. Regional menu and traditional roasts cooked in a wood fired oven. Madrid-style chickpea stew a speciality.

Botín, Cuchilleros 17, ✉ 28005, ☎ 91 366 42 17, *Fax 91 366 84 94* – ▤. AE ◑ MC VISA JCB. ✻ KY n
Meals a la carte 28/40.
◆ Founded in 1725 and said to be the oldest restaurant in the world. The old-style décor, traditional wine-cellar and wood fired oven all convey a strong feeling of the past.

Zerain, Quevedo 3, ✉ 28014, ☎ 91 429 79 09, *Fax 91 429 17 20,* Basque cider press – ▤. AE ◑ MC VISA JCB. ✻ MY x
closed Holy Week, August and Sunday – **Meals** a la carte 27/30.
◆ A Basque cider house with huge barrels. Friendly atmosphere and attractive décor with pictures of the Basque Country. Traditional cider house menu at reasonable prices.

Retiro, Salamanca, Ciudad Lineal : Paseo de la Castellana, Velázquez, Serrano, Goya, Príncipe de Vergara, Narváez, Don Ramón de la Cruz

Ritz, pl. de la Lealtad 5, ✉ 28014, ☎ 91 701 67 67, *reservations@ritz.es, Fax 91 701 67 76,* ☂, Ꝉ – |‡| ▤ TV ♿ – 🏛 25/250. AE ◑ MC VISA JCB. ✻ NY k
Meals a la carte 71/90 – ☕ 30 – **137 rm** 480, 30 suites.
◆ A hotel of international renown in a former 19C palace which had diplomatic connections. Sumptuous décor in the bedrooms and beautiful public areas. The well-known restaurant has attractive lounges and a pleasant terrace.

Villa Magna, paseo de la Castellana 22, ✉ 28046, ☎ 91 587 12 34, *hotel@villamagna.es, Fax 91 431 22 86,* ☂, Ꝉ – |‡| ▤ TV 🚗 – 🏛 25/400. AE ◑ MC VISA. ✻ rest GV y
Meals 39,50 - ***Le Divellec*** *(closed August and Sunday)* **Meals** a la carte 45/58 - ***Tsé Yang*** *(Chinese rest.)* **Meals** a la carte 34/40 – ☕ 26 – **164 rm** 465/520, 18 suites.
◆ Luxury, elegance and décor in the style of the time of Charles IV. Spacious rooms. Le Divellec restaurant is tasteful and has fine wood furnishings.

Wellington, Velázquez 8, ✉ 28001, ☎ 91 575 44 00, *wellington@hotel-wellington.com, Fax 91 576 41 64,* ⛱ – |‡| ▤ TV 🚗 – 🏛 25/200. AE ◑ MC VISA JCB. ✻ HX t
Meals see rest. ***Goizeko Wellington*** below – ☕ 25 – **259 rm** 250/325, 25 suites.
◆ In an elegant area of Madrid close to the Retiro. Classic style which has been updated in public rooms and bedrooms. Bullfighting aficionados meet here regularly.

Gran Meliá Fénix, Hermosilla 2, ✉ 28001, ☎ 91 431 67 00, *gran.melia.fenix@solmelia.com, Fax 91 576 06 61* – |‡| ▤ TV ♿ 🚗 – 🏛 25/100. AE ◑ MC VISA JCB. ✻ NV c
Meals a la carte 36/46 – ☕ 20 – **199 rm** 265/376, 16 suites.
◆ A distinguished hotel. Large public areas such as the elegant foyer with its cupola. Rooms comfortably furnished.

Meliá Galgos, Claudio Coello 139, ✉ 28006, ☎ 91 562 66 00, *melia.galgos@solmelia.es, Fax 91 561 76 62,* Ꝉ – |‡| ▤ TV 🚗 – 🏛 25/300. AE ◑ MC VISA JCB. ✻ GU a
Diábolo : **Meals** a la carte 36/48 – ☕ 18 – **350 rm** 144,50/305, 6 suites.
◆ Modern but traditional in style and frequented by business travellers and executives. Large and attractive public areas and bedrooms refurbished to a high level of comfort. Pleasant décor in the restaurant and excellent service.

Foxá M-30, Serrano Galvache 14, ✉ 28033, ☎ 91 384 04 00, *foxam30@foxa.com, Fax 91 384 04 02,* Ꝉ, ⛱, ⛱ – |‡|, ⊁ rm, ▤ TV ♿ 🚗 – 🏛 25/650. AE MC VISA. ✻ JR x
Meals a la carte 29/35 – ☕ 10 – **73 rm** 158/180, 2 suites.
◆ A magnificent hotel with works of art and antique furnishings. A grand staircase in the foyer and light and airy rooms, individually decorated. The elegant dining room offers traditional specialities and international dishes.

Adler, Velázquez 33, ✉ 28001, ✆ 91 426 32 20, *hoteladler@iova-sa.com, Fax 91 426 32 21* – |♦| ▤ TV 🚗. AE ⓓ ⓜ VISA. ✻ HV x
Meals a la carte 40/48 – ☕ 22 – **45 rm** 290/360.
◆ An exclusive hotel with an elegant décor. High-quality furnishings and comfortable and very well-appointed rooms. A pleasant restaurant with a friendly atmosphere.

Puerta Madrid, Juan Rizi 5, ✉ 28027, ✆ 91 743 83 00, *booking.puertamadrid@hoteles-silken.com, Fax 91 743 83 01* – |♦| ▤ TV 🚗 – 25/350. AE ⓓ ⓜ VISA. ✻ East : by Av. de América JT
Meals a la carte 29/62 – ☕ 15 – **188 rm** 228/270, 6 suites.
◆ A recently constructed hotel. Large public areas with concrete pillars and walls and modern and functional rooms with excellent bathrooms. Contemporary-style restaurant.

Sofitel Madrid Airport, av. de la Capital de España Madrid 10, ✉ 28042, ✆ 91 721 00 70, *h1606@accor-hotels.com, Fax 91 721 05 15,* – |♦|, rm, ▤ TV ♿ 🚗 – 50/120. AE ⓓ ⓜ VISA. ✻ rest North-East : by Av. de América JT
Mare Nostrum : **Meals** a la carte approx. 60 – ☕ 22,50 – **176 rm** 265/285, 3 suites.
◆ Near the Recinto Ferial. Fine hall, well-fitted rooms and an attractive dining room styled like a southern patio. Inventive à la carte in the stylish Mare Nostrum restaurant.

NH Príncipe de Vergara, Príncipe de Vergara 92, ✉ 28006, ✆ 91 563 26 95, *nhprincipedevergara@nh-hotels.com, Fax 91 563 72 53,* – |♦| ▤ TV ♿ 🚗 – 25/300. AE ⓓ ⓜ VISA. ✻ HU c
Meals 29 – ☕ 17 – **170 rm** 180/214, 3 suites.
◆ A hotel in an area well-served by public transport and with all the facilities and style of the NH chain. Practical, functional and with well-lit bedrooms.

NH Sanvy, Goya 3, ✉ 28001, ✆ 91 576 08 00, *nhsanvy@nh-hotels.com, Fax 91 575 24 43* – |♦| ▤ TV 🚗 – 25/160. AE ⓓ ⓜ VISA. ✻ NV r
Meals see rest. ***Sorolla*** below – ☕ 18 – **139 rm** 185/224, 10 suites.
◆ A functional though comfortable building and with attractive modern décor. Professional management and good service.

Bauzá, Goya 79, ✉ 28001, ✆ 91 435 75 45, *info@hotelbauza.com, Fax 91 431 09 43,* – |♦| ▤ TV ♿ 🚗 – 25/425. AE ⓓ ⓜ VISA. ✻ HV c
Meals a la carte approx. 37 – ☕ 12 – **169 rm** 174/251, 1 suite, 7 apartamentos.
◆ This is the refurbished former Hotel Pintor Goya. Modern facilities and elegant comfort. A beautiful lounge/library with a fireplace and a light and airy modern dining room.

Quinta de los Cedros, Allendesalazar 4, ✉ 28043, ✆ 91 515 22 00, *reservas@quintadeloscedros.com, Fax 91 415 20 50,* – |♦| ▤ TV 🚗 – 25/40. AE ⓓ ⓜ VISA JCB. ✻ JS x
Los Cedros *(closed Sunday dinner)* **Meals** a la carte 32/46 – ☕ 9 – **32 rm** 167/210.
◆ This modern building, in the style of a Tuscan villa, is surrounded by lawns and adorned with attractive decorative features. An extensive main floor, with personalised, fully equipped bedrooms. The classical-style restaurant comprises three separate rooms.

Agumar, paseo Reina Cristina 7, ✉ 28014, ✆ 91 552 69 00, *hotelagumar@h-santos.es, Fax 91 433 60 95* – |♦| ▤ TV ♿ 🚗 – 25/250. AE ⓓ ⓜ VISA JCB. ✻ HY a
Meals 22 – ☕ 11 – **239 rm** 170/210, 6 suites.
◆ Pleasant public areas and a renovated cafeteria, albeit soberly furnished. Well-equipped bedrooms and marble bathrooms. Classic dining room offering menus and à la carte.

Novotel Madrid Puente de La Paz, Albacete 1, ✉ 28027, ✆ 91 724 76 00, *h0843@accor-hotels.com, Fax 91 724 76 10,* – |♦|, rm, ▤ TV ♿ 🚗 – 25/250. AE ⓓ ⓜ VISA JT t
Claravía : **Meals** a la carte 22/29 – ☕ 13 – **240 rm** 125.
◆ A functional-style hotel with a modern façade and welcoming rooms with simple decor. The comfortable dining room has a terrace for the summer months.

NH Parque Avenidas, Biarritz 2, ✉ 28028, ✆ 91 361 02 88, *nhparque@nh-hotels.com, Fax 91 361 21 38,* – |♦| ▤ TV ♿ 🚗 – 25/500. AE ⓓ ⓜ VISA JCB. ✻ rest JU a
Meals a la carte 35/40 – ☕ 13,90 – **198 rm** 184/248, 1 suite.
◆ Near the bullring, with all the functionality and comfort you would expect from the NH chain. Well-maintained, with an abundance of wood decor.

Zenit Conde de Orgaz, Moscatelar 24, ✉ 28043, ✆ 91 748 97 60, *condeorgaz@zenithoteles.com, Fax 91 388 00 09* – |♦| ▤ TV 🚗 – 25/140. AE ⓓ ⓜ VISA. ✻ rest North-East : by José Silva JS
Bouquet : **Meals** a la carte 23/31 – ☕ 10 – **90 rm** 144/170.
◆ A cheerful, welcoming hotel in a residential district with good communications to the airport. Functional bedrooms, plus several private rooms for business meetings. A glass-topped terrace provides the setting for the modern dining room.

Rafael H. Ventas, Alcalá 269, ✉ 28027, ✆ 91 326 16 20, *ventas@rafaelhoteles.com,* *Fax 91 326 18 19* – |‡| ▤ TV ♿ 🚗 – 🎓 25/165. AE ◑ MC VISA. ✈ JV a
Meals 16,50 – ☕ 11,50 – **110 rm** 118/138, 1 suite.
◆ Modern in both facilities and decoration. The comfortable bedrooms have recently been refurbished with the emphasis on wood. A large traditional dining room with attractive oil paintings on the walls.

AC Avenida de América coffee shop dinner only, Cartagena 83, ✉ 28028, ✆ 91 724 42 40, *acamerica@ac-hoteles.com, Fax 91 724 42 41* – |‡| ▤ TV 🚗 – 🎓 25/50. AE ◑ MC VISA JCB. ✈ JU b
☕ 11 – **145 rm** 168.
◆ Ideal for business executives and with good communications. Modern and functional and with a coffee shop that is also a bar depending on the time of day.

Jardín de Recoletos, Gil de Santivañes 4, ✉ 28001, ✆ 91 781 16 40, *Fax 91 781 16 41,* 🌳 – |‡| ▤ TV 🚗. AE ◑ MC VISA JCB. ✈ NV p
Meals 23,50 – **43 rm** ☕ 184,18/191,41.
◆ A hotel with an attractive façade embellished with balustraded balconies. An elegant glass-crowned foyer-reception area, large studio-type bedrooms and an attractive patio-terrace. The walls of the pleasant dining room are adorned with landscape murals.

NH Lagasca, Lagasca 64, ✉ 28001, ✆ 91 575 46 06, *nhlagasca@nh-hotels.com, Fax 91 575 16 94* – |‡| ▤ TV – 🎓 25/60. AE ◑ MC VISA. ✈ GHV k
Meals *(closed August, Saturday and Sunday)* a la carte approx. 30 – ☕ 14,50 – **100 rm** 205.
◆ Good and comfortable rooms in a functional hotel where great thought is given to the needs and comfort of guests. Professional management.

Novotel Madrid Campo de las Naciones, Amsterdan 3, ✉ 28042, ✆ 91 721 18 18, *h1636@accor-hotels.com, Fax 91 721 11 22,* 🌳, 🏊 – |‡|, 🚭 rm, ▤ TV ♿ 🚗 – 🎓 25/200. AE ◑ MC VISA. ✈ rest
***Claravía* : Meals** a la carte 24/40 – ☕ 14 – **240 rm** 128/155, 6 suites.
◆ A classic-modern hotel near the Parque Ferial. Sufficiently large public rooms and comfortable bedrooms with functional furniture. A bright dining room with a summer terrace. North-East : by Av. de América JT

Acis y Galatea 🐌 without rest, Galatea 6, ✉ 28042, ✆ 91 743 49 01, *hotel@acisygalatea.com, Fax 91 741 76 97* – ▤ TV P. AE MC VISA. ✈ North-East : by Av. de América JT
☕ 10 – **16 rm** 115/120.
◆ The charm of this family-run hotel is enhanced by its friendly feel and the modern decor of contrasting light and dark tones. Comfortable, well-equipped bedrooms.

Zenit Abeba, Alcántara 63, ✉ 28006, ✆ 91 401 16 50, *abeba@zenithoteles.com, Fax 91 402 75 91* – |‡| ▤ TV 🚗. AE ◑ MC VISA. ✈ JV k
Meals a la carte approx. 28 – ☕ 11 – **90 rm** 142/190.
◆ In the Salamanca district of Madrid. A functional and modern hotel with refurbished rooms, contemporary furniture and up-to-date bathrooms.

NH Sur without rest, paseo Infanta Isabel 9, ✉ 28014, ✆ 91 539 94 00, *nhsur@nh-hotels.com, Fax 91 467 09 96* – |‡| ▤ TV – 🎓 25/30. AE ◑ MC VISA JCB. ✈ NZ a
☕ 11,50 – **68 rm** 110/133.
◆ A hotel with décor in keeping with modern hotel standards and the small lounge is complemented by a breakfast room. Comfortable bedrooms.

Club 31, Alcalá 58, ✉ 28014, ✆ 91 531 00 92, *club31@club31.net, Fax 91 531 00 92* – ▤. AE ◑ MC VISA. ✈ NX e
closed August – **Meals** a la carte 43/53.
◆ A long-established and well-respected restaurant which successfully combines classical style and modern decor. International cuisine and an excellent wine-list.

El Amparo, Puigcerdá 8, ✉ 28001, ✆ 91 431 64 56, *rte.elamparo@terra.es, Fax 91 575 54 91* – ▤. AE ◑ MC VISA. ✈ GX h
closed Saturday lunch and Sunday – **Meals** a la carte 58/67.
◆ A distinguished restaurant with neo-rustic décor and dining areas on different levels and skylights in the roof. Good wine-list and attentive staff.

Combarro, José Ortega y Gasset 40, ✉ 28006, ✆ 91 577 82 72, *combarro@combarro.com, Fax 91 435 95 12* – ▤. AE ◑ MC VISA JCB. ✈ HV e
closed Holy Week, August and Sunday dinner – **Meals** - Seafood - a la carte 44/58.
◆ Large and rather magnificent restaurant with a fish-tank and granite and wood décor.

Pedro Larumbe, Serrano 61-2nd floor, ✉ 28006, ✆ 91 575 11 12, *info@larumbe.com, Fax 91 576 60 19* – |‡| ▤. AE ◑ MC VISA. ✈ GV r
closed Holy week, 15 days in August, Saturday lunch and Sunday – **Meals** a la carte 48/58.
◆ In an elegant palace with three grand dining rooms, each individually decorated with great taste. Interesting menu of dishes elaborated with a creative touch.

XXX **Goizeko Wellington** - *Hotel Wellington*, Villanueva 34, ✉ 28001, ☎ 91 577 01 38, *goizeko@goizekowellington.com, Fax 91 555 16 66* – ▤. AE ⓓ MC VISA JCB. ✂ HX t
closed Saturday lunch in Summer and Sunday – **Meals** a la carte 57/80.
◆ An exquisite atmosphere characterised by a fusion of the contemporary and traditional. Refined cuisine which mirrors the ambience.

XXX **Sorolla** - *Hotel NH Sanvy*, Hermosilla 4, ✉ 28001, ☎ 91 576 08 00, *Fax 91 431 83 75* – ▤. AE ⓓ MC VISA. ✂ NV r
closed August, Saturday and Sunday – **Meals** a la carte 35/48.
◆ Excellent, traditional-style restaurant with four private rooms. International cuisine plus dishes prepared on a charcoal grill. A fine selection of coffees, teas and cigars.

XXX **Shiratori,** paseo de la Castellana 36, ✉ 28046, ☎ 91 577 37 34, *jarmas@todocep.es, Fax 91 577 44 55* – ▤ 🚗. AE ⓓ MC VISA JCB. ✂ GU d
closed Holy Week, Sunday and Bank Holidays – **Meals** - Japanese rest - a la carte 44/55.
◆ Japanese specialities and elegant traditional atmosphere in a large restaurant. Dishes prepared in front of the diner.

XXX **Balzac,** Moreto 7, ✉ 28014, ☎ 91 420 01 77, *restaurantebalzac@yahoo.es, Fax 91 429 83 70* – ▤. AE ⓓ MC VISA. ✂ NY a
closed 1 to 15 August, Saturday lunch and Sunday – **Meals** a la carte 52/66.
◆ An ideal place to rest after visiting the nearby museums. Classic comfortable style with modern and innovative cuisine.

XXX **Ponteareas,** Claudio Coello 96, ✉ 28006, ☎ 91 575 58 73, *Fax 91 431 99 57* – ▤ 🚗. AE ⓓ MC VISA JCB. ✂ GV w
Meals - Galician rest - a la carte 34/52.
◆ Traditional Galician dishes in large traditional dining rooms with wood décor and chandeliers. Private bar at the front of the restaurant. Many regular customers.

XXX **Paradis Casa de América,** paseo de Recoletos 2, ✉ 28001, ☎ 91 575 45 40, *casa-america@paradis.es, Fax 91 576 02 15*, 🏠 – ▤. AE ⓓ MC VISA. ✂ NX n
closed Saturday lunch and Sunday – **Meals** a la carte 36/42.
◆ An attractive restaurant with elegant decor inside the Palacio de Linares. A minimalist feel pervades the restaurant, where the emphasis is on innovative cuisine.

XXX **Castelló 9,** Castelló 9, ✉ 28001, ☎ 91 435 00 67, *castello9@castello9.com, Fax 91 435 91 34* – ▤. AE ⓓ MC VISA. ✂ HX e
closed Holy Week, August, Sunday and Bank Holidays – **Meals** a la carte approx. 43.
◆ Classic elegance in the Salamanca district. Intimate dining rooms offering an international à la carte choice plus a tasting menu featuring a variety of shared dishes.

XX **La Paloma,** Jorge Juan 39, ✉ 28001, ☎ 91 576 86 92, *Fax 91 575 51 41* – ▤. AE ⓓ MC VISA. ✂ HX g
closed Christmas, Holy Week, August, Sunday and Bank Holidays – **Meals** a la carte 39/47.
◆ A well-established and successful restaurant with a dining room on two levels and excellent service. An interesting menu and good wine-list.

XX **La Torcaz,** Lagasca 81, ✉ 28006, ☎ 91 575 41 30, *Fax 91 431 83 88* – ▤. AE ⓓ MC VISA. ✂ GHV t
closed Holy Week, August and Sunday – **Meals** a la carte 33/43.
◆ A friendly restaurant with a display of different wines near the entrance, a dining room divided into two areas and mirrors on the walls. Excellent service.

XX **Montana,** Lagasca 5, ✉ 28001, ☎ 91 435 99 01, *restaurantemontana@hotmail.com, Fax 91 426 04 18* – ▤. AE ⓓ MC VISA. ✂ GX s
closed 7 to 21 August and Sunday – **Meals** a la carte 28/36.
◆ The restaurant's atmosphere is best defined by its wood flooring and minimalist decor. A modern take on traditional cuisine, with an emphasis on presentation and natural products.

XX **Al Mounia,** Recoletos 5, ✉ 28001, ☎ 91 435 08 28, *Fax 91 575 01 73* – ▤. AE ⓓ MC VISA. ✂ NV u
closed Holy Week, August, Sunday and Monday – **Meals** - North African rest - a la carte 23/34.
◆ An exotic restaurant near the National Archaeological Museum. Moroccan décor with carved wood, plaster work and low tables. Traditional Arab dishes.

XX **Teatriz,** Hermosilla 15, ✉ 28001, ☎ 91 577 53 79, *Fax 91 431 69 10* – ▤. AE ⓓ MC VISA. ✂ GV u
Meals a la carte 27/37.
◆ In the stalls of the former Teatro Beatriz. A tapas bar near the entrance and a dining area and a bar on the stage, all with attractive Modernist décor.

XX **La Miel,** Maldonado 14, ✉ 28006, ☎ 91 435 50 45, *manuelcoto@restaurantelamiel.com* – ▤. AE ⓓ MC VISA. ✂ HU x
closed Holy Week, August and Sunday – **Meals** a la carte 34/42.
◆ A traditional, comfortable restaurant run by the proprietors. Attentive service, a good menu of international dishes and an impressive wine cellar.

XX **El Chiscón de Castelló,** Castelló 3, ✉ 28001, ✆ 91 575 56 62, *Fax 91 575 56 05* – ▤. AE ⓓ MC VISA HX e
closed August, Sunday and Bank Holidays – **Meals** a la carte 32/41.
♦ Hidden behind the typical façade is a warmly decorated interior that gives it the feel of a private house, particularly on the first floor. Well-priced traditional cuisine.

XX **El Asador de Aranda,** Diego de León 9, ✉ 28006, ✆ 91 563 02 46, *Fax 91 556 62 02* – ▤. AE ⓓ MC VISA. ✻ HU s
closed August and Sunday dinner – **Meals** - Roast lamb - a la carte approx. 25.
♦ Classic Castilian décor and a wood fired oven for roasting meat. The main dining room, with stained-glass windows, is on the 1st floor.

XX **Nicolás,** Villalar 4, ✉ 28001, ✆ 91 431 77 37, *jam@mail.ddnet.es, Fax 91 577 86 65* – ▤. AE ⓓ MC VISA. ✻ NX t
closed August, Sunday and Monday – **Meals** a la carte 27/37.
♦ A restaurant with minimalist décor. The traditional menu does not have many dishes but the quality of the food more than compensates for this.

XX **Guisando,** Núñez de Balboa 75, ✉ 28006, ✆ 91 575 10 10, *Fax 91 575 09 00* – ▤. AE ⓓ MC VISA JCB. ✻ HV f
closed Holy Week, 15 days in August and Sunday dinner – **Meals** a la carte approx. 33.
♦ Very popular with a younger clientele and very good prices. Bar near the entrance and also a spacious and light dining room. Different dishes available on a daily basis.

X ✿ **Casa d'a Troya,** Emiliano Barral 14, ✉ 28043, ✆ 91 416 44 55, *Fax 91 416 42 80* – ▤. ⓓ MC VISA. ✻ JS f
closed Christmas, Holy Week, 15 July-1 September, Sunday and Bank Holidays – **Meals** - Galician rest, Seafood - 25 and a la carte 31/37.
Spec. Pulpo a la gallega. Merluza a la gallega. Tarta de Santiago.
♦ A family-run restaurant offering excellent Galician food prepared in a traditionally simple way. A bar-entrance area and traditional furnishings in the dining room.

X **Asador Velate,** Jorge Juan 91, ✉ 28009, ✆ 91 435 10 24, *catering@velatecatering.com, Fax 91 576 12 40* – ▤. AE ⓓ MC VISA JCB. ✻ JX x
closed August and Sunday – **Meals** - Basque rest - a la carte 35/46.
♦ A traditional Basque-Navarrese grill-restaurant specialising in grilled hake and T-bone steaks. Dining areas with décor resembling a farmhouse of the region. Traditional menu.

X **Pelotari,** Recoletos 3, ✉ 28001, ✆ 91 578 24 97, *informacion@asador-pelotari.com, Fax 91 431 60 04* – ▤. AE ⓓ MC VISA. ✻ NV u
closed Sunday – **Meals** a la carte 29/43.
♦ A traditional Basque grill-restaurant which has improved both its service and its décor which is in the classic style of the Basque region.

X **La Trainera,** Lagasca 60, ✉ 28001, ✆ 91 576 05 75, *resta@latrainera.es, Fax 91 575 06 31* – ▤. AE ⓓ MC VISA JCB. ✻ GHV k
closed August and Sunday – **Meals** - Seafood - a la carte 39/53.
♦ A fish restaurant which is just about comfortable enough. Simple dining rooms with décor with a maritime feel which offer very high quality food. No tablecloths.

X **El Pescador,** José Ortega y Gasset 75, ✉ 28006, ✆ 91 402 12 90, *Fax 91 401 30 26* – ▤. MC VISA. ✻ JV t
closed Holy Week, August and Sunday – **Meals** - Seafood - a la carte 43/55.
♦ A modest restaurant with simple décor with a maritime feel which looks a little outdated. Excellent fish and seafood.

X **La Castela,** Doctor Castelo 22, ✉ 28009, ✆ 91 574 00 15 – ▤. AE ⓓ MC VISA. ✻
closed August and Sunday – **Meals** a la carte approx. 33. HX r
♦ An establishment in the tradition of Madrid taverns with a tapas bar and a simple traditional dining room offering traditional dishes.

Y/ **José Luis,** General Oráa 5, ✉ 28006, ✆ 91 561 64 13, *joseluis@nexo.es*, ☂ – ▤. AE ⓓ MC VISA. ✻ GU z
Tapa 1,40 – **Ración** approx. 10.
♦ A well-known establishment with a wide range of canapés, Basque-style tapas and servings of different dishes in elegant surroundings with traditional décor.

Y/ **Mesón Cinco Jotas,** Puigcerdá, ✉ 28001, ✆ 91 575 41 25, *m5jjorgejuan@osborne.es, Fax 91 575 56 35*, ☂ – ▤. AE ⓓ MC VISA. ✻ GX v
Tapa 2,20 – **Ración** - Ham specialities - approx. 10,50.
♦ Well-known for the high quality of its hams and other fine pork products. A wonderful terrace where you can enjoy well-made and appetising tapas.

Y/ **Tasca La Farmacia,** Diego de León 9, ✉ 28006, ✆ 91 564 86 52, *Fax 91 556 62 02* – ▤. AE ⓓ MC VISA. ✻ GHU s
closed 9 August-5 September and Sunday – **Tapa** 2,10 – **Ración** - Cod specialities - approx. 4,35.
♦ A traditional establishment with a beautiful tiled bar. Don't miss the opportunity to try the tapas or larger servings of salt-cod dishes.

Mesón Cinco Jotas, Serrano 118, ✉ 28006, ✆ 91 563 27 10, *m5jserrano@osborne.es, Fax 91 561 32 84,* – ▤. AE ⓓ MC VISA. ✻ GU a
Tapa 2,20 – **Ración** - Ham specialities - approx. 10,50.
• Good service in a modern establishment with a variety of tapas and larger portions of different dishes. The hams and fine pork products are very good.

El Barril, Goya 86, ✉ 28009, ✆ 91 578 39 98 – ▤. AE ⓓ MC VISA JCB. ✻ JVX r
closed Sunday dinner – **Tapa** 3 – **Ración** - Shellfish specialities - approx. 18.
• A good fish restaurant with a bar with a wide display of fish and seafood. Eat at the bar or enjoy the food in greater comfort in the dining room.

José Luis, Serrano 89, ✉ 28006, ✆ 91 563 09 58, *joseluis@nexo.es, Fax 91 563 31 02,* – ▤. AE ⓓ MC VISA. ✻ GU u
Tapa 1,40 – **Ración** approx. 10.
• This was first bar opened in Madrid by this chain and it is in a very good location. A wide variety of Basque and traditional-style tapas.

Taberna de la Daniela, General Pardiñas 21, ✉ 28001, ✆ 91 575 23 29, *Fax 91 409 07 11* – ▤. AE MC VISA. ✻ HV s
Tapa 2 – **Ración** approx. 5.
• Behind the tiled façade of this typical Madrid tavern are a number of dining rooms where you can enjoy a range of creative tapas, raciones, stews and fish dishes.

El Barril, Don Ramón de la Cruz 91, ✉ 28006, ✆ 91 401 33 05 – ▤. AE ⓓ MC VISA. ✻ JV n
closed 1 to 15 August – **Tapa** 7 – **Ración** - Shellfish - approx. 15.
• A fish restaurant which is both well-known and popular as much for the service as for the quality of the food. A bar specialising in different beers near the entrance.

Jurucha, Ayala 19, ✉ 28001, ✆ 91 575 00 98 – ▤. ✻ GV a
closed August, Sunday and Bank Holidays – **Tapa** 1,40 – **Ración** approx. 3,50.
• Delicious Basque-style tapas along with the Spanish omelette and croquettes have made this bar very popular with anybody enjoying an evening of tapas in Madrid.

Arganzuela, Carabanchel, Villaverde : Antonio López, Paseo de Las Delicias, Paseo Santa María de la Cabeza

Rafael H. Atocha, Méndez Álvaro 30, ✉ 28045, ✆ 91 468 81 00, *atocha@rafaelhoteles.com, Fax 91 468 81 20* – ▤ TV ♿ – 25/450. AE ⓓ MC VISA. ✻ GZ t
Meals 20,25 – ☕ 10,80 – **245 rm** 169/205.
• A modern hotel with elegant décor, good furnishings and tasteful paintings. Very good service and rooms with every mod con.

Rafael H. Pirámides, paseo de las Acacias 40, ✉ 28005, ✆ 91 517 18 28, *piramides@rafaelhoteles.com, Fax 91 517 00 90* – ▤ TV ♿ – 25/80. AE ⓓ MC VISA. ✻ DZ r
Meals 18 – ☕ 10,90 – **84 rm** 130/164, 9 suites.
• A hotel with exposed brickwork and sufficient public areas and a light and airy foyer-reception. Refurbished rooms with attractive curtains and wooden bathroom floors.

Carlton, paseo de las Delicias 26, ✉ 28045, ✆ 91 539 71 00, *carlton@hotelcarlton.com, Fax 91 527 85 10* – ▤ TV – 25/200. AE ⓓ MC VISA JCB. ✻ FZ n
Meals 26,30 – ☕ 12,80 – **105 rm** 158/196, 7 suites.
• A 1970s hotel with a traditional atmosphere and modernised, carpeted rooms with contemporary furnishings and welcoming lounges. It has an elegant restaurant.

Aramo, paseo de Santa María de la Cabeza 73, ✉ 28045, ✆ 91 473 91 11, *reservas-aramo@abbahoteles.com, Fax 91 473 92 14* – ▤ TV – 25/200. AE ⓓ MC VISA. ✻ rest EZ e
Meals 18 – ☕ 11,50 – **108 rm** 117/129.
• Refurbished rooms with carpets and wallpaper. The bathrooms are a little small. Well-equipped conference rooms and a modern restaurant with a wooden floor.

Hontoria, pl. del General Maroto 2, ✉ 28045, ✆ 91 473 04 25 – ▤. AE ⓓ MC VISA. ✻ EZ v
closed Holy Week, August, Sunday and Bank Holidays – **Meals** a la carte 27/37.
• A restaurant well-run by its chef-owner. A small traditional-style dining room. Lots of regular customers.

Moncloa : Princesa, Paseo del Pintor Rosales, Paseo de la Florida, Casa de Campo

Husa Princesa, Princesa 40, ✉ 28008, ✆ 91 542 21 00, *husaprincesa@husa.es, Fax 91 542 73 28,* – ▤ TV ♿ – 25/500. AE ⓓ MC VISA JCB. ✻ rest
Meals *(closed 1 to 15 August, Sunday and Monday dinner)* a la carte 36/46 – ☕ 22 – **263 rm** 275/345, 12 suites. DV z
• A magnificent hotel situated on one of the principal arteries of the city, with expansive lounge areas and spacious rooms offering high levels of comfort. An intimate, modern dining room offering a choice of traditional and international cuisine.

Meliá Madrid Princesa, Princesa 27, ✉ 28008, ☎ 91 541 82 00, *melia.madrid.princesa@solmelia.com, Fax 91 541 19 88,* – |♦| ▤ TV ♿ – 25/350. AE ⓓ ⓜ VISA JCB. ✂ KV t
Meals a la carte approx. 45 – ☕ 19 – **253 rm** 254/289, 23 suites.
• This hotel's location and facilities make it ideal for conferences and other group functions. Politicians, business executives and artists frequent this modern and refurbished hotel. There is a very good restaurant where you can enjoy fine cuisine.

Sofitel Madrid Plaza de España without rest, Tutor 1, ✉ 28008, ☎ 91 541 98 80, *h1320@accor.com, Fax 91 542 57 36* – |♦|, ✂ rm, ▤ TV ♿. AE ⓓ ⓜ VISA JCB. ✂ KV d
☕ 22,50 – **97 rm** 160/165.
• Well refurbished with high-quality furnishings in the bedrooms and marble fittings in the bathrooms. A perfect balance of elegance and comfort.

Monte Real ⑤, Arroyofresno 17, ✉ 28035, ☎ 91 316 21 40, *montereal@hotelmontereal.com, Fax 91 316 39 34,* ⛱ – |♦| ▤ TV 🚗 P – 25/250. AE ⓓ ⓜ VISA. ✂ North-West : by Av. de la Victoria DU
Meals 33,06 – ☕ 15,08 – **76 rm** 130/160, 4 suites.
• A hotel with a refreshing swimming pool surrounded by lawns. Refurbishment of the bedrooms, lounges and reception have made it much more comfortable. The pleasant and well-lit dining room is in traditional style and has decor in shades of vanilla.

Sal Gorda, Beatriz de Bobadilla 9, ✉ 28040, ☎ 91 553 95 06 – ▤. AE ⓓ ⓜ VISA. ✂
closed August and Sunday – **Meals** a la carte 25/28. DT e
• What a find ! Well-known professionals run this friendly and attractive restaurant. Traditional décor and good furnishings and an interesting menu at reasonable prices.

Neo, Quintana 30, ✉ 28008, ☎ 91 540 04 98 – ▤. AE ⓓ ⓜ VISA. ✂ DV c
closed Holy Week, August, Saturday lunch, Sunday and Bank Holidays – **Meals** a la carte 30/38.
• An attractive minimalist-style restaurant popular with a younger crowd. One room on two levels with wood floors and numerous design features. Excellent at-table service.

El Molino de los Porches, paseo Pintor Rosales 1, ✉ 28008, ☎ 91 548 13 36, *Fax 91 547 97 61,* ⛱ – ▤. AE ⓓ ⓜ VISA. ✂ DV e
Meals - Roast specialities - a la carte 43/56.
• A hotel located in the Parque del Oeste with several lounges and a pleasant glazed-in terrace. The meat produced from the wood fired oven and charcoal grill is delicious.

Currito, av. de las Provincias - Casa de Campo, ✉ 28011, ☎ 91 464 57 04, *curritomadrid@telefonica.net, Fax 91 479 72 54,* ⛱ – ▤ P. AE ⓓ ⓜ VISA. ✂ West : by Av. de Portugal DX
closed Sunday dinner – **Meals** - Basque rest - a la carte 45/51.
• A spacious and well-known restaurant located in the Vizcaya Pavilion of the Casa de Campo. Traditional Basque cuisine. A pleasant terrace and a public bar at the entrance.

Chamberí : San Bernardo, Fuencarral, Alberto Aguilera, Santa Engracia

AC Santo Mauro, Zurbano 36, ✉ 28010, ☎ 91 319 69 00, *santo-mauro@ac-hotels.com, Fax 91 308 54 77,* ⛱, Fб, ⛱ – |♦| ▤ TV ♿ 🚗 – 25/50. AE ⓓ ⓜ VISA JCB. ✂ FV e
Santo Mauro : **Meals** a la carte 46/55 – ☕ 20 – **43 rm** 255/307, 8 suites.
• A hotel in a beautiful French-style palace with garden situated in a classy district of Madrid. Elegant and with touches of luxury in the rooms. The restaurant is in a beautiful library-room which lends distinction to the food.

Miguel Ángel, Miguel Ángel 31, ✉ 28010, ☎ 91 442 00 22, *comercial.hma@oh-es.com, Fax 91 442 53 20,* ⛱, Fб, ⛱ – |♦| ▤ TV ♿ 🚗 – 25/200. AE ⓓ ⓜ VISA JCB. ✂ FU c
Arco : **Meals** a la carte 34/40 – ☕ 22 – **243 rm** 340, 20 suites.
• A prestigious and up-to-date hotel located in the Castellana district of Madrid. Well-appointed rooms and large public areas with classically elegant decor. Superb restaurant with a terrace for the summer months.

Intercontinental Castellana, paseo de la Castellana 49, ✉ 28046, ☎ 91 700 73 00, *madrid@interconti.com, Fax 91 308 54 23,* ⛱, Fб – |♦| ▤ TV ♿ 🚗 – 25/450. AE ⓓ ⓜ VISA JCB. ✂ GU v
Meals a la carte 45/80 – ☕ 28 – **270 rm** 335/365, 27 suites.
• Right in the heart of the banking and financial district. Totally refurbished and offering a high level of comfort and elegant décor.

Hesperia Madrid, paseo de la Castellana 57, ✉ 28046, ☎ 91 210 88 00, *hotel@hesperia-madrid.com, Fax 91 210 88 99* – |♦| ▤ TV ♿ – 25/300. AE ⓓ ⓜ VISA JCB. ✂ rest FU b
Meals see also rest. ***Santceloni*** below - 25 – ☕ 25 – **139 rm** 310/340, 32 suites.
• A hotel with modern décor and attractive design. A large lounge and light and airy foyer and reception area and a patio in the middle. Traditional bedrooms. A good dining room with many very tasteful details of décor.

Orfila, Orfila 6, ✉ 28010, ☎ 91 702 77 70, *inforeservas@hotelorfila.com, Fax 91 702 77 72,* – – . NV d
Meals 60 – 25 – **28 rm** 297/365, 4 suites.
◆ A hotel in a late 19C palace situated in an exclusive residential zone. A grand atmosphere and rooms with traditional and elegant furnishings. A welcoming dining room and interior garden where you can enjoy the à la carte menu.

NH Zurbano, Zurbano 79-81, ✉ 28003, ☎ 91 441 45 00, *nhzurbano@nh-hotels.com, Fax 91 441 32 24* – – 25/180. FU x
Meals a la carte approx. 35 – 13,40 – **255 rm** 153/184, 11 suites.
◆ A hotel divided into two buildings each with its own facilities. Tasteful décor in a functional style. Regular guests are business travellers and well-known sports teams.

NH Embajada, Santa Engracia 5, ✉ 28010, ☎ 91 594 02 13, *nhembajada@nh-hotels.com, Fax 91 447 33 12* – – 25/60. MV r
Meals *(closed August)* a la carte approx. 25 – 12,90 – **101 rm** 190.
◆ A hotel with a refurbished interior that leans towards the avant-garde in contrast to the very traditional façade. Contemporary and practical feel.

NH Alberto Aguilera, Alberto Aguilera 18, ✉ 28015, ☎ 91 446 09 00, *nhalbertoaguilera@nh-hotels.com, Fax 91 446 09 04* – – 25/100. DV b
Meals *(closed August)* a la carte approx. 35 – 14 – **148 rm** 154/180, 5 suites.
◆ Modern and welcoming although the public areas are limited to a lounge-coffee shop and the dining room. Comfort and well-equipped rooms are the hallmarks of this chain.

NH Prisma, Santa Engracia 120, ✉ 28003, ☎ 91 441 93 77, *nhprisma@nh-hotels.com, Fax 91 442 58 51* – – 25/70. EU g
Meals *(closed August, Saturday and Sunday)* - lunch only - a la carte approx. 31 – 13,50 – **103 suites** 190, 7 hab.
◆ In three separate buildings with the reception and lounge-coffee shop in the main one. The majority of the rooms are apartments with a sitting room.

Tryp Alondras coffee shop dinner only, José Abascal 8, ✉ 28003, ☎ 91 447 40 00, *tryp.alondras@solmelia.com, Fax 91 593 88 00* – . EU a
11,50 – **72 rm** 125/134.
◆ A traditional-style hotel with spacious, bright rooms which have all been refurbished. A good foyer-reception with a coffee shop on one side offering a limited menu.

Santceloni - *Hotel Hesperia Madrid,* paseo de la Castellana 57, ✉ 28046, ☎ 91 210 88 40, *santceloni@hesperia-madrid.com, Fax 91 210 88 99* – . FU b
closed Holy Week, August, Saturday lunch, Sunday and Bank Holidays – **Meals** 98 and a la carte 79/89.
Spec. Mero marinado con puré de manzana ahumado. Jarrete de ternera blanca con puré de patata. Sorpresas de fruta de la pasión.
◆ A restaurant with a modern façade and neo-rustic beams in the entrance. A spacious room with décor in minimalist style and designer tableware. Quite a culinary experience.

La Broche, Miguel Ángel 29, ✉ 28010, ☎ 91 399 34 37, *info@labroche.com, Fax 91 399 37 78* – . FU c
closed Holy Week, August, Saturday and Sunday – **Meals** 75 and a la carte 66/82.
Spec. Ensalada de sardinas ahumadas y trompeta de los muertos. Lubina asada con tapenade, cebollita, pimienta rosa y berros. Arroz basmati guisado y pichón de Navaz al aroma de las brasas (invierno-primavera).
◆ A spacious restaurant with bare white walls which allow all attention to be focused on the very innovative cuisine.

Las Cuatro Estaciones, General Ibáñez de Íbero 5, ✉ 28003, ☎ 91 553 63 05, *Fax 91 535 05 23* – . DT r
closed Holy Week, August, Saturday lunch and Sunday – **Meals** a la carte 45/68.
◆ A classic-style restaurant with a carpeted floor and fibre-optic lighting. The exclusive bar and waiting area lead into a pleasant and intimate dining room.

Il Gusto, Espronceda 27, ✉ 28003, ☎ 91 535 39 02, *Fax 91 535 08 61* – . FTU d
closed 15 days in August – **Meals** - Italian rest - a la carte 37/47.
◆ Discover the delicious nuances of Italian cuisine in this modern restaurant with an entrance hall and elegant restaurant, where the decor is a combination of wood and marble.

Annapurna, Zurbano 5, ✉ 28010, ☎ 91 319 87 16, *rteannapurna@yahoo.com, Fax 91 308 32 49* – . MV w
closed Saturday lunch, Sunday and Bank Holidays – **Meals** - Indian rest - a la carte approx. 30.
◆ A spacious restaurant with a private garden. Traditional Hindu decorative motifs and some colourful dishes with all the aromas and sensuousness of India.

XXX **Lur Maitea,** Fernando el Santo 4, ✉ 28010, ✆ 91 308 03 50, *restaurante@lurmaitea.com, Fax 91 308 62 25* – ▤. AE ⓓ ⓜ VISA. ✻ MV u
closed August, Saturday lunch, Sunday and Bank Holidays – **Meals** - Basque rest - a la carte 36/46.
◆ A carriage entrance is the way in to one of the best known places to try Basque cuisine. Traditional, with a large menu and a delicatessen.

XXX **Soroa,** Modesto Lafuente 88, ✉ 28003, ✆ 91 553 17 95, *soroa@restaurantesoroa.com, Fax 91 553 17 98* – ▤. AE ⓓ ⓜ VISA. ✻ FT x
closed Sunday – **Meals** a la carte approx. 39.
◆ An interesting menu of innovative dishes. Modern décor with a spacious dining room in light shades and a private dining area with wine-cellar décor in the basement.

XX **La Vendimia,** pl. del Conde del Valle de Suchil 7, ✉ 28015, ✆ 91 445 73 77, *Fax 91 448 86 72* – ▤. AE ⓓ ⓜ VISA JCB. ✻ DV b
closed Sunday – **Meals** a la carte 28/38.
◆ A menu offering traditional and Basque dishes in a classic contemporary restaurant. Good service. Regular customers from nearby offices.

XX **El Fogón de Zein,** Cardenal Cisneros 49, ✉ 28010, ✆ 91 593 33 20, *info@elfogondezein.com, Fax 91 591 00 34* – ▤. AE ⓓ ⓜ VISA. ✻ EU t
closed Holy Week and Sunday – **Meals** a la carte 28/37.
◆ A highly professional restaurant with a bar near the entrance leading to a small private room and the redecorated dining room, hung with contemporary paintings.

XX **Odriozola,** Zurbano 13, ✉ 28010, ✆ 91 319 31 50, *Fax 91 319 12 93* – ▤. AE ⓓ ⓜ VISA JCB MV d
closed August, Saturday lunch and Sunday – **Meals** - Basque rest - a la carte 33/57.
◆ A restaurant with a bar and a pleasant but small dining area. Traditional furnishings, slate floor and a private dining area on the mezzanine.

XX **Gala,** Espronceda 14, ✉ 28003, ✆ 91 442 22 44 – ▤. AE ⓓ ⓜ VISA. ✻ EU n
closed 10 to 25 August and Sunday – **Meals** a la carte 40/55.
◆ A pleasant modern restaurant with avant-garde decor which is in contrast to the wine-cellar-style private dining area. Very popular with a younger clientele.

XX **Tsunami,** Caracas 10, ✉ 28010, ✆ 91 308 05 69, *tsunamicaracas@telefonica.net, Fax 91 308 05 69* – ▤. AE ⓜ VISA. ✻ FV a
closed Saturday lunch, Sunday and Bank Holidays – **Meals** - Japanese rest - a la carte 33/37.
◆ A western-style bar near the entrance, modern dining rooms with designer furniture and a back bar where sushi is prepared in front of the customer.

XX **Alborán,** Ponzano 39-41, ✉ 28003, ✆ 91 399 21 50, *alboran@alboran-rest.com, Fax 91 399 21 50* – ▤. AE ⓓ ⓜ VISA. ✻ EU g
closed Sunday dinner – **Meals** a la carte 27/38.
◆ A coffee shop with tapas near the entrance and two dining areas with high-quality furnishings. Decor on a maritime theme with wooden floors and walls.

XX **La Plaza de Chamberí,** pl. de Chamberí 10, ✉ 28010, ✆ 91 446 06 97, *Fax 91 594 21 20* – ▤. AE ⓓ ⓜ VISA JCB. ✻ FV k
closed Sunday – **Meals** a la carte 29/31.
◆ A restaurant which deserves the success it now has. A private bar and a pleasant dining room on two levels. A select menu of traditional dishes.

X **Villa de Foz,** Gonzálo de Córdoba 10, ✉ 28010, ✆ 91 446 89 93 – ▤. AE ⓜ VISA. ✻ EV e
closed Sunday – **Meals** - Galician rest - a la carte 30/34.
◆ Good traditional Galician cuisine in a modern dining room. The menu is limited but the food is of very high quality.

X **Enzo,** Orfila 2, ✉ 28010, ✆ 91 308 16 47, *restaurante@pinocchio.es, Fax 91 662 18 65* – ▤. AE ⓓ ⓜ VISA. ✻ NV d
closed August, Saturday lunch and Sunday – **Meals** - Italian rest - a la carte approx. 30.
◆ An intimate and welcoming Italian restaurant with an attractive menu. Decorative features include exposed brickwork, wood flooring and modern furniture.

X **La Despensa,** Cardenal Cisneros 6, ✉ 28010, ✆ 91 446 17 94 – ▤. AE ⓓ ⓜ VISA. ✻ EV p
closed August, Sunday dinner and Monday – **Meals** a la carte approx. 24.
◆ A pleasant and friendly restaurant offering simple home cooking at reasonable prices. An intimate setting, functionally refurbished in classical style.

🍷 **Mesón Cinco Jotas,** paseo de San Francisco de Sales 27, ✉ 28003, ✆ 91 544 01 89, *m5jsfsales@osborne.es, Fax 91 549 06 51*, 🏠 – ▤. AE ⓓ ⓜ VISA. ✻ DT h
Tapa 2,20 – **Ración** - Ham specialities - approx. 10,50.
◆ In the style of this chain with two areas where you can have a single dish or eat à la carte. Also a variety of tapas, fine hams and pork products.

José Luis, paseo de San Francisco de Sales 14, ✉ 28003, ✆ 91 441 20 43, *joseluis@nexo.es*, – ▤. AE ⓓ ⓜ VISA. ✂ DU v
Tapa 1,40 – **Ración** approx. 10.
◆ One of the more simple establishments in this well-known chain. A variety of Basque-style tapas and larger portions of dishes. Also a terrace.

Zubia, Espronceda 28, ✉ 28003, ✆ 91 441 04 32, *info@restaurantezubia.com, Fax 91 441 10 43* – ▤. AE ⓓ ⓜ VISA. ✂ FU h
closed August, Saturday lunch and Sunday – **Tapa** 1,50 – **Ración** approx. 7,50.
◆ This professionally run bar is known for its high-quality Basque-style tapas and raciones. The reasonable menu on offer here is served in two small dining rooms.

La Taberna de Don Alonso, Alonso Cano 64, ✉ 28003, ✆ 91 533 52 49 – ▤. ✂ EFT r
closed Holy Week, August and Sunday dinner – **Tapa** 1,90 – **Ración** approx. 11.
◆ A tavern with a selection of Basque-style tapas and a blackboard listing tapas prepared to order and larger servings of dishes available. Wine by the glass.

Taberna El Maño, Vallehermoso 59, ✉ 28015, ✆ 91 448 40 35, , Bullfighting theme – ⓓ ⓜ VISA DU e
closed Sunday dinner and Monday – **Tapa** 2,50 – **Ración** approx. 12.
◆ A popular bar with a taurine atmosphere with lots of tapas and larger servings of dishes. Good seafood and ham. Relaxed atmosphere.

Chamartín, Tetuán : Paseo de la Castellana, Capitán Haya, Orense, Alberto Alcocer, Paseo de la Habana

Meliá Castilla, Capitán Haya 43, ✉ 28020, ✆ 91 567 50 00, *melia.castilla@solmelia.com, Fax 91 567 50 51*, – |‡| ▤ TV ♿ – 25/800. AE ⓓ ⓜ VISA. ✂ FR c
Meals see rest. ***L'Albufera*** and rest. ***La Fragata*** below – ☕ 19 – **904 rm** 253/262, 12 suites.
◆ An entrance with lots of plants and large and attractive rooms. A large hotel popular for social functions and conventions.

NH Eurobuilding, Padre Damián 23, ✉ 28036, ✆ 91 353 73 00, *nheurobuilding@nh-hoteles.es, Fax 91 345 45 76*, , , – |‡|, ✗ rm, ▤ TV ♿ – 25/900. AE ⓓ ⓜ VISA. ✂ GS a
Magerit *(closed August and Sunday)* **Meals** a la carte 35/44 – ☕ 18,50 – **421 rm** 246, 39 suites.
◆ Recently refurbished in keeping with this chain's usual standards of comfort. Spacious, modern and well-appointed bedrooms plus a variety of meeting areas. An attractive, high-quality restaurant in welcoming surroundings.

Mirasierra Suites H., Alfredo Marquerie 43, ✉ 28034, ✆ 91 727 79 00, *msh@jubanhoteles.com, Fax 91 727 79 08*, , , , – |‡| ▤ TV ♿ – 25/600. AE ⓓ ⓜ VISA JCB. ✂
North : by Av. de Monforte de Lemos GR
Meals 17 – ☕ 6 – **182 rm** 295/335.
◆ Key features at this hotel include a roomy reception standing beneath an open cupola, and well-appointed, apartment-style rooms with bath tubs and showers. The simply styled restaurant has the bonus of a small terrace.

Holiday Inn Madrid, pl. Carlos Trías Beltrán 4 (entrance by Orense 22-24), ✉ 28020, ✆ 91 456 80 00, *Fax 91 456 80 01*, , – |‡| ▤ TV ♿ – 25/400. AE ⓓ ⓜ VISA JCB. ✂ rm FS z
Big Blue : **Meals** a la carte 31/39 – **282 rm** ☕ 283/300, 31 suites.
◆ A good location near the Azca Complex with its many offices and leisure facilities. A classic foyer, shops and Internet facilities. The Big Blue restaurant has unusual modern décor and a good menu.

AC Aitana, paseo de la Castellana 152, ✉ 28046, ✆ 91 458 49 70, *aitana@ac-hotels.com, Fax 91 458 49 71*, – |‡| ▤ TV ♿. AE ⓓ ⓜ VISA JCB. ✂ GS c
Meals 20 – ☕ 14 – **109 rm** 191/215, 2 suites.
◆ Completely refurbished and with the latest mod cons. The décor and furnishings are very modern in style and with wood decoration.

NH La Habana, paseo de La Habana 73, ✉ 28036, ✆ 91 443 07 20, *nhhabana@nh-hotels.com, Fax 91 457 75 79* – |‡|, ✗ rm, ▤ TV – 25/250. AE ⓓ ⓜ VISA JCB. ✂ HS f
Meals *(closed August)* a la carte 20/32 – ☕ 14,45 – **155 rm** 165/198, 1 suite.
◆ A modern hotel with an excellent reception and very comfortable rooms, although they are a little on the small side. A regular clientele of business travellers.

Confortel Pío XII, av. Pío XII-77, ✉ 28016, ✆ 91 387 62 00, *com.confortel@once.es, Fax 91 302 65 22* – |‡| ▤ TV ♿ – 25/350. AE ⓓ ⓜ VISA JCB. ✂ JR t
Meals 18,50 – ☕ 12,50 – **214 rm** 170.
◆ Comfortable rooms decorated in soft tones with modern furnishings and wooden floors. Well-adapted for handicapped guests. A good restaurant with minimal decoration.

Orense, Pedro Teixeira 5, ✉ 28020, ℘ 91 597 15 68, *reservas@hotelorense.com, Fax 91 597 12 95* – 25/50. AE VISA JCB. FS q
Meals 18,50 – 12,60 – **140 rm** 202,65/236,25.
◆ A modern hotel featuring comfortable well-appointed rooms with attractive decor. Small lounge area but a good range of meeting rooms.

Confortel Suites Madrid, López de Hoyos 143, ✉ 28002, ℘ 91 744 50 00, *info@confortelsuitesmadrid.com, Fax 91 415 30 73* – 25/350. AE VISA. JT y
Meals *(closed August, Saturday and Sunday)* 15 – 12 – **120 suites** 175/195.
◆ A modern and not very luxurious hotel with good facilities which has a regular clientele of business customers. Suite-type rooms, but not very large.

Don Pío without rest, av. Pío XII-25, ✉ 28016, ℘ 91 353 07 80, *hoteldonpio@hoteldonpio.com, Fax 91 353 07 81* – AE VISA. HR s
13 – **40 rm** 120/130.
◆ An attractive patio foyer with a classic-modern skylight which runs through the building. The bedrooms are quite large and have facilities such as hydro-massage.

Cuzco coffee shop only, paseo de la Castellana 133, ✉ 28046, ℘ 91 556 06 00, *hotelcuzco@mundivia.es, Fax 91 556 03 72,* – 25/450. AE VISA JCB. FS a
12 – **322 rm** 162/203, 8 suites.
◆ A traditional hotel a few metres from the Palacio de Congresos. Spacious, well-maintained bedrooms with somewhat old-fashioned decor. Popular with business travellers.

Castilla Plaza, paseo de la Castellana 220, ✉ 28046, ℘ 91 567 43 00, *castilla-plaza@abbahoteles.com, Fax 91 315 54 06* – 25/150. AE VISA JCB. GR u
Meals 20,50 – 14,80 – **139 rm** 118/133.
◆ A beautiful glass building which is part of the Puerta de Europa complex. Comfortable and very much in accord with modern tastes. An attractive restaurant specialising in traditional cuisine.

Foxá 32, Agustín de Foxá 32, ✉ 28036, ℘ 91 733 10 60, *foxa32@foxa.com, Fax 91 314 11 65* – 25/250. AE VISA. GR e
Meals 10,50 – 10 – **63 rm** 174/195, 98 suites.
◆ Although the foyer-reception is on the small side, the hotel's apartment-type rooms are elegantly decorated and furnished with high-quality antiques. The restaurant has an attractive covered terrace.

Chamartín, Agustín de Foxá, ✉ 28036, ℘ 91 334 49 00, *chamartin@husa.es, Fax 91 733 02 14* – 25/500. AE VISA JCB. HR
Meals see rest. ***Cota 13*** below – 11,44 – **360 rm** 152/180, 18 suites.
◆ Situated at Chamartín train station and with a very busy foyer. Functional bedrooms and some lounges which are used for more than one purpose.

La Residencia de El Viso, Nervión 8, ✉ 28002, ℘ 91 564 03 70, *reservas@residenciadelviso.com, Fax 91 564 19 65,* – AE VISA JCB. HT c
Meals a la carte approx. 45 – 10 – **12 rm** 77/129.
◆ A charming little hotel with a lounge that encompasses the bar and reception. Cheerful rooms and a garden which offers peace and tranquillity in the middle of the city. The dining room is in a glass pavilion beside an interior terrace which is used in summer.

Aristos, av. Pío XII-34, ✉ 28016, ℘ 91 345 04 50, *hotelaristos@elchaflan.com, Fax 91 345 10 23* – AE VISA. JR d
Meals see rest. ***El Chaflán*** below – 8,75 – **22 rm** 102,15/138,85, 1 suite.
◆ A functional hotel with very well-equipped rooms and décor reminiscent of the 1980s. Good management and service.

Zalacain, Álvarez de Baena 4, ✉ 28006, ℘ 91 561 48 40, *Fax 91 561 47 32* – AE VISA JCB. GU b
closed Holy Week, August, Saturday lunch, Sunday and Bank Holidays – **Meals** 82 and a la carte 48/70.
Spec. Carpaccio de brevas con hígado de oca. Ravioli de botillo con salsa de vino de Mencia y trufas. Ragout de langostinos con albóndigas de acelgas.
◆ A refined restaurant with traditional and intimate dining rooms and highly-trained staff. An elegant atmosphere enhanced by decor showing fine attention to detail.

Príncipe de Viana, Manuel de Falla 5, ✉ 28036, ℘ 91 457 15 49, *principeviana@ya.com, Fax 91 457 52 83* – AE VISA. GS c
closed August, Saturday lunch, Sunday and Bank Holidays – **Meals** - Basque rest - a la carte 58/68.
◆ Well-known restaurant serving Basque-Navarrese inspired cooking. Traditional dining areas and excellent service.

XXXX **El Bodegón,** Pinar 15, ✉ 28006, ✆ 91 562 88 44, *Fax 91 562 97 25* – ▤. AE ◑ MC VISA. ⚘ GU q
closed August, Saturday lunch, Sunday and Bank Holidays – **Meals** a la carte 53/65.
◆ A rather grand and elegant restaurant with a private bar and a dining room on various levels with windows overlooking a pleasant garden.

XXX **L'Albufera** - *Hotel Meliá Castilla,* Capitán Haya 45, ✉ 28020, ✆ 91 567 51 97, *Fax 91 567 50 51* – ▤ 🚗. AE ◑ MC VISA JCB. ⚘ FR c
Meals - Rice dishes - a la carte 36/49.
◆ A restaurant with three attractive dining rooms and another in a conservatory in a central patio with numerous plants.

XXX **Combarro,** Reina Mercedes 12, ✉ 28020, ✆ 91 554 77 84, *combarro@combarro.com, Fax 91 534 25 01* – ▤. AE ◑ MC VISA JCB. ⚘ ES a
closed Holy Week, August and Sunday dinner – **Meals** - Seafood - a la carte 44/58.
◆ Galician cuisine based on good quality seafood and fish. Public bar, dining room on the 1st floor and two more rooms in the basement all in distinguished traditional style.

XXX ✿ **El Chaflán** - *Hotel Aristos,* av. Pío XII-34, ✉ 28016, ✆ 91 350 61 93, *restaurante@elchaflan.com, Fax 91 345 10 23,* 🏠 – ▤. AE ◑ MC VISA. ⚘ JR d
closed 15 days in August, Saturday lunch and Sunday – **Meals** 60 and a la carte 51/63.
Spec. Alcachofas con vieiras, tuétano y toffe de naranja. Salmonetes de trasmayo con tartar de pepino y menta, cous-cous de calamarcillos y escabeche de aceitunas. Lomo de buey del Valle del Esla con migas trufadas, royal de foie y chutney de alcachofas.
◆ A restaurant in minimalist style which prides itself on its service. An olive tree has pride of place in the centre of the room. Interesting and innovative cuisine.

XXX **La Fragata** - *Hotel Meliá Castilla,* Capitán Haya 45, ✉ 28020, ✆ 91 567 51 96, *Fax 91 567 50 51* – ▤ 🚗. AE ◑ MC VISA. ⚘ FR c
closed August and Bank Holidays – **Meals** a la carte 44/56.
◆ A separate entrance and an elegant private bar. The dining area surrounds a central patio with lots of plants. A good traditional menu.

XXX **Aldaba,** av. de Alberto Alcocer 5, ✉ 28036, ✆ 91 345 21 93, *Fax 91 345 21 93* – ▤. AE ◑ MC VISA. ⚘ GS e
closed Holy Week, August, Saturday lunch, Sunday and Bank Holidays – **Meals** a la carte 50/60.
◆ A bar near the entrance from which follows a pleasant dining room in classic-modern style. There are also private rooms. Excellent wine-list.

XXX **José Luis,** Rafael Salgado 11, ✉ 28036, ✆ 91 457 50 36, *joseluis@nexo.es, Fax 91 344 10 46* – ▤. AE ◑ MC VISA. ⚘ GS m
closed August – **Meals** a la carte approx. 46.
◆ A well-known restaurant in front of the Santiago Bernabeu Stadium. A pleasant dining room with a tapas bar and two glass covered terraces. International and Basque dishes.

XXX **Goizeko Kabi,** Comandante Zorita 37, ✉ 28020, ✆ 91 533 01 85, *Fax 91 533 02 14* – ▤. AE ◑ MC VISA JCB. ⚘ ES a
closed Saturday lunch in July-August and Sunday – **Meals** - Basque rest - a la carte 46/65.
◆ A Basque restaurant with prestige in the city. Elegant and comfortable although the tables are a little close together.

XXX **El Olivo,** General Gallegos 1, ✉ 28036, ✆ 91 359 15 35, *bistrotelolivosl@retemail.es, Fax 91 345 91 83* – ▤. AE ◑ MC VISA JCB. ⚘ GR c
closed 15 to 31 August, Sunday and Monday – **Meals** a la carte 38/63.
◆ Modern décor in shades of green and attractive decorative details alluding to olive oil. Carefully prepared cosmopolitan and Mediterranean dishes.

XXX **El Foque,** Suero de Quiñones 22, ✉ 28002, ✆ 91 519 25 72, *restaurante@elfoque.com, Fax 91 561 07 99* – ▤. AE ◑ MC VISA. ⚘ HT r
closed Sunday – **Meals** - Cod dishes specialities - a la carte 33/40.
◆ An intimate restaurant near the Auditorio Nacional de Música. A dining room on two levels decorated in maritime style. An interesting menu which specialises in cod dishes.

XX **De Vinis,** paseo de la Castellana 123, ✉ 28046, ✆ 91 556 40 33, *vic.vino@teleline.es, Fax 91 556 08 58* – ▤. AE ◑ MC VISA. ⚘ GS h
closed Saturday lunch and Sunday – **Meals** a la carte 35/48.
◆ Modern and intimate dining areas and excellent service. An innovative menu and a wide selection of wines served by the glass.

XX **La Tahona,** Capitán Haya 21 (side), ✉ 28020, ✆ 91 555 04 41, *Fax 91 556 62 02* – ▤. AE ◑ MC VISA. ⚘ FS u
closed August and Sunday dinner – **Meals** - Roast lamb - a la carte approx. 25.
◆ A bar near the entrance with a wood fired oven and wood ceiling from which lead off several dining areas. Traditional roast meat accompanied by the house rosé is delicious.

XX **O'Pazo,** Reina Mercedes 20, ✉ 28020, ✆ 91 553 23 33, *Fax 91 554 90 72* – ▤. MC VISA. ⚘
closed Holy Week, August and Sunday – **Meals** - Seafood - a la carte 39/69. EFS p
◆ Although the decor is a little out of date, O'Pazo has a large dining room and a library-lounge for private meetings. A good choice of fish and seafood always on display here.

XX **Pedralbes,** Basílica 15, ✉ 28020, ☎ 91 555 30 27, *Fax 91 570 95 30,* 🏠 – ▤. AE ⓓ ⓜ VISA. ⅋ FT z
Meals - Catalonian rest - a la carte 33/44.
◆ Restaurant with Mediterranean feel with lots of plants and pictures, evoking the palace after which it is named. Dining areas on three levels and traditional Catalan cuisine.

XX **Rianxo,** Oruro 11, ✉ 28016, ☎ 91 457 10 06, *Fax 91 457 22 04* – ▤. AE ⓓ ⓜ VISA. ⅋ HS h
closed 15 August-15 September and Sunday – **Meals** - Galician rest - a la carte approx. 48.
◆ Galician cuisine prepared in the classic way and based more on the quality of ingredients than elaborate preparation. A bar and attractive traditional dining room.

XX **Carta Marina,** Padre Damián 40, ✉ 28036, ☎ 91 458 68 26, *Fax 91 458 68 26* – ▤. AE ⓓ ⓜ VISA. ⅋ GS k
closed August and Sunday – **Meals** - Galician rest - a la carte 36/55.
◆ A restaurant with wood decor and an attractive private bar. Pleasant dining rooms with terrace. Traditional Galician cooking.

XX **Gaztelupe,** Comandante Zorita 32, ✉ 28020, ☎ 91 534 90 28, *Fax 91 554 65 66* – ▤. AE ⓓ ⓜ VISA JCB. ⅋ ES p
closed Sunday dinner in July-August and Sunday the rest of the year – **Meals** - Basque rest - a la carte 50/60.
◆ A bar at the entrance, refurbished dining areas with decor in regional style, and two private rooms in the basement. An extensive menu of traditional Basque dishes.

XX **El Comité,** pl. de San Amaro 8, ✉ 28020, ☎ 91 571 87 11, *Fax 91 435 43 27*, Bistrot – ▤. AE ⓓ ⓜ VISA. ⅋ FS x
closed Saturday lunch and Sunday – **Meals** a la carte approx. 36.
◆ Restaurant in a welcoming bistro-style, with café-type furniture and lots of old photos on the walls. French cuisine.

XX **Cota 13** - *Hotel Chamartín*, Chamartín railway station, ✉ 28036, ☎ 91 334 49 00, *chamartin@husa.es, Fax 91 733 02 14* – ▤. AE ⓓ ⓜ VISA JCB. ⅋ HR
closed August – **Meals** a la carte 27/35.
◆ A dining room with a ceiling like the roof of an old railway station. Décor in the style of a restaurant-car, circa 1900. Simple international cuisine and fixed-price menu.

XX **Sayat Nova,** Costa Rica 13, ✉ 28016, ☎ 91 350 87 55 – ▤. AE ⓓ ⓜ VISA. ⅋ JS a
Meals - Armenian rest - a la carte 25/34.
◆ A good address to discover the gastronomics merits of Armenian cuisine. Two rooms with parquet flooring and decor alluding to the minstrel who gives the restaurant its name.

X **Kabuki,** av. Presidente Carmona 2, ✉ 28020, ☎ 91 417 64 15, *Fax 91 556 02 32,* 🏠 – ▤. AE ⓓ ⓜ VISA JCB. ⅋ FS t
closed 1 to 23 August, Saturday lunch, Sunday and Bank Holidays – **Meals** - Japanese rest - a la carte 42/60.
◆ An intimate Japanese restaurant with tasteful, minimalist decor. A modern terrace, in addition to a bar/kitchen serving popular dishes such as sushi.

X **Fass,** Rodríguez Marín 84, ✉ 28002, ☎ 91 563 74 47, *info@fassgrill.com, Fax 91 563 74 53* – ▤. AE ⓓ ⓜ VISA. ⅋ HS t
Meals - German rest - a la carte 19/32.
◆ A bar at the front but a separate entrance for the restaurant. Rustic décor with lots of wood in pure Bavarian style. German cuisine.

X **El Asador de Aranda,** pl. de Castilla 3, ✉ 28046, ☎ 91 733 87 02, *Fax 91 556 62 02* – ▤. AE ⓓ ⓜ VISA. ⅋ GR b
closed 9 August-6 September and Sunday dinner – **Meals** - Roast lamb - a la carte approx. 25.
◆ A restaurant in a good location near the Kio towers. Typical Castilian charm with sober yet elegant decor. The suckling pig is one of several house specialities.

Y/ **Tasca La Farmacia,** Capitán Haya 19, ✉ 28020, ☎ 91 555 81 46, *Fax 91 556 62 02* – ▤. AE ⓜ VISA. ⅋ FS r
closed 9 August-5 September and Sunday – **Tapa** 2,10 – **Ración** - Cod specialities - approx. 4,35.
◆ A beautiful restaurant with décor of exposed brickwork, tiles, wood and wonderful stained glass. A wide selection of tapas although cod dishes are the house speciality.

Y/ **Mesón Cinco Jotas,** Padre Damián 42, ✉ 28036, ☎ 91 350 31 73, *m5jpdamian@osborne.es, Fax 91 345 79 51,* 🏠 – ▤. AE ⓓ ⓜ VISA. ⅋ GS s
Tapa 2,20 – **Ración** - Ham specialities - approx. 10,50.
◆ This establishment belongs to a chain specialising in ham and other pork products. Two attractive eating areas plus a limited choice of set menus.

Y/ **José Luis,** paseo de La Habana 4, ✉ 28036, ☎ 91 562 75 96, *joseluis@nexo.es, Fax 91 562 31 18* – ▤. AE ⓓ ⓜ VISA. ⅋ GT h
Tapa 1,40 – **Ración** approx. 10.
◆ Well-known to lovers of tapas. A relaxed and youthful ambience and a good selection of various dishes served in an adjoining room.

Environs

by motorway N II :

Meliá Barajas, av. de Logroño 305 - N II and detour to Barajas city, ✉ 28042, ✆ 91 747 77 00, *reservas.tryp.barajas@solmelia.com, Fax 91 747 87 17,* ☂, Fö, ⛱, 🌳 - |\$| ▤ TV ♿ P - 🏛 25/675. AE ⓓ MC VISA JCB. ✂ rest
Meals 25 - ☕ 17 - **220 rm** 196/242, 9 suites.
◆ Comfortable and traditional with extremely well-equipped rooms and refurbished bathrooms. A number of conference/meeting rooms around the swimming pool and garden. One dining room serves à la carte cuisine, the other food prepared on a charcoal grill.

Tryp Alameda Aeropuerto, av. de Logroño 100 - N II and detour to Barajas city, ✉ 28042, ✆ 91 747 48 00, *tryp.alameda.aeropuerto@solmelia.com, Fax 91 747 89 28* - |\$| ▤ TV P - 🏛 25/280. AE ⓓ MC VISA JCB. ✂
Meals 23,74 - ☕ 14 - **145 rm** 140/180, 3 suites.
◆ Bright and comfortable guest rooms furnished in modern style with cherry tones and well-equipped bathrooms. The hotel's lounges and meeting areas are in the process of being refurbished.

Aparthotel Convención Barajas without rest, no ☕, Noray 10 - N II, detour to Barajas city and industrial zone, ✉ 28042, ✆ 91 371 74 10, *aparthotel@hotel-convencion.com, Fax 91 371 79 01* - |\$| ▤ TV 🚗 - 🏛 25. AE ⓓ MC VISA. ✂
95 suites 140/175.
◆ Two towers with few areas in common although they have spacious apartment-type bedrooms with a small sitting room and kitchen.

NH Barajas without rest, Catamarán 1 - N II, detour to Barajas city and industrial zone, ✉ 28042, ✆ 91 742 02 00, *exbarajas@nh-hoteles.es, Fax 91 741 11 00* - |\$| ▤ TV 🚗. AE ⓓ MC VISA JCB. ✂
☕ 8 - **173 rm** 94.
◆ This budget hotel, part of the NH chain, offers reasonable comfort and value for money, although its lounges and public areas are somewhat on the small side.

by motorway N VI :

AC Forum Aravaca, Camino de la Zarzuela 23 - Aravaca : 10,2 km - exit 10 motorway, ✉ 28023, ✆ 91 740 07 10, *forum@ac-hotels.com, Fax 91 740 07 11* - |\$| ▤ TV 🚗 - 🏛 30/210. AE ⓓ MC VISA JCB. ✂
Meals 12 - ☕ 11 - **78 rm** 101.
◆ Functionality, design and good décor and furnishings in this hotel with comfortable bedrooms with wooden floors and modern bathrooms. A pleasant lounge area.

XX **Los Remos,** Sopelana 13 - La Florida : 13 km - exit 12 motorway, ✉ 28023, ✆ 91 307 72 30, *Fax 91 372 84 35* - ▤ P. AE ⓓ MC VISA. ✂
Meals - Seafood - a la carte approx. 50.
◆ A bar with a maritime feel with fish-tank and a glazed-in dining room. Fish and seafood a speciality.

XX **Gaztelubide,** Sopelana 13 - La Florida : 12,8 km - exit 12 motorway, ✉ 28023, ✆ 91 372 85 44, *gaztelubide@teleline.es, Fax 91 372 84 19,* ☂ - |\$| ▤ P. AE ⓓ MC VISA. ✂
closed Sunday dinner - **Meals** - Basque rest - a la carte 35/39.
◆ A rustic-style restaurant with one à la carte dining room and one private room. Simpler set-menu options on the first floor. A glass-covered terrace, plus banqueting suites.

by motorway N I *North : 13 km :*

La Moraleja coffee shop only, av. de Europa 17 - Parque Empresarial La Moraleja, ✉ 28108, ✆ 91 661 80 55, *info@hotellamoraleja.com, Fax 91 661 21 88,* Fö, ⛱ - |\$| ▤ TV 🚗 P - 🏛 25. AE ⓓ MC VISA. ✂
☕ 16,50 - **37 suites** 170.
◆ This hotel's location in a business district and excellent facilities make it an ideal choice for the business traveller. Magnificent suite-type rooms.

Moralzarzal *28411 Madrid* 576 J 18 575 J 18 121 G 5 - *pop. 2 248 alt. 979.*
Madrid 44.

XXXX ✿ **El Cenador de Salvador** 🐌 with rm, av. de España 30 ✆ 91 857 77 22, *cenador@infonegocio.com, Fax 91 857 77 80,* ☂ - ▤ TV P. AE ⓓ MC VISA. ✂
closed 10 January-10 February - **Meals** *(closed Sunday dinner and Monday)* 82 and a la carte 60/77 - ☕ 15 - **7 rm** 150/210,35.
Spec. Bourguignonne de caracoles y manitas de lechal. Consomé de tórtolas asadas y trufa de verano. Asado de pluma ibérica con puré de patatas raff.
◆ An elegant villa with dining rooms on two levels with classic furnishings and excellent service. Garden-terrace and charming rooms.

BARCELONA 08000 P 574 H 36 122 D 8 – pop. 1 505 325.

See : Gothic Quarter★★ (Barri Gòtic : Ardiaca House★ MX**A**, Cathedral★ (≤ from the tile roof★★) MX, No 10 Carrer Paradis (Roman columns★) MX**133**, Plaça del Rei★★ MX**150**, Museum of the City's History★★ (The Roman City★★★) MX**M1**, Santa Àgata Chapel★★ (Altarpiece of the Constable★★) MX**F**, Rei Martí Belvedere ≤★★ MX**K** – Frederic Marès Museum★ MX**M2**, La Rambla★★ : Barcelona Contemporary Art Museum★★ (MACBA) (building★★) HX**M10**, Barcelona Contemporary Culture Centre (CCCB) : patio★ HX**R**, (Former) Hospital of Santa Creu (Gothic patio★) LY, Santa Maria del Pi Church★ LX, Virreina Palace★ LX, Güell Palace★★ LY, Plaça Reial★★ MY – The Sea Front★ : Shipyards (Drassanes) and Maritime Museum★★ MY, Old Harbour★ (Port Vell) : Aquarium★ NY, Mercè Basilica★ NY, La Llotja★ (Gothic Hall★★) NX, França Station★ NVX, Ciutadella Park★ NV, KX (Waterfall★, Three Dragons Pavilion★★ NV**M7**, Zoology Museum★ NV**M7**, Zoo★ KX) – La Barceloneta★ KXY, Museum of the Catalonian History★ KY**M9**, Vila Olímpica★ (marina★★, twin towers ☀★★★) East : by Av. d'Icària KX, Carrer de Montcada★★ : Picasso Museum★ NV, Santa Maria del Mar Church★★ (rose window★) NX – Montjüic★ (≤★ from castle terraces) South : by Av. de la Reina María Cristina GY : Mies van der Rohe Pavilion★★, National Museum of Catalonian Art★★★, Spanish Village★ (Poble Espanyol), Anella Olímpica★ (Olympic Stadium★, Sant Jordi Sports Centre★★) – Joan Miró Foundation★★★, Greek Theatre★, Archaeological Museum★ – Eixample District★★ : La Sagrada Familia Church★★★ (East or Nativity Façade★★, ≤★★ from east spire) JU, Hospital Sant Pau★ North : by Padilla JU, Passeig de Gràcia★★ HV (Lleó Morera House★ HV**Y**, Amatller House★ HV**Y**, Batlló House★★★ HV**Y**, La Pedrera or Milà House★★★ HV**P**) – Terrades House (les Punxes★) HV**Q**, Güell Park★★ (rolling bench★★, Gaudí House-Museum★) North : by Padilla JU – Catalonian Concert Hall★★ (Palau de la Mùsica Catalana : façade★, inverted cupola★★) MV - Antoni Tàpies Foundation★★ HV**S**.

Additional sights : Santa Maria de Pedralbes Monastery★★ (Church★, Cloister★, Sant Miquel Chapel frescoes★★★ – Pedralbes Palace (Decorative Arst Museum★ EX, Güell Stables★ (Pabellones) EX, Sant Pau del Camp Church (Cloister★) LY.

18 Sant Cugat, North-West : 20 km ☎ 93 674 39 08.

✈ of El Prat - Barcelona, South-West : 18 km ☎ 93 298 38 38 – Iberia : Gran Via de les Corts Catalanes 629, ✉ 08010, ☎ 902 400 500 HV.

Sants ☎ 902 240 202.

. to the Balearic Islands : Cía. Trasmediterránea, Moll de Sant Beltrà - Estació Marítima, ✉ 08039, ☎ 93 295 91 00, Fax 93 295 91 34.

pl. de Catalunya 17-S ✉ 08002 ☎ 906 301 282 teltur@barcelonaturisme.com Fax 93 304 31 55 passeig de Gràcia 107 (Palau Robert) ✉ 08008 ☎ 93 238 40 00 Fax 93 238 40 10, Sants Estació ✉ 08014 ☎ 807 11 72 22 teltur@barcelonaturisme.com and at Airport ☎ 93 478 47 04 (Terminal A) and ☎ 93 478 05 65 (Terminal B) – R.A.C.E. Muntaner 81-bajo, ✉ 08011 ☎ 93 451 15 51 Fax 93 451 22 57.

Madrid 627 – Bilbao 607 – Lleida/Lérida 169 – Perpignan 187 – Tarragona 109 – Toulouse 388 – València 361 – Zaragoza 307.

Plans on following pages

Old Town and the Gothic Quarter : Ramblas, Pl. de Catalunya, Via Laietana, Pl. St. Jaume, Passeig de Colom, Passeig de Joan Borbó Comte de Barcelona

Le Méridien Barcelona, La Rambla 111, ✉ 08002, ☎ 93 318 62 00, *info.barcelona@lemeridien.com, Fax 93 301 77 76* – |♦|, ⇔ rm, ▤ TV ♿ 🚗 – 🏛 25/150. AE ⓓ MC VISA. ✄ rest LX b
Meals a la carte 36/56 – ☕ 23 – **202 rm** 390, 10 suites.
♦ This elegant, traditional hotel combines local flavour and a cosmopolitan contemporary look in a superb location right on the Ramblas. The patio-style restaurant, partly illuminated by natural light, offers a lunchtime buffet as well as à la carte choices.

Colón, av. de la Catedral 7, ✉ 08002, ☎ 93 301 14 04, *info@hotelcolon.es, Fax 93 317 29 15* – |♦| ▤ TV – 🏛 25/120. AE ⓓ MC VISA JCB. ✄ rest MV e
Meals 20 – ☕ 14,50 – **140 rm** 155/220, 5 suites.
♦ The Colón enjoys an enviable position opposite the cathedral, enhanced by the pleasant terrace at its entrance. Traditional in style with comfortable, well-appointed rooms. The dining room has a welcoming and intimate feel.

Rivoli Rambla, La Rambla 128, ✉ 08002, ☎ 93 481 76 76, *reservas@rivolihotels.com, Fax 93 317 50 53,* 🌳, Lδ – |♦|, ⇔ rm, ▤ TV ♿ – 🏛 25/100. AE ⓓ MC VISA JCB. ✄
Meals a la carte approx. 40 – ☕ 15 – **114 rm** 218/260, 15 suites. LX r
♦ This historic building has an avant-garde interior embellished with Art Deco touches, elegant bedrooms, plus a terrace offering panoramic views of the city. The restaurant menu offers a range of international dishes.

Royal, La Rambla 117, ✉ 08002, ☎ 93 301 94 00, *hotelroyal@hroyal.com, Fax 93 317 31 79* – |♦|, ⇔ rm, ▤ TV ♿ 🚗 – 🏛 25/100. AE ⓓ MC VISA JCB. ✄
***La Poma* : Meals** a la carte 22/35 – ☕ 13 – **108 rm** 175/215. LX e
♦ Located in the liveliest part of the city, the Royal is a pleasant hotel with classic style, attentive service and high levels of comfort. The restaurant, specialising in grilled meats, has a separate entrance.

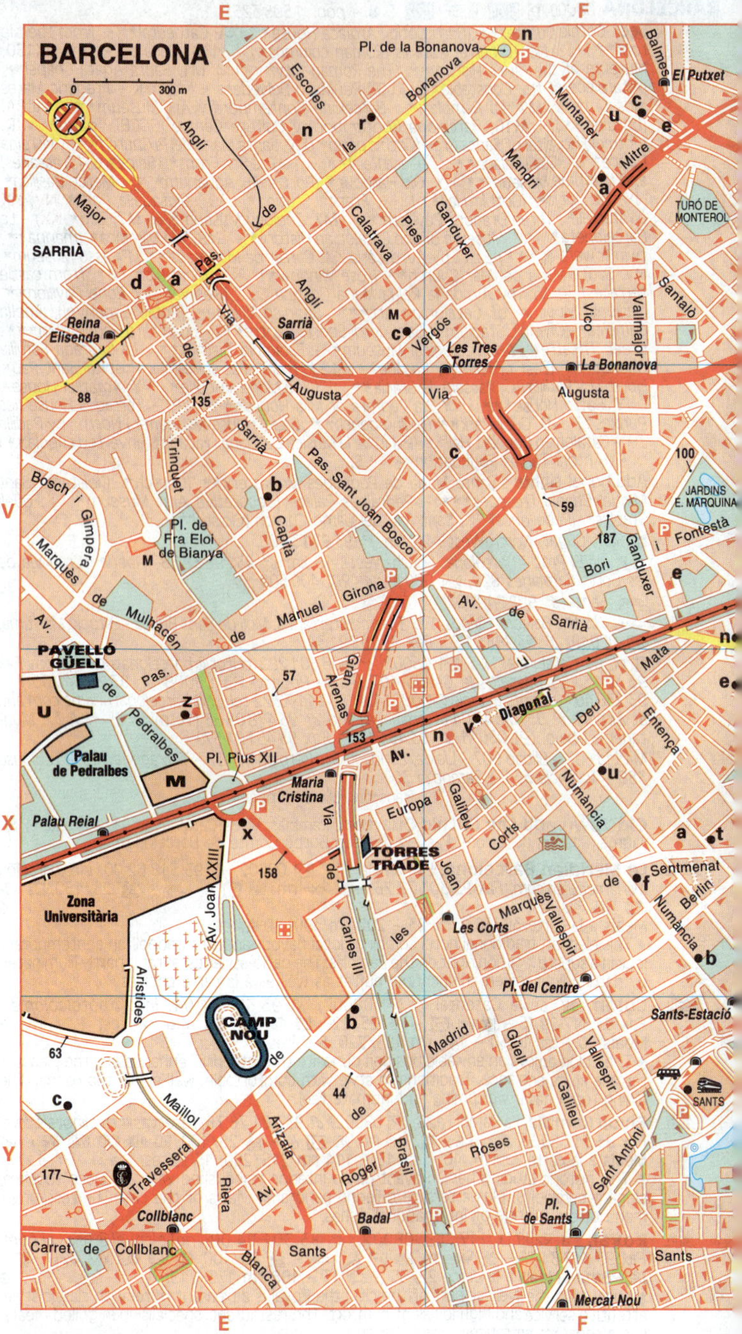
BARCELONA
0
300 m
E
F
U
V
X
Y
SARRIÀ
Major
Anglí
Escoles
la
de
Bonanova
Pl. de la Bonanova
Muntaner
Balmes
El Putxet
Mitre
Mandri
Calatrava
Pies
Ganduxer
TURÓ DE MONTEROL
Santaló
Vallmajor
Vico
Reina Elisenda
Pas.
Via
Sarrià
Vergós
Les Tres Torres
La Bonanova
Augusta
Via
Augusta
88
135
de
Sarrià
Trinquet
Pas. Sant Joan Bosco
100
JARDINS E. MARQUINA
59
187
Fontestà
Bosch
i
Gimpera
Marquès
Pl. de Fra Eloi de Bianya
Capità
Girona
Bori
Ganduxer
de
Mulhacén
Av.
Manuel
de
Av.
de
Sarrià
PAVELLÓ GÜELL
Pas.
de
Pedralbes
57
Gran Via
Arenas
Mata
Diagonal
Deu
Entença
Palau de Pedralbes
Pl. Pius XII
153
Av.
Maria Cristina
Europa
Galileu
Numància
Palau Reial
158
TORRES TRADE
Joan
Corts
Sentmenat
Berlin
Numància
de
Zona Universitària
Av. Joan XXIII
de
Carles III
les
Les Corts
Marquès
Vallespir
Pl. del Centre
Aristides
Sants-Estació
CAMP NOU
63
Madrid
Güell
Vallespir
Galileu
de
44
de
Maillol
Arizala
SANTS
Brasil
Roses
Sant Antoni
177
Travessera
Riera
Av.
Roger
Collblanc
Badal
Pl. de Sants
Carret. de Collblanc
Blanca
Sants
Sants
Mercat Nou

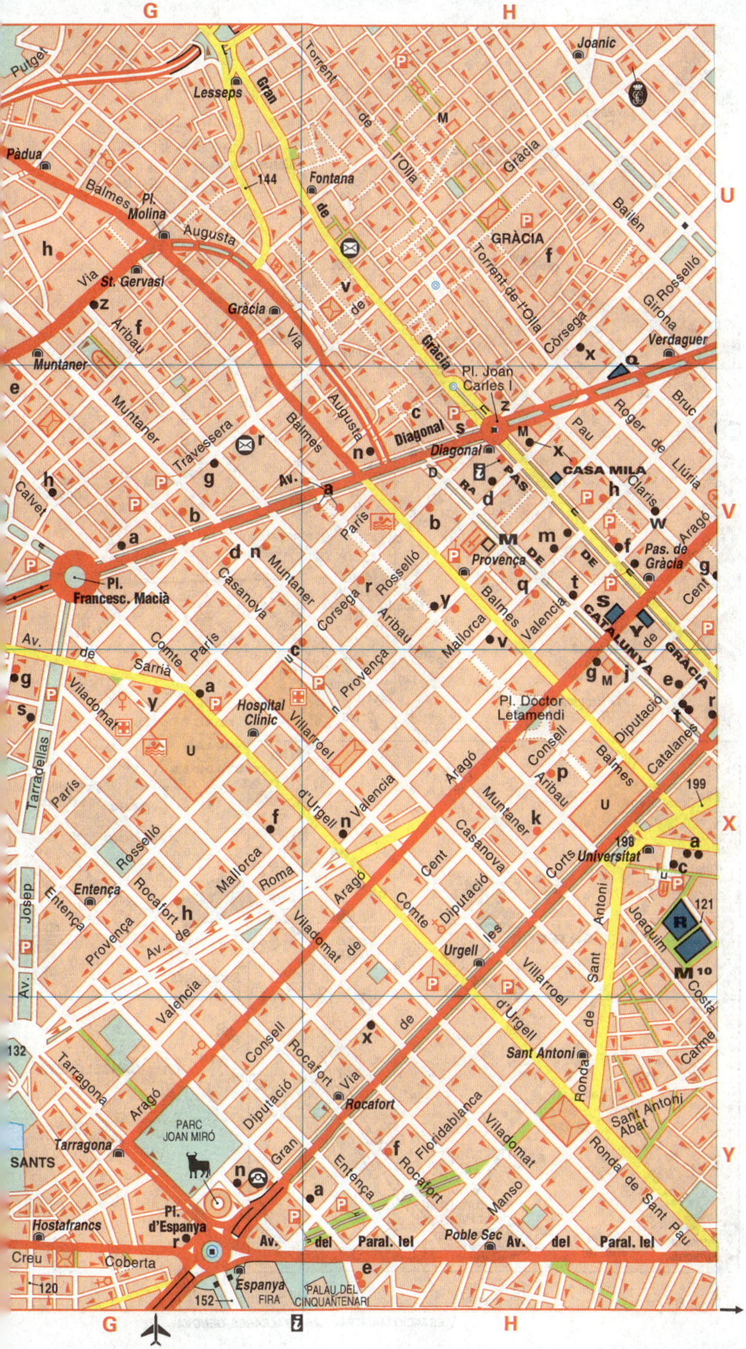
G
H
U
V
X
Y
Joanic
Putget
Lesseps
Gran
Torrent
de
l'Olla
Gràcia
Pàdua
Balmes
Pl.
Molina
Augusta
144
Fontana
de
Bailèn
GRÀCIA
Torrent de l'Olla
Via
St. Gervasi
Gràcia
Aribau
Via
Augusta
Gràcia
Rosselló
Girona
Verdaguer
Còrsega
Muntaner
Pl. Joan
Carles I
Bruc
Roger
de
Llúria
Muntaner
Travessera
Balmes
Diagonal
Diagonal
Pau
Claris
CASA MILA
Calvet
Av.
París
PAS
DE
GRÀCIA
Aragó
Provença
Pas. de
Gràcia
Cent
Pl.
Francesc. Macià
Casanova
Muntaner
Còrsega
Rosselló
Aribau
Balmes
Valencia
Mallorca
CATALUNYA
de
GRACIA
Av.
de
Sarrià
Comte
París
Provença
Viladomat
Hospital
Clinic
Villarroel
Pl. Doctor
Letamendi
Consell
Diputació
Catalanes
Tarradellas
París
d'Urgell
Valencia
Aragó
Muntaner
Aribau
Balmes
199
Rosselló
Casanova
Corts
Universitat
198
Entença
Rocafort
Mallorca
Roma
Cent
Antoni
Joaquim
121
Josep
Entença
Provença
Av.
de
Viladomat
de
Comte
Diputació
Urgell
les
Sant
M 10
Costa
Av.
Valencia
Villarroel
d'Urgell
132
Tarragona
Aragó
Consell
Rocafort
Via
de
Sant Antoni
Ronda
de
Carme
Diputació
Rocafort
Floridablanca
Viladomat
Sant Antoni
Abat
PARC
JOAN MIRÓ
Tarragona
SANTS
Gran
Entença
Rocafort
Manso
Ronda de Sant Pau
Pl.
d'Espanya
Hostafrancs
Av.
del
Paral. lel
Poble Sec
Av.
del
Paral. lel
Creu
Coberta
Espanya
FIRA
120
152
PALAU DEL
CINQUANTENARI

J
K
U
V
X
Y
Sardenya
Marina
Padilla
Lepant
València
Aragó
Cent
Còrsega
Sagrada Familia
SAGRADA FAMILIA
Nàpols
Rosselló
Roger
Mallorca
Provença
Sicília
Diagonal
Pl. de les Glòries Catalanes
TORRE AGBAR
Glòries
Diputació
Ribes
Monumental
Auditori
Av.
de
Aragó
Pas.
Bailèn
València
Girona
Consell
Flor
Corts
Catalanes
Casp
Marc
Lepant
Meridiana
Zamora
Almogàvers
Pallars
Marina
Bogatell
Girona
Diputació
Tetuán
Pl. de Tetuán
de
les
Roger
Ausiàs
Sant
Joan
Ribes
Nàpols
PARC ESTACIÓ DEL NORD
Gran
Via
Bailèn
Casp
Girona
Marc
Bruc
Arc de Triomf
Flor
Almogàvers
Buenaventura Muñoz
Av.
Pujadas
Llòria
Ausiàs
Urquinaona
Sant
Pere
Pas.
de
Wellington
PARC DE LA CIUTADELLA
Ronda
Pl. de Catalunya
CIUTAT VELLA
Pas. de Picasso
Comerç
Via
Princesa
Av. Marquès de l'Argentera
Ciutadella Vila Olímpica
PARC ZOOLOGIC
FRANÇA
Doctor
Aiguader
Pelai
LA RAMBLA
CATEDRAL
STA MARIA
Carme
Laietana
Ferrán
Barceloneta
Colom
Hospital
Pau
Rambla
MARINA
LA BARCELONETA
Almirall Cervera
Sant
de
la
Pas.
de
Nou
de
la
Rambla
Pl. Portal de la Pau
Paral. lel Funicular
Av. del Paral. lel
Pl. de les Drassanes
PORT VELL
PLATJA DE SANT SEBASTIÀ
ESTACIÓ MARÍTIMA BALEARES, GENOVA

INDEX OF STREET NAMES IN BARCELONA

Almirall Cervera . . . . KY
Almogàvers . . . . KV
Ample . . . . MY
Àngel (Pl. de l') . . . . MX
Àngel LX
Anglí . . . . EU
Antóni López (Pl. d') . . . . . . MY
Antóni Maura (Pl. d') . . . . . MV
Aragó . . . . HX
Argenteria . . . . NX
Aribau . . . . HX
Aristides Maillol . . . . EY
Arizala . . . . EY
Armes (Pl.) . . . . KX 3
Assaonadors . . . . NV
Augusta (Via) . . . . FV
Ausiàs Marc . . . . JV
Avinyó . . . . MY
Bacardí (Ptge de) . . . . MY 5
Badal . . . . FY
Bailèn . . . . JV
Balmes . . . . HV
Banys Nous . . . . MX 7
Bergara . . . . LV 10
Berlín . . . . FX
Bisbe . . . . MX 15
Bonanova (Pas. de la) . . . . EU
Bonanova (Pl. de la) . . . . . FU
Boqueria (Pl. de la) . . . . . . LY
Bori i Fontestà . . . . FV
Bòria . . . . MV 18
Born (Pas. del) . . . . NX 20
Bosch i Alsina (Moll de) . . . NY
Bosch i Gimpera . . . . EV
Boters . . . . MX 23
Brasil (Rambla del) . . . . . . EY
Bruc . . . . HV
Buenaventura Muñoz . . . . . KV
Calatrava . . . . EU
Calvet . . . . GV
Canaletes (Rambla de) . . . . LV 27
Canonge Colom (Pl. del) . . . LY 28
Canuda LX
Canvis Vells . . . . NX 32
Capità Arenas . . . . EV
Caputxins (Rambla dels) . . MY 35
Cardenal Casañas . . . . LX 36
Carders . . . . NV
Carles III (Gran Via de) . . . . EX
Carme LX
Casanova . . . . HX
Casp . . . . JV
Catalunya (Pl. de) LV
Catalunya (Rambla de) . . . . HX
Catedral (Av. de la) . . . . . . MV 40
Circumval.lació (Pas. de) . . . KX 41
Ciutat . . . . MX 43
Colom (Pas. de) . . . . NY
Comandant Benítez . . . . . . EY 44
Comerç . . . . NV
Comercial (Pl. de) . . . . NV 45
Comte d'Urgell . . . . HX
Consell de Cent . . . . HX
Còrsega . . . . HU
Corts (Travessera de les) . . . EY
Corts Catalanes (Gran Via de les) . . . . HX
Creu Coberta . . . . GY
Cucurulla . . . . LX 55
Déu i Mata . . . . FX
Diagonal (Av. de) . . . . HV
Dipósit (Moll del) . . . . NY
Diputació . . . . HX
Doctor Aiguader . . . . KX
Doctor Ferran . . . . EX 57
Doctor Fleming . . . . FV 59
Doctor Joaquím Pou . . . . . MV 61
Doctor Letamendi (Pl. del) . HX
Doctor Marañón (Av. del) . . EY 63
Drassanes (Av. de les) . . . . LY
Drassanes (Pl. de les) . . . . JY
Duc de Medinaceli (Pl. del) . NY
Elisabets LX
Entença . . . . GX
Escoles Pies . . . . EU
Escudellers . . . . MY
Espanya (Moll d') . . . . NY
Espanya (Pl. d') . . . . GY
Estudis (Rambla dels) LX
Europa . . . . EX
Ferrán . . . . MY
Floridablanca . . . . HY
Fontanella LV
Fra Eloi de Bianya (Pl. de) . . EV
Francesc Cambó (Av. de) . . MV 79
Francesc Macià (Pl. de) . . . GV
Galileu . . . . FX
Ganduxer . . . . FV
Garriga i Bachs (Pl. de) . . . . MX 83
Gavà . . . . BT 84
General Mitre (Ronda del) . . FU
Girona . . . . JV
Glòries Catalanes (Pl. de les) . . . . KU
Gràcia (Pas. de) . . . . HV
Gràcia (Travessera de) . . . . HU
Gran de Gràcia . . . . HU
Hospital . . . . LY
Ictíneo (Pl. del) . . . . NY
Isabel II (Pas. d') . . . . NX 98
Joan Carles I (Pl. de) . . . . . HV
Joan de Borbó Comte de Barcelona (Pas. de) . . . . KY 99
Joan Güell . . . . FY
Joan XXIII (Av. de) . . . . EX
Joaquín Costa . . . . HX
Johann Sebastian Bach . . . . FV 100
Josep Anselm Clavé . . . . . . MY
Laietana (Via) . . . . MX
Lepant . . . . JU
Lluís Companys (Pas. de) . . KX 108
Madrid (Av. de) . . . . EFY
Major de Sarrià . . . . EV
Mallorca . . . . HV
Mandri . . . . FU
Manso . . . . HY
Manuel Girona (Pas. de) . . EVX
Marina . . . . JU
Marquès de l'Argentera (Av. del) . . . . NX
Marquès de Mulhacén . . . . EV
Marques de Sentmenat . . . FX
Mata . . . . FX
Méndez Núñez . . . . JX 118
Mercaders . . . . MV
Meridiana (Av.) . . . . KV
Mirallers . . . . NX
Moianés . . . . GY 120
Montalegre . . . . HX 121
Montcada . . . . NV 122
Montjuïc del Bisbe . . . . MX 123
Muntaner . . . . GV
Nàpols . . . . JU
Nou de la Rambla . . . . LY
Nou Sant Francesc . . . . MY 126
Nova (Pl.) . . . . MX 128
Numància . . . . FX
Odisea (Pl. de la) . . . . NY
Ortigosa . . . . JX 130
Padilla . . . . KU
Països Catalans (Pl. dels) . . . FY 132
Palau (Pl. del) . . . . NX
Palla . . . . MX
Pallars . . . . KV
Paradis . . . . MX 133
Paral.lel (Av. del) . . . . HJY
París . . . . GX
Pau Claris . . . . HV
Pau Vila (Pl. de) . . . . KYX 134
Pedralbes (Av. de) . . . . EX
Pedró de la Creu . . . . EV 135
Pelai LV
Pi (Pl. del) . . . . LX 137
Pi i Suñer (Pl. de) LV
Picasso (Pas. de) . . . . NV
Pintor Fortuny . . . . LX 140
Pius XII (Pl. de) . . . . EX
Portaferrissa LX
Portal de la Pau (Pl. del) . . . MY
Portal de l'Àngel (Av. del) . . LV
Portal Nou . . . . KX 143
Portal Santa Madrona . . . . MY 142
Príncep d'Astúries (Av. del) GU 144
Princesa . . . . NV
Provença . . . . GX
Pujades (Pas. de) . . . . KX
Putget . . . . GU
Ramon Albó . . . . CS 147
Ramon Berenguer el Gran (Pl. de) . . . . MX 148
Rec Comtal . . . . JX 149
Rei (Pl. del) . . . . MX 150
Reial (Pl.) . . . . MY
Reina Elisenda de Montcada (Pas. de la) . . . . EUV 151
Reina Maria Cristina (Av. de la) . . . . GY 152
Reina Maria Cristina (Pl. de la) . . . . EX 153
Ribes . . . . KV
Rocafort . . . . HY
Roger de Flor . . . . JU
Roger de Llúria . . . . HV
Roger . . . . EY
Roma (Av. de) . . . . GX
Roses . . . . FY
Rosselló . . . . HV
Sabino Arana . . . . EX 158
Sant Antoni (Ronda de) . . HXY
Sant Antoni Abat . . . . HY
Sant Antoni . . . . FY
Sant Felip Neri (Pl. de) . . . MX 163
Sant Jaume (Pl. de) . . . . . . MX
Sant Joan (Pas. de) . . . . . . JV
Sant Joan Bosco (Pas. de) . EV
Sant Josep (Rambla de) . . . LX 168
Sant Josep Oriol (Pl. de) . . . LX 171
Sant Iu (Pl. de) . . . . MX 172
Sant Miquel (Pl. de) . . . . . . MX 173
Sant Pau (Ronda de) . . . . . HY
Sant Pau . . . . LY
Sant Pere (Ronda de) . . . . . JX
Sant Pere Més Alt . . . . MV
Sant Pere Més Baix . . . . . . MV
Sant Rafael . . . . LY
Sant Ramon Nonat (Av. de) . EY 177
Sant Sever . . . . MX 181
Santa Anna LV
Santa Fe de Nou Mèxic . . . FV 187
Santa Maria (Pl. de) . . . . . . NX 189
Santa Mònica (Rambla de) . MY
Santaló . . . . FU
Sants . . . . FY
Sardenya . . . . JU
Sarrià (Av. de) . . . . FV
Serra . . . . MY
Seu (Pl. de la) . . . . MX 192
Sicília . . . . JU
Tapineria . . . . MX 193
Tarragona . . . . GY
Teatre (Pl. del) . . . . MY
Tetuan (Pl. de) . . . . JV
Torrent de l'Olla . . . . HU
Trinquet . . . . EV
Universitat (Pl. de la) . . . . . HX 198
Universitat (Ronda de la) . . . LV 199
Urquinaona (Pl. d') . . . . . . JX
València . . . . HX
Vallespir . . . . FY
Vallmajor . . . . FU
Vergós . . . . FU
Vico . . . . FU
Viladomat . . . . HY
Villarroel . . . . GX
Wellington . . . . KX
Zamora . . . . KV

BARCELONA

Bacardí (Ptge de)	MY	5
Banys Nous	MX	7
Bergara	LV	10
Bisbe	MX	15
Bòria	MV	18
Born (Pas. del)	NX	20
Boters	MX	23
Canaletes (Rambla de)	LV	27
Canonge Colom (Pl. del)	LY	28
Canvis Vells	NX	32
Caputxins (Rambla dels)	MY	35
Cardenal Casañas	LX	36
Catalunya (Pl. de)	LV	
Catedral (Av. de la)	MV	40
Ciutat	MX	43
Comercial (Pl. de)	NV	45
Cucurulla	LX	55
Doctor Joaquím Pou	MV	61
Estudis (Rambla dels)	LX	
Francesc Cambó (Av. de)	MV	79
Garriga i Bachs (Pl. de)	MX	83
Isabel II (Pas. d')	NX	98
Montcada	NV	122
Montjuïc del Bisbe	MX	123
Nou Sant Francesc	MY	126
Nova (Pl.)	MX	128
Paradis	MX	133
Pi (Pl. del)	LX	137
Pintor Fortuny	LX	140
Portal Santa Madrona	MX	142
Ramon Berenguer el Gran (Pl. de)	MX	148
Rei (Pl. del)	MX	150
Sant Felip Neri (Pl. de)	MX	163
Sant Josep (Rambla de)	LX	168
Sant Josep Oriol (Pl. de)	LX	171
Sant Iu (Pl. de)	MX	172
Sant Miquel (Pl. de)	MX	173
Sant Sever	MX	181
Santa Maria (Pl. de)	NX	189
Santa Mònica (Rambla de)	MY	
Seu (Pl. de la)	MX	192
Tapineria	MX	193
Universitat (Ronda de la)	LV	199

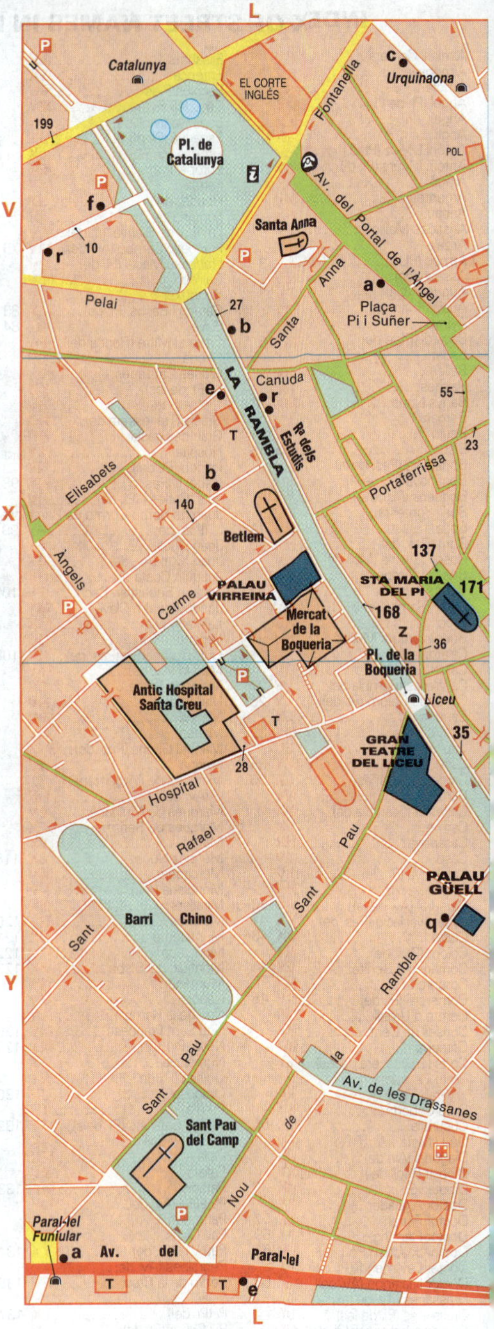

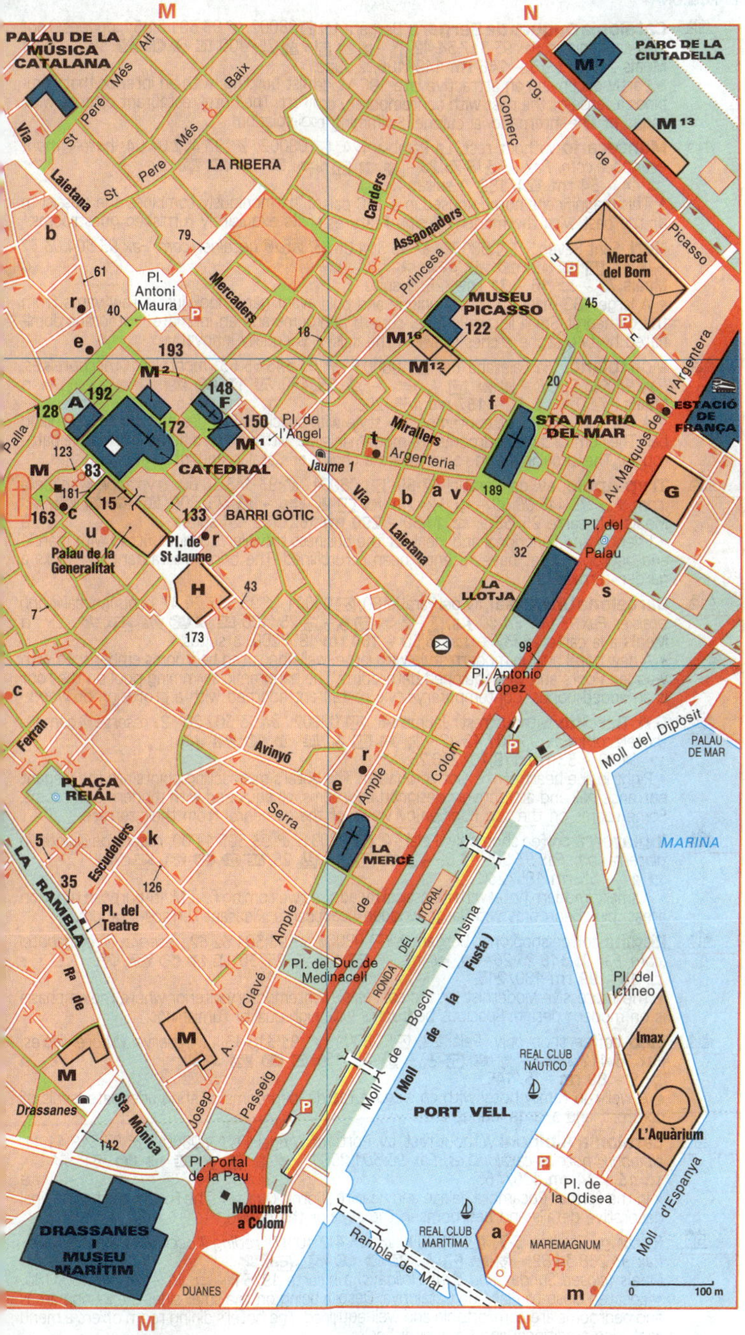
M
N
PALAU DE LA MÚSICA CATALANA
Via
Laietana
St Pere Més Alt
St Pere Més Baix
St Pere
LA RIBERA
PARC DE LA CIUTADELLA
M 7
M 13
Pg. de Picasso
Comerç
Carders
Assaonadors
Princesa
Mercaders
Pl. Antoni Maura
Mercat del Born
MUSEU PICASSO
122
M 16
M 12
79
61
40
18
45
b
r
e
193
M 2
192
A
148
F
150
M 1
128
172
Pl. de l'Àngel
Jaume 1
Palla
123
M
83
CATEDRAL
181
15
133
BARRI GÒTIC
163
c
u
Palau de la Generalitat
Pl. de St Jaume
r
H
43
173
7
Miralles
Argenteria
t
a
v
Via
Laietana
f
20
STA MARIA DEL MAR
189
e
ESTACIÓ DE FRANÇA
Av. Marquès de l'Argentera
G
r
Pl. del Palau
32
LA LLOTJA
s
98
Pl. Antonio López
V
X
Y
c
Ferran
PLAÇA REIAL
Avinyó
r
e
Ample
Colom
Serra
Moll del Dipòsit
PALAU DE MAR
MARINA
5
k
Escudellers
LA RAMBLA
35
126
Pl. del Teatre
LA MERCÈ
de
Ample
Pl. del Duc de Medinaceli
RONDA DEL LITORAL
Alsina
Bosch i
Moll de la Fusta
Clavé
Rª de
M
M
Drassanes
Sta Mònica
142
Josep A.
Passeig
Moll de
PORT VELL
REAL CLUB NÁUTICO
Pl. del Ictineo
Imax
L'Aquàrium
Moll d'Espanya
Pl. Portal de la Pau
Monument a Colom
DRASSANES I MUSEU MARÍTIM
DUANES
Rambla de Mar
REAL CLUB MARITIMA
a
Pl. de la Odisea
MAREMAGNUM
m
0
100 m
M
N

Catalonia Duques de Bergara, Bergara 11, 08002, 93 301 51 51, *duques@hoteles-catalonia.es, Fax 93 317 34 42,* – 25/400. LV f
Meals 20 – 13 – **146 rm** 149/186, 2 suites.
• Partly occupying an attractive late-19C Modernist building, with an interior that combines a sense of the past with contemporary comfort. The hotel restaurant offers a wide range of fine international cuisine. Swimming pool-solarium.

Montecarlo without rest, La Rambla 124, 08002, 93 412 04 04, *hotel@montecarlobcn.com, Fax 93 318 73 23* – LX r
14 – **54 rm** 124/182, 1 suite.
• This magnificent hotel, housed in a 19C palace, harmoniously combines the classicism of the past with the modern design features of its exquisitely furnished guestrooms.

Neri, Sant Sever 5, 08002, 93 304 06 55, *info@hotelneri.com, Fax 93 304 03 37* – MX c
Meals 70 – 16 – **21 rm** 225, 1 suite.
• A large 18C mansion with a unique and bold avant-garde look just a few yards from the cathedral. Small library-lounge, superb bedrooms and an intimate restaurant dominated by two stone arches in which the cuisine is equally innovative.

Montblanc, Via Laietana 61, 08003, 93 343 55 55, *montblanc@hcchotels.es, Fax 93 343 55 58* – 25/450. LV c
Meals 17,50 – 14 – **157 rm** 165/206.
• A hotel in classic yet contemporary style with spacious lounges and an elegant piano bar. The comfortable bedrooms are modern in style with carpeted floors and marble bathrooms. The circular dining room offers a choice of Catalan and international dishes.

Tryp Apolo, av. del Paral.lel 57-59, 08004, 93 343 30 00, *tryp.apolo@solmelia.com, Fax 93 443 00 59* – rm, – 25/500.
Meals a la carte 25/38 – 14,50 – **290 rm** 162/192, 24 suites LY e
• Friendly and functional and ideal for the business traveller. Lounges fitted with marble and bedrooms that have recently been refurbished. The bright restaurant overlooks a garden terrace.

Barcelona Universal, av. del Paral.lel 80, 08001, 93 567 74 47, *bcnuniversal@nnhotels.es, Fax 93 567 74 40,* – 25/100. LY a
Meals a la carte 25/37 – 13,50 – **164 rm** 180/200, 3 suites.
• A new hotel built in modern style with large, well-appointed bedrooms embellished with wooden floors and well-equipped bathrooms. The panoramic swimming pool on the roof is an added bonus. Contemporary-style restaurant adorned with a profusion of wood.

G.H. Barcino without rest, Jaume I-6, 08002, 93 302 20 12, *reserve@gargallo-hotels.com, Fax 93 301 42 42* – MX r
14,30 – **53 rm** 178,70/216,25.
• Right in the heart of the Gothic Quarter. The hotel's main selling points are the elegant entrance hall and attractively designed bedrooms, all equipped with modern bathrooms. Some rooms on the top floor enjoy views of the cathedral from their terrace.

Inglaterra coffee shop only, Pelai 14, 08001, 93 505 11 00, *recepcion@hotel-inglaterra.com, Fax 93 505 11 09* – 25. HX c
11 – **55 rm** 185/230.
• A smart, modern hotel with a classical façade and welcoming feel. Multi-purpose function areas, plus bedrooms with large wooden headboards. Pleasant terrace-solarium.

Regina coffee shop only, Bergara 2, 08002, 93 301 32 32, *reservas@reginahotel.com, Fax 93 318 23 26* – rm, – 25/30. LV r
15 – **99 rm** 180/215.
• The impressive Modernist façade conceals a contemporary interior where the emphasis is on modern design. Spacious bedrooms with high-quality furnishings.

Lleó coffee shop only, Pelai 22, 08001, 93 318 13 12, *reservas@hotel-lleo.es, Fax 93 412 26 57* – 25/150. HX a
9 – **89 rm** 115/145.
• A well-run family hotel with an elegant façade, bedrooms offering adequate levels of comfort, and a large lounge area.

Catalonia Albinoni without rest, av. Portal de l'Àngel 17, 08002, 93 318 41 41, *albinoni@hoteles-catalonia.es, Fax 93 301 26 31* –
13 – **74 rm** 129/165. LV a
• In the former Rocamora Palace and near the Gothic Quarter. The foyer area has original decorative details and bedrooms in the style of the period.

Reding, Gravina 5-7, 08001, 93 412 10 97, *reding@occidental-hoteles.com, Fax 93 268 34 82* – HX d
Meals *(closed Sunday and Bank Holidays)* a la carte 19/31 – 11 – **44 rm** 160/180.
• Located close to Plaça de Catalunya. Despite being on the small side, the lounge areas and bedrooms are comfortable and well-equipped. The hotel's dining room offers a menu featuring traditional and Catalan dishes.

Banys Orientals, L'Argenteria 37, ✉ 08003, ☎ 93 268 84 60, *reservas@hotelbanysorientals.com, Fax 93 268 84 61* – AE VISA JCB. NX t
Meals see rest. ***Senyor Parellada*** – ☕ 10 – **43 rm** 80/95.
• Comfortable minimalist rooms with design features galore, wooden floors and four-poster-style beds. No lounge area.

Catalonia Princesa, Rec Comtal 16, ✉ 08003, ☎ 93 268 86 00, *princesa@hoteles-catalonia.es, Fax 93 268 84 91* – – 25. AE VISA. KX b
Meals a la carte approx. 30 – ☕ 10 – **90 rm** 105/125.
• Functionality reigns supreme behind the attractive façade of this contemporary-style hotel. Pleasant reception and lounge area, plus guestrooms which have every essential. The basement restaurant offers a fixed menu as well as a small à la carte choice.

Atlantis without rest, Pelai 20, ✉ 08001, ☎ 93 318 90 12, *inf@hotelatlantis-bcn.com, Fax 93 412 09 14* – AE VISA. HX a
50 rm ☕ 108,18/138,23.
• Somewhat functional in feel, but with a reasonably central location. Pleasant rooms with marble bathrooms, in addition to a small bar next to the breakfast room.

Park H. without rest, av. Marquès de l'Argentera 11, ✉ 08003, ☎ 93 319 60 00, *parkhotel@parkhotelbarcelona.com, Fax 93 319 45 19* – AE VISA.
91 rm ☕ 126/160. NX e
• A modern, avant-garde feel permeates this well-maintained hotel with a friendly atmosphere and large breakfast room. Pleasant entrance-cum-reception area with adjoining bar.

Gaudí coffee shop only, Nou de la Rambla 12, ✉ 08001, ☎ 93 317 90 32, *gaudí@hotelgaudí.es, Fax 93 412 26 36,* – – 25. AE VISA JCB
☕ 10 – **73 rm** 115/150. LY q
• The Gaudí's main features are its Modernist fountain in the foyer and an attractive cafeteria. The hotel's bedrooms, some with balcony, are gradually being refurbished.

Regencia Colón without rest, Sagristans 13, ✉ 08002, ☎ 93 318 98 58, *info@hotelregenciacolon.com, Fax 93 317 28 22* – AE VISA JCB MV r
☕ 10 – **50 rm** 130/160.
• A great base from which to explore one of the city's most distinctive districts. Functional bedrooms with modern bathrooms and wood flooring.

Hesperia Metropol without rest, Ample 31, ✉ 08002, ☎ 93 310 51 00, *hotel@hesperia-metropol.com, Fax 93 319 12 76* – AE VISA. NY r
☕ 10 – **68 rm** 135/150.
• Situated in the old town with comfortable and well-decorated rooms. Friendly atmosphere and pleasant staff.

Continental without rest, Rambles 138-2º, ✉ 08002, ☎ 93 301 25 70, *barcelona@hotelcontinental.com, Fax 93 302 73 60* – AE VISA LV b
35 rm ☕ 70/100.
• Friendly hotel located close to the Plaza Catalunya square which gets much of its character from the bedrooms which are furnished in an English style.

Àbac (possible transfer to Av. del Tibidabo 7), Rec 79-89, ✉ 08003, ☎ 93 319 66 00, *abac12@telefonica.net, Fax 93 319 45 19* – AE VISA. NX e
closed 6 to 13 January, 3 weeks in August, Sunday and Monday lunch – **Meals** 84,14 and a la carte 60/82.
Spec. Calamares con ensalada y guisantes. Atún al comino de Marrakech y jugo de cochinillo. Charlota de manzana, caramelo y azafrán.
• Modern restaurant with minimalist design details. Excellent service and creative Mediterranean cuisine. Popular with a young clientele.

Hofmann, L'Argenteria 74-78 (1º), ✉ 08003, ☎ 93 319 58 89, *hofmann@ysi.es, Fax 93 319 58 82* – AE VISA. NX v
closed Christmas, Holy Week, August, Saturday and Sunday – **Meals** a la carte 43/60.
Spec. Raviolis de gambas sin pasta rellenos de setas, con su glace y aceite verde. Foie de pato salteado con blinis de cerezas y su salsa. Lasaña de manzana y arroz cremoso con helado de trufa y leche de gallina trufada.
• Housed in an old building which doubles as a catering school, the Hofmann is known for its classical design and innovative, imaginatively presented cuisine.

Reial Club Marítim, Moll d'Espanya, ✉ 08039, ☎ 93 221 71 43, *Fax 93 221 44 12,* ≤, – AE VISA JCB. NY a
closed 15 to 31 August, Sunday dinner and Monday – **Meals** a la carte 27/39.
• A large, attractively laid out dining room with wonderful views of the marina through the extensive windows. The culinary emphasis here is on the traditional.

Senyor Parellada, L'Argenteria 37, ✉ 08003, ☎ 93 310 50 94, *fondaparellada@hotmail.com, Fax 93 268 31 57* – AE VISA JCB. NX t
Meals a la carte 15/24.
• A pleasant restaurant with classic-contemporary decor, bar and several attractive dining rooms. The small central patio, crowned by a glass roof, is worthy of particular note.

XX **7 Portes,** passeig d'Isabel II-14, ✉ 08003, ✆ 93 319 30 33, *reservas@7portes.com, Fax 93 319 30 46* – ▤. AE ⓓ MC VISA JCB. ✂ NX s
Meals a la carte 23/31.
◆ A venerable Barcelona institution dating back to 1836, whose dining areas retain their old-fashioned feel. The traditional menu is strong on fish, seafood and rice dishes.

XX **La Nau,** Manresa 4-6, ✉ 08003, ✆ 93 268 77 47, *artgoldplus.sl@passadis.com, Fax 93 310 15 66* – ▤. AE ⓓ MC VISA. ✂ NX b
closed 8 to 29 August and Sunday – **Meals** a la carte 35/51.
◆ Housed in an old chocolate factory, La Nau has a cocktail bar near the entrance and two traditional-style dining areas serving traditional cuisine.

XX **Comerç 24,** Comerç 24, ✉ 08003, ✆ 93 319 21 02, *info@comerc24.com, Fax 93 268 39 57* – AE VISA. ✂ KX c
closed 7 days in Christmas, 21 days in August, Sunday and Monday – **Meals** a la carte 29/38.
◆ A modern restaurant with avant-garde décor offering different menus of creative cuisine. Popular with a younger clientele.

XX **L'Elx al Moll,** Moll d'Espanya-Maremagnun, Local 9, ✉ 08039, ✆ 93 225 81 17, *Fax 93 225 81 20,* ≤, 🏖 – ▤. AE MC VISA NY m
Meals - Rice dishes - a la carte 17/28.
◆ A restaurant with impressive views of the marina, a modern-rustic dining room and pleasant covered terrace. Popular for its fish, seafood and good choice of rice-based dishes.

X **Pitarra,** Avinyó 56, ✉ 08002, ✆ 93 301 16 47, *Fax 93 301 85 62* – ▤. AE ⓓ MC VISA JCB NY e
closed August, Sunday and Bank Holidays dinner – **Meals** a la carte 24/35.
◆ A pleasant and welcoming interior adorned with old clocks and mementoes of the poet Pitarra. The comprehensive, moderately priced menu is strong on traditional cuisine.

X **Can Majó,** Almirall Aixada 23, ✉ 08003, ✆ 93 221 54 55, *majocan@terra.es, Fax 93 221 54 55,* 🏖 – ▤. AE ⓓ MC VISA JCB KY x
Meals - Seafood - a la carte 27/55.
◆ This popular, family-run restaurant is renowned for its impressive fish and seafood menu. Attractive seafood counter plus a panoramic terrace.

🍷 **Estrella de Plata,** pl. del Palau 13, ✉ 08003, ✆ 93 319 60 07, *tapas@estrella-de-plata.es, Fax 93 268 10 01* – ▤. MC VISA. ✂ NX r
closed Sunday and Monday lunch – **Tapa** 8.
◆ A well-known restaurant managed by a team of young professionals offering excellent service and delicious traditional-style tapas and "raciones" with a modern twist.

🍷 **Sagardi,** L'Argenteria 62, ✉ 08003, ✆ 93 319 99 93, *sagardi@sagardi.es, Fax 93 268 48 86,* 🏖, Basque cider press – ▤. AE ⓓ MC VISA JCB. ✂ NX a
Tapa 1,30 - Basque tapas.
◆ A Basque cider house situated near the historic church of Santa María del Mar. A very wide range of Basque-style tapas and dining room with cider barrels and charcoal grill.

🍷 **Irati,** Cardenal Casanyes 17, ✉ 08002, ✆ 93 302 30 84, *sagardi@sagardi.es, Fax 93 412 73 76* – ▤. AE ⓓ MC VISA JCB. ✂ LX z
Tapa 1,30 - Basque tapas.
◆ This traditional-style Basque tavern close to the Liceo theatre offers a good choice of typical Basque dishes with an innovative touch.

🍷 **El Xampanyet,** Montcada 22, ✉ 08003, ✆ 93 319 70 03 – MC VISA NX f
closed Holy Week, August, Sunday dinner, Monday and Bank Holidays dinner – **Tapa** 3 – **Ración** - Preserves and salted foods - approx. 6.
◆ This well-established family-run tavern is attractively adorned with typical azulejo panelling. A varied selection of tapas, with the emphasis on fish and meat.

South of Av. Diagonal : Gran Via de les Corts Catalanes, Passeig de Gràcia, Balmes, Muntaner, Aragó

🏨 **Arts** 🐚, Marina 19, ✉ 08005, ✆ 93 221 10 00, *rc.barcelonareservations@ritzcarlton.com, Fax 93 221 10 70,* ≤, 🏖, 🏋, 🏊 – 🛗 ▤ 📺 ♿ 🚗 – 🏛 25/900. AE ⓓ MC VISA. ✂ rest East : by Doctor Aiguader KX
Arola *(closed January, Monday and Tuesday)* **Meals** a la carte approx. 50 – ☕ 25 – **397 rm** 495, 86 suites.
◆ Housed in one of the two towers overlooking the Olympic port, this superb hotel is justifiably renowned for the luxurious design of its guestrooms and lounges. The Arts has several restaurants, most notably the Arola, renowned for its creative cuisine.

Rey Juan Carlos I, av. Diagonal 661, ✉ 08028, ✆ 93 364 40 40, *hotel@hrjuancarlos.com, Fax 93 364 42 32*, ≤, , , heated, , – |♦|, ▤ TV ♿ 🚗 P – 25/1000. AE ⓓ ⓜ VISA JCB. West : by Av. Diagonal EX
The Garden *(closed 1 to 9 January, Sunday and Monday)* **Meals** a la carte 55/72 - ***Café Polo*** *(buffet)* **Meals** a la carte approx. 29 - ***Tati*** *(closed August, Sunday and Monday)* **Meals** a la carte 34/53 – ☕ 19 – **375 rm** 315/420, 37 suites.
◆ A hotel with impressive modern facilities surrounded by an area of parkland with a small lake and swimming pool. An exclusive atmosphere pervades this hotel, which is tastefully decorated throughout. The Garden restaurant has a pleasant terrace.

Eurostar Grand Marina H., Moll de Barcelona (World Trade Center), ✉ 08039, ✆ 93 603 90 00, *info@grandmarinahotel.com, Fax 93 603 90 90*, , , – |♦| ▤ TV ♿ 🚗 – 25/500. AE ⓓ ⓜ VISA. East : by Doctor Aiguader KX
Meals 65 – ☕ 20 – **258 rm** 375/400, 15 suites.
◆ A circular building in a very modern style with a patio in the middle. Rooms with a high level of comfort, attractive design details and original works of art. A well-lit restaurant with good service.

Ritz, Gran Via de les Corts Catalanes 668, ✉ 08010, ✆ 93 510 11 30, *ritz@ritzbcn.com, Fax 93 318 01 48* – |♦|, rm, ▤ TV – 25/280. AE ⓓ ⓜ VISA JCB. JV p
Caelis *(closed August, Saturday lunch and Sunday)* **Meals** a la carte 63/86 – ☕ 21 – **119 rm** 355/380, 6 suites.
◆ This famous, distinguished hotel, set in a beautiful building surrounded by wide boulevards and theatres, is defined by luxury, elegance and traditional, exquisite taste. The hotel's restaurant is a haven of modern minimalism amid more classical surroundings.

Claris, Pau Claris 150, ✉ 08009, ✆ 93 487 62 62, *claris@derbyhotels.es, Fax 93 215 79 70*, , , – |♦| ▤ TV 🚗 – 25/120. AE ⓓ ⓜ VISA. rest HV w
East 47 **: Meals** a la carte 40/54 – ☕ 19 – **80 rm** 335/372, 40 suites.
◆ An elegant hotel with an aristocratic feel in the former Palacio Vedruna, where tradition and modernity combine in perfect harmony.

Majestic, passeig de Gràcia 68, ✉ 08007, ✆ 93 488 17 17, *recepcion@hotelmajestic.es, Fax 93 488 18 80*, , – |♦|, rm, ▤ TV ♿ 🚗 – 25/400. AE ⓓ ⓜ VISA. HV f
Meals see rest. ***Drolma*** below - 30 – ☕ 20 – **273 rm** 350, 31 suites.
◆ A well-established and modern hotel on the Paseo de Gràcia. Good facilities for business meetings and conferences. Attractive, spacious and well-equipped rooms. Functional dining room with both an à la carte menu and a buffet.

Fira Palace, av. Rius i Taulet 1, ✉ 08004, ✆ 93 426 22 23, *sales@fira-palace.com, Fax 93 425 50 47*, , – |♦|, rm, ▤ TV ♿ 🚗 – 25/1300. AE ⓓ ⓜ VISA. South : by Lleida HY
Meals 23 - ***El Mall*** **: Meals** a la carte 27/34 – ☕ 15 – **258 rm** 242/282, 18 suites.
◆ Close to the exhibition and trade fair sector. Modern-style hotel with very well-equipped rooms. Ideal for conventions, conferences and social functions. Restaurant with a rustic feel, exposed brickwork and pleasant furnishings.

Hilton Barcelona, av. Diagonal 589, ✉ 08014, ✆ 93 495 77 77, *barcelona@hilton.com, Fax 93 495 77 00*, , – |♦|, rm, ▤ TV ♿ 🚗 P – 25/600. AE ⓓ ⓜ VISA JCB. FX v
Mosaic **: Meals** a la carte 32/36 – ☕ 20 – **275 rm** 320/350, 11 suites.
◆ Situated on one of the main arteries of the city, the Hilton has a spacious lobby, well-equipped meeting rooms and comfortable rooms in contemporary style. Its bright restaurant is enhanced by a pleasant terrace during the summer months.

G.H. Havana, Gran Via de les Corts Catalanes 647, ✉ 08010, ✆ 93 412 11 15, *granhotelhavana@hoteles-silken.com, Fax 93 412 26 11*, , – |♦|, rm, ▤ TV ♿ 🚗 – 25/150. AE ⓓ ⓜ VISA JCB. rest JV e
Meals 25,25 - ***Grand Place*** **: Meals** a la carte 22/34 – ☕ 16 – **141 rm** 155/168, 4 suites.
◆ This centrally located hotel has retained the building's original façade, dating from 1882. The refurbished interior includes a modern entrance hall, guestrooms which are contemporary in style, and an elegant restaurant serving international cuisine.

Meliá Barcelona, av. de Sarrià 50, ✉ 08029, ✆ 93 410 60 60, *melia.barcelona@solmelia.com, Fax 93 410 77 44*, ≤, – |♦|, rm, ▤ TV ♿ 🚗 – 25/500. AE ⓓ ⓜ VISA JCB. FV n
Meals a la carte 24/39 – ☕ 20 – **299 rm** 300, 15 suites.
◆ A traditional-style hotel in the city's most modern district. Large, well-equipped rooms, excellent services and facilities, plus a spacious and welcoming restaurant.

Princesa Sofía, pl. Pius XII-4, ✉ 08028, ✆ 93 508 10 00, *psofia@expogrupo.com, Fax 93 508 10 01*, ≤, , , – |♦| ▤ TV ♿ 🚗 – 25/1000. AE ⓓ ⓜ VISA.
Meals 32 – ☕ 20 – **475 rm** 390, 25 suites. EX x
◆ In the city's main business and commercial district. The hotel's excellent facilities, luxurious lounges and comfortable rooms make it an ideal location for business trips and conventions. The modern-style restaurant offers à la carte and buffet options.

AC Diplomatic, Pau Claris 122, ✉ 08009, ☎ 93 272 38 10, *diplomatic@ac-hotels.com, Fax 93 272 38 11*, – 25/70. AE VISA JCB. HV g
Meals 24 – 16 – **209 rm** 190, 2 suites.
• Located at the heart of the Ensanche district, this functional hotel offers guests comfortable, contemporary bedrooms with modern bathrooms and good sound-proofing.

NH Calderón, Rambla de Catalunya 26, ✉ 08007, ☎ 93 301 00 00, *nhcalderon@nh-hoteles.es, Fax 93 412 41 93*, – 25/200. AE VISA JCB. HX t
Meals 21 – 17,50 – **224 rm** 227, 29 suites.
• This hotel's location in the city's main financial district makes it an ideal base for business travellers. Excellent facilities and high levels of comfort.

Fiesta H. Caspe, Casp 103, ✉ 08013, ☎ 93 246 70 00, *caspe@fiesta-hotels.com, Fax 93 246 70 01*, rm, – 25/200. AE VISA. JV v
***3 Plats** (closed August and Sunday)* **Meals** a la carte approx. 15 – 14 – **141 rm** 200/230.
• The hotel's lounge area and modern foyer are both embellished with design furniture. Wide choice of meeting rooms and guest bedrooms, with a shower and bathtub as standard. A combination of Mediterranean and international cuisine is on offer in the restaurant.

Catalonia Barcelona Plaza, pl. d'Espanya 6, ✉ 08014, ☎ 93 426 26 00, *plaza@hoteles-catalonia.es, Fax 93 426 04 00*, heated – 25/600. AE VISA. GY r
Gourmet Plaza **: Meals** a la carte approx. 30 – 13 – **338 rm** 149/186, 9 suites.
• A modern hotel facing Barcelona's main exhibition centre, with excellent facilities aimed mainly at business clientele, as well as a functional restaurant decorated in minimalist style.

Barceló H. Sants, pl. dels Paûsos Catalans, ✉ 08014, ☎ 93 503 53 00, *sants@bchoteles.com, Fax 93 490 60 45*, rm, – 25/1500. AE VISA JCB. FY
Meals *(closed August and Sunday)* 26,50 – 12 – **364 rm** 185, 13 suites.
• Located within the confines of the Sants railway station with views of the city. Functional in style with good facilities and a spacious lobby. The well-lit dining room offers two contrasting sections, one for à la carte, the other a more relaxed buffet.

Condes de Barcelona *(Monument i Centre)*, passeig de Gràcia 75, ✉ 08008, ☎ 93 467 47 80, *reservas@condesdebarcelona.com, Fax 93 467 47 85* – rm, – 25/200. AE VISA JCB HV m
Thalassa **: Meals** a la carte 33/46 – 15,75 – **181 rm** 225, 2 suites.
• A hotel set in two well-known and emblematic Barcelona buildings, the Casa Batlló and the Casa Durella. The rooms are comfortable and the décor has many period details. A charming restaurant with a wide variety of dishes.

Avenida Palace, Gran Via de les Corts Catalanes 605, ✉ 08007, ☎ 93 301 96 00, *avpalace@husa.es, Fax 93 318 12 34* – 25/300. AE VISA JCB.
Meals 23 – 20 – **136 rm** 235/255, 14 suites. HX r
• An elegant, traditional-style hotel in which the attention to detail is evident throughout and the recently refurbished rooms offer high levels of comfort. The restaurant has a distinguished atmosphere, pleasant furnishings and impeccable service.

Ritz Barcelona Roger de Llúria, Roger de Llúria 28, ✉ 08010, ☎ 93 343 60 80, *ritzbcn@rogerdelluria.com, Fax 93 343 60 81* – 25/60. AE VISA. JV b
Meals *(closed Sunday)* a la carte approx. 43 – 16,50 – **46 rm** 165/247, 2 suites.
• A hotel with a welcoming and intimate feel, a small foyer, and large, extremely comfortable and well-appointed bedrooms. The spacious restaurant is traditionally furnished in elegant style.

Omm, Rosselló 265, ✉ 08008, ☎ 93 445 40 00, *reservas@hotelomm.es, Fax 93 445 40 04*, – 25/30. AE VISA JCB. HV x
Moo **: Meals** a la carte 40/52 – 18 – **59 rm** 250.
• Hiding behind the original façade is a boutique hotel with a bright and spacious lounge area with a designer feel laid out in three parts. Contemporary rooms with restrained decor, plus a restaurant serving varied and inventive cuisine.

Abba Sants, Numància 32, ✉ 08029, ☎ 93 600 31 00, *abba-sants@abbahoteles.com, Fax 93 600 31 01* – rm, – 25/200. AE VISA. FX b
Amalur **: Meals** a la carte 26/35 – 14,50 – **140 rm** 125/143.
• A newly constructed hotel of modern design. Adequate public areas and bedrooms, which are smallish but comfortable. Functional dining room where the menu is a mix of traditional and Basque cuisine.

Gallery H., Rosselló 249, ✉ 08008, ☎ 93 415 99 11, *email@galleryhotel.com, Fax 93 415 91 84*, – 25/200. AE VISA JCB. HV d
Meals 20 – 16 – **108 rm** 168/198, 5 suites.
• This spacious, modern hotel has a roomy foyer, a number of meeting rooms and comfortable bedrooms with attractive, fully equipped bathrooms. The pleasant atmosphere in the restaurant is enhanced by the large windows, interior patio and welcoming terrace.

St. Moritz, Diputació 264, ✉ 08007, ☎ 93 412 15 00, *stmoritz@hocchotels.com, Fax 93 412 12 36,* – rm, – 25/200. AE VISA. JV g
Meals 23 – 17,50 – **91 rm** 206/247.
• A well-run hotel with a traditional façade, well-appointed rooms and a number of private rooms suitable for any social function.

Prestige Paseo de Gràcia without rest, passeig de Gràcia 62, ✉ 08007, ☎ 93 272 41 80, *reservas@prestigehotels.com, Fax 93 272 41 81* – . AE VISA JCB. HV f
16,50 – **45 rm** 275.
• The design concept figures strongly here, with aesthetically pleasing pure lines and minimalist decor which is most evident in the hotel's bedrooms.

Gran Derby without rest, Loreto 28, ✉ 08029, ☎ 93 322 32 15, *info@derbyhotels.es, Fax 93 419 68 20,* – – 25/100. AE VISA GX g
14 – **29 rm** 195/215, 12 suites.
• A small, traditional-style hotel with a welcoming atmosphere and spacious, well-lit bedrooms, many of which have wooden floors.

Barceló H. Atenea Mar, passeig Garcia Faria 47, ✉ 08019, ☎ 93 531 60 40, *ateneamar@bchoteles.com, Fax 93 531 60 90,* – – 25/400. AE VISA JCB. East : by Doctor Aiguader KX
***El Comedor* : Meals** a la carte 31/36 – 12 – **191 rm** 150.
• On an avenue facing out to sea, the Atenea Mar offers a number of modular meeting rooms, reasonable fitness area and functional bedrooms, the majority with Mediterranean views. Restaurant with a separate entrance and menu based on traditional seasonal cuisine.

Rafael H. Diagonal Port, Lope de Vega 4, ✉ 08005, ☎ 93 230 20 00, *diagonalport@rafaelhoteles.com, Fax 93 230 20 10* – , rm, – 25/175. AE VISA. East : by Doctor Aiguader KX
Meals 15 – 12 – **115 rm** 158/180 – PA 48.
• A modern, functional hotel with spacious public areas, comfortable, carpeted bedrooms, bathrooms fitted with marble, and good sound-proofing.

NH Podium, Bailén 4, ✉ 08010, ☎ 93 265 02 02, *nhpodium@nh-hotels.com, Fax 93 265 05 06,* , – – 25/240. AE VISA JCB. JV n
***Corella* : Meals** a la carte 28/40 – 15,50 – **140 rm** 150/201, 5 suites.
• In the Modernist part of the Ensanche area. A traditional façade with a modern interior with avant-garde design details. Welcoming and well-lit rooms. Intimate restaurant with pleasant décor and contemporary paintings.

Balmes, Mallorca 216, ✉ 08008, ☎ 93 451 19 14, *balmes@derbyhotels.es, Fax 93 451 00 49,* – – 25/30. AE VISA JCB. HV v
Meals 13,50 – 13 – **93 rm** 184/205, 8 suites.
• A modern-style hotel with pleasantly furnished rooms with wooden floors and exposed brick walls. One of the hotel's main features is its pleasant pool and terrace.

Derby coffee shop only, Loreto 21, ✉ 08029, ☎ 93 322 32 15, *info@derbyhotels.es, Fax 93 410 08 62* – – 25/60. AE VISA FX e
15 – **111 rm** 180/200, 4 suites.
• A classic hotel in the business district of the city. Spacious public areas and a coffee shop with a separate entrance, an English-style bar and comfortable rooms.

Hesperia del Mar, Espronceda 6, ✉ 08005, ☎ 93 502 97 00, *hotel@hesperia-delmar.com, Fax 93 502 97 01,* – – 25/175. AE VISA. East : by Doctor Aiguader KX
Meals 16,50 – 13,38 – **78 rm** 176,55/187,25, 6 suites.
• This hotel is located close to the sea in an area in the process of redevelopment. Facilities here include spacious lounge areas, well-equipped guest rooms with modern, practical furnishings, and a bright, airy restaurant.

Vincci Marítimo, Llull 340, ✉ 08019, ☎ 93 356 26 00, *maritimo@vinccihoteles.com, Fax 93 356 06 69,* – – 25/250. AE VISA. East : by Doctor Aiguader KX
Meals 12 – 6 – **144 rm** 156/180.
• A good level of general comfort, although the hotel's outstanding feature is its designer decor, with original avant-garde features in the bathrooms and on the bed headboards. The restaurant is bright and simply designed.

AC Vilamarí, Vilamarí 34-36, ✉ 08015, ☎ 93 289 09 09, *acvilamari@ac-hotels.com, Fax 93 289 05 01,* – – 25/35. AE VISA. HY a
Meals a la carte approx. 28 – 11 – **90 rm** 170.
• Meticulous in style, this hotel is successfully combines functionality with the world of design. Comfortable bedrooms, half of which have bathtubs, the remainder showers. The subtly lit restaurant is modern yet intimate.

Alexandra, Mallorca 251, ✉ 08008, ☎ 93 467 71 66, *informacion@hotel-alexandra.com, Fax 93 488 02 58* – 25/100. AE VISA JCB. HV v
Meals - only set meal - 19,85 – 16 – **106 rm** 260/300, 3 suites.
• A modern and welcoming hotel with spacious, well-equipped rooms, pleasant furnishings, carpeted floors and bathrooms with marble fittings. Pleasant public areas.

NH Master, València 105, ✉ 08011, ☎ 93 323 62 15, *nhmaster@nh-hotels.com, Fax 93 323 43 89* – 25/100. AE VISA JCB. rest HX n
Meals *(closed 24 December-2 January, August, Saturday and Sunday)* 13 – 13 – **80 rm** 140/170, 1 suite – PA 24.
• Both central and modern, with the characteristic style of this hotel chain. Pleasantly decorated and functional bedrooms which are ideal for business travellers.

Cristal Palace, Diputació 257, ✉ 08007, ☎ 93 487 87 78, *reservas@hotelcristalpalace.com, Fax 93 487 90 30* – rm, 25/100. AE VISA JCB. HX e
Meals 19,25 – 12 – **147 rm** 220/255, 1 suite.
• Modern in design with a glass façade and well-equipped rooms offering a high levels of comfort. Efficiently managed by friendly staff.

NH Numància, Numància 74, ✉ 08029, ☎ 93 322 44 51, *nhnumancia@nh-hotels.com, Fax 93 410 76 42* – 25/65. AE VISA. FX f
Meals 22 – 12,50 – **140 rm** 116/155.
• Close to Sants train station. Pleasant public areas and comfortable bedrooms with modern décor and furnishings.

Senator Barcelona, Cardenal Reig 11, ✉ 08028, ☎ 93 260 99 00, *senator.bcn@playasenator.com, Fax 93 449 30 30,* – rm, 25/300. AE VISA. EY c
Meals 18 – 12 – **213 rm** 170/200 – PA 48.
• The Senator offers guests spacious, quiet and well-appointed rooms as well as a fitness and beauty centre. A varied buffet is available in the dining room.

América without rest, Provença 195, ✉ 08008, ☎ 93 487 62 92, *america@hotel-america-barcelona.com, Fax 93 487 25 18,* – 25/50. AE VISA JCB. HV y
15 – **60 rm** 180/229.
• A modern and spacious hotel with a combined reception and public areas. Comfortable bedrooms with minimalist décor and personalised service.

Núñez Urgell without rest, Comte d'Urgell 232, ✉ 08036, ☎ 93 322 41 53, *nunezurgell@nnhotels.es, Fax 93 419 01 06* – 25/150. AE VISA JCB GX a
12 – **106 rm** 160/175, 2 suites.
• A hotel with a welcoming foyer, coffee shop and comfortable bedrooms, most of which are pleasantly furnished and have a terrace-balcony.

Capital, Arquitectura 1, ✉ 08908 L'Hospitalet de Llobregat, ☎ 93 298 05 30, *info@hotel-capital.com, Fax 93 298 05 31* – 26/60. AE VISA. South : by Gran Via de les Corts Catalanes GY
Meals 12,60 – 9 – **103 rm** 151/163.
• Behind the glass of this contemporary hotel are pleasant rooms decorated in grey and beige, with standard furnishings and modern bathrooms. Popular with business travellers.

Regente without rest, Rambla de Catalunya 76, ✉ 08008, ☎ 93 487 59 89, *regente@hcchotels.es, Fax 93 487 32 27,* – 25/120. AE VISA JCB. HV t
18 – **79 rm** 197/240.
• A central hotel with a Modernist façade, small foyer and lounge area, comfortable, recently renovated bedrooms and a compact bar adorned with attractive decorative glass.

Hesperia Carlit without rest, Diputació 383, ✉ 08013, ☎ 93 505 26 00, *hotel@hesperia-carlit.com, Fax 93 505 26 10* – AE VISA. JV x
10 – **38 rm** 110/167.
• Despite lacking overall space, this hotel is both functional and modern in style. Well-appointed guest rooms, most of which come with a shower rather than a bath.

Onix Rambla coffee shop only, Rambla de Catalunya 24, ✉ 08007, ☎ 93 342 79 80, *reservas.hotelsonix@icyesa.es, Fax 93 342 51 52,* – 25/80. AE VISA. HX t
10 – **40 rm** 144/154.
• The Onix Rambla's seigniorial exterior contrasts with its welcoming, contemporary interior, with reasonably spacious and functionally furnished rooms with wood flooring.

Zenit Borrell, Comte Borrell 208, ✉ 08029, ☎ 93 452 55 66, *borrell@zenithoteles.com, Fax 93 452 55 60* – 25/60. AE VISA. GX f
Meals 12 – 11 – **73 rm** 170/190, 1 suite.
• The emphasis here is on impeccable taste, with bedrooms that have contemporary furnishings, wood floors and top-notch bathrooms. Small, Modernist-style lounge area.

NH Forum, Ecuador 20, ✉ 08029, ✆ 93 419 36 36, *nhforum@nh-hotels.com, Fax 93 419 89 10* – |₿|, ⇹ rm, ▤ TV 🚗 – 🏛 25/50. AE ⓓ ⓜ VISA. ⚘ rest FX t
Meals *(closed Christmas, August, Saturday and Sunday)* 21 – ☕ 12,50 – **47 rm** 141/155, 1 suite – PA 56,50.
• A modern hotel with the characteristic style of the NH chain. Pleasant and well-equipped rooms.

Open without rest, Diputació 100, ✉ 08015, ✆ 93 289 35 00, *open@hcchotels.es, Fax 93 289 35 05* – |₿| ▤ TV ♿ 🚗 – 🏛 25/100. AE ⓓ ⓜ VISA JCB. ⚘ HY x
☕ 14,50 – **100 rm** 165/206.
• A functional, centrally located hotel offering a good level of comfort and fully-equipped bedrooms which, despite being somewhat compact in size, have a contemporary feel.

NH Rallye, Travessera de les Corts 150, ✉ 08028, ✆ 93 339 90 50, *nhrallye@nh-hotels.com, Fax 93 411 07 90,* 🏋, 🏊 – |₿| ▤ TV ♿ 🚗 – 🏛 25/250. AE ⓓ ⓜ VISA JCB. ⚘ EY b
Meals a la carte 21/35 – ☕ 12,50 – **105 rm** 129/170, 1 suite.
• A modern, functional hotel with the characteristic style of the NH chain. Comfortable, well-equipped rooms, plus an attractive terrace-bar on the top floor.

NH Les Corts coffee shop dinner only, Travessera de les Corts 292, ✉ 08029, ✆ 93 322 08 11, *nhlescorts@nh-hotels.com, Fax 93 322 09 08* – |₿| ▤ TV ♿ 🚗 – 🏛 25/80. AE ⓓ ⓜ VISA FX u
☕ 13 – **80 rm** 128/175, 1 suite.
• Pleasant rooms, each with a terrace, furnished in brightly coloured modern decor. Multi-functional meeting rooms are also available. Efficiently managed by friendly staff.

Onix Fira without rest, Llançà 30, ✉ 08015, ✆ 93 426 00 87, *reservas.hotelsonix@icyesa.es, Fax 93 426 19 81,* 🏊 – |₿| ▤ TV ♿ 🚗 – 🏛 25/80. AE VISA. ⚘ GY n
☕ 9 – **80 rm** 104/129.
• Close to the old bullring. An intimate and comfortable hotel with a large coffee shop and functional rooms. Décor with an attractive use of marble.

La Dama, av. Diagonal 423, ✉ 08036, ✆ 93 202 06 86, *reservas@ladama-restaurant.com, Fax 93 200 72 99* – ▤. AE ⓓ ⓜ VISA JCB. ⚘ HV a
Meals a la carte 46/62.
• An elegant restaurant with Modernist decorative details both inside and on the façade. Professional staff.

Drolma - *Hotel Majestic,* passeig de Gràcia 68, ✉ 08007, ✆ 93 496 77 10, *drolma@hotelmajestic.es, Fax 93 445 38 93* – |₿| ▤ 🚗. AE ⓓ ⓜ VISA JCB. ⚘ HV f
closed 3 to 8 January and Sunday – **Meals** - dinner only in August - a la carte 77/110.
Spec. Caldereta de langosta en tres servicios (julio-septiembre). Puré de patata, zabaione y tuber magnatum (octubre-noviembre). Verduras y tuber melanosporum en cocota (diciembre-marzo).
• Traditional style, predominantly wood, décor creating an elegant and refined atmosphere. Professional staff.

Beltxenea, Mallorca 275 entlo, ✉ 08008, ✆ 93 215 30 24, *Fax 93 487 00 81,* 🌳 – ▤. AE ⓓ ⓜ VISA. ⚘ HV h
closed Holy Week, August, Christmas, Saturday lunch and Sunday – **Meals** a la carte 47/58.
• An elegant restaurant in a historic building with an atmosphere of the past. A dining room with views of the garden and an attractive, carved wooden fireplace.

Casa Calvet, Casp 48, ✉ 08010, ✆ 93 412 40 12, *restaurant@casacalvet.es, Fax 93 412 43 36* – ▤. AE ⓓ ⓜ VISA JCB. ⚘ JVX r
closed Holy Week, Sunday and Bank Holidays – **Meals** a la carte 43/53.
• A restaurant in an attractive building designed by Gaudí. The dining room is welcoming and there is an excellent à la carte menu.

Jaume de Provença, Provença 88, ✉ 08029, ✆ 93 430 00 29, *Fax 93 439 29 50* – ▤. AE ⓓ ⓜ VISA JCB. ⚘ GX h
closed Holy Week, August, Sunday dinner and Monday – **Meals** a la carte 36/50.
• A traditional-style restaurant with a small bar, which leads to a spacious dining room with an intimate atmosphere and attentive service.

Windsor, Còrsega 286, ✉ 08008, ✆ 93 415 84 83, *restaurantwindsor@minorisa.es, Fax 93 238 66 08* – ▤. AE ⓓ ⓜ VISA JCB. ⚘ HV b
closed Holy Week, August, Saturday lunch and Sunday – **Meals** a la carte 34/60.
• An elegant restaurant with a beautiful interior patio, several dining areas and a private bar. An interesting menu and a good wine-list.

Gargantua i Pantagruel, Còrsega 200, ✉ 08036, ✆ 93 453 20 20, *gipa@gargantuaipantagruel.com, Fax 93 419 29 22* – ⇹ rest, ▤. AE ⓓ ⓜ VISA. ⚘ GHV c
Meals a la carte 27/44.
• The main restaurant and private rooms are classic in style, enhanced by contemporary design features. Traditional cuisine with a modern twist, including dishes from Lérida.

XXX **Oliver y Hardy,** av. Diagonal 593, ✉ 08014, ☎ 93 419 31 81, *oliveryhardy@husa.es, Fax 93 419 18 99,* – ▤. AE ⓓ ⓜ VISA. ✻ FX n
closed Holy Week, Saturday lunch and Sunday – **Meals** a la carte 33/41.
◆ A renowned dinner venue divided between a night-club and restaurant. Refined dining room with a terrace used for private functions.

XXX **Talaia Mar,** Marina 16 (C.C. Moda Shopping), ✉ 08005, ☎ 93 221 90 90, *talaia@talaia-mar.es, Fax 93 221 89 89,* ⇚ – ▤ ⇔. AE ⓓ ⓜ VISA. ✻ East : by Doctor Aiguader KX
closed Monday – **Meals** a la carte 33/43.
◆ In the Olympic Village. An original circular and glazed-in dining area. Creative cuisine.

XXX **Maria Cristina,** Provença 271, ✉ 08008, ☎ 93 215 32 37, *Fax 93 215 83 23* – ▤. AE ⓓ ⓜ VISA. ✻ HV x
closed Saturday lunch and Sunday – **Meals** a la carte 33/52.
◆ The attractive opaque glass frontage leads to a small foyer and several dining rooms with a mixed classic-modern ambience. Traditional cuisine based on high-quality products.

XX **Orotava,** Consell de Cent 335, ✉ 08007, ☎ 93 487 73 74, *nuriaposo@terra.es, Fax 93 488 26 50* – ▤. AE ⓓ ⓜ VISA JCB HX j
closed Sunday – **Meals** a la carte 32/49.
◆ A classic-style restaurant close to the Fundació Tàpies with contemporary paintings hanging on the walls and a cosmopolitan menu.

XX **Rías de Galicia,** Lleida 7, ✉ 08004, ☎ 93 424 81 52, *info@riasdegalicia.com, Fax 93 426 13 07* – ▤. AE ⓓ ⓜ VISA. ✻ HY e
Meals - Seafood - a la carte 51/63.
◆ Close to the city's main exhibition centre, this restaurant has a bar, seafood counter and dining areas on two levels. High quality produce, plus an extensive wine list.

XX **Els Pescadors,** pl. Prim 1, ✉ 08005, ☎ 93 225 20 18, *contacte@elspescadors.com, Fax 93 224 00 04,* – ▤. AE ⓓ ⓜ VISA JCB East : by Doctor Aiguader KX
closed Holy Week – **Meals** a la carte 33/55.
◆ This restaurant has one dining room in the style of an early-20C café-bar and two with more modern decor. A varied menu of fish and seafood, including cod and rice dishes.

XX **El Asador de Aranda,** Londres 94, ✉ 08036, ☎ 93 414 67 90, *Fax 93 414 67 90* – ▤. AE ⓓ ⓜ VISA. ✻ GV n
closed Sunday dinner – **Meals** - Roast lamb - a la carte approx. 35.
◆ In a street off the Avenida Diagonal. A spacious restaurant with traditional Castilian-style décor, bar and a wood fired oven for roasting suckling pig and lamb.

XX **La Provença,** Provença 242, ✉ 08008, ☎ 93 323 23 67, *restofi@laprovenza.com, Fax 93 451 23 89* – ▤. AE ⓓ ⓜ VISA HV y
Meals a la carte 21/25.
◆ A fusion of the traditional and modern restaurant close to the Paseo de Gràcia in a comfortable, cheerful setting. The well-priced menu is based on fresh market produce.

XX **El Asador de Aranda,** Pau Claris 70, ✉ 08010, ☎ 93 342 55 78, *asador@asadoraranda.com, Fax 93 342 55 78* – ▤. AE ⓓ ⓜ VISA. ✻ JX b
closed Holy Week and Sunday dinner – **Meals** - Roast lamb - a la carte 30/35.
◆ The standard features of this chain are evident here, with a bar at the entrance, a roasting oven in open view, and two inviting dining rooms with elegant Castilian decor.

XX **El Túnel D'en Marc Palou,** Bailén 91, ✉ 08009, ☎ 93 265 86 58, *Fax 93 246 01 14* – ▤. AE ⓓ ⓜ VISA. ✻ JV t
closed August, Saturday lunch and Sunday – **Meals** a la carte 32/36.
◆ In a glass-fronted corner building with three small and contemporary dining rooms on various levels. A refined setting for cuisine that is interestingly inventive.

XX **Vinya Rosa-Magí,** av. de Sarrià 17, ✉ 08029, ☎ 93 430 00 03, *info@vinyarosamagi.com, Fax 93 430 00 41* – ▤. AE ⓓ ⓜ VISA GX y
closed Saturday lunch and Sunday – **Meals** a la carte 34/52.
◆ This small restaurant has an intimate and welcoming atmosphere and attractive décor details. Cosmopolitan cuisine.

XX **Gorría,** Diputació 421, ✉ 08013, ☎ 93 245 11 64, *info@restaurantegorria.com, Fax 93 232 78 57* – ▤. AE ⓓ ⓜ VISA JCB. ✻ JU a
closed Holy Week, August, Sunday and Bank Holidays dinner – **Meals** - Basque rest - a la carte 35/46.
◆ A well-established and pleasant restaurant with good service. Very good menu and cuisine.

XX **Casa Darío,** Consell de Cent 256, ✉ 08011, ☎ 93 453 31 35, *casadario@casadario.com, Fax 93 451 33 95* – ▤. AE ⓓ ⓜ VISA JCB. ✻ HX p
closed August and Sunday – **Meals** a la carte 34/59.
◆ A classic-style restaurant with a bar near the entrance leading to three pleasantly furnished dining areas and a private room upstairs. Cuisine based on quality ingredients.

Anfiteatro, av. Litoral (Parc del Port Olímpic), 08005, 659 69 53 45, *anfiteatrobcn@telefonica.net, Fax 93 457 14 19,* – . AE MC VISA East : by Doctor Aiguader KX
closed Sunday dinner and Monday – **Meals** a la carte 40/57.
• This modern restaurant has a friendly atmosphere, an abundance of natural light and careful attention to detail. A large fountain adds to the overall charm.

El Túnel del Port, Moll de Gregal 12 (Port Olímpic), 08005, 93 221 03 21, *info@eltuneldelport.com, Fax 93 221 35 86,* <, – . AE MC VISA East : by Doctor Aiguader KX
closed Sunday dinner and Monday – **Meals** a la carte 28/43.
• A traditional restaurant in an elegant setting with service in keeping with its reputation. Two dining rooms, one private section and two large-capacity terraces.

Saüc, passatge Lluís Pellicer 12, 08036, 93 321 01 89, *sauc@saucrestaurant.com* – . MC VISA GV d
closed 1 to 10 January, 9 to 30 August, Sunday and Monday – **Meals** a la carte 26/40.
• The couple who run this restaurant, functional in style but with the occasional avant-garde touch, offer a personal slant on regional cuisine based on high-quality products.

Nervión, Còrsega 232, 08036, 93 218 06 27 – . AE MC VISA JCB. HV r
closed Holy Week, August, Sunday and Bank Holidays – **Meals** - Basque rest - a la carte 21/40.
• A small and well-managed restaurant. Delicious traditional Basque dishes and friendly service.

Elche, Vila i Vilà 71, 08004, 93 441 30 89, *Fax 93 329 40 12* – . AE MC VISA
Meals - Rice dishes - a la carte 21/30.
• A welcoming restaurant with service in keeping with its category. Traditional Catalan dishes and a good range of rice dishes. JY a

Cañota, Lleida 7, 08004, 93 325 91 71, *info@riasdegalicia.com, Fax 93 426 13 07,* – . AE MC VISA. HY e
Meals - Braised meat specialities - a la carte 21/28.
• A well-lit and functional-style restaurant with a charcoal grill offering very good meat dishes at reasonable prices.

Mesón Cinco Jotas, Rambla de Catalunya 91-93, 08008, 93 487 89 42, *m5jrambla@osborne.es, Fax 93 487 91 21,* – AE MC VISA. HV q
Tapa 2,20 – **Ración** - Ham specialities - approx. 10,50.
• A spacious bar with traditional wood décor where customers can sample a good selection of fine hams and other pork products. Beyond the bar there is a dining room.

ba-ba-reeba, passeig de Gràcia 28, 08007, 93 301 43 02, *btap01@retemail.es, Fax 93 342 55 39,* – . AE MC VISA JX z
Tapa 3,50 – **Ración** approx. 8.
• In one of the tourist areas of Barcelona near the Plaza Catalunya square. A good range of tapas and a variety of other dishes. Popular with a younger clientele.

El Trobador, Enric Granados 122, 08008, 93 416 00 57, *Fax 93 238 61 45,* – . AE MC VISA. HV a
Tapa 3,25 – **Ración** approx. 9.
• Spacious and comfortable with tasteful decor and a kitchen in full view of diners. A great variety of delicious tapas to whet the appetite, plus a choice of grilled dishes.

Txapela, passeig de Gràcia 8-10, 08007, 93 412 02 89, *txapela@augrup.com, Fax 93 412 24 78,* – . AE MC VISA JCB. JV s
Tapa 1,50 - Basque tapas.
• A Basque-style bar and restaurant situated on the Paseo de Gràcia. Spacious and with a pleasant terrace.

Cervecería Catalana, Mallorca 236, 08008, 93 216 03 68, *jahumada@62online.com, Fax 93 488 17 97,* – . AE VISA. HV q
Tapa 3 – **Ración** approx. 5.
• A bar specialising in different beers with wood décor and a wide range of well-presented tapas made from carefully selected ingredients.

North of Av. Diagonal : Via Augusta, Capità Arenas, Ronda General Mitre, Passeig de la Bonanova, Av. de Pedralbes

G.H.La Florida , carret. Vallvidrera al Tibidabo 83-93, 08035, 93 259 30 00, *reservas@hotellaflorida.com, Fax 93 259 30 01,* < city and El Vallès, , , , , – , rm, – 25/80. AE MC VISA. North-West : by Via Augusta EU
L'Orangerie **: Meals** a la carte 52/75 – 25 – **55 rm** 350, 19 suites.
• This deluxe hotel on top of Mount Tibidabo carries the signature of the world's leading interior designers, as witnessed in the subtle combination of elegance, the avant-garde, and high levels of comfort. Superb views from the attractively laid-out restaurant.

Sansi Pedralbes, av. Pearson 1-3, ✉ 08034, ☎ 93 206 38 80, *pedralbes@sansihotels.com, Fax 93 206 38 81* – ▮ ▤ TV ♿ – 25/60. AE VISA. rest — West : by Av. de Pedralbes EV
Meals *(closed Saturday and Sunday)* a la carte 31/54 – 14 – **65 rm** 146/166.
• A top-notch modern hotel close to the famous monastery of Pedralbes. Excellent bedrooms with quality furnishings and modern bathrooms. The restaurant offers a good menu of carefully prepared dishes.

Hesperia Sarrià, Vergós 20, ✉ 08017, ☎ 93 204 55 51, *hotel@hesperia-sarria.com, Fax 93 204 43 92* – ▮, rm, ▤ TV – 25/300. AE VISA. EU c
Meals 19,60 – 13 – **134 rm** 168/198 – PA 38.
• A modern hotel with a spacious foyer and reception area and comfortable and very well-appointed bedrooms. Large meeting rooms.

Balmoral coffee shop only, Via Augusta 5, ✉ 08006, ☎ 93 217 87 00, *info@hotelbalmoral.com, Fax 93 415 14 21* – ▮ ▤ TV – 25/150. AE VISA. HV n
12 – **106 rm** 175/245.
• A comfortable, traditional-style hotel offering professional service. Bright, well-appointed bedrooms and a choice of panelled-off function rooms.

AC Irla, Calvet 40-42, ✉ 08021, ☎ 93 241 62 10, *acirla@ac-hotels.com, Fax 93 241 62 11*, – ▮ ▤ TV – 25/30. AE VISA. GV h
Meals a la carte approx. 28 – 13 – **36 rm** 221.
• Quality materials, design features and a sense of the functional add to the overall charm of this welcoming hotel. Spacious bathrooms with showers rather than baths.

Catalonia Suite, Muntaner 505, ✉ 08022, ☎ 93 212 80 12, *suite@hoteles-catalonia.es, Fax 93 211 23 17* – ▮ ▤ TV ♿ – 25/90. AE VISA. FU a
Meals 16 – 13 – **117 rm** 116/149.
• Located in an exclusive residential and business district, the Catalonia Suite offers guests functional, elegantly decorated rooms in a welcoming, restful atmosphere.

Catalonia Córcega, Còrsega 368, ✉ 08037, ☎ 93 208 19 19, *corcega@hoteles-catalonia.es, Fax 93 208 08 57* – ▮ ▤ TV ♿. AE VISA JCB. HU x
Meals 15 – 13 – **77 rm** 124/159, 2 suites.
• A modern hotel with attractive, spacious rooms, a mix of contemporary and traditional furniture and facilities in keeping with its rating, although the hotel lounge is on the small side. Fixed menu in the restaurant, with a small à la carte choice.

Victoria H. Suites coffee shop only, Beltran i Rózpide 7-9, ✉ 08034, ☎ 93 206 99 00, *victoria@victoriabcn.com, Fax 93 280 52 67*, – ▮ ▤ TV. AE VISA. EX z
9 – **67 rm** 97/116, 7 suites.
• A classic-style hotel with a welcoming atmosphere, comfortable, well-furnished bedrooms with quality linen, and marble bathrooms.

Turó de Vilana coffee shop only except Week End, Vilana 7, ✉ 08017, ☎ 93 434 03 63, *hotel@turodevilana.com, Fax 93 418 89 03* – ▮ ▤ TV – 25/40. AE VISA. EU r
12 – **20 rm** 120/145.
• A charming hotel in a residential area. Good spacious public areas and well-equipped rooms with attractive design details.

St. Gervasi, Sant Gervasi de Cassoles 26, ✉ 08022, ☎ 93 253 17 40, *stgervasi.booking@hoteles-silken.com, Fax 93 253 17 41* – ▮ ▤ TV ♿ – 25/50. AE VISA. FU c
Meals 13 – 10 – **51 rm** 150/180.
• This comfortable, well-managed hotel offers guests carpeted bedrooms with functional furniture in light tones and fully-equipped bathrooms.

NH Cóndor, Via Augusta 127, ✉ 08006, ☎ 93 209 45 11, *nhcondor@nh-hotels.es, Fax 93 202 27 13* – ▮ ▤ TV – 25/50. AE VISA GU z
Meals *(closed August)* 10 – 12,50 – **66 rm** 141/170, 12 suites.
• A functional and comfortable hotel with all the characteristic style of this hotel chain. Modern furnishings and wood décor creating an intimate atmosphere.

Husa Pedralbes, Fontcuberta 4, ✉ 08034, ☎ 93 203 71 12, *hotelpedralbes@husa.es, Fax 93 205 70 65* – ▮ ▤ TV. AE VISA JCB. EV b
Meals *(closed Saturday, Sunday and Bank Holidays)* 12 – 11,50 – **30 rm** 137/168.
• The minimalist, wood-inspired lobby provides a welcoming introduction to this hotel. Well-equipped rooms, characterised by the high quality of their furnishings.

Covadonga without rest, av. Diagonal 596, ✉ 08021, ☎ 93 209 55 11, *covadonga@hcchotels.com, Fax 93 209 58 33* – ▮ ▤ TV – 25/50. AE VISA JCB. GV a
15 – **101 rm** 165/206.
• A good location in a lively shopping area. A classical façade, intimate ambience, and bright rooms with all creature comforts. Popular with groups.

Condado without rest, Aribau 201, ✉ 08021, ☎ 93 200 23 11, *hotel@condadohotel.com, Fax 93 200 25 86* – ▮ ▤ TV ♿. AE ① MC VISA. ✈ GV g
☕ 10,50 – **81 rm** 105/130.
• At the heart of the city's financial and shopping district, the Condado has a glitzy marble lobby and functional rooms with the type of small detail that sets it apart.

Colors without rest, Campoamor 79, ✉ 08031, ☎ 93 274 99 20, *gruptravi@hotelcolors.com, Fax 93 427 42 20* – ▮ ▤ TV. AE ① MC VISA. ✈ North : by Padilla JU
25 rm ☕ 70/94.
• An intimate little hotel in the Horta area. Basic but pleasant with simple décor which changes in colour from floor to floor. Friendly service.

Neichel, Beltran i Rózpide 1, ✉ 08034, ☎ 93 203 84 08, *neichel@relaischateaux.com, Fax 93 205 63 69* – ▤. AE ① MC VISA JCB EX z
closed August, Sunday, Monday and Bank Holidays – **Meals** 57 and a la carte 58/70.
Spec. Ravioli de trufa fresca, taco de foie y ostra. Rodaballo asado, calçots, bacon, desglasado al vinagre de Chardonnay. Magret de pichón lacado a la miel, regalíz y puré de apio.
• Creative and innovative cuisine to satisfy even the most demanding palate. An elegant and pleasant restaurant with a garden.

Via Veneto, Ganduxer 10, ✉ 08021, ☎ 93 200 72 44, *pmonje@adam.es, Fax 93 201 60 95* – ▤. AE ① MC VISA. ✈ FV e
closed 1 to 20 August, Saturday lunch and Sunday – **Meals** 68 and a la carte 45/58.
Spec. Langostinos al vapor con brioche crujiente, aceitunas de Kalamata y pequeña ensalada. Hígado de pato fresco macerado al moscatel "Casta Diva" con bizcocho de miel. Massini de chocolate negro y maíz tostado con helado de yema.
• A restaurant with elegant Belle Epoque décor and impeccable service with an interesting menu. A highly professional staff.

Jean Luc Figueras, Santa Teresa 10, ✉ 08012, ☎ 93 415 28 77, *jlf@jeanlucfigueras.com, Fax 93 218 92 62* – ▤. AE ① MC VISA JCB. ✈ HV z
closed Sunday – **Meals** 70 and a la carte 62/92.
Spec. Raviolis de ostras y manitas, pequeña polenta de pasas y aceite de picada. Lubina de playa con tripa de bacalao, butifarra negra y alcachofa. Cochinillo confitado con tatín de melocotón y salsa agridulce.
• A very pleasant setting in which to enjoy creative and innovative dishes. Several elegant dining areas and décor with exquisitely tasteful design details.

Reno, Tuset 27, ✉ 08006, ☎ 93 200 91 29, *reno@restaurantreno.com, Fax 93 414 41 14* – ▤. AE ① MC VISA JCB. ✈ GV r
closed August, Saturday lunch and Sunday – **Meals** a la carte 44/58.
• A traditional-style restaurant with a welcoming atmosphere and a menu firmly rooted in the gastronomic culture of the region but with a modern twist. A very good wine-list.

Gaig (possible transfer to Aragón 214), passeig de Maragall 402, ✉ 08031, ☎ 93 429 10 17, *restaurantegaig@hotmail.com, Fax 93 429 70 02* – ▤ P. AE ① MC VISA. ✈ North : by Travessera de Gràcia HU
closed Holy Week, August and Sunday – **Meals** 74,20 and a la carte 47/64.
Spec. Tartar de lubina, gamba y caviar de trucha. Cochinillo lechal deshuesado y crujiente con fresones y cebolla tierna. Lubina a la sartén con verduritas de temporada.
• A refined setting with professional service of the highest order. Creative cuisine which takes its inspiration from the Mediterranean and Catalunya.

El Racó d'en Freixa, Sant Elies 22, ✉ 08006, ☎ 93 209 75 59, *info@elracodenfreixa.com, Fax 93 209 79 18* – ▤. AE ① MC VISA. ✈ GU h
closed Holy Week, 21 days in August, Sunday and Monday – **Meals** 60,70 and a la carte 52/58.
Spec. El estudio del huevo, habas, guisantes y espárragos (primavera). Liebre a la Royal (invierno). Chocolate 2005.1, contrastes dulces, ácidos, salados y amargos.
• Recently redecorated in a more contemporary style with pure, minimalist lines and designer touches to mirror the excellent service and interestingly creative cuisine.

Botafumeiro, Gran de Gràcia 81, ✉ 08012, ☎ 93 218 42 30, *info@botafumeiro.es, Fax 93 217 13 05* – ▤. AE ① MC VISA JCB. ✈ HU v
Meals - Seafood - a la carte 38/56.
• A well-known restaurant in the Gràcia district of the city with a maritime feel to it and a menu to match.

Roig Robí, Sèneca 20, ✉ 08006, ☎ 93 218 92 22, *roigrobi@roigrobi.com, Fax 93 415 78 42,* 🌳 – ▤ 🚗. AE ① MC VISA JCB HV c
closed 3 weeks in August, Saturday lunch and Sunday – **Meals** a la carte 48/68.
• A modern restaurant in a splendid setting with a pleasant garden-terrace. A very varied and original menu.

XX **El Asador de Aranda,** av. del Tibidabo 31, ✉ 08022, ✆ 93 417 01 15, *asador@asadoraranda.com, Fax 93 212 24 82,* – ▤ P. AE ⓓ MC VISA. ✗ North-West : by Balmes FU
closed Holy Week, Sunday in August and Sunday dinner the rest of the year – **Meals** - Roast lamb - a la carte approx. 33.
◆ A wonderful setting in the Modernist Casa Roviralta. Traditional Castilian cooking with very good suckling pig and young lamb.

XX **Tram-Tram,** Major de Sarrià 121, ✉ 08017, ✆ 93 204 85 18, – ▤. AE ⓓ MC VISA JCB. ✗ EU d
closed 24 to 31 December, Holy Week, 15 days in August, Saturday lunch, Sunday and Monday lunch – **Meals** a la carte 35/52.
◆ An intimate and welcoming restaurant in a historic residential building in an uptown area of the city. Creative and innovative contemporary cuisine.

XX ✿ **Alkimia,** Indústria 79, ✉ 08025, ✆ 93 207 61 15, *alkimia@telefonica.net* – ▤. ⓓ MC VISA JCB. ✗ JU v
closed Holy Week, 3 weeks in August, Saturday lunch and Sunday – **Meals** a la carte 28/38.
Spec. Lomo de atún con habitas, bacon y concentrado de frambuesa. Rabo de buey con tripitas de bacalao, calabaza y pipas garrapiñadas. Piña con sopa de lichis, apio confitado y helado de eucalipto.
◆ Dining room with soothing, minimalist decor, very good service and individual lighting. Modern cuisine based on Catalonian traditions and a "sampler" menu for tasting a variety of dishes.

XX **Laurak,** La Granada del Penedès 14-16, ✉ 08006, ✆ 93 218 71 65, *Fax 93 218 98 67* – ▤. AE ⓓ MC VISA. ✗ HV e
closed 22 December-3 January and Sunday – **Meals** - Basque rest - a la carte 55/61.
◆ A modern restaurant which is efficiently run by the owner-chef. Airy dining room with a wooden floor, design features and two private sections.

XX **Hisop,** passatge de Marimon 9, ✉ 08021, ✆ 93 241 32 33, *hisop@hisop.com* – ▤. AE ⓓ MC VISA. ✗ GV b
closed 13 to 22 August, Saturday lunch and Sunday – **Meals** a la carte 49/59.
◆ Hisop enjoys an excellent local reputation based upon its highly creative cuisine and good service. A minimalist look with floral decoration on the walls.

XX **Can Cortada,** av. de l'Estatut de Catalunya, ✉ 08035, ✆ 93 427 23 15, *gruptravi@cancortada.com, Fax 93 427 02 94,* – ▤ P. AE ⓓ MC VISA. ✗ North : by Padilla JU
Meals a la carte approx. 32.
◆ A restaurant in an old Catalan farmhouse with stone walls and wooden beams. A pleasant atmosphere and good regional cooking.

XX **St. Rémy,** Iradier 12, ✉ 08017, ✆ 93 418 75 04, *Fax 93 434 04 34* – ▤. AE ⓓ MC VISA JCB EU n
closed Sunday dinner – **Meals** a la carte 23/30.
◆ A restaurant on two levels with two spacious and well-lit dining rooms and contemporary-style furniture. Catalan dishes at reasonable prices.

XX **Le Quattro Stagioni,** Dr. Roux 37, ✉ 08017, ✆ 93 205 22 79, *restaurante@4stagioni.com, Fax 93 205 78 65,* – ▤. AE ⓓ MC VISA JCB. ✗ FV c
closed Holy Week, Sunday and Monday lunch (July-August), Sunday dinner and Monday the rest of the year – **Meals** - Italian rest - a la carte 24/30.
◆ A well-run restaurant with comfortable dining areas with modern décor and a pleasant patio-terrace. Cuisine in the Italian tradition.

XX **Silvestre,** Santaló 101, ✉ 08021, ✆ 93 241 40 31, *Fax 93 241 40 31* – ▤. AE ⓓ MC VISA. ✗ GV e
closed Holy Week, 2 weeks in August, Saturday lunch, Sunday and Bank Holidays – **Meals** a la carte approx. 26.
◆ The couple who own this restaurant have created a popular eatery with several sections which add intimacy to this classic setting. Good value-for money and seasonal produce.

XX **La Petite Marmite,** Madrazo 68, ✉ 08006, ✆ 93 201 48 79, *Fax 93 202 23 43* – ▤ . AE ⓓ MC VISA. ✗ GU f
closed Holy Week, August, Sunday and Bank Holidays – **Meals** a la carte 20/31.
◆ An old, traditional-style restaurant with a loyal following in the central business district. An attractive setting in which to enjoy a cosmopolitan menu with subtle twists.

X **Vivanda,** Major de Sarrià 134, ✉ 08017, ✆ 93 203 19 18, *vivanda1@yahoo.es, Fax 93 212 48 85,* – ▤. ⓓ MC VISA. ✗ EU a
closed Sunday and Monday lunch – **Meals** a la carte approx. 30.
◆ A restaurant situated in the residential area of Sarrià with a modern dining room, wicker furniture and adequate service. An interesting menu at reasonable prices.

La Venta, pl. Dr. Andreu, ✉ 08035, ☎ 93 212 64 55, *Fax 93 212 51 44*, – ▤. AE ⓓ ⓜ VISA North-West : by Balmes FU
closed Christmas and Sunday – **Meals** a la carte 32/40.
◆ A former Modernist-style café with a terrace and delightful views. A second restaurant, El Mirador de La Venta, can be found inside, offering a more innovative menu.

OT, Torres 25, ✉ 08012, ☎ 93 284 77 52, *otrestaurant@hotmail.com, Fax 93 284 77 52* – ▤. ⓜ VISA. HU f
closed Christmas, 3 weeks in August, Saturday lunch and Sunday – **Meals** - Set monthly menu - 45.
◆ An informal restaurant decorated in bright colours with artwork on the walls. Appetising tasting menu with dishes changing on a monthly basis.

La Taula, Sant Màrius 8-12, ✉ 08022, ☎ 93 417 28 48, *Fax 93 434 01 27* – ▤. AE ⓓ ⓜ VISA JCB. FU u
closed August, Saturday lunch, Sunday and Bank Holidays – **Meals** a la carte 14/29.
◆ A small, welcoming restaurant where the focus is on attention to detail. A lively atmosphere in which to enjoy the two types of menus and chef's recommendations.

José Luis, av. Diagonal 520, ✉ 08006, ☎ 93 200 83 12, *joseluis@nexo.es, Fax 93 200 83 12*, – ▤. AE ⓓ ⓜ VISA. HV a
Tapa 1,40 – **Ración** approx. 10.
◆ On the city's main artery. A tapas bar with tables and on the first floor two pleasant dining areas.

Casa Pepe, pl. de la Bonanova 4 ☎ 93 418 00 87, *casa_pepe@eresmas.com, Fax 93 418 95 53* – ▤. ⓜ VISA. FU n
closed 3 weeks in August and Monday – **Tapa** 10 – **Ración** approx. 20.
◆ An unusual meeting place where you can enjoy tapas and servings of a variety of dishes or buy gourmet food products in a relaxed and cheerful atmosphere.

Casa Pepe, Balmes 377, ✉ 08022, ☎ 93 417 11 76, *casa_pepe@eresmas.com, Fax 93 418 95 53* – ▤. ⓜ VISA. FU e
closed 7 days in August and Monday – **Tapa** 10 – **Ración** approx. 20.
◆ A somewhat atypical family-run tapas bar which is more akin to a delicatessen. A list of daily specials is available in addition to an extensive selection of wines.

Typical atmosphere :

Can Culleretes, Quintana 5, ✉ 08002, ☎ 93 317 64 85, *Fax 93 412 59 92* – ▤. ⓜ VISA JCB MY c
closed 3 weeks in July, 1 week in August, Sunday dinner and Monday – **Meals** a la carte 16/24.
◆ A family-run restaurant going back to 1786. Traditional décor with beams and lots of paintings, creating a welcoming atmosphere.

Los Caracoles, Escudellers 14, ✉ 08002, ☎ 93 302 31 85, *caracoles@versin.com, Fax 93 302 07 43* – ▤. AE ⓓ ⓜ VISA JCB. MY k
Meals a la carte 30/41.
◆ Established in 1835, this typically rustic restaurant in the city's old quarter has retained all its old charm. Interesting menu and as popular as ever.

Environs

at Esplugues de Llobregat *West : 5 km :*

La Masía, av. Paûsos Catalans 58-60, ✉ 08950 Esplugues de Llobregat, ☎ 93 371 00 09, *lamasia@lamasia-rte.com, Fax 93 372 84 00*, – ▤ P. AE ⓓ ⓜ VISA JCB.
closed Sunday dinner – **Meals** a la carte 26/39.
◆ Classically arranged dining room with two distinct atmospheres. Large function rooms and a pleasant terrace shaded by pine trees. Professionally run by a dedicated team.

at Sant Just Desvern *West : 6 km :*

Hesperia Sant Just, Frederic Mompou 1, ✉ 08960 Sant Just Desvern, ☎ 93 473 25 17, *hotel@hesperia-santjust.com, Fax 93 473 24 50*, – ▤ TV – 25/550. AE ⓓ ⓜ VISA JCB.
Meals see rest. ***Alambí*** below – 12 – **138 rm** 179/210, 12 suites.
◆ In an industrial area on the city's outskirts. Large public areas and comfortable rooms in classically modern style characterised by high-quality furniture and bed linen.

Alambí - *Hotel Hesperia Sant Just*, Frederic Mompou 1, ✉ 08960 Sant Just Desvern, ☎ 93 473 25 17, *hotel@hesperia-santjust.com, Fax 93 473 24 50* – ▤ . AE ⓓ ⓜ VISA JCB.
Meals - Braised meat specialities - a la carte approx. 34.
◆ Alambí's spacious contemporary dining room is the setting for a menu featuring innovative international cuisine, grilled meats and dishes roasted in a wood-fired oven.

El Mirador de Sant Just, av. Indústria 12, ✉ 08960 Sant Just Desvern, ☎ 93 499 03 42, *elmirador@elmirador.org, Fax 93 499 03 42,* ← - |‡|, ▤. AE ⓓ ⓜⓒ VISA
closed 14 August-September and Sunday dinner – **Meals** a la carte 30/38.
◆ An unusual restaurant built on a metal structure suspended in the chimney of an old factory. Enjoy impressive views from the panoramic dining room, at a height of 105m/345ft.

at Sant Joan Despí *West : 7 km :*

Novotel Barcelona Sant Joan Despí, de la TV3-2, ✉ 08970 Sant Joan Despí, ☎ 93 475 58 00, *H3289@accor-hotels.com, Fax 93 373 52 13,* , - |‡|, rm, ▤ TV ♿ - 25/200. AE ⓓ ⓜⓒ VISA. rest
Meals a la carte approx. 31 - 13,91 - **161 rm** 115.
◆ A modern and functional hotel with warm toned décor which creates a welcoming feel. Large function rooms.

Hesperia Sant Joan Suites coffee shop only, Josep Trueta 2, ✉ 08970 Sant Joan Despí, ☎ 93 477 30 03, *hotel@hesperia-santjoansuites.com, Fax 93 477 33 88,* , - |‡| ▤ TV ♿ - 25/90. AE ⓓ ⓜⓒ VISA.
9,50 - **128 suites** 130/152.
◆ A modern-style hotel with spacious studios and apartments, each with a small kitchen. Small lounge area and fully-equipped gym.

at Sant Cugat del Vallès *North-West : 18 km :*

Novotel Barcelona Sant Cugat, pl. Xavier Cugat, ✉ 08190, ☎ 93 589 41 41, *h1167@accor-hotels.com, Fax 93 589 30 31,* ←, , - |‡|, rm, ▤ TV ♿ P - 25/300. AE ⓓ ⓜⓒ VISA JCB
Meals 14 - 13,91 - **146 rm** 115, 4 suites.
◆ Located in a business district, this Novotel has several conference rooms, spacious lounge areas, including a cafeteria, and comfortable bedrooms with bathrooms that are on the small side. Well-lit dining room with a profusion of plants and views of the pool.

Girona or **Gerona** *17000* P *Girona* 574 G 38 122 G 5 – *pop. 75 256 alt. 70.*
See : *The Old town (Força Vella)★★ – Cathedral★ (nave★★, main altar★, Tresor★★ : Beatus★★, Tapestry of the Creation★★★, Cloister★) – Museum of Art★★ : Beam Cruilles★, Púbol Altar★, Sant Miquel of Cruilles alatar★★ – Collegiate Church of Sant Feliu★ : tomb★ – Sant Pere of Galligants Monastery★ : Archaeological Museum (Season'stomb)★ – Moorish Baths★.*
Envir. : *Pùbol (Castell Gala Dalí House Museum★) East : 16 km by C 255.*
Girona, Sant Julià de Ramis - North : 4 km ☎ 972 17 16 41 Fax 972 17 16 82.
of Girona, by ② : 13 km ☎ 972 18 66 00.
Rambla de la Llibertat 1 ✉ 17004 ☎ 972 22 65 75 oficinadeturismo@ajgirona.org Fax 972 22 66 12 – R.A.C.C. carret. de Barcelona 22 ✉ 17002 ☎ 972 22 36 62 Fax 972 22 15 57.
Madrid 708 – Barcelona 97.

El Celler de Can Roca, carret. Taialà 40, ✉ 17007, ☎ 972 22 21 57, *Fax 972 48 52 59* - ▤ P. AE ⓓ ⓜⓒ VISA JCB.
closed Christmas, 1 to 15 July, Sunday and Monday – **Meals** 57 and a la carte 41/56.
Spec. Fideua de gambas sin fideos y muselina de ajos tiernos. Cochinillo ibérico con almendras y genciana. Viaje a La Habana.
◆ A well-known restaurant with classic-modern design and stucco walls which is run with great professionalism by three members of one family. Comfortable furnishings.

Roses or **Rosas** *17480 Girona* 574 F 39 122 J 3 – *pop. 13 594 – Seaside resort.*
See : *City★ – Ciudadela★.*
Av. de Rhode 101 ☎ 972 25 73 31 otroses@ddgi.es Fax 972 15 11 50.
Madrid 763 – Barcelona 153 – Girona/Gerona 56.

at Cala Montjoi *South-East : 7 km :*

El Bulli, ✉ 17480 apartado 30 Roses, ☎ 972 15 04 57, *bulli@elbulli.com, Fax 972 15 07 17,* ←, - ▤ P. AE ⓓ ⓜⓒ VISA JCB.
April-October – **Meals** *(closed Monday and Tuesday except July-September)* - dinner only - 145.
Spec. "Espardenyes" al jamón, gelée de yogur, "llardons" de jamón. Gambas al natural. Tierra de chocolate.
◆ A gastronomic mecca in a hidden cove. Rustic and with a beautiful terrace. Highly professional staff and an abundance of imagination.

Sant Celoni 08470 Barcelona 574 G 37 122 E 6 – pop. 11 937 alt. 152.
Envir. : North-West : Sierra de Montseny★ : itinerary★★ from Sant Celoni to Santa Fé del Montseny – Road★ from Sant Celoni to Vic by Montseny.
Madrid 662 – Barcelona 51 – Girona/Gerona 54.

XXXX ✿✿✿ **Can Fabes** with rm, Sant Joan 6 ✆ 93 867 28 51, canfabes@canfabes.com, Fax 93 867 38 61 – AE VISA JCB. rm
closed 1 to 14 February and 27 June-11 July – **Meals** (closed Sunday dinner and Monday) 118 and a la carte 96/112 – 30 – **5 rm** 180/280.
Spec. Verduras en cocotte al aceite de setas. Pichón a la brasa con foie a las pimientas. Fresas con mascarpone y flores de acacia.
◆ The rustic dining room is in striking contrast to the minimalist design of the guestrooms, with their contemporary feel and pure lines. Creative cuisine with local roots.

Sant Pol de Mar 08395 Barcelona 574 H 37 122 F 7 – pop. 2 383 – Seaside resort.
Madrid 679 – Barcelona 46 – Girona/Gerona 53.

XXXX ✿✿ **Sant Pau,** Nou 10 ✆ 93 760 06 62, santpau@ruscalleda.com, Fax 93 760 09 50 – P. AE VISA JCB.
closed 2 to 23 May and 1 to 21 November, Sunday dinner, Monday and Thursday lunch – **Meals** 96 and a la carte 84/94.
Spec. Espardeñas-parmentier con aceite, calabacín y perejil (invierno). Capicúa de ternera-cuatro texturas cárnicas, fruta y verdura especiada. Postres temáticos en dos servicios.
◆ The restaurant's sophisticated dining rooms offer the perfect setting in which to enjoy the creative dishes on offer here. Interesting tasting menu and excellent wine list.

BILBAO 48000 P Bizkaia 573 C 20 – pop. 353 943.
See : Guggenheim Bilbao Museum★★★ DX – Fine Arts Museum★ (Museo de Bellas Artes : Antique Art Collection★★) DY M.
18 Laukariz, urb. Monte Berriaga-carret de Munguía, North-East by railway BI 631 FYZ ✆ 94 674 08 58 Fax 94 674 08 62.
✈ de Bilbao, Sondica, North-East : 11 km by railway BI 631 ✆ 94 486 96 64 – Iberia : Ercilla 20 ✉ 48009 ✆ 902 400 500 DY.
Abando ✆ 902 24 02 02.
Vapores Suardiaz. Bilbao, Colón de Larreátegui 30 ✉ 48009 ✆ 94 423 43 00 Telex 32056 Fax 94 424 74 59 EY.
Rodriguez Arias 3 ✉ 48008 ✆ 94 479 57 60 bit@ayto.bilbao.net Fax 94 479 57 61 and av. de Abandoibarra 2 ✉ 48001 ✆ 94 479 57 60 bit@ayto.bilbao.net Fax 94 479 57 61 – R.A.C.V.N. (R.A.C. Vasco Navarro) Rodríguez Arias 59 bis ✉ 48013 ✆ 94 442 58 08 Fax 94 442 52 56.
Madrid 393 – Barcelona 613 – A Coruña 567 – Lisboa 899 – Donostia-San Sebastián 102 – Santander 103 – Toulouse 449 – València 600 – Zaragoza 305.

Plans on following pages

López de Haro, Obispo Orueta 2, ✉ 48009, ✆ 94 423 55 00, lh@hotellopezdeharo.com, Fax 94 423 45 00 – 25/40. AE VISA JCB. EY r
Club Náutico (closed 21 days in August, Saturday, Sunday and Bank Holidays) **Meals** a la carte 50/59 – 15,25 – **49 rm** 159,14/209,69, 4 suites.
◆ An exclusive hotel in a quiet area of Bilbao with elegant décor. Excellent restaurant where the very good service raises Basque cuisine to an art form.

G.H. Domine Bilbao, Alameda Mazarredo 61, ✉ 48009, ✆ 94 425 33 00, reservas@granhoteldominebilbao.com, Fax 94 425 33 01, – 25/300. AE VISA. DX a
Beltz The Black (closed 1 to 15 August and Sunday dinner) **Meals** a la carte 38/49 – 17 – **139 rm** 200/230, 6 suites.
◆ This hotel shows the characteristic hallmarks of the designer Javier Mariscal. Modern design details throughout, particularly in the magnificent bedrooms, many with views of the Guggenheim. The restaurant combines subtle decor with contemporary cuisine.

Sheraton Bilbao, Lehendakari Leizaola 29, ✉ 48001, ✆ 94 428 00 00, bilbao@sheraton.com, Fax 94 428 00 01, heated – 25/340. AE VISA JCB
Aizian (closed 1 to 15 August and Sunday) **Meals** a la carte 40/64 – 18 – **199 rm** 205/240, 12 suites. CX b
◆ An impressive cube-shaped building incorporating the very latest in architectural and technical avant-garde design. Panoramic lifts, numerous works of art, and a varied restaurant menu with a slant towards traditional dishes.

Carlton, pl. de Federico Moyúa 2, ✉ 48009, ✆ 94 416 22 00, carlton@aranzazu-hoteles.com, Fax 94 416 46 28 – 25/200. AE VISA JCB.
Meals a la carte approx. 38 – 15 – **137 rm** 153/208, 7 suites. DY x
◆ A historic hotel with a warm welcome and traditional and spacious rooms. Famous guests have included Federico García Lorca, Einstein and King Alfonso XIII. A small but elegant dining room, although its location could be better.

BILBAO

Arenal (Puente) . . . . EY 2
Arriaga (Pl.) . . . . EYZ 3
Arriquíbar (Pl.) . . . . DYZ 4
Ayuntamiento (Puente) . . . . EY 5
Bidebarrieta . . . . EZ 7
Bilbao la Vieja . . . . EZ 8
Bombero Echániz (Pl.) . . . . CDZ 9
Correo . . . . EZ
Cosme Echevarrieta . . . . DY 14
Cruz . . . . EZ 15
General Latorre (Pl.) . . . . CZ 22
Gran Vía de López de Haro CEY
Jado (Pl. de) . . . . DY 28
Juan Antonio Zunzunegui . . CY 30
Ledesma . . . . EY 32

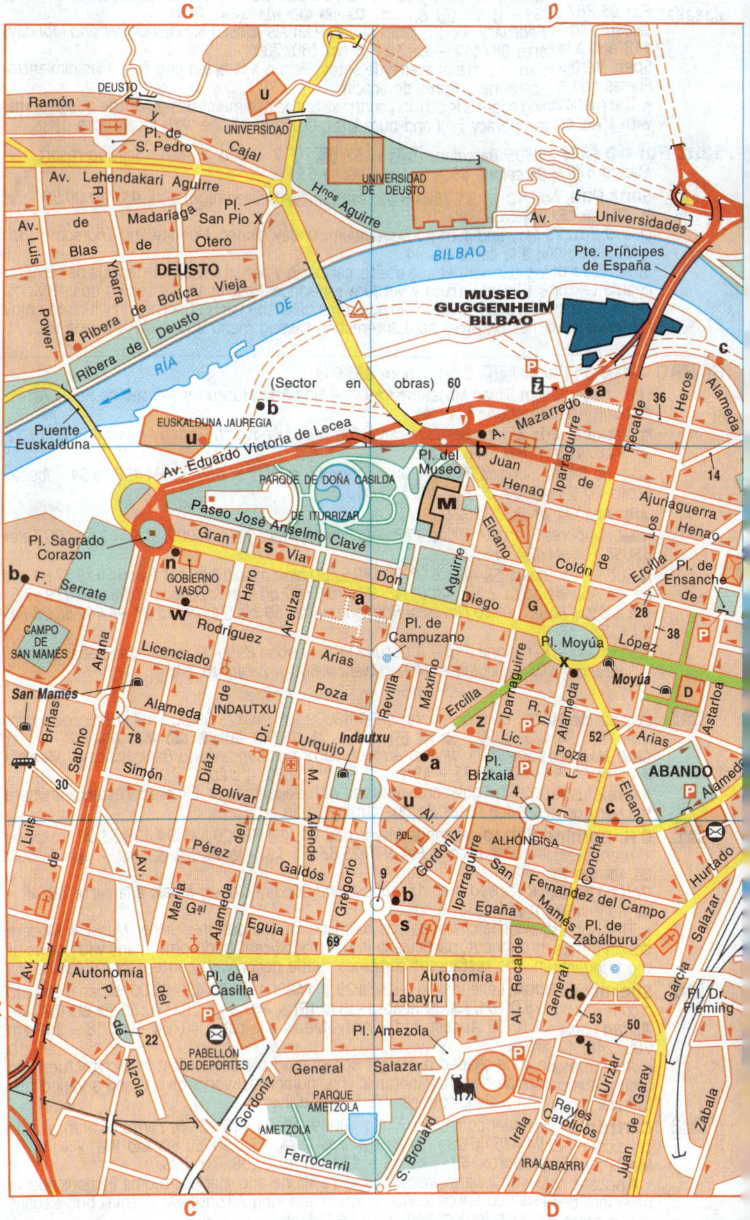

Lersundi	DX	36
Marqués del Puerto	DY	38
Merced (Muelle)	EZ	40
Merced (Puente)	EZ	41
Moraza (Pl. de)	EX	45
Pablo Picasso	DZ	50
Pedro Eguillor (Pl.)	DY	52
Pedro Martínez Artola	DZ	53
Pío Baroja (Pl.)	EZ	55
Plaza Nueva	EZ	57
Puerto de la Paz (Av.)	DX	60
Ribera (Puente)	EZ	65
San Francisco Javier (Pl.)	CZ	69
Santiago (Pl.)	EZ	71
Santos Juanes (Pl.)	EZ	73
Sombrerería	EZ	75
Victor Chávarri (Pl.)	CY	78
Viuda de Epalza	EY	80

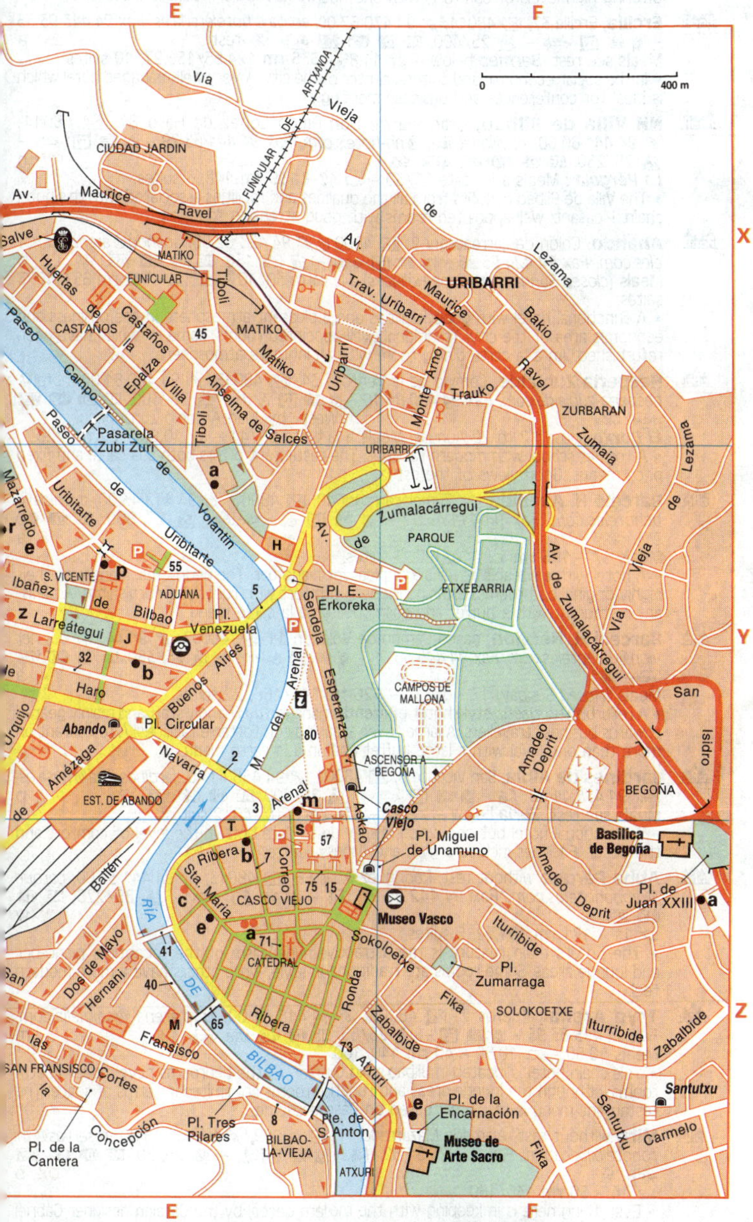

Indautxu, pl. Bombero Etxaniz, ✉ 48010, ☎ 94 421 11 98, *reservas@hotelindautxu.com, Fax 94 422 13 31* – |♦| ▤ TV ♿ 🚗 – 🏛 25/400. AE ⓓ MC VISA. 🚫 DZ b
Meals see rest. ***Etxaniz*** below – ☕ 12 – **181 rm** 135/155, 3 suites.
• A modern, functional hotel in a busy shopping district. Well-equipped, pleasant rooms offering high levels of comfort, with one floor reserved for business travellers.

Ercilla, Ercilla 37, ✉ 48011, ☎ 94 470 57 00, *ercilla@hotelercilla.es, Fax 94 443 93 35* – |♦| ▤ TV 🚗 – 🏛 25/400. AE ⓓ MC VISA JCB. 🚫 rest DY a
Meals see rest. ***Bermeo*** below – ☕ 11,85 – **335 rm** 124,95/156,97, 10 suites.
• In the social, economic and cultural centre of the city. A very well-managed hotel which is ideal for conferences and business meetings.

NH Villa de Bilbao, Gran Vía de Don Diego López de Haro 87, ✉ 48011, ☎ 94 441 60 00, *nhvilladebilbao@nh-hotels.com, Fax 94 441 65 29* – |♦| ▤ TV 🚗 – 🏛 25/250. AE ⓓ MC VISA JCB. 🚫 CY n
La Pérgola **: Meals** a la carte 25/30 – ☕ 12 – **139 rm** 148, 3 suites.
• The Villa de Bilbao benefits from all the qualities and facilities associated with this hotel chain. Pleasant, well-appointed rooms with good attention to detail.

Abando, Colón de Larreátegui 9, ✉ 48001, ☎ 94 423 62 00, *abando@aranzazu-hoteles.com, Fax 94 424 55 26* – |♦| ▤ TV 🚗 – 🏛 25/150. AE ⓓ MC VISA. 🚫 EY b
Meals *(closed Sunday and Bank Holidays)* a la carte 30/40 – ☕ 11 – **142 rm** 85/140, 3 suites.
• A functional hotel with good facilities and a pleasant atmosphere in the business and economic area of the city. Traditional, well-appointed rooms, some of which have been refurbished. An à la carte dining room with an intimate atmosphere.

Hesperia Zubialde, Camino de la Ventosa 34, ✉ 48013, ☎ 94 400 81 00, *hotel@hesperia-zubialde.com, Fax 94 400 81 10* – |♦| ▤ TV ♿ P – 🏛 25/300. AE ⓓ MC VISA JCB. 🚫
West : by Juan Antonio Zunzunegui CY
El Botxo *(closed 2 to 29 August)* **Meals** a la carte 29/41 – ☕ 10,80 – **82 rm** 128.
• A former school with modern facilities. The restaurant offers both à la carte and fixed price menus. Good views of the estuary.

Barceló H. Avenida, av. Zumalacárregui 40, ✉ 48006, ☎ 94 412 43 00, *avenida@bchoteles.com, Fax 94 411 46 17* – |♦| ▤ TV ♿ 🚗 P – 🏛 25/800. AE ⓓ MC VISA. 🚫 FZ a
Meals 17 – **186 rm** ☕ 110/120, 3 suites.
• A hotel with a sizeable foyer and a pleasant piano-bar. The bedrooms, along with their highly original bathrooms, combine modern comfort with functional furnishings. A pleasant restaurant with a buffet and cosmopolitan à la carte menu.

Barceló H. Nervión, paseo Campo de Volantín 11, ✉ 48007, ☎ 94 445 47 00, *nervion@bchoteles.com, Fax 94 445 56 08* – |♦| ▤ TV ♿ 🚗 – 🏛 25/350. AE ⓓ MC VISA JCB. 🚫 EY a
Meals *(closed Sunday)* 17 – ☕ 12 – **326 rm** 113/166, 22 suites.
• A refurbished, classic-style hotel, efficiently managed by friendly staff and mainly geared towards business travellers. A large foyer area and comfortable facilities. A restaurant on more than one level with a large buffet and an à la carte menu.

Jardines de Albia, San Vicente 6, ✉ 48001, ☎ 94 435 41 40, *jardinesalbia@husa.es, Fax 94 435 41 42*, Fɑ – |♦| ▤ TV 🚗 – 🏛 25/100. AE ⓓ MC VISA. 🚫 EY p
Meals see rest. ***Zuria*** below – ☕ 12 – **136 rm** 120/140, 2 suites.
• A functional hotel but one which is very up-to-date both in the level of comfort and the décor. Facilities include a gym and fitness centre.

Abba Parque without rest, Rodríguez Arias 66, ✉ 48013, ☎ 94 441 31 00, *parque@abbahoteles.com, Fax 94 442 21 97*, Fɑ – |♦| ▤ TV 🚗 – 🏛 25/225. AE ⓓ MC VISA CY w
☕ 11 – **171 rm** 101,72, 5 suites.
• The hotel's main feature is the attractive minimalism of the reception, piano-bar and lounge areas. Some rooms are traditional in style, while others have a more modern feel.

Tryp Arenal, Fueros 2, ✉ 48005, ☎ 94 415 31 00, *tryp.arenal@solmelia.com, Fax 94 415 63 95* – |♦| ▤ TV – 🏛 25/65. AE ⓓ MC VISA JCB. 🚫 EYZ m
Meals 10,50 – ☕ 10,50 – **40 rm** 140/160.
• This chain hotel is located in Bilbao's old quarter. All the bedrooms have modern bathrooms, although the lounge areas and function rooms are limited in terms of space. The restaurant menu is resolutely based on Basque cuisine.

Miró without rest, Alameda Mazarredo 77, ✉ 48009, ☎ 94 661 18 80, *reservas@mirohotelbilbao.com, Fax 94 425 51 82*, Fɑ – |♦| ▤ TV ♿ – 🏛 25/50. AE ⓓ MC VISA JCB. 🚫 DX b
☕ 14 – **50 rm** 130/160.
• Everything here is in keeping with the modern decor, by the Catalan designer Gabriel Miró. A successful combination of comfort and practicality, particularly in the bathrooms.

Petit Palace Arana without rest, Bidebarrieta 2, ✉ 48005, ☎ 94 415 64 11, *petit.palace.arana@hthotels.com, Fax 94 416 12 05* – EZ b
12 – **64 rm** 85/95.
◆ An old building with vestiges of its past, including exposed beams and the staircase, which combine harmoniously with its unusual minamalist style. Limited communal areas.

Iturrienea without rest, Santa María 14, ✉ 48005, ☎ 94 416 15 00, *Fax 94 415 89 29* – EZ e
6 – **21** hab 45,08/54,09.
◆ A friendly hotel right in the heart of the old town. The social areas are not very large although the bedrooms are well-appointed and with pleasant décor.

Vista Alegre without rest, Pablo Picasso 13, ✉ 48012, ☎ 94 443 14 50, *info@hotelvistaalegre.com, Fax 94 443 14 54* – DZ t
4,50 – **35 rm** 50/70.
◆ A well-managed hotel with functional rooms and standard furnishings. The pleasant, friendly ambience makes this hotel popular with a regular clientele of business travellers.

Zabálburu without rest, Pedro Martínez Artola 8, ✉ 48012, ☎ 94 443 71 00, *reservas@hotelzabalburu.com, Fax 94 410 00 73* – DZ d
6 – **38 rm** 49/63.
◆ A small, comfortable and friendly hotel with adequate facilities, rooms of varying sizes and a renovated lounge area.

Zortziko, Alameda de Mazarredo 17, ✉ 48001, ☎ 94 423 97 43, *zortziko@zortziko.es, Fax 94 423 56 87* – EY e
closed 15 August-15 September, Sunday and Monday dinner – **Meals** 68 and a la carte 42/65.
Spec. Cigala a la plancha con semillas de amapola y crujientes de callos de cordero servido con una infusión reducida de cigalas. Pintada sobre tirabeques con canelón de hinojo y aceite de cítricos. Molleja de ternera lechal asada en punto rosa con manzana, patata y reducción de txakolí.
◆ This centrally located, traditional and elegant restaurant has two dining rooms each with its own ambience. Pleasant décor and furnishings.

Bermeo - *Hotel Ercilla,* Ercilla 37, ✉ 48011, ☎ 94 470 57 00, *ercilla@hotelercilla.es, Fax 94 443 93 35* – DY a
closed 1 to 15 August, Saturday and Sunday in July, Saturday lunch and Sunday dinner the rest of the year – **Meals** a la carte 36/53.
◆ An excellent and very well-known restaurant with its own individual style. The décor has a maritime feel and the menu features traditional dishes of the region.

Etxaniz - *Hotel Indautxu,* Gordoniz 15, ✉ 48010, ☎ 94 421 11 98, *reservas@hotelindautxu.com, Fax 94 422 13 31* – DZ b
closed Holy Week, 1 to 15 August and Sunday – **Meals** a la carte 33/38.
◆ A tastefully furnished restaurant with wooden flooring, where the colour scheme is based on reds and blues. The menu here is a good mix of traditional and innovative cuisine.

Guria, Gran Vía de Don Diego López de Haro 66, ✉ 48011, ☎ 94 441 57 80, *guria@restauranteguria.com, Fax 94 441 85 64* – CY s
closed Sunday dinner – **Meals** a la carte 41/64.
◆ Close to the San Mamés football stadium. A pleasant restaurant with classic elegance and leather covered armchairs.

Goizeko Kabi, Particular de Estraunza 4, ✉ 48011, ☎ 94 442 11 29, *gkabi.bi@telefonica.net, Fax 94 441 50 04* – CDY a
closed 31 July-14 August and Sunday – **Meals** a la carte 41/57.
Spec. Risotto de hongos trufados con kokotxa de bacalao. Chuleta de atún gigante con espárragos naturales y salsa de soja. Canutillo con chocolate relleno de mousse de arroz y su cenefa.
◆ Centrally located in a lively area of the city. A comfortable restaurant with friendly staff and decor of the region. Basque cuisine.

Gorrotxa, Alameda Urquijo 30 (galería), ✉ 48008, ☎ 94 443 49 37, *Fax 94 422 05 35* – DY r
closed 19 March-3 April, 27 August-8 September and Sunday – **Meals** a la carte 39/50.
◆ An elegant setting for classic cuisine created from carefully selected ingredients. Good service in a comfortable atmosphere. The entrance is through a shopping centre.

Etxanobe, av. de Abandoibarra 4-3º, ✉ 48009, ☎ 94 442 10 71, *etxanobe@etxanobe.com, Fax 94 442 10 23,* ← – CXY u
closed Holy Week, 1 to 15 August, Sunday and Bank Holidays dinner – **Meals** 56 and a la carte 37/52.
Spec. Vieiras en dos cocciones con salsa especiada de yogurt. Bacalao confitado con hongos, crema de calabaza y regaliz. Flan de almendras y crema fría de esencia de café.
◆ Inside the Palacio Euskalduna, with access via a panoramic lift. The fine interior, furnished in modern style, provides a pleasant backdrop for Etxanobe's innovative cuisine.

XX **Víctor,** pl. Nueva 2-1º, ✉ 48005, ☎ 94 415 16 78, *victor@cyl.com, Fax 94 415 06 16* – ▤. AE ⓓ MC VISA. ✈ EZ s
closed 8 to 18 January, 23 August-7 September and Sunday – **Meals** a la carte 26/46.
◆ An intimate and friendly restaurant with a tapas bar and a traditional-style dining room on the first floor. A wine-list with a good range of Rioja wines.

XX **Guggenheim Bilbao,** av. de Abandoibarra 2, ✉ 48001, ☎ 94 423 93 33, *info@restauranteguggenheim.com, Fax 94 424 25 60,* Modern decor – ▤. AE ⓓ MC VISA. ✈ DX
closed 15 days in January, Sunday dinner, Monday and Tuesday dinner – **Meals** a la carte 53/62.
◆ A restaurant with modern décor in keeping with its location within the famous Guggenheim Museum. Contemporary cuisine and designer furnishings.

XX **Zuria** - *Hotel Jardines de Albia,* Uribitarte 7, ✉ 48001, ☎ 94 424 60 80, *zuria@zuria.biz, Fax 94 435 50 27* – ▤. AE ⓓ MC VISA. ✈ EY p
closed Sunday dinner – **Meals** a la carte 34/43.
◆ This restaurant has a separate entrance to the Hotel Jardines de Alba. A spacious split-level dining room with modern décor, a wooden floor and many attractive design details.

XX **La Cuchara de Euskalduna,** Ribera de Botica Vieja 27, ✉ 48014, ☎ 94 448 01 24, *joseba@restaurantelacuchara.com, Fax 94 476 15 59* – ▤. AE ⓓ MC VISA. ✈ CX a
closed Holy Week, 1 to 15 August and Sunday – **Meals** a la carte 34/57.
◆ A busy and lively restaurant near the Palacio Euskalduna. Modern decor, a comfortable atmosphere, with dishes rooted in the cuisine of northern Spain.

XX **El Asador de Aranda,** Egaña 27, ✉ 48010, ☎ 94 443 06 64, *Fax 94 443 06 64* – ▤. AE ⓓ MC VISA. ✈ DZ s
closed Sunday dinner – **Meals** - Roast lamb - a la carte 22/30.
◆ A central restaurant with tasteful décor. Three dining rooms with beautiful wooden ceilings and another private room. Delicious roast meats.

XX **Baita Gaminiz,** Alameda Mazarredo 20, ✉ 48009, ☎ 94 424 22 67, *Fax 94 431 81 92,* ☂ – ▤. AE MC VISA JCB. ✈ DX c
closed Holy Week, 1 to 15 September, Sunday and Monday dinner – **Meals** - Cod specialities - a la carte 37/44.
◆ A bar for guests at the entrance, a glass-adorned dining room serving traditional cuisine, including cod specialities, and a terrace overlooking the estuary. Small wine shop.

X **Rogelio,** carret. de Basurto a Castrejana 7, ✉ 48002, ☎ 94 427 30 21, *Fax 94 427 17 78* – ▤. ⓓ MC VISA. ✈ West : by Av. Autonomía CZ
closed 23 July-3 September and Sunday – **Meals** a la carte approx. 30.
◆ A renowned local restaurant accessed through a rustic-style public bar, with a dining room of similar style on the first floor. Simple cuisine based on quality products.

X **Serantes,** Licenciado Poza 16, ✉ 48011, ☎ 94 421 21 29, *restauranteserantes@telefonica.net, Fax 94 444 59 79* – ▤. AE ⓓ MC VISA. ✈ DY z
closed 25 August-15 September – **Meals** - Seafood - a la carte 38/44.
◆ Centrally located and with an entrance through a public bar. Attentive service and cuisine based on carefully selected fish and seafood.

Colmado Ibérico, Alameda de Urquijo 20, ✉ 48008, ☎ 94 443 60 01, *colmado@colmadoiberico.com, Fax 94 470 30 39* – ▤. AE ⓓ MC VISA. ✈ DYZ c
closed Sunday – **Tapa** 1,40 – **Ración** - Ham specialities - approx. 8,50.
◆ A spacious establishment with a bar with a wide range of Basque-style tapas. There is also a dining area with a menu of selected hams and other fine pork products.

Gatz, Santa María 10, ✉ 48005, ☎ 94 415 48 61 – ▤. ✈ EZ c
closed 15 to 31 September and Sunday dinner – **Tapa** 1,40 – **Ración** approx. 6.
◆ In the heart of the old town. Excellent management and professional staff. Carefully prepared and well-presented food make this a pleasant meeting place.

Xukela, El Perro 2, ✉ 48005, ☎ 94 415 97 72 – ▤. MC VISA. ✈ EZ a
Tapa 1,50 – **Ración** - Cheeses and patés - approx. 7.
◆ A well-run establishment and a pleasant place to sample tapas. Good atmosphere.

Rio-Oja, El Perro 4, ✉ 48005, ☎ 94 415 08 71 – ▤. ⓓ MC VISA. ✈ EZ a
closed 28 March-3 April, 21 days in September and Monday – **Tapa** 5 – **Ración** approx. 7.
◆ In the old-town area of the city. A recently refurbished establishment which is run professionally and offers good service. Delicious food in a friendly atmosphere.

Donostia-San Sebastián *20000* P *Gipuzkoa* 573 C 24 – *pop. 181 064 – Seaside resort.*
See : *Location and bay★★★ – Monte Igueldo ≤★★★ – Monte Urgull ≤★★ – Aquarium-Palacio del Mar★.*
Envir. : *Monte Ulía ≤★ North-East : 7 km by N I – Chillida-Leku Museum★, South-East : 6 km by Gi 131.*
18 of San Sebastián Jaizkibel, East : 14 km by N I ☎ 943 61 68 45.
of San Sebastián, Fuenterrabia, North-East : 20 km ☎ 943 66 85 00 – Iberia : Bengoetxea 3 ✉ 20004 ☎ 902 400 500 and airport ☎ 943 66 85 19.
Erregina Erregentearen 3 ✉ 20003 ☎ 943 48 11 66 cat@donostia.org Fax 943 48 11 72 – R.A.C.V.N. (R.A.C. Vasco Navarro) Foruen pasealekua 4 ✉ 20005 ☎ 943 43 08 00 Fax 943 42 91 50.
Madrid 453 – Bayonne 54 – Bilbao 102 – Pamplona 79 – Vitoria-Gasteiz 95.

María Cristina, Okendo 1, ✉ 20004, ☎ 943 43 76 00, *hmc@westin.com, Fax 943 43 76 76,* ≤ – ⬍ ▤ TV – 25/300. AE ⓓ MC VISA JCB. rest
Easo : **Meals** a la carte 33/53 – 21 – **108 rm** 405/615, 28 suites.
◆ San Sebastián's flagship hotel. An early 20C building with a very elegant interior. Magnificent and very well-equipped rooms. A distinguished restaurant with a glazed-in terrace.

XXXX ✿✿✿ **Arzak,** alto de Miracruz 21, ✉ 20015, ☎ 943 27 84 65, *restaurante@arzak.es, Fax 943 27 27 53* – ▤ P. AE ⓓ MC VISA JCB.
closed 12 to 29 June, 6 to 30 November, Tuesday except July-December, Sunday dinner and Monday – **Meals** 105 and a la carte 90/103.
Spec. Carabineros exprés. Cordero con café cortado. Vapor de cassia con bizcocho de cítricos.
◆ Elegant and traditional with a friendly atmosphere. Creative cooking with Basque roots. A treat for all the senses.

XXXX ✿✿ **Akelare,** paseo del Padre Orcolaga 56 (barrio de Igueldo) : 7,5 km, ✉ 20008, ☎ 943 31 12 09, *restaurante@akelarre.net, Fax 943 21 92 68,* ≤ – ▤ P. AE ⓓ MC VISA.
closed February, 1 to 15 October, Tuesday except July-December, Sunday dinner and Monday except Bank Holidays weekends – **Meals** 110 and a la carte 72/105.
Spec. Ostras a las uvas. Buey con lentejas en colores. Pantela de manzana y miel, helado de vainilla y pimienta.
◆ A house on a hillside with views of the sea. Great professionalism, creative cuisine and very good service.

Ganbara, San Jerónimo 21, ✉ 20003, ☎ 943 42 25 75, *Fax 943 43 08 09* – ▤. AE ⓓ MC VISA. – *closed 15 to 30 June, 15 to 30 November, Sunday dinner and Monday* – **Tapa** 1,80 – **Ración** approx. 10.
◆ The efficient staff and the quality of the tapas have made this establishment extremely successful. There is a pleasant and intimate dining room in the basement.

Martínez, Abutzuaren 31-13, ✉ 20003, ☎ 943 42 49 65 – ▤.
closed 15 to 31 January, 15 to 30 June, Thursday and Friday lunch – **Tapa** 1,50 – **Ración** approx. 8.
◆ This pleasant family-run bar in the city's old quarter has been serving tapas of the highest quality for several generations. One of the city's best-known landmarks.

Txepetxa, Arrandegui 5, ✉ 20003, ☎ 943 42 22 27, *bartxepetxa@yahoo.es* – ▤
closed 15 to 30 June, 15 to 31 October, Monday and Tuesday lunch – **Tapa** 1,70 – **Ración** approx. 10.
◆ A well-established bar renowned for its superb anchovies and other delicious tapas. A relaxed, friendly atmosphere.

Aloña Berri, Bermingham 24 (Gros), ✉ 20001, ☎ 943 29 08 18 – ▤. MC VISA.
closed Holy Week, 1 to 15 November, Sunday dinner and Monday – **Tapa** 2 – **Ración** approx. 6.
◆ This stylish bar offers a wide selection of Basque-style tapas, including a tasting menu featuring 12 different hot and cold specialities.

Bergara, General Arteche 8 (Gros), ✉ 20002, ☎ 943 27 50 26, *tapasbarbergara@eresmas.com* – ▤
closed 15 to 31 October – **Tapa** 3 – **Ración** approx. 9.
◆ This excellent bar prides itself on the high quality of its tapas, which can be enjoyed at the bar or at one of a number of tables.

Lasarte-Oria *20160 Gipuzkoa* 573 C 23 – *pop. 18 165 alt. 42.*
Madrid 491 – Bilbao 98 – Donostia-San Sebastián 8.

XXXX ✿✿✿ **Martín Berasategui,** Loidi 4 ☎ 943 36 64 71, *martin@martinberasategui.com, Fax 943 36 61 07,* ≤, – ▤ P. AE ⓓ MC VISA.
closed 15 December-15 January, Saturday lunch, Sunday lunch, Monday and Tuesday – **Meals** 112 and a la carte 85/94.
Spec. Bocadillo de vieira y hierbas en infusión de centolla con ensalada cruda de apio, nabo y alcachofas. Lubina con crema de algas, castañas al jengibre y leche de limón verde. Txakolí con fresas, crema helada de cáscara de cítricos y granizado de sanguina.
◆ A restaurant in a modern version of the Basque type farmhouse. A large entrance area from which follows an elegant and spacious glazed-in room with pleasant décor.

Oiartzun or Oyarzun 20180 Gipuzkoa 573 C 24 – pop. 8 393 alt. 81.

Madrid 481 – Bilbao 113 – Donostia-San Sebastián 11.

Zuberoa, pl. Bekosoro 1 (barrio Iturriotz) - 2,2 km ☎ 943 49 12 28, *Fax 943 49 26 79*, – ▤ P. AE ⓓ MC VISA. ✂
closed 30 December-16 January, 28 March-10 April, 12 to 30 October, Sunday and Wednesday – **Meals** 93 and a la carte 69/78.
Spec. Caldereta templada de bogavante. Cochinillo confitado, frutas al jengibre y puré de patata. Helado de mamia, bizcocho de nuez, compota de pera y crema de queso (noviembre-15 junio).
◆ A very well-known restaurant with very professional staff. In a 15C farmhouse with a pleasant terrace and elegant rustic dining room.

MÁLAGA 29000 P 578 V 16 124 H 5 – pop. 534 207 – Seaside resort.

See : *Gibralfaro* : ≤★★ EY – *Alcazaba*★★ ≤★ *(Archaeological Museum*★*)* EY – *Cathedral*★ DY – *El Sagrario Church (marienista altarpiece*★*)* DYF – *Sanctuary of the Virgin of Victory*★ *North : by Victoria st.* EY – *Picasso Museum*★★ EY **M3.**
Envir. : *Finca de la Concepción*★ *North : 7 km.*
Málaga, South-West : 9 km ☎ 95 237 66 77 Fax 95 237 66 12 – El Candado, East : 5 km ☎ 95 229 93 40 Fax 95 229 48 12.
Málaga, South-West : 9 km ☎ 95 204 88 44 – Iberia : Molina Larios 13, ✉ 29015, ☎ 95 212 01 97 CY *and airport ☎ 902 400 500.*
☎ 902 240 202.
to Melilla : Cía Trasmediterránea, Estación Marítima, Local E-1 ✉ 29016 CZ, *☎ 95 206 12 06 Fax 95 206 12 21.*
Pasaje de Chinitas 4 ✉ 29015 ☎ 95 221 34 45 otmalaga@andalucia.org Fax 95 222 94 21 and av. Cervantes 1 ✉ 29016 ☎ 95 213 47 30 info@malagaturismo.com Fax 95 221 41 20 – R.A.C.E. Córdoba 17 (bajo) ✉ 29001 ☎ 95 222 98 36 Fax 95 260 83 83.
Madrid 494 – Algeciras 133 – Córdoba 175 – Sevilla 217 – València 651.

Plans on following pages

Parador de Málaga Gibralfaro ♨, Castillo de Gibralfaro, ✉ 29016, ☎ *95 222 19 02, gibralfaro@parador.es, Fax 95 222 19 04,* ≤ Málaga and sea, ⛱ – |♦| ▤ TV ♿ P – 🏛 25/60. AE ⓓ MC VISA JCB. ✂ FY a
Meals 27 – ☕ 11 – **38 rm** 108/135.
◆ Overlooking the bay and the city lying at the foot of the Alcazaba. An elegant compromise between tradition and modernity in the well-equipped rooms. The restaurant has attractive décor and a refined atmosphere.

AC Málaga Palacio, Cortina del Muelle 1, ✉ 29015, ☎ 95 221 51 85, *mpalacio@achoteles.com, Fax 95 222 51 00,* ≤, Fб, ⛱ – |♦| ▤ TV ♿ – 🏛 25/110. AE ⓓ MC VISA. ✂ DZ n
Meals 17 – ☕ 13 – **195 rm** 180, 19 suites.
◆ Minimalist decor, carefully chosen materials and modern fittings throughout, plus a roomy entrance-cum-reception area and good soundproofing. Warm atmosphere in the restaurant where the focus is on international cuisine.

NH Málaga ♨, av. Río Guadalmedina, ✉ 29007, ☎ 95 207 13 23, *nhmalaga@nh-hotels.com, Fax 95 239 38 62,* Fб – |♦| ▤ TV ♿ 🚗 – 🏛 25/900. AE ⓓ MC VISA. ✂ CZ y
Meals 40 – ☕ 12,60 – **129 rm** 160, 4 suites.
◆ Minimalist decor, good furnishings and modern facilities. A spacious foyer-reception and bedrooms with good soundproofing. Renewed focus in the restaurant has resulted in a more innovative menu.

Larios, Marqués de Larios 2, ✉ 29005, ☎ 95 222 22 00, *info@hotel-larios.com, Fax 95 222 24 07* – |♦| ▤ TV – 🏛 25/150. AE ⓓ MC VISA. ✂ DY s
Meals *(closed Sunday)* a la carte 24/34 – ☕ 10 – **40 rm** 200.
◆ Elegance and comfort in the heart of the city. Bedrooms have light coloured lacquered furniture and well-equipped bathrooms fitted with marble.

Tryp Alameda without rest, av. de la Aurora (C.C. Larios), ✉ 29002, ☎ 95 236 80 20, *tryp.alameda@solmelia.com, Fax 95 236 80 24* – |♦|, ⇔ rm, ▤ TV ♿. AE ⓓ MC VISA. ✂ West : by Av. de Andalucía CZ
☕ 12 – **130 rm** 126/140, 2 suites.
◆ A traditional city-hotel, modern and well-equipped with large bedrooms, pleasant furnishings and modern bathrooms. A good breakfast room.

Don Curro coffee shop only, Sancha de Lara 7, ✉ 29015, ☎ 95 222 72 00, *reservas@hoteldoncurro.com, Fax 95 221 59 46* – |♦| ▤ TV – 🏛 25/60. AE ⓓ MC VISA JCB. ✂ DZ e
☕ 6 – **118 rm** 73/105, 6 suites.
◆ A very traditional hotel with a refined elegance. Bedrooms with wood décor and some have been refurbished and are more modern in style.

Monte Victoria without rest, Conde de Ureña 58, ✉ 29012, ☎ 95 265 65 25, *info@hotelmontevictoria.com, Fax 95 265 65 24* – ▮ ▤ TV ♿. MC VISA. ✗
☕ 5,95 – **8 rm** 52/78. North-East : by Victoria EY
• This cosy hotel is housed in a charming villa-type mansion. Antique furniture in the lounge, plus spacious bedrooms furnished with the personal touch.

Los Naranjos without rest, paseo de Sancha 35, ✉ 29016, ☎ 95 222 43 19, *reser@hotel-losnaranjos.com, Fax 95 222 59 75* – ▮ ▤ TV 🚗 – 🏛 25. AE ⓓ MC VISA. ✗ East : by Paseo de Reding FY
☕ 6,25 – **41 rm** 67,50/98,50.
• Friendly service in this pleasant and well-managed hotel. Attractively maintained and well-appointed bedrooms with marble fitted bathrooms.

California without rest, paseo de Sancha 17, ✉ 29016, ☎ 95 221 51 64, *info@hotel-california.net, Fax 95 222 68 86* – ▮ ▤ TV. AE ⓓ MC VISA. ✗ East : by Paseo de Reding FY
☕ 6,03 – **24 rm** 51,55/74,77.
• In a modernised old house. Small lounges with an old fashioned feel and pleasant rooms. A professionally-run family business.

Don Paco without rest, Salitre 53, ✉ 29002, ☎ 95 231 90 08, *recepcion@hotel-donpaco.com, Fax 95 231 90 62* – ▮ ▤ TV. AE ⓓ MC VISA. ✗
☕ 3,20 – **31 rm** 54,10/72,12. South-West : by Av. Manuel Agustín Heredia DZ
• A friendly and well-managed hotel with functional rooms and modern bathrooms around an internal patio.

Café de París, Vélez Málaga 8, ✉ 29016, ☎ 95 222 50 43, *cafedeparis@rcafedeparis.com, Fax 95 260 38 64* – ▤ 🚗. AE ⓓ MC VISA JCB. ✗ FZ x
closed July, Sunday and Monday – **Meals** 60 and a la carte 38/51.
Spec. Canelón de cigalitas de Málaga con caldo de queso y setas de temporada. Gazpachuelo aireado con lubina 65° y conchas finas. Chocolate (mousse-coulant-sorbete, etc.).
• A charming friendly and well-run establishment with pleasantly elegant décor and attentive service. Imaginative cooking.

Adolfo, paseo Marítimo Pablo Ruiz Picasso 12, ✉ 29016, ☎ 95 260 19 14, *infor@restauranteadolfo.com, Fax 95 222 67 63* – ▤. AE ⓓ MC VISA. ✗
closed 1 to 23 June and Sunday – **Meals** a la carte 35/44.
• A restaurant with a relaxed atmosphere and pleasant traditional décor with rustic detail. A good menu and a select and regular clientele.
East : by Paseo Cánovas del Castillo FZ

Doña Pepa, Vélez Málaga 6, ✉ 29016, ☎ 95 260 34 89, *paquitoreg@hotmail.com, Fax 95 260 34 89* – ▤. AE ⓓ MC VISA. ✗ FZ a
closed 22 August-19 September and Sunday – **Meals** a la carte 23/32.
• The bar and simply furnished dining room are adorned with bullfighting and flamenco mementoes plus photos of celebrities who have eaten here. Excellent banqueting facilities.

Figón de Juan, pasaje Esperanto 1, ✉ 29007, ☎ 95 228 75 47, *Fax 95 228 75 47* – ▤. AE MC VISA. ✗ West : by Av. de Andalucía CZ
closed August and Sunday – **Meals** a la carte 19/30.
• The rather unassuming appearance of this restaurant is compensated for by the attentive service. A mid-priced menu of quality dishes.

El Trillo, Don Juan Díaz 4, ✉ 29015, ☎ 95 260 39 20, *chaportorre@hotmail.com, Fax 952 60 23 82,* 🌳 – ▤. AE VISA. ✗ DZ r
closed Sunday – **Tapa** 1,60 – **Ración** approx. 7,80.
• An establishment with a tapas bar and a pleasant dining area with rustic décor. Numerous waiting staff and good service.

La Posada de Antonio, Granada 33, ✉ 29015, ☎ 95 221 70 69, *franquicia@laposadadeantonio.es, Fax 95 221 70 69* – ▤. AE ⓓ MC VISA. ✗ DY n
Tapa 1,50 – **Ración** - Meat specialities - approx. 3.
• A friendly tapas bar with traditional décor where you can sample a range of delicious foods in a youthful and relaxed ambience. Pleasant staff.

at El Palo *East : 6 km by Paseo Cánovas del Castillo :*

Mamé, av. Juan Sebastián Elcano 146, ✉ 29017, ☎ 95 229 34 66, *Fax 95 260 94 74* – ▤. AE MC VISA
closed Monday – **Meals** a la carte approx. 30.
• Mamé is best defined by its contemporary design and blue-influenced colour scheme. Efficient service, innovative menu and pleasant terrace.

El Cobertizo, av. Pío Baroja 25 (urb. Echeverría), ✉ 29017 Málaga, ☎ 95 229 59 39, 🌳 – ▤. AE ⓓ MC VISA. ✗
closed September and Wednesday except Bank Holidays – **Meals** a la carte 20/30.
• This small but well-maintained family-run establishment has a fine wine-cellar to complement its interesting cuisine. Typical decor and furnishings.

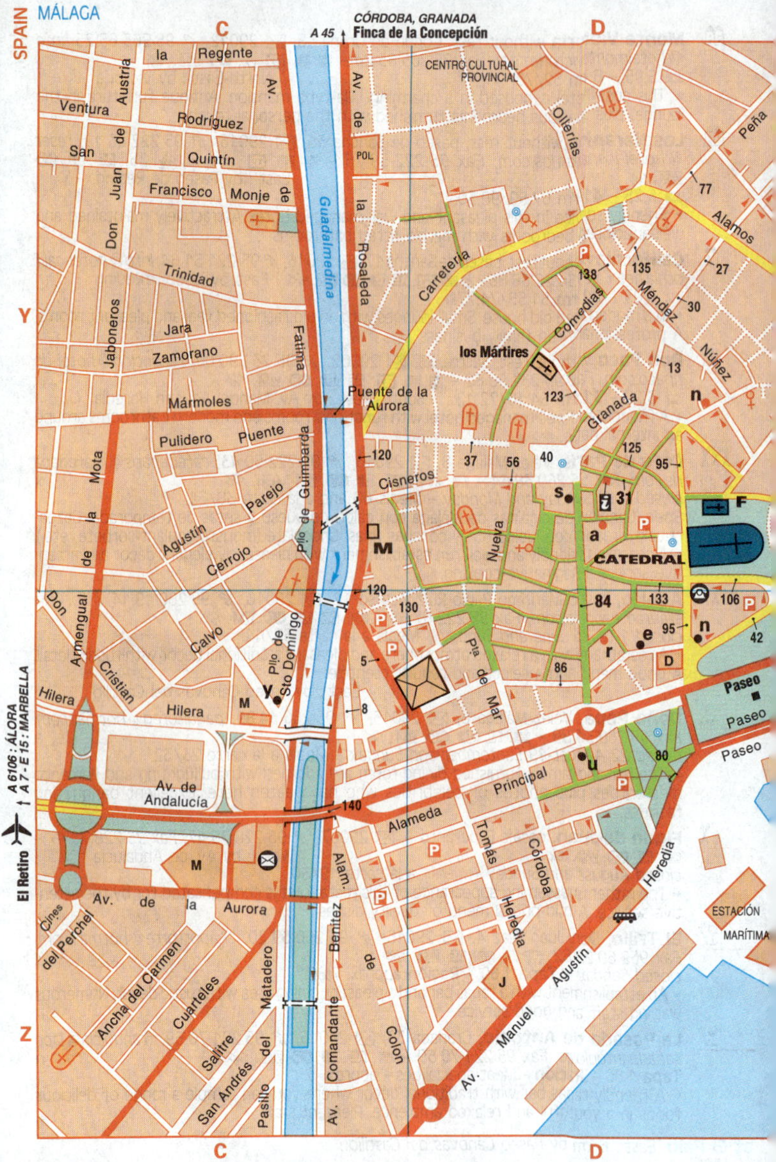

Aduana (Pl. de la)	EY	2	Casapalma	DY	30	Especerías	DY	56
Arriola (Pl. de la)	CZ	5	Chinitas (Pasaje)	DY	31	Frailes	EY	61
Atocha (Pasillo)	CZ	8	Cólon (Alameda de)	CZ	32	Granada	DEY	
Calderería	DY	13	Compañía	DY	37	Huerto del Conde	EY	67
Cánovas del Castillo (Pas.)	FZ	18	Constitución	DY	40	Mariblanca	DY	77
Cárcer	DY	27	Cortina del Muelle	DZ	42	Marina (Pl. de la)	DZ	80

Read the introduction carefully: it is the key to the Guide.

Marqués de Larios . . . . . . DYZ 84
Martínez . . . . DZ 86
Molina Larios . . . . DZ 95
Nueva . . . . DY
Postigo de los Abades . . . . DY 106
Santa Isabel (Pasillo de) . . . . CYZ 120
Santa Lucía . . . . DY 123
Santa María . . . . CY 125
Sebastián Souvirón . . . . . CDZ 130
Strachan . . . . DYZ 133
Teatro (Pl. del) . . . . DY 135
Tejón y Rodríguez . . . . DY 138
Tetuán (Puente de) . . . . CZ 140

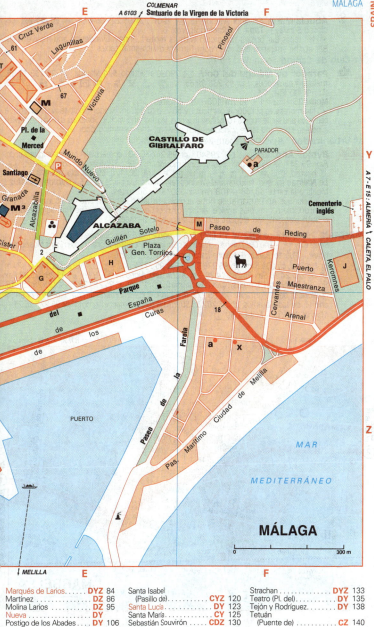

Abuela María, Salvador Allende 15, ✉ 29017, ✆ 95 229 96 87 – AE MC VISA.
closed Sunday – **Tapa** 3 – **Ración** approx. 6.
• This tapas bar breaks the mould with its modern, innovative design and mauve walls. Bar at the entrance and one room furnished with small tables.

at Club de Campo *South-West : 9 km :*

Parador de Málaga del Golf, ✉ 29080 apartado 324 Málaga, ✆ 95 238 12 55, *malaga@parador.es, Fax 95 238 89 63,* ←, , , , 18 – TV P – 25/320. AE MC VISA.
Meals 25 – 11 – **56 rm** 100/125, 4 suites.
• This impressive parador is particularly geared to golfers. Modern in style with extensive terraces and large rooms furnished in wood, leather and wicker. Spacious dining room with a gabled roof and large windows with views of the swimming pool.

at Urbanización Mijas Golf *South-West : 30 km by N 340 :*

Byblos Andaluz , ✉ 29640, ✆ 95 247 30 50, *comercial@byblos-andaluz.com, Fax 95 247 67 83,* ← golf course and mountains, , Thalassotherapy facilities, , heated, , , , 18 18 – TV P – 20/170. AE MC VISA.
Le Nailhac *(closed January and Wednesday)* **Meals** a la carte 42/65 - ***Byblos Andaluz :*** **Meals** a la carte 38/48 – **108 rm** 280/335, 36 suites.
• A luxurious Andalusian-style hotel complex situated between two golf courses. Large, comfortable rooms plus a wide variety of facilities and services. The Nailhac restaurant is both pleasant and elegant and has a poolside terrace.

Marbella *29600 Málaga* 578 **W 15** 124 **E 6** – *pop. 115 871 – Seaside resort.*
See : *City★★ – The Old Town★ – Naranjos Square★ – Contemporary Spain Print Museum★.*
Envir. : *Puerto Banús (Pleasure harbour★★) by ② : 8 km.*
18 *Río Real, by ① : 5 km ✆ 95 276 57 33 Fax 95 277 21 40 –* 18 *Los Naranjos, by ② : 7 km ✆ 95 281 24 28 Fax 95 281 14 28 –* 18 *Aloha, urb. Aloha by ② : 8 km ✆ 95 281 23 88 Fax 95 281 23 89 –* 18 *Las Brisas, Nueva Andalucía by ② : 11 km, ✆ 95 281 08 75 Fax 95 281 55 18.*
Glorieta de la Fontanilla ✆ 95 277 14 42 info@turismomarbella.com Fax 95 277 94 57 and Pl. de los Naranjos ✆ 95 282 35 50 info@turismomarbella.com Fax 95 277 36 21.
Madrid 602 ① – Málaga 59 ①

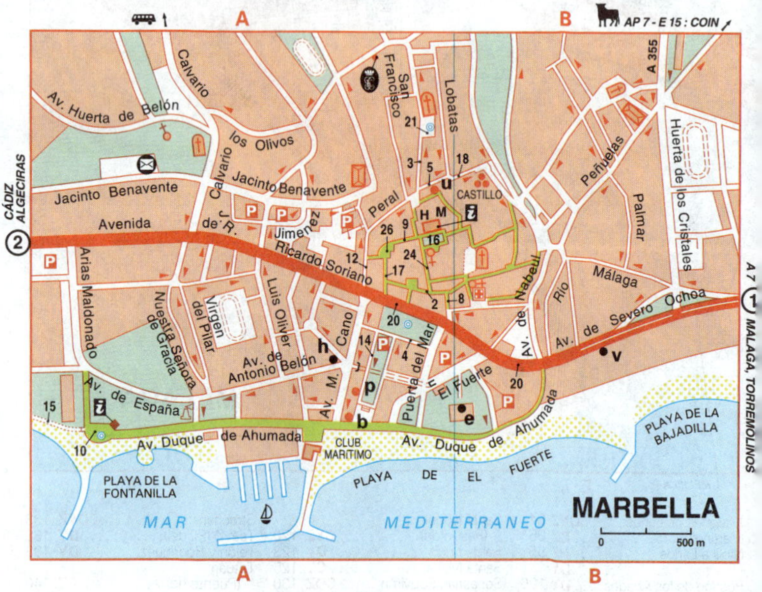

Alameda	A 2	Fontanilla (Glorieta de la)	A 10	Portada	AB 18
Ancha	A 3	Huerta Chica	A 12	Ramón y Cajal (Av.)	AB 20
Carlos Mackintosch	A 4	Mar (Av. del)	A 14	Santo Cristo (Pl. de)	A 21
Chorrón	A 5	Marítimo (Pas.)	A 15	Valdés	A 24
Enrique del Castillo	AB 8	Naranjos (Pl. de los)	A 16	Victoria (Pl. de la)	A 26
Estación	A 9	Pedraza	A 17		

Gran Meliá Don Pepe, José Meliá ☎ 95 277 03 00, *gran.melia.don.pepe@solmelia.com*, *Fax 95 277 99 54*, < sea and mountains, – AE MC VISA JCB. by ②
Grill La Farola **: Meals** a la carte 58/65 – 22 – **184 rm** 335/377, 17 suites.
• An oasis of peace and beauty beside the sea, surrounded by a carefully tended sub-tropical garden. Excellent, comfortable and well-appointed rooms. The Grill La Farola offers interesting dishes in an elegant ambience.

El Fuerte, av. El Fuerte ☎ 95 286 15 00, *elfuerte@fuertehoteles.com*, *Fax 95 282 44 11*, <, heated, – 25/400. AE MC VISA. B e
Meals - dinner only except July and August - a la carte 34/43 - ***Beach Club*** *(lunch only, closed January)* **Meals** a la carte 27/39 – **261 rm** 130/189, 2 suites.
• Pleasant rooms with harmonious decor and classically designed public areas perfect for relaxation. A good location beside the beach with areas of garden and palm trees. The Beach Club restaurant has a balcony overlooking the sea.

Fuerte Miramar, pl. José Luque Manzano ☎ 95 276 84 00, *miramarspa@fuertehoteles.com*, *Fax 95 276 84 14*, <, Therapeutic facilities, heated, – 25/320. AE MC VISA. B v
Meals - buffet dinner only except July and August - 34 – **217 rm** 131/189, 9 suites.
• Near to the city centre but away from its hustle and bustle. Modern and very comfortable, with a small swimming-pool beside the beach and well-equipped bedrooms. Dining room with buffet service.

Lima without rest, av. Antonio Belón 2 ☎ 95 277 05 00, *LIMAHOTEL@terra.es*, *Fax 95 286 30 91* – AE MC VISA. A h
5 – **64 rm** 80/99.
• A centrally located hotel with a good level of comfort for its category. The small social area is compensated for by the refurbished rooms with rustic décor.

Ruperto de Nola, av. de Antonio Belón 3 ☎ 95 276 55 50, *Fax 95 276 66 13* – . AE MC VISA JCB. A a
closed 15 January-15 February – **Meals** a la carte 49/57.
• Named after the author of the first treaty on Spanish cooking, written in 1520. Traditional dining rooms where the focus is on dishes with creative flair.

Santiago, av. Duque de Ahumada 5 ☎ 95 277 00 78, *reservas@restaurantesantiago.com*, *Fax 95 282 45 03*, – . AE MC VISA JCB. A b
closed November – **Meals** - Seafood - a la carte 36/49.
• This is considered to be one of the best restaurants in the city. Good management and attentive staff. Fish and seafood a speciality. An impressive wine-list.

El Balcón de la Virgen, Remedios 2 ☎ 95 277 60 92, *Fax 95 277 60 92*, – AE MC VISA. A u
Meals - dinner only - a la carte approx. 31.
• A restaurant in a 16C building named after the Virgin Mary, an altar to whom is on its façade. Simple and rustic. The secret of this restaurant is its reasonable prices.

La Taberna de Santiago, av. del Mar 20 ☎ 95 277 00 78, *Fax 95 282 45 03*, – . AE MC VISA JCB. A p
closed November – **Tapa** 1,20 – **Ración** approx. 5.
• A tapas bar with a tile covered façade, a small bar where tapas are displayed and several marble topped tables.

by the motorway to Málaga ① :

Don Carlos, exit Elviria : 10 km, ✉ 29600, ☎ 95 276 88 00, *info@hoteldoncarlos.com*, *Fax 95 283 34 29*, <, heated, – 25/1200. AE MC VISA.
closed 7 December-10 January - ***Los Naranjos*** *(dinner only)* **Meals** a la carte 40/55 – 19,20 – **229 rm** 239/279, 12 suites.
• An impressive building with all the luxury and comfort expected of a hotel in its category. The relaxing tropical area and swimming pools extending to the beach are a major plus. A delightful traditional dining room with views of the garden and beach.

Los Monteros, 5,5 km, ✉ 29600, ☎ 95 277 17 00, *hotel@losmonteros.com*, *Fax 95 282 58 46*, <, – 25/400. AE MC VISA.
Meals a la carte approx. 68 - ***El Corzo*** *(dinner only)* **Meals** a la carte 57/79 – 20 – **28 rm** 230/306, 149 suites.
• A tourist complex with a beautiful subtropical garden and elegant social and leisure areas. Good rooms with a high level of comfort. The El Corzo restaurant has a traditional and refined atmosphere.

Río Real Golf H., urb. Río Real - exit Torre Real : 3,5 km and detour 1,5 km, 29600, 95 276 57 32, *comercial@rioreal.com, Fax 95 277 21 40*, 25/55.
Meals a la carte 30/43 – **30 rm** 209/258, 2 suites.
• A modern hotel beside a golf course with comfortable rooms and décor by the well known interior designer Pascua Ortega. A pleasant restaurant in minimalist style.

Artola without rest, 12,5 km, 29600, 95 283 13 90, *hotelartola@inves.es, Fax 95 283 04 50*,
8 – **31 rm** 70/105, 2 suites.
• This hotel in a former inn is situated on a golf course and retains its regional characteristics. Good comfort and facilities. Various sports facilities available.

La Hacienda, exit Las Chapas : 11,5 km and detour 1,5 km, 29600, 95 283 12 67, *info@restaurantelahacienda.com, Fax 95 283 33 28*,
closed Monday and Tuesday (except July) – **Meals** - dinner only in July and August - a la carte approx. 50.
• A rustic villa which retains all the charm and tradition of another era along with very good and attentive service. Terrace-patio with an arcade.

El Lago, Av. Las Cumbres - urb. Elviria Hills - exit Elviria : 10 km and detour 2 km, 29600, 95 283 23 71, *ellago@restauranteellago.com, Fax 95 283 90 82*,
closed 8 to 24 December and Monday except August – **Meals** - dinner only - a la carte 39/46.
• In an attractive location on a golf course beside an artificial lake. Attractive dining rooms and interesting cuisine.

Las Banderas, urb. El Lido-Las Chapas : 9,5 km and detour 0,5 km, 29600, 95 283 18 19,
closed Monday – **Meals** a la carte 30/45.
• The awkward location of this restaurant is compensated for by its pleasant setting in an attractive house with a terrace and lawn. Good menu.

by the motorway to Cádiz ② :

Marbella Club, Boulevard Príncipe Alfonso von Hohenlohe : 3 km, 29600, 95 282 22 11, *hotel@marbellaclub.com, Fax 95 282 98 84*, Therapeutic facilities, heated, 25/120.
Meals a la carte 60/82 – 28 – **84 rm** 370/425, 53 suites.
• A classic and very elegant hotel with Andalusian charm, great comfort and attractive beachside areas. The sophisticated dining room has a pleasant terrace.

Puente Romano, 3,5 km, 29600, 95 282 09 00, *reservas@puenteromano.com, Fax 95 277 57 66*, heated, 25/650. rest
Roberto *(dinner only)* **Meals** a la carte 45/60 – 25 – **175 rm** 324/370, 99 suites.
• An elegant Andalusian-style complex in a magnificent subtropical garden which lends it a certain intimacy. Bungalow-type rooms that are spacious and very comfortable. The Roberto restaurant with wood décor offers Italian dishes.

G.H. Guadalpín, Boulevard Príncipe Alfonso von Hohenlohe : 2 km, 29600, 95 289 94 00, *info@granhotelguadalpin.com, Fax 95 289 94 01*, Therapeutic facilities, heated – 25/200.
Meals see rest. ***Mesana*** below - 73 – 20 – **30 rm** 240/300, 97 suites.
• The hotel's pleasant entrance hall leads to an attractive lobby bar to the rear. All the guest rooms are embellished with high-quality, classic furnishings, as well as a terrace. The restaurant offers a varied and cosmopolitan à la carte menu.

Coral Beach, 5 km, 29600, 95 282 45 00, *reservas.coral@oh-es.com, Fax 95 282 62 57*, 25/200.
15 March-October - ***Florencia*** *(dinner only)* **Meals** a la carte approx. 40 – 18 – **148 rm** 225/255, 22 suites.
• A complex designed in modern-Mediterranean style around a central swimming pool. Comfortable and spacious rooms each with its own balcony and beautiful sea views. The Florencia restaurant boasts an Arab-style watercourse with plants.

Mesana - *Hotel G.H. Guadalpín,* Boulevard Príncipe Alfonso von Hohenlohe : 2 km, 29600, 95 289 94 00, *info@granhotelguadalpin.com, Fax 95 289 94 01* –
closed Sunday dinner – **Meals** - dinner only - a la carte 57/70.
• This fine restaurant has an entrance separate from the hotel. The refined classical-cum-modern style here is matched by the inventive menu created by the renowned chef.

La Meridiana, camino de la Cruz : 3,5 km, 29600, 95 277 61 90, *Fax 95 282 60 24*,
closed 7 January-11 February – **Meals** - dinner only - a la carte 53/62.
• A pleasant hotel with elegant décor, attractive conservatory-type lounges and a pleasant terrace with palm trees and ponds.

XXX **Villa Tiberio,** 2,5 km, ✉ 29600, ✆ 95 277 17 99, *Fax 95 282 47 72,* – P. AE ⓓ ⓜⓒ VISA. ✻
closed Sunday except August – **Meals** - dinner only - a la carte approx. 48.
• An Italian-style restaurant with an attractive garden-terrace. A traditional dining room with comfortable furnishings and decorative details in refined taste.

XXX **El Portalón,** 3 km, ✉ 29600, ✆ 95 282 78 80, *restaurante@elportalonmarbella.com, Fax 95 277 71 04* – ▤ P. AE ⓓ ⓜⓒ VISA. ✻
closed Sunday except August – **Meals** a la carte approx. 55.
• Restaurant with wood décor in an attractive rustic cabin-style house. A good menu with traditional Castilian roast meats and creative touches.

at Puerto Banús *West : 8 km :*

XXX **Cipriano,** av. Playas del Duque - edificio Sevilla, ✉ 29660 Nueva Andalucía, ✆ 95 281 10 77, *rtecipriano@infonegocio.com, Fax 95 281 10 77,* – ▤ P. AE ⓓ ⓜⓒ VISA. ✻
Meals a la carte 44/59.
• Magnificent traditional-style restaurant with décor incorporating high quality wood and elegant details. A good bar and a spacious dining room on two levels.

SEVILLE (SEVILLA) *41000* P 578 T 11 y 12 – *pop. 702 520 alt. 12.*

See : *La Giralda*** (※**) BX – Cathedral*** (Capilla Mayor altarpiece***, Capilla Real**) BX – Real Alcázar*** BXY (Admiral Apartment : Virgin of the Mareantes altarpiece* ; Pedro el Cruel Palace*** : Ambassadors room vault*** ; Carlos V Palace : tapestries**, gardens* : grutesco gallery*) – Santa Cruz Quarter*** BCX (Venerables Hospital*) – Fine Arts Museum*** (room V***, room X**) AV – Pilate's House** (Azulejos**, staircase** : dome*) CX – Maria Luisa Park** (España Square*, Archaeological Museum* : Carambolo tresor*, roman collection*) South : by Paseo de las Delicias BY.*
Other curiosities : *Charity Hospital* (church**)* BY *- Santa Paula Convent* CV (front* church) – Salvador Church* BX (baroque altarpieces**, Lebrija Countess Palace* BV) – San José Chappel* BX – Town Hall (Ayuntamiento) : east front* BX – Santa María la Blanca Church* CX - Isla Mágica* North : by Torneo AV - San Luis de los Franceses Church* (inside**) North : by Bustos Tavera CV.*
18 Pineda, South-East : 3 km ✆ 95 461 14 00.
✈ Sevilla-San Pablo, North-East : 14 km ✆ 95 444 90 00 – Iberia : Av. de la Buhaira 8, (edificio Cecofar) ✉ 41018, ✆ 95 498 82 08.
Santa Justa ✆ 902 240 202.
Av. de la Constitución 21-B ✉ 41004 ✆ 95 422 14 04 otsevilla@andalucia.org Fax 95 422 97 53, Paseo de las Delicias 9 ✉ 41013 ✆ 95 423 44 65 Fax 95 422 95 66, Santa Justa station ✉ 41018 ✆ 95 453 76 26 and airport ✆ 95 444 91 28 – R.A.C.E. Av. Eduardo Dato 22, ✉ 41018 ✆ 95 463 13 50, Fax 95 465 96 04.
Madrid 531 – A Coruña 917 – Lisboa 410 – Málaga 211 – València 659.

Plans on following pages

Alfonso XIII, San Fernando 2, ✉ 41004, ✆ 95 491 70 00, *Fax 95 491 70 99,* – ▤, ⇸ rm, ▤ TV – 25/500. AE ⓓ ⓜⓒ VISA JCB. ✻ BY c
San Fernando **: Meals** a la carte 42/53 - ***Kaede*** *(Japanese rest)* **Meals** a la carte 28/39 – ☕ 20 – **127 rm** 347/455, 19 suites.
• A majestic Andalusian-style building with an exquisite interior combining arches, mosaics and arabesques, and bedrooms showing Moorish, Castilian and Baroque influence. The San Fernando restaurant provides a lavish setting for a refined dining experience.

Meliá Colón, Canalejas 1, ✉ 41001, ✆ 95 450 55 99, *melia.colon@solmelia.com, Fax 95 422 09 38* – ▤, ⇸ rm, ▤ TV ♿ – 25/200. AE ⓓ ⓜⓒ VISA JCB. ✻ AX s
Meals see rest. ***El Burladero*** below – ☕ 18 – **204 rm** 269/345, 14 suites.
• All the advantages of a central location. Very professional management and service and excellent bedrooms.

Sevilla Center, av. de la Buhaira, ✉ 41018, ✆ 95 454 95 00, *sevilla@hotelescenter.es, Fax 95 453 37 71,* – ▤, ⇸ rm, ▤ TV ♿ – 25/440. AE ⓓ ⓜⓒ VISA. ✻ South-East : by Av. de Carlos V CY
Meals 30 – ☕ 12 – **207 rm** 185/220, 23 suites.
• The Sevilla Center offers two styles of rooms : traditional executive and contemporary design, all of which are outward facing with spectacular views. Spacious lounge area with piano-bar, and an elegant restaurant enhanced by a pleasant summer terrace.

Meliá Lebreros, Luis Morales 2, ✉ 41018, ✆ 95 457 94 00, *melia.lebreros@solmelia.com, Fax 95 458 23 09,* – ▤, ⇸ rm, ▤ TV ♿ – 25/480. AE ⓓ ⓜⓒ VISA JCB. ✻ East : by La Florida CX
Meals see rest. ***La Dehesa*** below – ☕ 17 – **431 rm** 180, 6 suites.
• Located in a business district, this hotel has excellent facilities, including a floor for business travellers and several meeting rooms.

SEVILLA

Street	Grid	No.
Agua (Callejón del)	CY	4
Alemanes	BX	12
Alfaro (Pl. de)	CXY	15
Alianza (Pl.)	BX	19
Almirante Apodaca	CV	20
Almirante Lobo	BY	21
Álvarez Quintero	BX	22
Amador de los Ríos	CX	23
Antillano Campos	AX	26
Aposentadores	BV	29
Arco de la Judería	BY	30
Argote de Molina	BX	31
Banderas (Patio de)	BXY	35
Capitán Vigueras	CY	42
Cardenal Spínola	AV	47
Castelar	AX	55
Chapina (Puente)	AX	59
Doña Elvira (Pl. de)	BX	95
Doña Guiomar	AX	97
Escuelas Pías	CV	112
Farmacéutico E. Murillo Herrera	AY	115
Feria	BV	
Francisco Carrión Mejías	CV	126
Francos	BX	
Fray Ceferino González	BX	127
García de Vinuesa	BX	130
General Polavieja	BX	135
Gloria	BXY	137
Gonzalo Bilbao	CV	138
Jesús de la Vera Cruz	AV	147
José Laguillo	CV	302
José María Martínez Sánchez Arjona	AY	150
Julio César	AX	152
Júpiter	CV	153
Luis Montoto	CX	160
Marcelino Champagnat	AY	172
Martín Villa	BV	190
Mateos Gago	BX	192
Mesón del Moro	BX	197
Murillo	AV	202
Museo (Pl.)	AV	205
Navarros	CVX	207
O'Donnell	BV	210
Pascual de Gayangos	AV	220
Pastor Landero	AX	222
Pedro del Toro	AV	227
Pimienta o Susona	BCY	228
Ponce de León (Pl.)	CV	234
Puente y Pellón	BV	242
Puerta de Jerez	BY	243
República Argentina (Av.)	AY	255
Reyes Católicos	AX	260
Rodrigo Caro (Callejón de)	BX	261
Romero Morube	BX	264
San Gregorio	BY	272
San Juan de la Palma	BV	277
San Pedro (Pl.)	BV	286
San Sebastián (Pl.)	CY	287
Santa Isabel (Pl. de)	CV	296
Santa María La Blanca	CX	297
Santa Marta (Pl. de)	BX	298
Santa Teresa	CX	299
Santander	BY	300
Sierpes	BVX	
Temprado	BY	304
Tetuán	BX	
Tres Cruces (Pl. de las)	CX	306
Triunfo (Pl.)	BX	307
Velázquez	BV	310
Venerables (Pl.)	BCX	312
Virgen de los Reyes (Pl. de la)	BX	324
Viriato	BV	329

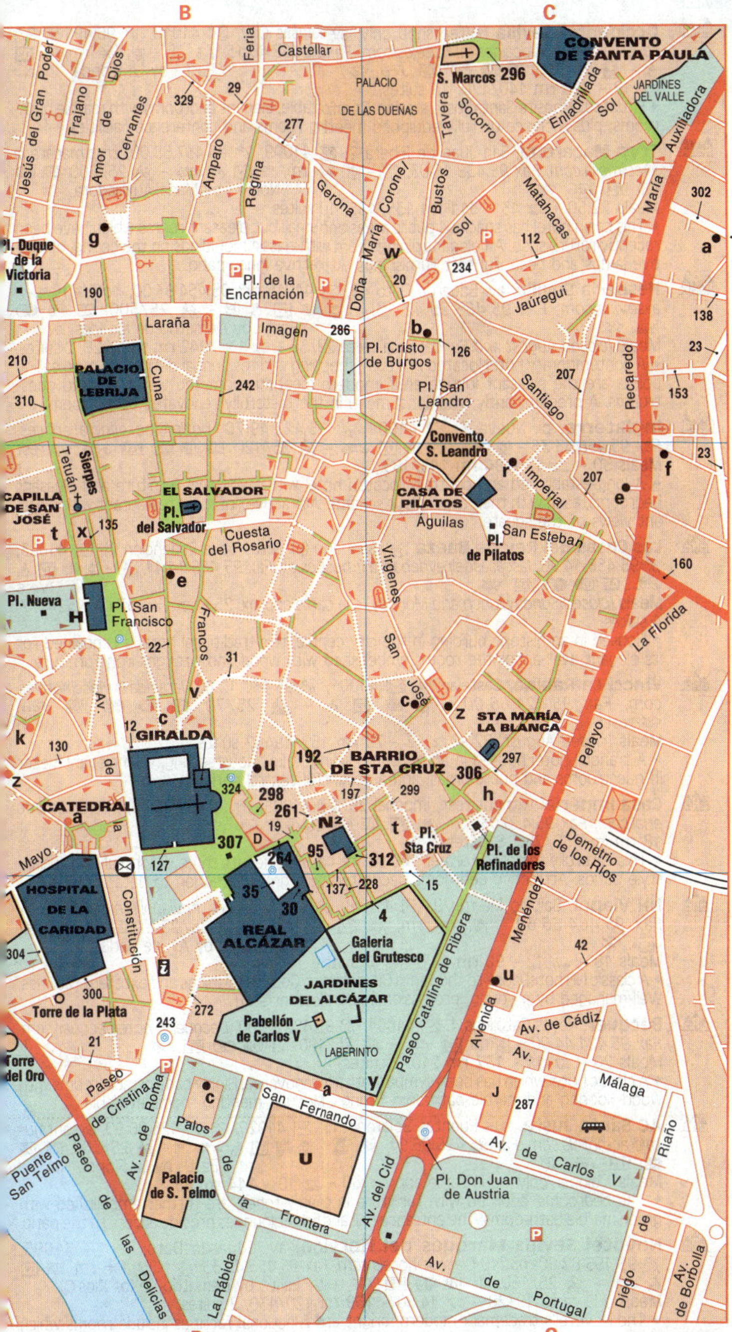
B
C
V
X
Y
CONVENTO DE SANTA PAULA
JARDINES DEL VALLE
PALACIO DE LAS DUEÑAS
S. Marcos 296
Castellar
Feria
Dios
Trajano
Jesús del Gran Poder
Amor de Cervantes
329
29
277
Amparo
Regina
Gerona
Doña María Coronel
Tavera
Bustos
Socorro
Enladrillada
Sol
Auxiliadora
Matahacas
María
302
a
112
234
Jáuregui
138
23
153
Recaredo
207
Santiago
Pl. Duque de la Victoria
g
190
Pl. de la Encarnación
w
20
b
126
Laraña
Imagen
286
Pl. Cristo de Burgos
Pl. San Leandro
210
PALACIO DE LEBRIJA
Cuna
242
310
Convento S. Leandro
r
Imperial
207
e
f
23
Sierpes
Tetuán
CAPILLA DE SAN JOSÉ
EL SALVADOR
Pl. del Salvador
CASA DE PILATOS
Águilas
Pl. de Pilatos
San Esteban
t
x
135
Cuesta del Rosario
Vírgenes
160
La Florida
Pl. Nueva
H
Pl. San Francisco
e
Francos
22
31
San José
v
c
z
STA MARÍA LA BLANCA
Pelayo
Av.
12
GIRALDA
k
130
z
de
192
BARRIO DE STA CRUZ
306
297
u
324
298
197
299
h
CATEDRAL
a
261
19
N²
t
Pl. Sta Cruz
Pl. de los Refinadores
Demetrio de los Ríos
307
D
264
95
312
Mayo
127
HOSPITAL DE LA CARIDAD
Constitución
35
30
137
228
15
4
Menéndez
REAL ALCÁZAR
Galeria del Grutesco
42
304
JARDINES DEL ALCÁZAR
Paseo Catalina de Ribera
300
Torre de la Plata
272
u
Pabellón de Carlos V
Avenida
Av. de Cádiz
Av.
243
21
Torre del Oro
LABERINTO
Málaga
Paseo de Cristina
Roma
c
a
y
J
287
Palos
San Fernando
Riaño
Puente San Telmo
Paseo de las Delicias
Av. de
Palacio de S. Telmo
de la Frontera
U
Av. del Cid
Pl. Don Juan de Austria
Av. de Carlos V
La Rábida
Av. de Portugal
Diego de
Av. de Borbolla

Occidental Sevilla coffee shop only, av. Kansas City, 41018, 95 491 97 97, *reservas-sevilla@occidental-hoteles.com, Fax 95 458 46 15*, – , rm, – 25/450. East : by La Florida CX
12 – **228 rm** 140/170, 13 suites.
• Situated opposite Santa Justa station. Comfortable, elegant bedrooms with marble bathrooms, plus a choice of fully-equipped meeting rooms and conference facilities.

Tryp Macarena, San Juan de Ribera 2, 41009, 95 437 58 00, *tryp.macarena@solmelia.com, Fax 95 438 18 03*, – , rm, – 25/600. North : by María Auxiliadora CV
Meals 22,50 – 13 – **311 rm** 135/155, 10 suites.
• This chain hotel has spacious public areas and small but pleasant rooms which have been recently refurbished. An elegant dining room with classic mouldings on the ceiling, attractive lamps and beautiful soft furnishings. Attractive inner patio.

Hesperia Sevilla, av. Eduardo Dato 49, 41018, 95 454 83 00, *hotel@hesperia-sevilla.com, Fax 95 453 23 42*, – – 25/500. East : by Demetrio de los Ríos CXY
Meals *(closed August and Sunday)* a la carte 29/36 – 13 – **242 rm** 180/228, 2 suites.
• A contemporary hotel located in a busy shopping and residential district. Its main selling points are the pleasant lounge area, modern meeting room and well-appointed guestrooms. A predominantly traditional menu in the tastefully renovated dining room.

Inglaterra, pl. Nueva 7, 41001, 95 422 49 70, *hotin@hotelinglaterra.es, Fax 95 456 13 36* – , rm, – 25/120. rest
Meals 30 – 12 – **94 rm** 148/185. AX r
• A long-established and centrally located hotel with traditional furniture and pleasant bedrooms, each with their own colour scheme. Attractive, intimate restaurant with pleasant views of the square.

Las Casas del Rey de Baeza, Santiago (pl. Jesús de la Redención 2), 41003, 95 456 14 96, *lascasasdelreydebaeza@hospes.es, Fax 95 456 14 41*, – . CV s
Meals *(closed Sunday lunch and Monday)* a la carte approx. 25 – 12 – **37 rm** 152/177, 4 suites.
• Housed in an historic building in the city centre, this traditional hotel is renowned for its elegant, well-appointed rooms embellished with wood and wrought-iron furniture.

Vincci La Rábida, Castelar 24, 41001, 95 450 12 80, *larabida@vinccihoteles.com, Fax 95 421 66 00* – – 25/70. rest AX b
Meals *(closed August)* 22 – 12 – **79 rm** 162/194, 2 suites.
• A tranquil hotel housed in an historic building. A luxurious setting, with elegant decor in guestrooms and public areas, and a delightful central patio.

Casa Imperial without rest, Imperial 29, 41003, 95 450 03 00, *info@casaimperial.com, Fax 95 450 03 30* – . CX r
18 rm 230/250, 8 suites.
• This carefully restored former 16C palace has retained its three delightful Andalusian-style patios. Attractive bedrooms decorated with great attention to detail.

NH Viapol, Balbino Marrón 9, 41018, 95 464 52 54, *nhviapol@nh-hotels.com, Fax 95 464 66 68* – , rm, – 25/250. East : by Av. de Carlos V CY
Meals 18 – 12 – **90 rm** 121/143, 6 suites.
• A classic NH hotel close to the Santa Cruz district. Good furnishings and excellent facilities. Well-managed by a young, professional and pleasant staff.

Bécquer, Reyes Católicos 4, 41001, 95 422 89 00, *becquer@hotelbecquer.com, Fax 95 421 44 00* – – 25/180. AX v
Meals 20 – 11 – **137 rm** 210, 2 suites.
• A classic hotel which has been sympathetically renovated. Highly comfortable rooms with wood flooring and marble bathroom fittings. Modular meeting rooms available.

AC Santa Justa, Luis Fuentes Bejarano 15, 41020, 95 426 06 90, *acsantajusta@ac-hotels.com, Fax 95 426 06 91*, , – – 25/500. East : by La Florida CX
Meals - dinner only - a la carte approx. 30 – 10 – **144 rm** 89.
• The bedrooms, adorned with furniture in cherry tones, are further embellished with green marble bathrooms. The entrance hall and bright lounges provide access to the patio.

Novotel Sevilla Marqués del Nervión, av. Eduardo Dato 71, 41005, 95 455 82 00, *h3210@accor-hotels.com, Fax 95 453 42 33*, – , rm, – 25/160. rest East : by Demetrio de los Ríos CXY
Meals a la carte 19/28 – 14,50 – **169 rm** 120/130, 2 suites.
• The Novotel's trademark modern, bright and functional facilities include rooms which all feature a double bed and sofa-bed. Panoramic swimming pool on the top floor.

Las Casas de los Mercaderes without rest, Álvarez Quintero 9, ✉ 41004, ☎ 95 422 58 58, *mercaderes@intergrouphoteles.com, Fax 95 422 98 84* – |‡| ▤ TV. AE ⓓ ⓜ VISA. ✻ BX e
☕ 13 – **47 rm** 88/128.
• In the heart of the commercial centre of the city with a pleasant covered patio and bedrooms which are adequately equipped. Those on the 1st floor are particularly large.

Doña María without rest, Don Remondo 19, ✉ 41004, ☎ 95 422 49 90, *reservas@hdmaria.com, Fax 95 421 95 46*, ←, ⛱ – |‡| ▤ TV. AE ⓓ ⓜ VISA. ✻ BX u
☕ 12 – **64 rm** 100/190.
• A traditional hotel with a magnificent terrace facing the Giralda. Grand bedrooms with décor in varied styles each named after a different famous woman from Seville.

G.H. Lar, pl. Carmen Benítez 3, ✉ 41003, ☎ 95 441 03 61, *larhotel@vianwe.com, Fax 95 441 04 52* – |‡| ▤ TV – 🎤 25/300. AE ⓓ ⓜ VISA JCB. ✻ CX f
Meals 19 – ☕ 7,90 – **129 rm** 86,50/120, 8 suites.
• Although the decor is a little dated the level of comfort in this well-managed hotel is consistently high. Traditional functionality throughout, plus a spacious restaurant.

Zenit Sevilla ⚲, Pagés del Corro 90, ✉ 41010, ☎ 95 434 74 34, *sevilla@zenithoteles.com, Fax 95 434 27 07* – |‡| ▤ TV – 🎤 25/160. AE ⓓ ⓜ VISA. ✻ AY a
Meals a la carte 24/38 – ☕ 12 – **112 rm** 155/165, 16 suites.
• A modern hotel with rustic furniture. The public areas are adequate and the bedrooms functional and there are three well-equipped function rooms. Good management. The charming traditional restaurant offers interesting cuisine.

Catalonia Emperador Trajano, José Laguillo 8, ✉ 41003, ☎ 95 441 11 11, *trajano@hoteles-catalonia.es, Fax 95 453 57 02* – |‡| ▤ TV – 🎤 25/150. AE ⓓ ⓜ VISA. ✻ CV a
Meals a la carte approx. 30 – ☕ 10 – **76 rm** 99/109.
• Named after the famous Roman emperor Trajan, who was born in Seville, this functional hotel has comfortable, well-equipped bedrooms ensuring a relaxing stay.

Catalonia Giralda, Sierra Nevada 3, ✉ 41003, ☎ 95 441 66 61, *giralda@hoteles-catalonia.es, Fax 95 441 93 52* – |‡| ▤ TV – 🎤 25/250. AE ⓓ ⓜ VISA. ✻ CX e
Meals a la carte approx. 30 – ☕ 10 – **110 rm** 99/109.
• A centrally located modern hotel with well-appointed bedrooms. An ideal location for conferences and business meetings.

Monte Triana coffee shop only, Clara de Jesús Montero 24, ✉ 41010, ☎ 95 408 50 00, *hmtreservas@hotelesmonte.com, Fax 95 433 89 07* – |‡|, ⊁ rm, ▤ TV – 🎤 25/40. AE ⓓ ⓜ VISA. ✻ West : by Puente Isabel II AX
☕ 8,80 – **117 rm** 107/117.
• A good choice in the ever-popular Triana district. Pleasant, soberly decorated lounge areas, plus renovated functional bedrooms with wood flooring and traditional furnishings.

Monte Carmelo coffee shop only, Virgen de la Victoria 7, ✉ 41011, ☎ 95 427 90 00, *montecarmelo@hotelesmonte.com, Fax 95 427 10 04* – |‡|, ⊁ rm, ▤ TV – 🎤 25/35. AE ⓓ ⓜ VISA. ✻ South : by Pl. de Cuba AY
☕ 8,50 – **68 rm** 107/117.
• A restful hotel in the quiet Los Remedios district. The gradual renovation has included the introduction of the very latest technology in the comfortable bedrooms.

Fernando III, San José 21, ✉ 41004, ☎ 95 421 77 08, *reservas@fernando3.com, Fax 95 422 02 46*, ⛱ – |‡| ▤ TV ♿ – 🎤 25/250. AE ⓓ ⓜ VISA JCB. ✻ CX z
Meals 18 – ☕ 13 – **154 rm** 198/220, 1 suite.
• A top location in the Santa Cruz district. Traditional in style, with renovated bedrooms with modern bathrooms and restored furniture. and fine views from the roof terrace.

Alcázar without rest, Menéndez Pelayo 10, ✉ 41004, ☎ 95 441 20 11, *reservas@hotelalcazar.com, Fax 95 442 16 59* – |‡| ⊁ ▤ TV. ⓓ ⓜ VISA. ✻ CY u
93 rm ☕ 134/166.
• Recent renovation has brought improvements throughout, including more modern comforts. The best rooms are those on the top floor with views of the Alcázar from the terrace.

Puerta de Triana without rest, Reyes Católicos 5, ✉ 41001, ☎ 95 421 54 04, *reservashotel@hotelpuertadetriana.com, Fax 95 421 54 01* – |‡| ▤ TV. AE ⓓ ⓜ VISA JCB. ✻ AX t
65 rm ☕ 65/85.
• An impressive lounge and reception area but with less striking bedrooms. A very pleasant, elegant and traditional hotel.

Casona de San Andrés without rest, Daoíz 7, ✉ 41003, ☎ 95 491 52 53, *info@casonadesanandres.com, Fax 95 491 57 65* – |‡| ▤ TV ♿. ⓓ ⓜ VISA. ✻ BV g
25 rm ☕ 50/90.
• Occupying a 19C building with two internal patios surrounded by the majority of the hotel's rooms. Antique wrought-iron work and glassware add charm to the overall decor.

Adriano without rest, Adriano 12, ✉ 41001, ☎ 95 429 38 00, *info@adrianohotel.com, Fax 95 422 89 46* – 25. AX d
3,60 – **34 rm** 104/130.
◆ Reception and coffee bar in the spacious foyer, leading to guestrooms with good facilities and sober yet high-quality decoration. Roof-top sun terrace.

Amadeus Sevilla without rest, Farnesio 6, ✉ 41004, ☎ 95 450 14 43, *reservas@hotelamadeussevilla.com, Fax 95 450 00 19* – . CX c
7 – **14 rm** 63/90.
◆ The main philosophy of this attractive house, now converted into a theme hotel, is based around classical music. Soundproofed, personalised rooms, some with their own piano.

Montecarlo, Gravina 51, ✉ 41001, ☎ 95 421 75 03, *hotel@hotelmontecarlosevilla.com, Fax 95 421 68 25* – . AX e
Meals 16,95 – 7 – **49 rm** 60/90.
◆ Two buildings with two central patios and one reception area. Differing level of comfort with the bedrooms in the annex more modern than those in the older section.

La Casa del Maestro without rest, Almudena 5, ✉ 41003, ☎ 95 450 00 07, *reservas@lacasadelmaestro.com, Fax 95 450 00 06* – . CV b
closed August – **11 rm** 111/138.
◆ The famous flamenco guitarist Niño Ricardo was born and grew up in this small house, which is nowadays a hotel with individually furnished bedrooms with plush decor.

Reyes Católicos without rest, no , Gravina 57, ✉ 41001, ☎ 95 421 12 00, *hotel@hotelreyescatolicos.info, Fax 95 421 63 12* – . AX z
29 rm 60/90.
◆ A charming little hotel with a friendly atmosphere and good management and service. Well-appointed rooms with fully equipped bathrooms.

Egaña Oriza, San Fernando 41, ✉ 41004, ☎ 95 422 72 54, *reservas@restauranteoriza.es, Fax 95 450 27 27* – . CY y
closed August, Saturday lunch and Sunday – **Meals** a la carte 45/55.
◆ A distinguished restaurant beside the old city walls with very good food. An attractive conservatory-style dining room with a wooden floor.

Taberna del Alabardero with rm, Zaragoza 20, ✉ 41001, ☎ 95 450 27 21, *rest.alabardero@esh.es, Fax 95 456 36 66* – . AX n
closed August – **Meals** a la carte approx. 47 – **7 rm** 118/145.
◆ Do try this beautiful restaurant in a former palace, now restored. Fine cuisine, exquisitely tasteful décor and very good and attentive service.

El Burladero - *Hotel Melia Colón,* Canalejas 1, ✉ 41001, ☎ 95 450 55 99, *melia.colon@solmelia.com, Fax 95 422 09 38* – . AX a
closed 15 June-August – **Meals** a la carte 36/49.
◆ A unique restaurant with a decor inspired by the world of bullfighting. A small bar at the entrance and a single dining room, serving traditional cuisine with modern flair.

La Dehesa - *Hotel Meliá Lebreros,* Luis Morales 2, ✉ 41018, ☎ 95 457 62 04, *melia.lebreros@solmelia.com, Fax 95 458 23 09* – .
Meals - Braised meat specialities - a la carte 33/42. East : by La Florida CX
◆ Traditional Andalusian décor and a pleasant atmosphere. Wooden ceilings and white walls and a small tapas bar. Grilled meat a speciality.

Marea Grande, Diego Angulo Íñiguez 16 - edificio Alcázar, ✉ 41018, ☎ 95 453 80 00, *Fax 95 453 80 00* – . East : by Demetrio de los Ríos CXY
closed 15 to 31 August and Sunday – **Meals** - Seafood - a la carte 33/40.
◆ A tapas bar and comfortable dining room with interesting cuisine. Elegant furniture and very good service.

Al-Mutamid, Alfonso XI-1, ✉ 41005, ☎ 95 492 55 04, *modesto@andalunet.com, Fax 95 492 25 02* – . East : by Demetrio de los Ríos CXY
closed 15 days in August – **Meals** a la carte 31/38.
◆ On three levels with a tapas bar at the entrance, a traditional dining room on the first floor and several private rooms on the second. Basement cellar for group bookings.

La Albahaca, pl. Santa Cruz 12, ✉ 41004, ☎ 95 422 07 14, *la-albahaca@terra.es, Fax 95 456 12 04,* – . CX t
closed Sunday – **Meals** a la carte 33/42.
◆ The flavour of good regional ingredients. A fine old house situated in the old part of Seville with a bar and three well-furnished dining areas.

San Fernando 27, San Fernando 27, ✉ 41004, ☎ 95 422 09 66, *Fax 95 422 09 66,* – . BY a
closed August and Sunday – **Meals** a la carte approx. 35.
◆ Located opposite the university, this restaurant has a modern interior where the designer decor provides a perfect backdrop in which to enjoy creative regional cuisine.

XX **El Asador de Aranda,** Luis Montoto 150, ✉ 41005, ✆ 95 457 81 41, *Fax 95 457 81 41,* 🏞 – ▤ 🅿. AE ⓓ MC VISA. ✂ East : by La Florida CX
closed August and Sunday dinner – **Meals** - Roast lamb - a la carte 22/27.
◆ A restaurant in an old and well-restored Castilian-style palace, with décor that has touches of local tradition. Well-prepared traditional food.

XX **Az-Zait,** pl. San Lorenzo 1, ✉ 41002, ✆ 95 490 64 75, *Fax 95 490 65 15* – ▤. AE ⓓ MC VISA. ✂ North : by Torneo AV
closed August and Sunday dinner – **Meals** a la carte 25/30.
◆ The Az-Zait's owner-chef has succeeded in endowing this restaurant, spread over several rooms, with characteristic Andalucian style. Impeccable and attentive service.

XX **La Isla,** Arfe 25, ✉ 41001, ✆ 95 421 26 31, *laisla@restaurantelaisla.com, Fax 95 456 22 19* – ▤. AE ⓓ MC VISA. ✂ BX a
closed August – **Meals** a la carte 39/45.
◆ The entrance is through a bar with a refrigerated cabinet displaying seafood. Well-cooked fish, professionalism and a pleasant atmosphere.

XX **Casa Robles,** Álvarez Quintero 58, ✉ 41004, ✆ 95 456 32 72, *info@roblesrestaurantes.com, Fax 95 456 44 79,* 🏞 – ▤. AE ⓓ MC VISA JCB. ✂ BX c
Meals a la carte 25/35.
◆ Decorated in typical style and popular with tourists. Bar and terrace followed by a traditional dining room. The remaining rooms are on the upper floor and in the annex.

X **Horacio,** Antonia Díaz 9, ✉ 41001, ✆ 95 422 53 85, *horacio@andalunet.com, Fax 95 421 79 27* – ▤. AE ⓓ MC VISA. ✂ AX c
closed 15 to 31 August and Sunday in July-15 August – **Meals** a la carte 20/31.
◆ A simple, friendly and well-managed establishment with a public bar and two dining rooms on different levels with wicker furniture.

𝕐/ **El Rinconcillo,** Gerona 40, ✉ 41003, ✆ 95 422 31 83, *elrinconcillo1670@elrinconcillo1670.e.telefonica.net* – ▤. AE ⓓ MC VISA. ✂ CV w
closed 17 July-9 August – **Tapa** 1,65 – **Ración** approx. 4.
◆ Professionally run and in the oldest tavern in the city. A pleasant ambience, regional décor and home cooking.

𝕐/ **Mesón Cinco Jotas,** Albareda 15, ✉ 41001, ✆ 954 21 05 21, *m5jalbareda@osborne.es, Fax 954 56 41 44* – ▤. AE ⓓ MC VISA. ✂ BX t
Tapa 2 – **Ración** - Ham specialities - approx. 9.
◆ Centrally located and with a wide variety of tapas and tables to sit at. There is also small dining room.

𝕐/ **José Luis,** pl. de Cuba 3, ✉ 41011, ✆ 95 427 20 17, *joseluis@nexo.es, Fax 95 427 64 80,* 🏞 – ▤. AE ⓓ MC VISA. ✂ AY e
Tapa 1,40 – **Ración** approx. 10.
◆ An establishment in classic José Luis chain style. A variety of tapas and servings of other dishes or if you prefer choose from the menu offered in the dining room.

𝕐/ **Robles Placentines,** Placentines 2, ✉ 41004, ✆ 95 421 31 62, *info@roblesrestaurantes.com, Fax 95 456 44 79,* 🏞 – ▤. AE ⓓ MC VISA JCB. ✂ BX v
Tapa 2,10 – **Ración** approx. 12,95.
◆ A typical tavern serving an enticing selection of tapas. A profusion of wood and attractive decor inspired by the world of bullfighting.

𝕐/ **Modesto,** Cano y Cueto 5, ✉ 41004, ✆ 95 441 68 11, *modesto@andalunet.com, Fax 95 492 25 02,* 🏞 – ▤. AE ⓓ MC VISA JCB. ✂ CX h
Tapa 2 – **Ración** - Seafood - approx. 10,50.
◆ A recommended address

𝕐/ **España,** San Fernando 41, ✉ 41004, ✆ 95 422 72 11, *reservas@restauranteoriza.es, Fax 95 450 27 27,* 🏞 – ▤. AE ⓓ MC VISA. ✂ CY y
closed August and Sunday dinner – **Tapa** 2,10 – **Ración** approx. 9.
◆ The tapas bar for the restaurant Egaña Oriza. A large bar filled with a wide range of tapas. A pleasant atmosphere and an attractive terrace beside the old city walls.

𝕐/ **Bodeguita Romero,** Harinas 10, ✉ 41001, ✆ 95 421 41 78, *sabenye@hotmail.com* – ▤. AE MC VISA. ✂ BX k
closed August and Monday except Bank Holidays – **Tapa** 1,80 – **Ración** approx. 21.
◆ Well-known and well-established with a large variety of delicious tapas. Very good management in a very pleasant bar.

𝕐/ **O'Tapas Albahaca,** Pagés del Corro 119, ✉ 41010, ✆ 95 427 41 63, *Fax 95 427 41 63,* 🏞 – ▤. AE ⓓ MC VISA. ✂ AY t
closed 14 to 31 August and Sunday – **Tapa** 2 – **Ración** approx. 7,50.
◆ This popular meeting-place in the charming Triana district has a bar at the entrance and a large dining room with a friendly atmosphere serving tasty tapas. Unusual wine list.

Casa La Viuda, Albareda 2, ✉ 41001, ☎ 95 421 54 20, *hostelse@eresmas.com, Fax 95 422 38 00,* – ▤. VISA. ✻ BX x
closed Sunday in July and August – **Tapa** 1,65 – **Ración** approx. 7,50.
◆ A centrally located bar with all the atmosphere of a good tapas bar. A wide choice of well made tapas. A lively and youthful ambience.

Mesón Cinco Jotas, Castelar 1, ✉ 41001, ☎ 954 21 07 63, *Fax 95 421 27 86,* – ▤. AE ⓓ ⓜ VISA. ✻ BX z
Tapa 2 – **Ración** - Ham specialities - approx. 9.
◆ A spacious, attractive bar and adjoining restaurant in which to taste an excellent selection of typical Spanish tapas. Pleasant terrace.

at Castilleja de la Cuesta *West : 7 km :*

Hacienda San Ygnacio, Real 190, ✉ 41950, ☎ 954 16 92 90, *reservas@haciendasanygnacio.com, Fax 95 416 14 37,* , , – ▤ TV P – 25/300. AE ⓓ ⓜ VISA JCB. ✻ rest
Almazara *(closed Sunday and Monday lunch)* **Meals** a la carte 28/32 – ☕ 8 – **16 rm** 105/150, 1 suite.
◆ A typical hacienda-style building with a whitewashed façade. Comfortable rooms with wooden floors, well-equipped bathrooms and rustic decoration. The Almazara restaurant is housed in what was once the property's olive mill.

at Sanlúcar la Mayor *West : 18 km :*

Hacienda Benazuza , Virgen de las Nieves, ✉ 41800, ☎ 95 570 33 44, *hbenazuza@elbullihotel.com, Fax 95 570 34 10,* ←, , , ✻ – |‡| ▤ TV P – 25/400. AE ⓓ ⓜ VISA. ✻
closed 6 to 31 January - ***La Alquería*** *(dinner only, closed Monday)* **Meals** a la carte 67/83 – ☕ 32 – **26 rm** 400, 18 suites.
Spec. Gazpacho de bogavante perfumado a la albahaca (abril-septiembre). Pañuelos de pan y trufa de verano. Cinta ibérica con pinzas de buey de mar y cilantro fresco.
◆ A magnificent hotel housed in a 10C farmhouse. The luxurious rooms harmoniously combine antique furniture, exquisite decor and a high degree of contemporary comfort. Elegant, rustic-style restaurant with a wooden ceiling and impeccable service.

VALÈNCIA *46000* P 577 N 28 y 29 – *pop. 746 612 alt. 13.*

See : *The Old Town★ : Cathedral★ (El Miguelete★, Capilla del Santo Cáliz★)* EX – *Palacio de la Generalidad★ (golden room : ceiling★)* EXD – *Lonja★ (silkhall★★)* DY – *City of Arts and Sciences★★ (The Oceanographic★★, Museum of Sciences Príncipe Felipe★★, The Hemispheric★, L'Umbrade★) by Av. Jacinto Benavente* FZ.
Other curiosities : *Ceramic Museum★★ (Palacio del Marqués de Dos Aguas★★)* EY **M1** - *Fine Arts San Pío V Museum★ (Valencian primitifs★★)* FX – *Patriarch College or of the Corpus Christi★ (Passion triptych★)* EY **N** – *Serranos Towers★* EX – *I.V.A.M.★* DX.
9 Club de Golf Manises, East : 12 km, ☎ 96 153 40 69 – 18 Club Escorpión, North-West : 19 km by road to Liria ☎ 96 160 12 11 – 18 El Saler-Parador de El Saler, South-East : 19 km ☎ 96 161 03 84.
✈ Valencia-Manises, East : 11 km ☎ 96 159 85 00 – Iberia : Paz 14, ✉ 46003, ☎ 902 400 500 EFY.
⛴. To the Balearic Islands : Cía Trasmediterránea, Muelle de Poniente ✉ 46024 ☎ 96 316 48 59 Fax 96 316 48 55 by Av. Regne de València FZ.
ℹ Pl. del Ayuntamiento 1, ✉ 46002 ☎ 96 351 04 17 aytovalencia@touristinfo.net Fax 96 352 58 12, Paz 48 ✉ 46003 ☎ 96 398 64 22 valencia@touristinfo.net Fax 96 398 64 21 Xàtiva 24 (North Station) ✉ 46007 ☎ 96 352 85 73 renfe@touristinfo.net Fax 96 352 85 73 and Poeta Querol ✉ 46002 ☎ 96 351 49 07 dipuvalencia@touristinfo.net Fax 96 351 99 27 – R.A.C.E. (R.A.C. de València) Gran Vía Marqués del Turia 79, ✉ 46005, ☎ 96 334 39 89 Fax 96 334 39 89.
Madrid 352 – Albacete 183 – Alacant/Alicante (by coast) 174 – Barcelona 355 – Bilbao 600 – Castelló de la Plana/Castellón de la Plana 75 – Málaga 608 – Sevilla 659 – Zaragoza 318.

Meliá Valencia Palace, paseo de la Alameda 32, ✉ 46023, ☎ 96 337 50 37, *melia.valencia.palace@solmelia.com, Fax 96 337 55 32,* ←, Fs, – |‡| ▤ TV ♿ – 25/800. AE ⓓ ⓜ VISA JCB. ✻ East : by Puente de Aragón FZ
Meals 35 – ☕ 14 – **243 rm** 188/227, 5 suites.
◆ A hotel in the 18C palace of The Dukes of Cardona. Extremely comfortable and with traditional details of décor. A spectacular entrance hall. The restaurant is in classic modern-style with minimalist details of décor.

Astoria Palace, pl. Rodrigo Botet 5, ✉ 46002, ☎ 96 398 10 00, *info@hotel-astoria-palace.com, Fax 96 398 10 10,* Fs – |‡| ▤ TV ♿ – 25/500. AE ⓓ ⓜ VISA JCB. ✻ EY p
Meals see rest. ***Vinatea*** below – ☕ 12 – **196 rm** 110/146, 8 suites.
◆ An unforgettable stay in a very modern and luxurious hotel. An elegant lounge, excellent bedrooms and a fitness centre.

Hesperia Parque Central, pl. Manuel Sanchís Guarner, ✉ 46006, ☎ 96 303 91 00, *hotel@hesperia-parquecentral.com, Fax 96 303 91 30*, – – 25/250. AE VISA JCB. South : by Alicante EZ
Meals 18 – 9 – **178 rm** 160/200, 14 suites.
◆ A classic modern city hotel. Large, comfortable and well-equipped rooms. Several lounges.

Vincci Lys, Martínez Cubells 5, ✉ 46002, ☎ 96 350 95 50, *lys@vinccihoteles.com, Fax 96 350 95 52* – – 25/70. AE VISA. EZ s
Meals *(closed August)* 26 – 11,80 – **95 rm** 245, 5 suites.
◆ Elegant and traditional with a spacious foyer and reception area which also serves as lounge and bar area. Magnificent bedrooms. A very good restaurant with a young chef in charge.

Puerta Valencia, Cardenal Benlloch 28, ✉ 46021, ☎ 96 393 63 95, *puertavalencia@hoteles-silken.com, Fax 96 393 63 96* – – 25/400. AE VISA. East : by Puente de Aragón FZ
Meals 15 – 10 – **150 rm** 120/140, 7 suites.
◆ Contemporary in style with tasteful designer decor, stunning guestrooms and a spacious foyer. Facilities include an excellent conference hall. Avant-garde restaurant with high ceilings and a traditional à la carte menu.

Meliá Plaza, pl. del Ayuntamiento 4, ✉ 46002, ☎ 96 352 06 12, *melia.plaza@solmelia.com, Fax 96 352 04 26*, – – 25/80. AE VISA JCB. EY d
Meals 23 – 9,50 – **100 rm** 165, 1 suite.
◆ A hotel which has been slowly refurbished to a high level of comfort with elegant décor and well-chosen furnishings. Excellently equipped rooms.

Abba Acteón, Vicente Beltrán Grimal 2, ✉ 46023, ☎ 96 331 07 07, *acteon@abbahoteles.com, Fax 96 330 22 30*, – – 25/400. AE VISA JCB. East : by Av. Regne de València FZ
Meals 21 – 11,75 – **182 rm** 140/150, 5 suites.
◆ A hotel with trademark quality and design features, including thoughtfully decorated, well-equipped bedrooms with marble bathrooms, and a bright, contemporary and elegant restaurant.

NH Center, Ricardo Micó 1, ✉ 46009, ☎ 96 347 50 00, *nhcenter@nh-hotels.com, Fax 96 347 62 52*, , heated, – – 25/400. AE VISA JCB. North : by Gran Vía Fernando el Católico DY
Meals 20 – 11,50 – **190 rm** 113, 3 suites.
◆ A classic chain hotel which is above average thanks to little touches like bathrobes being provided in the bathrooms. A covered swimming-pool which can be made open air in summer. A spacious and airy dining room with a pleasant atmosphere.

Holiday Inn Valencia, paseo de la Alameda 38, ✉ 46023, ☎ 96 303 21 00, *reservas@holidayinnvalencia.com, Fax 96 303 21 26*, – – 25/55. AE VISA East : by Puente de Aragón FZ
Meals 12 – 12 – **200 rm** 225/255.
◆ A hotel of modern design with comfortable, well-equipped bedrooms geared towards business travellers. Terrace-bar with fine views and a restaurant which adjoins the coffee-shop in the foyer.

AC València coffee shop dinner only, av. de Francia 67, ✉ 46023, ☎ 96 331 70 00, *acvalencia@ac-hotels.com, Fax 96 331 70 01*, – – 25/100. AE VISA JCB. East : by Puente de Aragón FZ
10 – **181 rm** 140, 2 suites.
◆ Modern, functional and clearly aimed at the business market, this hotel has pleasant lounge and meeting areas, a spacious cafeteria and rooms with the usual creature comforts.

Jardín Botánico without rest, Dr. Peset Cervera 6, ✉ 46008, ☎ 96 315 40 12, *inf-reservas@hoteljardinbotanico.com, Fax 96 315 34 08* – . AE VISA. West : by Gran Vía Fernando el Católico DY
9 – **16 rm** 240.
◆ A very well-refurbished 100-year-old building with modern interior décor. Well-appointed rooms with hydro-massage baths.

Dimar coffee shop only, Gran Vía Marqués del Turia 80, ✉ 46005, ☎ 96 395 10 30, *hdimar@terra.es, Fax 96 395 19 26* – – 25/50. AE VISA. FZ q
103 rm 110/134, 1 suite.
◆ A traditional hotel right in the heart of the city. Very comfortable and well-appointed rooms with pleasant décor and well-equipped bathrooms.

Reina Victoria, Barcas 4, ✉ 46002, ☎ 96 352 04 87, *hreinavictoriavalencia@husa.es, Fax 96 352 27 21* – – 25/75. AE VISA. EY s
Meals 22,25 – 10,50 – **94 rm** 130/185, 3 suites.
◆ A beautiful façade and a splendid location just a stone's throw from the principal museums. Elegant and with an attractive lounge area and modern rooms. The dining room is on the 1st floor beside the English-style bar.

D
E
0
200 m
Castro
Blanquerías
Jardín
Pte Serranos
Cronista
Rivelles
Pont de Fusta
Pas. de la Pechina
Na Jordana
Museo del Siglo XIX
I.V.A.M.
TORRES DE SERRANOS
Pl. de los Fueros
Conde Trenor
Pte Trinidad
Pintor
Roteros
Ripalda
Baja
Corona
Alta
Serranos
Navellos
Salvador
Trinitarios
Turia
Guillem
Jardín Botánico
PAL. DE LA GENERALITAT
Caballeros
Quart
San Nicolás
Torres de Quart
Murillo
EL MIGUELETE
CATEDRAL
Pl. del
LONJA
Carda
Pl. de la Reina
Santos Juanes
Santa Catalina
San Juan de los Hospitalarios
Mar
Carniceros
Mercado Central
Mercado
Plaza Redonda
Paz
Lepanto
Recaredo
Av.
Linterna
Moratín
Poeta
Comedias
Maldonado
Barón
Mártir
Salvá
Querol
Gran Vía Fernando el Católico
Guillem
Hospital
Vicente
Barcas
Pintor
Don Juan
Ángel Guinerá
Gran
de
Quevedo
Plaza del Ayuntamiento
Pascual
San
Cárcer
POL
Castro
Roger de Lauria
Av. Marqués de Sotelo
Paseo Ruzafa
Genís
Colón
Cuenca
Vía
Jesús
Xàtiva
Xàtiva
Félix
Jerusalén
Ramón
Vicente
Estación del Norte
Cirilo
Pizcueta
Plaza España
Convento
San F. de Borja
Pintor Benedito
Bailén
Castellón
Gal Sanmartín
Ruzafa
Gran
Germanías
San
Jesús
Cajal
Alicante
Gran Vía
Ruzafa
PALAU DE CONGRESSOS
X
Y
Z

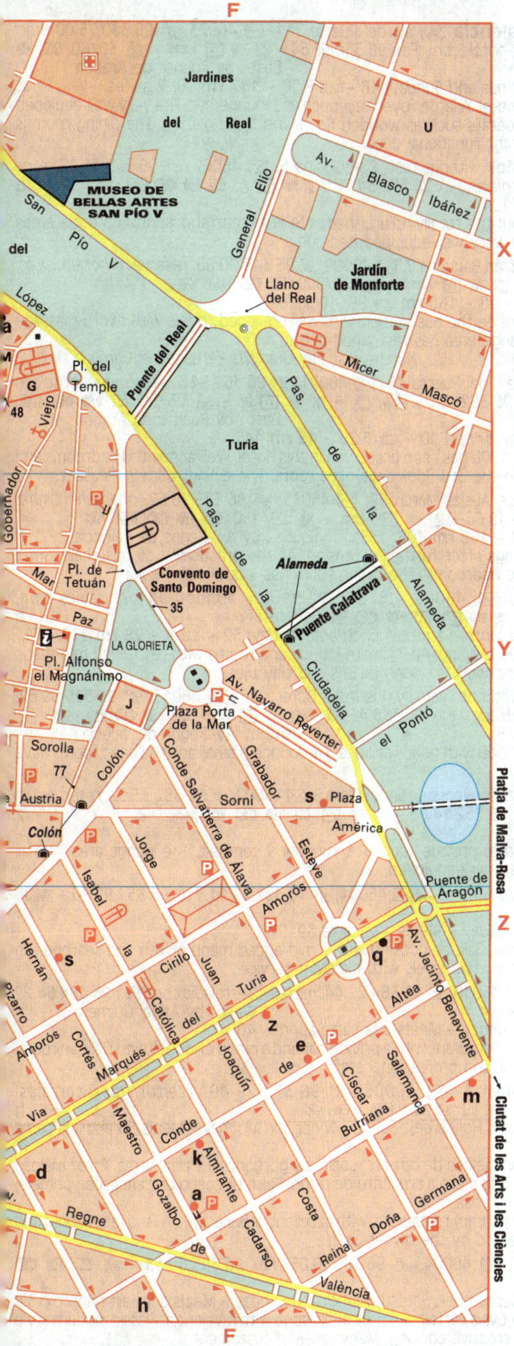

VALÈNCIA

Almirante	EX	3
Almudín	EX	4
Ángel Guimerá	DY	7
Ayuntamiento (Pl. del)	EY	
Bolsería	DX	8
Carmen (Pl. del)	DX	13
Doctor Collado (Pl.)	EY	18
Doctor Sanchís Bergón	DX	19
Embajador Vich	EY	23
Esparto (Pl. del)	DX	24
Garrigues	DY	30
General Palanca	FY	35
Guillem Sorolla	DY	41
Maestres	FX	48
Maestro Palau	DY	49
María Cristina (Av.)	EY	54
Marqués de Dos Aguas	EY	55
Marqués de Sotelo (Av.)	EZ	
Micalet	EX	59
Moro Zeit	DX	61
Músico Peydró	DY	64
Nápoles y Sicilia (Pl.)	EX	65
Padre Huérfanos	EX	66
Palau	EX	67
Pascual y Genís	EYZ	
Paz	EFY	
Periodista Azzati	DY	70
Pie de la Cruz	DY	74
Poeta Quintana	FY	77
Salvador Giner	DX	81
San Vicente Ferrer (Pl.)	EY	83
San Vicente Mártir	DY	
Santa Ana (Muro)	EX	87
Santa Teresa	DY	88
Santo Tomás	DX	89
Transits	EY	93
Universidad	EY	94
Virgen (Pl. de la)	EX	95
Virgen de la Paz (Pl.)	EY	98

NH Ciudad de Valencia, av. del Puerto 214, ✉ 46023, ☎ 96 330 75 00, *nhciudaddevalencia@nh-hotels.com, Fax 96 330 98 64* – |‡| ▤ TV – 30/80. AE ⓓ MC VISA JCB. East : by Puente de Aragón FZ
Meals *(closed Christmas and Sunday)* 16 – ☕ 9,50 – **147 rm** 90, 2 suites.
• A classic NH chain hotel. A large foyer-reception and lounge-bar. The very well-equipped rooms have design details such as wooden floors and triple glazing. The dining room is large and with pleasant functional décor.

Catalonia Excelsior without rest, Barcelonina 5, ✉ 46002, ☎ 96 351 46 12, *excelsior@hoteles-catalonia.es, Fax 96 352 34 78* – |‡| ▤ TV ♿. AE ⓓ MC VISA. EY a
☕ 10 – **81 rm** 99/124.
• The best thing about this totally refurbished hotel is its central location. Few social areas and rather small but very well-equipped bedrooms.

Turia, Profesor Beltrán Baguena 2, ✉ 46009, ☎ 96 347 00 00, *reservas@hotelturia.es, Fax 96 347 32 44* – |‡| ▤ TV – 25/300. AE MC VISA.
Meals - dinner only - 18 – **160 rm** ☕ 88, 10 suites.
• A modern hotel beside the bus station with well-equipped rooms with hydro-massage baths. The foyer-lounge area has restrained décor.
North-West : by Gran Vía Fernando el Católico DY

Cónsul del Mar, av. del Puerto 39, ✉ 46021, ☎ 96 362 54 32, *reservas@hotelconsuldelmar.com, Fax 96 362 16 25,* – |‡| ▤ TV P – 25/50. AE ⓓ MC VISA. rest East : by Puente de Aragón FZ
Meals *(closed Sunday dinner)* 10 – ☕ 6,25 – **45 rm** 145.
• The grand style of 1900 has been preserved in this hotel. Well-appointed bedrooms and bathrooms. Those on the 3rd floor have attic roofs. The dining room is pleasant.

NH Abashiri, av. de Ausias March 59, ✉ 46013, ☎ 96 373 28 52, *nhabashiri@nh-hotels.es, Fax 96 373 49 66* – |‡| ▤ TV – 30/250. AE ⓓ MC VISA.
Meals 22 – ☕ 9,50 – **168 rm** 103/135. South : by Av. Regne de València FZ
• Now in two buildings after further extension. All the practicality of this chain. Small lounges and intimate bedrooms. The dining room has lots of natural light.

Ad-Hoc, Boix 4, ✉ 46003, ☎ 96 391 91 40, *adhoc@adhochoteles.com, Fax 96 391 36 67* – |‡| ▤ TV. AE ⓓ MC VISA. rest FX a
Meals *(closed Friday lunch, Saturday lunch and Sunday)* 32 – ☕ 9 – **28 rm** 139/171.
• In an attractive 19C building. An intimate lounge and rooms with restrained neo-rustic décor of exposed brickwork, wooden beams and clay tiles.

NH Las Artes II without rest, av. Instituto Obrero 26, ✉ 46013, ☎ 96 335 60 62, *exlasartes@nh-hotels.com, Fax 96 333 46 83* – |‡| ▤ TV. AE ⓓ MC VISA.
☕ 8,50 – **121 rm** 88. South : by Av. Regne de València FZ
• A functional-style hotel with good facilities. The lounge is small and the basic rooms have cheerful decor.

Sorolla without rest, Convento de Santa Clara 5, ✉ 46002, ☎ 96 352 33 92, *reservas@hotelsorolla.com, Fax 96 352 14 65* – |‡| ▤ TV. AE ⓓ MC VISA JCB. EZ z
58 rm ☕ 99/142.
• Totally refurbished to provide adequate, functional comfort. The lounge area is small but the bedrooms are well-equipped.

Rías Gallegas, Cirilo Amorós 4, ✉ 46004, ☎ 96 352 51 11, *Fax 96 351 99 10* – ▤ P. AE ⓓ MC VISA. EZ r
closed August and Sunday – **Meals** a la carte 39/57.
• Faultless ! Traditional Galician cooking with a mid-priced menu of fish and seafood. An elegant dining room on two levels with excellent service.

Eladio, Chiva 40, ✉ 46018, ☎ 96 384 22 44, *michel@resteladio.com, Fax 96 384 64 21* – ▤. AE ⓓ MC VISA. West : by Ángel Guimerá DY
closed August and Sunday – **Meals** a la carte approx. 40.
• Elegant, traditional restaurant with a private bar and a menu of dishes with Galician roots. Efficient management and professional staff.

Torrijos, Dr. Sumsi 4, ✉ 46005, ☎ 96 373 29 49, *rte.torrijos@terra.es, Fax 96 373 29 49* – ▤. AE ⓓ MC VISA JCB. FZ h
closed 7 to 17 January, Holy Week, Sunday dinner and Monday – **Meals** 55 and a la carte 37/52.
Spec. Langostino con meloso de ternera, sopita de gorgonzola y alcaparras. Arroz meloso de ventresca de congrio y oreja crujiente de cerdo. Falso bizcocho de canela con pomelo, helado de membrillo y rosas.
• An elegant, contemporary restaurant with excellent service and an innovative, bold and attractive menu created by the owner-chef.

Albacar, Sorní 35, ✉ 46004, ☎ 96 395 10 05, *Fax 96 395 60 55* – ▤. AE ⓓ MC VISA. FY s
closed 6 August-6 September, Saturday lunch and Sunday – **Meals** a la carte approx. 37.
• This restaurant enjoys a certain amount of prestige within Valencia. Classic modern style and innovative and creative cooking. Many satisfied customers.

XXX **La Sucursal,** Guillém de Castro 118, ✉ 46003, ✆ 96 374 66 65, *Fax 96 392 41 54* – ▤. AE VISA. ✱ DX a
closed 15 to 31 August, Saturday lunch and Sunday – **Meals** a la carte 40/51.
◆ Part of the same building as the IVAM, with a cafeteria on the ground floor and a minimalist dining room on the first offering a fusion of the innovative and the traditional.

XXX **Vinatea** - *Hotel Astoria Palace,* Vilaragut 4, ✉ 46002, ✆ 96 398 10 00, *Fax 96 398 10 10* – ▤. AE ⊕ MC VISA JCB. ✱ EY p
Meals a la carte approx. 35.
◆ An excellent restaurant with a separate entrance where there is high quality food. Elegant traditional décor with good furnishings.

XXX **Riff,** Conde de Altea 18, ✉ 46005, ✆ 96 333 53 53, *restaurante@restaurante-riff.com* – ▤. AE ⊕ MC VISA. ✱ FZ k
closed August, Sunday and Monday – **Meals** a la carte 42/63.
◆ This establishment follows the current trends in restaurant cooking and provides creative cuisine in a setting that is minimalist in design. Efficient staff.

XX **Kailuze,** Gregorio Mayáns 5, ✉ 46005, ✆ 96 335 45 39, *Fax 96 335 48 93* – ▤. AE MC VISA. ✱ FZ d
closed Holy Week, August, Saturday lunch and Sunday – **Meals** - Basque rest - a la carte 51/61.
◆ Pleasant design and excellent service in an establishment with an entrance hall and a charming lounge. Good, traditional Basque-Navarrese cuisine.

XX **El Gastrónomo,** av. Primado Reig 149, ✉ 46020, ✆ 96 369 70 36 – ▤ 🚗. AE MC VISA. ✱ North-East : by Puente del Real FX
closed 1 to 7 January, Holy Week, August, Sunday and Monday dinner – **Meals** a la carte 30/40.
◆ A restaurant that is old fashioned both in how it is run and in its wide gastronomic offerings. Pleasant and adequately-equipped dining room.

XX **El Ángel Azul,** Conde de Altea 33, ✉ 46005, ✆ 96 374 56 56, *restaurante@angelazul.com, Fax 96 374 56 56* – ▤. ✱ FZ e
closed 15 August-15 September, Sunday and Monday – **Meals** a la carte 35/45.
◆ The owner of this restaurant, formerly its chef, is continuing the good work with an interesting menu of creative dishes. Modern traditional decor.

XX **Joaquín Schmidt,** Visitación 7, ✉ 46009, ✆ 96 340 17 10, *info@joaquinschmidt.com, Fax 96 340 17 10,* 🏠 – ▤. MC VISA. ✱ North : by Cronista Rivelles EX
closed 15 days in Holy Week, 15 to 31 August, Sunday and Monday lunch – **Meals** a la carte approx. 50.
◆ A welcoming restaurant, in an old house with a patio, that enjoys great prestige in the city. Good décor in its dining rooms and attentive service.

XX **Civera,** Lérida 11, ✉ 46009, ✆ 96 347 59 17, *civera@ole.com, Fax 96 346 50 50* – ▤. AE ⊕ MC VISA. ✱ North : by Cronista Rivelles EX
closed Holy Week, 15 to 31 August, 1 to 7 September, Sunday dinner and Monday – **Meals** - Seafood - a la carte 28/57.
◆ A well-known fish and seafood restaurant with a lively bar from which follow several dining areas in traditional regional style. A large menu of quality fish and seafood.

XX **Civera Centro,** Mosén Femades 10, ✉ 46002, ✆ 96 352 97 64, *civeracentro@marisqueriascivera.com, Fax 96 346 50 50,* 🏠 – ▤. AE ⊕ MC VISA. ✱ EZ a
closed Holy Week, 15 to 31 June and 1 to 7 July – **Meals** - Seafood - a la carte 32/53.
◆ A popular and well-known restaurant. Friendly staff and attentive service and good food.

XX ✿ **Ca'Sento,** Méndez Núñez 17, ✉ 46024, ✆ 96 330 17 75 – ▤. AE VISA. ✱
closed Holy Week, August, Sunday and Monday dinner – **Meals** - booking essential - 60 and a la carte 37/51. East : by Puente de Aragón FZ
Spec. Cornetes de yuca y changurro. Rodaballo con su piel crujiente y jugo de rustido de carne. Cochinillo confitado en su piel crujiente, y salsa de naranja y clavo.
◆ A family-run restaurant. Good fish and seafood dishes. Creative cuisine influenced by contemporary restaurant cooking.

XX ✿ **Alejandro,** Amadeo de Saboya 15, ✉ 46010, ✆ 96 393 40 46, *Fax 96 393 40 46* – ▤. AE MC VISA. ✱ East : by Puente de Aragón FZ
closed Saturday lunch and Sunday – **Meals** a la carte 39/43.
Spec. Vieiras con sorbete de pomelo rosa. Solomillo de buey con verduritas y cremoso de patata al aceite de trufa blanca. Drácula.
◆ A restaurant with future promise run by its talented chef-proprietor. A pleasant traditional-style dining room with minimalist design details.

XX **Chust Godoy,** Boix 6, ✉ 46003, ✆ 96 391 38 15, *Fax 96 392 22 39* – ▤. AE ⊕ MC VISA. ✱ FX a
closed Holy Week, August, Saturday lunch and Sunday – **Meals** a la carte 35/46.
◆ Personal attention from the chef who runs this restaurant with his wife. A neo-rustic dining room with exposed brickwork and wooden beams and excellent service.

Montes, pl. Obispo Amigó 5, ✉ 46007, ☎ 96 385 50 25 – ▤. AE ⓓ ⓜⓒ VISA. ✂ DZ v
closed August, Sunday dinner and Monday – **Meals** a la carte 20/27.
◆ A restaurant with a main dining room with pleasant décor and better than average service. Enter through an entrance hall area and bar which lead into a long dining room.

Mey Mey, Historiador Diago 19, ✉ 46007, ☎ 96 384 07 47 – ▤. AE ⓓ ⓜⓒ VISA. ✂ DZ e
closed Holy Week and the last 3 weeks in August – **Meals** - Chinese rest - a la carte 19/25.
◆ Good and traditional Chinese restaurant décor. It has a circular fountain with gold fish, an extensive menu and a youthful ambience.

Eguzki, av. Baleares 1, ✉ 46023, ☎ 96 337 50 33, *Fax 96 337 50 33* – ▤. ⓓ ⓜⓒ VISA. ✂ East : by Puente de Aragón FZ
closed Holy Week, August and Sunday – **Meals** - Basque rest - a la carte 26/34.
◆ A Basque restaurant run with friendly enthusiasm and with a lovely stone façade. There is a bar and the pleasant dining room is on the 1st floor.

Palace Fesol, Hernán Cortés 7, ✉ 46004, ☎ 96 352 93 23, *palacefesol@palacefesol.com, Fax 96 353 00 68,* Regional decor – ▤. AE ⓓ ⓜⓒ VISA. ✂ FZ s
closed Holy Week, Saturday and Sunday in Summer and Monday – **Meals** a la carte 28/37.
◆ A fairly basic and long-established restaurant. A public bar near the entrance and a dining room with simple décor in regional style. An unpretentious menu.

Bazterretxe, Maestro Gozalbo 25, ✉ 46005, ☎ 96 395 18 94 – ▤. VISA. ✂ FZ a
closed August and Sunday dinner – **Meals** - Basque rest - a la carte 18/23.
◆ A pleasant restaurant offering a fairly simple menu of traditional Basque cuisine. A large bar and a dining room with rather small tables.

El Romeral, Gran Vía Marqués del Turia 62, ✉ 46005, ☎ 96 395 15 17 – ▤. AE ⓓ ⓜⓒ VISA. ✂ FZ z
closed 28 March-4 April, August, Sunday dinner and Monday – **Meals** a la carte approx. 30.
◆ A city institution ! Old fashioned décor in the two dining rooms and a mid-priced menu offering simple dishes made from good ingredients.

by road C 234 *North-West : 8,5 km :*

NH Jardines del Turia, Pintor Velázquez, ✉ 46100 Burjassot, ☎ 96 390 54 60, *nhjardinesdelturia@nh-hotels.com, Fax 96 364 63 61* – |‡| ▤ TV ⇔ – 🏛 25/100. AE ⓓ ⓜⓒ VISA JCB. ✂ North-West : by Gran Vía Fernando el Católico DY
Meals 17 – ☕ 9,50 – **97 suites** 90/130, 15 hab.
◆ Pleasant and functional in the style of the chain. The apartment-type rooms have a kitchen and a sitting room. Lifts from which there are views of the beautiful interior patio. A pleasant and well-lit dining room.

at Alboraia *North-East : 8 km :*

Olympia, Maestro Serrano 5, ✉ 46120 Alboraia, ☎ 902 30 01 32, *reservas@olympiagrupo.com, Fax 902 30 01 42,* Thermal spa, ⅃₆, ▭ – |‡| ▤ TV ⇔ – 🏛 25/600. AE ⓓ ⓜⓒ VISA. ✂
Meals 16,25 – ☕ 9 – **164 rm** 120/140, 3 suites.
◆ Wonderful facilities which include a gym and thermal baths. An attractive terrace beneath a coloured glass dome. A classic modern-style restaurant offering rice dishes of the region.

at Almàssera *North-East : 9 km :*

Lluna de València, Camí del Mar 56, ✉ 46132 Almàssera, ☎ 96 185 10 86, *Fax 96 185 10 06* – ▤ P. AE ⓓ ⓜⓒ VISA. ✂ by Puente del Real FX
closed Holy Week, Saturday lunch and Sunday – **Meals** a la carte approx. 28.
◆ A thousand-year-old olive tree presides over the entrance to this restaurant, a former farmhouse. Attractive dining rooms ; the main one has a pleasant rustic atmosphere.

at El Saler *South : 12 km :*

Parador de El Saler ♨, av. Pinares 151, ✉ 46012 València, ☎ 96 161 11 86, *saler@parador.es, Fax 96 162 70 16,* <, ⅃₆, ▭, 18 – |‡| ▤ TV P – 🏛 25/200. AE ⓓ ⓜⓒ VISA JCB. ✂
Meals 27 – ☕ 11 – **58 rm** 108/135.
◆ A hotel situated on a golf course with the sea in the background. The splendid facilities invite you to relax and the attractive bedrooms have all mod cons. The Pleasant dining room offers cuisine anchored in tradition.

at Manises *on the airport road - East : 10 km :*

Tryp Azafata, autopista del aeropuerto 15, ✉ 46940, ☎ 96 154 61 00, *tryp.azafata@solmelia.com, Fax 96 153 20 19,* – TV P – 25/300. AE VISA JCB. rest

Meals a la carte 24/35 – 11 – **124 rm** 112/134,25, 4 suites.

◆ A traditional-style hotel close to the airport. Good social areas and rooms of adequate comfort.

at Puçol *North : 23 km by motorway A 7 :*

Monte Picayo, urb. Monte Picayo, ✉ 46530, ☎ 96 142 01 00, *Fax 96 142 21 68,* – TV P – 25/500. AE VISA.

Meals a la carte approx. 37 – **79 rm** 192/240, 3 suites.

◆ On a mountainside with magnificent vistas over the Valencian fertile plain. Spacious rooms such as the elegant lounge. A traditional restaurant with faultless service.

Sweden

Sverige

STOCKHOLM – GOTHENBURG

PRACTICAL INFORMATION

LOCAL CURRENCY

Swedish Kronor: *100 SEK = 11,23 euro (€) (Dec. 2004)*

TOURIST INFORMATION

In Stockholm, the Tourist Centre is situated in Sweden House, entrance from Kungsträdgården at Hamngatan. Open Mon-Fri 9am-6pm. Sat. and Sun. 9am-3pm. Telephone weekdays (08) 789 24 00, weekends to Excursion Shop and Tourist Centre (08) 789 24 90. For Gothenburg, see information in the text of the town under **i**.

National Holiday in Sweden: *6 June.*

FOREIGN EXCHANGE

Banks are open between 10am and 3pm on weekdays only. Most large hotels and the Tourist Centre have exchange facilities. Arlanda airport has banking facilities between 7am to 10pm seven days a week.

SHOPPING

In the index of street names, those printed in red are where the principal shops are found.
The main shopping streets in the centre of Stockholm are: Hamngatan, Biblioteksgatan, Drottninggatan, Sturegallerian.
In the Old Town mainly Västerlånggatan.

THEATRE BOOKINGS

Your hotel porter will be able to make your arrangements or direct you to Theatre Booking Agents.

CAR HIRE

The international car hire companies have branches in Stockholm, Gothenburg, Arlanda and Landvetter airports. Your hotel porter should be able to give details and help you with your arrangements.

TIPPING

Hotels and restaurants normally include a service charge of 15 per cent. Additionally cloakroom attendants are normally tipped 10 SEK. Doormen, baggage porters etc. are generally given a gratuity.
Taxis include 10 % tip in the amount shown on the meter.

SPEED LIMITS - SEAT BELTS

The maximum permitted speed on motorways and dual carriageways is 110 km/h 68 mph, 90 km/h - 56 mph on other roads except where a lower speed limit is indicated and in built up areas 50 km/h - 31 mph.
The wearing of seat belts is compulsory for drivers and all passengers.
In Sweden, drivers must not drink alcoholic beverages at all.

BREAKDOWN SERVICE

A 24 hour breakdown service is operated ☎ 112.

STOCKHOLM

Sverige 711 M 15 – pop. 674 459 Greater Stockholm 1 491 726.

Hamburg 935 – Copenhagen 630 – Oslo 522.

Stockholm Visitors Board, Tourist Centre, Sverigehuset, Hamngatan 27 ☎ (08) 50828 508.

Svenska Golfförbundet (Swedish Golf Federation) ☎ (08) 622 15 00.

Stockholm-Arlanda NW : 40 km ☎ (08) 797 61 00 – SAS : Reservations (0770) 727 727 – Air-Terminal : opposite main railway station – Arlanda Express rail link : departs Central Station every 15 mins – journey time 20 mins.

Motorail for Southern Europe : Ticket Travel-Agency, Sturegatan ☎ (08) 400 51 00.

To Finland : contact Silja Line ☎ (08) 22 21 40 or Viking Line ☎ (08) 452 40 00 – Excursions by boat : contact Stockholm Visitors Board (see above).

See: Old Town★★★ (Gamla Stan) AZ – Vasa Museum★★★ (Vasamuseet) DY – Skansen Open-Air Museum★★★ DY.

Royal Palace★★ (Kungliga Slottet) AZ ; Royal Apartments★★ ; Royal Armoury★ ; Royal Treasury★★ – Stockholm Cathedral★★ (Storkyrkan) AZ – City Hall★★ (Stadhuset) : Blue Hall★★★, Golden Hall★★★ ; ※★★★ BY H – Prins Eugens Waldemarsudde★★ (house and gallery) DY – Thiel Gallery★★ (Thielska Galleriet) DZ.

House of the Nobility★ (Riddarhuset) AZ R – Riddarholmen Church★ (Riddarholmskyrkan) AZ K[1] – Österlånggatan★ AZ.

Kaknäs TV Tower (Kaknästornet) ※★★★ DY – Stigberget : Fjällgatan ※★ DZ – Skinnerviksberget : ※★ BZ.

Museums: National Art Gallery★★ (Nationalmuseum) DY M[5] – Nordic Museum★★ (Nordiska Museet) DY – Museum of National Antiquities★★ (Historiska Museet) DY – Museum of Medieval Stockholm★★ (Stockholms Medeltidsmuseet) CY M[1] – Museum of Far Eastern Antiquities★ (Östasiatiska Museet) DY M[6] – Hallwyl Collection★ (Hallwylska Museet) CY M[3] – Museum of Modern Art (Moderna Museet) (collections★★) DY M[4] – Strindberg Museum★ (Strindbergsmuseet) BX M[2] – Junibacken★ DY.

Outskirts : Drottningholm Palace★★★ (Drottningholm Slott) W : 12 km BY – Stockholm Archipelago★★★ – Millesgården★★ (house and gallery) E : 4 km BX – Skogskyrkogården (UNESCO World Heritage Site).

Excursions : Gripsholms Slott★★ – Skokloster★★ – Ulriksdal★ – Birka★ – Strängnas★ – Sigtuna★ – Uppsala★★.

STOCKHOLM

Biblioteksgatan	CY	2
Birger Jarlsgatan	CXY	3
Brunnsgränd	AZ	6
Bryggargatan	BY	7
Brända Tomten	AZ	8
Djurgårdsbron	DY	9
Drottninggatan	BX, CY	10
Evert Taubes Terrass	AZ	13
Gallerian	CY	14
Grev Turegatan	CY	18
Gustav Adolfs Torg	CY	16
Hamngatan	CY	
Herkulesgatan	CY	19
Hötorget	CY	20
Järntorget	AZ	21
Järntorgsgatan	AZ	23
Kindstugatan	AZ	24
Klarabergsgatan	CY	25
Klarabergsviadukten	BY	27
Klaratunnel	CY	28
Kornhamnstorg	AZ	29
Kungsgatan	BCY	
Kungsträdgårdsgatan	CY	32
Köpmangatan	AZ	35
Lilla Nygatan	AZ	36
Mosebacke Torg	CZ	39
Munkbrogatan	AZ	40
Myntgatan	AZ	41
Mäster Mikaels Gata	DZ	42
Norrbro	CY	43
Norrlandsgatan	CY	44
Nybroplan	CY	45
Olof Palmes Gata	BY	47
Österlånggatan	AZ	
Prästgatan	AZ	48
Riddarhusgränd	AZ	49
Riddarhustorget	AZ	50
Rädhusgränd	AZ	52
Sergelgatan	CY	53
Sergels Torg	CY	54
Sista Styverns Trappor	DZ	55
Slottskajen	AZ	56
Slussplan	AZ	57
Stallgatan	CY	59
Stigbergsgatan	DZ	60
Storkyrkobrinken	AZ	61
Strömbron	CY	62
Södermalmstorg	CZ	64
Södra Blasieholmshamnen	CY	66
Tegelbacken	CY	67
Tegnérlunden	BX	69
Triewaldsgränd	AZ	70
Tyska Brinken	AZ	73
Urvädersgränd	CZ	74
Västerlånggatan	AZ	
Östermalmstorg	DY	76
Östra Järnvägsgatan	BY	78

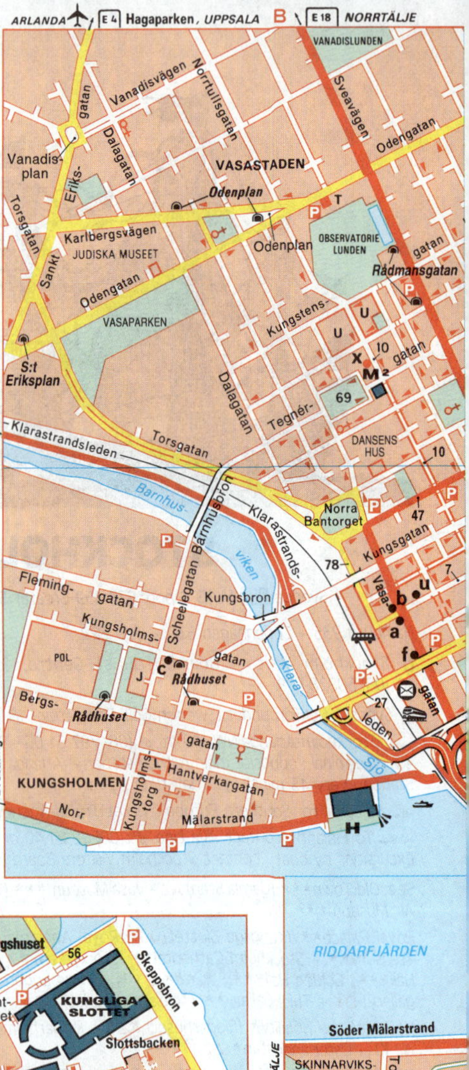

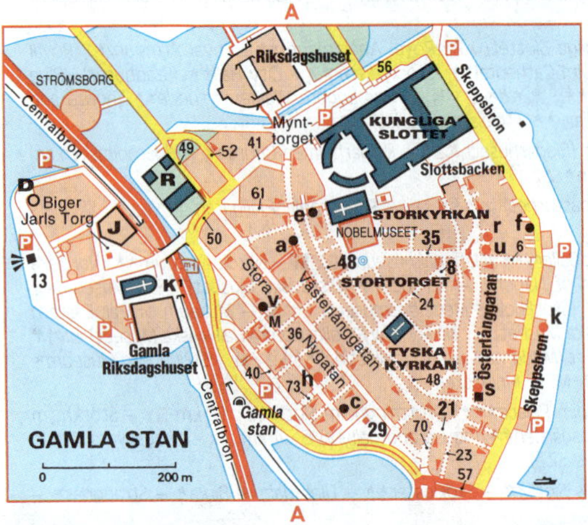

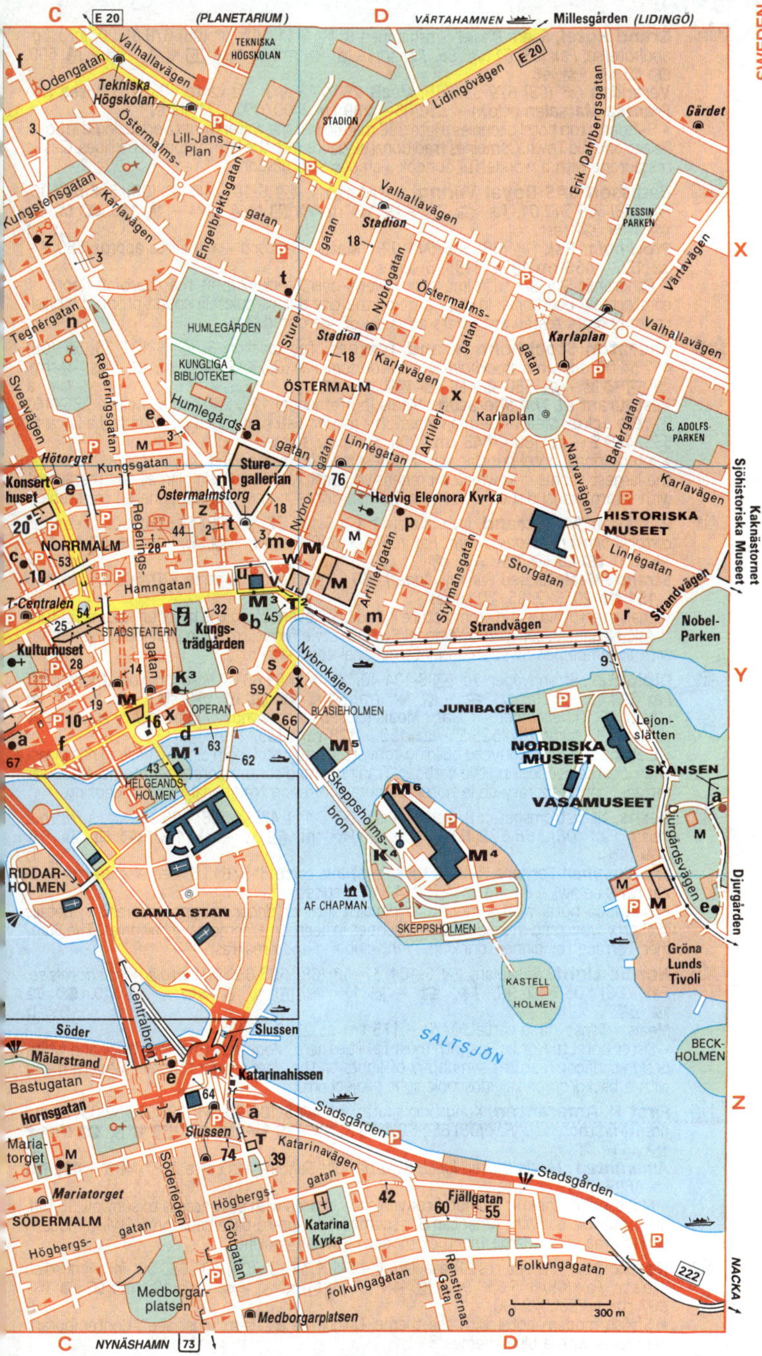
C
E 20
(PLANETARIUM)
D
VÄRTAHAMNEN
Millesgården (LIDINGÖ)
TEKNISKA HÖGSKOLAN
Valhallavägen
Odengatan
Tekniska Högskolan
Östermalms-
Lill-Jans Plan
STADION
Lidingövägen
E 20
Erik Dahlbergsgatan
Gärdet
Kungstensgatan
Karlavägen
Engelbrektsgatan
gatan
Valhallavägen
Stadion
TESSIN PARKEN
Värtavägen
X
Nybrogatan
Östermalms-
gatan
Tegnérgatan
HUMLEGÅRDEN
Sture
Stadion
Karlaplan
Valhallavägen
KUNGLIGA BIBLIOTEKET
ÖSTERMALM
Karlavägen
Artilleri-
gatan
Sveavägen
Regeringsgatan
Humlegårds-
gatan
Linnégatan
Karlaplan
Banérgatan
Narvavägen
G. ADOLFS-PARKEN
Hötorget
Kungsgatan
Sture-gallerian
Hedvig Eleonora Kyrka
Karlavägen
Konserthuset
Östermalmstorg
Nybro-
HISTORISKA MUSEET
NORRMALM
Regerings-
Artillerigatan
Styrmansgatan
Storgatan
Linnégatan
Hamngatan
Strandvägen
T-Centralen
STADSTEATERN
Kungs-trädgården
Strandvägen
Nobel-Parken
Kulturhuset
gatan
Nybrokajen
Y
OPERAN
BLASIEHOLMEN
JUNIBACKEN
Lejon-slätten
NORDISKA MUSEET
HELGEANDS-HOLMEN
Skeppsholms-
bron
SKANSEN
VASAMUSEET
Djurgårdsvägen
RIDDAR-HOLMEN
GAMLA STAN
AF CHAPMAN
SKEPPSHOLMEN
Gröna Lunds Tivoli
KASTELL HOLMEN
SALTSJÖN
BECK-HOLMEN
Söder
Slussen
Mälarstrand
Centralbron
Bastugatan
Katarinahissen
Z
Hornsgatan
Stadsgården
Slussen
Katarinavägen
Maria-torget
Mariatorget
gatan
Stadsgården
Högbergs-
Fjällgatan
SÖDERMALM
Katarina Kyrka
Högbergs-
gatan
Söderleden
Götgatan
Folkungagatan
Renstiernas Gata
Medborgar-platsen
Folkungagatan
0
300 m
222
NACKA
Medborgarplatsen
C
NYNÄSHAMN
73
D
Kaknästornet
Sjöhistoriska Museet
Djurgården

Grand Hôtel, Södra Blasieholmshamnen 8, S-111 47, (08) 679 35 00, *info@grandhotel.se, Fax (08) 611 86 86,* – rm, rest, – 600. CY r
Verandan** ((08) 679 35 86) :* **Meals** 280/445 and a la carte 405/575 (see also ***Franska Matsalen below) – 205 – **289 rm** 2400/4500, 21 suites.
• Sweden's top hotel occupies a late 19C mansion on the waterfront overlooking the Royal Palace and Old Town. Combines traditional elegance with the latest modern facilities. Classic restaurant with a wonderful outlook. Famous Smörgåsbord.

Radisson SAS Royal Viking, Vasagatan 1, S-101 24, (08) 506 540 00, *Fax (08) 506 540 01,* – rm, – 130. rest BY f
***Stockholm Fisk** ((08) 506 541 02) :* **Meals** - Seafood - a la carte approx 550 – 125 – **456 rm** 1995/2195, 3 suites.
• Panoramic Sky Bar with impressive views over Stockholm, at the top of 9 floors of comfortable bedrooms. In busy part of the city but completely sound-proofed. Stylish contemporary restaurant offers an array of seafood dishes.

Sheraton Stockholm H. and Towers, Tegelbacken 6, S-101 23, (08) 412 34 00, *sheraton.stockholm@sheraton.com, Fax (08) 412 34 09,* – rm, – 380. CY a
***Restaurant at The Sheraton** :* **Meals** (buffet lunch) 195/250 and a la carte 285/440 – ***Die Ecke** :* **Meals** - German Bierstub - *(closed Saturday lunch and Sunday)* a la carte 335/485 – 180 – **445 rm** 2900/3100, 17 suites.
• International hotel popular with business people, overlooking Gamla Stan and offering the largest rooms in town. Comprehensive guest facilities. Open plan all-day restaurant with international dishes. Authentic German dishes in classic wood panelled bierstube.

Radisson SAS Strand, Nybrokajen 9, S-103 27, (08) 506 640 00, *sales.strand.stockholm@radissonsas.com, Fax (08) 506 640 01,* – rm, – 100. CDY x
***Strand** :* **Meals** *(closed Sunday dinner)* 535 (dinner) and a la carte 370/505 – 180 – **131 rm** 2050/2395, 20 suites.
• Characterful old world architecture in red brick overlooking the harbour. Rooms feature classic elegant décor with traditional Swedish style furniture. Open plan lobby restaurant with accomplished Swedish and international cooking.

Diplomat, Strandvägen 7c, S-104 40, (08) 459 68 02, *info@diplomathotel.com, Fax (08) 459 68 20,* – rm, . DY m
closed 23-30 December – ***T Bar** :* **Meals** *(closed lunch Monday-Friday in July and Sunday dinner)* a la carte 282/525 – 150 – **128 rm** 1995/4495.
• Elegant 1911 Art Nouveau building converted into hotel from diplomatic lodgings pleasantly located overlooking the harbour. Traditional and contemporary bedrooms. A popular terrace, contemporary style hotel restaurant offering traditional Swedish cooking.

Berns, Näckströmsgatan 8, Berzelii Park, S-111 47, (08) 566 322 00, *info@berns.se, Fax (08) 566 322 01,* – rm, – 180. CY b
The Summer Terrace** :* **Meals** (grill rest.) a la carte 315/615 (see also ***Berns Restaurant below) – **61 rm** 2200/4100, 4 suites.
• Boutique hotel with a modern minimalist interior décor verging on trendy ; details in cherry wood and marble. Modern facilities in bedrooms, some have balconies. The Summer Terrace for dinner, drinking, night clubbing and breakfast.

Nordic Light, Vasaplan, S-101 37, (08) 505 630 00, *info@nordichotels.se, Fax (08) 505 630 90,* – – 40. BY b
Meals - Tapas - a la carte 30/70 – **175 rm** 2500/2900.
• Sister hotel to Nordic Sea with most facilities here. Modern harmonious black and white designer décor features symphony of lights on the Nordic Lights theme. Modern menu with a backdrop of kaleidoscopic light projections.

First H. Amaranten, Kungsholmsgatan 31, S-104 20, (08) 692 52 00, *amaranten@firsthotels.se, Fax (08) 652 62 48,* – , rest, . BY c
***Amaranten** :* **Meals** *(closed lunch Saturday and Sunday)* a la carte 268/448 – **422 rm** 1699/2399, 1 suite.
• Modernised, commercial hotel conveniently located with easy access to subway. Stylish, quiet public areas with American Bar ; compact but up-to-date bedrooms. Stylish modern eating area with a large menu of modern Swedish cooking.

Nordic Sea without rest., Vasaplan, S-101 37, (08) 505 630 00, *info@nordichotels.se, Fax (08) 505 630 90* – rm, – 100. BY a
367 rm 2000/2400.
• Stylish modern hotel with sea theme. Unique Ice Bar is a "must see". Contemporary bedrooms with a blue theme.

Birger Jarl, Tulegatan 8, ✉ S-104 32, ☎ (08) 674 18 00, *info@birgerjarl.se, Fax (08) 673 73 66,* – rest, – 150. **Meals** *(closed lunch Saturday and Sunday)* a la carte 267/365 – **229 rm** 1695/2450, 6 suites. CX z
◆ Modern hotel building in quieter part of city. Lobby features many art and sculpture displays. Some rooms decorated by local artists of international reputation. Simple and stylish restaurant with unfussy Swedish cooking.

Scandic H. Park, Karlavägen 43, ✉ S-102 46, ☎ (08) 517 348 00, *park@scandic-hotels.com, Fax (08) 517 348 11,* – – 60. rest CX t
Park Village : **Meals** 298 (dinner) and a la carte 213/415 – **190 rm** 1890/2490, 8 suites.
◆ Convenient location by one of the city's prettiest parks (view from suites). All rooms are a good size, modern and comfortable with good range of facilities and comforts. Modern restaurant with small summer terrace ; traditional Swedish and international fare.

Elite H. Stockholm Plaza, Birger Jarlsgatan 29, ✉ S-103 95, ☎ (08) 566 220 00, *info.stoplaza@elite.se, Fax (08) 566 220 20,* – rm, – 50. CX e
closed Christmas – **Meals** (see ***Vassa Eggen*** below) – **147 rm** 1895/2395, 4 suites.
◆ Well preserved 1884 building with up-to-date comforts. Compact well run commercial hotel with conference rooms, basement sauna and high percentage of single rooms.

Lydmar, Sturegatan 10, ✉ S-114 36, ☎ (08) 566 113 00, *info@lydmar.se, Fax (08) 566 113 01* – rm, . rest CX a
The Dining Room : **Meals** a la carte 400/650 – **61 rm** 1950/3950, 1 suite.
◆ Well located in the shopping and night life area, this boutique hotel overlooking the park offers style : bar with regular light music ; individually furnished bedrooms. Stylish, informal dining with original, modern cooking with eclectic influences.

Rica City H. Stockholm, Slöjdgatan 7, ✉ S-111 57, ☎ (08) 723 72 00, *info.stockholm@rica.se, Fax (08) 723 72 09,* – – 120. CY c
Oasen : **Meals** *(closed Saturday, Sunday and Bank Holidays)* (lunch only) a la carte 90/160 – **292 rm** 1705/2135.
◆ Conveniently located at heart of shopping district so popular with tourists. Rooms distributed around Atrium, beneath which is a winter garden. Stylish modern bedrooms. Eclectic range of international dishes in restaurant overlooking the street.

Comfort Hotel Wellington without rest., Storgatan 6, ✉ S-114 51, ☎ (08) 667 09 10, *info.wellington@comfort.choicehotels.se, Fax (08) 667 12 54,* – . rest DY p
closed 23 December-4 January – **58 rm** 1845/2245, 2 suites.
◆ Apartment block converted into hotel in late 1960s, well placed for shopping and night life. Compact but well-equipped bedrooms ; city views from upper floor balconies.

Hotel Riddargatan without rest., Riddargatan 14, ✉ S-114 35, ☎ (08) 555 730 00, *hotelriddargatan@profilhotels.se, Fax (08) 555 730 11* – .
56 rm 1745/2095, 2 suites. CY m
◆ Modern style hotel in quiet location behind the Royal Dramatik Theatre, near shops and restaurants. Swedish design bedrooms with good internet facilities.

Freys, Bryggargatan 12, ✉ S-101 31, ☎ (08) 506 213 00, *freys@freyshotels.com, Fax (08) 506 213 13,* – rm, – 50. rest BY u
closed 5 days Christmas – ***Hörnans Kok :*** **Meals** *(closed lunch Saturday and Sunday)* (light lunch)/dinner 295 and a la carte 190/322 – **123 rm** 1595/2200, 1 suite.
◆ Well located near central station. Paintings by local artists for sale. First-floor terrace. Fairly compact bedrooms with informal furnishings, superior rooms with balconies. Short, exclusive menu offers traditional fare and also some Belgian specialities.

Operakällaren, Operahuset, Karl XII's Torg, ✉ S-111 86, ☎ (08) 676 58 00, *info@operakallaren.se, Fax (08) 676 58 72,* – . CY d
closed mid July-mid August, 25 December-9 January, Monday and Tuesday – **Meals** (dinner only) 895/1100 and a la carte 765/898.
Spec. Symphony of crustaceans. Roast rib of beef, shallot gravy and duck foie gras. Pina Colada maison.
◆ Magnificent dining room with original 19C carved wood décor and fresco paintings situated in the historic Opera House. Extensive menu of well prepared gourmet dishes.

Franska Matsalen (at Grand Hôtel), Södra Blasieholmshamnen 8, ✉ S-103 27, ☎ (08) 679 35 84, *niclas.ohlsson@grandhotel.se, Fax (08) 611 86 86,* ← Royal Palace and Old Town – . CY r
closed 24-26 December, first week January, Sunday and Saturday lunch – **Meals** 295/1200 and a la carte 540/1160.
◆ Classic comfortable restaurant which is part elegant historic dining room with mahogany and crystal decor, part window terrace overlooking Royal Palace and Old Town.

XXX ✿ **Bon Lloc** (Dahlgren), Regeringsgatan 111, ✉ S-111 39, ✆ (08) 660 60 60, *bonlloc@telia.com, Fax (08) 10 76 35* – ▤. MC AE ⓓ VISA. ✻ CX n
closed Easter, 4-31 July, Christmas-New Year and Sunday – **Meals** (booking essential) (dinner only) a la carte 385/755 ♀.
Spec. Crema quemada of duck liver. Salad of tuna, quail egg and oscietre caviar. Goat's cheese pizza, figs, truffle and honey.
◆ Highly regarded, innovative restaurant where the owner draws inspiration from French, Italian and Spanish cuisines. Exacting service, relaxed surroundings. Booking a must.

XXX **Vassa Eggen** (at Elite H. Stockholm Plaza), Birger Jarlsgatan 29, ✉ S-114 25, ✆ (08) 21 61 69, *info@vassaeggen.com, Fax (08) 20 34 46,* 🏠 – ⅔. MC AE ⓓ VISA. ✻ CX e
closed July, Sunday and Saturday lunch – **Meals** a la carte approx 650 ♀.
◆ Refined restaurant popular with those in the know. Modern style reflected in both the décor and the cuisine, which is original and innovative.

XX ✿ **Fredsgatan 12** (Couet), Fredsgatan 12, ✉ S-111 52, ✆ (08) 24 80 52, *info@fredsgatan12.com, Fax (08) 23 76 05* – ▤. MC AE ⓓ VISA JCB. ✻ CY f
closed 2 weeks July, 2 weeks August, Christmas-New Year, Saturday and Sunday – **Meals** (booking essential) 325/995 and a la carte approx 700 ♀.
Spec. Figs 'en gelée', foie gras and port. 'Paupiette' of pike perch, water chestnut and lemongrass. Chocolate 'Bounty', coconut and exotic fruit.
◆ Stylish retro interior design with predominant 1970's theme in a wing of the Academy of Arts. Good value business lunch offered. Creative and original modern cuisine.

XX **Paul and Norbert,** Strandvägen 9, ✉ S-114 56, ✆ (08) 663 81 83, *restaurang.paul.norbert@telia.se, Fax (08) 661 72 36* – MC AE ⓓ VISA. ✻ DY m
closed Easter, 24-27 June, 23 December-9 January, Sunday, lunch Saturday, Monday and in summer and Bank Holidays – **Meals** (booking essential) 350/1050 and a la carte 350/660 ♀.
◆ Small sophisticated well run restaurant on harbour with stylish modern décor and artwork. Some tables in booths. Numerous menus featuring seasonal produce.

XX **Berns Restaurant** (at Berns H.), Berzelii Park, ✉ S-111 47, ✆ (08) 566 322 22, *info@berns.se, Fax (08) 566 323 23* – MC AE ⓓ VISA JCB. ✻ CY b
Meals a la carte 315/615 ♀.
◆ A stunningly restored 19C rococo ballroom with galleries overlooking the dining room. Modern international cuisine. Live music. The place to be seen in.

XX ✿ **Wedholms Fisk,** Nybrokajen 17, ✉ S-111 48, ✆ (08) 611 78 74, *info@wedholmsfisk.se, Fax (08) 678 60 11,* 🏠 – ⅔ ▤. MC AE ⓓ VISA JCB. ✻ CY s
closed Sunday and Saturday lunch – **Meals** - Seafood - a la carte 475/855 ♀.
Spec. Fricassée of sole, turbot, lobster and scallops with Champagne sauce. Boiled turbot with butter and horseradish. Swedish shellfish and seafood.
◆ Classic 19-20C building near harbour. Classic style restaurant serving superb quality fresh fish and shellfish, simply but accurately prepared ; similar dishes in the bar.

XX **Per Lei,** Artillerigatan 56, ✉ 114 45, ✆ (08) 411 38 11, *info@operlei.se, Fax (08) 662 64 45* – MC AE ⓓ VISA. ✻ DX x
closed mid July-mid August, 1 week Christmas, Sunday, Monday dinner and Saturday lunch – **Meals** - Italian influences - (booking essential) 395 (dinner) and a la carte 505/525.
◆ Popular neighbourhood restaurant in converted boutique ; elegant décor with crystal chandelier. Italian-inspired menu ; 2 dinner menus of 3 or 5 courses ; refined cooking.

XX **Café Opera,** Operahuset, Karl XII's Torg, ✉ S-111 86, ✆ (08) 676 58 07, *info@cafeopera.se, Fax (08) 676 58 71,* 🏠 – ▤. MC AE ⓓ VISA JCB. ✻ CY x
closed 24 December – **Meals** (booking essential) (dinner only) (music and dancing after 12pm) a la carte 360/530 ♀.
◆ Characterful rotunda style historic restaurant with ceiling painted in 1895, Corinthian pillars, fine mouldings and covered terrace. Swedish-influenced, international menu.

XX **Teatergrillen,** Nybrogatan 3, ✉ S-111 48, ✆ (08) 545 035 62, *riche@riche.se, Fax (08) 545 035 69* – ▤. MC AE ⓓ VISA. ✻ CY w
closed 24-25 December, 1 and 5-6 January, 9 April, 20 May, 20-21 and 31 June, Sunday and Monday dinner – **Meals** a la carte 225/494 ♀.
◆ Most pleasant in the evening and with an intimate, traditional atmosphere - an institution in the city. Same menu as Riche ; traditional cooking of Scandinavian classics.

XX **Clas På Hörnet** with rm, Surbrunnsgatan 20, ✉ S-113 48, ✆ (08) 16 51 30, *hotel@claspahornet.com, Fax (08) 612 53 15,* 🏠 – 🛗 ⅔, ▤ rm, TV ✆. MC AE ⓓ VISA. ✻ CX f
closed 24-26 December and Saturday lunch – **Meals** 395/550 and a la carte 350/565 ♀ – **10 rm** ☕ 1295/2395.
◆ Well established and busy restaurant in part-18C inn with character. Simple traditional rustic cooking using good quality local produce. Cosy, well-equipped bedrooms.

X **Restaurangen,** Oxtorgsgatan 14, ✉ S-111 57, ☎ (08) 22 09 52, *reservation.restaurangen@telia.com, Fax (08) 22 09 54,* – MC AE DC VISA. CY e
closed 4 weeks in summer, 1 week Christmas, Sunday and Saturday lunch – **Meals** (booking essential) (light lunch)/dinner 275/475 and a la carte.
• Contemporary interior with clean-cut minimalist décor and modern furnishings. Unusual menu concept based on a tasting of several small dishes.

X **Grill,** Drottninggatan 89, ✉ S-113 60, ☎ (08) 31 45 30, *info@grill.se, Fax (08) 31 45 80* – MC AE DC VISA JCB BX x
closed lunch Saturday and Sunday – **Meals** (light lunch)/dinner 175/335 and a la carte approx 206.
• Stylish city centre restaurant with spacious lounge area ; modern minimalist décor. Open plan kitchen. Menu based on different cooking methods - grilling, rotisserie, BBQ etc.

X **Halv Trappa Plus Gård,** Lästmakargatan 3, ✉ 111 36, ☎ (08) 678 10 50, *info@halvtrappaplusgard.se, Fax (08) 678 10 51* – MC AE DC VISA JCB. CY z
closed 22 December-3 January, Sunday and Monday – **Meals** - Chinese-Szechuan - (booking essential) (dinner only) a la carte 450/645.
• Busy basement restaurant without external sign or menu. Authentic Chinese cooking from Szechuan : hot and spicy. Well presented balanced set menus or individual dishes.

BRASSERIES AND BISTRO

XX **KB,** Smålandsgatan 7, ✉ S-111 46, ☎ (08) 679 60 32, *info@konstnarsbaren.se, Fax (08) 611 39 32* – MC AE DC VISA. CY u
closed Christmas, Sunday and Bank Holidays – **Meals** a la carte 190/650.
• 19C building with impressive façade and original wall frescoes in bar - a home of Swedish artists with interesting modern art on the walls. Traditional Swedish cooking.

X **Prinsen,** Mäster Samuelsgatan 4, ✉ S-111 44, ☎ (08) 611 13 31, *kontoret@restaurangprinsen.se, Fax (08) 611 70 79,* – MC AE DC VISA. CY t
closed 24-25 and 31 December, dinner 20 June and Sunday lunch – **Meals** (booking essential) a la carte 383/626.
• Long standing and classic, busy but well-run brasserie with literary associations. Exhibition of graphic art renewed monthly in basement room. Classic Swedish cooking.

X **Sturehof,** Stureplan 2-4, ✉ S-114 46, ☎ (08) 440 57 30, *info@sturehof.com, Fax (08) 678 11 01,* – MC AE DC VISA JCB. CY n
Meals - Seafood - a la carte 365/600.
• Very popular classic café-brasserie with closely packed tables and a busy atmosphere due to the steady stream of local business clientele. Good choice of seafood dishes.

X **Eriks Bakficka,** Fredrikshovsgatan 4, ✉ S-115 23, ☎ (08) 660 15 99, *info.bakfickan@eriks.se, Fax (08) 663 25 67,* – MC AE DC VISA. DY r
closed 23-26 December, 1 January and lunch Saturday and Sunday – **Meals** 395/520 and a la carte 365/570.
• Quiet residential situation, offering small terrace, bistro, bar-counter and more conventional dining room. Interesting choice of traditional Swedish dishes.

X **Riche,** Birger Jarlsgatan 4, ✉ S-114 53, ☎ (08) 545 035 60, *riche@riche.se, Fax (08) 545 035 69* – MC AE DC VISA. CY v
closed 1 and 6 January, 9 and 12 April, 20-21 June, 24-25 December and Sunday – **Meals** a la carte 225/494.
• The lively bar and bustling restaurant, very different from but with same menu as its sister Teatergrillen. Serves classic Scandinavian as well as international dishes.

at Gamla Stan (Old Stockholm) :

First H. Reisen, Skeppsbron 12, ✉ S-111 30, ☎ (08) 22 32 60, *reisen@firsthotels.se, Fax (08) 20 15 59,* – rm, TV. MC AE DC VISA JCB. AZ f
Reisen Bar and Dining Room : **Meals** a la carte 313/528 – 160 – **137 rm** 2199/5499, 7 suites.
• 19C hotel on waterfront with original maritime décor. Popular piano bar. Sauna in 17C vault. Deluxe and superior rooms offer quayside view and small balconies. Maritime interior and a warm and welcoming atmosphere. Traditional Swedish and international menu.

Victory, Lilla Nygatan 5, ✉ S-111 28, ☎ (08) 506 400 00, *info@victory-hotel.se, Fax (08) 506 400 10,* – rm, TV P – 80. MC AE DC VISA JCB.
closed 23 December-2 January – **Meals** (see ***Leijontornet*** below) – 170 – **45 rm** 1990/2990, 4 suites. AZ v
• Pleasant 17C hotel with Swedish rural furnishings and maritime antiques. Rooms named after sea captains with individually styled fittings, mixing modern and antique.

Rica City H. Gamla Stan without rest., Lilla Nygatan 25, ✉ S-111 28, ☎ (08) 723 72 50, *info.gamlastan@rica.se, Fax (08) 723 72 59* – TV. MC AE DC VISA
50 rm 1695/1945, 1 suite. AZ c
• Conveniently located 17C house with welcoming style. Well-furnished rooms with traditional décor and antique style furniture. Pleasant top-floor terrace with rooftop outlook.

Lady Hamilton without rest., Storkyrkobrinken 5, ✉ S-111 28, ℘ (08) 506 401 00, *info@lady-hamilton.se, Fax (08) 506 401 10,* – |♦| ⇔ TV P. MC AE ⊕ VISA JCB. AZ e
140 **34 rm** 1790/2290.
• 15C houses of character full of fine Swedish rural furnishings. Rooms boast antique pieces and modern facilities. Sauna and 14C well plunge pool in basement.

Lord Nelson without rest., Västerlånggatan 22, ✉ S-111 29, ℘ (08) 506 401 20, *info@lord-nelson.se, Fax (08) 506 401 30,* – |♦| ⇔ TV. MC AE ⊕ VISA JCB. AZ a
closed Christmas-New Year – **29 rm** 1690/2090.
• Charming late 17C house located in lively Old Town, with ship style interior and maritime antiques. Small cabin style rooms with good level of comfort and compact bathrooms.

Pontus in the Green House, Österlånggatan 17, ✉ S-111 31, ℘ (08) 545 273 00, *info@pontusfrithiof.com, Fax (08) 796 60 69* – MC AE ⊕ VISA AZ u
closed Sunday and Bank Holidays – **Meals** (booking essential) a la carte 540/1075 ♀.
• Restaurant with charm and style in 15C house. Classic décor and some booths in more formal upstairs room. Modern innovative or 'classic rustique' menu; accomplished cuisine.

Leijontornet (at Victory H.), Lilla Nygatan 5, ✉ S-111 28, ℘ (08) 506 400 80, *info@leijontornet.se, Fax (08) 506 400 85* – ⇔. MC AE ⊕ VISA JCB. AZ v
closed 23 December-2 January – **Meals** (booking essential) 295/725 and a la carte approx 575 ♀.
• Characterful dining room features remains of a 14C fortified tower and a glass fronted wine cellar sunk into floor. Main menu offers good range of original modern dishes.

Mistral (Andersson), Lilla Nygatan 21, ✉ S-111 28, ℘ (08) 10 12 24, *rest.mistral@telia.com* – MC AE ⊕ VISA. AZ h
closed 24 June-2 August, 23 December-4 January, Saturday-Monday and Bank Holidays – **Meals** (booking essential) (dinner only) (set menu only) 655/855 ♀.
Spec. Ginger pickled mackerel, fried pig's skin, oyster liaison. Tartare of langoustine with pistachio nuts. Braised brisket of milk fed lamb, roasted coffee beans and cardemom.
• Small personally-run restaurant with modern décor. Open plan kitchen preparing original and creative dishes; degustation menu of 8 courses.

Den Gyldene Freden, Österlånggatan 51, ✉ S-103 17, ℘ (08) 24 97 60, *info@gyldenefreden.se, Fax (08) 21 38 70* – ⇔. MC AE ⊕ VISA. AZ s
closed Christmas, 31 December-1 January, Sunday, Saturday lunch and Bank Holidays – **Meals** a la carte 355/645 ♀.
• Restaurant in early 18C inn with fine vaulted cellars owned by Swedish Academy. Traditional, Swedish, robust cooking incorporating plenty of flavours and good local produce.

Brasserie by the Sea, Skeppsbrokajen, Tullhus 2, ✉ S-111 31, ℘ (08) 20 20 95, *bythesea@pontusfrithiof.com, Fax (08) 22 08 28,* ≤ Stockholm harbour and islands, – MC AE VISA AZ k
closed lunch September-April – **Meals** 275/550 and a la carte 295/550 ♀.
• Quayside view of shipping, harbour and islands. Good value modern dishes, including shellfish. Dine on the attractive covered and heated terrace, followed by a game of boules.

Fem Små Hus, Nygränd 10, ✉ S-111 30, ℘ (08) 10 87 75, *fem.sma.hus@telia.com, Fax (08) 14 96 95* – ⇔. MC AE ⊕ VISA JCB AZ r
closed 25 December – **Meals** (dinner only) 375/545 and a la carte 365/625 ♀.
• Characterful restaurant located in 17C cellars of five adjacent houses and filled with antiques. Popular with tourists. Several menus available offering traditional cuisine.

at Djurgården :

Scandic H. Hasselbacken, Hazeliusbacken 20, ✉ S-100 55, ℘ (08) 517 343 00, *hasselbacken@scandic-hotels.com, Fax (08) 517 343 11,* – |♦|, ⇔ rm, ▤ rm, TV ♿ – 250. MC AE ⊕ VISA. rest DZ e
Restaurang Hasselbacken : **Meals** (booking essential) 395 (dinner) and a la carte – **110 rm** 1790/2090, 2 suites.
• Modern hotel situated on island in former Royal park, close to the Vasa Museum. Up-to-date bedrooms, some with views. Regular musical events. Restaurant with ornate mirrored ceilings, attractive terrace and pleasant outlook; traditional Swedish cooking.

Ulla Winbladh, Rosendalsvägen 8, ✉ S-115 21, ℘ (08) 663 05 71, *ulla.winbladh@telia.com, Fax (08) 663 05 73,* – MC AE ⊕ VISA. DY a
closed 24-25 December – **Meals** (booking essential) a la carte 295/515 ♀.
• Pleasant late 19C pavilion in former Royal hunting ground houses several welcoming dining rooms and extensive terraces in summer. Traditional Swedish cuisine.

at Södermalm :

Hilton Stockholm Slussen, Guldgränd 8, ✉ S-104 65, ☎ (08) 517 353 00, *stockholm-slussen@hilton.com, Fax (08) 517 353 11,* <, 🏞, Fo, ≘ – |‡|, ⊁ rm, ▤ TV ☎ ♿ 🚗 – 🎓 300. MC AE ⓓ VISA. ✻ rest CZ e
Eken : **Meals** *(closed lunch Saturday and Sunday)* (buffet lunch) 235/460 and dinner a la carte 292/550 ♀ – ☕ 135 – **174 rm** 2290/2490, 15 suites.
◆ Busy commercial hotel, overlooking Old Town and surrounding water, housed in three buildings with central lobby. Caters well for groups and conferences. Modern style restaurant with excellent view of Old Town and water. Traditional and modern Swedish cuisine.

Clarion, Ringvägen 98, ✉ S-104 60, South : by Götgatan ☎ (08) 462 10 00, *stockholm@clarion.choicehotels.se, Fax (08) 462 10 99,* ≘ – |‡| ⊁, ▤ rest, TV ☎ ♿ 🚗 – 🎓 500. MC AE ⓓ VISA. ✻
Gretas Kök : **Meals** a la carte approx 350 – **522 rm** ☕ 1895/2545, 10 suites.
◆ Large modern glass-fronted building. Décor includes contemporary Swedish artwork ; also live music. Stylish bedrooms with wood floors ; good views to west and south. Contemporary style restaurant serving Swedish dishes with a modern influence.

The Rival, Mariatorget 3, ✉ S-118 91, ☎ (08) 545 789 00, *reservations@rival.se, Fax (08) 545 789 24,* 🏞 – |‡|, ⊁ rm, TV ☎ ♿ – 🎓 700. MC AE ⓓ VISA. ✻ CZ r
The Bistro : **Meals** (residents only Sunday) (dinner only) a la carte 298/505 – ☕ 145 – **97 rm** 1990/2290, 2 suites.
◆ Modern boutique hotel and Art Deco cinema in 1930's building. Stylish bedroooms with cinema theme décor and high-tech facilities. First floor open plan bar and bistro/restaurant. Classic Swedish cooking in the bistro ; more modern dishes in the restaurant.

Eriks Gondolen, Stadsgården 6 (11th floor), ✉ S-104 56, ☎ (08) 641 70 90, *info@eriks.se, Fax (08) 641 11 40,* ✻ Stockholm and water, 🏞 – |‡| ▤. MC AE ⓓ VISA. ✻
closed Easter Monday, Whit Monday, 4 weeks July, Sunday and lunch 2 weeks in August – **Meals** 295/535 and a la carte 365/645 ♀. CZ a
◆ Glass enclosed suspended passageway, renowned for stunning panoramic view of city and water. Open-air dining and barbecue terraces on 12th floor. Traditional Swedish fare.

Gässlingen, Brännkyrkagatan 93, ✉ S-117 26, ☎ (08) 669 54 95, *gasslingen@telia.com, Fax (08) 84 89 90* – ⊁. MC AE ⓓ VISA. ✻ BZ
closed 23 June-6 August, 23 December-9 January, Sunday, Monday and Saturday lunch – **Meals** (booking essential) 165/395 and a la carte 428/688 ♀.
◆ Personally-run neighbourhood restaurant with rustic beamed interior ; ceramic tiles, wood and paintings with ducks and geese motif. Classic and modern influenced dishes.

to the North :

Stallmästaregården, Norrtull, ✉ S-113 47, North : 2 km by Sveavägen (at beginning of E 4) ☎ (08) 610 13 00, *info@stallmastaregarden.se, Fax (08) 610 13 40,* 🏞, 🌳 – |‡|, ⚓ ⊁ TV ☎ ♿ P – 🎓 200. MC AE ⓓ VISA JCB. ✻
closed 23-31 December – **Meals** (see below) – **36 rm** ☕ 1995/2400, 13 suites.
◆ Attractive 17C inn with central courtyard and modern bedroom wing. Quieter rooms overlook waterside and park. 18C style rustic Swedish décor with modern comforts.

Stallmästaregården (at Stallmästaregården H.), Norrtull, ✉ S-113 47, North : 2 km by Sveavägen (at beginning of E 4) ☎ (08) 610 13 00, *info@stallmastaregarden.se, Fax (08) 610 13 40,* <, 🏞, 🌳 –, ⚓ ⊁ P. MC AE ⓓ VISA. ✻
closed 23-31 December – **Meals** 425 (dinner) and a la carte 325/485 ♀.
◆ Part 17C inn with elegant 18C Swedish décor. Beautiful waterside terrace in summer. Open kitchen. Modern Swedish cuisine.

to the East :

at Ladugårdsgärdet :

Villa Källhagen ⛰ with rm, Djurgårdsbrunnsvägen 10, ✉ S-115 27, East : 3 km by Strandvägen ☎ (08) 665 03 00, *villa@kallhagen.se, Fax (08) 665 03 99,* <, 🏞, ≘, 🌳 – |‡|, ⚓, ⊁ rm, TV P – 🎓 55. MC AE ⓓ VISA. ✻ rest
closed 22-30 December – **Meals** 445/625 and a la carte ♀ – **18 rm** ☕ 1700/2400, 2 suites.
◆ Modern building in lovely waterside setting. Contemporary bedrooms, all with view of water. Extensive open-air terraces amid trees. Traditional modern Scandinavian cuisine.

at Fjäderholmarna Island *25 mn by boat, departure every hour (½ hour in season) from Nybrokajen* CY *:*

Fjäderholmarnas Krog, Stora Fjäderholmen, ✉ S-100 05, ☎ (08) 718 33 55, *fjaderholmarna@atv.se, Fax (08) 716 39 89,* < neighbouring islands and sea, 🏞 –, ⚓ ⊁. MC AE ⓓ VISA JCB. ✻
May-September and December – **Meals** - Seafood - *(closed dinner 20 June)* (booking essential) 147/565 and a la carte 420/590 ♀.
◆ Delightful waterside setting on archipelago island with fine view. Fresh produce, mainly fish, delivered daily by boat. Wide selection of traditional Swedish dishes.

to the Southeast :

at Nacka Strand *Southeast : 10 km by Stadsgården DZ or by boat from Nybrokajen :*

Hotel J, Ellensviksvägen 1, S-131 27, (08) 601 30 00, *nackastrand@hotelj.com, Fax (08) 601 30 09,* sea, – , 30. rest *restricted opening Christmas and New Year* – **Meals** (see ***Restaurant J*** below) – **41 rm** 1395/3195, 4 suites.

• Former politician's early 20C summer residence in quiet waterside setting. 'Boutique' style hotel with maritime theme. Stylish spacious rooms, some with sea view.

Restaurant J, Augustendalsvägen 52, S-131 27, (08) 601 30 25, *info@restaurantj.com, Fax (08) 601 30 09,* Sea, –, .
Meals 215/290 and a la carte approx 400.

• Bright, informal restaurant with sleek maritime décor and attractive terrace beside marina. Selective menu of Swedish and international dishes.

to the South :

at Johanneshov (Globen City) :

Quality H. Globe, Arenaslingan 7, S-121 26, South : 1 ½ km by Rd 73 (08) 686 63 00, *globe@quality.choicehotels.se, Fax (08) 686 63 01,* , – , rm, – 220. rest
Tabac : **Meals** *(closed Christmas and New Year)* a la carte 300/480 – **280 rm** 1695/1895, 7 suites.

• Located in industrial office complex and well equipped for conferences. Functional rooms with good facilities. Friendly staff. Modern informal eatery in conservatory overlooking small lake and fountain. Swedish cuisine with popular international dishes.

to the West :

at Lilla Essingen *West : 5 ¼ km by Norr Mälarstrand BY :*

Lux Stockholm (Norström), Primusgatan 116, S-112 62, (08) 619 01 90, *info@luxstockholm.com, Fax (08) 619 04 47,* , – .
closed Monday and lunch Saturday and Sunday – **Meals** a la carte 510/600.
Spec. Chicken soup, truffle and quail egg. Venison fillet with spiced sausage, pickled chanterelles. Caramelised apple, vanilla cream and Calvados.

• Converted brick warehouse overlooking waterways. Light and airy with green and white décor. Large window into kitchen ; innovative Swedish cooking with distinctive twists.

at Bromma *West : 5 ½ km by Norr Mälarstrand BY and Drottningholmsvägen :*

Sjöpaviljongen, Tranebergs Strand 4, Alvik, 167 40, East : 1 ½ km (08) 704 04 24, *info@paviljongen.se, Fax (08) 704 82 40,* , –, .
closed Christmas and New Year – **Meals** (booking essential) 275/375 and a la carte 287/434.

• Modern pavilion in attractive lakeside setting. Swedish style décor. Good value classic Swedish cuisine at lunch ; more modern dishes at dinner.

to the Northwest :

Ulriksdals Wärdshus, 170 79 Solna, Northwest : 8 km by Sveavägen and E 18 towards Norrtälje, taking first junction for Ulriksdals Slott (08) 85 08 15, *info@ulriksdalswardshus.se, Fax (08) 85 08 58,* , , – .
closed 11-25 July, 24-26 December, Monday and Tuesday January-April and September-November and Sunday dinner – **Meals** (booking essential) 300/550 and a la carte 350/670.

• 19C former inn in Royal Park with classic winter garden style décor. Wine cellar features in Guinness Book of Records. Extensive smorgasbord at weekends.

at Sollentuna *Northwest : 15 km by Sveavägen BX and E 4 (exit Sollentuna c) :*

Edsbacka Krog (Lingström), Sollentunavägen 220, 191 35, (08) 96 33 00, *info@edsbackakrog.se, Fax (08) 96 40 19,* – .
closed 25 March, 16 May, midsummer, 10 July-4 August, 23 December-5 January and Sunday-Monday except May, June and December – **Meals** 775 and a la carte 690/835.
Spec. Salmon and whitebait with cheese biscuits and vanilla. Saddle of roe deer with blackcurrant sauce. Chocolate palette with apricots.

• Charming part 17C inn in small park with elegant rustic Swedish décor. Superb range of menus offering highly accomplished and original modern dishes.

Bistro Edsbacka, Sollentunavägen 223, 191 35, (08) 631 00 34, *info@svenskasmaker.se, Fax (08) 96 40 19,* – .
closed 24-26 June, 1 week July and 23-26 December – **Meals** (booking essential) 385/395 and a la carte 265/502.

• Simple modern bistro, contrasting with hotel opposite, with black and white décor. Attractive rear terrace shielded from traffic. Good value menu of classic Swedish dishes.

at Arlanda Airport *Northwest : 40 km by Sveavägen* BX *and E 4 – ✉ Arlanda :*

Radisson SAS Sky City, at Terminals 4-5, 2nd floor above street level, ✉ 190 45 Stockholm-Arlanda, Sky City ☎ (08) 506 740 00, *sales.skycity.stockholm@radissonsas.com, Fax (08) 506 740 01,* – rm, . **Stockholm Fish : Meals** - Seafood - *(closed Friday-Sunday and Bank Holidays)* a la carte 253/494 – **229 rm** 1995, 1 suite.
◆ The perfect place not to miss your plane : modern, corporate airport hotel. Three décor styles : standard Scandinavian ; Art Deco or superior business style. Balcony restaurant overlooking airport terminal offering fish-based menu.

Radisson SAS Arlandia, Benstocksvägen, ✉ 190 45 Stockholm-Arlanda, Southeast : 1 km ☎ (08) 506 840 00, *reservations.arlandia.stockholm@radissonsas.com, Fax (08) 506 840 01,* – rm, rest, – 240. rest
closed 23 December-3 January – **Cayenne : Meals** (buffet lunch) 197 and a la carte approx 250 – **327 rm** 1400/1800, 8 suites.
◆ A short shuttle ride from the terminal. Bright and modern corporate hotel and congress hall. Ecological, maritime and Scandinavian themed bedrooms. Contemporary styled restaurant and adjacent bar for light snacks, pastas and traditional Scandinavian fare.

GOTHENBURG (GÖTEBORG) *Sverige* 711 O 8 – *pop. 437 313.*

See : *Art Gallery★★ (Göteborgs Konstmuseet)* CX **M1** – *Castle Park★★ (Slottsskogen)* AX – *Botanical Gardens★★ (Botaniska Trädgården)* AX – *East India House★★ (Ostindiska Huset : Göteborgs stadmuseum)* BU **M2** *Museum of Arts and Crafts★★ (Röhsska Konstlojdmuseet)* BV **M3** – *Liseberg Amusement Park★★ (Liseberg Nöjespark)* DX *Horticultural Gardens★★ (Trädgårdsföreningen)* CU – *Natural History Museum★ (Naturhistoriska museet)* AX – *Maritime Museum★ (Sjöfartsmuseet)* AV – *Kungsportsavenyn★* BCVX **22** – *Götaplatsen (Carl Milles Poseidon★★)* CX – *Seaman's Tower (Sjömanstornet) (※★★)* AV *Göteborgs-Utkiken (※★★)* BT – *Masthugg Church (Masthuggskyrkan) (interior★)* AV.

Envir. : *Öckerö Archipelago★ by boat or by car : N : 17 km by E 6 and road 155 – New Älvsborg Fortress★ (Nya Älvsborgs Fästning)* AU – *Bohuslan★★ (The Golden Coast) N : - Halland coast to the south : Äskhult Open-Air Museum★ ; Tjolöholms Slott★* AX.

Albatross, Lillhagsvägen Hisings Backa ☎ (031) 55 19 01 – Delsjö, Kallebäck ☎ (031) 40 69 59 – Göteborgs, Golfbanevägen, Hovås ☎ (031) 28 24 44.

Scandinavian Airlines System : Reservations ☎ (770) 727727 Landvetter Airport : ☎ (031) 94 10 00.

To Denmark : contact Stena Line A/B ☎ (031) 775 00 00, Fax (031) 85 85 95 – To Continent : contact DFDS Seaways ☎ (031) 65 06 50, Fax (031) 53 23 09.

Kungsportplatsen 2 ☎ (031) 61 25 00, Fax (031) 61 25 01.

Copenhagen 279 – Oslo 322 – Stockholm 500.

Radisson SAS Scandinavia, Södra Hamngatan 59-65, ✉ S-401 24, ☎ (031) 758 50 00, *reservations.scandinavia.gothenburg@radissonsas.com, Fax (031) 758 50 01,* – rm, – 450. **Atrium Bar & Restaurant : Meals** (buffet lunch) 110 and dinner a la carte – 125 – **332 rm** 1870/1970, 17 suites. BU b
◆ Grand commercial hotel with impressive atrium courtyard complete with water features and glass elevators. Spacious rooms with a choice of décor and good modern facilities. A range of international dishes offered in restaurant housed within the atrium.

Gothia Towers, Mässans Gata 24, ✉ S-402 26, ☎ (031) 750 88 00, *hotelreservations@gothiatowers.com, Fax (031) 750 88 82,* – rm, – 1500. rest DX k
Heaven 23 : Meals (buffet lunch) 264/475 and dinner a la carte 330/540 – **Incontro : Meals** *(closed 20 December-1 January and dinner Sunday and Monday)* (buffet lunch) 115/335 and dinner a la carte 235/375 – **696 rm** 1690/1990, 8 suites.
◆ Large twin tower hotel owned by Gothenburg Exhibition Centre, popular with conference delegates and business people. Elegant modern Scandinavian décor. Top floor restaurant, Heaven 23, for spectacular city views and modern cuisine. Buffet lunch in Incontro.

Elite Plaza, Västra Hamngatan 3, ✉ S-404 22, ☎ (031) 720 40 00, *info@gbgplaza.elite.se, Fax (031) 720 40 10,* – – 50. **Meals** (see **Swea Hof** below) - **141 rm** 1665/2850, 2 suites. BU s
◆ Discreet and stylishly converted late 19C building. Rooms embody understated luxury with those overlooking the atrium sharing its lively atmosphere. Smart cocktail bar.

Odin Residence without rest., Odinsgatan 6, ✉ S-411 03, ☎ (031) 745 22 00, *info@hotelodin.se, Fax (031) 711 24 60,* – rm,
112 rm 1395/1895, 24 suites.
◆ Central location near railway station. Smart, Scandic style well equipped, serviced apartments, with mini-kitchen ; also spacious and appealing suites.

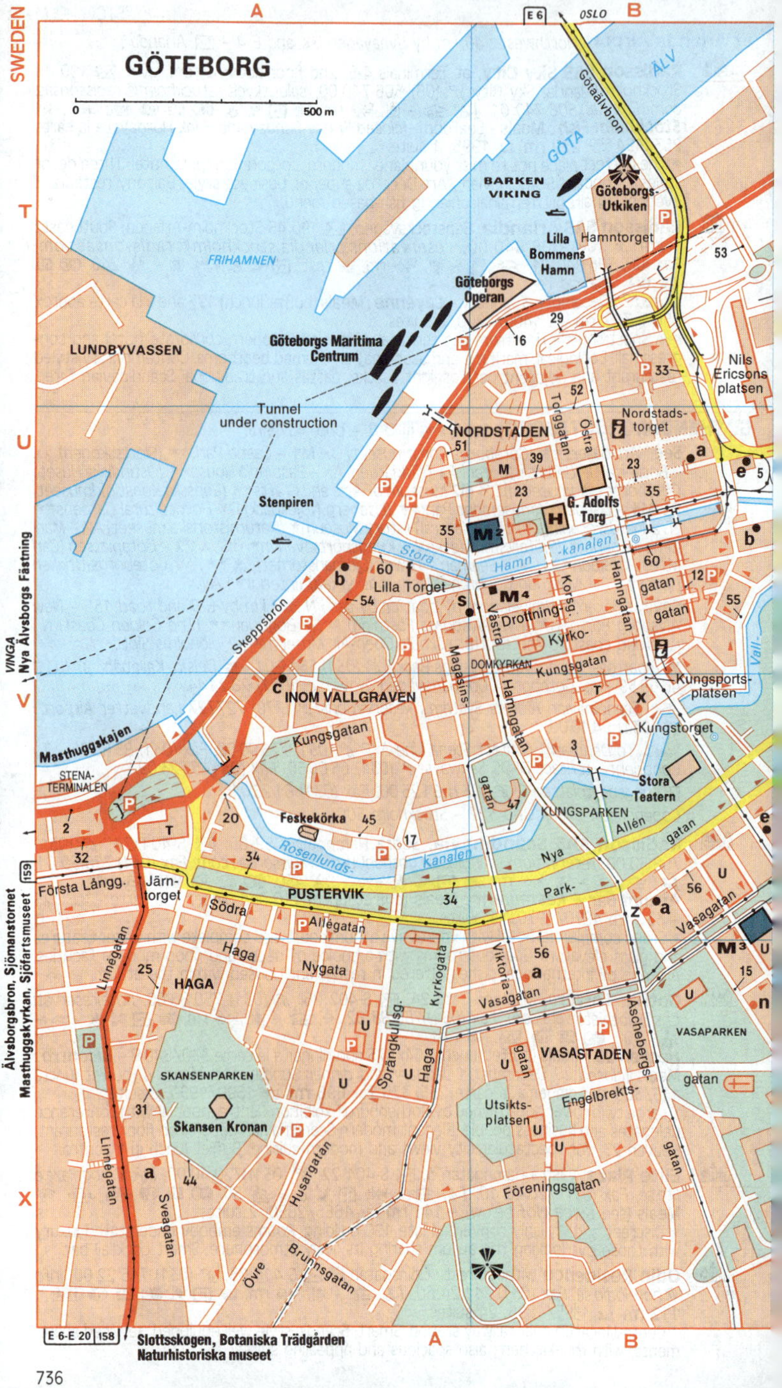
GÖTEBORG
0
500 m
A
B
E 6
OSLO
T
U
V
X
GÖTA
ÄLV
Götaälvbron
BARKEN
VIKING
Göteborgs-
Utkiken
Lilla
Bommens
Hamn
Hamntorget
53
FRIHAMNEN
Göteborgs
Operan
29
16
Göteborgs Maritima
Centrum
LUNDBYVASSEN
Nils
Ericsons
platsen
33
52
Torggatan
Östra
Nordstads-
torget
Tunnel
under construction
NORDSTADEN
51
39
M
23
35
Stenpiren
G. Adolfs
Torg
H
M²
Stora
Hamn
-kanalen
60
f
Lilla Torget
b
54
Skeppsbron
S
M⁴
Västra
Drottning-
Korsg.
Hamngatan
gatan
12
55
Kyrko-
Magasins-
DOMKYRKAN
Kungsgatan
Kungsports-
platsen
Vall-
VINGA
Nya Älvsborgs Fästning
c
INOM VALLGRAVEN
T
x
Kungstorget
Masthuggskajen
Kungsgatan
3
STENA-
TERMINALEN
Stora
Teatern
20
Feskekörka
45
47
KUNGSPARKEN
Allén
2
T
17
Rosenlunds-
kanalen
Nya
gatan
32
34
159
Första Långg.
Järn-
torget
PUSTERVIK
34
Park-
56
Södra
Allégatan
Z
Vasagatan
M³
Älvsborgsbron, Sjömanstornet
Masthuggskyrkan, Sjöfartsmuseet
Haga
Nygata
Kyrkogata
Viktoria-
56
15
Linnégatan
25
HAGA
Vasagatan
n
Sprängkullsg.
Haga
VASAPARKEN
VASASTADEN
Aschebergs-
SKANSENPARKEN
gatan
Engelbrekts-
Utsikts-
platsen
31
Skansen Kronan
Linnégatan
a
44
Sveagatan
Husargatan
gatan
Föreningsgatan
Övre
Brunnsgatan
E 6-E 20
158
Slottsskogen, Botaniska Trädgården
Naturhistoriska museet

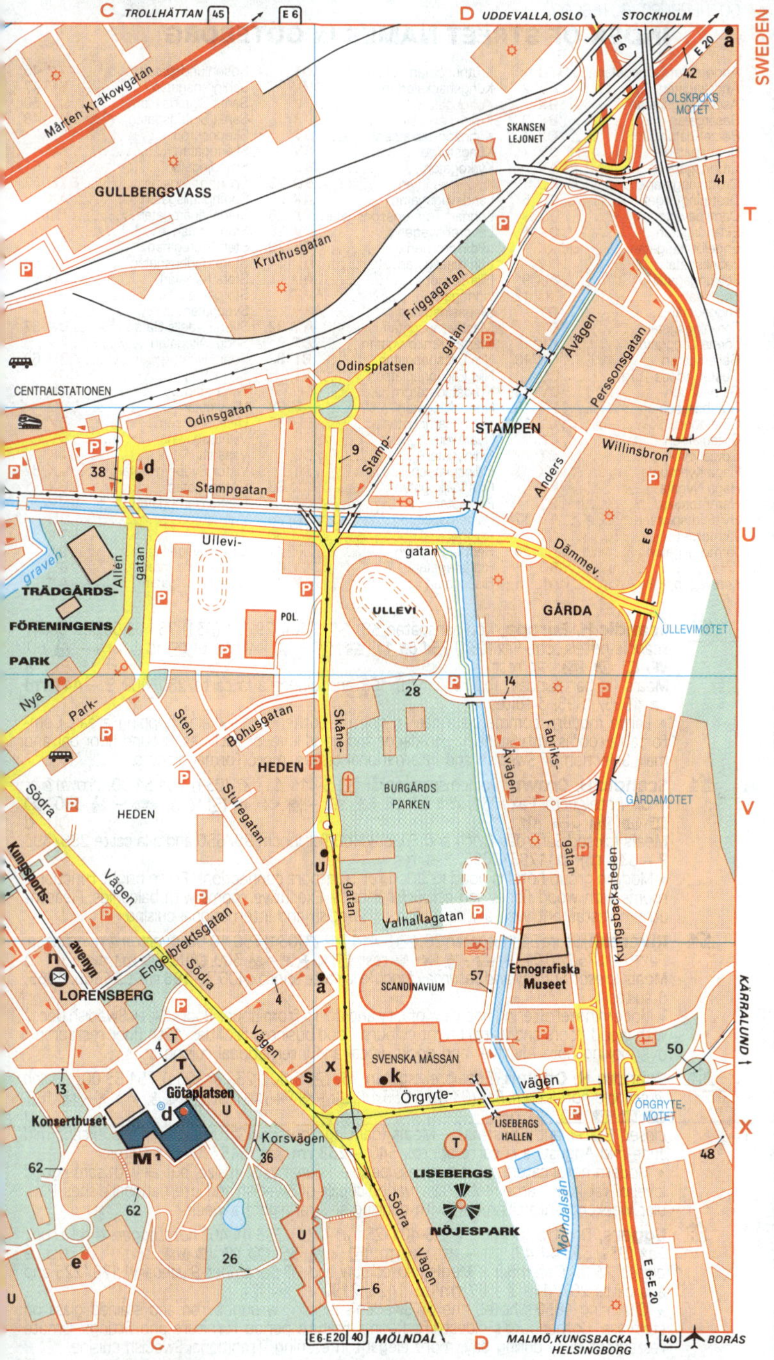

C TROLLHÄTTAN 45 E 6
D UDDEVALLA, OSLO
STOCKHOLM
SWEDEN
E 6
E 20
42
OLSKROKS MOTET
SKANSEN LEJONET
41
Mårten Krakowgatan
GULLBERGSVASS
Kruthusgatan
T
Friggagatan
Odinsplatsen
Åvägen
Perssonsgatan
CENTRALSTATIONEN
Odinsgatan
STAMPEN
9
Stamp-gatan
Willinsbron
Anders
38
d
Stampgatan
Ullevi-gatan
U
graven
Allén
gatan
Dämmev.
TRÄDGÅRDS-FÖRENINGENS PARK
POL.
ULLEVI
GÅRDA
ULLEVIMOTET
n
28
14
Nya Park-
Sten
Bohusgatan
Skåne-gatan
Fabriks-gatan
HEDEN
Södra Vägen
Sturegatan
BURGÅRDS PARKEN
Åvägen
GÅRDAMOTET
V
Kungsports-avenyn
u
Valhallagatan
Kungsbackaleden
Engelbrektsgatan
Södra Vägen
a
SCANDINAVIUM
57
Etnografiska Museet
KÄRRALUND
LORENSBERG
4
T
SVENSKA MÄSSAN
k
50
13
s
x
Götaplatsen
Örgryte-vägen
ÖRGRYTE-MOTET
X
Konserthuset
d
LISEBERGS HALLEN
48
M1
Korsvägen
36
62
LISEBERGS NÖJESPARK
Södra Vägen
Mölndalsån
26
e
6
E 6-E 20
E6-E20 40 MÖLNDAL
MALMÖ, KUNGSBACKA HELSINGBORG
40 BORÅS

INDEX OF STREET NAMES IN GÖTEBORG

Anders Perssonsgatan . . . DTU
Andréegatan . . . AV 2
Aschebergsgatan . . . BX
Basargatan . . . BV 3
Berzeliigatan . . . CX 4
Bohusgatan . . . CV
Brunnsgatan . . . AX
Drottninggatan . . . BU
Drottningtorget . . . BU 5
Dämmevägen . . . DU
Eklandagatan . . . DX 6
Engelbrektsgatan . . . BCVX
Fabriksgatan . . . DV
Folkungagatan . . . DU 9
Fredsgatan . . . BU 12
Friggagatan . . . DT
Föreningsgatan . . . BX
Första Långgatan . . . AV
Geijersgatan . . . CX 13
Gustaf Adolfs Torg . . . BU
Gårdavägen . . . DV 14
Götabergsgatan . . . BX 15
Götaleden . . . BT 16
Götaplatsen . . . CX
Götaälvbron . . . BT
Haga Kyrkogata . . . AX
Haga Nygata . . . AX
Hamntorget . . . BT
Hvitfeldtsplatsen . . . AV 17
Järntorget . . . AV
Järntorgsgatan . . . AV 20
Korsgatan . . . BU
Korsvägen . . . CDX
Kruthusgatan . . . CDT
Kungsbackaleden . . . DVX
Kungsgatan . . . ABV
Kungsportsavenyn . . . BCVX
Kungsportsplatsen . . . BV
Kungstorget . . . BV
Kyrkogatan . . . BU
Köpmansgatan . . . BU 23
Landsvägsgatan . . . AX 25
Lennart Torstenssonsgatan . CX 26
Levgrensvägen . . . DV 28
Lilla Bommen . . . BT 29
Lilla Risåsgatan . . . AX 31
Lilla Torget . . . AU
Linnégatan . . . AVX
Magasinsgatan . . . ABV
Masthamnsgatan . . . AV 32
Mårten Krakowgatan . . . CT
Nils Ericsonsgatan . . . BT 33
Nils Ericsonsplatsen . . . BT
Nordstadstorget . . . BU
Norra Allégatan . . . AV 34
Norra Hamngatan . . . ABU 35
Nya Allén . . . BCV
Odinsgatan . . . CU
Odinsplatsen . . . DT
Olof Wijksgatan . . . CX 36
Parkgatan . . . BCV
Polhemsplatsen . . . CU 38
Postgatan . . . BU 39
Redbergsvägen . . . DT 41
Riddaregatan . . . DT 42
Risåsgatan . . . AX 44
Rosenlundsgatan . . . AV 45
Sahlgrensgatan . . . BV 47
Sankt Sigfrids Plan . . . DX 50
Sankt Sigfridsgatan . . . DX 48
Skeppsbron . . . AU
Skånegatan . . . DV
Smedjegatan . . . AU 51
Spannmålsgatan . . . BTU 52
Sprängkullsgatan . . . AX
Stadstjänaregatan . . . BT 53
Stampgatan . . . CDU
Sten Sturegatan . . . CV
Stora Badhusgatan . . . AU 54
Stora Nygatan . . . BU 55
Storgatan . . . BVX 56
Sveagatan . . . AX
Sven Rydells Gata . . . DX 57
Södra Allégatan . . . AV
Södra Hamngatan . . . ABU 60
Södra Vägen . . . CDX
Torggatan . . . BTU
Ullevigatan . . . CDU
Utsiktsplatsen . . . BX
Valhallagatan . . . DV
Vasagatan . . . BVX
Viktor Rydbergsgatan . . . CX 62
Viktoriagatan . . . BVX
Västra Hamngatan . . . BUV
Willinsbron . . . DU
Åvägen . . . DTV
Örgrytevägen . . . DX
Östra Hamngatan . . . BU
Övre Husargatan . . . AX

Scandic H. Europa, Köpmansgatan 38, S-404 29, (031) 751 65 00, *europa@scandic-hotels.com, Fax (031) 751 65 11,* – rm, – 60. rest BU a
Meals (in bar Sunday) (buffet lunch) 108 and dinner a la carte 280/400 – **447 rm** 1595/1895, 3 suites.
• Large modern commercial hotel in one of Gothenburg's main shopping areas. Comfortable rooms with Scandinavian décor and good level of facilities. Ground floor bar and mall. Selection of Swedish and international dishes, more formal dinners.

Scandic H. Crown, Polhemsplatsen 3, S-411 11, (031) 751 51 00, *crown@scandic-hotels.com, Fax (031) 751 51 11,* – – 300. CU d
Meals *(closed Saturday lunch and Sunday)* (buffet lunch) 98/650 and a la carte 286/393 – **336 rm** 1795/2095, 2 suites.
• Modern group hotel in good location for transport connections. Fresh bright functional rooms with wood floors and colourful fabrics. Executive rooms with balconies. Pleasant atrium restaurant with a wide range of Swedish and international cuisine.

Riverton, Stora Badhusgatan 26, S-411 21, (031) 750 10 00, *riverton@riverton.se, Fax (031) 750 10 01,* – , rest, – 300. AV c
Meals *(closed Sunday and Saturday lunch)* a la carte approx 400 – **186 rm** 1365/1865, 5 suites.
• Modern hotel offering fine view of city and docks from upper floors. Sleek Swedish décor with wood floors and warm bright colours. Good business facilities. 12th floor restaurant, overlooking Göta Älv river and docks. Local and international cuisine.

Scandic H. Opalen, Engelbrektsgatan 73, S-402 23, (031) 751 53 00, *opalen@scandic-hotels.com, Fax (031) 751 53 11,* – , rest, – 180. rest DV u
closed Easter and Christmas – **Meals** (dancing Thursday-Saturday evenings except mid June-mid August) a la carte approx 340 – **238 rm** 1545/2045, 4 suites.
• Modern hotel catering for business people. Rooms vary in size, but all with same good level of facilities. Large restaurant, varied choice of Swedish and international dishes. Popular weekend entertainment, with dancing several nights a week.

Eggers, Drottningtorget, S-401 25, (031) 333 44 40, *hotel.eggers@telia.com, Fax (031) 333 44 49,* – rm, – 55. BU e
closed 23-26 December – **Meals** *(closed July and 20 December-9 January)* 179/225 and a la carte 207/449 – **67 rm** 1425/2190.
• Charming 1850's hotel, one of Sweden's oldest : wrought iron and stained glass on staircase, Gothenburg's oldest lift. Rooms feature period furniture and fittings. Ornate restaurant busy during day, more elegant in evening. Traditional Swedish cuisine.

Novotel Göteborg, Klippan 1, ⊠ S-414 51, Southwest : 3 ½ km by Andréeg taking Kiel-Klippan Ó exit, or boat from Lilla Bommens Hamn ✆ (031) 720 22 00, *info@novotel.se, Fax (031) 720 22 99,* ≤, – 120. rest
***Carnegie Kaj* : Meals** (buffet lunch) 149 and a la carte 237/352 – **143 rm** ⩦ 1390/1520, 5 suites.
◆ Converted brewery on waterfront with view of Göta Älv. Central atrium style lobby. Spacious rooms with international style décor and sofabeds. Restaurant overlooking the harbour. International cooking to appeal to all tastes.

Mornington, Kungsportsavenyn 6, ⊠ S-411 36, ✆ (031) 76 73 400, *goteborg@mornington.se, Fax (031) 711 34 39,* rm, – 45. rest BV e
***Brasserie Lipp* : Meals** *(closed Sunday)* 105/497 and a la carte – **91 rm** ⩦ 1420/2240.
◆ Modern office block style façade conceals hotel on one of the city's most famous shopping streets. Rooms are compact with comfortable functional furniture and bright décor. Pleasant brasserie-style restaurant, hearty home cooking and international fare.

Quality H. Panorama, Eklandagatan 51-53, ⊠ S-400 22, ✆ (031) 767 70 00, *info.panorama@quality.choicehotels.se, Fax (031) 767 70 75,* ≤, rm, – 100. rest DX
Meals 395/595 (dinner) and a la carte 247/468 – **339 rm** ⩦ 1450/1850.
◆ Commercial hotel popular with business people and conferences. Compact functional rooms, larger on top floors. First floor hotel restaurant in Scandinavian brasserie style. International menu.

Victors, Skeppsbroplatsen 1 (4th floor), ⊠ S-411 18, ✆ (031) 17 41 80, *info@victors-hotel.com, Fax (031) 13 96 10,* ≤ Göta Älv river and harbour, rm, – 40. rest AU b
closed 24-26 December – **Meals** *(closed Friday-Sunday)* (dinner only) a la carte 315/465 – **31 rm** ⩦ 1350/1700, 13 suites.
◆ Hotel occupies floors 4-6 of an office block on busy intersection but overlooking harbour. Compact reception and all-purpose dining/breakfast/coffee area. Functional rooms. Good view from restaurant. Choice of international cuisine.

Ramada Tidbloms, Olskroksgatan 23, ⊠ S-416 66, Northeast : 2 ½ km by E 20 ✆ (031) 707 50 00, *info@tidbloms.ramadasweden.se, Fax (031) 707 50 99,* rm, – 70. DT a
Meals *(closed Saturday and Sunday lunch)* 245 (dinner) and a la carte – **42 rm** ⩦ 1190/1500.
◆ Old red brick hotel in quiet residential area. Quaint turret and semi-circular veranda cum conservatory. Room décor in simple traditional style with standard comforts. Rustic circular restaurant. Hunting trophies adorn the walls. Simple steak-house style menu.

Poseidon without rest., Storgatan 33, ⊠ S-411 38, ✆ (031) 10 05 50, *info@hotelposeidon.com, Fax (031) 13 83 91* – BV a
closed 23 December-2 January – **49 rm** ⩦ 980/1250.
◆ Informal hotel in residential area not far from main shopping street. Comfortable neutral décor and functional furnishings in rooms. Accommodation for families available.

Sjömagasinet, Klippans Kulturreservat 5, ⊠ S-414 51, Southwest : 3 ½ km by Andréeg taking Kiel-Klippan Ó exit, or boat from Lilla Bommens Hamn ✆ (031) 775 59 20, *info@sjomagasinet.se, Fax (031) 24 55 39,* ≤, –
closed midsummer, 24-25 and 31 December, Sunday and Saturday lunch – **Meals** - Seafood - (booking essential) (buffet lunch in summer) 325/495 and a la carte 620/945.
Spec. Lobster soup, carpaccio of langoustines. Pan-fried cod, scallops and truffles. Milk chocolate panna cotta, vanilla ice cream.
◆ Delightful 18C former East India Company waterfront warehouse. Forever busy restaurant on two floors with ship's mast and charming terrace. Accomplished seafood cooking.

Swea Hof (at Elite Plaza H.), Västra Hamngatan 3, ⊠ S-404 22, ✆ (031) 720 40 40, *Fax (031) 720 40 10* – BU s
closed 24-26 December and Sunday – **Meals** 295/670 and a la carte 485/670.
◆ Striking atrium style restaurant in heart of hotel with glass roof on metal framework and open plan kitchen. Dinner menu offers elaborate, modern cuisine.

Thörnströms Kök, Teknologgatan 3, ⊠ S-411 32, ✆ (031) 16 20 66, *info@thornstromskok.com, Fax (031) 16 40 17* – CX e
closed 22 June-9 August, Sunday and Monday dinner and Bank Holidays – **Meals** (booking essential) (dinner only) 385/545 and a la carte 430/540.
◆ Restaurant in quiet residential area near university. Stylish elegant ambience and décor. Formal service. Menu offers gourmet international dishes.

28 + (Lyxell), Götabergsgatan 28, ✉ S-411 34, ☎ (031) 20 21 61, *28plus@telia.com*, *Fax (031) 81 97 57* – MC AE DC VISA JCB. ✻ BX n
closed 24-29 March, 3 July-21 August, 23-26 December, 31 December-1 January and Sunday – **Meals** (dinner only) a la carte 500/725 ♀.
Spec. Pan fried scallops with calamari and cockles. Breast of duck, cep cannelloni and duck foie gras. Cherry soufflé, Tahitian vanilla ice cream.
◆ Cellar restaurant down a steep flight of steps. Fine wine cellar accessible to diners. Special chef to describe cheeses. Modern Swedish cuisine with emphasis on seafood.

Linnéa, Södra Vägen 32, ✉ S-412 54, ☎ (031) 16 11 83, *info@restauranglinnea.com*, *Fax (031) 18 12 92* – MC AE DC VISA JCB. ✻ CX s
closed Christmas, New Year, Sunday, Saturday lunch and Bank Holidays – **Meals** 395/595 (dinner) and a la carte 503/559 ♀.
◆ Well run restaurant ; changing summer and winter décor. Simple lunch venue ; more formal and elaborate for dinner - stylish place settings. Well prepared modern Swedish cuisine.

Basement (Wagner), Götabergsgatan 28, ✉ S-411 34, ☎ (031) 28 27 29, *bokning@restbasement.com*, *Fax (031) 28 27 37* – MC AE DC VISA. ✻ BX n
closed 4 July-18 August, 23 December-6 January and Sunday – **Meals** (dinner only) 395/825 and a la carte 390/540 ♀.
Spec. Porcini consommé. Roast cod, anchovy potato. Chocolate biscuit, espresso ice cream.
◆ Restaurant below street level with white walls enlivened by contemporary paintings and lithographs. Imaginative modern cuisine using Swedish produce ; speciality tasting menus.

Hos Pelle, Djupedalsgatan 2, ✉ S-413 07, ☎ (031) 12 10 31, *hos.pelle@swipnet.se*, *Fax (031) 775 38 32* – MC AE DC VISA JCB AX a
closed 5 weeks in summer, 25 December, 1 January and Sunday – **Meals** (dinner only) a la carte 375/595 ♀.
◆ Popular local restaurant with comfortable atmosphere, displaying Swedish art. Serves classic and modern Swedish cuisine prepared to high standard. Ground floor bistro.

Fiskekrogen, Lilla Torget 1, ✉ S-411 18, ☎ (031) 10 10 05, *info@fiskekrogen.com*, *Fax (031) 10 10 06* – ⇔ ▤. MC AE DC VISA. ✻ AU f
closed July, 22 December-7 January and Sunday – **Meals** - Seafood - (buffet lunch) 195/795 and a la carte 455/730 ♀.
◆ Busy 1920's restaurant with reputation for its seafood. Striking rooms with high ceilings, wood panelling, columns and modern Scandinavian art.

Kock & Vin, Viktoriagatan 12, ✉ 411 25, ☎ (031) 701 79 79, *info@kockvin.se*, *Fax (031) 711 49 60* – ▤. MC AE DC VISA. ✻ BX a
closed 10 July-14 August, 23-26 December and Sunday – **Meals** (dinner only) 495/695 and a la carte 335/585 ♀.
◆ Attractive candlelit neighbourhood restaurant. Modern paintings but 19C painted ceiling. A la carte or set menu with complementary wines ; best of Swedish ingredients.

Fond, Götaplatsen, ✉ S-412 56, ☎ (031) 81 25 80, *fond@fondrestaurang.com*, *Fax (031) 18 37 90*, 佘 – ⇔ ▤. MC AE DC VISA. ✻ CX d
closed 4 weeks in summer, 2 weeks Christmas, Sunday, Saturday lunch and Bank Holidays – **Meals** 655 and a la carte 530/675 ♀.
Spec. Deep fried crayfish, orange cream sauce. Fillet of venison, glazed pearl onions and blue cheese croquettes. Milk chocolate and cinnamon mousse.
◆ Bright semi-circular glass structure outside Art Museum houses contemporary restaurant. Traditional Swedish fixed lunch as lighter option and modern elaborate dinner menus.

La Cucina Italiana, Skånegatan 33, ✉ S-412 52, ☎ (031) 16 63 07, *pietro@swipnet.ie*, *Fax (031) 16 63 07* – ⇔. MC AE DC VISA JCB DX x
closed Christmas-New Year – **Meals** - Italian - 99 (lunch) and dinner a la carte 400/550.
◆ Intimate snug authentic Italian restaurant, away from city centre, with real rustic décor. Good value modern menus, changed daily.

Trädgår'n, Nya Allén, ✉ S-411 38, ☎ (031) 10 20 80, *info@trakanten.se*, *Fax (031) 774 08 80*, 佘 – ⇔ rest,. MC AE DC VISA. ✻ CV n
closed 24-25 June, 23-24 December and Sunday lunch – **Meals** 245/595 and a la carte 365/575 ♀.
◆ A modern complex backing onto a charming park. Coolly decorated restaurant with large terrace with a lighter menu and a separate Cabaret/night club. International cooking.

BRASSERIES

Tvåkanten, Kungsportsavenyn 27, ✉ S-411 36, ☎ (031) 18 21 15, *info@tvakanten.se*, *Fax (031) 20 13 93*, 佘 – ⇔ ▤. MC AE DC VISA. ✻ CX n
closed 24-25 June, 23-24 December and Sunday lunch – **Meals** 245/595 and a la carte 365/575 ♀.
◆ Busy characterful restaurant in city centre setting attracting varied clientele. Spacious dining rooms with oak floors and large bar. Swedish fare.

Herr Dahls, Kungstorget 14, ✉ S-411 10, ✆ (031) 13 45 55, *info@herrdahls.nu, Fax (031) 13 45 59,* – . BV x
closed 24-25 December and 31 December-1 January – **Meals** 445 (dinner) and a la carte 355/630 ♀.
◆ Centrally located restaurant with terrace and adjoining shop. Large hatch giving view of kitchen. Set menu or à la carte for dinner ; good quality Swedish produce.

Ivy Grill, Vasaplatsen 2, ✉ -411 28, ✆ (031) 711 44 04, *info@ivygrill.com, Fax (031) 711 29 55,* – . BV z
closed Sunday-Monday – **Meals** (dinner only) 350/485 and a la carte 330/460 ♀.
◆ Step down from the lively bar to this trendy restaurant with its unusual décor. Menu specialises in grills ; simple lunch on the terrace in summer only.

at Eriksberg *West : 6 km by Götaälvbron* BT *and Lundbyleden, or boat from Lilla Bommens Hamn*

Quality Hotel 11, Maskingatan 11, ✉ S-417 64, ✆ (031) 779 11 11, *info.hotel11@quality.choicehotels.se, Fax (031) 779 11 10,* ← – – 1200. rest
closed Christmas-New Year – ***Kök & Bar 67 :*** **Meals** *(closed lunch Saturday and Sunday)* 206 (lunch) and dinner a la carte 311/399 – **177 rm** 1455/1850, 7 suites.
◆ Striking former shipbuilding warehouse, part see-through there is so much glass ! Rooms feature stylish modern Scandinavian interior design with pale wood and bright fabrics. Upper floor restaurant, waterway views. International cooking.

at Landvetter Airport *East : 30 km by Rd 40* DX – ✉ *S-438 13 Landvetter :*

Landvetter Airport H., ✉ S-438 13, ✆ (031) 97 75 50, *info@landvetterairporthotel.se, Fax (031) 94 64 70,* , – , rm, .
Meals 198 (lunch) and a la carte 190/436 ♀ – **103 rm** 1295/1445, 1 suite.
◆ Airport hotel a short walk from the terminal. Rooms are bright and welcoming and feature typical Swedish décor in bright colours. Full modern and business facilities. Relaxed restaurant and terrace off the main lobby. Offers popular Swedish fare.

Switzerland

Suisse
Schweiz
Svizzera

BERN – BASLE – GENEVA – ZÜRICH

PRACTICAL INFORMATION

LOCAL CURRENCY – PRICES

Swiss Franc: *100 CHF = 65,54 euro (€) (December 2004)*

National Holiday in Switzerland: *1st August.*

LANGUAGES SPOKEN

German, French and Italian are usually spoken in all administrative departments, shops, hotels and restaurants.

AIRLINES

SWISS International Air Lines Ltd.: *Genève-Airport, 1215 Genève 15, ✆ 0848 852 000, Unique Zürich airport, 8058 Zürich 58, ✆ 0848 852 000.*

AIR FRANCE: *15 rte de l'Aéroport, 1215 Genève 15, ✆ 0228 278 787, Fax 0228 278 781.*
Europastr. 31, 8152 Glattbrugg, ✆ 014 391 818.

ALITALIA: *Genève-Airport, 1215 Genève 15, ✆ 0227 982 080, Fax 0227 885 630.*
Neugutstr. 66, 8600 Dübendorf, ✆ 018 244 550, Fax 018 244 510.

AMERICAN AIRLINES: *Löwenstr. 2, 8001 Zürich, ✆ 016 545 256, Fax 016 545 259.*

BRITISH AIRWAYS: *Chantepoulet 13, 1201 Genève, ✆ 0848 801 010, Fax 0229 061 223.*
Löwenstr. 29, 8001 Zürich, ✆ 0848 845 845, Fax 0848 845 849.

LUFTHANSA: *29 rte de Pré-Bois, 1215 Genève-Cointrin, ✆ 0229 295 151, Fax 0229 295 150.*
Gutenbergstr. 10, 8002 Zürich, ✆ 014 479 966, Fax 012 867 205.

POSTAL SERVICES

In large towns, post offices are open from 7.30am to noon and 1.45pm to 6pm, and Saturdays until 11am. The telephone system is fully automatic.
Many public phones are equipped with phone card or credit card facilities. Prepaid phone cards are available from post offices, railway stations and tobacconist's shops.

SHOPPING

Department stores are generally open from 8.30am to 6.30pm, except on Saturdays when they close at 4 or 5pm. They are closed on Monday mornings.
In the index of street names, those printed in red are where the principal shops are found.

TIPPING

In hotels, restaurants and cafés the service charge is generally included in the prices.

SPEED LIMITS – MOTORWAYS

The speed limit on motorways is 120 km/h - 74 mph, on other roads 80 km/h - 50 mph, and in built up areas 50 km/h - 31 mph.
Driving on Swiss motorways is subject to the purchase of a single rate annual road tax (vignette) obtainable from border posts, tourist offices and post offices.

SEAT BELTS

The wearing of seat belts is compulsory in all Swiss cantons for drivers and all passengers.

BERN

3000 Bern 729 G 5, 551 J 7 – *pop. 122 707 – alt. 548.*

Basle 100 – Lyons 315 – Munich 435 – Paris 556 – Strasbourg 235 – Turin 311.

Tourist Center, Bahnhofplatz 10 A – Tourist Center, at Bärengraben ✆ 0313 281 212, info-res@bernetourism.ch, Fax 0313 281 277 – T.C.S., Thunstr. 63, ✆ 0313 563 434, Fax 0313 563 435 – A.C.S., Theaterplatz 13, ✆ 0313 113 813, Fax 0313 112 637.

27 Bern/Moossee, ✉ 3053 Münchenbuchsee, ✆ 0318 685 050, Fax 0318 685 049, North : 11 km.

18 Blumisberg, ✉ 3184 Wünnewil (mid March-mid November), ✆ 0264 963 438, Fax 0264 963 523, Southwest : 18 km.

9 at Oberburg, ✉ 3414 (March-November), ✆ 0344 241 030, Fax 0344 241 034, Northeast : 20 km.

9 Aaeretal, ✉ 3629 Kiesen, ✆ 0317 820 000, Fax 0317 812 641, South : 22 km.

Bern-Belp, ✆ 0319 602 111.

See: *Old Bern★★ : Marktgasse★* DZ *; Clock Tower★* EZ **C** *; Kramgasse★* EZ *; views★ from the Nydegg Bridge* FY *; Bear Pit★* FZ *; Cathedral of St Vincent★* EZ *: tympanum★★, panorama★★ from the tower* EZ *– Rosengarden* FY *: view★ of the Old Bern – Botanical Garden★* DY *– Dählhölzli Zoo★ – Church of St Nicholas★.*

Museums: *Fine Arts Museum★★ : Paul Klee Collection★★* DY *– Natural History Museum★★* EZ *– Bernese Historical Museum★★* EZ *– Alpine Museum★★* EZ *– Communication Museum★* EZ.

Excursions: *The Gurten★★.*

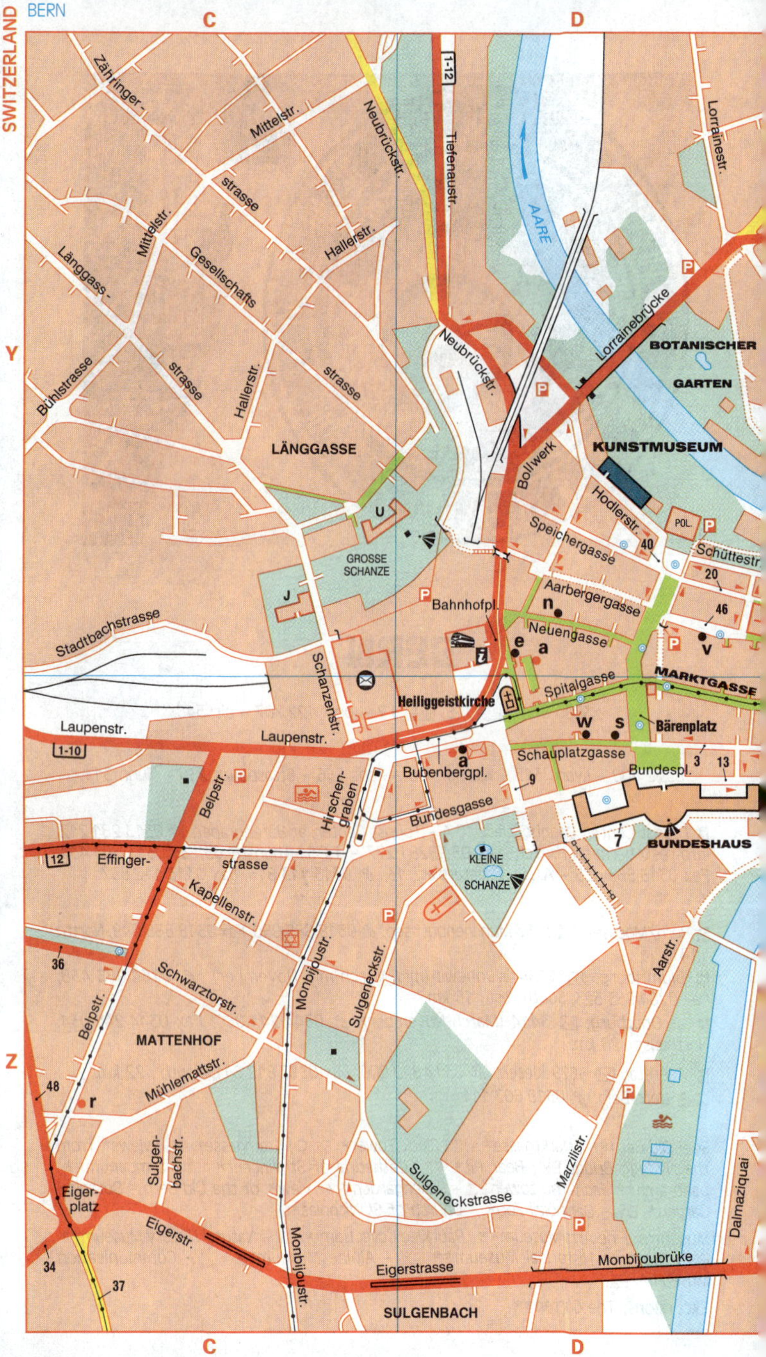
C
D
Y
Z
Zähringer-
Mittelstr.
strasse
Neubrückstr.
Tiefenaustr.
1-12
AARE
Lorrainestr.
Mittelstr.
Hallerstr.
Länggass-
Gesellschafts
strasse
Hallerstr.
strasse
Bühlstrasse
Neubrückstr.
Lorrainebrücke
BOTANISCHER
GARTEN
LÄNGGASSE
Bollwerk
KUNSTMUSEUM
Hodlerstr.
POL.
Speichergasse
Schüttestr.
GROSSE
SCHANZE
Aarbergergasse
Bahnhofpl.
Neuengasse
Stadtbachstrasse
MARKTGASSE
Spitalgasse
Schanzenstr.
Heiliggeistkirche
Bärenplatz
Laupenstr.
Laupenstr.
1-10
Schauplatzgasse
Bundespl.
Bubenbergpl.
Belpstr.
Hirschengraben
Bundesgasse
BUNDESHAUS
12
Effinger-
strasse
KLEINE
SCHANZE
Kapellenstr.
Aarstr.
Schwarztorstr.
Monbijoustr.
Sulgeneckstr.
Belpstr.
MATTENHOF
Mühlemattstr.
Sulgenbachstr.
Marzilistr.
Dalmaziquai
Sulgeneckstrasse
Eigerplatz
Eigerstr.
Monbijoustr.
Eigerstrasse
Monbijoubrüke
SULGENBACH

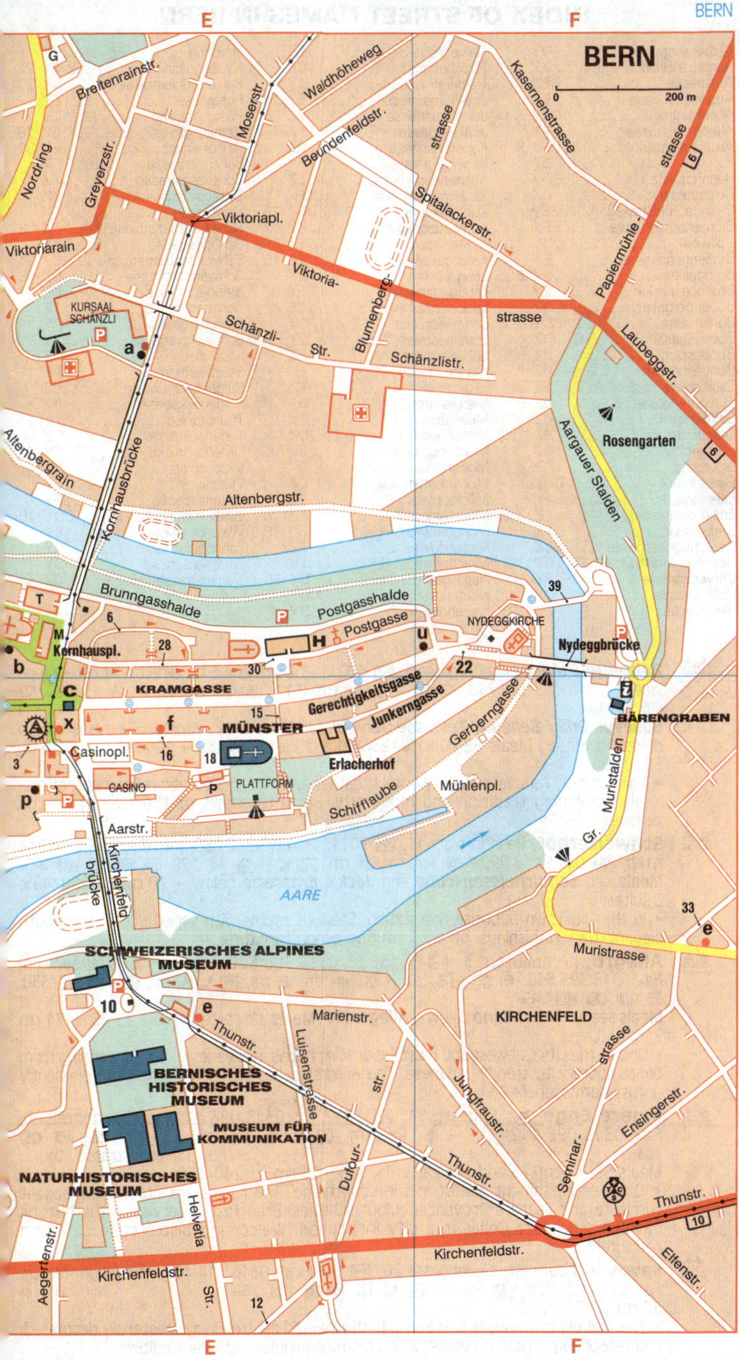
BERN
0
200 m
E
F
Y
Z
G
Breitenrainstr.
Nordring
Greyerzstr.
Moserstr.
Waldhöheweg
Beundenfeldstr.
strasse
Kasernenstrasse
strasse
6
Viktoriarain
Viktoriapl.
Spitalackerstr.
Viktoria-
Blumenberg-
strasse
Papiermühle-
Laubeggstr.
KURSAAL SCHÄNZLI
P
a
Schänzli-
Str.
Schänzlistr.
Rosengarten
Aargauer Stalden
6
Altenbergrain
Kornhausbrücke
Altenbergstr.
39
Brunngasshalde
Postgasshalde
T
6
P
Postgasse
NYDEGGKIRCHE
M
Kornhauspl.
28
H
u
Nydeggbrücke
b
30
22
P
C
KRAMGASSE
Gerechtigkeitsgasse
Junkerngasse
x
15
f
MÜNSTER
Gerberngasse
BÄRENGRABEN
3
Casinopl.
16
18
Erlacherhof
Muristalden
p
CASINO
P
PLATTFORM
Mühlenpl.
P
Schifflaube
Aarstr.
Gr.
Kirchenfeld
brücke
AARE
33
e
Muristrasse
SCHWEIZERISCHES ALPINES MUSEUM
P
10
e
Marienstr.
KIRCHENFELD
Thunstr.
strasse
Luisenstrasse
BERNISCHES HISTORISCHES MUSEUM
str.
Jungfraustr.
Ensingerstr.
MUSEUM FÜR KOMMUNIKATION
Dufour-
Thunstr.
Seminar-
NATURHISTORISCHES MUSEUM
Thunstr.
Helvetia
10
Aegertenstr.
Kirchenfeldstr.
Elfenstr.
Kirchenfeldstr.
Str.
12
E
F

INDEX OF STREET NAMES IN BERN

Aarbergergasse . . . . DY
Aargauer Stalden . . . . FY
Aarstrasse . . . . DEZ
Aegertenstrasse . . . . EZ
Altenbergrain . . . . DEY
Altenbergstrasse . . . . EFY
Amthausgasse . . . . DEZ 3
Bärenplatz . . . . DZ
Bahnhofplatz . . . . DY
Belpstrasse . . . . CZ
Beundenfeldstrasse . . . . EFY
Blumenbergstrasse . . . . EFY
Bollwerk . . . . DY
Breitenrainstrasse . . . . EY
Brunngasse . . . . EY 6
Brunngasshalde . . . . EY
Bubenbergplatz . . . . DZ
Bühlstrasse . . . . CY
Bundesgasse . . . . DZ
Bundesplatz . . . . DZ
Bundesterrasse . . . . DZ 7
Casinoplatz . . . . EZ
Christoffelgasse . . . . DZ 9
Dalmaziquai . . . . DZ
Dufourstrasse . . . . EZ
Effingerstrasse . . . . CZ
Eigerplatz . . . . CZ
Eigerstrasse . . . . CDZ
Elfenstrasse . . . . FZ
Ensingerstrasse . . . . FZ
Gerberngasse . . . . FZ
Gerechtigkeitsgasse . . . . EYZ
Gesellschaftsstrasse . . . . CY
Greyerzstrasse . . . . EY
Hallerstrasse . . . . CY
Helvetiaplatz . . . . EZ 10
Helvetiastrasse . . . . EZ
Hirschengraben . . . . CZ
Holderstrasse . . . . DY
Jubiläumsstrasse . . . . EZ 12
Jungfraustrasse . . . . FZ
Junkerngasse . . . . EFZ
Kapellenstrasse . . . . CZ
Kasernenstrasse . . . . FY
Kirchenfeldbrücke . . . . EZ
Kirchenfeldstrasse . . . . EFZ
Kochergasse . . . . DEZ 13
Kornhausbrücke . . . . EY
Kramgasse . . . . EZ
Kreuzgasse . . . . EZ 15
Längassstrasse . . . . CY
Laubeggstrasse . . . . FY
Laupenstrasse . . . . CZ
Lorrainebrücke . . . . DY
Lorrainestrasse . . . . DY
Luisenstrasse . . . . EZ
Marienstrasse . . . . EZ
Marktgasse . . . . DEZ
Marzilistrasse . . . . DZ
Mittelstrasse . . . . CY
Monbijoubrücke . . . . DZ
Monbijoustrasse . . . . CZ
Moserstrasse . . . . EY
Mühlemattstrasse . . . . CZ
Mühlenplatz . . . . FZ
Münstergasse . . . . EZ 16
Münsterplatz . . . . EZ 18
Muristalden . . . . FZ
Muristrasse . . . . FZ
Nägeligasse . . . . DY 20
Neubrückstrasse . . . . CDY
Neuengasse . . . . DY
Nordring . . . . EY
Nydeggasse . . . . FY 22
Papiermühlestrasse . . . . BX 27
Postgasse . . . . EY
Postgasshalde . . . . EY
Rathausgasse . . . . EY 28
Rathausplatz . . . . EY 30
Schänzlistrasse . . . . EY
Schanzenstrasse . . . . CYZ
Schauplatzgasse . . . . DZ
Schifflaube . . . . EY
Schosshaldenstrasse . . . . FZ 33
Schüttestrasse . . . . DEY
Schwarzenburgstrasse . . . . CZ 34
Schwarztorstrasse . . . . CZ 36
Seftigenstrasse . . . . CZ 37
Seminarstrasse . . . . FZ
Speichergasse . . . . DY
Spitalackerstrasse . . . . EFY
Spitalgasse . . . . DZ
Stadtbachstrasse . . . . CY
Sulgenbachstrasse . . . . CZ
Sulgeneckstrasse . . . . CDZ
Thunstrasse . . . . EFZ
Tiefenaustrasse . . . . DY
Untertorbrücke . . . . FY 39
Viktoriaplatz . . . . EY
Viktoriarain . . . . EY
Viktoriastrasse . . . . EFY
Waisenhausplatz . . . . DY 40
Waldhöheweg . . . . EY
Zähringerstrasse . . . . CY
Zeughausgasse . . . . DY 46
Zieglerstrasse . . . . CZ 48

Bellevue Palace, Kochergasse 3, ✉ 3001, ☎ 0313 204 545, *direktion@bellevue-palace.ch, Fax 0313 114 743,* – rm, rm, rm, rest, – 15/350. EZ p

Bellevue Grill / Bellevue Terrasse : *(Grill : closed lunch and in summer ; Terrasse : closed dinner in winter)* **Meals** 68 (lunch)/125 and a la carte 75/135 – **100 rm** 350/540, 30 suites.

◆ This recently renovated luxury hotel breathes an air of aristocratic refinement, effortlessly combining tradition and modernity. Beautiful views of the river from the terrace.

Schweizerhof, Bahnhofplatz 11, ✉ 3011, ☎ 0313 268 080, *info@schweizerhof-bern.ch, Fax 0313 268 090* – rm, rm, – 15/120. DY e

Meals see ***Schultheissenstube*** and ***Jack's Brasserie*** below – **78 rm** 290/495, 6 suites.

◆ In the Old Town opposite the station. Spacious rooms with varied décor, some with elegant, dark furnishings, others featuring period furniture.

Allegro, Kornhausstr. 3, ✉ 3013, ☎ 0313 395 500, *allegro@kursaal-bern.ch, Fax 0313 395 510,* – rm, rm, rm, – 15/350. EY a

Meals see also ***Meridiano*** below – ***Allegretto :*** **Meals** a la carte 44/83 – 25 – **171 rm** 215/450.

◆ One of the city's newest and most fascinating hotels, in a variety of styles ranging from contemporary to trendy Japanese. The Allegretto has an open kitchen and pleasantly unfussy atmosphere.

Innere Enge, Engestr. 54, ✉ 3012, ☎ 0313 096 111, *info@zghotels.ch, Fax 0313 096 112,* – rm, rm, – 20. by Tiefenaustrasse DY

Meals 50 (lunch)/75 and a la carte 45/103 – **26 rm** 240/360.

◆ Quiet establishment almost in the countryside. The rooms are fitted with elegant furniture and feature Provençal colour schemes. Breakfast is served in the historic Pavillon. The Jazz Cellar is a city institution. Welcoming bistro-style café and restaurant.

Savoy without rest, Neuengasse 26, ✉ 3011, ☎ 0313 114 405, *info@zghotels.ch, Fax 0313 121 978* – DY n

56 rm 225/290.

◆ This fine old town house is in Bern's pedestrianised centre. Bright, tastefully decorated, and reasonably spacious rooms, with up-to-the-minute technical facilities.

Bristol without rest, Schauplatzgasse 10, ✉ 3011, ☎ 0313 110 101, *reception@bristolbern.ch, Fax 0313 119 479,* – ▮ ✈ TV ☎. AE ⓓ MC VISA JCB DZ w
92 rm ☕ 190/300.
◆ This old town house has been completely refurbished and accommodates its guests in modern rooms with massive wooden furniture. Small sauna shared with the Hotelbern.

Bären without rest, Schauplatzgasse 4, ✉ 3011, ☎ 0313 113 367, *reception@baerenbern.ch, Fax 0313 116 983* – ▮ ✈ TV ☎. AE ⓓ MC VISA JCB DZ s
57 rm ☕ 190/300.
◆ Just a stone's throw from the Bundesplatz, a hotel with rooms furnished in contemporary style with a good range of technical facilities for business travellers.

Belle Epoque, Gerechtigkeitsgasse 18, ✉ 3011, ☎ 0313 114 336, *info@belle-epoque.ch, Fax 0313 113 936* – ▮, ✈ rm, TV ☎. AE ⓓ MC VISA JCB FY u
Meals 29 (lunch)/68 and a la carte 48/95 – ☕ 19 – **17 rm** 245/340.
◆ A charming hotel in Bern's beautiful Old Town. From the lovely foyer to the tasteful rooms, there is a wealth of Art Nouveau details and original pieces. Light lunches and speciality roasts in the evening.

Hotelbern, Zeughausgasse 9, ✉ 3011, ☎ 0313 292 222, *hotelbern@hotelbern.ch, Fax 0313 292 299,* – ▮, ✈ rm, TV ♿ rm, – 15/120. AE ⓓ MC VISA JCB EY b
***Kurierstube** : (closed July and Sunday)* **Meals** 33 (lunch)/68 and a la carte 52/111 –
7 Stube **: Meals** a la carte 36/92 – **100 rm** ☕ 255/335.
◆ This establishment in the heart of the Old Town is proud to bear the name of city and canton. Rooms with functional furniture and fittings, plus good facilities for seminars. Classically elegant Kurierstube. Traditional cuisine in the 7-Stube.

Novotel, Guisanplatz 2, ✉ 3014, ☎ 0313 390 909, *H5009@accor.com, Fax 0313 390 910* – ▮, ✈ rm, ▤ TV ☎ ♿ rm, – 15/120. AE ⓓ MC VISA Northeast by Papiermühlestrasse FY
Meals a la carte 42/89 – ☕ 25 – **112 rm** 169/230.
◆ Modern rooms with good technical mod cons, plus a light, contemporary restaurant, right next to the Bern Expo complex. The bar pays tribute to Germany's 1954 World Cup win - "The Miracle of Bern" - at the now rebuilt Wankdorf Stadium nearby.

City without rest, Bubenbergplatz 7, ✉ 3011, ☎ 0313 115 377, *city-ab@fhotels.ch, Fax 0313 110 636* – ▮ TV. AE ⓓ MC VISA JCB DZ a
☕ 18 – **58 rm** 135/210.
◆ This hotel is located right by the station. Contemporary rooms with decent, timeless furnishings and parquet floors throughout.

Kreuz, Zeughausgasse 41, ✉ 3011, ☎ 0313 299 595, *info@hotelkreuz-bern.ch, Fax 0313 299 596,* – ▮, ✈ rm, TV ☎ – 15/120. AE ⓓ MC VISA JCB DY v
Meals *(1st floor) (closed 2 July - 14 August, 18 December - 10 January, Saturday and Sunday)* a la carte 32/62 – **100 rm** ☕ 155/210.
◆ This hotel specialises in meetings and conferences. Most rooms are in contemporary style with dark wooden furniture. Seminar rooms of various types are available.

Ibis without rest, Guisanplatz 4, ✉ 3014, ☎ 0313 351 200, *H5007@accor.com, Fax 0313 351 210* – ▮ ▤ TV ☎ ♿ rm, . AE ⓓ MC VISA
☕ 14 – **96 rm** 109. Northeast by Papiermühlestrasse FY
◆ Simple, practical and affordable, the bedrooms here are clean and bright. A snack menu is available around the clock at the bar.

Schultheissenstube - Hotel Schweizerhof, Bahnhofplatz 11, ✉ 3011, ☎ 0313 268 080, *info@schweizerhof-bern.ch, Fax 0313 268 090* – AE ⓓ MC VISA JCB
closed July - August, Saturday lunch, Sunday and Bank Holidays – **Meals** (1st floor) 75 (lunch)/150 and a la carte 91/166. DY e
◆ On the first floor of the Schweizerhof, a small restaurant with lovely place settings. Beyond is the cosy Simmertalerstube with its authentically rustic atmosphere.

Meridiano - Hotel Allegro, Kornhausstr. 3, ✉ 3013, ☎ 0313 395 245, *allegro@kursaal-bern.ch, Fax 0313 395 510,* ← Bern and mountains, – ▤ P. AE ⓓ MC VISA JCB EY a
closed 10 July - 8 August, Saturday lunch, Sunday and Monday – **Meals** 56 (lunch)/135 and a la carte 70/138.
◆ The highlights of this restaurant on the fifth floor of the Hotel Allegro are the stylish modern ambience and the striking panorama of Bern and the mountains from the terrace.

Scala, Schweizerhofpassage 7, ✉ 3011, ☎ 0313 264 545, *antimo@ristorante-scala.ch, Fax 0313 264 546,* – AE ⓓ MC VISA JCB DY a
closed mid July - mid August and Sunday – **Meals** a la carte 60/98.
◆ Bright, modern restaurant in elegant Italian style on the first floor of one of Bern's shopping arcades. Parquet floors add to the congenial ambience.

Jack's Brasserie - Hotel Schweizerhof, Bahnhofplatz 11, ✉ 3011, ✆ 0313 268 080, *info@schweizerhof-bern.ch, Fax 0313 268 090* – ▤. AE ⓓ MC VISA JCB DY e
Meals 75 (lunch) and a la carte 62/98.
◆ On the ground floor of the Hotel Schweizerhof, this eating place is in refined brasserie style with nicely upholstered benches. Separate entrance, contemporary menu.

Mille Sens, Bubenbergplatz 9, in the market hall, ✉ 3011, ✆ 0313 292 929, *info@millesens.ch, Fax 0313 292 991* – AE ⓓ MC VISA DZ a
closed 18 - 31 July, Sunday and Bank Holidays ; from July - August also Monday dinner and Saturday lunch – **Meals** 59 (lunch)/98 and a la carte 69/101 – ***Marktplatz* : Meals** a la carte 50/95.
◆ A modern restaurant in the midst of busy shops : black leather chairs, smart white tablecloths, parquet beneath your feet and air ducts along the ceiling. The no-nonsense Marktplatz bistro serves a concise and well-priced menu.

Kirchenfeld, Thunstr. 5, ✉ 3005, ✆ 0313 510 278, *Fax 0313 518 416,* – AE ⓓ MC VISA EZ e
closed Sunday and Monday – **Meals** 46 (lunch)/62 and a la carte 50/92.
◆ This neo-Baroque edifice contains within its walls a garden café and a separate main room, both of which serve contemporary-style meals.

Wein und Sein (Blum), Münstergasse 50, ✉ 3011, ✆ 0313 119 844, *blum@weinundsein.ch* – ▤. MC VISA. EZ f
closed 17 July - 8 August, 24 December - 4 January, Sunday and Monday – **Meals** *(dinner only)* (set menu only) (booking essential) 88.
Spec. Berner Trüffel (October-November). Reh aus der Sommerjagd (June - July). Gebackene Desserts (winter).
◆ This is a typical Bern cellar restaurant, newly refurbished and with a wine bar. Gourmets come here in the evenings for a fascinating menu, changed daily.

Felsenau, Fährstr. 2, ✉ 3004, ✆ 0313 012 254, *felsenau@bluewin.ch, Fax 0313 052 258,* – P. AE ⓓ MC VISA North by Tiefenaustrasse DY
closed Sunday – **Meals** 75 and a la carte 43/88.
◆ This listed inn, a little way out of the centre, serves seasonal cuisine with a Mediterranean note. Pretty garden terrace.

Frohegg, Belpstr. 51, ✉ 3007, ✆ 0313 822 524, *Fax 0313 822 527,* – AE ⓓ MC VISA CZ r
Meals *(closed Sunday)* (booking essential) 49 (lunch)/58 and a la carte 45/92.
◆ In an outer part of town, this is a local restaurant with an attractive, subdivided interior and a terrace off the rear courtyard. Sensibly-priced plain food.

Schosshalde, Kleiner Muristalden 40, ✉ 3006, ✆ 0313 524 523, *Fax 0313 521 091,* – P. AE ⓓ MC VISA FZ e
closed 18 July - 14 August, Saturday lunch and Sunday – **Meals** - Italian rest. - (booking essential) 60 and a la carte 43/96.
◆ Diners are made to feel welcome in this inviting little restaurant with its Italian decor. Wide range of dishes including fish specialities.

at Muri *Southeast : 3,5 km by Thunstrasse – alt. 560 – ✉ 3074 Muri bei Bern :*

Sternen, Thunstr. 80, ✆ 0319 507 111, *info@sternenmuri.ch, Fax 0319 507 100,* – ⇅ TV P – 15/120. AE ⓓ MC VISA
Meals 37 (lunch) and a la carte 42/90 – **44 rm** 180/235.
◆ Village centre hotel in typical Bernese country style. Bright, functional rooms in the original house and annex. The "Läubli" and the lounge bar serve traditional dishes.

at Liebefeld *Southwest : 3 km direction Schwarzenburg – alt. 563 – ✉ 3097 Liebefeld :*

Landhaus, Schwarzenburgstr. 134, ✆ 0319 710 758, *landhausliebefeld@freesurf.ch, Fax 0319 720 249,* – P. AE ⓓ MC VISA.
Meals (booking essential) – ***Rôtisserie* : Meals** 88 and a la carte 61/118 – ***Taverne Alsacienne* : Meals** 47 (dinner) and a la carte 49/85.
◆ This governor's residence of 1641 houses a bright and cheerful rotisserie serving modern cuisine. The former prison cells downstairs are now stocked with fine wines. The rustic Taverne Alsacienne offers regional specialities, including tartes flambées.

Write to us...
If you have any comments on the contents of this Guide.
Your praise as well as your criticisms will receive careful consideration and, with your assistance, we will be able to add to our stock of information and, where necessary, amend our judgments.
Thank you in advance!

BASLE (BASEL) 729 G3 551 K3 315 J11 – *165 051 – alt. 277.*

See : *Old Town★ : Cathedral★★ (Münster) : ≤★ "Pfalz" terrace* CY *– Fish Market Fountain★ (Fischmarktbrunnen)* BY *– Old Streets★* BY *– Zoological Garden★★★* AZ *– The Port (Hafen) ✻★, "From Basle to the High Seas"★ Exhibition – City Hall★* BY **H.**

Museums : *Fine Arts★★★ (Kunstmuseum)* CY *– Historical★★ (Historisches Museum)* BY *– Ethnographic★ (Museum der Kulturen)* BY **M**[1] *– Antiquities★★ (Antikenmuseum)* CY *– Paper Museum★ (Basler Papiermühle)* DY **M**[6] *– Haus zum Kirschgarten★* BZ *– Jean Tinguely Museum★.*

Envir : *✻★ from Bruderholz Water Tower South : 3,5 km – Chapel of St.-Chrischona★ Northeast : 8 km – Augst Roman Ruins★★ Southeast : 11 km – Beyeler Foundation★★ Northwest : 6 km at Riehen.*

18 at Hagenthal-le-Bas, ✉ F-68220 (April - October), Southwest : 10 km, ✆ (0033) 389 68 50 91, Fax (0033) 389 68 55 66

18 Markgräferland at Kandern, ✉ D-79400 (March - November), North : 23 km, ✆ (0049) 7626 97 79 90, Fax (0049) 7626 97 79 922.

✈ EuroAirport, ✆ 0613 253 111, Basle (Switzerland) by Flughafenstrasse 8 km and – at Saint-Louis (France).

ℹ Tourist Office, Barfüsserplatz, Steinenberg 14 ; Tourist Office, in the station, ✆ 0612 686 868, info@baseltourismus.ch, *Fax 0612 686 870 – T.C.S., Steinentorstr. 13, ✆ 0612 059 999, Fax 0612 059 970 – A.C.S., Birsigstr. 4, ✆ 0612 723 933, Fax 0612 813 657.*

Bern 100 – Freiburg im Breisgau 72 – Lyons 401 – Mulhouse 35 – Paris 554 – Strasbourg 145.

Plans on following pages

Swissôtel Le Plaza, Messeplatz 25, ✉ 4005, ✆ 0615 553 333, *emailus.basel@swissotel.com, Fax 0615 553 970,* ⅃, ⇒, ▣ – ⇧, ⅔ rm, ▤ TV ✆ ♿ rm, ⇐ – 🏔 15/35. AE ⓞ MC VISA JCB DX r

Meals a la carte 42/92 – ☕ 30 – **231 rm** 520/570, 7 suites.

◆ Right by the trade fair centre, this extensive establishment offers business travellers an up-to-the-minute level of comfort, particularly in the recently refurbished de-luxe rooms. Contemporary bistro-style restaurant.

Hilton, Aeschengraben 31, ✉ 4002, ✆ 0612 756 600, *info.basel@hilton.com, Fax 0612 756 650,* ⇒, ▣ – ⇧ ⅔ ▤ TV ✆ ♿ rm, ⇐ – 🏔 15/300. AE ⓞ MC VISA JCB CZ d

Wettstein : **Meals** a la carte 60/111 – ☕ 30 – **205 rm** 550/660, 9 suites.

◆ This purpose-built establishment not far from the station harmonises well with the neighbouring buildings. Contemporary rooms designed with the needs of the business traveller in mind. Dine in the English-style Wettstein at basement level.

Radisson SAS, Steinentorstr. 25, ✉ 4001, ✆ 0612 272 727, *info.basel@radissonsas.com, Fax 0612 272 828,* ⅃, ⇒, ▣ – ⇧, ⅔ rm, ▤ TV ✆ ♿ rm, ⇐ – 🏔 15/150. AE ⓞ MC VISA JCB BZ b

Steinenpick (Brasserie) : **Meals** a la carte 50/105 – ☕ 29 – **205 rm** 470/550.

◆ In common with the majority of the rooms, the recently renovated foyer radiates a cool elegance. The inside rooms are quiet, the outside rooms well soundproofed. Welcoming ambience in the Steinenpick restaurant.

Victoria, Centralbahnplatz 3, ✉ 4002, ✆ 0612 707 070, *hotel-victoria@balehotels.ch, Fax 0612 707 077,* 🌴, ⅃ – ⇧ ⅔ ▤ TV ✆ ⇐ – 🏔 15/80. AE ⓞ MC VISA JCB BZ d

Le Train Bleu : **Meals** 45 (lunch)/75 and a la carte 51/92 – ☕ 25 – **107 rm** 340/460.

◆ This lovely hotel right by the station welcomes its guests with a splendidly spacious open-plan foyer. Rooms with up-to-the-minute comfort and tasteful décor. Le Train Bleu in elegant contemporary style, further enhanced with works of art.

Europe, Clarastr. 43, ✉ 4005, ✆ 0616 908 080, *hotel-europe@balehotels.ch, Fax 0616 908 880* – ⇧, ⅔ rm, ▤ TV ✆ ⇐ – 🏔 15/120. AE ⓞ MC VISA JCB CX k

Meals see also ***Les Quatre Saisons*** below – ***Bajazzo*** (Brasserie) : **Meals** 38 and a la carte 45/80 – ☕ 25 – **158 rm** 350/450.

◆ This business hotel by the trade fair centre has air-conditioned, functionally designed rooms with contemporary furniture. Plenty of room for meetings and conferences. Brasserie Bajazzo with fresh, contemporary décor.

Basel, Münzgasse 12, Spalenberg, ✉ 4001, ✆ 0612 646 800, *reception@hotel-basel.ch, Fax 0612 646 811,* 🌴 – ⇧, ⅔ rm, ▤ rm, TV ✆ P – 🏔 25. AE ⓞ MC VISA BY x

Brasserie Steiger : **Meals** 50 and a la carte 39/103 – ☕ 17 – **72 rm** 260/440.

◆ In a tranquil location in the central pedestrian area with parking facilities and elegant, up-to-the-minute rooms. Admirably suited to both business travellers and other guests. Dine in the Basler Keller under a vaulted stone ceiling.

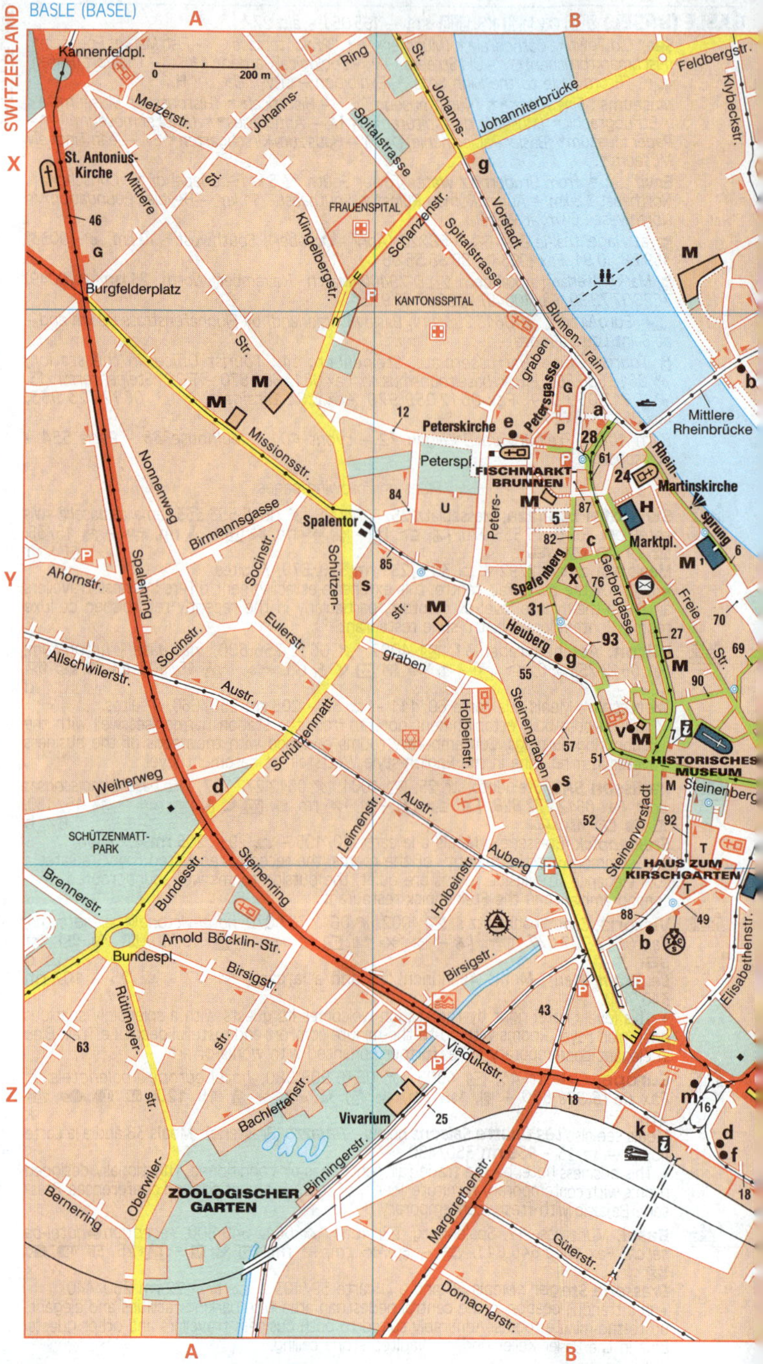
A
B
X
Y
Z
0
200 m
Kannenfeldpl.
Metzerstr.
Johanns-
Ring
St.
Johanns
Vorstadt
Johanniterbrücke
Feldbergstr.
Klybeckstr.
St. Antonius-
Kirche
Mittlere
Spitalstrasse
Klingelbergstr.
FRAUENSPITAL
Schanzenstr.
KANTONSSPITAL
Burgfelderplatz
Blumen-
rain
graben
Petersgasse
Mittlere
Rheinbrücke
Missionsstr.
Nonnenweg
Birmannsgasse
Spalenring
Peterskirche
Peterspl.
FISCHMARKT-
BRUNNEN
Martinskirche
Rhein-
sprung
Marktpl.
Spalentor
Schützen-
graben
Peters-
Spalenberg
Gerbergasse
Freie
Str.
Heuberg
Ahornstr.
Socinstr.
Eulerstr.
Allschwilerstr.
Austr.
Schützenmatt-
Holbeinstr.
Steinengraben
HISTORISCHES
MUSEUM
Steinenberg
Weiherweg
SCHÜTZENMATT-
PARK
Leimenstr.
Auberg
Steinenvorstadt
HAUS ZUM
KIRSCHGARTEN
Brennerstr.
Bundesstr.
Steinenring
Bundespl.
Arnold Böcklin-Str.
Birsigstr.
Elisabethenstr.
Rütimeyer-
str.
Viaduktstr.
Vivarium
Bachlettenstr.
Binningerstr.
ZOOLOGISCHER
GARTEN
Margarethenstr.
Bernerring
Oberwiler-
Güterstr.
Dornacherstr.

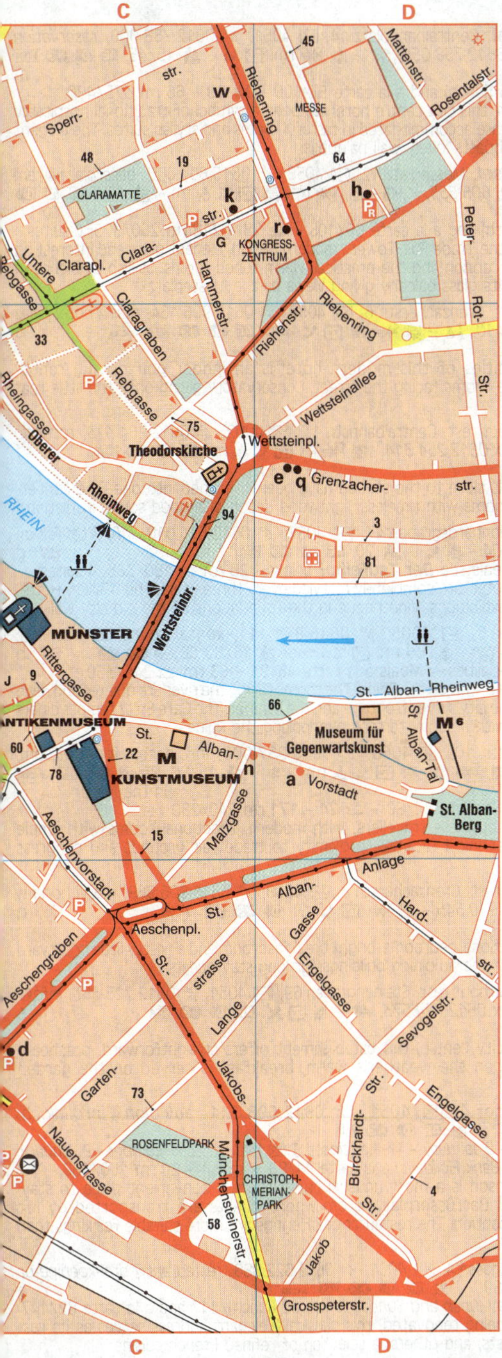

BASEL

Aeschenvorstadt . . . . . CYZ
Alemannengasse . . . . . . DY 3
Andreas-Heusler-Strasse DZ 4
Andreasplatz . . . . BY 5
Augustinergasse . . . . BY 6
Bäumleingasse . . . . CY 9
Barfüsserplatz . . . . BY 7
Bernoullistrasse . . . . . . ABY 12
Brunngässlein . . . . CYZ 15
Centralbahnplatz . . . . . . BZ 16
Centralbahnstrasse . . . . . BZ 18
Claraplatz CX
Drahtzugstrasse . . . . CX 19
Dufourstrasse . . . . CY 22
Eisengasse . . . . BY 24
Erdbeergraben . . . . BZ 25
Falknerstrasse . . . . BY 27
Fischmarktplatz . . . . BY 28
Freie Strasse . . . . BY
Gemsberg . . . . BY 31
Gerbergasse . . . . BY
Greifengasse . . . . BCY 33
Innere-Margarethen-strasse . . . . BZ 43
Isteinerstrasse . . . . DX 45
Kannenfeldstrasse . . . . . AX 46
Klingentalstrasse . . . . . . CX 48
Klosterberg . . . . BZ 49
Kohlenberg . . . . BY 51
Kohlenberggasse . . . . . . BY 52
Leonhardsgraben . . . . . . BY 55
Leonhardsstrasse . . . . . . BY 57
Lindenhofstrasse . . . . . . CZ 58
Luftgässlein . . . . CY 60
Marktgasse . . . . BY 61
Marktplatz . . . . BY
Marschalkenstrasse . . . . AZ 63
Messeplatz . . . . DX 64
Mühlenberg . . . . CDY 66
Münsterberg . . . . BY 69
Münsterplatz . . . . BY 70
Peter Merian-Strasse . . . CZ 73
Riehentorstrasse . . . . . . CY 75
Rümelinsplatz . . . . BY 76
St. Alban-Graben . . . . . . CY 78
Schaffhauserrheinweg . . DY 81
Schneidergasse . . . . BY 82
Spalengraben . . . . BY 84
Spalenvorstadt . . . . BY 85
Stadthausgasse . . . . BY 87
Steinentorstrasse . . . . . BZ 88
Steinenvorstadt . . . . . . BYZ
Streitgasse . . . . BY 90
Theaterstrasse . . . . BY 92
Unterer Heuberg . . . . . . BY 93
Wettsteinstrasse . . . . . . CY 94

Euler und Central, Centralbahnplatz 14, ✉ 4051, ✆ 0612 758 000, *reservation @hoteleuler.ch, Fax 0612 758 050,* – rm, 15/45. AE VISA JCB BZ m

Le Jardin : **Meals** 45 (lunch) and a la carte 57/100 – 28 – **66 rm** 375/490.

◆ Right by the station, this city centre hotel has been a symbol of traditional hospitality for 135 years. Guests are accommodated in tasteful rooms and stylish suites. The elegant Le Jardin restaurant boasts lovely wall paintings.

Ramada Plaza Basel, Messeplatz 12, ✉ 4058, ✆ 0615 604 000, *basel.plaza@ramada-treff.ch, Fax 0615 605 555,* – rm, rm – 15/500. AE VISA DX h

Filou : **Meals** 28 (lunch) and a la carte 60/108 – 28 – **218 rm** 260/320, 6 suites.

◆ A business hotel in the Trade Fair Tower : modern design, elegant glass and interesting light effects in the reception and the practical, warm-toned rooms. Stylish ambience in the Filou restaurant, its glass balcony giving views of the Messeplatz.

Palazzo without rest, Grenzacherstr. 6, ✉ 4058, ✆ 0616 906 464, *mail@hotel-palazzo.ch, Fax 0616 906 410,* – . AE VISA JCB DY e

36 rm 220/320.

◆ Among the amenities of this modern hotel is an indoor golf-driving range. Air-conditioning in the rooms facing the street. Conservatory giving onto the little rear garden.

St. Gotthard without rest, Centralbahnstr. 13, ✉ 4002, ✆ 0612 251 313, *reception@st-gotthard.ch, Fax 0612 251 314* – rm. AE VISA BZ f

103 rm 220/360.

◆ Two adjoining hotels close to the station have been combined into one. The conversion has resulted in rooms with timeless, lightwood décor with good sound insulation.

Der Teufelhof, Leonhardsgraben 47, ✉ 4051, ✆ 0612 611 010, *info@teufelhof.com, Fax 0612 611 004* – – 20. AE VISA BY g

closed Christmas – **Meals** see ***Der Teufelhof*** below – **28 rm** 180/365, 4 suites.

◆ Rooms in the "Art Hotel" are completely restyled every three years. The "Gallery Hotel" stages changing art exhibitions. Vinotheque in the foundations of the old city walls.

Merian, Rheingasse 2, ✉ 4005, ✆ 0616 851 111, *kontakt@merian-hotel.ch, Fax 0616 851 101,* – rm, – 15/80. AE VISA BY b

Café Spitz - Fish specialities - : **Meals** a la carte 46/91 – **63 rm** 245/350.

◆ Historic establishment right on the Rhine. The rooms facing the river are quieter and have a wonderful view of the city's river frontage and the Minster. The Café Spitz tempts diners with fish dishes and with a sunny terrace overlooking the Rhine.

Novotel, Schönaustr. 10, ✉ 4058, ✆ 0616 957 000, *info.basbas@dorint.com, Fax 0616 957 100* – rm, rm, – 15/80. AE VISA JCB. rest in the North DX

Olive Tree : **Meals** a la carte 44/80 – 24 – **171 rm** 240/289.

◆ An ideal hotel for business travellers, with modern, functional rooms with ample work desks and all technical facilities, proximity to trade fair grounds and congress centre.

Wettstein without rest, Grenzacherstr. 8, ✉ 4058, ✆ 0616 906 969, *mail@hotel-wettstein.ch, Fax 0616 910 545* – . AE VISA JCB DY q

40 rm 190/270.

◆ Contemporary, functional bedrooms, bright breakfast room and a pretty little courtyard garden. Apartments in the adjoining buildings for long-stay guests.

Steinenschanze without rest, Steinengraben 69, ✉ 4051, ✆ 0612 725 353, *info@steinenschanze.ch, Fax 0612 724 573,* – . AE VISA BY s

54 rm 180/250.

◆ Not far from the city centre, this establishment offers straightforward, practically furnished rooms. When the weather's warm, breakfast is served on the garden terrace.

Au Violon, Lohnhof 4, ✉ 4051, ✆ 0612 698 711, *auviolon@iprolink.ch, Fax 0612 698 712,* – . AE VISA BY v

closed 23 December - 9 January – **Meals** *(closed 3 to 13 July, 23 December - 9 January, Monday, Sunday and Bank Holidays)* a la carte 44/83 – 14 – **20 rm** 100/180.

◆ The old remand prison is a most unusual but extremely convenient place to stay, right on the central Barfüsserplatz, from where guests are transported by lift straight up to the reception. The restaurant's offerings are more suitable for kings than convicts.

Drei Könige, Marktgasse 4, ✉ 4001, ✆ 0612 622 888, *restaurant@drei-koenige-basel.ch, Fax 0612 622 890* – . AE VISA JCB BY a

Meals *(closed Saturday lunch and Sunday lunch)* 62 (lunch)/117 and a la carte 82/147.

◆ While the hotel is being renovated, this classically elegant address serves as its restaurant, offering guests, and others, a selection of refined French cuisine.

Bruderholz, Bruderholzallee 42, ✉ 4059, ✆ 0613 618 222, *bruderholz@bluewin.ch, Fax 0613 618 203,* – P. AE ⓓ MC VISA JCB
closed 7 to 21 February, Sunday and Monday (except major fairs) – **Meals** 68 (lunch)/198 and a la carte 118/217. South by Margarethenstrasse BZ
Spec. Le fin velouté d'asperges vertes et morilles farcies avec sa petite crème brûlée au foie gras (spring). La fricassée de langoustines sur une tapenade, nage parfumée à la mélisse et coriandre fraîche (summer). La poularde de Bresse poêlée, jus de cuisson au foie gras, coussinets maigres aux épinards
◆ This imposing mansion high up above the city is furnished in classically comfortable style and boasts a lovely flower garden. Creative cuisine for the committed gourmet.

Les Quatre Saisons - *Hotel Europe*, Clarastr. 43, ✉ 4005, ✆ 0616 908 720, *hotel-europe@balehotels.ch, Fax 0616 908 883* – ▤. AE ⓓ MC VISA JCB. ✂ CX k
closed 17 July - 7 August and Sunday (except major fairs) – **Meals** (1st floor) 63 (lunch)/145 and a la carte 84/145.
Spec. Carpaccio vom Lachs und Seeteufel mit rotem Pfeffer auf Kartoffelmousseline. Mit Trüffel braisiertes Kaninchen. Warme Apfel-Banane mit Limone und Bitterschokoladensorbet
◆ A light, pleasantly styled restaurant on the first floor of the Europa, where diners are treated to creative international delicacies by friendly, well-drilled staff.

Rest. Der Teufelhof - *Hotel Der Teufelhof*, Leonhardsgraben 47, ✉ 4051, ✆ 0612 611 010, *info@teufelhof.com, Fax 0612 611 004,* – ⅍. AE ⓓ MC VISA
closed Christmas – ***Bel Etage** : (closed 1 to 6 January, Saturday lunch, Sunday and Monday except major fairs)* **Meals** 77 (lunch)/180 and a la carte 93/148 – ***Weinstube** :* **Meals** 70/75 and a la carte 60/109. BY g
Spec. Geräuchertes Gänseleberparfait mit Apfel-Chartreuse und Aceto Balsamicosauce. Gegrilltes Steinbuttfilet mit Artischokennage und Safranspaghettini. Moorhuhnbrüstchen im Wirsingmantel mit Wacholder-Specksauce und Schupfnudeln
◆ Contemporary, strikingly creative cuisine served in tasteful rooms with lovely parquet floors. The dining experience is enhanced by a superb array of well-chosen wines. Beyond the courtyard, the congenial wine cellar offers a more straightforward menu.

Zum Schützenhaus, Schützenmattstr. 56, ✉ 4051, ✆ 0612 726 760, *restaurant@schuetzenhaus-basel.ch, Fax 0612 726 586,* – 🚗. AE ⓓ MC VISA AY d
***Gartensaal** :* **Meals** 61 and a la carte 77/139.
◆ The historic guilds building houses the country-style Gartensaal with wooden tables and cheerful décor as well as the straightforward Brasserie - both with a terrace.

Chez Donati, St. Johanns-Vorstadt 48, ✉ 4056, ✆ 0613 220 919, *Fax 0613 220 981,* BX g
closed 10 July - 8 August, 13 to 21 February, Sunday and Monday – **Meals** - Italian rest. - a la carte 72/127.
◆ The interior of this old building is in classic late-19C style, with chandeliers, pictures, stucco and woodwork all helping to produce an ambience of great elegance.

Charon, Schützengraben 62, ✉ 4051, ✆ 0612 619 980, *Fax 0612 619 909* – ▤. ⓓ MC VISA JCB AY s
closed 25 to 28 March, 16 July - 14 August, 24 to 27 December, Monday from October - April, Saturday from May - September, Sunday and Bank Holidays – **Meals** 100 (dinner) and a la carte 62/122.
◆ Appealing little restaurant with a bistro-style ambience and beautifully decorated with plants. Ever-changing menu based on the choicest and freshest ingredients.

Hong Kong, Riehenring 91, ✉ 4058, ✆ 0616 918 814, *info@restaurant-hongkong.ch, Fax 0616 918 836,* – AE ⓓ MC VISA JCB CX w
closed Easter, July and Christmas – **Meals** - Chinese rest. - 50 (lunch)/86 and a la carte 51/89.
◆ The offerings here cover the spectrum of Chinese cuisine from Canton to Szechwan, and are served up in a setting effectively evoking the Orient.

St. Alban-Stübli, St. Alban-Vorstadt 74, ✉ 4052, ✆ 0612 725 415, *Fax 0612 740 488,* – AE ⓓ MC VISA DY a
closed 31 July - 8 August, 24 December - 9 January, Saturday (except dinner from September - June) and Sunday – **Meals** (at lunch small carte only) (booking essential) 48 (lunch) and a la carte 60/108.
◆ Solid, traditional dishes served up in the cosy parlour or in the garden. Afterwards, it's up the staircase to the smoking room to savour a good cigar.

Zur Schuhmachernzunft, Hutgasse 6, ✉ 4001, ✆ 0612 612 091, *mschneiter@digi-com.ch, Fax 0612 612 591* – ▤. AE ⓓ MC VISA BY c
closed 25 June - 14 August, 24 to 31 December, Saturday (except November - December) and Sunday (except major fairs and carnival) – **Meals** (1st floor) (booking essential) 87 and a la carte 68/112.
◆ This welcoming restaurant is on the first floor of an old city residence. Venerable wood panelling, lots of pictures, a grand piano and lovely place settings set the tone.

Sakura, Centralbahnstr. 14, ✉ 4051, ☎ 0612 720 505, *info@bahnhofrestaurants.ch, Fax 0612 953 988* – AE ⓓ ⓜⓒ BZ k
closed 4 July - 14 August, Saturday lunch, Sunday and Bank Holidays – **Meals** - Japanese rest. - ***Teppanyaki :*** **Meals** 55/85 and a la carte 40/95 – ***Sushi-Kappoh :*** **Meals** 48 and a la carte 48/101.
◆ This establishment in the station building stands under the sign of the Rising Sun. It smilingly invites guests to savour its delicately presented teppan-yaki specialities. Japanese hospitality and the chance to see the chefs deploy their well-honed skills.

St. Alban-Eck, St. Alban-Vorstadt 60, ✉ 4052, ☎ 0612 710 320, *pluess@st-alban-eck.ch, Fax 0612 738 609* – AE ⓓ ⓜⓒ VISA CY n
closed 18 July - 7 August, Saturday lunch, Sunday and Bank Holidays – **Meals** 43 (lunch)/91 and a la carte 56/115.
◆ This old corner building with its half-timbered façade is located in a quiet residential area close to the Rhine. Congenial, rustic interior with lots of wood and panelling.

at Riehen *by ② : 5 km – alt. 288 – ✉ 4125 Riehen :*

Schürmann's, Äussere Baselstr. 159, ☎ 0616 431 210, *mail@schuermanns.ch, Fax 0616 431 211,* – AE ⓓ ⓜⓒ VISA
closed 26 July - 6 August, 18 to 29 October, 15 to 19 February, Sunday and Monday (except major fairs) – **Meals** *(dinner only)* 95 and a la carte 80/132.
Spec. Spezialitäten mit weissem Albatrüffel (November - December). Badische Spargeln (April - June). Ormalinger Jungschwein
◆ A modern restaurant with changing picture exhibitions and a garden terrace on which to enjoy a creative, tasty menu fashioned from ultra-fresh ingredients.

at Birsfelden *East by ④ : 3 km – alt. 260 – ✉ 4127 Birsfelden :*

Alfa, Hauptstr. 15, ☎ 0613 156 262, *info@alfa-hotel-birsfelden.ch, Fax 0613 156 263* – 15/80. AE ⓓ ⓜⓒ VISA
Meals 28 (lunch)/78 and a la carte 37/110 – **51 rm** ☕ 105/200.
◆ Located only 15 minutes from the city centre by tram. Functional and sensibly-priced rooms offering a useful alternative to a stay in a city centre establishment.

at Muttenz *by ⑤ : 4,5 km – alt. 271 – ✉ 4132 Muttenz :*

Baslertor, St. Jakobs-Str. 1, ☎ 0614 655 555, *hotel-baslertor@balehotels.ch, Fax 0614 655 550,* – rm, – 15/20. AE ⓓ ⓜⓒ VISA
Meals *(closed 3 weeks July - August, Saturday and Sunday) (dinner only)* a la carte approx. 43 – ☕ 15 – **43 rm** 270/330, 4 suites.
◆ Spacious rooms in a large-scale complex that also includes a shopping centre. Also available are apartments with fully equipped kitchens.

at Binningen *South : 2 km by Oberwilerstrasse AZ – alt. 284 – ✉ 4102 Binningen :*

Schloss Binningen, Schlossgasse 5, ☎ 0614 212 055, *wdammann@schloss-binningen.ch, Fax 0614 210 635,* – AE ⓓ ⓜⓒ VISA JCB
closed 29 January - 14 February, Sunday and Monday (except fairs and Bank Holidays) – **Meals** 50 (lunch)/98 and a la carte 68/126.
◆ Dinner in the Empire Salon, an intimate tête-à-tête in the Castle Parlour - pleasurable experiences abound in this stylishly decorated manor house set in parkland.

The Castle, Hasenrainstr. 59, ☎ 0614 212 430, *welcome@thecastle.ch, Fax 0614 217 709,* ≤, – AE ⓓ ⓜⓒ VISA
closed 25 to 30 December, Saturday lunch, Sunday and Monday – **Meals** 55 (lunch)/138 and a la carte 83/130 – ***Bistrot :*** **Meals** a la carte 45/87.
◆ Parquet floors, paintings and lovely place settings lend character to this elegant, English-style establishment divided up by arcades. Superb views over the city.

Gasthof Neubad with rm, Neubadrain 4, ☎ 0613 020 705, *gasthof.neubad@datacomm.ch, Fax 0613 028 116,* – rm, AE ⓜⓒ VISA
closed 5 to 20 February – **Meals** *(closed Wednesday)* 50 (lunch)/85 and a la carte 49/114 – **6 rm** ☕ 125/240.
◆ This lovely building of 1742 was originally an inn with a little spa attached. Good plain food is served here, as well as in the pretty garden restaurant.

In this guide a symbol or a character, printed in red or black does not have the same meaning.
Pay particular attention to the explanatory pages.

GENEVA 729 C7 552 B11 – *177 535 – alt. 375.*

See : *The Shores of the lake★★ : ≤★★★* FGY *– Parks★★ : Mon Repos* GX*, La Perle du Lac and Villa Barton – Botanical Garden★ : alpine rock-garden★★ – Cathedral St-Pierre★ : north Tower ※★★* FZ *– Old Town★ : Reformation Monument★* FZ **D** *; Archaeological Site★★ – Palais des Nations★★ – Parc de la Grange★ – Parc des Eaux-Vives★ – Nave★ of Church of Christ the King – Woodwork★ in the Historical Museum of the Swiss Abroad – Baur Collection★ (in 19C mansion)* GZ *– Maison Tavel★* FZ.

Museums : *Ariana★★ – Art and History★★* GZ *– Natural History★★* GZ *– International Automobile Museum★ – Petit Palais : Modern Art★★* GZ *– International Red Cross and Red Crescent Museum★★ –* **Excursions** *by boat on the lake, Information : Cie Gén. de Nav., Jardin Anglais ☎ 0848 811 848- Mouettes genevoises, 8 quai Mont-Blanc, ☎ 0227 322 944 - Swiss Boat, 4 quai Mont-Blanc, ☎ 0227 324 747.*

18 at Cologny ✉ 1223 (March - December), ☎ 0227 074 800, Fax 0227 074 820 ;

18 at Bossey ✉ F-74160 (March - December), ☎ (0033) 450 43 95 50, Fax (0033) 450 95 32 57 by road to Troinex ;

27 at Esery ✉ F-74930 Reignier (March - December), ☎ (0033) 450 36 58 70, Fax (0033) 450 36 57 62, Southeast : 15 km.

18 Maison Blanche at Echenevex-Gex ✉ F-01170 (March - mid December) ☎ (0033) 450 42 44 42, Fax (0033) 450 42 44 43, Northwest : 17 km.

✈ Genève-Cointrin, ☎ 0227 177 111.

Tourist Office, 18 r.du Mont Blanc ; Info Airport, Arrival ; 1 Pont-de-la-Machine, ☎ 0229 097 000, info@geneve-tourisme.ch, Fax 0229 097 011 – T.C.S., 8 cours de Rive, 1204 Genève, 4 ch. de Blandonnet, 1214 Vernier, ☎ 0224 172 030, Fax 0224 172 042 – A.C.S., 17 r. F.-Dussaud, ☎ 0223 422 233, Fax 0223 013 711.

Bern 164 – Bourg-en-B. 101 – Lausanne 60 – Lyons 151 – Paris 538 – Turin 252.

Plans on following pages

Right Bank (Cornavin Railway Station - Les Quais) :

Mandarin Oriental du Rhône, 1 quai Turrettini, ✉ 1201, ☎ 0229 090 000, *reserve-mogva@mohg.com, Fax 0229 090 010,* ≤, rm, rm, – 15/150. AE MC VISA. FY r
Meals see also ***Le Neptune*** below – ***Café Rafael :*** ☎ 0229 090 005 **Meals** 58 (lunch) and a la carte 64/111 – ☕ 39 – **180 rm** 510/940, 12 suites.
◆ Central location on the right bank of the Rhone. Sumptuous rooms with Art Deco furnishings and sparkling marble bathrooms. The Café Rafael offers a choice of traditional recipes showing occasional local influence.

Président Wilson, 47 quai Wilson, ✉ 1201, ☎ 0229 066 666, *resa@hotelpwilson.com, Fax 0229 066 667,* ≤, rm, – 15/600. AE MC VISA JCB. GX d
Spice's : *(closed 17 July - 14 August, Saturday lunch and Sunday)* **Meals** 55 (lunch)/128 and a la carte 96/143 – ***L'Arabesque :*** - Lebanese rest. - **Meals** 55 (lunch)/95 and a la carte 52/78 – ***Pool Garden :*** *(May - September)* **Meals** 49 (lunch)/60 and a la carte 74/114 – ☕ 40 – **219 rm** 670/990, 11 suites.
◆ Wood and marble abound in this hotel whose finest rooms look onto the lake. The Spice's has "World Cuisine" in a modern setting, while the Arabesque offers mouthwatering Lebanese delights. Try eating al fresco in the Pool Garden in summer.

Richemond, 8 - 10 r. Adhémar-Fabri, ✉ 1201, ☎ 0227 157 000, *reservation@richemond.ch, Fax 0227 157 001,* – 15/160. AE MC VISA JCB
Le Gentilhomme : - Lebanese rest. - *(closed Saturday lunch, Monday lunch and Sunday)* **Meals** a la carte 64/97 – ***Le Jardin :*** - Italian rest. - **Meals** 55 (lunch) and a la carte 78/134 – ☕ 48 – **86 rm** 580/890, 12 suites. FY u
◆ A 19C palace close to the lake with elegant public areas, personalised rooms with antique furnishings and several suites that have been tastefully renovated. Lebanese cuisine in the Gentilhomme brasserie and an Italian menu in Le Jardin.

Noga Hilton, 19 quai du Mont-Blanc, ✉ 1201, ☎ 0229 089 081, *reservations.geneva@hilton.com, Fax 0229 089 090,* ≤, rm, rm – 15/800. AE MC VISA JCB. rest GY y
Le Cygne : (1st floor) (☎ 0229 089 085) *(closed 25 March - 3 April, 13 to 28 August, 1 to 9 January, Saturday and Sunday)* **Meals** 61 (lunch) / 159 and a la carte 88/166 – ***La Grignotière :*** **Meals** a la carte 50/110 – ☕ 40 – **401 rm** 425/790, 9 suites.
◆ An imposing modern hotel on Lake Geneva with spacious bedrooms, a number of which are somewhat "eighties" in style. Other facilities include a casino, boutiques and swimming pool. Chic brasserie with a panoramic terrace, typical menu and oyster bar.

Angleterre, 17 quai du Mont-Blanc, ✉ 1201, ☎ 0229 065 555, *angleterre@rchmail.com, Fax 0229 065 556,* ≤, rm, video – 15/35. AE MC VISA FGY n
Windows : **Meals** 38 (lunch) / 95 and a la carte 80/121 – ☕ 39 – **45 rm** 620/920.
◆ A lakeside hotel with a calm, distinguished air offering spacious, welcoming guest rooms. Relaxed atmosphere and attentive service in the Leopard Lounge. Cosy veranda-restaurant with a contemporary menu and views of the lake.

GENÈVE
0 200 m
LAC LÉMAN
PARC MON REPOS
LE PRIEURÉ
LES PÂQUIS
PORT DES PÂQUIS
PARC DES CROPETTES
CORNAVIN
CASINO
Jet d'eau
PIERRE DU NITON
ÎLE J. J. ROUSSEAU
RHÔNE
Jardin Anglais
MAISON TAVEL
Musée Rath
CATH. ST-PIERRE
VIEILLE VILLE
MUSÉE D'ART ET D'HISTOIRE
MUSÉE D'HISTOIRE NATURELLE
Bibliothèque universitaire
COLLECTIONS BAUR
PETIT PALAIS
LES TRANCHÉES
PLAINE DE PLAINPALAIS
PLAINPALAIS
Pl. Ed. Claparède
Rd Point de Plainpalais
Pl. Neuve
AUTO TRAIN
Quai Wilson
Quai du Mont-Blanc
Quai Gustave Ador
Quai du Gal Guisan
Bd Helvétique
Bd des Philosophes
Bd du Pont d'Arve
Av. Henri Dunant
Av. du Mail
Bd Georges Favon
Bd James Fazy
Prom. de St-Jean
Prom. des Bastions
R. de la Croix Rouge
Grand' Rue
R. de Rive
R. de Lausanne
R. de Berne
R. des Pâquis
R. Rousseau
R. de Montbrillant
R. des Gares
Rte de Florissant
R. de Contamines
R. de la Scie
R. des Eaux-Vives
Pl. du Mont-Blanc
F
G
X
Y
Z

INDEX OF STREET NAMES IN GENEVE

22-Cantons (Pl. des) . . . . FY 142
Alpes (R. des) . . . . FY
Bastions (Prom. des) . . . . FZ
Bel Air (Pl.) . . . . FY 10
Bergues (Quai des) . . . . FY 12
Berne (R. de) . . . . FY
Bourg de Four (Pl. du) . . . . FZ 14
Buis (R. des) . . . . FX
Candolle (R. de) . . . . FZ 21
Chantepoulet (R. de) . . . . FY 28
Cirque (Pl. du) . . . . FZ 37
Confédération (R. de la) . . . . . FY 42
Contamines (R. de) . . . . GZ
Cornavin (Pl. de) . . . . FY 43
Corraterie (R. de la) . . . . FY 45
Coulouvrenière (Pont de la) . . FY 48
Croix d'Or (R. de la) . . . . FY 49
Croix Rouge (R. de la) . . . . FZ
Eaux Vives (Pl. des) . . . . GZ 52
Eaux Vives (R. des) . . . . GY
Edouard-Claparède (Pl.) . . . . FGZ
Ferdinand-Hodler (R.) . . . . GZ
Fort-Barreau (R. du) . . . . FX 58
Frontenex (Av. de) . . . . GZ 61
Gares (R. des) . . . . FX
Général-Guisan (Quai) . . . . . FGY
Georges-Favon (Bd) . . . . FZ
Grand'Rue . . . . FZ
Granges (R. des) . . . . FZ 65
Gustave-Ador (Quai) . . . . GY
Helvétique (Bd) . . . . FGZ
Henri-Dunant (Av.) . . . . FZ
Italie (R. d') . . . . GZ 72
Jacques-Dalcroze (Bd) . . . . FGZ
James-Fazy (Bd) . . . . FY
Lausanne (R. de) . . . . FX
Longemalle (Pl.) . . . . FY 76
Mail (Av. du) . . . . FZ
Malagnou (Rte de) . . . . GZ 79
Marché (R. du) . . . . FY 81
Molard (Pl. du) . . . . FY 84
Mont-Blanc (Pont du) . . . . FY
Mont-Blanc (Quai du) . . . . . . FGY
Mont-Blanc (R. du) . . . . FY 85
Montbrillant (R. de) . . . . FX
Monthoux (R. de) . . . . FXY 87
Neuve (Pl.) . . . . FZ
Pâquis (R. des) . . . . FXY
Pépinière (R. de la) . . . . FY 90
Philippe-Plantamour (R.) . . . . GX
Philosophes (Bd des) . . . . FZ
Pictet-de-Rochemont (Av.) . . . GZ 93
Pierre-Fatio (R.) . . . . GYZ 94
Plainpalais (Rond-Point de) . . . FZ
Pont d'Arve (Bd du) . . . . FZ
Rhône (R. du) . . . . FGY
Rive (R. de) . . . . FGZ
Rive (Rond-Point de) . . . . GZ 105
Rousseau (R.) . . . . FY
St-Léger (R.) . . . . FZ 118
Scie (R. de la) . . . . GY
Temple (R. du) . . . . FY 120
Terrassière (R. de la) . . . . GZ 121
Terreaux du Temple (R. des) . FY 123
Théâtre (Bd du) . . . . FZ 124
Tour (Bd de la) . . . . FZ 126
Tranchées (Bd des) . . . . GZ
Turrettini (Quai) . . . . FY 127
Valais (R. du) . . . . FX
Versonnex (R.) . . . . GY 133
Villereuse (R. de) . . . . GZ 139
Voltaire (R.) . . . . FY 140
Wilson (Quai) . . . . GX

Beau-Rivage, 13 quai du Mont-Blanc, ✉ 1201, ☎ 0227 166 666, *info@beau-rivage.ch, Fax 0227 166 060*, ←, 🏞 – 🛗, ⚹ rm, ▤ TV ☎ 🚗 – 🏛 15/120. AE ⓓ MC VISA JCB
Le Chat Botté **: Meals** 60 (lunch)/175 and a la carte 99/161 🍇 – ***Le Patara*** **:** ☎ 0227 315 566 - Thai rest. - *(closed 25 to 28 March, 23 December - 5 January, Saturday lunch and Sunday lunch)* **Meals** 34 (lunch) / 85 and a la carte 66/130 – ☕ 37 – **86 rm** 495/1080, 7 suites. FY d

◆ Facing the lake, this atmospheric establishment has been in the family since 1865. The bedrooms have a refined retro feel. Elegant atrium with fountain and colonnades. Experience the flavours of Thailand in the inviting atmosphere of the Patara restaurant.

De la Paix, 11 quai du Mont-Blanc, ✉ 1201, ☎ 0229 096 000, *reservation@hoteldelapaix.ch, Fax 0229 096 001*, ← – 🛗, ⚹ rm, ▤ TV video ☎ – 🏛 15/50. AE ⓓ MC VISA JCB. ⚹ rm FY e
Vertig'O **: Meals** 40 (lunch)/80 and a la carte 60/95 – ☕ 40 – **89 rm** 700/800, 11 suites.

◆ A new lease of life for this grand hotel built in the early years of the 20C : today's guests can enjoy elegant public rooms, various categories of bedrooms in classic-modern style, and a contemporary bar-brasserie with a menu to match.

Bristol, 10 r. du Mont-Blanc, ✉ 1201, ☎ 0227 165 700, *bristol@bristol.ch, Fax 0227 389 039*, 🏋, ♨ – 🛗, ⚹ rm, ▤ TV ☎ – 🏛 15/100. AE ⓓ MC VISA JCB. ⚹
Meals 48 (lunch)/85 and a la carte 62/104 – ☕ 32 – **95 rm** 390/585, 5 suites. FY w

◆ An opulent entrance hall leads to the reception area of this hotel near the lake. Spacious, refurbished rooms, fitness centre, sauna, steam room and collection of old canvasses. The bright dining room with its Louis XV decor overlooks a small garden.

Epsom, 18 r. de Richemont, ✉ 1202, ☎ 0225 446 666, *epsom@manotel.com, Fax 0225 446 699*, 🏋 – 🛗, ⚹ rm, ▤ TV ☎ ♿ rm – 🏛 15/60. AE ⓓ MC VISA JCB
Portobello **:** *(closed 25 December - 2 January)* **Meals** a la carte 50/100 – **153 rm** ☕ 350/510. FX d

◆ Very contemporary hotel on a quiet city-centre street. Relaxing atmosphere, homely rooms and high-tech conference facilities. Modern rotisserie with a glass roof.

Royal, 41 r. de Lausanne, ✉ 1201, ☎ 0229 061 414, *royal@manotel.com, Fax 0229 061 499*, 🏞, 🏋, ♨ – 🛗, ⚹ rm, ▤ TV ☎ ♿ rm, ♿ rest, 🚗 – 🏛 15/30. AE ⓓ MC VISA JCB FX i
Rive Droite **: Meals** 52 and a la carte 44/94 – ☕ 25 – **166 rm** 355/550, 6 suites.

◆ Situated between the station and the lake, the Royal classically furnished rooms are elegant and plush ; it also has several luxury suites. Parisian brasserie-style restaurant offers a good value menu chalked up on the slate board.

Warwick, 14 r. de Lausanne, ✉ 1201, ☎ 0227 168 000, *res.geneva@warwickhotels.com, Fax 0227 168 001* – 🛗, ⚹ rm, ▤ TV video ☎ – 🏛 15/150. AE ⓓ MC VISA JCB
La Bonne Brasserie **: Meals** 25 and a la carte 47/80 – ☕ 27 – **167 rm** 445/525.

◆ Located in front of the station, the Warwick is ideal for tourists and conference guests travelling by train. Contemporary, functional rooms. Paris bistro atmosphere in the Bonne Brasserie, next to the hotel bar. FY c

Sofitel, 18-20 r. du Cendrier, ✉ 1201, ☎ 0229 088 080, *h1322@accor-hotels.com, Fax 0229 088 081*, 🏞 – 🛗, ⚹ rm, ▤ TV video ☎. AE ⓓ MC VISA JCB. ⚹ FY t
Meals 48 and a la carte 64/92 – ☕ 35 – **95 rm** 450/600.

◆ A city-centre hotel with a choice of rustic- or Louis XVI-style rooms awaiting refurbishment. Lounge with an open fire and pianist in the evening. Classic/traditional fare in the restaurant, which has a terrace for those lazy summer days.

Novotel Genève Centre, 19 r. de Zürich, ✉ 1201, ✆ 0229 099 000, *H3133@accor-hotels.com, Fax 0229 099 001* – |♦|, ⇎ rm, ▤ TV ✆ ⇔ – 🏛 25. AE ⓓ MC VISA JCB
Meals 29 (lunch)/46 and a la carte 44/78 – ☕ 27 – **192 rm** 250/370, 14 suites. FX s
◆ A chain hotel recognisable by its glass façade, ideally located close to both the train station and lake. Good-sized, well-appointed bedrooms, in the process of being renovated. Contemporary-style "spice"-themed decor in the restaurant. Traditional cuisine.

Melia Rex Hotel, 42-44 av. Wendt, ✉ 1203, ✆ 0225 447 474, *melia.rex@solmelia.com, Fax 0225 447 499,* 🌳 – |♦|, ⇎ rm, ▤ rest, TV ✆. AE ⓓ MC VISA
Meals *(closed Saturday and Sunday)* (snack carte) 32 (lunch) and a la carte approx. 40 – ☕ 25 – **70 rm** 295. in the West FY
◆ Built in 2004 in a residential area, this hotel offers opulent reception areas and rooms of various sizes : at its best, the accommodation is bright, spacious and stylishly furnished. The restaurant serves a concise menu of lighter dishes.

Le Montbrillant, 2 r. de Montbrillant, ✉ 1201, ✆ 0227 337 784, *contact@montbrillant.ch, Fax 0227 332 511,* 🌳 – |♦|, ⇎ rm, TV ✆ ♿ rm, P – 🏛 15/50. AE ⓓ MC VISA JCB
***gastro* : Meals** 48/158 and a la carte 66/116 – ***Café de la Gare* : Meals** a la carte 43/84 – **82 rm** ☕ 190/350. FY b
◆ Invaluable accommodation for those who want to be near the station. Similar to a mountain retreat, with angular rooms and studios with kitchenette. The restaurant with its veranda feels like a bistro and offers contemporary fare.

Les Nations without rest, 62 r. du Grand-Pré, ✉ 1202, ✆ 0227 480 808, *info@hotel-les-nations.com, Fax 0227 343 884* – |♦| ⇎ TV video ✆. AE ⓓ MC VISA
71 rm ☕ 250/300. in the West FX
◆ Popular with business travellers and EU officials, Les Nations has been totally refurbished. The rooms, though on the small side, are as charming as they are smart.

Auteuil without rest, 33 r. de Lausanne, ✉ 1201, ✆ 0225 442 222, *auteuil@manotel.com, Fax 0225 442 299* – |♦| ⇎ ▤ TV video ✆ ⇔ – 🏛 25. AE ⓓ MC VISA JCB
104 rm ☕ 310/395. FX m
◆ A contemporary reception hall with Warhol-style portraits of the stars leads on to modern rooms in dark wood, designer bathrooms and a very trendy breakfast room.

Cornavin without rest, Cornavin Station, ✉ 1201, ✆ 0227 161 212, *cornavin@fhotels.ch, Fax 0227 161 200* – |♦| ⇎ ▤ TV ✆ – 🏛 60. AE ⓓ MC VISA FY a
☕ 18 – **162 rm** 375/425.
◆ Patronised by Tintin in "The Calculus Affair", this hotel is home to the world's biggest clock. Modern guest rooms with Le Corbusier armchairs, and a panoramic breakfast room.

Kipling without rest, 27 r. de la Navigation, ✉ 1201, ✆ 0225 444 040, *kipling@manotel.com, Fax 0225 444 099* – |♦| ⇎ ▤ TV ✆ P – 🏛 10. AE ⓓ MC VISA. ✂ FX x
62 rm ☕ 240/315.
◆ A delicate waft of incense greets you as you enter this colonial-styled hotel dedicated to the author of "The Jungle Book".

Du Midi, 4 pl. Chevelu, ✉ 1201, ✆ 0225 441 500, *info@hotel-du-midi.ch, Fax 0225 441 520,* 🌳 – |♦| ▤ TV ✆ ♿ rm. AE ⓓ MC VISA FY v
Meals *(closed Saturday and Sunday)* 35 (lunch)/50 and a la carte 59/90 – ☕ 24 – **89 rm** 240/400.
◆ On a little square by the Rhône, this spacious hotel has great rooms. In the evenings, a pianist plays relaxing melodies in the lounge. Comfortable modern restaurant with summer terrace.

Edelweiss, 2 pl. Navigation, ✉ 1201, ✆ 0225 445 151, *edelweiss@manotel.com, Fax 0225 445 199* – |♦|, ⇎ rm, ▤ TV ✆. AE ⓓ MC VISA JCB. ✂ rest FX a
Meals *(closed 1 to 24 January)(dinner only)* 55 and a la carte 43/90 – **42 rm** ☕ 270/330.
◆ The outside of this establishment gives a good idea of the pleasures within. It's a real Swiss chalet, with cosy bedrooms and a congenial galleried dining room where you can enjoy traditional fare and typical cheese dishes to the accompaniment of music.

Ambassador, 21 quai des Bergues, ✉ 1201, ✆ 0229 080 530, *info@hotel-ambassador.ch, Fax 0227 389 080,* 🌳 – |♦| ▤ TV video ✆ – 🏛 30. AE ⓓ MC VISA FY m
Meals *(closed Sunday lunch and Saturday)* 39/58 and a la carte 45/92 – ☕ 24 – **82 rm** 270/450.
◆ Traffic hurries by outside, following the river Rhône, but excellent soundproofing in the bedrooms keeps out all but a murmur. Traditional meals served in wood-fitted dining room or on the terrace in summer.

Eden, 135 r. de Lausanne, ✉ 1202, ✆ 0227 163 700, *eden@eden.ch, Fax 0227 315 260* – |♦| ▤ TV video ✆ – 🏛 20. AE ⓓ MC VISA JCB in the North FX
Meals *(closed 23 July - 14 August, 24 December - 9 January, Saturday and Sunday)* 31/43 and a la carte 39/62 – **54 rm** ☕ 225/300.
◆ This establishment facing the Palais des Nations is regularly refurbished. Bright and functional classically furnished rooms. Traditional restaurant where local people rub shoulders with guests and passers-by.

Strasbourg - Univers without rest, 10 r. Pradier, ✉ 1201, ☎ 0229 065 800, *info@hotel-strasbourg-geneva.ch, Fax 0227 384 208* – AE MC VISA. FY q
51 rm 190/250.
◆ Close to the station and the Cornavin car park, this refurbished establishment has small, functional rooms with cosy public areas.

Ibis without rest, 10 r. Voltaire, ✉ 1201, ☎ 0223 382 020, *h2154@accor-hotels.com, Fax 0223 382 030* – rm,. AE MC VISA in the West FY
14 – **65 rm** 129.
◆ This completely refurbished establishment is typical of the new generation of Ibis hotels. Contemporary comfort in rooms with modern, no-nonsense furnishings.

Le Neptune - Hotel Mandarin Oriental du Rhône, 1 quai Turrettini, ✉ 1201, ☎ 0229 090 006, *reserve-mogva@mohg.com, Fax 0229 090 010,* – . AE MC VISA. FY r
closed August, Saturday, Sunday and Bank Holidays – **Meals** 72/98 and a la carte 124/201.
Spec. Foie gras frais de canard pressé en croûte de tomates, réduction de Banuyls. Homard bleu rôti à l'éclatée, timbale de macaronis aux légumes et Maille. Cochon de lait laineux, de la tête aux pieds, cannelloni aux blettes. **Wines** Dardagny, Lully
◆ Culinary artistry and modern cuisine from the Mandarin Oriental du Rhône "Le Neptune restaurant" the god himself appears in the wall-paintings.

Tsé Yang, 19 quai du Mont-Blanc, ✉ 1201, ☎ 0227 325 081, *Fax 0227 310 582,* – . AE MC VISA JCB GY e
Meals (1st floor) - Chinese rest. - 45 (lunch)/139 and a la carte 71/170.
◆ Elegant restaurant with oriental décor and carved wooden partitions. Savour Chinese specialities while admiring the view over Lake Geneva.

La Perle du Lac, 128 r. de Lausanne, ✉ 1202, ☎ 0229 091 020, *info@perledulac.ch, Fax 0229 091 030,* lake, , , – . AE MC VISA.
closed 25 December - 25 January and Monday – **Meals** 58 (lunch)/115 and a la carte 87/133. in the North FX
◆ Established over a century ago, this chalet with a spacious panoramic terrace is located in a park facing the lake. Bold colours in the more modern of the two dining rooms.

Green, 5 r. Alfred Vincent, ✉ 1201, ☎ 0227 311 313, *Fax 0227 381 345* – AE MC VISA FY h
closed 8 to 21 August, Christmas, New Year, Saturday lunch and Sunday – **Meals** 48 (lunch) and a la carte 87/137.
◆ Hidden behind the leafy façade is this cosy, contemporary restaurant whose decor is dominated by the colour mauve and enhanced by paintings hanging from its walls.

Thai Phuket, 33 av. de France, ✉ 1202, ☎ 0227 344 100, *Fax 0227 344 240* – . AE MC VISA JCB. rest in the North FX
Meals - Thai rest. - *(closed Saturday lunch)* 35 (lunch)/90 and a la carte 43/102 .
◆ A respected address with attentive service from waitresses dressed in traditional costume. Vintage wines, including top clarets, and a superb aquarium of exotic fish.

Bistrot du Boeuf Rouge, 17 r. Alfred-Vincent, ✉ 1201, ☎ 0227 327 537, *Fax 0227 314 684* – AE MC VISA JCB FY z
closed 24 December - 3 January, Saturday and Sunday – **Meals** - Specialities of Lyons - 38 (lunch)/52 and a la carte 53/92.
◆ A typically French brasserie ornamented with mirrors, a bar and comfortable benches. The menu features specialities from the city of Lyon, local dishes and daily specials.

Sagano, 86 r. de Montbrillant, ✉ 1202, ☎ 0227 331 150, *Fax 0227 344 240,* – . AE MC VISA JCB in the North FX
Meals - Japanese rest. - *(closed Saturday lunch and Sunday)* 23 (lunch)/90 and a la carte 49/109 .
◆ Hungry for a taste of the exotic with a little zen? Head for this Japanese restaurant with its tatami mats and low tables. A culinary voyage from the Land of the Rising Sun.

L'Entrecôte Couronnée, 5 r. des Pâquis, ✉ 1201, ☎ 0227 328 445, *Fax 0227 328 446* – AE MC VISA JCB FY j
closed 23 December - 3 January, Saturday lunch and Sunday – **Meals** 58 and a la carte 59/84.
◆ This is the place to experience the real Geneva. Bistro-style ambience with contemporary food. Plenty of prints and paintings evoke the spirit of this old city.

Left Bank (Commercial Centre) :

Swissôtel Genève Métropole, 34 quai Général-Guisan, ✉ 1204, ☎ 0223 183 200, *reservations.geneva@swissotel.com, Fax 0223 183 300,* , , – , rm, video – 15/90. AE MC VISA GY a
Le Grand Quai **: Meals** a la carte 52/120 – 36 – **118 rm** 530/850, 9 suites.
◆ Built in 1854 overlooking the landmark Jet d'Eau. Attractive, traditional guest rooms, many with lake views, plus new king-size suites and a panoramic roof terrace and fitness centre. Le Grand Quai, with its trompe l'oeil frescoes, serves traditional fare.

Les Armures, 1 r. du Puits-Saint-Pierre, 1204, 0223 109 172, *armures@span.ch, Fax 0223 109 846*, – video . FZ g
Meals *(closed Easter, Christmas and New Year)* 58 and a la carte 45/90 – **28 rm** 360/510.
◆ An elegant 17C town house tucked away in the heart of the old town. Attractive bedroom decor with antique furniture and exposed beams. A choice of traditional dishes in the newly renovated restaurant, including fondue served in the "carnotset" (drinking den).

De la Cigogne, 17 pl. Longemalle, 1204, 0228 184 040, *cigogne@relaischateaux.com, Fax 0228 184 050* – . FGY j
Meals *(closed Sunday lunch and Saturday from July - August)* 59 (lunch)/105 and a la carte 72/107 – **46 rm** 360/570, 6 suites.
◆ The early-20C façade overlooks a busy square. Elegant decor, public areas adorned with objets d'art, and bedrooms and suites embellished with personal touches and antique furniture. Traditional cuisine beneath the glass roof of the Art Deco-style restaurant.

Tiffany, 1 r. des Marbriers, 1204, 0227 081 616, *info@hotel-tiffany.ch, Fax 0227 081 617* – , rm, . FZ v
Meals *(closed Easter, Christmas and New Year)* a la carte 59/88 – 18 – **46 rm** 230/410.
◆ Built on the site of a late-19C monument. Modern facilities with bedrooms, cosy lounge and bar all showing Belle Époque influence. Retro-style dining room which fits perfectly with the house style. A la carte menu featuring salads and low-calorie dishes.

Sagitta without rest, 6 r. de la Flèche, 1207, 0227 863 361, *sagitta@span.ch, Fax 0228 498 110* – . GZ c
42 rm 209/269.
◆ In the commercial district but secluded, this establishment has rooms, studios, apartments and numerous kitchenettes. The uninspiring façade belies renovated facilities.

Parc des Eaux-Vives with rm, 82 quai Gustave-Ador, 1207, 0228 497 575, *info@parcdeseauxvives.ch, Fax 0228 497 570*, , , – , rm, rest, – 15/80. . by quai Gustave-Ador GY
Meals (1st floor) *(closed 3 weeks January, Sunday except May - September and Monday)* 79 (lunch)/210 and a la carte 148/236 – **Meals** (see also ***Brasserie*** below) – 29 – **7 rm** 550/850.
Spec. L'omble chevalier du Lac Léman (May - August). Les huîtres de chez Gillardeau (October - April). Le lièvre à la royale (September - December). **Wines** Dardagny, Satigny
◆ Housed in a lavish 18C building in a public park. Fine Art Deco-style dining room, mouth-watering, creative cuisine, summer restaurant and high-tech guest rooms.

Le Béarn (Goddard), 4 quai de la Poste, 1204, 0223 210 028, *Fax 0227 813 115* – . FY x
closed 11 July - 22 August, 7 to 13 February, Saturday (except dinner from October - May) and Sunday – **Meals** 65 (lunch)/195 and a la carte 120/176.
Spec. Soufflé de truffes fraîches (winter). Oursins de Bretagne et coquilles Saint-Jacques à la coque (autumn - winter). Géline de Racan "truffé au beurre d'asperge" et jabugo aux pommes nouvelles (spring)
◆ Geneva's gourmets have been coming to this elegant eatery for more than 20 years to savour its fine cuisine. The menu is constantly updated.

Brasserie - Parc des Eaux-Vives, 82 quai Gustave-Ador, 1207, 0228 497 575, *info@parcdeseauxvives.ch, Fax 0228 497 570*, , – rest, . . by quai Gustave-Ador GY
Meals 49 (lunch) and a la carte 57/98.
◆ Elegant modern brasserie on the ground floor of the pavilion of the Parc des Eaux-Vives. Contemporary cuisine, a beautiful view of the lake and an inviting teak-decked terrace.

Roberto, 10 r. Pierre-Fatio, 1204, 0223 118 033, *Fax 0223 118 466* – . GZ e
closed 24 December - 1 January, Saturday dinner and Sunday – **Meals** - Italian rest. - a la carte 59/128.
◆ Vast restaurant made to look even more spacious by the mirrors on the walls. Intimate ambience for Italian cuisine showing Milanese influence.

Le Patio, 19 bd Helvétique, 1207, 0227 366 675, *Fax 0227 864 074* – GZ b
closed 23 December - 4 January, Saturday and Sunday – **Meals** 52 (lunch) and a la carte 63/103.
◆ This establishment has two modern dining rooms, one of them designed as a winter garden. A selection of seasonal recipes and Provençal specialities make easy bedfellows.

Buffet de la Gare des Eaux-Vives (Labrosse), 7 av. de la Gare des Eaux-Vives, ✉ 1207, ☎ 0228 404 430, *Fax 0228 404 431*, – AE MC VISA
closed 18 December - 2 January, Monday lunch from July - August, Saturday and Sunday – **Meals** 48 (lunch)/120 and a la carte 84/125. East direction Annemasse Z
Spec. Bruschetta de homard et tomate confite, vinaigrette au piment doux, millefeuille de légumes. Dos de cabillaud en risotto tomate, supions à la plancha, jus réduit au balsamique (summer). Filet de boeuf en croûte persillée, cannelloni farci de queue de boeuf braisée. **Wines** Satigny, Peissy
◆ Not your ordinary station buffet, here is a boldly contemporary yet sober interior with a railway fresco, a waterside summer terrace and an inventive up-to-the-minute menu.

Environs

to the North :

Palais des Nations : *by quai Wilson* FGX *:*

Intercontinental, 7-9 ch. du Petit-Saconnex, ✉ 1209, ☎ 0229 193 939, *geneva@interconti.com, Fax 0229 193 838*, ≤, – rm, rm, video rm, – 15/400. AE MC VISA JCB
Rest : expected change of concept in January 2005 – 28 – **264 rm** 450/800, 63 suites.
◆ Next door to the Palais des Nations and ideal for conferences, this hotel counts heads of state among its guests. Elegant public areas, spotless rooms and a respected gastronomic restaurant which has benefited from a total facelift.

at Chambésy *North : 5 km – alt. 389 – ✉ 1292 Chambésy :*

Relais de Chambésy, 8 pl. de Chambésy, ☎ 0227 581 105, *Fax 0227 580 230*, – AE MC VISA JCB
closed 24 December - 10 January, Saturday and Sunday – **Meals** 38 (lunch)/90 and a la carte 62/119 – ***Le Bistrot :*** **Meals** 34 (lunch) and a la carte 41/75.
◆ An authentic country inn on the village square with three charming dining rooms offering traditional dishes showing creative flair. The Bistrot's more traditional menu includes simpler, more budget-conscious fare.

at Bellevue *by rte de Lausanne : 6 km – alt. 380 – ✉ 1293 Bellevue :*

La Réserve , 301 rte de Lausanne, ☎ 0229 595 959, *info@lareserve.ch, Fax 0229 595 960*, ≤, , – rm, video rm, AE MC VISA
Tsé-Fung : - Chinese rest. - **Meals** 70/120 and a la carte 71/143 – ***Le Loti :*** **Meals** 59 (lunch) and a la carte 65/135 – 30 – **85 rm** 550/990, 17 suites.
◆ Most of the modern rooms of this luxury hotel have a terrace overlooking the park with its swimming pool. Splendid Garcia décor. Sample fine Chinese cuisine at the Tsé Fung or contemporary food at the Loti.

to the East by road to Evian :

at Cologny *by Quai Gustave Ador* GY *: 3,5 km – alt. 432 – ✉ 1223 Cologny :*

Auberge du Lion d'Or (Byrne/Dupont), 5 pl. Pierre-Gautier, ☎ 0227 364 432, *Fax 0227 867 462*, ≤, – rest, AE MC VISA JCB
closed 2 weeks Easter, 23 December - 10 January, Saturday and Sunday – **Meals** 70 (lunch)/160 and a la carte 102/161 – ***Le Bistro de Cologny :*** **Meals** 45 (lunch) and a la carte 62/106.
Spec. Ris de veau doré, laqué d'un jus d'oignons, caramélisé au tamarin, laitue sucrine croquante. Filets de rouget à la plancha, poêlée de courgette aux amandes, fleurs de câpres et tomate. Filet mignon de veau "élevage naturel" en aitre-doux au miel, confiture de tomate au jasmin, sésame et pistaches. **Wines** Genève
◆ The superb backdrop to this elegant, contemporary-style restaurant encompasses both the lake and surrounding mountains. Enticing menu and chef's recommendations.

at Anières *by road to Hermance : 7 km – alt. 410 – ✉ 1247 Anières :*

Auberge de Floris (Legras), 287 rte d'Hermance, ☎ 0227 512 020, *contact@auberge-de-floris.com, Fax 0227 512 250*, ≤ lake, – AE MC VISA
closed 8 to 12 September, 24 December - 10 January, Sunday and Monday – **Meals** 58 (lunch)/135 and a la carte 97/163 – **Meals** (see also ***Le Bistrot*** below).
Spec. Coussinet d'omble du Lac Léman à la chicorée. Plein cœur de côte de bœuf du Simmenthal, sauce Foyot. Soufflé chaud au pain d'épices. **Wines** Anières
◆ Elegant auberge serving contemporary cuisine, with a lovely view over the lake. Totally refurbished panoramic dining room and comfortable observatory-style summer restaurant.

Le Bistrot - Auberge de Floris, 287 rte d'Hermance, ☎ 0227 512 020, *contact@auberge-de-floris.com, Fax 0227 512 250*, – AE MC VISA
closed 8 to 12 September, 24 December - 10 January, Sunday and Monday – **Meals** (booking essential) 45 and a la carte 53/98.
◆ Banish hunger at the bistro of the Floris inn, which offers diners a wonderful menu of contemporary dishes. Interesting themed fortnights throughout the year.

to the East by road to Annemasse :

at Thônex *by rte de Chêne* GZ *: 5 km – alt. 414 – 1226 Thônex :*

Le Cigalon (Bessire), 39 rte d'Ambilly, at the customs border of Pierre-à-Bochet, 0223 499 733, *jmbessire@le-cigalon.ch, Fax 0223 499 739,* – AE VISA
closed 27 March - 4 April, 17 July - 9 August, 24 December - 4 January, Sunday and Monday – **Meals** 44 (lunch)/99 and a la carte 77/124.
Spec. Huîtres creuses de Marennes en trois préparations gourmandes (in season). Cassolette de chanterelles aux saveurs marines. Rouget en filet sur peau croustillante, risotto à l'encre de seiche. **Wines** Satigny, Jussy
• Lovers of seafood should pause here before crossing the border and allow themselves a gastronomic interlude. Fish dishes have pride of place on the limited modern menu.

to the South :

at Conches *Southeast : 5 km – alt. 419 – 1231 Conches :*

Le Vallon, 182 rte de Florissant, 0223 471 104, *vallon@chateauvieux.ch, Fax 0223 463 111,* – AE VISA
closed 24 December - 2 January, Saturday and Sunday – **Meals** 46 (lunch)/78 and a la carte 67/118.
• Charming bistro-style establishment where you can see into the kitchen as a range of dishes are prepared. Little easels propping up the menu, a nice touch. Secluded terrace.

at Vessy *by road to Veyrier : 4 km – alt. 419 – 1234 Vessy :*

Alain Lavergnat, 130 rte de Veyrier, 0227 842 626, *Fax 0227 841 334,* – AE VISA
closed 24 July - 15 August, 19 December - 3 January, Sunday and Monday – **Meals** 52/101 and a la carte 64/133.
• An old Geneva villa is the setting for this restaurant serving elegant and traditional cuisine in a rustic-style dining room with an adjoining winter garden.

at Carouge *by Av. Henri-Dunant* FZ *: 3 km – alt. 382 – 1227 Carouge :*

Ramada Encore, 12 rte des Jeunes, 0223 095 000, *geneve.encore@ramada-treff.ch, Fax 0223 095 005* – rm, video rm, rest, – 15/240. AE VISA JCB. rest
Meals *(closed Saturday, Sunday and Bank Holidays)* 32 and a la carte 42/66 – 18 – **130 rm** 170/230.
• Modern building by a motorway exit, between a stadium and a shopping centre. Conference centre, neat and tidy rooms and good breakfasts. Meals are buffets or a concise international selection à la carte.

Auberge de Pinchat with rm, 33 ch. de Pinchat, 0223 423 077, *Fax 0223 002 219,* – AE VISA p. 4 CV k
closed 24 December - 3 January, 20 to 28 March and 7 to 29 August – **Meals** *(closed Sunday and Monday)* 45 (lunch)/98 and a la carte 70/124 – **5 rm** 120/145.
• Sobriety and tradition are the watchwords of this homely inn with its charming outside terrace for summer dining. Limited number of bedrooms available.

at Petit-Lancy *by Av. Henri-Dunant* FZ *: 3 km – alt. 426 – 1213 Petit-Lancy :*

Hostellerie de la Vendée, 28 ch. de la Vendée, 0227 920 411, *info@vendee.ch, Fax 0227 920 546,* – – 15/60. AE VISA JCB
closed Easter and 23 December - 2 January – **Meals** *(closed also 30 July - 14 August, 3 to 7 January, Saturday lunch, Sunday and Bank Holidays)* 57 (lunch)/150 and a la carte 67/156 – ***Bistro :*** *(closed also Saturday lunch, Sunday and Bank Holidays)* **Meals** 39/54 and a la carte 50/83 – **34 rm** 185/340.
Spec. Huîtres de Jersey en gelée d'eau de mer, tartare de champignons aux miettes d'araignée (winter). Barbue de l'Atlantique à la plancha, spaghetti de courgette au pistou (summer). Soufflé glacé aux marrons, poire rôtie au sucre brun, sauce anglaise au whisky (autumn). **Wines** Satigny
• In a quiet residential area, this hotel is just the place for a good night sleep. The elegant dining room of the gourmet restaurant is extended outwards in the form of a delightful winter garden-style conservatory. Classic French meals much loved by foodies.

at Lully *South-West : 8 km by road to Bernex – alt. 430 – 1233 Bernex :*

La Colombière (Lonati), 122 rte de Soral, 0227 571 027, *Fax 0227 576 549,* – AE VISA
closed 20 August - 11 September, 19 December - 9 January, Saturday and Sunday – **Meals** (number of covers limited - booking essential) 48 (lunch)/142 and a la carte 74/124.
Spec. Crème de haricots blancs, févettes et foie gras rôti, petites ravioles à la truffe noire. Désossé gourmand de pigion des Deux-Sèvres, coulis de petits pois et crème fumée. Blanc-manger aux fraises, jus de pistaches caramélisées, gaufre et sucre glace. **Wines** Lully
• This picturesque old farmhouse with its lovely country-style interior owes its success to its cuisine, which is both refined and innovative.

to the West :

at Peney-Dessus *by road to Satigny and private lane : 10 km – ✉ 1242 Satigny :*

XXXX ✿✿ **Domaine de Châteauvieux** (Chevrier) with rm, 16, ch. de Châteauvieux, ✆ 0227 531 511, *info@chateauvieux.ch, Fax 0227 531 924*, ←, – ▤ rm, – 15. AE MC VISA
closed 27 March - 4 April, 31 July - 15 August and 24 December - 10 January – **Meals** *(closed Sunday and Monday)* 88 (lunch)/240 and a la carte 166/226 – **12 rm** 210/400.
Spec. Porcelet laineux d'Aire-La-Ville. Bison de Collex Bossy. Menu truffe noire (January - February). **Wines** Satigny
◆ This former farm surrounded by vineyards has been transformed into an elegant hotel-restaurant renowned for its exquisite cuisine and prestigious vintage wines.

at Cointrin *by road to Lyons : 4 km – alt. 428 – ✉ 1216 Cointrin :*

Mövenpick Genève, 20 rte Pré-Bois, ✆ 0227 171 111, *hotel.geneva@moevenpick.com, Fax 0227 171 122*, – rm, ▤ rm, – 15/400. AE MC VISA JCB
Meals a la carte 45/93 – ***Kamome :*** - Japanese rest. - *(closed 30 July - 21 August, Saturday lunch, Monday lunch and Sunday)* **Meals** 37 (lunch)/112 and a la carte 61/95 – 32 – **344 rm** 430/560, 6 suites.
◆ A chain hotel close to the airport. Facilities include lounges, bars, casino, conference rooms, business centre and various categories of bedrooms. Classic cuisine in the Brasserie, plus Japanese specialities at the Kamome, including teppanyaki and sushi bar.

Ramada Park Hotel, 75-77 av. Louis-Casaï, ✆ 0227 103 000, *resa@ramadaparkhotel.ch, Fax 0227 103 100*, – rm, ▤ rm, – 15/550. AE MC VISA JCB. rest
La Récolte : **Meals** 31 and a la carte 43/107 – 30 – **302 rm** 195/440, 6 suites.
◆ Next door to the airport, a hotel with a wide range of amenities including a newspaper kiosk, a hairdresser's, a sauna and fitness centre, and meeting rooms. The bedrooms are modern. Some weeks the contemporary restaurant stages a themed menu.

Express by Holiday Inn without rest, 16 rte de Pré-Bois, ✆ 0229 393 939, *info@expressgeneva.com, Fax 0229 393 930* – ▤ video rm, – 15/25. AE MC VISA JCB – **154 rm** 225.
◆ Intended to be modern and practical, this new addition to the Holiday Inn chain is tailor-made for business travel. Good triple-glazed rooms.

Ibis, 10 ch. de la Violette, ✆ 0227 109 500, *H3535@accor-hotels.com, Fax 0227 109 595*, – rm, ▤ rm, rest, . AE MC VISA
Meals 35 and a la carte approx. 41 – 14 – **109 rm** 129.
◆ Near the motorway and Geneva airport, you can find the whole range of the Ibis chain hotel services. Standard rooms with bathroom units. The restaurant has a slightly globe-trotting menu and a comfortable terrace.

at Meyrin *by road to Meyrin : 5 km – alt. 445 – ✉ 1217 Meyrin :*

NH Geneva Airport Hotel, 21 av. de Mategnin, ✆ 0229 899 000, *nhgenevaairport@nh-hotels.ch, Fax 0229 899 999* – rm, ▤ – 15/60. AE MC VISA JCB
Meals a la carte 51/92 – 25 – **190 rm** 290/320.
◆ A circular red-brick construction whose outer appearance provides a foretaste of the contemporary interior. Functional bedrooms, all of which have been recently refurbished. New, modern restaurant with a Mediterranean-influenced menu.

at Palais des Expositions *by quai Wilson* FGX *: 5 km – alt. 452 – ✉ 1218 Grand-Saconnex :*

Crowne Plaza, 26 voie de Moëns, ✆ 0227 470 202, *reservations@cpgeneva.ch, Fax 0227 470 303*, – rm, ▤ rm, – 15/180. AE MC VISA JCB
L'Olivo : *(closed Saturday and Sunday except in summer)* **Meals** 39 (lunch) and a la carte 48/108 – 32 – **500 rm** 470/680.
◆ The facilities at this American-style hotel close to the airport include modern bedrooms, conference halls and a fitness centre. Contemporary cuisine in the restaurant whose decor is inspired by the south of France.

Vufflens-le-Château *1134 Vaud* 729 D6 552 D10 – 636 – *alt. 471.*

Bern 118 – Geneva 53 – Lausanne 14 – Morges 3 – Pontarlier 72 – Yverdon-les-Bains 41.

XXXX ✿✿ **L'Ermitage** (Ravet) with rm, 26 rte du Village, ✆ 0218 046 868, *ermitage@ravet.ch, Fax 0218 022 240*, – AE MC VISA
closed 7 to 23 August, 24 December - 18 January, Sunday and Monday – **Meals** 68 (lunch)/225 and a la carte 183/235 – **9 rm** 380/420.
Spec. Dinette des quatre foies gras d'oie et de canard. Poissons du Lac Léman cuit à basse température (summer). Jarret de veau rôti longuement à la broche. **Wines** Morges sur lie, Féchy
◆ Food and pleasure in perfect harmony in this delightful residence with its garden and lake. Exquisite rooms, plus everything necessary for a superlative dining experience.

Cossonay *1304 Vaud* **729** D6 **552** D9 *- 2 487 - alt. 565.*
Bern 107 - Lausanne 16 - Fribourg 78 - Geneva 62 - Yverdon-les-Bains 28.

XXX **Le Cerf** (Crisci), 10 r. du Temple, ✆ 0218 612 608, *lecerf@swissonline.ch, Fax 0218 612 627* – AE MC VISA JCB
✿✿ *closed 10 July - 4 August, 23 December - 7 January, Sunday and Monday* – **Meals** (see also ***La Fleur de Sel*** below) 80 (lunch)/230 and a la carte 122/208.
Spec. Parmentier de caviar. Pot-au-feu de foie gras au gingembre et vin jaune (summer). Filet d'agneau aux escargots (spring). **Wines** Echichens
◆ This 16C establishment offers a gorgeous blend of venerable décor (pillar room with Louis XIII chairs) and inventive cuisine. Visual delight allied to gastronomic pleasure.

X **La Fleur de Sel** - *Le Cerf*, 10 r. du Temple, ✆ 0218 612 608, *lecerf@swissonline.ch, Fax 0218 612 627* – ▤. AE MC VISA JCB
closed 10 July - 4 August, 23 December - 7 January, Sunday and Monday – **Meals** 55 and a la carte 58/106.
◆ This tiny bistro shares an entrance with the Restaurant du Cerf. Simple but attractive interior. Tempting menu with a choice selection of local specialities.

Crissier *1023 Vaud* **729** D6 **552** E9 *- 5 756 - alt. 470.*
Bern 112 - Geneva 71 - Lausanne 6 - Montreux 40 - Nyon 50 - Pontarlier 64.

XXXX **Hôtel de Ville - Philippe Rochat,** 1 r. d'Yverdon, ✆ 0216 340 505, *restaurant.p.rochat@bluewin.ch, Fax 0216 342 464* – 15. AE ⓓ MC VISA
✿✿✿ *closed 24 July - 16 August, 23 December - 11 January, Sunday and Monday* – **Meals** 170 (lunch)/280 and a la carte 127/265.
Spec. Yin et Yang de tourteaux de Belle Ile aux pointes d'asperges violettes du Valais (spring). Ormeaux de la Côte du Trégor et petits coquillages façon marinière aux artichauts violets (spring). Caneton croisé aux baies rouges vinaigrées (spring). **Wines** Féchy, Viognier
◆ Behind the venerable façade of this restaurant is an elegantly refurbished interior harmonising perfectly with the refinement and excellence of the cuisine.

Cully *1096 Vaud* **729** E6 **552** E10 *- 1 748 - alt. 391.*
Bern 93 - Geneva 77 - Lausanne 8 - Montreux 15 - Pontarlier 77 - Yverdon-les-Bains 45.

XXX **Le Raisin** (Blokbergen) with rm, 1 pl. de l'Hôtel de Ville, ✆ 0217 992 131, *raisin@worldcom.ch, Fax 0217 992 501,* – |‡|, ▤ rest, TV. AE ⓓ MC VISA
✿ **Meals** 89 (lunch)/198 and a la carte 92/198 – ***La Pinte*** : **Meals** 50/89 and a la carte 67/126 – **9 rm** 280/350.
Spec. Opéra de foie gras. Homard cuit sur gros sel. Couronne de noix de Saint-Jacques au caviar (winter). **Wines** St. Saphorin, Aigle
◆ A building full of character with two dining rooms, one contemporary, the other more rustic in style, serving inventive dishes showing regional influence. La Pinte offers good, traditional cooking with no frills. Bedrooms furnished with a personal touch.

Brent *Vaud* **729** E6 **552** F10 *- alt. 569.*
Bern 85 - Geneva 89 - Lausanne 25 - Martigny 47 - Montreux 5.

XXX **Le Pont de Brent** (Rabaey), 4 rte de Blonay, ✆ 0219 645 230, *rabaey@bluewin.ch, Fax 0219 645 530* – ▤ P. AE MC VISA
✿✿✿ *closed 10 July - 1 August, 24 December - 6 January, Sunday and Monday* – **Meals** 90 (lunch)/250 and a la carte 127/220.
Spec. Marbré de truite du lac, sauce cresson (January - October). Tourte de grenouilles aux asperges vertes, tagliatelles à la farine de châtaignes (May - June). Porcelet d'Ormalingen au miel et aux épices (September - March). **Wines** Yvorne, Villeneuve
◆ Gracious building in local style with an elegant interior, a fine setting for a sumptuous cuisine abounding in exquisite flavours. A gastronomic experience to be savoured !

Vevey *1800 Vaud* **729** E6 **552** F10 *- 15 420 - alt. 386.*
Bern 85 - Geneva 90 - Montreux 7 - Lausanne 16 - Yverdon-les-Bains 53.

XXX **Denis Martin,** 2 r. du Château, ✆ 0219 211 210, *chateau2@bluewin.ch, Fax 0219 214 552,* – AE ⓓ MC VISA
✿✿ *closed 1 to 10 May, 25 December - 11 January, Sunday and Monday* – **Meals** 68 (lunch)/220 and a la carte 141/196.
Spec. Truite du lac, huile de persil et pastille de vinaigre. Saint-Jacques au croquant de cacahuètes (September - May). L'eau d'une tomate, bille de menthe (June - October). **Wines** Lavaux, Chablais
◆ On the ground floor of the former seat of the brotherhood of wine-producers. Vaulted rooms, a fine summer terrace in the garden, and cuisine as original as it is innovative.

ZÜRICH 729 J3 551 P5 – 342 518 – alt. 409.

See : *The Quays*★★ : ≤★ FZ ; *Mythenquai* : ≤★ CX – *Fraumünster cloisters*★ *(Alter Kreuzgang des Fraumünsters), windows*★ EZ – *Church of SS. Felix and Regula*★ – *Cathedral*★ *(Grossmünster)* FZ – *Fine Arts Museum*★★ *(Kunsthaus)* FZ – *Zoological Gardens*★ *(Zoo Zürich)* – *Bührle Collection*★★ *(Sammlung Bührle).*

Museums : *Swiss National Museum*★★★ *(Schweizerisches Landesmuseum)* EY – *Rietberg Museum*★★ CX M².

Envir : *Uetliberg*★★ *South-West : by rail* – *Albis Pass Road*★ *Southwest by the Bederstrasse* – *Former Abbey of Kappel*★ *Southwest : 22 km* – *Eglisau : site*★ *North : 27 km.*

Excursions : *Boat Trips, Information : Zürichsee-Schiffahrtsgesellschaft, Mythenquai 333, ℘ 014 871 333, Fax 014 871 320.*

9 Dolder (late March-late Sept.), ℘ 012 615 045, Fax 012 615 302 ; 18 at Zumikon, ✉ 8126 (April-October), ℘ 0432 881 088, Fax 0432 881 078, SE : 9 km ; 18 at Hittnau, ✉ 8335 (April-October), ℘ 019 502 442, Fax 019 510 166 E : 33 km, 18 at Breitenloo, ✉ 8309 Nürensdorf (April-October), ℘ 018 364 080, Fax 018 371 085 N : 22 km.

Unique Zürich airport, ℘ 0438 162 211.

Tourist Office, in the main station, ℘ 044 154 000, information@zuerich.com, Fax 044 154 044 – T.C.S., Alfred Escher-Str. 38, ℘ 012 868 686, Fax 012 868 687, Uraniastr. 14, ℘ 012 173 070, Fax 012 173 061 – A.C.S., Forchstr. 95, ℘ 013 877 500, Fax 013 877 509.

Bern 125 – Basle 109 – Geneva 278 – Innsbruck 288 – Milan 304.

Plans on following pages

On the right bank of the river Limmat (University, Fine Arts Museum) :

Zürich Marriott, Neumühlequai 42, ✉ 8006, ℘ 013 607 070, *marriott.zurich@marriotthotels.com, Fax 013 607 777,* ≤, – 15/250. AE VISA. rest EY c
White Elephant : - Thai rest. - *(closed Saturday lunch and Sunday lunch)* **Meals** 38 (lunch)/85 and a la carte 52/96 – ***La Brasserie*** : **Meals** a la carte 45/93 – 34 – **252 rm** 295/335, 9 suites.
◆ This tall building with basement parking and riverside location offers comfortable, modern, recently renovated rooms varying in size and décor. The White Elephant restaurant transports diners to far-off Siam, while the Brasserie is somewhat less exotic.

Eden au Lac, Utoquai 45, ✉ 8008, ℘ 0442 662 525, *info@edenaulac.ch, Fax 0442 662 500,* ≤, – 20. AE VISA JCB. rest DX a
Meals 48 (lunch)/145 and a la carte 66/137 – **48 rm** 420/710, 5 suites.
◆ Having set the architectural tone for Zürich's lakeside in 1909, this neo-Baroque hotel is now a listed cultural monument. Inside you will find everything you expect from a luxury hotel. The menu sets out a fine selection of classic international cuisine.

Steigenberger Bellerive au Lac, Utoquai 47, ✉ 8008, ℘ 012 544 000, *bellerive@steigenberger.ch, Fax 012 544 001,* ≤, rm, rm, – 15/25. AE VISA DX e
Meals 48 (lunch) and a la carte 51/115 – **51 rm** 300/490.
◆ With its elegant décor in the style of the 1920s, this establishment stands on the lakeside. State-of-the-art design, comfort, and technical facilities in every room. Small, stylish restaurant with classic décor and beautifully upholstered seating.

Sofitel, Stampfenbachstr. 60, ✉ 8006, ℘ 0443 606 060, *h1196@accor.com, Fax 0443 606 061,* – rm, rm, rest, – 15/40. AE VISA JCB FY b
Bel Etage : **Meals** 32 (lunch) and a la carte 54/108 – 32 – **149 rm** 400/480, 4 suites.
◆ Attractive décor throughout, based on the use of wood and warm colours, from the foyer in the style of an elegant Swiss chalet to the soundproofed rooms. A wide-ranging menu is served in the Bel Etage restaurant.

Dolder Waldhaus , Kurhausstr. 20, ✉ 8032, ℘ 0442 691 000, *reservations@doldenwaldhaus.ch, Fax 0442 691 001,* ≤ Zurich and lake, – rm, rest, – 15/30. AE VISA JCB by Gloriastrasse DV
Meals a la carte 55/106 – 20 – **70 rm** 240/460.
◆ In a quiet location, this hotel offers rooms in modern style, all with balcony and fine views over city and lake, plus apartments for families or longer stays There's a traditional atmosphere in the restaurant, which has a pleasant terrace.

Central Plaza, Central 1, ✉ 8001, ℘ 0442 565 656, *info@central.ch, Fax 0442 565 657,* – rm, rm, . AE VISA JCB FY z
King's Cave : - Grill room - **Meals** a la carte 42/91 – 18 – **94 rm** 288/308, 6 suites.
◆ This establishment is right on the River Limmat directly opposite the main station. Rooms are all in the same modern and comfortable style, calculated to meet guests' every need. The vaulted cellars house the King's Cave grill.

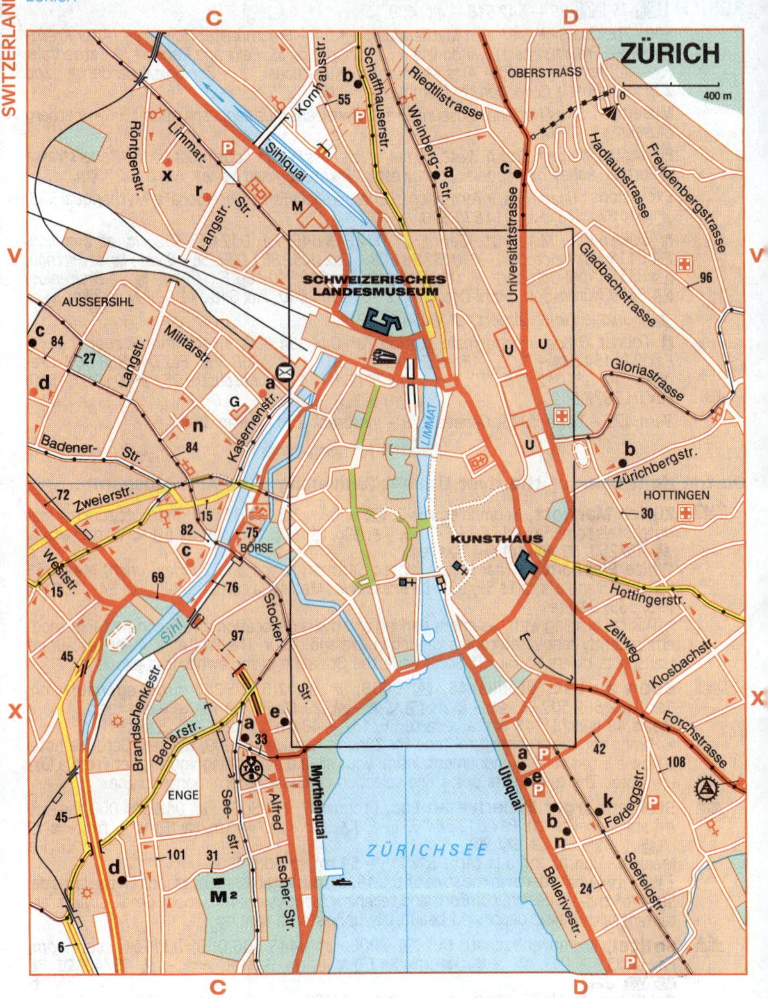

Allmendstrasse	CX	6
Augustinergasse	EZ	9
Bärengasse	EZ	10
Bahnhofstrasse	EYZ	
Beethovenstrasse	EZ	12
Bellevueplatz	FZ	
Birmensdorfer Strasse	CX	15
Claridenstrasse	EZ	18
Clausiusstrasse	FY	19
Culmannstrasse	FY	21
Dufourstrasse	DX	24
Feldstrasse	CV	27
Fraumünsterstrasse	EZ	28
Freiestrasse	DVX	30
Gablerstrasse	CX	31
General Wille-Strasse	CX	33
Hafnerstrasse	EY	36
Kantonsschulstrasse	FZ	39
Konradstrasse	EY	40
Kreuzstrasse	DX	42
Limmatquai	FYZ	
Löwenstrasse	EY	
Manessestrasse	CX	45
Marktgasse	FZ	46
Münsterhof	EZ	48
Museumstrasse	EY	49
Nelkenstrasse	FY	52
Neumarkt	FZ	54
Nordstrasse	DV	55
Paradeplatz	EZ	
Peterstrasse	EZ	57
Poststrasse	EZ	58
Rathausbrücke	EFZ	60
Rennweg	EYZ	63
Rindermarkt	FZ	64
Schimmelstrasse	CX	69
Seebahnstrasse	CX	72
Selnaustrasse	CX	75
Sihlhölzlistrasse	CX	76
Stadelhoferstrasse	FZ	78
Stampfenbachplatz	FY	79
Stampfenbachstrasse	EFY	81
Stauffacherplatz	CX	82
Stauffacherstrasse	CVX	84
Storchengasse	EZ	85
Strehlgasse	EZ	87
Sumatrastrasse	FY	88
Talacker	EZ	90
Tannenstrasse	FY	91
Theaterstrasse	FZ	93
Toblerstrasse	DV	96
Tunnelstrasse	CX	97
Uraniastrasse	EYZ	
Usteristrasse	EY	100
Waffenplatzstrasse	CX	101
Weinbergfussweg	FY	103
Zollikerstrasse	DX	108

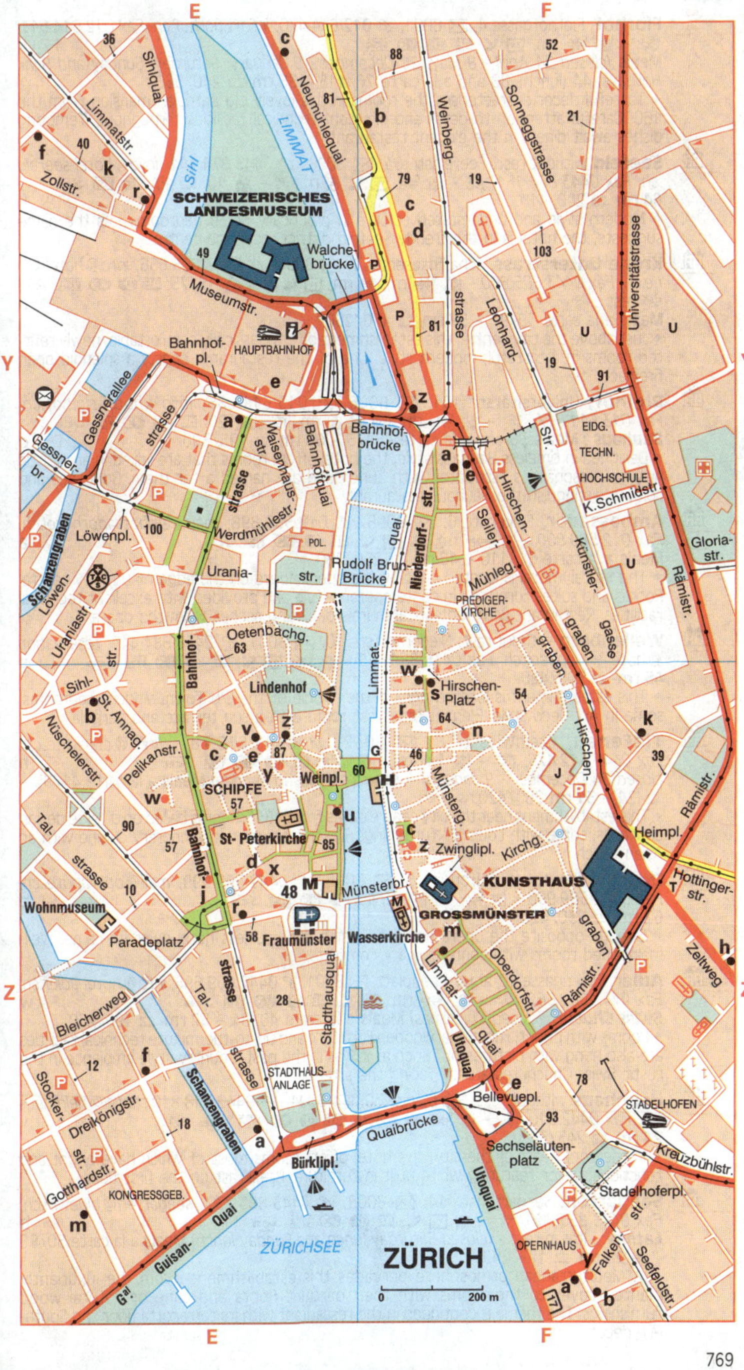
E
F
Y
Z
SCHWEIZERISCHES LANDESMUSEUM
Sihl
LIMMAT
Sihlquai
Limmatstr.
Zollstr.
Neumühlequai
Weinberg-
strasse
Sonneggstrasse
Universitätstrasse
Leonhard-
Str.
Walche-
brücke
Museumstr.
HAUPTBAHNHOF
Bahnhof-
pl.
Gessnerallee
Gessner-
br.
strasse
Waisenhaus-
str.
Bahnhofquai
Bahnhof-
brücke
EIDG.
TECHN.
HOCHSCHULE
K.Schmidstr.
Gloria-
str.
Hirschen-
Seiler
Künstler-
gasse
Rämistr.
Niederdorf-
str.
quai
Schanzengraben
Löwenpl.
Werdmühlestr.
POL.
Urania-
str.
Rudolf Brun-
Brücke
Mühleg.
PREDIGER-
KIRCHE
graben
Löwen-
Uraniastr.
str.
Oetenbachg.
Bahnhof-
Limmat-
Lindenhof
Hirschen-
Platz
Sihl-
St. Annag.
Nüschelerstr.
Pelikanstr.
SCHIPFE
Weinpl.
Münsterg.
Hirschen-
graben
Heimpl.
Tal-
strasse
St-Peterkirche
Zwinglipl.
Kirchg.
KUNSTHAUS
Hottinger-
str.
Wohnmuseum
Münsterbr.
GROSSMÜNSTER
Paradeplatz
Fraumünster
Wasserkirche
Oberdorfstr.
Zeltweg
Bleicherweg
Tal-
strasse
Stadthausquai
Limmat-
quai
Utoquai
Rämistr.
Stocker-
Dreikönigstr.
str.
Schanzengraben
strasse
STADTHAUS-
ANLAGE
Bellevuepl.
STADELHOFEN
Quaibrücke
Sechseläuten-
platz
Kreuzbühlstr.
Bürklipl.
Gotthardstr.
KONGRESSGEB.
Gal. Guisan-
Quai
ZÜRICHSEE
Utoquai
Stadelhoferpl.
OPERNHAUS
Falken-
str.
Seefeldstr.
ZÜRICH
0
200 m
36
40
49
88
81
79
52
21
19
103
19
91
100
63
54
64
9
87
46
60
57
85
90
57
10
48
58
28
12
18
78
93
39
17

Florhof, Florhofgasse 4, ✉ 8001, ☎ 012 614 470, *info@florhof.ch, Fax 012 614 611,* – rm, AE VISA FZ k
Meals *(closed 24 April - 8 May, 24 December - 9 January, Saturday, Sunday and Bank Holidays)* 44 (lunch)/88 and a la carte 76/115 – **35 rm** 240/360.
◆ Tasteful décor characterises the rooms in this lovely old patrician mansion from the 16C. Careful attention to detail and excellent technical facilities throughout. Tempting dishes await diners in the elegant restaurant.

Seefeld without rest, Seefeldstr. 63, ✉ 8008, ☎ 0443 874 141, *info@hotel-seefeld.ch, Fax 0443 874 151,* – rm, – 10. AE VISA JCB
64 rm 200/410. DX k
◆ Modern style and understated colours in practically fitted bedrooms : as the name suggests, the hotel is in the trendy Seefeld district, near the centre

Krone Unterstrass, Schaffhauserstr. 1, ✉ 8006, ☎ 0443 605 656, *info@hotel-krone.ch, Fax 0443 605 600* – rm, rm, – 15/75. AE VISA JCB. rest CV b
Meals a la carte 39/97 – **57 rm** 170/250.
◆ Just above the city centre, this establishment offers classically comfortable, newly refitted rooms in a tasteful, modern style. One of the restaurants boasts a splendid open fireplace.

Rigihof, Universitätstr. 101, ✉ 8006, ☎ 013 611 685, *info@hotel-rigihof.ch, Fax 013 611 617,* – rm, rm, – 20. AE VISA JCB
***Bauhaus* : Meals** 36 and a la carte 45/75 – **66 rm** 195/390. DV c
◆ Designed in timeless Bauhaus style, the hotel offers rooms that are linked in an artistic way to personalities associated with Zürich and are named after them. Bold lines and colours distinguish the Bauhaus restaurant.

Ambassador, Falkenstr. 6, ✉ 8008, ☎ 012 589 898, *mail@ambassadorhotel.ch, Fax 012 589 800* – rm, AE VISA JCB FZ a
Meals a la carte 51/116 – **45 rm** 250/480.
◆ This stately hotel is located right by the opera house on the edge of the city centre. Rooms and suites furnished in contemporary style and provided with excellent technical facilities. Restaurant with fantastical murals depicting scenes from the opera.

Wellenberg without rest, Niederdorfstr. 10, ✉ 8001, ☎ 0438 884 444, *reservation@hotel-wellenberg.ch, Fax 0438 884 445* – AE VISA JCB FZ s
45 rm 305/420.
◆ This establishment is located right in the middle of the Old Town. Modern bedrooms, some in Art Deco style. Elegant breakfast room with a sun terrace and pergola.

Tiefenau, Steinwiesstr. 8, ✉ 8032, ☎ 0442 678 787, *info@claridge.ch, Fax 0442 512 476,* – rm, AE VISA JCB FZ h
closed 24 December - 9 January – ***Orson's* :** *(closed Sunday)* **Meals** a la carte 41/95 – 24 – **31 rm** 280/420.
◆ This establishment near the city centre dates from 1835. Rooms based on diverse design concepts, some with Louis XV furnishings. Orson's serves contemporary cuisine with an Asian touch.

Opera without rest, Dufourstr. 5, ✉ 8008, ☎ 0442 589 999, *mail@operahotel.ch, Fax 0442 589 900* – AE VISA JCB FZ b
62 rm 230/420.
◆ Directly opposite the opera house to which this business hotel owes its name. Well-maintained rooms with contemporary comforts.

Adler, Rosengasse 10, at Hirschenplatz, ✉ 8001, ☎ 0442 669 696, *info@hotel-adler.ch, Fax 0442 669 669,* – rm, AE VISA JCB FZ w
***Swiss Chuchi* :** *(closed Christmas)* **Meals** a la carte 40/84 – **52 rm** 190/250.
◆ Rooms with bright, functional wooden furniture and up-to-the-minute technical facilities are also hung with pictures of Zürich as it was in the past. Country-style ambience in the rustic Swiss-Chuchi restaurant facing the street.

Helmhaus without rest, Schifflände 30, ✉ 8001, ☎ 0442 518 810, *hotel@helmhaus.ch, Fax 0442 510 430* – AE VISA JCB. FZ v
24 rm 245/342.
◆ In the very heart of the city, this hotel offers rooms most of which have bright and functional décor featuring white built-in furniture. Breakfast on the first floor.

Seegarten, Seegartenstr. 14, ✉ 8008, ☎ 0443 883 737, *seegarten@bluewin.ch, Fax 0443 833 738,* – AE VISA JCB DX b
***Latino* :** - Italian rest. - *(closed Saturday lunch and Sunday lunch)* **Meals** a la carte 50/86 – **28 rm** 179/299.
◆ A Mediterranean atmosphere pervades this establishment, from the luxuriantly planted foyer to the rooms with their parquet floors and cane or natural wood furnishings. The theme is continued in the restaurant with its terracotta floor and Southern decor.

Rex, Weinbergstr. 92, ✉ 8006, ☎ 013 602 525, *rex@zuerich-hotels.ch, Fax 013 602 552*, – |‡|, ⇹ rm, TV. AE MC VISA JCB DV a
Blauer Apfel : *(closed Saturday and Sunday)* **Meals** a la carte 48/79 – **38 rm** 145/195.
◆ On the edge of the city centre, this hotel offers colourful bedrooms, some larger than others, but all designed with functional simplicity. The Blauer Apfel restaurant is cheerful and inviting.

Lady's First without rest, Mainaustr. 24, ✉ 8008, ☎ 0443 808 010, *info@ladysfirst.ch, Fax 0443 808 020*, – |‡| TV rm,. AE MC VISA DX n
closed 24 December - 3 January – **28 rm** 195/280.
◆ The upper floors and the spa, with its spacious roof terrace, are exclusively for women travellers. Guests sleep in contemporary style rooms with built-in furniture.

Hirschen without rest, Niederdorfstr. 13, ✉ 8001, ☎ 0432 683 333, *info@hirschen-zuerich.ch, Fax 0432 683 334* – |‡| ⇹ TV rm,. MC VISA FY g
– **27 rm** 135/200.
◆ The 300 year-old Hirschen offers practical, modern rooms and a wine bar in the vaulted cellars, which date back to the 16C.

Plattenhof, Plattenstr. 26, ✉ 8032, ☎ 012 511 910, *hotel@plattenhof.ch, Fax 012 511 911* – |‡|, ⇹ rm, TV rm, rest, – 20. AE MC VISA DV b
Sento : - Italian rest. - *(closed Saturday lunch and Sunday lunch)* **Meals** a la carte 54/95 – **37 rm** 165/305.
◆ This hotel is in a residential area on the edge of the city centre : stylishly decorated designer rooms and personal service are its two strong suits. The trendy Sento restaurant specialises in fresh-tasting Piedmontese cuisine.

Rütli without rest, Zähringerstr. 43, ✉ 8001, ☎ 0442 545 800, *info@rutli.ch, Fax 0442 545 801*, – |‡| ⇹ TV rm,. AE MC VISA JCB FY a
closed 23 December - 3 January – **62 rm** 195/290.
◆ Located near the station, this hotel has a prettily furnished lobby, bedrooms with straightforward modern furnishings, and a generous breakfast buffet.

Sonnenberg, Hitziweg 15, ✉ 8032, ☎ 012 669 797, *restaurant@sonnenberg-zh.ch, Fax 012 669 798*, Zürich and lake, – rest, P. AE MC VISA
Meals - veal and beef specialities - (booking essential) a la carte 79/141.
◆ High up in the FIFA Building with a grandstand view of city, lake, and Alps. Classic French dishes served in the half-moon-shaped panoramic restaurant. by Gloriastrasse DV

Wirtschaft Flühgass, Zollikerstr. 214, ✉ 8008, ☎ 013 811 215, *info@fluehgass.ch, Fax 014 227 532* – P. AE MC VISA by Zollikerstrasse DX
closed 16 July - 14 August, 24 December - 2 January, Saturday (except dinner from November - December) and Sunday – **Meals** (booking essential) 62/135 and a la carte 56/121.
◆ The old 16C wine bar is now a congenial restaurant serving cuisine with a traditional French flavour.

Haus zum Rüden, Limmatquai 42 (1st floor), ✉ 8001, ☎ 0442 619 566, *info@hauszumrueden.ch, Fax 0442 611 804* – |‡|. AE MC VISA JCB FZ c
closed Christmas, Saturday and Sunday – **Meals** 59 (lunch)/135 and a la carte 72/135.
◆ This restaurant, with an amazing wooden ceiling, is in a 13C guild house. The elegant, historical atmosphere in keeping with a classic menu.

Riesbächli, Zollikerstr. 157, ✉ 8008, ☎ 014 222 324, *Fax 014 222 941* – rest, AE MC VISA by Zollikerstrasse DX
closed 16 July - 14 August, 24 December - 3 January, Saturday (except dinner from November - March) and Sunday – **Meals** 110 and a la carte 70/139.
◆ This traditional restaurant is divided up into three visually separate dining areas. Remarkable choice of wines to go with a range of classic dishes.

Conti-da Bianca, Dufourstr. 1, ✉ 8008, ☎ 012 510 666, *Fax 012 510 686* – AE MC VISA FZ y
Meals - Italian rest. - a la carte 53/118.
◆ On the edge of the city centre. Tastefully decorated and elegantly lit, this establishment consists of a long dining room with a stucco ceiling. Classic Italian cuisine.

Zunfthaus zur Zimmerleuten, Limmatquai 40, ✉ 8001, ☎ 0442 505 363, *zimmerleuten-zurich@bluewin.ch, Fax 0442 505 364*, – |‡|. AE MC VISA FZ z
closed 24 July - 7 August, Christmas and New Year – ***Restaurant :*** (1st floor) **Meals** a la carte 56/111 – ***Küferstube :*** **Meals** 58/88 and a la carte 38/82.
◆ Built in 1708 as a carpenters' guildhall : carved beams set a welcoming tone in the first floor restaurant ; with old barrels and dark wood fittings in the "Coopers' Bar".

Casa Ferlin, Stampfenbachstr. 38, ✉ 8006, ☎ 013 623 509, *casaferlin@bluewin.ch, Fax 013 623 534* – . AE MC VISA FY c
closed mid July - mid August, Saturday and Sunday – **Meals** - Italian rest. - (booking essential) 52 (lunch)/105 and a la carte 63/124.
◆ This classically styled restaurant, with its open fireplace and rustic furnishings, has been family run since 1907 : it's one of the oldest Italian restaurants in the city.

Lake Side, Bellerivestr. 170, ✉ 8008, ✆ 013 858 600, *info@lake-side.ch, Fax 013 858 601,* ≤ Zürichsee, 🏠 – ▤. AE ⓓ MC VISA. ⚹
Meals a la carte 60/127. South by Bellerivestrasse DX
◆ Choose from contemporary cooking or sushi at this modern restaurant in Seepark Zürichhorn. The large lakefront terrace is particularly appealing in summer.

Vorderer Sternen, Theaterstr. 22, ✉ 8001, ✆ 012 514 949, *info@vorderer-stern en.ch, Fax 012 529 063,* 🏠 – AE ⓓ MC VISA JCB FZ e
Meals (1st floor) a la carte 42/106.
◆ Straightforward café on the ground floor, above it a homely restaurant with dark wood décor. Good modern dishes at reasonable prices.

Blue Monkey Cocostin, Stüssihofstatt 3, ✉ 8001, ✆ 012 617 618, *koenigstuhl@ bluewin.ch, Fax 012 627 123,* 🏠 – AE ⓓ MC VISA FZ r
closed Sunday from January - March, Saturday lunch and Sunday lunch – **Meals** (1st floor) - Thai rest. - 50 (dinner) and a la carte 56/92.
◆ A Thai restaurant has been established on two floors of the historic guildhall called the Zunfthaus zur Schneidern. Ground floor bar-bistro, fine dining above.

Oepfelchammer, Rindermarkt 12, ✉ 8001, ✆ 012 512 336, *Fax 012 627 533,* 🏠 – AE ⓓ MC VISA FZ n
closed 18 July - 16 August, 23 December - 4 January, Monday, Sunday and Bank Holidays – **Meals** (1st floor) 61 (lunch)/110 and a la carte 53/93.
◆ The famous 19C Swiss writer Gottfried Keller was a regular in the wine bar in this 14C establishment. Good solid fare in the restaurant including local specialities.

Rosaly's, Freieckgasse 7, ✉ 8001, ✆ 012 614 430, *info@rosalys.ch, Fax 012 614 413,* 🏠 – AE ⓓ MC VISA JCB FZ e
Meals *(closed Saturday lunch and Sunday lunch)* a la carte 44/79.
◆ Contemporary, simply furnished restaurant with relaxed atmosphere, offering interesting international dishes prepared in a refined traditional style.

Frieden, Stampfenbachstr. 32, ✉ 8006, ✆ 012 531 810, *Fax 012 531 812,* 🏠 – AE ⓓ MC VISA. ⚹ rest FY d
closed 24 March - 10 April, 2 to 16 October, Saturday and Sunday – **Meals** a la carte 53/99.
◆ Housed in a municipal building, this is a bistro-style restaurant with plain wooden furnishings and parquet flooring. Friendly service.

Blaue Ente, Seefeldstr. 223 (mill Tiefenbrunnen), ✉ 8008, ✆ 013 886 840, *info@b laue-ente.ch, Fax 014 227 741,* 🏠 – AE ⓓ MC VISA by Zollikerstrasse DX
closed 24 July - 7 August and 24 December - 2 January – **Meals** (booking essential) a la carte 57/116.
◆ This trendy establishment with lots of glass, pipework, and gigantic gearwheels is housed in an old mill. Cheerful atmosphere and good, unfussy cooking in a modern style.

Ban Song Thai, Kirchgasse 6, ✉ 8001, ✆ 0442 523 331, *bansong@bluewin.ch, Fax 0442 523 315* – AE MC VISA FZ m
closed 21 July - 11 August, 19 December - 3 January, Saturday lunch and Sunday – **Meals** - Thai rest. - (booking essential) 59 and a la carte 48/101.
◆ This restaurant is very close to Kunsthaus and Cathedral. Its name evokes its offerings - you are cordially invited by your hosts to take a gastronomic trip to Thailand.

On the left bank of the river Limmat (Main railway station, Business centre) :

Baur au Lac, Talstr. 1, ✉ 8001, ✆ 0442 205 020, *info@bauraulac.ch, Fax 0442 205 044,* 🏠, 🏋, 🌳 – 🛗, ▤ rm, 📺 ✆ ♿ rm, 🚗 – 🏛 15/60. AE ⓓ MC VISA JCB. ⚹ EZ a
Le Pavillon/Le Français : **Meals** 90 (lunch)/140 and a la carte 78/178 – ***Rive Gauche*** : *(closed 3 weeks July - August and Sunday)* **Meals** a la carte 62/118 – ☕ 38 – **104 rm** 520/720, 20 suites.
◆ Elegant is the only word for this imposing 19C hotel, its grand entrance hall, lovely garden and luxurious rooms. Diners are treated to classic cuisine in the Pavillon in summer and in the Français in winter. The Rive Gauche has a touch of colonial style.

Savoy Baur en Ville, Paradeplatz, ✉ 8001, ✆ 0442 152 525, *welcome@savoy-zu erich.ch, Fax 0442 152 500* – 🛗 ▤ 📺 ✆ ♿ rm, ♿ rest, – 🏛 15/70. AE ⓓ MC VISA JCB. ⚹ EZ r
Savoy : (1st floor) **Meals** 64 (lunch) and a la carte 70/144 – ***Orsini*** : (in front of the cathedral) - Italian rest. - **Meals** (booking essential) 59 (lunch)/98 and a la carte 76/153 – **104 rm** ☕ 470/720, 8 suites.
◆ In the heart of town, the grandiose 19C architecture of this establishment offers guests the most stylish of settings. Exemplary service and an elegant, modern interior. The first-floor Savoy is classically elegant ; the Orsini provides an Italian alternative.

Widder, Rennweg 7, ✉ 8001, ✆ 012 242 526, *home@widderhotel.ch, Fax 012 242 424,* , - , rest, - 15/120. AE VISA. rest EZ v
Meals 88 (dinner) and a la carte 73/126 – **42 rm** 450/810, 7 suites.
• Ten historic Old Town houses have been renovated and combined to form this hotel. Distinguished interior, superlative comfort, contemporary architectural features. The two restaurants are full of charm and character.

Schweizerhof, Bahnhofplatz 7, ✉ 8001, ✆ 0442 188 888, *info@hotelschweizerhof.com, Fax 0442 188 181* - , rm, - 15/40. AE VISA. rest EY a
La Soupière : (1st floor) *(closed Saturday from mid July - mid August and Sunday)* **Meals** 72 (lunch) and a la carte 83/145 – **115 rm** 400/700.
• This historic establishment stands in the very heart of town directly opposite the main station. Beyond the imposing façade is an interior of contemporary elegance and great comfort. The La Soupière restaurant has a classically tasteful ambience.

Ascot, Tessinerplatz 9, ✉ 8002, ✆ 012 081 414, *info@ascot.ch, Fax 012 081 420,* - , rm, - 15/30. AE VISA JCB CX a
Lawrence : *(closed Saturday and Sunday)* **Meals** 62 (lunch) / 82 and a la carte 62/127 – **74 rm** 390/580.
• This stylishly decorated establishment offers rooms with furniture in either mahogany or limewashed oak. The Lawrence decorated in Tudor style

Zum Storchen, Weinplatz 2, ✉ 8001, ✆ 0442 272 727, *info@storchen.ch, Fax 0442 272 700,* <, - , rm, rm, - 15/20. AE VISA. rest EZ u
Rôtisserie : (1st floor) **Meals** 68 and a la carte 68/112 – **73 rm** 330/690.
• This traditional hotel - one of the city's oldest - stands right on the Limmat. Elegant, comfortable rooms, with tasteful toile de Jouy fabrics, ensure a relaxing stay. The restaurant's lovely riverside terrace offers a fine view of the Old Town.

ArabellaSheraton Neues Schloss, Stockerstr. 17, ✉ 8002, ✆ 0442 869 400, *neuesschloss@arabellasheraton.com, Fax 0442 869 445* - , rm, - 20. AE VISA JCB EZ m
Le Jardin : *(closed Saturday lunch, Sunday and Bank Holidays to non-residents)* **Meals** 57 (lunch)/75 and a la carte 66/106 – 30 – **60 rm** 425/475.
• Not far from the lakeside, this establishment makes an excellent base for your stay in Zürich. The recently renovated rooms have elegant wooden furnishings in contemporary style. The ground floor restaurant is lavishly decorated with indoor plants.

Alden Hotel Splügenschloss (Suitenhotel), Splügenstr. 2, ✉ 8002, ✆ 0442 899 999, *welcome@alden.ch, Fax 0442 899 998,* - , rm, rest, - 20. AE VISA JCB. rest CX e
Gourmet : *(closed Saturday and Sunday)* **Meals** 60 (lunch) / 150 and a la carte 93/147 – ***Bar / Bistro :*** **Meals** a la carte 51/89 – **10 rm** 700/1100, 12 suites.
• Up-to-the-minute suites decorated in elegant designer style, behind a splendidly imposing late 19C façade. The tasteful formal restaurant serves contemporary dishes.

Inter-Continental Zurich, Badenerstr. 420, ✉ 8004, ✆ 0444 044 444, *zurich@interconti.com, Fax 0444 044 440,* , , , - , rm, rm, - 15/300. AE VISA JCB by Badenerstrasse CV
Relais des Arts : *(closed Bank Holidays)* **Meals** 45 (lunch) and a la carte 53/91 – 30 – **364 rm** 280/350.
• Among the amenities of this hotel - as well as its comfortable and functional contemporary style rooms - is its accessibility to the airport and the motorway. Guests are invited to dine in the bright and elegant surroundings of the Relais des Arts.

Glärnischhof, Claridenstr. 30, ✉ 8002, ✆ 0442 862 222, *info@glaernischhof.com, Fax 0442 862 286* - , rm, rest, - 25. AE VISA JCB EZ f
Le Poisson : - Fish specialities - *(closed Saturday and Sunday)* **Meals** 59 (lunch)/95 and a la carte 72/115 – ***Vivace :*** - Italian rest. - **Meals** a la carte 43/92 – **62 rm** 340/490.
• This building on the edge of the city centre has functional rooms with fine wood furnishings and fresh and bright colour schemes. The restaurants' names spell out their wares : fish dishes in Le Poisson, Italian cuisine in Vivace.

Glockenhof, Sihlstr. 31, ✉ 8001, ✆ 012 259 191, *info@glockenhof.ch, Fax 012 259 292,* - , rm, rest, rm, - 15/40. AE VISA JCB EZ b
Meals 48 (lunch) and a la carte 45/86 – **100 rm** 260/450.
• Its city centre location is only one of the advantages of this well-run hotel. Choose from traditionally decorated rooms or tasteful modern ones. Enjoy the pleasantly relaxed terrace of the traditional Glogge-Stube restaurant or Bistro Glogge-Egge.

Engimatt, Engimattstr. 14, ✉ 8002, ✆ 0442 841 616, *info@engimatt.ch*, *Fax 0442 012 516*, , – | rm, – 15/25. AE MC VISA JCB CX d
Meals 43 (lunch)/75 and a la carte 44/84 – **80 rm** 220/370.
• Close to the city centre but nevertheless in an attractively leafy setting. Rooms solidly furnished in contemporary style, some with a tastefully rustic touch. The Orangerie restaurant is a modern interpretation of a winter garden in steel and glass.

Mercure Hotel Stoller, Badenerstr. 357, ✉ 8003, ✆ 0444 054 747, *info@stoller.ch*, *Fax 0444 054 848*, – – 15/25. AE MC VISA JCB
Ratatouille : **Meals** a la carte 46/95 – 17 – **78 rm** 199/220. by Badenerstrasse CV
• On the edge of the city centre close to a tram stop. Rooms in similar style with furnishings in grey veneer. Quieter rooms with balcony to the rear. The two-room Ratatouille is furnished in dark wood : it opens up its street café in summer.

Greulich, Herman Greulich-Str. 56, ✉ 8004, ✆ 0432 434 243, *mail@greulich.ch*, *Fax 0432 434 200*, – rm, rm, rest, – 20. AE MC VISA JCB CV c
Meals a la carte 69/101 – 18 – **18 rm** 195/275.
• Trim, modern, practically equipped rooms and mini-suites face a courtyard garden shaded by birches. Simple styling, warm colours, parquet floors and Spanish cuisine set the tone in the restaurant.

Novotel Zürich City-West, Schiffbaustr. 13, ✉ 8005, ✆ 0442 762 222, *H2731@accor-hotels.com*, *Fax 0442 762 323*, , , – , rm, rm, – 15/120. AE MC VISA by Seebahn-, Hard- and Pfingstweidstrasse CV
Meals 39 (lunch) and a la carte 35/102 – 25 – **142 rm** 195.
• This newly-built hotel with its cladding of black glass offers identical, contemporary style and reasonably spacious rooms featuring white built-in furniture.

Kindli, Pfalzgasse 1, ✉ 8001, ✆ 0438 887 676, *reservations@kindli.ch*, *Fax 0438 887 677*, – . AE MC VISA. rm EZ z
Zum Kindli : *(closed Sunday and Bank Holidays)* **Meals** a la carte 42/85 – **20 rm** 240/380.
• This historic town house with a friendly, informal ambience is decorated in English country-house style ; Laura Ashley design sets the tone in its individually styled rooms. Discreetly elegant Zum Kindli restaurant offers contemporary cooking.

Walhalla without rest, Limmatstr. 5, ✉ 8005, ✆ 014 465 400, *walhalla-hotel@bluewin.ch*, *Fax 014 465 454* – – 15/20. AE MC VISA JCB EY r
15 – **48 rm** 170/220.
• Good public transport access, by a tram stop behind the main station. Rooms with dark wood furniture and paintings of gods disporting themselves.

Montana, Konradstr. 39, ✉ 8005, ✆ 0433 666 000, *reservation@hotelmontana.ch*, *Fax 0433 666 010* – , rm, rm, AE MC VISA JCB EY f
Bistro Le Lyonnais : *(closed Sunday and Bank Holidays)* **Meals** 25 (lunch)/45 and a la carte 50/91 – **74 rm** 180/300.
• Located behind the station, this hotel is particularly good for short stopovers. A glass lift rises through the covered courtyard to take guests to their practically laid-out rooms. Le Lyonnais bistro has its own entrance and appropriate décor.

Ibis, Schiffbaustr. 11, ✉ 8005, ✆ 012 762 100, *h2942@accor-hotels.com*, *Fax 012 762 101*, – , rm, rm, . AE MC VISA
Meals *(closed Saturday lunch and Sunday lunch)* a la carte 33/63 – 14 – **155 rm** 139. by Seebahn-, Hard- and Pfingstweidstrasse CV
• This hotel is on the site of the old shipbuilding sheds : practical rooms provide all the essentials for what is a very reasonable price. The Swiss Park bistro offers specialities from all four of the country's language communities.

Kaiser's Reblaube, Glockengasse 7, ✉ 8001, ✆ 012 212 120, *rest.reblaube@bluewin.ch*, *Fax 012 212 155*, – AE MC VISA. EZ y
closed 12 July - 15 August – **Meals** (booking essential) ***Goethe-Stübli :*** (1st floor) *(closed Monday from mid April - August, Saturday lunch and Sunday)* **Meals** 58 (lunch)/134 and a la carte 72/117 – ***Weinstube :*** *(closed Monday dinner from mid April - August, Saturday lunch and Sunday)* **Meals** 39 (lunch) and a la carte 64/110.
• Historic townhouse hidden in a maze of streets. Modern cooking in the first floor Goethe-Stübli ; traditional favourites in the lively wine bar and bistro, which has a garden.

Il Giglio, Weberstr. 14, ✉ 8004, ✆ 0442 428 597, *Fax 0442 910 183* – AE MC VISA CX c
closed 23 July - 15 August, 25 December - 3 January, Saturday lunch, Sunday and Bank Holidays – **Meals** - Italian rest. - 47 (lunch)/105 and a la carte 59/102.
• The little white-ceilinged restaurant with walls covered in modern art is a short distance from the city centre. Choice of Italian dishes.

Carlton, Bahnhofstr. 41, ✉ 8001, ☎ 012 271 919, *info@carlton-zuerich.ch, Fax 012 271 927,* – AE VISA EZ w
Meals *(closed Sunday and Bank Holidays)* 49 (lunch)/99 and a la carte 60/111.
• A spacious restaurant, elegantly decorated in Art Deco style. The kitchen produces modern dishes, the wine cellar is open to diners and they also serve afternoon tea.

Zunfthaus zur Waag, Münsterhof 8, ✉ 8001, ☎ 0442 169 966, *zunfthaus-zur-waag@bluewin.ch, Fax 0442 169 967,* – AE VISA EZ x
Meals (1st floor) 65/85 and a la carte 52/98.
• The first floor of the hatters' and weavers' guildhall now houses a well-stocked restaurant with Biedermeier-style décor. Traditional offerings on the menu.

Accademia, Rotwandstr. 62, ✉ 8004, ☎ 012 414 202, *Fax 012 414 207* – AE VISA. CV n
closed Saturday (except dinner from November - December) and Sunday – **Meals** - Italian rest. - a la carte 68/129.
• Traditionally decorated restaurant in two sections. As well as Italian dishes and appropriate wines it also offers grilled specialities. Garage parking in the evening.

Sala of Tokyo, Limmatstr. 29, ✉ 8005, ☎ 012 715 290, *sala@active.ch, Fax 012 717 807,* – AE VISA JCB EY k
closed 25 to 28 March, 23 July - 8 August, 24 December - 10 January, Saturday lunch, Sunday and Monday – **Meals** - Japanese rest. - 68/120 and a la carte 48/112.
• Wood-panelled interior with sushi-bar and restaurant, to the rear a section in contemporary style with yakitori grills. The kitchen is sure to bring a smile to your lips.

Casa Aurelio, Langstr. 209, ✉ 8005, ☎ 012 727 744, *Fax 012 727 724,* – . AE VISA. rest CV r
closed 1 to 14 August, 20 December - 3 January and Sunday – **Meals** - Spanish rest. - 48 and a la carte 70/100.
• Frescoes decorate the walls of the visually separate rooms of this restaurant in old Spanish-villa style. Guests are served with dishes from the Iberian repertory.

Cantinetta Antinori, Augustinergasse 25, ✉ 8001, ☎ 012 117 210, *cantinetta-antinori@bindella.ch, Fax 012 211 613,* – AE VISA EZ c
Meals - Italian rest. - a la carte 51/124.
• Sophisticated dining room with original décor and lovely wainscoting on the first floor. Plainer fare served in the ground floor restaurant. Italian cuisine.

Josef, Gasometerstr. 24, ✉ 8005, ☎ 0442 716 595, *welcome@josef.ch, Fax 0444 405 564* – AE VISA. CV x
closed Christmas, New Year, Saturday lunch and Sunday – **Meals** a la carte 54/107.
• This contemporary place with a relaxed atmosphere offers a convincing blend of well-sourced modern cooking and helpful, personable service.

Caduff's Wine Loft, Kanzleistr. 126, ✉ 8004, ☎ 012 402 255, *caduff@wineloft.ch, Fax 012 402 256* – AE VISA CV d
closed 24 to 28 December, Saturday lunch and Sunday – **Meals** (booking essential) 52 (lunch)/115 and a la carte 50/118.
• This former wholesale flower market now serves tasty morsels at the long bar and well-sourced dishes accompanied by a fine wine from the famous cellars.

Heugümper, Waaggasse 4, ✉ 8001, ☎ 012 111 660, *info@restaurantheuguemper.ch, Fax 012 111 661* – – 15/40. AE VISA EZ d
closed 9 July - 21 August, Christmas, New Year, Saturday (except from October - December) and Sunday – **Meals** a la carte 69/122.
• In the part of the Old Town around the Fraumünster this restaurant consists of a smart bistro and an elegant dining room, both serving dishes with a modern twist.

Zentraleck, Zentralstr. 161, ✉ 8003, ☎ 014 610 800, *restaurant@zentraleck.ch, Fax 014 610 801* – AE VISA by Badenerstrasse CVX
closed 25 July - 6 August, 3 to 8 January, Saturday and Sunday – **Meals** 78 and a la carte 56/101.
• Pale walls and wood floors both add to the pleasantly smart, up-to-date feel of the Zentraleck, where little pots of kitchen herbs decorate the tables. Modern menus.

Ciro, Militärstr. 16, ✉ 8004, ☎ 012 417 841, *ciro@swissonline.ch, Fax 012 911 424,* – AE VISA CV a
Meals - Italian rest. - *(closed Sunday)* a la carte 52/80.
• In the welcoming interiors of this restaurant close to the station guests are served with a variety of Italian dishes and the wines to accompany them.

Strozzi's Più, Bahnhofstr. 25, ✉ 8001, ☎ 012 256 025, *strozzispiu@strozzis.ch, Fax 012 256 026,* – AE VISA EZ j
closed Sunday and Bank Holidays – **Meals** 36 (lunch) and a la carte 54/106.
• The long bar and lilac club chairs match the clean-lined interior of the Credit Suisse building. Trendy modern cuisine prepared in the old bank vaults.

at Zürich-Oerlikon *North : by Universitätstrasse* DV *: 5 km – alt. 442 – ✉ 8050 Zürich-Oerlikon :*

Swissôtel Zürich, Marktplatz, ✆ 0443 173 111, *reservations.zurich@swissotel.com*, *Fax 0443 124 468*, <, ⛱, Ⓛ, ⌂, ▢ – |‡|, ▤ rm, ▢ ✆ ♿ rm, P – 🚗 15/400. AE ⓘ ⓜ VISA. ✂
Dialog : **Meals** 60 (lunch) and a la carte 61/122 – ***Szenario :*** **Meals** 30 (lunch) / 50 and a la carte 44/105 – ☕ 28 – **334 rm** 250/310, 10 suites.
◆ Tall building on the market place in the centre of town. Rooms with timeless lightwood furnishings. Swimming-pool on the 32nd floor with view over the whole town. Open-plan dining area with two sections, one serving plain food, the other more refined dishes.

at Zürich-Seebach *North : by Schaffenhauserstrasse* CV *– alt. 442 – ✉ 8052 Zürich-Seebach :*

Landhus, Katzenbachstr. 10, ✆ 013 083 400, *info@landhus-zuerich.ch*, *Fax 013 083 451*, ⛱ – |‡| ▢ ✆ P – 🚗 15/300. AE ⓘ ⓜ VISA
Meals a la carte 47/78 – **28 rm** ☕ 120/150.
◆ On the edge of town, reached via the Schaffhausen road. Reasonably spacious rooms with contemporary furnishings in dark wood. Colourful, up-to-the-minute restaurant serving good plain food.

at Höngg *Northwest :* CV *: 5 km – ✉ 8049 Zürich-Höngg :*

WEIN & DEIN, Regensdorferstr. 22, ✆ 0433 115 633, *info@weinunddein.ch*, *Fax 0433 115 634*, ⛱ – ⊬ ♿ rest,. AE ⓘ ⓜ VISA
closed 10 July - 15 August, 24 December - 2 January, Saturday lunch, Sunday and Monday – **Meals** 48 (lunch) and a la carte 63/117 🍇.
◆ The name says it all : this charming vintner's shop with its own wine cellar now has a modern restaurant in what was once the barn.

at Glattbrugg *North : by Universitätstrasse* DV *: 8 km – alt. 432 – ✉ 8152 Glattbrugg :*

Renaissance Zürich Hotel, Talackerstr. 1, ✆ 018 745 000, *renaissance.zurich@renaissancehotels.com*, *Fax 018 745 001*, Ⓛ, ⌂, ▢ – |‡| ⊬ ▤ ▢ ✆ ♿ rm, 🚗 – 🚗 15/300. AE ⓘ ⓜ VISA. ✂ rest
Asian Place : *- Asian rest. - (closed 10 July - 15 August, Saturday lunch and Sunday)* **Meals** a la carte 55/117 – ***Brasserie :*** **Meals** a la carte 44/98 – ☕ 30 – **196 rm** 245/345, 8 suites.
◆ In a building complex with an extensive basement-level leisure area, this establishment offers rooms nearly all of which have tasteful, dark furnishings. To the rear of the foyer, the brasserie offers a range of contemporary cuisine.

Hilton, Hohenbühlstr. 10, ✆ 0448 285 050, *zurich@hilton.ch*, *Fax 0448 285 151*, Ⓛ, ⌂ – |‡|, ⊬ rm, ▤ ▢ ✆ P – 🚗 15/280. AE ⓘ ⓜ VISA JCB. ✂ rest
Market Place : **Meals** 59 and a la carte 52/105 – ☕ 35 – **310 rm** 329/439, 13 suites.
◆ Close to the airport, this establishment offers freshly refurbished rooms with bright maplewood furnishings. New executive rooms have been provided on two floors. Open kitchen in the Marketplace restaurant.

Mövenpick, Walter Mittelholzerstr. 8, ✆ 0448 088 888, *hotel.zurich.airport@moevenpick.ch*, *Fax 0448 088 877* – |‡|, ⊬ rm, ▤ ▢ ✆ ♿ rm, P – 🚗 15/220. AE ⓘ ⓜ VISA JCB
Appenzeller Stube : *(closed Saturday lunch)* **Meals** 45 (lunch)/85 and a la carte 53/121 – ***Mövenpick Rest. :*** **Meals** a la carte 38/104 – ***Dim Sum :*** - Chinese rest. - *(closed Saturday lunch and Sunday lunch)* **Meals** a la carte 42/97 – ☕ 28 – **335 rm** 340/400.
◆ This hotel is right by the exit off the motorway. All of the rooms have been refurbished, some have exercise equipment. Enjoy the typically Swiss atmosphere in the Appenzeller Stube or try International dishes in the Mövenpick restaurant.

Novotel Zürich Airport Messe, Talackerstr. 21, ✆ 018 299 000, *h0884@accor-hotels.com*, *Fax 018 299 999*, ⛱, Ⓛ, ⌂ – |‡|, ▤ rm, ▢ ✆ ♿ rm, 🚗 P – 🚗 15/150. AE ⓘ ⓜ VISA JCB. ✂ rest
Meals a la carte 41/86 – ☕ 25 – **255 rm** 240.
◆ On the edge of the town centre and just a few minutes from the new trade fair centre, this hotel offers convenient parking and functional rooms with lightwood furnishings.

NH Zurich Airport, Schaffhauserstr. 101, ✆ 018 085 000, *nhzurich.airport@nh-hotels.com*, *Fax 018 085 100*, Ⓛ, ⌂ – |‡|, ⊬ rm, ▤ ▢ ✆ ♿ rm, 🚗 – 🚗 15/45. AE ⓘ ⓜ VISA. ✂ rest
Meals *(closed Saturday lunch and Sunday lunch)* 26 (lunch)/70 and a la carte 54/92 – ☕ 26 – **140 rm** 180/255.
◆ The rooms of this airport hotel with their contemporary, functional décor and furnishings are above all suitable for business travellers. Shuttle service to the airport.

XX **Vivendi,** Europastr. 2, ☎ 0432 113 242, *info@restaurant-vivendi.ch, Fax 0432 113 241,* – AE VISA
closed 24 December - 2 January, Saturday, Sunday and Bank Holidays – **Meals** a la carte 51/100.
◆ Clean lines and a pleasantly muted colour scheme set the tone in this modern restaurant, which serves traditionally presented cuisine with modern touches.

at Kloten *North : by Universitätstrasse* DV *: 12 km – alt. 447 – ✉ 8302 Kloten :*

Allegra, Hamelirainstr. 3, ☎ 0448 044 444, *reservation@hotel-allegra.ch, Fax 0448 044 141,* – rm, – 15/30. AE VISA
Meals a la carte 32/73 – 15 – **132 rm** 160/190.
◆ New business hotel offers spacious, well-soundproofed rooms with colourful built-in furniture. Free airport bus service. Modern restaurant : Swiss favourites and a salad bar.

Fly away, Marktgasse 19, ☎ 0448 044 455, *reservation@hotel-flyaway.ch, Fax 0448 044 450,* – rm, rm, rm, P. AE VISA JCB
closed 24 December - 4 January (Hotel only) – ***Mercato :*** - Italian rest. - **Meals** a la carte 31/81 – 15 – **42 rm** 155/202.
◆ Close to the station, this hotel has spacious rooms all similar in décor and layout and all with timeless, functional furnishings.The Mercato restaurant is Mediterranean in style with contemporary décor and wooden furnishings.

X **Rias,** Gerbegasse 6, ☎ 018 142 652, *info@rias.ch, Fax 018 135 504,* – AE VISA
Meals *(closed Saturday dinner and Sunday)* 45/95 and a la carte 43/100.
◆ This contemporary style restaurant is tucked away rather unobtrusively down a little street. Separate bar and à la carte dining room offering reliable traditional fare.

at Küsnacht *Southeast : by Bellerivestrasse* DX *: 8 km – alt. 415 – ✉ 8700 Küsnacht :*

XXX ✿ **Ermitage am See** with rm, Seestr. 80, ☎ 019 144 242, *info@ermitage.ch, Fax 019 144 243,* ≤ Zurich lake, , , – AE VISA
Meals *(closed January, Sunday and Monday except June - August)* 140/195 and a la carte 102/191 – **22 rm** 210/430, 4 suites.
Spec. Medaillons von Bretonischen Hummer mit grünem Spargel und gefüllten Morcheln (end March - begin May). Gegrillter Atlantik-Steinbutt mit Schalottenconfit und glasiertem, jungen Lauch. Gratinierter Sisteron-Lammrücken mit Artischoken und Bohnenkrautjus.
◆ In a beautiful waterside location, this country house with its terrace, garden, and delightful interior, offers its guests a lovely view over Lake Zürich.

XXX ✿✿ **Petermann's Kunststuben,** Seestr. 160, ☎ 019 100 715, *petermannskunstuben @bluewin.ch, Fax 019 100 495,* – AE VISA.
closed 21 August - 12 September, 10 to 26 February, Sunday and Monday – **Meals** (booking essential for dinner) 78 (lunch)/195 and a la carte 121/202.
Spec. Noix de Saint-Jacques avec confit d'endives et jus de pommes vertes à la vanille. Les dos de lotte légèrement fumés et confit de tomates aux aubergines. Le grenadin de filet de veau et ris de veau aux écrevisses "Pattes Rouges". **Wines** Freisamer.
◆ Imaginatively created classic dishes, perfectly presented in elegant interiors or in the lovely little garden : there's no mistaking Petermann's prestigious restaurant.

at Gattikon *South by motorway A3* CX *: 11 km – alt. 510 – ✉ 8136 Gattikon :*

XX ✿ **Sihlhalde** (Smolinsky), Sihlhaldenstr. 70, ☎ 017 200 927, *Fax 017 200 925,* – AE VISA
closed 18 July - 8 August, 23 December - 4 January, Sunday and Monday – **Meals** (booking essential) 118 and a la carte 70/125.
Spec. Makkaronikrone mit Pilzen und Trüffeln (October - December). Alfonsino auf Linsen und Echalotten-Konfitüre (March - August). Rehrückienlende an Porto-Extrakt (June - July).
◆ Tucked away on the edge of town, this establishment with its three individually styled dining rooms pampers clients with an array of delectable dishes from its classic menu.

at Uetikon am See *Southeast by Bellerivestrasse : 18 km – alt. 414 – ✉ 8707 Uetikon am See :*

XX ✿✿ **Wirtschaft zum Wiesengrund** (Hussong), Kleindorfstr. 61, ☎ 019 206 360, *huss ong@wiesengrund.ch, Fax 019 211 709,* – AE VISA.
closed 31 July - 22 August, 6 to 21 February, Sunday and Monday – **Meals** (booking essential) 68 (lunch)/165 and a la carte 102/168.
Spec. Kleine Calamari "à la minute" gebraten mit Kapern und Oliven. Variation von Kalbsmilken, Gänseleber und Perigord-Trüffel. Gebackene Valrhôna-Schokolade mit Nüssen und weissem Kaffeeeis. **Wines** Meilener.
◆ An inconspicuous exterior hardly hints at the culinary masterpieces being served in the contemporary style restaurant or on the lovely little garden terrace.

United Kingdom

LONDON – BELFAST – BIRMINGHAM – EDINBURGH
GLASGOW – LEEDS – LIVERPOOL
MANCHESTER

PRACTICAL INFORMATION

LOCAL CURRENCY

Pound Sterling: *1 GBP = 1,44 euro (€) (Dec. 2004)*

TOURIST INFORMATION

Tourist information offices exist in each city included in the Guide. The telephone number and address is given in each text under 🅱

FOREIGN EXCHANGE

Banks are usually open between 9.00am and 4.30pm on weekdays only and some open on Saturdays. Most large hotels have exchange facilities. Heathrow and Gatwick Airports have 24-hour banking facilities.

SHOPPING

In London: *Oxford St/Regent St (department stores, exclusive shops) Bond St (exclusive shops, antiques)*

Knightsbridge area (department stores, exclusive shops, boutiques)

For other towns see the index of street names; those printed in red are where the principal shops are found.

THEATRE BOOKINGS IN LONDON

Your hotel porter will be able to make your arrangements or direct you to Theatre Booking Agents.
In addition there is a kiosk in Leicester Square selling tickets for the same day's performances at half price plus a booking fee. It is open 12 noon-6.30pm.

CAR HIRE

The international car hire companies have branches in each major city. Your hotel porter should be able to give details and help you with your arrangements.

TIPPING

Many hotels and restaurants include a service charge but where this is not the case an amount equivalent to between 10 and 15 per cent of the bill is customary. Additionally doormen, baggage porters and cloakroom attendants are generally given a gratuity.
Taxi drivers are customarily tipped between 10 and 15 per cent of the amount shown on the meter in addition to the fare.

SPEED LIMITS

The maximum permitted speed on motorways and dual carriageways is 70 mph (113 km/h.) and 60 mph (97 km/h.) on other roads except where a lower speed limit is indicated.

SEAT BELTS

The wearing of seat belts in the United Kingdom is compulsory for drivers, front seat passengers and rear seat passengers where seat belts are fitted. It is illegal for front seat passengers to carry children on their lap.

CONGESTION CHARGING

The congestion charge is £5 per day on all vehicles (except motor cycles and exempt vehicles) entering the central zone between 7.00 and 6.30pm Monday to Friday except on bank holidays.
Payment can be made in advance, on the day, by post, on the Internet, by telephone 0845 900 1234, or at retail outlets.
A charge of up to £80 will be made for non-payment.
Further information is available on the Transport for London website-www.cclondon.com

LONDON

504 folds ㊷ to ㊹ – pop. 7 651 634

Major sights in London and the outskirts .... pp 1 and 2
Maps .... pp 4 to 17
Hotels and Restaurants
Establishments with stars and "Bib Gourmand" Meals .... p 18
Restaurants classified according to type .... pp 19 to 22
Hotels and Restaurants listed by boroughs .... pp 23 to 77

Britain Visitor Centre, I Regent Street, WI, ✆ (020) 8846 9000.

Heathrow, ✆ 08700 000123 – **Terminal** *: Airbus (A1) from Victoria, Airbus (A2) from Paddington – Underground (Piccadilly line) frequent service daily.*

Gatwick, ✆ 08700 002468, by A 23 and M 23 – **Terminal** *: Coach service from Victoria Coach Station (Flightline 777, hourly service) – Railink (Gatwick Express) from Victoria (24 h service).*

London City Airport, ✆ (020) 7646 0000.

Stansted, at Bishop's Stortford, ✆ 08700 000303, NE : 34 m. by M 11 and A 120.

British Airways, Ticket sales and reservations *: 213 Piccadilly W1, ✆ 0845 606 0747.*

SIGHTS

HISTORIC BUILDINGS AND MONUMENTS

Palace of Westminster★★★ : House of Lords★★, Westminster Hall★★ (hammerbeam roof★★★), Robing Room★, Central Lobby★, House of Commons★, Big Ben★, Victoria Tower★ 39 ALX *– Tower of London★★★ (Crown Jewels★★★, White Tower or Key★★★, St-John's Chapel★★, Beauchamp Tower★, Tower Hill Pageant★)* 34 ASU *– British Airways London Eye (views★★★)* 32 AMV *– Banqueting House★★* 31 ALV *– Buckingham Palace★★ (Changing of the Guard★★, Royal Mews★★* 38 AIX *– Kensington Palace★★* 27 ABV *– Lincoln's Inn★★* 32 AMT *– London Bridge★* 34 ARV *– Royal Hospital Chelsea★★* 37 AGZ *– St. James's Palace★★* 30 AJV *– Somerset House★★* 32 AMU *– South Bank Arts Centre★★ (Royal Festival Hall★ National Theatre★, Country Hall★)* 32 AMV *The Temple★★ (Middle Temple Hall★)* 32 ANU *– Tower Bridge★★* 34 ASV *– Albert Memorial★* 36 ADX *– Apsley House★* 30 AHV *– Burlington House★*

30 AIV – *Charterhouse*★ 19 UZD – *George Inn*★, *Southwark* 33 AQV – *Cray's Inn*★ 32 AMV – *Guildhall*★ (*Lord Mayor's show*★★) 33 AQT – *International Shakespeare Globe Centre*★ 33 APV – *Dr Johnson's House*★ 32 ANT – *Lancaster House*★ 30 AIV – *Leighton House*★ 35 AAX – *Linley Sambourne House*★ 35 AAX – *Lloyds Building*★★ 34 ARU – *Mansion House*★ (*plate and insignia*★★) 33 AQV – *The Monument*★ (⁂★) 34 ARU – *Old Admiralty*★ 31 AKV – *Royal Albert Hall*★ 36 ADX – *Royal Exchange*★ 34 ARU – *Royal Opera House*★ (*Covent Garden*) 31 ALU – *Spencer House*★★ 30 AIV – *Staple Inn*★ 32 ANT – *Theatre Royal*★ (*Haymarket*) 31 AKV – *Westminster Bridge*★ 39 ALX.

CHURCHES

The City Churches – *St. Paul's Cathedral*★★★ (*Dome* ≤★★★) 33 APU – *St. Bartholomew the Great*★★ (*choir*★) 33 APT – *St. Dunstan-in-the-East*★★ 34 ARU – *St. Mary-at-Hill*★★ (*woodwork*★★, *plan*★) 34 ARU – *Temple Church*★★ 32 ANU – *All Hallows-by-the-Tower* (*font cover*★★, *brasses*★) 34 ARU – *Christ Church*★ 33 APT – *St. Andrew Undershaft* (*monuments*★) 34 ARU – *St. Bride*★ (*steeple*★★) 32 ANU – *St. Clement Eastcheap* (*panelled interior*★★) 34 ARU – *St. Edmund the King and Martyr* (*tower and spire*★) 34 ARU **B** – *St. Giles Cripplegate*★ 33 AQT – *St. Helen Bishopsgate*★ (*monuments*★★) 34 ART – *St. James Garlickhythe* (*tower and spire*★, *sword rests*★) 33 AQU – *St. Magnus the Martyr* (*tower*★, *sword rest*★) 34 ARU – *St. Margaret Lothbury*★ (*tower and spire*★, *woodwork*★, *screen*★, *font*★) 33 AQT – *St. Margaret Pattens* (*spire*★, *woodwork*★) 34 ARU *St. Martin-within-Ludgate* (*tower and spire*★, *door cases*★) 33 APU – *St. Mary Abchurch*★ (*reredos*★★, *tower and spire*★, *dome*★) 33 AQU – *St. Mary-le-Bow* (*tower and steeple*★★) 33 AQU – *St. Michael Paternoster Royal* (*tower and spire*★) 33 AQU **D** – *St. Nicholas Cole Abbey* (*tower and spire*★) 33 APU – *St. Olave*★ 34 ARU – *St. Peter upon Cornhill* (*screen*★) 34 ARU **L** – *St. Stephen Walbrook*★ (*tower and steeple*★, *dome*★), 33 AQU – *St. Vedast* (*tower and spire*★, *ceiling*★), 33 APT.

Other Churches – *Westminster Abbey*★★★ (*Henry VII Chapel*★★★, *Chapel of Edward the Confessor*★★, *Chapter House*★★, *Poets' Corner*★) 39 ALX – *Southwark Cathedral*★★ 33 AQV – *Queen's Chapel*★ 30 AJV – *St. Clement Danes*★ 32 AMU – *St. James's*★ 30 AJV – *St. Margaret's*★ 39 ALX – *St. Martin in-the-Fields*★ 31 ALV – *St. Paul's*★ (*Covent Garden*) 31 ALU – *Westminster Roman Catholic Cathedral*★ 39 ALX.

PARKS

Regent's Park★★★ (*Terraces*★★), *Zoo*★★ – *Hyde Park* 29 AFV – *Kensington Gardens*★★ 28 ACV (*Orangery*★) 27 ABV – *St. James's Park*★★ 31 AKV.

STREETS AND SQUARES

The City★★★ 33 AQT – *Bedford Square*★★ 31 AKT – *Belgrave Square*★★ 37 AGX – *Burlington Arcade*★★ 30 AIV – *Covent Garden*★★ (*The Piazza*★★) 31 ALU – *The Mall*★★ 31 AKV – *Piccadilly*★ 30 AIV – *The Thames*★★ 32 ANU – *Trafalgar Square*★★ 31 AKV – *Whitehall*★★ (*Horse Guards*★) 31 ALV – *Barbican*★ 33 AQT – *Bond Street*★ 30 AIU *Canonbury Square*★ – *Carlton House Terrace*★ 31 AKV – *Cheyne Walk*★ – *Fitzroy Square*★ – *Jermyn Street*★ 30 AJV – *Leicester Square*★ 31 AKU *Merrick Square*★ – *Montpelier Square*★ 37 AFX – *Neal's Yard*★31 ALU – *Piccadilly Arcade*★ 30 AIV – *Portman Square*★ 29 AGT – *Queen Anne's Gate*★ 39 AKX – *Regent Street*★ 30 AIU – *Royal Opera Arcade*★ 31 AKV – *Piccadilly Circus*★ 31 AKU – *St. James's Square*★ 31 AJV – *St. James's Street*★ 30 AIV – *Shepherd Market*★ 30 AHV – *Soho*★ 31 AKU – *Trinity Church Square*★ – *Victoria Embankment gardens*★ 31 ALV – *Waterloo Place*★ 31 AKV.

MUSEUMS

British Museum★★★ 31 AKL – *National Gallery*★★★ 31 AKV – *Science Museum*★★★ 36 ADX – *Tate Britain*★★★ 39 ALY – *Victoria and Albert Museum*★★★ 36 ADY – *Wallace Collection*★★★ 29 AGT – *Courtauld Institute Galleries*★★ (*Somerset House*) 32 AMU – *Gilbert Collection*★★ (*Somerset House*) 32 AMU – *Museum of London*★★ 33 APT – *National Portrait Gallery*★★ 31 AKU – *Natural History Museum*★★ 36 ADY – *Sir John Soane's Museum*★★ 32 AMT – *Tate Modern*★★ (*views*★★★ *from top floors*) 33 APV – *Clock Museum*★ (*Guildhall*) 33 AQT – *Imperial War Museum*★ 40 ANY – *London's Transport Museum*★ 31 ALU – *Madame Tussaud's*★ 17 QZD – *Museum of Mankind*★ 33 DM – *National Army Museum*★ 37 AGZ – *Percival David Foundation of Chinese Art*★ 18 SZD – *Planetarium*★ 15 HV **L** – *Wellington Museum*★ (*Apsley House*) 30 AHV.

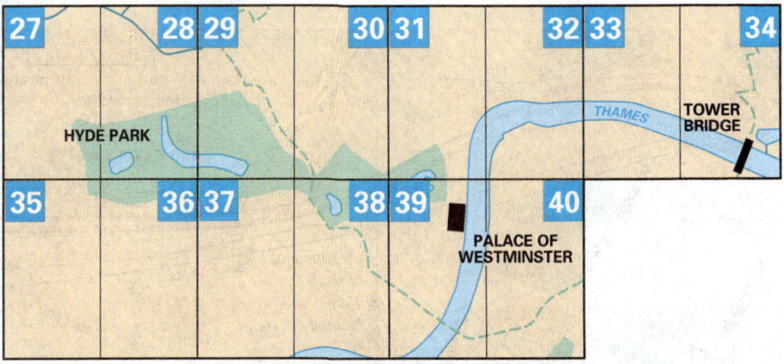

INDEX OF STREET NAMES IN LONDON CENTRE

Albemarle St 30 AIU 225
Aldford St 30 AHV 2
Arlington St 30 AIV 6
Artillery Row 39 AKX 8
Avery Row 30 AHU 12
Bankside 33 APV 291
Bateman St 31 AKU 18
Bayley St 31 AKT 260
Bedfordbury 31 ALU 243
Berwick St 31 AJT 26
Bessborough St 39 AKZ 30
Bevis Marks 34 ART 34
Bloomsbury Way 31 ALT 9
Bray Pl. 37 AFY 45
Bream's Buildings 32 ANT 47
Broad Sanctuary 39 ALX 52
Bryanston Square 29 AFT 14
Bute St 36 ADY 59
Cadogan Gardens 37 AGY 23
Cadogan Gate 37 AGY 220
Cambridge Square 29 AET 67
Camomile St 34 ART 71
Carlos Pl. 30 AHU 35
Carlton Gardens 31 AKV 74
Carting Lane 31 ALU 245
Chandos St 30 AIT 36
Charterhouse Square 33 APT 475
Chepstow Crescent 27 AAU 84
Cherries St 31 AKT 256
Clarendon Pl. 29 AEU 93
Clifford St 30 AIU 38
Cockspur St 31 AKV 39
Collingham Gardens 35 ABY 99
Collingham Rd 35 ABY 101
Coopers Row 34 ASU 318
Cornhill 34 ARU 309
Cranbourn St 31 AKU 115
Cranley Pl. 36 ADY 215
Cromwell Crescent 35 AAY 119
Cromwell Pl. 36 ADY 120
Crucifix Lane 34 ARV 125
Deanery St 30 AHV 132
Denman St 31 AKU 133
Denmark St 31 AKT 134
Devonshire St 30 AHT 48
Devonshire Terrace 28 ACU 136
Duke of Wellington Pl. 38 AHX 142
Duke of York St 31 AJV 143
Duke's Pl. 34 AST 145
Duncannon St 31 ALV 147
Dunraven St 29 AGU 149
Durham St 40 AMZ 150
Eardley Crescent 35 AAZ 151
Eccleston Bridge 38 AHY 157
Egerton Gardens Mews 37 AFY 162
Egerton Gardens 37 AFY 160
Egerton Terrace 37 AFY 161
Finsbury Square 33 AQT 310
Fish Street Hill 34 ARU 319
Foulis Terrace 36 ADZ 170
Furnival St 32 ANT 278
Garden Row 40 AOX 173
Gerrard St 31 AKU 174
Glasshouse St LAMBETH 39 ALZ 108
Glasshouse St SOHO 31 AJU 179
Glendower Pl. 36 ADY 180
Grafton St 30 AIU 62
Granville Pl. 29 AGU 476
Great Castle St 30 AIT 189
Great George St 39 AKX 193
Great Windmill St 31 AKU 261
Greycoat Pl. 39 AKY 200
Guildhouse St 38 AIY 201
Half Moon St 30 AHV 81
Hamilton Pl. 30 AHV 205
Hanway St 31 AKT 210
Harcourt Terrace 36 ACZ 477
Harriet St 37 AGX 214
Harrow Pl. 34 AST 317
Henrietta St 31 ALU 217
Holbein Mews 37 AGZ 223
Howland St 30 AIT 232
John Adam St 31 ALV 238
John Carpenter St 32 ANU 17
John St 33 APT 299
Kensington Court Pl. 35 ABX 242
Kensington Court 35 ABX 241
King Edward St 33 APT 247
King William St 34 ARU 250
Lancaster Terrace 28 ADU 257
Launceston Pl. 36 ACX 259
Lennox Gardens Mews 37 AFY 263
Limeburner Lane 33 AOT 298
Little Britain 33 APT 264
Little Portland St 30 AIT 228
Lombard St 34 ARU 268
Lower Grosvenor Pl. 38 AIX 274
Maiden Lane 31 ALU 83
Manchester Square 29 AGT 281
Market Pl. 30 AIT 286
Marylebone Lane 30 AHT 287
Monmouth St 31 ALU 88
Montagu Square 29 AGT 90
Montague St 33 APT 292
Neville Terrace 36 ADZ 300
New St Square 32 ANT 282
North Audley St 29 AGU 314
Old Burlington St 30 AIU 322
Orme Court 27 ABU 328
Ormonde Gate 37 AGZ 329
Oxford Square 29 AFU 332
Parry St 39 ALZ 341
Pembrocke Gardens 35 AAY 342
Porchester Square 27 ABT 197
Prince's Gardens 36 ADX 356
Procter St 32 AMT 273
Queen Anne's Gate 28 ACU 94
Queen's Gate Gardens 36 ACY 198
Queen's Gate Pl. 36 ACY 363
Queen Street Pl. 33 AQU 301
Queensberry Pl. 36 ADY 360
Ravensdon St 40 ANZ 219
Redesdale St 37 AFZ 367
Reeves Mews 29 AGV 103
Richmond Terrace 31 ALV 234
Romilly St 31 AKU 368
St. Andrews St 32 ANT 372
St. James's Pl. 30 AIV 116
St Bride St 32 ANT 376
St Martin's-le-Grand 33 APT 380
St Swithin's Lane 33 AQU 308
Sardinia St 32 AMT 381
Savoy St 32 AMU 270
Shepherd St 30 AHV 153
Snows Fields 34 ARV 386
South Pl. 34 ART 391
Southampton Row 31 ALT 473
Southampton St 31 ALU 388
Southwick St 29 AET 156
Spital Square 34 AST 399
Stanhope Pl. 29 AFU 400
Stanhope Terrace 28 ADU 158
Stratton St 30 AIV 168
Sumner St 33 APV 169
Surrey St 32 AMU 175
Sydney Pl. 36 ADY 405
Symons St 37 AGY 407
Templeton Pl. 35 AAY 410
Terminus Pl. 38 AIY 412
Thayer St 30 AHT 413
Thirleby Rd 39 AJY 416
Throgmorton St 34 ART 418
Tilney St 30 AHV 421
Tinworth St 39 ALZ 129
Upper St. Martin's Lane 31 ALU 430
Walbrook Crescent 33 AQU 304
Warwick Lane 33 APT 294
Warwick St 31 AJU 444
Waverton St 30 AHV 178
Wellington St 31 ALU 187
Westbourne Crescent 28 ADU 448
Westbourne Terrace Rd 28 ACT 452
Weston St 34 ARV 188
Whitehall Court 31 ALV 460
William IV St 31 ALV 467
William St 37 AGX 468
Wormwood St 34 ART 472

AA
AB
27
Grand Union Canal
Harrow Road
Bourne Terrace
BAYSWATER AND MAIDA VALE
Harrow
A 40
Westway
Westbourne Park
Great Western Road
Tavistock Rd
St Luke's Rd
Westbourne Park Road
Westbourne Park Villas
Royal Oak
Porchester Road
Gloucester
Westbourne Park Road
Chepstow Rd
Talbot Road
Ledbury Road
Westbourne Gdns
197
NORTH KENSINGTON
Talbot
Colville Ter.
Artesian Road
Hereford Road
Newton Rd
Bishop's Bridge
Westbourne Grove
Colville Rd
Garway Road
Queensway
Inverness
Gdns
Kensington Gdns Sq.
Leinster Sq.
Porchester
Queensborough Terrace
Westbourne Grove
Villas
Chepstow Villas
Pembridge Villas
Chepstow Pl.
Moscow Road
Bayswater
Portobello Road
84
Dawson Place
Pembridge Cres.
St Petersburgh Pl.
Bark Place
Queensway
Kensington Park Road
Pembridge Square
Ossington St
Palace Court
Pembridge Rd
Pembridge Gdns
Linden Gdns
Queensway
328
Ladbroke Square
Ladbroke Road
Notting Hill Gate
Bayswater Road
Broad Walk
Holland Park Ave
Notting Hill Gate
Uxbridge St
Kensington Palace Gardens
Kensington Church St
Campden Hill Square
Campden Hill Rd
Kensington Place
ORANGERY
Aubrey Walk
Bedford Gardens
Sheffield Terrace
Palace Gardens Terrace
Kensington Church St
Holland
KENSINGTON AND CHELSEA
Campden Hill
Campden Gro.
KENSINGTON PALACE
Palace
T
U
V
35
200 m
200 yards

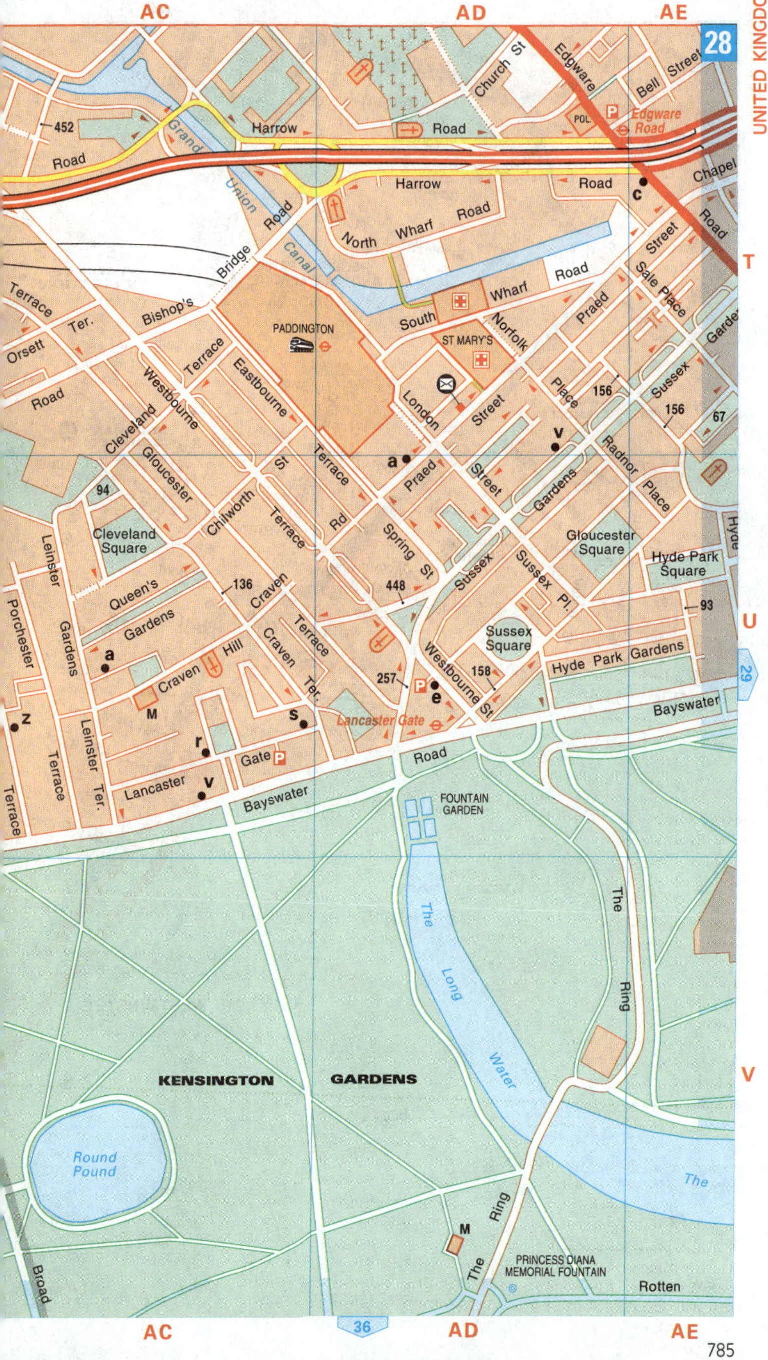
AC
AD
AE
28
Harrow
Road
Road
Grand
Union
Canal
Harrow
Road
North
Wharf
Road
Edgware
Road
Church St
Bell
Street
Edgware
Road
POL
Chapel
Street
Road
Sale
Place
Bishop's
Bridge
Road
Terrace
Orsett
Ter.
Road
PADDINGTON
South
Wharf
Road
ST MARY'S
Norfolk
Praed
Sussex
Garde
156
156
67
Westbourne
Terrace
Eastbourne
London
Street
Place
Cleveland
Gloucester
94
Terrace
Praed
Street
Gardens
Radnor
Place
Cleveland
Square
Chilworth
St
Terrace
Rd
Spring
St
Sussex
Sussex
Pl.
Gloucester
Square
Hyde Park
Square
Hyde
Leinster
Gardens
Porchester
Terrace
Queen's
Gardens
136
Craven
Terrace
448
Sussex
Square
93
Hyde Park
Gardens
Craven
Hill
Craven
Ter.
Westbourne
St
158
257
Lancaster Gate
29
Bayswater
Leinster
Ter.
Lancaster
Gate
Road
Bayswater
FOUNTAIN
GARDEN
The
Long
Water
The
Ring
KENSINGTON
GARDENS
Round
Pound
The
M
The
Ring
PRINCESS DIANA
MEMORIAL FOUNTAIN
Rotten
Broad
T
U
V
36
AC
AD
AE

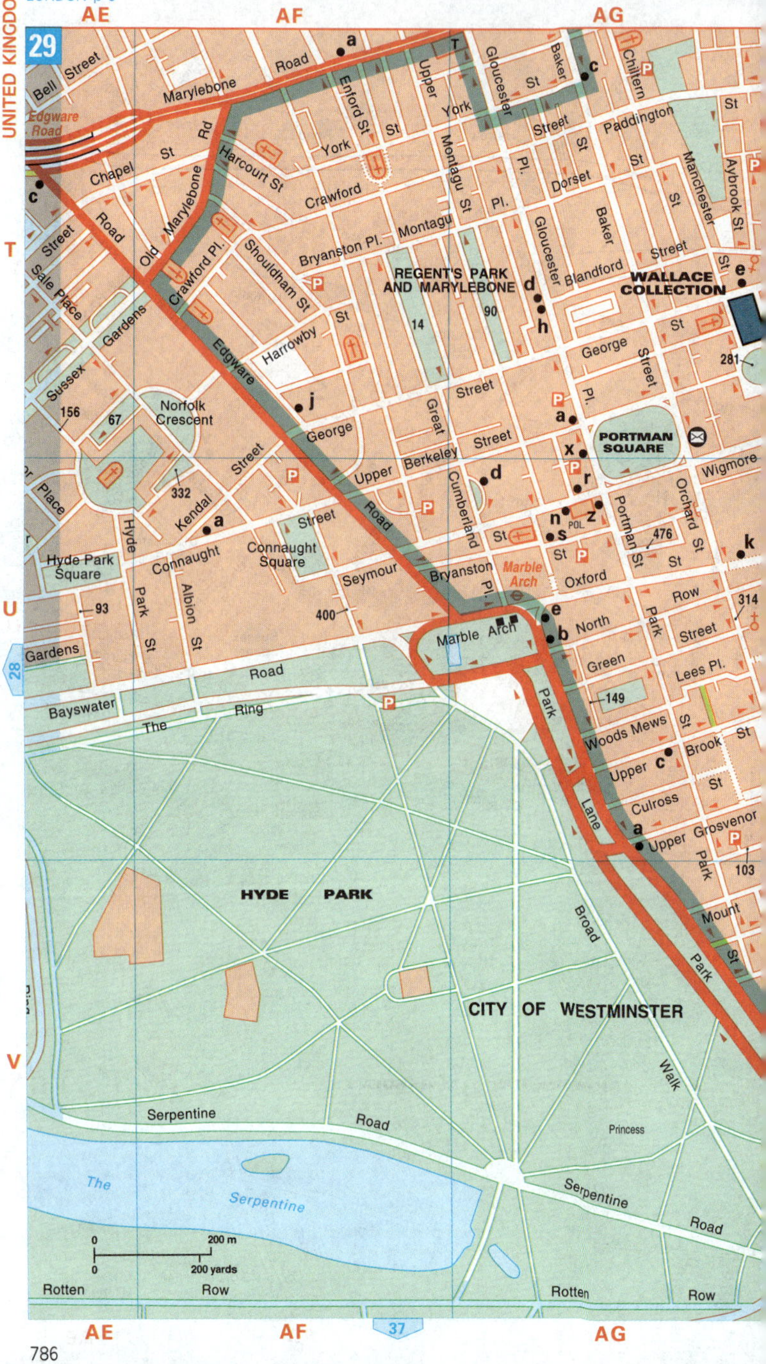
AE
AF
AG
29
T
U
V
28
37
Bell Street
Edgware Road
Marylebone Road
Enford St
Upper York St
Gloucester Pl.
Baker Street
Chiltern St
Paddington St
Manchester St
Aybrook St
Chapel St
Harcourt St
York St
Crawford St
Montagu St
Montagu Pl.
Dorset St
Old Marylebone Rd
Crawford Pl.
Shouldham St
Bryanston Pl.
Gloucester Pl.
Baker St
Blandford Street
Sale Place
Sussex Gardens
REGENT'S PARK AND MARYLEBONE
WALLACE COLLECTION
Harrowby St
George St
Great Cumberland Pl.
Upper Berkeley Street
Portman Square
Portman St
Orchard St
Wigmore St
Norfolk Crescent
Kendal Street
Connaught Street
Connaught Square
Hyde Park Square
Hyde Park Gardens
Albion St
Hyde Park St
Seymour Pl.
Bryanston St
Marble Arch
Oxford St
North Row
Park Street
Lees Pl.
Green St
North Row
Bayswater Road
The Ring
Park Lane
Woods Mews
Upper Brook St
Culross St
Upper Grosvenor St
Mount St
Park St
HYDE PARK
Broad Walk
CITY OF WESTMINSTER
Serpentine Road
Princess
The Serpentine
Rotten Row
0 200 m
0 200 yards
POL
14
67
90
93
103
149
156
281
314
332
400
476

AH
AI
AJ
30
31
38
T
U
V
BRITISH TELECOM TOWER
MIDDLESEX
Cavendish Sq.
Oxford Circus
Hannover Sq.
MAYFAIR
Grosvenor Square
Golden Sq.
Berkeley Square
BURLINGTON HOUSE
BURLINGTON ARCADE
PICCADILLY ARCADE
ST JAMES SQUARE
SHEPHERD MARKET
Green Park
GREEN PARK
SPENCER HOUSE
QUEEN'S CHAPEL
ST JAMES PALACE
LANCASTER HOUSE
APSLEY HOUSE WELLINGTON MUSEUM
Bond St
Marylebone High St
Weymouth St
New Cavendish Street
Wimpole Street
Harley Street
Welbeck Street
Queen Anne Street
Wigmore St
Henrietta Pl.
Portland Place
Great Portland St
Langham Place
Mortimer St
Great Titchfield Street
Foley St
Cleveland St
Charlotte St
Goodge St
Newman St
Berners St
Wells St
Eastcastle St
Margaret St
Holles St
Regent St
Oxford St
Princes St
Argyll St
Poland St
Noel St
D'Arblay St
Great Marlborough St
Marshall St
Carnaby St
Kingly St
Broadwick St
Lexington St
Beak St
Vere St
New Bond St
South Molton St
Davies St
Gilbert St
Binney St
Duke St
James St
Brook St
Brook's Mews
Grosvenor Street
Hanover St
Maddox St
George St
Conduit St
Savile Row
Bruton Street
Vigo St
Cork St
Old Bond St
Dover St
Berkeley St
Sackville St
Piccadilly
Jermyn St
Duke St
Bury St
King St
St James's St
Pall Mall
Mount Row
Adam's Row
South Audley Street
Mount Street
Farm St
Hay's Mews
Hill St
Charles Street
Curzon St
Bolton Street
Queen's Walk
Hertford St
Brick St
Old Park La.
Park Lane

31
AJ
AK
AL
T
U
V
30
39
BRITISH MUSEUM
BLOOMSBURY
BEDFORD SQUARE
Bloomsbury Sq.
Goodge St
Tottenham Court Rd
St Giles Circus
Soho Sq.
SOHO
NEAL'S YARD
ROYAL OPERA HOUSE
Covent Gdn
COVENT GARDEN
ST PAUL'S
Cambridge Circus
Leicester Sq.
LEICESTER SQUARE
NATIONAL PORTRAIT GALLERY
PICCADILLY CIRCUS
Golden Sq.
ST MARTIN-IN-THE-FIELDS
THEATRE ROYAL
ST JAMES'S
TRAFALGAR SQUARE
NATIONAL GALLERY
ROYAL OPERA ARCADE
WATERLOO PLACE
CARLTON HOUSE TERRACE
ST JAMES'S SQUARE
CHARING CROSS
Charing Cross
Embankment
VICTORIA EMBANKMENT GARDENS
OLD ADMIRALTY
WHITEHALL
HORSE GUARDS
BANQUETING HOUSE
QUEEN'S CHAPEL
ST JAMES'S PALACE
ST JAMES' PARK
THE MALL
STRAND
REGENT ST
Oxford Street
New Oxford Street
Great Russell Street
Shaftesbury Ave
Charing Cross Rd
Haymarket
Pall Mall
Northumberland Ave
Horse Guards Ave
Embankment
Golden
200 m
200 yards

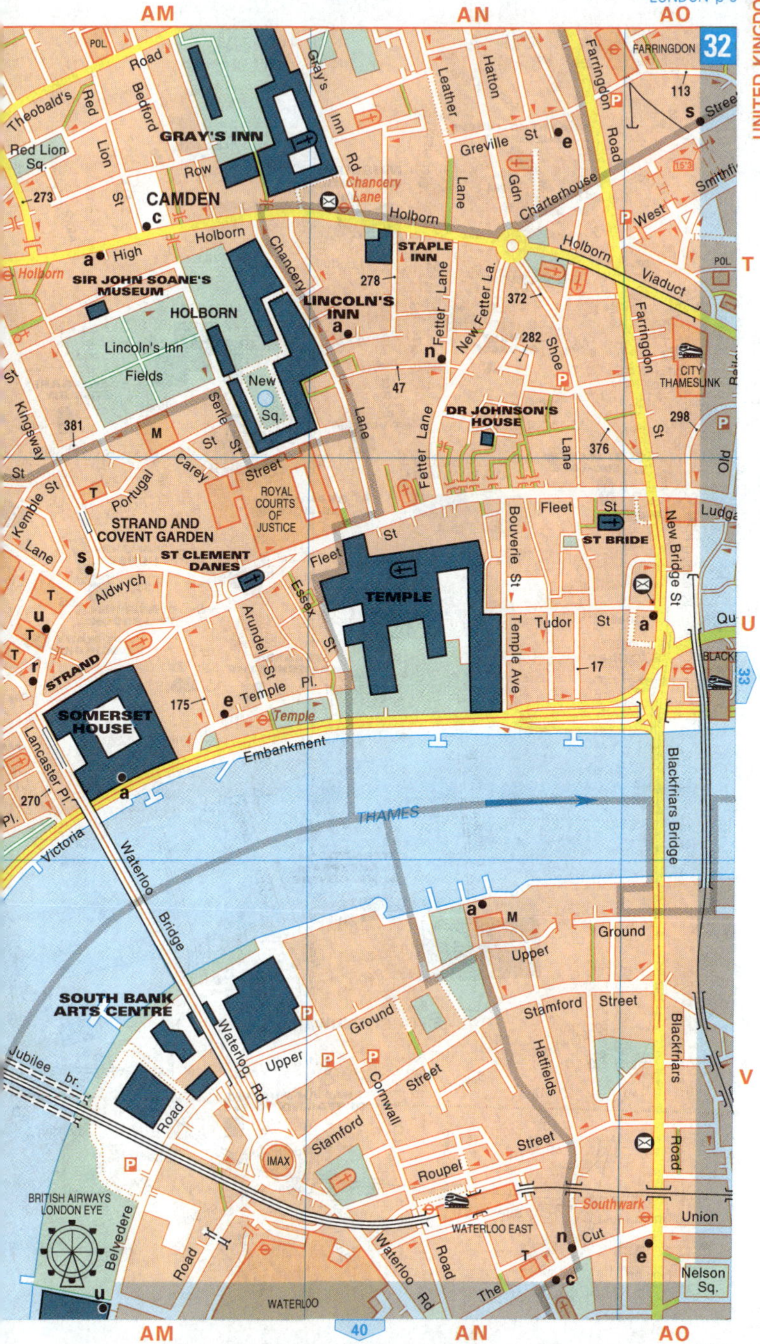
AM
AN
AO
32
FARRINGDON
113
POL.
Theobald's
Road
Red
Bedford
Gray's
Inn
Rd
Leather
Lane
Hatton
Gdn
Greville
St
Farringdon
Road
Street
Smithfield
Red Lion Sq.
Lion
St
GRAY'S INN
Row
CAMDEN
273
Chancery Lane
Holborn
Charterhouse
West
Holborn
Viaduct
High
Holborn
STAPLE INN
SIR JOHN SOANE'S MUSEUM
278
LINCOLN'S INN
HOLBORN
Chancery
Lane
Fetter
New Fetter La.
372
282
Shoe
Lincoln's Inn
Fields
New
Sq.
Serle
47
CITY THAMESLINK
Kingsway
381
M
Carey
Street
DR JOHNSON'S HOUSE
376
298
Old
Portugal
ROYAL COURTS OF JUSTICE
Fleet
Ludgate
Kemble St
Lane
STRAND AND COVENT GARDEN
ST CLEMENT DANES
ST BRIDE
New Bridge St
Bouverie St
Aldwych
Essex
Arundel
TEMPLE
Tudor
Temple Ave
Qu
BLACKFRIARS
33
STRAND
17
175
Temple
Pl.
SOMERSET HOUSE
Embankment
Lancaster Pl.
270
Pl.
Victoria
THAMES
Waterloo
Bridge
Blackfriars Bridge
Ground
Upper
SOUTH BANK ARTS CENTRE
Stamford
Street
Hatfields
Blackfriars
Road
Waterloo
Rd
Upper
Ground
Cornwall
Street
Jubilee
br.
Road
Stamford
Street
IMAX
Roupel
Southwark
Union
BRITISH AIRWAYS LONDON EYE
WATERLOO EAST
Cut
Belvedere
Road
Waterloo
Rd
Road
The
Nelson Sq.
WATERLOO
40
AM
AN
AO

AO
AP
AQ
T
U
V
33
32
Barbican
BARBICAN CENTRE
Long Lane
Ropemaker St
Silk St
ST BARTHOLOMEW THE GREAT
Aldersgate
MUSEUM OF LONDON
ST GILES CRIPPLEGATE
Fore St
Moor La.
Moorgate
BARBICAN
Smithfield
West
ST BARTHOLOMEW'S
London Wall
Viaduct
Farringdon
Giltspur
Newgate
CHRIST CHURCH
GUILDHALL
Basinghall
Gresham
Wood St
St Paul's
CITY THAMESLINK
Bailey
Old
Paternoster Sq.
Foster La.
ST VEDAST
CITY OF LONDON
ST MARGARET LOTHBURY
Lothbury
BANK OF ENGLAND
Princes St
Old Jewry
King St
Poultry
ST MARTIN LUDGATE
ST PAUL'S CATHEDRAL
Cheapside
New Change
ST MARY-LE-BOW
Bow Lane
Ludgate Hill
New Bridge St
St Paul's Churchyard
Cannon
Victoria St
MANSION HOUSE
Bank
COLE ABBEY PRESBYTERIAN
Queen Victoria St.
Queen
Mansion House
ST STEPHEN WALBROOK
ST MARY ABCHURCH
BLACKFRIARS
ST JAMES GARLICKHYTHE
Queen
Cannon Street
Upper Thames Street
CANNON STREET
Millennium Bridge
Blackfriars Bridge
Southwark Bridge
INTERNATIONAL SHAKESPEARE GLOBE CENTRE
TATE MODERN
Park St
Road
SOUTHWARK
Stoney St
SOUTHWARK CATHEDRAL
Southwark Street
Blackfriars Road
Great
Bridge
Suffolk St
Ewer
Guildford St
BRAMAH MUSEUM OF TEA AND COFFEE
Southwark Street
Union Street
Way
High
Borough
Redcross
GEORGE INN
London Bridge St
GUY'S AND ST THOMAS'S
Newcomen St
Nelson Sq.
Great
Southwark St
Union Street
310
299
113
475
264
292
247
380
294
298
304
308
250
301
291
169

AR
AS
Sun Street
Wilson St
Broadgate
Passage
LIVERPOOL STREET
Bishopsgate
Brushfield
Street
Commercial
Princelet St
Brick Lane
391
Eldon St
Sun Street
Finsbury Circus
Blomfield St
Liverpool St
Middlesex
Bell Lane
New St
Wentworth
Street
TOWER HAMLETS
Throgmorton Ave
Wall
Broad St
472
Bishopsgate
71
Axe
Houndsditch
317
Street
Goulston St
Whitechapel High St
Broad
Old
St
ST HELEN BISHOPSGATE
34
145
St Botolph St
Aldgate
Aldgate East
St
418
Threadneedle
Mary
St
ST ANDREW UNDERSHAFT
High St
Braham
Leman St
ROYAL EXCHANGE
Leadenhall
Street
Aldgate
309
LLOYD'S BUILDING
Minories
Mansell Street
268
Gracechurch St
Street
Lloyd's Ave
Fenchurch
ST CLEMENT EAST CHEAP
Lane
Prescot St
FENCHURCH STREET
Goodman's Yd
ST MARGARET PATTENS
ST OLAVE'S
Eastcheap
Mark
Pepys St
318
Monument
319
MONUMENT
ST MARY AT HILL
Gt Tower
Tower Hill
Shorter St
Royal Mint Rd
ST DUNSTAN-IN-THE-EAST
St
Byward St
Tower Hill
Lower Thames Street
ST MAGNUS THE MARTYR
ALL HALLOWS BY THE TOWER
Tower Hill
TOWER OF LONDON
Tower Bridge Approach
East Smithfield
Lower Thames St
LONDON BRIDGE
ST KATHARINE DOCK
THAMES
H.M.S. BELFAST
HAY'S GALLERIA SHOPPING CENTRE
Duke St Hill
18
TOWER BRIDGE
Tooley
Street
0
200 m
200 yards
LONDON BRIDGE
CITY HALL
Thomas
Street
Tooley
Tower Bridge Rd
Shad
Thames
St Thomas St
188
Druid St
St
Gainford St
125
POL
386
T
U
V

35
27
AA
AB
X
Y
Z
0 200 m
0 200 yards
KENSINGTON
HOLLAND PARK
LINLEY SAMBOURNE HOUSE
LEIGHTON HOUSE
High Street Kensington
Kensington Square
Edwardes Square
Kensington High Street
Holland Walk
Campden Hill
Holland St
Hornton Street
Kensington Church St
Phillimore Gdns
Argyll Rd
Earls Court Road
Abingdon Rd
Scarsdale Villas
Marloes Road
Young Street
St Alban's Grove
Cornwall Gdns
Cornwall
Lexham Gdns
Lexham Gardens
Cromwell Road
Warwick Gardens
Warwick Road
Pembroke Road
Logan Place
Longridge Road
Nevern Pl.
Nevern Square
Trebovir Road
Kenway Rd
Knaresborough Pl.
Earl's Court Gdns
Courtfield Gdns
Barkston Gdns
Bramham Gdns
Earl's Court
EARL'S COURT
Penywern Rd
Earl's Court Sq.
Bolton Gardens
Old Brompton Road
Redcliffe Gardens
Redcliffe Square
Finborough Road
Ifield Road
The Boltons
Philbeach Gardens
EARL'S COURT EXHIBITION BLDG
WEST KENSINGTON
North End Road
Lillie Road
Seagrave Rd
West Brompton
BROMPTON CEMETERY
Melbury Road
POL
342
119
410
101
99
151
241
242

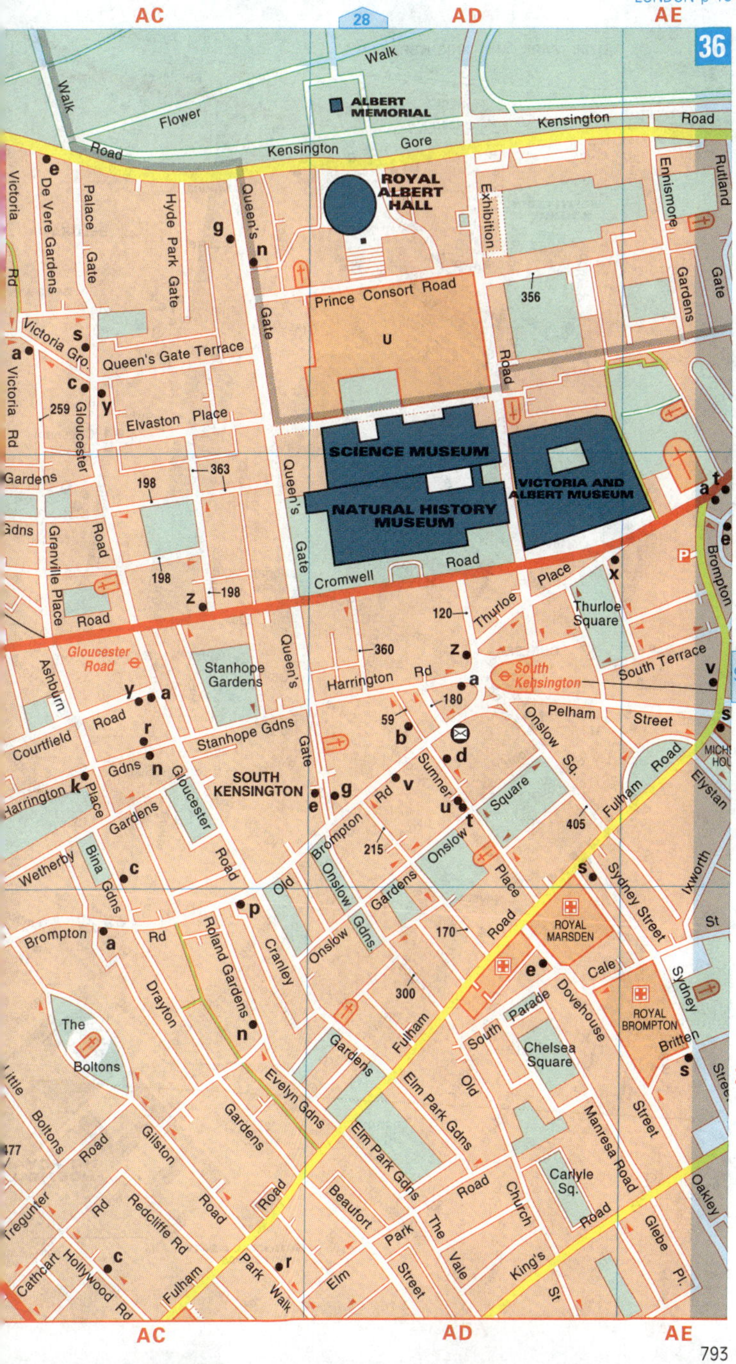
AC
28
AD
AE
36
Walk
Flower
ALBERT MEMORIAL
Kensington
Road
Gore
Kensington
Road
ROYAL ALBERT HALL
Exhibition
Ennismore
Rutland
Gardens
Gate
Victoria
Rd
De Vere Gardens
Palace
Gate
Hyde Park Gate
Queen's
Gate
Prince Consort Road
356
Road
U
X
Victoria Gro.
Queen's Gate Terrace
Victoria Rd
259
Gloucester
Elvaston Place
SCIENCE MUSEUM
NATURAL HISTORY MUSEUM
VICTORIA AND ALBERT MUSEUM
Gardens
198
363
Gdns
Grenville Place
Road
198
198
Cromwell
Road
Queen's
Gate
Place
Brompton
Road
Gloucester Road
Ashburn
Stanhope Gardens
120
Thurloe
Thurloe Square
Y
360
Harrington
Rd
South Kensington
South Terrace
37
180
59
Pelham
Street
Courtfield
Road
Stanhope Gdns
Onslow
Sq.
Road
Harrington
Gdns
Place
Gloucester
SOUTH KENSINGTON
Sumner
Rd
Square
Fulham
Elystan
Gardens
Brompton
Road
215
405
Wetherby
Bina Gdns
Onslow
Gardens
Ixworth
Old
Onslow
Road
Place
Sydney Street
St
Brompton
Rd
Roland Gardens
Cranley
Onslow
Gdns.
170
Road
ROYAL MARSDEN
Cale
The
Boltons
Drayton
300
South
Parade
Dovehouse
ROYAL BROMPTON
Sydney
Britten
Chelsea Square
Z
Fulham
Gardens
Old
Evelyn Gdns
Elm Park Gdns
Street
Little
Boltons
477
Road
Gilston
Gardens
Elm Park Gdns
Manresa Road
Carlyle Sq.
Oakley
Tregunter
Rd
Redcliffe Rd
Road
Road
Beaufort
Road
Church
Road
Glebe
Pl.
Cathcart
Hollywood
Rd
Fulham
Park
Walk
Elm
Street
Park
The
Vale
King's
St
AC
AD
AE

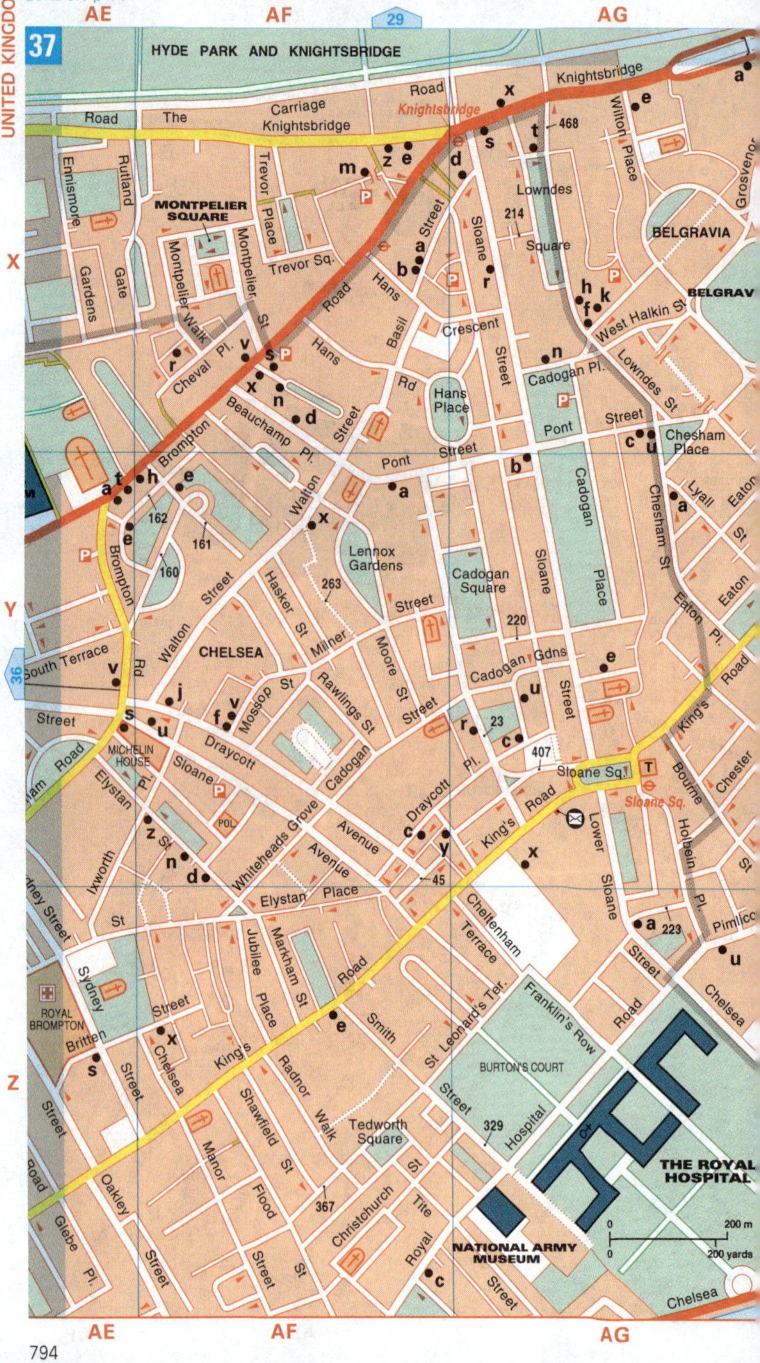
AE
AF
29
AG
37
HYDE PARK AND KNIGHTSBRIDGE
Road
The
Carriage
Knightsbridge
Road
Knightsbridge
Knightsbridge
468
Ennismore
Gardens
Rutland
Gate
MONTPELIER SQUARE
Montpelier Walk
Montpelier St
Trevor Place
Trevor Sq.
Brompton Road
Hans Road
Basil Street
Hans Crescent
Sloane Street
Lowndes Square
214
Wilton Place
Grosvenor
BELGRAVIA
BELGRAV
West Halkin St
Lowndes St
Cheval Pl.
Hans Place
Hans Rd
Beauchamp Pl.
Cadogan Pl.
Pont Street
Pont Street
Chesham Place
Chesham St
Lyall
Eaton
Eaton Pl.
Eaton
Walton Street
Lennox Gardens
Cadogan Place
Sloane Street
162
161
160
Brompton Rd
Hasker St
263
Milner Street
Cadogan Square
220
Cadogan Gdns
CHELSEA
South Terrace
Street
36
Walton
Mossop St
Rawlings St
Moore St
Street
23
407
Sloane Sq.
Sloane Sq.
King's Road
Bourne
Holbein Pl.
Chester
Road
St
MICHELIN HOUSE
Road
Elystan Pl.
Sloane Avenue
Draycott Avenue
Draycott Pl.
Cadogan
Whiteheads Grove
POL
King's Road
Lower Sloane Street
Pimlico
Ixworth
Elystan Place
45
Cheltenham Terrace
223
Sydney Street
St
Jubilee Place
Markham St
Road
Franklin's Row
Chelsea
ROYAL BROMPTON
Britten Street
Chelsea
Smith St
St Leonard's Ter.
Road
King's
Radnor Walk
BURTON'S COURT
Street
Hospital Road
329
Tedworth Square
THE ROYAL HOSPITAL
Shawfield St
Manor
Flood Street
367
Christchurch St
Tite St
Oakley Street
Glebe Pl.
Royal
NATIONAL ARMY MUSEUM
Street
Chelsea
0
200 m
0
200 yards
X
Y
Z
AE
AF
AG

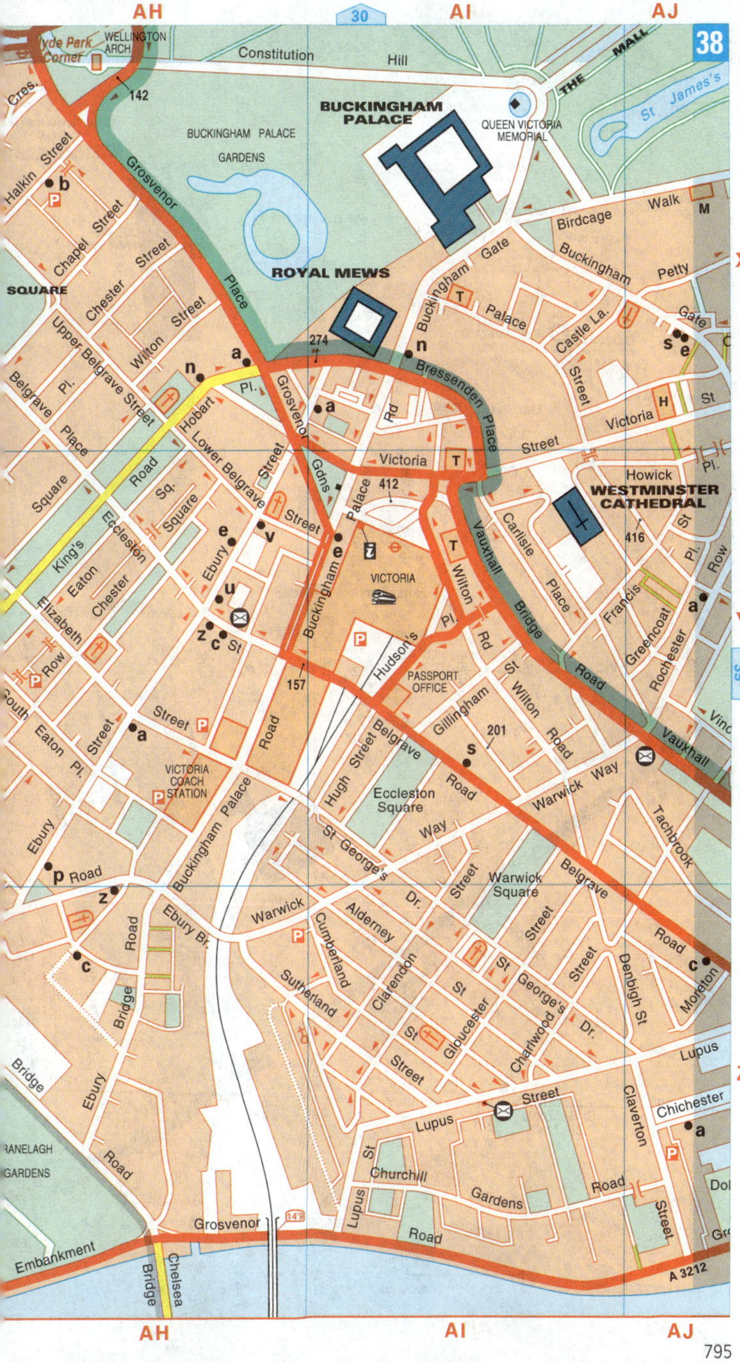
AH
AI
AJ
30
38
39
X
Y
Z
Hyde Park Corner
WELLINGTON ARCH
Constitution Hill
THE MALL
St James's
BUCKINGHAM PALACE
QUEEN VICTORIA MEMORIAL
BUCKINGHAM PALACE GARDENS
ROYAL MEWS
WESTMINSTER CATHEDRAL
VICTORIA
PASSPORT OFFICE
VICTORIA COACH STATION
Grosvenor Place
Birdcage Walk
Buckingham Gate
Petty France
Buckingham Palace Rd
Bressenden Place
Castle La.
Palace Street
Victoria Street
Howick Pl.
Vauxhall Bridge Road
Carlisle Place
Francis St
Greencoat Pl.
Rochester Row
Wilton Rd
Hudson's Pl.
Gillingham St
Belgrave Road
Eccleston Square
Warwick Way
Warwick Square
Tachbrook
St George's Dr.
Denbigh St
Moreton
Lupus Street
Chichester
Claverton Street
Churchill Gardens Road
Grosvenor Road
A 3212
Embankment
Chelsea Bridge
RANELAGH GARDENS
Ebury Bridge Road
Ebury Br.
Ebury Street
Eccleston Street
Elizabeth Street
Chester Square
Eaton Square
King's Road
Lower Belgrave Street
Hobart Pl.
Grosvenor Gdns
Upper Belgrave Street
Belgrave Place
Wilton Street
Chester Street
Chapel Street
Halkin Street
Cres.
SQUARE
Eaton Pl.
South Eaton Pl.
Hugh Street
Cumberland
Sutherland Street
Alderney Street
Clarendon Street
Gloucester St
Charlwood Street
Warwick
Vincent
142
274
412
157
201
416

39
AJ
AK
AL
31
38
X
Y
Z
St James's Park Lake
King Charles St
Parliament St
Victoria
Road
193
Westminster
WESTMINSTER BRIDGE
Birdcage Walk
Walk
M
QUEEN ANNE'S GATE
Storey's Gate
Parliament Sq.
52
Bridge St
Tothill Street
ST MARGARET'S
PALACE OF WESTMINSTER
France
Petty France
St James's Park
Palmer
a
Gate
Caxton St
NEW SCOTLAND YARD
Great Smith
Street
WESTMINSTER ABBEY
s
e
St
Victoria Street
St Anne's St
Great College St
Abingdon St
H
toria St
Old Pye Street
c
Tufton St
8
Street
Peter
Howick Pl.
200
Great
Monck Street
Marsham St
Street
Millbank
WESTMINSTER CATHEDRAL
Greycoat
Horseferry
T
416
St
Pl.
Row
P
J
Horseferry Road
Lambeth Bridge
Rd
Vincent Square
Thorney Street
Page Street
a
Greencoat
Rochester
VICTORIA
Regency
Marsham
z
Vincent Sq.
Street
St
Street
Embankment
Vincent Sq.
Vauxhall
Vincent
Street
Millbank
Islip
Tachbrook
Bridge
Douglas St
Street
Erasmus
TATE BRITAIN
Albert
c
Atterbury St
John
Street
St
Rd
Ponsonby Pl.
Road
Street
Rampayne
14'0
129
c
Pimlico
Bessborough Gdns
Millbank
THAMES
14'6
Moreton
108
Denbigh St
Street
30
Lupus
Aylesford
Vauxhall Bridge
13'3
Embankment
Chichester St
Albert
Claverton
a
St George's Square
Street
49
VAUXHALL
P
Dolphin Sq.
Road
Vauxhall
Street
Grosvenor
154
A 3212
0
200 m
0
200 yards
Nine Elms Lane
341

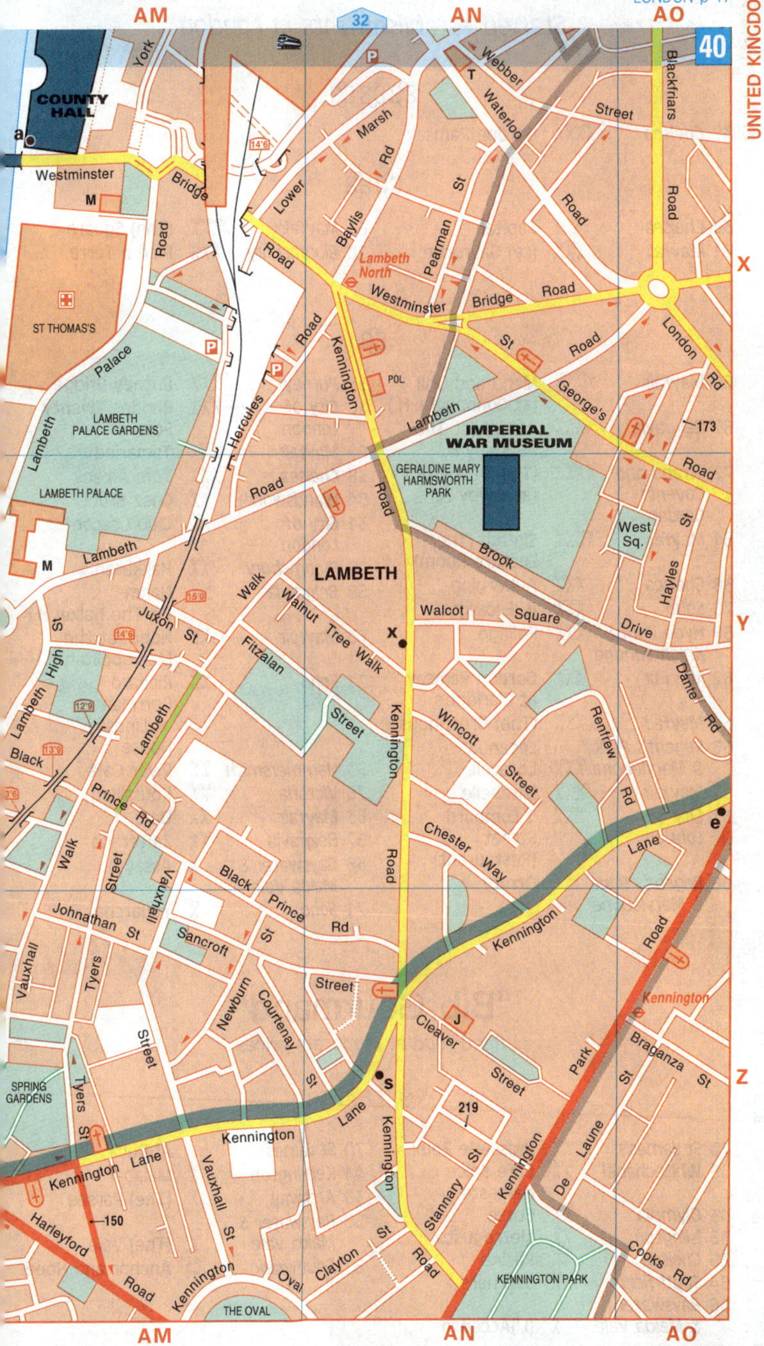
AM
AN
AO
32
40
X
Y
Z
COUNTY HALL
Westminster
Bridge
Road
York
M
ST THOMAS'S
Palace
Lambeth
LAMBETH PALACE GARDENS
LAMBETH PALACE
Lower
Marsh
Rd
Baylis
Lambeth North
Westminster
Bridge
Road
Pearman
St
Webber
Waterloo
Street
Blackfriars
Road
Kennington
Road
POL
Hercules
Lambeth
IMPERIAL WAR MUSEUM
GERALDINE MARY HARMSWORTH PARK
St
George's
Road
London
Rd
173
West Sq.
Brook
Hayles
St
LAMBETH
Walk
Walnut
Tree
Walk
Juxon
St
Fitzalan
Street
Walcot
Square
Drive
Dante
Rd
High
Black
Prince
Rd
Wincott
Street
Renfrew
Rd
Chester
Way
Lane
Walk
Street
Vauxhall
Johnathan
St
Sancroft
Black
Prince
Rd
Kennington
Road
Street
Newburn
Courtenay
Cleaver
Street
J
Kennington
Park
Braganza
St
Tyers
SPRING GARDENS
Kennington
Lane
219
Stannary
Laune
De
Kennington
Lane
Vauxhall
St
Harleyford
Road
150
Kennington
Oval
Clayton
St
THE OVAL
Road
KENNINGTON PARK
Cooks
Rd
x
s
e
a
T

Starred establishments in London

✿✿✿

38	*Chelsea*	XXXX	Gordon Ramsay

✿✿

36	*Chelsea*	🏨	Capital
61	*Mayfair*	XXX	(Le) Gavroche
61	*Mayfair*	XXXX	(The) Square
26	*Bloomsbury*	XXX	Pied à Terre

✿

61	*Mayfair*	XXXX	Menu and Grill (at Connaught H.)
57	*Belgravia*	XXXX	Pétrus (at The Berkeley H.)
72	*Strand and Covent Garden*	XXXX	(The) Savoy Grill (at Savoy H.)
61	*Mayfair*	XXXX	Sketch (The Lecture Room)
38	*Chelsea*	XXX	Aubergine
70	*Soho*	XXX	(L')Escargot
58	*Hyde Park & Knightsbridge*	XXX	Foliage
62	*Mayfair*	XXX	Gordon Ramsay at Claridge's
61	*Mayfair*	XXX	(The) Greenhouse
66	*Regent's Park & Marylebone*	XXX	Locanda Locatelli
62	*Mayfair*	XXX	Mirabelle
31	*City of London*	XXX	1 Lombard Street (Restaurant)
66	*Regent's Park & Marylebone*	XXX	Orrery
53	*Putney*	XXX	Putney Bridge
30	*City of London*	XXX	Rhodes Twenty Four
62	*Mayfair*	XXX	Tamarind
38	*Chelsea*	XXX	Tom Aikens
54	*Wandsworth*	XX	Chez Bruce
31	*City of London*	XX	Club Gascon
26	*Bloomsbury*	XX	Hakkasan
58	*Belgravia*	XX	Nahm (at The Halkin H.)
63	*Mayfair*	XX	Nobu (at the Metropolitan H.)
71	*Soho*	XX	Richard Corrigan at Lindsay House
33	*Hammersmith*	XX	River Café
76	*Victoria*	XX	Roussillon
63	*Mayfair*	XX	Umu
57	*Belgravia*	XX	Zafferano
56	*Bayswater & Maida Vale*	X	Assaggi
71	*Soho*	X	Yauatcha

"Bib Gourmand"

Good food at moderate prices

Meals

70	*St James's*	XX	Brasserie Roux
53	*Whitechapel*	XX	Cafe Spice Namaste
33	*Olympia*	XX	Cotto
36	*Islington*	XX	Metrogusto
39	*Chelsea*	XX	Racine
54	*Southfields*	XX	Sarkhel's
56	*Bayswater & Maida Vale*	X	(L')Accento
70	*St James's*	X	Al Duca
44	*Kensington*	X	Malabar
33	*Archway*	X	(The) Parsee
56	*Bayswater & Maida Vale*	X	(The) Vale
51	*Southwark*	🍺	Anchor and Hope

Restaurants classified according to type

Bangladeshi

56	*Bayswater & Maida Vale*	X	Ginger

Chinese

62	*Mayfair*	XXX	Kai
41	*Chelsea*	XX	Good Earth
26	*Bloomsbury*	XX	✿ Hakkasan
76	*Victoria*	XX	Ken Lo's Memories of China
40	*Chelsea*	XX	Mao Tai
32	*Fulham*	XX	Mao Tai
44	*Kensington*	XX	Memories of China
58	*Hyde Park & Knightsbridge*	XX	Mr Chow
28	*Hampstead*	XX	ZeNW3
72	*Soho*	X	Fung Shing
71	*Soho*	X	✿ Yauatcha

Danish

47	*South Kensington*	XX	Lundum's

English

61	*Mayfair*	XXXX	Grill Room (at Dorchester H.)
62	*Mayfair*	XXX	Brian Turner Mayfair
76	*Victoria*	XXX	Shepherd's
73	*Strand & Covent Garden*	XX	Rules

French

61	*Mayfair*	XXXX	✿✿ (Le) Gavroche
31	*City of London*	XXX	Coq d'Argent
36	*Islington*	XX	Almeida
68	*Regent's Park & Marylebone*	XX	(L') Aventure
70	*St James's*	XX	☺ Brasserie Roux
40	*Chelsea*	XX	(Le) Cercle
31	*City of London*	XX	✿ Club Gascon
40	*Chelsea*	XX	(Le) Colombier
53	*Battersea*	XX	(The) Food Room
26	*Bloomsbury*	XX	Mon Plaisir
40	*Chelsea*	XX	Poissonnerie de l'Avenue (Seafood)
39	*Chelsea*	XX	☺ Racine
76	*Victoria*	XX	✿ Roussillon
48	*Kennington*	X	Lobster Pot (Seafood)
76	*Victoria*	X	(La) Poule au Pot
71	*Soho*	X	(La) Trouvaille

Indian & Pakistani

57	*Belgravia*	XXX	Amaya
62	*Mayfair*	XXX	Benares
47	*South Kensington*	XXX	Bombay Brasserie
39	*Chelsea*	XXX	Chutney Mary
75	*Victoria*	XXX	(The) Cinnamon Club
71	*Soho*	XXX	Red Fort
62	*Mayfair*	XXX	✿ Tamarind
75	*Victoria*	XXX	Quilon (at Crowne Plaza St James H.)
50	*Bermondsey*	XX	Bengal Clipper
53	*Spitalfields*	XX	Bengal Trader
71	*Soho*	XX	Café Lazeez
53	*Whitechapel*	XX	☺ Cafe Spice Namaste
64	*Mayfair*	XX	Chor Bizarre

Indian & Pakistani

Page	Area		Restaurant
66	*Regent's Park & Marylebone*	XX	Deya
41	*Chelsea*	XX	Haandi
31	*City of London*	XX	Kasturi
47	*South Kensington*	XX	Khan's of Kensington
27	*Bloomsbury*	XX	Malabar Junction
48	*South Kensington*	XX	Memories of India
69	*St James's*	XX	Mint Leaf
40	*Chelsea*	XX	Painted Heron
48	*Kennington*	XX	Painted Heron
67	*Regent's Park & Marylebone*	XX	(La) Porte des Indes
67	*Regent's Park & Marylebone*	XX	Rasa Samudra (Seafood) (Vegetarian)
39	*Chelsea*	XX	Rasoi Vineet Bhatia
54	*Southfields*	XX	☺ Sarkhel's
48	*Herne Hill*	XX	3 Monkeys
40	*Chelsea*	XX	Vama
43	*Kensington*	XX	Zaika
48	*South Kensington*	X	Café Lazeez
35	*Finsbury*	X	Café Lazeez City
54	*Southfields*	X	Calcutta Notebook
54	*Tooting*	X	Kastoori (Vegetarian)
44	*Kensington*	X	☺ Malabar
27	*Bloomsbury*	X	Mela
33	*Archway*	X	☺ (The) Parsee
64	*Mayfair*	X	Veeraswamy

Italian

Page	Area		Restaurant
62	*Mayfair*	XXX	Cecconi's
39	*Chelsea*	XXX	Floriana
75	*Victoria*	XXX	(L') Incontro
66	*Regent's Park & Marylebone*	XXX	✿ Locanda Locatelli
71	*Soho*	XXX	Quo Vadis
75	*Victoria*	XXX	Santini
62	*Mayfair*	XXX	Sartoria
39	*Chelsea*	XXX	Toto's
63	*Mayfair*	XX	Alloro
56	*Bayswater & Maida Vale*	XX	Al San Vincenzo
44	*Kensington*	XX	(The) Ark
67	*Regent's Park & Marylebone*	XX	Bertorelli
67	*Regent's Park & Marylebone*	XX	Caldesi
40	*Chelsea*	XX	Caraffini
76	*Victoria*	XX	(Il) Convivio
39	*Chelsea*	XX	Daphne's
45	*North Kensington*	XX	Edera
53	*Putney*	XX	Enoteca Turi
67	*Regent's Park & Marylebone*	XX	Latium
36	*Islington*	XX	☺ Metrogusto
26	*Bloomsbury*	XX	Neal Street
40	*Chelsea*	XX	Pellicano
33	*Hammersmith*	XX	✿ River Café
67	*Regent's Park & Marylebone*	XX	Rosmarino
26	*Bloomsbury*	XX	Sardo
70	*St James's*	XX	Shumi
63	*Mayfair*	XX	Teca
50	*Bermondsey*	XX	Tentazioni
44	*Kensington*	XX	Timo
57	*Belgravia*	XX	✿ Zafferano
56	*Bayswater & Maida Vale*	X	☺ (L') Accento
70	*St James's*	X	☺ Al Duca
56	*Bayswater & Maida Vale*	X	✿ Assaggi
71	*Soho*	X	Bertorelli
68	*Regent's Park & Marylebone*	X	Caffè Caldesi
27	*Bloomsbury*	X	Camerino
50	*Bermondsey*	X	Cantina Del Ponte
44	*Kensington*	X	Cibo
56	*Bayswater & Maida Vale*	X	Green Olive
41	*Chelsea*	X	Manicomio
76	*Victoria*	X	Olivo
27	*Bloomsbury*	X	Passione
71	*Soho*	X	Vasco and Piero's Pavillion

Japanese

40 *Chelsea* XX Benihana
29 *Swiss Cottage* XX Benihana
29 *Holborn* XX Matsuri-High Holborn
70 *St James's* XX Matsuri-St James's
63 *Mayfair* XX ✿ Nobu (The Metropolitan H.)
67 *Regent's Park & Marylebone* XX Roka
64 *Mayfair* XX Sumosan
32 *City of London* XX Tatsuso
52 *Canary Wharf* XX Ubon by Nobu
63 *Mayfair* XX ✿ Umu
58 *Hyde Park & Knightsbridge* XX Zuma
27 *Bloomsbury* XX Abeno
47 *Chelsea* X itsu
71 *Soho* X itsu
48 *Clapham* X Tsunami

Kosher

31 *Bloomsbury* XX Bevis Marks
66 *Regent's Park & Marylebone* XX Six 13

Lebanese

63 *Mayfair* XX Fakhreldine
67 *Regent's Park & Marylebone* XX Levant
58 *Belgravia* XX Noura Brasserie

Moroccan

64 *Mayfair* XX Momo
47 *South Kensington* XX Pasha
68 *Regent's Park & Marylebone* X Momo

North African

33 *Hammersmith* X Azou

Polish

44 *Kensington* X Wódka

Pubs

68 *Regent's Park & Marylebone* (The) Abbey Road
41 *Chelsea* Admiral Codrington
51 *Southwark* Anchor and Hope
33 *Hammersmith* Anglesea Arms
36 *Islington* (The) Barnsbury
41 *Chelsea* Builders Arms
34 *Canonbury* Centuria
41 *Chelsea* Chelsea Ram
42 *Chelsea* Cross Keys
36 *Islington* Drapers Arms
29 *Primrose Hill* (The) Engineer
32 *Fulham* (The) Farm
49 *Wimbledon* (The) Fire Stables
52 *Canary Wharf* (The) Gun
33 *Shepherd's Bush* Havelock Tavern
42 *Earl's Court* Hollywood Arms
29 *Tufnell Park* Junction Tavern
42 *Chelsea* Lots Road Pub and Dining Room
28 *Hampstead* (The) Magdala
36 *Islington* (The) Northgate
35 *Finsbury* (The) Peasant
29 *Primrose Hill* (The) Queens
34 *Archway* St John's
32 *Hammersmith & Fulham* (The) Salisbury Tavern
36 *Islington* (The) Social
41 *Chelsea* Swag and Tails
56 *Bayswater and Maida Vale* (The) Waterway
28 *Hampstead* (The) Wells

Scottish

- 76 *Victoria* XX Boisdale
- 31 *City of London* XX Boisdale of Bishopgate

Seafood

- 39 *Chelsea* XXX One-O-One (at Sheraton Park Tower H.)
- 52 *St Katherine's Dock* XX (The) Aquarium
- 64 *Mayfair* XX Bentley's
- 32 *City of London* XX Chamberlain's
- 73 *Strand & Covent Garden* XX J. Sheekey
- 40 *Chelsea* XX Poissonnerie de l'Avenue (French)
- 67 *Regent's Park & Marylebone* XX Rasa Samudra (Indian) (Vegetarian)
- 41 *Chelsea* X Bibendum Oyster Bar
- 51 *Southwark* X Fish!
- 51 *Southwark* X Livebait
- 48 *Kennington* X Lobster Pot (French)

South East Asian

- 73 *Strand & Covent Garden* XXX East@West
- 26 *Bloomsbury* XX Crazy Bear
- 41 *Chelsea* XX Eight over Eight
- 63 *Mayfair* XX Taman Gang

Spanish

- 47 *South Kensington* XX Cambio de Tercio
- 26 *Bloomsbury* XX Fino
- 27 *Bloomsbury* X Cigala

Thai

- 32 *Fulham* XX Blue Elephant
- 53 *Battersea* XX Chada
- 58 *Belgravia* XX Mango Tree
- 58 *Belgravia* XX ✿ Nahm (at The Halkin H.)
- 56 *Bayswater & Maida Vale* XX Nipa (at Royal Lancaster H.)
- 48 *South Kensington* X Bangkok
- 68 *Regent's Park & Marylebone* X Chada Chada
- 54 *Tooting* X Oh Boy

Turkish

- 67 *Regent's Park & Marylebone* XX Ozer

Vegetarian

- 67 *Regent's Park & Marylebone* XX Rasa Samudra (Indian) (Seafood)
- 54 *Tooting* X Kastoori (Indian)

Vietnamese

- 35 *Highbury* X Au Lac

Greater London is divided, for administrative purposes, into 32 boroughs plus the City; these sub-divide naturally into minor areas, usually grouped around former villages or quarters, which often maintain a distinctive character.

of Greater London: 020.

LONDON AIRPORTS

Heathrow

Middx. West : 17 m. by A 4, M 4 **Underground** *Piccadilly line direct.*

(020) 8759 4321 – **Terminal :** Airbus (A 1) from Victoria, Airbus (A 2) from Paddington.

Terminals 1, 2 and 3, Underground Station Concourse, Heathrow Airport (0839) 123456.

London Heathrow Marriott, Bath Rd, Hayes, UB3 5AN, (020) 8990 1100, *reservations.heathrow@marriotthotels.co.uk, Fax (020) 8990 1110,* – rm, – 540.
Tuscany : **Meals** - Italian - (dinner only) a la carte 31.25/39.40 – ***Allie's grille :*** **Meals** a la carte 19.25/27.30 – 14.95 – **391 rm** 199.75, 2 suites.
◆ Built at the end of 20C, this modern, comfortable hotel is centred around a large atrium, with comprehensive business facilities : there is an exclusive Executive floor. Tuscany is bright and convivial. Grill favourites at Allie's.

Crowne Plaza London Heathrow, Stockley Rd, West Drayton, UB7 9NA, (0870) 400 9140, *reservations.cplhr@ichotelsgroup.com, Fax (01895) 445122,* – rm, – 200.
Concha Grill : **Meals** a la carte 23.75/41.75 **s.** (see also ***Simply Nico Heathrow*** below) – 17.00 – **457 rm** 179.00, 1 suite.
◆ Extensive leisure, aromatherapy and beauty salons make this large hotel a popular stopover for travellers. Club bedrooms are particularly well-equipped. Bright, breezy Concha Grill with juice bar.

Radisson Edwardian, 140 Bath Rd, Hayes, UB3 5AW, (020) 8759 6311, *Fax (020) 8759 4559,* – rm, – 550.
Henleys : **Meals** *(closed lunch Friday-Sunday)* a la carte 25.00/45.00 – 15.00 – **442 rm** 185.65/237.40, 17 suites.
◆ Capacious group hotel with a huge atrium over the leisure facilities. Plenty of comfortable lounges, well-appointed bedrooms and attentive service. Henleys boasts oil paintings and cocktail bar.

Sheraton Skyline, Bath Rd, Hayes, UB3 5BP, (020) 8759 2535, *res268skyline@sheraton.com, Fax (020) 8750 9150,* – – 500.
Sage : **Meals** 16.00/35.00 and a la carte 30.00/40.00 – 15.50 – **348 rm** 199.00, 2 suites.
◆ Well known for its unique indoor swimming pool surrounded by a tropical garden which is overlooked by many of the bedrooms. Business centre available. Classically decorated dining room.

Hilton London Heathrow Airport, Terminal 4, TW6 3AF, (020) 8759 7755, *gmheathrow@hilton.com, Fax (020) 8759 7579,* – rm, – 250.
Brasserie : **Meals** 25.50/31.50 and dinner a la carte 29.50/41.00 – ***Zen Oriental :*** **Meals** - Chinese - 28.80 and a la carte 19.80/34.00 – 19.50 – **390 rm** 222.00/258.50, 5 suites.
◆ Group hotel with a striking modern exterior and linked to Terminal 4 by a covered walkway. Good sized bedrooms, with contemporary styled suites. Spacious Brasserie in vast atrium. Zen Oriental offers formal Chinese experience.

Holiday Inn London Heathrow, Sipson Rd, West Drayton, UB7 0JU, (0870) 4008595, *rmheathrowm4@ichotelsgroup.com, Fax (020) 8897 8659,* – rm, – 140.
Sampans : **Meals** - Asian - (dinner only) a la carte 17.00/27.00 – ***Rotisserie :*** **Meals** (buffet meals) 18.50 – 14.95 – **606 rm** 179.00, 4 suites.
◆ Busy group hotel where the Academy conference suite attracts the business community. Bedrooms come in a variety of styles. Popular Irish bar. Sampans offers regional Chinese dishes. Spacious Rotisserie with chef carving to order.

Renaissance London Heathrow, Bath Rd, TW6 2AQ, ✆ (020) 8897 6363, *lhrrenaissance@aol.com, Fax (020) 8897 1113,* Ls, ≘s – |$|, ⇹ rm, ▤ TV ✆ ♿ P – 🛆 400. MC AE ① VISA. ✂
Meals *(closed lunch Saturday and Sunday)* 19.50/23.50 and a la carte 28.50/38.00 **s.** ♀ – ☕ 15.95 – **643 rm** 146.90, 6 suites.
◆ Low level façade belies the size of this easily accessible hotel. Large lounge and assorted shops in the lobby. Some of the soundproofed bedrooms have views of the runway. Open-plan restaurant with buffet or à la carte.

Holiday Inn Heathrow Ariel, 118 Bath Rd, Hayes, UB3 5AJ, ✆ (0870) 4009040, *reservations-heathrow@ichotelsgroup.com, Fax (020) 8564 9265* – |$|, ⇹ rm, ▤ rest, TV ✆ P – 🛆 55. MC AE ① VISA
Meals (bar lunch Saturday) (buffet lunch)/dinner a la carte 25.00/30.00 **s.** – ☕ 14.95 – **186 rm** 134.00.
◆ Usefully located hotel in a cylindrical shape. Modern bedrooms with warm colours. Third floor executive rooms particularly impressive. Conference rooms available. Subtly-lit, relaxing restaurant.

Premier Travel Inn, 15 Bath Rd, TW6 2AB, ✆ (0870) 6075075, *Fax (0870) 2419000* – |$|, ⇹ rm, ▤ TV ✆ ♿ P – 🛆 30. MC AE ① VISA JCB. ✂
Meals (grill rest.) – **590 rm** 74.95.
◆ Well-priced Travel Inn with modern, wood-panelled exterior and huge atrium. Well-equipped meeting rooms. Bedrooms are of good quality with triple glazing. Bright, airy, informal grill restaurant.

Simply Nico Heathrow (at Crowne Plaza London Heathrow H.), Stockley Rd, West Drayton, UB7 9NA, ✆ (01895) 437564, *heathrow.simplynico@corushotels.com, Fax (01895) 437565* – ▤ P. MC AE ① VISA
closed Saturday lunch and Sunday – **Meals** a la carte 25.40/36.25 **s.** ♀.
◆ Located within the hotel but with its own personality. Mixes modern with more classically French dishes. Professional service in comfortable surroundings.

Gatwick *W. Sussex South : 28 m. by A 23 and M 23 -* **Train** *from Victoria : Gatwick Express* 504 T 30 – ✉ *Crawley.*

✈ ✆ (0870) 0002468.

Hilton London Gatwick Airport, South Terminal, RH6 0LL, ✆ (01293) 518080, *londongatwick@hilton.com, Fax (01293) 528980,* Ls – |$|, ⇹ rm, ▤ TV ✆ ♿ P – 🛆 500. MC AE ① VISA. ✂
Meals 21.95/24.95 and a la carte 25.00/33.00 ♀ – ☕ 17.50 – **791 rm** 199.00.
◆ Large, well-established hotel, popular with business travellers. Two ground floor bars, lounge and leisure facilities. Older rooms co-ordinated, newer in minimalist style. Restaurant enlivened by floral profusions.

Renaissance London Gatwick, Povey Cross Rd, RH6 0BE, ✆ (01293) 820169, *Fax (01293) 820259,* Ls, ≘s, 🏊, squash – |$|, ⇹ rm, ▤ TV ✆ ♿ P – 🛆 180. MC AE ① VISA
Meals (bar lunch)/dinner 19.50 and a la carte 25.45/36.45 **s.** ♀ – ☕ 13.50 – **252 rm** 119.00, 2 suites.
◆ Large red-brick hotel. Good recreational facilities including indoor pool, solarium. Bedrooms are spacious and decorated in smart, chintzy style. Small brasserie area open all day serving popular meals.

Premier Travel Inn, Longbridge Way, Gatwick Airport (North Terminal), RH6 0NX, ✆ (0870) 2383305, *Fax (01293) 568278* – |$|, ⇹ rm, ▤ rest, TV ♿ P. MC AE ① VISA. ✂
Meals (grill rest.) – **219 rm** 48.95/54.95.
◆ Consistent standard of trim, simply fitted accommodation in contemporary style. Family rooms with sofa beds. Ideal for corporate or leisure travel.

In this guide a symbol or a character, printed in red or black does not have the same meaning. Pay particular attention to the explanatory pages.

CAMDEN

Bloomsbury – ✉ *W1/WC1/WC2.*

Russell, Russell Sq, WC1B 5BE, ✆ (020) 7837 6470 Ⓜ *Russell Square, sales.russell@lemeridien.com,* Fax (020) 7837 2857 – |$|, ⇹ rm, ▤ TV ✆ – 🛆 400. MC AE ① VISA. ✂
Meals a la carte 22.90/29.00 ♀ – ☕ 14.95 – **369 rm** 182.10/211.50, 2 suites.
◆ An impressive Victorian building dominating Russell Square. Boasts many original features including the imposing marbled lobby and staircase. Traditional or modern rooms. Restaurant has noticeable feel of grandeur.

UNITED KINGDOM

Marlborough, 9-14 Bloomsbury St, WC1B 3QD, (020) 7636 5601 *Tottenham Court Road, resmarl@radisson.com,* Fax (020) 7636 0532 – rm, rest, – 200. VISA JCB. 31 AKT k
***Glass :* Meals** *(closed lunch Friday-Sunday)* a la carte 25.00/45.00 – 15.00 – **171 rm** 171.50/238.50, 2 suites.
• A Victorian building around the corner from the British Museum. The lobby has been restored to its original marbled splendour and the bedrooms offer good comforts. Bright, breezy restaurant with suitably modish cooking.

Mountbatten, 20 Monmouth St, WC2H 9HD, (020) 7836 4300 *Covent Garden, Fax (020) 7240 3540,* – rm, – 90. VISA JCB. 31 ALU d
***Dial :* Meals** *(closed lunch Friday-Sunday)* a la carte 25.00/45.00 – 15.00 – **149 rm** 240.80/297.00, 2 suites.
• Photographs and memorabilia of the eponymous Lord Louis adorn the walls and corridors. Ideally located in the heart of Covent Garden. Compact but comfortable bedrooms. Bright, stylish restaurant.

Covent Garden, 10 Monmouth St, WC2H 9HB, (020) 7806 1000 *Covent Garden, covent@firmdale.com,* Fax (020) 7806 1100, – – 50. VISA. 31 ALU x
***Brasserie Max :* Meals** (booking essential) a la carte 31.00/41.00 – 18.00 – **56 rm** 246.75/358.40, 2 suites.
• Individually designed and stylish bedrooms, with CDs and VCRs discreetly concealed. Boasts a very relaxing first floor oak-panelled drawing room with its own honesty bar. Informal restaurant.

Grafton, 130 Tottenham Court Rd, W1P 9HP, (020) 7388 4131 *Warren Street, resgraf@radisson.com,* Fax (020) 7387 7394, – rm, – 100. VISA JCB.
***Aston's :* Meals** *(closed lunch Friday-Sunday)* a la carte 25.00/45.00 – 15.00 – **326 rm** 171.50/238.50, 4 suites.
• Just yards from Warren Street tube. Discreet Edwardian charm that belies its location in one of London's busier streets. Bedrooms to becalm in soft beige tones. Open-plan restaurant and bar.

Kenilworth, 97 Great Russell St, WC1B 3BL, (020) 7637 3477 *Tottenham Court Road, resmarl@radisson.com,* Fax (020) 7631 3133, – rm, – 100. VISA JCB. 31 AKT a
Meals - Asian - *(closed lunch Friday-Sunday)* a la carte 25.00/45.00 – 15.00 – **186 rm** 171.50/238.50.
• Usefully placed for the shops of Oxford Street. Stylish interiors and modern designer hi-tech bedrooms, equipped to meet the needs of the corporate traveller. Smart dining room with a modern style.

Jurys Gt Russell St, 16-22 Gt Russell St, WC1B 3NN, (020) 7347 1000 *Tottenham Court Road, gtrussellstreet@jurysdoyle.com,* Fax (020) 7347 1001 – rm, – 220. VISA. 31 AKT n
***Lutyens :* Meals** a la carte approx 29.00 – 16.00 – **168 rm** 225.00, 1 suite.
• Neo-Georgian building by Edward Lutyens, built for YMCA in 1929. Smart comfortable interior decoration from the lounge to the bedrooms. Facilities include a business centre. Restaurant has understated traditional style.

Montague on the Gardens, 15 Montague St, WC1B 5BJ, (020) 7637 1001 *Holborn, bookmt@rchmail.com,* Fax (020) 7637 2516, , , , – rm, – 120. VISA JCB 31 ALT a
***Blue Door Bistro :* Meals** a la carte 29.75/37.50 – 16.50 – **98 rm** 229.10/246.75, 6 suites.
• A period townhouse with pretty hanging baskets outside. The hushed conservatory overlooks a secluded garden. The clubby bar has a Scottish golfing theme. Rich bedroom décor. Restaurant divided into two small, pretty rooms.

Holiday Inn Bloomsbury, Coram St, WC1N 1HT, (0870) 4009222 *Russell Square, reservation-bloomsbury@ichotelsgroup.com,* Fax (020) 7713 5954 – rm, – 300. VISA JCB.
Meals 19.95 and a la carte 18.85/31.85 **s.** – 14.95 – **310 rm** 159.00.
• Bright, modern bedrooms in warm, neutral tones. Have a drink in either the stylish bar with leather chairs or Callaghans Irish themed bar. Relaxed and contemporary dining.

Thistle Bloomsbury, Bloomsbury Way, WC1A 2SD, (020) 7242 5881 *Tottenham Court Road, bloomsbury@thistle.co.uk,* Fax (020) 7831 0225 – rm, rest, – 80. VISA 31 ALT r
Meals 18.95 and dinner a la carte 18.85/29.35 – 14.95 – **138 rm** 252.60/320.30.
• Established over 100 years ago and retains much charm. Quiet and discreet lobby. An old fashioned lift leads up to the bedrooms that have a very English feel. Combined bar and dining room.

Myhotel Bloomsbury, 11-13 Bayley St, Bedford Sq, WC1B 3HD, ✆ (020) 7667 6000 Ⓜ *Tottenham Court Road, res@myhotels.co.uk*, Fax (020) 7667 6001, – – 40. 31 AKT x
Yo! Sushi **: Meals** - Japanese - a la carte 16.00/21.00 **s.** – 18.00 – **78 rm** 242.00/270.25.
◆ The minimalist interior is designed on the principles of feng shui ; even the smaller bedrooms are stylish and uncluttered. Mybar is a fashionable meeting point. Diners can enjoy Japanese food from conveyor belt.

Bonnington in Bloomsbury, 92 Southampton Row, WC1B 4BH, ✆ (020) 7242 2828 Ⓜ *Holborn, sales@bonnington.com*, Fax (020) 7831 9170, – , rm, – 250. 31 ALT s
Meals *(closed Sunday)* (bar lunch)/dinner 21.75 and a la carte approx 24.00 **s.** – **239 rm** 140.00/170.00, 8 suites.
◆ Built in 1911 and providing easy access to a number of tourist attractions. Functional, but well-kept, bedrooms offer traditional comforts with many modern extras. Classically decorated dining room.

Pied à Terre, (temporarily closed due to a fire, expected to reopen spring 2005), 34 Charlotte St, W1T 2NH, ✆ (020) 7636 1178 Ⓜ *Goodge Street, p-a-t@dircon.co.uk*, Fax (020) 7916 1171 – . 31 AJT e
closed last week December, first week January, Sunday and lunch Monday and Saturday – **Meals** 26.50/54.50.
Spec. Seared and poached foie gras in a Sauternes consommé. Rib of veal, ragoût of mousserons, broad beans and sage sauce. Chocolate tart with stout ice cream.
◆ Frosted glass front hints at the understated, cool interior. The kitchen offers an elaborate and adventurous, yet refined take on modern French cuisine. Well-chosen wine list.

Incognico, 117 Shaftesbury Ave, WC2H 8AD, ✆ (020) 7836 8866 Ⓜ *Tottenham Court Road, Fax (020) 7240 9525* – . 31 AKU q
closed 4 days Easter, 10 days Christmas, Sunday and Bank Holidays – **Meals** 19.50/24.00.
◆ Opened in 2000 with its robust décor of wood panelling and brown leather chairs. Downstairs bar has a window into the kitchen, from where French and English classics derive.

Neal Street, 26 Neal St, WC2H 9QT, ✆ (020) 7836 8368 Ⓜ *Covent Garden, Fax (020) 7240 3964* – 31 ALU s
closed 24 December-2 January and Sunday – **Meals** - Italian - 25.00 (lunch) and a la carte 28.50/52.00.
◆ Light, bright and airy ; tiled flooring and colourful pictures. Dishes range from the simple to the more complex. Mushrooms a speciality. Has its own shop next door.

Sardo, 45 Grafton Way, W1T 5DQ, ✆ (020) 7387 2521 Ⓜ *Warren Street, info@sardo-restaurant.com*, Fax (020) 7387 2559.
closed Saturday lunch and Sunday – **Meals** - Italian (Sardinian specialities) - a la carte 24.90/31.00.
◆ Simple, stylish interior run in a very warm and welcoming manner with very efficient service. Rustic Italian cooking with a Sardinian character and a modern tone.

Hakkasan, 8 Hanway Pl, W1T 1HD, ✆ (020) 7907 1888 Ⓜ *Tottenham Court Road, mail@hakkasan.com*, Fax (020) 7907 1889 – . 31 AKT c
closed 25 December and 1 January – **Meals** - Chinese (Canton) - a la carte 19.50/59.50.
Spec. Dim sum. Grilled Wagyn beef with soya. Peking duck with Royal Beluga caviar.
◆ A distinctive, modern interpretation of Cantonese cooking in an appropriately contemporary and cavernous basement. The lively, bustling bar is an equally popular nightspot.

Fino, 33 Charlotte St (entrance on Rathbone St), W1T 1RR, ✆ (020) 7813 8010 Ⓜ *Goodge Street, info@finorestaurant.com*, Fax (020) 7813 8011 – 31 AJT a
closed 25 December, Sunday and Bank Holidays – **Meals** - Spanish - 14.00 (lunch) and a la carte 18.00/32.00.
◆ Spanish-run basement Tapas bar with modern style décor and banquette seating. Wide-ranging menu of authentic dishes ; 2 set-price selections offering an introduction to tapas.

Mon Plaisir, 21 Monmouth St, WC2H 9DD, ✆ (020) 7836 7243 Ⓜ *Covent Garden, eatafrog@mail.com*, Fax (020) 7240 4774 – 31 ALU g
closed 25 and 31 December, 1 January, Saturday lunch, Sunday and Bank Holidays – **Meals** - French - 15.95 (lunch) and a la carte 20.75/36.65.
◆ London's oldest French restaurant and family-run for over fifty years. Divided into four rooms, all with a different feel but all proudly Gallic in their decoration.

Crazy Bear, 26-28 Whitfield St, W1T 2RG, ✆ (020) 7631 0088 Ⓜ *Goodge Street, enquiries@crazybeargroup.co.uk*, Fax (020) 7631 1188 – . 31 AKT b
closed Saturday lunch, Sunday and Bank Holidays – **Meals** - South East Asian - a la carte 24.00/39.50.
◆ Exotic destination : downstairs bar geared to fashionable set ; ground floor dining room is art deco inspired. Asian flavoured menus, with predominance towards Thai dishes.

XX **Archipelago,** 110 Whitfield St, W1T 5ED, ✆ (020) 7383 3346 Ⓜ *Goodge Street, archipelago@onetel.com,* Fax (020) 7383 7181 – MC AE ⓓ VISA JCB
closed 25 December, Saturday lunch, Sunday and Bank Holiday Mondays – **Meals** 21.50 (lunch) and a la carte 29.00/37.00.
◆ Eccentric in both menu and décor and not for the faint hearted. Crammed with knick-knacks from cages to Buddhas. Menu an eclectic mix of influences from around the world.

XX **Malabar Junction,** 107 Great Russell St, WC1B 3NA, ✆ (020) 7580 5230 Ⓜ *Tottenham Court Road,* Fax (020) 7436 9942 – ▤. MC AE VISA 31 AKT y
closed 25-27 December – **Meals** - South Indian - a la carte 15.00/23.50.
◆ Specialising in dishes from southern India. Bright restaurant with a small fountain in the centre of the room below a large skylight. Helpful and attentive service.

X **Passione,** 10 Charlotte St, W1T 2LT, ✆ (020) 7636 2833 Ⓜ *Tottenham Court Road, Liz@passione.co.uk,* Fax (020) 7636 2889 – MC AE ⓓ VISA JCB 31 AKT u
closed 2 weeks Christmas, Saturday lunch and Sunday – **Meals** - Italian - (booking essential) a la carte 36.50/40.00.
◆ Compact but light and airy. Modern Italian cooking served in informal surroundings, with friendly and affable service. Particularly busy at lunchtime.

X **Cigala,** 54 Lamb's Conduit St, WC1N 3LW, ✆ (020) 7405 1717 Ⓜ *Holborn, tasty@cigala.co.uk,* Fax (020) 7242 9949 – MC AE ⓓ VISA
closed 25-26 December – **Meals** - Spanish - 18.00 (lunch) and a la carte 21.50/31.00 ♀.
◆ Spanish restaurant on the corner of attractive street. Simply furnished with large windows and open-plan kitchen. Robust Iberian cooking. Informal tapas bar downstairs.

X **Camerino,** 16 Percy St, W1T 1DT, ✆ (020) 7637 9900 Ⓜ *Tottenham Court Road, info@camerinorestaurant.com,* Fax (020) 7637 9696 – ▤. MC AE ⓓ VISA JCB 31 AKT f
closed 1 week Christmas, Saturday lunch and Sunday – **Meals** - Italian - 21.50/26.50 ♀.
◆ Wood floored restaurant with intimate basement and brighter ground floor dining rooms. Authentic, rustic Italian dishes with a predominantely Northern Italian style.

X **Mela,** 152-156 Shaftesbury Ave, WC2H 6HL, ✆ (020) 7836 8635 Ⓜ *Leicester Square, info@melarestaurant.co.uk,* Fax (020) 7379 0527 – MC AE ⓓ VISA JCB 31 AKU e
closed 25 December – **Meals** - Indian - 10.95/34.95 and a la carte 11.70/16.20 **s.**.
◆ Vibrantly decorated dining room with a simple style in a useful location close to Theatreland. Enjoy thoroughly tasty Indian food in a bustling, buzzy environment.

X **Abeno,** 47 Museum St, WC1A 1LY, ✆ (020) 7405 3211 Ⓜ *Tottenham Court Road, okonomi@abeno.co.uk,* Fax (020) 7405 3212 – ▤. MC AE ⓓ VISA JCB 31 ALT e
closed 24-26 and 31 December and 1 January – **Meals** - Japanese (Okonomi-Yaki) - 6.50/16.80 (lunch) and a la carte 11.10/30.80.
◆ Specialises in Okonomi-yaki : little Japanese "pancakes" cooked on a hotplate on each table. Choose your own filling and the size of your pancake.

Euston – ✉ *NW1/WC1.*

Novotel London Euston, 100-110 Euston Rd, NW1 2AJ, ✆ (020) 7666 9000 Ⓜ *Euston, h5309@accor.com,* Fax (020) 7666 9100, Fā, ≘s – |♦|, ⇔ rm, ▤ TV ✆ ♿ – 🔑 450. MC AE ⓓ VISA JCB. ✂
Meals *(closed lunch Saturday and Sunday)* 18.00 (lunch) and a la carte 20.50/31.90 ♀ – ☕ 14.50 – **311 rm** 160.00, 1 suite.
◆ Extensive conference facilities that include the redeveloped Shaw theatre. Large marbled lobby. Modern bedrooms that offer views of London's rooftops from the higher floors. Lobby-based restaurant and bar look onto busy street.

Hilton London Euston, 17-18 Upper Woburn Pl, WC1H 0HT, ✆ (020) 7943 4500 Ⓜ *Euston,* Fax (020) 7943 4501, Fā, ≘s – |♦|, ⇔ rm, ▤ TV ✆ ♿ – 🔑 150. MC AE ⓓ VISA. ✂
***Three Crowns* : Meals** *(closed Saturday and Sunday lunch)* (dinner only) 19.95 and a la carte ♀ – ***Terrace* : Meals** 25.00 and a la carte 19.85/23.85 **s.** ♀ – ☕ 13.95 – **150 rm** 179.00/239.00.
◆ Nearby transport links make this a useful location. Scandinavian styled bedrooms. Executive rooms are particularly well-equipped. Three Crowns has smart basement location. Lighter fare in Terrace conservatory.

Premier Travel Inn, 141 Euston Rd, WC1H 9PJ, ✆ (0870) 2383301 Ⓜ *Euston,* Fax (020) 7554 3419 – |♦|, ⇔ rm, ▤ rest, TV ♿. MC AE ⓓ VISA. ✂
Meals (grill rest.) – **220 rm** 82.95.
◆ Budget accommodation with clean and spacious bedrooms, all with a large workspace. Double glazed but still ask for a quieter room at the back.

Hampstead – ✉ NW3.

Winnington Rd, Hampstead ☎ (020) 8455 0203.

The House without rest., 2 Rosslyn Hill, NW3 1PH, ☎ (020) 7431 8000, *reception@thehousehotel.co.uk, Fax (020) 7433 1775* – TV. MC AE D
23 rm 100.00/220.00.
◆ Large Victorian house close to the shops and not far from Hampstead Heath. Pleasant breakfast room/bar. Individually styled, well appointed rooms, with smart marbled bathrooms.

Langorf without rest., 20 Frognal, NW3 6AG, ☎ (020) 7794 4483 Ⓜ *Finchley Road, info@langorfhotel.com*, Fax (020) 7435 9055 – TV. MC AE D VISA JCB.
51 rm 82.00/110.00, 5 suites.
◆ Converted Edwardian house in a quiet residential area. Bright breakfast room overlooks secluded walled garden. Fresh bedrooms, many of which have high ceilings.

ZeNW3, 83-84 Hampstead High St, NW3 1RE, ☎ (020) 7794 7863 Ⓜ *Hampstead Heath, info@zenw3.com*, Fax (020) 7794 6956 – MC D VISA
closed 24-25 December – **Meals** - Chinese - 14.80/26.00 and a la carte 22.00/32.50.
◆ Contemporary interior provided by the glass topped tables and small waterfall feature on the stairs. Professional service. Carefully prepared Chinese food.

Cucina, 45a South End Rd, NW3 2QB, ☎ (020) 7435 7814 Ⓜ *Hampstead Heath, postmaster@cucinahampstead.co.uk*, Fax (020) 7435 7815 – MC AE VISA
Meals 21.95 and a la carte 21.85/34.85 ♀.
◆ The small deli at the front gives few clues to the large room inside. Eclectic mix of artwork scattered around the room. Modern menu with influences from around the globe.

The Wells, 30 Well Walk, NW3 1BX, ☎ (020) 7794 3785 Ⓜ *Hampstead Heath, info@thewellshampstead.co.uk*, Fax (020) 7794 6817, – MC AE VISA
closed 25-26 December and 1 January – **Meals** 25.00/29.50 ♀.
◆ Attractive 18C inn with modern interior. Ground floor bar and a few tables next to open-plan kitchen ; upstairs more formal dining rooms. Classically-based French cooking.

The Magdala, 2A South Hill Park, NW3 2SB, ☎ (020) 7435 2503 Ⓜ *Belsize Park, Fax (020) 7435 6167*, – MC VISA JCB
closed 25 December – **Meals** a la carte 17.50/26.00 ♀.
◆ Located on the edge of the Heath. Two bars popular with locals, one with open-plan kitchen. Upstairs dining room, open at weekends, offers robust cooking. Simpler lunch menu.

Hatton Garden – ✉ EC1.

Bleeding Heart, Bleeding Heart Yard, EC1N 8SJ, off Greville St ☎ (020) 7242 8238 Ⓜ *Farringdon, bookings@bleedingheart.co.uk*, Fax (020) 7831 1402, – MC AE D VISA 32 ANT e
closed 10 days Christmas-New Year, Saturday, Sunday and Bank Holidays – **Meals** a la carte 25.95/34.50 ♀.
◆ Wood panelling, candlelight and a heart motif ; a popular romantic dinner spot. By contrast, a busy City restaurant at lunchtime. French influenced menu. Weighty wine list.

Holborn – ✉ WC1/WC2.

Renaissance Chancery Court, 252 High Holborn, WC1V 7EN, ☎ (020) 7829 9888 Ⓜ *Holborn, sales.chancerycourt@renaissancehotels.com*, Fax (020) 7829 9889, – rm, TV – 400. MC AE D VISA. 32 AMT a
Meals (see ***Pearl*** below) – 20.95 – **354 rm** 252.60, 2 suites.
◆ Striking building built in 1914, converted to a hotel in 2000. Impressive marbled lobby and grand central courtyard. Very large bedrooms with comprehensive modern facilities.

Kingsway Hall, Great Queen St, WC2B 5BX, ☎ (020) 7309 0909 Ⓜ *Holborn, reservations@kingswayhall.co.uk*, Fax (020) 7309 9129, – rm, TV – 150. MC AE D VISA. 31 ALT b
***Harlequin* : Meals** *(closed lunch Saturday, Sunday and Bank Holidays)* 14.95/17.95 **s.** and dinner a la carte – 15.25 – **168 rm** 185.00, 2 suites.
◆ Large, corporate-minded hotel. Striking glass-framed and marbled lobby. Stylish ground floor bar. Well-appointed bedrooms with an extensive array of mod cons. Relaxing restaurant in warm pastel colours.

Pearl (at Renaissance Chancery Court H.), 252 High Holborn, WC1V 7EN, ☎ (020) 7829 7000 Ⓜ *Holborn, Fax (020) 7829 9889* – MC AE D VISA JCB 32 AMT a
closed Saturday lunch and Sunday – **Meals** 24.50/42.50 and a la carte 38.50/88.50 ♀.
◆ Impressive dining room with walls clad in Italian marble ; Corinthian columns. Waiters provide efficient service at well-spaced tables ; original menus.

Matsuri - High Holborn, Mid City Pl, 71 High Holborn, WC1V 6EA, (020) 7430 1970 *Holborn, eat@matsuri-restaurant.com,* Fax (020) 7430 1971 – . VISA JCB 32 AMT c
closed 25 December, Sunday and Bank Holidays – **Meals** - Japanese - 15.00/25.00 and a la carte 23.50/43.00.
• Spacious, airy Japanese restaurant. Authentic menu served in main dining room, in basement teppan-yaki bar and at large sushi counter, where chefs demonstrate their skills.

Primrose Hill – *NW1.*

Odette's, 130 Regent's Park Rd, NW1 8XL, (020) 7586 5486 *Chalk Farm, Fax (020) 7586 0508* – VISA
closed Monday lunch – **Meals** 19.00 (lunch) and a la carte 28.00/36.00.
• Identified by the pretty hanging baskets outside. A charming interior with mirrors of various sizes covering the walls. Detailed service. Contemporary cuisine.

The Queens, 49 Regent's Park Rd, NW1 8XD, (020) 7586 0408 *Chalk Farm, Fax (020) 7586 5677,* – VISA
Meals a la carte 22.00/30.00.
• One of the original "gastropubs". Very popular balcony overlooking Primrose Hill and the high street. Robust and traditional cooking from the blackboard menu.

The Engineer, 65 Gloucester Ave, NW1 8JH, (020) 7722 0950 *Chalk Farm, Fax (020) 7483 0592,* – VISA
closed 25 December – **Meals** a la carte 20.75/28.75.
• Busy pub that boasts a warm, neighbourhood feel. Dining room, decorated with modern pictures, has modish appeal. Informal, chatty service. Modern cuisine.

Swiss Cottage – *NW3.*

Marriott Regents Park, 128 King Henry's Rd, NW3 3ST, (020) 7722 7711 *Swiss Cottage, Fax (020) 7586 5822,* , , – , rm, – 300. VISA.
Meals (bar lunch)/dinner 18.00 and a la carte 19.00/30.00 – 16.95 – **298 rm** 193.90, 5 suites.
• Large writing desks and technological extras attract the corporate market to this purpose-built group hotel. The impressive leisure facilities appeal to weekend guests. Large, open-plan restaurant and bar.

Swiss Cottage without rest., 4 Adamson Rd, NW3 3HP, (020) 7722 2281 *Swiss Cottage, reservations@swisscottagehotel.co.uk,* Fax (020) 7483 4588 – – 35. VISA JCB.
53 rm 65.00/125.00, 6 suites.
• Made up of four Victorian houses in a residential conservation area. Bedrooms vary in size and shape, reflecting the age of the house. Basement breakfast room.

Bradley's, 25 Winchester Rd, NW3 3NR, (020) 7722 3457 *Swiss Cottage, ssjbradleys@aol.com,* Fax (020) 7435 1392 – . VISA JCB
closed 1 week Christmas, Saturday lunch, Sunday dinner, Monday and Bank Holidays – **Meals** 16.00/22.00 and a la carte 23.00/35.50.
• Warm pastel colours and modern artwork add a Mediterranean touch to this neighbourhood restaurant. The theme is complemented by the cooking of the chef patron.

Benihana, 100 Avenue Rd, NW3 3HF, (020) 7586 9508 *Swiss Cottage, info@benihana.co.uk,* Fax (020) 7586 6740 – . VISA
closed 25 December – **Meals** - Japanese (Teppan-Yaki) - 16.50/29.50.
• An entertaining experience where Japanese chefs chop, juggle and cook in front of you. Be prepared to talk with strangers as guests are seated in groups around the counters.

Globe, 100 Avenue Rd, NW3 3HF, (020) 7722 7200 *Swiss Cottage, globerella@aol.com,* Fax (020) 7722 2772 – . VISA
closed Saturday lunch and Sunday – **Meals** a la carte 19.00/25.50.
• Next to the Hampstead Theatre, which opened in 2003, so this airy, conservatory establishment tends to be busier earlier and later in the evening. Stylish upstairs bar.

Tufnell Park *Gtr London* – *NW5.*

Junction Tavern, 101 Fortess Rd, NW5 1AG, (020) 7485 9400 *Tufnell Park, Fax (020) 7485 9401,* – VISA
closed 24-26 December and 1 January – **Meals** a la carte 17.50/26.50.
• Typical Victorian pub with wood panelling. Eat in the bar or in view of the open plan kitchen. Robust cooking using good fresh ingredients, served in generous portions.

CITY OF LONDON – ✉ E1/EC2/EC3/EC4.

Great Eastern, Liverpool St, EC2M 7QN, ✆ (020) 7618 5000 Ⓜ *Liverpool Street, info@great-eastern-hotel.co.uk*, Fax (020) 7618 5001, – |$|, ⇔ rm, ▤ TV ✆ ♿ – 🏛 250. MC AE ⓓ VISA 34 ART t
***Fishmarket* : Meals** - Seafood - *(closed Saturday-Sunday)* a la carte 27.00/49.00 **s.** ♀ – ***Miyabi* : Meals** - Japanese - *(closed Sunday)* (booking essential) a la carte 19.50/
29.50 **s.** (see also ***Aurora*** below) – ☕ 16.00 – **264 rm** 264.30/334.80, 3 suites.
◆ A contemporary and stylish interior hides behind the classic Victorian façade of this railway hotel. Bright and spacious bedrooms with state-of-the-art facilities. Fishmarket based within original hotel lobby. Miyabi is compact Japanese restaurant.

Crowne Plaza London - The City, 19 New Bridge St, EC4V 6DB, ✆ (0870) 4009190 Ⓜ *Blackfriars, loncy.res@ichotelsgroup.com*, Fax (020) 7438 8080, – |$|, ⇔ rm, ▤ TV ✆ ♿ – 🏛 180. MC AE ⓓ VISA JCB. 32AOU a
***Refettorio* : Meals** - Italian - *(closed Sunday and Saturday lunch)* a la carte 33.00/39.00 – ***Benugo* : Meals** a la carte 25.50/29.50 – ☕ 15.00 – **201 rm** 346.60/522.90, 2 suites.
◆ Art deco hotel by the river ; interior enhanced by classical chocolate, cream and brown palette. Compact meeting room ; well equipped fitness centre. Sizable, stylish rooms. Modish Refettorio for Italian cuisine. Informal, all-day dining at Benugo.

Threadneedles, 5 Threadneedle St, EC2R 8AY, ✆ (020) 7657 8080 Ⓜ *Bank, resthreadneedles@theetongroup.com*, Fax (020) 7657 8100 – |$| ⇔ ▤ TV ✆ ♿ – 🏛 35. MC AE ⓓ VISA JCB. 34ARU y
Meals (see ***Bonds*** below) – ☕ 22.00 – **68 rm** 358.40, 1 suite.
◆ A converted bank, dating from 1856, with a stunning stained-glass cupola in the lounge. Rooms are very stylish and individual featuring CD players and Egyptian cotton sheets.

The Chamberlain, 130-135 Minories, EC3 1NU, ✆ (020) 7680 1500 Ⓜ *Aldgate, thechamberlain@fullers.co.uk*, Fax (020) 7702 2500 – |$|, ⇔ rm, ▤ TV ✆ ♿ – 🏛 40. MC AE ⓓ VISA. 34ASU n
closed Christmas – **Meals** (in bar Saturday and Sunday) a la carte 13.20/18.90 ♀ – ☕ 12.95 – **64 rm** 195.00/225.00.
◆ Modern hotel aimed at business traveller, two minutes from the Tower of London. Warmly decorated bedrooms with writing desks. All bathrooms have inbuilt plasma TVs. Popular range of dishes.

Novotel London Tower Bridge, 10 Pepys St, EC3N 2NR, ✆ (020) 7265 6000 Ⓜ *Tower Hill, h3107@accor-hotels.com*, Fax (020) 7265 6060, – |$|, ⇔ rm, ▤ TV ✆ ♿ – 🏛 95. MC AE ⓓ VISA. 34ASU b
***The Garden Brasserie* : Meals** (bar lunch Saturday-Sunday) 18.50 (lunch) and a la carte 22.75/27.50 **s.** ♀ – ☕ 13.00 – **199 rm** 169.00/189.00, 4 suites.
◆ Modern, purpose-built hotel with carefully planned, comfortable bedrooms. Useful City location and close to Tower of London which is visible from some of the higher rooms. Informally styled brasserie.

Travelodge without rest., 1 Harrow Pl, E1 7DB, ✆ (08700) 850950 Ⓜ *Liverpool Street, Fax (020) 7626 1105* – |$| ⇔ TV ✆ ♿. MC AE ⓓ VISA JCB. 34 AST s
142 rm 89.00.
◆ Suitable for both corporate travellers and families alike. Spacious, carefully designed, bright and modern rooms with sofa beds and ample workspace.

Aurora (at Great Eastern H.), Liverpool St, EC2M 7QN, ✆ (020) 7618 7000 Ⓜ *Liverpool Street, restaurants@great-eastern-hotel.co.uk*, Fax (020) 7618 5035 – ▤. MC AE ⓓ VISA JCB 34 ART t
closed Saturday, Sunday, Christmas and Bank Holidays – **Meals** 28.00 (lunch) and a la carte 31.00/49.00 ♀.
◆ Vast columns, ornate plasterwork and a striking glass dome feature in this imposing dining room. Polished and attentive service of an elaborate and modern menu.

Rhodes Twenty Four, 24th floor, Tower 42, 25 Old Broad St, EC2N 1HQ, ✆ (020) 7877 7703 Ⓜ *Liverpool Street, reservations@rhodes24.co.uk*, Fax (020) 7877 7788, ← London – |$| ▤. MC AE ⓓ VISA 34 ART v
closed Christmas-New Year, Saturday, Sunday and Bank Holidays – **Meals** a la carte 26.60/51.50 ♀.
Spec. Braised oxtail cottage pie. Skate wing with langoustines, soft leeks and ham. Bread and butter pudding.
◆ Modern restaurant on the 24th floor of the former Natwest building with panoramic views of the city. Modern, refined cooking of classic British recipes. Booking advised.

XXX **Coq d'Argent,** No.1 Poultry, EC2R 8EJ, ✆ (020) 7395 5000 Ⓜ *Bank, coqdargent @conran-restaurants.co.uk580,* Fax (020) 7395 5050, – ≣. MC AE Ⓓ VISA 33AQU c
closed 25-26 December, 1 January and Sunday dinner – **Meals** - French - (booking essential) 28.00 (lunch) and a la carte 29.25/39.25 ♀.
◆ Take the dedicated lift to the top of this modern office block. Tables on the rooftop terrace have city views ; busy bar. Gallic menus highlighted by popular shellfish dishes..

XXX ✿ **1 Lombard Street (Restaurant),** 1 Lombard St, EC3V 9AA, ✆ (020) 7929 6611 Ⓜ *Bank, hb@1lombardstreet.com,* Fax (020) 7929 6622 – ≣. MC AE Ⓓ VISA 33AQU r
closed Saturday, Sunday and Bank Holidays – **Meals** (lunch booking essential) 39.00 (lunch) and a la carte approx 57.50 ♀.
Spec. Carpaccio of tuna with Oriental spices, ginger and lime vinaigrette. Poached lamb, sweetbreads and tongue, summer vegetables. Feuillantine of apple, Guinness ice cream.
◆ A haven of tranquillity behind the forever busy brasserie. Former bank provides the modern and very comfortable surroundings in which to savour the accomplished cuisine.

XXX **Prism,** 147 Leadenhall, EC3V 4QT, ✆ (020) 7256 3875 Ⓜ *Aldgate, Fax (020) 7256 3876* – ≣. MC AE Ⓓ VISA JCB 34ARU u
closed Christmas, New Year, Saturday and Sunday – **Meals** a la carte 21.50/42.00 ♀.
◆ Enormous Corinthian pillars and a busy bar feature in this capacious and modern restaurant. Efficient service of an eclectic menu. Quieter tables in covered courtyard.

XXX **Bonds** (at Threadneedles H.), 5 Threadneedle St, EC2R 8AY, ✆ (020) 7657 8088 Ⓜ *Bank, bonds@theetongroup.com,* Fax (020) 7657 8089 – ≣. MC AE Ⓓ VISA JCB 34ARU y
closed Saturday and Sunday – **Meals** 29.50/70.00 and a la carte 31.50/51.50 ♀.
◆ Modern interior juxtaposed with the grandeur of a listed city building. Vast dining room with high ceiling and tall pillars. Attentive service of hearty, contemporary food.

XX ✿ **Club Gascon** (Aussignac), 57 West Smithfield, EC1A 9DS, ✆ (020) 7796 0600 Ⓜ *Barbican, Fax (020) 7796 0601* – ≣. MC AE VISA 33 APT z
closed 1-3 January, Saturday lunch, Sunday and Bank Holidays – **Meals** - French (Gascony specialities) - (booking essential) 35.00/60.00 and a la carte 21.50/74.50 ♀.
Spec. Lamb delicacies with creamy morels. Duck foie gras "pop corn". Rabbit with calamari and chorizo brunoise.
◆ Intimate and rustic restaurant on the edge of Smithfield Market. Specialises in both the food and wines of Southwest France. Renowned for the foie gras tasting dishes.

XX **The Chancery,** 9 Cursitor St, EC4A 1LL, ✆ (020) 7831 4000 Ⓜ *Chancery Lane, reservations@thechancery.co.uk,* Fax (020) 7831 4002 – ≣. MC AE Ⓓ VISA JCB 32 ANT a
closed Saturday-Sunday, Christmas and Bank Holidays – **Meals** 19.50 (lunch) and a la carte 26.25/32.25 ♀.
◆ Near Law Courts, a small restaurant with basement bar. Floor to ceiling windows give impression of size. Quality ingredients put to good use in accomplished, modern dishes.

XX **Boisdale of Bishopgate,** Swedeland Court, 202 Bishopgate, EC2M 4NR, ✆ (020) 7283 1763 Ⓜ *Liverpool Street, Fax (020) 7283 1664* – ≣. MC AE VISA 34 ART a
closed 25 December-3 January, Saturday, Sunday and Bank Holidays – **Meals** - Scottish - a la carte 22.95/40.50 ♀.
◆ Through ground floor bar, serving oysters and champagne, to brick vaulted basement with red and tartan décor. Menu featuring Scottish produce. Live jazz most evenings.

XX **Bevis Marks,** Bevis Marks, EC3 5DQ, ✆ (020) 7283 2220 Ⓜ *Aldgate, enquiries@bevismarkstherestaurant.com,* Fax (020) 7283 2221, – ⇹. MC AE VISA 34 ART x
closed Saturday-Sunday – **Meals** - Kosher - a la carte 27.50/35.00 ♀.
◆ Glass-roofed extension to city's oldest synagogue : limestone flooring, modern murals on wall. Regularly changing Kosher menus ; influences from Mediterranean and Middle East.

XX **Searcy's,** Barbican Centre, Level 2, Silk St, EC2Y 8DS, ✆ (020) 7588 3008 Ⓜ *Barbican, searcys@barbican.org.uk,* Fax (028) 7382 7247 – ≣. MC AE Ⓓ VISA JCB 33 AQT n
closed 24-26 December, Saturday lunch and Sunday – **Meals** 21.00/25.00 ♀.
◆ Stylish modern surroundings, smooth effective service and seasonal modern British cooking. Unique location ideal for visitors to Barbican's multi-arts events.

XX **Kasturi,** 57 Aldgate High St, EC3N 1AL, ✆ (020) 7480 7402 Ⓜ *Aldgate, reservation@kasturi-restaurant.co.uk,* Fax (020) 7702 0256 – ≣. MC AE VISA 34ASU a
closed 24 December-1 January, Sunday and Bank Holidays – **Meals** - Indian - a la carte 18.00/24.00.
◆ Spacious wooden floored restaurant enhanced by mirrors ; modern art on walls. Good service. Varied menu with original and authentic dishes.

XX **Chamberlain's,** 23-25 Leadenhall Market, EC3V 1LR, ✆ (020) 7648 8690 Ⓜ *Bank, info@chamberlains.org,* Fax (020) 7648 8691 – ▤. MC AE ◑ VISA 34ARU v
closed 25 December, Saturday, Sunday and Bank Holidays – **Meals** - Seafood - a la carte 34.40/49.00 ♀.
◆ Bright, modern restaurant in ornate Victorian indoor market. Top quality seafood from fish and chips to mousse of lobster. There's even a fish tank in the lavatories !

XX **Tatsuso,** 32 Broadgate Circle, EC2M 2QS, ✆ (020) 7638 5863, *Fax (020) 7638 5864* – ▤. MC AE ◑ VISA JCB 34 ART u
closed Christmas-New Year, Saturday, Sunday and Bank Holidays – **Meals** - Japanese - (booking essential) 38.00/97.00 and a la carte 50.00/100.00 **s.**
◆ Dine in the busy teppan-yaki bar or in the more formal restaurant. Approachable staff in traditional costume provide attentive service of authentic and precise dishes.

XX **The White Swan,** 1st Floor, 108 Fetter Lane, EC4A 1ES, ✆ (020) 7242 9696 Ⓜ *Temple, info@thewhiteswanlondon.com,* Fax (020) 7242 9122 – ▤. ✈ 32 ANT n
closed Saturday, Sunday and Bank Holidays – **Meals** 25.00/28.00 ♀.
◆ Smart dining room above pub just off Fleet Street : mirrored ceilings, colourful paintings on wall. Modern, daily changing menus, are good value for the heart of London.

XX **Novelli in the City,** London Capital Club, 15 Abchurch Lane, EC4N 7BW, ✆ (020) 7717 0088 Ⓜ *Bank, membership@londoncapitalclub.com,* Fax (020) 7717 0099 – ▤. MC AE ◑ VISA 33AQU v
closed 24 December-4 January, Saturday and Sunday – **Meals** (dinner only) 18.50 and a la carte 27.50/38.50 ♀.
◆ Set in the windowless basement of a private members' club ; bright, contemporary interior with linen-clad tables. Good sized dishes with a firm classical base.

HAMMERSMITH AND FULHAM

Fulham – ✉ *SW6.*

Premier Travel Inn, 3 Putney Bridge Approach, SW6 3JD, ✆ (020) 7471 8300 Ⓜ *Putney Bridge, Fax (020) 7471 8315* – |‡|, ⇹ rm, ▤ rest, TV ♿. MC AE ◑ VISA. ✈
Meals (grill rest.) – **154 rm** 76.95.
◆ Converted office block offering clean, well-priced accommodation. All rooms have sofa beds and large worktops.

XX **Blue Elephant,** 4-6 Fulham Broadway, SW6 1AA, ✆ (020) 7385 6595 Ⓜ *Fulham Broadway, london@blueelephant.com,* Fax (020) 7386 7665 – ▤. MC AE ◑ VISA
closed 23-25 December and Saturday lunch – **Meals** - Thai - (booking essential) 15.00/33.00 and a la carte 26.00/49.00.
◆ Elaborately ornate, unrestrained décor : fountains, bridges, orchids and ponds with carp. Authentic Thai food served by attentive staff in national costumes.

XX **Mao Tai,** 58 New Kings Rd, Parsons Green, SW6 4LS, ✆ (020) 7731 2520 Ⓜ *Parsons Green, info@maotai.co.uk,* Fax (020) 7471 8994 – ▤. MC AE ◑ VISA
closed 25-26 December – **Meals** - Chinese (Szechuan) - 12.50/24.70 and a la carte 26.00/41.80 ♀.
◆ A light and modern interior with wood flooring and framed artwork with an eastern theme. Well organised service. Chinese cuisine with Szechuan specialities.

X **Zinc Bar and Grill,** 11 Jerdan Pl, Fulham Island, SW6 1BE, ✆ (020) 7386 2250 Ⓜ *Fulham Broadway, zincfulham-reservations@conran-restaurants.co.uk,* Fax (020) 7386 2260,
– ▤. MC AE ◑ VISA
closed 25 December – **Meals** a la carte 15.00/32.00 ♀.
◆ Bright modern bar ; informal chic restaurant. Grills, seafood and modern international fare. No bookings accepted for the heated terrace so arrive early for a table.

The Farm, 18 Farm Lane, SW6 1PP, ✆ (020) 7381 3331 Ⓜ *Fulham Broadway, info@thefarmfulham.co.uk* – ▤. MC AE VISA
Meals a la carte 23.50/31.00 ♀.
◆ Red brick pub with leather sofas and contemporary fireplaces. Rear dining room is ultra stylish, and the menus are suitably modern British with a French accent.

The Salisbury Tavern, 21 Sherbrooke Rd, SW6 7HX, ✆ (020) 7381 4005 Ⓜ *Fulham Broadway, thesalisburytavern@longshotplc.com,* Fax (020) 7381 1002 – ▤. MC AE VISA JCB
closed 25-26 and 31 December – **Meals** (live jazz Monday evening) 18.50 and a la carte 22.50/30.00 ♀.
◆ Its residential location attracts a local crowd to the stylish bar. Separate, and equally à la mode, dining room with pleasant young staff. Wide ranging traditional menu.

Hammersmith *Gtr London* – ✉ *W6.*

River Café (Ruth Rogers/Rose Gray), Thames Wharf, Rainville Rd, W6 9HA, ☎ (020) 7386 4200 Ⓜ *Barons Court, info@rivercafe.co.uk*, Fax (020) 7386 4201, – MC AE ⓓ VISA
closed Christmas-New Year, Sunday dinner and Bank Holidays – **Meals** - Italian - (booking essential) a la carte 41.00/55.00 ♀.
Spec. Chargrilled squid with red chilli and rocket. Tranche of turbot, capers and marjoram. "Chocolate nemesis".
• Warehouse conversion with full length windows on one side, open plan kitchen the other. Canteen-style atmosphere. Accomplished rustic Italian cooking, uses the finest produce.

Snows on the Green, 166 Shepherd's Bush Rd, Brook Green, W6 7PB, ☎ (020) 7603 2142 Ⓜ *Hammersmith, sebastian@snowsonthegreen.freeserve.co.uk*, Fax (020) 7602 7553 – ▤. MC AE ⓓ VISA
closed 4 days Christmas, Saturday lunch, Sunday and Bank Holiday Mondays – **Meals** 13.50/16.50 (lunch) and a la carte 25.00/28.50 ♀.
• Name refers to the chef patron, not the inclement weather found in west London. Mediterranean influenced decoration matched by the style of the cooking.

The Brackenbury, 129-131 Brackenbury Rd, W6 0BQ, ☎ (020) 8748 0107 Ⓜ *Ravenscourt Park, Fax (020) 8748 6159*, – MC AE VISA
closed Easter, August Bank Holiday, 25-28 December, 1-3 January, Saturday lunch and Sunday dinner – **Meals** 13.50 (lunch) and a la carte 18.00/28.00 ♀.
• The closely set wooden tables, pavement terrace and relaxed service add to the cosy, neighbourhood feel. Cooking is equally unfussy ; modern yet robust.

Azou, 375 King St, W6 9NJ, ☎ (020) 8536 7266 Ⓜ *Stamford Brook, azourestaurant@artserve.net*, Fax (020) 8748 1009 – ▤. MC ⓓ VISA
closed 25 December, lunch Saturday and Sunday and Bank Holidays – **Meals** - North African - (lunch booking essential) 15.00 and a la carte 14.50/24.00.
• The North African theme is not confined to the menu ; the room is decorated with hanging lanterns, screens and assorted knick-knacks. Friendly service and well priced dishes.

Anglesea Arms, 35 Wingate Rd, W6 0UR, ☎ (020) 8749 1291 Ⓜ *Ravenscourt Park, Fax (020) 8749 1254*, – MC VISA
closed 23-31 December – **Meals** (bookings not accepted) 12.95 (lunch) and a la carte 19.00/24.00 ♀.
• The laid-back atmosphere and local feel make this pub a popular venue. Worth arriving early as bookings are not taken. Modern cooking from blackboard menu.

Olympia *Gtr London* – ✉ *W14.*

Cotto, 44 Blythe Rd, W14 0HA, ☎ (020) 7602 9333 Ⓜ *Kensington Olympia, bookings@cottorestaurant.co.uk*, Fax (020) 7602 5003 – ▤. MC AE VISA JCB
closed 25-30 December, Saturday lunch, Sunday and Bank Holidays – **Meals** 16.50/19.50 ♀.
• On two floors, with vivid abstract paintings on white walls, chrome-framed chairs and music. Efficient service from black-clad staff. Modern cooking with some originality.

Shepherd's Bush – ✉ *W14.*

K West, Richmond Way, W14 0AX, ☎ (020) 7674 1000 Ⓜ *Kensington Olympia, bookit@k-west.co.uk*, Fax (020) 7674 1050, ▤ TV ♿ – 60. MC AE ⓓ VISA.
Meals a la carte 36.00/53.50 **s.** ♀ – ☕ 19.00 – **222 rm** 205.60/276.10.
• Former BBC offices, the interior is decorated in a smart, contemporary fashion. Bedrooms in understated modern style, deluxe rooms with work desks and DVD and CD facilities. Modish menus in trendy dining room.

Havelock Tavern, 57 Masbro Rd, W14 0LS, ☎ (020) 7603 5374 Ⓜ *Kensington Olympia, Fax (020) 7602 1163*, – ▤
closed 22-26 December and Easter Sunday – **Meals** (bookings not accepted) a la carte 18.00/24.00 **s.** ♀.
• Typical new wave London pub where the kitchen produces generously portioned modern food. Pine tables and chairs, and a large central bar. Privately owned.

ISLINGTON *Gtr London.*

Archway – ✉ *N19.*

The Parsee, 34 Highgate Hill, N19 5NL, ☎ (020) 7272 9091 Ⓜ *Archway, dining@theparsee.co.uk*, Fax (020) 7687 1139 – ▤. MC AE ⓓ VISA
closed Christmas-New Year, Saturday lunch, Sunday and Bank Holidays – **Meals** - Indian (Parsee) - a la carte 16.00/23.95 ♀.
• Two brightly painted rooms, one non smoking and featuring a painting of a Parsee Angel. Good value, interesting, carefully spiced cuisine, Persian and Indian in inspiration.

St John's, 91 Junction Rd, N19 5QU, ✆ (020) 7272 1587 Ⓜ *Archway, Fax (020) 7687 2247* – MC AE VISA
closed Monday lunch – **Meals** a la carte 20.00/25.00 ♀.
◆ Busy front bar enjoys a lively atmosphere ; dining room in a large rear room. Log fire at one end, open hatch into kitchen the other. Blackboard menu ; rustic cooking.

Barnsbury – ✉ *N1.*

Morgan M, 489 Liverpool Rd, N7 8NS, ✆ (020) 7609 3560 Ⓜ *Highbury and Islington, Fax (020) 8292 5699* – ⇎ ▤. MC ⓓ VISA
closed 24-30 December, lunch Tuesday and Saturday, Sunday dinner and Monday – **Meals** 23.50/30.00 ♀.
◆ Simple restaurant in a converted pub. Smartly-laid tables complemented by formal service. Modern dishes based on classical French combinations.

Fig, 169 Hemingford Rd, N1 1DA, ✆ (020) 7609 3009, 舒 – MC VISA
closed 24 December-4 January, 2 weeks August, Sunday dinner and Monday – **Meals** (dinner only and Sunday lunch) a la carte 21.50/26.30 ♀.
◆ Simple, attractive and cosy neighbourhood restaurant with fawn colours and mirrors. Open hatch into kitchen. Asian-influenced cooking at a fair price.

Canonbury *Gtr London* – ✉ *N1.*

Centuria, 100 St Paul's Rd, N1 2QP, ✆ (020) 7704 2345 Ⓜ *Highbury and Islington, Fax (020) 7704 2204* – MC VISA
closed 25 December, 1 January and lunch Monday-Friday – **Meals** a la carte 20.00/30.00 ♀.
◆ Large pub in a residential area, with the dining room separate from the busy bar. Open-plan kitchen produces a modern menu, with influences ranging from Italy to Morocco..

Clerkenwell – ✉ *EC1.*

Malmaison, Charterhouse Sq, EC1M 6AH, ✆ (020) 7012 3700 Ⓜ *Barbican, london@malmaison.com,* Fax (020) 7012 3702, ⛹ – |♦|, ⇎ rm, ▤ TV ✆ ♿. MC AE ⓓ VISA JCB
Meals - Brasserie - 14.95/17.55 and a la carte 25.70/38.20 ♀ – ☕ 16.95 – **95 rm** 193.90, 2 suites.
◆ Striking early 20C redbrick building overlooking pleasant square. Stylish, comfy public areas. Bedrooms in vivid, bold colours, with extras such as stereo and free broadband. Modern brasserie employing meats from Smithfield.

The Rookery without rest., 12 Peters Lane, Cowcross St, EC1M 6DS, ✆ (020) 7336 0931 Ⓜ *Barbican, reservations@rookery.co.uk,* Fax (020) 7336 0932 – ⇎ TV ✆. MC AE ⓓ VISA JCB. ✻ 33 AOT p
☕ 9.75 **32 rm** 252.60/287.85, 1 suite.
◆ A row of charmingly restored 18C houses. Wood panelling, stone-flagged flooring, open fires and antique furniture. Highly individual bedrooms, with Victorian bathrooms.

Smiths of Smithfield, Top Floor, 67-77 Charterhouse St, EC1M 6HJ, ✆ (020) 7251 7950 Ⓜ *Barbican, smiths@smithfield.co.uk,* Fax (020) 7236 5666, ⇐, 舒 – |♦| ▤. MC AE ⓓ VISA 33 AOT s
closed 25-26 December and Saturday lunch – **Meals** a la carte 21.50/37.50 ♀ – ***The Dining Room* : Meals** *(closed Saturday lunch and Sunday)* a la carte 18.50/21.45 ♀.
◆ On three floors where the higher you go the more formal it becomes. Busy, bustling atmosphere and modern menu. Good views of the market from the top floor terrace. The Dining Room with mirrors and dark blue walls.

St John, 26 St John St, EC1M 4AY, ✆ (020) 7251 0848 Ⓜ *Barbican, reservations@stjohnrestaurant.com,* Fax (020) 7251 4090 – ▤. MC AE ⓓ VISA 33 APT c
closed 2 weeks Christmas, Saturday lunch, Sunday and Bank Holidays – **Meals** a la carte 26.10/36.80 ♀.
◆ Deservedly busy converted 19C former smokehouse. Popular bar, simple comforts. Menu specialises in offal and an original mix of traditional and rediscovered English dishes.

Finsbury – ✉ *EC1.*

The Zetter, 86-88 Clerkenwell Rd, EC1M 5RJ, ✆ (020) 7324 4444 Ⓜ *Farringdon, info@thezetter.com,* Fax (020) 7324 4445 – |♦|, ⇎ rm, ▤ TV ✆ ♿ – 🏛 40. MC AE VISA
closed 24-29 December – **Meals** - Italian - a la carte 25.00/31.00 ♀ – **59 rm** 152.75/305.50.
◆ Discreetly trendy modern design in the well-equipped bedrooms and rooftop studios of a converted 19C warehouse : pleasant extras from old paperbacks to flat-screen TV/DVDs. Light, informal restaurant serves modern Mediterranean dishes and weekend brunches.

XX **The Clerkenwell Dining Room,** 69-73 St John St, EC1M 4AN, ✆ (020) 7253 9000 Ⓜ *Farringdon, zak@theclerkenwell.com,* Fax (020) 7253 3322 – ▤. MC AE ① VISA
closed 24-26 December, 1 January, Saturday lunch and Sunday dinner – **Meals** 17.00 (lunch) and a la carte 27.00/36.00 ♀.
◆ Former pub, now a stylish modern restaurant with etched glass façade. Three adjoining dining areas with bar provide setting for contemporary British cooking.

X **Café Lazeez City,** 88 St John St, EC1M 4EH, ✆ (020) 7253 2224 Ⓜ *Farringdon, clerkenwell@cafelazeez.com,* Fax (020) 7253 2112 – ▤. MC AE ① VISA JCB
closed Saturday lunch and Sunday – **Meals** - North Indian - a la carte 19.85/25.85.
◆ Past the busy bar into this modern Indian restaurant. Has a certain warehouse feel, with a high ceiling and wood flooring. North Indian cooking from the open-plan kitchen.

X **Quality Chop House,** 94 Farringdon Rd, EC1R 3EA, ✆ (020) 7837 5093 Ⓜ *Farringdon, qualitychophouse@clara.co.uk,* Fax (020) 7833 8748 – ▤. MC AE VISA
closed 25-26 December and Saturday lunch – **Meals** a la carte 17.45/28.40.
◆ On the window is etched "Progressive working class caterers". This is borne out with the individual café-style booths and a menu ranging from jellied eels to caviar.

X **Moro,** 34-36 Exmouth Market, EC1R 4QE, ✆ (020) 7833 8336 Ⓜ *Farringdon, info@moro.co.uk,* Fax (020) 7833 9338 – ▤. MC AE ① VISA
closed Christmas, New Year, Saturday lunch, Sunday and Bank Holidays – **Meals** (booking essential) a la carte 22.50/30.50 ♀.
◆ Daily changing menu an eclectic mix of Mediterranean, Moroccan and Spanish. Friendly T-shirted staff. Informal surroundings with bare tables and a large zinc bar.

The Peasant, 240 St John St, EC1V 4PH, ✆ (020) 7336 7726 Ⓜ *Farringdon, eat@thepeasant.co.uk,* Fax (020) 7490 1089 – MC AE VISA
closed 1 week after Christmas, Saturday lunch, Sunday dinner and Bank Holiday Mondays – **Meals** (booking essential) a la carte 15.00/30.00 ♀.
◆ Large, busy pub with half of the ground floor given over as a bar. Dining continues in the high-ceilinged room upstairs. Robust and rustic cooking with generous portions.

Highbury – ✉ *N5.*

X **Au Lac,** 82 Highbury Park, N5 2XE, ✆ (020) 7704 9187 Ⓜ *Arsenal, Fax (0207) 704 9187* – ▤. MC ① VISA
closed lunch Saturday, Sunday and Bank Holidays – **Meals** - Vietnamese - 16.00 and a la carte 8.20/20.00.
◆ Cosy Vietnamese restaurant, with brightly coloured walls and painted fans. Large menus with authentic dishes usefully highlighted. Fresh flavours ; good value.

Islington *Gtr London* – ✉ *N1.*

Hilton London Islington, 53 Upper St, N1 0UY, ✆ (020) 7354 7700 Ⓜ *Angel, reservations.islington@hilton.com,* Fax (020) 7354 7711, ☂, Fб, ≘s – |♦|, ⇔ rm, ▤ TV ✆ ♿ – 🅐 35. MC AE ① VISA JCB. ✈
Meals 25.00 and a la carte 25.95/33.95 ♀ – ☕ 17.50 – **178 rm** 198.60, 6 suites.
◆ Benefits from its location adjacent to the Business Design Centre. A purpose-built hotel with all bedrooms enjoying the appropriate creature comforts. Open-plan brasserie with small bar.

Jurys Inn Islington, 60 Pentonville Rd, N1 9LA, ✆ (020) 7282 5500 Ⓜ *Angel, jurysinnislington@jurysdoyle.com,* Fax (020) 7282 5511 – |♦|, ⇔ rm, ▤ TV ✆ ♿ – 🅐 55. MC AE ① VISA. ✈
closed 24-26 December – **Meals** (bar lunch)/dinner 16.95 – ☕ 9.50 – **229 rm** 105.00.
◆ A corporate group hotel with good local transport links. Large lobby leads off to the characterful Irish themed pub. Uniform-sized bedrooms, all well-equipped. Popular dishes in restaurant.

XX **Lola's,** The Mall, 359 Upper St, N1 0PD, ✆ (020) 7359 1932 Ⓜ *Angel, lolas@lolas.co.uk,* Fax (020) 7359 2209 – ▤. MC AE ① VISA
closed Christmas, 1 January and Easter Monday – **Meals** 15.75 (lunch) and a la carte 25.50/34.50 ♀.
◆ On the first floor of a converted tram shed above the antique shops. Bright and airy, with glass ceiling and assorted artwork : an ideal setting to enjoy modern British dishes.

XX **Frederick's,** Camden Passage, N1 8EG, ✆ (020) 7359 2888 Ⓜ *Angel, eat@fredericks.co.uk,* Fax (020) 7359 5173, ☂, 🌳 – ▤. MC AE ① VISA JCB
closed Sunday and Bank Holidays – **Meals** 15.50 (lunch) and a la carte 28.50/34.50 ♀.
◆ Long-standing restaurant among the antique shops of Camden Passage. Attractive garden and al fresco dining ; main room with large, plant-filled conservatory.

Almeida, 30 Almeida St, N1 1AD, (020) 7354 4777 *Old Street, oliviere@conran-restaurants.co.uk*, Fax (020) 7354 2777 – . MC AE VISA JCB
closed 25 December and 1-2 January – **Meals** - French - 17.50 (lunch) and a la carte 20.50/38.50
◆ Spacious, open plan restaurant with pleasant contemporary styling adjacent to Almeida Theatre. Large à la carte : a collection of classic French dishes.

Metrogusto, 13 Theberton St, N1 0QY, (020) 7226 9400 *Highbury and Islington, Fax (020) 7226 9400* – . MC AE VISA JCB
closed Christmas, Bank Holidays and lunch Monday-Thursday – **Meals** - Italian - 18.50 (lunch) and a la carte 24.95/29.50
◆ Stylish and smart with a contemporary feel. Dining in two rooms with striking modern art on the walls and a relaxed atmosphere. Modern, carefully prepared Italian food.

Drapers Arms, 44 Barnsbury St, N1 1ER, (020) 7619 0348 *Highbury and Islington, Fax (020) 7619 0413,* – MC AE VISA
closed 25 December, 1 January and Sunday dinner – **Meals** a la carte 21.00/30.00
◆ Real presence to the the façade of this Georgian pub tucked away in a quiet residential area. Spacious modern interior where competent, contemporary dishes are served.

The Northgate, 113 Southgate Rd, N1 3JS, (020) 7359 7392, *Fax (020) 7359 7393,* – MC VISA JCB
closed 24-26 December and 1 January – **Meals** (dinner only and lunch Saturday and Sunday) a la carte 17.50/26.50
◆ Corner pub with wood flooring and modern art on display. Rear dining area with a large blackboard menu offering a cross section of internationally influenced modern dishes.

The Social, 33 Linton St, N1 7DU, (020) 7354 5809, *managers@thesocialn1.com, Fax (020) 7354 8087* – MC AE VISA JCB
closed 25-30 December and lunch Monday-Friday – **Meals** (booking essential) a la carte 15.00/20.00
◆ The former Hanbury Arms has a youthful clientele attracted by the DJ and music in the bar. The open plan kitchen and restaurant serve from a modern, sensibly priced menu.

The Barnsbury, 209-211 Liverpool Rd, N1 1LX, (020) 7607 5519 *Highbury and Islington, info@thebarnsbury.co.uk*, Fax (020) 7607 3256, – MC AE VISA
closed 25-26 December – **Meals** a la carte 25.00/35.00
◆ Former public house with pine tables and chairs arranged round central counter bar ; art work for sale on the walls. Robust and hearty food in generous portions.

KENSINGTON and CHELSEA *(Royal Borough of).*

Chelsea – *SW1/SW3/SW7/SW10.*

The Carlton Tower, Cadogan Pl, SW1X 9PY, (020) 7235 1234 *Knightsbridge, contact@carltontower.com*, Fax (020) 7235 9129, <, – , rm, – 400. MC AE VISA JCB. 37 AGX n
***Rib Room* :** **Meals** 27.00 (lunch) and a la carte 37.50/61.00 – 22.00 – **190 rm** 381.80, 30 suites.
◆ Imposing international hotel overlooking a leafy square. 'The Peak' health club is particularly well-equipped. Generously proportioned rooms have every conceivable facility. Rib Room restaurant has a clubby atmosphere.

Conrad London, Chelsea Harbour, SW10 0XG, (020) 7823 3000, *lonchrs@hilton.com, Fax (020) 7351 6525,* <, – , rm, – 250. MC AE VISA JCB
Meals (see ***Aquasia*** below) – 21.10, **160 suites** 387.75.
◆ Modern, all-suite hotel within an exclusive marina and retail development. Many of the spacious and well-appointed rooms have balconies and views across the Thames.

Sheraton Park Tower, 101 Knightsbridge, SW1X 7RN, (020) 7235 8050 *Knightsbridge, central.london.reservations@sheraton.com*, Fax (020) 7235 8231, <, – , rm, – 100. MC AE VISA JCB. 37 AGX t
Meals (see ***One-O-One*** below) – 20.75 – **258 rm** 446.50/587.50, 22 suites.
◆ Built in the 1970s in a unique cylindrical shape. Well-equipped bedrooms are all identical in size. Top floor executive rooms have commanding views of Hyde Park and City.

Capital, 22-24 Basil St, SW3 1AT, (020) 7589 5171 *Knightsbridge, reservations@capitalhotel.co.uk*, Fax (020) 7225 0011 – , rm, – 25. MC AE VISA JCB 37 AFX a
Meals (booking essential) 28.50/48.00 – 16.50 – **49 rm** 229.10/500.00.
Spec. Langoustine with pork belly and sweet spice. Saddle of rabbit with deep-fried calamari and tomato risotto. Ravioli of mango with chilli and coconut cream.
◆ Discreet and privately owned town house with distinct English charm. Individual, opulently decorated rooms with plenty of thoughtful touches. Elegant and intimate restaurant.

The Cadogan, 75 Sloane St, SW1X 9SG, (020) 7235 7141 *Knightsbridge, reservations@cadogan.com*, Fax (020) 7245 0994, – rm, – 40. 37 AGY b
Meals 18.00 (lunch) and a la carte 33.50/42.50 – 16.50 – **61 rm** 188.00/323.00, 4 suites.
• An Edwardian town house, where Oscar Wilde was arrested ; modernised and refurbished with a French accent. Wood panelled drawing room. Stylish bedrooms ; latest facilities. Discreet, stylish restaurant.

Basil Street, 8 Basil St, SW3 1AH, (020) 7581 3311 *Knightsbridge, info@thebasil.com*, Fax (020) 7581 3693 – rm, – 30. 37 AGX d
Meals 21.00/28.50 – 16.50 – **80 rm** 177.00/263.00.
• Classic English hotel in a pleasant residential road between Harrods and Harvey Nichols. Exclusive ladies only lounge. Traditionally furnished rooms with modern amenities. Dining room boasts rich style of a bygone era.

Draycott, 26 Cadogan Gdns, SW3 2RP, (020) 7730 6466 *Sloane Square, reservations@draycotthotel.com*, Fax (020) 7730 0236, – , rm, 37 AGY c
Meals (room service only) – 18.50 – **31 rm** 141.00/300.00, 4 suites.
• Charming Victorian house in an exclusive residential area. Elegant sitting room overlooks the tranquil communal garden. Individually decorated rooms in a country house style.

Millennium Knightsbridge, 17-25 Sloane St, SW1X 9NU, (020) 7235 4377 *Knightsbridge, reservations.knightsbridge@mill-cop.com*, Fax (020) 7235 7125 – – 120. 37 AGX r
Meals (see ***Mju*** below) – 18.00 – **218 rm** 246.75/270.25, 4 suites.
• Modern, corporate hotel in the heart of London's most fashionable shopping district. Executive bedrooms are well-appointed and equipped with the latest technology.

Franklin, 22-28 Egerton Gdns, SW3 2DB, (020) 7584 5533 *South Kensington, bookings@franklinhotel.co.uk*, Fax (020) 7584 5449, – . 37 AEY e
Meals a la carte 26.00/33.50 **s.** – 17.50 – **47 rm** 188.00/381.90.
• Attractive Victorian town house in an exclusive residential area. Charming drawing room overlooks a tranquil communal garden. Well-furnished rooms in a country house style. Elegantly appointed dining room offering traditional meals.

Knightsbridge, 10 Beaufort Gdns, SW3 1PT, (020) 7584 6300 *Knightsbridge, knightsbridge@firmdale.com*, Fax (020) 7584 6355 – . 37 AFX s
Meals (room service only) – **44 rm** 176.25/305.50.
• Attractively furnished town house with a very stylish, discreet feel. Every bedroom is immaculately appointed and has an individuality of its own ; fine detailing throughout.

The London Outpost of Bovey Castle without rest., 69 Cadogan Gdns, SW3 2RB, (020) 7589 7333 *Sloane Square, info@londonoutpost.co.uk*, Fax (020) 7581 4958, – . 37 AGY r
closed 24-26 December – 16.95 – **11 rm** 188.00/317.25.
• Classic town house in a most fashionable area. Relaxed and comfy lounges full of English charm. Bedrooms, named after local artists and writers, full of thoughtful touches.

The Sloane, 29-31 Draycott Pl, SW3 2SH, (020) 7581 5757 *Knightsbridge, reservations@sloanehotel.com*, Fax (020) 7584 1348 – rm, . 37 AFY c
Meals (room service only) – 12.00 – **20 rm** 193.80/329.00.
• Intimate and discreet Victorian town house with an attractive rooftop terrace. Individually styled and generally spacious rooms with antique furniture and rich fabrics.

Eleven Cadogan Gardens, 11 Cadogan Gdns, SW3 2RJ, (020) 7730 7000 *Sloane Square, reservations@number-eleven.co.uk*, Fax (020) 7730 5217, , – . 37 AGY u
Meals a la carte 27.00/40.00 – 13.00 – **56 rm** 155.00/325.00, 4 suites.
• Occupying four Victorian houses, one of London's first private town house hotels. Traditionally appointed bedrooms vary considerably in size. Genteel atmosphere. Light and airy basement restaurant.

Egerton House, 17-19 Egerton Terrace, SW3 2BX, (020) 7589 2412 *Knightsbridge, bookings@egertonhousehotel.co.uk*, Fax (020) 7584 6540 – . 37 AFY e
Meals (room service only) – 17.00 – **29 rm** 188.00/293.75.
• Stylish redbrick Victorian town house close to the exclusive shops. Relaxed drawing room popular for afternoon tea. Antique furnished and individually decorated rooms.

Beaufort without rest., 33 Beaufort Gdns, SW3 1PP, (020) 7584 5252 Knightsbridge, reservations@thebeaufort.co.uk, Fax (020) 7589 2834 – 37 AFX n
29 rm 182.00/305.50.
◆ English floral watercolours adorn the walls throughout this elegant Victorian town house. Modern and co-ordinated rooms. Tariff includes all drinks and continental breakfast.

Parkes without rest., 41 Beaufort Gdns, SW3 1PW, (020) 7581 9944 *Knightsbridge, info@parkeshotel.com*, Fax (020) 7581 1999 – 10.00 – **19 rm** 229.00/282.00, 14 suites 381.00/487.00.
◆ Behind the portico entrance one finds a well-kept private hotel. The generally spacious and high ceilinged rooms are pleasantly decorated. Friendly and personally run. 37 AFX x

Myhotel Chelsea, 35 Ixworth Pl, SW3 3QX, (020) 7225 7500 *South Kensington, mychelsea@myhotel.co.uk*, Fax (020) 7225 7555, – 60. 37 AFY z
Meals a la carte 13.00/19.00 **s.** – 18.00 – **43 rm** 242.05/297.75, 2 suites.
◆ Restored Victorian property in a fairly quiet and smart side street. Conservatory breakfast room. Modern and well-equipped rooms are ideal for the corporate traveller. Smart dining room for modern menus.

Sydney House, 9-11 Sydney St, SW3 6PU, (020) 7376 7711 *South Kensington, info@sydneyhousechelsea.com*, Fax (020) 7376 4233 – 36 ADY s
closed 24-28 December – **Meals** (room service only) – 9.95 – **21 rm** 145.00/210.00.
◆ Two usefully located Victorian town houses. Basement breakfast room ; small lounge near entrance. Compact contemporary style bedrooms ; one on top floor with own roof terrace.

57 Pont Street without rest., 57 Pont St, SW1X 0BD, (020) 7590 1090 *Knightsbridge, no57@no57.com*, Fax (020) 7590 1099 – – 30. 37 AFY a
10.00 – **20 rm** 146.00/194.00.
◆ Small, friendly, modern townhouse with discreet plaque at the end of Pont Street. Basement breakfast room and sitting room with deep brown suede chairs. Snug, modern rooms.

L'Hotel, 28 Basil St, SW3 1AS, (020) 7589 6286 *Knightsbridge, reservations@lhotel.co.uk*, Fax (020) 7823 7826 – rest,
Le Metro : **Meals** *(closed Sunday)* a la carte 15.50/21.00 – **12 rm** 182.10/211.50.
◆ Discreet town house a short walk from Harrods. Wooden shutters, pine furniture and stencilled walls provide a subtle rural theme. Well-appointed, comfy and informally run. Basement café dining. 37 AFX b

Gordon Ramsay, 68-69 Royal Hospital Rd, SW3 4HP, (020) 7352 4441 *Sloane Square, reservations@gordonramsay.com*, Fax (020) 7352 3334 – 37 AFZ c
closed 2 weeks Christmas-New Year, Saturday and Sunday – **Meals** (booking essential) 40.00/70.00
Spec. Roast langoustine tails with braised pork belly and lettuce. Lamb cooked three ways with aubergine, braised potatoes and thyme jus. Chocolate cylinder with coffee granite and ginger mousse.
◆ Elegant and sophisticated room. The eponymous chef creates some of Britain's finest, classically inspired cooking. Detailed and attentive service. Book one month in advance.

Tom Aikens, 43 Elystan St, SW3 3NT, (020) 7584 2003 *South Kensington, info@tomaikens.co.uk*, Fax (020) 7584 2001 – 37 AFY n
closed Easter, last 2 weeks August, 2 weeks Christmas-New Year, Saturday, Sunday and Bank Holidays – **Meals** 29.00/60.00
Spec. Foie gras with red pepper chutney and pickled raisins. Breast of pigeon with leg confit, foie gras beignets and onion tart. Coffee and hazelnut cake, coffee parfait.
◆ Smart restaurant ; minimalist style decor with chic tableware. Highly original menu of individual and inventive dishes ; smooth service. Book one month in advance.

Aubergine, 11 Park Walk, SW10 0AJ, (020) 7352 3449 *South Kensington, Fax (020) 7351 1770* – 36 ACZ r
closed 24 December-2 January, Saturday lunch, Sunday and Bank Holidays – **Meals** (booking essential) 32.00/55.00
Spec. Carpaccio of scallops, Jerusalem artichoke and truffle. Best end of lamb, sweetbreads, garlic purée. Poached peaches, lemon verbena sorbet.
◆ Intimate, refined restaurant where the keen staff provide well drilled service. French influenced menu uses top quality ingredients with skill and flair. Extensive wine list.

XXX **Drones,** 1 Pont St, SW1X 9EJ, ✆ (020) 7235 9555 Ⓜ *Sloane Square, sales@whitestarline.org.uk*, Fax (020) 7235 9566 – ▤. MC AE ⓓ VISA 37 AGX c
closed 26 December, 1 January, Saturday lunch and Sunday dinner – **Meals** 17.95 (lunch) and a la carte 23.50/39.00 ♀.
◆ Smart exterior with etched plate-glass window. L-shaped interior with moody film star photos on walls. French and classically inspired tone to dishes.

XXX **Bibendum,** Michelin House, 81 Fulham Rd, SW3 6RD, ✆ (020) 7581 5817 Ⓜ *South Kensington, manager@bibendum.co.uk*, Fax (020) 7823 7925 – ▤. MC AE ⓓ VISA
closed dinner 24-26 December – **Meals** 28.50 (lunch) and dinner a la carte 39.25/63.50 ♀. 37 AEY s
◆ A fine example of Art Nouveau architecture ; a London landmark. 1st floor restaurant with striking stained glass 'Michelin Man'. Attentive service of modern British cooking.

XXX **Floriana,** 15 Beauchamp Pl, SW3 1NQ, ✆ (020) 7838 1500 Ⓜ *Knightsbridge, info@floriana.co.uk*, Fax (020) 7584 1464 – ▤. MC AE ⓓ VISA JCB 37 AFX d
closed 25 December, 1 January, Easter Monday and Sunday – **Meals** - Italian - 19.00 (lunch) and a la carte 24.00/41.00 ♀.
◆ Behind the busy bar is a refined and contemporary restaurant. Approachable service of an elaborate, modern Italian menu. 1st floor room, with atrium roof, is more relaxing.

XXX **Fifth Floor** (at Harvey Nichols), Knightsbridge, SW1X 7RJ, ✆ (020) 7235 5250 Ⓜ *Knightsbridge, Fax (020) 7235 7856* – |‡| ▤. MC AE ⓓ VISA JCB 37 AGX s
closed 25 December, 1 January and Sunday dinner – **Meals** a la carte 30.50/48.00 ♀.
◆ Elevated style, sporting a pink-hued oval shaped interior with green frosted glass. Chic surroundings with food to match and smoothly run, attentive service.

XXX **One-O-One** (at Sheraton Park Tower H.), William St, SW1X 7RN, ✆ (020) 7290 7101 Ⓜ *Knightsbridge, Fax (020) 7235 6196* – ▤. MC AE ⓓ VISA JCB 37 AGX t
Meals - Seafood - 25.00 (lunch) and a la carte 44.50/50.50 ♀.
◆ Modern and very comfortable restaurant overlooking Knightsbridge decorated in cool blue tones. Predominantly seafood menu offers traditional and more adventurous dishes.

XXX **Toto's,** Walton House, Walton St, SW3 2JH, ✆ (020) 7589 0075 Ⓜ *Knightsbridge, Fax (020) 7581 9668* – MC AE ⓓ VISA 37 AFY x
closed 3 days Christmas – **Meals** - Italian - 23.00 (lunch) and a la carte 34.50/43.00 ♀.
◆ Converted mews house in tucked away location. Ornately decorated and bright restaurant with additional balcony area. Professional service of an extensive Italian menu.

XXX **Chutney Mary,** 535 King's Rd, SW10 0SZ, ✆ (020) 7351 3113 Ⓜ *Fulham Broadway, info@realindianfood.com*, Fax (020) 7351 7694 – ▤. MC AE ⓓ VISA JCB
Meals - Indian - (dinner only and lunch Saturday and Sunday) 16.50 (lunch) and dinner a la carte 30.25/52.40 ♀.
◆ Soft lighting and sepia etchings hold sway at this forever popular restaurant. Extensive menu of specialities from all corners of India. Complementary wine list.

XX **Daphne's,** 112 Draycott Ave, SW3 3AE, ✆ (020) 7589 4257 Ⓜ *South Kensington, office@daphnes-restaurant.co.uk*, Fax (020) 7225 2766 – ▤. MC AE ⓓ VISA 37 AFY j
closed 29 August – **Meals** - Italian - (booking essential) 18.75 (lunch) and a la carte 27.00/43.00 ♀.
◆ Positively buzzes in the evening, the Chelsea set gelling smoothly and seamlessly with the welcoming Tuscan interior ambience. A modern twist updates classic Italian dishes.

XX **Aquasia** (at Conrad London H.), Chelsea Harbour, SW10 0XG, ✆ (020) 7300 8443, *Fax (020) 7351 6525*, ≤, 🏠 – ▤ P. MC AE ⓓ VISA JCB
Meals 25.00/35.00 and a la carte 23.75/45.65 ♀.
◆ Modern restaurant located within Conrad International hotel. Views over Chelsea Harbour. Cuisine captures the essence of the Mediterranean and Asia.

XX **Racine,** 239 Brompton Rd, SW3 2EP, ✆ (020) 7584 4477 Ⓜ *South Kensington, Fax (020) 7584 4900* – ▤. MC AE ⓓ VISA JCB 37 AEY t
closed 25 December – **Meals** - French - 17.50 (lunch) and a la carte 24.50/34.50 ♀.
◆ Dark leather banquettes, large mirrors and wood floors create the atmosphere of a genuine Parisienne brasserie. Good value, well crafted, regional French fare.

XX **Rasoi Vineet Bhatia,** 10 Lincoln St, SW3 2TS, ✆ (020) 7225 1881 Ⓜ *Sloane Square, Fax (020) 7581 0220* – ✂ ▤. MC AE VISA 37 AFY y
closed Saturday lunch, Sunday and Bank Holidays – **Meals** - Indian - 24.00 (lunch) and a la carte 37.00/61.00 ♀.
◆ Elegant mid-19C townhouse just off the Kings Road. Compact interior with L-shaped dining room and attractive friezes. Classic favourites outweighed by original Indian dishes.

XX **Bluebird,** 350 King's Rd, SW3 5UU, ✆ (020) 7559 1000, *Fax (020) 7559 1111* – |‡| ▤. MC AE ⓓ VISA
closed 25 December – **Meals** a la carte 21.50/37.25 ♀.
◆ A foodstore, café and homeware shop also feature at this impressive skylit restaurant. Much of the modern British food is cooked in wood-fired ovens. Lively atmosphere.

XX **Poissonnerie de l'Avenue,** 82 Sloane Ave, SW3 3DZ, ✆ (020) 7589 2457 Ⓜ *South Kensington, info@poissonnerie.co.uk,* Fax (020) 7581 3360 – ▤. MO AE ⓓ VISA 37 AFY u
closed Christmas-New Year, Sunday and Bank Holidays – **Meals** - French Seafood - 24.00 (lunch) and a la carte 27.00/34.00.
◆ Long-established and under the same ownership since 1965. Spacious and traditional French restaurant offering an extensive seafood menu. An institution favoured by locals.

XX **Le Cercle,** 1 Wilbraham Pl, SW1X 9AE, ✆ (020) 7901 9999 Ⓜ *Sloane Square, info@lecercle.co.uk,* Fax (020) 7901 9111 – ▤. MO AE VISA 37 AGY e
closed Sunday-Monday – **Meals** - French - a la carte 12.50/30.60 ♀.
◆ Discreetly signed basement restaurant down residential side street. High, spacious room with chocolate banquettes. Tapas style French menus ; accomplished cooking.

XX **Le Colombier,** 145 Dovehouse St, SW3 6LB, ✆ (020) 7351 1155 Ⓜ *South Kensington, Fax (020) 7351 5124,* 🏛 – MO AE VISA 36 ADZ e
Meals - French - 19.00 (lunch) and a la carte 25.20/35.10 ♀.
◆ Proudly Gallic corner restaurant in an affluent residential area. Attractive enclosed terrace. Bright and cheerful surroundings and service of traditional French cooking.

XX **Mao Tai,** 96 Draycott Ave, SW3 3AD, ✆ (020) 7225 2500 Ⓜ *South Kensington, info@maotai.co.uk,* Fax (020) 7225 1965 – ▤. MO AE ⓓ VISA 37 AFY f
Meals - Chinese (Szechuan) - 12.50/24.70 and a la carte 23.00/59.00 **s.** ♀.
◆ Spacious Chinese restaurant in the heart of Chelsea. Modern, stylish décor with distinctive Eastern feel. Unique Szechuan menus, boasting some highly original dishes.

XX **Painted Heron,** 112 Cheyne Walk, SW10 0DJ, ✆ (020) 7351 5232 Ⓜ *Gloucester Road, Fax (020) 7351 5313,* 🏛 – ▤. MO AE VISA
closed 25 December and Saturday lunch – **Meals** - Indian - a la carte 28.50/41.50 ♀.
◆ Just off Cheyne Walk near the river. Contemporary in style, exemplified by oil paintings. Modern Indian dishes with eclectic ingredients drawn from around the sub-continent.

XX **Pellicano,** 19-21 Elystan St, SW3 3NT, ✆ (020) 7589 3718 Ⓜ *South Kensington, pellicanor@aol.com,* Fax (020) 7584 1789, 🏛 – ▤. MO AE ⓓ VISA 37 AFY d
closed 24 December-2 January – **Meals** - Italian - 16.50 (lunch) and a la carte 19.00/33.50 ♀.
◆ Attractive neighbourhood restaurant with dark blue canopy over pavement terrace. Contemporary interior with wood floors. Tasty and interesting modern Italian dishes.

XX **Mju** (at Millennium Knightsbridge H.), 17-25 Sloane St, SW1X 9NU, ✆ (020) 7201 6330 Ⓜ *Knightsbridge, mju@mill-cop.com,* Fax (020) 7235 3705 – ⅔ ▤. MO AE ⓓ VISA JCB 37 AGX r
closed Saturday lunch, Sunday and Bank Holidays – **Meals** a la carte 32.00/44.00 ♀.
◆ On the first floor of the Millennium Knightsbridge Hotel, a large glass ceiling provides plenty of light. Original mix of flavours underpinned by a classical French base.

XX **Brasserie St Quentin,** 243 Brompton Rd, SW3 2EP, ✆ (020) 7589 8005 Ⓜ *South Kensington, reservations@brasseriestquentin.co.uk,* Fax (020) 7584 6064 – ▤. MO AE ⓓ VISA 37 AEY a
closed 1 week Christmas – **Meals** 16.50 (lunch) and a la carte 23.65/30.70 ♀.
◆ Authentic Parisien brasserie, with rows of closely set tables, banquettes and ornate chandeliers. Attentive service and a lively atmosphere. French classics aplenty.

XX **Benihana,** 77 King's Rd, SW3 4NX, ✆ (020) 7376 7799 Ⓜ *Sloane Square, info@benihana.co.uk,* Fax (020) 7376 7377 – ▤. MO AE ⓓ VISA 37 AFZ e
closed 25 December – **Meals** - Japanese (Teppan-Yaki) - 33.00/45.00 **s.**
◆ Vast basement restaurant. Be prepared to share your table with other guests ; teppanyakis sit up to eight. Theatrical preparation and service of modern Japanese cooking.

XX **Caraffini,** 61-63 Lower Sloane St, SW1W 8DH, ✆ (020) 7259 0235 Ⓜ *Sloane Square, info@caraffini.co.uk,* Fax (020) 7259 0236, 🏛 – ▤. MO AE VISA 37 AGZ a
closed 25 December, Easter, Sunday and Bank Holidays – **Meals** - Italian - a la carte 23.20/33.90.
◆ The omnipresent and ebullient owner oversees the friendly service in this attractive neighbourhood restaurant. Authentic and robust Italian cooking ; informal atmosphere.

XX **Vama,** 438 King's Rd, SW10 0LJ, ✆ (020) 7351 4118 Ⓜ *Sloane Square, andy@vama.co.uk,* Fax (020) 7565 8501 – MO AE ⓓ VISA JCB – *closed 25-26 December and 1 January* – **Meals** - Indian - (booking essential) 7.95 (lunch) and a la carte 16.25/38.45 ♀.
◆ Adorned with traditional artefacts, a modern and bright restaurant. Keen and eager service of an elaborate and seasonally changing menu of Northwest Indian specialities.

XX **The Collection,** 264 Brompton Rd, SW3 2AS, ✆ (020) 7225 1212 Ⓜ *South Kensington, office@thecollection.co.uk,* Fax (020) 7225 1050 – ▤. MO AE VISA JCB 37 AEY v
closed 25-26 December, 1 January and Bank Holidays – **Meals** (dinner only) 15.00/40.00 and a la carte approx 35.00 ♀.
◆ Beyond the impressive catwalk entrance one will find a chic bar and a vast split level, lively restaurant. The eclectic and global modern menu is enjoyed by the young crowd.

XX **Eight over Eight,** 392 King's Rd, SW3 5UZ, ✆ (020) 7349 9934 Ⓜ *Gloucester Road, Fax (020) 7351 5157* – ▤. MC AE ① VISA
closed Christmas and Sunday lunch – **Meals** - South East Asian - a la carte 21.00/38.00 ♀.
◆ Lively modern restaurant in converted theatre pub ; bar in front and dining room at rear. Enthusiastic service. Eclectic Asian menu : strong flavours and unusual combinations.

XX **Good Earth,** 233 Brompton Rd, SW3 2EP, ✆ (020) 7584 3658 Ⓜ *Knightsbridge, goodearthgroup@aol.com*, Fax (020) 7823 8769 – ▤. MC AE VISA JCB 37 AFY h
closed 23-31 December – **Meals** - Chinese - 12.25/30.00 (dinner) and a la carte 17.00/27.00 ♀.
◆ Ornately decorated, long-established and comfortable restaurant. Polite and efficient service. Extensive and traditional Chinese menu.

XX **Dan's,** 119 Sydney St, SW3 6NR, ✆ (020) 7352 2718 Ⓜ *South Kensington, Fax (020) 7352 3265*, 🏖 – MC AE VISA 37 AEZ s
closed 25 December-2 January and Sunday dinner – **Meals** 19.50 (lunch) and a la carte 27.50/34.50.
◆ The eponymous owner oversees the operation in this long established neighbourhood restaurant. Eclectic menu with global influences. Private dining available.

XX **Haandi,** 136 Brompton Rd, SW3 1HY, ✆ (020) 7823 7373 Ⓜ *Knightsbridge, haandirestaurant@btconnect.com*, Fax (020) 7823 9696 – ▤. MC AE ① VISA JCB 37 AFX v
closed 25 December – **Meals** - Indian - 13.95 (lunch) and a la carte 14.05/29.60 ♀.
◆ Spacious basement restaurant, though with natural light in some sections. Live jazz in the bar and chefs very much on display. Flavoursome, succulent north Indian food.

X **Manicomio,** 85 Duke of York Sq, King's Rd, SW3 4LY, ✆ (020) 7730 3366 Ⓜ *Sloane Square, Fax (020) 7730 3377*, 🏖 – ▤. MC AE VISA JCB 37 AGY x
closed 25-26 December and 1 January – **Meals** - Italian - a la carte 27.00/34.00.
◆ Outside, a delightful terrace overlooks the trendy Square. Inside, a clean, modern, informal style prevails. Rustic Italian menus. Next door, a café and superbly stocked deli.

X **Bibendum Oyster Bar,** Michelin House, 81 Fulham Rd, SW3 6RD, ✆ (020) 7589 1480 Ⓜ *South Kensington, manager@bibendum.co.uk*, Fax (020) 7823 7148 – MC AE ① VISA
closed dinner 24-26 December – **Meals** - Seafood specialities - (bookings not accepted) a la carte 22.00/52.50. 37 AEY s
◆ Dine in either the busy bar, or in the light and relaxed foyer of this striking landmark. Concise menu of mainly cold dishes focusing on fresh seafood and shellfish.

X **itsu,** 118 Draycott Ave, SW3 3AE, ✆ (020) 7590 2400 Ⓜ *South Kensington, Fax (020) 7590 2403* – ▤. MC AE VISA 37 AFY j
closed 25 December and 1 January – **Meals** - Japanese - (bookings not accepted) a la carte 15.00/20.00 ♀.
◆ Sit at the conveyor belt and select your dishes from it. Cosmopolitan 'euro sushi' selection with Asian specialities. Fashionable and willing staff. Busy bar upstairs.

🍺 **Admiral Codrington,** 17 Mossop St, SW3 2LY, ✆ (020) 7581 0005 Ⓜ *South Kensington, Fax (020) 7589 2452* – ▤. MC AE VISA JCB 37 AFY v
closed 25-26 December – **Meals** a la carte 22.75/35.00 ♀.
◆ Aproned staff offer attentive, relaxed service in this busy gastropub. A retractable roof provides alfresco dining in the modern back room. Cosmopolitan menu of modern dishes.

🍺 **Chelsea Ram,** 32 Burnaby St, SW10 0PL, ✆ (020) 7351 4008 Ⓜ *Gloucester Road, pint@chelsearam.com*, Fax (020) 7349 0885 – MC VISA
closed 25 December – **Meals** a la carte 16.85/25.85 ♀.
◆ Wooden floors, modern artwork and books galore feature in this forever popular pub. Concise menu of modern British cooking with daily changing specials. Friendly atmosphere.

🍺 **Swag and Tails,** 10-11 Fairholt St, SW7 1EG, ✆ (020) 7584 6926 Ⓜ *Knightsbridge, theswag@swagandtails.com*, Fax (020) 7581 9935 – MC AE VISA JCB 37 AFX r
closed Christmas-New Year, Saturday, Sunday and Bank Holidays – **Meals** a la carte 26.00/30.00 ♀.
◆ Attractive Victorian pub close to Harrods and the fashionable Knightsbridge shops. Polite and approachable service of a blackboard menu of light snacks and seasonal dishes.

🍺 **Builders Arms,** 13 Britten St, SW3 3TY, ✆ (020) 7349 9040 Ⓜ *South Kensington* – ▤. MC VISA 37 AFZ x
closed 25-26 December and 1 January – **Meals** (bookings not accepted) a la carte 17.00/28.00 ♀.
◆ Modern 'gastropub' favoured by the locals. Eclectic menu of contemporary dishes with blackboard specials. Polite service from a young and eager team.

Cross Keys, 1 Lawrence St, SW3 5NB, (020) 7349 9111 *South Kensington, xkeys@fsmail.net,* Fax (020) 7349 9333 – . *closed 25 December, 1 January and Bank Holidays* – **Meals** 15.00 and a la carte 22.00/31.00.
• Hidden away near the Embankment, this 18C pub has period furniture and impressive carved stone fireplaces. Interesting, modern menus include blackboard of daily specials.

Lots Road Pub and Dining Room, 114 Lots Rd, SW10 0RJ, (020) 7352 6645 *Gloucester Road, lotsroad@thespiritgroup.com,* Fax (020) 7376 4975 – .
Meals a la carte 15.00/25.00.
• Traditional corner pub with an open-plan kitchen, flowers at each table and large modern pictures on the walls. Contemporary menus change daily.

Earl's Court – SW5/SW10.

K + K George, 1-15 Templeton Pl, SW5 9NB, (020) 7598 8700 *Earl's Court, hotelgeorge@kkhotels.co.uk,* Fax (020) 7370 2285, – . 35 AAY s
Meals (in bar) a la carte 15.90/22.30 **s.** – **154 rm** 175.00/210.00.
• Converted Victorian house overlooking its own large rear garden. Scandinavian style to the bedrooms with low beds, white walls and light wood furniture. Smart business centre. Informal dining in the bar.

Twenty Nevern Square without rest., Nevern Sq, SW5 9PD, (020) 7565 9555 *Earl's Court, hotel@twentynevernsquare.co.uk,* Fax (020) 7565 9444 – . 35 AAY u
10.00 – **20 rm** 110.00/120.00.
• In an attractive Victorian garden square, an individually designed, privately owned town house. Original pieces of furniture and some rooms with their own terrace.

Mayflower without rest., 26-28 Trebovir Rd, SW5 9NJ, (020) 7370 0991 *Gloucester Road, info@mayflower-group.co.uk,* Fax (020) 7370 0994 – . 35 ABY n
7.00 – **47 rm** 69.00/99.00.
• Conveniently placed, stylish establishment with a secluded rear garden, juice bar and breakfast room. Modern, individual bedrooms have an Indian and Asian influence.

Henley House without rest., 30 Barkston Gdns, SW5 0EN, (020) 7370 4111 *Earl's Court, reservations@henleyhousehotel.com,* Fax (020) 7370 0026 – . 35 ABY e
3.40 – **21 rm** 69.00/89.00.
• Located in a pleasant redbricked square, just yards from the high street. Bedrooms all styled similarly, with floral designs and good extras. Conservatory breakfast room.

Amsterdam without rest., 7 and 9 Trebovir Rd, SW5 9LS, (020) 7370 2814 *Earl's Court, reservations@amsterdam-hotel.com,* Fax (020) 7244 7608, – . 35 ABY c
2.75 **19 rm** 65.00/89.00, 8 suites.
• Basement breakfast room and a small secluded garden. The boldly decorated bedrooms dazzle with vivid colour schemes ; some boast their own balcony.

Rushmore without rest., 11 Trebovir Rd, SW5 9LS, (020) 7370 3839 *Earl's Court, rushmore-reservations@london.com,* Fax (020) 7370 0274 – . 35 ABY a
22 rm 59.00/79.00.
• Behind its Victorian façade lies an hotel popular with tourists. Individually decorated bedrooms in a variety of shapes and sizes. Piazza-styled conservatory breakfast room.

Langan's Coq d'Or, 254-260 Old Brompton Rd, SW5 9HR, (020) 7259 2599 *Earl's Court, admin@langansrestaurant.co.uk,* Fax (020) 7370 7735 – . 35 ABZ e
closed Bank Holidays – **Meals** 19.50.
• Classic, buzzy brasserie and excellent-value menu to match. Walls adorned with pictures of celebrities : look out for more from the enclosed pavement terrace. Smooth service.

Hollywood Arms, 45 Hollywood Rd, SW10 9HX, (020) 7349 7840 *Earl's Court,* Fax (020) 7349 7841 – . 36 ACZ c
closed 25 December – **Meals** a la carte 20.00/30.00.
• Period pub in smart residential area with stylish interior furnished in rich autumnal colours. Efficient service. Concise menu with Mediterranean influences and flavours.

Kensington – ✉ SW7/W8/W11/W14.

Royal Garden, 2-24 Kensington High St, W8 4PT, ✆ (020) 7937 8000 Ⓜ *High Street Kensington, sales@royalgarden.co.uk,* Fax (020) 7361 1991, <, **Fo**, – \|\$\|, ⇔ rm, ▤ TV ✆ ♿ P – 🕴 600. MO AE ⓓ VISA JCB. ✂ 35 ABX c
Park Terrace : Meals a la carte 20.50/30.25 (see also ***The Tenth*** below) – ☕ 18.00 – **376 rm** 287.80/393.60, 20 suites.
• A tall, modern hotel with many of its rooms enjoying enviable views over the adjacent Kensington Gardens. All the modern amenities and services, with well-drilled staff. Bright, spacious, large-windowed restaurant.

Baglioni, 60 Hyde Park Gate, SW7 5BB, ✆ (020) 7368 5700 Ⓜ *Gloucester Road, info@baglionihotellondon.com,* Fax (020) 7368 5701, ☂, **Fo**, ≘ – \|\$\| ▤ TV ✆ – 🕴 80. MO AE ⓓ VISA. ✂ 36 ACX e
Brunello : Meals - Italian - a la carte 33.00/55.00 – ☕ 25.00 – **53 rm** 270.00/458.00, 15 suites.
• Opposite Kensington Palace : ornate interior, trendy basement bar. Impressively high levels of service. Small gym/sauna. Superb rooms in cool shades boast striking facilities. Restaurant specialises in rustic Italian cooking.

Hilton London Kensington, 179-199 Holland Park Ave, W11 4UL, ✆ (020) 7603 3355 Ⓜ *Holland Park, sales.kensington@hilton.com,* Fax (020) 7602 9397 – \|\$\|, ⇔ rm, ▤ TV ✆ ♿ P – 🕴 200. MO AE ⓓ VISA JCB. ✂
Imbue : Meals *(closed lunch Saturday and Sunday)* 24.95 and a la carte 30.00/45.00 ♀ – ***Zen Oriental : Meals*** - Chinese - *(closed Sunday)* a la carte 21.50/37.00 – ☕ 16.95 – **602 rm** 175.00.
• The executive bedrooms and the nearby exhibition centres make this a popular business hotel. Equally useful spot for tourists ; it has all the necessary amenities. Warm, pastel coloured Imbue. Zen Oriental serving authentic classic Chinese cooking.

Hilton London Olympia, 380 Kensington High St, W14 8NL, ✆ (020) 7603 3333 Ⓜ *Kensington Olympia, reservations.olympia@hilton.com,* Fax (020) 7603 4846, **Fo** – \|\$\|, ⇔ rm, ▤ TV ✆ ♿ P – 🕴 250. MO AE ⓓ VISA
Meals a la carte 18.00/28.00 **s.** ♀ – ☕ 17.50 – **395 rm** 186.80/198.60, 10 suites.
• Busy, corporate hotel, benefiting from being within walking distance of Olympia. Bedrooms of a good size, with light wood furniture and fully tiled bathrooms. Bright dining room with large windows.

The Milestone, 1-2 Kensington Court, W8 5DL, ✆ (020) 7917 1000 Ⓜ *High Street Kensington, bookms@rchmail.com,* Fax (020) 7917 1010, **Fo**, ≘ – \|\$\|, ⇔ rm, ▤ TV ✆. MO AE ⓓ VISA JCB 35 ABX u
Meals (booking essential to non-residents) a la carte 28.50/68.25 ♀ – ☕ 21.50 – **52 rm** 352.50, 5 suites.
• Elegant 'boutique' hotel with decorative Victorian façade and English feel. Charming oak panelled lounge and snug bar. Meticulously decorated bedrooms with period detail. Panelled dining room with charming little oratory for privacy seekers.

Holland Court without rest., 31-33 Holland Rd, W14 8HJ, ✆ (020) 7371 1133 Ⓜ *Kensington Olympia, reservations@hollandcourt.com,* Fax (020) 7602 9114, ☘ – \|\$\| ⇔ TV. MO VISA. ✂
22 rm ☕ 75.00/120.00.
• Privately owned and run terraced house. Pretty little garden next to the conservatory extension of the breakfast room. Well-kept bedrooms benefit from the large windows.

The Tenth (at Royal Garden H.), 2-24 Kensington High St, W8 4PT, ✆ (020) 7361 1910 Ⓜ *High Street Kensington, Fax (020) 7361 1921,* < Kensington Palace and Gardens, London skyline – ▤ P. MO AE ⓓ VISA JCB 35 ABX c
closed Saturday lunch and Sunday – **Meals** (live music Saturday) 23.00 (lunch) and a la carte 38.70/48.50 ♀.
• Named after the hotel's top floor where this stylish yet relaxed room is situated. Commanding views of Kensington Palace and the Park. Well-structured service ; modern menu.

Belvedere, Holland House, off Abbotsbury Rd, W8 6LU, ✆ (020) 7602 1238 Ⓜ *Holland Park, sales@whitestarline.org.uk,* Fax (020) 7610 4382, ☂, 🌳 – ▤. MO AE ⓓ VISA
closed Sunday dinner – **Meals** 17.95 (lunch) and a la carte 26.40/34.45 ♀.
• Former 19C orangery in a delightful position in the middle of the Park. On two floors with a bar and balcony terrace. Huge vases of flowers. Modern take on classic dishes.

Zaika, 1 Kensington High St, W8 5NP, ✆ (020) 7795 6533 Ⓜ *High Street Kensington, info@zaika-restaurant.co.uk,* Fax (020) 7937 8854 – ▤. MO AE ⓓ VISA JCB
closed 25 December and Saturday lunch – **Meals** - Indian - 18.00 (lunch) and a la carte 28.45/46.45 ♀. 35 ABX r
• A converted bank, sympathetically restored, with original features and Indian artefacts. Well organised service of modern Indian dishes.

XX **Clarke's,** 124 Kensington Church St, W8 4BH, ✆ (020) 7221 9225 Ⓜ *Notting Hill, restaurant@sallyclarke.com,* Fax (020) 7229 4564 – ⅍ ▤. MC AE Ⓓ VISA JCB 27 ABV c
closed 10 days Christmas-New Year, Sunday and Bank Holidays – **Meals** (set menu only at dinner) 28.50/44.00 ♀.
◆ Open-plan kitchen, personally overseen by the owner, provides modern British cooking. No choice, set menu at dinner. Comfortable and bright, with a neighbourhood feel.

XX **Babylon** (at The Roof Gardens), 99 Kensington High St (entrance on Derry St), W8 5SA, ✆ (020) 7368 3993 Ⓜ *High Street Kensington, babylon@roofgardens.virgin.co.uk,* Fax (020) 7938 2774, ≤, 🏠 – ▤. MC AE VISA JCB 35 ABX n
closed Saturday lunch and Sunday dinner – **Meals** 16.00 (lunch) and a la carte 29.75/45.75 ♀.
◆ Situated on the roof of this pleasant London building affording attractive views of the London skyline. Stylish modern décor in keeping with the contemporary, British cooking.

XX **Launceston Place,** 1a Launceston Pl, W8 5RL, ✆ (020) 7937 6912 Ⓜ *Gloucester Road, LPR@place-restaurants.co.uk,* Fax (020) 7938 2412 – ▤. MC AE Ⓓ VISA 35 ACX a
closed 25-26 December, 1 January and Saturday lunch – **Meals** 22.50 (lunch) and a la carte 30.50/36.50 ♀.
◆ Divided into a number of rooms, this corner restaurant is lent a bright feel by its large windows and gilded mirrors. Chatty service and contemporary cooking.

XX **Memories of China,** 353 Kensington High St, W8 6NW, ✆ (020) 7603 6951 Ⓜ *High Street Kensington, Fax (020) 7603 0848* – ▤. MC AE Ⓓ VISA 35 AAY v
closed 25 December and 1 January – **Meals** - Chinese - (booking essential) a la carte 19.80/40.00 ♀.
◆ Subtle lighting and brightly coloured high-back chairs add to the modern feel of this Chinese restaurant. Screens separate the tables. Plenty of choice from extensive menu.

XX **Timo,** 343 Kensington High St, W8 6NW, ✆ (020) 7603 3888 Ⓜ *High Street Kensington, Fax (020) 7603 8111* – ▤. MC AE Ⓓ VISA 35 AAY c
closed 24 December-2 January – **Meals** - Italian - 21.50/29.50 ♀.
◆ Modern restaurant with unadorned lime green walls and comfortable seating in brown suede banquettes. Italian menus of contemporary dishes and daily changing specials.

XX **The Ark,** 122 Palace Gardens Terr, W8 4RT, ✆ (020) 7229 4024 Ⓜ *Notting Hill Gate, mail@thearkrestaurant.co.uk,* Fax (020) 7792 8787, 🏠 – ▤. MC AE VISA 27 ABV r
closed Sunday dinner, Monday lunch and Bank Holidays – **Meals** - Italian - a la carte 23.00/31.50 ♀.
◆ The hut-like external appearance belies the contemporary interior of this Italian restaurant. Comfortable, bright feel with bar and lounge. Smoothly run, rustic cooking.

X **Kensington Place,** 201 Kensington Church St, W8 7LX, ✆ (020) 7727 3184 Ⓜ *Notting Hill Gate, kpr@placerestaurants.co.uk,* Fax (020) 7229 2025 – ▤. MC AE Ⓓ VISA 27 AAV z
closed 24-26 December – **Meals** (booking essential) 16.50/24.50 and a la carte 28.50/46.00 ♀.
◆ A cosmopolitan crowd still head for this establishment that set the trend for large, bustling and informal restaurants. Professionally run with skilled modern cooking.

X **Cibo,** 3 Russell Gdns, W14 8EZ, ✆ (020) 7371 6271 Ⓜ *Kensington Olympia, Fax (020) 7602 1371* – MC AE Ⓓ VISA
closed Easter, Christmas, Saturday lunch and Sunday dinner – **Meals** - Italian - a la carte 23.40/34.40.
◆ Smoothly run Italian restaurant that combines style with the atmosphere of a neighbourhood favourite. Unaffected service with robust and tasty food.

X **Malabar,** 27 Uxbridge St, W8 7TQ, ✆ (020) 7727 8800 Ⓜ *Notting Hill Gate, feedback@malabar-restaurant.co.uk* – MC VISA 27 AAV e
closed 3 days September and 1 week Christmas – **Meals** - Indian - (booking essential) (buffet lunch Sunday) 20.00 and a la carte 18.95/31.25.
◆ Indian restaurant in a residential street. Three rooms with individual personalities and informal service. Extensive range of good value dishes, particularly vegetarian.

X **Wódka,** 12 St Albans Grove, W8 5PN, ✆ (020) 7937 6513 Ⓜ *High Street Kensington, info@wodka.co.uk,* Fax (020) 7937 8621 – MC AE Ⓓ VISA 35 ABX c
closed 25-26 December, 1 January, Easter Sunday, lunch Saturday and Sunday – **Meals** - Polish - 14.50 (lunch) and dinner a la carte 23.30/26.90 ♀.
◆ Unpretentious Polish restaurant with rustic, authentic menu. Assorted blinis and flavoured vodkas a speciality. Simply decorated, with wooden tables and paper napkins.

North Kensington – ✉ W2/W11.

Pembridge Court without rest., 34 Pembridge Gdns, W2 4DX, ✆ (020) 7229 9977 Ⓜ *Notting Hill Gate, reservations@pemct.co.uk*, Fax (020) 7727 4982 – MC AE VISA 27 AAU n
20 rm ☕ 125.00/195.00.
◆ Privately owned 19C town house ; very charmingly run, with comfortable sitting room, small lounge and flowery breakfast room. Bright, light bedrooms, some particularly large.

Abbey Court without rest., 20 Pembridge Gdns, W2 4DU, ✆ (020) 7221 7518 Ⓜ *Notting Hill Gate, info@abbeycourthotel.co.uk*, Fax (020) 7792 0858 – MC AE VISA JCB. 27 AAV u
22 rm 139.00/175.00.
◆ Five-storey Victorian town house with individually decorated bedrooms, with many thoughtful touches. Breakfast served in a pleasant conservatory. Friendly service.

Portobello without rest., 22 Stanley Gdns, W11 2NG, ✆ (020) 7727 2777 Ⓜ *Notting Hill Gate, info@portobello-hotel.co.uk*, Fax (020) 7792 9641 – MC AE VISA
closed 25-26 December – ☕ 12.00 **24 rm** 120.00/275.00.
◆ An attractive Victorian town house in an elegant terrace. Original and theatrical décor. Circular beds, half-testers, Victorian baths : no two bedrooms are the same.

Notting Hill Brasserie, 92 Kensington Park Rd, W11 2PN, ✆ (020) 7229 4481 Ⓜ *Notting Hill Gate, enquiries@nottinghillbrasserie.com*, Fax (020) 7221 1246 – MC AE VISA JCB 27 AAU a
closed Sunday – **Meals** 19.50 (lunch) and dinner a la carte appprox 26.00 ♀.
◆ Modern, comfortable restaurant with quiet, formal atmosphere set over four small rooms. Authentic African artwork on walls. Contemporary dishes with European influence.

Edera, 148 Holland Park Ave, W11 4VE, ✆ (020) 7221 6090 Ⓜ *Holland Park, Fax (020) 7313 9700* – MC AE VISA
closed 24 December-2 January – **Meals** - Italian - 29.50 (dinner) and lunch a la carte 19.00/27.50 ♀.
◆ Split level restaurant with 4 outdoor tables. Attentive service by all staff. Interesting menus of modern Italian cooking with some unusual ingredients and combinations.

Notting Grill, 123A Clarendon Rd, W11 4JG, ✆ (020) 7229 1500 Ⓜ *Holland Park, nottinggrill@aol.com*, Fax (020) 7229 8889, – MC AE VISA JCB
closed 24 December-2 January and Good Friday – **Meals** - Steak specialities - (dinner only and lunch Saturday, Sunday and December) a la carte 30.00/42.00 ♀.
◆ Converted pub that retains a rustic feel, with bare brick walls and wooden tables. Specialises in well sourced, quality meats.

South Kensington – ✉ SW5/SW7.

The Bentley Kempinski, 27-33 Harrington Gdns, SW7 4JX, ✆ (020) 7244 5555 Ⓜ *Gloucester Road, info@thebentley-hotel.com*, Fax (020) 7244 5566, – 60. MC AE VISA JCB 36 ACY k
Peridot : **Meals** 26.00/45.00 (see also ***1880*** below) – ☕ 21.00 – **52 rm** 293.75/675.60, 12 suites.
◆ A number of 19C houses have been joined to create this opulent, lavish, hidden gem, decorated with marble, mosaics and ornate gold leaf. Bedrooms with gorgeous silk fabrics. Airy, intimate Peridot offers brasserie menus.

Millennium Gloucester, 4-18 Harrington Gdns, SW7 4LH, ✆ (020) 7373 6030 Ⓜ *Gloucester Road, gloucester@mill-cop.com*, Fax (020) 7373 0409, – rm, – 650. MC AE VISA JCB. 36 ACY r
Meals *(closed Sunday-Monday)* (dinner only) 19.95 **s.** – ***Bugis Street :*** **Meals** - Singaporean - 7.95/20.00 and a la carte 17.45/35.90 – ☕ 16.50 – **604 rm** 250.00/350.00, 6 suites.
◆ A large international group hotel. Busy marbled lobby and vast conference facilities. Smart and well-equipped bedrooms are generously sized, especially the 'Club' rooms. Informal, compact Bugis Street.

The Pelham, 15 Cromwell Pl, SW7 2LA, ✆ (020) 7589 8288 Ⓜ *South Kensington, pelham@firmdale.com*, Fax (020) 7584 8444 – MC AE VISA. 36 ADY z
Kemps : **Meals** a la carte 22.00/31.00 ♀ – ☕ 17.50 – **48 rm** 176.20/293.70, 3 suites.
◆ Attractive Victorian town house with a discreet and comfortable feel. Wood panelled drawing room and individually decorated bedrooms with marble bathrooms. Detailed service. Warm basement dining room.

Blakes, 33 Roland Gdns, SW7 3PF, ✆ (020) 7370 6701 Ⓜ *Gloucester Road, blakes@blakeshotels.com*, Fax (020) 7373 0442, – rest, MC AE VISA.
Meals *(closed 25-26 December and 1 January)* a la carte 56.00/70.00 – ☕ 25.00 – **43 rm** 200.00/323.00, 5 suites. 36 ACZ n
◆ Behind the Victorian façade lies one of London's first 'boutique' hotels. Dramatic, bold and eclectic décor, with oriental influences and antiques from around the globe. Fashionable restaurant with bamboo and black walls.

Harrington Hall, 5-25 Harrington Gdns, SW7 4JW, (020) 7396 9696 *Gloucester Road, sales@harringtonhall.co.uk*, Fax (020) 7396 9090, – rm, – 200. 36 ACY n
Wetherby's : **Meals** *closed Saturday lunch* 17.95/19.95 and a la carte 20.45/31.40 – 15.95 – **200 rm** 185.00/200.00.
• A series of adjoined terraced houses, with an attractive period façade that belies the size. Tastefully furnished bedrooms, with an extensive array of facilities. Classically decorated dining room.

Millennium Bailey's, 140 Gloucester Rd, SW7 4QH, (020) 7373 6000 *Gloucester Road, breservations@mill-cop.com*, Fax (020) 7370 3760 – rm, – 460. 36 ACY a
Olives : **Meals** (bar lunch)/dinner 19.95 and a la carte 26.25/31.20 – 16.50 – **212 rm** 155.00/250.00.
• Elegant lobby, restored to its origins dating from 1876, with elaborate plasterwork and a striking grand staircase. Victorian feel continues through into the bedrooms. Modern, pastel shaded restaurant.

Vanderbilt, 68-86 Cromwell Rd, SW7 5BT, (020) 7761 9013 *Gloucester Road, Fax (020) 7761 9003*, – rm, – 120.
Meals *(closed lunch Friday-Sunday)* 25.00/45.00 and a la carte – 13.50 – **215 rm** 171.50/238.50. 36 ACY z
• A Victorian town house, once home to the Vanderbilt family. Retains many original features such as stained glass windows and fireplaces. Now a modern, group hotel. Restaurant has unusual objets d'art and striking cracked glass bar.

Rembrandt, 11 Thurloe Pl, SW7 2RS, (020) 7589 8100 *South Kensington, rembrandt@sarova.co.uk*, Fax (020) 7225 3476, – rm, rest, – 200. 36 ADY x
Meals (carving lunch) 18.95 and a la carte 14.70/27.40 **s.** – **195 rm** 240.00.
• Built originally as apartments in the 19C, now a well-equipped hotel opposite the Victoria and Albert museum. Comfortable lounge, adjacent leisure club, well appointed rooms. Spacious dining room.

London Marriott Kensington, 147 Cromwell Rd, SW5 0TH, (020) 7973 1000 *Gloucester Road, events.kensington@marriotthotels.co.uk*, Fax (020) 7370 1685, – – 200. 35 ABY n
Fratelli : **Meals** - Italian - 14.95 (lunch) and a la carte 19.00/47.00 – 16.95 – **216 rm** 175.00.
• Modern seven-storey hotel around atrium with good leisure centre. Coffee bar and Spanish tapas bar. Spacious, comfortable, well-equipped bedrooms with many extras. Informal Italian restaurant with open kitchen and wide ranging menu.

Jurys Kensington, 109-113 Queen's Gate, SW7 5LR, (020) 7589 6300 *South Kensington, kensington@jurydoyle.com*, Fax (020) 7581 1492 – rm, – 80. 36 ADY g
Meals (dinner only) 17.50 – 16.00 – **173 rm** 215.00.
• A row of 18C town houses that were converted into a hotel in the 1920s. Spacious lobby lounge and busy basement Irish pub. Well-equipped, comfortable bedrooms. Dining room exudes a traditional appeal.

Regency, 100 Queen's Gate, SW7 5AG, (020) 7373 7878 *South Kensington, info@londonregency.com*, Fax (020) 7370 5555, – rm, – 100. 36 ADY e
Meals *(closed lunch Saturday and Sunday)* (carvery lunch)/dinner a la carte 20.00/26.50 **s.** – 15.00 – **199 rm** 186.80, 11 suites.
• Impressive Regency house in an elegant tree lined street and close to the museums. Bedrooms vary from rather compact singles to spacious duplex suites. Basement restaurant with cocktail bar.

Gore, 190 Queen's Gate, SW7 5EX, (020) 7584 6601 *Gloucester Road, reservations@gorehotel.co.uk*, Fax (020) 7589 8127 – rm,
closed 24-25 December – ***Bistrot 190 :*** **Meals** (booking essential) a la carte 24.95/35.95 – 15.95 – **46 rm** 176.25/223.25. 36 ACX n
• Opened its doors in 1892 ; has retained its individual charm. Richly decorated with antiques, rugs and over 4,000 pictures that cover every inch of wall. Bistrot 190 boasts French-inspired décor.

John Howard, 4 Queen's Gate, SW7 5EH, (020) 7808 8400 *Gloucester Road, info@johnhowardhotel.co.uk*, Fax (020) 7808 8402 – rm, 36 ACX g
Meals *(closed Sunday)* (dinner only) 15.00 and a la carte 15.25/20.00 **s.** – 12.50 – **45 rm** 99.00/129.00, 7 suites.
• Occupies the site of three mid-19C houses, just a short walk from Kensington Palace. Some rooms with floor to ceiling windows and balconies, others look onto a quiet mews. Candlelit basement dining room.

Number Sixteen without rest., 16 Sumner Pl, SW7 3EG, ✆ (020) 7589 5232 Ⓜ *South Kensington, sixteen@firmdale.com,* Fax (020) 7584 8615, – |‡| ▤ TV ✆. MC AE VISA
☕ 13.00 – **42 rm** 111.60/293.75. 36 ADY d
◆ Four Victorian town houses in a smart part of town. Discreet entrance, comfortable sitting room and charming breakfast terrace. Bedrooms in English country house style.

The Cranley, 10 Bina Gdns, SW5 0LA, ✆ (020) 7373 0123 Ⓜ *Gloucester Road, info@thecranley.com,* Fax (020) 7373 9497 – |‡|, ⇔ rm, ▤ TV ✆. MC AE ⓓ VISA JCB. ✈ 36 ACY c
Meals (room service only) – ☕ 9.95 – **36 rm** 182.10/258.50, 3 suites.
◆ Attractive Regency town house that artfully combines charm and period details with modern comforts and technology. Individually styled bedrooms ; some with four-posters.

Five Sumner Place without rest., 5 Sumner Pl, SW7 3EE, ✆ (020) 7584 7586 Ⓜ *South Kensington, reservations@sumnerplace.com,* Fax (020) 7823 9962 – |‡| ⇔ TV. MC AE ⓓ VISA JCB. ✈ 36 ADY u
13 rm ☕ 85.00/150.00.
◆ Part of a striking white terrace built in 1848 in this fashionable part of town. Breakfast served in bright conservatory. Good sized bedrooms.

Aster House without rest., 3 Sumner Pl, SW7 3EE, ✆ (020) 7581 5888 Ⓜ *South Kensington, asterhouse@btinternet.com,* Fax (020) 7584 4925, – ⇔ ▤ TV ✆. MC AE VISA JCB. ✈ 36 ADY t
13 rm ☕ 106.00/153.00.
◆ End of terrace Victorian house with a pretty little rear garden and first floor conservatory. Ground floor rooms available. A wholly non-smoking establishment.

XXXX **1880** (at The Bentley Kempinski H.), 27-33 Harrington Gdns, SW7 4JX, ✆ (020) 7244 5555 Ⓜ *Gloucester Road, info@thebentley-hotel.com,* Fax (020) 7244 5566 – ⇔ ▤. MC AE ⓓ VISA JCB 36 ACY k
closed Sunday – **Meals** (dinner only) 45.00 and a la carte.
◆ Luxurious, opulently decorated room in Bentley basement : silk panels, gold leaf, Italian marble, chandeliers. Choose à la carte or extensive "grazing" menu up to 10 courses.

XXX **Bombay Brasserie,** Courtfield Rd, SW7 4QH, ✆ (020) 7370 4040 Ⓜ *Gloucester Road, bombay1brasserie@aol.com,* Fax (020) 7835 1669 – ▤. MC AE ⓓ VISA JCB
closed 25-26 December – **Meals** - Indian - (buffet lunch) 18.95 and dinner a la carte 30.00/37.00 ♀. 36 ACY y
◆ Something of a London institution : an ever busy Indian restaurant with Raj-style décor. Ask to sit in the brighter plant-filled conservatory. Popular lunchtime buffet.

XX **Lundum's,** 119 Old Brompton Rd, SW7 3RN, ✆ (020) 7373 7774 Ⓜ *Gloucester Road, Fax (020) 7373 4472,* – ▤. MC AE ⓓ VISA JCB 36 ACZ p
closed 23 December-5 January and Sunday dinner – **Meals** - Danish - 15.50/21.50 and a la carte 23.25/44.50.
◆ A family run Danish restaurant offering an authentic, traditional lunch with a more expansive dinner menu. Comfortable room, with large windows. Charming service.

XX **L'Etranger,** 36 Gloucester Rd, SW7 4QT, ✆ (020) 7584 1118 Ⓜ *Gloucester Road, sasha@etranger.co.uk,* Fax (020) 7584 8886 – ▤. MC AE VISA 35 ACX c
closed Saturday lunch – **Meals** (booking essential) 16.50 (lunch) and a la carte 24.00/74.00.
◆ Corner restaurant with mosaic entrance floor and bay window. Modern décor. Tables extend into adjoining wine shop. French based cooking with Asian influences.

XX **Khan's of Kensington,** 3 Harrington Rd, SW7 3ES, ✆ (020) 7584 4114 Ⓜ *South Kensington, Fax (020) 7581 2900* – ▤. MC AE VISA 36 ADY a
closed 25 December – **Meals** - Indian - a la carte 16.55/26.55.
◆ Bright room with wood flooring and a large mural depicting scenes from old India. Basement bar in a colonial style. Authentic Indian cooking with attentive service.

XX **Cambio de Tercio,** 163 Old Brompton Rd, SW5 0LJ, ✆ (020) 7244 8970 Ⓜ *Gloucester Road, Fax (020) 7373 8817* – MC AE VISA 36 ACZ a
closed 10 days Christmas – **Meals** - Spanish - a la carte 25.75/32.75 ♀.
◆ The keen young owners have created a vibrant room with rich red walls decorated with assorted bullfighting accessories. Sophisticated Spanish cooking.

XX **Pasha,** 1 Gloucester Rd, SW7 4PP, ✆ (020) 7589 7969 Ⓜ *Gloucester Road, Fax (020) 7581 9996* – ▤. MC AE ⓓ VISA JCB 36 ACX y
closed 25-26 December and Sunday lunch – **Meals** - Moroccan - 15.75 (lunch) and a la carte 22.45/31.05 ♀.
◆ A marble fountain, lanterns, spice boxes and silk cushions help create a theatrical Moroccan atmosphere. Service is helpful and able : the menu is more extensive at dinner.

Memories of India, 18 Gloucester Rd, SW7 4RB, (020) 7589 6450 *Gloucester Road, Fax (020) 7584 4438* – . MC AE VISA JCB 36 ACX s
closed 25 December – **Meals** - Indian - a la carte 11.85/15.40.
• A long-standing local favourite, decorated in traditional style with whicker chairs and pink linen tablecloths. Polite and able service. Authentic Indian cooking.

Café Lazeez, 93-95 Old Brompton Rd, SW7 3LD, (020) 7581 6996 *South Kensington, southkensington@cafelazeez.com,* Fax (020) 7581 8200 – . MC AE VISA JCB 36 ADY v
Meals - North Indian - a la carte 20.40/26.85.
• Glass-topped tables and tiled flooring add an air of modernity to this Indian restaurant; reflected in the North Indian cooking. Willing service. Upstairs room more formal.

Bangkok, 9 Bute St, SW7 3EY, (020) 7584 8529 *South Kensington* – . MC VISA 36 ADY b
closed Christmas-New Year and Sunday – **Meals** - Thai Bistro - a la carte 22.50/30.00.
• This simple Thai bistro has been a popular local haunt for many years. Guests can watch the chefs at work, preparing inexpensive dishes from the succinct menu.

LAMBETH

Clapham Common – *SW4.*

Windmill on the Common without rest., Clapham Common South Side, SW4 9DE, (020) 8673 4578 *Clapham Common, windmill@youngs.co.uk,* Fax (020) 8675 1486 – TV P. MC AE VISA.
29 rm 99.00/115.00.
• A former Victorian pub that has been sympathetically extended over the years. Pleasant spot on the Common. Well-kept and comfortable rooms of assorted sizes.

Tsunami, Unit 3, 1-7 Voltaire Rd, SW4 6DQ, (020) 7978 1610 *Clapham North, Fax (020) 7978 1591* – MC AE VISA
closed 1 week Christmas and Sunday – **Meals** - Japanese - (dinner only and Saturday lunch) a la carte 14.40/39.85.
• Trendy, mininalist-style restaurant. Interesting Japanese menu with many dishes designed for sharing and plenty of original options. Good Sushi and Sashimi selection.

Herne Hill – *SE24.*

3 Monkeys, 136-140 Herne Hill, SE24 9QH, (020) 7738 5500, *info@3monkeysrestaurant.com, Fax (020) 7738 5505* – . MC AE VISA JCB
closed 25-26 December – **Meals** - Indian - 10.00/25.00 and a la carte 11.50/25.35.
• 'New wave' Indian restaurant in a converted bank. Dining room in bright white reached via a bridge over the bar and kitchen. Menu uses influences from all over India.

Kennington *Gtr London* – *SE11.*

Painted Heron, 205-209 Kennington Lane, SE11 5QS, (020) 7793 8313 *Kennington, Fax (020) 7793 8323,* – . MC AE VISA 40 ANZ s
closed 25 December – **Meals** - Indian - a la carte 28.50/41.50.
• Attractive, predominantly glass-fronted restaurant with pleasant courtyard terrace. Linen-clad tables and an interesting modern Indian menu with touches of invention.

Lobster Pot, 3 Kennington Lane, SE11 4RG, (020) 7582 5556 *Kennington* – . MC AE VISA JCB 40 AOY e
closed Christmas-New Year, Sunday and Monday – **Meals** - French Seafood - 14.50/39.50 and a la carte 26.30/39.30.
• A nautical theme so bold you'll need your sea legs : fishing nets, shells, aquariums, portholes, even the sound of seagulls. Classic French seafood menu is more restrained.

Waterloo *Gtr London* – *SE1.*

Channel Tunnel : Eurostar information and reservations (08705) 186186.

London Marriott H. County Hall, SE1 7PB, (020) 7928 5200 *Westminster, salesadmin.countyhall@marriotthotels.co.uk,* Fax (020) 7928 5300, ≤, , , – , rm, TV – 70. MC AE VISA JCB. 40 AMX a
County Hall : **Meals** 26.50 (lunch) and a la carte 26.50/44.00 **s.** – 18.95 – **195 rm** 292.60, 5 suites.
• Occupying the historic County Hall building. Many of the spacious and comfortable bedrooms enjoy river and Parliament outlook. Impressive leisure facilities. Famously impressive views from restaurant.

Premier Travel Inn, Belvedere Rd, SE1 7PB, (0870) 2383300 *Waterloo, london.county.hall.mti.@whitbread.com*, Fax (020) 7902 1619 – rest, 32AMV u
Meals (grill rest.) – **313 rm** 86.95.
◆ Adjacent to the London Eye and within the County Hall building. Budget accommodation in a central London location that is the envy of many, more expensive, hotels.

Days without rest., 54 Kennington Rd, SE1 7BJ, (020) 7922 1331, Reservations (Freephone) 0800 0280400 *Lambeth North, reservations.waterloo@dayshotel.co.uk*, Fax (020) 7922 1441 – 40 ANY x
5.95 – **162 rm** 89.00.
◆ Useful lodge accommodation, opposite the Imperial War Museum. Identical bedrooms are well-equipped and decorated in warm colours. Competitively priced.

MERTON

Colliers Wood – SW19.

Express by Holiday Inn without rest., 200 High St, SW19 2BH, on A 24 (020) 8545 7300 *Colliers Wood, Fax (020) 8545 7301* – 50.
83 rm 92.00.
◆ Modern, corporate budget hotel. Spacious and well-equipped bedrooms ; power showers in en suite bathrooms. Ideal for the business traveller. Continental breakfast included.

Wimbledon – SW19.

Cannizaro House, West Side, Wimbledon Common, SW19 4UE, (0870) 333 9124 *Wimbledon, cannizarohouse@thistle.co.uk*, Fax (0870) 3339224, rm, – 120.
Meals a la carte 30.50/41.50 – 14.50 – **43 rm** 288.00/370.00, 2 suites.
◆ Part Georgian mansion in a charming spot on the Common. Appealing drawing room popular for afternoon tea. Rooms in original house are antique furnished, some with balconies. Refined restaurant overlooks splendid formal garden.

Light House, 75-77 Ridgway, SW19 4ST, (020) 8944 6338 *Wimbledon, lightrest@aol.com*, Fax (020) 8946 4440 –
closed 25 December, 2 days Easter and Sunday dinner – **Meals** - Italian influences - 16.50 (lunch) and a la carte 23.20/30.20.
◆ Bright and modern neighbourhood restaurant with open plan kitchen. Informal service of a weekly changing and diverse menu of progressive Italian/fusion dishes.

The Fire Stables, 27-29 Church Rd, SW19 5DQ, (020) 8946 3197 *Wimbledon, thefirestables@thespiritgroup.com*, Fax (020) 8946 1101 –
closed 25 December – **Meals** 15.50/23.00 and a la carte 18.00/30.00.
◆ Modern "gastropub" in village centre. Open-plan kitchen. Polished wood tables and banquettes. Varied modern British dishes. Expect fishcakes, duck confit salad or risotto.

SOUTHWARK

Bermondsey – SE1.

London Bridge, 8-18 London Bridge St, SE1 9SG, (020) 7855 2200 *London Bridge, sales@london-bridge-hotel.co.uk*, Fax (020) 7855 2233, – rm, – 100. 33 AQV a
Georgetown **: Meals** 12.50/15.00 (lunch) and a la carte 17.50/21.75 **s.** – 13.95 – **135 rm** 195.00, 3 suites.
◆ In one of the oldest parts of London, independently owned with an ornate façade dating from 1915. Modern interior with classically decorated bedrooms and an impressive gym. Restaurant echoing the colonial style serving Malaysian dishes.

Premier Travel Inn, 159 Tower Bridge Rd, SE1 3LP, (0870) 2383303 *Borough, Fax (020) 7940 3719* – rm,
Meals (grill rest.) – **195 rm** 79.95.
◆ Ideal for tourists by being next to a tube station and the famous bridge. Clean and spacious budget accommodation, with uniform-sized bedrooms.

Le Pont de la Tour, 36d Shad Thames, Butlers Wharf, SE1 2YE, (020) 7403 8403 *London Bridge, Fax (020) 7403 0267*, – 34 ASV c
closed Saturday lunch – **Meals** 29.50 (lunch) and dinner a la carte 27.50/46.00.
◆ Elegant and stylish room commanding spectacular views of the Thames and Tower Bridge. Formal and detailed service. Modern menu with an informal bar attached.

Bengal Clipper, Cardamom Building, Shad Thames, Butlers Wharf, SE1 2YR, (020) 7357 9001 *London Bridge, mail@bengalclipper.co.uk,* Fax (020) 7357 9002 – . MC AE VISA 34 ASV e
Meals - Indian - a la carte 13.65/24.90 **s.**
◆ Housed in a Thames-side converted warehouse, a smart Indian restaurant with original brickwork and steel supports. Menu features Bengali and Goan dishes. Evening pianist.

Tentazioni, 2 Mill St, Lloyds Wharf, SE1 2BD, (020) 7237 1100 *Bermondsey, tentazioni@aol.com,* Fax (020) 7237 1100 – MC AE VISA JCB
closed Sunday, lunch Saturday and Monday – **Meals** - Italian - 18.00/28.00 and a la carte 27.00/37.50.
◆ Former warehouse provides a bright and lively environment. Open staircase between the two floors. Keenly run, with a menu offering simple, carefully prepared Italian food.

Blueprint Café, Design Museum, Shad Thames, Butlers Wharf, SE1 2YD, (020) 7378 7031 *London Bridge, Fax (020) 7357 8810,* < Tower Bridge – MC AE VISA 34 ASV u
closed 25-26 December and Sunday dinner – **Meals** a la carte 24.00/37.50.
◆ Above the Design Museum, with impressive views of the river and bridge : handy binoculars on tables. Eager and energetic service, modern British menus : robust and rustic..

Cantina Del Ponte, 36c Shad Thames, Butlers Wharf, SE1 2YE, (020) 7403 5403 *London Bridge, Fax (020) 7403 4432,* <, – MC AE VISA 34 ASV c
closed 25 December – **Meals** - Italian - a la carte 15.85/27.95.
◆ Quayside setting with a large canopied terrace. Terracotta flooring ; modern rustic style décor, simple and unfussy. Tasty, refreshing Mediterranean-influenced cooking.

Butlers Wharf Chop House, 36e Shad Thames, Butlers Wharf, SE1 2YE, (020) 7403 3403 *London Bridge, Fax (020) 7403 3414,* < Tower Bridge, – MC AE VISA 34 ASV n
closed Sunday dinner – **Meals** 23.75 (lunch) and dinner a la carte 24.50/37.50.
◆ Book the terrace in summer and dine in the shadow of Tower Bridge. Rustic feel to the interior, with obliging service. Menu focuses on traditional English dishes.

Dulwich – *SE21.*

Belair House, Gallery Rd, Dulwich Village, SE21 7AB, (020) 8299 9788, *info@belairhouse.co.uk, Fax (020) 8299 6793,* , – P. MC AE VISA
closed Sunday dinner – **Meals** 22.00/32.00.
◆ A striking Georgian summer house, floodlit at night, and surrounded by manicured lawns. By contrast, interior is bright and modern with summery colours. Eclectic menu.

Rotherhithe – *SE16.*

Hilton London Docklands, 265 Rotherhithe St, Nelson Dock, SE16 5HW, (020) 7231 1001, *sales-docklands@hilton.com, Fax (020) 7231 0599,* <, , , , – , rm, P – 350. MC AE VISA
closed 23-28 December – ***Traders Bistro* : Meals** *(closed Sunday)* (dinner only) a la carte 20.00/30.00 – ***Terrace* : Meals** (dinner only) 23.00 **s.** – 14.00 – **361 rm** 185.00, 4 suites.
◆ Redbrick group hotel with glass façade. River-taxi from the hotel's own pier. Extensive leisure facilities. Standard size rooms with all mod cons. Eat on board Traders Bistro, a reconstructed galleon moored in dry dock. The Terrace for buffet style dining.

Southwark *Gtr London* – *SE1.*

Novotel London City South, 53-61 Southwark Bridge Rd, SE1 9HH, (020) 7089 0400 *London Bridge, h3269@accor.com,* Fax (020) 7089 0410, , – , rm, – 100. MC AE VISA JCB 34 AQV c
***The Garden Brasserie* :** **Meals** 18.95 and a la carte 15.70/30.80 **s.** – 12.95 – **178 rm** 150.00/170.00, 4 suites.
◆ The new style of Novotel with good business facilities. Triple glazed bedrooms, furnished in the Scandinavian style with keyboard and high speed internet. Brasserie style dining room with windows all down one side.

Premier Travel Inn, Anchor, Bankside, 34 Park St, SE1 9EF, (0870) 7001456 *London Bridge, Fax (0870) 7001457* – , rm, . MC AE VISA.
Meals (grill rest.) – **56 rm** 82.95.
◆ A good value lodge with modern, well-equipped bedrooms which include a spacious desk area, ideal for the corporate and leisure traveller. Popular, tried-and-tested menus. 33 AQV b

Express by Holiday Inn without rest., 103-109 Southwark St, SE1 0JQ, (020) 7401 2525 *Southwark, stay@expresssouthwark.co.uk,* Fax (020) 7401 3322 – P. MC AE VISA. 33 APV e
88 rm 120.00.
◆ Useful location, just ten minutes from Waterloo. Purpose-built hotel with modern bedrooms in warm pastel shades. Fully equipped business centre.

Southwark Rose without rest., 43-47 Southwark Bridge Rd, SE1 9HH, ☎ (020) 7015 1480 Ⓜ *London Bridge, info@southwarkrosehotel.co.uk*, Fax (020) 7015 1481 – 34 AQV c
8.95 **78 rm** 125.00, 6 suites.
◆ Purpose built budget hotel south of the City, near the Globe Theatre. Top floor breakfast room with bar. Uniform style, reasonably spacious bedrooms with writing desks.

Oxo Tower, (8th floor), Oxo Tower Wharf, Barge House St, SE1 9PH, ☎ (020) 7803 3888 Ⓜ *Southwark, oxo.reservations@harveynichols.co.uk*, Fax (020) 7803 3838, < London skyline and River Thames, – 32 ANV a
closed 25-26 December – **Meals** 29.50 (lunch) and dinner a la carte 34.75/54.25 ♀ (see also ***Oxo Tower Brasserie*** below).
◆ Top of a converted factory, providing stunning views of the Thames and beyond. Stylish, minimalist interior with huge windows. Smooth service of modern cuisine.

Baltic, 74 Blackfriars Rd, SE1 8HA, ☎ (020) 7928 1111 Ⓜ *Southwark, info@balticrestaurant.co.uk*, Fax (020) 7928 8487 – 33 AOV e
Meals - East European with Baltic influences - 13.50 (lunch) and a la carte 18.50/26.50 ♀.
◆ Set in a Grade II listed 18C former coach house. Enjoy authentic and hearty east European and Baltic influenced food. Interesting vodka selection and live jazz on Sundays.

Oxo Tower Brasserie, (8th floor), Oxo Tower Wharf, Barge House St, SE1 9PH, ☎ (020) 7803 3888 Ⓜ *Southwark, Fax (020) 7803 3838*, < London skyline and River Thames, – 32 ANV a
closed 25-26 December – **Meals** 21.50 (lunch) and a la carte 20.45/35.00 ♀.
◆ Same views but less formal than the restaurant. Open-plan kitchen, relaxed service, the modern menu is slightly lighter. In summer, try to secure a table on the terrace.

Cantina Vinopolis, No.1 Bank End, SE1 9BU, ☎ (020) 7940 8333 Ⓜ *London Bridge, cantina@vinopolis.co.uk*, Fax (020) 7940 8334 – 33 AQV z
closed Christmas, New Year and Sunday dinner – **Meals** 17.50 (lunch) and a la carte 19.20/28.15 ♀.
◆ Large, solid brick vaulted room under Victorian railway arches, with an adjacent wine museum. Modern menu with a huge selection of wines by the glass.

Livebait, 43 The Cut, SE1 8LF, ☎ (020) 7928 7211 Ⓜ *Southwark, livebaitwaterloo@groupchezgerard.co.uk*, Fax (020) 7928 2279 – 32 ANV c
closed 25 December and 1 January – **Meals** - Seafood - 18.50 (lunch) and a la carte 24.45/40.45 ♀.
◆ Slight Victorian feel with wall tiles and booths. Lively atmosphere is distinctly modern. Helpful and obliging service. Comprehensive seafood menu from the on-view kitchen.

Tate Cafe (7th Floor), Tate Modern, Bankside, SE1 9TG, ☎ (020) 7401 5020 Ⓜ *Southwark, Fax (020) 7401 5171*, < London skyline and River Thames – 33 APV s
closed 24-26 December – **Meals** (lunch only and dinner Friday-Saturday) a la carte 19.50/32.15 ♀.
◆ Modernity to match the museum, with vast murals and huge windows affording stunning views. Canteen-style menu at a sensible price with obliging service.

Fish!, Cathedral St, Borough Market, SE1 9AL, ☎ (020) 7407 3803 Ⓜ *London Bridge, borough@fishdiner.co.uk*, Fax (020) 7387 8636, – 33 AQV s
closed 25 December and 1 January – **Meals** - Seafood - a la carte 25.00/33.00 ♀.
◆ Under railway arches, an unusual structure made entirely of glass and metal. Seafood menu where diners choose the fish as well as the accompanying sauce.

Anchor and Hope, 36 The Cut, SE1 8LP, ☎ (020) 7928 9898 Ⓜ *Southwark, anchorandhope@bt.connect.com* – 32 ANV n
closed Christmas-New Year, 2 weeks August, Sunday, Monday lunch and Bank Holidays – **Meals** (bookings not accepted) a la carte 21.00/35.00 ♀.
◆ Close to Waterloo, the distinctive dark green exterior lures visitors in droves. Bare floorboards, simple wooden furniture. Seriously original cooking with rustic French base.

TOWER HAMLETS

Canary Wharf *Gtr London* – ✉ *E14.*

Four Seasons, Westferry Circus, E14 8RS, ☎ (020) 7510 1999 Ⓜ *Canary Wharf (DLR), Fax (020) 7510 1998*, <, – – 200.
Meals (see ***Quadrato*** below) – 20.00 – **128 rm** 376.00/458.25, 14 suites.
◆ Stylish hotel opened in 2000, with striking river and city views. Atrium lobby leading to modern bedrooms boasting every conceivable extra. Detailed service.

Marriott London West India Quay, 22 Hertsmere Rd, E14 4ED, ✆ (020) 7093 1000 Ⓜ *West India Quay (DLR), reservations@marriott.com*, Fax (020) 7093 1001, Fō, ≘s – |≑| ⇎ ▤ TV ✆ ♿ – 🏛 300. MC AE ① VISA. ✻
Curve : **Meals** a la carte 20.00/26.95 ♀ – ☕ 19.00 – **294 rm** 287.87, 7 suites.
◆ Spacious, very well-equipped bedrooms, classic or modern, plus a 24-hour business centre in this glass-fronted high-rise hotel on the quay. Champagne and oyster bar and informal, American-style seafood inn serving fish from nearby Billingsgate market.

Circus Apartments without rest., 39 Westferry Circus, E14 8RW, ✆ (020) 7719 7000 Ⓜ *Canary Wharf, res@circusapartments.co.uk*, Fax (020) 7719 7001, Fō, ≘s, ▭ – |≑| ⇎ ▤ TV ✆ 🚗. MC AE ① VISA JCB. ✻
45 suites 293.00/346.00.
◆ Smart, contemporary, fully serviced apartment block close to Canary Wharf : rooms, comfortable and spacious, can be taken from one day to one year.

Plateau (Restaurant), Canada Pl, E14 4QS, ✆ (020) 7715 7100 Ⓜ *Canary Wharf, Fax (020) 7715 7110* – |≑|. MC AE ① VISA
closed 24-25 December, Saturday lunch and Sunday – **Meals** a la carte 28.50/45.00.
◆ Fourth floor restaurant overlooking Canada Square and The Big Blue art installation. Glass-sided kitchen ; well-spaced, uncluttered tables. Modern menus with classical base.

Ubon by Nobu, 34 Westferry Circus, E14 8RR, ✆ (020) 7719 7800 Ⓜ *Canary Wharf, ubon@noburestaurants.com*, Fax (020) 7719 7801, ≤ River Thames and city skyline – |≑| ▤ P. MC AE ① VISA JCB
closed Saturday lunch, Sunday and Bank Holidays – **Meals** - Japanese - a la carte 50.00/70.00 ♀.
◆ Light, airy, open-plan restaurant, with floor to ceiling glass and great Thames views. Informal atmosphere. Large menu with wide selection of modern Japanese dishes.

Quadrato (at Four Seasons H.), Westferry Circus, E14 8RS, ✆ (020) 7510 1999 Ⓜ *Canary Wharf (DLR), Fax (020) 7510 1998*, 🏕 – ▤ 🚗. MC AE ① VISA
Meals - Italian - 27.00 (lunch) and a la carte 31.00/42.00 ♀.
◆ Striking, modern restaurant with terrace overlooking river. Sleek, stylish dining room with glass-fronted open-plan kitchen. Menu of northern Italian dishes ; swift service.

Plateau (Grill), Canada Pl, E14 5ER, ✆ (020) 7715 7100 Ⓜ *Canary Wharf, Fax (020) 7715 7110* – |≑| ▤. MC AE ① VISA
closed 24-25 December and Sunday dinner – **Meals** 20.00 and a la carte 23.50/30.50.
◆ Situated on fourth floor of 21C building ; adjacent to Plateau Restaurant, with simpler table settings. Classical dishes, with seasonal base, employing grill specialities.

The Gun, 27 Coldharbour, E14 9NS, ✆ (020) 7515 5222 Ⓜ *Blackwall (DLR), info@thegundocklands.com*, 🏕 – MC AE VISA
Meals a la carte 26.00/33.00 ♀.
◆ Restored historic pub with a terrace facing the Dome : tasty dishes, including Billingsgate market fish, balance bold simplicity and a bit of French finesse. Efficient service.

East India Docks – ✉ *E14.*

Travelodge, A 13 Coriander Ave, off East India Dock Rd, E14 2AA, ✆ (08700) 850950 Ⓜ *East India (DLR), Fax (020) 7515 9178*, ≤ – |≑|, ⇎ rm, ▤ rest, TV ♿ P. MC AE ① VISA. ✻
Meals (grill rest.) – **232 rm** 60.00.
◆ Overlooking the Millennium Dome, a larger than average lodge-style hotel with uniform sized bedrooms. Acres of parking and an informal café-bar on the ground floor.

St Katherine's Dock – ✉ *E1.*

The Aquarium, Ivory House, E1W 1AT, ✆ (020) 7480 6116 Ⓜ *Tower Hill, info@theaquarium.co.uk*, Fax (020) 7480 5973, ≤, 🏕 – MC AE ① VISA 34 ASV a
closed 2 weeks Christmas, Saturday lunch, Sunday dinner and Bank Holidays – **Meals** - Seafood - a la carte 30.00/70.00 ♀.
◆ Seafood restaurant in a pleasant marina setting with views of the boats from some tables. Simple, smart modern décor. Menu of market-fresh, seafood dishes.

Shoreditch *Gtr London* – ✉ *E1.*

St John Bread and Wine, 94-96 Commercial St, E1 6LZ, ✆ (020) 7247 8724 Ⓜ *Shoreditch* – ▤. MC AE VISA
closed 24 December-4 January and Bank Holidays – **Meals** a la carte 21.30/29.90.
◆ Very popular neighbourhood bakery providing wide variety of home-made breads. Appealing, intimate dining section : all day menus that offer continually changing dishes.

Spitalfields - ✉ E1.

Bengal Trader, 44 Artillery Lane, E1 7NA, ✆ (020) 7375 0072 Ⓜ *Liverpool Street, mail@bengalclipper.co.uk, Fax (020) 7247 1002* – ▤. MO AE VISA 34 AST x
closed Saturday, Sunday and Bank Holidays – **Meals** - Indian - a la carte 11.90/24.00.
◆ Contemporary Indian paintings feature in this stylish basement room beneath a ground floor bar. Menu provides ample choice of Indian dishes.

Wapping - ✉ E1.

Wapping Food, Wapping Wall, E1W 3ST, ✆ (020) 7680 2080 Ⓜ *Wapping, wappingfood@wapping-wpt.com,* – P. MO AE D VISA
closed 24 December-2 January and Sunday dinner – **Meals** a la carte 22.50/34.00.
◆ Something a little unusual ; a combination of restaurant and gallery in a converted hydraulic power station. Enjoy the modern menu surrounded by turbines and TV screens.

Whitechapel - ✉ E1.

Cafe Spice Namaste, 16 Prescot St, E1 8AZ, ✆ (020) 7488 9242 Ⓜ *Tower Hill, info@cafespice.co.uk,* Fax (020) 7481 0508 – ▤. MO AE D VISA JCB 34 ASU z
closed 1 week Christmas-New Year, Sunday, Saturday lunch and Bank Holidays – **Meals** - Indian - 30.00 and a la carte 17.75/29.40 ♀.
◆ A riot of colour from the brightly painted walls to the flowing drapes. Sweet-natured service adds to the engaging feel. Fragrant and competitively priced Indian cooking.

WANDSWORTH

Battersea - ✉ SW8/SW11/SW18.

Express by Holiday Inn without rest., Smugglers Way, SW18 1EG, ✆ (020) 8877 5950, *wandsworth@oreil-leisure.co.uk, Fax (020) 8877 0631* – ▤. TV & P – 35. MO AE D VISA
148 rm 92.00.
◆ Modern, purpose-built hotel on major roundabout, very much designed for the cost-conscious business guest or traveller. Adjacent steak house. Sizeable, well-kept bedrooms.

The Food Room, 123 Queenstown Rd, SW8 3RH, ✆ (020) 7622 0555, *Fax (020) 7622 9543* – ▤. MO VISA
closed 1-7 January, 25-26 December, Sunday and lunch Monday and Saturday – **Meals** - French - 16.50 (lunch) and a la carte 20.65/29.90.
◆ Attractive eatery with a relaxed feel and attentive service. Concise French/Mediterranean menus with Italian and North African flavours, utilising very good quality produce.

Chada, 208-210 Battersea Park Rd, SW11 4ND, ✆ (020) 7622 2209, *enquiry@chadathai.com, Fax (020) 7924 2178* – ▤. MO AE D VISA JCB
closed Bank Holidays – **Meals** - Thai - (dinner only) a la carte 17.35/35.15 ♀.
◆ Weather notwithstanding, the Thai ornaments and charming staff in traditional silk costumes transport you to Bangkok. Carefully prepared and authentic dishes.

Ransome's Dock, 35-37 Parkgate Rd, SW11 4NP, ✆ (020) 7223 1611, *chef@ransomesdock.co.uk, Fax (020) 7924 2614,* – MO AE D VISA JCB
closed 24-26 December, 1 January, August Bank Holiday and Sunday dinner – **Meals** a la carte 23.50/35.00 ♀.
◆ Secreted in a warehouse development, with a dock-side terrace in summer. Vivid blue interior, crowded with pictures. Chef patron produces reliable brasserie-style cuisine.

Putney - ✉ SW15.

Putney Bridge, Lower Richmond Rd, SW15 1LB, ✆ (020) 8780 1811 Ⓜ *Putney Bridge, information@putneybridgerestaurant.com,* Fax (020) 8780 1211, ← – ▤. MO AE D VISA JCB
closed Sunday dinner and Bank Holidays – **Meals** 22.50 (lunch) and a la carte 34.50/49.00 ♀.
Spec. Slow-cooked pork belly, squid and chorizo. Roast lobster, spaghetti and tomato vinaigrette. Chocolate fondant, barley milk ice cream.
◆ Winner of architectural awards, this striking glass and steel structure enjoys a charming riverside location. Exacting service ; accomplished and detailed modern cooking.

Enoteca Turi, 28 Putney High St, SW15 1SQ, ✆ (020) 8785 4449 Ⓜ *Putney Bridge, Fax (020) 8780 5409* – ▤. MO AE D VISA
closed 25-26 December, 1 January and Sunday – **Meals** - Italian - a la carte 22.75/31.25 ♀.
◆ A friendly neighbourhood Italian restaurant, overseen by the owner. Rustic cooking, with daily changing specials. Good selection of wine by the glass.

The Phoenix, Pentlow St, SW15 1LY, ✆ (020) 8780 3131, *phoenix@sonnys.co.uk*, *Fax (020) 8780 1114*, – . MC AE VISA
closed Bank Holidays – **Meals** - Italian influences - 19.50 (lunch) and a la carte 22.00/33.00 ♀.
◆ Light and bright interior with French windows leading out on to a spacious terrace. Unfussy and considerate service. An eclectic element to the modern Mediterranean menu.

Southfields – ✉ SW18.

Sarkhel's, 199 Replingham Rd, SW18 5LY, ✆ (020) 8870 1483 Ⓜ *Southfields, veronica@sarkhels.co.uk* – . MC VISA
closed 25-26 December – **Meals** - Indian - 9.95 (lunch) and a la carte 12.45/34.35 ♀.
◆ Recently expanded Indian restaurant with a large local following. Authentic, carefully prepared and well-priced dishes from many different Indian regions. Obliging service.

Calcutta Notebook, 201 Replingham Rd, SW18 5LY, ✆ (020) 8874 6603 Ⓜ *Southfields, info@sarkhels.com* – . MC VISA
closed 25-26 December – **Meals** - Indian (Bengali) - 5.00/18.00 and a la carte 14.50/22.85.
◆ Simple little eatery next to Sarkhel's, from whose kitchen the meals are served. East Indian cooking reflecting three generations of Sarkhel family ; also several street foods.

Tooting – ✉ SW17.

Kastoori, 188 Upper Tooting Rd, SW17 7EJ, ✆ (020) 8767 7027 Ⓜ *Tooting Bec* – . MC VISA
closed 25-26 December and lunch Monday and Tuesday – **Meals** - Indian Vegetarian - a la carte 12.75/15.50.
◆ Specialising in Indian vegetarian cooking with a subtle East African influence. Family-run for many years, a warm and welcoming establishment with helpful service.

Oh Boy, 843 Garratt Lane, SW17 0PG, ✆ (020) 8947 9760 Ⓜ *Broadway*, *Fax (020) 8879 7867* – . MC AE VISA JCB
closed Monday – **Meals** - Thai - (dinner only) a la carte 12.25/20.90.
◆ Long-standing neighbourhood Thai restaurant. Extensive menu offers authentic and carefully prepared dishes, in simple but friendly surroundings.

Wandsworth – ✉ SW17.

Chez Bruce (Poole), 2 Bellevue Rd, SW17 7EG, ✆ (020) 8672 0114 Ⓜ *Tooting Bec, chezbruce2@aol.com*, Fax (020) 8767 6648 – . MC AE VISA
closed 25-26 December and 1 January – **Meals** (booking essential) 23.50/32.50 ♀.
Spec. Foie gras and chicken liver parfait, toasted brioche. Roast cod with olive oil mash and grilled courgette. Strawberry and Champagne trifle.
◆ An ever-popular restaurant, overlooking the Common. Simple yet considered modern British cooking. Convivial and informal, with enthusiastic service.

WESTMINSTER (City of)

Bayswater and Maida Vale – ✉ E14/W2

Hilton London Paddington, 146 Praed St, W2 1EE, ✆ (020) 7850 0500 Ⓜ *Paddington, paddington@hilton.com*, Fax (020) 7850 0600, , – , rm, – 400. MC AE VISA JCB. 28 ADU a
***The Brasserie* : Meals** *(closed Saturday lunch)* 26.00/35.00 and a la carte 22.75/38.45 ♀ – 19.50 – **335 rm** 264.40, 20 suites.
◆ Early Victorian railway hotel, sympathetically restored in contemporary style with Art Deco details. Co-ordinated bedrooms with high tech facilities continue the modern style. Contemporarily styled brasserie offering a modern menu.

Royal Lancaster, Lancaster Terrace, W2 2TY, ✆ (020) 7262 6737 Ⓜ *Lancaster Gate, sales@royallancaster.com*, Fax (020) 7724 3191, – , rm, – 1400. MC AE VISA JCB. 28 ADU e
Meals (see ***Island*** and ***Nipa*** below) – 15.00 – **394 rm** 290.00/378.00, 22 suites.
◆ Imposing purpose-built hotel overlooking Hyde Park. Some of London's most extensive conference facilities. Well-equipped bedrooms are decorated in an Asian style.

Hilton London Metropole, Edgware Rd, W2 1JU, ✆ (020) 7402 4141 Ⓜ *Edgware Road, Fax (020) 7724 8866*, , , , – , rm, – 2000. MC AE VISA. 28 AET c
Meals a la carte 19.85/31.85 **s.** ♀ – 17.00 – **1033 rm** 222.00, 25 suites.
◆ One of London's most popular convention venues by virtue of both its size and transport links. Well-appointed and modern rooms have state-of-the-art facilities. Vibrant restaurant and bar.

The Hempel, 31-35 Craven Hill Gdns, W2 3EA, (020) 7298 9000 *Queensway, hotel@the-hempel.co.uk*, Fax (020) 7402 4666, – ⫶ TV. MC AE VISA JCB. 28 ACU a
I-Thai **: Meals** - Italian-Japanese-Thai - *(closed Sunday dinner)* a la carte 29.50/32.00 – 17.50 – **40 rm** 323.00/346.60, 6 suites.
◆ A striking example of minimalist design. Individually appointed bedrooms are understated yet very comfortable. Relaxed ambience. Modern basement restaurant.

Marriott, Plaza Parade, NW6 5RP, (020) 7543 6000 *Maida Vale, reservations.maidavale@marriotthotels.co.uk*, Fax (020) 7543 2100, , , – ⫶, rm, TV – 200. MC AE VISA.
Fratelli **: Meals** - Italian - (dinner only) a la carte 17.00/25.00 – 16.95 – **221 rm** 170.40, 16 suites.
◆ A capacious hotel, a short walk from Marble Arch and Oxford Street. Well-equipped with both business and leisure facilities including 12m pool. Suites have small kitchens. Informal restaurant and brasserie.

Thistle Hyde Park, Bayswater Rd, 90-92 Lancaster Gate, W2 3NR, (020) 7262 2711 *Lancaster Gate, hydepark@thistle.co.uk*, Fax (020) 7262 2147 – ⫶ TV P – 25. MC AE VISA JCB. 28 ACU v
Meals (bar lunch Saturday) a la carte 20.85/25.85 **s.** – 14.95 – **52 rm** 211.50/282.00, 2 suites.
◆ Behind the ornate pillared façade sits an attractively restored hotel. Appealing to the corporate and leisure traveller, the generally spacious rooms retain a period feel. Aperitifs in relaxed conservatory before formal dining.

Colonnade Town House without rest., 2 Warrington Crescent, W9 1ER, (020) 7286 1052 *Warwick Avenue, Fax (020) 7286 1057* – ⫶ TV. MC AE VISA.
closed 25-26 December – 15.00 – **43 rm** 164.50/241.00.
◆ Two Victorian townhouses with comfortable well-furnished communal rooms decorated with fresh flowers. Stylish and comfortable bedrooms with many extra touches.

Mornington without rest., 12 Lancaster Gate, W2 3LG, (020) 7262 7361 *Lancaster Gate, london@mornington.co.uk*, Fax (020) 7706 1028 – ⫶ TV. MC AE VISA 28 ACU s
closed 24-29 December – **66 rm** 125.00/150.00.
◆ The classic portico facade belies the cool and modern Scandinavian influenced interior. Modern bedrooms are well-equipped and generally spacious. Duplex rooms available.

Commodore, 50 Lancaster Gate, Hyde Park, W2 3NA, (020) 7402 5291 *Lancaster Gate, reservations@commodore-hotel.com*, Fax (020) 7262 1088, – ⫶, rm, TV. MC AE VISA JCB. 28 ACU r
Meals *(closed Sunday)* (dinner only) a la carte 25.50/32.50 **s.** – 7.50 – **79 rm** 105.00/165.00, 2 suites.
◆ Three converted Georgian town houses in a leafy residential area. Bedrooms vary considerably in size and style. Largest rooms decorated with a Victorian theme. Relaxed, casual bistro.

Hilton London Hyde Park, 129 Bayswater Rd, W2 4RJ, (020) 7221 2217 *Queensway, reservations.hydepark@hilton.com*, Fax (020) 7229 0557 – ⫶, rest, TV – 100. MC AE VISA JCB. 27 ABU c
Meals (bar lunch)/dinner 29.95 and a la carte approx 27.00 **s.** – 16.95 – **128 rm** 163.30/175.00, 1 suite.
◆ Classical Victorian hotel on busy main road. Well-appointed bedrooms enjoy up to date facilities. Rooms to front have Park views. Intimate dining room or relaxed bar for meals.

Delmere, 130 Sussex Gdns, W2 1UB, (020) 7706 3344 *Paddington, delmerehotel@compuserve.com*, Fax (020) 7262 1863 – ⫶, rm, TV. MC AE VISA JCB. 28 ADT v
Meals *(closed August and Christmas)* (dinner only) 19.00 **s.** – 9.00 – **36 rm** 97.00/120.00.
◆ Attractive stucco fronted and porticoed Victorian property. Now a friendly private hotel. Compact bedrooms are both well-equipped and kept. Modest prices. Bright, relaxed restaurant and adjacent bar.

Miller's without rest., 111A Westbourne Grove, W2 4UW, (020) 7243 1024 *Bayswater, enquiries@millersuk.com*, Fax (020) 7243 1064 – TV. MC AE VISA JCB. 27 ABU a
8 rm 176.25/270.25.
◆ Victorian house brimming with antiques and knick-knacks. Charming sitting room provides the setting for a relaxed breakfast. Individual, theatrical rooms named after poets.

Byron without rest., 36-38 Queensborough Terrace, W2 3SH, (020) 7243 0987 *Queensway, byron@capricornhotels.co.uk*, Fax (020) 7792 1957 – 28ACU z
44 rm 78.00/120.00, 1 suite.
◆ Centrally located and refurbished in the late 1990's - an ideal base for tourists. Bright and modern bedrooms are generally spacious and all have showers ensuite.

Island (at Royal Lancaster H.), Lancaster Terrace, W2 2TY, (020) 7551 6070 *Lancaster Gate, eat@islandrestaurant.co.uk*, Fax (020) 7551 6071 – 28ADU e
Meals 19.50 (lunch) and a la carte 24.00/37.00.
◆ Modern, stylish restaurant with buzzy open kitchen. Full length windows allow good views of adjacent Hyde Park. Seasonally based, modern menus with wide range of dishes.

Nipa (at Royal Lancaster H.), Lancaster Terrace, W2 2TY, (020) 7262 6737 *Lancaster Gate, Fax (020) 7724 3191* – 28ADU e
closed Saturday lunch, Sunday and Bank Holidays – **Meals** - Thai - 14.90/28.00 and a la carte 29.40/44.00 **s.**
◆ On the 1st floor and overlooking Hyde Park. Authentic and ornately decorated restaurant offers subtly spiced Thai cuisine. Keen to please staff in traditional silk costumes.

Al San Vincenzo, 30 Connaught St, W2 2AF, (020) 7262 9623 *Marble Arch* – 29 AFU a
closed Saturday lunch and Sunday – **Meals** - Italian - (booking essential) a la carte 23.50/35.50 ♀.
◆ A traditional Italian restaurant that continues to attract a loyal clientele. Rustic, authentic cooking and a wholly Italian wine list. Attentive service overseen by owner.

Green Olive, 5 Warwick Pl, W9 2PX, (020) 7289 2469 *Warwick Avenue, Fax (020) 7289 2463* –
closed 25-26 December and 1 January – **Meals** - Italian - (booking essential) 21.50/26.00 ♀.
◆ Attractive neighbourhood restaurant in a smart residential area. Modern Italian food served in the bright street level room or the more intimate basement.

Assaggi (Sassu), 39 Chepstow Pl, (above Chepstow pub), W2 4TS, (020) 7792 5501 *Bayswater, nipi@assaggi1.demon.co.uk* – 27AAU c
closed 2 weeks Christmas, Sunday and Bank Holidays – **Meals** - Italian - a la carte 26.15/39.15.
Spec. Insalatadi gamberoni. Tagliolini alle erbe. Fritto misto.
◆ Polished wood flooring, tall windows and modern artwork provide the bright surroundings for this forever busy restaurant. Concise menu of robust Italian dishes.

The Vale, 99 Chippenham Rd, W9 2AB, (020) 7266 0990 *Maida Vale, thevale@hotmail.com*, Fax (020) 7286 7224 –
closed 1 week Christmas, Easter, Sunday dinner and lunch Monday and Saturday – **Meals** 15.00/18.50 and a la carte 19.75/25.50 ♀.
◆ Dine in either the light and spacious conservatory, or in the original bar of this converted pub. Modern British food with Mediterranean influences. Destination bar below.

Ginger, 115 Westbourne Grove, W2 4UP, (020) 7908 1990 *Bayswater, info@gingerrestaurant.co.uk*, Fax (020) 7908 1991 – 27ABU v
closed 25 December – **Meals** - Bangladeshi - (dinner only and lunch Saturday and Sunday) a la carte 17.00/27.00.
◆ Bengali specialities served in contemporary styled dining room. True to its name, ginger is a key flavouring ; dishes range from mild to spicy and are graded accordingly.

L'Accento, 16 Garway Rd, W2 4NH, (020) 7243 2201 *Bayswater, laccentorest@aol.com*, Fax (020) 7243 2201 – 27ABU b
closed 25-26 December and Sunday – **Meals** - Italian - 18.50 and a la carte 22.50/28.00.
◆ Rustic surroundings and provincial, well priced, Italian cooking. Menu specialises in tasty pasta, made on the premises, and shellfish. Rear conservatory for the summer.

Formosa Dining Room (at Prince Alfred), 5A Formosa St, W9 1EE, (020) 7286 3287 *Warwick Avenue, theprincealfred@thespiritgroup.com*, Fax (020) 7286 3383 –
Meals a la carte 21.50/33.00 ♀.
◆ Traditional pub appearance and a relaxed dining experience on offer behind the elegant main bar. Contemporary style of cooking.

The Waterway, 54 Formosa St, W9 2JU, (020) 7266 3557 *Warwick Avenue, info@thewaterway.co.uk*, Fax (020) 7266 3547, –
closed 25-26 December – **Meals** a la carte 22.00/30.00 ♀.
◆ Pub with a thoroughly modern, metropolitan ambience. Spacious bar and large decked terrace overlooking canal. Concise, well-balanced menu served in open plan dining room.

Belgravia - ✉ SW1.

The Berkeley, Wilton Pl, SW1X 7RL, ☎ (020) 7235 6000 Ⓜ *Knightsbridge, info@the-berkeley.co.uk*, Fax (020) 7235 4330, Ⓜ, ⅼⅆ, ⇔, ⌂ - |‡|, ⇔ rm, ▤ TV ☏ ⇔ - ⛺ 220. MC AE Ⓓ VISA JCB. ✈ 37 AGX e
Boxwood Café (☎ *(020) 7235 1010)* **: Meals** a la carte approx 43.00 ♀ (see also **Pétrus** below) - ☕ 27.00 - **189 rm** 376.00/475.90, 25 suites.
• A gracious and discreet hotel. Relax in the gilded and panelled Lutyens lounge or enjoy a swim in the roof-top pool with its retracting roof. Opulent bedrooms. Split-level basment restaurant, divided by bar, with modern stylish décor ; New York-style dining.

The Lanesborough, Hyde Park Corner, SW1X 7TA, ☎ (020) 7259 5599 Ⓜ *Hyde Park Corner, info@lanesborough.com*, Fax (020) 7259 5606, ⅼⅆ - |‡|, ⇔ rm, ▤ TV ☏ ♿ P - ⛺ 90. MC AE Ⓓ VISA JCB 37 AGX a
The Conservatory **: Meals** 24.00/48.00 and a la carte 27.50/49.50 **s.** ♀ - ☕ 27.00 - **86 rm** 334.80/558.10, 9 suites.
• Converted in the 1990s from 18C St George's Hospital. A grand and traditional atmosphere prevails. Butler service offered. Regency-era decorated, lavishly appointed rooms. Ornate, glass-roofed dining room with palm trees and fountains.

The Halkin, 5 Halkin St, SW1X 7DJ, ☎ (020) 7333 1000 Ⓜ *Hyde Park Corner, res@halkin.como.bz*, Fax (020) 7333 1100 - |‡| ⇔ ▤ TV ☏. MC AE Ⓓ VISA JCB. ✈ 38 AHX b
closed 25-26 December and 1 January - **Meals** (see **Nahm** below) - ☕ 23.00 - **37 rm** 376.00, 4 suites.
• One of London's first minimalist hotels. The cool, marbled reception and bar have an understated charm. Spacious rooms have every conceivable facility.

Sheraton Belgravia, 20 Chesham Pl, SW1X 8HQ, ☎ (020) 7235 6040 Ⓜ *Knightsbridge, central.london.reservations@sheraton.com*, Fax (020) 7201 1926 - |‡|, ⇔ rm, ▤ TV ☏ ♿ P - ⛺ 25. MC AE Ⓓ VISA JCB. ✈ 37 AGX u
The Mulberry **: Meals** a la carte 18.90/44.00 ♀ - ☕ 17.50 - **82 rm** 329.00, 7 suites.
• Modern corporate hotel overlooking Chesham Place. Comfortable and well-equipped for the tourist and business traveller alike. A few minutes' walk from Harrods. Modern, international menus.

The Lowndes, 21 Lowndes St, SW1X 9ES, ☎ (020) 7823 1234 Ⓜ *Knightsbridge, contact@lowndeshotel.com*, Fax (020) 7235 1154, ☂ - |‡|, ⇔ rm, ▤ TV ☏ P - ⛺ 25. MC AE Ⓓ VISA JCB. ✈ 37 AGX h
Citronelle **: Meals** 15.95 and a la carte 23.00/36.00 ♀ - ☕ 17.50 - **77 rm** 305.50, 1 suite.
• Compact yet friendly modern corporate hotel within this exclusive residential area. Good levels of personal service offered. Close to the famous shops of Knightsbridge. Modern restaurant opens onto street terrace.

Diplomat without rest., 2 Chesham St, SW1X 8DT, ☎ (020) 7235 1544 Ⓜ *Sloane Square, diplomat.hotel@btinternet.com*, Fax (020) 7259 6153 - |‡| TV. MC AE Ⓓ VISA JCB. ✈
26 rm ☕ 95.00/170.00. 37 AGY a
• Imposing Victorian corner house built in 1882 by Thomas Cubitt. Attractive glass-domed stairwell and sweeping staircase. Spacious and well-appointed bedrooms.

Pétrus (Wareing) (at The Berkeley H.), Wilton Pl, SW1X 7RL, ☎ (020) 7235 1200 Ⓜ *Knightsbridge, petrus@marcuswareing.com*, Fax (020) 7235 1266 - ⇔ ▤. MC AE VISA JCB 37 AGX e
closed Christmas-New Year except 31 December, Saturday lunch, Sunday and Bank Holidays - **Meals** 30.00/90.00 ♀.
Spec. Trio of foie gras on Sauternes jelly plate, figs and quince purée. Poached turbot with crushed new potatoes and langoustine tails with morels. Gâteau Opéra, espresso ice cream and caramelised hazelnuts.
• Elegantly appointed restaurant named after one of the 40 Pétrus vintages on the wine list. One table in the kitchen to watch the chefs at work. Accomplished modern cooking.

Amaya, Halkin Arcade, 19 Motcomb St, SW1X 8JT, ☎ (020) 7823 1166 Ⓜ *Knightsbridge, info@realindianfood.com*, Fax (020) 7259 6464 - MC AE Ⓓ VISA JCB 37 AGX k
Meals - Indian - 14.50/30.00 and a la carte 28.00/38.00.
• Light, piquant and aromatic Indian cooking specialising in kebabs from a tawa skillet, sigri grill or tandoor oven. Chic comfortable surroundings, modern and subtly exotic.

Zafferano, 15 Lowndes St, SW1X 9EY, ☎ (020) 7235 5800 Ⓜ *Knightsbridge, Fax (020) 7235 1971* - ▤. MC AE Ⓓ VISA 37 AGX f
closed 24 December-2 January and Bank Holidays - **Meals** - Italian - 28.50/37.50 ♀.
Spec. Langoustine risotto. Veal shank ravioli. Almond and apricot tart, amaretto ice cream.
• Forever busy and relaxed. No frills, robust and gutsy Italian cooking, where the quality of the produce shines through. Wholly Italian wine list has some hidden treasures.

XX ✿ **Nahm** (at The Halkin H.), 5 Halkin St, SW1X 7DJ, ✆ (020) 7333 1234 Ⓜ *Hyde Park Corner, Fax (020) 7333 1100* – ▤. MC AE ① VISA JCB 38 AHX b
closed 25-26 December, 1 January, lunch Saturday and Sunday and Bank Holidays – **Meals** - Thai - (booking essential) 26.00/47.00 and a la carte 37.00/39.00 ♀.
Spec. Wild salmon with lime juice, chillies and shredded ginger. Aromatic curry of chicken with pumpkin and cucumber relish. Double-steamed chicken with bamboo and sour chilli sauce.
◆ Wood floored restaurant with uncovered tables and understated decor. Menu offers the best of Thai cooking with some modern interpretation and original use of ingredients.

XX **Mango Tree,** 46 Grosvenor Pl, SW1X 7EQ, ✆ (020) 7823 1888 Ⓜ *Victoria, mangotree@mangotree.org.uk*, Fax (020) 7838 9275 – ▤. MC AE ① VISA JCB 38 AHX a
closed 25-26 December and 1 January – **Meals** - Thai - 35.00/50.00 and a la carte approx 35.00 ♀.
◆ Thai staff in regional dress in contemporarily styled dining room of refined yet minimalist furnishings sums up the cuisine : authentic Thai dishes with modern presentation.

XX **Noura Brasserie,** 16 Hobart Pl, SW1W 0HH, ✆ (020) 7235 9444 Ⓜ *Victoria, Fax (020) 7235 9244* – ▤. MC AE ① VISA 38 AHX n
Meals - Lebanese - 14.50/23.00 and a la carte 23.00/30.00.
◆ Dine in either the bright bar or the comfortable, contemporary restaurant. Authentic, modern Lebanese cooking specialises in char-grilled meats and mezzes.

Hyde Park and Knightsbridge – ✉ *SW1/SW7.*

Mandarin Oriental Hyde Park, 66 Knightsbridge, SW1X 7LA, ✆ (020) 7235 2000 Ⓜ *Knightsbridge, molon-reservations@mohg.com*, Fax (020) 7235 2001, ≤, Ⓦ, Fδ, ≘s – |‡|, ⇜ rm, ▤ TV ✆ ♿ – 🅰 220. MC AE ① VISA JCB. ✂ 37 AGX x
The Park :* Meals** 25.00 (lunch) and a la carte 47.50/50.00 (see also ***Foliage below) – **177 rm** 405.40/581.60, 23 suites.
◆ Built in 1889 this classic hotel, with striking façade, remains one of London's grandest. Many of the luxurious bedrooms enjoy Park views. Immaculate and detailed service. Smart ambience in The Park.

Knightsbridge Green without rest., 159 Knightsbridge, SW1X 7PD, ✆ (020) 7584 6274 Ⓜ *Knightsbridge, reservations@thekghotel.co.uk*, Fax (020) 7225 1635 – |‡| ⇜ ▤ TV ✆. MC AE ① VISA. ✂ 37 AFX z
☕ 10.50 – **16 rm** 90.00/145.00, 12 suites 170.00.
◆ Privately owned hotel, boasting peaceful sitting room with writing desk. Breakfast - sausage and bacon from Harrods ! - served in the generously proportioned bedrooms.

XXXX ✿ **Foliage** (at Mandarin Oriental Hyde Park H.), 66 Knightsbridge, SW1X 7LA, ✆ (020) 7201 3723 Ⓜ *Knightsbridge, Fax (020) 7235 4552* – ▤. MC AE ① VISA JCB 37 AGX x
Meals 25.00 (lunch) and a la carte 47.50/50.00 ♀.
Spec. Duo of foie gras with caramelised endive tarte Tatin. Roast turbot with pork, langoustine and horseradish cream. Chocolate fondant, amaretto parfait, pearl barley sorbet.
◆ Reached via a glass-enclosed walkway that houses the cellar. Hyde Park outside the window reflected in the foliage-themed décor. Gracious service, skilled modern cooking.

XX **Zuma,** 5 Raphael St, SW7 1DL, ✆ (020) 7584 1010 Ⓜ *Knightsbridge, info@zumarestaurant.com*, Fax (020) 7584 5005 – ▤. MC AE ① VISA JCB 37 AFX m
Meals - Japanese - a la carte 24.60/46.10 ♀.
◆ Strong modern feel with exposed pipes, modern lighting and granite flooring. A theatrical atmosphere around the Sushi bar and a varied and interesting modern Japanese menu.

XX **Mr Chow,** 151 Knightsbridge, SW1X 7PA, ✆ (020) 7589 7347 Ⓜ *Knightsbridge, mrchow@aol.com*, Fax (020) 7584 5780 – ▤. MC AE ① VISA JCB 37 AFX e
closed 24-26 December, 1 January and Easter Monday – **Meals** - Chinese - 20.00 (lunch) and a la carte 36.00/45.00 ♀.
◆ Cosmopolitan Chinese restaurant with branches in New York and L.A. Well established ambience. Walls covered with mirrors and modern art. House specialities worth opting for.

Mayfair – ✉ *W1.*

Dorchester, Park Lane, W1A 2HJ, ✆ (020) 7629 8888 Ⓜ *Hyde Park Corner, reservations@dorchesterhotel.com*, Fax (020) 7409 0114, Ⓦ, Fδ, ≘s – |‡|, ⇜ rm, ▤ TV ✆ ♿ 🚗 – 🅰 550. MC AE ① VISA JCB. ✂ 30 AHV a
Meals (see ***Grill Room*** below) – ☕ 24.50 – **200 rm** 358.40/546.40, 49 suites 646.25/2497.00.
◆ A sumptuously decorated, luxury hotel offering every possible facility. Impressive marbled and pillared promenade. Rooms quintessentially English in style. Faultless service.

Claridge's, Brook St, W1A 2JQ, ✆ (020) 7629 8860 Ⓜ *Bond Street, info@claridges.co.uk*, Fax (020) 7499 2210, – rm, – 200. MC AE VISA JCB. 30 AHU c

Meals 32.50 and a la carte 32.50/50.00 (see also ***Gordon Ramsay at Claridge's*** below) – 24.50 – **143 rm** 457.00/562.80, 60 suites.

◆ The epitome of English grandeur, celebrated for its Art Deco. Exceptionally well-appointed and sumptuous bedrooms, all with butler service. Magnificently restored foyer. Relaxed, elegant restaurant.

Grosvenor House, Park Lane, W1K 7TN, ✆ (020) 7499 6363 Ⓜ *Marble Arch, Fax (020) 7493 8512*, – rm, – 2000. MC AE VISA JCB. 29 AGU a

La Terrazza **: Meals** - Italian influences - *(closed Saturday lunch)* a la carte 25.00/50.00 – 21.95 – **378 rm** 240.90, 74 suites.

◆ Over 70 years old and occupying an enviable position by the Park. Edwardian style décor. The Great Room, an ice rink in the 1920s, is Europe's largest banqueting room. Bright, relaxing dining room with contemporary feel.

Four Seasons, Hamilton Pl, Park Lane, W1A 1AZ, ✆ (020) 7499 0888 Ⓜ *Hyde Park Corner, fsh.london@fourseasons.com*, Fax (020) 7493 1895, – rm, – 500. MC AE VISA JCB. 30 AHV b

Lanes **: Meals** 28.00/35.00 and a la carte 33.50/62.50 **s.** – 23.00 – **185 rm** 364.25/440.60, 35 suites.

◆ Set back from Park Lane so shielded from the traffic. Large, marbled lobby; its lounge a popular spot for light meals. Spacious rooms, some with their own conservatory. Restaurant's vivid blue and stained glass give modern, yet relaxing, feel.

Le Meridien Piccadilly, 21 Piccadilly, W1J 0BH, ✆ (020) 7734 8000 Ⓜ *Piccadilly Circus, lmpiccres@lemeridien-hotels.com*, Fax (020) 7437 3574, squash – rm, – 250. MC AE VISA JCB. 31 AJV a

Terrace **: Meals** 22.50 and a la carte 24.00/41.50 – 22.50 – **248 rm** 376.00, 18 suites.

◆ Comfortable international hotel, in a central location. Boasts one of the finest leisure clubs in London. Individually decorated bedrooms, with first class facilities.

London Hilton, 22 Park Lane, W1K 1BE, ✆ (020) 7493 8000 Ⓜ *Hyde Park Corner, reservations@hilton.com*, Fax (020) 7208 4142, London, – rm, – 1000. MC AE VISA. 30 AHV e

Trader Vics *(✆ (020) 7208 4113)* **: Meals** *(closed 25 December and lunch Saturday and Sunday)* 19.50 (lunch) and a la carte 30.00/48.00 – ***Park Brasserie*** **: Meals** 25.00 (lunch) and a la carte 35.00/50.00 (see also ***Windows*** below) – 22.00 – **395 rm** 210.30/393.60, 55 suites.

◆ This 28 storey tower is one of the city's tallest hotels, providing impressive views from the upper floors. Club floor bedrooms are particularly comfortable. Exotic Trader Vics with bamboo and plants. A harpist adds to the relaxed feel of Park Brasserie.

Connaught, 16 Carlos Pl, W1K 2AL, ✆ (020) 7499 7070 Ⓜ *Bond Street, info@the-connaught.co.uk*, Fax (020) 7495 3262, – MC AE VISA JCB. 30 AHU e

Meals (see ***Menu and Grill*** below) – 26.50 – **68 rm** 352.50/499.40, 23 suites.

◆ 19C quintessentially English hotel, with country house ambience. The grand mahogany staircase leads up to antique furnished bedrooms. One of the capital's most exclusive addresses.

Inter-Continental, 1 Hamilton Pl, Hyde Park Corner, W1J 7QY, ✆ (020) 7409 3131 Ⓜ *Hyde Park Corner, london@interconti.com*, Fax (020) 7493 3476, – rm, – 700. MC AE VISA. 30 AHV s

Meals 26.00/30.00 and a la carte 36.50/50.50 – ***Le Souffle*** **: Meals** *(closed Saturday lunch, Sunday, Monday and Bank Holidays)* 23.50/39.50 and a la carte 41.50/57.50 – 20.50 – **418 rm** 376.00/470.00, 40 suites.

◆ A large, purpose-built, international group hotel that dominates Hyde Park Corner. Spacious marbled lobby and lounge. Well-equipped bedrooms, many of which have Park views. Informal café style dining or more intimate Soufflé.

Park Lane, Piccadilly, W1J 7BX, ✆ (020) 7499 6321 Ⓜ *Green Park, 00105.central.london.reservations@sheraton.com*, Fax (020) 7499 1965, – rm, – 500. MC AE VISA JCB. 30 AHV x

Citrus *(✆ (020) 7290 7364)* **: Meals** 18.00/22.00 and a la carte 21.00/30.50 – 18.95 – **285 rm** 305.50, 20 suites.

◆ The history of the hotel is reflected in the elegant 'Palm Court' lounge and ballroom, both restored to their Art Deco origins. Bedrooms vary in shape and size. Summer pavement tables in restaurant opposite Green Park.

London Marriott Park Lane, 140 Park Lane, W1K 7AA, (020) 7493 7000 *Marble Arch, mhrs.parklane@marriotthotels.com*, Fax (020) 7493 8333, – – 75. 29AGU b
***140 Park Lane* : Meals** (bar lunch Saturday) 18.50 (lunch) and a la carte 24.50/37.00 – 20.95 – **148 rm** 311.40/358.40, 9 suites.
◆ Superbly located 'boutique' style hotel at intersection of Park Lane and Oxford Street. Attractive basement health club. Spacious, well-equipped rooms with luxurious elements. Attractive restaurant overlooking Marble Arch.

Westbury, Bond St, W1S 2YF, (020) 7629 7755 *Bond Street, sales@westburymayfair.com*, Fax (020) 7495 1163, – , rm, – 120. 30 AIU a
Meals 20.00 and a la carte 41.50/54.50 – 23.00 – **233 rm** 311.40, 21 suites.
◆ Surrounded by London's most fashionable shops ; the renowned Polo bar and lounge provide soothing sanctuary. Some suites have their own terrace. Bright, fresh restaurant enhanced by modern art.

The Metropolitan, Old Park Lane, W1Y 1LB, (020) 7447 1000 *Hyde Park Corner, res.lon@metropolitan.com.bz*, Fax (020) 7447 1100, , – , rm, . 30 AHV c
Meals (see ***Nobu*** below) – 22.00 – **147 rm** 305.50/411.25, 3 suites.
◆ Minimalist interior and a voguish reputation make this the favoured hotel of pop stars and celebrities. Innovative design and fashionably attired staff set it apart.

Athenaeum, 116 Piccadilly, W1J 7BS, (020) 7499 3464 *Hyde Park Corner, info@athenaeumhotel.com*, Fax (020) 7493 1860, , – , rm, – 55. 30 AHV g
***Bulloch's at 116* : Meals** *(closed lunch Saturday and Sunday)* 15.00/40.00 and a la carte approx. 35.35 – 21.00 – **124 rm** 311.00/346.60, 33 suites.
◆ Built in 1925 as a luxury apartment block. Comfortable bedrooms with video and CD players. Individually designed suites are in an adjacent Edwardian townhouse. Conservatory roofed dining room renowned for its mosaics and malt whiskies.

Chesterfield, 35 Charles St, W1J 5EB, (020) 7491 2622 *Green Park, bookch@chmail.com*, Fax (020) 7491 4793 – , rm, – 110. 30 AHV f
Meals 24.00 and a la carte 28.70/38.95 – 18.50 – **106 rm** 264.30/381.90, 4 suites.
◆ An assuredly English feel to this Georgian house. Discreet lobby leads to a clubby bar and wood panelled library. Individually decorated bedrooms, with some antique pieces. Classically decorated restaurant.

Washington Mayfair, 5-7 Curzon St, W1J 5HE, (020) 7499 7000 *Green Park, info@washington-mayfair.co.uk*, Fax (020) 7495 6172, – , rm, – 90. 30 AHV d
Meals 27.35/30.35 and a la carte – 16.95 – **166 rm** 252.60, 5 suites.
◆ Successfully blends a classical style with modern amenities. Relaxing lounge with traditional English furniture and bedrooms with polished, burred oak. Piano bar annex to formal dining room.

London Marriott Grosvenor Square, Grosvenor Sq, W1K 6JP, (020) 7493 1232 *Bond Street, Fax (020) 7491 3201*, – , rm, – 600. 30AHU s
***Diplomat* : Meals** *(closed Saturday lunch)* a la carte 24.85/39.85 – 22.50 – **209 rm** 311.40, 12 suites.
◆ A well-appointed international group hotel that benefits from an excellent location. Many of the bedrooms specifically equipped for the business traveller. Formal dining room with its own cocktail bar.

Hilton London Green Park, Half Moon St, W1J 7BN, (020) 7629 7522 *Green Park, reservations.greenpark@hilton.com*, Fax (020) 7491 8971 – – 130. 30 AIV a
Meals *(closed lunch Saturday and Sunday)* (bar lunch)/dinner 21.95 and a la carte 21.00/30.00 – 18.95 – **162 rm** 222.00/234.00.
◆ A row of sympathetically adjoined townhouses, dating from the 1730s. Discreet marble lobby. Bedrooms share the same décor but vary in size and shape. Monet prints decorate light, airy dining room.

Flemings, Half Moon St, W1J 7BH, (020) 7499 2964 *Green Park, sales@flemings-mayfair.co.uk*, Fax (020) 7491 8866 – , rm, – 55. 30 AIV z
Meals 25.00 – 18.00 – **121 rm** 198.60/233.85, 10 suites.
◆ A Georgian town house where the oil paintings and English furniture add to the charm. Apartments located in adjoining house, once home to noted polymath Henry Wagner. Candlelit basement restaurant with oil paintings.

Hilton London Mews, 2 Stanhope Row, W1J 7BS, (020) 7493 7222 Ⓜ *Hyde Park Corner, reservations.mews@hilton.com*, Fax (020) 7629 9423 – 50. 30 AHV u
closed 22-30 December – **Meals** (dinner only) 25.00 and a la carte 25.00/34.00 – 17.50 – **72 rm** 205.60/217.40.
◆ Tucked away in a discreet corner of Mayfair. This modern, group hotel manages to retain a cosy and intimate feel. Well-equipped bedrooms to meet corporate needs. Meals in cosy dining room or lounge.

No.5 Maddox St without rest., 5 Maddox St, W1S 2QD, (020) 7647 0200 Ⓜ *Oxford Circus, no5maddoxst@living-rooms.co.uk*, Fax (020) 7647 0300 – 30 AIU c
12 suites 287.80/705.00.
◆ No grand entrance or large foyer, just a discreet door bell and brass plaque. All rooms are stylish and contemporary suites, with kitchenettes and every conceivable mod con.

Le Gavroche (Roux), 43 Upper Brook St, W1K 7QR, (020) 7408 0881 Ⓜ *Marble Arch, bookings@le-gavroche.com*, Fax (020) 7491 4387 –
closed Christmas-New Year, Sunday, Saturday lunch and Bank Holidays – **Meals** - French - (booking essential) 44.00 (lunch) and a la carte 59.60/111.00. 29AGU c
Spec. Foie gras chaud et pastilla de canard à la cannelle. Râble de lapin et galette au parmesan. Le palet au chocolat amer et praline croustillant.
◆ Long standing renowned restaurant with a clubby, formal atmosphere. Accomplished classical French cuisine, served by smartly attired and well-drilled staff.

Grill Room (at Dorchester H.), Park Lane, W1A 2HJ, (020) 7317 6336 Ⓜ *Hyde Park Corner*, Fax (020) 7317 6464 – 30 AHV a
Meals - English - 25.00/42.00 and a la carte 40.50/72.50 **s.**
◆ Ornate Spanish influenced, baroque decoration with gilded ceiling, tapestries and highly polished oak tables. Formal and immaculate service. Traditional English cooking.

Menu and Grill (at Connaught H.), 16 Carlos Pl, W1K 2AL, (020) 7592 1222 Ⓜ *Bond Street, reservations@angelahartnett.com*, Fax (020) 7592 1223 – 30AHU e
Meals (booking essential) 30.00/70.00
Spec. Pea tortellini with roast girolles and braised chicory. Roast lamb with tomato compote, baby fennel and black olive jus. Chocolate millefeuille with pear purée.
◆ Refined Italian influenced cooking can be enjoyed in the elegant panelled 'Menu'. The more intimate 'Grill' also offers a selection of traditional British favourites.

The Square (Howard), 6-10 Bruton St, W1J 6PU, (020) 7495 7100 Ⓜ *Green Park, info@squarerestaurant.com*, Fax (020) 7495 7150 –
closed 24-26 December and lunch Saturday, Sunday and Bank Holidays – **Meals** 30.00/55.00 30 AIU v
Spec. Lasagne of crab with shellfish and basil cappuccino. Roast foie gras with caramelised endive tart, late picked Muscat grapes. Saddle of lamb with herb crust, rosemary and shallot purée.
◆ Marble flooring and bold abstract canvasses add an air of modernity. Extensive menus offer French influenced cooking of the highest order. Prompt and efficient service.

Sketch (The Lecture Room), First Floor, 9 Conduit St, W1S 2XG, (0870) 7774488 Ⓜ *Oxford Street*, Fax (0870) 7774400 – 30 AIU h
closed Saturday lunch, Sunday, Monday, Christmas and Bank Holidays – **Meals** (booking essential) 35.00/65.00 and a la carte 57.00/139.00.
Spec. Chilled Dover sole, Champagne and celery jelly, mango and French beans. Saddle of lamb, lamb dumplings with apricots and figs, breaded cutlets. Peach and almond shot.
◆ Stunning venue, combining art and food, creating an experience of true sensory stimulation. Vibrant dining options : Lecture Room or Library. Highly original, complex cooking.

Windows (at London Hilton H.), 22 Park Lane, W1Y 1BE, (020) 7208 4021 Ⓜ *Hyde Park Corner*, Fax (020) 7208 4142, London – 30 AHV e
closed Saturday lunch and dinner Sunday and Bank Holidays – **Meals** 30.00 (lunch) and a la carte 49.00/69.00
◆ Enjoys some of the city's best views. The lunchtime buffet provides a popular alternative to the international menu. Formal service and a busy adjoining piano bar.

The Greenhouse, 27a Hay's Mews, W1X 7RJ, (020) 7499 3331 Ⓜ *Hyde Park Corner, reservations@greenhouserestaurant.co.uk*, Fax (020) 7499 5368 – 30 AHV m
closed 25-26 December, Saturday lunch and Sunday – **Meals** 32.00/55.00
Spec. Seared foie gras, espresso syrup, amaretto foam. Pig's trotter with salt-cured foie gras and apple en gêlée. Grilled rib of beef with baby spring vegetables.
◆ A pleasant courtyard, off a quiet mews, leads to this well established restaurant. Original British cooking and inventive touches ensure an enjoyable dining experience.

XXXX ✿ **Gordon Ramsay at Claridge's,** Brook St, W1A 2JQ, ✆ (020) 7499 0099 Ⓜ *Bond Street, reservations@gordonramsay.com,* Fax (020) 7499 3099 – ⇔ ▤. MC AE ⓓ VISA JCB 30 AHU c
Meals (booking essential) 30.00/70.00 ♀.
Spec. Scallops with Jerusalem artichoke risotto, Sherry vinaigrette. Pan-fried fillet of veal with spring greens and root vegetables. Caramelised apple tart Tatin, vanilla ice cream.
◆ A thoroughly comfortable dining room with a charming and gracious atmosphere. Serves classically inspired food executed with a high degree of finesse.

XXXX ✿ **Mirabelle,** 56 Curzon St, W1J 8PA, ✆ (020) 7499 4636 Ⓜ *Green Park, sales@whitestarline.org.uk,* Fax (020) 7499 5449, 余 – ▤. MC AE ⓓ VISA 30 AIV x
closed 26 December and 1 January – **Meals** 19.50 (lunch) and a la carte 31.50/53.50 ♀.
Spec. Omelette Arnold Bennett, Mornay sauce. Braised pig's trotter with morels and pomme purée. Soufflé of mirabelles.
◆ As celebrated now as it was in the 1950s. Stylish bar with screens and mirrors, leather banquettes and rows of windows. Modern interpretation of some classic dishes.

XXXX **Benares,** 12 Berkeley House, Berkeley Sq, W1J 6BS, ✆ (020) 7629 8886 Ⓜ *Green Park, enquiries@benaresrestaurant.com,* Fax (020) 7491 8883 – ▤. MC AE ⓓ VISA
closed Christmas, 1 January, lunch Saturday and Sunday and Bank Holidays – **Meals** - Indian - 15.00 (lunch) and a la carte 22.20/35.45 ♀. 30 AIU q
◆ Indian restaurant where pools of water scattered with petals and candles compensate for lack of natural light. Original Indian dishes ; particularly good value at lunch.

XXXX **Embassy,** 29 Old Burlington St, W1S 3AN, ✆ (020) 7851 0956 Ⓜ *Green Park, embassy@embassylondon.com,* Fax (020) 7734 3224, 余 – ▤. MC AE VISA 30 AIU u
closed 25-26 December, 1 January, Saturday lunch, Sunday and Monday – **Meals** 19.95 (lunch) and a la carte 26.40/48.40 ♀.
◆ Marble floors, ornate cornicing and a long bar create a characterful, moody dining room. Tables are smartly laid and menus offer accomplished, classic dishes.

XXXX ✿ **Tamarind,** 20 Queen St, W1J 5PR, ✆ (020) 7629 3561 Ⓜ *Green Park, tamarind.restaurant@virgin.net,* Fax (020) 7499 5034 – ▤. MC AE ⓓ VISA JCB 30 AHV h
closed 24-27 December, 1 January and lunch Saturday – **Meals** - Indian - 16.95 (lunch) and a la carte 36.50/52.50 ♀.
Spec. Tandoor grilled mushrooms with pickled onions, curry leaf dressing. Lamb with onion garlic, red chillies and pickling spices. Sea bass with spinach, sauce of coconut, garlic and ground spices.
◆ Gold coloured pillars add to the opulence of this basement room. Windows allow diners the chance to watch the kitchen prepare original and accomplished Indian dishes.

XXXX **Sartoria,** 20 Savile Row, W1X 1AE, ✆ (020) 7534 7000 Ⓜ *Green Park, sartoriareservations@conran-restaurants.co.uk,* Fax (020) 7534 7070 – ▤. MC AE ⓓ VISA
closed 25-26 December and Sunday lunch – **Meals** - Italian - 21.00 and a la carte 27.50/41.50 ☺ ♀. 30 AIU b
◆ In the street renowned for English tailoring, a coolly sophisticated restaurant to suit those looking for classic Italian cooking with modern touches.

XXXX **Brian Turner Mayfair** (at Millennium Mayfair H.), 44 Grosvenor Sq, W1K 2HP, ✆ (020) 7596 3444 Ⓜ *Bond Street, turner.mayfair@mill-cop.com,* Fax (020) 7596 3443 – ⇔. MC AE ⓓ VISA JCB 30 AHU x
closed 25-26 December, Saturday lunch, Sunday and Bank Holidays – **Meals** - English - 25.50 (lunch) and a la carte 31.75/51.25 ♀.
◆ Located within the Millennium Mayfair overlooking Grosvenor Square. Restaurant on several levels with sharp modern décor. Good English dishes with modern twist.

XXXX **Cecconi's,** 5a Burlington Gdns, W1S 3EP, ✆ (020) 7434 1500 Ⓜ *Green Park, info@cecconis.co.uk,* Fax (020) 7494 2440 – ▤. MC AE ⓓ VISA 30 AIU d
closed 23 December-3 January – **Meals** - Italian - a la carte 25.00/48.50 ♀.
◆ A chic bar and a stylish, modern dining venue, invariably busy ; the menus call on the Italian classics with unusual touches.

XXXX **Berkeley Square,** 7 Davies St, W1K 3DD, ✆ (020) 7629 6993 Ⓜ *Bond Street, info@theberkeleysquare.com,* Fax (020) 7491 9719, 余 – MC AE ⓓ VISA JCB 30 AHU w
closed Christmas, last 2 weeks August, Saturday lunch, Sunday and Bank Holidays – **Meals** 19.95/45.00 ♀.
◆ Smart contemporary restaurant with pavement terrace and recordings of famous novels in the loos ! Modern British food with original touches.

XXXX **Kai,** 65 South Audley St, W1K 2QU, ✆ (020) 7493 8988 Ⓜ *Hyde Park Corner, kai@kaimayfair.com,* Fax (020) 7493 1456 – ▤. MC AE ⓓ VISA JCB 30 AHV n
closed Christmas and New Year – **Meals** - Chinese - 39.00 and a la carte 33.00/54.00 ♀.
◆ Marble flooring and mirrors add to the opulent feel of this smoothly run Chinese restaurant. Extensive menu offers dishes ranging from the luxury to the more familiar.

XXX **Umu,** 14-16 Bruton Pl, W1J 6LX, ✆ (020) 7499 8881 Ⓜ *Bond Street, enquiries@umurestaurant.com* – ✈ ▤. MC AE DC VISA JCB 30 AIU k
closed 25-26 December, Sunday and Bank Holidays – **Meals** - Japanese - 32.00/75.00 and a la carte 40.00/70.00.
Spec. Marinated sardine with grated radish. Classic and modern sushi. Deep-fried seabass with sesame and miso sauce.
◆ Exclusive neighbourhood location : stylish, discreet interior with central sushi bar. Japanese dishes, specialising in Kyoto cuisine, employing highest quality ingredients.

XXX **Patterson's,** 4 Mill St, W1S 2AX, ✆ (020) 7499 1308 Ⓜ *Oxford Street, pattersonmayfair@btconnect.com*, Fax (020) 7491 2122 – ▤. MC AE VISA 30 AIU p
closed 25 December, Saturday lunch, Sunday and Bank Holidays – **Meals** 25.00 (lunch) and a la carte 30.00/40.00 ♀.
◆ Stylish modern interior in black and white. Elegant tables and attentive service. Modern British cooking with concise wine list and sensible prices.

XXX **Deca,** 23 Conduit St, W1S 2XS, ✆ (020) 7493 7070 Ⓜ *Oxford Circus*, *Fax (020) 7493 7090* – ▤. MC AE DC VISA 30 AIU x
closed 10 days Christmas, 4 days Easter, Sunday and Bank Holiday Mondays – **Meals** 19.50/24.00 ♀.
◆ Attractively styled and comfortable, personally-run restaurant. Menu offers an appealing mix of modern French and traditional English dishes.

XXX **Teca,** 54 Brooks Mews, W1Y 2NY, ✆ (020) 7495 4774 Ⓜ *Bond Street*, *Fax (020) 7491 3545* – ▤. MC AE DC VISA 30 AHU f
closed 24 December-2 January, Sunday, Saturday lunch and Bank Holidays – **Meals** - Italian - 31.50 (dinner) and lunch a la carte 21.00/31.00 ♀.
◆ A glass-enclosed cellar is one of the features of this modern, slick Italian restaurant. Set price menu, with the emphasis on fresh, seasonal produce.

XXX **Alloro,** 19-20 Dover St, W1S 4LU, ✆ (020) 7495 4768 Ⓜ *Green Park*, *Fax (020) 7629 5348* – ▤. MC AE DC VISA 30 AIV r
closed 24 December-2 January, Saturday lunch, Sunday and Bank Holidays – **Meals** - Italian - 26.00/31.00 ♀.
◆ One of the new breed of stylish Italian restaurants, with contemporary art and leather seating. A separate, bustling bar. Smoothly run, with modern cooking.

XXX **Hush,** 8 Lancashire Court, Brook St, W1S 1EY, ✆ (020) 7659 1500 Ⓜ *Bond Street, info@hush.co.uk*, Fax (020) 7659 1501, 🏠 – |♦| ▤. MC AE DC VISA JCB 30 AHU v
closed 24-27 December, 29 December-3 January and Sunday – ***Brasserie*** 🏠 **: Meals** a la carte 28.50/43.50 ♀ – ***hush up* : Meals** (booking essential) a la carte 37.00/50.00 ♀.
◆ Tucked away down a side street : spacious, informal hush down brasserie with a secluded courtyard terrace. Serves tasty modern classics. Join the fashionable set in the busy bar or settle down on the banquettes at hush up. Serves robust, satisfying dishes.

XXX **Fakhreldine,** 85 Piccadilly, W1J 7NB, ✆ (020) 7493 3424 Ⓜ *Green Park, info@fakhreldine.co.uk*, Fax (020) 7495 1977 – ▤. MC AE DC VISA JCB 30 AIV e
closed 25 December and 1 January – **Meals** - Lebanese - 25.00 (lunch) and a la carte 23.00/40.00 ♀.
◆ Long-standing Lebanese restaurant with great view of Green Park. Large selection of classic mezze dishes and more modern European styled menu of original Lebanese dishes.

XXX **Noble Rot,** 3-5 Mill St, W1S 2AU, ✆ (020) 7629 8877 Ⓜ *Oxford Street, info@noblerot.com*, Fax (020) 7629 8878 – ▤. MC AE DC VISA 30 AIU r
closed 24-29 December, 31 December-4 January, Saturday lunch and Sunday – **Meals** 19.75 (lunch) and a la carte 36.00/60.00 ♀.
◆ A modern room with framed photographs, tiled flooring and venetian blinds. Ambient lighting and music. Modern cooking with some French regional specialities.

XXX **Nobu** (at The Metropolitan H.), 19 Old Park Lane, W1Y 4LB, ✆ (020) 7447 4747 Ⓜ *Hyde Park Corner, confirmations@noburestaurants.com*, Fax (020) 7447 4749, ← – ▤. MC AE VISA JCB 30 AHV c
closed Bank Holiday lunch – **Meals** - Japanese with South American influences - (booking essential) 50.00/60.00 and a la carte approx 62.25 **s.** ♀.
Spec. "New style" sashimi. Black cod with miso. Sashimi salad.
◆ Its celebrity clientele has made this one of the most glamorous spots. Staff are fully conversant in the unique menu that adds South American influences to Japanese cooking.

XXX **Taman Gang,** 140a Park Lane, W1K 7AA, ✆ (020) 7518 3160 Ⓜ *Marble Arch, info@tamangang.com*, Fax (020) 7518 3161 – ▤. MC AE VISA 29 AGU e
closed lunch Saturday, Sunday and Bank Holidays – **Meals** - South East Asian - 20.00 (lunch) and a la carte 28.50/75.00 ♀.
◆ Basement restaurant with largish bar and lounge area. Stylish but intimate décor. Informal and intelligent service. Pan-Asian dishes presented in exciting modern manner.

Sumosan, 26 Albemarle St, W1S 4HY, ✆ (020) 7495 5999 Ⓜ *Green Park, info@sumosan.co.uk*, Fax (020) 7355 1247 – ▤. MC AE ⓓ VISA 30 AIU e
closed 25 and 31 December, lunch Saturday and Sunday and Bank Holidays – **Meals** - Japanese - 19.50/65.00 and a la carte 15.50/38.25 **s.** ♀.
◆ A very smart interior in which diners sit in comfy banquettes and armchairs. Sushi bar to the rear with some semi-private booths. Extensive menus of Sushi and Sashimi.

Chor Bizarre, 16 Albemarle St, W1S 4HW, ✆ (020) 7629 9802 Ⓜ *Green Park, chorbizarrelondon@oldworldhospitality.com*, Fax (020) 7493 7756 – ▤. MC AE ⓓ VISA JCB 30 AIV s
closed 25 December, 1 January, Sunday lunch and Bank Holidays – **Meals** - Indian - 14.50/24.00 and a la carte 15.50/23.00.
◆ Translates as 'thieves market' and the décor is equally vibrant ; antiques, curios, carvings and ornaments abound. Cooking and recipes chiefly from north India and Kashmir.

Bentley's, 11-15 Swallow St, W1B 4DG, ✆ (020) 7734 4756 Ⓜ *Green Park*, Fax (020) 7287 2972 – ▤. MC AE ⓓ VISA JCB 30 AJV e
closed 24-27 December and 1 January – **Meals** - Seafood - a la carte 36.00/45.00 ♀.
◆ One of London's oldest restaurants. Ground floor oyster bar leads to the upstairs dining room. Booth seating and walls adorned with oil paintings. Specialises in seafood.

Sketch (The Gallery), 9 Conduit St, W1S 2XG, ✆ (0870) 7774488 Ⓜ *Oxford Street, info@sketch.uk.com*, Fax (0870) 7774400 – ▤. MC AE ⓓ VISA 30 AIU h
closed 25 December, Sunday and Bank Holidays – **Meals** (booking essential) (dinner only) a la carte 31.50/50.50.
◆ On the ground floor of the Sketch building : daytime video art gallery metamorphoses into evening brasserie with ambient wall projections and light menus with eclectic range.

Momo, 25 Heddon St, W1B 4BH, ✆ (020) 7434 4040 Ⓜ *Oxford Circus, info@momoresto.com*, Fax (020) 7287 0404, 🏠 – ▤. MC AE ⓓ VISA 30 AIU n
closed Sunday lunch – **Meals** - Moroccan - 17.00 (lunch) and a la carte 26.50/36.50.
◆ Elaborate adornment of rugs, drapes and ornaments mixed with Arabic music lend an authentic feel to this busy Moroccan restaurant. Helpful service. Popular basement bar.

The Cafe (at Sotheby's), 34-35 New Bond St, W1A 2AA, ✆ (020) 7293 5077 Ⓜ *Bond Street*, Fax (020) 7293 5920 – ⊭. MC AE ⓓ VISA 30 AIU y
closed 23 December-3 January, last 2 weeks August, Saturday, Sunday and Bank Holidays – **Meals** (booking essential) (lunch only) a la carte 19.95/30.50 ♀.
◆ A velvet rope separates this simple room from the main lobby of this famous auction house. Pleasant service from staff in aprons. Menu is short but well-chosen and light.

Veeraswamy, Victory House, 99 Regent St, W1B 4RS, entrance on Swallow St ✆ (020) 7734 1401 Ⓜ *Piccadilly Circus, info@realindianfood.com*, Fax (020) 7439 8434 – ▤. MC AE ⓓ VISA JCB 30 AIU t
Meals - Indian - 16.50 (lunch) and a la carte 23.00/36.25 ♀.
◆ The country's oldest Indian restaurant boasts a new look with vivid coloured walls and glass screens. The menu also combines the familiar with some modern twists.

Zinc Bar and Grill, 21 Heddon St, W1B 4BG, ✆ (020) 7255 8899 Ⓜ *Piccadilly Circus*, Fax (020) 7255 8888 – MC AE ⓓ VISA 30 AIU f
closed 24-26 December and Sunday – **Meals** a la carte 17.00/28.50 ♀.
◆ The eponymous bar takes up half the room and is a popular after-work meeting place. Parquet flooring and laminated tabletops. Offers a wide selection of modern cooking.

Regent's Park and Marylebone – ✉ *NW1/NW8/W1.*

Landmark London, 222 Marylebone Rd, NW1 6JQ, ✆ (020) 7631 8000 Ⓜ *Edgware Rd, reservations@thelandmark.co.uk*, Fax (020) 7631 8080, ⓦ, Fō, ≘s, ⛆ – |ǂ|, ⊭ rm, ▤ TV ✆ ♿ ⇔ – 🏛 350. MC AE ⓓ VISA JCB. ✂ 29 AFT a
Winter Garden : **Meals** 25.75 (lunch) and a la carte 28.85/47.40 ♀ – ☕ 22.00 – **290 rm** 387.75/417.10, 9 suites.
◆ Imposing Victorian Gothic building with a vast glass enclosed atrium, overlooked by many of the modern, well-equipped bedrooms. Winter Garden popular for afternoon tea.

Langham, 1c Portland Pl, Regent St, W1B 1JA, ✆ (020) 7636 1000 Ⓜ *Oxford Circus, langham@hilton.com*, Fax (020) 7323 2340, ⓦ, Fō, ≘s, ⛆ – |ǂ|, ⊭ rm, ▤ TV ✆ ♿ – 🏛 250. MC AE ⓓ VISA JCB. ✂ 30 AIT e
Memories : **Meals** 19.00/27.50 and a la carte 34.10/62.50 ♀ – ☕ 23.00 – **409 rm** 300.00, 20 suites.
◆ Opposite the BBC, with Colonial inspired décor. Polo themed bar and barrel vaulted Palm Court. Concierge Club rooms offer superior comfort and butler service. Memories is bright, elegant dining room.

Hyatt Regency London The Churchill, 30 Portman Sq, W1A 4ZX, (020) 7486 5800 *Marble Arch, london.churchill@hyattintl.com*, Fax (020) 7486 1255, – , rm, – 250. VISA JCB. 29 AGT x

Terrace on Portman Square **: Meals** a la carte 29.50/45.00 – 20.75 – **405 rm** 229.00, 40 suites.

◆ Modern property overlooking attractive square. Elegant marbled lobby.Cigar bar open until 2am for members. Well-appointed rooms have the international traveller in mind. Restaurant provides popular Sunday brunch entertainment.

Charlotte Street, 15 Charlotte St, W1T 1RJ, (020) 7806 2000 *Goodge Street, charlotte@firmdale.com*, Fax (020) 7806 2002, – , – 65. VISA. 31 AKT e

Meals (see ***Oscar*** below) – 18.50 – **44 rm** 229.10/334.90, 8 suites.

◆ Interior designed with a charming and understated English feel. Welcoming lobby laden with floral displays. Individually decorated rooms with CDs and mobile phones.

Sanderson, 50 Berners St, W1T 3NG, (020) 7300 1400 *Oxford Circus, sanderson@morganshotelgroup.com*, Fax (020) 7300 1401, , – , rm, . VISA. 31 AJT c

Spoon+ **: Meals** a la carte 38.00/58.00 – 20.00 – **150 rm** 370.00/393.60.

◆ Designed by Philipe Starck : the height of contemporary design. Bar is the place to see and be seen. Bedrooms with minimalistic white décor have DVDs and striking bathrooms. Stylish Spoon+ allows diners to construct own dishes.

The Leonard, 15 Seymour St, W1H 7JW, (020) 7935 2010 *Marble Arch, theleonard@dial.pipex.com*, Fax (020) 7935 6700, – . VISA JCB. 29 AGU n

Meals (room service only) – 18.50 – **24 rm** 200.00/258.50, **20 suites** 329.00/646.00.

◆ Around the corner from Selfridges, an attractive Georgian townhouse : antiques and oil paintings abound. Informal, stylish café bar offers light snacks. Well-appointed rooms.

Radisson SAS Portman, 22 Portman Sq, W1H 7BG, (020) 7208 6000 *Marble Arch, sales.london@radissonsas.com*, Fax (020) 7208 6001, , , – , rm, – 650. VISA. 29 AGT a

Talavera **: Meals** (buffet lunch)/dinner a la carte 28.50/36.00 – 15.00 – **265 rm** 150.00/185.00, 7 suites.

◆ This modern, corporate hotel offers check-in for both British Midland and SAS airlines. Rooms in attached towers decorated in Scandinavian, Chinese and Italian styles. Restaurant renowned for its elaborate buffet lunch.

Montcalm, Great Cumberland Pl, W1H 7TW, (020) 7402 4288 *Marble Arch, montcalm@montcalm.co.uk*, Fax (020) 7724 9180 – , rm, – 80. VISA JCB. 29 AGU d

Meals (see ***The Crescent*** below) – 17.95 – **110 rm** 270.25/293.75, 10 suites.

◆ Named after the 18C French general, the Marquis de Montcalm. In a charming crescent a short walk from Hyde Park. Spacious bedrooms with a subtle oriental feel.

London Marriott Marble Arch, 134 George St, W1H 5DN, (0870) 400 7255 *Marble Arch, salesadmin.marblearch@marriott.co.uk*, Fax (020) 7402 0666, , , – – 150. VISA JCB. 29 AFT j

Mediterrano **: Meals** (dinner only) a la carte 24.00/30.00 **s.** – 16.95 – **240 rm** 198.50/245.50.

◆ Centrally located and modern. Offers comprehensive conference facilities. Leisure centre underground. An ideal base for both corporate and leisure guests. Mediterranean-influenced cooking.

Berkshire, 350 Oxford St, W1N 0BY, (020) 7629 7474 *Bond Street, Fax (020) 7629 8156* – , rm, – 40. VISA JCB. 30 AHU n

Ascots **: Meals** *(closed lunch Friday-Sunday)* a la carte 25.00/45.00 – 15.00 – **146 rm** 231.50/297.25, 2 suites.

◆ Above the shops of Oxford St. Reception areas have a pleasant traditional charm. Comfortably appointed modern bedrooms have plenty of style. Personable staff. Stylish, relaxed dining room.

Durrants, 26-32 George St, W1H 5BJ, (020) 7935 8131 *Bond Street, enquiries@durrantshotel.co.uk*, Fax (020) 7487 3510 – , rest, – 55. VISA. 29 AGT e

Meals 17.50 (lunch) and a la carte 32.00/42.00 – 13.50 – **88 rm** 92.50/165.00, 4 suites.

◆ First opened in 1790 and family owned since 1921. Traditionally English feel with the charm of a bygone era. Cosy wood panelled bar. Attractive rooms vary somewhat in size. Semi-private booths in quintessentially British dining room.

Dorset Square, 39-40 Dorset Sq, NW1 6QN, (020) 7723 7874 Ⓜ *Marylebone, reservations@dorsetsquare.co.uk*, Fax (020) 7724 3328, – AE VISA.
closed 25-26 December – ***The Potting Shed :*** **Meals** *(closed Saturday lunch and Sunday dinner)* (booking essential) 19.50/24.50 and a la carte 32.00/36.00 – 14.00 – **37 rm** 164.50/296.10.
◆ Converted Regency townhouses in a charming square and the site of the original Lord's cricket ground. A relaxed country house in the city. Individually decorated rooms. The Potting Shed features modern cuisine and a set business menu.

Sherlock Holmes, 108 Baker St, W1U 6LJ, (020) 7486 6161 Ⓜ *Baker Street, info@sherlockholmeshotel.com*, Fax (020) 7958 5211, – – 45. AE VISA JCB 29 AGT c
Meals 16.50 (lunch) and a la carte 26.00/30.50 – 12.50 – **116 rm** 252.60/270.25, 3 suites.
◆ A stylish building with a relaxed contemporary feel. Comfortable guests' lounge with Holmes pictures on the walls. Bedrooms welcoming and smart, some with wood floors. Brasserie style dining.

Hart House without rest., 51 Gloucester Pl, W1U 8JF, (020) 7935 2288 Ⓜ *Marble Arch, reservations@harthouse.co.uk*, Fax (020) 7935 8516 – . AE VISA JCB. 29 AGT d
15 rm 75.00/105.00.
◆ Once home to French nobility escaping the 1789 Revolution. Now an attractive Georgian, mid-terraced private hotel. Warm and welcoming service. Well kept bedrooms.

St George without rest., 49 Gloucester Pl, W1U 8JE, (020) 7486 8586 Ⓜ *Marble Arch, reservations@stgeorge-hotel.net*, Fax (020) 7486 6567 – . AE VISA JCB. 29 AGT h
19 rm 95.00/135.00.
◆ Terraced house on a busy street, usefully located within walking distance of many attractions. Offers a warm welcome and comfortable bedrooms which are spotlessly maintained.

Orrery, 55 Marylebone High St, W1M 3AE, (020) 7616 8000 Ⓜ *Regent's Park, Fax (020) 7616 8080* – . AE VISA JCB
closed 25 December and 1-2 January – **Meals** (booking essential) 23.50/55.00 and a la carte 42.00/56.50 .
Spec. Pan-fried foie gras, beetroot, pain d'épices. Baked salmon, sorrel, fennel and hollandaise. Roast saddle of lamb, aubergine, capers and braised shank.
◆ Contemporary elegance : a smoothly run 1st floor restaurant in converted 19C stables, with a Conran shop below. Accomplished modern British cooking.

Locanda Locatelli, 8 Seymour St, W1H 7JZ, (020) 7935 9088 Ⓜ *Marble Arch, info@locandalocatelli.com*, Fax (020) 7935 1149 – . AE VISA 29AGU r
closed Sunday and Bank Holidays – **Meals** - Italian - a la carte 25.00/45.00 .
Spec. Roast rabbit wrapped in Parma ham with polenta. Scallops with saffron vinaigrette. Tasting of Amedei chocolate.
◆ Very stylishly appointed restaurant with banquettes and cherry wood or glass dividers which contribute to an intimate and relaxing ambience. Accomplished Italian cooking.

Deya, 34 Portman Sq, W1H 7BY, (020) 7224 0028 Ⓜ *Marble Arch, reservation@deya-restaurant.co.uk*, Fax (020) 7224 0411 – . AE VISA JCB 29AGU z
closed 25 December, Sunday and Saturday lunch – **Meals** - Indian - 18.00/29.00 and a la carte 20.00/27.75 .
◆ Has its own pillared entrance, though part of Mostyn hotel. Grand 18C Grade II listed room with ornate ceiling. Modern, stylish makeover. Interesting, original Indian menus.

The Crescent (at Montcalm H.), Great Cumberland Pl, W1H 7TW, (020) 7402 4288 Ⓜ *Marble Arch, reservations@montcalm.co.uk*, Fax (020) 7724 9180 – . AE VISA JCB 29AGU d
closed lunch Saturday, Sunday and Bank Holidays – **Meals** 25.00/27.50 .
◆ Discreetly appointed room favoured by local residents. Best tables overlook a pretty square. Frequently changing fixed price modern menu includes half bottle of house wine.

Six13, 19 Wigmore St, W1H 9UA, (020) 7629 6133 Ⓜ *Bond Street, enquiries@six13.com*, Fax (020) 7629 6135 – . AE VISA 30 AHT n
closed Jewish holidays and Friday-Sunday – **Meals** - Kosher - 24.50 (lunch) and a la carte 26.25/37.25 .
◆ Stylish and immaculate with banquette seating. Strictly kosher menu supervised by the Shama offering interesting cooking with a modern slant.

Oscar (at Charlotte Street H.), 15 Charlotte St, W1T 1RJ, (020) 7907 4005 Ⓜ *Goodge Street, charlotte@firmdale.com*, Fax (020) 7806 2002 – . AE VISA 31 AKT e
closed Sunday lunch – **Meals** (booking essential) a la carte 31.50/42.50 .
◆ Adjacent to hotel lobby and dominated by a large, vivid mural of contemporary London life. Sophisticated dishes served by attentive staff : oysters, wasabi and soya dressing.

XX **The Providores,** 109 Marylebone High St, W1U 4RX, ✆ (020) 7935 6175 Ⓜ *Bond Street, anyone@theprovidores.co.uk,* Fax (020) 7935 6877 – ⇜ ▤. MC AE VISA JCB 30 AHT s
closed 25-26 December, 1 January and Easter – **Meals** a la carte 21.40/36.20 ♀.
• Swish, stylish restaurant on first floor ; unusual dishes with New World base and fusion of Asian, Mediterranean influences. Tapas and light meals in downstairs Tapa Room.

XX **La Porte des Indes,** 32 Bryanston St, W1H 7EG, ✆ (020) 7224 0055 Ⓜ *Marble Arch, london@laportedesindes.com,* Fax (020) 7224 1144 – ▤. MC AE ⓓ VISA JCB 29 AGU s
closed 24-26 December and Saturday lunch – **Meals** - Indian - 34.00/52.00 and a la carte 21.70/47.50 ♀.
• Don't be fooled by the discreet entrance : inside there is a spectacularly unrestrained display of palm trees, murals and waterfalls. French influenced Indian cuisine.

XX **Rosmarino,** 1 Blenheim Terrace, NW8 0EH, ✆ (020) 7328 5014 Ⓜ *St John's Wood, Fax (020) 7625 2639,* 斋 – ▤. MC AE ⓓ VISA
closed 25 December and 1 January – **Meals** - Italian - 24.50/27.50 ♀.
• Modern, understated and relaxed. Friendly and approachable service of robust and rustic Italian dishes. Set priced menu is carefully balanced.

XX **Ozer,** 4-5 Langham Pl, Regent St, W1B 3DG, ✆ (020) 7323 0505 Ⓜ *Oxford Circus, Fax (020) 7323 0111* – ▤. MC AE VISA JCB 30 AIT z
Meals - Turkish - 18.00 (lunch) and a la carte 15.35/23.60 ☺ ♀.
• Behind the busy and vibrantly decorated bar you'll find a smart modern restaurant. Lively atmosphere and efficient service of modern, light and aromatic Turkish cooking.

XX **Roka,** 37 Charlotte St, W1T 1RR, ✆ (020) 7580 6464 Ⓜ *Tottenham Court Road* – ⇜ ▤. MC AE ⓓ VISA 31 AJT k
closed 24-26 December and Sunday lunch – **Meals** - Japanese - a la carte 35.00/70.00 ♀.
• Striking glass and steel frontage. Airy, atmospheric interior of teak, oak and paper wall screens. Authentic, flavoursome Japanese cuisine with variety of grill dishes.

XX **Rasa Samudra,** 5 Charlotte St, W1T 1RE, ✆ (020) 7637 0222 Ⓜ *Goodge Street, Fax (020) 7637 0224* – ⇜. MC AE VISA JCB 31 AKT r
closed 24-29 December, 1 January and Sunday lunch – **Meals** - Indian Seafood and Vegetarian - 22.50/30.00 and a la carte 13.25/23.45.
• Comfortably appointed, richly decorated and modern Indian restaurant. Authentic Keralan (south Indian) cooking with seafood and vegetarian specialities.

XX **Levant,** Jason Court, 76 Wigmore St, W1U 2SJ, ✆ (020) 7224 1111 Ⓜ *Bond Street, Fax (020) 7486 1216* – ▤. MC AE ⓓ VISA JCB 30 AHT c
Meals - Lebanese - 8.50/39.50 and a la carte ♀.
• The somewhat unpromising entrance leads down to a vibrantly decorated basement. Modern Lebanese cooking featuring subtly spiced dishes.

XX **Latium,** 21 Berners St, Fitzrovia, W1T 3LP, ✆ (020) 7323 9123 Ⓜ *Oxford Circus, info@latiumrestaurant.com,* Fax (020) 7323 3205 – ▤. MC AE VISA 31 AJT n
closed 25 December, Saturday lunch, Sunday and Bank Holidays – **Meals** - Italian - 25.50 ♀.
• Latium, the Latin for Lazio, reflects the patrons' interest in football. The minimalist décor is enlivened by colourful artwork. Italian country cookery ; daily specials.

XX **Caldesi,** 15-17 Marylebone Lane, W1U 2NE, ✆ (020) 7935 9226 Ⓜ *Bond Street, Fax (020) 7935 9228* – ▤. MC AE ⓓ VISA 30 AHT e
closed 25 December, Saturday lunch and Sunday – **Meals** - Italian - a la carte approx 30.50.
• A traditional Italian restaurant that continues to attract a loyal clientele. Robust and authentic dishes with Tuscan specialities. Attentive service by established team.

XX **Bertorelli,** 19-23 Charlotte St, W1T 1RL, ✆ (020) 7636 4174 Ⓜ *Goodge Street, bertorellisc@groupechezgerard.co.uk,* Fax (020) 7467 8902 – ▤. MC AE VISA 31 AJT v
closed 25 December, 1 January, Sunday and Bank Holidays – **Meals** - Italian - 18.50 (lunch) and a la carte 19.20/28.75 ☺ ♀.
• Above the informal and busy bar/café. Bright and airy room with vibrant décor and informal atmosphere. Extensive menu combines traditional and new wave Italian dishes.

XX **Blandford Street,** 5-7 Blandford St, W1U 3DB, ✆ (020) 7486 9696 Ⓜ *Bond Street, info@blandford-street.co.uk,* Fax (020) 7486 5067 – ▤. MC AE ⓓ VISA 30 AHT v
closed Christmas, Easter, Monday lunch and Bank Holidays – **Meals** 18.50 (lunch) and a la carte 24.00/34.00 ☺ ♀.
• Understated interior with plain walls hung with modern pictures and subtle spot-lighting. Contemporary menu with a notably European character.

L'Aventure, 3 Blenheim Terr, NW8 0EH, (020) 7624 6232 *St John's Wood, Fax (020) 7625 5548,* – *VISA*
closed first 2 weeks January, Easter, Sunday and Saturday lunch – **Meals** - French - 18.50/32.50.
◆ Behind the pretty tree lined entrance you'll find a charming neighbourhood restaurant. Relaxed atmosphere and service by personable owner. Authentic French cuisine.

Villandry, 170 Great Portland St, W1W 5QB, (020) 7631 3131 *Regent's Park, bookatable@villandry.com,* Fax (020) 7631 3030 – *VISA* JCB 30 AIT s
closed 25 December-3 January and Bank Holidays – **Meals** a la carte 22.00/35.75 ♀.
◆ The senses are heightened by passing through the well-stocked deli to the dining room behind. Bare walls, wooden tables and a menu offering simple, tasty dishes.

Union Café, 96 Marylebone Lane, W1U 2QA, (020) 7486 4860 *Bond Street, unioncafe@brinkleys.com,* Fax (020) 7486 4860 – *VISA* 30 AHT d
closed 2 weeks Christmas, Sunday and Bank Holidays – **Meals** a la carte 25.00/30.00 ♀.
◆ No standing on ceremony at this bright, relaxed restaurant. The open kitchen at one end produces modern Mediterranean cuisine. Ideal for visitors to the Wallace Collection.

Momo (at Selfridges), 400 Oxford St (2nd floor), W1A 1AB, (020) 7318 3620 *Bond Street, Fax (020) 7318 3228* – *VISA* JCB 29AGU k
closed 25 December and Easter Day – **Meals** - Moroccan - (lunch only) 20.00 and a la carte 15.00/29.00 ♀.
◆ Unique open-plan restaurant boasting Moroccan rugs, authentic furskin chairs and tasty North African dishes. There's also a tea room for Arabic snacks and a tent for drinks.

Caffè Caldesi, 1st Floor, 118 Marylebone Lane, W1U 2QF, (020) 7935 1144 *Bond Street, people@caldesi.com,* Fax (020) 7935 8832 – *VISA* 30 AHT s
closed 25 December and Sunday dinner – **Meals** - Italian - a la carte approx 29.50 ♀.
◆ Converted pub with a simple modern interior in which to enjoy tasty, uncomplicated Italian dishes. Downstairs is a lively bar with a deli counter serving pizzas and pastas.

Chada Chada, 16-17 Picton Pl, W1M 5DE, (020) 7935 8212 *Bond Street, enquiry@chadathai.com,* Fax (020) 7924 2178 – *VISA* JCB 30AHU b
closed Sunday and Bank Holidays – **Meals** - Thai - a la carte 17.35/35.15 ♀.
◆ Authentic and fragrant Thai cooking ; the good value menu offers some interesting departures from the norm. Service is eager to please in the compact and cosy rooms.

No.6, 6 George St, W1U 3QX, (020) 7935 1910 *Bond Street, Fax (020) 7935 6036* – *VISA* 30 AHT a
closed 2 weeks August, 2 weeks Christmas, Saturday and Sunday – **Meals** (lunch only) a la carte 25.40/30.95.
◆ To the front is a charming delicatessen offering fresh produce and behind is a simple, well-kept dining room. Daily changing menu with good use of fresh ingredients.

The Abbey Road, 63 Abbey Rd, NW8 0AE, (020) 7328 6626 *St John's Wood, abbey.road@btconnect.com,* Fax (020) 7625 9168, – *VISA*
closed 31 December – **Meals** *(closed Monday lunch)* 25.00 (dinner) and a la carte 17.00/30.00 ♀.
◆ Grand Victorian pub appearance in bottle green. Busy bar at the front ; main dining room, in calm duck egg blue, to the rear. Modern menus boast a distinct Mediterranean style.

St James's – *W1/SW1.*

Ritz, 150 Piccadilly, W1J 9BR, (020) 7493 8181 *Green Park, enquire@theritzlondon.com,* Fax (020) 7493 2687, – rm, – 50. *VISA* JCB. 30 AIV c
Meals (see ***The Restaurant*** below) – 28.00 – **116 rm** 352.50/505.25, 17 suites.
◆ Opened 1906, a fine example of Louis XVI architecture and decoration. Elegant Palm Court famed for afternoon tea. Many of the lavishly appointed rooms overlook the park.

Sofitel St James London, 6 Waterloo Pl, SW1Y 4AN, (020) 7747 2200 *Piccadilly Circus, h3144@accor-hotels.com,* Fax (020) 7747 2210, – rm, – 180. *VISA* 31 AKV a
Meals (see ***Brasserie Roux*** below) – 19.50 – **179 rm** 376.00/423.00, 7 suites.
◆ Grade II listed building in smart Pall Mall location. Classically English interiors include floral Rose Lounge and club-style St. James bar. Comfortable, well-fitted bedrooms.

Stafford , 16-18 St James's Pl, SW1A 1NJ, (020) 7493 0111 *Green Park, info@thestaffordhotel.co.uk,* Fax (020) 7493 7121 – – 40. *VISA* JCB. 30 AIV u
Meals *(closed lunch Saturday and Bank Holidays)* 25.50 (lunch) and dinner a la carte 49.50/58.50 **s.** ♀ – 16.50 – **75 rm** 252.60/323.10, 6 suites.
◆ A genteel atmosphere prevails in this elegant and discreet country house in the city. Do not miss the famed American bar. Well-appointed rooms created from 18C stables. Refined, elegant, intimate dining room.

Dukes, 35 St James's Pl, SW1A 1NY, (020) 7491 4840 Ⓜ *Green Park, bookings @dukeshotel.com*, Fax (020) 7493 1264, – |‡|, rest, – 50. MO AE VISA JCB. 30 AIV f
Meals a la carte 29.50/43.00 – 18.50 – **82 rm** 232.65/329.00, 7 suites.
◆ Privately owned, discreet and quiet hotel. Traditional bar, famous for its martini's and Cognac collection. Well-kept spacious rooms in a country house style.

Trafalgar Hilton, 2 Spring Gdns, SW1A 2TS, (020) 7870 2900 Ⓜ *Charing Cross, lontshirm@hilton.com*, Fax (020) 7870 2911 – |‡|, rm, – 50. MO AE VISA JCB. 31 AKV b
Jago **: Meals** *(closed Saturday lunch and Sunday)* a la carte 35.00/50.00 – 20.50 – **127 rm** 304.30, 2 suites.
◆ Enjoys a commanding position on the square of which the deluxe rooms, some split-level, have views. Bedrooms are in pastel shades with leather armchairs or stools ; mod cons. Low-lit restaurant with open-plan kitchen.

De Vere Cavendish, 81 Jermyn St, SW1Y 6JF, (020) 7930 2111 Ⓜ *Piccadilly Circus, cavendish.reservations@devere-hotels.com*, Fax (020) 7839 2125 – |‡|, rm, – 100. MO AE VISA. 30 AIV v
Meals *(closed lunch Saturday and Sunday)* a la carte 16.50/28.00 **s.** – 17.95 – **227 rm** 276.10/287.90, 3 suites.
◆ Modern hotel in heart of Piccadilly. Contemporary, minimalist style of rooms with moody prints of London ; top five floors offer far-reaching views over and beyond the city. Classic styled restaurant overlooks Jermyn Street.

22 Jermyn Street, 22 Jermyn St, SW1Y 6HL, (020) 7734 2353 Ⓜ *Piccadilly Circus, office@22jermyn.com*, Fax (020) 7734 0750 – |‡| MO AE VISA JCB. 31 AKV e
Meals (room service only) – 12.65 – **5 rm** 246.75, **13 suites** 346.60/393.60.
◆ Discreet entrance amid famous shirt-makers' shops leads to this exclusive boutique hotel. Stylishly decorated bedrooms more than compensate for the lack of lounge space.

The Restaurant (at Ritz H.), 150 Piccadilly, W1V 9DG, (020) 7493 8181 Ⓜ *Green Park, Fax (020) 7493 2687*, – . MO AE VISA JCB 30 AIV c
Meals (dancing Friday and Saturday evenings) 39.00/60.00 and a la carte 57.50/88.00 **s.**
◆ The height of opulence : magnificent Louis XVI décor with trompe l'oeil and ornate gilding. Delightful terrace over Green Park. Refined service, classic and modern menu.

The Wolseley, 160 Piccadilly, W1J 9EB, (020) 7499 6996 Ⓜ *Green Park, Fax (020) 7499 6888* – . MO AE VISA 30 AIV q
closed dinner 24 December, 25 December and 1 January – **Meals** (booking essential) a la carte 26.75/54.75
◆ Has the feel of a grand European coffee house : pillars, high vaulted ceiling, mezzanine tables. Menus range from caviar to a hot dog. Also open for breakfasts and tea.

Osia, 11 Haymarket, SW1Y 4BP, (020) 7976 1313 Ⓜ *Piccadilly Circus, Fax (020) 7976 1919* – . MO AE VISA 31 AKV n
closed 1 week Christmas, Saturday lunch and Sunday – **Meals** 23.00 (lunch) and a la carte 34.00/40.00
◆ Converted bank with high ornate ceilings ; dining hall separated by wine display case from long bar in leather boothed lounge. Interesting menus of Asian and Australian dishes.

Quaglino's, 16 Bury St, SW1Y 6AL, (020) 7930 6767 Ⓜ *Green Park, Fax (020) 7839 2866* – . MO AE VISA 30 AIV j
closed 25-26 December – **Meals** (booking essential) 19.00 (lunch) and a la carte 26.50/40.50
◆ Descend the sweeping staircase into the capacious room where a busy and buzzy atmosphere prevails. Watch the chefs prepare everything from osso bucco to fish and chips.

Mint Leaf, Suffolk Pl, SW1Y 4HX, (020) 7930 9020 Ⓜ *Piccadilly Circus, reservations@mintleafrestaurant.com*, Fax (020) 7930 6205 – . MO AE VISA 31 AKV k
closed Sunday and Bank Holidays – **Meals** - Indian - a la carte 25.00/40.00
◆ Basement restaurant in theatreland. Cavernous dining room incorporating busy, trendy bar with unique cocktail list and loud music. Helpful service. Contemporary Indian dishes.

Criterion Grill Marco Pierre White, 224 Piccadilly, W1J 9HP, (020) 7930 0488 Ⓜ *Piccadilly Circus, sales@whitestarline.org.uk*, Fax (020) 7930 8380 – . MO AE VISA 31 AKU c
closed 25 December, 1 January and Sunday – **Meals** 17.95 (lunch) and a la carte 29.25/48.25
◆ A stunning modern brasserie behind the revolving doors. Ornate gilding, columns and mirrors aplenty. Bustling, characterful atmosphere, Pre and post-theatre menus.

Brasserie Roux, 8 Pall Mall, SW1Y 5NG, ☎ (020) 7968 2900 Ⓜ *Piccadilly Circus, h3144-fb4@accor-hotels.com,* Fax (020) 7747 2242 – ▤. MC AE ⓓ VISA 31 AKV a
Meals - French - a la carte 19.00/42.50 ♀.
◆ Informal, smart, classic brasserie style with large windows making the most of the location. Large menu of French classics with many daily specials ; comprehensive wine list.

Le Caprice, Arlington House, Arlington St, SW1A 1RT, ☎ (020) 7629 2239 Ⓜ *Green Park,* Fax (020) 7493 9040 – ▤. MC AE ⓓ VISA 30 AIV h
closed 25-26 December, 1 January and August Bank Holiday – **Meals** (Sunday brunch) a la carte 23.00/47.50 ♀.
◆ Still attracting a fashionable clientele and as busy as ever. Dine at the bar or in the smoothly run restaurant. Food combines timeless classics with modern dishes.

Shumi, 23 St James's St, SW1A 1HA, ☎ (020) 7747 9380 Ⓜ *Green Park, info@shumilondon.com,* Fax (020) 7747 9389 – |‡| ▤. MC AE ⓓ VISA JCB 30 AIV k
closed Sunday and Bank Holidays – **Meals** - Italian - 23.50 (lunch) and a la carte 25.50/36.00 ♀.
◆ Listed 1960s building : get the lift up to the main restaurant and dine with the fashionable set on tasty, modern Italian dishes ; renowned for delicate presentation.

The Avenue, 7-9 St James's St, SW1A 1EE, ☎ (020) 7321 2111 Ⓜ *Green Park, avenue@egami.co.uk,* Fax (020) 7321 2500 – ▤. MC AE ⓓ VISA 30 AIV y
closed 25-26 December and 1 January – **Meals** 19.95 and dinner a la carte 25.50/46.00 ♀.
◆ The attractive and stylish bar is a local favourite. Behind is a striking, modern and busy restaurant. Appealing and contemporary food. Pre-theatre menu available.

Matsuri - St James's, 15 Bury St, SW1Y 6AL, ☎ (020) 7839 1101 Ⓜ *Green Park, dine@matsuri-restaurant.com,* Fax (020) 7930 7010 – ▤. MC AE ⓓ VISA JCB 30 AIV w
Meals - Japanese (Teppan-Yaki, Sushi) - 15.00/35.00 and a la carte 19.00/28.50 ♀.
◆ Specialising in theatrical and precise teppan-yaki cooking. Separate restaurant offers sushi delicacies. Charming service by traditionally dressed staff.

Al Duca, 4-5 Duke of York St, SW1Y 6LA, ☎ (020) 7839 3090 Ⓜ *Piccadilly Circus, info@alduca-restaurants.co.uk,* Fax (020) 7839 4050 – ▤. MC AE ⓓ VISA JCB
closed 25-26 December, Sunday and Bank Holidays – **Meals** - Italian - 20.50/24.00 ♀.
◆ Relaxed, modern, stylish restaurant. Friendly and approachable service of robust and rustic Italian dishes. Set priced menu is good value. 31 AJV r

Inn the Park, St James's Park, SW1A 2BJ, ☎ (020) 7451 9999 Ⓜ *Charing Cross, info@innthepark.co.uk,* Fax (020) 7451 9998, ←, 🏡 – MC AE VISA 31 AKV n
closed 25 December – **Meals** a la carte 22.50/39.50 ♀.
◆ Eco-friendly restaurant with grass covered roof ; pleasant views across park and lakes. Super-heated dining terrace. Modern British menus of tasty, wholesome dishes.

Soho – ✉ *W1/WC2.*

Hampshire, Leicester Sq, WC2H 7LH, ☎ (020) 7839 9399 Ⓜ *Leicester Square,* Fax (020) 7930 8122, 🏡, F₆ – |‡|, ⇔ rm, ▤ TV ☏ – 🎪 100. MC AE ⓓ VISA JCB. ✂
***The Apex* : Meals** *(closed lunch Friday-Sunday)* a la carte 25.00/45.00 – ☕ 16.00 – **119 rm** 309.00/405.40, 5 suites. 31 AKU s
◆ The bright lights of the city are literally outside and many rooms overlook the bustling Square. Inside, it is tranquil and comfortable, with well-appointed bedrooms.

The Soho, 4 Richmond Mews, W1D 3DH, ☎ (020) 7559 3000 Ⓜ *Tottenham Court Road, soho@firmdale.com,* Fax (020) 7559 3003, F₆ – |‡| ▤ TV ☏ ♿ – 🎪 100. MC AE VISA
***Refuel* : Meals** a la carte 31.00/40.50 – **88 rm** 276.00/440.50, 4 suites. 31 AKU n
◆ Opened in autumn 2004 : stylish hotel with two screening rooms, comfy drawing room, and up-to-the-minute bedrooms, some vivid, others more muted, all boasting hi-tec extras. Contemporary bar and restaurant.

Hazlitt's without rest., 6 Frith St, W1D 3JA, ☎ (020) 7434 1771 Ⓜ *Tottenham Court Road, reservations@hazlitts.co.uk,* Fax (020) 7439 1524 – TV ☏. MC AE ⓓ VISA JCB
22 rm 205.60/240.80, 1 suite. 31 AKU u
◆ A row of three adjoining early 18c town houses and former home of the eponymous essayist. Individual and charming bedrooms, many with antique furniture and Victorian baths.

L'Escargot, 48 Greek St, W1D 5EF, ☎ (020) 7437 2679 Ⓜ *Tottenham Court Road, sales@whitestarline.org.uk,* Fax (020) 7437 0790 – ▤. MC AE ⓓ VISA JCB 31 AKU b
***Ground Floor* : Meals** *(closed 25-26 December, 1 January, Sunday, lunch Saturday and Bank Holidays)* 17.95 (lunch) and a la carte approx 26.00 ♀ – ***Picasso Room* : Meals** *(closed 2 weeks Christmas-New Year, August, Sunday, Monday and Saturday lunch)* 21.00/42.00.
Spec. Salad of caramelised sweetbread, truffle vinaigrette. Squab pigeon "en vessie" with ravioli of wild mushroom, thyme jus. Milk chocolate soufflé.
◆ Ground Floor is chic, vibrant brasserie with early-evening buzz of theatre-goers. Finely judged modern dishes. Intimate and more formal upstairs Picasso Room famed for its limited edition art.

XXX **Quo Vadis,** 26-29 Dean St, W1D 3LL, ✆ (020) 7437 9585 Ⓜ *Tottenham Court Road, whitestarline@org.uk*, Fax (020) 7734 7593 – ▤. MC AE Ⓓ VISA JCB 31 AKU v
closed 25 December, Sunday and lunch Saturday and Bank Holidays – **Meals** - Italian - 30.00/60.00 and a la carte 29.45/36.00 ♀.
◆ Stained glass windows and a neon sign hint at the smooth modernity of the interior. Modern artwork abounds. Contemporary cooking and a serious wine list.

XXX **Red Fort,** 77 Dean St, W1D 3SH, ✆ (020) 7437 2525 Ⓜ *Tottenham Court Road, info@redfort.co.uk*, Fax (020) 7434 0721 – ▤. MC AE VISA 31 AKU x
closed Saturday lunch and Sunday – **Meals** - Indian - 12.00 (lunch) and a la carte 30.50/42.00 ♀.
◆ Smart, stylish restaurant with modern water feature and glass ceiling to rear. Seasonally changing menus of authentic dishes handed down over generations.

XX ✿ **Richard Corrigan at Lindsay House,** 21 Romilly St, W1D 5AF, ✆ (020) 7439 0450 Ⓜ *Leicester Square, richardcorrigan@lindsayhouse.co.uk*, Fax (020) 7437 7349 – ▤. MC AE Ⓓ VISA JCB 31 AKU f
closed 1 week Christmas, first week September, Sunday and Saturday lunch – **Meals** 25.00/48.00 ♀.
Spec. Deep-fried crubeens and Jabugo ham. Rack of lamb, confit of garlic and moussaka. Cherries with Banyuls, bitter chocolate and buttermilk sorbet.
◆ One rings the doorbell before being welcomed into this handsome 18C town house, retaining many original features. Skilled and individual cooking with a subtle Irish hint.

XX **Café Lazeez,** 21 Dean St, W1V 5AH, ✆ (020) 7434 9393 Ⓜ *Tottenham Court Road, soho@cafelazeez.com*, Fax (020) 7434 0022 – ▤. MC AE Ⓓ VISA JCB 31 AKU d
closed 24-26 December and 1 January – **Meals** - North Indian - a la carte 20.40/26.85 ♀.
◆ In the same building as Soho Theatre ; the bar hums before shows, restaurant is popular for pre- and post-theatre meals of modern Indian fare. Refined décor ; private booths.

X ✿ **Yauatcha,** 15 Broadwick St, W1F 0DL, ✆ (020) 7494 8888 Ⓜ *Tottenham Court Road, mail@yauatcha.com* – ⚟ ▤. MC AE VISA 31 AJU k
closed 25 December – **Meals** - Chinese (Dim Sum) - a la carte 25.00/30.00.
Spec. Salt and pepper quail. Baked venison puff. Prawn cheung fun.
◆ Converted 1960s post office in heart of Soho. Below smart, cool tea room is spacious restaurant serving Chinese cuisine that's original, refined, authentic and flavoursome.

X **Bertorelli,** 11-13 Frith St, W1D 4RB, ✆ (020) 7494 3491 Ⓜ *Tottenham Court Road, bertorelli-soho@groupechezgerard.co.uk*, Fax (020) 7439 9431, 🏠 – ▤. MC AE VISA
closed 25 and 31 December and 1 January – **Meals** - Italian - 18.50 (lunch) and a la carte 15.85/30.00 ♀. 31 AKU t
◆ A haven of tranquilllity from the bustling street below. Discreet and professionally run first floor restaurant with Italian menu. Popular ground floor café.

X **La Trouvaille,** 12A Newburgh St, W1F 7RR, ✆ (020) 7287 8488 Ⓜ *Piccadilly Circus, Fax (020) 7434 4170*, 🏠 – MC AE Ⓓ VISA 30 AIU g
closed 25-26 December, Sunday dinner and Bank Holidays – **Meals** - French - 19.75/29.50 and a la carte 22.70/26.55.
◆ Atmospheric restaurant located just off Carnaby Street. Hearty, robust French cooking with a rustic character. French wine list with the emphasis on southern regions.

X **Alastair Little,** 49 Frith St, W1D 5SG, ✆ (020) 7734 5183 Ⓜ *Tottenham Court Road, Fax (020) 7734 5206* – ▤. MC AE Ⓓ VISA JCB 31 AKU y
closed 24-26 December, 1 January, Sunday, Saturday lunch and Bank Holidays – **Meals** (booking essential) 29.00/38.00.
◆ The eponymous owner was at the vanguard of Soho's culinary renaissance. Tasty, daily changing British based cuisine ; the compact room is rustic and simple.

X **Vasco and Piero's Pavilion,** 15 Poland St, W1F 8QE, ✆ (020) 7437 8774 Ⓜ *Tottenham Court Road, vascosfood@hotmail.com*, Fax (020) 7437 0467 – ▤. MC AE Ⓓ VISA 31 AJU b
closed Sunday, Saturday lunch and Bank Holidays – **Meals** - Italian - (lunch booking essential) 21.00/25.00 and lunch a la carte 25.00/32.50.
◆ A long standing, family run Italian restaurant with a loyal local following. Pleasant service under the owners' guidance. Warm décor and traditional cooking.

X **itsu,** 103 Wardour St, W1F 0UQ, ✆ (020) 7479 4790 Ⓜ *Piccadilly Circus, angela@itsu.co.uk*, Fax (020) 7479 4795 – ⚟ ▤. MC AE VISA 31 AKU m
closed 25 December – **Meals** - Japanese - (bookings not accepted) a la carte 15.00/25.00.
◆ Japanese dishes of Sushi, Sashimi, handrolls and miso soup turn on a conveyor belt in a pleasingly hypnotic fashion. Hot bowls of chicken and coconut soup also appear.

X **Aurora,** 49 Lexington St, W1F 9AP, ✆ (020) 7494 0514 Ⓜ *Piccadilly Circus*, 🏠 – MC VISA 31 AJU e
Meals (booking essential) a la carte 19.45/24.90.
◆ An informal, no-nonsense, bohemian style bistro with a small, but pretty, walled garden terrace. Short but balanced menu ; simple fresh food. Pleasant, languid atmosphere.

Fung Shing, 15 Lisle St, WC2H 7BE, (020) 7437 1539 *Leicester Square, Fax (020) 7734 0284* – . 31 AKU j
closed 24-26 December and lunch Bank Holidays – **Meals** - Chinese (Canton) - 17.00/30.00 and a la carte 17.50/27.05.
◆ A long-standing Chinese restaurant on the edge of Chinatown. Chatty and pleasant service. A mix of authentic, rustic dishes and the more adventurous chef's specials.

Strand and Covent Garden – WC2.

Savoy, Strand, WC2R 0EU, (020) 7836 4343 *Charing Cross, info@the-savoy.co.uk,* Fax (020) 7240 6040, , , – , rm, – 500. 31 ALU a
Banquette* : Meals** a la carte 30.50/56.50 (see also ***The Savoy Grill below) – 24.50 – **236 rm** 352.50/458.25, 27 suites.
◆ Famous the world over, since 1889, as the epitome of English elegance and style. Celebrated for its Art Deco features and luxurious bedrooms. Banquette is bright, airy, upmarket American diner.

Swissôtel The Howard, Temple Pl, WC2R 2PR, (020) 7836 3555 *Temple, reservations.london@swissotel.com,* Fax (020) 7379 4547, , – , rm, – 150. 32AMU e
Meals (see ***Jaan*** below) – 23.50 – **148 rm** 346.60/499.30, 41 suites.
◆ Cool elegance is the order of the day at this handsomely appointed hotel. Many of the comfortable rooms enjoy balcony views of the Thames. Attentive service.

The Waldorf Hilton, Aldwych, WC2B 4DD, (020) 7836 2400 *Covent Garden, waldorflondon@hilton.com,* Fax (020) 7836 7244, , , – , rm, – 400. 32AMU u
***Homage* : Meals** a la carte 20.00/44.00 – 19.50 – **290 rm** 327.80, 10 suites.
◆ Impressive curved and columned façade : an Edwardian landmark. Basement leisure club. Ornate meeting rooms. Two bedroom styles : one contemporary, one more traditional. Large, modish brasserie with extensive range of modern menus.

One Aldwych, 1 Aldwych, WC2B 4RH, (020) 7300 1000 *Covent Garden, reservations@onealdwych.com,* Fax (020) 7300 1001, , , – , rm, – 50. 32AMU r
Indigo* : Meals** a la carte 25.95/40.95 (see also ***Axis below) – 19.75 – **96 rm** 370.00/476.00, 9 suites.
◆ Decorative Edwardian building, former home to the Morning Post newspaper. Now a stylish and contemporary address with modern artwork, a screening room and hi-tech bedrooms. All-day restaurant looks down on fashionable bar.

St Martins Lane, 45 St Martin's Lane, WC2N 4HX, (020) 7300 5500 *Trafalgar Square, sml@ianschragerhotels.com,* Fax (020) 7300 5501, , – , rm, – 40. 31 ALU e
***Asia de Cuba* : Meals** - Asian - a la carte 25.00/50.00 – 20.00 – **200 rm** 311.30/334.80, 4 suites.
◆ The unmistakable hand of Philippe Starck evident at this most contemporary of hotels. Unique and stylish, from the starkly modern lobby to the state-of-the-art rooms. 350 varieties of rum at fashionable Asia de Cuba.

Thistle Charing Cross, Strand, WC2N 5HX, (0870) 3339105 *Charing Cross, charingcross@thistle.co.uk,* Fax (0870) 3339205 – , rm, – 150. 31 ALV c
***The Strand Terrace* : Meals** 19.95 and a la carte 26.40/31.90 – 16.50 – **239 rm** 311.40/390.00.
◆ Classic Victorian hotel built above the station. In keeping with its origins, rooms in the Buckingham wing are traditionally styled whilst others have contemporary décor. Watch the world go by from restaurant's pleasant vantage point.

The Savoy Grill (at Savoy H.), Strand, WC2R 0EU, (020) 7592 1600 *Charing Cross, savoygrill@marcuswareing.com,* Fax (020) 7592 1601 – . 31 ALU a
Meals 30.00/65.00.
Spec. Baked Pithiviers of forest mushrooms and foie gras. Châteaubriand with glazed turnips and shallots, Madeira truffle sauce. Pineapple with vanilla and rum, mascarpone, passion fruit ice cream.
◆ Redesigned in 2003 to conserve its best traditions, the Grill buzzes at midday and in the evening. Formal service ; menu of modern European dishes and the Savoy classics.

Ivy, 1 West St, WC2H 9NQ, (020) 7836 4751 *Leicester Square, Fax (020) 7240 9333* – . 31 AKU p
closed 25-26 December, 1 January and August Bank Holiday – **Meals** a la carte 23.75/50.75.
◆ Wood panelling and stained glass combine with an unpretentious menu to create a veritable institution. A favourite of 'celebrities', so securing a table can be challenging.

XXX **Axis,** 1 Aldwych, WC2B 4RH, ☎ (020) 7300 0300 Ⓜ *Covent Garden, sales@onealdwych.co.uk*, Fax (020) 7300 0301 – ▤. MC AE ① VISA JCB 31AMU r
closed Saturday lunch and Sunday – **Meals** (live jazz at dinner Tuesday and Wednesday) 19.95 (lunch) and a la carte 27.75/37.40 ♀.
◆ Lower-level room overlooked by gallery bar. Muted tones, black leather chairs and vast futuristic mural appeal to the fashion cognoscenti. Globally-influenced menu.

XXX **Jaan** (at Swissôtel The Howard), Temple Pl, WC2R 2PR, ☎ (020) 7300 1700 Ⓜ *Temple, jaan.london@swissotel.com*, Fax (020) 7240 7816, 舎 – ▤. MC AE ① VISA JCB 32AMU e
closed Saturday lunch – **Meals** 29.00/31.00 ♀.
◆ Bright room on the ground floor of the hotel with large windows overlooking an attractive terrace. Original cooking - modern French with Cambodian flavours and ingredients.

XXX **East@West** with rm, 15 West St, WC2H 9NE, ☎ (020) 7010 8600 Ⓜ *Leicester Square, east.west@egami.co.uk*, Fax (020) 7010 8601 – |‡|, ⇔ rest, ▤ TV ℭ. MC AE ① VISA 31AKU a
closed 1 week Christmas, Sunday and Bank Holidays – **Meals** - South East Asian influences - (dinner only) 40.00 – ☕ 10.00 – **3 rm** 147.00/264.00.
◆ Enter into a dimly lit, leather furnished bar. Climb the stairs to minimalistic dining room for Asian influenced cuisine with Antipodean twists. Stylish rooms available.

XX **J. Sheekey,** 28-32 St Martin's Court, WC2N 4AL, ☎ (020) 7240 2565 Ⓜ *Leicester Square, Fax (020) 7240 8114* – ▤. MC AE ① VISA 31 ALU v
closed 25-26 December, 1 January and August Bank Holiday – **Meals** - Seafood - (booking essential) a la carte 24.50/47.75 ♀.
◆ Festooned with photographs of actors and linked to the theatrical world since opening in 1890. Wood panels and alcove tables add famed intimacy. Traditional British cooking.

XX **Rules,** 35 Maiden Lane, WC2E 7LB, ☎ (020) 7836 5314 Ⓜ *Leicester Square, info@rules.co.uk*, Fax (020) 7497 1081 – ⇔ ▤. MC AE ① VISA JCB 31 ALU n
closed 4 days Christmas – **Meals** - English - (booking essential) a la carte 29.15/37.85 ♀.
◆ London's oldest restaurant boasts a fine collection of antique cartoons, drawings and paintings. Tradition continues in the menu, specialising in game from its own estate.

XX **Adam Street,** 9 Adam St, WC2N 6AA, ☎ (020) 7379 8000 Ⓜ *Charing Cross, info@adamstreet.co.uk*, Fax (020) 7379 1444 – ▤. MC AE ① VISA 31 ALU c
closed 24 December-4 January, Sunday and Bank Holidays – **Meals** (lunch only) 17.95 and a la carte 22.50/41.50 ♀.
◆ Set in the striking vaults of a private members club just off the Strand. Sumptuous suede banquettes and elegantly laid tables. Well executed classic and modern English food.

XX **The Admiralty,** Somerset House, The Strand, WC2R 1LA, ☎ (020) 7845 4646 Ⓜ *Temple, Fax (020) 7845 4658* – ⇔. MC AE ① VISA JCB 32AMU a
closed 25-26 December and dinner Sunday and Bank Holidays – **Meals** a la carte 30.30/40.00 ♀.
◆ Interconnecting rooms with bold colours and informal service contrast with its setting within the restored Georgian splendour of Somerset House. 'Cuisine de terroir'.

XX **Bank,** 1 Kingsway, Aldwych, WC2B 6XF, ☎ (020) 7379 9797 Ⓜ *Covent Garden, aldres@bankrestaurants.com*, Fax (020) 7379 5070 – ▤. MC AE ① VISA JCB 32AMU s
closed Saturday lunch, Sunday and Bank Holidays – **Meals** 15.00 (lunch) and a la carte 29.90/41.90 ♀.
◆ Ceiling decoration of hanging glass shards creates a high level of interest in this bustling converted bank. Open-plan kitchen provides an extensive array of modern dishes.

XX **Le Deuxième,** 65a Long Acre, WC2E 9JH, ☎ (020) 7379 0033 Ⓜ *Covent Garden, Fax (020) 7379 0066* – ▤. MC AE VISA 31 ALU b
closed 24-25 December – **Meals** 14.50 (lunch) and a la carte 24.50/30.00 ♀.
◆ Caters well for theatregoers : opens early, closes late. Buzzy eatery, quietly decorated in white with subtle lighting. Varied International menu : Japanese to Mediterranean.

XX **Maggiore's,** 33 King St, WC2 8JD, ☎ (020) 7379 9696 Ⓜ *Leicester Square, enquiries@maggiores.uk.com*, Fax (020) 7379 6767 – ▤. MC AE VISA 31 ALU z
closed 24-26 December and 1 January – **Meals** - Bistro - 17.50 (lunch) and dinner a la carte 25.30/37.30 ♀.
◆ Narrow glass-roofed dining room with distinctive lighting and greenery creating a woodland atmosphere. Quick service and good value wide-ranging pre-theatre menu.

X **Le Café du Jardin,** 28 Wellington St, WC2E 7BD, ☎ (020) 7836 8769 Ⓜ *Covent Garden, Fax (020) 7836 4123* – ▤. MC AE VISA 31 ALU f
closed 24-25 December – **Meals** 14.50 (lunch) and a la carte 24.50/30.50 ♀.
◆ Divided into two floors with the downstairs slightly more comfortable. Light and contemporary interior with European-influenced cooking. Ideally placed for the Opera House.

Victoria - ✉ SW1.

Victoria Station Forecourt.

The Goring, 15 Beeston Pl, Grosvenor Gdns, SW1W 0JW, ✆ (020) 7396 9000 Ⓜ *Victoria, reception@goringhotel.co.uk*, Fax (020) 7834 4393, – ▯ ▤ TV ✆ – 🏛 50. MC AE ⓓ VISA. ✂ 38 AIX a

Meals *(closed Saturday lunch)* 29.50/40.00 ♀ – ☕ 17.50 – **67 rm** 246.75/311.40, 6 suites.

◆ Opened in 1910 as a quintessentially English hotel. The fourth generation of Goring is now at the helm. Many of the attractive rooms overlook a peaceful garden. Elegantly appointed restaurant provides memorable dining experience.

Crowne Plaza London St James, 45 Buckingham Gate, SW1E 6AF, ✆ (020) 7834 6655 Ⓜ *St James's, sales@cplonsj.co.uk*, Fax (020) 7630 7587, Lõ, ≘s – ▯, ⇔ rm, ▤ TV ✆ ♿ – 🏛 180. MC AE ⓓ VISA JCB. ✂ 39 AJX e

Bistro 51 **: Meals** 15.00/18.50 and a la carte 20.25/50.35 ♀ (see also ***Quilon*** and ***Bank*** below) – ☕ 15.70 – **323 rm** 293.70, 19 suites.

◆ Built in 1897 as serviced accommodation for visiting aristocrats. Behind the impressive Edwardian façade lies an equally elegant interior. Quietest rooms overlook courtyard. Bright and informal café style restaurant.

Royal Horseguards, 2 Whitehall Court, SW1A 2EJ, ✆ (0870) 333 9122 Ⓜ *Charing Cross, royalhorseguards@thistle.co.uk*, Fax (0870) 333 9222, , Lõ – ▯, ⇔ rm, ▤ TV ✆ – 🏛 200. MC AE ⓓ VISA JCB. ✂ 31 ALV a

One Twenty One Two **: Meals** *(closed lunch Saturday, Sunday and Bank Holidays)* 19.50/25.50 and dinner a la carte 27.50/34.50 ♀ – ☕ 17.50 – **276 rm** 309.00/329.00, 4 suites.

◆ Imposing Grade I listed property in Whitehall overlooking the Thames and close to London Eye. Impressive meeting rooms. Some of the well-appointed bedrooms have river views. Stylish restaurant, sub-divided into intimate rooms.

51 Buckingham Gate, 51 Buckingham Gate, SW1E 6AF, ✆ (020) 7769 7766 Ⓜ *St James's, info@51-buckinghamgate.co.uk*, Fax (020) 7828 5909, Lõ, ≘s – ▯ ▤ TV ✆. MC AE ⓓ VISA JCB. ✂ 39 AJX s

Meals (see ***Quilon*** and ***Bank*** below) – ☕ 19.50 –, **82 suites** 370.00/528.75.

◆ Canopied entrance leads to luxurious suites : every detail considered, every mod con provided. Colour schemes echoed in plants and paintings. Butler and nanny service.

41 without rest., 41 Buckingham Palace Rd, SW1W 0PS, ✆ (020) 7300 0041 Ⓜ *Victoria, book41@rchmail.com*, Fax (020) 7300 0141 – ▯ ▤ TV ✆. MC AE ⓓ VISA JCB 38 AIX n

19 rm 346.60/370.10, 1 suite.

◆ Discreet appearance ; exudes exclusive air. Leather armchairs ; bookcases line the walls. Intimate service. State-of-the-art rooms where hi-tec and fireplace merge appealingly.

The Rubens at The Palace, 39 Buckingham Palace Rd, SW1W 0PS, ✆ (020) 7834 6600 Ⓜ *Victoria, bookrb@rchmail.com*, Fax (020) 7828 5401 – ▯ ⇔ ▤ TV ✆ – 🏛 90. MC AE ⓓ VISA JCB 38 AIX n

Meals *(closed lunch Saturday and Sunday)* (carvery) 17.95 ♀ – ***The Library*** **: Meals** (dinner only) a la carte approx 37.00 ♀ – ☕ 16.50 – **170 rm** 229.10/287.90, 2 suites.

◆ Traditional hotel with an air of understated elegance. Tastefully furnished rooms : the Royal Wing, themed after Kings and Queens, features TVs in bathrooms. Smart carvery restaurant. Intimate, richly decorated Library restaurant has sumptuous armchairs.

Dolphin Square, Dolphin Sq, Chichester St, SW1V 3LX, ✆ (020) 7834 3800 Ⓜ *Pimlico, reservations@dolphinsquarehotel.co.uk*, Fax (020) 7798 8735, Lõ, ≘s, , , , squash – ▯ ⇔, ▤ rest, TV ✆ 🚗 – 🏛 85. MC AE ⓓ VISA. ✂ 39 AJZ a

The Brasserie **: Meals** 15.00 and a la carte 17.45/23.75 (see also ***Allium*** below) – ☕ 13.50 – **30 rm** 185.00/205.00, **118 suites** 205.00/450.00.

◆ Built in 1935 and shared with residential apartments. Art Deco influence remains in the Clipper bar overlooking the leisure club. Spacious suites with contemporary styling. Brasserie overlooks the swimming pool.

Jolly St Ermin's, Caxton St, SW1H 0QW, ✆ (020) 7222 7888 Ⓜ *St James's, stermins@jollyhotels.co.uk*, Fax (020) 7222 6914 – ▯, ⇔ rm, ▤ rm, TV ✆ – 🏛 150. MC AE ⓓ VISA. ✂ 39 AKX a

Cloisters Brasserie **: Meals** 22.50/26.50 and a la carte ♀ – ☕ 15.95 – **282 rm** 212.00/235.00, 8 suites.

◆ Ornate plasterwork to both the lobby and the balconied former ballroom are particularly striking features. Club rooms have both air conditioning and a private lounge. Grand brasserie with ornate ceiling.

Thistle Victoria, 101 Buckingham Palace Rd, SW1W 0SJ, (0870) 3339120 *Victoria, victoria@thistle.co.uk,* Fax (0870) 3339220 – rm, rm, – 200. 38 AIY e
***Harvard Bar & Grill* : Meals** *(closed lunch Saturday and Sunday)* 15.00 (lunch) and a la carte 22.00/39.00 – 13.95 – **354 rm** 211.50/317.25, 3 suites.
◆ Former Victorian railway hotel with ornate front entrance and grand reception. Harvard bar particularly noteworthy. Well-furnished rooms are generally spacious. Elegantly appointed dining room.

City Inn, 30 John Islip St, SW1P 4DD, (020) 7630 1000 *Pimlico, westminster.res@cityinn.com,* Fax (020) 7233 7575, – – 100. 39 ALY a
***City Cafe* : Meals** 17.50/30.00 and a la carte 22.75/35.75 – 19.00 – **444 rm** 264.40, 16 suites.
◆ Modern hotel five minutes' walk from Westminster Abbey and Tate Britain. Well-appointed bedrooms with high-tech equipment and some with pleasant views of London. Brasserie serving modern style food next to a glass covered terrace with artwork feature.

Tophams Belgravia, 28 Ebury St, SW1W 0LU, (020) 7730 8147 *Victoria, tophamsbelgravia@compuserve.com,* Fax (020) 7823 5966 – – 30. 38 AHY e
closed 24 December-2 January – **Meals** (dinner only) a la carte 21.50/26.00 **s.** – **37 rm** 115.00/170.00.
◆ Family owned and run since 1937, this hotel has a certain traditional charm. Cosy lounges, roaring fires and antique furniture aplenty. Individually decorated bedrooms. Homely basement dining room.

Winchester without rest., 17 Belgrave Rd, SW1V 1RB, (020) 7828 2972 *Victoria, winchesterhotel17@hotmail.com,* Fax (020) 7828 5191 – . 38 AIY s
closed 24-26 December – **18 rm** 75.00/125.00.
◆ Behind the portico entrance one finds a friendly, well-kept private hotel. The generally spacious rooms are pleasantly appointed. Comprehensive English breakfast offered.

Express by Holiday Inn without rest., 106-110 Belgrave Rd, SW1V 2BJ, (020) 7630 8888 *Pimlico, info@hiexpressvictoria.co.uk,* Fax (020) 7828 0441 – . 39 AJZ c
52 rm 119.00.
◆ Converted Georgian terraced houses a short walk from station. Despite property's age, all rooms are stylish and modern with good range of facilities including TV movies.

Allium (at Dolphin Square H.), Dolphin Sq, Chichester St, SW1V 3LX, (020) 7798 6888 *Pimlico, info@allium.co.uk,* Fax (020) 7798 5685 – . 39 AJZ a
closed 26 December, Saturday lunch, Sunday dinner and Monday – **Meals** 22.50/32.50 and a la carte 30.00/44.30 .
◆ A calm atmosphere prevails in this richly decorated room. Raised tables to rear with sumptuous banquettes for more privacy. Interesting and assured modern British cooking.

The Cinnamon Club, Great Smith St, SW1P 3BU, (020) 7222 2555 *St James's, info@cinnamonclub.com,* Fax (020) 7222 1333 – . 39 AKX c
closed Saturday lunch, Sunday and Bank Holidays – **Meals** - Indian - 19.00/22.00 (lunch) and a la carte 33.00/48.00 .
◆ Housed in former Westminster Library : exterior has ornate detail, interior is stylish and modern. Walls are lined with books. New Wave Indian cooking with plenty of choice.

Quilon (at Crowne Plaza London St James H.), 45 Buckingham Gate, SW1 6AF, (020) 7821 1899 *St James's, Fax (020) 7828 5802* – . 39 AJX e
closed Sunday, Saturday lunch and Bank Holidays – **Meals** - Indian - 15.95 (lunch) and dinner a la carte 16.95/35.20 .
◆ A selection of Eastern pictures adorn the walls in this smart, modern and busy restaurant. Specialising in progressive south coastal Indian cooking.

L'Incontro, 87 Pimlico Rd, SW1W 8PH, (020) 7730 6327 *Sloane Square, cristiano@lincontro-restaurant.com,* Fax (020) 7730 5062 – . 37 AGZ u
closed Easter, 25-26 December, 1 January and Sunday – **Meals** - Italian - 19.50 (lunch) and a la carte 28.50/47.50.
◆ Cool, understated and comfortable with attentive service. Simple, unfussy, traditional Italian cooking ; set lunch good value. Private dining downstairs for 30 people.

Santini, 29 Ebury St, SW1W 0NZ, (020) 7730 4094 *Victoria, info@santini-restaurant.com,* Fax (020) 7730 0544 – . 38 AHY v
closed 25-26 December, lunch Saturday, Sunday and Bank Holidays – **Meals** - Italian - 19.50 (lunch) and a la carte 29.50/49.00 .
◆ Discreet, refined and elegant modern Italian restaurant. Assured and professional service. Extensive selection of modern dishes and a more affordable set lunch menu.

XXX **Shepherd's,** Marsham Court, Marsham St, SW1P 4LA, ☎ (020) 7834 9552 Ⓜ *Pimlico, admin@langansrestaurants.co.uk,* Fax (020) 7233 6047 – ▤. MC AE ⓓ VISA JCB
closed Saturday, Sunday and Bank Holidays – **Meals** - English - (booking essential) 29.00.
◆ A truly English restaurant where game and traditional puddings are a highlight. Popular with those from Westminster - the booths offer a degree of privacy. 39 AKY z

XX ✿ **Roussillon,** 16 St Barnabas St, SW1W 8PE, ☎ (020) 7730 5550 Ⓜ *Sloane Square, alexis@roussillon.co.uk,* Fax (020) 7824 8617 – ▤. MC AE VISA JCB 38 AHZ c
closed 1 week Christmas, last week August, first week September, Sunday, lunch Saturday-Tuesday and Bank Holidays – **Meals** - French - 30.00/45.00 ♀.
Spec. Lightly battered calf's sweetbread, morels, lettuce and veal jus. Smoked eel and scrambled eggs, peas and hollandaise sauce. Lemon financier with lemon pepper sorbet.
◆ Tucked away in an smart residential area. Cooking clearly focuses on the quality of the ingredients. Seasonal menu with inventive elements and a French base.

XX **The Ebury (Dining Room),** 1st Floor, 11 Pimlico Rd, SW1W 8NA, ☎ (020) 7730 6784 Ⓜ *Sloane Square, info@theebury.co.uk,* Fax (020) 7730 6149 – ▤. MC AE VISA 38 AHZ z
closed 25-26 December and 1 January – **Meals** (dinner only July-August) 19.50/29.50 ♀.
◆ Mount the spiral stair to the formal restaurant with tall windows overlooking the street. Open-plan kitchen provides set gastronomic style menu using first-class ingredients.

XX **Il Convivio,** 143 Ebury St, SW1W 9QN, ☎ (020) 7730 4099 Ⓜ *Sloane Square, comments@etruscagroup.co.uk,* Fax (020) 7730 4103, 🏛 – ▤. MC AE ⓓ VISA JCB
closed Easter, 25-26 December, Sunday and Bank Holidays – **Meals** - Italian - 19.50/38.50 and a la carte 22.00/38.50 ♀. 38 AHY a
◆ A retractable roof provides alfresco dining to part of this comfortable and modern restaurant. Contemporary and traditional Italian menu, with home-made pasta specialities.

XX **Simply Nico,** 48a Rochester Row, SW1P 1JU, ☎ (020) 7630 8061 Ⓜ *St James's, westminster@simplynico.co.uk,* Fax (020) 7828 8541 – MC AE ⓓ VISA 39 AJY a
closed Easter, 25-26 December, 1 January, Saturday lunch and Sunday – **Meals** (booking essential) a la carte 24.50/35.50 ♀.
◆ Relaxed and discreet restaurant with a certain bistro atmosphere. Lunch is especially busy. Short, Anglo-French menu. One of a small chain.

XX **Bank,** 45 Buckingham Gate, SW1E 6BS, ☎ (020) 7379 9797 Ⓜ *St James's, westres@bankrestaurants.com,* Fax (020) 7379 5070, 🏛 – ▤. MC AE ⓓ VISA JCB 39 AJX e
closed 25-26 December, 1-2 January and Bank Holidays – **Meals** 15.00 (lunch) and a la carte 23.95/38.95 🍷 ♀.
◆ The understated entrance belies the vibrant contemporary interior. One of Europe's longest bars has a lively atmosphere. Conservatory restaurant, modern European cooking.

XX **Boisdale,** 15 Eccleston St, SW1W 9LX, ☎ (020) 7730 6922 Ⓜ *Victoria, info@boisdale.co.uk,* Fax (020) 7730 0548, 🏛 – ▤. MC AE ⓓ VISA 38 AHY c
closed Saturday lunch and Sunday – **Meals** - Scottish - (live jazz at dinner) a la carte 23.45/42.50 ♀.
◆ Popular haunt of politicians ; dark green, lacquer red panelled interior. Run by a Scot of Clanranald, hence modern British dishes with Scottish flavour : Crofter's pie.

XX **Tate Britain,** Tate Gallery, Millbank, SW1P 4RG, ☎ (020) 7887 8825 Ⓜ *Pimlico, tate.restaurant@tate.org.uk,* Fax (020) 7887 8902 – ▤. MC AE ⓓ VISA JCB 39 ALY c
closed 24-26 December – **Meals** (booking essential) (lunch only) a la carte 25.50/31.00 ♀.
◆ Continue your appreciation of art when lunching in this basement room decorated with original Rex Whistler murals. Forever busy, it offers modern British fare.

XX **Ken Lo's Memories of China,** 65-69 Ebury St, SW1W 0NZ, ☎ (020) 7730 7734 Ⓜ *Victoria, Fax (020) 7730 2992* – ▤. MC AE ⓓ VISA 38 AHY u
closed 25 December and 1 January – **Meals** - Chinese - a la carte 20.80/48.50 ♀.
◆ An air of tranquillity pervades this traditionally furnished room. Lattice screens add extra privacy. Extensive Chinese menu : bold flavours with a clean, fresh style..

X **The Ebury (Brasserie),** Ground Floor, 11 Pimlico Rd, SW1W 8NA, ☎ (020) 7730 6784 Ⓜ *Sloane Square, info@theebury.co.uk,* Fax (020) 7730 6149 – ▤. MC AE VISA
closed 25-26 December and 1 January – **Meals** a la carte 22.00/35.00 ♀. 38 AHZ z
◆ Victorian corner pub restaurant with walnut bar, simple tables and large seafood bar. Friendly service. Wide-ranging menu from snacks to full meals.

X **Olivo,** 21 Eccleston St, SW1W 9LX, ☎ (020) 7730 2505 Ⓜ *Victoria, maurosanna@olivo.fsnet.co.uk,* Fax (020) 7823 5377 – ▤. MC AE ⓓ VISA JCB 39 AHY z
closed 25 December, 1 January, lunch Saturday and Sunday and Bank Holidays – **Meals** - Italian - 18.50 (lunch) and a la carte 26.50/30.50.
◆ Rustic, informal Italian restaurant. Relaxed atmosphere provided by the friendly staff. Simple, non-fussy cuisine with emphasis on best available fresh produce.

X **La Poule au Pot,** 231 Ebury St, SW1W 8UT, ☎ (020) 7730 7763 Ⓜ *Sloane Square, Fax (020) 7259 9651,* 🏛 – ▤. MC AE ⓓ VISA JCB 38 AHY p
Meals - French - 16.50 (lunch) and a la carte 25.50/41.00.
◆ The subdued lighting and friendly informality make this one of London's more romantic restaurants. Classic French menu with extensive plats du jour.

Bray-on-Thames *Windsor & Maidenhead* 504 R 29 – *Maidenhead.*

London 34 – Reading 13.

Waterside Inn (Roux) with rm, Ferry Rd, SL6 2AT, (01628) 620691, *reservations @ waterside-inn.co.uk, Fax (01628) 784710,* Thames-side setting –, P. MC AE VISA JCB.
closed 26 December-27 January and 30-31 March – **Meals** - French - *(closed Tuesday except dinner June-August and Monday)* (booking essential) 40.00/85.00 and a la carte 75.00/126.50 – **8 rm** 165.00/205.00, 1 suite.
Spec. Tronçonnettes de homard poêlées minute au Porto blanc. Filets de lapereau grillés aux marrons glacés. Péché Gourmand.
• Thames-side idyll still delights : opulent dining room, drinks in the summer houses, exquisite French cuisine and matchless service. Bedrooms are restful and classically chic.

Fat Duck (Blumenthal), High St, SL6 2AQ, (01628) 580333, *Fax (01628) 776188* – P. MC AE VISA
closed 2 weeks Christmas, Sunday dinner and Monday – **Meals** 35.00/65.00 ♀.
Spec. Roast foie gras, almond fluid gel and cherry. "Nitro" poached green tea and lime mousse. Macerated Mara des Bois, purée of black olive, pistachio scrambled eggs.
• History and science combine in an innovative alchemy of contrasting flavours and textures. Modern art, stylish, relaxing milieu, confident service.

Cambridge *Cambs.* 504 U 27 – *pop. 117 717.*

The Old Library, Wheeler St (01223) 457581.
London 55 – Oxford 100.

Midsummer House (Clifford), Midsummer Common, CB4 1HA, (01223) 369299, *reservations@midsummerhouse.co.uk, Fax (01223) 302672,* – MC AE VISA
closed 2 weeks Christmas, 2 weeks August-September, 1 week Easter, Sunday and Monday – **Meals** 26.00/48.50 ♀.
Spec. Terrine of apple, smoked eel and foie gras with sultanas. Poached and grilled Anjou pigeon, cherry pastilla and sweet potato purée. Banana parfait, caramelised banana ice cream.
• A river Cam idyll. Chic conservatory dining room and first-floor lounge with pleasant views from three perspectives over the city. Refined cooking with a French base.

Oxford *Oxon.* 503 504 Q 28 – *pop. 143 016.*

15-16 Broad St (01865) 726871.
London 59 – Birmingham 63 – Bristol 73.

Le Manoir aux Quat' Saisons (Blanc), Church Rd, OX44 7PD, (01844) 278881, *lemanoir@blanc.co.uk, Fax (01844) 278847,* – rest, rest, P – 50. MC AE VISA.
Meals - French - 45.00 (lunch weekdays) and a la carte 84.00/98.00 **s.** ♀ – 24.00 – **25 rm** 275.00/495.00, 7 suites 670.00/1250.00.
Spec. Ceviche of scallops, tuna and shaved fennel salad. Confit of foie gras, rhubarb compote, ginger brioche. Anjou squab, cappuccino of coco beans, Madeira scented jus.
• World famous and picture perfect, its beauty lies in its refinement. Sumptuous lounges and rooms, classic and modern, surrounded by Japanese, ornamental and kitchen gardens. Virtuoso classic French menu of precision and flair, inspired by the seasons.

Stansted Airport *Essex* 504 U 28 – *Stansted Mountfitchet.*

Stansted International Airport : (0870) 0000303 – **Terminal :** to Liverpool Street Station, London.
London 37 – Cambridge 29.

Radisson SAS, Waltham Close, CM24 1PP, (01279) 661012, *info.stansted@radissonsas.com, Fax (01279) 661013,* – P – 400. MC AE VISA.
New York Grill Bar : **Meals** a la carte 23.40/31.40 **s.** – ***Wine Tower :*** **Meals** a la carte 10.70/13.00 **s.** – ***Filini :*** **Meals** - Italian - a la carte 15.70/24.95 **s.** – **484 rm** 140.00, 16 suites.
• Impressive hotel just two minutes from main terminal ; vast open atrium housing 40 foot wine cellar. Extensive meeting facilities. Very stylish bedrooms in three themes. Small, formal New York Grill Bar. Impressive Wine Tower. Filini for Italian dishes.

Hilton London Stansted Airport, Round Coppice Rd, CM24 1SF, (01279) 680800, *reservations.stansted@hilton.com, Fax (01279) 680890,* – rm, rest, P – 250. MC AE VISA JCB.
Meals *(closed lunch Saturday, Sunday and Bank Holidays)* a la carte 25.85/33.40 ♀ – 14.95 – **237 rm** 145.00, 2 suites.
• Bustling hotel whose facilities include leisure club, hairdressers and beauty salon. Modern rooms, with two of executive style. Transport can be arranged to and from terminal. Restaurant/bar has popular menu ; sometimes carvery lunch as well.

BELFAST *Antrim* 712 O 4 *Ireland G.* – *pop. 277 391.*

See : *City★ - Ulster Museum★★ (Spanish Armada Treasure★★, Shrine of St Patrick's Hand★) – City Hall★* BY *– Donegall Square★* BY **20** *– Botanic Gardens (Palm House★) – St Anne's Cathedral★* BX *– Crown Liquor Saloon★* BY *– Sinclair Seamen's Church★* BX *– St Malachy's Church★* BY.

Envir. : *Belfast Zoological Gardens★★ AC, N : 5 m. by A 6* BX.

Exc. : *Carrickfergus (Castle★★ AC, St Nicholas' Church★) NE : 9 ½ m. by A 2* BX *– Talnotry Cottage Bird Garden, Crumlin★ AC, W : 13 ½ m. by A 52* BX.

Balmoral, 518 Lisburn Rd ℘ (028) 9038 1514 – Belvoir Park, Church rd, Newtonbreda ℘ (028) 9049 1693 – Fortwilliam, Downview Ave ℘ (028) 9037 0770 – The Knock Club, Summerfield, Dundonald ℘ (028) 9048 2249 – Shandon Park, 73 Shandon Park ℘ (028) 9079 3730 – Cliftonville, Westland Rd ℘ (028) 9074 4158 – Ormeau, 50 Park Rd ℘ (028) 9064 1069.

Belfast International Airport, Aldergrove : ℘ (028) Belfast City Airport : ℘ (028) 9093 9093 – **Terminal :** *Coach service (Ulsterbus Ltd) from Great Victoria Street Station (40 mn).*

to Liverpool (NorseMerchant Ferries Ltd) daily (11 h).

47 Donegal Pl ℘ (028) 9024 6609, info@nitic.com – Belfast International Airport, Information desk ℘ (028) 9442 2888 – Belfast City Airport, Sydenham Bypass ℘ (028) 9093 9093.

Dublin 103 – Londonderry 70.

Plans on following pages

Hilton Belfast, 4 Lanyon Pl, BT1 3LP, ℘ (028) 9027 7000, *hilton.belfast@hilton.com, Fax (028) 9027 7277,* – rm, – 400. VISA BY s

Sonoma : **Meals** *(closed lunch Saturday and Sunday)* 16.95/21.00 and dinner a la carte 25.15/38.00 **s.** – ***Cables :*** **Meals** a la carte 26.00/31.50 **s.** – 17.25 – **189 rm** 160.00, 6 suites.

◆ Modern branded hotel overlooking river and close to concert hall. Spacious and brightly decorated rooms with all mod cons. Upper floors with good city views. Striking California-style décor and good city views from Sonoma. Contemporary Cables bar-restaurant.

Europa, Great Victoria St, BT2 7AP, ℘ (028) 9027 1066, *res@eur.hastingshotels.com, Fax (028) 9032 7800* – rm, – 750. VISA BY e

closed 24-25 December – ***Gallery :*** **Meals** (dinner only) a la carte 22.50/29.50 **s.** – ***The Brasserie :*** **Meals** a la carte 17.40/25.95 – 16.00 – **235 rm** 120.00/175.00, 5 suites.

◆ Busy hotel in the heart of the lively Golden Mile area. Extensive meeting facilities. Most executive rooms are well-equipped with hi-fis. Formal Gallery restaurant and immaculate bar. Pleasant feel suffuses Brasserie ; fish and chips a favourite here.

Radisson SAS, 3 Cromac Pl, Cromac Wood, BT7 2JB, ℘ (028) 9043 4065, *info.belfast@radissonsas.com, Fax (028) 9043 4066* – rm, – 175. VISA.

Filini's : **Meals** *(closed Sunday dinner)* a la carte 17.50/23.50 – 14.95 – **119 rm** 140.00, 1 suite.

◆ New hotel, completed late 2004, in Cromac Park. Smart, up-to-date facilities in public areas. Two room styles - Urban or Nordic - with floor-to-ceiling windows for fine views. Restaurant/bar has vista to park's stylish water feature.

Stormont, Upper Newtownards Rd, BT4 3LP, East : 3 ½ m. on A 20 ℘ (028) 9065 1066, *res@stor.hastingshotels.com, Fax (028) 9048 0240* – rm, – 400. VISA.

Shiraz : **Meals** *(closed Sunday)* (dinner only) a la carte 23.65/29.35 **s.** – ***La Scala Bistro :*** **Meals** a la carte 19.35/23.85 **s.** – 16.00 – **105 rm** 118.00/148.00.

◆ In a suburb opposite the gardens of Stormont castle ; an up-to-date conference and exhibition oriented hotel. Brightly decorated, modern bedrooms. Comfortable, split-level Shiraz. All-day La Scala has appealing ambience.

Malmaison, 34-38 Victoria St, BT1 3GH, ℘ (028) 9022 0200, *belfast@malmaison.com, Fax (028) 9022 0220* – rm, – 60. VISA. BY v

Meals 13.95 (lunch) and a la carte 23.85/32.40 – 11.75 – **64 rm** 135.00/155.00.

◆ An unstuffy, centrally located hotel hides behind its intricate Victorian façade. Originally two warehouses, many original features remain. Modern, comfortable rooms. Vibrantly decorated restaurant offers an eclectic menu.

Ramada Belfast, Shaws Bridge, BT8 7XA, South : 3 ¾ m. on A 55 (by Malone rd) ℘ (028) 9092 3500, *reservations@ramadabelfast.com, Fax (028) 9092 3600,* – rm, – 1000. VISA.

closed 11-13 July – ***Belfast Bar and Grill :*** **Meals** (bar lunch)/dinner 15.00/25.00 and a la carte 21.50/29.50 **s.** – 10.50 – **118 rm** 115.00/135.00, 2 suites.

◆ Good leisure, and Belfast's most extensive conference facilities ; situated on city bypass. Modern bedrooms are well equipped for business travellers. First floor restaurant offering modern-style classics.

Tensq, 10 Donegall Square South, BT1 5JD, ✆ (028) 9024 1001, *reservations@tensquare.co.uk*, Fax *(028) 9024 3210* – |‡|, ⇔ rm, ▤ TV ✆ ♿ P. MC AE VISA JCB. ✂ BY x
Porcelain **: Meals** - Asian specialities - a la carte 14.00/38.00 – **23 rm** ☕ 160.00.
◆ Victorian mill building in heart of city renovated to a thoroughly contemporary standard. Notably spacious deluxe bedrooms. Access to private bar for guests. Restaurant décor maintains the modern style of the hotel.

Holiday Inn Belfast, 22 Ormeau Ave, BT2 8HS, ✆ (028) 9032 8511, *belfast@ichotelsgroup.com*, Fax *(028) 9062 6546*, Lδ, ≘s, ⊠ – |‡|, ⇔ rm, ▤ TV ✆ ♿ – 🏠 140. MC AE ⓓ VISA. ✂ BY u
The Junction **: Meals** *(closed Saturday and Sunday lunch)* 15.95/21.95 and dinner a la carte 24.15/28.15 **s.** ♀ – ☕ 13.95 – **168 rm** 155.00, 2 suites.
◆ Convenient city-centre location, up-to-date conference facilities and trim, well-equipped rooms in modern colours make this an good business choice. Plenty of choice from the menu of modern cooking.

Malone Lodge, 60 Eglantine Ave, BT9 6DY, ✆ (028) 9038 8000, *info@malonelodgehotel.com*, Fax *(028) 9038 8088*, Lδ, ≘s – |‡|, ⇔ rm, ▤ rest, TV ✆ ♿ P – 🏠 120. MC AE ⓓ VISA JCB. ✂
The Green Door **: Meals** *(closed Sunday dinner)* 11.50/22.50 and dinner a la carte 13.50/27.00 – **50 rm** ☕ 95.00/109.00, 8 suites.
◆ Imposing hotel in Victorian terrace in quiet residential area. Elegant lobby lounge and smart bar. Conference facilities. Basement gym. Stylish, modern rooms with big beds. Restaurant provides a comfortable, contemporary environment.

The Crescent Townhouse, 13 Lower Crescent, BT7 1NR, ✆ (028) 9032 3349, *info@crescenttownhouse.com*, Fax *(028) 9032 0646* – ▤ rest, TV. MC AE VISA. ✂ BZ x
closed 12-13 July, 24-25 December and 1 January – ***Metro Brasserie*** **: Meals** *(closed Sunday lunch)* 13.50 (dinner) and a la carte 18.65/29.65 ♀ – **17 rm** ☕ 70.00/145.00.
◆ Intimate Regency house that blends original features with modern amenities. Relaxed, discreet atmosphere. Spacious and luxurious rooms with interior designed period feel. Modern classic brasserie with a lively and relaxed ambience.

Madison's, 59-63 Botanic Ave, BT7 1JL, ✆ (028) 9050 9800, *info@madisonshotel.com*, Fax *(028) 9050 9808* – |‡|, ⇔ rm, ▤ rest, TV ♿. MC AE VISA. ✂ BZ s
The Restaurant **: Meals** a la carte 15.40/23.40 – **35 rm** ☕ 70.00/80.00.
◆ Contemporary hotel in a lively and fashionable area packed with bars and restaurants. Spacious bedrooms with up-to-date facilities. Brightly decorated with modern art. Vibrantly decorated bar and restaurant with a busy and buzzy atmosphere.

Benedicts, 7-21 Bradbury Pl, Shaftsbury Sq, BT7 1RQ, ✆ (028) 9059 1999, *info@benedictshotel.co.uk*, Fax *(028) 9059 1990* – |‡|, ▤ rest, TV ♿. MC AE ⓓ VISA. ✂ BZ c
closed 12 July and 25 December – ***Benedicts Restaurant*** **: Meals** 12.00/22.00 and a la carte 20.65/24.65 **s.** ♀ – **32 rm** ☕ 60.00/75.00.
◆ A lively, strikingly designed bar with nightly entertainment can be found at the heart of this busy commercial hotel. Well-appointed bedrooms above offer modern facilities. Relaxed, popular restaurant.

Jurys Inn Belfast, Fisherwick Pl, Great Victoria St, BT2 7AP, ✆ (028) 9053 3500, *jurysinnbelfast@jurysdoyle.com*, Fax *(028) 9053 3511* – |‡|, ⇔ rm, TV ✆ ♿ – 🏠 30. MC AE ⓓ VISA. ✂ BY c
closed 24-26 December – **Meals** a la carte approx 16.95 – ☕ 8.00 – **190 rm** 78.00.
◆ Beside the opera house and convenient for the shops. Modern and functional hotel suitable for both corporate and leisure travellers. Generously proportioned family rooms. Restaurant offers popular international menu with subtle Asian touches.

Express by Holiday Inn without rest, 106A University St, BT7 1HP, ✆ (028) 9031 1909, *mail@exhi-belfast.com*, Fax *(028) 9031 1910* – |‡|, ⇔ rm, TV ✆ ♿ P – 🏠 120. MC AE ⓓ VISA. ✂ BZ z
114 rm ☕ 64.95.
◆ Good value and ideal for business travellers. Spacious, bright and modern bedrooms with plenty of work space. Complimentary Continental breakfast.

Days H., 40 Hope St, BT12 5EE, ✆ (028) 9024 2494, *reservations@dayshotelbelfast.com*, Fax *(028) 9024 2495* – |‡| ⇔, ▤ rest, TV ✆ ♿ P – 🏠 30. MC AE VISA. ✂ BY a
Meals a la carte 12.15/24.85 **s.** – **244 rm** ☕ 75.00.
◆ Centrally located, with the bonus of free parking. Large, "no frills", low cost hotel designed for business traveller or tourist. Sizable, bright, modern rooms with mod cons.

Ravenhill House without rest., 690 Ravenhill Rd, BT6 0BZ, ✆ (028) 9020 7444, *info@ravenhillhouse.com*, Fax *(028) 9028 2590* – ⇔ TV P. MC VISA
closed 1 week Christmas – **5 rm** ☕ 42.00/65.00.
◆ Personally run detached 19C house, attractively furnished in keeping with its age. The largely organic breakfast is a highlight. Good sized rooms with bold shades predominant.

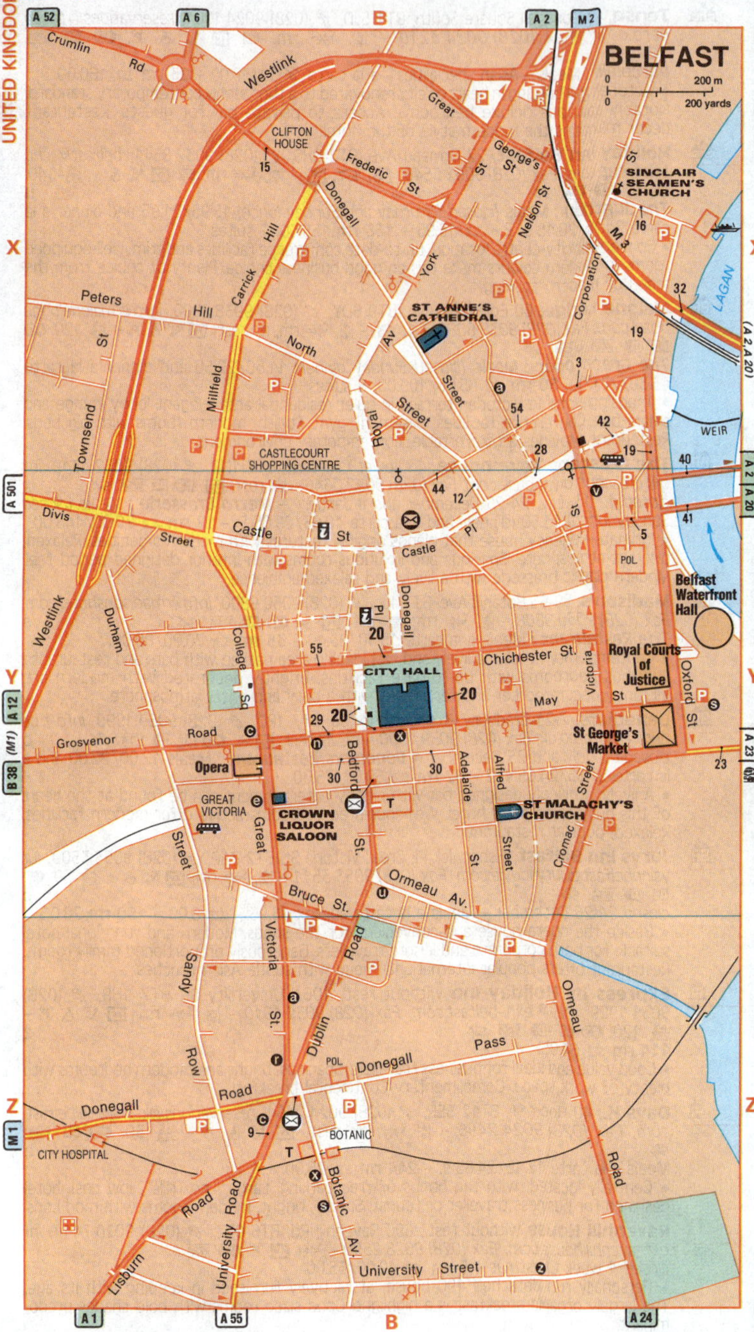
BELFAST
0
200 m
0
200 yards
A 52
A 6
B
A 2
M 2
X
Y
Z
A 501
A 12
B 38
(M1)
M 1
A 1
A 55
A 24
A 23
A 2
A 20
(A 2, A 20)
Crumlin
Rd
Westlink
CLIFTON HOUSE
Frederic St
Donegall
Great George's St
Nelson St
SINCLAIR SEAMEN'S CHURCH
M 3
LAGAN
Carrick Hill
Peters Hill
North Street
York St
ST ANNE'S CATHEDRAL
Corporation
Royal Av
Street
Millfield
Townsend
CASTLECOURT SHOPPING CENTRE
WEIR
Divis Street
Castle St
Castle Pl
Donegall Pl
Durham
College Sq
CITY HALL
Chichester St.
Victoria St
May St
Royal Courts of Justice
Oxford St
Belfast Waterfront Hall
POL.
St George's Market
Grosvenor Road
Opera
GREAT VICTORIA
Great Victoria Street
CROWN LIQUOR SALOON
Bedford St.
Adelaide St
Alfred Street
ST MALACHY'S CHURCH
Cromac Street
Ormeau Av.
Bruce St.
Sandy Row
Dublin Road
Ormeau Road
POL
Donegall Pass
Donegall Road
CITY HOSPITAL
BOTANIC
Botanic Av.
University Road
University Street
Lisburn Road
15
16
32
19
3
54
42
28
19
40
41
44
12
5
20
55
29
30
23
9
T

INDEX OF STREET NAMES IN BELFAST

In Northern Ireland traffic and parking are controlled in the town centres. No vehicle may be left unattended in a Control Zone.

Adelaïde St . . . BY
Albert Square . . . BX 3
Alfred St . . . BY
Ann St . . . BY 5
Bedford St . . . BY
Belmont Rd . . . BZ 7
Botanic Ave . . . BZ
Bradbury Pl. . . . BZ 9
Bridge St . . . BY 12
Castle Pl. . . . BY
Castle St . . . BY
Castlecourt Shopping Centre . . . BXY
Chichester St . . . BX
City Hospital St . . . BZ
Clifton St . . . BX 15
College Square . . . BY
Corporation Square . . . BX 16
Corporation St . . . BX
Cromac St . . . BY
Crumlin Rd . . . BX
Divis St . . . BY
Donegall Pass . . . BZ
Donegall Pl. . . . BY
Donegall Quay . . . BXY 19
Donegall Rd . . . BZ
Donegall Square . . . BY 20
Donegall St . . . BX
Dublin Rd . . . BZ
Durham St . . . BY
Frederic St . . . BX
Great George's St . . . BX
Great Victoria St . . . BY, BZ
Grosvenor Rd . . . BY
High St . . . BXY 28
Howard St . . . BY 29
Ladas Drive . . . BY 31
Lagan Bridge . . . BX 32
Lisburn Rd . . . BZ
May St . . . BX
Millfield Carrick Hill . . . BXY
Nelson St . . . BX
North St . . . BX
Ormeau Ave . . . BZ
Ormeau Rd . . . BZ
Oxford St . . . BY
Peters Hill . . . BX
Queen Elizabeth Bridge . . . BY 40
Queen's Bridge . . . BY 41
Queen's Square . . . BX 42
Rosemary St . . . BY 44
Royal Ave . . . BXY
Sandy Row . . . BZ
Townsend St . . . BX
University Rd . . . BZ
University St . . . BZ
Victoria St . . . BY
Waring St . . . BX 54
Wellington Pl. . . . BY 55
Westlink . . . BY
York St . . . BX

Ash Rowan Town House, 12 Windsor Ave, BT9 6EE, ✆ (028) 9066 1758, *Fax (028) 9066 3227,* – *closed 2 weeks Christmas* – **Meals** (by arrangement) 35.00 – **5 rm** 52.00/96.00.
◆ Late 19C house in quiet tree-lined avenue. Personally run; interestingly "cluttered" interior. Comfy conservatory sitting room. Well-judged bedrooms with thoughtful touches.

The Old Rectory, 148 Malone Rd, BT9 5LH, ✆ (028) 9066 7882, *info@anoldrectory.co.uk, Fax (028) 9068 3759,* – *closed 25 December-1 January* – **Meals** (by arrangement) 19.50 – **6 rm** 36.00/60.00.
◆ Former Victorian rectory in residential area; period charm retained. Attractive drawing room. Traditionally furnished rooms. Hot Irish whiskey served as guests retire to bed.

Roseleigh House without rest., 19 Rosetta Park, BT6 0DL, South : 1 ½ m. by A 24 (Ormeau Rd) ✆ (028) 9064 4414, *info@roseleighhouse.co.uk* – **9 rm** 50.00/60.00.
◆ Imposing Victorian house close to the Belvoir Park golf course and in a fairly quiet residential suburb. Brightly decorated and well-kept bedrooms with modern amenities.

Restaurant Michael Deane, 34-40 Howard St, BT1 6PF, ✆ (028) 9033 1134, *info@michaeldeane.co.uk, Fax (028) 9056 0001* – BY n
closed 1 week July, Easter, Christmas, New Year and Sunday-Tuesday – **Meals** (dinner only) 40.50 ♀ (see also ***Deanes Brasserie*** below).
Spec. Squab pigeon with fig compote, foie gras and cauliflower. Beef fillet with black pudding, carrot custard, cinnamon and rosemary. "Yellow" fruit dessert.
◆ Elegant 1st floor restaurant with rich, plush décor. Polished and professional service by approachable team. Concise menu of refined, classically based modern Irish dishes.

James Street South, 21 James Street South, BT2 7GA, ✆ (028) 9043 4310, *info@jamesstreetsouth.co.uk, Fax (028) 9043 4310* – BY o
closed Easter, 12-13 July, 25-26 December and Sunday lunch – **Meals** 15.50 (lunch) and a la carte 19.95/26.15.
◆ Tucked away down back alley in heart of the city. 19C façade hides distinctly modish interior. Good value menus; modern cooking based upon well-sourced, fine quality produce.

Aldens, 229 Upper Newtownards Rd, BT4 3JF, East : 2 m. on A 20 ✆ (028) 9065 0079, *info@aldensrestaurant.com, Fax (028) 9065 0032* –
closed 2 weeks July, Saturday lunch, Sunday and Bank Holidays – **Meals** (booking essential) a la carte 17.50/26.85 ♀.
◆ Personally run, spacious and contemporary restaurant in "up-and-coming" suburb. Extensive selection of confident, modern dishes. Moderately priced midweek menu also offered.

Cayenne, 7 Ascot House, Shaftesbury Sq, BT2 7DB, ✆ (028) 9033 1532, *reservations@cayennerestaurant.com, Fax (028) 9026 1575* – BZ r
closed 25-26 December, 1 January, 12 July and lunch Saturday and Sunday – **Meals** (booking essential) 15.50 (lunch) and a la carte 19.75/37.75 ♀.
◆ Striking modern artwork and a lively atmosphere feature in this busy, relaxed and stylish restaurant. Carefully prepared selection of creative Asian influenced dishes.

Shu, 253 Lisburn Rd, BT9 7EN, ☎ (028) 9038 1655, *eat@shu-restaurant.com, Fax (028) 9068 1632* – ▤. MC AE VISA
closed 1 May, 11-13 July, 24-27 December and Sunday – **Meals** a la carte 19.00/30.00 **s.** ♀.
◆ Trendy, modern restaurant on the Lisburn Road. Converted from terraced houses, it is spacious and uncluttered with neutral and black décor. Eclectic, contemporary dishes.

The Wok, 126 Great Victoria St, BT2 7BG, ☎ (028) 9023 3828 – ▤. MC VISA
closed 25-26 December – **Meals** - Chinese - 17.00/23.00 (dinner) and a la carte 13.80/19.00 **s.** BZ a
◆ Smart, modern Chinese restaurant with pleasant ambience. Menus feature classic interpretations and less well-known authentic dishes : most regions of China are represented.

Deanes Brasserie, 36-40 Howard St, BT1 6PF, ☎ (028) 9056 0000, *info@michaeldeane.co.uk, Fax (028) 9056 0001* – ▤. MC AE VISA BY n
closed 1 January, Easter, 12-13 July, 25-26 December and Sunday – **Meals** a la carte 24.00/34.45 ♀.
◆ Ornately decorated, lively and modern street level brasserie continues to attract a loyal regular following. Robust and cosmopolitan cooking with a traditional Irish base.

Nick's Warehouse, 35-39 Hill St, BT1 2LB, ☎ (028) 9043 9690, *info@nickswarehouse.co.uk, Fax (028) 9023 0514* – ▤. MC AE ① VISA BX a
closed 2 days Easter, 1 May, 12 July, 24-27 December, 1 January, Saturday lunch, Monday dinner and Sunday – **Meals** a la carte 15.55/27.90 ♀.
◆ Built in 1832 as a bonded whiskey store. On two floors, the ground floor Anix is relaxed and buzzy. Upstairs more formal. Well informed service of an eclectic menu.

at Belfast International Airport *West : 15 ½ m. by A 52* BX – ✉ *Belfast*

Fitzwilliam International, Aldergrove, BT29 4ZY, ☎ (028) 9445 7000, *reception@fitzwilliaminternational.com, Fax (028) 9442 3500* – |‡|, ⇆ rm, ▤ TV ☎ ♿ P – 🏛 250. MC AE ① VISA JCB. ✈
The Terrace *:* **Meals** (booking essential) (buffet lunch)/dinner 18.95 **s.** – ☕ 12.00 – **106 rm** 95.00/140.00, 2 suites.
◆ Imposingly up-to-date hotel with sun-filled lobby, 50 metres from terminal entrance. Terrace, secluded garden, cocktail bar ; conference facilities. Distinctively modern rooms. Formal restaurant with smart, cosmopolitan ambience.

Write to us...
If you have any comments on the contents of this Guide.
Your praise as well as your criticisms will receive careful consideration and, with your assistance, we will be able to add to our stock of information and, where necessary, amend our judgments.
Thank you in advance!

BIRMINGHAM *W. Mids.* 503 504 O 26 *Great Britain G.* – *pop. 970 892.*

See : *City★ – Museum and Art Gallery★★* LY **M2** – *Barber Institute of Fine Arts★★ (at Birmingham University)* EX **U** – *Cathedral of St Philip (stained glass portrayals★)* LMY – *Thinktank★, Millennium Point* FV.

Envir. : *Aston Hall★★* FV **M.**

Exc. : *Black Country Museum★, Dudley, NW : 10 m. by A 456 and A 4123 – Bourneville★, SW : 4 m. on A 38 and A 441.*

Edgbaston, Church Rd ☎ (0121) 454 1736 FX – *Hilltop, Park Lane, Handsworth ☎ (0121) 554 4463 – Hatchford Brook, Coventry Rd, Sheldon (0121) 743 9821* HX – *Brandhall, Heron Rd, Oldbury, Warley ☎ (0121) 552 2195 – Harborne Church Farm, Vicarage Rd, Harborne (0121) 427 1204* EX.

✈ *Birmingham International Airport : ☎ (08707) 335511, E : 6 ½ m. by A 45.*

ℹ *Convention & Visitor Bureau, 2 City Arcade ☎ (0121) 643 2514, Fax (0121) 616 1038 – Convention & Visitor Bureau, National Exhibition Centre ☎ (0121) 202 5099 – Birmingham Airport, Information Desk ☎ (0121) 767 7145 Visitor Information Centre, 130 Colmore Row ☎ (0121) 693 6300.*

London 122 – Liverpool 103 – Manchester 86.

Plans on following pages

Malmaison, Mailbox, 1 Wharfside St, B1 1RD, (0121) 246 5000, *birmingham@malmaison.com, Fax (0121) 246 5002,* - rm, - 45. LZ e
Brasserie : **Meals** 12.95/13.95 and a la carte 22.15/37.65 - 11.75 - **186 rm** 129.00, 3 suites.
◆ Modern hotel near shops and nightlife. Ground floor leisure centre. Stylish bar. Spacious contemporary bedrooms with every modern facility; good view from upper floors. First floor brasserie serving contemporary French influenced cooking at reasonable prices.

Hyatt Regency, 2 Bridge St, B1 2JZ, (0121) 643 1234, *birmingham@hyattintl.com, Fax (0121) 616 2323,* - rm, - 240. KZ a
Court Cafe : **Meals** 13.50/16.75 and a la carte 25.00/45.00 - 15.00 - **315 rm** 180.00, 4 suites.
◆ Striking mirrored exterior. Glass enclosed lifts offer panoramic views. Sizeable rooms with floor to ceiling windows. Covered link with International Convention Centre. Large dining room with Impressionist prints.

Birmingham Marriott, 12 Hagley Rd, B16 8SJ, (0121) 452 1144, *reservations.birmingham@marriotthotels.co.uk, Fax (0121) 456 3442,* - rm, - 80. JZ c
West 12 : **Meals** (bar lunch Saturday) 14.00/26.00 and a la carte 24.00/32.00 **s.** - 14.95 - **100 rm** 129.00, 4 suites.
◆ Edwardian grand foyer with Italian marble and mahogany. Drawing room popular for afternoon tea. Egyptian theme fitness centre. Individually appointed, sizeable rooms. Stylish, modern restaurant.

Hotel Du Vin, 25 Church St, B3 2NR, (0121) 200 0600, *info@birmingham.hoteldu vin.com, Fax (0121) 236 0889,* - rm, rest, - 85. LY e
Bistro : **Meals** a la carte 30.50/33.70 - 13.50 - **66 rm** 125.00/225.00.
◆ Former Victorian eye hospital with striking, wine themed interiors. "Cave du Vin" for wine, cigar purchases. Low lighting in rooms of muted tones; one has 8ft bed and gym. Champagne in "bubble lounge"; Parisian style brasserie.

Crowne Plaza Birmingham, Central Sq, B1 1HH, (0870) 4009150, *reservations.bhamcity@ichotelsgroup.com, Fax (0121) 643 9018,* - rm, - 150. LZ z
closed 24-26 December – **Meals** *(closed Sunday dinner)* 14.95/19.50 and dinner a la carte 19.85/29.40 **s.** - 15.95 - **281 rm** 175.00, 3 suites.
◆ Ideal for both corporate and leisure guests. Extensive leisure facilities include children's pool. Well-equipped bedrooms with air-conditioning and triple glazing. Conservatory restaurant with views across city.

The Burlington, Burlington Arcade, 126 New St, B2 4JQ, (0121) 643 9191, *mail@burlingtonhotel.com, Fax (0121) 643 5075,* - rm, rest, - 400. LZ a
closed 25-26 December - ***Berlioz :*** **Meals** 22.95 (dinner) and a la carte 22.85/25.50 - 13.95 - **107 rm** 130.00/165.00, 5 suites.
◆ Approached by a period arcade. Restored Victorian former railway hotel retains much of its original charm. Period décor to bedrooms yet with fax, modem and voice mail. Elegant dining room : ornate ceiling, chandeliers and vast mirrors.

Copthorne, Paradise Circus, B3 3HJ, (0121) 200 2727, *reservations.birmingham@mill-cop.com, Fax (0121) 200 1197,* - rm, rest, - 180. LZ v
Goldsmiths : **Meals** (dinner only) 25.00 and a la carte 26.00/36.00 - ***Goldies :*** **Meals** 10.95/18.95 and a la carte 20.95/33.95 - 15.25 - **209 rm** 160.00/180.00, 3 suites.
◆ Overlooking Centenary Square. Corporate hotel with extensive leisure club and cardiovascular gym. Cricket themed bar. Connoisseur rooms offer additional comforts. Flambé dishes offered in intimate Goldsmiths. Goldies is all-day relaxed brasserie.

Jonathan's, 16-24 Wolverhampton Rd, Oldbury, B68 0LH, West : 4 m. by A 456 (0121) 429 3757, *enquiries@jonathans-birmingham.com, Fax (0121) 434 3107* - , rest, - 100.
closed 1 January - ***Victorian Restaurant :*** **Meals** - English - (booking essential) 12.60/16.50 and a la carte 22.40/34.20 - **43 rm** 98.00/125.00, 2 suites.
◆ Unique property decorated with Victorian furnishings and memorabilia. Country house ambience. Reconstructed Victorian street. Individual bedrooms with antiques. 19C artefacts in Victorian Restaurant.

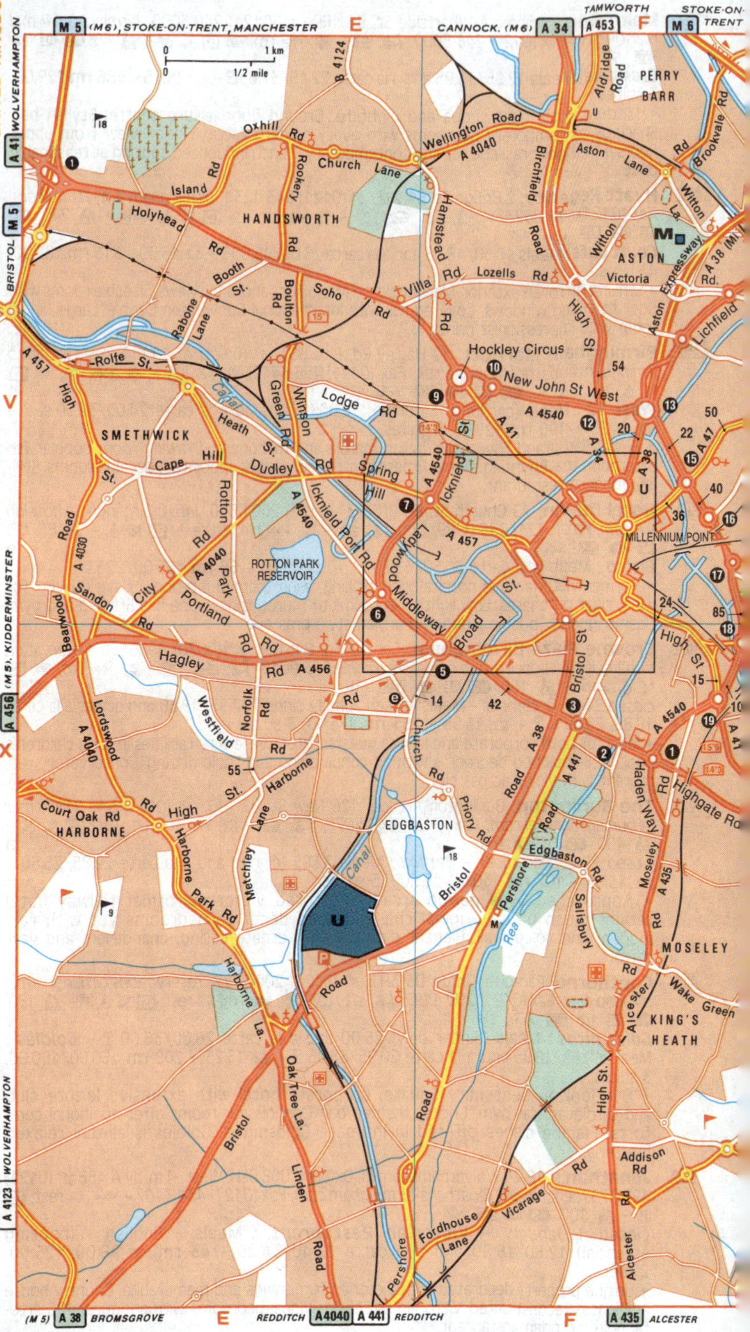
M 5 (M6), STOKE-ON-TRENT, MANCHESTER
E
CANNOCK, (M6) A 34
A 453 TAMWORTH
F
M 6 STOKE-ON-TRENT
A 41 WOLVERHAMPTON
M 5 BRISTOL
A 456 (M5), KIDDERMINSTER
A 4123 WOLVERHAMPTON
(M 5) A 38 BROMSGROVE
REDDITCH A4040 A 441 REDDITCH
A 435 ALCESTER
V
X
0 1 km
0 1/2 mile
PERRY BARR
HANDSWORTH
ASTON
SMETHWICK
HARBORNE
EDGBASTON
MOSELEY
KING'S HEATH
Hockley Circus
New John St West
MILLENNIUM POINT
ROTTON PARK RESERVOIR
Oxhill Rd
Church Lane
Wellington Road
A 4040
Birchfield Road
Aldridge Road
Aston Lane
Brookvale Rd
Witton Rd
Witton La.
Aston Expressway
A 38 (M)
Lichfield
Victoria Rd.
Lozells Rd
Villa Rd
Hamstead Rd
Rookery Rd
Island Rd
Holyhead Rd
Booth St.
Soho Rd
Boulton Rd
Rabone Lane
Rolfe St.
A 457
High St.
Canal
Heath St.
Green Rd
Winson Rd
Lodge Rd
Icknield St
A 41
A 4540
A 34
A 38
A 47
Cape Hill
Dudley Rd
Spring Hill
Icknield Port Rd
Ladywood Middleway
Rotton Park Rd
City Rd
Sandon Rd
Portland Rd
Bearwood Road
A 4030
Hagley Rd
A 456
Broad St.
Bristol St
Westfield Rd
Norfolk Rd
Lordswood
A 4040
Court Oak Rd
High St.
Harborne Rd
Church Rd
Priory Rd
Pershore Road
A 441
Edgbaston Rd
Haden Way
Highgate Rd
Moseley Rd
A 435
Salisbury Rd
Harborne Park Rd
Metchley Lane
Bristol Rd
Rea
Harborne La.
Oak Tree La.
Linden Road
Bristol Road
Alcester Rd
Wake Green Rd
High St.
Addison Rd
Vicarage Rd
Fordhouse Lane
Pershore Road
Alcester Rd
B 4124
U
M
P
54 20 22 50 40 36 24 85 15 42 14 55 10
1 2 3 5 6 7 9 10 12 13 15 16 17 18 19
14'3 15'9 15'

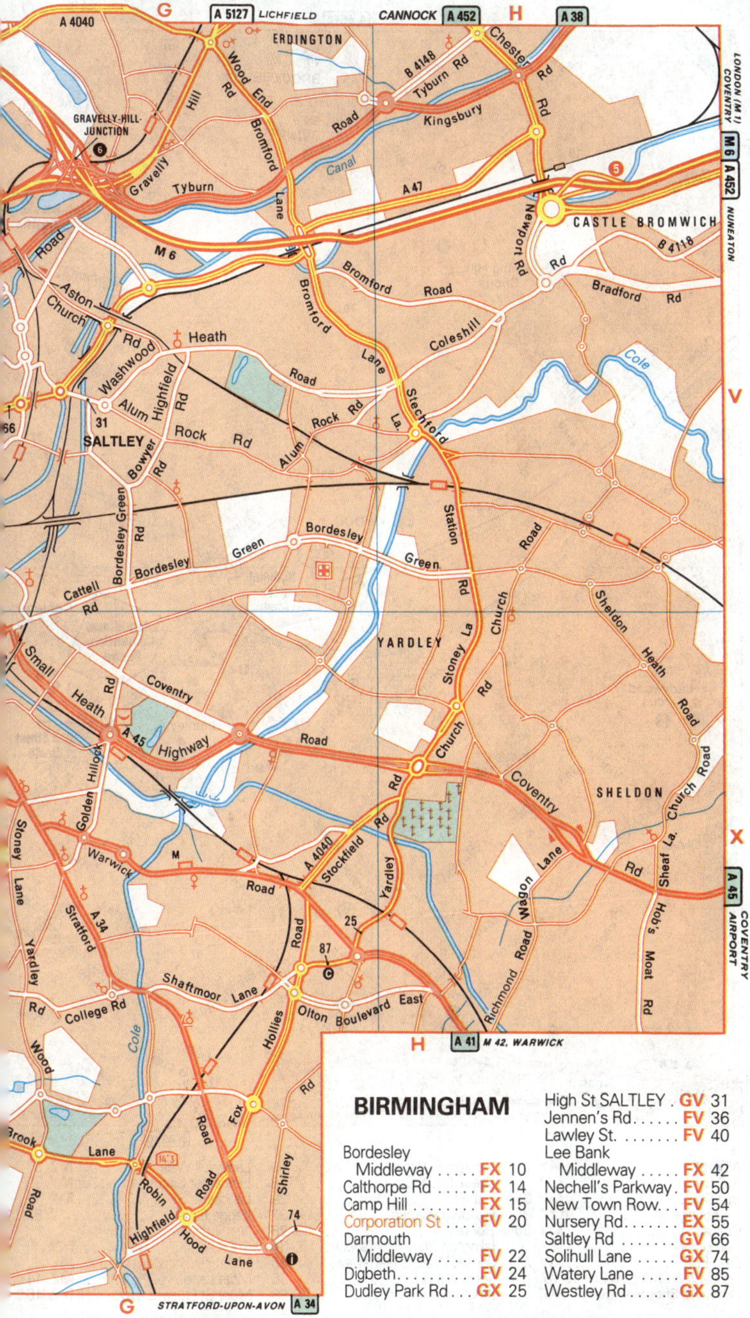

BIRMINGHAM

Bordesley Middleway	FX	10
Calthorpe Rd	FX	14
Camp Hill	FX	15
Corporation St	FV	20
Darmouth Middleway	FV	22
Digbeth	FV	24
Dudley Park Rd	GX	25
High St SALTLEY	GV	31
Jennen's Rd	FV	36
Lawley St.	FV	40
Lee Bank Middleway	FX	42
Nechell's Parkway	FV	50
New Town Row	FV	54
Nursery Rd	EX	55
Saltley Rd	GV	66
Solihull Lane	GX	74
Watery Lane	FV	85
Westley Rd	GX	87

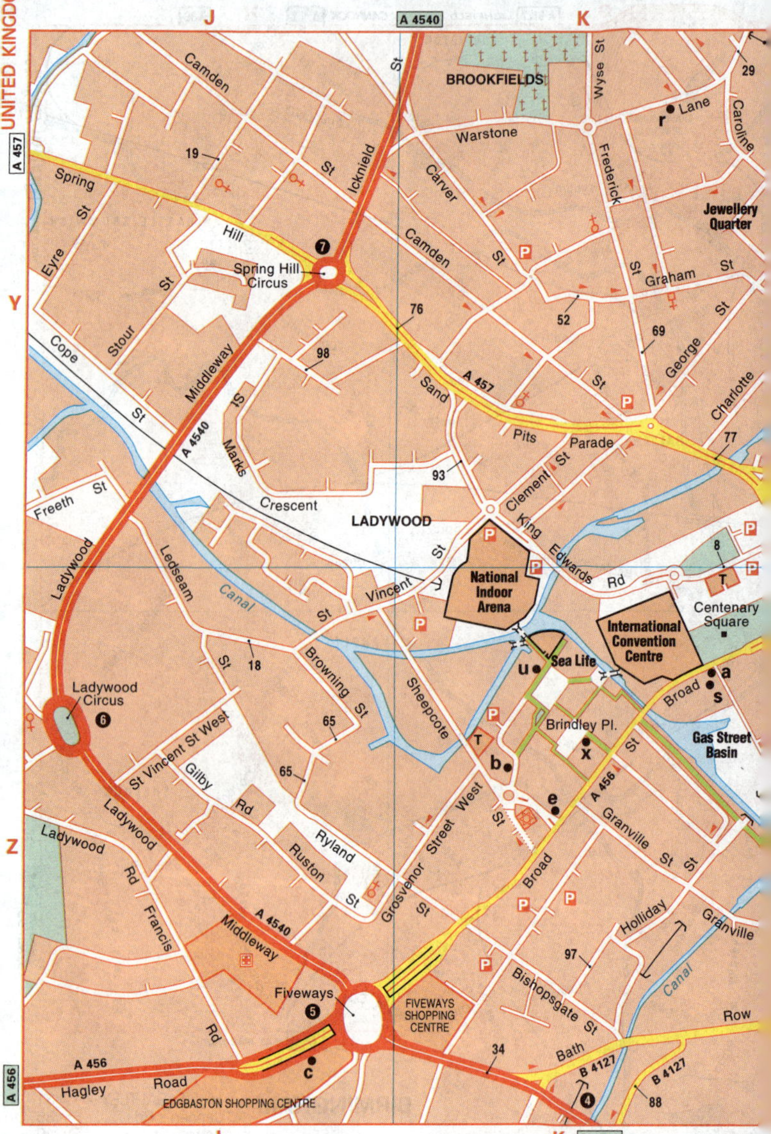

Albert St . . . . MY 2
Bull Ring Centre . . . . MZ
Bull St . . . . MY 3
Cambridge St . . . . KYZ 8
Chapel St . . . . MY 30
Corporation St . . . . MYZ
Dale End . . . . MY 21
Edgbaston Shopping Centre JZ
Fiveways Shopping Centre . KZ
George St West . . . . JY 19
Great Tindal St . . . . JZ 18
Hall St . . . . KY 29
Holloway Circus . . . . LZ 32
Horse Fair . . . . LZ 28
Islington Row Middleway . . KZ 34
James Watt Queensway . . MY 35
Jennen's Rd . . . . MY 36
King Edwards Rd . . . . JY 98
Ladywell Walk . . . . MZ 37
Lancaster Circus . . . . MY 39
Lancaster St . . . . MY 41
Legge Lane . . . . KY 52
Martineau Place Shopping Centre . . . . MY
Minories Shopping Centre . MY
Moat Lane . . . . MZ 44
Moor St Queensway . . . . MYZ 46

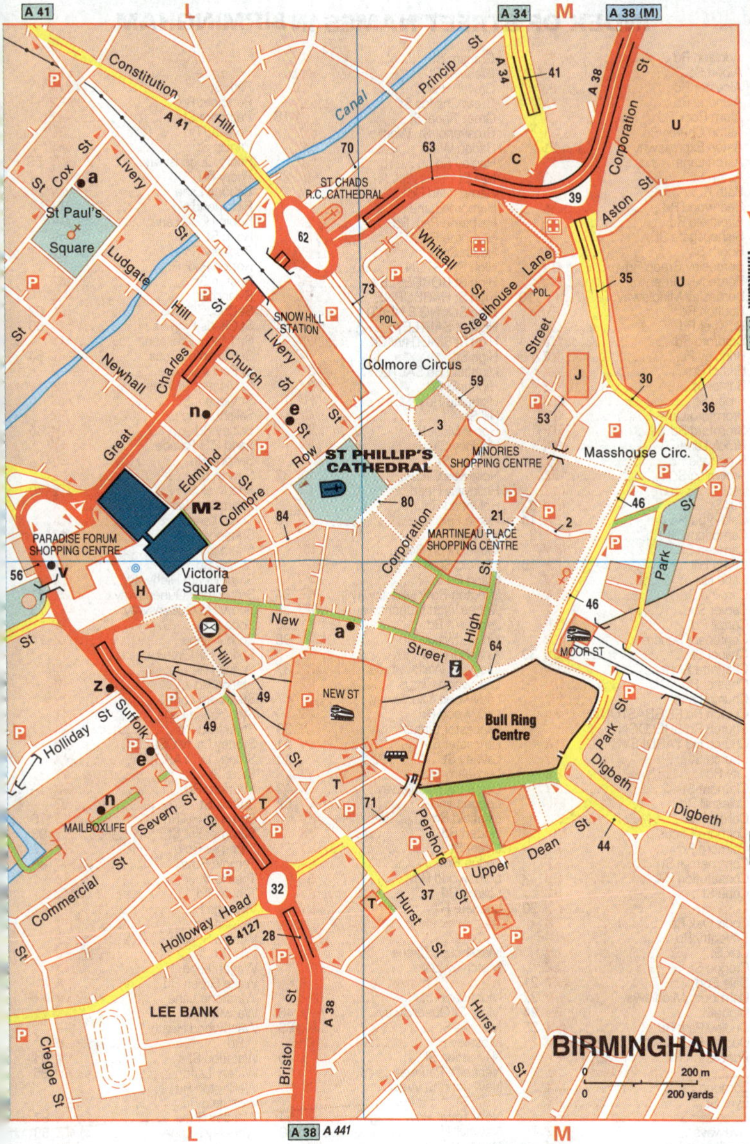

Morville St . . . . JZ 65
Navigation St . . . . LZ 49
New St . . . . LMZ
Newhall Hill . . . . KY 69
Newton St . . . . MY 53
Paradise Circus . . . . LYZ 56
Paradise Forum Shopping Centre . . . . LYZ
Priory Queensway . . . . MY 59
St Chads Circus . . . . LY 62
St Chads Ringway . . . . MY 63
St Martin's Circus . . . . MZ 64
Shadwell St . . . . LMY 70
Smallbrook Queensway . . . . LMZ 71
Snow Hill Queensway . . . LMY 73
Summer Hill Rd . . . . JKY 76
Summer Hill St . . . . KY 93
Summer Row . . . . KY 77
Temple Row . . . . MY 80
Waterloo St . . . . LY 84
Wheeley's Lane . . . . KZ 88
William St . . . . KZ 97

INDEX OF STREET NAMES IN BIRMINGHAM

Addison Rd . . . FX
Albert St . . . MY 2
Alcester Rd . . . FX
Aldridge Rd . . . FV
Alum Rock Rd . . . GV
Aston Church Rd . . . GV
Aston Expressway . . . FV
Aston Lane . . . FV
Aston St . . . MY
Bath Row . . . KZ
Bearwood Rd . . . EV
Birchfield Rd . . . FV
Bishopsgate St . . . KZ
Booth St . . . EV
Bordesley Green Rd . . . GV
Bordesley Green . . . GV
Bordesley Middleway . . . FX 10
Boulton Rd . . . EV
Bowyer Rd . . . GV
Bradford Rd . . . HV
Brindley Pl. . . . KZ
Bristol Rd . . . EFX
Bristol St . . . LZ
Broad St . . . KLZ
Bromford Lane . . . GV
Bromford Rd . . . HV
Brook Lane . . . GX
Brookvale Rd . . . FV
Browning St . . . JZ
Bull Ring Centre . . . MZ
Bull St . . . MY 3
Calthorpe Rd . . . FX 14
Cambridge St . . . KYZ 8
Camden St . . . JKY
Camp Hill . . . FX 15
Cape Hill . . . EV
Caroline St . . . KLY
Carver St . . . KY
Cattell Rd . . . GV
Centenary Square . . . KZ
Chapel St . . . MY 30
Charlotte St . . . KLY
Chester Rd . . . HV
Church Lane . . . EV
Church Rd EDGBASTON . . . FX
Church Rd SHELDON . . . HX
Church Rd YARDLEY . . . HX
Church St . . . LY
City Rd . . . EV
Clement St . . . KY
Coleshill Rd . . . HV
College Rd . . . GX
Colmore Circus . . . MY
Colmore Row . . . LY
Commercial St . . . LZ
Constitution Hill . . . LY
Cope St . . . JY
Corporation St . . . FV 20
Court Oak Rd . . . EX
Coventry Rd . . . GHX
Cox St . . . LY
Cregoe St . . . LZ
Dale End . . . MY 21
Darmouth Middleway . . . FV 22
Digbeth . . . FV 24
Dudley Park Rd . . . GX 25
Dudley Rd . . . EV
Edgbaston Rd . . . FX
Edgbaston Shopping Centre . . . JZ
Edmund St . . . LY
Eyre St . . . JY
Fiveways Shopping Centre . . . KZ
Fiveways . . . JZ
Fordhouse Lane . . . FX
Fox Hollies Rd . . . GX
Francis Rd . . . JZ
Frederick St . . . KY
Freeth St . . . JY
George St West . . . JY 19
George St . . . KY
Gilby Rd . . . JZ
Golden Hillock Rd . . . GX
Graham St . . . KY
Granville St . . . KLZ
Gravelly Hill . . . GV
Great Charles St . . . LY
Great Tindal St . . . JZ 18
Grosvenor St West . . . JKZ
Haden Way . . . FX
Hagley Rd . . . JZ
Hall St . . . KY 29
Hampstead Rd . . . FV
Harborne Lane . . . EX
Harborne Park Rd . . . EX
Harborne Rd . . . EX
Heath St . . . EV
High St ASTON . . . FV
High St BORDESLEY . . . FX
High St HARBORNE . . . EX
High St KING'S HEATH . . . FX
High St SALTLEY . . . GV 31
High St SMETHWICK . . . EV
High St . . . MZ
Highfield Rd SALTLEY . . . GV
Highfield Rd . . . GX
Highgate Rd . . . FX
Hill St . . . LZ
Hob's Moat Rd . . . HX
Hockley Circus . . . FV
Holliday St . . . KLZ
Holloway Circus . . . LZ 32
Holloway Head . . . LZ
Holyhead Rd . . . EV
Horse Fair . . . LZ 28
Hurst St . . . MZ
Icknield Port Rd . . . EV
Icknield St . . . JKY
Island Rd . . . EV
Islington Row Middleway . . . KZ 34
James Watt Queensway . . . MY 35
Jennen's Rd . . . MY 36
King Edwards Rd . . . JY 98
Kingsbury Rd . . . HV
Ladywell Walk . . . MZ 37
Ladywood Circus . . . JZ
Ladywood Middleway . . . JYZ
Ladywood Rd . . . JZ
Lancaster Circus . . . MY 39
Lancaster St . . . MY 41
Lawley St . . . FV 40
Ledseam St . . . JYZ
Lee Bank Middleway . . . FX 42
Legge Lane . . . KY 52
Lichfield Rd . . . FV
Linden Rd . . . EX
Livery St . . . LY
Lodge Rd . . . EV
Lordswood Rd . . . EX
Lozells Rd . . . FV
Ludgate Hill . . . LY
Martineau Place Shopping Centre . . . MY
Masshouse Circus . . . MY
Metchley Lane . . . EX
Minories Shopping Centre . . . MY
Moat Lane . . . MZ 44
Moor St Queensway . . . MYZ 46
Morville St . . . JZ 65
Moseley Rd . . . FX
Navigation St . . . LZ 49
Nechell's Parkway . . . FV 50
New John St West . . . FV
New St . . . LMZ
New Town Row . . . FV 54
Newhall Hill . . . KY 69
Newhall St . . . MY
Newport Rd . . . HV
Newton St . . . MY 53
Norfolk Rd . . . EX
Nursery Rd . . . EX 55
Oak Tree Lane . . . EX
Olton Bd East . . . GX
Oxhill Rd . . . EV
Paradise Circus . . . LYZ 56
Paradise Forum Shopping Centre . . . LYZ
Park St . . . MYZ
Pershore Rd . . . FX
Pershore St . . . MZ
Portland Rd . . . EV
Princip St . . . MY
Priory Queensway . . . MY 59
Priory Rd . . . FX
Rabone Lane . . . EV
Richmond Rd . . . HX
Robin Hood Lane . . . GX
Rolfe St . . . EV
Rookery Rd . . . EV
Rotton Park Rd . . . EV
Ruston St . . . JZ
Ryland St . . . JKZ
St Chads Circus . . . LY 62
St Chads Ringway . . . MY 63
St Marks Crescent . . . JY
St Martin's Circus . . . MZ 64
St Paul's Square . . . LY
St Vincent St West . . . JZ
St Vincent St . . . JKZ
Salisbury Rd . . . FX
Saltley Rd . . . GV 66
Sand Pits Parade . . . KY
Sandon Rd . . . EV
Severn St . . . LZ
Shadwell St . . . LMY 70
Shaftmoor Lane . . . GX
Sheaf Lane . . . HX
Sheepcote St . . . KZ
Sheldon Heath Rd . . . HX
Shirley Rd . . . GX
Small Heath Highway . . . GX
Smallbrook Queensway . . . LMZ 71
Snow Hill Queensway . . . LMY 73
Soho Rd . . . EV
Solihull Lane . . . GX 74
Spring Hill Circus . . . JY
Spring Hill . . . JY
Station Rd . . . HV
Stechford Lane . . . HV
Steelhouse Lane . . . MY
Stockfield Rd . . . GX
Stoney La. MOSELEY . . . GX
Stoney La. YARDLEY . . . HX
Stour St . . . JY
Stratford Rd . . . GX
Suffolk St . . . LZ
Summer Hill Rd . . . JKY 76
Summer Hill St . . . KY 93
Summer Row . . . KY 77
Temple Row . . . MY 80
The Row . . . MZ
Tyburn Rd . . . GHV
Vicarage Rd . . . FX
Victoria Rd . . . FV
Victoria Square . . . LZ
Villa Rd . . . FV
Wagon Lane . . . HX
Wake Green Rd . . . FX
Warstone Lane . . . KY
Warwick Rd . . . GX
Washwood Heath Rd . . . GV
Waterloo St . . . LY 84
Watery Lane . . . FV 85
Wellington Rd . . . FV
Westfield Rd . . . EX
Westley Rd . . . GX 87
Wheeley's Lane . . . KZ 88
Whittall St . . . MY
William St . . . KZ 97
Winson Green Rd . . . EV
Witton Lane . . . FV
Witton Rd . . . FV
Wood End Rd . . . GV
Wyse St . . . KY
Yardley Rd . . . HX
Yardley Wood Rd . . . GX

Asquith House without rest., 19 Portland Rd, Edgbaston, B16 9HN, (0121) 454 5282, *tina@totelapartment.co.uk, Fax (0121) 456 4668* – JX c
closed 25 December – **1 rm, 9 suites** 65.00/95.00.
◆ 19C house converted into comfortable, spacious fully-serviced apartments, individually styled with modern facilities. Friendly service. Continental breakfast served in room.

City Inn, 1 Brunswick Sq, Brindley Pl, B1 2HW, (0121) 643 1003, *birmingham.reservations@cityinn.com, Fax (0121) 643 1005,* – rm, – 80. KZ b
City Café : **Meals** 12.50/16.50 and a la carte 25375/30.85 – 11.50 – **238 rm** 129.00.
◆ Vast hotel ; the spacious atrium with its bright rugs and blond wood sets the tone for equally stylish rooms. Corporate friendly with many meeting rooms. Eat in restaurant, terrace or bar.

Novotel, 70 Broad St, B1 2HT, (0121) 643 2000, *hlo77@accor-hotels.com, Fax (0121) 643 9796,* – rm, rest, – 300. KZ e
Meals 14.95 and a la carte 13.40/25.40 **s.** – 11.50 – **148 rm** 140.00/155.00.
◆ Well located for the increasingly popular Brindleyplace development. Underground parking. Modern, well-kept, branded bedrooms suitable for families. Modern, open-plan restaurant.

Simpson's (Antona) with rm, 20 Highfield Rd, Edgbaston, B15 3DX, (0121) 454 3434, *info@simpsonsrestaurant.co.uk, Fax (0121) 454 3399,* – rest, – **Meals** 20.00/30.00 and a la carte 28.50/37.95 – **4 rm** 80.00/180.00. EX e
Spec. Seared foie gras, roast banana, pain d'épice. Squab pigeon with its own pastilla, aromatic cous cous, apricots, pigeon jus. Praline soufflé, turron ice cream.
◆ Restored Georgian residence ; its interior a careful blend of Victorian features and contemporary style. Refined, classically based cooking. Elegant bedrooms.

Jessica's (Purnell), 1 Montague Rd, B16 9HU, (0121) 455 0999, *Fax (0121) 455 8222* – EX c
closed last 2 weeks July, 1 week Easter, 24 December-2 January, Sunday and lunch Saturday and Monday – **Meals** 21.50/29.95.
Spec. Terrine of smoked ham and crab with celeriac and pineapple. Roast saddle and shoulder of lamb, roast pear and artichoke. Crème brûlée with coffee ice cream.
◆ Restaurant with conservatory facing garden and fountain. Contemporary décor and furniture. Good value menu offering accomplished modern British cooking.

Paris, 109-111 Wharfside St, The Mailbox, B1 1RF, (0121) 632 1488, *paris.restaurant@virgin.net, Fax (0121) 632 1489,* – LZ n
closed 1 week Christmas – New Year, 2 weeks summer, Sunday and Monday – **Meals** 21.50 (lunch) and a la carte 21.50/48.50.
◆ Located in fashionable Mailbox area, and painted in a deep chocolate brown palette with stylish tan leather chairs. Fine dining, with chef's gourmand menu also available.

Bank, 4 Brindleyplace, B1 2JB, (0121) 633 4466, *birmres@bankrestaurants.com, Fax (0121) 633 4465,* – KZ u
Meals 14.00 (lunch) and a la carte 18.30/33.00.
◆ Capacious, modern and busy bar-restaurant where chefs can be watched through a glass wall preparing the tasty modern dishes. Pleasant terrace area.

La Toque D'Or, 27 Warstone Lane, Hockley, B18 6JQ, (0121) 233 3655, *didier@latoquedor.co.uk, Fax (0121) 233 3655* – KY r
closed Easter, 2 weeks August, Christmas-New Year, Sunday, Monday, Tuesday after Bank Holidays and Saturday lunch – **Meals** - French - (booking essential) 19.50/24.50 **s.**
◆ A different type of gem in the Jewellery Quarter. Personally run former rolling mill : bare brick and stained glass. Well-judged seasonal menu bears classic French hallmarks.

Metro Bar and Grill, 73 Cornwall St, B3 2DF, (0121) 200 1911, *Fax (0121) 200 1611* – LY n
closed 25-26 December, Saturday lunch, Sunday and Bank Holidays – **Meals** (booking essential) a la carte 19.90/28.40.
◆ Gleaming chrome and mirrors in a bright, contemporary basement restaurant. Modern cooking with rotisserie specialities. Spacious, ever-lively bar serves lighter meals.

Zinc Bar and Grill, Regency Wharf, Gas Street Basin, Broad St, B1 2DS, (0121) 200 0620, *zinc-birmingham@conran-restaurants.co.uk, Fax (0121) 200 0630,* – KZ s
closed 25-26 December and Sunday dinner – **Meals** a la carte 17.00/33.50.
◆ Purpose-built restaurant in lively pub and club area of city. Spiral staircase leads to dining area, including terrace overlooking canal. Modern, classically toned, dishes.

Henry's, 27 St Paul's Sq, B3 1RB, (0121) 200 1136, *enquiries@henrysrestaurant.co.uk, Fax (0121) 200 1190* – LY a
closed Bank Holidays – **Meals** - Chinese (Canton) - 8.50 (lunch) and a la carte 13.10/36.50.
◆ An extensive range of Cantonese dishes offered in this well-established and personally run restaurant. Private dining rooms available for 40. Opposite the 18C square.

at Birmingham Airport *Southeast : 9 m. by A 45 HX – ✉ Birmingham :*

Novotel, Passenger Terminal, B26 3QL, ☎ (0121) 782 7000, *h1158@accor.com, Fax (0121) 782 0445* – |‡|, ⇆ rm, TV ☎ ♿ – 🎭 35. MC AE ⊙ VISA
Meals (bar lunch Saturday, Sunday and Bank Holidays) 15.00/21.50 and a la carte 16.65/28.95 ♀ – ☕ 12.95 – **195 rm** 119.00.
◆ Opposite main terminal building : modern hotel benefits from sound proofed doors and double glazing. Mini bars and power showers provided in spacious rooms with sofa beds. Open-plan garden brasserie.

at National Exhibition Centre *Southeast : 9 ½ m. on A 45 HX – ✉ Birmingham :*

Hilton Birmingham Metropole, Bickenhill, B40 1PP, ☎ (0121) 780 4242, *Fax (0121) 780 3923*, Fб, ≘s, 🏊 – |‡|, ⇆ rm, ▤ rest, TV ♿ P – 🎭 2000. MC AE ⊙ VISA
closed 24-29 December – **Meals** (carvery) 18.00/29.95 **s.** ♀ – ***Primavera :* Meals** - Italian - (booking essential) (dinner only) a la carte 26.50/35.25 ♀ – ***Millers :* Meals** - American grill - (dinner only) a la carte 19.35/27.80 ♀ – ☕ 14.95 – **787 rm** 190.00/235.00, 15 suites.
◆ Imposing, modern conference oriented hotel beside lake. NEC within walking distance. Well-equipped rooms, some with the benefit of a balcony. Conservatory restaurant. Bright, Mediterranean influenced Primavera. Busy, bustling, American-styled Millers.

Crowne Plaza, Pendigo Way, B40 1PS, ☎ (0870) 400 9160, *Fax (0121) 781 4321*, Fб, ≘s – |‡|, ⇆ rm, ▤ TV ☎ ♿ P – 🎭 180. MC AE ⊙ VISA. ⇎
***Brian Turners :* Meals** (bar lunch Saturday) a la carte 23.40/34.95 ♀ – ☕ 14.50 – **242 rm** 195.00.
◆ Modern hotel adjacent to NEC. Small terrace area overlooks lake. Extensive conference facilities. State-of-the-art bedrooms with a host of extras. Basement dining room : food with a Yorkshire twist.

Chagford *Devon* 503 I 31.

London 218 – Bath 102 – Birmingham 186.

Gidleigh Park 🍃, TQ13 8HH, Northwest : 2 m. by Gidleigh Rd ☎ (01647) 432367, *gidleighpark@gidleigh.co.uk, Fax (01647) 432574*, ← Teign Valley, woodland and Meldon Hill, 🎣, 🏑, 🌳, ✂ – ⇆ rest, TV P. MC AE ⊙ VISA
✿✿
Meals (booking essential) 28.00/80.00 ♀ – **12 rm** ☕ (dinner included) 275.00/575.00, 3 suites.
Spec. Terrine of lobster, red mullet, monkfish and scallops. Best end of lamb, tomato fondue and roast garlic. Poached peach, vanilla mousse and blackcurrants.
◆ Spectacular hotel of sensual delights. Outstanding rooms decorated in a flourish of style. Oak panelled lounge with watercolours. Water garden, herb beds and croquet lawn. Culinary specialities abound, full of exquisitely prepared local produce.

Cheltenham *Glos.* 503 504 N 28 – *pop. 98 875.*

ℹ 77 Promenade ☎ (01242) 522878.
London 99 – Birmingham 48 – Bristol 40 – Oxford 43.

Le Champignon Sauvage (Everitt-Matthias), 24-26 Suffolk Rd, GL50 2AQ, ☎ (01242) 573449, *Fax (01242) 254365* – MC AE ⊙ VISA JCB
✿✿
closed 3 weeks June, 1 week Christmas, Sunday and Monday – **Meals** 25.00/44.00 ♀.
Spec. Pan-fried foie gras with walnuts and quince, Maury syrup. Braised veal with snails and nettles. Chocolate marjolaine.
◆ Cheerful restaurant with artwork on yellow walls ; intimate feel with nine well-spaced tables. Masterful cooking : ingredients combined with inventiveness to seduce the palette.

Ludlow *Shrops.* 503 L 26 – *pop. 9 548.*

ℹ Castle St ☎ (01584) 875053.
London 162 – Birmingham 39.

Hibiscus (Bosi), 17 Corve St, SY8 1DA, ☎ (01584) 872325, *Fax (01584) 874024* – ⇆ P. MC VISA JCB
✿✿
closed 3 weeks Christmas, 1 week May, 1 week August, Sunday and Monday – **Meals** (booking essential) 25.00/42.50 ♀.
Spec. Foie gras ice cream with emulsion of brioche and caramel. Pork belly with eel in truffle jus, pineapple confit. Hazelnut millefeuille with butternut squash ice cream.
◆ Two dining rooms, one with 17C oak panelling and the other with exposed stone walls. Precise cooking with some original and innovative touches ; attentive formal service.

EDINBURGH *Edinburgh* **501** K 16 *Scotland G.* – *pop. 430 082.*

See: *City*** Edinburgh International Festival*** (August) – Royal Museum of Scotland*** EZ* **M2** *National Gallery of Scotland** DY Royal Botanic Garden*** – The Castle** AC DYZ : Site*** Palace Block (Honours of Scotland***) St Margaret's Chapel (※***) Great Hall (Hammerbeam Roof**) – St Margaret's Chapel (※***) Great Hall (Hammerbeam Roof**) ≤** from Argyle and Mill's Mount DZ Abbey and Palace of Holyroodhouse** AC – (Plasterwork Ceilings***, ※** from Arthur's Seat) BV Royal Mile** : St Giles' Cathedral** (Crown Spire***) EYZ – Gladstone's Land* AC EYZ* **A** *Canongate Talbooth* EY* **B** *– New Town** (Charlotte Square*** CY* **14** *The Georgian House* CY* **D** *– Scottish National Portrait Gallery* EY* **M6** *Dundas House* EY* **E**) *– Scottish National Gallery of Modern Art* Victoria Street* EZ* **84** *Scott Monument* (≤*) AC EY* **F** *– Craigmillar Castle* AC, SE : 3 m. by A 7 BX Calton Hill (※*** AC from Nelson's Monument) EY.*

Envir.: *Edinburgh Zoo** AC – Hill End Ski Centre (※**) AC, S : 5 ½ m. by A 702 – The Royal Observatory (West Tower ≤*) AC – Ingleston, Scottish Agricultural Museum*, W : 6 ½ m. by A 8.*

Exc.: *Rosslyn Chapel** AC (Apprentice Pillar***), S : 7 ½ m. by A 701 and B 7006 – Forth Bridges**, NW : 9 ½ m. by A 90 – Hopetoun House** AC, NW : 11 ½ m. by A 90 and A 904 – Dalmeny* Dalmeny House* AC, St Cuthbert's Church* (Norman South Doorway**), NW : 7 m. by A 90 – Crichton Castle (Italianate courtyard range*) AC, SE : 10 m. by A 7 and B 6372.*

18, 18 Braid Hills, Braid Hills Rd ☎ (0131) 447 6666 – 18 Carrick Knowe, Glendevon Park ☎ (0131) 337 1096 – 18 Duddingston, Duddingston Road West ☎ (0131) 661 7688 – 18 Silverknowes, Parkway ☎ (0131) 336 3843 – 18 Liberton, 297 Gilmerton Rd ☎ (0131) 664 3009 – 18, 18 Marriott Dalmahoy H. & C.C., Kirknewton ☎ (0131) 335 8010.

Edinburgh Airport : ☎ (0131) 333 3342, W : 6 m. by A 8 – **Terminal** : *Waverley Bridge.*

Edinburgh & Scotland Information Centre, 3 Princes St ☎ (0845) 2255121, info@visitscotland.co.uk – Edinburgh Airport, Tourist Information Desk ☎ (0845) 2255121.

Glasgow 46 – Newcastle upon Tyne 105.

Plans on following pages

Balmoral, 1 Princes St, EH2 2EQ, ☎ (0131) 556 2414, *reservations@thebalmoralhotel.com, Fax (0131) 557 8740,* – 350. MC AE D VISA JCB. EY n
closed first week January – **Meals** (see ***Number One*** and ***Hadrian's*** below) – 18.00 – **167 rm** 205.00/340.00, 21 suites.
• Richly furnished rooms in grand baronial style complemented by contemporary furnishings in the Palm Court exemplify this de luxe Edwardian railway hotel and city landmark.

Caledonian Hilton, Princes St, EH1 2AB, ☎ (0131) 222 8888, *guest.caledonian@hilton.com, Fax (0131) 222 8889,* – rm, rest, – 250. MC AE D VISA JCB. CY n
The Pompadour : **Meals** *(closed Saturday lunch, Sunday and Monday)* 19.95/25.50 and a la carte 37.00/49.00 ♀ – ***Chisholms*** : **Meals** (dinner only and lunch Saturday-Monday) 19.95 and a la carte 29.00/39.00 ♀ – 16.50 – **238 rm** 195.00/225.00, 13 suites.
• A city landmark, affectionately known locally as "The Cally". Overlooked by the castle, with handsomely appointed rooms and wood-panelled halls behind an imposing 19C façade. The Pompadour boasts elegant dining. Informal Chisholms serves popular brasserie fare

Sheraton Grand, 1 Festival Sq, EH3 9SR, ☎ (0131) 229 9131, *grandedinburgh.sheraton@sheraton.com, Fax (0131) 229 6254,* – rm, – 500. MC AE D VISA. CDZ v
Terrace : **Meals** (buffet only) 19.95/20.95 ♀ (see also ***Grill Room*** and ***Santini*** below) – 17.00 – **244 rm** 225.00/265.00, 16 suites.
• A modern, centrally located and smartly run hotel. A popular choice for the working traveller, as it boasts Europe's most advanced urban spa. Comfy, well-kept rooms. Glass expanse of Terrace restaurant overlooks Festival Square.

The George Intercontinental, 19-21 George St, EH2 2PB, ☎ (0131) 225 1251, *Fax (0131) 226 5644* – rm, – 200. MC AE D VISA JCB. DY z
Le Chambertin (☎ *(0131) 240 7178)* : **Meals** *(closed Saturday lunch and Sunday)* 19.95 (lunch) and a la carte 23.50/30.25 **s.** ♀ – ***Carvers*** (☎ *(0131) 459 2305)* : **Meals** a la carte 13.50/20.95 **s.** ♀ – 16.00 – **192 rm** 185.00/240.00, 3 suites.
• An established classic that makes the most of Robert Adam's listed 18C design. Welcoming marble-floored lobby, convivial Clans bar and well-proportioned bedrooms. Le Chambertin is light, spacious and stylish. Carvers is set in magnificent glass-domed room.

The Howard, 34 Great King St, EH3 6QH, ☎ (0131) 623 9303, *reserve@thehoward.com, Fax (0131) 623 9306* – rest, – 30. MC AE D VISA. DY s
closed Christmas – ***The Atholl*** : **Meals** (booking essential for non-residents) 28.00/32.50 ♀ – **13 rm** 145.00/295.00, 5 suites.
• Crystal chandeliers, antiques, richly furnished rooms and the relaxing opulence of the drawing room set off a fine Georgian interior. An inviting "boutique" hotel. Elegant, linen-clad tables for sumptuous dining.

EDINBURGH

Bernard Terrace	EZ	3
Bread St	DZ	6
Bristo Pl.	EZ	7
Candlemaker Row	EZ	9
Castle St	DY	
Castlehill	DZ	10
Chambers St	EZ	12
Chapel St	EZ	13
Charlotte Square	CY	14
Deanhaugh St	CY	23
Douglas Gardens	CY	25
Drummond St	EZ	27
Forrest Rd	EZ	31
Frederick St	DY	
Gardner's Crescent	CZ	32
George IV Bridge	EZ	33
George St	DY	
Grassmarket	DZ	35
Hanover St	DY	
High St	EYZ	37
Home St	DZ	38
Hope St	CY	39
Johnston Terrace	DZ	42
King's Bridge	DZ	44
King's Stables Rd	DZ	45
Lawnmarket	EYZ	46
Leith St	EY	47
Leven St	DZ	48
Lothian St	EZ	51
Mound (The)	DY	55
North Bridge	EY	61
North St Andrew St	EY	66
Princes St	DY	
Raeburn Pl.	CY	69
Randolph Crescent	CY	71
St Andrew Square	EY	73
St James Centre	EY	
St Mary's St	EY	75
Shandwick Pl.	CYZ	77
South Charlotte St	DY	78
South St David St	DEY	79
Spittal St	DZ	83
Victoria St	EZ	84
Waterloo Pl.	EY	87
Waverley Bridge	EY	89
Waverley Market	EY	
West Maitland St	CZ	92

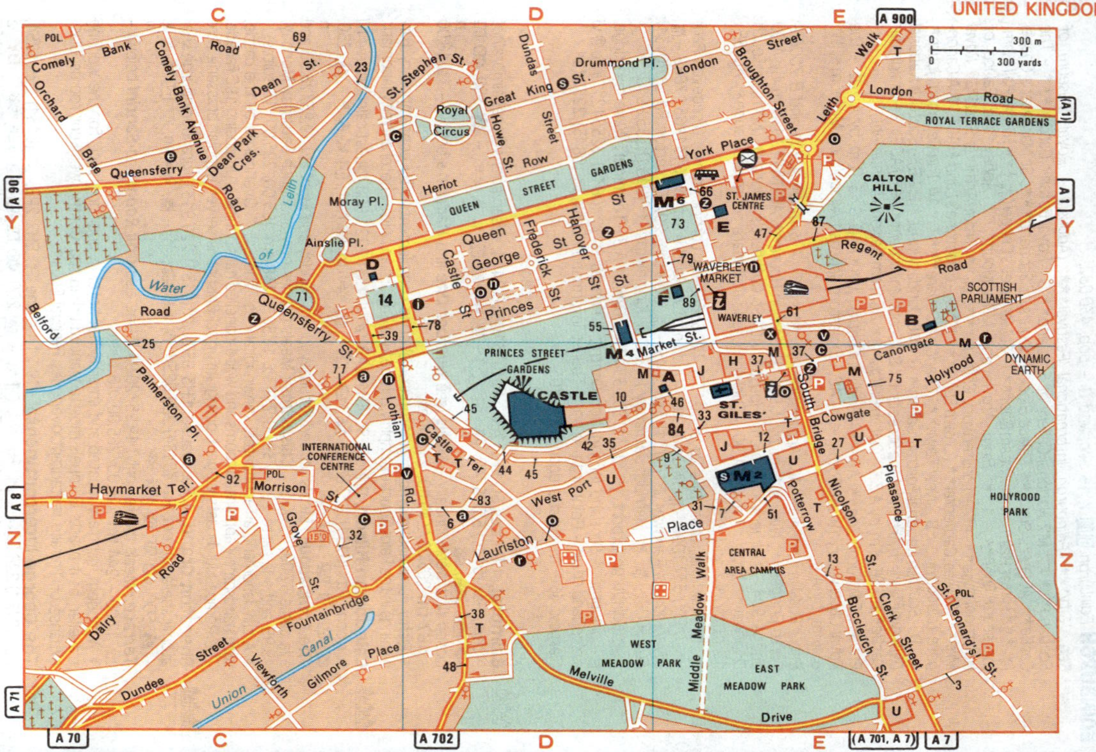

The Scotsman, 20 North Bridge, EH1 1YT, ☎ (0131) 556 5565, *reservations@thescotsmanhotelgroup.co.uk, Fax (0131) 652 3652*, – rm, – 80. EY x

Vermilion : **Meals** (dinner only) 35.00/50.00 and a la carte 31.00/46.00 – ***North Bridge Brasserie :*** **Meals** 9.95 (lunch) and a la carte 18.00/31.00 – 17.50 – **57 rm** 250.00/295.00, 12 suites.

◆ Imposing former offices of "The Scotsman" newspaper, with marble reception hall and historic prints. Notably impressive leisure facilities. Well-equipped modern bedrooms. Vibrant, richly red Vermilion. North Bridge Brasserie boasts original marble pillars.

Prestonfield, Priestfield Rd, EH16 5UT, ☎ (0131) 225 7800, *reservations@prestonfield.com, Fax (0131) 220 4392*, – rm, – 900. by A 7 EZ

Rhubarb : **Meals** a la carte 30.85/35.40 – **22 rm** 195.00/225.00, 2 suites.

◆ Superbly preserved interior, tapestries and paintings in the main part of this elegant country house, built in 1687 with modern additions. Set in parkland below Arthur's Seat. Two-roomed, period-furnished 18C dining room with fine views of the grounds.

Channings, 15 South Learmonth Gdns, EH4 1EZ, ☎ (0131) 623 9302, *reserve@channings.co.uk, Fax (0131) 623 9306*, – – 35. CY e

Ochre Vita : **Meals** 7.50/9.50 (lunch) and a la carte 15.00/24.50 (see also ***Channings*** below) – **43 rm** 140.00/225.00, 3 suites.

◆ Sensitively refurbished rooms and fire-lit lounges blend an easy country house elegance with original Edwardian character. Individually appointed bedrooms. Informal conservatory dining room with summer terrace.

The Bonham, 35 Drumsheugh Gdns, EH3 7RN, ☎ (0131) 623 9301, *reserve@thebonham.com, Fax (0131) 623 9306* – – 50.

Meals 13.50/16.00 (lunch) and dinner a la carte 23.05/38.10 – **46 rm** 145.00/225.00, 2 suites. CY z

◆ A striking synthesis of Victorian architecture, eclectic fittings and bold, rich colours of a contemporary décor. Numerous pictures by "up-and-coming" local artists. Chic dining room with massive mirrors and "catwalk" in spotlights.

The Glasshouse without rest., 2 Greenside Pl, EH1 3AA, ☎ (0131) 525 8200, *resglasshouse@theetongroup.com, Fax (0131) 525 8205*, – – 70. EY o

16.50 – **65 rm** 195.00.

◆ Glass themes dominate the discreet style. Modern bedrooms, with floor to ceiling windows, have views of spacious roof garden or the city below. Breakfast room to the rear.

The Roxburghe, 38 Charlotte Sq, EH2 4HG, ☎ (0131) 240 5500, *roxburghe@csmm.co.uk, Fax (0131) 240 5555*, – rest, – 350. DY i

The Melrose : **Meals** *(closed Saturday lunch)* (dinner only and Sunday lunch) 24.50 and a la carte 16.00/30.00 – 14.50 – **197 rm** 145.00/210.00, 1 suite.

◆ Attentive service, understated period-inspired charm and individuality in the British style. Part modern, part Georgian but roomy throughout ; welcoming bar. Restaurant reflects the grandeur of architect Robert Adam's exterior.

Radisson SAS, 80 High St, EH1 1TH, ☎ (0131) 557 9797, *reservations.edinburgh@radissonsas.com, Fax (0131) 557 9789*, – rm, – 250. EY z

closed 24-26 December – **Meals** 20.95 and a la carte 20.85/38.65 **s.** – 14.50 – **228 rm** 105.00/230.00, 10 suites.

◆ Recreates the look of a baronial Great House. Rooms are pleasantly spacious, some looking down on the Royal Mile. Compact leisure centre with jet stream swimming pool. Basement restaurant flaunts eye-catching suspended lighting.

Hilton Edinburgh Grosvenor, Grosvenor St, EH12 5EF, ☎ (0131) 226 6001, *reservations.edinburghgros@hilton.com, Fax (0131) 220 2387* – rest, – 300. CZ a

Meals (bar lunch)/dinner 22.45/31.90 **s.** – 15.50 – **187 rm** 220.00, 2 suites.

◆ Company hotel in an attractive 19C row, with some rooms in the annex across the road. Relax in the welcoming lounge and bar after a day in the main shopping streets nearby. Scottish themed restaurant.

Edinburgh Marriott, 111 Glasgow Rd, EH12 8NF, West : 4 ½ m. on A 8 ☎ (0870) 400 7293, *edinburgh@marriotthotels.co.uk, Fax (0870) 400 7393*, – – 250.

Mediterrano : **Meals** (lunch booking essential) a la carte 20.00/30.00 **s.** – 14.95 – **241 rm** 120.00, 4 suites.

◆ Excellent road connections for the airport and Glasgow and well-equipped rooms make this large, group-operated hotel a practical choice for business travel. Modern restaurant with Mediterranean twist.

Point, 34 Bread St, EH3 9AF, ✆ (0131) 221 5555, *info@point-hotel.co.uk, Fax (0131) 221 9929* – |‡|, ⇎ rm, TV ✆ ♿ – 100. MC AE ⦿ VISA DZ a
Meals *(closed Saturday lunch and Sunday)* 12.90/16.90 ♀ – **136 rm** ☐ 125.00/165.00, 4 suites.
• Formerly the Co-operative offices, converted in daring minimalist style. Boldly toned lobby and light, clean-lined rooms. Castle views over the rooftops from the upper floors. Strikingly lit avant-garde restaurant.

Holyrood Aparthotel without rest., 1 Nether Bakehouse (via Gentles entry), EH8 8PE, ✆ (0131) 524 3200, *mail@holyroodaparthotel.com, Fax (0131) 524 3210* – |‡| ⇎ TV ✆ ♿ ⇔. MC AE ⦿ VISA EY r
41 suites 160.00/250.00.
• These two-bedroomed apartments are neat and up-to-date with well-stocked kitchens. Located in a booming area of the city, not far from the Palace of Holyrood.

Christopher North House, 6 Gloucester Pl, EH3 6EF, ✆ (0131) 225 2720, *reservations@christophernorth.co.uk, Fax (0131) 220 4706* – ⇎ rm, TV ✆. MC AE ⦿ VISA JCB. ✈ CY c
Meals *(closed Sunday)* (dinner only) a la carte 16.50/25.50 **s.** – **18 rm** ☐ 75.00/140.00.
• Georgian house on cobbled street in quiet residential area ; a chintzy feel overlays the contemporary interior. Eclectically styled bedrooms feature homely extra touches. Classic Scottish cooking in formally styled dining room.

Novotel Edinburgh Centre, 80 Lauriston Pl, EH3 9DE, ✆ (0131) 656 3500, *h3271@accor.com, Fax (0131) 656 3510,* Ꮀ, ≘, ⊡ – |‡|, ⇎ rm, ▤ TV ✆ ♿. MC AE ⦿ VISA JCB DZ o
Meals a la carte 14.00/28.00 – ☐ 13.00 – **180 rm** 129.00.
• 21C hotel in a smart, contemporary style. Well-equipped leisure club. Modern bedrooms : two top-floor suites have private balconies, while 40 rooms look towards the castle. Informal dining room, open 18 hours a day.

Clarendon, 25 Shandwick Pl, EH2 4RG, ✆ (0131) 229 1467, *res@clarendonhoteledi.com, Fax (0131) 229 7549* – |‡| ⇎ TV ♿. MC AE ⦿ VISA JCB. ✈ CZ a
Meals *(closed Sunday)* (dinner only) a la carte 16.00/29.00 – **66 rm** ☐ 65.00/105.00.
• Two minutes' walk from Princes Street, and completely refurbished in 2004, this smart hotel boasts bright, vivid colours, a cosy, contemporary bar and well-presented rooms. Modish dining room specialisng in Asian menus.

Edinburgh City, 79 Lauriston Pl, EH3 9HZ, ✆ (0131) 622 7979, *reservations@bestwesternedinburghcity.co.uk, Fax (0131) 622 7900* – |‡| ⇎, ▤ rest, TV ✆ ♿. MC AE ⦿ VISA JCB. ✈ DZ r
closed 24-26 December – **Meals** (bar lunch)/dinner a la carte 15.00/30.00 – ☐ 9.50 – **51 rm** 140.00/190.00, 1 suite.
• Tidily run hotel, converted from Scotland's first maternity hospital, an easy stroll from the centre. A listed Victorian building, it boasts bright, good-sized bedrooms. Smart, comfortable restaurant.

Ibis without rest., 6 Hunter Sq, EH1 1QW, ✆ (0131) 240 7000, *h2039@accor.com, Fax (0131) 240 7007* – |‡| ⇎ TV ✆ ♿. MC AE ⦿ VISA JCB EZ o
☐ 4.75 **99 rm** 52.95.
• Interior design reflects the group's ethos - compact and functional, yet comfortable. A super position just off the High Street will appeal to tourists throughout the year.

XXXX ✿ **Number One** (at Balmoral H.), 1 Princes St, EH2 2EQ, ✆ (0131) 622 8831, *Fax (0131) 557 8740* – ▤. MC AE ⦿ VISA JCB EY n
closed Saturday and Sunday lunch – **Meals** 18.50/22.50 (lunch) and a la carte 40.95/50.40 ♀.
Spec. Isle of Skye crab with pasta, avocado and tomato. Roast fillet of beef, curried oxtail, spinach and woodland mushrooms. Trio of chocolate surprise, hot cherry sauce.
• Edinburgh's nonpareil for polished fine dining and immaculate service ; spacious basement setting. Original dishes with a well-balanced flair showcase Scottish produce.

XXX **Oloroso,** 33 Castle St, EH2 3DN, ✆ (0131) 226 7614, *info@oloroso.co.uk, Fax (0131) 226 7608,* ≤, 斎 – ▤. MC AE VISA DY o
Meals a la carte 17.95/31.00 **s.** ♀.
• Modish third floor restaurant in heart of city. Busy, atmospheric bar. Lovely terrace with good castle views to the west. Stylish, modern cooking with Asian influence.

XXX **Grill Room** (at Sheraton Grand H.), 1 Festival Sq, EH3 9SR, ✆ (0131) 221 6422, *Fax (0131) 229 6254* – ⇎ ▤ P. MC AE ⦿ VISA JCB CDZ v
closed Saturday lunch, Sunday and Monday – **Meals** 29.00 and a la carte 38.00/45.00 ♀.
• Ornate ceilings, wood panels and modern glass make an ideal setting for imaginative, well presented cooking. Local ingredients with a few European and Pacific Rim elements.

XXX **Santini** (at Sheraton Grand H.), 8 Conference Sq, EH3 8AN, ✆ (0131) 221 7788, *Fax (0131) 221 7789* – ▤ P. MC AE ⓓ VISA CDZ v
closed Saturday lunch and Sunday – **Meals** - Italian - 25.00/29.00 and a la carte 27.00/37.50.
◆ The personal touch is predominant in this stylish restaurant appealingly situated under a superb spa. Charming service heightens the enjoyment of tasty, modern Italian food.

XX **Off The Wall,** 105 High St, EH1 1SG, ✆ (0131) 558 1497, *otwedinburgh@aol.com* – MC AE VISA EY c
closed 24-26 December, 1-2 January and Sunday – **Meals** 16.50/19.95 (lunch) and dinner a la carte 26.85/30.90 ♀.
◆ Located on the Royal Mile, though hidden on first floor away from bustling crowds. Vividly coloured dining room. Modern menus underpinned by a seasonal Scottish base.

XX **Channings** (at Channings H.), 12-16 South Learmonth Gdns, EH4 1EZ, ✆ (0131) 623 9302, *Fax (0131) 623 9306*, ⛱ – ⚟. MC AE ⓓ VISA CY e
closed Sunday-Monday – **Meals** 19.00/35.50 ♀.
◆ A warm, contemporary design doesn't detract from the formal ambience pervading this basement restaurant in which classic Gallic flavours hold sway.

XX **Forth Floor (at Harvey Nichols),** 30-34 St Andrew Sq, EH2 2AD, ✆ (0131) 524 8350, *Fax (0131) 524 8351*, ≤ Castle and city skyline, ⛱ – |♦| ▤. MC AE ⓓ VISA JCB EY z
closed Christmas and Sunday and Monday dinner except August and Bank Holidays – **Meals** a la carte 26.45/37.45 ☺ ♀.
◆ Stylish restaurant with delightful outside terrace affording views over the city. Half the room in informal brasserie-style and the other more formal. Modern, Scottish menus.

XX **Atrium,** 10 Cambridge St, EH1 2ED, ✆ (0131) 228 8882, *eat@atriumrestaurant.co.uk, Fax (0131) 228 8808* – ▤. MC AE ⓓ VISA JCB DZ c
closed 25-26 December, 1-2 January, Sunday and Saturday lunch except during Edinburgh Festival – **Meals** 17.50/25.00 and a la carte 28.50/38.50 ♀.
◆ Located inside the Traverse Theatre, an adventurous repertoire enjoyed on tables made of wooden railway sleepers. Twisted copper lamps subtly light the ultra-modern interior.

XX **Duck's at Le Marche Noir,** 2-4 Eyre Pl, EH3 5EP, ✆ (0131) 558 1608, *enquiries@ducks.co.uk, Fax (0131) 556 0798* – ⚟. MC AE ⓓ VISA JCB by A 1 EY
closed 25-26 December and lunch Saturday-Monday – **Meals** a la carte 23.10/38.25 ♀.
◆ Confident, inventive cuisine with a modern, discreetly French character, served with friendly efficiency in bistro-style surroundings - intimate and very personally run.

XX **Rogue,** 67 Morrison St, EH3 8HH, ✆ (0131) 228 2700, *info@rogues-uk.com, Fax (0131) 228 3299* – MC AE VISA CZ c
closed 25-26 December, 1 January and Sunday – **Meals** a la carte 17.50/22.50.
◆ Stylish, bright venue with beautiful wooden stripped bar. Contemporary feel highlighted by chrome and leather chairs. Modern international menu with substantial choice.

XX **The Marque,** 19-21 Causewayside, EH9 1QF, ✆ (0131) 466 6660, *Fax (0131) 466 6661* – ⚟. MC AE VISA by A 701 EZ
closed Christmas, first week January, Monday and Tuesday – **Meals** 15.00 and a la carte 21.95/28.40 ☺ ♀.
◆ Arresting yellow decor and modern art won't distract attention from an original menu and smart service. A good lunch or pre-theatre choice ; expect subtle Provençal touches.

XX **Hadrian's** (at Balmoral H.), 2 North Bridge, EH1 1TR, ✆ (0131) 557 5000, *Fax (0131) 557 3747* – ▤. MC AE ⓓ VISA JCB EY n
Meals 11.00 and a la carte 13.75/24.75 ☺ ♀.
◆ Drawing on light, clean-lined styling, reminiscent of Art Deco, and a "British new wave" approach ; an extensive range of contemporary brasserie classics and smart service.

XX **Martins,** 70 Rose St, North Lane, EH2 3DX, ✆ (0131) 225 3106, *martinirons@fsbdial.co.uk* – ⚟. MC AE ⓓ VISA JCB DY n
closed 1 week May, 1 week September, 24 December-late January, Saturday lunch, Sunday and Monday – **Meals** (booking essential) 20.00 (lunch) and a la carte 29.50/37.00 ♀.
◆ A concise menu of tasty, well-prepared options from local, mostly organic produce behind an unprepossessing façade. An impressive cheeseboard.

XX **Marque Central,** 30b Grindley St, EH3 9AX, ✆ (0131) 229 9859, *Fax (0131) 221 9515* – MC AE VISA DZ i
closed first week September, Christmas, Sunday and Monday – **Meals** 15.00 and a la carte 21.95/28.40 ☺ ♀.
◆ Modern restaurant, incorporated into the Lyceum Theatre. Generous, reasonably priced dishes which draw on contemporary Scottish and Italian traditions with equal facility.

XX **La Garrigue,** 31 Jeffrey St, EH1 1DH, ✆ (0131) 557 3032, *jeanmichel@lagarrigue.co.uk, Fax (0131) 5573032* – MO AE VISA EY v
closed 1-3 January and Sunday lunch – **Meals** - French - 15.50/21.50 and a la carte 20.50/29.50.
• Very pleasant restaurant near the Royal Mile : beautiful handmade wood tables add warmth to rustic décor. Authentic French regional cooking with classical touches.

XX **The Tower,** Museum of Scotland (fifth floor), Chambers St, EH1 1JF, ✆ (0131) 225 3003, *mail@tower-restaurant.com, Fax (0131) 220 4392*, <, – |♦| ✈ ▤. MO AE ① VISA EZ s
closed 25-26 December – **Meals** a la carte 20.20/40.45 ♀.
• Game, grills and seafood feature in a popular, contemporary brasserie style menu. On the fifth floor of the Museum of Scotland - ask for a terrace table and admire the view.

Leith *Edinburgh.*

Malmaison, 1 Tower Pl, EH6 7DB, ✆ (0131) 468 5000, *edinburgh@malmaison.com, Fax (0131) 468 5002*, , Fб – |♦|, ✈ rm, TV ✆ ♿ P – 🏛 70. MO AE ① VISA JCB. ✂ by A 900 EY
Brasserie **: Meals** 9.95 (lunch) and a la carte 18.40/44.40 ♀ – ☕ 11.75 – **95 rm** 135.00, 5 suites.
• Imposing quayside sailors' mission converted in strikingly elegant style. Good-sized rooms, thoughtfully appointed, combine more traditional comfort with up-to-date overtones. Sophisticated brasserie with finely wrought iron.

Express by Holiday Inn without rest., Britannia Way, Ocean Drive, EH6 6JJ, ✆ (0131) 555 4422, *info@hiex-edinburgh.com, Fax (0131) 555 4646* – |♦| ✈ TV ✆ ♿ P – 🏛 30. MO AE ① VISA by A 900 EY
145 rm 86.00.
• Modern, purpose-built hotel offering trim, bright, reasonably-priced accommodation. Convenient for Leith centre restaurants and a short walk from the Ocean Terminal.

XXX ✿ **Martin Wishart,** 54 The Shore, EH6 6RA, ✆ (0131) 553 3557, *info@martin-wishart.co.uk, Fax (0131) 467 7091* – ✈. MO AE VISA by A 900 EY
closed 25-26 December, 1 January, Sunday and Monday – **Meals** (booking essential) 18.50/22.00 (lunch) and a la carte 42.00/52.00 **s.** ♀.
Spec. Roast halibut and braised pig's trotter with caramelised endive. Soufflé of lobster and smoked haddock. Assiette of oysters.
• Simply decorated dockside conversion with a growing reputation. Modern French-accented menus characterised by clear, intelligently combined flavours.

XX **The Vintners Rooms,** The Vaults, 87 Giles St, EH6 6BZ, ✆ (0131) 554 6767, *enquiries@thevintnersrooms.com, Fax (0131) 555 5653* – ✈. MO AE VISA JCB
closed 1-15 January, Sunday dinner and Monday – **Meals** 16.50 (lunch) and dinner a la carte 25.00/33.00 ♀. by A 900 EY
• Atmospheric 18C bonded spirits warehouse with high ceilings, stone floor, rug-covered walls and candlelit side-room with ornate plasterwork. Modern British cooking.

at Bonnyrigg *(Midlothian) Southeast : 8 m. by A 70 EZ and A 7 on A 6094* – ✉ *Edinburgh :*

Dalhousie Castle ⛰, EH19 3JB, Southeast : 1 ¼ m. on B 704 ✆ (01875) 820153, *info@dalhousiecastle.co.uk, Fax (01875) 821936*, <, ≘s, , , – ✈ TV P – 🏛 100. MO AE ① VISA
Dungeon **: Meals** (booking essential to non-residents) (dinner only) 34.00 **s.** – ***The Orangery*** **: Meals** a la carte 22.75/33.05 **s.** – **34 rm** ☕ 120.00/170.00.
• 13C castle in woodland on the South Esk. Period-style furnishing in the spacious rooms, eclipsed by the library's 19C panelling and rococo ceiling. Falconry centre in grounds. Classic menus in characterful Dungeon. Orangery overlooks river and parkland.

at Kirknewton *Southwest : 7 m. on A 71 CZ* – ✉ *Edinburgh*

Dalmahoy H. & Country Club ⛰, EH27 8EB, ✆ (0870) 400 7299, *reservations.dalmahoy@marriotthotels.co.uk, Fax (0870) 400 7399*, <, , Fб, ≘s, , 18, , , – |♦| ✈, ▤ rest, TV ✆ ♿ P – 🏛 350. MO AE ① VISA. ✂
Pentland **: Meals** (dinner only) 37.50 and a la carte 30.25/50.50 ♀ – ***The Long Weekend*** **: Meals** *(closed Christmas and New Year)* (grill rest.) a la carte 17.25/25.40 ♀ – ☕ 14.95 – **212 rm** 135.00/150.00, 3 suites.
• Extended Georgian mansion in 1000 acres with 2 Championship golf courses. Comprehensive leisure club, smart rooms and a clubby cocktail lounge. Tranquil atmosphere with elegant comfort in Pentland restaurant. Informal modern dining at The Long Weekend.

at Edinburgh International Airport *West : 7 ½ m. by A 8* CZ – ✉ *Edinburgh :*

Hilton Edinburgh Airport, 100 Eastfield Rd, EH28 8LL, ✆ (0131) 519 4400, *Fax (0131) 519 4422,* – rest, – 240. MC AE VISA
Meals (carvery lunch)/dinner 26.00 **s.** – 15.50 – **150 rm** 195.00.
◆ Busy, purpose-built hotel offering large, well-equipped rooms designed with working travellers in mind. Shuttle service to the terminal and excellent road links to the city. A large modern restaurant, comfortable and informal.

GLASGOW *Glasgow* 501 502 H 16 *Scotland G.* – *pop. 624 501.*

See : *City★★★ – Cathedral★★★ (<★)* DZ *The Burrell Collection★★★ – Hunterian Art Gallery★★ (Whistler Collection★★★ Mackintosh Wing★★★) AC* CY **M4** *– Museum of Transport★★ (Scottish Built Cars★★★, The Clyde Room of Ship Models★★★) – Art Gallery and Museum Kelvingrove★★* CY *– Pollok House★ (The Paintings★★) – Tolbooth Steeple★* DZ *Hunterian Museum (Coin and Medal Collection★)* CY **M5** *– City Chambers★* DZ **C** *– Glasgow School of Art★ AC* CY **M3** *– Necropolis (<★ of Cathedral)* DYZ *– Gallery of Modern Art★ – Glasgow (National) Science Centre★, Pacific Quay.*

Envir. : *Paisley Museum and Art Gallery (Paisley Shawl Section★), W : 4 m. by M 8.*

Exc. : *The Trossachs★★★, N : 31 m. by A 879, A 81 and A 821 – Loch Lomond★★, NW : 19 m. by A 82 – New Lanark★★, SE : 20 m. by M 74 and A 72* BX.

18 Littlehill, Auchinairn Rd ✆ (0141) 772 1916 – 18 Rouken Glen, Stewarton Rd, Thornliebank ✆ (0141) 638 7044 – 18 Linn Park, Simshill Rd ✆ (0141) 633 0377 – 18 Lethamhill, Cumbernauld Rd ✆ (0141) 770 6220 – 9 Alexandra Park, Dennistoun ✆ (0141) 556 1294 – 9 King's Park, 150a Croftpark Ave, Croftfoot ✆ (0141) 630 1597 – 9 Knightswood, Lincoln Ave ✆ (0141) 959 6358 9 Ruchill Park, Brassey St ✆ (0141) 946 7676.

Access to Oban by helicopter.

Erskine Bridge (toll).

Glasgow Airport : ✆ (0870) 0400008, W : 8 m. by M 8 – **Terminal :** *Coach service from Glasgow Central and Queen Street main line Railway Stations and from Anderston Cross and Buchanan Bus Stations Prestwick International Airport : ✆ (01292) 511000* **Terminal :** *Buchanan Bus Station.*

11 George Sq ✆ (0141) 204 4400, enquiries@seeglasgow.com – Glasgow Airport, Tourist Information Desk, Paisley ✆ (0141) 848 4440.

Edinburgh 46 – Manchester 221.

Plans on following pages

Hilton Glasgow, 1 William St, G3 8HT, ✆ (0141) 204 5555, *reservations.glasgow@hilton.com, Fax (0141) 204 5004,* – 1000. MC AE VISA. CZ s
Minsky's : **Meals** 18.95/24.95 and a la carte 29.40/36.85 – ***La Primavera :*** **Meals** - Italian - *(closed Sunday-Monday)* (dinner only) a la carte 28.65/56.85 (see also ***Camerons*** below) – 17.50 – **315 rm** 190.00, 4 suites.
◆ A city centre tower with impressive views on every side. Comfortable, comprehensively fitted rooms. Extensive leisure and conference facilities. Spacious, modern Minsky's has the style of a New York deli. La Primavera boasts authentic Italian cooking.

Radisson SAS, 301 Argyle St, G2 8DL, ✆ (0141) 204 3333, *reservations.glasgow@radissonsas.com, Fax (0141) 204 3344,* – rm, – 800. MC AE VISA. DZ o
Collage : **Meals** - Mediterranean - a la carte 20.00/40.00 **s.** – ***TaPaell'Ya :*** **Meals** - Tapas - *(closed Saturday lunch and Sunday)* a la carte 10.00/25.00 **s.** – 13.75 – **249 rm** 190.00, 1 suite.
◆ A stunning, angular, modish exterior greets visitors to this consummate, modern commercial hotel. Large, stylish, eclectically furnished bedrooms. Collage is a bright modern restaurant. TaPaell'Ya serves tapas.

One Devonshire Gardens without rest., 1 Devonshire Gdns, G12 0UX, ✆ (0141) 339 2001, *reservations@onedevonshiregardens.com, Fax (0141) 337 1663* – – 50. MC AE VISA by A 82 CY
17.00 – **32 rm** 145.00, 3 suites.
◆ Collection of adjoining 19C houses in terrace, furnished with attention to detail. Elegantly convivial drawing room, comfortable bedrooms and unobtrusive service.

Malmaison, 278 West George St, G2 4LL, ✆ (0141) 572 1000, *glasgow@malmaison.com, Fax (0141) 572 1002,* – rm, – 25. MC AE VISA CY c
The Brasserie *(✆ (0141) 572 1001) :* **Meals** a la carte 20.85/30.85 – 11.95 – **64 rm** 135.00, 8 suites.
◆ Visually arresting former Masonic chapel. Comfortable, well-proportioned rooms seem effortlessly stylish with bold patterns and colours and thoughtful extra attentions. Informal Brasserie with French themed menu and Champagne bar.

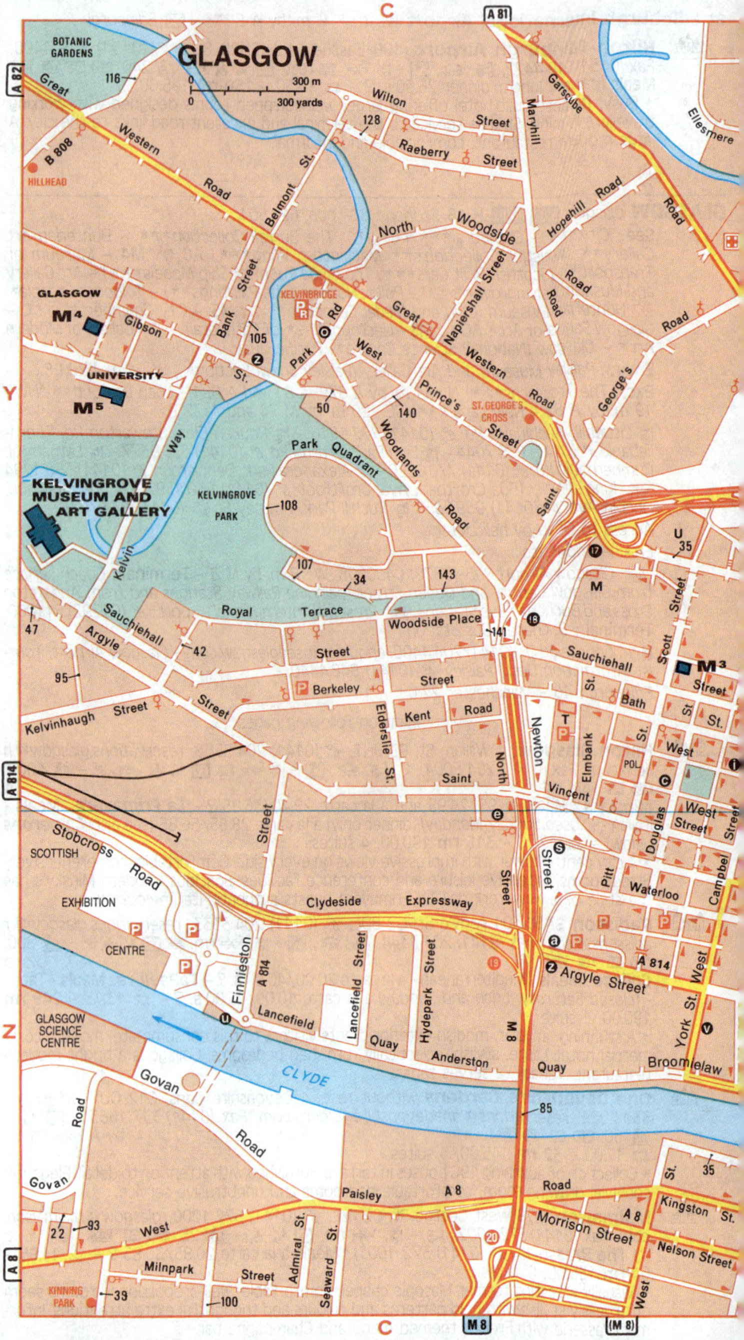
GLASGOW
0 300 m
0 300 yards
C
Y
Z
A 81
A 82
A 814
A 8
M 8
(M 8)
BOTANIC GARDENS
HILLHEAD
B 808
Great Western Road
Belmont St.
Wilton Street
Raeberry Street
Maryhill
Garscube Road
Ellesmere
Hopehill Road
North Woodside Road
Napiershall Street
Road
George's Road
KELVINBRIDGE
Bank Street
Park Rd
West Prince's Street
ST. GEORGE'S CROSS
GLASGOW UNIVERSITY
M 4
M 5
Gibson St.
University Way
KELVINGROVE MUSEUM AND ART GALLERY
KELVINGROVE PARK
Kelvin Way
Park Quadrant
Woodlands Road
Saint
Royal Terrace
Woodside Place
Sauchiehall Street
Argyle Street
Kelvinhaugh Street
Berkeley Street
Kent Road
Elderslie St.
North
Newton
Elmbank St.
Saint Vincent
Scott Street
M 3
Bath St.
West St.
Douglas
West Street
Pitt Street
Waterloo
Campbell
Stobcross Road
SCOTTISH EXHIBITION CENTRE
Clydeside Expressway
Finnieston Street
Street
Lancefield Quay
Lancefield Street
Hydepark Street
Anderston Quay
Argyle Street
A 814
York St.
West
Broomielaw
GLASGOW SCIENCE CENTRE
CLYDE
Govan Road
Govan
Road
Paisley Road West
A 8
Kingston St.
Morrison Street
Nelson Street
West St.
Milnpark Street
Admiral St.
Seaward St.
KINNING PARK
116
128
105
50
140
108
107
34
143
141
47
42
95
35
85
22
93
39
100
U
M
T
POL
17
18
19
20

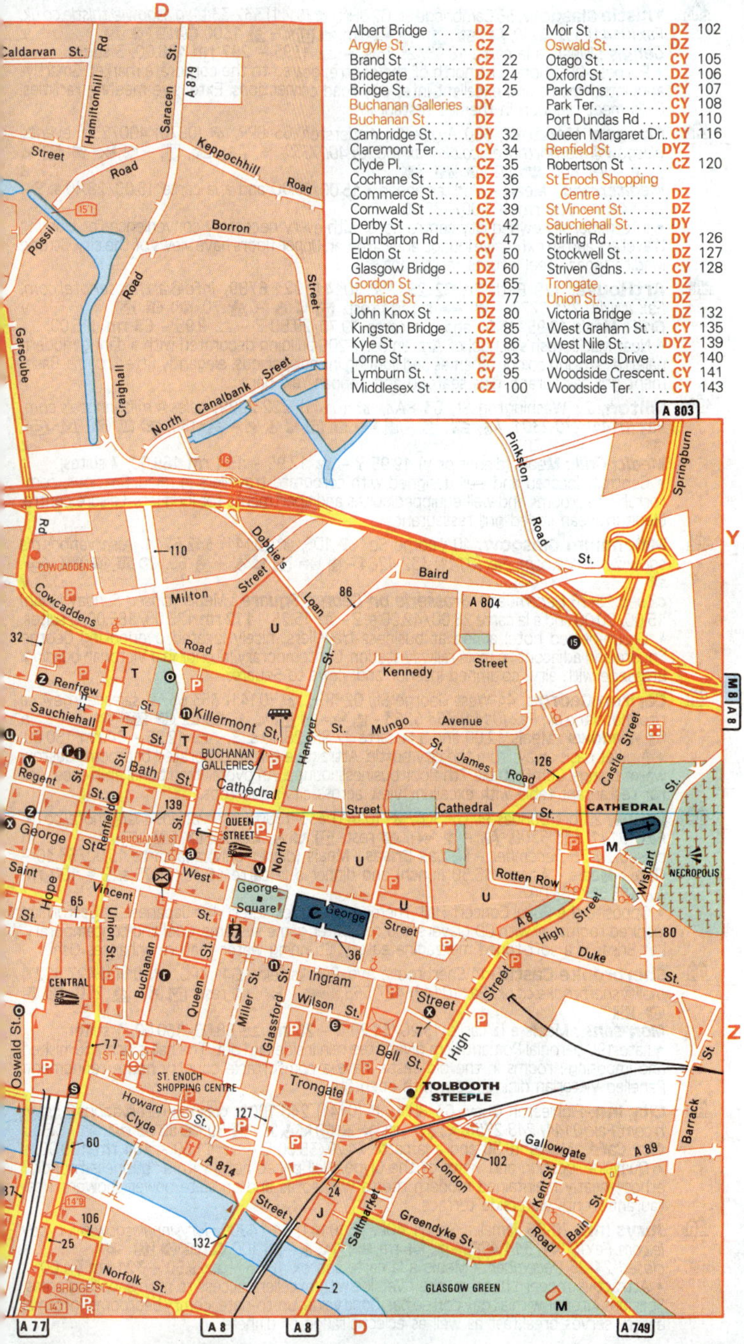

Albert Bridge	DZ	2	Moir St	DZ	102
Argyle St	CZ		Oswald St	DZ	
Brand St	CZ	22	Otago St	CY	105
Bridegate	DZ	24	Oxford St	DZ	106
Bridge St	DZ	25	Park Gdns	CY	107
Buchanan Galleries	DY		Park Ter	CY	108
Buchanan St	DZ		Port Dundas Rd	DY	110
Cambridge St	DY	32	Queen Margaret Dr	CY	116
Claremont Ter	CY	34	Renfield St	DYZ	
Clyde Pl	CZ	35	Robertson St	CZ	120
Cochrane St	DZ	36	St Enoch Shopping Centre	DZ	
Commerce St	DZ	37	St Vincent St	DZ	
Cornwald St	CZ	39	Sauchiehall St	DY	
Derby St	CY	42	Stirling Rd	DY	126
Dumbarton Rd	CY	47	Stockwell St	DZ	127
Eldon St	CY	50	Striven Gdns	CY	128
Glasgow Bridge	DZ	60	Trongate	DZ	
Gordon St	DZ	65	Union St	DZ	
Jamaica St	DZ	77	Victoria Bridge	DZ	132
John Knox St	DZ	80	West Graham St	CY	135
Kingston Bridge	CZ	85	West Nile St	DYZ	139
Kyle St	DY	86	Woodlands Drive	CY	140
Lorne St	CZ	93	Woodside Crescent	CY	141
Lymburn St	CY	95	Woodside Ter	CY	143
Middlesex St	CZ	100			

Thistle Glasgow, 36 Cambridge St, G2 3HN, (0141) 332 3311, *glasgow@thistle.co.uk, Fax (0141) 332 4050,* – rm, – 1300. VISA DY z
Gengis : **Meals** a la carte 18.95/25.75 **s.** – 13.95 – **297 rm** 198.00, 3 suites.
◆ Purpose-built hotel just north of the centre, geared to the corporate market. Smartly-appointed rooms and excellent inter-city road connections. Extensive meeting facilities. Grills meet tandoori in themed restaurant.

Glasgow Marriott, 500 Argyle St, Anderston, G3 8RR, (0870) 4007230, *events.glasgow@marriotthotels.co.uk, Fax (0870) 4007330,* – – 600. VISA. CZ a
Mediterrano : **Meals** - Mediterranean - 15.00/30.00 and a la carte 15.00/28.40 **s.** – 14.95 – **300 rm** 145.00/185.00.
◆ Internationally owned city centre hotel with every necessary convenience for working travellers and an extensive lounge and café-bar. Upper floors have views of the city. Strong Mediterranean feel infuses restaurant..

ArtHouse, 129 Bath St, G2 2SZ, (0141) 221 6789, *info@arthousehotel.com, Fax (0141) 221 6777* – , rm, rest, – 70. VISA DY v
Grill : **Meals** 12.95/15.00 and a la carte 19.70/29.80 – 9.95 – **63 rm** 115.00.
◆ Near Mackintosh's School of Art, an early 20C building decorated with a daring modern palette : striking colour schemes and lighting in the spacious, elegantly fitted rooms. Basement grill restaurant, plus seafood and Teppan-Yaki bar.

Milton, 27 Washington St, G3 8AZ, (0141) 222 2929, *sales@miltonhotels.com, Fax (0141) 270 2301,* – – 150. VISA JCB. CZ z
Medici Grill : **Meals** (dinner only) 19.95 – 12.95 – **134 rm** 169.00, 7 suites.
◆ Centrally located and well designed with corporate travellers in mind. Spacious, comfortable bedrooms and well-equipped suites and apartments for long lets. Leisure centre. Mediterranean styled grill restaurant.

Millennium Glasgow, 40 George Sq, G2 1DS, (0141) 332 6711, *reservations.glasgow@mill-cop.com, Fax (0141) 332 4264* – – 60. VISA JCB. DZ v
closed 25-26 December – ***Brasserie on George Square :*** **Meals** *(closed Sunday lunch)* 15.00/20.00 and a la carte 25.00/42.00 **s.** – 15.25 – **112 rm** 175.00/185.00, 5 suites.
◆ Group-owned hotel aimed at business travellers, nicely located overlooking George Square and adjacent to main railway station. Contemporary interior in a Victorian building. Brasserie with airy, columned interior and views to Square.

Carlton George, 44 West George St, G2 1DH, (0141) 353 6373, *salesgeorge@carltonhotels.co.uk, Fax (0141) 353 6263* – . VISA. DZ a
Windows : **Meals** 12.00 and a la carte 17.95/28.40 **s.** – 12.95 – **64 rm** 150.00.
◆ A quiet oasis away from the city bustle. Attractive tartan decorated bedrooms bestow warm tidings. Comfortable 7th floor business lounge. An overall traditional ambience. Ask for restaurant table with excellent view across city's rooftops.

Langs, 2 Port Dundas Pl, G2 3LD, (0141) 333 1500, *reservations@langshotel.co.uk, Fax (0141) 333 5700,* – , rest, . VISA JCB DY n
closed 24-26 December – ***Las Brisas :*** **Meals** (dinner only) a la carte 15.00/33.30 – ***Oshi :*** **Meals** - Asian - 13.50 (lunch) and dinner a la carte 16.45/25.75 **s.** – **100 rm** 155.00/165.00.
◆ Opposite the Royal Concert Hall. Themed loft suites and stylish Japanese or Californian inspired rooms, all with CD players and computer game systems. Cool and contemporary. Las Brisas is a soft-toned mezzanine eatery. Stunning water feature enhances Oshi.

Sherbrooke Castle, 11 Sherbrooke Ave, Pollokshields, G41 4PG, (0141) 427 4227, *mail@sherbrooke.co.uk, Fax (0141) 427 5685,* – , rest, – 250. VISA by M 8 CZ
Morrisons : **Meals** a la carte 15.20/31.20 – **20 rm** 68.00/150.00, 1 suite.
◆ Late 19C baronial Romanticism given free rein inside and out. The hall is richly furnished and imposing ; rooms in the old castle have a comfortable country house refinement. Panelled Victorian dining room with open fire.

City Inn, Finnieston Quay, G3 8HN, (0141) 240 1002, *glasgow.reservations@cityinn.com, Fax (0141) 248 2754,* – – 50. VISA. CZ u
City Café : **Meals** 16.50 and a la carte 24.20/35.60 – 11.50 – **164 rm** 109.00.
◆ Quayside location and views of the Clyde. Well priced hotel with a "business-friendly" ethos ; neatly maintained modern rooms with sofas and en suite power showers. Restaurant fronts waterside terrace.

Jurys Inn, 70-96 Jamaica St, G1 4QE, (0141) 314 4800, *jurysinnglasgow@jurydoyle.com, Fax (0141) 314 4888* – , rm, – 100. VISA. DZ s
closed 24-26 December – **Meals** a la carte approx 16.95 – 9.50 – **321 rm** 74.00.
◆ Attractive modern hotel on the riverside with excellent access to main shopping areas. Spacious interior with all day coffee bar. Good value, up-to-date, comfy bedrooms. Informal eatery serves breakfast as well as eclectic range of dinners.

Bewley's, 110 Bath St, G2 2EN, ✆ (0141) 353 0800, *gla@bewleyshotels.com*, *Fax (0141) 353 0900* – |‡|, ⇹ rm, ▤ rest, TV ✆ ♿. MC AE ① VISA. ✂ DY i
closed 24-26 December – ***Loop*** **: Meals** a la carte 18.00/25.00 – ☕ 6.95 – **103 rm** 59.00.
◆ A well-run group hotel, relaxed but professional in approach, in the middle of Glasgow's shopping streets. Upper rooms boast rooftop views and duplex apartments. People-watch from glass-walled eatery.

Tulip Inn, 80 Ballater St, G5 0TW, ✆ (0141) 429 4233, *info@tulipinnglasgow.co.uk*, *Fax (0141) 429 4244*, 🏋 – |‡| ⇹, ▤ rest, TV ✆ ♿ P – 🏛 180. MC AE ① VISA
Bibo Bar and Bistro **: Meals** (dinner only) a la carte 14.40/22.15 **s.** – ☕ 6.95 – **114 rm** 69.50.
◆ Sensibly priced hotel appealing to cost-conscious business travellers. Good access to motorway and city centre. Bedrooms have working space and most modern conveniences. Informal, bright eatery serves a varied menu.

Express by Holiday Inn without rest., Theatreland, 165 West Nile St, G1 2RL, ✆ (0141) 331 6800, *express@higlasgow.com*, *Fax (0141) 331 6828* – |‡| ⇹ TV ✆ ♿. MC AE ① VISA JCB DY o
closed 25-26 December – **88 rm** 75.00.
◆ Modern accommodation - simple and well arranged with adequate amenities. Equally suitable for business travel or leisure tourism.

Camerons (at Hilton Glasgow H.), 1 William St, G3 8HT, ✆ (0141) 204 5511, *Fax (0141) 204 5004* – ⇹ ▤ P. MC AE VISA CZ s
closed Saturday lunch, Sunday and Bank Holidays – **Meals** 19.50 (lunch) and dinner a la carte 29.85/56.85 ♀.
◆ Carefully prepared and full-flavoured modern cuisine with strong Scottish character. Very formal, neo-classical styling and smart staff have advanced its local reputation.

Buttery, 652 Argyle St, G3 8UF, ✆ (0141) 221 8188, *ia.fleming@btopenworld.com*, *Fax (0141) 204 4639* – ⇹ P. MC AE VISA CZ e
closed 25-26 December, 1-2 January, Sunday and Monday – **Meals** 16.00/38.00 and lunch a la carte 22.00/25.50 🎭 ♀.
◆ Established, comfortable restaurant away from the bright lights ; red velour and ageing bric-a-brac reveal its past as a pub. Ambitiously composed modern Scottish repertoire.

étain, The Glass House, Springfield Court, G13 3JN, ✆ (0141) 225 5630, *etain@conran.com*, *Fax (0141) 225 5640* – |‡| ▤. MC AE ① VISA DZ r
closed 25 December and Sunday dinner – **Meals** 17.00/29.00 ♀.
◆ Comfortable, contemporary restaurant in unusual glass extension to Princes Square Centre. Well-sourced Scottish ingredients prepared in a modern, interesting way.

Rococo, 202 West George St, G2 2NR, ✆ (0141) 221 5004, *rococo@onetel.net*, *Fax (0141) 221 5006* – ▤. MC AE ① VISA DYZ z
closed 1 January and Sunday – **Meals** 18.00/36.50 and lunch a la carte 28.80/40.50 🎭 ♀.
◆ In style, more like studied avant-garde : stark, white-walled cellar with vibrant modern art and high-backed leather chairs. Accomplished, fully flavoured contemporary menu.

Lux, 1051 Great Western Rd, G12 0XP, ✆ (0141) 576 7576, *luxstazione@btconnect.com*, *Fax (0141) 576 0162* – ⇹ ▤ P. MC AE VISA by A 82 CY
closed 25-26 December, 1-2 January and Sunday – **Meals** (dinner only) 26.50/30.50.
◆ 19C railway station converted with clean-lined elegance : dark wood, subtle lighting and vivid blue banquettes. Fine service and flavourful, well-prepared modern menus.

Brian Maule at Chardon d'Or, 176 West Regent St, G2 4RL, ✆ (0141) 248 3801, *info@brianmaule.com*, *Fax (0141) 248 3901* – ⇹. MC AE VISA CY i
closed 2 weeks January, 2 weeks July, 25-26 December, 1-2 January, Saturday lunch, Sunday and Bank Holidays – **Meals** 18.50 (lunch) and a la carte 30.00/41.50 🎭 ♀.
◆ Large pillared Georgian building. Airy interior with ornate carved ceiling and hung with modern art. Modern dishes with fine Scottish produce ; substantial wine list.

Gamba, 225a West George St, G2 2ND, ✆ (0141) 572 0899, *info@gamba.co.uk*, *Fax (0141) 572 0896* – ⇹. MC AE VISA DZ x
closed 25-26 December, 1-2 January, Sunday and Bank Holidays – **Meals** - Seafood - 17.95 (lunch) and a la carte 32.00/42.00 🎭.
◆ Seafood specialists : an enterprising diversity of influences and well-priced lunches. Compact, brightly decorated basement in hot terracotta with a pleasant cosy bar.

La Parmigiana, 447 Great Western Rd, Kelvinbridge, G12 8HH, ✆ (0141) 334 0686, *s.giovanazzi@btclick.com*, *Fax (0141) 357 5595* – ▤. MC AE ① VISA JCB CY r
closed 25-26 December, 1-2 January, Sunday and Easter Monday – **Meals** - Italian - 10.50 (lunch) and a la carte 20.70/34.50 **s.** 🎭.
◆ Compact, pleasantly decorated traditional eatery with a lively atmosphere and good local reputation. Obliging, professional service and a sound, authentic Italian repertoire.

Quigley's, 158-166 Bath St, G2 4TB, ✆ (0141) 331 4060, *Fax (0141) 331 4065* – ▤. MC AE VISA DY u
closed 25-26 December, 1-2 January, Sunday and Monday – **Meals** (dinner only) a la carte 21.50/31.00 ☏ 𝕐.
◆ A converted Victorian building that retains many original features and has an open, contemporary feel. Deep banquettes and subtle lighting. Good, modern menus.

Papingo, 104 Bath St, G2 2EN, ✆ (0141) 332 6678, *info@papingo.co.uk, Fax (0141) 332 6549* – MC AE D VISA DY r
closed 25-26 December, 1-2 January and Sunday lunch – **Meals** 9.95 (lunch) and a la carte 21.00/32.00 ☏ 𝕐.
◆ Parrot motifs recur everywhere, even on the door handles! Well-spaced tables and mirrored walls add a sense of space to the basement. A free-ranging fusion style prevails.

Zinc Bar and Grill, Princes Sq, G1 3JN, ✆ (0141) 225 5620, *zincglasgow@conran.com, Fax (0141) 225 5640* – |♿| ▤. MC AE D VISA DZ r
closed 25 December and Sunday dinner – **Meals** a la carte 14.50/23.00 **s.** 𝕐.
◆ Contemporary dining on second floor atrium of Princes Square Centre. Stylish décor and tableware. Modern menu offering popular dishes ; good value lunches.

Corinthian, 191 Ingram St, G1 1DA, ✆ (0141) 552 1101, *corinthian@g1group.co.uk, Fax (0141) 552 3730* – MC AE VISA DZ n
Meals (dinner only) 12.95 and a la carte 21.40/31.85 ☏ 𝕐.
◆ Breathtaking example of grand 19C design : a glass-domed bar and spacious, supremely elegant dining room serving solid, competently prepared dishes with a light modern touch.

Ho Wong, 82 York St, G2 8LE, ✆ (0141) 221 3550, *ho.wong@amserve.com, Fax (0141) 248 5330* – ▤. MC AE D VISA JCB CZ v
Meals - Chinese (Peking) - 27.00 (dinner) and a la carte 16.00/20.95.
◆ In an up-and-coming part of town, a long-established restaurant with a modern style. Authentic Chinese cuisine with the emphasis on Peking dishes.

Amber Regent, 50 West Regent St, G2 2QZ, ✆ (0141) 331 1655, *Fax (0141) 353 3398* – ▤. MC AE D VISA DY e
closed Chinese New Year and Sunday – **Meals** - Chinese - 9.95/38.95 and a la carte 22.25/42.90.
◆ Traditional Chinese dishes served by conscientious staff. Comfy, personally managed restaurant in a 19C office building in the heart of the city. Good value lunch.

Bouzy Rouge Seafood and Grill, 71 Renfield St, G2 1LP, ✆ (0141) 333 9725, *reservations@bouzy-rouge.com, Fax (0141) 354 0453.* MC AE D VISA DY e
closed 1 January – **Meals** 14.95 (lunch) and a la carte 28.85/38.95 ☏.
◆ Wonderfully atmospheric former bank with original tiled interior reflecting a superb Moorish style. Fresh Scottish seafood and fish with carefully sourced Aberdeen Angus beef.

Shish Mahal, 60-68 Park Rd, G4 9JF, ✆ (0141) 3398256, *reservations@shishmahal.co.uk, Fax (0141) 572 0800* – ▤. MC AE VISA JCB CY o
closed 25 December and Sunday lunch – **Meals** - Indian - 6.75/16.95 and a la carte 11.15/15.40.
◆ Tandoori specialities in a varied pan-Indian menu, attentive service and an evocative modern interior of etched glass, oak and Moorish tiles have won city-wide recognition.

The Ubiquitous Chip, 12 Ashton Lane, G12 8SJ, off Byres Rd ✆ (0141) 334 5007, *mail@ubiquitouschip.co.uk, Fax (0141) 337 1302* – ▤. MC AE D VISA JCB
closed 25 December and 1 January – **Meals** 21.50/37.50 and a la carte 14.05/26.15 𝕐. by B 808 CY
◆ A long standing favourite, "The Chip" mixes Scottish and fusion styles. Well known for its glass-roofed courtyard, with a more formal but equally lively warehouse interior.

Mao, 84 Brunswick St, G1 1ZZ, ✆ (0141) 564 5161, *info@cafemao.com, Fax (0141) 564 5163* – ▤. MC AE VISA DZ e
closed 24-26 December and 1 January – **Meals** - South East Asian - a la carte 17.00/22.50 **s.** 𝕐.
◆ Eatery located over two floors which are decorated in bright, funky style with vivid, modern colours ; centrally located, buzzy atmosphere. Thoroughly tasty South East Asian food.

Shimla Pinks, 777 Pollokshaws Rd, G41 2AX, ✆ (0141) 423 4488, *Fax (0141) 423 2434* – ▤. MC AE D VISA by A 77 DZ
closed 1 January and lunch Saturday and Sunday – **Meals** - Indian - 6.95 (lunch) and a la carte 10.40/24.85.
◆ Simple, modern interior with white walls and contemporary lighting. Sound repertoire of Indian cuisine. A well-run restaurant to south of city. Good value set lunch menu.

Babbity Bowster, 16-18 Blackfriars St, G1 1PE, ✆ (0141) 552 5055, *fraser@babbity.com, Fax (0141) 552 7774,* – MC AE D VISA. DZ x
closed 25 December – **Meals** a la carte 12.95/25.85 𝕐 – ☕ 6.00 – **6 rm** 40.00/60.00.
◆ Well regarded pub of Georgian origins with columned façade. Paradoxically simple ambience : gingham-clothed tables, hearty Scottish dishes, slightly more formal in evenings.

LEEDS *W. Yorks.* **502** **P 22** *Great Britain G.* – *pop. 443 247.*

See : *City★ - Royal Armouries Museum★★★* GZ *City Art Gallery★ AC* GY **M.**

Envir. : *Kirkstall Abbey★ AC, NW : 3 m. by A 65* FY *– Temple Newsam★ (decorative arts★) AC, E : 5 m. by A 64 and A 63.*

Exc. : *Harewood House★★ (The Gallery★) AC, N : 8 m. by A 61 – Nostell Priory★, SE : 18 m. by A 61 and A 638 – Yorkshire Sculpture Park★, S : 20 m. by M 1 to junction 38 and 1 m. north off A 637 – Brodsworth Hall★, SE : 25 m. by M 1 to junction 40, A 638 and minor rd (right) in Upton.*

18, 18 Temple Newsam, Temple Newsam Rd, Halton (0113) 264 5624 – 18 Gotts Park, Armley Ridge Rd (0113) 234 2019 – 18 Middleton Park, Ring Rd, Beeston Park, Middleton (0113) 270 9506 – 18, 9 Moor Allerton, Coal Rd, Wike (0113) 266 1154 – 18 Howley Hall, Scotchman Lane, Morley (01924) 472432 – 9 Roundhay, Park Lane (0113) 266 2695.

Leeds - Bradford Airport : (0113) 250 9696, NW : 8 m. by A 65 and A 658.

The Arcade, City Station (0113) 242 5242, tourinfo@leeds.golf.uk.

London 204 – Liverpool 75 – Manchester 43.

Plans on following pages

Radisson SAS without rest., No.1 The Light, The Headrow, LS1 8TL, (0113) 236 6000, *Fax (0113) 236 6100* – – 50. MC AE VISA. GY a
12.95 – **147 rm** 135.00/170.00.

♦ Impressive hotel in heart of city. Open atrium and individually styled furnishings throughout. State-of-art meeting rooms. Ultra modern, very well appointed bedrooms.

Devere Oulton Hall, Rothwell Lane, Oulton, LS26 8HN, Southeast : 5 ½ m. by A 61 and A 639 on A 654 (0113) 282 1000, *oulton.hall@devere-hotels.com, Fax (0113) 282 8066,* 18, 9, – rest, – 330. MC AE VISA

Bronte : **Meals** 16.00 (lunch) and dinner a la carte 25.75/32.46 **s.** – **150 rm** 150.00/160.00, 2 suites.

♦ Once home to Leeds' Calverley family ; neo-Classical mansion set in woodland with PGA standard golf course. The drawing room and main house bedrooms exemplify elegant style. Pictures of the famous sisters adorn walls of Bronte restaurant.

Thorpe Park H. and Spa, 1150 Century Way, LS15 8ZB, East : 6 m. by A 64 and A 63 on B 6120 (0113) 264 1000, *thorpepark@shirehotels.co.uk, Fax (0113) 264 1010,* – – 200. MC AE VISA JCB.
Meals a la carte 21.00/27.00 **s.** – **119 rm** 145.00/185.00, 4 suites.

♦ Handily placed hotel, close to motorways. Open-fired reception and richly toned central atrium. Fully equipped leisure centre with spa. Immaculate rooms with host of extras. Spacious, modern restaurant.

Leeds Marriott, 4 Trevelyan Sq, Boar Lane, LS1 6ET, (0870) 4007260, *events.leeds@marriotthotels.co.uk, Fax (0870) 4007360,* – rm, – 320. MC AE VISA. GZ x
John T's : **Meals** *(closed Sunday lunch)* 15.00/24.00 and a la carte 20.00/28.00 – 14.95 – **243 rm** 140.00, 1 suite.

♦ Between Corn Exchange and station with smart, modern bedrooms behind its Victorian façade. Extensive business facilities and a good leisure centre. Relax in informal bar/bistro.

Park Plaza, Boar Lane, City Sq, LS1 5NS, (0113) 380 4000, *pplinfo@parkplazahotels.co.uk, Fax (0113) 380 4100,* – rm, – 150. MC AE VISA JCB GZ d
closed 24-27 December – ***China Latino :*** **Meals** - Asian - *(closed Sunday)* 9.95/35.00 and a la carte 18.95/34.95 **s.** – 14.50 – **182 rm** 160.00, 4 suites.

♦ Located in city centre, directly opposite railway station, with some great views. Oriented for the business traveller. Rooms are minimalistic with a stylish, neutral feel. Modern restaurant with popular Asian-based menus.

Malmaison, Sovereign Quay, LS1 1DQ, (0113) 398 1000, *leeds@malmaison.com, Fax (0113) 398 1002* – rm, – 45. MC AE VISA JCB. GZ n
Meals 11.95 (lunch) and a la carte 30.95/44.45 – 11.95 – **100 rm** 99.00/135.00, 1 suite.

♦ Relaxed, contemporary hotel hides behind imposing Victorian exterior. Small spa. Vibrantly and individually decorated rooms are thoughtfully furnished with CD players. Dine in modern interpretation of a French brasserie.

Quebecs without rest., 9 Quebec St, LS1 2HA, (0113) 244 8989, *res-quebecs@etontownhouse.com, Fax (0113) 244 9090* – MC AE VISA JCB FZ a
closed 24-26 December – 13.50 – **45 rm** 125.00/250.00.

♦ Ex-19C Liberal Club, now a stylish, intimate city centre hotel. Original features include oak staircase and stained glass window depicting Yorkshire cities. Very comfy rooms.

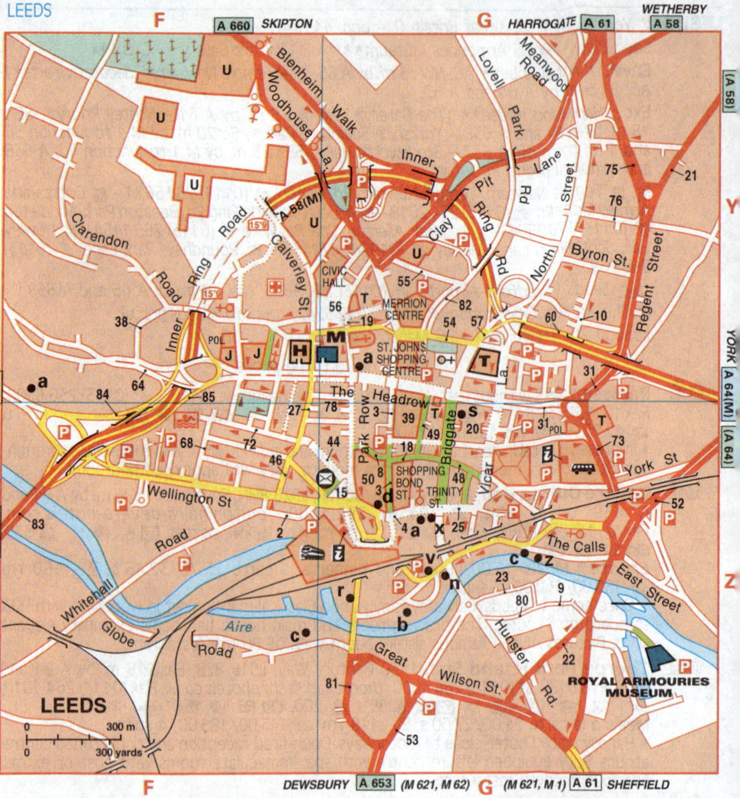

Aire St	FZ	2
Albion St	GZ	3
Bond St	GZ	8
Bowmane Lane	GZ	9
Bridge St	GY	10
Briggate	GZ	
City Square	GZ	15
Commercial St	GZ	18
Cookridge St	GY	19
County Arcade	GZ	20
Cross Stamford St	GY	21
Crown Point Rd	GZ	22
Dock St	GZ	23
Duncan St	GZ	25
East Parade	FGZ	27
Eastgate	GZ	31
Hanover Way	FY	38
Headrow (The)	GY	
Headrow Centre	GZ	39
Infirmary St	GZ	44
King St	FZ	46
Kirkgate	GZ	48
Lands Lane	GZ	49
Leeds Shopping Plaza	GZ	50
Marsh Lane	GZ	52
Meadow Lane	GZ	53
Merrion Centre	GY	
Merrion St	GY	54
Merrion Way	GY	55
Millennium Square	GY	56
New Briggate	GY	57
New York Rd	GY	60
Park Lane	FY	64
Queen St	FZ	68
St John's Centre	GY	
St Paul's St	FZ	72
St Peter's St	GZ	73
Sheepscar St South	GY	75
Skinner Lane	GY	76
South Parade	FGZ	78
Trinity St Shopping Centre	GZ	
Victoria Rd	GZ	81
Wade Lane	GY	82
Waterloo St	GZ	80
Wellington Rd	FZ	83
West St	FZ	84
Westgate	FZ	85

42 The Calls, 42 The Calls, LS2 7EW, ✆ (0113) 244 0099, *hotel@42thecalls.co.uk, Fax (0113) 234 4100,* ← - ▯ - 85. GZ z
closed 4 days Christmas – **Meals** (see ***Pool Court at 42*** and ***Brasserie Forty Four*** below) – 13.75 – **38 rm** 140.00/210.00, 3 suites.
◆ Stylish, contemporary converted quayside grain mill retaining many of the original workings. Rooms facing river have best views ; all have CD players and host of extras.

Weetwood Hall, Otley Rd, LS16 5PS, Northwest : 4 m. on A 660 ✆ (0113) 230 6000, *sales@weetwood.co.uk, Fax (0113) 230 6095,* , squash – – 180.
***The Woodlands* : Meals** (bar lunch Monday-Saturday)/dinner 21.00 and a la carte approx 30.15 s. – 12.50 – **106 rm** 115.00/130.00.
◆ Extended 17C sandstone manor farm ; popular business venue as it boasts some of the region's finest meeting and leisure facilities. Well-appointed, comfortable bedrooms. Dining options : main restaurant or welcoming pub in former 16C stables.

Hilton Leeds City, Neville St, LS1 4BX, ✆ (0113) 244 2000, *Fax (0113) 243 3577*, ≤, 🏋, ≘s, 🏊 - |⇕|, ⇹ rm, ▤ rm, TV ✆ ♿ P - 🏛 400. MC AE ① VISA GZ r
***New World* : Meals** (bar lunch)/dinner a la carte 22.85/36.50 ♀ - ☕ 14.50 - **186 rm** 140.00, 20 suites.
• Proximity to station, business and commercial districts make this 1970s tower block a favourite for the corporate traveller. Neat and spacious rooms have views of city. Blackboard menus or international cuisine.

Haley's, Shire Oak Rd, Headingley, LS6 2DE, Northwest : 2 m. by A 660 ✆ (0113) 278 4446, *info@haleys.co.uk, Fax (0113) 275 3342* - ⇹, ▤ rest, TV ✆ P - 🏛 25. MC AE VISA. ✂
closed 25-30 December - **Meals** *(closed Sunday dinner to non-residents)* (dinner only and Sunday lunch)/dinner 35.00 ♀ - **27 rm** ☕ 120.00/150.00, 1 suite.
• Named after a prominent stonemason, this part 19C country house in a quiet area is handy for cricket fans. Antique furnished public areas. Individually styled bedrooms. Elegant, relaxed dining room with collection of original local artwork.

Novotel, 4 Whitehall, Whitehall Quay, LS1 4HR, ✆ (0113) 242 6446, *h3270@accor-hotels.com, Fax (0113) 242 6445*, 🏋 - |⇕|, ⇹ rm, ▤ TV ✆ ♿ P - 🏛 80. MC AE ① VISA FZ x
***The Garden Brasserie* : Meals** 16.95/18.95 and a la carte ♀ - ☕ 12.00 - **194 rm** 109.00, 1 suite.
• Just a minute's walk from the main railway station. Ideally suited to the business traveller, with desk modems and meeting rooms. Compact exercise facility. Functional rooms. Informal brasserie adjacent to lobby.

No.3 York Place, 3 York Pl, LS1 2DR, ✆ (0113) 245 9922, *dine@no3yorkplace.co.uk, Fax (0113) 245 9965* - ▤. MC AE VISA FZ e
closed 25-30 December, Saturday lunch, Sunday and Bank Holidays - **Meals** 18.50 (lunch) and a la carte 25.85/46.85 🎭.
• Striking, stylish, minimalist interior keeps the spotlight on the accomplished cuisine. Classic flavours reinterpreted in an imaginative repertoire of seafood and game dishes.

✿ **Pool Court at 42** (at 42 The Calls H.), 44 The Calls, LS2 7EW, ✆ (0113) 244 4242, *info@poolcourt.com, Fax (0113) 234 3332*, 🌳 - ⇹ ▤. MC VISA GZ z
closed Saturday lunch, Sunday and Bank Holidays - **Meals** 30.00/45.00.
Spec. Gâteau of salmon and scallops, guacamole sorbet. Young grouse with bread pudding, Savoy cabbage. Poached apricot and peach Savarin, Champagne sabayon.
• Book early for the small terrace overlooking the Aire. Sophisticated, modern menus with seasonal dishes and attentive service make for formal yet intimate armchair dining.

Anthony's, 19 Boar Lane, LS1 6EA, ✆ (0113) 245 5922, *dineatanthonys@aol.com* - ⇹ ▤. MC VISA GZ a
closed 1-3 January, 1 week February, Sunday, Monday and Tuesdays after Bank Holidays. - **Meals** (booking essential) 23.95 (lunch) and a la carte 28.50/35.00.
• Converted 19C property ; ground floor lounge with red leather Chesterfields ; minimalist basement dining room offers innovative menus with some intriguing combinations.

Simply Heathcotes, Canal Wharf, Water Lane, LS11 5PS, ✆ (0113) 244 6611, *leeds@simplyheathcotes.co.uk, Fax (0113) 244 0736*, ≤ - ▤. MC AE VISA FZ c
closed 25 December and Bank Holidays - **Meals** 15.50 (lunch) and a la carte 18.75/33.50 ♀.
• Converted grain warehouse by the canal. Distinctive modern feel with rich black banquettes. Effective contemporary cooking with prominent "northern" slant.

Leodis, Victoria Mill, Sovereign St, LS1 4BJ, ✆ (0113) 242 1010, *Fax (0113) 243 0432*, 🌳 - MC AE ① VISA GZ b
closed 26 December, Sunday and lunch on Saturday and Bank Holidays - **Meals** 16.95 (lunch) and a la carte 22.45/29.95 ♀.
• Appealing converted riverside storehouse offers hearty roasts, carving trolley and other generous British-style favourites in a bustling atmosphere. Friendly service.

Quantro, 62 Street Lane, LS8 2DQ, ✆ (0113) 288 8063, *info@quantro.co.uk, Fax (0113) 288 8008*, 🌳 - ⇹ ▤. MC AE VISA by A 58 GY
closed 25-26 December, 1 January and Sunday - **Meals** 12.95 (lunch) and a la carte 15.80/28.90 🎭 ♀.
• Modern restaurant in suburban parade. Stylish décor : the smart atmosphere is augmented by friendly service. Excellent value lunches ; modern dishes with international twists.

🙂 **Brasserie Forty Four** (at 42 The Calls H.), 44 The Calls, LS2 7EW, ✆ (0113) 234 3232, *info@brasserie44.com, Fax (0113) 234 3332* - ▤. MC VISA GZ z
closed Sunday, Saturday lunch and Bank Holidays - **Meals** a la carte 23.15/29.25 🎭.
• Former riverside warehouse with stylish bar ; exudes atmosphere of buzzy informality. Smokehouse and char-grilled options in an eclectic range of menu dishes.

XX **Fourth Floor** (at Harvey Nichols), 107-111 Briggate, LS1 6AZ, ☎ (0113) 204 8000, Fax (0113) 204 8080, – ▤. MC AE ⊕ VISA JCB GZ s
closed 25-26 and 31 December, 1 January, Easter Sunday and dinner Sunday-Wednesday – **Meals** (lunch bookings not accepted) 18.00 (lunch) and a la carte 20.50/27.50 ♀.
• Watch the chefs prepare the modern food with world-wide influences in these bright, stylish, buzzy, contemporary surroundings. Advisable to get here early at lunch.

XX **Maxi's,** 6 Bingley St, LS3 1LX, off Kirkstall Rd ☎ (0113) 244 0552, *info@maxi-s.co.uk, Fax (0113) 234 3902* – ▤ P. MC AE ⊕ VISA by Burley Rd FY a
closed 25-26 December – **Meals** - Chinese (Canton, Peking) - 17.80 and a la carte 14.90/42.70.
• Savour the taste of the Orient in this ornately decorated and busy pagoda style restaurant. Specialises in the rich flavours of Canton and hot and spicy Peking dishes.

X **The Calls Grill,** Calls Landing, 38 The Calls, LS2 7EW, ☎ (0113) 245 3870, *Fax (0113) 243 9035* – ▤. MC AE ⊕ VISA JCB GZ c
closed 1 week Christmas-New Year – **Meals** (dinner only) 18.50 and a la carte 19.95/30.40 ♀.
• Restored Aireside textile mill with rustic ambience : exposed brickwork and timbers. Well-priced modern British cooking ; bustling informality. Steaks a speciality.

at Garforth *East : 6 m. by A 64 GY and A 63 at junction with A 642 – ✉ Leeds :*

XX **Aagrah,** Aberford Rd, LS25 1BA, on A 642 (Garforth rd) ☎ (0113) 287 6606 – ▤ P. MC AE VISA
closed 25 December – **Meals** - Indian (Kashmiri) - (booking essential) (dinner only) 14.00/15.00 and a la carte 14.95/21.05 **s.**
• Part of a family owned and personally run expanding group. Classic regional Indian cooking, specialising in the fragrant and subtly spiced dishes of the Kashmir region.

at Pudsey *West : 5 ¾ m. by M 621 FZ and A 647 – ✉ Leeds :*

XX **Aagrah,** 483 Bradford Rd, LS28 8ED, on A 647 ☎ (01274) 668818 – ▤ P. MC AE VISA
closed 25 December – **Meals** - Indian (Kashmiri) - (booking essential) (dinner only) 14.00/15.00 and a la carte 14.95/21.05 **s.**
• Advance booking most definitely required here ; a very busy and bustling traditional Indian restaurant. Offers an extensive range of carefully prepared authentic dishes.

Winteringham *North Lincolnshire* 502 S 22 – ✉ *Scunthorpe.*
London 176 – Leeds 62.

XXXX ✿✿ **Winteringham Fields** (Schwab) with rm, Silver St, DN15 9PF, ☎ (01724) 733096, *wintfields@aol.com, Fax (01724) 733898* – TV P. MC AE VISA
closed 10 days Christmas, first 10 days August, first 4 days October and last week March – **Meals** *(closed Sunday-Monday)* (booking essential to non-residents) 31.00/38.00 and a la carte 65.00/72.00 **s.** – ☕ 12.00 – **8 rm** 95.00/200.00, 2 suites.
Spec. Poached turbot, tagliatelli, fish velouté with lavender and caviar. Breast of pigeon with truffle polenta and walnuts. Nougatine bowl of raspberries, meringue and lime sorbet.
• Cosy 16C house : beamed ceilings, narrow passages, original range with fire. Conservatory or lounges for drinks. Exceptional, original food superbly prepared. Elegant bedrooms.

LIVERPOOL *Mersey.* 502 503 L 23 *Great Britain G.* – *pop. 469 017.*
See : *City★ - The Walker★★ DY* **M3** *– Liverpool Cathedral★★ (Lady Chapel★) EZ – Metropolitan Cathedral of Christ the King★★ EY – Albert Dock★ CZ (Merseyside Maritime Museum★ AC* **M2** *- Tate Gallery Liverpool★).*
Exc. : *Speke Hall★ AC, SE : 8 m. by A 561.*
18, 9 *Allerton Municipal, Allerton Rd ☎ (0151) 428 1046 – 18 Liverpool Municipal, Ingoe Lane, Kirkby ☎ (0151) 546 5435 – 9 Bowring, Bowring Park, Roby Rd, Huyton ☎ (0151) 489 1901.*
Mersey Tunnels (toll).
✈ *Liverpool Airport : ☎ (0870) 7508484, SE : 6 m. by A 561 –* **Terminal :** *Pier Head.*
⛴ *to Isle of Man (Douglas) (Isle of Man Steam Packet Co. Ltd) (2 h 30 mn/4 h) – to Northern Ireland (Belfast) (NorseMerchant Ferries Ltd) 1-2 daily (11 h) – to Dublin (NorseMerchant Ferries Ltd) 2 daily (approx 7 h 45 mn) – to Dublin (P & O Irish Sea) daily (8 h) – to Dublin (Seacat) daily February-November (3 h 45 mn).*
⛴ *to Birkenhead and Wallasey (Mersey Ferries) frequent services daily.*
ℹ *Queens Square ☎ (0906) 680 6886, askme@visitliverpool.com –* Atlantic Pavilion, Albert Dock ☎ (0906) 680 6886.
London 219 – Birmingham 103 – Leeds 75 – Manchester 35.

Radisson SAS, 107 Old Hall St, L3 9BD, ✆ (0151) 966 1500, *info.liverpool@radissonsas.com, Fax (0151) 966 1501,* – 130. CY c
***Filini* : Meals** - Italian influences - *(closed Sunday)* 13.50 (lunch) and a la carte 18.50/26.50 **s.** – 14.95 – **189 rm** 130.00, 5 suites.
• Waterfront style : state-of-the-art meeting rooms and very well equipped leisure facilities. Chic bar in two Grade II listed cottages. Modern rooms themed "ocean" or "urban". Spacious dining room with Italian influenced menus.

Crowne Plaza Liverpool, St Nicholas Pl, Princes Dock, Pier Head, L3 1QN, ✆ (0151) 243 8000, *sales@cpliverpool.co.uk, Fax (0151) 243 8008,* rm, – 700. CY a
closed 24-26 December – ***Plaza Brasserie* : Meals** a la carte 23.45/28.40 – 13.95 – **155 rm** 175.00, 4 suites.
• A busy conference venue within the popular dockside development. Enjoys views of the Mersey and the Liver Building. Well-appointed and very comfortable rooms. Spacious, informal ground floor brasserie.

Hope Street, 40 Hope St, L1 9DA, ✆ (0151) 709 3000, *sleep@hopestreethotel.co.uk, Fax (0151) 709 2454* – rest, – 25. EZ o
The London Carriage Works *(✆ (0151) 705 2222)* **: Meals** *(closed Sunday dinner and Bank Holidays)* 25.00/34.00 – 14.50 – **41 rm** 115.00/175.00, 7 suites.
• Converted 19C city centre property with modern, stylish interior : leather furniture prominent. Trendy basement lounge bar. Contemporary rooms with state-of-the-art facilities. Modern glass feature at heart of dining room.

Racquet Club, Hargreaves Buildings, 5 Chapel St, L3 9AA, ✆ (0151) 236 6676, *info@racquetclub.org.uk, Fax (0151) 236 6870,* squash – – 80. CY e
closed Bank Holidays – **Meals** (see ***Ziba*** below) – 10.00 – **8 rm** 135.00.
• Ornate Victorian city centre building converted into club offering unusual accommodation. Good leisure facilities open to residents. Simple well equipped rooms.

Travelodge without rest., 25 Old Haymarket, L1 6ER, ✆ (08700) 850950, *Fax (0151) 227 5835* – . DY a
105 rm 47.00.
• Purpose-built hotel providing a handy central location for visitors to the city. Dependable standard of accommodation : compact and functional, yet comfortable.

60 Hope Street, 60 Hope St, L1 9BZ, ✆ (0151) 707 6060, *info@60hopestreet.com, Fax (0151) 707 6016* – . EZ x
closed 25-26 December, 1 January, Saturday lunch, Sunday and Bank Holidays – **Meals** 15.95 (lunch) and a la carte 28.85/43.85 .
• Modern restaurant within an attractive Grade II Georgian house. Informal basement café-bar, brightly decorated dining room and private room above. Modern European cooking.

Simply Heathcotes, Beetham Plaza, 25 The Strand, L2 0XL, ✆ (0151) 236 3536, *liverpool@simplyheathcotes.co.uk, Fax (0151) 236 3534,* – . CY s
closed 25-26 December, 1 January and Bank Holiday Mondays – **Meals** 15.50 (lunch) and a la carte 17.25/24.00 .
• Behind a sloping glass façade is a modish dining room where staff in emblemed shirts serve variations on the classics : hash brown of black pudding. Views of water sculpture.

Ziba (at Racquet Club), Hargreaves Buildings, 5 Chapel St, L3 9AA, ✆ (0151) 236 6676, *info@racquetclub.org.uk, Fax (0151) 236 6870* – . CY e
closed Saturday lunch, Sunday and Bank Holidays – **Meals** a la carte 19.85/36.85 **s.** .
• Modern restaurant in old Victorian building with huge windows and artwork on walls. Small lunch menus, more extensive dinner menus, offering classic-based modern dishes.

The Other Place Bistro, 29a Hope St, L1 9BQ, ✆ (0151) 707 7888, *Fax (0151) 707 7888* – . EZ a
closed 25-26 December, 1 January, Sunday, Monday, Saturday lunch and Bank Holidays – **Meals** 14.95 (dinner) and a la carte 19.40/25.85 .
• Victorian end of terrace ground floor and basement eatery with green painted brick and wood floors. Good value dishes are supplemented by a concise wine list.

at Knowsley Industrial Park *Northeast : 8 m. by A 59 DY and A 580 – ✉ Liverpool*

Suites H., Ribblers Lane, L34 9HA, ✆ (0151) 549 2222, *enquiries@suiteshotelgroup.com, Fax (0151) 549 1116,* – 300.
Meals *(closed lunch Saturday and Sunday)* a la carte 17.75/25.75 **s.**, **80 suites** 97.00/107.00.
• Adjoins a business park, with smartly designed work areas. A well-equipped, privately owned hotel, ideal for corporate clients. All rooms are comfortably furnished suites. Upbeat, vibrantly decorated dining room.

LIVERPOOL

Argyle St	DZ	6
Blackburne Pl.	EZ	10
Bold St	DZ	
Brunswick Rd	EY	19
Canada Boulevard	CYZ	22
Canning Pl.	CZ	23
Church St	DY	
Churchill Way	DY	26
Clarence St	EYZ	27
Clayton Square Shopping Centre	DY	
College Lane	DZ	28
Commutation Row	DY	30
Cook St	CY	32
Crosshall St	DY	36
Daulby St	EY	40
Erskine St	EY	45
Fontenoy St	DY	48
Forrest St	DZ	49
George's Dock Lane	CY	51
Grafton St	DZ	53
Great Charlotte St	DY	54
Great Howard St	CY	56
Hatton Garden	DY	57
Haymarket	DY	58
Hood St	DY	62
Houghton St	DY	65
Huskisson St	EZ	66
James St	CY	68
King Edward St	CY	69
Knight St	EZ	72
Leece St	EZ	73
Lime St	DY	
Liver St	CZ	76
London Rd	DEY	
Lord St	CDY	
Mansfield St	DEY	80
Mathew St	CDY	81
Moss St	EY	86
Mount St	EZ	88
Myrtle St	EZ	89
New Quay	CY	93
Newington St	DZ	92
North John St	CY	96
Norton St	EY	97
Parker St	DY	103
Prescot St	EY	105
Prince's Rd	EZ	107
Queen Square	DY	
Ranelagh St	DY	108
Renshaw St	DEZ	
Richmond St	DY	109
Roe St	DY	114
St James Pl.	EZ	117
St John's Centre	DY	
St John's Lane	DY	118
School Lane	DYZ	122
Scotland Pl.	DY	123
Sefton St	DZ	129
Seymour St	EY	130
Skelhorne St	DY	133
Stanley St	CDY	135
Suffolk St	DZ	137
Tarleton St	DY	139
Victoria St	DY	143
Water St	CY	150
William Brown St	DY	156
York St	DZ	157

D
E
A 59
123
Leeds St.
Byron St
U
St
Anne St.
80
William
Henry St.
Soho Street
Shaw St
19
A 580
A 5049
45
Y
Hunter St.
Great Crosshall St.
Islington
48
57
26
M3
M
86
105
30
London
97
Road
40
J
QUEENSWAY TUNNEL
12'9
58
156
St George's Hall
Pembroke
Place
St.
36
T
130
A 5047
118
QUEEN SQUARE
Lime
Hill
Great Newton St.
143
M
114
LIME STREET
U
135
T
ST JOHN'S
Russell St.
62
T
CENTRE
133
TOWER St.
109
65
Elliot
St.
Copperas
Hill
St
139
103
CLAYTON SQUARE SHOPPING CENTRE
54
Brownlow
U
Church St
122
METROPOLITAN CATHEDRAL
T
108
Mount
27
M
Renshaw
Pleasant
28
St.
Bold
CENTRAL
Oxford St.
Street
92
U
Hanover
Seel
St.
Street
Street
T
U
Street
Duke
73
Hardman
U
Paradise
Slater
St.
Street
157
Rodney
St.
Berry
T
T
49
Upper
Gilbert
137
72
89
(A 562)
Park
Frederick
St.
88
Falkner
Street
Upper
Duke
St.
U
Street
10
St.
N
Lane
St.
St.
Street
Canning
St.
Wapping
Nelson
A 5038
LIVERPOOL CATHEDRAL
St.
Upper
Pitt
George
66
Blundell
St.
66
Catharine
A 5039
Chaloner
Jamaica
James
St.
Hope
A 562
Great
St.
St.
Parliament
Berkley
107
St.
Upper
Windsor
B 5175
St.
St.
Parliament
Stanhope
St.
St.
St.
53
129
117
AIRPORT
A 561
WIDNES
D
E

at Huyton *East : 8 ¼ m. by A5047* EY *and A 5080 on B 5199 – ✉ Liverpool :*

Village H. and Leisure Club, Fallows Way, L35 1RZ, Southeast : 3 ¼ m. by A 5080 off Whiston rd ☎ (0151) 449 2341, *village.liverpool@village-hotels.com, Fax (0151) 449 3832,* squash – rest, – 280.
Meals 18.50 and a la carte 18.65/26.00 **s.** – 9.95 – **62 rm** 100.00/145.00.
◆ Modern, corporate hotel with unrivalled high-tech leisure facilities. A favourite with families at weekends. The spacious bedrooms are comfy and well equipped. Airy restaurant and conservatory.

at Grassendale *Southeast : 4 ½ m. on A 561* EZ *– ✉ Liverpool :*

Gulshan, 544-548 Aigburth Rd, L19 3QG, on A 561 ☎ (0151) 427 2273, *Fax (0151) 427 2111* –
Meals - Indian - (dinner only) a la carte approx. 17.50.
◆ A richly decorated and comfortable traditional Indian restaurant within a parade of shops. Smart and efficient service of an extensive menu of authentic dishes.

at Woolton *Southeast : 6 m. by A 562* EZ *, A 5058 and Woolton Rd – ✉ Liverpool :*

Woolton Redbourne, Acrefield Rd, L25 5JN, ☎ (0151) 421 1500, *reception@woolton redbourne.fsnet.co.uk, Fax (0151) 421 1501,* – rest,
Lady Catherine : **Meals** (dinner only and Sunday lunch)/dinner a la carte 29.15/41.90 – **17 rm** 68.00/99.00, 1 suite.
◆ Imposing Grade II listed Victorian mansion built by Sir Henry Tate in 1884. Period antiques throughout. Many of the spacious rooms overlook the attractive terraced gardens. Partly wood-panelled restaurant.

at Speke *Southeast : 8 ¾ m. by A 561* EZ *– ✉ Liverpool*

Liverpool Marriott H. South, Speke Aerodrome, Speke Rd, L24 8QD, West : 1 ¾ m. on A 561 ☎ (0870) 4007269, *events.liverpoolsouth@marriotthotels.co.uk, Fax (0870) 4007369,* squash – – 350.
Starways : **Meals** 25.00 (dinner) and a la carte approx 25.00 **s.** – 14.95 – **163 rm** 105.00, 1 suite.
◆ Converted Art Deco airport terminal building, built 1937. Aviation and 1930s era the prevailing themes throughout. The modern, well-equipped bedrooms have a stylish appeal. Smart brasserie within original airport terminal ; in keeping with hotel's style.

MANCHESTER *Gtr Manchester* 502 503 504 N 23 *Great Britain G.* – *pop. 394 269.*

See : *City★ - Castlefield Heritage Park★* CZ *– Town Hall★* CZ *– Manchester Art Gallery★* CZ **M2** *– Cathedral★ (stalls and canopies★)* CY *– Museum of Science and Industry★* CZ **M** *– Urbis★* CY *– National War Museum North★, Trafford Park.*

Envir. : *Whitworth Art Gallery★, S : 1 ½ m.*

Exc. : *Quarry Bank Mill★, S : 10 m. off B 5166, exit 5 from M 56 – Bramall Hall★, SE : 13 m. by A 6 and A 5102.*

Heaton Park, Prestwich ☎ (0161) 654 9899 – Houldsworth Park, Houldsworth St, Reddish, Stockport ☎ (0161) 442 9611 – Chorlton-cum-Hardy, Barlow Hall, Barlow Hall Rd ☎ (0161) 881 3139 – William Wroe, Pennybridge Lane, Flixton ☎ (0161) 748 8680.

Manchester International Airport : ☎ (0161) 489 3000, S : 10 m. by A 5103 and M 56 – **Terminal :** *Coach service from Victoria Station.*

Manchester Visitor Centre, Town Hall Extension, Lloyd St ☎ (0161) 234 3157, manchestervisitorcentre@notes.manchester.gov.uk – Manchester Airport, International Arrivals Hall, Terminal 1 ☎ (0161) 436 3344 – Manchester Airport, International Arrivals Hall, Terminal 2 ☎ (0161) 489 6412 Salford T.I.C., 1 The Quays, Salford ☎ (0161) 848 8601.

London 202 – Birmingham 86 – Glasgow 221 – Leeds 43 – Liverpool 35.

Plan on next page

The Lowry, 50 Dearmans Pl, Chapel Wharf, Salford, M3 5LH, ☎ (0161) 827 4000, *enquiries@thelowryhotel.com, Fax (0161) 827 4001,* – – 400. CY n
Meals (see ***River Room*** below) – 16.50 – **158 rm** 209.00/239.00, 7 suites.
◆ Stylish contemporary design with a minimalist feel. Smart spacious bedrooms have high levels of comfort and facilities ; some overlook River Irwell. State-of-the-art spa.

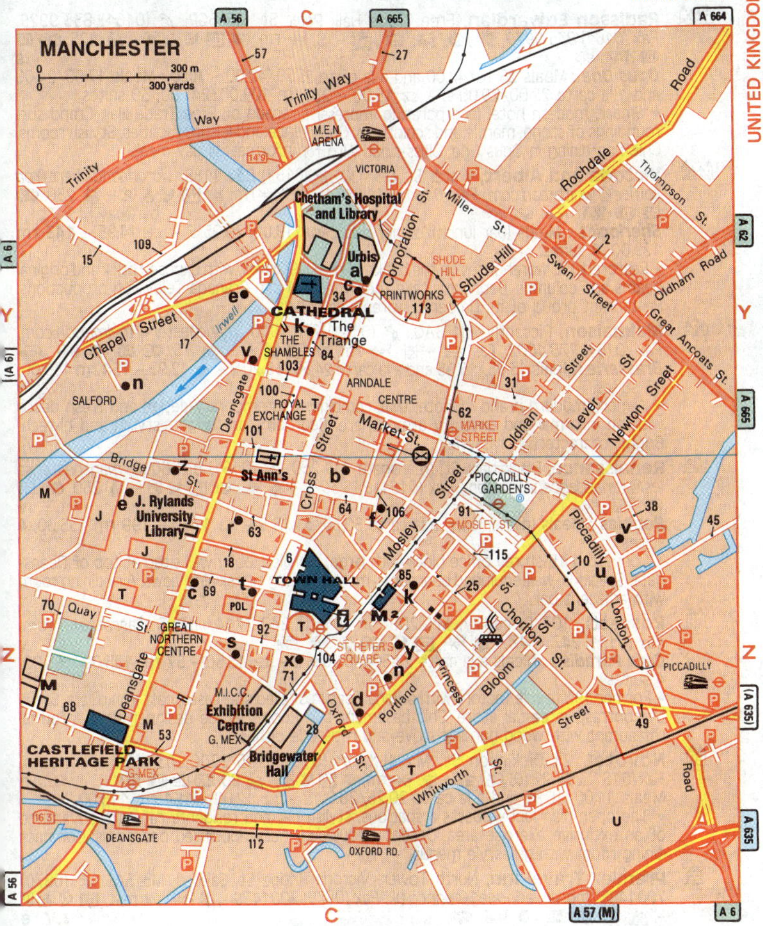

Addington St	CY	2
Albert Square	CZ	6
Aytoun St	CZ	10
Blackfriars Rd	CY	15
Blackfriars St	CY	17
Brazennoze St	CZ	18
Charlotte St	CZ	25
Cheetham Hill Rd	CY	27
Chepstow St	CZ	28
Church St	CY	31
Corn Exchange	CY	34
Dale St	CZ	38
Deansgate	CYZ	
Ducie St	CZ	45
Fairfield St	CZ	49
Great Bridgewater St	CZ	53
Great Ducie St	CY	57
Great Northern centre	CZ	
High St	CY	62
John Dalton St	CZ	63
King St	CZ	64
Liverpool Rd	CZ	68
Lloyd St	CZ	69
Lower Byrom St	CZ	70
Lower Mosley St	CZ	71
Mosley St	CZ	
New Cathedral St	CY	84
Nicholas St	CZ	85
Parker St	CZ	91
Peter St	CZ	92
Princess St	CZ	
St Ann's Square	CY	100
St Ann's St	CY	101
St Mary's Gate	CY	103
St Peter's Square	CZ	104
Shambles Shopping Centre (The)	CY	
Spring Gardens	CZ	106
Viaduct St	CY	109
Whitworth St West	CZ	112
Withy Grove	CY	113
York St	CZ	115

The Midland, Peter St, M60 2DS, ☎ (0161) 236 3333, *midlandreservations@paramount-hotels.co.uk, Fax (0161) 932 4100*, Ⓕ, ⓢ, ⓟ, squash – ⓑ, ⓧ rm, ▤ ⓣⓥ ✆ ♿ ⓟ – 🏛 450. ⓜⓒ ⓐⓔ ⓞ ⓥⓘⓢⓐ CZ x

Trafford Room* : Meals** (carving rest.) 18.95/26.95 (see also ***The French and ***Nico Central*** below) – ☐ 14.95 – **289 rm** 165.00, 14 suites.

◆ Edwardian splendour on a vast scale in the heart of the city. Period features and a huge open lobby combine with up-to-date facilities to create a thoroughly grand hotel. Classically proportioned restaurant with carvery based menu.

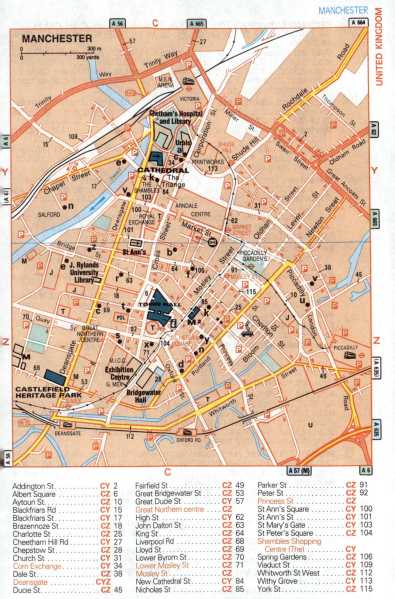

Radisson Edwardian, Free Trade Hall, Peter St, M2 5GP, (0161) 835 9929, *Fax (0161) 835 9979,* , , , , – , rm, – 425. CZ s
Opus One : **Meals** 25.10/42.00 and a la carte 25.50/42.00 – ***Alto :*** **Meals** 17.00/24.00 and a la carte 22.00/29.00 **s.** – 15.00 – **233 rm** 109.00/241.00, 30 suites.
• Smart, modern hotel incorporating impressive façade of Free Trade Hall. Grand surroundings of stone, marble and sculptures. Conference and leisure facilities. Stylish rooms. Chic fine dining in Opus One. Glass-sided Alto for informal, all day meals.

Victoria and Albert, Water St, M3 4JQ, (0161) 832 1188, *victoriaandalbert.frontoffice@whitbread.com, Fax (0161) 834 2484* – , rm, – 250. by Quay St CZ
Sherlock's : **Meals** (bar lunch)/dinner a la carte 19.00/29.95 – 14.95 – **143 rm** 129.00, 4 suites.
• Restored 19C warehouses on the banks of the River Irwell, with exposed brick and original beams and columns. Bedrooms take their themes from Granada Television productions. Restaurant proud of its timbered warehouse origins.

Malmaison, Piccadilly, M1 3AQ, (0161) 278 1000, *manchester@malmaison.com, Fax (0161) 278 1002,* , – , rm, – 75.
Brasserie : **Meals** 13.95/15.95 and a la carte 24.30/39.20 – 12.95 – **154 rm** 135.00, 13 suites. CZ u
• A more modern brand of hotel that combines contemporary design and fresh décor with an informal and unstuffy atmosphere. Bedrooms are bright, stylish and hi-tech. Bright, characterful brasserie.

Renaissance, Blackfriars St, Deansgate, M3 2EQ, (0161) 831 6000, *manchester.sales@renaissancehotels.com, Fax (0161) 835 3077* – – 250. CY v
Robbies : **Meals** (dinner only) a la carte 30.35/33.15 – 12.50 – **199 rm** 135.00, 4 suites.
• Converted 15-storey office block with large, marbled lobby well sited at top of Deansgate. Spacious, well-equipped bedrooms, most enjoying city skyline views. Airy dining room with adjacent bar.

Rossetti, 107 Piccadilly, M1 2DB, (0161) 247 7744, *info@aliasrossetti.com, Fax (0161) 247 7747* – . CZ v
Cafe Paradiso : **Meals** a la carte 22.50/28.00 **s.** – 13.50 – **57 rm** 105.00/155.00, 4 suites.
• Former 19C textile factory with original features : tiled staircases, cast iron pillars. Staff, by contrast, in casual attire. Chic basement bar. Rooms exude designer style. Informal restaurant with wood-burning stove and rotisserie dishes.

Novotel, 21 Dickinson St, M1 4LX, (0161) 235 2200, *h3145@accor.com, Fax (0161) 235 2210,* , – , rm, – 90. CZ n
Meals 11.00/16.95 and a la carte 20.25/26.95 – 12.00 – **164 rm** 115.00.
• The open-plan lobby boasts a spacious, stylish bar and residents can take advantage of an exclusive exercise area. Decently equipped, tidily appointed bedrooms. Compact dining room with grill-style menus.

Premier Travel Inn, North Tower, Victoria Bridge St, Salford, M3 5AS, (0870) 7001488, *mpremierlodge1@snr.co.uk, Fax (0870) 7001489* – , rest, – 35. CY e
Meals (grill rest.) – **170 rm** 48.95/54.95.
• Modern accommodation with bright, well-planned rooms. Convenient city centre location close to Deansgate and Victoria station. The higher the room the better the view. Popular dishes in airy restaurant.

Premier Travel Inn, 112-114 Portland St, M1 4WB, (0870) 2383315, *Fax (0161) 233 5299* – , rest, . CZ d
Meals (grill rest.) – **225 rm** 48.95/54.95.
• Maintains the group's reputation for affordable accommodation and simple contemporary styling. Neat, bright rooms, spacious and carefully designed.

The French (at The Midland H.), Peter St, M60 2DS, (0161) 236 3333 – CZ x
closed Sunday and Bank Holidays – **Meals** (dinner only) a la carte 38.95/52.85 .
• As grand as the hotel in which it is housed, with gilded paintings, large mirrors and heavy drapes. Attentively formal service, classically French-based cooking.

Le Mont, Urbis, Levels 5 and 6, Cathedral Gardens, M4 3BG, (0161) 605 8282, *robert@urbis.org.uk, Fax (0161) 605 8283,* – . CY a
closed 24 December-7 January, Saturday lunch and Sunday – **Meals** a la carte 31.65/39.40 .
• Set on top of the Urbis Museum, boasting spectacular views of the city : formal dining in dramatic surroundings. Imaginative modern cuisine based around a classic French style.

XXX **River Room** (at The Lowry H.), 50 Dearmans Pl, Chapel Wharf, Salford, M3 5LH, ✆ (0161) 827 4003, *enquiries@thelowryhotel.com, Fax (0161) 827 4001*, – ▤ P. MO AE ① VISA CY n
Meals 18.50 (lunch) and a la carte 34.70/45.20 **s.** ♀.
◆ Matching its surroundings, this is a stylish modern restaurant serving, in a precise manner, classic dishes that have stood the test of time. Irwell views, for good measure.

XX **Establishment,** 43-45 Spring Gdns, M2 2BG, ✆ (0161) 839 6300, *Fax (0161) 839 6353* – ✈. MO AE VISA CZ f
closed 1 week Christmas, Sunday and Bank Holidays – **Meals** 16.95 (lunch) and a la carte 26.50/44.85 ♀.
◆ Converted Victorian building in city centre : marble columns, ornate glass domed ceilings. Precise, modern dishes, with a classical base, cooked in accomplished fashion.

XX **Second Floor - Restaurant** (at Harvey Nichols), 21 New Cathedral St, M1 1AD, ✆ (0161) 828 8898, *Fax (0161) 828 8570* – ✈ ▤. MO AE ① VISA JCB CY k
closed 25-26 December, 1 January, Easter Sunday and dinner Sunday and Monday – **Meals** 21.50 (lunch) and a la carte 22.00/35.00 ♀.
◆ Central location on second floor of a department store. Well-designed restaurant with immaculate linen-clad tables. Brasserie style cooking.

XX **Yang Sing,** 34 Princess St, M1 4JY, ✆ (0161) 236 2200, *info@yang-sing.com, Fax (0161) 236 5934* – ▤. MO AE VISA CZ y
closed 25 December – **Meals** - Chinese - a la carte 20.00/30.00.
◆ This most renowned of Chinese restaurants continues to provide some of the most authentic, carefully prepared and varied cooking of its kind to be found in the country.

XX **Nico Central** (at The Midland H.), 2 Mount St, M60 2DS, ✆ (0161) 236 6488, *manchester.nicocentral@corushotels.com, Fax (0161) 236 8897* – ▤. MO AE ① VISA CZ x
closed 25 December, 1 January and Sunday – **Meals** 13.95 (lunch) and a la carte 21.70/35.35 ♀.
◆ Contemporary in style with high ceilings, bold colours and an array of mirrors that add to the subtle Art Deco feel. Cooking has its roots in classic Continental techniques.

XX **Hurricane Bar & Grill,** King St, Spring Gardens, M2 4ST, ✆ (0161) 835 2785, *manchester@hurricanerestaurants.com, Fax (0161) 834 6364* – ✈. MO AE VISA CZ n
closed 24-26 December, 1 January, Sunday and Bank Holidays – **Meals** a la carte 21.70/32.45 ♀.
◆ Former Victorian club in city centre with original fireplace and windows contrasting with elegant modern tables. Attractive menu of modern grill-based dishes ; very flexible.

XX **Pacific,** 58-60 George St, M1 4HF, ✆ (0161) 228 6668, *enquiries@pacificrestaurant.co.uk, Fax (0161) 236 0191* – ▤ ▤. MO AE ① VISA CZ k
Meals - Chinese and Thai - 9.50/38.00 and a la carte 17.50/23.50.
◆ Located in Chinatown : Chinese cuisine on first floor, Thai on the second ; modern décor incorporating subtle Asian influences. Large menus boast high levels of authenticity.

XX **Simply Heathcotes,** Jackson Row, M2 5WD, ✆ (0161) 835 3536, *manchester@simplyheathcotes.co.uk, Fax (0161) 835 3534* – ▤ ✈ ▤. MO AE ① VISA CZ c
closed 25 December, 1 January and Bank Holiday Mondays – **Meals** 15.50 (lunch) and a la carte 15.70/25.00 ♀.
◆ Contemporary interior, with live jazz in the wine bar, contrasts with the original oak panels of this Victorian former register office. Robust menu is equally à la mode.

XX **Koreana,** Kings House, 40a King St West, M3 2WY, ✆ (0161) 832 4330, *alexkoreana@aol.com, Fax (0161) 832 2293* – MO AE ① VISA CZ z
closed 25-26 December, 1 January, 1 week August, Sunday, lunch Saturday and Bank Holidays – **Meals** - Korean - 12.40 and a la carte 10.50/26.50.
◆ Family run basement restaurant, bustling yet still relaxed, offers authentic, balanced Korean cuisine. Novices are guided gently through the menu by staff in national dress.

X **The Restaurant Bar and Grill,** 14 John Dalton St, M2 6JR, ✆ (0161) 839 1999, *manchester@rbgltd.co.uk, Fax (0161) 835 1886* – ▤. MO AE ① VISA JCB CZ r
closed 25 December – **Meals** a la carte 14.00/30.00 ♀.
◆ Stylish ground floor lounge bar and lively first floor eatery. Extensive international repertoire from an open kitchen. Very busy with business community at lunch.

X **Second Floor - Brasserie** (at Harvey Nichols), 21 New Cathedral St, M1 1AH, ✆ (0161) 828 8898, *secondfloor.reservations@harveynichols.com, Fax (0161) 828 8815* – ✈ ▤. MO AE ① VISA CY k
closed 25-26 December, 1 January, Easter Sunday and dinner Sunday and Monday – **Meals** 13.50 (dinner) and a la carte 19.00/24.50 ♀.
◆ Open and lively restaurant with minimalist décor. Wide range of cocktails available at the large bar. Attractive menu with a European eclectic mix of dishes.

X **Le Petit Blanc,** 55 King St, M2 4LQ, ✆ (0161) 832 1000, *manchester@lepetitblanc.co.uk, Fax (0161) 832 1001* – ▤. MO AE VISA CZ b
closed 25-26 December – **Meals** 14.50 (lunch) and a la carte 20.95/31.45 ♀.
◆ Busy, group-owned brasserie with large bar and polished tables. Extensive menus of classic and modern British dishes as well as regional French options. Attentive service.

Palmiro, 197 Upper Chorlton Rd, M16 0BH, South : 2 m. by A 56 off Chorlton Rd ✆ (0161) 860 7330, *bookings@palmiro.net, Fax (0161) 861 7464,* – MC VISA JCB
Meals - Italian - (dinner only and Sunday lunch)/dinner a la carte 19.15/22.95.
• Spartan interior with grey mottled walls and halogen lighting : a highly regarded neighbourhood Italian eatery boasting good value rustic dishes cooked with maximum simplicity.

Livebait, 22 Lloyd St, Albert Sq, M2 5WA, ✆ (0161) 817 4110, *lbmanchester@groupechezgerard.co.uk, Fax (0161) 817 4111* – MC AE VISA CZ t
closed 25 December and 1 January – **Meals** - Seafood - 16.50 (lunch) and a la carte 21.20/37.95.
• A friendly atmosphere in which to dine at linen-clad tables amid Art Deco styling. Plenty of choice from seafood oriented menus ; indeed, crustacea are on display.

Shimla Pinks, Dolefield Crown Sq, M3 3HA, ✆ (0161) 831 7099, *enquiries@shimlapinksmanchester.com, Fax (0161) 832 2202* – MC AE VISA CZ e
closed 25-27 December, 1-2 January and lunch Saturday and Sunday – **Meals** - Indian - 14.95/19.95 and a la carte 20.00/28.00.
• Centrally located Indian restaurant. Colourful artwork and murals and a bustling modern ambience. Extensive menus of authentic Indian dishes and regional specialities.

Zinc Bar and Grill, The Triangle, Hanging Ditch, M4 3ES, ✆ (0161) 827 4200, *zincmanchester-reservations@conran-restaurants.co.uk, Fax (0161) 827 4212,* – MC AE VISA CY c
closed 25 December – **Meals** a la carte 15.00/26.00.
• Converted 19C corn exchange with bustling atmosphere, background jazz and a late-night bar. Tables available on pavement and in shopping centre. Modern international menu.

at Crumpsall *North : 3 ½ m. on A 56* CY *and A 576* – ✉ *Manchester*

Premier Travel Inn, Middleton Rd, M8 4NB, ✆ (0161) 720 6171, *Fax (0161) 740 9142* – rm, rest, MC AE VISA JCB.
Meals (grill rest.) – **45 rm** 45.95/48.95.
• Good value, group owned, purpose-built lodge set on a main road in the city's suburbs. Bedrooms decorated in a uniform fitted modern style. Rear rooms quietest.

at Didsbury *South : 5 ½ m. by A 5103* CZ *on A 5145* – ✉ *Manchester*

Didsbury House, Didsbury Park, M20 5LJ, South : 1 ½ m. on A 5145 ✆ (0161) 448 2200, *enquiries@didsburyhouse.co.uk, Fax (0161) 448 2525,* – MC AE VISA.
Meals (room service only) – 13.50 – **23 rm** 145.00/185.00, 4 suites.
• Grade II listed 19C house : grand wooden staircase, superb stained glass window. Otherwise, stylish and modern with roof-top hot tubs. Spacious, individually designed rooms.

Eleven Didsbury Park, 11 Didsbury Park, M20 5LH, South : ½ m. by A 5145 ✆ (0161) 448 7711, *enquiries@elevendidsburypark.com, Fax (0161) 448 8282,* – MC AE VISA.
Meals (room service only) – 13.50 – **20 rm** 145.00/185.00.
• The cool contemporary design in this Victorian town house creates a serene and relaxing atmosphere. Good-sized bedrooms decorated with flair and style. Personally run.

Café Jem &I, 1c School Lane, M20 6SA, ✆ (0161) 445 3996, *jemosullivan@aol.com* – MC AE VISA
closed 25-26 December, 1 January, Monday lunch and Bank Holidays – **Meals** a la carte 17.85/28.25.
• Simple, unpretentious cream coloured building tucked away off the high street. Open-plan kitchen ; homely, bistro feel. Good value, tasty modern classics.

at Manchester Airport *South : 9 m. by Lower Mosley St.* CZ *and A 5103 off M 56* – ✉ *Manchester :*

Radisson SAS Manchester Airport, Chicago Ave, M90 3RA, ✆ (0161) 490 5000, *sales.airport.manchester@radissonsas.com, Fax (0161) 490 5100,* – rm, – 250. MC AE VISA.
Phileas Fogg : Meals *(closed Saturday lunch)* (buffet lunch) 20.00/26.00 – ***Runway Brasserie :*** **Meals** a la carte – 16.50 – **354 rm** 145.00, 6 suites.
• Vast, modern hotel linked to airport passenger walkway. Four room styles with many extras. Ideal for business clients or travellers. Phileas Fogg is curved restaurant with eclectic menus and runway views. All-day Runway with arrivals/departures info.

Hilton Manchester Airport, Outwood Lane (Terminal One), M90 4WP, ✆ (0161) 435 3000, *Fax (0161) 435 3040,* – rm, – 300. MC AE VISA JCB
Meals 25.00 and a la carte – ***Lowry's : Meals*** *(closed Saturday lunch)* 14.95/25.00 and dinner a la carte – 17.50 – **224 rm** 139.00/189.00, 1 suite.
• Popular with corporate travellers for its business centre and location 200 metres from the airport terminal. Comfortable, soundproofed bedrooms. Restaurant exudes pleasant, modern style. Open-plan bar leads to informal Lowry's.

Etrop Grange, Thorley Lane, M90 4EG, (0161) 499 0500, *etropgrange@corushotels.com, Fax (0161) 499 0790* – TV P – 80. VISA
The Restaurant : **Meals** 14.00/36.95 and a la carte 21.70/31.95 **s.** – 13.50 – **62 rm** 129.00/169.00, 2 suites.
◆ Sympathetically extended Georgian house that retains a period feel. Rooms vary in size ; all are pleasantly decorated with some boasting four-posters, others cast-iron beds. Intimate, traditionally styled dining room.

Bewley's, Outwood Lane, (Terminal One), M90 4HL, (0161) 498 0333, *man@bewleyshotels.com, Fax (0161) 498 0222* – rm, rest, TV P – 90. VISA.
Meals (bar lunch)/dinner a la carte 14.85/25.40 ♀ – 6.95 – **365 rm** 59.00.
◆ Good value, four-storey, purpose-built group hotel with modern, open lobby. Brightly decorated bedrooms that all have either one double bed and sofa or two double beds. Main restaurant or lobby café dining options.

Moss Nook, Ringway Rd, Moss Nook, M22 5WD, East : 1 ¼ m. on Cheadle rd (0161) 437 4778, *Fax (0161) 498 8089,* – P. VISA
closed 2 weeks Christmas, Saturday lunch, Sunday and Monday – **Meals** 19.50/36.50 and a la carte 32.00/43.75.
◆ Decorated in a combination of Art Nouveau, lace and panelling. Long-standing owners provide polished and ceremonial service ; cooking is robust and classically based.

at Trafford Park *Southwest : 2 m. by A 56 CZ and A 5081 – ✉ Manchester*

Golden Tulip, Waters Reach, M17 1WS, (0161) 873 8899, *info@goldentulipmanchester.co.uk, Fax (0161) 872 6556* – TV P – 180. VISA JCB.
Meals (see ***Watersreach*** below) – 12.00 – **157 rm** 115.00, 3 suites.
◆ Manchester United fans will not only appreciate the proximity to the ground but also the football paraphernalia in the lobby. Uniformly decorated bedrooms are a good size.

Old Trafford Lodge without rest., Lancashire County Cricket Club, Talbot Rd, Old Trafford, M16 0PX, (0161) 874 3333, *lodge@lccc.co.uk, Fax (0161) 282 4068,* – TV P. VISA.
closed 1 week Christmas-New Year – **68 rm** 56.00/64.00.
◆ Purpose-built lodge within Lancashire County Cricket Club ; half the rooms have balconies overlooking the ground. Good value accommodation in smart, colourful bedrooms.

Watersreach, Waters Reach, M17 1WS, (0161) 868 1900, *watersreach@goldentulipmanchester.co.uk, Fax (0161) 868 1901* – P. VISA JCB
closed lunch Saturday, Sunday and Bank Holidays – **Meals** 15.50 (lunch) and a la carte 19.00/28.00 ♀.
◆ Modern, stylish, David Collins designed restaurant, adjacent to Old Trafford. Smart bar area has comfortable seating. Good, eclectic mix of precisely cooked dishes.

at Salford Quays *Southwest : 2 ¼ m. by A 56 CZ off A 5063 – ✉ Manchester*

Copthorne Manchester, Clippers Quay, M50 3SN, (0161) 873 7321, *roomsales.manchester@mill-cop.com, Fax (0161) 877 1639* – rm, rest, TV P – 150. VISA. by A 56 CZ
Chandlers : **Meals** *(closed Saturday lunch and Sunday)* (dinner only) 25.00 and a la carte 25.05/41.20 **s.** ♀ – ***Clippers :*** **Meals** (carving rest.) (bar lunch Saturday) 15.00/23.00 and a la carte 18.40/30.70 **s.** ♀ – 15.25 – **166 rm** 155.00/215.00.
◆ Part of the redeveloped Quays, overlooking the waterfront, with a Metrolink to the City. Connoisseur bedrooms are particularly well-appointed.

Express by Holiday Inn without rest., Waterfront Quay, M5 2XW, (0161) 868 1000, *managersalfordquays@expressholidayinn.co.uk, Fax (0161) 868 1068,* – TV P – 25. VISA JCB.
120 rm 75.00.
◆ Its pleasant quayside position and modern, well-equipped bedrooms make it a popular choice with both business and leisure travellers. Complimentary breakfast provided.

at Worsley *West : 7 ¼ m. by A 6 CY , A 5063, M 602 and M 62 (eastbound) on A 572 – ✉ Manchester :*

Marriott Worsley Park Hotel & Country Club, Worsley Park, M28 2QT, on A 575 (0870) 4007270, *events.worsley@marriotthotels.co.uk, Fax (0870) 4007370,* , , , , 18, – , rm, rest, TV P – 250. VISA
Brindley's : **Meals** *(closed Saturday lunch)* (carving lunch) 15.00/25.00 and dinner a la carte 27.45/29.45 **s.** ♀ – 14.95 – **153 rm** 119.00, 5 suites.
◆ Built around restored Victorian farm buildings in over 200 acres. Excellent leisure facilities including a championship standard golf course. Large, well-equipped bedrooms. Restaurant is former farm building with high beamed ceiling.

Calendar of main tradefairs and other international events in 2005

AUSTRIA

Vienna	Wiener Festwochen	13 May to 19 June
Salzburg	Salzburg Festival (Festspiele)	19 to 28 March 23 July to 31 August

BENELUX

Amsterdam	Holland Festival	15 to 20 February
Bruges	The Holy Blood Procession	Ascension
Brussels	Guild Procession (Ommegang)	first Thursday of July and the previous Tuesday
	Holiday and Leisure Activities International Show	3 to 7 February
	Belgian Antique Dealers Fair	21 to 30 January
	Eurantica (Antiques Show)	17 to 22 March

CZECH REPUBLIC

Prague	Verdi Festival	16 Aug. to 3 Sept.
	Dance Festival	8-23 June
	Spring International Music Festival	12 May to 13 June
	International Book Fair	5 to 8 May

DENMARK

Copenhagen	Hans Christian Andersen 200th anniversary	All year
	Official opening of new Opera House	15 January
	International Fashion Fair	10 to-13 February & 11 to 14 August
	Tivoli Gardens Summer Season	Mid April to mid September
	Scandinavian Furniture Fair	18 to 22 May
	August Bournonville Festival	3 to 11 June
	Copenhagen Jazz Festival	1 to 10 July
	Night of Culture	14 October
	Tivoli Christmas Market	Mid November to 23 December

FINLAND

Helsinki	*Finnish Boat Fair*	*11 to 20 February*
	Helsinki Festival	*19 August to 4 Sept.*
	Helsinki International Horse Show	*14 to 17 October*

FRANCE

Paris	*Paris Fair*	*12 to 22 May*
	World Tourism Show	*17 to 20 March*
	Book Fair	*18 to 23 March*
Cannes	*International Film Festival*	*11 to 22 May*
Lyons	*Lyons Fair*	*18 to 28 March*
Marseilles	*Santons crib Figurines Fair*	*Last weekend November to 31 December*
Monte Carlo	*Spring Art Festival*	*1 to 17 April*
Nice	*Carnival*	*12 to 27 February*
Strasbourg	*Christmas Market*	*End of November to Christmas*
	European Fair	*2 to 12 September*

GERMANY

Berlin	*Berlin Fair (Grüne Woche)*	*21 to 30 January*
Frankfurt	*International Fair*	*11 to 15 Feb. and 26 to 30 August*
	Frankfurt Book Fair	*19 to 24 October*
Hanover	*Hanover Fair*	*10 to 16 March*
Leipzig	*International Book Fair*	*17 to 20 March*
Munich	*Beer Festival (Oktoberfest)*	*17 Sept. to 2 Oct.*

GREECE

Athens	*Athens Festival*	*June to Oct.*

HUNGARY

Budapest	*Budapest Funfair*	*1 April to 31 October*
	Spring Festival	*17 March to 3 April*
	Summer Opera and Ballet Festival	*2 July to 18 August*
	International Wine and Champagne Festival	*2 to 14 Sept.*
	Autumn Festival	*21 Oct. to 30 Oct.*
	Christmas Market	*1 to 24 December*

IRELAND

Dublin	*St Patrick's Festival*	*17 March*
	Dublin International Film Festival	*11 to 20 February*
	Dublin Horse Show	*3 to 7 August*

ITALY

Milan	Bit (International Tourism Exchange)	12 to 15 February
	Fashion Fair (Moda Milano)	19 to 28 February
		24 September to 3 October
	SMAU (International Exhibition of Information and Communication Technology)	20 to 24 October
Florence	Pitti Bimbo	1 to 3 July
	Fashion Fair (Pitti Immagine Uomo)	23 to 26 June
Turin	International Book Fair	6 to 10 May
Venice	International Film Festival	last week August-first week September
	The Carnival	29 January to 8 February

NORWAY

Oslo	World Cup Nordic Skiing and Ski Jumping	12 to 13 March
	International Jazz Festival	9 to 16 August
	Fashion Fair	19 to 22 August
	Horse Show	14 to 16 October
	International Film Festival	November

POLAND

Warsaw	Ludwig van Beethoven Easter Festival	15 to 25 March
	International Book Fair	19 to 22 May
	Mozart Festival	15 June to 26 July
	Frederick Chopin International Piano Competitions	23 September to 24 October
	Jazz Jamboree	21 to 23 October

PORTUGAL

Lisbon	Contemporary Art Fair	24 to 28 November

SPAIN

Madrid	Fitur	25 to 29 January 2006
	International Book Fair	12 to 15 October
Barcelona	International Tourism Show in Catalonia	26 to 29 May
	Barcelona International Motor Show	7 to 15 May
Seville	April Fair	12 to 17 April
València	Fallas	15 to 19 March

SWEDEN

Stockholm	*International Furniture Fair*	*9 to 13 February*
	International Antique Fair	*27 to 30 January*
	Festival of Steam Boats	*7 to 11 August*
	Jazz Festival	*16 to 24 July*
	International Film Festival	*mid. November*
	Nobel Prize Day	*10 December*
Gothenburg	*Boat Show*	*4 Feb. to 13 Feb.*
	Motor Show	*February*
	International Horse Show	*8 to 11 April*
	International Book Fair	*29 Sept. to 2 Oct.*
	Gothenburg Film Festival	*28 Jan. to 7 Feb.*

SWITZERLAND

Bern	*BEA : Exhibition for Handicraft, Agriculture, Trade and Industry*	*29 April to 8 May*
Basle	*Baselworld European Watch, Clock and Jewellery Fair*	*31 March to 7 April*
Geneva	*International Exhibition of inventions, new technologies and products*	*6 to 10 April*
	International Motor Show	*2 to 12 March 2006*
Zürich	*Züspa : Zurich Autumn Show for Home and Living, Sport and Fashion*	*22 September to 2 October*

UNITED KINGDOM

London	*Book Fair*	*13 to 15 March*
	Fine Art and Antiques Fair	*9 to 19 June*
	International Map Fair	*10 to 11 June*
	International Film Festival	*2 weeks October*
Birmingham	*Antiques for Everyone*	*April and November*
	International Motorcycle & Scooter Show	*27 October to 6 November*
	Toy Collectors Fair	*27 February, 29 May, 21 August, 9 October*
	Horse of the Year	*12 to 16 Oct.*
Edinburgh	*Military Tattoo*	*5 to 27 August*
	Fringe Festival	*14 August to 4 Sept.*
	International Book Festival	*13 to 29 August*
	International Film Festival	*17 to 28 August*
	International Festival	*14 August to 4 Sept.*
Glasgow	*West End Festival*	*10 to 26 June*
	International Jazz Festival	*17 to 26 June*
	Antiques for Everyone	*13 to 14 May*
Leeds	*International Film Festival*	*October to November*

International Dialling Codes

Note : when making an international call, do not dial the first "0" of the city codes (except for calls to Italy).

Indicatifs Téléphoniques Internationaux

Important : Pour les communications internationales, le zéro (0) initial de l'indicatif interurbain n'est pas à composer (excepté pour les appels vers l'Italie).

from \ to	A	B	CH	CZ	D	DK	E	FIN	F	GB	GR
A Austria		0032	0041	00420	0049	0045	0034	00358	0033	0044	0030
B Belgium	0043		0041	00420	0049	0045	0034	00358	0033	0044	0030
CH Switzerland	0043	0032		00420	0049	0045	0034	00358	0033	0044	0030
CZ Czech Republic	0043	0032	0041		0049	0045	0034	00358	0033	0044	0030
D Germany	0043	0032	0041	00420		0045	0034	00358	0033	0044	0030
DK Denmark	0043	0032	0041	00420	0049		0034	00358	0033	0044	0030
E Spain	0043	0032	0041	00420	0049	0045		00358	0033	0044	0030
FIN Finland	0043	0032	0041	00420	0049	0045	0034		0033	0044	0030
F France	0043	0032	0041	00420	0049	0045	0034	00358		0044	0030
GB United Kingdom	0043	0032	0041	00420	0049	0045	0034	00358	0033		0033
GR Greece	0043	0032	0041	00420	0049	0045	0034	00358	0033	0044	
H Hungary	0043	0032	0041	00420	0049	0045	0034	00358	0033	0044	0030
I Italy	0043	0032	0041	00420	0049	0045	0034	00358	0033	0044	0030
IRL Ireland	0043	0032	0041	00420	0049	0045	0034	00358	0033	0044	0030
J Japan	00143	00132	00141	001420	0149	00145	00134	001358	00133	00144	00130
L Luxembourg	0043	0032	0041	00420	0049	0045	0034	00358	0033	0044	0030
N Norway	0043	0032	0041	00420	0049	0045	0034	00358	0033	0044	0030
NL Netherlands	0043	0032	0041	00420	0049	0045	0034	00358	0033	0044	0030
PL Poland	0043	0032	0041	00420	0049	0045	0034	00358	0033	0044	0030
P Portugal	81043	0032	0041	00420	0049	0045	0034	00358	0033	0044	0030
RUS Russia	81043	81032	81041	810420	81049	81045	81034	810358	81033	81044	81030
S Sweden	0043	0032	0041	00420	0049	0045	0034	00358	0033	0044	0030
USA	01143	01132	01141	011420	01149	01145	01134	011358	01133	01144	01130

* *Direct dialing not possible**

* *Pas de sélection automatique*

Internationale Telefon-Vorwahlnummern

Wichtig : bei Auslandsgesprächen darf die Null (0) der Ortsnetzkennzahl nicht gewählt werden (ausser bei Gesprächen nach Italien).

Indicativi Telefonici Internationali

Importante: per le comunicazioni internazionali, non bisogna comporre lo zero (0) iniziale dell'indicativo interurbano (escluse le chiamate per l'Italia).

Prefijos telefónicos internacionales

Importante: para las llamadas internacionales, no se debe marcar el cero (0) inicial del prefijo interurbano (excepto para llamar a Italia).

H	I	IRL	J	L	N	NL	PL	P	RUS	S	USA	
0036	0039	00353	0081	00352	0047	0031	0048	00351	007	0046	001	**Austria A**
0036	0039	00353	0081	00352	0047	0031	0048	00351	007	0046	001	**Belgium B**
0036	0039	00353	0081	00352	0047	0031	0048	00351	007	0046	001	**Switzerland CH**
0036	0039	00353	0081	00352	0047	0031	0048	00351	007	0046	001	**Czech Republic CZ**
0036	0039	00353	0081	00352	0047	0031	0048	00351	007	0046	001	**Germany D**
0036	0039	00353	0081	00352	0047	0031	0048	00351	007	0046	001	**Denmark DK**
0036	0039	00353	0081	00352	0047	0031	0048	00351	007	0046	001	**Spain E**
0036	0039	00353	0081	00352	0047	0031	0048	00351	007	0046	001	**Finnland FIN**
0036	0039	00353	0081	00352	0047	0031	0048	00351	007	0046	001	**France F**
0036	0039	00353	0081	00352	0047	0031	0048	00351	007	0046	001	**United Kingdom GB**
0036	0039	00353	0081	00352	0047	0031	0048	00351	007	0046	001	**Greece GR**
	0039	00353	0081	00352	0047	0031	0048	00351	007	0046	001	**Hungary H**
0036		00353	0081	00352	0047	0031	0048	00351	*	0046	001	**Italy I**
0036	0039		0081	00352	0047	0031	0048	00351	007	0046	001	**Ireland IRL**
00136	00139	001353		001352	00147	00131	00148	001351	*	00146	0011	**Japan J**
0036	0039	00353	0081		0047	0031	0048	00351	007	0046	001	**Luxembourg L**
0036	0039	00353	0081	00352		0031	0048	00351	007	0046	001	**Norway N**
0036	0039	00353	0081	00352	0047		0048	00351	007	0046	001	**Netherlands NL**
0036	0039	00353	0081	00352	0047	0031		00351	007	0046	001	**Poland PL**
0036	0039	00353	0081	00352	0047	0031	0048		007	0046	001	**Portugal P**
81036	81039	810353	81081	810352	81047	81031	81048	810351		81046	8101	**Russia RUS**
0036	0039	00353	0081	00352	0047	0031	0048	00351	007		001	**Sweden S**
01136	01139	011353	01181	011352	01147	01131	01148	011351	*	01146		**USA**

* *Automatische Vorwahl nicht möglich* * *Selezione automatica impossibile* * *No es posible la conexión automática*

Manufacture française des pneumatiques Michelin

Société en commandite par actions au capital de 304 000 000 EUR
Place des Carmes-Déchaux – 63 Clermont-Ferrand (France)
R.C.S. Clermont-Fd B 855 200 507

Michelin et Cie, propriétaires-éditeurs, 2005
Dépôt légal : mars 2005 – ISBN 2.06.710947-2

Printed in Belgium : 02-2005/3-1

Compogravure : MAURY Imprimeur S.A., Malesherbes

Impression-Reliure : AUBIN, Ligugé

Illustrations : Nathalie Benavides, Patricia Haubert, Cécile Imbert/MICHELIN Narratif Systèmes/Genclo, Rodolphe Corbel.